W9-CPH-236

THE GUINNESS ENCYCLOPEDIA

~of~

POPULAR MUSIC

Edited by
COLIN LARKIN

VOLUME 5
• • • • • • •
Primitives –
Three's A Crowd

GUINNESS PUBLISHING

First edition published in 1992
Second impression 1994
Second edition published in 1995 by
GUINNESS PUBLISHING LTD
33 London Road, Enfield, Middlesex EN2 6DJ, England

Published in the United States by
STOCKTON PRESS
an imprint of Grove's Dictionaries Inc.
345 Park Avenue South, New York, NY 10010, USA

British Library Cataloguing-in-Publication data
A catalogue record for this book is available from the British Library

ISBN 0-85112-662-6 (UK)

Library of Congress Cataloging-in-Publication Data
A catalog record for this book is available from the Library of Congress

ISBN 1-56159-176-9 (USA)

Conceived and edited by Colin Larkin for
SQUARE ONE BOOKS LTD
to whom all editorial correspondence should be sent
Iron Bridge House, 3 Bridge Approach, Chalk Farm, London NW1 8BD
Production Editor: Susan Pipe
Desk Editor: Miles Hutchinson
Senior contributors: Alex Ogg, John Martland and Brian Hogg
Special thanks to John Reiss and to David Roberts of Guinness Publishing
This book has been designed on Apple Macintosh computers
using 4th Dimension, Quark XPress and Microsoft Word

Printed and bound in Great Britain by the Bath Press

Contents

Primitives

This highly-melodic group, from Coventry, England, formed in the summer of 1985, with a line-up that featured Kieron (vocals), Paul Court (b. 27 July 1965; vocals/guitar), Steve Dullaghan (b. 18 December 1966; bass) and Pete Tweedie (drums). However, Kieron was soon replaced by Tracy Tracy (b. Tracy Cattell, 18 August 1967, Australia). The group set up their own label, Lazy Records, and achieved a modicum of success on the UK independent circuit with the singles 'Thru The Flowers', 'Really Stupid' and 'Stop Killing Me'. Despite the label now being effectively a subsidiary of the major **RCA Records** set-up, the Primitives maintained their roots in the 'indie' scene and were, for a time, the darlings of the pop press. With echoes of early **Blondie** and the **Ramones**, the Primitives' jangling guitar work brought them national fame in early 1988, when 'Crash', a classic piece of 'indie' pop, reached the UK Top 5. The accompanying album, *Lovely*, reached the UK Top 10, but any chance of their consolidating on this position was brought to a halt by personnel changes. The acrimonious ousting of Pete Tweedie led to the subsequent inclusion of Tig Williams, and there were further line-up changes when Andy Hobson replaced Dullaghan. The new line-up's subsequent singles failed to emulate the success of 'Crash' and the follow-up album, *Pure*, was only a partial success. The Primitives ended the 80s touring the USA and returned to UK to undergo extensive touring around Britain, hoping to regenerate those brief glory days. Both Dullahan and Tweedie went on to join Hate, while Hobson's tenure in the bass position was a fleeting one, being replaced in 1989 by Paul Samspon. When *Galore* failed to sell, the Primitives disbanded.

Albums: *Lovely* (Lazy 1988), *Pure* (Lazy/RCA 1989), *Galore* (Lazy/RCA 1992). Compilation: *Lazy 86-88* (Lazy 1989).

Primus

The vast majority of reviewers can generally agree on one word to describe the US band Primus, and that word is 'weird'. Formed in San Francisco, USA in 1984 by the former **Blind Illusion** bassist Les Claypool, seven drummers passed through their ranks before Tim 'Herb' Alexander settled in, with Claypool's Blind Illusion colleague, ex-**Possessed** guitarist Larry Lalonde replacing the original guitarist Todd Huth shortly before the band recorded their debut album. Musically, the band are highly talented and original, mixing together funk, punk, thrash, metal and rock in their own intense manner, which was once described by Claypool as 'psychedelic polka'. Claypool and Alexander produce quirky, sometimes hypnotic rhythms, accentuating each other's playing, while former **Joe Satriani** pupil Lalonde creates and colours

within the framework, although his playing owes more to **Frank Zappa** than to that of his old teacher. Claypool's vocals lean towards cartoonish narrative, with lyrics of a suitably abstract and humorous nature, drawing from both life and his film and literary influences. A common theme to all their albums is marine life, reflecting the band's passion for sea-fishing (they have played with fish-shaped covers on their vocal microphones). Their debut, *Suck On This*, was a self-financed live set successfully released on their own Prawn Song label, and much of the material was to feature on *Fizzle Fry*, an independent studio release which won a Bay Area Music Award and, helped by touring with **Faith No More**, **Jane's Addiction**, **24-7 Spyz** and **Living Colour**, a major record deal. *Sailing The Seas Of Cheese* further raised their profile, with their reworking of 'Tommy The Cat' from the debut (with a **Tom Waits** guest vocal) featuring in hit movie *Bill & Ted's Bogus Journey*. A lengthy world tour in support of **Rush** was then followed by stadium dates with **U2**. Any doubts as to the band being a sufficient draw for the closing (effectively headlining) slot on the 1993 Lollapalooza extravanganza in the USA were completely dispelled when their fourth album *Pork Soda* went straight into the US charts at number 7, and produced the hit single 'My Name Is Mud'. Claypool would also hook up with Huth and former Primus drummer Jay Lane to form side-project Sausage, recording *Riddles Are Abound Tonight* for Interscope in 1994.

Albums: *Suck On This* (Prawn Song 1990), *Frizzle Fry* (Caroline 1990), *Sailing The Seas Of Cheese* (Interscope 1991), *Pork Soda* (Interscope 1993), *Tales From The Punchbowl* (Interscope 1995).

Prince

b. Prince Rogers Nelson, 7 June 1958, Minneapolis, Minnesota, USA. A prodigiously talented singer-songwriter, multi-instrumentalist and producer, the genre-defying pop maverick Prince was named after the Prince Roger Trio, of whom his father, John Nelson, was a member. After running away from his mother and step-father Prince Rogers Nelson briefly joined up with John, who bought him his first guitar. He was later adopted by the Andersons, and became a close friend of Andre Anderson (later Andre Cymone). Prince was already conversant with piano and guitar and had written his own material from an early age. Together with Andre he joined Anderson's cousin Charles Smith in a junior high school band titled Grand Central. As Prince progressed to high school, Grand Central became Champagne, and he introduced original material into his sets for the first time. His musical development continued with the emergence of 'Uptown', a musical underground scene which included Flyte Time as well as other important influences Jellybean Johnson, Terry Lewis and

Alexander O'Neal. Prince's first demos were recorded in 1976 with Chris Moon, who gave Prince guidance in the operation of a music studio, and free reign to experiment at weekends. Moon also introduced him to backer Owen Husney, after which Prince provided interested parties with a superior quality demo. Husney and partner Levinson set about a massive 'hyping' campaign, the results of which secured him a long term, flexible contract with **Warner Brothers** after a great deal of scrambling amongst the majors.

Debuting with *For You*, Prince sent shock waves through his new sponsors by spending double his entire advance on a single album. It sold moderately, with the single 'Soft And Wet' making a big impact in the R&B charts. The album's blend of deep funk and soul was merely an appetizer in comparison to his later exploits, but enough to reassure his label that their investment had been a solid one. By 1979 Prince had put together a firm band (his debut was recorded almost exclusively by himself). This featured Cymone (bass), Gayle Chapman and Matt Fink (both keyboards), Bobby Z (drummer) and Dez Dickerson (guitar). Despite lavishing considerably less time and money on it than its predecessor, *Prince* nevertheless charted (number 22) and boasted two successful singles, 'Why You Wanna Treat Me So Bad?' and 'I Wanna Be Your Lover'. A succession of live dates promoting the new album *Dirty Mind* saw Chapman replaced by Lisa Coleman. The album was the first fully to embody Prince's sexual allure, and the phallic exhortations on his Telecaster and explicit material like 'Head' appalled and enticed in equal proportions. Artists like **Rick James**, whom Prince supported in 1980, were among those who mistrusted Prince's open, androgynous sexuality. Returning to Minneapolis after an aborted UK tour, Cymone departed for a solo career while former members of Flyte Time and others released a self-titled album under the band name the **Time**. It transpired later that their songs had been written by Prince, who was the motivation behind the entire project. Prince was nothing if not prolific, and both *Controversy* and *1999* followed within 12 months. *Controversy* attempted to provide a rationale for the sexual machinations which dominated *Dirty Mind*, falling unhappily between the two stools of instinct and intellect. It was a paradox not entirely solved by *1999*, a double album which had enough strong material to make up two sides of excellence but no more.

The promotional tour featured a special revue troupe. Prince And The Revolution headlined above the Time and **Vanity 6** (an all-girl Prince creation). The single 'Little Red Corvette' was lifted from the album and was the first to gain significant airplay on **MTV**. The song was almost entirely constructed for this purpose, using a strong 'white' metaphor as leverage. After internal disputes with the Time, Prince began work on the *Purple Rain* film, a glamorized autobiographical piece in which he would star. The potent social commentary of 'When Doves Cry' was lifted from the soundtrack and became the first Prince song to grace the top of the US charts. 'Let's Go Crazy' and 'Purple Rain' (numbers 1 and 2 respectively) further established him as a figurehead for the 80s. After the finish of a huge tour, Prince returned to the studio for a duet with Apollonia, the latest in a seemingly endless succession of female protegées. He also found time to revitalize the career of Scottish singer **Sheena Easton** by composing her US Top 10 effort 'Sugar Walls'. When *Around The World In A Day* emerged in 1985 it topped the US charts for a three-week run, despite a deliberate lack of promotion. Drowning in quasi-psychedelia and 60s optimism, it was a diverting but strangely uneventful, almost frivolous jaunt. It preceded the announcement that Prince was retiring from live appearances. Instead he had founded the studio/label/complex Paisley Park in central Minneapolis, which would become the luxurious base for his future operations. As work began on a second movie, *Under The Cherry Moon*, 'Kiss' was released to become his third US number 1. Held one place beneath it was the **Bangles**' 'Manic Monday', written by Prince under one of his numerous pseudonyms, in this case, Christopher.

He quickly overturned his decision not to perform live, and set out on the *Parade* tour to promote the number 1 album of the same name. Unfortunately, if 'Kiss' and 'Girls And Boys' represented classic Prince innuendo, the rest of the album lacked focus. The shows, however, were spectacular even by Prince standards, but his backing band the Revolution were nevertheless disbanded at the end of the tour. 1987 saw a new line-up for the latest live engagements. While retaining the backbone of the Revolution (Fink, Leeds, Brooks and Safford) he added **Sheila E**, Marco Weaver, and Seacer. The new album was to be a radical departure from the laconic, cosseted atmosphere which pervaded *Parade*. 'Sign 'O' The Times', the title track, was a hard-hitting testimony to urban dystopia, drug-related violence and human folly. The vast majority of tracks on the double album revisited the favoured territory of sex and sensuality. The follow-up album would elaborate on the darker shades of *Sign 'O' The Times*' apocalyptic vision. However, the *Black Album* was recalled by Prince before it reached the shops. Combining primal funk slices with sadistic overtones, Prince's decision to suspend it ensured that it would become the 80s' most coveted bootleg. The mythology surrounding its non-release has it that the *Black Album* was the work of Prince's 'dark' side - 'Spooky Electric'. This was given credence by the subsequent *Lovesexy*, apparently the result of the pre-eminence of 'Camille' - Prince's 'good' side. Playing both albums side by side certainly reveals a sharp dichotomy of approach.

His next tour, meanwhile, saw the inclusion of a huge

Pink Cadillac as a mobile part of the set. Exhausted musicians testified to the difficulty of backing their leader, rushing from orchestrated stadium performances to private club dates where entire sets would be improvised. All of which Prince, naturally, took in his stride. 1989 closed with a duet with **Madonna**, who, alongside **Michael Jackson**, was the only artist able to compete with Prince in terms of mass popularity. The following year was dominated by the soundtrack album for the year's biggest film, *Batman*. If the album was not his greatest artistic success, it proved a commercial smash, topping the US charts for six weeks. He had also written and produced an album for singer **Mavis Staples**. At first glance it seemed an unlikely combination, but Prince's lyrics tempered the sexual with the divine in a manner that was judged acceptable by the grand lady of gospel. *Graffiti Bridge* would prove his first commercial let-down for some time, peaking at number 6 in the US (though it made number 1 in the UK). Prince, as usual, was already busy putting together new projects. These included his latest backing outfit the New Power Generation, featuring Tony M (rapper), Rosie Gaines (vocals), Michael Bland (drums), Levi Seacer (guitar), Kirk Johnson (guitar), Sonny T (bass) and Tommy Barbarella (keyboards). They were in place in time for the sessions for *Diamonds And Pearls*, a comparatively deliberate and studied body of work. Although Prince has yet to provide the definitive album he is so obviously capable of, the continued flow of erratic, flawed gems suggests the struggle will continue to captivate his audience through the 90s.

Albums: *For You* (1978), *Prince* (1979), *Dirty Mind* (1980), *Controversy* (1981), *1999* (1982), *Purple Rain* (1984, film soundtrack), *Around The World In A Day* (1985), *Parade - Music From Under The Cherry Moon* (1986, film sountrack), *Sign 'O' The Times* (1987), *Lovesexy* (1988), *Batman* (1989, film soundtrack), *Graffiti Bridge* (1990), *Diamonds And Pearls* (1991), and The New Power Generation *Symbol* (1993), *Come* (Paisley Park 1994). Compilations: *The Hits: Volume I & II* (1993).

Videos: *Double Live* (1986), *Prince And The Revolution; Live* (1987), *Sign O' The Times* (1988), *Lovesexy Part 2* (1989), *Lovesexy Part 1* (1989), *Get Off* (1991), *Prince: The Hits Collection* (1993), *3 Chains O' Gold* (Warner Reprise 1994), *Billboards* (Warner Vision 1994).

Further reading: *Prince: A Pop Life*, Dave Hill. *Prince - A Documentary*, Per Nilsen. *Prince: Imp Of The Perverse*, Barney Hoskyns. *Prince By Controversy*, The 'Controversy' Team. *Prince: An Illustrated Biography*, John W. Duffy. *Prince*, John Ewing.

Prince Buster

b. Cecil Bustamante Campbell, 28 May 1938, Kingston, Jamaica, West Indies. Buster was named after Alexandra Bustamante, the leader of the Jamaican Labour Party, and began his career as a boxer, but soon found his pugilistic talents being put to use as a bouncer/strong arm man and minder for **Coxsone Dodd**'s Down Beat **sound system**. Competition was fierce in those early days, with fights often breaking out between the supporters of rival sounds with wires (and people) being cut regularly, and Buster still carries the scars (literally). He claims, like so many others, to have personally invented the **ska** sound, and he was certainly involved from the very early stages - at first with his work for Coxsone and after they had parted company with his own Voice Of The People sound system, record label and shop. His very first recording session produced one of the all-time classics of Jamaican music, 'Oh Carolina', with vocals by the **Folks Brothers** and musical accompaniment from **Count Ossie**. Inventive and innovative at the time, the record still sounds every bit as exciting now as it did then. Buster released countless records both by himself and other top acts on his Wild Bells, Voice Of The People and Buster's Record Shack labels, which were subsequently released in the UK on the Blue Beat imprint. They proved as popular there as they had been in Jamaica, firstly with the Jamaican community and secondly with the mods, who took the Prince to their hearts with songs such as 'Al Capone' and 'Madness'. He toured the UK in the mid-60s to ecstatic crowds and appeared on the hugely popular *Ready, Steady, Go* television show.

He recorded in many different styles but his talking records were the most popular, including the hilarious 'Judge Dread' where he admonishes rude boys and sentences them to 400 years; the wildly misogynistic 'Ten Commandments'; the evocative 'Ghost Dance' - a look back at his early Kingston dancehall days; the confused and confusing 'Johnny Cool'; and the not so well known but equally wonderful 'Shepherd Beng Beng'. He also claims to have taught **Georgie Fame** to do the ska and he influenced other white pop acts - **Madness** named themselves after his song (debuting with a tribute, 'The Prince') and inspired doorman/bouncer Alex Hughes to adopt the name **Judge Dread** and have UK chart hits with variations on Prince Buster's lewd original 'Big Five'. Buster had tended towards 'slack' or rude records towards the end of the 60s which were only mildly risqué compared with what was to follow but caused a sensation at the time. He wisely invested his money in record shops and juke box operations throughout the Caribbean and, in the early 70s, took to recording many of the current top names including **Big Youth**, **Dennis Alcapone**, **John Holt**, **Dennis Brown** and **Alton Ellis** with varying degrees of success. He soon realised that his older recordings would outsell his newer efforts every time and he turned to re-pressing his extensive back catalogue on single and releasing his old albums both in Jamaica and the UK. He also put together some brilliant compilations where the superb sleevenotes, written by the Prince himself, attack in no uncertain terms the music of the day: 'They have used guns to spoil the fun and force tasteless and meaningless music upon the land.'

Throughout the rest of the 70s and on into the 80s he lived on his shops, his juke boxes and his past glories but he returned to live work in the latter half of the 80s. He has become a crowd puller again for, as he says: 'The people know my songs and loved them.' He even started, for the first time in years, to record new music again (1992). While it is impossible to forecast if this will prove successful or not one cannot ever take away the fact that Prince Buster's music has already inspired generations of performers. He is respected abroad - probably more than in his native Jamaica - but he will always have his place as one of the few Jamaican artists to reach directly to the international audience. Many more have played their part indirectly but his name was known both through his own recordings ('Al Capone' reached the lower regions of the UK national charts) and his work with other people. It is unlikely that any other Jamaican artist (apart from **Bob Marley**) still has his records so regularly played in clubs and dances throughout the world.

Selected albums: *Judge Dread Rock Steady* (Blue Beat 1967), *I Feel The Spirit* (1968), *Wreck A Pum Pum* (Blue Beat 1968), *She Was A Rough Rider* (Melodisc 1969), *Big Five* (Melodisc 1972), *On Tour* (1966, reissued 1988), *Judge Dread* (1968, reissued Blue Beat 1991), *Tutti Fruitti* (Melodisc). Various: *Pain In My Belly* (Islam/Blue Beat 1966). Compilations: *Prince Buster's Fabulous Greatest Hits* (Fab 1968), *Original Golden Oldies Vol. 1 & 2* (Prince Buster 1989).

Prince Far I

b. Michael Williams, c.1944, Spanish Town, Jamaica, d. 15 September 1983. Prince Far I, the voice of thunder, was originally a bouncer at the premises of **Studio One**, Jamaica's premier record label of the 60s and early 70s. A huge, muscular figure with impressive facial scars, he was known as a gentle giant with hidden depths. One day in 1970 **King Stitt**, the regular DJ at Studio One, had failed to turn up to voice a track, and Michael the bouncer persuaded the producer, **Coxsone Dodd**, to give him a try. Impressed, Dodd named the new artist King Cry-Cry and a legend was born. After a couple of records as Cry-Cry, he renamed himself Prince Far I. A gruff, deep, slow-burning rhymer, his talents at first appeared limited although Far I was built to last: while other DJs' careers fizzled like firecrackers, Far I retained his status throughout his life. When he really let rip, as on his 1977 album *Under Heavy Manners*, he was awesome. His *Psalms For I* (1976) remains a roots classic today, and his **Trojan Records** albums, *Free From Sin*, *Jamaican Heroes* and *Voice Of Thunder*, were all of a high standard. A brief liaison with **Virgin Records** brought him a wider,

rockier audience, as did his *Cry Tuff Dub Encounter* (1976-79) series of dub albums, originally cut for his own Jamaican label Cry Tuff. Eventually Far I spent a fair portion of his time in England, where he recorded as part of Singers And Players for Adrian Sherwood's **On-U Sound** label. The pair worked together well, particularly on the 'Virgin' single, an undisguised swipe at Far I's previous label. UK gigs were frequent, with Far I, dressed in biblical robes, 'chanting down babylon' with the help of hundreds of white kids, whom he genially met and signed autographs for after the show. However, just as he was starting to build this new following, he was shot dead in Jamaica, yet another victim of Kingston's regular street violence, one year short of his 40th birthday.

Albums: *Psalms For I* (Carib Gems 1976), *Under Heavy Manners* (Joe Gibbs 1977), *Message From The King* (Front Line 1978), *Long Life* (Front Line 1978), *Cry Tuff Dub Encounter* (Cry Tuff/Hit Run 1978), *Free From Sin* (Trojan 1979), *Cry Tuff Dub Encounter Chapter 3* (Cry Tuff/Daddy Kool 1979), *Livity* (Pre 1979), *Cry Tuff Dub Encounter, Part 2* (Cry Tuff/Front Line 1979), *Jamaican Heroes* (Trojan 1980), *Showcase In A Suitcase* (Pre 1980), *Cry Tuff Dub Encounter Chapter 4* (Cry Tuff/Trojan 1981), *Voice Of Thunder* (Trojan 1981), *Musical History* (Trojan 1983), *Spear Of The Nation* (Kingdom 1984). With the Suns Of Arqa: *The Musical Revue* (1989, live 1983 recording - cassette only). Compilations: *Black Man Land* (Front Line 1990), *Dubwise* (Front Line 1991).

Prince Hammer

b. Beresford Simpson, c.1962, Kingston Jamaica, West Indies. Simpson began his recording career with Glen Brown who produced, 'Daughter A Whole Lotta Sugar Down Deh', which surfaced in the UK as the b-side to 'Two Wedden Skank'. Other singles appeared notably 'Tel Aviv Skank'. His early recordings were in his own name but he chose the pseudonym Prince Hammer for his own production, 'King Of Kings'. The film *Rockers* included cameo appearances from nearly all Jamaica's top performers including Prince Hammer, although he did not contribute to the soundtrack. He gained international notoriety when produced by Blacka Morwell who licensed his work to **Virgin Records** in the UK. The result, *Bible*, was a popular compilation with liner notes from dub poet, **Linton Kwesi Johnson** who stated, 'There is no doubt in my mind that *Bible* will win a large following for the Prince and we will be hearing a lot more from him'. The album featured the title track, 'B - I - B - L - E, Bible who no like it bite it' and 'Sister Bella' a lament of lost love. The consequence of his success led to a visit to the UK and a move to the forerunner of **On U Sound**, Hit Run. In 1979 he was featured in a reggae showcase called, Roots Encounter although some of the gigs were cancelled at the last minute. Those lucky enough to witness the events were able to enjoy performances from Prince Hammer along with **Bim Sherman** and **Prince Far I**. While in the UK he released his production of Rod Taylor's, 'If Jah Should Come Now' and enjoyed a big hit, although the album of the same name did not achieve the same success. He also released, '10,000 Lions' which featured his singing and DJ style on the same discomix. He continued producing other artists enjoying moderate success with, **Echo Minott**, Jennifer Lara, Toyan, George Nooks, and he was one of the first producers to record DJ **Trinity** singing. Many of Prince Hammer's early productions surfaced on the compilation, *Africa Iron Gate Showcase*.

Albums: *Bible* (Front Line 1978), *Roots And Roots* (Hit Run 1979), *Roots Me Roots* (Little Luke 1980), *World War Dub Part 1* (Baby Mother 1980), *Dancehall Style* (Hit Run 1981), *World War Dub Part 2* (Baby Mother 1981).

Prince Jazzbo

b. Linval Carter, c.1950, Jamaica, West Indies. Prince Jazzbo is one of the survivors of reggae music. While he has never been as important as other 70s DJs such as **U-Roy** or **Big Youth**, it is Jazzbo who retains a charismatic personal style and a reasonably healthy following through his label, Ujama, for which he produces and occasionally records. Like many others, Jazzbo first recorded for the **Studio One** label in the early 70s. Legend has it that Jazzbo had come in from the countryside and was kept waiting in the yard all day by **Coxsone Dodd**, the studio and label owner, because no one was expecting much from the skinny youth. However, Jazzbo eventually pestered his way into the studio and took the microphone. Dodd ran a backing track at random - **Horace Andy**'s 'Skylarking' - and Jazzbo delivered what was to become a monster hit first-take, 'Crabwalking'. For the next 18 months or so, Jazzbo stuck with Dodd, cutting a string of flawless roots records: 'Crime Don't Pay', 'Pepper Rock', 'School' and 'Imperial I'. However, a much-promised album for Dodd failed to materialize, so Jazzbo, disillusioned, began to record for other producers, **Glen Brown** and **Bunny Lee**. A liaison with **Lee Perry** on the expected one-off single 'Penny Reel' eventually turned into the superb 1976 album *Natty Passing Thru*, AKA *Ital Corner*, for which he was paid a mere $1,000 Jamaican (about £100 at the time). Other albums from this time include *Kick Boy Face* and *Step Forward Youth*, the latter shared with **I Roy**. By 1977 Jazzbo had launched Ujama, recording as a singer for the label, under the name Johnny Cool. Neither his *alter-ego* or his label worked, sales-wise. Jazzbo reached the start of the 80s and the impending **dancehall** boom in much the same state as his fellow DJ pioneers I Roy, U-Roy and Big Youth: he still had talent but reggae's styles were changing fast. Jazzbo decided that Ujama must become a viable operation, and from around 1983 onwards it has been - even if his

idiosyncratic production style and somewhat off-the-wall ideas have held it back in the larger marketplace. Besides offering a shelter for older DJs like U-Roy and I Roy, Ujama specialises in finding the sort of reggae acts other producers overlook: Zebra, Manchez and Horace Ferguson. None of them have made it to the status of Jazzbo's most famous ally, **Frankie Paul**, but that is wholly in keeping with Ujama's symbol of a donkey, because, as Jazzbo never tires of telling people: 'a donkey may not arrive quickly, but it was good enough to carry Jesus and will not suffer a mechanical breakdown on the way'. The cheaply produced sleeves of his albums nearly always feature a cartoon donkey carrying Jazzbo or taking part in a horse race. While Jazzbo is unlikely ever to make it big internationally, his career received an unexpected fillip in 1991 when Studio One finally deigned to release his album, *Choice Of Version*, some 18 years late, to ecstatic reviews and considerable excitement. If it had happened in 1973, Jazzbo might have been in a far stronger position today.

Selected albums: *Kick Boy Face* (Third World 1975), *Natty Passing Thru* aka *Ital Corner* (Black Wax 1976), *Choice Of Version* (Studio One 1990). With I Roy: *Step Forward Youth* (1976). With Jah Stitch: *Straight To Babylon Chest* (1979). With I Roy: *Head To Head Clash* (1990).

Prince La La

b. Lawrence Nelson. The brother of Walter 'Papoose' Nelson, a respected session musician, this New Orleans-based singer/guitarist was signed to AFO ('All For One'), a local label owned by **Harold Battiste**. The Prince enjoyed a US R&B Top 30 hit with 'She Put The Hurt On Me' (1961), an enchanting slice of classic Crescent City back beat, originally intended for singer **Barbara George**. It was later recorded by the **Spencer Davis Group**. Prince La La's promising career was tragically cut short when he was murdered shortly after the release of his second single. He nevertheless remained an influential figure and his voodoo, 'night-tripper' persona was later adopted by **Dr. John**.

Prince Lincoln (The Royal Rasses)

b. Lincoln Thompson. Lincoln Thompson's solo career began at **Studio One**, where he made three singles in the early 70s which failed to make any impact but established his name amongst the committed following for 'roots' music. He had been involved in the music business in the 60s as a member of the Tartans, and their 'Dance All Night' on Merritone Records was a big **rocksteady** hit, but they disbanded soon after this early taste of success. 'Live Up To Your Name', 'True Experience' and 'Daughters Of Zion' are still sought-after records which sell out immediately every time **Coxsone Dodd** re-presses them. Prince Lincoln left Studio One to establish his own label, God Sent, and released three more singles - this time as the Royal Rasses (Royal Princes) which were effectively solo efforts with harmonies provided by an assortment of back-up singers including Cedric Myton (of **Congos** fame), Keith Peterkin and Studio One stalwart, Jennifer Lara. 'Love The Way It Should Be', 'Kingston 11' - a musical tour of the ghetto and 'Old Time Friend' were all good sellers both in Jamaica and the UK, and attracted the attention of Ballistic Records who signed them and heavily promoted their debut, *Humanity*. The album contained the three hit singles and songs of the same calibre including 'San Salvador', a hugely in-demand **dub plate** popularised on **Lloydie Coxsone**'s London-based **sound system**. The set was issued in a full colour (and very expensive) sleeve with lyric sheet and backed up with a lengthy European tour in 1979. The group were poised on the brink of international stardom and Prince Lincoln's carefully-crafted thoughtful songs and soaring vocals were just right for the time. Sadly, it all went wrong. Although the Royal Rasses were making music that Lincoln defined as 'inter-reg' or crossover music, their follow-up album, *Experience*, failed to scale the heights that *Humanity* had reached and was not particularly popular with either the reggae audience or the pop audience it was aimed at. The third album release, a very brave step and one that brought Lincoln much critical acclaim, but failed to sell in any quantity, was a collaboration with English singer **Joe Jackson**. The cost of these admirable ventures was borne by Ballistic Records, who went out of business in the process, and Thompson returned to Jamaica in 1981. There was nothing from Prince Lincoln for the rest of the decade but the early 90s have seen a handful of interesting UK releases on God Sent which might signal a return to the business for one of reggae's most gifted singers, songwriters and arrangers. He is one of the few with the vision the music needs.

Albums: *Humanity* (Ballistic 1979), *Experience* (Ballistic 1980), *Ride With The Rasses* (God Sent 1981), with Joe Jackson *Roots Man Blues* (Ballistic 1981).

Prince Paul

b. Paul E. Huston, 2 April 1967, Amityville, Long Island, New York, USA. Alongside **Daddy-O**, Prince Paul is the second of **Stetsasonic**'s founding members to enjoy notable extra-curricular activities. Similarly his production credits take pride of place in his list of achievements. Probably his proudest moment came in helming **De La Soul**'s *3 Feet High And Rising*, though other credits included the **Fine Young Cannibals**. His other notable productions included the anti-crack 'You Still Smoking That Shit?', and 'Don't Let Your Mouth Write A Check That Your Ass Can't Cash'. He set up his own Doo Dew label in the 90s, with signings including Resident Alien. However, by 1994 the contract with the label's sponsors had turned sour and

he embarked instead on a collaboration with old-Stetsasonic hand Fruitkwan as part of the rap super group **Gravediggaz**.

Prince, Harold

b. 30 January 1928, New York, USA. A distinguished director and producer - the supreme Broadway showman - whose career has lasted for nearly 40 years, and is still going strong. Prince served his theatrical apprenticeship in the late 40s and early 50s with the esteemed author, director, and producer **George Abbott**. In 1954, he presented his first musical, *The Pajama Game*, in collaboration with Robert Griffith and Frederick Brisson. His association with Griffith continued until the latter's death in 1961, mostly with hits such as *Damn Yankees*, *New Girl In Town*, *West Side Story*, and *Fiorello!* (1959). *Tenderloin* (1960) was a disappointment, as was Prince's first assignment as a director, *A Family Affair* (1962). From then on, he has been the producer or co-producer and/or director for a whole range of (mostly) successful musicals such as *A Funny Thing Happened On The Way To The Forum* (1962), *She Loves Me* 1963), *Fiddler On The Roof* (1964), *Baker Street* (1965), *Flora, The Red Menace* (1965), *It's A Bird, It's A Plane, It's Superman* (1966), *Cabaret* (1966), *Zorba* (1968), *Company* (1970), *Follies* (1971), *A Little Night Music* (1973), *Candide* (1974), *Pacific Overtures* (1976), *On The Twentieth Century* (1978), *Evita* (1978), *Sweeney Todd* (1979), *Merrily We Roll Along* (1981), *A Doll's Life* (1982), *Grind* (1985), *The Phantom Of The Opera* (1986), *Roza* (1987), and *Kiss Of The Spider Woman* (1992). The list does not include re-staging and directing the original productions in several different countries, nor his work with American opera companies such as the New York Opera, the Houston Opera, and the Chicago Lyric Opera. For his innovative concepts, the ability to find the exact visual framework for the musical-narrative content, and his role, notably with **Stephen Sondheim**, in the drastic reshaping of the modern theatre musical, Prince has received more **Tony Awards** than anyone else. The latest came in 1995 for his superb direction of the Broadway revival of *Show Boat*.

Further reading: *Contradictions*, Harold Prince. *Harold Prince And The American Musical Theatre*, Foster Hirsch. *From Pajama Game To The Phantom Of The Opera And Beyond*, Carol Ilson.

Princess Pang

This New York-based rock quintet was formed in 1986 around the nucleus of Jeni Foster (vocals), Ronnie Roze (bass) and Brian Keats (drums). The line-up was finally completed a year later by the addition of guitarists Jay Lewis and Andy Tyernon. Signing to Metal Blade Records, they were introduced to Ron St. Germain (of

Bad Brains fame) who eventually handled the production of their debut. Released in 1989, it was a gutsy hard rock album, full of tales of New York's low-life. Foster, with her aggressive delivery, drew comparisons to **Guns N' Roses**' Axl Rose, though the band failed to capitalise on the attentive press they initially received.

Album: *Princess Pang* (Roadrunner 1989).

Princess Theatre Musicals

A short but legendary series of significant musical productions presented at the tiny 299-seater house in New York in the period leading up to the Roaring Twenties. The Princess Theatre was built in 1913 at the corner of 39th Street and Sixth Avenue as a home for intimate one-act plays. However, in 1915 the theatre's owner, F. Ray Comstock, decreed that there should be musicals, so **Jerome Kern**, **Guy Bolton** and lyricist Schuyler Greene created *Nobody Home*, which, although it contained several interpolated numbers, was the first of what were subsequently regarded as landmarks in the history of American musical comedy. Instead of the usual old-fashioned, scarcely credible operettas, the new shows were funny and fast-moving, with the stylish, contemporary songs and situations integrated to an extent never attempted before. Kern, Bolton and Greene came together later that year for *Very Good Eddie*, before Schuyler was replaced by **P.G. Wodehouse** and the magic really began. Not straight away though, because the new team considered that it would be inappropriate to add music and lyrics to Charles Hoyt's play, *A Milk White Flag*, and so the third Princess Theatre musical, *Go To It* (1916), had a score by John Golden and Anne Caldwell. However, Kern, Bolton and Wodehouse came into their own with *Oh, Boy!* (1917) and *Oh, Lady! Lady!!* (1918). Another of their shows, *Leave It To Jane* (1917), was also a contender for the Princess Theatre but was unable to play there because *Oh, Boy!* was in residence for over a year. When it was finally withdrawn, Bolton and Wodehouse collaborated with composer Louis Hirsch for *Oh, My Dear!* (1918), and the final show in the Princess series was *Toot Sweet*, a revue with a score by **Richard Whiting** and Raymond B. Egan. Some 75 years later it is hardly credible that just a few small productions had such an influence on the future course of Broadway, and by definition, world musical theatre, but it is said to be so. In later years the Princess Theatre presented straight plays, and was also used for extended periods as a cinema. In 1936 the theatre was re-named the Labor Stage when it was taken over by the International Ladies Garment Workers Union who produced the popular revue *Pins And Needles* there, and was finally demolished in the 50s.

Principal Edwards

This UK group was formed in 1968 at Essex University, England, and originally known as Principal Edwards Magic Theatre. The artistic hippie co-operative revolved around Belinda 'Bindy' Borquin (vocals/recorder/violin/piano), Root Cartwright (guitar/mandolin/recorder) and David Jones (percussion) who were initially joined by Jeremy Ensor (bass) and vocalists Martin Stellman, Monica Nettles and Vivienne McAuliffe. Numerous dancers, technicians and stage hands took the line-up number into double figures and, having recorded *Soundtrack* for **John Peel**'s Dandelion label, the group abandoned university to establish a commune. *The Asmoto Running Band*, produced by **Pink Floyd** drummer Nick Mason, preceded an ambitious season at London's Hampstead Theatre Club. The residency exacerbated an internal dispute over ultimate direction, and the unit disintegrated in December 1971. Bourquin, Cartright and Jones reshaped the group around Nick Pallett (guitar/vocals), Richard Chipperfield-Jones (bass/vocals) and Geoff Nicholls (drums) and, having dropped the 'Magic Theatre' suffix, completed the rock orientated *Round One*, again under the aegis of Mason.

Albums: *Soundtrack* (1969), *The Asmoto Running Band* (1971), *Round One* (1974).

Principle, Jamie

Famed for his breathy, **Smokey Robinson**-styled delivery, USA-born Principle's classic early house recordings were 'Waiting On My Angel' and 'Baby Wants To Ride'. The latter gave this Chicago house master and innovator a hit after a long time in the shadows (although a more or less identical version appeared at the same time from **Frankie Knuckles**). Following 'Rebels' there was a long absence from the nation's dancefloors punctuated only by US tracks 'Cold World' (during a brief liaison with **Atlantic** Records) and 'Date With The Rain' on a **Steve 'Silk' Hurley** compilation. He re-emerged with a US smash in 1991 with 'You're All I've Waited 4', self-written and co-produced with Hurley again.

Prine, John

b. 10 October 1946, Maywood, Illinois, USA. John came from a musical background in that his Grandfather had played with **Merle Travis**. Prine started playing guitar at the age of 14. He then spent time in College, worked as a postman for five years, and spent two years in the Army. He began, around 1970, by singing in clubs in the Chicago area. Prine signed to **Atlantic** in 1971, releasing the powerful *John Prine*. The album contained the excellent Vietnam veteran song 'Sam Stone' with the wonderfully evocative line 'There's a hole in daddy's arm where all the money goes, and Jesus Christ died for nothing I suppose'. Over the years Prine achieved cult status, his songs being increasingly covered by other artists. 'Angel From Montgomery', 'Speed Of The Sound Of Loneliness', and 'Paradise' being three in particular. He was inevitably given the unenviable tag 'the new Dylan' at one stage. His last album for Atlantic, *Common Sense* (produced by **Steve Cropper**) was his only album, to make the US Top 100. Whilst the quality and content of all his work has been quite excellant his other albums only scratched the US Top 200. His first release for **Asylum**, *Bruised Orange*, was well received, but the follow up, *Pink Cadillac*, was not so well accommodated by the public or the critics. However, *The Missing Years* changed everything with massive sales at home, and a Grammy nomination, making Prine almost a household name. His outstanding songs had been covered by the likes of **Bonnie Raitt**, and **John Denver**, over the years, and his career would appear to have taken on a new lease of life in the 90s. Prine presented *Town And Country* for Channel 4 Television in 1992, a series of music programmes featuring singers such as **Nanci Griffith**, and **Rodney Crowell**. In keeping with his career upswing *The Missing Years* is a faultless work containing some of his strongest songs in many years.

Albums: *John Prine* (1971), *Diamonds In The Rough* (1972), *Sweet Revenge* (1973), *Common Sense* (1975), *Bruised Orange* (1978), *Pink Cadillac* (1979), *Storm Windows* (1980), *Aimless Love* (1986), *German Afternoons* (1987), *John Prine Live* (1988), *The Missing Years* (1992), *Live* (1993). Compilations: *Prime Prine* (1976), *Anthology: Great Days* (Rhino 1994).

Prior, Maddy

A dedicated and thoroughly professional performer who worked as a roadie for **Rev. Gary Davis** during the 60s folk scene, Prior went on to form a successful duo with the traditionalist, Tim Hart. Both were absorbed into **Steeleye Span** in 1969, and Prior quickly became the group's focal point and ambassador. When Steelye Span disbanded in 1978, she signed to **Chrysalis**, and launched her solo career with *Woman In The Wings* and *Changing Winds*. Both albums contained several 'historical ballads' written by Prior herself. After an unsuccessful tour, for which she was backed by several prominent musicians, she worked with a basic four piece unit, which included her husband Rick Kemp (bass), and former Steeleye Span drummer, Nigel Pegrum. During the 80s, she also sang with the re-formed Steeleye Span. Her songs became more intimate and rootsy, and, with her backing group, the Answers, she recorded the poppy, *Going For Glory*, which included work with the **Eurythmics**, and Kemp's impressive 'Deep In The Darkest Night'. Prior's schedule involved television, a cappella folk concerts, world tours with Steeleye Span (she was the last original member), and smaller gigs with Kemp. In 1984, a broadcast with the early music specialists, the Carnival Band, led to three mutual albums of richly varied music, and annual tours. With Rick Kemp, she recorded *Happy Families*, a loose, swinging album, featuring his guitar playing. Just after its release, he was forced into temporary retirement because of an arm injury. Prior was subsequently accompanied by a 'jazz/shuffle' unit, and later toured with the sympathetic Nick Holland on keyboards, rediscovering much of her early influences. Of her own Radio 2 series *In Good Voice*, she says: 'I sit there and play all this wonderful music, and then tell people why I like it. Can you think of a better job?'. Prior remains one of the most diverse characters on the folk scene.

Albums: *Woman In The Wings* (1978), *Changing Winds* (1978), *Hooked On Winning* (1981), *Going For Glory* (1983), *Happy Families* (1990), *Year* (1993). With the Carnival Band: *Tapestry Of Carols* (1986), *Sing Lustily & With Good Courage* (1986), *Carols & Capers* (1991).

Priority Records

A record company which was stablished in 1985, originally to piece together compilation records, Priority has established itself in the intervening period as one of America's most pre-eminent rap stable. Former **Captiol** employee Bryan Turner (b. Canada), the label's president, acknowledges the hit-and-miss nature of their business plan: We didn't sit down and decide to have a rap label, it just sort of happened. Rap was exciting - it was music that kids really wanted'. However, the label has never been strictly a one-genre affair. They still package compilations, and alongside their high-profile hip hop acts, who have included **NWA**, **Ice-T** (following his departure from **Warners**) and **Ice Cube**, their most recent signings include **Carole King**. However, they would lose their deal with **Eazy-E**'s **Ruthless** nest when their contract expired in 1993, allowing the latter to move to **Relativity** Records.

Selected albums: NWA: *Straight Outta Compton* (Ruthless/Priority 1988). Ice Cube: *Amerikkka's Most Wanted* (Priority 1989).

Prism

This Canadian rock group has always proved difficult to categorize in terms of musical style, and major commercial success has proven similarly elusive. Their most stable line-up comprised Ron Tabak (vocals - replaced by Henry Small in 1981), Lindsay Mitchell (guitar), Al Harlow (bass) and Rocket Norton (drums). Their first two releases on the Ariola label were lightweight pop rock workouts with layered keyboards fills, while *Armageddon* saw the band, now signed to the **Capitol** label, move towards a heavier, grandiose style. with several lengthy compositions. Their next two recordings saw further line-up changes and resulted in a more typical American rock sound, ideal for radio consumption. In the process they found considerable success as a live act on the US circuit. However, just as long-term rewards seemed within reach, Ron Tabak was killed in a car crash during 1984. Prism died with him.

Albums: *Prism* (Ariola 1977), *See Forever Eyes* (Ariola 1978), *Armageddon* (Ariola 1979), *Young And Restless* (Capitol 1980), *Small Change* (Capitol 1981), *Beat Street* (Capitol 1983). Compilation: *The Best Of Prism* (Phonogram 1988).

Prisoners

This mod-influenced group came from the UK's Medway Valley in Kent. Chief songwriter Graham Day (guitar/vocals), Allan Crockford (bass), James 'Jamie' Taylor (Hammond organ) and Johnny Symons (drums) emerged in 1982 with a rough and raucous debut, *A Taste Of Pink*, on their Own Up label. A deal with the Ace Records subsidiary, Big Beat, yielded *The Wisermiserdemelza* in 1983, a far more laid back, considered effort that ranged from powerful, 60s-influenced rock (the single, 'Hurricane') to tranquil ballads. The EP, *Electric Fit*, followed in 1984 and was notable for the excellent 'Melanie'. The band were featured on television's *The Tube* with other Big Beat acts, celebrated on the EP, *Four On Four: Trash On The Tube*, the Prisoners contributing the awesome 'Reaching My Head'. The group were unhappy with the sound on their second album and returned to Own Up for *The Last Fourfathers*, a less slick production, but a more mature offering. It was enough to secure a deal with **Stiff Records**/Countdown, but from the start relations between band and label were poor. Although *In From The Cold* was an impressive album, it was far poppier and cleaner than the Prisoners had wished. Preceded by 'Whenever I'm Gone' (a re-recording from *The Last Fourfathers*), the album was badly promoted and the band, disillusioned with proceedings, split soon after. Aside from two live albums shared with the Milkshakes, there has since been an album's worth of rarities, *Rare And Unissued*. As to the Prisoners themselves, Taylor has since carved out a niche with his originally **Booker T. Jones**-influenced, and now rare groove-inspired, **James Taylor Quartet**. Crockford joined him for a while before re-uniting with Graham Day (after his spell with Milkshakes offshoot, Thee Mighty Caesars) in the Prime Movers. The Prisoners lasting influence can clearly be detected in many of the later Manchester bands, notably the **Charlatans** and the **Inspiral Carpets**, who also utilised the Hammond organ to propel their quasi-psychedelic pop songs.

Albums: *A Taste Of Pink* (Own Up 1982), *The Wisermiserdemelza* (Big Beat 1983), *The Last Fourfathers* (Own Up 1985), with the Milkshakes *The Last Night At The MIC Club* (Empire 1986), *In From The Cold* (54321 Countdown 1986), *Milkshakes V Prisoners Live* (Media Burn 1987). Compilations: *Revenge Of The Prisoners* (Pink Dust 1984), *Rare And Unissued* (Hangman 1988).

Private Lives

This UK group was originally formed in 1980 and featured John Adams (vocals/drums), Rick Lane (keyboards) and John Reed (bass). They signed to **Chrysalis** and gained a strong live following, but poor record sales precipitated their break-up. In 1984, they re-emerged on **EMI** where Adams, the sole surviving original member, teamed up with Morris Michael (vocals/guitar) and several session musicians. This time a single 'Living In A World' made a minor impression on the UK charts, helped by a support slot on the UK tour of **Hall And Oates**. However, they failed to capitalize on their exposure and were left without a recording contract.

Album: *Prejudice And Pride* (1984).

Privilege

This enigmatic British film starred former **Manfred Mann** vocalist **Paul Jones** as a pop singer who becomes a Christ-like figure following a highly-successful, but contentious, publicity campaign. Written by Johnny Speight, later famed for the television series *Till Death Us Do Part*, *Privilege* was directed by the controversial Peter Watkins, creator of *The War Game*, a chilling view of Britain following nuclear war, banned by the BBC. Watkins' political leanings doubtlessly attracted him to the underlying theme of manipulation permeate this feature, but such ambitions were only partially realised. Segments of *Privilege* were genuinely powerful, particularly when Jones is manacled and jailed onstage by authoritarian figures. Yet where the singer copes well with his role, co-star Jean Shrimpton, famed as a model, is an unconvincing actress. The cast also featured George Bean, a former protégé of **Rolling Stones**' manager **Andrew Loog Oldham**. The soundtrack for *Privilege* was composed by Mike Leander, who later scored success as musical director for **Gary Glitter**. Although the attendant album did not chart, Paul Jones enjoyed a Top 5 hit single with one of the songs from the film, 'I've Been A Bad, Bad, Boy'. Such success, however, did not help the fate of *Privilege*, which is now viewed only as a period-piece curio.

Privin, Bernie

b. 12 February 1919, New York City, New York, USA. A self-taught musician, by his late teens Privin was playing trumpet professionally in dance bands and quickly graduated to some of the best big bands of the swing era, including those of **Bunny Berigan**, **Tommy Dorsey** and **Artie Shaw** (with whom he was featured soloist). In the early 40s he was with **Charlie Barnet** and **Benny Goodman** and during World War II played in **Glenn Miller**'s Army Air

Force band. After the war he made a brief return to Goodman but then entered studio work, where he remained until the late 60s. In later years he worked in Europe, seizing many opportunities to show that despite his advancing years he still retained much of the biting tone that had characterized his earlier work.

Selected albums: *Bernie Privin And His Orchestra* (1956), *The Bernie Privin Quintet In Sweden* (1969). Compilation: with Artie Shaw *Deux Grandes Annees - In The Blue Room/In The Cafe Rouge (1938-39)* (1983).

Pro-Ject X

Very much in the vein of the **Lifers Group** in the USA, Pro-Ject X was started in England in 1994 to allow a musical platform for the inmates of Strangeways prison, Manchester. A soul/hip hop/reggae collective, the idea was formulated by Headley Aylock, an MA student in pop/jazz and the proprietor of Summit Records, alongside Phil Ellis, who has also worked in prisons in East Anglia. In 1994 he organised the first Pro-Ject X gig alongside the BBC Philharmonic Orchestra. The rest of the group were all prisoners and included Andy Miller and Mark Beckett (both serving six years on separate armed robbery offences), Harvey Black (two years for robbery and blackmail) and the two middle-aged front men - Prince Hammer and Prince Marley. Hammer claimed to have preached as a street poet in the Bronx and Jamaica, while Hammer prided himself on being the father of 27 children. With members drawn from tough Manchester areas such as Withenshawe and Moss Side, the group conveyed their concerns to the outside world with a 1995 single, 'The Summit', recorded with **A Guy Called Gerald** and **Justin Robertson**, two highly prominent dance artists with strong personal sympathies for the inmates. The future of the project was limited, however, by the impending release dates for several members.

Pro-Pain

This New York hardcore outfit was assembled by the former **Crumbsuckers** rhythm section of Gary Meskil (bass/vocals) and Dan Richardson (drums) after the demise of their old band. Tom Klimchuck provided the guitars on *Foul Taste Of Freedom*, a full-blooded and aggressive hardcore blast given a brutally heavy sound by producer Alex Perialas, and matched by typically challenging lyrics, an approach which drew **Pantera** and **Biohazard** comparisons. It also impressed **Roadrunner Records** sufficiently to gain the band a deal. However, Klimchuck departed shortly after the release to be replaced by Nick St Dennis, with a second guitarist in Mike Hollman (ex-**Possessed**) added later. Pro-Pain ran into problems over the original cover for *The Truth Hurts*, which depicted a stitched-up female torso after an autopsy, while the inner artwork featured a series of disturbing police photographs of street crime

victims from the early 90s. Despite the fact that the cover was from an art exhibit in a prominent Indiana gallery and that the police photos were public domain, the cover was obscured by a large sticker in the USA, while it was replaced entirely in the UK, with the original available by mail order. The music, meanwhile, had acquired a new groove from the band's touring experience, while Meskil's lyrics remained true to his roots, with the social decay in his Long Island home a favourite subject.

Albums: *Foul Taste Of Freedom* (Energy 1992), *The Truth Hurts* (Roadrunner 1994).

Proby, P.J.

b. James Marcus Smith, 6 November 1938, Houston, Texas, USA. This iconoclastic singer spent his early career in Hollywood, recording demos for song publishing houses. Several low-key singles ensued, credited to Jett Powers and a number of bit parts as an actor ensued, before the Proby appellation surfaced on 'So Do I' (1963). 'Powers' had already demonstrated a songwriting talent, his most notable composition being 'Clown Shoes' for **Johnny Burnette** in 1962. The artist came to Britain the following year, at the behest of producer **Jack Good**, to appear on the *Around The Beatles* television special. An ebullient revival of 'Hold Me', originally a gentle ballad, brought Proby a UK Top 3 hit, while the similarly raucous 'Together' reached number 8. Proby completely changed direction following a move to **Liberty Records** and, again, reached the UK Top 10 with a memorable version of 'Somewhere' from *West Side Story*. This record started a series of epic ballads featuring Proby's strong but affected vocal. Both 'I Apologise' (complete with **Billy Eckstine** paraphrasing) and 'Maria' (again from *West Side Story*) became big hits. Proby's biggest hit, however, was with the popular UK press. Following a 'split trousers' incident, Proby was accused of obscenity. He then made an act of regularly splitting his crushed blue velvet jumpsuit. He completed his attire during the mid-60s with a **Tom Jones** wig and black bow tie and baggy nightshirts. Prior to 'Maria' (4 months earlier) his chart career suddenly floundered with **John Lennon** and **Paul McCartney**'s 'That Means A Lot', and although further immaculate productions followed after 'Maria' with 'To Make A Big Man Cry' and the **Righteous Brothers**' sounding 'I Can't Make It Alone', Proby was relegated to the cabaret circuit. Although he continued to record, the press were more interested in his tax problems and subsequent bankruptcy. *Three Week Hero* won retrospective acclaim when the singer's backing group achieved fame as **Led Zeppelin**. In 1970, Proby took the role of Iago in *Catch My Soul*, former mentor Good's rock adaptation of *Othello*. Proby's subsequent work was more sporadic; he appeared on the UK nightclub circuit, played **Elvis Presley** in the stage production *Elvis On Stage* until he was sacked, and continued to court publicity for erratic behaviour. In 1985 he completed two suitably eccentric versions of 'Tainted Love', previously a hit for **Soft Cell** which became the first of a series of contentious singles for a Manchester-based independent label. Recreations of songs by **Joy Division** ('Love Will Tear Us Apart') and **David Bowie** ('Heroes') followed, but further releases were marred by poor production and the artist's often incoherent intonation. Although years of apparent self-abuse has robbed the singer of his powers of old, he retains the ability to enthral and infuriate. In 1993 Proby made an unannounced appearance in **Jack Good**'s *Good Rockin' Tonite* at the Liverpool Empire. Further Proby sightings were made in June 1995 when he began a 15 minute spot during each performance of the London production of the **Roy Orbison** musical *Only The Lonely*.

Albums: *I Am P.J. Proby* (1964), *P.J. Proby* (1965), *P.J. Proby In Twon* (1965), *Enigma* (1966), *Phenomenon* (1967), *Believe It Or Not* (1968), *Three Week Hero* (1969), *I'm Yours* (1973), *The Hero* (1981), *Clown Shoes* (1987). Compilations: as Jet Powers *California License* (1969), *Somewhere* (1975), *The Legendary P.J. Proby At His Very Best* (1986), *The Legendary P.J. Proby At His Very Best, Volume 2* (1987), *Rough Velvet* (1992).

Proclaimers

This Scottish folk duo, who specialized in belligerent harmonies, consisted of identical twins Craig and Charlie Reid from Auchtermuchty. They had an early hit in 1987 with the **Gerry Rafferty** produced 'Letter From America'. Follow-ups included the typically boisterous 'Make My Heart Fly' and 'I'm Gonna Be'. **Pete Wingfield** was brought in to produce *Sunshine On Leith*, after which they took a two-year sabbatical. Writing for the third album was disrupted, however, when they spent much energy and money ensuring that their beloved, debt-ridden Hibernian Football Club did not close down. In common with many fans, they are now shareholders. They reappeared in 1990 with the *King Of The Road* EP. The title track, a cover of the old **Roger Miller** song, came from the film *The Crossing*. Other tracks on the EP, which reached the UK Top 10, included the folk/country classic 'Long Black Veil'. Hit The Highway became a major selling record in the USA where they unexpectedly became hugely popular during 1994.

Albums: *This Is The Story* (1987), *Sunshine On Leith* (1988), *Hit The Highway* (Chrysalis 1994).

Procol Harum

This UK group was formed in Essex, England following the demise of the R&B pop unit, the **Paramounts**, Procol Harum comprised: **Gary Brooker** (b. 29 May 1945, Southend, Essex, England; piano/vocals), Matthew Fisher (b. 7 March 1946, London, England; organ), Bobby Harrison (b. 28 June 1943, East Ham, London, England; drums), Ray Royer (b. 8 October 1945; guitar) and Dave Knights (b. 28 June 1945, Islington, London, England; bass). Their debut with the ethereal 'A Whiter Shade Of Pale' made them one of the biggest successes of 1967. The record has now achieved classic status with continuing sales, which now run to many millions. The long haunting Bach-influenced introduction takes the listener through a sequence of completely surreal lyrics, which epitomized the 'Summer Of Love'. 'We skipped the light fandango, turned cart-wheels across the floor, I was feeling kind of seasick, the crowd called out for more'. It was followed by the impressive Top 10 hit 'Homburg'. By the time of the hastily thrown together album, (only recorded in mono), the band were falling apart. Harrison and Royer departed to be replaced with Brooker's former colleagues Barrie 'B.J.' Wilson (b. 18 March 1947, Southend, Essex, England) and **Robin Trower** (b. 9 March 1945, London, England) respectively. The other unofficial member of the band was lyricist Keith Reid (b. 10 October 1946), whose penchant for imaginary tales of seafaring appeared on numerous albums. The particularly strong *A Salty Dog*, with its classic John Player cigarette pack cover, was released to critical acclaim.

Fisher and Knights departed and the circle was completed when Chris Copping (b. 29 August 1945, Southend, Essex, England; organ/bass) became the last remaining ex-Paramount to join. On *Broken Barricades*, in particular, Trower's **Jimi Hendrix**-influenced guitar patterns began to give the band a heavier image which was not compatible with Reid's introspective fantasy sagas. This was resolved by Trower's departure, to join **Frankie Miller** in Jude, and following the recruitment of Dave Ball (b. 30 March 1950) and the addition of Alan Cartwright (bass), the band pursued a more symphonic direction. The success of *Live In Concert With The Edmonton Symphony Orchestra* was unexpected. It marked a surge in popularity, not seen since the early days. The album contained strong versions of 'Conquistador' and 'A Salty Dog', and was a Top 5, million-selling album in the USA. Further line-up changes ensued with Ball departing and Mick Grabham (ex-**Plastic Penny** and **Cochise**) joining in 1972. This line-up became their most stable and they enjoyed a successful and busy four years during which time they released three albums. *Grand Hotel* was the most rewarding, although both the following had strong moments. 'Nothing But The Truth' and 'The Idol' were high points of *Exotic Birds And Fruit*; the latter showed traces of Keith Reid's epic work. 'Pandora's Box' was the jewel in *Procol's Ninth*, giving them another surprise hit single. By the time their final album was released in 1977 the musical climate had dramatically changed and Procol Harum were one of the first casualties of the punk and new wave movement. Having had a successful innings Gary Brooker initiated

a farewell tour and Procol quietly disappeared. In the words of Keith Reid; 'they fired the gun and burnt the mast'. During 1991 the band re-formed, and unlike many reformed 'dinosaurs' the result was a well-received, album *The Prodigal Stranger*. Silence ensued once again until 1995 when they reformed once again.
Albums: *Procol Harum* (1967), *Shine On Brightly* (1968), *A Salty Dog* (1969), *Home* (1970), *Broken Barricades* (1971), *In Concert With The Edmonton Symphony Orchestra* (1972), *Grand Hotel* (1973), *Exotic Birds And Fruit* (1974), *Procol's Ninth* (1975), *Something Magic* (1977), *The Prodigal Stranger* (1991). Compilations: *The Best Of Procol Harum* (1973), *Platinum Collection* (1981), *Collection: Procol Harum* (1986), *The Early Years* (1993).

Procope, Russell

b. 11 August 1908, New York City, New York, USA, d. 21 January 1981. A neighbour of **Benny Carter**, **Rudy Powell** and **Bobby Stark**, Procope played clarinet and alto saxophone in New York clubs in his late teens and when he was 20 years old recorded with **Jelly Roll Morton**. A year later he was a member of Carter's big band, then was successively with **Chick Webb**, **Fletcher Henderson**, **Tiny Bradshaw**, **Teddy Hill** and **Andy Kirk**. His apprenticeship well and truly served, Procope had to wait until the end of World War II and his army discharge before entering the post for which he had been unconsciously grooming himself. From 1946 until 1974 he was a member of the **Duke Ellington** orchestra, with only a brief aside in the **Wilbur De Paris** band in 1961. After Ellington's death, Procope worked in a number of Ellington-inspired small groups and also in the pit band for the show *Ain't Misbehavin'*. His long spell with Ellington was unspectacular, he was a section man rather than a soloist and as such provided the kind of solid base the Ellington band sometimes lacked when its less reliable members had other things on their minds. When he did solo, on such features as 'Mood Indigo', he revealed a warm and full-toned clarinet style that recalled New Orleans rather than New York.
Selected albums: with Duke Ellington *Masterpieces* (1950), *Russell Procope And His Orchestra* (1956), *Duke Ellington's Seventieth Birthday Concert* (1969). Compilation: *John Kirby And His Orchestra (1941-42)* (1988).

Prodigy

The Prodigy represent the vanguard of the UK's rave scene, and are one of the few collectives operating in these waters not to be cloaked in anonymity. The band, based in Essex, comprised MC Maxim, dancers Keith and Leeroy, plus mastermind Liam Howlett (b. c.1971). Howlett, a former breakdancer and DJ with Cut To Kill, handles most of the compositions and governs the band's style. They began their career with *The Android* EP, which showcased their speeded up hip hop twists (the band are all rap fans). The big time beckoned

when they scored a UK number 3 with 'Charly', a children's public information film sample overlaying a pulsating backbeat. It would start a huge trend of rave singles incorporating signature tunes to popular kids television tunes, notably *The Magic Roundabout, Sesame Street*, etc. More importantly it signified the crossover of rave music from the clubs to the chart. Another side-effect was that the Prodigy were derided by the underground as the group that killed rave: "Charly' did seem a bit corny but all it was was a mad rave record. That's all I set out to do'. They followed up with the equally impressive *G-Force* EP. In 1992 they became, as one magazine put it, 'The only techno outfit with the legs to be able to put together a whole album', though perhaps that comment was a little prejudicial. Certainly Howlett had moved on from the heady days of rave music, dropping some of the breakbeats, and he was now a real force in techno, two strains of music that were originally conceived as oppositional. The single, 'Fire'/'Jericho' also won many fans, the topside utilising the famous opening of **Crazy World Of Arthur Brown**'s 'I am the god of hell fire'. By 1993 he was using MC Keeti to cover the hip hop angle, and built his own home studio in his native Braintree, Essex. He also occupied himself with remixes for **Front 242** and **Jesus Jones**, among several others. Acknowledging his weighty and sometimes unwarranted reputation, he then released 'One Love', putting it out initially on white label only, so that underground DJs, who had foresworn the Prodigy once they had become a chart act, might give it needle time. 1994 saw the release of an accomplished double set which confirmed the group's ability to operate outside of club waters as a standalone music project, and also put on record their response to their numerous critics. The set opened with the words 'So I've decided to take my work back underground, To stop if falling into the wrong hands'. 'Their Law' (which featured a guest appearance from **Pop Will Eat Itself**), maintained links to the rave scene which broke the Prodigy by attacking the Criminal Justice Bill which sought to legislate against such events.
Albums: *The Prodigy Experience* (XL 1992), *Music For The Jilted Generation* (XL 1994, double album).
Further reading: *The Prodigy: Electronic Punks*, Martin Roach.

Production House

London record label set up in 1987 by Phil Fearon, formerly of Brit-funk act **Galaxy,** with help from Laurie Jago. Primarily orientated towards hardcore and rave music, the self-distributed imprint rose to prominence in 1992 via the success of Acen ('Trip II The Moon') and **Baby D** ('Let Me Be Your Fanstasy'), both of which reached the top of the national dance charts and also broke the mainstream listings. Solo artist Acen (b. c.1972, Tottenham, London, England) had been unlucky not to do so previously with 'Close Your Eyes', which sold 25,000 copies without ever entering the charts. In the event 'Trip II To The Moon', Production House's 42nd release, would be the one to bring them their first hit. Other notable signings include the **House Crew** ('Keep The Fire Burning' and 'We Are Hardcore'), Nino ('Future Of Latin', from Terry 'The Chocolate Prince' Jones), Brothers Grimm's ('Field Of Dreams' and 'Exodus' - which sampled **Mike Oldfield**'s 'Tubular Bells') and X Static ('Ready To Go'). A subsidiary outlet, Special Reserve, was also founded to house swingbeat and soul material, beginning with MC Juice's 'Freak In Me'.

Professionals

This UK group was an offshoot from the notorious **Sex Pistols** and featured Paul Cook (drums/vocals) and Steve Jones (guitar/vocals) plus Ray McVeigh (guitar/vocals) and Paul Myers (bass, ex-**Vic Goddard And The Subway Sect**). The band received plenty of press attention thanks to the involvement of Cook and Jones but their debut album proved disappointing. A second album followed, plus a handful of singles, which still could not convince either the critics or the record-buying public that they had anything to offer.

Albums: *The Professionals* (1980), *I Didn't See It Coming* (1981).

Professor Griff

Brought up in Long Island New York along with 13 brothers and sisters, Griff (b. Richard Griffin, Long Island, New York, USA) formed The Universal Revolutionary Freedom Fighters Society (TUFFS) in his youth, providing study groups and martial arts training for young people. It was while he was offering a security service that he first met Chuck D of **Public Enemy**. Griff's CV subsequently included a residency as part of Public Enemy's 'Security Of The First World' team, before, in the best traditions of hip hop, he managed to stoke huge controversy before he ever performed his first rap. As Public Enemy's 'Minister Of Information', Griff went on record to state that the Jewish people were responsible for the majority of the world's wickedness, including the selling of his own race into slavery. The quote's explosive value had little to do with the fact that Griff's historical vision so obviously lacked substance, but it served instead to bring rap right into the mainstream of racial debate, highlighting the danger of allowing a platform to those neither gifted nor educated enough to use it (it is worth noting, however, that Griff inists he was misquoted). His role as Public Enemy's diplomat ended when he was unceremoniously ejected, but Griff persevered with a solo career that has produced music of some note. Fuelled by what many commentators have ascribed as paranoia theory, his second album, after signing with **Luther Campbell**'s record label, revealed tight,

harsh funk backing to his incendiary polemic, backed by his own band, the Asiastic Disciples.

Albums: *Pawns In The Game* (Skywalker 1990), *Kao's II Wiz *7* Dome* (Luke 1991), *Disturb N Tha Peace* (Luke 1992).

Professor Longhair

b. Henry Roeland Byrd, 19 December 1918, Bogalusa, Louisiana, USA, d. 30 January 1980. Byrd grew up in New Orleans where he was part of a novelty dance team in the 30s. He also played piano, accompanying **John Lee 'Sonny Boy' Williamson**. After wartime service, Byrd gained a residency at the Caldonia club, whose owner christened him Professor Longhair. By now, he had developed a piano style that combined rumba and mambo element with more standard boogie-woogie and barrelhouse rhythms. Particularly through his most ardent disciple, **Dr John** Longhair's has become recognised as the most influential New Orleans R&B pianist since **Jelly Roll Morton**. In 1949 he made the first record of his most famous tune, 'Mardi Gras In New Orleans' for the Star Talent label, which credited the artist as Professor Longhair & his Shuffling Hungarians. He next recorded 'Baldhead' for **Mercury** as Roy Byrd and his Blues Jumpers and the song became a national R&B hit in 1950. Soon there were more singles on **Atlantic** (a new version of 'Mardi Gras' and the well-known 'Tipitina' in 1953) and Federal. A mild stroke interrupted his career in the mid-50s and for some years he performed infrequently apart from at Carnival season when a third version of his topical song, 'Go To The Mardi Gras' (1958) received extensive radio play. Despite recording **Earl King**'s 'Big Chief' in 1964, Longhair was virtually inactive throughout the 60s. He returned to the limelight at the first New Orleans Jazz & Heritage Festival in 1971 when, accompanied by **Snooks Eaglin**, he received standing ovations. (A recording of the concert was finally issued in 1987). This led to European tours in 1973 and 1975 and to recordings with **Gatemouth Brown** and for Harvest. Longhair's final album, for Alligator, was completed shortly before he died of a heart attack in January 1980. In 1991 he was posthumously inducted into the Rock 'n' Roll Hall Of Fame.

Selected albums: *New Orleans Piano* (reissue, 1972), *Rock 'N' Roll Gumbo* (1977), *Live On The Queen Mary* (1978), *Crawfish Fiesta* (1980), *The London Concert* (1981), *The Last Mardi Gras* (1982), *Houseparty New Orleans Style* (1987), *Live In Germany* (1993).

Further reading: *A Bio-discography*, John Crosby.

Proffitt, Frank

b. Frank Noah Proffitt, 1913, Laurel Bloomery, Tennessee, USA, d. 24 November 1965. Proffitt was a tobacco farmer, part-time carpenter, singer, guitarist, banjo player, dulcimer player and song collector. He is

mainly remembered for 'Tom Dooley' made popular by the **Kingston Trio** and **Frank Warner**. This song appears on *Frank Proffitt Of Reese, North Carolina*, and was 'collected' by Frank Warner from Proffitt in 1938. It was only one of over a hundred songs that the Warners collected from Proffitt. During lean times on the farm, he worked in a spark plug factory, in Toledo, Ohio, and even on road construction. He also made and sold mountain dulcimers and fretless banjos. Proffitt's acknowledged importance lies in his collection of the traditional material of America, in particular North Carolina. Many of the songs were picked up from his father, Wiley Proffitt, and his aunt Nancy Prather. Many were sung while working in the fields, and Frank absorbed all that he heard. His first public appearance was at the First Annual Folk Festival in Chicago. This had been brought about by the publicity that had accompanied the success of the Kingston Trio's recording of 'Tom Dooley'. *Frank Proffitt Of Reese, North Carolina*, was recorded at his home during the winter of 1961 by Sandy Paton. Considering his importance, it is surprising that Proffitt contributed only 11 songs to the *Frank C. Brown Collection Of North Carolina Folklore*. He died on Thanksgiving Day, 1965. In addition to his own recordings for Folk Legacy, Proffitt also contributed a number of tracks, in particular 'Cumberland Gap' and 'Satan, Your Kingdom Must Come Down', to a compilation album, *High Atmosphere - Ballads And Tunes From Virginia And North Carolina* (1974).
Albums: *Frank Proffitt Sings Folk Songs* (1961), *Frank Proffitt Of Reese, North Carolina* (1962), *North Carolina Songs And Ballads* (1962), *Memorial Album* (1969).

Profile Records

One of the earliest of hip hop labels, formed in 1981 in New York by Steve Plotnicki and Cory Robbins with a loan from their parents of $70,000. The catalogue began with a single by **Grace Kennedy**, before their second release, and first rap record, 'Young Ladies' by Lonnie Love. They were down to the last $2,000 of their parents' investment when they scored their first hit, with 'Genius Rap' by **Dr. Jeckyll and Mr. Hyde** (namely Andre Harrell, now president of Uptown Enterpises, and Alonzo Brown, who was also 'Lonnie Love', respectively). Another significant benchmark was **Run DMC**'s 'Sucker MCs' 1983 cut, a ruffhouse hit which helped to establish the 'new school' tradition, as well as enlarging rap's vocabulary. Run DMC continued to provide the label with their greatest successes throughout the decade. In January 1994 Plotnicki bought out Robbins to take sole ownership of the label.
Selected albums: Run DMC: *Raising Hell* (Profile 1986). Special Ed: *Youngest In Charge* (Profile 1989). Poor Righteous Teachers: *Holy Intellect* (Profile 1990). Various: *Diggin' In The Crates Volume One* (Profile 1994).

Profit, Clarence

b. 26 June 1912, New York City, New York, USA, d. 22 October 1944. By his late teenage years, Profit had played piano with several bands, small and large, performed with **Edgar Sampson**, a school friend, and formed his own big band. In 1930 he joined **Teddy Bunn**, touring and playing residencies in various Caribbean locations, but by the middle of the decade was resident in New York as leader of a trio. It was a format which best suited his powerful stride piano style and the next few years saw him achieve a substantial measure of popularity. Before he could take full advantage of the public's liking for his piano-bass-guitar line-up, he died in 1944.
Selected compilations: *Complete 1939-40* (Meritt 1988), *Solo And Trio Sides* (Memoir 1993).

Promises, Promises

Although they had previously enjoyed enormous success writing popular songs, and music for television shows and films, *Promises, Promises* was the first Broadway musical with a score by **Burt Bacharach** and **Hal David**. The show, which opened at the Shubert Theatre in New York on 1 December 1968, was adapted by Neil Simon from the successful Billy Wilder film *The Apartment* (1960). The story follows the tormented love affair of Chuck Baxter (Jerry Orbach), a clerk who achieves promotion by renting his room to his bosses for their extra-marital affairs. In the course of his career rise, Chuck learns that one of these 'temporary tenants', J. D. Sheldrake (Edward Winter), is having an affair with Fran Kubelik (Jill O'Hara), the girl he loves. Marian Mercer, A. Larry Haines, Paul Reed, Dick O'Neill. and Norman Shelly, were also among the strong cast which included the future Broadway star Donna McKechnie. The score contained many delightful songs, including 'Whoever You Are', 'Knowing When To Leave', 'You'll Think Of Something', 'Wanting Things', 'Upstairs', 'She Likes Basketball', 'Our Little Secret', and 'I'll Never Fall in Love Again', which became a hit for **Dionne Warwick** in the US, and was a UK number 1 for **Bobby Gentry**. *Promises, Promises* won **Tony Awards** for best actor (Orbach) and supporting actress (Mercer), and ran for a remarkable 1,281 performances. **Betty Buckley**, Anthony Roberts, and James Congdon starred in the 1969 London production which was in residence at the Prince of Wales Theatre for well over a year, a total of 560 performances. Evan Pappas led a well received 1993 revival at the Goodspeed Opera House, Connecticut, and a year later, 60s pop star-turned jazz singer **Helen Shapiro** co-starred with Christopher Ryan when the show was presented briefly at London's Bloomsbury Theatre.

Prong

This US thrash-hardcore rock trio was formed in the mid-80s. Hailing from New York's Manhattan lower east side, the band comprised Tommy Victor (vocals/guitar), Mike Kirkland (vocals/bass) and Ted Parsons (drums), and caused an immediate stir with their first release on the independent Spigot label. Emotionally angry, lyrically brutal, Prong partnered a relentless assault with some fierce guitar-riffing. Their second album for **Epic Records**, *Prove You Wrong*, in 1991, was their most significant work to date. By the advent of *Cleansed* the group had expanded to a four-piece. First they had added ex-**Flotsam & Jetson** bass player Tony Gregory, before recruiting **Killing Joke** musician Raven, who had previously worked with the band on their *Whose Fist Is It Anyway* remix EP. John Bechdel of **Murder Inc.** additionally expanded the band's sound with his programming and sampling skills.

Albums: *Primitive Origins* (Spigot 1987), *Force Fed* (Spigot 1988), *Beg To Differ* (Epic 1990), *Prove You Wrong* (Epic 1991), *Cleansed* (Epic 1994).

Propaganda

This Euro pop/synthesizer band left their native Germany to arrive in England in 1983. Comprising Claudia Brücken (ex-Eggolinos; vocals), Michael Mertens (ex-Dusseldorf Symphony Orchestra; percussion), Susanne Freytag and Ralf Dorper (keyboards), they found an early advocate in Paul Morley of **ZTT Records**. Their first release, 'Dr. Mabuse', rallied well in the UK charts, reaching number 27. However, due to the label, and Trevor Horn's commitment to **Frankie Goes To Hollywood**, the follow-up would not be released until over a year later. 'Duel'/'Jewel' was more successful still as Brücken moved permanently to England to wed Morley. The group's first live performance in June 1985 saw their line-up bolstered by Derek Forbes (ex-**Simple Minds**) on bass and Steve Jansen (ex-**Japan**, brother of **David Sylvian**) on drums. *A Secret Wish* and the single from it, 'P-Machinery', emerged a month later. Their European tour saw another line-up shuffle with Brian McGee (also ex-Simple Minds) taking over drums, and Kevin Armstrong on guitar, alongside Brücken, Mertens, Freytag and Forbes. Dorper had departed on the advent of the tour, and eventually only Mertens remained from the original line-up. They became involved in a huge legal battle with ZTT, and Brücken decided to stay with her husband's label. She formed Act with Thomas Leer in 1987. When the litigation had finished in 1988 the new Propaganda line-up featured Besti Miller, an American expatriate based in Germany on vocals. They released *1-2-3-4* in 1990, with contributions from old hands Freytag and Dorper, as well as **Howard Jones** and **David**

Gilmour. Meanwhile, Brücken had embarked on a solo career.

Albums: *A Secret Wish* (1985), *1-2-3-4* (1990). Solo: Claudia Brücken *Love; And A Million Other Things* (1991).

Prophet, Chuck

US-born guitarist Prophet first attracted attention in March 1983 on joining Los Angeles band **Green On Red**. His exciting, highly skilled, technique added a new dimension to this already excellent group, although critics initially dubbed his work derivative of **Neil Young**. Successive releases by the group have established Prophet as one of the era's finest musicians, whose skills have been enhanced through jams with the cream of San Francisco's rock fraternity. In 1990 the artist released *Brother Aldo*, a largely country-rock selection. This superior set featured several vocal duets with Stephanie Finch and included support from R&B pianist **Spooner Oldham** and **Durocs**' drummer Scott Matthews. Prophet's guitar work was, however, also prominent, particularly on 'Scarecrow', the album's most intense offering.

Albums: *Brother Aldo* (1990), *Balinese Dancer* (1992).

Prophet, Michael

b. Michael George Haynes, 1957, Kingston, Jamaica, West Indies. Prophet's singular crying vocal style was first heard in 1977 when he was discovered by Vivian '**Yabby You**' Jackson, who took him to **Channel One** for his debut, 'Praise You Jah Jah', written some five years earlier. 'Fight It To The Top' was his first hit. With Yabby he made several highly regarded roots albums inevitably featuring the Gladiators in support and mixed by either **Scientist** or **King Tubby**, **Island** releasing *Serious Reasoning* in 1980.

By then Prophet had left for **Henry 'Junjo' Lawes**, who successfully steered him towards **dancehall** popularity. 'Gunman', voiced in response to the violent Jamaican elections of that year, becoming his biggest ever hit. After two albums with Lawes he freelanced with varying results; recording *Blood Stain* for Satta Blue and tunes for Don Mais, Al Campbell, **Sugar Minott**, **Winston 'Niney' Holness**, **Soul Syndicate**, **Winston Riley** and others. All helped maintain his presence throughout the early 80s. By 1986 he was recording for Delroy Wright's Live & Learn label then left Jamaica for Miami, where he briefly voiced for Skengdon. In 1988 he moved to England and within two years had teamed up with former Stur-Mars and Coxsone Outernational DJ, Ricky Tuffy. Their debut single, 'Your Love', was a number 1 hit in 1990 and preceded the best-selling *Get Ready* album for Brixton label Passion a year later. The self-produced *Bull Talk* was released in 1993. Since then Prophet has recorded solo singles with a variety of UK producers including **General Saint**, Ruff Cutt and Lloydie Crucial. He remains one of the most enduring singers to emerge from the roots era.

Selected albums: *Serious Reasoning* (Island 1980), *Righteous Are The Conqueror* (Greensleeves 1980), *Michael Prophet* (Greensleeves 1981), *Love Is An Earthly Thing* (CSA 1983), *Blood Stain* (Satta Blue 1984), *Cease Fire* (Move 1985), *Settle Yu Fe Settle* (Live & Love 1986), *Certify* (Burning Sounds 1988), *Get Ready* (Greensleeves 1991), *Bull Talk* (Greensleeves 1993). With Half Pint: *Joint Favourites* (Greensleeves 1986). Compilation: *Gunman* (Greensleeves 1991, comprises *Righteous Are Conqueror* and *Michael Prophet*).

Prophet, Ronnie

b. 26 December 1937, Calumet, Quebec, Canada. Prophet, whose second cousin is Canadian country singer, Orvel Prophet, was raised on a farm but spent his adolescence playing clubs in Montreal. In the late 60s Ronnie, deciding that this Prophet needed more than honour in his own country, established himself at the Carousel Club in Nashville. With his comedy and impressions, he stood apart from other country performers. **Chet Atkins** called him 'the greatest one-man show I've seen' and Prophet himself comments, 'I believe that if an audience goes to a live show, then they should get a *live* show. I'm irritated by artists who are walking jukeboxes.' In truth, Prophet has not had enough country hits to be a walking jukebox, and he has only had five minor successes on the US country charts - 'Sanctuary' (number 26), 'Shine On' (number 36). His serious records resemble **Conway Twitty** at his most mannered. In 1978, Prophet was a major success in the UK at the Wembley Country Music Festival, which led to further appearances, UK tours and his own television programmes. Although he is an excellent MC, Prophet has not sustained his popularity, possibly because 'Harry The Horny Toad' and 'The Phantom Of The Opry' wear thin.

Albums: *Ronnie Prophet Country* (1976), *Ronnie Prophet* (1977), *Just For You* (1978), *Faces And Phrases* (1980), *Audiograph Alive* (1982), *I'm Gonna Love Him Out Of You* (1983), *Ronnie Prophet And Glory-Anne* (80s), *Ronnie Prophet* (1987).

Protheroe, Brian

b. Salisbury, Wiltshire, England. This showbusiness jack-of-all-trades was a trainee laboratory technician, moonlighting in a provincial folk group, before becoming a professional thespian. Earnings as a recording artist were an adjunct to those in repertory acting, but his mid-70s albums were more pleasant and less coyly self-centred than those of others more famous who had cornered the student bedsit market. The title track of *Pinball* - wracked flashes of London's Soho low-life - was his only UK hit. Backed on record by Barry Morgan (drums) and Brian Odgers (bass), Protheroe was a proficient guitarist and pianist, and a tuneful vocalist both in the studio - and onstage as shown by his success in 1976's West End rock musical *Leave Him To Heaven*. He has also appeared as 'Macheath' in a London production of John Gay's *The Beggar's Opera* in 1980, and, later, in Dublin, Eire as 'Captain Von Trapp' in **The Sound Of Music**. He has also composed music for many pantomimes at his local Stratford East theatre. By the 90s, he was better known as an excellent actor appearing in British television drama appearances which included leading roles in *Not A Penny More Not A Penny Less*, *Shrinks* and *Natural Lies*. He has also been seen in films, notably *Superman* and *A Nightingale Sang In Berkeley Square*.

Albums: *Pinball* (1974), *Pick Up* (1975), *I/You* (1976).

Provine, Dorothy

b. 20 January 1937, Deadwood, South Dakota, USA. An actress and singer who made a number of films in the late 50s and early 60s, including *The Bonnie Parker Story*, *It's A Mad Mad Mad Mad World*, *That Darn Cat*, *The Great Race*, *One Spy Too Many* and *Kiss The Girl And Make Them Die*, but gained her greatest success on television. She played opposite Rex Reason in *The Roaring Twenties* which ran for 45 episodes on the 1960-61 season. Her depiction of the singing, dancing flapper was outstanding, and her interpretations of songs of the era led to her making a number of briefly popular records, including 'Don't Bring Lulu', 'Crazy Words Crazy Tune', and the catchy 'Frankfurter Sandwiches'. By the late 60s, her film career had stalled and she drifted from public view.

Album: *The Roaring 20s* (1961).

Pruett, Jeanne

b. Norma Jean Bowman, 30 January 1937, Pell City, Oklahoma, USA. Pruett, one of 10 children, used to listen to the *Grand Ole Opry* with her parents and she harmonized with her brothers and sisters. She married Jack Pruett and, in 1956, they settled in Nashville where he became **Marty Robbins**' long-standing lead guitarist. She wrote several songs for Robbins, and 'Count Me Out' was a US country hit in 1966. After some unsuccessful records for **RCA**, she made the US country charts with 'Hold On To My Unchanging Love' for **Decca** in 1971. It was followed by a country number 1 in 1973, 'Satin Sheets', which was also a US pop hit. Another Top 10 country single, 'I'm Your Woman', was on the charts at the same time as a Robbins' single she had written, 'Love Me'. (After Robbins' death, a duet version of the same song was also a country hit.) Although she did not repeat the success of 'Satin Sheets', she generated interest in 1979 with 'Please Sing Satin Sheets For Me'. Although she regularly appears at *Grand Ole Opry*, Pruett has never been fully committed to her career as she values her home life and is a prize cook and gardener.

Albums: *Love Me* (1972), *Satin Sheets* (1973), *Welcome To The Sunshine* (1974), *Honey On His Hands* (1975), *Encore*

(1980), *Country* (1982), *Star Studded Nights* (1982), *Audiograph Alive* (1983), *Stand By Your Man* (1984), *Jeanne Pruett* (1985).

Pryor, Snooky

b. James Edward Pryor, 15 September 1921, Lambert, Mississippi, USA. After settling in Chicago in 1945 after US Army service, Pryor joined the Maxwell Street group of blues singers which included **Johnny Young**, **Floyd Jones** and **Moody Jones**, with whom he recorded in 1948. Their records were harbingers of the amplified downhome sound of post-war Chicago blues, although at this time Pryor's singing and harmonica were heavily influenced by **John Lee 'Sonny Boy' Williamson**. Pryor made his first record, 'Telephone Blues' with guitarist Moody Jones in 1949. There were later singles for J.O.B. ('Boogy Fool' 1950), Parrot (1953), Blue Lake (1954) and **VeeJay Records** ('Someone To Love Me' 1956). During the 50s Pryor also frequently toured the South. After making the dance novelty 'Boogie Twist', Pryor left the music business in 1963 but returned in the early 70s, touring and recording in Europe in 1973. A 1974 album was made with a New Orleans rhythm section including guitarist Justin Adams. In recent years he has benefited from the revived interest in blues, recording his 1992 album for Texas label Antone's.
Albums: *Snooky Pryor* (1969), *Snooky Pryor And The Country Blues* (1973), *Do It If You Want To* (1973), *Homesick James And Snooky Pryor* (1974), *Shake Your Moneymaker* (1984), *Too Cool To Move* (1992), with Johnny Shines *Back To The Country* (1993).

Prysock, Arthur

b. 2 January 1929, Spartanburg, South Carolina, USA. After singing with a number of small bands, in 1945 Prysock joined **Buddy Johnson**, with whom he appeared at many Harlem clubs and ballrooms. Subsequently, he worked as a soloist, recording for numerous small labels. In 1964 he broke into the big time via a recording contract with Verve and record dates with **Count Basie**'s orchestra. He had some success thereafter, performing at Carnegie Hall in 1966 and hosting his own television show. Although not a jazz singer in the real sense, Prysock has a broad vocal sound and his deep voice sometimes resembles **Billy Eckstine**, some of whose hits he covered. He also sang R&B and it might well be that his eclecticism has harmed his wider acceptance.
Albums: *Coast To Coast* (1963), *A Portrait Of Arthur Prysock* (1963), *Everlasting Songs For Everlasting Lovers* (1964), *A Double Header For Arthur Prysock* (1965), *Arthur Prysock/Count Basie* (1965), *Art & Soul* (1966), *Love Me* (1967), *To Love Or Not To Love* (1967), *Love Me* (1967), *Arthur Prysock* i (1968), *I Must Be Doing Something Right/Funny Thing* (1968), *This Is My Beloved* (1968), *Arthur Prysock* ii (1969), *Where The Soul Trees Grow* (1969),

Arthur Prysock iii (1970), *All My Life* (1977), *A Rockin' Good Way* (1985), *This Guy's In Love With You* (1986).

Prysock, Wilbert 'Red'

b. 2 February 1926, Greensboro, North Carolina, USA. After attempting to learn piano, organ, clarinet and trumpet, Prysock received a tenor saxophone from his sister for his 17th birthday. He learned to play the instrument during his military service during World War II. Prysock turned professional upon his demobilization in 1947 and joined **Tiny Grimes**' Rocking Highlanders, with whom he recorded for the fledgling **Atlantic Records**. He left them in 1950 to join **Roy Milton**'s Solid Senders before finding fame with **Tiny Bradshaw**'s band and such recordings as 'Soft', 'Off And On' and 'Free For All' (which became known as 'Go, Red, Go') on King Records. Prysock formed his own band in 1953, after experimenting with three releases on **Bobby Robinson**'s Red Robin label, Prysock was signed by **Mercury** the following year for whom he notched up many big sellers, among them 'Hand Clappin'', 'Jump, Red, Jump' and 'Finger Tips'. He played with the **Alan Freed** Big Band, backing all the top rock 'n' roll artists of the 50s, and was able to switch styles with the advent of soul music in the 60s, recording for King and **Chess** and supporting many of the era's big names. In 1971, Red teamed up with his famous elder brother, **Arthur Prysock**, and they continue touring and performing together - the sax and the voice.
Selected albums: *Rock 'N' Roll* (1956, reissued 1988), *Cryin' My Heart Out* (1983).

Psychedelic Furs

Until the recruitment of a drummer (Vince Ely) in 1979, Richard Butler (b. 5 June 1956, Kingston-upon-Thames, Surrey, England; vocals), Roger Morris (guitar), ex-Photon John Ashton (b. 30 November 1957; guitar), Duncan Kilburn (woodwinds) and Tim Butler (b. 7 December 1958; bass) had difficulties finding work. The group were also dogged by an unprepossessing sullenness in interview, an equally anachronistic group name - inspired by the 1966 **Velvet Underground** track, 'Venus In Furs' - and Richard Butler's grating one-note style. It was not until a session on **John Peel**'s BBC Radio 1 programme that they were invested with hip credibility - and a **CBS Rcords** recording contract. Under **Steve Lillywhite**'s direction, their bleak debut album was followed by minor singles chart entries with 'Dumb Waiter' and 'Pretty In Pink', both selections from 1981's more tuneful and enduring *Talk Talk Talk*. Creeping even closer to the UK Top 40, 'Love My Way' was the chief single from *Forever Now*, produced in the USA by **Todd Rundgren**. On replacing Ely with Philip Calvert (ex-**Birthday Party**) in 1982, the outfit traded briefly as just 'the Furs' before *Mirror Moves* bore a UK Top 30 hit with 'Heaven' (which was underpinned with a fashionable disco rhythm). Lucrative too were 'Ghost In You' and a re-recording of 'Pretty In Pink' for inclusion on 1986's film of the same title. That same year, they appeared at the mammoth Glastonbury Fayre festival - which, to many of their fans, remains the most abiding memory of the Psychedelic Furs as performers. By 1990, Ashton, the Butler brothers and hired hands were all that remained of a band that had become mostly a studio concern. Three years later the band were just a very fond memory, with Richard Butler moving on to recapture 'the spark of surprise' with new outfit, Love Spit Love.

Albums: *Psychedelic Furs* (Columbia 1980), *Talk Talk Talk* (Columbia 1981), *Forever Now* (Columbia 1982), *Mirror Moves* (Columbia 1984), *Midnight To Midnight* (Columbia 1987), *Book Of Days* (Columbia 1989), *World Outside* (Columbia 1991). Compilations: *All Of This And Nothing* (Columbia 1988), *The Collection* (CBS 1991).

Psychic TV

This somewhat misrepresented UK *avant garde* collective have seen their aural experimentalism overshadowed by their connections with the literary underworld, or simply the underworld itself. They were formed by Genesis P. Orridge (b. c.1950; ex-Pork Dukes and **Throbbing Gristle**) and Peter Christopherson (ex-Throbbing Gristle). The line-up also included P. Orridge's long-term lover, Cosey Fanni Tutti and Geoff Rushton (former editor of *Stabmental* fanzine). However, Christopherson and Rushton soon left to form **Coil**. P. Orridge has been portrayed in much of the media as a deranged and dangerous madman. He had first come to the attention of the media and authorities as the organizer of the 'Prostitution' exhibition at London's ICA gallery in the late 70s. His shock tactics continued with his work in Throbbing Gristle and Psychic TV, and much use was made of fascinating/disturbing slide and film back projection at gigs. Alternatively, Genesis has repeatedly been revealed as a most personable and charming a character as the music industry has thrown up, albeit a little mischievous. P. Orridge takes his inspiration from the works of the Maquis De Sade, Charles Manson and particularly William Burroughs. Burroughs reciprocated the respect, and has stated of Psychic TV that they provide: 'the most important work with communication that I know of in the popular medium'. This is central to the band, and the philosophical congregation which backs them, the Temple Ov Psychick Youth. Their use of guerrilla tactics in the information war follows on from Throbbing Gristle's work, and makes use of broad readings of situationist and deconstructionist thought. P. Orridge's respect for 60s stars **Brian Wilson** and Brian Jones were revealed with two minor UK chart singles in 1986. The surprisingly poppy 'Godstar' celebrated the former

Rolling Stones' guitarist, while the tribute to Wilson was a cover of 'Good Vibrations'. In an ambitious project, from 1986, the group aimed to issue 23 live albums on the 23rd of each month (23 being a statistically, symbolic number), each from a different country from their world tour. After walking out of their deal with **Some Bizarre** (who released their debut single 'Just Driftin') the band no longer involve themselves with the business concerns of music, like promotion. The ranks of the band have been swelled by a variety of members, including John Gosling (ex-Zos Kia), Alex Ferguson (ex-**Alternative TV**), Daniel Black, Matthew Best, Dave Martin and many others. They have also branched out in to other media such as film and literature. (They made available recordings of Burroughs speeches for the first time.) Although the mainstream music press have continually painted a black picture of Psychic TV's music (and activities), it can at times be surprisingly bright and accessible. Conventional *society's* inability to come to terms with Psychic TV's message was demonstrated early in 1992 when police seized videos, books and magazines from Genesis P. Orridge's Brighton home after a performance art video was, it was claimed, shown out of context on a television programme about child abuse. The Orridges reportedly since fled the USA.

Albums: *Force The Hand Of Chance* (1982), *Dreams Less Sweet* (1983), *New York Scum Haters* (1984), *Themes* (1985), *Mouth Of The Night* (1985), *Live In Tokyo* (1986), *Pagan Day* (1987), *Live En Suisse* (1987), *Berlin Atonal, Vol. 1* (1987), *Live In Heaven* (1987), *Live In Reyjavik* (1987), *Live At Gottingen* (1987), *Temporary Temple* (1988), *Live At Mardi Gras* (1988), *Allegory And Self* (1988), *Live At Thee Circus* (1988), *Live In Glasgow* (1989), *Themes 3* (1989), *Live In Paris* (1989), *Live In Toronto* (1989), *Live At The Ritz* (1989), *Live At The Pyramid* (1989), *Kondole/Copycat* (1989), *Towards Thee Infinite Beat* (1990).

Psychick Warriors Ov Gaia

Ethnic trance team from the low countries, often featuring 'organic' live percussion, whose main man is Bobby Reiner. Their debut single, 'Exit 23', appeared in 1991, followed by 'Maenad', both on Belgian label KK. Their most widely-renowned release, however, was 'Obsidian'. They also joined the throngs in the Midi Circus tour. As for their musical ethos, Reiner would note: 'One of our main ideas about making dance music is the deconstruction of old values, deconstruction of what music is about and re-establishing ritual and trance states'. Former member Robert Heyman would go on to form Exquisite Corpse.

Album: *Ov Biospheres And Sacred Grooves (A Document Ov New Edge Folk Classics)*.

Public Enemy

Hugely influential and controversial New York rap act,

frequently referred to as 'The Black **Sex Pistols**'. Public Enemy were initially viewed either as a radical and positive avenging force, or a disturbing manifestation of the guns 'n' violence-obsessed, homophobic, misogynist, anti-Semitic attitudes of a section of the black American ghetto underclass. The group's origins can be traced to 1982 and the Adelphi University, Long Island, New York. There college radio DJ Chuck D (b. Carlton Douglas Ridenhour, 1 August 1960, Roosevelt, Long Island, New York City, USA) and Hank Shocklee were given the chance to mix tracks for the college station, WBAU, by Bill Stephney. Together they produced a collection of aggressive rap/hip hop cuts under the title *Super Special Mix Show* in January 1983. They were eventually joined by **Flavor Flav** (b. William Drayton, 16 March 1959, Roosevelt, Long Island, New York City, USA), who had previously worked alongside Chuck D and his father in their V-Haul company in Long Island, and rang the station incessantly until he too became a host of their show. 1984 saw Shocklee and Chuck D mixing their own basement hip hop tapes, primarily for broadcast on WBAU, which included 'Public Enemy Number 1', from which they took their name. By 1987 they had signed to Rick Rubin's **Def Jam** label (he had first approached them two years earlier) and increased the line-up of the group for musical and visual purposes - **Professor Griff** 'Minister Of Information' (b. Richard Griffin), DJ Terminator X (b. Norman Rogers) and a four-piece words/dance/martial arts back-up section (Security Of The First World). Shocklee and Chuck D were also to be found running a mobile DJ service, and managed Long Island's first rap venue, the Entourage. The sound of Public Enemy's debut, *Yo! Bum Rush The Show*, was characteristically hard and knuckle bare, its title-track a revision of the original 'Public Enemy Number 1' cut. With funk samples splicing **Terminator X**'s turntable sequences, a guitar solo by **Living Colour**'s Vernon Reid (on 'Sophisticated Bitch'), and potent raps from Chuck D assisted by Flav's grim, comic asides, it was a breathtaking arrival. That Public Enemy were not only able to follow-up, but also improve on that debut set with *It Takes A Nation Of Millions To Hold Us Back*, signified a clear division between them and the gangsta rappers. Their nearest competitors, **NWA**, peaked with *Straight Outta Compton*, their idea of progress seemingly to become more simplisticly hateful with each subsequent release. Public Enemy, on the other hand, were beginning to ask questions. And if America's white mainstream audience chose to fear rap, the invective expressed within 'Black Steel In The House Of Chaos', 'Prophets Of Rage' and 'Bring The Noise' gave them excellent cause. That anxiety is cleverly exploited in the title of the band's third set, *Fear Of A Black Planet*. Despite their perceived antagonistic stance, they proved responsive to some criticism, evident in the

necessary ousting of Professor Griff in 1989 for an outrageous anti-Semitic statement made in the US press. He would subsequently be replaced by James Norman, then part-time member **Sister Souljah**. *Fear Of A Black Planet*, their first record without Griff's services, nevertheless makes use of samples of the news conferences and controversy surrounding his statements, enhancing the bunker mentality atmosphere which pervades the project. The 45, '911 Is A Joke', an attack on emergency service response times in ghetto areas, became the subject of a barely credible **Duran Duran** cover version, strangely confirming Public Enemy's mainstream standing. *Apocalypse 91* was almost as effective, the band hardly missing a beat musically or lyrically with black pride cuts like 'I Don't Wanna Be Called Yo Nigga' and 'Bring The Noise', performed with thrash metal outfit **Anthrax**. In September 1990 it was revealed that they actually appeared in an FBI report to Congress examining 'Rap Music And Its Effects On National Security'. Despite their popularity and influence, or perhaps because of it, there remains a large reservoir of antipathy directed towards the band within sections of the music industry (though more thoughtful enclaves welcomed them; Chuck D would guest on **Sonic Youth**'s 1990 album, *Goo*, one of several collaborative projects). Either way, their productions in the late 80s and early 90s have been hugely exciting - both for the torrents of words and the fury of the rhythm tracks, and in the process they have helped to write rap's lexicon. 1988's 'Don't Believe The Hype' has become as powerful a slogan in the late 80s/early 90s as 'Power To The People' was almost 20 years earlier. Similarly, the use of 'Fight The Power' in Spike Lee's 1989 film *Do The Right Thing* perfectly expressed supressed anger at the Eurocentric nature of American culture and history. In recent times several members of the band have embarked on solo careers, while Hank Shocklee and his brother Keith established Shocklee Entertainment in 1993, a production firm and record label. They released their first album in three years in 1994 with *Muse Sick N Hour Message* (Music And Our Message), though touring arrangments were delayed when Terminator X broke both his legs in a motorcycle accident. The album was released on July 4th - American Independence Day. Again it proved practically peerless, with cuts like 'So Watcha Gone Do Now' putting the new breed of gangsta rappers firmly in their place. Public Enemy's legacy extends beyond rap, and has attained a massive cultural significance within black communities. The effect on the consciousness (and consciences) of white people is almost as considerable.

Albums: *Yo! Bum Rush The Show* (Def Jam 1987), *It Takes A Nation Of Millions To Hold Us Back* (Def Jam 1988), *Fear Of A Black Planet* (Def Jam 1990), *Apocalypse '91 The Enemy Strikes Black* (Def Jam 1991), *Muse Sick N Hour*

Mess Age (Def Jam 1994). Compilations: *Greatest Misses* (Def Jam 1992, features six 'new' tracks), *Twelve Inch Mixes* (Def Jam 1993).

Public Image Limited

Public Image Ltd (PiL) was the 'company' formed by John Lydon (b. 31 January 1956, Finsbury Park, London, England) when he left behind both the **Sex Pistols** and previous moniker, Johnny Rotten, in January 1978. With Lydon on vocals, classically trained pianist and early **Clash** guitarist Keith Levene on guitar, reggae influenced bass player **Jah Wobble** (b. John Wordle), and Canadian drummer Jim Walker (ex-Furies), the band were put together with the working title of the Carnivorous Buttock Flies. By the time the debut single - the epic 'Public Image' - was released in its newspaper sleeve in September, they had adopted the less ridiculous name. Their live debut followed in Paris on 14 December, and they played the UK for the first time on Christmas Day. In January 1979 ex-**101ers** and **Raincoats**' drummer Richard Dudanski replaced Walker, who went on to punk band the Straps. The *Metal Box* set came out later that year as a set of 12-inch records housed in tin 'film' cans (it was later re-issued as a normal album). One of the most radical and difficult albums of its era, its conception and execution was a remarkable blend of Lydon's antagonism and Levene's climatic guitar. The single, 'Death Disco', also reached the UK charts. With Dudanski leaving, **Fall** drummer Karl Burns was enlisted until Martin Atkins (b. 3 August 1959, Coventry, England) from Mynd, joined in time to tour the USA in the spring of 1980. A live album, *Paris Au Printemps*, was recorded after which both Wobble and Atkins left. Wobble went on to record solo material and work for London Transport as a train guard while Atkins joined Brian Brain. In May 1981 Lydon and Levene, augmented by hired musicians, played from behind an onstage screen at the New York Ritz. The crowd failed to grasp the concept and 'bottled' the band. After *Flowers Of Romance* Pete Jones (b. 22 September 1957) became bass player, and Atkins returned on drums. Around this time subsidiary members Dave Crowe and Jeanette Lee, who had been with the band since the beginning in business roles, both departed and the group started a new era as Lydon decided to settle in Los Angeles. In 1983 Jones left as the hypnotic 'This Is Not A Love Song' became PiL's Top 5 hit, and Levene also departed as it was climbing the chart. In a relatively quiet period when Lydon collaborated with **Afrika Bambaataa** on the Time Zone single, 'World Destruction', PiL released only the 1984 album *This Is What You Want, This Is What You Get*, and another set of live recordings from foreign fields. Lydon also made his first feature film appearance in *Order Of Death*. They returned to the forefront with 1986's *Album*, from which came 'Single'

aka 'Rise', featuring the drumming talents of **Ginger Baker**. The album included numerous guest/session musicians such as **Steve Vai**, **Ryûichi Sakamoto** and **Tony Williams**. The next year, Lydon assembled a permanent band once again, this time drawing on guitarists John McGeogh (ex-**Magazine**, **Siouxsie And The Banshees**, **Armoury Show**) and Lu Edmunds (ex-**Damned**, **Mekons**, **3 Mustaphas 3**), bass player Allan Dias from America (formerly in nightclub backing bands and working with stars such as **Tyrone Ashley** and the *avant garde* **Sun Ra**), and drummer Bruce Smith (ex-**Pop Group** and various sessions). Lu Edmunds was forced to leave because he was suffering from tinnitus (Ted Chau was a temporary replacement) and Smith left as the band fell into inactivity again after 1988. The three remaining members came back to life in 1990 when **Virgin Records** put out a *Greatest Hits ... So Far* compilation, confidently including the new single 'Don't Ask Me' - Lydon's nod to the environmental problems of the world. After several years and countless line-ups, Lydon has remained the *enfant terrible* of the music industry, a constant irritant and occasional source of brilliance: 'I've learnt to manipulate the music business. I have to deal with all kinds of stupid, sycophantic people. I've just learnt to understand my power. Everyone should learn that, otherwise they lose control'. PiL then recruited new drummer Mike Joyce (ex-**Smiths**, **Buzzcocks**), but Lydon concentrated more on his autobiography and other musical projects (such as the **Leftfield** collaboration, 'Open Up') than PiL in the 90s.

Albums: *Public Image* (Virgin 1978), *Metal Box* (Virgin 1979), *Paris Au Printemps* (Virgin 1980), *Flowers Of Romance* (Virgin 1981), *Live In Tokyo* (Virgin 1983), *This Is What You Want, This Is What You Get* (Virgin 1984), *Album* (Virgin 1986), *Happy?* (Virgin 1987), *9* (Virgin 1989), *That What Is Not* (Virgin 1992). Compilation: *Greatest Hits ... So Far* (Virgin 1990).

Further reading: *Public Image Limited: Rise Fall*, Clinton Heylin.

Puckett, Gary, And The Union Gap

Originally known as the Outcasts, a San Diego act renowned for cover versions, this popular group took the name Union Gap in January 1967. Although burdened by a *passé* image - they dressed in American Civil War uniforms - 'General' Gary Puckett (b. 17 October 1942, Hibbing, Minnesota, USA; vocals), 'Sergeant' Dwight Benett (b. December 1945, San Diego, California, USA; tenor saxophone), 'Corporal' Kerry Chater (b. 7 August 1945, Vancouver, British Columbia, Canada; bass), 'Private' Gary 'Mutha' Withem (b. 22 August 1946, San Diego, California, USA; woodwind/piano) and 'Private' Paul Whitbread (b. 8 February 1946, San Diego, California, USA; drums) enjoyed considerable success through their relationship with songwriter/producer Jerry Fuller. 'Woman Woman' achieved gold status in 1967, and the following year the quintet scored three more million-sellers with 'Young Girl', a chart-topper in the US and UK, 'Lady Willpower' and 'Over You', each of which were marked by Puckett's soaring vocal line. However, the formula appeal of their highly-polished sound gradually waned and the unit disbanded in 1971.

Albums: *Woman Woman* (1968), *Young Girl* (1968), *Incredible* (1968), *The New Gary Puckett And The Union Gap Album* (1970). Compilation: *Gary Puckett And The Union Gap's Greatest Hits* (1970). Solo: *The Gary Puckett Album* (1971).

Puckett, Riley

b. George Riley Puckett, 7 May 1894, near Alpharetta, Georgia, USA, d. 13 July 1946. Due to the accidental use of overly strong medication to treat a minor eye infection, he was blinded as a baby. In 1912, after graduating from the Georgia Academy for the Blind in Macon, where he first learned to play the banjo and piano, he sought the life of a musician and moved to Atlanta. He appeared at the Georgia Old Time Fiddler's Convention in 1916, drawing good reviews as 'the blind banjoist'. (He made further appearances at the conventions, the last being in 1934, when he won the banjo contest.) He also took to playing the guitar and singing and worked local dances and busked on the streets. In 1922, he made his radio debut on WSB as a special guest with the Hometown Band - a local band led by fiddler Clayton McMichen. The programmes of the powerful WSB could be heard over most of the United States and Puckett's performance attracted attention. He was a fine singer and listeners were also greatly impressed by his excellent yodelling. In 1923, he, McMichen and Gid Tanner began to play together as the Skillet Lickers. Puckett made his first recordings in New York in March 1924, when he and Tanner became the first hillbilly artists to appear on the **Columbia** label. He recorded such solo numbers as 'Little Old Log Cabin In The Lane' and 'Rock All My Babies To Sleep'. By yodelling on the latter, he probably became the first hillbilly singer to yodel on record - preceding the blue yodels of **Jimmie Rodgers** by three years. (It has never been established just where he first learned this art.) He was badly injured in a car crash in 1925 and subsequently married his nurse. (They had one daughter, Blanche but later parted.)

His recordings proved so popular that, by the end of the year, only the recordings of **Vernon Dalhart** received more orders among Columbia artists. The Skillet Lickers, who underwent various changes in line-up during their existence, made their first recordings in 1926 and proved very successful. Their 1927 recording of 'A Corn Licker Still In Georgia' very quickly sold a quarter of a million copies. During the years that Puckett played with the Skillet Lickers, he still made solo concert and recording appearances. When, because of the Depression, the Skillet Lickers disbanded in 1931, he was still much in demand as a solo artist. They re-formed briefly in 1934, when he and Tanner recorded together for the last time. (Tanner tired of the music business and returned to chicken farming.) During the 30s and early 40s, Puckett travelled extensively making personal appearances and for some time he also had his own very popular tent show, which toured the mid-west, Texas, Oklahoma and the southern states. He was featured on various radio stations and at times ran his own bands. In 1945, he was a regular member of the *Tennessee Barn Dance* on WNOX Knoxville, where he appeared with the **Delmore Brothers, Chet Atkins** and **Sam And Kirk McGee**. After leaving Columbia in 1934, he made recordings for **RCA**-Victor and **Decca**. His final recordings were made for RCA in 1941, in a session that included the pop oriented 'Where The Shy Little Violets Grow' and **Carson Jay Robison**'s 'Railroad Boomer'. The undoubted secret of Puckett's success, quite apart from his instrumental abilities, was his large repertoire. He could sing (and play) equally well any songs ranging from old time folk ballads like 'Old Black Joe' and 'John Henry' (his 1924 version is in all probability the first time the song was recorded) through to vaudeville numbers such as 'Wait Till The Sun Shines Nellie' and 'Red Sails In The Sunset'. His fine banjo playing included standards such as 'Cripple Creek' and 'Oh Susanna' and his unique guitar style, with its very fast thumb played bass string runs, has been equalled by very, very few other guitarists: one exception being another blind musician, **Doc Watson**. Prior to his untimely death in 1946, he was appearing regularly on WACA Atlanta, with a band called the Stone Mountain Boys. A boil on his neck caused blood poisoning and though he was rushed to hospital, it was too late and he died on 13 July. One of the pallbearers at his funeral was his old associate, Gid Tanner. It seems ironic that, as with his blindness, the correct treatment at the appropriate time could no doubt have effected a proper cure. Puckett is one of country music's most interesting and talented but, unfortunately, now overlooked characters.

Compilations: with Gid Tanner And The Skillet Lickers *Gid Tanner And His Skillet Lickers* (1973), *The Skillet Lickers* (1973), *Gid Tanner And His Skillet Lickers, Volume 2* (1975), *Kickapoo Medicine Show* (1977), *A Day A The County Fair* (1981), *A Corn Licker Still In Georgia* (80s). Solo compilations: *Waitin' For The Evening Train* (1977), *Old Time Greats, Volume 1* (1978), *Old Time Greats, Volume 2* (1986), *Red Sails In The Sunset* (1988).

Further reading: *Riley Puckett (1894-1946)*, Charles K.Wolfe, with *Discography* by John Larson, Tony Russell, Richard Weize.

Pudgee The Phat Bastard

Having already written part of MC Fatal's verse on the **Main Source** track 'Live At The BBQ', and providing material for both **Roxanne Shanté** and the **Ghetto Girls**, Pudgee came to his solo career with something of a reputation. Insisting on a formulaic blend of sexual boasting, the predictability of his rhymes, though occasionally amusing, were tempered effectively by the funky backing of Trickmasterz. His debut album boasted a head to head clash with **Kool G Rap**, with whom Pudgee's voice has often been compared.
Album: *Give 'Em The Finger* (Giant 1993).

Puente, Tito

b. Ernesto Antonio Puente Jnr., 20 April 1923, Harlem Hospital, New York City, New York, USA. Born of Puerto Rican parentage, Tito began piano lessons when he was seven years old and around the age of 10 he started tuition in drums and percussion, which became his forte. Around 1936, Puente commenced his professional career as a drummer with the orchestra of Noro Morales. In 1941 he played with the **Machito** band. World War II intervened and Tito was drafted into the US Navy for three years service. After his discharge he took courses at New York's Juilliard School of Music and did stints with the bands of José Curbelo and Fernando Alvarez between 1946 and 1947. With Curbelo, Puente performed alongside **Tito Rodríguez**, who later became his arch-rival. Tito's reputation as a sizzling arranger quickly grew and led to numerous assignments from prominent bandleaders. Even Rodríguez hired him to write the charts for four numbers he recorded with his Mambo Devils on Gabriel Oller's SMC (Spanish Music Center) label. In the late 40s, whilst Tito was performing the roles of contractor, arranger and timbales player with Pupi Campo's orchestra, he organized a group which promoter Federico Pagani dubbed the Picadilly Boys ('Picadillo' meaning: beef or pork hash) after being impressed by their performance of the latin jam style (descarga). With them, Puente recorded a number of sides for SMC. Shortly afterwards, he renamed his aggregation Tito Puente And His Orchestra. Tito used two lead vocalists, Angel Rosa and then Paquito Sosa, before settling for Cuban Vicentico Valdés as his resident lead singer.

In late 1949, Puente organized a line-up of four trumpets, three trombones, four saxophones and a full rhythm section for a recording session for Tico Records. One recording from this session, leaving out the trombones and saxophones, resulted in a fiery version of 'Abaniquito'. With the help of English translation by disc jockey Dick 'Ricardo' Sugar, the song became one of the first crossover mambo hits. Between the late 40s and mid-50s, Puente issued recordings on Tico. During a suspension of recording

by the company in 1950 - due to a wrangle between the co-founders, George Goldner and Art 'Pancho' Raymond - Tito recorded for the Seeco, Verne and **RCA** labels. Along with Tito Rodríguez and Machito, Puente became one of the kings of the 50s mambo era. His consistent top billing at New York's Palladium Ballroom, the famed 'Home of the Mambo', became one of the areas of friction between himself and Rodríguez. Puente switched to **RCA** Victor Records and between 1956 and 1960 he released a string of albums on the label, including the notable *Cuban Carnival* and his all-time best-seller, *Dance Mania*. The album marked debut of Santos Colón (b. 1 November, Mayagüez, Puerto Rico) as Puente's new lead singer. Colón arrived in New York in 1950 and performed with the bands of Jorge Lopés, Tony Novos and José Curbelo before joining Tito. He remained with Puente until 1970, when he departed to pursue a solo career and released a series of albums on Fania Records.

Several of Puente's Tico and RCA Victor releases between the mid to late 50s were entirely devoted to the cha cha chá rhythm, which was enjoying considerable popularity at the time. At the beginning of the 60s, the pachanga style took over. One of the prime-movers of the dance craze was Afro-Cuban singer Rolando La Serie's 1960 smash hit recording of 'La Pachanga' with the Bebo Valdés band. The following year, whilst the fad was still raging at full force, Puente teamed up with La Serie to make *Pachanga In New York* for Gema Records.

In 1960, Tito and His Orchestra journeyed to the west coast of America to record *Exciting Band In Hollywood* (aka *Puente Now!*) for GNP Records. Upon his arrival, Puente contacted Los Angeles-based flautist Rolando Lozano (b. José Calazan Lozano, 27 August 1931, Cienfuegos, Santa Clara Province, Cuba), an alumnus of Orquesta Aragón, Orquesta América, Orquesta Nuevo Ritmo, **Mongo Santamaría** and **Cal Tjader**. Puente re-joined Tico Records (and remained with them until the mid-80s) to make *Pachanga Con Puente*, which yielded the big hit 'Caramelos'. 1962's *El Rey Bravo* was essentially a descarga set: an untypical Puente album, it stands as one of his strongest recordings. The disc featured Cuban violinist/flautist **Pupi Legarreta** and spawned the original version of Puente's perennial classic 'Oye Como Va', which was given a latin-rock treatment by **Santana** in 1970. Around 1965, Tito linked up with Alegre Records for *Y Parece Bobo*, which was produced by the label's founder **Al Santiago** and featured Chivirico Dávila on lead vocals. Santiago also co-produced *Cuba Y Puerto Rico Son...* on Tico, Puente's first in a series of collaborations with the 'Queen of Salsa' **Celia Cruz**. Tito also recorded a string of successful albums with **La Lupe** between 1965 and 1967, and made a couple of albums with **Beny Moré**'s widow, Noraida, at the beginning of the 70s. On his late 60s releases, *20th Anniversary* and

The King Tito Puente, Tito was obliged to bow to the overwhelming popularity of the R&B/Latin fusion form called boogaloo. 'The Boogaloo meant nothing to me. It stunk,' he said forthrightly in 1977. 'It hurt the established bandleaders. It was a dance **Eddie Palmieri**, I and other bandleaders didn't want to record but had to in order to keep up with the times' (quote from *Latin Times*).

Panamanian vocalist Miguel 'Meñique' Barcasnegras, who worked previously with **Kako** and **Willie Rosario**, did a brief stint with Puente's band in the early 70s. After performing on Tito's *Pa'Lante!/Straight!* and *Para Los Rumberos*, Meñique departed to work as a solo artist (Puente arranged and directed his 1972 solo debut *Meñique*) and with Santos Colón, **Charlie Palmieri**, Charanga Sensación de Rolando Valdés and Conjunto Chaney. In 1977, Tito and Santos Colón reunited on *The Legend*, the title track of which was written by **Rubén Blades**. The album, which was nominated for a Grammy Award, was produced by 'The Genius of Salsa' **Louie Ramírez**. The following year, Puente's first tribute album to Beny Moré (in a series of three volumes) won a Grammy Award. The trio of albums featured a galaxy of vocalists from the Fania Records stable, including Cruz, Colón, Cheo Feliciano, **Ismael 'Pat' Quintana**, **Adalberto Santiago**, Héctor Lavoe, **Pete 'El Conde' Rodríguez**, **Ismael Miranda** and **Justo Betancourt**. In 1979 and 1980, Puente toured Europe and recorded with the Latin Percussion Jazz Ensemble (LPJE), members of which included Argentinian pianist Jorge Dalto (1948-1987), violinist **Alfredo De La Fé** and conga player Carlos 'Patato' Valdez. This group was a precursor of his own Latin jazz outfit, which debuted on the Concord Picante label in 1983 with *Tito Puente And His Latin Ensemble On Broadway*. He garnered another Grammy Award for the album. Tito released a further seven albums with his Latin Ensemble on Concord Picante between 1984 and 1991, two of which: *Mambo Diablo* and *Goza Mí Timbal*, received Grammy's. However, Puente's work with his Latin Ensemble woefully sank into tired recycling of his earlier material. He has more than paid his dues, so probably he was entitled to. At concerts Tito and his high-calibre musicians often appeared just to be 'going through the motions'. For 1991's *The Mambo King: 100th LP* on RMM Records, Tito returned to a full big band line-up to back an assortment of the label's vocalists (including **Oscar D'León**, **Tito Nieves**, **Tony Vega**, **José Alberto** and Domingo Quiñones) plus Santos Colón and Celia Cruz. Although the album is purported to be his 100th, the actual total of his recordings in 1992 exceeded that figure. In addition to those mentioned, Puente has recorded with an array of Latin music and jazz names, including the Tico All-Stars, Fania All Stars, Bobby Capó, **Ray Barretto**, **Camilo Azuquita**, Gilberto Monroig, Sophy, Myrta

Silva, Manny Roman, **Doc Severinsen**, **Woody Herman**, **Buddy Morrow**, Cal Tjader, **Terry Gibbs**, **George Shearing**, **Phil Woods**, Pete Escovedo and **Sheila E.** (Escovedo's daughter).

Selected albums: *Cha Cha Chá For Lovers* (mid-50s), *Dance The Cha Cha Chá* (mid-50s), *Cuban Carnival* (1956), *Puente Goes Jazz* (1956), *Mambo On Broadway* (1957), *Let's Cha-Cha With Puente* (1957), with Doc Severinsen *Night Beat* (1957), *Mucho Puente* (1957), *Top Percussion* (1958), *Dance Mania* (1958), with Vicentico Valdés *Tito Puente Swings, Vicentico Valdés Sings* (1958), *Puente In Love* (late 50s), with Woody Herman *Herman's Heat & Puente's Beat* (late 50s), *Dancing Under Latin Skies* (1959), *Mucho Cha-Cha* (1959), *Cha Cha With Tito Puente At Grossinger's* (1960), *Tambo* (1960), with Rolando La Serie *Pachanga In New York* (1961), *The Most Exciting Band In Hollywood* aka *Puente Now!* (1961), *Pachanga Con Puente* (1961), *Vaya Puente* (1961), *El Rey Bravo* (1962), *Bossa Nova By Puente* (1962), *Tito Puente In Puerto Rico - Recorded Live* (1962), *Bailables* (1963), *More Dance Mania* (1963, rec. 1959), *Excitante Ritmo de Tito Puente/The Exciting Rhythm Of Tito Puente* (1964), Puente's rhythm section, featuring Mongo Santamaría, Willie Bobo, Carlos 'Patato' Valdez *Puente In Percussion* (1964), *Mucho Puente* (1964), with La Lupe *La Excitante Lupe Canta Con El Maestro Tito Puente /Tito Puente Swings, The Exciting Lupe Sings* (1965), with La Lupe *Tú y Yo/You 'N' Me* (1965), *My Fair Lady Goes Latin* (1965), *Carnaval En Harlem* (1965), with Chivirico Dávila *Y Parece Bobo* (1965), with La Lupe *Homenaje A Rafael Hernández* (1966), with Tico All-Stars *Descargas At The Village Gate-Live, Volumes 1-3* (1966), with Celia Cruz *Cuba Y Puerto Rico Son...* (1966), *20th Anniversary* (1967), with La Lupe *The King And I//El Rey y Yo* (1967), *The King Tito Puente/El Rey Tito Puente* (1968), *En El Puente/On The Bridge* (1969), with Cruz *Quimbo Quimbumbia* (1969) *Pa'Lante!/Straight!* (1971), with Cruz *Alma Con Alma/The Heart And Soul Of Celia Cruz* (1971), with Noraida *Tito Puente Presents Noraida: La Barbara del Mundo Latino* (1971), with Cruz *Celia Cruz y Tito Puente en España* (1971), with Noraida *Me Voy A Desquitar* (1971), *Para Los Rumberos* (1972), with Cruz *Algo Especial Para Recordar/Something Special To Remember* (1972), *Tito Puente And His Concert Orchestra* (1973), *Tito Unlimited* (1974), *The Tico-Alegre All Stars Recorded Live At Carnegie Hall, Volume 1* (1974), with Cal Tjader *Primo* (1974), *The Legend* (1977), *Homenaje A Beny* (1978), with La Lupe *La Pareja* (1979), *Homenaje A Beny, Volume 2* (1979), with the Latin Percussion Jazz Ensemble (LPJE), *Just Like Magic* (1979), *LPJE Live At The Montreux Jazz Festival 1980* (1980), with Frankie Figueroa *Dancemania 80's* (1980) with Camilo Azuquita *Ce' Magnifique* (1981), *Tito Puente And His Latin Ensemble On Broadway* (1983), *El Rey* (1984), with various artists *Super All Star* (1984), with George Shearing *Mambo Diablo* (1985), with Cruz *Homenaje A Beny Moré Volume 3* (1985), with Terry Gibbs *Sensación* (1986), *Un Poco Loco* (1987), with guest Phil Woods *Salsa Meets Jazz* (1988), *Goza Mí Timbal* (1989), with Sheila E., Pete

Escovedo *Latina Familia* (1989), *Out Of This World* (1991), *The Mambo King: 100th LP* (1991), *Mambo Gozon* (1993), with His Jazz Allstars *Master Timabelero* (Concord 1994), with His Golden Jazz Allstars *In Session* (Bellaphon 1994). Compilations: *The Latin World Of Tito Puente* (1965, UK release), *No Hay Mejor - There Is No Better* (1975), *The Best Of The Sixties* (1988), *Rumbas And Mambos* (1991, CD release - contains late 40s Seeco recordings), *Mamborama!* (1990, contains 50s Tico recordings), *Royal 'T'* (1993).

Pugh, Joe Bennie

b. Joe Bennie Pugh, 10 July 1926, Hughes, Arkansas, USA, d. 3 April 1960, Horseshoe Lake, Arkansas, USA. An admirer of **John Lee (Sonny Boy) Williamson,** Joe Pugh aka Forest City Joe only recorded two sessions 11 years apart, but these were enough to create a significant reputation. He lived most of his life in Crittenden County, which encompasses the sites of his birth and death. Like many other harmonica players growing up in the 30s, his idolisation of Williamson led to an imitation not only of his instrumental style but also of the speech impediment that affected his 'tongue-tied' vocals. In the late 40s he travelled north to Chicago several times, earning a reputation in the clubs that he played. On 2 December 1948, six months after Williamson had been murdered with an ice-pick, Joe recorded eight titles for Aristocrat with a guitarist tentatively identified as J.C. Cole. Only one single was issued at the time, combining 'Memory Of Sonny Boy' and 'A Woman On Every Street'. The complete session was released in the late 80s. Returning to Arkansas, nothing was heard of him until August 1959, when **Alan Lomax r**ecorded him for the *Southern Folk Heritage* series, both solo and with a band including guitarist **Sonny Boy Rodgers,** performing Williamson songs and 'Red Cross Store', a piano blues. Nine months later, he died when the lorry in which he was travelling home from a dance overturned, killing him instantly.
Album: *Memory Of Sonny Boy* (1988).

Pukwana, Dudu

b. Mtutuzel Pukwana, 2 September 1941, Port Elizabeth, South Africa, d. 29 June 1990, London, England. Although for the majority of his career Pukwana specialized in the alto saxophone, playing a wild, passionate style which owed more or less equal measures to South African township mbaqanga and sax jive, **Charlie Parker** and **King Curtis**, his first instrument was the piano, which he began learning from his father when he was 10 years old. Moving to Cape Town, and still playing piano, he joined his first band, Tete Mbambisa's Four Yanks, in 1957. It was around this time that he began playing saxophone, learning the rudiments from friend and fellow sideman Nick Moyake, and spending a lot of time listening to

imported records by Curtis, Parker, **Louis Jordan**, **Sonny Rollins** and **Ben Webster**. In Cape Town, he became friends with the white jazz pianist and bandleader **Chris McGregor**, who in 1960 invited Pukwana to join his Blue Notes band as saxophonist. He spent the next three years touring South Africa with the Blue Notes, under increasingly difficult conditions, until apartheid legislation made it practically impossible for a mixed race band to appear in public. The group's opportunity to leave the country came in 1963, when they were invited to appear at the annual jazz festival held in Antibes, France. Once the festival was over, the band spent a few months working in Switzerland, until, with the help of London musician and club owner **Ronnie Scott**, they were able to acquire work permits and entry visas for the UK.
Pukwana remained with McGregor until 1969 (by which time the Blue Notes had been renamed the Brotherhood Of Breath), when he took up an offer to join **Hugh Masekela**'s fledgling Union Of South Africa in the USA. When that band fell apart in 1970, he returned to London and formed his own band, **Spear**, shortly afterwards renamed Assegai. Pukwana also gigged and recorded with, inter alia, **Keith Tippett**'s Centipede, **Jonas Gwangwa**, **Traffic**, the **Incredible String Band**, Gwigwi Mrwebi, Sebothane Bahula's Jabula, **Harry Miller**'s Isipingo and the **Louis Moholo** Unit. He made memorable contributions to **John** and **Beverly Martyn**'s *Road To Ruin* in 1970, and the same year co-led a sax jive/kwela album, *Kwela*, with fellow South African saxophonist Gwigwi Mrwebi. With Assegai, he recorded two albums - *Assegai* and *Assegai Zimbabwe* - before launching the second Spear in 1972. That year, he was also a featured artist on Masekela's London-recorded album *Home Is Where The Music Is*. The new Spear included in its line-up fellow ex-Blue Notes **Mongezi Feza** (trumpet) and Louis Moholo (drums), along with South Africans **Harry Miller** (bass) and Bixo Mngqikana (tenor saxophone). Their first album was the superb *In The Townships*, in 1973, which like its follow-up, *Flute Music*, took the mbaqanga/sax jive/jazz fusion into previously uncharted depths of emotional and creative intensity. In 1978, Pukwana disbanded Spear to form the larger band **Zila**, a horns and percussion dominated outfit whose album debut was *Diamond Express*. He continued leading Zila, recording the occasional album and working the UK and European jazz club and festival circuit, until his death from liver failure in 1990 deprived the jazz and African music scene of one of its most consistently inventive players.
Albums: *In The Townships* (Earthworks 1973), *Flute Music* (1974), with Assegai *Zimbabwe* (1974), *Blue Notes For Mongezi* (1976), *Diamond Express* (1977), *Blue Notes In Concert* (1978), with Zila *Sounds - Live At The 100 Club* (Jika 1981), with Zila *Live At Bracknell & Willisau* (Jika 1984), *Zila '86* (Jika 1986), with John Stevens *Radebe -*

They Shoot To Kill (Affinity 1987), *Blue Notes For Johnny* (1987), with Zila *Cosmics Chapter 90* (Ah-Um 1990).

Pullen, Don

b. 25 December 1941, Roanoke, Virginia, USA, d. 22 April 1995. After playing piano in church, accompanying gospel singers, Pullen worked in various R&B bands before turning to jazz. In the early 60s he studied with **Muhal Richard Abrams**, and Giuseppe Logan, with whom he made his recording debut in 1964. Pullen also continued to work in R&B and related fields, occasionally working with **Albert Ayler** and saxophonist Syl Austin but usually as accompanist to singers often playing organ, and in 1970 joined **Nina Simone** for a year. In the meantime, he led his own small bands and formed a long-standing partnership with **Milford Graves**, recording with him on the SRP label they ran together. In the early 70s he joined **Charles Mingus** appearing on *Mingus At Carnegie Hall* and *Changes* vol 1 and vol 2 and played briefly with **Art Blakey**. Later in the decade he played with **Sam Rivers** and the **Art Ensemble Of Chicago**. Towards the end of the 70s he formed a lasting musical partnership with **George Adams**, with whom he co-led as the Pullen/George Adams Quartet and additionally featured Cameron Brown (bass) and Dannie Richmond (drums), and also worked with Mingus Dynasty. A vibrant, eclectic and usually exciting pianist that often resulted in bruised and blistered knuckles, Pullen has the technique to match his questing imagination and his playing, whether as soloist or as accompanist, is always interesting. In particular, his interplay with Adams, with whom he worked until Adams death in 1979, displayed his talent to the full. In recent times he formed the African Brazilian Connection but lost the battle with a lymphoma in 1995.

Selected albums: with Milford Graves *Live At Yale University* (1966), with Graves *Nommo* (1967), *Solo Piano Album* (1975), *Five To Go* (1976), *Capricorn Rising* (Black Saint 1976), *Healing Force* (1976), *Montreaux Concert* (Atlantic 1978), *Don't Lose Control* (1979), with Mingus Dynasty *Chair In The Sky* (1979), *Warriors* (Black Saint 1979), with George Adams *Don't Lose Control* (1979), *Milano Strut* (Black Saint 1979), with Adams *Life Line* (1981), with Adams *Melodic Excursions* (1982), with Adams *Live At The Village Vanguard, Vols 1 & 2* (1983), *Evidence Of Things Unseen* (Black Saint 1983), with Adams *City Gates* (1983), with Adams *Decisions* (1984), *Plays Monk* (Paddle Wheel 1985), *The Sixth Sense* (Black Saint 1985), with Adams *Breakthrough* (1986), *Life Line* (Timeless 1986), *New Beginnings* (Blue Note 1988), *Random Thoughts* (Blue Note 1990), *Kele Mou Bana* (Blue Note 1992), *Ode To Life* (1993), *Live...Again* (Blue Note 1995).

Pulp

Camp pop troupe headed up by the inimitable Jarvis Cocker. Based in Sheffield, England, Cocker actually put the first version of Pulp together whilst still at school, recording a sole **John Peel** radio session in November 1981. That line-up boasted Cocker (vocals, guitar), Peter Dalton (keyboards), Jamie Pinchbeck (bass) and Wayne Furniss (drums). Bullied as a child for his angular, national health-bespectacled looks, Cocker went on to work in a nursery for deaf children. Certainly his Pulp project could hardly be described as an overnight success. After the mini-album *It*, the first real evidence of Cocker's abilities as a lyricist arrived with 'Little Girl (With Blue Eyes)' ('There's a hole in your heart and one between your legs, you'll never have to wonder which one he's going to fill despite what he says'). Though singles like this and the subsequent 'Dogs Are Everywhere' and 'They Suffocate At Night' should have broken the band, it took a third chapter in their history, and a new line-up, to provide the impetus. Cocker's desire for success was always explicit: 'Until I've been on *Top Of The Pops* I will always consider myself a failure' (in fact by 1994 he was to be seen presenting an edition). By 1992 the group had coalesced to its current line-up, featuring Russell Senior (guitar, violin), Candida Doyle (keyboards), Stephen Mackay (bass) and Nicholas Banks (drums). The group's early 1994 single, 'Do You Remember The First Time?', was accompanied by a short film in which famous celebrities were quizzed on this very subject (the loss of their virginity). The *Sunday Times* described such songs as being like 'Mike Leigh set to music'. Which was ironic, given that the mother of Pulp member Doyle, who starred in the movie, had previously appeared in two Leigh films. She had also, more famously, played posh employer to Hilda Ogden's cleaner lady in *Coronation Street*. As well as this *His 'N' Hers*, nominated for the 1994 Mercury Prize, also contained minor hits in 'Lipgloss' and 'Babies'. It was their debut album for major label **Island**, with production supervised by Ed Buller, and offered a supreme evocation of the 'behind the net curtains' sexual morés of working class Britons.

Albums: *It* (Red Rhino 1983, mini-album), *Freaks* (Fire 1987), *Separations* (Fire 1992), *His 'N' Hers* (Island 1994). Compilations: *Intro - The Gift Recordings* (Island 1993), *Masters Of The Universe - Pulp On Fire 1985-86* (Fire 1994).

Pulse 8 Records

Pulse 8 is, by accident or design, the British home of the female vocalist, with label personnel seemingly unable to resist signing or licensing a belting diva performance on garage or house discs. As A&R director Steve Long pointed out: 'We are quite keen to sign male vocalists. But there don't seem to be many about'. Managed by Frank Sansom, the duo behind the label had originally promoted artists like **New Kids On The Block**, **Foster & Allen** and even **Max Bygraves**. They moved to dance because they believed 'the real artists, the future artists, album artists, are going to come from the dance area'. The label's most prominent artist was arguably **Rozalla**, whose 1991 cut 'Faith (In The Power Of Love)' brought them chart success. Other releases included 4T Thieves' 'Etnotechno' in 1991, licensed from Italy's Calypso imprint and Friends Of Matthew's 'The Calling' from the same year, a follow-up to 'Out There'. Other pivotal artists were **Sue Chaloner** ('Answer My Prayer' and 'I Wanna Thank You'), Rave Nation ('Stand Up') and Clubland (introducing Zemya Hamilton) ('Hold On (Tighter To Love)'), both from 1991. Their major hits of 1992 included **Reckless** ('Reckless Karnage'), Debbie Malone ('Rescue Me (Crazy About Your Love)'), and Rozalla ('Are You Ready To Fly?'). Rage (Pierson Grange, Angela Lupino, Tony Jackson, Jeffrey Sayadian and Toby Sadler) would take them into the Top 10 with, of all things, a **Bryan Adams** song - 'Run To You'. It was produced by Barry Lang and Duncan Hannant. Lang had previously overseen **Amii Stewart**'s 'Light My Fire', Hannant having worked with **Bomb The Bass** and **Betty Boo**. However, the lynchpin producers behind the label's output are **Band Of Gypsies**. They recorded cuts like 'Take Me Higher' in their own right, as well as providing Australian singer Juliette Jaimes with hits in 'Stand Up' and 'Summer Breeze' (and working with Chaloner and Rozalla). Other material arrived from Lee Rogers (formerly of Temper and her own group, Suspect, and also a Hollywood actor, with 'Love Is The Most'). Sadly the label fell out with Rozalla when she attempted to release her debut album, recorded at Pulse 8's expense, on **Epic**. Pulse 8 won the subsequent court case in February 1992, despite Rozalla having at no time signed a contract. Their quest for a talented male vocalist alighted on Keith Nunnally, who, fronting Intuition, provided 'Greed (When Will The World Be Free)', a revision of the same artist's DJ International oldie. Pulse 8 is also the mother label to the Faze 2 subsidiary, famed for its contribution to the world of toytown techno with Urban Hype (Bobby D and Mark Lewis) and 'A Trip To Trumpton'. That group had previously scored with the more sober 'Teknologi'. Faze 2 also provided a home for **Visions Of Shiva** and others.

Pungent Stench

A Viennese death metal band, Pungent Stench began as a musical project in February 1988. In this form they released a split album with the Disharmonic Orchestra and an EP entitled *Extreme Deformity* in 1989. Their increasing popularity among fans of extreme, grotesque music soon convinced them to become a permanent unit, comprising Alex Wank (drums), Jacek Perkowski (bass) and bositerous frontman Martin Schirenc (vocals/guitar). After an undistinguished first album they released *Been Caught Buttering*, a strong development in Pungent Stench's distinctive style. The death metal genre has always been fixated with blood and guts, but Pungent Stench took things further with a level of sickness which showed a certain morbid panache. They also have a rampant sense of humour which runs throughout their gross lyrics and nauseating artwork, while touring committments with **Type O Negative**, **Brutal Truth** and **Soldom** helped spread their warped messages around the world. Later releases, such as the 1993 EP *Dirty Rhymes and Psychotronic Beats*, highlighted the funk or even dance-related elements in their death metal cocktail. *Club MONDO BIZARRE For Members Only* revealed an increasing tendency towards material concerning sexual deviance (fitting, perhaps, for a band hailing from the same city as Freud).
Albums: *For God Your Soul... For Me Your Flesh* (Nuclear Blast 1990, remixed and re-released in 1993), *Been Caught Buttering* (Nuclear Blast 1991), *Club MONDO BIZARRE For Members Only* (Nuclear Blast 1994).
Video: *La Muerte* (1993).

Punk In London

Shot by German film director Wolgang Bilt in September 1977, *Punk In London* caught the flavour of the contemporary atmosphere but failed to fully expose its excitement. Balancing copious interview material with onstage performances, the film was made too late to enshrine the scene's prime movers and thus included footage of second generation bands the **Adverts**, **X-Ray Spex** and the Killjoys. The **Jam** are also featured but their Mod sympathies were the antithesis of the true punk flame and their inclusion suggested commercial rather than artistic concerns. *Sniffin' Glue* editor Mark Perry, **Police** manager Miles Copeland and **Stranglers**' bassist Jean-Jacques Burnell were among the others featured while the **Sex Pistols**, **Boomtown Rats** and **Lurkers** can be heard on the soundtrack. Film of the **Clash** was reportedly removed at the group's behest, but in the absence of a classic punk documentary, *Punk In London* at least provides a glimpse of the era.

Purdie, Bernard 'Pretty'

b. 11 June 1939, Elkton, Maryland, USA. Purdie, the 11th of 15 children, began to learn drums at the age of six. During the 60s he became a highly respected session drummer, and played on numerous releases ranging from **Nina Simone** to **Tim Rose** and **Jack Jones**. He is, however, better remembered for his work in the New York-based houseband put together for the **Atlantic** label by saxophonist **King Curtis**. Purdie was thus present on several of **Aretha Franklin**'s finest recordings. The self-proclaimed 'world's greatest drummer' also played on jazz sessions, including **Albert Ayler**'s controversial *New Grass*. Such work anticipated the direction Purdie took when he embarked on a solo career.

Albums: *Soul Drums* (1968), *Soul Fingers* (1968), *Stand By Me* (1971), *Purdie Good* (1971), *Soul Is...Pretty Purdie* (1972), *Shaft* (1974), *Delights Of The Garden* (mid-70s).

Pure Prairie League

Formed in 1971, this US country rock group comprised Craig Lee Fuller (vocals/guitar), George Powell (vocals/guitar), John Call (pedal steel guitar), Jim Lanham (bass) and Jim Caughlin (drums). Their self-titled debut album was a strong effort, which included the excellent 'Tears', 'You're Between Me' (a tribute to McKendree Spring) and 'It's All On Me'. The work also featured some novel sleeve artwork, using Norman Rockwell's portrait of an ageing cowboy as a symbol of the Old West. On *Pure Prairie League*, the figure was seen wistfully clutching a record titled 'Dreams Of Long Ago'. For successive albums, the cowboy would be portrayed being ejected from a saloon, stranded in a desert and struggling with a pair of boots. The image effectively gave Pure Prairie League a brand name, but by the time of their *Bustin' Out*, Fuller and Powell were left to run the group using session musicians. This album proved their masterwork, one of the best and most underrated records produced in country rock. Its originality lay in the use of string arrangements, for which they recruited the services of former **David Bowie** acolyte **Mick Ronson**. His work was particularly effective on the expansive 'Boulder Skies' and 'Call Me Tell Me'. A single from the album, 'Amie', was a US hit and prompted the return of John Call, but when Fuller left in 1975 to form American Flyer, the group lost its major writing talent and inspiration. Powell continued with bassist Mike Reilly, lead guitarist Larry Goshorn and pianist Michael Connor. Several minor albums followed and the group achieved a surprise US Top 10 hit in 1980 with 'Let Me Love You Tonight'. Fuller is now with **Little Feat**, while latter-day guitarist **Vince Gill**, who joined Pure Prairie League in 1979, has become a superstar in the country market in the 90s.

Albums: *Pure Prairie League* (1972), *Bustin' Out* (1972), *Two Lane Highway* (1975), *If The Shoe Fits* (1976), *Dance* (1976), *Live!! Takin' The Stage* (1977), *Just Fly* (1978), *Can't Hold Back* (1979), *Firin' Up* (1980), *Something In The Night* (1981). Compilation: *Pure Prairie Collection* (1981).

Purify, James And Bobby

Formed in 1965, this high-powered soul duo consisted of James Purify (b. 12 May 1944, Pensacola, Florida, USA) and Robert Lee Dickey (b. 2 September 1939, Tallahassee, Florida, USA). Unfairly tarnished as a surrogate **Sam And Dave**, the duo's less frenetic style was nonetheless captivating. During the early 60s

Dickey worked as a singer/guitarist in the Dothan Sextet, a group fronted by **Mighty Sam** McClain. When Florida disc jockey 'Papa' Don Schroeder offered Sam a solo career, Dickey introduced his cousin, James Purify, as a replacement. Their onstage duets became so popular that Schroeder added them to his fast-growing roster. Their first single, 'I'm Your Puppet', was recorded at Fame in **Muscle Shoals** and released on Bell. Written by **Dan Penn** and **Spooner Oldham**, this simple, poignant ballad became the duo's only US Top 10 hit in September 1966. Rather than follow their own path, the cousins were tempted towards cover versions including 'Shake A Tail Feather' and 'I Take What I Want'. In spite of the undoubted quality of these releases, many critics dubbed them 'contrived'. In 1967 'Let Love Come Between Us' became their last US Top 30 hit, although several strong records followed. When Dickey retired in 1970 James found another 'Bobby' in Ben Moore and it was this new combination which secured a 1976 British hit with a remake of 'I'm Your Puppet'. Unable to sustain this rejuvenation, the duo parted, although Moore resurfaced in 1979 with a solo album, *Purified*. The pick of the original duo's Bell recordings can be found on *100% Purified Soul*.

Albums: *James And Bobby Purify* (1967), *The Pure Sound Of The Purifys* (1968), *James And Bobby Purify* (1976), *You And Me Together Forever* (1978). Compilation: *100% Purified Soul* (1988).

Purim, Flora

b. 6 March 1942, Rio de Janeiro, Brazil. Purim was raised in a musical atmosphere (her parents were classical musicians) and she played several instruments before settling on a career as a singer. While studying percussion she met and later married **Airto Moreira**. After moving to the USA in the late 60s she worked with musicians including **Stan Getz**, **Duke Pearson**, **Gil Evans** and **George Duke** before becoming a member of **Chick Corea**'s **Return To Forever** unit which also included Moreira. In the early and mid-70s Purim and Moreira had their own band; the singer also made several solo albums, which broadened her appeal into more popular areas of music. In the late 70s and early 80s Purim recorded with **David Sanborn** and a few years later was again working with Moreira. Purim scats interestingly, and frequently vocalizes wordlessly, her light captivating voice floating over the improvisations of the accompanying musicians. Her sister, Yana Purim, is also a singer.

Albums: *Milestone Memories* (70s), *Butterfly Dreams* (Original Jazz Classics 1973), *Stories To Tell* (1974), *Open Your Eyes You Can Fly* (1976), *500 Miles High At Montreux* (1976, rec. 1974), *Nothing Will Be As It Was...Tomorrow* (1977), *Encounter* (1977), *That's What She Said* (1977), *Everyday, Everynight* (1978), *Humble People* (1985), *The Magicians* (Crossover 1986), *Love Reborn* (Fantasy 1986), with Airto Moreira *The Colours Of Life* (1987), *The Midnight Sun* Venture (1988), *The Sun Is Out* (Crossover 1989).

Purlie

With a score by two newcomers to the New York musical theatre, Gary Geld (music) and Peter Udell (lyrics), this amusing satire on the serious subject of racial bigotry opened at the Broadway Theatre on 15 March 1970. The book, by Ossie Davis, Philip Rose, and Peter Udell, was based on Davis's 1961 play *Purlie Victorious*, and set in southern Georgia. It deals mainly with the struggle between the young evangelist, Purlie (Cleavon Little), who wants to take over the Big Bethel Church, and the intolerant plantation owner, Cap'n Cotchipee (John Heffernan). Fortunately, the Cap'n's son, Charlie (C. David Colson), has not inherited his father's twisted views, and he defects to Purlie's cause. In the end, the new preacher man not only gets the church - but the girl as well Her name was Lutiebelle, and she was played by **Melba Moore**, an actress who made a big impression in *Hair* (1968), and has since had several hits in the wider world of pop music. In *Purlie*, Moore gave a beautiful, understated performance, and introduced the tender 'I Got Love'. There was also the spirited 'New Fangled Preacher Man', which celebrates the Cap'n's death early on (the story is told in flashback), and sets the scene for one of those feel-good, 'hallelujah'-style evenings complete with songs such as 'Walk Him Up The Stairs', 'Purlie', 'Skinnin' A Cat', 'First Thing Monday Mornin', 'He Can Do It', 'Big Fish, Little Fish', 'The Harder They Fall', and 'God's Alive'. Cleavon Little and Melba Moore won **Tony Awards** for their work in a show that, naturally enough, attracted more black audiences than usual to Broadway, and ran for 688 performances. Gary Geld and Peter Udell went on to further success with *Shenandoah* (1975), another show with a relevant, contemporary theme. Melba Moore was joined by Ron Richardson (a 1985 Tony winner for his performance in *Big River*) in the 1993 US revival tour of *Purlie*.

Purnell, Alton

b. 16 April 1911, New Orleans, Louisiana, USA, d. 14 January 1987. Starting out as a singer, Purnell took up piano in his youth and became a professional musician in his mid-teens. He worked with a number of well-known bands in his home town including those led by **Alphonse Picou** and **Big Eye Louis Nelson** before moving to New York in the mid-40s. He played in various bands, including those led by **Bunk Johnson** and **George Lewis**. In the mid-50s he moved out to the west coast where he played with many leading New Orleans and Dixieland jazzmen including **Kid Ory**, **Teddy Buckner**, **Ben Pollack** and **Barney Bigard**. From the mid-60s onwards, Purnell toured

extensively, sometimes in bands such as the Legends of Jazz, the Young Men Of New Orleans and **Kid Thomas**'s band. He also toured as a soloist. A strong player who ably blended the traditional New Orleans style of piano playing with elements of Harlem stride, Purnell proved very popular in the later years of his career. His singing was always engaging and entertaining.

Albums: with George Lewis *New Orleans Stompers* (1955), *Alton Purnell Quartet* (1958), *Live With Keith Smith's Climax Jazz Band* (1965), *Tribute To Louis* (1971), *Kid Thomas* (1975), *In Japan* (GHB 1977), *Alton Purnell Meets Houlind* (Nathan 1988), *Alton Purnell Live* (CSA 1989).

Purple Gang

Formed in Manchester, England, the original line-up comprised of Lucifer (b. Peter Walker; vocals/kazoo), Deejay Robinson (harmonica/mandolin), Ank Langley (jug), Geoff Bourjer (piano/washboard) and James 'Joe' Beard (guitar). All were students at Stockport College of Art. The Purple Gang achieved notoriety when 'Granny Takes A Trip', their debut single, was adopted by the English 'underground' as an unofficial anthem. Although a gentle, happy, jugband song, the 'trip' reference was taken to be about LSD, despite fervent claims by the group that this was not their intention. Joe Beard (12-string guitar), Gerry Robinson (mandolin), Geoff Bowyer (keyboards) and Lucifer completed an attendant album in the space of two days, but had split up by the time of its release. Continued interest in their anthemic single inspired a reformation in 1969, but with George Janken (bass) and Irish Alex (washboard/drums) replacing Lucifer. However, the heavy style embraced by the new unit lacked the charm of earlier acoustic, goodtime music and failed to generate interest.

Album: *The Purple Gang Strikes* (1968).

Purple Hearts

This UK group was one of a wave of late 70s UK mod revivalists, hailing from Romford, Essex. Previously they had been Jack Plug And The Sockets, who were closer to punk than mod. By May 1978 however, they had changed their name to the Purple Hearts (after a drug much favoured by mods in the 60s). The line-up featured Robert Manton (vocals), Simon Stebbing (guitar), Jeff Shadbolt (bass) and Gary Sparks (drums). They signed to Fiction, the new label formed by Chris Parry. The group came to prominence on the *March Of The Mods* tour with **Secret Affair** and Back To Zero. Their debut single came in September 1979 with 'Millions Like Us', with 'Frustration' and 'Jimmy' following shortly afterwards. The first and last of the trio brushed the lower regions of the charts. By 1980 they had moved on to the Safari label and released 'My Life's A Jigsaw' and 'Plane Crash', after which they split up. They reformed in 1982 for a one-off single,

'Scooby Doo', on Roadrunner Records. They returned once more in 1986 to record their second album for Razor.

Albums: *Beat That* (1980), *Pop-Ish Frenzy* (1986).

Pursell, Bill

b. Oakland, California, and raised in Tulare, California, USA. Bill Pursell had one US Top 10 hit in 1963 before going on to a successful career as a session pianist. Pursell's main claim to fame was 'Our Winter Love', a number 9 single for **Columbia Records**. Before that, he studied music composition in Baltimore and worked as an arranger for the US Air Force Band during World War II. Further musical education following his discharge led to a position with the Nashville Symphony Orchestra and a teaching position at Nashville's Vanderbilt University. He signed with Columbia in 1962 and recorded an album which included his version of the instrumental 'Our Winter Love'. After its chart run, and that of the album of the same title (with arrangements by **Bill Justis** and an orchestra conducted by **Grady Martin**), Pursell continued to record, for such labels as Epic, Alton and **Dot Records**, but he never made the charts again.

Album: *Our Winter Love* (1963).

Pursuit Of Happiness, The

This Canadian rock group was formed in Toronto during the mid-80s and comprised; Mole Berg (guitar, lead vocal), Dave Gilburg (drums), Kris Abbott (guitar), Johnny Sinclair (bass) and Leslie Stanwyck (vocals). Their brand of accesible rock mixed a variety of styles, they describe themselves as '**AC/DC** meets **Abba**', although many other influences are heard on their debut. The band gained a following in their home country and worldwide by supporting **Duran Duran** and **Eurythmics**. They released *Love Junk* in 1988 which was produced by their biggest influence **Todd Rundgren**, who was also retained for *One Sided Story*. It was this release that gained them some minor success in Europe with the single 'She's So Young'. This was also marked a change in personnel when Sinclair and Stanwyck were replaced by Bran Barker (bass) and Susan Murumets (vocals).

Albums: *Love Junk* (1988), *One Sided Story* (1990).

Purvis, Jack

b. 11 December 1906, Kokomo, Indiana, USA, d. 30 March 1962. In the early 20s Purvis played trumpet and trombone with the Original Kentucky Night Hawks, then began a life which, as jazz musician and writer **Digby Fairweather** has observed, 'makes a ripping jazz yarn' - even if only a tenth of it is true. In the late 20s Purvis played in various bands, made records, including a remarkable take-off of **Louis Armstrong**, and sat in with **Fletcher Henderson**'s band. In the 30s he made more records with the likes of

Coleman Hawkins and **J.C. Higginbotham**, played the harp with **Fred Waring**, arranged music for motion pictures, became a smuggler in his own small aircraft, fought as a mercenary and was a hotel chef. By the end of the decade he was reputedly playing in a Texas prison band while serving time for robbery. He served 10 years, vanishing from sight on his release but was later believed to be serving time again for second-degree murder. He died in 1962, his body being found in a gas-filled room. Whether he killed himself - at the time of his death he was an unemployed radio repair-man - or died accidentally was made uncertain when an autopsy showed a substantial level of alcohol in his blood. Highly regarded by fellow musicians, Purvis's few records suggest an enormously talented trumpet player with a flamboyant and sometimes erratic style.

Compilation: with Louis Armstrong *Satchmo Style (1929-30)* (1988).

Pussy Galore

Formed in Washington, DC, USA in 1985, this controversial act centred on Jon Spencer (guitar/vocals) and Julie Cafritz (guitar/vocals). Their debut EP, *Feel Good About Your Body*, recorded with the aid of drummer John Hammill, was completed after only two rehearsals. Its marriage of garage, industrial and hardcore fury set the tone for the group's subsequent releases. Having added two more guitarists, Neil Haggerty and Cristina Martinez, Pussy Galore released another EP, *Groovy Hate Fuck*, which confirmed their uncompromising, often carnal, obsessions. The group decamped to New York in 1986, where they were joined by ex-**Sonic Youth** percussionist, Bob Bert, in place of Hammill. A cassette-only rendition of the **Rolling Stones**' *Exile On Main Street* ensued, inspired by Sonic Youth's often-quoted desire to record the **Beatles**' *White Album*. Martinez left the line-up prior to the release of two limited-issue pressings, *1 Yr Live* and *Pussy Galore 5000*, and the group's first full-length album, *Right Now*. Produced by Steve Albini (**Big Black**) with the aid of fellow maverick **Kramer** (**Bongwater**), it stands as one of the definitive 80s' 'noise' collections. Neil Haggerty was replaced by Kurt Wolf prior to *Sugarshit Sharp*, which includes a cover of art terrorists **Einsturzende Neubaten**'s 'Yu Gung'. Confrontation between Spencer and Cafritz led to the latter's departure in 1989. Haggerty rejoined the fold for *Dial M For Motherfucker*, much of which was produced by Albini in London during Pussy Galore's final tour. A version of **Black Flag**'s 'Damaged', recorded for the **Sub Pop** label's singles' club purported to be the group's last recording, but in 1990 Spencer re-enlisted Haggerty and Bert for *La Historia De La Musica Rock*, a blues-soaked selection which included versions of **Elvis Presley**'s 'Crawfish' and **Howlin' Wolf**'s 'Little Red Rooster', herein titled 'Eric Clapton

Must Die'. The LP cover was a priceless pastiche of exploitative mid-70s European progressive rock collections. Pussy Galore folded following the album's release. Spencer subsequently formed the **Jon Spencer Blues Explosion** and occasionally features in Boss Hogg, Cristian Martinez' new venture. Neil Haggerty founded the abrasive **Royal Trux**, while Julie Cafritz joined Sonic Youth's Kim Gordon in the abrasive **Free Kitten**. The legacy of Pussy Galore continues to flourish.

Albums: *Exile On Main Street* (1986), *Right Now* (1987), *Dial M For Motherfucker* (1989), *La Historia De La Musica Rock* (1990). Compilations: *Groovy Hate Fuck* (1989), *Corpse Love: The First Year* (1992).

Pussycat

Although Pussycat were a soft rock band from Limburg in Holland, three of their members, Theo Wetzels, Theo Coumans and John Theunissen, were previously in hard rockers Scum. They joined with husband and wife Lou and Tony Wille plus Tony's two sisters Marianne Hewson and Betty Dragstra. Lou Wille was previously in Ricky Rendell And His Centurions, and later Sweet Reaction alongside Tony. Sweet Reaction signed to **EMI** (Holland) and producer Edy Hilberts changed their name to Pussycat. They recorded 'Mississippi', which became a surprise UK number 1 on Sonet Records. The follow-up, 'Smile', was a minor hit, after which the band failed to chart.

Album: *First Of All* (1976).

PWL

Hardly the coolest record label on the dance scene, owned as it is by the **Stock Aitken & Waterman** triad, PWL has nevertheless made a massive contribution to the subculture by licensing mainstream successes (on PWL Continental) from Europe, including DJ Professor, **2 Unlimited**, **Capella** and **RAF**, while PWL International has offered the Toxic Two ('Rave Generator'), **Opus III** ('It's A Fine Day'), Vision Masters ('Keep On Pumpin' It') and **Undercover** ('Never Let Her Slip Away', 'Baker Street' etc.). In addition there was a rave offshoot/promo label Black Diamond which originally housed tunes like 'Rave Generator' and 2 Unlimited's 'Workaholic', until they crossed over. However, Black Diamond disappeared in 1992 to be replaced by 380, headed by John Barratt, and named after its address at a converted church on Manchester's Deansgate. Its career began with **Family Foundation**'s 'Xpress Yourself', then Ultracynic's 'Nothing Is Forever'.

Pye Records

The Pye label was established in the UK in 1955 as the record division of an electronics firm. Initially known as Pye/Nixa, the new venture enjoyed almost immediate success with hit singles by **Petula Clark**, who enjoyed a lengthy spell with the label, and **Lonnie Donegan**. By the end of the 50s Pye was, alongside **EMI**, **Decca** and **Phillips**, one of the four major companies operating in the UK, boasting its own, nationwide distribution system. Between 1956 and 1958 it held the rights to US Mercury and in 1960 a subsidiary, Pye International, was inaugurated for US licensees. The **Marcels** 'Blue Moon', derived from the **Colpix** label, gave the new venture a UK chart-topper. Having secured the rights to **Chess** in 1963, Pye International was responsible for seminal releases from **Muddy Waters**, **Chuck Berry**, **Bo Diddley** and **Howlin' Wolf** at the height of the British R&B boom. The US outlet was later given its own imprint, while Pye International continued to issue material from the **Wand** label, including **Dionne Warwick**, A&M (**Herb Alpert**, **Chris Montez**) and **Kama Sutra** (the **Lovin' Spoonful** and **Captain Beefheart**). The last-named pair were also granted their own logo later, with the parent company still marketing releases.

Emile Ford And The Checkmates and **Kenny Ball**'s Jazzmen were among Pye's most successful pre-Beatles signings, while the **Searchers** were undoubtedly the cream of their Liverpool acts. The **Undertakers**, **Tommy Quickly** and Remo Four failed to emulate their appeal, although the **Kinks** emerged from R&B roots to become one of the quintessential 60s groups with a string of stellar, timeless recordings. Meanwhile producer John Schroeder took the **Rockin' Berries** into the UK charts on another Pye subsidiary, Piccadilly, while the rights to French Vogue brought **Françoise Hardy** to the parent outlet's roster. During the mid-60s **Donovan** was one of company's prime attractions, but Pye was slow to capture the emergent 'underground' market. This, coupled with a curious reticence to issue many albums in stereo and an eagerness to promote budget-price lines, rather than new releases, helped foster an 'old fashioned' image. By 1968 Pye International was all but a spent force with the loss of its chief licensees and the company was dealt another blow when **Warner Brothers/Reprise** removed their catalogues. Although these companies had remained autonomous, they had relied on Pye for pressing, sleeve manufacture and distribution. A short-lived 'progressive' outlet, Dawn, did not convince the counter-culture, although one signing, **Mungo Jerry**, scored international hits with 'In The Summertime' and 'Baby Jump'. Pye was unable to retain **Status Quo**, who moved to **Vertigo** in 1973 where they became one of the UK's most popular acts. Over the ensuing decade their former outlet looked increasingly towards the MOR market and during the 80s the company, and its back-catalogue, were sold to Precision, where it re-emerged as PRT.

Pyewackett

This dance and concert outfit drew on John Playford's *English Dancing Master*, first published in 1651, for a good deal of their material. The group included vocalist Rosie Cross (b. 6 October 1954, Leeds, Yorkshire, England; bassoon, tambourine, hammer dulcimer), Ian Blake (b. 9 December 1955, Finchley, London, England; clarinet, recorder, saxophone, bass, keyboards, vocals), Mark Emerson (b. 15 August 1958, Ruislip, Middlesex, England; violin, viola, keyboards, drum, vocals), Laurie Harper (b. 22 November 1953, Lambeth, London, England; violin, mandolin, mandola, bass, vocals) and Bill Martin (b. 3 May 1955, Woolwich, London, England; guitar, accordion, keyboards, vocals). The group formed in 1975, when Ian, Rosie and Bill were students together, and became the resident band at their university folk club. They played their first professional date in 1977, having already undergone numerous personnel changes. By 1977, both Emerson and Harper had joined the line-up. After the release of *Pyewackett*, on Dingle's Records in 1981, the group issued the single 'The Lambeth Walk'/'Poor Little Angelina', under the pseudonym of Des Dorchester And His Dance Orchestra. They employed the services of a number of drummers over the years, including session musician Ralph Salmins (b. 4 June 1964, Farnborough, Kent, England) but the first permanent drummer came in 1983, when Micky Barker joined them. He left the group around 1985, eventually joining **Magnum**. From then on the unit used drummers only on larger tours. Many of the tours were for the British Council, and took them the the Middle East, North Africa and Europe. Pyewackett mostly used Mike Barraclough as caller, and from the mid-80s, until 1991, they were the resident band for the BBC radio school programme *The Song Tree*. The group were very popular for their reworking of old dance tunes, utilizing a number of modern instruments supplemented by synthesizers. Owing to outside commitments Pyewackett ceased working regularly from 1989. Cross took up the post of Folk Development Worker for Humberside in 1987; Martin became involved in production work, and also arranged and recorded with the Firm for the hit single 'Star Trekkin'' and Emerson regularly tours with **June Tabor**. However, Pyewackett still get together for occasional appearances.

Albums: *Pyewackett* (1981), *The Man In The Moon Drinks Claret* (1983), *7 To Midnight* (1985), *This Crazy Paradise* (1987).

Pyne, Chris

b. 14 February 1939, Bridlington, Yorkshire, England, d. 12 April 1995. Pyne was a self-taught trombonist whose initial band experience was with a Royal Air Force band during his National Service (1960-1961).

He later appeared in a succession of units throughout the 60s, which included John Cox's band, **Alexis Korner**'s **Blues Incorporated**, **Humphrey Lyttelton**, **John Dankworth**, **Ronnie Scott**, **Tubby Hayes** and **Maynard Ferguson**. Pyne was a consummately professional studio musician who has recorded with **Ella Fitzgerald** and **Tony Bennett** and has played on many of **Frank Sinatra**'s UK tours. Pyne had a polished, accurate playing style which reflects an early liking for **J.J. Johnson**. During the 70s and 80s he worked with, among others: **John Taylor**, **Mike Gibbs**, **Kenny Wheeler**, **Gordon Beck** and **John Surman**. Pyne's brother, **Mike Pyne**, was also a jazz musician.

Selected albums: with Alexis Korner *Blues Incorporated* (1967), with John Dankworth *Million Dollar Collection* (1967), with John Stevens' SME *The Source* (1970), with John Taylor *Pause And Think Again* (1971) with Pete Hurt *Lost For Words* (1984), with Kenny Wheeler *Music For Large And Small Ensembles* (1990).

Pyne, Mike

b. 2 September 1940, Thornton-le-Dale, Yorkshire, England, d. 24 May 1995. Pyne's father was a pianist and he encouraged him to play from the age of three. He came to London in 1961 and played piano regularly in a succession of bands - with drummer **Tony Kinsey**, **Alexis Korner**'s Blues Incorporated, **Tubby Hayes** and **Humphrey Lyttelton**. Pyne sometimes got the chance to play his second instrument, the trumpet, but more regularly contributed his strong solo lines or accompaniments on piano. He worked with **Philly Joe Jones**, saxophonists **Stan Getz**, **Rahsaan Roland Kirk**, **Dexter Gordon** and **Ronnie Scott**, with the **Mike Gibbs** Orchestra and the **Cecil Payne** Quintet. In the 80s he also played with **Georgie Fame**'s Stardust Road show and **Keith Smith**'s Hefty Jazz. Pyne's brother, **Chris Pyne**, was also a jazz musician.

Albums: with Philly Joe Jones *Trailways Express* (1968), with John Stevens' SME *The Source* (1970), with Humphrey Lyttelton *21 Years On* (1969), with Lyttelton *Once In A While* (Black Lion 1976), with Lyttelton *Alone Together* (Spotlite 1977), with Jon Eardley *Two Of A Kind* (1977), with Tubby Hayes *Mexican Green* (1981), with Lyttelton *Humph At The Bull's Head* (1984), with Tommy Whittle *Straight Eight* (1985), *A Little Blue* (Miles Music 1988).

Pyramids

The Pyramids were a seven-piece, UK-based **ska/rocksteady** band, although they began their career as a straight 'pop' group, consisting of Josh Roberts, Ray Knight, Roy Barrington, Monty Naismith, Ray Ellis, Mick Thomas and Frank Pitter. A popular live attraction in Britain in the late 60s, they hit with 'Train Tour To Rainbow City', an appropriately chugging piece written and produced by **Eddy Grant,** which ran through many of the period's most popular records and bore a close resemblance to **Prince Buster**'s 'Train To Girls Town'. As rock steady gave way to reggae, elements of the band, including Ellis, Naismith and Thomas, resurfaced in 1969 as Symarip with 'Skinhead Moon Stomp', based on **Derrick Morgan**'s 'Moon Hop' hit, which was one of the anthems of the skinhead era but which had to wait until its 1980 re-issue to gain a chart placing.

Albums: *Pyramids* (1968), as Symarip *Skinhead Moon Stomp* (Trojan 1970).

Film: *Bikini Beach* (1964).

Q

Q Magazine

At once iconoclastic and orthodox, *Q* has changed the nature of UK-based rock journalism and become a pillar of the music business since its appearance in 1986. In the hands of founding editors David Hepworth and Mark Ellen and designer Andy Cowles it rapidly established a strong identity at a time when established journals such as *Melody Maker* and *New Musical Express* were losing theirs. Hepworth and Ellen persuaded ambitious publishers EMAP that an up-market mélange of rock, lifestyle, films and books would work, and set about creating *Q*.

The monthly publication interval and new power of desktop publishing removed the restrictions which confined their rivals. With great good fortune they secured an interview with **Paul McCartney** for the first issue, after which UK circulation grew steadily from an initial 41,000 to 173,000 by the end of 1990. A period of stagnation followed, due partly to the advent of the recession, and partly to the appearance of *Vox* from rival publisher IPC (home of *NME*). From mid-1992 the upward trend was resumed, and *Q* had reached worldwide sales of nearly 205,000 by the end of 1994.

In the course of this growth it has shed or diluted some of the peripheral coverage to concentrate on rock. Inevitably, its success has also led to some compromise in the tone and range of its content. Record companies recognised its influence on the CD market with a resulting increase in the correspondence between featured artists and their CD releases. Nevertheless, it still succeeds in attracting buyers across a wide range of musical tastes, and even those whose primary interest is not the music but the personality. The founders went on to establish *Mojo* in 1993, aimed at the slightly older reader. Since 1992 *Q* has been edited by Danny Kelly.

Q-Tips

Fronted by **Paul Young** (b. 17 January 1956, Luton, Bedfordshire, England), Q-Tips was one of the most renowned live bands on the UK club circuit in the early 80s, playing an estimated 800 gigs in under three years. The group was formed in 1979 by Young and other ex-members of **Streetband**, John Gifford (guitar/vocals) and Mick Pearl (bass/vocals). In place of their former band's rock sound, Q-Tips was organized as a classic soul group with an experienced brass section of Tony Hughes (trumpet),and saxophonists Steve Farr and Stewart Blandamer who had worked with Johnny Wakelin's Kinshasa Band, **Jimmy James And The Vagabonds** and the Flirtations. Other members were Barry Watts drums and **Ian Kewley** (keyboards) from **Samson** and latterly hard rock band Limey. With matching suits and arrangements out of the Tamla/**Motown** and **Stax** songbooks, Q-Tips were seen as part of a mod revival. After releasing a frantic version of **Joe Tex**'s 'SYSLJFM (The Letter Song)' on the independent Shotgun label, the group signed to **Chrysalis** and covered the **Miracles**' 'Tracks Of My Tears'. By now Clifford had been replaced by Garth Watt-Roy, whose career had included spells with **Greatest Show On Earth**, Fuzzy Duck, **Marmalade** and Limey. The debut album included Blandamer originals like 'A Man Can't Lose' as well as cover versions, but its lack of sales led to Chrysalis dropping the band. The group then signed to Rewind Records which chose a version of **Boudleaux Bryant**'s 'Love Hurts' as a single. Although this failed to sell, it brought Young to the notice of **CBS**, which signed him as a solo artist at the start of 1982. This was the signal for the break-up of Q-Tips, and they disbanded after a farewell tour and the release of a live album. *Live At Last* included 'Broken Man', the first song co-written by Young and Kewley, who would continue their partnership during the first phase of the singer's triumphant solo career.

Albums: *Q-Tips* (1980), *Live At Last* (1982), *BBC Radio 1 Live In Concert* (1991).

Q5

This US group was formed in Seattle, Washington, in 1983 by the innovative guitarist Floyd Rose. He is otherwise best known for being the inventor of the locking tremelo system, the now indispensable device that ensures the guitar stays in tune even after the heaviest of tremelo use. Joining Floyd Rose in Q5 were Jonathan K (vocals), Rick Pierce (guitar), Evan Sheeley (bass/keyboards) and Gary Thompson (drums), all previously with **TKO**. Signing to the small independent label Albatross Records, the band released their debut, *Steel The Light*, in 1984. It was later released in Europe on the **Roadrunner Records** label in 1985. The album was typically Americanized melodic hard rock and in a glut of such releases passed largely unnoticed. Floyd Rose built his own recording studio at his home which the band then used for the recording of a second

album. With virtually unlimited studio time available, *When The Mirror Cracks* was released on the **Music For Nations** label in 1986. Full of strong, melodic compositions, it did, however, tend to sound slightly over-produced. The band fell apart in 1987, and Floyd Rose will be remembered more for his contribution to guitar technology than his recordings with Q5.
Albums: *Steel The Light* (Albatross 1984), *When The Mirror Cracks* (Music For Nations 1986).

QDIII

b. Quincy Jones III. British-born, Los Angeles, California, USA-based early 90s hip hop producer. The son of **Quincy Jones**, QD got the rap bug as a breakdancer for Nike, before attending jams and street parties. There he was introduced to the work of the new rap kings, which built on his abiding love of soul legends like S**tevie Wonder**. However, it was the production work of Mantronik (**Mantronix**) which really caught his attention, especially a track entitled 'Cold Getting Dumb' by Just Ice. Among his earliest commissions as a producer/remixer was a cut for **T La Rock**, 'Nitro', while he was still living in New York. He next approached **Warner Brothers**, who suggested he put together a compilation album to showcase new talent. The resultant *Soundlab* eventually led to **Justin Warfield** being signed - whose expansive debut album was helmed by QDIII. It also spurred QD on to further production work, most notably with **LL Cool J** and **Ice Cube**. These two heavyweights anchored his reputation via the highly successful *14 Shots To The Dome* (three tracks) and *Lethal Injection* (four tracks) respectively. He has gone on to produce and remix for a myriad of other talents, including **Tairrie B**, **Naughty By Nature**, **Da Lench Mob**, **Yo Yo** (both the latter two out of Ice Cube's stable), **En Vogue**, **Special K**, **Queen Latifah** and the **Whooliganz**. He continues to run his own company, Soundlab productions, titled after the compilation album that made his reputation.

Quadrophenia

Released in 1979, *Quadrophenia* is based upon the **Who** album of the same title in which **Pete Townshend** paid tribute to the Mod movement inspiring his group. **Phil Daniels** starred as Jimmy, rootless and disillusioned, who seeks solace and thrills in this vibrant sub-culture. Director Francis Roddam captures the atmosphere of the time to perfection, whether it is parties, fumbled sex, clubs or fights. Realistic and unflinchingly unsentimental, *Quadrophenia* portrays amphetamine-fuelled aggression, the Bank Holiday skirmishes between Mods and Rockers on seaside beaches and an intoxicating love of fashion and scooters. The Who's musical contributions apart, the soundtrack features bluebeat star **Derrick Morgan**, **James Brown**, **Marvin Gaye** and **Booker T And The MGs**, whose seminal 'Green Onions' scaled the UK Top 10 following the film's release, 17 years after it was first issued. Leslie Ash and **Toyah** Willcox are among the supporting cast, while **Sting** excels as the 'Ace Face', later reduced to the role of bellboy, much to Jimmy's chagrin. Rodham's evocative settings apart, *Quadrophenia* main strength is derived from Daniels' remarkable portrayal of a pained, frustrated teenager. It remains one of the most powerful films in rock music history.

Quaker Girl, The

Lionel Monkton was one of the most successful composers for the London musical stage at the turn of the century and for several years afterwards. He wrote the score for this show with lyricists Adrian Ross and Percy Greenbank just 18 months after one of his biggest hits, *The Arcadians*, began its West End run. Presented by George Edwardes, *The Quaker Girl* opened at London's Adelphi Theatre on 5 November 1910. The book was by James T. Tanner, and Gertie Millar starred as Prudence Pym, an English girl who has been brought up in the Quaker faith by her strict aunt and uncle. She is entranced by a visiting American, Tony Chute (Joseph Coyne), and he tempts her to taste some of the 'forbidden' champagne at a wedding reception. Disowned by her family for the dreadful act, she travels to Paris where Tony is a naval attaché at the American Embassy, and works for a time as a mannequin at a fashion house. She attracts the attention of a well-known roué, Prince Carlo (George Carvey), who tries to seduce her, and she and Tony part for a time, before meeting up again at a masked ball when all their misunderstandings are forgotten as they go into 'The First Dance'. The happy and melodious score was full of delightful numbers such as 'Take A Step', 'Tony From America', 'The Quaker Girl', 'A Bad Boy And A Good Girl', 'I Wore A Little Grey Bonnet', 'Tip Toe', and the ravishing 'Come Come The Ball', which was introduced by George Carvey. *The Quaker Girl* played for a remarkable 536 performances in London, and added another 240 to that total in New York, when Ina Claire took the role of Prudence. One London revival was presented in 1938, and two more in the 40s. Since then, *The Quaker Girl* has been kept alive through many amateur productions.

Qualls, Henry

b. 1934, Elmo, Texas, USA. As the elder statesmen of Texas blues have almost all died, it falls to individuals such as Qualls to represent, in a less than competent way, a tradition that has all but succumbed to the passage of time. While performing songs first recorded by artists such as **Lightnin' Hopkins** and **Li'l Son Jackson,** his faltering guitar technique, including a very wayward slide style, is more reminiscent of **Smokey Hogg**, an artist who built a reputation on his

incapacity to observe the formalities of 12-bar blues. Taught as a youth by Emmitt Williams, Qualls supplemented his instruction by making regular visits to Dallas to watch Hopkins, Jackson and **Frankie Lee Sims** in action. Through most of his adult life, music was an intermittent hobby as he earned his living ploughing fields and mowing the lawns of the Dallas elite. Found by Dallas Blues Society men Scottie Ferris and Chuck Nevitt, Qualls became a reluctant local celebrity. His album contains the expected material from the Hopkins and Jackson songbooks, along with **Big Boy Crudup**'s 'Death Valley Blues' and fumbled versions of 'Motherless Children' and 'I Shall Not Be Moved'. The touchstone of his importance as a Texas bluesman is his ability to place the **Newbeats**' 'Bread And Butter' alongside **Lowell Fulson**'s 'Reconsider Baby'.
Album: *Blues From Elmo, Texas* (Dallas Blues Society 1994).

Quarterflash

This band were most renowned for their massive US/UK hit single 'Harden My Heart'. This track was a prime example of the group's sound, delivering passionate guitars, wailing saxophone, emotive vocals and an enormous chorus. Primarily described as AOR, Quarterflash boasted the talents of Cindy Ross (vocals/saxophone), Marv Ross (guitar), Jack Charles (vocals/guitar), Rich Gooch (bass), Rick DiGiallonardo (keyboards) and Brian Willis (drums). They recorded three strong albums, although their debut met with most commercial success, particularly in the USA. The group split in 1985 after the release of *Black Into Blue* but re-formed in 1990 much to the delight of classic AOR fans.
Albums: *Quarterflash* (1982), *Take Another Picture* (1983), *Black Into Blue* (1985).

Quartz

Quartz were formed in Birmingham, England, in 1974 by ex-**Idle Race** guitarist Mike Hopkins and local singer Mike Taylor, initially taking the name Bandylegs. Two years later they joined forces with Geoff Nicholls (guitar/keyboards), Dek Arnold (bass/vocals) and Mal Cope (drums) to become Quartz. It was their friendship with **Black Sabbath**'s Tony Iommi that helped get them a deal with Jet Records, and Iommi agreed to produce their first album as well as taking them on Sabbath's 1977 tour. *Quartz* should have been a stepping stone to stardom but the group were deluged by press accusations of plagiarism of their sponsors. By 1978 they had been dropped by Jet, and found themselves moving from label to label in search of commercial success. Indie imprint Reddingtons Rare Records offered a new bolthole in 1980 as Quartz had a crack at the singles market with their version of **Mountain**'s classic, 'Nantucket Sleighride', which was

used as the theme to UK television's *Weekend World* current affairs programme. The band soldiered on, releasing a 12-inch red vinyl single, 'Satan's Serenade', also on Reddingtons, and had a track featured on **EMI**'s *Mutha's Pride* EP showcase after becoming caught up in the **New Wave Of British Heavy Metal**. Jet reissued their debut album in a large brown paper bag with a competition which allowed the winning entrant to fill said recepticle at a famous record shop. This promotion was backed up with a mini-tour followed by support slots to **Gillan** on his UK tour. **MCA** finally picked up their contract and released *Stand Up And Fight*, which contained one of their best-loved numbers in 'Stoking Up The Fires Of Hell'. Nicholls began to moonlight by playing keyboards for Black Sabbath and later joined them on a full-time basis when Quartz ground to a halt in 1984.
Albums: *Quartz* (Jet 1977), *Live Songs* (Logo 1980), *Stand Up And Fight* (MCA 1980), *Against All Odds* (Heavy Metal 1983).

Quatermass

Pete Robinson (keyboards), John Gustafson (bass/vocals) and Mick Underwood (drums) were members of **Episode Six** during that renowned pop group's final incarnation. They disbanded to form Quatermass in September 1969 and, over the ensuing 18 months, forged a career as a tight progressive power-trio. Their lone album was an impressive example of this genre, but failed to achieve a significant commercial breakthrough. Quatermass broke up in 1971. Gustafson, a former member of the **Big Three** and the **Merseybeats**, pursued a similar direction with **Hard Stuff**, while Robinson reverted to session work. Underwood joined several subsequent groups, including **Strapps** and **Gillan**.
Album: *Quatermass* (1970).

Quatro, Suzi

b. 3 June 1950, Detroit, Michigan, USA. From patting bongos at the age of seven in her father's jazz band, she graduated to go-go dancing in a pop series on local television. With an older sister, Patti (later of **Fanny**) she formed the all-female Suzi Soul And The Pleasure Seekers in 1964 for engagements that included a tour of army bases in Vietnam. In 1971, her comeliness and skills as bass guitarist, singer and chief show-off in Cradle were noted by **Mickie Most** who persuaded her to record **Nicky Chinn**-**Mike Chapman** songs for his **RAK** label in England. Backed initially by Britons Alastair McKenzie (keyboards), Dave Neal (drums) and her future husband, ex-**Nashville Teens** member Len Tuckey (guitar), a second RAK single, 1973's 'Can The Can', topped hit parades throughout the world at the zenith of the glam-rock craze - of which rowdy Suzi, androgynous in her glistening biker leathers, became an icon. Her sound hinged mostly on a hard rock chug beneath lyrics in which scansion overruled meaning ('the 48 crash/is a silken sash bash'). The team's winning streak with such as '48 Crash', 'Daytona Demon' and 'Devil Gate Drive' - a second UK number 1 - faltered when 'Your Mama Won't Like Me' stuck outside the Top 30, signalling two virtually hitless years before a mellower policy brought a return to the Top 10 with 'If You Can't Give Me Love'. Quatro's chart fortunes in Britain have since lurched from 'She's In Love With You' at number 11 to 1982's 'Heart Of Stone' at a lowly 68. 'Stumblin' In' - a 1978 duet with **Smokie**'s Chris Norman - was her biggest US Hot 100 strike (number 8) but barely touched the UK Top 40. By the late 80s, her output had reduced to pot-shots like teaming up with Reg Presley of the **Troggs** for a disco revival of 'Wild Thing'. More satisfying than tilting for hit records, however, was her development as a singing actress - albeit in character as 'Leather Tuscadero' in *Happy Days*, a cameo in ITV's *Minder* and as the quick-drawing heroine of a 1986 London production of **Irving Berlin**'s *Annie Get Your Gun*.

Selected albums: *Suzi Quatro* (1973), *Suzi Quatro's Greatest Hits* (1980), *Main Attraction* (1983), *Saturday Night Special* (1987), *Rock 'Til Ya Drop* (1988).

Further reading: *Suzi Quatro*, Margaret Mander.

Quattlebaum, Doug

b. 22 January 1927, Florence, South Carolina, USA. It was after moving to Philadelphia in the early 40s that Quattlebaum took up the guitar seriously, and toured with a number of gospel groups, claiming to have recorded with the Bells Of Joy in Texas. In 1952, he recorded solo as a blues singer for local label Gotham. By 1961, he was accompanying the Ward Singers but, when discovered by a researcher, was playing blues and popular tunes through the PA of his ice-cream van, hence the title of his album. *Softee Man Blues* showed him to be a forceful singer, influenced as a guitarist by **Blind Boy Fuller**, and with an eclectic repertoire largely derived from records. Quattlebaum made some appearances on the folk circuit, but soon returned to Philadelphia, where he recorded a single in the late 60s. He is thought to have entered the ministry soon afterwards.

Albums: *Softee Man Blues* (1962), *East Coast Blues* (1988).

Quebec, Ike

b. 17 August 1918, Newark, New Jersey, USA, d. 16 January 1963. Quebec played piano at first, then took up the tenor saxophone in 1940. He worked in several well-known bands, including outfits led by **Benny Carter**, **Coleman Hawkins**, **Roy Eldridge** and, later, **Cab Calloway**, with whom he stayed from 1944-51. He also led his own small groups in the 40s, recording several sessions for **Blue Note**, the first of which produced the hit 'Blue Harlem'. A close friend of

the label's co-founder, Alfred Lion, Quebec advised Blue Note on the bebop scene, recommending that they record both **Thelonious Monk** and **Bud Powell**. For much of the 50s, Quebec struggled against heroin addiction and worked various day jobs, including a stint as a taxi driver. He returned to the music business in 1959, becoming an A&R man for Blue Note and also recording for them again - first making several jukebox singles, then a series of albums that showcased his expertise at slow blues and soulful ballads. He also guested on albums by **Sonny Clark**, **Grant Green**, **Jimmy Smith** and vocalist Dodo Green. In January 1963, he died of lung cancer; and, for many years, appeared to be one of the forgotten men of jazz. Then, in the 80s, Blue Note issued some previously unreleased sessions while Mosaic Records produced lavishly-packaged compilations both of his 40s Blue Note recordings and the later jukebox singles. The appearance of this material sparked a new interest in, and welcome re-evaluation of, Quebec's shapely, affecting, big-toned tenor playing.

Selected albums: *Heavy Soul* (1961), *Blue And Sentimental* (Blue Note 1961), *It Might As Well As Spring* (1962), *Soul Samba* (1962), *With A Song In My Heart* (1980, rec. 1962), *Congo Lament* (1981, rec. 1962), *Easy Living* (Blue Note 1987, rec. 1962). Compilations: *The Complete Blue Note Forties Recordings Of Ike Quebec And John Hardee* (1987, rec. 40s, 4-album box-set), *The Complete Blue Note 45 Sessions Of Ike Quebec* (1987, rec. 1959-62, 3-album box-set).

Queen

Arguably Britain's most consistently successful group of the past two decades, Queen began life as a glam rock unit in 1972. **Brian May** (b. 19 July 1947, Twickenham, Middlesex, England; guitar) and **Roger Taylor** (b. Roger Meddows-Taylor, 26 July 1949, Kings Lynn, Norfolk, England; drums) had been playing in a college group called Smile with bassist Tim Staffell. When the latter left to join Humpty Bong (featuring former **Bee Gees** drummer Colin Petersen), May and Taylor elected to form a new band with vocalist **Freddie Mercury** (b. Frederick Bulsara, 5 September 1946, Zanzibar, Africa, d. 24 November 1991). Early in 1971 bassist John Deacon (b. 19 August 1951, Leicester, England) completed the line-up. Queen were signed to **EMI** late in 1972 and launched the following spring with a gig at London's Marquee club. Soon after the failed single, 'Keep Yourself Alive', they issued a self-titled album, which was an interesting fusion of 70s glam and late 60s heavy rock (it had been preceded by a Mercury 'solo' single, credited to Larry Lurex). Queen toured extensively and recorded a second album which fulfilled their early promise by reaching the UK Top 5. Soon after, 'Seven Seas Of Rhye' gave them their first hit single, while *Sheer Heart Attack* consolidated their commercial standing. The title-track from the album was also the band's first US hit. The pomp and circumstance of Queen's recordings and live act were embodied in the outrageously camp theatrics of the satin-clad Mercury, who was swiftly emerging as one of rock's most notable showmen during the mid-70s. 1975 was to prove a watershed in the group's career. After touring the Far East, they entered the studio with producer Roy Thomas Baker and completed the epic 'Bohemian Rhapsody', in which Mercury succeeded in transforming a seven-minute single into a mini-opera. The track was both startling and unique in pop and dominated the Christmas charts in the UK, remaining at number 1 for an astonishing nine weeks. The power of the single was reinforced by an elaborate video production, highly innovative for its period and later much copied by other acts. An attendant album, *A Night At The Opera*, was one of the most expensive and expansive albums of its period and lodged at number 1 in the UK, as well as hitting the US Top 5. Queen were now aspiring to the superstar bracket. Their career thereafter was a carefully marketed succession of hit singles, annual albums and extravagantly produced stage shows. *A Day At The Races* continued the bombast, while the catchy 'Somebody To Love' and anthemic 'We Are The Champions' both reached number 2 in the UK. Although Queen seemed in danger of being stereotyped as over-produced glam rock refugees, they successfully brought eclecticism to their singles output with the 50s rock 'n' roll panache of 'Crazy Little Thing Called Love' and the disco-influenced 'Another One Bites The Dust' (both US number 1s). Despite this stylistic diversity, each Queen single seemed destined to become an anthem, as evidenced by the continued use of much of their output on US sporting occasions. The group's soundtrack for the movie *Flash Gordon* was another success, but was cited by many critics as typical of their pretentious approach. By the close of 1981, Queen were back at number 1 in the UK for the first time since 'Bohemian Rhapsody' with 'Under Pressure' (a collaboration with **David Bowie**). After a flurry of solo ventures, the group returned in fine form in 1984 with the satirical 'Radio Gaga', followed by the histrionic 'I Want To Break Free' (and accompanying cross-dressing video). A performance at 1985's **Live Aid** displayed the group at their most professional and many acclaimed them the stars of the day, though there were others who accused them of hypocrisy for breaking the boycott of apartheid-locked South Africa. Coincidentally, their next single was 'One Vision', an idealistic song in keeping with the spirit of Live Aid. Queen's recorded output lessened during the late 80s as they concentrated on extra-curricular ventures. The space between releases did not affect the group's popularity, however, as was proven in 1991 when *Innuendo* entered the UK chart at number 1. By this time they had become an institution. Via faultless musicianship, held together by May's guitar virtuosity

and the spectacular Mercury; Queen were one of the great theatrical rock acts. The career of the group effectively ended with the death of lead singer Freddie Mercury on 24 November 1991. 'Bohemian Rhapsody' was immediately reissued to raise money for AIDS research projects, and soared to the top of the British charts. A memorial concert for Mercury took place at London's Wembley Stadium in the spring of 1992, featuring an array of stars including **Liza Minnelli**, **Elton John**, **Guns N'Roses**, **George Michael,** David Bowie and Annie Lennox (**Eurythmics**). Of the remaining members Brian May's solo career would enjoy the highest profile, while Roger Taylor would work with the **Cross**.

Albums: *Queen* (EMI 1973), *Queen II* (EMI 1974), *Sheer Heart Attack* (EMI 1974), *A Night At The Opera* (EMI 1975), *A Day At The Races* (EMI 1976), *News Of The World* (EMI 1977), *Jazz* (EMI 1978), *Live Killers* (EMI 1979), *The Game* (EMI 1980), *Flash Gordon* (EMI 1980), *Hot Space* (EMI 1982), *A Kind Of Magic* (EMI 1986), *Live Magic* (EMI 1986), *The Miracle* (EMI 1989), *Queen At The Beeb* (Band Of Joy 1989), *Innuendo* (EMI 1991). Compilations: *Greatest Hits* (EMI 1981), *The Works* (EMI 1984), *The Complete Works* (EMI 1985), *Greatest Hits Vol. 2* (EMI 1991).

Videos: *Greatest Flix* (1981), *We Will Rock You* (1984), *Live In Rio* (1985), *Live In Budapest* (1987), *Magic Years* (1987), *Rare Live - A Concert Through Time And Space* (1989), *Rare Live* (1989), *The Miracle EP* (1989), *Queen At Wembley* (1990), *Greatest Flix II* (1991), *Box Of Flix* (1991).

Further reading: *Queen*, Larry Pryce. *The Queen Story*, George Tremlett. *Queen: The First Ten Years*, Mike West. *Queen's Greatest Pix*, Jacques Lowe. *Queen: An Illustrated Biography*, Judith Davis. *Queen: A Visual Documentary*, Ken Dean. *Freddie Mercury: This Is The Real Life*, David Evans and David Minns. *Queen: As It Began*, Jacky Gun and Jim Jenkins. *Queen Unseen*, Michael Putland. *Queen And I, The Brian May Story*, Laura Jackson. *Queen & I - The Brian May Story*, Laura Jackson.

Queen Ida (Guillory)

b. Ida Lewis, 15 January 1930, Lake Charles, Louisiana, USA. Lewis grew up singing Louisiana French songs and began playing accordion shortly after the World War II. When the family moved to San Francisco and Ida married, she had little to do with music until 1976. Ida and her brother Al Rapone played at parties, and she was then invited to perform at a Mardi Gras celebration, which subsequently led to more bookings. She signed with GNP Records in 1976 and has made numerous albums since then, and has been a frequent visitor to Europe with her Bon Ton Zydeco Band. Ida's brand of zydeco is more accessible than that of many Louisiana artists, and she enjoys huge popularity among the non-Louisiana audience. Selected albums: *Zydeco* (1976), *Cooking With Queen Ida* (1989).

Queen Latifah

Rap's first lady, Queen Latifah (b. Dana Owens, March 18 1970, East Orange, New Jersey, USA) broke through in the late 80s with a style which picked selectively from jazz and soul traditions. The former Burger King employee has maintained her early commitment to answer the misognyist armoury of her male counterparts, and at the same time impart musical good times to all genders. After working as the human beatbox alongside famale rapping crew Ladies Fresh, she was just 18 years old when she released her debut single, 'Wrath Of My Madness', in 1988. A year later her debut long player enjoyed fevered reviews: an old, wise head was evident on the top of her young shoulders. Production expertise from **Daddy-O**, **KRS-1**, **DJ Mark the 45 King** and members of **De La Soul** doubtlessly helped as well. By the time of her third album she had moved from **Tommy Boy** to a new home, **Motown**, and revealed a shift from the soul and ragga tones of *Nature Of A Sista* to sophisticated, sassy hip hop. She has subsequently embarked on a career as an actor, notably in the hit streetwise black comedy, *Living Single*, where she plays magazine boss Khadijah James. He film credits already include *Juice*, *Jungle Fever* and *House Party 2*. As if that wasn't enough, she additionally set up her own Flavor Unit record label and management company in 1993, as an outlet for new rap acts as well as her own recordings. The first release on it, 'Roll Wit Tha Flava', featured an all-star cast including **Naughty By Nature**'s Treach, **Fu-Schnickens**' Chip-Fu, **Black Sheep**'s Dres and **D-Nice**. She also guested on the **Shabba Ranks**' single, 'Watcha Gonna Do'. Previous collaborations had included those with De La Soul ('Mama Gave Birth To The Soul Children', in that band's infancy) and **Monie Love** (the agenda-setting 'Ladies First'). Queen Latifah represents an intelligent cross-section of hip hop influences. Though she is a forthright advocate of her race's struggle, she is also the daughter of and brother to policemen. *Black Reign*, in fact, is dedicated to the death of that same brother: 'I see both sides. I've seen the abuse and I've been the victim of police who abuse their authority. On the other side you've got cops getting shot all the time, you got people who don't respect them at all'. Whilst a little too strident to live up to the Arabic meaning of her name (Latifah equates to delicate and sensitive), Queen Latifah is one of the most positive role models for young black women (and men) in hip hop culture: 'Aspire to be a doctor or a lawyer, but not a gangster'. As one of the singles lifted from *Black Reign* advocates: 'UNITY (Who You Calling A Bitch?)'.

Albums: *All Hail The Queen* (Tommy Boy 1989), *Nature Of A Sista* (Tommy Boy 1991), *Black Reign* (Motown 1993).

Queen Of Hearts

After the successful teaming of handsome Old Etonian John Loder with the far more down-to-earth **Gracie Fields** in *Love Life And Laughter* (1933) and *Sing As We Go* (1934), producer Basil Dean brought them together again for this Associated Talking Pictures release which eager British audiences enjoyed in 1936. Early in the film there is a famous scene in which seamstress Grace Perkins (Fields) pursues the famous (inebriated) actor Derek Cooper (Loder) for his autograph, and gets involved in a hair-raising car drive through London streets, during which she is thrown 'from the running board into the dicky seat'. Next day, at the theatre where Cooper is appearing in *Queen Of Hearts*, Grace is mistaken for the wealthy Mrs. Vandeleur who has promised to invest money in the show if she can have a small part in it. The ensuing events are even more complicated than usual, with Grace appearing as La Perkinosa (she has to do an apachè dance), and the whole thing ending with a wild police chase through the theatre, after which Derek takes Grace into his own personal custody. At intervals amid the chaos, Gracie Fields managed to sing three appealing ballads, 'My First Love Song', 'Why Did I Have To Meet You?', 'Queen Of Hearts', along with the amusing 'One Of The Little Orphans Of The Storm'. A strong supporting cast included Enid Stamp-Taylor, Fred Duprez, Jean Lister, Edward Rigby, Julie Suedo, Jean Lister, Hal Gordon, Madelaine Seymour, Syd Crossley, Tom Payne, and Vera Hilliard. Monty Banks, who subsequently married Gracie Fields, had a small role, and he also directed the picture. The screenplay was written by Anthony Kimmins, Douglas Furber and Gordon Wellesley. It was another box-office success for 'Our Gracie', the most popular British entertainer of her time.

Queensrÿche

Queensrÿche were formed in Seattle, USA, by Geoff Tate (vocals), Chris DeGarmo (guitar), Michael Wilton (guitar), Eddie Jackson (bass), and Scott Rockenfield (drums), from the ashes of club circuit band the Mob and, in Tate's case, the Myth. Immediately Tate offered them a distinctive vocal edge, having studied opera but turned to hard rock because of the lyrical freedom it offered. A four track demo tape recorded in the basement of Rockenfield's parents house in June 1982 led to record store owners Kim and Diana Harris offering to manage the band. The tape itself took on a life of its own, circulating throughout the north west of America, and in May 1983 the band launched their own 206 Records label to house the songs on a self-titled 12-inch EP (lead track, 'Queen Of The Reich', had long since given them their name). The EP caused quite a stir in rock circles and led to **EMI** offering them a seven album deal. The record was quickly re-released and grazed the UK Top 75, although the band's sound was still embryonic and closer to Britain's **N.W.O.B.H.M.** than the progressive rock flavour which would become their hallmark. Their first full album for EMI, *The Warning*, was comparatively disappointing, failing to live up to the promise shown on the EP, particularly in the poor mix which was the subject of some concern for both the record company and band. Only 'Road To Madness' and 'Take Hold Of The Flame', two perennial live favourites, met expectations. *Rage For Order* followed in 1986 and saw the band creating a more distinctive style, making full use of modern technology, yet somehow the production (this time from Neil Kernon) seemed to have over-compensated. Although a dramatic improvement, and the first genuine showcase for Tate's incredible vocal range and the twin guitar sound of DeGarmo and Wilton, the songs emerged as clinical and neutered. 1988 saw the Peter Collins-produced *Operation Mindcrime*, a George Orwell-inspired concept album which was greeted with enthusiastic critical acclaim on its release. With some of the grandiose futurism of earlier releases dispelled, and additional orchestration from Michael Kamen, worldwide sales of over one million confirmed this as the album to lift the band into rock's first division. In the wake of its forerunner, there was something positively minimal about *Empire*, which boasted a stripped-down but still dream-like rock aesthetic best sampled on the single, 'Silent Lucidity', a Top 5 US hit, which was also nominated for a Grammy. The album itself earned Top 10 placings on both sides of the Atlantic. Only single releases broke a four year recording gap between *Empire* and 1994's *Promised Land*, the most notable of which was 1993's 'Real World', included on the soundtrack to the Arnold Schwarzenegger flop *Last Action Hero*. Though a more personal and reflective set, *Promised Land* continued the band's tradition of dramatic song structures, this time without Kamen's arranging skills. Over a decade into a career which at first seemed of limited appeal, Queensrÿche's popularity continues to grow.

Albums: *The Warning* (EMI 1984), *Rage For Order* (EMI 1986), *Operation Mindcrime* (EMI 1988), *Empire* (EMI 1990, double album), *Promised Land* (EMI 1994). Compilation: *Queensrÿche* (EMI 1988; includes *Queensrÿche* and *Prophecy* EPs).
Videos: *Live In Tokyo* (1985), *Video Mindcrime* (1989), *Operation Live Crime* (1991), *Building Empires* (1992).

Quest

This USA jazz group emerged in 1978 and have since diminished to a quartet consisting of David Liebman (saxophone/flute), Richard Beirach (piano), **Ron McClure** (bass) and **Billy Hart** (drums). Earlier versions of the group included **George Mraz** (bass) and **Al Foster** (drums) as substitutes in the rhythm section. The group's music is primarily centred on Liebman and Beirach. Since the early 70s they have worked together, both as instrumentalists and composers. Liebman's approach is clearly influenced by **John Coltrane**, but he has a strong and easily recognized style of his own. Beirach can be equally powerful in this region, but also shows influences from classical music. The rhythm section is as competent and creates the rhythmic drive that this group's music requires. These different influences give the group a wide range of expressive possibilities that include hard swinging uptempo jazz, more introspective tone-painting pastiches and occasionally free improvisation.
Albums: *Quest* (1984), *Quest II* (1986), *Midpoint, Quest III Live At The Montmartre Copenhagen Denmark* (1988), *Natural Selection* (1988), *Of One Mind* (1990).

? And The Mysterians

Formed 1963 in Texas, USA as XYZ, ? and the Mysterians entered rock 'n' roll immortality as the band which first popularized the punk-rock classic '96 Tears' in 1966 (number 1 USA, number 37 UK). ? (Question Mark) was vocalist Rudy Martinez (b. 1945, Mexico) and, after numerous line-up changes, the Mysterians became Frankie Rodriguez, Jnr. (b. 9 March 1951, Crystal City, Texas, USA; keyboards), Robert Lee 'Bobby' Balderrama (b. 1950, Mexico; lead guitar), Francisco Hernandez 'Frank' Lugo (b. 15 March 1947, Welasco, Texas, USA; bass) and Eduardo Delgardo 'Eddie' Serrato (b. 1947, Mexico; drums). '96 Tears' was initially intended as the b-side of their debut single, first issued on the tiny Pa-Go-Go label. However, disc jockeys in Michigan, where the group had now settled, turned it over and began playing the three-chord rocker with the now-infamous lead organ line (played on a Vox, not Farfisa as legend dictates). The record was sold to the **Cameo** label and re-released, whereupon it became a number 1 single. The group's name invited further publicity, with ? (Martinez had changed his name legally) refusing to divulge his true identity and opaque sunglasses shielding him from recognition. The group charted with three more Cameo singles of which only 'I Need Somebody', in 1966, made any significant impact, reaching number 22 in the US charts. That single is notable in that the b-side, '8-Teen' was later a hit for **Alice Cooper** in 1971 after undergoing a slight title change to 'Eighteen'. Despite success with their singles and their first album, ? And The Mysterians never again came close to recapturing their brief moment of fame. '96 Tears' was incorporated into the live sets of countless 'garage bands' during the 60s, and was later revived by such artists as **Eddie And The Hot Rods** (1976), **Garland Jeffreys** (1981) and the **Stranglers** (1990).
Albums: *96 Tears* (1966), *Action* (1967). Compilation: *96 Tears Forever* (1985).

Questions

Stephen Lennon (vocals/guitar), John Robertson (vocals/guitar), Paul Barry (vocals/bass) and Chris Kowalski (drums) were all pupils at a secondary school in Edinburgh, Scotland when their home-recorded demo tape secured a recording deal with Zoom, a local independent label. The group's two singles betrayed an obvious immaturity, but they also unveiled the germ of a songwriting talent. Voted 'Best Young Band' on television's *Saturday Banana* show, the Questions then came to the attention of **Jam/Style Council** leader Paul Weller who signed the quartet to his Respond label. When Lennon left the line-up, Paul Barry emerged as the group's principal songsmith and his melodic, soul-tinged direction was apparent on the unit's three minor hits, 'Price You Pay', 'Tear Soup' (both 1983) and 'Tuesday Sunshine' (1984). However, they were unable to secure a significant breakthrough and when Weller's own commercial fortunes declined, so did those of his several proteges, including the Questions.
Album: *Belief* (1984).

Quick

This UK studio-based duo featured Col Campsie (vocals/guitar), George McFarlane (synthesizers/bass/guitar). They not only worked on their own material but also wrote for **Chaka Khan** and produced Haywoode, **Blue Zoo** and Second Image. The Quick debuted in 1980 and instantly became club favourites with a string of singles aimed at the dancefloor. Only one single 'Rhythm Of The Jungle' managed to cross over to the singles chart, just missing the UK Top 40 position by one place. On the strength of the hit an album containing all the singles to date plus some of the b-sides was released to little success. By 1983 they had found club success in the USA, but the limited following in the UK had dwindled so much that all future releases sank without trace. In 1988 the duo re-emerged as Giant Steps along with Gardner Cole (keyboards), Edie Lehmann (backgrounds), Bruce Gaitsch (guitar) and David Boruff (saxophone). The debut album and a single 'Another Lover' were both Top 20 hits in the USA.
Albums: *Fascinating Rhythm* (1982), *International Thing* (1984), *Wah Wah* (1986), as Giant Steps *The Book Of Pride* (1988).

Quickly, Tommy

b. 7 July c.1943, Liverpool, England. A popular singer in his native Liverpool, Quickly started performing in the Challengers, a band formed with his sister. He joined **Brian Epstein**'s management stable in 1963. A highly-publicized launch ensued, including a prestigious slot on the **Beatles** concurrent package tour, while his debut single, 'Tip Of My Tongue', was an exclusive, if undistinguished, **John Lennon/Paul McCartney** song. Quickly was subsequently teamed with the Remo Four, but although 'Kiss Me Now' echoed the chirpy pop of **Gerry And The Pacemakers**, the singer was unable to repeat their success. A 1964 release, 'The Wild Side Of Life', reached the Top 40, but the artist's recording career was brought to an end when the follow-up, 'Humpty Dumpty', failed to chart. During the mid-60s he became involved in drugs and developed a strong dependency. Some years ago Quickly fell from a ladder and suffered serious head injuries, causing brain damage which has severely restricted his life.

Quicksand

This band grew from roots in the 80s New York hardcore scene, but evolved towards an intense, cerebral delivery akin to that of **Prong**, **Tool** and **Helmet**. The line-up of Walter Schriefels (guitar/vocals), Sergio Vega (bass), Tom Capone (guitar) and Alan Cage (drums) made their debut with an independently released EP, stimulating enough interest to gain both major recording and management deals. *Slip* was a strong full debut, built on Quicksand's ability to blend melodic songwriting with dense riffing, and drew **Fugazi** comparisons amid considerable music press acclaim. The band's low-key approach and anti-image made a major breakthrough difficult, however, despite an extensive touring schedule which included dates with **Rage Against The Machine**.
Album: *Slip* (Polygram 1993).

Quicksilver Messenger Service

Of all the bands that came out of the San Francisco area during the late 60s Quicksilver typified most, the style, attitude and the sound. The original band in 1964 comprised: **Dino Valenti** (vocals), **John Cipollina** (guitar), David Freiberg (b. 24 August 1938, Boston, Massachusetts, USA; bass/vocals), Jim Murray (vocals/harmonica), Casey Sonoban (drums) and, very briefly, Alexander 'Skip' Spence (b. 18 April 1946, Windsor, Ontario, Canada; guitar/vocals), before being whisked off to join the **Jefferson Airplane** as drummer. Another problem which would prove to be significant in Quicksilver's development was the almost immediate arrest and imprisonment of Valenti for a drugs offence. He did not rejoin the band until late 1969. In 1965 the line-up was strengthened by the arrival of Gary Duncan (b. Gary Grubb, 4 September 1946, San Diego, California, USA; guitar) and, replacing Sonoban, Greg Elmore (b. 4 September 1946, San Diego, California, USA). Murray departed soon after their well-received appearance at the **Monterey Pop Festival** in 1967. The quartet of Cipollina, Duncan, Elmore and Freiberg recorded the first two albums; both are important in the development of San Francisco rock music, as the twin lead guitars of Cipollina and Duncan made them almost unique. The second collection *Happy Trails* is now regarded as a classic. George Hunter and his Globe Propaganda company were responsible for some of the finest album covers of the 60s and *Happy Trails* is probably their greatest work. Likewise the live music within showed a spontaneity that the band were never able to recapture on subsequent recordings. The side-long suite of **Bo Diddley**'s 'Who Do You Love' has some incredible dynamics and extraordinary interplay between the twin guitarists. Duncan departed soon after and was replaced by UK session pianist and ex-**Steve Miller** Band member, **Nicky Hopkins**. His contributions breathed some life into the disappointing *Shady Grove*, notably with the frantic 'Edward, The Mad Shirt Grinder'. *Just For Love* shows a further decline, with Valenti, now back with the band, becoming overpowering and self-indulgent. 'Fresh Air' gave them a Top 50 US hit in 1970. Cipollina departed, as did Freiberg following his arrest in 1971 for drug possession (he found a lucrative career later with **Jefferson Starship**). Various incarnations have appeared over the years with little or no success. As recently as 1987, Gary Duncan recorded an album carrying the Quicksilver name, but by then old Quicksilver fans were more content to purchase copies of the first two albums on compact disc.

Albums: *Quicksilver Messenger Service* (1968), *Happy Trails* (1969), *Shady Grove* (1969), *Just For Love* (1970), *What About Me* (1971), *Quicksilver* (1971), *Comin' Thru* (1972), *Solid Silver* (1975), *Maiden Of The Cancer Moon* (1983), *Peace By Piece* (1987). Compilations: *Anthology* (1973), *Sons Of Mercury* (1991).

Quiet Five

The UK-based Quiet Five had nothing to do with Bradford's Quiet Three, Kris Ife (guitar), Roger McKew (guitar), John Howell (keyboards), Richard Barnes (bass) and Roger Marsh (drums) backed Bournemouth singer Patrick Dane before Barnes assumed lead vocals framed by lush harmonies reminiscent of the **Searchers**. Released by **Parlophone**, the Five's 'When The Morning Sun Dries The Dew' - co-written by Ife - and its follow-up (a 1966 arrangement of **Paul Simon**'s 'Homeward Bound') were both minor UK hits but a cover of **Rolling Stones** album track, 'I Am Waiting' was a flop - as was 1967's 'Goodnight Sleep Tight', a one-shot single on **CBS**. With the group's consequent split, Barnes recorded several solo singles of which two ('Take To The Mountains' and 'Go North') crept into 1970's Top 40.

Quiet Riot

Heavy metal band Quiet Riot had their 'five minutes' of fame in 1983 with a remake of a **Slade** song, 'Cum On Feel The Noize', and a US number 1 album, *Metal Health* - the first metal album to reach that position in the US charts. However, they were unable to maintain that momentum with subsequent releases. The band formed in 1975 with lanky vocalist Kevin DuBrow (b. 1955), **Randy Rhoads** (guitar), Drew Forsyth (drums) and Kelly Garni (bass), taking their name from a suggestion made by **Status Quo**'s Rick Parfitt. They recorded two albums with that line-up, released only in Japan, which are now collector's items. Rudy Sarzo then replaced Garni. Rhoads left in 1979 to join **Ozzy Osbourne** and was later tragically killed in a plane crash in March 1982. At that point the band briefly split up, with some members joining the vocalist in a band called DuBrow, Sarzo also working with Ozzy. Quiet Riot regrouped around DuBrow, Sarzo, guitarist Carlos Cavazo and drummer Frankie Banali and signed to the Pasha label for their breakthrough album and single in 1983, their musical and visual style fashioned after the harder rocking glam acts of the 70s. Friction within the group followed their quick success and resultant publicity affected sales of the follow-up, *Condition Critical*, which reached number 15 in the US charts but was considered disappointing. After several personnel changes Quiet Riot recorded another album in 1986, which reached number 31 but showed a marked decline in the group's creativity. DuBrow was subsequently ejected from the band and a self-titled 1988 album, with new vocalist Paul Shortino (ex-**Rough Cutt**), barely made the charts. The group then disbanded, with DuBrow going on to form **Little Women**. Banali would later work with **W.A.S.P.**

Albums: *Quiet Riot* (Columbia Japan 1977), *Quiet Riot II* (Columbia Japan 1978), *Metal Health* (Epic 1983), *Condition Critical* (Epic 1984), *QRIII* (Epic 1986), *Quiet Riot* (Pasha 1988). Compilation: *Wild Young And Crazee* (Raw Power 1987).

Film: *Footloose - (Soundtrack Song)* (1984).

Quijano, Joe

b. 27 September 1935, Puerta De Tierra, San Juan, Puerto Rico. The versatile Latin bandleader/vocalist/percussionist/composer Quijano was seven years of age when his family settled in the Bronx, New York City, USA. In 1950, while at school he sang and played maracas with a teenage group organized by Orlando Marín (b. 1934, Bronx, New York City, USA, of Puerto Rican parentage; timbales) and pianist **Eddie Palmieri**. Three trumpets were later added and they became the Orlando Marín Conjunto. Marín had become leader after Palmieri's departure to Johnny Seguí's group. Accounts conflict about the next stage in the band's history. Quijano states he inherited the outfit when Marín was drafted into the US Army, whereas Orlando maintains that Joe left and was replaced by another vocalist prior to his military stint. In 1956, Quijano travelled to Cuba, where he saw and met many of his idols. He later recalled, ' . . . I also heard a different sound - the Senen Suarez Group, that consisted of one trumpet and a flute, as a free form . . . I returned with an idea for a new sound for the band. I worked with my friend **Charlie Palmieri**, and asked him if he could make musical arrangements using a combination of two trumpets, flute, and a rhythm section playing a charanga feel with the singers in unison . . . Charlie argued that since the two instruments tune differently, there would be a clash, but I insisted, and he persisted, and a few months later, he came up with the instrumental version of '"Amor". It was then that the sound of the Conjunto Cachana was born . . .' (quote from sleeve notes to *La Pachanga Se Baila Asi*, 1990). He named his band 'Cachana' after his grandfather's nickname. He persuaded his employers, who ran a wholesale record distributors, to finance the recording of a single with pianist Héctor Rivera. The success of the release led to an album deal with Spanoramic Records. Conjunto Cachana's two releases on the label, *A Cataño* and *Volvi A Cataña*, were big hits in Latin America.

In 1960, Quijano managed to secure a contract with **Columbia Records**. He made three albums on the label between c.1961 and 1963. The lyrics to the title track of the first, *La Pachanga Se Baila Asi*, co-written by Quijano and Charlie Palmieri, were intended to end the confusion dancers made between the terms 'pachanga' and 'charanga': 'There is a lot of discussion in the Latin communities that everyone is dancing the pachanga. There is talk that a charanga is the orchestra that plays it . . . that everyone is dancing the pachanga, the dance rage of the moment . . .' (translated lyrics from the article 'Remembering Charlie Palmieri' by Max Salazar). Joe's lead vocalists at this stage were Paquito Guzmán and Willie Torres (see **Joe Cuba**). Guzmán later joined **Tommy Olivencia**'s band in Puerto Rico, where he also recorded with the Puerto Rico All Stars and now works as a solo artist. In 1965, Quijano participated in the second descarga (Latin jam session) album by the Alegre All-Stars. Joe founded his own Cesta Records label, named after the basket used in the game of Jai-Alai. Two notable releases on the label were the Cesta All-Stars descarga workouts, *Live Jam Session* and *Salsa Festival*, both directed by Charlie Palmieri and featuring **Cheo Feliciano**, **Kako**, **Louie Ramírez**, **Willie Rosario**, Orlando Marín, and others. Quijano also had the distinction of being the first artist to record a composition by the great Puerto Rican composer, C. Curet Alonso. The song was titled 'Efectivamente', and Joe re-recorded it for *Cositas Sueltas* in 1980.

Selected albums: *A Cataño, Volvi A Cataño, La Pachanga Se Baila Asi* (c.1961), *Latin Joe* (1962), *Everything Latin, Yeah Yeah* (1963), *Mr Pachanga N'Changa, The Fiddler On The Roof Goes Latin* (1965), *Joe Quijano y su Fantastico Conjunto Cachana, Swings Uptown And Downtown, Joe Quijano*

Shingalings (late 60s), *The Joe Quijano Party Album, Joe Quijano With Strings, Joe Quijano y su Conjunto Cachana Do Their Own Thing*, with the Cesta All-Stars *Live Jam Session* (late 60s), *Joe Quijano Christmas Album, El Nuevo Joe Quijano, Joe Quijano En Puerto Rico, Joe Quijano Christmas LP 'Para Las Parejas'*, with the Cesta All-Stars *Salsa Festival* (early 70s), *Ahora* (1975), *Cositas Sueltas* (1980), *Joe Quijano: Nosotros 2* (early 80s), *Joe Quijano: El Conjunto Cachana, 83-84, The World's Most Exciting Latin Orchestra & Review* (1988). Selected compilations: *La Lancha: Los Exitos De Joe Quijano, Exitos De Oro/Golden Hits* (1976), *La Pachanga Se Baila Asi* (1990, double album). The latter contains one new tune: 'El Tema De Charlie', a tribute to the late Charlie Palmieri.

Quill, Greg

Quill started out as a folk singer in Sydney, Australia in the 60s, running venues as well as performing, before moving to music journalism with the *GoSet* magazine. Essentially a singer/songwriter with the emphasis on lyrics, Quill's band Country Radio (1971-73) is regarded as among the best country rock groups Australia has produced along with the **Dingoes**. He wrote two classic Australian-sounding songs, 'Gypsy Queen' and 'Wintersong', both Australian hit singles for the band, before their move to Canada where they eventually split up. While the members moved on to other bands, Quill recorded a solo album which did not live up to expectations, and formed another outfit featuring expatriate Australians, Southern Cross. He resumed work in Canada as a freelance journalist, writing biographies about **Michael Jackson** in 1989, and the **Rolling Stones** in 1990.

Albums: with Country Radio *Fleetwood Plain* (1971), with Country Radio *Gypsy Queen* (1974), *Outlaw's Reply* (1975).

Quillian, Rufus And Ben

Rufus (b. 2 February 1900, Gainesville, Georgia, USA, d. 31 January 1946; piano/vocals) and Ben (b. 23 June 1907, Gainesville, Georgia, USA; vocals). They worked in various combinations, but mostly in a group named the Blue Harmony Boys. This group, which also included other singers or musicians at various times, such as guitarist James McCrary, was very rare in that they sang blues and related material in sweet, close harmonies. Ben was not with them at their first recording session in 1929, but was present at sessions in the following two years. The brothers were well-known as performers around Atlanta at this time and they had a regular spot on a local radio station. Although their material on record was of a good-time nature, Rufus was also known for composing religious songs.

Album: *Complete Recordings In Chronological Order* (1985).

Quilter, Roger

b. 1 November 1877, Brighton, Sussex, England, d. 21

September 1953, England. Quilter's best-known work was his 'Children's Overture' which was first performed in London at a Promenade Concert on 18 September 1919, conducted by Sir Henry Wood. He is also remembered for his songs, particularly his settings of poems by Shakespeare (notably a 1921 production of *As You Like It*) and Herrick. His parents' considerable wealth meant that there was no need for Quilter to earn a living, but he chose to gain recognition as a composer in his own right, and he was particularly generous to his musical friends. His financial assistance helped to launch the career of Australian composer Percy Grainger, who achieved fame for his 'Country Gardens', 'Handel In The Strand', and 'Molly On The Shore'. Like many writers, he was attracted to folk music, and his 'Three English Dances' (1910) were orchestrated by Derby-born Percy Fletcher (1879-1932). Quilter provided the music for the fairy tale for children *Where The Rainbow Ends* which was first performed at London's Savoy Theatre on 21 December 1911. The cast largely consisted of children from stage schools, among them the 12 year old **Noël Coward**, who is reported to have congratulated Quilter on his score. Although an accomplished pianist, Quilter wrote little solo music for piano, an exception being his 'Country Pieces' (1923) which transferred well to full orchestra when orchestrated by **Ernest Tomlinson** in 1991. The paths of Coward and Quilter crossed again when both contributed material for Charles B. Cochrnan's 1927 revue *The Rake*. For most of his life Quilter was plagued with ill health - both physical and mental, leading to long bouts of depression, which stifled his creativity. Rare later works included the concert waltz 'Rosme' and the arrangement of 16 folksongs in 1947 for the book *The Arnold Book Of Old Songs*. Quilter helped to found the Musicians' Benevolent Fund in 1921.
Selected album: *British Light Music - Roger Quilter* (Marco Polo 1994).

Quin-Tones

Formed in 1957 in Philadelphia, Pennsylvania, USA, the Quin-Tones were a doo-wop sextet (five vocalists and a pianist) with one Top 20 single to its name, 1958's 'Down The Aisle Of Love'. The group consisted of lead singer Roberta Haymon and back-up vocalists Phyllis Carr, Jeannie Crist, Carolyn Holmes and Kenny Sexton, plus piano player Ronnie Scott, who also arranged their material. Originally called the Quinteros, they were taken under the wing of disc jockey Paul Landersman, who secured the group a recording contract, under their new name Quin-Tones (the hyphen was to avoid confusion with another Quintones group), with **Chess Records**. Their first single, 1958's 'Ding Dong', did not catch on, and neither did the follow-up, the ballad 'Down The Aisle Of Love', on Red Top. But after **Dick Clark** aired the

song on *American Bandstand* and agreed to purchase the song's publishing rights, it was re-released on Hunt Records. This time, it sold, giving the group its one taste of success. Subsequent recordings failed and the group disbanded in 1960. There were no albums.

Quinichette, Paul

b. 17 May 1916, Denver, Colorado, USA, d. 25 May 1983. After formally studying clarinet and alto saxophone, Quinichette switched to tenor saxophone. He played in a number of local and **territory bands**, notably that led by Nat Towles. Amongst the outfits with which he played in the early 40s were those led by **Jay McShann**, **Benny Carter** and **Johnny Otis**. Later in the decade he was active in New York, playing and recording with **Louis Jordan**, **Dinah Washington**, **Lucky Millinder** and others and in the early 50s he worked with **Count Basie**. Included in his recordings of this period are concert performances with Washington released as *The Jazz Sides* (1954-58). In the mid-50s Quinichette played briefly with **Benny Goodman**, **John Coltrane** and **Nat Pierce** but then drifted out of music for several years. In the 70s he was back on the jazz scene but, plagued by poor health, he made little impact. During the late 40s and early 50s Quinichette attracted attention because of similarities in tone and style to **Lester Young**, even picking up the nickname 'Vice-Pres'. The resemblance was deliberate and when he was at his best was more than merely superficial. Nevertheless, such comparisons were damaging to Quinichette's career and he rarely overcame the link for long enough to establish a strong personal identity. In retrospect he can be seen as a fine, lyrical and always swinging player; had he not suffered a hiatus in his career, he might well have been able to overcome the disadvantage of following so closely upon Young's unique path.
Albums: *A Look At Yesterday* (Mainstream 1950), *The Vice Pres* (1952-53), *Six Classics Tenors* (EPM 1953), *The Kid From Denver* (Fresh Sounds 1956), *Paul Quinichette's New Stars* (1957), *On The Sunny Side* (RCA 1957), with Charlie Rouse *The Chase Is On* (1957), *Cattin' With John Coltrane And Paul Quinichette* (1957), *For Basie* (1957), *Basie Reunion* (1958), *Like Who?* (1959), *Paul Quinichette/Paul Gonsalves* (1974), with Buddy Tate, Jay McShann *Kansas City Joys* (1976). Compilation: with McShann *Early Bird* (1940-43).

Quinn, Freddy

b. Manfred Petz, 1932, Vienna, Austria. His family fled from the city in 1945 at the approach of the Red Army. While a civilian worker with occupying US forces in Belgium, Petz was taught guitar and a repertoire of popular songs. This stood him in good stead when, after 18 months with a travelling circus, he busked his way as far south as North Africa. From 1951-1953, he was a deckhand with Finland's merchant navy before returning to Germany as nightclub entertainer 'Freddy Quinn'. After radio and television appearances, he was contracted by **Polydor**. His first major hit was with a German translation of **Dean Martin**'s 'Memories Are Made Of This' in 1956 but, for most of his subsequent output - such as 'Heimatlos' (his second million-seller), 'Unter Treemden Sternen' and 1964's 'Vergangen Vergessen Vorueber' - he relied on European composers, particularly the Aldo Pinelli-Lotar Olias team. If not a prolific recording artist, he still enjoyed at least one smash per year until the late 60s. His debut album, *Sailors Ballads*, sold 100,000 copies in West Germany alone, and 'Die Guitarre Und Das Meer', the title theme of the first of many movies featuring Quinn, was on Teutonic radio turntables throughout 1959 - as was his vocal version of the well-known 19th century tango, 'La Paloma', in 1961. The following year, he starred in the Berlin musical *Homesick For St. Pauli*. Its most wildly applauded number, 'Junge Komm Bald Wieder', trod a well-beaten path up the domestic singles chart and, with English lyrics co-written by Quinn, was even issued as an afterthought in the UK and the USA - territories that would figure but little in his continued career as a mid-European megastar.

Quintana, Ismael 'Pat'

b. 3 July 1937, Ponce, Puerto Rico. This influential salsa singer was only 15-days-old when his family moved to New York City. While attending high school he organized a band with some friends, playing bongos. After graduating, he gigged in clubs in the Bronx. **Eddie Palmieri** heard Ismael at an audition with Orlando Marín. He was so impressed with his singing style that when he formed his band in 1961, he invited Quintana to be lead vocalist. Ismael performed with Palmieri between 1961 and 1973 and returned in 1981 to sing two tracks on *Eddie Palmieri*. Ismael is also a composer and co-wrote a number of hit songs with Eddie. In 1966, he won a trophy for the most popular Latin singer of the year, which was presented to him at New York's Palladium. Ismael made his solo recording debut on United Artists Records in 1968 with *Punto y Aparte*, which contained his great composition 'La Oportunidad', arranged by pianist Javier Vázquez. This was followed by *Dos Imagenes*. His solo career began in earnest when he signed to Vaya Records and between 1974 and 1983, he issued five albums on the label. The first, *Ismael Quintana*, included his hit composition 'Mi Debilidad', which featured a fine piano solo by Mark 'Markolino' Dimond. **Louie Ramírez** contributed arrangements to *Ismael Quintana* and the 1976 follow-up, *Lo Que Estoy Viviendo*, and was the recording director on *Amor, Vida y Sentimiento/Love, Life And Feelings* (1977). In 1979, Ismael sang lead vocals on one track of Louie's own *Salsa Progresiva*. Quintana's 1979 collaboration with Ricardo Marrero

and the Group, entitled *Jessica* (after his recently born daughter), proved to be a perfect combination. The album contained the outstanding 'No Se Compara'; Marrero's superb arrangement of this Johnny Ortiz composition demonstrated how well salsa and jazz mix together. **Papo Lucca** played piano and wrote arrangements on Ismael's first three Vaya releases. In 1983, the two artists teamed up to record *Mucho Talento*, which contained an excellent cover of **Adalberto Alvarez**'s composition 'Vamos, Hablame Ahora', arranged by Lucca. Ismael became a member of the **Fania All Stars** in 1975 and recorded with them up to 1984. With the Fania All Stars, he toured Africa, Japan, France, Central and South America, the USA and the UK (where he made his only appearance in 1976) and appeared in the film *Salsa* (1976). He performed 'Mi Debilidad' with Fania All Stars on *Live At Yankee Stadium Vol.2*, 1975. The same recording of the song is included on the 1976 double album soundtrack *Salsa. Fania All Stars Live In Japan 1976*, issued in 1986, contains another version. Quintana appeared on **Tito Puente**'s first two tribute albums to **Beny Moré**, released in 1978 and 1979. He also sessioned extensively as a coro (chorus) singer and percussionist (maracas and güiro) with many New York based Latin artists and bands. Lamentably, after the Fania All Stars 1984 album *Lo Que Pide La Gente*, he faded from the scene. In 1991, Quintana reunited with Eddie Palmieri at New York's Club Broadway for a dance organized to pay tribute to the singer. Also on the bill were **Johnny Pacheco**, **José Alberto** and **Tito Nieves.**
Selected albums and solo on which he sang lead vocals: with Eddie Palmieri *Eddie Palmieri And His Conjunto La Perfecta* (1962), *El Molestoso Vol. II* (1963), *Lo Que Traigo Es Sabroso* (1964), *Echando Pa'lante (Straight Ahead)* (c.1964), *Azucar Pa'Ti (Sugar For You)* (1965), *Mozambique* (c.1965), *Molasses* (1966), *Champagne* (1968), *Punto y Aparte* (1968), with Palmieri *Justicia* (1969), *Superimposition* (c.1969), *Vamonos Pa'l Monte* (c.1971), *Live At Sing Sing* (1972), *Sentido* (1973), *Eddie Palmieri & Friends In Concert At The University Of Puerto Rico* (1973), *Live At Sing Sing Vol.2* (1974), *Ismael Quintana* (1974), *Lo Que Estoy Viviendo* (1976), *Amor, Vida y Sentimiento/Love, Life And Feelings* (1977), with Ricardo Marrero and the Group *Jessica* (1979), one track with Louie Ramírez *Salsa Progresiva* (1979), with Palmieri *Eddie Palmieri* (1981), with Papo Lucca *Mucho Talento* (1983).

Quintessence

Although formed by virtue of advertisements in *Melody Maker*, this briefly-popular act encapsulated the spiritual ambitions prevalent among sections of the UK 60s 'underground' movement. The original line-up - Raja Ram (b. Ron Rothfield; vocals/flute), Shiva Shankar (aka Shiva Jones; vocals/keyboards), Alan Mostert (lead guitar), Maha Dev (rhythm guitar), Sambhu Babaji (bass) and Jake Milton (drums) - was forged following rehearsals at London's Notting Hill's All Saints Hall and their ensuing debut, *In Blissful Company*, captured the sextet's rudimentary blend of jazz/rock and Eastern philosophies. Mostert's powerful guitar style endeared the group to the progressive audience, but a commitment to religious themes was maintained on *Dive Deep* and *Self*. The departures of Shankar and Maha Dev - the former resurfaced in the similarly-styled Kala - robbed Quintessence of a sense of purpose and the group split up following the release of *Indweller*.

Albums: *In Blissful Company* (1969), *Quintessence* (1970), *Dive Deep* (1970, *Self* (1971), *Indweller* (1972).

Quireboys

After violent incidents at early live shows, this UK band altered their name from Queerboys to Quireboys, to avoid further trouble. Comprising Spike (vocals), Nigel Mogg (bass; brother of Phil Mogg of **UFO**), Chris Johnstone (keyboards), Guy Bailey (guitar), Ginger (guitar) and Coze (drums), they were originally all drinking buddies in London pubs. Drawing musical inspiration from the **Faces**, **Rolling Stones** and **Mott The Hoople**, they specialized in bar-room boogie, beer-soaked blues and infectious raunch 'n' roll. Spike's rough-as-a-gravel-path vocal style, closely resembling **Rod Stewart**'s, added fuel to accusations of the band being little more than Faces copyists. After releasing two independent singles they signed to **EMI** and immediately underwent a line-up re-shuffle. Coze and Ginger were removed and replaced by Ian Wallace and Guy Griffin, respectively. They recorded *A Bit Of What You Fancy* in Los Angeles, under the production eye of Jim Cregan (former Rod Stewart guitarist). It was an immediate success, entering the UK album charts at number 2. 'Hey You', lifted as a single, also met with similar success, peaking at number 14 in January 1990. An eight-track live album followed, which duplicated most of the numbers from their first album, as a stop-gap measure to bridge the long period between successive studio releases. However, when *Bitter Sweet & Twisted* failed to ignite Spike would leave to form his own band, God's Hotel, denying rumours that he had been invited to replace Axl Rose in **Guns N'Roses** (after having contributed to Slash's solo album). The Quireboys had come to a natural conclusion, or, as Spike prefers to put it - 'we were past our sell-by-date'. Bassist Nigel Mogg put together his own project, the Nancy Boys, in New York.

Albums: *A Bit Of What You Fancy* (Parlophone 1989), *Live Around The World* (Parlophone 1990), *Bitter Sweet & Twisted* (Parlophone 1992). Compilation: *From Tooting To Barking* (Castle 1994).

Video: *A Bit Of What You Fancy* (1990).

Quiver

This under-rated group evolved from the ruins of **Junior's Eyes**, one of UK's more inventive progressive rock bands. Tim Renwick (guitar) and Honk (bass) founded the new unit, but when the latter dropped out, the line-up was completed by Pete Thomas (bass), formerly of Village, ex-**Cochise** drummer John 'Willie' Wilson' and guitarist/songwriter Cal Batchelor. Quiver hold the distinction of being the first group to play at London's famous Rainbow Theatre. Their two albums showcase a grasp of melodic rock, similar to American acts such as the **Doobie Brothers**, while sharing an affinity with the early **Brinsley Schwarz**. Neither release made a commercial impact and in 1973 all of the group, except Batchelor, agreed to amalgamate with the **Sutherland Brothers**. Renwick, meanwhile, joined 747, a short-lived pub-rock band, before forming Kicks, an equally brief ensemble.

Albums: *Quiver* (1971), *Gone In The Morning* (1972).

R

R&S Records

Ghent Belgium techno label/talent pool founded by Renaat Vanderpapeliere and Sabine Maes in the early 80s. R&S's high profile has been earned on the back of some of the dance scene's most innovative aritsts: **Kevin Saunderson/Derrick May**, **Dave Angel** ('Planet Function', 'Stairway To Heaven') **Joey Beltram** ('Vol 1-2' etc.), **C.J. Bolland** ('Ravesignal 1-3'), **Jam & Spoon** ('Stella') and the **Aphex Twin** ('Didgeridoo') - a who's who of techno in itself, have all seen their vinyl bedecked by the familiar R&S enblem of a reering steed. In 1987 Code 61 provided the label with 'Drop The Deal', which became an early balearic hit and established R&S' credentials. From their roots in the much-maligned 'Belgian new beat' scene, the label picked up the Detroit sound and nurtured it into a hard house style best recalled on tracks like Spectrum's 'Brazil'. Subsequent records like Human Resource's 'Dominator' and Beltram's 'Mentasm' proved hugely important to the UK's rave generation. However, it is far more than a one horse stable, as can be discerned by its subsidiary operations. These include Apollo (ambient), Global Cuts (uplifting club house), Outrage (experimental) and Diatomyc (acid). Notable also have been two series of compilations, *TZ* (Test Zone) and *In Order To Dance*. The latter gathers highlights from the R&S roster at more or less regular intervals, providing DJs and clubbers with the most important cuts. The label set up a UK outlet in the beginning of 1993, which co-ordinates releases and promotion in tandem with the six person team in Ghent, while former employee Marcus Graham left to form ITP with DJ Eddie Love Chocolate. Among the label's most satisfying current projects have been **Jaydee** ('Plastic Dreams'), **Biosphere** ('Microgravity'), C.J. Bolland ('The 4th Sign'), **Source** ('Organized Noise') and **Locust**, whose album project for Apollo was produced in association with a documentary. R&S planned to delve further into multi-media projects with a MTV tie-up party and the inclusion of a computer game, film and subliminal artwork as part of *In Order To Dance 5*. Plans for a 'helicopter shuttle service' for staff members between Ghent and London were probably an exaggeration, but it would be unwise to rule anything out bearing in mind R&S' formidable former achievements and appetite for dance music.

Selected albums: Various: *In Order To Dance Volumes 1-5* (R&S 1990 - 1994).

R. Cajun And The Zydeco Brothers

R. Cajun were formed in 1979 by Chris Hall, a former member of Shufflin' Sam and a keen enthusiast of Cajun music. The original line-up was Chris Hall (b. 2 July 1952, Sheffield, Yorkshire, England; accordion/vocals), Tony Dark (fiddle), Alf Billington (guitar/vocals), and Veronica Matthews (triangle). The following year, Trevor Hopkins (bass) joined the line-up, but was soon replaced by Beeds (b. 13 October 1947, Derby, Derbyshire, England; guitar/harmonica). The line-up, which started to make some impact on the folk circuit in 1982, consisted of Hall, Billington, John Squire (fiddle/guitar/mandolin), who joined that year, as did Beeds, and Jan Hall (b. 17 January 1953, Sheffield, Yorkshire, England; triangle/percussion). *Bayou Rhythms* included the Zydeco Brothers, Graham Jones (bass) and Neil 'Freddy' Hopwood (b. 23 April 1947, Lichfield, Staffordshire, England; drums). Hopwood had formerly been a member of **Dr. Strangely Strange**, and the **Sutherland Brothers** bands. The album contained some infectious pieces such as 'Cajun Two-Step', and 'Bayou Pom Pom Special', as well as standards such as 'Jambalaya' and 'Deportees', and quickly established them as a popular group at festivals. In 1984, Dave Blant (b. 27 November 1949, Burton Upon Trent, Staffordshire, England; bass/vocals) joined, replacing Graham Jones. Having previously left the group, Tony Dark re-joined them in 1986, in turn replacing John Squire. The same year, Clive Harvey (b. 27 November 1945, Watford, Hertfordshire, England; guitar/vocals), was added. It was this line-up that recorded *Pig Sticking In Arcadia*. Three years later, Dark again left the group, to be replaced by Derek Richardson (fiddle), then Dave 'Mitch' Proctor (b. 8 December 1952, Heanor, Derbyshire, England; fiddle) joined in 1990, replacing Richardson. Despite the various personnel changes, the overall sound of the group has remained remarkably constant. Their blend of cajun and zydeco, apart from being unusual, has added to the band's original sound and style. They are currently playing festivals, both at home and abroad, where they are equally popular.

Albums: *Bayou Rhythms* (1984), *Pig Sticking In Arcadia* (1987), *Out Of The Swamp* (1990), *No Known Cure* (1993), *That Cajun Thing* (Bearcat 1994).

R.A.F.

This Scottish-based group revolved around David

Valentine (vocals/keyboards) and Douglas Bogie (guitar). A set of superior demos engendered a recording deal with **A&M Records** which resulted in the melodic *R.A.F.* Billy McGhee (bass) and Tom Annan (percussion) completed the featured line-up, but by the release of *Restless Spirit*, the group had become synonymous with Valentine. A veteran of Edinburgh's beat group scene, this accomplished musician pre-produced the set in his own recording studio, before completing it with the aid of London-based session musicians. Despite interest in US musical circles, the album was not a commercial success, and the R.A.F. name has since been shelved.

Albums: *R.A.F.* (1980), *The Heat's On* (1981), *Restless Spirit* (1986).

R.E.M.

R.E.M. played their first concert in Athens, Georgia, USA on 19 April 1980. Their line-up, then as now, consisted of four drop-outs from the University of Georgia; Michael Stipe (vocals), Peter Buck (guitar), Mike Mills (bass) and Bill Berry (drums). Without the charisma of Stipe and his eccentric onstage behaviour, hurling himself about with abandon in between mumbling into the microphone, they could easily have been overlooked as just another bar band, relying on the harmonious guitar sound of the **Byrds** for their inspiration. Acquiring a healthy following among the college fraternity in their hometown, it wasn't long before they entered the studio to record their debut single 'Radio Free Europe', to be released independently on Hibtone Records. This was greeted with considerable praise by critics who conceded that the band amounted to more than the sum of their influences. Their country/folk sound was contradicted by a driving bassline and an urgency that put the listener more in mind of the **Who** in their early mod phase. Add to this the distinctive voice of Stipe and his, on the whole, inaudible, perhaps even non-existent, lyrics, and R.E.M. sounded quite unlike any other band in the USA, in the post-punk era of the early 80s. Gaining further favourable notices for the *Chronic Town* mini-LP, their debut full-length album was now eagerly anticipated; when it arrived in 1983 it surpassed all expectations, and was eventually made Album Of The Year by **Rolling Stone** magazine. As in the USA, the band earned a devoted cult following in Europe, largely comprised of college students, as a result of *Murmur*.

Reckoning appeared the following year and was permeated by a reckless spontaneity that had been missing from their earlier work. Recorded in only 12 days, the tracks varied in mood from frustration, as on 'So. Central Rain', to the tongue-in-cheek singalong '(Don't Go Back To) Rockville'. The songs were accessible enough but, as would be the case for most of the 80s, the singles culled from R.E.M.'s albums were generally deemed uncommercial by mainstream radio programmers. However, their cult reputation benefited from a series of flop singles on both sides of the Atlantic. Although received enthusiastically by critics, *Fables Of The Reconstruction* was a stark, morose album that mirrored a period of despondency within the band. Peter Buck summed it up in the 90s - 'If we were to record those songs again, they would be very different'. *Life's Rich Pageant*, in 1986, showed the first signs of a politicization within the band that would come to a head, and coincide with their commercial breakthrough, in the late 80s. Stipe's lyrics began to dwell increasingly on the prevailing amorality in the USA and question its inherited ethics, whilst still retaining their much vaunted obliqueness. Tracks like 'These Days' and 'Cuyahoga' were rallying cries to the young and disaffected; although the lyrics were reflective and almost bitter, the music was the most joyous and uplifting the band had recorded to date. This ironic approach to songwriting was typified by 'It's The End Of The World As We Know It (And I Feel Fine)', from the equally impressive *Document*. Released also as a single, it intentionally trivialized its subject matter with a witty and up-tempo infectiousness, more characteristic of the **Housemartins**.

Green arrived in 1988 and sold slowly but steadily in the USA, the attendant single 'Stand' reaching number 6 there, while 'Orange Crush' entered the UK Top 30. Apart from demonstrating their environmental awareness, particularly in 'You Are The Everything', the album laid more emphasis than previously on Stipe's vocals and lyrics. This, to the singer's dismay, led to his elevation as 'spokesman for a generation'. Already hero-worshiped by adoring long-term fans, Stipe insists 'Rock 'n' roll is a joke, people who take it seriously are the butt of the joke'. The world tour that coincided with the album's release saw R.E.M. making a smooth transition from medium-size venues to the stadium circuit, due as much to Stipe's individual choreography as to the elaborate, projected backdrops. After a break of two years the band re-emerged in 1991 with *Out Of Time*. Their previous use of horns and mandolins to embroider songs did not prepare their audience for the deployment of an entire string section, nor were the contributions from **B-52s** singer Kate Pierson and Boogie Down Productions' KRS-1 expected. Ostensibly all love songs, the album was unanimously hailed as a masterpiece and entered the UK Top 5 on its release, topping both US and UK album charts shortly afterwards. The accompanying singles from that album 'Losing My Religion', 'Shiny Happy People', and 'Near Wild Heaven' gave them further hits. After picking up countless awards during the early 90s the band has maintained the high standard set by *Out Of Time*. *Automatic For The People* was released in October 1992, to universal favour. It reached the top of the charts in the UK and USA. Michael Stipe was seen both as pin-up and creative genius. The album produced a number of memorable singles including the moody 'Drive' and the joyous 'Man In The Moon', with its classic **Elvis Presley** vocal inflections from Stipe and an accompanying award-winning monochrome video. *Monster* showed the band in grungelike mode, not letting any accusations of selling out bother them, and certainly letting fans and critics alike know that they had not gone soft. 'What's The Frequency Kenneth?' started a run of further hit singles taken from the album and further awards were heaped upon them. Following the collapse of Bill Berry in Switzerland while on a major tour the band were forced to rest up. Berry was operated on for a ruptured aneurysm and it is expected that he will make a full recovery without any brain damage. The critical praise heaped upon the band has been monumental, through all the attention the band appear united, reasonably unaffected and painfully modest. They are one of the most important and popular groups to appear over the past three decades, and still retain massive credibility together with fresh ideas.

Albums: *Chronic Town* (IRS 1982, mini-LP), *Murmur* (IRS 1983), *Reckoning* (IRS 1984), *Fables Of The Reconstruction* (IRS 1985), *Life's Rich Pageant* (IRS 1986), *Document* (IRS 1987), *Dead Letter Office* (IRS 1987, outtakes and b-sides), *Green* (Warner 1988), *Out Of Time* (Warner 1991), *Automatic For The People* (Warner 1992), *Monster* (Warner 1994). Compilation: *Eponymous* (IRS 1988).

Videos: *Succumbs* (1987), *Pop Screen* (1990), *This Film Is On* (1991), *Tourfilm* (1991), *Parallel* (1995).

Further reading: *Remarks: Story Of R.E.M.*, Tony Fletcher. *R.E.M.: File Under Water, The Definitive Guide To 12 Years Of Recordings And Con*, Jon Storey. *An R.E.M. Companion: It Crawled From The South*, Marcus Gray. *R.E.M.: Behind The Mask*, Jim Greer. *Talk About The Passion: R.E.M. An Oral History*, Denise Sullivan. *R.E.M. Documental*, Dave Bowler and Bryan Dray.

Rabbitt, Eddie

b. Edward Thomas Rabbitt, 27 November 1944, Brooklyn, New York City, USA. Rabbitt, whose name is Gaelic, was raised in East Orange, New Jersey. His father, Thomas Rabbitt, a refrigeration engineer, played fiddle and accordion and is featured alongside his son on the 1978 track, 'Song Of Ireland'. On a scouting holiday, Rabbitt was introduced to country music and he soon became immersed in the history of its performers. Rabbitt's first single was 'Six Nights And Seven Days' on 20th Century Fox in 1964, and he had further singles for **Columbia**, 'Bottles' and 'I Just Don't Care No More'. Rabbitt, who found he could make no headway singing country music in New York, decided to move to Nashville in 1968. Sitting in a bath in a cheap hotel, he had the idea for 'Working My Way Up From The Bottom', which was recorded by **Roy Drusky**. At first, he had difficulty in placing other

songs although **George Morgan** recorded 'The Sounds Of Goodbye' and **Bobby Lewis** 'Love Me And Make It All Better'. He secured a recording contract and at the same time gave Lamar Fike a tape of songs for **Elvis Presley**. Presley chose the one he was planning to do himself, 'Kentucky Rain', and took it to number 16 in the US country charts and number 21 in th UK. Presley also recorded 'Patch It Up' and 'Inherit The Wind'. In 1974 **Ronnie Milsap** topped the US country charts with 'Pure Love', which Rabbitt had written for his future wife, Janine, the references in the song being to commercials for Ivory soap ('99 44/100th per cent') and 'Cap'n Crunch'. Rabbitt also recorded 'Sweet Janine' on his first album. He had his first US country success as a performer with 'You Get To Me' in 1974, and, two years later, topped the US country charts with 'Drinkin' My Baby (Off My Mind)', a good time drinking song he had written with Even Stevens.

He often wrote with Stevens and also with his producer, David Molloy. Rabbitt followed his success with the traditional-sounding 'Rocky Mountain Music' and two more drinking songs, 'Two Dollars In The Jukebox (Five In A Bottle)' and 'Pour Me Another Tequila'. Rabbitt was criticized by the Women's Christian Temperance Union for damaging their cause. Further number 1s came with 'I Just Want To Love You', which he had written during the session, 'Suspicions' and the theme for the Clint Eastwood film, *Every Which Way But Loose*, which also made number 41 in the UK. Rabbitt harmonized with himself on the 1980 country number 1, 'Gone Too Far'. Inspired by the rhythm of **Bob Dylan**'s 'Subterranean Homesick Blues', he wrote 'Drivin' My Life Away', a US Top 5 pop hit as well as a number 1 country hit, for the 1980 film *Roadie*. A fragment of a song he had written 12 years earlier gave him the concept for 'I Love A Rainy Night', which topped both the US pop and country charts. He had further number 1 country hits with 'Step By Step' (US pop 5) and the **Eagles**-styled 'Someone Could Lose A Heart Tonight' (US pop 15). He also had chart-topping country duets with **Crystal Gayle** ('You And I') and **Juice Newton** ('Both To Each Other (Friends And Lovers)'), the latter being the theme for the television soap opera, *Days Of Our Lives*. Rabbitt's son, Timmy, was born with a rare disease in 1983 and Rabbitt cut back on his commitments until Timmy's death in 1985. Another son, Tommy, was born in good health in 1986. Rabbitt topped the US country charts by reviving a pure rock 'n' roll song from his youth in New York, **Dion**'s 'The Wanderer'. During his son's illness, he had found songwriting difficult but wrote his 1988 US country number 1, 'I Wanna Dance With You'. His ambition is to write 'a classic, one of those songs that will support me for the rest of my life'.

Albums: *Eddie Rabbitt* (1975), *Rocky Mountain Music* (1976), *Variations* (1978), *Loveline* (1979), *Horizon* (1980),

Step By Step (1981), *Radio Romance* (1982), *Rabbitt Trax* (1986), *I Wanna Dance With You* (1988), *Jersey Boy* (1990), *Ten Rounds* (1991).

Rabin, Oscar

b. Oscar Rabinowitz, 26 April 1899, Latvia, Russia, d. 20 June 1958, England. An extremely popular figure on the British dance band scene from the 30s through to the 50s. After emigrating to England with his parents when he was a small child, Rabin won a scholarship to the Guildhall School of Music and led his own outfit while in his teens. In the late 20s he formed a small dance band with singer and actor Harry Davis, and their association lasted for some 25 years. Davis fronted the bands, and Rabin, who was a fine musician and an astute businessman but did not have the extrovert personality necessary to lead on the stand, concentrated on playing the saxophone. They spent most of the 30s resident at two prestige London venues, the Astoria, Charing Cross Road and the Hammersmith Palais, and their first recordings to be released were made early in 1933. A hectic touring schedule during the 40s was followed by a long spell at Mecca's Lyceum Ballroom in the Strand in the 50s. Harry Davis left the organization in 1951, and was replaced by David Ede, who continued to lead the band for some years after Rabin's death in 1958. Many talented artists have reason to be grateful for the showcase Rabin afforded them over the years, including musicians **Don Rendell**, Arthur Greenslade, Eddie Harvey, Bill Geldard, Don Pashley, **Kenny Clare**, Bernie Fenton, Laurie Gold, and vocalists Alan Dean, Bob Dale, Annabelle Lee, Cyril Shane, Marion Williams and Harry Davis's daughter Beryl Davis, amongst many others. Rabin also nurtured future top bandleaders and arrangers such as **Wally Stott**, **Ken Mackintosh** and **Tito Burns**. Rabin's attractive and familiar signature tune, 'Dancing Time', was written by **Jerome Kern** and George Grossmith for the highly successful 1921 London musical *The Cabaret Girl*.
Selected albums: *Especially For You* (Decca 1981), *Try A Little Tenderness* (Burlington 1988).

Rabin, Trevor

b. 1955, South Africa. Trevor Rabin learned classical piano and guitar from an early age, forming his first band, Rabbit, when he was aged only 14. Rabbit were a short-lived teenybop sensation in South Africa during the early 70s, releasing two albums which reached gold status. Moving to England in 1977, he signed to **Chrysalis Records** and polished up some demos he had previously recorded in South Africa for release as his first solo album. This featured a mixture of styles, and included jazz, rock, blues and AOR numbers. Future releases pursued a more mainstream melodic rock approach, with *Wolf*, released in 1981, being his *tour-de-force*. He also ventured into production with

Wild Horses and **Manfred Mann**. He accepted the invitation to join **Yes** in 1983, and it was not until there was a major conflict in this camp that he managed to find enough time to record another solo effort. *Can't Look Away*, surfacing in 1989, had more in common with Yes than with his previous solo work. In 1990 he helped contribute to **Seal**'s big-selling debut album.
Albums: *Trevor Rabin* (Chrysalis 1978), *Face To Face* (Chrysalis 1979), *Wolf* (Chrysalis 1981), *Can't Look Away* (Elektra 1989).

Rabinowitz, Harry

b. 26 March 1916, Johannesburg, South Africa. Trained as a classical pianist, Rabinowitz was educated at Athlone High School and Witwatersrand University and made his first radio broadcast in 1933. After service with the South African Army, he studied composition and conducting, and moved to London in 1946 to continue his studies at the Guildhall School of Music. He played the piano on several BBC popular radio programmes, including *Variety Bandbox*, and spent some time as house pianist at **EMI Records**. His first conducting jobs were with the show, *Golden City* (1950), followed by four ice spectaculars at London's Empress Hall, and as musical director for **Alan Jay Lerner** and **Frederick Loewe**'s 1953 hit, *Paint Your Wagon*. In the same year he joined the BBC staff and was conductor of the BBC Revue Orchestra until 1960, working on programmes such as *Take It From Here*, *Henry Hall's Guest Night*, *Variety Playhouse* and *Just Fancy*. He also featured as a pianist on *Piano Playtime*, *Rendezvous* and *Midday Music Hall*. In 1960, he moved to BBC Television as Head Of Music for Light Entertainment, and was responsible for programmes such as the *Val Doonican Show*, *Michael Bentine Show*, *Billy Cotton Band Show* and *Not Only But Also*, featuring Peter Cook and **Dudley Moore**. Rabinowitz moved to the rival London Weekend Television as Head of Music in 1968, and during the next nine years his projects included *Black Beauty*, *Upstairs, Downstairs* and several David Frost programmes. He also composed many themes to successful television programmes such *The Agatha Christie Hour* and *Love For Lydia*, which was nominated for an **Ivor Novello** Award in 1977. In the same year he won the Television And Radio Industries Council Celebrity Award for 'Best Television Theme Music Of The Year' for his music to *Reilly, Ace Of Spies*. Since returning to freelance work in 1977, Rabinowitz has been musical director for many feature films, such as *The Greek Tycoon* (1978), *Mon Oncle D'Amerique* (1980), *Chariots Of Fire* (1981), *Time Bandits* (1981), *Heat And Dust* (1982), *Maurice* (1987), *Queen Of Hearts* (1989), *Music Box* (1989), *Lord Of The Flies* (1990), and *The Ballad Of The Sad Cafe* (1990). In the early 80s, he conducted the first six weeks of the London runs of **Andrew Lloyd Webber**'s *Cats* and

Song And Dance, and travelled to the USA to conduct the Los Angeles Philharmonic Orchestra in concerts at the Hollywood Bowl. In the UK, he frequently conducts the Royal Philharmonic, the London Symphony, and the London Concert Orchestras at venues such as London's Barbican Centre and the Royal Festival Hall. In 1977, he was awarded an MBE for services to music.

Race, Steve

b. 1 April 1921, Lincoln, England. Race is a prolific broadcaster, pianist, writer and composer, with tastes and skills ranging from jazz to classical music. He studied at the Royal Academy of Music in London before playing piano with various dance bands. He made his first broadcast with Willie Wilson's Band from the Criterion Theatre, Piccadilly Circus, on 8 March 1941. Later that year Race joined the Royal Air Force, and organized his own musical ensembles, writing arrangements for name bands such **Ted Heath**, **Eric Winstone**, **Phil Green** and Paul Fenoulhet and the Skyrockets. After his demobilization in 1946, Race played on broadcasts with **Lew Stone**, **George Elrick** and **Jack Jackson**, and also spent six years as an audition pianist for the newly-formed BBC Television Service. From 1955-60, he was Light Music Advisor to the Associated Rediffusion Television company, and worked on several of their top-rated shows including *Opportunity Knocks*. In 1966 Race became chairman, and compiled the questions for the musical panel game *My Music*. First on radio, then television, the show ran for over 500 editions, and into the 90s. Other programmes during an extremely varied broadcasting career included *Talk Of The Town, Centre Show, The Forces Show, Jazz In Perspective, Musician At Large, Kaleidoscope, Look What They've Done To My Song, Jazz Record Requests* and current affairs programmes such as *Any Questions* and *PM*. He appeared regularly on BBC radio programmes hosted by great comedians such as Tony Hancock, Peter Sellers, Arthur Askey and Dickie Henderson. A contributor to numerous magazines and periodicals, he had a regular column in the *Melody Maker* for 12 years. His other publications include *Musician At Large* (an autobiography), *My Music, Dear Music Lover, Steve Race's Music Quiz, You Can't Be Serious* and *The Two Worlds Of Joseph Race*. In 1962 Race won the **Ivor Novello** Award for the Outstanding Orchestral Composition of the Year with the latin-styled 'Nicola', named after his daughter. His other compositions include 'Pied Piper (The Beeje)' (which entered the UK Top 30 in 1963), 'Faraway Music', 'My Music - My Songs', 'The Day Of The Donkey', in addition to countless pieces of mood music and incidental music for television and radio programmes such as *Cyrano de Bergerac, Twelfth Night, Richard III*, plus music for many television commercials. In 1987 he was awarded the Wavendon Allmusic

Media Personality Of The Year Award, and in the following year his *Steve Race Presents The BBC Radio Orchestra* on Radio 2 won a major award. After celebrating 50 years of broadcasting in 1991, a year later his contribution to popular music was rewarded with an O.B.E.

Further reading: *Musician At Large*, Steve Race. *Dear Music Lover*, Steve Race.

Racer X

This Los Angeles, California, USA band earned a reputation for guitar-orientated melodic rock, delivered with precision despite the blurring speed. Featuring Jeff Martin (vocals; ex-Surgical Steel), Paul Gilbert (guitar), John Alderete (bass) and Harry Gschoesser (drums; ex-Nobros) they released *Street Lethal*, a high-tech fusion of relentless guitar work and some memorable songs. Scott Travis (ex-Hawk) took over the drum stool and Bruce Bouillet was added as a second guitarist in 1986. By the time *Second Heat* was issued the following year the band had matured considerably, with the music more accomplished on several levels, most notably in arrangement and production. Paul Gilbert left in 1988 to join **Mr. Big**, and was replaced by Chris Arvan. Jeff Martin broke ranks shortly afterwards and Scott Travis understandably accepted the offer to join his heroes, **Judas Priest**. The band ground to a halt in 1990.

Albums: *Street Lethal* (Roadrunner 1986), *Second Heat* (Roadrunner 1987), *Extreme Volume...Live* (Roadrunner 1988), *Live...Extreme Vol. 2* (Roadrunner 1992).

Racey

One of **Mickie Most**'s numerous UK successes on the **RAK** label in the 70s, this pop outfit originated from Weston Super Mare, Somerset, England. The line-up featured Phil Fursdon (vocals/guitar), Richard Gower (vocals/keyboards), Pete Miller (vocals/bass) and Clive Wilson (vocals/drums). After playing extensively round the pub circuits, an early supporter called Steve Matthews brought them to the attention of Most in London. He quickly signed them after hearing a demo, and they released their debut 'Baby It's You', written by Chris Norman and Pete Spencer of **Smokie**, which narrowly missed the charts. However, they got their hit with second single, 'Lay Your Love On Me', which rose to number 3 in the UK charts in 1979. 'Some Girls' went one place better in March, but after two more hits, including a cover of **Dion**'s 'Runaround Sue', the race was over.

Album: *Smash And Grab* (1979).

Rachell, James 'Yank'

b. 16 March 1910, Brownsville, Tennessee, USA. Yank Rachell learned mandolin from his uncle Daniel Taylor and later extended his talents to include guitar, harmonica and violin. He worked on the L&N railroad as a track hand in his early years, supplementing his

income by playing local dances and parties in the company of local artists such as **Hambone Willie Newbern**. Rachell seems to have been doubling as a talent scout when he recorded with **Sleepy John Estes** in 1929. Later, he formed a partnership with Dan Smith and worked on record with **John Lee Sonny Boy Williamson**. Recordings under his own name appeared on labels such as Victor, Vocalion and Banner and between 1938 and 1941 he recorded 24 titles for the famous Bluebird label. Despite all this activity Yank was never able to survive as a full-time musician and often worked as a farmer. He returned to music, along with Estes and **Hammie Nixon,** with the revival of interest in blues in the early 60s. During that period he appeared at festivals, clubs and concerts, and recorded again for Delmark in 1964.
Albums: *Complete Recordings In Chronological Order Volume 1 (1934-1938) Vol 2 (1938-1941)* (1986), *Yank Rachell* (1964).

Racing Cars

From his Manchester, England audio shop, ex-**Mindbenders** Bob Land (bass) was persuaded to re-enter showbusiness in 1975 with Graham Headley Williams (guitar), Gareth Mortimer (guitar), Roy Edwards (keyboards) and Robert Wilding (drums). Released by **Chrysalis**, their records included bit-parts for session pianist Geraint Watkins, American saxophonist Jerry Jumonville, the Bowles Brothers Band (on vocal harmonies) and **Swinging Blue Jeans** guitarist Ray Ennis. Reaching number 39 in the UK album list, the band's debut *Downtown Tonight* also produced an unexpected Top 20 entry with the ballad 'They Shoot Horses Don't They'. No more hits were forthcoming but the group were sufficiently established in the colleges to issue two further albums.
Albums: *Downtown Tonight* (1976), *Weekend Rendezvous* (1977), *Bring On The Night* (1978).

Radcliff, Bobby

b. 22 September 1951, Bethesda, Maryland, USA. Radcliff started to play guitar at 12 years old. In the 60s and 70s he worked on the Washington DC blues scene, associating with veterans such as **Thomas 'TNT' Tribble** and **Bobby Parker.** By the end of the 60s he spent some time in Chicago, meeting and absorbing the music of bluesmen such as **Magic Sam**, **Otis Rush**, and **Jimmy Dawkins**. Radcliff moved to New York in 1977 and in the early 80s he recorded a little edition album for the A-OK label. Towards the end of the decade he was recommended to his present label, Black Top Records, by **Ronnie Earl,** and his first album for them was highly acclaimed. Radcliff is a strong singer and a powerful, rhythmic guitarist who utilizes elements of soul and funk in his playing.
Albums: *Dresses Too Short* (Black Top 1989), *Universal Blues* (Black Top 1991).

Radiants

An R&B vocal group from Chicago, Illinois, USA. The Radiants were a typical transitional group of the early 60s who brought doo-wop harmonies into the soul era with gospel-inspired vocal treatments. The group began in 1960 when Maurice McAlister (b. 11 January 1940, Mississippi, USA) distilled a vocal group from members of the Greater Harvest Baptist Church choir. The original group besides McAlister (lead) were Wallace Sampson (baritone), Jerome Brooks (second tenor), Elzie Butler (bass), and Green McLauren (first tenor), and their first hit (and disc) for **Chess Records** was a **Miracles**-styled 'Father Knows Best' (1962), but the superior b-side, 'One Day I'll Show You', received much regional play. 'Heartbreak Society' and 'Shy Guy', both 1963, failed to generate sales outside the Chicago and the group reorganized as a trio - Maurice McAlister, Wallace Sampson, and Leonard Caston Jnr. The trio format introduced a unique pronounced switch-off lead style in which the vocal interplay worked like a constant flux of voices slipping in and out of the musical mix, most evident on 'Voice Your Choice' (number 16 R&B), from 1964, and 'It Ain't No Big Thing' (number 14 R&B), from 1965. Another reorganization took place in 1965, in which McAlister left the group, and the Radiants then hit with 'Feel Kind Of Bad' (number 47 R&B), and yet after another reorganization got a hit with 'Hold On' (number 35 R&B). The Radiants broke up in 1972. McAlister and McLauren, meanwhile, formed in 1966 a duo, Maurice And Mac, that received several southern R&B hits recording in Muscle Shoals, Alabama, notably with 'You Left The Water Running' (number 43 R&B) in 1968.

Radiator

A replica of the folk/rock band **Lindisfarne** in everything but name. Led by **Alan Hull**, the band had two drummers, and operated directly before Lindisfarne reformed. Members were recruited from Lindisfarne and **Snafu**, and their music was more uptempo than much of Hull's often intospective work, revealing something of his thinking at the time.
Album: *Isn't It Strange?* (1977).

Radiators (UK)

During the punk uprising in Eire during the 70s, two bands with similar aspirations and backgrounds became highly popular locally. The **Boomtown Rats** went on to huge success, while their equal rivals did not. Formed as Greta Garbage And The Trashcans in 1972 the band evolved from the two original members Peter Holidai (b. 19 May 1954, Dublin, Eire; guitar/vocals) and Stephen Rapid (vocals). Known as the Radiators From Space they were joined by Phillip Chevron (guitar/vocals), Jimmy Crashe (bass) and

Mark Megaray (bass). Their debut single 'Television Screen' was released in April 1977, an energetic power pop song which preceeded the album *Radiators From Space*.

The band relocated to London in September 1977, although they were frustrated by the delay in the release of **Tony Visconti** produced *Ghostown*, which had been completed. 'Million Dollar Hero' was given heavy radio exposure and the single entered the UK chart, just outside the then crucial Top 75. The band were geared up for an appearance on *Top Of The Pops* the following week, providing the single broached the Top 75. The single dropped the following week and vital exposure was missed. The delay in the release of *Ghostown* found the band at a low ebb. Shortly afterwards following a gig at London's Electric Ballroom. In 1980 'Stranger Than Fiction' was released (produced by *Hans Zimmer*) and the band folded in 1981.
Albums: *Radiators From Space* (1977), *Ghostown* (1979).

Radiators (USA)

Formed in New Orleans, Louisiana, USA in 1978, the Radiators became one of that city's most popular rock bands by the late 80s, developing a national following in the process. Keyboardist/vocalist Ed Volker and guitarist/vocalist Camile Baudoin began playing together in the 60s. Drummer Frank Bua started accompanying them in 1970. Guitarist/vocalist Dave Malone and bassist Reggie Scanlon played with another New Orleans band, Roadapple, in the 70s and the five musicians fused as the Rhapsodizers in the mid-70s. The name was changed to the Radiators in 1978 and *Work Done On Premises,* was released two years later on their own Croaker label. *Heat Generation* followed a year later. Percussionist Glenn Sears joined in the 80s. By that time the band had built up a local following, particularly among college students, due to its tireless live performances and multi-hour sessions featuring long improvisations in a style comparable to that of **Little Feat** and the **Allman Brothers Band**. Their concerts were highlights of the annual New Orleans Jazz & Heritage Festival and an audience cropped up in places as far away as New York and Chicago. In 1987, after a six-year recording absence, the Radiators signed to Epic Records and released *Law Of The Fish*, a critically-acclaimed album. *Zig-Zaggin' Through Ghostland*, followed in 1989, by which time the band was able to sell out medium-sized concert halls in several US cities.
Albums: *Work Done On Premises* (1980), *Heat Generation* (1981), *Law Of The Fish* (1987), *Zig-Zaggin' Through Ghostland* (1989).

Radiators From Space

(see **Radiators** (UK))

Radical Dance Faction

Formed from the ashes of UK anarchic reggae band Military Surplus, RDF, as they are commonly abbreviated, set out in 1987. Their line-ups have been erratic but are based around the one constant, lyricist and vocalist Chris Bowsher. Using beat poetry, with its imagery of modern decay and capitalism gone wrong, their chosen musical outlet is reggae and ska. Bowsher was a veteran of the early punk explosion, and was particularly enamoured of bands like the **Clash** and **Ruts** who attempted to bridge the gap between rock and black music. Alongside the **Levellers**, they became prime movers in the media-christened 'crusty' movement (ie their following comprises largely the dispossessed and homeless, bonded by a political consciousness which has its roots in hippiedom, beatnik romanticism and early 80s anarcho-punk).
Albums: *Borderland Cases* (1989), *Wasteland* (1991).

Radics, Jack

b. Jordan Bailey, Kingston, Jamaica, West Indies. As a teenager Radics had become involved with the New World **sound system** in 1975, responsible for running a little soul selection at their uptown Kingston gigs before trying his hand as a singer. He made one recording, a cover of **Kool And The Gang**'s 'Get Down On It', before moving to London in the early 80s. There he met up with producer Blacker Dread who released 'Easy' (a duet with Debbie Ryvers) and 'Walk On By' in 1985, the year he was signed to **Island** under his real name. Despite recording an album for them only a handful of tracks ever emerged. When the contract expired in 1988 he returned to Jamaica and promptly scored two local hits with 'Dream Merchant' and 'Conversation'. It was at the Sting '90 festival that he made his reputation for singing in a dramatic and exaggerated baritone which, once harnessed to **dancehall** rhythms, provided a barrage of releases for a variety of Jamaican producers. 'Set My Heart On Fire' for Shocking Vibes, 'All Of Me' on **Freddie McGregor**'s Big Ship label, 'Good Loving' for boxer Lloyd Honeyghan and 'I'll Be Sweeter' and 'My Love Is On Fire' for **Penthouse** were all substantial hits in 1991, the year Castro Brown released Radics' debut album, *Jack*.

The following year he repeated the process all over again, increasing his volume of cover versions and also his producers, who by now had grown to include numerous labels in Jamaica, England and America. The list increased throughout 1993 when there was a growing shift towards more self-penned, cultural material, resulting in several fine sides for Star Trail, Shocking Vibes, **Bobby Digital** and Taxi. That summer the Montego Bay label Top Rank released his second album *Something*, which was followed by his belated Penthouse set, *I'll Be Sweeter*, in October. In

December 1993 **Sly And Robbie** teamed Radics with **Chaka Demus And Pliers** on a version of 'Twist And Shout' which became an international hit, reaching number 1 on the UK chart in January 1994. Selected albums: *Jack* (New Name 1991), *Something* (Top Rank 1993), *I'll Be Sweeter* (Penthouse 1993).

Radio Birdman

This highly-rated Australian group was formed in Sydney, New South Wales in 1974. Its Detroit/**MC5** guitar-based sound was propelled by two American medical students Deniz Tek (b. Detroit, Michigan, USA; guitar) and Phillip 'Pip' Hoyle (guitar/keyboards), plus Rob Younger (vocals), Gilbert Warwick (guitar), Ron Keely (drums), Carl Rourke (bass) and, joining later, Chris Masuak (guitar). Because of study commitments the band was very much a part-time affair. This heightened the mystique which surrounded the band as they forged their own niche on the outer fringe of the Sydney music circuit from the mid-70s. A trip to the UK in 1978 saw a short tour and an album, but the band dissolved shortly afterwards. Radio Birdman have inspired many bands since, to the extent that Sydney is regarded as a nurturing ground for guitar-based bands. Lead singer Rob Younger has become one of the most important producers of underground and alternative bands in the past few years. One of the direct descendants of Radio Birdman was the hard rock band, the Hitmen of which comprised of Warwick, Masuak and former **Saints'** drummer Ivor Hay. Rob Younger, has lead his own group the New Christs since 1983. Another interesting chapter of the Birdman legend was the one-off band New Race in 1981, which comprised: Tek, Younger, and Gilbert with Ron Asheton (ex-**Stooges**) and Dennis Thompson of MC5 for a short tour and a live album.
Albums: *Radios Appear* (1978), *Living Eyes* (1981).

Radio Luxembourg

The Compagnie Luxembourgeoise de Radiodiffusion was set up in 1931 to broadcast in German and French and two years later began Sunday broadcasts in English on 208 metres medium wave. Until 1939, programmes of dance music were punctuated with commercials. Sponsored shows included *The Palmolive Hour* and *The Ovaltineys*. After World War II, the English service was broadcast daily and most of its programming was records, although the station broadcast a Top 20 compiled from sheet music sales until 1959. Until the arrival of **pirate radio** ships in 1964, Radio Luxembourg's evening shows were the most important source of pop music broadcasting for British listeners. While the BBC Light Programme devoted only a few hours a week to record shows, Luxembourg played new releases for six hours a night. Beginning with **Teddy Johnson** (1948) and Pete Murray (1950), virtually every disc jockey from that era had a show on Lux. Among those who made their broadcasting debut there were **Jimmy Young**, Alan Freeman and Jimmy Savile, who made his first broadcast in 1957 and hosted the *Teen And Twenty Disc Club*. For a period, a *Fab 208* magazine was also published. From 1946-68, record companies paid for 15-minute shows on the station, plugging their latest releases. These were pre-recorded in London by name disc jockeys such as Young, Kent Walton, Barry Aldis, Ray Orchard and Savile. In 1968, Radio Luxembourg abolished these slots in favour of 'mixed' programmes and the sponsored plays were spread throughout the schedule. In 1971, the station became 'all live' with every show presented by disc jockeys based in Luxembourg itself. By now, strong competition from BBC Radio 1, and after 1973, from Capital Radio and other UK-based commercial stations was affecting Luxembourg's listening figures. At the end of 1991, the English-language service was moved from 208 metres to a satellite waveband and was reorganized. By then, however, the company had set up Atlantic 252, a highly successful long-wave pop station based in Ireland but transmitting to the western side of Britain. 'Lux' as it was known had a massive part to play in every UK 60s pop fan's life, even with the maddening fade in and fade out, owing to poor reception and the disc jockey's habit of often only playing part of the record (presumably due to the programme's sponsor).

Radio On

Released in 1979 and directed by Christopher Petit, *Radio On* is a low-key British film, shot in black and white, indebted in equal terms to road movies and contemporary German cinema. David Beams stars as a disc jockey who travels from London to Bristol to investigate the death of his brother. Engaging, if wilfully obscure, *Radio On* also features **Sting** as a garage mechanic, obsessed by the life and work of **Eddie Cochran**. Sting performs a rendition of 'Three Steps To Heaven' in the film. The soundtrack also features music by **David Bowie**, **Kraftwerk**, **Robert Fripp** and a succession of new-wave starts including **Devo**, **Lene Lovich**, **Ian Dury** and **Wreckless Eric**. These contributions emanate from jukeboxes and radios Beams encounters on his journey. Critically well-received upon release, *Radio On* captures something of the uncertainty pervading late 70s culture and life.

Radio Stars

This UK group was formed in 1977 by Andy Ellison (vocals), Ian McLeod (guitar) and Martin Gordon (bass), all of whom were previously members of **Jet**. Drummer Steve Parry completed the line-up of a group engendering considerable interest through its association with **John's Children** (Ellison) and

Sparks (Gordon). A series of tongue-in-cheek singles, including 'Dirty Pictures' and 'Nervous Wreck', captured the quartet's brand of quirky pop/punk, but although the latter reached the fringes of the Top 40, the group was unable to achieve consistent success. Trevor White, also ex-Sparks, was later added to the line-up but Gordon's departure in 1978 undermined any lingering potential and Radio Stars disbanded the following year. Ellison and White subsequently undertook several low-key projects and the singer later revived the group's name, but to little success.
Albums: *Songs For Swinging Lovers* (1977), *Radio Stars' Holiday Album* (1978).

Radiohead
The five members of Radiohead, widely tipped to steal **U2**'s crown as the 90s progressed, first met at a private boys school in Abingdon, a small, picturesque town on the outskirts of Oxford. Thom Yorke (b. 7 October 1968, Wellingborough, Northamptonshire, England; vocals/guitar) had been given his first instrument, a Spanish guitar, at age eight by his mother. He formed his first band two years later, then joined an existing school punk band, TNT. Singing for the first time, he realised he would require more sympathetic band members and formed what would become Radiohead with school friends Ed O'Brien (b. Edward John O'Brien, 15 April 1968, Oxford, Oxfordshire, England; guitar) 'who looked cool' and Colin Greenwood (b. Colin Charles Greenwood, 26 June 1969, Oxford, Oxfordshire, England; bass) 'because he was in my year and we always ended up at the same parties'. They shared an interest in **Joy Division** and the **Smiths** and Greenwood earned Yorke's sympathy for joining TNT after him. Mild-mannered drummer Phil Selway (b. Philip James Selway, 23 May 1967, Hemmingford Grey, England; drums) bound the group, titled On A Friday, together. The addition of Colin's brother and jazz fanatic, Jonny Greenwood (b. 5 November 1971, Oxford, Oxfordshire, England; guitar/keyboards) completed the line-up, originally on harmonica, after he pestered his elder brother and friends continually to let him join. A week after his first rehearsal with the band, On A Friday played their debut gig at the now defunct Jericho Tavern in Oxford. With a musical canon resembling a youthful **Talking Heads**, they added two saxophone-playing sisters to fill out the band. However, the band were then put on hold while the members pursued their academic careers, in an effort to appease already frantic parents (Jonny finished his schooling). Colin became entertainment's officer at Peterhouse College, Cambridge University, and helped get his friends together for occasional gigs there. At Exeter University Yorke played guitar in a techno band, Flickernoise, while Selway drummed for various theatrical productions (*Blood Brothers, Return To The Forbidden Planet*) while studying at Liverpool

Polytechnic. The band finally regrouped in Oxford in the summer of 1991, deciding to dispense with the brass section and concentrate squarely on the band, now entitled Radiohead (after a Talking Heads song). Playing their first gig at the Hollybush Inn in July 1991, it was not long before they made a lasting impression. Their first commercial broadcast followed when 'Prove Yourself' was voted Gary Davies' 'Happening Track Of The Week' on BBC Radio 1. 'Creep' then became *the* alternative rock song in the UK during 1993, its self-loathing lyric ('I'm a creep, I'm a weirdo, I don't belong here') stretched over driven guitars that at one point simply explode. Ignored when it was first released in September 1992, its re-release sparked enormous interest as the group toured with **Kingmaker** and **James**. Taking the band in to the UK Top 10, it also announced a Top 30 debut album, *Pablo Honey*. Unlike other celebrated UK indie hopefuls such as **Suede**, Radiohead also translated well to international tastes, from the US to Egypt. Two years of promotional activity followed, before the release of *The Bends* in March 1995. With the pressure on following the plaudits, the recording process was not easy. With hardly a note recorded over two months, producer **John Leckie** ordered all bar Yorke out of the studio and told the singer to 'just fucking play it'. The songs came, and he and the rest of the band relocated to Abbey Road Studios to finish off the album in a mere three weeks. *The Bends* did not disappoint, with a vibrant mood range encouraging Yorke's prosaic yet affecting lyrics: 'When your insides fall to pieces, You just sit there wishing you could still make love'.
Albums: *Pablo Honey* (Parlophone 1993), *The Bends* (Parlophone 1995).
Video: *27.5.94* (1995).

Radle, Carl
Having completed a series of sessions with pop act **Gary Lewis And The Playboys**, bassist Radle became a founder member of Los Angeles group, Colours. In 1969 he joined **Delaney And Bonnie** at the behest of producer/pianist **Leon Russell**, who subsequently introduced the artist to **Joe Cocker**'s expanded touring ensemble, Mad Dogs And Englishmen. Radle was also associated with Russell in the latter's backing group, the Shelter People, but achieved greater fame in **Derek And The Dominoes**, alongside guitarist **Eric Clapton**. Although this highly talented group was doomed to a premature demise, the two musicians retained their working relationship throughout the 70s. Radle also made notable contributions to releases by **J.J. Cale**, **Dr. John** and **Freddy King**, and remained a respected figure in music circles until his death in 1989.

Rae, Jesse
An unashamed champion of Scottish culture and

independence, Jesse Rae has produced an idiosyncratic brand of Caledonian funk. In the 70s he moved to the USA and through work in Cleveland and Los Angeles studios, became acquainted with several leading soul artists, including Bernie Worrell and Michael Hampton from the **Funkadelic/Parliament** enclave. Back in the UK, Rae was unable to secure a deal despite offering several superior demos, and his debut single, 'D.E.S.I.R.E', was latterly issued via the Miami-based TK organization. In 1981 he worked with Worrell on the eccentric *Space Cadets*, and the following year Rae's excellent composition, 'Inside Out', was a UK Top 3 hit for **Odyssey**. That same year he released 'I Feel Liberal-Alright!', with politician David Steel on vocals, in the hope of securing a Scottish Prime Minister during an election year. In 1985 Rae was signed to WEA and although the anthem-like 'Over The Sea' was only a minor hit, its attendant video was highly praised. Rae has since become a respected director, partially through the need for video and audio tapes to support his live appearances. Yet his novelty-bound garb - kilt, helmet and claymore are sported on all personal appearances - has detracted from his undoubted musical skills.
Album: *The Thistle* (1987).

Raeburn, Boyd

b. 27 October 1913, Faith, South Dakota, USA, d. 2 August 1966, Layfayette, Indiana, USA. Raeburn attended the University of Chicago, where he led a campus band before becoming a professional musician leading a small, light music band, but in the 30s turned his attention to swing. In 1944 he formed a high class band that featured some fine young musicians including **Dizzy Gillespie**, **Sonny Berman** (trumpets), Earl Swope, Tommy Pederson (trombones), **Al Cohn**, Johnny Bothwell (saxophones), while older stars such as **Roy Eldridge** and **Trummy Young** played with the band that recorded for the V Disc label. Raeburn was unlucky - a fire at New Jersey's Palisades Amusement Park destroyed the band's library together with many of its instruments. Undeterred, Raeburn put together an astonishing outfit that seemed, in 1945, years ahead of its time. It played numbers like 'Dalvatore Sally', 'Yerxa' and 'Boyd Meets Stravinsky', and the music was as impressionistic as the titles suggest. Vocalists **David Allyn** and Raeburn's wife Ginny Powell found their songs placed in Debussy-like settings and although the critics loved it all, the public did not take to a band that played non-danceable music. In 1947, although signed to the up and coming **Atlantic Records**, Boyd broke up the band. The man who fronted the band holding an ungainly bass saxophone had become disenchanted with the scene, and moved on to part ownership of a Fifth Avenue shop, later moving to Nassau in the Bahamas for more business interests. He died of a heart

attack in 1966, having outlived his wife Ginny by seven years.
Selected albums: *Teen Rock* (1957), *Boyd Raeburn And His Musicians (1943-48)* (1977), *Rhythms By Raeburn* (Aircheck 1978), *Boyd Raeburn 1945* (1979), *Boyd Raeburn Orchestra - On The Air, Volume One* (1981), *Memphis In June* (1981), *Boyd Raeburn Orchestra - On The Air, Volume Two* (1981), *Jewels* (1985), *Airshots 1944-1946* (IAJRC 1990), *Boyd Meets Stravinsky* (Savoy 1992), *Transcription Performances 1946* (Hep 1993).

Raelettes

The Raelettes was formed in the USA around Margie Hendrix and previously known as the **Cookies**, whose R&B backing voices appeared on numerous 50s sessions and inspired the new group's inception. Founded to provide the responsive vocals to singer **Ray Charles**, this female trio has provided the launching pad for several careers. **Merry Clayton**, **Mable John**, **Minnie Riperton**, Clydie King and Estella Yarbrough were all members at some point, although Hendrix has provided a long-serving consistency. The Raelettes did have several minor hits via Charles' Tangerine label, but their constantly changing personnel denied them a more constructive recording career. Hendrix, though, who had had early solo exposure on the Lamp label, also recorded on her own in the 60s, for Tangerine, **Mercury** and Sound Stage 7.
Albums: *Souled Out* (late 60s), *Yesterday, Today And Tomorrow* (1972).
Film: *Blues For Lovers* aka *Ballad In Blue* (1964).

Rafferty, Gerry

b. 16 April 1947, Paisley, Scotland. The lengthy career of the reclusive Rafferty started as a member of the **Humblebums** with **Billy Connolly** and Tam Harvey in 1968. After its demise through commercial indifference, Transatlantic Records offered him a solo contract. The result was *Can I Have My Money Back?*, a superb blend of folk and gentle pop music, featuring one of the earliest cover paintings from the well-known Scottish artist 'Patrick' (playwright John Byrne). Rafferty showed great promise as a songwriter with the rolling 'Steamboat Row' and the plaintive and observant, 'Her Father Didn't Like Me Anyway', but the album was a commercial failure. Rafferty's next solo project came after an interruption of seven years, four as a member of the brilliant but turbulent **Stealers Wheel**, and three through litigation over managerial problems. Much of this is documented in his lyrics both with Stealers Wheel and as a soloist. *City To City* in 1978 raised his profile and gave him a hit single that created a classic song with probably the most famous saxophone introduction in pop music, performed by Raphael Ravenscroft. 'Baker Street' became a multi-million seller and narrowly missed the top of the charts. The album sold similar numbers and Rafferty became a reluctant star. He declined to perform in the USA even though his album was number 1. The follow-up *Night Owl* was almost as successful, containing a similar batch of strong songs with intriguing lyrics and haunting melodies. Rafferty's output has been sparse during the 80s and none of his recent work has matched his earlier songs. He made a single contribution to the film *Local Hero* and produced the Top 3 hit for the **Proclaimers** with 'Letter From America' in 1987. *North And South* continued the themes of his previous albums, although the lengthy introductions to each track made it unsuitable for radio play. During the early 90s Rafferty's marriage broke up, and, as is often the case this stimulates more songwriting creativity. *On A Wing And A Prayer* was certainly a return to form, but although the reviews were favourable it made little impression on the charts. *Over My Head* in 1995 was a lacklustre affair, interestingly the only songs which offered something original were re-recorded Stealers Wheel tracks, written with his former songwritng partner Joe Egan. 'Over My Head' and 'Late Again' are the highpoints on an album which Rafferty seems bereft of ideas.

Albums: *Can I Have My Money Back* (1971), *City To City* (1978), *Night Owl* (1979), *Snakes And Ladders* (1980), *Sleepwalking* (1982), *North And South* (1988), *On A Wing And A Prayer* (1992), Over My head (Polydor 1995). Selected compilations: *Early Collection* (1986), *Blood And Glory* (1988).

Raga

This 1971 documentary charted the life and work of Indian master musician, **Ravi Shankar**. His stellar early 60s recordings were largely responsible for introducing the sitar to Western audiences, partly through the patronage of several pop musicians, notably **George Harrison**, who makes a brief appearance in *Raga*, as does ex-**Monkees** drummer/vocalist Mickey Dolenz. Their cameos are, however, incidental as the film charts Shankar's evolution from Oriental classicist to his adoption by rock audiences at such events as the **Monterey Festival**, **Woodstock** and the Concert For Bangladesh. A sumptuously-packaged soundtrack album was issued in the US by the Beatles' record label Apple, but the set was denied a UK pressing.

Rage

Formerly known as Avenger, this German power trio changed their name to Rage in 1985, to avoid confusion with the British **Avenger** (and thereby get confused with the British band Rage). A series of line-up changes ensued before the combination of vocalist Peavey Wagner, guitarist Manni Schmidt and drummer Chris Efthimiadis gelled. Their first two albums were rather one-dimensional, being competent, but uninspiring techno-thrash affairs. With the recording of *Perfect Man*, they experimented more with song structures and had improved considerably as musicians. Future releases combined the technical prowess and subtle melodies of **Rush**, with the unbridled aggression of **Megadeth**. Their reputation in Germany has grown rapidly, but they have yet to make any significant impression outside their homeland.

Albums: *Reign Of Fear* (Noise 1986), *Execution Guaranteed* (Noise 1987), *Perfect Man* (Noise 1988), *Secrets In A Weird World* (Noise 1989), *Reflections Of A Shadow* (Noise 1990), *Beyond The Wall* (Noise 1992), *Saviour* (Noise 1993).

Rage Against The Machine

The name says everything about Rage Against The Machine. The aggressive musical blend of metal guitar and hip-hop rhythms is an appropriate background to the rap-styled delivery of angry, confrontational, political lyrics, addressing the band's concerns over inner city deprivation, racism, censorship, propaganda, the plight of Native Americans and many other issues as the band strive to be more than mere entertainment. Formed in Los Angeles in 1991 by former Lock Up guitarist Tom Morello and ex-Inside Out vocalist Zack de la Rocha, with bassist Timmy C and drummer Brad Wilk, Rage Against The Machine signed a major record deal with, importantly, creative control on the strength of a demo tape and some impressive early live shows. Further live work with **Pearl Jam**, **Body Count**, **Tool** and **Suicidal Tendencies** ensued, with the band encountering trouble with the French government during the Suicidal tour over t-shirts which showed a genuine CIA instructional cartoon on how to make a Molotov cocktail, taken from documents made for the Nicaraguan Contra rebels. The t-shirts were confiscated and destroyed by French Customs. The band subsequently released a self-titled debut, with a stunning cover photograph of a Buddhist monk burning himself to death in protest at the Vietnam War, and rose rapidly to fame, **Henry Rollins** describing them as 'the most happening band in the US'. The album was a hit on both sides of the Atlantic, and Rage Against The Machine scored single success with 'Killing In The Name', although de la Rocha was distinctly unhappy with a radio edit which removed all expletives and 'completely shut down the whole purpose of that song'. A sell-out UK tour in 1993 was followed by further powerful performances on the **Lollapalooza** festival tour in the USA.

Album: *Rage Against The Machine* (Epic 1992).

Raggamuffin/Ragga

It's not often that an entire genre of music can be traced to one record, but Ragga was single-handedly started by one single, Wayne Smith's 'Under Me Sleng Teng' (1985). Legend states that one of the musicians working in **Prince Jammy**'s studio in Waterhouse, Kingston 11, was messing about with a Casio electronic keyboard, and found a pre-set demo rhythm. With the addition of a keyboard bassline, he provided the basis for Wayne Smith to 'voice' it, and the 'digital' era of reggae began. More than 200 other versions of the backing track were recorded, such was its popularity.

Ragga is, therefore, barely distinguishable from the earlier **dancehall**, other than a slightly more aggressive attitude, and an alignment with the kind of concerns of its youthful audience - one-upmanship, guns, sex - and an all-important, rocking electronic beat. The early years of the genre (1986-89) were dominated by **King Jammy**'s production house, **Donovan Germain**'s Penthouse Studio and a variety of other producers, such as Mixing Lab, **Exterminator**, Black Scorpio and **King Tubby**'s. Veteran producer **Gussie Clarke** added a roots edge at his Music Works studio, and released the next biggest watershed record in **Gregory Isaacs**' 'Rumours'. Leading ragga musicians include **Steely & Clevie**, **Mafia & Fluxy** and the Firehouse Crew. Just like dancehall before it, ragga has also created its own set of stars, including **Cutty Ranks**, **General Levy**, **Tiger**, and, the biggest of them all, **Shabba Ranks**. The music is still 'running t'ings' in Jamaica at the time of writing.

Selected albums: Various: *Ragga Clash Vol. 1* (Fashion 1990), *Ragga Clash Vol. 2* (Fashion 1990), *Just Ragga Vol. 5* (Charm 1994), *Ragga Ragga Ragga* (Greensleeves 1994). Cutty Ranks: *The Stopper* (Fashion 1990).

Raging Slab

Greg Strzempka (vocals/guitar) and Elyse Steinman (bottleneck guitar) formed Raging Slab in 1983, picking up lead guitarist Mark Middleton and bassist Alec Morton while going through numerous drummers, including ex-**Whiplash/Slayer** percussionist T.J. Scaglione and future **Warrior Soul** frontman Kory Clarke. The three-guitar frontline gave a definite Southern rock flavour to the Slab's basic rock 'n' roll, but gigging around the New York hardcore scene of the 80s also added a hard, contemporary edge. The band made their debut with *Assmaster*, which was elaborately packaged with a comic drawn by friends at *Marvel Comics*, and was followed by *True Death* as the band supported themselves with constant touring before a major deal emerged. *Raging Slab*, with latest drummer Bob Pantella, was excellent, with 'Geronimo', a sensitive lament to the fall of the Native American nation, as its centrepiece,. However, despite support tours with everyone from **Mötley Crüe** to the **Butthole Surfers**, it sold poorly. The band at last found a spiritual home and more creative freedom at **Def American**, and moved to a Pennsylvania farm where they built their own studio to record the acclaimed *Dynamite Monster Boogie Concert*. This was

Raging Slab's most consistent work as they freely extended their talents in new directions, and finally felt at home with their 14th drummer, Paul Sheenan. The live shows were as hot as ever as the Slab toured America with **Monster Magnet** and undertook their first European tour.

Albums: *Assmaster* (Buy Our Records 1987), *True Death* (Buy Our Records 1988, mini-album), *Raging Slab* (RCA 1989), *Dynamite Monster Boogie Concert* (Def American 1993).

Ragovoy, Jerry

b. 4 September 1930, Philadelphia, Pennsylvania, USA. Ragovoy's career as a songwriter and producer began in the doo-wop era of the early 50s. His first successful act was the **Castelles**, who had a hit with 'My Girl Awaits Me' in 1953. In 1959 he began a partnership with entrepreneur Bill Fox which resulted in several collaborations with the **Majors**, one of the latter's successful acts. Ragovoy produced several of the group's releases, including the US Top 30 hit 'A Wonderful Dream', co-writing them under the pseudonym 'Norman Meade'. This appellation also appeared on 'Time Is On My Side', recorded by **Irma Thomas** in 1964 and later revived successfully by the **Rolling Stones**. Ragovoy also enjoyed a fruitful partnership with fellow black music producer **Bert Berns** and together the duo guided the career of deep soul singer **Garnet Mimms**. In 1966 Ragovoy wrote and produced 'Stay With Me Baby' for **Lorraine Ellison**, one of the decade's most compulsive vocal performances, before supervising a series of excellent releases by **Howard Tate**. His anthem-like recording, 'Get It While You Can', was later adopted by **Janis Joplin**, who covered several Ragovoy compositions including 'Piece Of My Heart', originally written for **Erma Franklin**. In the mid-60s he also became east coast A&R chief for **Warner Brothers**' then recently formed soul subsidiary, Loma, where he wrote songs for and produced artists including the **Olympics**, the Enchanters (ex-Garnet Mimms), Carl Hall, Lonnie Youngblood, Roy Redmond, Ben Aiken and (once again) Lorraine Ellison. Then in 1973 Ragovoy formed his own Rags production company and leased product to Epic, most notably that by Howard Tate and Lou Courtney, the latter's *I'm In Need Of Love*. In the late 70s/early 80s, Ragovoy began writing for and producing artists as diverse as **Bonnie Raitt**, **Dionne Warwick**, Essra Mohawk, **Major Harris** and Peggi Blu. In 1988 he produced some songs for Irma Thomas' album that year for Rounder and his name still apears occasionally on the credits of songs performed by many different artists. In his book, *Off The Record*, Joe Smith (ex-Warner President and then President of Capitol/EMI) gave Ragovoy's major contribution to soul music long-overdue recognition when he said: 'You might not know him but he produced and wrote some of the best rhythm and blues of the sixties - and he's not black - he's a man with a sense of soul.'

Rah Band

This fictitious studio group was masterminded by Richard A. Hewson (b. 17 November 1943, Stockton-on-Tees, Teeside, England). In the late 60s arranger, conductor and multi-instrumentalist Hewson worked with **James Taylor** and **Herbie Hancock** and arranged hits such as the **Beatles** 'The Long And Winding Road' and **Mary Hopkin**s' 'Those Were The Days'. His fame as an arranger spread and in the next decade he worked with artists including **Supertramp**, **Diana Ross**, **Carly Simon**, **Art Garfunkel**, **Leo Sayer**, **Al Stewart**, **Chris DeBurgh**, **Fleetwood Mac** and **Chris Rea**. In 1976 he decided to produce, write and play on his own records under the name RAH Band. In 1977 the instrumental 'The Crunch' on Good Earth climbed into the UK Top 10. Three years later 'Falcon' hit the Top 40 and started a long string of dance hits for the band. In 1985 'Clouds Across The Moon', with vocals by his wife Liz, gave him a second Top 10 single. Over the years the band have chalked up seven UK hits and have had records on a myriad of labels including **DJM**, KR, TMT, Sound, **RCA**, Supreme and Creole. Hewson, who in the 80s worked with **Toyah** and **Five Star** and produced big hits for **Cliff Richard** and **Shakin' Stevens**, now concentrates on writing and producing music for UK television shows and advertisements.
Albums: *Going Up* (1983), *Mystery* (1985).

Raheem

From the **Geto Boys**' Houston, Texas stable, Raheem embraces that group's familiar offensiveness, but has no little musical dexterity to offer. His debut album spanned reggae ('Punks Give Me Respect') and rock ('Shotgun'), but some of the words on the follow-up were so nasty that he was elevated to the level of 'the new Scarface'. A dubious honour but one which Raheem would doubtless relish.
Albums: *The Vigilante* (Rap-A-Lot 1988), *The Invincible* (Rap-A-Lot 1992).

Railroad Gin

This Australian pop group emerged out of a loose collection of Brisbane musicians in 1968, and by 1973 had settled to a steady eight-piece line-up comprising Carol Lloyd (vocals), two bassists Dim Janson and Jim Dickson, Bob Brown (percussion/brass), Gary Evans (drums), Peter Evans (flute/percussion/brass), Phil Shields (guitar) and Laurie Stone (keyboards). The music was a mixture of covers and originals written by Stone and was busy, brassy, percussive rock with a funk-jazz feel. But most important was the stunning voice of Carol Lloyd - a voice that was raw, stretched and soared in a manner comparable to **Janis Joplin**. The band was one of the few Australian acts that was signed to Polygram and a couple of singles in 1974 charted in their home city, and were followed by an album in 1975. Lloyd left and was replaced by Judee Ford. A second album was recorded without the strings and brass of *A Matter Of Time*. The band released several more singles and toured extensively, but within a year it disbanded, sales of the albums not being high enough to support such a large group. Lloyd continued with her own rock band for several years, releasing two albums; Ford became a well known radio disc jockey and Stone formed a songwriting duo with Peter Moscos and provided hits for other artists as well as several charting singles and two albums of their own.
Albums: *A Matter Of Time* (1975), *Journeys End* (1976).

Railway Children

Formed in 1985 by Gary Newby (b. 5 June 1966, Australia), Brian Bateman (b. 3 August 1966, Wigan, Lancashire, England), Stephen Hull (b. 7 July 1966, Wigan, Lancashire, England) and Guy Keegan (b. 16 June 1966, Wigan, Lancashire, England), the Railway Children started playing small gigs around the north west of England. After a batch of demo tapes the four 19-year-olds found themselves being feted by numerous record companies, eventually settling on a contract-free deal with **Factory Records**. A brace of graceful singles which fused 60s harmonies with the early 80s pop sensibility of Liverpool paved the way for the fine *Reunion Wilderness* in 1987, and the Railway Children appeared set to follow guitar-based contemporaries the **Smiths** onto greater things. The band signed to **Virgin Records** that same year, and suddenly sounded a lot neater for it. The expensive production polish eradicated the quartet's rougher edges, and with pivotal creative force Gary Newby content to have his instinct smoothed by studio techniques, *Recurrence* appeared in 1988 to an uncertain audience confused by the band's independent beginnings and the new, mellower sound. Although singles regularly entered the Top 75 of the UK charts and the Railway Children flirted with fashionable dance beats with particularly encouraging results in America, it was not until the start of 1991 that a re-released version of 'Every Beat Of The Heart' took the band into the upper echelons of the UK chart and thus validated their efforts of five years. However, when follow-up shots 'Something So Good' and 'Music Stop' failed to emboss their new chart status, the band repaired to Lancashire to lick their wounds. Rumours of a final split were hardly dispelled by a complete absence of new material until Virgin's compilation of their finer moments confirmed their demise.
Albums: *Reunion Wilderness* (Factory 1987), *Recurrence* (Virgin 1988), *Native Place* (Virgin 1990), *The Radio 1*

Evening Show Sessions (Nighttracks 1993). Compilation: *Listen On - The Best Of* (Virgin 1995).

Rain

This group originated in Liverpool, England in the late 80s and adopted the heritage of harmony pop in the vein of the **Byrds**. Rain were initially notable by dint of having three good harmony singers to back up their **Rickenbacker** guitar sound. They formed at the Merseyside Trade Union Community And Unemployed Resource Centre in Liverpool, set up with a £100,000 grant. The band's original locale was the severely depressed Huyton area, but eight months later they were signed to **CBS** and worked on album sessions with **Nick Lowe**. After a debut single, 'Lemonstone Desired', they courted controversy with the provocative nudity featured on the cover of 'Taste Of Rain'. Their debut album was honed by months of rehearsal with guest appearances by **Green On Red** and blues musician **Joe Louis Walker**. The band comprise Ned Clark, Colin Murphy (singers, guitarists and songwriters), Martin Campbell and Tony McGuigan (bass and drums).
Album: *A Taste Of Rain* (1991).
Film: *Birth Of The Beatles* (1979).

Rain Parade

Part of Los Angeles' rock renaissance of the early 80s, the Rain Parade drew from late 60s influences to forge a new brand of psychedelia-tinged rock. After a promising debut single, 'What She's Done To Your Mind', on their own Llama label, the band - David Roback (vocals/guitar/percussion), brother Steve (vocals/bass), Matthew Piucci (vocals/guitar/sitar), Will Glenn (keyboards/violin) and Eddie Kalwa (drums) - issued *Emergency Third Rail Power Trip* to critical acclaim in 1983, followed by the excellent 'You Are My Friend' in 1985. Such was their impetus that the Rain Parade signed with **Island Records**, despite the loss of key figure David Roback (who then formed Opal with partner and original Rain Parade bassist Kendra Smith, eventually re-emerging in **Mazzy Star**). His replacement, John Thoman, arrived alongside new drummer Mark Marcum in time for *Beyond The Sunset*, drawn from live performances in Japan. A second studio set, *Crashing Dream*, emerged later in the year, but some of the original Rain Parade's other-worldly, evocative nature had been lost. Piucci would go on to form Gone Fishin'. He would also record an album with **Neil Young**'s Crazy Horse.
Albums: *Emergency Third Rail Power Trip* (Enigma 1983), *Beyond The Sunset* (Restless 1985), *Crashing Dream* (Island 1985).

Rainbow

In 1975 guitarist Ritchie Blackmore (b. 14 April 1945, Weston-Super-Mare, England; guitar) left **Deep Purple**, forming Rainbow the following year. His earlier involvement with American band **Elf** led to his recruitment of the latter's **Ronnie James Dio** (vocals), Mickey Lee Soule, (keyboards), Craig Gruber on bass and Gary Driscoll as drummer. Their debut, *Ritchie Blackmore's Rainbow*, was released in 1975, and was undeservedly seen by some as a poor imitation of Deep Purple. The constant turnover of personnel was representative of Blackmore's quest for the ultimate line-up and sound. Dissatisfaction with the debut album led to new personnel being assembled. Jimmy Bain took over from Gruber, and **Cozy Powell** replaced Driscoll. With Tony Carey on keyboards, *Rainbow Rising* was released, an album far more confident than its predecessor. Shortly after this Bain and Carey left, being replaced by Bob Daisley and David Stone respectively. It was when Rainbow moved to America that difficulties between Dio and Blackmore came to a head, resulting in Dio's departure from the band in 1978. His replacement was **Graham Bonnet**, whose only album with Rainbow, *Down To Earth*, saw the return as bassist of Roger Glover, the man Blackmore had forced out of Deep Purple in 1973. The album was a marked departure from the Dio days, and while it is often considered one of the weaker Rainbow collections, it did provide an enduring single, 'Since You've Been Gone', written and originally recorded by **Russ Ballard**. Bonnet and Powell soon became victims of another reorganization of Rainbow's line-up. Drummer Bobby Rondinelli and particularly new vocalist **Joe Lynn Turner** brought an American feel to the band, a commercial sound introduced on *Difficult To Cure*, the album which produced their biggest hit in 'I Surrender'. Thereafter the group went into decline as their increasingly middle-of-the-road albums were ignored by fans (former **Brand X** drummer Chuck Burgi replaced Rondinelli for 1983's *Bent Out Of Shape*). In 1984 the Rainbow project was ended following the highly popular Deep Purple reunion. The group played its last gig on 14 March 1984 in Japan, accompanied by a symphony orchestra as Blackmore, with a typical absence of modesty, adapted Beethoven's 'Ninth Symphony'. A compilation, *Finyl Vinyl*, appeared in 1986, and (necessarily) featured several different incarnations of Rainbow as well as unreleased recordings.
Albums: *Ritchie Blackmore's Rainbow* (Oyster 1975), *Rainbow Rising* (Polydor 1976), *Live On Stage* (Polydor 1977), *Long Live Rock And Roll* (Polydor 1978), *Down To Earth* (Polydor 1979), *Difficult To Cure* (Polydor 1981), *Straight Between The Eyes* (Polydor 1982), *Bent Out Of Shape* (Polydor 1983). Compilations: *Best Of* (Polydor 1983), *Finyl Vinyl* (Polydor 1986, double album), *Live In Germany* (Connoisseur 1990, rec. 1976).
Videos: *The Final Cut* (1986), *Live Between The Eyes* (1988).
Further reading: *Rainbow*, Peter Makowski.

Rainbow Bridge

Chuck Wein directed this 1971 feature which blended fact and fiction. At the heart of the film was an occult research centre, sited in Hawaii, but any interest *Rainbow Bridge* generated was due to the presence of **Jimi Hendrix**. Mitch Mitchell (drums) and Buddy Cox (bass) accompany the guitarist on footage shot at a concert held on the side of the Haleakala Volcano. However, a large portion of the soundtrack was recorded the previous year at Hendrix' New York studio, Electric Ladyland. 'Ezy Rider', 'Star Spangled Banner', 'Purple Haze', 'Dolly Dagger' and 'Voodoo Chile' are among the songs on offer, many of which were enshrined on a later soundtrack album. *Rainbow Bridge* also features interview material with Hendrix, including a chilling passage wherein he discusses his death - an event which transpired some three months later. Although hardly a cinematic landmark, *Rainbow Bridge* does at least afford the chance to watch one of rock music's greatest talents in action.

Raincoats

This female outfit epitomized the experimental approach that characterized much of punk's aftermath. The group were formed at Hornsea Art College, London, in 1976 by Gina Birch and Ana Da Silva. Augmented by Vicky Aspinall and manager Shirley O'Loughlin, they were originally joined by Palmolive before she left to concentrate on the **Slits**. This line-up was merely a nucleus for a flexible structure that involved numerous other musicians. As Birch recalls: 'We didn't exactly ignore the audience, but for us, playing was an emotional thing. We would struggle, we would cry, we didn't really know what we were doing half the time'. The Raincoats' debut, 'Fairytale In The Supermarket', appeared on **Rough Trade Records** (a label that shared their ground-breaking stance) in 1979. It would sell a healthy 25,000 copies. A self-titled album that same year boasted a similarly distinctive sound and both were revered by critics and a hardcore of admirers alike. *Odyshape* followed in 1981, but was less direct than their debut. Two further singles, a cover of **Sly Stone**'s 'Running Away' (1982) and 'Animal Rhapsody' (1983) both hinted at unfulfilled potential. The Raincoats eventually delivered their swansong in 1984 with *Moving*. However, as fitting an epitaph as any can be found on *The Kitchen Tapes*, on the ROIR label, originally released in 1983. The group may have remained of historical interest only had not one of their biggest US fans, Kurt Cobain of **Nirvana**, tracked down Ana Da Silva to an antique shop in Notting Hill, London. In exchange for a customized original of the band's debut album, Cobain offered the Raincoats the chance to reform and support Nirvana on upcoming UK dates (he would also write sleevenotes for the CD reissues of their albums). Thus the 1994 model

Raincoats, who featured Da Silva with Birch, joined by violinist Anne Wood and drummer Steve Shelley (a stand-in on loan from **Sonic Youth**). Palmolive was said to have departed for a life of religious evangelicism in Texas, while Aspinall was busy running a dance label.

Albums: *The Raincoats* (Rough Trade 1979), *Odyshape* (Rough Trade 1981), *The Kitchen Tapes* (ROIR 1983), *Moving* (Rough Trade 1984).

Raindance

A reel 'n' reggae troupe from Oxford, England, they wrote their own material, but still played some jigs. Much more of a draw in France, the band were quite surprised to discover they had made a folk record. They just thought it was Raindance music.

Album: *Raindance* (1987).

Raindrops

This rock 'n' roll girl group came from New York City, New York, USA. The group was actually the songwriting/producing team of **Ellie Greenwich** (b. 23 October 1940, Brooklyn, New York, USA) and **Jeff Barry** (b. 3 April 1938). As part of the golden age of girl groups, the Raindrops presented a grating teenage-orientated sound with undeniable rock 'n' roll energy in their three 1963 hits: 'What A Guy' (number 25 R&B and number 41 pop), 'The Kind Of Boy You Can't Forget' (number 27 R&B and number 17 pop), and 'That Boy John' (number 64 pop). A Raindrops album track, 'Hanky Panky', later proved to be a big hit for **Tommy James And The Shondells**. Greenwich grew up in Levittown on Long Island and while in college at 1958 recorded her first single as Ellie Gaye. She found the world of songwriting more intriguing and by 1961 was teamed up with Tony Powers, writing songs for such acts as **Bobby B. Soxx And The Bluejeans** and the **Exciters**. In 1963 she turned to a new writing partner, Jeff Barry, and the soon-to-married pair began writing for **Phil Spector**, creating such classic girl group hits as 'Then He Kissed Me' and 'Da Doo Ron Ron' for the **Crystals** and 'Be My Baby' and 'Baby, I Love You' for the **Ronettes**. At the same time, Greenwich and Barry were signed as the Raindrops to Jubilee Records, after a demo of 'What A Guy' was picked up by the label for release. For public appearances Bobby Bosco was substituted for Barry and Greenwich's sister or other girls were added. By 1964 the Raindrops were history and Greenwich and Barry joined Red Bird Records, writing and producing such hits as 'Leader Of The Pack' and 'Give Us Your Blessings' for the **Shangri-Las** and the 'Chapel Of Love' and 'People Say' for the **Dixie Cups**.

Album: *The Raindrops* (1963).

Rainer

b. Rainer Ptacek, 7 June 1951, East Berlin, Germany.

A taste for seclusion and a penchant for unstructured imaginative slide guitar playing made Rainer something of a cult figure before his records became generally available. His parents fled to West Berlin three years after his birth and in 1956 the family emigrated to America and settled in Chicago. While studying at the Saint Rita High School, Rainer heard blues players like **Muddy Waters**, **Paul Butterfield** and **Charlie Musselwhite** at the Aragon Ballroom and the Electric Circus. He moved west in 1972 and ended up in Tucson. For the next 20 years, his principal employment was as a guitar repairman after periods as a cab driver, janitor and cabinet maker. He was also a founding member of bands such as **Naked Prey**, the Giant Sandworms and the Band Of Blacky Ranchette. He formed Das Combo with Nick Augustine and Ralph Gilmore in 1984. A year later their initial cassette release, *The Mush Mind Blues*, was reviewed in ***Rolling Stone*** by Kurt Loder, followed in 1986 by *Barefoot Rock*, which was only released in England. *Worried Spirits* was a solo effort recorded in two days direct to DAT, incorporating natural sounds and effects machinery. *The Texas Tapes* was a long-standing project with **Z.Z. Top** guitarist Billy Gibbons. Rainer has also recorded with **Robert Plant**.

Albums: with Das Combo *Barefoot Rock* (Making Waves 1986), *Worried Spirits* (Demon 1992), with Das Combo *The Texas Tapes* (Demon 1993), *Nocturnes (The Instrumentals)* (Glitterhouse 1995).

Rainey, Gertrude 'Ma'

b. Gertrude M. Pridgett, 26 April 1886, Columbus, Georgia, USA, d. 22 December 1939. After working as a saloon and tent show singer around the turn of the century, Rainey began singing blues. She later claimed that this occurred as early as 1902 and however much reliance is placed upon this date she was certainly amongst the earliest singers to bring blues songs to a wider audience. By the time of her first recordings, 1923, she was one of the most famous blues singers in the deep south and was known as the 'Mother of the Blues'. Although many other singers recorded blues songs before her, she eschewed the refining process some of them had begun, preferring instead to retain the earthy directness with which she had made her name. Her recordings, sadly of generally inferior technical quality, show her to have been a singer of great power, while her delivery has a quality of brooding majesty few others ever matched. A hard-living, rumbustious woman, Rainey influenced just about every other singer of the blues, notably **Bessie Smith** whom she encouraged during her formative years. Although Rainey continued working into the early 30s her career at this time was overshadowed by changes in public taste. She retired in 1935 and died in 1939. In the late 80s a musical show, *Ma Rainey's Black Bottom*, was a success on Broadway and in London.

Compilations: *Blues The World Forgot* (1923-24), *Complete Recordings Vol. 1* (1923-24), *Oh My Babe Blues* (1923-24), *Complete Recordings Vol. 2* (1924-25).

Further reading: *Ma Rainey And The Classic Blues Singers*, Derrick Stewart-Baxter, *Mother Of The Blues: A Study Of Ma Rainey*, S. Lieb.

Rainger, Ralph

b. 7 October 1901, New York City, New York, USA, d. 23 October 1942, near Palm Springs, California, USA. After studying classical music as a child Rainger won a scholarship to New York's Institute of Musical Art. Despite his academic success and enthusiasm, his family disapproved and persuaded him to study law. By the mid-20s, however, he had become a professional pianist, playing in dance and jazz bands. He was also in several pit orchestras in Broadway theatres and worked briefly with **Paul Whiteman**. While playing in a revue, *Little Show*, in 1929, Rainger wrote 'Moanin' Low' (lyrics by **Howard Dietz**), which was sung in the show by **Libby Holman**. After the success of this song, Rainger and Dietz continued their collaboration with 'Got A Man On My Mind' and 'I'll Take An Option On You', and Rainger also wrote 'Breakfast Dance' (lyrics by Edward Eliscu). In the early 30s Rainger was drawn to Hollywood, where he wrote 'When A Woman Loves A Man' (lyrics by **Billy Rose**) and began a fruitful collaboration with **Leo Robin**. Many of their joint efforts were sung by **Bing Crosby**, among them 'Please', 'Love In Bloom', 'June In January', 'With Every Breath I Take' and 'Blue Hawaii'. The team's 'Thanks For The Memory' won the Oscar after it was sung by **Bob Hope** and Shirley Ross in *Big Broadcast Of 1938*. Robin and Rainger's film work included ***The Big Broadcast*** (1932), ***Little Miss Marker***, *She Loves Me Not*, *Here Is My Heart*, *The Big Broadcast Of 1937*, *Palm Springs*, *Three Cheers For Love*, *Rhythm On The Range*, *College Holiday*, *Waikiki Wedding*, *Ebb Tide*, *Artists And Models*, *Give Me A Sailor*, *Paris Honeymoon*, ***Moon Over Miami***, *Tall, Dark And Handsome*, ***My Gal Sal***, *Footlight Serenade*, ***Coney Island***, and *Riding High* (1943). Rainger was killed in a flying accident in October 1942 shortly before the last film was released.

Rainwater, Marvin

b. Marvin Karlton Percy, 2 July 1925, Wichita, Kansas, USA. A big-voiced, rockabilly singer-songwriter, who is a quarter Cherokee Indian (using his mother's maiden name on stage). He became a regular on **Red Foley**'s *Ozark Mountain Jubilee* in the early 50s and after being spotted on Arthur Godfrey's Talent Scouts television show in the mid-50s was signed to Coral. The first of his two singles for them 'I Gotta Go Get My Baby' became a hit for the label when their top act **Teresa Brewer** covered his record. Rainwater then joined **MGM** and his second release, the self

composed 'Gonna Find Me A Bluebird', in 1957 gave him his only US Top 40 hit. Later that year a duet with **Connie Francis** (before her string of hits), 'Majesty Of Love', graced the US Top 100. In 1958 another of his songs 'Whole Lotta Woman', which only reached number 60 in his homeland, topped the UK chart and his UK recorded follow-up 'I Dig You Baby' also entered the British Top 20. He later recorded without success for Warwick, **Warner Brothers**, United Artists, Wesco, his own label Brave, as well as UK labels Philips, Sonet and Westwood. In subsequent years, the man who performed in full American Indian regalia, has played the rockabilly and country circuit on both sides of the Atlantic.
Albums: *Marvin Rainwater Sings* (1958), *Marvin Rainwater* (1962). Compilations: *Classic Recordings* (1992), *Whole Lotta Woman* (Bear Family 1994).

Raise The Roof

This is reputed to be the first British musical comedy film - as opposed to the revue-style **Elstree Calling** which was simply a collection of songs and sketches not linked by a story; both features were released in 1930 by British International Pictures. Walter Summers and Philip MacDonald's simple screenplay concerns Rodney Langford (Maurice Evans) whose ambitions to enter show business are realised when he becomes the owner of an unsuccessful touring company. One of its members, Maisie Gray (Betty Balfour), is on his side from the start, but his parents (played by Sam Livesey and Ellis Jeffreys) are totally opposed to this new venture. Their efforts to ruin the show with the assistance of the company's corrupt leading man, Atherley Armitage (Jack Raine), fail miserably and inspire the company to even greater success. On the opening night, Rodney is reconciled with his father, and he and Maisie embark on their own (personal) long-running partnership. The attractive and tuneful score was complemented by a supporting cast which included Arthur Hardy, Louie Emery, the Plaza Tiller Girls, and specialities Dorothy Minto and Malandrinos, and Josephine Earle. Betty Balfour, who enjoyed a successful career as a comedienne in 20s silent films, proved to be a pleasing singer and dancer, and had one of the best numbers, 'I'm Trembling On The Brink Of Love'. The director, Walter Summers, also worked on silents, and he went on to write and direct the unconventional and highly acclaimed *The Return Of Bulldog Drummond*, starring Ralph Richardson.

Raisin

During a Broadway season in which good original musicals were scarce, and one-person shows by such as **Sammy Davis Jnr.**, **Liza Minnelli**, and **Sammy Cahn** proliferated, *Raisin* came as a welcome relief. It opened at the 46th Street Theatre on 18 October 1973, with a book by Robert Nemiroff and Charlotte

Zaltzburg which was based on Lorraine Hansbury's 1959 play *A Raisin In The Sun*. Set in a Chicago ghetto during the 50s, the story told of the efforts of a black family to change their lives once and for all. Newly widowed Lena Younger (Virginia Capers), decides to use her late husband's inheritance to buy a liquor store for her son Walter (Joe Morton), put her daughter Beneatha (Deborah Allen), through medical school, and buy a house somewhere away from the ghetto. Lena's plans are in jeopardy for a time when Walter's sometime business partner flees with part of the money, but her ambitious plans eventually come to fruition, and the family moves into the house of their dreams. It was a moving, heart-warming story, complemented perfectly by a score from Broadway newcomers, Judd Woldin (music) and Robert Brittan (lyrics). Songs such as 'Sweet Time', 'He Come Down This Morning', 'Whose Little Angry Man', 'Not Anymore', 'Measure The Morning', and 'A Whole Lotta Sunlight', were put over with a great deal of verve and zeal by a high-quality cast, which also included Ernestine Jackson, Ralph Carter, Ted Ross, and Robert Jackson. Virginia Capers won a **Tony Award** for her outstanding performance, and the show itself won for best musical. No doubt the kudos helped *Raisin* to surprise a lot of people, and stay in New York for two years.

Raitt, Bonnie

b. 8 November 1949, Burbank, California, USA. Born into a musical family, her father, **John Raitt**, starred in Broadway productions of **Oklahoma!** and **Carousel**. Having learned guitar as a child, Bonnie became infatuated with traditional blues, although her talent for performing did not fully flourish until she attended college in Cambridge, Massachusetts. Raitt initially opened for **John Hammond**, before establishing her reputation with prolific live appearances throughout the east coast circuit on which she was accompanied by longtime bassist, Dan 'Freebo' Friedberg. Raitt then acquired the management services of Dick Waterman, who guided the career of many of the singer's mentors, including **Son House**, **Mississippi Fred McDowell** and **Sippie Wallace**. She often travelled and appeared with these performers and *Bonnie Raitt* contained material drawn from their considerable lexicon. Chicago bluesmen **Junior Wells** and A.C. Reed also appeared on the album, but its somewhat reverential approach was replaced by the contemporary perspective unveiled on *Give It Up*. This excellent set included versions of **Jackson Browne**'s 'Under The Falling Sky' and Eric Kaz's 'Love Has No Pride' and established the artist as an inventive and sympathetic interpreter. *Taking My Time* features assistance from **Lowell George** and Bill Payne from **Little Feat** and included an even greater diversity, ranging from the pulsating 'You've Been In Love Too Long' to the traditional 'Kokomo Blues'. Subsequent releases followed a similar pattern, and although *Streetlights* was a minor disappointment, *Home Plate*, produced by veteran **Paul A. Rothchild**, reasserted her talent. Nonetheless Raitt refused to embrace a conventional career, preferring to tour in more intimate surroundings. Thus the success engendered by *Sweet Forgiveness* came as a natural progression and reflected a genuine popularity. However its follow-up, *The Glow*, although quite commercial, failed to capitalize on this newfound fortune and while offering a spirited reading of **Mable John**'s 'Your Good Thing', much of the material was self-composed and lacked the breadth of style of its predecessors. Subsequent releases, *Green Light* and *Nine Lives* proved less satisfying and Raitt was then dropped by **Warner Brothers**, her outlet of 15 years. Those sensing an artistic and personal decline were proved incorrect in 1989 when *Nick Of Time* became one of the year's most acclaimed and best-selling releases. Raitt herself confessed to slight amazement at winning a Grammy award. The album was a highly accomplished piece of work, smoothing some of her rough, trademark blues edges for an AOR market. The emotional title track became a US hit single while the album, produced by Don Was of **Was (Not Was)**, also featured sterling material from **John Hiatt** and Bonnie Hayes. Raitt also garnered praise for her contributions to **John Lee Hooker**'s superb 1990 release, *The Healer*, and that same year reached a wider audience with her appearance of the concert for Nelson Mandela at Wembley Stadium. She continued in the same musical vein with the excellent *Luck Of The Draw* featuring strong material from **Paul Brady**, Hiatt and Raitt herself. The album was another multi-million seller and demonstrated Raitt's new mastery in singing smooth emotional ballads; none better than the evocative 'I Can't Make You Love Me'. Her personal life also stabilized following her marriage in 1991 (to Irish actor/poet Martin O'Keefe), and after years of singing about broken hearts, faithless lovers and 'no good men', Raitt entered the 90s at the peak of her powers. She was also growing in stature as a songwriter: on her 1994 album she displayed the confidence to provide four of the songs herself, her first nine albums having yielded only eight of her own compositions. Although that album *Longing In Their Hearts* spawned further US hits and reached 2 million sales it was a record that trod water. Maybe Raitt is so happily married she finds it hard to get mean and sound dirty any more. Even her US hit version of **Roy Orbison**'s 'You Got It' from the movie *Boys On The Side* sounded strangely lacking. All this aside, she is an outstanding slide guitarist and possesses one of the finest voices in rock music.

Albums: *Bonnie Raitt* (Warners 1971), *Give It Up* (Warners 1972), *Takin' My Time* (Warners 1973), *Streetlights* (Warners 1974), *Home Plate* (Warners 1975), *Sweet Forgiveness* (Warners 1977), *The Glow* (Warners 1979), *Green Light* (Warners 1982), *Nine Lives* (Warners 1986), *Nick Of Time* (Capitol 1989), *Luck Of The Draw* (Capitol 1991), *Longing In Their Hearts* (Parlophone 1994). Compilation: *The Bonnie Raitt Collection* (Warners 1990).

Raitt, John

b. John Emmett Raitt, 19 January 1917, Santa Ana, California, USA. An actor and singer with a fine baritone voice, Raitt sang in light opera and concerts before playing the lead in a Chicago production of *Oklahoma!* (1944). In the following year he made his Broadway debut, playing Billy Bigelow, and introducing immortal songs such as 'If I Loved You' and 'Soliloquy' in **Richard Rodgers** and **Oscar Hammerstein II**'s magificent *Carousel*. Three years later, he appeared on Broadway again in the short-lived and 'unconventional' *Magdelana*. This was followed in 1952 by the 'whimsical' *Three Wishes For Jamie*, which was 'too treacly' to run for long. *Carnival In Flanders* (1953), despite a score by **Johnny Burke** and **Jimmy Van Heusen** which contained 'Here's That Rainy Day', provided less than a week's employment, but his next job, as the factory superintendent in *The Pajama Game* (1954), lasted nearly two-and-a-half years. Raitt's spirited and sensitive renditions of **Richard Adler** and **Jerry Ross**'s 'There Once Was A Man' and 'Small Talk' (both with Janis Paige), plus 'Hey There', a duet with a dictaphone machine, made sufficient impact in Hollywood for him to be cast opposite **Doris Day** in the 1957 film version, despite him being a complete newcomer to the big screen. In the 50s and 60s Raitt appeared frequently on US television, and in 1960 toured with the satirical musical *Destry Rides Again*. In the spring of 1966 he re-created his original role in a New York Music Theater revival of *Carousel* and, later in the year, dwelt for a brief spell amid the 'newly created folk songs' of *A Joyful Noise*. Thereafter, Raitt devoted much of his time to touring, and in 1975 was back on Broadway, along with Patricia Munsell, Tammy Grimes, Larry Kert, Lillian Gish and Cyril Ritchard, in *A Musical Jubilee*, a 'potpourri' claiming to demonstrate the development of the American musical. By then, his daughter, **Bonnie Raitt**, was gaining recognition as one of the best female singer/guitarists of the 70s and 80s. John Raitt himself continued to be active, and in 1992 he received an Ovation Award in Hollywood for services to the Los Angeles theatre scene. A year later he was inducted into New York's Theater Hall Of Fame, and celebrated the 50th anniversary of *Oklahoma!* by singing the show's title song on the stage of the St. James Theatre in New York (the theatre in which *Oklahoma!* first opened in 1943) prior to a performance of a very different kind of musical - *The Who's Tommy*.

Selected albums: *Mediterranean Magic* (50s), *Songs The Kids Brought Home* (50s), and Original Cast recordings.

Rak Records

Mickie Most (b. Michael Peter Hayes, June 1938, Aldershot, Surrey, England) started out in the music business as a performer who had a string of successes in South Africa in the 60s (with Mickie Most And The Playboys). He came home from constant touring of that country and became a producer, working with everyone from the **Animals** to **Donovan**. In the late 60s he decided to introduce the American selling style of rack-jobbing to the UK. This is where the salesman sets up a rack of albums for sale in places outside of record shops such as garages and supermarkets. To achieve this he formed Rak Records - the 'c' dropped from Rack as he thought it looked less harsh. Unfortunately supermarkets were not keen on the idea - although within a decade it was a commonplace outlet - but Most chose to keep the company name. In 1970 he decided to form a production company but initially he had no artists signed as all the people he was working with were already on the books of other companies. However, this changed in 1970 when he released Rak's first single - **Julie Felix** singing the **Paul Simon**-penned 'If I Could (El Condor Pasa)'. This was followed by a release from **Peter Noone** whom Most knew from producing **Herman's Hermits**. Rak quickly became big business, picking up **Hot Chocolate** from **Apple**, **Alexis Korner**'s **CCS** - Collective Consciousness Society (whose version of 'Whole Lotta Love' was the theme music to *Top Of The Pops* for the best part of a decade), the Australian folk group **New World** (soon to be implicated in the **Janie Jones** 'sex for airplay' scandal), and dozens of teenybop groups like **Kenny**, **Suzi Quatro**, **Mud**, the **Arrows** and **Smokie**. Songwriters and producers like **Nicky Chinn** and **Mike Chapman** had many hits through Rak, and at one point the company was situated in Charles Street, Mayfair, next door to the equally successful **Bell Records** (**Gary Glitter**, **Bay City Rollers**, etc.) causing some people to dub it 'teen-pan alley'. At the same time as running Rak, Most also became famous as a panelist on the talent show *New Faces*. As the teeny bop era passed into punk, Rak became less prolific with the hits though they bounced back briefly in the 80s with **Kim Wilde**.

Raksin, David

b. 4 August 1912, Philadelphia, Pennsylvania, USA. A composer, lyricist, and arranger for film background music, whose career has spanned more than 50 years. Raksin was originally taught to play the clarinet by his father, and, after further studying at Pennsylvania University, where he was a soloist with the band, he performed and arranged for society outfits, and on the radio station WCAU. After further stints as a sideman-arranger with New York bands, and a spell with Harms Publishing House in the early 30s, he broke into the movie business in 1936 when he arranged Charlie Chaplin's music for *Modern Times*. In the late 30s and early 40s he worked on several films as co-composer, including *San Quentin*, *Suez*, *Hollywood Cavalcade*, *Stanley And Livingstone*, *The Magnificent Dope* and *The Undying Monster*, and had a few solo credits such as *The Man In Her Life* and *Tampico*. In 1944, Raksin's score for Otto Preminger's highly acclaimed murder mystery *Laura* included the haunting title theme, which, complete with a later lyric by **Johnny Mercer**, became popular for **Dick Haymes**, Johnnie Johnston and **Freddie Martin**, among others, and endured as an all-time standard. Raksin's other 40s film music included another Preminger project *Fallen Angel* (1945) (which contained 'Slowly', a hit for **Kay Kyser**), and *Where Do We Go From Here?*, *Smoky*, ***The Shocking Miss Pilgrim***, *The Secret Life Of Walter Mitty*, *Apartment For Peggy*, *Force Of Evil* and *Forever Amber* (1947), for which Raksin was nominated for an Academy Award. Johnny Mercer again added words to Raksin's title theme. In the 50s and 60s Raksin scored movies with a wide variety of themes, such as courtroom dramas (*The Magnificent Yankee* and *Until They Sail*), boxing (*Right Cross*), Frank Sinatra as an assassin (*Suddenly*), gangsters galore (*Al Capone* and *Pay Or Die*), Westerns (*Invitation To A Gunfighter*), a Jerry Lewis comedy (*The Patsy*), and others such as *The Girl In White*, *Carrie*, *Seven Wonders Of The World (Cinerama)*, *Love Has Many Faces*, including some of the most highly acclaimed productions of their time, such as *The Bad And The Beautiful*, (containing 'Love Is For The Very Young', with Dory Previn), *Two Weeks In Another Town*, *Sylvia*, *A Big Hand For The Little Lady*, *Will Penny* and *Separate Tables* for which Raksin won another Oscar nomination. In 1962 Raksin contributed a jazz-oriented score to *Too Late Blues*, in which John Cassavetes made his Hollywood debut. It featured musicians such as **Benny Carter**, **Shelly Manne** and **Red Mitchell**, and numbers like 'Sax Raises Its Ugly Head' and 'Benny Splits, While Jimmy Rowles'. In the 70s and 80s, apart from occasional feature films such as *What's The Matter With Helen?* and *Glass Houses*, Raksin worked more and more in television on such as *The Over-The Hill Gang Rides Again*, *The Ghost Of Flight 401*, *The Day After* and *Lady In A Corner*. His earlier work for the small screen had included music for *Ben Casey* and *The Breaking Point*. He also scored several movie cartoons including *Sloppy Jalopy*, *Madeline*, *Giddyap* and *The Unicorn In The Garden*, and has written several serious works.

Ralphs, Mick

b. 31 May 1944, Hereford, England. Ralphs was a member of the Hereford-based act known variously as the Shakedown Sound, the Doc Thomas Group and Silence. They took the name **Mott The Hoople** in 1969 upon securing a recording deal with **Island Records** and Ralphs remained with the group for the next four years. This underrated lead guitarist then became a founding figure of the supergroup **Bad Company** and has remained at the helm throughout its turbulent history. In 1985 Ralphs released *Take This*, a low-key solo album, before resuming his role in the parent unit he has done much to fashion and maintain. Album: *Take This* (1985).

Ram Jam

Formed in the mid-70s, Ram Jam was an east coast of America group best known for its one Top 20 single, 'Black Betty', in 1977. That song was the focus of a boycott by several groups who considered it offensive to black women, even though it had originally been written by Huddie '**Leadbelly**' Ledbetter, the legendary black folk and blues singer. The group consisted of guitarist Bill Bartlett (b. 1949), bassist Howie Blauvelt (formerly a member of **Billy Joel**'s early group the Hassles), singer Myke Scavone and drummer Pete Charles. Bartlett had earlier been lead guitarist with the **Lemon Pipers**. After leaving that group, Bartlett retired from music for some time, before recording a demo of the Leadbelly song. Released on **Epic Records**, it reached number 18, but the group never had another hit. In the UK they succeeded twice, in 1977 (number 7) and in 1990 a re-mix version made number 13 making them a quite extraordinary one-hit-wonder.
Albums: *Ram Jam* (Epic 1977), *Portrait Of An Artist As A Young Ram* (Epic 1978).

Rambeau, Eddie

b. Edward Cletus Fluri, 30 June 1943, Hazleton, Pennsylvania, USA. Rambeau became a footnote in pop music history owing to his lone chart single, 'Concrete And Clay', US number 35 in 1965, which was also a hit that year for the UK's **Unit Four Plus Two**. Rambeau's career stretched back to the early 60s. His first record, 'Skin Divin'', the first of five for Swan Records, was released in 1961 and became a local hit, turning Rambeau into a teen idol in Pennsylvania. His first national success occurred in 1964, not as an artist but as a songwriter, who co-authored the US Top 10, 'Navy Blue' by **Diane Renay**. His other compositions were recorded by such performers as **Frank Sinatra Jnr.** and **Dee Dee Sharp**. 'Concrete And Clay' appeared on the DynoVoice label, owned by the record's producer, **Bob Crewe**. Rambeau continued to record until the end of the 60s and then left recording behind to produce. In the late 70s he switched careers to acting. Album: *Concrete And Clay* (1965).

Ramblers International Dance Band

Formed in 1962 as a result of the big band highlife boom instigated by **E.T. Mensah**, the Ramblers was one of Ghana's most popular touring and recording groups throughout the 60s and 70s. Under the leadership of tenor saxophonist/arranger Jerry Hansen the band developed a highly individual style, featuring two lead vocalists singing in close harmony over a lush 15-piece orchestral backing, and mixing highlife with soul and Latin material. By the end of the 60s they had won large followings in neighbouring Nigeria, Sierra Leone and Ivory Coast. During the 70s, they were the featured house band at the dancehall operated by leading Accra hotel The Ambassador. In 1974, Hansen was elected president of the Musicians Union of Ghana (the organization which succeeded the pioneering union established by E.T. Mensah in the mid-50s). By this time, the market for big band highlife was fast diminishing, although the band managed to scrape a living until the early 80s, when they finally broke up. Hansen emigrated, settling in New York, with the result that when the big band highlife revival occurred in the mid-80s, the group - lacking an effective alternative leader were unable to make a successful comeback. In 1986, vocalist Charles Kodjo emigrated to London, where he joined **Hi-Life International**.
Albums: *The Fabulous Ramblers* (1964), *Ramblers Dance Band* (1968), *Doin' Our Own Thing* (1970), *The Hit Sounds Of The Ramblers Dance Band* (1974).

Ramey, Gene

b. 4 April 1913, Austin, Texas, USA, d. 8 December 1984. A student of **Walter Page**, bass player Ramey briefly led his own band in Kansas City before joining **Jay McShann**. This was in 1938 and he remained with McShann until the band broke up in 1943. During the rest of the 40s Ramey became a regular at numerous club and recording dates in New York, playing with a wide range of top-flight swing and bop stars including **Charlie Parker**, **Coleman Hawkins** and **Lester Young**. In the 50s he freelanced with mainstreamers and beboppers, comfortably fitting in with the musical concepts of **Buck Clayton** and **Art Blakey** while also making the transition to dixieland with **Muggsy Spanier**. Ramey's skills were highly regarded and his musical range meant that he was in demand throughout his musical career and appeared on countless albums with musicians as diverse as **Thelonious Monk**, **Teddy Wilson**, **Horace Silver**, **Lennie Tristano**, **Count Basie** and **Stan Getz**. In the 60s he retired to become a bank security guard but later returned to the jazz scene to play at international festivals with his old comrade McShann. He retired in 1975, moving to Texas to run a smallholding.
Album: *The Count Basie Sextet* (1952).

Ramírez, Louie

b. 24 February 1938, Manhattan, New York, USA; of Puerto Rican parentage. Probably the most sought after and prolific arranger and producer during salsa's

70s boom years, the versatile Ramírez, who leads his own band, composes and plays timbales, vibraphone and keyboards, has justifiably been compared to **Quincy Jones** and described as 'El Genio de la Salsa' (The Genius of Salsa). The arranger is an important figure in salsa, who is always expected to be creative, original and usually progressive within the strict structure of the genre, the band's style and its front-line (the two are inextricable). Ramírez began classical piano tuition at the age of seven and later studied at the Juilliard School of Music. Seeing the pianist/bandleader **Noro Morales** perform made a great impression on the young Ramírez and he decided to devote his energies to Latin music. He made his professional debut in 1956 when he replaced Pete Terrace as the vibraphonist in a quintet led by his uncle, Joe Loco. Before becoming a leader in 1946, pianist Loco worked with **Xavier Cugat**, Enric Madriguera and Pupi Campo, amongst others, and wrote arrangements for artists including **Tito Rodríguez**, **Machito**, Noro Morales and **Tito Puente**. Also in the mid-50s, Ramírez did a stint with the Vicentico Valdés band, which at the time included pianist **Eddie Palmieri** and percussionist Manny Oquendo (see **Conjunto Libre**).

In 1960, Ramírez co-wrote and arranged the smash hit 'El Güiro De Macorina' from **Johnny Pacheco**'s debut *Pacheco y su Charanga Vol.I* on the Alegre label. The album achieved the largest sales in the history of Latin music up to that point. Ramírez played timbales and wrote some of the arrangements on the album, which was described by musicologist John Storm Roberts as ' . . . one of the tightest Latin jazz recordings ever made . . . ' (quote from *The Latin Tinge*, 1979). In 1961 Ramírez was the timbalero on *The Latin Jazz Quintet* on United Artists Records (reissued by Palladium Records in 1990). The group was led by vibes player Felipe Díaz and featured jazz musician **Eric Dolphy** on flute, bass clarinet and alto saxophone. Louie wrote songs and arrangements for La Playa Sextet and also recorded with the band. He composed the magnificent 'Pachanga Con La Playa' from their early 60s release *La Playa Sextet Vol.11* on the Mardi Gras label. In the mid-60s Ramírez made his recording debut as a bandleader with *Introducing Louie Ramírez* on Remo Records. 1965's *Good News* was his debut on the new Fania Records label, founded in 1964 by Jerry Masucci and Johnny Pacheco. Ramírez performed a superb vibes solo on a descarga (Latin jam) interpretation of the Noro Morales composition 'Ponce' on *Tributo A Noro* (Tribute To Noro Morales) by **Kako**'s New York After Hours Orchestra, which was effectively an Alegre All-Stars album produced by Al Santiago. Santiago produced Ramírez's *Vibes Galore* on Alegre in c.1966, which featured lead vocalist Willie Torres. Ramírez embraced the boogaloo and Latin soul fad with a vengeance on *In The Heart Of Spanish*

Harlem issued by the major record company **Mercury**. He included more Latin soul material on *Ali Baba* in 1968, his second Fania outing. That year he appeared on the debut recording by the Fania All Stars at New York's Red Garter club and on the Al Santiago produced *Salsa All-Stars*.

Between 1965 and 1968, Ramírez did stints with **Charlie Palmieri** and **Joe Cuba**. In late 1968 he teamed up with ex-**Ray Barretto** vocalist Pete Bonet (b. Santurce, San Juan, Puerto Rico; singer, composer, co-bandleader, promoter) to co-lead a 12-piece band with a front line of three trumpets and three saxophones (alto, tenor and baritone). For the next two years the band became a regular fixture at New York's Corso club. In 1972 Ramírez and the great singer/bandleader Tito Rodríguez collaborated on *Algo Nuevo* for Rodríguez's own TR label. Ramírez became the company's vice-president. 1974's *Típico* (meaning typical, rootsy salsa) on UA Latino (a division of United Artists) featured ex-Charlie Palmieri lead vocalist Victor Velázquez, and was one of Ramírez's strongest albums. His 1976 debut on Cotique Records, which by that time was controlled by the Fania empire, was a bland disco-orientated crossover project called *A Different Shade Of Black*. He made three more albums on the label between 1978 and 1980. In 1977 he participated in the 17th anniversary recording by the Alegre All-Stars. The melange of styles he employed on his 1978 Cotique follow-up, *Louie Ramírez y sus Amigos*, served to showcase his skill and experimentalism as an arranger and musician. **Camilo Azuquita**, **Adalberto Santiago** and **Rubén Blades** were the album's lead vocalists. The latter composed and sang the smash hit track 'Paula C', for which Ramírez wrote a progressive Brazilian tinged arrangement. Isidro Infante arranged one track on Ramírez's final Cotique release, *Salsero*, in 1980. The two artists had worked on Azuquita's *Llego y Dijo* in 1979, and up to the mid-80s, their names appeared together on numerous New York salsa recordings, including albums by Orlando Watusi, Raúl Marrero, **Bobby Rodríguez** Carlos Santos, Conjunto Granada, Junior González and Salsa Latina. Infante worked as Louie's regular pianist between the early and mid-80s, contributing arrangements to Ramírez's albums during that period. From the latter half of the 80s into the 90s, Infante has been one of the busiest and most prolific arrangers, producers and musical directors on the New York salsa scene.

In 1982, Ramírez was responsible for *Noche Caliente*, which gave ballads an uptempo salsa style and spawned the hit 'Estar Enamorado'. The album, which went gold, has been cited as the precursor of the salsa romántica style. New York born Latino, Ray de la Paz, performed lead vocals on the record. Formerly with Conjunto Melao, Guarare and Ray Barretto, de la Paz appeared on Ramírez's 1983 release *Super Cañonalos Con Louie Ramírez*. The two artists became co-leaders of a four trumpet band and recorded three successful albums between 1984 and 1986 on Sergio Bofill and Humberto Corredor's Caimán Records label. de la Paz misguidedly split from Ramírez and made the disappointing *Estoy Como Nunca* on BC Records in 1987. After having a low profile for a while, he re-emerged in 1990 and had a medium-sized hit with *Como Tu Quieras* on Ralph Mercado's RMM label. Infante handled the album's production and musical direction, played keyboards and wrote half the charts. Meanwhile, Louie put together a Latin jazz ensemble for 1987's *Tribute To Cal Tjader*, his last release on Caimán. The personnel included **José Fajardo**, flute; **Paquito D'Rivera**, alto saxophone and Mario Rivera, flute, tenor and soprano saxophone, who all took solos. de la Paz sang in the chorus and provided lead vocals to 'El Titere', which was the third occasion Ramírez recorded this self-penned tune; it appeared previously on *Vibes Galore* and *Ali Baba*. He was awarded a gold disc for sales of the album at New York's Copacabana club in 1988. He added baritone saxophone to his four trumpet frontline on his next four releases. 1987's *Louie Ramírez y Super Banda* on Faisán Records (out of the same stable as Caimán) featured two lead singers: Jorge Maldonado and **Tony Vega**. The latter performed 'Feo Pero Sabroso', a remake of Ramírez's composition 'Feo Como El Oso' from 1974's *Tipico*. Ramírez indulged in an ironic piece of recycling on his 1989 release *El Genio*: he took the tune of the title track of *Tipico*, had new lyrics written and re-arranged it to create the hit 'Salsa Romántica'. The number was performed by Carlos 'El Grande' (see **Nati**), who shared lead vocals with **Tito Allen**, Sammy González (see **Roberto Roena**) and Willie Gómez. Allen and González were joined by Adalberto Santiago and Efrain Morales on 1990's *Louie Ramírez y sus Amigos* on the new Caché label founded by Alex Masucci, the brother of Fania co-founder Jerry Masucci. Ramírez returned to Latin jazz on 1991's *The King Of Latin Vibes* on Sugar Records, which contained two tracks recorded at the 1988 Montreal Jazz Festival. In addition to the artists and bands mentioned above, Ramírez has lent his talents to countless recordings by such salsa names as **Celia Cruz**, Tito Puente, Cesta All-Stars (see **Joe Quijano**), **Willie Rosario**, **Roberto Torres**, Típica Novel (aka Orquesta Novel), **Ismael Miranda**, Raúl Marrero, Kako, Fania All Stars, **Ismael Rivera**, **Cheo Feliciano**, **Típica 73**, Sonora Ponceña (see **Papo Lucca**), **Pete 'El Conde' Rodríguez**, **Ricardo 'Richie' Ray** (and Bobby Cruz), Adalberto Santiago, Sociedad 76, Tito Allen, **Justo Betancourt**, Jimmy Sabater (see **Joe Cuba**), Santiago Ceron, **Héctor Lavoe**, **Mongo Santamaría**, Ray Barretto, **Willie Colón**, **Larry Harlow**, **Conjunto Clásico**, José Bello, Héctor Casanova, Roberto Lugo, **Grupo Fascinación**, Ralphy Santi, **Ismael Quintana**, Daniel Santos and **Pupi Legarreta**.

Albums: *Introducing Louie Ramírez* (c.1964), *Good News* (1965), *Latin Au Go Go* (c.1966), *Vibes Galore* (c.1966), *In The Heart Of Spanish Harlem/En El Corazón De Harlem Español* (c.1967), *Ali Baba* (1968), with Pete Bonet *The Odds Are On* (c.1969), *Pete & Louie/The Beautiful People* (c.1970), with Tito Rodríguez *Algo Nuevo* (1972), *Tipico* (1974), *A Different Shade Of Black* (1976), *Louie Ramírez y sus Amigos* (1978), *Salsa Progresiva* (1979), *Salsero* (1980), *Noche Caliente* (1982), *Super Cañonalos Con Louie Ramírez* (1983), *Con Caché!* (1984), *Alegres y Romanticos* (1985), *Sabor Con Clase!* (1986), *A Tribute To Cal Tjader* (1987, issued in the UK in 1988), *Louie Ramírez y Super Banda* (1987), *El Genio* (1989), *Louie Ramírez y sus Amigos* (1990), *The King Of Latin Vibes* (1991). Compilation: *Various States Of Mind* (1978).

Ramirez, Roger 'Ram'

b. 15 September 1913, Puerto Rico, d. 11 January 1994, New York, USA. Raised in New York City, Ramirez displayed a prodigious talent as a pianist and at the age of 13 became a member of the American Federation of Musicians. During the mid- and late 30s he worked with various artists, including Monette Moore, the **Spirits Of Rhythm**, **Putney Dandridge**, Stew Pletcher and **Willie Bryant**. He recorded with Dandridge and Bryant in 1936. Mostly working in the New York area, he occasionally led small groups in the early 40s, but was also with **Ella Fitzgerald** in 1940, in the band she took over after the death of **Chick Webb**. He next played in bands led by **Frankie Newton** and **Ike Quebec**, appearing with the latter on some early Blue Note records. In the mid-40s he was with **John Kirby**, playing and recording with his reformed sextet. Ramirez also recorded under his own name in 1946, leading a trio with guitarist Jimmy Shirley and bassist Al Hall. In 1944 **Billie Holiday** recorded Ramirez's composition, 'Lover Man', a song which subsequently became a jazz standard. In the late 40s and early 50s he continued to play in and around New York, and towards the end of this period began to play organ. In the 60s he worked with **'T-Bone' Walker**, and the following decade was with the Harlem Blues And Jazz Band. He continued to make appearances with this group into the early 80s. A blues-orientated pianist and organist, Ramirez is perhaps less well known than his skills warrant. Although he visited Europe in 1937 and toured with the Harlem Blues And Jazz band, his decision to spend much of his career in a small geographical area has meant that his international reputation rests largely upon numerous recordings of his most famous composition.

Albums: *Lover Man* (1966-67), *Rampant Ram* (1973-74), *Harlem Blues And Jazz Band, 1973-80* (1973-80).

Ramones

The Ramones, comprising Johnny Ramone (b. John

Cummings, 8 October 1951, Long Island, New York, USA; guitar), Dee Dee Ramone (b. Douglas Colvin, 18 September 1952, Vancouver, British Columbia, Canada; bass) and Joey Ramone (b. Jeffrey Hyman, 19 May 1952; drums) made their debut at New York's Performance Studio on 30 March 1974. Two months later manager Tommy Ramone (b. Tommy Erdelyi, 29 January 1952, Budapest, Hungary) replaced Joey on drums, who then switched to vocals. The quartet later secured a residency at the renowned **CBGB's** club where they became one of the city's leading proponents of punk rock. The fever-paced *Ramones* was a startling first album. Its high-octane assault drew from 50s kitsch and 60s garage-bands, while leather jackets, ripped jeans and an affected dumbness enhanced their music's cartoon-like quality. The group's debut appearance in London in July 1976 influenced a generation of British punk musicians, while *The Ramones Leave Home*, which included 'Suzie Is A Headbanger' and 'Gimme Gimme Shock Treatment', confirmed the sonic attack of its predecessor. *Rocket To Russia* was marginally less frenetic as the group's novelty appeal waned, although 'Sheena Is A Punk Rocker' gave the group their first UK Top 30 hit in 1977. In May 1978 Tommy Ramone left to pursue a career in production and former **Richard Hell** drummer Marc Bell, remodelled as Marky Ramone, replaced him for *Road To Ruin*, as the band sought to expand their appealing, but limited, style. They took a starring role in the trivial *Rock 'N' Roll High School* film, a participation which led to their collaboration with producer **Phil Spector**. The resultant release, *End Of The Century*, was a curious hybrid, and while Johnny baulked at Spector's laborious recording technique, Joey, whose penchant for girl-group material gave the Ramones their sense of melody, was less noticeably critical. The album contained a sympathetic version of the **Ronettes**' 'Baby I Love You', which became the group's biggest UK hit single when it reached the Top 10. The Ramones entered the 80s looking increasingly anachronistic, unable or unwilling to change. *Pleasant Dreams*, produced by **Graham Gouldman**, revealed a group now outshone by the emergent hardcore acts they had inspired. However, *Subterranean Jungle* showed a renewed purpose which was maintained sporadically on *Animal Boy* and *Halfway To Sanity*, the former containing 'Bonzo Goes To Bitburg', a hilarious riposte to Ronald Reagan's ill-advised visit to a cemetery containing graves of Nazi SS personnel. Although increasingly confined to pop's fringes, a revitalized line-up - Joey, Johnny, Marky and newcomer C.J. - undertook a successful 1990 US tour alongside fellow CBGB's graduate **Deborah Harry** and **Talking Heads**' offshoot **Tom Tom Club**. 1992 brought *Mondo Bizarro*, from which 'Censorshit', an attack on Tipper Gore, head of the PMRC, was the most notable moment. By 1995 and *Adios Amigos*, rumours inferred

that the two-minute buzzsaw guitar trail may have finally run cold, with the impression of a epitaph exacerbated by the album's title. As Johnny conceded: 'I know that you have to deal with a life without applause, and I'm looking forward to trying it. A lot of musicians are addicted to it and won't get out.'
Albums: *Ramones* (Sire 1976), *The Ramones Leave Home* (Sire 1977), *Rocket To Russia* (Sire 1977), *Road To Ruin* (Sire 1978), *It's Alive* (Sire 1979, UK only, double album), *End Of The Century* (Sire 1980), *Pleasant Dreams* (Sire 1981), *Subterranean Jungle* (Sire 1983), *Too Tough To Die* (Sire 1984), *Animal Boy* (Sire 1986), *Halfway To Sanity* (Sire 1987), *Brain Drain* (Sire 1989), *Loco Live* (Chrysalis 1991), *Mondo Bizarro* (Chrysalis 1992), *Acid Eaters* (Chrysalis 1993), *Adios Amigos* (Chrysalis 1995). Compilations: *Ramones Mania* (Sire 1988), *All The Stuff And More (Volume One)* (Sire 1990), *End Of The Decade* (Beggars Banquet 1990).
Further reading: *The Ramones: An Illustrated Biography*, Miles. *Ramones: An American Band*, Jim Bessman.

Rampling, Danny

Former bank manager Rampling (b. 15 July 1961, London, England) is a staple of the Manchester **DeConstruction** label, a member of the Kiss FM team, and a hugely popular DJ the world over. DJing since the age of 18, he was pre-eminent in the balearic movement in the late 80s, and has successfully negotiated dozens of shifts in dance music's climate since. He was pivotal in importing the acid sound, after playing legendary sets at Ibiza clubs like Koo and Pacha. His nights at south London's legendary Shoom Club, which he opened with his wife Jenny in 1988, are now legendary. Shoom introduced many of the 'Phuture' tracks imported from Chicago, though Rampling also mixed this up with other dance sounds, he himself having come from a soul background. He waited some time before releasing his first record, Sound Of Shoom's 'I Hate Hate' in 1990, a cover of an obscure soul cut from Razzy Bailey sung by Stephen Eusebe. In the meantime he had remixed for the **B-52's**, **Beloved**, **Erasure** and **James Taylor Quartet**, among many others. He went on to form the Millionaire Hippies, who have released strong singles like 'I Am The Music, Hear Me!', featuring the vocals of Das Strachen and Gwen Dupree, with remixes from **Farley And Heller**.

Ramrods

This instrumental rock quartet from Connecticut, USA featured lead guitarist Vincent Bell Lee (b. Gambella), female drummer and singer Claire Lane, her brother tenor saxophonist Richard and their cousin, guitarist Eugene Moore. The family group was formed in 1956 by Claire, who had originally played in the C&W group, Gino & The Homesteaders. Lee, who as a soloist had previously recorded a rock version of the cowboy song 'Mule Train', helped music student Claire arrange the old **Vaughn Monroe** 1949 million-seller '(Ghost) Riders in The Sky'. They gave this old cowboy song a **Duane Eddy**-ish treatment, complete with cattle noises and various special effects. The record, which they placed with Amy, went into the UK Top 10 and made the US Top 40 in 1961. The group's follow-up 'Take Me Back My Boots & Saddles' and another similar record 'Cry Of The Wild Goose', by Lee with another group, the Challengers, both failed to click. Lee later became a very in-demand session man and also recorded solo on **Verve**, Musicor and **Decca** where his version of 'Airport Theme' in 1970 sold a million copies worldwide.

Ran-Dells

This group was formed in the early 60s in Villas, New Jersey, USA. The Ran-Dells are recalled only for their 1963 novelty hit, 'Martian Hop', one of numerous songs during the 50s and 60s to capitalize on the exploration of space and the possibility of alien visitors. The group was a trio comprised of brothers Bob and John Rappaport (both b. 1943) and John Spirt, their cousin (b. 1949). 'Martian Hop' was composed by all three and theorized that Martians were probably great dancers. Released on the small Chairman label, it reached number 16 in the autumn of 1963. Two follow-up singles, 'Sound Of The Sun' and 'Beyond The Stars', did not chart and the Ran-Dells subsequently split up.

Rance Allen Group

Family vocal and instrumental soul ensemble from Monroe, Michigan, USA, near Detroit. The group consisted of brothers Rance (lead vocals/piano/guitar), Tom (vocals/drums), Steve (vocals/electric guitar). In the early years of the group brother Esau (congas) also participated. The Rance Allen Group with Rance's soaring falsetto lead epitomized the secularized gospel sound of soul music, in which the only aspect that defined the music as R&B was the secular themes of its lyrics. The group first recorded in 1969 for the tiny Reflect label in their hometown of Monroe. In 1971 they were discovered by Memphis-based **Stax**, which began recording them on its Gospel Truth (later Truth) label. The group's first releases were in the gospel vein, notably 'Just My Salvation' (a spiritual version of the **Temptations**' 'Just My Imagination'). The Rance Allen Group's first chart record, 'I Got To Be Myself' (number 31 R&B) in 1973 established their name in soul music. The group next recorded for **Capitol**, but the label only produced only one single to make the charts, 'Truth Is Marching On' (number 100 R&B) in 1977. After Fantasy picked up the catalogue of Stax in 1976, it revived the label for several years in the late 1970s. The Rance Allen Group were signed in 1978, getting their biggest hits with 'I Belong To You'

(number 24 R&B) and 'Smile' (number 41 R&B), both in 1979. After recording their third album for the revived Stax in 1980, the group joined a gospel company, Word, and recorded for several years on Word's subsidiary label, Myrrh. In 1991 the Rance Allen Group returned to secular music when they recorded for Al Bell's Bellmark.
Albums: *Truth Is Where It's At* (Gospel Truth 1972), *A Soulful Experience* (Truth 1975), *The Way It Is* (Capitol 1979), *Straight From The Heart* (Stax 1978), *Smile* (Stax 1979), *I Feel Like Going On* (Myrrh 1980), *Hear My Voice* (Myrrh 1983), *I Give Myself To You* (Myrrh 1984), *Phenomenon* (Bellmark 1991). Compilations: *The Best Of The Rance Allen Group* (Stax 1991), *Up Above My Head* (Stax 1995).

Randall, Freddy

b. 6 May 1921, London, England. Randall began playing trumpet in the late 30s and led his own small band in 1939. By the mid-40s he was one of the most respected dixieland trumpeters in the UK, appearing on radio and at clubs and concerts. He was therefore well placed to take advantage of the trad boom which swept the UK from the late 40s and on through the 50s. Randall's band became one of the most popular of the era and he also toured the USA. Ill health forced his retirement in the late 50s but he was back, part-time, in 1963, and thereafter continued to make occasional and usually unscheduled appearances at London clubs and pubs. These gigs found him playing as well as ever and delighting an army of fans which seemed to grow stronger and more numerous as the years passed. A band he formed in the early 70s in collaboration with **Dave Shepherd** played at international festivals to great acclaim. Reissues of his earlier records confirmed that his qualities were not the result of nostalgic glow. Randall played hard-driving Chicago-style jazz with verve and great skill, and the many fine musicians who played in his band at one time or another responded to his enthusiastic lead.
Albums: *His Great Sixteen* (1951-56), *Something Borrowed, Something Blue* (Alamo 1978, 50s recordings), *Wild Bill Davison With Freddy Randall's Band* (1965), *Freddy Randall-Dave Shepherd All Stars* (1972), *Freddy Randall-Dave Shepherd All Stars 'Live' At Montreux Jazz Festival* (1973), *Freddie Randall And His Band* (Dormouse 1986).

Randall, Jon

b. Duncanville, Dallas, Texas, USA. Randall grew up in Dallas suburb Duncanville, where his influences included **Elvis Presley** and **Z.Z. Top** as well as old and new bluegrass artists. During his high school days he toured surrounding states in a battered Cadillac as part of bluegrass combo Southern Heritage. After completing his studies, he moved to Nashville in an attempt to make an impact in the country music industry. By day holding down jobs including courier

and process server for a law firm, he also found time to continue playing the guitar and sing. He passed his first audition for Holly Dunn's band, playing the *Grand Ole Opry* on its 20th anniversary celebrations, before touring Alaska and Japan. From thence came occasional gigs with **Vince Gill** and **Steve Wariner**, before **Carl Jackson** introduced him as a new member of **Emmylou Harris**' Nash Ramblers. Randall began his solo career as an **RCA Records**' artist in 1994 with *What You Don't Know*. This featured compositions by respected artists and writers including Russell Smith, Carl Jackson, Jim Lauderdale, Vince Melamend, Kevin Welch and Jeff Black, as well as Randall's own material. Guest appearances from Harris, the Nash Ramblers, **Trisha Yearwood** and Vince Gill confirmed his standing in the country community. As the singer/guitarist commented: 'What you hear on the album is what I am. And what I am is a little bit mainstream, a little bit left field, a little bit bluegrass and a little bit rock 'n' roll.' Randall had already toured and/or recorded with **Sam Bush**, Carl Jackson and Steve Wariner in addition to Emmylou Harris, with whom he had participated in the 1992 Grammy Award winning live album, *At The Ryman*. He insisted that he wanted his solo career to carry on both the intensity and musical integrity of his work with the Nash Ramblers. To promote it he set out on as support act to **Mary-Chapin Carpenter**'s 1994 UK tour.
Album: *What You Don't Know* (RCA 1994).

Randazzo, Teddy

b. 20 May 1937, New York City, New York, USA. Randazzo was an accomplished child accordion player. His singing career started with the Three Chuckles, whose other members were Tom Romano (guitar) and Russ Gilberto (bass). The group had small hits with 'Two Times I Love You' (1955) and 'And The Angels Sing' (1956). The group also appeared in **Alan Freed**'s film *Rock Rock Rock*, performing 'Cinnamon Sinner'. A versatile singer who could move from R&B to rock 'n' roll to florid balladry, Randazzo went solo in 1957, recording 'Next Stop Paradise'. 'Little Seranade' was a minor hit a year later. He moved to **ABC Records** in 1960, when 'The Way Of A Clown' reached the Top 50. He joined in the dance crazes of 1962 with 'Dance To The Locomotion', tried folk with a version of 'Cotton Fields' and made an album of standards, **Frank Sinatra**-style, but his only subsequent hit was 'Big Wide World' (1963). The following year Randazzo joined **Don Costa**'s DCP company, concentrating on songwriting and production, notably for **Little Anthony And The Imperials**. Among the group's hits with which he was involved were 'I'm On The Outside Lookin' In', 'Goin' Out Of My Head' (revived by the **Lettermen** in 1968) and 'Hurts So Bad', with which **Linda Ronstadt** had a 1980 hit. Randazzo briefly resumed his own recording career with **Buddah**

in the late 60s. His later songwriting successes included 'Feels So Good To Be Loved So Bad', a 1977 hit for the **Manhattans**.
Albums: *Teddy Randazzo Twists* (1962), *Journey To Love* (1963), *We're Gonna Rock Tonight* (1988, reissue).
Film: *Hey Let's Twist* (1961).

Randolph, Boots

b. Homer Louis Randholph III, 3 June 1925, Paducah, Kentucky, USA. Known as 'Mr. Saxophone', he was of that self-contained caste that improvised the orthodox 'Nashville sound' from a notation peculiar to city studios, and thus had first refusal on countless daily record dates in 'Music City USA' until well into the 60s. Though the 'Western Swing' element of C&W had always admitted woodwinds, his employment was vital in widening the genre's range of instrumentation as the country capital beckoned purveyors of more generalized pop. Indeed, as a solo star, Randolph entered the US pop charts himself with 1963's 'Yakety Sax' *tour de force*. As well as refashioning on disc the diverse likes of 'Tequila', 'Hi Heel Sneakers', 'Willie And The Hand Jive' and 'Bridge Over Troubled Waters', he also ventured into the soul field with a version of **Phil Upchurch** Combo's 'You Can't Sit Down'. Though 'Yakety Sax' resurfaced as the traditional closing theme to UK television's **Benny Hill** Show, Randolph will be remembered chiefly as an accompanist heading horn sections for artists of such immeasurable fame as **Elvis Presley** - notably on 1960's *Elvis Is Back* - and **Roy Orbison** for whom he became a 'good luck charm. I'd pay him even if he didn't play'.
Selected albums: *Boots Randolph's Yakety Sax* (1963), *Boots Randolph Plays More Yakety Sax* (1965), *Boots With Strings* (1967), *Boots Randolph With The Knightsbridge Strings And Voices* (1968), *Sunday Sax* (1968), *The Sound Of Boots* (1968), *...With Love; The Seductive Sax Of Boots Randolph* (1969), *Yakety Revisited* (1970), *Hit Boots 1970* (1970), *Boots With Brass* (1971), *Homer Louis Randolph III* (1971), *The World Of Boots Randolph* (1971), *Boots Randolph Plays The Great Hits Of Today* (1972). Compilation: *Yakety Sax* (1989).

Randolph, Mouse

b. Irving Randolph, 22 January 1909, St. Louis, Missouri, USA. After serving a long apprenticeship in numerous **territory bands** including those led by **Fate Marable** and **Alphonso Trent**, trumpeter Randolph joined **Andy Kirk** in 1931. After leaving Kirk in 1934 he played in big bands led by **Fletcher Henderson**, **Benny Carter**, **Luis Russell** and **Cab Calloway**, the former **Chick Webb** band under the nominal leadership of **Ella Fitzgerald** and **Don Redman**. During this period he also recorded with pick up groups, including **Teddy Wilson**'s band, and after leaving Redman in 1943 he then began a round of small groups, including the sextet led by **Edmond Hall**. Throughout the 50s and 60s he worked for long periods in relatively unknown and undistinguished orchestras, occasionally recording with jazz groups. He later drifted into retirement. Highly regarded by fellow musicians, Randolph's career, although taking him into many fine swing era bands, suggests that he lacked the ambition which brought fame and fortune to lesser musicians.

Album: *The Chronological Teddy Wilson And His Orchestra 1936-1937* (1936-37).

Randy And The Rainbows

This rock 'n' roll vocal group came from Queens, New York, USA. The members were brothers Dominick (lead) and Frank Safuto (baritone), brothers Mike (first tenor) and Sal Zero (second tenor), and Ken Arcipowski (bass). Randy and the Rainbows came out of the thriving New York Italian-American vocal group scene and were one of the last to get a national hit before self-contained bands began dominating popular music. The group can be traced back to 1959 and the formation of the Dialtones, which consisted of the Safuto brothers, a cousin Eddie Scalla, and their lead, Rosalie Calindo. In 1960 they recorded for George Goldner's Goldisc label. Around 1962 the Safuto brothers joined with the Zero brothers and Arcipowski to form Randy And The Rainbows. They hooked up with the **Tokens**' production company and recorded 'Denise', which when it came out on a Laurie Records subsidiary became a Top 10 hit. Despite a lack of subsequent chart success the group managed to continue in the business for decades afterwards, recording in the late 60s as Them And Us, in the early 70s as Triangle, and in the late 70s as Madison Street. The group under their original name recorded two albums for the Ambient Sound label in the early 80s. 'Denise' was revived successfully by **Blondie** in the late 70s.

Albums: *C'Mon Let's Go* (1982), *Remember* (1984). Compilation: *Joy Ride* (1979).

Raney, Jimmy

b. 20 August 1927, Louisville, Kentucky, USA, d. 10 May 1995, Louisville, Kentucky, USA. After working in the New York and Chicago areas, in bands led by Jerry Wald and **Lou Levy**, guitarist Raney joined **Woody Herman** in 1948. Thereafter he played and recorded with a number of leading swing era veterans and up-and-coming stars including **Artie Shaw**, **Stan Getz**, **Terry Gibbs** and **Red Norvo**. Throughout the 60s he worked in studios, making occasional jazz club appearances. This pattern continued into the 70s with the bias gradually swinging towards jazz work. A relaxed and highly proficient technician, Raney's solo work displayed a cool, lambent style which is much admired, although his attraction was often cerebral

rather than emotional. His son, Doug, also plays guitar. Albums: *The Jimmy Raney Quintet* i (1953), *The Jimmy Raney Quartet* ii (1954), *Jimmy Raney Visits Paris* (1954), *Too Marvellous For Words* (1954), *A* (Original Jazz Classics 1955), *Jimmy Raney In Three Attitudes* (1956), *Strings And Swings* (1957-69), *Two Jims And Zoot* (Original Master Recordings 1964), *Momentum* (1974), *The Influence* (1975), *Live In Tokyo* (1976), *The Complete Jimmy Raney In Tokyo* (Xanadu 1977), with Doug Raney *Stolen Moments* (Steeplechase 1979), with Doug Raney *Duets* (Steeplechase 1979), *Here's That Raney Day* (Black And Blue 1980), with Doug Raney *Raney '81* (1981), *The Date* (1981), *The Master* (Criss Cross 1983), with Doug Raney *Nardis* (1983), *Visits Paris* (Fresh Sounds 1988), *Wisteria* (Criss Cross 1985-90), *But Beautiful* (Criss Cross 1993).

Raney, Sue

b. Raelene Claire Claussen, 18 June 1940, McPherson, Kansas, USA. Raised in New Mexico, as a small child Raney was trained by her mother, a professional singer and music teacher. Raney began singing at the age of four and a age eight was singing professionally. Four years on, she had regular radio and television spots including appearances with country singer **Glen Campbell**. Her early singing idols were in the popular field, although some were jazz-inflected, but by her mid-teens had begun to direct her style more firmly into jazz. She gained some valuable early experience working with the **Ray Anthony** band. In the early 60s she sang with **Nelson Riddle** in the UK and made several albums that were critically successful but failed to find a wide audience. She continued to perform, her career remaining regrettably low-key although musical partnerships with **Stan Kenton**, **Michel Legrand**, **Henry Mancini** and others continued to attract critical favour. Further fine albums in the mid-80s and an outstanding 1990 release, *In Good Company*, on which she was backed by jazzmen such as **Conte Candoli**, **Bob Cooper**, **Bill Watrous** and **Alan Broadbent**, attracted wider attention. Raney is also an accomplished songwriter, contributing lyrics to several songs including 'Statue Of Snow'. Singing with a finely-textured voice, beautifully pitched, always displaying impeccable timing and taste, and with effortless swing, Raney is an exceptionally gifted performer. She is one of the finest living interpreters of the great standards and is an excellent jazz singer. Sadly, even following her most recent albums, she remains relatively little known outside a small circle of justifiably devoted admirers. Her husband is flügelhorn player Carmen Falzone.

Albums: *Sue Raney Sings The Music Of Johnny Mandel* (Discovery 1982), with Bob Florence *Ridin' High* (Discovery 1984), *Flight Of Fancy* (Discovery 1985), with Florence *Quietly There* (Discovery 1988), *In Good Company* (Discovery 1990).

Raney, Wayne

b. 17 August 1921, Wolf Bayou, near Batesville, Arkansas, USA. Raney became interested in music at an early age, due to the fact that a crippled foot prevented him playing games. He learned to play the harmonica and listened intently to the playing of Lonnie Glosson on Border radio station XEPN. In 1934, at the age of 13, he hitchhiked to the station's studios in Eagle Pass and recorded some transcription records. He returned home, but when he was 17 he teamed up with Glosson and in 1938, the pair became favourites on KARK Little Rock and continued to play together on many occasions throughout the 40s. In 1941, Raney had his own show on WCKY in Cincinnati and sold a great many 'talking harmonicas' by mail order through the programme. In the late 40s, he became friendly with the **Delmore Brothers** and between 1946 and 1952, made many King recordings with them as the Delmore Brothers, the Brown's Ferry Four or under his own name. (Some recordings also included Glosson.) One of his most popular was the 1946 recording of 'Harmonica Blues'. He obtained two Top 20 US country chart hits in 1948 with 'Lost John Boogie' and 'Jack And Jill Boogie'. In 1949, his recording of 'Why Don't You Haul Off And Love Me', which he co-wrote with Glosson, became a country number 1 and also made number 22 in the US pop charts. In the mid-50s, he left the King label and spent some time as a member of the *Grand Ole Opry* and toured with its shows. He recorded contributions to rock 'n' roll in 1957, such as his **Decca** version of 'Shake Baby Shake'. He left WCKY in 1961 and moved back to his native Arkansas, where he relocated to Concord, opened his own Rimrock recording studio and became involved with promotion work.

Albums: *Songs From The Hills* (1958), *Wayne Raney And The Raney Family* (1960), *Don't Try To Be What You Ain't* (1964), *Gathering In The Sky* (60s), *We Need A Lot More Of Jesus* (60s), *Early Country Favorites* (1983).

Ranger, Shorty

b. Edwin Haberfield, 9 October 1925, Kempsey, New South Wales, Australia. He grew up on the adjoining farm at Nulla Nulla Creek to that occupied by the family of **Slim Dusty**. After first meeting at school, they became firm friends with a mutual love of music. Especially attracted to the songs and yodels that they heard on the recordings of such artists as **Wilf Carter** and **Tex Morton**, they aimed for a singing career. They learned to play guitar and performing as a duo, at one time briefly as Buddy Bluebird and Buddy Blackbird, they entertained in their local area. During the 40s, they toured further afield, including Adelaide and Sydney, without lasting success. Although their careers separated in 1951, their friendship has continued throughout the years. Shorty gained recognition and a recording contract with Rodeo Records that year, by his appearance on a national talent show organised by **Tim McNamara** and Slim went on to international stardom. Shorty married in 1952 and the following year, when the first of four sons and two daughters arrived, he decided to concentrate on his family. From the mid-50s through to the early 70s, limiting his personal appearances, he made some recordings but mainly concentrated on his songwriting. In 1969, the legendary Australian singer **Buddy Williams**, who recorded almost 50 of Shorty's songs, released a tribute album called *Buddy And Shorty*. After 1973, with his family grown, he became more active both as a performer and as a recording artist. He released six albums on Hadley and later a series of 12 on his own Wildwood label. During the late 80s, he suffered a stroke and also a period of ill-health as a result of poisoning from pest control chemicals. He survived and in 1989, he won the Songmaker of the Year award at the prestigious Tamworth Country Music Awards. In 1992, he celebrated 50 years of country by appearing on stage with old friend, Slim Dusty. His health caused concern again in August 1994, which led to a brief hospital stay. In October, he was involved in a serious road accident but by December, he was working on his first CD release. Since 1942, Shorty Ranger has written over 360 other songs, many of which have been recorded by other artists. 'Winter Winds', written in 1943, is undoubtedly the best known, owing to its use as his signature tune and to Slim Dusty's 1957 recording of it. The song, now rated as an Australian country classic, won Shorty a gold award in 1992. Over the years, he has received many other awards including a golden guitar. He has been honoured several times as a Pioneer of Country Music in Australia and in 1993, he was elected to the Country Music Roll Of Renown - the Australian equivalent to Nashville's Country Music Hall of Fame.

Albums: *Heaven Country Style* (Hadley 1973), *The Man From Nulla Nulla* (Hadley 1976), *Sugarloaf Mountain Country* (Hadley 1978), *From Bullock Team To Diesels* (Hadley 1980), *A Tribute To Wilf Carter* (Hadley 1982), *38 Years Of Country Music* (Hadley 1983), *Heaven Country Style* (Wildwood 1984), *The Land Where Time Stands Still* (Wildwood 1985), *Bush Balladeer* (Wildwood 1986), *I'm In Love With The Country* (Wildwood 1987), *Shorty Ranger, The Singing Wanderer* (EMI 1987), *Drifting Along With A Song* (Wildwood 1988), *Hillbilly Memories* (Wildwood 1989), *The Vintage Collection* (Wildwood 1990), *True Country Style* (Wildwood 1990), *Wildwood Country Gospel* (Wildwood 1991), *Riding The Trail To My Home* (Wildwood 1992), *Take Me Back To The Country* (Wildwood 1993). (All Australian releases).

Ranglin, Ernest

b. 1932, Manchester, Jamaica, West Indies. Ranglin had two uncles who played guitar and ukelele, and as a

child would pick up their instruments and try to imitate their playing. He was also influenced by the recordings of **Charlie Christian**, and by Cecil Hawkins, an unrecorded local guitarist. At the age of 15, Ranglin joined his first group, the Val Bennett band, and subsequently played with Eric Deans and Count Boysie. By the early 50s, he had developed into a proficient jazz guitarist, and started to tour overseas. Around 1959, he joined bassist Cluett Johnson in a studio group called **Clue J And His Blues Blasters**, who recorded several instrumentals for **Coxsone Dodd** at JBC studio. The first of these recordings, 'Shuffling Jug', is widely regarded as one of the first **ska** recordings. Ranglin's beautiful, versatile guitar playing ensured that he was in demand as a session musician throughout the ska era, and he provided the musical accompaniment for **Millie**'s world-wide smash, 'My Boy Lollipop'. In the mid-60s he recorded two jazz albums for the Merritone label, *Wranglin* (1964) and *Reflections* (1965). Around this time, **Duke Reid** employed him as musical director at his Treasure Isle recording studio, where he worked for several years. From the late 60s and all through the 70s he worked as a studio musician and arranger for many of the island's top producers such as Coxsone Dodd, **Lee Perry** and **Clancy Eccles**. His most recent albums have been *Ranglin Roots* (1977) and *From Kingston JA To Miami USA* (1982). He continues to record, but spends most of his time playing live, both locally and abroad.
Albums: *Wranglin* (Island 1964), *Reflections* (Island 1965), *Ranglin Roots* (Water Lily 1977), *From Kingston JA To Miami USA* (1982).

Rank And File

Formed in Los Angeles in 1981, Rank And File comprised of former members of the **Dils**, Chip Kinman (guitar/vocals) and Tony Kinman (bass/vocals), and ex-**Nuns**' guitarist/vocalist Alejandro Escovedo. Drummer Slim Evans completed the line-up featured on *Sundown*, an exemplary blend of new wave and country. The album included 'Amanda Ruth', later recorded by the **Everly Brothers**. The Kinman brothers then took control of the group and, having moved to Austin, Texas, completed *Long Gone Dead* with session musicians, including **Richard Greene** (fiddle) and Stan Lynch, drummer with **Tom Petty And The Heartbreakers**. The new set emphasized the duo's love of pop melody, but the contents were still infused with C&W. A long hiatus ensued, but their third album proved a major disappointment, lacking the verve and charm of its predecessors. Rank And File was then disbanded with the Kinmans later founding Blackbird. Escovedo reappeared leading the acclaimed True Believers before embarking on a solo career.
Albums: *Sundown* (1982), *Long Gone Dead* (1984), *Rank And File* (1987).

Rank, Bill

b. 8 June 1904, Lafayette, Indiana, USA, d. 20 May 1979. During the mid-20s trombonist and arranger Rank played with **Jean Goldkette** alongside **Bix Beiderbecke**. In 1928 he was one of several former Goldkette sidemen who joined **Paul Whiteman** where he led the trombone section and was for a while featured soloist. Respected by fellow musicians, Rank's career was frequently overshadowed by other trombone luminaries such as **Jack Teagarden**, with whom he played in the Whiteman band and who took over solo duties. In the late 30s he began working in film studios and thereafter divided his time between playing, mostly in Cincinnati where he led his own band, and non-musical activities.
Album: *Bix Beiderbecke And His Gang* (1927-28).

Rankin Family

This Canadian folk quintet (all of whom are indeed members of the same family) consist of John Morris (b. 28 March 1959, Mabou, Nova Scotia, Canada), Raylene (b. 15 September 1960, Mabou, Nova Scotia, Canada), Jimmy (b. 28 May 1964, Mabou, Nova Scotia, Canada), Cookie (b. 4 May 1965, Mabou, Nova Scotia, Canada) and Heather (b. 24 October 1967, Mabou, Nova Scotia, Canada). The group was formed when they all gave up their respective careers to concentrate on music in the autumn of 1989. With instruments that include guitar, bass, piano, synthesizer, violin, mandolin and percussion, the Rankin Family produce a blend of traditional and contemporary music dominated by the sweet vocals of the family sisters. The *Daily News* described their sound as 'the unpretentious good time charm of a maritime kitchen ceilidh with tight, lilting harmonies, dynamic musicianship and strong original songwriting'. Indeed, the 'wholesome' image of the band was supported by their appearance at the 1993 **Cambridge Folk Festival** at which they played two sets - one specially for children. The group's first album was released independently in 1989, and was followed by *Fare Thee Well Love* a year later. (It was eventually repressed by **EMI Records**.) *North Country* helped launch the band internationally, while their growing domestic profile was rewarded with four Canadian JUNO Awards: Single Of The Year; Canadian Entertainer Of The Year; Best Group; and Best Country Group.
Albums: *The Rankin Family* (Independent 1989), *Fare Thee Well Love* (Independent/EMI 1990), *North Country* (EMI 1993).

Rankin, R.S.

b. 22 February 1933, Royse City, Texas, USA. Rankin's uncle was **'T-Bone' Walker**, who encouraged the youngster to play blues guitar and then took him on the road as a valet in the late 40s. He

worked and recorded with Walker during the 50s, and was dubbed 'T-Bone' Walker Jnr. around 1955, and it was under this name that he recorded for the Midnite label in 1962. He has been less active on the music scene since the mid-60s but did surface to play at the T-Bone Walker Memorial Concert in Los Angeles, California in May 1975, when *Blues Unlimited* reported that 'he did a fantastic job on his uncle's classics'.
Compilation: (one 1962 recording only) *Texas Guitar - From Dallas To L.A.* (1972).

Ranking Dread

b. Winston Brown, Kingston, Jamaica, West Indies. Ranking Dread established his reputation as a live DJ for **Lloydie Coxsone**'s London based **sound system** as yet another in that long line of eccentric, idiosyncratic microphone men associated with reggae music. His particular style of delivery was based around a slurring, almost whining vocal constantly interrupted by comments and interjections, and was definite proof that it was not what you said but how you said it that mattered. His early recordings were inauspicious and failed to make any impact, but *Lots Of Loving* was among the most played records in UK reggae in 1979/1980 where the combination of the Dread's delivery coupled with some of **Sly And Robbie**'s and **Sugar Minott**'s best current rhythms assured his popularity. A number of big selling 12-inch singles followed, a couple of which hovered in the lower reaches of the national charts. He is now believed to be residing in Canada but no longer records or works live.
Album: *Lots Of Loving* (Stand Firm/Freedom Sounds 1980).

Ranking Joe

b. Joe Jackson, c.1960, Kingston, Jamaica. Ranking Joe cut his musical teeth toasting on a **sound system** known as Smith The Weapon. Working his way up through the ranks he became resident DJ on the El Paso ssound, performing as Little Joe. His name was inspired by DJ Big Joe, who had enjoyed a hit with 'Selassie Skank', and not, as many believed, by the character from Western television series *Bonanza*. As with so many of his Jamaican counterparts he began recording with **Clement 'Coxsone' Dodd** at Studio One. His first session resulted in 'Gun Court', which saw him toasting over the **Heptones**' 'Love Me Girl', but this did not make an impression on the charts. He subsequently studied electronics before pursuing his recording career. Encouraged by his father, he was to enjoy a major breakthrough when he went back to the studio to record the highly infectious '750'. The hit resulted in many recordings for a number of producers, notably 'Don't Give Up', 'Psalm 54', 'Natty Don't Make War', 'Tradition', and a tribute to the bionic man, 'Steve Austin'. He also returned to the sound system circuit as resident DJ for **U Roy's** King

Sturgav, alongside **Jah Screw**, before it was destroyed in the violent election campaign of 1980. Later in the same year the Jamaican sound system Ray Symbolic Hi Fi toured the UK, giving British audiences their first taste of a real 'yard' sound. As he had become the resident DJ with the system Ranking Joe featured on the tour and a new wave of enthusiasm for his recordings followed. By 1982 he had become an international figure with the release of *Weakheart Fadeaway* and *Saturday Night Jamdown Style*. Tracks featured included the popular 'Natty The Collie Smoker', 'Nine Month Belly' and 'Step It Down A Shepherds Bush'. The popularity of the lewd slackness style of 'Lift Up Your Frock', 'Rub Sister Rub It' and 'Sex Maniac' ensured an enthusiastic response to his output. The release of *Dub It In A Dance* included 'Clarks Booty Style', 'Slackness Style' and the title-track, but was not as successful. In 1983 he enjoyed renewed success with *Disco Skate* and the reissued *Armageddon*. Shortly after Ray Symbolic's system returned to Jamaica the promoter's life was bought to a sudden end in the streets of Kingston. The tragedy cut short Ranking Joe's career, but many of his albums are still available and remain cherished by the discerning reggae fan.
Albums: *Best Of Ranking Joe* (TR International 1977), *Round The World* (Ital 1978), *Weakheart Fadeaway* (Greensleeves 1982), *Showcase* (Tads 1982), *Armageddon* (Kingdom 1982), *Saturday Night Jamdown Style* (Cha Cha 1982), *Disco Skate* (Copasetic 1982), *Dub It In A Dance* (Trojan 1983), *Check It Out* (Vista 1983), *Natty Superstar* (Joe Gibbs 1983).

Ranks, Cutty

b. Philip Thomas, 12 February 1965, Kingston, Jamaica, West Indies. Thomas began his working life as a butcher, and it is tempting to state that he continued his DJing career as if he was still working with his cleaver - cutting through rhythms and rivals like so many slices of meat. Off the microphone, Cutty is as friendly and personable a character as you're likely to meet in the reggae business, but his style is strictly no holds barred, and his career during the 90s has progressed from strength to strength due to this uncompromising musical stance.
He first took up the microphone for local **sound system** Feathertone, and moved on to Stereo Mars, Arrows and Metro Media - all top ranking sounds. He began his recording career for **Winston Riley** of Techniques Records and then moved to Miami with Skeng Don, learning his craft from **Super Cat** and Nicodemus. He then moved on to Patrick Roberts at Shocking Vibes where he made his first - and highly influential - hit, 'The Bomber'. His next move to **Donovan Germain**'s Penthouse set-up further consolidated his popularity, and he hit again with 'Pon Me Nozzle'. His 'rock-stone' ranting attracted the

attention of London-based **Fashion** Records, and his 1990 recording, 'The Stopper', became a huge international reggae hit both in the original and hip hop remix versions. The album of the same name still sells some four years after its release like a new outing, while its catch phrases and hooklines have been endlessly sampled and reworked.

Cutty had arrived and he has now established his position as one of the foremost exponents of the 90s DJing style. He was even able to deal with a falling-off in his popularity on record in 1992 with 'A Who Seh Me Dun', where he dusted out rivals with his customary blend of venom and humour and came out on top again. He's only ever worked with the best producers in the business, such as **Sly & Robbie**, Roof International and the aforementioned Donovan Germain, Fashion and Shocking Vibes, and has always resisted the ever present temptation for Jamaican DJs to 'voice out' too many tunes for too many producers. It can only be a matter of time before he crosses over in the same way that fellow travellers **Buju** (**Banton**) and **Shabba** (**Ranks**) have done already, as his 'Limb By Limb', a massive hit in the US in 1993, suggests he will.
Albums: *The Stopper* (Fashion 1991), *Lethal Weapon* (Penthouse 1991), *From Mi Heart* (Shanachie 1992). With Tony Rebel: *Die Hard (Volumes One And Two)* (Penthouse 1991), *20 Man Dead* (Charm 1991).
Video: *Champions Of The Dance* (1992).

Ranks, Shabba

b. Rexton Gordon, 1965, St. Ann's, Jamaica, West Indies. Although born in a country parish his family moved to Kingston when he was eight; by the age of 12 he was studying DJs like **General Echo**, **Brigadier Jerry**, **Yellowman** and especially **Josey Wales**, who took him to **King Jammys** after Shabba had served his apprenticeship on the Roots Melody **sound system** alongside **Admiral Bailey**, recording his debut 'Heat Under Sufferers Feet' in 1985. 'Original Fresh' a year later was his first for Jammys. Unable to really establish himself despite an album shared with **Chakademus** (*Rough And Rugged*) his initial notoriety for 'slackness' came with hits for Wittys ('Needle Eye Punany'), voiced while visiting New York in 1988. Shortly afterwards he left King Jammys for **Bobby Digital**'s new label and Heatwave sound system, scoring immediately with 'Mama Man', 'Peanie Peanie' and then 'Wicked In Bed', which proved highly successful in 1989. Digital, after being engineer with Jammys had known Shabba since he was 15 and this special relationship between the two is still very much in evidence today.
Mike 'Home T' Bennett had also worked for Jammys and first teamed Shabba with **Cocoa Tea** and his vocal group, Home T4 for 'Who She Love' then 'Stop Spreading Rumours'. They took the formula to **Gussie Clarke**, who produced a subsequent album,

Holding On, and big hits like 'Pirate's Anthem', 'Twice My Age' (with Krystal) and 'Mr Loverman' (with **Deborahe Glasgow**). Later the song would be re-voiced with Chevelle Franklin and become an international success in 1993. Throughout 1989 however, Shabba's presence dominated reggae music, although he recorded for few producers outside of Bobby Digital and Gussie Clarke. His personal appearances in London resulted in riots and, in one tragic case, a shooting. He also attracted the attention of the hip hop fraternity, which had previously forged strong links with reggae before breaking into the mainstream. He was signed to **Epic** Records in late 1990, the year his duet with **Maxi Priest** on 'Housecall' became a major crossover hit. The first Epic album, *Raw As Ever*, wisely continued to use the top Jamaican producers and won him a US Grammy in 1991. By now his gruff, commanding voice had become known world-wide and the follow-up album, *X-tra Naked*, repeated the feat; Shabba becoming the first DJ to win two consecutive Grammy Awards. After releasing a number of commercially successful singles in 1993 he returned to the **dancehall** arena with a flourish; 'Shine And Criss', and 'Respect' pleasing his still fanatical reggae following immensely, and further hits with 'Mr Loverman' and 'Family Affair'. In 1995 he released the excellent 'Let's Get It On' as a trailer for his 1995 album *A Mi Shabba*.
Selected albums: *Best Baby Father* (John John/Blue Mountain 1989), *Just Reality* (Blue Mountain 1990), *Star Of The 90s* (King Jammys 1990), *Rappin' With The Ladies* (Greensleeves 1990), *As Raw As Ever* (Epic 1991), *Rough & Ready Vol. 1* (Epic 1992), *Mr Maximum* (Greensleeves 1992), *X-Tra Naked* (Epic 1992), *Rough & Ready Vol. 2* (Epic 1993), *A Mi Shabba* (Epic 1995). With Chakademus: *Rough & Rugged* (King Jammys 1988). With Home T4 and Cocoa T: *Holding On* (Greensleeves 1989).
Videos: *Fresh And Wild X Rated* (1992). With Ninjaman: *Reggae Sting Vol. 1* (1992).

Rap-A-Lot Records

Houston, Texas-based rap label run by James Smith (b. c.1964), who has seen considerable financial reward for his efforts in promoting ultra-hardcore rappers like the **Geto Boys** and sundry spin-off projects. One of several items of real estate to his name is a 30 acre ranch where he hosted *Source Magazine*'s debate about gangsta rap. His opinion: 'This rap shit is the biggest challenge to this government in a long-ass time. It's bigger than Martin Luther King and all them'. His empire has expanded to include new talent like **5th Ward Boys** and **Raheem**, though they hardly provide stylistic diversity.
Selected albums: Geto Boys: *We Can't Be Stopped* (Rap-A-Lot 1991). Scarface: *The World Is Yours* (Rap-A-Lot 1993).

Rapeman

This controversially-named US act was created when Steve Albini (ex-**Big Black**; guitar/vocals) joined forces with two former members of **Scratch Acid**, David Wm. Sims (bass) and Rey Washam (drums). The trio was short-lived and their output comprised of a single, 'Inkis' Butt Crack', released on the cult **Sub Pop** label, *Budd*, a 4-track set, and *Two Nuns And A Pack Mule*. The album maintained the loud, uncompromising sound the two previous groups had offered - tight, crashing drums, pounding bass and sheets of metallic guitarwork - and included a startling interpretation of **Z.Z. Top**'s 'Just Got Paid'. However, the group was unable to shake off criticism of its repellent name which Albini took from a character in contemporary Japanese comics. Several distributors objected to handling the album and many venues were forced under pressure, particularly at colleges and universities, to cancel appearances, which in part explained the trio's demise. Sims subsequently resurfaced in the **Jesus Lizard**, which Albini produced.
Album: *Two Nuns And A Pack Mule* (1988).

Rapino Brothers

Italian producers, remixers and writers, the Rapino Brothers are Marco Sabiu and Charlie Mallozzi. Sabiu is a keyboard player and programmer, who admits to being classically trained ('though trying to forget it'). Former drummer Mallozzi, meanwhile, provides the musical knowledge behind the group, and most of its strategy. After working initially in their native Bologna, Italy, the duo 'got bored', and decided to pack up and relocate to London in May 1992. Their career since then has boomed, becoming fixtures on the club remix circuit via work with **Vegas** ('She'), **Freaky Realistic** ('Something New'), **Heaven 17** ('Fascist Groove Thing'), **Candyland** ('Rainbow'), **Dayeene** ('Around The World'), **London Boys** ('Baby Come Back') and Milan ('Affectionately Mine'), among others. As artists they also employ their own act, Rapination, which features assorted vocalists, and they quickly scored a UK Top 40 success in January 1993 with the aid of **Kym Mazelle**'s vocals on 'Love Me The Right Way'.

Rappin' Is Fundamental

Among the forerunners of one of rap's many clashes with different genres, in this case doo-wop. The trio consists of Easy Mo Bee (b. Osten Harvey, brother of producer 'LG' Harvey), JR and AB Money, all Brooklyn neighbours, raised under the paternal wing of their local church. JR (b. Darron Strand) decided to put on hold his career in Wall Street for the music business in 1987. There is little to dislike about Rappin' Is Fundamental and their mix of funky beats with breezy a cappella breaks and doo wop harmonies, with the possible exception of their rather laborious name. Influenced by vocal harmony groups like the Flamingos, they were certainly among the more sophisticated members of New York's hip hop culture. They were keen to differentiate themselves from anything so one-dimensional: 'We don't want to be looked on as just rappers. We're born singers, we're *bona fide* dancers and natural rappers. We're all round entertainers.' However, they were dropped by **A&M**, after their debut album stiffed, but were still active in 1994, independently releasing 'Helluva Guy'.
Album: *The Doo Hop Legacy* (A&M 1991).

Rare Bird

Steve Gould (vocals/saxophone/bass) and Dave Kaffinette (keyboards) fronted this British group throughout its recording career. Graham Field (organ) and Mark Ashton (drums) completed the line-up featured on *Rare Bird*, which included their memorable 1970 hit single, 'Sympathy'. Although this atmospheric protest ballad only reached the lower reaches of the UK Top 30, it proved highly popular on the Continent and has since become a cult favourite. The group came under the wing of **Tony Stratton-Smith**, but failed to translate their European charm into further success at home. Gould and Kaffinette were joined by Andy Curtis (guitar) and Fred Kelly (percussion) for *Epic Forest*, but despite initial promise, this restructured line-up failed to revitalize Rare Bird's increasingly ailing fortunes.
Albums: *Rare Bird* (1969), *As Your Mind Flies By* (1970), *Epic Forest* (1972), *Somebody's Watching* (1973), *Born Again* (1974), *Rare Bird* (1975). Compilations: *Sympathy* (1976), *Rare Bird - Polydor Special* (1977).

Rare Earth

Saxophonist Gil Bridges and drummer Pete Rivera formed their first R&B band, the Sunliners, in Detroit in 1961. Bassist John Parrish joined in 1962; guitarist Rod Richards and keyboards player Kenny James followed in 1966. After years of playing in local clubs, they were signed to **Motown** in 1969, where they were renamed Rare Earth after the label's newly-formed progressive rock subsidiary. They scored immediate success with a rock-flavoured version of the **Temptations**' hit 'Get Ready', which reached the US Top 10. The single was edited down from a 20-minute recording which occupied one side of their debut album: it showcased the band's instrumental prowess, but also typified their tendency towards artistic excess. A cover of another Temptations' classic, '(I Know) I'm Losing You', brought them more success in 1970, as did original material like 'Born To Wander' and 'I Just Want To Celebrate'. But Rare Earth had already suffered the first in a bewildering series of personnel changes which dogged their progress over the next decade, as Rod Richards and Kenny James were replaced by Ray Manette and Mark Olson respectively, and Ed Guzman (b. c.1944, d. 29 July 1993) was added on percussion. This line-up scored several minor US hits in the early 70s, until internal upheavals in 1973 led to a complete revamp of the band's style. The Temptations' mentor, **Norman Whitfield**, produced the highly-regarded *Ma* that year, with new band leader Peter Hoorelbeke on vocals. By the release of *Back To Earth* in 1975, he in turn had been supplanted by Jerry La Croix. Subsequent releases proved commercially unsuccessful, though the band continued to record and tour into the 80s. Former members Peter Hoorelbeke, Gil Bridges and Michael Urso later combined as Hub for an album on **Capitol Records**. At the turn of the decade the line-up comprised, Gil Bridges, Ray Monette, Edward Guzman, Wayne Baraks, Rick Warner, Dean Boucher, Randy Burghdoff. They joined **Ian Levine**'s Motor City label in 1990 and issued 'Love Is Here And Now You've Gone'. The band continue to be hugely successful in Germany.

Albums: *Get Ready* (1969), *Ecology* (1970), *One World* (1971), *In Concert* (1971), *Willie Remembers* (1972), *Ma* (1973), *Back To Earth* (1975), *Midnight Lady* (1976), *Rare Earth* (1977), *Band Together* (1978), *Grand Slam* (1978).

Ras Michael And The Sons Of Negus

b. Michael George Henry, c.1943, Kingston, Jamaica, West Indies. Michael grew up in a Rastafarian community at St. Mary where he learned hand-drumming, eventually becoming a master-drummer. In the early 60s, he formed the Sons Of Negus, a Rastafarian group of drummers and singers. In the mid-60s he founded his own Zion Disc label, and started to release a series of singles including 'Lion Of Judah', 'Ethiopian National Anthem' and 'Salvation'. These recordings, on which the group is usually augmented by guitar and bass, show a remarkable degree of invention and subtlety. Around 1966, he recorded at **Studio One** as a percussionist, playing with **Jackie Mittoo** And The Soul Vendors in exchange for studio time. In the early 70s he recorded *Dadawah Peace And Love*, on which his group was augmented by studio musicians, a blend of Rastafarian chant, reggae, Southern soul and psychedelia greatly enhanced by its imaginative arrangements. *Nyahbinghi* was a collection of chants and hymns in the style of his Zion disc singles. In 1975, he recorded *Rastafari*, on which his group was augmented by several well-known reggae musicians. The album's tight arrangements and excellent songs brought him into the reggae mainstream, but the momentum was lost with 1976's *Tribute To The Emperor* with Jazzboe Abubaka and *Freedom Sounds*. He augmented his group again for 1978's *Kabir Am Lak* (Glory To God) and *Movements*, both of which are strong albums. In 1979, *Rastafari In Dub* was issued, an excellent collection of material

culled from *Rastafari* and *Kibir Am Lak*. Further releases included *Promised Land Sounds Live* (1980), *Disarmament* and *Revelation* (1982). His last outstanding album was *Love Thy Neighbour*, whose imaginative production is the work of **Lee Perry**. During the late 80s Michael spent a great deal of time teaching drumming. He returned to recording with *Zion Train* (1988), a mediocre album made without the Sons Of Negus, followed by *Know How* (1990), a disappointing set which tried to incorporate world music elements.

Albums: *Dadawah Peace And Love* (Trojan 1975), *Nyahbinghi* (1975), *Rastafari* (Grounation 1975), *Freedom Sounds* (Dynamic 1976), *Irations Of Ras Michael* (Top Ranking 1977), *Kibir Am Lak* (Rastafari 1978), *Movements* (Dynamic 1978), *Rastafari In Dub* (Grounation 1979), *Promised Land Sounds Live* (Lions Gate 1980), *Revelation* (Trojan 1982), *Disarmament* (Trojan 1983), *Love Thy Neighbour* (Live & Love 1984), *Rally Round* (Shanachie 1985), *Know How* (Shanachie 1990). With Jazzboe Abubaka: *Tribute To The Emperor* (Trojan 1976). With HR: *Zion Train* (SST 1988).

Raspberries

Formed in 1970, this popular 70s US group evolved from several aspiring Ohio-based bands. The original line-up included two former members of Cyrus Erie, **Eric Carmen** (b. 11 August 1949, Cleveland, Ohio, USA; vocals, guitar, keyboards) and Marty Murphy (guitar), as well as ex-Choir drummer Jim Bonfanti (b. 17 December 1948, Windber, Pennsylvania, USA). Murphy was quickly replaced by Wally Bryson (b. 18 July 1949, Gastonia, North Carolina, USA), a veteran of both groups, who in turn introduced John Alleksic. However the latter was removed in favour of Dave Smalley (b. 10 July 1949, Oil City, Pennsylvania, USA; guitar, bass), another ex-Choir acolyte. The Raspberries' love of the **Beatles** was apparent on their debut 'Don't Wanna Say Goodbye'. Its melodic flair set the tone of 'Go All The Way', a gorgeous slice of Anglophilia which rose to number 5 in the US chart. *Raspberries* confirmed the quartet's undoubted promise, but it was on *Fresh*, released a mere four months later, that their talent fully blossomed. Here the group's crafted harmonies recalled those of the **Beach Boys** and **Hollies**, while a buoyant *joie de vivre* was apparent on such memorable songs as 'Let's Pretend' and 'I Wanna Be With You'. This cohesion, sadly, was not to last and while *Side 3* included wider influences drawn from the **Who** and **Small Faces**, it also reflected a growing split between Carmen and the Bonfanti/Smalley team who were summarily fired in 1973. Scott McCarl (guitar) and Michael McBride (drums, ex-Cyrus Erie) completed the new Raspberries' line-up which debuted the following year with the gloriously ambitious 'Overnight Sensation'. The attendant album, cheekily entitled *Starting Over*, contained several equally memorable songs, but it was clear that Carmen now required a broader canvas for his work. He disbanded the group in 1975 and embarked on an intermittently successful solo career, while Bryson resurfaced in two disappointing pop/rock bands, Tattoo and Fotomaker.

Albums: *Raspberries* (1972), *Fresh* (1972), *Side 3* (1973), *Starting Over* (1974). Compilations: *Raspberries' Best Featuring Eric Carmen* (1976), *Overnight Sensation - The Very Best Of The Raspberries* (1987).

Further reading: *Overnight Sensation: The Story Of The Raspberries*, Ken Sharp.

Rasta Music

By which is meant the 'burru' or 'nyabhingi' drumming, as practised by outfits like **Count Ossie** & The Mystic Revelation Of Rastafari, and **Ras Michael And The Sons Of Negus**. There are three drums used in such music, the large bass drum of between two to three feet diameter, played by striking with a stick, the end of which is padded. This is used to mark time and keep the pace with a deeply resonant, almost sub-frequency thump. The smaller funde and repeater hand drums lay down the rhythm, with the repeater improvising across the top. These are often complemented by a selection of percussion instruments and home-made bottle horns or saxes. Rasta music derives from the Afro-Jamaican burru and kumina traditions, themselves said to have descended from traditional West African dances. Prior to the late 50s, such music was confined to Rastafarian strongholds at Wareika Hill, Dungle, and other locations. Count Ossie was instrumental in bringing such music to wider public attention, especially when he agreed to provide the backing for **Prince Buster**'s production of the **Folks Brothers**' 'Oh Carolina'. Count Ossie and his drummers were subsequently used on a number of recordings throughout the next ten years, including 'Babylon Gone' aka 'Going Home' (c.1961), featuring saxophonist Wilton Gatnair, producer **Harry Mudie**'s first record; 'Lumumba' (1961) by Bonny & Skitter, and 'Another Moses' (1961) by the Mellowcats for **Coxsone Dodd**. 'Cassavubu' (1961) aka 'Chubby' provided another hit for Buster. Other notable releases included 'Ducksoup' (1962) by Drumbago's Orchestra, 'Down The Train Line' (1967) by **Stranger Cole** & Patsy, and 'Pata Pata Rock Steady' (1967) by Patsy, both for **Sonia Pottinger**. They managed to cut a few singles under their own steam too, including 'So Long Rastafari Calling' (1971) for **Studio One**, 'Rasta Reggae' for Arnold Wedderburn's Right On label, 'Whispering Drums' (1969) for Harry Mudie and 'Blacker Black' (1968), wrongly credited to the **Ethiopians**, and released on **Pama**'s Crab label in the UK in 1968.

In 1973 Count Ossie linked up with Rasta saxophonist **Cedric Brooks** to record the classic triple set, *Grounation*, released in the UK on the Ashanti label.

This remains the essential Rasta music artefact, a compelling *tour de force* of heartbeat drumming, dread philosophy and free jazz-styled horn playing. Count Ossie died in 1975, crushed when a storm panicked the crowd during a cricket match at Kingston's National Stadium. Cedric Brooks carried out further experimentation with the basic Rasta music structure, with some satisfying results on *United Africa* (1977), and went on to form the Light Of Saba, of whom 'Lambs Bread Collie' (1978) is a fine example. Ras Michael follows much in the tradition of Count Ossie, though his music often fits more easily into the orthodox reggae format. His early albums, *Peace & Love* (1975) and *Freedom Sounds*(1976), remain fairly conventional examples of Rasta music. Later albums such as *Rastafari* (1976) and *Irations Of Ras Michael* (1977) combined burru drumming and standard reggae rhythms to good effect. While Rasta music has never been at the forefront of reggae music itself, it is a uniquely Jamaican aspect that was incorporated into the earliest R&B derived, pre-**ska** forms. Its influence has been felt in subtle ways ever since.

Albums: Count Ossie: *Grounation* (Ashanti 1973), *Tales Of Mozambique* (Dynamic 1975). Ras Michael & The Sons Of Negus: *Dadawah Peace & Love* (Trojan 1975), *Freedom Sounds* (Dynamic 1976).

Rastafarianism

Rastafari emerged out of the ghettos of Kingston, Jamaica, West Indies during the 30s. Its rise in popularity among Jamaica's youth in the late 60s and 70s facilitated its worldwide recognition as the driving philosophical force behind the music of prominent reggae artists such as **Burning Spear**, **Culture**, **Big Youth**, **Black Uhuru** and of course the three main **Wailers**; **Bunny Wailer**, **Peter Tosh** and **Bob Marley**. So strongly has Rasta been associated with reggae music that for many people the one is unthinkable without the other. But reggae reflects all the aspects and concerns of Jamaican life, whether spiritual, temporal, or purely hedonistic, whatever affects or is held dear by the youth from which it so often springs, and to whom it speaks loudest, is a fit subject for eulogisation in reggae. In this way Rastafarianism was felt most keenly in the 70s, but though it is less crucial to the music's identity nowadays, its reverberations are still felt.

Religion has always played a large part in the lives of Jamaicans. Part of the process of slavery was to ingrain the Bible deeply into the slave psyche in order to provide Holy justification for the superior stance of the slave masters and to reinforce the inevitability of the slaves' bondage and backbreaking toil. The African religions and traditions practised prior to enslavement were severely discouraged, and yet means were found in which they were retained in coded forms, through music, dance and folk tales. These survive in modern

Jamaica through such forms as Kumina, and Obeah, and adapted with Christianity, in Pocomania (aka Pukkumania). The majority of the island's population though, adhere to Christian forms such as Anglican, Methodist, Roman Catholic, and The Church of God, as well as a strong following for the Ethiopian Orthodox Church. More than 80 per cent of Jamaica's population is Christian.

The roots of Rasta may be found in the rise of black awareness in Jamaica during the early part of the 20th century. Some African-Jamaicans began to feel increasingly dissatisfied with the Caucasian bias of the Christian churches, and the image of God as a white man. A new interest in African affairs also burgeoned. This new found consciousness was manifested in many ways by as many different individuals and organisations, but in particular in the activities and speeches of Marcus Mosiah Garvey (b. 17 August 1887, St. Ann's Bay, Jamaica, West Indies, d. 1940). Garvey had established the Universal Negro Improvement Association (UNIA) in Jamaica in 1914 with the aim of providing an impetus for disenfranchised blacks to learn about their history, their African roots, and to make provision for a hopeful future despite their humble present. The limitations of working within the confines of Jamaica soon prompted Garvey's relocation to America where UNIA soon blossomed among the black ghettos and tenements of Harlem and naturally attracted the attention of the authorities. Garvey attempted to launch a steamship company, the Black Star Line, that would hopefully establish a firm business base for the organisation and with which he hoped to provide free passage back to Africa for those African-Americans who wished to return. This eventually proved to be his undoing when he was jailed in Atlanta and deported to Jamaica on trumped-up charges of fraud. Garvey died in obscurity in London in 1940, but when his body was returned to Jamaica for burial he was received as a hero.

Garvey was an important figure in what eventually became the Civil Rights Movement in the US, but his importance to this story lies in certain pronouncements he is said to have made, in particular the famous 'Look to Africa, when a black king shall be crowned, for the day of deliverance is near.' In Jamaica, among his followers (known as Graveyites) this was received literally as prophecy, and when in November 1930 Haile Selassie, the latest in the Ethiopian line of royalty, whose birthright is said to trace back to the Biblical marriage between King Solomon and the Queen of Sheba, was crowned Ras Tafari, King of Kings, Lord of Lords, Conquering Lion of the Tribe of Judah, Emperor of Ethiopia, many Garveyites and sympathisers felt that Garvey's prophecy had been fulfilled.

Another key figure in this story is preacher Leonard P. Howell, who was arrested in 1933 for sedition and blasphemy. Howell had been selling postcards of Emperor Haile Selassie and claiming him to be 'the spirit of our Lord . . . returned'. Howell also claimed that blacks in the west were really Jews, the Biblical lost tribe of Israel. To Howell, Selassie, Ras Tafari, was literally the same man as Jesus, and therefore God made flesh on earth. Citing Selassie's coronation attended by 72 nations paying homage and bearing gifts, Selassie was 'Christ returned to earth to kill Nebuchadnezzar's image'. Other factors and individuals were involved in these early stages, and the Rastafarian movement began to flourish in the ghettos, its followers marked out, in accordance with certain Old Testament passages, by the adoption of dreadlocks, in which the hair is not combed or otherwise teased into submission, but is allowed to grow in wild coils frequently tucked into knitted tams adorned with the colours of the Ethiopian flag; red, green and gold. Frowned upon by the authorities, life was made difficult for the Rastas during these early years. Howell's stronghold in Pinnacle, where hundreds of Rastas lived in quite reflective isolation from the rest of Jamaican society, was raided twice, and finally closed down by police after which the faithful settled in the ghetto districts of Kingston. This was probably the catalyst for the movement's greater influence among Jamaica's poor. By the mid-60s it was established that there were at least 70,000 Rastafarians living in Jamaica.

True Rastafarians are deeply spiritual individuals who hold their faith uppermost in their lives. There are many misconceptions and seemingly mysterious aspects of their faith in terms of behaviour and speech, the headline grabbing use of marijuana (aka ganga, the holy herb), the dreadlocks (though neither ganga smoking or dreadlocks are necessary requirements), the purposeful lack of an organised church and hierarchy (until the inauguration of the Twelve Tribes in the early 70s), the grounations (gatherings where brethren would partake of the herb by way of the chalice, sit and reason, play drums, chant, and sing adapted hymns) (see **Rasta Music**), the desire for repatriation back to Africa, and the apocalyptic view of the world's present state of affairs. Throughout the 60s interest in Rasta had been growing among Jamaica's youth and this was naturally reflected in the popular music of the day on records such as 'Oh Carolina' by the **Folks Brothers** which utilised the burru drumming of master Rasta musician **Count Ossie** and his group, and 'Beardman Ska' (1965) by the **Skatalites**. This influence found its fullest flowering in the 70s with Rasta sentiments expressed clearly in popular records such as 'Beat Down Babylon' and 'A Place Called Africa' (both 1971) by **Junior Byles**, and 'Satta Massa Gana' (recorded in 1969 but only becoming a hit in 1971) by the **Abyssinians**.

The movement came to worldwide recognition in the

mid-70s with the success of Bob Marley And The Wailers. Marley, like many of his contemporaries, had been interested in the faith since the mid-60s, finally capitulating fully at the turn of the 70s, his guidance coming through Rasta elder Mortimer Planno, the dread who stood on the steps of the plane with the Emperor during his tumultuous visit to Jamaica in 1966. The release of the epochal *Natty Dread* (1976), and the extensive touring Marley undertook subsequently, brought Rasta to the attention of the world's media, and also alerted many in Europe and America to the faith. Rastafarianism's influence waned to some extent during the 80s, many of those attracted to the faith found it hard to adhere to the strict moral, dietary, and philosophical guidelines of fundamental Rastafarianism, and in some cases its practitioners adapted and compromised the faith, to a more easily assimilated lifestyle. Rastafari still has a struggle to be recognised as a 'proper' religion, and this is probably because many Rastas practise their faith in a personal way rather than adhering to any organisation. Its popularity in the 70s among Jamaica's youth was for many a transitionary phase, later dropped when it became unfashionable. It has also suffered from the bad publicity it has received at the hands of criminals affecting the outward appearance of Rastafarians. It has survived the 'death' of its Godhead Haile Selassie (who never officially recognised, nor denounced, the faith) in 1976 after Ethiopia had endured a communist backed military coup. Nevertheless Rasta has been and still remains a strong and positive influence for many people, of all races, all over the world.

Rat Race, The

Better than its original reception suggests, this downbeat tale of a jazz musician and his dancehall girl has a quirky charm. Directed by Robert Mulligan and staring Tony Curtis and **Debbie Reynolds**, this 1960 film was based upon the stage play by Garson Kanin who also wrote the screenplay. In the forefront of the jazz musicians taking part is **Gerry Mulligan**.

Ratcat

Emerging in 1986 from Australia's thrash metal scene and based in Sydney, Ratcat relocated to the UK to promote their **Ramones** tinged pop rock. The trio comprises Simon Day (vocals, guitar), Amr Zaid (bass and occasional vocals) and Andrew Polin (drums). If UK audiences were surprised to see them occupy support slots for **INXS**, it was less of a shock in their homeland, where they regularly top the charts and appear on the covers of teenage magazines. Despite the obvious commercial validity of the band, their music remains rooted in pure garage group aesthetics: 'We've always said that, at heart, we're basically scuzz rats. We're at our best when we're at our scuzziest'.
Albums: *Tingles* (1991), *Blind Love* (1991).

Ratt

This heavy metal group formed in Los Angeles, California, USA, and featured Stephen Pearcy (vocals), Robbin Crosby (guitar), Warren DeMartini (guitar), Juan Croucier (bass) and Bobby 'The Blotz' Blotzer (drums). They evolved out of 70s band Mickey Ratt, transmuting into their present form in 1983, with a hint of pop about their brand of metal similar to **Cheap Trick** or **Aerosmith**. They released a self-titled mini-album in 1983 on a local label, and struck up a close personal friendship with members of **Mötley Crüe** which no doubt helped them to sign to **Atlantic** the following year. They made their breakthrough with their first full album, *Out Of The Cellar*, which stayed in the *Billboard* Top 20 for six months. They toured with **Ozzy Osbourne** before joining a **Billy Squier** jaunt where they were apparently 'thrown off' because they were more popular than the headline act. Their subsequent output has seen them follow a familiar heavy metal route with accusations over sexist videos contrasting with their ability to sell out concert halls and produce recordings that regularly received gold discs. *Decimater* featured several songs co-written with **Desmond Child** and proved their most adventurous recording to date, though Crosby would depart after *Rat 'n' Roll*. In 1993 Pearcy unveiled his new outfit, Arcade, confirming the dissolution of the band.
Albums: *Ratt* (Time Coast 1983, mini-album), *Out Of The Cellar* (Atlantic 1984), *Invasion Of Your Privacy* (Atlantic 1985), *Dancing Undercover* (Atlantic 1986), *Reach For The Sky* (Atlantic 1988), *Decimater* (Atlantic 1990), *Rat 'n' Roll* (East West 1991).
Video: *The Video* (1986).

Rattle 'N' Reel

A group formed by Irish expatriots in Manchester, England, with **Mike Harding**'s brother in charge. Their debut comprised melodic folk-rock, and mainly featured their own songs when many of their contemporaries were covering traditional material. A good, promising live act.
Albums: *Not Just Anyone* (1992), *Outrageous* (Rattle'n'Reel 1994).

Rattles

Guided by the late Manfred Weissleder, proprietor of the city's Star-Club, Hamburg teenagers Achim Reichel (guitar/vocals), Hajo Kreutzfeldt (guitar), Herbert Hildebrandt (bass/vocals) and Reinhard Tarrach (drums) modelled their group on the British beat image in 1962. Among their first recordings was a version of 'The Hippy Hippy Shake', and they often shared bills with **Tony Sheridan, Cliff Bennett**, the **Beatles** and **Kingsize Taylor**. Later, morale was boosted by a successful fortnight's residency in Liverpool's Cavern, and appearances on British television. However, shortly after a domestic chartbuster with 'The Witch' (written by Hilderbrandt) in 1968, the quartet was halted by compulsory army service and other external factors. Hilderbrandt rallied by taking a back seat as producer, composer and general *eminence grise* to a new Rattles enlisted in Italy and consisting of Frank Mille (guitar), Sotto Lumgen (bass), Herbert Bornhold (drums) and a personable Israeli singer with the stage name 'Edna'. 'The Witch' was remade with English lyrics to fly into the UK Top 10. The Rattles also became the first German group to enter the US Hot 100. They were, however, unable to secure a lasting place in foreign hearts, and soon returned to the West German orbit of engagements where they are remembered as one of the leading beat groups of the era.

Rattlesnake Annie

b. Rosanne Gallimore, 26 December 1941, Puryear, Tennessee, USA. Rattlesnake Annie, of Cherokee heritage, was born into a poor family of tobacco farmers. They had no electricity or modern conveniences, apart from a radio, on which Gallimore would hear country music from Nashville. Many of her songs ('Cotton Mama', 'Bulger Wilson', 'Good Ole Country Music') are about those years. As part of the Gallimore sisters, she appeared on the *Junior Grand Ole Opry* in 1954 but when she married Max McGowan, her ambitions were put on hold while she raised a family. **David Allan Coe** recorded her song, 'Texas Lullaby' and she became Rattlesnake Annie by wearing a rattlesnake's tail on her right ear. Her first album, although self-financed, featured top Nashville musicians and established her as both a performer and a songwriter. Because she shares the same love of traditional country music as **Boxcar Willie**, she has been accepted in the UK and even more so in Czechoslovakia where her album with local country star, Michal Tuny, was a best-seller. She recorded 'Long Black Limousine' with **Willie Nelson**, a performer who favours the same casual approach to stage wear.

Albums: *Rattlesnakes And Rusty Water* (1980), with Michal Tuny *Rattlesnake Annie And The Last Cowboy* (1983), *Country Livin'* (1985), *Rattlesnake Annie* (1987), *Indian Dreams* (1991), *Crossroads* (1990), *Rattlesnake Annie Sings Hank Williams* (1991).

Rattlesnake Kiss

Birmingham, UK-based heavy metal quintet, formed in 1990 by vocalist Sean Love and guitarists Ralph Cardall and Bill Carroll. Influenced by American bands such as **Queensrÿche**, **Van Halen** and **Rush**, their speciality was in highly sophisticated and technically accomplished hard rock. The songs, which came over more powerfully in a live setting than in the studio, combined power with musical precision. Picked up by the independent Sovereign label they released a self-titled debut album in early 1992, though this did not fully reflect the band's musical prowess or energy due to thin production.

Album: *Rattlesnake Kiss* (Sovereign 1992).

Rava, Enrico

b. 20 August 1943, Trieste, Italy. Rava's mother was a classical pianist, but he began on trombone in bands playing New Orleans jazz and then graduated to trumpet. He studied with Carmine Caruso in New York and joined **Gato Barbieri**'s quintet in 1964. Between 1965 and 1968 he toured with **Steve Lacy**, then left to join trombonist **Roswell Rudd,** with whom he worked until 1972 (also fitting in stints with the **Jazz Composers Orchestra** and **Bill Dixon**). Later in the 70s he worked with **Abdullah Ibrahim**, **Giorgio Gaslini** and the **Globe Unity Orchestra** amongst others. In 1975 he formed a group with guitarist **John Abercrombie** and has led his own groups ever since (Rudd played in his quartet in 1978-79). In 1980 he collaborated with classical composer Morton Feldman and visual artist Michelangelo Pistoletto for a project in Atlanta, Georgia. In 1982 he played with **Gil Evans** and he toured with **Cecil Taylor**'s Segments II big band in 1984. In 1984 and 1985 he worked with English drummer **Tony Oxley** and in 1988 renewed his acquaintance with Taylor, playing in the European Orchestra assembled in Berlin by FMP to perform with the pianist. Enrico Rava's name has become synonymous with Italian jazz, though he is now increasingly involved in straight composing and has also written the score for Bertolucci's film *Oggetti Smarriti*.

Selected albums: *Il Giro Del Giorno In 80 Mondi* (1972), *Katcharpari Rava* (1973), *Pupa O Crisalide* (1974), *Quotation Marks* (1974), *Jazz A Confronto* (1974), *The Pilgrim And The Stars* (1975), *The Plot* (1976), *Enrico Rava Quartet* (1978), *AH* (1979), *Opening Night* (1982), *Andanada* (1983), *Rava String Band* (1984), *Secrets* (1986).

Ravan, Genya

b. Genya Zelkowitz, Poland. Ravan's family fled from the Nazis to New York. By the early 60s, she was leading **Goldie And The Gingerbreads** and although they did not chart in the US, they enjoyed a UK Top 30 entry with 'Can't You Hear My Heartbeat', and they were also appreciated for their exacting musical standards. After disbandment in 1969, Zelkowitz sang in various jazz combos before joining the otherwise all-male Ten Wheel Drive who combined jazz with progressive rock. She released three solo albums attributed to Goldie Zelkowitz before reverting to Goldie Ravan for two further recordings. From the late 70s to the present, the former name has been the one most used for sleeve credits for session work on albums by Gamma and **Lou Reed** among others, and for her duet with **Ellen Foley** 'Mr. Music'. As a record producer she has been responsible for **Dead Boys**' *Young Loud And Snotty* and an attempt to relaunch **Ronnie Spector** as a punk star with 1980's *Siren*.

Albums: *With Baby* (1972), *They Love Me/They Love Me Not* (1973), *Goldie Zelkowitz* (1974), *Urban Desire* (1978), *...And I Mean It!* (1979).

Rave

Specifically a one-off gathering for late night consumption of pre-recorded dance music in the late 80s early 90s, a musical definition of rave is more problematic. Descending from the acid house sound and ethos, the main fare tends to be fast techno and hardcore records, pitched between 125 and 140 bpm and often released on tiny independent labels with little background information. Some of rave's established anthems include Toxic Two's 'Rave Generator' and Human Resource's 'Dominator'. Like other forms of dance music, rave has its favoured DJs and remixers. However, arguably the most recognisable and popular of the 'rave' acts are Liam Howlett's **Prodigy**. Other acts venerated include **Altern 8**, **Bizarre Inc**, **Basshead**s and early **K Klass** material.

Raven

Formed in 1980, Raven were one of the first bands to be associated with the **New Wave Of British Heavy Metal** movement. Hailing from Newcastle, the group comprised the Gallagher brothers; John (vocals/bass) and Mark (guitar), plus drummer Rob 'Wacko' Hunter. Unleashing a three-component wall of noise punctuated by searing guitar work and shattering vocals, they signed to local independent label, Neat Records. Their reputation grew with the release of a single, 'Don't Need Your Money', and the ensuing live shows which promoted it. John Gallagher's trademark high-pitched vocals and the group's before-its-time speed metal were heard to best effect on four albums for Neat Records, including the excellent *Live At The Inferno*. They then relocated to America and secured a deal with **Atlantic Records**. Adopting a more melodic approach, *Stay Hard* emerged in 1985 and sold well, but only in their adopted territory - the home-grown fan base was left somewhat aghast. Since then the band has reverted back to its former blitzkrieg style, releasing a string of competent, but rather dated and pedestrian albums. Drummer Rob Hunter moved into production work in 1988, to be replaced by Joe Hasselvander.

Albums: *Rock Until You Drop* (Neat 1981), *Wiped Out* (Neat 1982), *All For One* (Neat 1983), *Live At The Inferno* (Neat 1984), *Stay Hard* (Atlantic 1985), *The Pack Is Back* (Atlantic 1986), *Life's A Bitch* (Atlantic 1987), *Nothing Exceeds Like Excess* (Under One Flag 1989). Compilation: *The Devil's Carrion* (Castle 1985, double album).

Raven, Eddy

b. Edward Garvin Futch, 19 August 1944, Lafayette, Louisiana, USA. Eddy, one of 11 children, was raised in bayou country. His father, a truck driver and blues guitarist, would take him to honky tonks. He was given a guitar, and by the time he was 13 years old, he was playing in a rock 'n' roll band. When the family moved to Georgia in 1960, he worked for a radio station and recorded his own song, 'Once A Fool', as Eddy Raven for the small Cosmo label. They returned to Lafayette in 1963 and Eddy worked in La Louisianne record store and also made singles for the owner's label. In 1969 he recorded *That Crazy Cajun Sound*, which impressed **Jimmy C. Newman**, who secured Raven a songwriting contract in Nashville with **Acuff-Rose**. He also worked as lead singer for **Jimmie Davis**' band and toured with him during an election campaign for Governor of Louisiana. In 1971 **Don Gibson** had a Top 5 US country hit with Raven's 'Country Green', which was followed by **Jeannie C. Riley**'s 'Good Morning, Country Rain'. He also wrote 'Back In The Country' (**Roy Acuff**), 'Sometimes I Talk In My Sleep' (Randy Cornor) and 'Touch The Morning' (**Don Gibson**). He had his first US country chart entry with 'The Last Of The Sunshine Cowboys' in 1974 for **ABC** and then recorded for Monument ('You're A Dancer') and Dimension ('Sweet Mother Texas', 'Dealin' With The Devil'). He had four country hits from his **Elektra** album, *Desperate Dreams*, including 'Who Do You Know In California?' and 'She's Playing Hard To Forget'. A second album for Elektra was never released and Raven spent two years resolving management problems. He wrote a Top 5 country record for the **Oak Ridge Boys**, 'Thank God For Kids'. He came back on RCA in 1984 with the escapist theme of 'I Got Mexico', a style he returned to in 1988 for 'Joe Knows How To Live'. He followed it with other hits, including 'I Could Use Another You', 'Shine Shine Shine' and 'You're Never Too Old For Young Love'. He went to number 1 with a bluesy song written by Dennis Linde and first recorded by **Billy Swan**, 'I'm Gonna Get You'. Linde also wrote his 1989 number 1, 'In A Letter To You', for the new Universal label. That year he also returned to the cajun sounds of his youth for 'Bayou Boys' in a mixture he describes as 'electric cajun'. In 1991 he moved to the ninth label of his career, **Capitol**.

Albums: *That Cajun Country Sound* (1969), *This Is Eddy Raven* (1976), *Eyes* (1980), *Desperate Dreams* (1981), *I Could Use Another You* (1984), *Love And Other Hard Times* (1985), *Right Hand Man* (1987), *Temporary Sanity* (1989), *Right For The Flight* (1991).

Ravens

An African-American vocal group from New York City, New York, USA. Formed in 1945, the Ravens are

considered the first of the 'bird groups' and their success was highly influential in ushering in an avalanche of vocal groups in the post World War II R&B revolution. Original members were Ollie Jones (tenor), Leonard Puzey (tenor), Warren Suttles (baritone), and Jimmy Ricks (bass). After Maithe Marshall replaced Jones in 1946, the Ravens featured two leads, Jimmy Ricks, who used his outstanding bass with terrific rhythmic bounce on the mid-tempo tunes, and Maithe Marshall, whose soaring falsetto tenor lent great poignancy to the ballads. The group also used with great effectiveness the switchover lead between Marshall and Ricks, which gave the Ravens a unique sound until it was widely imitated by other vocal ensembles. The Ravens first recorded for the Hub label in 1946, but only after they signed with National did they get on the charts, with a Ricks-led 'Write Me A Letter' (number 5 R&B) in 1948. Memorable recordings by the group at this time also included the Maithe Marshall-led songs 'September Song' and 'Searching For Love'. Their 1948 hit versions of 'Silent Night' (number 8 R&B) and 'White Christmas' (number 9 R&B) paved the way for later R&B vocal groups to interpret Christmas standards with an R&B flavour. (the Ravens' vocal arrangement of 'White Christmas' was lifted for **Clyde McPhatter** And The **Drifters**' version from 1955). The Ravens' last chart record was in 1952 on **Mercury** with 'Rock Me All Night Long' (number 4 R&B). The group's last notable recording was 'Give Me A Simple Pray' in 1955 on the Argo label. With Rick's departure for a solo career in 1956 the group faded from the scene.
Selected compilations: *The Ravens* (Harlem Hit Parade 1973) *The Greatest Group Of Them All* (Savoy 1978), *Old Man River* (Savoy Jazz 1985). ·

Raw Breed

Alongside **Onyx**, with whom Raw Breed are all too frequently compared, this Bronx, New York troupe encapsulate the 'Nastee nigga' term which has been coined to address their sound. After a brief sojourn with Jam Master Jay of **Run DMC**, Raw Breed hooked up with **Ice-T**'s Rhyme Syndicate to launch their career. The band comprise Mark Rippin (cousin of **Ultramagentic MCs'** Kook Keith) and four others, and kicked off their career with the 'Rabbit Stew' 45, which dissed 'all the wack MCs, and wack groups that came out in '93'.
Album: *Loon Tunz* (1993).

Raw Fusion

Comprising **Digital Underground** members DJ Fuze and Money B, who opened their account with 'Throw Your Hands In The Air'. Instead of following the **P-Funk** fixation of their erstwhile employers, as Raw Fusion the duo concentrated instead on a more mellow, reggae tinged delivery. Despite the presence on

their debut of old sparring partners Shock G. and Shmoovy Shomoov, along with **Tupac Shakur**, the resulting album was no classic. A second set introduced filthy rhymes from Money B, dubbed up by Fuze, on 'Freaky Note', but again failed to capture the magic of Digital Underground at their best.
Albums: *Live From The Styletron* (Hollywood Basic 1992), *Hoochiefied Funk* (Hollywood Basic 1994).

Raw Stylus

Signed to **Acid Jazz Records** on the basis of 1992's 'Pushin' Against The Flow', Raw Stylus have undergone a comparatively long incubation. Their early career was as a covers band on the north London circuit. Then the singer Jules Brookes, a former *Boxing Weekly* journalist, and Ron Aslan, his songwriting partner and production wizard, began to write their own material. Inspired not only by **Marvin Gaye** and **Curtis Mayfield**, they also looked to the clean-cut production of **Steely Dan** for a lead. Their first release was the white label 12-inch, 'Bright Lights Big City', in 1989, before 'Pushin'' announced their arrival properly. **Paul Weller** was so impressed he offered to play guitar on the song. On the back of hugely successful gigs at the Brixton Fridge in London they signed to James Lavelle's **Mo Wax Records** label. However, after the club hit, 'Many Ways', problems arose, and they switched to Acid Jazz instead. They began their career there with a **Bill Withers**' cover, 'Use Me'. By this time female vocalist Donna Gadye had become a semi-permanent fixture, replacing Marcella (aka Debbie French). However, soon after they changed labels again, this time to Wired, an offshoot of Michael Levy's M&G Records. The studio chosen for the band's debut album, River Sound in New York, was owned by producer Gary Katz, who produced the early Steely Dan albums so admired by the band.

Rawls, Lou

b. 1 December 1935, Chicago, Illinois, USA. Briefly a member of the acclaimed gospel group, the Pilgrim Travellers, this distinctive singer began forging a secular career following his move to California in 1958. An association with **Sam Cooke** culminated in 'Bring It On Home To Me', where the Rawls' throaty counterpoint punctuated his colleague's sweet lead vocal. Lou's own recordings showed him comfortable with either small jazz combos or cultured soul, while an earthier perspective was shown on his 1965 release, *Live!*. He scored two Top 20 singles with 'Love Is A Hurtin' Thing' (1966) and 'Dead End Street' (1967), and enjoyed further success with a 1969 reading of **Mable John**'s 'Your Good Thing (Is About To End)'. Several attempts were made to mould Rawls into an all-round entertainer, but while his early 70s work was generally less compulsive, the singer's arrival at

Philadelphia International signalled a dramatic rebirth. 'You'll Never Find Another Love Like Mine', an international hit in 1976, matched the classic Philly sound with Rawl's almost plumby delivery and prepared the way for a series of exemplary releases including 'See You When I Git There' (1977) and 'Let Me Be Good To You' (1979). The singer maintained his association with producers **Gamble And Huff** into the next decade. His last chart entry, 'I Wish You Belonged to Me', came in 1987 on the duo's self-named label, since when he has recorded for the jazz outlet, **Blue Note**. Rawls has also pursued an acting career and provided the voice for several Budweiser beer commercials.

Albums: *Lou Rawls Sings, Les McCann Ltd Plays Stormy Monday* (1962), *Black And Blue* (1963), *Tobacco Road* (1963), *Nobody But Lou Rawls* (1965), *Lou Rawls And Strings* (1965), *Live!* (1966), *Soulin'* (1966), *Merry Christmas Ho! Ho!* (1965), *Carryin' On* (1966), *Too Much!* (1967), *That's Lou* (1967), *Merry Christmas Ho! Ho! Ho!* (1967), *Feeling Good* (1968), *You're Good For Me* (1968), *The Way It Was - The Way It Is* (1969), *Your Good Thing* (1969), *You Made Me So Very Happy* (1970), *Bring It On Home To Me* (1970) *Natural Man* (1971), *Silk And Soul* (1972), *All Things In Time* (1976), *Unmistakably Lou* (1977), *When You Hear Lou, You've Heard It All* (1977), *Live* (1978), *Let Me Be Good To You* (1979), *Sit Down And Talk To Me* (1980), *Shades Of Blue* (1981), *Now Is The Time* (1982), *When The Night Comes* (1983), *Close Company* (1984), *Love All Your Blues Away* (1986), *At Last* (1989), *Portrait Of The Blues* (1992), *Greatest Hits In Concert* (1993). Selected compilations: *'Live' The Best Of Lou Rawls* (1968), *Soul Serenade* (1985), *Stormy Monday* (1985), *Classic Soul* (1986), *For You My Love* (1994).

Ray, Dave

As a member of Koerner, Ray And Glover, with **John 'Spider' Koerner** and Tony Glover, Dave 'Snaker' Ray was in the vanguard of the folk revival of the 60s. An accomplished six- and 12-string guitarist, the artist pursued a concurrent solo career with two compulsive country blues albums. The first included interpretations of material by, among others, **Muddy Waters**, **Robert Johnson** and **Leadbelly**, while the follow-up featured a greater emphasis on original material. The rise of electric styles obscured Ray's progress and it was 1969 before he re-emerged in Bamboo, a country-based duo he had formed with pianist Will Donight. Their eccentric album made little impression and Ray's subsequent profile was distinctly low-key. However, in 1990 Ray and Glover teamed up to record *Ashes In My Whiskey* for the **Rough Trade** label, winning critical acclaim.

Albums: *Fine Soft Land* (1967). As Koerner, Ray And Glover *Blues, Rags And Hollers* (1963), *More Blues, Rags And Hollers* (1964), *The Return Of Koerner, Ray And Glover* (1965), *Live At St. Olaf Festival* (60s/70s), *Some American Folk Songs Like They Used To Be* (1974), with Tony Glover *Ashes In My Whiskey* (1990), with Glover *Picture Has Faded* (Tim/Kerr 1994).

Ray, Goodman And Brown

Al Goodman (b. 31 March 1947, Jackson, Mississippi, USA), Harry Ray (b. 15 December 1946, Longbranch, New Jersey, USA) and William Brown (b. 30 June 1946, Perth Amboy, New Jersey, USA). This smooth soul trio had 27 R&B hits as the **Moments**. While waiting for the outcome of legal wranglings with **Sylvia** Robinson's Stang Records, they recorded backing vocals on two successful **Millie Jackson** albums. When it was decided that Stang owned the name the Moments, the trio joined **Polydor** in 1979 under their own surnames. Their first single, their own composition 'Special Lady', reached the US Top 5 and their debut album, which they co-produced with Vince Castellano, made the Top 20. *Ray, Goodman & Brown II* made the US Top 100 and their revival of the **Platters**' 'My Prayer' narrowly missed the Top 40. Ray left in 1982 and made an unsuccessful solo album on Sylvia Robinson's Sugar Hill label. He rejoined the trio in 1983 and they had some success with Panoramic Records. In 1986 they signed to **EMI** America when they had their last R&B Top 10 hit with 'Take It To The Limit'.

Albums: *Ray, Goodman & Brown* (1980), *Ray, Goodman & Brown II* (1980).

Ray, Harmon

b. 1914, Indianapolis, Indiana, USA. Ray grew up in St. Louis, where he took up blues singing in the 30s, adopting the vocal style of **Peetie Wheatstraw,** with whom he worked as a double act from 1935 until Wheatstraw's death in 1941. In 1942, Ray recorded as 'Peetie Wheatstraw's Buddy'. After military service he settled in Chicago, singing in clubs, and recording for **J. Mayo Williams,** who may have been the source of a Hy-Tone 78 release. Ray's last recordings were made in 1949, one song being in the manner of **Charles Brown**, and the other three in Wheatstraw's style; two of these were covers of Wheatstraw songs, but 'President's Blues' was an original tribute to Truman. Ray continued to work in Chicago clubs until the early 60s, when cancer forced him to retire.

Album: *Chicago Blues* (1985).

Ray, Johnnie

b. 10 January 1927, Dallas, Oregon, USA, d. 24 February 1990, Los Angeles, California, USA. Known at various times in his career as the Prince of Wails, the Nabob of Sob, and the Howling Success because of his highly emotional singing and apparent ability to cry at will, Ray is rated an important influence in the development of 50s and early 60s popular music. Of North American Indian origin, he became deaf in his right ear at the age of 12, which caused him to wear a hearing-aid throughout his career. He was heavily influenced by gospel and R&B music and performed in bars and clubs around Detroit in the late 40s, singing to his own piano accompaniment. Signed by **Columbia Records** in 1951, his first two releases were on their small **OKeh** label, usually reserved for black artists. His first record, 'Whiskey And Gin', was followed by 'Cry'. Unsophisticated, full of anguish, despair and a good deal of sobbing, it shocked a pop world accustomed to male singers crooning in front of big bands, and streaked to the top of the US charts, complete with Ray's own composition, 'The Little White Cloud That Cried', on the b-side. 'Cry' became his 'identity' song, and a multi-million-seller.

Ray was then transferred to the Columbia label, and during the next couple of years, had several massive US hits including 'Please Mr Sun', 'Here Am I - Broken Hearted', 'Walkin' My Baby Back Home' and 'Somebody Stole My Gal'. His stage performances, with their overt sexuality and hysterical audience reaction, made him *persona non grata* to parents of teenagers, worldwide. For a few years during the 50s, he enjoyed phenomenal success, revolutionizing popular music and symbolizing teenagers' frustrations and desires. Always acknowledging his gospel roots, Ray recorded several tracks associated with black artists, including the **Drifters**' R&B hit, 'Such a Night' (1954), which was banned on several USA radio stations, and 'Just Walkin' In the Rain' (1956), which climbed to number 2 in the US charts, and was originally recorded by the Prisonaires. By contrast, in 1954, he played a young singer who decides to be a priest in **Irving Berlin**'s musical film, ***There's No Business Like Show Business***. Ray sang the gospel-styled 'If You Believe' and 'Alexander's Ragtime Band'. During the late 50s in the USA, rumours were rife concerning his possible homosexuality and of drug-taking, and as a result he became more popular abroad than at home. In the UK, in-person and on-record, he had been a favourite since 1952. Three of his US hits reached UK number 1, including 'Yes Tonight Josephine' (1957). Other UK successes included 'Faith Can Move Mountains', 'Hey There' and 'Look Homeward Angel'. Ray also duetted with **Doris Day** ('Ma Says Pa Says', 'Full Time Job', 'Let's Walk That-Away') and **Frankie Laine** ('Good Evening Friends'). In the early 60s, suffering from financial problems and alcoholism, and left behind as the musical climate rapidly changed, he turned to cabaret in the USA. During the 70s he began to revive his career, leaning heavily on his old material for its nostalgic appeal. Always in demand in the UK, he was headlining there until the late 80s. His last performance is said to have been in his hometown on 7 October 1989, and he died of liver failure a few months later in Los Angeles. As to his influence and effect, one writer concluded: 'Ray was

the link between **Frank Sinatra** and **Elvis Presley**, re-creating the bobby-sox mayhem that elevated "The Voice" while anticipating the sexual chaos that accompanied Presley.'

Selected albums: *Johnnie Ray Sings The Big Beat* (1957), *Johnnie Ray At The Desert Inn In Las Vegas* (1959), *A Sinner Am I* (1959), *'Til Morning* (1959), *Johnnie Ray On The Trail* (1959), *I Cry For You* (1960), *Johnnie Ray* (1962), *Yesterday, Today And Tomorrow* (1980), *Yesterday - The London Sessions 1976* (1993). Compilations: *Johnnie Ray's Greatest Hits* (1959), *An American Legend* (1979), *Portrait Of A Song Stylist* (1989).

Further reading: *The Johnnie Ray Story*, Ray Sonin.

Ray, Ricardo 'Richie', And Bobby Cruz

Salsa's beautiful duo comprised Ray (b. Ricardo Maldonado, 15 February 1945, Brooklyn, New York, USA, of Puerto Rican parentage; co-bandleader/composer/multi instrumentalist). Cruz (b. Roberto Cruz, 26 February 1941, Hormigueros, Puerto Rico; co-bandleader, singer, composer, arranger, güiro, maracas). Ray and Cruz have been partners for over 25 years. Ray began playing the piano at the age of seven. In 1957 he played bass in a group led by Cruz. Richie attended the Brooklyn Conservatory of Music, High School of Performing Arts and Juilliard School of Music. He left the latter after a year to devote himself fully to his newly formed band, which included Cruz on lead vocals. Ray signed with Fonseca Records and debuted on *Ricardo Ray Arrives/Comején* in 1964. The title track 'Comején' (co-written by Ray and Cruz) was a hit and the album included the outstanding 'Mambo Jazz', which the two performers reworked on several future releases. The duo recorded some of their very finest work during their period with the label. The follow-up, *On The Scene With Ricardo Ray*, contained a delightful version of **Bud Powell**'s 'Parisian Thoroughfare', which changed midway through from a cool Latin jazz piece to a driving mambo. Notable accompanists on these early releases included Richie's brother, trumpeter Ray Maldonado, bassist/arranger Russell 'Skee' Farnsworth and vocalist Chivirico Dávila. Ray had a crossover hit in the black American community with 'Jango' from 1966's *3 Dimensions*.

Richie switched to Alegre Records and released nine albums (including a compilation) on the label between 1966 and 1970. He was one of the first artists to record the R&B/Latin fusion style called boogaloo. Ray described his Alegre debut, *Se Soltó/On The Loose/Introducing The Bugaloo*, as 'too musical' and 'ahead of its time' (quoted in *Latin NY* magazine, c.1968). The more deliberately commercial follow-up, *Jala Jala Y Boogaloo*, contained one of his greatest hits 'Richie's Jala Jala', co-written by Richie and Bobby. While still under contract to Alegre, Ray recorded *Viva Ricardo* and *El Diferente* for UA Latino, which was a division of United Artists Records. The latter included the marvellous

'Feria En Manizales'. In 1968, *Los Durísimos/The Strong Ones/Salsa Y Control* was the first album on which Cruz shared equal billing with Ray. At this stage, the band had an eight piece line-up of Venezuelan Pedro Rafael Chaparro and jazz musician Adolphus '**Doc**' **Cheatham**, trumpets; Farnsworth, bass/co-arranger; José 'Candido' Rodríguez, timbales; Jackie 'El Conde' Dillomis, conga; Harry 'Bongo' Rodríguez, bongo; Ray, piano/co-arranger; and Cruz, lead vocals. Richie and Bobby continued to use an all trumpet frontline, and later added flugelhorn on occasions. The two-some enjoyed considerable success in Colombia in the late 60s and their sound had a significant influence on the country's own variant of salsa. Their fifth Alegre release, *Let's Get Down To The Real Nitty Gritty*, featured the single 'Nitty Gritty' which had some success in the UK.

In 1970 the duo relocated from New York to Puerto Rico. 'The competitiveness of the Latin bands in New York was becoming too rough and we had grown tired of this city's circuit . . . (and Bobby) just didn't want his children to develop in this city's environment', Ray explained in *Latin NY* in 1976. Meanwhile their former trumpeter, Pedro Rafael Chaparro, who worked previously with **Pérez Prado**, **Tito Puente**, **Machito** and **Tito Rodríguez**, made his recording debut as leader on *Este Es Chaparro* (1971) on Ralph Cartagena's Rico Records. His band on the album included three ex-Ray and Cruz players: Cheatham, Farnsworth and Dillomis. Only Cheatham remained on Chaparro's *Gozando* in 1974, which featured **Israel 'Cachao' López** on bass. Richie and Bobby experienced some initial hardships after their arrival in Puerto Rico, but the bookings soon came pouring in. Their financial success enabled them to open a night-club in Santurce, a district of Puerto Rico's sprawling capital, San Juan. However, running the club in addition to their heavy gigging schedule proved to be too great a strain. So they sold the club and concentrated on playing the island circuit.

Richie and Bobby signed with the newly created Vaya Records, a subsidiary of Jerry Masucci and **Johnny Pacheco**'s Fania Records. Their output on Vaya during the 70s and 80s was uneven in quality, but there was the occasional redeeming moment of interest. The Puerto Rico-recorded *El Bestial Sonido de . . . Ricardo Ray Y Bobby Cruz* (1970), the first ever release on Vaya, was one of their better albums on the label. It featured 18-year-old female vocalist Miki Vimarí and contained the **Rubén Blades** composition 'Guaguanco Triste'. The 1972 Vimarí showcase, *Ricardo Ray Presenta A La Vimarí*, was a disappointing set of slow sentimental numbers. However, 1973's *Jammin' Live*, with Vimarí as co-lead singer, was a commendable album. In 1974, Ray entered a period of emotional turmoil, which led to alcohol and drug abuse. He had several religious experiences and announced in August of that year that

he had converted to a brand of evangelical Christianity. Richie's new spiritual concerns took precedence over gigging and initially caused friction with Bobby, but after a short while, he too became a convert. They began to make specifically religious recordings, as well as proselytize through their 'regular' salsa recordings - what UK salsa broadcaster Tomek called 'salsa with beatitude'. They also started crusading via concerts. 1975's *Reconstrucción* won them their ninth gold disc, which was presented at Madison Square Garden, New York, in June 1980. The recording was directed by **Louie Ramírez**, who also arranged one track. The album contained their smash hit single 'Juan En La Ciudad', which they co-wrote. 1977's *Viven!* included the exciting 'El Rey David', another joint composition. Their second release in 1980, *De Nuevo 'Los Durísimos' Again*, included the swinging 'Yo Soy La "Zarza"', which they co-penned. Doc Cheatham returned to provide trumpet solos to the duo's three albums issued in 1981 and 1982. Richie and Bobby's final release on Vaya, the Miami recorded *Los Inconfundibles* (1987), featured the magnificent 'Sipriano', composed by Cruz. Unlike most of their peers, the extent of Ray and Cruz's work with other Latin artists and bands had been very limited, especially since their conversion. Richie appeared on the 1966 Tico All-Star's descarga (Latin jam session) recordings at New York's Village Gate and on the Fania All Stars' 1968 album debut (two volumes). Between 1971 and 1976, the duo recorded with the Fania All Stars and appeared in the Jerry Masucci movies *Our Latin Thing (Nuestra Cosa)*, 1972, and *Salsa* (1976). The pair produced Chivirico Dávila's 1978 release *Nuevos Conceptos/New Concepts*. Ray guested on a cover of **Joe Jackson**'s 'Cancer' on **Héctor Lavoe's** *Revento* in 1985. In 1991, Ray and Cruz appeared on the bill of a tribute concert at El Campín Stadium, Bogotá, Colombia, to mark superstar **Joe Arroyo**'s 20th anniversary in the music business. That year, the pair made their farewell appearance at the first part of the annual New York Salsa Festival at Madison Square Garden.

Selected albums: *Ricardo Ray Arrives/Comején* (1964), *On The Scene With Ricardo Ray* (1965), *3 Dimensions* (1966), *A Go-Go-Go/Ricardo Ray Introduces Bobby Cruz*, (Christmas album) *Bobby Cruz En Fiesta Navideña, Bobby Cruz Sings For Lovers And Swingers Con Ricardo Ray, Se Soltó/On The Loose/Introducing The Bugaloo* (1966), *Jala, Jala Y Boogaloo* (1966), *Jala, Jala Y Boogaloo Volume II* (1967), *Viva Ricardo* (c.1968), *Los Durísimos/The Strong Ones/Salsa Y Control* (1968), with Nydia Caro *Los Durísimos Y Yo!* (c.1969), *Let's Get Down To The Real Nitty Gritty* (c.1969), *Agúzate* (c.1969), *El Diferente*, various artists *Lluvia De Estrellas* (c.1970), *In Orbit* (1970), *El Bestial Sonido de...Ricardo Ray Y Bobby Cruz* (1970), (Christmas release) *Felices Pascuas* (1971), Bobby Cruz showcase i *Canta Para Ti* (1972), with Miki Vimarí *Ricardo Ray Presenta A La Vimarí* (1972), *Jammin' Live* (1973), Cruz showcase ii *Amor En La Escuela*

(1974), *1975* (1974), *10 Aniversario* (*10th Anniversary*) (1975), *Reconstrucción* (1975), *Viven!* (1977), *El Sonido De La Bestia* (1980), *De Nuevo 'Los Durísimos' Again* (1980), *Pinturas* (1981), *Los Aguilas - The Eagles* (1982), *Back To Back* (1982), *Los Inconfundibles* (1987). Compilations: *The Best Of/Lo Mejor de Ricardo Ray & Bobby Cruz* (c.1969), *Ricardo Ray & Bobby Cruz, Lo Mejor de/ The Best Of Ricardo Ray & Bobby Cruz* (1977, double album).

Rayber Voices

This early **Motown** backing vocal group came from Detroit, Michigan, USA. The ensemble was established in 1958 and directed by **Berry Gordy**'s second wife, Raynoma Gordy (b. Raynoma Mayberry, 8 March 1937, Detroit, Michigan, USA). There was no established line-up, but the most common participants were Robert Bateman (bass), Sonny Sanders (b. William Sanders, 6 August 1939, Chicago Heights, Illinois, USA; tenor), Brian Holland (b. 15 February 1941, Detroit, Michigan, USA; baritone) and Raynoma Gordy (soprano). The group made their debut on Herman Griffin's 'I Need You' (1958), and toured with **Marv Johnson** the following year after his 'Come To Me' achieved a modicum of success. Joining the voices at this time was Gwendolyn Murray. As Gordy's Motown empire grew the Rayber Voices would eventually include members of the **Temptations**, **Martha And The Vandellas**, and the **Miracles**. But the days of using *ad hoc* ensembles soon ended and by the early 60s the Rayber Voices was replaced by a full-time back-up group, the Andantes.

Rayburn, Margie

b. Madera, California, USA. Her first significant professional experience was as vocalist for the **Ray Anthony** Orchestra. She later sang with **Gene Autry** and as a member of the **Sunnysiders**, on their sole Top 20 hit, 'Hey, Mr. Banjo' in 1955. Going solo after the Sunnysiders' fortunes dimmed, Rayburn released 'I'm Available', written by Dave Burgess, later of the **Champs**, for **Liberty Records**, eventually peaking at number 9 in the *Billboard* pop charts in 1957. She was unable to follow the single with another hit and gave up her recording career by the mid-60s.

Raydio

Raydio was the creation of **Ray Parker Jnr.** (b. 1 May 1954, Detroit, Michigan, USA), a songwriter who taught himself to play guitar as a teenager when laid up with a broken leg. His first group came in 1968 with Ollie Brown and Nathan Watts, and the following year he toured with the **Detroit Spinners**. He then joined Jeep Smith And The Troubadours who did the 'weddings, parties, bar mitzvahs' circuit. Their residency at the Twenty Grand in Detroit was in support of a variety of visiting soul stars. Afterwards, he became a studio musician mainly for Invictus and Hot

Wax. In 1982 he played with **Stevie Wonder** on the **Rolling Stones** tour, and Wonder also recorded some of his songs. Afterwards he journeyed to Hollywood to concentrate on his songwriting. He scored his first big hit with 'Rufus' You've Got The Love', co-written with **Chaka Khan**. As a session musician he was also playing on a plethora of hits, mainly in the USA, for **Marvin Gaye**, **Boz Scaggs**, **Labelle**, **Stevie Wonder**, **Barry White**, and **Love Unlimited**. Clive Davis signed him to **Arista** and he assembled Raydio, with himself on vocals and guitar, Arnell Carmichael (synthesizer), Jerry Knight (bass) and Vincent Bonham (piano). He scored a hit with 'Jack And Jill', and found minor success with subsequent releases 'You Can't Change That', and 'Betcha Can't Love Just Once'. The band changed its name to Ray Parker Jnr. And Raydio, and then simply Ray Parker Jnr. He would have a massive hit (US number 1, UK number 2) with 'Ghostbusters', the theme to the film of the same name, the similarity of which to **Huey Lewis And The News**' 'Power Of Love' was the subject of litigation. His other solo hits include: 'Girls Are More Fun', and 'I Don't Think A Man Should Sleep Alone'.
Albums: *Raydio* (1978), *Rock On* (1979), *Two Places At The Same Time* (1980), *A Woman Needs Love* (1981), *The Very Best Of Ray Parker Jnr* (1982), *The Other Woman* (1982), *Woman Out Of Control* (1983), *Sex And The Single Man* (1985), *After Dark* (1987).

Raye, Collin

b. 1960, Arkansas, USA. Raye was raised in Texas, where his mother often opened shows for visiting star performers. For many years he and his brother Scott worked in Oregon and then in casinos in Las Vegas and Reno, but their contract to record for Warner Brothers as the Wray Brothers led nowhere. The brothers split and Collin was signed as a solo act to Epic by producer Bob Montgomery. A collection of romantic songs, *All I Can Be*, was a best-selling country album in the USA and 'Love Me' topped the US country chart, and was featured on BBC Radio 2.
Albums: *In This Life* (80s), *All I Can Be* (1991), *Extremes* (Epic 1994).
Videos: *My Kind Of Girl* (1994), *Little Rock* (Sherman Halsey 1994).

Raye, Don

b. Donald McRae Wilhoite Jnr., 16 March 1909, Washington, D.C., USA, d. January 1985. A popular songwriter from the 30s through to the 50s, Raye was as accomplished dancer as a boy, and won the Virginia State Dancing Championship. From the mid-20s he worked as a singer and dancer in vaudeville, and later toured theatres and nightclubs in France and England, whilst also writing songs for himself and other performers. In 1935 he collaborated with **Sammy Cahn**, **Saul Chaplin** and band leader **Jimmie**

Lunceford on 'Rhythm In My Nursery Rhymes' and in the late 30s worked for a New York music publishing house. After moving to Hollywood in 1940, Raye was commissioned to write the songs for *Argentine Nights*, in which the **Andrews Sisters** made their screen debut. Together with Hughie Prince and the Sisters' arranger, Vic Schoen, Raye wrote 'Hit The Road' and 'Oh! How He Loves Me'. Another collaboration with Prince resulted in 'Rhumboogie', the first of a series of 'boogie woogie' numbers, several of which became hits for the Andrews Sisters, pianist **Freddie Slack**, and **Will Bradley** and his Orchestra. Raye and Prince's next assignment was *Buck Privates*, which also featured the Andrews Sisters, and rocketed the comedy duo Abbott And Costello to movie stardom. The songs included 'You're A Lucky Fellow, Mr Smith', 'Bounce Me Brother With A Solid Four' and 'Boogie Woogie Bugle Boy From Company B'. The latter number was nominated for an Academy Award, and revived successfully in 1973 by **Bette Midler**. Raye's other boogie ballads included 'Beat Me Daddy (Eight To The Bar)', 'Rock-A-Bye The Boogie', 'Down The Road A Piece' and 'Scrub Me, Mamma, With A Boogie Beat'. His long partnership with **Gene De Paul**, which began in the early 40s, resulted in songs for films such as *In The Navy, San Antonio Rose, Moonlight In Hawaii, Keep 'Em Flying, Hellzapoppin', What's Cookin', Ride 'Em Cowboy, Almost Married, Pardon My Sarong, Behind The Eight Ball, When Johnny Comes Marching Home, Hi Buddy, Reveille With Beverley*, *What's Buzzin' Cousin?*, *Larceny With Music, Crazy House, I Dood It, Hi Good Lookin'* and *Stars On Parade*. The team also enjoyed success in 1944 with 'Who's That In Your Love Life?', 'Irresistible You', 'Solid Potato Salad', and 'Milkman, Keep Those Bottles Quiet' from *Broadway Rhythm*. Towards the end of World War II De Paul spent two years in the Armed Forces, before he and Don Raye resumed writing their movie songs in 1947 with 'Who Knows?' for *Wake Up And Dream* and 'Judaline' for *A Date With Judy*. In 1948 they contributed to *A Song Is Born* and also wrote 'It's Whatcha Do With Whatcha Got' for the **Walt Disney** live-action feature *So Dear To My Heart*. De Paul and Raye's last film work together was for the highly acclaimed Disney cartoon *The Adventures Of Ichabod And Mr Toad* (1949). During the time he worked with De Paul, Raye also collaborated with others on 'Yodelin' Jive', 'Why Begin Again?', 'This Is My Country', 'I Love You Too Much', 'Music Makers', 'The House Of Blue Lights', 'Your Home Is In My Arms', 'Domino', 'They Were Doin' The Mambo' (a US hit for **Vaughn Monroe**), 'Roses And Revolvers', 'I'm Looking Out The Window' and 'Too Little Time'. Although he wrote just the occasional song after the mid-50s, Raye's 'Well, All Right' (with Frances Faye and Dan Howell) became a hit for the Andrews Sisters in 1959, and was also interpolated into the 1978 bio-pic *The Buddy Holly Story*.

Raye, Susan

b. 8 October 1944, Eugene, Oregon, USA. In 1961, with no personal thoughts of being a country singer, she found her mother had entered her in a talent show. She won and was soon singing and working as a disc jockey on local radio. By the mid-60s, she was a regular on the Portland television show *Hoedown*, where she was seen by **Buck Owens**' manager. Between 1968 and 1976, she worked with Owens, became a **Capitol** recording artist in her own right and was a regular performer on the top television show *Hee Haw*, which Owens co-hosted. Between 1970 and 1977, she registered 21 solo country hits, including 'I've Got A Happy Heart' and her version of **Kay Starr**'s pop hit 'Wheel Of Fortune'. During this time she also recorded duets with Owens, six of which charted including a Top 10 with 'The Great White Horse'. She retired for a time but reappeared in the country charts in 1986 with 'I Just Can't Take The Leaving Anymore'.
Albums: *One Night Stand* (1970), *Willy Jones* (1971), *Pitty Pitty Patter* (1971), *I've Got A Happy Heart* (1972), *Wheel Of Fortune/L.A International Airport* (1972), *My Heart Has A Mind Of It's Own* (1972), *Plastic Trains, Paper Planes* (1973), *Singing Susan Raye* (1974), *Love Sure Feels Good In My Heart* (1973), *Hymns By Susan Raye* (1973), *The Cheating Game* (1973), *Whatcha Gonna Do With A Dog Like That* (1975), *Honey Toast And Sunshine* (1976), *Susan Raye* (1977), *There And Back* (1985), *Then And Now* (1986). With Buck Owens: *The Great White Horse* (1970), *We're Gonna Get Together* (1970), *Merry Christmas From Buck Owens & Susan Raye* (1971), *The Best Of Buck & Susan* (1972), *The Good Old Days Are Here Again* (1973).

Rays

This R&B group consisted of Harold Miller (b. 17 January 1931), tenor Walter Ford (b. 5 September 1931), second tenor Davey Jones (b. 1931), and baritone Harry James (b. 1932). It was formed in New York in 1955, when two refugees from the Four Fellows (of 'Soldier Boy' fame), Miller and Jones, got together with James and Ford. They first recorded for **Chess** with no success, then moved to the Philadelphia-based Cameo in 1957 and achieved lasting fame, albeit as one-hit-wonders, with 'Silhouettes.' The song went to number 3 both R&B and pop in late 1957. The flip, the rousing jump led by Ford, 'Daddy Cool', received solid play and briefly charted. These songs are much better known than the Rays, having been remade innumerable times. **Herman**'s **Hermits** in 1965 and **Cliff Richard** in 1990 both took 'Silhouettes' up the charts; while British revivalist band, **Darts**, in 1977, and **Boney M** in 1976 each took 'Daddy Cool' into the UK Top 10.

Razaf, Andy

b. Andrea Menentania Razafinkeriefo, 16 December

1895, Washington, D.C., USA, d. 3 February 1973, Hollywood, California, USA. Related to the Queen of Madagascar but raised in the USA, Razaf was lyricist to several leading ragtime and jazz pianists of the late 20s and early 30s. Among his collaborations were those with **Eubie Blake** and **James P. Johnson** although he is best remembered for his work with **Fats Waller**. On the Broadway show *Keep Shufflin'* (1928), Razaf was co-lyricist with Henry Creamer, and the music was by Waller and Johnson. Among the Razaf-Waller songs from this show was 'Willow Tree', and in 1928 the duo wrote 'Honeysuckle Rose' and 'My Fate Is In Your Hands'. In the following year Razaf contributed to *Hot Chocolates*, again with Waller, who this time was teamed with Harry Brooks. The hit of the show was 'Ain't Misbehavin'', which was taken up by **Louis Armstrong,** who joined the cast during its early days. Another song from the show, 'What Did I Do To Be So Black And Blue?', was also popular. Apart from this show, 1929 also saw another Razaf hit, 'I've Got A Feeling I'm Falling' (music by Waller and Harry Link). With Blake, Razaf wrote 'Memories Of You' for *Blackbirds Of 1930*. He also wrote lyrics for 'In The Mood', the popular instrumental hit by Joe Garland, collaborated with Paul Denniker on 'S'posin'', and wrote a seldom-heard lyric for the **Edgar Sampson** composition 'Stompin' At The Savoy'. Apart from his song lyrics, Razaf also wrote and published poetry. From the 50s onwards he lived in California but worked less and less in music.
Further reading: *Black And Blue: The Life And Lyrics Of Andy Razaf*, Barry Singer.

Raze

US house group from Washington D.C. whose mainman was Vaughn Mason, aided by singer Keith Thompson (b. Bronx, New York, USA). Raze perfected the house formula with club classics (and crossover hits) 'Jack The Groove', originally released in 1986, which re-entered and broke the UK Top 20 in January the following year. 'Let The Music Move U', and particulary 'Break 4 Luv' (a US dance number 1) also became house standards. Controversy followed the latter when Thompson alleged that Mason had wrongly appropriated all the writing and publishing credits. 'During that time', Thompson recounts, "Break 4 Love' sold one million copies worldwide and it was tough when people didn't believe I was the vocalist or had anything to do with it'. A settlement was finally reached and Thompson starting releasing solo product and founded his own Level 10 label. Happily for him, when the record was restored via the **Mastercuts** series *Classic House* compilation, this time his name featured. Raze persevered with tracks like 1991's 'Bass Power' (**Champion**), with vocals by Pamela Frazier and rapper **Doug Lazy**.

Razorblade Smile

This indie band formed in Newcastle, Tyne & Wear, England, in the summer of 1990 when the quartet became bored with their college courses. The band consist of Jim James (vocals/guitar), Pete Lofty (vocals/guitar), Chris Scott (drums) and Dave Chary (bass), and they released their debut single, 'This Accurate Pain', the following year, through a friend's record label, Chocolate Narcotic. It revealed a band capable of writing intense, persuasive rock pop songs, influenced by the lo-fi alternative scene in the US. 'They seem to have a better idea of the indie ethic in America,' says James. 'They do things for the hell of it and not for some kind of career motive.' In keeping with this the band released a series of limited-edition 7-inch singles, including the well-received 'Vertical Orange'/'What's The Point', before their debut mini-album and support slots with **Heavenly**.
Album: *Fastest Wide-Eyed Implement* (Chocolate Narcotic 1993, mini-album).

Razorcuts

Revolving around the songwriting talents of vocalist/guitarist Gregory Webster and bassist Tim Vass, the Razorcuts emerged at the tail end of the UK independent scene's melodic mid-80s phase. It was a time when bands wore their influences on their sleeves, from the **Byrds** to the **Buzzcocks**, and the Razorcuts were no exception. 'Big Pink Cake', issued on the Subway Organisation label in 1986, had all the familiar trademarks of the period; a simple melody, a childlike theme sung in a childlike, out-of-tune voice, a hand-drawn sleeve and jangly guitars. The songs possessed a certain charm, particularly evident on November's *Sorry To Embarrass You* EP. The presence of New Zealand drummer and music journalist David Smith led the band to antipodean label Flying Nun Records for their third single, 'I Heard You The First Time', released in June 1987. When the label ceased operations in the UK, the Razorcuts relocated, ending up at **Creation Records**, a label which sympathized with the band's 60s influences. And it was the Byrds' early sound which dominated *The Storyteller*. Issued in February 1988, it benefited from its musical intricacies, but did little to avoid accusations of plagiarism. A year later, *The World Keeps Turning* found a band struggling to develop their folk rock sound, despite the added clout of a second guitarist, Pete Momtchiloff, to beef up Webster's 12-string, a new drummer, Struan Robertson, backing vocals from Richard Mason and some attractive Hammond organ from producer John Rivers. When the Razorcuts split shortly afterwards, Vass formed Red Chair Fadeaway and combined folk elements with a laid-back psychedelic feel.
Albums: *The Storyteller* (Creation 1988), *The World Keeps Turning* (Creation 1989).

RCA Records

The Radio Corporation of America entered the record business in 1929, when they bought the Victor Talking Machine Company. Victor had been formed by Ernie Berliner and Eldridge R. Johnson, inventors of the gramophone, and had been the USA's most important record company until the Depression caused sales to plummet. Victor owned part of **HMV**, and scored right across the board. They had the first million-seller with **Enrico Caruso**; they issued the first jazz records (the **Original Dixieland Jazz Band**); they were one of the first to record blues and country music. They even recorded the USA presidents, from Roosevelt to Harding. Popular acts included **Al Jolson** and **Fats Waller**. After RCA took over, the Victor and Bluebird labels dominated the swing era with names like **Benny Goodman**, **Artie Shaw**, **Glenn Miller**, **Tommy Dorsey** (with **Frank Sinatra**) and **Duke Ellington**. They had the good sense to record **Dizzy Gillespie**'s Big Band in the late 40s, even though pop singers were taking over. Victor had **Perry Como**, **Dinah Shore**, **Eddie Fisher** and **Mario Lanza**, but **Columbia** recovered its earlier lead, and RCA hit the relative doldrums in the early 50s. The C&W division had **Jim Reeves**, **Hank Snow** and **Arthur Crudup**; recordings were made in 1951-52 with a young R&B singer called **Little Richard**; in October 1955 came their first rock 'n' roll signing. Buying **Elvis Presley** from **Sun Records** for the record transfer fee of $35,000 - plus a Cadillac for Elvis - proved to be the turning point, as well as the soundest investment in rock history. Next year he charted with 'Heartbreak Hotel' and 'Hound Dog' and went on to be one of the most successful and consistently best-selling artists in popular music history. In the late 50s RCA was one of the first to issue stereo records. As rock 'n' roll merged into pop, RCA had hits with **Duane Eddy** and **Neil Sedaka**, and thanks to **Chet Atkins,** the country-pop roster blossomed. There was also **Harry Belafonte** and some successful soundtrack recordings. In the late 60s they released American rock from **Jefferson Airplane**, and bubblegum music from the **Monkees** and the **Archies**. Other stars were **John Denver**, **Hall And Oates**, **David Bowie**, **Sweet**, then **Diana Ross** and the **Eurythmics**. RCA's crown slipped again in the 80s, but they acquired Ariola/**Arista** in 1985, labels that had scored with **Gary Glitter**, the **Bay City Rollers** and **Barry Manilow**, only to be themselves taken over by General Electric and renamed BMG.

Re-Animator

Formed in Hull, England, in 1987, Re-Animator consisted of Kevin Ingleson (guitar/vocals), Mike Abel (guitar), John Wilson (bass) and Mark Mitchell (drums). Strongly influenced by the legacy of the **New Wave Of British Heavy Metal**, and armed with the new thrash metal musical attitude this had helped to inspire, the band signed to the **Music For Nations** subsidiary label, Under One Flag. They released their debut mini-album, *Deny Reality*, in 1989, a harsh barrage of guitars that stood them in good stead for their full album debut, *Condemned To Eternity*. This offered no great departure in musical style but was still regarded as a solid statement. The release of *Laughing* in 1991 saw a major change in direction for the band. Gone were the guitar set-pieces as the band incorporated funk elements in a manner approximating **Red Hot Chili Peppers**. Added to other stylistic experiments it resulted in an album which was neither one thing nor another. However, the new approach gelled better on 1993's agenda-setting *That Was Then, This Is Now*.
Albums: *Deny Reality* (Under One Flag 1989, mini-album), *Condemned To Eternity* (Under One Flag 1990), *Laughing* (Under One Flag 1991), *That Was Then, This Is Now* (Under One Flag 1993).

Rea, Chris

b. 4 March 1951, Middlesborough, Cleveland, England. Rea is a songwriter, singer and guitarist with a wide following throughout Europe. Of Irish/Italian parentage, he grew up in the northeast of England where his family owned an ice cream parlour. Rea's first group was Magdalene, a local band in which he replaced David Coverdale, who had joined **Deep Purple**. As Beautiful Losers, the band won a national talent contest in 1975 but remained unsuccessful. Rea went solo, signing to Magnet Records where **Gus Dudgeon** produced his first album. With a title referring to a suggested stage-name for Rea, it included the impassioned 'Fool (If You Think It's Over)' which reached the Top 20 in the US and was later covered successfully in Britain by **Elkie Brooks**. With the UK in the grip of punk and new wave, Rea's earliest supporters were in Germany, and throughout the first part of the 80s he steadily gained in popularity across the Continent through his gruff, bluesy singing and rock guitar solos, notably the instrumental track, 'Deltics'. His backing group was led by experienced keyboards player Max Middleton. Rea's most successful record at this time was 'I Can Hear Your Heartbeat' from *Water Sign*. In Britain, the breakthrough album proved to be *Shamrock Diaries*. Both it and 'Stainsby Girls' (a slice of nostalgia for the northern England of his adolescence) reached the Top 30 in 1985. Two years later, *Dancing With Strangers* briefly went to number 2 in the UK charts although the gritty 'Joys Of Christmas' was commercially unsuccessful. In 1988, WEA acquired Rea's contract through buying Magnet, and issued a compilation album which sold well throughout Europe. The album reached the Top 5 in the UK and suddenly Rea was fashionable, something that this unpretentious artist has been trying to live down ever since. This was followed by his first UK number 1, *The Road To Hell*, one of the most successful albums of 1989-90. The powerful title track told of an encounter with the ghost of the singer's mother and a warning that he had betrayed his roots. Like its predecessor, *Auberge* topped the UK chart while its title track reached the UK Top 20. 'Julia' a track from *Espresso Logic* became his 27th UK hit in November 1993. Rea remains loyal to his roots and refuses to join the rock *cognoscenti*.

Albums: *Whatever Happened To Benny Santini* (1978), *Deltics* (1979), *Tennis* (1980), *Chris Rea* (1982), *Water Sign* (1983), *Wired To The Moon* (1984), *Shamrock Diaries* (1985), *On The Beach* (1986), *Dancing With Strangers* (1987), *New Light Through Old Windows* (1988), *The Road To Hell* (1989), *Auberge* (1991), *God's Great Banana Skin* (1992), *Espresso Logic* (1993).

React Records

UK label established by former **Rhythm King** director James Horrocks with new partner Thomas Foley. After Rhythm King had gone overground in a big way, Horrocks bailed out, and kicked around for a couple of years before taking up an A&R job for Really Useful's short-lived dance label (also called React). Afterwards he moved on to his own project, initially packaging compilations like *Deep Heat*, *Thin Ice* and *Megabass*. The first single proper came about via ex-bootlegger John Truelove, who, as the Source featuring Candi Station, recorded 'You Got The Love'. It would sell over 200,000 copies in the UK. It was at this point that Horrocks made the acquaintence of Foley, who introduced him to the house scene (establishing the React-backed Garage night at Heaven). He has gone on to be the prime mover behind the label's highly successful *Reactivate* compilation series. On the single front React maintains an enviable reputation. Their biggest releases include Age Of Love's classy 'Age Of Love', arguably the perfect example of trance house, remixed by **Jam And Spoon**. In 1991 React were joined by scene stalwarts Fierce Ruling Diva, a duo of Amsterdam DJ's Jeroen Flamman and Jeffrey 'DJ Abraxas' Porter (famous for hosting the Planet E club in Amsterdam and an after hours barge club, Subtopia). In 1991 they released 'Rubb It In' for the label, then 'You Gotta Believe' a year later. The label also signed Italian producer Alex Lee, releasing his 'Take It' in June. The latter artist was drafted for national service in Italy for two years just as his career was beginning to take off. They also provided a home to **GTO** (who recorded two of the earliest singles on the React catalogue in 'Listen To The Rhythm Flow' and 'Elevation'), Ether Real ('Zap'), Elevator ('Shinny') and MASH ('U Don't Have To Say U Love Me').

Reader, Eddi

b. Sadenia Reader, c.1959, Glasgow, Scotland.

Formerly lead singer of **Fairground Attraction**, Reader gradually has developed an increasingly prominent solo career throughout the 90s, always taking care to select complementary musicians and material, partly as a result of her previous chastening experience of the music industry. Having spent eight years as a session singer (nicknamed 'Ever Ready' because of her willingness to accept any offer of work, ranging from **Gang Of Four** and the **Eurythmics** to Tesco adverts), Reader eventually reached number 1 in the UK charts with Fairground Attraction's 'Perfect' in 1988. Disbanding after only one album (*The First Of A Million Kisses*) because of internal tensions between the band and songwriter Mark Nevin, Reader bided her time before embarking on a solo career at the turn of the decade. She relocated to Kilmarnock with Fairground drummer Roy Doods, where her brother Frank's group, the **Trash Can Sinatras**, have their studio. The two of them took the demos they recorded down to London, where they met guitarist Neil MacColl (son of **Ewan MacColl** and half-brother of **Kirsty MacColl**) and his multi-instrumentalist brother, Calum. With the addition of bass player Phil Steriopulos, Reader's new 'backing' band, The Patron Saints Of Imperfection, was complete. **RCA Records** invested heavily in the artist, resulting in several expensive sessions, including stints at **Jools Holland**'s studio in Greenwich, London. When the album eventually emerged after several re-recordings, it was given impetus by a strong suite of covers, including **Loudon Wainwright III**'s 'Swimming Song', **Fred Neil**'s 'Dolphins', **Steve Earle**'s 'My Friend The Blues' and **John Prine**'s 'Hello In There'. Its title, *Mirmama*, was taken from the Yugoslavian word for peace, 'mir', and arose because of a story Reader had encountered about a speaking Madonna which had appeared in Hercegovina. However, sales failed to match RCA's expectations. Afterwards Reader appeared live with the Trash Can Sinatras, sung at 1993's Virago Women's Day celebration, and presented a BBC 2 Scottish music television series. She also acted for the first time, in a London theatre production of *The Trick Is To Keep Breathing*. A second, self-titled album, now for **Warner Brothers**' subsidiary Blanco Y Negro, followed in June 1994. Produced by Greg Penny (behind **k.d. Lang**'s *Ingenue*), it included a Top 40 hit in 'Patience Of Angels', one of three compositions by **Boo Hewerdine**. Other credits included four songs co-written with Teddy Borowiecki, and four from Mark Nevin of Fairground Attraction, now the two parties had buried their past. The only retained musician was Roy Dodds, joining Dean Parks (guitar), Penny (drums), Nevin (guitar) and Borowiecki (accordion). This time she was rewarded with a Top 5 album.

Albums: *Mirmama* (RCA 1992), *Eddi Reader* (Blanco Y Negro 1994).

Real Kids

This American quartet, originally from Boston, gained recognition amid the punk-rock explosion in New York during the late 70s. Formed by vocalist/guitarist and part-time **Modern Lover** John Felice in 1975, they pre-dated the punk movement, but jumped on the bandwagon as soon as it started to roll. With bassist Allen 'Alpo' Paulino, Billy Borgioli (guitar) and Howard Ferguson (drums) completing the line-up, they were nevertheless a talented outfit. Delivering a varied and classy selection of predominantly high-energy rockers, they infused reggae, rock 'n' roll and pop influences into their songs, making them instantly memorable. Their self-titled debut, released in 1978, is one of the great unheralded classics of this genre. However, a big-seller it was not, and Felice moved over to a career as a **Ramones** roadie. He also worked as part of the Taxi Boys back in Boston. Borgioli and Ferguson departed to be replaced by Billy Cole and Robby 'Morocco' Morin before the recording of a second album. *Outta Place* was a disappointment, for Felice's new compositions lacked the infectious sparkle that made their debut so special. A shambolic live album, recorded in Paris in 1983, was their final offering before disbanding. Paulino and Borgioloi would form the Primitive Souls (one EP), while their former leader would resurface with John Felice And The Lowdowns. Albums: *The Real Kids* (Red Star 1978), *Outta Place* (Star-Rhythm 1982), *All Kindsa Jerks Live* (New Rose 1983), *Hit You Hard* (New Rose 1983). Compilation: *Girls! Girls! Girls!* (Lolita 1983; comprises Real Kids and Taxi Boys recordings).

Real Life

This Australian band formed in the early 80s, had a hugely successful hit in their home land with their debut single 'Send Me An Angel' in 1983. This success was continued in the USA reaching the Top 30 early the next year The group however had difficulties coping with this instant stardom and only managed to consolidate their success in the US with the Top 40 hit 'Catch Me I'm Falling'. Comprising David Sterry (lead vocals), Alan Johnson (bass), Danny Simcic (drums), Steve Williams (keyboards) and Richard Zatorski (violin/keyboards), the band had its image and sound rooted in the British new romantic movement, **Spandau Ballet** and **Duran Duran** being major influences, and were hence able to sustain their career in dance clubs, both in Australia and the USA. Albums: *Heartland* (1983), *Flame* (1985).

Real People

Living down a previous incarnation as Jo Jo And The Real People, which featured a working dalliance with the infamous disco production team of **Stock, Aitken And Waterman**, the freshly-named Real People were born in 1989 by brothers Tony (b. 7 April 1966, Liverpool, England; bass/vocals) and Chris Griffiths (b. 30 March 1968, Liverpool, England; guitar/vocals). Augmented by Sean Simpson (b. 9 October 1969, Liverpool, England; guitar) and Tony Elson (b. 2 January 1966, Liverpool, England; drums), the foursome started playing local pub gigs in the Bootle area of Merseyside and soon found themselves embroiled in a scene with fellow Scousers, **Rain**, Top and the **La's** as all four bands carried the mantle of classic Liverpool pop as instigated three decades earlier by the **Beatles**. Unfortunately, the Real People's natural instinct for muscular tunes and powerful melodies was undermined by the demands of the music industry. So although the quartet signed to **CBS Records** (soon to be Sony) at the end of 1989, and had enormous fun spending their advance on a trip to India, it was to be a whole year before any product reached the public. In an environment which thrived on a quick turnover, the Real People suffered a loss of impetus, reaching number 60 in the UK charts with 'Windowpane' when a more hasty work rate could have ensured richer dividends. Album: *The Real People* (1991).

Real Roxanne

b. Adelaida Martinez. One of a strange flurry of rapping namesakes to emerge in the late 80s, after the release of **U.T.F.O.**'s 'Roxanne Roxanne'. This Puerto Rican female MC, based in New York, was arguably the most talented, releasing a powerful debut album aided by the production genius of Jam Master Jay (**Run DMC**), **Howie Tee** and **Full Force**, who were behind U.T.F.O.'s original 'Roxanne Roxanne', and discovered Martinez when she was waitressing in Brooklyn. Sadly, when the 'Roxanne' fracas finally died down, she was left without a bandwagon to hitch her career to. Album: *The Real Roxanne* (Select 1988), *Go Down (But Don't Bite It)* (Select 1992).

Real Sounds

Despite the emergence of artists such as the **Bhundu Boys** with their jit jive style, and **Thomas Mapfumo** with chimurenga, imported music - especially Zairean rumba - remains hugely popular in Zimbabwe. The Real Sounds, an eleven-piece line-up based in the Zimbabwean capital of Harare and consisting entirely of Zairean musicians, are the most successful proponents of the rumba outside Zaire itself. The group was founded by guitarist Ghaby Mumba, who was born in Kinshasa and played with a variety of local bands before joining the Government-sponsored Orchestre Diables Noirs, playing a mixture of jazz, rock 'n' roll and rumba in the **OK Jazz** mould. In 1967, two years after the end of the civil war, Mumba left for Zambia, capitalizing on the local interest in

Congolese music with a soukous band called OC Jazz. His second outfit, Les Elite Bantous, with its less-than-subtle reference to the influential Congolese band Bantous De La Capitale, took the name game even further. He formed the Real Sounds in 1975. The band moved from Zambia to Zimbabwe in 1978, when they were invited to take up a residency in a hotel in Umtali. As the Zimbabwean war of independence hotted up, they left Umtali, the centre of regular fire fights between guerrillas and the army, and moved to Harare. In the capital, the Real Sounds found an eager audience for their own brand of soukous, which resulted in two hit albums, *Harare* and *Funky Lady* - and a string of top singles. Of these, 'Dynamos Versus Caps', about the competition between two leading national football teams, followed by 'Dynamos Versus Tornados' on the 1987 album *Wende Zako*, showed the extent to which they had become involved in local issues. Their rhythms changed too. In the late 70s, the Real Sounds experimented with sungura, but soon changed back to the mellower, Zairean rumba sound. By 1986, the band had moved one step forward, one step back. The single 'Non Aligned Movement', commemorating the meeting in Harare of delegates from the non-aligned nations, extolled the Mugabe government over a smooth rumba beat. The b-side dug into a mixture of rumba with Zimbabwe's mbira sound, which by now the band had titled rhumbira. The same year, the band took another surprise step by re-recording the 1973 OK Jazz hit 'Azada' - further proof of the continuing appeal of Zairean rumba in Zimbabwe. The Real Sounds made their first European tour in 1986, and have since returned several times.

Albums: *Harare* (1984), *Funky Lady* (1985), *Wende Zako* (1987), *Real Sounds Of Africa* (1989).

Real Thing

This Liverpool-based group has its origins in the Mersey boom. Lead singer Eddie Amoo was a former member of the **Chants**, whose excellent beat singles garnered considerable praise. Although they failed to chart, the Chants continued to record for various labels until the name was ultimately dropped. The Real Thing emerged in 1976 with 'You To Me Are Everything' which reached number 1 in the UK. Their next release, 'Can't Get By Without You' continued their brand of commercial sweet soul, but later singles were less successful until a more forthright performance in 1979 with the *Star Wars*-influenced, 'Can You Feel The Force', took the group back into the Top 5 establishing their popularity with the British disco audience. Since then the Real Thing's new material has fared less well, although remixes of those first two hits charted 10 years after their initial release.

Albums: *The Real Thing* (1976), *Four From Eight* (1977), *Step Into Our World* (1978), *Can You Feel The Force* (1979).

Real World Records

As a result of their excitement for world music, **Peter Gabriel** and some business friends set up WOMAD (a World Of Music, Arts and Dance) in 1980. The organization, though financially shaky at the start, went on to promote a vast array of ethnic acts over the decade via festivals and sporadic album releases in the WOMAD *Talking Book* series. The next step on from *Talking Book*, Real World was officially launched on 5 June 1989 with the simultaneous release of five albums. The first was *Passion* by Peter Gabriel, who had helped to finance both the label and its hi-tech studios in Wiltshire, England with royalties from his best-selling *So*. With contributions from a host of world musicians, *Passion* and the companion compilation *Passion Sources* were a clear taste of things to come. In the following two years the label released a total of 18 albums of artists from Cuba (**Orquesta Reve**) to India (**K Sridhar And K Shivakumar**), Zaire (**Tabu Ley**) to Russia (**Dmitri Pokrovsky**), much of it recorded at the Real World studios by resident engineer David Bottril. Through these releases the label has given a worldwide audience to a plethora of talent that would otherwise remain unheard of outside of their native countries.

Realm

This Milwaukee, USA-based hi-tech thrash metal quintet was formed by guitarists Takis Kinis and Paul Laganowski in 1985. By a process of trial and error they finally completed the line-up with Mark Antoni (vocals), Steve Post (bass) and Mike Olson (drums). Following a string of successful club shows they landed support slots to **Wendy 'O' Williams** and **Megadeth** tours in 1986. Signing to Roadracer Records they released *Endless War* in 1988. This was a complex fusion of hard rock, thrash and jazz influences and included a remarkable cover of the **Beatles**' 'Eleanor Rigby'. Their second album saw them becoming arguably too complex with a multitude of unnecessary time-changes, rendering much of the material incoherent and unmelodic.

Albums: *Endless War* (Roadracer 1988), *Suiciety* (Roadracer 1990).

Reardon, Caspar

b. 15 April 1907, Little Falls, New York, USA, d. 9 March 1941. One of only a handful of harpists to make any impact on the jazz scene (the others being Adele Girard, Corky Hale and Dave Snell), Reardon was a classically-trained musician who played with the Philadelphia and Cincinnati Symphony Orchestras. In the early 30s he made some records with **Paul Whiteman** and **Jack Teagarden**, the latter being the most interesting. Any aspirations he might have had to enhance the peripheral role his chosen instrument had in jazz ended with his premature death in 1941. Albums: with Jack Teagarden *A Hundred Years From Today* (1931-34 recordings).

Rebel MC

After leaving his Double Trouble partners (Michael Menson and Leigh Guest), famed for the bubblegum ska hit 'Street Tuff', London based former electronics student Rebel MC (b. Michael Alec Anthony West, 27 August 1965, Tottenham, London, England) has earned greater plaudits as a solo artist. Double Trouble would go on to score minor hits with 'Love Don't Live Here Anymore' and 'Rub-A-Dub', without their former leader. Originally considered the UK's **Hammer**, the Rebel's more recent work is characterised by ragga beats, fast rhymes and roots harmonics. It was heartfelt music with a solid Rastafarian message. It was learned, no doubt, from his earlier stints on the live reggae circuit, having set up the Beat Freak sound system with jungle innovator DJ Ron. The single 'Rich An' Getting Richer' was an excellent social commentary rant with dub synchronized, orchestral mixes. On *Black Meaning Good* he was joined by **Tenor Fly**, **Barrington Levy**, **P.P. Arnold**, and **Dennis Brown**, the more political agenda emphasized by its sleeve dedication to: 'scapegoats of the British judicial system'. 'Rebel Music', meanwhile, was remixed by Pasemaster Mase of **De La Soul**. The son of a semi-pro cricketer, West helped start the 'People Against Poverty And Oppression Movement', and joined with 'Musicians Against The War' in the days of the Gulf conflict. More lastingly, he helped establish his own Tribal Bass label, working with homegrown UK rap talent like the **Demon Boyz** and others.
Albums: *Black Meaning Good* (Desire 1991), *Word, Sound And Prayer* (Desire 1992). With Double Trouble: *21 Mixes* (Desire 1990).

Rebel, Tony

b. Patrick Barrett, Manchester, Jamaica, West Indies. Rebel is one of the few dreadlocked 'cultural' DJs of the **ragga** era, but actually started out as a singer, winning local talent competitions as Papa Tony or Tony Ranking on **sound systems** such as Destiny Outernational, Thunderstorm, Wha Dat and finally **Sugar Minott**'s Youth Promotion. In 1988 he recorded 'Casino' for the MGB label, his first ever release. Sides for Delroy 'Callo' Collins and Shocking Vibes followed, but it was at **Penthouse** where his true potential began to be realised. 'Fresh Dee-Jay', 'Music Fraternity' and 'Mandella Story' announced his arrival, before he was matched with **Cutty Ranks** for *Die Hard*. It contained two of his first hit singles, 'The Armour' and 'Instant Death'. Although notable for their combative zeal both revealed an uncompromisingly spiritual approach, and were voiced

in a melodic sing-jay fashion that was unique. 'Fresh Vegetable' was the unlikeliest love song of 1990, but proved a sizeable hit; so too 'D.J. Unity' (with Macka B), 'The Herb', 'War And Crime' and 'Hush', the latter voiced for **Bobby Digital**. Throughout 1991-92 he recorded for a number of different producers, including **Exterminator**, Redman, Star Trail and the Two Friends label, who teamed him with first Anthony Red Rose ('Gun Talk') and then **Judy Mowatt** ('Guilty'). Penthouse released his debut album, *Rebel With A Cause*, in 1992 and this was followed by *Rebellious*, a more rootsy set produced by Sky High which included duets with **Half Pint** and **Garnett Silk**. 'Chatty Chatty Mouth' continued his winning habits with Penthouse before he recorded the anthemic 'Reggae On Top' for **Steely And Clevie**. By the end of the year he had signed to **Columbia Records** for *Vibes Of The Times*, released in 1993. 'Sweet Jamaica', a song voiced for Bobby Digital, was chosen for the soundtrack of the film *Cool Runnings* that November.
Albums: *Rebel With A Cause* (Penthouse 1992), *Rebellious* (RAS 1992), *Vibes Of The Times* (Columbia 1993). With Cutty Ranks: *Die Hard (Vols. 1 & 2)* (Penthouse 1990).

Rebello, Jason

b. 1969, London, England; of mixed Indian-Portuguese and English ancestry. In 1988, pianist Rebello was one of the most talked-about young musicians on the London jazz scene, having just won the **Pat Smythe** Award for the most promising young player of that year. Unlike a purely bebop-based performer, Rebello's technique was as strong in either hand, and he was as liable to play snatches of boogie and stride as in a fast, linear improvising style. Rebello's interests as a piano student lay equally in classical music and jazz, but the earliest music he heard was by **Jimi Hendrix** and the **Beatles**, and in his mid-teens, exposure to **Herbie Hancock**'s pop-funk Rockit band turned him on to dance music with a strong improvisational flavour. Through Hancock's antecedents, Rebello discovered the jazz piano tradition, went to London's Guildhall School of Music to pursue it, and was soon working with younger UK jazz celebrities such as **Courtney Pine**, **Jean Toussaint**, **Steve Williamson** and **Cleveland Watkiss**. In the late 80s he was a member of **Tommy Smith**'s group and in 1990 he released his first album as leader, with **Wayne Shorter** producing and has since built a considerable following, aware of his extraordinarily mature style. In the summer of 1995 he played at the Festival Hall, London, after which he spent some time in a monastery.
Albums: *A Clearer View* (Novus 1990), *Permanent Love* (1993), *Keeping Time* (Novus 1993), *Make It Real* (RCA 1994).

Rebennack, Mac

(see **Dr. John**)

Reckless

This Canadian pop-metal act was formed by guitarist Steve Madden with Jan Melanson (vocals), Gene Stout (bass) and Gil Roberts (drums), originally under the name Harlow. *Reckless* emerged to a generally positive reception, with commercial guitar-led metal in a **Van Halen** vein given individual identity by Melanson's quirky vocal delivery. Coupled with the frontwoman's striking blond looks, this seemed to give Reckless a chance to stand out from the crowd. However, the album bombed, and the band broke up. Madden tried again with a new line-up featuring Doug Adams (vocals), Todd Pilon (bass) and Steve Wayne Lederman (drums), but while *Heart Of Steel* was another good effort based around Madden's stylish guitar work, it lacked the distinctive qualities of its predecessor, and the band faded.
Albums: *Reckless* (EMI 1981), *Heart Of Steel* (Heavy Metal America 1984).

Reco, Ezz, And The Launchers

Reco's band have the distinction of being the first artists to hit the UK charts with a ska record. In March 1964 their infectious rework of **Jimmy Cliff**'s 'King Of Kings', fronted by the band's singer Boysie Grant, reached the Top 50 one week before **Millie** pierced the public's eardrums with 'My Boy Lollipop'. 'Kings Of Kings' spent four weeks in the hit parade, as it was then known, but follow-ups 'Little Girl' and 'Please Come Back' did not match its success and the band was not heard from again though trombonist **Emmanuel 'Ezz Reco' Rodriguez** has pursued an active career both as a leader and as featured soloist with the **Specials** and **Paul Young**.

Records

Will Birch (b. c.1950, Essex, England) started out on his drumming career in the 60s with local Southend band the Geezenstacks. He then moved on to the Tradewinds who performed two songs and appeared in a BBC television documentary about young people screened in June 1965. Next up came a stint in the Flowerpots with **Wilko Johnson**, before he played with Surly Bird, Glory, Cow Pie, the Hot Jets, and even a few gigs with **Dr. Feelgood**. He later joined the **Kursaal Fliers** when they formed in October 1973. When the Kursaals split in November 1977 Birch formed a partnership with John Wicks who had been the Kursaals' lead singer for the last few months of their existence (and also played rhythm guitar). In February 1978 they recruited bassist Phil Brown (ex-the Janets) and guitarist Huw Gower, whom Birch spotted playing a one-off gig with Peter Perret's (**Only Ones**) old band, the Ratbites From Hell. This completed the Records, who made their live debut at Bristol Granary Club in March 1978. The debut single, 'Starry Eyes',

was released in November, becoming a minor pop classic in the process. The band then used their connections to join the *Be Stiff* tour ostensibly to back **Rachel Sweet,** but they also opened the show (the only non **Stiff** act on board). They signed to **Virgin** and released further quality pop singles all co-written by Birch, mostly with Wicks as his partner. The best were gathered together on the debut *Shades In Bed* which included an old song dating from Kursaal days, 'Girls That Don't Exist', plus 'Starry Eyes', and 'Teenerama'. Initial copies of the album also included a free 12-inch single featuring Records' cover versions of various well known songs. Ian Gibbons was drafted in to play keyboards on the album. Birch also wrote 'Hearts In Her Eyes' for the **Searchers**' 1979 comeback album. Gower left just before the second album to be replaced by Judy Cole. He joined **David Johannson**'s band before going solo. By the time of their final album in 1982 the line-up was Birch, Wicks and Brown plus Dave Whelan (guitar) and Chris Gent (vocals).
Albums: *Shades In Bed* (1979), *Crashes* (1980), *Music On Both Sides* (1982). Compilation: *Smashes, Crashes & Near Misses* (1988).

Recycle Or Die

German record label associated with the **Harthouse Records**/Eye Q group, whose managing director is Heinz Roth. They had the sum total of their product, six albums, released in the UK for the first time in 1994. Each CD arrived in a cover painted by a cult German artist, packaged in recyclable cardboard. The albums were: *Straylight* (Dominic Woosey), *Looking Beyond* (Ralf Hildenbeutel), *Constellation* (Oliver Lieb), *Baked Beans* (Helmut Zerlett), *Archaic Modulation* (Stevie Be Zet) and *Rhythm & Irrelevance* (#9 Dream). Roth: 'It's very much like a community project...Recycle Or Die is not an ambient label. It's more experimental. It's not like putting together a couple of sounds and smoking a joint'. Recycle Or Die took a stage in the 1994 Montreaux Jazz Festival, where Ralph Hildenbeutel, **Sven Vath**'s engineer, played.

Red Bird Records

Formed in 1963 by famed record producers and songwriters **Leiber And Stoller**, Red Bird Records was the label on which such classic hits as the **Dixie Cups**' 'Chapel Of Love' and the **Shangri-Las**' 'Leader Of The Pack' first appeared. Red Bird was one of the most successful independent labels of the mid-60s, although it lasted a mere four years. Leiber and Stoller decided to form their own company in 1962 and launched Tiger Records that year, without success. Daisy Records followed in 1963 but also failed to get off the ground. In late 1963 they hooked up with another legendary record executive, **George Goldner**, and started Red Bird. The first single on the new label was the unsuccessful 'Mira Mira' by the Latin Quarters. The Dixie Cups' 'Chapel Of Love', written by **Ellie Greenwich, Phil Spector** and **Jeff Barry** was next, however, and rose to number 1 in the US in mid-1964. Red Bird concentrated on the 'girl group' sound of the early 60s even as the British beat groups gained in popularity. Such Red Bird hits as the **Jellybeans** 'I Wanna Love Him So Bad' and the Dixie Cups' second hit, 'People Say', kept the new label riding high. In August 1964 the Shangri-Las had their first hit with 'Remember (Walkin' In The Sand)', followed two months later by their biggest hit, the 'bad girl' classic 'Leader Of The Pack', another number 1 single. Red Bird did not maintain its high level of success for long, however, and by 1965 Leiber and Stoller were anxious to return to their first love, rhythm and blues music. They briefly revived the Tiger label and then started a Red Bird spin-off, Blue Cat Records, whose greatest success was the **Ad Libs**' hit 'The Boy From New York City'. In 1966 Leiber and Stoller sold their interests in the two labels to Goldner, who kept them going for another year. Among other memorable Red Bird/Blue cat hits were the Shangri-Las' 'Give Him A Great Big Kiss' and 'I Can Never Go Home Anymore', the Dixie Cups' 'Iko Iko', the **Trade Winds**' 'New York's A Lonely Town' and the Butterflys' 'Good Night Baby'. Other artists to record for the company included **Alvin Robinson,** Bessie Banks (the original version of 'Go Now', later popularized by the **Moody Blues**), disc jockey Murray The K, blues guitarist **John Hammond**, rockabilly singer **Ral Donner** and songwriters Jeff Barry and **Barry Mann**.

Red Box

This UK band was formed in 1982 with a line-up comprising Simon Toulson-Clark (vocals/guitar), Julian Close (saxophone), Martin Nickson (drums), Rob Legge (bass), Paddy Talbot (keyboards). The group enjoyed minor success with the independently issued 'Chenko' and subsequently signed to WEA Records. This coincided with a reduction in the line-up, from which Clark and Close emerged as a duo. In the summer of 1985, they enjoyed a UK Top 3 hit with the catchy 'Lean On Me (Ah-Li-Ayo)'. Its Top 10 success was repeated the following year with 'For America'. Their first album *The Circle And The Square* reached number 73, but a long gap in recording saw Red Box lose ground. Four years passed before the follow-up *Motive*, was issued and none of its attendant singles reached, the charts.
Albums: *The Circle And The Square* (1986), *Motive* (1990).

Red Crayola

Despite several contrasting line-ups, Red Crayola remains the vision of Mayo Thompson. He formed the Houston, Texas-based group in July 1966 with drummer Rick Barthelme, although several other individuals, including future country star **Guy Clark**, were temporary members until Steve Cunningham (bass) joined two months later. The group's set initially featured cover versions, but these were soon supplanted by their own remarkable, original compositions. In addition the Crayola were renowned for free-form pieces, during which they were augmented by an assortment of friends known as the Familiar Ugly. This improvisatory unit was featured on the trio's debut *The Parable Of Arable Land*, where their erratic contributions punctuated the main body of work. Tommy Smith replaced Barthelme for *God Bless Red Krayola And All Who Sail With It*, the altered spelling in deference to objections from the US crayon company. Shorn of the Familiar Ugly, the album displayed an impressive discipline while maintaining a desire to challenge. Thompson disbanded the Crayola when 'obscurity hit us with great force'. He completed the solo *Corky's Cigar* aka *Corky's Debt To His Father*, before engaging in several projects including Art And Language, an *ad hoc* gathering responsible for a 1976 release, *Corrected Slogans*. Mayo then moved to the UK where he re-established Red Crayola in the light of the musical freedom afforded by punk. *Soldier Talk* featured assistance from several members of **Pere Ubu**, a group Thompson subsequently joined. He continued to pursue his own direction with *Kangaroo*, which also featured a billing for Art And Language, and despite a somewhat lower profile, Mayo Thompson remains one of rock's most imaginative and challenging figures.
Albums: *The Parable Of Arable Land* (1967), *God Bless Red Krayola And All Who Sail With It* (1968), *Soldier Talk* (1979), *Kangaroo* (1981), *Black Snakes* (1983), *malefactor, ade* (1989).

Red Devils

Intrinsic to the rise of blues hard rockers the Red Devils has been the King King venue in their home town of Los Angeles, California, USA. Beginning in 1988, the Red Devils' Monday night residencies at the former Chinese Restaurant, including its inception as a live entertainment venue on 19 December, steadily brought approving nods among the club's celebrated clientele (**Bruce Willis**, etc.). The band's original line-up featured Lester Butler (vocals/harp), Jonny Ray Bartel (bass) and Bill Bateman (drums) among others, although only these three graduated to the 90s line-up which additionally housed Paul Size (lead guitar) and Dave Lee Bartel (rhythm guitar). They began as an informal jam session when King King was still called Snooty Ho's, and Bateman recalls their first audience as 'nine champion skateboarders sitting at the bar'. Butler had first learned blues harp at age six, because the instrument was the only one within his budget. Later he became a confidante of urban blues guitar maestro Hollywood Fats, who contributed to groups including the **Blasters** and the **James Harman**

Band. When Fats died in 1986 it gave Butler the impetus to enter the music industry that he needed. After performing regularly at high school parties and other informal events, he eventually made the acquaintance of Bateman and Bartel, both fellow travellers on the Los Angeles roots rock scene (Bateman had, of course, also played on three albums with the Blasters). The Red Devils finally came to the attention of **Def American Records** and **Rick Rubin** in the early 90s, who saw an opening for their dense, excitable blues rock sound. Rubin was also on hand to record the band's debut album, a glimpse of the Red Devils in their natural, live setting. The previous year they had appeared on sessions with another King King regular, **Mick Jagger**, though he elected not to include the results on his *Wandering Spirit* album.

Album: *King King* (Def American 1993).

Red Dogs

This blues-based UK rock 'n' roll quintet was formed in 1989 by Mickey 'The Vicar' Ripley (vocals) and Chris John (guitar). Enlisting the services of Mick Young (bass), Paul Guerin (guitar) and Stow (drums), the band signed to Episode Records the following year. They debuted with *Wrong Side Of Town*, a six-track offering which took the **Rolling Stones** as its primary influence. The Red Dogs raised their profile by supporting **Cheap And Nasty** and **UFO** on their 1991 UK tours. Taking their infectious brand of bar-room boogie to a larger stage proved initially successful, though afterwards they failed to heighten their profile significantly.

Album: *Wrong Side Of Town* (Episode 1989, mini-album).

Red Dragon

b. Leroy May, Kingston, Jamaica, West Indies. One of the most enduring and dependable DJs to emerge from Jamaica, Dragon - or rather Redman as he was then known - learnt his trade on Barrington Hi-Fi in 1981, progressing to Stone Love, Small Axe, Rambo Mango (which he owned) and People's Choice **sound systems**, before changing his name in 1984 after the popularity of his 'Laughing Dragon' lyric on a **dub plate**. Fellow DJ Charlie Chaplin had also passed through the ranks of People's Choice and produced his debut tune, 'Computer', in 1985. The following year Dragon went to **Harry J** who released 'Nah Get Nutten' and 'Commander' to a welcoming **dancehall** audience. In 1987 'Hol A Fresh' was a massive hit for **Winston Riley**, but failed to crossover as predicted owing to poor promotion. Nevertheless its local success ensured a wealth of releases for the late **King Tubby** ('Canter Mi Horse'), Redman, Vena and **King Jammys**, where 'Duck Dance' and 'Della Skank' confirmed his ability to define the latest dancehall moves. In 1989 Riley's Techniques label issued an

album pairing him with his DJ brother, Flourgon. That same year witnessed the birth of his own Dragon imprint, on which he released tunes by young artists such as John Mouse as well as himself: 'Old', 'Love Unuh' and 'My Anthem' achieving the most recognition. Throughout 1990-91 he recorded very little; concentrating instead on encouraging fresh talent coming up through Rambo Mango and Flourgon's Sweet Love set. **Buju Banton** and Terry Ganzie both started their careers with Dragon. In 1992 he made a return to the dancehall market with the uncharacteristic *Pum Pum Shorts*, and then several sides for Shang, **Steely And Clevie**, **Mafia & Fluxy** and Parrish. The momentum increased during 1993 and there were a proliferation of hits for the likes of **Bobby Digital**, Danny Browne, Winston Riley, **Fashion** and **Sly And Robbie**'s Taxi label, all capturing his deep, rolling vocals and adept rhythm-riding to perfection.

Selected albums: *Red Dragon Vs Flourgon* (Techniques 1989), *Pum Pum Shorts* (Dragon 1992).

Red Fox

b. c.1970, St. Catherine, Jamaica, West Indies. An artist who un-self-consciously mixes hip hop and reggae, Red Fox was initially compared to **Yellowman** when he appeared at sound systems in his native country, due to his light complexion. However, it wasn't until he moved to New York (still at the tender age of 16) that his musical career found its feet. Following stage shows alongside dancehall stars like **Shabba Ranks** and **Buju Banton**, he hooked up with producer Peter McKenzie to record 'Come Boogie Down' on FM Records. It quickly became a cult item both in his adopted home of Brooklyn and back in Jamaica. In 1992 he teamed with **Brand Nubian** to duet on the memorable 'Black Star Liner' cut. That outfit returned the compliment to Red Fox on 'Hey Mr. Rude Boy', from his debut album, *As A Matter Of Fox*. It was preceded by the roughneck 'Dem A Murderer' 45, which, like the album, entwined dancehall and rap into a presentable cocktail. Further singles 'Born Again Black Man', a straight reggae song, and 'Ghetto Gospel', sandwiched an appearance at Jamaica's annual Sting festival.

Album: *As A Matter Of Fox* (Elektra 1993).

Red Fun

A band from Stockholm, Sweden, formed in 1992, consisting of four veterans of that country's metal scene. Thomas Persson (vocals), whose mane of red hair gives the band their name, was formerly part of **Alien**. Tobbe Moen (bass) is an experienced session player, while Freddy von Gerber (drums) had appeared in a number of groups including Intermezzo, Bam Bam Boys, Rat Bat Blue and Easy Action. Kee Marcello (guitar) was also a member of the last-named band, as well as, more famously, **Europe**. Having been built around Marcello and Persson's lifelong friendship, Red Fun recorded a self-titled debut album during the winter of 1992 as well as a promotional single, 'My Baby's Coming Back'. With press statements about putting some of the hedonism back in to hard rock following grunge's domination, and support slots to **Guns N'Roses** and **Neil Young** in the summer of 1993, Red Fun were set firm to appeal to traditionalists. Album: *Red Fun* (Cheiron/Music For Nations 1993).

Red Guitars

This Hull, Yorkshire based guitar pop band featured Jerry Kidd (vocals), Louise Barlow (bass), Hallam Lewis (lead guitar), John Rowley (rhythm guitar), and Matt Higgins (drums). Formed in 1982 by Lewis and Kidd, they released two superb singles, 'Good Technology' and 'Fact', before scoring a number 1 on the independent charts with 'Marimba Jive'. The latter was included on *Slow To Fade* which emerged on Kidd's own Self Drive Records in November 1984. A highly polished and original pop album, with Kidd's analytical lyrics to the fore: 'I said that I love you/God knows I tried/You say you still love me/But you're always saying goodbye'. Fittingly, Kidd himself was to leave barely two months after the album's release. He issued a press statement to the effect that 'Technically we improved a lot during the last year but musically, from my point of view, we were standing still. New ideas and songs I had for the group no longer seemed to fit in. I still favour independence within the record industry and shall continue to look for success, both artistic and commercial, with releases on my own Self Drive Record label.' He was quickly replaced by Robert Holmes, who played his first gig with the band at the University of London Union on 24 May 1985. Lou Howard replaced Barlow on bass as *Tales Of The Expected* saw the band move to One Way Records, through **Virgin**. Although the lyrical focus of the band had changed, they were still capable of producing highly individual and moving music, notably on singles 'National Avenue' and the yearning 'Be With Me'. Interestingly, both album sleeves featured quotes from poet Sean O'Brien. Hallam and Howard left to form the Planet Wilson in 1987, with drummer Jonah Oxburrow (ex-That Noble Porpoise), and released the album *Not Drowning But Waving*. Hallam now runs his own studio in Hull, while Holmes released his solo album, *Age Of Swing*, for Virgin in 1989.
Albums: *Slow To Fade* (Self Drive 1984), *Tales Of The Expected* (Virgin 1985).

Red Hot Chili Peppers

These engaging Hollywood ruffians mixed funk and punk in the mid-80s and encouraged a legion of other bands to regurgitate the formula. Led by 'Antwan The Swan' (b. Anthony Kiedis; vocals), the band's original line-up also featured 'Flea' (b. Michael Balzary,

Melbourne, Australia), Hillel Slovak (b. 31 March 1962, Israel, d. 25 June 1988; guitar) and Jack Irons (b. California, USA; drums). They began life as garage band Anthem before Balzary departed for seminal 80s punks **Fear**. When Irons and Slovak moved on to join the less notable What Is This?, the nails appeared to be firmly in place on the Anthem coffin. However, under their new name, the Red Hot Chili Peppers acquired a speculative recording deal with **EMI** America. Unfortunately, as Irons and Slovak were under contract with their new band, their debut album had to be recorded with Jack Sherman on guitar and Cliff Martinez (ex-**Captain Beefheart**, **Weirdos**) on drums. Production was handled, somewhat surprisingly, by the **Gang Of Four**'s Andy Gill. The band set about building their considerable reputation as a live outfit, much of which was fuelled by their penchant for appearing semi-naked or worse. Slovak returned to guitar duties for the second album, this time produced by **George Clinton**. Also featured was a horn section comprising **Maceo Parker** and **Fred Wesley**, veterans of **James Brown** among others. Martinez returned shortly after to reinstate the original Anthem line-up, and their third album saw a shift back to rock from the soul infatuation of its predecessors. 1988 brought the release of their renowned *Abbey Road* EP, featuring a pastiche of the famous **Beatles** album pose on the cover (the band were totally naked save for socks covering their genitalia). However, the mood was darkened when Slovak took an accidental heroin overdose and died in June. Deeply upset, Irons left, while the band recruited John Frusciante (guitar) and Chad Smith (drums). After the release of *Freaky Styley* the single, 'Knock Me Down', was released as a tribute to Slovak. Of their most commercially successful excursion, 1991's *Blood, Sex, Sugar, Magik*, they accurately diagnosed their motivation, and much of their attraction: 'Just recognizing that I was a freak, but knowing that was a cool place to be.' Producer **Rick Rubin**, usually associated with the harder end of the metal and rap spectrum (**Slayer**, **Danzig**), nevertheless brought out the Peppers' first ballads. Such sensitivity has done little to deter the vanguard of critics who have long since raged at what they saw as the band's innate sexism. Frusciante was replaced in June 1992 by Arik Marshall, who in turn was sacked one year later. 1994 saw new guitarist Dave Navarro (ex-**Jane's Addiction**) perform his live UK debut as the band headlined the Reading Festival, before joining the **Rolling Stones** on their US tour.
Albums: *Uplift Mofo Party Plan* (EMI 1988), *Mother's Milk* (EMI 1989), *The Red Hot Chili Peppers* (EMI 1990), *Freaky Styley* (EMI 1990), *Blood, Sex, Sugar, Magik* (Warners 1991). Compilations: *What Hits!?* (EMI 1992), *Plasma Shaft* (Warners 1994, double album), *Greatest Hits* (CEMA/EMI 1995).
Video: *What Hits!?* (1992).

Further reading: *True Men Don't Kill Coyotes*, Dave Thompson.

Red House Painters

Once described by the ***New Musical Express*** as 'the most intensely sad and beautiful new band of 1992', the Red House Painters' carefully sculpted, highly impressive work has hardly been over publicised. Band leader Mark Kozelek hates to do interviews, and is even less fond of having his picture taken, despite which he has continually basked in critical adoration. Addicted to drugs at the age of 10, he was admitted to a rehab centre at 14. His way out of this misery was music, though he still remained an outsider to whatever community he lived in, spending most of his time in his bedroom. He had previously formed his first band, God Forbid, in Massilon, Ohio, USA, before moving to Atlanta. There he met drummer Anthony Koutsos and formed the Red House Painters. When they relocated to San Francisco together, the band was fleshed out with the addition of Gordon Mack (guitar) and Jerry Vessel (bass). Via the intervention of **American Music Club**'s Mark Eitzel, a tape of demos recorded between 1989 and 1990 was passed on to **4AD Records**, who promptly signed the band. Six of the demo cuts were remixed and released as *Down Colorful Hill* in September 1992. By November they had played their first UK gig at London's Borderline club with Earwig. Given an outlet for his work, there then came a flood of Kozelek's meandering guitar and introspective travelogue lyrics in the double album, *Red House Painters*, which, confusingly, was followed by a single album of the same title. In the wake of these two albums, and despite his reluctance to talk to them, Kozelek became venerated by UK critics, one describing his band's style as 'desolate music that's fragile but oddly warming.' Songs such as 'Cabezon' on *Ocean Beach* saw a reflective, earnest **Jeff Buckley**-like delivery allied to the familiar aching song structures, but also the departure of long-time bass player Vessel, a man of highly unusual, strangely unmusical technique. A version of **Yes**' 'Long Distance Runaround' confirmed the band had not also lost its humour (previous cover versions had included material by both **Wings** and **Kiss**).
Albums: *Down Colourful Hill* (4AD 1992, mini-album), *Red House Painters* (4AD 1993, double album), *Red House Painters* (4AD 1993), *Ocean Beach* (4AD 1995).

Red Jasper

Led by 'screaming' Davey Dodds, Red Jasper mix folkist sentiments with out and out heavy metal. A kind of **Anthrax**-go-rustic, they are restricted, but when 'live', the stops are pulled out and it's all guitars, leather and thunder.
Selected album: *Sting In The Tale* (1990).

Red Letter Day

This Portsmouth, England-based pop punk band formed in 1983, with a line-up consisting of Ade (vocals/guitar), Ian Campbell (lead guitar), Pete White (bass) and Brian Lee (drums). However, nine months and two demos later, Ade was joined by Daryn Price (drums), Keith Metcalfe (bass) and Davie Egan (guitar) in the band's second incarnation. After the single 'Wherever You May Run' they found favour with BBC disc jockey **John Peel** who secured a session for them on his show. The 12-inch EP *Released Emotions* followed on Quiet Records (they would, confusingly, join a record company with the same title, so called because its boss was a fan of the band). Metcalfe was replaced by a temporary bass player before Steve (ex-Original Mirrors) took over on bass. The highlight of 1987 was one of the support slots at the Polderock Festival in Belgium alongside the **Mission**, **Primitives** and **Sonic Youth**. Now on the Released Emotions label, they recorded a joint album with the Sect, titled *Soft Lights And Loud Guitars*. This picked up a series of good reviews and they also appeared on the Link Records sampler *Underground Rockers*, alongside other bands of a similar persuasion like **Mega City Four** and the **Price**. Egan left shortly afterwards, to be replaced by their present guitarist Ray. After a double a-sided single they completed work on their first full long player, *More Songs About Love And War*, in a rockier vein.
Albums: with the Sect *Soft Lights And Loud Guitars* (Released Emotions 1988), *More Songs About Love And War* (Released Emotions 1991).

Red Lorry Yellow Lorry

This post punk gothic band formed in Leeds, England, in 1982, and their first single was 'Take It All Away'. The line-up consisted of Chris Reed (vocals/rhythm guitar), Wolfie (b. Dane Wolfenden; lead guitar, replacing Martin Fagen), Paul Southern (bass; replacing Steve Smith) and Mick Brown (drums). The debut album *Talk About The Weather*, included 'Hollow Eyes', which proved popular in Gothic circles following its regular airing on BBC disc jockey **John Peel**'s BBC Radio 1 show. The album was an intoxicating mix of musical aggression and lyrical minimalism ('It was a strange dream/He stood and stared/Those shining faces/Those darkened eyes/And alone he ran/Alone he ran', comprised the entire scope of the track 'Strange Dream'). After seven singles on **Red Rhino Records** the band moved on to Situation 2. By this time their material had been revitalized by a broader approach to songwriting: 'People are surprised to find that we have a sense of humour. We do see the irony of things in life', commented Reed. 1988's 'Only Dreaming' attested to this, being their first ballad. In early 1990 the band was forced to cancel four gigs when the current drummer, Chil, was hospitalized for a wrist operation. After eight years' service Wolfie was also absent, leaving Reed as the only surviving original member. His replacement was Gary Weight, alongside bassist Martin Scott.

Albums: *Talk About The Weather* (Red Rhino 1985), *Paint Your Wagon* (Red Rhino 1986), *Nothing's Wrong* (Beggars Banquet 1988), *Blow* (Beggars Banquet 1989), *Drop* (Beggars Banquet 1989), *Blasting Off* (Beggars Banquet 1992). Compilation: *Smashed Hits* (Red Rhino 1988).

Red Mill, The

As an operetta with a sense of humour, this has to be one of the most cherished productions of its time. *The Red Mill* opened at the Knickerbocker Theatre in New York on 24 September 1906, and was a vehicle for the ex-vaudeville comedy duo of David Montgomery and Fred Stone who had made their first impact on Broadway in **The Wizard Of Oz** (1903). Their adventures as a couple of naïve American tourists, Kid Connor and Con Kidder, stranded without money in Katwyk-aan-Zee, Holland, involve them in some hair-raising situations, and force them to adopt a number of disguises, one of which finds them masquerading as Sherlock Holmes and Doctor Watson. Henry Blossom's book and lyrics, and **Victor Herbert**'s fine music combined in a score that is generally considered to have crossed the divide from operetta into musical comedy. Romantic and engaging songs such as 'Every Day Is Ladies Day With Me', 'Because You're You', 'When You're Pretty And The World Is Fair', 'The Isle Of Our Dreams', 'Moonbeams', and 'The Streets Of New York' (which became a hit for Billy Murray), ensured a run of 274 performances, the longest for any of Victor Herbert's book musicals. The 1945 revival, which starred Eddie Foy Jnr. and Michael O'Shea, and had additional lyrics by Forman Brown, did even better and stayed at the **Ziegfeld** Theatre for well over a year. A 1919 London production, with Little Tich as Kid Connor, folded after only 64 performances. A 1947 radically revised revival with 'a tedious new libretto', and starring one of Britain's top comedy double acts, Jewel And Warriss, lost a lot of money in a very short time.

Red Nelson

b. Nelson Wilborn, 31 August 1907, Sumner, Mississippi, USA. Red Nelson was a Chicago based vocalist, and possibly a guitarist, but not a pianist, despite frequent reports to that effect. He was given interesting and varied accompanists during his recording career, which began in 1935, and was a fine singer with a telling falsetto, although he often held himself emotionally in check, possibly to accommodate the 30s fashion for the laconic. His 1935/6 **Decca** recordings with **Cripple Clarence Lofton,** though less considered, are outstanding, with 'Crying Mother Blues' an unquestionable masterpiece, while his 1947

titles for Aladdin, with **James Clark** on piano are almost as good. Last seen working with **Muddy Waters** in the 60s, Nelson was an amiable alcoholic with a penchant for *double entendres*, as might be inferred from the ebullient 'Dirty Mother Fuyer', which he recorded in 1947 under the pseudonym 'Dirty Red'.

Albums: *Blues Uptown* (1969), *The Piano Blues Vol. 9 Lofton/Noble* (1979), *Red Nelson* (1989).

Red River Dave

(see **McEnery, David**)

Red Shoes, The (Film Musical)

One of the most outstanding films in the history of the British cinema. *The Red Shoes*, which was produced and directed by Michael Powell and Emeric Pressburger, was released in 1948 to worldwide acclaim. Pressburger also wrote the screenplay which was based on a story by Hans Christian Andersen. It told the tragic and romantic tale of Vicky Page (Moira Shearer in her film debut), a gifted young dancer who is forced by the Svengali-like impresario Boris Lermontov (Anton Walbrook), to choose between a glittering career in the ballet and her love for the brilliant composer Julian Craster (Marius Goring). After enjoying spectacular success in *The Red Shoes* ballet, Vicky assures Lermontov that dancing will be the sole purpose of her life. However, her conceptions change as soon as she falls in love with the ballet's composer. When Lermontov discovers their liaison, Julian is immediately dismissed from the company, and, despite the impresario's protestations, Vicky goes with him. Some time later, still intoxicated by glamour of the theatre, she returns to dance *The Red Shoes* ballet once more. She is still torn between going on stage or re-joining Julian, but the shoes themselves seem to take control and they whisk her out of the theatre where she falls to her death under the wheels of a passing train. Opinions in the film world are divided as to whether she committed suicide. Robert Helpmann plays Boleslawsy, the company's leading dancer, and he was also responsible for the film's outstanding choreography which was so skilfully integrated into the story. The part of the shoemaker was created and danced by Leonide Massine, and the remainder of the fine supporting cast included Albert Basserman, Ludmilla Tcherina, Esmond Knight, Irene Browne, Austin Trevor, Jerry Verno, Marcel Poncin, and Hay Petrie. Brian Easdale, who first came to prominence for his work on GPO film shorts, composed, arranged and conducted the music, which was played by the Royal Philharmonic Orchestra. Sir Thomas Beecham conducted the orchestra for *The Red Shoes* ballet. Easdale won an Academy Award for his memorable score, and other Oscars went to Hein Heckroth and Arthur Lawson for colour art direction-set direction. The film was also nominated for best picture, story, and film editing, although not, strangely, for Jack Cardiff's stunning Technicolor photography. This exquisite and thrilling picture, which has inspired so many young people over the years with its revealing glimpse of the backstage world of ballet, is still viewed with a mixture of awe and admiration to this day. Not so the Broadway musical which was based on the film and Hans Christian Andersen's original story. It opened on 16 December 1993, and closed three days later.

Red Shoes, The (Stage Musical)

'Cobbling' and 'cobbled', two words that are dangerously close to 'cobblers' - which does not perhaps have the same connotations in America as is it does in Britain - were prominent in several US critics' reviews of this 'mishmash musical version of the beloved 1948 ballet film **The Red Shoes**', which opened at the Gershwin Theatre in New York on 16 December 1993. The score was mostly the work of veteran composer **Jule Styne** and his lyricist and librettist Marsha Norman, but Styne brought in Paul Stryker (a *nom de guerre* for his **Funny Girl** collaborator **Bob Merrill**) at a late hour to help out with the lyrics. Other pre-Broadway changes resulted in director Susan Schulman being replaced by Hollywood legend **Stanley Donen**, and the departure of Roger Rees, one of the principals. The well-known story tells of a young dancer, Victoria Page (Margaret Illman), who is torn between the impresario who has made her a star, Boris Lermontov (Steve Barton), and the young and dashing composer Julian Craster (Hugh Panaro). He falls passionately in love while creating her 'role of a lifetime', The 'banal and melodramatic' score included 'Swan Lake', 'Corps de Ballet', 'When It Happens To You', 'It's A Fairy Tale', 'Be Somewhere', 'The Rag', 'Come Home', and 'When You Dance For A King'. Lyric lines such as 'Now we learn what no one's known/The shoes have passions of their own', and 'Most of us are bound to a lifetime on the ground/You won't stop 'til you reach the top of the sky', were seized upon with derisory glee by the critical fraternity. The meeting of classical dance and musical comedy just did not work, although Margaret Illman was applauded for her performance overall (in a role that was immortalised in the film by Moira Shearer), and in particular for her elegance and style in the second-act showpiece, 'The Red Shoes Ballet' - the longest dance sequence of its kind since **Richard Rodgers**' 'Slaughter On Tenth Avenue' for **On Your Toes** (1936). Heidi Landesman's sets, which featured a baroque false proscenium, were complimented too. But the knives were out, and *The Red Shoes* was withdrawn after only three days. At the time, the reported loss of $8 million was reported to be a Broadway record.

Red, Hot And Blue!

This attempt to repeat the success of **Anything Goes**

(1934), went wrong somewhere on the road to the Alvin Theatre in New York, where it opened on 20 October 1936. Victor Moore and William Gaxton, two of the reasons for the earlier show's appeal, were absent this time, but librettists Howard Lindsay and Russel Crouse (who wrote a very amusing book) and songwriter **Cole Porter** were on hand, and **Ethel Merman**'s presence ensured that the audience heard every word and note. Her co-star was comedian **Jimmy Durante,** and disagreement over top billing resulted in a design in which their names formed a cross, with 'Jimmy' appearing on the upper left-hand diagonal arm, and 'Merman' on the right. **Bob Hope**'s name was below and in the middle, and a good deal easier to read. Together with Merman, he introduced 'You've Got Something', as well as one of Porter's most durable standards, 'It's De-Lovely'. Merman had the first stab at two more of the composer's most memorable songs, the exuberant 'Ridin' High', and 'Down In The Depths (On the Ninetieth Floor)' ('When the only one you wanted wants another/What's the use of swank and cash in the bank galore?/Why, even the janitor's wife/Has a perfectly good love life/And here am I/Facing tomorrow/Down in the depths on the ninetieth floor'). Durante had 'A Little Skipper From Heaven Above', as part of his role as 'Policy' Pinkle, the captain of the polo team at Lark's Nest Prison. 'Policy' is one of several inmates who are released in an effort to assist with a national lottery organized by 'Nails' O'Reilly Duquesne (Ethel Merman) and her lawyer, Bob Hale (Bob Hope). The winner of the lottery has to find the whereabouts of Hale's childhood sweetheart. The search is made easier by the knowledge that the girl sat on a waffle iron when she was four, so identification should prove to be a fairly simple matter. The whole thing becomes academic anyway when the Supreme Court rules that any such contest which benefits the American people is unconstitutional. The show's political overtones and other aspects of the production, meant that *Red, Hot And Blue!* was often compared to the 1931 political musical satire **Of Thee I Sing**. It was not nearly as successful though, and closed after only 183 performances.

Redbone

A North American Indian band formed in 1968, Redbone included brothers Pat and Lolly Vegas (both b. Fresno, California, USA), who had already pursued minor performing careers. Lolly had recorded as early as 1961, while together the brothers completed *At The Haunted House*, as well as several singles. The duo were also successful songwriters, and a compulsive dance-based composition, 'Niki Hoeky', was interpreted by such diverse acts as **P.J. Proby** and **Bobbie Gentry**. Redbone, an Anglicized cajun epithet for half-breed, was completed by Tony Bellamy (b. Los Angeles, California, USA; rhythm guitar/vocals) and Peter

DePoe (b. Neah Bay Reservation, Washington, USA; drums). DePoe, whose native name was 'Last Walking Bear', had been for some time a ceremonial drummer on his reservation. With Pat on bass and Lolly on guitar and vocals, the group initially backed several different artists, including **Odetta** and **John Lee Hooker**, before embarking on an independent direction. The quartet scored an international hit with 'Witch Queen Of New Orleans', which owed much to the then-popular southern, or Cajun 'swamp-rock' style. In 1974 they enjoyed their sole million-seller, 'Come And Get Your Love', but the group was unable to transform their taught, but rhythmic, style into a consistent success.

Albums: *Redbone* (1970), *Potlatch* (1970), *Witch Queen Of New Orleans* (1971), *Message From A Drum* (1972), *Already Here* (1972), *Wovoka* (1974), *Beaded Dreams Through Turquoise Eyes* (1974), *Cycles* (1978). Compilations: *Come And Get Your Redbone* (1975), *Best Of Redbone* (1976), *Rock Giants* (1982).

Redbone, Leon

Believed to have been born in Canada, this enigmatic, gravelly-voiced singer ('I am a performer, but only in the metaphysical sense') resolutely declines to divulge his origins. He was first heard of in Toronto during the early 70s, and achieved some popularity on the US television show *Saturday Night Live*. Even then he maintained an air of strict privacy, so much so that the contact number he gave to the legendary jazz and rock producer **John Hammond Jnr.** turned out to be a 'Dial-A-Joke' line. With his trademark fedora, dark glasses, and Groucho Marx moustache, Redbone celebrates a pre-World War II era of ragtime, jazz, blues, and minstrel shows, resurrecting the work of his heroes, who include **'Jelly Roll' Morton**, **Lonnie Johnson**, **Joe Venuti**, the young **Bing Crosby**, and vaudeville performer Emmett Miller. Jazz violinist Venuti was featured on Redbone's *On The Track* in 1976, along with **Don McLean**, who played the banjo. The album is said to have sold more than 100,000 copies, and his next release, *Double Time*, made the US Top 40. Redbone is joined by well-known musical personalities on most of his albums, and for *Whistling In The Wind*, he duetted with **Merle Haggard** on 'Settin' By The Fire' and **Ringo Starr** on 'My Little Grass Shack'. Joe Venuti was present too, and the other tracks on this varied and entertaining set included 'Bouquet Of Roses', 'If I Could Be With You', 'Love Letters In The Sand', and 'I'm Crazy 'Bout My Baby' Redbone's distinctive baritone became familiar to British television viewers in the late 80s/early 90s when he sang 'Relax', 'Sleepy Time', and 'Untwist Again' in a series of commercials with nostalgic themes for British Rail's Inter-City service.

Selected albums: *On The Track* (Warners 1976), *Double Time* (Warners 1977), *Champagne Charlie* (Warners 1978),

From Branch To Branch (ATCO/Emerald 1981), *Red To Blue* (August 1986), *No Regrets* (Sugar Hill 1988), *Christmas Island* (Private Music 1990), *Sugar* (Private Music 1990), *Up A Lazy River* (Private Music 1992), *Whistling In The Wind* (Private Music 1994).

Redd Kross

This Los Angeles, California, USA band was formed in 1979. Redd Kross melded elements of 70s glam-rock, 60s psychedelia and 80s heavy metal to become a popular 'alternative' act in the 80s. Originally called the Tourists, the band changed its name to Red Cross. (They were later forced to change the spelling after the International Red Cross organization threatened to sue.) At the beginning, the band consisted of 15-year-old Jeff McDonald as singer, his 11-year-old brother Steve on bass, Greg Hetson on guitar and Ron Reyes on drums. After gaining local recognition opening for such punk outfits as **Black Flag**, Red Cross made its first recordings in 1980 for a compilation album on the punk label, Posh Boy Records. Shortly afterwards Hetson left to form the **Circle Jerks** and Reyes joined Black Flag. Other musicians came and went throughout the band's history, the McDonald brothers being the only mainstay. The group's popularity grew steadily, particularly among those who listened to college radio stations, and by the end of the 80s they had recorded three albums in addition to the debut. Some featured covers of songs by such influences as the **Rolling Stones** and **Kiss**, while elsewhere the group's originals seemed to cross 70s punk with the bubblegum hits of the 60s. The group resurfaced in the autumn of 1990 with *Third Eye*, their first album for a major label, **Atlantic Records**. However, it was 1993's *Phaseshifter* which brought about their commercial breakthrough, with the band signing with **Nirvana** manager John Silva and continuing to record catchy post-punk homages to 70s kitsch.

Albums: *Born Innocent* (Smoke 7 1982), *Teen Babes From Monsanto* (Gasatanka 1984), *Neurotica* (Big Time 1987), *Third Eye* (Atlantic 1990), *Phaseshifter* (Atlantic 1993).

Redd, Vi

b. Elvira Redd, 10 September 1928, Los Angeles, California, USA. As a child, Redd took up the saxophone and was directed into jazz through the influence of her father, professional jazz drummer Alton Redd. Concentrating on the alto but also playing soprano and singing, Redd's career moved slowly at first but she blossomed in the 60s, appearing nationally and internationally with **Earl 'Fatha' Hines**, **Max Roach**, **Dizzy Gillespie** and other distinguished jazz stars. At the end of the decade she turned to teaching but throughout the 70s and 80s continued to make occasional appearances as a performer. Like most alto saxophonists of her generation, she was deeply influenced by **Charlie Parker** and, like her idol, her playing is redolent with a strong feeling for the blues, as is her singing.

Albums: *Bird Call* (1962), with Al Grey *Shades Of Grey* (1965), with Gene Ammons, Dexter Gordon *The Chase!* (1973), with Marian McPartland *Now's The Time!* (1977).

Redding, Otis

b. 9 September 1941, Dawson, Georgia, USA, d. 10 December 1967. The son of a Baptist minister, Redding assimilated gospel music during his childhood and soon became interested in jump blues and R&B. After resettling in Macon, he became infatuated with local luminary, **Little Richard**, and began singing on a full-time basis. A high-school friend and booking agent, Phil Walden, then became his manager. Through Walden's contacts Redding joined Johnny Jenkins And The Pinetoppers as a sometime singer and occasional driver. Redding also began recording for sundry local independents and his debut single, 'She's Alright', credited to Otis And The Shooters, was quickly followed by 'Shout Bamalama'. Both performances were firmly in the Little Richard mould. The singer's fortunes blossomed when one of his own songs, 'These Arms Of Mine', was picked up for the **Stax** subsidiary, Volt. Recorded at the tail end of a Johnny Jenkins session, this aching ballad crept into the American Hot 100 in May 1963. Further poignant releases, 'Pain In My Heart', 'That's How Strong My Love Is' and 'I've Been Loving You Too Long', were balanced by brassy, uptempo performances including 'Mr. Pitiful', 'Respect' and 'Fa Fa Fa Fa Fa Fa (Sad Song)'. He remained something of a cult figure until 1965 and the release of the magnificent *Otis Blue* in which original material nestled beside the **Rolling Stones**' 'Satisfaction' and two songs by a further mentor, **Sam Cooke**. Redding's version of the **Temptations**' 'My Girl' then became a UK hit, while the singer's popularity was further enhanced by the visit of the *Hit The Road Stax* revue in 1967. 'Tramp', a duet with **Carla Thomas**, also provided success while Redding's production company, Jotis, was responsible for launching **Arthur Conley**. A triumphant appearance at the **Monterey Pop Festival** suggested that Redding was about to attract an even wider following but tragedy struck on 10 December 1967. The light aircraft in which he was travelling plunged into Lake Monona, Madison, Wisconsin, killing the singer, his valet, the pilot and four members of the **Bar-Kays**. The wistful '(Sittin' On) The Dock Of The Bay', a song Redding recorded just three days earlier, became his only million-seller and US pop number 1. The single's seeming serenity, as well as several posthumous album tracks, suggested a sadly unfulfilled maturity. Although many now point to Redding's limited range, his emotional drive remains compelling, while the songs he wrote, often with guitarist **Steve Cropper**, stand among soul's most lasting moments. Redding is rightly regarded as a giant of soul music.

Albums: *Pain In My Heart* (1964), *The Great Otis Redding Sings Soul Ballads* (1965), *Otis Blue/Otis Redding Sings Soul* (1965), *The Soul Album* (1966), *Complete And Unbelievable ... The Otis Redding Dictionary Of Soul* (1966), *Live In Europe* (1967), with Carla Thomas *The King & Queen* (1967), *Here Comes Some Soul From Otis Redding And Little Joe Curtis* (1967, pre-1962 recordings), *The Dock Of The Bay* (1968), *The Immortal Otis Redding* (1968), *Otis Redding In Person At The Whiskey A Go Go* (1968), *Love Man* (1969), *Tell The Truth* (1970), shared with Jimi Hendrix *Monterey International Pop Festival* (1970), *Live Otis Redding* (1982), *Remember Me* (1992), *Good To Me* (1993). Selected compilations: *The History Of Otis Redding* (1967), *The Best Of Otis Redding* (1972), *Pure Otis* (1979), *Come To Me* (1984), *Dock Of The Bay-The Definitive Collection* (1987), *The Otis Redding Story* (1989, 4-album box-set), *Remember Me* (US title) *It's Not Just Sentimental* (UK title) (1992, previously unissued recordings), *Otis!: The Definitive Otis Redding* (1993, 4-CD boxed-set).

Further reading: *The Otis Redding Story*, Jane Schiesel.

Reddy, Helen

b. 25 October 1942, Melbourne, Victoria, Australia, A big-voiced interpreter of rock ballads, with a reputation as a high-profile feminist and campaigner on social issues, Helen Reddy came from a show business family. She was a child performer and had already starred in her own television show before winning a trip to New York in an Australian talent contest in 1966. There, an appearance on the influential *Tonight Show* led to a recording contract with **Capitol**, and a 1971 hit single with 'I Don't Know How To Love Him' from **Andrew Lloyd Webber** and **Tim Rice**'s *Jesus Christ Superstar*. The following year, the powerful feminist anthem, 'I Am Woman', which she co-wrote with **Peter Allen**, went to number 1 in the US, and sold over a million copies. It also gained Reddy a Grammy for best female vocal performance (part of her acceptance speech went: 'I want to thank God because she makes everything possible'), and was adopted by the United Nations as its theme for International Women's Year. Over the next five years, she had a dozen further hit singles, including 'Leave Me Alone (Ruby Red Dress), 'Keep On Singing', 'You And Me Against The World', 'Emotion', and two contrasting number 1s, **Alex Harvey**'s modern country ballad 'Delta Dawn' (1973), and the chilling, dramatic 'Angie Baby' in 1974. Her 1976 hit, 'I Can't Hear You No More', was composed by **Carole King** and **Gerry Goffin,** while Reddy's final Top 20 record (to date) was a revival of **Cilla Black**'s 1964 chart-topper, 'You're My World', co-produced by **Kim Fowley**. Reddy also became a well-known television personality, hosting the *Midnight Special* show for most of the 70s, taking a cameo role in *Airport 75* and starring in the

1978 film *Pete's Dragon*. She also sang 'Little Boys', the theme song for the film *The Man Who Loved Women* (1983). Disenchanted with life in general during the 80s, she performed infrequently, but made her first major showcase in years at the Westwood Playhouse, Los Angeles, in 1986. Since then she has appeared in concert and cabaret around the world. In 1995 she was performing at London's Café Royal in the evenings, while rehearsing during the day to take over from **Carole King** in the hit musical ***Blood Brothers*** on Broadway.

Albums: *I Don't Know How To Love Him* (1971), *Helen Reddy* (1971), *I Am Woman* (1972), *Long Hard Climb* (1973), *Love Song For Jeffrey* (1974), *Free And Easy* (1974), *No Way To Treat A Lady* (1975), *Music Music* (1976), *Ear Candy* (1977), *We'll Sing In The Sunshine* 1978, *Live In London* (1979), *Reddy* (1979), *Take What You Find* (1980), *Play Me Out* (1981), *Imagination* (1983), *Take It Home* (1984). Compilations: *Helen Reddy's Greatest Hits* (1975), *The Very Best Of...* (1993).

Redeye

Redeye was formed in 1970 by guitarist Douglas 'Red' Mark, a former member of the Los Angeles, USA, pop-psychedelic group **Sunshine Company**. Mark teamed with David Hodgkins (guitar/vocals), Bill Kirkham (bass) and Bobby Bereman (drums). The rock group signed to the small Pentagram label and released the single 'Games' in late 1970; it eventually landed in the Top 30 nationally. A second single, 'Redeye Blues', was issued in the spring of 1971, although it was banned in many radio markets due to its lyrical content - some programmers objected to the song's story-line about a person getting stoned and then unable to find his drug stash. Nevertheless, the single charted. The group was unable to follow it with another hit and split up in 1972.

Album: *Redeye* (1970).

Redgum

Formed in Adelaide, Australia in 1975, the success of Redgum's brand of folk/rock political satire has since been regarded as an anomaly, albeit thoroughly deserved. The core members comprised university students John Schumann (vocals/guitar), Verity Truman (vocals/tin whistle/saxophone), Michael Atkinson (vocals/guitar/mandolin), and have in the past included 15 other musicians. After going professional the band built up their support base by constant touring featuring an excellent live show, with stage wit provided by Schumann, whose droll voice was the antithesis of the traditional rock hero. Their debut album provides some of their best material, comprising typically astute observations on the rich, the hypocritical, politicians and the plight of the under privileged, but it was only originally available on a small independent label. National mainstream success

was not achieved until the release of 'I Was Only 19', in 1983, a song written about a survivor of the Vietnam war, which compares favourably with three other poignant anti-war songs by fellow Australians - 'Jungle Green' by **Broderick Smith**, 'The Band Played Waltzing Matilda' by **Eric Bogle** and 'Khe Sahn' by **Cold Chisel**. A second hit single, the reggae-flavoured 'I've Been To Bali Too' (1984) hit home with many Australian tourists. As the band lost more original members, they began to lack their characteristic bite even though their albums became better produced. A third Australian chart single in 1987, 'Roll It On Robbie', caused outrage amongst the conservative elements of the country because it encouraged the use of condoms to promote safe-sex. At their peak, Redgum were among the top five live acts in Australia despite not having a national hit for some time. Schumann has since recorded two solo albums, his collection of children's music is probably the more popular of the two. He has also worked in record production and children's television.

Albums: *If You Don't Fight You Lose* (1978), *Virgin Ground* (1978), *Brown Rice And Kerosene* (1983), *Caught In The Act* (1983), *Frontline* (1985), *Midnight Sun* (1987).

Redhead

Composer **Albert Hague** and veteran lyricist and librettist **Dorothy Fields** came together for the first time to write the score for this musical which opened at the 46th Street Theatre in New York on 5 February 1959. Fields, together with her brother, Herbert, and their fellow authors, Sydney Sheldon and David Shaw, came up with what was an unusual subject for a Broadway musical - a murder mystery. Set in Victorian London at around the time of the Jack the Ripper killings, the story has Essie Whimple (**Gwen Verdon**) and Tom Baxter (Richard Kiley) chasing suspects around various parts of the metropolis, including a waxworks museum bearing a remarkable resemblance to Madame Tussaud's emporium. Hague and Fields's score is not considered to be remarkable, but any show that contains such engaging songs as 'I Feel Merely Marvellous', 'The Right Finger Of My Right Hand', and 'Look Who's In Love', merits serious consideration. Add to those, Gwen Verdon's music hall version of 'Erbie Fitch's Twitch', and several other bright numbers, including 'I'm Back In Circulation', The Uncle Sam Rag', 'My Girl Is Just Enough Woman For Me', and 'We Loves Ya, Jimmy', and it certainly was not all bad news. The **Tony Awards** committee certainly did not think so, and their kudos went to Verdon, Kiley, and Hague, along with others for best musical, libretto, and **Bob Fosse**'s brilliant choreography. The public gave the show their vote, too, and it ran for well over a year, a total of 452 performances.

Redhead Kingpin And FBI

b. David Guppy, c.1970, Englewood, New Jersey, New York State, USA, and nicknamed after his bright red hair. Guppy is a polite, dignified humourist whose raps mingle coy allusion without lapses into vulgar detail. After all, his mother is a serving member of the police force, and he refused to swear on his albums in case she heard the cussing. His career began when he hooked up with Gene Griffin's Sutra Records, via an introduction from his former camp counsellor. He determindedly set out his stall against B-boy culture, insisting instead on moral rectitide in all matters. If that seeemed a little boring, then the message was rescued by his excellent breakthrough single, 'Do The Right Thing'. Although he has gone on to score several minor hits with songs like '3-2-1 Pump', he has yet to equal that moment of artistic and chart success. His backing band, the FBI (For Black Intelligence), consisted of DJ Wildstyle, Bo Roc, Lt. Squeak, Buzz and Poochie. The group later changed its name to Private Investigations.
Albums: *A Shade Of Red* (Virgin 1989), *The Album With No Name* (Virgin 1991), *React Like You Know* (Virgin 1993).

Redman

New Jersey-based rapper whose debut album broke the Top 50 of the US Billboard album charts, failing to get a UK release until much later in the year, after it had moved over 300,000 copies on home turf. Enshrining the new ethos of cannabis as the drug of choice ('How To Roll A Blunt'), there was also room for the traditional braggadacio ('Day Of Sooperman Lover', 'I'm A Bad'). As superb an album as it was, from the cover shot of the artist up to his elbows in blood onwards, many critics also noted it was a little close to **EPMD**. Not surprising considering that he was a member of .their Hit Squad, alongside **K-Solo** and **Das EFX**, and that Erick Sermon had produced it. In fact Redman had spent two years living with the latter when both his parents chucked him out of their respective homes because he was 'selling drugs and shit'.
Albums: *Whut? Thee Album* (RAL 1992), *Dare Iz A Darkside* (Def Jam 1995).

Redman, Dewey

b. 17 May 1931, Fort Worth, Texas, USA. After first playing clarinet at school, where one of his musical companions was **Ornette Coleman**, Redman turned to alto saxophone and later still took up the tenor. One of many well-versed students at North Texas State University, Redman became a professional musician on graduation. In the late 60s and through into the mid-70s he played and recorded with Coleman, **Charlie Haden**, **Roswell Rudd**, **Keith Jarrett** and **Carla Bley**. In 1976 he formed Old and New Dreams, a

quartet completed by **Don Cherry**, **Ed Blackwell** and Haden, touring and recording into the mid-80s. An eclectic musician, seamlessly linking the blues with freeform music over a hard bop base, Redman's playing style constantly demonstrates his technical mastery of his instruments which sometimes include the Arabian musette. He also composes and arranges much of the material he performs and records, drawing inspiration from eastern music as well as that of his own heritage.
Albums: *Look For The Black Star* (1966), with Ornette Coleman *New York Is Now* (1968), *Ear Of The Behearer* (1973), *Coincide* (1974), *Old And New Dreams* i (1976), *Soundsigns* (1978), *Old And New Dreams* ii (1979), *Redman And Blackwell In Willisau* (Black Saint 1980), *The Struggle Continues* (ECM 1982), *Living On The Edge* (Black Saint 1989), *Choices* (Enja 1992).

Redman, Don

b. 29 July 1900, Piedmont, West Virginia, USA, d. 30 November 1964. A gifted child, alto saxophonist Redman studied extensively and by his graduation had mastered most of the wind instruments and was also adept at arranging. He then joined a **territory band** based in Pittsburgh, Pennsylvania, with whom he visited New York. This was in 1923 and by the following year he had begun a musical relationship with **Fletcher Henderson** that was to alter perceptions of big band jazz. In 1927 he took over leadership of **McKinney's Cotton Pickers**, continuing to develop the arranging style with which he had experimented while with Henderson. In 1931 Redman formed his own band which remained in existence for almost a decade. During this period Redman wrote charts for numerous other big bands and after his own unit folded he pursued this aspect of his career, writing for **Jimmy Dorsey**, **Count Basie**, **Jimmie Lunceford**, **Harry James** and many others. In 1946 he formed a new band, taking it to Europe and subsequently worked in radio and television. For several years he was musical director for **Pearl Bailey**, occasionally recording and dedicating what time he could spare to composing. Originally inspired by the creative genius of **Louis Armstrong** who joined the Henderson band while he was arranger, Redman went on to lay many of the ground rules for much of what is today regarded as 'big band music'. In his work for Henderson, the Cotton Pickers and his own band he consistently demonstrated his confident grasp of all arranging techniques in use up to his time, extending them to prove that an arranged format need not lose the spontaneity of an improvised performance and, indeed, could enhance the work of a good jazz soloist. In particular, his writing for the reed and brass sections, in which he set up call-and-response passages, while polished to perfection by such successors as **Sy Oliver**, has rarely been improved upon.

Selected albums: *For Europeans Only* (1946), *Don Redman's Park Avenue Patters* (1957), *July 22nd And 26th, 1957* (1957), *Don Redman And The Knights Of The Round Table* (1959), *Shakin' The African* (Hep Jazz 1986). Selected compilations: *Don Redman And His Orchestra 1931-1933* (1931-33), *Doin' The New Low Down* (Hep Jazz 1984, 1932-33 recordings), *Redman's Red Book* (1932-36), *Smoke Rings* (Nostalgia 1988), *Don Redman* (1932-37), *1936-1939* (Classics 1991), *Doin' What I Please* (1993).

Redman, Joshua

b. 1 February 1969, Berkeley, California, USA. The latest in a long line of intensively marketed young jazz musicians, Joshua Redman saw his star rise dramatically in 1991, when he burst suddenly into the international arena in his (very) early 20s with all the right credentials (a hard-bop influenced style, good looks, a Harvard education, a famous saxophone playing father [see **Dewey Redman**] and a compelling fluency and originality that captured the imagination of the older generation of jazz musicians). Despite the inevitable media tag lines, Redman was influenced less by his famous father, whom he saw infrequently, than by his mother, who always encouraged an awareness of music, and enrolled him at Berkeley's Centre For World Music at the age of five, to study Indian and Indonesian music. Whilst his flair for music was obvious, his flair for practise was less clear, and although he played in the jazz big band and combo while at school, he displayed little genuine commitment. Concentrating, instead, on a glittering academic career, he won a place at Harvard to study social sciences. It was there that he began to listen to jazz in earnest, studying records by the post-war master saxophonists, and spending summer breaks in Boston with the **Berklee College Of Music** jazz students. Graduating in 1991 (with highly distinguished grades), he accepted a place at Yale Law School, but took a year off to dabble in the New York music scene. He began attending jam sessions and playing the odd sideman gig, and then, in the Autumn of 1991, won the **Thelonious Monk** International Saxophone Competition. This prestigious award threw Redman into the limelight, and he soon found himself working with a host of jazz legends, including **Elvin Jones**, **Jack DeJohnette**, **Red Rodney**, **Paul Motian**, **Roy Hargrove** and John Hicks, and winning *Jazz Times* readers' poll Best New Jazz Artist in 1992, **Rolling Stone**'s Hot Jazz Artist Of 1993 and *Down Beat*'s critics' poll's Number 1 Tenor Saxophonist Deserving Of Wider Recognition (1993). Signed to Warners, his eponymous debut album was released in March 1993 to widespread critical acclaim, but never reached the UK. *Wish*, his all-star second featuring **Pat Metheny**, **Charlie Haden** and **Billy Higgins**, helped spread the word to the UK, and serves as a good introduction to his warm and swinging style. In 1994 he joined older saxophone star **Joe Lovano** on a lively and extrovert two tenor date for the **Blue Note** label.

Albums: *Joshua Redman* (Warners 1993), *Wish* (Warners 1993), with Joe Lovano *Tenor Legacy* (Blue Note 1994), *Mood Swings* (Warners 1994).

Rednex

In the wake of the **Grid**'s innovative coupling of down home hillbilly with techno, there were bound to be those waiting in the wings to duplicate the formula. Rednex were ostensibly a five-piece family affair, comprising Mary Joe (vocals), Ken Tacky (vocals/banjo), Bobby Sue (violin) and Billie Ray (violin). The press story conjured up to describe their evolution was entertaining enough to repeat: drawing personnel from Brunkeflo City, Idaho, where Mary Joe's ancestors moved to from Sweden (where she grew up) two centuries ago. 'Billie Ray and Ken Tacky are cousins, Billie Ray and Bobbie Sue are half-brothers cos they have the same father. My cousin's aunt is sister to Bobbie Sue's cousin's uncle. Since my family moved there, no one has come in from the outside, so everyone in the town is related in some way'. However, *Waltons* shenanigans aside, there was doubtless more truth in the fact that Euro-dance producer Pat Reniz had a large hand in the project. Rednex enjoyed massive success with 'Cotton-Eye Joe', a UK number 1, following up with the near-identikit 'Old Pop In An Oak'.

Album: *Sex And Violins* (Internal Affairs 1995).

Redpath, Jean

b. 28 April 1937, Edinburgh, Scotland. This traditional singer and guitar player is well-known for her children's songs and her extensive collection of the works of Robert Burns. Redpath emigrated to the USA in 1961. After an indifferent start, she moved to New York, and within six weeks had played the renowned Gerde's Folk City. Although *Skipping Barefoot Through The Heather* was recorded on Prestige International before *Scottish Ballad Book*, on Elektra, the latter was released first. The Robert Burns project began in 1976, but was different from another series of Burns songs produced for Scottish Records. For *The Scottish Fiddle - The Music And The Songs*, Jean had wanted to combine the violin and cello as they have long been associated with Scottish traditional music. The blend was successful, giving a classic, almost mournful, feel to the music. During the latter part of the 70s, Jean was lecturing in the music department of the Wesleyan University. Always productive, Redpath continues to perform and record traditional folk music.

Albums: *Scottish Ballad Book* (c.1964), *Skipping Barefoot Through The Heather* (c.1965), *Songs Of Love, Lilt And Laughter* (1966), *Laddie Lie Near Me* (1967), *Frae My Ain Country* (1973), *Jean Redpath* (1975), with Lisa Neustadt

Shout For Joy (1975), *There Were Minstrels* (1976), *The Songs Of Robert Burns Vol.1* (1976), *Jean Redpath With Guests* (1977), *Song Of The Seals* (1978), with Abby Newton *Father Adam* (1979), with Newton *Lowlands* (1980), *The Songs Of Robert Burns Vol.2* (1980), *The Songs Of Robert Burns Vol.3* (1982), *The Songs Of Robert Burns Vol.4* (1983), with the Angel Band *Anywhere Is Home* (1984), with Neustadt and the Angel Band *Angels Hovering Round* (c.1984), with Newton *Lady Nairne* (1986), *The Songs Of Robert Burns Vol.5* (1985), with Newton, Alistair Hardie *The Scottish Fiddle - The Music And The Songs* (1985), *The Songs Of Robert Burns Vol.6* (1987), with Abby *Lady Naime* (1987), with Newton *A Fine Song For Singing* (1987), *Leaving The Land* (1990), *The Songs Of Robert Burns Vol.7* (c.1990).

Redskins

This politically-motivated English trio united the left-wing skinhead movement with a volatile mix of punk and northern soul, aggression and belligerence. Originally formed in York as No Swastikas, they relocated to London where singer/guitarist and **New Musical Express** writer Chris Dean (b. c.1963) assumed the identity of X. Moore. The other original members were Martin Hewes (bass) and Nick King (drums). They were joined in the studio and on stage by a fluid brass section, the most permanent members of which were Lloyd Dwyer and Steve Nicol. After the strident debut, 'Peasant Army', on Leeds based independent CNT Records in 1982, they secured a session for the **John Peel** BBC Radio 1 programme which would be repeated five times. The follow-up, 'Lean On Me' was voted Single Of The Year by *Sounds* journalist Gary Bushell. Given a high media profile by dint of their exclusively political lyrics (they were all members of the Socialist Workers Party), interest from major record companies soon followed, leading to a deal with **London Records**. After personal disagreements, King was replaced by Paul Hookham (ex-English Subtitles, Lemons, **Woodentops**) on the eve of the band's second major tour. By 1984 they had become vigorous supporters of the striking National Union of Miners, playing a host of benefits on their behalf, though 'Keep On Keeping On' and subsequent singles were no match for their earlier promise. The debut album, *Neither Washington Nor Moscow*, was impressive, but critics still cited the band as under-achievers, a fate they condemned themselves to when they broke up in 1986. Hewes returned to life as a motorcycle despatch rider.
Album: *Neither Washington Nor Moscow* (London 1986).

Redwing

Redwing originated in a Colorado trio, Tim Tom And Ron, which featured Timothy B. Schmit (b. 30 October 1947, Sacramento, California, USA; guitar/bass/vocals), Tom Phillips (guitar/pedal steel/vocals) and Ron Flogel (guitar/vocals). They developed into the Contenders with the addition of George Hullin (drums), but this surf-based unit took the name the New Breed when the group embraced a garage-cum-folk/rock direction. The same quartet moved to Sacramento, California where they were later known as both Never Mind and Glad. Schmit joined **Poco** as bassist in 1970 and was replaced by Andrew Samuels. Securing a permanent bass player would plague the band for years, and while Samuels, normally a lead guitarist, often performed the bass duties in the studio, this role was tackled by various personnel and on occasion calling upon the erstwhile member Schmit to stand in. This reshaped line-up evolved to become Redwing, and the masters of a self-financed album secured a deal with **Fantasy Records**. The band's sound embraced a taut, melodic style, based on country-rock which was to become identifiable with California in the ensuing years. However their five albums were marred by inconsistency. The group was unable to garner a significant following, and split up following the release of *Beyond The Sun And Stars*.
Albums: *Redwing* (1971), *What This Country Needs* (1972), *Take Me Home* (1973), *Dead Or Alive* (1974), *Beyond The Sun And Stars* (1975).

Reece, Dizzy

b. Alphonso Reece, 5 January 1931, Kingston, Jamaica. After playing in Jamaica as a young teenager, trumpeter Reece moved to the UK in 1948. During the next few years he established a reputation in the UK and throughout Europe, working mostly with bop musicians like **Kenny Graham**, **Victor Feldman** and **Tubby Hayes**. Reece also occasionally played with such leading swing era figures as **Don Byas**. At the end of the 50s, an especially active period of creative work, Reece settled in the USA. There he played with **Duke Jordan**, **Philly Joe Jones** and others, and made occasional and usually well-spaced return trips to Europe with bands such as that led by **Dizzy Gillespie** and the Paris Reunion Band. A technically-gifted player with an eclectic yet distinctive playing style, Reece has not been recorded as often or as well as his talent deserves.
Albums: *Progress Report* (Jasmine 1956), *Victor Feldman In London* (1956), *Blues In Trinity* (1958), *Star Bright* (1959), *Soundin' Off* (1960), with Duke Jordan *Flight To Jordan* (1960), *Asia Minor* (Original Jazz Classics 1962), with Philly Joe Jones *'Round Midnite* (1966), *From In To Out* (1970), *Possession, Exorcism, Peace* (Honeydew 1972), *Manhattan Project* (Beehive 1978), *Moose The Mooche* (Discovery 1978), *Blowin' Away* (Interplay 1979).

Reed, A.C.

b. Aaron Corthen Reed, 9 May 1926, Wordell, Missouri, USA. Reed was attracted to the saxophone by hearing a **Jay 'Hootie' McShann** record. On moving to Chicago at the age of 15, he bought a saxophone and studied music, although he was tutored in the blues by J.T. Brown. He spent much of the 50s touring the southwestern states with blues musician Dennis Binder. The following decade he re-established himself in Chicago, recording in his own right for several small labels, even enjoying a minor hit with 'Talkin' 'Bout My Friends' on Nike Records in the mid-60s. He became an in-demand session musician for over three decades. He has had long spells in the bands of **Buddy Guy** and **Albert Collins** but now has a successful solo career. Reed's vocals, powerful saxophone playing and often witty songwriting have been recorded for the white collector market by Alligator and Wolf, and he also runs his own Ice Cube label.

Album: *Take These Blues And Shove 'Em* (1984).

Reed, Dan, Network

Along with **Living Colour**, this band led the way in the late 80s growth of funk-rock. Formed in Oregon, USA, the Network featured Dan Reed (vocals), Melvin Brannon II (b. 6 July 1962; bass), Brion James (lead guitar), Daniel Pred (drums), and Blake Sakamoto (keyboards). Signed to **Mercury Records**, they released their first, self-titled album in 1988, which contrasted the commercial rock of artists such as **Bon Jovi** with the funk rhythms of **Prince**. The album was enthusiastically received by those craving rock music with a difference, as tracks such as 'Get To You' and 'Ritual' soon became dance floor hits at rock club bastions. That debut was followed by *Slam*, produced by **Nile Rodgers** of **Chic** fame, who gave the album a slightly harder edge while still retaining the funk element of its predecessor. A single, 'Rainbow Child', provided the band with its first minor UK hit single, briefly entering the Top 40 in 1989. Prestigious support slots were gained in 1990 in Europe with Bon Jovi and the **Rolling Stones**, which helped to raise their profile and bring their music to much larger audiences. In 1991 *The Heat* was released, which saw them reunited with Bruce Fairburn, producer of their first album. This included a highly original version of **Pink Floyd**'s 'Money' as well as the singles 'Mix It Up' and 'Baby Now I', neither of which made an impression in the charts. Despite critical acclaim, support slots on major tours and a fair degree of radio exposure, Dan Reed Network have yet to achieve their big commercial break and have had to watch contemporaries such as Living Colour and **Faith No More** achieve platinum status.

Albums: *Dan Reed Network* (Mercury 1988), *Slam* (Mercury 1989), *The Heat* (Mercury 1991). Compilation: *Mixing It Up - The Best Of* (Mercury 1993).

Reed, Jerry

b. Jerry Hubbard, 20 March 1937, Atlanta, Georgia, USA. Reed has had three distinct careers: as a respected country guitarist, as a composer and singer of clever pop/country hits and as a genial, jokey television personality and film actor. A cotton mill worker, he was one of many youths brought up on country music who played rockabilly in the mid-50s. His own records for **Capitol** were unsuccessful but Reed's songs were taken up by **Gene Vincent** ('Crazy Legs') and **Brenda Lee**. After army service, Reed moved to Nashville working as a session guitarist and scoring minor hits with 'Hully Gully Guitars' and the traditional 'Goodnight Irene'. He also wrote songs for **Porter Wagoner** ('Misery Loves Company') and **Johnny Cash** ('A Thing Called Love') Reed's skill at the finger-picking guitar style was showcased on two duet albums with **Chet Atkins** in the 70s. Atkins also produced Reed's albums and singles. Reed's career gathered momentum after he signed a recording contract with **RCA** in 1965. Two years later he recorded the boastful 'Guitar Man' and 'U.S. Male' both of which were covered successfully by **Elvis Presley** in 1968. Reed had two big US pop hits in 1971 with the swamp-rock styled 'Amos Moses' and 'When You're Hot, You're Hot' (based on his television catch-phrase), but his continuing popularity was with country audiences; the latter was a US country chart number one for five weeks. Another country number 1 followed with 'Lord Mr Ford' in 1973, a humorous attack on the cost of running a car in the 70s. During the late 70s he was less successful but he returned to prominence with the recording of the Tim DuBois song 'She Got The Goldmine (I Got The Shaft)' for **RCA** in 1982. Produced by **Rick Hall**, it was a country number 1. Reed became well known to television viewers with appearances on **Glen Campbell**'s show in the early 70s. This led to cameo roles in several Burt Reynolds movies including *W.W. And the Dixie Dance Kings* (1975), *Gator* (1976) and *Smokey And The Bandit* (1977).

Albums: *Tupelo Mississippi Flash* (1967), *Alabama Wild Man* (1969), *Cookin'* (1970), *Georgia Sunshine* (1971), *When You're Hot You're Hot* (1971), *Ko Ko Joe* (1972), *Jerry Reed* (1972), *Hot A Mighty* (1973), *Lord Mr Ford* (1973), *Half And Half* (1974), *Live At Exit Inn - Hot Stuff* (1974) *Red Hot Picker* (1975), *Uptown Poker Club* (1975), *Smell The Flowers* (1975), *Me And Chet* (1976), *Sweet Love Feelings A Good Woman's Love* (1977), *Sings Jim Croce* (1977), *Eastbound And Down* (1977), *Both Barrels* (1978), *In Concert* (1980), with Chet Atkins *Sneakin' Around* (1992). Compilations: *The Best Of Jerry Reed* (1972), *20 Of The Best* (1982).

Reed, Jimmy

b. Mathis James Reed, 6 September 1925, Leland, Mississippi, USA, d. 29 August 1976, Oakland, California, USA. Jimmy Reed was a true original, he sang in a lazy mush-mouthed ramble, played limited, if instantly recognizable harmonica, and even more minimal guitar. He produced a series of hits in the 50s that made him the most successful blues singer of the era. He was born into a large sharecropping family and spent his early years on Mr. Johnny Collier's plantation situated near Dunleith, Mississippi. Here, he formed a childhood friendship with **Eddie Taylor** which was to have a marked effect on his later career. Reed sang in church and learned rudimentary guitar along with Taylor, but while Eddie progressed Jimmy never became more than basically competent on the instrument. Jimmy left school in 1939 and found work farming around Duncan and Meltonia, Mississippi. Around 1943-44 he left the south to find work in Chicago where opportunities abounded due to the war effort. He was drafted in 1944 and served out his time in the US Navy. Discharged in 1945 he returned briefly to Mississippi before gravitating north once more to the Chicago area. Working in the steel mills, Reed gigged around in his leisure time with a friend named Willie Joe Duncan, who played a one-string guitar, or Diddley-bow. He also re-established contact with Eddie Taylor who had also moved north to try his luck. This led to his becoming known on the local club scene and after appearances with **John** and **Grace Brim** Reed secured a recording contract with **VeeJay Records** in 1953. His initial sessions, though highly regarded by collectors, produced no hits and VeeJay were considering dropping him from their roster when in 1955 'You Don't Have To Go' took off. From then on, his success was phenomenal as a string of hits such as 'Ain't That Lovin' You Baby', 'You've Got Me Dizzy', 'Bright Lights Big City', 'I'm Gonna Get My Baby' and 'Honest I Do' carried him through to the close of the decade. Many of these timeless blues numbers were adopted by every white R&B beat group during the early 60s. Two of his songs are now standard and often used as rousing encores by name bands; 'Baby What You Do You Want Me To Do' closed the **Byrds**' live performances for many years and 'Big Boss Man' is arguably the most performed song of its kind. Much of the credit for this success must be attributed to his friend Eddie Taylor, who played on most of Reed's sessions, and his wife, Mama Reed, who wrote many of his songs and even sat behind him in the studio reciting the lyrics into his forgetful ear as he sang. On some recordings her participation is audible. Jimmy's songs had little to do with the traditional blues, but they were eminently danceable and despite employing the basic blues line-up of harmonica, guitars and drums were generally classed as R&B. His hits were 'crossovers' appealing to whites as well as blacks. Perhaps this contributed to his continuing success as the blues entered its post-rock 'n' roll hard times. In his later days at VeeJay, various gimmicks were tried such as dubbing an album's worth of 12-string guitar solos over his backing tracks, faking live performances and introducing a commentary between album cuts; none

were too successful in reviving his flagging sales. To counter the positive elements in his life, Reed was continually undermined by his own unreliability, illness (he was an epileptic) and a fascination for the bottle. He visited Europe in the early 60s by which time it was obvious that not all was well with him. He was supremely unreliable and prone to appear on stage drunk. By the mid-60s his career was in the hands of the controversial Al Smith and his recordings were appearing on the Bluesway label. Inactive much of the time due to illness, Reed seemed on the road to recovery and further success, having controlled his drink problem. Ironically he died soon after of respiratory failure. He was buried in Chicago. Reed is an important figure who has influenced countless artists through his songs. **Steve Miller** recorded *Living In The 20th Century* with a segment of Reed songs and dedicated the album to him. The **Rolling Stones**, **Pretty Things** and the **Grateful Dead** also acknowledge a considerable debt to him.
Albums: *I'm Jimmy Reed* (VeeJay 1958), *Rockin' With Reed* (VeeJay 1959), *Found Love* (VeeJay 1960), *Now Appearing* (VeeJay 1960), *At Carnegie Hall* (VeeJay 1961), *Just Jimmy Reed* (VeeJay 1962), *T'ain't No Big Thing...But He Is!* (VeeJay 1963), *The Best Of The Blues* (VeeJay 1963), *The 12-String Guitar Blues* (VeeJay 1963), *Jimmy Reed At Soul City* (VeeJay 1964), *The Legend, The Man* (VeeJay 1965), *The New Jimmy Reed Album* (Bluesway 1967), *Soulin'* (Bluesway 1967), *Big Boss Man* (Bluesway 1968), *Down In Virginia* (Bluesway 1969), *As Jimmy Is* (Roker 1970), Let *The Bossman Speak!* (Blues On Blues 1971). Compilations: *The Best Of Jimmy Reed* (VeeJay 1962), *More Of The Best Of Jimmy Reed* (VeeJay 1964), *The Soulful Sound Of Jimmy Reed* (Upfront 1970), *I Ain't From Chicago* (Bluesway 1973), *The Ultimate Jimmy Reed* (Bluesway 1973), *Cold Chills* (Antilles 1976), *Jimmy Reed Is Back* (Roots 1980), *Hard Walkin' Hanna* (Versatile 1980), *Greatest Hits* (Hollywood 1992), *Speak The Lyrics To Me, Mama Reed* (VeeJay 1993).

Reed, Les

b. 24 July 1935, Woking, Surrey, England. A pianist, conductor, arranger, musical director, and highly succesful composer, particularly in the 60s and 70s. Reed's father, a semi-professional mouth-organist with a local troupe, the Westfield Kids, was eager to formalize his son's interest in music. Keyboard lessons from the age of six, and a spell as the Kids' accordionist prefaced a Royal College of Music scholarship and National Service in the Royal East Kent Regiment. As well as learning clarinet, he also played piano in a mess dance band that included saxophonist **Tony Coe** who, years on, would assist Reed and **Robert Farnon** on *Pop Makes Progress*. On demobilization in 1956, Reed became a freelance session player, then joined the **John Barry** Seven who, as well as playing in concerts and on records in their own right, backed other artists -

notably those appearing on **Jack Good**'s *Oh Boy!* television series. Among them was **Adam Faith**, for whom Reed wrote a b-side. From this small beginning as a pop composer, Reed's 60-odd major hits since have earned numerous gold discs, **Ivor Novello** awards and, in 1982, the British Academy Gold Badge Of Merit. In the mid-60s, it was unusual for a British singles chart not to list a Les Reed song (usually with collaborators like **Gordon Mills,** Geoff Stephens or Barry Mason). Among numerous Top 30 acts indebted to Reed as writer and arranger are the **Applejacks** ('Tell Me When'), **Tom Jones** ('It's Not Unusual', 'Delilah'), **P.J. Proby**, **Mirielle Mathieu**, **Engelbert Humperdinck** ('The Last Waltz'), **Des O'Connor** ('I Pretend') and the **Dave Clark Five** (Everybody Knows', 1967). In 1969, towards the end of their regular partnership, Reed and Mason wrote 'Love Is All', a powerful ballad with which **Malcolm Roberts** triumphed at the San Remo Song Festival. Reed subsequently became one of the best known faces at annual song festivals all over the world, and his contributions as a conductor, arranger and soloist were recognized in 1977 when he accepted an invitation to become President of The International Federation of Festivals (FIDOF) for one year, and then served as its Ambassador. His work in the late 60s included two songs with Robin Conrad, 'Don't Bring Me Your Heartaches', a hit for **Paul and Barry Ryan**, and 'Leave A Little Love', which received a compelling treatment from **Lulu**. Reed also collaborated with comedian Jackie Rae for 'When There's No You', another of Humperdinck's US hits, and 'Please Don't Go', which provided veteran singer **Donald Peers** with his first chart entry. Both songs were adapted from classical pieces. Reed's renewed working association with Geoff Stephens in the late 60s and early 70s resulted in 'There's A Kind Of Hush' for **Herman's Hermits**, 'Daughter Of Darkness' for Tom Jones, and a Leeds United football song. 'There's a Kind Of Hush' was successfully revived by the **Carpenters** in 1976. Reed and Stephens also won the Silver Prize at the 1973 Tokyo Music Festival for their composition 'Sandy Sandy' which was sung by Frankie Stephens. Four years later, Reed and Tony Macaulay won the International Song Contest at Mallorca with 'You And I'. And in 1980, together with lyricist **Roger Greenaway** and singer Marilyn Miller, Reed carried off the Grand Prix Award in Seoul for 'Everytime You Go'. Other artists who have recorded Reed's songs over the years have included **Elvis Presley** ('Girl Of Mine'), **Shirley Bassey** ('Does Anybody Miss Me') and **Bing Crosby** ('That's What Life Is All About', said to be the last recording he made before his death in 1977). Reed has also composed several film scores including *Crossplot, Girl On A Motor Cycle, One More Time, My Mother's Lovers, Bush Baby*, and *Creepshow 2*, and has written for stage musicals such as *The Magic Show,*

American Heroes and *And Then I Wrote*. When Reed celebrated 30 years in the music business in 1989, he was estimated to have written more than 2,000 songs. In the summer of 1994 he produced a CD with **Max Bygraves** and the Children of Arnhem which they hoped would raise money for the old Veterans who were returning to Arnhem in September. The titles included his 1973 composition 'Lest We Forget'. All his artist's royalties from this piece are donated in perpetuity to the 'Lest We Forget' Association. In the same year he was made a Freeman of the City of London for his 'contribution to the music industry'. Still resident in Surrey, Reed has executive interests in a Guildford radio station (County Sound) and his daughter Donna's publishing company, Rebecca Music Ltd.

Selected albums: *Fly Me To The Sun* (Deram 60s), *New Dimensions* (Deram 60s), *The New World Of Les Reed* (Chapter One), *The Hit Making World Of Les Reed* (Decca).

Reed, Lou

b. Louis Firbank, 2 March 1942, Freeport, Long Island, New York, USA. A member of several high-school bands, Reed made his recording debut with the Shades in 1957. Their 'So Blue' enjoyed brief notoriety when played by influential disc jockey Murray The K, but was lost in the plethora of independent singles released in this period. Having graduated from Syracuse University, Reed took a job as a contract songwriter with Pickwick Records which specialized in cash-in, exploitative recordings. His many compositions from this era included 'The Ostrich' (1965), a tongue-in-cheek dance song which so impressed the label hierarchy that Reed formed the Primitives to promote it as a single. The group also included a recent acquaintance, **John Cale**, thus sewing the early seeds of the **Velvet Underground**. Reed led this outstanding unit between 1966 and 1970, contributing almost all of the material and shaping its ultimate direction. His songs, for the most part, drew on the incisive discipline of R&B, while pointed lyrics displayed an acerbic view of contemporary urban life. Reed's departure left a creative vacuum within the group, yet he too seemed drained of inspiration following the break. He sought employment outside of music and two years passed before *Lou Reed* was released. Recorded in London with British musicians, including **Steve Howe** and **Rick Wakeman**, the set boasted some excellent songs - several of which were intended for the Velvet Underground - but was marred by an indistinct production. Nonetheless, an attendant UK tour with the Tots, a group of New York teenagers, was an artistic success.

David Bowie, a longtime Velvets' aficionado, oversaw *Transformer*, which captured a prevailing mood of decadence. Although uneven, it included the classic

'Walk On The Wild Side', a homage to transsexuals and social misfits drawn to artist/film-maker Andy Warhol. This explicit song became a surprise hit, reaching the UK Top 10 and US Top 20 in 1973, but Reed refused to become trapped by the temporary nature of the genre and returned to the dark side of his talents with *Berlin*. By steering a course through sado-masochism, attempted suicide and nihilism, the artist expunged his newfound commerciality and challenged his audience in a way few contemporaries dared. Yet this period was blighted by self-parody and while a crack back-up band built around guitarists Dick Wagner and Steve Hunter provided undoubted muscle on the live *Rock 'N' Roll Animal*, *Sally Can't Dance* showed an artist bereft of direction and purpose. Having sanctioned a second in-concert set, Reed released the stark *Metal Machine Music*, an electronic, atonal work spaced over a double album. Savaged by critics upon release, its ill-synchronized oscillations have since been lauded by elitist sections of the *avant garde* fraternity, while others view its release as a work of mischief in which Reed displayed the ultimate riposte to careerist convention. It was followed by the sedate *Coney Island Baby*, Reed's softest, simplest collection to date, the inherent charm of which was diluted on *Rock 'N' Roll Heart*, a careless, inconsequential collection which marked an artistic nadir. However its successor, *Street Hassle*, displayed a rejuvenated power, resuming the singer's empathy with New York's subcultures. The title track, later revived by **Simple Minds**, was undeniably impressive, while 'Dirt' and 'I Wanna Be Black' revealed a wryness missing from much of the artist's solo work. Although subsequent releases, *The Bells* and *Growing Up in Public*, failed to scale similar heights, they offered a newfound sense of maturity. Reed entered the 80s a stronger, more incisive performer, buoyed by a fruitful association with guitarist Robert Quine, formerly of **Richard Hell**'s Void-Oids. *The Blue Mask* was another purposeful collection and set a pattern for the punchy, concise material found on *Legendary Hearts* and *Mistrial*. However, despite the promise these selections offered, few commentators were prepared for the artistic rebirth found on *New York*. Here the sound was stripped to the bone, accentuating the rhythmic pulse of compositions which focused on the seedy low-life that Reed excels in chronicling. His lyrics, alternately pessimistic or cynical, reasserted the fire of his best work as the artist regains the power to paint moribund pictures which neither ask, nor receive, pity. *New York* was a splendid return to form and created considerable interest in his back catalogue. *Songs For 'Drella*, was a haunting epitaph for Andy Warhol on which Reed collaborated with John Cale. Its showed another facet of the dramatic regeneration that places this immensely talented artist back at rock's cutting edge. In 1993 Reed joined together with his legendary colleagues for a high-profile Velevet Underground reunion. Although it was short

lived (rumours of old fueds with Cale) Reed has the benefit on being able to fall back on his solo work at any given time.

Albums: *Lou Reed* (1972), *Transformer* (1972), *Berlin* (1973), *Rock 'N' Roll Animal* (1974), *Sally Can't Dance* (1974), *Metal Machine Music* (1975), *Lou Reed Live* (1975), *Coney Island Baby* (1976), *Rock 'N' Roll Heart* (1976), *Street Hassle* (1978), *Live - Take No Prisoners* (1978), *The Bells* (1979), *Growing Up In Public* (1980), *The Blue Mask* (1982), *Legendary Hearts* (1983), *New Sensations* (1984), *Live In Italy* (1984), *Mistrial* (1986), *New York* (1989), *Magic And Loss* (1992), with John Cale *Songs For 'Drella* (1990). Selected compilations: *Walk On The Wild Side - The Best Of Lou Reed* (1977), *Rock 'N' Roll Diary 1967-1980* (1980), *I Can't Stand It* (1983), *New York Superstar* (1986), *Magic And Loss* (1992).

Further reading: *Lou Reed & The Velvets*, Nigel Trevena. *Lou Reed*, Diana Clapton. *Lou Reed: Growing Up In Public*, Peter Doggett. *Between Thought And Expression: Selected Lyrics*, Lou Reed. *Waiting For the Man: A Biography Of Lou Reed*, Jeremy Reed. *Lou Reed: The Biography*, Victor Bockris. *Between The Lines*, Michael Wrenn.

Reed, Ola Belle

b. 1915, in the mountains of western North Carolina, USA. Reed learned the clawhammer-style of banjo playing as a child and grew up singing the old time songs of her local area. She played with the North Carolina Ridge Runners in the 30s and after World War II, with their band the New River Boys And Girls, she and her brother played at many North Carolina events. She featured on numerous radio stations and became an acknowledged authority on Appalachian tunes, as well as her old time gospel, bluegrass and folk music. Later she appeared with her husband Bud and son David, with whom she established the New River Ranch country park at Oxford, Pennsylvania. This venue attracted a great many lovers of her music from the New England area. In the late 70s, she recorded an album that ensured she would be correctly remembered, although she perhaps tempted fate somewhat prematurely by calling it *My Epitaph*.

Albums: *Ola Belle Reed* (1975), *Ola Belle & Bud Reed, All In One Evening* (c.1976), *My Epitaph* (1977), *Ola Belle Red & Family* (1978).

Reef

The line-up comprises; Kenwyn House (b. 1 August 1970, Tiverton, Devon, England; guitar), Gary Stringer (18 June 1973, Litchfield, Staffordshire, England; vocals), Dominic Greensmith (b. 2 June 1970, Denby, Derbyshire, England; drums) and Jack Bessant (b. 19 March 1971, Wells, Somerset, England; bass) came to fame via an advert for the Mini-Disc portable stereo system. This depicted them as a heavy metal band touting for a deal, presenting their song, 'Naked', to an unimpressed A&R man, who throws the offending demo out of the window only for it to be retrieved and played by a passing skateboarder. Despite the impression given of them being a US band (the video was filmed in New York), Reef come from England. Signed to the **Sony** empire, their first release was 'Good Feeling' in late 1994. The group, anxious to avoid a '**Stiltskin** situation', were keen not to be perceived as a one-horse operation and to this end declined to offer 'Naked' as a single release, often not even playing it live. Their debut album was well received although the **Pearl Jam** comparisons they could probably do without.

Album: *Replenish* (Sony 1995).

Reegs

One of two splinter groups from the ashes of underrated UK group the **Chameleons**, the Reegs was formed by guitarists Dave Fielding and Reg Smithies after they split in 1987. They were joined by vocalist Gary Lavery and a drum machine for their 1991 debut under their new title, *The Return Of The Sea Monkeys*. 'We didn't do anything for a while after the Chameleons split, I think we both needed to take some time out. There was never any question of us not working together again.' Fielding had kept busy with production work, the most successful of which was with the **Inspiral Carpets**. Following the enthusiasm shown by Imaginary Records, they made their first recording with 'See My Friend', for a **Kinks**' tribute album. The first of their own material came in the shape of two EPs, which formed the basis of the album.

Album: *The Return Of The Sea Monkeys* (Imaginary 1991).

Reel 2 Real

Featuring the antics of The Mad Stuntman (b. c.1969, Trinidad, West Indies), whose vocals towered over the house ragga breakthrough 'I Like To Move It'. A resident of Brooklyn, New York, since the age of nine, Stuntman took his name from the Lee Majors' television series *The Fall Guy*. He met prolific producer **Erick 'More' Morillo** through a friend and the two combined on tracks for **Strictly Rhythm** which they never envisioned to be crossover material. They were proved emphatically wrong by the sustained sales of 'I Like To Move It', when it was licensed to **Positiva** in the UK. Its chart life was an erratic one, running a sequence of weekly positions which read 10, 12, 12, 10, 9, 7, 5, 8, 7, 7, boosted by a 40-date club tour. That and the fact that at no stage was it playlisted by Radio 1 DJs. They followed up with 'Go On Move'.

Album: *Move It* (Positiva 1994).

Reels

Dubbo, a large provincial city in New South Wales, Australia, provided one exception to the rule that most bands in Australia originate from the large state capitals. Perhaps this helps to explain the Reels, whose musical direction has been erratic, however brilliant. Based around Dave Mason (vocals) and Colin 'Polly' Newman (keyboards/saxophone) with Paul Abrahams (bass), John Bliss (drums) and Craig Hooper (guitar), the band was the first to utilize backing tapes, organize a national tour by train and to do a show based solely on requests, gathered by the band before the show. The band began as a quirky post new wave outfit achieving notice with the single and album 'Quasimodo's Dream' which remains their outstanding song. National success came with an album of MOR covers, *Beautiful*, marketed by the K-Tel label on television, but by 1978 the band was reduced to a duo, performing with backing sequencers and a computer. Their 1988 album consisted entirely of covers of well-known Australian bands. The band's two homeland hit singles have been a straight cover of **Burt Bacharach**'s 'This Guy's In Love With You' in 1982 and a slow whimsical version of **Creedence Clearwater Revival**'s 'Bad Moon Rising' in 1986.

Albums: *The Reels* (1979), *Quasimodo's Dream* (1981), *Beautiful* (1981), *Unreel* (1982), *Neighbours* (1988).

Reese Project

Along with **Inner City**, the Reese Project is the other regular home to Detroit techno guru **Kevin Saunderson** (b. Kevin Maurice Saunderson, 9 May 1964, Brooklyn, New York, the second syllable of his middle name provided the term Reese). He had relocated to Detroit at the age of 15, and was a proficient running back in college football until he became a DJ. His musical inspirations were his mother, a former member of the **Marvelettes**, and his brother, a road manager for rock bands. His first release would be 'Triangle Of Love' on **Juan Atkins'** **Metroplex** imprint, before breaking through with 'The Sound'. With techno in its infancy, Reese's 'Rock To The Beat' (1987) was a hugely influential, hypnotic marvel. His other early releases came as either Reese or Reese Santonio (Saunderson with DJ Tone aka Antonio Eccles). The Reese Project was incorporated in 1991 to allow a venue for his more soul-inspired techno outings. It was specifically geared towards productions of around 120bpm (making it 'in tune' with the human heartbeat, and also, apparently, the abilities of his vocalists). However, as Saunderson recounts: 'The Reese Project is not about me, myself and I. It's not about indulging myself musically. It's my chance to take a back seat, and give the platform up to talented people who only need a break, but give back as much as they get'. The three main vocalists on the album - Raechel Kapp, LaTrece and Terence FM - who featured on the single 'I Believe' (Kapp taking the honours on 'Direct Me', LaTrece on 'So Deep'), are part of a family environment overseen by Saunderson's wife Ann, who also writes the words and melodies. They met after Saunderson recorded his first remix for

Wee Girl Papa Rappers' 'Heat It Up' for **Jive**, where she formerly worked. 'I Believe' was one of two minor UK hits in 1992 (number 74), the other being 'The Colour Of Love' (with Kapp on vocals, number 52). A further single, 'Miracle Of Life', featured Kapp alongside Byron Stingily of **Ten City**. In furtherance of his ambitions to give Detroit musicians a chance, he also reactivated the **KMS** label to expose undiscovered talent. A new line-up of guest artists was recruited for the group's 1994 tour, though Kapp was retained after returning from having her child.

Album: *Faith Hope And Clarity* (Network 1992, also issued as a double remix set in 1993).

Reese, Della

b. Dellareese Taliaferro, 6 July 1932, Detroit, Michigan, USA. Reese is a renowned gospel singer, working with **Mahalia Jackson** and **Clara Ward** before becoming lead singer with the Meditation Singers. Her place was taken by **Laura Lee** when she left to join the **Erskine Hawkins** orchestra in 1956. Reese began a solo recording career with Jubilee in 1957, releasing the Top 20 hit 'And That Reminds Me' and a version of **Cole Porter**'s 'In The Still Of The Night'. Now established as a gospel-influenced ballad singer, she signed to **RCA** in 1959 where Hugo And Luigi produced 'Don't You Know', based on an aria from Puccini's opera *La Bohème*. It reached number 2 and was followed by the Top 20 single 'Not One Minute More'. Later RCA singles included revivals of 'Someday (You'll Want Me To Want You)' (1960) from 1946 and the 20s standard 'Bill Bailey' (1961). During the 60s and 70s, she worked frequently in cabaret, recording for **ABC** and Avco, where she had a small disco hit with 'If It Feels Good Do It' in 1972. In 1980, Reese returned to RCA to record an album of songs adapted from the classics.

Selected albums: *Della Della Cha-Cha-Cha* (1960), *Special Delivery* (1961), *The Classic Della* (1962), *Della On Stage* (1962), *Waltz With Me Della* (1964), *Della Reese Live* (1966), *Let Me Into Your Life* (1975), *The Classical Della* (1980), *Della By Starlight* (1982), *I Like It Like That* (1984), *Sure Like Lovin' You* (1985). Compilation: *The Best Of* (1973).

Reeves, Del

b. Franklin Delano Reeves, 14 July 1933, Sparta, North Carolina, USA. A singer, songwriter and multi-instrumentalist who had his own radio show at the age of 12. Reeves moved to California, where by the late 50s, he had his own television show. He first charted in 1961 with 'Be Quiet Mind' on **Decca**, but in 1965, he registered a US country number 1 with 'Girl On A Billboard' after moving to United Artists, with whom he stayed until 1980. A number 4 hit with 'The Belles Of Southern Bell' followed and he moved to Nashville. He became a regular on the *Grand Ole Opry* (having first

guested on it 1958) and remained on the roster through to the 80s. Between 1966 and 1986, he registered almost 50 country chart hits, including 'Looking At The World Through A Windshield', 'Good Time Charlies' and 'The Philadelphia Phillies'. He also achieved chart success with duet recordings with **Bobby Goldsboro**, **Penny DeHaven** and **Billie Jo Spears**. Reeves has appeared in several films including *Second Fiddle To An Old Guitar*, as well as hosting many television shows. He has toured extensively and with his wife written many popular country songs. A fine entertainer who also is noted for his comedy and impressions of other artists, his casual manner has led to him being called The **Dean Martin** Of Country Music. He later moved into management and in 1992, he discovered **Billy Ray Cyrus**.

Albums: *Girl On The Billboard* (1965), *Doodle-OO-Doo-Doo* (1965), *Getting Any Feed For Your Chickens* (1966), *Sings Jim Reeves* (1966), *Mr Country Music* (1966), *Special Delivery* (1966), *Santa's Boy* (1966), *Struttin' My Stuff* (1967), *Six Of One, Half A Dozen Of The Other* (1967), *Little Church In The Dell* (1967), with Bobby Goldsboro *Our Way Of Life* (1967), *Looking At The World Through A Windshield* (1968), *Running Wild* (1968), *Down At Good Time Charlie's* (1969), *Wonderful World Of Country Music* (1969), *Big Daddy Del* (1970), *Country Concert - Live* (1970), *Out In The Country* (1970), *Del Reeves Album* (1971), *Friends & Neighbours* (1971), *Before Goodbye* (1972), *Trucker's Paradise* (1973), *Live At The Palomino Club* (1974), *With Strings And Things* (1975), *Tenth Anniversary* (1976), with Billie Jo Spears *By Request* (1976), *Del Reeves* (1979), *Baby I Love You* (1988), with Liz Lyndell *Let's Go To Heaven Tonight* (1980).

Reeves, Dianne

b. 1956, Detroit, Michigan, USA. A vocalist with an international reputation and following, Dianne Reeves made her name in the late 80s, when she was discovered by the **Blue Note** label during a worldwide revival of interest in jazz. A gifted technician with a genuine swing feel, Reeves' career has tended to reflect the difficult fortunes of the singer trying to find a voice in contemporary jazz, without succumbing to the financially dominant worlds of soul or R&B. Born in Detroit but raised from the age of two in Denver, Reeves was still in high school, singing with the high school big band, when she was spotted by swing trumpeter **Clark Terry** at the National Association of Jazz Educators Conference in Chicago. Terry's encouragement and advice led her to study at the University of Colorado, where she was able to perform with him, and later to move to California and pursue music full time. In Los Angeles in the mid-70s, Reeves' range and rich, expressive natural voice, led her quickly into the west coast's famous studio scene, where she became very much in demand, recording for drummer **Lenny White**, saxophonist **Stanley Turrentine** and drummer Alphonzo Johnson. Between 1978 and 1980, she worked full-time with Los Angeles-based pianist Billy Childs, whom Reeves still credits for giving her a chance to experiment and grow, whilst working almost nightly. Still studying (under vocal coach Phil Moore), she got her first big international exposure in 1981, touring with **Sergio Mendes**. Reeves recorded her first album a year later. *Welcome To My Love*, co-produced by Childs and released on Palo Alto Jazz, set the trend for the original material that helped distinguish much of Reeves' work in later years. But it was in 1987 that she got her biggest break, when Blue Note Records president Bruce Lundvall spotted her at an Echoes Of Ellington concert in Los Angeles, and wasted no time in setting up her first major session. The resulting *Dianne Reeves* features **George Duke**, **Freddie Hubbard**, **Herbie Hancock**, **Tony Williams**, **Stanley Clarke** and her old friend Billy Childs, and rocketed Reeves onto the international festival circuit. Despite a long-running flirtation with R&B and soul (her discography is split almost exactly down the middle), Reeves has managed to retain her jazz credibility, most recently releasing *Quiet After The Storm*, a superb world music-influenced jazz record with guest contributions by saxophonist **Joshua Redman**, trumpeter **Roy Hargrove**, flautist **Hubert Laws**, guitarist **Kevin Eubanks** and percussionist **Airto Moreira**.

Albums: *Welcome To My Love* (Palo Alto Jazz 1982), *For Every Heart* (Palo Alto Jazz 1985), *Dianne Reeves* (Blue Note 1987), *Never Too Far* (EMI 1989), *I Remember* (1990), *Art And Survival* (EMI 1994), *Quiet After The Storm* (Blue Note 1995).

Reeves, Goebel

b. Goebel Leon Reeves, 9 October 1899, Sherman, Texas, USA, d. 26 January 1959, Long Beach, California, USA. One of the true characters of country music, who managed to reverse the rags to riches story and from his nomadic life style, he acquired the nickname of the Texas Drifter. He received his early training from his mother, a talented musician, who taught both piano and singing. His father, once a salesman, was elected to State legislature and when the family relocated to Austin, he got the boy a page boy's job in the government buildings. Reeves' long association with hobos started one cold night when, as he left work wearing an expensive new overcoat given to him for Christmas, he met a hobo. He subsequently arrived home, coatless, but engrossed by tales of hobo life. He began to spend more and more time talking to any hobo that he found in the neighbourhood. His parents provided a tutor to improve his education and though intelligent, his interests turned to music after hearing a vaudeville artist called Al Wilson and to the life style of the hobo. He was impressed by Wilson's singing and yodelling and it was probably Wilson who first taught him the yodel that he used so proficiently.

He already played piano and trumpet but now turned to the guitar and began singing cowboy songs such as 'Little Joe the Wrangler'. In 1917, he joined the Army (initially as a bugler) and saw action in Europe, where he was wounded and returned to the USA for discharge. Soon after, he left home and adopted the life of a hobo. He eked a living by singing on street corners and from that point many aspects of his life are unclear. He was known to fabricate facts - an early one being that he was born west of the Pecos and had been a hell-raising cowboy. On occasions, Reeves has been branded a liar, given the benefit of the doubt on others and yet sometimes his outlandish stories were found to be true. He certainly played WFAA Dallas in the early 20s and his claim to have befriended and worked with **Jimmie Rodgers** was not disproved by Nolan Porterfield in his definitive book on Rodgers. He apparently even claimed to have taught Rodgers how to yodel. However, Reeves was infinitely the more accomplished exponent of the art and since their yodels are dissimilar, this may have been just one of his inventions. Around 1921, he joined the Merchant Navy and spent several years in Europe, some in Italy but by the late 20s, he was back in Galvaston, Texas. Spurred by hearing a recording of Jimmie Rodgers, he sought the opportunity to record himself and made his first recordings for **OKeh**, in San Antonio, on 25 June 1929. This proved to be the first of many recordings that he made during the 30s. He moved to New York and heeded advice not to commit himself to one label. His recordings subsequently appeared on numerous labels including Gennett, Challenge, Conqueror, Oriole, Banner and Perfect and in the UK and Ireland on Panachord and Irish Rex. He avoided **RCA**-Victor, professing that he did not wish his recordings to clash with those of his friend Rodgers. Reeves also used the pseudonyms George Riley, Bert Knowles (Burton Knolds), Johnny Fay, the Broadway Wrangler and his own favourite, the Texas Drifter. He wrote most of the songs that he sang, many are biographical of his own life as a hobo and, in 1934, he even published a book containing the words to some of them. He drifted all over America and after playing network radio in New York (billed as the Singing Bum), he gained a contract with NBC, which saw him appear on the networked **Rudy Vallee** show. However, his rough country songs and his singing were totally unsuited to Vallee's more upper class audiences and he soon quit. He played on Nashville's *Grand Ole Opry* and did programmes on numerous Canadian and American stations. His stories (true or invented) made him a most popular entertainer, although his refusal to settle in one place for more than a few months did not endear him to promoters. He appeared at the 1933 World's Fair in Chicago and played the WLS *National Barn Dance* in that city. He married in the mid-30s, but not surprisingly, because of his nomadic life style, the marriage soon ended. Many of his later songs recounted stories of loneliness and lack of family life, again no doubt biographical. 'The Kidnapped Baby', recorded for **Decca** in January 1935, would seem to be his last professional recording which, for some reason, received a UK release but not a USA one. The final Reeves' recordings were the transcription discs that he made in 1938/9 for the Macgregor Company of California. Soon afterwards, tired of the same routines, he took a ship to Japan, where he quickly learned enough of the language to be actively employed with The Industrial Workers of the World. He returned to America before the start of World War II, but his entertaining career was basically over. He gave as his reason the fact that 'the songs were poor and current styles were artificial and insincere'. Becoming something of a recluse, he made his home in Bell Gardens, a small Los Angeles suburb and worked in connection with the community's Japanese-American problems. He had lost all contacts with family and friends, in fact, a sister lived within 30 miles of him for some years with neither knowing of the other's existence. In August 1957, Fred Hoeptner (writing in the booklet accompanying a 1994 **Bear Family** CD release of Reeves recordings), after initial work by John Edwards (the late Australian country authority), describes finally tracking Reeves down and gaining a taped interview with him. He found the Texas Drifter, still a showman and still inclined to bend the truth, when it suited his purpose. In the 50s, Reeves had suffered heart problems and he eventually died of a heart attack in the Long Beach Veterans Hospital on 26 January 1959 and was buried in the Veteran's Cemetery five days later. Reeves made an important contribution to country music and his style influenced many other artists. Many of his songs, especially 'Hobo's Lullaby' (later also popularised by **Woody Guthrie**) and 'The Tramp's Mother', have been recorded by countless other artists while many people rate his amusing 'Station HOBO Calling' to be one of his best songs. Any genre of music needs characters and, in Reeves, country music had one, which is why he is still so popular because, as Hoeptner states, 'he had the intellectual capacity to convert his experiences to recorded accounts, which were both artistically and commercially successful'.

Albums: *The Texas Drifter* (Glendale 1978), *Goebel Reeves - In Story And Song* (Glendale 1979), *Goebel Reeves - Hobo's Lullaby* (Bear Family 1994).

Reeves, Jim

b. James Travis Reeves, 20 August 1923, Galloway, Texas, USA, d. 31 July 1964. (Reeves' plaque in the Country Music Hall Of Fame mistakenly gives his date of birth as 1924.) Reeves' father died when he was 10 months old and his mother was left to raise nine children on the family farm. Although only aged five,

Reeves was entranced when a brother brought home a gramophone and a **Jimmie Rodgers** record, 'Blue Yodel No. 5'. When aged nine, he traded stolen pears for an old guitar he saw in a neighbour's yard. A cook for an oil company showed him the basic chords and when aged 12, he appeared on a radio show in Shreveport, Louisiana. Because of his athletic abilities, he won a scholarship to the University of Texas. However, he was shy, largely because of a stammer, which he managed to correct while at university. (Reeves' records are known for perfect diction and delivery.) His first singing work was with **Moon Mullican**'s band in Beaumont, Texas and he worked as an announcer and singing disc jockey at KGRI in Henderson for several years. (Reeves bought the station in 1959.) He recorded two singles for a chain store's label in 1949. In November 1952 Reeves moved to KWKH in Shreveport, where his duties included hosting the *Louisiana Hayride*. He stood in as a performer when **Hank Williams** failed to show and was signed immediately to Abbott Records. In 1953, Reeves received gold discs for two high-voiced, country novelties, 'Mexican Joe' and 'Bimbo'. In 1955 he joined the *Grand Ole Opry* and started recording for **RCA** in Nashville, having his first hit with a song based on the 'railroad, steamboat' game, 'Yonder Comes A Sucker'. **Chet Atkins** considered 'Four Walls' a 'girl's song', but Reeves persisted and used the song to change his approach to singing. He pitched his voice lower and sang close to the microphone, thus creating a warm ballad style which was far removed from his hillbilly recordings. 'Four Walls' became an enormous US success in 1957, crossing over to the pop market and becoming a template for his future work. From then on, Atkins recorded Reeves as a mellow balladeer, giving him some pop standards and replacing fiddles and steel guitar by piano and strings. (Exceptions include an album of narrations, *Tall Tales And Short Tempers*.)

Reeves had already swapped his western outfit for a suit and tie, and, in keeping with his hit 'Blue Boy', his group, the Wagonmasters, became the Blue Boys. He always included a religious section in his stage show and also sang 'Danny Boy' to acknowledge his Irish ancestry. 'He'll Have To Go', topped the US country charts for 14 weeks and made number 2 in the US pop charts. In this memorable song Reeves conveyed an implausible lyric with conviction, and it has now become a country standard. A gooey novelty, 'But You Love Me Daddy', recorded at the same session with Steve, the nine-year-old son of bass player Bob Moore, was a UK Top 20 hit 10 years later. Having established a commercial format, 'Gentleman Jim' had success with 'You're The Only Good Thing', 'Adios Amigo', 'Welcome To My World' (UK number 6) and 'Guilty', which features French horns and oboes. His records often had exceptional longevity; 'I Love You Because' (number 5) and 'I Won't Forget You' (number 3) were

on the UK charts for 39 and 25 weeks, respectively. He became enormously popular in South Africa, recording in Afrikaans, and making a light-hearted film there, *Kimberley Jim*, which became a local success. Reeves did not like flying but after being a passenger in a South African plane which developed engine trouble, he obtained his own daytime pilot's license. On 31 July 1964 pilot Reeves and his pianist/manager, Dean Manuel, died when their single-engine plane ran into difficulties during a storm and crashed into dense woods outside Nashville. The bodies were not found until 2 August despite 500 people, including fellow country singers, being involved in the search. Reeves was buried in a specially-landscaped area by the side of Highway 79 in Texas, and his collie, Cheyenne, was buried at his feet in 1967. Reeves continued to have hits with such ironic titles as 'This World Is Not My Home' and the self-penned 'Is It Really Over?'. Although Reeves had not recorded 'Distant Drums' officially - the song had gone to **Roy Orbison** - he had made a demo for songwriter Cindy Walker. Accompaniment was added and, in 1966, 'Distant Drums' became Reeves' first UK number 1. He had around 80 unreleased tracks and his widow followed a brilliant, if uncharitable, marketing policy whereby unheard material would be placed alongside previously issued tracks to make a new album. Sometimes existing tracks were remastered and duets were constructed with Deborah Allen and the late **Patsy Cline**. Reeves became a best-selling album artist to such an extent that *40 Golden Greats* topped the album charts in 1975. Both the Blue Boys and his nephew John Rex Reeves have toured with tribute concerts. Although much of Jim Reeves' catalogue is available, surprisingly there is still no biography of Reeves, who was the first crossover star. Reeves' relaxed style has influenced **Don Williams** and **Daniel O'Donnell** but the combination of pop balladry and country music is more demanding than it appears, and Reeves remains its father figure.
Albums: *Jim Reeves Sings* (1956), *Singing Down The Lane* (1956), *Bimbo* (1957), *Jim Reeves* (1957), *Girls I Have Known* (1958), *God Be With You* (1958), *Songs To Warm The Heart* (1959), *He'll Have To Go* (1960), *According To My Heart* (1960), *The Intimate Jim Reeves* (1960), *Talking To Your Heart* (1961), *Tall Tales And Short Tempers* (1961), *The Country Side Of Jim Reeves* (1962), *A Touch Of Velvet* (1962), *We Thank Thee* (1962), *Good 'N' Country* (1963), *Gentleman Jim* (1963), *The International Jim Reeves* (1963), *Twelve Songs Of Christmas* (1963), *Have I Told You Lately That I Love You?* (1964), *Moonlight And Roses* (1964), *Kimberley Jim* (1964), *The Jim Reeves Way* (1965), *Distant Drums* (1966), *Yours Sincerely* (1966), *Blue Side Of Lonesome* (1967), *My Cathedral* (1967), *A Touch of Sadness* (1968), *Jim Reeves On Stage* (1968), *Jim Reeves - And Some Friends* (1969), *Jim Reeves Writes You A Record* (1971), *Young And Country* (1971), *My Friend* (1972), *Missing You* (1972), with

Deborah Allen *Don't Let Me Cross Over* (1979), *Abbott Recordings, Volume 1* (1982), *Abbott Recordings, Volume 2* (1982), *Live At The Opry* (1987), *The Definitive Jim Reeves* (1992), *Dear Hearts & Gentle People* (1992), *Country Clasics* (1993, 3-CD), *Welcome To My World* (Bear Family 1994, 16—CD set). Compilations are always available and the Bear Family boxed-set *Gentleman Jim, 1955-59* includes previously unreleased material.
Further reading: *The Saga Of Jim Reeves: Country And Western Singer And Musician*, Pansy Cook.

Reeves, Martha

b. Martha Reeves, 18 July 1941, Alabama, USA. Reeves was schooled in both gospel and classical music, but it was vocal group R&B that caught her imagination. She began performing in the late 50s under the name Martha Lavaille, briefly joining the **Fascinations** and then the Del-Phis. In 1961 she joined the fledgling **Motown** organization in Detroit, where she served as secretary to **William Stevenson** in the A&R department. Her other duties included supervising Little **Stevie Wonder** during office hours, and singing occasional backing vocals on recording sessions. Impressed by the power and flexibility of her voice, **Berry Gordy** offered her the chance to record for the label. She reassembled the Del-Phis quartet as the Vels for a single in 1962, and later that year she led the group on their debut release under a new name, **Martha And The Vandellas**. From 1963 onwards, they became one of Motown's most successful recording outfits, and Reeves' strident vocals were showcased on classic hits like 'Heat Wave', 'Dancing In The Street' and 'Nowhere To Run'. She was given individual credit in front of the group from 1967 onwards, but their career was interrupted the following year when she was taken seriously ill, and had to retire from performing. Fully recovered, Reeves emerged in 1970 with a new line-up of Vandellas. After two years of episodic success, she reacted bitterly to Motown's decision to relocate from Detroit to Hollywood, and fought a legal battle to be released from her contract. The eventual settlement entailed that she lost the use of the Vandellas' name, but left her free to sign a solo contract with MCA in 1973. Her debut album was the result of lengthy recording sessions with producer **Richard Perry**. It gained much critical acclaim but was commercially disappointing, failing to satisfy either rock or soul fans with its hybrid style. Moving to **Arista Records** in 1977, she was submerged by the late 70s disco boom on a series of albums that allowed her little room to display her talents. Her subsequent recording deals have been unproductive, and since the early 80s she has found consistent work on package tours featuring former Motown artists. During the late 80s she toured with a 'fake' Vandellas before being reunited with the original group (Annette Sterling and Rosalind Holmes) on Ian Levine's Motor City label.

They released 'Step Into My Shoes' in 1989 while ex-Vandella Lois Reeves also recorded for Levine's label.
Albums: *Martha Reeves* (1974), *The Rest Of My Life* (1977), *We Meet Again* (1978), *Gotta Keep Moving* (1980). Compilation: *We Meet Again/Gotta Keep Moving* (1993).

Reeves, Vic
b. Jim Moir, 21 January 1959, Darlington, England. During the late 70s top alternative comic Reeves played in a group of **King Crimson** clones. Later he teamed up with comic sidekick Bob Mortimer and produced the highly successful comedy show *Vic Reeves Big Night Out*. His peculiar brand of humour earned him cult popularity among many sectors of the musical community. As a result of this, he teamed up with the **Wonderstuff** to record a magnificently camp revival of 'Dizzy', which went to number 1 in the UK charts. He would later record imposing solo versions of 'Born Free' and 'Abide With Me', and his first album, which would become a fixture of student record collections the country over.
Album: *I Will Cure You* (1991).

Reflections
Formed in Detroit in the early 60s, the Reflections comprised vocalists Tony 'Spaghetti' Micale (b. 23 August 1942, Bronx, New York, USA), Phil 'Parrot' Castrodale (b. 2 April 1942, Detroit, Michigan, USA), Daniel 'Danny' Bennie (b. 13 March 1940, Johnstone, Strathclyde, Scotland), Raymond 'Razor' Steinberg (b. 29 October 1942, Washington, Pennsylvania, USA) and John Dean (b. 1942, Detroit, Michigan, USA). All four were previously members of two other local groups, the Parisians and the Del Prados. After some local recognition, the group was signed in 1964 to Golden World Records. The group originally disliked the bouncy rocker '(Just Like) Romeo And Juliet', which the company chose for them to record, but it became their only hit that same year, peaking at number 6 in the US pop charts. The group found difficulty in duplicating their success and later recordings for Golden World and then **ABC Records** did nothing. They briefly changed their name to the High And The Mighty, but still a change of fortune eluded them. The group disbanded but reformed in the 80s around two original members.
Album: *Just Like Romeo And Juliet* (1964).

Reflex
This UK pop group comprised Baxter (guitar/lead vocals), Paul Fishman (keyboards/vocals), Roland Vaughan Kerridge (drums), Nigel Ross-Scott (bass). After signing with **EMI**, they enjoyed minor hit success with their second single the cleverly titled 'The Politics Of Dancing' in Europe, and also the USA. Afterwards they enjoyed limited success abroad, but all subsequent singles failed to make any impact on home territory.

After nearly a year away they re-appeared in 1985 to find all attention had dwindled. The band was then dropped by their record company.
Albums: *The Politics Of Dancing* (1983), *Humanication* (1985).

Refugee
After growing restless with the direction in which his group **Jackson Heights** was heading, Lee Jackson saw in Patrick Moraz (b. 24 June 1948, Morges, Switzerland) the chance to rekindle the style of music that he and drummer, **Brian 'Blinky' Davidson**, had pursued successfully in the **Nice**. Signed by **Charisma Records**, Refugee was launched with a blaze of publicity in the summer of 1973, but their sole album drew inevitable, and often unfavourable, comparisons with the band it attempted to emulate. Ironically, this promising combination was dealt a blow very similar to the one Jackson and Davidson had experienced when **Keith Emerson** had left the Nice. With **Yes** scouting around for a new member to replace **Rick Wakeman**, their eyes fell upon Moraz and by August 1974 he had accepted their offer, leaving Refugee in tatters, after which Jackson and Davidson parted company.
Album: *Refugee* (1974).

Regal Zonophone
A part of the **EMI** group of companies, Regal Zonophone was originally established as an outlet for material related to the Salvation Army. As such there have been several periods when the label has been suspended. It was reactivated successfully in 1964 when the **Joystrings** took their beat-inspired benediction, 'It's An Open Secret', into the UK Top 40. A further period of inactivity ensued until 1967, when producers **Denny Cordell** and **Tony Visconti** and manager **Tony Secunda** switched to the label from **Deram** for releases under their Straight Ahead production company. 'Flowers In The Rain' by the **Move** was the first single under this arrangement. It was followed by recordings by **Procol Harum**, **Joe Cocker** and **Tyrannosaurus Rex**, but Zonophone's brief period as a pop/underground outlet ended in 1970 when the Straight Ahead triumvirate joined forced with **Who** manager **Kit Lambert** to create the **Fly** label. Regal Zonophone not only lost all its roster, but also its back catalogue and once again EMI discontinued its use. In ensuing years its has reappeared on a temporary basis - as simply Zonophone - for acts wishing to share autonomy with an awareness of pop's heritage.

Regan, Joan
b. 19 January 1928, Romford, Essex, England. A popular singer in the UK during the 50s and early 60s, with a particularly glamorous image. It was after working at various jobs, which included a

photographer's re-toucher, that Regan first made an impression on the music scene in 1953. Her private recordings of 'Too Young' and 'I'll Walk Alone' gained her a contract with **Decca Records**, partly because it was thought she had a '**Vera Lynn** sound'. Her first releases, 'Till I Waltz Again With You' and 'I'll Always Be Thinking Of You', were followed by 'Ricochet', on which she was backed by **Ronnie Aldrich**'s **Squadronaires**. It made the UK Top 10, and led to the nationwide fame she achieved when she became the resident singer on producer Richard Afton's television series *Quite Contrary*, followed later by four series of her own *Be My Guest* programmes. After being knocked out by a descending safety curtain during her first appearance in variety, she developed her act to include effective impressions of artists such as **Gracie Fields**, **Judy Garland**, and actress **Anna Neagle**, to whom Regan bore a remarkable facial resemblance. During the late 50s and early 60s, Regan appeared in several shows at the London Palladium, including *We're Having A Ball* with **Max Bygraves**; *Stars In Your Eyes* with **Russ Conway**, **Cliff Richard**, **Edmund Hockridge** and Billy Dainty; in pantomime with **Frankie Vaughan** and Jimmy Edwards; and several Royal Command Performances. Her other record hits, through to 1961, included 'Someone Else's Roses', 'If I Give My Heart To You', 'Prize Of Gold', 'Open Up Your Heart', 'May You Always', 'Happy Anniversary', 'Papa Loves Mama', 'One Of The Lucky Ones', 'Must Be Santa', 'Wait For Me' (with the Johnston Brothers). She also recorded several duets, such as 'Seven And A Half Cents'/'Good Evening Friends', with Max Bygraves; 'Cleo And Me-O', with **Dickie Valentine**; and 'Open Up Your Heart', with her son, Rusty. In July 1957 Regan married Harry Claff, the joint general manager and box office manager of the London Palladium. In November, the *Daily Herald* reported that she was to have a baby in February of the following year - seven months after the wedding. After receiving 'abusive and wounding letters from people who were personally unknown to her', Regan successfully sued the newspaper for libel, and her daughter was born in April. In 1963, she was involved in a far more serious court case, when her husband was sentenced to five years' imprisonment for 'frauds on his employers involving £62,000'. Regan, who had known nothing about the deceptions, suffered a nervous breakdown, and divorced him later on the grounds of adultery. She resumed work later, and in 1968 married a doctor, Martin Cowan, eventually settling in Florida, USA. In 1984 she slipped in the shower, hit her head on the tiles, and suffered a brain haemorrhage. After an emergency operation she was left paralysed and speechless. Her recovery, which entailed much physical and speech therapy, was aided by her miming to her old records. In 1987, some of those tracks, together with others by various 'Stars Of The Fifties', Dickie

Valentine, **Lita Roza** and **Jimmy Young**, were issued on the double album *Unchained Melodies*. In the same year, while on holiday in the UK, Regan was invited by her old accompanist, Russ Conway, to sing on stage again. Such was the response, that she has become a familiar figure in UK shows in the 90s.
Selected albums: *The Girl Next Door* (Decca 1955), *Just Joan* (Decca 1957), with Edmund Hockridge *Joan And Ted* (Pye-Nixa 1961). Compilations: *The World Of Joan Regan* (1976), *Joan Regan Collection* (Nectar 1989).

Regan, Russ
(see **Dancer, Prancer & Nervous**)

Regents
A rock 'n' roll vocal group from the Bronx, New York, New York. The Regents were a part of the explosion of the Italian-American vocal groups from the New York area that made their impact during the early 60s, before the British invasion and the rise of self-contained bands made them passe. Members were Guy Villari (lead), Sal Cuomo, Charles Fassert, Don Jacobucci, and Tony Gravagna. The group was formed in 1958 and recorded a demo of 'Barbara-Ann', but when no company showed interest in the song they broke up. Three years later, the small Cousins label released the demo with some bass dubbing and the record became a hit (number 13 pop). The Regents reformed without their lead, Villari, and gained a moderate hit with 'Runaround' (number 28 pop) in 1961, but could not sustain themselves beyond that. Villari and Fassert with Ronnie Lapinsky and Sal Corrente formed the Runarounds in 1964 and found some local success with 'Carrie'. The memory of the Regents was sustained in 1966 when the **Beach Boys** made 'Barbara-Ann' a hit all over again, and during the 70s the Regents reformed and became regulars on the east coast revival doo-wop circuit.
Albums: *Barbara-Ann* (Gee 1961), *Live At The AM/PM Discotheque* (Capitol 1964).

Reggae
Although used as the generic title for all Jamaican music, reggae really first arrived in 1968, with Larry & Alvin's 'Nanny Goat' and the Beltones' 'No More Heartaches' fighting it out for the status of first reggae record. The beat was distinctive from **rocksteady** in that it dropped any of the pretensions to a smooth, soulful sound which characterised slick American R&B, and instead was perhaps closer in kinship to US southern funk, being heavily dependent on the rhythm section to drive it along. Reggae's great advantage was its almost limitless flexibility: from the early, jerky sound of **Lee Perry**'s 'People Funny Boy' to the uptown sounds of **Third World**'s 'Now That We've Found Love' was an enormous leap through the years and styles, yet both are instantly recognisable as reggae.

Like **ska** before it, reggae found favour in the UK with the mods' successors, skinheads. They supported the music to a degree that enabled a roll-call of reggae acts to hit the charts between 1968-72, among them **Desmond Dekker**, **Dave & Ansell Collins**, **Jimmy Cliff** and **Bob & Marcia**. Many similar acts also received a bite of the commercial cherry. By 1970-72 skinheads had begun to tire of the Jamaican sound, which had diversified away from the quirky love songs (**Clancy Eccles**, **Pat Kelly**) and the stomping organ instrumentals (**Upsetters**, Lloyd Charmers) of its early days to embrace Rasta philosophy (**Junior Byles**, **Bob Marley**, **Abyssinians** etc.), DJ music (**U-Roy**, **I Roy**, **Dennis Alcapone**) and black rights (**Burning Spear**, **Heptones**). Other sub-genres such as skank, dub, rockers, steppers etc. unfolded through the 70s, before all were more or less supplanted by **dancehall** and **ragga** for the 80s. Each style, however, remained under the collective banner of reggae, a flag of convenience that never seems to outstay its welcome Albums: *The Story Of Jamaican Music* (1993).

Reggae George

b. George Daley, c.1950, Kingston, Jamaica. With Neville Beckford Daley would attend auditions as one half of the duo, Neville and George. His partner went on to record in the DJ style as **Jah Woosh**, whilst George recorded 'Babylon Kingdom Fall' as Prince George - an alias he used only once. His second release, 'Fig Root', credited to Reggae George, was produced by **Sonia Pottinger** for her High Note label. The success of 'Fig Root' led to recording sessions with producer Hartnell Henry, featuring Eric '**Bingy Bunny**' Lamont and Noel 'Sowell Radics' Bailey, who later formed part of the **Roots Radics** session band. The most notable release was 'Read The Bible', which was followed by 'Vision', 'Stop Push The Fire' and a version of the classic **Dennis Walks**' hit, 'Drifter'. The big break came with producer **Winston 'Niney' Holness** and the release of 'Trodding', which achieved international acclaim and an appearance in the reggae chart. Then came 'Three Wicked Men' for 56 Hope Road, an offshoot label of **Bob Marley's** Tuff Gong empire. It was in the studio which gave the imprint its title that **Rita Marley** engineered the recording, ably assisted by Sylvan Morris who had worked on much of Marley's output, notably *Rastaman Vibration*. With such an impressive track record **Trojan** were keen to release *Mix Up*, which included the hit 'Stop Push The Fire', alongside 'No Fuss Nor Fight', 'Sister Dawn', 'Gimme Gimme Your Love' and a version of **John Holt's** 'My Eyes'. The set was produced by the late **Prince Far I** and musicians on the set included **Jah Lloyd**, Sowell Radics, Errol 'Flabba Holt' and Professor Larry. Despite critical acclaim and the obvious pedigree, *Mix Up* was to make little impression on the album charts. In 1983 his Tuff

Gong recordings surfaced on **Dennis Brown's** Yvonne's Special label in the UK, whilst **Greensleeves Records** released 'Walla Walla' and the more popular 'You'll Never Know'/'We Still Survive'. A follow-up to *Mix Up* was scheduled, but due to the untimely death of Prince Far I, the project was abandoned. By the mid 80s, reunited with his old friend Neville Beckford and employing a host of the island's top session men, he released *Fight On My Own*.
Albums: *Mix Up* (Trojan 1981), *Fight On My Own* (Sky Juice 1985).

Reggae Philharmonic Orchestra

Formed by original **Steel Pulse** member Mykaell S. Riley, the Reggae Philharmonic was a noble and bizarre experiment which crossed reggae rhythms with orchestral themes, despite the fact that Riley can neither read nor write music. The idea was to employ the most talented black classical musicians, with Riley adding vocals on top of these arrangements to surprisingly good effect.
Albums: *Reggae Philharmonic Orchestra* (Mango/Island 1988), *Time* (Mango/Island 1990).

Reggae Sunsplash

A joint Jamaican/West German company was responsible for this 1980 film that documented the previous year's *Sunsplash II* Festival. Held in Jamaica's Montego Bay, the event, which attracted an audience of 40,000, featured some of the island's premier talents, including **Bob Marley And The Wailers**, **Peter Tosh**, **Burning Spear** and **Third World**. Sadly, poor lighting and a grainy texture detracted from the power of the performances, which is particularly galling with reference to **Burning Spear**, who were rarely captured on film.

Reich, Steve

b. 3 October 1936, New York City, USA. Reich studied philosophy at Cornell University and composition at Juilliard School of Music and, moving to California, at Mills College with *avant garde* composers Luciano Berio and Darius Milhaud. He supported himself while at college by working as a drummer, but declined to follow an academic career and became a taxi-driver in 1963. In 1966 he formed a group, Steve Reich And Musicians, to play his compositions. In the 70s he studied African drumming in Ghana and gamelan music and Hebrew cantillation in the USA. One of the founders of the Minimalist/Systems/Process/Repetitive (choose your own label) school, his music is deeply rooted in African, Balinese and Baroque music, having less overt connections with (and less influence on) rock and new age than, say, **Terry Riley**, **Louis Andriessen** or **Philip Glass**. However, his astonishing early tape works, *My Name Is*, *Come Out* and *It's Gonna Rain*, anticipated techniques now in common use in scratch and hip-hop by a good 15 years, as well as using them in ways which rock has never caught up with. His work has ranged from the most minimalist (*Clapping Music*, which is just that, two people clapping, working through a pre-determined rhythmic process, and *Pendulum Music*, for microphones which are set swinging over amplifiers until the feedback pulses resolve into a continuous tone) to *The Four Sections*, a concerto for orchestra, and *The Desert Music* for orchestra and choir, which examines the premise that humankind has only survived because it has been unable to realise its ambitions: now that it is able to do so it must change its ambitions or perish. Desert Music characterized Reich's move towards a fuller, more conventional orchestration, a development which had the consequence that performances of his music would have to involve resources beyond those of his own ensemble. (In fact, Reich had never restricted the use of his scores in the way that Philip Glass had done.) However, he still composed for small forces as well, and in 1988 he wrote *Electric Counterpoint* for jazz guitarist **Pat Metheny**. This was coupled on record with *Different Trains*, a remarkable work reflecting on the Holocaust and devised for live string quartet, pre-recorded string quartet and sampled voices. He is currently nearing completion of a music theatre piece about the prophet Abraham, important to Judaism, Christianity and Islam, called *The Cave*, which will incorporate a video film by his wife, Beryl Corot.

Selected albums: *Drumming* (1970), *Music For 18 Musicians* (1978), *Octet - Music For A Large Ensemble - Violin Phase* (1980), *Tehillim* (1982), *Eight Lines - Vermont Counterpoint* (1985), *The Desert Music* (1986), *Early Works* (1987), *Different Trains - Electric Counterpoint* (1989), *The Four Sections* (1990).

Reichel, Hans

b. 10 May 1949, Hagen, Germany. Reichel has described himself as the cuckoo's egg in the catalogue of Berlin's FMP label. In between all the hard core free jazz, much of it a cheerfully barbaric yawp, Reichel's records nestle: albums of glittering, pretty, fragile electric guitar music in which silence has a role to play. Trained as a classical musician - he still occasionally reverts to violin or cello - Reichel took to rock in the 1960s until contact with the music of **Derek Bailey** changed his thinking totally; henceforth he was a free improviser and instrument builder. Multi-necked guitars became a speciality and on these he developed a technique of two-handed tapping long before **Stanley Jordan** appeared on the jazz scene. Recent Reichel innovations have included the development of a new bowed instrument, the daxophon. Because his music, with its subtleties and nuances, needs space for its proper development, Reichel has mostly worked as a solo performer or in duo settings. However, the formation in 1987 of the X-Communication band ('spiritual leader': **Butch Morris**) showed that the guitarist's individualism could function profitably inside a carefully-controlled group context.

Albums: *Wichlinghauser Blues* (1973), *Bonobo* (1976), with Derek Bailey, Fred Frith *Guitar Solos* (1976), with Achim Knispel *Erdmännchen* (1977), *The Death Of The Rare Bird Ymir* (1979), with Rüdiger Carl *Buben* (1980), *Bonobo Beach* (1981), with Eroc *Kino* (1985), *The Dawn Of Dachsman* (1987), *Coco Bolo Nights* (1989), with Tom Cora *Angel Carver* (1990), with Butch Morris, Shelley Hirsch and others *X-Communication* (1991), with Wädi Gysi *Show-Down* (1991), with Frith, Kazuhisha Uchihashi *Stop Complaining / Sundown* (1991).

Reid, Billy

b. William Gordon Reid, 19 September 1902, Southampton, Hampshire, England, d. 12 December 1974, Southampton, Hampshire, England. A popular composer and lyricist in the 40s, Reid was a self-taught pianist who also played the piano accordion in the band which featured on the *Stars Of Luxembourg* radio show in the mid-30s. Reid also ran a tango band with violinist Eugene Pini, and in 1938 successfully auditioned a young singer, **Dorothy Squires**, who subsequently recorded most of his songs. Together they formed one the UK's most popular double acts from the mid-40s to 1951, when Squires went on to concentrate on her solo career. In the late 30s his first song was published: the Irish influenced 'When The Rose Of Tralee Met Danny Boy'. In the early 40s Reid wrote 'Out Of The Blue', which was often played by the wartime bands of the Royal Air Force, the **Squadronaires** and Paul Fenoulhet's band, the Skyrockets. In 1945 he had his first big hit with 'The Gypsy'. Dorothy Squires' recording was successful in the UK, and the **Ink Spots**' version went to number 1 in the USA, the first time a British song had reached that top spot, and sold over a million copies. It is generally regarded as his best-known number, with estimated total record sales of over 10 million, and was one of the songs selected by **Frank Sinatra** in 1962 for inclusion on his *Great Songs From Great Britain*. The late 40s was Reid's most prolific period, with songs such as 'I'll Close My Eyes', 'Coming Home', 'It's A Pity To Say Goodnight' (recorded by **Ella Fitzgerald** and **June Christy**), 'When China Boy Meets China Girl', 'Danger Ahead! (Beware)', 'My First Love, My Last Love For Always', 'This Is My Mother's Day', 'Anything I Dream Is Possible', 'Reflections On The Water', 'Too-Whit! Too-Whoo!' and 'Snowy White Snow And Jingle Bells'. In 1948, **Margaret Whiting**, daughter of songwriter **Richard Whiting**, had a US number 1 and a million-seller with Reid's 'A Tree In The Meadow (I Love You Till I Die)'. Although his songs were extremely popular in Britain - **David Whitfield** made the UK Top 10 in 1953 with 'Bridge

Of Sighs' - it seemed that the US versions of his songs gave Reid his biggest hits. In that same year, **Eddie Fisher**'s record of 'I'm Walking Behind You' spent seven weeks at the top of the US chart, and sold a million copies. Frank Sinatra also sang it on his first single released to launch an impressive career with **Capitol Records**. In spite of receiving substantial royalties from his songs, Reid was declared bankrupt in 1956, and that, coupled with the threatening rock 'n' roll revolution, persuaded him to retire from the music scene. Ironically, one of Reid's earliest numbers, 'I'll Close My Eyes', was sung by **Joan Regan** in *Six-Five Special*, the 1958 movie version of one of BBC television's first attempts to reflect the changing face of popular music in the 50s. Shortly after Reid died in 1974, Dorothy Squires presented a concert at the London Palladium as a tribute to her former partner.

Reid, Duke

b. c.1915, Jamaica, West Indies, d. 1974. Perhaps the single biggest influence on reggae music after his close rival, **Coxsone Dodd**, Duke Reid's marvellous productions were, at their best, reggae at its absolute peak. Reid spent 10 years as a Kingston policeman, a sometimes dangerous profession that enabled him to develop the no-nonsense style he displayed while conducting business negotiations in later life. He and his wife Lucille bought the Treasure Isle Liquor Store in the 50s, and in a sponsorship deal Reid hosted his own radio show, *Treasure Isle Time*, airing US R&B: his theme song was Tab Smith's 'My Mother's Eyes'. Reid also ran his own **sound system**, Duke Reid The Trojan, for which he visited America to find obscure R&B tunes with which to baffle rivals like Coxsone Dodd's Downbeat sound system. After flirting with the record business for three years, recording tunes such as 'Duke's Cookies', 'What Makes Honey' and 'Joker', he seriously took up record production in 1962, scoring **ska** hits galore with **Stranger Cole**, the **Techniques**, **Justin Hinds** & the Dominoes and **Alton Ellis** & the Flames, issuing them on three labels; Treasure Isle, Duke Reid, and Dutchess. Reid did not exactly dominate the music business, but his was a formidable presence: he was notorious for carrying a loaded gun and letting his ammunition belt be clearly visible. However, he was more than mere muscle and had an astute musical sensibility, as the fast approaching **rocksteady** era would prove beyond doubt.

By 1966 ska was evolving into a slower, more stately beat, and with help from guitarist **Ernest Ranglin** and the band of sax player **Tommy McCook** & the Supersonics, Reid's productions at his own Treasure Isle Studio epitomised the absolute peak of the style. Hits such as the **Paragons** 'Ali Baba' and 'Wear You To the Ball', **Alton Ellis**' 'Cry Tough', 'Breaking Up', 'Rock Steady' and 'Ain't That Loving You', the **Melodians**' 'You Don't Need Me', 'I Will Get Along', 'I Caught You' and 'Last Train To Expo '67', the Jamaicans' 'Things You Say You Love' and the Techniques' 'Queen Majesty' were only the tip of an impressive iceberg. All are tasteful, irresistibly danceable, soul-soaked rocksteady classics, released on Reid's own labels in Jamaica and on **Trojan** (the label was named after his sound) or its imprints (including Treasure Isle and Duke) in the UK. By 1969 rocksteady had died, and Reid was apparently struggling, stuck in a musical revolution he had created. However, in 1970 he did it again, taking a sparsely-recorded toaster named **U-Roy** and single-handedly founded the modern DJ era. At one point U-Roy held four out of the top five Jamaican chart positions and both he and Reid were watching them swap places over a period of months: 'Wake The Town', 'Wear You To the Ball', 'Everybody Bawlin'', 'Version Galore': Reid simply dropped the chatter over his old rocksteady hits to start an entire new genre of reggae music. He also had hits with other DJs, such as **Dennis Alcapone** and Lizzy. Reid's legend in the reggae pantheon was assured. By 1973 Reid's fortunes had again begun to wane, perhaps because he was notorious for not wanting to record rasta lyrics in an era dominated by roots themes, and was considered to be an establishment figure as the senior reggae producer in Jamaica. He died in 1974, his extensive back catalogue going on to sell thousands of singles and albums through a variety of licensees, his name on a record virtually a guarantee of sheer joy for the duration of its playing time.

Albums: Various: *Golden Hits* (Trojan 1969, covers 1966-69), *The Birth Of Ska* (Trojan 1972, covers 1962-65), *Hottest Hits* (Front Line 1979, covers 1966-69), *Hottest Hits Volume Two* (Front Line 1979, covers 1966-69), *Ba Ba Boom Time* (Trojan 1988, covers 1967-68). The Skatalites: *Tribute To The Skatalites* (1991). Alton Ellis: *Greatest Hits* (1977, covers c.1967-70). Paragons: *On The Beach* (Treasure Isle 1968). Justin Hinds And The Dominoes: *From Jamaica With Reggae* (High Note 1984), *Early Recordings* (Esoldun/Treasure Isle 1991). U-Roy: *Version Galore* (Trojan 1971).

Reid, Eileen

This Irish singer came to prominence during the early 60s in the showband, the Cadets. With her extraordinary beehive hairdo and the group's distinctive naval style uniforms they were one of the more colourful bands of the period. In 1963, they appeared on the UK television show *Thank Your Lucky Stars* and enjoyed some airplay with their debut single for **Decca**, 'Hello Trouble'. 1964 proved a big year for the group in Eire. They topped the charts with 'Fallen Angel' and were given their own radio series, *Carnival Time With The Cadets*. With 'I Gave My Wedding Dress Away', Reid found the perfect song for the romantic dancehalls. She appeared on-stage in a full wedding dress, which was much commented on at the time. Further hits followed with 'Right Or Wrong', 'Jealous Heart' and 'If I Had My Life Over'. The group broke up at the end of the 60s when the showband scene entered a period of decline.

Reid, Junior

b. Delroy Reid, 1965, Kingston, Jamaica, West Indies. Born in the Tower Hill area of Kingston, Junior grew up in the infamous Waterhouse ghetto. He made his first recording in 1979 at the age of 13 for the equally youthful singer **Hugh Mundell**, entitled 'Speak The Truth', and released through **Augustus Pablo**'s Rockers label. Another Mundell production, 'Know Myself', a version of Dennis Walks' classic, 'Drifter', appeared on **Greensleeves** in 1981. After Mundell's untimely death - Reid was in the car when he was murdered - he achieved some success as part of the Voice Of Progress group, with a single and album entitled *Mini-Bus Driver* for producer Robert Palmer's Negus Roots label. Recording throughout the rest of the early 80s as a solo artist, Reid scored with tracks like 'Jailhouse', 'Sister Dawn', 'Pallaving Street' and 'Give Thanks & Praise' for **Prince Jammy**. Other 45s included 'The Original Foreign Mind', which was actually a self-production, for which he adopted a fast delivery similar to that of the new wave of UK DJs like **Papa Levi** and **Smiley Culture**, on **Sugar Minott**'s Youth Promotion label. Other notable recordings included 'Babylon Release The Chain' for **Errol Thompson**, 'Chanting' for **Delroy Wright** and the monster 'Boom Shack A Lack' for Prince Jammy, released in the UK on Greensleeves.

In 1985 Reid's solo career was interrupted when he was enlisted into the ranks of Grammy Award winners **Black Uhuru**, after lead singer Michael Rose's departure. The first release with Uhuru, 'Fit You A Fe Fit', met with approval from the reggae audience. However, subsequent material, particularly the experimental, rock influenced **Arthur Baker** production, 'Great Train Robbery', and Grammy-nominated *Brutal* album, made more of an impact on the international market, only serving to alienate the grass roots following he had worked so hard to build up. Aware of this credibility gap, Reid inaugurated his own label, JR Productions, and began to issue roots tunes like 'Pain On The Poor Man's Brain' and 'Nah Get Rich And Switch', credited to Black Uhuru, but far more in the vein of his previous solo material. After recording Uhuru's *Positive* in 1988, Junior left the group to concentrate once more on his own career. Teaming up with English dance outfit **Coldcut** for 'Stop This Crazy Thing', he reached number 21 in the UK pop chart in September 1988. In 1990, he made another appearance in the singles chart when he joined forces with the indie-dance band the **Soup Dragons**, for a

version of the **Rolling Stones**' 'I'm Free', hitting number 5 in August of that year.

Back in the reggae world, Reid's return to grass roots favour came in 1989 with the anthemic 'One Blood', followed by the well received album of the same title. Its raw digital rhythms and roughneck ragga production firmly re-established his name at the forefront of the reggae scene. Since then he has issued a flood of tunes on his own label, including 'Married Life', 'Good Man Scarce', 'Can't Tek the Gun Gun', a new version of 'Mini-Bus Driver', 'Friend Enemy', 'Banana Boat Man', 'Strong Survive', and the popular 'All Fruits Ripe', as well as producing other artists like Junior Demus, **Ninjaman**, **Dennis Brown**, and **Gregory Isaacs**. He has also opened his own studio, one more step towards complete artistic independence. Junior Reid, like that other Waterhouse singer, **Yammie Bolo**, is an artist who has continued to display his commitment to roots reggae music, and looks set to carry the winning formula on into the millennium.

Albums: *Boom Shack A Lack* (Greensleeves 1983), *Back To Back* (Volcano 1985), *Original Foreign Mind* (Black Roots 1985), *One Blood* (JR Music 1989), *Visa* (Greensleeves 1993). With Voice Of Progress: *Mini Bus Driver* (Negus Roots 1982).

Reid, Mike

b. 24 May 1947, Altoona, Pennsylvania, USA. Reid obtained a degree in music from Penn State University but he was also an outstanding football player, becoming a professional for the Cincinnati Bengals. He won a national award as Defensive Rookie of the Year. Although he became a football star, he quit in 1975 to play keyboards for the Apple Butter Band in Cincinnati. He then became a solo performer with most bookings based on his previous fame including some performances as a guest pianist with symphony orchestras. In 1980, he moved to Nashville. He befriended **Ronnie Milsap** and wrote several US country hits for him including 'Inside' (a number 1), 'Stranger In My House', 'Lost In The Fifties' and 'Old Folks', which was a duet. Since then, he has written numerous country successes including 'One Good Well' (**Don Williams**), 'Tell Him I'm Crazy' (**Shelby Lynne**), 'Love Without Mercy' (**Lee Roy Parnell**), 'Born To Be Blue' (**Judds**) and 'He Talks To Me' (**Lorrie Morgan**). A contender for one of the best country records of all-time must be **Willie Nelson**'s 'There You Are', an ultra-sensitive love song which he penned. He wrote all the songs on his first album, *Turning For Home*, which was produced by Steve Buckingham, and topped the US country charts with 'Walk Of Faith'.

Albums: *Turning For Home* (Columbia 1991), *Twilight Town* (Columbia 1992).

Reid, Neil

b. 1960, Motherwell, Scotland. By the age of eight Reid was already singing in public, at a Christmas party for Old Age Pensioners. His uncle played keyboards in Scottish Working Men's clubs and from the age of 10 Reid joined him as a singer. A teacher encouraged him to enter the television talent contest *Opportunity Knocks*, a contest he would go on to win three times. He recorded the weepy 'Mother Of Mine' (written by Bill Parkinson of the band P.A.T.C.H.) which became a massive hit in 1972 while Reid was not yet a teenager. Follow-ups included 'That's What I Want To Be' and 'With Every Passing Day'. For the remaining years of his youth he was a big attraction to both young teens and their parents and toured the UK, Europe and South Africa. The death of his grandfather coincided with his increasing interest in Christianity, and he became disillusioned with the fickle world of showbusiness where producers consistently expected him to sing like a 12-year-old. He took a break and worked in a fast food restaurant before a brief return during the 80s. He turned his back on performance once again, and is now an insurance salesman living in Blackpool, Lancashire, with his family.
Albums: *Neil Reid* (1972), *Smile* (1972), *I'll Walk With God* (1973).

Reid, Rufus

b. 10 February 1944, Sacramento, California, USA. After starting out on trumpet, Reid switched to playing bass during his miltary service. He played and studied in California for some years, often working in company with leading bop musicians. He also played in Chicago, toured internationally and, in the mid-70s, settled in New York. During the 80s Reid was active as a teacher and writer of tutors. Throughout his professional career Reid has appeared on numerous record dates, playing with musicians such as **Kenny Burrell, Art Farmer, Jack DeJohnette, Dexter Gordon, Jimmy Heath, Lee Konitz, Thad Jones-Mel Lewis** and **Howard McGhee**. An outstandingly talented bass player, Reid has begun to attract wider attention since forming a successful and superbly swinging hard bop band, TanaReid, with drummer **Akira Tana**.
Albums: *Perpetual Stroll* (1980), *Seven Minds* (1984), with TanaReid *Yours And Mine* (1990).

Reid, Terry

b. 13 November 1949, Huntingdon England. Reid first attracted attention in **Peter Jay And The Jaywalkers** where his ragged voice helped transform their *passé* beat-group image into something more contemporary. Reid's debut single, 'The Hand Don't Fit The Glove', was issued in 1967, but he achieved a greater recognition upon forming a trio with Pete Solley (keyboards) and Keith Webb (drums). Having turned down **Jimmy Page**'s overtures to join the embryonic **Led Zeppelin**, Reid became a popular figure in the USA following a tour supporting **Cream**. His debut *Bang Bang You're Terry Reid* produced by **Mickie Most**, emphasized the artist's exceptional vocal talent and impassioned guitar style, while a second collection featured soaring versions of **Donovan**'s 'Superlungs My Supergirl' and **Lorraine Ellison**'s 'Stay With Me Baby'. Terry's own compositions included the excellent 'Speak Now Or Forever Hold Your Peace' and 'Friends', which later became a hit for **Arrival**. Much of Reid's *River*, was recorded in America, where the singer had settled. More introspective than his earlier work, its meandering tunes enraged some critics but enthralled others, who drew parallels with **Van Morrison**'s *Astral Weeks*. However, the consensus viewed its follow-up, *Seed Of Memory*, a major disappointment while a fifth collection, *Rogue Waves*, which featured several undistinguished cover versions, was equally frustrating. Following a long period out of the limelight, Reid re-established his recording career with *The Driver*, which featured able support from **Joe Walsh**, Tim Schmidt and **Howard Jones**.
Albums: *Bang Bang You're Terry Reid* (1968), *Terry Reid* (1969), *River* (1973), *Spring Of Memory* (1976), *Rogue Waves* (1979), *The Driver* (1991). Selected compilations: *The Most Of Terry Reid* (1971), *The Hand Don't Fit The Glove* (1985).

Reign

Reign are a thrash/doom metal band from South Shields in the North East of England, culling influences from bands such as **Paradise Lost**, **Carcass** and others. Comprising John Cook (vocals/bass), Mark Robinson (rhythm and acoustic guitar), Ronnie McLean (drums) and Mick Storrie (rhythm and lead guitar), they initially rose to prominence via a final appearance in BBC Radio 1's *Rock War* competition, where they were unarguably the most extreme group on offer. Signing to European record label Mausoleum Records, the obvious next step was the recording of a debut album. *Embrace* combined brutal riffs with selective displays of melody. Positively reviewed in most of the genre magazines, Reign set about UK touring to promote the album during the spring of 1995.
Album: *Embrace* (Mausoleum 1995).

Reinforced Records

This USA hardcore label begun in 1990 by Gus Lawrence, Mark, Dego, and Ian, who collectively record as 4 Hero. It was their debut, 'Mr Kirk's Nightmare', which opened the label's catalogue. After consistently innovative releases from Nebula II ('Seance'/'Atheama'), Manix ('Oblivion (Head In The Crowds)') and others from One II One and Basic Rhythm, the quartet were joined by a fifth member,

former New York-based graffiti artist Goldie, who took on the A&R, Graphic Design and spokesperson roles. He had previously recorded as the Ajaz Project before his first outings on Reinforced as Rufige Cru. He is also behind the **Metalheads** project. Other early releases on the label included material by Doc Scott (as Nasty Habits - 'As Nasty As I Wanna Be'), Internal Affairs and Primary Sources. As with that other mainstay of hardcore music, **Suburban Base**, Reinforced recognise the contribution hip hop and breakbeats have made to the foundation of the music. The label closely observed the shifts in techno during the 90s, being a staple source of 'darkside' hardcore in 1992. So too the arrival of ambient techno, or what they preferred to describe as 'a blues for the 90s kind of ambient', previewed on their continuing 'Enforcers' series of experimental EPs. These used newer signings AK47, Covert Operations, Peshay (Coventry's Neil Trix), Open Skies (Norwegian techno crew Bjorn Torske, Ole J Mjos and Rune Hindback) and Myserson, a Philadelphian import.
Selected album: 4 Hero: *Parallel Universe* (Reinforced 1994). Various: *The Definition Of Hardcore* (Reinforced 1994).

Reinhardt, Django

b. Jean Baptiste Reinhardt, 23 January 1910, Liberchies, near Luttre, Belgium, d. 16 May 1953. Reinhardt first played violin but later took up the guitar. Living a nomadic life with his gypsy family, he played in a touring show before he was in his teens. Following serious injuries which he suffered in a caravan fire in 1928 he lost the use of two fingers on his left hand. To overcome this handicap, he devised a unique method of fingering and soon embarked on a solo career in Parisian clubs. He was hired as accompanist to the popular French singing star, Jean Sablon, and in 1934 teamed up with **Stéphane Grappelli** to form a band they named the Quintette Du Hot Club De France. Reinhardt was a popular sitter-in with visiting American jazzmen, recording with **Eddie South**, **Benny Carter**, **Coleman Hawkins** and others. It was, however, the recordings by the Quintet that made him an international name. His remarkable playing caused a sensation and it is not an exaggeration to state that he was the first non-American to make an impact upon jazz and become an important influence upon the development of the music. His distinctive, flowing lines were filled with inventive ideas and couched in a deeply romantic yet intensely rhythmic style. Above all, Reinhardt's was an original talent, revealing few if any precedents but becoming a major influence upon other jazz guitarists of the 30s.
With the outbreak of war in 1939, the Quintet folded and Reinhardt returned to his nomadic life, playing in various parts of Europe and ensuring that he kept well

clear of the German army. At the end of the war, (by which time he had switched from acoustic to electric guitar) Reinhardt was invited by **Duke Ellington** to visit the USA and duly turned up in New York. The visit was less than successful and some of the blame might well be laid at Reinhardt's door as he approached the tour with a measure of arrogance out of place with his status as a guest instrumentalist. Some reports of the time suggest that he was eager to pursue the new concepts of jazz created by the bebop revolution: musically, however, the guitarist's gloriously romantic style fitted uneasily into the new music and his efforts in this field were overshadowed by those of another guitarist, the late **Charlie Christian**. Back in Europe he led his own small band and was occasionally reunited with Grappelli in a reformed Quintet. He continued to tour and record during the late 40s and early 50s, simultaneously pursuing a career as a composer. Reinhardt remains one of the outstanding figures in jazz, and although Christian ultimately became the more profound influence, echoes of Reinhardt's style can be heard today in many musicians, some of whom were born after his death. His brother, Joseph, was also a guitarist and his two sons, Lousson and Babik, are also gifted players of the instrument. In the early 90s Babik Reinhardt was featured at an international jazz and gypsy guitar festival in France.
Selected albums: *Rare Django* (1928-38), *50th Anniversary* (1934-35), *Django Reinhardt And Stéphane Grappelli With The Quintet Of The Hot Club Of France* (1938-46), *The Story* (1947-51), *Rome 1949-50 Vols 1 & 2* (1949-50), *Django Reinhardt Et Ses Rhythmes* (1953), *The Chronological Django Reinhardt 1934-1935* (Classics, c.80s), *Djangology Vols 1-20* (EMI 1983), *Swing In Paris 1936-1940* (Affinity 1991), *Rare Recordings* (1993), *Jazz Portraits* (Jazz Portraits 1993).
Further reading: *Django Reinhardt*, Charles Delauney. *La Tristesse De Saint Louis: Swing Under The Nazis*, Mike Zwerin. *The Book Of Django*, M. Abrams.

Reisman, Leo

b. 11 October 1897, Boston, Massachusetts, USA, d. 18 December 1961, Miami, Florida, USA. After being presented with a violin at the age of 10, Reisman attended the New England Conservatoire of Music. At the age of 18, he joined the Baltimore Symphony Orchestra, while simultaneously leading a local dance orchestra. By 1919, he had formed his own dance band playing at Boston's Hotel Brunswick. Two years later his quartet featured in **Jerome Kern**'s Broadway musical *Good Morning Dearie*. Based in New York, Reisman became resident at the Central Park Casino. His featured pianists there, **Johnny Green**, Nat Brandwynne and **Eddie Duchin** all went on to lead their own bands. As depicted in the movie *The Eddie Duchin Story*, Duchin took over from Reisman at the casino when he moved on to the Waldorf Astoria. Although basically a society dance band, Reisman did record the occasional 'hot' track, particularly with **Duke Ellington** trumpeter **Bubber Miley**. His more conventional output gave him hits with 'The Wedding Of The Painted Doll', 'Paradise', 'The Continental', 'Stormy Weather' (with a vocal by its composer, **Harold Arlen**), and 'Night And Day'/'I've Got You On My Mind', featuring vocalist **Fred Astaire**. Other singers with his orchestra included Lee Wiley and actor Clifton Webb. Reisman, Astaire and his sister Adele, also recorded the first **RCA** Victor long playing record, featuring songs from the Broadway musical *The Band Wagon*. Reisman remained popular in radio and on the hotel circuit into the 50s. Selected album: *Three Little Words* (50s).

Relativity

An occasional Celtic folk group, formed in the 80s, the lineup consisted of the youngsters, Triona Ni Dhomhnaill (vocals, keyboards), Michael O Dhomhnaill (vocals, guitar) and **Phil Cunningham** (accordion), along with **Johnny Cunningham** (fiddle) from the **Bothy Band** and Silly Wizard. The members of the quartet each had flourishing solo careers, but cross-fertilised their Irish Scots heritage with absorbing results. A top line draw in the USA, where three of them lived, their British debut was a coup for the small salt-town of Northwich, Cheshire, who presented them in a packed marquee in the local park. Their music is an energetic Celtic force with some graceful rockist touches.
Albums: *Relativity* (1985), *Gathering Pace* (1987).

Relativity Records

New York-based label which originally preached the word of rock guitar ala **Joe Satriani** and **Steve Vai**, initially as part of Important Record Distributors in 1979. Come the 80s and the label was licensing 'alternative' UK rock like the **Cocteau Twins** and **Gene Loves Jezebel**, while Sony purchased a 50% stake in the company in 1990. However, in 1991 the musical climate was changing, and president Barry Kobrin and his staff noted the commercial progress of rap and hip hop records. Their first tentative signing was 2 Black 2 Strong, which never worked out. A&R chief Peter Kang was subsequently given a wider brief, and the company brought rap label Violator under their wing. The first successful release was Chi Ali's debut album in March 1992, which inspired confidence throughout the label with its 70,000 sales (in half the time it would have taken an established rock outfit to move that many copies). Together with its distribution company, Relativity Entertainment Distribution, the company then signed a deal in 1993 with **Ruthless** Records, and also established the new Lifestyle imprint. Which effectively meant that under one company HQ

there existed no less than three powerful hip hop camps: Ruthless (**Eazy-E**, **Hoez With Attitude**, **Kokane**, **Blood Of Abraham**, **MC Ren**), Violator (**Fat Joe**, **Beatnuts**, **Chi Ali**) and Lifestyle (Black Caesar). In addition Relativity signed its first 'own brand' artist, Common Sense. Their biggest initial success came with Fat Joe's 'Flow Joe' single, a Billboard Rap number 1 hit, while Alan Grumblatt, vice president of marketing, wished aloud in 1994 that Relativity would become 'the number 1 rap label in the country' by the end of the millenium.

Reload

UK band based in Yeovil, Somerset featuring former DJ Mark Pritchard and one-time **Aphex Twin** collaborator Tony Middleton (the 'other' twin, who shares the same date of birth as Richard James). The duo also record under several different monikers including Global Communications, Link, E621 and Rebos. They have their own label, Evolution, though their debut album came via the **Infonet** imprint. Their work blends dark hardcore with ambient strains, augmented by multi-media presentations drawing in environmental sounds like the ticking of clocks. *A Collection Of Short Stories* arrived with a book of accompanying essays written by their friend Dominic Fripp. Some of the text was designed to be read in-sync with the music. Both Pritchard and Middleton actually draw on a strong musical devotion to the likes of **Peter Gabriel**, **Jean-Michel Jarre** and even the **Smiths**, as well as the more anticipated Detroit techno and Eurobeat. Their *Auto Reload* EP late in 1993 continued to cement their profile with the more demanding club-goers. In 1993 they signed with indie label **Dedicated**, for whom they had previously remixed the **Cranes** and **Chapterhouse**.
Albums: *A Collection Of Short Stories (Soundtracks Without Films)* (Infonet 1993). As Global Communications: *76:14* (Dedicated 1994).

Remains

This Boston, USA-based garage band was formed in 1964 by guitarist/vocalist Barry Tashian. Inspired by a trip to London, where he heard British groups playing material he loved - **Jimmy Reed**, **Little Walter**, **Chuck Berry** and **John Lee Hooker** - Tashian put together the Remains with Bill Briggs (keyboards), Vern Miller (bass) and Chip Damiani (drums). They made their debut in 1965 with 'Why Do I Cry', a melodic slice of R&B. It was succeeded by the equally persuasive 'I Can't Get Away' and an assured reading of 'Diddy Wah Diddy', but the Remains' crowning moment came with their fourth single, 'Don't Look Back'. This engaging slice of riff-laden pop was later immortalised on Lenny Kaye's seminal 60s punk compilation, *Nuggets*. The Remains moved from Boston to New York in 1966, shedding Damiani in the process.

Tashian now feels this undermined the dynamics of the group. N.D. Smart joined the line-up which enjoyed a support slot on the final **Beatles**' tour before splitting up later that year. *The Remains* was compiled and issued following the break. Tashian and Briggs then forged the original **Flying Burrito Brothers**, a name later appropriated by his friend, **Gram Parsons**. Barry accompanied the latter on his classic *GP* and *Grievous Angel* albums - N.D. Smart also surfaced in Parsons' 'road' band - and subsequently performed with Gram's erstwhile partner, **Emmylou Harris**. He now works with his wife in a country duo, Barry And Holly Tashian.
Album: *The Remains* (Epic 1966, reissued with extra tracks, Spoonfed 1978). Compilation: *The Remains* (Columbia Legacy 1991).

Rembrandts

The Rembrandts are a Los Angeles, California, USA duo of Danny Wilde and Phil Solem, who rose to prominence when 'I'll Be There For You', their theme song to the hit NBC-TV comedy series *Friends*, became a major radio success in 1995. However, previously they had scored significant success with their 1991 self-titled debut, which included a Top 15 *Billboard* hit in the sparkling 'Just The Way It Is Baby'. The album itself peaked at number 88 in the US charts, and brought the Rembrandts a significant following for their gritty AOR. Among those attracted to the group's multi-layered songs was *Friends* co-producer Kevin Bright. He asked the group to write and record the theme for his proposed new series about the young clientele of a New York coffee house. Wilde and Solem cut a 42 second version of 'I'll Be There For You' on a single Saturday, mixing it in the same session for delivery on the following Monday. Radio demand for the song escalated, long before a full version of the song had been completed. A full-length version was finally added during recording sessions for the group's second album, *L.P.* (some copies of the record were shipped without the song being mentioned on the track-listing). The song continued to enjoy healthy radio response (though it was never actually issued as a single), partly due to a hastily convened video featuring the cast of the television show including Courtney Cox, Jennifer Ariston, Matthew Perry, Lisa Kudrow, David Schwimmer and Matt LeBlanc playing various instruments. *L.P.* meanwhile has already dwarfed the success of their debut
Albums: *Rembrandts* (East West 1991), *L.P.* (East West 1995).

Remingtons

James Griffin (b. Memphis, Tennessee, USA), although overshadowed by **David Gates**, was a singer-songwriter with **Bread**. After leaving the group, Griffin made an album with Terry Sylvester of the **Hollies** and was part of Black Tie with **Billy Swan** and **Randy Meisner**, who made a superb, goodtime album, *When The Night Falls*, in 1990. Griffin then teamed up with Rick Yancey (b. 1948) and Richard Mainegra (b. 1948, New Orleans, Louisiana, USA), who had had a US pop hit with 'Rings' as part of **Cymarron** in 1971. Yancey had played guitar for **Willie Nelson** and **Waylon Jennings**, while Mainegra had written **Elvis Presley's** hit single, 'Separate Ways'. As the Remingtons, they released a close harmony single, 'A Long Time Ago' and an album which, in some respects, sounded similar to Bread.
Album: *Blue Frontier* (RCA 1992).

Remler, Emily

b. 18 September 1957, New York City, New York, USA, d. 4 May 1990. Emily Remler began playing guitar as a small child and her early preference for rock was superseded by jazz while studying at **Berklee College Of Music**. After leaving Berklee in 1976 she began performing professionally, playing club, concert and festival engagements across the USA. A residency in New Orleans attracted attention when she was called upon to accompany important visiting instrumentalists and singers. She was heard by **Herb Ellis**, who actively encouraged her career, helping her to obtain her first recording date, for Concord, and an appearance at the Concord Jazz Festival. She continued to tour, particularly with **Astrud Gilberto**, and made a fine duo album, *Together*, with **Larry Coryell**. Other guitarists with whom she worked were **Barney Kessel** and **Charlie Byrd**. A strikingly gifted performer with eclectic musical tastes, she played with flair and her dazzling technique was built upon a deep knowledge and understanding of all forms of jazz. Appealing alike to audiences, critics and her fellow musicians, she rapidly gained respect and admiration for her dedication enthusiasm and remarkable skills. That someone as gifted as this should have died so young (though she was addicted to heroin) and so unexpectedly was a major loss to the jazz world. Her death, at the age of 32, came while she was on tour in Australia. Remler had played on **David Benoit**'s *Waiting For Spring* and he wrote the beautiful 'Six String Poet' in her memory on his *Inner Motion*.
Albums: *The Firefly* (Concord 1981), *Take Two* (Concord 1982), *Transitions* (Concord 1983), *Catwalk* (Concord 1985), *Together* (1985) *East To West* (Concord 1988). Compilations: *Retrospective Vols 1 & 2* (Concord 80s), various artists *Just Friends: A Gathering In Tribute To Emily Remler Vol. 2* (1992), *This Is Me* (Justice 1992).

Rena, Kid

b. Henry René, 30 August 1898, New Orleans, Louisiana, USA, d. 25 April 1949. Like **Louis Armstrong**, trumpeter Rena was a 'graduate' of

Joseph Jones's Colored Waifs' Home band. In 1919 he succeeded Armstrong in the **Kid Ory** band, quitting in 1921 to form his own group. Thereafter, he mostly led his own bands but also played in a number of marching bands. He made his first and only records in 1940 but was unable to participate fully in the **Revival** because ill health sent him into early retirement. According to the testimony of other musicians, in his prime Rena was a forceful player with a remarkably wide range and melodious style. Unfortunately, his recordings display only the vestiges of his talent, affected as they are by his fast-deteriorating physical condition.
Album: *Down On The Delta* (1940).

Renaissance

In 1968, former **Yardbirds Jim McCarty** (b. 25 July 1943, Liverpool, England; drums) and Keith Relf (b. 22 March 1943, Richmond, Surrey, England; vocals/acoustic guitar) reunited as **Together** for two self-composed singles that in their pastoral lyricism and acoustic emphasis anticipated the more lucrative Renaissance in which they were joined by ex-**Nashville Teens** John Hawken (keyboards), Louis Cennamo (bass/vocals) and Relf's sister Jane (vocals). Produced by **Paul Samwell-Smith** (another Yardbirds veteran), their promising debut album embraced folk, classical and *musique concrète* reference points. However, though McCarty played and co-wrote tracks on *Prologue*, he and the others had abandoned Renaissance who continued with Annie Haslam (vocals), Robert Hendry (guitar/vocals), John Tout (keyboards), Jonathan Camp (bass/vocals) and Terry Slade (drums). As the last was replaced by Terence Sullivan in 1975, so Hendry was two years earlier by Mike Dunford, who provided melodies to poet Betty Thatcher's lyrics for *Ashes Are Burning* and later records which met with greater commercial acclaim in North America than Europe - so much so that the group found it more convenient to take up US residency. Indeed, *Turn Of The Cards* was not available in Britain until a year after its release in the USA, and the group's only concert recording was from Carnegie Hall with the New York Philharmonic. An orchestra had also augmented a Renaissance interpretation of Rimsky-Korsakov's *Scheherazade* featuring the stunning vocal harmonies that were to enliven *A Song For All Seasons* which became their biggest UK seller in the wake of a Top 10 entry for its 'Northern Lights' (1978). Haslam recorded the solo *Annie In Wonderland* but 1979's *Azur D'Or* was the only other album by Renaissance or its associates to make even a minor impression in the UK. In 1980, the band weathered the departures of Sullivan and Tout as pragmatically as they had worse upheavals in the past - and, indeed, Renaissance's considerable cult following has since taken many years to dwindle.
Albums: *Renaissance* (1969), *Prologue* (1972), *Ashes Are Burning* (1973), *Turn Of The Cards* (1974), *Scheherazade And Other Stories* (1975), *Live At Carnegie Hall* (1976), *Novella* (1977), *A Song For All Seasons* (1978), *Azur D'Or* (1979), *Camera Camera* (1981), *Time Line* (1983), *The Other Woman* (HTD 1995).

Renaldo And Clara

Having completed recording sessions for what became *Desire*, **Bob Dylan** began rehearsals for an informal cavalcade-style tour, later dubbed the Rolling Thunder Revue. **Joan Baez**, **Roger McGuinn**, **Mick Ronson**, **T-Bone Burnette** and Scarlet Rivera were among the featured artists on a venture which suggested the camaraderie of the 60s coffee-house era inspiring the venture's leading participants. The revue lasted from October 1975 until the following January, before being reconvened between April and May 1976. Several concerts were filmed and, when intercut with acted sequences, the results were released as this intriguing film. First screened in January 1978, *Renaldo And Clara* is still the subject of fierce debate. Many critics pronounced it over-long and self-indulgent, particularly with respect to Dylan's confused 'plotline'. Taking a cue from Spanish director Louis Bunuel, he cast two women, Joan Baez and Ronee Blakely, as 'Mrs. Dylan' while his 'part' was played by rock 'n' roll singer **Ronnie Hawkins**. This surreal role-playing was enhanced by Dylan's increasing use of white face paint during live performances, but any intended metaphor was either confused or too trite to be of relevance. Stung by the negative response, Dylan re-edited the film later in the year, in the process trimming a version of 'Knockin' On Heaven's Door' recorded at New Jersey's Clinton Correctional Institution For Women, two songs from an appearance at Boston's Music Hall and an informal reading of 'House Of The Rising Sun' undertaken in a Quebec hotel room. However, despite unwieldly qualities, both versions of *Renaldo And Clara* reward the patient viewer with many memorable scenes. Former folksinger **David Blue** is a joy as the narrator and cameo appearances by **Ramblin' Jack Elliott**, **Gordon Lightfoot**, **Arlo Guthrie** and **Allen Ginsberg** accentuate the notion of friendship which binds the project. The last-named's beard is symbolically shaven during the film and the portion where the poet joins Dylan for an informal threnody at the grave of novelist Jack Kerouac is highly moving. The musical highlights are many, notably Roger McGuinn's powerful rendition of the **Byrds**' classic 'Eight Miles High', although the bulk of Dylan's contributions were taped in New York during rehearsals for the tour. Curiously, the film did not inspire a soundtrack album, although four songs were culled from its soundtrack to provide a promotional EP. *Renaldo And Clara* is a frustrating feature, yet is sits alongside the **Band**'s *The Last Waltz* as a tribute to a generation of musicians about to feel the blast of punk rock.

Renaud, Henri

b. 20 April 1925, Villedieu-sur-Indre, France. From the mid-40s and on into the middle of the following decade, pianist and record producer Renaud was active in Paris where he often accompanied visiting American jazzmen. Among the visitors with whom he worked and occasionally recorded were **Don Byas**, **Milt Jackson**, **J.J. Johnson**, **Zoot Sims**, **Al Cohn**, **Lester Young** and **Clifford Brown**. From the early 50s he was often the producer of the record dates on which he played and he was also active on radio and television. In the late 50s he was briefly resident in the USA, continuing to organize and play on record dates. In the mid-60s he was back in Paris where he became head of French **CBS Records**. He has also written about jazz and was a consultant for the highly successful jazz feature film *Round Midnight* (1986). A sound pianist and able accompanist, Renaud's playing career has been overshadowed by the success and importance of his parallel career as a record company executive. One of few musicians in the field, certainly at such an exalted level, he has masterminded many fine recording dates as well as instigating an interesting reissue programme.

Albums: *Henri Renaud And His Orchestra* i (1952), *The Henri Renaud All Stars* i (1953), *The Henri Renaud Trio* i (1953), *The Henri Renaud Quintet* (1953), *Clifford Brown Quartet: Paris Sessions* (1953), *Zoot Sims Sextet* (1953), *The Henri Renaud-Al Cohn Quartet* (1954), *The Henri Renaud All Stars* ii (1954), *The Henri Renaud Sextet* (1955), *The Henri Renaud Trio* ii (1957), *Henri Renaud And His Orchestra* ii (1957), *Henri Renaud And His Orchestra* iii (c.1962).

Renbourn, John

Renbourn received his first guitar at the age of 13, insisting on the present because he wished to emulate the singing cowboys he had seen in American movies. After a brief dalliance with classical music he turned his attention to folk. Having flirted with various part-time electric bands (including the blues-inclined Hogsnort Rupert And His Famous Porkestra), Renbourn began his folk-singing career on London's club circuit. Startling guitarwork compensated for his less assured vocals and he quickly established a reputation as a leading traditionalist, whose interpretations of classic country blues and Elizabethan material provided a remarkable contrast to the freer styles of **Davey Graham** and **Bert Jansch**. Friendship with the latter resulted in Renbourn's debut album, but it was on the following collection, *Another Monday*, that the artist's talent truly flourished. The two guitarists were the inspiration behind the **Pentangle**, but Renbourn, like Jansch, continued to record as a solo act during the group's existence. When the individual musicians went their separate ways again in 1973, John maintained his unique, eclectic approach and further excursions into medieval music contrasted with the eastern styles or country blues prevalent on later albums. His 1988 album was recorded with the assistance of **Maggie Boyle** and Steve Tilson under the collective title of 'John Renbourn's Ship Of Fools'. Although his studio releases are now less frequent, the guitarist remains a popular figure on the British and international folk circuit, and is often to be found double-heading with fellow maestro **Isaac Guillory**.

Albums: *John Renbourn* (1965), with Bert Jansch *Bert And John* (1966), *Another Monday* (1967), *Sir John A Lot Of Merrie Englandes Musik Thynge And Ye Grene Knyghte* (1968), *The Lady And The Unicorn* (1970), *Faro Annie* (1972), *The Hermit* (1977), *Maid In Bedlam* (1977), *John Renbourn And Stefan Grossman* (1978), *Black Balloon* (1979), *Enchanted Garden* (1980), *Live In Concert* (1985), *Three Kingdoms* (1987), *Nine Maidens* (1988), *Ship Of Fools* (1988), with Robin Williamson *Wheel Of Fortune* (Demon Fiend 1994). Compilations: *The John Renbourn Sampler* (1971), *Heads And Tails* (1973), *The Essential Collection Volume 1: The Soho Years* (1987) *The Essential Collection Volume 2: Moon Shines Bright* (1987), *The Folk Blues Of John Renbourn* (1988), *The Mediaeval Almanac* (1989), *The Essential John Renbourn (A Best Of)* (1992).

Rendell, Don

b. 4 March 1926, Plymouth, Devon, England. Rendell began playing alto saxophone as a child but later switched to tenor. He played in a number of dance bands during the late 40s, and in 1950 became a member of **John Dankworth**'s septet. After leaving Dankworth in 1953 he formed his own small group but also worked with bands led by **Tony Crombie, Ted Heath** and others. In 1956 he joined **Stan Kenton** for a European tour, appearing on *Live At The Albert Hall*. In the late 50s he played with **Woody Herman**. During the 60s Rendell was again leading his own bands, featuring musicians such as **Graham Bond, Michael Garrick** and **Ian Carr**, with whom he was co-leader of a successful band. Rendell has also recorded with **Stan Tracey**, (*The Latin American Caper*), and Neil Ardley (*Greek Variations*). A fluent improviser, with hints of post-bop styling overlaying a deep admiration for the earlier work of **Lester Young**, Rendell has long been one of the most admired of British jazz artists. For many years he has been tireless in the promotion of jazz through his activities as a sought-after teacher.

Albums: *Meet Don Rendell* (1955), *Recontre A Paris* (1955), *Playtime* (1958), *Roarin'* (1961), *Shades Of Blue* (1964), *Phase III* (1967), *Don Rendell Live* (1968), *Change Is* (1969), *Spacewalk* (1971), *Live At The Avgarde Gallery, Manchester* (1973), *Just Music* (1974), *Earth Music* (1979), *Set Two* (1979).

René Brothers

Otis (b. 1898, New Orleans, Louisiana, USA, d. 1968) and Leon (b. 1902, Covington, Louisiana, USA, d.

1982). Formed their Exclusive Records in Los Angeles, California, in 1942. Otis generally worked outside the music business before the 30s, whereas Leon had studied music and piano at night school and formed his own orchestra, the Southern Syncopators, in the mid-20s. The brothers' greatest successes came in the 30s when, as songwriters, they composed **ASCAP** standards such as 'When It's Sleepy Time Down South' (1931) and 'When The Swallows Come Back To Capistrano' (1939), the royalties from which helped to fund their new venture in 1942. They continued to pen big sellers such as 'Gloria', 'Someone's Rocking My Dreamboat' and 'I Left My Sugar in Salt Lake City'. Exclusive had early successes with ex-**Duke Ellington** band balladeers **Ivie Anderson** and **Herb Jeffries**, but hit its stride in 1945 with the inauguration of the 200 R&B series, resulting in some of the earliest R&B hits by **Joe Liggins** ('the **Honeydripper**'), **Ivory Joe Hunter** ('Blues At Sunrise'), and **Johnny Moore's Three Blazers** ('Sunny Road', 'Merry Christmas Baby', 'Soothe Me'). Otis formed a companion label, Excelsior, in 1944 which issued records by **Nat 'King' Cole**, **Johnny Otis**, and **Big Joe Turner**, but by 1949 both Excelsior and Exclusive were in difficulties and the masters were sold to fund new projects - the short-lived Excellent and Selective labels. In 1953, Leon returned to incorporate his new label, Class, which had big hits in the rock 'n' roll era by Oscar McLollie, Richard Berry and **Bobby Day** - Leon penned the classic 'Rockin' Robin' - and lasted until 1962.

Renees

This UK London-based pop group was loosely formed in 1987, in the aftermath of the break-up of the **Gymslips** a year earlier. Paula Richards (b. 1 August 1963, Kent, England; guitar/vocals), who had in the meantime been working with the ska/R&B outfits, the Deltones and Potato 5, reunited with Karen Yarnell (b. 2 April 1961; drums) using various friends to perform at gigs, often alongside contemporaries, **Coming Up Roses**. By 1989 the group had gone full-time with the recruitment of Katrina Slack (b. 14 July 1962; bass), Jacqui Callis (vocals, ex-**Delta 5**) and the lone male, Paul Seacroft (lead guitar, ex-Potato 5). The single, 'He Called Me A Fat Pig (And Walked Out On Me)', suitably impressed reviewers and the group signed to the French independent label, Squale, releasing their only album, *Have You Got It!*, in 1990. This included an impressive version of **'Mama' Cass Elliot**'s 'California Earthquake' and the more English-flavoured 'Valerie'. However, with the dissolution of the label the following year, the group broke up, tired of battling against the growing tide of insularity within the capital's live club scene.
Album: *Have You Got It!* (Squale 1990).

Renegade Soundwave

London born and bred esoteric dance trio whose recordings have been variously described as 'Dance-Noise-Terror' and '**Chas 'n' Dave** with a beatbox'. The group originally consisted of three multi-faceted instrumentalists, Danny Briotett (ex-**Mass**), Carl Bonnie and Gary Asquith (ex-**Rema Rema**, Mass). 'We're a by-product of punk. It forged the way we think, though the sound is nothing to do with it.' Their first single 'Kray Twins' emerged on **Rhythm King Records**, the sound of a television documentary set to a throbbing bass undertow. After the equally notorious 'Cocaine Sex' they switched to **Mute Records** because of the greater eclecticism of their catalogue. A series of dancefloor singles like 'Biting My Nails' and 'Probably A Robbery' prefaced a debut album which included an unlikely cover of the **Beat**'s 'Can't Get Used To Losing You'. Their aggressive dancefloor attack was continued the same year with *In Dub*, on which 'Holgertron' made use of the theme music to television's *Doctor Who*. The group re-emerged in 1994 with another fine album, one of the tracks, 'Last Freedom Fighter', announcing that 'We've all been asleep for a very long time'. It was a welcome return, though Bonnie had long since left for a solo career. Briotett also worked alongside his wife, Linda X, as half of Planet X (who recorded the James Bond tribute, 'I Won't Dance', and 'Once Upon A Dancefloor').
Albums: *Soundclash* (Mute 1990), *In Dub* (Mute 1990), *HowYa Doin?* (Mute 1994), *The Next Chapter Of Dub* (Mute 1995, remix album).

Renk Records

Although jungle music generated much of the heat in 1994's UK music industry, only two records from the genre broke into the mainstream charts. Both of those, **M Beat** featuring **General Levy**'s 'Incredible' and M Beat featuring Nazlyn's 'Sweet Love' were housed on Renk Records, a label formed in east London by Junior Hart (b. c.1958) in 1989. Both had been passed over by major record companies (**Island Records** and **ffrr, London Records**' dance subsidiary). Hart was previously a pop promotions director, launching H Jam Productions in 1988 to promote acid house parties. By 1989 he had put by enough money from previous parties to launch the label and sign its principal act, M Beat, who launched the label with the release of the timely 'Let's Pop An E'. M Beat predicted the rise of jungle with two singles, 1992's 'Booyaka' and 1993's 'Junglistic Bad Boy'. Renk Records' relationship with jungle extended to its first live concert in May 1994 held at the Walthamstow Assembly Hall. After 'Incredible' reached number 8 in the UK charts in September, the first jungle record to abandon samples in favour of a live MC, a record shop was set up in Tottenham. 'Sweet Love's rise to number 18 in

December helped make possible the building of a jungle production studio in January 1995.

Reno, Don

b. 21 February 1927, Spartanburg, South Carolina, USA, d. 16 October 1984. Reno who began his career on local radio at the age of 12 and was playing professionally with the **Morris Brothers** at 14, went on to become one of the world's greatest five-string banjo players. A fine tenor vocalist, he also played mandolin, guitar and harmonica. In 1941, he worked with **Arthur Smith** but between 1944 and 1946, his career was interrupted by army service. He and **Earl Scruggs**, (who he replaced in **Bill Monroe**'s band in 1948) popularized the three finger roll technique of playing initially introduced by Snuffy Jenkins in the late 30s. In 1949, Reno left Monroe to start his own band, the Tennessee Cut-Ups. Soon after guitarist Red Smiley (b. Arthur Lee Smiley, Asheville, North Carolina, USA, d. 2 January 1972) joined him and the two recorded and worked together at various major venues including the *Wheeling Jamboree* and the *Old Dominion Barn Dance*. Although still recording together, they semi-disbanded in the early 50s when Reno, wishing to expand the market for his playing, again worked with Arthur (Guitar Boogie) Smith until May 1955. In 1955, with Smith playing a tenor banjo, they recorded the definitive version of 'Feuding Banjoes'. The tune was later used (without their consent) under the the title of 'Duelin' Banjoes' as the soundtrack of the film, *Deliverance*. Smith and Reno sued the film company and won. Reno and Smiley resumed their touring in 1955 and it lasted until 1964, when the worsening effects of wounds received during war-time service forced Smiley to give up the travelling. He continued to appear on a Roanoke television show and still recorded and made some special appearances with Reno. In 1966, Reno began working with bluegrass singer/guitarist Bill Harrell. In 1969, Smiley returned to more full time work with Reno until his death in 1972. They are remembered for their fine version of Reno's song 'I'm Using My Bible For A Road Map' and in 1961, they achieved a Top 20 US country hit with 'Don't Let Your Sweet Love Die' and also charted the novelty number, 'Jimmy Caught The Dickens (Pushing Ernest In The Tubb)', under the pseudonym of Chick & His Hot Rods. After Smiley's death, Reno continued to work with Harrell until 1976 and made further recordings for CMH. He moved to Lynchburg, Virginia to semi-retirement but still worked on occasions with his three sons until his death in 1984. Reno wrote many country songs including the standard 'I Know You're Married But I Love You Still', (a chart hit for both **Bill Anderson** and **Jan Howard** and **Red Sovine**).
Albums: *Mr 5-String Plays Bluegrass* (1965), *A Song For Everyone* (1966), with Benny Martin *Bluegrass Gospel Favorites* (1967), *Fastest Five String Alive* (1969), with Eddie Adcock *Bluegrass Super Session* (1970), *Mr 5-String Banjo* (1973), *Magnificent Bluegrass Band* (1978), *30th Anniversary Album* (1979), *Arthur Smith & Don Reno Feudin' Again* (1979), *Still Cutting Up* (1983), with Bobby Thompson *Banjo Bonanza* (1983), *The Final Chapter* (1986), *Family & Friends* (1989). With Red Smiley: *Instrumentals* (1958), *Folk Ballads & Instrumentals* (1958), *Good Ole Country Ballads* (1959), *Someone Will Love Me In Heaven* (1959), *A Variety Of Country Songs* (1959), *Hymns & Sacred Songs* (1960), *New & Original Folk Songs Of The Civil War* (1961), *Wanted* (1961), *Country Songs* (1961), *Banjo Special* (1962), *Another Day* (1962), *Country Folk Sing & Instrumentals* (1962), *World's 15 Greatest Hymns* (1963), *World's Best 5-String Banjo* (1963), *Bluegrass Hits* (1963), *Sweet Ballads Of The West* (1963), *True Meaning Of Christmas* (1963), *Tribute To Cowboy Copas* (1964), *On The Road* (1964), *Variety Show* (1966), *24 Country Songs* (1967), *Emotions* (1969), *I Know You're Married But I Love You Still* (1969), *Together Again* (1971), *Last Time Together* (1973), *Songs For My Many* (1976), *Live At The Lone Star Festival* (1977), *16 Greatest Hits* (1977), *16 Gospel Greats* (1978), *A Day In The Country* (1989). With Red Smiley & Bill Harrell: *Letter Edged In Black* (1971). With Bill Harrell: *Bluegrass Favorites* (1967), *Reno & Harrell* (1967), *Yellow Pages* (1967), *All The Way To Reno* (1968), *Most Requested Songs* (1968), *A Variety Of Sacred Songs* (1968), *I'm Using My Bible For A Road Map* (1970), *Bluegrass On My Mind* (1973), *Rivers & Roads* (1974), *Tally Ho* (1974), *Spice Of Life* (1975), *Bi-Centennial Bluegrass* (1975), *Dear Old Dixie* (1976), *The Don Reno Story* (1976), *Home In The Mountains* (1977).

Reno, Jack

b. 30 November 1930, near Bloomfield, Iowa, USA. Reno, a singer/guitarist, first worked on radio at the age of 16 and, from 1955, was a regular member of the *Ozark Jubilee*. He continued working on radio, both in and out of the forces, and had his first record success in the US country charts with 'Repeat After Me' on the JAB label. His best-known single was 'I Want One' for **Dot Records,** but he also charted with country versions of pop hits, 'Hitchin' A Ride', 'Do You Want To Dance?', 'Beautiful Sunday' and 'Let The Four Winds Blow', with his last chart entry 'Jukebox' in 1974. His awards include the Country Music Association's Disc Jockey Of The Year in 1978, but his career was curtailed by Hodgkin's disease. He recovered but, apart from duets with his daughter Sheila in 1986, he has become more involved in management and production.
Albums: *Meet Jack Reno* (1968), *I Want One* (1968), *I'm A Good Man In A Bad Frame Of Mind* (1969), *Hitchin' A Ride* (1970), *Interstate 7* (1978), *The Best Of Jack Reno* (1990), *Hitchin' A Ride To The Country* (1990).

REO Speedwagon

Formed in Champaign, Illinois, USA, in 1970 when

pianist Neal Doughty (b. 29 July 1946, Evanston, Illinois, USA) and drummer Alan Gratzer (b. 9 November 1948, Syracuse, New York, USA) were joined by guitarist and songwriter Gary Richrath (b. 10 October 1949, Peoria, Illinois, USA). Although still in its embryonic stage, the group already had its unusual name which was derived from an early American fire-engine, designed by one Ransom E. Olds. Barry Luttnell (vocals) and Greg Philbin (bass) completed the line-up featured on *REO Speedwagon*, but the former was quickly replaced by Kevin Cronin (b. 6 October 1951, Evanston, Illinois, USA). The quintet then began the perilous climb from local to national prominence, but despite their growing popularity, particularly in America's mid west, the band was initially unable to complete a consistent album. Although *REO Two* and *Ridin' The Storm Out* eventually achieved gold status, disputes regarding direction culminated in the departure of their second vocalist. Michael Murphy took his place in 1974, but when ensuing albums failed to generate new interest, Cronin rejoined his former colleagues. Bassist Bruce Hall (b. 3 May 1953, Champaign, Illinois, USA) was also brought into a line-up acutely aware that previous releases had failed to reflect their in-concert prowess. The live summary, *You Get What You Play For*, overcame this problem to become the group's first platinum disc, a distinction shared by its successor, *You Can Tune A Piano, But You Can't Tuna Fish*. However, sales for *Nine Lives* proved disappointing, inspiring the misjudged view that the band had peaked. Such impressions were banished in 1980 with the release of *Hi Infidelity*, a crafted, self-confident collection which topped the US album charts and spawned a series of highly-successful singles. An emotive ballad, 'Keep On Lovin' You', reached number 1 in the US and number 7 in the UK, while its follow-up, 'Take It On The Run', also hit the US Top 5. However, a lengthy tour in support of the album proved creatively draining and *Good Trouble* is generally accepted as one of REO's least worthy efforts. The quintet withdrew from the stadium circuit and, having rented a Los Angeles warehouse, enjoyed six months of informal rehearsals during which time they regained a creative empathy. *Wheels Are Turning* recaptured the zest apparent on *Hi Infidelity* and engendered a second US number 1 in 'Can't Fight This Feeling'. *Life As We Know It* and its successor, *The Earth, A Small Man, His Dog And A Chicken*, emphasized the group's now accustomed professionalism, by which time the line-up featured Cronin, Doughty, Hall, Dave Amato (b. 3 March 1953; lead guitar; ex-**Ted Nugent**), Bryan Hitt (b. 5 January 1954; drums; ex-**Wang Chung**) and Jesse Harms (b. 6 July 1952; keyboards). Too often lazily dubbed 'faceless', or conveniently bracketed with other in-concert 70s favourites **Styx** and **Kansas**, REO Speedwagon have proved the importance of a massive, secure, grass roots following.

Albums: *REO Speedwagon* (Epic 1971), *REO Two* (Epic 1972), *Ridin' The Storm Out* (Epic 1973), *Lost In A Dream* (Epic 1974), *This Time We Mean It* (Epic 1975), *REO* (Epic 1976), *REO Speedwagon Live/You Get What You Play For* (Epic 1977), *You Can Tune A Piano But You Can't Tuna Fish* (Epic 1978), *Nine Lives* (Epic 1979), *Hi Infidelity* (Epic 1980), *Good Trouble* (Epic 1982), *Wheels Are Turning* (Epic 1984), *Life As We Know It* (Epic 1987), *The Earth, A Small Man, His Dog And A Chicken* (Epic 1990). Compilations: *A Decade Of Rock 'N' Roll 1970-1980* (Epic 1980), *Best Foot Forward* (Epic 1985), *The Hits* (Epic 1988), *A Second Decade Of Rock 'N' Roll 1981-1991* (Epic 1991).
Videos: *Wheels Are Turnin'* (1987), *REO Speedwagon* (1988).

Reparata And The Delrons

Schoolfriends Mary Aiese, Nanette Licari, Anne Fitzgerald and Regina Gallagher began performing together in 1962. Dubbed the Del-Rons in honour of the **Dell-Vikings** and Del-Satins, they appeared at dances in their Brooklyn neighbourhood before Mary realigned the group around Carol Drobinicki, Sheila Reille, Kathy Romeo and Margi McGuire. The last was asked to leave when the unit acquired a recording deal which in turn engendered 'Whenever A Teenager Cries'. This light, but plaintive offering topped the local New York chart, but although it only rose to number 60 nationally, the single - credited to Reparata And The Delrons - nonetheless secured the trio's reputation. With Mary taking the lead spot, the group underwent further alterations when original member Licari and newcomer Lorraine Mazzola replaced Reille and Romeo. Although commercial success eluded them, the revitalized trio recorded a series of excellent singles, including the **Jeff Barry**-penned 'I'm Nobody's Baby Now' and 'I Can Hear The Rain', which featured **Melba Moore** on backing vocals. Despite continued apathy at home the trio enjoyed a major UK hit when the excellent 'Captain Of Your Ship' reached number 13 in 1968. Paradoxically the vocal line featured Mazzola, who assumed the name Reparata when Mary Aiese retired in 1970. Mazzola, Licari and newcomer Cookie Sirico completed the concept album, *1970 Rock 'N' Roll Revolution*, which contained various 'girl-group' classics, before disbanding in 1973. Mazzola later appeared in Lady Flash, the backing group to **Barry Manilow**, but her continued use of the name Reparata was challenged by Aiese who reclaimed the appellation for a series of solo singles, of which 'Shoes' reached the UK Top 50 in 1975.
Albums: *Whenever A Teenager Cries* (1965), *1970 Rock 'N' Roll Revolution* (1970).

Rephlex

Record label set up by the **Aphex Twin** and Grant Wilson-Claridge, a friend from school. The idea was to offer local Cornish DJs some new material to play, and the first releases were all the Aphex Twin under various guises; Caustic WIndow, Blue Calx etc. New signings, however, include the intriguing **u-Ziq**. Other artists signed for one-off or longer deals included **Seefeel**, Kosmic Kommando (eponymous debut EP) and Kinesthesia.

Selected album: Various: *The Philosophy Of Sound And Machine* (Rephlex 1992).

Replacements

This pop-punk group was formed in Minneapolis, Minnesota, USA, in 1979, with **Paul Westerburg** (b. 31 December 1960, Minneapolis, USA; guitar/vocals), Tommy Stinson (b. 6 October 1966, San Diego, California, USA; bass), Bob Stinson (b. 17 December 1959, Mound, Minnesota, USA; guitar) and **Chris Mars** (b. 26 April 1961, Minneapolis, USA; drums). Originally the Impediments, their early shambolic, drunken gigs forced a name change to secure further work. Their debut album for the local Twin/Tone label showcased their self-proclaimed power trash style, earning comparisons with hardcore legends **Hüsker Dü**. Subsequent albums saw the group diversifying to encompass influences from folk, country, and blues without straying far from their winning formula of rock 'n' roll married to the raw passion of punk rock. Beloved by critics on both sides of the Atlantic, the group appeared on the verge of mainstream success in America with the release of *Pleased To Meet Me*. Bob Stinson was replaced by Slim Dunlap (keyboards) and Westerburg was at the height of his songwriting powers on the suicide anthem, 'The Ledge', and the achingly melodic 'Skyway'. Greater success somehow eluded them and *All Shook Down* was a largely subdued affair, hinting at an impending solo career for Westerburg. However, it was Mars who would become the first ex-Replacement to record following the band's dissolution in 1990. Westerburg too would go on to sign under his own name, while Tommy Stinson formed his own band, Bash And Pop. Dunlap would re-appear on former **Georgia Satellites** mainman **Dan Baird**'s debut solo album. Bob Stinson died on 18 February 1995 of a suspected drug overdose.

Albums: *Sorry Ma, Forgot To Take Out The Trash* (Twin/Tone 1981), *Hootenanny* (Twin/Tone 1983), *Let It Be* (Twin/Tone 1984), *The Shit Hits The Fans* (Twin/Tone 1985, cassette only), *Tim* (Sire 1985), *Pleased To Meet Me* (Sire 1987), *Don't Tell A Soul* (Sire 1989), *All Shook Down* (Sire 1990). Compilation: *Boink!!* (Glass 1986).

Represent Records

Collective rap troupe/record label formed in the early 90s, based in Nottingham, England. The group numbers four DJs and five rappers, who include label head and general spokesperson Parks. However, it was one of his fellow rapping crew, Mr 45, who first brought the label to the wider public's attention via his 'Radford (You Get Me)' cut on the *Ruffneck EP*. Also part of the operation is a soul band and a reggae artist, D-Link. The collective was set up on the back of an enterprise allowance grant, which allowed them to build their own DIY studio having previously recorded demo tapes on more primitive equipment. There is no connection between Represent and the well-thought of UK hip hop fanzine of similar name.

Reprise Records

Among the earliest artist-owned companies, the label was founded in 1961 by **Frank Sinatra** and a group of business associates, with Mo Ostin as managing director. Sinatra's *Ring-A-Ding-Ding* was the first Reprise release. The company quickly built up a formidable roster of artists which included **Trini Lopez**, **Bing Crosby** and **Dean Martin**. However, Sinatra's previous label, **Capitol**, retaliated by cutting the price of his records and within two years Reprise was $2m in debt. When **Warner Brothers** negotiated for Sinatra's acting services in 1963, it purchased a majority share of Reprise as part of the deal. Ostin remained head of the label, eventually becoming president of the Warner-Reprise group. During the 60s and early 70s, Reprise became a mainstream rock company, issuing material by **Frank Zappa**, **Joni Mitchell**, **Neil Young**, **Moby Grape**, **Ry Cooder**, **Fleetwood Mac**, **Gordon Lightfoot** and **Randy Newman**. From the UK, the label gained USA rights to the Pye catalogue (**Petula Clark**, the **Kinks**) and to **Jimi Hendrix**'s output. In 1967 Reprise signed a distribution agreement with Brother Records, the **Beach Boys**' own label. During the mid-70s, however, Warners began to run down the Reprise roster and when Neil Young left to join **Geffen Records** in 1982, the Reprise name was discontinued. It was revived four years later to issue material by country singer **Dwight Yoakam** and soon afterwards rock artists such as Taja Seville, **Enya** and **Dream Academy** were added. By the early 90s, the Reprise roster had been rebuilt as a broad-based mix of country, rock and gospel acts. Among its artists were **Carlene Carter**, **Take 6**, **Chris Isaak**, **Kenny Rogers**, **Chicago** and, once again, Neil Young.

Republic Records

Record label founded by Ian 'Tommy' Tomlinson in association with Dave Lee (aka **Joey Negro**), both of whom formerly worked for **Rough Trade** Records. Together they approached Geoff Travis of that label in February 1989 to suggest the instigation of a dance subsidiary, and by May of the same year Republic had released its first record (by M-D-Emm). Lee was given the A&R say, as the label follwed up with material by Blaze, Phaze II and Turntable Orchestra (many of which were Lee in disguise). As well as the occasional licensing deal (notably **Kym Mazelle**), they pressed on with a catalogue of material distinguished by releases from the aforementioned M-D-Emm ('Can't Win For Losing') and Phaze II ('I Wanna Do It' and 'Burning To The Boogie').

Residents

Despite a recording career spanning two decades, the Residents have successfully - and deliberately - achieved an air of wilful obscurity. Mindful of the cult of personality, they studiously retain an anonymity and refuse to name personnel, thus ensuring total artistic freedom. Their origins are shrouded in mystery and mischief, although common currency agrees the group was founded in Shrieveport, Louisiana, USA. They later moved to San Mateo, California, where a series of home-recorded tapes was undertaken. In 1971 the group collated several of these performances and sent the results to Hal Haverstadt of **Warner Brothers**, who had signed **Captain Beefheart**. No name had been included and thus the rejected package was returned marked 'for the attention of the residents', which the collective accepted as a sign of distinction. In 1972 the group was resettled in San Francisco where they launched Ralph Records as an outlet for their work. *Meet The Residents* established their unconventional style, matching bizarre reconstructions of 60s pop favourites with ambitious original material. Critics drew comparisons with the **Mothers Of Invention**, but any resemblance was purely superficial as the Residents drew reference from a wider variety of sources and showed a greater propensity to surprise. *Third Reich Rock 'N' Roll* contained two suites devoted to their twisted vision of contrasting cover versions, whereas *Not Available* comprised material the group did not wish to release. It had been recorded under the Theory Of Obscurity, whereby a record should not be issued until its creators had forgotten its existence, but appeared as a stop-gap release during sessions for the ambitious *Eskimo*. *The Commercial Album* consisted of 40 tracks lasting exactly 1 minute and contrasted the Residents' next project, the *Mole Trilogy*, which comprised *Mark Of The Mole*, *The Tunes Of Two Cities* and *The Big Bubble*. The group undertook extensive live appearances in the US and Europe to promote this expansive work, which in turn spawned several in-concert selections and an EP devoted to music played during the shows' intermission. Their subsequent *American Composers Series* has included *George And James*, a homage to **George Gershwin** and **James Brown**, *Stars And Hank Forever*, a celebration of **Hank Williams** and **John Phillip Sousa**, and *The King And Eye*, an album of **Elvis Presley** hits. If this suggests a paucity of original material, it is worth recalling the Residents' strength lies in interpretation and use of cultural icons as templates for their idiosyncratic vision. Albums: *Meet The Residents* (Ralph 1974), *Blorp Esette*

(Ralph 1975), *Third Reich Rock 'N' Roll* (Ralph 1976), *Fingerprince* (Ralph 1976), *Not Available* (Ralph 1978), *Duck Stab/Buster And Glen* (Ralph 1978), *Eskimo* (Ralph 1979), *The Commercial Album* (Ralph 1980), *Mark Of The Mole* (Ralph 1981), *Intermission* (Ralph 1982), *The Tunes Of Two Cities* (Ralph 1982), *The Big Bubble* (Ralph 1983), *The Mole Show Live In Holland* (Ralph 1983), *George And James* (Ralph 1984), *Vileness Fats* (Ralph 1984), *13th Anniversary Show Live In Holland* (Torso 1986), *13th Anniversary Show Live In Japan* (Ralph 1986), *Stars And Hank Forever* (Ralph 1986), *God In Three Persons* (Rykodisc 1988), *The King And Eye* (Enigma 1989), *Freakshow* (Official Product 1991), *The Residents Present Our Finest Flowers* (Ralph 1993). Compilations: *Nibbles* (Virgin 1979), *Ralph Before '84 Volume 1* (Ralph 1984), *Ralph Before '84 Volume 2* (Ralph 1985), *Buster And Glen/Duck Stab* (Ralph 1995).

Further reading: *Meet The Residents*, Ian Shirley.

Restless Heart

John Dittrich (b. 7 April 1951, Union, New Jersey, USA; drums, vocals), Paul Gregg (b. 3 December 1954; bass, vocals), Dave Innis (b. 9 April 1959, Bartlesville, Oklahoma, USA; keyboards, vocals), Greg Jennings (b. 2 October 1954, Oklahoma City, Oklahoma, USA; guitar, vocals), Larry Stewart (b 2 March 1959, Paducah, Kentucky, USA; lead vocals, guitar, keyboards), Restless Heart are a latter-day **Eagles** continuing with the soft-rock sounds and harmonies of one of their favourite groups. They were formed by producers Tim DuBois and Scott Hendricks in 1983, originally as the Okie Project, but it took them two years to develop their sound and obtain a record contract. Their first single, 'Let The Heartache Ride', gained them some attention and then, between 1986 and 1988 they topped the US country charts six times; 'That Rock Won't Roll', 'I'll Still Be Loving You' (also a pop hit and now much requested at weddings), 'Why Does It Have To Be (Wrong Or Right)', 'Wheels' (their best-known record, written by **Dave Loggins**, and in the same vein as the Eagles' 'Take It Easy'), 'Bluest Eyes In Texas' and the emotion-packed ballad, 'A Tender Lie'. Stewart left for a solo career and his first solo album, *Down The Road* (RCA 1993), included guest appearances from **Vince Gill** and **Suzy Bogguss**. Restless Heart decided to remain as a quartet and won the **ASCAP** song of the year with 'When She Cries'. In the early 90s Innis left the band and *Matters Of The Heart* just shows the remaining members on the cover.

Albums: *Restless Heart* (RCA 1985), *Wheels* (RCA 1987), *Big Dreams In A Small Town* (RCA 1988), *Fast Movin' Train* (RCA 1990), *Big Iron Horses* (RCA 1991), *Matters Of The Heart* (BMG 1994). Compilation: *The Best Of Restless Heart* (RCA 1991).

Return To Forever

This jazz group featured **Chick Corea** (b. 12 June

1941, Chelsea, Massachusetts, USA; keyboards), **Joe Farrell** (b. 16 December 1937, Chicago Heights, Illinois, USA, d. 10 January 1986; soprano saxophone/flute), **Flora Purim** (b. 6 March 1942, Rio de Janeiro, Brazil; vocals), **Stanley Clarke** (b. 30 June 1951, Philadelphia, USA; bass/electric bass), and **Airto Moreira** (b. 5 August 1941, Itaiopolis, Brazil; percussion). Formed by Chick Corea in 1971, Return To Forever began as a Latin-influenced fusion band, mixing the wild vocals of Purim with the tight, funk-edged slapping bass of Clarke to create a new sound. The group toured and made two commercially successful albums before disbanding in 1973. Keeping Clarke, Corea immediately put together the second of what was to be three successive Return To Forever bands. Hiring Bill Connors to play electric guitar (soon replaced by **Earl Klugh** and then **Al DiMeola**), and drummer **Lenny White**, the second band was much more of a rock-orientated outfit. Producing a harder overall sound, and aided by Corea's adoption of various electronic keyboard gadgetry, the new band achieved massive popularity, particularly with rock audiences, and its 1976 *Romantic Warrior* quickly became its best-selling album. The third and final Return To Forever was a huge but not altogether successful departure from what had come before. Corea put together a 13-piece band that included small string and brass sections, as well as Clarke and Farrell from the original band. A soft, unchallenging music resulted, and Return To Forever refined itself out of existence in 1980. Corea, Clarke, DiMeola, and White joined up for a single tour in 1983.

Albums: *Light As A Feather* (1972), *Return To Forever* (1973), *Hymn Of The Seventh Galaxy* (1973), *Where Have I Known You Before?* (1974), *No Mystery* (1975), *Romantic Warrior* (1976), *Musicmagic* (1977), *Live: The Complete Concert* (1977). Compilation: *The Best Of* (1980).

Return To The Forbidden Planet

Based very loosely on the 1956 film *Forbidden Planet* which was a sci-fi version of William Shakespeare's play, *The Tempest*, this show - 'it's all a-Bard for an intergalactic rock extravaganza' - opened at the Cambridge Theatre in London on 18 September 1989. It was written and directed by Bob Carlton, who had mounted a miniature production for the Bubble Theatre Company in the mid-80s. The story, which retains only three names from the original source, Prospero, Miranda, and Ariel, is set on a spaceship that lands on the uncharted planet D'Illyria, the very place that the mad scientist Doctor Prospero (Christian Roberts) and his daughter Miranda (Allison Harding) had ended up several years previously, after the Doctor's wife had rather carelessly tinkered with his formula which was about to change the world. The spaceship's commander is Captain Tempest (John Ashby), 'a square-jawed, *Boys Own*-paper-hero and

pipe-smoker', and the antithesis of the devilishly devious Prospero. Examples of the fractured Shakespearean dialogue included 'Two bleeps, or not two bleeps? That is the question', and 'Shall I compare thee to a chemist's shop?' But it was the music and the high-tech effects (credited to *Thunderbirds* creator Gerry Anderson) that gave the show its wide appeal. Rock classics such as 'Wipeout', 'Telstar', 'Great Balls Of Fire', 'Don't Let Me Be Misunderstood', 'Good Vibrations', 'A Teenager In Love', 'Go Now', 'We've Gotta Get Out Of This Place', and many more, accompanied the crazy antics aboard the space vehicle. Patrick Moore, the doyen of the high-powered telescope and star of UK television's long-running *The Sky At Night*, materialised in video form as a galactic guide, and, of all the comic-book characters, Kraig Thornbar excelled as Ariel, the roller-skating robot. The show won the 1990 **Laurence Olivier Award** for best musical and went on to become a tremendous success, running for 1,516 performances before its closure in January 1993. A 1991 Off Broadway production stayed at the Variety Arts Theatre for six months.

Reunion

Reunion was a studio group created around songwriters Norman Dolph and Paul DiFranco, which scored one US Top 10 single in 1974 with the novelty song 'Life Is A Rock (But The Radio Rolled Me)'. The group had already released a number of singles on **RCA Records** with no luck when writer/producer DiFranco approached writer/singer **Joey Levine** to work on the song which ultimately became their only hit. The song had been written two years previously but had remained unfinished. Levine, Dolph and DiFranco took final writing credit and it was recorded in a bubblegum style (Levine had had success writing hit songs in the 60s for studio bubblegum outfits such as the **Ohio Express**, and was a member of the **Third Rail**). 'Life Is A Rock (But The Radio Rolled Me)' reached number 8 in the US in late 1974 but further releases under the Reunion name failed to chart. They did not record any albums and the project was soon shelved.

Rev, Martin

(see **Suicide**)

Reveille With Beverly

Fluffy but engaging US war-time musical, made in 1943, about a radio station DJ, Ann Miller, who plays swing music for the boys in local army camps. Several leading musicians of the era appear including the orchestras of **Count Basie**, **Bob Crosby** and **Duke Ellington**. Amongst the singers on hand are the **Mills Brothers**, **Ella Mae Morse**, **Betty Roché** and **Frank Sinatra**.

Revel, Harry

b. 21 December 1905, London, England, d. 3 November 1958, New York City, New York, USA. An important composer, mostly remembered for the series of appealing songs that he and his chief collaborator **Mack Gordon** contributed to movie musicals of the 30s. After demonstrating a remarkable ability on the piano as a young child, Revel studied at the Guildhall School of Music and seemed destined for a career as a classical musician. Instead, he went to Europe at the age of 15 and toured with dance orchestras, later composing light and operatic music. In 1929 he moved to America where he met vaudevillian Mack Gordon, and in the early 30s they contributed some songs to mostly unsuccessful Broadway shows such as *Fast And Furious* (with **Harold Adamson**), the 1931 *Ziegfeld Follies* (with **Harry Richman**), *Everybody's Welcome*, *Marching By*, and *Smiling Faces*. In 1932, Joe Rines, **Don Redman**, Chick Bullock and **Fletcher Henderson** all had hits with Revel and Gordon's 'Underneath The Harlem Moon', and in the following year they wrote the score for their first movie, *Broadway Thru A Keyhole*. This was followed during the remainder of the 30s by scores or single songs for a string of mostly entertaining features which included *Sitting Pretty*, *We're Not Dressing*, *Shoot The Works*, *She Loves Me Not*, **The Gay Divorcee**, *College Rhythm*, *Love In Bloom*, *Paris In The Spring*, *Two For Tonight*, *Stowaway*, *Collegiate*, **Poor Little Rich Girl**, *You Can't Have Everything*, *Head Over Heels In Love*, *Wake Up And Live*, *Thin Ice*, *Ali Baba Goes To Town*, *My Lucky Star*, *Rebecca Of Sunnybrook Farm*, *Sally, Irene And Mary*, *In Old Chicago*, *Thanks For Everything*, *Josette*, *Tailspin*, *Love Finds Andy Hardy*, *Love And Hisses*, and **Rose Of Washington Square** (1939). From out of those pictures came many popular and appealing numbers such as 'Did You Ever See A Dream Walking?', 'Good Morning Glory', 'You're Such A Comfort To Me', 'It Was A Night In June', 'May I?', 'Love Thy Neighbour', 'She Reminds Me Of You', 'With My Eyes Wide Open, I'm Dreaming', 'Don't Let It Bother You', 'Stay As Sweet As You Are', 'My Heart Is An Open Book', 'Here Comes Cookie', 'Without A Word Of Warning', 'I Feel Like A Feather In The Breeze', 'When I'm With You', 'Oh, My Goodness', 'Goodnight, My Love', 'One Never Knows, Does One?', 'Never In A Million Years', 'There's A Lull In My Life', 'You Can't Have Ev'rything', 'An Old Straw Hat', 'I've Got A Date With A Dream', 'Meet The Beat Of My Heart', 'It Never Rains But It Pours', and 'I Never Knew Heaven Could Speak'. After working on *The Rains Came* in 1939, the team split up and Gordon went off to write with **Harry Warren**. Revel worked in an administrative capacity for US Forces entertainment units during World War II and continued to write film songs in the 40s, mostly with lyricist Mort Greene, although he was unable to match his previous success.

He provided several numbers, including 'You Go Your Way (And I'll Go Crazy)' and 'I'm In Good Shape (For The Shape I'm In)', for the **Ray Bolger** picture *Four Jacks And A Jill*, and also worked on *Call Out The Marines*, *Joan Of Arzak*, *Midnight Masquerade*, *Hit The Ice*, **The Dolly Sister**s, *I'll Tell The World*, *It Happened On Fifth Avenue*, and *The Stork Club*. Two of Revel and Greene's songs, 'There's A Breeze On Lake Louise' (from *The Mayor Of Forty-Fourth Street*) and 'Remember Me To Carolina' (from *Minstrel Man*) were nominated for Oscars. There were no awards for Revel and Arnold B. Horwitt's score for the 1945 Broadway show *Are You With It?*, but it enjoyed a reasonable run. Revel's other collaborators included **Paul Francis Webster**, Bennie Benjamin and George Weiss with whom he wrote one of his last songs, 'Jet', in 1951. It became a modest hit for **Nat 'King' Cole**.

Further reading: *Meet The Musikids-They Wrote Your Songs*, Harry Revel.

Revenants

The core of Ireland band the Revenants are Stephen Ryan (guitar/vocals), Doug Steen (guitar), Jeremy Irvin (bass), Chris Heaney (drums) and Don Ryan (keyboards), although ex-Would Be's singer Eileen Gogan and Something Happens! drummer Eamonn Ryan and bass player Ray Harman also contributed to the group's debut album. Stephen Ryan had formerly played with the much-loved **Stars Of Heaven**, a band who never quite conquered the public the way they did the press. After their break up Ryan retreated to the studio to work on a new collection of songs with fellow Dublin native Steen. These songs and a band to play them finally came to fruition at the end of 1992 with the advent of debut album, *Horse Of A Different Colour*. With Ryan's plangent, almost unforthcoming vocals, and patent lyrical wit, it was a fine collection of songs which spanned territory somewhere between **R.E.M.** and **10,000 Maniacs**. One theme, alcohol, was poignantly revisited in several lyrics, notably 'Let's Get Falling Down (Drunk Tonight)' and 'The Drinking Side Of Me', though Ryan professed that 'Most of the songs are love songs of one kind or another.'
Album: *Horse Of A Different Colour* (1993).

Revenge

Formed in Manchester in 1987, and now one of three offshoots featuring 'resting' members of **New Order**. Peter Hook (b. 13 February 1956, Salford, Manchester, England) was initially joined by David Hicks (ex-Southern Death Cult, Lavolta Lakota; guitar) and CJ (Hook's studio engineer, who had previously worked with the **Chameleons** and the **Fall**). The band was started because: 'Hooky likes playing gigs', and they performed their debut at London's Skin 2 Bondage Club in 1990. By this time they featured drummer Ashley Taylor and bassist David Potts, who had worked in Hook's Suite 16 studio. Unlike the more successful **Electronic**, the first releases by Revenge have garnered mediocre reviews at best. The album was prefaced by disappointing singles '7 Reasons' and 'Pineapple Face'. The third single, 'I'm Not Your Slave', came closest to familiar New Order territory and was the best of the bunch, with Hook's characteristic tugging bass. However, like its predecessors, it failed to make the UK charts. *One True Passion* garnered mixed reviews. Some critics pointed to song titles like 'Surf Nazi' and the recent 'Slave...' single as recalling the flirtation with fascist imagery which had dogged **Joy Division** and New Order. In spite of this, Hook has repeated his intention that Revenge should be an ongoing project.

Album: *One True Passion* (1990).

Revere, Paul, And The Raiders

Formed in Portland, Oregon, USA in 1961, when pianist Revere added Mark Lindsay (vocals/saxophone) to the line-up of his club band, the Downbeats. Drake Levin (guitar), Mike Holliday (bass) and Michael Smith (drums) completed a group later known as Paul Revere And The Nightriders, before settling on their Raiders appellation. Several locally-issued singles ensued, including 'Beatnik Sticks' and 'Like Long Hair', the latter of which rose into the US Top 40. Group manager and disc jockey Roger Hart then financed a demonstration tape which in turn engendered a prestigious recording deal with **CBS/Columbia**. Their version of bar-band favourite 'Louie Louie' was issued in 1963, but although highly successful regionally, was outsold by local rivals the **Kingsmen** who secured the national hit. A year passed before the Raiders recorded a new single, during which time Phil Volk had replaced Holliday. 'Louie Go Home' showed their confidence remained undiminished, but it was 1965 before the Raiders hit their commercial stride with the punky 'Steppin' Out'. By this point the group was the resident act on *Where The Action Is*, **Dick Clark**'s networked, daily television show. The attendant exposure resulted in a series of classic pop singles, including 'Just Like Me' (1965) 'Kicks', 'Hungry', 'Good Things' (all 1966) and 'Him Or Me - What's It Gonna Be' (1967), each of which were impeccably produced by **Terry Melcher**. However, the Raiders' slick stage routines and Revolutionary War garb - replete with thigh-boots, tights, frilled shirts and three-cornered hats - was frowned upon by the emergent underground audience. The departures of Smith, Levin and Volk made little difference to the Raiders' overall sound, enhancing suspicion that session musicians were responsible for the excellent studio sound. Later members Freddie Weller (guitar), Keith Allison (bass) and Joe (Correro) Jnr. (drums) were nonetheless accomplished musicians, and thus enhanced the professional approach marking *Hard & Heavy (With Marshmallow)* and *Collage*. Despite inconsistent chart places, the group maintained a high television profile as hosts of *Happening 68*. In 1969 Lindsay embarked on a concurrent solo career, but although 'Arizona' sold over 1 million copies, later releases proved less successful. Two years later the Raiders scored an unexpected US chart-topper with 'Indian Reservation', previously a UK hit for **Don Fardon**, but it proved their final Top 20 hit. Although Weller forged a new career in country music, Revere and Lindsay struggled to keep the group afloat, particularly when dropped by their longstanding label. The former eventually became the act's custodian, presiding over occasional releases for independent outlets. The Raiders flourished briefly during the US Bicentennial celebrations, before emerging again in 1983 mixing old favourites and new songs on their Raiders America label. This regeneration proved short-lived, although Revere still fronts a version of the group for the nostalgia circuit.

Albums: *Paul Revere And The Raiders* aka *In The Beginning* (1961), *Like, Long Hair* (1961), *Here They Come* (1965), *Just Like Us* (1965), *Midnight Ride* (1966), *The Spirit Of 67* aka *Good Thing* (1967), *Revolution* (1967), *A Christmas Present....And Past* (1967), *Goin' To Memphis* (1968), *Something Happening* (1968), *Hard And Heavy (With Marshmallow)* (1969), *Alias Pink Puzz* (1969), *Collage* (1970), *Indian Reservation* (1971), *Country Wine* (1972). Compilations: *Greatest Hits* (1967), *Greatest Hits Volume 2* (60s), *All-Time Greatest Hits* (70s), *Kicks* (1982).

Revillos

Formed in March 1979 by Eugene Reynolds and Fay Fife, previously vocalists with the **Rezillos**. HiFi Harris (guitar), Rocky Rhythm (drums) and three backing singers - Jane White, Jane Brown and Tricia Bryce - completed the group's original line-up, but within months the latter trio had been replaced by Babs and Cherie Revette. The Revillos made their debut with 'Where's The Boy For Me' (1979), but although this exciting performance recalled the best of the previous group, it failed to emulate their success. Internal friction undermined the unit's undoubted potential - guitarists, bassists and singers were replaced with regularity as Reynolds, Fife and Rhythm pursued their uncompromising vision. An album, *Rev-Up*, captured the Revillos' enchanting mixture of girl-group, beat and science-fiction, but they were subsequently dropped by their record company. Undeterred the group inaugurated Superville for ensuing releases and embarked on two gruelling tours of the USA and Canada which they financed themselves. However an anticipated deal failed to materialize and this ebullient act later disintegrated.

Albums: *Rev Up* (1980), *Attack* (1983).

Revival Movement

Around 1940, at the height of the swing era when commercialism was affecting jazz, adversely so by most standards, many musicians sought alternatives forms of expression. Strikingly, this produced two massively dissimilar views. One, bebop, looked forward and wrought fundamental changes to jazz; the other looked back and revived interest in New Orleans-style jazz. Heading this latter movement in the USA were **Lu Watters,** with his Yerba Buena Jazz Band, and his colleagues **Bob Scobey** and **Turk Murphy**. Amongst the forgotten masters who rose again to public acclaim were **Bunk Johnson** and **George Lewis**. Musicians were not the only people who generated new interest in this early jazz. Many writers helped bring the movement to the attention of the jazz, and sometimes general, public, amongst them Frederick Ramsey, Rudi Blesh and William Russell. In the UK the revivalist movement made its first major impact in the closing years of World War II. One of the most influential of the bandleaders active at this time was **George Webb** and his example was followed by **Humphrey Lyttelton, Wally Fawkes** (both of whom played in Webb's band), **Chris Barber, Freddy Randall** and a succession of others, many of whom followed a significantly more commercial path, unlike **Ken Colyer**, who remained utterly dedicated to the first principles of New Orleans jazz. All these musicians found audiences and their once-removed pioneering efforts found their reward in the continuation around the world, but notably in the UK, of a persistent strain of dixieland. Many of these dixieland bands owed more to early Chicago music than that of New Orleans while even more missed the point of revivalism by basing themselves upon the style and format of the **Louis Armstrong** All Stars of the late 40s and 50s. Despite these dilutions of revivalist principles, the standards set by New Orleans advocates such as Watters and Colyer helped to retain interest in early forms of jazz and their records demonstrate that imitation can be more than sincere flattery and retain much of the enthusiasm and skills of the music's progenitors.

Revolting Cocks

Endearingly titled industrial funk metal band, the name occasionally shortened to RevCo when propriety demands. The Revolting Cocks history stretches back to the mid-80s when Al Jourgenson (also **Ministry**) met Belgians Richard 23 and Luc Van Acker in a Chicago pool hall. Legend has it that a drunken Van Acker stumbled in to Jourgenson when the latter was attempting to make a winning shot in a $500 game. However, Jourgenson recovered his composure to win, and the three celebrated by wrecking the club. On their exit the manager was heard to remark 'Get out, you revolting cocks!'. The group's first single under their new moniker would be 'No Devotion', housed on Chicago's infamous **Wax Trax** label. When it made the PMRC's 'Naughty 9' list for its blasphemy something of a noble tradition was born. The lyrical scope of the group's debut offered no respite. Subject matter included rioting soccer fans, sitcom junkies and industrial accidents. Joined in 1987 by multi-instrumentalist William Rieflin, the next single, 'You Often Forget', featured both 'malignant' and 'benign' versions in tribute to the prevalent media fascination with Betty Ford's breasts. Richard 23 then departed for **Front 242**, to be replaced by **Chris Connelly** of **Finitribe** fame. Paul Barker of Ministry was also on hand to guest and co-produce the half-live *You Goddamned Son Of A Bitch*, recorded at a Chicago show in September 1987. However, *Beers, Steers And Queers* would be the group's second album proper, its title-track a hilarious machismo pile-up of cowboy kitsch and dialogue stolen from the homo-erotic scenes of *Deliverance*. A 'cover' of **Olivia Newton John**'s '(Let's Get) Physical' was also on hand to startle the casual browser - basically consisting of a loop of someone screaming the title. Afterwards the band would move away from Wax Trax (as had Ministry, from whom RevCo would now additionally absorb Roland Barker, Mike Scaccia and Louie Svitek). The madness continued unabated at their new label, with *Linger Ficken' Good* this time seizing **Rod Stewart**'s 'Do You Think I'm Sexy' and righteously deflowering it with additional lyrics from Connelly concerning dentistry. Afterwards RevCo took a break from inflaming moral umbrage while Jourgenson concentrated on Ministry activities.

Albums: *Big Sexy Land* (Wax Trax 1986), *You Goddamned Son Of A Bitch* (Wax Trax 1988), *Beers, Steers + Queers* (Wax Trax 1990), *Linger Ficken' Good And Other Barnyard Oddities* (Devotion 1993).

Revolution

This rarely-screened 1969 film was directed by Jack O'Connell who 'discovered' its star, Today Malone, dancing at San Fransciso's Avalon Ballroom. Taking its cue from that city's 'flower-power' era, *Revolution* focuses on such hippie-styled tracts as a back-to-the-woods commune, a Krishna temple, a celebration of the Summer Solstice and a ballet performed by the San Franciscan Workshop in which the participants are naked. Bay Area musicians are also very much in evidence and the soundtrack includes material by three groups in their formative stages. A five-piece **Quicksilver Messenger Service** contribute 'Babe I'm Gonna Leave You' and 'Codine', the only tracks this line-up recorded. The **Steve Miller Band** offer the equally nascent 'Mercury Blues', 'Superbyrd' and 'Your Old Lady', while Texan act **Mother Earth** provide 'Without Love', 'Stranger In My Home Town' and the title track. None of these performances are available on other contemporary releases, inspiring interest in the attendant soundtrack album. Indeed, when the lustre of the film ebbed, the set was repackaged as a release showcasing three fascinating acts in their formative years. An interesting view of west coast alternative lifestyles, *Revolution* is interesting, if only for the rare music on offer.

Revolutionaries

The Revolutionaries were formed in 1976 and consisted of the in-house session band at Channel One Recording Studio, Maxfield Avenue, Kingston. The line-up featured **Sly Dunbar**, **Robbie Shakespeare**, Earl 'Wire' Lindo, Rad Bryan and **Ansell Collins**. If any of the musicians were unavailable others would step in. These included **Lloyd Parkes**, Uziah 'Sticky' Thompson, Barnabus, Bo Peep, Errol 'Tarzan' Nelson and Skully. They were accompanied by the horn section which consisted of ex-**Skatalite Tommy McCook**, 'Deadly' Headly Bennett and Vin Gordon. The line-up evolved from Skin, Flesh And Bones who were the resident band at the Tit For Tat club. Their notoriety spread and they were considered to be the island's top session band. They accompanied **Al Brown** on his track 'Here I Am Baby (Come And Take Me)' which led to them supporting him and others on the Jamaica Showcase tour in 1974. Dunbar's drumming, with its innovative beat, helped the group provide hits for the **Mighty Diamonds** ('Right Time'), **Junior Byles** ('Fade Away'), **Johnny Osbourne** ('Kiss Somebody') and **Dillinger** ('CB 200'). The Mighty Diamonds cut led to an album of the same name which was released through **Virgin Records** in the UK. The Revolutionaries recording style became known as Rockers and the other studios in Jamaica emulated the band's winning formula. The ensemble were criticized for utilizing **Coxsone Dodd**'s old Studio One rhythms but the record-buying public loved it. The group also recorded a number of dub and instrumental albums *Vital Dub, Goldmine Dub, Black Ash Dub* and *Negrea Love Dub*, all of which were greeted with enthusiasm and sold in good quantities. The group's demise occurred when **Sly And Robbie**'s services were enroled by **Peter Tosh** for his backing band, Word Sound And Power, whilst the other members joined forces with **Bunny Lee**'s **Aggrovators**. Ironically a dub compilation *The Revolutionaries Meet The Aggrovators At Channel One* surfaced which has proved to be the most enduring set.

Albums: *Vital Dub* (Virgin 1976), *Goldmine Dub* (Greensleeves 1978), *Guerilla Dub* (Burning Sounds 1978), *Negrea Love Dub* (Trojan 1978), *Black Ash Dub* (Trojan 1978), *Macca Roots Man Dub* (GG 1978), *Outlaw Dub* (Trojan 1978), *Junkanoo Dub* (Cha Cha 1978), Compilations: *Revolutionaries Part One* (United Artists 1981), *Revolutionaries Part Two* (United Artists 1981), *Hit Bound The Revolutionary Sound Of Channel One* (Heartbeat 1990, covers 1976-79).

Revolutionary Ensemble

Leroy Jenkins, **Sirone** and **Jerome Cooper**. Violinist Leroy Jenkins was dispatched to New York in 1970 as a representative for Chicago's **AACM**. On the east coast, the musicians, by and large, still viewed performance in the competitive terms of the 'cutting contest' and 'fighting for your space'. Chicago's music had been geared toward collective endeavour; to get the message across, Jenkins needed a band. The Revolutionary Ensemble explored chamber-music textures in an unstuffy way, was often the most subtle band in the new music, used multi-instrumentation undemonstratively, juxtaposed broken-time nerve-pulse playing with drummer/pianist Cooper's often tribal-sounding rhythms, while Jenkins's acid-edged violin skirled on and on. Bassist Sirone saw the group as 'interpreters of Nature's Music. We find that everything on the earth contributes to its harmony.' The group's example was a big influence on the 'Loft movement' of the mid-70s but, by 1978, the Ensemble players were pulling in different directions and the group disbanded. At Sirone's instigation, the Revolutionary Ensemble re-formed for a one-off appearance at the Nickelsdorf Festival in Austria in 1990.

Albums: *Vietnam I & II* (1972), *Manhattan Cycles* (1974), *The Psyche* (1975), *The People's Republic* (1976), *Revolutionary Ensemble* (1978).

Revolver

This three piece UK 90s independent label pop group comprised Mat Flint (vocals/guitar), Nick Dewey (drums) and Hamish Brown (bass). Flint and Dewey were both from Winchester, had played in several bands for the previous three years, and met Brown in London in September 1990. Influenced in their efforts by the **Beach Boys**, **Beatles**, **Byrds**, **My Bloody Valentine**, and the **Jesus And Mary Chain**, they played their first gig in December 1990. Soon after came the EP, *Heaven Sent An Angel*, after which the media, keen to establish some form of clearly defined trend, picked up on them and numerous others with a similar approach. They were clearly taken unawares by the glare of attention: 'We don't have a desire as individuals to be famous, but we want the band to be a famous name so we can grin down from bedroom walls and get to play in New York.' Possibly due to the fact that all three members of the band were still attempting to pursue a parallel academic career, it would be 1993 before a debut album was released. Its basic rock energy took many journalists, who had written the band off as part of the much reviled 'shoegazing' scene, by surprise.

Album: *Cold Water Flat* (Hut 1993).

Revolving Paint Dream

The Revolving Paint Dream was not only the most mysterious act on **Creation Records**' original roster back in 1984, but also one of the most inventive. After a memorable psychedelia-tinged single, 'Flowers In The Sky'/'In The Afternoon', in February, the band disappeared for three years before a strange collection of what seemed like out-takes, *Off To Heaven*, reached the shelves in June 1987. 60s-influenced pop sat alongside weird, distorted soundscapes to create an album that lacked any overall identity but was stacked full with ideas. It transpired that the band comprised **Primal Scream**'s second guitarist Andrew Innes, **Nico**-like vocalist Christine Wanless (also present on several **Biff Bang Pow!** recordings) and Luke Hayes, with probable involvement from label organizers Alan McGee and Richard Green. January 1989's *Mother Watch Me Burn* was even more experimental and the listener was hard pushed to believe that it was the same band performing the fragrant pop tune, 'Sun, Sea, Sand' and the ferocious instrumentals.
Albums: *Off To Heaven* (Creation 1987), *Mother Watch Me Burn* (Creation 1989).

Rey, Alvino

b. Al McBurney, 1 July 1911, Cleveland, Ohio, USA. An accomplished guitarist, Rey played with various dancebands, including those of Phil Spitalney, **Russ Morgan**, **Freddy Martin** and **Horace Heidt,** before forming his own band in the winter of 1938/9. With Heidt, Rey had been featured on the steel Hawaiian guitar and also on an early form of electronically-amplified guitar. He continued to play guitar in his own band, and also brought from Heidt the vocal group, the **King Sisters**, one of whom, Louise, he married. Rey toured extensively in the early 40s and eventually became popular with dancers across the USA. The band featured comedy, lots of vocals and highly competent musicianship. All this, allied to the unusual effect Rey created by miking Louise King's vocals through the guitar amplifier, helped build a following for the band. Towards the end of 1942, however, Rey changed to a more jazz-orientated policy, commissioning arrangements from **Billy May**, **Johnny Mandel**, **Neal Hefti** and others. He also hired top flight musicians, including at one time or another saxophonists **Zoot Sims**, **Al Cohn** and **Herbie Steward** and a succession of excellent drummers, amongst whom were **Nick Fatool**, **Mel Lewis**, **Dave Tough** and **Don Lamond**. During the early years of World War II, Rey managed to keep the band going while also engaging himself and his sidemen in factory work for the war effort. The band eventually folded in 1944 and Rey entered the US Navy where he led a band. In the post-war years Rey formed a new band, even more strongly committed to playing jazz, but his attempts to sustain a big band met with increasing difficulties. By the 50s he was leading a small group and in the following decade drifted into television as a producer and occasional performer. One of the shows with which he was associated was *The King Family Show*, which featured his wife and her sisters. By the 70s, Rey was in semi-retirement.
Albums: *The Uncollected Alvino Rey Vols 1-3* (1940-46), *Alvino Rey And His Orchestra 1946* (1946).

Reynolds, Allen

In the USA during the late 50s, Reynolds started his professional career as a record producer when he worked with his friend, country singer, **Dickey Lee**, and they had a regional hit with 'Dream Boy'. He then worked at **Sun Records** in Memphis, becoming friends with producer **Jack Clement**, who recorded him singing 'Through The Eyes Of Love' for **RCA** in 1960. Reynolds was drafted and began a banking career, but he then wrote a pop hit, 'Five O'Clock World', for the **Vogues**. He was soon an established writer and produced **Crystal Gayle** ('Don't It Make My Brown Eyes Blue' and 'When I Dream'). Because of his production commitments, Reynolds has never been a prolific songwriter but his small output is of a high standard and includes, 'Dreaming My Dreams' (**Waylon Jennings**, **Don Williams**), 'I Recall A Gypsy Woman' (Waylon Jennings, Don Williams), 'Somebody Loves You' (Crystal Gayle) and 'We Should Be Together' (Don Williams). Crystal Gayle is associated with 'Wrong Road Again', but Reynolds' own version made the US country charts, albeit number 95, in 1978. Some of his songs are written with Bob McDill, whose work is frequently performed by Reynolds' artists. In the late 80s, he established **Kathy Mattea** with his productions of 'Love At The Five And Dime' and 'Walk The Way The Wind Blows'. He had his biggest successes with **Garth Brooks** and has also produced **Daniel O'Donnell**.

Reynolds, Blind Joe

b. 1900, Arkansas, USA, d. 10 March 1968, Monroe, Louisiana, USA. Reynolds also recorded as Blind Willie Reynolds. He was a wild and violent man with an extensive criminal record, who carried a gun even after he was blinded by a shotgun during an argument in the mid-20s. He played widely in Mississippi and Louisiana, and recorded in 1929 and 1930; the two 78s on which he recorded feature fierce singing and slide guitar, closely allied to the blues styles of Mississippi. His lyrics are caustic, misogynistic, bawdy and sometimes hastily self-censored. His signature tune, 'Outside Woman Blues' was recorded by **Cream** in the 60s, at which time Reynolds, was still performing in his original milieu, perhaps the last important blues singer of his generation to do so.
Album: *Son House And The Great Delta Blues Singers* (1990).

Reynolds, Debbie

b. Mary Frances Reynolds, 1 April 1932, El Paso, Texas, USA. A popular actress and singer, particularly in movies. After moving to California in 1940 she became a majorette and played French horn with the Burbank Youth Orchestra. It was there she was spotted by talent scouts at a Miss Burbank competition in 1948. She quickly became a leading light in film musicals such as *The Daughter Of Rosie O'Grady* (1950), *Three Little Words* (as 'Boop-Boop-A-Doop' girl **Helen Kane**), *Two Weeks With Love*, ***Singin' In The Rain*** (perhaps her most memorable role), *Skirts Ahoy!*, *I Love Melvin*, *The Affairs Of Dobie Gillis*, *Athena*, *Give A Girl A Break*, ***Hit The Deck***, *The Tender Trap* (comedy with music), *Bundle Of Joy*, *Meet Me In Las Vegas*, *Say One For Me*, *Pepe*, and *The Unsinkable Molly Brown* (1964, Oscar nomination). In 1966 Reynolds appeared in *The Singing Nun* (a fictionalized story about Soeur Sourire), and three years later starred in her own television series *Debbie*. In 1951 she recorded her first million-selling single, 'Aba Daba Honeymoon' (from the film *Two Weeks With Love*), on which she duetted with Carleton Carpenter. She also went to the top of the US charts in 1957 with the million-selling 'Tammy' (from *Tammy And The Bachelor*). She married the singer and actor **Eddie Fisher** in September 1955, and their daughter Carrie has since become an established actress and writer. They divorced in 1959 when Fisher married Elizabeth Taylor. As her film career declined, she made an acclaimed Broadway debut in the 1973 revival of the much-loved American musical ***Irene***, and appeared in her own television series and nightclub revue. In later years, she survived severe financial problems when her second husband's business failed, and she and Carrie were estranged after Carrie's hard-hitting novel, *Postcards From The Edge*, which was supposedly based on their lives together, was filmed in 1990. Always the trouper, she bounced right back, launching two keep-fit videos, and headlining at venues such as Harrah's in Reno, and Caesar's Palace in Las Vegas, often in the company of her former film co-stars, such as Harve Presnell (*The Unsinkable Molly Brown*) and **Donald O'Connor** (*Singin' In The Rain*). In 1993 she opened the Debbie Reynolds Hotel on the fringe of the Las Vegas Strip, where she presents her two-hour autobiographical one-woman show which contains often bawdy impressions of Zsa Zsa Gabor, Mae West, and **Barbra Streisand.** The complex also houses Reynolds' museum of Hollywood memorabilia.

Albums: *Debbie Reynolds* (Dot 1959), *Am I That Easy To Forget* (Dot 1960), *Fine & Dandy* (Dot 1960), *From Debbie With Love* (Dot (1960), *Tammy* (Dot 1963), *Raising A Ruckus* (Metro (1965), *Debbie* (Jasmine 1985), and film soundtrack recordings.

Further reading: *Debbie - My Life*, Debbie Reynolds with David Patrick Columba.

Reynolds, Donn

b. Winnipeg, Canada. Little seems known of Reynolds' early life or where he first learned his country music, but during World War II, he served in the Canadian Navy. In the late 40s, he spent two years touring Australia and New Zealand, where he worked on the radio and played the theatre circuit in New South Wales. He was initially attracted to yodelling by the recordings of Harry Torrani but soon developed his own style, which includes traces of both normal country and Bavarian yodels. On 16 September 1947, during his Australian tour, he recorded six sides for Regal-Zonophone, including his own composition 'The Stockman's Lullaby'. An urge to travel then prompted him return to the USA where, apart from his singing, he also appeared in films that starred **Roy Rogers**, **Gene Autry** and John Wayne. He later toured very successfully in South Africa. In the mid-50s, he played venues in the UK and Europe and in 1960, on a further UK visit, he married his wife, Cindy, a member of the Skylarks trio. They played venues together in the UK and he recorded tracks for Pye and HMV, before returning to Winnipeg in 1961, where he became popular on CTV's *Cross Country Barndance*. In the early 60s, he recorded two albums for the Canadian ARC label, one being a yodelling album. Reynolds is equally at home with gentle ballads or with yodelling. It may be, however, that to some people, he is better known for his yodelling ability since in 1956, this talent won him both the National and the World Yodelling Championship in the USA. In 1976, he also got his name into the *Guinness Book Of Records*, when he yodelled non-stop for seven hours and twenty-nine minutes. Reynolds is still singing and yodelling and often performs now for charities.

Albums: *Springtime In The Rockies* (ARC 60s), *Blue Canadian Rockies* (ARC 60s), *The Wild One* (Banff 60s), *Song Of The West* (Marathon 60s), *King Of The Yodellers* (Grand Slam 1979).

Reynolds, Jody

b. 3 December 1938 in Denver, Colorado, USA. Reynolds grew up in Oklahoma and formed his first band, the Storms, in 1952. He played guitar in the group and worked various jobs until he could make a living playing music. In 1958 the band went to Los Angeles and was there signed to the new Demon label. The label did not use the Storms but did record Reynolds backed with a number of professional session musicians on his 1958 single 'Endless Sleep' (covered in the UK by **Marty Wilde**), a song Reynolds had written with George Brown (credited under the pseudonym Delores Nance). The song reached number 5 and became one of the first of the so-called 'death rock' hits of the 50s and 60s (others in that category included 'Tell Laura I Love Her', 'Terry', 'Teen Angel' and 'Leader Of The Pack'). Reynolds made the charts once more, with 'Fire Of Love' (also in 1958) but none of his subsequent recordings for Demon, Smash or other labels charted. Reynolds continued to perform with the Storms for much of the 60s, but by the 70s had retired to a non-musical career. His only album was a 1978 set on the Tru-Gems label including a remake of his only hit.

Album: *Endless Sleep* (Tru-Gems 1978).

Reynolds, Malvina

b. 23 August 1900, San Francisco, California, USA, d. 17 March 1978, Berkeley, California, USA. Reynolds was primarily a songwriter who later took to performing her material on guitar. She did not begin writing until as late as the 50s. Prior to this she had worked in various jobs. In 1925, Malvina gained her BA in English Language and Literature, and, two years later, her MA. In 1939, she was awarded a PhD. During the Depression days, Reynolds had been able to findwork as a teacher. Such classic as 'Little Boxes' made popular by **Pete Seeger**, and 'What Have They Done To The Rain' brought Reynolds to public attention. The latter composition achieved hit status in 1965 when recorded by the **Searchers**. The following year the **Seekers** reached number 2, in the UK charts with their version of Reynolds' 'Morningtown Ride'. Reynolds' popularity increased when **Joan Baez**, **Bob Dylan**, and **Judy Collins** began to record her songs. Reynolds recorded two albums for children, *Artichokes, Griddle Cakes*, and *Funnybugs*, as well as writing for, and appearing on, television's *Sesame Street*. Reynolds died in March 1978. *Mama Lion* was a posthumous release.

Albums: *Another County Heard From* (1960), *Malvina Reynolds...Sings The Truth* (1968), *Malvina Reynolds* (1970), *Artichokes, Griddle Cakes* (1970), *Malvina* (1972), *Funnybugs* (1972), *Malvina..Held Over* (1975), *Magical Songs* (1978), *Mama Lion* (1980).

Further reading: *Tweedles And Foodles For Young Noodles*, Malvina Reynolds. *Little Boxes And Other Handmade Songs*, Malvina Reynolds. *The Muse Of Parker Street*, Malvina Reynolds. *Cheerful Tunes For Lutes And Spoons*, Malvina Reynolds. *The Malvina Reynolds Songbook*, Malvina Reynolds. *There's Music In The Air*, Malvina Reynolds

Rezillos

Formed in Edinburgh, Scotland, in March 1976, the Rezillos were initially an informal aggregation consisting of Eugene Reynolds (b. Alan Forbes; vocals), Fay Fife (b. Sheila Hynde; vocals), Luke Warm aka Jo Callis (lead guitar), Hi Fi Harris (b. Mark Harris; guitar), Dr. D.K. Smythe (bass), Angel Patterson (b. Alan Patterson; drums) and Gale Warning (backing vocals). Their irreverent repertoire consisted of pre-beat favourites by **Screaming Lord Sutch** and the **Piltdown Men**, judicious material from the **Dave Clark Five** and glam-rock staples by the **Sweet**.

Their image, part Marlon Brando, part **Shangri-Las**, allied them with the punk movement, although their love of pop heritage denied wholesale involvement. The Rezillos' debut single, 'I Can't Stand My Baby', encapsulated their crazed obsessions, but its success introduced a discipline at odds with their initial irreverence. Harris, Smythe and Warning left the line-up, while auxiliary member William Mysterious (b. William Donaldson; bass/saxophone) joined the group on a permanent basis. Now signed to a major label, **Sire Records**, the quintet undertook several tours and scored a UK Top 20 hit with the satirical 'Top Of The Pops' in August 1978. The group's debut album, *Can't Stand The Rezillos*, also charted, before internal pressures began pulling them apart. Mysterious was replaced by Simon Templar, but in December 1978 the Rezillos folded following a brief farewell tour. Fife and Reynolds formed the **Revillos**, while the rest of the band became known as Shake. Callis later found fame in the **Human League**. In the 90s the Revillos/Rezillos reformed for tours in Japan, from which a live album was culled to bookmark their fifteen year career.

Albums: *Can't Stand The Rezillos* (Sire 1978), *Mission Accomplished ... But The Beat Goes On* (Sire 1979). Compilations: *Can't Stand The Rezillos, The (Almost) Complete Rezillos* (Sire 1995), *Live And On Fire In Japan* (Vinyl Japan 1995).

Rhapsody In Blue

Yet another film biography which bears little resemblance to reality. Fortunately, in this case the subject is composer **George Gershwin** and so the music more than makes up for the inadequacies and fantasies of the screenplay. Robert Alda, the well-known Broadway and radio actor, made his film debut as Gershwin, and Joan Leslie and Alexis Smith played two of the important women in his life. Leslie, whose singing voice was dubbed by Louanne Hogan, handled several of the songs in a predictably glorious score which included 'Fascinating Rhythm', 'I Got Rhythm', 'Love Walked In', 'Embraceable You', 'An American In Paris', 'Someone To Watch Over Me', 'Mine', 'The Man I Love', 'Oh, Lady, Be Good', 'Bidin' My Time', and 'Clap Yo' Hands' (all with lyrics by **Ira Gershwin**); and 'Summertime' (Du Bose Heyward), 'Swanee' (**Irving Caesar**), 'Somebody Loves Me' (**Buddy De Sylva**-Ballard Macdonald), 'Do It Again' (DeSylva), and 'I'll Build A Stairway To Paradise' (DeSylva-Ira Gershwin). **Oscar Levant** played the celebrated 'Concerto In F' and 'The Rhapsody In Blue' (conducted by **Paul Whiteman**), and among the other artists who appeared as themselves were **Al Jolson**, Hazel Scott, George White and Anne Brown. Rosemary DeCamp and Morris Carnovsky played Gershwin's mother and father, and other roles were taken by Charles Coburn (as music publisher Max Dreyfuss), Albert Basserman, Julie Bishop, Herbert

Rudley, Mickey Roth, Darryl Hickman, Johnny Downs, Tom Patricola, Stephen Richard, Martin Noble, and Will Wright. Howard Koch and Elliot Paul dreamed up the screenplay, and LeRoy Prinz was responsible for the choreography which, like the rest of the picture, benefited from some fine black and white photography by Sol Polito. Irving Rapper was the director, and *Rhapsody In Blue*, which was produced for Warner Brothers in 1945 by Jesse L. Lasky, still retains its appeal to this day.

Rhino Records

The Los Angeles-based record company was launched in 1978 by Richard Foos and Harold Bronson as an outgrowth of their Rhino Records retail store. At first the fledgling company specialized in novelty records, including an all-kazoo version of **Led Zeppelin**'s 'Whole Lotta Love' by the Temple City Kazoo Orchestra and an album by one-time **Frank Zappa** protege **Wild Man Fischer**. During the 80s the label took to reissuing out-of-print recordings from rock's 'golden era' including the catalogues of the **Monkees** and the **Turtles** and hits collections from a diverse list of artists including **Jerry Lee Lewis**, **Nancy Sinatra** and the **Neville Brothers**. Rhino also made an impact with its inventive various artists compilations, including two volumes of nothing but the song 'Louie, Louie' and collections of soul music, novelty records, early 70s AM radio hits, British Invasion, 'Frat Rock' and many others. By the mid-80s Rhino was recognized as the leading repackager in the USA.
Compilations: *Rhino Teen Magazine* (1984), *Rhino Brothers Greatest Flops* (1988).

Rhinoceros

A rock band that promised more than it was able to deliver, Rhinoceros was an **Elektra Records**' signing of the late 60s. The group looked a formidable line-up on paper with Michael Fonfara, ex-**Electric Flag** (keyboards), Billy Mundi, ex-**Mothers Of Invention** (drums), Doug Hastings, ex-**Buffalo Springfield** (guitar), Danny Weis, ex-**Iron Butterfly** (guitar) and John Finlay (vocals). The spectacular fold out cover artwork on their debut by G. Sazaferin showed a brightly colourful, beaded Rhinoceros. Unfortunately the music was disappointing, only the **Buddy Miles** influenced 'You're My Girl (I Don't Want To Discuss It)' and their 'greatest hit' the instrumental 'Apricot Brandy' stood out. The BBC adopted the latter as a Radio 1 theme. Two more albums followed, but by now the ponderous Rhinoceros had turned into a dodo.
Albums: *Rhinoceros* (1968), *Satin Chickens* (1969), *Better Times Are Coming* (1970).

Rhoads, Randy

Possibly one of the best hard rock guitarists to come out of America during the past two decades, Randy Roads (b. Randall William Rhoads, 6 December 1956, Santa Monica, California, USA, d. 19 March 1982) would, had his life not been so tragically curtailed in a freak aeroplane accident, be talked about in the same breath as **Eddie Van Halen** and **Jimmy Page**. Certainly, there are many sterile technicians in the metal world whose celebrated virtuosity offers no match to Rhoads' flair. At an early age Rhoads began to study the guitar and in 1972 formed his first band, **Quiet Riot**, who, by 1975, with vocalist Devin Dubrow and drummer Drew Forsyth, began to earn a good live reputation. By 1978 (when they were joined by bassist Rudy Sarzo), this had earned them a recording contract with **Columbia Records**, who pushed them (successfully) into the Japanese market. In October 1979 Sarzo joined American legends **Angel** and Rhoads became a guitar tutor. With **Ozzy Osbourne** finally free of **Black Sabbath** he began to put together a new band called Blizzard Of Ozz, having recruited a bassist and drummer. Ozzy then held auditions for a guitarist in Los Angeles. At the end of a day spent listening to rehashed Sabbath riffs he fell asleep. Later that evening he awoke to hear a gripping and original style. Half-conscious, he turned to his manager/wife Sharon and asked who the girl with the guitar was. From out of his mass of long blonde hair Rhoads appeared to take the post. It is with Ozzy that Rhoads is best remembered for his stunning live performances and excellence in the studio. The first Ozzy album contained his powerful signature on tracks like 'Crazy Train' and 'Suicide Solution', as well as the more sensitive 'Dee', a track written by Rhoads for his mother. The title-track to the second album, *Diary Of A Madman*, contains a superb mixture of acoustic and electric guitar, while 'You Can't Kill Rock And Roll' moved one reviewer to say that 'Randy is at his most eloquent, spacey and rich'. Not satisfied with being merely a rock guitarist, Rhoads also concentrated on his masters degree in classical guitar, eventually hoping to melt the two styles to create new wonders. It was not to be. Whilst *en route* to Florida for further live shows the tour bus made an unscheduled stop where the driver's friend had a small aeroplane. After taking up a couple of band members for a joy ride Rhoads and a make-up girl were persuaded to enlist. The pilot, high on cocaine, seemingly aimed the aircraft at the empty tour bus and all passengers were killed. Ozzy and his wife have never fully recovered from the tragedy. Nor, for that matter, has his music. In 1987 Ozzy and Rhoads' mother put together a tribute album containing live recordings and a studio outtake of 'Dee'.
Albums: with Quiet Riot *Quite Riot* (Columbia 1978), *Quiet Riot 2* (Columbia 1979); with Ozzy Osbourne *Blizzard Of Ozz* (Jet 1980), *Diary Of A Madman* (Jet 1981); *Randy Rhoads Tribute Album* (Epic 1987).

Rhoda With The Special AKA

Rhoda Daker (a former member of UK group the **Bodysnatchers**) briefly teamed up with the **Special AKA** in 1981. The following year, they backed her in the above collaboration on 'The Boiler'. This extraordinary song about sexual attitudes towards women, chillingly evoked an attempted rape, ending with a blood-curdling scream. Because of its controversial subject matter and impassioned performance, moves were made to ban it, but it subsequently climbed into the UK Top 40.

Rhodes, Emitt

b. February 1948, Hawthorne, California, USA. Rhodes first attracted attention as drummer in the Palace Guard, a Los Angeles-based septet which recorded several superior British-influenced singles, notably 'All Night Long' and 'Like Falling Sugar'. Emitt left the line-up in 1966, tiring of its conservative image, and having switched to guitar, pieced together the **Merry-Go-Round**. This superb anglophile quartet completed an album and a handful of singles, before Rhodes left to record as a solo act. *An American Dream* combined several Merry-Go-Round masters with new material, and his career did not flourish fully until the release of *Emitt Rhodes*. He wrote, arranged and co-produced the entire selection as well as playing all the instruments. The results offered a grasp of melodic pop similar to that of **Paul McCartney**, and invoked a kinship with contemporaries **Badfinger** and the **Raspberries**. *Mirror* was burdened by an unfocused production and thus lacked the immediacy of its predecessor. Rhodes was also under pressure to fulfil contractual obligations, which may well explain the artistic decline that marked *Farewell To Paradise*. Emitt abandoned his recording career in the wake of 'Tame The Lion', an anti-war single, and opted instead for an A&R/production post at **Elektra/Asylum**. Despite completing several demo tapes during the 80s, Rhodes has since remained in relative seclusion.
Albums: *Emitt Rhodes* (1970), *The American Dream* (1971, recordings from 1967-68), *Mirror* (1972), *Farewell To Paradise* (1973).

Rhodes, Eugene

Rhodes' blues singing and guitar were recorded in the Indiana State Penitentiary in the early 60s. As a youth, he had been a travelling one-man-band, and claimed to have met **Blind Lemon Jefferson**, **Buddy Moss** and **Blind Boy Fuller**, being particularly impressed and influenced by the latter pair. Rhodes' repertoire consisted largely of the commercially recorded blues of the late 20s and the 30s, with a few well-known spirituals; his performance of them was marred by his erratic timing and uncertain pitch.
Album: *Talkin' About My Time* (1963).

Rhodes, Sonny

b. Clarence Edward Smith, 3 November 1940, Smithville, Texas, USA. Rhodes received his first electric guitar at the age of nine and began emulating **'T-Bone' Walker**, **Chuck Willis** (Rhodes still wears a turban), **Junior Parker** and **Bobby Bland**. He first recorded in 1961 in Austin, then moved to California two years later and recorded for Galaxy in 1965. In the 70s and 80s he made several mediocre albums for European companies and some interesting singles for Blues Connoisseur, Cleve White's Cherrie label, and his own Rhodes-Way label. In 1991 Rhodes made the best album of his career for Ichiban, highlighting his vocals and songwriting skills in addition to his prowess on both regular and lap steel guitars.
Selected albums: *I Don't Want My Blues Colored Bright* (1978), *Just Blues* (1985), *Disciple Of The Blues* (1990), *Living Too Close To The Edge* (Ichiban 1992).

Rhodes, Todd Washington

b. 31 August 1900, Hopkinsville, Kentucky, USA, d. 4. June 1965, Detroit, Michigan, USA. Pianist Rhodes first came to prominence in the late 20s as a founder member of **McKinney's Cotton Pickers**, recording several dozen tracks for **RCA** Victor between 1928 and 1931. Leaving the Cotton Pickers in 1934, Rhodes became a popular act in the Detroit jazz scene and formed his own band in the early 40s, recording for the local Sensation label between 1947 and 1950. He hit the R&B charts with 'Bell Boy Boogie', and gave **Alan Freed** his famous signature tune 'Blues For The Red Boy'. Rhodes' material was leased to Vitacoustic in Chicago and King in Cincinnati. In 1951, Todd Rhodes And His Toddlers began recording for King Records proper and for the following three years laid down some of the best R&B of the 50s, both alone and as backing band for artists including **Wynonie Harris** and **Dave Bartholomew**. Rhodes was also instrumental in given R&B singer **LaVern Baker** her big break. Rhodes disbanded his group in 1957, although he continued to play as a solo act until his death in 1965. Many of his sidemen and associates progressed to become respected jazz musicians or session players for the mighty **Motown** empire.
Albums: *Dance Music That Hits The Spot* (50s, reissued 1988), *Your Daddy's Doggin' Around* (1985).

Rhodes, Walter

Reportedly from Cleveland, Mississippi, USA, Rhodes was unusual, possibly unique, coming from that state, to be a blues singing accordionist. He had one record issued, cut in 1927, and it seems certain that **Charley Patton** knew either Rhodes personally or his record; for Patton's 'Banty Rooster Blues' is a cover of Rhodes' 'The Crowing Rooster'. Rhodes played in a band that included two guitars and a fiddle, though only a guitar duo backs him on record. He is said to have died in the 40s after being struck by lightning.

Albums: *Memphis Blues* (1987), *Giving You The Blues* (Swingmaster 1989).

Rhythm albums

Rhythm albums are reggae LPs that are all based on one backing track. The first such artefact was Rupie Edwards' 'Yamaha Skank', which featured a dozen different mixes and vocals over the 'My Conversation' rhythm in 1975. Gradually rhythm albums increased in popularity until, by 1990, they constituted around a third of all Jamaican LP releases. Their advantages were obvious: once you like a rhythm, chances are you'll like more of it. To producers it represents the minimum outlay in terms of musicians and studio time. It is also cheaper to buy one LP containing 10 versions of a track than 10 singles.

Selected albums: *Various: Yamaha Skank* (1975), *Stalag 17, 18, 19* (1987), *Music Works Showcase '88* (1988), *Funky Punany* (Fashion 1991).

Rhythm Heritage

The pseudonym of producers **Steve Barri** and Michael Omartian (ex-**Loggins And Messina** band), Rhythm Heritage was a studio group specially created to record the 'Theme From S.W.A.T.' This top-rated American television series, dealing with the adventures of the Special Weapons And Tactics Team, had an arresting theme written by Barry De Vorzon that was unavailable on record. Sensing its commercial potential, Barri recorded his own version, aided by studio musicians including Jeff Porcaro (later of **Toto**) and **Ray Parker Jnr**. 'Theme From S.W.A.T.' went on to become the first theme from a television series ever to top the US charts. Barri, already a songwriter with his illustrious former partner, **P.F. Sloan**, was no stranger to the film theme game, having previously scored a hit with **Johnny Rivers**' 'Secret Agent Man' (from the UK series *Danger Man*). Using the group title Rhythm Heritage again, Barri and Omartian found success with another television tie-in 'Barretta's Theme (Keep Your Eye On The Sparrow)'. Remarkably, a third television-related theme brought Barri back to number 1 late in 1976, this time as producer rather than artist. The song was 'Welcome Back', performed by **John Sebastian**, and adapted from the series *Welcome Back Kotter*.

Rhythm Invention

Rhythm Invention are a UK duo of Nick Simpson and Richard Brown. Together they offered one of the better examples of the 'trance dance' formula, or deep house without the sexuality, or rave without the front running electronics. Their early singles 'Crunch' and 'I Can't Take It' caught the media's attention with their simple but irresistible percussion effects. Typically their 1993

effort, 'Ad Infinitum', was fairly uneventful, but produced a tangible hypnotic effect.

Album: *Inventures In Wonderland* (Warp 1993).

Rhythm King

One of the UK's largest and most successful mainstream dance labels, Rhythm King was an idea originally mooted in 1976 by two friends, Martin Heath and James Horrocks, who shared a love of **Motown** and soul music. An initial parent deal with a major was abandoned when that label refused to pay a minimal advance to licence an American track, 'Love Can't Turn Around'. They hooked up instead with Daniel Miller's highly successful independent label, **Mute**, who granted them the necessary artistic freedom and budget. One of their first signings was **3 Wise Men**, arguably the first ever British rap group. Another notable early rapper, **Schoolly D**, was licensed from the US to their Flame subsidiary. Other signings included **Chuck Brown** and **Gwen McCrae**. The other subsidiary, Transglobal - was a disco-styled operation, which delivered a hit with **Taffy**'s 'I Love My Radio'. It had been popular in clubs for several months before Transglobal gave it a stock release, their reward coming with a number 6 national chart success. 1987 was a quiet year for the label, though **King Sun**/D Moet's 'Hey Love!' picked up lots of airplay (but few sales), and Shawnie G's 'Mission Impossible' and Denise Motto's 'Tell Jack', licensed from the *Chicago Jackbeat* compilations, kept things ticking over. It was 1988 before Rhythm King re-established itself with the **Beatmasters**' featuring the **Cookie Crew**'s 'Rok Da House', which had ironically been a flop when released in its original version a year previously. It was at this point that Horrocks' growing dissatisfaction with the label's direction forced him to leave, going on to establish **React Records**. Undeterred, Adele Nozedar stepped in and new commercial heights were achieved with **Bomb The Bass** hitting number 5 in the charts, and **S'Express** (Mark Moore having originally brought Taffy, the Cookie Crew and Beatmasters to RK's attention) bringing them a first number 1 with 'Theme From S'Express' in the summer of 1988. This triumvirate of bands (S'Express, Bomb The Bass and the Beatmasters) continued their ascent throughout the year, both in albums and singles sales. The 1989 signings were a less viable crop, however. Rapper **Merlin**, who had originally appeared on Bomb The Bass's 'Megaton', proved a disappointment, as did Hotline, a house duo from Huddersfield. The saving grace was **Baby Ford**, who provided a run of hits, while the label expanded in opening the **Outer Rhythm** subsidiary, ostensibly to license tracks. Their major success of the 90s would prove to be **D:Ream**, though other artists included bhangra house duo **Joi**, industrial dance groups **KMFDM** and **Sheep On**

Drugs, and indie pop outfit **Sultans Of Ping**.
Selected albums: Bomb The Bass: *Into The Dragon*
(Rhythm King 1988). S'Express: *Original Soundtrack*
(Rhythm King 1989). Beatmasters: *Anywayawanna*
(Rhythm King 1989). Baby Ford: *Ooo The World Of Baby
Ford* (Rhythm King 1990). D:Ream: *Dream On Vol. 1*
(Rhythm King 1993).

Rice, Bobby G.

b. Robert Gene Rice, 11 July 1944, on a farm at
Boscobel, Wisconsin, USA. The Rice Family were
musical and all six siblings were taught an instrument
as children. After first playing for local parties, the
family progressed to running the local Circle D
Ballroom. Rice, who plays guitar and banjo, made his
first appearances there with the family at the age of
five. From the mid-50s, for almost seven years, the
family also presented their own show on WRCO
Richmond, Wisconsin, on which Bobby became the
featured vocalist. In 1962, after graduation and after
the family group disbanded, Bobby pursued a musical
career. He formed the Rock-A-Teens band, which
played rock 'n' roll locally and on its own programme
on WIST-TV. After two years, missing country music,
he began to sing as a duo with his sister Lorraine. They
proved popular in their area, hosted their own
television show and sang backing harmonies on others.
After Lorraine retired, he formed his own band, began
songwriting and played what he termed modern
country, which included country arrangements of pop
songs. He moved to Nashville in the late 60s and
recorded for Royal American. In the early 70s, his first
five chart entries were all minor hits with songs that
had been pop hits of the early 60s, including 'Sugar
Shack' and 'Hey Baby'. Further hits followed, including
Top 10s with 'You Lay So Easy On My Mind' (self-
penned; a UK pop hit for **Andy Williams** in 1975),
'You Give Me You' and 'Freda Comes, Freda Goes'.
Between 1976 and 1988, he charted 19 hits but only
'The Softest Touch In Town' made the Top 30; the
last being 'Clean Livin' Folk' - a duet with Perry
LaPointe in 1988. He recorded albums for several
different labels but has seemingly failed to maintain the
popularity he established in the 70s.
Albums: *Hit After Hit* (1972), *You Lay So Easy On My
Mind* (1973), *She Sure Laid The Lonelies On Me* (1974),
Write Me A Letter (1975), *Instant Rice* (1976), *Bobby G. Rice*
(1982). Compilation: *Greatest Hits* (1980).

Rice, Tim

b. Timothy Miles Bindon Rice, 10 November 1944,
Amersham, Buckinghamshire, England. A lyricist,
librettist, journalist, broadcaster and cricket captain.
Around the time he was briefly studying law, Rice met
the 17-year-old **Andrew Lloyd Webber**, and in
1965, they collaborated on *The Likes Of Us*, a musical
version of the Dr. Barnardo story. Lloyd Webber then
went off to concentrate on serious music, and Rice
worked for **EMI Records**, progressing later to the
Norrie Paramor Organization. In 1968 they
resumed their partnership with *Joseph And The
Amazing Technicolor Dreamcoat*, a 20-minute
'pop cantata' based on the biblical character of Joseph,
for an end-of-term concert at Colet Court boys' school
in the City of London. Subsequently, the piece reached
a wider audience with performances at the Edinburgh
Festival, and venues such as the Old Vic, St. Paul's
Cathedral, and the Central Hall, Westminster, where
Rice played the part of Pharaoh. In 1970, Rice and
Lloyd Webber raided the 'good book' again for the
score of *Jesus Christ Superstar*, a 'rock opera',
presented on a double album, which, when exploited
by producer **Robert Stigwood**, topped the US chart,
and spawned successful singles by **Murray Head**
('Superstar'), and **Yvonne Elliman** ('I Don't Know
How To Love Him'). After several concert
performances of the piece in the USA, some of them
unauthorized and unlicensed the show was
'extravagantly' staged on Broadway in 1972, and ran
for over 700 performances despite some reviews such as
'nearer to the rock bottom than rock opera', and a
good deal of flak from the religious lobby. It did even
better in London, running for a total of 3,358
performances over a period of eight years. In 1992 a
concert version, celebrating the show's 20th
anniversary, toured the UK, starring **Paul Nicholas**
and Claire Moore. The 1973 film version, in one
critic's opinion, was 'one of the true fiascos of modern
cinema'.

Meanwhile, *Joseph And The Amazing Technicolor Dreamcoat*
had risen again, and when extended, and paired with a
new one-act piece, *Jacob's Journey*, played in the West
End for nearly 250 performances during 1973.
Lengthened even further, it became extremely popular
throughout the world, and stayed on Broadway for 20
months in 1981, during which time Joseph was
personified by pop stars such as **Andy Gibb** and
David Cassidy. Hardly any subject could have been
further from Joseph, Jesus and Jacob, than Rice and
Lloyd Webber's next collaboration, *Evita*, 'an opera
based on the life of Eva Peron'. Conceived as an album
in 1976, **Julie Covington**, who sang the part of Eva,
went to number 1 in the UK with 'Don't Cry For Me
Argentina', and 'Another Suitcase, Another Hall' was
successful for **Barbara Dickson**. When the project
reached the West End in 1978, **Elaine Paige** became
a star overnight as Eva, and **David Essex**, in the role
of Che, made the Top 10 with 'Oh What a Circus'.
Four years later, Essex climbed to the UK number 2
spot with Rice's 'A Winter's Tale', written in
collaboration with **Mike Batt**. The original
production of *Evita* was 'a technical knockout, a
magnificent earful, a visual triumph', which stayed at
the Prince Edward Theatre for nearly eight years, and

spent almost half that time on Broadway. Rice's next musical, with composer Stephen Oliver, was **Blondel** (1983), 'a medieval romp' which ran for eight months. Three years later Rice was back in the West End with **Chess** (1986), which replaced *Evita* at the Prince Edward Theatre. Written with Benny Andersson and Bjorn Ulvaeus, both ex-members of **Abba**, the score was released two years earlier on an album which produced 'You Know Him So Well', a UK number 1 for Elaine Paige And Barbara Dickson, and 'One Night In Bangkok', a Top 20 entry for Murray Head. *Chess* ran for three years in London, but was 'a £5 million flop' in New York. Over the years, Rice tinkered with various aspects of the show, and the 1992 off-Broadway version had a drastically revised book. At that stage of his career, *Chess* remained Rice's last major production. In the same year, his first, albeit small theatrical effort, *Joseph And The Amazing Technicolor Dreamcoat* was re-staged at the London Palladium, starring, at various times, the children's television entertainer **Phillip Schofield**, and actor/pop star **Jason Donovan**. The latter topped the UK chart with the show's big number, 'Any Dream Will Do'. Schofield also had a UK chart hit with another song from the show, 'Close Every Door'. It was estimated that Rice and Lloyd Webber were each receiving £16,000 each week from the box office, besides the peripherals.

Rice's projects on a rather smaller scale have included *Cricket* (1986) (with Andrew Lloyd Webber) and *Tycoon*, an English-language version of Michel Berger's hit French musical *Starmania* (1991). He has also contributed songs to several non-musical films, including *The Fan, The Odessa File, Gumshoe* and *The Entertainer*, and worked with composers such as **Francis Lai**, **Vangelis**, **Rick Wakeman** and **Marvin Hamlisch**. In 1993, Rice took over from the late **Howard Ashman** as Alan Menken's lyricist on the **Walt Disney** movie **Aladdin**, and won a Golden Globe Award and an Academy Award for 'A Whole New World'. The number went to the top of the US charts in a version by **Peabo Bryson** and Regina Belle. In the early 90s Rice's worked again with Alan Menken on additional songs for the Broadway stage production of **Beauty And The Beast**, and his collaboration with **Elton John** on the score for the Disney film **The Lion King**, earned him a second Oscar, a Golden Globe, and an **Ivor Novello** Award for the charming 'Circle Of Life'. He has won several other 'Ivors', along with **Tony** and Grammy awards and gold and platinum records. A tribute album, *I Know Them So Well*, containing a selection of his most successful songs performed by various artists, was released in 1994.

As a journalist, Rice has written regular columns for UK national newspapers and for cricket magazines, reflecting his abiding interest in the game which manifested itself in him forming and leading his own regular side, the Heartaches, complete with team colours and year-book. His other more lucrative publications include co-authorship, with his brother Jonathan, and Paul Gambaccini, of the *The Guinness Book Of British Hit Singles* and over 20 associated books. His interest in, and knowledge of, popular music was rewarded with the title of 'Rock Brain Of The Year' on BBC Radio in 1986. He also wrote the script for a 15-part series on the history of Western popular music. His other radio and television work includes *The Musical Triangle, Many A Slip, American Pie, Lyrics By Tim Rice, Just A Minute* and *Three More Men In A Boat*. In 1994, Rice was awarded a Knighthood for services to the arts, particularly music, and sport.

Rich Kids
Formed in London, England, during September 1977, the Rich Kids were the subject of exceptional initial interest. Centred on bassist Glen Matlock (b. 27 August 1956), a former member of the seminal **Sex Pistols**, his eminent role was emphasized by the inclusion of two 'unknown' musicians, Steve New (guitar/vocals) and Rusty Egan (drums). The group was later completed by **Midge Ure**, disillusioned frontman of struggling pop group, **Slik**, and this unusual mixture engendered criticism from unsympathetic quarters. The Rich Kids distanced themselves from punk, and their meagre releases were generally mainstream in execution. Indeed the group's ebullience recalled a 60s bonhomie, but this merely compounded criticism of their 'power pop' approach. The quartet was unable to transform their energy to record, while tension between Matlock and Ure increased to the extent that they were constantly squabbling. The group broke up in November 1978, but denied the fact until free of contractual obligations. Egan and Ure later formed **Visage**, while their former colleagues pursued several low-key projects. Ure would find the greatest subsequent success as singer with **Ultravox**, also playing a significant part in the launch of **Band Aid**. Album: *Ghosts Of Princes In Towers* (EMI 1978).

Rich, Buddy
b. Bernard Rich, 30 September 1917, New York City, New York, USA, d. 2 April 1987. In showbusiness from the age of two, Rich achieved considerable fame as a drummer and tap dancer, performing on Broadway when he was four-years-old as a member of his parents' act. Two years later he was touring as a solo artist, playing the USA vaudeville circuit and also visiting Australia. At the age of 11 he formed his own band and within a few more years was attracting attention sitting in with bands in New York clubs. In 1937 he was hired by **Joe Marsala** and soon thereafter began to rise in critical estimation and public popularity. In quick succession he played in several important bands of the swing era including those of **Bunny Berigan**, **Harry**

James, **Artie Shaw** and **Tommy Dorsey**. After military service he again played with Dorsey, then formed his own big band which survived for a few years in the late 40s. He next worked with **Les Brown** and also became a regular with **Jazz At The Philharmonic**. In the early 50s he led his own briefly re-formed big band and also became a member of the Big Four, led by **Charlie Ventura**. He also recorded extensively for **Norman Granz**, not only with the impresario's JATP but also with **Art Tatum**, **Lionel Hampton**, **Ray Brown**, **Oscar Peterson**, **Flip Phillips**, **Dizzy Gillespie**, **Roy Eldridge**, **Louis Armstrong**, **Lester Young**, **Gene Krupa** and many others.

Return stints with James and Dorsey followed, but by the late 50s, despite a heart attack, he was appearing as a singer and leading his own small bands. He continued to make records with, amongst others, **Max Roach**. In the early 60s, Rich was once more with James, but by 1966 had decided to try again with his own big band. He continued to lead a big band for the next dozen years, spent a while leading a small group, then re-formed a big band in the 80s, continuing to lead this band for the rest of his life. His later bands frequently featured young, recently-graduated musicians, towards whom he displayed an attitude which resembled that of a feudal lord. Nevertheless, whether through awareness of these musicians' interests or the demands of audiences, the repertoire of many of Rich's 60s and 70s bands contained elements of rock without ever becoming a true fusion band. Rich's playing was characterized by his phenomenal speed and astonishing technical dexterity. His precision and clarity were legendary even if, at times, the band's charts were specifically designed to better display his remarkable skills. During his bandleading years, Rich continued to make records in many settings, in these he would usually revert to the drummer's traditional role of supporting player. In such contexts Rich was a subtle accompanist, adept with brushes but always swinging and propulsive. Early in his career Rich was notorious for his short temper, and during his stint with Dorsey frequently clashed with the band's singer, **Frank Sinatra**, a similarly short-fused artist. A caustically witty man, later in his life Rich became popular on television chat shows, where his put-downs of ill-equipped pop singers often bordered upon the slanderous. Rich came back frequently from illness and accident (once playing one-handed when his other arm was in a sling, without any noticeable diminution of his ability) but was finally diagnosed as having a brain tumour. Even during his final illness, his wit did not desert him. When a nurse preparing him for surgery asked if there was anything to which he was allergic he told her, 'Only country music.'

Selected albums: with Nat 'King' Cole *Anatomy Of A Jam Session* (1945), *The Lionel Hampton-Art Tatum-Buddy Rich Trio* (1955), *The Monster* (1955), *Gene Krupa Meets Buddy Rich* (1955), with Harry Edison *Buddy And Sweets* (1955), *Buddy Rich Sings Johnny Mercer* (1956), *Big Band Shout* (1956), *Buddy Just Sings* (1957), *The Buddy Rich Quartet In Miami* (1957), *Buddy Rich Versus Max Roach* (1959), *Richcraft* (1959), *The Voice Of Buddy Rich* (1959), *The Driver* (1960), *The Electric Sticks Of Buddy Rich* (1960), *Playmates* (1960), *Blues / Caravan* (1962), *Krupa And Rich / The Burning Beat* (1962), *Swingin' New Big Band* (1966), *Big Swing Face* (1967), *The New One!* (1967), *Rich A La Rakha* (1968), *Mercy, Mercy* (1968), *Buddy And Soul* (1969), *Keep The Customer Satisfied* (1970), incl. on *Jazz Monterey 1958-1980* (1970), *A Different Drummer* (1971), *Buddy Rich-Louie Bellson-Kenny Clare With The Bobby Lamb-Ray Premru Orchestra* (1971), *Very Alive At Ronnie Scott's* (1971), *Time Being* (1971-72), *Stick It* (1972), *The Roar Of '74* (1973), *Ease On Down The Road* (1973-74), *The Last Blues Album Vol. 1* (1974), *Speak No Evil* (1976), *Buddy Rich Plays And Plays* (1977), *Killing Me Forcefully* (1977), *Jam Session* (1977), *Giants Of Jazz Vol. 1* (1977), *Class Of '78* (1977), *Lionel Hampton Presents Buddy Rich* (Kingdom Gate 1977), *The Man From Planet Jazz* (1980), *Rich And Famous* (c.1980), *The Legendary Buddy Rich* (c.1982), *The Magic Of Buddy Rich* (1984), *Tuff Dude* (LRC 1984), *Live On King Street* (c.1985), *The Cinch* (1985). Compilations: *A Man And His Drums* (1945), *Riot* (1946), *Great Moments* (1946), *Buddy Rich And His Greatest Band* (1946), *Buddy Rich '47-'48* (1947-48), *No Jive* (Novus 1992).

Further reading: *Improvising*, Whitney Balliett.

Rich, Charlie

b. 14 December 1932, Colt, Arkansas, USA, d. 25 July 1995. One of Rich's country hits is 'Life Has Its Little Ups And Downs', and the ups and downs of his own life have been dramatic. Rich's parents were cotton farmers and he heard the blues from the pickers and gospel music from his parents as his father sang in a choir and his mother played organ. Rich himself developed a passion for **Stan Kenton**'s music, so much so that his friends nicknamed him 'Charlie Kenton'. He played piano and saxophone and studied music at the University of Arkansas. While in the US Air Force, he formed a small group in the vein of the **Four Freshmen**, the Velvetones, with his wife-to-be, Margaret Ann. After the forces, they bought a farm but following bad weather, he opted for playing in Memphis clubs for $10 a night. At first, **Sam Phillips** felt that Rich was too jazz-orientated for his **Sun** label, but arranger **Bill Justis** gave him some **Jerry Lee Lewis** records and told him to return 'when he could get that bad'. Soon Rich was working on sessions at Sun including some for Lewis ('I'll Sail My Ship Alone'), Bill Justis and Carl Mann. He wrote 'The Ways Of A Woman In Love', 'Thanks A Lot' (both recorded by **Johnny Cash**), 'Break Up' (**Ray Smith** and Lewis), 'I'm Comin' Home' (Mann and then covered by **Elvis Presley**) and the continuation of

'Don't Take Your Guns To Town', 'The Ballad Of Billy Joe' (Lewis and Rich himself). His first single, 'Whirlwind', was issued in the USA in August 1958 on the Sun subsidiary, Phillips International. His first US hit came in 1960 when 'Lonely Weekends', a bright, echoey rock 'n' roll song which he had intended for Jerry Lee Lewis, made number 22 in the US charts. Time has shown it to be a fine rock 'n' roll standard but Rich's original recording was marred by heavy-handed chorus work from the Gene Lowery Singers.

Rich recorded 80 songs at Sun although only 10 singles and one album were released at the time. Many of the tracks have been issued since, some even being doctored to include an Elvis soundalike. Rich was not able to consolidate the success of 'Lonely Weekends' but some of his songs from that period, 'Who Will The Next Fool Be?', an R&B success for **Bobby 'Blue' Bland** and later Jerry Lee Lewis, 'Sittin' And Thinkin'' and 'Midnight Blues', have remained in his act. Rich's heavy drinking caused his wife to leave with the children, but he convinced her that he would change. In 1962 Rich, like Elvis before him, went from Sun to **RCA**, albeit to their subsidiary, Groove. From then on, Rich recorded in Nashville although Groove were grooming him as a performer of jazz-slanted standards ('I've Got You Under My Skin', 'Ol' Man River', 'Nice 'N' Easy'). He had no hits at the time but his reflective ballad, 'There Won't Be Anymore', was a US Top 20 hit 10 years later; similarly, 'I Don't See Me In Your Eyes Anymore' and 'Tomorrow Night' were to become US country number 1s. Many regard Rich's period with producer Jerry Kennedy at Smash as his most creative, particularly as Margaret Ann was writing such excellent material as 'A Field Of Yellow Daisies'. He almost made the US Top 20 with **Dallas Frazier**'s **Coasters**-styled novelty about a hippie, 'Mohair Sam', but he says, 'One hit like 'Mohair Sam' wasn't much use. What I needed was a string of singles that would sell albums. I was also unlucky in that I put 'I Washed My Hands In Muddy Water' on the b-side. **Johnny Rivers** heard it, copied my arrangement and sold a million records.' His next label, Hi, adopted another approach by putting Rich with familiar country songs, but the album's sales were poor and he seemed destined to play small bars forever, although salvation was at hand. **Billy Sherrill**, who had worked as a recording engineer with Rich at Sun, signed him to Epic in 1967. He knew Rich's versatility but he was determined to make him a successful country singer. Choosing strong ballads, often about working-class marriage in the over-30s, and classy middle-of-the-road arrangements, he built up Rich's success in the US country charts, although it was a slow process. In 1968 his chart entries were with 'Set Me Free' (number 44) and 'Raggedly Ann (number 45) and even Margaret Ann's cleverly written but thinly-veiled comment on their own marriage, 'Life Has Its Little Ups And

Downs', only reached number 41. His first substantial US country hit was with 'I Take It On Home' in 1972. In view of the material, Rich's lined face and grey hair became assets and he was dubbed 'The Silver Fox'. Although Rich's piano was often relegated to a supporting role, it complements his voice on **Kenny O'Dell**'s ballad, 'Behind Closed Doors'. The 1973 song gave Rich a number 1 country and Top 20 pop hit and became the Country Song of the Year. Rich's recording was used to amusing effect for Clyde's love affair in the Clint Eastwood film, *Every Which Way But Loose*. The follow-up, 'The Most Beautiful Girl', partly written by Sherrill, was a US Number 1, and the b-side 'Feel Like Goin' Home' was almost as strong. (Rich had chosen the title after being the subject of the opening essay in Peter Guralnick's study of blues and rock 'n' roll, *Feel Like Going Home*.) In the UK, 'The Most Beautiful Girl' made number 2 and was quickly followed by a Top 20 placing for 'Behind Closed Doors'. His *Behind Closed Doors* which contained both hits and songs written by himself, his wife and son Allan, was a smash and he topped the US country charts with 'There Won't Be Anymore' (number 18, pop), 'A Very Special Love Song' (number 11), 'I Don't See Me In Your Eyes Anymore', 'I Love My Friend' (number 24) and 'She Called Me Baby'. Also, 'Everytime You Touch Me (I Get High)' was number 3, country and 19 in the pop chart. Allan Rich, a member of his father's road band, recorded his father's 'Break Up', while Rich's evocative composition 'Peace On You' was also the title song of a **Roger McGuinn** album.

In 1974 Rich was voted the Entertainer of the Year by the Country Music Association of America. The next year, instead of announcing the winner (**John Denver**) on a live television show, he burnt the envelope. He says, 'I was ill and I should never have been there' but country fans were not so sympathetic and Rich lost much support. His records too were starting to sound stale as Sherrill had difficulty in finding good material and put too much emphasis on the strings. Nevertheless, there were gems including 'Rollin' With The Flow', which returned Rich to the top of the US country charts, and a duet with **Janie Fricke**, 'On My Knees', also a country number 1. Rich made a gospel album, *Silver Linings*, with Billy Sherrill and says, 'We had a similar background of gospel music. His father was a Baptist preacher and he used to preach on horseback. That's him in the left-hand corner of the cover. I regard 'Milky White Way' as one of my best recordings.' In 1978 Rich moved to United Artists where **Larry Butler** continued in the same vein. Occasionally the material was right - 'Puttin' In Overtime At Home', 'I Still Believe In Love' and the bluesy 'Nobody But You' - but, by and large, the records found Rich on automatic pilot. In 1980 he moved to **Elektra** where he recorded a fine version of

Eric Clapton's 'Wonderful Tonight' and had a country hit with 'I'll Wake You Up When You Get Home'. There followed a long decade or more of silence from Rich, amid rumours that his occasionally self-destructive lifestyle had taken its toll. But he returned triumphantly in 1992 with *Pictures And Paintings*, an album overseen by his long-time champion, journalist Peter Guralnick. Mixing jazzy originals with reinterpretations of songs from his past, the album proved to be Rich's most satisfying work since *The Fabulous Charlie Rich* 22 years earlier.

Albums: *Lonely Weekends With Charlie Rich* (1960), *That's Rich* (1965), *The Many New Sides Of Charlie Rich* (1965), *The Best Years* (1966), *Charlie Rich Sings Country And Western* (1967), *Set Me Free* (1968), *The Fabulous Charlie Rich* (1970), *Boss Man* (1970), *Behind Closed Doors* (1973), *Very Special Love Songs* (1974), *The Silver Fox* (1974), *Everytime You Touch Me (I Get High)* (1975), *Silver Linings* (1976), *Take Me* (1977), *Rollin' With The Flow* (1977), *I Still Believe In Love* (1978), *The Fool Strikes Again* (1979), *Nobody But You* (1979), *Once A Drifter* (1980), *Pictures And Paintings* (1992), *Charlie Rich Sings The Songs Of Hank Williams Plus The R&B Sessions* (Diablo 1994). Compilations are available.

Further reading: *Charlie Rich*, Judy Eton.

Rich, Freddy

b. 3 January 1898, Warsaw, Poland, d. 8 September 1956. A leader of successful dancebands from the early 20s, Rich toured Europe late in the decade. In the 30s and early 40s he was active in radio and films, appearing in such musical shorts as *Song Hits On Parade* (1936) leading a band which featured **Bunny Berigan** and **Adrian Rollini**. His studio work continued into the 50s despite partial paralysis following an accident. Although he was primarily a very commercial leader, Rich made several interesting records and radio broadcasts, some of which were recorded, on which he augmented his regular band with leading jazz performers like Berigan, **Benny Goodman**, **Joe Venuti**, **Eddie Lang**, **Mannie Klein**, **Jimmy** and **Tommy Dorsey**, **Roy Eldridge** and **Benny Carter**.

Albums: *Freddy Rich On The Air Vol. 1* (1931), *Freddy Rich On The Air Vol. 2* (1931). Compilations: *Dance The Depression Away* (1929-31), *Freddy Rich And His Orchestra Vols 1 & 2* (1931).

Rich, Paul

b. 20 August 1921, London, England. A dance band vocalist/guitarist and music publisher, Rich is the son of Greek parents who emigrated to Britain from Russia. His first job in the music business was as a singer and guitarist with the **Oscar Rabin** Band in 1941. Shortly afterwards he joined **Lou Preager**, just as the bandleader was beginning his remarkable 18-year residency at London's popular Hammersmith Palais.

Another vocalist who joined Preager around the same time was Edna Kaye, and she duetted with Rich on the novelty 'The Quack Quack Song', which was recorded in June 1944. Rich was also the featured singer with Preager on many other sides, including 'You're In Love', 'No-One Else Will Do', 'Waiting In Sweetheart Valley', 'Coming Home', 'I'm Beginning To See The Light', 'The Cokey Cokey' (a novelty dance, which became all the rage, and is still a popular party favourite), 'I'll Always Be With You', 'I'd Rather Be Me', 'Lonely Footsteps', 'I'll Close My Eyes', 'Let's Keep it That Way', 'Two Can Dream As Cheaply As One', 'Carolina', and 'Cruising Down The River', 'You're In Love', 'No-One Else Will Do', 'Waiting In Sweetheart Valley', 'Coming Home', 'I'm Beginning To See The Light', 'The Cokey Cokey', 'I'll Always Be With You', 'I'd Rather Be Me', 'Lonely Footsteps', 'I'll Close My Eyes', 'Let's Keep It That Way', 'Two Can Dream As Cheaply As One', 'Carolina', 'Cruising Down The River', 'Until', 'Don't Be A Baby', 'I Heard You Cried Last Night' (with Edna Kaye), 'Hey! Good Lookin'', and 'Mairzy Doats And Doazy Doats'. 'Cruising Down The River', which was written by two amateurs, Eily Beadell and Nell Tollerton, won the Palais's immensely popular songwriting contest 'Write A Tune For £1000' in 1945. It headed the sheet music bestsellers lists in the UK and US, and was featured in the Hollywood movie *Cruisin' Down The River*, starring **Dick Haymes**. With the advent of rock 'n' roll, Rich left Preager in February 1955 after 13 years to supervise a chain of retail shops. He then took a job as a song plugger, eventually working in various capacities for a number of music publishers, before becoming general manager for **Freddy Bienstock**'s **Carlin Music** in 1967. During his time with the company it expanded and prospered, and was the top publisher in the *Record Retailer* charts for 11 consecutive years. He retired in 1989, and devotes much of his time to hobbies such as sailing and photography. He also paints in oils, and has held a joint exhibition with his barrister son Clive.

Selected albums: with Lou Preager *et al On the Sunny Side Of The Street* (President).

Richard(s), Keith

b. Keith Richards, 18 December 1943, Dartford, Kent, England. As founding member and principal guitarist of the **Rolling Stones**, Richards occupies a unique place in rock's pantheon. Although not a recognized frontman, his incisive rhythm work, initially modelled on **Chuck Berry**, has provided the template for many of his group's finest moments. He became the partner of **Mick Jagger** when a need for original material arose, and although their early efforts betrayed an immaturity, their work flourished on completing 'The Last Time' in 1965. The first in a series of excellent singles, including '(I Can't Get No) Satisfaction', 'Get

Off Of My Cloud' (both 1965) and 'Paint It Black' (1966), Richards' riffs provided the cornerstone to a sound which relied on atmosphere, rather than melody, for effect. Despite this, his name was attached to *Today's Pop Symphony*, wherein the Aranbee Pop Symphony Orchestra performed contemporary pop hits under his 'direction'. The project was doubtlessly inspired by manager **Andrew Loog Oldham**, as it mirrored his own similar ventures, but the album was nonetheless the first to bear Richards' name without the Stones. The group survived what was, for the Stones, an awkward psychedelic era (and its attendant arrests) by reconnecting with R&B, which had provided their initial inspiration. Richards' riffs for 'Jumping Jack Flash' (1968), 'Honky Tonk Women' (1969) and 'Brown Sugar' (1971) were instantly recognizable and their international success enhanced an artistically fertile period. Richards' drug dependency, which would bedevil the guitarist throughout the 70s, blighted his private life, but musically there continued to be several highlights including *Exile On Main Street*, a much-lauded album recorded at his French villa, and *Some Girls*, the group's controversial post-punk set. His obligatory vocal tracks included 'Happy' and 'Before They Make Me Run', and such performances were eagerly awaited by a loyal core of aficionados. Richards completed several solo studio sessions during 1976 and 1977, but their sole product was the belated Christmas single, 'Run Rudolph Run' (1979). That same year he was convicted of heroin charges by a Toronto court. His penance was a charity concert for which he formed the New Barbarians with **Ron Wood**, **Stanley Clarke**, **Ian McLagan** and saxophonist Bobby Keys. The group also undertook a tour of the USA and at the Knebworth Festival in England, before Richards resumed his commitment to the Rolling Stones. He appeared at **Live Aid** in 1985 as part of the ramshackle trio of **Bob Dylan** and **Ron Wood** A feud with Mick Jagger reached its peak in 1986, threatening the future of the group. Richards subsequently worked with Chuck Berry and **Aretha Franklin** before beginning his first official solo album. *Talk Is Cheap* offered the sparkle and commitment missing from several latter-day Stones' releases, and in 'Don't Take It So Hard' Keith offered an invective to his estranged partner. However, the pair were later reconciled and worked on the parent group's *Steel Wheels* and the mammoth USA and European tour which followed. Richards has always argued that the Stones should be his prime vehicle, but their increasingly disparate status would suggest that the guitarist's solo career may yet assume paramount importance. If Jagger decides to call it a day, it is Richards the man with ten lives that will prosper.

Albums: directing the Aranbee Pop Symphony Orchestra *Today's Pop Symphony* (1966), *Talk Is Cheap* (1988), *Main Offender* (1992).

Further reading: *Keith Richards: The Biography*, Victor Bockris. *In His Own Words*, Mick St Michael.

Richard, Belton

b. Rayne, Louisiana, USA. A noted performer of Cajun music. His father, Cleby Richard, was a popular accordionist and exponent of the music, who fronted a Cajun band called the Welcome Playboys, which played venues around his local area. Learning accordion from his father, Richard first played rock 'n' roll with his Cajun Rockers before changing to Cajun music around 1959. He formed his Musical Aces and played regularly at major clubs in Breaux Bridge, Crowley and Lafayette, soon building a considerable reputation. He made his first recordings for Chamo, a small company based in Crowley but soon joined the more prestigious Swallow label. His recordings for that label soon established him as a top Cajun artist and won him his own television show. His most successful recordings were 'Just En Reve', recorded for Chamo in 1962, and two Swallow releases, 'Un Autre Soir D'Ennui' (Another Sleepless Night) (1967), and in 1974, 'The Cajun Streak', a Cajun version of the **Ray Stevens** hit.

Album: *Modern Sounds In Cajun Music* (Swallow 70s).

Richard, Cliff

b. Harry Roger Webb, 14 October 1940, Lucklow, India. One of the most popular and enduring talents in the history of UK showbusiness, Richard began his career as a rock 'n' roll performer in 1957. His fascination for **Elvis Presley** encouraged him to join a skiffle group and several months later he teamed up with drummer Terry Smart and guitarist Ken Payne to form the Drifters. They played at various clubs in the Cheshunt/Hoddesdon area of Hertfordshire before descending on the famous 2Is coffee bar in London's Old Compton Street. There they were approached by lead guitarist Ian Samwell and developed their act as a quartet. In 1958, they secured their big break in the unlikely setting of a Saturday morning talent show at the Gaumont cinema in Shepherd's Bush. It was there that the senatorial theatrical agent George Ganyou recognized Cliff's sexual appeal and singing abilities and duly financed the recording of a demonstration tape of 'Breathless' and 'Lawdy Miss Clawdy'. A copy reached the hands of **EMI** producer **Norrie Paramor** who was impressed enough to grant the ensemble an audition. Initially, he intended to record Richard as a solo artist backed by an orchestra, but the persuasive performer insisted upon retaining his own backing group. With the assistance of a couple of session musicians, the unit recorded the American teen ballad 'Schoolboy Crush' as a projected first single. An acetate of the recording was paraded around Tin Pan Alley and came to the attention of the influential television producer **Jack Good**. It was not the juvenile

'Schoolboy Crush' which captured his attention, however, but the Ian Samwell b-side 'Move It'. Good reacted with characteristically manic enthusiasm when he heard the disc, rightly recognizing that it sounded like nothing else in the history of UK pop. The distinctive riff and unaffected vocal seemed authentically American, completely at odds with the mannered material that usually emanated from British recording studios. With Good's ceaseless promotion, which included a full-page review in the music paper *Disc*, Cliff's debut was eagerly anticipated and swiftly rose to number 2 in the UK charts. Meanwhile, the star made his debut on Good's television showcase *Oh Boy!*, and rapidly replaced **Marty Wilde** as Britain's premier rock 'n' roll talent. The low-key role offered to the Drifters persuaded Samwell to leave the group to become a professional songwriter, and by the end of 1958 a new line-up emerged featuring **Hank B. Marvin** and **Bruce Welch**. Before long, they changed their name to the **Shadows**, in order to avoid confusion with the black American R&B group, the **Drifters**.

Meanwhile, Richard consolidated his position in the rock 'n' roll pantheon, even outraging critics in true Elvis Presley fashion. The *New Musical Express* denounced his 'violent, hip-swinging' and 'crude exhibitionism' and pontificated: '**Tommy Steele** became Britain's teenage idol without resorting to this form of indecent, short-sighted vulgarity'. Critical mortification had little effect on the screaming female fans who responded to the singer's boyish sexuality with increasing intensity.

1959 was a decisive year for Richard and a firm indicator of his longevity as a performer. With management shake-ups, shifts in national musical taste and some distinctly average singles his career could easily have been curtailed, but instead he matured and transcended his Presley-like beginnings. A recording of **Lionel Bart**'s 'Living Doll' provided him with a massive UK number 1 and three months later he returned to the top with the plaintive 'Travellin' Light'. He also starred in two films, within 12 months. *Serious Charge*, a non-musical drama, was banned in some areas as it dealt with the controversial subject of homosexual blackmail. The Wolf Mankowitz directed *Expresso Bongo*, in which Richard played the delightfully named Bongo Herbert, was a cinematic pop landmark, brilliantly evoking the rapacious world of Tin Pan Alley. It remains one of the most revealing and humorous films ever made on the music business and proved an interesting vehicle for Richard's varied talents.

From 1960 onwards Richard's career progressed along more traditional lines leading to acceptance as a middle-of-the-road entertainer. Varied hits such as the breezy, chart-topping 'Please Don't Tease', the rock 'n' rolling 'Nine Times Out Of Ten' and reflective 'Theme For A Dream' demonstrated his range, and in 1962 he hit a new peak with 'The Young Ones'. A glorious pop anthem to youth, with some striking guitar work from Hank Marvin, the song proved one of his most memorable number 1 hits. The film of the same name was a charming period piece, with a strong cast and fine score. It broke box office records and spawned a series of similar movies from its star, who was clearly following Elvis Presley's cinematic excursions as a means of extending his audience. Unlike the King, however, Richard supplemented his frequent movie commitments with tours, summer seasons, regular television slots and even pantomime appearances. The run of UK Top 10 hits continued uninterrupted until as late as mid-1965. Although the showbiz glitz had brought a certain aural homogeneity to the material, the catchiness of songs like 'Bachelor Boy', 'Summer Holiday', 'On The Beach' and 'I Could Easily Fall' was undeniable. These were neatly, if predictably, complemented by ballad releases such as 'Constantly', 'The Twelfth Of Never' and 'The Minute You're Gone'.

The formula looked likely to be rendered redundant by the British beat boom, but Richard expertly rode that wave, even improving his selection of material along the way. He bravely, though relatively unsuccessfully, covered a **Rolling Stones** song, 'Blue Turns To Grey', before again hitting top form with the beautifully melodic 'Visions'. During 1966, he had almost retired after converting to fundamentalist Christianity, but elected to use his singing career as a positive expression of his faith. The sparkling 'In The Country' and gorgeously evocative 'The Day I Met Marie' displayed the old strengths to the full, but in the swiftly changing cultural climate of the late 60s, Richard's hold on the pop charts could no longer be guaranteed. The 1968 Eurovision Song Contest offered him a chance of further glory, but the jury placed him a close second with the 'oom-pah-pah'-sounding 'Congratulations'. The song was nevertheless a consummate Eurovision performance and proved one of the biggest UK number 1s of the year. Immediately thereafter, Cliff's chart progress declined and his choice of material proved at best desultory. Although there were a couple of solid entries, **Raymond Froggatt**'s 'Big Ship' and a superb duet with Hank Marvin 'Throw Down A Line', Richard seemed a likely contender for Variety as the decade closed.

The first half of the 70s saw him in a musical rut. The chirpy but insubstantial 'Goodbye Sam, Hello Samantha' was a Top 10 hit in 1970 and heralded a notable decline. A second shot at the Eurovision Song Contest with 'Power To All Our Friends' brought his only other Top 10 success of the period and it was widely assumed that his chart career was spent. However, in 1976 there was a surprise resurgence in his career when Bruce Welch of the Shadows was assigned to produce his colleague. The sessions resulted in the best-selling album *I'm Nearly Famous*, which included two major hits 'Miss You Nights' and 'Devil Woman'. The latter was notable for its decidedly un-Christian imagery and the fact that it gave Richard a rare US chart success. Although Welch remained at the controls for two more albums, time again looked as though it would kill off Richard's perennial chart success. A string of meagre singles culminated in the dull 'Green Light' which stalled at number 57, his lowest chart placing since he started singing. Coincidentally, his backing musicians, Terry Britten and Alan Tarney, had moved into songwriting and production at this point and encouraged him to adopt a more contemporary sound on the album *Rock 'N' Roll Juvenile*. The most startling breakthrough however was the attendant single 'We Don't Talk Anymore', written by Tarney and produced by Welch. An exceptional pop record, which gave the singer his first UK number 1 hit in over a decade and also reached the Top 10 in the US. The 'new' Richard sound, so refreshing after some of his staid offerings in the late 70s, brought further well arranged hits, such as 'Carrie' and 'Wired For Sound', and ensured that he was a chart regular throughout the 80s.

Although he resisted the temptation to try anything radical, there were subtle changes in his musical approach. One feature of his talent that emerged during the 80s was a remarkable facility as a duettist. Collaborations with **Olivia Newton-John**, Phil Everly, **Sarah Brightman**, Sheila Walsh, **Elton John** and **Van Morrison** added a completely new dimension to his career. It was something of a belated shock to realize that Richard may be one of the finest harmony singers working in the field of popular music. His perfectly enunciated vocals and the smooth texture of his voice have the power to complement work that he might not usually tackle alone.

The possibility of his collaborating with an artist even further from his sphere than Van Morrison remains a tantalizing challenge. Throughout his three decades in the pop charts, Cliff has displayed a valiant longevity. He parodied one of his earliest hits with comedy quartet the Young Ones and registered yet another number 1; he appeared in the stage musical *Time*; he sang religious songs on gospel tours; he sued the ***New Musical Express*** for an appallingly libellous review far more vicious than their acerbic comments back in 1958; he was decorated by the Queen; and he celebrated his 50th birthday with a move into social commentary with the anti-war hit 'From A Distance'. Richard was nominated to appear at the celebrations in 1995 for VE day appearing with **Vera Lynn**, he now has been adopted as her male equivalent. It was no surprise to find that he was knighted for his services to popular music in June 1995. And so he goes on. Sir Cliff Richard has outlasted every musical trend of the past four decades with a sincerity and commitment that may well be unmatched in his field. He is British pop's most celebrated survivor.

Selected albums: *Cliff* (1959), *Cliff Sings* (1959), *Me And My Shadows* (1960), *Listen To Cliff* (1961), *21 Today* (1961), *The Young Ones* (1961), *32 Minutes And 17 Seconds With Cliff Richard* (1962), *Summer Holiday* (1963), *Cliff's Hit Album* (1963), *When In Spain* (1963), *Wonderful Life* (1964), *Aladdin And His Wonderful Lamp* (1964), *Cliff Richard* (1965), *More Hits By Cliff* (1965), *When In Rome* (1965), *Love Is Forever* (1965), *Kinda Latin* (1966), *Finders Keepers* (1966), *Cinderella* (1967), *Don't Stop Me Now* (1967), *Good News* (1967), *Cliff In Japan* (1968), *Two A Penny* (1968), *Established 1958* (1968), *The Best Of Cliff* (1969), *Sincerely Cliff* (1969), *It'll Be Me* (1969), *Cliff 'Live' At The Talk Of The Town* (1970), *All My Love* (1970), *About That Man* (1970), *Tracks 'N' Grooves* (1970), *His Land* (1970), *Cliff's Hit Album* (1971), *The Cliff Richard Story* (1972), *The Best Of Cliff Volume 2* (1972), *Take Me High* (1973), *Help It Along* (1974), *The 31st Of February Street* (1974), *Everybody Needs Somebody* (1975), *I'm Nearly Famous* (1976), *Cliff Live* (1976), *Every Face Tells A Story* (1977), *Small Corners* (1977), *Green Light* (1978), *Thank You Very Much* (1979), *Rock 'N' Roll Juvenile* (1979), *40 Golden Greats* (1979), *Rock On With Cliff* (1980), *The Cliff Richard Songbook* (1980), *Listen To Cliff* (1980), *I'm No Hero* (1980), *Love Songs* (1981), *Wired For Sound* (1981), *Now You See Me, Now You Don't* (1982), *Dressed For The Occasion* (1983), *Silver* (1983), *Cliff In The 60s* (1984), *Cliff And The Shadows* (1984), *Walking In The Light* (1984), *The Rock Connection* (1984), *Time* (1986), *Hymns And Inspirational Songs* (1986), *Always Guaranteed* (1987), *Private Collection* (1988), *The Album* (1993). Compilation: *The Hit List* (EMI 1994).

Videos: *The Video Connection* (1984), *Together* (1984), *Thank You Very Much* (1984), *Rock In Australia* (1986), *We Don't Talk Anymore* (1987), *Video EP* (1988), *Take Me High* (1988), *Summer Holiday* (1988), *Private Collection* (1988), *Always Guaranteed* (1988), *Live And Guaranteed* (1989), *From A Distance Vols 1and 2* (1990), *Together With Cliff Richard* (1991), *Access All Areas* (1993), *The Event* (1993), *The Story So Far* (1994).

Films: *Expresso Bongo* (1959), *Finders Keepers* (1967).

Further reading: *Driftin' With Cliff Richard: The Inside Story Of What Really Happens On Tour*, Jet Harris and Royston Ellis. *Cliff, The Baron Of Beat*, Jack Sutter. *It's Great To Be Young*, Cliff Richard. *Me And My Shadows*, Cliff Richard. *Top Pops*, Cliff Richard. *Cliff Around The Clock*, Bob Ferrier. *The Wonderful World Of Cliff Richard*, Bob Ferrier. *Questions: Cliff Answering Reader And Fan Queries*, Cliff Richard. *The Way I See It*, Cliff Richard. *The Cliff Richard Story*, George Tremlett. *New Singer, New Song: The Cliff Richard Story*, David Winter. *Which One's Cliff?*, Cliff Richard with Bill Latham. *Happy Christmas From Cliff*, Cliff Richard. *Cliff In His Own Words*, Kevin St. John. *Cliff*, Patrick Doncaster and Tony Jasper. *Cliff Richard*, John Tobler. *Silver Cliff: A 25 Year Journal 1958-1983*, Tony Jasper. *Cliff Richard: The Complete Recording*

Sessions, 1958-1990, Peter Lewry and Nigel Goodall. *Cliff: A Biography*, Tony Jasper. *Cliff Richard, The Complete Chronicle*, Mike Read, Nigel Goodhall And Peter Lewry. *Cliff Richard: The Autobiography*, Steve Turner.

Richards, Cynthia

b. 1944, Duhaney Park, Jamaica, West Indies. Richards' voice was to win the adoration of fellow pupils at the Denham Town Primary school where she impressed them at end-of-term concerts. At one of her teachers suggestion she appeared on the Vere John's Talent Show, and utilized the financial rewards to further her career. Aware of the pitfalls in the music business she worked as a magistrates clerk as well as with veteran guitarist **Bobby Aitken**'s Carib Beats Band. Following her departure from the group her vocal skills were employed by the **Falcons**, **Byron Lee**'s **Dragonaires** and the **Mighty Vikings**. In 1969 she recorded her first single, 'How Could I', for **Coxsone Dodd** at Studio One. The song did not make any waves but, encouraged by what he had heard, **Clancy Eccles** recorded her and 'Foolish Fool' was a smash hit in Jamaica. The single was also released in the UK where it bubbled under the pop chart. Continuing with her live performances in 1970 she also linked up with **Skin Flesh And Bones** performing at the Tit For Tat club while maintaining her solo career. Frustrated with the lack of financial reward for her recordings she did not return to the studio until summoned by **Duke Reid**. She recorded a version of 'Clean Up Woman', 'Sentimental Reason' and the more rootsy 'Aily I', the latter proving a UK reggae smash when released on the Attack label in 1972. With other producers, including **Alvin GG Ranglin** and Larry Lawrence, she released the minor hits, 'Place In My Heart' and 'Change Partners'. With the business side of the industry thwarting her efforts, Richards decided to go it alone. By 1972 she had recorded 'Mr Postman', which, assisted by **Al Brown**, was written, produced and arranged by Richards. By 1973 she had finally triumphed over the music industry's inadequacies and enjoyed a hit with the **Staple Singer**'s, 'If You're Ready (Come Go With Me)'. The success of the single led her to be voted Top Female Artist Of 1973 and she toured as part of the Jamaica showcase alongside **Dennis Brown**, **Toots And The Maytals**, **Sharon Forrester** and Al Brown, all backed by Skin Flesh And Bones.
Album: with friends *Foolish Fool* (Trojan 1972).

Richards, Johnny

b. John Cascales, 2 November 1911, Schenectady, New York, USA, d. 7 October 1968. This most progressive of modern jazz arrangers began his musical career at the age of 10 playing trumpet, violin and banjo in a vaudeville act called 'The Seven Wonders Of The World'. Taking up the saxophone when 17-years-old, he was in London in 1931 working in films, then went to Hollywood as an arranger. Forming a big band in the 40s, he had trouble finding musicians who could cope with his involved scores, so he gave it up to write for **Boyd Raeburn**'s forward-looking band. Oddly enough, considering the reputations of both men, Richards's contributions to the Raeburn library were pretty, romantic, woodwind scores for *inter alia*, 'Prelude To The Dawn', 'Love Tales' and 'Man With The Horn'. He scored and conducted the first *Dizzy Gillespie With Strings* album, and in a more commercial vein wrote (with **Carolyn Leigh**) 'Young At Heart' for the **Frank Sinatra** film (1954). He later joined the **Stan Kenton** arranging staff, which gave scope for his progressive writing (eg 1957's *Cuban Fire* album). That year he formed a new band for recording, resulting in the *Wide Range, I'm Shooting High, Experiments In Sound* albums for **Capitol**, *Something Else By Richards* (Bethlehem), *Walk Softly - Run Wild* (Coral) and *Rites Of Diavolo* (Roulette). Hardly a commercial success, Richards was nevertheless a musical, if sometimes misused asset to any employer.
Selected albums: *Cuban Fire* (1957), *Wide Range* (1957), *I'm Shooting High* (1957), *Experiments In Sound* (1957).

Richards, Red

b. Charles Coleridge Richards, 19 October 1912, New York City, New York, USA. After playing classical piano as a child, Richards was moved to turn to jazz after hearing **Fats Waller**. He played in and around the city of his birth for several years as both soloist and band pianist. In the late 40s and early 50s he worked with several leading jazz musicians including periods in bands led by **Tab Smith** and **Sidney Bechet**. During the 50s he worked in the USA and in Europe, playing with diverse artists including **Mezz Mezzrow** and **Frank Sinatra**, but spent most of this decade in **Muggsy Spanier**'s band. After a brief stint with **Wild Bill Davison** he teamed up with **Vic Dickenson** to form a band they named the Saints And Sinners. This band remained in existence until the early 70s after which Richards returned to New York where he worked in various clubs as soloist and leader of small groups. Towards the end of the decade he began touring internationally, an activity he continued throughout the 80s, sometimes as soloist but also as a member of the Savoy Sultans led by **Panama Francis**. Richards' best work has always been heard in his role as a band player where he adds swing and drive to any rhythm section.
Albums: *Saints And Sinners In Europe* (1968), *Soft Buns* (1978), *In A Mellow Tone* (1979).

Richards, Ron

From a UK music publishing background, Richards entered the realm of record production in the 50s as **George Martin**'s A&R lieutenant at **Parlophone**.

Although the label specialized in variety and comedy, Richards and his boss strove to transform it into a viable pop label. Among discoveries given specifically to Richards were **Shane Fenton** And The **Fentones**, Judd Proctor, Paul Raven (later, **Gary Glitter**) and the Clyde Valley Stompers. Some of these artists had hits, but a bigger feather in Richards' cap during this period was overseeing an **Ella Fitzgerald** session. Plus, a fact not greatly appreciated at the time, taking charge of the **Beatles** recording debut for **EMI**, until an intrigued Martin assumed responsibility. Entirely Richards' doing was the 1963 signing to Parlophone of the **Hollies** who, under his aegis, survived Merseybeat's collapse as the most distinguished northern group (other than the Beatles) - and the vehicle on 1965's 'I'm Alive'. That year, he also produced **P.J. Proby** and, while remaining a stalwart of EMI's Abbey Road complex, left the firm to join Martin's Associated Independent Recording (AIR) company, with whom **CBS**'s **New Seekers** emerged as his most renowned clients as, gradually, he came to work more as an administrator.

Richardson, Clive

b. 23 June 1909, Paris, France, of British parents. Pianist and composer of light orchestral music. Early career during 30s included working in André Charlot reviews in London's West End, with artists such as Bea Lillie, **Lupino Lane** and Hermione Gingold. As Hildegarde's accompanyist, he spent several years touring Britain and Europe, culminating in a triumphant season at New York's prestigious Rainbow Room. In 1936 joined Gaumont-British Films as arranger and assistant musical director to Louis Levy, working alongside **Charles Williams,** Leighton Lucas, Jack Beaver, Bretton Byrd and Mischa Spoliansky, although almost every film gave screen credits to Levy who did little conducting and no composing at all. With Charles Williams, Richardson wrote the scores for most of the Will Hay comedies, including *Oh Mr Porter* (1937), and he also scored *French Without Tears* (1939) which was officially credited to **Nicholas Brodszky**. Served in Royal Artillery Regiment during World War II, but managed to keep musical career active. Contributed arrangements to BBC radio's most popular show *ITMA*; novel arrangements by leading writers of folk songs, nursery rhymes and traditional melodies, played by the BBC Variety Orchestra conducted by Charles Shadwell, were a popular feature of each programme. Richardson's scores for this feature included 'A-Hunting We Will Go', 'Baa! Baa! Black Sheep', 'British Grenadiers', 'Camptown Races', 'Come Lassies And Lads', 'Grand Old Duke Of York', 'Irish Washerwoman', 'John Peel', 'Lincolnshire Poacher', 'Little Brown Jug', 'Oh Susannah', 'O Where O Where Has My Little Dog Gone', 'On Ilka Moor Baht' At',

'Polly-Wolly-Doodle' and 'Sing A Song Of Sixpence'. Following the success of **Richard Addinsell**'s 'Warsaw Concerto', Richardson's publisher asked him to compose a sequel, which was originally called 'The Coventry Concerto', as a tribute to the Midlands city which had suffered from saturation bombing. Eventually in 1944 this work emerged as 'London Fantasia', and it was recorded by **Sidney Torch** (**Parlophone Records**) and **Charles Williams** (**Columbia Records**) - both with the composer at the piano, and also by the **Mantovani** Orchestra with Monia Liter (**Decca Records**). Other major works at this time included 'Salute To Industry' (1945) and a nautical overture 'White Cliffs' (1946). Between numerous composing assignments, Richardson developed a performing career with fellow pianist Tony Lowry as Four Hands In Harmony, which topped variety bills and notched up over 500 broadcasts. Today Richardson is best remembered for his light orchestral works: 'Holiday Spirit', 'Shadow Waltz' (written under the *nom de plume* Paul Dubois), 'Running Off The Rails', 'Melody On The Move', 'Road To Rio', 'Tom Marches On' (the ITMA march), 'Chiming Strings', 'Continental Galop', 'Elixir Of Youth', 'Valse Bijou', 'Romantic Rhapsody' and many others. In 1988 he received a BASCA Gold Award for lifetime services to the music business.

Richardson, Jerome

b. 15 November 1920, Sealy, Texas, USA. Raised in California, Richardson began playing alto saxophone in local bands in his early teens. In 1941 he was briefly with the **Jimmie Lunceford** band, then, after military service during World War II he played in bands led by **Marshal Royal**, **Lionel Hampton** and **Earl 'Fatha' Hines**. In 1953 he relocated in New York City, working at Minton's Playhouse with his own group. Later in the decade he worked with such leading swing and bop musicians as **Lucky Millinder**, **Kenny Burrell**, **Gerry Mulligan** and **Oscar Pettiford**. In 1959 he began an association with **Quincy Jones** and also accompanied several leading song stylists. In 1965 he was a founder member of the **Thad Jones-Mel Lewis** big band at New York's Village Vanguard. In 1971 he settled in Los Angeles, working mostly in film studios but also appearing with Quincy Jones, **Art Pepper**, **Bill Berry** and others. In the 80s he continued to combine studio work with jazz gigs, the former paying the rent while the latter consistently demonstrated his great versatility and talent as both soloist and section musician.

Albums: *The Oscar Pettiford Orchestra In Hi-Fi* (1956), *The Jerome Richardson Sextet* (1958), *The Great Wide World Of Quincy Jones* (1959), *Roamin' With Jerome Richardson* (1959), *Going To The Movies* (1962), *Midnight Oil* (Original Jazz Classics 1963), *Groove Merchant* (1967), with Thad Jones-Mel Lewis *Central Park North* (1969).

Richie, Lionel

b. 20 June 1949, Tuskegee, Alabama, USA. Richie grew up on the campus of Tuskegee Institute, where he formed a succession of R&B groups in the mid-60s. In 1968 he became the lead singer and saxophonist of the **Commodores**. They signed to **Atlantic** in 1968 for a one-record deal, before moving to **Motown**, being schooled as support act to the Jackson Five. The Commodores became established as America's most popular soul group of the 70s, and Richie was responsible for writing and singing many of their biggest hits, specializing in romantic, easy-listening ballads such as 'Easy', 'Three Times A Lady' and 'Still'. His mellifluous vocal tones established him as the most prominent member of the group, and by the late 70s he had begun to accept songwriting commissions from other artists. He composed **Kenny Rogers**' 1980 number 1 'Lady', and produced his *Share Your Love* the following year. Also in 1981, he duetted with **Diana Ross** on the theme song for the film *Endless Love*. Issued as a single, the track topped the UK and US charts, and became one of Motown's biggest hits to date. Its success encouraged Richie to branch out into a fully-fledged solo career in 1982. His debut *Lionel Richie*, produced another chart-topping single, 'Truly', which continued the style of his ballads with the Commodores. In 1983, he released *Can't Slow Down*, which catapulted him into the first rank of international superstars, eventually selling more than 15 million copies world-wide. The set also won two Grammy Awards, including Album Of The Year. It spawned the number 1 hit 'All Night Long', a gently rhythmic dance number which was promoted by a startling video, produced by former **Monkee**, **Michael Nesmith**. Several more Top 10 hits followed, the most successful of which was 'Hello', a sentimental love song which showed how far Richie had moved from his R&B roots. Now described by one critic as 'the black **Barry Manilow**', Richie wrote and performed a suitably anodyne theme song, 'Say You, Say Me', for the film *White Nights* - winning an Oscar for his pains. He also collaborated with **Michael Jackson** on the charity single 'We Are The World' by **USA For Africa**. In 1986, he released *Dancing On The Ceiling*, another phenomenally popular album which produced a run of US and UK hits. The title track, which revived the sedate dance feel of 'All Night Long', was accompanied by another striking video, a feature which has played an increasingly important role in Richie's solo career. The critical consensus was that this album represented nothing more than a consolidation of his previous work, though Lionel's collaboration with the country group **Alabama** on 'Deep River Woman' did break new ground. Since then, his ever more relaxed schedule has kept his recording and live work to a minimum.
Albums: *Lionel Richie* (1982), *Can't Slow Down* (1983), *Rockin And Romance* (1985), *The Composer* (1985), *Dancing On The Ceiling* (1986), *Back To Front* (1992).
Further reading: *Lionel Richie: An Illustrated Biography*, David Nathan.

Richman, Boomie

b. Abraham S. Richards, 2 April 1921, Brockton, Massachusetts, USA. In the early and mid-40s Richman played tenor saxophone in bands led by Jerry Wald, **Muggsy Spanier** and **Tommy Dorsey**. This last engagement lasted five years and was followed by a long spell of studio work during which he also played and recorded with **Benny Goodman**, **Neal Hefti**, **Ruby Braff**, the **Sauter-Finegan** Orchestra, **Red Allen** and **Cootie Williams**. By the 60s his studio work considerably outweighed his jazz appearances, a fact which did not alter during succeeding decades. As the quality of his musical leaders indicates, Richman is a sound player with considerable versatility and a great sense of swing.
Albums: with Benny Goodman *B.G. In Hi-fi* (1954), *Muggsy Spanier* (1954).

Richman, Harry

b. Harry Reichman, 10 August 1895, Cincinnati, Ohio, USA, d. 3 November 1972, Hollywood, California, USA. An actor, singer, and nightclub entertainer, Richman was a flamboyant character, with a debonair 'man-about-town' image, complete with top hat, or straw boater and cane, he had an uninhibited vocal style which was often compared to that of **Al Jolson**. At the age of 12, together with a friend, he formed a musical act, Remington and Reichman, and appeared at the Casino Theatre, Chicago. When he was 18 he changed his name to Richman and played regular cafe engagements in San Francisco as a comedian, then appeared in vaudeville as a song and dance man, and as a pianist for headliners such as the **Dolly Sisters**, Mae West and Nora Bayes. In 1922 he made his Broadway debut, with Bayes, in *Queen O' Hearts*, which ran for only 39 performances. Much more successful was *George White's Scandals Of 1926*, in which Richman introduced the songs 'Lucky Day' and 'The Birth Of the Blues' which was one of his biggest hits. Richman also starred in the 1928 edition of the *Scandals*, in which he sang 'I'm On the Crest Of A Wave'. His next Broadway appearance was in Lew Leslie's lavish *International Revue* in 1930, which was another comparative flop, despite the presence of England's **Gertrude Lawrence**, dance director **Busby Berkeley**, and Richman's renditions of two of **Dorothy Fields** and **Jimmy McHugh**'s best songs, 'Exactly Like You' and 'On The Sunny Side Of The Street'. He introduced another all-time standard, **Joseph McCarthy** and **Jimmy Monaco**'s 'You Made Me Love You', in the *Ziegfeld Follies* of 1931, which also had **Helen Morgan** and **Ruth Etting** in the cast. A year later, in *George White's Musical Hall Varieties*, his big numbers were 'I Love A Parade' and **Herman Hupfeld**'s 'Let's Put Out The Lights And Go To Sleep'. Richman's last 30s Broadway musical was *Say When*, in 1934.

From early in his career he had co-written songs and made hit recordings of some of them, including 'Walking My Baby Back Home', 'There's Danger In Your Eyes, Cherie', 'Singing A Vagabond Song', 'Miss Annabelle Lee', 'C'est Vous (It's You)' and 'Muddy Water'. As well as records and stage appearances, he was enormously popular during the 30s in cabaret and on radio. He also made a few films, including *Putting On The Ritz* (1930), *The Music Goes Round* (1936) and *Kicking The Moon Around* (1938). The latter movie was made in England, and co-starred top bandleader **Ambrose** and his Orchestra. Richman was very popular in the UK, playing the London Palladium and other theatres several times. During the 40s, he appeared in the revue *New Priorities Of 1943*, and continued to play clubs and theatres. By the late 40s he had become semi-retired, but emerged to give the occasional performance until the early 60s. Always a high-living individual, it is said that, at the peak of his career, he drove along Broadway in his Rolls Royce, dispensing 10 dollar gold pieces to his admirers. He also owned a speak-easy establishment, Club Richman, in New York. In his leisure time he was an accomplished pilot, and in 1935 set the world altitude record for a single-engine amphibious plane. A year later, with his partner Dick Merrill, he created another record by flying from New York to the UK, and back again, in a single-engine plane. They reputedly packed the aircraft with 50,000 ping-pong balls as an aid to buoyancy in case they ditched in the sea. After all that, the title of Richman's autobiography, *A Hell Of A Life*, would seem to be a reasonable one. Still remembered in 1993, a cabararet entertainment entitled *Puttin' On the Ritz: An Evening At The Club Richman*, starring Joe Tonti, was presented at Don't Tell Mama in New York.
Album: *Harry Richman And Sophie Tucker* (1979).
Further reading: *A Hell Of A Life*, Harry Richman.

Richman, Jonathan

b. 16 May 1951, Boston, Massachusetts, USA. Richman rose to prominence during the early 70s as leader of the **Modern Lovers**. Drawing inspiration from 50s pop and the **Velvet Underground**, the group initially offered a garage-band sound, as evinced on their UK hit 'Roadrunner' and the infectious instrumental 'Egyptian Reggae' in 1977. However, Richman increasingly distanced himself from electric music and latterly embraced an acoustic-based direction. He disbanded the group in 1978 to pursue an idiosyncratic solo career in which his naive style was deemed charming or irritating according to taste. His songs, including 'Ice Cream Man', 'My Love Is A

Flower (Just Beginning To Bloom)', showed a child-like simplicity which seemed oblivious to changes in trends around him. Richman exhumed the Modern Lovers' name during the 80s without any alteration to his style and the artist continues to enjoy considerable cult popularity.
Albums: *Jonathan Richman And The Modern Lovers* (1977), *Back In Your Life* (1979), *The Jonathan Richman Songbook* (1980), *Jonathan Sings* (1984), *Its Time For Jonathan Richman And The Modern Lovers* (1986), *Jonathan Richman & Barence Whitfield* (1988), *Modern Lovers 88* (1988), *Jonathan Richman* (1989), *Jonathan Sings Country* (1990), *I, Jonathan* (1993). Compilation: *23 Great Recordings* (1990).

Richmond, Dannie

b. 15 December 1935, New York City, New York, USA, d. 16 March 1988. After starting out as an R&B tenor saxophonist, Richmond switched to drums and direction in the early 50s. His success was such that by 1956 he was a member of **Charles Mingus**'s band, a role he maintained until 1970. After a spell working in rock bands, backing **Joe Cocker** and **Elton John**, Richmond returned to Mingus. After Mingus's death in 1979 he became a founder member of the Mingus Dynasty. He also worked in small groups with **George Adams** and **Don Pullen**. A powerful drummer with a playing style that allowed him to range widely in music, from jazz to jazz-rock fusion and straight rock, Richmond's long service with Mingus led to his appearing on many seminal recording dates.
Selected albums: with Charles Mingus *Mingus Ah Um* (1958), with Mingus *Town Hall Concert* (1962), *The Great Concert Of Charles Mingus* (1964), with Don Pullen *Jazz A Confronto 21* (1975), with Mingus *Three Or Four Shades Of Blue* (1977), with Pullen *Don't Lose Control* (1979), *Ode To Mingus* (1979), *Dannie Richmond Plays Charles Mingus* (Timeless 1980), *Three Or Four Shades Of* (Tutu 1992).

Rickenbacker

Following the hand-tooling of an acoustic prototype guitar by Swiss artisan Adolph Rickenbacker in the 1890s, a further breakthrough embraced the development of a semi-acoustic guitar (the Electro Spanish) and an electric steel instrument (the Frying Pan). Next came the solid-body R. Electro Model B when Rickenbacker emigrated to North America to establish a Los Angeles-based manufacturing firm in 1925. Among the most lucrative of the firm's early commissions was to make metal parts for National resonator guitars - purchased mostly by blues and C&W musicians. The more streamlined modern company evolved after a 1953 takeover by a Californian conglomerate headed by Francis Hall. The next decade was its period of greatest prosperity after **John Lennon** became a conspicuous player of the short-armed Model 1996 - actually renamed 'The John Lennon' in 1964 - having acquired an imported

Rickenbacker three years before. More publicity-gaining **Beatles** endorsement emerged after **George Harrison** was credited with introducing the 12-string version to pop consumers mainly via the resounding *bis* passage in 'A Hard Day's Night'. If employed but rarely for soloing, its uniquely jangling effect as rhythm arpeggio was seized upon by the **Searchers** and the **Byrds**. However, because of its synonymity with the 60s, the Rickenbacker had declined in popularity by the time of its inventor's death in 1976. Nonetheless, during the high summer of punk (1977), a vintage model was employed by the **Jam**'s Paul Weller - an admirer of the **Who**'s **Pete Townshend**, another Rickenbacker user. It resurfaced again with the **Pretenders** and in a fleeting revival of the mod movement, and with the later and more substantial impact of general 60s nostalgia on both the charts and concert stage. **Roger McGuinn** arguably the most famous endorser of Rickenbacker and certainly its most distinctive player, co-operated with the company during the late 80s to market a 'Roger McGuinn' 12-string model. This replica of the legendary sound created by McGuinn for the Byrds, has the tone pre-set to sound 'Byrdslike'. The guitar has retained its popularity in the 90s being favoured by the guitar-based indie pop scene.

Further reading: *The Complete History Of Rickenbacker Guitars*, Richard Smith.

Ricotti, Frank

b. 31 January 1949, London, England. Ricotti was born into a musical family and followed in his drummer-father's footsteps by taking up percussion. Educational facilities were limited but fortunately Ricotti came to the attention of **Bill Ashton**, then a teacher in London. With Aston's encouragement, Ricotti was able to extend his studies (and, inspired by Ricotti, Ashton embarked on a project which eventually became the **National Youth Jazz Orchestra**). Although adept on most percussion instruments, Ricotti concentrated upon the vibraphone and also developed his talents as a composer and arranger. In the late 60s and early 70s Ricotti played and recorded with Neil Ardley, Dave Gelly, **Graham Collier**, **Mike Gibbs**, **Stan Tracey** and **Gordon Beck**. By the late 70s Ricotti had become established as a studio musician; during the following decade he was deeply involved in the soundtrack music for a succession of popular British television series by Alan Plater, including *The Beiderbecke Affair*. Also in the 80s he was co-leader, with **Chris Laurence** and **John Taylor**, of Paragonne.

Albums: *Aspects Of Paragonne* (1985), *The Beiderbecke Collection* (1986-88).

Riddle, Leslie

b. 13 June 1905, Burnsville, North Carolina, USA, d. 1980. Although not discovered until the 60s, Riddle was one of the few remaining exponents of the music prevalent among black communities before the blues held sway. His association with the **Carter Family** during the 30s served to highlight the interaction of black and white musicians in the area bounded by Tennessee, Virginia and North Carolina. At the age of 10, Riddle learned to play guitar in open tuning from his uncle Ed Martin, who taught him traditional pieces such as 'John Henry', 'Casey Jones' and a train piece, 'KC'. Moving to Kingsport, Tennessee, he met another guitarist, John Henry Lyons, and also George McGhee, father of Brownie. In August 1927, Riddle lost his left leg in an accident at the cement plant where he worked. Thereafter, he turned increasingly to music, often partnering **Brownie McGhee**. In 1934, Lyons introduced him to A.P. Carter, who took him on trips around Tennessee and Virginia collecting songs. Riddle also taught about a dozen of his own pieces, including 'The Cannon Ball', to the Carter family, with whom he associated for several years. He moved to Rochester, New York, in 1942 where he remained until approached by **Mike Seeger**, then researching the Carter family. *Step By Step* consists of recordings made by Seeger between 1965 and 1978 which combine sacred and secular material encapsulating a bygone era. Album: *Step By Step* (Rounder 1994).

Riddle, Nelson

b. Nelson Smock Riddle, 1 June 1921, Oradell, New Jersey, USA, d. 6 October 1985. After studying piano, Riddle took up the trombone when in his early teens and in the late 30s played in a number of big bands, including those led by Jerry Wald, **Charlie Spivak**, **Tommy Dorsey** and **Bob Crosby**. After a stint in the army, he settled in California and studied arranging with Mario Castelnuovo-Tedesco and conducting with Victor Bay. In the late 40s Riddle joined NBC, but was lured to **Capitol Records** and registered immediately with a driving arrangement of 'Blacksmith Blues' for **Ella Mae Morse**. He confirmed his outstanding ability when he began to arrange and conduct for recordings by **Nat 'King' Cole** and **Frank Sinatra**. Among these were some of Cole's most engaging and memorable sides, such as 'Unforgettable', 'Somewhere Along The Way' and 'Ballerina', along with a good many of his best-selling albums. Riddle also worked with Sinatra on his important early Capitol albums, such as *Songs For Young Lovers*, *Swng Easy*, *Songs For Swingin' Lovers*, *In the Wee Small Hours*, and many other later ones. In additiona, he served as musical director on most of the singer's popular television specials. To a considerable extent, Riddle's easy swinging charts, with their echoes of the big band music of an earlier era (and the distinctive solos of George Roberts (trombone) and **Harry Edison** (trumpet)), were of considerable importance in re-establishing Sinatra as a major star of

popular music. Riddle also worked extensively with **Ella Fitzgerald** on such as *Ella Swings Brightly With Nelson*, and the highly acclaimed *Songbook* series. Other artists to benefit from the distinctive Riddle touch were **Judy Garland** (*Judy*), **Rosemary Clooney** (*Rosie Solves The Swinging Riddle*), **Sammy Davis Jnr.**, (*That's Entertainment*), **Eddie Fisher** (*Games That Lovers Play*), **Jack Jones** (*There's Love*), **Peggy Lee** (*Jump For Joy*), **Dean Martin** (*This Time I'm Swinging*), **Johnny Mathis**, (*I'll Buy You A Star*), **Antonio Carlos Jobim** (*The Brazilian Mood*), **Shirley Bassey** (*Let's Face The Music*), **Dinah Shore** (*Yes Indeed*) and many more. In 1954, Riddle had some success with 'Brother John', adapted from the French song, 'Frere Jacques', and, in the following year his instrumental version of 'Lisbon Antigua' topped the US chart. He made some fine, non vocal albums too, which contrasted the lush ballads of *The Tender Touch* and *The Joy Of Living* with the up-tempo exuberance of *Hey...Let Yourself Go* and *C'mon...Get Happy*. Although under contract to Capitol at the time, he is usually credited with conducting and arranging another label's *Phil Silvers Swings Bugle Calls For Big Band*, which contained Riddle compositions (with US Army/Sgt. Bilko connotations) such as 'Chow, A Can Of Cow And Thou' and 'The Eagle Screams'. Another unusual record item was *Sing A Song With Riddle*, a set of genuine Riddle arrangements, complete with sheet music, and an invitation to the listener to become the featured vocalist. From the mid-50s Riddle was also active in television and feature films: he wrote the theme for the long-running series *Route 66*, and received Oscar nominations for his background scores for the movies **Li'l Abner**, **Can-Can**, *Robin And The Seven Hoods*, and **Paint Your Wagon**, and won an Academy Award in 1974 for his music for *The Great Gatsby*. Among his other film credits were **The Pajama Game**, **St. Louis Blues**, *Merry Andrew* and several Sinatra movies such as **The Joker Is Wild** and **Pal Joey**. After attempting retirement, Riddle made an unexpected and hugely successful comeback in the early 80s, when he recorded three albums with **Linda Ronstadt**: *What's New*, *Lush Life*, and *For Sentimental Reasons*. A gentle, self-effacing man, he was in poor heath for some years before he died.
Selected albums: *Oklahoma!* (Capitol 1955), *Moonglow* (Capitol 1955), *Lisbon Antigua* (Capitol 1956), *Hey...Let Yourself Go!* (Capitol 1957), *The Tender Touch* (Capitol 1957), *Conducts Johnny Concho* (Capitol 1957), *C'mon...Get Happy!* (1958), *Gold Record* (Capitol 1958), *Pal Joey* soundtrack (Capitol 1958), *Sea Of Dreams* (Capitol 1958), *The Girl Most Likely* soundtrack (Capitol 1958), *Merry Andrew* soundtrack (Capitol (1959), *Sing A Song With Riddle* (Capitol 1959), *The Joy Of Living* (Capitol 1959), *Can-Can* soundtrack (Capitol 1960), *Love Tide* (Capitol 1961), *The Gay Life* (Capitol 1961), *Tenderloin* (Capitol 1961), *Magic Moments* (1962), *Route 66 And Other Great TV Themes* (Capitol 1962), *Love Is Just A Game Of Poker* (Capitol 1962), *Come Blow Your Horn* soundtrack (1962), *Lolita* soundtrack (MCA 1962), *British Columbia Suite* (1963), *Paris When It Sizzles* soundtrack (Reprise 1963), *Robin And the Seven Hoods* soundtrack (Reprise (1964), *Hits Of 1964* (Reprise (1964), *A Rage To Live* soundtrack United Artists (1965), *Harlow* soundtrack (Warner (1965), *Great Music, Great Films, Great Sounds* (Reprise 1965), *Batman* (20th Century-Fox 1966), *Music For Wives And Lovers* (United Artists 1967), *El Dorado* soundtrack (CBS 1967), *How To Succeed In Business Without Even Trying* soundtrack (United Artists 1967), *Bright And The Beautiful* (1967), *Riddle Of Today* (1968), *The Today Sound Of Nelson Riddle* (Sunset 1969), *Nat - An Orchestral Portait* (CBS 1969), *The Look Of Love* (Bulldog (1970), *On A Clear Day You Can See Forever* soundtrack CBS 1970), *Nelson Riddle Conducts The 101 Strings* (Marble Arch 1970), *Communication* MPS 1972), *Changing Colours* MPS 1972), *Vivé Legrand!* (Daybreak 1973), *The Great Gatsby* (Paramount 1974), *Romance Fire And Fancy* (Intersound 1983). Selected compilations: *The Silver Collection* (1985), *The Capitol Years* (1993).

Ride

Formed at Art School in Oxfordshire, England, in 1988 by Mark Gardener (vocals/guitar), Andy Bell (guitar/vocals), Stephan Queralt (bass) and Laurence Colbert (drums), Ride had a rapid impact on the alternative music scene. Initially described as 'The **House Of Love** with chainsaws', within a year the quartet's serrated guitar melodies were attracting unusual amounts of attention. At the start of 1990 their debut EP reached number 71 in the UK charts - the first time their label, **Creation Records**, had ever registered such a placing. By the end of the spring, Ride had transcended their independent parameters and entered the Top 40 of the UK chart with the *Play* EP, helped by their youthful good looks and large-scale touring. The success continued with *Nowhere* reaching number 14 in the UK charts before the close of the year. Tours of Japan, Australia and America showed just how impressively swift the band's rise had been, especially when a third EP went straight into the Top 20 of the UK chart. Their success was sealed by a headlining appearance at 1991's Slough Music Festival in front of 8,000 fans. In 1992 Ride consolidated their position as one of the most interesting new bands with the excellent *Going Blank Again* and the hypnotic UK hit single, 'Leave Them All Behind'. *Carnival Of Light* witnessed something of a backlash, however, with the group stalling artistically, seemingly lacking the ideas which had come so quickly at their inception. 1995's *Tarantula* was recorded by the band in London with producer Richard 'Digby' Smith, a veteran of work with **Bob Marley** and **Free**.
Albums: *Nowhere* (Creation 1990), *Going Blank Again* (Creation 1992), *Carnival Of Light* (Creation 1994), *Tarantula* (Creation 1995).

Ride The Wild Surf

Pop singers **Fabian**, **Tab Hunter** and **Shelley Fabares** feature alongside television's *I Dream Of Genie* star Barbara Eden in this 1964 outing. The plot involved three friends who travel to Ohahu in Hawaii to tackle some of the world's biggest heads of surf. True love and dexterity naturally triumph by the close of this lacklustre vehicle, which lacks the guest appearances by hit artists salvaging similar films from the American International Pictures group. Surf singing duo **Jan And Dean**, who were managed by Ms. Fabares' husband **Lou Adler**, provide the rousing title song. This **Brian Wilson**/Jan Berry/Roger Christian composition brought the duo their final US Top 20 hit. It provides *Ride The Wild Surf*'s sole saving grace.

Riders In The Sky

A Nashville-based trio consisting of Ranger Doug (b. Douglas B. Green, 20 March 1946, Great Lakes, Illinois, USA; guitar/baritone vocals), Woody Paul (b. Paul Woodrow Chrisman, 23 August 1949, Nashville, Tennessee, USA; fiddle/guitar/banjo/tenor vocals) and Too Slim (b. Fred LaBour, 3 June 1948, Grand Rapid, Michigan, USA; string bass/lead vocals). The group was initially founded in 1977 and before Woody Paul joined, both Bill Collins and Tommy Goldsmith had played as lead guitarists. The present trio formed their act to re-create (perhaps a little tongue-in-cheek) the music and entertaining facets of western groups such as the **Sons Of The Pioneers** and Riders Of The Purple Sage. Their fine harmonies and yodels are supported by sketches, humour and even rope spinning and similar tricks. Their repertoire varies from old favourites like 'Cool Water' and 'Tumbling Tumbleweeds', to a great deal of newer material of their own writing (often very humorous) but maintains their avowed intent to re-produce the music and songs of the Old West. In 1982, they became members of the **Grand Ole Opry** and the following year, they commenced their *Tumbleweed Theater* series, each episode of which featured a comedy skit, a few songs and a classic b-western movie, on the Nashville Network television channel. In 1988, National Public Radio began broadcasting *Riders Radio Theater* and in 1991-92, they had a Saturday morning children's show, *Riders In The Sky*, on CBS television. They have toured extensively in the USA and were very well received on UK visits to festivals at Peterborough (1985) and Wembley (1987). Outside of the act, Green is a respected Nashville historian and writer, who has edited several country music publications and is the author of *Country Roots (The Origins of Country Music)*.
Albums: *Three On The Trail* (Rounder 1979), *Cowboy Jubilee* (Rounder 1980), *Prairie Serenade* (Rounder 1981), *Weeds And Water* (Rounder 1982), *Live* (Rounder 1983), *Saddle Pals* (Rounder 1984), *New Trails* (Rounder 1986), *The Cowboy Way* (MCA 1987), *Best Of The West* (Rounder 1987), *Best Of The West Rides Again* (Rounder 1987), *Riders Radio Theater* (MCA 1988), *Riders Go Commercial* (MCA 1988), *Horse Opera* (MCA 1990), *Harmony Ranch* (Columbia 1991), *Saturday Morning With Riders In The Sky* (MCA 1992), *Merry Christmas From Harmony Ranch* (Columbia 1992), *Cowboys In Love* (Columbia 1994).
Further reading: *Riders In The Sky*, Ranger Doug, Woody Paul and Too Slim with Texas Bix Bender.

Ridgley, Tommy

b. 30 October 1925, New Orleans. Originally a pianist, Ridgley played with a dixieland group and Earl Anderson's band in 1949 before his powerful R&B voice made him one of New Orleans most respected singers for nearly three decades. His first record was 'Shrewsbury Blues', named after a district of the city and produced by **Dave Bartholomew** for **Imperial** in 1949. He also recorded the humorous 'Looped' before **Ahmet Ertegun**'s **Atlantic** label came to record in New Orleans in 1953. The label recorded Ridgley singing 'I'm Gonna Cross That River' and 'Ooh Lawdy My Baby', with **Ray Charles** on piano. Both were highly popular locally. 'Jam Up', an instrumental with Ridgley on piano, later appeared on anthology albums. In 1957, it was the turn of Al Silver of the New York-based Ember label to fish in the New Orleans talent pool. He recorded Ridgley in a more mellow blues ballad style on 'When I Meet My Girl' and 'I've Heard That Story Before'. At this point, Ridgley turned down a booking at New York's **Apollo** because 'the money they was offering didn't match up to the money down here'. By now, Ridgley and his band the Untouchables were resident at the New Orleans Auditorium, backing touring rock 'n' roll package shows when they reached Louisiana. Several young singers also started their careers with his group, notably **Irma Thomas**. In the early 60s, Ridgley recorded for the local Ric label, owned by Joe Ruffino. Among his singles were 'In The Same Old Way' and and **Ivory Joe Hunter**'s 'I Love You Yes I Do'. Later tracks were produced by Wardell Quezergue while in 1973, Ridgley turned to production, having a local hit with 'Sittin' And Drinkin'' by Rose Davis. He remained a familiar figure on the New Orleans music scene throughout the 70s and 80s when Rounder recorded him.
Albums: *Through The Years* (reissue 1984), *New Orleans King Of The Stroll* (1988).

Ridgway, Stan

b. Stanard Ridgway, 1954, Los Angeles, California, USA. Ridgway was brought up as a Christian Scientist and his mother's tendency to bring Kirlian photographs home for her son to look at may have contributed to his love of the more perverse elements of

life. At school he was nicknamed Mr. Monster and formed the Monster Club. He also admits to being the 'man who cried when Bela Lugosi died!'. A sometime cab driver, Ridgway's first major musical venture was the soundtrack company - Acme - he formed with Marc Morehand. They became **Wall Of Voodoo** in 1977, the name taken with deference to **Phil Spector**'s 'Wall Of Sound' recording techniques. In 1984 Ridgway collaborated with Stewart Copeland on the soundtrack for Francis Ford Coppolla's movie *Rumblefish*, but Ridgway enjoyed success in 1986 when his wacky 'death disc' 'Camouflage', became a surprise UK hit. The follow-up 'The Big Heat' was equally strong but failed to chart. An album of the same name-recorded with Chapter II, including wife Pietra on keyboards, was highly acclaimed. Ridgway's narrative songs such as 'Drive She Said' were particularly striking. Career problems were compounded when contractual disputes with Miles Copeland at IRS effectively put him out of action for two years. The resultant *Mosquitoes* featured 'Heat Takes A Walk', co-written with **Beach Boys** collaborator **Van Dyke Parks**, as well as 'Newspapers', which partially summed up his frustration with his career so far.
Albums: *Camouflage* (1986), *The Big Heat* (1986), *Mosquitoes* (1989).

Riel, Axel

b. 13 September 1940, Copenhagen, Denmark. After drum lessons in his teens, Riel started playing with local trad jazz bands in the 50s. He soon moved on to modern jazz and became the house drummer at the Montmatre Jazzhus, Copenhagen (1963-5). He spent a short time at the **Berklee College Of Music** in 1966. Although he was playing with Danish Radiojazzgruppen (1965-68), he had become very committed to free jazz and worked with saxophonists **John Tchicai** and **Archie Shepp** and bassist **Gary Peacock**. He formed a quintet with **Palle Mikkelborg**, which won first prize at the **Montreux Jazz Festival** (1968), and then played Newport. Meanwhile he was playing with rock group Savage Roses (1968-72). In the 70s he co-led a group called V8 with Mikkelborg and has since freelanced throughout Europe.
Albums: with Dexter Gordon *Billie's Bounce* (1964), *Alex Riel Trio* (1965), with Jackie McLean *Live At Montmatre* (1972), with McLean, Gordon *The Meeting* (1973), with Ken McIntyre *Hindsight* (1974).

Riff Raff

Featuring Doug Lubahn (vocals/bass), Ned Lubahn (guitar/keyboards), Werner Fritzching (guitar) and Mark Kaufman (drums), this group from New York, USA, released just one album of above-average melodic heavy rock. *Vinyl Futures* represents a mixture of styles, the closest approximation of which might be early **Rush** crossed with **Foreigner**. They are not to be confused with the Finnish band of the same title. Lubahn would go on to work with **Billy Squier** when Riff Raff bit the dust.
Album: *Vinyl Futures* (Atco 1981).

Rifkin, Joshua

b. 22 April 1944, New York, USA. A pianist, musicologist, arranger and conductor, Rifkin was instrumental in reviving interest in the important composer of ragtime music, **Scott Joplin**. During the 60s, Rifkin studied at the Juilliard School of Music, New York University, Gottingen University and Princeton; and worked on composition with Karl-Heinz Stockhausen in Darmstadt. At the same time, he played ragtime and piano jazz, and recorded for **Elektra** as a member of the **Even Dozen Jug Band**. Also for Elektra, he conducted *The Baroque **Beatles***, classical-style versions of **John Lennon** and **Paul McCartney** songs. He also arranged and conducted *Wildflowers*, and other recordings for **Judy Collins**. In 1970 he was appointed Professor of Music at Brandeis University in Massachusetts, and musical director of the Elektra ancillary, Nonesuch Records. The following year, the Lincoln Centre produced the highly successful *An Evening With Scott Joplin*, at which Rifkin was a featured artist. From 1970-74, he released a series of three *Piano Rags By Scott Joplin*, which won *Stereo Review* and ***Billboard*** awards as records of the year, and coincided with the release of the film, *The Sting* (1973), whose soundtrack featured 'The Entertainer' and several other Joplin tunes, arranged by another Juilliard 'old boy', **Marvin Hamlisch**. The film won seven Academy Awards, and, together with Rifkin's albums, sparked off a nationwide revival of Joplin's works. Subsequently, Rifkin worked a good deal in the classical field, conducting concerts and releasing several albums. He was also at the forefront of the move to revitalize vintage recordings of ragtime music by the digital process.
Albums: *The Baroque Beatles Book* (1965), *Piano Rags By Scott Joplin, Volumes 1 & 2* (1974), *Piano Rags By Scott Joplin, Volume 3* (1974), *Digital Ragtime* (1980).

Riggins, J., Jnr.
(see **Dixon, Floyd**)

Riggs

This Californian quartet was founded by vocalist/guitarist Jerry Riggs in 1981. With Jeremy Graf (guitar), David Riderick (bass) and Stephen Roy Carlisle (drums) completing the line-up, they specialized in hard-edged, metallic pop, with considerable crossover potential. Riggs on vocals was particularly distinctive, sounding not dissimilar to **Bryan Adams**. Their debut and only release remains an undiscovered gem of infectious and classy AOR.

They were unfortunate in that they lacked a strong visual image and, without a strong promotional push, the project was doomed. Disillusioned, they disbanded, with Jerry Riggs later going on to play with **Pat Travers**.

Album: *Riggs* (Full Moon 1982).

Right Said Fred

This camp UK pop trio features the bald pated brothers Richard (b. c.1953) and Fred Fairbrass (b. c.1964), plus Rob Manzoli (b. c.1955, despite claims to the contrary that he is some 10 years younger). Fred, who failed trials for Chelsea and Fulham football clubs, had formerly toured with **Bob Dylan** and played with **Then Jerico** in 1989. He had also appeared in the film *Hearts Of Fire*. Lead vocalist Richard was originally a bass player who had served time with several prominent artists including **Boy George**, and, allegedly, **David Bowie** and **Mick Jagger**. Following their divergent paths, the brothers came together to form their own band in the late 80s, touring New York and signing to **Capitol** records. By 1988 they were back in London working as a duo. They eventually met up with collaborator Manzoli, a guitarist whose history includes live work with **Z.Z. Top**, **Geno Washington**, the **Platters**, **Muddy Waters** and **Captain Sensible**. The son of an established London restauranter, he is also a qualified chef. His colleagues in Right Said Fred are responsible for a gymnasium called the Dance Attic in Putney, London. To raise money for their first recording foray, the band had to secure a £100 loan from their bank manager. They lied, stating they were about to purchase a car. Initial names for the band included Trash Flash And Money, the Actors and the Volunteers. They finally settled on Right Said Fred after the novelty 1962 Bernard Cribbins hit of the same name. Their initial success was embedded in the slow-burning kitsch classic 'I'm Too Sexy', with equally lascivious follow-ups 'Deeply Dippy' and 'Don't Talk Just Kiss'. Almost overnight Right Said Fred had become the coolest pop band in the UK, cornering the pop market while adult audiences found them impossible to dislike. 1991 saw them sell more singles than any other artist in the UK, (excluding **Bryan Adams**). They were heavily involved in the 1993 Comic Relief fund raising effort 'Stick It Out' with the help of several celebrities. The title is a typically obvious double entendre.

Albums: *Up* (1992), *Sex And Travel* (1993).

Righteous Brothers

Despite their professional appellation, **Bill Medley** (b. 19 September 1940, Santa Ana, California, USA) and Bobby Hatfield (b. 10 August 1940, Beaver Dam, Wisconsin, USA) were not related. They met in 1962 at California's Black Derby club, where they won the approbation of its mixed-race clientele. By blending Medley's sonorous baritone to Hatfield's soaring high tenor, this white duo's vocal style invoked that of classic R&B, and a series of excellent singles, notably 'Little Latin Lupe Lu', followed. They achieved national fame in 1964 following several appearances on US television's highly-popular *Shindig*. Renowned producer **Phil Spector** then signed the act to his Philles label and proceeded to mould his 'Wagerian' sound to their dramatic intonation. 'You've Lost That Lovin' Feelin'' justifiably topped the US and UK charts and is rightly lauded as one the greatest pop singles of all time. A similar passion was extolled on 'Just Once In My Life' and 'Ebb Tide', but the relationship between performer and mentor rapidly soured. The Righteous Brothers moved outlets in 1966, but despite gaining a gold disc for '(You're My) Soul And Inspiration', a performance modelled on their work with Spector, the duo was unable to sustain the same success. They split in 1968, with Medley beginning a solo career and Hatfield retaining the name with new partner Jimmy Walker, formerly of the **Knickerbockers**. This short-lived collaboration ended soon afterwards, but the original pair were reunited in 1974 for an appearance on *The Sonny And Cher* Comedy Hour. They scored a US Top 3 hit that year with the maudlin 'Rock 'n' Roll Heaven', but were unable to regain former glories and have subsequently separated and reformed on several occasions. In 1987 Medley enjoyed an international smash with '(I've Had) The Time Of My Life', a duet with **Jennifer Warnes** taken from the film *Dirty Dancing*, while a reissue of 'Unchained Melody', a hit for the Righteous Brothers in 1965, topped the UK chart in 1990 after it featured in the film *Ghost*.

Albums: *The Righteous Brothers - Right Now* (1963), *Blue-Eyed Soul* (1965), *This Is New* (1965), *You've Lost That Lovin' Feelin'* (1965), *Just Once In My Life* (1965), *Back To Back* (1966), *Go Ahead And Cry* (1966), *Soul And Inspiration* (1966), *Sayin' Somethin'* (1967), *Souled Out* (1967), *Standards* (1967), *One For The Road* (1968), *Rebirth* (1970), *Kingston Rock* (1974), *Give It To The People* (1974), *Sons Of Mrs Righteous* (1975). Compilations: *The Best Of The Righteous Brothers* (1965), *In Action* (1966), *Greatest Hits* (1967), *Greatest Hits Volume 2* (70s), *2 By 2* (1973), *Best Of The Righteous Brothers* (1987).

Film: *Beach Ball* (1964).

Riley, Howard

b. John Howard Riley, 16 February 1943, Huddersfield, Yorkshire, England. Riley began playing piano at the age of six, although it was another 10 years before he began to play jazz. At university he studied under Bernard Rands at Bangor, North Wales (1961-66) gaining BA and MA degrees, then with David Baker at Indiana, adding M.Mus to his name in 1967. From 1967-70 he studied for his Ph.D at York University under Wilfred Mellers, who wrote a piece (Yeibichai) for symphony orchestra, scat singer and jazz trio which was performed by the BBC Symphony Orchestra, Frank Holder and Riley's trio at the 1969 Proms. Riley had led a trio, at Bangor, then joined **Evan Parker**'s quartet. On his return from Indiana he formed a trio with **Barry Guy** (or sometimes Ron Rubin) and **Jon Hiseman** (or **Tony Oxley** or, later, Alan Jackson) and began writing for bands like the **Spontaneous Music Ensemble** and the **Don Rendell-Ian Carr** Quintet. At this time he also began to have his chamber and orchestral pieces performed in concert, and was a founder member of the Musicians' Co-Operative. He has composed for Barry Guy's London Jazz Composers' Orchestra and the New Jazz Orchestra and played with **Keith Tippett**, **John McLaughlin** (who had also occasionally sat in with the late 60s trio), **Jaki Byard**, **Elton Dean**, the LJCO (being the featured soloist on their *Double Trouble*), **Barbara Thompson**, Tony Oxley and many others. He has also taught at the Guildhall and Goldsmith's schools of music in London and at the Center Of The Creative And Performing Arts in Buffalo. In the late 80s he began to release both old and new recordings on his own cassette label, Falcon Tapes; and in 1990 he and Elton Dean co-lead a quartet of improvisers on a set of jazz standards, *All The Tradition*.

Selected albums: *Discussions* (1967), *Angle* (1969), *The Day Will Come* (1970), *Flight* (1971), *Synopsis* (1976), *Singleness* (1976), *Interwine* (1977), *Shaped* (Mosaic 1977), *Toronto Concert* (1979, rec 1976), *Facets* (Impetus 1981, rec 1979-81, three album box-set), *Duality* (1982), *The Other Side* (1983), *For Four On Two Two* (Affinity 1984), with Keith Tippett *In Focus* (Affinity 1985), with Jaki Byard *Live At The Royal Festival Hall* (1987, rec 1984), with Elton Dean *All The Tradition* (1990), *Procession* (Wondrous 1991), *The Heat Of Moments* (Wondrous 1993), with Tippett *The Bern Concert* (Future Music 1994), *Beyond Category* (Wondrous 1993).

Riley, Jeannie C.

b. Jeannie Carolyn Stephenson, 19 October 1944, Anson, Texas, USA. Riley wanted to be a country singer, and, after marrying her childhood sweetheart, Mickey Riley, she persuaded him to move to Nashville. He worked in a filling station while she became a secretary on Music Row for music publisher, Jerry Chesnut. She also recorded demo records for his writers and her voice appealed to record producer, **Shelby Singleton**, who felt that Alice Joy's voice was too smooth on the demo for **Tom T. Hall**'s song of small town hypocrisy, 'Harper Valley PTA', which owed much to **Bobbie Gentry**'s 'Ode To Billie Joe', and was more suited to a female singer than Hall himself. Riley recorded the song in one take and then rang her mother to tell her she had recorded a million-seller. It was an understatement as 'Harper Valley PTA' topped the USA charts and sold over six million. It was a UK hit but only made number 12. With her

mini-skirts and knee-length boots, Riley acted out the central character of 'Harper Valley PTA' and she recorded a concept album about others in Harper Valley. Her singles include 'The Girl Most Likely To', 'There Never Was A Time' and 'The Back Side Of Dallas', but she had no other substantial hits. She started drinking and her marriage ended in 1970. By 1976, she was a born-again Christian and she and Mickey had remarried. A successful film based on the song was produced in 1978 and led to a television series, both starring Barbara Eden. Riley will not work in clubs which serve alcohol and although she has made Christian albums, everyone remembers the day she 'socked it to the PTA', hence her record, 'Return To Harper Valley' in 1987.

Albums: *Harper Valley PTA* (1968), *Sock Soul* (1968), *Yearbooks And Yesterdays* (1968), *The Songs Of Jeannie C. Riley* (1969), *Things Go Better With Love* (1969), *Country Girl* (1970), *The Generation Gap* (1970), *Jeannie* (1972), *Down To Earth* (1972), *Give Myself A Party* (1972), *When Love Has Gone Away* (1973), *Just Jeannie* (1974), *Sunday After Church* (1975), *Fancy Friends* (1977), *Wings To Fly* (1979), *From Harper Valley To The Mountain Top* (1981), *On The Road* (1982), *Pure Country* (1982), *Total Woman* (1987).

Further reading: *From Harper Valley To The Mountain Top*, Jeannie C. Riley with Jamie Buckingham.

Riley, Marc, And The Creepers

b. Manchester, England. Riley started playing in a band when he was aged 15, 'then I sort of wormed my way into the **Fall** when I was 16'. He left to form the Creepers, with Eddie Fenn (drums), Paul Fletcher (guitar) and Pete Keogh (bass). The last two were later replaced by Mark Tilton (guitar) and Phil Roberts (bass). The records that followed were full of hard-hitting humour and remained as opinionated as those of Riley's former boss, Mark E. Smith (who apparently wrote the sarcastic 'Middle Mass' about Riley). Examples included the anti-**Paul Weller** rallying cry, 'Bard Of Woking'. Riley formed In Tape records with keyboardist Jim Khambatta, who also managed the Creepers. Starved of commercial success, and burdened by his heritage, Riley disbanded the Creepers in 1987 and formed the Lost Soul Crusaders, later undertaking a career in radio.

Albums: *Cull* (In Tape 1984), *Gross Out* (In Tape 1984), *Fancy Meeting God* (In Tape 1985), *Warts 'n' All* (In Tape 1985). The Creepers: *Miserable Sinners* (In Tape 1986), *Rock 'N' Roll Liquorice Flavour* (Red Rhino 1987). Compilation: *Sleeper: A Retrospective* (Bleed 1989).

Riley, Mike

(see **Farley And Riley**)

Riley, Teddy

Widely regarded as not only the originator, but the

whole motivating force behind New Jack Swing, Riley remains arguably the most successful and revered producer in commercial dance music. His writing, remixing and production credits include numerous **Bobby Brown** records, and work with **Keith Sweat**, **Jazzy Jeff And The Fresh Prince**, Wreckx-N-Effect, **James Ingram** and **Michael Jackson** (*Dangerous*). Despite this profusion, he maintains that 'I don't work with anyone who isn't a real singer. I've turned down a lot of artists who are big but who I reckon don't have the ability.' His 'swing' groups included the originals, **Guy**, on which he sang vocals, as well as **Jodeci**, **Mary J. Blige** and soundtrack work on *New Jack City* and *Do The Right Thing*. His origins were in the R&B group, Kids At Work, and his step-father was Gene Griffin, who released one of the earliest rap tracks in Trickeration's 'Rap, Bounce, Rollerskate'. Riley's own rap connections included an uncredited appearance on **Doug E. Fresh**'s 'The Show', but by the turn of the decade he would be a multi-millionaire. He returned to the group format in 1994 as vocalist for his latest projectm Blackstreet, who also boasted Chauncey 'Black' Hannibal (an original member of Jodeci), Levi Little (bass, guitar, keyboards) and David Hollister (formerly backing vocalist for Mary J. Blige, **Al B. Sure**, **Patti LaBelle** and 2Pac).
Selected albums: Guy: *Guy* (Uptown 1989). Blackstreet: *Blackstreet* (East West 1994).

Riley, Terry

b. 24 June 1935, Colfax, California, USA. A former ragtime pianist on San Francisco's Barbary Coast, Riley forged an exceptional, *avant garde* minimalist style while performing in Europe. Having studied with fellow radical LaMonte Young, he completed his revolutionary piece, 'In C', in 1964. Here Riley's piano part, the pulse, strikes a uniform tempo as an ensemble plays 53 separate figures. Each musician moves at his/her own pace and the composition is only complete when every player reaches figure 53. Riley found a more widespread audience with *A Rainbow In Curved Air* which comprised of two lengthy compositions, the title track and 'Poppy Nogood And The Phantom Band'. Electric organ and electric harpsichord ebb and flow in cyclical patterns, creating a mood adopted by the **Soft Machine**, **Brian Eno**, **Philip Glass** and a host of new age practitioners. *Church Of Anthrax*, a joint effort with **John Cale**, which for the most part was a unsatisfying collaboration, brought Riley a small degree of commercial success, but he preferred to pursue an irregular release schedule rather than capitalize on any new-found fame. Indeed, it was 1980 before he recorded for the American market, although intermediate releases had been undertaken for European outlets. Riley has since garnered plaudits and his work has been interpreted successfully by the acclaimed Kronos Quartet.

Albums: *Reed Streams* (1967), *In C* (1968), *A Rainbow In Curved Air* (1969), with John Cale *Church Of Anthrax* (1971), *Persian Surgery Dervishes* (1972), *Happy Ending* (1973), *Le Secret De La Vie* (1974), *Ten Voices Of The Two Prophets* (70s), *Shri Camel* (1980), *Descending Moonshine Dervishes* (1982), *The Ethereal Time Shadow* (1985), *No Man's Land* (1990).

Riley, Winston

Riley started out as a singer, forming the legendary **rocksteady** outfit the **Techniques** as a schoolboy in 1962. In 1968 the group broke away from their producer **Duke Reid**, and Riley, with his brother Buster, borrowed enough money from his mother to form his own label. Their first production, **Johnny Osbourne**'s 'Come Back Darling', was an immediate success followed by an album of the same name. Other early productions include Osbourne's 'See And Blind' and 'Purify Your Heart', **Alton Ellis**' 'I'll Be Waiting', Lloyd Young's 'High Explosion', **Dennis Alcapone**'s 'Look Into Yourself', Jimmy Riley's 'Prophecy', the **Ethiopians**' 'Promises', and various Techniques sides. These appeared on a variety of labels in Jamaica; Techniques, Wind, Serpent, Romax and Riley Inc. and a licensing deal with the B&C group resulted in the appearance of many of them on release on the Techniques label in the UK. He scored a number 1 UK hit in May 1971 with 'Double Barrel' by **Dave And Ansell Collins**, which spawned an album of the same title in 1971. The follow-up, 'Monkey Spanner', reached number 7 in July of the following year.
In 1973 he enjoyed a huge Jamaican hit with his production of Ansell Collins' 'Stalag 17', DJ versions by **Big Youth**; 'Jim Screechy' and 'All Nations', were also popular. During the mid-70s other fine productions appeared in the then popular roots style, including the Interns' (aka the **Viceroys**) 'Missions Impossible' and two melodica cuts of the rhythm both entitled 'Black Out', by **Augustus Pablo** and Ansell Collins, 'Cheer Up Blackman' by former Technique Morvin Brooks, 'Don't Mock Jah' by Donovan Addams and a pair of fine dub albums; *Meditation Dub* and *Concrete Jungle Dub* (both 1976). As the decade drew to a close, Riley was responsible for producing one of the first and most influential of the new breed of **dancehall** DJs; **General Echo**, scoring a big reggae hit with 'Arleen' which rode the original 'Staleg' rhythm, and releasing the popular *Ranking Slackness* (1980), which more or less inaugurated the whole trend for lewd lyrics that has prospered since. When quizzed on this in an interview in Canada's *Reggae Quarterly* in 1986, he remarked, with admirable candour; 'Let's face it, that record was a big seller! People would pass by the shop (Techniques Records situated at 2 Chancery Lane, Kingston) and say "You don't have to make a record like that!" But somebody have to do it.' This period also saw numerous sides by Johnny Osbourne including

'Politician', 'Inflation' and a re-cut of 'Purify Your Heart'. In 1982 Riley revived the Techniques with Morvin Brooks and ex-**Paragon** Tyrone (aka Don) Evans to record an album, *Never Fall In Love*.

In 1985 Riley resurrected the durable 'Stalag' rhythm once more for **Tenor Saw**'s massive dancehall hit, 'Ring The Alarm', which begat the classic one rhythm album, *Stalag 17, 18 And 19* (1985), and brought the rhythm back in a big way. The following year another of his productions; 'Boops' (Jamaican slang for a sugar daddy) by DJ **Supercat**, went massive, breaking the artist internationally, and starting another trend for records dealing with the same subject. Riley has been among the most successful Jamaican producers of the last 25 years, and many artists have benefitted from his expertise including **Frankie Paul** (*Strange Feeling* 1984), **Michael Prophet**, Don Evans (*Don Evans* 1983), **Admiral Tibet** (*Leave People's Business* 1988), Sister Nancy, **Red Dragon** ('Hol' A Fresh' 1987), Courtney Melody (*Bad Boy* 1988), Ernest Wilson, **Gregory Isaacs**, Papa San & Lady G ('Legal Rights' 1989), **Cutty Ranks, Yammie Bolo**, who recorded his debut 'When A Man's In Love' (1985) for Riley, and many others.

Rimington, Sammy

b. 29 April 1942, London, England. Rimington began playing clarinet and alto saxophone professionally in his mid-teens as a member of Barry Martyn's band and by 1960 was with **Ken Colyer** where he remained for four years. In 1965 he visited the USA, playing in New Orleans with several leading veterans including **George Lewis** and **Zutty Singleton**. In the late 60s he was back in the UK working with Martyn and touring Americans, such as **Kid Thomas** and **John Handy**, but was also experimenting with jazz rock. He was, however, most at home in New Orleans-style music and since the mid-70s has played with many leading exponents of traditional jazz including **George Webb**, **Keith Smith** and **Chris Barber**. On clarinet, Rimington is an exceptionally fine performer in the tradition originating in the style of Lewis whom he clearly admires and he has great flair on this instrument. Like Barber, Rimington has constantly sought to expand the boundaries of his chosen area of jazz and this is most apparent when he plays alto saxophone. On this instrument he plays with great emotional depth, creating fascinating and highly rhythmic solos using a quirky distinctive style that faintly echoes the sound of **Pete Brown**. Despite his comparative youthfulness, Rimington is one of the outstanding exponents of New Orleans jazz playing today, and thanks to his broad-based musical outlook he can appeal to a much wider audience than this might at first suggest.

Albums: with Kid Thomas *The December Band* (1965), with Zutty Singleton *Zutty And The Clarinet Kings* (1967), with Keith Smith *Way Down Yonder In New Orleans, Then And Now* (1977), *And Red Beans* (1977), *Sammy Rimington And His New Orleans Quartet* (1977), *Reed All About It* (Hefty Jazz 1978), *The Sammy Rimington Band* (1980), *Exciting Sax* (Progressive 1986-91), *In Town With Sam Lee* (GHB 1988), *A New Orleans Session With* (GHB 1989), *One Swiss Night* (Music Mecca 1993).

Rinehart, Cowboy Slim

b. Nolan Rinehart, 12 March 1911, near Gustine, Texas, USA, d. 28 October 1948. Little is known of Rinehart, especially of his early life but he grew up in a ranching area. A natural singer, he learned to play guitar and probably made his first broadcasts on local radio in Brady. In the 30s, his down-to-earth cowboy singing saw him become one of the most popular artists ever to appear on XEPN, a border radio station situated at Piedras Negras, just inside the Mexican border. In his early days at XEPN, he worked for a time with the then established **Patsy Montana**. She toured the east coast of America with Rinehart and was amazed to find how many people regularly listened to the powerful border radio broadcasts. His ability to sell his sponsor's products over the air led to him becoming known as the King Of Border Radio. He recorded many transcription discs, sometimes under differing names, which were broadcast as live programmes on various stations. A strong willed person, he was difficult to pin down, as singing cowboy **Ken Maynard** discovered, when he tried to arrange for Rinehart to audition for some appearances in his cowboy films. Maynard rated Rinehart the greatest cowboy singer that he had heard in his life. When eventually Rinehart went to Hollywood, he later maintained that the studio did not want him to perform with his guitar but as a crooner fronting an orchestra. They also wanted him to use Nolan, instead of the German-sounding Rinehart. It seems probable, since his prospected film career never happened, that Rinehart told the studio what to do with the job. He remained with border radio, where he sold vast numbers of his songbooks to his many fans, until his death. It has been written that, at the time, he was about to become involved more with the administrative side of border radio but this was never to happen. On 28 October 1948, he was killed in a car crash in Detroit, Michigan. He may have been making a few rare appearances away from border radio but it is also possible, since he had a recording contract from **Decca** in his pocket, that he was on his way to make his first commercial recordings.

Further reading: *Cowboy Slim Rinehart's Folio Of Country Song Hits*, Dallas Turner.

Rink, The

Considered by many of the US critics to be simply a vehicle for the singing and dancing talents of **Chita Rivera** and **Liza Minnelli**, *The Rink* made its debut at the Martin Beck Theatre in New York on 9 February 1984. Terrence McNally's story, much of it told in flashback, deals with the tussle between the hard-hearted Anna (Rivera) and her confused daughter Angel (Minnelli) over the fate of the family-owned run-down seaside roller skating rink. Anna has sold it for development, and the arrival of the demolition men drives the two women into a frenzy of bitter regrets and recriminations about the past and what might have been - and the immediate future. **John Kander** and **Fred Ebb**'s fine - and at times, often touching and wryly amusing - score, gets off to a flyer with Minnelli's rousing 'Coloured Lights', which is followed splendidly by 'Chief Cook And Bottle Washer', 'Don't "Ah, Ma" Me', 'Blue Crystal', 'Under The Roller-Coaster', 'Not Enough Magic', 'We Can Make It', 'After All These Years', 'Angel's Rink And Social Centre', 'What Happened To The Old Days?', 'Marry Me', 'Mrs. A.', 'The Rink', 'Wallflower' and 'All The Children In A Row'. 'The Apple Doesn't Fall', a rare moment of harmony between mother and daughter, is a particular delight. The members of the supporting cast, Jason Alexander, Mel Johnson Jnr., Scott Holmes, Scott Ellis, Frank Mastrocola and Ronn Carroll, each played several roles, and the inevitable - and highly entertaining - roller skating scene was choreographed by Graciela Daniele. The director was A.J. Antoon. Chita Rivera won the best actress Tony Award, but audiences dwindled rapidly following Minnelli's departure, and *The Rink* closed after 204 performances. A UK production, directed and choreographed by Paul Kerryson which originated at Manchester's Library Theatre, transferred to the Cambridge Theatre in London on 17 February 1988. Starring Diane Langton and Josephine Blake, it was acclaimed by the critics but immediately began to lose money. In spite of an all-night sit-in at the theatre by members of the cast and sympathetic actors and actresses from musicals such as *Starlight Express* and *Les Misérables*, *The Rink* was withdrawn on 19 March.

Rinzler, Ralph

b. 20 July 1934, New York, USA, d. 2 July 1994, Washington, DC, USA. A leading exponent of American folklore, Rinzler became acquainted with traditional music while in his teens. He studied in London under **A.L. Lloyd** and, in 1959, replaced Eric Weissberg in the **Greenbriar Boys**. An accomplished mandolin player, Rinzler performed with this influential bluegrass attraction until 1964. He then became director of field research for the Newport Folk Festival, and as such undertook several recording trips with archivist **Alan Lomax**. Three years later Rinzler became director of the Festival Of American Folklife at the Smithsonian Institution and embarked on a concurrent filming career. His documentaries have included two studies of traditional pottery, while he has published books about handicraft work and several folk artists, including **Doc Watson** and **Uncle Dave Macon**.

Rio Rita

An historic show, in that it was the first to be presented at New York's brand new Ziegfeld Theatre, on 2 February 1927. **Florenz Ziegfeld** himself produced this hybrid of musical comedy and operetta, so it goes without saying that it was a colourful and spectacular affair, populated by lots of beautiful girls. **Guy Bolton** and Fred Thomson's story is firmly in the operetta tradition, and concerns the hunt for a desperado known as the Kinkajou. The search across the Rio Grande is led by Capt. James Stewart (J. Harold Murray), with his Texas Rangers. Captain Stewart is in love with the wild and passionate Rita Ferguson (Ethelind Terry), but has to wait for her hand until her other suitor, General Esteban (Vincent Serrano), has been revealed as the Kinkajou. Composer **Harry Tierney** and lyricist **Joseph McCarthy** were collaborating on their third, and last, successful Broadway musical, following *Irene* and *Kid Boots*. Their score was notable for the rousing 'Rangers' Song' and the delightful 'If You're In Love, You'll Waltz'. Terry and Murray combined on another lovely ballad, 'Rio Rita', and the rest of the songs included the lively 'The Kinkajou', 'Following The Sun Around', and 'You're Always In My Arms'. *Rio Rita* was an enormous hit, and ran for 494 performances - even longer than *The Desert Song* which had opened earlier in that same season. Coincidentally, when the show reached London, where it starred Edith Day, it inaugurated yet another theatre, the Prince Edward, but only stayed there for 59 performances. Many more people had the opportunity to enjoy the early-talkie film version, with Bebe Daniels and John Boles, which was released in 1929.

Rios, Miguel

b. 1944, Grenada, Spain. Rios was a juvenile soloist in a church choir and on leaving school, he formed a rock 'n' roll outfit that played locally. In 1969, he was singled out by a Hispanvox Records talent scout to sing lead on a grandiloquent pop adaptation of the last movement of Beethoven's Ninth Symphony, by orchestra conductor Waldo De Los Rios (no relation). After 'Himno A La Alegria' ('Song Of Joy') reached number 3 in Spain, and topped the charts in South America and Germany, it was re-recorded with an English libretto (by Ross Parker) for leasing to UK and North American companies as a commemoration of the German composer's bi-centennial. Although it became a Top 10 entry in Canada and then the US, progress in the UK was sluggish and the record peaked at number 16 in the summer of 1970. Miguel Rios had no further international hits.

Riot

Riot's career has forever been dogged by record company problems and a general lack of interest from press quarters - a surprising epitaph for a New York band who formed in 1976 and were the subject of a petition to get one of their albums released in Europe. Signed in 1977 to Ariola, the band comprised L.A. Kouvaris (guitar), Mark Reale (guitar), Peter Bitelli (drums), Jimmy Iommi (bass) and vocalist Speranza. Constant touring brought them little success and by 1979 Kouvaris was replaced by Rick Ventura. **Capitol Records** signed them and released *Narita* - still hailed as a hard rock classic, it brought them widespread attention in the UK which led to an appearance at the Donington Festival in 1980. The following year they returned to the studio and recorded *Fire Down Under*. Capitol refused to release it and fans in the UK started the aforementioned petition to force their hand. Capitol stuck fast and dropped them, but **Elektra** were quick to see their potential. The album was eventually released to critical acclaim. However, Iommi and Bitelli quit, to be replaced by Kip Leming and Sandy Slavin, while former **Rachel** vocalist Rhett Forrester replaced Speranza. The next album, *Restless Breed*, was a mixed affair, but contained an excellent version of **Eric Burden**'s 'When I Was Young'. After a badly produced live album they were dropped by Elektra. They released one final album to a total absence of industry or fan interest in 1984. A brief but unsuccessful reformation with most of the original line-up ensued in 1986, before Reale emerged with an all-new band, featuring Tony Moore (vocals), Don Van Stavern (bass) and Bobby Jarzombek (drums) and made an acclaimed comeback with *Thundersteel*, although *Privilege Of Power* and *Nightbreaker*, with new vocalist Michael Dimeo and guitarist Mike Flyntz, saw the band's sound fail to progress with the times. Forrester had a short-lived solo career before he too disappeared from view. Later it emerged he was murdered during an attempted robbery in January 1994.

Albums: *Rock City* (Ariola 1977), *Narita* (Capitol 1979), *Fire Down Under* (Elektra 1981), *Restless Breed* (Elektra 1982), *Riot Live* (Elektra 1982), *Born In America* (Grand Slam 1984), *Thundersteel* (CBS 1988), *Privilege Of Power* (CBS 1989), *Riot Live* (CBS 1989, rec. 1980), *Nightbreaker* (Rising Sun 1994).

Riot On Sunset Strip

Released in 1967, *Riot On Sunset Strip* was one of several films, alongside *The Wild Angels*, in which the notorious American International Pictures company used story-lines drawn from California's emergent underground sub-cultures. Famed for a lengthy series of 'beach' films starring **Annette** Funicello, AIP brought the same exploitative, 'quickie' practices to these new features, grafting moral punchlines to plots involving drugs and sex on the same surface level as their predecessors had shown 'bad guys' and kissing. *Riot On Sunset Strip* was inspired by real-life events on the fabled Los Angeles thoroughfare when curfews and legislation prohibiting assembly resulted in an infamous demonstration. Indeed, newsreel footage of the event was dropped into film near its close. Whereas the fall-from-grace and retribution of 'Andy' (Mimsy Farmer) - the daughter of a police lieutenant and an alcoholic mother - provides a cardboard framework, *Riot On Sunset Strip* is revered for appearances by US garagebands the **Standells**, who sing the title theme, and **Chocolate Watchband**. The latter's second contribution, 'Sitting There Standing', was actually written in the on-set bathroom during a break in shooting. Both groups are featured playing in a reconstruction of the Strip's fabled club, Pandora's Box. Their cameos lift the entire film although wooden acting, laughable script and sterotypical scenes ensure its cult status. Entrepreneur **Mike Curb** assembled a soundtrack which included the aforementioned acts as well as several who did not feature in the final print. These included the Mugwumps, the Sidewalk Sounds and Mom's Boys although contractual obligations precluded an appearance by the Enemies, who are in the film. Unpretentious at the outset, *Riot On Sunset Strip* still retains its charm.

Riot Squad

A group of young UK session musicians formed by producer **Larry Page**, the Riot Squad consisted of **Graham Bonney** (vocals), Ron Ryan (lead guitar), Bob Evans (saxophone), Mark Stevens (organ), Mike Martin (bass) and John 'Mitch' Mitchell (drums). They made their recording debut in January 1965 with the gritty 'Anytime', while subsequent releases explored contrasting strands of R&B. The group completed seven singles over the ensuing two years, but was plagued by internal dissent. Bonney subsequently enjoyed momentary success with his second solo release, 'Supergirl', but it was Mitchell who gained the highest profile, first with **Georgie Fame**, then with the **Jimi Hendrix** Experience. By that point **Joe Meek** had assumed the Riot Squad reins from Page, but this made little difference to their fortunes. A group bearing their name struggled on into 1968, but by this point none of the original line-up remained.

Album: *Anytime* (1988, all of the group's releases).

Rip Chords

One of the first rock groups signed to **Columbia Records** in the USA, the Rip Chords were best known for a 'hot rod' hit in early 1964, 'Hey Little Cobra', which reached the Top 5 just as the **Beatles** broke through in the USA. The group's records were actually the work of singer/producer **Terry Melcher**, and singer **Bruce Johnston**, later of the **Beach**

Boys. However, that duo did not represent the Rip Chords in concerts; a completely different set of musicians was sent out on the road. The Rip Chords were an already-existing group in 1963, including Phil Stewart, Ernie Bringas, Arnie Marcus and Rich Rotkin. Stewart and Bringas approached Melcher, a staff producer at Columbia, and were signed to the label. Their first single, 'Here I Stand', was a minor chart hit in 1963, as was 'Gone', written by Melcher and Johnston and featuring the latter on background vocals. Melcher and Johnston heard 'Hey Little Cobra', written by former **Teddy Bears** member Annette Kleinbard under the name Carol Connors, and recorded it themselves. Although the pair had planned to record under the name Bruce and Terry, they decided to release the record under the Rip Chords' name, since that group already had appeared in the charts. The single shot to number 4. *Hey Little Cobra And Other Hot Rod Hits*, was recorded in 1964, featuring Melcher and Johnston singing on nearly half the tracks. Another car-orientated single, 'Three Window Coupe', by Jan Berry of **Jan And Dean** and Roger Christian, was a Top 30 hit in the summer of 1964 and was followed with an album of the same name, which also featured Melcher and Johnston on most of the tracks. After one final chart single, 'One Piece Topless Bathing Suit', Melcher turned down the **Brian Wilson** composition 'Help Me Rhonda' for the Rip Chords and took on more production for Columbia, most notably for **Paul Revere And The Raiders** and the **Byrds**. From that point on the Rip Chords ceased to exist.

Albums: *Hey Little Cobra And Other Hot Rod Hits* (1964), *Three Window Coupe* (1964).

Rip Rig And Panic

Evolving out of Bristol's the **Pop Group**, Rip Rig And Panic was formed in 1981 as a conceptual musicians' collective, taking its name from an album by **Roland Rahsaan Kirk**. The group's prime movers were multi-instrumentalist and songwriter Gareth Sager, jazz trumpeter **Don Cherry**'s stepdaughter **Neneh Cherry** (b. Stockholm, Sweden; vocals), Cherry's partner and drummer Bruce Smith, Sean Oliver (bass) and Mark Springer (piano). Powerful and disturbing live, their playful, anarchic jazz-funk was well-captured on the irreverent 1981 debut album, *God*, which appeared as two 45rpm discs, but was too radical for daytime airplay or significant sales. They performed at the first WOMAD festival in 1982 shortly before Cherry returned to Sweden to have her first baby. Sean Oliver's sister Andrea temporarily took over vocals, and **Louis Moholo** joined on drums. The equally experimental second album, *I Am Cold*, appeared in 1982, followed by the more accessible *Attitude* in 1983. Unwilling to compromise further, but feeling the strain of constant innovation, they split in 1985, only to re-

align as the smaller outfit, Float Up CP and, briefly, God Mother And Country, before Cherry went on to a successful solo career with Andrea Oliver contributing to some of her songs.

Albums: *God* (1981), *I Am Cold* (1982), *Attitude* (1983).

Riperton, Minnie

b. 8 November 1947, Chicago, Illinois, USA, d. 12 July 1979. A former singer with the **Gems**, Riperton recorded under the name 'Andrea Davis' prior to joining the **Rotary Connection**. She remained with this adventurous, black pop/psychedelic group between 1967 and 1970, before embarking on a solo career. In 1973 the singer began working with Wonderlove, **Stevie Wonder**'s backing group. Two years later he returned this compliment, producing Minnie's *Perfect Angel*, and contributing two original compositions to the selection. However, it was 'Loving You', a song written by Riperton and her husband, Richard Rudolph, which brought international success, (US number 1/UK number 2) in 1975. This delicate performance featured the artist's soaring multi-octave voice, but set a standard later releases found hard to emulate. Riperton died from cancer in July 1979.

Albums: *Come To My Garden* (1969), *Perfect Angel* (1974), *Adventures In Paradise* (1975), *Stay In Love* (1977), *Minnie* (1979), *Love Lives Forever* (1980). Compilation: *The Best Of Minnie Riperton* (1981).

Rippingtons

Russ Freeman (b. 11 February 1960, Nashville, Tennessee, USA; guitar), **Kenny G.** (b. Kenneth Gorelick, 1959, Seattle, Washington, USA; saxophone), **David Benoit** (b. 1953, Bakersfield, California, USA; keyboards). The man generally recognised as the founder of the Rippingtons, Russ Freeman discovered the guitar with the kind of inevitability that comes from growing up in Nashville. In fact, it was a studio guitarist friend of Russ' father that gave him his initial encouragement. He studied at Cal Arts and at UCLA, developing the essential studio skills, releasing a debut album (*Nocturnal Playground*) in 1985. *Moonlighting* came the following year, after Freeman got together with Kenny G., David Benoit and a group of friends, to record some of his own new compositions, in an unambitious project he lightheartedly called The Rippingtons, and the record was an instant hit. One of the GRP label's most coveted acts, the band specialises in a smooth instrumental pop fusion, featuring element of Latin music and R&B.

Albums: *Moonlighting* (Passport 1987), *Kilimanjaro* (Passport 1988), *Tourist In Paradise* (GRP 1989), *Welcome To The St. James' Club* (GRP 1992), *Curves Ahead* (GRP 1991), *Weekend In Monaco* (GRP 1992), *Live In L.A.* (GRP 1993), *Sahara* (GRP 1995).

Riptides

Formed in Brisbane, Australia in 1979, the Riptides became a cult band along the coast with surf audiences, eventually arriving in Sydney where they became the 'next big thing'. The initial line-up comprised Mark Callaghan (vocals), Dennis Cantwell (drums), Scott Matheson (guitar, replaced in 1981 by Michael Hiron) and Andrew Leitch (keyboards/guitar). Their melodies and pop songs were gems, but somehow the band failed to take the next step to the top rung and, by 1983, had split up after several line-up changes. Main songwriter Mark Callaghan later formed GANGgajang in 1984 and produced an excellent solo album, *Sailors And Mermaids* (1988). Riptides reform occasionally for national tours, which are well attended, suggesting that the band had charisma if only lacking in commercial success.

Albums: *Last Wave* (1983), *The Riptides* (1983), *Resurface* (1987).

Rising High Collective

Namely one Casper Pound (b. c.1970), of **The Hypnotist** fame, and also the man who formed **Rising High Records**, and vocalist Plavka (b. Los Angeles, California, USA). Pound's ancestry extends to spells in **A Homeboy, A Hippie, And A Funki Dred**, before he found Top 75 success no less than seven times in his own right, and also navigated three Top 40 remixes into the charts, including the **Shamen**'s number 1, 'Progen'. Plavka came to fame via the former group, gracing their first Top 30 cut, 'Hyperreal'. She came to London in 1989, immersing herself in the rave scene and passing herself off as a journalist in order to make the acquaintance of the Shamen. But ater they broke through toghether she quit the group to concentrate on projects where she could have more input into the songwriting, in addition to her much-admired operatic soprano range. She met Pound in 1991, the duo releasing their first single, 'Fever Called Love', in December of that year, for **R&S**. It was a stunning cut, above and beyond the novelty value of hearing a genuine techno track with genuine vocals. It was not until the summer of 1993 and a **Hardfloor** remix that the song really took off, however. After slightly misfiring with 'Reach', which was neverthless a minor hit, 'There's No Deeper Love' (whose lyrics quietly provided a text on astrology and the formation of the universe) proved another club hit, this time with the progressive house faction. They made an acclaimed appearance at the 1993 Reading Festival, as well as many PA's at venues like the **Ministry Of Sound**, Heaven and Camden Palace. 1994's *Liquid Thoughts* EP provided further well-received slices of deep trance. They additionally recorded togetether as Dominatrix (two EPs, *Possession* and *Discipline*) while Plavka released a solo single, 'Maximum Motion' (all on Rising High or their Ascension/Sappho subsidiaries), and guested for **Jam And Spoon** ('Right In The Middle').

Rising High Records

Record label founded in London, England, in February 1991 by Casper Pound, initially as an outlet for his own material, having recently disengaged from chart act **A Homeboy, A Hippie And A Funki Dred**. Having spent time living in Italy he returned to England bluffing his way into studio work with reggae producer **Mad Professor** and hi-NRG man **Ian Levine**. Soon he had learned enough to give his own operation a shot. Since its inception (the honour of first release going to Pound as **The Hypnotist**, with 'Rainbows In The Sky'), the label has grown to be much more than an inventive young man's hobby. Rising High has been at the forefront, if not beyond it, in all of the major developments of dance music in the 90s. Pound has developed a second sense in recognising or anticipating trends such as jungle/breakbeat, trance and finally ambient. Their early hardcore techno is best sampled on **Aural Assault**, Earth Leakage Trip and **Project One** releases. As Pound asserted, unrepentently, at the time: 'I like nosebleed techno, the more nosebleedy the better'. A good example was Earth Leakage Trip's techno rave anthems on the *Neopolitan* EP, which featured the improbably bombastic 'The Ice Cream Van From Hell' - a furious rhythm track anchored by coy samples. A regular feature of the label has been the artistic growth of **Mixmaster Morris** (aka the Irresistible Force). After making his debut for the label with 'Space Is The Place' his recordings have continued to be a prominent fixture of Rising High's release schedule. As Rising High has grown it has spawned its own subsidiary imprints. Sappho (specialising in the harder, experimental end of the techno spectrum, set up in conjunction with RH A&R scout Pypee) and Ascension. They also brought the exciting sounds being developed in Germany at **Harthouse**/Eye Q via a link-up as Harthouse UK (earning significant kudos for giving the British public **Hardfloor**'s 'Hardtrance Acperience'). Yet Rising High has also retained an endearing self-mockery and unfettered approach to dance music. Their slogans: 'You're going home in a fuckin' ambience', or Mixmaster Morris' 'I Think Therefore I Ambient' notwithstanding. Most of 1993/94's innovations were in the latter sector, flooding the market with a noble array of compilations such as *Chill Out Or Die* and *Definitive Ambient Collection* - the former specially packaged by Mixmaster Morris, the latter by German ambient meister **Peter Namlock**. That duo also recorded together for the label under the title Dreamfish.

Selected albums: Various: *Techno Anthems Vol. 1 & 2* (Rising High 1991), *Chill Out Or Die 1 & 2* (Rising High

1993), *Secret Life Of Trance 1, 2 & 3* (Rising High 1993 - 1994). The Hypnotist: *The Complete Hypnotist* (Rising High 1992). Peter Namlook & Mixmaster Morris: *Dreamfish* (Rising High 1993).

Rising Sons

A group of almost legendary proportions, the Rising Sons were formed in Los Angeles, California, USA in 1964. Founding members **Taj Mahal** and Jesse Lee Kincaid met while performing folk and blues at the Club 47 in Cambridge, Massachusetts. Having travelled together to the West Coast, they were joined by guitarist **Ry Cooder**. Bassist Gary Marker and drummer Ed Cassady completed the original line-up, although the latter left to join his stepson, **Randy California**, in the Red Roosters, and later, **Spirit**. Cassady was replaced by Kevin Kelly, a cousin of **Byrds**' bassist, **Chris Hillman**. Indeed the Rising Sons were also signed to the latter group's label, **CBS**, and were assigned to the same producer, **Terry Melcher**. Despite a high-powered campaign, the quintet's lone single, 'Candy Man'/'Devil Got My Woman', was released in February 1966, was not a commercial success. The Rising Sons did complete an album, encompassing traditional material, choice cover versions and Kincaid's marvellous **Beatles**'-styled originals, but it was deemed too eclectic for release. The group split up later that year. Mahal embarked on a solo career - his early releases feature several songs first recorded by his former group - and he remains a highly respected folk/blues performer. Cooder joined **Captain Beefheart** before establishing his reputation as a session musician. He later recorded successfully under his own name. Kelly joined the Byrds and **Fever Tree**, Marker founded the aptly-titled Fusion and Kincaid recorded three haunting singles. He also composed the memorable 'She Sang Hymns Out Of Tune', popularised by **Nilsson**, the **Dillards** and **Hearts And Flowers**. The eminence of the Rising Sons' former members prompted the release of their long-lost recordings, which confirmed the visionary aspect of their work.
Album: *Rising Sons* (1993).

Ritchie, Jean

b. 8 December 1922, Viper, Kentucky, USA. Ritchie was the youngest of 14 children from a well-known family of traditional singers. Her parents, Balis and Abigail Ritchie were of Scottish-Irish descent. Jean's father taught her to play the mountain dulcimer. The family were visited by **Cecil Sharp** in 1917 during one of his song-collecting expeditions to the Appalachian Mountains. Jean was first recorded in 1948 when she was heard by **Mitch Miller** as she demonstrated a dulcimer in a store. Miller was impressed enough to produce *Round And Roundelays*. Later, having gained a degree in social work, she went to New York where she was introduced to **Alan Lomax**, the well-known, and equally well-respected, folklorist. Lomax recorded Ritchie's songs, both for his own collection and for the Library Of Congress Folksong Archives. She has performed all over the USA and given recitals at universities and colleges. In 1952 Ritchie travelled to the UK after winning a Fulbright scholarship. This also gave her the chance to trace the origins of her family's songs. While in the UK she appeared at the Royal Albert Hall and Cecil Sharp House, the headquarters of the English Folk Dance And Song Society. Jean's 1952 release, *Jean Ritchie Singing Traditional Songs Of Her Kentucky Mountain Family*, was the first folk recording to be issued on the **Elektra** label. In 1953 she attended the International Conference of Folk Music held in Biaritz-Pamplona, and appeared at many folk seminars countrywide. Numerous television and radio appearances, and a wealth of recorded material have ensured her place in her country's folk heritage. Her light voice and simple arrangements have gained the appeal of a wide audience. Many folk song collectors have sought the Ritchie family as a source of traditional tunes and songs. Ritchie's book, *The Singing Family Of The Cumberlands*, recounts the history of her family growing up in the Cumberland mountains. 'My Dear Companion' was recorded by **Linda Ronstadt**, **Emmylou Harris** and **Dolly Parton** on their album *Trio* in 1987. Ritchie's sister Edna also recorded on Jean's own Greenhays label.
Selected albums: *Round And Roundelays* (1948), *Jean Ritchie Singing Traditional Songs Of Her Kentucky Mountain Family* (1952), with Tony Kraber *Valleys In Colonial America* (1953), with Oscar Brand *Shivaree!* (1955), *Saturday Night And Sunday Too* (1956), *A Folk Concert* (1959), *Field Trip-England* (1960), *As I Roved Out-Field Trip Ireland* (1960), *Child Ballads Of The Southern Mountains Vol. 1* (1961), *Child Ballads Of The Southern Mountains Vol. 2* (1961), *Come On In, We're Pickin' And Singin'* (1962), with various artists *Folk Songs At The Limelight* (1962), *The Appalachian Dulcimer* (1963), *Marching Across The Green Grass And Other American Children's Game Songs* (1968), *None But One* (1977). Compilations: *Courtin's A Pleasure* (1957), *The Best Of Jean Ritchie* (1962).
Further reading: all Jean Ritchie *Singing Family Of The Cumberlands. The Swapping Song Book*, Henry Z. Walck Inc. *A Garland Of Mountain Song*, Broadcast Music. *From Fair To Fair*, Henry Z. Walck Inc. *Loves Me Loves Me Not*, Henry Z. Walck Inc. *Jean Ritchie's Dulcimer People*, Oak Publications. *The Dulcimer Book*, Jean Ritchie Oak Publications.

Ritenour, Lee

b. 1 November 1953, Los Angeles, California, USA. The prolific Ritenour has established himself as one of the world's leading jazz fusion guitarists with a series of accessible albums over the past two decades. Known as 'Captain Fingers' Ritenour became a sought-after session player in the mid-70s and like **Larry Carlton** (both regularly play a **Gibson** 335) has developed his own solo career. Although heavily influenced in his early days by the relaxed styles of **Wes Montgomery**, **Joe Pass** and **Barney Kessel** he now has his own distinctive sound and fluid style. His list of session work is awesome, but some of his notable performances were with **Herbie Hancock, Steely Dan** and **Stanley Clarke**. Since the mid-80s Ritenour has been strongly influenced by Brazilian music. He joined GRP Records around this time, having worked with stablemate **Don Grusin** in the band Friendship. He recorded the magnificent *Harlequin* with GRP co-owner **Dave Grusin** in 1985. In the early 90s Ritenour teamed up with **Bob James, Harvey Mason** and bassist Nathan East under the name of Fourplay, and released two soul/jazz/funk fusion albums, *Fourplay* and *Between The Sheets*, for **Warner Brothers**. In 1993 Ritenour topped the **Billboard** jazz chart with his accomplished tribute to Wes Montgomery, *Wes Bound* and followed it in 1995 with an excellent joint album with **Larry Carlton**.

Albums: *First Course* (c.1974), *Guitar Player* (c.1975), *Captain Fingers* (1975), *The Captain's Journey* (Elektra 1978), *Gentle Thoughts* (JVC 1978), with Kazume Watanbe *Sugarloaf Express* (Elite 1978), *Feel The Night* (1979), *Friendship* (JVC 1979), *Rit* (Asylum 1981), *Rio* (GRP 1982), *Rit 2* (GRP 1983), *Banded Together* (1983), *On The Line* (1984), with Dave Grusin *Harlequin* (GRP 1985), *American Flyers* (1986), *Earth Run* (GRP 1986), *Portrait* (1987), *Festival* (GRP 1988), *Wes Bound* (GRP 1993), with Larry Carlton *Larry And Lee* (GRP 1995).

Ritter, Tex

b. Maurice Woodward Ritter, 12 January 1905, near Murvaul, Panola County, Texas, USA, d. 2 January 1974. The youngest of the six children, he grew up on the farm that the Ritter family had worked for over 70 years. He attended High School in Beaumont and then entered the University of Texas in Austin. Here he began his studies for a law degree in Government and Political Science. He was active in the debating societies and sang with the University Glee Club. During this period, he developed a lasting interest in cowboy songs, being greatly influenced by the research of such authorities as **John A. Lomax** and J. Frank Dobie. He financed himself during his time at the University by working menial jobs but finally left in 1928, having completed the first year of his Law School course. He sang cowboy and folk songs on KPCR Houston and struggled to make a living selling insurance. After meeting members of a touring operetta company in Austin, he joined them, finally arriving with the company in a Depression-gripped New York. He possibly sang on *Broadway in The New Moon* in September 1928, although some accounts place his arrival in the city a year later. After visiting Chicago, he

decided to continue his studies for his Law degree and entered Northwestern University Law School in Evanston, Illinois in September 1929. Without financial backing, he soon found himself unable to continue with the course and left to join a touring production of The New Moon in 1930. Late in 1930, he successfully auditioned for the part of Cord Elam, in *Green Grow The Lilacs*. The producer said he wanted real cowboys who could sing but farm boy Woodward reckoned he qualified. (It was around this time that he acquired his nickname 'Tex'.) After a test run in Boston, the company opened on Broadway, on 26 January 1931, with Tex not only singing four songs as Elam but also understudying leading actor Franchot Tone. The play was very successful (it was later converted into the musical *Oklahoma*) and Tex stayed with it, until it finally closed in Detroit. He sang on NBC radio and in 1932, he played the part of Sagebrush Charlie in a Broadway production of *The Roundup* and later appeared in *Mother Lode*. In the early 30s, he also worked on various radio programmes. He sang songs and told tales of the Old West in *Lone Star Rangers* and appeared in several radio dramas including *Death Valley Days* and CBS's networked *Bobby Benson's Adventures* (later appearing in the music version *Songs Of The B-Bar-B*). In 1933, he starred in a daily children's cowboy radio show on WINS New York called *Cowboy Tom's Roundup*. His popularity saw him also appear on WHN radio with *Tex Ritter's Campfire* and *The WHN Barn Dance*. He made four recordings for ARC (American Record Corporation) in March 1933 but only 'Rye Whiskey' was released and he subsequently moved to **Decca**, where he made his first recordings 'Sam Hall' and 'Get Along Little Dogie', on 21 January 1935. He went on to record a further 28 songs for the label, the last being in January 1939, in a session in Los Angeles, billed as Tex Ritter And His Texans, which produced four recordings including his version of the **Vagabonds**' hit 'When It's Lamp Lighting Time In The Valley'. Actually his 'Texans' were the **Sons Of The Pioneers**, a group more associated with **Roy Rogers** than Ritter. Many of the songs recorded were featured in his films plus one or two popular numbers like 'Nobody's Darling But Mine'. In 1936, Grand National Pictures decided that they, like other companies, should make some singing cowboy westerns. Their problem being that they had no singing cowboy under contract but Edward Finney, a producer working with the company, promised he would find one. Ritter was drawn to his attention and Finney signed him to a personal contract, thus becoming his producer-agent. Ritter soon accepted a contract which promised to pay him, as the star, $2,400 per picture. New York had been reasonably good to him but the challenge of Hollywood was too good to refuse. He found himself a horse, White Flash and although more than competent with the singing aspect of his new career, he was coached by one-time outlaw Al Jennings on how to look equally convincing with a gun and his fists. The first of his 12 Grand National B-western's, *Song Of The Gringo*, was shot in five days and was released in November 1936. Before the year was out *Headin' For The Rio Grande* had followed. In his fourth film, *Trouble In Texas* (1937), his co-star was Rita Cansino, who later found fame as Rita Hayworth. In 1938, after *Utah Trail*, Grand National's financial problems saw Finney move Ritter to Monogram, where by 1941, he had made 20 films. The critics were often unkind about some of them, but Ritter escaped most of the comments. When his contract with Finney expired, Ritter decided to look after his own affairs and signed with Columbia Pictures. Financially, things improved and in 1941, he co-starred with Bill Elliott in eight more films. When Elliott left for Republic, Ritter assumed that he would then become the studio's only cowboy star and was totally surprised when Columbia released him. He and White Flash moved to Universal, where he starred in seven films with Johnny Mack Brown and once again suffered by the double billing. In 1943, Brown moved on leaving Ritter to star alone in his next three films, the last being *Oklahoma Raiders*. Financial problems then forced Universal to drop the series but many rate these as three of Ritter's best pictures. In 1944, he joined PRC (Producers Releasing Corporation), where he made a series of eight films that were later described as being little better than the low budget Grand National series. On 15 October 1945, Tex Ritter's last singing cowboy film, *Flaming Bullets*, was released. In his private life, Ritter married Dorothy Fay Southworth, on 14 June 1941. She was the promising actress Dorothy Fay, who had been his leading lady four times and also appeared in *The Philadelphia Story*. After their marriage, she gave up her career and subsequently raised their two sons, Thomas (Tom) and John (Jonathan Southworth Ritter). During his singing cowboy years, Ritter made countless personal appearances to promote his films and his stage shows with White Flash which were very popular. There were books of songs released such as the *Tex Ritter Cowboy Song Folio* (1937) and *Tex Ritter: Mountain Ballads And Cowboy Songs* (1941). When he realised the film career was over, he concentrated more on his touring show, which he combined with his recording work. After his Decca contract ended, he did not actually resume his recording career until 1942, when he became the first C&W singer signed to the newly formed **Capitol Records**, with whom he stayed until his death. He achieved considerable success with 'Jingle Jangle Jingle', which topped the Hit Parade chart for several weeks in July and August 1942. In 1944, *Capitol 174* proved a smash hit for him with 'I'm Wastin' My Tears On You' (a country number 1/pop number 11) and 'There's A New Moon Over My Shoulder' (number 2 in the country chart and number 21 in the

pop chart). Between 1945 and 1946, he registered seven successive Top 5 hits, including 'You Two Timed Me One Time Too Often', a country number 1 for 11 weeks. In 1948, 'Rye Whiskey' and his version of 'Deck Of Cards' both made the Top 10, whilst 'Pecos Bill' from the **Walt Disney** movie *Melody Time* also reached number 15. In 1950, 'Daddy's Last Letter (Private First Class John H McCormick)', based on an actual letter from a soldier killed in Korea, became a surprising hit for him. In the early 50s, the chart hits had dried up and it seemed that his career was nearing an end. He maintained his touring but was unable to gain television exposure other than guest appearances. The situation suddenly changed, when he was asked to record the soundtrack song for the Fred Zinnemann film *High Noon* (which starred gary Cooper and Grace Kelly). Ritter's US recording was made on 14 May 1952 without the drum beat so prominent in the film; it was dubbed on in August. In September or October, whilst touring the UK, he recorded a version in Decca's London studios, with an orchestra directed by Johnny Douglas, that contained the drumbeat and which is arguably Ritter's best recording of the song. This version was not released in the USA but was included on a Bear Family album in 1992. The resultant success of the film and the popularity of Ritter's recording relaunched his career. Surprisingly, he was not too keen on the song and had to be persuaded to sing it at the Academy Awards ceremony where it won an Oscar for Best Title Song. (Perhaps surprisingly, Ritter's recording of the song never actually made the country charts and in the UK it was **Frankie Laine**'s version that became a Top 10 pop hit.) Following the success of 'High Noon', Ritter became the star of the Los Angeles television show *Town Hall Party* which ran until 1961. He also guested on various western adventure programmes such as *Zane Grey Theatre* but one writer has been unkind enough to comment that 'none of the roles were memorable and his extra heft and advancing age, unfortunately, took away somewhat from the memory of his movie singing roles of previous years'. The success of 'High Noon' led to him singing other movie or television themes, including 'The Marshal's Daughter', 'Trooper Hook', 'Gunsmoke' and 'The Searchers'. In 1963, Ritter was a founder member of the Country Music Association and in 1964, he became only the fifth person and first singing cowboy to be elected to the Country Music Hall Of Fame. The plaque stated 'One of America's most versatile stars of radio, television, records, motion pictures and Broadway stage. Untiring champion of the country and western music industry'. The following year when the **Grand Ole Opry** granted him life membership, he finally moved his home from California to Nashville. He played himself in *What Am I Bid?* (1967), in which he sang 'I Never Got To Kiss The Girl' - an amusing number based on fact, since he never did in any of his westerns. In 1970, Ritter was persuaded to run for election to the Senate but as a writer later reported 'maybe the electorate did not want to lose him to Washington, they wanted him to stay at the Opry' and he was not elected. He made his last film appearance, in 1972, in *The Nashville Story*. Suggestions that he slowed down had little effect and he was still in great demand for personal appearance tours. He toured the UK in May 1973 and played three concerts in Scotland and 28 in England on successive days. He had first toured the UK and Europe with his Wild West Show in 1952. On 2 January 1974, at a time when he was working on arrangements for a further tour, he was told that one of his band members was in Nashville's jail over the matter of unpaid child support. He immediately went to the jail to arrange bail and whilst there, he suffered a heart attack from which he died within minutes. His final chart hit, 'The Americans', entered the charts a few days after his death. Although he starred in 58 B-westerns and appeared in over 20 other films, to a great many people Ritter was much more than just a one time singing cowboy. He was a very respected statesman and his vast knowledge of the history of folk, country and cowboy music made him a popular figure wherever he went.

Albums: *Cowboy Favorites* (Capitol 50s, 10-inch), *Songs From The Western Screen* (Capitol 1958), *Psalms* (Capitol 1959), *The Texas Cowboy* (Capitol 1960), *The Lincoln Hymns* (Capitol 1961), *Hillbilly Heaven* (Capitol 1961), *Stan Kenton-Tex Ritter* (Capitol 1962), *Border Affair* (Capitol 1963), *The Friendly Voice Of Tex Ritter* (Capitol 1965), *Blood On The Saddle* (Capitol 1966), *Sings His Hits* (Hilltop 1966), *Just Beyond The Moon* (Capitol 1967), *Sweet Land Of Liberty* (Capitol 1967), *Tennessee Blues* (Hilltop 1967), *Tex Ritter's Wild West* (Capitol 1968), *Love You Big As Texas* (Hilltop 1968), *Bump Tiddil Dee Bum Bum* (Capitol 1968), *Chuck Wagon Days* (Capitol 1969), *Tex* (Hilltop c.1970), *Green Green Valley* (Capitol 1971), *Super Country Legendary Tex Ritter* (Capitol 1972), *An American Legend* (Capitol 1973, triple album), *Fall Away* (Capitol 1974), *Comin' After Ginny* (Capitol 1976), *High Noon* (Bear Family 1983, covers 40s-50s), *Lady Killin' Cowboy* (Bear Family 1986, Picture Disc, covers 1935-36), *Singing In The Saddle* (Bear Family 1986, Picture Disc, covers 1937-39), *High Noon* (Bear Family 1992, covers 1942-1957).

Further reading: *The Tex Ritter Story*, Johnny Bond.

River City People

Tim Speed (b. 17 November 1961, Chester, Cheshire, England; guitar/vocals), Paul Speed (b. 27 October 1964, Chester, Cheshire, England; drums) and Dave Snell (bass), were all studying at Liverpool Polytechnic in 1987 when they got together with Siobhan Maher (b. 11 January 1964, Liverpool, England; vocals), who had previously played with Snell in Peep Show and was now working as a researcher for the BBC. After the fortuitous break of an all-expenses-paid video for '(What's Wrong With) Dreaming', commissioned by the British independent television programme, *The Chart Show*, they signed to **EMI** and found themselves recording in Los Angeles with producer Don Gehman. The results of this collaboration can be heard on their debut *Say Something Good* released in September 1989, which spawned a number of successful pop-rock singles: '(What's Wrong With) Dreaming', 'Say Something Good', 'Walking On Ice' and the double a-side hit 'Carry The Blame'/'California Dreamin'', the latter being a remake of the classic **Mamas And The Papas** track, which reached number 13 in the UK charts. Between extensive touring throughout the UK and abroad, they recorded their follow-up *This Is The World*. Released in October 1991 and recorded at **Peter Gabriel**'s Real World Studios, it demonstrated a new 'harder edge' but still retained their more sensitive side, so evident on 'Say Something Good'.

Albums: *Say Something Good* (1989), *This Is The World* (1991).

Rivera, Chita

b. Dolores Conchita Figueroa del Rivero, 23 January 1933, Washington, DC, USA. A vivacious singer, dancer, and actress - an exciting and explosive performer - Rivera was born to Puerto Rican parents and grew up in the Bronx. She started dancing when she was seven, and from the age of 11, trained for a career in classical ballet. After studying at the New York City Ballet via a scholarship from choreographer George Balanchine, in 1952 she turned from classical dance and joined the chorus of **Call Me Madam** on Broadway. Further chorus work in **Guys And Dolls** and **Can-Can**, was followed by appearances in *Shoestring Revue*, *Seventh Heaven*, and *Mr. Wonderful* (1956). She rocketed to stardom in 1957 as Anita in **West Side Story**, and stopped the show nightly by singing and dancing herself into a frenzy to the whooping rhythms of 'America'. She caused even more of a sensation when *West Side Story* opened in London on 12 December 1958; it is still regarded by many as the most exciting first night of the post-year years. Two years later she was back on Broadway as Dick Van Dyke's secretary Rose, in the first successful rock 'n' roll musical, **Bye Bye Birdie**, and she recreated her role in London in the following year. A musical adaptation of the *The Prisoner Of Zenda* (1963) in which she starred with **Alfred Drake** folded before it reached New York, but a year later, Rivera was acclaimed for her role as a gypsy princess in *Bajour* on Broadway. In the late 60s, she toured in various productions including **Sweet Charity**, and also appeared in the 1969 film version with Shirley MacLaine. After more national tours in the early 70s in musicals such as **Jacques Brel Is Alive And Well And Living In Paris** and **Kiss, Me Kate**, in addition to several straight roles, she co-starred with **Gwen Verdon** in the 'sinfully seductive' *Chicago* (1975). **John Kander** and **Fred Ebb** wrote the score, and they also devised and developed Chita Rivera's cabaret act which included a number called 'Losing', a reference to the number of **Tony Award** nominations she had received. She gained one more nomination for her performance in *Bring Back Birdie* (1981) which closed after only four nights, and *Merlin* (1983) was unsuccessful too. Rivera was finally awarded the coveted Tony - and a Drama Desk Award - when she co-starred with **Liza Minnelli** in *The Rink* (1984), another of Kander and Ebb's projects. Shortly afterwards, she was was involved in a serious car accident which: 'mangled my leg from the knee down'. After having 12 bolts inserted in the bones, she was back on Broadway, along with Leslie Uggams, Dorothy Loudon, and others, in *Jerry's Girls*, a tribute to the composer **Jerry Herman**. During the rest of the 80s, she performed in cabaret and continued to tour in America and other countries including the UK. In 1988/9, she joined the Radio City Music Hall Rockettes in a national tour of *Can-Can* which lasted for over a year. In 1991, she was inducted into New York's Theatre Hall Of Fame, along with - nice touch - Kander and Ebb. She was subsequently widely applauded - and won London *Evening Standard* and **Tony Awards** - for her outstanding dual performance as the movie star Aurora and the Spider Woman in Kander and Ebb's musical *Kiss Of the Spider Woman*. After 749 performances in Toronto, London and New York, in November 1994 she set out on the show's two-year road tour of North America. Her outstanding contribution to the musical theatre was recognized in the early 90s by the Drama Desk's Annual Achievement Award, and the first annual Bandai Musical Award for Excellence in Broadway Theatre.

Rivera, Ismael

b. 1931, Santurce, San Juan, Puerto Rico, d. 13 May 1987, Santurce, San Juan, Puerto Rico. Firmly fixed in the Latin music firmament as 'El Sonero Mayor' (The Greatest Latin Singer) Rivera has been showered with superlatives and made the subject of numerous tribute songs. He was blessed with a gloriously husky voice, which he honed into a unique improvisational instrument. Rivera gained his musical education in the streets of Santurce. 'I've been singing since I had the use of reason.' At the age of 10 he regularly went to the beach with his conga and jammed all day. He sang with small local bands and, on the advice of former school friend, **Rafael Cortijo**, he turned professional as a member of Orquesta Panamericana in 1951. Their friendship led to Ismael becoming lead vocalist with Cortijo's Combo from the 1953-62. After Rivera served a 43-month prison sentence for cocaine possession, the two masters reunited on two mid-60s releases:

Bienvenido!/Welcome!, which contained seven of Ismael's own compositions, and *Con Todo Los Hierros (Everything But The Kitchen Sink!)*. To escape the stigma of being an ex-prisoner, Ismael relocated to New York. In 1967, while visiting the home of the Black Christ in Portobello, Panama, Rivera had a profound religious experience. At the end of the year he decided to form his own band, called Cachimbos. The following year he debuted with them on *De Colores*. The follow-up, *Controversia* (c.1969), was produced by **Tito Puente**. Ismael became a major star, but his fame precipitated depression. Afterwards he reflected, 'when I was punishing myself. I thought that I was hurting no one but myself'. Apparently, his religious outlook and a will to survive, helped him recover and successfully resume his musical career.

In 1971, Ismael teamed up with **Kako** and his band on *Lo Ultimo En La Avenida*. Javier Vázquez (b. 8 April 1936, Matanzas Province, Cuba; piano, arranger, composer) became a regular accompanist with Rivera and Cachimbos. He wrote the arrangements on their 1972 release *Esto Fué Lo Que Trajo El Barco* and supervised both arranging and direction chores on *Vengo Por La Maceta* (1973). The nine-piece line-up of Cachimbos on *Traigo de Todo* (1974) included a horn section of trumpet (played by **Alfredo 'Chocolate' Armenteros**), alto saxophone and trombone, and a rhythm section of timbales, conga, bongo, bass and piano (played by Vázquez). Javier wrote all the charts and composed one track. In May 1974, Ismael and Cachimbos appeared on *Tico-Alegre All Stars Recorded Live At Carnegie Hall, Vol.1*. In August the same year, he participated in a reunion by original members of Cortijo's Combo on *Juntos Otra Vez*. This was later reissued as the re-mixed *Ismael Rivera Sonero No.1* (1982). Vázquez composed the title track of Ismael's 1975 release *Soy Feliz*. His Christmas album *Feliz Navidad* was produced by **Louie Ramírez**, who also wrote and arranged the stand-out track 'Bomba De Navidad'. In 1977, Rivera and Ramírez co-produced *De Todas Maneras Rosas*. Ismael produced his *Esto Si Es Lo Mio* in 1978. The same year, Rivera and **Celia Cruz** performed 'Cucala' together with the Fania All Stars on *Fania All Stars Live*. The song had been a hit for both of them, first for Ismael with Cortijo on 1959's *Cortijo En New York*, then for Celia and **Johnny Pacheco** in the mid-70s (from *Tremendo Caché*, 1975).

The final album by Rivera and Cachimbos was *Maelo* (1980). Ismael produced and Vázquez played piano, composed two songs and was arranger and musical director. In 1981, Rivera reached the Top 5 in the *Farándula* Puerto Rican chart with a notable version of Guillermo Rodríguez Fiffe's Latin standard 'Bilongo', from the Fania All Stars' *Latin Connection*; the track was arranged by Vázquez and featured **Roberto Roena** and **Luis 'Perico' Ortiz**. Ismael developed polyps in his vocal chords and had to cease singing. He returned to Puerto Rico, where he underwent surgery and treatment; but barely a month before a planned tribute concert, he died of a massive heart attack. Puerto Rico virtually stood still during his funeral.

In October 1991, the second Ismael Rivera Festival was held over three nights in Santurce, Puerto Rico, and featured the bands of **Andy Montañez**, **Tony Vega**, Don Perignon, Ismael Rivera Jnr. and others. The same year, Ismael Rivera Jnr. released *Termina Lo Que Su Padre Empezó*, which comprised of material his father had prepared in 1981, for what was going to be his Puerto Rican recording debut with Cachimbos (with their front-line changed to four trumpets and four trombones), but did not record.

Selected albums: with Orquesta Panamericana *Orquesta Panamericana Vol.1*; with Cortijo *Invites You To Dance/Los Invita A Bailar*, *Baile Con Cortijo y su Combo*, *Cortijo y su Combo*, *El Alma De Un Pueblo* (issued 1977), *Cortijo En New York* (1959), *Fiesta Boricua, Bueno, Y Qu... ?* (1960), *Quitate de la Via, Perico* (1961), *Danger* (1961), *Los Internacionales, Bienvenido!/Welcome!* (c.1966) *Con Todo Los Hierros (Everything But The Kitchen Sink!)* (c.1967); *De Colores* (1968), *Controversia* (c.1969); with Kako *Lo Ultimo En La Avenida* (1971); *Esto Fué Lo Que Trajo El Barco* (1972), *Vengo Por La Maceta* (1973), *Traigo de Todo* (1974); various artists *Tico - Alegre All Stars Recorded Live At Carnegie Hall, Vol.1* (1974); with Cortijo *Juntos Otra Vez* (1974, aka *Ismael Rivera Sonero No. 1*, 1982); *Soy Feliz* (1975), *Feliz Navidad* (1975), *De Todas Maneras Rosas* (1977), *Esto Si Es Lo Mio* (1978), *Maelo* (1980). Selected compilations: with Cortijo *Ismael y Cortijo - Los Dos Grandes de Siempre 'Sus 16 Exitos'* (1982); *Eclipse Total* (1975), *Oro* (1979), *Legend* (1984).

Rivera, Mon

b. Efrain Rivera Castillo, 1925, Mayagüez, Puerto Rico, d. 12 March 1978, Manhattan, New York City, USA. Bandleader, singer, composer, multi-instrumentalist Rivera was a pioneer of the trombone front-line in Latin music; some say he was *the* pioneer, whereas others maintain that **Eddie Palmieri** was the originator. However, it is arguably their record producer at the time, **Al Santiago** (founder of Alegre Records), who deserves the credit. Whoever it was, the all trombone sound influenced bandleaders like **Willie Colón** and others, and has been described as the symbol of urban salsa. Rivera was known as 'El Rey del Trabalengua' (The Tongue Twister King) because ' . . . his improvised quips would delight fans with his clear enunciation of rhymes and alliterations conjured up at bullet speed and perfectly weaved in the timing and circumstances of the music' (quote from Aurora Flores, 1978). Rivera was always closely associated with the plena and bomba forms of his island of birth. His father, Ramón Rivera Alers, wrote popular plenas. Rivera began his professional career at the age of 16 and joined the band of William Manzano. He was also

a professional baseball player and played with Los Indios in Mayagüez between 1943 and 1945. In the early 50s, he relocated to the USA with the band of Héctor Pellot, which was later led by Moncho Leña. After Leña disbanded, he organized his own band with its famous trombone front-line. His debut on the Alegre Records label, *Que Gente Averigua*, contained the delicious instrumental 'Lluvia Con Nieve' (Rain With Snow), which Mon composed himself. No musician credits were given on the sleeve, however the album's producer, Al Santiago, revealed that a stellar line-up had been assembled for the recording, which included **Charlie Palmieri**, piano (eight tracks); Eddie Palmieri, piano (two tracks); **Kako**, timbales; Barry Rogers, Mark Weinstein and Manolin Pazo, trombones. Rivera had a big hit with the self-penned 'Karacatis-Ki', a plena dengue, which was the title track of his first volume on Ansonia Records.

Rivera's 1975 collaboration with Willie Colón, *There Goes The Neighborhood/Se Chavó El Vecindario*, helped connect him with the younger Latino audience. He arranged the hit track, the plena 'Ya Llego'. An impressive line-up was congregated for the session, including Lewis Kahn and Jose Rodrigues, trombones; **Papo Lucca**, piano; Kako, timbales and conga; **Rubén Blades** and **Héctor Lavoe**, chorus. 'Mon was not immortal and fell victim to the vices of life. But in his realization, he struggled and became free of the "monkey" that sucked at his lifeline', wrote Aurora Flores, in that typically oblique manner found in accounts on Latin artists. He died, in his Manhattan residence on 12 March 1978, from a heart attack. The posthumously released *Forever*, was produced by **Johnny Pacheco**. In addition to singing lead vocals and composing one track, Rivera shared arranging chores with Colón and Ernie Agosto.

Selected albums: with Moncho Leña *A Night At The Palladium With Moncho Leña, Dance*; *Que Gente Averigua* (1963, reissued as *Mon y sus Trombones* in 1976), *Karacatis-Ki* (c.1964), *Mon Rivera y su Orquesta Vol. 2 'Kijis Konar'*, *Mon Rivera y su Orquesta Vol. 3* (mid-60s), with Willie Colón *There Goes The Neighborhood/Se Chavó El Vecindario* (1975), *Forever* (1978), *Todo Exitos/El Rey del Trabalengua* (issued 1982), with Moncho Leña *Mas Exitos Inolvidables Vol. 3* (collection of 1955 and 1956 recordings issued in 1985).

Rivers, Johnny

b. John Ramistella, 7 November 1942, New York, New York State, USA. Johnny Rivers scored a long streak of pop hits in the 60s and 70s, initially by remaking earlier R&B songs and eventually with his own compositions. His singles were spirited creations, some recorded live in front of an enthusiastic, hip Los Angeles audience. His father moved the family to Baton Rouge, Louisiana, in 1945, where Rivers began playing guitar at the age of eight. By the age of 13, having become enamoured of the local rock 'n' roll and R&B artists, he was fronting his own group. In 1958 he ventured to New York to make his first recording. Top disc jockey **Alan Freed** met the singer and gave him his new name, Johnny Rivers, and also recommended to the local Gone Records label that they sign Rivers. They did, and his first single, 'Baby Come Back', was issued that year. At 17 Rivers moved to Nashville, where he wrote songs with another aspiring singer, **Roger Miller**, and recorded demo records for **Elvis Presley**, **Johnny Cash** and others, including **Ricky Nelson**, who recorded Rivers' 'Make Believe' in 1960. Rivers relocated to Los Angeles at that time. Between 1959 and his 1964 signing to **Imperial Records** he recorded singles for such small labels as Guyden, Cub and Dee Dee, as well as the larger Chancellor, **Capitol Records**, **MGM Records**, Coral Records and United Artists Records, none with any chart success. In late 1963 Rivers began performing a three-night stand at the LA club Gazzari's, which was so successful it was extended for weeks. He then took up residency at the popular discotheque the Whisky A Go Go, where his fans began to include such stars as Johnny Carson, Steve McQueen and Rita Hayworth. His first album for Imperial, *Johnny Rivers At The Whisky A Go Go*, was released in the summer of 1964 and yielded his first hit, **Chuck Berry**'s 'Memphis', which reached number 2. Further hits during 1964-65 included Berry's 'Maybelline', **Harold Dorman**'s 'Mountain Of Love', the traditional folk song 'Midnight Special', **Willie Dixon**'s 'Seventh Son' and **Pete Seeger**'s 'Where Have All The Flowers Gone', each delivered in a rousing, loose interpretation that featured Rivers' nasal vocal, his concise, soulful guitar-playing and sharp backing musicians. Relentlessly rhythmic, the tracks were produced by **Lou Adler**, working his way toward becoming one of the city's most formidable hitmakers. Rivers started 1966 with 'Secret Agent Man', the theme song from a popular television spy thriller. Later that year he achieved his only number 1 record with his own 'Poor Side Of Town' (co-written with Adler), an uncharacteristic ballad using top studio musicians such as **Hal Blaine**, **James Burton** and Larry Knechtel. Rivers also launched his own Soul City record label in 1966, signing the popular **Fifth Dimension**, who went on to score four Top 10 singles on the label. Retreating from the party atmosphere of his earlier recordings for Imperial, Rivers had hits in 1967 with two **Motown** covers, the **Four Tops**' 'Baby I Need Your Lovin'' and **Smokey Robinson**'s 'The Tracks Of My Tears'. Following an appearance at the **Monterey Pop Festival**, another soulful ballad, the James Hendricks-penned 'Summer Rain', became Rivers' last major hit of the 60s. The latter also appeared on Rivers' best-selling album, the *Realization*. Early 70s albums such as *Slim Slo Slider*, *Home Grown* and *LA Reggae* were critically lauded but not commercially

successful, although the latter gave Rivers a Top 10 single with **Huey 'Piano' Smith**'s 'Rockin' Pneumonia - Boogie Woogie Flu'. A version of the **Beach Boys**' 'Help Me Rhonda' (with backing vocal by **Brian Wilson**) was a minor success in 1975, and two years later Rivers landed his final Top 10 single, 'Swayin' To The Music (Slow Dancin')'. Rivers recorded a handful of albums in the 80s, including a live one featuring the old hits, but none reached the charts.

Albums: *Johnny Rivers At The Whisky A Go Go* (1964), *The Sensational Johnny Rivers* (1964), *Go, Johnny, Go* (1964), *Here We A-Go-Go Again* (1964), *Johnny Rivers In Action!* (1965), *Meanwhile Back At The Whisky A Go Go* (1965), *Johnny Rivers Rocks The Folk* (1965), *...And I Know You Wanna Dance* (1966), *Golden Hits* (1966), *Changes* (1966), *Rewind* (1967), *Realization* (1968), *A Touch Of Gold* (1969), *Slim Slo Slider* (1970), *Home Grown* (1971), *L.A. Reggae* (1972), *Johnny Rivers* (1972), *Blue Suede Shoes* (1973), *Last Boogie In Paris* (1974), *Rockin' Rivers* (1974), *Road* (1974), *New Lovers And Old Friends* (1975), *The Very Best of* (1975), *Outside Help* (1978), *Borrowed Time* (1980), *The Johnny Rivers Story* (1982), *Portrait Of* (1982), *Not A Through Street* (1983), *Greatest Hits* (1985), *The Best Of* (1987).

Rivers, Mavis

b. c.1930, Apia, Upolu, Western Samoa. As a child Rivers sang with a small band led by her father, entertaining USA troops based on Samoa during World War II. After the war her family moved to New Zealand where she worked in clubs and on radio, and for three years from 1949 she was voted the country's most popular singer. In 1954 she moved to the USA where her first album, *Take A Number*, was nominated for a Grammy. She continued to record and in 1962 became the regular singer with **Red Norvo**'s small group. Thereafter, she sang with various small bands including those led by **Terry Gibbs** and Page Cavanaugh. She has also performed in concert and recorded with her son, **Matt Catingub**. A tuneful singer with a light, airy vocal sound, Rivers is most at ease in a small group setting.

Albums: *Take A Number* (c.1959), *Hooray For Love* (c.1960), *Mavis Rivers Sings About The Simple Life* (c.1960), *Mavis Rivers i* (1961), *Sing Along With Mavis* (c.1961), *Mavis Rivers ii* (c.1962), *Mavis Rivers iii* (1962), *Mavis Rivers iv* (c.1964), with Matt Catingub *It's A Good Day* (1983), with Catingub *My Mommy And Me* (1983).

Rivers, Sam

b. 25 September 1930, El Reno, Oklahoma, USA. Alto, soprano and tenor saxophones, flute, piano and composer. After extensive studies, Rivers began playing in and around Boston, Massachusetts in the late 40s. (His first professional engagement had been with **Jimmy Witherspoon** during his military service.) During the next few years he played mostly in the

Boston area with **Jaki Byard**, **Nat Pierce**, **Herb Pomeroy** and the very young **Tony Williams**. He also worked in Florida in a band led by Don Wilkerson. It was not until 1964 that he achieved prominence when he joined **Miles Davis** thanks to the recommendation of Williams, then a member of Davis's band. In the mid-60s he worked in New York, recording for **Blue Note** with Williams, Byard, **Ron Carter** and others. In the late 60s he continued recording with such artists as **Donald Byrd**, **Bobby Hutcherson** and **Julian Priester**. Around this time he also began teaching and established a five-year association with **Cecil Taylor** with whom he visited Europe. Since that time he has continued to teach, compose and perform with a wide variety of musical groups including the San Francisco Symphony Orchestra, his own small groups and has had a lasting relationship with **Dave Holland**. A highly acclaimed musician, Rivers' concentration on teaching and on developing original musical concepts has tended to make him less accessible to the wider audience. Those who have persevered with his music have found it rewarding in its imaginative blending of many jazz styles, ranging from blues to the *avant garde*. Rivers is particularly effective on flute and soprano, instruments on which he displays a light, dancing style. Whether as performer or composer, it is the remarkably sustained inventiveness which most characterizes his work.
Selected albums: *Fuchsia Swing Song* (Blue Note 1964), with Miles Davis *Miles In Tokyo* (1964), *Streams* (MCA 1973), *Sam Rivers/Dave Holland* (Improvising Artists 1976), *The Tuba Trio Vols 1-3* (1976), *Waves* (Tomato 1978), *Colours* (Black Saint 1983), *Lazuli* (Timeless 1990).

Riverside Records

Beginning life as an important US label for traditional jazz, Riverside later became a major presenter of modern jazz. Founded in 1953 by Bill Graner and Orrin Keepnews, early Riverside albums provided long-playing compilations of many classic early jazz labels, including Gennett, HRS, QRS, and Circle. The following year Riverside tested current waters with an album by **Randy Weston** and soon added **Thelonious Monk**, **Bill Evans** and **Cannonball Adderley** to its roster. Later, **Wes Montgomery** signed and, in the early 60s, **Barry Harris**. The early interest in traditional jazz was not forgotten and new recordings were made, also in the 60s by **Kid Thomas Valentine**, **Peter Bocage** and, before his rediscovery and promotion as a mainstream giant, **Earl 'Fatha' Hines**. Soon after Graner's death at the end of 1963, Riverside folded but the following decade saw many of the company's best albums reissued by Fantasy on their Milestone and OJC (Original Jazz Classics) labels.

Rivieras (R&B)

This R&B vocal group came from Englewood, New Jersey, USA. The members were, Homer Dunn (lead), Charles Allen (bass), Ronald Cook (tenor) and Andrew Jones (baritone). The group specialized in singing doo-wop versions of old big band hits, especially those of **Glenn Miller**. Homer Dunn formed his first group, the Bob-O-Links, in 1952 in Hackensack, New Jersey. Moving to Englewood, New Jersey, Dunn formed the Rivieras in 1955, and they managed to stay together for three years playing local gigs before being eventually signed to the Coed label. The Rivieras' principal hits were 'Count Every Star' (1958), which was previously a 1950 hit for **Ray Anthony** and 'Moonlight Seranade' (1959) a Miller hit in 1939. Other outstanding releases put out before the group disbanded in 1961 were 'Our Love' (1959) and 'Moonlight Cocktail' (1960), previously hits for **Tommy Dorsey** and, Miller respectively.
Albums: with the Duprees *Jerry Blavat Presents Drive-In Sounds* (Lost Nite mid-60s), *The Rivieras Sing* (Post early 70s). Compilation: *Moonlight Cocktails* (Relic 1992).

Rivieras (rock 'n' roll)

This rock 'n' roll band came from South Bend, Indiana, USA. The members comprised lead vocalist and guitarist Marty Fortson, organist Otto Nuss, guitarist Joe Pennell, bassist Doug Gean, and drummer Paul Dennert. The group's manager Bill Dobson sang and played keyboards. Fortson was the lead on their giant hit, 'California Sun', which went to US number 5 in 1964. The song had earlier been recorded by **Joe Jones** as a slow bluesy number, but the band speeded it up and gave it a happy California surf-music sound. Before the record was released, however, Pennell and Fortson had gone into national service, and manager Dobslaw stepped in and sang the lead on subsequent records, but the group had no further success. Dobslaw kept the group which went through various membership changes to the middle of 1965.
Albums: *Let's Have A Party* (1964), *Campus Party* (1965).

Rivingtons

Formed in the early 60s in Los Angeles, California, USA, the Rivingtons placed two songs in the US pop charts, both of which rank among the best top rock 'n' roll novelty records of all time: 'Papa-Oom-Mow-Mow' and 'The Bird's The Word'. The group consisted of lead vocalist Carl White, Al Frazier, Sonny Harris and Rocky Wilson Jnr all of whom had previously worked as backing vocalists on recordings by **Paul Anka**, **Duane Eddy** and **Thurston Harris**, as the Sharps. The phrase 'Papa-Oom-Mow-Mow' reportedly came to Wilson while in jail, following a fight a fellow inmate supposedly whispered it in his ear. Upon his release the group worked the phrase into a song and they offered it

to various record labels. **Liberty Records** accepted and recorded it in the summer of 1962, resulting in a number 48 single later it was covered by the **Beach Boys**. 'The Bird Is The Word', the 1963 follow-up, was less successful, but both songs were worked into a new hit, 'Surfin' Bird', by the Minneapolis group the **Trashmen** in 1964, which reached US number 4 and was later covered by such artists as Pee Wee Herman and the **Ramones**. A re-formed version of the Rivingtons, featuring all the original members except for White who died in 1980, performed in the Los Angeles area in the late 80s.
Album: *Doin' The Bird* (1963).

Roach, Max

b. 10 January 1924, New Land, North Carolina, USA. Beginning to play drums in his pre-teen years, Roach later studied in New York and by 1942 was active in the bebop revolution. As a member of the house rhythm section at Monroe's Uptown House and a regular at Minton's Playhouse, he backed all the leading practitioners of the new art. Along with **Kenny Clarke** he established a new drummers' vocabulary, and his work with **Charlie Parker** and **Dizzy Gillespie** from this period demonstrates his inventiveness and masterly technique. In addition to playing bebop, the 40s also found him working in small and big bands led by such swing era veterans as **Coleman Hawkins** and **Benny Carter**. Towards the end of the decade, however, he abandoned the older style and was henceforth one of bebop's major voices. He was with **Miles Davis** for two years from 1948, participating in the seminal *Birth Of The Cool* recording dates. In 1954 Roach formed a quintet with **Clifford Brown**, a band which was one of the most musically inventive of the period. Brown's accidental death in 1956 was a devastating loss to Roach and it took many years for him to fully shake off the traumatic effect it had upon him. From the late 50s Roach began to take a political stance and was active in many black cultural projects. Inevitably, his work of this period took on elements of his commitment to Civil Rights issues. His compositions included the *We Insist! Freedom Now Suite*. He also experimented with unusual line-ups, sometimes abandoning conventional time structures. In these respects he was in line with concurrent developments in free jazz, but was never a true part of that movement. His own small groups saw an impressive array of talented musical partners including **Freddie Hubbard**, **Sonny Rollins**, **George Coleman** and **Stanley Turrentine**. He also worked with a variety of singers and vocal groups, including performances with his wife **Abbey Lincoln**. In the 70s, although he was by then becoming an elder statesman of jazz, Roach continued to associate with musicians of the *avant garde*, recording duo albums with **Abdullah Ibrahim**, **Archie Shepp**, **Cecil Taylor**

and **Anthony Braxton**. One of few drummers to perform and record extended solo works, Roach achieved a remarkably high standard of performance and overcame the customary negative critical response to such works. Throughout the 80s and into the early 90s, Roach continued to perform and compose, finding time to teach and to maintain his activism in black politics. One of the most technically-gifted musicians in jazz, Roach has long been a major figure in the development of the music and his consistently high standard of performance has never faltered. As a drummer, he is a master of all aspects of his work, a mastery which he demonstrated during his 1990 UK tour by playing as an encore a thoroughly absorbing ten-minute solo using only the hi-hat cymbal. If there is another jazz drummer capable of such feats he has yet to appear in public.

Selected albums: with Miles Davis *The Complete Birth Of The Cool* (1949-50), *The Max Roach-Clifford Brown Quintet* (1954-6), *Study In Brown* (1955), *At Basin Street* (1956), *Max Roach Plus Four* (1956), *Jazz In 3/4 Time* (1957), *Drummin' The Blues* (1957), *Max Plays Charlie Parker* (1957-58), *Max* (1958), *Max Roach Plus Four, Newport 1958 Jazz Festival* (1958), *Deeds, Not Words* (1958), *Sessions, Live* (1958), *The Many Sides Of Max Roach* (1959), *Award-Winning Drummer* (1959), *Quiet As It's Kept* (1960), *Drum Conversation/Long As You're Living* (1960), *Parisian Sketches* (1960), *Again* (1960), *We Insist! Freedom Now Suite* (1960), *Moon-Faced And Starry-Eyed* (1960), *Percussion Bitter Suite* (1961), *It's Time* (1961-62), *Speak, Brother, Speak* (1962), *Paris Concert* (1962-63), *The Legendary Hasaan* (1964), *Members Don't Get Weary* (1968), *Lift Every Voice And Sing* (1971), *Force-Sweet Mao-Suid Afrika '76* (1976), *Max Roach Quartet Live In Tokyo Vols 1 & 2* (1977), *The Loadstar* (1977), *Live In Amsterdam* (1977), *Solos* (1977), *Confirmation* (1978), *Birth And Rebirth* (Black Saint 1978), with Archie Shepp *The Long March* (1979), *One In Two-Two In One* (Hat Art 1979), *Pictures In A Frame* (Soul Note 1979), *Historic Concerts* (1979), *Chattahoochee Red* (1981), *Swish* (1982), *In The Light* (Soul Note 1982), *Live At Vielharmonie, Munich* (Soul Note 1983), *Scott Free* (Soul Note 1984), *Survivors* (Soul Note 1984), *Easy Winners* (Soul Note 1985), *Bright Moments* (Soul Note 1987), *To The Max!* (Enja 1992). Compilation: *The Max Roach Quintet* (1949).

Roach, Steve

The music of California-born electronic composer Steve Roach is nurtured by the earth around him. Having been performing live since 1978, Roach is essentially an electronic landscape painter, but his work also concerns itself with the relationships between time and space. After founding the synthesizer group Moebius, Roach became known as a leader of the west coast electronic scene while living in Santa Monica. His first two albums were relatively conventional, energetic and dynamic, but with 1984's *Structures From Silence* he took a quantum leap, creating chiming patterns held in computer memory to induce a feeling of time suspended. Inspired by Peter Weir's film *The Last Wave*, Roach abandoned purism in order to complete *Dreamtime Return*, based on Aborignal beliefs, in 1988. He not only travelled to Australia to make field recordings on DAT, but augmented his electronic instruments with acoustic percussion. By now, rich swirling textures and trance-like rhythms were hallmarks of his style. 1988's *The Leaving Time*, recorded for **RCA**'s Novus label with former **Santana** percussionist Michael Shrieve and guitarist **David Torn** found Roach in an atypically mainstream setting, bordering on ambient jazz. After trekking through the Mojave Desert with composer friend Kevin Braheny, the pair recorded 1987's *Western Spaces*, a set of 'evocations of the American Southwest', whose theme was continued by the duo on *Desert Solitaire*, in 1989. That year, Roach moved to Tucson and established his own Timeroom Studio. With Australian composer Sarah Hopkins, Roach embellished improvisations by Aboriginal didgeridoo virtuoso David Hudson to create *Australia: Sound Of The Earth*. 1990 also brought *Strata*, a collaboration with Robert Rich for the *Hearts Of Space* radio show and record label. 1993's *Origins* explored 'the cracks between conscious and unconscious awareness' and then, inspired by William Lesch's remarkable desert photographs, 1994's *Artifacts* dramatically expanded Roach's use of esoteric acoustic instruments. Roach has frequently performed live, as a solo act and with his trio, Suspended Memories, as well as producing works for other composers.

Albums: *Now* (Fortuna 1982), *Traveller* (Fortuna 1983), *Structures From Silence* (Fortuna 1984), *Empetus* (Fortuna 1986), *Dreamtime Return* (Fortuna 1988), *Origins* (1993), *Artifacts* (Fortuna 1994).

Roachford

This UK rock band is comprised of Andrew Roachford (vocals/keyboards/percussion), Chris Taylor (drums), Hawi Gondwe (guitars), Derrick Taylor (bass). Andrew Roachford has performed since the age of 14 when he played in London's Soho jazz clubs. The band was put together in 1987, and by early 1988 were touring with **Terence Trent D'Arby** and the **Christians**, and gaining a reputation for excellent live shows. Strong live support was instrumental to their breakthrough and **CBS Records** beat many other labels to sign the band. Two singles and an album came outin late 1988, but it was not until early 1989 that 'Cuddly Toy' was re-released to become a massive hit, then closely followed by 'Family Man'. The self-titled album was also rediscovered and the band started to make inroads into the American market. Sessions for their second album took place in Britain and at **Prince**'s Paisley Park studios. Although named after Andrew Roachford, he has always maintained that, 'Roachford

is a whole band, not a group of session guys backing me up'.

Albums: *Roachford* (1988), *Get Ready!* (1991), *Permanent Shades Of Blue* (Columbia 1994).

Road To Singapore

The first in the enormously successful Paramount series starring **Bing Crosby**, **Bob Hope** and **Dorothy Lamour** was released in 1940. Frank Butler and Don Hartman's screenplay concerns Josh Mallon (Crosby), the easy-going heir to a shipping fortune, and his buddy Ace Lannigan (Hope), who decide to get away from it all. After ending up in Singapore, they rescue the lovely Mima (Lamour) from a seedy nightspot act in which she has a lighted cigarette removed from her mouth every night by Caesar (Anthony Quinn), her swarthy South American partner. After the usual complications, Lamour chooses Crosby for her romantic partner as she did in all the 'Road' trips, although Hope was in there pitching right up to the final episode in 1962. The main reason for Crosby's continued success with the lady in the sarong may well be that he always had the big love ballad - in this case, 'Too Romantic'. **Johnny Burke** and **Jimmy Monaco** wrote that one, along with 'Sweet Potato Piper' and 'Kaigoon', while Burke and the film's director, **Victor Schertzinger**, contributed 'Captain Custard' and 'The Moon And The Willow Tree'. LeRoy Prinz handled the choreography, and the producer was Harlan Thompson. The general critical opinion at the time was that this film was nothing special, although it rated highly at the box-office. However, subsequent journeys to *Zanzibar* 1941, *Morocco* 1942, *Utopia* 1945, *Rio* 1947, and *Bali* 1952, were acclaimed for the outrageous laid-back humour and zany antics of the two male stars. Generally cast as a couple of likeable swindlers, with Crosby as the 'brains' and Hope in the role of the incredibly gullible fall guy, they were able to extricate themselves from any scrape simply by facing each other and going into their 'Patta-cake' routine which always ended with one of their captors, or similar adversaries, being knocked to the ground. As well as the fun and games, each of the above films in the series had some good songs by **Jimmy Van Heusen** and Johnny Burke, an engaging mixture of ballads and lively comedy numbers. Over the years these included 'You Lucky People You', 'It's Always You', 'Birds Of A Feather', 'Road To Morocco', 'Ain't Got A Dime To My Name (Ho-Hum)', 'Constantly', 'Moonlight Becomes You', 'Personality', 'Put It There, Pal', 'But Beautiful', 'You Don't Have To Know The Language', 'Experience', 'The Merry Go Runaround', 'Chicago Style', 'Hoot Mon', and 'To See You'. After *Road To Bali* there was a gap of 10 years before the trio were reunited for *The Road To Hong Kong* (1962) which was made in England by Melnor Pictures (producer Melvin Frank and director Norman Panama). At the time,

Hope and Crosby were both 59, and in spite of the inclusion of the young and attractive Joan Collins (Lamour still came along for the ride - as herself), as well as a starry list of guest artists such as **Frank Sinatra**, **Dean Martin**, Peter Sellers, David Niven, and Jerry Colonna, it was too much to ask that things would be the same. The magic just was not there any more, and it was obviously the end of the 'Road' - and of an era - although the film did well financially. Even the songs, by Van Heusen and **Sammy Cahn**, were not in the previous class, but the veteran performers did their best with 'Let's Not Be Sensible', 'Teamwork', 'It's The Only Way To Travel', 'We're On The Road To Hong Kong', and 'Warmer Than A Whisper.' No matter, the memories of that historic, much-loved series still remain, and still bring a smile to the lips in the 90s.

Roadhouse

This melodic UK hard rock quintet was assembled in 1991 around former **Def Leppard** guitarist Pete Willis. Utilizing the talents of Wayne Grant (bass), Richard Day (guitar), Paul Jackson (vocals) and Trevor Brewis (drums), the band were signed by **Phonogram** largely on the strength of the guitarist's connections. Their self-titled debut album was a major disappointment, however, featuring an average collection of commercial AOR-styled songs. The band lacked identity and have so far been unable to inject drive or spontaneity into their uptempo numbers, while the ballads lacked sincerity, emotion or class.
Album: *Roadhouse* (Phonogram 1991).

Roadie

Ebullient vocalist **Meat Loaf** rose to stardom thanks to *Bat Out Of Hell*, one of the most successful albums in rock history. Its standing inspired the singer's starring role in this 1980 film, in which he plays the roadie. *Roadie* was not Meat Loaf's first on-screen venture, he previously played a part in *The Rocky Horror Picture Show*, but this venture was built around his amiable personality. As the Meat Loaf character rises through rock's multi-layered echelons, he encounters various performers including **Alice Cooper**, **Blondie**, **Roy Orbison** and **Ramblin' Jack Elliott**. Many were featured on the soundtrack which also contained contributions from **Cheap Trick**, **Teddy Pendergrass**, **Pat Benetar**, **Styx** and **Asleep At The Wheel**. Comedian Art Carney co-starred in this engaging feature and proved an excellent foil. *Roadie* remains an amusing picture, taking a wry view of life on the road.

Roadnight, Margret

b. Australia. An imposing figure on stage, Roadnight possesses an amazing voice and a large repertoire of blues and folk music. Well known throughout the Australian folk circuit Roadnight also toured extensively in the USA and Europe. Her strength lies in her interpretations of other people's songs, although Bob Hudson's 'Girls Of Our Town' is virtually regarded as her signature song. She has shown a willingness to explore different directions in ethnic music, women's music and 'world' music.
Albums: *People Get Ready* (1973), *Ice* (1978), *Bluesmakers* (1980), *Out Of Fashion Not Out Of Style* (1981), *Moving Target* (80s), *People In Concert* (80s), *Living In The Land Of Oz* (80s).

Roadside Picnic

This UK group is comprised of Dave O'Higgins (tenor saxophone/soprano saxophone/EWI), John Smith (piano/keyboards), Mario Castronari (bass), and Mike Bradley (drums/percussion). Despite the considerable press coverage given to the saxophonist O'Higgins, it was the compositional and conceptual strength of Castronari which gave Roadside Picnic its initial impetus. Formed during the British jazz boom of the mid-80s, it is a strong four-piece fusion band featuring some of the young British talent presently securing a niche in the jazz scene. Their popular debut, *Roadside Picnic*, was recorded in 1988 and released to an enthusiastic reception. In 1990 they followed up with their concept set *For Mad Men Only*. Intended as a musical representation of scenes from Herman Hesse's novel *Steppenwolf*, it was accompanied by another burst of media attention. The group's repertoire consists of carefully arranged original material. Smith's futuristic keyboard sounds are played over complex rhythmic patterns and shifting time signatures, leaving a fairly strict framework for O'Higgins' **Michael Brecker**-influenced saxophone solos.
Albums: *Roadside Picnic* (1988), *For Mad Men Only* (1990).

Roar Of The Greasepaint-The Smell Of The Crowd, The

Leslie Bricusse and **Anthony Newley**'s follow-up to their smash-hit *Stop The World - I Want To Get Off* floundered in the UK provinces with the popular knockabout comedian **Norman Wisdom** in the leading role. Adjudged unfit to face the West End critics in its present condition, producer David Merrick persuaded Newley to take over from Wisdom, and sent the show on a successful three month tryout tour of the USA and Canada before the Broadway opening at the Shubert Theatre on 16 May 1965. It proved to be very similar in style to its predecessor - an allegorical piece in which the irrepressible Cocky (Newley) and the imperious Sir (Cyril Ritchard) play the 'game' (of life) in a small arena-like area. Cocky, the little man, always plays by the rules, while the conniving Sir simply ignores them and goes his own way. Towards the end of the piece, Cocky, with the help of the Negro (Gilbert Price), begins to assert himself, and eventually he and Sir agree that the 'game' should be a tie. The British actress Sally Smith made her Broadway debut as The Kid, and Murray Tannenbaum was pretty scarey as The Bully. Bricusse and Newley's score was full of good things, not all of them immediately appreciated. 'Who Can I Turn To? (When Nobody Needs Me)', which was introduced by Newley, emerged as the biggest hit, particularly in a version by **Tony Bennett**. Price created quite an impact with 'Feeling Good', and Ritchard, with a group of 'urchins', sang 'A Wonderful Day Like Today'. The remainder of the fine score consisted of 'The Beautiful Land', 'It Isn't Enough', 'Things To Remember', 'Put It In The Book', 'This Dream', 'Where Would You Be Without Me', 'Look At That Face', 'My First Love Song', 'The Joker', 'A Funny Funeral', 'That's What It's Like To Be Young', 'What A Man', 'Nothing Can Stop Me Now', and 'Sweet Beginning'. Several them were recorded by **Sammy Davis Jnr.**, an enthusiastic promoter of the composers' work. Newley directed the show himself, and the musical staging was by **Gillian Lynne**, the choreographer and director, whose subsequent credits included **Andrew Lloyd Webber**'s mega-hits *Cats* and *The Phantom Of The Opera*. *The Roar Of The Greaspaint* could only manage a disppointing run of 232 performances, but, fortunately for David Merrick, most of the show's original costs had been recouped during the pre-Broadway tour. A West End production in the near future would seem unlikely.

Roaring Jelly

This UK comedy-folk trio comprised Clive Harvey (b. 27 November 1945, Watford, Hertfordshire, England; guitar/vocals/ukelele/harmonica), Derek Pearce (b. Birmingham, Warwickshire, England; vocals/multi-instrumentalist), and Mick Hennessey (b. Derby, Derbyshire, England; acoustic and electric bass/vocals). Harvey met Pearce in 1970 at Trent Polytechnic, Nottingham, where they played the college folk club and won a local talent contest. This led to folk club gigs in the Derby/Nottingham area. Hennessey joined the line-up soon after. The group took their name from a famous Irish jig. Even though their act was moving away from folk and increasingly towards comedy, the group continued playing folk clubs in and around the midlands. They played the Sidmouth International Festival in 1975, which led to concerts and dates on a national scale. The the group split in 1985, while still at the height of their popularity. Harvey, along with Ian Carter, formed the short-lived Beverley Brothers, then joined **R. Cajun And The Zydeco Brothers** in December 1985. He also plays with another trio, the Back Seat Jivers. Pearce is now a furniture maker and sculptor. Roaring Jelly re-formed, briefly, in 1986 for a reunion tour titled Pay The Tax Bill Tour. Still spoken of with affection, the group were considered pioneers of alternative comedy before the term became fashionable.

Albums: *Roaring Jelly's Golden Grates* (1977), *In The Roar* (1981).

Rob Base And DJ E-Z Rock

Light-hearted, New York-based rap unit distinctive through its exploration of musical genres, and an aversion to speech-only raps. Samples and lifts from **Motown**, **James Brown** (particularly on the latter's production of **Lyn Collins**' 'Think (About It)', which gave them a breakthrough hit in 1988 with 'It Takes Two') and others set the tone for the duo, while Base's lyrics, although tending to highlight his romantic prowess, do so in a way which doesn't reach the listener as egotistical. He got into trouble for sampling **Maze**'s 'Joy And Pain', however, when he neglected to credit its source. Base (b. Robert Ginyard, Harlem, New York) jettisoned DJ E-Z Rock (b. Rodney Bryce, Harlem, New York) in time for his second album, which this time round hoisted choruses from **Marvin Gaye**, **Edwin Starr** and even native American rock band, **Redbone**. The most effective slice of the action was a reworking of Starr's classic 'War' cut.
Albums: *It Takes Two* (Profile 1988). As Rob Base: *The Incredible Base* (Profile 1989).

Robbins, Jerome

b. Jerome Rabinowitz, 11 October 1918, New York, USA. An important director, choreographer, and dancer, Robbins began his career with the celebrated Ballet Theatre in New York, and subsequently appeared as a dancer on Broadway in shows such as *Great Lady*, *The Straw Hat Revue*, and *Stars In Your Eyes*. In 1944, he and composer **Leonard Bernstein** conceived a short ballet, *Fancy Free*, which, with the participation of **Betty Comden** and **Adolph Green**, evolved into the musical *On The Town* - and Robbins was off and running (or rather, dancing). During the 40s and early 50s he was constantly acclaimed for his stylish and original choreography for shows such as *Billion Dollar Baby* (1945), ***High Button Shoes*** (**Tony Award**), *Look Ma, I'm Dancing*, ***Miss Liberty***, ***Call Me Madam***, ***The King And I***, and *Two's Company* (1952). From then on, he also served as the director on series of notable productions: ***The Pajama Game***, ***Peter Pan***, ***Bells Are Ringing***, ***West Side Story*** (Tony Award), ***Gypsy***, ***A Funny Thing Happened On The Way To The Forum***, ***Funny Girl***, and ***Fiddler On The Roof***. For the last-named show, one of his greatest achievements, he won Tony Awards for choreographer and director. He and Robert Wise were also awarded Oscars when they co-directed the film version of ***West Side Story*** in 1961. After working on the London productions of *Funny Girl* and *Fiddler On The Roof* in 1966 and 1967, Robbins turned away from the Broadway musical theatre and announced that he was devoting his life to ballet. He returned to the popular field in February 1989 to direct a celebratory revue of his work entitled *Jerome Robbins' Broadway*. In a season which was so bereft of original musicals that *Kenny Loggins On Broadway* and *Barry Manilow At The Gershwin* were catagorized as such, this reminder of Broadway's glory days was greeted with relief and rejoicing (and six Tony Awards). It featured extended sequences from *West Side Story* and *Fiddler On The Roof*, along with other delights such as the gloriously incongruous 'You Gotta Have A Gimmick' from *Gypsy*, and the famous Keystone Cops chase from *High Button Shoes*, all sandwiched between excerpts from Robbins' first hit, *On The Town*, which opened and closed the show. An enormously expensive investment at $8 million, the show reportedly lost around half of that, even though it ran for 538 performances.

Robbins, Marty

b. Martin David Robinson, with twin sister, Mamie, 26 September 1925, near Glendale, Arizona, USA, d. 8 December 1982. He later maintained that his father hated him and that his early childhood was unhappy. Reports indicate that John Robinson (originally a Polish immigrant named Mazinski) suffered from a drink problem that led to him abusing his family before eventually leaving his wife, Emma, to cope alone with their seven children plus the two from her previous marriage. At one time they lived in a tent in the desert, but in 1937 his parents divorced and Emma and the children moved to a shack in Glendale, where she took in laundry to support the family. In his early teens, Marty spent some time with an elder brother breaking wild horses on a ranch near Phoenix. Consequently his education suffered; he attended high school in Glendale but never graduated, and by the early 40s he was becoming involved in a life of petty crime. He left home to live the life of a hobo until he joined the US Navy in May 1943. It was during his three years in the service, where he saw action in the Pacific, that he learned to play the guitar and first started songwriting and singing. He also acquired a love of Hawaiian music which would show several times during his career. After discharge in February 1946, he returned to Glendale, where he tried many jobs before starting to sing around the clubs and on local radio under the names of either Martin or Jack Robinson. (His mother strongly disapproved of him singing in clubs and he used the name 'Jack' to try to prevent her finding out.) By 1950, he had built a local reputation and was regularly appearing on KTYL Mesa and on both radio and in his own television show *Western Caravan* on KPHO Phoenix. He married Marizona Baldwin on 27 September 1948; a marriage that lasted until Marty's death. A son, Ronald Carson Robinson, was born in 1949 and 10 years later their daughter Janet. (Ronald eventually became a singer, performing both as Ronnie Robbins and as Marty Robbins Jnr.)
Through the assistance of **Little Jimmy Dickens**,

and by now known as Marty Robbins, he was signed by **Columbia**, for whom he first recorded in November 1951. In December 1952, 'I'll Go On Alone' became his first US country hit. It charted for 18 weeks, two of which were spent at number 1. (Marty wrote the song because initially his wife disliked his showbusiness life.) He moved to Nashville in January 1953 and became a member of the *Grand Ole Opry*. Early in his career, he acquired the nickname of 'Mr Teardrop' and later wrote and recorded a song with that title. In 1955, his career, which by the end of 1954 appeared somewhat becalmed, received a welcome boost by the success of his recordings of rockabilly numbers, 'That's All Right' (originally written and recorded by **Arthur 'Big Boy' Crudup** in 1947 but more recently a hit for **Elvis Presley**) and 'Maybelline' both became Top 10 country hits. He had always realised that it would be advantageous to record in differing styles and accordingly his recordings varied from country to pop, from Hawaiian, to gospel and even some with his own guitar providing the sole accompaniment. In 1956, he achieved another country number 1 with his version of Melvin Endsley's 'Singing The Blues'. The song also made number 17 in the US pop charts, where **Guy Mitchell**'s version was number 1. The following year, Marty turned Endsley's song 'Knee Deep In The Blues' into a number 3 country hit but again lost out in the pop charts to Mitchell, who had immediately covered Robbins' recording. Somewhat frustrated Robbins made his next recordings in New York with **Ray Conniff** and his orchestra and during 1957-58, with what may be best termed teenage love songs, he registered three more country number 1s with his own song, 'A White Sports Coat (And A Pink Carnation)' (a million-seller), the **Hal David-Burt Bacharach** song, 'The Story Of My Life' and 'Stairway Of Love'. The first two were also major US pop hits for him. (In the UK, the former was a hit for the **King Brothers** and **Terry Dene**, while **Michael Holliday** had Top 3 successes with the latter two.)
During the late 50s, he formed a talent and booking agency and launched his own record label. Robbins had always had a love of the old west. He always rated the cowboy state of Arizona as his home (his maternal grandfather had once been a Texas Ranger), and in the late 50s he appeared in three b-westerns, *Raiders Of Old California*, *Badge Of Marshal Brennan* and *Buffalo Gun*. The first two were straight acting roles but the latter co-starred **Webb Pierce** and **Carl Smith** and included several songs. It was also at this time that he began to record the material that would see release on albums such as his now legendary *Gunfighter Ballads And Trail Songs*. (He actually recorded the whole album in one day.) In 1959, he wrote and charted the title track of the film *The Hanging Tree*, which starred Gary Cooper, before his classic 'El Paso' became a number 1 country and pop hit. It gave him a second million-seller and was

also the first country music song to be awarded a Grammy. The success of this song established Marty once and for all and songs such as 'Big Iron' and 'Running Gun' became firm favourites with audiences the world over.

During the 60s, he registered 31 USA country hits, 13 of which also found success in the pop charts. The country number 1s included 'Don't Worry', (which has the distinction of being the first song to include the 'fuzz' sound on the recording. Unknown to all at the time, a fuse had blown in the control room channel carrying Grady Martin's lead guitar with the result that it came out fuzzy. Robbins liked the effect and left it in), 'Devil Woman' (a UK Top 5 pop hit for him), 'Ruby Ann', 'Ribbon Of Darkness', 'Tonight Carmen' and 'I Walk Alone'. In 1964, Robbins supported Barry Goldwater in his bid for President and also wrote, 'Ain't I Right' and 'My Own Native Land', two protest songs against Communism and anti-American war protesters. He felt the first would be a hit but Columbia, fearing racial repercussions, would not let him release them. However, his guitarist and backing vocalist, Bobby Sykes's recordings of the songs were released on the Sims label. He used the pseudonym Johnny Freedom, but sounded so much like his boss that for years many people have believed the recordings were by Robbins himself. (Marty's own recordings were later released by Bear Family on the album *Pieces Of Your Heart*.)

In 1969, **Frankie Laine** scored a pop hit with Robbins' semi-autobiographical song 'You Gave Me A Mountain', while **Johnny Bush** had the country version. Surprisingly Marty's own recording was never released as a single. He also had a great interest in stock-car racing and during the 60s he began driving at the Nashville Speedway, an occupation that later saw him fortunate to survive several serious crashes. Also during the 60s, he filmed a television series called *The Drifter*, appeared in eight films, including *Hell On Wheels*, *The Nashville Story*, *Ballad Of A Gunfighter*, *Road To Nashville* and *From Nashville With Music*, and wrote a Western novel *The Small Man*. In August 1969, he suffered a heart attack on his tour bus near Cleveland and in January 1970 he underwent bypass surgery. He soon returned to his punishing schedules and in April he was starring in Las Vegas. The same year his moving ballad 'My Woman, My Woman, My Wife' became his second Grammy winner and the *Academy Of Country Music* voted him The Man of the Decade. (Originally it had been intended that Frankie Laine should have the song but Robbins' wife told him to keep it for himself.) He left Columbia for **Decca** in 1972 but returned in December 1975 and immediately registered two number 1 country hits with 'El Paso City' (a look back at his previous hit) and the old pop ballad 'Among My Souvenirs'. He had previously returned to El Paso with the nine-minute long 'Feleena

(From El Paso)'. During the 70s, he had further 30 country hits, made film appearances in *Country Music*, *Guns Of A Stranger*, *Country Hits* and *Atoka* as well as starring in his network television series *Marty Robbins Spotlight*.

His songwriting talents saw him elected to the Nashville Songwriters International Hall Of Fame in 1975. His extensive touring schedules included crowd pleasing appearances at the 1975 and 1976 Wembley Festivals in London. He continued with these punishing schedules into the 80s but was again hospitalized following a second heart attack in January 1981. He returned to London for the April 1982 Festival, before making a tour in Canada. 'Some Memories Just Won't Die' became his biggest hit since 1978 and on 11 October 1982 he was inducted into the Country Music Hall Of Fame in Nashville. He toured on the west coast but in Cincinnati, on 1 December 1982, he played what turned out to be his last concert. The following day he suffered his third heart attack. He underwent major surgery but died of cardiac arrest on 8 December and was buried in Nashville three days later. A few days after his funeral his recording of 'Honky Tonk Man', the title track of a Clint Eastwood film in which he had made a cameo appearance, entered the charts, eventually peaking at number 10. A quiet and withdrawn man offstage, Robbins possessed an on-stage ability to communicate with and hold his audience and his clever use of in-jokes, asides and sheer personality made him one of the finest entertainers to grace any genre of music. His tally of 94 **Billboard** country chart hits places him in eighth position in the list of most-charted country artists. He actually charted at least one song every year from 1952 (when he first recorded) to 1983 and during this period he also registered 31 pop hits.

Albums: *Rock 'N' Rollin' Robbins* (Columbia 1956), *The Song Of Robbins* (Columbia 1957), *Song Of The Islands* (Columbia Columbia 1957), *Marty Robbins* (1958), *Gunfighter Ballads And Trail Songs* (Columbia 1959), *Marty's Greatest Hits* (Columbia 1959), *More Gunfighter Ballads And Trail Songs* (Columbia 1960), *More Greatest Hits* (Columbia 1961), *Just A Little Sentimental* (Columbia 1961), *Devil Woman* (Columbia 1962), *Marty After Midnight* (Columbia 1962), *Portrait Of Marty* (Columbia 1962), *Hawaii's Calling Me* (Columbia 1963), *Return Of The Gunfighter* (Columbia 1963), *R.F.D. Marty Robbins* (Columbia 1964), *Island Woman* (Columbia 1964), *Turn The Lights Down Low* (Columbia 1965), *What God Has Done* (Columbia 1965), *Saddle Tramp* (Columbia 1966), *The Drifter* (Columbia 1966), *Christmas With Marty Robbins* (Columbia 1967), *My Kind Of Country* (Columbia 1967), *Tonight Carmen* (Columbia 1967), *By The Time I Get To Phoenix* (Columbia 1968), *Bend In The River* (Columbia 1968), *I Walk Alone* (Columbia 1968), *Heart Of Marty Robbins* (Columbia 1969), *It's A Sin* (Columbia 1969), *Singing The Blues* (Columbia 1969), *My Woman,*

My Woman, My Wife (Columbia 1970), *The Story Of My Life* (Columbia 1970), *From The Heart* (Columbia 1971), *Today* (Columbia 1971), *Marty Robbins Favorites* (Columbia 1972), *Song Of The Islands* (1972), *I've Got A Woman's Love* (1972), with his Friends *Joy Of Christmas* (1972), *This Much A Man* (1972), *Bound For Old Mexico* (1973), *Marty Robbins* (1973), *Good 'N' Country* (1974), *Have I Told You Lately That I Love You* (1974), *No Sign Of Loneliness Here* (1976), *El Paso City* (1976), *Two Gun Daddy* (1976), *Adios Amigo* (1977), *Don't Let Me Touch You* (1977), *All Around Cowboy* (1979), *The Performer* (1979), *With Love* (1980), *Encore* (1981), *Everything I've Always Wanted* (1981), *The Legend* (1981), *Come Back To Me* (1982), *Some Memories Just Won't Die* (1982), *Sincerely* (1983), *Forever Yours* (1983), *Twentieth Century Drifter* (1983), *Just Me And My Guitar* (1983), *Rockin' Rollin' Robbins Volumes 1, 2, 3* (1983-85), *Hawaii's Calling Me* (1983), *Marty Robbins Files Volumes 1-5* (1983-85), *In The Wild West Parts 2, 4, 5* (1984-85), *Pieces Of Your Heart* (1985), *Marty Robbins Country 1951-58* (1991, Bear Family 5-CD boxed set), *Lost And Found* (Columbia 1994).

Video: *The Best Of The Marty Robbins Show Vol. 3* (1993).

Further reading: *Marty Robbins: Fast Cars And Country Music*, Barbara J. Pruett.

Robert And Elizabeth

A musical adaptation of the 1930 play *The Barretts Of Wimpole Street* by Rudolph Besier, with music by **Ron Grainer** and a book and lyrics by Ronald Millar. The source of this piece was an unproduced musical, *The Third Kiss*, by the American composer and lyricist Fred G. Moritt. *Robert And Elizabeth*, which opened at the Lyric theatre in London on 20 October 1964, was set in 1845-46 and based on the true story of two poets, the bed-ridden Elizabeth Moulton-Barrett (June Bronhill) and Robert Browning (Keith Michell). After corresponding with each other for some time, they fall in love and eventually marry in spite of stern opposition from Elizabeth's tyrannical father, Edward Moulton-Barrett (John Clements). The production, directed and choreographed by Wendy Toye, captured the period perfectly, with Bronhill and Michell leading an outstanding cast. They made the most of Grainer and Millar's highly romantic score which included 'The Girls That Boys Dream About', 'I Know Now', 'The World Outside', 'Escape Me Never', 'In A Simple Way', and 'I Said Love'. *Robert And Elizabeth* ran for well over two years, a total of 948 performances. The show has never played Broadway, but was presented in Chicago (1974), Maine (1978), and at the Paper Mill Playhouse (1982). An acclaimed production was mounted in England at the Chichester Festival Theatre in 1987, starring **Mark Wynter** and Gaynor Miles.

Robert And Johnny

This R&B duo came from the Bronx, New York, USA. Robert Carr and Johnny Mitchell grew up in the same neighbourhood and attended high school together, in a centre of doo-wop culture. Thus, upon their signing to Old Town Records in 1956, their duets captured the sound of the doo-wop groups then currently popular. 'I Believe in You' with the duo's trademark approach of sighing and pausing, where one takes the lead and then the two come together on the choruses, established their name in New York City, but not much further west than the Hudson River. 'We Belong Together', however, established the duo as rock 'n' roll immortals, going to number 12 R&B and number 32 pop in 1958. Robert and Johnny, alas, were fated to be one-hit-wonders and ended their recording career in 1962. 'We Belong Together' fared far better, getting revived on the charts in 1966 by Dee Brown and Lola Grant and in 1968 by the Webs.

Album: *We Belong Together* (1986).

Robert, Yves

b. 17 January 1958, Clermont-Ferrand, France. Robert received a classical training at the Conservatoire de Vichy where he studied the flute before concentrating on the trombone. In 1981 he joined the Lyon-based experimental music collective ARFI (Association a la recherche d'un folklore imaginaire) and was particularly influenced by its co-founder, the eclectic jazz saxophonist and clarinettist **Louis Sclavis**. During the 80s he worked with Sclavis' quartet, the **Didier Levallet** Quintet, **Chris McGregor**'s afro-free jazz ensemble, the Brotherhood Of Breath, **Steve Lacy**'s music-dance project Futurities and La Marmite Infernale big band. He also led his own improvising quartet and gave solo trombone concerts. In 1991 he made an impressive debut at **Derek Bailey**'s Company Week festival of improvised music in London. Robert is a versatile and highly inventive trombone player with a strong sense of timing and a Tatiesque eye for humour, should the opportunity arise.

Albums: with La Marmite Infernale *Moralité Surprise* (1983), *Yves Robert Trombone Solo* (1983), with Didier Levallet Quintet *Quiet Days* (1985).

Roberta (Film Musical)

The **Fred Astaire** and **Ginger Rogers** bandwagon gathered pace with this 1935 adaptation of another successful Broadway musical. Naturally, the original libretto, which itself was based on Alice Duer Miller's book *Gowns By Roberta*, was tinkered with by screenwriters Jane Murfin, Sam Mintz, Glen Tryon and Allan Scott, but the basic plot remained. This concerned all-American fooballer John Kent (played by Randolph Scott without a horse), who inherits his aunt's Parisian dress salon and falls in love with her assistant, a Russian princess (Irene Dunne). The latter lady was top-billed, but, as usual, Astaire and Rodgers dominated proceedings - in the nicest possible way.

Four of **Jerome Kern** and **Otto Harbach**'s songs from the show were retained: 'Smoke Gets In Your Eyes', 'Let's Begin', 'Yesterdays', and 'I'll Be Hard To Handle' - the latter number being given a new lyric by Bernard Dougall. Three other numbers were added: 'Indiana' (written by Ballard MacDonald and James F. Hanley in 1917), the delightful ballad 'Lovely To Look At' (Kern-**Dorothy Fields**), which was introduced by Irene Dunne and decorated the film's gigantic fashion parade finale, and 'I Won't Dance' (Kern-Fields-**Oscar Hammerstein II**) - an Astaire *tour de force*. He also served as the film's (uncredited) dance director with **Hermes Pan**, and this RKO production was directed by Willam A. Seiter. Another version of *Roberta* entitled *Lovely To Look At*, starring **Howard Keel** and **Kathryn Grayson**, was released in 1952.

Roberta (Stage Musical)

Opening at the New Amsterdam Theatre in New York on 18 November 1933, this show was based on Alice Duer Miller's novel *Gowns By Roberta*, and set, appropriately enough, in the high fashion capital of the world - Paris. **Otto Harbach**'s book concerned John Kent (Ray Middleton), who used to be an All-American full-back before he inherited an interest in a dress shop named Roberta, which is operated by his Aunt Minnie (Fay Templeton). He takes on a partner, Stephanie (Tamara), who leaves it until they are almost married before revealing that she is a Russian Princess. This was a visually stunning production, the highlight of which was an elegant, lavishly mounted fashion show. **Jerome Kern** and Otto Harbach's score was pretty spectacular, too. It contained a ravishing trio of songs 'Smoke Gets In Your Eyes', 'The Touch Of Your Hand', and 'Yesterdays' which was introduced by Fay Templeton, who was making her final Broadway appearance in a career that had lasted for 50 years. Most of the laughs were provided by **Bob Hope** and George Murphy, prior to them both going off to Hollywood. They were involved in 'Let's Begin' (with Tamara), and Hope also had the amusing 'You're Devastating', and 'Something Had To Happen' with Ray Middleton and Lyda Roberti. The latter, who was described as 'a supple, Polish-accented blond', also registered strongly with 'I'll Be Hard To Handle' (lyric by Bernard Dougall). This was Jerome Kern's last Broadway hit, and although 295 performances was alright, it could have been better The composer who had been the catalyst for what became accepted as America's own popular music, as opposed to the European imported variety, was to spend most of the rest of his life writing music for films. Hollywood had two attempts at filming *Roberta*. The first, in 1935, starred Irene Dunne, **Fred Astaire** and **Ginger Rogers**, and the second, retitled *Lovely To Look At*, had **Howard Keel**, **Kathryn Grayson** and **Ann Miller**.

Roberts, Andy

b. 12 June 1946, Harrow, Middlesex, England. Guitarist Roberts', solo achievements have been overshadowed by the work he has done for other artists. He first came to public attention after meeting BBC disc jockey **John Peel** in 1967. From 1966-67, Roberts had accompanied the **Scaffold** and later joined the **Liverpool Scene** from 1968-70. He recorded *Everyone* in 1971 with Everyone, and then concentrated on session and solo work. In 1972, with **Plainsong**, he recorded the highly regarded *In Search Of Amelia Earhart*. He then joined Grimms from 1973-76, during which time he appeared on their final two albums. In 1974, he featured in his first stage musical *Mind Your Head*. Roberts then joined **Roy Harper**'s, Band. In 1980, he performed with the **Hank Wangford** Band, with whom he recorded - *Hank Wangford* (1980) and *Live At The Pegasus* (1982) - and toured until 1984. He still continued with other session commitments, including playing guitar on **Pink Floyd**'s *The Wall*, in 1981. Roberts also provided a singing voice for television's satirical puppet series *Spitting Image* from 1983-84. Since then he has released two solo albums, and has been heavily involved in composing music for the theatre, film and television. His flexibility is reflected in the diversity of the programmes he has composed for, ranging from television drama series such as *The Men's Room* (excellent theme song sung by Sarah Jane Morris, 'I Am A Woman') to *Madhur Jaffrey's Far Eastern Cookery*. In his capacity as composer, Roberts has been involved with *Z Cars*, *Bergerac*, and more recently, the six-part television documentary series, *Where On Earth Are We Going*. He has also played on countless sessions by a wealth of artists.

Albums: *Homegrown* (1970), *Nina And The Dream Tree* (1971), *Urban Cowboy* (1971), *Andy Roberts And The Great Stampede* (1973), with Grimms *Rockin' Duck* (1973), with Grimms *Sleepers* (1976), with Roger McGough *Summer With Monika* (1978), *Loose Connections* (1984, film soundtrack), *From Time To Time* (1985). Compilation: *Recollections* (1972).

Roberts, Hank

b. 1954, Terre Haute, Indiana, USA. Cellist - and until recently, professional chef - Roberts has become one of the busiest musicians in New York's 'downtown' scene. His music is wide-open experimental and heedless of idiomatic boundaries. It acknowledges his hillbilly roots with a comic barn dance or two, but moves out towards sleek rock, free sound exploration, anything and everything. First heard amongst the massed strings of **Michael Mantler**'s Orchestra on *13* (1975), Roberts began to attract rave notices for his work with guitarist **Bill Frisell**. The cellist leads his own group Birds Of Prey and co-leads two others: Miniature (with **Tim**

Berne and Joey Baron), and Arcado, a string trio with **Mark Dresser** and Mark Feldman. Roberts is also a distinctive singer, his vocals having an ethereal quality that has prompted critics to make comparisons with **Milton Nascimento** and **Robert Wyatt**. Often doctoring his voice with echo and tape-delay, Roberts uses it to expand the sound of his cello, 'to make the chords bigger'.

Albums: *Black Pastels* (JMT 1988), *Miniature* (1988), *Arcado* (1989), *Hank Robert & Birds Of Prey* (JMT 1990), with Arcado *Behind The Myth* (1990), with Miniature *I Can't Put My Finger On It* (1991), with Arcado *For Three Strings And Orchestra* (1992), *Little Motor People* (JMT 1993).

Roberts, James

b. 10 February 1918, Madison County, Kentucky, USA. The mandolin playing son of legendary fiddler Doc Roberts. He first sang on recordings with his father and Asa Martin at the age of 10 and continued to work with Martin until, in 1937, tiring of the music, he joined the Navy. He later returned to performing and whilst working at WLAP Louisville, on Asa Martin's *Morning Roundup*, he met **Martha Lou Carson**. They married and singing as a duo played various stations, including WHIS Bluefield, *The Renfro Valley Barn Dance* and in 1940, WSB Atlanta where, specialising in country gospel material and using the stage name of James And Martha Carson, the Barn Dance Sweethearts, they were a very popular act. In 1950, they moved to WNOX Knoxville's *Mid-Day Merry-Go-Round*. Between 1946 and 1950, they recorded 30 sides, initially with just their own guitar and mandolin accompaniment but on the latter backing vocals and hand clapping were added. Their 1947 recording of 'The Sweetest Gift' and Robert's self-penned 'Man Of Galilee' are very highly rated. In 1951, they divorced and Roberts moved to WWVA Wheeling where he worked with **Wilma Lee And Stoney Cooper** and also led the station staff band, the Country Harmony Boys. Between 1952 and 1960, he returned to Knoxville. He recorded with the Lonesome Pine Fiddlers and the Masters Family and also, at times, played as a studio musician. He eventually retired to Lexington but made some personal appearances usually of an evangelical nature.

Album: with Martha Lou Carson *James & Martha Early Gospel Greats* (ACM 70s, covers 40s).

Roberts, Joe

Manchester-based soul-dance vocalist, and an ex-mod who was brought up in a commune (when his parents moved from London to Karling in Norfolk, his father switching jobs from economist to carpenter). This can be guaged in his lyrics, which come heavily laden peace 'n' luv metaphors, but also reflect the early influence of **Sly Stone**, **Al Green** and **Marvin Gaye**, who were

introduced to him by later collaborator Eric Gooden. He had been also been learning the piano from the age of eight, and this was reflected in the musicianship of his club music. After moving to Manchester in 1981 he became a member of local covers band the Risk, who evenutally used Roberts' own songs. He hit sprightly single form on cuts like 'Love Is Energy' - recorded with the aforementioned Eric Gooden, whom he had met at college, and is his current songwriting partner - and 'Back In My Life'.

Album: *Looking For The Here And Now* (London 1994).

Roberts, Juliet

The term house diva does not fully cover the career or capabilities of Juliet Roberts, who is in addition a proficient singer/songwriter, and a veteran of the early days of British soul. Unlike many in the field, she did not learn her craft at the church choir, having instead been brought up in the more restrained Catholic faith. However, music was still in her blood. Her father was formerly a member of the calypso band the Nightingales, and took her to various concerts. Her first performances came as a member of reggae band Black Jade, before she signed solo to Bluebird Records in 1980, a label set up by her local record shop in Paddington, North London. Two tracks, a cover of the **Police**'s 'The Bed's Too Big Without You' and 'Fool For You' emerged, while she was still engaged in her day job as a sports' tutor. They were enough to attract the attention of fellow Londoners the Funk Masters. She appeared as lead singer on their Top 10 hit, 'It's Over', in 1983. After a year's sabbatical in the US she embarked on her music career proper, and, within a week of returning to British shores, was enlisted as singer for Latin jazz band **Working Week**. When that group floundered (after several noble releases) she finally signed to **Cooltempo** as a solo artist.

Album: *Natural Thing* (Cooltempo 1994).

Roberts, Kane

Kane Roberts first came to prominence as machismo lead guitarist in **Alice Cooper**'s band, during his mid-80s comeback, when he was lured from **Lone Justice** to add musical and visual muscle to Cooper's theatrical live show. With the help of Cooper's management he secured a solo deal with **MCA Records** in 1987. His debut release, however, was somewhat at odds with his tough-guy image, featuring a collection of AOR and ballads. He quit Cooper's band the following year to concentrate on his solo career. Playing down the muscleman image, he teamed up with **Desmond Child** to write material for *Saints And Sinners*. This was a highly polished melodic rock album in a **Bon Jovi** meet **Kiss** vein, with John McCurry (guitar), Steven Steele (bass), Myron Grombacher (drums) and Chuck Kentis (keyboards) being recruited as permanent band members.

Albums: *Kane Roberts* (MCA 1987), *Saints And Sinners* (Geffen 1991).

Roberts, Kenny

b. 14 October 1927, Lenoir City, Tennessee, USA. After Roberts' mother died when he was a child, the family relocated to a farm near Athol, Massachusetts. He learned guitar, harmonica and fiddle and grew up listening to the music of the singing cowboys and the yodelling of Elton Britt. He won a talent competition when he was 13 years old and first played with the Red River Rangers on WHAI Greenfield in 1942. He moved to WKNE Keene, New Hampshire the following year, where he became a member of the Down Homers. In 1946, the group moved to Fort Wayne, Indiana, where they regularly played the Barn Dance programme known as the *Hoosier Hop*. When the group relocated to Connecticut, Roberts decided it was time to launch his solo career. He had first recorded as a member of the group, but in early 1947 he recorded some solo tracks for Vita-Coustic. When these were not released, he moved to Coral. He worked regularly on stations in Fort Wayne and also KMOF St Louis, before moving to WLW Cincinnati in 1948. He acquired many nicknames during his career not least of which was the title of The Jumping Cowboy, which he got for a strange ability to jump several feet in the air while singing. He performed this feat regularly on his WLW children's television programme. He was an outstanding yodeller and naturally many of his recordings demonstrate this talent with such fine examples as 'She Taught Me How To Yodel' and 'Yodel Polka'.

Experts in the art rate that his speciality 'galloping yodel' made him the world's fastest yodeller. In 1949, he achieved his greatest hit when his recording of 'I Never See Maggie Alone' became a million seller. It was a Top 10 hit in both US pop and country charts and also has the distinction of possibly being the first British composition to make the Top 10 in the US country charts. (It dated from 1926 and was written by Harry Tilsley (words) and Everett Lynton (music).) In 1949-1950, he had further US country chart hits with 'Wedding Bells', 'Jealous Heart' and 'Choc'late Ice Cream Cone'. During the 50s and mid-60s, he recorded for various labels, though few releases appeared but in the late 60s, he recorded four complete albums for Starday. In the 70s, he recorded a tribute album to his idol Elton Britt and was asked to take Britt's place on a concert in 1972 in New Jersey on the night that Britt died. He semi-retired for a time in the late 50s but soon returned and has maintained an active participation ever since. He has fronted his own shows on radio and television on many stations and has appeared at all the major venues, including the *Wheeling Jamboree* and the *Grand Ole Opry*. With his wife Bettyanne (who writes some of his songs), he has toured in Australia, the Far East and throughout Europe. He is especially popular in the British country clubs, where he is still rated by his best-known nickname of King Of The Yodelers.

Albums: *Indian Love Call (Kenny Roberts, America's King Of The Yodelers)* (1965), *Yodelin' Kenny Roberts Sings Country Songs* (1966), *Country Music Singing Sensation* (1969), *Jealous Heart* (1970), *I Never See Maggie Alone* (1971), *Yodelin' With Kenny Roberts* (1971), *Tribute To Elton Britt* (1972), *Feelings Of Love* (1978), *Just Call Me Country* (1988), *You're My Kind Of People* (1991).

Roberts, Luckey

b. Charles Luckyeth, 7 August 1887, Philadelphia, Pennsylvania, USA, d. 5 February 1968. After working in vaudeville as a child, Roberts moved to New York where he established a minor reputation as a composer and a major one as a performer of rags and, later, stride piano. In the years between the wars, Roberts's composing talents were recognized more and several of his musical shows were produced. During the 40s and early 50s he owned and regularly played at a Harlem bar. Roberts made few records and most of these were early piano rolls while his later records were made after he had suffered strokes and injuries in a road accident. Nevertheless, it is possible to understand the awe felt by such pianists as **Fats Waller**, **James P. Johnson** and **Willie 'The Lion' Smith** at his astonishing technique, a technique which was greatly facilitated by his remarkably large hands.

Album: *Harlem Piano Solos* (1958).

Roberts, Malcolm

b. 31 March 1944, Manchester, England. This powerful vocalist has had most of his success outside the UK. Roberts studied interior design at a local art college, and went to music and drama classes in the evenings. After a spell with the National Youth Theatre as an actor, he appeared in several programmes on UK television, including *Coronation Street*. In 1964 he understudied the part of Eric Dooley in **Lionel Bart**'s West End musical **Maggie May**, and later took over the role. He also appeared in a Manchester revival of **West Side Story**, along with other diverse productions such as *The Hunchback Of Notre Dame* and *Julius Caesar* (with Timothy Dalton). After a period out of showbusiness, during which he worked as an ice cream salesman and a 'bouncer' in a Soho strip club in London, Roberts was offered a contract with **RCA Records**. His first release, 'Time Alone Will Tell', entered the UK charts in 1967, and was followed by the **Tobias Brothers**' 'May I Have The Next Dream With You', which reached the Top 10. In the late 60s Roberts was a familiar figure on UK television, guesting on shows such as *Words And Music*, *International Cabaret* and *London Palladium Show*. In 1969 he triumphed at the San Remo Song Festival in Rio de

Janeiro with **Les Reed** and Barry Mason's 'Love Is All'. The song became a smash hit in Brazil, and stayed near the top of the charts for a reputed six months, elevating Roberts to superstar status in that part of the world. For several years afterwards, he returned annually, playing to audiences of 50,000 or more. His popularity with the female population there is reflected in a bizarre incident in which 50 beauty queens are reported to have queued outside his dressing room for the privilege of being kissed by him. His success in South America generated interest from the USA, and Roberts appeared on Jack Benny's show in Las Vegas, and also featured on television with Johnny Carson and David Frost. In 1972 he captained the winning British team at the Knokke le Zoute Song Festival, and found a fresh audience for himself in Belgium, Spain, Germany, and other parts of Europe. During the following year he re-launched his career in the UK, attempting to present a more raunchy image. The sleeve of his new single, 'Never Get Back Home', announced 'A New Malcolm Roberts'. In 1986 Roberts returned to the musical theatre, and appeared as Alencon in *Jeanne*, Shirlie Roden's rock opera on Joan of Arc, at Sadler's Wells in London. The home breakthrough has not yet arrived, and he divides his time between performing in the UK and abroad, especially in Brazil and Australia where he is especially popular.

Selected albums: *Voice Of Malcolm Roberts* (70s), *Sounds Like Malcolm Roberts* (70s), *This Is Malcolm Roberts* (1981), *The Best Of The EMI Years* (1993).

Roberts, Marcus

b. 7 August 1963, Jacksonville, Florida, USA. If **Thelonious Monk** frequently pursued improvisation through harmonic as well as (or sometimes instead of) melodic routes, Roberts is an appropriate inheritor of the method. Like **Wynton Marsalis**, later to be his employer, Roberts is a dedicated respecter of earlier jazz traditions, and his technique comfortably encompasses stride, many variations of blues, and bebop. He took up the instrument early, exposed to a mixture of classical and gospel music, and studied piano at Florida State, winning competitions on the instrument by the mid-80s. Roberts's vitality, knowledge, technique and admiration for his keyboard predecessors brought him a place in the Wynton Marsalis group by 1985 and - as with Marsalis - a series of albums as leader took him further back into the archives, albeit with a continuing grace and swing. 1990's *Alone With Three Giants* demonstrated Roberts's singleminded determination to subjugate self-expression to interpretation of classic works, including pieces by **Jelly Roll Morton** and Monk.

Albums: *The Truth Is Spoken Here* (Novus 1989), *Deep In The Shed* (Novus 1990), *Alone With Three Giants* (Novus 1990), *Prayer For Peace* (Novus 1991), *As Serenity Approaches* (Novus 1992), *If I Could Be With You* (Novus 1993).

Roberts, Paddy

b. 1910, South Africa, d. September 1975, England. A songwriter, pianist and singer, Roberts' early education took place in England. He subsequently attended university in South Africa before joining a law practice. Intent on becoming a songwriter, he returned to the UK where he had some success in the late 30s with songs such as 'Angel Of The Great White Way' (written with Elton Box, Desmond Cox and Don Pelosi), and 'Horsey, Horsey' (with Box, Cox and Ralph Butler) which became popular for Jack Jackson, **Billy Cotton** and **Henry Hall**. During World War II Roberts flew with the RAF, and when peace came he became an airline captain on BOAC Constellations. Subsequently, he returned to songwriting, and, during the 50s, had several UK chart hits, including 'The Book' (**David Whitfield**), 'Heart Of A Man' (**Frankie Vaughan**), 'Lay Down Your Arms' (**Anne Shelton**), 'Meet Me On The Corner' (**Max Bygraves**), 'Pickin' A Chicken' (**Eve Boswell**); and 'Evermore', 'Softly, Softly' (number 1), and 'You Are My First Love' (the last three sung by **Ruby Murray**). The latter song was featured in the British musical film *It's Great To Be Young*, and Roberts wrote several other movie songs, including 'In Love For The Very First Time' (for *An Alligator Named Daisy*', starring Diana Dors) and the title number to *The Good Companions*. His other 50s compositions included 'Johnny Is The Boy For Me', 'It's A Boy', 'That Dear Old Gentleman', 'Send For Me', and 'The Three Galleons (Las Tres Carabelas)'. Most of the above songs were written in collaboration with others, such as Hans Gottwald, C.A. Rossi, Geoffrey Parsons, Peggy Cochran, Jack Woodman, Gerry Levine, Ake Gerhard, Leon Land, Peter Hart, Garfield De Mortimer, Derek Bernfield, Augusto Alguego, G. Moreu, and Lester Powell. However, towards the end of the decade, he was beginning to write more and more unaided, and during the 60s he included several of his own often wry, witty and sophisticated numbers in an accomplished cabaret act. Probably the best-known of these is 'The Ballad Of Bethnal Green' which enjoyed a good deal of airplay, but there were many others too, including 'The Belle Of Barking Creek', 'The Big Dee-Jay', 'Follow Me', 'Country Girl', 'I Love Mary', 'The Tattooed Lady', 'What's All This Fuss About Love?', 'The Lavender Cowboy', and 'Don't Upset The Little Kiddywinks'. Roberts won several **Ivor Novello** Awards, and held high office in the Performing Right Society and the Song Writers Guild.

Selected albums: *Paddy Roberts At The Blue Angel* (Decca 1961), *Best Of Paddy Roberts* (Music For Pleasure 1968).

Robertson, B.A.

b. Brian Robertson, Glasgow, Scotland. This gregarious vocalist achieved notoriety when, as Brian Alexander Robertson, his debut *Wringing Applause*, was accompanied by excessive hype. He nonetheless survived the ensuing backlash to secure an international deal with **Asylum** through which he enjoyed three UK Top 10 singles with 'Bang Bang', 'Knocked It Off' (both 1979) and 'To Be Or Not To Be' (1980). His tongue-in-cheek delivery was also apparent on 'Hold Me', a duet with **Maggie Bell**, and 'We Have A Dream', on which he fronted the 1982 Scotland World Cup Squad. The following year Robertson scored a minor hit with 'Time' a collaboration with former **Abba** member **Frida**, and although chart success has since proved elusive, the artist has pursued a successful and financially rewarding career as a songwriter. He composed the theme tune to *Wogan*, BBC television's thrice-weekly chat show. His on-camera foolishness belies a considerable talent.

Albums: *Wringing Applause* (1973), *Initial Success* (1980), *Bully For You* (1981), *B.A. Robertson* (1982).

Robertson, Eck

b. Alexander Campbell Robertson, 20 November 1887, Delaney, Madison County, Arkansas, USA. He grew up in Texas and as a boy learned to play the fiddle, guitar and banjo, although it was as a fiddler that he established himself. The story exists that, as a boy who badly wanted a fiddle, he once made himself a substitute by skinning the family cat and stretching the skin over a gourd. In 1903, he toured with medicine shows but after his marriage in 1906, he confined his playing to more local venues some times even providing musical backing for the silent western films. His love of the western image not only saw him become the first country musician to wear cowboy dress but, in 1918, he was known as the Cowboy Fiddler. In June 1922, he and fellow fiddler Henry Galliland, a 76 year old Civil War veteran from Altus, Oklahoma, were engaged to play at a reunion of Old Confederate Soldiers in Richmond, Virginia. After the reunion, both men decided, without invitation, to head for New York to make records. They arrived at **RCA**-Victor's studios with Robertson still dressed as a cowboy and his colleague still wearing his Confederate uniform. Although shocked by their effrontery and dress, RCA-Victor did record them. They made duet recordings of well known fiddle tunes 'Arkansas Traveller' and 'Turkey In The Straw' on 30 June and the following day, Robertson made solo recordings of 'Ragtime Annie' and 'Sallie Gooden' (a version now rated as a classic fiddle recording), plus two further recordings accompanied by the studio pianist. (Galliland returned to his home in Altus, where he died a few years later). When RCA-Victor released a record containing 'Arkansas Traveller' and 'Sallie Gooden' on 1 September 1922, it seemingly became the first known hillbilly recording. When Robertson played these two tunes on WBAP Fort Worth on 23 March 1923, in theory, he became the first country artist to promote his own records on the radio. He acquired legendary status throughout the southwest by his regular successes at fiddle contests, where his version of 'Ragtime Annie' was respected by all. (His 1922 recording of this number appears on the RCA-Victor *Early Rural String Bands*). He often competed against **Bob Wills** and his father John and the rivalry between Robertson and the two Wills became known throughout the area. In later years Bob related 'I could never beat Eck in a fiddle contest. Papa beat him lots of times but I never did'. After one monumental battle, where the elder Wills had augmented his playing with more than his usual volume of hollering which seemingly pleased that day's judge, a bystander asked Robertson if Wills had outfiddled him. The reply was 'Hell, no. He didn't outfiddle me. That damned old man Wills outhollered me'. Robertson and wife, Nettie (also a talented musician who played piano, guitar and mandolin), raised 10 children. Robertson made no further recordings until 1929 when, accompanied by Nettie, son Eck Jnr. (banjo/guitar), a guitar playing daughter and fiddler Dr. J.B. Cranfill (who played in the style of Galliland), they recorded 15 numbers, some of which contain vocals by Robertson. He continued to play for local events but also worked as a piano tuner. His fiddle playing provided great inspiration to many other musicians. In 1964, at the age of 76, he made a very successful appearance at the UCLA Folk Festival in Amarillo. Several of Robertson's recordings have appeared on County and RCA compilation albums. His noted 'Sallie Gooden' may be found on *The Smithsonian Collection Of Classic Country Music*, while Sonyatone reportedly released an album of his work.

Robertson, Jeannie

b. Regina Christina Robertson, 1908, Aberdeen, Scotland, d. March 1975. This Scottish traditional singer was the youngest of five children of Donald Robertson and Maria Stewart. Her parents were both from tinker families, who would travel in caravans, selling goods from house-to-house during the summer, and then spend the winter living in Aberdeen. It was from her mother that Jeannie learned a lot of her repertoire. Robertson was 'discovered' in Aberdeen by Hamish Henderson in 1953, when it was apparent that she possessed an outstanding voice and capacity for story-telling. Riverside Records, in the USA, were the first to offer a recording contact to Robertson. The recordings were made by Bill Leader, in April 1956, and featured a guitar accompaniment of the late **Josh MacRae**. *Songs Of A Scots Tinker Lady* was re-released in the UK in 1965 by **Topic Records** and retitled

Jeannie Robertson. They also removed the accompanying guitar tracks. A series of EPs were brought out in 1959 by Collector Records which included: *The Gallowa' Hills*, *The Twa Brothers*, *I Know Where I'm Going*, and *Jeannie's Merry Muse*. Robertson was awarded the MBE in 1968 for her services to traditional music, and continued singing until her death in 1975.

Albums: *Songs Of A Tinker Lady* (1956), *Lord Donald* (1959), *Jeannie Robertson, The World's Greatest Folksinger* (1960), *The Cuckoo's Nest* (1960).

Robertson, Justin

Robertson (b. c.1968) is a UK songwriter, producer and remixer who has worked on tracks by the likes of **Talk Talk** ('Dum Dum Girl') **Yargo** ('Love Revolution') **Finitribe** ('Forevergreen'), **Erasure** ('Snappy'), **React 2 Rhythm** ('Intoxication'), **Inspiral Carpets** ('Caravan And Skidoo'), **Shamen** ('Boss Drum'), **Coco Steel & Lovebomb** ('Feel It'), **Gary Clail** ('These Things Are Worth Fighting For'), **Sugarcubes** ('Birthday' and 'Motorcrash'), **Happy Mondays** ('Sunshine And Love') and the rather less-celebrated **Candy Flip** ('Red Hills Road') He was even asked to do his thing for the **Fall**. On his remixing ethos: 'With me its always a case of to butcher or not to butcher. Usually its the former'. His first remix was actually housed on **Eastern Bloc**'s Creed operation (Mad Jacks' 'Feel The Hit'), and he is one of a number of famous people to have staffed that record shop's counters. He started DJing while at Manchester University, playing parties because, more or less, he had the best record collection. It was through his purchases at Eastern Bloc that he eventually landed a job there (establishing the Spice club with fellow internee, Greg Fenton). Robertson is now the motivating force behind hip Manchester outfit Lionrock, who specialise in warm, uplifting house. The group's singles include 'Packet Of Peace' (which cracked the charts and featured a rap from **MC Buzz B**) and 'Carnival' in 1993, which again collared numerous Single Of The Week awards. The band's full line-up boasts Justin Robertson (keyboards) and Mark Stagg (keyboards). Robertson was also behind the label which housed Lionrock's first record, MERC. This was formed with Ross McKenzie, and stood for Most Excellent Record Company. Other releases included Life Eternal's 'Come Into The Light' and **Dub Federation**'s 'Space Funk' and 'Love Inferno' releases, prior to that group splitting in 1994. Robertson later abdicated much of his responsibility for the imprint, signing to **DeConstruction** as a solo artist. The mid-90s saw him raise his profile outside of dance music by touring with **Primal Scream**.

Robertson, Robbie

b. Jaime Robbie Robertson, 5 July 1943, Toronto, Canada. Robertson's professional career began in 1960 when he replaced guitarist James Evans in **Ronnie Hawkins**' backing group, the Hawks. Robertson's rough, but exciting style prevails on several of Hawkins' releases, including 'Matchbox', 'Bo Diddley' and 'Who Do You Love', the last of which boasts an arresting solo. The group then left Hawkins and by 1964 was barnstorming tiny American venues, firstly as the Canadian Squires, then as Levon And The Hawks. They recorded a handful of singles including Robertson's 'The Stones I Throw', which showed the genesis of a remarkable compositional talent. The compulsive backing the Hawks had provided on sessions by blues singer **John Hammond** led to their association with **Bob Dylan**. Their emphatic drive underscored Robertson's raging guitar work and helped complete the one-time folksinger's transformation from acoustic sage to electric guru. Robertson's songwriting blossomed during their relationship. His lyrics assumed a greater depth, suggesting a pastoral America, while the music of the group, now dubbed simply the **Band**, drew its inspiration from a generation of rural styles, both black and white, as well as contemporary soul music peers. Such skill resulted in a body of work which, by invoking the past, created something familiar, yet original. The Band broke up in 1976 following a farewell concert at San Francisco's Winterland Ballroom. The event was captured in the celebratory film *The Last Waltz*, directed by Martin Scorsese, which in turn inspired Roberston's cinematic ambitions. *Carny*, which he also produced, provided his sole starring role to date, although he maintained a working relationship with Scorsese by scoring several of his films, including *Raging Bull* and *The Color Of Money*.

A 1983 collaboration, *King Of Comedy*, was notable for Robertson's solo track, 'Between Trains'. This understated performance was the prelude to the artist's 'comeback' album. *Robbie Robertson*, released in 1987, was an exceptional collection and offered a full, state-of-the-art production and notable guest contributions by U2, **Peter Gabriel**, **Daniel Lanois** and the late **Gil Evans**, as well as his former Band colleagues Rick Danko and Garth Hudson. Such appearances enhanced a work which compared favourably with Robertson's previous recordings and included two exceptional compositions in 'Fallen Angel' and 'Broken Arrow'. This artistic rebirth bodes well for the 90s, although *Storyville* was a disappointing album for those expecting a repeat of his solo debut. His most interesting project to date (although uncommercial) was in 1994 with the Red Road Ensemble, a group of native Americans. Robertson is passionate about their continuing plight and much of his time in the mid-90s was working on their behalf.

Albums: *Robbie Robertson* (1987), *Storyville* (1991), *Music For The Native Americans* (Capitol 1994).

Robertson, Sherman

b. 27 October 1948, Breaux Bridge, Louisiana, USA.
Already a veteran of zydeco, Texas R&B and swamp
blues, Robertson is a seasoned entertainer who rarely
writes his own material but knows how to sell a song.
Like many of his generation, he was initially inspired by
country music and asked his father for a guitar after
watching **Hank Williams** on television. He learned
about blues from Floyd London, who also lived in the
Fifth Ward of Houston where Robertson grew up.
Conrad Johnson was music director of his high school
band and recruited him to play in his group, Connie's
Combo. Later, Robertson formed the Crosstown Blues
Band, with whom he made his first albums, but broke
them up when **Clifton Chenier**, a friend of his
father's, asked him to work with him. In the next five
years, he visited Europe and recorded with Chenier for
Arhoolie and Maison De Soul. He then joined
Rockin' Dopsie's band and took part in the **Paul
Simon** session that became part of Simon's *Gracelands*
album. He next joined Terrence Simien's Mallet
Playboys, where he stayed for two and a half years. In
1992 he was contacted by blues producer **Mike
Vernon**, who eventually signed him to Indigo Records
and recorded *I'm The Man* with him in February 1993.
Robertson became a regular visitor to Europe,
undertaking lengthy tours and appearing at most
European blues festivals, where his energy regularly
won over audiences. His album was re-released on
Code Blue in 1994.
Albums: *Bad Luck And Trouble* (Lunar 2 1981), *Married
Blues* (Lunar 2 1983), *Sherman & Friends* (Lunar 2 1985),
I'm The Man (Indigo/Code Blue 1993/4).

Robertson, Zue

b. C. Alvin Robertson, 7 March 1891, New Orleans,
Louisiana, USA, d. 1943. After learning to play piano,
Robertson switched to trombone and first played
professionally in his early teenage. He worked with
such leading New Orleans musicians as **Manuel
Perez**, **John Robichaux** and **Richard M. Jones**.
He was also a member of the band accompanying a
touring wild west show which featured frontiersman Kit
Carson. Dividing his time between New Orleans and
Chicago, Robertson became a proficient performer and
by the early 20s had recorded with **Jelly Roll Morton**
and **King Oliver**. After spending most of the 20s on
the road he settled in New York where he reverted to
piano and also played organ, giving up the trombone
entirely. He played on through the 30s, relocating in
California, and took up yet another instrument, the
bass.

Robeson, Paul

b. 9 April 1898, Princeton, New Jersey, USA, d. 23
January 1976, Philadelphia, Pennsylvania, USA.

Robeson's father was born into slavery, but he escaped
at the age of 15 and eventually studied theology and
became a preacher. His mother was a teacher, but she
died in 1904. Education was of paramount importance
to the Robeson family, one son became a physician,
and the daughter was a teacher. Of all the family, Paul
Robeson was by far the most gifted. In 1911 he was one
of only two black students at Somerville High School in
New Jersey, yet maintained a potentially dangerous
high profile. He played the title role in *Othello*, sang in
the glee club and also played football. He graduated
with honours and won a scholarship to Rutgers
University. A formidable athlete, he played football at
All-American level and achieved scholastic success. In
the early 20s, while studying law at Columbia
University, he took part in theatrical productions and
sang. In 1922 he visited England where he toured in
the play *Taboo* with the noted actress Mrs Patrick
Campbell. During this visit he also met pianist
Lawrence Brown, with whom he was to have a close
professional relationship for the rest of Brown's life. In
1923 Robeson was in the chorus of Lew Leslie's
Plantation Revue, which starred Florence Mills, and the
following year made his first film, *Body And Soul*, for
Oscar Micheaux, one of the earliest black film-makers.
He appeared in prestigious stage productions, including
All God's Chillun Got Wings (1924) and *The Emperor Jones*
(1925).
In 1924 he had his first brush with the Ku Klux Klan
over a scene in *All God's Chillun* in which he was
required to kiss the hand of a white woman. In 1925 he
made his first concert appearance as a singer. The
impact of this concert, which awakened Americans to
the beauty of his rich bass-baritone voice, was such that
he was invited to tour Europe, appearing in London in
1928 in ***Show Boat*** with **Alberta Hunter**. Also in
1928 he played the title role of Porgy in the play by
DuBose and Dorothy Heyward which formed the basis
of **George Gershwin**'s *Porgy And Bess*. In 1930 he
was again in London, where he took the leading role in
Othello, playing opposite Peggy Ashcroft and Sybil
Thorndike. During the 30s he made a number of films
including, *The Emperor Jones* (1933) and several in the
UK, among them *Sanders Of The River* (1935) and *The
Proud Valley* (1939) and in 1936 he made the screen
version of *Show Boat*. As in the stage production, his
part was small but his rendition of 'Ol' Man River' was
one of the outstanding features. The 30s also saw his
first visit to Russia and he travelled to Spain to sing for
the loyalist troops. He also developed an amazing
facility with languages, eventually becoming fluent in
25, including Chinese and Arabic. He incorporated folk
songs of many nations in his repertoire, singing them in
the appropriate language. This same period saw
Robeson's political awareness develop and he extended
his studies into political philosophy and wrote on many
topics. In 1939 he again played Othello in England,

this time at Stratford-upon-Avon, and also played the role in Boston, Massachusetts, in 1942 and on Broadway in 1943. In the 40s Robeson's politicization developed, during another visit to Russia he embraced communism, although he was not blind to the regime's imperfections and spoke out against the anti-Semitism he found there. Reaction in his home country to his espousal of communism was hostile and a speech he delivered in Paris in 1949, in which he stated that although he loved America he loved Russia more than he loved those elements of America which discriminated against him because of his colour, was predictably misunderstood and widely misquoted. Also in 1949, Robeson led protests in London against the racist policies of the government of South Africa.

The FBI began to take an interest in Robeson's activities and conflict with right-wing elements and racists, especially during a rally at Peekskill in upstate New York, which drew the attention of the media away from his artistic work. An appearance before the Un-American Activities Committee drew even more attention to his already high political profile. In 1950 his passport was withdrawn because the State Department considered that his 'travel abroad at this time would be contrary to the best interests of the United States'. Ill health in the mid-50s allied to the withdrawal of his passport, severely damaged his career when he was in his vocal prime. He continued to address rallies, write extensively on political matters and make occasional concert performances by singing over telephone links to gatherings overseas. Repeated high-level efforts by other governments eventually caused the US State Department to reconsider and during his first New York concert in a decade, to a sell-out audience at Carnegie Hall, he was able to announce that his passport had been returned. This was in May 1958 and later that year he appeared on stage and television in the UK and in Russia. His comeback was triumphant and he made several successful tours of Europe and beyond. He was away for five years, returning to the USA in 1963 for more concerts and political rallies. However, pressures continued to build up and he suffered nervous exhaustion and depression. His wife of 44 years died in 1965.

Another comeback, in the late 60s, was greeted with considerable enthusiasm, but the power and quality of his voice had begun to fade. During the final years of his life Robeson toured, wrote and spoke, but his health was deteriorating rapidly and he died on 23 January 1976. Although Robeson possessed only a limited vocal range, the rich coloration of his tone and the unusual flexibility of his voice made his work especially moving. He brought to the 'Negro spiritual' an understanding and a tenderness that overcame their sometimes mawkish sentimentality, and the strength and integrity of his delivery gave them a quality no other male singer

has equalled. His extensive repertoire of folk songs from many lands was remarkable and brought to his concert performances a much wider scope than that of almost any regular folk singer. Although beyond the scope of this work, Robeson's career as actor, writer and political activist cannot be ignored. His independence and outspokenness against discrimination and political injustice resulted in him suffering severely at the hands of his own government. Indeed, those close to him have intimated a belief that his final illness was brought about by the deliberate covert action of government agents. Perhaps as a side-effect of this, he is frequently omitted from reference works originating in his own country, even those which purport to be black histories. For all the dismissiveness of his own government, Robeson was highly regarded by his own people and by audiences in many lands. His massive intellect, his powerful personality and astonishing charisma, when added to his abilities as a singer and actor, helped to make him one of the outstanding Americans of the 20th century. In 1995, the Missouri Repertory Company in Missouri, Kansas, presented a play 'illustrating the extent of the man's talent and life of controversy', entitled *Paul Robeson*, which starred Don Marshall in the title role.

Selected albums: all various dates *Green Pastures, A Lonesome Road, Songs Of Free Men, Songs Of The Mississippi, The Essential Paul Robeson*, with Elisabeth Welch *Songs From Their Films 1933-1940* (Conifer 1994).

Further reading: *Here I Stand*, Paul Robeson. *Paul Robeson Speaks: Writings Speeches Interviews 1918-1974*, Paul Robeson. *Paul Robeson*, Martin Bauml Duberman.

Robey, Don

b. 1 November 1903, Houston, Texas, USA, d. 16 June 1975, Houston, Texas, USA. Houston businessman and impresario Don Robey bought his nightclub, the Bronze Peacock, in 1945, and it soon became a centre for developing local talent as well as bringing in big names from across the country. Soon after, he opened a record shop, which was also to become the base of operations for his Peacock Records, one of the first labels ever in the US to have a black owner. Peacock developed as one of the most important R&B and gospel labels, featuring artists such as **Gatemouth Brown**, **Johnny Ace** and **Big Mama Thornton**, as well as the Dixie Hummingbirds and Five Blind Boys. Robey then bought the Duke label from Memphis, which became another major outlet, especially for **Bobby Bland** and **Junior Parker**. Another label, Songbird, also issued gospel records for many years.

Robichaux, John

b. 16 January 1886, Thibodaux, Louisiana, USA, d. 1939. Resident in New Orleans from the last years of the 19th century, violinist and drummer Robichaux formed a dance orchestra in 1893 and thereafter continuously led a band until his death. He worked with many noted New Orleans musicians including **Lorenzo Tio** and **Manuel Perez**. Although he was active during the birth and early development of jazz, Robichaux mostly, apart from this musical trend, concentrated instead on providing dance music for the wider audiences of the day. His nephews include **Joseph Robichaux** and John Robichaux, a drummer, who worked on into the 70s.

Robichaux, Joseph

b. 8 March 1900, New Orleans, Louisiana, USA, d 17 January 1965. A nephew of **John Robichaux**, he played piano in New Orleans and Chicago in the years immediately after World War I. In the early 20s he was a member of the Black Eagle Band and also worked with the Davey Jones-**Lee Collins** Astoria Hot Eight. In the early 30s he played with **Kid Rena** and also formed his own band, the New Orleans Rhythm Boys which stayed in existence until 1939. During the 40s Robichaux worked as a soloist in New York. In the 50s he was accompanist to **Lizzie Miles** and then joined the **George Lewis** band, touring internationally and recording. He remained with Lewis until 1964, then returned to New Orleans where he died in 1965. He was a solid ensemble pianist with a lively solo style.
Albums: *Joe Robichaux And His New Orleans Boys* (1933), with George Lewis *The Perennial George Lewis* (1958), *The Perennial George Lewis* (1958). Compilations: *Joe Robichaux And His New Orleans Boys* (1933), *1933* (Classic Jazz Masters 1986), *The Complete* (Blu-Disc 1988).

Robillard, Duke

b. Michael Robillard, 4 October 1948, Woonsocket, Rhode Island, USA. Although associated in most minds with **Roomful Of Blues**, the band he formed with pianist Al Copley in 1967, Robillard's ambitions reach beyond the rigorous guidelines of the blues. This is reflected in the number of times he has left a blues-based band in order to pursue more personal musical goals. In its first 12 years, Roomful Of Blues extended its gig sheet beyond Boston and Rhode Island and down the east coast to New York and Washington. After signing with **Island Records** and recording two albums, Robillard left the band in 1979 to form the Pleasure Kings with Thomas Enright and Tom DeQuattro. He also worked with **Robert Gordon** and the **Legendary Blues Band**. In 1990 he replaced **Jimmie Vaughan** in the **Fabulous Thunderbirds**, which at the time featured two ex-Roomful musicians, Preston Hubbard and Fran Christina. In 1992, he left the Thunderbirds to once again form a new band with Marty Ballou and ex-**Lonnie Mack** drummer, Jeff McAllister. *Temptation* featured a set of original songs, except for Sugar Boy Crawford's 'What's Wrong?', that illustrated Robillard's creative potential without establishing a persona as convincing as that he assumes when playing blues.
Albums: *Duke Robillard & The Pleasure Kings* (Rounder/Demon 1984), *Too Hot To Handle* (Rounder/Demon 1985), *You Got Me* (Rounder 1988), *Swing* (Rounder 1990), *Turn It Around* (Rounder 1991), *After Hours Swing Session* (Rounder 1992), *Temptation* (PointBlank 1994).

Robin, Leo

b. 6 April 1895, Pittsburgh, Pennsylvania, USA, d. 29 December 1984. After studying law, Robin turned to writing lyrics for songs. In the mid-20s, in collaboration with various composers, he had a number of minor successes including 'Looking Around' (music by Richard Myers) and one major hit with 'Hallelujah' (**Vincent Youmans**), written for the 1927 show, *Hit The Deck*. After a few uncertain years on Broadway, Robin went to Hollywood where he came into his own. Amongst his songs written for films during the next few years were 'Louise', 'Beyond The Blue Horizon' (both with **Richard Whiting**), 'My Ideal' (Newell Chase), 'True Blue Lou' (Sam Coslow), 'If I Were King' (Chase and Coslow), 'Prisoner Of Love' (Clarence Gaskill and **Russ Columbo**), 'Whispers In The Dark' (Frederick Hollander), 'Zing A Little Zong', 'No Love, No Nothin'' (both **Harry Warren**) and an often-overlooked little gem, written with **Jerome Kern**, 'In Love In Vain'. Many of Robin's best Hollywood songs were written with composer **Ralph Rainger**. This collaboration produced 'Please', 'Here Lies Love', 'Give Me Liberty Or Give Me Love', 'June In January', 'With Every Breath I Take', 'Here's Love In Your Eye', 'Blue Hawaii', 'Here You Are' and two songs which became theme songs for two of America's best-known comedians, Jack Benny and **Bob Hope**, 'Love In Bloom' and 'Thanks For The Memory'. They were featured in pictures such as *The Big Broadcast* (1932), *International House*, *Little Miss Marker*, *Shoot The Works*, *She Loves Me Not*, *Here Is My Heart*, *The Big Broadcast Of 1936*, *The Big Broadcast Of 1937*, *Palm Springs*, *Three Cheers For Love*, *Rhythm On The Range*, *Artists And Models*, *College Holiday*, *St. Louis Blues*, *The Big Broadcast Of 1938*, *Give Me A Sailor*, *Paris Honeymoon*, *Moon Over Miami*, *My Gal Sal*, *Footlight Serenade*, and *Coney Island* (1943). After Rainger's death in 1943, Robin collaborated with other composers including **Jule Styne**, Harry Warren, **Arthur Schwartz** and **Sigmund Romberg**. With Styne he wrote the score for the memorable stage musical *Gentlemen Prefer Blondes*, which included songs such as 'Bye Bye, Baby', 'A Little Girl From Little Rock' and 'Diamonds Are A Girl's Best Friend'. He also worked on several films including *The Gang's All Here*, *Centennial Summer*, *The Time, The Place And The Girl*, *Casbah*, *Meet Me After The Show*, *Just For You*, *Latin Lovers*, and *Small Town Girl*. Out of these came notables songs such as

'Paducah', 'The Lady In The Tutti-Frutti Hat', 'Oh, But I Do', 'A Gal In Calico', A Rainy Night In Rio', 'What's Good About Goodbye?', 'It Was Written In The Stars', 'My Flaming Heart', 'Lost In Loveliness', and Love Is The Funniest Thing'. The last two numbers were the result of a partnership with **Sigmund Romberg** on the stage show *The Girl In Pink Tights* (1954), although the score had to be completed by Don Walker after Romberg's death. In 1982, in sprightly disregard of his age, Robin appeared in New York in a presentation of many of his songs.

Robins

An R&B vocal group from Los Angeles, California, USA, formed in 1947. Original members were 'Ty' Terrell Leonard, twins Billy and Roy Richard, and Bobby Nunn. The group recorded some tracks for Aladdin before they hooked up with bandleader **Johnny Otis** in 1949, when they won second place at a talent contest at his club, The Barrelhouse. Their first chart record, in 1950 for Savoy Records, was the mid-tempo 'If It's So, Baby' (number 10 R&B), recorded with the Johnny Otis Orchestra. It's excellent ballad b-side, 'If I Didn't Love You So', received much more airplay in many areas. Otis also used the Robins to back his young prodigy, **Little Esther**, on the hit 'Double Crossing Blues' in 1950. The Savoy recordings were done in a bluesy modulated style of the period and did not set the Robins apart from other groups. During 1950-52 the group recorded for Modern, RPM (as the Nic Nacs), and Recorded In Hollywood without notable success. In 1953 the Robins with the addition of tenor lead Grady Chapman were signed to **RCA** and came under the production aegis of an upcoming songwriting team of **Leiber And Stoller**. Jerry Leiber and Mike Stoller began to radically transform the Robins into a proto-rock 'n' roll group with an exuberant beat-infected sound. No hits resulted on **RCA**, but in 1954 with a move to Leiber and Stoller's own Spark label, and with Carl Gardner having replaced Grady Chapman, the Robins found success with 'Riot In Cell Block No. 9'. The song using the menacing bass of **Richard Berry** and machine-gun sound-effects was one of the most controversial records of 1954. It sold well in California and a few other locales but failed to chart nationally because of poor distribution. The group successfully followed with another regional hit, 'Framed' (1954), and in 1955 hit with 'Smokey Joe's Cafe'. Fast rising independent **Atlantic Records** took notice of sales in California and assumed distribution and made it a national hit (number 10 R&B) on their **Atco** subsidiary. The Robins, however, split up, with Gardner and Nunn joining with Billy Guy and Leon Hughes to form the **Coasters** to record for Atlantic. Under the aegis of producers Leiber And Stoller the Coasters flourished. The Robins - with newcomer H.B. Barnum and with

returning Grady Chapman - continued to record, on the Whippet and other labels, albeit unsuccessfully, until breaking up sometime in the early 60s.
Album: *Rock 'N' Roll With The Robins* (Whippet 1958). Compilations: *The Best Of The Robins* (GNP-Crescendo 1975, collects their Whippet recordings), *The Roots Of Rock 'N Roll* (Savoy Jazz 1987, collects their Savoy recordings).

Robinson, 'Lonesome' Jimmy Lee

b. 30 April 1931, Chicago, Illinois, USA. In the 40s, Robinson played blues guitar on Chicago's Maxwell Street, occasionally working with **Eddie Taylor**. In the 50s he worked in the clubs, associating with artists including **Freddie King**, **Elmore James**, and **Magic Sam**. He became an in-demand session player, both as a bassist and guitarist, and recorded under his own name for the Bandera label in the early 60s. He toured Europe with the *American Folk Blues Festival* in 1965 and again in 1975 with the *American Blues Legends*, recording on both occasions.
Albums: *Chicago Jump* (1979, Bandera recordings), two tracks, plus backing other artists *American Blues Legends '75* (1975).

Robinson, Alvin

b. 1937, d. 24 January 1989. Robinson was a New Orleans-based session guitarist, Robinson secured a minor hit in 1964 with a recording of a **Chris Kenner** song, 'Something You Got'. The single was released on Tiger Records, a short-lived outlet owned by **Jerry Leiber** and **Mike Stoller**, who then took Robinson to their next venture, **Red Bird**. His first release there, 'Down Home Girl', was an inspired amalgamation of New York pop and Crescent City R&B. Later covered by the **Rolling Stones**, Robinson's single was one of the finest to appear on this impressive label. It was followed by a reshaped version of 'Let The Good Times Roll', but the artist was unable to score another success. Robinson moved to the west coast in 1969 and was one of several expatriot musicians who played on **Dr. John**'s New Orleans 'tribute' album, *Gumbo*. He returned to New Orleans in 1985 and died in 1989.
Album: *Shine On* (1989).

Robinson, Banjo Ikey

b. 28 July 1904, Dublin, Virginia, USA. Despite a brief stint with **Jelly Roll Morton**, recording with **Clarence Williams**, and providing superb single-string guitar on the records of **Georgia White**, most of Robinson's work was on the borderline between jazz and popular music. He worked for **Wilbur Sweatman** and **Noble Sissle** in New York, and was a member of the **Hokum Boys**. In Chicago, he played with **Carroll Dickerson** and Erskine Tate before forming his own band in the 40s. He has continued to be active in music, though on a diminishing scale.

Robinson's guitar and banjo work is fast, precise and elaborate, and his singing is likewise clearly enunciated. An all-round entertainer, Robinson, though black, is reminiscent of such black-influenced white musicians as Ukulele Ike (**Cliff Edwards**).
Album: *Banjo Ikey Robinson* (1986).

Robinson, Bill 'Bojangles'

b. 25 May 1878, Richmond, Virginia, USA, d. 25 November 1949. As a child Robinson worked in racing stables, nursing a desire to become a jockey. He danced for fun and for the entertainment of others, first appearing on stage at the age of eight. Three years later he decided that dancing was likely to prove a more lucrative career than horseback riding. He became popular on the black vaudeville circuit and also appeared in white vaudeville as a 'pick', from pickaninny, where his dancing skills gave a patina of quality to sometimes second-rate white acts. As his reputation grew so did his prominence in showbusiness. In 1921 while working at the Palace in New York, he danced up and down the stairs leading from the stage to the orchestra pit and out of this developed his famous 'stair dance'. Although Robinson was not the first to dance on stairs, he refined the routine until it was one of the most spectacular events in the world of vernacular dance. Towards the end of the decade, though he was now 60-years-old, he was a huge success in the smash-hit production of Lew Leslie's *Blackbirds Of 1928*. In the mid-30s he appeared at nightclubs in revues, musical comedies and other stage shows, amongst which was *The Hot Mikado*. He was so active in these years that he sometimes played different shows in different theatres on the same night. Robinson had no doubts that he was the best at what he did, a self-confidence that some took to be arrogance and which was mixed with a sometimes brooding depression at the fact that, because he was black, he had to wait until he was in his 60s before he could enjoy the fame and fortune given to less talented white dancers. In fact, he appears to have been a remarkably generous man and in addition to his massive work-load, he never refused to appear at a benefit for those artists who were less successful or ailing. It has been estimated that in one year he appeared in a staggering 400 benefits. In 1930 Robinson had made a film, *Dixiana*, but it was not until he went to Hollywood in the middle of the decade that he made a breakthrough in this medium.
He danced in a string of popular films, including some with **Shirley Temple**. By 1937 Robinson was earning $6,600 a week for his films, a strikingly high sum for a black entertainer in Hollywood at the time. In 1943 he played his first leading role in *Stormy Weather*, an all-black musical in which he starred opposite **Lena Horne**. Despite being in his early 70s when he made the film he performed his stair dance and even if he was outglossed by the **Nicholas Brothers**, his was a remarkable performance. In addition to dancing, Robinson also sang in a light, ingratiating manner, memorably recording 'Doing The New Low Down' in 1932 with **Don Redman** And His orchestra. Although his high salary meant that he was estimated to have earned more than $2 million during his career, Robinson's generosity was such that when he died in November 1949 he was broke. Half a million people lined the funeral route of the man who was known with some justification as the Mayor of Harlem. In 1993, a potential Broadway show entitled *Bojangles*, with a book by Douglas Jones and a score by **Charles Strouse** and the late **Sammy Cahn**, was being workshopped in various provincial theatres.
Further reading: *Mister Bojangles*, Jim Haskins and N.R Mitgang.

Robinson, Bobby

Robinson opened a record shop in Harlem, New York City, USA shortly after World War II, and became an authority on the music scene. His advice was sought by many independent labels. In November 1951 he formed his first record company, Robin Records - which swiftly became Red Robin Records when a southern independent of the same name threatened legal action. He began producing and releasing records by such artists as Morris Lane, **Tiny Grimes** and **Red Prysock**, but found greater success with the birth of the New York doo-wop groups, and such acts as the Mello Moods, Vocaleers and the Du Droppers. Red Robin was dissolved in 1956, but many more labels were to follow through to the 60s - Whirlin Disc, Fury, Fire, Fling, Enjoy, and Everlast - mainly issuing classic vocal group numbers by such as the Channels, **Velvets**, Scarlets, Teenchords, the **Delfonics** and **Gladys Knight And the Pips**. These labels occasionally achieved success with single R&B stars like **Wilbert Harrison** ('Kansas City'), Buster Brown ('Fannie Mae'), **Bobby Marchan** ('There Is Something On Your Mind'), **Lee Dorsey** ('Ya Ya'), **Lightnin' Hopkins**, **Elmore James** and **King Curtis**.
In the early 70s Bobby Robinson started a new label, Front Page Records and reactivated his Enjoy label.

Robinson, Fenton

b. 23 September 1935, Greenwood, Mississippi, USA. Although held in high regard by both his peers and audiences, Robinson's mellow voice and jazz-oriented guitar-playing remains a rare pleasure. Robinson took an interest in guitar on hearing **T-Bone Walker's** Black & White records in 1946 and was helped by local musician, Sammy Hampton. In 1951 he moved to Memphis and received tuition from Charles McGowan, guitarist in Billy 'Red' Love's band. In 1953 he moved to Little Rock, Arkansas to play with Love and Eddie Snow. He formed a band with Larry Davis, then a drummer but later a bass player and guitarist. Robinson made his recording debut in Memphis in 1955, 'Tennessee Woman', for **Lester Bihari's** Meteor. Two years later, he and Davis recorded for Duke Records in Houston, playing on each other's tracks. Robinson's four Duke records included a remake of 'Tennessee Woman', 'Mississippi Steamboat' and the first version of his most famous song, 'As The Years Go By'. In the 60s, he moved to Chicago and made singles for U.S.A., Palos (his other blues standard, 'Somebody Loan Me A Dime'), Giant and Sound Stage 7. During the 70s, he made two critically-acclaimed albums for Alligator, *Somebody Loan Me A Dime* and *I Hear Some Blues Downstairs*, before personal problems and disillusionment kept him out of music. One album, *Blues In Progress* was made in 1984 with guitarist/arranger Reggie Boyd. In 1989, he headlined the Burnley Blues Festival and recorded the *Special Road* in Holland. Not just a bluesman, Robinson seems too individual a musician to pander to blunatic audiences and his career suffers thereby.

Selected albums: *Somebody Loan Me A Dime* (1974), *I Hear The Blues Downstairs* (1977), *Special Road* (1989), *Mellow Fellow* (1993).

Robinson, Freddie

b. c.30s, Arkansas, USA. As 'Fred Robertson' he recorded with **Little Walter** (Jacobs) in the late 50s and by the early 60s he had become a noted guitarist in Chicago, where he recorded for the Queen, M-Pac/One-Der-Ful, and **Chess** labels. After moving to Los Angeles around 1968, he maintained his links with producer/musician Milton Bland (aka Monk Higgins) and recorded in a jazz context for World Pacific in 1969 and as blues and soul guitarist for Enterprise (the **Stax** subsidiary label) a few years later. In 1977 he recorded for ICA, with which he also worked as a session guitarist, writer, and arranger, mostly in a soul vein. In the 80s he toured and record with **Louis Myers**.

Albums: *The Coming Atlantis* (1969), *At The Drive-In* reissued as *Black Fox* (1972), *Off The Cuff* (1973).

Robinson, Jim

b. 25 December 1890, Deer Range, Louisiana, USA, d. 4 May 1976. After playing guitar for a number of years, Robinson took up the trombone while serving in the US Army during World War I. In the immediate post-war years he played regularly in New Orleans, and was good enough to be hired by such leading New Orleans musicians as **Kid Rena** and **Sam Morgan**. He later played in the bands of **John Handy** and **Kid Howard** but, like many other New Orleans jazzmen, he retained his 'day job'. In his case he worked as a longshoreman well into the 30s. The **Revival Movement** persuaded him that he could make his

living playing jazz and in the 40s he played with **Bunk Johnson** and in the 50s was a regular member of **George Lewis**'s band. He toured extensively in the 60s, with **Billie** and **De De Pierce**, Percy Humphrey and the Preservation Hall Jazz Band. An outstanding ensemble player, Robinson played with great attack and brought drive and enthusiasm to any band of which he was a member.

Albums: *George Lewis At The San Jacinto Hall* (1964), *Robinson's Jacinto Ballroom Orchestra* (1964), with Percy Humphrey *Climax Rag* (1965), *Economy Hall Breakdown* (1965), *Jim Robinson And Tony Fougerat* (1967), *Living New Orleans Jazz* (1976). Compilations: *Bunk Johnson With George Lewis* (1944), *Jim Robinson And His New Orleans Band* (Center 1992), *Classic New Orleans Jazz Vol 2* (Biograph 1993).

Robinson, John

b. Australia. Robinson's place in Australian rock history is secured as co-writer of the **Blackfeather** song 'Seasons of Change', generally considered an Australian 70s rock classic. However, Robinson's inventive guitar work featured on several other recordings such as the Dave Miller Set (1966-69), Hunger (1971-72), Duck (1972), Tramp (1973), Current (1974-76) and E.G.O. (1979-80). His solo album remains his only output for many years although he is still active, teaching guitar in Sydney (many of his students progressed to well-known Australian bands of the 70s and 80s), and recording at home.

Album: *Pity the Victim* (1974).

Robinson, L.C. 'Good Rockin''

b. Louis Charles Robinson, 15 May 1915, Brenham, Texas, USA, d. 26 September 1976. Robinson began playing guitar at nine years old, and was reputedly taught to play bottleneck style by **Blind Willie Johnson**. Western swing musician **Leon McAuliffe** introduced him to the steel guitar, and Robinson was also a blues fiddler of note and gave **Sugarcane Harris** some lessons on the instrument. L.C. moved to the San Francisco area around 1939, where he often played together with his brother A.C. Robinson. They recorded for the Black And White label in 1945 as the Robinson Brothers. L.C. recorded for Rhythm in the early 50s, for World Pacific in the 60s, and for **Arhoolie** and Bluesway in the 70s, and he accompanied **Mercy Dee Walton** and **John Lee Hooker** on records. He died of a heart attack in September 1976.

Albums: *Ups And Down* (1971), *House Cleanin' Blues* (1974).

Robinson, Perry

b. 17 August 1938, New York City, New York, USA. Robinson grew up in a musical family, his father Earl being a well-known filmscore composer. He started

playing clarinet at the age of eight, graduated from the New York High School Of Music and Art in 1956. From there he went to the School of Jazz at Lennox in Massachusetts (1959), to the Manhattan School of Music between 1961 and 1962 and then studied clarinet with Kalman Black (first clarinettist with the LA Philharmonic) and Eric Simon (at the Mannes Music School). He toured Spain in 1959-60, where he met and played with **Tete Montoliu**. Returning to New York, he formed a trio with **Paul Bley** and **Sunny Murray** in 1962, although his debut recording, *Funk Dumpling*, from the same year, featured **Kenny Barron**, **Henry Grimes** and **Paul Motian**. Robinson next played with **Bill Dixon** and **Archie Shepp**, recording on the latter's classic *Mama Too Tight* (1967), then he joined **Roswell Rudd**'s Primordial Quartet in 1968. He also appeared in a trio with bassist **David Izenzon** and drummer Randy Kaye. He was a member of **Charlie Haden**'s Liberation Music Orchestra, recording on their 1969 debut album and, as an occasional member of the **Jazz Composer's Orchestra**, he played on **Carla Bley**'s *Escalator Over The Hill* in 1974. In 1973 he played with **Dave Brubeck** and also performed regularly with German vibes player **Gunter Hampel** and his Galaxie Dream Band (1972-78). In 1978 he recorded *Kundalini* with Brazilian percussionist **Nana Vasconcelos** and Indian tabla-player Badal Roy, a particularly successful encounter between jazz dexterity and world music textures. Robinson is the missing link between the clarinet playing of **Pee Wee Russell** and new bloods like Don Byron: an essential musician.
Albums: *Funk Dumpling* (1962), with Archie Shepp *Mama Too Tight* (1967), with Gunter Hampel *Cosmic Dancer* (1975), *The Traveller* (1977), with Nana Vasconcelos, Badal Roy *Kundalini* (1978).

Robinson, Prince

b. 7 June 1907, Portsmouth, Virginia, USA, d. 23 July 1960. An exceptionally gifted tenor saxophonist, Robinson was a close contemporary of **Coleman Hawkins** and was consequently overshadowed for much of his career. Doubling on clarinet, Robinson played with several bands in New York in the 20s, including those led by **Elmer Snowden** and **Duke Ellington** before joining **McKinney's Cotton Pickers** where he remained, with a short break, for seven years. In the late 30s and early 40s he worked in a succession of bands including those of Blanche Calloway, **Willie Bryant**, **Roy Eldridge**, **Louis Armstrong** and **Lucky Millinder**. He also played in one of **Teddy Wilson**'s bands accompanying **Billie Holiday** on a 1937 record date. From the mid-40s until 1952 he was with the **Claude Hopkins** band. Thereafter he led his own groups and also played with **Red Allen**. A gifted player on both instruments with an especially robust and exciting tenor style, Robinson

has had only limited opportunities to play solos on his many record dates. He died in 1960.
Albums: *McKinney's Cotton Pickers Vols 1/2* (1928-29), *The Chronological Teddy Wilson And His Orchestra 1936-1937* (1936-37), *Roy Eldridge At The Arcadia Ballroom, August/September 1939* (1939).

Robinson, Roscoe

b. 22 May 1928, Dumont, Alabama, USA. Robinson was a soul and gospel singer in the mid-60s and 70s. After moving to Gary, Indiana at the age of 10, Robinson's singing career began in the early 40s with the gospel group Joiner's Five Trumpets and he became a member of various gospel groups throughout the rest of the decade. He first recorded for Trumpet Records in 1951 with the Southern Sons. In the early 50s, after a spell in the army, he continued working with gospel groups including the Five Blind Boys Of Mississippi. Switching to secular music in 1965, Robinson first recorded 'What Makes A Man Do Wrong' for Tuff Records. His biggest hit came in 1966 with 'That's Enough', a Top 10 R&B single for Wand Records. Moving over to the Sound Stage 7 label in 1967 did not yield any chart successes and there was one final R&B chart single in 1969 on **Atlantic Records**. In 1971, Robinson signed Stan Lewis' Jewel/Paula/Ronn concern, and six singles for Paula appeared over the next two years, while a fine gospel album was released on Jewel in 1972. It was gospel which reclaimed Robinson after this with outings on Gospel Roots in 1977, a re-association with the Original Five Blind Boys on their 1982 Peace International album, and a fine solo gospel set for Savoy the following year.
Albums: *He Still Lives In Me* (1972), *Time To Live* (1977), *High On Jesus* (1983). Compilation: *Why Must It End* (1987, Sound Stage 7 and Paula secular recordings).

Robinson, Smokey

b. William Robinson, 19 February 1940, Detroit, USA. A founding member of the **Miracles** at Northern High School, Detroit, in 1955, Robinson became one of the leading figures in the local music scene by the end of the decade. His flexible tenor voice, which swooped easily into falsetto, made him the group's obvious lead vocalist, and by 1957 he was composing his own variations on the R&B hits of the day. That year he met **Berry Gordy**, who was writing songs for R&B star **Jackie Wilson**, and looking for local acts to produce. Vastly impressed by Robinson's affable personality and promising writing talent, Gordy took the teenager under his wing. He produced a series of Miracles singles in 1958 and 1959, all of which featured Smokey as composer and lead singer, and leased them to prominent R&B labels. In 1960 he signed the Miracles to his **Motown** stable, and began to groom Robinson as his second-in-command. In Motown's early days, Robinson was involved in every facet of the company's operations, writing, producing and making his own records, helping in the business of promotion and auditioning many of the scores of young hopefuls who were attracted by Gordy's growing reputation as an entrepreneur. Robinson had begun his career as a producer by overseeing the recording of the Miracles' 'Way Over There', and soon afterwards he was charged with developing the talents of **Mary Wells** and the **Supremes**. Wells soon became Robinson's most successful protegee: Smokey wrote and produced a sophisticated series of hit singles for her between 1962 and 1964. These records, like 'You Beat Me To The Punch', 'Two Lovers' and 'My Guy', demonstrated his growing confidence as a writer, able to use paradox and metaphor to transcend the usual banalities of the teenage popular song. A measure of Robinson's influence over Wells' career is the fact that she was unable to repeat her chart success after she elected to leave Motown, and Robinson, in 1964.

Although Robinson was unable to turn the Supremes into a hit-making act, he experienced no such failure in his relationship with Motown's leading male group of the mid-60s, the **Temptations**. Between 1964 and 1965, Smokey was responsible for the records that established their reputation, writing lyrical and rhythmic songs of a calibre which few writers in pop music have equalled since. 'The Way You Do The Things You Do' set the hit sequence in motion, followed by the classic ballad 'My Girl' (later equally popular in the hands of **Otis Redding**), the dance number 'Get Ready', 'Since I Lost My Baby' and the remarkable 'It's Growing', which boasted a complex lyric hinged around a series of metaphorical images. During the same period, Robinson helped to create two of **Marvin Gaye**'s most enduring early hits, 'Ain't That Peculiar' and 'I'll Be Doggone'. Throughout the 60s, Smokey Robinson combined this production and A&R work with his own career as leader of the Miracles. He married fellow group member Claudette Rogers in 1959, and she provided the inspiration for Miracles hits like 'You've Really Got A Hold On Me' and 'Oooh Baby Baby'. During the mid-60s, Robinson was apparently able to turn out high-quality songs to order, working with a variety of collaborators including fellow Miracle Ronnie White, and Motown guitarist Marv Tarplin. As the decade progressed, **Bob Dylan** referred to Robinson apparently without irony, as 'America's greatest living poet': as if to justify this assertion, Robinson's lyric writing scaled new heights on complex ballads like 'The Love I Saw In You Was Just A Mirage' and 'I Second That Emotion'. From 1967 onwards, Robinson was given individual credit on the Miracles' releases. For the next two years, their commercial fortunes went into a slide, which was righted when their 1965 recording of 'The Tracks Of My Tears' became a major hit in Britain in 1969, and

the four-year-old 'The Tears Of A Clown' achieved similar success on both sides of the Atlantic in 1970. At the end of the decade, Smokey briefly resumed his career as a producer and writer for other acts, collaborating with the **Marvelettes** on 'The Hunter Gets Captured By The Game', and the **Four Tops** on 'Still Water'. Business concerns were occupying an increasing proportion of his time, however, and in 1971 he announced that he would be leaving the Miracles the following year, to concentrate on his role of Vice-President of the Motown corporation. A year after the split, Smokey launched his solo career, scoring a hit single with 'Sweet Harmony', an affectionate tribute to his former group, and issuing the excellent *Smokey*. The album included the epic 'Just My Soul Responding', a biting piece of social comment about the USA's treatment of blacks and American Indians.

Robinson maintained a regular release schedule through the mid-70s, with one new album arriving every year. Low-key and for the most part lushly produced, they made little impact, though Robinson's songwriting was just as consistent as it had been in the 60s. He continued to break new lyrical ground, striking the banner for non-macho male behaviour on 1974's 'Virgin Man', and giving name to a new style of soft soul on 1975's *A Quiet Storm*. Singles like 'Baby That's Backatcha' and 'The Agony And The Ecstasy' sold well on the black market, but failed to achieve national airplay in the States, while in Britain Robinson was recorded as a left-over from the classic era of Motown. His first film soundtrack project, *Big Time* in 1977, won little praise, and it appeared as if his creative peak was past. Instead, he hit back in 1979 with 'Cruisin', his biggest chart success since 'The Tears Of A Clown' nine years earlier. A sensuous ballad in the musical tradition of his 60s work, the record introduced a new eroticism into his writing, and restored faith in his stature as a contemporary performer. Two years later, he scored his first UK number 1 with 'Being With You', a touching love song which came close to equalling that achievement in the States. 'Tell Me Tomorrow' enjoyed more Stateside success in 1982, and Robinson settled into another relaxed release schedule, which saw him ride out the 80s on a pattern of regular small hits and consistent album sales. Smokey was contributing significantly less new material, however, and his 1988 autobiography, *Smokey*, revealed that he had been battling against cocaine addiction for much of the decade. Although his marriage to Claudette failed, he returned to full health and creativity, and enjoyed two big hits in 1987, 'Just To See Her' and 'One Heartbeat'. Voted into the Rock And Roll Hall Of Fame in 1988, Smokey Robinson is now one of the senior figures in popular music, a writer and producer still best remembered for his outstanding work in the 60s, but who has seldom betrayed the responsibility of that legacy since then.

Albums: *Smokey* (1973), *Pure Smokey* (1974), *A Quiet Storm* (1975), *Smokey's Family Robinson* (1976), *Deep In My Soul* (1977), *Big Time* (1977), *Love Breeze* (1978), *Smokin'* (1978), *Where There's Smoke?* (1979), *Warm Thoughts* (1980), *Being With You* (1981), *Yes It's You Lady* (1982), *Touch The Sky* (1983), *Blame It On Love* (1984), *Essar* (1984), *Smoke Signals* (1985), *One Heartbeat* (1987), *Love, Smokey* (1990). Compilation: with the Miracles *The Greatest Hits* (1992).

Further reading: *Smokey*, Smokey Robinson with David Ritz.

Robinson, Spike

b. Henry Berthold Robinson, 16 January 1930, Kenosha, Wisconsin, USA. Beginning on alto saxophone in his early teenage years, Robinson soon discovered that it was hard to make a living playing the kind of music he wanted to play. So, in 1948 he joined the US Navy as a musician and by 1950 was based in the UK. He was soon regularly jamming at London's Club Eleven, Downbeat Club and Studio 51 with leading UK beboppers, including Tommy Pollard and **Victor Feldman**. He made a few records for Carlo Krahmer's Esquire label but eventually was transferred home and demobilized. Unhappy with the music scene in the Chicago area, he took advantage of the GI Bill to study electronic engineering at university. For most of the next 30 years he lived and worked in Colorado, eventually taking up music again, this time playing tenor saxophone and working nights at local clubs. A constant musical companion of these times was **Dave Grusin**. In 1981 Robinson recorded for the first time since his London sessions, in a band led by Feldman. Encouraged to visit the UK by a British fan, in 1984 Robinson began a series of tours which were so successful that he took early retirement from his engineering job to turn to a full-time career in music. Throughout the rest of the 80s and into the early 90s, he has played at clubs and festivals throughout the UK, Europe and in various parts of the USA, making his New York debut at Christmas 1990. A succession of superb record albums, most as leader but some with artists such as **Louis Stewart**, **Harry Edison**, **Al Cohn**, **Roy Williams** and **Claude Tissendier**, have attracted high critical and public praise. Despite his bebop beginnings, the mature musician who emerged in the 80s from self-imposed exile is a consummate ballad player who eagerly explores the endless archives of the Great American Song Book. His rhapsodic, breathy style is instantly identifiable and the effortless loping swing of everything he plays has helped to make Robinson into one of the outstanding tenor saxophonists of his generation. In the early 90s Robinson was touring extensively from a UK base, recording many albums and headlining at clubs and festivals in Europe and the USA.

Selected albums: *The Guv'nor* (1951), with Victor Feldman *The Music Of Harry Warren* (1981), *Spike Robinson At Chesters Vols 1 & 2* (Hep 1984), *London Reprise* (1984), with Roy Williams *It's A Wonderful World* (1985), *The Gershwin Collection* (1987), with Al Cohn *Henry B. Meets Alvin G.* (1987), with Elaine Delmar *In Town* (Hep 1987), *The Odd Couple* (Capri 1988), with Louis Stewart *Three For The Road* (Hep 1989), with Harry Edison *Jusa Bit O' Blues Vols 1 & 2* (Capri 1989), with Claude Tissendier *Saxomania Presenting Spike Robinson* (1989), *Stairway To The Stars* (Hep 1990), *One Man In His Time* (1991), *Spike Robinson And George Masso Play Arlen* (Hep 1992), *Reminiscin'* (Capri 1993).

Robinson, Sugar Chile

b. c.1940, Detroit, Michigan, USA. Robinson was essentially a novelty act. His precocious feel for boogie and his squeaky, pre-pubescent voice singing incongruously salacious lyrics charmed audiences on both sides of the Atlantic. His earliest appearances were with **Frankie Carle**, leader of a highly successful big band. By 1946 Sugar Chile was playing for President Truman and jamming with **Lionel Hampton**. After signing to **Capitol** in 1949 he had hits both in the USA and the UK outselling competition such as **Louis Jordan** and **Wynonie Harris**. His cover of Jordan's 'Caldonia' was one of the biggest sellers in 1949. Throughout this time he broke box office records with attendances rivalling those drawn by **Duke Ellington**. In 1951 he appeared at the London Palladium. However, by 1952 the novelty had worn thin, and amid rumours that he was in reality a midget in his late teens, he sank into total obscurity.

Albums: *Go Boy Go* (1984), *Junior Jump* (1986).

Robinson, Tom

b. 1 July 1950, Cambridge, England. Robinson's wayward youth included the study of oboe, clarinet and bass guitar, and a spell in Finchden Manor, a readjustment centre in Kent, where he met guitarist Danny Kurstow with whom he formed his first group, Davanq, in 1971. Two years later Robinson formed **Café Society** with Hereward Kaye and Ray Doyle and they signed to the **Kinks**' Konk label. In 1974, *Café Society* was recorded with help from **Ray Davies** and Mick Avory. During the taping of an intended second album, administrative discord was manifested in what was now the Tom Robinson Band's on-stage mocking of Davies, and, later, the Kinks' reciprocal dig at Robinson in a 1977 b-side, 'Prince Of The Punks' - with whom Robinson's band had been categorized (not entirely accurately) when contracted by **EMI Records** the previous year. Konk, nevertheless, retained publishing interests in 13 Robinson numbers. Some of these were selected for TRB's *Power In The Darkness* debut and attendant UK Top 40 singles - notably the catchy '2468 Motorway'. Backed by keyboardist Mark Ambler, drummer 'Dolphin' Taylor plus the faithful

Kurstow, lead singer Robinson's active support of many radical causes riddled his lyrical output, but the gravity of 'Summer Of 79' and 'Up Against The Wall' was mitigated by grace-saving humour. The quartet's *Rising Free* EP, for example, contained the singalong 'Glad To Be Gay' anthem - which was also a highlight of both TRB's 1978 benefit concert for the Northern Ireland Gay Rights and One Parent Families Association, and Robinson's solo set during a Lesbian and Gay Rights March in Washington in 1979, shortly after parting with his band (Taylor going on to **Stiff Little Fingers**). This followed a disappointing critical and market reaction to *TRB2* (supervised by **Todd Rundgren**) - on which the sloganeering was overdone and the musical performance tepid. While Kurstow joined ex-**Sex Pistol** Glen Matlock in the Spectres, Robinson led the short-lived Section 27 and began songwriting collaborations with **Elton John** and **Peter Gabriel**. By 1981 he had relocated to Berlin to record the solo *North By Northwest* and work in alternative cabaret and fringe theatre. Professionally, this period proved fruitful - with 1982's strident 'War Baby' and evocative 'Atmospherics' in the UK Top 40, and a revival of **Steely Dan**'s 'Ricki Don't Lose That Number', from *Hope And Glory*, which fared as well as the original in the same chart. However, when *Still Loving You* produced no equivalent of even this modest triumph Robinson, now a contented father, regrouped his original band. Subsequent engagements were viewed by many as akin to a nostalgia revue - and certainly several old favourites were evident on the Berlin concert set, *Last Tango*. However, Robinson's lyrical eloquence argues that further solid work may lie ahead now he has returned to recording with **Cooking Vinyl Records**.

Albums: *Power In The Darkness* (Harvest 1978), *TRB2* (Harvest 1979). With Sector 27: *Sector 27* (Fontana 1980). Solo: *North By Northwest* (Fontana 1982), *Hope And Glory* (RCA 1984), *Still Loving You* (RCA 1986), *Last Tango* (Line 1989), with Jakko Jakzyk *We Never Had It So Good* (Musidisc 1990), *Living In A Boom Time* (Cooking Vinyl 1992), *Love Over Rage* (Cooking Vinyl 1994). Compilations: *Tom Robinson Band* (EMI 1981), *Cabaret '79* (Panic 1982).

Robison, Carson Jay

b. 4 August 1890, Oswego, near Chetopa, Labette County, Kansas, USA, d. 24 March 1957. Robison's father was a champion fiddle player and his mother a pianist and singer, and, by the age of 14, Robison was competent enough to play the guitar professionally. Robison left home and worked with various dance bands and radio stations developing into a multi-instrumentalist. **Victor Records** were impressed when he made his first recording as a backing musician for Wendell Hall and employed him on a regular basis.

They particularly liked his two-tone whistle which was used to good effect on Felix Arnolt's piano novelty, 'Nola'. Between 1924 and 1928, Robison was associated with **Vernon Dalhart**, singing tenor harmony and playing guitar. They recorded 'The Wreck Of The Number 9', 'Little Green Valley', 'My Blue Ridge Mountain Home', 'Golden Slippers' and many topical songs. Robison recorded with Frank Luther (b. Francis Luther Crow, 4 August 1905, Kansas, USA) as Bud And Joe Billings and released 'Will The Angels Play Their Harps For Me?' and 'The Wanderer's Warning', both of which became popular in Britain in 1929, and 'Barnacle Bill'. In 1932 Carson Robison And The Buckeroos became the first country band to tour the UK. They made records here, entertained royalty and played London's Berkeley Hotel for 13 weeks. Proud of his success, Robison changed his band's name to the Pioneers and, following a commercial series on **Radio Luxembourg**, they became Carson Robison And The Oxydol Pioneers. Robison also toured the UK in 1936 and 1939 and also played in Australasia. During World War II, Robison maintained his popularity by writing topical songs which ridiculed Hitler, Mussolini and Hirohito such as 'We're Gonna Have To Slap That Dirty Little Jap (And Uncle Sam's The Man That Can Do It)'. 'Turkey In the Straw' was rated the most popular song of 1942, and his songbooks included 'The Runaway Train', 'Carry Me Back To The Lone Prairie', 'Take Me Back To My Boots And Saddle' and 'Empty Saddles'. In 1947, Robison recorded his narration, 'Life Gets Tee-Jus, Don't It', which was also successful for Peter Lind Hayes. Robison recorded square dance music for **MGM** in the 50s as well as bringing himself up to date with 'Rockin' And Rollin' With Granmaw'. He died in New York on 24 March 1957. Vernon Dalhart was elected to the Country Music Hall Of Fame in 1981 and although Robison played a crucial part in his success, he has yet to be elected himself.

Albums: *Square Dance* (1955), *Life Gets Tee-Jus, Don't It* (1958), *The Immortal Carson Robison* (1978), *Just A Melody* (1980), *Carson J. Robison, The Kansas Jayhawk* (1987).

Robs' Records

UK record label overseen by **New Order** manager Rob Gretton. The breakthrough release was **Sub Sub**'s 'Ain't No Love, Ain't No Use', a storming house track that established both the artist and the company in the 90s. It would sell over 50,000 copies on pre-release alone. It would be followed by records from the **Flamingos** and old Manchester stalwarts **A Certain Ratio**. Despite their commercial rewards, Sub Sub remained happy with the informal nature in which Robs' Records conducted their business. 'There's no corporate cobblers. You're not talking to someone in a suit'.

Roché, Betty

b. 9 January 1920, Wilmington, Delaware, USA. After winning an amateur talent contest in the early 40s, Roché sang with Al Cooper's **Savoy Sultans**. Joining **Duke Ellington** in 1943 she appeared at Carnegie Hall, then, after a brief spell with the **Earl Hines** band, she drifted out of the big time. In 1952 she was back with Ellington, appearing at clubs and concerts and also broadcasting with the band. A further period out of the spotlight followed although she made several albums under her own name in the late 50s and early 60s. After this she again returned to obscurity. An attractive song stylist, Roche was one of the best to work for Ellington, who, after **Ivie Anderson**, was notoriously casual with his choice of vocalists.

Albums: with Duke Ellington *Carnegie Hall Concert: January 1943* (1943), with Ellington *The Duke Is On The Air* (1952), *Take The 'A' Train* (1956), *Singing' And Swingin'* (Original Jazz Classics 1961), *Lightly And Politely* (Original Jazz Classics 1961).

Rochell And The Candles

An R&B vocal group from Los Angeles, California, USA. Members were first tenor lead Johnny Wyatt (b. 1938, Texacali, Texas; d. 1983), tenor lead Rochell Henderson, baritone Melvin Sasso, and bass T. C. Henderson. Their one hit, 'Once Upon A Time' (number 20 R&B, number 26 pop), from 1961, was part of the early 60s neo-doowop phenomenon when doo-wop experienced a resurgence of interest on the charts. The novelty of the falsetto lead of Wyatt plus the name of 'Rochell' gave many listeners the false impression that the group was led by a female. The follow-up, 'So Far Away' (1961), likewise featured Wyatt's high pitched lead, but despite its excellence failed to dent the charts. Other singles followed, both on Swingin' and Challenge, but the Candles could not return to the charts. Their last recording, a sublime remake of the **Olympics**' 'Big Boy Pete' was released in 1964 to an indifferent world. Wyatt went on to become lead of the soul-era group, Johnny And The Expressions, who hit the charts with 'Something I Want To Tell You' in 1966. He also made some singles as a solo artist for Bronco during 1966-67.

Compilation: *The Golden Groups: The Best Of Swingin' Records* (Relic 1985, features 10 tracks by Rochell And The Candles, four by the Hollywood Saxons).

Roches

Sisters Maggie (b. 26 October 1951, Detroit, Michigan, USA) and Terre Roche (b. 10 April 1953, New York City, New York, USA) began singing a mixture of traditional, doo-wop and barbershop quartet songs in New York clubs in the late 60s. Their first recording was as backing singers on **Paul Simon**'s 1972 album, *There Goes Rhymin' Simon*. Through Simon, the duo recorded an album for **CBS** in 1975 which attracted little attention. The following year, the Roches became a trio with the addition of the distinctive voice of younger sister Suzzy (b. New York City, New York, USA) to Terre's soprano and Maggie's deep alto. With Maggie's compositions, by turns whimsical and waspish, featuring strongly they became firm favourites on New York's folk club scene. A **Warner Brothers** recording deal followed and **Robert Fripp** produced the self-titled album, which included compositions by each of the sisters and remains their strongest recording. Among the many lyrical extravaganzas were Maggie's best-known song of infidelity 'The Married Men' (later covered by **Phoebe Snow**), Terre's poignant and autobiographical 'Runs In The Family' and 'We', the trio's **a cappella** opening number at live performances. The highly commercial 'Hammond Song' was arguably the star track (featuring a fine Fripp solo). *Nurds* another Fripp production featured the extraordinary 'One Season' wherein the trio manage to sing harmony almost a cappella but totally (and deliberately) out of tune. (Harmony vocalists will appreciate that this is extremely difficult). *Keep On Doing*, maintained a high standard including a refreshing burst of Handel's 'Hallelujah Chorus' and Maggie's tragic love song 'Losing You'. If the Roches ever had strong desires on the charts *Another World* was potentially the album to do it. Featuring a full rock-based sound this remains an undiscovered gem including the glorious title track and a cover of the **Fleetwoods**' 'Come Softly To Me'. Throughout the 80s, the Roches continued to perform in New York and appeared occasionally at European folk festivals. They also wrote and performed music for theatre productions and the 1988 film *Crossing Delancy*. *Speak* went largely unnoticed in 1989. Their next album was a memorable Christmas gift, *Three Kings*. Containing traditional yuletide songs and carols it displayed clearly the Roches exceptional harmony. *A Dove* in 1992 featured the 'Ing' Song' a brilliant lyrical exercise with every word ending with ing. They remain a highly original unit with a loyal cult following.

Albums: *Seductive Reasoning* (1975), *The Roches* (1979), *Nurds* (1980), *Keep On Doing* (1982), *Another World* (1985), *Speak* (1989), *Three Kings* (1990), *A Dove* (1992).

Rock 'n' Roll High School

Directed by Alan Arkush and produced by exploitation king Roger Corman, *Rock 'n' Roll High School* starred P.J. Soles in yet another reworking of the 'campus' formula. Although released in 1979, the film bore the stylistic trappings of the 50s, grafting contemporary pop styles on a tired plot. Where the **Twist** and surfing had provided past genres, here it was punk, with the Soles' character's love of the **Ramones** the key to the plot. The US quartet played a succession of their best-known songs, including 'Sheena Is A Punk Rocker', 'Pinhead',

'Blitzkrieg Bop' and 'I Wanna Be Sedated', but *Rock 'n' Roll High School* frustratingly failed to exploit the cartoon-like qualities of the group's music and image. Such facets were equally drawn from the era inspiring the film itself. Records by **Devo**, the **Velvet Underground** and **MC5** were also heard on the soundtrack, alongside distinctly non-new wave acts **Fleetwood Mac**, **Wings** and **Chuck Berry**. *Rock 'n' Roll High School* failed to encapsulate punk nor invoke a cross-generation sense of rebellion.

Rock 'n' Roll Revue

Jazz and R&B performers were at the fore of this 1956 film, despite its grossly misleading title. Also known as *Harlem Rock 'n' Roll*, it was shot at New York's fabled **Apollo** Theatre. **Lionel Hampton**, **Duke Ellington** and **Nat 'King' Cole** headed a star-studded cast which also featured the **Clovers**, **Joe Turner** and **Ruth Brown**. Shot in sepia-inspired yellow and brown - known as Wondercolour - the film captures several performers at their peak and provides a fascinating insight to several acts inspiring, but not recording, rock 'n' roll. Curiously, the portion featuring **Dinah Washington** was cut from the UK print, but *Rock 'n' Roll Revue* remains highly interesting feature.

Rock Around The Clock

Fred Sears directed this 1956 second feature, inspired by the reaction generated by **Bill Haley And The Comets**' contribution to *The Blackboard Jungle*. Although not seen on-screen, the group's recording of 'Rock Around The Clock' was heard over the opening credits, provoking riots in cinemas. The same occurred when this film was screened, prompting several local authorities to ban it from municipal screens. The first feature wholly devoted to rock 'n' roll music, *Rock Around The Clock* cast Haley's group as a small-town act that a bank manager tries to turn into a national attraction, despite the efforts of a booking agent to sabotage his plans. The Comets naturally provide the lion's share of the material, including 'Rock A Beatin' Boogie', 'See You Later Alligator' and the title track. The **Platters**, **Little Richard** and **Freddie Bell And His Bellboys** are among the other acts included, as is disc jockey **Alan Freed** in the first of a string of roles in rock 'n' roll films. Although hardly innovatory in terms of plot or acting, for better or worse *Rock Around The Clock* opened the doors for celluloid pop.

Rock City Angels

This blues-based hard rock quintet from the USA were formed by vocalist Bobby Durango and bassist Andy Panik in 1982. After a series of false-starts under the names the Abusers and the Delta Rebels, they settled on the title Rock City Angels, adding guitarists Doug Banx and Mike Barnes and drummer Jackie D. Jukes to complete the line-up. *Young Man's Blues* was an impressive debut. Utilizing full digital technology, it was a double album which featured a superb amalgam of earthy rockers and honest blues numbers. Durango's vocals have a southern twang to them, while the songs themselves combined elements of **Lynyrd Skynyrd**, **Little Feat** and the **Georgia Satellites**. Despite this the album failed commercially and, disillusioned, the band broke-up in 1989. Durango immediately started a new band under his own name.

Album: *Young Man's Blues* (Geffen 1988, double album).

Rock Goddess

Formed by sisters Jody and Julie Turner at the tender age of 13 and nine respectively, even in such infancy Jody proved a good guitarist and Julie showed considerable promise as a drummer. Their father, ran a music shop in Wandsworth, London, which had a rehearsal room next to it. The sisters, along with school friend and budding bassist Tracey Lamb, soon started to put a set together. By 1981 they had recorded their first demo tape and began to play clubs in London, earning a reputation as schoolgirl rockers who could hold their own against more established outfits. They soon attracted the attention of Karine, singer with indie band **Androids Of Mu**, who invited them to contribute one track, 'Make My Night', which she produced, to the all-female compilation album, *Making Waves*. They then set out on tour with Androids Of Mu and the **Gymslips**, with their father now managing them. Through his efforts they acquired a deal with **A&M Records**, and spent most of 1982 writing songs and playing live. The following year they released their debut album, and a single entitled 'My Angel'. With **Girlschool** running out of steam they picked up much of their following and boosted their line-up with Kate Burbela on second guitar. Their follow-up album the same year was a better received product, yet Lamb decided to leave and was replaced by Dee O'Malley, who departed herself in 1986 to start a family. The final album was a good effort but interest in the band had long gone and Jody left to pursue a solo career. In 1988 Lamb joined Girlschool.

Albums: *Rock Goddess* (A&M 1983), *Hell Hath No Fury* (A&M 1983), *Young And Free* (Just In 1987).

Rock Rock Rock

Manifestly another formula 'quickie' made to cash-in on rock 'n' roll, *Rock Rock Rock* nonetheless contains several points of interest to pop historians. This 1957 film, reportedly shot in two weeks, starred Tuesday Weld as the girlfriend of an aspiring entrepreneur who organizes a concert. Famed disc jockey **Alan Freed** makes an obligatory appearance - herein leading an 18-piece band - but *Rock Rock Rock* is notable for the acts it enshrines. **Frankie Lymon And The Teenagers** offer the memorable 'I'm Not A Juvenile Delinquent', while doo-wop acts the **Flamingos** and **Moonglows** perform 'Would I Be Crying' and 'Over And Over Again' respectively. **Chuck Berry** makes his celluloid debut with 'You Can't Catch Me' and vibrant rockabilly act the **Johnny Burnette** Trio roar through 'Lonesome Train' in what was their only appearance on film. **LaVern Baker**, the Three Chuckles and the Bowties are among the others on offer. Ms. Weld contributes 'I Never Had A Sweetheart' and 'Little Blue Wren', but her 'voice' was provided by the then-unknown **Connie Francis**. Much of the material aired in *Rock Rock Rock* was released by the **Chess** label, who advertised the set as the first rock soundtrack album. Although not breaking new grounds as far as plot and style were concerned, the film showcases several seminal acts at the height of their creative powers.

Rock Workshop
Formed in 1970, this fluid but short-lived group featured several of the UK's leading young jazz musicians, and originally included **Harry Beckett**, Bob Downes (saxophone), Bud Parkes and Tony Roberts (woodwind), **Derek Wadsworth**, Alan Greed and Brian Miller (keyboards), Ray Russell (guitar), Daryl Runswick (bass), Alan Rushton and Robin Jones (drums). Several were involved in other, simultaneous projects, notably solo albums by Downes and Russell and session appearances for **Jack Bruce**, **Keef Hartley** and **Alex Harvey**. Wadsworth and Parkes appeared on the latter's solo album, *Roman Wall Blues*, and Harvey reciprocated by singing on *Rock Workshop*. The group's second set, *For The Very Last Time*, featured percussionists Phil Wainman and Tony Uter in place of Jones, while Ginger Harper was added on vocals. The individual members then went their separate ways. *Rock Workshop* in particular remains an underrated gem, featuring Russell's frantic 'Spoin Kop' and the evocative and brassy 'Primrose Hill'. Although both albums have long since been deleted, they represent a bold attempt at fusing what would be termed rock/jazz as opposed to jazz/rock.
Albums: *Rock Workshop* (1970), *For The Very Last Time* (1971).

Rock, Dickie
b. 1946, Cabra, Dublin, Eire. After a spell with Dublin's Melochords, Rock came to prominence on the Irish showband circuit, when he replaced Jimmy Harte as lead vocalist in the **Miami Showband**. With his thin frame and jug ears, Rock seemed the antithesis of the hunky showband pop star as personified by the **Royal Showband**'s **Brendan Bowyer**. However, Rock's deep tenor voice and romantic balladeering rapidly established him as one of the most popular singers in Irish showband history. During 1964, he catapulted to the top of Eire's charts three times with 'There's Always Me', 'I'm Yours' and 'From The

Candy Store On The Corner'. A further array of hits followed in 1965, including two more number 1s: 'Every Step Of The Way' and 'Wishing It Was You'. In 1966, he was chosen to represent Ireland in the Eurovision Song Contest with the plaintive 'Come Back To Stay'. In the wake of his Eurovision adventure, he was featured in an RTE documentary, *Dickie - Portrait Of An Artiste*. The focus of attention on Rock, coupled with his desire for better money, prompted a split in the Miami. By 1967, several of the originals went on to form the **Sands**. A second-generation Miami stayed with Rock until 1972, after which he continued as a soloist. In a chart career spanning 20 years, he achieved a staggering 25 Irish hit records. Despite his enormous popularity in his home country, Rock declined the opportunities to tour abroad. Instead, he continued to earn a substantial living on the lucrative Irish cabaret circuit.
Further reading: *Send 'Em Home Sweating*, Vincent Power.

Rock, Pete
One of rap's most respected producers, only **Marley Marl** is ahead of him on the quality/quantity thresholds. It was the latter that introduced Pete Rock to the world via his WBLS *Marley Marl In Control Show* in 1989. Rock has gone on to work with everyone from forerunners **Heavy D** (his cousin), **Slick Rick**, **EPMD** and **Run DMC** (including their first single, 'Down With The King') to new talents in the shape of **Lords Of The Underground** (actually offering vocals on their 'Flow On') Nas and K-Solo. Other projects include his soundtrack work on *Who's The Man* and *Menace II Society*. His remix roster is almost as impressive, with engagements with **Brand Nubian**, **Public Enemy, House Of Pain, Das EFX, Father** and non-rap artists like **Shabba Ranks** and **Johnny Gill**. Based in Mount Vernon, New York, he went on to join with **C.L. Smooth** for a release under his own name. The album housed the hit single (US 48) 'They Reminisce Over You (T.R.O.Y.)'. He also put together the Untouchables producer network/umbrella organisation for the activities of himself and co-conspirators Eddie F, Dave Hall and Nevelle Hodge.
Albums: With C.L. Smooth: *Mecca & The Soul Brother* (Elektra 1992). *The Main Ingredients* (Elektra 1994).

Rock, Salt And Nails
A product of the embryonic Shetland folk/rock scene, Rock, Salt And Nails are a young, energetic group who smoothly reel and jig. They are currently building up a dedicated, folksy following north of the border. Their island heritage influences everything they write.
Selected album: *Waves* (Iona (1994).

Rock-A-Bye Baby
Frank Tashlin, who directed the seminal rock film ***The***

Girl Can't Help It, took charge of this 1958 feature. It starred comedian Jerry Lewis, former partner of **Dean Martin**, who excelled in zany, 'misfit' roles, notably *The Nutty Professor*. In *Rock-A-Bye Baby* he plays a nanny, responsible for a film star's triplets, who finds time to satirize rock 'n' roll and USA television. The film is largely forgettable, although Lewis does perform a duet, 'In The Land Of La la La', with his 12-year old son, Gary. In the following decade, Gary Lewis became a pop star in his own right as leader of **Gary Lewis And The Playboys** who scored a number 1 US hit with 'This Diamond Ring', succeeding it with six further Top 10 entries.

Rock-A-Teens

Formed in the late 50s in Virginia, USA, the Rock-A-Teens were a sextet comprised of Vic Mizelle, Bill Cook, Bill Smith, Paul Evans, Boo Walke and Eddie Robinson. Best known for their Top 20 1959 semi-instrumental hit 'Woo-Hoo', the group was originally signed to the small Doran label, for which they recorded 'Woo-Hoo', (on which the only vocal sounds are the words 'woo-hoo' shouted repeatedly) and 'Untrue', a vocal number originally intended as the a-side. The record's distribution was overtaken by **Morris Levy** of **Roulette Records** and ascended to number 16 in the USA. The group recorded an album and released a second single called 'Twangy' before disappearing again. Member Bill Smith went on to record for **Chess Records** but the future endeavours of the others is unknown.
Album: *Woo-Hoo* (1960).

Rockers

The name given to the 'militant' double drumming style of reggae that dominated the music from 1975-78. Pioneered by **Sly Dunbar**, the drummer for **Channel One** Studio's in house band the Revolutionaries, it became immediately popular and Sly not only worked for Channel One but also laid rhythms for most of Jamaica's other top producers. Sly worked the drum kit like no-one else and made his presence felt on every tune he recorded, but it was not long before every other drummer in reggae had developed his own variation of the Sly Dunbar style. **Bunny Lee**, **Joe Gibbs**, **Yabby You** and ironically **Coxsone Dodd** (whose original rhythms many of the hit records were based on) all enjoyed success with their versions of the sound. In the ordinary scheme of things all of this would have been of purely parochial interest to reggae fans only, but the rise of Rockers coincided with the first real outside money to ever be invested in Jamaican music - notably from **Island Records** and **Virgin Records**. Both were anxious to capitalize on the then current international success of **Bob Marley And The Wailers**, and the subsequent interest and greater availability of 'roots' reggae meant that the 'Rockers'

sound became both well known and influential worldwide. Much of the musical output of the period sounds more dated now than the originals that were being 'updated' but, as always, the best still sounds as fresh and innovative as when it was first released.
Albums: The Revolutionaries: *Vital Dub, Strictly Rockers*. The Mighty Diamonds: *Right Time* (Well Charge/Virgin 1976). Joe Gibbs And The Professionals: *African Dub All Mighty Chapter Three*.

Rocket 88

This part-time attraction was drawn from the ranks of the UK's finest R&B/jazz musicians. Formed in 1979, the unit revolved around singer/guitarist **Alexis Korner**, bassist/vocalist **Jack Bruce** and three members of the **Rolling Stones**' circle, Ian Stewart (piano), **Bill Wyman** (bass) and Charlie Watts (drums). The unit took its name from a 1951 recording by Jackie Brenson, often cited as the first rock 'n' roll single, although the music offered by this *ad hoc* collective invoked the earlier, boogie-woogie style of **Meade Lux Lewis**. Their lone album, recorded live in Hannover, Germany, included versions of 'St. Louis Blues' and 'Roll 'Em Pete' and, while undeniably low-key, was nonetheless an enthralling glimpse into the artistic preferences of musicians freed from perceived commercial restraints. Korner's premature death ended speculation that Rocket 88 might blossom into a full-time commitment.
Album: *Rocket 88* (1981).

Rockets

Formed in Los Angeles, California in 1967 when Danny Whitten (guitar/vocals), Billy Talbot (bass/vocals) and Ralph Molina (drums/vocals), formerly of the Circle and Danny And The Memories, joined forces with Leon Whitsell (guitar), George Whitsell (guitar) and Sandy Notkoff (violin). *The Rockets* was produced by **Barry Goldberg** and featured a diverse selection of original material, including folk-rock, pop and soul styles. All of the songs, bar two, were written either by Whitten or Leon Whitsell and the contrasts between their approaches enhanced the eclectic nature of the set. The opening track, 'Hole In My Pocket', garnered local interest when issued as a single, and Goldberg subsequently recorded the song on his 1968 solo album. The Rockets had meanwhile disintegrated, but Whitten, Talbot and Molina resurfaced as **Crazy Horse**, backing **Neil Young** on *Everybody Knows This Is Nowhere* (1969). This excellent album included the track 'Running Dry', subtitled 'Requiem For The Rockets', which featured a sterling contribution from Notkoff. The violinist also appeared on several late-period Crazy Horse releases, while George Whitsell rejoined his former colleagues for *Loose* (1971).
Album: *The Rockets* (1968).

Rockhead

Rockhead were put together by producer Bob Rock (b. Robert Jens Rock, 19 April 1954, Winnipeg, Canada), famed for his work with **Bon Jovi**, **Aerosmith**, **Mötley Crüe** and **Metallica**, with Steve Jack (vocals), Jamey Kosh (bass) and Chris Taylor (drums). Rockhead (the producer/guitarist's nickname) had little difficulty in finding a recording deal, with **Richie Sambora** and the **Cult**'s Billy Duffy guesting on their debut, and landed a prestigious European tour support slot with Bon Jovi. All this made the band an easy target for sniping critics, but although *Rockhead* was hardly innovative, it was a solid and, naturally, superbly-produced collection of stadium hard rock which translated well to the stage. The band proved to be a capable live act too, providing Bob Rock with a pleasant diversion from studio work.
Album: *Rockhead* (EMI 1993).

Rockin' Berries

This early 60s UK pop quintet comprised Clive Lea (b. 16 February 1942, Birmingham, England; vocals), Geoffrey Turton (b. 11 March 1944, Birmingham, England; guitar), Bryan Charles 'Chuck' Botfield (b. 11 November 1943, Birmingham, England; guitar), Roy Austin (b. 27 December 1943, Birmingham, England; guitar) and Terry Bond (b. 22 March 1943, Birmingham, England; drums). After beginning as an R&B cover group, they fell under the spell of visiting American **Kim Fowley**, who suggested they cover the **Tokens**' US hit 'He's In Town'. The song hit the Top 5 in late 1964 and was followed by two other hits, 'What In The World's Come Over You' (not to be confused with the **Jack Scott** million seller of the same name) and an excellent reading of the **Reflections**' 'Poor Man's Son', with Lea and Turton on counter vocals. Like several of their contemporaries, the Berries quickly laid the foundations for a career in cabaret by including comedy sketches and parodic impressions of other artists into their act. A minor hit with 'The Water Is Over My Head' in July 1966 concluded their chart run. By 1968 Turton had embarked on a solo career as **Jefferson**, while the group continued on the timeless supper club circuit.
Album: *In Town* (1965). Compilation: *Bowl Of Rockin' Berries* (1988).

Rockin' Dopsie

b. Alton Jay Rubin, 10 February 1932, Carencro, Louisiana, USA, d. 26 August 1993. Following the death of **Clifton Chenier**, Dopsie was acclaimed the new King Of Zydeco and crowned as such by the mayor of Lafayette in January 1988. He taught himself accordion at the age of 14, and in 1955 teamed up with scrubboard player Chester Zeno to work the local club circuit, adapting his name from that of 'Doopsie', a

Chicagoan dancer. In 1969-70 he recorded for the Bon Temps and Blues Unlimited labels, and in 1973 began a successful collaboration with Sonet Records and producer Sam Charters. In 1986, **Paul Simon** featured Dopsie on his classic *Graceland*, and three years later, **Bob Dylan** hired him for another much-acclaimed set, *Oh Mercy*. In 1987, he made *Crowned Prince Of Zydeco* for Maison De Soul and in 1990 was rewarded with a major three-year contract with **Atlantic**. His band, the Twisters, featured his sons Alton (drums) and David Rubin (rub-board), and the legendary zydeco saxophone player John Hart. After his father's death in 1993 from a heart attack, David became known as Rockin' Dopsie Jnr.
Albums: *Clifton Chenier/Rockin' Dupsee* (1970), *Hold On* (1979), *Crowned Prince Of Zydeco* (1987), *Saturday Night Zydeco* (1988), *Zy-De-Co-In* (1989).

Rockin' Sidney

b. Sidney Semien, 9 April 1938, Lebeau, Louisiana, USA. The full range of black South Louisiana music - blues, R&B, swamp pop and zydeco - can be found in the work of Rockin' Sidney, who was born and grew up in the French-speaking part of that state. Many of his records are characterized by a light approach, even his blues tracks frequently opt for melody rather than emotional expression. Nevertheless, he has recorded regularly for over 30 years, from early singles on the local Jin and Goldband labels to albums self-produced in his own studio. In the early 80s, he achieved a wider profile through the success of his song 'Toot Toot'. So far he has not managed to recapture its novelty appeal, despite evident hard work his recent recordings have featured Semien playing all of the instruments. His infectious and accessible songs have done much to widen the appeal of zydeco music in Europe.
Albums: *They Call Me Rockin'* (1975), *Boogie Blues 'N' Zydeco* (1984), *My Toot Toot* (1986), *Creola* (1987), *Crowned Prince Of Zydeco* (1987), *Give Me A Good Time Woman* (1987), *A Celebration Holiday* (1987), *Hotsteppin'* (1987), *My Zydeco Shoes* (1987), *Live With The Blues* (1988), *Mais Yeah Chere* (1993).

Rockingbirds

Six-piece London band playing country rock in the best traditions of **Gram Parsons**. The unit were originally based in a Camden squat before eviction notices forced their departure. The initial line-up comprised Alan Tylor (vocals/guitar), Andy Hackett (guitar), Dave Golding (bass), Dave Morgan (drums; ex-**Loft**), Shaun Reid (percussion/backing vocals) and Patrick Harbuthnot (pedal steel guitar). Their second 45, 'Jonathan Jonathan', was a stirring tribute to **Jonathan Richman**, backed by a cover of the Parsons/**Chris Hillman** tune, 'Older Guys'. They also covered **Tammy Wynette** with guest vocals, unlikely as it may seem, by Leslie of **Silverfish**.

Another notable cover was 'Deeply Dippy' as part of their record company's tribute to the genius of **Right Said Fred**. At the beginning of 1993 they were showcasing material for their second album and taking part in the **Cambridge Folk Festival**, by which time they had already played a significant part in a new-found, critical accomodation of country music. However, the move from **Heavenly Records** proved unfortunate, and after line-up changes (losing Bill Prince to a solo career) they only re-emerged in 1995 with a self-deprecating album (produced by **Edwyn Collins**) for **Cooking Vinyl Records**, whose title said everything about their commercial malaise.

Albums: *The Rockingbirds* (Heavenly 1992), *Whatever Happened To The Rockingbirds* (Cooking Vinyl 1995).

Rockpile

The name Rockpile was derived from a 1972 album by founding vocalist/guitarist **Dave Edmunds**. In 1979 he suspended his solo career by officially joining forces with three musicians who had featured on several albums issued under his own name. Ex-**Brinsley Schwarz** frontman, **Nick Lowe**, bassist Billy Bremner (ex-**Lulu** And The Luvvers) and drummer Terry Williams (ex-**Love Sculpture** - with Edmunds - and **Man**), completed the founding line-up. *Seconds Of Pleasure* fused Edmunds' love of classic rock 'n' roll with Lowe's grasp of quirky pop, but although Rockpile members continued to guest on the pair's solo albums (*Twangin'*/Edmunds; *Nick The Knife*/Lowe), the quartet split up following internal disputes. The two vocalists subsequently pursued independent paths, while Williams eventually joined **Dire Straits**.

Album: *Seconds Of Pleasure* (F-Beat 1980).

Rocksteady

Rocksteady, among the most elegant and rhythmically pleasing of all pop music forms, grew out of **ska,** spanning a period c. 1966-68. Ska's furious high-tempo beat had driven dancers into frenzies in Jamaica for five years by then and a new, more confident breed of singers had emerged in Jamaica: the **Ethiopians**, the **Maytals**, **Ken Boothe**, **Alton Ellis** and the **Wailers**. Ska offered limited possibilities for a singer: you either fought with it or flowed through it, but the chances of you really stamping your personality on a song, in the same way that American soul stars could, were minimal. As Jamaica's singers began to offer more than just the icing on ska's cake, with the idea of being real songwriters with something to say, so the beat slowed to allow them the time to say it. The bass parts took a distinctive character for the first time, leaving a space in the rhythm that came to characterise all of Jamaican music from this point hence.

It is almost impossible to pinpoint when ska actually became rocksteady in the frantic currents of Jamaican music, though certain records such as **Peter Tosh**'s 'I'm The Toughest', the **Wailers**' 'Rasta Put It On' and **Alton Ellis** And The Flames' 'Cry Tough' were rocksteady in all but name before the genre was defined as such. By 1967 the rocksteady era was in full flood, perhaps best epitomised by the sounds emanating from **Duke Reid**'s Treasure Isle Studio in Bond Street, Kingston. Reid's productions were heavily dependent on the arrangements of saxophonist **Tommy McCook**, and together the pair of them created a pantheon of hits from the likes of Alton Ellis, the **Paragons**, the **Melodians** and Joya Landis, that remain unsurpassed today for their sheer melodic strength. Other producers who worked on distinctive rocksteady sides include **Coxsone Dodd**, **Sonia Pottinger** and **Prince Buster**. The shift of emphasis away from costly horn sections meant that more people could now afford to become involved in record production, and many new producers began to make their mark. The rocksteady bubble burst around 1968, when the new, faster, and more manic style of reggae began to emerge. However, the lines between new and old styles of Jamaican music were blurred, and remain so today - reggae's DJ boom was started by **U-Roy**'s use of old rocksteady backing tracks at Treasure Isle; and both **dancehall** and **ragga** styles owe plenty to the format.

Selected albums: Various: *Put It On - Its Rocksteady* (Island 1968), *Rocksteady Coxsone Style* (Studio One 1968), *Get Ready Rock Steady* (Studio One 1968), *Hottest Hits (Vols. 1, 2 & 3)* (Treasure Isle 1979), *Rocksteady Years* (Island 1980), *Mojo Rock Steady* (Heartbeat/Studio One 1994). Alton Ellis: *Best Of* (Studio One 1970).

Rocksteady Crew

These US-based breakdance/hip hop pioneers of the 80s were led by the celebrated Crazy Legs (b. Richie Colon) - one of the earliest examples of Latin influence in the hip hop genre - and Frosty Freeze (b. Wayne Frost). When B-boys first embraced 'The Freak' craze (inspired by **Chic'**s song of the same title), the Rocksteady Crew stayed true to their origins and became the most successful and widely respected of the breakdancers. They dealt firmly in old school hip hop culture which included grafitti, breakdancing, and tongue-twisting, call and response rhymes. They were as much acrobats as dancers, displaying their wares in Central Park alongside competing crews like the Incredible Breakers, Magnificent Force and **U.T.F.O.** As breakdancing evolved they threw new shapes, enlisting the developing cultures of dance, including moonwalking, bodypopping and robotics. Displaying a combination of the latter they were committed to celluloid history via a scene in the 1983 dance movie, *Flashdance*. They were also a huge influence on other crews, the **Kaliphz** being just one of the hip hop groups formed after seeing them perform.

Album: *Ready For Battle* (Charisma 1984).

Rockwell

Kenneth Gordy (b. 15 March 1964, Detroit, Michigan, USA) was the son of **Berry Gordy**, the head of **Motown Records**. Nepotism was not an immediate factor in his career, as he was signed to Motown as a soloist without his father's knowledge. Using the name of his school band, Rockwell made his debut in 1984 with the eerie funk song 'Somebody's Watching Me', which featured backing vocals by **Michael** and **Jermaine Jackson**. Only after the record reached number 2 in the US charts was Rockwell's identity revealed, as he was determined that his music should be judged on its merits, not his parentage. His second single, 'Obscene Phone Caller', was another Top 40 hit, but 'He's A Cobra' in 1985 failed to breach the Top 100, despite a cameo appearance by **Stevie Wonder**. Subsequent recordings have demonstrated the limitations of his synth-based arrangements and inflexible vocals.

Albums: *Somebody's Watching Me* (1984), *Captured* (1985), *Genie* (1986).

Rocky Horror Picture Show, The

Borrowing themes from Hammer Horror films and pop, *The Rocky Horror Show* was a huge success as a stage production. **Tim Curry** reprised his starring role as Frank N. Furter in this 1975 film version which also featured its author Richard O'Brien, Susan Sarondan (later in *Thelma And Louise*) and **Meat Loaf** in its cast. The premise - a young couple take refuge from a storm in a Gothic castle populated by aliens from the planet Transylvania - was a slight variation on a well-worn theme, but Curry's outrageously camp performance provided the film's memorable qualities. Released in the wake of rock's androgynous period, headed by **David Bowie**, *The Rocky Horror Picture Show* quickly became a cult favourite, a standing it has retained over the ensuing years. Many of the songs were peppered with sexual innuendo, tickling an audience imagining they were watching something daring. However, *The Rocky Horror Picture Show* is as traditional as the ideas inspiring it.

Rocky Horror Show, The

One of the phenomenons of the UK musical theatre in the 70s and 80s, this rock musical opened at the Royal Court Theatre Upstairs on 19 June 1973. The book, music and lyrics were by Richard O'Brien who had played a minor role in the London production of *Jesus Christ Superstar*. The abolition of theatrical censorship in Britain nearly five years previously, provided the opportunity to present what turned out to be a jumble of 50s and 60s sexual deviation, drug abuse, horror and science fiction movies, rock 'n' roll music, and much else besides. The story followed a young all-American couple, Brad (Christopher

Malcolm) and Janet (**Julie Covington**), who take refuge in a remote castle. It is the home of several weird characters, including Frank 'N' Furter (**Tim Curry**), a 'sweet transvestite from Transexual, Transylvania', Magenta (Patricia Quinn), an usherette, Columbia (Little Nell), who tap-danced a lot, and the satanic Riff Raff (Richard O'Brien). The outrageously charismatic Frank 'N' Furter, dressed in the obligatory black stockings and suspenders, creates his perfect man, Rocky Horror, when he is not ravishing both Brad and Janet, and the remainder of the plot has to be experienced to be believed. The mostly 50s-style songs included 'Science Fiction, Double Feature', 'Dammit, Janet', 'Over At The Frankenstein Place', 'Sweet Transvestite', 'Time Warp', 'Sword Of Damocles', 'Hot Patootie (Bless My Soul)', 'Touch-A-Touch-A-Touch-A-Touch Me', 'Once In A While', 'Rose Tint My World', 'I'm Going Home', and 'Superheroes'. This 'harmless indulgence of the most monstrous fantasies' caught on in a big way, especially when it moved in August 1973 to the ideal environment of a seedy cinema in the trendy King's Road, Chelsea. After an incredible period of five and a half years, Frank 'N' Furter and his pals finally made it to the West End's Comedy Theatre in April 1969, where they stayed until September of the following year. The total London run amounted to 2,960 performances, but New York audiences demurred, and that production closed after only 45 performances at the Belasco theatre in 1975. In the following year, several of the original cast reassembled to film the *The Rocky Horror Picture Show* which proved to be a critical and financial disaster in the UK, but, ironically, in the USA where the original show had flopped, the movie became a hot cult item on university campuses. However, legend has it that the Waverly Theatre in New York was the scene of the first example of the audience participation craze which has since become the norm. Fanatical fans in America and many other countries in the world, including Britain, who return again and again to see the movie, now dress up in clothes similar to those worn on the screen, and join in with the dialogue and lyrics, as well as constantly constantly heckling and introducing their own ad-lib material. The movie's success helped the stage show's survival in the UK, where, on various provincial tours, the audiences repeated the excesses of the cinema. One of the 'highspots' comes when Brad and Jane are married, and a barrage of rice and various other celebratory souvenirs are despatched from the auditorium, threatening the life and limbs of the participating thespians. It even happened when the show was revived briefly at the Piccadilly Theatre in London in 1990, where, when Frank 'N' Furter sang 'The chips are down, I needed a break', the audience tended to hurl bars of KitKat on to the stage. Two years later, in addition to *The Rocky Horror* fan clubs that have sprung up around the world, the first convention of the British version, snappily called 'Timewarp', was held in London. A 1991 Dublin production of the piece was halted when Frank 'N' Furter's costume fell foul of the Irish decency laws. The 21st Birthday Anniversary production of *The Rocky Horror Show* took place at the Duke of York's Theatre in 1994, with Jonathon Morris as Frank 'N' Furter, and the celebrations began all over again in the following year when the leading character, who 'teeters between Princess Margaret and an outrageous queen in black suspenders', was played by ex-ice skating champion Robin Cousins.

Further reading: *The Rocky Horror Show: Participation Guide*, Sal Piro and Michael Hess.

Roden, Jess

This former member of the respected 60s band the **Alan Bown** Set formed **Bronco** in 1970. Their brand of US-influenced rock was too derivative and they folded after two albums for **Island Records**. He then joined former **Doors'** members, John Densmore and Robby Krieger in the Butts Band. His solo debut *Jess Roden* in 1974 prompted him to form the Jess Roden Band, and he made the well-received *You Can Keep Your Hat On* in 1976. Roden returned in 1980 as part of the Rivets, who released an undistinguished album. Roden now lives in New York working as a graphic artist. In 1995 an album of live recordings made with **Robert Palmer** in the mid-70s was issued.

Albums: *Jess Roden* (1974), *You Can Keep Your Hat On* (1976), as Jess Roden And The Humans *Jess Roden And The Humans* (Arrangement 1995).

Rodford, Jim

b. 7 July 1945, St. Alban's, Hertfordshire, England. As **Rod Argent**'s bass-playing cousin, Rodford was well-placed to join the **Zombies** when a vacancy occurred in 1963. Instead, he enlisted with the jazzy **Mike Cotton** Sound who were often hired as an all-purpose backing group to artists including **Gene Pitney** and the **Four Tops** on round-Britain package tours. One such trek headlined by the **Kinks** in 1964 had an important bearing on Rodford's future. Towards the end of the decade he became more embroiled in session work - frequently in harness with Ian Gibbons (keyboards) - before his famous relation recruited him for **Argent** in 1969. When this band had run its course, he was among those ex-members who formed **Phoenix** with **Michael Des Barres** in 1976 but, after two albums, Rodford left for the Kinks - whose leader Ray Davies tended to compose very precise bass lines 'but he lets me embellish (them) a bit'. However, the respected Rodford's recommendations would lead to the group's enlistment of both Robert Henrit (ex-Phoenix) and Ian Gibbons. Still a Kink in the 90s, Rodford concluded that 'nothing that does any good is easy'.

Rodgers, Clodagh

b. 1947, County Down, Northern Ireland. After eight years in showbusiness, this Anglo-Irish singer unexpectedly climbed into the Top 10 with 'Come Back And Shake Me' in April 1969. With the backing of songwriter **Kenny Young** and husband Johnny Morris (a record plugger at **Decca**) Rodgers successfully followed up with 'Goodnight Midnight' and 'Biljo', and also walked off with the 'Best Legs In Show Business' trophy. She had the legs and her voice insured for £1 million. A veteran of continental song festivals, she was a natural choice as the British entrant for the Eurovision Song Contest in 1971, and although she failed to secure victory, the catchy 'Jack In The Box' brought her another Top 10 UK hit. In the same year her 'Lady Love Bug' made the Top 30, and since then she has toured in various productions and appeared in cabaret and pantomime. In 1985 she co-starred with **Joe Brown**, Lynsey de Paul, Jeremy Clyde, Peter Duncan and Chad Stewart in the West End musical *Pump Boys And Dinettes*.

Selected albums: *Clodagh* (1969), *Midnight Clodagh* (1969) *Clodagh Rodgers* (1969) I*t's Different Now* (RCA 1973).

Rodgers, Jesse

b. Jesse Otto Rodgers, 1911, Waynesboro, Mississippi, USA, d. 1973. Cousin of **Jimmie Rodgers**. A guitarist and singer, he may have worked with Jimmie in 1932 and so been influenced in a career as an entertainer himself. He worked on the powerful Border radio stations XERA, XEPN and XELO and recorded Rodgers-type material until the late 30s, when his interest turned to things Western. He made his recording debut for **RCA**-Victor in San Antonio in March 1934, singing and yodelling in the manner of his cousin. When in 1936, RCA released Jimmie's recording of 'My Good Gal's Gone Blues', Jesse's version of 'Leave Me Alone Sweet Mama' was on the b-side. This has raised the question as to whether it was a case of mistaken identity or an attempt by the record company to test public reaction to Jesse as a possible successor to the then dead Singing Brakeman?. In the late 40s, mainly based in Philadelphia, he recorded cowboy songs, appeared in the 1949 film *The Western Balladeer* and for some time, he had his own television show, *Ranger Jim*. In 1960, emphysema began to affect him and by 1963, he was forced to give up public performances. He wrote songs and cowboy stories until his death in 1973.

Album: *His Country And Western Yodelling Days* (Cowgirl Boy 80s, German release).

Rodgers, Jimmie (country)

b. James Charles Rodgers, 8 September 1897, Pine Springs, near Meridian, Mississippi, USA, d. 26 May 1933, New York, USA. The youngest of the three sons of Aaron Woodberry Rodgers, a tough but respected Alabama man, who had moved to Meridian to work as foreman of the maintenance crew on that section of the Mobile & Ohio Railroad. In 1904, his mother Eliza (Bozeman) died (most probably from tuberculosis) and he and elder brother Talmage lived for a time with relatives until their father remarried. Life with the new stepmother was far from happy and in 1906, he and Talmage moved out to live with their Aunt Dora (their mother's unmarried sister), who ran the Bozeman family farm at Pine Springs. A well educated woman, who held degrees in English and Music which she had previously taught, making it quite possible that Rodger's first real interest in music started during the time spent with his aunt. She also tried to curb his growing reputation for boyish activities, not least of all playing truant and smoking. In 1911, his father recalled him to Meridian but his long absences at work soon left Jimmie lacking parental control. He frequented the local pool halls and barbershops, often becoming involved in arguments. However, his ability to charm his way out of most problems usually kept him out of serious trouble. He may have taken his first steps towards playing some stringed instruments during the hours spent singing with others in the barbershops. At the age of 12, renderings of 'Steamboat Bill' and 'I Wonder Why Bill Bailey Don't Come Home' won him a local amateur talent contest. Flushed by this success, he decided to set up his own touring tent show. His father quickly followed him to a nearby venue and took him back home, where he then discovered that the boy had used his credit account at a local store to buy the tent. Soon afterwards, he ran away with a travelling medicine show but he quickly found the life was not what he expected and he was glad when eventually his father once again collected him. This time, he was given the choice of returning to school or working with his father's gang on the railroad. He chose the latter because it seemed more likely to offer adventure.

During the next decade, he worked on various railroad jobs including call boy, flagman, baggage master and brakeman, in places that ranged from Mississippi to Texas and the Pacific Coast. He became noted as a flashy dresser (when funds allowed) and for having an eye for the girls, although music was never far from his mind. On 1 May 1917, after only knowing her a few weeks, he married Sandra Kelly; by autumn although she was pregnant, they had separated. She said later 'He was sweet as could be but he never had any money. He would strum away on some instrument and fool away his time and his money'. She literally disappeared from the scene and Rodgers continued his nomadic existence but finally filed for and obtained his divorce from her on 17 November 1919. While working as a brakeman for the New Orleans & Northeastern Railroad, he had met Carrie Williamson (b. 8 August 1902, Meridian, Mississippi, USA), the daughter of a Meridian minister. On 7 April 1920, with Carrie still at high school, they were married. Soon afterwards, Rodgers was laid off by the railroad. He drove a truck and did many more menial tasks but never relinquished his hopes of a singing career. If the chance to entertain arose, he was likely to take it, even when it meant leaving Carrie for a time. They had many lodgings and the problems worsened on 30 January 1921, with the birth of their first daughter, Carrie Anita. When their second, June Rebecca (b. 20 June 1923, d. 22 December 1923), died of diphtheria, aged six months, Jimmie was away with a travelling show. He hitched a ride in boxcars and arrived in Meridian, broke and unable to pay for the funeral. Sometime during his travels in the early 20s, possibly in New Orleans, he met and probably worked with **Goebel Reeves**, who later claimed to have taught Rodgers to yodel. Reeves, known as the Texas Drifter, was noted for his tall tales and this may have been one of them. In any event, their yodels were totally dissimilar, the slow blues yodel that Rodgers used on his recordings being infinitely less complicated than the speed and triple yodels with which Reeves was so adept. It is also probable though that, during this time, Rodgers worked hard on his instrumental work. His health had never been good, he was often confined to bed and forced to rest. He frequently suffered from colds and a bad cough and late in 1924, a doctor diagnosed tuberculosis. Ignoring the fact that the disease usually proved fatal (as with his mother), he soon discharged himself from hospital. He formed a trio with his piano playing sister-in-law Elsie McWilliams and fiddler Slim Rozell and briefly played at local dances. He still worked on the railroad, played blackface comedy with a touring show and later worked on the Florida East Coast Line. In 1926, believing the climate would help the TB, he worked as a switchman for the Southern Pacific in Tucson, Arizona. He sang and played banjo and guitar at local venues, until this interfered with his work. He was fired and they moved, as they did many times, back to Meridian to live with his in-laws. In 1927, alone, he moved to Asheville, North Carolina, supposedly to work on the railroad but his health was poor. He could no longer do the hard work and he never actually worked on the railroads again. He drove a taxi, worked as a janitor and boosted his income by playing and singing at local functions and with a band on WWNC radio. He raised enough cash for his family to join him but he was soon on the road again. This time he went to Johnson City, Tennessee, where he became involved with Jack Pierce and brothers, Claude and Jack Grant. Known as the **Teneva Ramblers**, the trio were a string band struggling, like Rodgers, to make it as entertainers. He convinced the trio that he had a radio show in Asheville and they agreed to back him. The radio programme carried no pay but he used it to advertise himself, until the station dropped him. Leaving the family in Asheville, Rodgers and the trio took to the road. They played various venues as the Jimmie Rodgers Entertainers, before gaining a residency as a dance band at the affluent North Fork Mountain Resort. Rodgers then heard that Ralph Peer, a field representative equipped with portable recording equipment, for The Victor Talking Machine Company, was in Bristol, Tennessee, seeking local acts to record. Rodgers persuaded the others that they should go to Bristol, to try their luck. When they were offered an audition, they argued over the name of their act. The result being that the trio again became the Teneva Ramblers and Rodgers found himself minus his Entertainers. He convinced Peer that he should record as a solo artist and consequently on 4 August 1927, with only his own guitar accompaniment, Rodgers made his first recordings, 'The Soldier's Sweetheart' and 'Sleep Baby Sleep'. The two songs were released on 7 October 1927 (Vi 20864) and although the record did not become a major seller, it marked a step towards the successful stage of his career. When Rodgers knew the record had been released, he headed for New York, booked himself in at a hotel by telling them he was an **RCA**-Victor recording artist and contacted Peer. His impudence paid off and on 30 November 1927, he made four more recordings at RCA's Camden studios. It was the third recording 'Blue Yodel' (often referred to as 'T for Texas'), that proved to be the boost that Rodgers needed. It was coupled with Rodgers' version of Kelly Harrell's song 'Away Out On The Mountain' (Vi 21142). The wistful yodel, which eventually became a million seller, became so popular that it led to him recording a series of 'Blue Yodel' numbers during his career and won him the nickname of 'America's Blue Yodeler'. Late in 1927, Rodgers, who had moved to Washington, appeared on a weekly show on WTFF billed as the Singing Brakeman (he always dressed as a brakeman on stage) and to help with family expenses, Carrie worked as a waitress. The northern climate though did not suit him, he was regularly ill with colds and the medicines were expensive. In February 1928, Rodgers recorded eight more sides at Camden, including 'Blue Yodels #3 and #4' and a version of 'In The Jailhouse Now' that has become a country classic. Peer provided accompaniment from Julian Ninde (guitar) and Ellsworth T. Cozzens (steel guitar/mandolin/ukulele/banjo). Three further sessions were held that year, one at Camden and two in Atlanta, which produced 14 more sides. Peer constantly pressed him for new material and although Rodgers brazenly stated he had many songs ready, it was bluff, until Elsie McWilliams came to his rescue. In a week, she combined with Rodgers to write nine new songs. These included 'Daddy And Home', 'My Old Pal' and 'You And My Old Guitar', while Cozzens co-wrote 'Dear Old Sunny South By The Sea' and 'Treasures

Untold', both very successful Rodgers' recordings. By the end of the year, he was receiving a considerable sum in royalties and he had played major tours in the south, allegedly receiving a weekly wage of $600 dollars for a 20-minute spot each night. He was hailed a hero on a visit to Meridian but his health again gave cause for concern. By this time, he had forsaken his image and dress as the Singing Brakeman. He now dressed more normally, sometimes in tuxedo and bowler hat and gloried in his billing as 'America's Blue Yodeler'. The year 1929 would have proved hectic for a fit man and Rodgers was certainly not one. In February, he recorded 11 sessions (New York (two), Dallas (four) and Atlanta (five)). He also recorded the soundtrack for the short film *The Singing Brakeman* in Camden. He received backing on many of the recordings from Joe Kaipo (steel guitar), Billy Burkes (guitar) and Weldon Burkes (ukulele). Between the recording sessions, he played many venues, some of his own booking and many on the major Radio-Keith-Orpheum Interstate Circuit tour (RKO), which visited many cities in Texas, Oklahoma, Louisiana, Alabama and Georgia. In 12 days during June and July 1930, Rodgers recorded a total of 16 tracks. Some including 'Pistol Packin' Papa' and 'Blue Yodel #8' (Muleskinner Blues) featured only his guitar, whilst others had backing from Lani McIntire's Hawaiians ('Moonlight And Skies' and 'For The Sake Of Day's Gone By'). It is interesting, bearing in mind Rodger's love of and ability as a white man to sing the blues, to note the recording of 'Blue Yodel #9', whereon he was backed by **Lillian Armstrong** (piano) and the trumpet of a young **Louis Armstrong**. Away from the studios, he suffered health and other problems, including one caused by his first wife Stella's reappearance. She was accompanied by her daughter Kathryn (b. 16 February 1918), who everyone agreed looked like Rodgers. Stella, no doubt, impressed by her ex-husband's new found financial fame, obviously thought that she should receive some benefit for raising the child. On 3 February 1931, she launched a civil action, claiming Rodgers had not made proper provision for his daughter. Rodgers seemingly did not actually dispute the parentage but the staggering amounts claimed certainly frightened him. Carrie, understandably, was not amused by the development and for some time Jimmie headed west, while his lawyer brother-in-law sorted out the problem. (The delayed final judgement, on 9 June 1932, ordered Rodgers to pay $50 per month until Kathryn was 18 years old - a total of $2,650. Stella got nothing. Kathryn married but died aged 19, in 1938, which prevented Rodgers having any further claims made against him). In January and February 1931, Rodgers worked with Will Rogers on a Red Cross tour to raise funds for families affected by the drought and depression in Texas and Oklahoma. Rodgers also found the results of the Depression were affecting his bookings and, in consequence, he struggled to maintain his financial lifestyle. His health was worse but he managed to keep up with his recording schedules. In January, he cut seven sides in San Antonio, amongst which was his now famous 'T.B. Blues'. (Four including an alternative cut of that song were unissued by RCA-Victor and remained so until released by **Bear Family** in 1992). He moved his recording centre to Louisville, where, on 10 June, he made his only recordings with a female vocalist, one also being the only gospel number that he ever recorded. Sara Carter (a member of the **Carter Family**, who had also made their first recordings at the same Bristol sessions) duetted on 'Why There's A Tear In My Eye' and 'The Wonderful City', to the accompaniment of Mother Maybelle Carter's guitar. Two days later, Peer recorded two novelty items containing vocals and dialogue in 'Jimmie Rodgers Visits The Carter Family' and 'The Carter Family And Jimmy Rodgers In Texas'. Amongst the more serious songs were 'When The Cactus Is In Bloom', a self-penned number that suited Rodgers secret wish to be associated with things Western.

He made 12 recordings in Dallas, during a five-day period in February 1932, which included the prophetical 'My Time Ain't Long' and 'Blue Yodel #10'. Again health problems prevented him working at times and the bookings were still affected by the Depression. A plan for Rodgers to tour the UK was never finalized; in any event his health would not have allowed him to have made the trip. In August, he travelled to Camden and with a backing that included Clayton McMichen and **Slim Bryant**, he managed 12 further recordings. Two of the numbers, 'Mother The Queen Of My Heart' and 'Peach Picking Time In Georgia', were written by Bryant and McMichen respectively and both have become country standards through Rodgers' original recordings. He also recorded 'Whippin' That Old T.B.' - a brave but sadly an overly optimistic number. Two weeks later, after rest, Rodgers went to New York, insisting that Bryant accompanied him, and with other musicians, he made four recordings, including 'Prairie Lullaby' and his delightful version of 'Miss The Mississippi And You'. A promised network show on WEAF New York failed to happen and his health had so deteriorated that he was constantly taking painkillers and alcohol. He refused to quit and is quoted as telling McMichen that 'I want to die with my shoes on'. In late 1932 and the spring of 1933, Rodgers' desperate need for cash saw him alternate periods of enforced rest with some appearances in far from high class venues in Texas, even to appearing with vaudeville acts between films in nickelodeons. While living in San Antonio, he did for a time manage a weekly show on KMAC. In February 1933, he collapsed in Lufkin and was rushed to the Memorial Hospital, Houston. Rodgers realized that he had little time left to provide finance for his family. He contacted Peer and persuaded him to advance the proposed summer recording session to May. Peer well realised the financial and health problems and agreed to pay Rodgers $250 dollars a side for 12 recordings. Rodgers, accompanied by a nurse (Cora Bedell), sailed from Galveston on the *S.S. Mohawk* and reached New York on 14 May. On the 17th, with only his own guitar, he recorded four songs including 'Blue Yodel #12' and another Western-orientated number in 'The Cowhand's Last Ride'. The following day he added 'Dreaming With Tears In My Eyes', 'Yodeling My Way Back Home' and 'Jimmie Rodger's Last Blue Yodel'. Those present in the studio could only wonder how he managed to complete the recordings. At the end of the day, he was carried from the studio to a taxi and taken to his hotel. After two day's rest, he made recordings of 'The Yodeling Ranger' and 'Old Pal Of My Heart'. Four days later, he returned to the studios. On the first three recordings, 'Old Love Letters', 'Mississippi Delta Blues' (its bluesy sadness has led many devotees to rate this one of his finest works) and 'Somewhere Below The Dixon Line', he had Tony Colicchio (guitar) and John Cali (steel guitar/guitar/banjo) providing instrumental backing. He had rested on a cot after the second recording and he again rested on it before, with only his own guitar (just as he had made his first recording in 1927), he cut his final song, 'Years Ago'. When he had finished, he walked slowly from the studio to his taxi. He decided to have a little holiday in New York and the following day, he paid a visit to Coney Island pleasure beach. Returning, he told his driver to stop a little way from the hotel so that he could walk. After a short distance, he stopped, slumped on a fire hydrant and gasping for air told brother-in-law, Alex Nelson, 'Let me take a blow'. He was taken back to the hotel and put to bed. Just before midnight, he developed a deep cough and began to haemorrhage worse than ever before. A doctor was called but before he arrived, Rodgers had slipped into a coma. He died in the early hours of 26 May; he had literally drowned in his own blood. His body was taken by train to Meridian, carried in a specially adapted baggage car attached to one of the trains that he had always held in great affection; the engineer was Homer Jenkins, a man who had known Rodgers since his railroad days. Hundreds waited in Meridian, hearing the mournful sound of the locomotive's whistle blowing long before the train arrived at Union Station. On 29 May, his body lay in state and many filed past to mark their respect. After funeral services, he was buried in Oak Grove Cemetery, next to the grave of June, his baby daughter. Jimmie's relationship with Carrie during the latter part of his life may be a little unclear. She did not accompany him to New York, even though it was readily apparent to all that his time was very limited. She later said she was caring for her brother. No doubt, there were many problems during their marriage.

Rodgers was certainly no angel, he always had an eye for a pretty girl, he rarely refused a drink, perhaps because it helped him forget the pain that he suffered for much of his life. On countless occasions, when the going got tough at home, he literally got going himself, to find some other place where he could sing his songs, even if it was for little financial reward. However, there seems little doubt that in spite of his meanderings and dalliances, Rodgers dearly loved Carrie and daughter Anita. After his death, RCA-Victor released very few of the unissued recordings, the last single being in 1938, to mark the fifth anniversary of his death. In the early 50s, no doubt through Peer's efforts, RCA released four 10-inch albums of his recordings. In 1956, they released the first 12-inch album. The interest it raised and the sales led to the release of seven more by 1964. In 1987, the Smithsonian Institution produced a boxed set of 36 recordings and later RCA released a boxed set in Japan. In the early 90s, Rounder issued a series of compact discs and cassettes, which included some alternative takes. In 1992, Bear Family released a definitive set of six compact discs of Rodgers' work. They contained all of his original recordings, in the order they were recorded, some alternative takes issued for the first time, the soundtrack to his only film and eight recordings from 1955, that featured Rodgers' original vocals, overdubbed by **Hank Snow**'s Rainbow Ranch boys with **Chet Atkins**. The only thing not included, naturally, was the 1931 Jimmie Rodgers Puzzle Record. This novelty release contained three songs recorded in parallel grooves but with three different lead in points which meant that the person playing it never knew which of the three songs would be played. (Puzzle records were a gimmick, with early versions appearing as early as 1915). Amongst the countless tribute recordings that have been made over the years are those by **Gene Autry** (probably the first Rodgers soundalike in his early days), **Bradley Kincaid** and **Ernest Tubb**. In October 1936, even Mrs Carrie Rodgers got into the act when, with Ernest Tubb accompanying her on Rodgers' guitar, she rendered the rather maudlin 'We Miss Him When The Evening Shadows Fall'. Arguably the best is the rather long 'Jimmie Rodgers' Blues' by **Elton Britt**, which cleverly uses the titles of his songs within its lyrics. Later several artists, including Hank Snow, **Merle Haggard**, **Wilf Carter**, **Yodeling Slim Clark** and Australia's **Buddy Williams** all recorded albums of Rodgers' songs. Naturally, there has also been much written about him, most of it appearing in numerous articles in many different publications. In 1935, his widow, with some persuasion and assistance, privately published her account of Rodgers' life. The book attracted little attention then, nor in 1953, when it was reprinted to coincide with the first Jimmie Rodgers memorial celebration in Meridian. It was reprinted again by the Country Music Foundation Press in 1975.

(Both Ernest Tubb and Hank Snow were greatly influenced in their early careers by Rodgers and the two singers subsequently worked to start the annual Meridian memorial event). Carrie Rodgers' book tended to avoid any controversial matters but it does offer some insight to his family's life style. Mike Paris and Chris Comber published a far more interesting volume in 1977 but the definitive book on the artist is undoubtedly the 1979 volume (revised 1992), written by Nolan Porterfield and published by the University Of Illinois Press as a volume in their informative series Music In American Life.

In the late-50s, Carrie Rodgers had great hopes of a film being made of his life but the project was cancelled in 1960. Rodgers' death left his wife and daughter by no means financially secure. In his last two years, the medical expenses and medicines had made a severe in-road into their savings and although his royalties basically kept them, they hardly provided for any of life's luxuries. When it was discovered that Carrie had cancer and was in need of major surgery, friends started a fund to help with the costs. The treatment failed to halt the cancer and Carrie Williamson Rodgers died on 28 November 1961. His daughter, Carrie Anita Rodgers Court, died from emphysema in San Antonio on 5 December 1993 and was taken to Meridian, where she was buried next to her father. She requested that only Jimmie's recording of 'Sleep, Baby, Sleep' was to be played at her funeral. (The second song he had recorded in Bristol in 1927, it was one he had often sung to her in her childhood). Since his death, his influence on subsequent American artists is incalculable. Many of the top stars, including Gene Autry, **Jimmie Davis**, Hank Snow and Ernest Tubb started their careers almost as Rodgers' impersonators before developing their own styles. In more recent times other USA singers have openly admitted how they were influenced by Rodgers. His inspiration has not been confined to the USA. Australian legend, **Tex Morton**, made no secret that he was influenced by both Rodgers and Wilf Carter, nor did Buddy Williams. Both performed in the manner of Rodgers and sang his material, although Morton, in particular, mainly used the more intricate Goebel Reeves' type yodels. In the UK, Harry Torrani, an English vaudeville yodeler of the early 30s (who later moved to Australia), sang in a similar manner on his early recordings. **Brian Golbey**, a top British artist for many years, learned his first songs from hearing his father's recordings of Rodgers and later recorded several of the songs on his own first album in 1970. During his lifetime, Rodgers could not really be termed a country music singer, since the category did not then truly exist. He sang a mixture of folk ballads, blues and vaudeville and even semi-risqué numbers such as 'Frankie And Johnny' which in his hands, became the accepted fare of not only the first generations of country music listeners and record buyers but also those that have followed in the years since his death. Over the years, there has been a considerable amount of discussion concerning Rodgers' actual contribution to country music; a contribution that has seen him named as the 'Father Of Country Music' and elected as the first entrant to the Country Music Hall Of Fame in Nashville on its foundation in 1961. There is no doubt at all that, in his relatively short career, he set patterns that many have followed. He was one of the first to successfully master the art of recording, his mournful yodel was magnetic to many people's ears and he was a very proficient entertainer, who loved to be in front of an audience.

Albums: *Travellin' Blues* (RCA Victor 1952, 10-inch album), *Memorial Album Volume 1* (RCA Victor 1952, 10-inch album), *Memorial Album Volume 2* (RCA Victor 1952, 10-inch album), *Memorial Album Volume 3* (RCA Victor 1952, 10-inch album), *Never No Mo' Blues* (RCA Victor 1956), *Train Whistle Blues* (RCA Victor 1958), *My Rough And Rowdy Ways* (RCA Victor 1960), *Jimmie The Kid* (RCA Victor 1961), *Country Music Hall Of Fame* (RCA Victor 1962), *The Short But Brilliant Life Of Jimmie Rodgers* (RCA Victor 1963), *My Time Ain't Long* (RCA Victor 1964), *First Sessions 1927-28* (Rounder 1990), *The Early Years (1928-29)* (Rounder 1990), *On The Way Up (1929)* (Rounder 1991), *Riding High (1929-30)* (Rounder 1991), *America's Blue Yodeller (1930-31)* (Rounder 1991), *Down The Old Road (1931-32)* (Rounder 1991), *No Hard Times (1932)* (Rounder 1992), *Last Sessions (1933)* (Rounder 1992), *Jimmie Rodgers, The Singing Brakeman* (Bear Family 1992, 6-CD box set).

Further reading: *My Husband Jimmie Rodgers*, Mrs Jimmie Rodgers. *Jimmie The Kid (The Life Of Jimmie Rodgers)*, Mike Paris and Chris Comber. *Jimmie Rodgers (The Life And Times Of America's Blue Yodeler)*, Nolan Porterfield.

Rodgers, Jimmie (pop)

b. James Frederick Rodgers, 18 September 1933, Camus, Washington, USA. After being taught by his mother, the young Rodgers successfully auditioned for the Arthur Godfrey talent show and impressed Luigi Creatore and Hugo Peretti who signed him to their recently formed Roulette Records. Rodgers' creamy, effortless voice and blend of folk-tinged pop appealed to a post-war middle America, and over the next decade he made the *Billboard* singles chart 25 times. He never however, topped his debut, 'Honeycomb', which stayed at number 1 for four weeks in 1957 (number 30 in the UK). His early successes included 'Kisses Sweeter Than Wine' a Top 3 hit in 1957 which vied with **Frankie Vaughan** in the UK for the best position, (Rodgers number 7, Vaughan number 8). One of Rodgers' most memorable songs was the innocent but catchy 'English Country Garden', which although it became his biggest UK hit (reaching the

Top 5) it did not appear to warrant an American release, possibly because of its title. Rodgers suffered a serious mugging in 1967 which left him with a fractured skull. Although he eventually returned to performing full-time, his career had lost its momentum. He was still singing professionally in the late 80s.

Selected albums: *Jimmie Rodgers* (1957), *Its Over* (1966), *Child Of Clay* (1968), *Windmills Of Your Mind* (1969), *This Is Jimmie Rodgers* (1987). Compilations: *Best Of Jimmie Rodgers* (1988), *Kisses Sweeter Than Wine* (1988).

Rodgers, Richard

b. 28 June 1902, Hammells Station, Arverne, Long Island, USA, d. 30 December 1979, New York, USA. One of the all-time great composers for the musical theatre, Rodgers was raised in a comfortable middle-class family and developed an early love of music. Encouraged by his parents, he was able to pick out a tune on the piano at the age of four, and wrote his first songs, 'Campfire Days' and 'Auto Show Girl' (lyric: David Dyrenforth), when he was 14. Many years later, when he was asked what he had done before he began composing music, he is supposed to have said: 'I was a baby.' In 1919, Rodgers was introduced to the lyricist **Lorenz Hart**, and they collaborated on the scores for two well received Columbia University Varsity shows, *Fly With Me* and *You'll Never Know*, and on songs for other productions, such as the Broadway musicals *A Lonely Romeo* (1919, 'Any Old Place With You'), and *Poor Little Ritz Girl* (1920). The early 20s presented few further opportunities, and a frustrated Rodgers was contemplating taking a job as a wholesaler in the baby-wear business, when, in 1925, he and Hart were asked to write the score for a benefit show in aid of the Theatre Guild, the prestigious theatrical producing organization. The resulting revue, ***The Garrick Gaieties***, was so successful that it began a commercial run which lasted for 211 performances. Rodgers and Hart's lively and amusing score included the charming 'Sentimental Me' as well as one of their most enduring standards, 'Manhattan'. A second edition of the *Gaieties* in 1926, had another of the songwriters' brightest and inventive numbers, 'Mountain Greenery', which was associated in later years with the distinguished jazz singer **Mel Tormé**. From this point, Rodgers and Hart were off and running, and during the next few years, wrote some of their most romantic and innovative songs for a series of musical shows which met with varying degrees of success. They included ***Dearest Enemy*** (1925, 'Here In My Arms'), ***The Girl Friend*** (1926, 'The Blue Room', 'The Girl Friend'), *Lido Lady* (London 1926, 'Try Again Tomorrow'), ***Peggy-Ann*** (1926, 'Where's That Rainbow?', 'A Tree In The Park'), *Betsy* (a 39 performance flop in 1926, 'This Funny World'), ***One Dam Thing After Another*** (London 1927, 'My Heart Stood Still'), ***A Connecticut Yankee*** (1927,

'Thou Swell', 'On A Desert Island With Thee!', 'Nothing's Wrong'), *She's My Baby* (1928, 'You're What I Need'), *Present Arms!* (1928, 'You Took Advantage Of Me', 'A Kiss For Cinderella'), *Chee-Chee* (a 31-performance flop in 1928, 'Better Be Good to Me'), *Lady Fingers* (1929, 'I Love You More Than Yesterday'), *Spring Is Here* (1929, 'With A Song In My Heart', 'Why Can't I?', 'Baby's Awake Now'), *Heads Up!* (1929, 'A Ship Without A Sail'), *Simple Simon* ('Ten Cents A Dance', 'He Was Too Good To Me'), and *Ever Green* (London 1930, 'Dancing On The Ceiling', 'No Place But Home', 'The Colour Of Her Eyes'). When the team wrote the optimistic 'I've Got Five Dollars' for Ann Sothern and Jack Whiting to sing in *America's Sweetheart* in 1931, the US was in the middle of the Depression. Although more than 20 new musicals were being produced each season on Broadway, Rodgers and Hart's last five shows had been relatively unsuccessful, and they spent much of the early 30s in Hollywood writing some memorable songs for early film musicals such as *The Hot Heiress* (1931, 'You're The Cats'), *Love Me Tonight* (1932, 'Isn't It Romantic?', 'Mimi', 'Lover'), *The Phantom President* (1932, 'Give Her A Kiss'), *Hallelujah, I'm A Bum* (1933, 'You Are Too Beautiful'), *Hollywood Party* (1934, 'Hello'), Nana (1934, 'That's Love'), and *Mississippi* (1935, 'It's Easy To Remember', 'Soon', 'Down By The River'). They also contributed a song called 'The Bad In Every Man' (previously known as 'Prayer') to the Oscar-winning screen thriller *Manhattan Melodrama*. After Hart wrote a new lyric, it was re-titled 'Blue Moon', and became one of their biggest hits. That song, and many of their other successful numbers, was featured in the 1948 biopic, *Words And Music*, in which Rodgers was played by Tom Drake, and Hart by **Mickey Rooney**.

Rodgers and Hart returned to New York in 1935, and embarked on a body of work which even surpassed their previous achievements. *Jumbo* (1935), with a score containing three outstanding numbers, 'My Romance', 'Little Girl Blue', and 'The Most Beautiful Girl In The World', was followed by the splendid *On Your Toes* (1936, 'Glad To Be Unhappy', 'There's A Small Hotel', 'Too Good For The Average Man', 'Slaughter On Tenth Avenue'), *Babes In Arms* (1937, 'I Wish I Were In Love Again', 'The Lady Is A Tramp', 'My Funny Valentine', 'Where Or When', 'Johnny One Note'), *I'd Rather Be Right* (1937, 'Have You Met Miss Jones?'), *I Married An Angel* (1938, 'Spring Is Here', 'I Married An Angel', 'At The Roxy Music Hall'), *The Boys From Syracuse* (1938, 'Falling In Love With Love', 'This Can't Be Love', 'Sing For Your Supper', 'You Have Cast Your Shadow On The Sea'), *Too Many Girls* (1939, 'I Didn't Know What Time It Was', 'Give It Back To The Indians', 'I Like To Recognize The Tune', 'You're Nearer'), *Higher And Higher* (1940, 'It Never Entered My Mind'), *Pal Joey* ('Betwitched', 'I Could Write A

Book', 'Den Of Iniquity'), and *By Jupiter* (1942, 'Wait Till You See Her', 'Nobody's Heart', 'Careless Rhapsody'). *Pal Joey*, in particular, was regarded as a landmark in Broadway history, partly because it was the first musical in which the leading character, played by **Gene Kelly**, was a villain - an anti-hero. Rodgers and Hart's final work together was probably on the songs for a revised production of their 1927 hit, *A Connecticut Yankee*, which contained the witty 'To Keep My Love Alive'. By the time that show opened on 3 November 1943, Hart's physical condition, which had been worsening for several years, had deteriorated to such an extent that he was unable to work, and he died some two weeks later.

In the previous year, Rodgers had been asked by the Theatre Guild to write the score for what eventually turned out to be *Oklahoma!* (1943). With Hart unavailable, he began the collaboration with **Oscar Hammerstein II** which produced some of the biggest blockbusters in the (pre-**Andrew Lloyd Webber**) history of the musical theatre. Marvellous songs such as 'Oh, What A Beautiful Mornin'', 'People Will Say We're In Love', 'The Surrey With The Fringe On Top', and the rousing title number, were cleverly integrated into the story, and *Oklahoma!* won a special Pulitzer Prize, and ran for 2,212 performances in New York. Next came the magnificent *Carousel* (1945, 'If I Loved You', 'June Is Bustin' Out All Over', 'What's The Use Of Wond'rin'', 'You'll Never Walk Alone', 'Soliloquy'), which is often regarded as Rodgers and Hammerstein's best score. Also in 1945, the partners wrote their only original film score for the highly popular *State Fair*, which featured the exuberant 'It's A Grand Night For Singing' and the lovely ballad, 'It Might As Well Be Spring', Back on Broadway, the out-of-character *Allegro* (1947, 'A Fellow Needs A Girl', 'The Gentleman Is A Dope'), complete with its Greek chorus, was a disappointment. But there were more triumphs just around the corner in the shape of *South Pacific* (1949, 'I'm Gonna Wash That Man Right Outa My Hair', 'Bali Ha'i', 'Some Enchanted Evening', 'This Nearly Was Mine', 'There Is Nothin' Like A Dame'), which ran for nearly five years, and won the Pulitzer Prize for Drama; and *The King And I* (1951, 'Hello, Young Lovers', 'I Have Dreamed', 'Shall We Dance?', 'We Kiss In A Shadow', 'Getting To Know You').

In 1952, Richard Rodgers wrote the music for the NBC documentary television series *Victory At Sea*, for which he was awarded the US Navy's Distinguished Public Service Medal. A musical theme from one of the episodes entitled 'Beyond The Southern Cross', attracted a great deal of interest, and Rodgers used it, with a lyric by Hammerstein, as a part of the score for their next Broadway show, *Me And Juliet* (1953). The song was called 'No Other Love', and featured again in television and stage versions of *Cinderella*. Neither

Me And Juliet, or Rodgers and Hammerstein's Broadway follow-up, *Pipe Dream* (1955, 'All At Once You Love Her', 'The Next Time It Happens'), are considered to be among their best work. Nor, for that matter, is **Flower Drum Song** ('I Enjoy Being A Girl', 'Sunday', 'Love, Look Away'), but the show did stay around for 602 performances, and was still running when the final Rodgers and Hammerstein smash hit, **The Sound Of Music** ('Climb Ev'ry Mountain', 'Edelweiss', 'Do-Re-Mi', 'My Favourite Things', 'The Sound Of Music') opened in November 1959 and ran for nearly three and a half years in New York, and more than five and a half in London. The film versions of this and several other Rodgers and Hammerstein shows were among the highest-grossing movie musicals of the 50s and 60s. Less than a year after *The Sound Of Music* opened, Hammerstein was dead. Rodgers subsequently contributed five new songs (music and lyrics) to the 1962 remake of *State Fair*, and wrote the complete score for the Broadway musical **No Strings** ('The Sweetest Sounds'), which ran for 580 performances. For his work on that show he won a **Tony Award** for Outstanding Composer, and a Grammy for the Original Cast album. From then on, apart from providing both words and music for a US television adaptation of *Androcles And The Lion* (1967), starring **Noël Coward** and **Norman Wisdom**, for the remainder of his career Rodgers worked with established lyricists. These included **Stephen Sondheim** (1965, **Do I Hear A Waltz?**, 'We're Gonna Be All Right', 'Do I Hear A Waltz'), Martin Charnin (1970, *Two By Two*, 'I Do Not Know A Day I Did Not Love You'), **Sheldon Harnick** (1976, *Rex*), and Martin Charnin (1979, *I Remember Mama*). When he was working on the last two shows, which were both dismal failures at the box office, Rodgers was a sick man, and he died in December 1979.

The emotionally uplifting and often witty and sophisticated melodies he left behind - written in collaboration with two supremely gifted, but temperamentally opposite partners - played an important part in the development of American's own indigenous popular music, and in the acceptance of the musical as an important and respected art form. His honours included special Tonys in 1962 and 1972, a Trustee Grammy Award, and the 1979 Lawrence Langner Award for Distinguished Lifetime Achievement in the Theatre. In 1993, on the 50th anniversary of the birth of his second momentous partnership, a celebratory revue entitled *A Grand Night For Singing*, which was crammed with Rodgers and Hammerstein's songs, was presented in New York.

Selected album: *Mary Martin Sings Richard Rodgers Plays* (1958).

Further reading: *Musical Stages: His Autobiography*, Richard Rodgers. *With A Song In His Heart*, David Ewen. *The Rodgers And Hammerstein Story*, Stanley Green.

Rodgers And Hart: Bewitched, Bothered And Bedevilled, S. Marx and J. Clayton. *The Sound Of Their Music: The Story Of Rodgers And Hammerstein*, Frederick Nolan.

Rodgers, Sonny

b. Oliver Lee Rodgers, 4 December 1939, Hughes Arkansas, USA, d. 7 May 1990. He learned guitar from his father and was influenced by **B.B. King**, **Robert Nighthawk**, and **Muddy Waters**. After forming his first band at the age of 17, he recorded as accompanist to Forest City Joe Pugh in 1959. Two years later, Rodgers settled in Minneapolis, beginning a long association with Mojo Burford. He also recorded with Burford and Lazy Bill Lucas. In the early 70s Rodgers had a spell as guitarist in Muddy Waters' band, and after some years out of music, he formed his own band in the 80s, winning several music awards in Minnesota. His Blue Moon single 'Big Leg Woman/Cadillac Blues' was voted 'Blues Single Of 1990' in the international **W.C. Handy** awards. Rodgers only made one full album, which was highly-acclaimed on its release, which tragically coincided with his death on 7 May 1990, just prior to a tour of the UK.

Album: *They Call Me The Cat Daddy* (1990).

Rodin, Gil

b. Gilbert A. Rodin, 9 December 1909, Russia, d. 17 June 1974. Raised in Chicago, Rodin played clarinet and saxophones in a number of local dance bands before moving to California. In 1927 he became a member of the **Ben Pollack** band. He quickly became a key figure in the band as both player and administrator. He also wrote a number of arrangements. In 1935, following disagreements with Pollack, Rodin was one of the founders of a new co-operative band which was eventually fronted by **Bob Crosby**. Once again, Rodin assumed multiple roles, one of which was as president of the Crosby corporation, and was the mastermind of the band's huge popularity. After World War II he worked with another ex-Crosby sideman, **Ray Bauduc** and in a reconstituted Crosby band. At the end of the 40s he moved out of music and into radio and television where he worked as a programme producer.

Album: with Bob Crosby *South Rampart Street Parade* (1935-42).

Rodman, Judy

b. 23 May 1951, Riverside, California, USA. Rodman, the daughter of an air traffic controller, comes from a musical family that loved to entertain. She was raised in Miami and studied at Jacksonville University. In 1971 she moved to Memphis and shared rooms with **Janie Frickie**, with whom she recorded jingles and commercials. After marrying John Rodman and having a son, Peter, she moved to Nashville in 1980 and recorded many commercials. She sang background vocals on **George Strait**'s US country number ls, 'Let's Fall To Pieces Together' and 'You Look So Good In Love' as well as on **T.G. Sheppard**'s 'Only One You' and Janie Frickie's album, *It Ain't Easy*. While working for singer **Ed Bruce**, she impressed producer Tommy West and became the first signing to Mary Tyler Moore's new label, MTM, in 1984. Her first single, 'I've Been Had By Love Before', made the US country Top 40 and won **Bob Dylan**'s patronage. In the booklet accompanying his *Biograph* set, Dylan says, 'At the moment I like Judy Rodman's 'I've Been Had By Love Before' more than anything happening on the pop stations.' In 1986, she had a US country number l single with 'Until I Met You'. This was followed by 'She Thinks That She'll Marry', 'Girls Ride Horses Too' and, predictably, a revival of Bob Dylan's 'I'll Be Your Baby Tonight'. Unfortunately, her success could not prevent MTM from going into liquidation.

Albums: *Judy* (1986), *A Place Called Love* (1987), *Goin' To Work* (1988).

Rodney O And Joe Cooley

Street-orientated duo who, having lacked adequate repayment on their first three albums (each of which sold 200,000 copies), elected to go it alone on the fourth, *Fuck New York*. They had to sell their cars and possessions to get it done, but they were confident of a return having taken control of the means of production. On that album's provocative title, Rodney elaborates: 'The crux of the LP is about the people who are ripping off New York rap fans. It speaks about the reluctance of some New York people to break a West Coast artist because they feel that rap started in New York'. It was hardly the most diplomatic way to introduce themselves to East Coast hip hop fans, however.

Selected album: *Fuck New York* (Psychotic Records 1993).

Rodney, Red

b. Robert Chudnick, 27 September 1927, Philadelphia, Pennsylvania, USA, d. 27 May 1994, Boynton Beach, Florida, USA. Within a few years of taking up the trumpet (first presented to him by a great aunt at his Bar Mitzvah) Rodney was hired by dance band leader Jerry Wald. While still in his teens he also played with **Jimmy Dorsey**, **Elliot Lawrence** and **Benny Goodman**. By 1946, when he joined **Gene Krupa**, Rodney was a highly experienced big band trumpeter but was already experimenting with bebop. These inclinations were encouraged by Krupa, **Claude Thornhill** and **Woody Herman** with whom he also played in the late 40s. In 1949, with his reputation as a rising bop star fast gaining ground, he joined the **Charlie Parker** quintet (via an introduction from **Dizzy Gillespie**). For the next two years he was acclaimed as one of the best bebop trumpeters around and was certainly among the first white players to gain

credibility and acceptance in the field (he would go on to help record the soundtrack to Clint Eastwood's film tribute to Parker, *Bird*. Among the anecdotes to emerge from this time was the tale of Parker telling his agent that Rodney was in fact an albino, in order to ensure he wasn't barred from a tour of the South). Ill health and drug addiction nevertheless damaged his career and the 50s and 60s were bleak periods - despite arranging an elaborate fraud whereby he impersonated the similar-looking General Arnold T. MacIntyre in order to obtain money by deception. During the early 70s Rodney returned to the centre of the jazz stage, playing better than ever and displaying inventiveness and thorough mastery of his instrument in all bop and post-bop settings. He continued to be in demand playing in festivals, concerts and clubs around the world until his death, from lung cancer, in 1994.

Selected albums: *Georgie Auld / Red Rodney On The Air* (1947), with Charlie Parker *Live At Carnegie Hall* (1949), *The New Sounds* (1951), *Modern Music From Chicago* (1955), *Red Arrow* (1957), *The Red Rodney Quintet* (1958), *Fiery* (Savoy 1958), *Bird Lives!* (Muse 1973), *Superbop* (Muse 1974), *Red Rodney With The Bebop Preservation Society* (1975), *Red Rodney With The Danish Jazz Army* (1975), *The Red Tornado* (Muse 1975), *Yard's Pad* (Sonet 1976), *Red, White And Blues* (Muse 1976), *Home Free* (Muse 1977), *The Three Rs* (1979), *Hi Jinx At The Village Vanguard* (Muse 1980), *Live At The Village Vanguard* (1980), *Spirit Within* (1981), *Night And Day* (1981), *Sprint* (1982), *Red Giant* (Steeplechase 1988), *No Turn On Red* (Denon 1988), *One For Bird* (Steeplechase 1988), *Red Snapper* (Steeplechase 1988), *Then And Now* (Chesky 1992). Compilation: with Gene Krupa *Drummin' Man* (1945-49).

Rodríguez, Alfredo

b. 1936, Havana, Cuba. Unlike most salsa musicians of his generation, whose musical education was 'street schooling', virtuoso pianist, arranger and composer Rodríguez comes from a classical music background. When he was five or six years old he sang and played claves. At the time, there were lots of children's talent contests at theatres and on the radio. Alfredo participated in these and won a number of competitions. When he was seven years old, he began taking classical piano lessons with a concert pianist in Havana. He remembers seeing several classical pianists, including Rubinstein and Arrau, in Havana and he dreamed of becoming a classical pianist. Rodríguez relocated to New York in 1960. After his arrival, he resumed piano tuition and studied musical theory. He also started listening to Cuban music. Alfredo was influenced by Pedro 'Peruchín' Jústiz (b. 1913, d. 1977; who worked with **Beny Moré,** Orquesta Riverside, Julio Gutiérrez, Antobal and others, and as a leader), who he regards as 'the master of all contemporary salsa pianists', as well as Luis 'Lili' Martínez Grinan (who belonged to Félix Chapottín's band and was a prolific composer) and Jesús López (who was a sideman with Antonio Arcaño - see **Israel 'Cachao' López**). Rodríguez describes these keyboardists as 'the three pillars of Cuban piano playing of all time'. Currently he admires his contemporary compatriots Jesús 'Chucho' Valdés (leader of **Irakere**), Gonzalito Rubalcaba and Emiliano Salvador. Later on, his love for jazz led him to take private courses with Roland Hanna, Albert Dailey and **Bill Evans**, among others. In the mid-60s he began his professional career in Latin music as a member of the Vicentico Valdés band. This was followed by work with **Sonora Matancera** and the charanga (flute and strings band) of Belisario López. Alfredo made his recording debut in 1966 on *Swing* by Conjunto Sensación. This eight-piece group was led by Rey Roig and featured **Pete 'El Conde' Rodríguez** on lead vocals. In 1968, Rodríguez, who had been working in the printing trade for a number of years, became one of the rare salsa sidemen to give up his day job. This decision meant he had to suffer a big financial cut and it was a struggle for him to survive. **Willie Rosario** hired him to perform with his orchestra. **Bobby Valentín** also played bass with the band at the time. 'I really loved his playing very much,' said Rodríguez in 1990. 'Bass and piano is like two brothers . . . Bobby Valentín is a nice guy. He is fantastic.' After two years and two albums with Rosario, he moved to one of the big names of the 60s, **Joe Cuba**. He joined Cuba's sextet during its period of decline, replacing pianist Nick Jiménez, who had relocated to Puerto Rico. He was recommended to Joe Cuba by Lino Frías, the pianist with Sonora Matancera at the time. Frías was an old friend of Alfredo's father, who had built the pianist's house back in Cuba. Rodríguez went directly on a tour of California with the Joe Cuba Sextet. However, he did not know the group's repertoire and was further handicapped by the absence of piano charts, which Cuba had lost. Rodríguez and the bandleader became close friends. He later said of Cuba: 'he was a very shrewd man and he had a lot of charisma . . . That's what he used to sell, his image'. Rodríguez's spell with Joe Cuba was followed by a stint with Cuban sonero (improvising salsa singer) **Justo Betancourt**, who Alfredo describes as one of his idols. The two artists became good friends. Rodríguez performed on Betancourt's biggest hit, the title track of *Pa Bravo Yo*.

In the mid-70s, Alfredo moved to Miami and initially worked with a big band accompanying great vocalists like Rolando La Serie and Vicentico Valdés. After three months he broke his contract by agreement and went to work for **José Fajardo**, who needed a pianist for his quintet. Rodríguez had heard Fajardo on popular radio programmes in Cuba in the early 50s. Alfredo recorded two albums with Fajardo's charanga during his three-year tenure with the bandleader,

which finished in 1976. The two artists performed together again in Paris in 1989. 'The time spent with Fajardo's band was very important to me since my musical abilities were put to a big test. He is one of the best flautists of this music of all time', said Alfredo. In 1976, he was back in New York still mourning the death of his father and had not played piano for three months, when Cuban master percussionist Carlos 'Patato' Valdez invited him to perform on *Ready For Freddy*. The record, which also featured singer/percussionist **Papaíto**, was considered as 'one of the pillars of Cuban music done outside Cuba'. Rodríguez became a member of Charanga 76 and performed on several of the band's albums. In 1979, he sessioned on *Para Africa Con Amor*, one of the finest albums by violinist **Alfredo de la Fé**. At the beginning of the 80s, Justo Betancourt invited Rodríguez to come to Puerto Rico to perform with him, but he had already decided to settle in Paris, France. In 1981, Alfredo participated in *Afro-Charanga*, an interesting experiment fronted by African singer/composer Amadou Balake supported by a charanga ensemble of New York-based salsa musicians performing Cuban arrangements. Rodríguez played a particularly aggressive and intense solo on the track 'Whiskey Et Coca Cola', which became a London club favourite. Also in 1981, Alfredo toured as a member of **Tito Puente**'s Latin Ensemble, which included Patato.

In 1982 he completed a three-month stint with SAR Records (founded in 1979 by Sergio Bofill, Andriano García and **Roberto Torres**) as a replacement for the company's house pianist and musical director, Alfredo Valdes Jnr.. Rodríguez sessioned on SAR albums by Papaíto, **Alfredo 'Chocolate' Armenteros** and Lita Branda (the sister of Melcochita). That year, Alfredo acted as musical director, arranged two tracks and played on *Y Sigue La Cosa . . .* by the typical band Armando Sánchez y su Conjunto Son de la Loma. Additionally in 1982, Rodríguez toured with a quintet that included flautist Artie Webb, saxophonist/flautist Allen Hoist and Patato, who was living in Paris having become a key figure on the city's Latin scene. In 1983, he made his debut as a bandleader in collaboration with Patato and Totico (Eugenio Arango) on *Sonido Solido* recorded in New York. The track 'Para Africa Traigo Mí Son', which Alfredo composed and arranged, was a hit in New York, throughout France and in various parts of Africa.

In 1985, Rodríguez returned to New York to record *Monsieur Oh, La, La* for Caimán Records, a successor of SAR co-founded by Sergio Bofill and Humberto Corredor. The album featured **Adalberto Santiago** and Jimmy Sabater as co-lead vocalists. From 1987 onwards, Rodríguez and his group have had frequent residencies at London's Bass Clef club. Also in 1987, he performed with Papaíto in Paris and London. In 1989 he toured Europe and French Guiana with Patato. In addition to the artists and bands already mentioned, Rodríguez has gigged with **Ismael Rivera**, **Celia Cruz**, **Johnny Pacheco**, **Ray Barretto**, **Pupi Legarreta**, **Mongo Santamaría**, **Monguito**, **Rafael Cortijo**, **Camilo Azuquita**, Roberto Torres and Andy and Jerry González (see **Conjunto Libre**) amongst others, and sessioned with Louie Colón, **Dizzy Gillespie**, José Mangual Jnr., Orquesta Novel, Legarreta, Daniel Santos, Charanga La Reina and others. Rodríguez regards the salsa erótica/romántica trend of the second half of the 80s and early 90s as vulgar, unattractive and without swing, and prefers listening to the 'real masters' like Félix Chapottín (who was married to his cousin), Orquesta Aragón, Arcaño y sus Maravillas and others.

Selected albums Alfredo Rodríguez has performed on: with Conjunto Sensación *Swing* (1966), with Willie Rosario *El Bravo De Siempre* (c.1969) and *Mr Rhythm/Mr. Ritmo* (1971), with Joe Cuba Sextet *Recuerdos de mi Querido Barrio (Memories of My Beloved Neighborhood)* (c.1971), *Bustin' Out* (1972) and *Doin' It Right/Hecho y Derecho* (1973), with Justo Betancourt *Pa Bravo Yo* (1972) and *Leguleya No* (1982), with José Fajardo *Fajardo y sus Estrellas del 75* (1975) and *Fajardo '76: La Raiz De La Charanga 'Charanga Roots'* (1976), with Carlos 'Patato' Valdez *Ready For Freddy* (1976), with Alfredo de la Fé *Para Africa Con Amor* (1979), with Amadou Balake *Afro-Charanga* (1981), with Papaíto *Papaíto* (1982), with Alfredo 'Chocolate' Armenteros *Chocolate Dice* (1982), with Armando Sánchez y su Conjunto Son de la Loma *Y Sigue La Cosa...* (1982), with Irazu, guesting along with Lou Donaldson, Nicky Marrero *La Fiesta Del Timbalero* (1991). Solo albums: *Sonido Solido* (aka *Alfredo Rodríguez . Patato . Totico*, 1983), *Monsieur Oh, La, La* (1985), (Live set with Patato guesting *Cuba-New York-Paris* (1991).

Rodríguez, Arsenio

b. 30 August 1911, Güira de Macurije, Matanzas Province, Cuba, d. 31 December 1970, New York City, USA. Rodríguez was the third generation descendant of a slave from the Congo region of Africa. When he was seven years old he lost his eyesight and in his adult years he became known as 'El Ciego Maravilloso' (The Marvellous Blind Man). He is reputed to have begun his professional career at the age of eight, starting with African derived bass instruments and the conga. Later on, street soneros (performers of the Afro-Cuban form called son) helped him learn the tres (six or nine string Cuban guitar), which he favoured and became a celebrated exponent. Rodríguez began composing in 1927. His friend, the magnificent vocalist Miguelito Valdés (b. Eugenio Zacrias Miguel Valdés, 6 September 1910, Belén district, Havana, Cuba, d. 8 November 1978, Bogotá, Colombia), recorded a number of his songs during his career. The Valdés compilation *Mister Babalú ... Miguelito Valdés* (1978)

contained a fine interpretation of Rodríguez's prize winning composition 'Bruca Manigua' with **Chico O'Farrill**'s Orchestra.

During the late 30s he played tres with Sexteto Boston and Conjunto Bellamar. In 1940 he founded a new style of conjunto (group/band) which, by adding conga, cowbell, second and third trumpet and piano to the typical sexteto or septeto line-up of trumpet, tres, guitar, maracas, bass and bongo, created the mould for the modern salsa conjunto format. The copying of Antonio Arcaño's flute riffs (leader of Arcaño y sus Maravillas - see **López, Israel 'Cachao'**) by his trumpeter, Benetin Bustillo, inspired him to create the son montuno rhythm, which he initially called 'el diablo' (the devil). Amid the controversy about the invention of the mambo, Latin music historian Max Salazar, has cited Arsenio as one of the rhythms four possible creators, the other three are: **Pérez Prado**, Antonio Arcaño and Orestes López (pianist, cellist, bassist, composer; brother of Cachao). Many elderly Cubans maintain that the mambo and son montuno are identical.

Rodríguez and his conjunto scored a big hit in 1943 with the **RCA**-Victor release 'La Yuca de Catalina'. A number of his 40s recordings have been issued as compilation albums. While he was in New York City in February 1947 waiting to be examined to ascertain if his eyesight could be restored, he participated in a recording session by **Chano Pozo** for Gabriel Oller's SMC label, which included **Machito**'s orchestra, Miguelito Valdés and **Tito Rodríguez**. He left Cuba in 1950 and moved to New York City. He handed his band over to his trumpeter Félix Chapottín (1909-82), who played with a highly distinctive wailing style and was the brother of Chano Pozo. *En route* to New York he visited Miami, Florida, but he hated it there because of the anti-black discrimination he encountered. His contributions to the development of Latin music were particularly influential during the genres 'return to roots' típico revivals of the late 60s, early 70s and early 80s, many salsa bands included his compositions in their repertoires. For instance, Sonora Ponceña (see **Lucca, Papo**) had a big hit in c.1969 with a version of the Rodríguez classic 'Hay Fuego En El 23' (composed by Lucia Martínez) plucked from his mid-50s album *Sabroso y Caliente*. The band Rodríguez organized in New York included his two brothers, percussionist/composer/singer Raúl 'Caesar' Travieso and percussionist/composer Israel Moises 'Quique' Travieso. In April 1957, the three brothers and three other band members sessioned with **Sabú Martínez** on his mainly Afro-Cuban percussion and voices workout *Palo Congo* on **Blue Note.** Five years later Sabú contributed percussion to the album *Cumbanchando con Arsenio (Fiesta en Harlem)*, recorded by Gabriel Oller for SMC. Arsenio composed and arranged all the tracks and sang on one . His early 60s debut album on Ansonia, *Arsenio Rodríguez y su Conjunto*, featured vocalist/composer Candido Antomattei. Candido resurfaced in 1989 as leader of *Candido y las Super Estrellas* on La Plata Records, which contained an impressive cover of Rodríguez's 1943 hit composition 'La Yuca de Catalina'. In the mid-60s, mainstream pop songwriter **Bert Berns** (whose name was associated with 'Hang On Sloopy', 'Twist & Shout' and many other hits) produced Rodríguez's *Viva Arsenio!* for his Bang Records label, which he founded in 1965. Rodríguez performed his own unique version of 'Hang On Sloopy' on the album.

Unlike some of his imitators who tended towards a conservative defence of 'orthodoxy', the master himself was an experimentalist. For example, he dropped trumpets for two saxophones and emphasized the tres on *Quindembo/Afro Magic/La Magia de Arsenio Rodríguez* (1963, Epic) and used a trumpet/saxophone combination in his conjunto on *Arsenio Rodríguez y su Conjunto Vol.2* (mid-60s,) and *Arsenio Dice ... /Arsenio Says ...* (c.1968). He also developed a fusion form that he called Quindembo, which he claimed was a Congolese word for a mixture of many things. After his death, bandleader **Larry Harlow** paid homage with the *Tribute to Arsenio Rodríguez* (1971), which contained versions of Rodríguez compositions and new songs all done in the style of 'El Ciego Maravilloso'.

Selected albums: compilations of 40s RCA-Victor recordings *El Sentimiento de Arsenio* (1974, Cariño), *A Todo Los Barrios* (1974, Cariño) and *Arsenio Rodríguez y su Conjunto 1947-48* (1976, Cubitas), compilation of hits on Seeco *Exitos de Arsenio Rodríguez y su Conjunto* (50s), *Sabroso y Caliente* (mid-50s), with Sabú *Palo Congo* (1957), *Cumbanchando con Arsenio (Fiesta en Harlem)* (1962), *La Pachanga* (1962, Tico), *Arsenio Rodríguez y su Conjunto* (early 60s), *Quindembo/Afro Magic/La Magia de Arsenio Rodríguez* (1963), with Carlos 'Patato' Valdez, Eugenio Arango 'Totico' *Patato & Totico* (mid-60s), *Arsenio Rodríguez y su Conjunto Vol.2* (mid-60s), *Viva Arsenio!* (mid-60s), *Arsenio Dice ... /Arsenio Says ...* (c.1968), *Primitivo*.

Rodríguez, Bobby

b. El Barrio (Spanish Harlem), Manhattan, New York City, USA. Not to be confused with the veteran bass player of the same name, bandleader, saxophonist, flautist, clarinettist, pianist, vocalist, percussionist, arranger, composer, producer Rodríguez was a member of his brother Ray's band in the late 60s and at the beginning of the 70s. He was the band's musical director, arranger, composer and tenor saxophone player. The second release by Ray Rodríguez and his orchestra, *Delusion*, contained the exceptional 'Olvidame' (Forget Me), co-written by Bobby and the band's original vocalist, albino Nestor Sánchez 'El Albino Divino'. Sánchez (b. New York City, of Puerto Rican parents) left to join Tony Pabón's band La

Protesta; he later worked with Conjunto Candela, **Larry Harlow**, Julio Castro and as a solo artist. In 1974, Bobby organized his own brass and flute-led band, called La Compañia (the Company). They consistently worked the New York club circuit before debuting on *Lead Me To That Beautiful Band* in 1975. From the beginning, La Compañia's style, although firmly rooted in the Latin tradition, was heavily influenced by jazz, soul and funk, and their repertoire included English lyric songs. Second generation 'Nuyorican' (New Yorker of Puerto Rican descent), Eddie Iglesias Hernández, sang the English vocals and doubled on trombone. The Spanish lyric songs were performed by Puerto Rico-born Junior Cordova and José Acosta. Cordova had worked previously with Nelson Feliciano and **Rafael Cortijo**. A track from their first album, the **Rubén Blades** composition 'Numero 6' about delays on the subway, was a massive hit. Lyrics like: 'Hurry up, damn machine, I've been here for hours and still I cannot see that number six subway, number six . . .', really struck a chord with the Latino audience in New York. Blades also wrote the hit 'What Happened' from Bobby's 'live' 1976 follow-up *Salsa At Woodstock*.

In 1977, Rodríguez, Hernández, Acosta and La Compañia's timbales player, Charlie Salinas, participated in the 17th anniversary album by the Alegre All-Stars led by **Charlie Palmieri** and produced by **Al Santiago**. Bobby's namesake played bass on the session. In 1978, Rodríguez and La Compañia had a hit single with the title track of *Latin From Manhattan*. This cover version of the 30s song, originally recorded by **Al Jolson**, was given a salsa/dixieland jazz treatment with Rodríguez's clarinet playing very much to the fore. In 1984, Eddie Iglesias Hernández left La Compañia and took Acosta and Salinas with him to form the nine-piece, two-trombone band Los Amigos And The Bad Street Boys. Spanish lead vocals on their tremendously successful debut *Cheek To Cheek*, were handled by Frankie Morales, who went on to work with the **Lebron Brothers**, before turning solo. Meanwhile, after a gap of three years, Rodríguez renamed his band La Nueva Compañia (The New Company) and came back with the appropriately titled *Mi Regreso (My Return)* in 1984. The lead singer on the album was Orlando Castillo 'Watusi' (b. 23 March, San Felipe, Yaracuy State, Venezuela). Watusi worked with Los Satélites, Porfi Jiménez and Federico y su Combo Latino before becoming a solo artist; he made his first UK appearance in 1990 with **Tito Puente**. *Mi Regreso* contained an outstanding remake of 'Olvidame' and a fine version of the classic 'Maria Cristina', composed by Ñico Saquito (b. 13 February 1901, Santiago de Cuba, Cuba; d. 5 August 1982, Cuba). In 1987, Cordova, Iglesias and Salinas reunited with Bobby and La Nueva Compañia for *Juntos Otra Vez (Back Together Again)*.

Albums: with Ray Rodríguez And His orchestra *Introducing Ray Rodríguez And His Orchestra* (c.1968), *Delusion* (c.1969), *Ray Rodríguez y su Orquesta* (c.1970); *Lead Me To That Beautiful Band* (1975), *Salsa At Woodstock* (1976); with the Alegre All-Stars *The Alegre All-Stars 'Perdido' (Vol. 5)* (1977); *Latin From Manhattan* (1978), *Hay Que Cambiar La Rutina* (1980), *The Force Of The 80's* (1981), *Mi Regreso* (1984), *Juntos Otra Vez* (1987).

Rodriguez, Johnny

b. Juan Raul Davis Rodriguez, 10 December 1951, Sabinal, Texas, USA. Rodriguez grew up with a large family living in a shanty town 90 miles from the Mexican border. He was given a guitar when he was seven and, as a teenager, he sang with a beat group. His troubles with the law included goat rustling (he barbecued the goats). A Texas ranger, who heard him singing in his cell, found him a job at the Alamo village and he drove stagecoaches, rode horses and entertained tourists. **Tom T. Hall** recognized his talent and employed him as lead guitarist with his road band, the Storytellers. He was signed to **Mercury Records** who particularly liked the way he could switch from English to Spanish. Rodriguez went to number 9 in the US country chart with his first release, 'Pass Me By' in 1972 and he then had three consecutive number 1 records, 'You Always Come Back (To Hurting Me)', 'Riding My Thumb To Mexico' and 'That's The Way Love Goes'. He wrote many of his songs and occasionally wrote with Hall. In 1975 he had further number 1 country records with 'I Just Can't Get Her Out Of My Mind', 'Just Get Up And Close The Door' and 'Love Put A Song In My Heart'. In 1977, he had a Top 10 country hit with a revival of the **Eagles**' 'Desperado'. He moved to Epic Records in 1979 and scored by singing 'I Hate The Way I Love It' with newcomer Charly McClain. However, his drug addiction made him more erratic. He started to take less care over his records and, in 1983, he sacked his band. He realised he could only obtain a new one if he adopted a more responsible attitude. He moved to **Capitol** in 1988 and had a country hit with a classy ballad, 'I Didn't (Every Chance I Had)'.

Albums: *Introducing Johnny Rodriguez* (1973), *All I Ever Meant To Do Was Sing* (1973), *My Third Album* (1974), *Songs About Ladies In Love* (1974), *Just Get Up And Close The Door* (1975), *Love Put A Song In My Heart* (1975), *Reflecting* (1976) *Practice Makes Perfect* (1977), *Just For You* (1977), *Love Me With All Your Heart* (1978), *Rodriguez Was Here* (1979), *Rodriguez* (1979), *Sketches* (1979), *Gypsy* (1980), *Through My Eyes* (1980), *After The Rain* (1981), *For Every Rose* (1983), *Fooling With Fire* (1984), *Full Circle* (1986), *Gracias* (1988), *Run For The Border* (Intersound 1994).

Rodríguez, Lalo

b. Ubaldo Rodríguez, 16 May 1958, Puerto Rico. In 1970, 12-year-old Rodríguez joined the band Tempo Moderno and sang with them until 1974. He made his album debut at the age of 16 as lead singer on **Eddie Palmieri**'s *Sun Of Latin Music* (1974), the first Latin album to win a Grammy Award. It included his composition 'Deseo Salvaje'. He also appeared on Palmieri's *Unfinished Masterpiece* (1976), which won another Grammy. In 1976, he shared lead vocals on **Tommy Olivencia**'s *Introducing Lalo Rodríguez & Simon Pérez*. Lalo was special guest artist on **Machito**'s Grammy-nominated *Fireworks* (1977), on which he sang lead (on four tracks), chorus and provided three powerful but sensitive compositions. He sang his composition 'Alianza de Generales' on the Puerto Rico All Stars' *Los Profesionales* (1977) and sang 'Oyelo Que Te Conviene' ('Listen, It's Convenient' - which he originally performed on *Unfinished Masterpiece*) on the Puerto Rico All Stars' 1979 tribute album to Eddie Palmieri. Rodríguez made his solo debut in 1980 with *Simplemente Lalo*, which contained five self-penned songs. The album was produced by Frank Ferrer for his Tierrazo Records label. Ferrer formed the band Puerto Rico 2010 in the 70s. He renamed them Puerto Rico 2013 and released *Puerto Rico 2013* and *Band'alla* in 1989, both with lead vocalist Van Lester. In 1985, Lalo co-produced and wrote all the tracks on *El Niño, El Hombre, El Soñador, El Loco*.

In 1988 he jumped on the salsa romántica bandwagon and achieved massive success with the chart-topping album *Un Nuevo Despertar* on the TH-Rodven label, it was still riding high in the ***Billboard*** salsa Top 10 in mid-1989. The track 'Ven Devórame Otra Vez' (Come And Devour Me Again) was a smash hit during the summer of 1988. Lalo and **Eddie Santiago**, another leading romantic salsa star, were special attractions at the 1988 annual New York Salsa Festival - a traditional gathering of the year's best artists at Madison Square Garden. In 1990, Rodríguez was involved in music industry press speculation about multinational labels poaching top salsa romántica stars. Mid-year it was reported that he had renewed his contract for five more albums with TH-Rodven - the company that had successfully promoted him in Spain - but later in the year he handed over the previously independently distributed, *Una Voz Para Escuchar*, to the major label **Capitol/EMI** Latin for release.

Selected albums: *Simplemente Lalo* (1980), *El Niño, El Hombre, El Soñador, El Loco* (1985), *Punto y Coma* (1987), *Un Nuevo Despertar* (1988), *Sexsacional!* (1989), *Una Voz Para Escuchar* (1990).

Rodríguez, Pete 'El Conde'

b. Pedro Juan Rodríguez, 31 January, Ponce, Puerto Rico. Golden voiced salsa vocalist Rodríguez has a cool and inspired singing style and a regal stage presence that befits his nickname of 'El Conde' (The Count). He worked with local groups in Ponce before relocating to

New York. **Johnny Pacheco** hired him for *Pacheco y su Charanga Vol.IV - 'Suav'ito'* (c.1963), *Cañonazo* (1964, the first release on the Fania Records label) and *Pacheco at the N. Y. World's Fair*. In 1966 he sang lead vocals on *Swing* by Conjunto Sensación, a three-trumpet group led by Cuban Rey Roig, who also wrote the arrangements. Roig was a former member of Conjunto Casino in Havana. The pianist with Sensación was **Alfredo Rodríguez**. El Conde reunited with Pacheco in 1966 on *Pacheco y su Charanga - By Popular Demand*. Between 1967 and 1973 they recorded a further five albums together, including probably their best, *Tres de Café y Dos de Azúcar*, which contained the marvellous 'El Piro De Farra'. They produced several hits which became classics, such as C. Curet Alonso's composition 'La Esencia Del Guaguanco' (from *La Perfecta Combinación*) and 'Dulce Con Dulce' (from *Los Compadres*).

In 1974, Pete went solo under the new management of his wife, Frances, and made a series of albums which used the same typical Cuban trumpet and tres (six or nine-string Cuban guitar) conjunto format that he had worked in with Pacheco. The recording of his debut, *El Conde*, was directed by Pacheco, who also sang in the coro (chorus). The album was a best seller and won him the *Latin NY* magazine award for 'Best New Band' in 1975. José Febles arranged the hit tracks 'Catalina La O' (written by Johnny Ortiz) and 'Pueblo Latino' (composed by Alonso) on his 1976 follow-up *Este Negro Si Es Sabroso*. **Louie Ramírez** produced this album and El Conde's 1977 release, *A Touch Of Class*, which contained the **Rubén Blades** composition 'Tambo', arranged by Febles. Frances took over the role of producer on *Soy La Ley* in 1979. Febles handled all production and arrangement chores on *Fiesta Con 'El Conde'* (1982). A decade after *Tres de Café y Dos de Azúcar*, Rodríguez and Pacheco teamed up again for four albums between 1983 and 1989, which included their 25th anniversary release *Celebración*. Johnny was in the background as producer and musical director on El Conde's salsa romántica oriented *El Rey* in 1990. Pete was a founder member of the Fania All Stars and performed an exciting version of his hit 'Pueblo Latino' on their *Live At Yankee Stadium Vol.1* (1975). He recorded two interpretations of the **Beny Moré** classic 'El Conde Negro', first in 1974 on *El Conde*, and then on **Tito Puente**'s second tribute album to Moré in 1979. Albums on which he sang lead vocals: with Pacheco *Pacheco y su Charanga Vol. IV - 'Suav'ito'* (c.1963), *Cañonazo* (1964), *Pacheco At The N. Y. World's Fair* (1964); with Conjunto Sensación *Swing* (1966); with Pacheco *Pacheco y su Charanga - By Popular Demand* (1966), *Sabor Típico* (1967), *Volando Bajito* (1968), *La Perfecta Combinación* (c.1970), *Los Compadres* (1971); with Larry Harlow *Hommy - A Latin Opera* (1973); with Pacheco *Tres de Café y Dos de Azúcar* (1973); *El Conde* (1974); *Este Negro Si Es Sabroso* (1976); with Celia Cruz, Pacheco, Justo

Betancourt, Papo Lucca *Recordando El Ayer* (1978); *A Touch Of Class* (1978); *Soy La Ley* (1979); with Tito Puente *Homenaje A Beny, Vol. 2* (1979); with Cruz, Pacheco *Celia, Johnny and Pete* (1980); *Fiesta Con 'El Conde'* (1982); with Pacheco *De Nuevo Los Compadres* (1983), *Jicamo* (1985); with Cruz and Puente *Homenaje A Beny Moré, Vol. III* (1985); with Pacheco *Salsobita* (1987), *Celebración* (1989); *El Rey* (1990).

Rodriguez, Rico

b. Emmanuel Rodriguez, 17 October 1934, Kingston, Jamaica, West Indies. Apart from **Don Drummond**, Rico aka Reco aka El Reco, was undoubtedly the most gifted trombonist working in the early years of Jamaican music. In the 40s he attended the famous Catholic Alpha Boys School where, by the age of 10, he had learned to play the trombone under the strict tutelage of the Nuns, though he had originally wanted to play the saxophone. In the early 50s he began appearing at and winning local talent contests. He became a Rasta and formed a close musical association with master Rasta drummer **Count Ossie** at his encampment at Wareika Hill, to the east of Kingston. Rico's first recording session was for **Coxsone Dodd**, playing on the Jiving Juniors' 'Over The River' and **Theophilius Beckford**'s seminal 'Easy Snappin'', and his own 'Stew Peas And Cornflakes'. He went on to work on literally hundreds of sessions for Dodd and most of the top producers of the day including **Duke Reid** ('Let George Do It'), **Leslie Kong**, Vincent Chin (Randy's, for whom he cut 'Rico Special'), and **Prince Buster**, who released a few sides credited to Rico himself including 'Luke Lane Shuffle', 'August 1962', 'This Day', 'Blues From The Hills', and the amazing 'Soul Of Africa'. In an interview with Carl Gayle for *Black Music* magazine in 1977, Rico claimed that some records, issued after he moved to Britain but recorded years earlier ('Let George Do It', 'Salt Lane Shuffle') and credited to his successor Don Drummond, were really by him. In 1966 while resident in the UK, Rico joined Buster when the latter toured the country, and was enlisted to play on 'Barrister Pardon', the follow-up to the infamous 'Judge Dread', during recording sessions in London.

Rico left Jamaica in 1961 and settled in the UK where he continued recording as a session musician for artists such as **Laurel Aitken**, **Georgie Fame**, Joe 'Brixton Cat' Mansano and others, and also in his own right with many singles, including the popular 'The Bullet', and a number of albums released on various UK reggae labels throughout the 60s. In March 1964 he experienced a taste of pop chart success with a reworking of **Jimmy Cliff**'s 'King Of Kings' as Ezz Reco And The Launchers, with Boysie Grant on vocals. The record entered the chart one week before **Millie**'s 'My Boy Lollipop' and spent four weeks in the lower reaches of the UK Top 50, but follow-ups 'Little

Girl' and 'Please Come Back' failed to sell in any quantity and the band folded. He spent the early 70s in the doldrums, rarely recording, but passing the time by playing live with the Undivided, a band made up of ex-patriot Jamaican musicians. In 1976 he returned to Jamaica to record the well-received *Man From Wareika* utilising many of the key Jamaican session musicians of the day, including **Sly And Robbie**. With the arrival of **2-Tone** in the early 80s Rico enjoyed great success playing on stage and on record with the **Specials** upon whose label his next album, *That Man Is Forward* (1981) was released. This was followed by *Jama Rico* a year later. Since returning from a protracted stay in Jamaica, where he spent eight years living once more in Wareika, Rico has returned to London and appears regularly on stage with double bassist Gary Crosby's Jazz Jamaica.

Albums: *Reco In Reggae Land* (1969), *Blow Your Horn* (1969), *Brixton Cat* (1969), *Man From Wareika* (1976), *That Man Is Forward* (2-Tone 1981), *Jama Rico* (2-Tone 1982).

Rodríguez, Tito

b. Pablo Rodríguez, 4 January 1923, Santurce, San Juan, Puerto Rico, d. 28 February 1973, New York University Hospital, New York, USA. Vocalist, percussionist, bandleader, composer, producer, label boss Tito Rodríguez was 'equally talented as an uptempo improvising sonero (singer in the salsa style) and a romantic singer'. 'At its peak, the Rodríguez band's blend of Cuban-orientated numbers and tight, solo-filled instrumentals equalled any of his rivals' (quotes from *The Latin Tinge* by John Storm Roberts, 1979). Tito was born to a Cuban mother and Dominican father. At the age of 16 he played maracas and sang second voice with Cuarteto Mayari before relocating to New York to live with his older brother Johnny (b. 10 October 1912, Camuy, Puerto Rico), who had moved there in 1935. Popular vocalist/composer Johnny formed his own trio in 1940; recordings he made with his trio on the Seeco label were collected on *Encores de Johnny Rodríguez y su Trio* and *Siempre Favoritas de Johnny Rodríguez y su Trio*. Rodríguez's first job in the city was with Cuarteto Caney. After brief stints with Enric Madriguera and **Xavier Cugat** (as a singer and bongo player), a year in the US Army was followed by a spell singing with **Noro Morales**. *El Dinamico Tito Rodríguez* was a reissue of a Morales collection with Tito. In 1946 Cuban pianist/composer José Curbelo recruited Rodríguez and **Tito Puente** (on timbales) to his band, which became an 'incubator' for the future New York mambo sound. Recordings made by Curbelo's band during the two years of Tito's period of tenure were later compiled on *Los Reyes del Mambo*. In 1946, while Curbelo's band were appearing at the China Doll nightclub, Rodríguez met a Japanese American chorus girl called Tobi Kei (b. Takeku Kunimatzu, 23 January 1925, Bellingham,

Washington, USA), whom he married a few months later. In February 1947, while he was still with Curbelo, Tito participated in a recording session by **Chano Pozo** for Gabriel Oller's SMC label, which included the **Machito** band, **Arsenio Rodríguez** and Miguelito Valdés. Curbelo sacked Rodríguez in 1947. The bandleader had given him a day off to look after Tobi, who was sick, but someone informed Curbelo that Rodríguez spent the day drinking in a bar. Tito was unemployed for some months.

After leading a short-lived quintet, which he formed in late 1947, Rodríguez organized a trumpet conjunto (group) called the Mambo Devils in mid-1948. With them he recorded eight tunes for SMC, four of them arranged by Puente, who went on to become his musical antagonist. Tito later expanded his outfit to a big band, which he led until 1965. In 1949 he signed to Tico Records, formed in 1948 by two shirt label manufacturers, George Goldner and Art 'Pancho' Raymond. Rodríguez had to rename his band the Lobos del Mambo (Mambo Wolves) as the aggrieved Oller objected to the use of Mambo Devils. He did two stints with the label, between 1949 and 1953 and between 1956 and 1958, during which time he released 78s, six 10-inch volumes of mambos and various 12-inch albums. Material from both these periods was later compiled on *Nostalgia* (1972) and *Uptempo* (1978). Tito made no records during 1950 because a wrangle between Goldner and Raymond suspended all recording at Tico. He resumed recording the following year when Goldner took charge of the label. In pursuit of the crossover market, Rodríguez switched to **RCA** in 1953 and his records on the label sold well. *Ritmo y Melodia, 15 Joyas Tropicales* (1990) was the most recent compilation of material culled from his RCA period. On his return to Tico, he issued *Wa-Pa-Cha* (1956). His final release for them was *Señor Tito Rodríguez* (1958). In 1960 he signed to United Artists on the basis that he would be the only Latin bandleader to record for the company. His first album on the label, *Live At The Palladium*, was a great success. Conflict over top billing at New York's famous Palladium Ballroom and elsewhere was an aspect of the rivalry that existed between Puente and Rodríguez.

In 1962 Rodríguez had three massive hits in a row: 'Vuela La Paloma' (From *West Side Beat*), 'Cuando, Cuando' (from *Back Home In Puerto Rico*) and 'Cara De Payaso' (from *Tito Rodríguez' Hits*), which were all number 1 in Puerto Rico and other South American countries. Rodríguez and his band recorded *Back Home In Puerto Rico* during a two week stay on the island in June 1962. His return was marked by official government receptions and heavy media coverage. He tried to find fame in Las Vegas with a revue, but it flopped and he made a heavy financial loss. Tito also recorded as lead singer with La Playa Sextet, whose line-up substituted the electric guitar of their Puerto

Rican leader, Payo Alicea, for traditional piano. A compilation of La Playa Sextet cuts with Tito on lead vocals was issued under the title, *Tito Dice ... Separala Tambien!*. In 1963 he issued the Latin jazz *Live At Birdland*, which featured the jazz musicians **Zoot Sims**, **Clark Terry**, **Bob Brookmeyer**, **Al Cohen** and Bernie Leighton. The same year Tito had a huge hit of over one-and-a-half million sales with the smoochy string laden bolero 'Inolvidable' (Unforgettable), contained on *From Tito Rodríguez With Love*. The song was written by Cuban bandleader/pianist Julio Gutiérrez. He followed this with a series of soft romantic bolero albums, interspersed with uptempo collections like *Tito Tito Tito*, on which accompanist **Israel 'Cachao' López**'s championing of Latin jam sessions (descargas) was spotlighted on the opening track 'Descarga Cachao'. The Rodríguez/Puente feud was reflected on some of the recordings Tito made for Musicor Records, such as 'Avisale A Mi Contrario Que Aqui Estoy Yo' (Tell My Adversary I'm Here) from *Carnival of the Americas* (1964) and the album title *Tito No. 1*. Cuban vocalist Miguelito Valdés and Machito appealed to the two combatants in the Valdés-penned song 'Que Pena Me Da' (How Sorry I Feel) on their 1963 collaboration *Reunion*. Tito and his band accompanied singer Nelson Pinedo (b. Barranquilla, Colombia) on his Musicor release *A Latin In America*.

Bad deals and conflict with his colleagues over pay led him to disband and move to Puerto Rico in 1966. Negative attitudes towards 'Nuyoricans' (New York Puerto Ricans) initially prevented him from breaking into Puerto Rican television, but he managed to get a show when the parent company of United Artists acquired one of the island's channels. Guests like **Shirley Bassey**, **Tony Bennett** and **Sammy Davis Jnr.** appeared on his programme. He believed that anti-Nuyorican sentiment was also the reason why he did not receive an award for the show. Feeling rejected by his own people, Tito moved to Coral Gables in Miami, USA. He returned to New York and slayed the capacity audience at the Manhattan Center with the title track of *Estoy Como Nunca* (I'm As Good As Ever). *El Doctor* (1968) contained 'Esa Bomba', his last rivalry tune aimed at Puente. He was accompanied to Puerto Rico by arranger/saxophonist Ray Santos, who joined his band in 1963. A graduate of New York's Juilliard School of Music, Santos did stints with **Al Santiago**'s Chack-a-nunu Boys, Noro Morales (twice), Machito and Tito Puente between the early 50s and 1962. He remained in Puerto Rico to work as a contractor for shows in the major hotels until 1984, when he returned to the Big Apple and took up a teaching post at the City College of New York. In 1991, Santos was hired to work on the music for the Hollywood movie adaptation of the Oscar Hijuelos novel *The Mambo Kings Play Songs Of Love* (1989).

Rodríguez first displayed signs of illness in 1967 while making one of his last television shows. He decided to found his own TR Records label in 1969 and while waiting for medical test results in the UK, he used British musicians to record the music for his first TR album, *Involvidable/Unforgettable*. It was confirmed that he had leukaemia but he insisted that the results be kept secret. TR Records, Inc. was launched in August 1971 and his second album on the label, *Palladium Memories*, sold well. He teamed up with **Louie Ramírez** for the third release, *Algo Nuevo*. Tito's *25th Anniversary Performance*, recorded in a nightclub in Perú, was issued a month before his death. The album provoked speculation about whether he had intended it to be a farewell. Rodríguez's last appearance was with Machito and his band at Madison Square Garden on 2 February 1973. He finally lost the battle with leukaemia and 26 days later, Tito died in Tobi's arms.

Selected albums: with Noro Morales *El Dinamico Tito Rodríguez* aka *Bailemos con Noro Morales y su Orquesta* (40s), with José Curbelo *Los Reyes del Mambo* (1946-47), *Nostalgia* (50s), *Uptempo* (50s), *Ritmo y Melodia, 15 Joyas Tropicales* (1953-55), *Señor Tito Rodríguez* (1958), *Live At The Palladium* (1960), *Charanga Pachanga* (1961), *Returns To The Palladium - Live!*, *West Side Beat* (1962), *Latin Twist, Back Home In Puerto Rico* (1962), *Tito Rodríguez' Hits* (1962), with La Playa Sextet *Tito Dice ... Separala Tambien* (early 60s), *Let's Do The Bossa Nova, Live At Birdland* (1963), *En Puerto Azul, Venezuela* (1963), *From Tito Rodríguez With Love* (1963), *More Amor, Tito Tito Tito* (1964), *Carnival of the Americas* (1964), *Tito No. 1, En Escenario* (1967), *Big Band Latino* (1968), *Estoy Como Nunca* (1968), *El Doctor* (1968), *Involvidable/Unforgettable* (1971), *Palladium Memories*, with Louie Ramírez *Algo Nuevo* (1972), *25th Anniversary Performance* (1973). Selected compilations: two disc collection of United Artists hits *Tito Rodríguez Superpak*, double TR Records collection *Un Retrato*.

Rods

This New York power-trio exploded onto the heavy metal scene in 1980. Formed by ex-**Elf** guitarist David Feinstein, the line-up was completed by drummer Carl Canedy and bassist Stephen Farmer. Although heavily influenced by **Kiss**, **Ted Nugent** and **Deep Purple**, they transformed these influences into a unique sound that was at once aggressive, powerful and uncompromising. *Rock Hard*, released on the independent Primal label, was a terse and anthemic debut, which eventually led to the inking of a deal with **Arista**. Gary Bordonaro replaced Farmer before their first major label release (a re-mixed version of *Rock Hard*, with three additional tracks). *Wild Dogs* was a disappointing follow-up and sold poorly, which ensured the band would be dropped by their label. Consigned once more to the independent sector, *In The Raw* was a poorly-produced collection of demos, while the live album suffered from muddy sound and uninspired performances. By this stage the band had largely alienated their original fan base. *Let Them Eat Metal*, although a marked improvement, still failed to sell and they branched into more melodic rock, recruiting Andy McDonald (guitar), Rick Caudle (vocals), and Emma Zale (keyboards). In 1987 the band returned to a three-piece format again, with Craig Gruber (ex-Elf) replacing Bordonaro, before ex-**Picture** vocalist Shmoulic Avigal was added to record *Heavier Than Thou*. A third successive release to fail to make any impact, this increased existing internal pressures and the band imploded shortly thereafter.

Albums: *Rock Hard* (Primal 1980), *The Rods* (Arista 1981), *Wild Dogs* (Arista 1982), *In The Raw* (Shrapnel 1983), *Live* (Music For Nations 1983), *Let Them Eat Metal* (Music For Nations 1984), *Heavier Than Thou* (Zebra 1987).

Roe, Tommy

b. 9 May 1942, Atlanta, Georgia, USA. Vocalist Roe began his career with high school act, the Satins. The group performed several of his compositions, notably 'Sheila', which they recorded in 1960. The single was unsuccessful, but Roe revived the song two years later upon securing a solo deal. This **Buddy Holly**-influenced rocker topped the US chart, and reached the Top 3 in Britain where the artist enjoyed considerable popularity. Roe scored two Top 10 hits in 1963 with 'The Folk Singer' and 'Everybody' and, although not a major chart entry, 'Sweet Pea' garnered considerable airplay through the auspices of **pirate radio**. The song reached the US Top 10, as did its follow-up, 'Hooray For Hazel', but Roe's biggest hit came in 1969 when 'Dizzy' topped the charts on both sides of the Atlantic. The singer enjoyed further success with 'Heather Honey' and 'Jam Up Jelly Tight', but for much of the 70s he opted to pursue a low-key career in his home state. Roe did attempt a 'comeback' with *Energy* and *Full Bloom*, but subsequently plied the nostalgia circuit. Memories of his past success were resurrected when 'Dizzy' returned to the top of the UK charts in 1992 in a version by the **Wonder Stuff** and Vic Reeves.

Albums: *Sheila* (1963), *Something For Everybody* (1963), *Sweet Pea* (1966), *It's Now A Winter's Day* (1967), *Phantasia* (1967), *Dizzy* (1969), *We Can Make Music* (1970), *Energy* (1976), *Full Bloom* (1977). Compilations: *12 In A Roe* (1970), *Greatest Hits* (1970), *Beginnings* (1971), *16 Greatest Hits* (1976), *16 Greatest Songs* (1993).

Roena, Roberto

b. 16 January c.1940, Mayagüez, Puerto Rico; his last name is occasionally spelt as Rohena. A salsa bandleader for over 20 years, Roena began his musical career as a dancer with various bands in Puerto Rico - he later became known as 'El Gran Bailarín' (The Great Dancer). While performing as a dancer and chorus singer with Cortijo y su Combo, the band's leader **Rafael Cortijo** gave Roena his first percussion lessons. He settled for the bongo and became a member of Cortijo's band between 1957 and 1962. Roberto was amongst the seven accompanists, led by pianist Rafael Ithier, who defected from Cortijo's Combo in May 1962 to become the basis of **El Gran Combo**. During his tenure with Gran Combo he appeared on **Kako**'s classic Latin jam outing *Puerto Rican All-Stars Featuring Kako*, recorded in 1963, and 1967's *Los Mejores Mujsicos de Puerto Rico*, directed and arranged by Ray Santos. In 1966, Roena made his recording debut as leader with a band called Megatones on *Se Pone Bueno/It Gets Better* on Alegre Records. Panamanian **Camilo Azuquita** provided the lead vocals and El Gran Combo's lead vocalists at the time, **Andy Montañez** and Pellín Rodríguez, sang in the chorus. Roena left Gran Combo in mid-1969. He signed with Fania International (later called just International), a division of Jerry Masucci and **Johnny Pacheco**'s Fania Records, and debuted with his band Apollo Sound on *Roberto Roena y su Apollo Sound*. The great Puerto Rican composer, Catalino 'Tite' Curet Alonso, was the album's 'creative musical director' and wrote the smash hit track 'Tu Loco Loco, Y Yo Tranquilo'. From the outset, Apollo Sound featured a line-up of two trumpets, trombone, tenor saxophone (doubling on flute), rhythm section (bongo, conga, timbales, bass, piano) and voices (lead and chorus). A third trumpet was added in the mid-70s and the resultant front-line combination was retained into the 90s. While preserving their rhythmic integrity, Roena and Apollo Sound developed into one of salsa's more progressive and sophisticated outfits with their own highly distinctive style. To help achieve this, Roena hired some of Puerto Rico's most creative arrangers over the years, including **Bobby Valentín**, Elías Lopés, **Luis 'Perico' Ortiz,** Julio 'Gunda' Merced, **Papo Lucca**, Louis García, Tito Rivera and Humberto Ramírez.

The first three Apollo Sound albums all featured the same trio of vocalists, namely, Piro Mantilla, Dino Guy Casiano and Frankie Calderon. Trumpeter Elías Lopés acted as musical director on Apollo Sound's second and third releases. Tito Cruz replaced Mantilla on 1972's *Roberto Roena y su Apollo Sound 4*. Casiano was succeeded by Sammy González, a former **Tommy Olivencia** band member, on Apollo Sound's fifth release in 1973, which marked the recording debut of virtuoso trombonist/arranger Julio 'Gunda' Merced with the band. Luis 'Perico' Ortiz arranged the hits 'Traición' and 'Parece Mentira' from 1974's *Roberto Roena y su Apollo Sound 6*. In 1974 Roena participated in the reunion of original members of Cortijo's Combo on *Juntos Otra Vez*. Calderon and Cruz departed after Apollo Sound's sixth album and José 'Papo' Sánchez joined González as co-lead vocalist on *Lucky 7* in 1976.

This record contained another of Roena's greatest hits, 'Mi Desengaño', which was co-written and subtly arranged by Merced. **Rubén Blades** contributed his compositions 'Para Ser Rumbero' and 'Amistad Barata' to *La 8va. Maravilla* in 1977. Sammy González left and recorded as a leader on *Sammy González y Los Torbellinos con Samuel Serrano* (1978). Tito Cruz returned to replace González on *Roberto Roena y su Apollo Sound 9* in 1977. In mid-1978, Merced split from Apollo Sound taking five band members with him, including singer Papo Sánchez, to found Salsa Fever. In the late 80s, Merced became the house producer and musical director for Tony Moreno's Musical Productions label. Roena carried on to produce *El Progreso* in 1978, which was one of his strongest albums. It contained the C. Curet Alonso composition 'Lamento de Concepción' with a wonderful multi-layered arrangement by Papo Lucca, who played piano on the track and four other tracks. Tito Cruz was joined on lead vocals by Carlos Santos, who performed previously with Kako and Vilató y Los Kimbos (see **Típica 73**). Also in 1978, Roena produced *La Practica Hace La Perfección* for Apollo Sound founder member, trumpeter/vocalist Mickey Cora (Mario Alvarez Cora), leading his own band called Orquesta Cabala.

Roena switched to Fania and released four albums (including a compilation) on the label between 1980 and 1982. 1981's *Looking Out For 'Numero Uno'* contained the dark bitter-sweet 'Se Esconde Porque Me Debe', superbly arranged by Louis García, and three interpretations of songs written by Cuban composer/bandleader **Adalberto Alvarez**. Carlos Santos went solo and debuted on *Lo Mío* in 1982. The same year, Roberto teamed up with vocalist **Adalberto Santiago** for his last release on Fania, *Super Apollo 47:50*. Also in 1982, Roena participated in a reunion of some ex-members of El Gran Combo on *El Combo Del Ayer*, and again in 1983 on *Aquel Gran Encuentro*. Roena re-surfaced with Apollo Sound in 1985 on *Afuera y Contento* on Pa' Lante Records. Founder member of Apollo Sound, Piro Mantilla, and Sammy González, another former member, together with Junior Reynoso, comprised the album's trio of lead singers. Included was a gloriously understated, yet swinging version of Adalberto Alvarez's composition 'A Ver' (Let's See).

The album also featured an example of the short-lived Puerto Rican dance fad called zuky. The track in question, 'Apollo Zuky', was a latinized cover of the 1981 soca hit 'Soca Rhumba' by Montserrat's **Arrow.** After a brief gap, Roena released the aptly titled *Regreso* (Return) in 1987 on Up Records. The record also marked the comeback to Apollo Sound of Papo Sánchez, who shared lead vocals with Rubén La Hoz and two female vocalists: Johanie Robles and Aracelis Beltran. The album was a further top quality serving of sophisticated salsa and featured two more cover versions of Adalberto Alvarez songs, including a magnificent arrangement of his 'Reflexiones Mías' by Tito Rivera. Sánchez was the sole lead singer on 1990's *New Decade* on the Sonostar label.

Roena joined the Fania All Stars at the beginning of the 70s and has continued to record and gig with them up to the present day. With them he appeared in the films *Our Latin Thing (Nuestra Cosa)* (1972) and *Salsa* (1976), and made his UK debut in 1976. He can be seen performing as a percussionist and dancer with the band in the 1991 UK video release *Salsa Madness*, filmed in Zaire in 1974. Roena has sessioned on recordings by various other salsa artists and bands, including **Charlie Palmieri**, **Cheo Feliciano**, **Ismael Quintana**, Julio 'Gunda' Merced y su Salsa Fever, Pedro Arroyo, Roberto Lugo, Andy and Harold Montañez and Willie González.

Albums: *Se Pone Bueno / It Gets Better* (1966), *Roberto Roena y su Apollo Sound* (1969), *Roberto Roena y su Apollo Sound 2* (1970), *Roberto Roena y su Apollo Sound 3* (1971), *Roberto Roena y su Apollo Sound 4* (1972), *Roberto Roena y su Apollo Sound 5* (1973), *Roberto Roena y su Apollo Sound 6* (1974), *Lucky 7* (1976), *La 8va. Maravilla* (1977), *Roberto Roena y su Apollo Sound 9* (1977), *Roberto Roena y su Apollo Sound X / El Progreso* (1978), *Que Suerte He Tenido De Nacer* (1980), *Looking Out For 'Numero Uno'* (1980), with Adalberto Santiago *Super Apollo 47:50* (1982), *Afuera y Contento* (1985), *Regreso* (1987), *New Decade* (1990). Compilations: *Pa' Fuera* (1974), *Gold* (1980).

Roger, Roger

b. 5 August 1911, France. One of the most prolific composer/conductors to contribute scores to numerous French radio, television and film productions. He calculates that he has made over 2,000 recordings, half of which are his own compositions. He also claims to have worked on 500 French films, many shown overseas. Roger's father, Edmond Roger (who gave his son the same christian name as his surname to satisfy a personal whim) was a well-known conductor of opera, and a friend of Claude Debussy. He encouraged his son into the music profession, and arranged for him to conduct his first five-man orchestra at the age of 18 in a small French music hall. This encouraged him to work with singers, and develop his arranging skills. Roger has contributed works to many mood music publishers, notably Chappells of London, for whom he wrote 'New Town', 'Paris Fashions', 'The Toy Shop Window', 'Holiday Party', 'Clowneries', 'Along The Avenue', and 'City Movement' (used in the 60s BBC television soap *Compact*). His style of background music made it particularly suitable for situations such as television test card transmissions.

Selected albums: *Musique Aux 4 Vents* (Pacific), *Tourbillon de Paris* (Mode/Vogue), *American Flavour* (Pacific), *Varietes Pour Tous* (Vega), *Roger Roger* (MGM).

Rogers, Ce Ce

b. Kenny Rogers. The gentle giant from Cleveland, Ohio, Rogers is not actually a house artist *per se*, but certainly his records for Atlantic made him a hallowed name in those circles. 'Someday' sold over 100,000 copies on import before his record company finally had the good sense to release it in England as the b-side to 'Forever'. 'Someday' quickly became a house classic and was subsequently remixed and remodelled. It formed the basis for rave anthems like **Liquid**'s 'Sweet Harmony' and Urban Shakedown's 'Some Justice', among others. Ironically, when **Marshall Jefferson** first brought him 'Someday' the artist himself had little faith in it. Rogers was born the son of a music teacher, alongside three brothers and sisters, and was raised on a diet of gospel and soul. It was certainly a musical family. His rapping brother Marcski signed to **CBS**, while his sister Sonia is a backing vocalist (for Intense among others). Before Rogers left school he toured with the Jazz Messengers, before meeting up with the likes of **Branford Marsalis** at Berkeley. From there he moved to New York, where Marshall Jefferson spotted him in a club leading Ce Ce And Company (who included subsequent solo artist **Sybil**). It was Jefferson who introduced him to Atlantic Records at the age of 25. Following 'Someday' his other great moment came with 'All Join Hands', again later re-released, this time on East West. It came with a **David Morales** remix, and was a second all-consuming, passionate, pure house affair.

Album: *Ce Ce Rogers* (Atlantic 1989).

Rogers, David

b. 27 March 1936, Atlanta, Georgia, USA, d. 10 August 1993, Atlanta, Georgia, USA. From 1952, (military service excepted), his ambition to entertain saw him playing local venues, including almost six years at the Egyptian Ballroom until 1967, when he joined the *Wheeling Jamboree* on WWVA. Rogers made his US country chart debut on **Columbia** in 1968 with 'I'd Be Your Fool Again' and soon moved to Nashville. In 1972, his recording of 'Need You' reached number 9, a position equalled in 1974 by 'Loving You Has Changed My Life', after he became the first country artist on the **Atlantic** label. During the late 70s, he registered 13 minor hits on Republic but in the early 80s, he recorded for several minor labels. In total Rogers scored 37 country chart entries, the last 'I'm A Country Song', being a minor hit on the Hal Kat label in 1984. In 1991, in spite of failing health, he appeared at several country clubs during a UK visit, being warmly welcomed by his British fans. He died after a long illness in Atlanta, Georgia, on 10 August 1993, just a few days before he was scheduled to receive a Pioneer Award from the Georgia Country Music Hall Of Fame. Rogers is perhaps best remembered for his excellent 1973 album recalling the *Grand Old Opry's* years at the Ryman Auditorium.

Albums: *The World Called You* (Columbia 1970), *She Don't Make Me Cry* (Columbia 1971), *Need You* (Columbia 1972), *Just Thank Me* (1973), *Farewell To The Ryman* (Atlantic 1973), *Hey There Girl* (Atlantic 1974), *Country* (Hal Kat 1984).

Rogers, Ginger

b. Virginia Katherine McMath, 16 July 1911, Independence, Missouri, USA, d. 25 April 1995, Rancho Mirage, California, USA. A charming and vivacious actress, dancer and singer, Ginger Rogers became a movie legend after partnering **Fred Astaire** in a series of memorable musicals between 1933 and 1949. She grew up in Fort Worth, Texas, and, after winning a Charleston contest at the age of 15, worked in vaudeville for a time before making a big impression in the 1929 **Guy Bolton-Bert Kalmar-Harry Ruby** Broadway musical *Top Speed*. A year later she played the lovelorn postmistress Molly Gray, introducing **George** and **Ira Gershwin**'s lovely song 'But Not For Me', in *Girl Crazy*. Also in 1930, Rogers made her first feature film, *Young Man Of Manhattan*, which was followed by several others, in which she generally played streetwise blondes (after dying her hair), including *42nd Street* (as Anytime Annie) and *Gold Diggers Of 1933*. That was also the year in which she was teamed with Astaire in RKO's *Flying Down To Rio*, the first of 10 light-hearted and tuneful musicals, through which they became the most beloved dance duo in movie history. The films were *The Gay Divorcee*, *Roberta*, *Top Hat*, *Follow The Fleet*, *Swing Time*, *Shall We Dance*, *Carefree*, *The Story Of Vernon And Irene Castle*, and - after a break of 10 years - *The Barkleys Of Broadway* (1949). Even before the two stars went their separate ways in 1939, Ginger Rogers had been playing critically acclaimed dramatic roles in films such as *Stage Door*, and, during the rest of her film career, she continued to excel in both serious and comedy parts, winning the best actress Oscar for her outstanding performance in *Kitty Foyle* (1940). After making her last picture, *Harlow*, in 1964, she returned to the stage in the following year, taking over the leading role from **Carol Channing** on Broadway in *Hello, Dolly!*, and subsequently touring with the show. In 1969 she opened at London's Theatre Royal Drury Lane in another **Jerry Herman** musical, *Mame*, the first time British audiences had been given the opportunity to see the show. On her return to the USA she formed the *Rogue River Revues*, out of which came the *Ginger Rogers Show* which toured major cities in the USA in the late 70s and played two weeks at the London Palladium. In later years she became a fashion and beauty consultant and also spent a good deal of time pursuing her hobby of painting. In 1986 Rogers attempted to block the distribution of Federico Fellini's film *Ginger And Fred*, which told of two small-time entertainers who do an impression of Astaire and Rogers, because 'it depicted the film's dance team as having been lovers'. In real life Ginger Rogers was married five times, first to Jack Pepper with whom she danced for a time in the early days, and then to actor Lew Ayres, US marine Jack Briggs, actor Jacques Bergerac, and finally actor-director-producer William Marshall. In 1993, more than 60 years after she came to prominence when playing Molly in *Girl Crazy*, Ginger Rogers attended a performance of the hit Broadway production ***Crazy For You***, which was adapted from that very same Gershwin show. She made another rare public appearance in December 1994 to receive a dedication at the European launch of the annual International Achievement in Arts Awards at London's Dominion Theatre.

Selected albums: *Miss Ginger Rogers* (1978), *20 Golden Greats* (1986), *Curtain Calls* (1988), *Rare Recordings 1930-1972* (1989) *Fred Astaire And Ginger Rogers Story* (1989).

Further reading: *The Fred Astaire And Ginger Rogers Book*, Arlene Croce. *Ginger: My Story* (her autobiography).

Rogers, Jimmy

b. James A. Lane, 3 June 1924, Ruleville, Mississippi, USA. Self-taught on both harmonica and guitar, Rogers began working at local house parties in his early teens. He then followed an itinerant path, performing in Mississippi and St. Louis, before moving to Chicago in 1939. Rogers frequently took work outside of music, but having played for tips on the city's famed Maxwell Street, began appearing in several clubs and bars. Although he worked as a accompanist with pianist **Sunnyland Slim**, Rogers established his reputation with the **Muddy Waters** Band with whom he remained until 1960. The guitarist thus contributed to many of urban blues' finest performances, including 'Hoochie Coochie Man', 'I Got My Mojo Workin'' and the seminal *At Newport*. Rogers also enjoyed a moderately successful career in his own right. 'That's All Right' (1950), credited to Jimmy Rogers And His Trio, featured Waters, **Little Walter** (harmonica) and Big Crawford (bass) and its popularity around the Chicago area engendered a new group, Jimmy Rogers And His Rocking Four. Several more sessions ensued over the subsequent decade, but the guitarist only enjoyed one national R&B hit when 'Walkin' By Myself' reached number 14 in 1957.

By the 60s Rogers found himself eclipsed by a new generation of guitarists, including **Buddy Guy** and **Magic Sam**. Despite enjoying work supporting **Sonny Boy Williamson** and **Howlin' Wolf**, he spent much of the decade in seclusion and only re-emerged during the blues revival of the early 70s. He was signed to **Leon Russell**'s **Shelter** label for whom he completed *Gold Tailed Bird*, a low-key but highly satisfying set. It inspired a period of frenetic live activity which saw Rogers tour Europe on two occasions, with the American Folk Blues Festival (1972) and the Chicago Blues Festival (1973). Appearances in the USA were also well-received, but the artist retired from music during the middle of the decade to work as the manager of an apartment building. However Rogers rejoined Muddy Waters on *I'm Ready* (1977), one of the excellent selections recorded under the aegis of **Johnny Winter**. These releases brought Waters new dignity towards the end of his career and invested Rogers with a newfound confidence. He continues to perform on the contemporary blues circuit and his 1990 release, *Ludella*, named after the artist's guitar, was produced by Kim Wilson from the **Fabulous Thunderbirds**.

Albums: *Gold Tailed Bird* (1971), *That's All Right* i (1974), *Jimmy Rogers And Left Hand Frank* (1979), *Live: Jimmy Rogers* (1982), *Chicago Blues* (1982), *Feelin' Good* (1985), *Dirty Dozens* (1985), *Ludella* (1990). There have been several compilations and archive releases, including: *Chicago Bound, Golden Years* (1976), *Chess Masters* (1982), *Chicago Blues* (1982), *That's All Right* ii (1989), *Jimmy Rogers Sings The Blues* (1990).

Rogers, Julie

b. Julie Rolls, 6 April 1943, London, England. She left her Bermondsey secondary school in 1959 for a long working holiday as a dancer in Spain. Next, she worked as a secretary and then a ship's stewardess before becoming singer with a middle-of-the-road band led by Teddy Foster with whom she would later function in a cabaret duo, and, under a new stage surname, made a radio debut in 1962 on the BBC Light Programme's *Music With A Beat*. Following an audition for Philips A & R manager **Johnny Franz**, she recorded her first single 'It's Magic', in 1963. Her recording career touched its zenith the following year when 'The Wedding' - an orchestrated translation of a song (by Argentinian Joaquin Prieto) which she had first heard in Spain - rose to a UK number 3, triggered by an initial plug on the ITV television regional magazine, *Day By Day*. As well as generating huge sheet music sales, it also disturbed the US Top Ten, despite two previous hit versions in 1961 by **Anita Bryant** and **Malcolm Vaughan**. The yuletide follow-up, 'Like A Child' and 1965's 'Hawaiian Wedding Song' were only minor hits, but Rogers remained in demand on the variety circuit for the rest of the decade.

Rogers, Kenny

b. Kenneth David Rogers, 21 August 1938, Houston, Texas, USA. Rogers was the fourth of eight children, born in a poor area, where his father worked in a shipyard and his mother in a hospital. By sheer perseverance, he became the first member of his family to graduate. By 1955 Rogers was part of a doo-wop group, the Scholars, who recorded 'Poor Little Doggie',

'Spin The Wheel' and 'Kangewah', which was written by gossip columnist, Louella Parsons. At 19, he recorded 'That Crazy Feeling' as Kenneth Rogers for a small Houston label. Rogers' brother, Lelan, who had worked for US **Decca**, promoted the record and its limited success prompted the brothers to form their own label, Ken-Lee, although Rogers' single 'Jole Blon' was unsuccessful. Rogers also recorded 'For You Alone' for the Carlton label as Kenny Rogers The First. When Lelan managed **Mickey Gilley**, Rogers played bass on his 1960 single, 'Is It Wrong?' and he played stand-up bass with the Bobby Doyle Three and appears on their 1962 album of standards, *In A Most Unusual Way*. After recording solo for **Mercury**, Rogers joined the **New Christy Minstrels** and he appears on their 1967 album of pop hits, *New Kicks!*, while forming a splinter group with other Minstrels - Mike Settle, Thelma Camacho and Terry Williams. They took their name, the First Edition, from the flyleaf of a book and developed a newsprint motif, dressing in black and white and appearing on black and white sets. They signed with **Reprise** and Rogers sang lead on their first major hit, Mickey Newbury's song about the alleged pleasures of LSD, 'Just Dropped In (To See What Condition My Condition Was In)'. *The First Edition* was in the mould of the **Association** and **Fifth Dimension**, but they had developed their own style by *The First Edition's 2nd*. The album did not produce a hit single and was not released in the UK, but the First Edition returned to the US charts with Mike Settle's ballad, 'But You Know I Love You', which was also recorded by **Buddy Knox** and **Nancy Sinatra**.

The First Edition had heard **Roger Miller**'s low-key arrangement of 'Ruby, Don't Take Your Love To Town' and they enhanced it with an urgent drumbeat. **Mel Tillis**' song was based on an incident following the Korean war but it had implications for Vietnam. The record, credited to Kenny Rogers And The First Edition, reached number 6 in the US charts and number 2 in the UK. Its follow-up, 'Reuben James', about a coloured man who was blamed for everything, was only moderately successful, but they bounced back with **Mac Davis**' sexually explicit 'Something's Burning' (US number 11, UK number 8). The b-side, Rogers' own 'Momma's Waitin'', incorporates the major themes of country music - mother, prison, death, God and coming home - in a single song. The group had further US success with 'Tell It All Brother' and 'Heed The Call', performed the music for the Jason Robards film, *Fools*, and hosted a popular television series. In 1972 all stops were pulled out for the beautifully-packaged double album, *The Ballad Of Calico*, written by Michael Murphey and dealing with life in a silver mining town. After leaving Reprise, Rogers formed his own Jolly Rogers label which he has since described as 'a lesson in futility', and, when the group broke up in 1974, he owed $65,000. In 1975

Rogers signed with **United Artists** and his producer, Larry Butler, envisaged how he could satisfy both pop and country markets. Impotence was an extraordinary subject for a hit record, but 'Lucille' (US number 5, UK number 1) established Rogers as a country star. He wrote and recorded 'Sweet Music Man' but the song is more appropriate for female singers and has been recorded by **Billie Jo Spears**, **Anne Murray**, **Tammy Wynette**, **Dolly Parton** and **Millie Jackson**. Rogers, who had a second solo hit with 'Daytime Friends', toured the UK with **Crystal Gayle**, and, although plans to record with her did not materialize, he formed a successful partnership with **Dottie West**. Don Schlitz' story-song, 'The Gambler', was ideal for Rogers and inspired the television movies, *The Gambler*, *The Gambler II* and *The Gambler Returns* which featured Rogers. His love for poignant ballads about life on the road, such as 'She Believes In Me' (US number 5), is explained by his own life.

Rogers had the first of four marriages in 1958 and blames constant touring for the failure of his relationships. His fourth marriage was to Marianne Gorden, a presenter of the USA television series *Hee-Haw* and an actress who appeared in *Rosemary's Baby*. His stage show then promoted his happy, family life and included home movies of their child, Christopher Cody. (Rogers says the worst aspect of touring is being bombarded with grey-bearded lookalikes!) 'You Decorated My Life' was another US hit and then came 'Coward Of The County' (US number 3, UK number 1). This song too became a successful television movie and the album *Kenny*, sold five million copies. Rogers also made the documentary *Kenny Rogers And The American Cowboy*, and a concept album about a modern-day Texas cowboy, *Gideon*, led to a successful duet with one of its writers **Kim Carnes**, 'Don't Fall In Love With A Dreamer' (US number 4). Rogers' also had success with 'Love The World Away' from the soundtrack of the film, *Urban Cowboy*, and 'Love Will Turn You Around' from *Six Pack*, a lighthearted television movie in which he starred. Rogers' voice was ideal for **Lionel Richie**'s slow-paced love songs and 'Lady' topped the US charts for six weeks. This was followed by 'I Don't Need You' (US number 3) from the album Richie produced for Rogers, *Share Your Love*. Rogers and **Sheena Easton** revived the **Bob Seger** song, 'We've Got Tonight' (US number 6). Having sold 35 million albums for United Artists, Rogers moved to **RCA** and *Eyes That See In The Dark*, was produced by **Barry Gibb** and featured the **Bee Gees**. It included 'Islands In The Stream' (US number 1, UK number 7) with Dolly Parton, which was helped by her playful approach on the video. Further US hits include 'What About Me?' with **James Ingram** and Kim Carnes and 'Make No Mistake, She's Mine' with **Ronnie Milsap**. Surprisingly, Rogers has not recorded with his close friend **Glen Campbell**, although he took the cover photograph for his album, *Southern Nights*. Rogers was also featured on the most successful single ever made, **USA For Africa**'s 'We Are The World'. **George Martin** was an inspired choice of producer for *The Heart Of The Matter* album, which led to two singles which topped the US country charts, 'Morning Desire' and 'Tomb Of The Unknown Love'. The title track from *They Don't Make Them Like They Used To* was the theme song for the Kirk Douglas and Burt Lancaster film, *Tough Guys*, but overall, Rogers' services on RCA may have disappointed its management who had spent $20 million to secure his success. Rogers returned to Reprise but the opening track of his first album, 'Planet Texas', sounded like a joke. His son, Kenny Rogers Jnr, sang background vocals on his father's records and launched his own career in 1989 with the single, 'Take Another Step Closer'. Now, Rogers breeds Arabian horses and cattle on his 1,200-acre farm in Georgia and has homes in Malibu, Bel Air and Beverly Hills. He owns entertainment centres and recording studios and has 200 employees. This is impressive for someone who was described by *Rolling Stone* as an 'overweight lightweight'. He says, 'I've never taken my talent that seriously. At one time I had a three-and-a-half octave range and sang the high parts in a jazz group. Now I don't use it because I don't have to. If Muhammad Ali can beat anyone without training, why train?'

Albums: by the First Edition *The First Edition* (1967), *The First Edition's 2nd* (1968), *The First Edition '69* (1969), *Ruby, Don't Take Your Love To Town* (1969), *Something's Burning* (1970), *Fools* (1970, soundtrack), *Tell It All Brother* (1971), *Transition* (1971), *The Ballad Of Calico* (1972), *Backroads* (1972), *Monumental* (1973), *Rollin'* (1974). By Kenny Rogers *Love Lifted Me* (1976), *Kenny Rogers* (1976), *Daytime Friends* (1977), with Dottie West *Every Time Two Fools Collide* (1978), *Love Or Something Like It* (1978), *The Gambler* (1978), *Ten Years Of Gold* (1979), with West *Classics* (1979), *Kenny* (1979), *Gideon* (1980), *Share Your Love* (1981), *Christmas* (1981), *Love Will Turn You Around* (1982), *We've Got Tonight* (1983), *Eyes That See In The Dark* (1983), *What About Me?* (1984), with Dolly Parton *Once Upon A Christmas* (1984), *The Heart Of The Matter* (1985), *Short Stories* (1986), *They Don't Make Them Like They Used To* (1986), *I Prefer The Moonlight* (1987), *Something Inside So Strong* (1989), *Christmas In America* (1989), *The Very Best Of Kenny Rogers* (1991), *You're My Kind Of People* (1991), *Some Prisons Don't Have Walls* (1991), *Back Home Again* (1992), *If Only My Heart Had A Voice* (1993), with Dottie West *Duets* (Music For Pleasure 1994). Several compilations of Rogers' best-known tracks are available.

Video: with Dolly Parton *Real Love* (1988).

Further reading: *Making It In Music*, Kenny Rogers and Len Epand. *Kenny Rogers - Gambler, Dreamer, Lover*, Martha Hume.

Rogers, Paul

b. 1956, Luton, Bedfordshire, England. Bassist Rogers moved to London in 1974. A versatile player, he has worked with **Paul Rutherford**, **Art Themen**, **Keith Tippett**, **John Stevens**, **Elton Dean**, **Mike Osborne**, **Stan Tracey**, **Louis Moholo**, **Alan Skidmore**'s Tenor Tonic, and 7 RPM (with Tony Marsh and Simon Picard). Among European musicians, those he worked with include **Alexander von Schlippenbach** and **Joachim Kuhn**. In 1981 he played on the British debut recording of Brazilian saxophonist Andres Boiarsky (*Plays South Of The Border*). He took part in two notable foreign tours by British musicians: **Harry Beckett** (touring the Middle East in 1984) and **Evan Parker** (Rumania, Yugoslavia and Greece in 1985). Since the late 80s he has been working frequently with drummer **Mark Sanders**, and together they have provided a powerful and flexible engine for Atlas (with pianist John Law), Parker, **Dennis Gonzalez**, and the Elton Dean/**Howard Riley** Quartet (*All The Tradition*). Recently he has also been a member of Tippett's intense quartet Mujician and the **Louis Moholo** trio. An Arts Council grant led to the composition of a suite (Anglo American Sketches) for three saxophonists, flute, bass and drums, which was well received when it was toured nationally in 1990. In the same year Rogers also toured in a trio with **Andrew Cyrille**.

Album: with Atlas *Trio Improvisations* (1989).

Rogers, Roy (blues)

b. 28 July 1950, Redding, California, USA. Since producing a quartet of best-selling and award-winning albums with **John Lee Hooker**, Rogers' own career has become more of an indulgence than a necessity. By 13, he was playing guitar in a high school R&B band. A few years later, he began to study blues techniques and slide playing in particular. During the 70s, he formed a partnership with harmonica player David Bergin, making their recording debut with *A Foot In The Door*. In 1979, he formed the Delta Rhythm Kings, a trio which he has retained ever since. Between 1982 and 1986, he divided his time between them and being a member of John Lee Hooker's Coast To Coast Boogie Band. Rogers financed his own album, *Chops Not Chaps*, in 1986, later reissued on Blind Pig. *Slidewinder*, the following year, also featured Hooker and **Allen Toussaint**. Toussaint worked on *Slide Of Hand* six years later. Rogers teamed up with another harmonica player, **Steve Miller**'s sideman Norton Buffalo, on *R&B* and subsequently *Travelin' Tracks*. Hooker's *The Healer* was released in 1989, bringing both commercial success and a fistful of Grammy Awards. *Mr Lucky* and *Boom Boom* followed in 1991 and 1992, but it was not until 1995's *Chill Out* that Rogers established a firm presence on both sides of the microphone. His **Liberty** albums contain a shrewd mixture of the entertaining and the edifying, showing that Rogers now combines an understanding of the music with a commercial ear.

Albums: *A Foot In The Door* (Waterhouse 1976), *Slidewinder* (Blind Pig 1987), *Blues On The Range* (Blind Pig 1989), with Norton Buffalo *R&B* (Blind Pig 1991), *Chops Not Chaps* (Blind Pig 1992), with Buffalo *Travelin' Tracks* (Blind Pig 1993), *Slide Of Hand* (Liberty 1993), *The Slide Zone* (Liberty 1994).

Rogers, Roy (country)

b. Leonard Franklin Slye, 5 November 1911, Cincinnati, Ohio, USA. Rogers worked on the west coast picking fruit and, after several singing jobs, he formed the **Sons Of The Pioneers** in 1933. They performed in many western films, and, as a result of Republic's dispute with **Gene Autry**, Rogers received his first starring role, playing a singing congressman in the 1938 film, *Under Western Skies*. When he and John Wayne jumped off a cliff in *Dark Command*, Hollywood's treatment of horses was severely questioned, which led to the formation of the Society for Prevention of Cruelty to Animals. In 1946 his wife died shortly after giving birth to their son, Roy Jnr. On 31 December 1947 he married an actress from his film, *The Cowboy And The Senorita*, Dale Evans. His films include *King Of The Cowboys*, *Son Of Paleface* with **Bob Hope** and Jane Russell, and *Hollywood Canteen*, in which he sang 'Don't Fence Me In'. Rogers' four-legged friend, Trigger ('the smartest horse in the movies') had been ridden by Olivia de Havilland in *The Adventures Of Robin Hood* and cost Rogers $2,500. His films and television series (100 shows between 1951 and 1957) also featured a lovable, toothless and fearless old-timer George 'Gabby' Hayes. They contained no sex and little violence (he'd wing the baddies in black hats), and his wholesome image found favour when he toured UK theatres in the 50s. High prices are now paid for Roy Rogers memorabilia, be it cut-out dolls, thermos flasks or holster sets. Rogers' records include 'Blue Shadows On The Trail', 'These Are The Good Old Days', a tribute to the past, 'Hoppy, Gene And Me' and 'Ride, Concrete Cowboy, Ride' from the film *Smokey And The Bandit 2*. His palomino Trigger died in 1965 at the age of 33 and was stuffed and mounted, as referred to in **Jimmy Webb**'s song '**P.F. Sloan**'. Rogers became a successful businessman with a chain of restaurants, and he and Evans confined their appearances to religious ones. He made his first film in 16 years in 1975, *Mackintosh And T.J.*, while his son, Roy Rogers Jnr., made an album *Dusty* in 1983. **Don McLean** recorded Rogers' famous signature tune 'Happy Trails' and Rogers revived it with **Randy Travis** in 1990. San Francisco rock band the **Quicksilver Messenger Service** used Rogers' *Happy Trails* as the title of their album in 1968 as well as recording the song as the closing track. He returned to the US country chart with his album, *Tribute*, in 1991, which included guest appearances from contemporary country performers. **Clint Black** helped to revitalize his career, the first time Rogers had accepted help from a man in a black hat. In 1992, a feature-length documentary entitled *Roy Rogers, King Of The Cowboys*, was shown at the Rotterdam Film Festival, and in the same year Rogers was reported to have signed a deal with Republic Pictures which involved an animated film based on Hollywood's most famous 'good guy'.

Albums: *Souvenir Album* (1952), with Spade Cooley *Skip To My Lou And Other Square Dances* (1952), *Roy Rogers Roundup* (1952), with Dale Evans *Hymns Of Faith* (1954), with Evans *Sweet Hour Of Prayer* (1957), with Evans *Jesus Loves Me* (1959), with Evans *The Bible Tells Me So* (1962), with The Sons Of The Pioneers *Pacos Bill* (1964), *Lore Of The West* (1966), with Evans *Christmas Is Always* (1967), *The Country Side Of Roy Rogers* (1970), *A Man From Duck Run* (1971), *Take A Little Love And Pass It On* (1972), with Evans *In The Sweet Bye And Bye* (1973), *Happy Trails To You* (1975), with Evans *The Good Life* (1977), with The Sons Of The Pioneers *King Of The Cowboys* (1983), *Roy Rogers* (1984), with Evans, Roy Rogers Jnr. *Many Happy Trails* (1984), *The Republic Years* (1985), *Roll On Texas Moon* (1986), *Tribute* (1991).

Further reading: *Roy Rogers: King Of The Cowboys*, Morris, Georgia & Mark Pollard (1994).

Rogers, S.E.

b. Sooliman Rogie, 1927, Freetown, Sierra Leone. Vocalist and guitarist Rogers has played a similar role in preserving the traditional acoustic guitar music of Sierra Leone to **Konimo** in neighbouring Ghana. Originally a tailor, he began recording in the early 60s, with his band the Morning Stars. In 1967, he enjoyed a massive local hit with 'My Lovely Elizabeth', which was covered by dozens of bands and became enduringly popular throughout West Africa. In 1975, he visited the USA, where he released *African Lady*. In the mid-80s, the growth of interest in African music led to a revival in the popularity of Rogers' early recordings, some of which were released on *The Sixties Sounds Of S.E. Rogers*.

Albums: *African Lady* (1975), *Palm Wine Guitar Music* (1988), *The Palm Wine Sounds Of S.E. Rogers* (1989). Compilation: *The Sixties Sounds Of S.E. Rogers* (1986).

Further reading: *The Rolling Stone Story*, Robert Draper.

Rogers, Shorty

b. 14 April 1924, Great Barrington, Massachusetts, USA, d. 7 November 1994, Los Angeles, California, USA. After studying in New York, Rogers played trumpet in the bands of **Will Bradley**, where he first met **Shelly Manne**, and **Red Norvo**. Military service interrupted his career, but in 1945 he joined **Woody Herman** for a spell during which he also wrote a number of bop-flavoured big band charts. After Herman, he played with and arranged for the **Stan Kenton** band, thus increasing his public exposure still more. While with Kenton he also composed a number of features for fellow sidemen such as **Art Pepper** and **Maynard Ferguson**. During the 50s Rogers worked mostly in California, still writing hard-swinging charts for Kenton but trying to get work locally. He worked in films, appearing on-screen and on the soundtrack of *The Man With The Golden Arm* (1955). He also recorded with his own big band, effectively 'borrowing' most of the current Kenton band, but he was most often in a succession of important small groups. Rogers's involvement in the west coast scene was intense and he, more than any other single musician, is most readily identifiable as a prime mover in the movement's success. The first small group record date Rogers organized was in October 1951 and resulted in the influential *Modern Sounds*, on which he was joined by Manne, Pepper, **Jimmy Giuffre**, **Hampton Hawes** and others. He also appeared on the *Lighthouse All Stars*, then led his own groups through a succession of fine recordings including the big band *Cool And Crazy*, on which he used Kenton's men.

On these and his many other albums of the 50s, including *The Swinging Mr Rogers* and *Martians Come Back*, Rogers ably demonstrates his arranging gifts and magnificently showcases the musicians hired for the occasion. This use of several young veterans of the swing era tradition to play music that drew heavily upon the newer vocabularies of bebop created a perfect blending of all that was best of both forms. There was little or no evidence of the cliches which were, by then, adversely affecting the performances of many of the surviving big bands. While the Rogers brand of west coast jazz did not have the aggressive urgency of its east coast counterpart, it always swung lithely. Rogers was constantly on the lookout for new and unusual sounds and styles and was an early jazz experimenter with 12-tone writing. He continued playing and writing throughout the 60s, 70s and 80s, touring extensively and always eager to work with young musicians in the USA or UK and with old friends like **Bud Shank** and **Vic Lewis**. In the early 90s he most frequently played flügelhorn, the warmer, denser sound admirably suiting his expressive playing style.

Selected albums: *Modern Sounds* (Affinity 1951), *Popo* (1951), *Cool And Crazy* (1953), *Short Snort* (1953), *Blues Express* (RCA 1953-56), *Shorty Rogers Courts The Count* (1953), *Shorty Rogers And His Giants* (1954), *The Swinging Mr Rogers/Martians Stay Home* (Atlantic 1955), *Martians Come Back/Way Up There* (1955), *Clickin' With Clax* (Atlantic 1956), *Wherever The Five Winds Blow* (1956), *Shorty Rogers Plays Richard Rodgers* (1957), *Portrait Of Shorty* (1957), *Gigi In Jazz* (1958), *Afro-Cuban Jazz Inc.* (1958), *Chances Are, It Swings* (1958), *Wizard Of Oz* (1959), *Shorty Rogers Meets Tarzan* (1959), *The Swinging Nutcracker* (1960), *Fourth Dimension* (1961), *Bossa Nova* (1962), *Jazz Waltz* (Discovery 1962), *Gospel Mission* (1963), *West Coast Jazz* (Atlantic 1976), *Re-entry* (1983), *Yesterday, Today And Forever* (Concord 1983), *Shorty Rogers And The West Coast Giants* (1983), with Vic Lewis, Bud Shank *Back Again* (Concept 1984), *Shorty Rogers And Bud Shank Live At The Concorde Club, Southampton* (1984), *California Concert* (1985), with Shank *America The Beautiful* (Candid 1991), *Eight Brothers* (Candid 1992).

Rogers, Stan

b. 1949, Hamilton, Ontario, Canada, d. 2 June 1983. Singer-songwriter Rogers began as a bass player in a rock band before becoming a well-respected artist within the folk arena. In 1969, he turned professional and, the following year, released two singles for **RCA**. There followed a period of playing the coffee house circuit, with Nigel Russell (guitar), until Stan's brother, Garnet Rogers (violin/flute/vocals/guitar), joined them. Garnet worked with Stan for nearly 10 years. Stan Rogers' low-register voice exuded a warm sensitive sound, the perfect complement to his sensitive lyrics. Remembered for songs such as 'Northwest Passage' and 'The Lock-keeper', he is probably best known for 'The Mary Ellen Carter'. Writing for films and television, and having toured a number of countries, Rogers was poised for international success but was killed in an aeroplane fire in 1983. In 1976, he had composed 'Forty Five Years' for his wife Diane, and in fulfilment of his wishes, his ashes were scattered in Cole Harbour, Nova Scotia, the place where he had written the song. *Home In Halifax* was recorded 15 months before his death, for a radio programme on Canadian Broadcasting Corporation.

Albums: *From Fresh Water* (1975), *Fogarty's Cove* (1976), *Turnaround* (1978), *Between The Breaks-Live* (1979), *Northwest Passage* (1981), *For The Family* (1983), *The Great Lakes Project* (1983), *Home In Halifax* (1993).

Further reading: *Songs From Fogarty's Cove*, Stan Rogers. *An Unfinished Conversation: The Life And Music Of Stan Rogers*, Chris Gudgeon.

Rogue Male

Formed in London, England, in 1984, the band's original line-up consisted of Jim Lyttle (vocals/guitar), John Fraser Binnie (guitar), Kevin Collier (bass; ex-**Le Griffe**) and Steve Kingsley (drums). Signing to the **Music For Nations** label their debut, *First Visit*, was released in 1985, an album full of fast, tough, punk-influenced metal. With live gigs revealing mainman Jim Lyttle to be a charismatic bandleader they embarked on an ill-fated American tour. Blaming their American label **Elektra Records** for a lack of promotion, the band returned to England to begin work on a second album. At this point Steve Kingsley left to be replaced by session drummer Charlie Morgan, who played on the album recordings, but was replaced soon after by Danny Fury. *Animal Man* was released in 1986 but the band dissolved soon after release in the face of public indifference.

Albums: *First Visit* (Music For Nations 1985), *Animal Man* (Music For Nations 1986).

Roker, Mickey

b. 3 September 1932, Miami, Florida, USA. Raised in Philadelphia, Pennsylvania, Roker played drums with R&B bands but was attracted to jazz. He worked briefly with such visiting and local jazzmen as **Jimmy Heath**, **Lee Morgan** and **McCoy Tyner** and it was not until the end of the 50s that he went to New York. During the next few years he played in bands led by **Gigi Gryce**, **Ray Bryant**, **Duke Pearson**, **Art Farmer**, **Sonny Rollins**, **Milt Jackson**, **Clifford Jordan** and Morgan. He was for a while in the house band at **Blue Note Records** and played on many dates. In 1971 he began a long association with **Dizzy Gillespie** which lasted through the rest of the decade. Freelancing in the 80s has brought him into groups led by **Oscar Peterson**, Ray Bryant, **Zoot Sims**, **Jackson** and **Ray Brown**. A forceful, dynamic drummer, Roker's style is rooted in swing but has the urgent attack of the best of the beboppers.
Albums: with Gigi Gryce *Rat Race Blues* (1960), with Duke Pearson *Wahoo!* (1964), with Lee Morgan *Live at The Lighthouse* (1970), *Dizzy Gillespie's Big 4* (1974), with Gillespie *Dizzy's Party* (1976), with Ray Bryant *Potpourri* (1980).

Roland, Gene

b. 15 September 1921, New York City, New York, USA, d. 11 August 1982. In the early 40s many of Roland's arrangements played an important part in establishing the success of the **Stan Kenton** band. Among his arrangements was the **June Christy** hit, 'Tampico'. During this period he sometimes played trumpet in the band, later switching to trombone. Generally credited with **Jimmy Giuffre** as co-creator of the 'Four Brothers' sound of the **Woody Herman** band, Roland arranged for and played piano with **Stan Getz**, Giuffre (with whom he had studied at North Texas State Teachers' College, forerunner of NTSU), **Herbie Steward** and **Zoot Sims** in a small group which was heard by Herman in 1947. Later in the 40s Roland played in the bands of **Georgie Auld**, **Count Basie**, **Charlie Barnet** and **Lucky Millinder**, sometimes on trumpet, other times on trombone. He tried his hand at bandleading in 1950 with an adventurous but ill-fated bebop big band which featured **Charlie Parker**, **Don Fagerquist**, **Red Rodney**, **Jimmy Knepper**, Sims and **Al Cohn**. In the 50s he again wrote for Kenton and Herman, helping create the former's 'mellophonium band'. During the 60s Roland worked in Scandinavia, writing and directing a radio orchestra, and in the 70s, back in the USA, he continued to write challenging big band charts and to play on a variety of instruments.
Albums: *The Band That Never Was* (1950), *A Swinging*

Introduction To Jimmy Knepper (1957), *The Gene Roland Sextette* (1957), with Stan Kenton *Adventures In Blues* (1961), *Swinging Friends* (1963).

Roland, Walter

b. Birmingham, Alabama, USA, d. c.1970. Although a somewhat obscure character Walter Roland saw something like 40 recordings issued under his own name during the period 1933-35. He is also justly famous for the work he did accompanying **Lucille Bogan** (Bessie Jackson) and **Sonny Scott** around the same time. Roland was a skilled pianist, capable of providing sympathetic support to his own and other people's vocal performances as well as displaying a considerable ability in the 'barrel house' style. His own voice was expressive and his blues ran the whole gamut from the deeply introspective through to the cheerfully obscene. Although often only discussed in relationship to the outstanding Bogan, Roland stands on his own as a blues singer and pianist of the first rank whose work deserves to be much better known and appreciated. His 1933 recording 'Jook It, Jook It', a piano solo issued as by the Jolly Jivers, has appeared on many anthologies.
Selected albums: *The Piano Blues Volume 6: Walter Roland* (1978), *Walter Roland* (1988), with Lucille Bogan *1927 - 35* (1993).

Rolling Stone

Former student Jann Wenner founded *Rolling Stone* in partnership with Ralph J. Gleason, a seasoned jazz and rock columnist and a writer of beautiful prose. First published in San Francisco in 1967, the magazine drew its early inspiration from the city's considerable underground movement which encompassed both musical and visual arts. However, Wenner shrewdly avoided ephemeral trappings and, although chronicling the counter culture, his publication maintained an editorial distance bordering on ambivalence. *Rolling Stone* was also expertly designed and its conventional layout, mirroring that of the 'establishment' press, ascribed it an air of authority. It also demonstrated that hippies could actually deliver (the typography, notably its use of dropped capitals was quite brilliant). The magazine also exploited a niche in America's publishing market and while the UK boasted *New Musical Express* and *Melody Maker*, the US had no comparable outlet for pop and rock journalism. Wenner thus attracted a generation of writers, including Greil Marcus, Ed Ward and **Lester Bangs**, whose passion for music was matched by their literacy. *Rolling Stone* was uniquely informative, its record reviews were studious and well-argued, while the *Rolling Stone* Interview became a byword for lengthy, detailed examinations of musicians, their work and overall philosophies. Two interviews with **John Lennon**, wherein he demolished the sanctity surrounding the **Beatles**, established the format as a vehicle for controversial subjects and while helping generate wider interest in the publication, marked the end of its wholehearted dalliance with music. Being featured on the cover was as important as being on the front of *Time* or *Newsweek* and **Dr Hook** brilliantly capitalized on this with the amusing 'Cover Of The *Rolling Stone*' which reached the US Top 3. Not surprisingly they were featured a few weeks afterwards! Other facets, notably politics, began to encroach on its editorial space, particularly those surrounding the ill-fated McGovern presidential campaign of 1972, and the magazine drew plaudits for several examples of brave reportage, notably its dogged pursuit of the truth surrounding the death of nuclear worker Karen Silkwood (1974).

Although readers welcomed the amphetamine-paced writings of Hunter S. Thompson, long-time critics bemoaned an increasingly perfunctory coverage of rock - film stars and media figures began attracting a greater percentage of covers - but the flaccid state of US 70s music did little to inspire strong journalism. *Rolling Stone*'s relocation to New York in 1977 provided the final break with the past and while Wenner's brainchild had long-since achieved a respectability, the magazine had become merely a cypher rather than a kernel. By the 80s its most popular issues were devoted to single topics; fashion, live concerts, the 100 best albums.

Further reading: *The Rolling Stone Story*, Robert Draper. *Best Of Rolling Stone: Classic Writing From The World's Most Influential Music Magazine*, Robert Love. *Rolling Stone: The Photographs*, Laurie Kratochvil (ed.).

Rolling Stones

Originally billed as the Rollin' Stones, the first line-up of this immemorial English 60s group was a nucleus of **Mick Jagger** (b. Michael Philip Jagger, 26 July 1943, Dartford, Kent, England; vocals), **Keith Richard** (b. Keith Richards, 18 December 1943, Dartford, Kent, England; guitar), Brian Jones (b. Lewis Brian Hopkin-Jones, 26 February 1942, Cheltenham, Gloucestershire, England, d. 3 July 1969; rhythm guitar) and Ian Stewart (b. 1938, d. 12 December 1985; piano). Jagger and Richard were primary school friends who resumed their camaraderie in their closing teenage years after finding they had a mutual love for R&B and particularly the music of **Chuck Berry**, **Muddy Waters** and **Bo Diddley**. Initially, they were teamed with bassist Dick Taylor (later of the **Pretty Things**) and before long their ranks extended to include Jones, Stewart and occasional drummer Tony Chapman. Their patron at this point was the renowned musician **Alexis Korner**, who had arranged their debut gig at London's Marquee club on 21 July 1962. In their first few months the group met some opposition from jazz and blues aficionados for their alleged lack of musical 'purity' and the line-up remained unsettled for several months.

In late 1962 bassist **Bill Wyman** (b. William Perks, 24 October 1936, Plumstead, London, England) replaced Dick Taylor while drummers came and went including Carlo Little (from **Screaming Lord Sutch**'s Savages) and Mick Avory (later of the **Kinks**, who was billed as appearing at their debut gig, but didn't play). It was not until as late as January 1963 that Charlie Watts reluctantly surrendered his day job and committed himself to the group. After securing a residency at **Giorgio Gomelsky**'s Crawdaddy Club in Richmond, the Stones' live reputation spread rapidly through London's hip cognoscenti. One evening, the flamboyant **Andrew Loog Oldham** appeared at the club and was so entranced by the commercial prospects of Jagger's sexuality that he wrested them away from Gomelsky and, backed by the financial and business clout of agent Eric Easton, became their manager. Within weeks, Oldham had produced their first couple of official recordings at IBC Studios. By this time, record company scouts were on the prowl with **Decca**'s **Dick Rowe** leading the march and successfully signing the group. After re-purchasing the IBC demos, Oldham selected Chuck Berry's 'Come On' as their debut. The record was promoted on the prestigious UK television pop programme *Thank Your Lucky Stars* and the Stones were featured sporting matching hounds-tooth jackets with velvet collars. This was to be one of Oldham's few concessions to propriety for he would soon be pushing the boys as unregenerate rebels. Unfortunately, pianist Ian Stewart was not deemed sufficiently pop star-like for Oldham's purpose and was unceremoniously removed from the line-up, although he remained road manager and occasional pianist. After supporting the **Everly Brothers**, **Little Richard**, **Gene Vincent** and Bo Diddley on a **Don Arden** UK package tour, the Stones released their second single, a gift from **John Lennon** and **Paul McCartney** entitled 'I Wanna Be Your Man'. The disc fared better than its predecessor climbing into the Top 10 in January 1964. That same month the group enjoyed their first bill-topping tour supported by the **Ronettes**.

The early months of 1964 saw the Stones catapulted to fame amid outrage and controversy about the surliness of their demeanour and the length of their hair. This was still a world in which the older members of the community were barely coming to terms with the **Beatles** neatly-groomed mop tops. While newspapers asked 'Would you let your daughter marry a Rolling Stone?', the quintet engaged in a flurry of recording activity which saw the release of an EP and an album both titled *The Rolling Stones*. The discs consisted almost exclusively of extraneous material and captured the group at their most derivative stage. Already, however, there were strong signs of an ability to combine different styles. The third single, 'Not Fade Away', saw them fuse **Buddy Holly**'s quaint original with a chunky Bo Diddley beat that highlighted Jagger's vocal to considerable effect. The presence of **Phil Spector** and **Gene Pitney** at these sessions underlined how hip the Stones had already become in the music business after such a short time. With the momentum increasing by the month, Oldham characteristically over-reached himself by organizing a US tour which proved premature and disappointing. After returning to the UK, the Stones released a decisive cover of the **Valentinos**' 'It's All Over Now', which gave them their first number 1. A best-selling EP, *Five By Five*, cemented their growing reputation, while a national tour escalated into a series of near riots with scenes of hysteria wherever they played. There was an ugly strain to the Stones' appeal which easily translated into violence. At the Winter Gardens Blackpool the group hosted the most astonishing rock riot yet witnessed on British soil. Frenzied fans displayed their feelings for the group by smashing chandeliers and demolishing a Steinway grand piano. By the end of the evening over 50 people were escorted to hospital for treatment. Other concerts were terminated within minutes of the group appearing on-stage and the hysteria continued throughout Europe. A return to the USA saw them disrupt the stagey *Ed Sullivan Show* prompting the presenter to ban rock 'n' roll groups in temporary retaliation. In spite of all the chaos at home and abroad, America remained resistant to their appeal, although that situation would change dramatically in the New Year.

In November 1964, 'Little Red Rooster' was released and entered the *New Musical Express* chart at number 1, a feat more usually associated with the Beatles and, previously, **Elvis Presley**. The Stones now had a formidable fan base and their records were becoming more accomplished and ambitious with each successive release. Jagger's accentuated phrasing and posturing stage persona made 'Little Red Rooster' sound surprisingly fresh while Brian Jones's use of slide guitar was imperative to the single's success. Up until this point, the group had recorded cover versions as a-sides, but manager Andrew Oldham was determined that they should emulate the example of Lennon/McCartney and locked them in a room until they emerged with satisfactory material. Their early efforts, 'It Should Have Been You' and 'Will You Be My Lover Tonight?' (both recorded by the late George Bean) were bland, but Gene Pitney scored a hit with the emphatic 'That Girl Belongs To Yesterday' and Jagger's girlfriend **Marianne Faithfull** became a teenage recording star with the moving 'As Tears Go By'. 1965 proved the year of the international breakthrough and three extraordinary self-penned number 1 singles. 'The Last Time' saw them emerge with their own distinctive rhythmic style and underlined an ability to fuse R&B and pop in an enticing fashion. America finally succumbed to their

spell with '(I Can't Get No) Satisfaction', a quintessential pop lyric with the still youthful Jagger sounding like a jaundiced roué. Released in the UK during the 'summer of protest songs', the single encapsulated the restless weariness of a group already old before its time. The distinctive riff, which Keith Richard invented with almost casual dismissal, became one of the most famous hook lines in the entire glossary of pop and was picked up and imitated by a generation of garage groups thereafter. The 1965 trilogy of hits was completed with the engagingly surreal 'Get Off Of My Cloud' in which Jagger's surly persona seemed at its most pronounced to date. As well as the number 1 hits of 1965, there was also a celebrated live EP, *Got Live If You Want It* which reached the Top 10 and, *The Rolling Stones No. 2* that continued the innovative idea of not including the group's name on the front of the sleeve. There was also some well documented bad boy controversy when Jagger, Jones and Wyman were arrested and charged with urinating on the wall of an East London petrol station. Such scandalous behaviour merely reinforced the public's already ingrained view of the Stones as juvenile degenerates.

With the notorious **Allen Klein** replacing Eric Easton as Oldham's co-manager, the Stones consolidated their success by renegotiating their Decca contract. Their single output in the USA simultaneously increased with the release of a couple of tracks unavailable in single form in the UK. The sardonic put-down of suburban valium abuse, 'Mother's Little Helper' and the Elizabethan-styled 'Lady Jane', complete with atmospheric dulcimer, displayed their contrasting styles to considerable effect. Both these songs were included on their fourth album, *Aftermath*. A breakthrough work in a crucial year, the recording revealed the Stones as accomplished rockers and balladeers, while their writing potential was emphasized by **Chris Farlowe**'s chart-topping cover of 'Out Of Time'. There were also signs of the Stones' inveterate misogyny particularly on the cocky 'Under My Thumb' and an acerbic 'Stupid Girl'. Back in the singles chart, the group's triumphant run continued with the startlingly chaotic '19th Nervous Breakdown' in which frustration, impatience and chauvinism were brilliantly mixed with scale-sliding descending guitar lines. 'Paint It Black' was even stronger, a raga-influenced piece with a lyric so doom-laden and defeatist in its imagery that it is a wonder that the angry performance sounded so passionate and urgent. The Stones' nihilism reached its peak on the extraordinary 'Have You Seen Your Mother Baby, Standing In The Shadow?', a scabrous-sounding solicitation taken at breathtaking pace with Jagger spitting out a diatribe of barely coherent abuse. It was probably the group's most adventurous production to date, but its acerbic sound, lengthy title and obscure theme contributed to rob the song of sufficient commercial potential to continue the chart-topping run. Ever outrageous, the group promoted the record with a photo session in which they appeared in drag, thereby adding a clever, sexual ambivalence to their already iconoclastic public image.

1967 saw the Stones' anti-climactic escapades confront an establishment crackdown. The year began with an accomplished double a-sided single, 'Let's Spend The Night Together'/'Ruby Tuesday' which, like the Beatles' 'Penny Lane'/'Strawberry Fields Forever', narrowly failed to reach number 1 in their home country. The accompanying album, *Between The Buttons*, trod water and also represented Oldham's final production. Increasingly alienated by the Stones' bohemianism, he would move further away from them in the ensuing months and surrender the management reins to his partner Klein later in the year. On 12 February, Jagger and Richard were arrested at the latter's West Wittering home 'Redlands' and charged with drugs offences. Three months later, increasingly unstable Brian Jones was raided and charged with similar offences. The Jagger/Richard trial in June was a cause célèbre which culminated in the notorious duo receiving heavy fines and a salutary prison sentence. Judicial outrage was tempered by public clemency, most effectively voiced by *The Times*' editor William Rees-Mogg who, borrowing a phrase from Pope, offered an eloquent plea in their defence under the leader title, 'Who Breaks A Butterfly On A Wheel?' Another unexpected ally was rival group the **Who**, who rallied to the Stones' cause by releasing a single coupling 'Under My Thumb' and 'The Last Time'. The sentences were duly quashed on appeal in July, with Jagger receiving a conditional discharge for possession of amphetamines. Three months later, Brian Jones tasted judicial wrath with a nine-month sentence and suffered a nervous breakdown before seeing his imprisonment rescinded at the end of the year.

The flurry of drug busts, court cases, appeals and constant media attention had a marked effect on the Stones' recording career which was severely curtailed. During their summer of impending imprisonment, they released the fey 'We Love You', complete with slamming prison cell doors in the background. It was a weak, flaccid statement rather than a rebellious rallying cry. The image of the cultural anarchists cowering in defeat was not particularly palatable to their fans and even with all the publicity, the single barely scraped into the Top 10. The eventful year ended with the Stones' apparent answer to *Sgt Pepper's Lonely Hearts Club Band* - the extravagantly-titled *Their Satanic Majesties Request*. Beneath the exotic 3-D cover was an album of psychedelic/cosmic experimentation bereft of the R&B grit that had previously been synonymous with the Stones' sound. Although the album had some strong moments, it had the same inexplicably placid inertia of 'We Love You', minus notable melodies or a convincing direction. The overall impression conveyed

was that in trying to compete with the Beatles' experimentation, the Stones had somehow lost the plot. Their drug use had channelled them into laudable experimentation but simultaneously left them open to accusations of having 'gone soft'. The revitalization of the Stones was demonstrated in the early summer of 1968 with 'Jumpin' Jack Flash', a single that rivalled the best of their previous output. The succeeding album, *Beggars Banquet*, produced by **Jimmy Miller**, was also a return to strength and included the socio-political 'Street Fighting Man' and the brilliantly macabre 'Sympathy For The Devil', in which Jagger's seductive vocal was backed by hypnotic Afro-rhythms and dervish yelps.

While the Stones were re-establishing themselves, Brian Jones was falling deeper into drug abuse. A conviction in late 1968 prompted doubts about his availability for US tours and in the succeeding months he contributed less and less to recordings and became increasingly jealous of Jagger's leading role in the group. Richard's wooing and impregnation of Jones' girlfriend Anita Pallenberg merely increased the tension. Matters reached a crisis point in June 1969 when Jones officially left the group. The following month he was found dead in the swimming pool of the Sussex house that had once belonged to writer A.A. Milne. The official verdict was 'death by misadventure'. A free concert at London's Hyde Park two days after his death was attended by a crowd of 250,000 and became a symbolic wake for the tragic youth. Jagger released thousands of butterfly's and narrated a poem by Shelley for Brian. Three days later, Jagger's former love Marianne Faithfull attempted suicide. This was truly the end of the first era of the Rolling Stones.

The group played out the last months of the 60s with a mixture of vinyl triumph and further tragedy. The sublime 'Honky Tonk Women' kept them at number 1 for most of the summer and few would have guessed that this was to be their last UK chart topper. The new album, *Let It Bleed* (a parody of the Beatles' *Let It Be*) was an exceptional work spearheaded by the anthemic 'Gimme Shelter' and revealing strong country influences ('Country Honk'), startling orchestration ('You Can't Always Get What You Want') and menacing blues ('Midnight Rambler'). It was a promising debut from **John Mayall**'s former guitarist **Mick Taylor**, who had replaced Jones only a matter of weeks before his death. Even while *Let It Bleed* was heading for the top of the album charts, however, the Stones were singing out the 60s to the backdrop of a Hells Angels' killing of a black man at the **Altamont Festival** in California. The tragedy was captured on film in the grisly *Gimme Shelter* movie released the following year. After the events of 1969, it was not surprising that the group had a relatively quiet 1970. Jagger's contrasting thespian outings reached the screen in the form of *Performance* and *Ned Kelly* while Jean-Luc

Godard's tedious portrait of the group in the studio was delivered on *One Plus One*. For a group who had once claimed to make more challenging and gripping films than the Beatles and yet combine artistic credibility with mass appeal, it all seemed a long time coming.

After concluding their Decca contract with a bootleg-deterring live album, *Get Yer Ya-Ya's Out*, the Stones established their own self-titled label. The first release was a three track single, 'Brown Sugar'/'Bitch'/'Let It Rock', which contained some of their best work, but narrowly failed to reach number 1 in the UK. The lead track contained a quintessential Stones riff: insistent, undemonstrative and stunning, with the emphatic brass work of Bobby Keyes embellishing Jagger's vocal power. The new album, *Sticky Fingers* was as consistent as it was accomplished, encompassing the bluesy 'You Gotta Move', the thrilling 'Moonlight Mile', the wistful 'Wild Horses' and the chilling 'Sister Morphine', one the most despairing drug songs ever written. The entire album was permeated by images of sex and death, yet the tone of the work was neither self-indulgent nor maudlin. The group's playful fascination with sex was further demonstrated on the elaborately designed Andy Warhol sleeve which featured a waist-view shot of a figure clad in denim, with a real zip fastener which opened to display the lips and tongue motif that was shortly to become their corporate image. Within a year of *Sticky Fingers*, the group returned with a double album, *Exile On Main Street*. With Keith Richard firmly in control, the group were rocking-out on a series of quick-fire songs. The album was severely criticized at the time of its release for its uneven quality but was subsequently re-evaluated favourably, particularly in contrast to their later work.

The Stones' soporific slide into the 70s mainstream probably began during 1973 when their jet-setting was threatening to upstage their musical endeavours. Jagger's marriage and Richard's confrontations with the law took centre stage while increasingly average albums came and went. *Goat's Head Soup* was decidedly patchy but offered some strong moments and brought a deserved US number 1 with the imploring 'Angie'. 1974's 'It's Only Rock 'n' Roll' proved a better song title than a single, while the undistinguished album of the same name saw the group reverting to Tamla/**Motown** for the **Temptations**' 'Ain't Too Proud To Beg'.

The departure of Mick Taylor at the end of 1974 was followed by a protracted period in which the group sought a suitable replacement. By the time of their next release, *Black And Blue*, former *Faces* guitarist **Ronnie Wood** was confirmed as Taylor's successor. The album showed the group seeking a possible new direction playing variants on white reggae, but the results were less than impressive.

By the second half of the 70s the gaps in the Stones' recording and touring schedules were becoming wider. The days when they specially recorded for the singles market were long past and considerable impetus had been lost. Even big rallying points, such as the celebrated concert at Knebworth in 1976, lacked a major album to promote the show and served mainly as a greatest hits package.

By 1977, the British music press had taken punk to its heart and the Stones were dismissed as champagne-swilling old men, who had completely lost touch with their audience. The **Clash** effectively summed up the mood of the time with their slogan 'No Elvis, Beatles, Stones' in '1977'.

Against the odds, the Stones responded to the challenge of their younger critics with a comeback album of remarkable power. *Some Girls* was their most consistent work in years, with some exceptional high-energy workouts, not least the breathtaking 'Shattered'. The disco groove of 'Miss You' brought them another US number 1 and showed that they could invigorate their repertoire with new ideas that worked. Jagger's wonderful pastiche of an American preacher on the mock country 'Far Away Eyes' was another unexpected highlight. There was even an attendant controversy thanks to some multi-racist chauvinism on the title track, not to mention 'When The Whip Comes Down' and 'Beast Of Burden'. Even the cover jacket had to be re-shot because it featured unauthorized photos of the famous, most notably actresses Lucille Ball, Farrah Fawcett and Raquel Welch. To conclude a remarkable year, Keith Richard escaped what seemed an almost certain jail sentence in Toronto for drugs offences and was merely fined and ordered to play a couple of charity concerts. As if in celebration of his release and reconciliation with his father, he reverted to his original family name Richards. In the wake of Richards' reformation and Jagger's much-publicized and extremely expensive divorce from his model wife Bianca, the Stones reconvened in 1980 for *Emotional Rescue*, a rather lightweight album dominated by Jagger's falsetto and over-use of disco rhythms. Nevertheless, the album gave the Stones their first UK number 1 since 1973 and the title track was a Top 10 hit on both sides of the Atlantic. Early the following year a major US tour (highlights of which were included on *Still Life*) garnered enthusiastic reviews, while a host of repackaged albums reinforced the group's legacy. 1981's *Tattoo You* was essentially a crop of old outtakes but the material was anything but stale. On the contrary, the album was surprisingly strong and the concomitant single 'Start Me Up' was a reminder of the Stones at their 60s best, a time when they were capable of producing classic singles at will. One of the Stones' cleverest devices throughout the 80s was their ability to compensate for average work by occasional flashes of excellence. The workmanlike *Undercover*, for example, not only boasted a brilliantly menacing title

ROLLING STONES

track ('Undercover Of The Night') but one of the best promotional videos of the period. While critics continually questioned the group's relevance, the Stones were still releasing worthwhile work, albeit in smaller doses.

A three-year silence on record was broken by *Dirty Work* in 1986, which saw the Stones sign to **CBS Records** and team up with producer **Steve Lillywhite**. Surprisingly, it was not a Stones original that produced the expected offshoot single hit, but a cover of **Bob And Earl**'s 'Harlem Shuffle'. A major record label signing often coincides with a flurry of new work, but the Stones were clearly moving away from each other creatively and concentrating more and more on individual projects. Wyman had already tasted some chart success in 1983 with the biggest solo success from a Stones' number, 'Je Suis Un Rock Star' and it came as little surprise when Jagger issued his own solo album, *She's The Boss*, in 1985. A much publicized-feud with Keith Richards led to speculation that the Rolling Stones story had come to an anti-climactic end, a view reinforced by the appearance of a second Jagger album, *Primitive Cool*, in 1987. When Richards himself released the first solo work of his career in 1988, the Stones' obituary had virtually been written. As if to confound the obituarists, however, the Stones reconvened in 1989 and announced that they would be working on a new album and commencing a world tour. Later that year the hastily-recorded *Steel Wheels* appeared and the critical reception was generally good. 'Mixed Emotions' and 'Rock And A Hard Place' were radio hits while 'Continental Drift' included contributions from the master musicians of Joujouka, previously immortalized on vinyl by the late Brian Jones. After nearly 30 years in existence, the Rolling Stones began the 90s with the biggest grossing international tour of all time, and ended speculation about their future by reiterating their intention of playing on indefinitely. Voodoo Lounge in 1994 was one of their finest recordings, it was both lyrically daring and musically fresh. They sounded charged up and raring to go for the 1995 US tour. Monies taken at each gig could almost finance the national debt and confirmation (as if it were needed) that they are still the world's greatest rock band, a title that is likely to stick, even though Bill Wyman officially resigned in 1993.

Albums: *The Rolling Stones* (London/Decca 1964), *12X5* (London 1964), *The Rolling Stones* (London/Decca 1965), *The Rolling Stones Now!* (London 1965), *December's Children (And Everybody's* (London 1965), *Out Of Our Heads* (Decca/London 1965), *Aftermath* (Decca/London 1966), *Got Live If You Want It* (London 1966), *Between The Buttons* (London/Decca 1967), *Their Satanic Majesties Request* (Decca/London 1967), *Flowers* (London 1967), *Beggars Banquet* (1968), *Let It Bleed* (London/Decca 1969), *Get Yer Ya-Ya's Out!* (1970), *Sticky Fingers* (Rolling Stones 1971), *Exile On Main Street* (1972), *Goat's Head*

Soup (Rolling Stones 1973), *It's Only Rock 'N' Roll* (Rolling Stones 1974), *Black And Blue* (1976), *Love You Live* (1977), *Some Girls* (1978), *Emotional Rescue* (1980), *Tattoo You* (1981), *Still Life (American Concerts 1981)* (1982), *Undercover* (1983), *Dirty Work* (1986), *Steel Wheels* (1989), *Voodoo Lounge* (Virgin 1994). Selected compilations: *Big Hits (High Tide And Green Grass)* (London 1966), *Through The Past, Darkly* (London 1969), *Hot Rocks 1964-1971* (London 1972), *More Hot Rocks (Big Hits And Fazed Cookies)* (London 1972), *The Rolling Stones Singles Collection: The London Years* (Abko/London 1989, 3-CD box set). Many compilation and archive albums have also been issued.

Videos: *Gimme Shelter* (1993), *25 X 5, The Continuing Adventures Of The Rolling Stones* (1994).

Further reading: *The Rolling Stones File*, Tim Hewat. *The Stones*, Philip Carmelo Luce. *Uptight With The Rolling Stones*, Richard Elman. *Mick Jagger: The Singer Not The Song*, J. Marks. *Mick Jagger: Everybody's Lucifer*, Anthony Scaduto. *STP: A Journey Through America With The Rolling Stones*, Robert Greenfield. *Les Rolling Stones*, Philippe Contantin. *The Rolling Stones Story*, George Tremlett. *The Rolling Stones*, Cindy Ehrlich. *The Rolling Stones: A Celebration*, Nik Cohn. *The Rolling Stones*, Tony Jasper. *The Rolling Stones: An Illustrated Record*, Roy Carr. *The Rolling Stones*, Jeremy Pascall. *The Rolling Stones On Tour*, Annie Leibowitz. *Up And Down With The Rolling Stones*, Tony Sanchez with John Blake. *The Rolling Stones: An Annotated Bibliography*, Mary Laverne Dimmick. *Keith Richards*, Barbara Charone. *Rolling Stones In Their Own Words*, Rolling Stones. *The Rolling Stones: An Illustrated Discography*, Miles. *The Rolling Stones In Their Own Words*, David Dalton and Mick Farren. *The Rolling Stones: The First Twenty Years*, David Dalton. *Mick Jagger In His Own Words*, Miles .*The Rolling Stones In Concert*, Linda Martin. *The Rolling Stones: Live In America*, Philip Kamin and Peter Goddard. *Death Of A Rolling Stone: The Brian Jones Story*, Mandy Aftel. *Jagger*, Carey Schofield. *The Rolling Stones A To Z*, Sue Weiner and Lisa Howard. *The Rolling Stones*, Robert Palmer. *The Stones*, Philip Norman. *Satisfaction: The Rolling Stones*, Gered Mankowitz. *The Rolling Stones*, Dezo Hoffman. *On The Road With The Rolling Stones*, Chet Flippo. *The True Adventures Of The Rolling Stones*, Stanley Booth. *Heart Of Stone: The Definitive Rolling Stones Discography*, Felix Aeppli. *Yesterday's Papers: The Rolling Stones In Print*, Jessica MacPhail. *The Life And Good Times Of The Rolling Stones*, Philip Norman. *Stone Alone*, Bill Wyman and Ray Coleman. *The Rolling Stones 25th Anniversary Tour*, Greg Quill. *Blown Away: The Rolling Stones And The Death Of The Sixties*, A.E. Hotchner. *The Rolling Stones: Complete Recording Sessions 1963-1989*, Martin Elliott. *The Rolling Stones Story*, Robert Draper. *The Rolling Stones Chronicle: The First Thirty Years*, Massimo Bonanno. *Rolling Stones: Images Of The World Tour 1989-1990*, David Fricke and Robert Sandall. *The Rolling Stones: Behind The Buttons (Limited Edition)*, Gered Mankowitz and Robert Whitaker

(Photographers). *Golden Stone: The Untold Life And Mysterious Death Of Brian Jones*, Laura Jackson. *Rolling Stones: Das Weissbuch*, Dieter Hoffmann. *Not Fade Away: Rolling Stones Collection*, Geoffrey Giuliano. *Keith Richards: The Unauthorised Biography*, Victor Bockris. *Who Killed Christopher Robin*, Terry Rawlings. *A Visual Documentary*, Miles. *Complete Guide To The Music Of*, James Hector.

Rolling Stones Rock 'n' Roll Circus, The

The 60s most enigmatic rock film, *The Rolling Stones Rock 'n' Roll Circus*, although completed, has never been screened. Shot in 1968, it was the subject of considerable publicity, notably a lengthy feature in *Rolling Stone* magazine. Stills photographer Michael Cooper documented the proceedings, which were set in a carnival big top, with the participants dressed in costume as clowns and ringmasters. **John Lennon**, **Yoko Ono** and **Marianne Faithfull** are among the assembled cast; the first-named completed a ravaged reading of 'Yer Blues' with the aid of **Keith Richard** and **Eric Clapton**. Other musical contributions were drawn from **Jethro Tull**, **Taj Mahal**, **Dick Heckstall-Smith**, **Stephen Stills**, the **Who** and, of course, the **Rolling Stones** themselves. Part of the Who's set - a virulent version of their mini-opera, A Quick One While He's Away' - surfaced later on the group's own documentary, *The Kid's Are Alright*. So powerful was the Who's performance, it has been suggested the Stones withheld the *Rock 'n' Roll Circus*, as they feared being upstaged. In subsequent interviews they admitted giving a sub-par set as they were tired from the day's events. The film may yet surface; until then the Stones' last live show with Brian Jones sadly remains locked away.

Rollini, Adrian

b. 28 June 1904, New York City, New York, USA, d. 15 May 1956. After starting out on piano and xylophone, Rollini switched to bass saxophone in the early 20s. As a member of the prolific recording band, the **California Ramblers**, he played with many leading jazzmen of the day including **Bix Beiderbecke**, **Frank Trumbauer** and **Red Nichols**. His younger brother, **Arthur Rollini**, was also a sometime member of the Ramblers. Rollini had a great influence upon many young white jazzmen in the USA and also in the UK where he worked towards the end of the decade as a member of **Fred Elizalde**'s band. In the mid-30s and 40s he was mostly in New York where he held several long hotel residencies, at the time adding the vibraphone to the list of instruments on which he was adept. He continued playing into the 50s but in Florida where he had moved to run his own hotel. Despite the cumbersome nature of the bass saxophone, Rollini always played with great flair and swing and few other musicians in jazz have matched him on this instrument. He influenced **Harry Gold** and several baritone saxophonists including **Harry Carney**. He died in 1956.

Album: *The Adrian Rollini Quartet And Trio* (1938-40 recordings).

Rollini, Arthur

b. 13 February 1912, New York City, New York, USA. By his late teens, Rollini was playing tenor saxophone with various bands including the **California Ramblers**, where a fellow musician was his older brother, **Adrian Rollini**. He also played with Adrian in London in the **Fred Elizalde** band. In the 30s he worked mostly in New York, often in company with his brother. In 1934 he joined **Benny Goodman**, staying on through the early years of struggle to the successes of the swing era. He left Goodman in 1939 and thereafter played mostly as a freelance and studio musician, recording with **Brad Gowans** and others. By the 60s he had virtually stopped playing. A very musicianly player with a coolly elegant solo style, Rollini's jazz dates were tantalizingly infrequent. His autobiography was published in 1987.

Compilations: with Benny Goodman *Breakfast Ball* (1934), *Brad Gowans And His New York Nine* (1946).

Further reading: *Thirty Years With The Big Bands*, Arthur Rollini.

Rollins, Henry

Vocalist Henry Rollins (b. Henry Garfield, 13 February 1961, Washington DC, USA) quickly returned to action following the break-up of **Black Flag**, releasing *Hot Animal Machine*, followed by the *Drive-By Shooting* EP (under the pseudonym Henrietta Collins and the Wifebeating Childhaters). The Rollins Band was eventually formed in 1987 with Chris Haskett (guitar), Andrew Weiss (bass) and Sim Cain (drums). The group developed their own brand of hard rock, with blues and jazz influences, over several studio and live albums, building a considerable following with their heavy touring schedule. Rollins' lyrics dealt with social and political themes, often unashamedly exorcising personal demons from a troubled childhood. The sight of the heavily-muscled and tattooed frontman on stage, dripping sweat and roaring out his rage, is one of the most astonishing, memorable sights in hard rock music, topping off an enthralling live act. Their commercial rise began with the opening slot on the first Lollapalooza tour, exposing the band to huge audiences for the first time. *The End Of Silence* was a deserved success, and contained some of Rollins' most strikingly introspective lyrics. 'Just Like You' narrated his difficulty in dealing with his similarities to an abusive father: 'You should see the pain I go through, When I see myself I see you'. Rollins' spoken word and publishing activities (his regime is one which allows for little more than a few hours sleep each night) also drew major media interest. An accomplished and experienced spoken word performer with several albums to his credit, Rollins' often hilarious style is in distinct contrast to his musical persona, and has drawn comparisons to Lenny Bruce and Denis Leary (though, in contrast, he implores his audiences not to destroy themselves with 'poisons' like alcohol and tobacco). Despite the humour, there is a serious edge to his words, best animated in the harrowing story of the murder of his best friend, Joe Cole, within feet of him. Rollins' workaholic frame also levers his own publishing company, 2.13.61 (after his birthdate), which has grown from very small beginnings in 1984 to publish a wide range of authors, including Rollins' own prolific output. He also has a music publishing enterprise, Human Pitbull, and co-owns a record label with **Rick Rubin**, dedicated to classic punk reissues - Rollins himself having graduated from the infamous late 70s Washington DC 'straight edge' scene and bands like SOA. He has additionally broken into film acting, appearing in *The Chase* and *Johnny Mnemonic*. Back with the Rollins Band, *Weight*, produced by long-time soundman Theo Van Rock, saw the first personnel change since the band's inception, with Melvin Gibbs replacing Weiss, and adding a funkier spine to the band's still intense core.

Albums: Henry Rollins: *Hot Animal Machine* (Texas Hotel 1986). Rollins Band: *Life Time* (Texas Hotel 1988), *Do It* (Texas Hotel 1988), *Hard Volume* (Texas Hotel 1989), *Turned On* (Quarterstick 1990), *The End Of Silence* (Imago 1992), *Weight* (Imago 1994). Spoken word: *The Boxed Life* (Imago 1993).

Further reading: all titles by Henry Rollins *High Adventure In The Great Outdoors* aka *Bodyba*. *Pissing In The Gene Pool*. *Art To Choke Hearts*. *Bang!*. *One From None*. *See A Grown Man Cry*. *Black Coffee Blues*. *Now Watch 'Em Di*. *Get In The Van: On The Road With Black Flag*.

Rollins, Sonny

b. Theodore Walter Rollins, 7 September 1929, New York, USA. Although an older brother played violin and, at the age of nine, he took piano lessons, Rollins was destined for the saxophone. In 1944 he played alto saxophone in high school and when he left in 1947 he began gigging round New York on tenor. His first inspiration was **Coleman Hawkins**, but he was well aware of the beboppers, many of whom lived in his neighbourhood. His first recording date was with scat-singer **Babs Gonzalez** for **Capitol Records** in 1948. Soon he was recording with **Bud Powell**, **Fats Navarro** and **J.J. Johnson**, who recorded his first composition, 'Audubon'. Rollins's assured version of **Charlie Parker** on tenor was embraced by the top jazz artists: in 1949 he played with **Art Blakey**, in 1950 with **Tadd Dameron**, in 1951 with **Miles Davis** and in 1953 with **Thelonious Monk**. In 1954 Davis recorded with Rollins, including in the set three important Rollins compositions: 'Airegin' (Nigeria

backwards - a salute to the newly independent African state), 'Oleo' and 'Doxy'. However, Rollins left for Chicago and Davis chose **John Coltrane** when he formed his new quintet. In January 1956, when the **Clifford Brown/Max Roach** quintet lost its tenor (**Harold Land**) in Chicago, Rollins stepped in, and played with them for 18 months. After that, Rollins began leading his own groups. In May 1956 he recorded *Tenor Madness* for Prestige, with the **Paul Chambers/Philly Joe Jones** rhythm team from Coltrane's group. The title track consisted of a mighty 'tenor battle' with Coltrane himself, Rollins's melodious expansion contrasting with Coltrane's pressure-cooker angularity.

In April 1956 Rollins recorded *Saxophone Colossus*, generally regarded as his first masterpiece. However, the advent of **Ornette Coleman** caused a deal of self-reflection and he retired for two years (1959-1960), amidst rumours that he was practising on Williamsburg Bridge. In 1961 he re-emerged to work with **Jim Hall** and then with two musicians associated with Ornette: trumpeter **Don Cherry** and drummer **Billy Higgins**. *Our Man In Jazz* shows him taking on the new freedoms with confidence and passion: the 20-minute 'Oleo' was a *tour de force*. He then toured as a soloist, using local rhythm sections (European tours in 1965, 1966 and 1967). In 1966 he recorded *East Broadway Rundown* with the **Jimmy Garrison/Elvin Jones** rhythm section from Coltrane's classic quartet. The music, with its blistering title track and tremulous version of 'We Kiss In A Shadow' was superb, but it was indicative of Rollins's problems that it was a one-off group. Rollins found it difficult to deal with the possibilities opened up by the assaults on form of the *avant garde*. He again took a two-year sabbatical (1968-71), this time studying in India and Japan.

In 1973 he recorded *Horn Culture* using electric accompaniment. On electric bass **Bob Cranshaw** lacked the fire he had shown on *Our Man In Jazz* and despite Rollins's self-overdubs and characteristically ambitious solos, he seemed to be mired in pedestrian jazz-rock. *The Cutting Edge* (1974) had a bravura *a cappella* rendition of 'To A Wild Rose' but a similarly subdued band. In 1978 he toured with the Milestone All Stars. Here, a band of the stature of **McCoy Tyner**, **Ron Carter** and **Al Foster** could not fail to spark him, but these musicians were all leaders in their own right and could not work with him regularly. At this point Rollins refused all further nightclub performances and resolved to play festivals and concert halls exclusively. In 1985 Rollins attempted to do without rhythm sections altogether in *The Solo Album* and then toured Europe with a band featuring ex-**Weather Report** bassist Victor Bailey and drummer Tommy Campbell. In 1986 his *Concerto For Saxophone And Orchestra* was premiered in Japan. 1988 saw him linking up with some of the new names of the jazz revival: Marvin 'Smitty' Smith provided him with ferociously good drumming at live appearances. However, a rather tight and commercial sound made *Dancing In The Dark* unsatisfactory. Rollins is a soloist *par excellence*. His indecision about the form of his music - whether it is to be free/electric/acoustic - reflects the general quandary of jazz in the 80s. He is still capable of the solo flights that caused Davis to vote for him as 'greatest tenor ever' in a poll conducted by **Leonard Feather** at the end of the 60s.

Selected albums: *First Recordings* (1951), *Sonny And The Stars* (1953), *Movin' Out* (Original Jazz Classics 1954), *Worktime* (1956), *With The Modern Jazz Quartet* (Original Jazz Classics 1956), *Plus Four* (Original Jazz Classics 1956), *Tenor Madness* (Original Jazz Classics 1956), *Work Time* (Original Jazz Classics 1956), *Saxophone Colossus* (Original Jazz Classics 1956), *Sonny Rollins Vol 1* (Blue Note 1956), *Plays For Bird* (Original Jazz Classics 1957), *Tour De Force* (Original Jazz Classics 1957), *Sonny Rollins, Volume Two* (Blue Note 1957), *Newk's Time* (Blue Note 1957), *A Night At The Village Vanguard Vol 1* (Blue Note 1957), *The Sound Of Sonny* (Original Jazz Classics 1957), *Way Out West* (Blue Note 1957), *A Night At The Village Vanguard Vol 1* (1958), *A Night At The Village Vanguard Vol 2* (Blue Note 1958), *Meets The Big Brass* (1958), *Brass/Trio* (1958), *And The Contemporary Leaders* (1959), *The Bridge* (RCA 1962), *What's New* (1962), *Our Man In Jazz* (1962), *Sonny Meets Hawk* (1963), *Now's The Time!* (1964), *The Standard Sonny Rollins* (1965), *On Impulse* (Impulse 1965), *Plays Alfie* (Impulse 1966), *East Broadway Rundown* (Impulse 1966), *There Will Never Be Another You* (1967), *Next Album* (Original Jazz Classics 1972), *Horn Culture* (Original Jazz Classics 1973), *In Japan* (1974), *The Cutting Edge* (Original Jazz Classics 1974), *Nucleus* (Original Jazz Classics 1975), *More From The Vanguard* (1975, rec 1957), *The Way I Feel* (Original Jazz Classics 1976), *Easy Living* (1977), *Don't Stop The Carnival* (Milestone 1978), with others *Milestone Jazz Stars* (Milestone 1978), *Don't Ask* (1979), *Love At First Sight* (1980), *The Alternative Rollins* (1981, rec 1964), *No Problem* (1982), *Reel Life* (1982), *St Thomas: In Stockholm 1959* (1984, rec 1959), *Sunny Days, Starry Nights* (Milestone 1984), *In Paris* (1984, rec early 60s), *The Solo Album* (Milestone 1985), *Alternate Takes* (1986, rec 1957-58), *Plays G-Man* (Milestone 1986), *Dancing In The Dark* (Milestone 1988), *Falling In Love With Jazz* (Milestone 1990), *Here's To The People* (Milestone 1991), *What's New* (1993), *Old Flames* (Milestone 1994).

Further reading: *Sonny Rollins*, Charley Gerard (ed.). *Sonny Rollins: The Journey Of A Jazzman*, Charles Clement Blancq.

Roman Scandals

This **Eddie Cantor** vehicle, which was produced by Samuel Goldwyn and released by United Artists in 1933, proved to be one the most entertaining of all the comedian's 15 or so films. The screenplay, which was the work of William Anthony McGuire, George Oppenheimer, Nat Perrin, and Arthur Sheekman, cast Cantor as a law-abiding resident of a small town in Oklahoma. Concerned at the level of bribery and corruption all around him, he joins in the political process to try and change things for the better. Most of the film is concerned with a dream in which he is transported back in time to ancient Rome where he discovers what *real* corruption is all about! Cantor ran the full gamut of his energetic, eye-rolling shtick, and director Frank Tuttle managed to manoeuvre his star into blackface (even in ancient Rome), a chariot race, and a scene in which the modesty of a gaggle of gorgeous girls (including the 23-year-old Lucille Ball) is only maintained by their fashionably long tresses. Broadway torch singer **Ruth Etting**, making her movie debut, introduced the lovely ballad 'No More Love', and Cantor's high-pitched voice was heard to great effect on **Harry Warren** and **Al Dubin**'s other songs, 'Keep Young And Beautiful', 'Build A Little Home', and 'Put A Tax On Love' (lyric also with L. Gilbert Wolfe). Also among the cast were Gloria Stuart, David Manners, Edward Arnold, Veree Teasdale, and Alan Mowbray.

Roman, Murray

Briefly touted as a likely successor to Lenny Bruce, late-60s comedian Roman achieved a cult popularity in Britain through import copies of *You Can't Beat People Up And Have Them Say I Love You*. His routines centred chiefly on sex and drugs and were punctuated by discotheque soul as if to emphasize a party-like atmosphere. The UK rights were later acquired by Track Records, which also issued Roman's second set, *Blind Man's Movie*. The title was inspired by a remark attributed to **Ray Charles** and the album's fold-out sleeve was entirely matt black. The collection failed to emulate the popularity of its predecessor as it became clear that, despite surface similarities, Roman lacked Bruce's depth and sense of irony. *Busted*, which offered one side of old material and another chronicling the comedian's spell in prison, proved unrewarding and signalled the end of its creator's brief fame.

Albums: *You Can't Beat People Up And Have Them Say I Love You* (1968), *Blind Man's Movie* (1970), *Busted* (1971).

Romance On The High Seas

Songwriter **Sammy Cahn** used to claim much of the credit for bringing band singer **Doris Day** to the attention of the Warner Brothers studio which led to her feature film debut in this movie released in 1948. Whatever the facts of the case, Day just about stole the film from under the noses of top-billed stars Janis Paige, Jack Carson and Don DeFore. Her light comedy touch was evident right from the start of this slight and corny story about mistaken identities on a luxurious Caribbean cruise. **Oscar Levant** was in the supporting cast - which is always an encouraging sign - along with S.Z Sakall, Eric Blore, Fortunio Bonanova, William Bakewell, Franklin Pangborn, and guest artists the Page Cavanaugh Trio, Sir Lancelot, the Samba Kings and Avon Long. **Jule Styne** and that same Sammy Cahn produced an enjoyable score which gave Day two big record hits, 'It's Magic' and 'Put 'Em In A Box, Tie 'Em With A Ribbon', as well as 'I'm In Love' and 'It's You Or No One'. The rest of the score consisted of 'Run, Run, Run', 'The Tourist Trade', and 'Cuban Rhapsody' (Levant-Ray Heindorf). The musical numbers were created and directed by **Busby Berkeley** and the screenplay was written by Philip G. Epstein (with additional dialogue by I.A.L. Diamond) from a story by S. Pondal Rios and Carlos A. Olivari. Michael Curtiz directed this bright, entertaining Technicolor film which was re-titled *It's Magic* for UK distribution.

Romano, Aldo

b. 16 January 1941, Belluno, Italy. Moving to France as a child, Romano studied guitar before teaching himself drums. Employment with the local modern groups **Barney Wilen** and Michel Portal led to Romano playing with visiting Americans including **Jackie McLean**, **Bud Powell** and **Stan Getz**, but it was playing with the **Don Cherry** group in 1963 that convinced him that free jazz was to be his chosen path. During the late 60s Romano drummed for **Carla Bley**, **Gato Barbieri** and **Steve Lacy**. **Joachim Kuhn** and **Jean-Luc Ponty**, whose bands featured Romano at the turn of the decade, were both experimenting with jazz rock, and in 1971 Romano formed his own rock group in which he sang and played guitar. The 70s saw him with fusioneers, Pork Pie, and recording with Francois Jeanneau and Enrico Rava. During the 80s Romano has looked back to his earlier style, to the small group free music of the 60s. He expressed his fondness for this music in a recent sleevenote: 'I have said a number of times that if **Ornette** (**Coleman**) had been Italian, he would have composed *La Traviata*'.
Albums: with Steve Lacy *Disposability* (1965), with Pork Pie *Transitory* (1973), *Il Piacere* (1978), *To Be Ornette To Be* (1989).

Romano, Joe

b. 17 April 1932, Rochester, New York, USA. After playing alto and tenor saxophones with various bands in the north-eastern states, Romano joined **Woody Herman** in 1956. Subsequently, he worked with **Chuck Mangione**, Gus Mancuso, Sam Noto and others, returning frequently to Herman. In the late 60s and early 70s he played in bands led by **Buddy Rich** and **Les Brown**. In the mid-70s he was a member of **Chuck Israel**'s National Jazz Ensemble and in 1978 joined the **Louie Bellson** band which played in the USA and UK. He has also played with the **Thad Jones-Mel Lewis** band and has recorded with **Bill Watrous** and **Don Menza**. An aggressive, bebop-influenced player, Romano's career has rarely been settled for long periods, making it difficult to form an accurate assessment of his status in the jazz world. Nevertheless, the regularity with which important leaders have called upon his services is an indicator of his standing among fellow musicians. The power and dynamism of his section work is particularly impressive and his solos display fiery urgency and an impressive flow of ideas.
Albums: with Sam Noto *Act One* (1975), with Noto *Notes To You* (1977), with Bill Watrous *Watrous In Hollywood* (1978), with Louie Bellson *Matterhorn* (1978), *Louie Bellson's Big Band Explosion Live At Ronnie Scott's* (1979), with Bellson *London Scene* (1980), with Don Menza *Burnin'* (1980), *And Finally Romano* (Fresh Sounds 1988).

Romantics

A band whose career falls into two distinct halves; the **Knack**-like pop of the 70s dressed in tight red leather pants, and the near stadium rock-like success of the early 80s. The Romantics started out as four factory workers from Detroit, USA; Wally Palmer (vocals, guitar), Mike Skill (guitar, vocals), Rich Cole (bass, vocals) and Jimmy Marinos (drums, vocals). They originally formed in February 1977, releasing their debut single, 'Little White Lies', on their own Spider Records. It was followed by 'I Tell It To Carrie' on Greg Shaw's **Bomp** label in 1978. The music was uptempo and pop-like, much in the vein of the **Flamin' Groovies** or the **Raspberries**, but in the 80s they developed a much more sophisticated, and familiar, US rock sound, for which they were rewarded with a US Top 10 hit with 'Talking In Your Sleep'. However, despite their sudden success Jimmy Marinos left in 1983 and the band effectively disappeared with him.
Albums: *The Romantics* (1980), *National Breakout* (1981), *Strictly Personal* (1981), *In Heat* (1983).

Romao, Dom Um

b. 3 August 1925, Rio de Janeiro, Brazil. Romao's father was a drummer and Dom started playing in his youth. In the early 60s he joined the Bossa Rio Sextet with **Sergio Mendes**. After recording with saxophonist **Cannonball Adderley** at the Carnegie Hall in 1962 he settled in the USA and worked in Chicago with vocalist **Oscar Brown Jnr.** (1965). After moving to Los Angeles in 1966 he toured with Sergio Mendes before replacing **Airto Moreira** in **Weather Report** (1971-74). During the early 70s he established his own rehearsal studio in New York - Black Beans Studio. In 1976 he recorded with **George Gruntz**'s Band in Zurich and has since spent a lot of time in Europe with the Swiss band Om.

Albums: *Dom Um Romao* (1972), *Spirit Of The Times* (1973), with Weather Report *I Sing The Body Electric* (1972), with Weather Report *Sweetnighter* (1973), with Collin Walcott *Grazing Dreams* (1977).

Romberg, Sigmund

b. 29 July 1887, Nagykanizsa, Hungary, d. 9 November 1951. After formal training as a violinist, Romberg began writing music while in his late teens. Despite these early interests, Romberg's main studies were in engineering and it was not until 1909, after completing a period of service in the Hungarian army, most of which was spent in Vienna, that he decided to make his career in music. Romberg showed a practical streak by recognizing that he would do better away from the Viennese 'hot house', which already contained numerous important composers. He emigrated to the USA, taking up residence in New York City where he found work in a factory, supplementing his income playing piano in restaurants and bars. He graduated to leading an orchestra, which proved very popular but his heart was set on composing for the musical stage. His first show, written in collaboration with lyricist Harold Atteridge, was *The Whirl Of The World*, which opened in 1914, the year in which Romberg became an American citizen. Romberg and Atteridge continued their partnership for several years, creating numerous shows, few of which were especially successful despite starring such leading theatrical personalities as Marilyn Miller, Nora Bayes and **Al Jolson**. The shows that fared best were **The Blue Paradise** (1915) and **Maytime** (1917); for both Romberg drew upon his musical heritage, writing waltzes in the Viennese manner. This was a practice he untilised in 1921 with **Blossom Time**, which told a fanciful version of the life of classical composer Franz Schubert. The score included 'Song Of Love', by far Romberg's most popular song up to this time. Convinced that the operetta was where he was most at ease, Romberg turned increasingly to this form even though he was obliged to write in other contexts to make a living. It was not until 1924 and the opening of **The Student Prince**, that he was able to prove conclusively that he was right in his belief. *The Student Prince*, in which Romberg was joined by lyricist Dorothy Donnelly, included such major song successes as 'Deep In My Heart', 'Serenade', 'Golden Days' and the 'Drinking Song'. With the evidence of this show as his guide, he concentrated on operettas and, despite some failures, soon became America's leading exponent of this type of musical theatre. In 1926 he wrote **The Desert Song** (lyrics by **Otto Harbach** and **Oscar Hammerstein II**), from which came 'Blue Heaven', 'One Alone' and the rousing 'Riff Song'. Romberg followed this with **The New Moon** (1928, with Hammerstein). Both on stage and as a film, in 1930, *The New Moon* was hugely popular, with hit songs such as 'Lover, Come Back To Me', 'One Kiss', 'Stouthearted Men' and 'Softly, As In A Morning Sunrise'. Inevitably, Romberg's inclination towards operetta endangered his continuing popularity through the 30s. Changing musical tastes conspired against him, although he still wrote many engaging songs, among them 'When I Grow Too Old To Dream', written with Hammerstein for the 1934 film *The Night Is Young*. In 1935 he adapted to the vogue for musical comedy with *May Wine*, before settling in California to write for films. In the early 40s he was relatively inactive but he made a comeback on Broadway in 1945 with **Up In Central Park**. With lyrics by **Dorothy Fields**, the show included such songs as 'Close As Pages In A Book' and 'Carousel In The Park'. Despite this show's success, Romberg's subsequent work drifted between operetta and musical comedy and met with little interest from audiences.

Rome, Harold

b. 27 May 1908, Hartford, Connecticut, USA, d. 26 October 1993, New York, USA. While still attending school Rome played piano in local dance bands and was already writing music. Despite this early interest in music, he went on to study architecture and law at Yale. In 1934 he practised as an architect in New York City, but studied piano and composition in his spare time. This was a fortunate decision because by the following year, with work opportunities diminishing with the Depression, he was obliged to turn more and more to his second string activity for support. Much of the music Rome was writing at this time was socially-conscious and was thus of little interest to Tin Pan Alley. Nevertheless, he was engaged to write a revue for the International Garment Workers' Union. To everyone's surprise, the revue, **Pins And Needles** (1937), put on for members of the union, became a popular success and one song, 'Sunday In The Park', established a life outside the show. Rome was now much sought-after, although his next show displayed similarly political concerns. This was *Sing Out The News* (1939) and, once again, there was a universally-accepted hit song, 'F.D.R. Jones'. In the early 40s Rome wrote songs for several revues and shows, but it was not until after the end of World War II that he had his first major success. This was **Call Me Mister** (1946), from which came 'South America, Take It Away'. More revues followed until his first full-fledged musical show, **Wish You Were Here**, in 1952. Two years later he wrote **Fanny**, his most popular Broadway show, which included 'Love Is A Very Light Thing'. This was followed by **Destry Rides Again** (1959) and **I Can Get It For You Wholesale** (1962), in which **Barbra Streisand** made her Broadway debut. In the mid-60s Rome showed that the social conscience which had marked his early work was still intact when he wrote *The Zulu And The Zayda* (1965), which dealt with racial and religious intolerance. In

1970 he wrote *Scarlett*, based upon the novel *Gone With The Wind*, for a Japanese production in Tokyo. More than with any other American composer in the field of mainstream popular music, Rome's work consistently showed an awareness of social issues, often to the extent that it kept him from the massive successes enjoyed by many of his contemporaries. He was also a gifted painter and a dedicated art collector.

Romeo's Daughter

This UK AOR band were fronted by female vocalist Leigh Matty and expertly backed by songwriter and guitarist Craig Joiner, Tony Mitman on keyboards, Ed Poole on bass and drummer Andy Wells. The band came together under the direction of producer Robert 'Mutt' Lange in what seemed to be an attempt to recreate a similar project from the late 70s with his wife's band, Night. Lange, along with **John Parr** and Joiner, worked hard on the songs and production and armed with a deal with **Jive** Records issued the single, 'Heaven In The Back Seat', a minor hit that brought together elements of both **Heart** and **Belinda Carlisle** whilst retaining an 'English' sound. 1989's self-titled album sold well and the band proved a popular live attraction, receiving much attention from Radio 1's *Rock Show* who broadcast live concerts and an exclusive session. 'Heaven In The Back Seat', meanwhile, also turned up on the soundtrack to *Nightmare On Elm Street 5*: *The Dream Child*. The band went to ground but resurfaced in 1993 with another single, 'Attracted To The Animal', followed by a major tour and an album on **Music For Nations**. By this time they had lost much of their earlier impact and by 1994 had left both management and label in search of new ideas, and were contemplating a change of name.
Albums: *Romeos Daughter* (Jive 1989), *Delectable* (Music For Nations 1993).

Romeo, Max

b. Max Smith, c.1947, Jamaica, West Indies. It was Romeo who first introduced Britain to the concept of rude reggae with 'Wet Dream', which, despite a total radio ban, reached number 10 in the UK charts. He toured the UK several times in the space of a year and issued two albums: *A Dream* being the best selling. However, despite other similarly-styled singles like 'Mini Skirt Vision', he did not enjoy chart success again. Romeo was, essentially, something of a gospel singer with the ability to convey a revivalist fervour on his records such as 'Let The Power Fall' (a Jamaican political anthem in 1972) and 'Pray For Me'. Furthermore, he had an ability to get the trials, tribulations and amusements of Jamaican life into a song, as evinced by 'Eating Competition', 'Sixpence' and 'Aily And Ailaloo'. In 1972 Romeo began a liason with producers **Lee Perry** and **Winston 'Niney' Holness**, and from this point on his records had a

musical fire to match his apocalyptical vision and contrasting humour: 'Babylose Burning', 'Three Blind Mice', 'The Coming Of Jah' all maintained his star status in Jamaica between 1972 and 1975. *Revelation Time* was one of the best albums of 1975, and 1976's *War Ina Babylon* was hailed by the rock press as one of the all-time classic reggae albums. However, Perry had much to do with those records' artistic success, and following a much-publicised split between the pair - with Perry recording 'White Belly Rat' about Max, and scrawling 'Judas' over the singer's picture in Perry's studio - Romeo was cast adrift without musical roots. *I Love My Music*, recorded with the help of **Keith Richards** was a flop, and the stronger *Reconstruction* fared no better. A move to New York's Wackies' label in the early 80s did little to reverse his fortunes, and by the late 80s Max Romeo's name was forgotten in the mainstream reggae market. However, in the spring of 1992, London producer **Jah Shaka** recorded *Far I Captain Of My Ship* on Jah Shaka Records, an unabashed, Jamaican-recorded roots album generally reckoned to be Romeo's best for over 15 years.
Albums: *A Dream* (1970), *Let The Power Fall* (1972), *Revelation Time* (Tropical Sound Tracs 1975), *War Ina Babylon* (Island 1976), *Reconstruction* (1978), *I Love My Music* (1979), *Rondos* (1980), *Holding Out My Love For You* (Shanachie 1987), *Far I Captain Of My Ship* (Jah Shaka 1992), *On The Beach* (1993).

Ron C

b. Ronald Pierre Carey, Oakland, California, USA. Rapper Carey moved to Dallas at the age of 17. However, by the spring of 1990 he anticipated gangsta's rap's flirtation with unlawfulness by being convicted of 'Possession of a controlled dangerous substance with intent', ensuring an unseemly hiatus in his recording career.
Albums: *'C' Ya* (Profile 1990), *Back On The Street* (Profile 1992).

Ronald And Ruby

Ronald was teenage singer Lee Morris and Ruby was Beverly Ross (b. 1939, New Jersey, USA), his singing partner. Ross, who had already penned a hit for **Bill Haley And His Comets** ('Dim, Dim The Lights'), wrote a song in 1958 called 'Lollipop' and the pair, renamed Ronald and Ruby by their manager, recorded it for **RCA**-Victor. The irritating repeated lyric 'lollipop, lollipop ooh lolly lolly lolly' was hummed by millions over the next few months. The **Chordettes** immediately covered the song for Cadence Records, and that group's version outsold Ronald And Ruby's; the pair's rendition reached number 20 in the US charts while the Chordettes' made it to number 2. (In the UK the Mudlarks took it to number 2). Ross went on to become a successful songwriter, among her credits: **Roy Orbison**'s 'Candy Man', **Lesley Gore**'s

'Judy's Turn To Cry' and 'the **Earls**' 'Remember Then'. Ronald And Ruby never recorded an album and the act split up after their initial hit.

Ronco Records

For over a decade, Ronco was one of the UK's leading television marketing companies for pop albums. Originally a Canadian firm selling carpet cleaners and other household products it branched out into music in the 70s, arriving in the UK in 1972, shortly after its main rival **K-Tel**. The first Ronco success was *20 Star Tracks*, followed by *That'll Be The Day*, a compilation of 50s hits timed to coincide with the hit film starring **David Essex** and **Ringo Starr**. Released in 1973, it became the label's only number 1. Ronco later released soundtrack albums, having the greatest success with *Stardust*, the movie sequel to *That'll Be The Day* and *The Stud*, a Joan Collins vehicle. However, most of its 70s releases were collections of tracks from various musical styles - rock, black music, disco and military bands. Some of Ronco's biggest sellers came from single artist albums, by MOR stars. In 1976, its **Max Bygraves** release, *100 Gold Greats* reached the UK Top 10, while two **Lena Martell** albums were almost as successful. The increased competition from mainstream record companies in the television advertising sphere eventually caused the collapse of Ronco in 1984. Its former general manager Tony Naughton went on to found Stylus Music, another television merchandising label which in turn crashed after five years.

Ronettes

Veronica 'Ronnie' Bennett (b. 10 August 1943, New York, USA), her sister Estelle (b. 22 July 1944, New York, USA) and cousin Nedra Talley (b. 17 January 1946, New York, USA) began their career as a dance act the Dolly Sisters. By 1961 they had become the resident dance troupe at the famed Peppermint Lounge, home of the **twist** craze, and having taken tuition in harmony singing, later secured a recording deal. The trio's first single, 'I Want A Boy', was credited to Ronnie And The Relatives, but when 'Silhouettes' followed in 1962, the Ronettes appellation was in place. They recorded four singles for the Colpix/May group and appeared on disc jockey Murray The K's *Live From The Brooklyn Fox* before a chance telephone call resulted in their signing with producer **Phil Spector**. Their first collaboration, the majestic 'Be My Baby' defined the girl-group sound as Spector constructed a cavernous accompaniment around Ronnie's plaintive, nasal voice. The single reached the Top 5 in the US and UK before being succeeded by the equally worthwhile 'Baby I Love You', another Top 20 entrant in both countries. The producer's infatuation with Ronnie - the couple were later married - resulted in some of his finest work being reserved for her and although ensuing singles, including

'The Best Part of Breaking Up', 'Walking In The Rain' (both 1964) and 'Is This What I Get For Loving You' (1965), failed to emulate the Ronettes' early success, they are among the finest pop singles of all time. The group's career was shelved during Spector's mid-60s 'retirement', but they re-emerged in 1969 with 'You Came, You Saw You Conquered'. Credited to 'The Ronettes Featuring The Voice Of Veronica', this excellent single was nonetheless commercially moribund and Ronnie's aspirations were again sublimated. She separated from Spector in 1973 and joined **Buddah Records**, founding a new group with vocalists Denise Edwards and Chip Fields. Ronnie And The Ronettes made their debut that year with 'Lover Lover', before changing their name to **Ronnie Spector** and the Ronettes for 'I Wish I Never Saw The Sunshine', an impassioned remake of a song recorded by the original line-up, but which remained unissued until 1976. The unit's name was then dropped as its lead singer pursued her solo ambitions.
Album: *Presenting The Fabulous Ronettes Featuring Veronica* (1964). Compilations: *The Ronettes Sing Their Greatest Hits* (1975), *Their Greatest Hits - Vol. II* (1981), *The Colpix Years 1961-63* (1987), *The Best Of* (1992).

Roney, Wallace

b. 25 May 1960, Philadelphia, Pennsylvania, USA. He began playing trumpet at the age of seven and six years later was given some informal but invaluable tuition by **Clark Terry**. Later he studied briefly at both Howard University and **Berklee College Of Music**. In 1981 he was hired by **Art Blakey** and during the 80s he also met **Miles Davis**, whom he greatly admired, but did not have the chance to play with him until 1991, a few months before Davis' death. His recording career has included appearances with **Tony Williams**, **Dizzy Gillespie** and **Gerry Mulligan**. From the late 80s and on into the 90s he has made several well-received albums as leader. A fluent, melodic improviser, Roney's playing consistently displays imagination and it is self-evident why his fellow musicians hold him in such high regard even though his name is not yet as widely known amongst audiences.
Albums: *Verses* (Muse 1988), *Intuition* (Muse 1989), *The Standard Bearer* (Muse 1990), *Obsession* (Muse 1991), *Seth Air* (Muse 1992), *Crunchin'* (Muse 1993), *Misterios* (Warners 1994).

Ronnie And The Hi-Lites

Formed in Jersey City, New Jersey, USA in the early 60s, Ronnie and the Hi-Lites were a doo-wop group best remembered for one recording, the 1962 US Top 20 ballad 'I Wish That We Were Married'. The group, originally called the Cascades, initially consisted of tenors Sonny Caldwell and John Witney, bass singer Kenny Overby and baritone Stanley Brown. Adding 12-year-old Ronnie Goodson as their lead singer, they were soon introduced to songwriter Marian Weiss, who offered them 'I Wish That We Were Married'. The small Joy Records label picked up the demo recording the group had made and, renaming the ensemble, released the single. The group released only one other single for Joy and it was unsuccessful. They recorded a few more singles for Win Records, without success. Ronnie Goodson died 4 November 1980.

Ronny And The Daytonas

Ronny Dayton (b. 26 April 1946, Tulsa, Oklahoma, USA; guitar) formed this group with close friends Jimmy Johnson (guitar), Van Evans (bass) and Lynn Williams (drums). Avid fans of surf and hot rod music, the quartet scored with the latter genre when 'G.T.O.' reached the US Top 5 in 1964. This homage to a beloved stock car eventually sold in excess of 1 million, but the group was unable to repeat this success. They did enjoy minor hits with 'California Bound', 'Bucket T' (later covered by the **Who**), and 'Sandy', but had become too closely associated with a passing trend to enjoy a long career.
Albums: *GTO* (1964), *Sandy* (1965).

Ronson, Mick

b. 26 May 1945, Hull, Yorkshire, England, d. 30 April 1993. This UK guitarist, was originally a member of **David Bowie's** backing group Hype, in February 1970. Bowie later renamed the group, the Spiders From Mars and achieved international success, with Ronson playing lead on the pivotal albums, *The Man Who Sold The World*, *Hunky Dory*, *The Rise And Fall Of Ziggy Stardust And The Spiders From Mars* and *Aladdin Sane*. Ronson embarked on a short-lived and unsuccessful solo career towards the end of 1973, initiated by Bowie's decision to quit touring at the time. Recording two competent rock albums, he found it difficult to accept the lack of success as a solo artist and joined **Mott The Hoople** in 1974. They only recorded the single 'Saturday Gigs' with Ronson, before a major personnel change ensued. Lead vocalist, **Ian Hunter**, departed to start a solo career and Ronson followed. He subsequently appeared with **Bob Dylan** in the famous Rolling Thunder Revue. The remaining members shortened the name to **Mott** and recruited new members. The Hunter-Ronson partnership lasted over 15 years, but it was only on *YUIORTA*, that Ronson received equal billing on the sleeve with Hunter. In 1991, Ronson underwent treatment for cancer, and the following year he appeared with Bowie at the **Freddy Mercury** Aids Benefit concert. Just before Ronson's death in 1993 he was working on his third album with contributions from artists such as Chrissie Hynde, **John Mellencamp**, Joe Elliott and David Bowie.
Albums: *Slaughter On Tenth Avenue* (1974), *Play Don't Worry* (1975), *Heaven And Hull* (Epic 1994).

Ronstadt, Linda

b. Linda Maria Ronstadt, 15 July 1946, Tucson, Arizona, USA. The daughter of a professional musician, Ronstadt's first singing experience was gained with her sisters in the Three Ronstadts. She met guitarist Bob Kimmel at Arizona's State University and together the two aspirants moved to Los Angeles where they were joined by songwriter Kenny Edwards. Taking the name the **Stone Poneys**, the trio became popular among the city's folk fraternity and scored a US Top 20 hit with 'Different Drum'. Ronstadt embarked on a solo career in 1968. Her early solo albums, *Hand Sown, Home Grown* and *Silk Purse* signalled a move towards country-flavoured material, albeit of a more conservative nature. The singer's third album marked a major turning point and featured a core of excellent musicians, including **Don Henley**, **Glen Frey**, **Bernie Leadon** and **Randy Meisner** who subsequently formed the **Eagles**. The content emphasized a contemporary approach with songs by **Neil Young**, **Jackson Browne** and **Eric Anderson**, and the set established Ronstadt as a force in Californian rock. The artist's subsequent two albums showed the dichotomy prevalent in her music. *Don't Cry Now* was largely undistinguished, chiefly because the material was weaker, while *Heart Like A Wheel*, paradoxically given to Linda's former label to complete contractual obligations, was excellent.
This platinum-selling set included 'You're No Good', a US number 1 pop hit, and a dramatic version of **Hank Williams'** 'I Can't Help It', which won Ronstadt a Grammy award for best female country vocal. This highly successful release set the pattern for the singer's work throughout the rest of the decade. Her albums were now carefully constructed to appease both the rock and country audiences, mixing traditional material, singer/songwriter angst and a handful of rock 'n' roll/soul classics, be they from Tamla/**Motown** ('Heatwave'), **Roy Orbison** ('Blue Bayou') or **Buddy Holly** ('That'll Be The Day'). Despite effusive praise from the establishment media and a consistent popularity, this predictable approach resulted in lethargy, and although *Mad Love* showed a desire to break the mould, Ronstadt was increasingly trapped in an artistic cocoon.
The singer's work during the 80s has proved more divergent. Her performance in Joseph Papp's production of *Pirates Of Penzance* drew favourable reviews, although her subsequent role in the more demanding *La Boheme* was less impressive. Ronstadt also undertook a series of releases with veteran arranger/conductor **Nelson Riddle**, which resulted in three albums - *What's New*, *Lush Life* and *For Sentimental Reasons* - consisting of popular standards. In 1987 a duet with **James Ingram**, produced 'Somewhere Out There', the title track to the film *An*

American Tail, this gave her a number 2 US hit (UK Top 10) hit, while that same year her collaboration with **Dolly Parton** and **Emmylou Harris**, *Trio* and a selection of mariachi songs, *Canciones De Mi Padre*, showed an artist determined to challenge preconceptions. Her 1989 set, *Cry Like A Rainstorm*, revealed a crafted approach to mainstream recording and included 'Don't Know Much', a haunting duet with **Aaron Neville**, which gave Linda Ronstadt another number 2 hit in the USA (and the UK). The highly acclaimed *Winter Light* was produced by herself and George Massenburg, and came across as a personal and highly emotional album. Ronstadt, while hugely popular and successful, has never been truly recognised by the *cognoscenti*. Her change in styles may have been a contributing factor. She has courted (with great success), country/rock, country, rock 'n' roll, latin, standards, opera, light opera, AOR and white soul.

Albums: *Hand Sown, Home Grown* (1969), *Silk Purse* (1970), *Linda Ronstadt* (1971), *Don't Cry Now* (1973), *Heart Like A Wheel* (1974), *Prisoner In Disguise* (1975), *Hasten Down The Wind* (1976), *Simple Dreams* (1977), *Living In The USA* (1978), *Mad Love* (1980), with Kevin Kline, Estelle Parsons, Rex Smith *Pirates Of Penzance* (1981), *Get Closer* (1982), *What's New* (1983), *Lush Life* (1984), *For Sentimental Reasons* (1986), with Emmylou Harris, Dolly Parton *Trio* (1987), *Canciones De Mi Padre* (1987), *Cry Like A Rainstorm - Howl Like The Wind* (1989), *Winter Light* (Elektra 1993), *Feels Like Home* (WEA 1995). Compilations: *Different Drum* (1974, includes five Stone Poney tracks), *Greatest Hits: Linda Ronstadt* (1976), *Retrospective* (1977), *Greatest Hits: Linda Ronstadt Volume 2* (1980).

Further reading: *Linda Ronstadt: A Portrait*, Richard Kanakaris. *The Linda Ronstadt Scrapbook*, Mary Ellen Moore. *Linda Ronstadt*, Vivian Claire. *Linda Ronstadt: An Illustrated Biography*, Connie Berman. *Linda Ronstadt: It's So Easy*, Mark Bego.

Rooftop Singers

Cashing in on the folk music revival of the early 60s, the Rooftop Singers were a trio specifically assembled for the purpose of recording a single song, 'Walk Right In', originally recorded in 1930 by **Gus Cannon** And The Jugstompers. The Rooftop Singers consisted of Erik Darling (b. 25 September 1933, Baltimore, Maryland, USA), Bill Svanoe and former **Benny Goodman** band vocalist, Lynne Taylor. Darling had played in folk groups called the Tune Tellers and the Tarriers, the latter including future actor Alan Arkin, and replaced **Pete Seeger** in the **Weavers** in 1958, remaining with them for four years. In 1962 he heard 'Walk Right In' and adapted the lyrics for a more modern sound, utilizing two 12-string guitars and an irresistible rhythm; he then assembled the trio and signed with **Vanguard Records**. 'Walk Right In'

became that label's, and the group's, only number 1 record. The Rooftop Singers placed one album and two other folk songs in the US charts: 'Tom Cat' and 'Mama Don't Allow'. The group disbanded in 1967 and Taylor died the same year; Darling and Svanoe subsequently retired from the music business.
Albums: *Walk Right In!* (1963), *Goodtime* (1964), *Rainy River* (1965).

Roogalator

One of the first of the 70s UK R&B revivalist bands (along with **Dr Feelgood**), Roogalator were led by American **Danny Adler**. He left the USA in the early 70s having played guitar for **Bootsy Collins** and various jazz and blues musicians. He arrived in London and in 1972 put together the first line-up of Roogalator. Over the years numerous personnel were involved including key names like Paul Riley (of **Chilli Willi And The Red Hot Peppers**), and Bobby Irwin (of the Strutters, the Sinceros, and various **Nick Lowe** bands). They came under the management of Robin Scott (later the brains behind **M**) and in 1973 recorded their best-known track - 'Cincinatti Fat Back' - for a BBC radio session. This was eventually released as an EP by **Stiff** in 1976. Scott then formed the Do It label in order to release an album by the band whose new line-up was Adler (guitar/vocals), Nick Plytas (keyboards), Julian Scott (bass), and Justin Hilkdreth (drums). Adler also ran a simultaneous career with the De Luxe Blues Band.
Album: *Play It By Ear* (1978).

Room

An adventurous pop band formed in Liverpool, England, the Room quickly attracted strong support from the press with records variously acclaimed for their wit, irony, poise and intelligence. The line-up featured Dave Jackson (vocals), Paul Cavanagh (guitar), Becky Stringer (bass), and Alan Willis (drums). Early singles on Box records ('Bitter Reaction', 'Motion', 'In Sickness And In Health') revealed a talented band slipstreaming the innovations of **Echo And The Bunnymen**. More attractive still was their debut for Red Flame, 'Things Have Learnt To Walk That Should Only Crawl'. The band played several dates with **Tom Verlaine** in 1984, who went on to produce three tracks on *In Evil Hour*. Their first 'complete' album, it also featured John Porter (of **Smiths** fame) on production. Among the Verlaine slices was 'Jackpot Jack': 'You pulled the lever back/You hit the jackpot jack/And all the radios, are blaring new pop cack'. It was an ambitious statement of intent, and one not missed by critics of the day. However, the single 'New Dreams For Old', also included on the album, saw the band's best, and final, crack at the charts. By this time they had bolstered their line-up with the addition of Peter Baker (organ/synthesizer) and Phil Lucking (trombone/trumpet). However, the band 'just sort of fell out really. . .'. Jackson went on to front **Benny Profane** taking Stringer and Baker with him.

Albums: *Clear* (1983), *In Evil Hour* (1984), *Nemesis* (1986).

Roomful Of Blues

Formed as a seven-piece band in the Boston, Massachusetts, area in the late 70s. Roomful Of Blues quickly established first a national reputation in the USA with their very authentic-sounding, swing big band R&B, and then broke through on the international scene in the 80s. The group honed their first-hand knowledge of the music by playing with many of the originators, as well as having numerous recordings in their own right. The also recorded behind **Big Joe Turner**, **Eddie 'Cleanhead' Vinson**, and **Earl King**. The group's main successful alumni include guitarists Duke Robillard and Ronnie Earl, vocalist Curtis Salgado, pianist Al Copley, and saxophonist Greg Piccolo. Despite personnel changes, the group continues to work, though their impact has lessened, due to the plethora of similar groups that have followed in their wake.

Albums: *The First Album* (Island, rec.1977), *Hot Little Mama* (1981), *Dressed Up To Get Messed Up* (Rounder 1985), *Live At Lupo's Heartbreak Hotel* (1987).

Rooney, Mickey

b. Joe Yule Jnr., 23 September 1920, Brooklyn, New York, USA. A five feet three-high bundle of dynamite - an actor, singer, comedian, dancer, songwriter - and much else. The son of vaudevillian parents, Rooney made his stage debut when he was 18 months old, and was taken to Hollywood by his mother soon afterwards. He got his big break at the age of six when he made the first of over 50 two-reel comedies featuring the comic-strip character Mickey McGuire. For most of the 30s he was cast in mainly minor roles, but received critical acclaim for his performances in *Ah Wilderness!* and as Puck in *A Midsummer Night's Dream* (both 1935). The year 1937 marked the beginning of two important associations for Rooney. In *Thoroughbreds Don't Cry* (1937) he was teamed for the first time with **Judy Garland**, and he also made *A Family Affair*, the first in a highly successful series of 'Andy Hardy' pictures which continued until 1946. In 1938 he created 'cinema's first punk kid' in *Boys' Town*, with Spencer Tracy. In the same year Garland joined him in one of the Hardy pictures, *Love Finds Andy Hardy*, but their real impact together came in the enormously popular musicals **Babes In Arms** (1939), **Strike Up the Band** (1940), **Babes On Broadway** (1941), and **Girl Crazy** (1943). By then, Rooney was at the peak of his career, topping box-office charts in the US and all over the world. However, after an appearance in **Thousands Cheer**, MGM's tribute to the US Armed Forces - and then a stint in the real thing during World War II - he made only two more musicals, **Summer Holiday** and **Words and Music** (both 1948). After that, for many different reasons, his career declined rapidly, although he turned in fine dramatic performances in several films during the 50s. After filing for bankruptcy in 1962 his life hit rock bottom, but he continued to work in movies, nightclubs, dinner-theatres and on television, and in 1979, after being nominated for an Oscar for his role in the adventure movie *Black Stallion*, made a sensational comeback on Broadway with **Sugar Babies**. This celebration of the golden age of American burlesque with its old song favourites and many examples of classic schtick, was perfect for Rooney, and, with co-star **Ann Miller**, he toured with the show for several years following its New York run of nearly 1,500 performances, and took it to London in 1988. In 1981 he won an Emmy for the television film *Bill*, and a year later received an Honorary Oscar 'in recognition of his 60 years of versatility in a variety of memorable film performances'. He had received a special Academy Award 44 years earlier, when he and **Deanna Durbin** had been cited for 'their significant contribution in bringing to the screen the spirit and personification of youth, and as juvenile players setting a high standard of ability and achievement'. He continues to film in the 90s, and is estimated to have made in excess of 200 pictures. In 1990, he returned to Broadway, and played the role of Will Rogers' father Clem during the final weeks of the musical **The Will Rogers Follies**. He remains an immensely likeable character who has continually bounced back at every stage of adversity. A good deal of the money he earned from his films up until 1965 (estimated box-office taking $3, 000 million - Rooney's share $12 million) went on alimony to ex-wives. He has (to date) been married eight times: ranging from Ava Gardner ('We were both under contract to MGM, and I was dressed as **Carmen Miranda** at the time, so she could hardly refuse'), through Barbara Thomason (she was murdered by her lover), to his present wife for more than 15 years, C&W singer Jan Chamberlain. At the time of writing he is only in his early 70s, so much else can be expected of Mickey Rooney, especially if he abides by the US Mickey Rooney Old People's Association's principal motto which is: 'Never Retire But Inspire'.

Further reading: *The Nine Lives Of Mickey Rooney*, Arthur Marx. *I.E.* and *Life Is Too Short* (his autobiographies).

Film: *How To Stuff A Wild Bikini* (1965).

Roots (Rap)

Philadephia-based rap crew comprising rapper Tariq Trotter (aka Black Thought), rapper Malik B, bass player Hob and drummer Ahmir Thompson. Specialising in old school freestyling, many comparisons to **Digable Planets** or **Gang Starr**'s jazz-flavoured hip hop followed the release of their debut mini-album. However, the Roots are more of a self-contained musical unit, relying on their own talents rather than samples or session musicians. The band was started in 1987 when Trotter and Ahmir were students at Philadelphia High School For The Performing Arts. They learned to earn a crust on the busking circuit, until their manager arranged a European tour for them. They were spotted by **Geffen** while playing in Germany, who signed the group (for the US, **Talkin' Loud** taking responsibility for the UK). A second long playing set, *Do You Want More*, featured top jazz guests plus the Roots' own rap protégés, the Foreign Objects.

Albums: *From The Ground Up* (Geffen 1994, mini-album), *Do You Want More* (Geffen 1994).

Roots Radics

Jamaican session band centred around a nucleus of Errol 'Flabba' Holt (bass), Lincoln Valentine 'Style' Scott (drums) and Eric 'Bingy Bunny' Lamont (guitar). Other members at various times included Roy Hamilton (lead guitar), Noel 'Sowell' Bailey (lead guitar), Dwight Pinkney (formerly of the Sharks and Zap Pow, on lead guitar), Carlton 'Santz' Davis (drums), Fish Clarke (drums) and Steely Johnson (later of **Steely & Clevie** fame, on keyboards). Flabba and Bingy Bunny were previously active as part of Morris 'Blacker' Wellington's **Morwells** set up, recording such popular tunes as 'Swing & Dine' (1974), 'They Hold Us Down' (1978) and 'Kingston Twelve Tuffy' (1979). Before this Bunny had been teamed with bongo player Bongo Herman, the pair enjoying a big hit, 'Know Far I', in 1971 for producer/singer **Derrick Harriott**. He had also produced Peter Broggs' *Progressive Youth* LP, and played in the crack **Channel One** session band the Revolutionaries, whose demise at the end of the 70s was due to **Sly & Robbie**'s production for their Taxi label and live work with **Peter Tosh**, which had left a vacuum the Radics were only too pleased to fill. Errol Holt was previously noted for his many fine singles during the mid-70s including 'A You Lick Me First', 'Gimme Gimme' and 'Who Have Eyes To See'.

Their initial impact was to slow the beat down a notch from the militant rockers sound of the Revolutionaries. This is perhaps best showcased on an album they worked on for producer **Henry 'Junjo' Lawes**, the hottest producer of the early 80s. *Bounty Hunter* (1979) was **Barrington Levy**'s debut, as it was for the Radics, and it revolutionised reggae music in the same way that the **Mighty Diamond**'s *Right Time* did five years earlier. The similarities include the revival of old **Studio One** rhythms central to the success of both groups. The Radics worked on innumerable sessions for as many different producers, including Linval Thompson - it was with their rhythms that **Scientist**

destroyed space invaders and won the World Cup, as the titles of his LPs suggest - and worked for a while as **Gregory Isaacs**' backing band on tour and record, responsible for the rhythms on his classic *Night Nurse* (1982). They also did sessions for **Bunny Wailer** and **Israel Vibration** among many others. Whilst in the UK on tour with **Prince Far I** (for whom they recorded under the name the Arabs), the group forged a social and musical friendship with maverick reggae/rock producer Adrian Sherwood, for whom they worked on many sessions as part of the loose conglomerates Creation Rebel and Singers & Players. The Roots Radics came in at the birth of, and were partly responsible for, the **dancehall** style that dominated in the first half of the 80s. But as their commitments to live work grew, particularly in the States, they were eventually usurped by other outfits. The **digital/ragga** revolution sparked off by **Prince Jammy**'s production of **Wayne Smith**'s massive hit, 'Under Me Sleng Teng', virtually eradicated the need for live musicians overnight, and the Radics lost their position as Jamaica's number one session band, though they remain in demand for stage shows. Eric Lamont died of prostrate cancer in January 1994.

Albums: *Roots Radics Dub Session* (Solid Groove 1982), *Freelance* (Kingdom 1985), *Forwards Never Backwards* (Heartbeat 1990), *World Peace Three* (Heartbeat 1992). With Scientist: *Scientist Meets The Space Invaders* (Greensleeves 1981), *Scientist Wins The World Cup* (Greensleeves 1983), *Scientist And Jammy Strike Back* (Trojan 1983).

Roots, Rock And Reggae

Jeremy Marre's 1978 documentary about Jamaican music is a fine examination of reggae culture. He includes interviews, live material and **sound system** rivalry, interspersing these with brief histories of record company practices and the role of radio stations. The music is provided by **Bob Marley And The Wailers** (including 'Trenchtown Rock' and 'Lively Up Yourself'), **Junior Murvin**, **Third World** and **Jimmy Cliff**. The role of harmony groups in the development of Jamaican music is heard in the **Mighty Diamonds**' 'When The Right Time Comes' and the **Gladiators**' 'Hearsay', while the importance of Rastafarianism is captured in the **Abyssinians**' 'Satta Massanga'. **Toots And The Maytals** also contribute five wonderfully ebullient songs to a highly engaging film.

Rope Ladder To The Moon

This is the film biography of former **Cream** bassist/vocalist **Jack Bruce** and takes its title from a track on his first solo album, *Songs For A Tailor*. Director Tony Palmer, who was responsible for *All My Loving* and *Cream's Last Concert*, charted this stellar musician's rise from poverty in Glasgow's disingenuously-named

Harmony Row to millionaire status. Bruce, who won a scholarship to Edinburgh's Royal Academy Of Music, embraced jazz as a member of Jack McHarg's Band, before moving to London where he joined **Alexis Korner**'s Blues Incorporated, the **Graham Bond Organization** and **John Mayall**'s Bluesbreakers. Mayall is one of the musicians paying tribute to Baker, as is the jazz drummer **Tony Williams**, who later partnered Bruce in **Lifetime**. Baker's manager, **Robert Stigwood**, produced this fitting feature, which largely draws its soundtrack from *Goodbye Cream* and the aforementioned *Songs For A Tailor*.

Roppolo, Leon

b. 16 March 1902, Lutcher, Louisiana, USA, d. 14 October 1943. After being taught clarinet by his father, Roppolo began playing in bands in and around New Orleans including those led by **George Brunis** and **Santo Pecora**. After playing on riverboats he made his way to Chicago where, in 1921, he became a member of the Friars' Inn Society Orchestra. This band, led by Paul Mares and which included Brunis, later evolved into the **New Orleans Rhythm Kings**. In 1923 Roppolo and Mares quit and went to New York and the following year Roppolo was in Texas playing with Peck Kelley's Bad Boys. In 1925 he was back in New Orleans and was once again teamed with Mares in a reformed NORK. By this time Roppolo's bad habits, he was a heavy drinker and used marijuana, allied to ill-health had begun to take their toll. That same year he suffered a severe mental breakdown and was committed to a state asylum. Apparently he continued to play while in the institution, taking up the tenor saxophone. He was released in 1940 and died in 1943. Roppolo played clarinet with a full, rich tone and was always experimenting with technique and phrasing. His imaginative work influenced many of his contemporaries and the younger musicians who heard him.
Album: with NORK incl. on *Jazz Sounds Of The Twenties* (1922-25).

Ros, Edmundo

b. 7 December 1910, Port Of Spain, Trinidad. The leader of one of the most popular - if not the most popular - Latin American band in the UK for many years, spent his early life in Venezuela, before attending the Military Academy at Caracas, where, via the Academy's band, he became interested in music and learned to play the euphonium or 'bombardin'. Despite harbouring ambitions to become a criminal lawyer, he travelled to the UK in 1937 and studied composition and harmony at the Royal Academy of Music. Although he recorded with jazzman **Fats Waller** in 1938, Ros mainly sang and served as percussionist, with various Latin-styled bands, including one led by pianist Don Marino Barretto. He formed his own five piece unit, Rumba With Ros, in 1940, and, for the next 35 years, played and recorded with groups such as Ros's Rumba Romeos, his Rumba Band, and Edmundo Ros and his Orchestra. After making his London debut at the New Cosmos Club and St. Regis Hotel, he played all the smartest nightspots, including the Bagatelle, before opening his own Edmundo Ros Club, on the site of the Coconut Grove, in 1949. By then, with his gently rhythmic style and engaging vocals, he was enormously popular with the public generally, and a favourite of London's high society and some members of the Royal Family. Earlier in his career, he had decided that the best way to introduce complex Latin rhythms to his audiences would be to apply them to popular and familiar songs, and throughout the 40s and 50s, on radio and records, he had great success with numbers such as 'Enjoy Yourself', 'Melodie D'Amour', 'Tico, Tico', 'I Got The Sun In The Morning', 'South America, Take It Away', ' I'm Crazy For You', 'Her Bathing Suit Never Got Wet', 'The Coffee Song', 'No Can Do', 'The Maharajah Of Magador', his theme, 'The Cuban Love Song', and especially 'The Wedding Samba', which was also a hit in the US in 1949, although he wasn't allowed to perform there because of Musicians' Union regulations. His music was in demand in many other parts of the world too, particularly Japan. In the early 60s, he collaborated on an album with **Ted Heath** which exploited the relatively new stereo recording process. The shift in musical tastes during the decade affected Ros's standing but he played on into the 70s. Disillusioned with the business, he disbanded in 1975, and, so he says, destroyed most of the bands' arrangements, keeping just one set in case he received an offer he couldn't refuse. He retired to Spain, emerging occasionally for events such as his 80th birthday celebrations in 1990, and to introduce a series of record programmes for BBC Radio in 1992. Two years later, he joined another veteran musical personality, **Stanley Black**, in a 'Latin Reunion' at London's Royal Festival Hall. Often the butt of the musical élite, he was gently satirized by the **Bonzo Dog Doo-Dah Band** in 'Look Out There's A Monster Coming'.
Selected albums: *Calypsos* (1956), *Mambos* (1956), *Rhythms Of The South* (1957), *Calypso Man* (1958), *Perfect For Dancing* (1958), *Ros On Broadway* (1959), *Hollywood Cha Cha Cha* (1959), *Dance Again* (1963), *Sing And Dance With Edmundo Ros* (1963) *Heath Versus Ros* (1964), *Ros Remembers* (1974), *Edmundo Ros Today* (1978), *Latin Favourites* (1979), *Latin Song And Dance Men* (1980), *Music For The Millions* (1983), *Strings Latino* (1985), *Cuban Love Song* (1985), *Latin Magic* (1987), *Edmundo Ros & His Rumba Band, 1939-1941* (1992).

Rosalie

Two composers representing entirely different worlds of popular music contributed to this lavish **Florenz**

Ziegfeld production which opened at the New Amsterdam Theatre in New York on 10 January 1928. **George Gershwin** and **Sigmund Romberg** squeezed this show into their busy schedules, and were rewarded with an excellent run of 335 performances. The book, by William Anthony McGuire and **Guy Bolton**, capitalised on the American public's fascination with early aviators in general, and Captain Charles Lindbergh's record-breaking solo flight to Paris in particular. No doubt the latter's achievement pales in comparison with the exploits of West Point high flyer, Lieutenant Richard Fay (Oliver McLennan), who loves Princess Rosalie of Romanza (Marilyn Miller), and risks life and limb to make a trans-Atlantic flight to be near her. However, she is unable to marry a commoner unless her father, King Cyril (Frank Morgan), abdicates. As this appears to be the European thing to do, the King is pleased to oblige. One of the George Gershwin songs, a future standard, 'How Long Has This Been Going On?' (lyric: **Ira Gershwin**), which had been cut from *Funny Face*, resurfaced here, but did not catch on, and another other of the brothers' numbers, 'Ev'rybody Knows I Love Somebody', was also in the score. The rest of the songs included 'Say So!' and 'Oh Gee! Oh Joy!' (music: George Gershwin, lyrics: Ira Gershwin and **P.G. Wodehouse**), and 'West Point Song' (music: Sigmund Romberg, lyric: Wodehouse). The highly commercial combination of Ziegfeld's elegant production, a singable, danceable score, and the enormous box-office appeal of the petite and lovely Marilyn Miller, ensured that *Rosalie* stayed on Broadway for over 10 months. An attempt by Hollywood to make a film version with Marion Davies was never released, but some of the footage was used in the 1937 movie of *Rosalie* which starred **Nelson Eddy** and **Eleanor Powell**. Several pieces of classical music were incorporated, and the orginal stage score was neatly removed in favour of one by **Cole Porter** - and *Rosalie* got a title song at last.

Rosario, Willie

b. Fernando Luis Marín Rosario, 6 May 1930, Coamo, Puerto Rico. Exemplary salsa bandleader, timbales, composer Rosario has been drilling his band to perfection for over three decades. Spurred on by his mother, Rosario began studying guitar and saxophone at the age of seven, but he much preferred playing baseball. When he was 16 years old, his family migrated to New York in search of better opportunities. In New York, Rosario studied public relations and journalism and later worked as a radio newsreader. However, in 1951 he was so inspired by seeing **Tito Puente** play timbales at New York's famous Palladium Ballroom, that he decided to make music his vocation. He started to study the timbales seriously and worked with various bandleaders, including **Noro Morales**, Aldemaro Romero and Johnny Sequí. When Sequí

decided to return to Puerto Rico, Rosario organized his own band and made his debut with them in 1959 at the Club Caborrojeño in New York. He signed with Alegre Records and released the classic *El Bravo Soy Yo* in 1963, which was produced by the label's founder **Al Santiago**. Lead vocals were provided by Frankie Figueroa, who began his career as a conga player with **Kako** and later performed with various bandleaders, including César Concepción, Memo Salamanca and Tito Puente, and as a solo artist. While with Alegre, Rosario appeared on two of the legendary 60s' descarga (Latin jam session) albums by the Alegre All-Stars. In 1968, while the boogaloo craze was raging, Rosario was signed-up by the **Atlantic Records** subsidiary **Atco** to record *Boogaloo & Guaguanco*, which featured **Adalberto Santiago** on lead vocals. That year, Rosario released another boogaloo orientated set, *Two Too Much*, which was produced by Al Santiago on the Musicor label. He added baritone saxophone to his four-trumpet front-line on this album and has retained this combination until the present day. Lead singers Willie Torres and Pete Bonet handled the boogaloos and Figueroa returned to perform the typical Latin numbers. Rosario later admitted that he disapproved of boogaloo.

He signed with Inca Records and released a series of seven albums (including a compilation) on the label between 1969 and 1978. His Inca debut, *El Bravo De Siempre*, contained his first major hit 'La Cuesta De La Fama', sung by Panamanian Meñique. The follow-up, *Mr. Rhythm/Mr. Ritmo*, included his next big hit 'De Barrio Obrero A La 15', performed by Chamaco Rivera. Afro-Cuban pianist **Alfredo Rodríguez**, who played on both albums, later described his two-year stint as a Rosario accompanist in a 1990 interview: 'He is a very steady man . . . He hardly ever took solos. He has a very personal way of playing the timbales and he concentrated on the sound of the band; that the brass section be tight, that the rhythm section be tight. He's not the spectacular guy doing all kind of things on the timbales. He kept himself that way from the beginning to the end, it's his trademark.' Rosario relocated to Puerto Rico in 1972, but continued to record in New York until the mid-70s. Junior Toledo (d. 1990) replaced Rivera as lead vocalist on 1973's *Infinito. Otra Vez* in 1975 was dedicated to Al Santiago. In 1977, Rosario's good friend **Bobby Valentín** handled the production chores and contributed arrangements to his first Puerto Rico recorded album, *Gracias Mundo*. Valentín worked as an accompanists in Rosario's band in the 60s and wrote charts for Rosario's previous and future albums. *Gracias Mundo* marked the introduction of a pair of lead singers: Bobby Concepción and Guillo Rivera.

Rosario signed with TH (Top Hits) Records - who were lookin to 'beef-up' their salsa roster at the time - and issued seven albums (including a compilation) on the label between 1978 and 1985. Toledo returned to replace Concepción on 1978's *From The Depth Of My Brain* . . . In 1980 Rosario celebrated the 20th anniversary of the formation of his band with *El De A 20 De Willie*, which was dedicated to Latin music historian Max Salazar. On this album, the band's pianist, Javier Fernández, started contributing arrangements and a further turnover of lead singers occurred: Concepción came back and **Tony Vega** joined from **Raphy Leavitt**'s band. Ex-**Tommy Olivencia** lead vocalist **Gilberto Santa Rosa** joined Vega and Concepción on 1981's *The Portrait Of A Salsa Man*. This album marked the debut of José Madera (b. 1951, New York, USA; conga/arranger; son of Puerto Rico-born tenor saxophonist José 'Pin' Madera, who was a founder member of **Machito**'s band) as one of Rosario's regular arrangers; Madera was a member of Machito's band between 1969 and 1972, and has been an accompanist of Tito Puente's since 1972. Commencing on 1982's *Atizame El Fogón*, José Febles became another of Rosario's regular arrangers. Gifted trumpeter, David 'Piro' Rodríguez departed after 1983's *The Salsa Machine*. Piro first recorded with Rosario on 1980's *El De A 20 De Willie*. He later acted as his musical director and then musical consultant on the bandleader's 1982 and 1983 releases. From the mid-80s, Piro became a regular accompanist with Tito Puente. Rosario joined Bobby Valentín's Bronco Records and has released nine albums (including a compilation) on the label to date (1991) - the first three (1984 to 1986) are among his finest. Concepción departed, leaving Santa Rosa and Vega as co-lead singers on *Nuevos Horizontes* (1984) and *Afincando/25 Aniversario* (1985). Pianist/arranger Ricky Rodríguez made his debut on the 1984 release as Fernández's replacement. Both records featured notable arrangements by José Madera of compositions by Cuban composer/bandleader **Adalberto Alvarez**. Trumpeter/arranger/composer Humberto Ramírez put in his first album appearance with Rosario's band on *Afincando/25 Aniversario*. Rosario quickly promoted him to producer on 1986's *Nueva Cosecha*. Ramírez remained with the band a further two years as a producer and performed and arranged on *A Man Of Music* (1987) and *The Salsa Legend* (1988); his arranging skills became much in demand and he has written charts for **Roberto Roena**, Luis Enrique, Cano Estremera, Conjunto Chaney, Puerto Rican Power, Willie González, Tito Rojas, Pedro Conga, Roberto Lugo, Frank Ferrer, Tony Vega, Opus Orquesta, Kim de los Santos, Milagros Hernández, La Puertorriqueña, Andy and Harold Montañez, Nestor Sánchez, La Exclusiva, among others.

Ex-**Conjunto Libre** member, Tony 'Pupy Cantor' Torres, joined as a third lead vocalist on *Nueva Cosecha*, which was Vega and Santa Rosa's last with the band. Josué Rosado joined Cantor as co-lead singer on *A Man*

Of Music, which also marked the debut of trumpeter/arranger Julio Alvarado. Cantor departed and Rosario returned to a trio of vocalists with the inclusion of Primi Cruz (formerly with **Mario Ortiz**) and Bernie Pérez on *The Salsa Legend* and 1989's *Unique/30th Anniversary*; Rosado left after the latter, Alvarado replaced Ramírez as producer on *Unique*; he has also written charts for various artists and bands. Rosario took his first tentative step into salsa romántica/erótica waters on *Unique*. He waded in further with *Viva Rosario!*, which contained the massive erótica hit 'Anuncio Clasificado/Damelo'. However, it is evident that Rosario is not happy with the salsa romántica style - the softness and limpness of which runs counter to his usual progressive, solid and swinging approach - and he has dubbed it 'salsa monga', which politely translates as 'flaccid salsa'. He resumed the role of producer on *Viva Rosario!*. In 1991, Rosario won the Puerto Rican music industries Diplo award for 'Salsa Band Of The Year'. For his 1991 album, he largely turned his back on sexy salsa in favour of a project called *The Roaring Fifties* - a thoroughly modern, robust and swinging tribute to the mambo era - a concept he had talked about for some while.

Albums: *El Bravo Soy Yo* (1963, reissued 1978); with the Alegre All-Stars *The Alegre All-Stars Vol. 2 'El Manicero'* (c.1965), *The Alegre All-Stars Vol. 4 'Way Out'*; *Boogaloo & Guaguanco* (1968), *Two Too Much* (1968); with the Cesta All-Stars *Live Jam Session*; *El Bravo De Siempre* (c.1969), *Mr. Rhythm/Mr. Ritmo* (1971); with the Cesta All-Stars *Salsa Festival*; *Mas Ritmo* (1972), *Infinito* (1973), *Otra Vez* (1975), *Gracias Mundo* (1977), *From The Depth Of My Brain...1978*), *El Rey Del Ritmo!* (1979), *El De A 20 De Willie* (1980), *The Portrait Of A Salsa Man* (1981), *Atizame El Fogón* (1982), *The Salsa Machine* (1983), *Nuevos Horizontes* (1984), *Afincando/25 Aniversario* (1985), *Nueva Cosecha* (1986), *A Man Of Music* (1987), *The Salsa Legend* (1988), *Unique/30th Anniversary* (1989), *Viva Rosario!* (1990), *The Roaring Fifties* (1991), *Tradición Clásica* (1993). Compilations: culled from Rosario's Alegre and Inca back catalogue by Al Santiago *Campanero Rumbero* (1978), TH hits collection *15 Exitos De...Willie Rosario Y Su Orquesta* (1985), Bronco 'best of' selection *Lo Mejor De Willie Rosario* (1990).

Rose Marie

Previously filmed in 1928 as a silent, this MGM adaptation of the highly successful Broadway operetta was released in 1936. Starring **Jeanette MacDonald** and **Nelson Eddy**, it came to the screen with a radically revised plot and minus most of the original songs. In the new story, by Frances Goodrich, Albert Hackett, and Alice Duer Miller, MacDonald is a famous Canadian opera star whose brother (James Stewart) is on the run from the law. Nelson Eddy plays the Mountie intent on bringing him to justice, which interrupts his romance with MacDonald for a time, but the inevitable happy ending is always just around the bend. As for the score, there were four survivors from the stage show, 'Indian Love Call' and 'Rose Marie' (**Rudolph Friml-Oscar Hammerstein II-Otto Harbach**), and 'The Mounties' and 'Totem Tom-Tom' (Herbert Stothart-Hammerstein-Harbach). They were joined by several others including 'Just for You' (Friml-**Gus Kahn**), 'Pardon Me, Madame' (Stothart-Kahn), 'Some Of These Days' (**Shelton Brooks**), and 'Dinah' (**Sam M. Lewis-Joe Young**-Harry Akst). The names of two future film idols also appeared in the credits, **Allan Jones**, whose marvellous voice was heard in many a screen musical, and the young David Niven who went on to become the epitome of the dashing and debonair Englishman abroad. Other members of the large cast included Reginald Owen, Alan Mowbray, Una O'Connor, Robert Greig, George Regas, and Herman Bing. Chester Hale was the choreographer, and the film was directed by MGM stalwart W. S. Van Dyke. *Rose Marie* was re-made again in 1954 with **Howard Keel**, Ann Blyth, Fernando Lamas, Bert Lahr, and Marjorie Main. This version was choreographed by **Busby Berkeley** and directed by Mervyn LeRoy.

Rose Of Avalanche

This Yorkshire, England-based group came to the fore following heavy airplay from UK BBC disc jockey **John Peel**. The debut single, 'LA Rain', finished high in his 1985 'Festive Fifty', although it was released before the band had performed. The follow-up, 'Castles In the Sky', originated from overhearing a man in a pub asking a girl if she wanted to 'See my castle in the sky?'. 'Velveteen', meanwhile, was a tribute to **Nico**. The band's principals were Phillip Morris (vocals) and Paul James Berry (guitar), while a host of supporting musicians passed through their ranks. These included: Mark Thompson and Andrew Parker (drums), Alan Davis, Nicol Mackay and Daren Horner (bass) and Glenn Shultz (guitar). Horner and Parker then became encumbants of the rhythm section. After gaining early praise the band were stopped in their tracks for 18 months between 1987 and 1988 following disputes with their label, Fire Records. They responded by setting up their own Avalantic label. Their two most recent collections, *String A Beads* and *I.C.E.* have brought about a transformation in the band's sound. Gone are the heavy rhythms and chiming guitar which saw them pigeon-holed as 'gothic', replaced by material of a comparatively melodic and 'poppy' nature.
Albums: *Always There* (Fire 1986), *First Avalanche* (Fire 1987), *In Rock* (Avalantic 1988), *Never Another Sunset* (Avalantic 1989), *String A Beads* (Avalantic 1990), *I.C.E.* (Avalantic 1991).

Rose Of Washington Square

More than 30 years before **Barbra Streisand** shot to screen stardom in *Funny Girl* (1968), this unauthorised version of the **Fanny Brice** story starred **Alice Faye** and Tyrone Power - and attracted a successful writ for invasion of privacy from the subject herself. According to this story, As Power goes steadily downhill, eventually ending up in prison, Faye's career goes from strength to strength supported by a great bunch of songs which included 'I Never Knew Heaven Could Speak' (**Mack Gordon-Harry Revel**), 'The Curse Of An Aching Heart' (Al Piantadosi-Henry Fink), 'I'm Just Wild About Harry' (**Noble Sissle-Eubie Blake**), 'Rose Of Washington Square' (Ballard MacDonald-James F. Hanley) and 'My Man' (Channing Pollock-Maurice Yvain). The last two are especially associated with Fanny Brice. Although Faye and Power were top-billed, their star status was threatened by **Al Jolson**, who gave typically dynamic performances of favourites such as 'Toot Toot Tootsie' (**Gus Kahn**-Ernie Erdman-**Ted Fio Rito**-Robert A. King), 'California, Here I Come' (**Buddy De Sylva**-Jolson-**Joseph Meyer**), and 'Pretty Baby' (Kahn-Egbert Van Alstyne-Tony Jackson). Also in the cast were William Frawley, Hobart Cavanaugh, Joyce Compton, and **Louis Prima** with his band. The screenplay that caused all the legal problems was by Nunnally Johnson, and Gregory Ratoff directed this thoroughly entertaining film which was released by 20th Century-Fox in 1936.

Rose Royce

Formed in the USA as a multi-purpose backing group, the original nine-piece worked under a variety of names. In 1973 Kenji Brown (guitar), Victor Nix (keyboards), Kenny Copeland, Freddie Dunn (trumpets), Michael Moore (saxophone), Lequient 'Duke' Jobe (bass), Henry Garner and Terrai Santiel (drums) backed **Edwin Starr** as Total Concept Limited, before supporting **Yvonne Fair** as Magic Wand. This line-up later became the regular studio band behind the **Undisputed Truth** and **Temptations**, before embarking on their own recording career following the addition of singer Gwen Dickey. The group took the name Rose Royce in 1976 when they recorded the successful soundtrack to the motion picture *Car Wash*, the title song of which was a platinum-selling single. Two further songs from the film reached the R&B Top 10 before the band joined producer **Norman Whitfield**'s label. Two atmospheric releases, 'Wishing On A Star' and 'Love Don't Live Here Anymore' (both 1978) reached the Top 3 in the UK despite disappointing sales at home. This feature continued the following year with 'Is It Love You're After', another UK Top 20 record. Their popularity in Britain was verified in 1980 when the

Greatest Hits collection reached number 1 in the album charts. Since then the group has continued to record, but their releases have only reached the lower reaches of the charts.

Albums: *Car Wash* (1976), *In Full Bloom* (1977), *Rose Royce Strikes Again!* (1978), *Rainbow Connection IV* (1979), *Golden Touch* (1981), *Jump Street* (1981), *Stronger Than Ever* (1982), *Music Magic* (1984), *The Show Must Go On* (1985), *Fresh Cut* (1987). Compilations: *Greatest Hits* (1980), *Is It Love You're After* (1988).

Rose Tattoo

This legendary Australian band was formed by former **Buster Brown** members **Angry Anderson** (vocals) and Mick 'Geordie' Leech (bass) with Peter Wells (slide guitar/vocals), Michael Cocks (lead guitar) and Dallas 'Digger' Royall (drums) in Sydney in 1977. They released their classic self-titled debut (known as *Rock 'N' Roll Outlaws* outside Australia) the following year. *Rose Tattoo* was an aggressive blues-rock masterpiece packed with excellent songs, and the band's electric live performances and tough tattooed image drew support from punks and rockers alike. Their European debut in 1981, supporting **Rainbow,** and an appearance at the Reading Festival caused quite a stir, but a poor sound on *Assault & Battery* rather dulled their impact. This was despite the quality of the material, with Anderson characteristically offering political comment and true story narrative against a straightforward boogie background. *Scarred For Life*, with Robin Riley replacing Cocks, had a stronger production and yet more quality songs, but the band fell apart on their first US tour with **Aerosmith** and **Pat Travers** over numerous personal problems. Anderson and Leech assembled a new line-up with Greg Jordan (slide guitar), Robert Bowron (drums) and John Meyer (guitar) for *Southern Stars*, but the band later split. *Beats From A Single Drum* was released for contractual reasons under the name Rose Tattoo, but was in fact Anderson's solo debut as he expanded his horizons into film and television. However, the legend remained strong, and Rose Tattoo were persuaded to reform the original line-up (sadly without Royall, who had died in 1990) for an Australian support slot with **Guns N'Roses** (who had covered the group's 'Nice Boys' on their debut EP) in 1993, plus a small tour of their own, culminating in a biker festival headline slot. Despite an average age around 45, Rose Tattoo proved that the old fire still burned brightly with dazzling performances.

Albums: *Rose Tattoo* (Albert 1978), *Assault & Battery* (Albert 1981), *Scarred For Life* (Albert 1982), *Southern Stars* (Albert 1984), *Beats From A Single Drum* (Mushroom 1987). Compilation: *Nice Boys Don't Play Rock 'N' Roll* (Albert 1992).

Rose, Biff

Raconteur and songwriter, Biff Rose enjoyed a cult following in the USA during the early 70s for a series of albums mixing anodyne pop with distinctly satirical lyrics. Although some of his work was coyingly sentimental, reflecting the naive aspirations of the previous decade, his early releases, notably *The Thorn In Mrs Rose's Side*, managed to maintain a sense of balance. He achieved a measure of fame when **David Bowie** covered 'Fill Your Heart' on *Hunky Dory*, but in general Rose's songs, like his talent, remain too eccentric for large-scale consumption.

Albums: *Biff Rose* (late 60s), *The Thorn In Mrs Rose's Side* (1969), *Children Of Light* (1969), *Half Live At The Bitter End* (early 70s), *Uncle Jesus Aunty Christ* (early 70s).

Rose, Billy

b. William Samuel Rosenberg, 6 September 1899, New York, USA. d. 10 February 1966, Jamaica. An important lyricist and impresario, Rose was a small, dynamic man, once called 'the little Napoleon of showmanship'. He was married twice, firstly to star comedienne **Fanny Brice**, and then to champion swimmer Eleanor Holm. As a lyric writer, it is sometimes said that he often insisted on collaborating with songwriters who were contributing to shows that he was producing. His first successful songs came in the early 20s. 'Barney Google', based on the popular cartoon strip, and 'You've Got To See Mama Every Night', were both written with Con Conrad in 1923. 'Does The Spearmint Lose Its Flavor On The Bedpost Overnight?', on which Rose collaborated with Marty Bloom and Ernest Brever in 1924, was also hits, along with 'Spearmint', for US radio's popular tenor-baritone team of Ernest Hare and Billy Jones. With a slightly modified title, the latter song resurfaced in the US charts in 1961, sung by UK artist, **Lonnie Donegan**. Hare and Jones again, and Billy Murray (the 'Denver Nightingale'), also had success with 'Don't Bring Lulu', which Rose wrote with **Lew Brown** and **Ray Henderson**. Among Rose's other well known songs were 'The Night Is Young And You're So Beautiful' (Irving Kahal and Dana Suesse), 'I've Got A Feeling I'm Falling' (**Fats Waller** and Harry Link), 'That Old Gang Of Mine' (**Mort Dixon** and Ray Henderson), 'Clap Hands! Here Comes Charley' (Ballard MacDonald and **Joseph Meyer**), 'Tonight You Belong To Me' (Lee David), 'It Happened In Monterey' (**Mabel Wayne**), 'Back In Your Own Backyard', 'There's A Rainbow 'Round My Shoulder' and 'Me And My Shadow' (written with **Al Jolson** and Dave Dreyer).

In 1926 Rose started to contribute songs to Broadway shows and revues, including 'A Cup Of Coffee, A Sandwich And You', for **Gertrude Lawrence** to sing in the *Charlot Revue* of that year. Three years later he wrote his first Broadway score for *Great Day!*, with Edward Eliscu and **Vincent Youmans**. This included the songs 'More Than You Know', 'Happy Because

I'm In Love', 'Without A Song' and 'Great Day'. Rose's first Broadway production, in 1930, was the revue *Sweet And Low*, which also contained two of his songs, 'Cheerful Little Earful' (with **Ira Gershwin** and **Harry Warren**) and 'Would You Like To Take A Walk?' (with **Mort Dixon** and Warren). When the show was revised in 1931 as *Crazy Quilt*, Rose, Warren and Dixon had added another song, 'I Found A Million Dollar Baby (In A Five And Ten Cent Store)', which was sung by Rose's wife, Fanny Brice. Rose's 1935 Broadway project, ***Jumbo***, was not quite a 'million-dollar-baby', but it apparently did cost somewhere in the region of $350,000 to produce - a lot of money for a show in those days. For this musical comedy-vaudeville-circus extravaganza, much of the cash was spent in gutting Broadway's Hippodrome Theatre and refitting it to resemble a circus arena, with a circular revolving stage, and the audience seating sloping in grandstand fashion. *Jumbo* was spectacular in every way. The extravaganza featured **Jimmy Durante**, bandleader **Paul Whiteman** seated on a white horse, an elephant named Big Rosie, a human cast of around 90, and almost as many animals. Despite a book by Ben Hecht and Charles MacArthur, a **Richard Rodgers/Lorenz Hart** score (no Rose lyrics in this one) which featured songs such as 'The Most Beautiful Girl In The World', 'My Romance', and 'Little Girl Blue', and a healthy New York run of five months, *Jumbo* closed without getting near to recovering its costs. From the excesses of *Jumbo*, Rose's next production was Hecht and MacArthur's play *The Great Magoo*, the story of a Coney Island barker, which contained only one song, 'It's Only A Paper Moon', written by Rose, **E.Y. 'Yip' Harburg**, and **Harold Arlen**. Rose, in collaboration with Maceo Pinkard, also contributed one additional song, 'Here Comes The Showboat', to the original **Jerome Kern/Oscar Hammerstein II/P.G. Wodehouse** score for the 1936 film version of the musical ***Show Boat***. During the 40s, Rose's two main Broadway productions were ***Carmen Jones*** (1943) and *Seven Lively Arts* (1944). Despite his failure to get Sir Thomas Beecham, his first choice conductor for *Carmen Jones*, Oscar Hammerstein II's re-setting of Georges Bizet's opera *Carmen* was extremely well received by critics and public alike. In direct contrast, *Seven Lively Arts*, with a concept embracing opera, ballet, Broadway, vaudeville, jazz, concert music, and modern painting, along with a **Cole Porter** score which included 'Ev'ry Time We Say Goodbye', was thought to be somewhere between a 'disappointment' and a 'disaster'. As well as his Broadway projects, Rose produced aquacades at many locations including the *New York World's Fair* in 1937, and the *San Francisco World's Fair* in 1940. He also owned two top New York nightspots, (the New York Supper Club and the Diamond Horseshoe) and two Broadway theatres, the **Ziegfeld** and the Billy Rose

Theatre. One of the most colourful show business characters of his time, Rose retired in the 50s, and repeated his previous success, this time as a stock market speculator.

Further reading: *Billy Rose: Manhattan Primitive*, Earl Conrad. *The Nine Lives Of Billy Rose*, Pearl Rose Gottlieb (Billy Rose's sister). *Wine, Women And Words*, Billy Rose.

Rose, David

b. 15 June 1910, London, England, d. 23 August, 1990, Burbank, California, USA. A distinguished orchestra leader, composer, and arranger in the 40s and 50s, Rose was taken to the USA when he was just four-years-old. After graduating from the Chicago College of Music at the age of 16, he joined **Ted Fio Rito**'s dance band, and three years later became a pianist/arranger/conductor for NBC Radio. In 1936 he provided the arrangement for **Benny Goodman**'s big hit 'It's Been So Long', before moving to Hollywood, where he formed his own orchestra in 1938 for the Mutual Broadcasting System, and featured on the programme *California Melodies*. In the same year Rose married comedienne/singer Martha Raye and backed her on her hit record 'Melancholy Mood'. The marriage was later dissolved, and, after meeting **Judy Garland** when she was appearing on **Bob Hope**'s radio show, he became the first of her five husbands from 1941 until 1945. During military service in World War II Rose was composer/conductor for the Army/Air Force morale-boosting stage musical *Winged Victory*, which was filmed in 1944. In 1943 he had a big hit with his own composition 'Holiday For Strings' and, a year later, with 'Poinciana (Song Of The Tree)'. By the late 40s he was a regular on **Red Skelton**'s radio show, moving with him into television. He later wrote scores and themes for over 20 television series and won Emmy awards for his 14 year stint on *Bonanza*, 10 years with *Little House On The Prairie* and his work on three much-acclaimed **Fred Astaire** specials, beginning with *An Evening With Fred Astaire* in 1959.

Rose began working in movies in 1941, and is credited with scoring 36 films through to the 60s including *Texas Carnival* (1951), *Rich, Young And Pretty* (1951), *Everything I Have Is Yours* (1952), *Operation Petticoat* (1959), *Please Don't Eat The Daisies* (1960) and *Never Too Late* (1965). He received an Oscar nomination for his song 'So In Love', with a lyric by **Leo Robin**, which was featured in the 1944 **Danny Kaye** movie ***Wonder Man***. His other compositions included 'Our Waltz' (which he is said to have written for Judy Garland), 'Dance Of The Spanish Onion', 'Manhattan Square Dance', 'Deserted City', 'Holiday For Trombones', 'Rose Of Bel-Air', 'Holiday For Flutes', 'Four Twenty AM', 'Waltz Of The Bubbles', 'Like Young', 'Taco Holiday', 'The Tiny Ballerina', 'Gay Spirits', 'Parade Of The Clowns', 'The Christmas Tree' (familiar to millions of Americans through its traditional use each Yuletide on *The Red*

Skelton Show), and a collection of 32 piano solos entitled *Music For Moderns*. After chart success with 'Calypso Melody' in 1957 and his accompaniment for the **Connie Francis** 1959 hit 'My Happiness', Rose had a worldwide smash hit in 1962 with another of his own tunes, a humorous and satirical piece called 'The Stripper', which was written for a television show called *Burlesque*, starring **Dan Dailey**. Naturally, it was included on *The Stripper And Other Fun Songs For The Family*, which reached number 3 in the US album chart in 1962. Among Rose's other reported 50 or so albums, were the best-selling *Like Young* and *Like Blue*, recorded with **André Previn**. Apart from his record, film and television work, Rose was guest conductor with several symphony orchestras. His 'Concerto For Flute And Orchestra' was first played by the Los Angeles Philharmonic Orchestra and later by the Boston Pops. Selected albums: *Autumn Leaves* (1957), *Gigi* (1958), *Jamaica* (1958), *Reflections In The Water* (1958), *Songs Of The Fabulous 30s* (1958), *Great Waltzes* (1958), *Holiday For Strings* (1959), *Fiddlin' For Fun* (50s), *Let's Fall In Love* (50s), *Love Walked In* (50s), *Music From Motion Pictures* (50s), *Sentimental Journey* (50s), *Concert With A Beat* (1960), *Bonanza* (1961), *Spectacular Strings* (1961), *Box-Office Blockbusters* (1961), *Cimarron And Others* (1961), *21 Channel Sound* (1962), *The Stripper And Other Fun Songs For The Family* (1962), *Like Young, Like Blue* (1974), *In The Still Of The Night* (1976), *Melody Fair* (1977), *Great Orchestras Of The World* (1978), *Very Thought Of You* (1984). Compilation: *16 Original Hits* (1984).

Rose, Fred

b. 24 August 1897, Evansville, Indiana, USA, d. 1 December 1954, Nashville, Tennessee, USA. Rose was an important and influential figure in country music during the 40s and early 50s, and was known as a composer, singer, pianist, music publisher and record producer. He grew up in St. Louis, and at the age of the age of 15 played piano in Chicago honky-tonks. He recorded for **Brunswick Records** in the early 20s as a singer-pianist. After working for a short time with **Paul Whiteman**, he teamed with whistler Elmo Tanner on Chicago radio, and later had his own show. His early songs, in the 20s, included 'Doo Dah Blues', 'Honest And Truly', 'Charlestonette', 'Deep Henderson' and 'Deed I Do'. The latter, written with lyricist Walter Hirsch, was a hit for **Ruth Etting**. During the 30s Rose worked in Chicago, New York, and Nashville, before moving to Hollywood and collaborating with the enormously popular cowboy star, **Gene Autrey**. One of their songs, 'Be Honest With Me', from the movie, *Ridin' On A Rainbow*, was nominated for an Academy Award in 1941, only to be beaten by **Jerome Kern** and **Oscar Hammerstein II**'s, 'The Last Time I Saw Paris'. Having stumbled into the area of country music virtually by accident, previously not particularly caring for the genre, Rose

formed the first all-country music publishing company, **Acuff-Rose Music**, in 1942, with singer-fiddler-bandleader, **Roy Acuff**, who was known as 'The King Of Country Music'. In 1946 the company signed **Hank Williams** to a writer's contract although Williams could neither read or write music. All of Williams' hit records were produced by Rose, and he co-wrote several of them, including 'A Mansion On The Hill', 'Crazy Heart', 'Settin' The Woods On Fire', 'Kaw-Liga' and 'Take These Chains From My Heart'. The latter was subsequently given an agonized reading by **Ray Charles** in 1963. Rose's background was ideally suited to promote country hits across into the more popular field. His major successes included **Pee Wee King**'s compositions such as 'Slow Poke', a hit for **Ralph Flanagan**, **Helen O'Connell** and King himself; 'Bonaparte's Retreat', successful for **Kay Starr** and **Gene Krupa**; 'You Belong To Me', a US and UK number 1 hit for **Jo Stafford**; and 'Tennessee Waltz', recorded by several artists, and a smash hit, number 1, for **Patti Page** in 1950. Other big Acuff-Rose crossover hits included 'Your Cheatin' Heart' (**Joni James**), 'Hey, Good Lookin' (**Frankie Laine** and **Jo Stafford**) and 'Jambalaya' (the **Carpenters**). Rose's own compositions included 'Tears On My Pillow', 'I'm Trusting In You', 'You Waited Too Long', 'Blue Eyes Crying In The Rain', 'Sweet Kind Of Love', 'Texarkana Baby', 'Pins And Needles', 'Fire Ball Mail', No One Will Ever Know', 'We Live In Two Different Worlds', 'Home In San Antonio', 'Roly Poly', 'You'll Be Sorry When I'm Gone', and many more. His collaborators included Steve Nelson, Ed G. Nelson, and Hy Heath. After Fred Rose's death in 1954, his son Wesley took over his interest in Acuff-Rose
Further reading: *Fred Rose And The Development Of The Nashville Music Industry, 1942-1954*, John Woodruff Rumble.

Rose, Judy

b. 1938, Chicago, USA, d. 25 November 1990, California, USA. The youngest daughter of Patsy Montana, she naturally followed in her mother's country music footsteps. She made her first public appearance at the age of four, when she sang 'Danny Boy' on the *National Barn Dance* on WLS Chicago. Eventually, she joined her elder sister Beverley (b. 1935, New York) and mother, who were then singing on WLS and the three sang as a trio, until Beverley quit the music business. (Patsy and Beverley were probably the first mother-daughter duo to sing on national radio). Judy also retired for a time but returned to work with her mother during the 60s, singing modern country songs as opposed to Patsy's old time numbers. They played extensively in the USA and Judy also built herself some reputation as a solo artist and made appearances on the *Grand Ole Opry*. In the 70s and early 80s, she and Patsy made trips to Europe, during which they proved a popular act on several tours around the British country music clubs. In 1977, they even recorded an album together for Look Records in England. A September 1988 tour to Europe had to be cancelled, when Judy was found to be suffering with cancer. It seemed that the disease had successfully responded to treatment when sadly a recurrence resulted in her death in November 1990.

Albums: with Patsy Montana *Mum And Me* (Look 1977), *A Girl Nobody Knows* (Westwood 1978) (both UK releases).

Rose, Michael

Former **Black Uhuru** vocalist who left soon after they had earned a Grammy award for *Anthem*. His solo career kicked off with 'Demonstration' on his own Grammy Rose label. 'Bogus Badge', the follow-up, gained strong reviews, but it wasn't until he signed with **RCA** that he began to attract serious exposure. However, by this time Rose's music had transferred to a pop/soul direction. A cover of **Paul Simon**'s early 70s 'Mother And Child Reunion' cut was indicative of this, being closer to contemporary hip hop than the roots sound of Black Uhuru. It was undeniably effective whichever category critics decided to place it in. His singles for **Sly And Robbie**'s **Taxi** label heralded a return to roots reggae and 'Monkey Business', 'Visit Them' and 'One A We, Two A We' are already regarded as classics of 90s roots music, with promise of an album to come.

Selected album: *Free Yourself* aka *Proud* (RCA 1990).

Rose, The

This 1979 film starred **Bette Midler** in the role of a self-destructive singer, loosely based on the career of **Janis Joplin**. Midler was already renowned as a brassy interpreter who injected personality into her performances and parallels between the two artists' approach, as opposed to lifestyles, were not outlandish. Eschewing the blues-based métier marking Joplin's work, Midler performed material more akin to conventional 'show-biz' styles and *The Rose* thus functions as cautionary 'rise and fall' tale akin to *A Star Is Born*. British actor Alan Bates appears as the singer's manager, mavericks Harry Dean Stanton and Frederick Forrest are also featured, but the film revolves around Midler's powerful Oscar-nominated portrayal of a hedonistic, self-destructive individual but brilliant person.

Video: *1991: The Year Punk Broke* (1993).

Rose, Tim

b. 23 September 1940. A one-time student priest and navigator for the USAF Strategic Air Command, Rose began his professional music career playing guitar with the **Journeymen**, a folk group active in the early 60s which featured **John Phillips** and **Scott McKenzie**.

He subsequently joined **Cass Elliot** and James Hendricks in another formative attraction, the **Big Three**. Although initially based in Chicago, the trio later moved to New York, where Rose forged a career as a solo singer on the group's disintegration in 1964. A gruff stylist and individual, he was turned down by **Elektra** and **Mercury** before securing a deal with **Columbia**. A series of majestic singles then followed, including 'Hey Joe' (1966) and 'Morning Dew' (1967). Rose's slow, brooding version of the former was the inspiration for that of **Jimi Hendrix**, while the latter, written by Rose and folksinger Bonnie Dobson, was the subject of cover versions by, among others, **Jeff Beck** and the **Grateful Dead**.

Tim Rose was assembled from several different sessions, but the presence of several crack session musicians - **Felix Pappalardi** (bass/piano), **Bernard Purdie** (drums) and Hugh McCracken (guitar) - provided a continuity. The set included a dramatic reading of 'I'm Gonna Be Strong', previously associated with **Gene Pitney**, and the haunting anti-war anthem 'Come Away Melinda', already recorded by the **Big Three**, on which Rose's blues-soaked, gritty voice was particularly effective. The singer's next release, 'Long Haired Boys', was recorded in the UK under the aegis of producer **Al Kooper**, before Rose returned to the USA to complete *Through Rose Coloured Glasses* (1969). This disappointing album lacked the strength of its predecessor and the artist was never again to scale the heights of his early work. He switched outlets to **Capitol** for *Love, A Kind Of Hate Story*, before the disillusioned performer abandoned major outlets in favour of the Playboy label where his manager's brother was employed. The promise of artistic freedom was fulfilled when **Gary Wright** of **Spooky Tooth**, a group Rose revered, produced the ensuing sessions. The album, also entitled *Tim Rose*, contained a version of the **Beatles**' 'You've Got To Hide Your Love Away' performed at a snail's pace. It was not a commercial success and the singer again left for the UK where he believed audiences were more receptive. Resident in London, Rose undertook a series of live concerts with fellow exile **Tim Hardin**, but this ill-fated partnership quickly collapsed. *The Musician*, released in 1975, revealed a voice which retained its distinctive power, but an artist without definite direction. In 1976 Rose was recording a new album with help from **Andy Summers**, Snowy White, Raphael Ravenscroft, **B.J. Cole** and Michael D'Alberquerque. This country-tinged album was finally released on President in 1991 as *The Gambler*. Rose moved back to New York in the late 70s. Little has been heard from him for several years.

Albums: *Tim Rose* (Columbia 1967), *Through Rose Coloured Glasses* (Columbia 1969), *Love, A Kind Of Hate Story* (1970), *Tim Rose* (1972), *The Musician* (1975), *The Gambler* (President 1991).

Rose, Tony

b. Anthony Rose, 1 May 1941, Exeter, Devon, England. Rose specialises in songs of the west country of England. Performing on guitar and concertina, and often unaccompanied, Tony has established a reputation for quality translations of traditional songs. Rose found his interest in folk music through jazz, blues and skiffle via the American folk-song tradition. He started singing at the Oxford University Heritage Society in 1960 and was also a member of the resident group, the Journeymen. During the early 60s, he worked semi-professionally while still at Oxford, and from 1965-69 taught in London. He was a resident at a number of clubs during this time, including **Cecil Sharp** House, **Karl Dallas**'s Goodge Street Centre, and the Mercury Theatre (along with **Young Tradition**, **Andy Irvine**, and **Lou Killen**). Tony finally turned professional in September 1969, and based himself in London. He was asked by Bill Leader to record for Leader's own Trailer label and *Young Hunting* resulted. The following year, *Under The Greenwood Tree*, featuring songs of the west country, was released to critical acclaim from the folk press. He joined **Nic Jones**, **Pete Coe** and Chris Coe, in the short-lived group Bandoggs who released just one album. Despite its short life span, the group is still fondly remembered. Tony changed labels to Dingles Records for his fourth solo release, *Poor Fellows*, which featured contemporary material. He has latterly turned to journalism in addition to still performing.

Albums: *Young Hunting* (1970), *Under The Greenwood Tree* (1971), with Jon Raven, Nic Jones *Songs Of A Changing World* (70s), *On Banks Of Green Willow* (1977), with Raven, Harry Boardman *Steam Ballads* (70s), with Nic Jones, Pete, Chris Coe *Bandoggs* (1978), *Poor Fellows* (1982).

Rose, Wesley

b. 11 February 1918, Chicago, Illinois, USA, d. 26 April 1990, Nashville, Tennessee, USA. The son of **Fred Rose**, he lived with his mother when his parents divorced and after completing college, worked as an accountant in the Chicago offices of Standard Life. (He married Margaret Erdelyan on 16 November 1940 and they had one daughter, Scarlett). In April 1945, whilst visiting an aunt in St. Louis, he was persuaded to call on his father. They had not seen each other since 1933 and he did not recognise Fred, nor seemingly did the short-sighted Fred recognise his son. After this first reunion, Fred saw Wesley on his regular business trips to Chicago and tried to persuade him to work for the mighty **Acuff-Rose** Publishing company established by himself and **Roy Acuff** as Nashville's first publishing house on 13 October 1942. At the time, Wesley Rose had no interest at all in country music and certainly no desire to live in Nashville. After considerable discussions and much hesitation on Wesley's part, he finally accepted his father's offer of the post of general manager with responsibility for all business decisions. In December 1945, Wesley Rose became a most important part of the family business and his undoubted business skills and accountant's training freed his father to concentrate more on handling the music side of the business - not least of all the emerging talent of **Hank Williams**. Although Wesley had no love for country music in his early days, he had no hesitation in believing that a good country song such as those written by Hank could be a hit in popular music. He soon proved his point and made the initial break through when, under his careful guidance, 'Cold Cold Heart' became a million seller for **Tony Bennett** in 1951. Other crossover hits followed including 'Jambalaya' for **Jo Stafford** and 'Hey Good Lookin'' for **Frankie Laine**. When Fred Rose died in 1954, Roy Acuff immediately recognised Wesley as the natural successor and placed him in full charge of all the company's business. Under his guidance the successes are too numerous to mention but the company's list of talented songwriters included the **Everly Brothers** (who he also managed for seven years), **Don Gibson**, **Marty Robbins**, the **Louvin Brothers** and **Roy Orbison**. In spite of his work as the head of the organisation, Rose still became very active in record production of artists including **Bob Luman** and others on the company's Hickory Label, which he had founded. Exactly when Rose's opinion of country music changed is not clear but in later years, he was certainly a staunch supporter of traditional country singers like **Boxcar Willie** and, while he had no objections or qualms at all about using a country song for a crossover hit, he had a considerable abhorrence for rock 'n' roll. Several journalists have related the story of him advocating radio stations not to play a recording of **Elvis Presley** because he always maintained that Presley was not a country singer. It was a dedicated belief, when one takes into consideration that Acuff-Rose would benefit by Presley's record sales, since the song concerned was on their own roster. Over the years some of his dealings caused animosity and problems. In September 1982, Roy Orbison filed a $50 million suit accusing Wesley of mismanagement and fraud: Wesley had been his manager since 1958. It was settled out of court for around $3 million and then the law firm sued Orbison for non-payment of fees. The Everlys also had a row with him. In the early 60s, they began to record songs that were not Acuff-Rose and dropped Wesley Rose as manager. He sued them for lack of earnings and he refused to let **Felice** and **Boudleaux Bryant** give them any more songs. Don Everly took to writing songs under a pseudonym so that Wesley could not get them.

Over the years, Rose became connected with many aspects of the industry and also served on various boards, including the Nashville Chamber Of Commerce, Vanderbilt Medical Centre, First American National Bank and Boy Scouts Of America. He was the first Southern publisher elected to the board of **ASCAP** and also served as National President of NARAS. He was a founder member of the Country Music Association, being Chairman of the organisation on three different occasions and he also served on the board of the Country Music Foundation. In 1986, he was elected to the Country Music Hall Of Fame, thus joining his father, who had been one of the first three entrants (with **Jimmie Rodgers** and Hank Williams) when the award was first created in 1961. He remained active with Acuff-Rose, until the company was sold to Opryland USA in 1985. Wesley Rose, a highly respected gentleman, who was once the most powerful man in Nashville's whole music industry, died in the Edgefield Hospital, Nashville, after a long illness in April 1990. Mrs Margaret Rose died in Nashville in late December 1990.

Rosengarden, Bobby

b. 23 April 1924, Elgin, Illinois, USA. After starting to play drums while still a child, Rosengarden studied at university and played in military bands during his army service. In 1945 he played in a New York dance band with **Henry Busse** and during the next two decades played drums and percussion with many bands in a wide range of styles including jazz with **Miles Davis** and **Benny Goodman**, television studio bands, and symphony orchestras. In the 70s he was with the **World's Greatest Jazz Band** and the **Bob Wilber-Kenny Davern** group, **Soprano Summit**. With Davern and **Dick Wellstood** he formed the Blue Three and he also played with **Dick Hyman**'s New York Jazz Repertory Orchestra and at Dick Gibson's Colorado Jazz Parties. He has also played with **Gerry Mulligan** and led his own bands. A driving, enthusiastic drummer, Rosengarden's broad-based technique allows him to feel at home in most settings especially those with a traditional to mainstream bias. His deep interest in Brazilian music also makes its presence felt in his work.
Albums: *Colorado Jazz Party* (1971), *Soprano Summit* (1973), with Dick Hyman *Satchmo Remembered* (1974), *The World's Greatest Jazz Band Of Yank Lawson And Bob Haggart On Tour* (1975), *The Blue Three Live At Hanratty's* (1981), *By Request* (Statiras 1987).

Rosengren, Bernt

b. 24 December 1937, Stockholm, Sweden. Rosengren had already played the tenor saxophone professionally with the Swedish hard bop group Jazz Club '57 when he became a member of **Marshall Brown**'s International Youth Band in 1958. His earthy tenor playing was later influenced by the early sound of **John Coltrane**. In the early 60s he moved to Poland where

he played the tenor solos on the soundtrack of Polanski's film *Knife In The Water* (1962). The music had been written by **Krzysztof Komeda** with whom Rosengren had appeared at the Polish Jazz Jamboree in 1961. After his return to Sweden he worked and recorded with **George Russell**, **Don Cherry** and Lars Gullin (baritone saxophone) in the early 70s and has since led his own groups.
Albums: *Live In Stockholm* (1974), *Big Band* (1979), *Summit Meeting* (1984).

Rosenman, Leonard

b. 7 September 1924, Brooklyn, New York, USA. A composer and arranger for films and television, who only studied music seriously after serving in the US Air Force during World War II. His first film score, *East Of Eden* (1955), was followed in the same year by another James Dean vehicle, *Rebel Without A Cause*. Rosenman's other 50s scores included dramas like *Bombers B-52*, *Edge Of The City*, *The Young Stranger*, *Lafayett Escadrille*, *Pork Chop Hill* and *The Savage Eye*. After providing music for more of the same genre in the 60s, such as *The Rise And Fall Of Legs Diamond*, *The Bramble Bush*, *The Chapman Report*, *A Covenant With Death* and *Hellfighters*, plus essays into science-fiction with *Countdown* and *Fantastic Voyage*, Rosenman received much critical acclaim for his score to *A Man Called Horse* and *Beneath The Planet Of The Apes* (1970). He also scored two 'Apes' sequels. During the 70s Rosenman received two Academy Awards for his adaptation of the scores to *Barry Lyndon* (1975) and *Bound For Glory* (1976). Rosenman's original background scores around that time included *Birch Interval*, *The Car*, *Race With The Devil*, *Prophecy*, *Promises In The Dark* and the animated feature *The Lord Of The Rings*. In the 80s and early 90s, apart from the occasional feature film such as *Hide In Plain Sight*, *Making Love*, *Cross Creek* (Oscar nomination), *The Voyage Home - Star Trek IV*, *Robocop 2*, *Heart Of The Stag* and *Ambition* (1992), Rosenman wrote more and more for television, although he still managed to score the occasional big feature, such as ***The Jazz Singer*** and *Star Trek IV: The Voyage Home*. Rosenman's music for television included *Stranger On The Run*, *Shadow Over Elveron*, *Any Second Now*, *Banyon*, *Vanished*, *In Broad Daylight*, *The Bravos*, *The Cat Creature*, *The Phantom Of Hollywood*, *Nakia*, *Lanigan's Rabbi*, *Kingston: The Power Play*, *The Possessed*, *Friendly Fire*, *City In Fear*, *The Wall*, *Murder In Texas*, *Celebrity* (mini-series), *Heartsounds*, *First Steps*, *Promised A Miracle*, *Where Pigeons Go To Die*, the popular series, *The Defenders*, *Marcus Welby MD*, its sequel, *The Return Of Marcus Welby MD* and the telefilm *Keeper Of The City* (1991). He also composed several classical works.

Rosewoman, Michele

b. 19 March 1953, Oakland, California, USA. Rosewoman comes from a musical family: her parents ran a record shop and her elder brother is a musician,

so she was exposed to jazz and world music at an early age. She began playing piano at the age of six and when she was 17 years old she met pianist Edwin Kelly, who introduced her to hard bop and the music of **Thelonious Monk** and **John Coltrane** and gave her lessons. She also studied Cuban percussion with Orlando 'Puntilla' Rios and Shona (Zimbabwean) and Yoruba (Nigerian) traditional music. San Francisco's Keystone Korner was a centre for jazz, where she heard **Cecil Taylor**. She met trumpeter **Baikida Carrol** and altoist **Oliver Lake** from **BAG** (Black Artists Group) in St. Louis and also members of the **AACM**. In 1978 she relocated to New York - her first appearance was with Lake at Carnegie Hall. Since then she has performed regularly as sidewoman and leader. In 1981 she played on **Billy Bang**'s *Rainbow Gladiator*. She also worked with a number of Cuban groups, notably Los Kimy, with whom she recorded. Her interest in Afro-Cuban music led her to form the 15-piece New Yor-Uba: in December 1983 she premiered 'New Yor-Uba, A Musical Celebration Of Cuba In America' at the Public Theatre in New York to great acclaim. She made her recording debut as a leader in 1985 with *The Source* for **Soul Note**. In 1986 she formed a quintet, Quintessence, which has released *Quintessence* and *Contrast High*. In Summer 1991 she toured with **Carlos Ward**. 1991's *Occasion To Rise* was a trio recording with **Rufus Reid** on bass and Ralph Peterson Jnr. on drums. Michele Rosewoman's broad musical vision, welcome in a period of jazz neo-conservatism, is matched by the strength of her compositions and the energy of her playing.
Albums: *The Source* (1985), *Quintessence* (Enja 1987), *Contrast High* (Enja 1989), *Occasion To Rise* (1991), *Harvest* (Enja 1993).

Rosie And The Originals

Formed in 1960 in San Diego, California, USA, Rosie And The Originals were 15-year-old Rosalie 'Rosie' Hamlin (b. Alaska, USA), Noah Tafolla (guitar), Carl Van Guida (drums), Tony Gomez (saxophone) and David Ponci (guitar). Hamlin wrote their only hit song, 'Angel Baby' (wrongly credited to Ponci), as a poem to her first boyfriend, then set it to music on a piano. They recorded the doo-wop ballad and then found a local label, Highland Records, to issue it. The record became a local sensation on Los Angeles radio station KFWB before breaking nationally in late 1960, eventually climbing to the US Top 5. Rosie And The Originals recorded no albums but, with the assistance of **Jackie Wilson**, Hamlin later recorded for **Brunswick Records**, including *Lonely Blue Nights* in 1961. She subsequently married Tafolla, then divorced and later appeared in 'oldies' shows, performing with a band, the LA Rhythm Section.

Rosolino, Frank

b. 20 August 1926, Detroit, Michigan, USA, d. 26 November 1978. After dabbling with guitar, Rosolino took up the trombone while in his teens. After military service during World War II he played in a succession of big bands, including those of **Bob Chester** and **Glen Gray**. In 1948 he was one of several bebop-influenced musicians playing in **Gene Krupa**'s big band (contributing the scat vocalizing on the band's hit record of 'Lemon Drop'). After playing in several other dance bands he briefly led his own group before joining **Stan Kenton** in 1952. Two years later he left the band and settled in California, where he divided his time between studio and jazz work. He recorded with **Dexter Gordon**, **Stan Levey**, **Conte Candoli** and many of the musicians who frequented the Lighthouse. In the mid-70s Rosolino again worked with Candoli, visiting Europe, and he also played several times with **Benny Carter**, who was one of the trombonist's greatest admirers. Also in the 70s he played in **Med Flory**'s band, **Supersax**, and with **Quincy Jones**. A brilliant technician with a precisely articulated attacking style, Rosolino was one of the finest trombonists of his time and one of few practitioners on the instrument to fully adapt to bebop. His later work showed him to be a consummate section player whether in big bands or small groups. He died in 1978 in acutely tragic circumstances, shooting both of his children (one of whom survived) before shooting himself.
Albums: with Stan Kenton *New Concepts Of Artistry In Rhythm* (1952), one side only *The Trombone Album/Swing Not Spring* (1952), *Stan Kenton Presents: Frank Rosolino Sextet* (1954), *Frankly Speaking* (1955), with Stan Levey *This Time The Drum's On Me* (1955), with Levey *Grand Stan* (1956), *I Play Trombone* (1956), with Lighthouse All Stars *Double Or Nothin'* (1957), *The Most Happy Fella* (1957), with Benny Carter *Aspects* (1958-59), *Turn Me Loose!* (1961), *Conversations* (1975), *Just Friends* (1975), *Thinking About You* (1976), *In Denmark* (1978).

Ross, Annie

b. Annabelle Short Lynch, 25 July 1930, Mitcham, Surrey, England. After working as a child actress in Hollywood, she then toured internationally as a singer. She sang with both **Tony Crombie** and **Jack Parnell** during the 50s. Ross had recorded successful wordless jazz vocals before becoming a member of the famous scat (vocalese) trio, **Lambert, Hendricks And Ross** from 1958-62. Her song 'Twisted', written with Wardell Gray, was expertly covered by **Joni Mitchell**, among others. In the mid-60s Ross operated Annie's Room, a jazz club in London, and in later years worked in films and television as both actress and singer, at one point being briefly reunited with **Jon Hendricks**. Personal problems affected the continuity of Ross's career but despite the resulting irregularity of her public performances she maintained an enviably high standard of singing. Her scat singing was some of the finest ever heard. In the early 80s she found a compatible musical partner in **Georgie Fame** with whom she toured and recorded.

Selected albums: *Annie Ross Sings* (Original Jazz Classics 1953), *Annie By Candlelight* (1956), with Gerry Mulligan *Annie Ross Sings A Song With Mulligan* (EMI Manhattan 1958), *Gypsy* (1958-59), with Zoot Sims *A Gasser* (Pacific Jazz 1959), *You And Me Baby* (c.1964), *Annie Ross And Pony Poindexter With The Berlin All Stars* (1966), with Georgie Fame *In Hoagland '81* (Bald Eagle 1981), *Sings A Handful Of Songs* (Fresh Sounds 1988).

Ross, Diana

b. Diane Ernestine Ross, 26 March 1944, Detroit, USA. While still in high school Ross became the fourth and final member of the **Primettes**, who recorded for Lu-Pine in 1960, signed to **Motown Records** in 1961 and then changed their name to the **Supremes**. She was a backing vocalist on the group's early releases, until Motown supremo **Berry Gordy** insisted that she become their lead singer, a role she retained for the next six years. In recognition of her prominent position in the Supremes, she received individual billing on all their releases from 1967 onwards. Throughout her final years with the group, Ross was being groomed for a solo career under the close personal supervision of Gordy, with whom she was rumoured to have romantic links. In late 1969, he announced that Ross would be leaving the Supremes, and she played her final concert with the group in January 1970. Later that year Ross began a long series of successful solo releases, with the chart-topping 'Ain't No Mountain High Enough'. In April 1971, she married businessman Robert Silberstein, but they were divorced in 1976 after renewed speculation about her relationship with Gordy.

As she continued to enjoy success with lightweight love songs in the early 70s, Motown's plan to widen Ross's appeal led her to host a television special, *Diana!*, in 1971. In 1972, she starred in Motown's film biography of **Billie Holiday**, *Lady Sings The Blues*, winning an Oscar nomination for her stirring portrayal of the jazz singer's physical decline into drug addiction. But subsequent starring roles in *Mahogany* (1975) and *The Wiz* (1978) drew a mixed critical response. In 1973, Ross released an album of duets with **Marvin Gaye**, though allegedly the pair did not meet during the recording of the project. She scored another USA number 1 with 'Touch Me In The Morning', and repeated that success with the theme song from *Mahogany* in 1975. 'Love Hangover' in 1976 saw her moving into the contemporary disco field, a shift of direction that was consolidated on the 1980 album *Diana*, produced by Nile Rodgers and Bernard Edwards

of **Chic**. Her choice of hit material continued to be inspired and the 80s started with a major hit 'Upside Down', which rooted itself at the top of the US chart for a month, similar but lesser success followed with 'I'm Coming Out' and 'It's My Turn'. The following year the teaming up with **Lionel Richie** produced the title track to the film Endless Love, this tearjerker spent more than two months at the top of the US chart. By now, Ross was as much a media personality as a soul singer, winning column inches for her liaison with Gene Simmons of **Kiss**. There was also intense speculation about the nature of her relationship with **Michael Jackson**, whose career she had helped to guide since 1969.

After months of rumour about her future, Ross left Motown in 1981, and signed contracts with **RCA** for North America, and **Capitol** for the rest of the world. She formed her own production company and had further hits. A reworking of **Frankie Lymon**'s 'Why Do Fools Fall In Love' and Michael Jackson's 'Muscles' confirmed her pre-eminence in the field of disco-pop. During the remainder of the 80s only 'Missing You', a tribute to the late Marvin Gaye, brought her the success to which she had become accustomed. In Britain, however, she achieved a number 1 hit in 1986 with 'Chain Reaction', an affectionate re-creation of her days with the Supremes written and produced by the **Bee Gees**. In 1986, Ross married a Norwegian shipping magnate, effectively quashing renewed rumours that she might wed Berry Gordy and return to Motown. Since then, she has won more publicity for her epic live performances, notably an open-air concert in New York's Central Park in a torrential storm, than for her sporadic releases of new material, which continue to occupy the lighter end of the black music market.

Albums: *Reach Out* (Motown 1970), *Everything Is Everything* (Motown 1970), *Diana!* (Motown 1971), *Surrender* (Motown 1971), *Lady Sings The Blues* (Motown 1972), *Touch Me In The Morning* (Motown 1973), with Marvin Gaye *Diana And Marvin* (Motown 1973), *Last Time I Saw Him* (Motown 1973), *Live At Caesar's Palace* (Motown 1974), *Mahogany* (Motown 1975), *Diana Ross* (Motown 1976), *An Evening With Diana Ross* (Motown 1977), *Baby It's Me* (Motown 1977), *Ross* (Motown 1978), *The Boss* (Motown 1979), *Diana* (Motown 1980), *To Love Again* (Motown 1981), *Why Do Fools Fall In Love* (RCA 1981), *Silk Electric* (RCA 1982), *Ross* (RCA 1983), *Swept Away* (RCA 1984), *Eaten Alive* (RCA 1985), *Red Hot Rhythm 'N' Blues* (RCA 1987), *Working Overtime* (Motown 1989), *Greatest Hits Live* (Motown 1989), *Force Behind The Power* (Motown 1991), *Live, Stolen Moments* (1993), with Placido Domingo, José Carreras *Christmas In Vienna* (Sony 1993). Compilations: *All The Great Hits* (Motown 1981), *Diana Ross Anthology* (Motown 1983), *One Woman, The Ultimate Collection* (EMI 1993).

Videos: *Visions Of Diana Ross, The* (1986), *One Woman -*

The Video Collection (1993), *Stolen Moments* (1994).
Further reading: *Diana Ross*, Leonore K. Itzkowitz. *Diana Ross*, Patricia Mulrooney Eldred. *Diana Ross: Supreme Lady*, Connie Berman. *I'm Gonna Make You Love Me: The Story Of Diana Ross*, James Haskins. *Diana Ross: An Illustrated Biography*, Geoff Brown. *Dreamgirl: My Life As A Supreme*, Mary Wilson. *Call Her Miss Ross*, J. Randy Taraborrelli. *Call Her Miss Ross*, J. Randy Taraborrelli. *Supreme Faith: Someday We'll Be Together*, Mary Wilson with Patricia Romanowski. *Secrets Of The Sparrow*, Diana Ross.

Ross, Doctor

b. Charles Isiah Ross, 21 October 1925, Tunica, Mississippi, USA. Ross had American Indian ancestry. He learned harmonica at the age of nine and was performing with **Willie Love** and on radio stations in Arkansas and Mississippi in the late 30s. He served in the US Army from 1943-47. His paramedical training there earned Ross the soubriquet of Doctor when he returned to music, leading his Jump And Jive Band and appearing on radio in the *King Bicuit Time Show*. Ross also developed a one-man-band act, which he frequently performed in the 50s and 60s. His Memphis recordings for **Sam Phillips** in the early 50s included 'Country Clown' and 'The Boogie Disease'. In 1954, he moved to Flint, Michigan to work in an auto factory. Ross continued to perform and in 1958 set up his own DIR label. In the early 60s, Ross benefited from the growing white interest in blues, recording for Pete Welding's Testament label and touring Europe with the 1965 Folk Blues Festival. He returned there during the 70s, recording in London and performing at the **Montreux Jazz Festival** with **Muddy Waters**' band.
Albums: *The Flying Eagle* (1966), *Dr Ross, The Harmonica Boss* (1972), *Jivin' The Blues* (1974), *Live At Montreux* (1975), *First Recordings* (reissue 1981).

Ross, Jackie

b. 30 January 1946, St. Louis, Missouri, USA. This cool, stylish singer made her debut on **Sam Cooke**'s Sar label in 1962. 'Selfish One' (1964), her first single for **Chess**, showcased a mature delivery which further releases, including 'I've Got The Skill' (1964) and 'Take Me For A Little While' (1965), amplified. Tailor-made for producer **Billy Davis**'s imaginative arrangements, she found it hard to maintain this standard on the several labels – **Brunswick**, Scepter, **Mercury** and more – she had later turned to. An interlude on **Jerry Butler**'s Fountain label resulted in 'Who Could Be Loving You' (1969), an alluring mid-paced ballad subsequently revived by **Dusty Springfield**. Ross was last heard on a 1981 album by **Little Milton**.
Albums: *Full Bloom* (1964), *A New Beginning* (1980), shared with Little Milton *In Perspective* (1981).

Ross, Jerry
(see **Adler, Richard**)

Ross, Ronnie

b. 2 October 1933, Calcutta, India, d. 12 December 1991. Ross came to England in his early teens where he first took up the tenor saxophone. In the mid-50s he joined **Don Rendell** who persuaded him to change to baritone. Thereafter, Ross built a reputation as an outstanding player of the instrument, working in bands led by **Ted Heath**, **Marshall Brown** and **Woody Herman**. He was also co-leader with **Allan Ganley** of the Jazzmakers. In the early 60s he was leader of his own small band and also participated in numerous recording sessions, including some with **John Dankworth**. The 60s also saw him spending time in Europe where he played with the **Clarke-Boland Big Band**. Ross continued leading his own groups and recording under various leaders during the 70s and into the 80s, including an appearance on rock singer **Lou Reed**'s hit single 'A Walk On The Wild Side'. A forceful player, Ross's baritone has long been one of the treasures of the British jazz scene although he seldom achieved the recognition his talent deserves.
Albums: *The Ronnie Ross Quintet* (1958), *Swinging Sounds Of The Jazz Makers* (1959), *Beatle Music By The Session Men* (1967), *Cleopatra's Needle* (1968).

Ross, Spencer

USA-born Spencer Ross was a musical arranger during the 40s who went on to release a best-selling single, 'Tracy's Theme', under his own name in 1960. Ross was an arranger for the **Gordon Jenkins** orchestra in the 40s, before going to work for both Big Top and **Columbia Records** in the 50s. 'Tracy's Theme', written by Robert Ascher and featuring Jimmy Abato on saxophone, was recorded for Columbia in late 1959 and was used in the television special *The Philadelphia Story*. It then took off with the record-buying public, ultimately reaching number 13. Ross recorded an album and a handful of singles similar to his hit but never found his way up the charts again.

Rosselson, Leon

b. 22 June 1934, Harrow, Middlesex, England. Rosselson is well-known in UK folk circles for his incisive satirical and political songwriting. 'The World Turned Upside Down', from *That's Not The Way It's Got To Be*, has been recorded by **Billy Bragg** and **Dick Gaughan**. Earlier in his career, Rosselson had been a member of the Galliards, and later the 3 City 4, which included Roy Bailey and **Martin Carthy** in the line-up. The 60s television series *That Was The Week That Was* included songs written by Rosselson and, in 1962, he recorded an EP *Songs For City Squares*. *Songs For Sceptical Circles* was Rosselson's first solo album release.

As a part of the Campaign for Press and Broadcasting Freedom, he produced the popular 'Ballad Of A Spycatcher' in 1987. The record featured Billy Bragg and members of the **Oyster Band**. *I Didn't Mean It* included longstanding compatriots Carthy and Bailey and also **Frankie Armstrong** and **John Kirkpatrick**. One of his songs, 'Don't Get Married Girls', is a favourite among audiences and performers alike. Owing to the obvious feminist leaning in the lyric, many thought that it had been written by a woman. Rosselson continues to produce songs strong on social comment and his satirical edge shows no sign of blunting.

Albums: with the Galliards *Scottish Choice* (1962), *A-Roving* (1962), *The Galliards* (1963); with the 3 City 4 *The Three City Four* (1965), *Smoke And Dust* (1966); *Songs For Sceptical Circles* (1967), *A Laugh, A Song And A Hand Grenade* (1968), *The Word Is Hugga Mugga Chugga Lugga Humbugga Boom Chit* (1971), *That's Not The Way It's Got To Be* (1973), *Palaces Of Gold* (1975), with Roy Bailey *Love, Loneliness, Laundry* (1977), *If I Knew Who The Enemy Was* (1979), *For The Good Of The Nation* (1981), *Temporary Loss Of Vision* (1983), *Bringing The News From Nowhere* (1986), *I Didn't Mean It* (1989), *Wo Sind Die Elefanten?* (1991). Compilations: *Rosselsongs* (1990), *Guess What They're Selling At The Happiness Counter* (1992).

Further reading: *For The Good Of The Nation*, Leon Rosselson with Jeff Perks. *Bringing The News From Nowhere*, Leon Rosselson.

Rossington Collins

This US rock band was formed in 1979 by the four surviving members of the 1977 **Lynyrd Skynyrd** plane crash; Gary Rossington (guitars), Allen Collins (guitars), Billy Powell (keyboards) and Leon Wilkerson (bass), who joined with Dale Krantz (vocals), Barry Harwood (guitars) and Derek Hess (drums). They continued in the best traditions of Skynyrd, though the female lead vocals gave them a different sound. They broke up in 1983 after just two albums. Powell later joined the Christian rock band **Vision**, while Collins was paralysed from the waist down in a car accident in the mid-80s, and died of pneumonia on 23 January 1990. Krantz married Rossington and both they and Powell took their place in the Lynyrd Skynyrd reunion tour of 1987.

Albums: *Anytime, Anyplace, Anywhere* (MCA 1980), *This Is The Way* (MCA 1982).

Rosso, Nini

b. Celeste Rosso, 19 September 1926, Italy, d. 1994. As a teenager, Rosso ran away from home through parental pressure to pursue an academic career. After he was found playing trumpet in a Nice night spot, his parents relented, and he formed a small orchestra that garnered a work schedule beyond Italy to include, on one occasion, a tour of India. After a residency on Radio Turin, Rosso relocated to Rome where he became recognized as a formidable mainstream jazz player. Nevertheless, his fortune would be made in pop after he was contracted by Durium late in 1962. His debut single, 'La Ballenta Della Tromba', sold well nationally but 1963's 'Concerto Disperato' - also self-composed - entered charts as far afield as Japan. Rosso's biggest commercial moment, however, was with 'Il Silenzio' - theme tune to 1965's *The Legion's Last Patrol* starring Stewart Granger - which, co-written with Guglielmo Brazzo, was a variation on 'The Last Post'. Despite a UK cover by **Eddie Calvert** and another in the USA by **Al Hirt**, the Rosso original was an international smash for which he received the first Common Market Gold Disc award in Hamburg.

Rota, Nino

b. 3 December 1911, Milan, Italy, d. 10 April 1979, Rome, Italy. A prolific composer for films, from the early 30s to the late 70s. A child prodigy, Rota wrote an oratorio and an opera before he was aged 15. He studied at the Curtis Institute in Philadelphia, and, later, at the Liceo Musicale in Bari, eventually becoming its director from 1950-78. He began composing for Italian movies in 1933, but had enormous success in Britain in 1949 with his score for *The Glass Mountain* starring the husband and wife team, Michael Denison and Dulcie Gray. By 1950, when he started collaborating with Federico Fellini, he had composed the scores to some 30 films. His association with the influential Italian director lasted nearly 30 years and included movies such as *Lo Sceicco Bianco*, *I Vitelloni*, *La Strada* (including the 'Love Theme'), *Il Bidone*, *La Dolce Vita* (including 'The Sweet Life'), *Boccaccio*, *Eight And A Half* (with its popular 'Love Theme'), *Juliet Of The Spirits*, *Fellini-Satyricon*, *The Clowns*, *Casanova*, *The Orchestra Rehearsal* and more. Meanwhile, for other directors, Nino provided the music for *The Hidden Room* ('Obsession'), *Anna*, *The White Sheik*, *Star Of India*, *War And Peace*, *Rocco And His Brothers*, *Shoot Louder, Louder ... I Don't Understand*, Franco Zeffirelli's *Romeo And Juliet* (1968), and *Waterloo* (1970). In 1972 Rota composed the scores for Francis Ford Coppola's *The Godfather*, 'the 70s' answer to *Gone With The Wind*'. Oscar-laden as it was, Rota had to wait for the sequel, *The Godfather, Part Two* (1974), for his Academy Award. **Andy Williams** had a minor hit in the USA and UK with the 'Love Theme' from the original movie, entitled 'Speak Softly Love' (lyric by Larry Kusik). Rota's other 70s film music included *The Abdication, Boys From The Suburbs, Casanova, Hurricane* and *Death On The Nile* (1978), with Peter Ustinov as Agatha Christie's Poirot. Rota's last, of an impressive number of scores, was for Fellini's *Orchestra Rehearsal* (1979), which was originally made for television.

Rotary Connection

Formed in 1967, Rotary Connection was a Chicago, USA-based group mixing art-rock and soul. The group was assembled by Marshall Chess, son of **Chess Records** founder Leonard Chess. Looking to update the company's image, Marshall Chess chose several hip-looking singers and musicians, intending to keep the group's membership revolving with each new recording. The original Rotary Connection included pianist/arranger Charles Stepney, who co-produced with Chess, guitarist/vocalist Bobby Simms, bassist/vocalist Mitch Aliotta, drummer Kenny Venegas, and three vocalists: Sid Barnes, Judy Hauff and **Minnie Riperton**. Chess placed the group on his Cadet/Concept label and recorded a debut album largely consisting of covers of recent hits, re-done in a progressive/psychedelic style. Subsequent albums consisted of original material. The group, which underwent several personnel changes in its lifetime, ultimately recorded six albums up to 1971 but experienced only minor chart success. Riperton left in 1970 to pursue a solo career, but the group disbanded in the mid-70s and the others retreated into obscurity.
Albums: *Rotary Connection* (1967), *Aladdin* (1968), *Peace* (1968), *Songs* (1969), *Dinner Music* (1970), *Hey Love* (1971).

Roth, Dave Lee

Dave Lee Roth (b. 10 October 1955, Bloomington, Indeanapolis, USA), former lead vocalist with **Van Halen**, first expressed his desire to go solo during a period of band inactivity during 1985. He subsequently recorded a mini-album, *Crazy From The Heat*, featuring a varied selection of material that was a departure from the techno-metal approach of Van Halen. The album was favourably reviewed and after much speculation, he finally broke ranks in the autumn of 1985. Roth soon found himself in the US Top 3 with an unlikely version of the **Beach Boys**' 'California Girls' (complete with a suitably tacky video) and an even stranger cover of 'I Ain't Got Nobody'. This bizarre change must have baffled and bemused his fans, but he soon assembled an impressive array of musicians, notably guitar virtuoso **Steve Vai** (ex-**Zappa** and **Alcatrazz**), bassist Billy Sheehan (ex-**Talas**) and drummer Greg Bissonette to record *Eat 'Em And Smile*. This featured an amazing selection of blistering rockers and offbeat, big production numbers. It proved that Roth was still a great showman; the album was technically superb and infused with an irreverent sense of 'Yankee' humour. *Skyscraper*, released two years later, built on this foundation, but focused more on an elaborately produced hard rock direction. Billy Sheehan departed shortly after its release to be replaced by Matt Bissonette. Brett Tuggle on keyboards was also recruited to expand the line-up to a five piece and add an extra dimension to their sound. Steve Vai left in 1989 to pursue a solo career, but was only temporarily missed as **Jason Becker** stepped in, a new six-string whizz kid of the **Yngwie Malmsteen** school of guitar improvisation. *A Little Ain't Enough* emerged in 1991 and, although technically faultless, it tended to duplicate ideas from his previous two albums. *Your Filthy Little Mouth* saw him relocate to New York. This time, amid the histrionics about girls and cars, were odes to the Los Angeles riots, and the unutterably horrible pseudo reggae of 'No Big 'Ting'.
Albums: *Crazy From The Heat* (Warners 1985), *Eat 'Em And Smile* (Warners 1986), *Skyscraper* (Warners 1988), *A Little Ain't Enough* (Warners 1991), *Your Filthy Little Mouth* (Warners 1994).
Video: *David Lee Roth* (1987).

Rothchild, Paul A.

b. 18 April 1935, Brooklyn, New York, USA, d. 30 March 1995. A subtle, sympathetic producer, Rothchild first garnered attention for his work on the Prestige label. Here he oversaw sessions by folksingers **Tom Rush** and Eric Von Schmidt, before moving to a rival outlet, **Elektra**, in 1964. There he continued his association with Rush, while supervising other acoustic acts, including **Fred Neil**, **Tom Paxton**, **Phil Ochs** and Koerner, Ray And Glover. Rothchild eased the label's transition from folk to rock via work with their first electric signing, the **Paul Butterfield Blues Band**. His production skills were a crucial element in several of Elektra's most innovative releases, including **Love**'s *Da Capo* and **Tim Buckley**'s impressive debut album. However, it was Rothchild's relationship with the **Doors**, the company's premier act, which proved most fruitful. He produced the group's entire output, save their final selection, *LA Woman*. Paradoxically the finished album was a major success in the wake of singer Jim Morrison's death. Rothchild was also responsible for recordings by **Clear Light** and **Rhinoceros**, an in-house 'supergroup' he had instigated, but left the label in 1970 to pursue an independent career. His freelance productions included **Janis Joplin**'s final collection, *Pearl*, several of **John Sebastian**'s solo releases and **Bonnie Raitt**'s excellent *Home Plate*, but his wider ambitions were thwarted when his ill-fated Buffalo label collapsed. In 1978, Rothchild resumed his association with the Doors when the three surviving members re-grouped to provide backing on *An American Prayer*, a collection of Morrison's poetry readings initially recorded during the *LA Woman* sessions. This reconstituted partnership resulted in post-production work for other resurrected performances including *Alive She Cried* and *The Doors Live At Hollywood Bowl*. He was later involved in the music production for the 1991 Oliver Stone film, *The Doors*. In recent years he worked on a number of film sountracks and worked once again with Holzman on some jazz recordings including *Body Heat - Jazz At The Movies* and more recently the *Lost Elektra Paul Butterfield Tapes*. He died after a long battle against cancer in a career that had his professional involvement in over 150 albums.

Rothschilds, The

Six years after their smash-hit **Fiddler On The Roof**, **Jerry Bock** (music) and **Sheldon Harnick** (lyrics) collaborated with librettist Sherman Yellen on another tale which centred on the plight of oppressed Jews in Europe. *The Rothschilds* opened at the Lunt-Fontanne Theatre in New York on 19 October 1970. Yellen's book was based on a best-selling biography by Frederic Morton, which detailed the rise of the Rothschilds, the fabulously wealthy banking family, and, in particular, one of its driving influences, Mayer Rothschild (Hal Linden). Paul Hecht, as the son Nathan, and Keene Curtis, who took on several roles throughout the piece, both gained favourable notices. Unlike *Fiddler On The Roof*, *The Rothschilds'* score contained no durable hits, but apposite and engaging songs such as 'He Tossed A Coin', 'Rothschild And Sons', 'One Room', 'Sons', 'I'm In Love! I'm In Love!', 'In My Own Lifetime', 'Everything', and 'Pleasure And Privilege', ensured a run of 507 performances. Linden won a **Tony Award** for his vigorous performance, and Bock and Harnick split up after writing seven scores together.

Rough Cutt

Typical of its kind mid-80s Los Angeles, California, USA rock band following in the footsteps of **Ratt** and **Quiet Riot** but lacking originality. Led by vocalist Paul Shortino, they were proficient enough to gain support slots on American tours with **Accept** and **Krokus**, but generated little interest in the UK. **Warner Brothers** took a chance on them in 1985 and released the first of two average albums. In 1986 they were dropped by the company and Shortino left to join **Quiet Riot** leaving the rest of the band - Amir Derakh (guitar), David Alford (drums), Matt Thor (bass) - to form Jailhouse.
Albums: *Rough Cutt* (Warners 1985), *Wants You* (Warners 1986).

Rough Diamond

This highly-touted UK supergroup was formed to considerable fanfare in 1976. **Dave Clempson** (ex-**Bakerloo**, **Colosseum**, **Humble Pie**; guitar), Damon Butcher (keyboards; ex-**Steve Marriot**'s All Stars), Willie Bath (bass) and Geoff Britton (ex-**Wings**; drums) joined former **Uriah Heep** singer **David Byron**, but their launch was undermined by a court case brought by another group claiming the same name. The delay undermined the quintet's confidence and the ensuing album proved disappointing. Its appearance during the punk explosion exacerbated problems and although the band looked to the USA for

solace, friction between Byron and his colleagues proved insurmountable. The singer embarked on a solo career in October 1977 while the remaining members added Garry Bell and adopted a new name, **Champion**, releasing an album on **Epic** in 1978.
Album: *Rough Diamond* (Island 1977).

Rough Silk

Comprising Jan Barnett (vocals/guitar), Herbert Harman (drums), Ferdy Doernberg (piano/keyboards), Hilmer Staacke (guitar) and Ralf Schwertner (bass), Hannover, Germany based rock band Rough Silk represent part of the new wave of European rock music. With an easily detectable bent towards American AOR stylings, in the vein of bands such as **Rainbow**, **Bon Jovi** and **REO Speedwagon**, Rough Silk have struggled to throw off accusations of imitation. However, they are nevertheless competent at their craft, as has been proved by two albums for the Mausoleum label recorded at Dieter Dierks German studio. The second of these was the better, with songs such as 'Toxical Roses' and 'One More For The Ride' demonstrating the group's ability to tackle contrasting material without losing momentum.
Albums: *Rough Silk* (Mausoleum 1993), *Walls Of Never* (Mausoleum 1995).

Rough Trade Records

Initially based near west London's Portobello Road, the Rough Trade retail shop opened in February 1976, just months prior to the rise of the punk rock phenomenon. Owned by Geoff Travis (b. 2 February 1952, Stoke Newington, London, England), it was an important outlet for punk and independent releases from the UK and USA. Travis's empathy for this musical revolution helped build the shop's reputation as a leading source for import material, British independent releases, complimentary reggae releases and as a selling point for the proliferation of music fanzines. The demand for outlets generated by bands inspired the formation of a distribution network and label, and the Rough Trade record label was launched two years later with the release of 'Paris Maquis' by Metal Urbain, which anticipated the 'Industrial' style flourishing later in the decade. Subsequent releases by reggae artist **Augustus Pablo** and *avant garde* act **Cabaret Voltaire** confirmed Rough Trade's reputation as an outlet for diverse talent. **Stiff Little Fingers**, **Young Marble Giants**, **Aztec Camera**, the **Raincoats**, the **Go-Betweens**, the **Fall**, **Scritti Politti** and the **Pop Group** maintained the company's reputation as purveyors of challenging music, while a succession of excellent recordings by the **Smiths** combined perception with popular acclaim, making the group the company's biggest asset for much of its history. The label also became the natural outlet for several US acts, ranging from the guitar-orientated **Feelies**, **Dream**

Syndicate, the idiosyncratic **Jonathan Richman** and **Camper Van Beethoven**, to the experimental styles of **Pere Ubu** and the offbeat country/folk of **Souled American**. Many defections to major labels most notably Aztec Camera and Scritti Politti undermined the pitfalls bedevilling independent outlets and in 1984, under the aegis of the giant **Warner Brothers** corporation, Travis established Blanco Y Negro on which acts who preferred the security of a major company could nonetheless enjoy the intimacy of an independent. **Jesus And Mary Chain**, **Everything But The Girl** and Dinosaur Jnr have been among the label's signings, confirming Travis as one of Britain's most astute executives. Rough Trade Records continued to serve as the natural outlet for independently-minded acts throughout the 80s, but defection to **EMI** by the aforementioned Smiths was a significant loss. Hopes were then pinned on the **Sundays**, but the collapse of the Rough Trade distribution network in 1991 put the label's fate in jeopardy. However, a trimming down of staff and operations found the company steadying its position and subsequent recordings by artists such as **Robert Wyatt** suggest that its long-term future as a haven for adventurism is still assured.

Album: *Wanna Buy A Bridge?* (1980).

Round Midnight

A long step (if not exactly a leap) forward in the treatment of jazz and jazz musicians in feature films, this film released in 1986, loosely traces the life and times of **Bud Powell** in Paris. Centring upon the characters of an alcoholic American jazzman and his Parisian fan-cum-mentor, the film contains an excellent performance from **Dexter Gordon** as the saxophonist for which he was unsuccessfully nominated for an Oscar. The music, an approximation of late 50s bop, is generally well-realized by Gordon and musicians such as **Ron Carter**, **Billy Higgins**, **Bobby Hutcherson**, **Freddie Hubbard**, **John McLaughlin**, **Pierre Michelot**, **Wayne Shorter**, **Cedar Walton**, **Tony Williams** and **Herbie Hancock** (who was also responsible for the score). The mostly restrained, unmelodramatic development of an essentially tragic storyline is the responsibility of director Bernard Tavernier yet there is rather too much reliance upon stereotype and cliché to warrant the accolades heaped upon the film. Undoubtedly, it is an important improvement upon many jazz-based films but, as so often before, film-makers seem unwilling, or unable, to either leave historical context undamaged or acknowledge the fact that most musicians do what they do because they are musicians. They play to hear the music; film-makers apparently feel obliged to give them non-musical motivation which, as often or not, diminishes them when, presumably, the intention is to uplift.

Rounder Records

The label was founded in 1970 by Ken Irwin, Marina Leighton Levy and Bill Nowlin, three Boston-area college students, merely to further their common interest in traditional music and its contemporary offshoots. They released only two albums in their first year, 0001 George Pegram (a North Carolina banjoist) and 0002 Spark Gap Wonder Boys (a Cambridge old-timey String Band). Initially, with financial support from other employment, they operated mainly as a home-based mail order outlet and by investing any profits they raised from also selling their releases at festivals, they slowly built up the company. By the third year there were 19 releases. Now, with their ventures into varying types of music, the annual average is around 100. In the 70s, they became noted for releases of folk, blues and bluegrass music by such artists as Norman Blake and Del McCoury and achieved a major success with the first album by J.D. Crowe And The New South featuring **Ricky Skaggs**. In the late 70s, the label was boosted by sales of over 500,000 for two albums by blues guitarist **George Thorogood**. During the 80s, Rounder acquired the Philo label, which led to recordings by **Nanci Griffith** and **Iris Dement** and in 1982, they founded their Heartbeat label as an outlet for reggae. By the mid-80s, their Modern New Orleans Masters series had been launched and the label has now become one of the most active labels to record Cajun and Zydeco music by such exponents as D.L Menard, **Jo-El Sonnier** and Buckwheat Zydeco. Their Bullseye label deals with white blues music. Bluegrass has always been an important genre and Rounder have released material by such leading exponents as **Alison Krauss** and the Johnson Mountain Boys. Releases of important early days' country artists include series of the recordings of the **Carter Family**, **Jimmie Rodgers** and the **Louvin Brothers**. Their current catalogue exceeds 1,250 and they additionally represent 19 other labels on exclusive national and in many cases worldwide distribution. Their other business interests include Rounder Music (**ASCAP**), Happy Valley Music (BMI) (music publishing companies) and Roundup Records (mail order retailer). There are over 20 independent distributors representing the Rounder group in countries around the world. The original three founders are equal shareholders in a company which now has an annual turnover in excess of $20 million, employs over 100 people and operates from three adjacent warehouses in Cambridge, Massachusetts.

Rouse, Charlie

b. 6 April 1924, Washington, DC, USA, d. 30 November 1988. After learning to play clarinet, Rouse took up the tenor saxophone; by the end of his teens he was proficient enough to be hired by **Billy Eckstine** for his bebop-orientated big band. Thereafter, Rouse played with **Dizzy Gillespie**, **Tadd Dameron** and **Fats Navarro**. At the end of the 40s he worked in an R&B band but also subbed with **Duke Ellington** and **Count Basie**. In the early 50s he played and recorded with a number of important small groups, including those led by **Clifford Brown**, **Art Farmer**, **Paul Quinichette** and **Oscar Pettiford**. In the second half of the decade he led his own small bands, was briefly with **Buddy Rich** and the **Gerry Mulligan** Concert Band and then, at the end of 1958, began a long and fruitful relationship with **Thelonious Monk** which lasted until 1970. During this period he made records with others, including **Donald Byrd** and **Benny Carter**, appearing on the latter's fine *Further Definitions*. Throughout the 70s and 80s he freelanced, sometimes leading bands, including Sphere, touring as a single or playing as accompanist. A distinctively quirky player, Rouse's long musical partnership with Monk had the advantage of bringing his work to a very wide audience and the disadvantages of linking him with an often overpowering personality, and enclosing him in a very specific fairly limited area of bop.

Albums: with Thelonious Monk *5 By Monk By 5* (1959), *Takin' Care Of Business* (Original Jazz Classics 1960), with Benny Carter *Further Definitions* (1961), *Unsung Hero* (Columbia 1962), *Bossa 'N' Bacchanal* (1962) with Monk *Misterioso* (1963-65), *Two Is One* (Strata East 1974), *Cinnamon Flower* (Rykodisk 1976), *Moment's Notice* (1977), *The Upper Manhattan Jazz Society* (Enja 1981), *Flight Path* (1983), with Paul Quinichette *Chase Is On* (Affinity 1986), with Stan Tracey *Playin' In The Yard* (Steam1987), *Epistrophy* (Landmark 1988).

Roussos, Demis

b. 15 June 1947, Alexandria, Egypt. This multi-lingual Greek's father was a semi-professional classical guitarist, and his mother a singer. At music college in Athens, Roussos mastered trumpet, double bass, organ and bouzouki. These talents were put to commercial use with his founder membership of **Aphrodite's Child** in 1963. Following 1968's million-selling 'Rain And Tears', he began a career as a solo vocalist which, after a slow start, hit its stride with *Forever And Ever*, a chart success in Europe. 'Happy To Be On An Island In The Sun', climbed into the UK Top 5 but it seemed as if the new sensation had dwindled as both 'Can't Say How Much I Love You' the follow-up and the second album struggled in their respective listings. However, Roussos was to return with a vengeance in 1976 with self-produced *The Roussos Phenomenon*, the first EP to top the UK singles chart. That same year, 'When Forever Has Gone' peaked at number 2. Within months, he bade farewell to the Top 40 with the EP *Kyrila*. Although general consumer reaction to subsequent releases has been modest, the impact of their perpetrator on theatre box office takings has been

immense. Roussos has lent a high euphonious tenor to essentially middle-of-the-road material. Style transcends content when, with dramatic *son et lumiere* effects and garbed in billowing robes, his Grand Entrance - like Zeus descending from Olympus - still leaves an indelible impression on every packed audience before he sings even a note.

Selected albums: *Forever And Ever* (1974), *Souvenirs* (1975), *Happy To Be* (1976), *My Only Fascination* (1976), *The Magic Of Demis Roussos* (1977), *Man Of The World* (1980), *Love And Life* (1978), *Magic* (1981), *Demis* (1982), *Greatest Hits* (1984), *The Golden Voice Of Demis Roussos* (1988), *My Friend The Wind* (1989), *The Complete Collection* (1992), *Lost In Love* (1993).

Roustabout

Elvis Presley's Hollywood career had become a treadmill by the time this 1964 feature was completed. The obligatory early-reel fight-scene over, the plot took the singer into a travelling carnival where, following mishaps and misunderstandings, he finds the inevitable true love. Presley's punishing schedule left him little space to develop acting skills, but in *Roustabout* he is lifted from stupor by the craft of co-star Barbara Stanwyck. Rightfully feted for her performances in a string of excellent films, notably *Double Indemnity* and *Sorry, Wrong Number*, she uses her talent to great effect herein, despite its flimsy premise. Her presence gives the film status it would otherwise lack and Presley rose to the occasion by contributing two superior recordings; the title track and a reading of the **Coasters**' 'Little Egypt'. However, *Roustabout* proved but a temporary pause in the decline of his once-promising acting career.

Routers

A USA instrumental group formed in the early 60s in the Los Angeles area, the original Routers were not the same musicians that eventually secured its only hit in 1962 with 'Let's Go (Pony)'. The original group consisted of musicians Mike Gordon, Al Kait, Bill Moody, Lynn Frazier and a fifth musician (unknown). Signed to **Warner Brothers Records**, the group was assigned to producer Joe Saraceno, who then proceeded to use studio musicians and not the actual group on the recording of 'Let's Go (Pony)'. The single reached the US charts number 19 and *Let's Go With The Routers*, was released, but it too was apparently recorded by session musicians such as **Hal Blaine** and **Plas Johnson**. Warner Brothers continued to issue singles under the name Routers, one of which, 'Sting Ray', reached the charts in 1963. There were three other Warner albums, followed by later Routers singles on **RCA Records** and **Mercury Records** (which also released an album) as late as 1973, after which the name was apparently shelved and the remaining members disbanded.

Albums: *Let's Go With The Routers* (1963), *The Routers Play 1963's Great Instrumental Hits* (1963), *Charge!* (1964), *Go Go Go With The Chuck Berry Songbook* (1965), *Superbird* (1973).

ROVA Saxophone Quartet

Jon Raskin (baritone/alto and soprano saxophones/Bb clarinet), Larry Ochs (b. 3 May 1949, New York City, New York, USA; tenor, alto and sopranino saxophones), Andrew Voigt (alto, soprano, sopranino saxophones/flute), Bruce Ackley (Eb alto and Bb clarinets/soprano saxophone). Formed on America's west coast in 1977, ROVA soon established itself as the *avant garde* representative on the saxophone quartet front, seeking to link the new, improvised saxophone languages of players such as **Anthony Braxton** and **Steve Lacy** with both the world of contemporary composition (from Ives to Stockhausen) and extremely left-field rock (Fred Frith, **Henry Kaiser**). ROVA recorded at first on Kaiser's Metalanguage label, but later releases have been on European labels such as **Black Saint**, Hat Hut and Sound Aspects. In 1983 and 1989 they toured the Soviet Union (the former visit documented on *Saxophone Diplomacy*, the latter on *This Time We Are Both* while other projects have included albums with Braxton (*The Aggregate*) and electronics expert Alvin Curran (*Electric Rags II*) plus a record of Lacy tunes (*Favorite Street*). In 1986 they initiated a special concert series, PreEchoes, in the San Francisco area, in which the group commissioned and collaborated on pieces by composers from all genres of contemporary music: participants to date have included Braxton, Curran, Frith, Kaiser, **Butch Morris**, **Terry Riley**, Richard Teitelbaum and **John Zorn**. Although essentially an improvising group, ROVA's music is densely-textured and closely integrates composition with freer modes. Their music has often been influenced by literary sources - for example, the title-track of their double-set *The Crowd* takes its name from Elias Canetti's book *Crowds And Power* and a continuing series of pieces is called *Trobas Clus* after a spontaneous form of poetry sung by the medieval troubadours of southern France. In 1989 Steve Adams replaced Andrew Voigt in the quartet. Voigt has since recorded a duo album with Braxton (*Kol Nidre*) and Larry Ochs has guested on Chris Brown's *The Room*.
Albums: *Cinema Rovaté* (1978), with Henry Kaiser *Daredevils* (1979), *The Removal Of Secrecy* (1979), with Andrea Centazzo *The Bay* (1979), *This, This, This, This* (1981), *As Was* (1981), with others *The Metalanguage Festival Of Improvised Music, Volume One: The Social Set* (1981), *Invisible Frames* (1982), *Favorite Street* (1984), *Saxophone Diplomacy* (1985, rec 1983), *The Crowd* (1986), *Beat Kennel* (1987), with Anthony Braxton *The Aggregate* (1988), with Alvin Curran *Electric Rags II* (1990), *Long On Logic* (1990), *This Time We Are Both* (1991, rec 1989). Solo: Andrew Voigt with Braxton *Kol Nidre* (1990).

Rover Boys

Formed in 1950 in Toronto, Canada, the Rover Boys were originally a vocal trio fashioned after the **Four Aces**. First tenor Larry Amato, second tenor Doug Wells (b. Southampton, England) and bass Al Osten relocated to Long Island, New York, USA in the early 50s and added lead vocalist Billy Albert (b. Brooklyn, New York USA) to the group. In 1954 they were discovered by disc jockey Bill Silbert and signed to Coral Records without any success. They moved to the **ABC**-Paramount label in 1956 and finally hit with 'Graduation Day', a US Top 20 placing, that year. Further recordings for ABC, **RCA** and United Artists failed to return the group to the top of the charts. The **Beach Boys** later covered the Rovers' only hit.

Rowan, Peter

Rowan's long career began as a member of two influential groups, the **Charles River Valley Boys** and **Bill Monroe**'s Bluegrass Boys. For two years he led the critically acclaimed **Earth Opera** with fellow traditional acolyte **David Grisman**, before joining **Sea Train** in 1970. Although both units were rock-based, Rowan maintained his bluegrass roots as a member of Muleskinner and Old And In The Way, and his subsequent solo work has placed the performer firmly within America's folk heritage. A prolific and engaging artist, his recordings have embraced Tex-Mex, country and ethnic material, each of which has been performed with empathy and purpose. His vast catalogue also includes albums with his siblings, the Rowan Brothers.
Selected albums: *Peter Rowan* (1978), *Mediciane Trail* (1980), *Peter Rowan* (1980), *Hiroshima Mon Amour* (1980), *Peter Rowan, Richard Green And The Red Hot Pickers* (1980), *Texican Badman* (1981), *Walls Of Time* (1981), *The Usual Suspect* (1982), *Peter Rowan And The Wild Stallions* (1983), *Peter Rowan And The Red Hot Pickers* (1984), *Revelry* (1984), *Festival Tapes* (1985), *T Is For Texas* (1985), *The First Whipoorwill* (1985), *New Moon Rising* (1988), *All On A Rising Day* (1991), *Awake Me In The New World* (1993), as the Rowan Brothers *Tree On A Hill* (Sugar Hill 1994), with David Grisman, Keith, Greene And White *Muleskinner* (1987).
Video: *Muleskinner - Live The Video* (1991).

Rowe, Dick

After overseeing the Stargazers's 1953 number 1, 'Broken Wings', he became recognized as a key producer and talent spotter of the UK record industry. Later 50s singers who also thrived under his aegis as **Decca**'s head of A&R included **Lita Roza**, **Dickie Valentine** and **Billy Fury**. For a while, Rowe left Decca to work for Top Rank for whom he procured a chart entrant for **John Leyton** via **Joe Meek**. When the label folded, he returned to Decca to minister further hits including **Jet Harris And Tony Meehan**'s 'Diamonds' in 1963. Rowe had been instrumental in the signing of several acts of the 50s svengali **Larry Parnes**, and was also a favourite with other managers, including **Phil Solomon** and **Don Arden**. Unfortunately, one manager with whom he failed to establish any rapport was **Brian Epstein**. For all his Top 10 triumphs, Rowe has earned a historical footnote as 'The Man Who Turned Down The Beatles' on the grounds that 'four-piece groups with guitars are finished'. He preferred the more pliant Dagenham sound of **Brian Poole And The Tremeloes** who auditioned that same 1962 day - but, in fairness, executives with other companies were just as blinkered. Provoked by the quartet's infuriating success with **EMI**, a chastised but cynical Rowe saturated Decca with Merseybeat acts in the hope that one of them might be a New Beatles. In January 1963 alone, he made off from Liverpool with the **Big Three**, **Beryl Marsden**, Billy Butler and, because their drummer was ex-Beatle **Pete Best**, Lee Curtis And The All-Stars. On **George Harrison**'s recommendation, Rowe signed the **Rolling Stones** in May. **Dave Berry** And The Cruisers, the **Nashville Teens**, **John Mayall**'s Bluesbreakers, **Them**, **Unit Four Plus Two**, the **Moody Blues**, the **Applejacks** and the **Zombies** were among further acquisitions but for each such hitmaking unit, there was a Beat Six, a Bobby Cristo and the Rebels, a Gonks, a Falling Leaves . . . Although Rowe continued to strike lucky with outfits such as **Small Faces**, **Animals** and **Marmalade**, he was more at home with 'real singers' like some of his pre-Beatles finds had been - and so it was that **Tom Jones** and **Engelbert Humperdinck** led a counter revolution on behalf of middle-of-the-road music when contracted by Rowe in the mid-60s, before his calculated withdrawal from a business in which his critical prejudices no longer fitted.

Rowe, Normie

b. Norman Rowe, 1 February 1947, Melbourne, Victoria, Australia. Whereas **Johnny O'Keefe** took the rockier and more outrageous side of rock, Normie Rowe took the singer/idol/clean-cut image styled rock/pop of the mid-60s. While his early career with backing band the Playboys, was certainly more rock-orientated, Rowe's subsequent recordings put him in MOR and AOR territory with ballads and pop songs. 'Que Que Sera', 'It Ain't Necessarily So', 'Tell Him I'm Not Home' and 'Ooh La La' remain his best-known releases, but he also recorded good versions of classic numbers such as 'Shakin' All Over' (**Johnny Kidd And The Pirates**) although they were less popular. Rowe spent the latter part of 1966 and most of 1967 in the UK without making a big impression. On his return to Australia, call-up papers for National Service were waiting. The next two years, which

included active service in Vietnam, saw his career stymied, as he was not able to regain his former popularity, but he has remained in the limelight, performing at nostalgia 60s concerts, stage shows, television and club appearances, and releasing the occasional record.

Albums: *It Ain't Necessarily So, But It Is* (1965), *Normie Rowe A Go Go* (1965), *Wonderful Feeling* (1966), *So Much Love From...* (1966), *Normie's Happening Hits* (1967), *Everything's Alright* (1968), *Normie's Top Tunes* (1969), *Hello* (1970), *Come Hear My Song* (1974), *That's The Way I Am* (1975), *Out Of The Norm* (1979), *Out Of The Blue* (1983), *Shakin' All Over* (1985).

Rowland, Kevin

(see **Dexys Midnight Runners**)

Rowles, Jimmy

b. 19 August 1918, Spokane, Washington, USA. A self-taught pianist, Rowles first attracted wide attention in Southern California in the early 40s as a member of small groups led by **Slim Gaillard**, **Lester Young** and others. Later in the decade he was with big bands led by **Woody Herman**, **Tommy Dorsey**, **Les Brown** and **Benny Goodman**, and was also in great demand as accompanist to singers. His reputation in this last respect was enhanced by his work with **Peggy Lee**, **Billie Holiday**, **Sarah Vaughan**, **Carmen McRae** and **Ella Fitzgerald**. His long years as a studio musician in Los Angeles, and later in New York, failed to dampen either his own talent or the regard in which he was held by musicians. He has recorded with **George Mraz**, **Al Cohn**, **Zoot Sims**, **Stan Getz**, **Dexter Gordon**, Herbie Harper, **Pepper Adams** and **Mel Lewis** among many others. A highly gifted player, his deft touch and a seemingly endless store of ideas, which he imparts with wit and skill, combine to make Rowles one of the best mainstream pianists in jazz. As an accompanist to singers he has few, if any, superiors. His many record albums are ample testimony to his talent yet he remains one of the least known of jazz players. His daughter Stacy (b. 11 September 1955) is an accomplished jazz trumpeter, and the Rowleses worked together in Los Angeles during the early 80s, later recording *Tell It Like It Is* in 1984.

Selected albums: *Rare - But Well Done* (1954), with Billie Holiday *Music For Torching* (1955), with Pepper Adams, Mel Lewis *Critics' Choice* (1957), *The Upper Classmen* (1957), *The Jimmy Rowles Sextet* (1958), *The Jimmy Rowles Quartet* i (1960), *The Jimmy Rowles Quintet* (1962), *Some Other Spring* (c.1970), with Carmen McRae *The Great American Songbook* (1971), *Sarah Vaughan And The Jimmy Rowles Quintet* (1972), *Jazz Is A Fleeting Moment* (1974), *The Special Magic Of Jimmy Rowles* (1974), *Zoot Sims Party* (1974), *Music's The Only Thing That's On My Mind* (1976), *Grand Paws* (1976), *Paws That Refresh* (1976), with Stan

Getz *The Peacocks* (Columbia 1977), *If I'm Lucky* (1977), *I Remember Bebop* (1977), *Heavy Love* (1977), *Isfahan* (Sonet 1978), *Scarab* (1978), *As Good As It Gets* (1978), *We Could Make Such Beautiful Music Together* (Xanadu 1978), *Nature Boy* (1978), with Red Mitchell *Red 'N' Me* (1978), *My Mother's Love* (1979), *Jimmy Rowles At The Philharmonic, Warsaw* (1979), *Jimmy Rowles Plays Duke Ellington And Billy Strayhorn* (1981), *In Paris* (Columbia 1981), *Profile* (Columbia 1982), with Stacy Rowles *Tell It Like It Is* (1984), *The Jimmy Rowles Quartet* ii (1985), *Looking Back* (Delos 1989), *Remember When* (Mastermix 1989), *Trio* (Capril 1991).

Rox

Hailing from Manchester, England, Rox were a glam rock band heavily influenced by **Kiss** and **Angel**, who sprang to life in 1981 (as Venom) with Mark Anthony (vocals), Red Hot Red (b. Ian Burke; guitar), Paul Diamond (b. Paul Hopwood; guitar), Gary Maunsell (bass) and Tony Fitzgerald (drums). They soon built up a loyal following and received a great deal of attention from *Sounds*. A year later Fitzgerald left and was replaced by Bernie Emerald (b. Bernard Nuttall). With the departure of Anthony they recruited their roadie, Kevin Read, who took on the name of 'Kick Ass' Kevin Kozak. After reported threats from Newcastle's black metal merchants of the same name they decided to change theirs to Rox. Maunsell was then replaced by Billy Beaman before they set out on tour. After the release of the EP, *Hot Love In The City*, in August 1992 they signed to **Music For Nations**. The group released a 12-inch EP, *Krazy Kutz*, a year later, before a higher profile tour and album, *Violent Breed*. Soon after Kozak was replaced by Anthony again, this time using the name Mark Savage. Despite the fact that there were no new records to promote they managed to hitch a ride on the **Quiet Riot** tour of the UK in 1984. The following year Diamond quit and the band split up (Diamond later turning up in a new group, Torino). Album: *Violent Breed* (Music For Nations 1983).

Roxanne Shanté

b. Lolita Shanté Gooden, 9 November 1969, Queens, New York, USA. Shanté came to prominence at the tender age of 14 via her belated answer record to **U.T.F.O.**'s 1984 rap hit, 'Roxanne, Roxanne'. Gooden was walking outside a New York housing project when she overheard three men discussing U.T.F.O.'s cancellation of a show they were promoting. In turn Gooden offered them a reply record. The onlookers, DJ Mister Magic, Tyrone Williams and **Marley Marl**, took her up on the offer. Her version, 'Roxanne's Revenge', mixed sassy, indignant raps with a funky backbeat. It was a massive hit, which sold over a quarter of a million copies in the New York area alone, and spawned a flood of answerback records (well over a hundred at the final

count), as rappers queued to take up the challenge. U.T.F.O. replied by sueing her for using their b-side as the rhythm track. Shanté was still only 14 years old, and forced to stay away from school because of all the attention. Her arrival was cemented by further singles 'Have A Nice Day' and 'Go On Girl', produced by Marley Marl, with lyrics penned by **Big Daddy Kane**. Her debut album saw the conscious rhymes of songs like 'Independent Woman' (though it was written for her by a man) spliced by saucy narratives like 'Feelin' Kinda Horny'. By 1986, Shanté was being edged from the centre of the female rap stage by **The Real Roxanne** (Adelaida Martinez) and her turntable wizard Hitman Howie Tee. Perhaps her most infamous post-'Roxanne' moment came with the release of 'Big Mama', which would see her take out her frustrations by dissing other female rappers **Queen Latifah**, **MC Lyte**, **Yo Yo** and **Monie Love**.
Albums: *Roxanne's Revenge* (Pop Art 1987), *Bad Sister* (Cold Chillin' 1989), *The Bitch Is Back* (Livin' Large 1992).

Roxette

Roxette, Sweden's first pop export of the 90s with the striking image and catchy blend of pop and rock, consist of Marie Fredriksson (b. 30 May 1958 Sweden) and Per Gessle (b. 12 January 1965, Halmstad, Sweden). Gessle became a solo star in the early 80s having previously played in the new wave band Gyllene Fider. He was 'discovered' by former **Abba** manager Thomas Johannson who was looking for songs for a **Frida** album. Meanwhile Fredriksson was playing on the singer/songwriter circuit. Johansson teamed them up in 1985 and they became Roxette. Recording at Gessle's studio in Halmstad they soon conquered Sweden and broke through in the USA thanks to the inclusion of the ballad, 'It Must Have Been Love', which was used on the soundtrack of the film *Pretty Woman*. 'The Look' was also a massive hit on both sides of the Atlantic. Other singles like 'Dressed For Success' and 'Joyride' have continued to keep the band high in the charts.
Albums: *Look Sharp* (1988), *Joyride* (1991), *Tourism* (1992), *Crash! Boom! Bang!* (EMI 1994).

Roxy Music

This highly regarded and heavily influential UK group came together in January 1971 with a line-up comprising **Bryan Ferry** (b. 26 September 1945, Washington, Co. Durham, England; vocals, keyboards); **Brian Eno** (b. Brian Peter George St. Baptiste de la Salle Eno, 15 May 1948, Woodbridge, Suffolk, England; electronics, keyboards); Graham Simpson (bass) and Andy Mackay (b. 23 July 1946, England). Over the next year, several new members came and went including drummer Dexter Lloyd, guitarist Roger Bunn and former **Nice** guitarist David

O'List. By early 1972, a relatively settled line-up emerged with the recruitment of Paul Thompson (b. 13 May 1951, Jarrow, Northumberland, England; drums) and **Phil Manzanera** (b. Philip Targett Adams (b. 31 January 1951, London, England; guitar). Roxy's self-titled 1972 debut album for **Island Records** was a musical pot pourri, with Ferry's 50s-tinged vocals juxtaposed alongside distinctive 60s rhythms and 70s electronics. The novel sleeve concept underlined Roxy's art school background, while the group image (from 50s quiffs to futurist lurex jackets) emphasized their stylistic diversity. Reviews verged on the ecstatic, acclaiming the album as one of the finest debuts in living memory. Ferry's quirky love songs were often bleak in theme but strangely effervescent, fusing romanticism with bitter irony. On 'If There Was Something', for example, a quaint melody gradually descends into marvellous cliche ('I would do anything for you . . . I would climb the ocean blue') and bathos ('I would put roses round your door . . . growing potatoes by the score'). 'The Bob (Medley)' was another clever touch; a montage of war-time Britain presented in the form of a love song. As a follow-up to their first album, the group issued 'Virginia Plain', a classic single combining Ferry's cinematic interests and love of surrealistic art. During the same period, Simpson departed and thereafter Roxy went through a succession of bassists, including John Porter, John Gustafson, John Wetton, Rik Kenton, Sal Maida, Rick Wills and Gary Tibbs.

After failing to break into America, the group scored a second UK Top 10 hit with 'Pyjamarama' and released *For Your Pleasure*, produced by **Chris Thomas**. Another arresting work, the album featured the stunning 'Do The Strand', arguably the group's most effective rock workout, with breathtaking saxophone work from Mackay. 'Beauty Queen' and 'Editions Of You' were contrastingly strong tracks and the album's centrepiece was 'In Every Dream Home A Heartache', Ferry's paean to an inflatable rubber doll and a chilling evocation of consumerist alienation. On 21 June 1973, Eno left, following a series of disagreements with Ferry over his role in the group. The replacement was former **Curved Air** violinist Eddie Jobson, who willingly accepted the role of hired musician rather than taking on full membership. After taking time off to record a solo album of cover versions, Ferry took Roxy on a nation-wide tour to promote the excellent *Stranded*. 'Street Life', the first album track to be issued as a single, proved another Top 10 hit. The song neatly summed up his contradictory attitude to city life: 'You may be stranded if you stick around — and that's really something'. The epic 'A Song For Europe', with a melody borrowed from **George Harrison**'s 'When My Guitar Gently Weeps', was another tour of alienation. The most complex and rewarding piece on the album, however, was 'Mother Of Pearl', a

macrocosm of Ferry's lounge-lizard image, complete with plastic goddesses and lifeless parties.

Following his second solo album, Ferry completed work on Roxy's fourth album, *Country Life*, another strong set ranging from the uptempo single 'All I Want Is You' to the aggressive 'The Thrill Of It All' and the musically exotic 'Triptych'. In the USA, the album sleeve was withdrawn due to its risqué portrayal of two semi-naked women, and Roxy took advantage of the controversy by undertaking two consecutive US tours. Their hopes of capturing stadium-sized audiences ultimately remained unfulfilled. In spite of a challenging pilot single, 'Love Is The Drug', Roxy's next album, *Siren*, proved a major disappointment, lacking the charm and innovation of its predecessors. Only 'Both Ends Burning', which hinted at a disco direction, gave evidence of real vocal passion. The album was followed by a three-year gap during which the individual members pursued various solo projects. The 1979 comeback, *Manifesto*, received mixed reviews but included two excellent hit singles, 'Angel Eyes' and the fatalistic 'Dance Away'. The succeeding *Flesh And Blood* was a more accomplished work with some strong arrangements, including a reworking of **Wilson Pickett's** 'In The Midnight Hour' and an unusual interpretation of the **Byrds**' 'Eight Miles High'. Two UK hit singles were also in attendance: 'Over You' and 'Oh Yeah (On The Radio)'. In 1981 Roxy finally achieved their first number 1 single with 'Jealous Guy', an elegiac tribute to its recently assassinated composer **John Lennon**. The following year, Roxy released their final album *Avalon*, which topped the album charts and was praised by most critics. Roxy Music left behind a substantial body of work whose sheer diversity contributed significantly to the multifarious musical styles that followed in their wake.

Albums: *Roxy Music* (1972), *For Your Pleasure* (1973), *Stranded* (1973), *Country Life* (1974), *Siren* (1975), *Viva! Roxy Music* (1976), *Manifesto* (1979), *Flesh And Blood* (1980), *Avalon* (1981). Compilations: *Greatest Hits* (1977), *The First Seven Albums* (1981), *The Atlantic Years 1973-1980* (1983), *Street Life - 20 Great Hits* (1986), *The Ultimate Collection* (1988), *The Compact Collection* (1992, 3-CD box set).

Further reading: *Roxy Music: Style With Substance - Roxy's First Ten Years*, Johnny Rogan. *The Bryan Ferry Story*, Rex Balfour. *Bryan Ferry & Roxy Music*, Barry Lazell and Dafydd Rees.

Roy, Harry

b. Harry Lipman, 12 January 1900, London, England, d. 1 February 1971. Influenced by a visit to the UK by the **Original Dixieland Jazz Band** in 1919, Roy and his brother Sidney formed a dance band, the Darnswells, with Harry on saxophone and clarinet and Sidney on piano. During the 20s, under various names such as the Original Lyrical Five and the Original

Crichton Lyricals, the combination played prestige venues including the Alhambra, the London Coliseum, and spent three years at the Café de Paris. They also toured South Africa, Australia and Germany and had a four-month spell in Paris. By the early 30s Roy was fronting the band under his own name, broadcasting successfully from the Café Anglais and the Mayfair Hotel and working the variety circuit. In 1935 he married Miss Elizabeth Brooke, daughter of the white Rajah of Sarawak, nicknamed Princess Pearl, and appeared to good effect with her in two film-musicals, *Rhythm Racketeer* (1937) and *Everything Is Rhythm* (1940). In 1938, Harry Roy and his band toured South America, and during World War II played for the troops in the Middle East with ENSA. After the War he went to the USA, but was refused a work permit, so he re-formed his UK band and in 1949 had a big hit with his own composition, 'Leicester Square Rag'. During the 50s he recorded and appeared only spasmodically, and by 1960 was running a restaurant, the Diners' Club, which was ultimately destroyed by fire. In 1969, he led the orchestra for the successful musical *Oh, Clarence* at London's Lyric theatre, but his health was deteriorating and he died in London in 1971. The Harry Roy band did not appeal to the purists although musicians of the calibre of **Joe Daniels**, Nat Temple, **Stanley Black** and **Ray Ellington** passed through the ranks. However, the public appreciated the novelty numbers, the pseudo rags, and Roy's exuberant vocals, all of which made it one of the most popular and entertaining bands of its time.

Selected albums: *The Golden Age Of British Dance Bands* (1969), *The World Of Harry Roy* (1971), *Are You Listening?* (1973), *Raggin' The Rags* (1982), *Bugle Call Rag* (1982), *There Goes That Song Again* (1983), *The Golden Age Of Harry Roy And His Orchestra* (1983), *Hot-Cha-Ma-Cha-Cha* (1986), *Everybody's Swingin' It Now* (1987), *Truckin' On Down* (1988), *Let's Swing It* (1988), *Mayfair Nights* (1988), *Greetings From You* (1993).

Royal Court Of China

This Nashville, Tennessee quartet were formed in 1984 by Joe Blanton (vocals, rhythm guitar), Chris Mekow (drums), Robert Logue (bass) and Oscar Rice (guitar), taking their name from a reference to the highest form of Chinese opium, which had originally been the name chosen by **Jimmy Page** and **Paul Rodgers** for the group which became the **Firm**. Impressive local gigging and the self-financed *Off The Beat 'n' Path* EP led to a contract with **A&M**, but with Logue and Rice's penchant for a folkier sound, the album tended more towards **REM** in style than the hard rock direction which the other two preferred, and following a tour with **REO Speedwagon**, the band split. Blanton and Mekow retained both name and deal, and recruited bassist Drew Cornutt and guitarist Josh Weinberg, although the latter was replaced by Jeff Mays when he

failed to live up to expectations in the studio. *Geared And Primed*, produced by Vic Maile, was an impressively diverse album, following a harder direction while retaining the more rootsy guitar elements of their previous release, particularly on the lighter material. However, the album lacked the depth of quality material to make it a success, and the band faded from sight.

Albums: *The Royal Court Of China* (A&M 1987), *Geared And Primed* (A&M 1989).

Royal Guardsmen

As if to prove just about any topic could become a hit song, the Royal Guardsmen made a career in the mid-60s out of writing about Snoopy, the dog in the *Peanuts* comic strip. The group formed in 1966 in Ocala, Florida, USA and consisted of Chris Nunley (vocals), Tom Richards (lead guitar), Barry Winslow (rhythm guitar/vocals), Bill Balogh (guitar), Billy Taylor (organ) and John Burdette (drums). That same year, under the management of Phil Gernhard, the group signed to Laurie Records and recorded a novelty tune, 'Snoopy Vs. The Red Baron', which ultimately peaked at number 2 in the US chart in January 1967 and eventually reached number 8 in the UK chart that same year. Capitalizing on the debut's success, they recorded further Snoopy songs - 'The Return Of The Red Baron', 'Snoopy's Christmas' and 'Snoopy For President' - as well as other novelty songs. One 1967 single, 'Airplane Song (My Airplane)', was written by **Michael Martin Murphey**, who had his own US number 3 hit in 1975 with 'Wildfire'. The Royal Guardsmen disbanded in 1968.

Albums: *Snoopy Vs. The Red Baron* (1967), *Return Of The Red Baron* (1967), *Snoopy And His Friends* (1967), *Snoopy For President* (1968).

Royal Rasses
(see **Prince Lincoln**)

Royal Scots Dragoon Guards

One of the more unlikely records to top the UK charts during the 70s was an instrumental version of the traditional 'Amazing Grace', already a hit courtesy of **Judy Collins**' evocative reading. The Pipes, Drums And Military Band of the Royal Scots Dragoon Guards had first recorded their haunting version on the album *Farewell To The Greys* their tribute to the Royal Scots Greys. The stirring bagpipes caught the attention of BBC Radio 2, however, and they began playing 'Amazing Grace' which received a favourable response from radio listeners. By April 1972, the song was number 1, where it stayed for a lengthy five weeks. Two further hits followed that same year, 'Heykens Serenade/The Day Is Over' and 'Little Drummer Boy', before the Dragoon Guards ended their chart run.

Albums: *Farewell To The Greys* (1972), *Amazing Grace* (1972), *The Amazing Sound Of The Royal Scots Dragoon Guards* (1984), *Golden Sounds Of The Royal Scots Dragoon Guards* (1984), *Royal Scots Dragoon Guards* (1986). Compilation: *Spotlight On The Royal Scots Dragoon Guards* (1984).

Royal Showband

The most popular Irish showband of the 60s, the Royal originally formed in 1957 and turned fully professional two years later, with a line-up comprising Michael Coppinger (saxophone/accordion), **Brendan Bowyer** (vocals/trombone), Gerry Cullen (piano), Jim Conlan (guitar), Eddie Sullivan (saxophone), Charlie Matthews (drums) and Tom Dunphy (bass). After coming under the management of the astute T.J. Byrne, the Royal were poised to emerge as the biggest act in Eire, playing almost every night to audiences in excess of 2,000. Ballroom gods, they ushered in the era of the showband and in Brendan Bowyer boasted the genre's most potent sex symbol. In 1961, they toured the UK, were supported by the **Beatles** in Liverpool and received the Carl Alan Award for their prodigious box-office success. At some halls firemen were called upon to hose unruly crowds, as the group's popularity reached unforeseen proportions. Back in Ireland, they were the first showband to record a single, with Tom Dunphy singing lead on the infectious, quasi-traditional 'Come Down The Mountain Katie Daly'. That was just the start. The Royal soon notched up four successive number 1 hit singles: 'Kiss Me Quick', 'No More', 'Bless You' and 'The Hucklebuck'. The latter became one of the best-selling dance records in Irish chart history. Dunphy and Bowyer continued the chart-topping spree with 'If I Didn't Have A Dime' and the cash-in 'Don't Lose Your Hucklebuck Shoes', respectively. Having conquered Eire, the band switched their attention to Las Vegas where they became a regular attraction from the late 60s onwards. In 1971, Bowyer and Dunphy rocked the Irish music world by leaving Eire's most famous septet to form the showband supergroup, the **Big 8**. Although the star duo were briefly replaced by vocalists Lee Lynch and Billy Hopkins, the Royal collapsed within a year. Their founding member Tom Dunphy died tragically in a car accident on 29 July 1975. The abrupt dissolution of the Royal at the beginning of the 70s symbolically ended the showband domination of the previous era, to which they had provided an incalculable contribution.
Album: *The One Nighters* (HMV 1964).

Royal Teens

Formed 1956 in Bergen County, New Jersey, USA, the Royal Teens are remembered primarily for the 1958 rock 'n' roll novelty number 'Short Shorts'. The group was originally a quartet called the Royal Tones, including pianist Bob Gaudio, saxophonist Bill

Crandall, bassist Billy Dalton and drummer Tom Austin. Influenced by black music, the group worked as back-up band to travelling R&B artists, and Gaudio and Austin had written an instrumental dance song as a warm-up for their stage show. Adding the lyrics 'Who wears short shorts? We wear short shorts', the song was heard by an executive of **ABC**-Paramount Records, which signed the group; the single hit number 3 in the USA. At that time Crandall was replaced by Larry Quagliano and Dalton also left, to be replaced by **Al Kooper**. Joe Villa, formerly of the doo-wop group the Three Friends, was added as vocalist, making the group a quintet. The group scored one further chart single for ABC and one for **Capitol Records** before starting to disintegrate in 1960. Although some members continued with the unit until 1965, recording for such labels as Mighty, All New, Jubilee, Blue Jay and Swan, there was no further success. Gaudio went on to become a founding member of the **Four Seasons** and a top producer. Kooper later formed the **Blues Project** and **Blood, Sweat And Tears**. The Royal Teens never recorded an album.

Royal Trux

New York duo comprising Neil Hagerty (vocals/guitar), and Jennifer Herrema (vocals, sundry instruments), who specialise in a drug-addled, chemically fuelled dirty rock habit. Royal Trux was formed in 1985 while Hagerty was still playing guitar in **Pussy Galore**. He was behind the latter's idea to cover the **Rolling Stones**' *Exile On Main Street* in its entirety. The duo debuted with an untitled 1988 album, and a declared ambition of retracing the US noise scene back to its primal roots (**MC5** etc). Descriptions like 'garage psychobilly punk' proliferated in the press. 1990's *Twin Infinitives* double set saw songs based on the works of science fiction writer Philip K Dick, alongside the riffs of **Led Zeppelin**, **Rolling Stones** and **AC/DC**, music which had dominated their youth. Recorded in three months in a deserted warehouse, the touring schedule that ensued saw them physically and aurally confront their audience, *ala* the **Swans**. In truth Hagerty and Herrema were both heavily strung out on heroin. A third album, also untitled, was released in 1992, and largely essayed their heroin fixation/trials. One result of their ordeals is that they are currently based in Washington DC, having found the ethos of New York a little destructive. Their fourth album, and the first to see them garner serious UK and European press, was recorded in a Virginian country home in 1993. *Thank You* saw them arrange a more permanent band together, and also featured the help of producer David Briggs, a celebrated partner of **Neil Young**. It included the single 'Map Of The City', as well as confident R&B and rock numbers such as 'Shadow Of The Wasp' and 'Night To Remember'.
Albums: *Untitled* (1988), *Twin Infinitives* (1990, double

album), *Untitled* (1992), *Cats And Dogs* (1993), *Thank You* (Virgin 1995).

Royal Wedding

Inspired by the wedding of Princess Elizabeth to Philip Mountbatten in 1947, this film, which was released by MGM four years later in 1951, was also loosely based on the experiences of one of its stars, **Fred Astaire**. In 1928, he and his sister Adele appeared in the London production of the stage musical **Funny Face**. They were feted by the city's fashionable high society, and, eventually, Adele broke up their double act and married Lord Charles Cavendish in 1932. **Alan Jay Lerner**'s screenplay for *Royal Wedding* also concerns a brother and sister dance team, Tom and Ellen Bowen (Astaire and **Jane Powell**), who take their hit Broadway show, *Every Night At Seven*, to the British capital where Ellen marries her Lord John Brindale (Peter Lawford) and gives up her show business career. Tom also finds happiness in London with a music hall performer (played by Sarah Churchill, daughter of Britain's new Prime Minister in 1951), and all three couples (including Elizabeth and Philip) get married on the same November day. **Burton Lane** (music) and Alan Jay Lerner (lyrics) wrote the score which contained one of the longest song titles ever: 'How Could You Believe Me When I Said I Love You When You Know I've Been A Liar All My Life.' That number provided a humorous no-punches-pulled knockabout duet for Astaire and Powell, a young and up and coming singer-actress who surprised a lot of people with her all-round versatility in this film. She also had the tender 'Too Late Now' and 'Open Your Eyes', while Fred, amazingly innovative as usual, danced with a hat stand in 'Sunday Jumps', and appeared to dance on the floor, walls and ceiling of a room filled with furniture, accompanied by 'You're All The World To Me'. Illustrated lectures have since been given as to how that last feat was accomplished. Nick Castle (with an uncredited assist from Astaire, was responsible for the choreography). The rest of the score included 'I Left My Hat In Haiti', 'Open Your Eyes', 'Ev'ry Night At Seven', 'The Happiest Day Of My Life', and 'What A Lovely Day For A Wedding'. **Stanley Donen** directed the film, which was photographed in Technicolor and re-titled *Wedding Bells* when it was released in the UK.

Royal, Billy Joe

b. 3 April 1942, Valdosta, Georgia, USA. Raised in Marietta, Georgia, Royal's father owned a truck-driving company and the family moved to Atlanta when Royal was aged 10. At school he entertained in school concerts, and after graduation, worked for two years in a nightclub in Savannah, Georgia. Starting in 1962, Royal made several unsuccessful singles, but then teamed with a local songwriter/producer, **Joe South**.

In 1965 they made the US Top 20 with 'Down In The Boondocks' and 'I Knew You When', which in theme and vocal delivery was similar to **Gene Pitney**'s hits. Royal's subsequent records were not so successful but he failed to appreciate the potential of 'Rose Garden' as it later became a hit for **Lynn Anderson**. In 1969, he returned to the US Top 20 with 'Cherry Hill Park' and worked for several years in Las Vegas. Royal, whose early influences came from country musicians, turned to country music and his 1987 *Looking Ahead* spent a year on the US country albums chart. His US country hits include: 'Burned Like A Rocket', 'I'll Pin A Note On Your Pillow', 'I Miss You Already' and a duet with **Donna Fargo**, 'Members Only'. He has also revived **Aaron Neville**'s 'Tell It Like It Is' and **Johnny Tillotson**'s 'It Keeps Right On A-Hurtin''. Despite his return to the US charts, Royal has yet to improve in the UK on his Number 38 position for 'Down In The Boondocks'.

Albums: *Down In The Boondocks* (1965), *Billy Joe Royal* (1965), *Hush* (1967), *Cherry Hill Park* (1969), *Looking Ahead* (1987), *The Royal Treatment* (1987), *Tell It Like It Is* (1989), *Out Of The Shadows* (1990).

Royal, Ernie

b. 6 February 1921, Los Angeles, California, USA, d. 16 March 1983. Royal began playing trumpet as a child and while at Jefferson High School numbered among his fellow pupils future jazz artists such as **Dexter Gordon**, **Chico Hamilton**, Vi Redd, Jackie Kelso and **Melba Liston**. He played in a number of bands in Southern California in the late 30s and early 40s, including those led by **Les Hite** and **Lionel Hampton**, in both of which he followed in the footsteps of his older brother, **Marshal Royal**. In the post-war years he was with **Count Basie**, **Woody Herman** and, briefly, **Duke Ellington**. After a spell in Europe in the early 50s he returned to his home town and played in small groups with **Wardell Gray**, **Gerry Mulligan**, **Sonny Criss**, **Sonny Rollins**, **Cannonball Adderley**, **Jimmy Rowles**, Hamilton, **Red Mitchell** and others. He also played in **Stan Kenton**'s big band. From the late 50s to the early 70s he worked mostly in studios in New York but took time out to play with **Gil Evans**, **Quincy Jones**, **Oliver Nelson** and others on record dates and for special tours. An experienced musician with often under-used melodic gifts, Royal died in 1983.

Albums: *Accent On Trumpet* (1954), with Sonny Rollins *Brass/Trio* (1958), with Quincy Jones *The Birth Of A Band!* (1959), with Gil Evans *Blues In Orbit* (1969).

Royal, Marshal

b. 5 December 1912, Sapulpa, Oklahoma, USA, d. 8 May 1995, Los Angeles, Califotnia, USA. Royal learned several instruments as a child, finally concentrating on alto saxophone in his teenage years.

In the 30s he moved to Los Angeles and played there in several bands, including a long spell with **Les Hite**. Among his fellow musicians in this band, were his brother, **Ernie Royal**, and **Lionel Hampton**. When Hampton formed his own band in 1940 Royal joined and became the band's straw boss, ruthlessly drilling the younger musicians. One of them, **Dexter Gordon**, later paid tribute to Royal as being largely responsible for teaching him to breathe and phrase correctly. After military service in World War II, he played briefly in New York before returning to Los Angeles and work in the studios. In 1951 he joined **Count Basie**'s small group and when Basie reformed his big band Royal took on similar duties to those he had carried out for Hampton. Under his watchful eye, the Basie band became a crisp and efficient outfit. He remained in the band for 20 years, touring the world several times but then, while absent due to ill-health, was quietly replaced. Resident once more in Los Angeles, Royal became lead alto with the big bands of **Bill Berry** and **Frank Capp-Nat Pierce**. He also played many club and festival dates, recording with **Dave Frishberg**, **Snooky Young** and others. In 1989 he returned to Europe to play club and festival dates, sometimes alone, at other times with Berry and **Buster Cooper**. Also in 1989, Royal visited Japan with the Basie-style big band co-led by **Frank Wess** and **Harry Edison**, receiving a rapturous welcome from audiences who revelled in his soaring romanticism. Although Royal's main contribution to jazz may well have been his important, if relatively anonymous, work as lead alto in a succession of fine bands, for the fans it was the rich flowing solos, especially on romantic ballads, that made him universally popular.

Albums: with Count Basie *Basie* (1957), *Marshal Royal With Gordon Jenkins And His Orchestra* (1960), *Back To Basie* (1962), with Bill Berry *Hot & Happy* (1974), with Berry *Hello Rev* (1976), with Frank Capp-Nat Pierce *Juggernaut* (1976), with Dave Frishberg *Getting Some Fun Out Of Life* (1977), with Snooky Young *Snooky And Marshal's Album* (1978), with Berry *Shortcake* (1978), *First Chair* (1978), *Royal Blue* (1980), with Capp-Pierce *Juggernaut Strikes Again!* (1981), with Frank Wess-Harry Edison *Dear Mr Basie* (1989).

Royalettes

A female R&B vocal group from Baltimore, Maryland, USA. Members were sisters Anita and Sheila Ross (lead), Terry Jones, and Veronica Brown. The group was discovered in 1962 when they won a talent contest sponsored by Baltimore disc jockey legend Buddy Deane. Their prize was a recording contest on Chancellor Records, but the two releases did not click with the public. A single for **Warner Brothers** did nothing either. In 1964 the Royalettes were signed to **MGM** and were teamed up with arranger/producer

Teddy Randazzo, and he applied a little of the same magic that he used in recording all the **Little Anthony And The Imperials** hits for DCP during the 60s. The result was the girls' first national hit with 'It's Gonna Take A Miracle' (number 28 R&B, number 41 pop), from 1965, on which Randazzo created a sound that was indistinguishable from Little Anthony. The girls broke out of the Little Anthony mode with their second hit 'I Want To Meet Him' (number 26 R&B, number 72 pop), also from 1965. The Royalettes were not able to get on the charts again, despite the release of some excellent songs, notably 'Only When You're Lonely' (1966). It failed to chart perhaps because Chicago-based singer Holli Maxwell had already scored in several markets with her version of the song. After a single for Roulette in 1967 failed to attract an audience the Royalettes broke up.

Albums: *It's Gonna Take A Miracle* (MGM 1965), *The Elegant Sound Of The Royalettes* (MGM 1966).

Royals

Formed by Roy Cousins (b. c.1945, Jamaica, West Indies) in 1964, alongside Bertram Johnson, Keith Smith and Errol Wilson, though other than Cousins the line-up remained largely fluid. The Royals recorded for **Duke Reid** and Federal in the mid-60s, and for **Coxsone Dodd** in 1967, though no releases were forthcoming until 1968 when they cut 'Never See Come See' for producer **Joe Gibbs**, a dig at the **Pioneers**. The following year the group recorded 'Never Gonna Give You Up' for Byron Smith, 'Pick Out Me Eye', and, in 1969, '100 Pounds Of Clay' for Lloyd Daley. Though they achieved a measure of popular, if not fiscal success with these records, Cousins disbanded the group and took a two year sabbatical. He eventually saved enough money from his job in the Jamaican Post Office to finance a self-produced single, 'Down Comes The Rain', issued in Jamaica on his own Tamoki label. In 1973 the Royals again recorded the classic 'Pick Up The Pieces', the success of which prompted Coxsone to release his original version of the song, which had been languishing ignored since the group's stint with him in the late 60s. This too became very popular, particularly the rhythm which has been versioned countless times since.

More self-produced releases followed throughout the decade including 'Promised Land', 'When You Are Wrong', 'Ghetto Man', 'Blacker Black', 'Only For A Time' and 'Sufferer Of The Ghetto', all collected on the essential *Pick Up The Pieces*, which ranks alongside the finest works of contemporaries like the **Abyssinians**, the **Wailing Souls** and the **Mighty Diamonds**. Cousins also produced records by other artists, including 'Jah Jah Children' by the **Kingstonians**, 'Genuine Way' by Lloyd Ruddock (**King Tubby**'s brother), 'Heart In Pain' by Vinni O'Brien, 'Monkey Fashion' by **I Roy** and 'Way Of

Life' by **Gregory Isaacs**, many included on the various artists set, *Herb Dust Volume 1* (1983). In 1975, the Royals split yet again, the rest of the group going on to record for **Channel One** as the Jayes. Roy enlisted two new members with whom he recorded the single, 'Make Believe', followed by two more albums, *Ten Years After* and *Israel Be Wise*, featuring **Heptones** Barry Llewelyn and Naggo Morris on harmonies. Cousins has been resident in the UK since the early 80s, concentrating mainly on producing other artists for his Wambesi and Dove labels, including the **Gaylads**, Derrick Pitter, **Cornell Campbell**, **Earl Sixteen** (*Julia* and *Crazy Woman*), **Prince Far I**, Charlie Chaplin (*Diet Rock*) and **Don Carlos** (*Plantation*).
Albums: *Pick Up The Pieces* (Magnum 1977), *Ten Years After* (Ballistic 1978), *Israel Be Wise* (Ballistic 1978), *Moving On* (Kingdom 1983). Compilation: *Royals Collection* (Trojan 1983).

Royaltones
This rock 'n' roll instrumental group came from Dearborn, Michigan, USA. With its honking saxophone-dominated records, the Royaltones typified the sound of rock 'n' roll bands of the late 50s, before the guitar sound had become dominant. The group was formed in 1957 as the Paragons, and consisted of George Katsakis on tenor saxophone, Karl Kay on guitar, and two brothers, Mike Popoff on piano and Greg Popoff on drums. 'Bad Boy' was a US Top 20 hit in 1958. 'Flamingo Express' went to number 82 in 1961. The Royaltones broke up in the mid-60s long after their sound had become passe.

Roza, Lita
b. 1926, Liverpool, England. A popular singer, particularly during the 50s, whose name is forever associated with the renowned **Ted Heath** Orchestra. At the age of 12 she appeared in a Christmas pantomime in Norwich, and, at 15, took part in the revue *Black Velvet*, which starred top UK comedian Ted Ray. After working outside showbusiness for a while, she became the resident vocalist at the New York restaurant in the northern seaside resort of Southport. By the time she was 17 she had joined **Harry Roy**'s Band for a tour of the Middle East, and then sang with Art Thompson's group at London's Embassy Club. Later, she toured with **Edmundo Ros** before moving to the USA, where she stayed until 1950. On her return to the UK, Roza successfully auditioned for Ted Heath by singing on one of his popular London Palladium Swing Concerts, and was allocated the middle stool, between **Dickie Valentine** and **Dennis Lotis**. During her stay of over four years with Heath, she recorded with his band, and in her own right. In 1951 she had a big hit with Irving Gordon's 'Allentown Jail', followed by other successful sides, such as 'High Noon', 'Half As Much', 'Walkin' to Missouri', 'I Went To

Your Wedding', 'Why Don't You Believe Me' and 'Hi-Lili, Hi-Lo'. In 1953 she topped the UK chart with **Bob Merrill**'s novelty, '(How Much Is) That Doggie In The Window', a cover of **Patti Page**'s enormous US hit. Her other chart entries included 'Hey There', the big ballad from **The Pajama Game**, which was also successful in the UK for **Rosemary Clooney**, **Sammy Davis Jnr.** and **Johnnie Ray**; and, finally, 'Jimmy Unknown'. She also sang 'A Tear Fell' on *All Star Hit Parade*, a single record which also featured songs by **Joan Regan**, **David Whitfield**, Dennis Lotis, **Winifred Atwell** and **Dave King**. When Roza left Heath, she toured the UK variety circuit and appeared extensively on radio and television in shows such as *Off The Record*, *The Jack Jackson Show*, *Saturday Spectacular*, *Music Shop* and the top pop music programmes, *6.5 Special* and *Oh Boy!*; she also featured in the ITV series *The Ted Heath Story*. She recorded several albums, including one entitled *Drinka Lita Roza Day* (presumably a play on the television advertising slogan: 'Drinka Pinta Milka Day'), but eventually became yet another victim of the rapidly changing musical climate. In later years she has made television and concert appearances with her contemporaries, celebrating the good times of years gone by, and was one of the 'Four Stars Of The 50s', along with **Jimmy Young**, Dickie Valentine and Joan Regan, on the double album *Unchained Melodies*.
Selected albums: *Between The Devil And The Deep Blue Sea* (1958), *Me On A Carousel* (1959), *Drinka Lita Roza Day* (1961), *Love Songs For Night People* (1964), *You're Driving Me Crazy* (1983), *Somewhere, Somehow, Someday* (1990). Compilation: includes performances with Dennis Lotis and the Ted Heath Orchestra *Lita Roza* (1977).

Rozalla
Zambian born rave queen, whose singles like 'Are You Ready To Fly?' were surefire dancefloor meteorites. She began life singing over records at fashion shows and nightclubs at age 13. She then performed with a band in Zimbabwe, going on to become that nation's most famous famale singer. At the age of 18 she appeared as an extra (a prostitute) in Richard Chamberlain's *King Solomon's Mines*. Despite parental misgivings, she subsequently launched a recording career in England. Singles like 'Everybody's Free To Feel Good' (created by 3 Man Island/**Band Of Gypsies** duo Nigel Swanston and Tim Cox) duly apeared on **Pulse 8**, who released her debut ablum. This came after something of a legal squabble, with Rozalla attempting to take the studio tapes to **Epic**. Pulse 8 objected and won their day in court.
Albums: *Everybody's Free* (Pulse 8 1992), *Look No Further* (Epic 1995).

Rozsa, Miklos
b. 18 April 1907, Budapest, Hungary. An important composer for films from the early late 30s until the

early 80s, who had an equally distinguished career in the world of classical music. Rozsa began to play the piano at the age of five and soon added the violin to his studies. He gave his first public performance when he was seven, playing a movement from a Mozart violin concerto and conducting a children's orchestra in Haydn's 'Toy Symphony'. In his teens Rozsa attended Leipzig University and, during his four years there, completed his first serious compositions. His big breakthrough came in 1934 with his 'Theme, Variations, And Finale (Opus 13)'. A year later he moved to London to write a ballet, and was invited to compose the music for Alexandra Korda's film, *Knight Without Armour*, starring Robert Donat and **Marlene Dietrich**. The successful outcome marked the beginning of Rozsa's five-year association with Korda which, in the late 30s, produced *The Squeaker*, *The Divorce Of Lady X*, *The Spy In Black* and *The Four Feathers*. In 1940, Rozsa went to Hollywood to finish work on *The Thief Of Baghdad* and then scored *Sundown* and *The Jungle Book*. All three films gained him Oscar nominations, and together with *The Four Feathers*, were designated as his 'Oriental' period. Rozsa was nominated again, for *Lydia*, before Korda shut down London Films for the duration of World War II. Rozsa moved to Paramount where he provided the 'stark, powerful, dissonant score' for 'the archetypal film noir of the 40s', Billy Wilder's *Double Indemnity* (1944), followed by other Wilder movies such as *Five Graves To Caioro* and *The Lost Weekend* (1945). In the latter, Rozsa introduced a new instrument, the theremin, 'an ideal accompaniment to torture'. It was one of around 10 'psychological' movies with which Rozsa was involved during his career. Another, in the same year, was Alfred Hitchcock's *Spellbound*, for which Rozsa won his first Academy Award for a 'bleak and exciting' score.

In the late 40s, besides Paramount, Rozsa worked mostly for United Artists and Universal on films such as *Because Of Him*, *The Strange Love Of Martha Ivers*, *The Killers* (Burt Lancaster's first movie), *The Red House*, *The Macomber Affair*, *Brute Force*, *The Naked City* (with Frank Skinner) and *A Double Life* (1947), for which he won another Oscar. At the end of the decade Rozsa began to work for **MGM** and, embarked on his 'religious and historical epic' period, with 'majestic' scores for *Quo Vadis*, *Ivanhoe*, *Julius Caesar*, *Knights Of The Round Table*, *Valley Of The Kings*, *Ben Hur* (1959) (his third Academy Award, and his last major assignment for MGM). Rozsa pursued the epic into the 60s with blockbusters *King Of Kings* and *El Cid* (1961), both of which were made in Spain. By no means all of Rozsa scores in the 50s and 60s were of such gigantic proportions. He also provided the music for movies with a wide variety of subjects, such as *The Asphalt Jungle*, *Crisis*, *The Story Of Three Loves*, *Moonfleet*, *Tribute To A Bad Man*, *Bhowani Junction*, *Lust For Life*, *Something Of Value*, *The World*, *The Flesh And The Devil*, *The V.I.P's*, *The Power*, *The Green*

Berets, and many more. In 1970 Rozsa made his last film with Billy Wilder, *The Private Life Of Sherlock Holmes*, and played a cameo role as a ballet conductor. His other 70s film music included *The Golden Voyage Of Sinbad*, *The Secret Fifles Of J. Edgar Hoover*, *Fedora*, *The Last Embrace*, *Time After Time* and *Providence*, his 'most inspiring project for years'. Somewhat ironically, during the 70s and 80s, when the demand for elaborate orchestra movie scores had declined, to be replaced by a montage of pop records, renewed interest in Rozsa's earlier classic film works caused record companies to make new recordings of his scores. In 1981, Rozsa's music for *Eye Of The Needle*, was, for some, shades of Korda's *The Spy In Black* over 40 years earlier and, *Dead Men Don't Wear Plaid* (1982), a parody of 40s film noir which included footage from classics of the genre, found Rozsa writing music for scenes that he had originally scored many years ago. Even though he was partly paralysed by a stroke in 1982, he continued to compose classical works and, on his 80th birthday, was presented with a Golden Soundtrack Award by **ASCAP**. The anniversary was declared 'Miklos Rozsa Day' in Los Angeles, and the composer was presented with greetings from President Reagan, Queen Elizabeth, and other luminaries such as Margaret Thatcher and Pope John Paul II. Later in 1987 Rozsa was the guest of honour at a gala charity concert of his music given by the Royal Philharmonic Orchestra at London's Royal Festival Hall.

Selected albums: *Miklos Rozsa Conducts His Great Film Music* (Polydor 1975), *Spellbound-The Classic Film Scores Of Miklos Rozsa* (RCA 1975), *Miklos Rozsa Conducting The Royal Philharmonic Orchestra* (Polydor 1976).

Further reading: *Miklos Rozsa: A Sketch Of His Life And Work*, C. Palmer. *Double Life: The Autobiography Miklos Rozsa*, Miklos Rozsa.

RPLA

RPLA sprang to fame when they starred on an unlikely front cover of the Uk heavy metal bible *Kerrang!* magazine, who marketed them as a 'Pretty Boy' band similar to **Poison** and **Mötley Crüe**. Not long after this appearance they emerged with a different image and admitted that they were a 'gay' rock band. While this should have made no difference at all it knocked the macho metal press off its stride and suddenly the rave write-ups and gig reviews disappeared, with the band suffering as a result. They became the subject of a news item on UK television about sexism/homophobia in rock and *Kerrang!* were singled out. Within a few weeks a small piece on them became conspicuous by its appearance in said magazine. Whatever their press relationship was, the band did themselves no favours because the music content was never strong enough to overcome even the mildest prejudice.

Album: *Metal Queen Hijack* (EMI 1992).

Rub Ultra

Dub metal crossover artists formed in London in August 1993, comprising Will (vocals), Steve (guitar), Charlie (bass), Sarah (vocals/percussion; sister of Will) and Pete (drums). Together they released two EPs in 1994, *Combatstrengthsoap* and *Cosmyk Fynger Tactik*, the latter's cover featuring a holiday snap of a camel's posterior. Following support slots with **Headswim**, **S*M*A*S*H*** and **Therapy?** (whose Michael McKeegan was prepared to roadie for the band) rumours began to circulate that their debut album for **Virgin** indie subsidiary Hut would have none other than **John Leckie** as producer.

Rubella Ballet

Formed in the summer of 1979, the first stable line-up of this UK punk band comprised Zillah Minx (b. 31 March 1961, Birkenhead, Merseyside, England; vocals), Sid Attion (b. 18 April 1960, Sutton Coalfield, England; drums), Pete Fender (ex-**Honey Bane**, Fatal Microbes; guitar), and several bass players. Other early members included **Annie Anxiety**, Womble, Colin (**Flux Of Pink Indians**) and the strangely named 'It'. Anxiety was to be the singer, but when she dropped out drummer Sid, who would also work with Flux Of Pink Indians, suggested his girlfriend Zillah fill the position (at extremely short notice). Their first release was the cassette-only 'Ballet Bag', followed by a series of snappy punk pop singles. Gemma (also ex-Fatal Microbes, and brother of Fender) took over the bass position, although still a schoolgirl. The two, incidentally, are the children of the **Poison Girls**' Vi Subversa. The line-up would continue to be fluid however, with several guitarists passing through the ranks once Fender departed. He would go on to build his own studio, and record the solo single, '4 Formulas'. After spells with Xcentrix and Jungle Records, they formed their own Ubiquitous label with enterprising singles 'Money Talks' and 'Artic Flowers', and eventually three albums. In 1983, they launched a major tour with **Death Cult**, and were joined by Rachel Minx (b. 12 November 1964, Birkenhead, Merseyside, England; Zillah's sister) on bass. Zillah and Sid later recorded a techno dance track for the compilation *Beyond The Threshold*, under the name Xenophobia, and subsequent singles also appeared under that title.
Albums: *Ballet Bag* (Xentrix 1986), *If* (Ubiquitous 1986), *Cocktail Mix* (Ubiquitous 1987) *Birthday Box* (Ubiquitous 1988), *At The End Of The Rainbow* (Ubiquitous 1990). Video: *Freak Box* (1986).

Rubettes

Former songwriters of the **Pete Best** Four, Wayne Bickerton and Tony Waddington created the Rubettes from session musicians after their composition, 'Sugar Baby Love', was rejected by existing acts. A fusion of 50s revivalism and glam-rock, it gave the new group's career a flying start by topping the UK charts and climbing into the US Top 40 in 1974. The song was mimed on television and promoted in concert by Alan Williams (b. 22 December 1950, Welwyn Garden City, Hertfordshire, England; vocals/guitar), Tony Thorpe (b. 20 July 1947, London, England; guitar), Bill Hurd (b. 11 August 1946, London, England; keyboards), Mick Clarke (b. 10 August 1948, Grimsby, Humberside, England; bass) and John Richardson (b. 3 May 1947, Dagenham, Essex, England). Despite adverse publicity when it was revealed that a Paul Da Vinci had warbled the punishing falsetto lead vocal on 'Sugar Baby Love', the five stayed together and were able to continue as hit parade contenders and touring attractions - particularly in Britain and northern Europe - for another three years. 'Tonight', 'Juke Box Jive', 'I Can Do It' and lesser hits mixed mainly Waddington-Bickerton and band originals. Five years after their grand exit with 1977's countrified 'Baby I Know' in the domestic Top 10, Thorpe returned from obscurity to sing lead on the Firm's 'Arthur Daley (E's Alright)', a chartbusting paean to the main character in the television series *Minder*. This was followed in 1987 with the UK number 1, 'Star Trekkin''.
Albums: *We Can Do It*, (1975), *Impact* (1982). Compilations: *Best Of The Rubettes* (1983), *The Singles Collection 1974 - 1979* (1992), *Juke Box Jive* (1993). Further reading: *The Rubettes Story*, Alan Rowett.

Rubinoos

The Rubinoos carried on the great pop tradition of UK bands like the **Hollies** and the **Beatles** and that espoused by other American acts like the **Raspberries**. They were formed in the Bay Area of San Francisco, California, in 1973 by Tommy 'TV' Dunbar and Jon Rubin, who were thrown out of high school together and enrolled in a so-called Progressive School where they learnt to smoke illegal substances. They called themselves the Rubinoos after Jon's surname, Rubin acting as vocalist while Dunbar played guitar. They were joined by Royse Ader on bass and Donn Spindit on drums. Their early set consisted of covers including the **Archies**' 'Sugar Sugar'. The Rubinoos were often pelted with vegetables until the American new wave scene helped make 60s pop respectable again. Dunbar's brother Rob was in a band called Earthquake and their manager, Matthew Kaufman, helped get the Rubinoos gigs. He also added them to his impressive roster on **Beserkley Records**. Their debut single in 1977 (produced by Kaufman) was a version of **Tommy James And The Shondells** 'I Think We're Alone Now'. Both this, and their self-penned but similarly styled 'I Wanna Be Your Boyfriend', were much vaunted but not hits. They became a popular live attraction particularly for their showstopping 'Rock And Roll Is Dead (And We Don't

Care)'. Regardless of their lack of major success they ploughed on though Ader left in 1980 and by the time of their 1983 mini-album, *Party Of Two*, they were just a duo of Rubin and Dunbar. However, the four original members re-formed in 1988.

Albums: *The Rubinoos* (1977), *Rubinoos In Wax* (1979), *Back To The Drawing Board* (1979), *Party Of Two* (1983).

Ruby And The Romantics

Edward Roberts (first tenor), George Lee (second tenor), Ronald Mosley (baritone) and Leroy Fann (bass) had been working as the Supremes prior to the arrival of Ruby Nash Curtis (b. 12 November 1939, New York City, New York, USA) in 1962. Ruby had met the group in Akron, Ohio and took on the role as their lead singer. They subsequently secured a contract with the New York label Kapp and at the suggestion of the company, changed their name to Ruby And The Romantics. By the following year they had taken the evocative 'Our Day Will Come' to the top of the US pop chart, earning them a gold disc. Over the next 12 months the group scored a further six hits including the original version of 'Hey There Lonely Boy' which, with a change of gender, was later revived by **Eddie Holman**. After three years at Kapp, the group signed to the **ABC** label. In 1965 'Does He Really Care For Me', the Romantics' last chart entry, preceded a wholesale line-up change. Ruby brought in a new backing group; Richard Pryor, Vincent McLeod, Robert Lewis, Ronald Jackson and Bill Evans, but in 1968 the forthright Curtis replaced this version with Denise Lewis and Cheryl Thomas.

Albums: *Our Day Will Come* (1963), *Till Then* (1963), *Ruby And The Romantics* (1967), *More Than Yesterday* (1968). Compilation: *Greatest Hits Album* (1966).

Ruby Blue

A folk-pop group from Edinburgh, Scotland, Ruby Blue was formed in 1986 by drama student Rebecca Pidgeon (b Cambridge, Massachusetts, USA 1963 vocals) and Roger Fife (b 1963 guitar/bass). Adding Anthony Coote (bass) and Erika Spotswood (backing vocals), the group released 'Give Us Our Flag Back' on independent label Red Flame in 1987. The debut album was an enterprising mix of folk, blues, jazz and pop with Pidgeon's crystal-clear singing bringing comparisons with the late **Sandy Denny**. Adding a drummer (Chris Buck, replaced in 1990 by Karlos Edwards) Ruby Blue developed an electric sound for live shows and gained attention supporting **John Martyn**. Pidgeon also pursued a successful acting career, appearing at the National Theatre in London and in the film *The Dawning*. Both Anthony Coote and Rebecca Pidgeon departed at the end of 1990, following her marriage to the playwright David Mamet. Her replacement was Erika Woods (Spotswood); who took over lead vocals with a band that was still unable

to find commercial success, which belies their considerable talent as writers and performers.

Albums: *Glance Askances* (1988), *Down from Above* (1990), *Broken Water* (1992, early recordings), *Almost Naked* (1993). Solo: Rebecca Pidgeon *The Raven* (1994).

Ruby, Harry

b. Harry Rubinstein, 27 January 1895, New York, USA, d. 23 February 1974, Woodland Hills, California, USA. A successful composer for stage shows and films, mostly in collaboration with lyricist **Bert Kalmar**, Ruby played the piano in publishing houses, and accompanied vaudeville acts such as the Messenger Boys, before starting to write songs. He had an early hit in 1919 with 'And He'd Say Oo-La-La, Wee-Wee', written with comedian George Jessel, which became popular for specialist novelty singer Billy Murray. From 1918-28 Kalmar and Ruby wrote songs for Broadway shows, with Ruby sometimes contributing to the libretto. These included *Helen Of Troy, New York* ('I Like A Big Town', 'Happy Ending'); *The Ramblers* ('All Alone Monday', 'Just One Kiss', 'Any Little Tune'); *Five O'Clock Girl* ('Thinking Of You', 'Up In The Clouds'); *Good Boy* ('Some Sweet Someone', 'I Wanna Be Loved By You', the latter memorably revived by **Marilyn Monroe** in the 1959 Billy Wilder movie *Some Like It Hot*); and *Animal Crackers* ('Watching The Clouds Roll By, 'Who's Been Listening To My Heart?', 'Hooray For Captain Spaulding'). While working on *Animal Crackers*, Kalmar and Ruby formed a friendship with the Marx Brothers, and, after moving to Hollywood in 1928, supplied songs for some of the Brothers' early movies, including *Horse Feathers* (1932) and *Duck Soup* (1933), and the film version of *Animal Crackers*. Groucho Marx later used their 'Hooray For Captain Spaulding' as a theme for his radio and television shows. While in Hollywood, Kalmar and Ruby wrote what was probably their most popular song, 'Three Little Words', for the comedy film *Check And Double Check* (1930), featuring radio's famous double-act, Amos 'N Andy. The songwriting team continued to write consistently for films through the 30s, including *The Cuckoos* (1931, 'I Love You So Much', 'Dancing The Devil Away'), ***The Kid From Spain*** (1932, 'Look What You've Done', 'What A Perfect Combination'), *Hips, Hips, Hooray* (1934, 'Keep On Doin' What You're Doin''), and *Kentucky Kernels* (1934) ('One Little Kiss'). Their last film work together, in 1939, was for ***The Story Of Vernon And Irene Castle*** ('Only When You're In My Arms', 'Ain'tcha Comin' Out?'), starring **Fred Astaire** and **Ginger Rogers**, although their 1947 song 'A Kiss To Build A Dream On', written with **Oscar Hammerstein II**, featured in the 1951 movie *The Strip*, and was nominated for an Academy Award. In 1941, they also contributed to another Broadway show, *The High Kickers* ('You're On My Mind', 'A Panic In Panama', 'Time To Sing'). In the 1950 bio-pic *Three*

Little Words, **Red Skelton** played Ruby, and Fred Astaire was cast as Kalmar. The film featured most of their big hits including 'Who's Sorry Now', 'Nevertheless', and the novelty, 'So Long, Oo-Long (How Long You Gonna Be Gone?)'. During the 40s, Ruby also wrote songs with other lyricists, including **Rube Bloom** ('Give Me The Simple Life'), and provided both music and lyrics for the title song to the **Dick Haymes**-Maureen O'Hara film *Do You Love Me?* (1946). After the early 50s Ruby was semi-retired, emerging occasionally to appear on television programmes to celebrate songwriters and associated artists. In 1992, the Goodspeed Opera House in Connecticut presented a revival of *Animal Crackers*, with Frank Ferrante in the role of Groucho Marx.

Rucker, Ellyn

b. 29 July 1937, Des Moines, Iowa, USA. Coming from a very musical family, Rucker first took an interest in piano when she was eight years old. Later, she studied classical piano but by the age of 13 her brother had persuaded her to listen to jazz. She began playing clubs and hotels in her hometown area, but it was 1979 before she became a full-time professional musician. By this stage in her career, she had also begun to sing occasionally to her own accompaniment. She spent several years working in Denver, Colorado, where she was heard by **Mark Murphy** who advised her to try for the 'big time'. Although essentially a solo player, sometimes working with a rhythm section, she has occasionally worked with visiting jazzmen, including **Roy Eldridge**, **James Moody**, **Clark Terry**, **Richie Cole** and **Buddy Tate**. In 1986 she played at the Northsea Jazz Festival in Holland and in subsequent years toured Europe and the UK. Latterly, Rucker has continued to concentrate on solo tours but has also worked with **Spike Robinson** on a number of occasions. Her accompanists on records have included Robinson, **Pete Christlieb** and **John Clayton**. An eclectic pianist, with a wide-ranging repertoire, Rucker is gradually becoming accepted as an inventive and skilled jazz musician. Her playing style can be elegantly poised or dynamically forceful depending upon the material or the mood that she is in. Her singing, although less strongly promoted than her piano playing, is easy and natural.
Albums: with Spike Robinson *Nice Work* (Capri 1985), *Ellyn* (Capri 1987), *This Heart Of Mine* (Capri 1988).

Rudd, Mike

b New Zealand. Rudd relocated to Australia with the Chants R'N'B in 1966. In 1968 he joined another similar combo, Party Machine, containing future members of **Daddy Cool**. This band evolved into an 'underground' experimental band - the short-lived Sons Of The Vegetal Mother in 1969. Forming his own band **Spectrum** that same year, Rudd teamed up with long-term collaborator, bassist Bill Putt, and wrote most of the material. Rudd led the band (and their alter-ego, **Murtceps**), through the blues orientated heavy rock music period in Australia during 1971-73. Next came Ariel (1973-74), a band which was a more exotic spectacle consisting of weird and wonderful costumes, exotic light shows and smoke bombs. Instant Reply followed (1978-79), who later changed their name to the Heaters. As trends changed, the Heaters become Rudd's post punk, new wave band, touring frequently during 1979-1982 but not achieving any commercial success with *Unrealist*. Rudd briefly returned to his roots with the Living Legend Blues Band, subsequently forming W.H.Y. in 1983, which toured and recorded in Germany, and was a more experimental outfit, as was the similar Mike Rudd's No. 9. He now performs in the Suburban Blues Band, a good-time cover band. He later briefly reformed Spectrum in early 1990. His song, 'I'll Be Gone', recorded by Spectrum, remains one of the most recognizable Australian hits of the early 70s.

Rudd, Roswell

b. 17 November 1935, Sharon, Connecticut, USA. Rudd studied singing and French horn at college and theory at Harvard (1954-58). Like several other members of the 60s *avant garde* he began his jazz career playing dixieland, a fact which points up the line of evolution between the New Orleans roots and the New Thing, and his big, fulsome trombone sound strongly recalls the early 'tailgate' players, even when he is working in the most abstract surroundings. Rudd moved to New York in 1954 and played in various traditional bands. He began to work in a modern context with **Herbie Nichols** (1960-62) and in 1961 he joined **Steve Lacy** (who also started out playing traditional jazz). His conversion to free-form jazz began as a result of meeting **Bill Dixon**. In 1964 he formed the New York Art Quartet with **John Tchicai**, to whom he had been introduced by Dixon (*Mohawk, New York Art Quartet*). When the Quartet disbanded in 1965 he became a member of **Archie Shepp**'s highly-influential group until 1967 (*Four For Tranc, Mama Too Tight*). In 1968 he formed the Primordial Quintet (which ended up as a nine-piece band) with **Lee Konitz**. During the late 70s and 80s he toured extensively with his own groups, and in 1982 was reunited with Lacy in the Monk Project with **Misha Mengelberg**. He has also worked with **Cecil Taylor**, **Jazz Composers Orchestra** (who, in 1973, commissioned the *Numatik Swing Band* from him), **Albert Ayler**, **Karl Berger**, **Enrico Rava**, **Perry Robinson**, **Gato Barbieri**, Robin Kenyatta and **Charlie Haden**'s Liberation Music Orchestra, and in 1961 he appeared in the film *The Hustler*. He has also worked with the distinguished ethno-musicologist **Alan Lomax**, and became professor of Music Ethnology at the University of Maine. He has tried to show the connections between jazz, so-called ethnic music and the European classical tradition in his compositions. In the early 90s he was reportedly playing dixieland again in upstate New York.

Albums: *Roswell Rudd Quartet* (1965), *Everywhere* (1966), *Numatik Swing Band* (1973), *Flexible Flyer* (1974), with Steve Lacy *School Days* (1975, rec 1963), *Blown-bone* (1976), *Inside Job* (Freedom 1976), *Maxine* (1976), with Giorgio Gaslini *Sharing* (1978), *The Definitive Roswell Rudd* (1979), with Misha Mengelberg and others *Regeneration* (Soul Note 1982).

Ruegg, Matthias

b. 8 December 1952, Zurich, Switzerland. During the 70s Ruegg played piano with a variety of bands while studying composition and arranging in Graz and Vienna, where he eventually settled and formed the Vienna Art Orchestra (1977) and later the Vienna Art Choir (1983). He continues to play the piano with the Orchestra in a competent modern style but is best known for the music he has written and arranged. He has taken themes from the whole history of jazz and even produced a double album of arrangements of the music of Eric Satie. In his arrangements he fulfils his hopes that he has 'arranged, orchestrated, altered and alienated . . . added some parts, extended phrases, and exposed striking solos, always . . . following the sense of the composition and the composer's intention'.

Albums: *Suite For The Green Eighties* (1981), *From No Time To Rag Time* (1982), *The Minimalism Of Eric Satie* (1984), *Perpetuum Mobile* (1985).

Ruffhouse

Columbia's rap subsidiary, home to Joe 'The Butcher', which enjoys a primarily hardcore roster, including **Cypress Hill**, **Tim Dog** and **Nas**, though the A&R policy did extend to offering contracts to artists with strong commercial potential like **Kriss Kross** and the **Goats**. In 1994 they picked up on the then-homeless **Schoolly D**.

Ruffin, Bruce

b. Bernardo Constantine Balderamus, 17 February 1952, St Catherine, Jamaica. Ruffin served his vocal apprenticeship in 1968 alongside **Pat Kelly, Winston Riley** and Junior Menns as the **Techniques**. He also sang with Morvin Brooks on 'Travelling Man', credited to the same group. Other members of the Techniques included **Dave Barker**, who replaced Pat Kelly. Each went on to pursue successful solo careers and Ruffin was no exception. Working with **Leslie Kong** at Beverly's studio successful singles such as 'Dry Up Your Tears', 'I'm The One' and 'Bitterness Of Life' followed. With Kong licensing his recordings to **Trojan Records** the hits soon became international, appearing on the Summit offshoot. Following Kong's

death in 1971 Ruffin went on to record with **Herman Chin-Loy** for 'One Big Happy Family' and a cover of **Jose Felancio**'s 'Rain', which took him into the UK Top 20 in May 1971. The flip-side featured 'Geronimo', wrongly credited to Bruce Antony (Bruce White and Tony Cousins of Creole Records) and originally released in 1970 on the Duke label. The success led to a compilation set, *Rain*, which featured the overtly commercial 'Candida', 'C.C. Child', 'Heaven Child' and 'Bitterness Of Life', as well as the title track. In an effort to capitalize on the first hit, the release of 'Songs Of Peace', 'You Are The Best' and 'We Can Make It' as a maxi single failed to achieve a chart entry. In 1972 Ruffin switched to the Rhino label, a subsidiary of Creole, and enjoyed a Top 10 hit with the blatantly commercial 'I'm Mad About You'. The track featured squawking backing vocals and when he appeared on the television show **Top Of The Pops** with a parrot in the background, the purists were aghast. The hit was followed with the release of 'Coming On Strong', but this flopped. In an effort to regain chart status he returned to the style of 'Mad About You' with 'Tickle Me' and 'In The Thick Of It'. Further releases, including 'I Like Everything About You' and 'Little Boys And Little Girls' followed, but neither improved his profile in the reggae or pop charts. In 1976 Bruce was reunited with Dave Barker as part of the British soul group **Chain Reaction**. They released *Never Lose Never Win*, and the notable contributions from Ruffin included a cover of **Lamont Dozier**'s 'Why Can't We Be Lovers', and a self-composition, 'I'm Indebted To You'. Ruffin now runs his own Genius management and publishing companies in north London.

Albums: *Rain* (Trojan 1971), *Bruce Ruffin* (Rhino 1972). With Chain Reaction: *Never Lose Never Win* (Gull 1976), *Change Of Action* (Vista 1983), *Chase A Miracle* (Vista 1983). Compilations: With the Techniques: *Classics* (Techniques 1991), *Run Come Celebrate - Their Greatest Hits* (Heartbeat 1993).

Ruffin, David

b. 18 January 1941, Meridian, Mississippi, USA, d. 1 June 1991. The younger brother of **Jimmy Ruffin** and the cousin of Melvin Franklin of the **Temptations**, David Ruffin was the son of a minister, and began his singing career with the gospel group the Dixie Nightingales. He combined the roles of vocalist and drummer in the doo-wop combo the Voice Masters from 1958, before signing to the Anna label in Detroit as a soloist in 1960. His releases there and on Check-Mate in 1961 proved unsuccessful, though they demonstrated the raw potential of his vocal skills. In 1963, Ruffin replaced Eldridge Bryant as tenor vocalist in the Temptations. At first, he played a supporting role behind the falsetto leads of **Eddie Kendricks**. From 1965 onwards he was allowed to take the spotlight on

hits like 'My Girl' and 'I Wish It Would Rain', which illustrated his commanding way with a ballad, and raunchier R&B material like 'I'm Losing You' and 'Ain't Too Proud To Beg'. Adopting the role of front-man, Ruffin was soon singled out by the media as the key member of the group, though his erratic behaviour caused some tension within the ranks. The **Motown** hierarchy slowly began to ease him out of the line-up, achieving their aim when they refused to give him solo billing in front of the group's name in 1968. Still under contract to the label, he embarked on an episodic solo career. 'My Whole World Ended', a Top 10 hit in 1969, re-established his credentials as a great soul singer, under the tutelage of producers **Harvey Fuqua** and **Johnny Bristol**. Subsequent releases failed to utilize his talents to the full, and an album of duets with his brother Jimmy also proved disappointing. After three years of comparative silence, Ruffin re-emerged in 1973 with the first of a series of workmanlike albums which spawned one Top 10 single, the **Van McCoy**-produced 'Walk Away From Love', and a batch of minor hits. In 1979, he left Motown for **Warner Brothers**, where his career fell into decline. In the early 80's he was briefly jailed for tax evasion, and his slide was only halted when a Temptations reunion in 1983 brought him back into contact with Eddie Kendricks. After the project was complete, Ruffin and Kendricks established a regular partnership, which was boosted when they were showcased on a prestigious concert at New York's **Apollo** by long-time Temptations' fans, **Hall And Oates**. This event was captured on a 1985 live album, and Ruffin and Kendricks also joined the rock duo at the Live Aid concert in Philadelphia. They subsequently recorded a well-received album of duets for **RCA,** which revived memories of their vocal interplay with the Temptations two decades earlier. He recorded with Ian Levine's Motor City label in 1990 including 'Hurt The One You Love' and toured with Eddie Kendricks and Dennis Edwards as Tribute To The Temptations on a package tour in 1991. A few weeks after the last performance he died in tragic circumstances after an overdose of crack (cocaine).
Albums: *My Whole World Ended* (1969), *Feelin' Good* (1969), with Jimmy Ruffin *I Am My Brother's Keeper* (1970), *David Ruffin* (1973), *Me'n'Rock'n'Roll Are Here To Stay* (1974), *Who I Am* (1975), *Everything's Coming Up Love* (1976), *In My Stride* (1977), *So Soon We Change* (1979), *Gentleman Ruffin* (1980), with Kendrick *Ruffin And Kendrick* (1988).

Ruffin, Jimmy

b. 7 May 1939, Collinsville, Mississippi, USA. The son of a minister, Ruffin was born into a musical family: his brother, **David Ruffin**, and cousin, Melvin Franklin, both became mainstays of the **Temptations**. Ruffin abandoned his gospel background to become a session singer in the early 60s, joining the **Motown** stable in 1961 for a one-off single before he was drafted for national service. After leaving the US Army, he returned to Motown, turning down the opportunity to join the Temptations and instead recommending his brother for the job. His commercial breakthrough came in 1966 with the major US and UK hit 'What Becomes Of The Broken-Hearted', which displayed his emotional, if rather static, vocals. After three smaller hits, Ruffin found success in the USA hard to sustain, concentrating instead on the British market. 'I'll Say Forever My Love' and 'It's Wonderful' consolidated his position in the UK, and in 1970 he was voted the world's top singer in one British poll. Ruffin left Motown in the early 70s after an unsuccessful collaboration with his brother, and achieved minor success with singles on **Polydor** and **Chess**. Despite his popularity as a live performer in Britain, he enjoyed no significant hits until 1980, when 'Hold On To My Love', written and produced by **Robin Gibb** of the **Bee Gees**, brought him his first USA Top 30 hit for 14 years. A duet with **Maxine Nightingale**, 'Turn To Me', was a big seller in 1982, while Ruffin's only other success of note in the 80s was the British chart-contender 'There Will Never Be Another You' in 1985. He joined Ian Levine's Motor City label in 1988 and recorded two singles with **Brenda Holloway**.
Albums: *Top Ten* (1967), *Ruff'n'Ready* (1969), *The Groove Governor* (1970), with David Ruffin *I Am My Brother's Keeper* (1970), *Jimmy Ruffin* (1973), *Love Is All We Need* (1975), *Sunrise* (1980).

Rufus

This Chicago-based group evolved from the **American Breed** when three original members, Al Ciner (guitar), Charles Colbert (bass) and Lee Graziano (drums), were joined by Kevin Murphy (keyboards), Paulette McWilliams (vocals), Ron Stockard and Dennis Belfield. Initially known as Smoke, then Ask Rufus, it was several months before a stable unit evolved. Graziano made way for Andre Fisher, but the crucial change came when **Chaka Khan** (b. Yvette Marie Stevens, 23 March 1953, Great Lakes Naval Training Station, Illinois, USA) joined in place of McWilliams. The group, now known simply as Rufus, signed with the **ABC** label in 1973, but made little headway until a chance encounter with **Stevie Wonder** during sessions for a second album. Impressed by Khan's singing, he donated an original song, 'Tell Me Something Good' which, when issued as a single, became a gold disc. It began a run of exceptional releases, including 'You Got The Love' (1974), 'Sweet Thing' (1975) and 'At Midnight (My Love Will Lift You Up)' (1977), all of which topped the R&B chart. By this time Rufus had stabilized around Khan, Murphy, Tony Maiden (guitar), Dave Wolinski (keyboards), Bobby Watson (bass) and John Robinson (drums), but it was clear that the singer was the star attraction. She began recording as a solo act in 1978, but returned to the fold in 1980 for *Masterjam*, which contained 'Do You Love What You Feel', a further number 1 soul single. Khan continued to pursue her own career and perform with Rufus, who secured an international hit in 1983 with 'Ain't Nobody'. The song was written by Wolinski, by now an established figure in soul circles through his work on **Michael Jackson**'s *Off The Wall*. The distinction between Chaka Khan's successful solo recordings and her work with Rufus has become blurred over the years, but it remains arguable whether or not she achieved the same empathy elsewhere.

Albums: *Rufus* (1973), *Rags To Rufus* (1974), *Rufusized* (1974), *Rufus Featuring Chaka Khan* (1975), *Ask Rufus* (1977), *Street Player* (1978), *Numbers* (1979), *Masterjam* (1979), *Party 'Til You're Broke* (1981), *Camouflage* (1981), *Live - Stompin' At The Savoy* (1983).
Film: *Breakdance - The Movie* (1984).

Rugolo, Pete

b. 25 December 1915, San Piero, Sicily. After studying composing and arranging under classicist Darius Milhaud, Rugolo began writing arrangements for **Stan Kenton**. Many of Kenton's most successful recordings of the late 40s were Rugolo charts and of these a high proportion were also his compositions. After his full-time collaboration with Kenton ended in 1949, Rugolo produced a number of recording sessions for **Capitol Records** including some with **Miles Davis**, **Mel Tormé**, **Peggy Lee** and **Nat 'King' Cole**. He also recorded with a studio band under his own name. The period with Capitol also saw him writing additional material for Kenton and his Innovations in Modern Music Orchestra, and he was arranger and musical director for **June Christy**'s *Something Cool* album. In the 50s he joined Columbia Records and in the late 50s was with **Mercury Records**, writing for **Sarah Vaughan**, **Billy Eckstine** and others. From the 60s into the early 80s he worked in film and television studios, eventually retiring in 1985. Heavily influenced by Kenton, Rugolo's arrangements demonstrate his interest in developing ideas for the modern orchestra often as displays of technical virtuosity and as such sometimes leaving the jazz content behind.

Albums: *Music For Hi-Fi Bugs* (1956), *Out On A Limb* (1956), *Pete Rugolo And His Orchestra* i (1956), *Pete Rugolo And His Orchestra* ii (1958), *Pete Rugolo And His Orchestra* iii (1958), *The Music From Richard Diamond* (1959), *Pete Rugolo And His Orchestra* iv (1959), *The Thriller* (c.1960), *Pete Rugolo And His Orchestra* v (1960), *Ten Trumpets And Two Guitars* (1961), *Pete Rugolo And His Orchestra* vi (1961), *The Diamonds Meet Pete Rugolo* (c.1961), *TV Themes* (1962). Compilations: by Stan Kenton *The Kenton Era* (1940-53), *Rugolomania* (Fresh Sounds 1988).

Ruiz, Hilton

b. 29 May 1952, New York City, New York, USA. Ruiz studied piano from an early age, performing public recitals as a small child. In the mid- to late 60s he worked as a professional musician in bands playing Latin American music. In the early 70s he turned to jazz, studying with **Mary Lou Williams**. Later in the decade he played on numerous club, concert and recording dates with **Joe Newman**, **Freddie Hubbard**, **Clark Terry**, **Charles Mingus**, **Rahsaan Roland Kirk** (with whom he recorded *Return Of The 5000lb Man*), **Chico Freeman**, (on *Beyond The Rain*), **Betty Carter** and **Archie Shepp**. He continued an active career in the 80s, appearing with Terry's all-star big band at festivals and on television and making records, including some as a member of **Marion Brown**'s group. A strikingly inventive pianist, Ruiz's jazz style incorporates many elements from his continuing interest in Latin music.

Albums: *Piano Man* (Steeplechase 1975), *Excitation* (1977), *New York Hilton* (1977), *Fantasia* (1978), *The Hilton Ruiz Trio* (1978), *Cross Currents* (1984), *Vibration Society: The Music Of Rahsaan Roland Kirk* (1986), *El Camino* (1987), *Strut* (Novus 1988), *Cross Currents* (Stash 1987, 1984-86 recordings), *Doin' It Right* (Novus 1989), *A Moment's Notice* (Novus 1991), *Live At Birdland* (Candid 1993).

Rumour

Formed in 1975, the Rumour served as the backing group to **Graham Parker**. Brinsley Schwarz (guitar/vocals) and Bob Andrews (keyboards/vocals), both ex-**Brinsley Schwarz**, were joined by Martin Belmont (guitar, ex-**Ducks Deluxe**), Andrew Bonar (bass) and Steve Goulding (drums) in a unit supplying the necessary punch to the singer's R&B ambitions. Their own aspirations were realized in 1977 with the release of *Max*, but a sense of individuality only fully emerged on *Frogs, Sprouts, Clogs And Krauts* which included the single 'Emotional Traffic'. However, as the parent attraction fell from commercial favour, so too did the career of the Rumour whose independent recordings ended with *Purity Of Essence*.

Albums: *Max* (1977), *Frogs, Sprouts, Clogs And Krauts* (1979), *Purity Of Essence* (1980).

Rumpf, Inga

b. 2 August 1948, Hamburg, Germany. Rumpf, the daughter of a seafaring man, is widely accepted as the 'grand dame' of German rock music. Her first venture into recording (though she had always sung as a child) came in 1965 when she joined folk band the City Preachers. Later she teamed up with fellow singer Dagmar Krause (a **Kevin Coyne** associate) for an album, *I.D. Company*, which culled influences from both jazz and the Indian subcontinent and became a cult favourite among European audiences. In the same year, 1970, she went on to become lead vocalist for Frumpy, whose three years of performances (until 1972) were distinguished by Rumpf's raucous singing, to the accompaniment of organ-driven rock influenced by the late 60s California scene. She then joined a second rock outfit, Atlantis, who again enjoyed immense popularity within Germany. However, Atlantis too disbanded, in 1976, by which time Rumpf had recorded her debut solo album proper. The rest of that year was spent, sporadically, in the Herzbolzheimer Bigband, whose influence would be apparent in later work, before she retired from performance for a couple of years. She returned in 1978 with *My Life Is A Boogie*, recorded with Neil Hubbard (guitar), Robert Awaii (guitar), Alan Spenner (bass), Paul Carrack (keyboards) and Peddlers' drummer Trevor Morais. Unfortunately two subsequent albums, *I Know Who I Am* and *Reality*, were unsuccessful both critically and commercially. Rumpf then became music teacher at the Music Highschool in Hamburg, though she did continue to pursue various one-off recording projects. None of these were successful, however, and by the 90s she was to be found undergoing a patchwork schedule of gigs on the jazz, blues and big band circuits.

Albums: with Dagmar Krause *I.D. Company* (1970), *Second Hand Maedchen* (1975), *My Life Is A Boogie* (1978), *I Know Who I Am* (1979), *Reality* (1981), *Lieben, Leiden, Leben* (1984).

Rumsey, Howard

b. 7 November 1917, Brawley, California, USA. After briefly playing piano and drums, Rumsey took up the bass while still at school. In the late 30s he played in the **Vido Musso** band alongside **Stan Kenton** and went with the pianist when he formed his own band in 1941. From 1943 he mostly freelanced but played in the bands of **Freddy Slack** and **Charlie Barnet**. At the end of the decade he was directly responsible for establishing a jazz club at the Lighthouse Cafe at Hermosa Beach. He was himself a member of the house band at the Lighthouse, a venue which became the focus of the west coast jazz scene. Throughout the 50s Rumsey played at the Lighthouse, eventually taking over the running of the Café. During this period he played and recorded with many of the outstanding musicians of the day, among them **Teddy Edwards**, **Sonny Criss**, **Hampton Hawes**, **Shorty Rogers**, **Jimmy Giuffre**, **Conte Candoli**, **Rolf Ericson**, **Frank Rosolino**, **Bob Cooper**, **Art Pepper** and **Shelly Manne**. He continued his activities into the 60s but eventually ceased playing and severed his connection with the Lighthouse. In the early 70s he returned to the scene by opening another club, Concerts By the Sea. A solid player with a good ear for the best in musical talent, Rumsey's greatest

achievement in jazz remains the fact that he provided a setting and format that gave great encouragement to one of the most important areas of jazz in the 50s.

Selected albums: *At Last! Miles Davis And The Lighthouse All Stars* (1953), *Sunday Jazz A La Lighthouse* (Original Jazz Classics 1953), *Howard Rumsey And The Lighthouse All Stars* i (1954), *Howard Rumsey And The Lighthouse All Stars* ii (1955), *In The Solo Spotlight* (Original Jazz Classics 1954-57), *Music For Lighthouse-Keeping* (1956), *Jazz Rolls Royce* (Fresh Sounds 1957), with Max Roach *Drummin' The Blues* (1957), *Volume 6* (Original Jazz Classics 1957), *Lighthouse At Laguna* (Original Jazz Classics 1958).

Run C&W

Run C&W are country music's equivalent to the **Travelin' Wilburys**. Here four key musicians pretend to be a bluegrass band who know nothing of modern life and perform 60s soul standards as though they are traditional tunes. You can hear a herd of cows in **Ray Charles**' 'What'd I Say' and country stars are substituted for the soul brothers in 'Sweet Soul Music'. The group consists of Russell Smith (Rug Burns), Bernie Leadon (Crashen Burns), Vince Melamed (Wash Burns) and Jim Photoglo (Side Burns), collectively known as the Burns Brothers. With such backgrounds as the **Eagles** and the **Amazing Rhythm Aces**, the playing is immaculate and the results are often hilarious. The second album, dispensing with the dialogue from the first set, includes guest appearances from **George Jones** (Possum Burns) and **Vince Gill** (Sun Burns) on **Joe Tex**'s 'Hold What You Got'.

Albums: *Into The Twangy-First Century* (MCA 1993), *Row Vs Wade* (MCA 1994).

Run DMC

New York rappers Joe Simmons (b. 24 November 1966, New York, USA; the brother of **Russell Simmons**, their Rush Management boss), Darryl 'DMC' McDaniels (b. 31 May 1964, New York, USA) and DJ 'Jam Master Jay' (b. Jason Mizell, 1965, New York, USA) originally came together as Orange Crush in the early 80s, becoming Run DMC in 1982 after graduating from St. Pascal's Catholic School. They had known each other as children in Hollis, New York, Mizell and McDaniels even attending the same kindergarten. After circulating demos the group signed to **Profile** Records for an advance of $2,500, immediately scoring a US underground hit with 'It's Like That'. However, it was the single's b-side, 'Sucker MCs', which created the stir. It single-handedly gave birth to one of rap's most prevalent terms, and almost became a genre in its own right. Many critics signpost the single as the birth of modern hip hop, with its stripped down sound (no instruments apart from a drum machine and scratching from a turntable, plus the fashion image of the B-boy: street clothing, chiefly sportswear, and street language). In the wake of the single's success their debut album went gold in 1984, the first time the honour had been bestowed upon a rap act. They cemented their position as hip hop's men of the moment with furious touring, and appearances on the *Krush Groove* film, a fictionalised account of the life of Russell Simmons, who was now joint-head of **Def Jam** with Rick Rubin. They also took a hand at the prestigious King Holliday (a Martin Luther King tribute) and Sun City (Artists Against Apartheid) events. They broke further into the mainstream on both sides of the Atlantic in 1986 when, via Rubin's auspices, they released the heavy metal/rap collision 'Walk This Way' (featuring Steve Tyler and Joe Perry of **Aerosmith**). Its disinctive video caught the imagination of audiences on both sides of the Atlantic. The partnership had been predicted by earlier singles, 'Rock Box' and 'King Of Rock', both of which fused rap with rock. By 1987 *Raisin' Hell* had sold three million copies in the US, becoming the first rap album to hit the R&B number 1 mark, the first to enter the US Top 10, and the first to go platinum. Run DMC also became the first rap group to have a video screened by MTV, the first to feature on the cover of *Rolling Stone*, and the first non-athletes to endorse Adidas products (a sponsorship deal which followed rather than preceded their 'My Adidas' track). Sadly, a projected collaboration with **Michael Jackson** never took place, though they did duet with Joan Rivers on her television show, and held street seminars to discuss inter-gang violence. Subsequent efforts have been disappointing, although both *Tougher Than Leather* and *Back From Hell* contained a few tough-like-the-old-times tracks ('Beats To The Ryhme', 'Pause' etc.) among the fillers. The former album was tied to a disastrous film project of similar title. In the 90s Daniels and Simmons experienced religious conversion, after the former succumbed to alcoholism and the the latter was falsely accused of rape in Cleveland. Singles continued to emerge sporadically, notably 'What's It All About', which even sampled the **Stone Roses**. Despite an obvious effort to make *Down With The King* their major comeback album, with production assistance offered by **Pete Rock**, **EPMD**, the **Bomb Squad**, **Naughty By Nature**, **A Tribe Called Quest**, even **Rage Against The Machine**, and guest appearances from **KRS-1** and **Neneh Cherry**, it is hard to shake the view of Run DMC as a once potent, now spent force. Unsurprisingly, this is not their own outlook, and as Simmons is keen to point out: 'The Run DMC story is an exciting story. It's a true legend, its the sort of life you want to read about'.

Albums: *Run DMC* (Profile 1984), *King Of Rock* (Profile 1985), *Raising Hell* (Profile 1986), *Tougher Than Leather* (Profile 1988), *Back From Hell* (Profile 1990), *Down With The King* (Profile 1993). Compilation: *Together Forever: Greatest Hits 1983-1991* (Profile 1991).
Further reading: *Run DMC*, Adler, B (1987).

Runaways

Formed in 1975, the Runaways were initially the product of producer/svengali **Kim Fowley** and teenage lyricist Kari Krome. Together they pieced together an adolescent female-group following several auditions in the Los Angeles area. The original line-up consisted of **Joan Jett** (b. Joan Larkin, 22 September 1960, Philadelphia, Pennsylvania, USA; guitar/vocals), Micki Steele (bass - later of the **Bangles**) and Sandy West (drums), but was quickly bolstered by the addition of **Lita Ford** (b. 23 September 1959, London, England; guitar/vocals) and **Cherie Currie** (vocals). The departure of Steele prompted several replacements, the last of which was Jackie Fox (b. Jacqueline Fuchs) who had failed her first audition. Although originally viewed as a vehicle for compositions by Fowley and associate **Mars Bonfire** (b. Dennis Edmonton), material by Jett and Krome helped assert the quintet's independence. *The Runaways* showed a group indebted to the 'glam-rock' of the **Sweet** and punchy pop of **Suzi Quatro**, and included the salutary 'Cherry Bomb'. *Queens Of Noise* repeated the pattern, but the strain of touring - the quintet were highly popular in Japan - took its toll on Jackie Fox, who left the line-up and abandoned music altogether becoming an attorney practicing in intellectual property law. Personality clashes resulted in the departure of Cherie Currie, whose solo career stalled following the failure of her debut, *Beauty's Only Skin Deep*. Guitarist/vocalist Vicki Blue and bassist Laurie McAllister completed a revitalized Runaways, but the latter was quickly dropped. Subsequent releases lacked the appeal of the group's early work which, although tarred by novelty and sexual implication, nonetheless showed a sense of purpose. The Runaways split in 1980 but both Jett and Ford later enjoyed solo careers, the former engendering considerable commercial success during the 80s. In 1985 the mischievous Fowley resurrected the old group's name with all-new personnel. This opportunistic concoction split up on completing *Young And Fast*. 1994 brought reports that Fowley was being sued by Jett, Ford, Currie and West over unpaid royalties. Fox was not involved in the action, presumably because she is now herself a practising lawyer.

Albums: *The Runaways* (Mercury 1976), *Queens Of Noise* (Mercury 1977), *Live In Japan* (Mercury 1977), *Waitin' For The Night* (Mercury 1977), *And Now...The Runaways* (Phonogram 1979), *Young And Fast* (Allegiance 1987). Compilations: *Rock Heavies* (Mercury 1979), *Flamin' Schoolgirls* (Phonogram 1982).

Rundgren, Todd

b. 22 June 1948, Philadelphia, Pennsylvania, USA. One of rock's eccentric talents, Rundgren began his career in local bar-band Woody's Truck Stop, before forming the **Nazz** in 1967. This acclaimed quartet completed three albums of anglophile pop/rock before disintegrating in 1970. Rundgren sought solace as an engineer - his credits included *Stage Fright* by the **Band** - before recording *Runt*, a name derived from his nickname. Brothers Hunt and Tony Sales (drums and bass respectively), later of **Tin Machine**, joined the artist on a set deftly combining technical expertise with his love of melody. This exceptionally accomplished album spawned a US Top 20 hit in 'We Got To Get You A Woman' and paved the way for the equally charming *The Ballad Of Todd Rundgren*. However, it was with *Something/Anything?* that this performer truly flourished. The first three sides were entirely his own creation - as writer, singer, musician and producer - and contained some of Rundgren's most popular songs, including 'I Saw The Light' and 'It Wouldn't Have Made Any Difference'. Although the final side was devoted to an indulgent 'pop opera', the set is rightly regarded as one of the landmark releases of the early 70s. *A Wizard, A True Star* offered a similarly dazzling array of styles, ranging from a suite of short song-snippets to a medley of soul ballads, including 'I'm So Proud' and 'Ooh Baby Baby'. *Todd*, a second double-set, proved equally ambitious, although its erratic content suggested that Rundgren was temporarily bereft of direction. His riposte was Utopia, a progressive rock ensemble which initially featured three musicians on keyboards/synthesizers - Moogy Klingman, M. Frog Labat and Ralph Shuckett - John Segler, then Kasim Sulton, (bass) and John Wilcox (drums). Although Roger Powell latterly assumed all keyboard duties, the group's penchant for lengthy instrumental interludes and semi-mystical overtones remained intact.

A popular live attraction, Utopia taxed the loyalties of Rundgren aficionados, particularly when their unrepentant self-indulgence encroached into the artist's 'solo' work, notably on *Initiation*. *Faithful* did reflect a return to pop with 'Love Of The Common Man' and 'The Verb To Love', while acknowledging Todd's inspirational roots with note-for-note remakes of several 60s classics, including 'If Six Was Nine' (**Jimi Hendrix**), 'Good Vibrations' (the **Beach Boys**) and 'Strawberry Fields Forever' (the **Beatles**). In 1977 Utopia released *Ra* and *Oops! Wrong Planet*, the latter of which had Rundgren taking a less prominent role. He nonetheless maintained a frenetic workload and having already established his credentials as a producer with the **New York Dolls**, **Grand Funk Railroad** and **Hall And Oates**, commenced work on **Meatloaf**'s *Bat Out Of Hell*, which has since become one of the best-selling albums of all time. The artist also began recording *Hermit Of Mink Hollow*, a superb set recalling the grasp of pop offered on *Something/Anything?* and deservedly lauded by critics. Rundgren entered the 80s determined to continue his eclectic path. Utopia's

Deface The Music was a dazzling pastiche of Beatles' music from 'I Wanna Hold Your Hand' to 'Tomorrow Never Knows' while another 'solo' set, *Healing*, flirted with ambient styles. His earlier profligacy lessened as the decade progressed but retained the capacity to surprise, most notably on the inventive *Aceppella*. Production work for **XTC** joined later recordings in proving his many talents have remained as true as ever. In 1994 he scored the music for the movie *Dumb And Dumber*.

Albums: *Runt* (1970), *The Ballad Of Todd Rundgren* (1971), *Something/Anything?* (1972), *A Wizard, A True Star* (1973), *Todd* (1974), *Initiation* (1975), *Faithful* (1976), *Hermit Of Mink Hollow* (1978), *Back To The Bars* (1978), *Healing* (1981), *The Ever Popular Tortured Artist Effect* (1983), *A cappella* (1985), *POV* (1985), *Nearly Human* (1989), *Second Wind* (1991). Compilations: *Anthology: Todd Rundgren* (1988). With Utopia *Todd Rundgren's Utopia* (1974), *Another Live* (1975), *Ra* (1977), *Oops! Wrong Planet* (1977), *Adventures In Utopia* (1980), *Deface The Music* (1980), *Swing To The Right* (1982), *Utopia* (1982), *Oblivion* (1984).

Running Wild

This quartet from Hamburg, Germany, were strongly influenced by the **New Wave Of British Heavy Metal Movement** of the early 80s. Formed in 1983 by guitarist/vocalist Rockin' Rolf, a plethora of personnel changes occurred before Majik Moti (guitar), Jens Becker (bass) and Iain Finlay (drums) were recruited and a degree of stability was achieved. They initially pushed a black-metal image, but made little impact with their rigidly formularized, one-paced rantings. They changed course musically with their third album and tried to emulate the style of **Iron Maiden**, and also adopted a rather unfortunate swashbuckling pirate's image. However, Rolf's weak vocals and the repetitiveness of their material always hindered their chances of promotion to rock's upper echelons.

Albums: *Gates Of Purgatory* (Noise 1984), *Branded And Exiled* (Noise 1985), *Under Jolly Roger* (Noise 1987), *Ready For Boarding* (Noise 1988), *Port Royal* (Noise 1988), *Death Or Glory* (Noise 1990), *Blazin' Stone* (Noise 1991). Compilation: *The First Years Of Piracy* (Noise 1992). Video: *Death Or Glory* (1992).

Runrig

The phenomenon of Runrig is an extraordinary example of cultural differences. This premier Scottish group has emerged from a folk background to a higher profile in the pop/rock field and is arguably the most popular band north of Carlisle. The group made its debut - as the Run Rig Dance Band - at the Kelvin Hall, Glasgow in 1973. Initially a trio comprising of brothers Rory MacDonald (b. 27 July 1949, Dornoch, Sutherland, Scotland; guitar/bass/vocals, ex-Skyevers), Calum MacDonald (b. 12 November 1953,

Lochmaddy, North Uist, Scotland; drums/percussion/vocals) and Blair Douglas (accordion), the group was viewed as a part-time venture, 'Something to do during the holidays,' as Calum later stated. Donnie Munroe (b. 2 August 1953, Uig, Isle Of Skye, Scotland; vocals/guitar) joined the following year as the group took on a more serious perspective. At this point their repertoire comprised of cover versions - **Creedence Clearwater Revival** was a particular favourite - and traditional material played in a folk/rock manner, reminiscent of **Horslips** and **Fairport Convention**. Although the MacDonald siblings were writing material, Runrig demurred from playing them live until 1978 and the release of *Play Gaelic*. Issued on the Scottish Lismor Record label, this pastoral set introduced newcomer Robert MacDonald (no relation) who had replaced Blair Douglas. A higher profile ensued and, with the extra credibility of an album behind them, the group set up their own label, Ridge Records. Malcolm Jones (b. 12 July 1958, Inverness, Scotland; guitar/mandolin/accordion) replaced Robert MacDonald who was unwilling to turn professional. Sadly, Robert died of cancer in 1986. *Highland Connection* introduced a greater emphasis on electric styles and in 1980 Iain Bayne (b. 22 January 1960, St. Andrews, Fife, Scotland) took over as the drummer, freeing Calum to concentrate on vocals and percussion. By the release of *Recovery*, produced by Robert Bell of the **Blue Nile**, it was clear the band was more than just another folk/rock act. The music still retained its rural feel and traditions, with many songs being sung in Gaelic, but the sound took Runrig outside the narrow bounds of the traditional arena. English keyboard player Richard Cherns joined the group for its first European tour, but left following the release of *Heartland*. He was replaced by former **Big Country** member Peter Wishart (b. 9 March 1962, Dunfermline, Fife, Scotland). Runrig performed successful concerts in Canada and East Berlin in 1987 and played support to **U2** at Murrayfield, Edinburgh, Scotland. After the release of *The Cutter And The Clan*, the group signed to **Chrysalis Records**, who immediately re-released the album. Chart success followed in 1989 with *Searchlight* almost making the Top 10 in the UK charts. Constant touring - the secret of Runrig's appeal - ensued and in 1990 the *Capture The Heart* EP entered the UK Top 50. A television broadcast of a live performance elicited huge response from viewers to the extent that five concerts at Glasgow's Royal Concert Hall sold out. A subsequent video, *City Of Lights*, reached the Top 10-selling videos in the UK. The highly acclaimed *The Big Wheel* reached number 4 in the UK charts and an open-air concert at Loch Lomond was attended by 45,000 people. The EP *Hearthammer* broached the UK Top 30 in September 1991, followed by 'Flower Of The West' (UK number 43. The acceptance of Runrig outside Scotland now seems certain and having

combined their national and cultural pride with stadium rock, they have awoken the world to Scottish popular music and traditions, without hint of compromise.

Albums: *Play Gaelic* (Lismor 1978), *Highland Connection* (Ridge 1979), *Recovery* (Ridge 1981), *Heartland* (Ridge 1985), *The Cutter And The Clan* (Ridge 1987), *Once In A Lifetime* (Chrysalis 1988), *Searchlight* (Chrysalis 1989), *The Big Wheel* (Chrysalis 1991), *Amazing Things* (Chrysalis 1993), *Transmitting Live* (Chrysalis 1994).

Further reading: *Going Home: The Runrig Story*, Tom Morton.

RuPaul

A seven foot tall, trans-sexual American diva package. Raised in San Diego, at age 15 RuPaul took himself (as he then was) off to Atlanta, where he hung out with the **B-52's** and appeared on cable television. Moving to New York, he would become part of the Wigstock counter-culture that also gave birth to **Deee-Lite**. He subsequently became a figurehead for the US gay movement when his debut album crossed over to the mainstream, and was a chat show favourite. He has been keen to tackle the role, leading a demonstration against the Ku Klux Klan in full drag. He landed his own television series, and helped to present the 1994 BRIT Awards alongside a dwarfed **Elton John**.

Album: *Supermodel Of The World* (Tommy Boy 1993).

Rupe, Art

Originally from Pittsburgh and the son of Hungarian immigrants, Rupe had moved to Los Angeles as a teenager to attend University of California at Los Angeles. His first involvement in the record business was as a partner in the small Atlas Records, which was notable for being the first label to record **Johnny Moore**'s **Three Blazers** and **Frankie Laine**. Despite this, Atlas failed in its first year, and with diminished savings Rupe founded Jukebox Records in 1944. The first release on Jukebox, 'Boogie #1' by the Sepia Tones, sold about 70,000 copies. While the following year the label added Roy Milton's Solid Senders to its roster and had immediate success with 'R.M. Blues' in 1946, at which point Jukebox became Specialty Records. Specialty went from strength to strength throughout the late 40s with records by **Jimmy Liggins** And His Drops Of Joy, **Camille Howard** and, at the turn of the decade, **Joe Liggins** and **Percy Mayfield**. In early 1952 Rupe made his first trip to New Orleans to find a '**Fats Domino**' for **Specialty Records**, and instead he came away with **Lloyd Price** and 'Lawdy, Miss Clawdy', which shot to number 1 on the R&B charts and became one of the first funky R&B records to be bought in large quantities by white Americans. Later in the 50s, this New Orleans connection led to artists such as of **Larry Williams**, **Earl King**, **Art Neville**, **Guitar Slim** and, of course,

Little Richard. Owing mainly to the success of Little Richard and his many hit records, Specialty continued to flourish during the rock 'n' roll years with secular recordings by **Sam Cooke** among others, but after the departure of Richard and Cooke in the late 50s, Rupe began to direct his business acumen towards movies and real estate. However, he and his family have maintained the Specialty label, whose treasured reissues continue to sell to R&B, rock 'n' roll and gospel fans, to this day.

Rush

This Canadian heavy rock band comprised Geddy Lee (b. 29 July 1953, Willowdale, Toronto, Canada; keyboards/bass/vocals), Alex Lifeson (b. 27 August 1953, British Columbia, Canada; guitar) and John Rutsey (drums). From 1969-72 they performed in Toronto playing a brand of **Cream**-inspired material, honing their act on the local club and bar circuit. In 1973 they recorded a version of **Buddy Holly**'s 'Not Fade Away' as their debut release, backing it with 'You Can't Fight It', for their own label, Moon Records. Despite failing to grab the attention as planned, the group pressed ahead with the recording of a debut album, which was remixed by Terry 'Broon' Brown. Brown would continue to work with the band until 1984's *Grace Under Pressure*. With no bite from the majors, once again this arrived via Moon, with distribution by London Records. However, at least the quality of the group's live appointments improved, picking up support slots with the **New York Dolls** in Canada and finally crossing the US border to play gigs with **Z.Z. Top**. Eventually Cliff Burnstein of **Mercury Records** (who would later also sign **Def Leppard**) heard the band, and his label would reissue the group's debut. At this point Neil Peart (b. 12 September 1952, Hamilton, Ontario, Canada; drums; ex-Hush), who was to be the main songwriter of the band, replaced Rutsey, and Rush undertook their first full tour of the USA. Rush's music was typified by Lee's oddly high-pitched voice, a tremendously powerful guitar sound, especially in the early years, and a recurrent interest in science fiction and fantasy from the pen of Neil Peart. Later he would also conceptualise the work of authors like John Barth, Gabriel Garcia Marquez and John Dos Passos. This approach reached its zenith in the group's 1976 concept album, *2112*, based on the work of novelist/philosopher Ayn Rand, which had as its central theme the concept of individual freedom and will. Including a 20-minute title-track which lasted all of side one, it was a set which crystalised the spirit of Rush for both their fans and detractors. However, the band's most popular offering, *A Farewell To Kings*, followed by *Hemispheres* in 1978, saw Peart finally dispense with his 'epic' songwriting style. By 1979 Rush were immensely successful worldwide, and the

Canadian Government awarded them the title of official Ambassadors of Music. As the 80s progressed Rush streamlined their image to become sophisticated, clean-cut, cerebral music-makers. Some early fans denigrated their determination to progress musically with each new album, though in truth the band had thoroughly exhausted its earlier style. They enjoyed a surprise hit single in 1980 when 'Spirit Of Radio' broke them out of their loyal cult following, and live shows now saw Lifeson and Lee adding keyboards for a fuller sound. Lee's vocals had also dropped somewhat from their earlier near-falsetto. The best recorded example of the band from this period is the succinct *Moving Pictures* from 1981, a groundbreaking fusion of technological rock and musical craft which never relied on the former at the expense of the latter. However, their career afterwards endured something of a creative wane, with the band at odds with various musical innovations. Despite this, live shows were still exciting events for the large pockets of fans the band retained all over the world, and in the powerful *Hold Your Fire* in 1987 they proved they were still able to scale former heights. Often criticised for lyrical pretension and musical grandstanding - unkind critics have suggested that Rush is exactly what you get if you let your drummer write your songs for you, they nevertheless remain Canada's leading rock attraction.

Albums: *Rush* (Moon 1974), *Fly By Night* (Moon 1975), *Caress Of Steel* (Mercury 1975), *2112* (Mercury 1976), *All The World's A Stage* (Mercury 1976, double album), *A Farewell To Kings* (Mercury 1977), *Hemispheres* (Mercury 1978), *Permanent Waves* (Mercury 1980), *Moving Pictures* (Mercury 1981), *Exit: Stage Left* (Mercury 1981, double album), *Signals* (Mercury 1982), *Grace Under Pressure* (Mercury 1984), *Power Windows* (Mercury 1985), *Hold Your Fire* (Mercury 1987), *A Show Of Hands* (Mercury 1989, double album), *Presto* (Atlantic 1989), *Roll The Bones* (Atlantic 1991), *Counterparts* (Mercury 1993). Compilations: *Archives* (Mercury 1978, triple set comprising first three albums), *Rush Through Time* (Mercury 1980), *Chronicles* (Mercury 1990). Videos: *Grace Under Pressure* (1986), *Exit Stage Left* (1988), *Thru' The Camera's Eye* (1989), *A Show Of Hands* (1989), *Chronicles* (1991).

Further reading: *Rush*, Brian Harrigan. *Rush Visions: The Official Biography*, Bill Banasiewicz.

Rush, Bobby

b. Emmitt Ellis Jnr., 10 November 1940, Homer, Louisiana, USA. For most of his career, Rush has managed to forge an amalgam of blues, soul and R&B which allows him the widest scope for personal expression. The son of a preacher, he began performing in Pine Bluff, Arkansas with a band that included guitarist **Boyd Gilmore** and **Johnny 'Big Moose' Walker**. Moving to Chicago, he led a series of bands that at times included **Freddie King**,

Luther Johnson, **Bobby King** and **Luther Allison**. During the 60s, he made singles for small labels such as Jerry-O, Palos and Starville before recording 'Gotta Have Money' for **ABC**-Paramount, the earliest example of the Rush signature style. Six records for Salem made little impression before 'Chicken Heads' on Galaxy put Rush's name on the *Billboard* charts. Further singles for On Top, Jewel, **Warner Brothers** and **London Records** led to a contract with **Gamble And Huff**'s **Philadelphia International** label. *Rush Hour* was the first significant release of Rush's career but 'artistic differences' precluded any further collaboration. Throughout the 80s Rush recorded for James Bennett's LaJam label a series of albums which highlighted his skill at adapting traditional blues themes for a contemporary audience. This continued with his switch to Urgent! in the 90s, although *Instant Replay: The Hits* perhaps denoted that his career was marking time.

Albums: *Rush Hour* (Philadelphia International 1979), *Sue* (LaJam 1982), *Wearing It Out* (LaJam 1983), *Gotta Have Money* (LaJam 1984), *What's Good For The Goose Is Good For The Gander* (LaJam 1985), *A Man Can Give It But He Can't Take It* (LaJam 1989), *I Ain't Studdin' You* (Urgent! 1991), *Instant Replay: The Hits* (Urgent! 1992).

Rush, Jennifer

b. Heidi Stern, 29 September 1960, New York City, New York, USA. Rush originally studied classical piano, violin and singing before launching a belated pop career. She arrived in Europe for the first time in 1969, when her father, opera singer Maurice Stern, took an engagement at the Flensburg Opera in northern Germany. She subsequently settled in Wiesbaden, Germany, but decamped back to America in the early 70s. A return to Germany came at the beginning of the 80s, working as a secretary for the US Army in Harlaching, Bavaria. Her career in popular music was hallmarked by the spectacular 1986 success of 'Power Of Love', an emphatic MOR ballad which became a major world-wide hit. It reached number 1 in the UK charts in June 1985, re-entering the Top 60 nearly 18 months later in December 1986. Further success arrived via duets with **Elton John** and **Michael Bolton**, before teaming up with Placido Domingo, in many ways a salute to her operatic roots, for the 1989 hit, 'Till I Loved You'. She also enjoyed solo success with '25 Lovers', 'Ring Of Ice' and 'I Come Undone'. By the 90s she had become a fixture on US AOR radio, with each of her albums (which as well as balladeering revealed her wide stylistic heritage) selling strongly to an established market. She had also racked up over 50 gold records, and numerous platinum albums (four of which reached the 'double platinum' benchmark). With total sales of well over 12 million, Rush's career amounts to much more than the one hit wonder perception with which most of the public view her.

Albums: *Jennifer Rush* (CBS 1979), *Moving* (CBS 1985), *Passion* (CBS 1988), *Wings Of Desire* (CBS 1989), *Jennifer Rush* (CBS 1992).

Rush, Merrilee, And The Turnabouts

b. Seattle, Washington, USA. Merrilee Rush was the singer of the original 1968 hit version of 'Angel Of The Morning', a song later popularized again by country singer **Juice Newton**. Rush joined a band called the Aztecs at the age of 13 and the following year started her own band, Merrilee And Her Men. For a number of years she worked with numerous other bands and recorded several local singles, finally forming another band, Merrilee Rush and the Turnabouts, in the mid-60s, consisting of guitarist Carl Wilson (brother of **Heart**'s Ann and Nancy Wilson), saxophonist Neil Rush, bassist Terry Craig and drummer Pete Sack. With this band, in 1968, she recorded 'Angel Of The Morning', written by **Chip Taylor** and released on Bell Records it went to number 7 in the US charts. She continued to record throughout the 70s and early 80s but was unable to follow up her lone hit.

Albums: *Angel Of The Morning* (1968), *Merrilee Rush* (1977), *Merrilee Rush* (1982).

Rush, Otis

b. 29 April 1934, Philadelphia, Mississippi, USA. A left-handed blues guitarist, Rush moved to Chicago where his impassioned singing and playing on 'I Can't Quit You Baby' brought a Top 10 R&B hit in 1956. He became one of the 'young turks' of the Chicago scene together with **Buddy Guy**, **Freddie King** and **Magic Sam**. 'I Can't Quit You Baby' and other Cobra recordings ('Double Trouble', 'All Your Love') from the same era inspired British guitarists such as **Peter Green**, **Eric Clapton** and **Mick Taylor** who strived to re-create the starkly emotive quality of his solos. **John Mayall** opened the pivotal *Bluesbreakers* with 'All Your Love' and continued by making Rush more widely known in the UK with recordings of 'So many Roads', 'I Can't Quit You Baby' (also recorded by **Led Zeppelin**) and 'Double Trouble'.In the early 60s, Rush recorded for **Chess** and Duke where 'So Many Roads' and 'Homework' became his best-known songs. As blues declined in popularity with black audiences, he turned increasingly to college concerts and collaborations with white blues artists such as **Mike Bloomfield**, with whom he made an album for Cotillion in 1969. During the 70s, Rush toured Europe and Japan, recording in Sweden, France and Japan as well as making two albums for Chicago-based label **Delmark**. *Right Place Wrong Time* had been made in 1971 for **Capitol** with producer **Nick Gravenites**, but was only issued on the independent Bullfrog label five years later. He performed and toured less frequently in the 80s, although an album made at the 1985 San Francisco Blues Festival showed him to be on top form. The influence of Rush has always been greater than his commercial standing and like Buddy Guy, his former stablemate at Chess he has become a guitarist's guitarist. In keeping with the recent blues boom Rush seems destined to benefit in a similar way that **John Lee Hooker** and Buddy Guy have. John Porter the producer of Guy's excellent *Damn Right I Got the Blues* was enlisted to work on *Ain't Enoiugh Comin' In*. On this, his best work in many years Rush demonstrates total confidence and experience and is well supported by **Mick Weaver** (organ), Bill Payne (piano) and Greg Rzab (bass).

Albums: *Chicago - The Blues - Today !* (1964), *Mourning In The Morning* (1969), *Cold Day In Hell* (1975), *Right Place, Wrong Time* (1976), *So Many Roads* (1978), *Troubles, Troubles* (1978), *Screamin' And Cryin'* (1979), *Tops* (1985), *Ain't Enough Comin' In* (This Way Up 1994). Compilation: *Double Trouble - Charly Blues Masterworks Vol. 24* (1992).

Rush, Tom

b. 8 February, 1941, Portsmouth, New Hampshire, USA. Tom Rush began performing in 1961 while a student at Harvard University. Although he appeared at clubs in New York and Philadelphia, he became a pivotal figure of the Boston/New England circuit and such haunts as the Cafe Yana and the Club 47. *Live At The Unicorn*, culled from two sets recorded at another of the region's fabled coffee houses, was poorly distributed but its competent mixture of traditional songs, blues and **Woody Guthrie** compositions was sufficient to interest the renowned Prestige label. *Got A Mind To Ramble* and *Blues Songs And Ballads*, completed over three days, showcased an intuitive interpreter. Rush's exemplary versions of 'Barb'ry Allen' and 'Alabama Bound' were enough to confirm his place alongside **Dave Van Ronk** and Eric Von Schmidt, the latter of whom was an important influence on the younger musician. *Tom Rush*, his first release on the **Elektra** label, was one of the era's finest folk/blues sets. The artist had developed an accomplished bottleneck guitar style which was portrayed to perfection on 'Panama Limited', an 8-minute compendium comprising several different songs by **Bukka White**. *Take A Little Walk With Me* contained the similarly excellent 'Galveston Flood', but its high points were six electric selections drawn from songs by **Bo Diddley**, **Chuck Berry** and **Buddy Holly**. Arranged by **Al Kooper**, these performances featured musicians from **Bob Dylan**'s ground-breaking sessions and helped transform Rush from traditional to popular performer. This change culminated in *The Circle Game*, which contained material by **Joni Mitchell**, **James Taylor** and **Jackson Browne**, each of whom had yet to record in their own right. The recording also included the poignant 'No Regrets', the singer's own composition, which has since become a pop classic through hit versions by the

Walker Brothers (1976) and **Midge Ure** (1982).

Tom Rush, the artist's first release for **Columbia/CBS**, introduced his long-standing partnership with guitarist Trevor Veitch. Once again material by Jackson Browne and James Taylor was to the fore, but the album also contained compositions by **Fred Neil** and Murray McLaughlin's beautiful song of leaving home, 'Child's Song', confirming Rush as having immaculate taste in choice of material. However two subsequent releases, *Wrong End Of The Rainbow* and *Merrimack County*, saw an increased emphasis on material Rush either wrote alone, or with Veitch. By contrast a new version of 'No Regrets' was the sole original on *Ladies Love Outlaws*, a collection which marked a pause in Rush's recording career. It was 1982 before a new set, *New Year*, was released. Recorded live, it celebrated the artist's 20th anniversary while a second live album, *Late Night Radio*, featured cameos from **Steve Goodman** and **Mimi Farina**. Both were issued on Rush's Night Light label on which he also repackaged his 1962 debut. In 1990 his New Hampshire home and recording studio were totally destroyed by fire, and this cultured artist has since moved to Wyoming.

Albums: *Live At The Unicorn* (1962), *Got A Mind To Ramble* (later known as *Mind Rambling*) (1963), *Blues Songs And Ballads* (1964), *Tom Rush* (1965), *Take A Little Walk With Me* aka *The New Album* (1966), *The Circle Game* (1968), *Tom Rush* (1970), *Wrong End Of The Rainbow* (1970), *Merrimack County* (1972), *Ladies Love Outlaws* (1974), *New Year* (1982), *Late Night Radio* (1984). Compilations: *Classic Rush* (1970), *The Best Of Tom Rush* (1975).

Rushen, Patrice

b. 30 September 1954, Los Angeles, California, USA. Rushen grew up in Los Angeles and attended the University of Southern California. She started learning classical piano when she was three, and turned to jazz in her teens. A group with which she was playing, won an award for young musicians at Monterey in 1972. She played with a host of artists, including **Abbey Lincoln**, **Donald Byrd** and **Sonny Rollins**, before joining **Lee Ritenour**'s group in 1977.

Her career a solo singing artist which commenced in the late 70s as a pop/soul artist, bore fruit on the Elektra label. The US R&B Top 20 hit 'Hang It Up' (1978) was followed by 'Haven't You Heard' (US R&B number 7/US pop Top 30, 1979). The latter, plus 'Never Gonna Give You Up (Won't Let You Be)' were minor UK hits in the early 80s, but were eclipsed by the Top 10 'Forget Me Nots'. Despite a tailing off in UK/US pop chart action from then on, Rushen continued to score regularly on the US R&B/soul charts. She gained notable chart success with 'Feel So Real (Won't Let Go)' (number 3, 1984) and 'Watch Out (number 9, 1987). After a period of label change, to **Arista Records**, she has given increased attention to her singing, and her predominantly bop-based playing, has given way to a fusion style. In 1988 she played with the **Wayne Shorter/Carlos Santana** group.

Albums: *Prelusion* (1974), *Before The Dawn* (1975), *Shout It Out* (1977), with Sonny Rollins *The Way I Feel* (1976), with Lee Ritenour *Sugarloaf Express* (1977), with John McLaughlin *Johnny McLaughlin, Electric Guitarist* (1978), *Patrice* (1979), *Pizzazz* (1979), *Let There Be Funk* (1980), *Posh* (1980), *Straight From The Heart* (1982), *Now* (1984), *Breaking All The Rules* (1986), *Watch Out!* (1987).

Rushing, Jimmy

b. 26 August 1902, Oklahoma City, Oklahoma, USA, d. 8 June 1972. He began singing while still studying music at school in his home town. By 1923 he was a full-time professional singer, working in California with, among others, **Jelly Roll Morton** and Paul Howard. Back home in the mid-20s he teamed up with **Walter Page** and then joined **Bennie Moten** and by 1935 was a member of the **Count Basie** band. He remained with Basie until 1948 and then worked as a solo, sometimes leading a small band. During these later years he regularly worked with leading jazz artists including **Benny Goodman**, **Buck Clayton**, Basie, and, during tours of the UK, with **Humphrey Lyttelton**.

Rushing's voice was a slightly nasal high tenor which carried comfortably over the sound of a big band in full cry. The fact that he sang at a somewhat higher pitch than most other male blues singers gave his performances a keening, plaintive quality. In fact, his singing style and repertoire made him far more than merely a blues singer and he was comfortably at ease with romantic ballads. Nevertheless, he tinged everything he sang, from love songs to up-tempo swingers, with the qualities of the blues. Despite his extensive repertoire, in later years he favoured certain songs, including 'Going To Chicago', 'Every Day I Have The Blues' and 'Exactly Like You', but even repeated performances at clubs, concerts and record dates were infused with such infectious enthusiasm that he never palled. Known because of his build as 'Mr Five By Five', Rushing was at his best in front of a big band or a Kansas City-style small group but even when he stepped out of character, as on his final formal record date, he could enchant listeners. By the early 70s, and his last date, his voice was showing signs of decades of wear and tear but he retained his unflagging swing and brought to unusual material, such as 'When I Grow Too Old To Dream' and 'I Surrender Dear', great emotional depths and a sharp awareness of the needs of both music and lyrics. An exceptionally gifted artist, Rushing was always unmistakable and never imitated. He was original and unique and one of the greatest singers jazz has ever known. He died in 1972.

Selected albums: *Goin' To Chicago* (1954), *The Essential Jimmy Rushing* (1954-57), *The Jazz Odyssey Of James Rushing Esq* (1956), *If This Ain't The Blues* (1957), with Buck Clayton *Copenhagen Concert* (1959), *Little Jimmy Rushing And The Big Brass* (1958), *Rushing Lullabies* (1959), *The Smith Girls* (1960), *Gee, Baby, Ain't I Good To You* (1967), *Who Was It Sang That Song* (1967), *Every Day I Have The Blues* (1968), *The You And Me That Used To Be* (Bluebird 1971). Compilations: with Count Basie *Good Mornin' Blues* (1937-39 recordings), with Basie *Do You Wanna Jump...?* (1938 recordings), with Basie *The Jubilee Alternatives* (1943-44 recordings), *His Complete Vanguard Recordings* (Vanguard 1954-57 recordings), *The Essential Jimmy Rushing* (Vogue 1983).

Rushton, Joe

b. 7 November 1907, Evanston, Illinois, USA, d. 2. March 1964, San Francisco, California, USA. Rushton learned to play the drums, clarinet and saxophone but had settled on the bass saxophone by the time he was playing with the **California Ramblers** in the late 20s. He moved to Chicago in the 30s and though he later worked in the aircraft industry he had spells with **Jimmy McPartland** and **Bud Freeman** before returning to California. He worked with **Benny Goodman** and **Horace Heidt** in the mid-40s and in 1947 recorded with **Louis Armstrong**. In the same year he joined cornetist **Red Nichols** (1947) with whom he stayed until his death. His booming, rhythmically swinging bass saxophone parts make an important contribution to the success of the Five Pennies' later recordings. Rushton toured Europe with Nichols and took part in the film *The Five Pennies* (1958). Albums: *Rampart Street Paraders* (1954), *Meet The Five Pennies* (1959).

Russell, Andy

b. Andres Rabajos (or Rabago), 1920, Los Angeles, California, USA, d. 16 April 1992, Phoenix, Arizona, USA. The son of Mexican-Spanish parents, Russell was a popular singer in the USA during the 40s, with a romantic image and a penchant for Latin American numbers. In the early 40s he worked with several bands, including **Sonny Dunham**, **Gus Arnheim** and **Johnny Richards**, sometimes also playing drums. In 1942 he was one of seven vocalists with **Alvino Rey**'s big band, but was unable to record with the outfit because of union leader James Caesar Petrillo's infamous musicians recording ban. His own hits, for **Capitol Records**, began in 1944 with 'Besame Mucho' and 'Amor', and continued through until 1948, with romantic ballads such as 'What A Difference A Day Made', 'I Dream Of You', 'I Can't Begin To Tell You', 'Laughing On The Outside (Crying On The Inside)', 'They Say It's Wonderful', 'Pretending' and 'Anniversary Song'. He also recorded **Billy Reid**'s 'I'll Close My Eyes' and **Bud Flanagan**'s 'Underneath The Arches', on which he was accompanied by **Tommy Dorsey**'s old vocal group, the **Pied Pipers**. Russell was also successful with 'Je Vous Aime', which he sang in the film *Copacabana*, starring Groucho Marx. Russell's other movies included *The Stork Club*, in which he joined **Betty Hutton** on 'If I Had A Dozen Hearts', *Make Mine Music*, a series of short **Walt Disney** cartoons, for which Russell contributed 'Without You', and *Breakfast In Hollywood*, derived from a radio series of the same name, and featuring artists such as **Spike Jones** and his City Slickers, and the **Nat 'King' Cole** Trio. Russell was very popular on US radio during the mid-late 40s on the *Old Gold Show* and *Lucky Strike Hit Parade*. He also appeared at many top venues, including the Paramount Theatre in New York. In 1947 he was in Los Angeles, deputizing for **Frank Sinatra** who, with **Bing Crosby**, had declined to sing one of the nominated songs in the annual Academy Awards Ceremony. Russell moved to Mexico City, and became successful there on radio, television and in movies. In the late 60s he returned to the USA where he continued to sing, and appear on television.

Russell, Curley

b. 19 March 1917, Trinidad, d. 3 July 1986. After playing bass in several big bands of the early 40s, Russell directed his attention towards bop. As a member of the quintet led by **Dizzy Gillespie** and **Charlie Parker** in 1945, he attracted considerable attention and thereafter was much in demand for club and recording dates. In the late 40s and early 50s he played in bands led by **Tadd Dameron**, **Bud Powell**, **Horace Silver**, **Art Blakey**, **Thelonious Monk** and others. Despite his popularity with beboppers and his undoubted skills in this area of jazz, Russell appeared to be impervious to changing needs within later rhythm sections and by the end of the 50s he was playing in R&B bands. He died in 1986.
Albums: with Art Blakey *A Night At Birdland* (1954), *Thelonious Monk Quintet* (1954). Compilations: with Dizzy Gillespie and others *The Small Groups 1945-46* (1945-46), *The Bud Powell Trio Plays* (1947).

Russell, George

b. 23 June 1923, Cincinnati, Ohio, USA. One of modern jazz's leading composers, Russell started out as a drummer with **Benny Carter**, but first came to prominence in the mid-40s writing for **Dizzy Gillespie**, notably 'Cubano Be, Cubano Bop'. He also wrote for **Artie Shaw** and **Claude Thornhill** and his 'A Bird In Igor's Yard', combining elements of **Charlie Parker** and Stravinsky, was recorded by the **Buddy De Franco** big band in 1949. Periods of hospitalization for tuberculosis led to him developing his theoretical *The Lydian Chromatic Concept Of Tonal Organization*, first published in 1953 and a crucial influence on the later modal jazz of **Miles Davis** and

John Coltrane. In the 50s Russell wrote 'All About Rosie' on a commission from Brandeis University and taught both privately and at the School of Jazz in Lennox, Massachusetts: his students, then and later, included **Carla Bley**, **Rahsaan Roland Kirk**, **Don Ellis** and **Steve Swallow** (the later pair also recording with him). In the early 60s he led a sextet and made several celebrated recordings, often featuring *avant garde* artists such as **Sheila Jordan** ('You Are My Sunshine'), **Eric Dolphy** (*Ezz-Thetics*) and **Don Cherry** (*At Beethoven Hall*). In the mid- to late 60s, Russell was based in Sweden, where he experimented with electronic music and worked with upcoming players, such as **Jan Garbarek**, **Terje Rypdal** and **Palle Mikkelborg**. In 1969 he returned to the USA to teach at the New England Conservatory, but still continued to record in Sweden. (Many of the recordings he made in Scandinavia in the 60s and 70s have since reappeared on the **Soul Note** label in the 80s.) From the late 70s he began playing and recording regularly in the USA, often working with a big band. He was one of the first artists signed up by the reactivated **Blue Note** label, and in the mid- to late 80s he toured the UK with bands that included several well-known British players, for example, **Chris Biscoe**, **Ian Carr**, **Andy Sheppard** and **Kenny Wheeler**. Russell has continued with his theoretical work, completing a second volume of his *Lydian Chromatic Concept* in 1978. This stands as one of the central texts of modern jazz theory. A complex work, its basic premise is that traditional jazz structures, such as chord sequences, can be overlaid with scales or modes that introduce a degree of pan-tonality and so allow the player more choices for improvising.
Selected albums: *The Jazz Workshop* (Bluebird 1956), *New York, NY* (1959), *Jazz In The Space Age* (1960), *At The Five Spot* (1960), *In Kansas City* (1960), *Stratosphunk* (1960), *Ezz-thetic* (Original Jazz Classics 1961), *The Outer View* (Original Jazz Classics 1962), *At The Beethoven Hall Vols. 1 & 2* (1965), with Bill Evans *Living Time* (1972), *Electronic Sonata For Souls Loved By Nature 1980* (Soul Note 1980), with Jan Garbarek *Othello Ballet Suite* (Soul Note 1981, rec 1967), with Garbarek *Trip To Prillarguri* (Soul Note 1982, rec 1970), *New York Big Band* (Soul Note 1982, rec 1978), *Listen To The Silence* (1983, rec 1972), *The Essence Of George Russell* (1983, rec 1966-70), *Live In An American Time Spiral* (Soul Note 1983), *The African Game* (1985, rec 1983), *So What* (Blue Note 1986), *Time Space* (Polygram 1988), *The London Concert Vols 1-2* (Stash 1990).
Further reading: *The Lydian Chromatic Concept Of Tonal Organization*, George Russell.

Russell, Hal

b. Harold Russell Luttenbacher, 28 August 1926, Detroit, Michigan, USA, d. 5 September 1992. Russell grew up in Chicago and first became involved in music by playing drums. He attended the University of Illinois, receiving both bachelor and masters degrees in musical education. Although he had learned the trumpet as part of his degree course, he abandoned it for 30 years while he worked in jazz groups as a drummer and vibraphonist. In 1950 he played with **Miles Davis** and later in the decade performed with many leading jazz artists, such as **Sonny Rollins**, **Duke Ellington**, **Billie Holiday**, **Erroll Garner** and **Sarah Vaughan**. From 1961 he played drums in the Joe Daley Trio, one of Chicago's first free jazz groups, then in the late 60s, inspired by the high-energy music of *avant gardists*, such as **Albert Ayler** and **Sunny Murray**, he began to lead his own groups. From the late 70s Russell headed a quintet and a trio in what he called NRG Ensembles, and was perhaps most creative in the freedom granted him by the latter format. The incompetence of the group's original saxophonist led Russell to take up saxophone himself - at the age of 50 - and he became an enthusiastic performer on tenor and soprano. 'I thought God, what a fool I am! I should have been playing saxophone all along! I shouldn't have played drums at all!' In 1990 he released *Hal On Earth*, with an unusual quintet consisting of two saxophones, two basses and drums - with three members of the ensemble doubling on didjeridoo! Russell stated: 'I find that the more popular you become the less you like the music you are playing. This makes you search for new forms and ways of musical expression'. In 1991 **ECM Records** recognized what had previously been underground success by releasing the live *Finnish-Swiss Tour* by an NRG Ensemble that comprised Russell and longtime associates Mars Williams (best-known for his work with the **Psychedelic Furs**), Steve Hunt, Brian Sandstrom and Kent Kessler. In the summer of 1992 Russell became ill and was rushed into hospital for heart bypass surgery. The operation was considered a success, but he died three weeks later.

Albums: *The Hal Russell NRG Ensemble* (1981), with Mars Williams *EFT Soons* (1981), with Charles Tyler *Generation* (Chief 1982), *Conserving NRG* (Principally Jazz 1984), *Hal On Earth* (1990), *The Finnish-Swiss Tour* (ECM 1991), *Hal's Bells* (ECM 1992), *The Hal Russell Story* (ECM 1993).

Russell, Janet

b. 11 January 1958, Buckhaven, Fife, Scotland. Russell is as well-known for her work with **Sisters Unlimited** as for her solo performances. Following an early career singing in the clubs of Edinburgh, she went on to support to a number of major artists at the Edinburgh Folk and Fringe Festivals from 1981-83. In addition, Russell worked with Christine Kydd, performing on *Folk On 2* for BBC Radio. The pair released *Janet Russell And Christine Kydd*, on Greentrax. Russell's first solo outing on record emerged with *Gathering The Fragments*

on Harbourtown Records, a release that was well received and gained airplay on non-folk programmes on radio. She was one of a number of performers who took part in the **Les Barker** album, *The Stones Of Callanish*. Having taken some time out to have her first child she was inspired to write 'Breastfeeding Baby In The Park'. The following month saw the first broadcast, on BBC Radio, of a recording of a concert by Sisters Unlimited (*No Limits*) at the Purcell Room, on the South Bank, London. In March 1991, Janet appeared on the **McCalman**'s television series on BBC Scotland, taking time out to have a second child in December of the same year. Although still performing solo, more of Russell's time is now given to Sisters Unlimited.

Albums: *Janet Russell And Christine Kydd* (1988), *Gathering The Fragments* (Harbourtown 1988), with others *The Stones Of Callanish* (1989), with Sisters Unlimited *No Limits* (1991), *Bright Shining Morning?* (Harbourtown 1993).

Russell, Johnny

b. John Bright Russell, 23 January 1940, Sunflower County, Mississippi, USA. Russell's family moved to Fresno, California when he was 12 years old and his ambitions were centred around country music. He wrote his own songs and performed as a singer/guitarist. **Jim Reeves** heard his first record, 'In A Mansion Stands My Love' (for Radio Records when he was 18) and recorded the song as the b-side of 'He'll Have To Go'. Other early Russell compositions include **Loretta Lynn**'s 'Two Mules Pull This Wagon' and the **Wilburn Brothers**' 'Hurt Her Once For Me'. Russell was working on a song about Hollywood but a chance remark, 'They're gonna put me in the movies', enabled him to complete it as 'Act Naturally'. Russell's co-writer, Vonnie Morrison, placed the song with **Buck Owens** and it became a number 1 US country hit. 'Act Naturally' was recorded by the **Beatles** with **Ringo Starr** on lead vocals for their *Help!* album and was also the b-side of their US number 1, 'Yesterday'. Russell, who had recorded as a sideline for **MGM** and **ABC**-Paramount, took his own career seriously when he signed with **Chet Atkins** for **RCA** in 1971. He had US country hits with 'Catfish John', 'The Baptism Of Jesse Taylor', 'She's In Love With A Rodeo Man' and, most significantly, 'Rednecks, White Socks And Blue Ribbon Beer', which became an anthem in the south. 'I was appearing on **Charley Pride**'s road show,' says Russell, 'and he wouldn't let me sing the song 'cause he thought it was racial.' Strangely, Russell did not write his biggest RCA singles. He explains, 'I like singing people songs and as I tend to write hurting love songs, I never wrote the kind of songs that were right for me.' Russell's 1977 single 'Obscene Phone Call' was banned by several USA radio stations. In 1978 he moved to **Mercury** and his singles included 'While The Choir

Sang The Hymn, I Thought Of Her', 'You'll Be Back Every Night In My Dreams' and 'Song Of The South'. Russell married his second wife, Beverly Heckel, in 1977 when she was 17. She had her own chart success with 'Bluer Than Blue' and she joined his stage show. **George Strait** had a US country number 1 in 1984 with Russell's 'Let's Fall To Pieces Together' and **Gene Watson** did well with 'I Got No Reason Now For Going Home'. Although Johnny Russell's name was known only to die-hard fans in the UK, he was a showstopper at the 1985 Wembley country music festival with his **Burl Ives**-styled personality and humour. (Ives did, in fact, record a Russell song, 'Mean Mean Man'.) Russell weighs 25 stone and his opening remark, 'Can you all see me at the back?', was a winner and a successful UK tour with **Boxcar Willie** followed. A heart attack put Russell out of action for sometime but he is now back on the road and still remains one of Nashville's leading songwriters. As he says, 'I carry a lot of weight in this town.'
Albums: *Mr. And Mrs. Untrue* (1971), *Catfish John/Chained* (1972), *Rednecks, White Socks And Blue-Ribbon Beer* (1973), *She's In Love With A Rodeo Man* (1974), *Here Comes Johnny Russell* (1975), *Something Old Something New* (1991).

Russell, Leon

b. 2 April 1941, Lawton, Oklahoma, USA. The many talents of Russell include that of singer, songwriter, producer, arranger, entrepreneur, record company executive and multi-instrumentalist. While he tasted great honours as a solo star in the early 70s, it is his all-round contribution, much of it in the background, that has made him a vitally important figure in rock music for more than 30 years. His impressive career began, after having already mastered piano and trumpet as a child, when he played with **Ronnie Hawkins** and **Jerry Lee Lewis** in the late 50s. He became a regular session pianist for the pivotal US television show *Shindig* as well as being present on most of the classic **Phil Spector** singles, including the **Ronettes**, **Crystals** and the **Righteous Brothers**. **James Burton** is reputed to have taught him the guitar around this time. He has appeared on hundreds of major singles right across the music spectrum, playing with a plethora of artists, including **Frank Sinatra**, **Bobby Darin**, the **Byrds**, **Herb Alpert** and **Paul Revere**. He formed his own unit **Asylum Choir** in 1968 together with Marc Benno and formed a cultist duo that was a commercial disaster. He befriended **Delaney And Bonnie** and created the famous Mad Dogs And Englishmen tour, which included **Joe Cocker**. Cocker recorded Russell's 'Delta Lady' during this time, to great success. Russell founded his own label **Shelter Records** with UK producer Denny Cordell and released the self-titled debut which received unanimous critical approbation. His own session players included **Steve Winwood**, **George Harrison**, **Eric**

Clapton, Charlie Watts, **Bill Wyman** and **Ringo Starr**. Following further session work including playing with **Bob Dylan** and **Dave Mason**, he appeared at the historic Concert for Bangla Desh in 1971 and was forced to rest the following year when he suffered a nervous and physical breakdown.

He returned in 1972 with the poignantly stunning *Carney*. This US number 2, million seller, was semi-autobiographical using the circus clown theme as an analogy to his own punishing career. The following year Russell delivered a superb country album, *Hank Wilson's Back*, acknowledging his debt to classic country singers. That year he released an album by his future wife, Mary McCreary, and in 1974 an excellent version of **Tim Hardin**'s 'If I Were A Carpenter'. Leon concentrated on his own career more and more and in 1977 was awarded a Grammy for his song 'This Masquerade', which made the US Top 10 the previous year for **George Benson**. A partnership with **Willie Nelson** produced a superb country album in 1979; it became one of his biggest albums. The single 'Heartbreak Hotel' topped the US country chart, endorsing Russell's acceptance as a country singer. An excursion into bluegrass resulted in the 1981 live set with the **New Grass Revival**. Following *Hank Wilson's Volume II* in 1984 Leon became involved with his own video production company. Now white-haired, he resembles Tolkein's Gandalf. He returned in 1992 with the disappointing *Anything Will Happen*. Russell has already earned his retirement twice over and his place in the history books. If there were such a trophy he would be a contender for the 'most outstanding all-round contribution to rock' music award, yet sadly in recent years he has easily won the 'where on earth is he' nomination.
Albums: *Look Inside The Asylum Choir* (1968), *Leon Russell* (1970), *Leon Russell And The Shelter People* (1971), *Asylum Choir II* (1971), *Carney* (1972), *Leon Live* (1973), *Hank Wilson's Back, Vol.1* (1973), *Stop All That Jazz* (1974), *Looking Back* (1974), *Will O' The Wisp* (1975), *Wedding Album* (1976), *Make Love To The Music* (1977), *Americana* (1978), with Willie Nelson *One For The Road* (1979), *Live And Love* (1979), with the New Grass Revival *The Live Album* (1981), *Hank Wilson Vol.II* (1984), *Anything Will Happen* (1992). Compilation: *Best Of Leon* (1976).

Russell, Luis

b. 6 August 1902, Careening Clay, Bocas Del Toro, Panama, d. 11 December 1963. After playing various instruments in his homeland, Russell moved to New Orleans in 1919 and thereafter played piano in local saloons and clubs. In the early 20s he played with **Albert Nicholas** among others, and also led bands. He played with **King Oliver** in Chicago in 1925 and in 1927 became leader of a band in New York. For the next few years he led his band in the city and on tours, often backing **Louis Armstrong**. In 1935 the band became known as Armstrong's but Russell stayed on until the early 40s, when he formed a new band for touring. From the late 40s he ran a business outside music but continued to lead small bands for club dates. Russell's bands never had the impact on the jazz public achieved by many of his contemporaries. Nevertheless, he was a dedicated musician and made serious attempts to integrate some of the fundamental concepts of the New Orleans style into big band music. He died in 1963.

Albums: with others *Gut Bucket Blues And Stomps - Chicago* (1926-28), *New York Jazz* (1928-33), *1930-1934* (VJM 1986), *Luis Russell And His Orchestra 1929-30* (Swaggie 1988), *Savoy Shout* (JSP 1989).

Russell, Pee Wee

b. Charles Ellsworth Russell, 27 March 1906, Maple Wood, Missouri, USA, d. 15 February 1969. Russell began playing clarinet in the early 20s and by 1927, the year he came to New York, had already worked with luminaries such as **Jack Teagarden**, **Frank Trumbauer** and **Bix Beiderbecke**. In the late 20s and throughout the 30s and 40s, Russell played with numerous jazzmen working in the traditional sphere, among them **Bobby Hackett**, **Wild Bill Davison**, **Louis Prima**, **Billy Butterfield**, **Muggsy Spanier**, **George Wettling** and **Art Hodes**. He also enjoyed a long association with **Eddie Condon**, although enjoyed is perhaps an inappropriate term for what Russell later described as a time of sadness - because thanks to his hangdog expression and idiosyncratic style of playing, he was often treated as a clown. In the 50s Russell's health was suspect, he suffered from alcoholism, but by the 60s he was back playing at clubs, concerts and festivals around the world. One of the most endearing eccentrics in jazz, Russell's playing style was unique and at first and sometimes even second hearing might be thought primitive. Nevertheless, the sometimes grating sounds he produced on his instrument and the seemingly indecisive placing of notes during solo and ensemble passages had a cumulative effect which demonstrated the existence of an inquiring and adventurous musical mind. This became more overtly apparent when he blended easily with such diverse musical associates as **Thelonious Monk**, **Henry 'Red' Allen** and **Coleman Hawkins**. In the 60s he played in a pianoless quartet with **Marshall Brown** and on a big band album with **Oliver Nelson**, as well as working again in more traditional contexts. A totally original and often brilliant clarinettist, he inspired writer George Frazier to enthuse about 'the bliss and the sadness and the compassion and the humility that are there in the notes he plays'. Finally, the liver condition that had almost killed him in the 50s returned to finish the job, and he died in February 1969.

Selected albums: *The Definitive Pee Wee Russell* (1958),

The Pee Wee Russell Quintet i (1958), *Portrait Of Pee Wee Russell* (1958), *A Salute To Newport* (1959), *Swinging With Pee Wee* (1960), with Coleman Hawkins *Jazz Reunion* (Candid 1961), *Pee Wee Russell-Coleman Hawkins All Stars* (1961), *The Pee Wee Russell Quintet* ii (1962-63), *Thelonious Monk At Newport* (1963), *Hot Licorice* (c.1964), *Gumbo* (c.1964), *Ask Me Now* (1965), *The College Concert* (1966), with Oliver Nelson *The Spirit Of '67* (1967). Compilations: *The Great Soloists - Pee Wee Russell* (1932-35), *The Pied Piper Of Jazz* (1941-44), *Muggsy And Pee Wee* (1941-57), *The Individualism Of* (Savoy 1985), *Portrait Of Pee Wee* (Fresh Sounds 1991).

Further reading: *Pee Wee Russell: The Life Of A Jazzman*, Robert Hilbert. *Pee Wee Speaks: A Discography Of Pee Wee Russell*, Robert Hilbert with David Niven.

Russo, Bill

b. 25 June 1928, Chicago, Illinois, USA. After extensive studies in arranging, Russo wrote for **Lennie Tristano** and also occasionally played trombone. One of the earliest musicians to lead a rehearsal band, his experimental style came to the attention of **Stan Kenton** in the early 50s. In the mid-50s he concentrated on performing with a small group but by the end of the decade was again deeply involved in writing for larger jazz ensembles. He was also active as a teacher and this combination of work continued on throughout the 60s and early 70s. After spending some time in film and television work he returned to teaching in the 80s. He remains one of the more interesting of writers for the large modern jazz orchestra.

Albums: *Bill Russo And His Orchestra* i (1951), by Stan Kenton *New Concepts Of Artistry In Rhythm* (1952), by Kenton *Portraits On Standards* (1953-54), *The Wall Of Alcina* (1955), *Bill Russo Plus The Hans Koller Ensemble* (1955), *Bill Russo And The New Jazz Group, Hanover* (1955), *Bill Russo And His Orchestra* ii (1960), *The Seven Deadly Sins* (1960), *Suite No. 1 Opus 5 & Suite No. 2 Opus 8* (1962), *Bill Russo On The Air In London* (1963), *Bill Russo And The London Jazz Orchestra* (1964).

Rust Never Sleeps

Neil Young's cinematic excursions have proved the stuff of controversy. He withdrew a 1973 film, ***Journey Through The Past***, in the wake of adverse critical reaction, while *Human Highway* (1982), although several years in the making, received only a limited screening. *Rust Never Sleeps*, released in 1979 and directed by Young under his 'Bernard Shakey' alias, took its title from his album of the same name. The set not only rekindled interest in the singer's career, it also showed he empathised with the concurrent punk movement. Indeed, US new-wave act **Devo** were featured in *Rust Never Sleeps*, an elliptical movie combining compulsive live material with suitably obscure imagery. A road crew dressed in garb combining science-fiction and Ku Klux Klan-styled robes and outlandish stage props are but two of the unusual interludes peppering fiery renditions of material drawn from throughout Young's catalogue. 'Cinnamon Girl', 'Like A Hurricane', 'Hey Hey, My My (Out Of The Blue And Into The Black)', 'Cortez The Killer' and 'Tonight's The Night' are among the songs on offer, many of which are energized by the presence of his excellent backing band, **Crazy Horse**. The performances were later enshrined on *Live Rust*, but the appeal of the album has outlasted the film from which it comes. *Rust Never Sleeps* has become yet another rarely-seen epic from this mercurial character.

Rutherford, Mike

b. 2 October 1950. While working in **Genesis**, guitarist Rutherford has had a solo career broken into two distinct phases. *Smallcreep's Day* was a concept album based on Peter C. Brown's novel, featuring vocalist Noel McCalla, formerly with Moon who made two Epic albums in 1976-77. But neither that nor the follow-up were commercially successful. Rutherford resumed his solo activity in 1985, under the name **Mike And The Mechanics**. He had two new songwriting partners - producer Chris Neil and former hit-maker **B.A. Robertson**. The group also had twin lead vocalists in **Paul Carrack** (ex-**Ace** and **Squeeze**) and Paul Young from **Sad Cafe**. The new formation created two US hit singles, 'Silent Running' and 'All I Need Is A Miracle' and a million-selling album. The same line-up was retained for *Living Years*, whose title track was both an international best seller and an **Ivor Novello** award winner. Co-written by Rutherford and Robertson it was strongly autobiographical in its theme of the death of a parent. During the late 80s and 90s, the group was also a touring band, with the addition of Peter Van Hooke (drums) and Adrian Lee (bass).
Abums: *Smallcreep's Day* (1980), *Acting Very Strange* (1982), *Mike And The Mechanics* (1985), *Living Years* (1988), *Word Of Mouth* (1991), *Beggar On A Beach Of Gold* (Virgin 1995).

Rutherford, Paul

b. 29 February 1940, Greenwich, London, England. Rutherford began to play saxophone in the mid-50s, then changed to trombone, which he played in RAF bands from 1958-63. While in the RAF he met **John Stevens** and **Trevor Watts**, with whom he founded the **Spontaneous Music Ensemble** in 1965. From 1964-68 he studied at London's Guildhall School of Music in the day and played free jazz in The Little Theatre Club at night. In 1967 be began to work regularly in **Mike Westbrook**'s bands. In the early 70s he formed his own Iskra 1903 group, with **Derek Bailey** and **Barry Guy**, and also worked with the London Jazz Composers Orchestra the **Globe Unity** Orchestra and the **Tony Oxley** septet as well as with other freelance improvisers, such as **Evan Parker** and **Paul Lovens**. A major figure on the European

improvising scene, Rutherford's major contribution is probably the new language for solo trombone that he began to develop in the early 70s and best demonstrated on the 1976 classic *Gentle Harm Of The Bourgeoisie*. *Neuph*, from 1978, also showed his skills as a composer and euphonium player. In the 80s he formed a new line-up of Iskra 1903, with Guy and **Phil Wachsmann**, continued to work with LJCO, played in the Free Jazz Quartet with **Eddie Prevost** and recorded a set of solos and duos with baritone saxophonist George Haslam. A virtuoso trombonist, Rutherford's commitment to experimental, abstract and improvised music has earned him the respect of players all over the world.
Albums: *Iskra 1903* (1972), *Iskra 1903* (1974), *Gentle Harm Of The Bourgeoisie* (1976, rec 1974), *Old Moers Almanac* (1976), with Paul Lovens *And When I Say Slowly...*(1977), *Neuph* (1978), with Evan Parker, Barry Guy, John Stevens *Four Four Four* (1979), with others *The Ericle Of Dolphi* (1989, rec 1985, 1977), with George Haslam *1989 And All That* (1989), with free Jazz Quarter *Premonitions* (1989).

Ruthless Rap Assassins

Manchester, England-based, and self-styled 'North Hulme' soundsculptors comprising Dangerous 'C' Carsonova (vocals, turntables), MC Kermit Le Freak (vocals) and Paul Roberts (guitar). Ruthless Rap Assassins formed in that district in the mid-80s, earning their reputation via local gigs. They were signed by **EMI** in 1987 after they had heard their debut single, 'We Don't Care'. Placed on the Syncopate subsidiary, the first result was the *Killer Album*, whose 'Go Wild' effectively sampled **Steppenwolf**'s 'Born To Be Wild'. Even better was 'The Dream', which utilised the funked up groove of **Cynade**'s 'The Message' to underpin this tale of West Indians moving to England in the 50s, and the subsequent dashing of their hopes and spirits. The militant aesthetics of *Killer Album* came as something of a shock to those who still considered such daunting music the preserve of inner-city Americans. The follow-up selection, however, cut much deeper. Tracks like 'Down And Dirty' proved an effective parody of rap's pre-occupation with matters sexual, while 'No Tale, No Twist' observed some clever jazz touches. The group remained inventive and militant, the single 'Justice (Just Us)', proving a particularly defiant swipe at the majority white populace. Though they split afterwards due to record label and public indifference, the Ruthless Rap Assassins' legacy as the first worthwhile UK hip hop band remains.
Albums: *Killer Album* (Syncopate 1990), *Think - It Ain't Illegal Yet* (Murdertone 1991).

Ruthless Records

Eazy-E's record label, by legend founded on his illegal

activities, which for several years offered the rap world incisive, definitive gangsta hip hop documents. A hitch came when house producer **Dr Dre**, so central to much of the label's success (which at the time included nine gold albums), left in bitter acrimony in the early 90s. The public slanging match with Eazy-E and General Manager Jerry Holler did not abate until Dre persuaded Jimmy Iovine at Interscope to let him set up his own label, **Death Row**. In 1993 **Relativity** Records stepped in to bring Ruthless, whose stable now boasted **Hoez With Attitude**, **Kokane**, **Blood Of Abraham** and **MC Ren**, under their wing after the original deal with **Priority** expired. Yet, post-Dre, the label's fortunes have continued to flag.

Rutles

The product of satirists **Neil Innes** (ex-**Bonzo Dog Doo-Dah Band**) and Eric Idle, formerly of the comedy team *Monty Python's Flying Circus*, the Rutles, was an affectionate and perceptive parody of the **Beatles**' career, which emerged from the duo's *Rutland Weekend Television* BBC comedy series. Innes played Ron Nasty (Lennon), Idle played Dirk McQuickly (McCartney), while Rikki Fataar (ex-**Beach Boys**) and John Halsey (ex-**Patto**) completed the line-up as Stig O'Hara (Harrison) and Barry Wom (Starr) respectively. The Rutles' film, *All You Need Is Cash*, and attendant album deftly combined elements drawn from both founder members' past work. Innes' songs re-created the different, and indeed, contrasting, styles of music the Beatles offered, ranging from the Mersey pop of 'I Must Be In Love' and 'Ouch!' to the psychedelia of 'Piggy In The Middle'. **Mick Jagger** and **Paul Simon** made excellent cameo appearances while **George Harrison** enjoyed a small acting role. The project is now rightly regarded, alongside **Spinal Tap**, as one of rock's most lasting parodies and the Rutles were themselves lampooned in 1991 when maverick New York label Shimmy Disc produced *Rutles Highway Revisited* wherein its roster performed a unique interpretation of the original album.
Album: *The Rutles* (1978).

Ruts

This punk/reggae-influenced group comprised Malcolm Owen (vocals), Paul Fox (guitar/vocals), Dave Ruffy (drums) and John 'Segs' Jennings (bass). They first came to the fore in 1979 with the UK Top 10 single, 'Babylon's Burning'. Their gigs of that year were the most stunning of punk's second generaton, with one in Bradford cited by Justin Sullivan of **New Model Army** as the biggest influence on his career. Their style resembled that of the **Clash**, but while Owen was occasionally compared to **Joe Strummer**, there was something just as original sparking the group's songwriting. The strident 'Something That I Said' gave them another hit and their debut album, *The Crack*,

though not representing the band as well as their blistering singles, was well received. The rampaging 'Staring At The Rude Boys' neatly displayed their rock/dub talents, but their progress was arrested by Owen's drug-related death on 14 July 1980. On the run-out groove of their final single together the band scratched the legend 'Can I Use Your Bathroom?' in tribute - Owen having died in the bath. The remaining members were joined by Gary Barnacle and elected to continue as Ruts DC. They recorded two further albums under that name, moving towards funk-influenced reggae. Without Owen, however, the spirit of the group was not the same and they faded from prominence, though their influence lives on in bands such as the **Wildhearts** and the **Almighty**. Fox would go on to a successful production career.
Albums: *The Crack* (Virgin 1979), *Grin And Bear It* (Virgin 1980). As Ruts DC: *Animal Now* (Virgin 1981), *Rhythm Collision Vol 1* (Bohemian 1982). Ruts DC And The Mad Professor: *Rhythm Collision Dub Vol. 1* (ROIR 1987, cassette only). Compilations: *The Ruts Live* (Dojo 1987), *The Peel Sessions* (Strange Fruit 1990), *The Best Of The Ruts* (Virgin 1995).

Ryan, Marion

b. Middlesbrough, England. This popular singer, with a vivacious style, was successful in the UK on records, radio and television in the 50s and early 60s. In one sense Marion Ryan's contribution to the UK charts began in 1948 when she gave birth to twins, **Paul And Barry Ryan**, who had hits of their own in the late 60s. Barry's 'Eloise' went to number 2, which was three places higher than his mother's best effort. Marion Ryan first appeared on the UK music scene in 1953 after a spell singing with **Edmundo Ros**, and became a favourite on UK television with programmes such as *Off The Record*, *Music Shop*, *Festival Of British Song*, *Jack Jackson's Record Roundup*, *Gerry's Inn*, *Sunday Night At Blackpool*, *6.5 Special*, *Oh Boy* and *Two's Company*. She also starred in four series of *Spot The Tune* with Canadian vocalist-comedian Jackie Rae. She sang regularly with the **Ray Ellington** Quartet, and appeared with them in the 1956 movie *Eric Winstone's Stagecoach*. In the late 50s, Ryan covered several big hits, including **Perry Como**'s 'Hot Diggity', **Peggy Lee**'s 'Mr Wonderful' and **Rosemary Clooney**'s 'Mangos'. In 1958 she had chart success with 'Love Me Forever', which beat the **Eydie Gorme** version and rose to number 5. She also released some EPs (those four-track mini-albums), including *That Ryan Gal* and *Hit Parade*. In 1963 she featured in the **Tommy Steele** movie *It's All Happening*, with **Russ Conway**, **Danny Williams**, **John Barry** and **Shane Fenton**. Shortly afterwards, she retired from singing to live with her husband, impresario Harold Davison.
Selected album: *A Lady Loves* (1960 Pye-Nixa).
Film: *It's All Happening* (1963).

Ryan, Paul And Barry

b. Paul and Barry Sapherson, 24 October 1948, Leeds, England. Paul, d. 29 November 1992. The twin sons of popular singer **Marion Ryan**, Paul and Barry were launched as clean-cut act to attendant showbusiness publicity. Their debut single, 'Don't Bring Me Your Heartaches' reached the UK Top 20 in 1965, and over the ensuing months the siblings enjoyed respectable, if unspectacular, chart placings with 'Have Pity On The Boy' and 'I Love Her'. The Ryans shifted away from their tailored image with 'Have You Ever Loved Somebody' (1966) and 'Keep It Out Of Sight' (1967), penned, respectively, by the **Hollies** and **Cat Stevens**, but such releases were less successful. They split amicably in 1968 with Paul embarking on a songwriting career while Barry recorded as a solo act. Together they created 'Eloise', the latter's impressive number 2 hit and subsequent million seller, but ensuing singles failed to emulate its popularity. Paul's compositions included 'I Will Drink The Wine', which was recorded by **Frank Sinatra**, but neither brother was able to sustain initial impetus. During 1969 Barry had an accident which caused serious burns to his face. In the 70s Paul moved to the USA, but later left the music business and opened a chain of hairdressing salons.
Album: *The Ryans* (1967). Solo: Barry Ryan *Barry Ryan Sings Paul Ryan* (1968). Paul Ryan *Scorpio Rising* (1976).

Ryan, Tommy

This popular American band singer was known for his smooth tenor voice. Ryan worked with **Sammy Kaye**'s very successful 'swing and sway' orchestra from 1938-43. He sang on some of their biggest hits, including three chart toppers: 'Rosalie', 'Love Walked In' and 'Dream Valley'. He also enjoyed success with 'Sometimes I'm Happy', 'All Ashore', 'Carolina Moon', 'They Say', 'We've Come A Long Way Together', 'Last Night's Gardenias', 'Make Believe Island', 'A Nightingale Sang In Berkeley Square', 'Harbour Of Dreams', 'Minka', 'On The Street Of Regret', 'Johnny Doughboy Found A Rose In Ireland' and 'My Buddy'. When he left Kaye, Ryan joined Blue Barron's sweet orchestra, and took over the leadership for a while when Barron was in the US Armed Forces. He led his own outfit during the late 40s, and appeared in a song series on radio during the early 50s.

Rydell, Bobby

b. Robert Ridarelli, 26 April 1942, Philadelphia, Pennsylvania, USA. Probably the most musically talented of the late 50s Philadelphia school of clean-cut teen idols, Rydell first performed in public as a drummer at the age of seven. At nine he debuted on **Paul Whiteman**'s *Teen Club* amateur television show and was the show's regular drummer for three years.

He attended the same boys club as **Fabian** and **Frankie Avalon**, formed a duo with Avalon in 1954 and shortly after they both joined local group Rocco And The Saints. After several rejections from labels, he recorded his first solo single 'Fatty Fatty' for his manager's Veko label. In 1958 he joined **Cameo** and his fourth release for that label 'Kissin' Time' (which owed something to 'Sweet Little Sixteen') became the first of his 18 US Top 40 hits over the next four years. The photogenic pop/rock singer's best-known transatlantic hits are 'Wild One', 'Sway' and 'Volare' (only two years after the song first topped the charts) all in 1960 and 'Forget Him', a number written and produced in Britain by **Tony Hatch** in 1963. Rydell, whose ambition was always to be an all-round entertainer, starred in the movie *Bye Bye Birdie* and quickly, and initially successfully, moved into the cabaret circuit. The arrival of the British groups in 1964 was the final nail in his chart coffin. He later recorded without success for **Capitol**, **Reprise**, **RCA**, Perception and Pickwick International. Rydell has continued to work the club and oldies circuit and had some recognition for his role in rock when the high school in the hit 70s musical *Grease* was named after him.
Selected albums: *Bobby's Biggest Hits* (1961), *Rydell At The Copa* (1961), *Rydell/Chubby Checker* (1961), *All The Hits* (1962), *Biggest Hits Vol. 2* (1962), *Top Hits Of 1963* (1964), *Forget Him* (1964), *Greatest Hits* (1993).
Film: *Because They're Young* (1960).

Ryder, Mitch, And The Detroit Wheels

b. William Levise Jnr., 26 February 1945, Detroit, Michigan, USA. An impassioned singer, bearing an aural debt to **Little Richard**, Mitch Ryder spent his formative years frequenting the clubs on Woodward Avenue, watching many of Tamla/**Motown**'s star attractions. Having outgrown two high school bands, Levise formed Billy Lee And The Rivieras in 1963. Jim McCarty (lead guitar - later of **Buddy Miles** Express and **Cactus**), Joe Cubert (rhythm guitar), Earl Elliott (bass) and 'Little' John Badanjek (drums) completed the group's early line-up, which recorded two singles for local labels prior to their 'discovery' by producer **Bob Crewe**. The quintet was then given a sharper name - Mitch Ryder And The Detroit Wheels - and in 1965 secured their biggest hit with the frenzied 'Jenny Take A Ride', a raw and earthy performance which set new standards in 'blue-eyed' soul. Uninhibited at a time of increasing sophistication, Ryder successfully captured the power of his black inspirations. Subsequent releases showed a similar verve, but the group reached its zenith with the exceptional medley of 'Devil With A Blue Dress On' and 'Good Golly Miss Molly'. From there, however, the formula became predictable and more studied recreations failed to emulate its fire. The Wheels were summarily fired in 1967 as the singer was coaxed towards safer fare. He and Crewe split up in rancorous circumstances but a union with guitarist **Steve Cropper** resulted in the excellent *Detroit/Memphis Experiment*.

In 1971 Levise formed Detroit, a hard-edged rock band of great promise which disintegrated prematurely. The singer then abandoned music, nursing a throat ailment which threatened his one-time livelihood. He resumed performing in the late 70s and although later releases lack the overall passion of those initial recordings, there are moments when that erstwhile strength occurs. In the 90s Mitch Ryder is still a major concert attraction. A primary influence on **Bruce Springsteen**, the architect of Detroit's 'high-energy' performers, the **MC5** and the **Stooges**, Mitch Ryder's talent should not be under-estimated.

Albums: with the Detroit Wheels *Take A Ride* (New Voice 1966), *Breakout...!!!* (New Voice 1966), *Sock It To Me!* (New Voice 1967); Mitch Ryder solo *What Now My Love* (1967), *All The Heavy Hits* (1967), *Mitch Ryder Sings The Hits* (1968), *The Detroit-Memphis Experiment* (1969), *How I Spent My Vacation* (1978), *Naked But Not Dead* (1979), *Got Change For A Million* (1981), *Live Talkies* (1982), *Smart Ass* (1982), *Never Kick A Sleeping Dog* (1983), *In The China Shop* (1986), *Red Blood And White Mink* (1989), *La Gash* (1992). Compilations: *All Mitch Ryder Hits!* (1967), *Mitch Ryder And The Detroit Wheels' Greatest Hits* (1972), *Wheels Of Steel* (1983), *Rev Up* (1990), *The Beautiful Toulang Sunset* (1992), *Document Series Presents...* (1992).

Rypdal, Terje

b. 23 August 1947, Oslo, Norway. The son of a nationally famous conductor, Rypdal had piano lessons as a child, but taught himself the electric guitar.

Studying composition at Oslo University, he also studied **George Russell**'s theories of improvisation with Russell himself, and then played in his big band and sextet. In the late 60s he began to collaborate with **Jan Garbarek**, and played on Garbarek's first two albums for **ECM Records**; but he received more exposure in the 1969 German Free Jazz Festival, playing with musicians from the burgeoning Chicago free jazz scene in a band led by **Lester Bowie**. Forming Odyssey in the 70s, Rypdal, now recording, also began touring, which he has continued strenuously ever since. Odyssey made a highly successful tour which included the USA, and since then he has made annual appearances at the major European jazz festivals, leading a trio in the mid-80s with Bjorn Kjellemyr and Audun Kleive, and performing with **Palle Mikkelborg** in Norway. Rypdal is making an an important contribution to the European genre. Writing for orchestra as well as jazz ensemble, he is noted for his system of bowing the guitar in the manner of violin. On *If Mountains Could Sing* the violin is featured strongly, not by the guitarist but by Terje Tonnesen, Lars Anders Tomter and Oystein Birkland. It is however in rolling and uplifting pieces such as 'The Return Of Per Ulv' that Rypdal is renowned.

Albums: *What Comes After* (ECM 1974), with Jan Garbarek *Afric Pepperbird* (ECM 1974), *Odyssey* (ECM 1975), *Whenever I Seem To Be Far Away* (ECM 1975), *After The Rain* (ECM 1976), *Waves* (ECM 1978), *To Be Continued* (ECM 1981), *Eos* (ECM 1984), *Chaser* (ECM 1985), *Sunrise* (1985), *Terje Rypdal/Miroslav Vitous/Jack DeJohnette* (ECM 1985), *Descendre* (ECM 1986), *Blue* (ECM 1987), *The Singles Collection* (ECM 1989), *Undisonus* (1990), *Q.E.D.* (1993), *If Mountains Could Sing* (ECM 1995). Compilation: *Works* (ECM 1989).

S

1600 Pennsylvania Avenue

The title, of course, is the location of the White House in Washington, where, in 1974, the current resident, Richard Nixon, reluctantly vacated the premises. Two years later, on 4 May 1976, the show bearing that fancy address took up residence at the Mark Hellinger Theatre in New York - and was evicted after only seven performances. The early departure was all the more surprising because those mainly responsible for its existence were two of the American musical theatre's most illustrious names: **Leonard Bernstein** (music) and **Alan Jay Lerner** (book and lyrics). As usual in this kind of debacle, the book got most of the blame. It was a fascinating idea to tell the White House story - the first 100 years of its history from George Washington to Theodore Roosevelt - through the eyes of three generations of Lud Simmons, a family dynasty of black servants who worked at the White House. In this piece, they oversee the action, and represent the American people. Gilbert Price stood in for all the servants, and the presidents were played by one actor, Ken Howard. The British actress Patricia Routledge portrayed all The First Ladies. It is impossible to say where it all went wrong - after all, not many people saw it - but at least the score contained several engaging numbers such as 'Duet For One', 'Take Care Of This House', and 'We Must Have A Ball'. Sixteen years later, on 11 August 1992, a major revival opened - appropriately enough at the John F. Kennedy Centre for the Performing Arts in Washington.

1776

America's obsession with its own history had already resulted in at least two Broadway musicals based on momentous national events before this show opened at the 46th Street Theatre on 16 March 1969. Exactly 20 years before that, *Miss Liberty*, with a score by **Irving Berlin**, concerned itself with the period leading up to the dedication ceremony for the lady with the torch, and, in 1925, songwriters **Richard Rodgers** and **Lorenz Hart**, together with librettist Herbert Fields, offered *Dearest Enemy*, which was 'inspired' by the American Revolution. Naturally, with a title like *1776*, Peter Stone's book and Sherman Edwards's score relates to the culmination of that Revolution - the signing of the Declaration of Independence. Edwards, a newcomer to Broadway, had worked on the project for several years before

collaborating with the more experienced Stone on the final draft. It stayed closely to historical fact, both in regard to the dramatic circumstances, and the personalities involved in them. The performances of Howard Da Silva (Benjamin Franklin), William Daniels (John Adams), and Ken Howard (Thomas Jefferson) were particularly applauded. In many ways, the show was more like a straight play - a powerful and emotional piece of theatre. Edwards's sympathetic, and sometimes poignant score included songs such as 'Momma Look Sharp', 'Cool, Cool Considerate Man', 'Sit Down, John', 'But Mr. Adams', 'The Lees Of Old Virginia', 'He Plays The Violin', 'Is Anybody There?', 'Yours, Yours, Yours!', 'Molasses To Rum', and 'Till Then'. The show was acclaimed from the start, and became a tremendous success, running for 1,217 performances. It won three **Tony Award**s: for best musical, supporting actor (Ronald Holgate in the role of Richard Henry Lee) and director (Peter Hunt). There was a short-lived London production in 1970, and in 1991 the show was revived at the Williamstown Theatre Festival in the USA. The 1972 film version retained several of the Broadway cast.

2nd Heat

Drawn together in Bremerhaven, Germany, by Kai Braue (guitar), Marcel Robbers (vocals), Mathias Gonik (bass) and Frank Hoogestraat (guitar), 2nd Heat were formed in 1992 and soon earned their spurs on bills with **Phantom Blue**, **Tigertailz**, **Lee Aaron** and **Saga**. Soon after the group, who specialise in guitar-intensive traditional metal, raised their profile by recording a self-financed cassette, which would sell over 800 copies. This came to the attention of Rock The Nation Records, who signed the band and re-released the tape with the addition of a bonus track, 'Cyan Eyes', to generally strong reviews.
Album: *Shreddervision* (RTN 1994).

6.5 Special

BBC Television's *6.5 Special*, so-named after the time it was screened, was one of the first British attempts at a pop-based television show. The opening 'train' credits are fixed in the mind of a generation of rock music aficionados. Producer **Jack Good** used informal camera angles and unconventional methods to invest a sense of spontaneity and movement and although staid in comparison with its immediate successors, *Oh Boy* and *Boy Meets Girl*, *6.5 Special* began to link music's aural excitement with complementary visual effects. The show's success inspired this 1957 feature, which simply repeated the formula for the big screen. In keeping with its television counterpart, the film contained many acts of questionable quality, including MOR-styled singers **Dickie Valentine**, **Petula Clark** and **Joan Regan**. Comperes Pete Murray and Josephine Douglas did introduce a handful of homegrown, but polite, rock 'n' roll acts, **Jim Dale**, the **King Brothers** and the kilt-wearing **Jackie Dennis**, but their contributions were overtly sanitised. One of the brightest moments was provided by skiffle king, **Lonnie Donegan**, while studio houseband Don Lang And His Frantic Five injected a measure of pulse into the proceedings. Better still were the superb **John Barry** Seven, but *6.5 Special* is recalled for the doors it opened, rather than this film. It does, however, document the sterile nature of British 50s pop and helps explain why Good later left for the USA.

7 Seconds

Formed in 1980 in Reno, Nevada, USA, 7 Seconds consisted of Kevin Seconds (guitar/vocals), Steve Youth (bass) and Bix Bigler (drums). Earlier incarnations of the band had included the drummers Tom Borhino, also of the Cowskulls and Section 8, and Troy. 7 Seconds' recording career began with two cassettes on their own Vicious Scam label, and they made their vinyl debut with an EP, of hardcore punk tracks, *Skins, Brains And Guts*, one of the first releases on **Alternative Tentacles Records.** (Kevin Seconds, who only took over vocals after the initial cassettes, was also responsible for the writing and distribution of local fanzine, S.K.I.T.C.H.) *The Crew*, housed on their own BYO (Better Youth Organization) label, was much better recorded and received. Next came the *Walk Together, Rock Together* mini-album, recorded with Ian MacKaye of **Minor Threat** in Washington, which included an efficient demolition of **Nena**'s '99 Red Balloons'. Musically their songs had progressed to encompass tight harmonies and rhythmic diversions. Their developing musicianship resulted in considerable popularity in US punk circles, culminating in the award of two consecutive 'best band' polls in the Los Angeles hardcore bible, *Flipside*. By 1986 Troy was playing drums with a band who alienated their existing audience with material (the appropriately titled *New Wind*) that had more in common with **Simple Minds** than the **Circle Jerks**. 7 Seconds began to flounder, with Kevin Seconds working on his side project, the Acid Drops. The *Old School* album offered a good summary of the band's achievements, including re-recordings of their 1982 to 1983 material that were many times better than the originals.

Albums: *The Crew* (BYO 1984), *Walk Together Rock Together* (BYO 1985), *New Wind* (BYO/Positive Force

1986). Compilations: *Old School* (Head Hunter/Cargo 1988), *The Crew And 7 Live Tracks* (BYO 1989). Video: *I Still Believe (In These Words)* (1985).

70, Girls, 70

Another celebrated flop, this show closed some five weeks after it emerged into the lights of the Broadhurst Theatre on 15 April 1971. Some critics attributed its failure to **Stephen Sondheim**'s *Follies*, which had arrived on Broadway just 11 days earlier, and also concerned itself with the celebration of old troupers from the past. However, the glamorous settings of the 'Wiesmann Follies', and a group of veteran vaudevillians returning to Broadway, could hardly be compared to the more down-to-earth situation in *70, Girls, 70*, in which some equally venerable old-time performers live at The Sussex Arms, a senior Citizens' run-down hotel in New York City. One of that establishment's favourite residents, Ida Dodd (Mildred Natwick), forms a shop-lifting gang to get her own back on rude traders. The resulting profits enable the 'crooks' to refurbish their quarters and take in more poor, but deserving cases. After one job the aged criminals just make their getaway, but Ida gets caught. Before they can put her away, she escapes - by dying. The book, by **Fred Ebb** and Norman L. Martin, was based on the English comedy, *Breath Of Spring*, which was filmed as *One Touch Of Mink*. The show opened with a rousing, defiant anthem: 'Old Folks' . . . 'don't go out, strangers make them ill at ease/Old folks stay at home, nursing their infirmities' . . . 'So take a look at the old folks, they're quite an interesting sight/But if you want to see old folks/You're in the wrong hall tonight!'). From then on, Fred Ebb and composer **John Kander** cleverly interpolated numbers such as 'Broadway, My Street', 'Go Visit' and 'Coffee In A Cardboard Cup' by the old vaudeville performers, Melba (Lillian Hayman) and Fritzi (Goldye Shaw), among the 'plot' songs which included 'Home', 'The Caper', 'You And I, Love', 'Do We?', 'Hit It, Lorraine', 'See The Light', 'Boom Ditty Boom', 'Believe', 'The Elephant Song', and 'Yes'. Whatever the reason for the show's miserable run of 35 performances (*Follies* scooped the **Tony Awards**), it certainly was not the fault of the score, which was witty and entertaining throughout. Twenty years later, *70, Girls, 70* finally reached the West End, where Dora Bryan was 'irresistible' in the leading role.

707

US melodic pomp-rock group formed in 1979 by Kevin Russell (guitar/vocals), Jim McLarty (drums) and Phil Bryant (bass/vocals). However, the band's line-up was always in a constant state of flux. Tod Howarth (keyboards/guitar/vocals) and Felix Robinson (bass; ex-**Angel**) made important contributions during the group's lifetime. 707 debuted with a radio-friendly self-

titled album, characterized by strong musicianship and instantly contagious hooklines and choruses. Their next two albums adopted a more metallic approach, with *2nd Album* deservedly reaching the lower reaches of the US *Billboard* chart. *Megaforce*, produced by Keith Olsen, also provided the theme tune for the film of the same name. Unfortunately, the creative ideas had started to run dry by this stage, while the songs duplicated earlier ideas and were generally less immediate. Internal disputes became more and more common, and the band finally fell apart in 1983. Howarth went on to play with **Frehley's Comet**.
Albums: *707* (Casablanca 1980), *2nd Album* (Casablanca 1981), *Megaforce* (Broadwalk 1982).

7669

Four New York 'New Jill Swingers' (they prefer the term new ghetto revolutionary music) with rap's hardcore attitude, 7669 arrived on the scene in 1994 amid a swirl of deliberately provocative press shots, notably topless poses astride large motorcycles, which also graced the album cover. Less readily apparent was the fact that the backdrop of shrubbery was in fact a 'field of pot'. Their name was taken from the year of US indepedence (1776) crossed with the 'date' of the sexual revolution (1969). The members; Shorti-1-Forti, Big Angel, El Boog-E and Thickness, proferred songs with dubious titles like '69 Ways To Love A Black Man' and 'Cloud 69', the duplicity of lascivious titles being an obvious clue to the lack of imagination inherent in the project. However, the production, helmed by Kangol, Ali Dee and Forceful, was enough to make proceedings listenable.
Album: *East From A Bad Block* (Motown/Polydor 1994).

S'Express

Home to Mark Moore (b. 12 January 1965, London, England), who was aruably the best British interpretor of the late 80s Italo-house phenomenon. Moore is half-Korean, though his early claims that he had a twin brother in that nation's army were spurious. More factual were the revelations that he was put into care at the age of nine, when his mother had a breakdown. As a youth he ligged outside **Siouxsie & The Banshees** gigs begging 10 pence pieces to get in. After the punk explosion, the first time he felt he belonged to anything, he made his name on the domestic DJ circuit, notably the Mud Club. At one point his record collection was so large he was forced to have his flat strengthened. He broke through with a series of singles which combined Euro-pop stylings with a hard funk spine: 'Theme From S'Express', 'Superfly Guy', 'Hey Music Lover' and 'Mantra For A State Of Mind' among them. After which the chart action dissipated somewhat. 'Nothing To Lose', ironically one of his strongest singles, stalled at number 32, as dance music upped a gear and discovered hardcore. Moore set up the Splish label,

through Rhythm King, in the early 90s, opening with Canadian-born singer Tiziana's 'Seduce Me' and Yolanda's 'Living For The Nite', licensed from **Underground Resistance**. Former S'Express vocalist Linda Love would go on to record with Word Of Mouth ('What It Is (Ain't Losing Control)'). A delayed second album *Intercourse* failed to revive S'Express fortunes, despite the gifted vocal presence of Sonique. A sample of John Waters ('Bad taste is what entertainment is all about') preceded a demonstrably shabby, tongue in cheek rendition of 'Brazil' on the album's best track. Moore would continue to earn a crust as a remixer however, notably on **Malcolm McLaren**'s 'Something's Jumpin' In Your Shirt' (with **William Orbit**) and Saffron's 'Fluffy Toy' (with Peter Lorimer).
Albums: *Original Soundtrack* (Rhythm King 1989), *Intercourse* (Rhythm King 1992).

S-1000

The moniker of Spencer Williams, who had previously remixed for the **Sugarcubes** and the **Art Of Noise**, and, alongside Paul Gotel, was half of **Well Hung Parliament**. 'I'm Not Gonna Do It' was a typical bouncing dub 45, while he scored further club hits with 'Flatliner' and 'Look Inside'. Williams also has the distinction of having been 'on the ground', literally, when the Los Angeles earthquake struck. He was actually in the middle of a set at the Sketch Pad in Hollywood when the earth started moving. S-1000 has now moved from **Guerilla** to **Deep Distraxion**.

S-K-O

This US group comprised three songwriters, Thom Schuyler, Fred Knobloch and Paul Overstreet, who decided to work together as an occasional band. Schuyler (b. 1952, Bethlehem, Pennsylvania, USA) was, by trade, a carpenter, whose songwriting abilities were discovered by **Eddie Rabbitt** when he was making alterations to the latter's studio. Schuyler wrote '16th Avenue', 'Hurricane' and 'I Don't Know Where To Start' and had *Blue Heart*, released by **Capitol Records**, which led to some entries on the US country chart. With Paul Overstreet, he wrote 'I Fell In Love Again Last Night' (the **Forester Sisters**), and 'A Long Line Of Love' (**Michael Martin Murphey**), both US country number 1 hits. Knobloch, pronounced 'no-block', (b. Jackson, Mississippi, USA) worked in Atlanta, Georgia and Los Angeles, California, before moving to Nashville, Tennessee in 1983. He wrote 'The Whole World's In Love When You're Lonely' and 'Julianne' (the **Everly Brothers**). As Fred Knoblock (sic), he had a US pop hit with 'Why Not Me' and country hits with 'Memphis' and, with Susan Allanson, 'Killin' Time'. Overstreet (b. VanCleave, Mississippi, USA), a more traditional country songwriter, wrote both 'On The Other Hand' and

'Forever And Ever, Amen' with Don Schlitz (both US country number 1 hits for **Randy Travis**); 'Diggin' Up Bones' with Al Gore (also a number 1 for Travis); and 'You're Still New To Me' with Paul Davis (a US country number 1 for **Marie Osmond** and **Paul Davis**). Fred was briefly married to **Dolly Parton**'s sister, Freida. The first S-K-O release, 'You Can't Stop Love', made the US country Top 10. Their second single, 'Baby's Got A New Baby', topped the US country chart in 1987. At that time, Overstreet opted for a solo career and he had a further US country number 1 with **Tanya Tucker** and Paul Davis with a song he wrote with Don Schlitz, 'I Won't Take Less Than Your Love'. He also wrote 'You Again' (the Forester Sisters), 'When You Say Nothing At All' (**Keith Whitley**) and 'Deeper Than The Holler' (Randy Travis), all with Don Schlitz and all US country number 1 hits. His place was taken by songwriter, Craig Bickhardt (b. Pennsylvania, USA), thus making the group S-K-B. Bickhardt had a band, Wire And Wood, which opened for many well-known acts in the early 70s. He wrote or co-wrote 'Finally Found A Reason' (**Art Garfunkel**), 'I'm Falling In Love Tonight' (the **Judds**), 'Never Been In Love' (**Randy Meisner**), 'You're The Power' (**Kathy Mattea**), 'Give A Little Love To Me' (the Judds), 'I Know Where I'm Going' (the Judds), and songs for the film, *Tender Mercies*. S-K-B finally had a US Top 10 country single with 'Givers And Takers' before disbanding in 1989.

Albums: with Schuyler, Knobloch, Overstreet *S-K-O* (1987), with Schuyler, Knobloch, Bickhardt *No Easy Horses* (1987).

S.A.D.O.

This German group achieved a degree of notoriety during the mid-80s with their **Tubes**-like stage show which incorporated a selection of scantily-clad females in sado-masochistic uniform. Vocalist Andre Cook has been the only permanent member since the band's inception in 1983, losing original collaborators Matti Kaebs (drums), Wolfgang Eicholz (guitar), Matthias Moser (guitar) and Stepan Neumann (bass) - all of whom left to form V2 after the release of the erroneously-titled *Circle Of Friends*. Cook attempted to jump the thrash-metal bandwagon with *Dirty Fantasy*, attracting minimal attention, then adopted a more melodic AOR approach for *Sensitive*. Their final line-up included Cook, a returning Moser (guitar), Duncan O'Neill (bass) and Danny (drums), but all to little avail as the band disbanded shortly after release.

Albums: *Shout* (Noise 1984), *Circle Of Friends* (Noise 1987), *Dirty Fantasy* (Noise 1988), *Another Kind Of...*(Noise 1989, mini-album), *Sensitive* (Noise 1990).

S.O.B. Band

(see **Sons Of Blues**)

S.O.S.

(see **Skidmore, Alan**; **Osborne, Mike**; **Surman, John**)

S.O.S. Band

Formed in Atlanta, Georgia, USA, in 1977, the S.O.S. Band enjoyed a long run of hits on the US R&B charts during the 80s. The group originally consisted of Mary Davis (vocals/keyboards), Jason 'T.C.' Bryant (keyboards), Billy R. Ellis (saxophone) and James Earl Jones III (drums). They performed regularly, as Sounds Of Santa Monica, at Lamar's Regal Room in Atlanta where they were discovered by Milton Lamar, the club's owner, who later became their manager. The group were signed to the independent Tabu Records and soon added new members Willie 'Sonny' Killebrew (saxophone/flute), John Simpson III (bass/keyboards) and Bruno Speight (guitar). The group then changed its name to the S.O.S. Band. Performing in the then popular funk style, the band began to amass a catalogue of US hits in 1980, with 'Take Your Time (Do It Right) Part 1' rising to number 1 on the R&B chart and number 3 national pop chart. They returned to the pop singles chart four more times throughout their career, but never rose close to that initial position again. On the R&B chart, however, they were mainstays through 1987, returning to the Top 10 four more times: in 1983 with 'Just be Good To Me' (number 2) and 'Tell Me If You Still Care' (number 5), in 1984 with 'Just The Way You Like It' (number 6), and in 1986 with 'The Finest' (number 2). Five S.O.S. Band albums also charted in the US, the debut, *S.O.S.*, faring the best at number 12. There were a number of personnel changes throughout the decade, with vocalist Davis leaving for a solo career in 1987. The S.O.S. Band was still recording for Tabu and performing at the end of the 80s.

Albums: *S.O.S.* (1980), *Too* (1981), *S.O.S. III* (1982), *On The Rise* (1983), *Just The Way You Like It* (1984), *Sands Of Time* (1985), *Diamonds In the Raw* (1989).

Sabater, Jimmy

(see **Cuba, Joe**)

Sabbat

Formed in England in 1986, this group comprised Martin Walkyier (vocals), Andy Sneap (guitar), Frazer Craske (bass) and Simon Negus (drums). It was a demo tape, *Fragments Of A Faith Forgotten*, which first brought Sabbat to the attention of the press and public in 1986. Part of a new wave of thrash metal bands, Sabbat stood out for their skillful live displays and musical flair, and earned a two-page spread in *Kerrang!* magazine before releasing any vinyl. Lyrically they were preoccupied with pagan arts, witchcraft and the dark ages, elements of which were incorporated into a bizarre and theatrical stageshow. Their brand of thrash, meanwhile, was complex but forceful, and they quickly became a cult attraction on the metal circuit. *History Of A Time To Come* emerged soon afterwards and was well-received, reflecting the promise of earlier recordings. Its successor, *Dreamweaver,* was based on Brian Bates' novel *The Way Of Wyrd,* and demonstrated considerable musical development. After this Walkyier and Craske left, to replaced by Ritchie Desmond (vocals), Wayne Banks (bass) and extra guitarist Neil Watson. This line-up recorded the less taxing and ultimately inconsequential *Mourning Has Broken.* It was immediately followed by the break-up of Sabbat. Martin Walkyier has since formed **Skyclad**, while Sneap launched Godsend.

Albums: *History Of A Time To Come* (Noise 1988), *Dreamweaver (Reflections Of Our Yesterdays)* (Noise 1989), *Mourning Has Broken* (Noise 1991).

Sablon, Jean

b. 25 March 1906, Nogent-sur-Marne, Seine, France, d. 24 February 1994, Cannes-La-Bocca, France. The son of a composer, Jean Sablon studied music and piano at the Lyceé Charlemagne in Paris, but left before the end of his third term. Moving instead to the conservatoire, he found supporting roles in operettas, before making his professional bow at the Théâtre des Bouffes-Parisiens in *Trois Jeunes Filles Nues* (Three Naked Girls) in 1923. By this time Sablon was already writing songs, and he was encouraged in this pursuit when his first film appearance, *Chacun Sa Chance,* proved a flop. However, after a sojourn in Brazil he returned to Paris to work in cabaret. There he formed an alliance with **Jean Cocteau**, **Django Reinhardt** and **Stéphane Grappelli**. Together they played jazz at various clubs and cabarets. Following which Sablon was recruited by Mistinguett who installed him as partner in her Casino de Paris venture. There he was taught dance steps, and his voice was tutored by Damia (of Abel Gance's *Napoléon* fame). He scored his first single successes with material from his friend Mireille; 'La Petit Chemin' and 'Couché Dans Le Foin'. He eventually won the Grand Prix du disque Charles-Cros in 1937 for his signature tune, 'Vous Qui Passez Sans Me Noir', written by Charles Trenet and Johnny Hess. Afterwards he spent two years in America, singing on stage, radio and record, and his success there made him second only to **Maurice Chevalier** as France's most successful expatriate, known alternately as 'The French **Bing Crosby**' or the 'Latin Lover'. On his return to Paris he introduced the microphone to the stage - a discovery he had made in New York. Though he faced derision at the hands of purists, Sablon incorporated the microphone fully into his act, prefacing the swagger and theatre of rock 'n' roll. Though his influence continued to be felt in the work of his admirers, including **Sacha Distel** and **Charles Aznavour**,

Sablon became less prolific as the decades passed. By the 70s he was appearing regularly on television, and bought a ranch in Brazil. It was there he played his final concert in Rio De Janeiro in 1983, leaving the stage, as was his custom, with a rendition of 'Je Tire Ma Révérence' ('I Bow Myself Out').

Further reading: *De France Ou Bien D'ailleurs* (From France Or Anywhere You Like), Jean Sablon, 1979.

Sabres Of Paradise

Andy Weatherall's favoured dance emporium, whose releases include 'Smokebelch' - arguably *the* techno tune of the early 90s. In addition to Weatherall, Nina Walsh helms the ship, aided by Jagz Kooner and Gary Burns. Walsh was a regular at Weatherall's Shoom evenings during the heady days of 1988's acid scene. She in turn worked for the **Boys Own** stable. Before joining the Sabres she also worked with Youth's (ex-**Killing Joke**, **Brilliant** etc) WAU/Butterfly recordings. The duo set up their own label under the Sabres name, and released work from the likes of SYT, Blue, **Secret Knowledge**, Musical Science, Waxworth Industries, Jack O' Swords and the **Corridor**. The label operation eventually became known as Sabrettes. There was also a studio and club (based in a brick-dust cellar under London Bridge) both titled Sabresonic, as was the group's debut long player. This seamless collection of post-**Orb**, dreamscape dance, with a vaguely industrial edge, increased the avalanche of plaudits which usually accompany Weatherall's best work. Together with assistants Gary and Jagz, Weatherall has turned the Sabres into one of the UK's premier remix teams. Among their work are remixes of everyone worth noting in the dance scene, right through to hardcore rockers **Therapy?** Two other accomplices, Mick and Phil, help out with live work. The group have contributed one track, 'Sabres Them', to the film *Shopping*, and it seems likely that more soundtrack work will follow. Typically, despite the otherworldly grandeur of this music, the Sabres studio remains located above a Tandoori house in West Hounslow.

Albums: *Sabresonic* (Sabrettes 1993), *Haunted Dancehall* (Warp 1994).

Sabrettes

Originally titled **Sabres Of Paradise**, after **Andy Weatherall** and Nina Walsh's band of the same name, this emergent label has so far released Voodoo People's *Altitude* EP, the Cause's 'Through The Floor and Charged' (aka DJs Scott Braithwaite and Craig Walsh, Nina's brother), and two 12-inch techno opuses from **Inky Blacknuss** (DJ's Alex Knight and Andrea Parker). Future plans include a collaboration between Les from Holy Ghost and Anna Haigh (ex-**Bocca Juniors**). The label is stated to be based on Nina Walsh's personal taste. It gives her an outlet to escape the perennial 'DJ's girlfriend' tag she has found herself lumbered with, following her relationship with the much in demand Weatherall.

Album: Various: *Pink Me Up* (Sabrettes 1994).

Sabri Brothers

The name Sabri is the name given to members of a group of followers of Sufism, to which all the players belong. The group comprised Haji Ghuram Farid Sabri (b. India; vocals/harmonium), Haji Maqbool Ahmed Sabri (b. India; vocals/harmonium), Haji Kamal Sabri (b. India; vocals/chirya tarang), Mehmood Ghaznavi Sabri (b. India; vocals/bongo), Fazal Islam (b. India; chorus), Azmat Farad Sabri (b. India; chorus), Sarwat Farid (b. India; chorus), Javed Kamal Sabri (b. India; chorus), Haji Abdul Karim (b. India; dholak), Hoji Mohammed Anwar (b. India; tabla). After moving to Pakistan in 1947, the brothers first sang with their father and uncle. In the mid-50s they formed their own group whose first album was released in 1959 to critical acclaim across Pakistan. The band is nowadays based in Karachi and still enjoy immense popularity in their homeland. *Ya Habib* (Oh Beloved) is a forthright expression of their devotional qawwali performance.

Selected albums: *Ya Habib* (1990), *Qawwali Masterworks* (1993).

Sabrina

This curvaceous late 80s' Italian disco-pop diva, challenged the former UK 'page three model', turned pop-singer, **Samantha Fox** as Europe's favourite pop sex symbol. Her major UK chart hit was in the summer of 1988 with 'Boys (Summertime Love)' which reached number 3. Although the follow-up that same year with 'All Of Me' reached the UK Top 25, Sabrina's obvious visual attraction was not enough to sustain a successful chart career in the UK.

Album: *Sabrina* (1988).

Sabu

The son of actor Selar Sabu, vocalist/guitarist Paul Sabu (b. Burbank, California, USA) has carved out a successful career as a songwriter, producer/engineer and guitarist for a variety of major acts. He has also contributed to numerous film soundtracks, but his solo projects have been dogged by bad luck. The Sabu band, featuring bassist Rick Bozzo and drummer Dan Holmes, found some success with their soulful hard rock debut, but the album was lost in America in confusion with a disco album released by Sabu on the Ocean label: 'basically....for the money'. Sabu turned to studio work, putting the band on ice until **Motown** subsidiary Morocco offered him a deal. As Kidd Glove, the band adopted a harder style, showcasing Sabu's excellent vocals, reminiscent of a smokier **Sammy Hagar**, and rivetting guitar work. However, the album

didn't take off, and when Morocco folded the band followed suit. Sabu was joined by Bozzo, Dan Ellis (keyboards) and Charles Esposito (drums) for the critically-acclaimed *Heartbreak*, which did well until the label went into liquidation, and Sabu supported himself with an **Arista** songwriting contract while he put together his next project, **Only Child**.

Albums: *Sabu* (MCA 1980, mini-album), *Heartbreak* (Heavy Metal America 1985). Kidd Glove: *Kidd Glove* (Morocco 1984).

Sacred Reich

This Phoenix, Arizona, USA thrash band formed in 1985, with Jason Rainey (rhythm guitar) joined by Phil Rind (bass/vocals) and Greg Hall (drums), with Wiley Arnett replacing original lead guitarist Jeff Martinek in 1987. The band stuck together despite **Flotsam And Jetsam** wooing Arnett and Rind (who was also offered the **Dark Angel** vocal slot) and **Slayer** offering Greg Hall Dave Lombardo's then vacant drumstool, appearing on *Metal Massacre 8* before making a fine debut with *Ignorance*. This displayed considerable maturity and musicianship with hardcore political lyrics to match the ironic band name. Rind continued to work on political themes on *Surf Nicaragua*, while the band toured heavily, and the *Live At The Dynamo* EP followed an acclaimed 1989 performance at the Dutch festival. *The American Way* reaped the benefits of Scared Reich's experience, with Hall's performance particularly outstanding, while Rind's lyrics ranged across ecology (on the brilliant 'Crimes Against Humanity', the original album title), intolerance, apartheid and the ills of US society ('Lady Liberty rots away, No truth, no justice, The American way'). The band also preached musical tolerance with '31 Flavors', the funk-rock album closer. Hall, however, found the constant touring hard, and was later replaced by Dave McClain, who made his recording debut on *Independent*, ironically the band's first major label outing, which saw them stretch their musical abilities beyond straight thrash boundaries. *Independent* became the US metal radio's choice as the best album of 1993.

Albums: *Ignorance* (Metal Blade/Enigma 1987), *Surf Nicaragua* (Metal Blade/Enigma 1988, mini-album), *The American Way* (Metal Blade/Enigma 1990), *Independent* (Hollywood 1993).

Sad Cafe

Formed in 1976, Sad Cafe originally consisted of Paul Young (vocals), Ian Wilson (guitar), Mike Hehir (guitar), Lenni (saxophone), Vic Emerson (keyboards), John Stimpson (bass) and David Irving (drums). They evolved out of two Manchester groups, Gyro and Mandala, although Young had previously sung in an earlier beat group, the Toggery Five. Their debut *Fanx Ta Ra*, introduced the group's blend of hard-rock riffs and adult pop, but it was a second collection, *Misplaced*

Ideals, which brought them international success when one of its tracks, 'Run Home Girl', became a US hit. *Facades*, produced by **10cc** guitarist Eric Stewart, contained 'Every Day Hurts', a UK Top 3 single in 1979, and two further Top 40 entries the following year, 'Strange Little Girl' and 'My Oh My'. John Stimpson had became the group's manager in August 1980 and his place in the line-up was taken by Des Tong. However, despite enjoying a handful of minor hits, Sad Cafe were unable to sustain their early success although they continued to record, intermittently, throughout the 80s.

Albums: *Fanx Ta Ra* (1977), *Misplaced Ideals* (1978), *Facades* (1979), *Sad Cafe* (1980), *Live* (1981), *Ole* (1981), *The Politics Of Existing* (1986), *Whatever It Takes* (1989).

Sad Lovers And Giants

This UK post-punk group, based in Watford, Hertfordshire, England, featured a line-up comprising Grace Allard (vocals), Tristan Garel Funk (guitar), David Wood (keyboards), Cliff Silver (bass) and Nigel Pollard (drums). After the exposure of early singles 'Colourless Dream' and 'Lost In A Moment', it was the release of 'Man Of Straw' and the accompanying *Feeding The Flame* which really established the group as masters of the double-edged lyric and sweeping, emotional textures of guitar and keyboard: 'Like confession whispered slowly, Hate's a word that's spoken softly, Standing lonely trusting no one, In disarray with collar undone'. The band had already fallen apart by the time the *Total Sound* mini-album, recorded live for broadcast on Dutch radio in 1983, was released. Another posthumous release, *In the Breeze*, consisting of demos, live tracks and alternative versions recorded for BBC disc jockey **John Peel**, pre-dated its release. The group was briefly reactivated in 1987, releasing the disappointing 'White Russians', while only Pollard and Allard were still in place for the subsequent final albums.

Albums: *Epic Garden Music* (Midnight 1982), *Feeding The Flame* (Midnight 1983), *In The Breeze*, (Midnight 1984) *Total Sound* (Midnight 1986, mini-album), *The Mirror Test* (Midnight 1988), *Les Annes Vertes* (Midnight 1988).

Sade

b. Helen Folasade Adu, 16 January 1959, Ibadan, Nigeria. Sade's sultry jazz-tinged vocals made her one of the most successful international stars of the 80s. Of mixed Nigerian/English parentage, Sade grew up in Clacton, Essex, England, writing songs as a teenager. While as an art student in London, she joined Arriva where she met guitarist Ray St. John with whom she composed 'Smooth Operator'. From 1981-83, Sade fronted the funk band Pride, leaving the following year to form her own band with ex-Pride members Stewart Matthewman (saxophone), Andrew Hale (keyboards) and Paul Denman (bass). The line-up was completed by drummer Paul Cook. The group gained a following on the London club scene and in 1984 its first single, the lilting 'Your Love Is King' was a Top 10 hit. This was followed by the Robin Millar-produced *Diamond Life*, which was to become one of the biggest-selling debut albums of the decade, with over six million copies sold world-wide. Sade's next album, with all songs written by group members, included the US number 1 'Promise' as well as further hit singles, 'The Sweetest Taboo' and 'The First Time'. Sade also contributed music to the soundtrack of *Absolute Beginners*, a 1987 film in which she had a cameo role. With ex-**Wham!** backing singer Leroy Osbourne added to the group, Sade began a world tour in 1988 to coincide with the release of her third album, from which 'Paradise' headed the R&B chart in the USA. Sade took her time in delivering *Love Deluxe*. Although it was another mature work, and included two excellent hit singles, 'No Ordinary Love' and 'Feel No Pain'. The fickle British public were lukewarm. The album briefly dented the UK top 30, whilst in the USA it was a million seller peaking at number 3. A greatest hits package was released in 1994 indicating by implication that the artist's best compositions are already behind her.

Albums: *Diamond Life* (1984), *Promise* (1985), *Stronger Than Pride* (1988), *Love Deluxe* (1992). Compilation: *The Best Of Sade* (Epic 1994).

Videos: *Life Promise Pride Love* (1993), *Live Concert Home Video (Epic)* (1994).

Sadler, Barry, Staff Sgt.

b. 1941, New Mexico, USA. While stationed at Fort San Houston, Texas, Staff Sgt. Barry Sadler spent his spare time composing a number of songs and, after serving in Vietnam, decided to complete a lyric dedicated to his regiment. The result was submitted to a publisher who passed the composition on to author Robin Moore whose book, *The Green Berets*, was a best-seller. Together, Sadler and Moore refashioned the song into 'The Ballad Of The Green Berets' which, following its release on **RCA Records** surprisingly dominated the USA number 1 position for an astonishing five weeks. Sadler's repertoire was limited, but he managed to complete a follow-up, 'The A Team' and a best-selling album. His career thereafter was stormy and controversial. After re-enlisting in the Army and briefly pursuing an acting career, he was charged and acquitted of the murder of Nashville songwriter Lee Emerson Bellamy. Three years later, in 1981, he was found not guilty of a charge of shooting his former business partner. It was an extraordinary denouement to the career of one of the most unlikely chart-topping artists of all time.

Albums: *Ballads Of The Green Berets* (1966), *The 'A' Team* (1966).

Safaris

A rock 'n' roll vocal group from Los Angeles, California, USA. The Safaris typified the best of white vocal group rock n' roll of the early 60s, the marriage of soulful vocals and the perfect feeling of teen angst. Members were lead Jim Stephens, Sheldon Breier, Richard Clasky, and Marv Rosenberg. Their splendid ballad, 'Image Of A Girl' (number 6 pop), from 1960, was their only hit record, making the group a one-hit-wonder. The record was a huge international hit, and made a significant enough impact in the UK to generate two cover versions, by **Mark Wynter** (number 11) and **Nelson Keene** (number 37). The Safaris had one weak follow-up, 'The Girl With The Story In Her Eyes' (number 85 pop) and then broke up. Stephens continued the group's name with three new members, but could not make a return to the charts. Stephens rejoined the original members to record one more single on Valient under the name of Suddens, but after that record failed the members left the music business.

Safranski, Eddie

b. 25 December 1918, Pittsburgh, Pennsylvania, USA, d. 10 January, 1974. Safranski first played bass in high school but was in his early 20s before he joined a name band, that led by **Hal McIntyre**, with whom he played for four years, departing in 1945 to join a small group led by **Miff Mole**. Later that year he joined **Stan Kenton** and, from 1948, spent about a year with **Charlie Barnet**. From then onwards, a handful of jazz engagements apart, Safranski was mostly engaged in studio work in New York, teaching and working for a company which manufactured musical instruments. A powerful player with a good sense of the swing style, his bass playing with Kenton's band was exemplary.
Albums: with Stan Kenton *The Kenton Era (1940-53)* (1955), *Stan Kenton's Greatest Hits (1943-51)* (1983), *Loaded* (1946).

Saga

Drawing on a variety of influences from **Rush** to **Emerson, Lake And Palmer**, multi-talented musician Mike Sadler and drummer Steve Negus put together their first line-up in Toronto, Canada, in 1977, with the guitar/keyboard playing brothers Jim and Ian Crichton. A self-financed album was then released on their own label. In 1980 they signed to **Polydor Records** and, with additional musicians, produced *Images At Twilight*, which continued the science fiction themes of their debut. A 12-inch EP was released in the UK to promote the album and, receiving a good deal of positive reaction, they set out on tour, supported for many shows by **Magnum**. Later that year they added another keyboard player, Jim Gilmore, and began work on the next album.

Released in 1981, this elevated them into the major concert circuit where they proved a big attraction in America. Their record company lost interest, but **Epic** came to the rescue until a more lasting deal was set up with Portrait Records. However, the band lost direction and the founder members became disillusioned and soon left to pursue a new band under their own name. The rest of the group continued to little interest, but in one final attempt to recapture the imagination they returned to the sci-fi concept for their final album in 1989.
Albums: *Saga* (Maze 1978), *Images At Twilight* (Polydor 1980), *Silent Knight* (Polydor 1980), *Worlds Apart* (Polydor 1981), *In Transit* (Polydor 1982), *Head Or Tails* (Epic 1983), *Behaviour* (Portrait 1984), *Wildest Dreams* (Atlantic 1987), *The Beginners Guide To Throwing Shapes* (Bonaire 1989).

Sager, Carole Bayer

b. 8 March 1946, New York City, New York, USA. Sager's career as a hit songwriter stretches over three decades, from the catchy pop of 'A Groovy Kind Of Love' to the charity ballad 'That's What Friends Are For', which has raised over $1 million for AIDS research. She began writing songs in the early 60s while a student at New York's High School of Music and Art. Sager was subsequently spotted by **Don Kirshner** who signed her to his Screen Gems publishing company. She had her first big hit in 1966 with 'A Groovy Kind Of Love'. Co-written by Toni Wine, the song was first recorded by **Patti Labelle** And The Bluebelles, but it became an international best-seller in the version by the **Mindbenders**. It was equally successful when revived by **Phil Collins** for the soundtrack of *Buster* in 1989. In 1970, Sager provided the lyrics for the Off Broadway musical *Georgy*, before co-writing 'Midnight Blue' with **Melissa Manchester**, who took it into the US Top 10 in 1975. Her own recording career had begun in 1972, and, four years later, **Richard Perry** produced 'You're Moving Out Today', which she wrote with **Bette Midler** and Bruce Roberts. It was a UK Top 10 hit for Sager on **Elektra Records**. Even more impressive was the dramatic 'When I Need You' (with Albert Hammond), a chart-topper for **Leo Sayer** on both sides of the Atlantic. In the late 70s Sager collaborated with **Marvin Hamlisch** on the successful Broadway musical *They're Playing Our Song*, a semi-autobiographical piece about the romantic entanglement of a songwriting team. In 1981, she recorded for **CBS**, having her biggest US hit with 'Stronger Than Before'. Her most important partnership, with **Burt Bacharach**, produced the Oscar-winning 'Arthur's Theme (Best That You Can Do)', which was a US number 1 in 1981 for **Christopher Cross**, who collaborated on the number along with **Peter Allen**. She subsequently

married Bacharach (they parted in 1991) and worked with him on 'Love Is My Decision' (from *Arthur 2: On The Rocks*) and 'That's What Friends Are For', which became a US number 1 hit in 1986 when recorded by **Dionne Warwick** And Friends. Other notable Sager compositions include 'Don't Cry Out Loud' and 'I'd Rather Leave While I'm In Love' (both with Peter Allan); 'Better Days', 'Come In From The Rain' (with Melissa Manchester); two numbers with Hamlisch, 'Better Than Ever' and 'Nobody Does It Better' (the James Bond film theme recorded by **Carly Simon**), the Patti Labelle/**Michael McDonald** duet 'On My Own' (with Bacharach), and two 90s film songs, 'The Day I Fell In Love' (from *Beethoven's 2nd*, with James Ingram, and Cliff Magness) and 'Look What Love Has Done' (from *Junior*, with Ingram, **James Newton Howard**, and Patty Smyth).
Albums: *Carole Bayer Sager* (1977), *Too* (1978), *Sometimes Late At Night* (1981).

Sagittarius

Formed in Los Angeles, California, USA in 1967, Sagittarius was a studio group created by singer/songwriter **Curt Boettcher** and **Byrds'** producer **Gary Usher**. Its close-knit harmony sound and lush orchestration was similar to that of the **Millenium**, a concurrent project whose members provided the instrumental backing on *Present Tense*. **Bruce Johnston** and **Terry Melcher** added their vocals to a set best recalled for 'My World Fell Down', a gorgeous pop song reminiscent of the **Beach Boys**, written by British team John Carter and Ken Lewis for their own group, the **Ivy League**. The Sagittarius version drew considerable acclaim, but failed to chart when issued as a single. *The Blue Marble*, issued on the Usher/Boettcher outlet Together, continued in the vein of its predecessor, but when it too failed to reap due commercial rewards, the concept was discontinued.
Albums: *Present Tense* (1968), *The Blue Marble* (1969).

Sahko Recordings

Finnish purveyors of weird electronic music, whose releases are housed in silver sleeves drilled with tiny holes, or, in the case of CD's, cardboard envelopes. Headed by architect-cum-label-manager Tommi Gronlund, the two principal artists are techno animateur Mika Vainio (otherwise known as Ø) and ambient/easy listening vendor Jimi Tenor. The latter's *Sahkomies* was particularly well received in mainland Europe, while Vainio's *Metri* demonstrated a unique and incredibly sparse approach to techno. Indeed it was Vainio's music which had inspired Gronlund to set up the label in the first place. While big names such as **Richie Hawtin** and **Mixmaster Morris** all spoke highly of their efforts, the label remained completely anonymous within their native Finland. Undeterred, they entertained audiences with an all-nighter at London's Quirky club and announced a new UK distribution deal in 1994.

Sahm, Doug

b. 6 November 1941, San Antonio, Texas, USA. Born of Lebanese-American extraction, Sahm is highly knowledgeable and a superbly competent performer of Texas musical styles, whether they be blues, country, rock 'n' roll, western swing, cajun or polkas. He made his recording debut in 1955 with 'A Real American Joe', under the name of Little Doug Sahm and within three years was fronting the Pharoahs, the first of several rough-hewn backing groups. Sahm recorded a succession of singles for local labels, including his **Little Richard** pastiche 'Crazy Daisy' (1959), plus 'Sapphire' (1961) and 'If You Ever Need Me' (1964). For several years, Sahm had been pestering producer, **Huey P. Meaux**, to record him. Meaux, having success with **Barbara Lynn** and **Dale And Grace**, was not interested. However, the producer found himself without a market when Beatlemania hit America, and shut himself away in a hotel with the **Beatles'** records, determined to discover what made them sell. He then called Sahm, told him to grow his hair, form a group and write a tune with a Cajun two-step beat. Accordingly, Sahm assembled his friends, **Augie Meyers** (keyboards), Frank Morin (saxophone), Harvey Kagan (bass) and Johnny Perez (drums). Meaux gave them an English-sounding name, the **Sir Douglas Quintet** and subsequently scored an international hit in 1965 with the catchy 'She's About A Mover'.
The group also had success in the US charts with 'The Rains Came', but, after being arrested for possession of drugs, the group disbanded and Sahm moved to California to avoid a heavy fine. He formed the Honkey Blues Band, but had difficulty in getting it on the road. He then gathered the rest of the Quintet in California for another classic single, 'Mendocino', its spoken introduction being indicative of the hippie-era. The album, also called *Mendocino*, is a forerunner of country-rock. The Sir Douglas Quintet toured Europe and made the successful *Together After Five*, while Sahm made an excellent country single under the name of Wayne Douglas, 'Be Real'. He moved to Prunedale in northern California and befriended a Chicano band, Louie And The Lovers, producing their *Rise*. Sahm, having resolved his problems with the authorities, went back to Texas and released *The Return Of Doug Saldaña*, the name reflecting his affection for Chicanos. The album, co-produced with Meaux, included an affectionate tribute to **Freddy Fender**, 'Wasted Days And Wasted Nights', which prompted Meaux to resurrect Fender's career and turn him into a country superstar. Sahm appeared with **Kris Kristofferson** in the film, *Cisco Pike*, and told his record company that the song he performed, 'Michoacan', was about a state

in Mexico. Disc jockeys, however, realized that he was actually praising marijuana and airplay was restricted. **Atlantic Records**' key producer, **Jerry Wexler**, decided that progressive country was becoming fashionable and signed both **Willie Nelson** and Doug Sahm. Sahm's high-spirited *Doug Sahm And Band*, was made in New York with **Bob Dylan**, **Dr. John** and accordionist **Flaco Jiminez**, and Sahm achieved minor success with 'Is Anybody Going To San Antone?'. The Sir Douglas Quintet were resurrected intermittently which resulted in two fine live albums, *Wanted Very Much Alive* and *Back To The 'Dillo*. Although it might seem strange that the band should tour with the new wave band the **Pretenders**, Sahm's voice and style were arguably an influence on **Elvis Costello**. Sahm himself says, 'I'm a part of Willie Nelson's world and at the same time I'm a part of the **Grateful Dead**'s. I don't ever stay in one bag'. Among Sahm's finest albums are *Hell Of A Spell*, a blues album dedicated to Guitar Slim, and *The Return Of The Formerly Brothers*, with guitarist Amos Garrett and pianist Gene Taylor. In 1990, Doug re-used the name, the Texas Tornadoes, for an album with Meyers, Jiminez and Fender. The album, which included Sahm's witty 'Who Were You Thinkin' Of?' and Butch Hancock's 'She Never Spoke Spanish To Me', showed that he has lost none of his powers. In the UK, the Sir Douglas Quintet may be regarded as one-hit-wonders, but in reality Sahm has recorded a remarkable catalogue of Texas music. *Day Dreaming At Midnight* was a prime example. It was produced by ex-**Creedence Clearwater Revival** member Doug Clifford and was a rousing collection notably for 'Too Little Too Late' and the blistering **Bob Dylan** pastiche 'Dylan Come Lately'.
Albums: *Doug Sahm And Band* (1973), *Texas Tornado* (1973), *Groovers Paradise* (1974), *Texas Rock For Country Rollers* (1976), *Live Love* (1977), *Hell Of A Spell* (1980), *Texas Road Runner* (1986), *Live Doug Sahm* (1987), *Back To The 'Dillo* (1988), *Juke Box Music* (1989), *The Texas Tornadoes* (1990), as Texas Tornadoes *Zone Of Our Own* (1991), *Hangin' On By A Thread* (1992), with Amos Garrett, Gene Taylor *The Return Of The Formerly Brothers* (1992), *Day Dreaming At Midnight* (Elektra 1994), *The Last Real Texas Blues Band* (Antone's 1995). Compilations: *Sir Douglas - Way Back When He Was Just Doug Sahm* (1979), *Sir Douglas - His First Recordings* (1981), *Sir Doug's Recording Trip* (1989), *The Best Of Doug Sahm And The Sir Douglas Quintet* (1991).

Sailcat

Sailcat was the duo of Court Pickett and John Wyker, two guitarists-vocalists working in the Muscle Shoals, Alabama, USA area in the early 70s. Pickett and Wyker, along with local session musicians Chuck Leavell (keyboards, later of the **Allman Brothers Band**), Clayton Ivey (bass) and Pete Carr (guitar, half of the duo **LeBlanc And Carr**), put together the

debut Sailcat album on **Elektra Records** in 1972, although they never performed under that name. Wyker's song 'Motorcycle Mama' was included on that album and became a US number 12 single. With that success, the musicians converged to record songs for follow-up singles, but none reached the charts and the project was abandoned.
Album: *Sailcat* aka *Motorcycle Mama* (1972).

Sailing Along

Released in 1938, this was the last of the three films in which **Jessie Matthews** appeared under the direction of her husband **Sonnie Hale**. She plays 'water gypsy' Kay Martin, the ambitious step-daughter of bargemaster Skipper Barnes (Frank Pettingell), who is in love with Skipper's studious son, Steve (Barry Mackay). In an effort to attract his attention, she breaks into show business and is rapidly propelled to stardom by eccentric millionaire Victor Gulliver (Roland Young) and producer and song-and-dance-man Dick Randall (Jack Whiting). Meanwhile, Steve is also taking Victor's advice, and makes a killing on the Stock Exchange. It all ends with Kay fending off the advances of the pushy American press agent, Windy (Noel Madison), and sailing off to foreign climes with Steve in his new yacht. The frothy story, which was adapted by Lesser Samuels from a story by Selwyn Jepson, gave Jessie Matthews and Jack Whiting ample opportunity for some slick dance routines which were staged by Buddy Bradley. There were also several appealing songs by Arthur Johnston and Maurice Sigler, including 'My River', 'Souvenir Of Love', 'Trusting My Luck', 'Your Heart Skips A Beat', and the delightful 'Sailing Along'. Athene Seyler and Alastair Sim (the future star of Ealing comedies and St. Trinian's films), provided the comic relief, and also in the cast were Margaret Vyner, Peggy Novak, and William Dewhurst. The screenplay was adapted by Lesser Samuels from a story by Selwyn Jepson.

Sailor

Sailor were formed in 1974 by songwriter and acoustic guitarist George Kajanus (b. Georg Hultgren, Norway) who, apart from claiming to be a Norwegian prince, was a member of the folk rock group **Eclection**. The remainder of Sailor comprised Phil Pickett (b. Germany; nickleodeon) and Grant Serpell (b. Maidenhead, England; drums). They were signed to **CBS**/Epic Records who released their debut 'Traffic Jam'. A projected 1975 tour with **Mott** was expected to bring the group success; however, it was cancelled when Mott split. Subsequent tours with **Kiki Dee** and **Cockney Rebel** did have the desired effect. They reached number 2 in the UK charts with the sparkling 'A Glass Of Champagne'. They had two more hits with 'Girls Girls Girls' and 'One Drink Too Many' before the onset of punk overwhelmed them, but they continued gigging. The line-up underwent some changes but Marsh and Pickett were still on board by 1982. Kajanus formed the offshoot group Data in 1980 and they made three albums under that name. In 1983, Pickett acted as keyboard player and songwriter for **Culture Club** and his 'Karma Chameleon' was an international hit for them; though he was later sued by the writers of **Jimmy Jones**' 'Handy Man' for alleged plagiarism. Pickett went on to write and perform ITV's 'Olympic Games Theme' in 1984 and produce Thereze Bazaar's solo album that same year. The group reformed in 1991, releasing their first album in 13 years.

Albums: *Sailor* (1974), *Trouble* (1975), *The Third Step* (1976), *Checkpoint* (1977), *Hideaway* (1978), *Dressed For Drowning* (1980), *Sailor* (1991). Compilation: *Greatest Hits* (1978).

Sain (Recordiau) Cyf

Sain, Wales' leading record company, was founded in Cardiff, South Wales, in 1969, by Huw Jones, Dafydd Iwan and Brian Morgan Edwards. The company moved to Llandwrog, near Caernarfon, North Wales, in 1971, and a new studio was opened in 1980. A second studio was opened in 1987. With the resurgence in interest in Celtic folk music, it was apparent that Welsh folk music was under-represented, and extensive promotion was required. Responding to this market demand, Sain regularly issued approximately 40 albums a year in Welsh and English on their Sain/Cambrian label. Their Tryfan label handles private recordings of choirs, schools and clubs. Over the years, Sain has taken over the catalogues of Cambrian, Welsh Teledisc, and Ty ar y Graig, after those companies ceased trading. Sain have released a wide number of folk recordings from artists such as **Ar Log**, **4 Yn Y Bar**, **Plethyn**, **Calennig**, and **Mabsant**. The label now has a catalogue of music covering the gamut from folk to rock, pop and choral work;it released two compilations of Welsh folk artists and now has international distribution.

Albums: *'Gorau Gwerin' The Best Of Welsh Folk* (1984), *'Gorau Gwerin' The Best Of Welsh Folk 2* (1985), *Valley Lights-Folk Songs Of Wales Today* (1987).

Sain, Oliver

b. 1 March 1932, Dundee, Mississippi, USA. Working out of St. Louis, saxophonist Sain first established himself as a bandleader and producer, but later in his career made a name for himself as a disco star. After forming his band in St. Louis in 1960 he developed a considerable local reputation playing at all the clubs in the city and across the Mississippi in East St. Louis and other communities. Members of his band have included **Fontella Bass**, Bobby McClure, and **Little Milton**. He made his first records in 1962 for the tiny Bobbin label, featuring Fontella Bass on vocals and piano and Little Milton on guitar. In 1966 he founded Archway Studio and occasionally recorded himself as well as a host of St. Louis/East St. Louis acts. Sain never achieved any national recognition, however, until the early 70s, when he began recording hot instrumentals for the Nashville-based Abet label, establishing himself as an unlikely disco star. His most renowned hits were 'Bus Stop' (number 47 R&B) in 1974 and 'Party Hearty' (number 16 R&B) in 1976. His last chart record a year later was 'I Feel Like Dancin'' (number 74 R&B). Sain's albums, unlike his singles, were broader than disco in appeal, containing besides rousing dance grooves some warm southern-style soulful saxophone playing. During the 80s and 90s he established himself as a producer of blues acts, notably Larry Davis, **Eddie Kirkland**, David Dee, and **Johnnie Johnson**.

Albums: *Main Man* (Abet 1973), *Bus Stop* (Abet 1974), *Blue Max* (Abet 1975), *So Good In The Morning* (Houston Connection 1981). Compilations: *Disco King* (Soul Posters 1976), *At His Best* (Abet 1977).

Saint Etienne

By far the most dextrous of those bands cursed with the 'indie-dance' label, and one of the few to maintain genuine support in both camps. Pete Wiggs (b. 15 May 1966, Reigate, Surrey, England) and music journalist Bob Stanley (b. 25 December 1964, Horsham, Sussex, England) grew up together in Croydon, Surrey, England. In the early 80s, the pair began to experiment with party tapes, but did not make any serious inroads into the music business until forming Saint Etienne in 1988, taking their name from the renowned French football team. Relocating to Camden in north London, the pair recruited Moira Lambert of **Faith Over Reason** for a dance/reggae cover of **Neil Young**'s 'Only Love Can Break Your Heart'. Issued in May 1990 on the aspiring **Heavenly Records** label, the single fared well in the nightclubs and surfaced on a magazine flexidisc remixed by label mates **Flowered Up** (who appeared on the b-side) in July. Another cover, indie guitar band the **Field Mice**'s 'Kiss And Make Up', was given a similar dance pop overhaul for Saint Etienne's second single, fronted this time by New Zealand vocalist Donna Savage of **Dead Famous People**. Then came the infectious northern soul-tinged 'Nothing Can Stop Us' in May 1991. Its strong European feel reflected both their name, which helped attract strong support in France, and their logo (based on the European flag). It also benefited from Sarah Cracknell (b. 12 April 1967, Chelmsford, Essex, England)'s dreamy vocals, which would dominate Saint Etienne's debut, *Fox Base Alpha*, released in the autumn. Cracknell had formerly recorded with Prime Time. 'Only Love Can Break Your Heart' was reissued alongside the album, and provided them with a minor chart hit. Throughout the 90s the only critical barb that seemed to stick to Saint Etienne with any justification or regularity was that they were simply 'too clever for their own good'. A criticism which Stanley clearly could not abide: 'The image that the media has built up of us as manipulators really makes us laugh'. *So Tough* revealed a rich appreciation of the vital signs of British pop, paying homage to their forerunners without ever indulging in false flattery. *Tiger Bay*, toted as a folk-album, transcended a variety of musical genres with the sense of ease and propriety that Saint Etienne had essentially patented. The medieval folk/trance ballad, 'Western Wind', and the instrumental, 'Urban Clearway', redolent but not traceable to a dozen prime time television themes, were just two of the bookends surrounding one of the greatest albums of that year. It was followed by a fan club only release, *I Love To Paint*, limited to 500 copies. However, in 1995 Sarah Cracknell was said to be working on a solo album, having already recorded a duet with Tim Burgess of the **Charlatans**, 'I Was Born On Christmas Day', released at the end of 1993 in a failed attempt to mug the Christmas singles market.

Albums: *Fox Base Alpha* (Heavenly 1991), *So Tough* (Heavenly 1993), *You Need A Mess Of Help To Stand Alone* (Heavenly 1993), *Tiger Bay* (Heavenly 1994), *I Love To Paint* (Heavenly 1994, fan club only).

Sainte-Marie, Buffy

b. 20 February 1941, Piapot Reserve, Saskatchewan, Canada. An honours graduate from the University of Massachusetts, Buffy eschewed a teaching career in favour of a folksinger. She was signed to the **Vanguard** label in 1964, following her successful performances at Gerde's Folk City. Her debut *It's My Way*, introduced a remarkable compositional and performing talent. Sainte-Marie's impassioned plea for Indian rights, 'Now That The Buffalo's Gone', reflected her native- American parentage and was one of several standout tracks, along with 'Cod'ine' and 'The Universal Soldier'. The latter was recorded, successfully, by **Donovan**, which helped introduce Buffy to a wider audience. Her second selection included 'Until It's Time For You To Go', a haunting love song which was later recorded by **Elvis Presley**. However, Sainte-Marie was also a capable interpreter of other writer's material, as her versions of songs by **Bukka White**, **Joni Mitchell** and **Leonard Cohen** showed. Her versatility was also apparent on a superb C&W collection, *I'm Gonna Be A Country Girl Again*, and on *Illuminations*, which featured an electronic score on several tracks. A campaigner for Indian rights, Sainte-Marie secured an international hit in 1971 with the theme song to the film, *Soldier Blue*, but subsequent releases failed to capitalize on this success. Temporarily bereft of direction, Buffy returned to the Indian theme with *Sweet America*, but with the collapse of the **ABC** labels, she retired to raise her family and concentrate

on her work for children's foundations. She composed the 1982 **Joe Cocker/Jennifer Warnes'** hit, 'Up Where We Belong' which featured in the film *An Officer And A Gentleman*. Her welcome return in 1991, following her signing with **Chrysalis Records**, produced the warmly-received *Coincidence And Likely Stories*, which displayed her current interest in computer technology.

Albums: *It's My Way* (1964), *Many A Mile* (1965), *Little Wheel Spin And Spin* (1966), *Fire, Fleet And Candlelight* (1967), *I'm Gonna Be A Country Girl Again* (1968), *Illuminations* (1970), *She Used To Wanna Be A Ballerina* (1971), *Moonshot* (1972), *Quiet Places* (1973), *Buffy* (1974), *Changing Woman* (1975), *Sweet America* (1976), *Coincidence And Likely Stories* (1992). Compilations: *The Best Of Buffy Sainte-Marie* (1970), *Native North American Child: An Odyssey* (1974), *The Best Of Buffy Sainte-Marie, Volume 2* (1974).

Saints

Formed in Brisbane, Australia in 1975, the Saints were the first Australian punk band to be recognized as being relevant by the UK media. The band comprised Chris Bailey (vocals/guitar), Kym Bradshaw (bass, replaced by Alisdair Ward in 1977), **Ed Kuepper** (guitar) and Ivor Hay (drums). They were plucked from obscurity via their single 'I'm Stranded' being reviewed as single of the week by the now defunct UK weekly music paper, *Sounds*. Following this, and encouraging sales for their debut album, the band based itself in the UK. Although labelled a punk band, the Saints did not strictly conform to the English perception of punk, as their roots were more R&B-based. A refusal to imitate the punk fashion was certainly instrumental in their rapid fall from favour, although they have since attained considerable cult status. Co-founder Kuepper left the group in 1978 to form the **Laughing Clowns**. The band stayed together long enough, with various personnel, to record two more albums, disbanding in 1979. Chris Bailey performed with a variety of musicians during the 80s, using the Saints' name, as well as touring solo, playing acoustic guitar. He reformed the original line-up of the Saints in 1984 (minus Kuepper) and has recorded constantly over the ensuing decade. As a retaliation to Bailey's continued usage of Kuepper's songs in the latter-day Saints line-up, Kuepper formed the Aints in 1990.

Albums: *I'm Stranded* (1977), *Eternally Yours* (1978), *Prehistoric Sounds* (1978), *Monkey Puzzle* (1981), *Casablanca* (1982), *A Little Madness To Be Free* (1984), *Live In A Mud Hut* (1985), *All Fool's Day* (1986), *Prodigal Son* (1989). Compilation: *Songs Of Salvation 1976-1988* (1991).

Sakamoto, Kyu

b. 1941, Kawasaki, Japan, d. 12 August 1985. The original singer with the Paradise Kings, he signed to Toshiba Records in 1959 after being discovered singing in the tea rooms of his home town. He had a succession of hits in Japan, but his only major worldwide hit was

'Sukiyaki', in 1963. The reason for its international success was due to Louis Benjamin of Pye Records in England, who brought home a copy from Japan for popular trad-jazz clarinettist **Kenny Ball**. At this stage the record (written in 1962 by pianist Hachidai Nakamura and lyricist Rokusuke Ei) was called 'Ueo Muite Aruko' ('Walk With Your Chin Up'). This duly changed to 'Sukiyaki'. Ball's version reached the Top 10 in the UK and interest was stirred in the original which repeated the feat a few months later. Sakamoto never managed to duplicate his initial world-wide success (although the follow up, 'China Nights', was a minor US hit), but continued to be a star in his native country, appearing in many films and on television programmes. His career came to an abrupt end in 1985 when he was among the 524 passengers killed when a Japanese Boeing 747 civil aircraft crashed outside Tokyo.

Selected album: *Sukiyaki And Other Japanese Hits* (1963).

Sakamoto, Ryûichi

b. 17 January 1952, Tokyo, Japan. Sakamoto studied composition and electronic music at Tokyo College of Arts and took a Master of Arts degree in 1976 before forming the **Yellow Magic Orchestra** with Haruomi Hosono and Yukihiro Takahashi two years later. It was with the YMO that he first achieved international recognition with 'Computer Game (Theme From The Invaders)' reaching number 17 in the UK charts in 1980. Sakamoto's first solo *One Thousand Knives*, was recorded in 1978, but not released until 1982 and only then in the Netherlands. The first widely-distributed recording was *B-2 Unit*, made while he was still a member of the Yellow Magic Orchestra in 1980 with the help of **Andy Partridge** (**XTC**) and Dennis Bovell. **Robin Scott** was given equal billing on *Left Handed Dream* on which he provided vocals, with US session guitarist Adrian Belew (**Talking Heads**, **Frank Zappa** and **David Bowie**) also featured. *The End Of Asia* was recorded with Danceries, a Japanese classical ensemble which specialized in recreating medieval music. Working alongside **David Sylvian** (of who's work Sakamoto would become a key contributor), he scored two UK hit singles with 'Bamboo Houses' (1982) and 'Forbidden Colours' (1983). Since the mid-80s, Sakamoto has established a successful career as a solo recording artist, a film composer and an film actor. Sakamoto's evocative soundtrack to Nagisa Oshima's *Merry Christmas, Mr Lawrence* - in which he made his acting debut - received critical acclaim; his contribution to the soundtrack of Bernardo Bertolucci's *The Last Emperor* (with **David Byrne** and Cong Su), earned him an Academy Award. In September 1985 at the Tsukaba Expo, he collaborated with Radical TV on a spectacular live performance of *TV WAR*, a science fiction show involving music, video and computer graphics. He has constantly attracted a variety of leading musicians in studio work, varying from **Iggy Pop** to **Brian Wilson** and **Robbie Robertson** and was assisted by **Thomas Dolby** on *Musical Encyclopedia* and the single 'Field Work' (1986). He has also contributed to **Public Image Limited**'s *Album* and Arto Lindsey's *Esperanto*. His own solo albums have consistently displayed a hi-tech integration of western pop music with traditional music from Japan, the Middle East and Africa. After releasing *Beauty*, which incorporated Okinawan music, Sakamoto toured the USA and Europe and established his international fame with his highly eclectic style. He conducted and arranged the music at the opening ceremony for the 1992 Barcelona Olympic Games.

Albums: *B-2 Unit* (1980), *Hidariudeno (A Dream Of The Left Arm)* (1981), *Merry Christmas, Mr. Lawrence* (1983, film soundtrack), *Coda* (1983), *Ongaku Zukan (A Picture Book Of Music)* (1984), *Esperanto* (1985), *Miraiha Yarô (A Futurist Chap)* (1986), *Media Bahn Live* (1986), *Oneamisno Tsubasa (The Wings Of Oneamis)* (1986), *Illustrated Musical Encyclopedia* (1986), *Neo Geo* (1987), with David Byrne, Cong Su *The Last Emperor* (1987, film soundtrack), *Playing The Orchestra* (1988), *Gruppo Musicale* (1989), *Beauty* (1989), *Heartbeat* (1991), with Iggy Pop *Neo Geo* (1992), *Wild Palms* (1993, soundtrack), *Sweet Revenge* (1994). Compilations: *Tokyo Joe* (1988), *Sakamoto Plays Sakamoto* (1989).

Further reading: *Otowo Miru, Tokiwo Kiku (Seeing Sound And Hearing Time)*, Ryûichi Sakamoto and Shôzô Ômori. *Seldom-Illegal*, Ryûichi Sakamoto.

Salad

Fronted by ex-**MTV** presenter Marijne van der Vlugt, UK indie band Salad first took shape when she started writing songs with guitarist Paul Kennedy while working as a photographic fashion model. Signed to **Island Records** indie offshoot label Red, Salad offer a sparse sound which contrasts with the dense narratives of their lyrics. Both Vlugt and Kennedy, at one time romantically linked, are ex-film students. Kennedy's work includes *The Yoghurt Laugh*, while Vlugt used her own revolving, naked torso as the subject of her film project. Kennedy also worked for a design company before signing up with the band full time, painting betting shop windows. It was through van der Vlugt's original band, Merry Babes, that she was offered the MTV job, being asked for an audition after attempting to press the group's videos onto a member of staff. The song writing on their debut album, *Drink Me*, was split three ways, with Kennedy writing half the songs, Vlugt four and drummer Rob Wakeman (ex-**Colenso Parade**) three. Bass player Peter Brown is the final, non-writing member of the band. Following 'Your Ma', which explored illicit sexual desires à la *The Graduate*, 'Elixir', penned by Wakeman, gripped the charts in early 1995 portraying the destructiveness of the youth and beauty aesthetic associated with the shallow and glitzy world of fashion and advertising. Album: *Drink Me* (Red 1995).

Salad Days

Hastily assembled to fill a three-week gap in the schedule of the Bristol Old Vic in 1954, *Salad Days* was swiftly transferred to London where it opened at the Vaudeville Theatre on 5 August that same year. **Julian Slade** wrote the music and collaborated on the book and lyrics with Dorothy Reynolds. The simple story told of story of two young university graduates, Jane (Eleanor Drew) and Timothy (John Warner), He is trying to find a job, while Jane's mother is urging her to get married. They meet a tramp (Newton Blick) in the park, and agree to take care of his mobile piano for a month in return for a payment of £7 per week. The instrument is a magic one, and makes everybody dance. They lose the instrument, and their efforts to to find it involve blackmail, a flying saucer, and several of Timothy's uncles. Whimsical stuff, but some shrewd observers saw a serious underlying message decrying indolence and emphasising the desirability of work satisfaction. Also in the cast were James Cairncross, Michael Aldridge, Christine Finn, Pat Heywood, Michael Meacham, Yvonne Coulette, Joe Gregg, Bob Harris, and Dorothy Reynolds. The endearing score consisted of a mixture of lively and gentle songs, and included 'The Things That Are Done By A Don', 'It's Easy To Sing', 'We're Looking For A Piano', 'We Said We Wouldn't Look Back', 'Sand In My Eyes, 'I Sit In The Sun', 'Oh, Look At Me', 'Out Of Breath', 'Find Yourself Something To Do', 'Hush-Hush', 'The Saucer Song', 'Cleopatra', and 'The Time Of My Life'. Julian Slade himself played one of the two accompanying pianos, and *Salad Days* ran on and on for 2,283 performances - a remarkable achievement in the days long before the **Andrew Lloyd Webber** blockbusters. Sophisticated New Yorkers were not so impressed, and the 1958 US production folded after only 10 weeks. Londoners retained their enormous affection for this curiously British phenomenon, and there were West End revivals in 1961, 1964, and again in 1976. In 1983, a television version was screened in the UK. The 40th anniversary of this charming entertainment was celebrated in 1994 with a new production which was broadcast on BBC Radio 2.

Salas, Stevie, Colorcode

Guitarist/vocalist Stevie Salas was working in a Los Angeles recording studio when **George Clinton** turned him into a hot property by asking him to play on his 1986 album, *R&B Skeletons In The Closet*. Salas subsequently found himself in demand for his guitar and production skills, working with acts such as **Was (Not Was)**, **Andy Taylor**, the **Tubes** and **Eddie Money**, and contributing to the *Bill & Ted's Excellent Adventure* soundtrack. A lucrative and enjoyable stint in

Rod Stewart's touring band ensued before Salas was able to concentrate on his own project with bassist C.J. deVillar and drummer Winston A. Watson. *Stevie Salas Colorcode* was a sparkling debut, fusing raw hard rock and funk into excellent songs, from the anthemic 'Stand Up' to 'Indian Chief', a sensitive tribute to Salas' father. With airplay success for opening single 'The Harder They Come', the band were hotly tipped by the rock press. Live shows with **Joe Satriani** in the US and **24-7 Spyz** in the UK further enhanced Colorcode's reputation, but the momentum was lost, along with their recording deal, during the sale of **Island Records** to **Polygram**, when the majority of Island's hard rock acts were dropped. However, the band retained a Japanese deal, and released two further albums: *Stuff*, a collection of demo and live tracks with a superb acoustic reworking of 'Blind' from the debut, and the *Bootleg Like A Mug!!* live set, which displayed a distinct **Hendrix** influence with covers of 'Little Wing' and 'Hey Joe'. Salas went on to work with old friend **Bootsy Collins** and ex-**Band Of Gypsys** drummer Buddy Miles, releasing *Hardware* in 1992 under the Third Eye name (conversely packaged in the UK as *Third Eye Open* on Rykodisc by Hardware), before reuniting with the Colorcode band and a host of guest stars to record *Stevie Salas Presents The Electric Pow Wow*, a mixture of original material and largely obscure covers. The adaptable guitarist also played as part of **Terence Trent D'Arby**'s live band. Salas then put Colocode on ice for a time to work more closely with Sass Jordan on her *Rats* album, the pair having aleady collaborated on *Racine* and Salas' *Electric Pow Wow* set. Another Colorcode album, *Back From The Living Dead*, then emerged with the original line-up augmented by bassist T.M. Stevens, Pride And Glory/ex-Sass Jordan drummer Brian Tichy, and **24-7 Spyz** bassist Rick Skatore, and the material and performances matched the quality of the debut.

Albums: *Stevie Salas Colorcode* (Island 1990), *Stuff* (Polystar 1991), *Bootleg Like A Mug!!* (Polystar 1992), *Stevie Salas Presents The Electric Pow Wow* (Polystar 1993), *Back From The Living Dead* (Polystar 1994).

Salem, Kevin

Prominent New York-based rock singer/songwriter Kevin Salem (guitar/vocals) made best use of his dramatic surname by recruiting Dave Dunton (keyboards), Keith Levreault (drums; ex-Blood Oranges, Roscoe's Gang), Todd Novak (guitar/vocals; ex-Dragsters) and Scott Yoder (bass; ex-Blue Chieftains) to provide a 'going concern' rock group. Salem himself hailed from Johnstown, Pennsylvania, before moving to Boston where he joined **Dumptruck** for their acclaimed 1987 album, *For The Country*. He would stay with that band until the dawn of the 90s, when frustrations and legal complications saw him depart. Relocating to New York, Salem performed with

his own *ad hoc* band, also working as a sideman for **Freedy Johnston** and **Yo La Tengo**. His session contributions included tracks on Johnston's *Can You Fly*, the **Pooh Sticks**' *Million Seller* and **Chris Harford**'s *Be Headed*. As well as recording with **Miracle Legion** Salem also took the production mantle for **Madder Rose**'s debut album. His first album under his own name was actually completed in 1992, after he had recorded 11 songs in a variety of New York studios, sneaking in after-hours to lay down the tracks when cash flow problems arose. The resulting *Keep Your Crosses Fingered* would have to be postponed however. Instead Salem concentrated on putting together the current line-up of his band, who recorded *Soma City* in five days at Hoboken's Water Music studios. It was helped in no small part by the production tutelage of Niko Bolas (best known for his work with **Neil Young**) who fitted Salem in for free between commissions from **Billy Joel** and **Rod Stewart**. It included one song, 'Forever Gone', co-written with **Nirvana/Urge Overkill** producer Butch Vig.
Album: *Soma City* (Roadrunner 1994).

Sally

One of the most popular musicals of the 20s, this was really another version of the Cinderella rags-to-riches story which has been used in shows such as *Irene*, *Mlle. Modiste*, *My Fair Lady*, and *42nd Street*, amongst others. *Sally* opened at the New Amsterdam Theatre in New York on 21 December 1921, and was intended as a showcase for producer **Florenz Ziegfeld**'s current protegée, Marilynn (later Marilyn) Miller. **Guy Bolton**'s book portrayed Miss Miller as poor Sally Green, who dreams of becoming a famous dancer while washing dishes at a Greenwich Village cafe. One of the waiters (who, not surprisingly, is the exiled Duke of Czechogovinia in disguise) encourages her when a theatrical agent, Otis Hopper (Walter Catlett), suggests that she masquerades as prima ballerina Mme. Nookarova at an elegant party. Of course, it is her big chance, and leads to a starring role in the *Ziegfeld Follies*, where she dances the 'Butterfly Ballet' with music by **Victor Herbert**. Leon Errol, as the disguised Duke, provided most of the comedy, along with Walter Catlett. The score was rather a mixed-up affair. All the music was written by **Jerome Kern**, but several lyricists were involved. **P.G. Wodehouse**, who, at one stage, was to have written all the song lyrics, ended up by collaborating with Clifford Grey on just two: 'The Church 'Round The Corner' and 'You Can't Keep A Good Girl Down' (Joan Of Arc). Grey also wrote the words for 'Wild Rose', 'Sally', 'On With The Dance', and 'The Schnitza Komisski'. Two of the numbers, with lyrics by **Buddy De Sylva**, came from *Zip Goes A Million* which folded before it reached Broadway. One of them, 'Whip-Poor-Will', did not cause much of a stir, but the

other, 'Look For The Silver Lining', eventually became a sentimental standard. One more song, 'The Lorelei' (lyric: Anne Caldwell), was also 'borrowed' from an earlier Kern score for *The Night Boat*. It all added up to a tremendous hit. 570 performances in a season when 42 other musicals made their Broadway debut, was quite phenomenal. When *Sally* returned to New York in 1948 with Bambi Linn in the leading role, it was only for a brief run. London audiences took to the show in 1921, when it starred Dorothy Dickson and **Leslie Henson**, and stayed at the Winter Garden for nearly a year. They also enjoyed a revised version, entitled *Wild Rose*, which spent six months at the Prince's Theatre in 1942 with **Jessie Matthews** as Sally. There have been two films of the story: a silent version in 1925, and the 1929 early talkie, with Marilyn Miller.

Sally In Our Alley

Gracie Fields was already the talk of the north of England, when she made her film debut in this 1931 Basil Dean production for Associated Talking Pictures. The screenplay, by Miles Malleson, Archie Pitt, and Alma Reville, was based on the play *The Likes Of 'Er* by Charles McEvoy. Gracie Fields plays Sally Winch, a lively young lady who has left Rochdale in Lancashire for a job in a coffee shop in London's Mile End Road which is run by Sam Bilson (Ben Field). After many years of waiting she has given up all hope of seeing her true love, George Miles (Ian Hunter), again, fearing him lost in action during World War I. However, George's terrible wounds have healed, and, in spite of the efforts of jealous Florrie Small (Florence Desmond), 'a child of the gutter - cunning suspicious and pretty' - to keep them apart, he and Sally are eventually reunited. Renee Macready and Helen Ferrers play Lady Daphne and the Duchess of Wexford, a couple of toffs who try, without success, to turn Sally's head, and also among a strong supporting cast were Fred Groves, Gibb McLaughlin, Ivor Barnard, Barbara Gott, and Florence Harwood. Rising above the action was Gracie Fields's thrilling voice on songs such as 'Following The Sun Around' (**Joseph McCarthy-Harry Tierney**), 'Moonlight On The Alster' (Osacar Fetras), 'Lancashire Blues', 'Fred Fernackerpan', and the immortal 'Sally' (Will Haines-Harry Leon-Leo Towers), the number which became her life-long theme. This film, which was directed by Maurice Elvey, helped Gracie on her way to becoming one of the best-loved British entertainers of all time.

Sallyangie

This duo formed in 1968 featured **Mike Oldfield** (guitar/vocals) and his sister **Sally Oldfield** (vocals). Given the era it was recorded, there are definite shades of the **Incredible String Band** about the *Children Of The Sun*. Other musicians featured on the album were Terry Cox (drums), Ray Warleigh (flute) and John

Collins (guitar). Sallyangie was a short-lived affair with Mike destined to progress further, and Sally later to have moderate chart success in her own right.
Album: *Children Of The Sun* (1968).

Salt 'N' Pepa

Cheryl 'Salt' James (b. Brooklyn, New York, USA) and Sandra 'Pepa' Denton (b. 9 November 1969, Jamaica) grew up in the Queens district of New York City. They became telephone sales girls and envisioned a career in nursing until fellow workmate and part time producer **Hurby 'Luv Bug' Azor** stepped in. He got them to rap for his group the Super Lovers (credited on record as Supernature) on his answer record to **Doug E. Fresh**'s 'The Show'. They started recording as Salt 'N' Pepa (adapted from Super Nature recording 'Showstopper') under Azor's guidance and released singles such as 'I'll Take Your Man', 'It's My Beat', and 'Tramp', the latter a clever revision of the old **Otis Redding/Carla Thoma**s duet. They also used the female DJ Spinderella (aka Dee Dee Roper), backing singers and male erotic dancers to complete their act. Their big break came in 1988 when a re-issue of an earlier single - 'Push It' - reached the UK number 2 spot and was also a hit on the US R&B chart. Later that year a remake of the **Isley Brothers**' 'Twist And Shout' also went into the Top 10. In between those two they released 'Shake Your Thang' (once again a take on an Isley Brothers' track, 'It's Your Thing') which featured the instrumental group EU. Nominated for the first ever Rap Grammy in 1989, they refused to attend the ceremony when it was discovered that the presentation of that particular bauble would not be televised - withdrawing to show solidarity with hip hop's growing status. Their most confrontational release was the 1991 'Let's Talk About Sex' manifesto, something of a change of tack after the overtly erotic 'Push It'. 'Do You Want Me' was similarly successful, encouraging the record company to put out *A Blitz Of Salt 'N' Pepa Hits*, a collection of remixes, in their absence. Both Salt and Pepa were otherwise engaged having babies (Pepa in 1990, Salt in 1991. DJ Spinderella would make it a hat-trick of single mothers in the group a short time later). In the interim they could content themselves with being the most commercially successful female rap troupe of all time, and the first to go gold. They subsequently enjoyed an invitation to appear at President Clinton's inauguration party. They returned to the charts in 1994 with their highly successful collaboration with **En Vogue**, 'Whatta Man'. It was a return to their naughty/nice personas, typically suggestive and salacious. After all, the charts would indeed be a boring place without Salt 'N' Pepa.
Albums: *Hot Cool & Vicious* (Next Plateau 1987), *A Salt With A Deadly Pepa* (Next Plateau 1988), *Black's Magic* (Next Plateau 1990), *Very Necessary* (London 1993).

Compilations: *A Blitz Of Salt 'N' Pepa Hits* (London 1991), *The Greatest Hits* (London 1991).

Salt Tank

Internal Records' signings who, under the 'intelligent techo' mantle, have broke several musical barriers, notably supporting **Hawkwind** on live dates. Their sequence of releases runs chronilogically *ST1*, *ST2* and *ST3*, the latter EP comprising seven different 'stereotypical' approaches to modern techno, all of which are carried off with aplomb. They are a duo comprising Malcolm Stanners, who had worked with **Derrick May** and **Kevin Saunderson** in the late 80s, and partner David. They made their debut with 'Ease The Pressure'/'Charged Up", which sold well in mainland Europe, then 1993's 'Sweli'/'Meltdown' - a record packaged to resemble a **Djax-Up Beats** disc, with David's phone number on the label. The first person to ring up was **Andy Weatherall**. *ST3* also featured samples of **Simple Minds** and David Byrne (**Talking Heads**).

Salty Dog

This Los Angeles-based band were put together in late 1986 by bassist Mike Hannon (b. Columbus, Ohio, USA) and drummer Khurt Maier (b. Sacramento, California, USA), enlisting Youngstown, Ohio-born vocalist Jimmi Bleacher and replacing their original guitarist (Scott Lane) with Canadian Pete Reveen in early 1987. The band developed a blues-based style which drew immediate **Led Zeppelin** comparisons, but owed more to a mixture of influences from old bluesmen like **Memphis Slim**, '**Sonny Boy' Williamson** and **Willie Dixon** to the more contemporary sounds of **Black Flag** and **Motörhead**. *Every Dog Has Its Day*, recorded in Rockfield Studios in Wales with producer Peter Collins, demonstrated that the Zeppelin references were most apt due to the sheer variety of styles within Salty Dog's bluesy framework, from straightforward opener, 'Come Along', through the smouldering 'Slow Daze', to the tongue-in-cheek acoustic blues of 'Just Like A Woman'. The album received a flurry of good reviews, but Salty Dog were unable to capitalize, as Bleacher departed shortly after its release. The band struggled to find a replacement, locating Dallas native Darrel Beach (ex-**DT Roxx**) in late 1991, but the loss of momentum proved crucial and Salty Dog faded.
Album: *Every Dog Has Its Day* (Geffen 1990).

Saluzzi, Dino

b. Timoteo Saluzzi, 20 May 1935, Campo Santa, Argentina. Saluzzi was born into a family of folk musicians, and was taught bandoneon by his father. Despite subsequent classical training and forays into *avant garde* composition, 'Dino' Saluzzi insists that these folk roots are the most crucial ingredient in his music, his particular variety of impressionistic tango frequently making use of chants and percussive effects. At home, he is best known as the leader of his experimental chamber music group Musica Creativa, while in Europe his reputation is based upon his solo concerts and his collaborations with jazz musicians. Saluzzi has performed with **Charlie Haden**, the **George Gruntz** Concert Jazz Band, and **Edward Vesala**'s Sound & Fury.

Albums: *Kultrum* (1983); *Once Upon A Time - Far Away In The South* (1986), *Andina* (1988).

Salvador, Sal

b. 21 November 1925, Monson, Massachusetts, USA. Like so many other guitarists, Salvador was inspired by **Charlie Christian** and, by the late 40s, was making an impact on the New York scene. Briefly working with **Stan Kenton** in the early 50s, Salvador then worked mostly in small groups but formed a big band of his own late in the decade. After spending many years working in studios and teaching, with only occasional recording dates, Salvador returned to the jazz scene in the late 70s, making records with artists such as **Billy Taylor**, **Mel Lewis** and **Eddie Bert** and leading his own band.

Selected albums: *The Sal Salvador Quartet/Quintet* (1953), *Boo Boo Be Doop* (1954), *The Sal Salvador Quartet* (1956), *A Tribute To The Greats* (1957), *Colors In Sound* (1958), *Sal Salvador And His Orchestra* (1960), *The Sal Salvador Quartet* ii (1963), *Starfingers* (1978), *Parallelogram* (c.1978), *Juicy Lucy* (1978), *In Your Own Sweet Way* (1982), *The World's Greatest Jazz Standards* (1983), *Sal Salvador Plays Gerry Mulligan/Bernie's Tune* (1984), *Sal Salvador And Crystal Image* (c.1989).

Salvation

This progressive rock duo frrom Seattle, USA, were formed in the late 60s by Al Linde (vocals) and Joe Tate (guitar). This eclectic unit was completed by the addition of Art Resnick aka the US of Arthur (keyboards), Artie McLean (bass) and Teddy Stewart (drums). The group, initially dubbed the Salvation Army Banned, later moved south to San Francisco where they became a popular live attraction. The quintet then purchased a renovated school-bus and, having painted it the requisite psychedelic colours, travelled the USA playing wherever they could. *Salvation* showcased their divergent interests with extended workouts, straight rock, good-time music and humour. Rick Levin replaced Stewart for *Gypsy Carnival Caravan*, but this second album lacked the charm of its predecessor and the group broke up soon after its release.

Albums: *Salvation* (1968), *Gypsy Carnival Caravan* (1969).

Sam And Bill

An R&B vocal duo formed in Newark, New Jersey, USA, consisting of Bill Johnson (b. 16 October 1932, Augusta, Georgia, USA) and Sam Gary (b. Columbus, South Carolina, USA). Sam And Bill were fine representatives of interesting early 60s phenomenon in the soul revolution; that is, the emergence of the highly gospelized vocal duos such as **Sam And Dave**, **Righteous Brothers**, and **Knight Brothers**. Johnson first recorded for **Sun Records** in a group called the Steps Of Rhythm. Gary originally was the guitarist for a group called the Soul Brothers. The two teamed up in 1962. They had hits with deep soul reworkings of two pop ballads, 'For Your Love' (number 14 R&B, 1965), which was a remake of Ed Townsend's 1958 hit, and 'Fly Me To The Moon' (number 38 R&B, 1966). Their record company JoDa then folded and the duo broke up. Johnson recruited Sam Davis Jnr. (b. 10 December 1940, Winston-Salem, North Carolina, USA) to be the new Sam. This duo in 1967 recorded for **Brunswick Records** without success.

Sam And Dave

Samuel David Moore (b. 12 October 1935, Miami, Florida, USA) and David Prater (b. 9 May 1937, Ocilla, Georgia, USA, d. 11 April 1988). Sam And Dave first performed together in 1961 at Miami's King Of Hearts club. Moore originally sang in his father's Baptist church before joining the Melonaires, while Prater, who had worked with the Sensational Hummingbirds, was also gospel-trained. Club-owner John Lomelo became the duo's manager and was instrumental in securing their contract with Roulette. Five singles and one album subsequently appeared between 1962-64, produced by R&B veteran Henry Glover, but it was not until **Jerry Wexler** signed Sam And Dave to **Atlantic Records** that their true potential blossomed. For political reasons their records appeared on **Stax**; they used the Memphis-based houseband while many of their strongest moments came from the **Isaac Hayes/David Porter** staff writing team. 'You Don't Know Like I Know', 'Hold On I'm Comin' (both 1966), 'Soul Man' (1967) and 'I Thank You' (1968), featuring Prater's gritty delivery and Moore's higher interjections, were amongst the genre's finest. When Stax and Atlantic parted in 1968, Sam And Dave reverted to the parent company, but a disintegrating personal relationship seemed to mirror their now decaying fortune. The amazing 'Soul Sister, Brown Sugar' (1969) delayed the slide, but the duo split briefly the next year when Sam Moore began his own career. Three solo singles followed, but the pair were reunited by a deal with United Artists. A renewed profile, on the strength of the **Blues Brothers**' success with 'Soul Man', faltered when the gulf between the two men proved irreconcilable. By 1981, Moore was again pursuing an independent career direction, but his sole chart success came when he was joined by

Lou Reed for a remake of 'Soul Man' six years later. Prater found a new foil in the 'Sam' of Sam & Bill, but before they were able to consolidate this new partnership, Prater died in a car crash on 11 April 1988. Arguably soul's definitive duo, Sam And Dave released records that combined urgency with an unbridled passion.

Albums: *Sam And Dave* i (1963), *Hold On, I'm Comin'* (1966), *Double Trouble* (1966), *Double Dynamite* (1967), *Soul Men* (1967), *I Thank You* (1968), *Back At 'Cha* (1976), *Sweet And Funky Gold* (1978), *Sam And Dave* ii (Edsel 1994, rec. 1962/3). Compilations: *The Best Of Sam And Dave* (1969), *Can't Stand Up For Falling Down* (1984), *The Best Of* (1987), *Wonderful World* (1987), *Sweet Funky Gold* (1988), *Sam & Dave Anthology* (1993, double CD).

Sam Apple Pie

This irreverent group was formed in Walthamstow, London, England, where they ran their own blues club, the Bottleneck. A popular live attraction, Sam Apple Pie laced their 12-bar boogie with humour, although this quirkiness was difficult to capture on record. Sam 'Tomcat' Sampson (vocals/harmonica), Mike 'Tinkerbell' Smith (guitar), Steve Jolly (guitar), Bob 'Dog' Rennie (bass), Malcolm Morley (keyboards) and Dave Charles (drums) completed the unit's debut album, which included the cryptic 'Uncle Sam's Blues'. Morley and Charles soon departed to form **Help Yourself** and by 1972, Sampson was fronting a new line-up of Andy Johnson (guitar), Denny 'Pancho' Barnes (guitar), Mark DeMajo (bass) and Lee Baxter Hayes (drums). However, by the time the group's second album was issued, Barnes was absent altogether and Hayes had been replaced by Martin Bell. Despite such instability, the group were still active in the late 70s. The line-up featured Sampson, Johnson, Gary Fletcher (bass) and Jimmy Knox (drums). Fletcher subsequently joined the **Blues Band**.

Albums: *Sam Apple Pie* (1969), *East 17* (1973).

Sam Gopal's Dream

One of London's earliest 'underground' groups, Sam Gopal's Dream were enthusiastic practitioners of a prevailing fascination with Indian/eastern music. Eschewing an orthodox drummer, Gopal's tabla work provided a percussive element, irrespective of the song's complexion. The unit was later known simply as Sam Gopal. Ian 'Lemmy' Kilminster (vocals/guitar), Roger Delia (lead guitar) and Phil Duke (bass) completed the line-up responsible for *Escalator*, a promising set marred by its lacklustre production. Despite indications to the contrary, the quartet was reliant on Lemmy who contributed much of the material, including the powerful title song. Unsurprisingly, it was he who pursued a successful career in **Hawkwind**, and later, **Motorhead**, following the group's demise.

Album: *Escalator* (1969).

Sam The Sham And The Pharaohs

b. Domingo Samudio aka Sam Samudio, Dallas, Texas, USA. Although drawing inspiration from the Tex-Mex tradition, Sam's initial releases were made for Memphis-based outlets. Backed by the Pharaohs, which comprised Ray Stinnet (guitar), Butch Gibson (saxophone), David Martin (bass) and Jerry Patterson (drums) - he scored a US chart-topper in 1965 with 'Wooly Bully', a pulsating novelty-dance song which achieved immortality as a staple part of aspiring bar band repertoires. The single became the act's sole UK Top 20 hit, but they enjoyed further success in the USA with 'Lil' Red Riding Hood', which reached number 2 the following year. The group later mutated into the Sam The Sham Revue, but the singer dissolved the venture in 1970 to embark on a solo career under his own name. Although *Hard And Heavy* featured support from guitarist **Duane Allman**, the set was marred by inconsistency and failed to establish its proponent's talent. Domingo subsequently contributed to the soundtrack of the motion picture *The Border* (1982) and remains a popular talent in his native state.

Albums: *Sam The Sham And Wooly Bully* (1965), *Their Second Album* (1965), *When The Boys Meet The Girls* (1965, film soundtrack), *Sam The Sham And The Pharaohs On Tour* (1966), *Lil' Red Riding Hood* (1966), *The Sam The Sham Revue/Nefertiti* (1967), *Ten Of Pentacles* (1968). Compilation: *The Best Of Sam The Sham And The Pharaohs* (1967). As Sam Domingo *Hard And Heavy* (1970).

Samhain

Samhain were Glenn Danzig's second major project and formed a bridge between the macabre exuberance of USA punk legends the **Misfits** and the seductively menacing rock of his current band, **Danzig**. Samhain consisted of Glenn Danzig (vocals), ex-Misfits drummer Eerie Von (now bass), Steve Zing (drums), and Peter 'Damien' Marshall (guitars), with Lyle Preslar (ex-**Minor Threat**) and London May (drums) also recording under the banner. In Samhain Danzig stripped away a lot of the kitsch that had characterized the Misfits, and replaced it with a starker, less comic book approach. Sinister and predatory, Samhain's music was an exercise in lean, evocative rhythm and bleak mood. As with the Misfits, the production is very uneven, and the sound often feels too thin to sustain the bite the material demands. Nevertheless, at their best, most notably on their strongest album, *November Coming Fire*, Samhain could be hauntingly hungry and morbidly resonant. Their last recording, *Final Descent*, features a remastered version of the *Unholy Passion* material compiled with another session from 1987 with future Danzig band guitarist John Christ.

Albums: *Initium* (Plan 9 1984), *Unholy Passion* (Plan 9 1985, mini-album), *November Coming Fire* (Plan 9 1986). Compilation: *Final Descent* (Plan 9 1990).

Sammes, Mike

b. 19 February 1928, Reigate, Surrey, England. The son of a photographic equipment dealer, Sammes attended the local grammar school and played cello in its orchestra. However, his greater interest in vocal music led to the formation of the Michael (later, Mike) Sammes Singers in 1957, while he was working for a London publishing firm. The mixed choir's professional debut was at the London Palladium where they appeared frequently as accompanists to solo stars like **Judy Garland**. As well as being the name most readily mentioned whenever a BBC Light Entertainment producer requires a polished vocal group (and having their own Radio 2 series, *Sammes Songs*, the Singers have been employed on innumerable studio sessions for **Cliff Richard**, **Michael Holliday**, **Tommy Steele**, **Val Doonican**, **Engelbert Humperdinck**, **Tom Jones**, **Matt Monro**, **Julie Andrews**, **Cilla Black**, and even the **Beatles**. They have also recorded in their own right for **HMV Records**, and had a UK hit in 1966 with 'Somewhere My Love' ('Lara's Theme' from the film *Doctor Zhivago*) - which peaked at number 14 after overtaking a rival version by **Manuel And His Music Of The Mountains**. Sammes included many fascinating stories of the people he has worked with over the years in his autobiography, which was published in 1995.

Selected albums: *Sounds Sensational* (Columbia 1965), *Colour It Folksy* (EMI 1965), *Songs That Live Forever* (1973), *Cole* (1974), *Sammes Songs* (1976), *Double Take, Volumes 1 & 2* (1986), *Just For You* (1987), *The Songs We Love* (1988), *The Very Best Of* (1992).

Further reading: *Backing Into The Limelight*, Mike Sammes.

Sammy

Stars of the new 'lo-fi' breed of American artists, a pop format which accentuates the quality of songs above any production expertise and was partly coined in answer to **Beck**'s phenomenal rise, Sammy are a duo of Luke Wood (guitar/bass) and Jesse Hartman (vocals/guitar) who rose to prominence when supporting that artist in the US and UK. The pair met when Hartman noted Wood's **Velvet Underground** t-shirt in the late 80s, discovering a musical kindred spirit. Together they recorded a debut album, titled simply *Debut Album*, in their occasional drummer Corn's Long Island, New York basement. Though Wood originally worked in the New York press office of **Geffen Records**, he used the Smells Like Records subsidiary imprint of Geffen artist Steve Shelley (**Sonic Youth**) to release it. The duo's relationship has become somewhat strained by Woods' job, after he moved to a marketing position with Geffen in Los Angeles. Hartman, still located in New York and employed in his brother's pizza parlour was forced to write with his partner by sending tapes back and forth. However, the approach did not unduly damage the quality of compositions on the album, and both have brought their individual experiences to bear on their songs. 'Rudy', for instance, concerns a 'crack smoking Rastafarian dishwasher' employed at the restaurant, with Hartman's writing primarily influenced by his abiding interest in film. The Long Island lifestyle certainly seemed to offer ample scope: 'My piano teacher was a child molester, my high-school teacher was murdered by a gay prostitute and sometimes these characters find their way into my songs'. The album was followed by a 1995 EP, *Kings Of The Inland Empire*.

Album: *Debut Album* (Smells Like 1994).

Sample, Joe

b. 1 February 1939, Houston, Texas, USA. While still at high school, Sample co-founded a group that would dominate his working life. Known from 1960 as the Jazz Crusaders, the band, with its core of Sample on piano, Wayne Henderson, **Wilton Felder** and Nesbert 'Stix' Hooper, produced a series of popular albums that helped define the term soul jazz. A change of name, to the **Crusaders**, led to a change of direction in 1972, with increasing emphasis on a soul and funk repertoire. Sample stayed with the group throughout the 70s and, in a number of reformations, into the 80s, but throughout these periods, Sample, and the other group members, have maintained solo careers. Sample worked as an accompanist with the **Bobby Hutcherson/Harold Land** quintet in 1967 and during the late 60s became a regular **Motown** session musicians working with artists such as **Diana Ross** and the **Jackson Five**. Further session work in Hollywood studio bands followed until, in the early 70s, Sample joined **Tom Scott**'s group LA Express, an experience that led to more session work for many pop and folk musicians, notably **Joni Mitchell**. Recent interest in jazz funk of the early 70s has introduced the Crusaders to a new audience, and Sample continues to produce solo works.

Selected albums: as the Joe Sample Trio *Try Us* (1969), with Bobby Hutcherson *San Francisco* (1971), with Blue Mitchell *Blue's Blues* (1974), with Mitchell *Graffiti Blues* (1974), *Rainbow Seeker* (MCA 1978), *Carmel* (MCA 1979), *Fancy Dance* (Sonet 1979), *Voices In The Rain* (MCA 1981), with David T Walker *Swing Street Cafe* (MCA 1982), *The Hunter* (MCA 1983), *Oasis* (MCA 1985), *Spellbound* (WEA 1989), with Miles Davis *Amandla* (1989), *Ashes To Ashes* (WEA 1990), *Roles* (MCA 1992), *Invitation* (1993), *Did You Feel That?* (Warner Bros 1994). Compilation: *Joe Sample Collection* (GRP 1991).

Samples, Junior

b. Alvin Samples, 10 August 1926, Cumming Georgia, USA, d. 13 November 1983, Cumming, Georgia,

USA. Samples had worked for most of his life in a sawmill, when he became an unexpected star. Weighing in at well over 20 stone, he revelled in being called the 'world's biggest liar' - a title he acquired from relating what some have termed hilarious tales. One such story brought him to the attention of Chart Records and he scored a minor country hit in 1967, with 'World's Biggest Whopper'. He subsequently recorded a solo album and one with fellow comedian **Archie Campbell**. This record success saw him become a member of *Hee Haw* even though, in the words of Bill C. Malone, 'he was at the time a natural but semi-literate rural comedian with virtually no professional experience'. Samples died suddenly following a heart attack at his home in 1983.

Albums: *The World Of Junior Samples* (Chart 1968), with Archie Campbell *Bull Session At Bull's Gap* (Chart 1968).

Sampling

The art of sampling was first introduced to an international audience in 1979 when the **Sugarhill Gang** used a reconstructed **Chic** track, 'Good Times', as backing for their 'Rapper's Delight' success. Others followed, notably **Grandmaster Flash**' 'Adventures Of Grandmaster Flash On The Wheels Of Steel', which featured cut and paste segments from Chic, **Queen**, **Blondie** and other rap artists including **Spoonie Gee** and the Sugarhill Gang. Similarly **Afrika Bambaataa**'s 'Planet Rock', which many cite as the first real hip hop record, utilised the work of others, in this case **Kraftwerk**'s 'Trans-Europe-Express'. While hip hop and rap remained underground there was little interest taken by anyone in the format. However, as soon as corporations sniffed out profits half a dozen law suits were brought against those who had indulged in 'copyright violation'. Among the most notable sufferers were England's **Shut Up And Dance**. Long considered an act of plagiarism at best, it is only in recent years that sampling the work of older artists has been seen to be beneficial to both parties. Many artists, from **James Brown** to **Spandau Ballet**, have seen their work reassessed and reappraised in the wake of major hip hop aritsts sampling their work. By allowing **Us3** to ransack the **Blue Note** vaults the same label experienced a doubling in their US sales when *Hand On The Torch* broke big. In many ways it has become the stamp of approval to an artists' longevity: certainly all the major rock acts from the **Beatles** (**2 Live Crew** and others) to **Jimi Hendrix** (the **Pharcyde**) have experienced their wares being rehabilitated. Among the most-sampled catalogues are the works of James Brown (hugely influential in the initial development of rap) and **George Clinton** and **P-Funk/Parliament** (specifically in the West Coast traditions of **Ice Cube** and **Too Short**). Also popular have been more conventional rock sources like **Grand Funk Railroad** (**KRS-1** and **De La Soul**) and **Aerosmith** (**Run DMC**), reggae (**Bob Marley** in particular) and jazz. Like everything else, sampling cuts both ways: in September 1991 Chuck D of **Public Enemy** sued the marketing company promoting St. Ides Malt licquor for using his voice without permission. Public Enemy also took legal action against **Madonna** for using their rhythm to underscore her 'Justify My Love' single.

Sampson, Edgar

b. 31 August 1907, New York City, New York, USA, d. 16 January 1973. One of the outstanding arrangers in big band jazz, Sampson played alto saxophone and violin in a number of bands during the 20s and 30s, including those led by **Duke Ellington**, **Rex Stewart** and **Fletcher Henderson**, but his most notable period was a two-year spell with **Chick Webb** that began in 1934. Apart from writing many excellent arrangements of popular songs for the Webb band he also composed several tunes which became jazz standards, among them 'Stompin' At The Savoy', 'Don't Be That Way' (later adopted by **Benny Goodman** as his theme tune), 'If Dreams Come True' and 'Blue Lou'. After leaving Webb he continued to write for him and several other bandleaders, including Goodman, **Artie Shaw** and **Teddy Wilson**. He also resumed playing occasionally, sometimes on alto and also on tenor and baritone saxophones. He briefly led his own big band in the late 40s and early 50s, forming small groups thereafter. Although often overlooked in accounts of the development of big band arranging, Sampson's work was always of the very highest standard and bears favourable comparison with that of the better-known arrangers of the period. In the 50s and early 60s he showed his versatility by writing for **Tito Puente** and several other currently popular Latin bands.

Album: *Swing Softly Sweet Sampson* (Jasmine 1956).

Samson

This UK heavy metal group were formed in 1978 by guitarist Paul Samson, and have since been dogged by line-up changes, management disputes and record company problems. These have occurred at critical points in their career, just as major success seemed imminent. The first incarnation of the band comprised Paul Samson (guitar), Chris Aylmer (bass), Bruce Bruce (vocals) and Clive Burr (drums), the latter soon moving on to **Iron Maiden** and being replaced by the masked **Thunderstick**. Samson specialized in high energy blues-based rock and were among the leading lights of the **New Wave Of British Heavy Metal** movement, with each of their first four albums becoming minor classics of the genre. In 1981 Bruce Bruce and Thunderstick departed, the former assumed his real name, **Bruce Dickinson**, and joined Iron Maiden as lead vocalist. Thunderstick formed a new group under his own name. Nicky Moore (ex-**Tiger**) and Mel Gaynor (ex-**Light Of The World**) stepped in on vocals and drums respectively, but Gaynor soon moved on to **Simple Minds**, with Pete Jupp filling in as replacement (who would in turn later join **FM**). *Before The Storm* and *Don't Get Mad, Get Even* are Samson's most accomplished works, with Moore's gritty and impassioned vocals giving the band a sound that was both earthy and honest. Chris Aylmer left in 1984 and was replaced by ex-**Diamond Head** bassist, Merv Goldsworthy, before the recording of an excellent live album, *Thank You And Goodnight*. The band split soon after, with *Head Tactics* being a posthumous release comprising remixes of tracks from *Head On* and *Shock Tactics*. Nicky Moore went on to form **Mammoth**, while Paul Samson released a solo effort, *Joint Forces*, in 1986. The band reformed in 1988 and released *Refugee* two years later, a classy if slightly dated collection of bluesy hard rock numbers.

Albums: *Survivors* (Lazer 1979), *Head On* (Gem 1980), *Shock Tactics* (RCA 1981), *Before The Storm* (Polydor 1982), *Don't Get Mad, Get Even* (Polydor 1984), *Thank You And Goodnight* (Metal Masters 1984), *Refugee* (Communique 1990), *Live At Reading* (Raw Fruit 1991), *Joint Forces* (1993). Compilations: *Head Tactics* (Capitol 1986), *Pillars Of Rock* (Connoisseur 1990).
Video: *Biceps Of Steel* (1985).

Samuels, Dave

b. 1948, Chicago, Illinois, USA. Samuels played the drums from the age of six. While pursuing a degree in psychology at Boston University in 1971, he studied vibes with **Gary Burton** and went on to teach at the **Berklee College of Music** (1971-74). He moved to New York in 1974 and worked with **Gerry Mulligan** for three years as well as starting the group, Timepiece. In the late 70s he worked and recorded with **Frank Zappa** and the group Double Image, with which he toured Europe. He taught workshops at the Manhattan School of Music and played in a group called Gallery with Michael di Pasqua, **Paul McCandless** and **David Darling**. Throughout this period he had an increasing involvement with **Spyro Gyra**, becoming a full member in 1986.

Albums: with Gerry Mulligan *Carnegie Hall Concert* (1975), with Frank Zappa *Live In New York* (1976), with Double Image *Dawn* (1979) with Gallery *Gallery* (1981), with Spyro Gyra *Morning Dance* (1979), *Alternating Currents* (1985), *Breakout* (1986).

Samwell-Smith, Paul

b. 8 May, 1943. A founder member of the **Yardbirds**, Samwell-Smith's talents as a composer and arranger did much to shape their most successful era. He left the group in May 1966, incensed at what he perceived to be unprofessionalism during a particularly anarchic live performance. Briefly mooted as part of projected 'supergroup' with songwriter **Graham Gouldman** and former **Animals**' guitarist Hilton Valentine, Samwell-Smith preferred a career in production. He worked on several low-key releases (Washington DC's) before becoming established for his contributions to best-selling albums by **Cat Stevens**, **Carly Simon** and, more recently, **Jethro Tull**. Despite his reservations over live performances, Samwell-Smith was a member of **Box Of Frogs**, a new-styled Yardbirds formed in 1984. Samwell-Smith is now a leading record producer with a long and impressive list of credits.

San Francisco

Jeanette MacDonald arranged a temporary 'divorce' from her celebrated singing partner **Nelson Eddy**, and co-starred with Clark Gable in this film which must have qualified as one of the very first 'disaster' movies (at least with sound), when it was released by MGM in 1936. In Anita Loo's superb screenplay (based on a story by Robert Hopkins), Macdonald plays singer Mary Blake, whose association with Blackie Norton (Gable), a cabaret club owner in the rough, tough Barbary Coast area of San Francisco, leads to a career in opera and a temporary suspension of their romantic affair. They get back together again after the earth moves for them - and all the other residents of the city - in a spectacular earthquake sequence towards the end of the picture. Spencer Tracy gave an excellent performance as Gable's best buddy, and also in the cast were Jessie Ralph, Jack Holt, Shirley Ross, Ted Healy, Edgar Kennedy, Al Shean, and Richard Carle. The songs were a mixed bag of operatic excerpts and popular numbers, and included 'Would You?' (**Nacio Herb Brown-Arthur Freed**), 'Sempre Libera' (from Verdi's *La Traviata*), 'A Heart That's Free' (Alfred J. Robyn-T. Railey), 'The Holy City' (Stephen Adams-F.E. Weatherley), and the title song which was mercilessly lampooned by **Judy Garland** in her celebrated Carnegie Hall concert recording in 1961. *San Francisco*, which was produced by John Emerson and Bernard Hyman, and skilfully directed by W.S. Van Dyke, is considered to be a classic of its kind and a fine example of the film makers' art.

Sanborn, David

b. 30 July 1945, Tampa, Florida, USA. Sanborn's virtuosity has now spanned four decades, taking him from being a band member (with the seminal **Paul Butterfield**) to a leading session player for artists such as **David Bowie**, **James Taylor** and **Stevie Wonder**. His is the alto saxophone solo on Bowie's 'Young Americans'. He grew up in St Louis and played with some of the finest Chicago school bluesmen, including **Albert King**. Nowadays, under his own name, Sanborn records and performs regularly. His blistering alto saxophone style competes somewhere between **Junior Walker** and **Dick Heckstall-Smith**. and is all the more remarkable because for many years as a child he suffered from polio and had breathing difficulties. Sanborn does not flirt with his instrument, he blows it hard. His solo debut was in 1975 with *Takin' Off*. Over the next decade he produced a series of albums that were all successful, and won a Grammy for *Voyeur*. In 1985, *A Change Of Heart* proved to be a big hit in the jazz charts, although much of it was in the rock style, notably the unrelenting and powerful 'Tintin' along with the pure funk of 'High Roller'. *Close Up* featured a sensitive (though raucous) reading of the **Diana Ross** and **Marvin Gaye** hit 'You Are Everything'. In 1991 Sanborn made his first ever 'pure jazz album' and achieved the esteem of the jazz reviewers. *Another Hand* and more recently *Pearls* have lifted Sanborn to the peak of his already lengthy career. The latter album was lodged at the top of the *Billboard* Jazz chart for many weeks in 1995.

Albums: *Taking Off* (Warners 1975), *Sanborn* (1976), *David Sanborn Band* (1977), *Heart To Heart* (Warners 1978), *Hideaway* (1980), *Voyeur* (Warners 1981), *As We Speak* (Warners 1982), *Backstreet* (Warners 1983), *Let It Speak* (1984), *Love And Happiness* (1984), *Straight To The Heart* (Warners 1985), *A Change Of Heart* (Warners 1987), *Close Up* (Reprise 1988), *Another Hand* (Elektra 1991), *Upfront* (Elektra 1992), *Hearsay* (Elektra 1993), *Pearls* (Elektra 1995).

Sanchez

b. 28 November 1967, Kingston, Jamaica. In the autumn of 1987, record releases by a singer called Sanchez D first arrived in the reggae shops. His voice was distinctive but untutored. He was not afraid to wail with a roughness that matched the equally gritty **dancehall** rhythms of the time, and his first hit was 'Lady In Red' for Red Man. By November of that year he was drawing attention with 'Zim Bam Zim', riding a scorching, bizarre **Sly And Robbie** rhythm. A more traditional 'Tears' followed and almost immediately gave him his debut UK chart appearance, becoming the lead track on *Sanchez* a few months later. By the spring of 1988, Sanchez was the number one singer of love songs in reggae. He became highly popular with a strong female following and 60s-style screaming was *de rigeur* at his concerts. His skinny frame and boyish demeanour and exciting stage act appealed to the ladies. Hit followed hit, including 'Old Friend', 'Green Green Grass Of Home', 'Let It Be Me', 'Impossible', 'Joy', 'Hello Josephine', 'Let Me Love You Now', 'Lonely Won't Leave', 'My Girl' and 'Tell Him I'm Not Home' - in typical reggae style, every producer and label in Jamaica was demanding a piece of the singer. His first UK gigs in the summer of 1988 revealed a massive following there too: Sanchez mania brought screaming to every show. A second album, *Loneliness*,

orchestrated by veteran producer **Winston Riley**, dominated the reggae charts for months and the title cut, 'Loneliness Leave Me Alone', was a massive seller. *Sweetest Girl*, named after yet another hit, was his second 1988 album. Critically dismissed as a cover-singing fad whose own lyrics were slight, Sanchez was merely doing what was practical. When he felt the spirit he turned to writing serious songs such as 'South Africa', which became yet another hit. It was also said that as a singer he was limited, a jibe that he shattered when he recorded a superb version of 'End Of The World' in the spring of 1989, followed by *Wild Sanchez*. Hit singles continued to arrive: 'Me Love Me Girl Bad' with ragga DJ Flourgon; a cover of **Bobby Brown**'s (with whom Sanchez has often been compared) 'My Prerogative', 'Come To Rule' and **Tracy Chapman**'s 'Baby Can I Hold You Tonight' for his original producer **Philip 'Fatis' Burrell**. *Number One* was released in the UK on **Island Records** and 1990 saw the release of a 'clash' album with **Pinchers** (*Meets Pinchers*), to be followed by two sets with Wayne Wonder.

Albums: *Sanchez* (Vena 1987), *Loneliness* (Techniques 1988), *Sweetest Girl* (Dennis Star 1988), *Wild Sanchez!* (Greensleeves 1988), *Number One* (Mango/Island 1989), *In Fine Style* (Charm 1990), *I Can't Wait* (Blue Mountain 1991), *Bring Back The Love* (World Enterprise 1992), *The One For Me* (1993), *Boom Boom Bye Bye* (Greensleeves 1993), *Missing You* (VP 1994). With Pinchers: *Pinchers Meets Sanchez* (Exterminator 1989). With Wayne Wonder: *Penthouse Presents (Volume One & Two)* (Penthouse 1990, 1991).

Sanchez, Roger

Widely regarded as one of the hottest US remixers, New York-based Sanchez made his name with a series of devastating releases for **Strictly Rhythm**, such as Logic's 'One Step Beyond'. He finally made his solo long-playing bow with an album in January 1994. As might have been expected from the man who provided **Juliet Roberts**' with hits like 'Free Love' and 'Caught In The Middle', it preferred a blend of sweet soul and house. It was released under the acronym, Roger S already familiar through his remixes for **Michael Jackson** and others. Graced by the deep house vocals of Jay Williams, it reinstated his integrity in the underground dance scene at a time when he was handling more and more major league clients. It was released on **One Records**, which he jointly owns with Eddie Colon. He also set up a management company with UK partner Marts Andrups (who also represents **Benji Candelario** and **Danny Tenaglia** in Europe), titled Indeep, signing artists like vocalist Melodie Washington. Sanchez was also partly behind the Sound Of One hit, 'As I Am', for **Cooltempo**, and Logic's 'One Step Beyond'. He recently produced an album for Kathy Sledge, among sundry other projects.

Album: *Secret Weapons Vol. 1* (One Records 1994).

Sanctuary

Formed in Seattle, Washington, USA, in 1985, Sanctuary consisted of Warrel Dane (vocals), Lenny Rutledge (guitar/vocals), Sean Blosl (guitar/vocals), Jim Sheppard (bass) and Dave Budbill (drums/vocals). Through two early demo tracks included on a low budget compilation, *Northwest Metal Fest*, the band attracted the attention of **Megadeth** guitarist Dave Mustaine, who offered to oversee their next recordings. With this recommendation behind them the band signed to **CBS/Epic Records** and Mustaine was duly drafted as producer. *Refuge Denied* introduced Sanctuary's somewhat basic thrash sound, one of great intensity but little direction or scope. After extensive touring with Megadeth the band offered the slightly superior *Into The Mirror Black*, but broke up shortly afterwards.
Albums: *Refuge Denied* (CBS 1987), *Into The Mirror Black* (CBS 1990).

Sandals

Nouveau hippies the Sandals consist of Derek Delves (vocals; ex-Espresso 7, **A Man Called Adam**), John Harris (flute, vocals), Ian 'Easy' Simmonds and Wild Cat Will (ex-Batniks; drums). Signed to **Acid Jazz**, they confessed to being conceptual recording artists rather than musicians, specialising in a Latin-tinged trance-funk, and operating in the manner of a 60s collective. They came together initially in a seedy Soho bar in the summer of 1987, organising a 60s style 'happening' night (named Violets), with poetry readings, party games and jazz spots. Since then they have opened a shop, Rich And Strange, which sells their art and second-hand fashion. After which they also started their own club night, Tongue Kung Fu, which was exported to Los Angeles, Tokyo and Istanbul. They run their own label too, the appropriately titled Open Toe stable. Their debut performance as the Sandals came at the 1990 Soho Jazz Festival, while their first single, 'Profound Gas', was remixed by old friends **Leftfield** (Derek having been a one-time member of A Man Called Adam with Leftfield's Paul Daley). Their second effort, 'Nothing', was premiered on the opening of a new series of youth television programme, *The Word*. 1993 also brought excessive gigging across several festivals and continents, before sessions on their debut album began in earnest. Before which they released their third single, 'We Wanna Live'. This was produced as a 'live remix' by the **Disco Evangelists** and **Sabres Of Paradise** - with all three parties present on the studio take, 'jamming' together.
Album: *Rite To Silence* (Open Toe 1994).

Sandburg, Carl

b. 6 January 1878, Galesburg, Illinois, USA, d. 22 July 1967. Sandburg has been an author, historian, singer, poet, and folk song collector. He is predominantly remembered for his collection of American folk song and tradition. The son of Swedish immigrant parents, Sandburg left home in 1897, travelling and working in various cities throughout the USA for a year. Enrolling at Lombard College, he became Editor in Chief of the *Lombard Review*, before leaving in 1902. Sandburg later worked as a reporter, in New York, for the *Daily News*, but returned to his native Mid-west where he worked for the Social Democratic Party. Still working in journalism, Carl then worked for the *Daily Socialist* in Chicago, and later, from 1917-27 for the *Chicago Daily News*. In 1914, Sandburg's poem 'Chicago' received the Helen Haire Levinson prize after appearing in *Poetry* magazine. Sandburg wrote prolifically and his Pulitzer Prize winning *Abraham Lincoln: The War Years* was just part of a six- volume series on the past President. One of his earlier books *The American Songbag*, which was published in 1927, contains 280 songs. When his novel, *Remembrance Rock* was published, it received a lukewarm response. However, Sandburg received a Pulitzer Prize for his *Complete Poems* in 1951. *Honey And Salt*, another book of poems, was published on Sandburg's 85th birthday in 1963. He died on 22 July 1967 from a heart attack. A commemorative stamp was issued by the US Postal Service in 1973.
Albums: *Carl Sandburg Sings His American Songbag* (50s).
Further reading: *Old Troubadour-Carl Sandburg With His Guitar Friends*, Gregory d'Alessio.

Sanders, Ed

A veteran of New York's bohemian enclave, poet Sanders co-founded the Peace Eye Bookstore and edited the publication *Fuck You - A Magazine Of The Arts* before joining **Tuli Kupferberg** and Ken Weaver in the **Fugs**. Sanders wrote many of this irreverent group's best-known songs, including 'Frenzy', 'Wet Dream' and 'Ramses II Is Dead, My Love'. He embarked on a solo career following the Fugs' disintegration, completing two country-influenced albums which, if not commercially successful, did at leat inspire a cult following. However, Sanders is better known for his literary work, in particular his book *The Family* (1971), a widely acclaimed investigative account of the Charles Manson and Sharon Tate murder case. During the 80s Sanders collaborated with **Shockabilly** on *Nicaragua*, and reconvened the Fugs for a series of fascinating releases. In 1987 his poetry was anthologized in *Thirsting For Peace In A Raging Century*.
Albums: *Sanders' Truckstop* (1969), *Beer Cans On The Moon* (1973).

Sanders, Joe

(see **Coon-Sanders Nighthawks**)

Sanders, Mark

b. 31 August 1960, Beckenham, Kent, England. A self-taught drummer who combines power with agility and precision, Sanders began his career playing with a disco band at UK American Air Force bases. He turned to jazz in 1984, studying with Will Evans who, along with **Elvin Jones** and **Tony Oxley**, was a major influence. His first jazz engagements were with Lyn Dobson, Stu Brown, Pete Nu and **Elton Dean**. In 1987 he joined Mervyn Afrika's Kaap Finale and formed a duo with Phil Durrant. Since 1988 he has played in duos and trios with **Evan Parker**, and has often worked with bassist **Paul Rogers**. He and Rogers have provided an intense and versatile rhythm section for Atlas (with John Law on piano), Parker, **Dennis Gonzalez** and the Elton Dean Trio. He has recently been working with **Jon Lloyd** and **Spirit Level**, and was part of the Paul Rogers Sextet which toured Britain in 1990 with the Arts Council-commissioned Anglo American Sketches. He has also played with Dreamtime (with Nick Evans), **Dick Heckstall-Smith**'s DHSS, and in a quartet with Peter Cusack, Clive Bell and Dean Broderick.

Albums: with Atlas *Trio Improvisations* (1989), with Spirit Level *New Year* (1990), with Elton Dean/Howard Riley Quartet *All The Tradition* (1991), with Jon Lloyd *Syzygy* (1991).

Sanders, Pharoah

b. 13 October 1940, Little Rock, Arkansas, USA. By the time he left high school Sanders was proficient on several instruments, but eventually chose the tenor saxophone. After working in R&B bands he settled in New York in the early 60s where he became a frequent musical associate of **Don Cherry**, **Albert Ayler** and others active in the 'free jazz' movement and worked for a while in the **Sun Ra** Arkestra. For a couple of years beginning in 1965, he worked frequently with **John Coltrane**, playing on several influential recording dates during the period when Coltrane was extending the boundaries he had previously breached with his music. Sanders's playing with Coltrane was marked by a ferocious tone which sometimes growled, sometimes screeched and, within a limited range, he shaped intriguing and often adventurous phrases. In 1968, he played with the **Jazz Composers' Orchestra** led by **Mike Mantler** and **Carla Bley**. In his mid-career Sanders rarely extended the format of his earlier popular success and many of his 70s and 80s records were curious and unsuccessful mixtures of jazz, fusion, strings and vocals that offered fairly banal paeans to peace and love. In the late 80s, he reverted to a more purely instrumental jazz and later was a familiar figure at international festivals, playing in a style which displayed a clear understanding of bebop and which hinted only occasionally at his earlier

espousal of the sometimes less accessible aspects of the freedom principle.

Selected albums: *Pharoah's First* (ESP 1965), *Tauhid* (Impulse 1967), *The Jazz Composers' Orchestra* (1968), *Karma* (1969), *Thembi* (1971), *Love Will Find A Way* (1977), *Rejoice* (Evidence 1981), *Pharoah Sanders Live* (1982), *Heart Is A Melody* (Evidence 1982), *Black Unity* (Impulse 1985), *Africa* (Timeless 1987), *A Prayer Before Dawn* (Evidence 1989), *Moon Child* (Timeless 1989), *Welcome To Love* (Timeless 1990), *Shukuru* (Evidence 1992), *Izipho Zam* (1993, rec. 1969), *Tauhid* (1993), *Oh Lord Let Me Do No Wrong* (Dillion 1992), *Ed Kelly & Pharoah Sanders* (1993).

Sanders, Ric

b. Richard Sanders, 1952, Birmingham, Warwickshire, England. After appearing in local Birmingham bands, violinist Sanders briefly joined **Stomu Yamash'ta**'s touring group. Having been influenced by both folk and jazz, Sanders subsequently joined both the **Soft Machine** and the **Albion Band**. While with the latter he was involved heavily with theatre work, Ric formed Second Vision, along with former Soft Machine guitarist **John Etheridge**, Dave Bristow (keyboards), Jonathan Davie (b. 6 September 1954, Twickenham, Middlesex, England; bass), and Mickey Barker, later with **Magnum** (drums). They released *First Steps*, for **Chrysalis Records**, in 1980. Sanders returned to session work and released his first solo *Whenever*. He joined **Fairport Convention** in 1985, appearing on *Gladys' Leap*, and other subsequent releases, as well as touring with the group and taking part in the now legendary Annual Festival at Cropredy in Oxfordshire. Sanders has toured with **Simon Nicol**, as an acoustic duo, and with **Gordon Giltrap**. In addition, Ric regularly gives performance lectures in schools on playing violin. In 1991, he made a violin instruction video, and others are planned. He has contributed to many albums including those by **June Tabor**, **Andrew Cronshaw**, **All About Eve** and **Jethro Tull**.

Albums: with Soft Machine *Alive And Well* (1978), with Second Vision *First Steps* (1980), with the Albion Band *Rise Up Like The Sun* (1978), *Whenever* (1984), with Pete York and Steve Richardson *String Time* (mid-80s), with Gordon Giltrap *One To One* (1989), *Neither Time Nor Distance* (1991).

Sandpebbles

A vocal group from New York City, New York, USA. Members were Calvin White, Andrea Bolden, and Lonzine Wright. White had been a member of the Gospel Wonders in the early 60s and he brought some robust gospel-style singing to the Sandpebbles when he formed the group. Under the production aegis of New York producer Tony Vann, the Sandpebbles' scored big hits with 'Forget It' (number 10 R&B, number 81 pop) and 'Love Power' (number 14 R&B, number 22 pop) for the Calla label in 1967. The Sandpebbles changed their name to C & The Shells in 1968 and produced by Jerry Williams had a hit with a softer-styled 'You Are The Circus' (number 28 R&B) in 1969. C & The Shells left Cotillion in 1970, and joined the tiny Zanzee label, where they recorded with little success. The last release on the group was in 1973.

Sandpipers

Richard Shoff, Mike Piano and Jim Brady were members of the California-based Mitchell Boys Choir prior to forming a harmonic singing group known initially as the Four Seasons. When a New York attraction also laid claim to the name, the trio became the Grads and as such recorded several singles before securing a successful residency at a Lake Tahoe night-club. A mutual friend introduced the act to **Herb Alpert**, owner of **A&M Records**, but several unsuccessful releases, under both the Grads and Sandpipers' appellations, would follow before producer Tommy LiPuma suggested they record 'Guantanamera'. The Sandpipers' 1966 rendition of this South American folk song reached the Top 10 in both the US and UK, and set a pattern for several lesser hits, including similarly-sweet interpretations of 'Louie Louie' (1966), 'Quando M'Innamoro (A Man Without Love)' (1968), 'Kumbaya' (1969) and the posthumous 'Hang On Sloopy' (1976). Such MOR recordings, coupled with the trio's clean-cut image, has tended to obscure their undoubted vocal skill.
Albums: *Guantanamera* (1966), *The Sandpipers* (1967), *Misty Roses* (1967), *Softly* (1968), *The Wonder Of You* (1969), *Come Saturday Morning* (1970), *Second Spanish Album* (1974), *Overdue* (1977). Compilation: *Greatest Hits* (1970).

Sands

Formed in Eire in 1967, the Sands featured vocalist Tony Kenny, backed by a regular line-up of Murty Quinn (trombone), Clem Quinn (lead guitar), Martin Phelan (saxophone) and Tommy O'Rourke (trumpet). The latter four had previously achieved considerable fame on the showband circuit as lead players in the **Miami Showband**. Having effectively replaced **Dickie Rock** with Tony Kenny, they lost no time in re-establishing their name on the Irish dancehall circuit. Highly professional with a strong, dance-orientated repertoire, they briefly latched on to the US bubblegum music craze by covering such hits as the **Ohio Express**' 'Yummy Yummy Yummy' and the **1910 Fruitgum Company**'s 'Simon Says'. Like the **Freshmen**, however, they were noted for their vocal skills and among the songs they covered was a solid version of the **Beach Boys**' 'Help Me Rhonda'. A respectable run of Irish hits, including 'Dance Dance Dance' and 'Lend A Helpin' Hand', coincided with packed dancehalls, until they fell victim to the showband decline of the early 70s.

Sands, Tommy

b. 27 August 1937, Chicago, Illinois, USA. Tommy Sands' father was a pianist, and his mother was Grace Lou Dixon, a singer with the Art Keassel Band. He sang in a local folk music television series *Lady Of The Montain* when he was only five years old, and made his first recording, of 'Love Pains', on Freedom in 1949, when aged only 12. In 1952, with help from his new manager, **Colonel Tom Parker**, he joined **RCA Records** as a country artist. In the early and mid-50s Sands played many country shows including some with **Hank Williams**, **Elvis Presley** and **Johnny Cash**. His big break came when he got the part of a rock 'n' roll star in NBC's *The Singing Idol*, a role that was originally offered to **Elvis Presley**. The show was a smash hit, and its main song , 'Teen-Age Crush', totalled over a half-a-million advance orders and shot to number 2 in the US charts. The television show was snapped up by Hollywood and was adapted to become Sands' first film *Sing, Boy, Sing* (1958). The first of his five albums on **Capitol Records**, *Steady Date With Tommy Sands* and *Sing Boy Sing*, both made the US Top 20, and he was tipped by some as likely to replace Elvis. However, of his other eight singles that charted, only 'Goin' Steady' made the US Top 40 in 1957. That same year in the UK he was the subject of BBC television's *This Is Your Life*. He made a string of films including *Mardi Gras* with **Pat Boone**, *Love In A Goldfish Bowl* with **Fabian**, *Babes In Toyland* with **Annette**, the star-studded *The Longest Day*, and *None But The Brave* with his father-in-law **Frank Sinatra** (he was married to **Nancy Sinatra** from 1960-65). Together with his group the Raiders (aka the Sharks), which included the future number one session drummer **Hal Blaine**, he later recorded on **ABC**, Paramount, **Imperial** and **Liberty** without further chart success. In the late 60s he moved to Hawaii and opened a club. He tried to make a comeback between 1974-79, and again in 1987. He played his first UK dates in 1990.
Albums: *Steady Date With Tommy Sands* (1957), *Sing, Boy, Sing* (1958, film soundtrack), *Sands Storm* (1959), *Teenage Rock* (1959), *This Thing Called Love* (1959), *When I'm Thinking Of You* (1960), *Sands At The Sands* (1960), *Dream Of Me* (1961), *The Parent Trap* (1961, film soundtrack), *Babes In Toyland* (1961, film soundtrack), *Blue Ribbon Baby* (1987), *Down By Bendy's Lane* (1988), *Beyond The Shadows* (1992).

Sane, Dan

b. 22 September 1896, Hernando, Mississippi, USA, d. c.1971, Osceola, Arkansas, USA. Sane, sometimes identified as Dan Sain and also as Dan Sing, was an unobtrusive, but important member of the Memphis blues community up to the 50s. He only ever sang on an unissued recording, and it was as a ragtime-influenced guitarist that he made his mark. He recorded as a member of the band led by **Jack Kelly**, accompanying the singing of violinist **Will Batts**, a fellow band member, and guitarist **Frank Stokes**. He recorded fairly extensively, with the latter producing percussive but effortlessly nimble flat-picked figures that meshed with Stokes' rhythm guitar to form one of the most impressive series of two-guitar arrangements in blues.

Albums: *The Beale Street Sheiks* (1990), *Frank Stokes* (1990), *Jack Kelly & His South Memphis Jug Band* (1990).

Sangster, John

b. 17 November 1928, Melbourne, Australia. Sangster started off playing the trombone but switched to trumpet when he appeared in trad bands in 1948. In 1950, he learned enough about drumming to be able to tour overseas with **Graeme Bell**'s band. His interests have become increasingly progressive and he worked with Don Banks in the 60s playing at the Expos in Montreal and Tokyo. He now plays the vibraphone and marimbaphone and sees himself principally as a composer. *The Hobbit Suite* is typical of his eclectic style mixing hummable tunes with highly abstract or impressionistic passages. It has been followed by an eight album set *Lord Of The Rings* as well as tribute works to **Bix Beiderbeck** and **Duke Ellington**. Movie producers have been attracted by his colourful style and he has written numerous film scores including *Fluteman* (1982).

Albums: *Conjurman* (1967), *Australia & All That Jazz* (1971), *The Hobbit Suite* (1973), *Lord Of The Rings* (1974).

Santa Esmeralda

A studio group performing in the disco-style of the late 70s, Santa Esmeralda made the US charts in 1977-78 with dance-oriented remakes of two songs originally popularized by the British group the **Animals** in the 60s. Santa Esmeralda featured vocalist Leroy Gomez (b. Cape Cod, Massachusetts, USA), a multi-instrumentalist who had played with **Elton John**, **Tavares** and others before taking the Santa Esmeralda position. The group recorded two of Gomez's songs, a cover of **Van Morrison**'s 'Gloria' and the Animals hit 'Don't Let Me Be Misunderstood'. An album was built around those songs and itself reached number 25 on Casablanca Records in the US in late 1977, while 'Don't Let Me Be Misunderstood' made it to number 15. For the follow-up, the Animals' 'House Of The Rising Sun', Gomez was not involved, and the single peaked at number 78. No other singles charted, but a final album charted in late 1978 before the group's name was retired.

Albums: *Don't Let Me Be Misunderstood* (1977), *House Of The Rising Sun* (1978), *Beauty* (1978).

Santa Rosa, Gilberto

b. 21 August 1950, Puerto Rico. Since the mid-80s, the mainstream salsa recording industry in Puerto Rico and the USA has been largely preoccupied with developing and marketing the images of 'good looking' young male vocalists, rather than producing solid, stimulating music performed by swinging soneros (improvising salsa singers). Santa Rosa however, who was one of the first of this new crop of solo singers, is regarded as being amongst the small number who deserve to be called a sonero. His apprenticeship included stints with top Puerto Rican bandleaders, **Tommy Olivencia** and **Willie Rosario**, before he signed with Ralph Cartagena's Combo Records. In 1986, Santa Rosa debuted on *Good Vibrations* fronting his own salsa orquesta of two trumpets, two trombones, baritone saxophone, rhythm section (conga/bongo/timbales/bass/piano) and coro (chorus). After releasing three more albums on Combo, he switched to **CBS** and issued the chart-topping salsa romántica set *Punto De Vista* in 1990, which spawned the smash hits 'Vivir Sin Ella' and 'Perdoname'. Gilberto's 1991 **CBS**/Sony follow-up, *Perspectiva*, was another monster hit. In 1990, Santa Rosa was in the illustrious company of **Andy Montañez** and Pedro Brull (from **Mulenze**), as one of the contemporary soneros assembled by bandleader Don Perignon for his all-star La Puertorriqueña project. Between 1984-90, Gilberto acted as artistic assistant and sang coro on albums by Puerto Rican bandleader **Mario Ortiz**. In 1990, he won the ***Billboard*** Lo Nuestro award for 'Best Male Singer'. He has also performed at New York's prestigious annual salsa festival.

Albums: with Tommy Olivencia *Tommy Olivencia & His Orchestra* (1979); with Willie Rosario *The Portrait Of A Salsa Man* (1981), *Atízame El Fogón* (1982), *The Salsa Machine* (1983), *Nuevos Horizontes* (1984), *Afincando/25 Aniversario* (1985), *Nueva Cosecha* (1986); solo *Good Vibrations* (1986), *Keeping Cool!* (1987), *De Amor y Salsa* (1988), *Salsa En . . . Movimiento* (1989), *Punto De Vista* (1990); with La Puertorriqueña *Festival De Soneros* (1990). Compilation: *Perspectiva* (1991).

Santamaría, Mongo

b. Ramón Santamaría, 7 April 1927, Jesús María district, Havana, Cuba. 'Mongo stands for integrity, both personal and musical, throughout almost half a century in a mad, bad and dangerous to blow business. He, as much as any other individual, is responsible for whatever wider familiarity with the music exists today. Mambo, charanga, salsafunk, jazzlatino - he has brought taste, swing and sass to them all, his modesty alone denying the widest acclaim' (Tomek). Santamaría arrived in New York at the end of the 40s. There he performed with the first charanga (flute, violins, rhythm section and voices band) to be organized in the city, led by Gilberto Valdés (b. Matanzas Province, Cuba; multi-instrumentalist/composer), **Pérez Prado** (for a brief stint) and **Tito Puente** (between 1951 and 1957). In 1955 Mongo recorded *Changó* (aka *Drums And Chants*), an album of roots Afro Cuban music featuring the Cuban percussionists Silvestre Méndez (b. Jesús María district, Havana, Cuba; bongo/composer), Carlos 'Patato' Valdez and Julito Collazo. In 1991, Mongo commented: '*Changó* is the best album recorded in the USA, within that genre, and much better than *Yambú* and other albums which I recorded later for Fantasy Records' (quote from an interview with Luis Tamargo published in *Latin Beat* magazine). As Puente's conguero, Santamaría enjoyed celebrity status in the Latino community. However, in 1957 he and two other Puente sidemen, percussionist **Willie Bobo** and bassist Bobby Rodríguez, provoked the bandleader's wrath when they were credited as performers on *Más Ritmo Caliente* by Latin jazz vibes player **Cal Tjader**. Hurt by Puente's response, Mongo and Bobo informed Tjader of their intention to leave. Cal could not believe his luck, and offered to hire them. Early the following year, they both joined him in San Francisco. During their three-year tenure, Santamaría and Bobo contributed significantly to Tjader's sound on a string of classic albums recorded for **Fantasy Records**, and through their association with Cal, they attained more widespread fame.

Santamaría was still with Tjader when he recorded the Afro Cuban sets *Yambú* and *Mongo* on Fantasy. The second contained his hit composition 'Afro Blue', which became a much covered jazz standard. In 1960, Mongo and Willie took time out to visit Cuba, where they recorded the progressive típico album *Our Man In Havana* with local musicians, including the legendary tres guitarist/arranger/composer Niño Rivera and teenage pianist Paquito Echavarría. The latter relocated to Miami and worked there with bassist **Israel 'Cachao' López**. In 1961, Santamaría left Tjader (taking Bobo with him) to inherit former personnel from Armando Sánchez's Chicago-based charanga Orquesta Nuevo Ritmo (whose only album was 1960's *The Heart Of Cuba*), including violinist/composer Pupi Legarreta, flautist/composer Rolando Lozano, pianist René 'El Flaco' Hernández, vocalist/composer Rudy Calzado and bassist Victor Venegas (a good friend of Mongo who remained with him until the late 60s). Santamaría added the incredible violinist/tenor saxophonist José 'Chombo' Silva and others to form his own charanga, which debuted on the excellent *Sabroso!*. On this and his other charanga releases on Fantasy, including one with pianist Joe Loco, Mongo successfully managed to infuse the traditional Cuban flute and strings framework with jazz idioms.

In 1962, Santamaría returned to New York, leaving Bobo in San Francicso (however Willie rejoined him later on for a brief spell). Mongo put together a Latin fusion (although this nomenclature did not exist then) group with a view to securing a contract with Riverside Records. He succeeded and debuted on the label with *Go, Mongo!*. At the end of 1962, Santamaría recorded the crowd-pleaser 'Watermelon Man', written by keyboardist **Herbie Hancock**, who performed with Mongo's group that year. With negligible promotion, the single became a Top 10 hit in 1963. The song's R&B/jazz/Latin cocktail pretty much set Santamaría's stylistic compass for the rest of his career. After a few more albums on Riverside, he continued in the Latin fusion vein into the 90s with a string of releases on the **Columbia**, **Atlantic**, Vaya, Pablo, Roulette, Tropical Budda and Concord Picante labels. 1977's *Dawn (Amanecer)*, his sixth release on Vaya, won a Grammy Award, becoming the first album from the Fania Records stable to receive the accolade. From the mid-60s, Santamaría only rarely diverted from his fusion path to record typical Latin albums such as *El Bravo* and the **Justo Betancourt** collaboration *Ubane*. During his career as a bandleader, Mongo hired and developed such notable artists as **Chick Corea**, **La Lupe**, **Hubert Laws**, Marty Sheller and others. Sheller began his long association with Santamaría as a trumpeter on 1963's *Watermelon Man*. He switched to percussion because of a problem with his lower lip, then increasingly concentrated on arranging, composing, musical direction and production. Marty worked with various salsa names, including **Willie Colón**, Tito Puente, **Conjunto Libre**, **Louie Ramírez**, **Roberto Torres** and **Conjunto Clásico**.

Selected albums: with Tito Puente's rhythm section, featuring Willie Bobo, Carlos 'Patato' Valdez *Puente In Percussion* (mid-50s, reissued 1978), *Changó* (1955, reissued as *Drums And Chants* in 1978), with Cal Tjader *Más Ritmo Caliente* (1957), *Yambú* (1958), with Tjader *Cal Tjader's Latin Concert* (1958), *A Night At The Blackhawk* (1959) and *Tjader Goes Latin* (1959), *Mongo* (1959), with Tjader *Concert By The Sea, Volumes 1 & 2* (1959, reissued as *Monterey Concerts*), *Concert On The Campus* (1960), *Our Man In Havana* (1960), with Tjader *Demasiado Caliente* (c.1960), *Live And Direct* (c.1960)), with Joe Loco *Pachanga con Joe Loco, Arriba! La Pachanga* (1962), *Más Sabroso* (1962), *Viva Mongo!* (1962), *Go, Mongo!* (1962), *Watermelon Man* (1963), with La Lupe *Mongo Introduces La Lupe* (1963, aka *Mongo y La Lupe*), *Mongo At The Village Gate* (1963), *Mongo Explodes* (1964), *El Pussy Cat* (1965), *La Bamba* (1965), *Hey! Let's Party* (1966), *El Bravo!* (1966), *Mongo Santamaría Explodes At The Village Gate* (c.1967), *Soul Bag* (1968), *Stone Soul* (1969), *Workin' On A Groovy Thing* (1969), *Feelin' Alright* (1970), *Mongo '70* (1970), *Mongo At Montreux* (1971), *Mongo Santamaría At Yankee Stadium* (1974), with the Fania All Stars *Latin-Soul-Rock* (1974), *Live At Yankee Stadium, Voume. 2* (1975), with Justo Betancourt *Ubane* (1976), *Dawn (Amanacer)* (1977), with

Bob James, Charlie Palmieri *Red Hot* (1979), with Dizzy Gillespie, Toots Thielemans *'Summertime' Digital At Montreux* 1980 (1981), the Ensemble of Latin Music Legends featuring Palmieri, José 'Chombo' Silva, Barry Rogers, Johnny 'Dandy' Rodriguez, Nicky Marrero *Mambo Show* (1990), *Live At Jazz Alley* (1990).

Compilations: with Tjader *Latino* (1965), *Mongo's Greatest Hits* (1987), *Mongo's Groove* (1987), *Mongo Santamaría's Greatest Hits*, *Mongo Mongo* (1978), *Afro Roots* (1972, combined *Yambú* and *Mongo*), *The Watermelon Man* (1973, combined *Watermelon Man* and *Mongo At The Village Gate*), *Skins* (1976, combined *Go, Mongo!* and *Mongo Explodes*).

Santana

This US group were the pioneers of Afro-Latin rock, head and shoulders above all pretenders to the throne. Santana emerged as part of the late 60s San Francisco new wave scene, which they rapidly transcended. Over the past 25 years the leader Carlos Santana (b. 20 July 1947, Autlan de Navarro, Mexico) has introduced jazz and funk into his unique blend of polyrhythmic music. Carlos owns the name, and has maintained his role as leader through a constant change of personnel, yet fully maintaining the Santana sound of 1967. The original line-up consisted of Gregg Rolie, Michael Shrieve, David Brown, Marcus Malone and Mike Carabello. Later important members were José Chepito Areas, Neal Schon, Tom Coster, Armando Peraza, Raul Rekow, Graham Lear, Orestes Vilato and Coke Escovedo. Santana was a regional favourite by 1969 and Carlos appeared on **Al Kooper** and **Mike Bloomfield**'s *The Live Adventures Of. . .* The **Woodstock Festival** of 1969 was the band's major breakthrough; their performance gave rock fans a first taste of 'Cubano rock' and was one of the highlights. The first three albums are outstanding examples of the genre. *Santana*, *Abraxas* and *Santana III* spent months high in the US charts, the latter two staying at number 1 for many weeks. These albums included numerous, memorable and fiery tracks including 'Jingo', **Tito Puente**'s 'Oye Como Va', a definitive version of **Peter Green**'s 'Black Magic Woman' and possibly the most sensual rock instrumental of all time; 'Samba Pa Ti'. On this Carlos plays a solo that oozes sexuality over an irresistible slow Latin beat. *Caravanserai* marked a change of style as Rolie and Schon departed to form **Journey**. This important album is almost a single suite showing a move towards jazz in the mode of **Miles Davis**' *In A Silent Way*. At that time Carlos became a disciple of Sri Chimnoy and, after befriending fellow guitarist **John McLaughlin**, he released the glorious *Love Devotion And Surrender*. During that year he released a live album with soul/funk drummer **Buddy Miles**. All these albums were considerable hits. *Welcome* (featuring vocalist Leon Thomas and guest John McLaughlin) and *Borboletta* (with guests **Flora Purim**

and **Stanley Clarke**) were lesser albums. He returned to hard Latin rock with the excellent *Amigos* in 1977. A version of the **Zombies** 'She's Not There' became a hit single from *Moonflower* in 1977. In his parallel world Carlos was maintaining a jazz-fusion path with a series of fine albums, the most notable was *The Swing Of Delight* with **Herbie Hancock** and **Wayne Shorter**. *Zebop!* in 1981 was a *tour de force*, and Santana's guitar playing was particularly impressive, with a clarity not heard since the earliest albums. The hit single from this collection was the admirable **Russ Ballard** song 'Winning'. The solo *Havana Moon* featured guests, **Willie Nelson** and **Booker T. Jones**, although the difference between what is solo Santana and band Santana has become almost irrelevant as Carlos is such an iconoclastic leader. *Beyond Appearances* in 1985 maintained his considerable recorded output. The same year he toured with **Bob Dylan** to ecstatic audiences. He scored the music for *La Bamba* in 1986 and reunited with Buddy Miles in 1987 to record *Freedom*. During the summer of 1993 the band toured South America and a live album, *Sacred Fire*, was released. At the same time Carlos also put his own record company, Guts And Grace, on to the market, beginning with a compilation of classic live performances from original artists such as **Jimi Hendrix**, **Bob Marley** and **Marvin Gaye**. Any association with the name Santana continues to be a positive one; whether as the band or solo, Carlos Santana is an outstanding figure in rock music and has influenced countless aspiring guitarists.

Albums: *Santana* (1969), *Abraxas* (1970), *Santana III* (1971), *Caravanserai* (1972), *Carlos Santana And Buddy Miles! Live!* (1972), *Love Devotion Surrender* (1973), *Welcome* (1973), *Borboletta* (1974), *Illuminations* (1974), *Lotus* (1975), *Amigos* (1976), *Festival* (1977), *Moonflower* (1977), *Inner Secrets* (1978), *Marathon* (1979), *Oneness: Silver Dreams, Golden Reality* (1979), *The Swing Of Delight* (1980), *Zebop!* (1981), *Shango* (1982), *Havana Moon* (1983), *Beyond Appearances* (1985), *La Bamba* (1986), *Freedom* (1987), *Blues For Salvador* (1987), *Persuasion* (1989), *Spirits Dancing In The Flesh* (1990), *Sacred Fire* (1993), with the Santana Brothers *Santana Brothers* (Island 1994). Compilations: *Greatest Hits* (1974), *Viva Santana - The Very Best* (1986), *Viva Santana* (1988, triple album), *The Very Best Of Santana, Volumes 1 And 2* (1988).

Santers

Canadian heavy metal trio with a strong blues influence formed in 1980 by guitarist and vocalist Rick Santers and his brother Mark on drums together with their friend, Rick Lazaroff, on bass. Aside from playing numerous concerts and recording their debut album in 1981, Rick Santers was in demand as a session player and, in particular, helped fellow Canadian **Lee Aaron** with her demos and first album. In 1982 Santers the band picked up a European licensing deal with Heavy

Metal Records who released *Racing Time* in December. This featured some fine guitar work, especially on the tracks 'Mistreatin' Heart' and 'Hard Time Loving You'. Their last album was released two years later before Rick decided to return to session work.

Albums: *Shot Down In Flames* (Ready 1981), *Racing Time* (Ready/Heavy Metal 1982), *Guitar Alley* (Ready/Heavy Metal 1984).

Santiago, Adalberto

b. Ciales, Puerto Rico. Adalberto's relaxed and flawless lead vocals are amongst the best in salsa, and for over two decades he has sessioned as a coro (chorus) singer on countless New York recordings. His early influences included the great Cuban vocalists **Beny Moré** and Miguelito Cuní (b. 8 May 1920, Pinar del Río, Cuba; d. 5 March 1984, Havana, Cuba). Santiago started his professional career singing with trios and playing bass and guitar. After stints with the bands of Chuíto Vélez, Willie Rodríguez and **Willie Rosario**, his career really took off when he joined **Ray Barretto**'s band. Between 1966-72, Adalberto made seven albums (excluding compilations) with Barretto. In late 1972, Adalberto and four other members of Barretto's band departed to found **Típica 73**. He appeared on three of their albums before disagreement over musical direction led him, and three other band members, to split during the mid-70s to form Los Kimbos. Meanwhile, Santiago sang lead vocals on two critically-acclaimed charanga albums, *Fantasia Africana/African Fantasy* and *Our Heritage - Nuestra Herencia*, by flautist/composer/producer Lou Pérez.

Los Kimbos were reputed to be a tough working band and had a sound reminiscent of both the pre-split Barretto band and Típica 73. With them, Adalberto recorded 1976's *Los Kimbos* and *The Big Kimbos With Adalberto Santiago* in 1977. That year he made his solo debut on *Adalberto*, which was produced by Barretto and contained two of his own compositions. Los Kimbos continued under the leadership of timbales player Orestes Vilató and released two further albums- *Hoy y Mañana* (1978) and *Aquacero Ne Me Moja* (1979). Santiago sang lead on one track on *Louie Ramírez y sus Amigos* by **Louie Ramírez**. In 1979, Adalberto and Ramírez co-produced his solo follow-up, *Adalberto Featuring Popeye El Marino*. The same year, he reunited with Barretto on *Rican/Struction*. Ray produced Adalberto's next solo album, *Feliz Me Siento*, the following year. Sonora Matancera member, Javier Vázquez, produced, arranged, directed and played piano on the rootsy *Adalberto Santiago*, which was Adalberto's contribution to the early 80s tipico (typical) salsa revival. In 1982, he teamed up with bandleader/bongo player **Roberto Roena** for *Super Apollo 47:50*. Santiago co-produced *Calidad* with **Papo Lucca**, who also played piano, arranged one track and oversaw musical direction. His *Cosas Del Alma* was an album of lush boleros which included his third recorded version of the classic 'Alma Con Alma' (previously contained on Barretto's *The Message* and *Gracias*). He returned to harder-edged urban salsa in 1985 on *Mas Sabroso*.

Adalberto did his own mature version of salsa romántica on the classy *Sex Symbol*, with production, arrangements, musical direction and piano by the ubiquitous Isidro Infante. In 1990, he again performed 'Alma Con Alma', this time arranged by Infante in a salsa romántica style for Louie Ramírez's second album entitled *Louie Ramírez y sus Amigos*. Santiago has written songs for a number of the albums he has appeared on, both as bandleader and solo artist, and provided compositions for other artists to record, such as **Joe Cuba**. Adalberto has remained true to his Latin roots and a statement he made in 1977 is still relevant in the 90s: 'I want to bring a truly Latin message to the people; this is what I do best and the structure of Latin music is best suited to my singing style'.

Solo albums and selected albums on which he sang lead vocals: with Willie Rodríguez *Heat Wave* (mid-60s), with Ray Barretto *Latino Con Soul* (1966), *Acid* (1967), with Willie Rosario *Boogaloo & Guaguanco* (1968), with Barretto *Hard Hands* (1968), *Together* (1969), *Power* (1970), *The Message* (1971), *Que Viva La Musica* (1972), with Típica 73 *Típica 73* (1973), *Típica 73* (1974), with Típica 73 *La Candela* (1975), with Lou Pérez *Fantasia Africana/African Fantasy* (1975), with Los Kimbos *Los Kimbos* (1976), with Barretto *Barretto Live: Tomorrow* (1976), with Lou Pérez *Our Heritage - Nuestra Herencia* (1976), with Los Kimbos *The Big Kimbos With Adalberto Santiago* (1977), *Adalberto* (1977), with Barretto *Gracias* (1979), *Adalberto Featuring Popeye El Marino* (1979), with Barretto *Rican/Struction* (1979), *Feliz Me Siento* (1980), *Adalberto Santiago* (1981), with Roberto Roena *Super Apollo 47:50* (1982), *Calidad* (1982), with Celia Cruz and Barretto *Tremendo Trio!* (1983), *Cosas Del Alma* (1984), *Mas Sabroso* (1985), with Alfredo Rodríguez *Monsieur Oh, La, La* (1985), *Sex Symbol* (1989), with Charanga Ranchera *Charanga Ranchera* (1989), with Papaíto, Melcochita, Herman Olivera, Yayo El Indio and Isidro Infante *Valdesa Records Presenta Vol.1: Salsa Sudada* (1990), *Hay Algo En Ella* (1991).

Santiago, Al

b. Albert Santiago, 1932, Spanish Harlem, Manhattan, New York City, USA, of Puerto Rican parentage. Pianist, saxophonist, composer, arranger, bandleader, conductor, record producer, Latin retail record store owner/manager, Latin record label founder and boss, Al Santiago, describes himself as 'an extrovert of manic proportions, an over-achiever, pioneer, catalyst and innovator'. Santiago was born into a musical family. His father was a professional musician who played violin, saxophones, clarinet and trombone with various Latin dance bands and his uncle led a Latin big band.

His older sister studied piano with a female professional musician who worked on the New York Latin scene and frequently performed in the same band as his father. Al began piano tuition with the same teacher in the early 40s, but did not take to the instrument. 'I disliked piano so much that I used to play 'The Minute Waltz' in 30 seconds so I could get out to play softball', he later joked. He decided to switch to saxophone, which he found easier to play. Santiago became the band-boy for his uncle's big band. When he was 15 years old, his uncle told him to take over his tenor saxophone chair. In 1950, Al's uncle quit bandleading to open the Casa Latina, which became one of New York's leading Latin record shops. He handed his orchestra over to the 18-year-old Santiago, who found himself surrounded by 'old men' in their 30s and 40s, including his father on saxophone. Al gradually introduced new younger personnel, so that eventually only his father remained as an original member. He called the band the Chack-a-nunu Boys. 'Chack-a-nunu' was his attempt at a verbal interpretation of the sound made by a Latin rhythm section playing alone. Between 1948-60, Al also performed with Carlos Pizarro, El Combo Ponce, Jack Portalatin, Quique Monsanto and Pepi LaSalle. He also sat-in with various other orchestras including **Machito** and **Tito Puente**.

Santiago is a great admirer of **Buck Clayton**. When Al was about 19-years-old, an incident involving the jazz trumpeter/arranger occurred which proved to be a major turning point in his life. A skeleton version of the Chack-a-nunu Boys was booked for a Latin wedding. However, the band's regular trumpeter was unable to attend and telephoned Santiago to say he was sending a substitute. Al explained what happened on the night of the gig: 'Buck Clayton walks in. Now I'm stunned . . . (He) never had rehearsed, looks at the music as he's playing it, sight reads it to perfection. And my thoughts that night were: if a guy like Buck Clayton can come to play with an unknown kiddie band . . . for 20 bucks on a Saturday night, I've got to get out of the performing end of music. Because I know I am not an exceptional instrumentalist, and the only way you are going to make bucks is you have to be a superstar performer/leader, not a sideman. If Buck can play this gig - I don't want to perform!' Santiago remembered his uncle mentioning someone was selling a record store.

With money borrowed from his family, he acquired the premises. Al ran the shop, called Casa Latina del Bronx, between 1951-55 while studying at college. At his father's insistence, he switched subjects from music to business. Towards the end of his course, the demolition of local residential blocks caused him to lose virtually half of his trade. He sold the store and took jobs in various department stores until one day a record business friend told him of a large vacant shop on Prospect Avenue and Westchester in the Bronx. The following day he put a deposit on the property and signed a lease. He opened the premises under the name of Casalegre Record Store in November 1955, and ran it until 1975. Santiago achieved his goal of becoming 'the most famous, hippest, successful record shop in the Latin field' within the first year by using the gimmick of giving a record away free (from a cut-price stock he had acquired) with each disc purchased, and advertising this promotion heavily in a local movie-house and on the radio. He also placed advertisements in whatever Hispanic publication 'popped-up', including a television guide that later converted into the Latin music magazine *Farándula*, which its founder, Cuban Bernardo Hevia, still publishes in Puerto Rico in the 90s.

His next goal was to launch a record company, and in 1956 he went into partnership with the clothing entrepreneur, Ben Perlman, to co-found the Alegre Recording Corp. During the first four years of the firm, the label issued 44 singles, including recordings by Vitín Avilés, Joe Cotto, **Kako** and Cuarteto Mayari. Continued promotion, by way of 'freebie' records and radio advertisements for Casalegre featuring Alegre Records products, led to the success of the label.

In late 1959, a Casalegre shop assistant urged Santiago to visit the Tritons social club on Southern Boulevard in the Bronx to hear **Johnny Pacheco** and his charanga (violins and flute group). 'I don't think the band had reached its eighth bar, when I decided I'm recording this band', he later said. Suspecting that Pacheco would be a big hit, Santiago insisted that he sign a recording contract, otherwise he would not record him. Pacheco yielded, and 1960's *Johnny Pacheco y su Charanga Vol. 1* - Alegre's first album release - became the biggest selling album up to that point in the history of Latin music. A few months after the smash hit success of Pacheco's album, Al saw **Charlie Palmieri**'s Charanga 'La Duboney' performing. 'I assume Charlie has been signed up and I speak to him. My parents and his parents knew each other before Charlie, **Eddie** (**Palmieri**) and I were born. Charlie tells me he's not under contract to anybody. I cannot believe the stupidity of the record industry. And a lot of my success has to be contributed to a lack of competition and foresight. If I've got Pacheco who sold a 100,000 albums in six months, how come the other record companies don't say: "hey, Charlie may be the number 2 group, let's sign him up". So I end up with the two top charangas'. In total, Santiago produced 49 albums on Alegre between 1960-66, including further releases by Pacheco, the debut albums by Kako, Eddie Palmieri and **Willie Rosario**, recordings by Sabú Martínez, Charlie Palmieri, Dioris Valladares, Orlando Marín, César Concepción, Johnny Rodríguez (the older brother of **Tito Rodríguez**), **Mon Rivera** (Al's three trombone band instrumentation on *Que Gente*

Averigua gave new life to Rivera's career), Tito Puente, **Louie Ramírez**, Celio González and the legendary first four Alegre All-Stars volumes. 'The Alegre All-Stars was my baby', said Santiago in 1989, 'I conceived it. I had it in my mind two years before I put it into action, because I had heard the Panart releases, the *Cuban Jam Session*'s . . . the hippest Latin jazz thing I had ever heard in my life. And the same impact those records had on me, I was told later the Alegre All-Stars had on other musicians . . . I decided why don't I put all bandleaders together. Form a band, and whatever chairs are missing, get the best musicians in the bands that I have under contract . . . I knew it was going to be difficult for many reasons; one, Pacheco and Charlie already had a difference unto their musical visions. Dioris was the "King of the Merengue". Kako was an introvert. How do I get this band together. It was solved at the Tritons on Tuesday nights . . . There was no music. It was strictly improvised. There was no leader. I was like the supervisor . . . At the first things at the Tritons I had no musical input, other than I would suggest a tune or two. They worked it out among themselves. I heard them every Tuesday and then took them into the studio and we had a very easy time with the first album, because although there was no music written, the guys had been playing these things for the last six or eight Tuesdays.'

Album cover designer, MC and former *Latin NY* magazine publisher, Izzy Sanabria, came up with the idea of releasing *The Alegre All-Stars Vol. 4* before *Vol. 3*. They advertised in newspapers that the tapes to *Vol. 3* were lost. Santiago went to the dancehalls and the bands permitted him to stop the proceedings, and after a fanfare and drum-roll, he would announce: '"*The Alegre All-Stars Vol. 3* is lost in the subway, please there is a reward" . . . we got to the point where we got to believe it ourselves. And when we put out *Vol. 3*, the cover is that description of losing the tapes and we're blaming Kako.' In 1966, Santiago and Perlman sold Alegre to Branston Music, Inc., which was the umbrella organization that owned Roulette and Tico Records. Whilst remaining the owner and manager of Casalegre, Al worked for Tico, producing *Cuba Y Puerto Rico Son . . .* by **Celia Cruz** and Tito Puente (her first album with the bandleader), Celia's *Son Con Guaguanco*, one of her greatest albums, and *They Call Me La Lupe/A Mí Me Llaman La Lupe* by **La Lupe** with **Chico O'Farrill**. Next, Santiago and Perlman co-founded Futura Records, which put out a single for Kako as well as **Willie Colón**'s debut. In 1968, Al began a stint as staff producer with Musicor Records, producing albums by Bobby Capó (with Tito Puente), Kako (two albums- the first with **Camilo Azuquita**, the second with Meñique), **Orquesta Broadway**, Mark Weinstein (the avant-garde *Cuban Roots*), Willie Rosario, Dioris Valladares, Tito Rodríguez, La Playa Sextet (recorded in Puerto Rico) and Tato Díaz. After his spell with Musicor, Santiago freelanced with various companies. He continued the tradition of the Alegre All-Stars in the guise (for contractual reasons) of the *Salsa All-Stars*, which he produced for Salsa Records in 1968, and two albums by the Cesta All-Stars, which he co-produced for **Joe Quijano**'s Cesta Records. He also produced albums by Orquesta Capri and Orquesta Tentación on the Salsa label.

In 1970, Santiago began Mañana Records. In addition to producing albums by Capri and Tentación for the label, he conceived and produced the 1971 masterpiece *Saxofobia Vol. 1* by Orlando Marín's 'La Saxofonica'. The record was the first Latin album to be recorded on 16 tracks. The band 'La Saxofonica' featured a unique frontline of five saxophones (including Panamanian Mauricio Smith, who doubled on flute and arranged two tracks, and Mexican Dick 'Taco' Meza), with rhythm section and voices. Louie Ramírez wrote half the arrangements and composed one track. Charlie Palmieri and Paquito Pastor shared the piano playing chores. The album was a musical success, but regrettably not a commercial one.

In 1975, Al co-founded Montuno Records with two other partners, and produced three albums for the company, including the debut releases by Yambú and Saoco (co-produced by the band's co-leaders, **Henry Fiol** and William Millán, and released on Mericana Records). In 1976, he wrote the liner notes for the Alegre All-Stars compilation *They Just Don't Makim Like Us Any More*. The following year he returned to Alegre, which by that stage was controlled by Jerry Musucci's Fania Records empire, to produce *Pa' Bailar Na' Ma'* by Dioris Valladares and the Alegre All-Stars 17th anniversary reunion *Perdido (Vol. 5 or 6?)*. The All-Stars also marked the event with an appearance at New York's Madison Square Garden.

In 1978, Al became the Director of Special Projects for Fania Records and was responsible for the reissue of classic albums and/or immaculately selected compilations by the irreverent and controversial Dominican singer, bandleader/composer Frankie Dante and his Orquesta Flamboyán, Charlie Palmieri, Celia Cruz, Eddie Palmieri, Willie Colón and **Héctor Lavoe**, Willie Rosario, **Mongo Santamaría**, Tito Puente, **Ismael Rivera** and **Rafael Cortijo**, Sonora Ponceña (see **Papo Lucca**), Orlando Marín, **Típica 73** and **Tommy Olivencia**. Back with Alegre in 1978, Santiago acted as consultant on Charlie Palmieri's *The Heavyweight* and produced the self-titled debut album by the young band, Fuego '77.

In 1980, he prepared a compilation for the Miami-based company, Armada and Rodríguez (now Armado and Fernández), titled *Al Santiago Presents The Best of Cuba*, which was released on their Funny label. During the 80s, the mainstream salsa industry, which by the second half of the decade was predominantly pumping out bland and uninspired salsa romántica product, criminally neglected to employ Santiago's vast pool of skills and experience. In 1982, he produced and hosted the *Big Band Latino* radio show. In 1984 and 1985, Al worked as a music teacher for the New York City Board of Education. More radio work followed in 1989 and 1990, when he was the disc jockey on the programme *Jazz Retrospect*. At the end of the decade, the ever versatile Santiago attended graduate school to become a school psychologist.

Santiago, Eddie

b. c.1961, Puerto Rico. Santiago's record-breaking solo debut *Atrevido y Diferente* was full of saccharin sweet romantic vocals and hip arrangements over a driving yet laid-back beat. It triggered a revival of salsa's fortunes with a new wave - variously called salsa romántica, salsa erótica, salsa sensual or sexy salsa - and spawned a breed of new solo singers and bands and some comebacks, including Nicaraguan Luis Enrique, Willie González, Paquito Guzmán, **Lalo Rodríguez**, Roberto Lugo and Nino Segarra. *Billboard*'s former Latin music reporter, Carlos Agudelo, attempted a definition of salsa sensual: 'This Puerto Rican song-and-dance craze mixes the Spanish lyrics of romantic ballads - borrowed shamelessly from pop records even before they have exhausted their life span - with the traditional salsa beat. It's performed by a mostly new generation of soneros (salsa singers), all of them remarkably similar in the pitch of their voices, the moods and cadences of their sensually, or shall we say sexually, tinged tunes' (from New York's *Village Voice*, August 1988). Although Santiago's rapid rise to fame helped rescue salsa from the depths to which the Dominican merengue boom had pushed it, it was a massive set-back for the tradition of solid, progressive salsa associated with names like **Willie Rosario**, **Papo Lucca** and Sonora Ponceña, **Mulenze**, **Conjunto Libre**, **Angel Canales** and others. UK salsa broadcaster, Tomek, said in 1991: 'Eddie Santiago's success represents the nadir of salsa's commercialization. A thin voice made ludicrous by an impressive range of bum notes, even smokey reverb and echo failed to redeem its dismal squawk. But his true crime was the success of *that* album - it launched a tidal wave of palsied imitators. Credit to his producer Julio César Delgado, though; a cunningly crafted if deeply cynical and ultimately resounding success, now thankfully on the wane'.

Santiago started as a singer with various bands, including Generación 2000, Orquesta La Potente, Orquesta Opus and Orquesta Saragüey. In March 1984 he joined Willie González as co-lead vocalist of Conjunto Chaney, led by bongo player Nicolas Vivas. The band's self-titled album of the same year was a great success, spawning such hits as 'Desesperado' and 'Que Maravilla Fue Sentirte' performed by Santiago. He and González both departed to go solo. Santiago

signed with TH (later TH-Rodven) and released the famous (or infamous, depending on your point of view) *Atrevido y Diferente* in 1986, which catapulted him into the limelight. González signed with ex-TH executive producer Tony Moreno's Musical Productions company and issued the ***Billboard*** chart-topper *Willie González & Noche Sensual Orquesta* in 1986, which went platinum and earned him Diplo awards for 'Album of the Year' and 'Best New Salsa Artiste of the Year'. He continued with the diminishingly successful *Sin Comparación* (1989) and *Para Ustedes . . . 'El Publico'* (1990). Chaney, who previously released *Chaney Chaney Chaney* (1980), *Conjunto Chaney* (1983), carried on with *El Conjunto del Amor* (1986), *Mas Que Atrevido* (1988), *El Conjunto del Amor* (1989), which contained the superb 'Sera Que Estoy Soñando', and *Somos Amigos* (1991).

Atrevido y Diferente quickly went gold and caused Santiago to win the *Billboard* Bravo Award for 'Best Selling Album' and ACE Award for 'Band of the Year' in 1987. His chart-topping follow-up . . . *Sigo Atrevido!* was nominated for a Grammy Award in March 1989. 1988's *Invasión De La Privacidad* was another number 1 and attracted nominations for the *Billboard* Lo Nuestro awards for 'Album of the Year' and 'Artiste of the Year' in May 1990. In 1989, Eddie made a controversial move to the multinational label **Capitol/EMI** Latin.

The company also managed to acquire TH-Rodven's house recording and production director, Julio César Delgado, who worked on all Santiago's releases and albums by most of TH-Rodven's impressive past and present roster of salsa artists and bands, including Marvin Santiago (see **Bobby Valentín**), Willie Rosario, **Raphy Leavitt**, **Tommy Olivencia**, **Oscar D'León**, **Andy Montañez**, La Solución, Paquito Guzmán, Frankie Ruiz, Milagros Hernández, Alex León, Lalo Rodríguez, David Pabón and Héctor Tricoche. Baritone saxophonist Delgado was a key architect of the salsa romántica sound, however some regard **Louie Ramírez**'s early 80s *Noche Caliente* project as the true genesis of the style. In 1990, TH-Rodven and **CBS** collaborated to release the highly successful joint Eddie Santiago/Luis Enrique (a CBS signee) compilation *Los Príncipes De La Salsa*. Santiago's final TH-Rodven release, *El Rey De La Salsa Romántica*, was his least successful in chart terms. In April 1991, he made his UK debut with a lacklustre concert at London's Empire Ballroom. In late 1991: 'his stunning lack of insight into his own qualities was hilariously evident in the choice of title for his first album on the major, Capitol/EMI Latin: *Soy El Mismo/I'm Still The Same*. Oh dear. Depressingly, it reached number 1 in the *Billboard* chart.' (Tomek). However, the album did less well in his homeland of Puerto Rico.

Albums: with Conjunto Chaney *Conjunto Chaney* (1984), *Atrevido y Diferente* (1986), . . . *Sigo Atrevido!* (1988), *Invasión De La Privacidad* (1988), *New Wave Salsa* (1989), *El Rey De*

La Salsa Romántica (1991), *Soy El Mismo/I'm Still The Same* (1991). Compilation: with Luis Enrique *Los Príncipes De La Salsa* (1990).

Sapphires

A vocal trio from Philadelphia, Pennsylvania, USA, consisting of Carol Jackson (lead), George Gainer, and Joe Livingston. The group delivered an infectious pop-soul girl-group sound that was typical of east coast African-American acts during the early 60s. Their one big hit was 'Who Do You Love' (number 9 R&B, number 25 pop) in 1964, but they recorded other excellent numbers in 'Oh So Soon' and 'Where Is Johnny Now'. Moving to **ABC** later in the decade they failed to get back on the charts but created several cherished singles that later found favour in the UK on the northern soul scene such as 'Gotta Have Your Love' and 'Slow Fizz'.

Album: *Who Do You Love* (Swan 1964). Compilation: *Who Do You Love* (Collectables 1989).

Sarah Records

This fiercely independent UK Bristol-based label was formed in 1987 by Matt Haynes with Clare Wadd. Hayne's involvement with the UK independent music scene began with the fanzine publication, *Are You Scared To Get Happy?*, which supported the 'back-to-the-roots' idealism of the *New Musical Express*'s *C86* compilation. He and Wadd cultivated a label determined to resist the growing fashion for CDs and 12-inch singles by blatantly promoting the 7-inch single and the anti-hi tech flexi-disc. Despite the later deviation from this ideology, the label have continued to promote this format, ignoring industry claims of the death of vinyl and the single format. The musical content, quintessentially English pop, is aptly summed up in the sleeve notes for *Shadow Factory*: the songs are 'full of wrong notes and wrong chords, but crammed with right Everything Elses'. Often derided by their contemporaries for being too soft and twee, the average Sarah group's lyrical content has tended not to stray very far from the timeless subject of boyfriends and girlfriends. Sarah's biggest asset, and the finest exponents of the 'Sarah sound', were, until their break-up in late 1991, the **Field Mice**. Amongst the other groups who have recorded for the label are the **Sea Urchins** (who were responsible for the first Sarah release, the *Pristine Christine* EP), the Orchids, the Springfields, Another Sunny Day, St. Christopher, **14 Iced Bears**, the Wake, **Heavenly** and, from Australia, Even As We Speak. Periodically, Sarah issue compilations, containing previously released singles, with the album titles and sleeve artwork reflecting the label's fondness for the Bristol area. While not breaking down any barriers or creating any artistic revolution, Sarah quietly go about their business, ensuring an outlet for their type of music, treating it with love and

respect - and continuing to annoy their detractors.
Compilations: *Shadow Factory* (Sarah 1988), *Temple Cloud* (Sarah 1990), *Air Balloon Road* (Sarah 1991, CD only release), *Glass Arcade* (Sarah 1991).

Saraya

Formed in 1987 by vocalist Sandi Saraya and keyboard player Gregg Munier, this US rock band originally travelled under the title Alsace Lorraine. With the addition of Tony Rey (guitar), Gary Taylor (bass) and Chuck Bonfarte (drums), they changed their name to Saraya. Fusing influences such as **Heart**, the **Pretenders** and **Pat Benatar**, they recorded a self-titled debut for Polygram; a melodic and highly polished collection of AOR numbers characterized by Sandi's hammy but infectious vocal style. Following internal disputes Rey and Taylor quit in 1990 and were replaced by Tony Bruno and Barry Dunaway respectively. *When The Blackbird Sings*, released in 1991, built on their former style but again failed to find success.

Albums: *Saraya* (Polygram 1989), *When The Blackbird Sings* (Polydor 1991).

Sargeant, Bob

This freelance multi-instrumentalist and vocalist was a denizen of the British 'progressive' rock scene in the 70s. As well as serving in the **Mick Abrahams** Band from 1971-72, he was hired for albums by **Andy Roberts**, Junco Partners and Patrick Campbell-Lyons (ex-**Nirvana** (UK)), and, briefly, to play keyboards in **Curved Air**. In 1975, he recorded *First Starring Role*, for **RCA Records** on which he was assisted by **Herbie Flowers**, Mike Garson, **Cozy Powell** and former Abrahams sideman, Jack Lancaster. This move to centre stage was, however, short-lived as Sargeant found production work more artistically, if not financially, rewarding - with the **Monochrome Set** and the **Beat** among the more famous of his later employers.

Album: *First Starring Role* (1975).

Sargent, Kenny

(see **Casa Loma Orchestra**)

Sarkoma

Alternative metal band from the USA mid west staffed by 'a brotherhood of musicians' who include Brian Carter (vocals), Tony Chrisman (bass), Mike Hilleburg (guitar), Aaron Ingram (drums) and Stuart Johnson (guitar). Sarkoma made their debut in 1992 with the *Completely Different* EP, before regional and national touring. Lyrical content derived from the personal and imagined experiences of Johnson, including one song, 'Blue Horizon', written from a female perspective. Other issues explored on the group's debut album, *Integrity*, included evolution ('Universal Footsteps') and celebrity ('Mortamer'). With strong all-round songwriting it may not prove too long before the band are forced to become better acquainted with the latter sentiment.

Album: *Integrity* (Bulletproof 1994).

Sarmanto, Heikki

b. 22 June 1939, Helsinki, Finland. Sarmanto studied languages and music at Helsinki University and Sibelius Academy before going on to the **Berklee College of Music** (1968-71). He was named the best pianist at Montreux in 1971. He led his own bands from 1962 and in 1976 a workshop group he ran became the big band UMO. He has written *New Hope Jazz Mass*, a jazz ballet and a jazz opera and was chosen by saxophonist **Sonny Rollins** to arrange and orchestrate his *Saxophone Concerto* (1986). He continues to write vocal, orchestral and theatre works in a most assured style.

Album: *Suomi* (1983).

Sarony, Leslie

b. 22 January 1897, Surbiton, Surrey, England, d. 12 February 1985. a singer, songwriter and all-round entertainer, Sarony made his first stage appearance in a music hall act in 1911. He subsequently became one of Park's Eton Boys, and appeared in the revue *Hello Tango* at the London Hippodrome in 1913. He also toured the provincial music halls while they were enjoying their 'golden era'. During World War I, he served with the London Scottish Regiment in France and Salonika, spending much of his time entertaining in army concert parties. After the war he appeared in pantomime, and then in 20s revues such as *The Peep Show*, *His Girl*, *Dover Street To Dixie*, *Brighter London*, *The Whirl Of The World*, *Rat-A-Tat* and *Up With The Lark*, and an adaptation of the French operetta *Phi-Phi*.

In 1928, he played the role of Frank Schultz, with Edith Day and Howett Worster, in the London production of *Show Boat*. Two years later, he joined Day again in *Rio Rita*, at the Prince Edward Theatre. In the following year, Sarony had what was probably his best known song, 'I Lift Up My Finger And I Say "Tweet Tweet"', interpolated into the musical *Love Lies*, which starred **Stanley Lupino**. Sarony also contributed 'Far Away' to *Silver Wings*, in which he also appeared, and his 'How're You Getting On?' was included in the 'musical horse play' *Sporting Love* (1935). Sarony devoted himself more to variety shows in the early 30s and became a popular radio personality. In 1935 he teamed up with Leslie Holmes, a former danceband drummer, to form the Two Leslies, which became an extremely popular variety and radio act. They appeared in a Royal Command Performance, and toured North Africa and Italy, entertaining the Allied Forces in World War II. Holmes left the act in 1946, and Sarony worked with another partner for a

while, and then continued as a single, armed with a battery of monologues, songs, funny voices and eccentric sound effects that sustained him during the radical changes which took place in popular music. In his heyday, when he sang with top dance bands such as **Jack Hylton**, he had a knack of composing songs which appealed to ordinary people. Some of these songs had unusual or colloquial titles, such as 'Mucking About In The Garden', and 'Ain't It Grand To Be Bloomin' Well Dead'. Others included 'Forty Seven Ginger-Headed Sailors', 'Over The Garden Wall', 'Wheezy Anna', 'Coom Pretty One', 'Rhymes', 'When The Guards Are On Parade' (with Horatio Nicholls) and 'When A Soldier's On Parade'. In 1968, he appeared in the British musical film *Chitty Chitty Bang Bang*, and in the 70s undertook straight roles in the theatre, in productions ranging from Beckett's *Endgame* to Shakespeare's *As You Like It*. He was back in the musical theatre in 1977, appearing with **Roy Castle** in *The History Of Mr Polly*, for which he wrote 'Sweet Fanny Adams'. He appeared in another British film, *Yanks* (1979), and in the same year, in a nostalgic concert at London's Royal Festival Hall, he was as perky and vital as ever at the age of 82.

Selected album: *Roy Hudd Presents Leslie Sarony* (World 1980).

Sarstedt, Peter

Brother of 60s pop idol **Eden Kane**, this singer-songwriter was a denizen of the British folk scene when the hunt was on for a native riposte to **Bob Dylan**. Sarstedt was not chosen but, growing a luxuriant black moustache, he cultivated the image of a suave wanderer of global bohemia. Recording for United Artists, his 'I Am A Cathedral' was an airplay hit on pirate radio and university juke-boxes, but it was not until 1969 that he restored family fortunes with a UK number 1, 'Where Do You Go To My Lovely' which has since attained status as a pop classic and is a perennial on 'gold' format radio stations. That year, both an album and another single ('Frozen Orange Juice') also sold well throughout Europe. Yet, though a forerunner of the early 70s 'self-rock' school, his style was not solemn enough for its collegian consumers. In 1973, he teamed up on *Worlds Apart Together* with Kane and another sibling, Robin Sarstedt. Then came the resumption of his solo career with the issue of further albums, which was accompanied by the unexpected BBC airplay for 'Beirut' from *PS...*, and 'Love Among The Ruins' almost charting in 1982. Based in Copenhagen for several years, he settled down with his American wife, Joanna, on a Wiltshire farm. In the early 90s, he was seen on 60s nostalgia shows, often supporting **Gerry And The Pacemakers**.

Albums: *Peter Sarstedt* (1969), *PS...* (1979), *Up Date* (1981), *Asia Minor* (1987), *Never Say Goodbye* (1987). Compilation: *The Very Best Of Peter Sarstedt* (1987).

Sasha

Wales-born Manchester-based 'Top DJ pin-up' whose regular nights include Renaissance (Manchester) and La Cotta (Birmingham). A former fish-farm worker and grade eight pianist, after pioneering Italian house in 1989 and 1990 he made his name with a jazzy, garage style as a remixer on projects like **Mr Fingers**' 'Closer' and **Urban Soul**'s 'He's Always' and 'Alright'. Sasha moved to **DeConstruction** in 1993 in a three album deal. Most had expected him to sign with **Virgin** following the success of his BM:Ex (Barry Manilow Experience) cut, 'Appolonia', a double-pack 12-inch with a running time of over an hour, on their **Union City Recordings** subsidiary. 'Appolonia' originally emerged as an obscure Italian white label promo, and was a record Sasha played regularly at the end of his sets at Shelley's in Stoke without ever being able to discover the identity of its originators. As nobody could find out any further details he decided to re-record it himself. The first result of the liaison with DeConstruction was 'Higher Ground', recorded with production partner Tom Frederikse and vocalist Sam Mollison. He also provided a single, 'Quat', for **Cowboy**, who were originally set to release 'Feel The Drop', which ended up as the b-side to 'Appolonia'. Sasha was also signed up to PolyGram Music in 1993 for publishing, indicating that at last dance songwriters were beginning to be taken seriously by the music industry, rather than as short-term recording artists. As Sasha himself expounded: 'I've plans for bigger things. I don't want to be restricted by the dancefloor. That's where my inspiration is, but I want to do something with a little more longevity than the latest number 1 on the Buzz chart'. He has thus far, however, turned down interview opportunities with the *Daily Mirror* and *Sun*. Among his many other remix/production clients have been **Ce Ce Rogers**, **Unique 3** ('No More') and soundtrack composer Barrington Pheloung.

Sassafras

A band that never achieved major league success, they nevertheless built up a loyal following by extensively touring the UK during the 70s. Hailing from Wales, their line-up featured Terry Bennett (vocals), Dai Shell (guitar), Ralph Evans (guitar), Ricky John (bass) and Robert Jones (drums). They recorded three albums of straightforward boogie rock, similar in style to **Status Quo**.
Albums: *Expecting Company* (1973), *Whealin' And Dealin'* (1976), *Riding High* (1976).

Satan

Formed from the ashes of the band Blitzkrieg in Newcastle-upon-Tyne, England, in 1981, the original line-up of Satan comprised Trevor Robinson (vocals), Russ Tippins (guitar), Steve Ramsey (guitar), Graeme English (bass) and Andy Reed (drums). In 1981 the band recorded two tracks for a compilation, *Roxcalibur*, and a self-financed single entitled 'Kiss Of Death'. Soon after its release vocalist Robinson left the band to be replaced by Ian Swift who himself was soon supplanted by Brian Ross. Through numerous demos and a name built for themselves via the underground tape-trading scene, they attracted the attention of Noise Records. Their debut album, *Court In The Act*, followed in 1984. Typified by speed-metal riffs and strong lead guitar work, this was again well-received. However, the name of the band did not work to their advantage, and was atypical of their lyrical dimension. Not only did they alter the name to **Blind Fury** but once again changed vocalists, replacing the departed Ross with Lou Taylor. This line-up recorded one album using the Blind Fury appellation, *Out Of Reach*, in 1985. The band changed vocalists yet again replacing Taylor with Michael Jackson and reverted to the name Satan shortly thereafter. A new demo attracted the interest of the German-based Steamhammer Records and *Into The Future* was released in 1986. The album's poor production was parried by the power and quality of the material. *Suspended Sentence* followed in 1987. However, once again the name was causing problems and record company and managerial pressure now saw it changed to **Pariah**. After two further albums, *The Kindred* and *Blaze Of Obscurity*, the band in all its myriad guises folded in 1990.
Albums: *Court In The Act* (Neat 1984), *Into The Future* (Steamhammer 1986), *Suspended Sentence* (Steamhammer 1987).

Satan And Adam

Sterling Magee (b. 20 May 1936, Mount Olive, Mississippi, USA) and Adam Gussow (b. 3 April 1958, Congers, New York, USA). Magee almost had a career in the 60s when, managed by **Al Sears** and **Jesse Stone**, he made one single for Sylvia Records, 'Get In My Arms Little Girlie', and a pair for **Ray Charles**'s Tangerine label, 'Oh She Was Pretty' and 'I Still Believe In You'. By the mid-80s he had become a one-man-band on 125th Street in Harlem, playing guitar, two hi-hats, tambourines and a sounding board. In October 1986 Gussow, a 1979 Princeton graduate who had busked in Paris and Amsterdam, happened by and asked to play. Since then, the pair have toured Europe on several occasions and appeared in **U2**'s concert film, *Rattle & Hum*. Their first album was nominated for a **W.C. Handy** award, but its sequel added nothing to the impression made by *Harlem Blues*. Their dynamic blend of funk, blues and R&B intrigues the ear on first listening but the hybrid nature of their music leaves little room for creative development.
Albums: *Satan and Adam* (Duane Street Music Collective 1991, cassette), *Harlem Blues* (Flying Fish/Demon 1991), *Mother Mojo* (Flying Fish/Demon 1993).

Satchmo The Great

Made for television by Ed Murrow, this 1956 film follows **Louis Armstrong** on a tour of Europe and Africa. Intercut with scenes of live performance by Armstrong And His All Stars, and their welcome, often by tens of thousands of well-wishers, at airports, are interviews with Armstrong. Although one of the finest and most respected journalists of his, or any other era, Murrow's questions are sometimes a shade naïve but Armstrong takes it all in his stride. The film ends with a New York concert performance of 'St Louis Blues' in which Armstrong and his men are joined by **Leonard Bernstein** and the New York Philharmonic to play to a capacity audience which includes **W.C. Handy**. One moving moment shows Handy, then turned 80, removing his hat to take his handkerchief from his head to mop a tear from his blind eyes. The All Stars featured are **Trummy Young**, **Edmond Hall**, **Billy Kyle**, **Jack Lesberg** and **Barrett Deems** with singer **Velma Middleton**.

Satherley, Art

b. Arthur Edward Satherley, 19 October 1889, Bristol, England. Known as 'Uncle Art', Satherley was a pioneer in the US recording industry during the 20s and 30s. As a talent scout, producer and A&R person, he was credited with providing the American Recording Company with one of the strongest country music catalogues in the USA. After travelling to America in 1913, he worked for the Wisconsin Chair Company which also made phonograph cabinets. He soon moved into the recording business, promoting blues artists, such as **Ma Rainey**, **Blind Blake** and **Blind Lemon Jefferson** for the Paramount label. In 1929, he joined the newly formed ARC, and toured the US in search of new talent in the areas of country, hillbilly, blues and 'race' music, and was at the forefront in promoting new markets. During the 30s he recorded artists such as **Hank Penny**, **Roy Acuff**, **Bob Wills**, **Big Bill Broonzy**, Bill and Cliff Carlisle, **Blind Boy Fuller** and **Gene Autry**. The latter had enormous hits with 'Silver Haired Mother Of Mine', 'Yellow Rose Of Texas' and 'Tumbling Tumbleweeds'. When ARC became **Columbia** in 1938, Satherley stayed with the company as an A&R executive until his retirement in 1952. Among the artists whose careers he guided and influenced were **Marty Robbins**, **Lefty Frizzell**, **Bill Monroe**, **Carl Smith**, Spade Cooley, **Al Dexter** and **Little Jimmy Dickens**. Satherley's assistant for many years, David Law, eventually became a leading producer, and was responsible for the early recordings of **David Frizzell**, younger brother of the legendary Lefty. Satherley was elected to the Country Music Hall Of Fame in 1971 for his pioneering work in the genre.

Satintones

An R&B vocal group from Detroit, Michigan, USA. The Satintones are known not so much for their recordings, but for their early association with the famed **Motown** organization, and for producing future talents in the Detroit recording scene. The original members were Robert Bateman, Chico Laverett, James Ellis, and Sonny Sanders, who came together in 1957. They were the first group signed to one of **Berry Gordy**'s labels, when 'Going To The Hop' was issued on Tamla in 1959, followed by the first single on **Motown Records**, 'Sugar Daddy'. After three further singles for Motown, all in the R&B vocal group style of the late 50s, the group disbanded, with Robert Bateman becoming a producer for the label. He worked on the **Marvelettes**' hit single, 'Please Mr. Postman' in 1962, before leaving Motown and setting up an independent producer in Detroit. In 1967, Bateman produced the solo recordings by the former Supreme, **Florence Ballad**. Sonny Sanders had the most impressive post-Satintones career, working as an arranger, producer, and band leader in Detroit and later Chicago. In Detroit, he arranged and produced several big hits for **Ric Tic**, notably **Edwin Starr**'s 'Stop Her On Sight' and the **Reflections**' 'Just Like Romeo And Juliet'. In Chicago, working under producer **Carl Davis** he arranged such hits as **Mary Wells**'s 'Dear Lover', the **Artistics**' 'I'm Gonna Miss You', **Barbara Acklin**'s 'Love Makes A Woman', and **Gene Chandler**'s 'The Girl Don't Care'. Sanders was one of the key behind-the-scenes talents in the success of the **Brunswick** label during the late 60s and early 70s.

Satriani, Joe

Joe Satriani grew up in Long Island, New York, USA, and is a skilled guitarist responsible for teaching the instrument to, among others, Kirk Hammett of **Metallica**, and **Steve Vai**. After travelling abroad extensively in his youth he returned to the USA to form the Squares. This project folded in 1984 through an abject lack of commercial recognition, giving Satriani the opportunity to concentrate on his experimental guitar playing. The outcome of this was the release of an EP, *Joe Satriani*. Following a spell with the **Greg Kihn** band, appearing on *Love And Rock 'N' Roll*, Satriani released *Not Of This Earth*, an album which was less polished than its successor, *Surfing With The Alien*. Despite offering no vocal accompaniment, this set was a major seller and brought mainstream respect to an artist often felt to be too clinical or technical for such reward. In 1988 he was joined more permanently by Stu Hamm (bass) and Jonathan Mover (drums), also working for a spell on **Mick Jagger**'s late-80s tour. Never afraid to push his considerable musical skills to the limit, Satriani has played the banjo and harmonica on his albums, as well as successfully attempting vocals on *Flying In A Blue Dream*. In 1993 he released *Time Machine*, a double CD which contained a mixture of new and previously unreleased tracks dating back to 1984, and also live material from his 1993 Extremist world tour. The guitarist then replaced **Ritchie Blackmore** in **Deep Purple** in 1994.

Albums: *Not Of This Earth* (Relativity 1986), *Surfing With The Alien* (Relativity 1987), *Dreaming 11* (Relativity 1988), *Flying In A Blue Dream* (Relativity 1990), *Time Machine* (1993, double album).

Saturday Night Fever

One of the most popular films of the 1970s, *Saturday Night Fever* (1977) launched **John Travolta** as a teen idol. He starred as a member of a Brooklyn street gang, obsessed by dancing which provides a release from his impoverished background. Travolta's routines were remarkable - inspiring numerous pastiches - and his portrayal of the inarticulate central character is highly convincing. Sadly, several external factors have robbed *Saturday Night Fever* of its undoubted strengths. An expurgated version, undertaken to reach a younger audience, has become the print through which many encounter the film. This trimming robbed it of dramatic purpose, editing 'bad' language, sex scenes and violence integral to the plot. More crucially, disco music did not enjoy critical popularity and many disparaged *Saturday Night Fever* on this premise alone. This did not stop the soundtrack becoming, for a while, the best-selling album of all time, retaining the UK number 1 spot for 18 consecutive weeks. Despite contributions from **Tavares** and the **Trammps**, it is chiefly remembered for several excellent tracks by the **Bee Gees**. Four selections, 'How Deep Is Your Love', 'More Than A Woman', 'Staying Alive' and 'You Should Be Dancing' reached the UK Top 10 in their own right as singles, while 'Night Fever' held the top spot in 1978. Had *Saturday Night Fever* charted punk, it would probably have enjoyed greater approbation. As it stands, it remains a taught, absorbing teen-orientated film.

Saunders, Merl

b. 14 February 1934, San Mateo, California, USA. Merl Saunders was best known for his keyboard playing in a 70s band with **Jerry Garcia**, lead guitarist of the **Grateful Dead**. Saunders began playing keyboards professionally at the age of 13 in San Francisco, concentrating on the organ after hearing jazz organist **Jimmy Smith** in 1957. Saunders worked in jazz outfits with vibes player **Lionel Hampton** and vocalist **Billy Williams** in the early 60s and put together his own trio at the end of that decade. He recorded his first album with that trio and the **Ray Charles** Orchestra for Galaxy Records in 1968. That same year he served as musical director for a Broadway

musical in New York City, *Big Time Buck White*, with jazz vocalist **Oscar Brown Jnr**. Following that he stayed on Broadway as musical director for a show starring boxer Muhammad Ali, providing drummer **Billy Cobham** with one of his first professional gigs. After recording with **Harry Belafonte** Saunders returned to San Francisco and associated with the local rock and blues musicians such as **Mike Bloomfield** and **Nick Gravenites**. Introduced to Garcia in 1971, Saunders sat in with the Dead leader at small club dates and added keyboard parts to the Dead's 1971 live album. Following a brief spell with the **Paul Butterfield** blues band in New York, Saunders returned to San Francisco and formed a steadier liaison with Garcia. A band including second guitarist Tom Fogerty, formerly of **Creedence Clearwater Revival**, drummer Bill Vitt from **Sons Of Champlin** and bassist John Kahn (**New Riders Of The Purple Sage**) performed regular club dates whenever Garcia was free. They recorded two studio albums and one live for **Fantasy Records** in 1972-73, with former **Elvis Presley** drummer Ron Tutt replacing Vitt and Fogerty leaving the band during the latter stages of its career. Saunders and Garcia parted company in the mid-70s and the keyboardist continued to record and perform live with various bands of his own into the 80s and 90s. He also wrote music for the revitalized *Twilight Zone* television programme, bringing in Garcia and other Dead members. In 1984 he joined the **Dinosaurs**, a group consisting of former members of 60s San Francisco bands. Saunders' *Blues From The Rainforest*, reunited him with Garcia in 1990.

Albums: *Soul Groovin'* (1968), *Heavy Turbulence* (1972), *Fire Up* (1973), with Jerry Garcia *Live At Keystone* (1973), *Merl Saunders* (1974), *You Can Keep Your Hat On* (1976), *Do I Move You* (1979), *San Francisco After Dark* (1982), *Meridien Dreams* (1987), *Blues From The Rainforest* (1990).

Saunders, Red

b. Theodore Saunders, 2 March 1912, Memphis, Tennessee, USA, d. 4 March 1981, Chicago, Illinois, USA. One of the two claims to fame that Saunders had was his position as leader of the houseband in Chicago's Club DeLisa, a tenure that lasted two decades up to 1958. During that time, the prevailing taste in music ranged from jazz to blues and R&B and he worked with **Albert Ammons**, **Louis Armstrong**, **Duke Ellington** and **Woody Herman**. Saunders studied percussion at school in Milwaukee, principally drums also vibes and tympani. Before taking up his position at the Club DeLisa, he was with **Tiny Parham**'s Savoy Ballroom Orchestra. He recorded for **Savoy**, Sultan and Supreme before securing a contract with **OKeh**. The featured vocalist on his 1950/1 sessions was **Jumpin' Joe Williams**, some years and a coat of polish before his stint with **Count Basie**. Saunders' other claim to fame was a ramshackle 1952 novelty hit, 'Hambone'. The 'Hambone Kids', Sammy McGrier, Ronny Strong and Delecta Clark (who grew up to become **Dee Clark**), patted 'juba', slapping their bodies in syncopated rhythm, between singing childish verses that anticipated 'Bo Diddley', while Dolores Hawkins ejaculated 'Yeah!' at the end of each stanza.

Compilations: *Okeh Rhythm & Blues* (Epic 1982), *The OKeh Rhythm & Blues Story 1949-1957* (Epic/Legacy 1993).

Sauter, Eddie

b. 2 December 1914, New York City, New York, USA, d. 21 April 1981. After studying arranging and composition at the Juilliard School of Music, Sauter became staff arranger for **Red Norvo**. In 1939, after four years with Norvo, he freelanced, writing charts for several prominent big bands, including **Artie Shaw**, **Woody Herman** and **Tommy Dorsey**. He made his greatest impact with **Benny Goodman**, for whom he wrote 'Clarinet A La King' in the early 40s. He later worked for **Ray McKinley** where, unusually for an arranger at that time (or any other), he was given prominent billing. While hospitalized with tuberculosis Sauter began corresponding with **Bill Finegan** and in 1952 the two arrangers formed their own orchestra. The resulting 21-piece band was conceived as a studio band, but its records, which included the joyous 'The Doodletown Fifers' and the irresistible 'Midnight Sleigh Ride', were so popular that they took it on the road. In 1957, Sauter became musical director of the South-West German Radio Big Band in Baden-Baden. He later worked with **Stan Getz**, the New York Saxophone Quartet and in films and television.

Selected albums: *The Sauter-Finegan Orchestra* (1952), *Historic Donanschingen Jazz Concert 1957* (1957), by Stan Getz *Focus* (1961), *The New York Saxophone Quartet* (1980). Compilations: *Eddie Sauter In Germany (1975-58)* (1980), *The Return Of The Doodletown Fifers* (1985), *Directions In Music* (1989).

Sauter-Finegan Orchestra

(see **Sauter, Eddie**; **Finegan, Bill**)

Savage

Formed in Mansfield, England, in 1978, Savage's line-up consisted of Chris Bradley (bass/vocals), Andy Dawson (guitar), Wayne Redshaw (guitar) and Mark Brown (drums). Their debut album, *Loose 'N' Lethal*, won critical acclaim for its ultra-heavy riffs and was firmly rooted in the **New Wave Of British Heavy Metal**. The band then toured Europe where they quickly gained popularity, especially in Holland. Similar success in their homeland was not so forthcoming. In 1984 the band signed a new recording agreement with Zebra Records who released an EP, *We Got The Edge*. This revealed an amended approach with

a mellower, more cultured sound. Restraint was also in evidence on 1985's *Hyperactive*. After this, Savage seemed to lose both momentum and direction and they disbanded in 1986.

Albums: *Loose 'N' Lethal* (Ebony 1983), *Hyperactive* (Zebra 1985).

Savage Grace

No relation to the early 70s group who recorded for **Reprise Records**, this USA power-metal quartet, originally titled Maquis De Sade, were formed in Los Angeles, California, in 1981. Since then they have enjoyed a chequered career hindered by unstable line-ups, the first of which featured Mike Smith (vocals), Chris Logue (guitar/vocals), Brian East (bass) and Dan Finch (drums). They were signed on the strength of a track included on the *Metal Massacre* series of compilations and a self-financed EP, *The Dominatress*, which the band had released in 1983. *Master Of Disguise*, their full debut from 1985, preceded their first line-up changes; ex-**Agent Steel** guitarist Mark Marshall was added, while Mike Smith's departure left Chris Logue to handle the lead vocals. Drummer Dan Finch also quit to be replaced by Mark Markum. This incarnation of the band managed to stay together long enough to record 1986's *After The Fall From Grace*. Savage Grace then toured Europe with **Heir Apparent** and swapped bassist Brian East for that band's Derek Peace before beginning work on recordings for a projected third album. However, the continual line-up shuffles had taken their toll and Peace rejoined Heir Apparent as Savage Grace disappeared late in 1988.

Albums: *Master Of Disguise* (Metal Blade 1985), *After The Fall From Grace* (Black Dragon 1986).

Savage Resurrection

This late 60s, US group comprised John Palmer, Steve Lange, Bill Harper, Randy Hammon and Jeff Myer. Despite their brief lifespan, the band completed one of the most assured albums of their era. Palmer wrote most of the group's material, including the Eastern-tinged 'Expectations' and the fiery 'Thing In E', which was also issued as a single. However, it was Lange's guitar work which provided many highlights, with a style combining the urgency of garage-punk and the experimentation marking the era. Savage Resurrection broke up soon afterwards. Myer later became one of the Bay Area's renowned drummers, appearing with **Jesse Colin Young** and the ever-shifting **Terry And The Pirates**.

Album: *Savage Resurrection* (1968).

Savage Seven, The

Richard Rush, veteran of the American International Pictures' treadmill, directed this 1969 feature which drew upon the legacy of 'biker' movies *The Wild Angels* and *Hells Angels On Wheels*. A Californian shanty town provides the setting for battles between a motorcycle gang and Native Americans, paying lip-service to the former's standing as 'outlaws of America.' Guitarist **Duane Eddy**, responsible for a string of late 50s/early 60s hits, including 'Rebel Rouser', 'Cannonball' and 'Shazam', is unaccustomably featured in an acting role, portraying one of the unruly misfits. **Mike Curb**, whose Sidewalk company was responsible for scoring many of the exploitation movies from the AIP group and others, assembled a soundtrack which included 'Anyone For Tennis (The Savage Seven Theme)' by **Cream**. This lilting pop song, which grazed the UK Top 40 when issued as a single, had nothing to do with the film plot, suggesting it was a recording the group would otherwise have held in abeyance. Clearly inspired by *The Magnificent Seven*, the *Savage Seven* has little of the former's lasting qualities.

Savalas, Telly

d. January 1994. Although a successful actor in various film and television roles, Savalas will always be most closely identified with the title role of detective series *Kojak*, his bald head, liking for lollipops (boosting sales by 500% when the series was at its peak) and fondness for phrases like 'Who Loves Ya Baby?' building something approaching a 70s icon. However, he also enjoyed a briefly successful singing career, sending a sentimental cover of **David Gates**' 'If' to number 1 in the UK charts in February 1975. His croaky, melodramatic version seemed to capture some of Kojak's charisma, but its follow-up, a version of the **Righteous Brothers**' 'You've Lost That Lovin' Feeling', had even less appeal.
Album: *Telly* (MCA 1975).

Savatage

Previously known as Metropolis and **Avatar**, Savatage, a melodic, heavy rock quintet, were formed in Florida, USA, in 1983 by the Oliva brothers. The full band line-up comprised Jon Oliva (vocals/keyboards), Criss Oliva (guitar), Steve 'Doc' Wacholz (drums) and Keith Collins (bass), the latter eventually replaced by Johnny Lee Middleton. Their initial approach was strongly influenced by **Judas Priest** and **Iron Maiden**, a style demonstrated by their *City Beneath The Surface* EP from their year of formation. Savatage's first three albums also clearly reflect their influences, with a high-energy fusion of power-riffs and high-pitched vocals. *Fight For The Rock* marked a detour towards more melodic AOR, which was poorly received by their fans, before returning to their roots for the next album. Chris Caffery was added as a second guitarist in 1989, before the recording of *Gutter Ballet*. This, and *Streets*, represented the band's finest work to this point. Both were elaborate rock operas, featuring a mixture of dynamic hard rock and atmospheric ballads. Utilizing an orchestra and state-of-the-art production techniques, they also found themselves with a minor hit single on their hands in the shape of 'Jesus Saves'. Jon Oliva was then relegated to nominal backing vocals behind new frontman Zachary Stevens - having elected instead to concentrate on penning rock operas full time and working as part of **Doctor Butcher**. Stevens was ex-White Witch, and joined in time for 1993's *Edge Of Thorns*. That year also brought tragedy when founding member and guitarist Criss Oliva was killed in October in a car crash near his home in Clearwater, Florida. For *Handful Of Rain* the group recruited ex-**Testament** guitarist Alex Skolnick, whose former band had toured with Savatage in support of **Dio** in 1989. The set included one notable tribute to the late guitarist, 'Alone I Breathed'. 'Watching You Fall', meanwhile, discussed the war in Bosnia.
Albums: *Sirens* (Music For Nations 1985), *The Dungeons Are Calling* (Music For Nations 1985, mini-album), *Power Of The Night* (Atlantic 1985), *Fight For The Rock* (Atlantic 1986), *Hall Of The Mountain King* (Atlantic 1987), *Gutter Ballet* (Atlantic 1990), *Streets* (Atlantic 1991), *Edge Of Thorns* (Bullet Proof 1993), *Handfull Of Rain* (Bullet Proof 1994).

Savitt, Jan

b. 4 September 1913, St. Petersburg, Russia, d. 4 October 1948. A violin-playing leader of a well-drilled dance orchestra, Savitt's father played in Tsar Nicholas II's Imperial Regiment Band. When he was 18-months-old the family moved to the USA, and Savitt was raised in Philadelphia and attended the Curtis Institute. He studied the violin from the age of six, and at 15 was invited by Leopold Stokowski to join the Philadelphia Symphony Orchestra. After forming a string quartet and broadcasting nationwide, Savitt turned to popular music in 1937, creating his dance band, the Top Hatters, with its distinctive shuffle rhythm and theme, 'Quaker City Jazz'. Their first major hit, 'Hi-Yo, Silver' in 1938, featured a vocal by **Bon Bon** (George Tunnell), one of the first black singers to work with a white band. Other Savitt vocalists included Carlotta Dale, **Gloria De Haven** and Alan DeWitt. During the late 30s/early 40s Savitt had several other hits on Bluebird and **Decca** including 'Make Believe Island', 'Where Was I?', 'Tuxedo Junction' and his own compositions, '720 In The Books' (a swing era classic), 'Meadowbrook Shuffle' and 'It's A Wonderful World'. In the 40s he also recorded popular versions of well-known classical pieces, and made low-budget movies such as *Betty Coed* and *High School Hero*. Post-war, he led a smaller band of eight musicians and was still active until his death, from a cerebral haemorrhage, on the way to an engagement in Sacramento, California.
Albums: *In Disco Order, Volume 1* (1977), *Jan Savitt 1938, Volume 2 & 3* (1979), *Futuristic Shuffle 1938-41* (1988), *Jan Savitt And The Top Hatters* (1989).

Savoy Brown

Formed in 1966 as the Savoy Brown Blues Band, this institution continues to be led by founding guitarist Kim Simmonds. The original line-up comprising Simmonds (b. 6 December 1947), Brice Portius (vocals), Ray Chappell (bass), John O'Leary (harmonica), Bob Hall (piano) and Leo Mannings (drums), were featured on early sessions for producer **Mike Vernon**'s Purdah label, before a second guitarist, Martin Stone, joined in place of O'Leary. The re-shaped sextet then secured a recording deal with **Decca**. Their debut *Shake Down*, was a competent appraisal of blues favourites, featuring material by **Freddie King**, **Albert King** and **Willie Dixon**.

Unhappy with this reverential approach, Simmonds pulled the group apart, retaining Hall on an auxiliary basis and adding Chris Youlden (vocals), Dave Peverett (guitar/vocals), Rivers Jobe (bass) and Roger Earl (drums). The new line-up completed *Getting To The Point* before Jobe was replaced by Tone Stevens. The restructured unit was an integral part of the British blues boom. In Youlden they possessed a striking frontman, resplendent in bowler hat and monocle, whose confident, mature delivery added panache to the group's repertoire. Their original songs matched those they chose to cover, while the Simmonds/Peverett interplay added fire to Savoy Brown's live performances. 'Train To Nowhere', from *Blue Matter*, has since become one of the genre's best-loved recordings. Youlden left the group following *Raw Sienna*, but the inner turbulence afflicting the group culminated at the end of 1970 when Peverett, Stevens and Earl walked out to form **Foghat**.

Simmonds meanwhile toured America with a restructured line-up - Dave Walker (vocals), Paul Raymond (keyboards), Andy Pyle (bass) and Dave Bidwell (drums) - setting a precedent for Savoy Brown's subsequent development. Having honed a simple, blues-boogie style, the guitarist now seemed content to repeat it and the group's ensuing releases are of decreasing interest. Simmonds later settled in America, undertaking gruelling tours with musicians who become available, his determination both undeterred and admirable.

Albums: *Shake Down* (Deram 1967), *Getting To The Point* (Deram 1968), *Blue Matter* (Deram 1969), *A Step Further* (Deram 1969), *Raw Sienna* (Deram 1970), *Looking In* (Deram 1970), *Street Corner Talking* (Deram 1971), *Hellbound Train* (Deram 1972), *Lion's Share* (Deram 1972), *Jack The Toad* (Deram 1973), *Boogie Brothers* (1974), *Wire Fire* (1975), *Skin 'N' Bone* (1976), *Savage Return* (1978), *Rock 'N' Roll Warriors* (1981), *Just Live* (1981), *A Hard Way To Go* (1985), *Make Me Sweat* (1988). Compilations: *The Best Of Savoy Brown* (1977), *Blues Roots* (1978), *Highway Blues* (1985).

Savoy Sultans

The Savoy Sultans were a highly accomplished US small band (usually nine pieces) led by alto saxophonist/clarinettist Al Cooper. They were formed originally out of a band in which Cooper and trumpeter Pat Jenkins had played at New York's 101 Club and New Jersey's Harlem-on-the-Hudson. The band was heard by **John Hammond** and **Willie Bryant** who recommended them to Charles Buchanan, manager of the Savoy Ballroom in New York's Harlem. The band opened at the Savoy on Labor Day, 1937, and was an instant success with the Savoy's hyper-critical dancers.

The Sultans had excellent soloists in Sam Massenberg (trumpet), **George Kelly** (tenor saxophone) and **Rudy Williams** (alto saxophone), and had a fine rhythm section in pianist Cyril Haynes (piano), Grachan Moncur (bass, also Cooper's half-brother and father of trombonist **Grachan Moncur III**) and Razz Mitchell (drums). Despite its relatively small size and its occasionally rather rudimentary arrangements, the Sultans swung mightily and maintained their popularity, and a remarkably stable personnel, until they broke up in 1946. Stylistically, the Sultans' brand of swinging dance music was slightly aside from that offered by most big bands of the day and had greater affinity with the small jump bands of the same period. In 1974, **David 'Panama' Francis**, who had played drums with the **Lucky Millinder** band in the early 40s, formed a small band modelled on the original Sultans. From the late 70s and on into the 90s, Panama Francis And His Savoy Sultans, which regularly included Kelly in its ranks, revived the spirit of the original band while offering its own exciting brand of swinging jazz music.

Saw Doctors

Originating in Tuam, County Galway, Eire, the Saw Doctors continue the practice of rock reacquainting itself with traditional Gaelic music. Inspired by the madcap antics of the **Pogues** et al, the medium is a furious medley of traditional and modern instruments, meshing together in boozy singalongs or sombre ballads. They signed to **WEA** in 1992 for *All The Way From Tuam*, but they had made their mark with an independent debut featuring 'I Usta Love Her'. The latter would become Eire's biggest selling single of all time. Peviously Leo Moran (vocals) had been playing guitar with the local reggae-folk outfit Too Much For The White Man. Fellow Tuam 'sham'. Singer Davy Corton (guitar) was recruited - or perhaps brought out of retirement might be a more accurate description, the father of three having served time some years previously with local punk force Blase X. The duo next recruited mandolin player and traditional singer John 'Turps' Burke. Science student Pierce Doherty came in as bass player, the rhythm section filled out by the presence of ex-footballer John Donnelly. The startling sucess of 'I Usta Love Her' brought a re-release of debut single 'N17', and the band, fresh from supports to the **Waterboys**, were selling out venues on both sides of the Irish sea in their own right. They had been joined at this juncture by Tony Lambert (ex-**Racing Cars**, **Alex Harvey Band**; keyboards/piano accordion). Media assertions that these were 'designer bogmen' were enhanced by the choice of producer Phil Tennant (**Levellers**). However, support slots for bands such as **Genesis** at Knebworth demonstrated the breadth of their appeal.

Albums: *If This Is Rock 'n' Roll, I Want My Old Job Back* (1991), *All The Way From Tuam* (1992).

Sawyer Brown

The members of the band Sawyer Brown come from different parts of the USA: Mark Miller (b. Dayton, Ohio, USA vocals) and Gregg Hubbard (keyboards) were schoolfriends in Apopka, Florida: Bobby Randall (b. Midland, Michigan, USA, guitar) and Jim Scholten (b. Michigan, USA; bass) and Joe Smyth (drums) were part of the Maine Symphony Orchestra. They all came to Nashville around 1980 and took varying roles in singer Don King's band. In 1983 they decided to work together, without King, first as Savanna and then as Sawyer Brown, taking their name from a street in Nashville. In 1983, they took part in a US television talent show, *Star Search*. They won the first prize of $100,000 and a recording contract. Their first single, 'Leona', was a US country hit and they toured with **Kenny Rogers** and **Dolly Parton**. Miller wrote their second single, a country number l hit, 'Step That Step' (1985), about the perseverance needed in the music business. They established themselves as a goodtime country band and had further country hits with 'Used To Blue', 'Betty's Bein' Bad', 'This Missin' You Heart Of Mine' and a remake of **George Jones**' 'The Race Is On'. 'My Baby's Gone' made number 11 on the country charts in 1988, but they have since lost much of their impetus.

Albums: *Sawyer Brown* (1985), *Shakin'* (1986), *Out Goin' Cattin'* (1986), *Somewhere In The Night* (1987), *The Boys Are Back* (1989), *Dirt Road* (1992), *Cafe On The Corner* (1993), *Outskirts Of Town* (1993). Compilation: *Greatest Hits 1990-1995* (Curb 1995).

Videos: *Greatest Video Hits: Vol 2* (1993), *Outskirts Of Town (High Five)* (1994), *I Don't Believe In Goodbye (Curb)* (1995).

Saxon

Formed in the north of England in the late 70s, Saxon were originally known as Son Of A Bitch and spent their early days paying dues in clubs and small venues up and down the UK, with Peter 'Biff' Byford (vocals), Graham Oliver (guitar), Paul Quinn (guitar), Steve Dawson (bass) and Pete Gill (drums) building a strong live reputation. After the name switch they signed a deal with French label Carrere, better known for its disco productions than its work with heavy metal bands. During the late 70s many young metal bands were emerging in a UK scene which became known as the **New Wave Of British Heavy Metal**. These bands challenged the supremacy of the old guard of heavy metal bands, and Saxon were at the head of this movement along with **Iron Maiden** and **Diamond Head**. The first album was a solid, if basic heavy rock outing, but the release of *Wheels Of Steel* turned the tide. Saxon's popularity soared, earning themselves two UK Top 20 hits with 'Wheels Of Steel' and '747 (Strangers In The Night)'. They capitalized on this success with the release in the same year of *Strong Arm Of The Law*, another very heavy, surprisingly articulate, metal album. A further Top 20 hit arrived with 'And The Bands Played On', drawn from the following year's *Demin And Leather*, which also produced 'Never Surrender'. They toured the USA to great acclaim and appeared at the Castle Donington 'Monsters Of Rock' festival. By the time of 1982's *The Eagle Has Landed*, which gave Saxon their most successful album, reaching the UK Top 5, the group were at their peak. That same year, Pete Gill was replaced by drummer Nigel Glockler, who had previously worked with **Toyah**. At this point Saxon counted among their rivals only the immensely popular Iron Maiden. The release of *Power And The Glory* enforced their credentials as a major rock band. The follow-up, *Innocence Is No Excuse*, was a more polished and radio-friendly production but it stalled just inside the Top 40. It heralded an uncertain time for the band and a resulting slide in their popularity. The departure of Steve Dawson contributed to their malaise. *Rock The Nations* was as punishing as old, but the chance to recapture former glories had now expired. In 1990 Saxon returned to the public eye with a UK tour that featured a set-list built on their popular older material. *Solid Ball Of Rock* was their most accomplished album for some time, but any return to their previous status seems unlikely.

Albums: *Saxon* (Saxon Carrere 1979), *Wheels Of Steel* (Saxon Carrere 1980), *Strong Arm Of The Law* (Carrere 1980), *Denim And Leather* (Carrere 1981), *The Eagle Has Landed* (Carrere 1982), *Power And The Glory* (Carrere 1983), *Crusader* (Carrere 1984), *Innocence Is No Excuse* (Parlophone 1985), *Rock The Nations* (EMI 1986), *Destiny* (EMI 1988), *Rock 'N' Roll Gypsies* (Roadrunner 1990), *Solid Ball Of Rock* (Virgin 1991), *Dogs Of War* (HTD 1995). Compilations: *Anthology* (Raw Power 1988), *Back On The Streets* (Connoisseur 1990), *Greatest Hits Live* (Essential 1990), *Best Of* (EMI 1991).

Videos: *Live Innocence* (1986), *Power & The Glory - Video Anthology* (1989), *Saxon Live* (1989), *Greatest Hits Live* (1990).

Saxon, Sky

b. Richard Marsh. Saxon emerged from the nascent Los Angeles music circle during the early 60s. He recorded 'Goodbye' as Little Richie Marsh, before taking his above sobriquet as the frontperson of two groups, the Soul Rockers and the Electra Fires. In 1965 he formed the **Seeds**, arguably the city's finest punk/garage group, which later evolved into a psychedelic/flower-power attraction. Although the quartet split up officially in 1969, Saxon retained the name for a series of increasingly deranged singles, including 'Love In A Summer Basket' and 'Shucking And Jiving'. The singer, who variously dubbed himself Sky Sunlight, Sunstar, or Sky Sunlight Saxon, subsequently founded several groups, known either as the Universal Stars Band or Star's New Seeds Band. A series of self-mythologizing, yet engaging, releases ensued, many of which featured cohort guitarist Rainbow. *Firewall* was a collaboration with Mars Bonfire, who wrote **Steppenwolf**'s million-seller, 'Born To Be Wild'. It featured cameos from several luminaries from the 'new psychedelic' movement, including members of the **Dream Syndicate**, **Yard Trauma** and the Plimsouls, in turn confirming Sky's revered status among this particular group of musicians. Now domiciled in Hawaii, Saxon remains an idiosyncratic figure, yet one who, in common with **Roky Erickson**, still commands a considerable cult following.

Albums: *Sunlight And The New Seeds* (1976), *In Love With Life* (1978), *Heavenly Earth - Live* (1978), *Starry Ride* (1983), *Masters Of Psychedelia* (1984), *A Groovy Thing* (1986), *Firewall* (1986), as Sky Sunlight Saxon And Firewall *In Search Of Brighter Colours* (1988). Compilation: *Retrospective* (1986).

Saxophone

Invented by Belgian-born Adolphe Sax around 1840, the saxophone is usually constructed from brass but employs a reed in the mouthpiece. The instrument thus combines some of the elements of brass and woodwinds. The body of the saxophone is made from brass tubing which tapers conically. Holes in the tube are covered by movable keys which can be operated singly or in groups by the player. The mouthpiece, made of wood in Sax's day, is fitted with a detachable reed over which the player breathes air into the body of the instrument. Vibration of the reed produces variations in sound that can incorporate further individual characteristics desired by the player. Some saxophones have been made of plastic instead of metal but have not proved popular with musicians. Designed as an addition to the range of instruments available for use by classical composers, the saxophone made little impact upon the genre - although Debussy, Ibert and Ravel were amongst the handful who did incorporate the instrument in their scores. However, it was generally regarded as something of a novelty by musicians and audiences in most fields; the exception being military bands in several European countries and in the USA, which adopted it enthusiastically. In the early years of the 20th century the saxophone was used by the popular bandleader **John Philip Sousa** and also by an entertainer named Rudy Wiedoeft, who used a saxophone in his vaudeville act in the USA. Wiedoeft also made records and through this medium attracted the attention of some jazz and danceband musicians. Broad similarities in construction and fingering between the saxophone and the clarinet, a genuine woodwind, made it an instrument that was relatively easy for these players to take up. Saxophones are made in a variety of sizes, each with its own characteristic sounds and range. Although the soprano saxophone was the first to make a significant impact on jazz, thanks to the decision by clarinettist **Sidney Bechet** to adopt the instrument, it was the alto and tenor saxophones which proved to be the most popular in jazz and dance bands and, through them, popular music at large. Eventually, the sound of the saxophone became synonymous with jazz and replaced the trumpet as the instrument upon which most musical innovations were wrought. The stronger, more robust sound of the tenor saxophone found favour first through the playing of **Coleman Hawkins** and a great tradition of players came in his wake, amongst them **Herschel Evans**, **Chu Berry**, **Buddy Tate**, **Ben Webster**, **Arnett Cobb**, **Illinois Jacquet** and **Joe 'Flip' Phillips**. Although he also played tenor, **Lester Young** displayed the versatility of the instrument and its propensity for allowing a musician to develop his own characteristic sound. In his turn, Young spawned a succession of fine players, including **Al Cohn**, **Stan Getz**, **Warne Marsh** and **Zoot Sims**. Jazz saxophonists who drew elements from both Hawkins and Young included **Dexter Gordon**, **John Coltrane** and **Sonny Rollins**, while more recent outstanding proponents include **Albert Ayler**, **Wayne Shorter** and **David Murray**.

The alto saxophone had its own early exponents in jazz and dance music, notably **Jimmy Dorsey** (a virtuoso performer), **Johnny Hodges**, **Benny Carter** and **Willie Smith**. However, it was not until the appearance of **Charlie Parker** that the alto challenged the tenor as a major instrument in jazz. Parker revolutionized jazz and in his wake came many major players, such as **Art Pepper** and **Sonny Stitt**. Other important jazz alto saxophonists, some of whom forged their own distinctive style, included **Lee Konitz**, **Ornette Coleman**, **Paul Desmond**, **Jackie McLean**, **Eric Dolphy** and **Anthony Braxton**. Although the alto and tenor are the most popular of the many instruments in the saxophone family, the baritone has found its jazz champions, notably **Harry Carney**, **Serge Chaloff**, **Gerry Mulligan**, **Cecil Payne**, **Ronnie Ross**, **John Barnes, John Surman** and **Alan Barnes**. For many years Bechet remained unchallenged on soprano but one of his pupils, **Bob Wilber**, subsequently attained enormous success, as did **Kenny Davern** and **Steve Lacy**, while several important jazzmen doubled on the instrument, amongst them Coltrane, Braxton, Shorter and **Andy Sheppard**. Less popular but still used from time is the bass saxophone, amongst the players of which are **Adrian Rollini** and **Harry Gold**. The C-melody saxophone is a rarity today but in the 20s and early 30s found a distinctive exponent in **Frankie Trumbauer**.

Contemporaneously with its rise in popularity in jazz, the saxophone found its niche in the world of popular dance music. The sound of the instrument lent itself to the melodic and harmonic needs of arrangers writing for 20s dancebands and by the early 30s the saxophone section was an established part of all big bands. Eventually, the section settled down to a standard form at two altos, two tenors and one baritone saxophone. With some musicians doubling on two or more saxophones and on clarinet, a five-piece section could have at the disposal of the arranger as many as a dozen instrumental sounds. The section thus became the most useful of the arranger's tools and in time its sound was also the most redolent of the 20s, the so-called 'Jazz Age', and the 30s and early 40s, the swing era. Stylistically, the music played by the saxophone section could vary enormously. There was the biting, gritty sound of the **Jimmie Lunceford** band, the sweetness of **Glenn Miller** and **Guy Lombardo**, and the power and volume of **Stan Kenton**. There was also the coy corn of **Sammy Kaye** and, light-years away, the highly individualistic sound of the **Duke Ellington** saxophone section.

By the 40s changes had begun to make their appearance in popular music, amongst them the advent of R&B. The possibilities of the saxophone, probably never even imagined by its inventor, included 'honking' and 'screaming' and such vocalizations fitted into the highly charged atmosphere generated by R&B singers. One of the early stars of the genre, and a major factor in popularizing the music, was **Louis Jordan**, who not only sang but also played alto saxophone, having begun his career in the big bands. Many R&B bands featured saxophonists, usually tenors because their harder, more rasping sound, suited the music. Players such as **King Curtis**, **Sam 'The Man' Taylor**, **Bullmoose Jackson**, **Big Jay McNeely** and **Earl Bostic** appeared on records, sometimes named, sometimes anonymous contributors to their success: **Boots Randolph** even had a hit with the riffing instrumental, 'Yakety Sax'. As R&B merged into rock 'n' roll the saxophonists lost some of their popularity, although a few bands, such as **Bill Haley**'s Comets, retained a

tenor player. Clarence Clemmons continued to incorporate this hard blowing R&B style with **Bruce Springsteen** during the 70s and 80s. Over the past thirty years the saxophone has been by far the most popular instrument in jazz but has not found comparable favour in the wider world of popular music, where the guitar has been predominant. However, a few performers saw the possibilities of the saxophone as a backing for their vocals. For example, **Billy Joel** included saxophone soloist **Phil Woods** on his hit 'I Love You Just The Way You Are', and **Gerry Rafferty**'s hit 'Baker Street' owed much to its accompanying saxophone riff, performed by Raphael Ravenscroft. Recent exponents have combined a rock background with a progression through to jazz, such as **David Sanborn**, Nelson Rangell, **Kenny G** and **Candy Dulfer**. Moreover, of all the instruments used in the performance of popular music, the saxophone is the one that has become most often synonymous with the form. Even the appearance of the instrument has found its way into art and design as a symbol of the ultimate in fashionable music.

Sayer, Leo

b. 21 May 1948, Shoreham-on-Sea, Sussex, England. Sayer fronted the Terraplane Blues Band and Phydeaux while a Sussex art student before moving to London, where he supplemented his wages as a typographic designer (during this time he designed 3 of his own typefaces) by street busking and via floor spots in folk clubs. In 1971, he formed Patches in Brighton who were managed by Dave Courtney to whose melodies he provided lyrics. Speculating in artist management, Courtney's former employer, **Adam Faith** found the group ultimately unimpressive and chose only to promote its animated X-factor - Sayer. During initial sessions at **Roger Daltrey**'s studio, the **Who**'s vocalist was sufficiently impressed by the raw material to record some Courtney-Sayer numbers himself. These included 'Giving It All Away', Daltrey's biggest solo hit. After a miss with 'Why Is Everybody Going Home', Sayer reached the UK number 1 spot with 1973's exuberant 'The Show Must Go On' but immediate US success was thwarted by a chart-topping cover by **Three Dog Night**. Seeing him mime the song in a clown costume and pan-caked face on BBC television's *Top Of The Pops*, some dismissed Sayer as a one-shot novelty, but he had the last laugh on such detractors when his popularity continued into the next decade. After 'One Man Band' and 'Long Tall Glasses' - the US Hot 100 breakthrough - came the severing of Sayer's partnership with Courtney in 1975 during the making of *Another Year*. With a new co-writer in Frank Furrell (ex-**Supertramp**) from his backing group, Sayer rallied with the clever 'Moonlighting'. Though the year ended on a sour note with an ill-advised version of the **Beatles**' 'Let It Be', 1976 brought a US million-seller in 'You Make Me Feel Like Dancing' just as disco sashayed near its *Saturday Night Fever* apogee. Sayer and Faith parted company shortly after the 'Let It Be' release. From 1977's *Endless Flight* (produced by fashionable **Richard Perry**), the non-original ballad, 'When I Need You', marked Sayer's commercial peak at home - where the BBC engaged him for two television series. However, with the title track of *Thunder In My Heart* halting just outside the UK Top 20, hits suddenly became harder to come by with 1978's 'I Can't Stop Lovin' You' and telling revivals of **Buddy Holly**'s 'Raining In My Heart' and **Bobby Vee**'s 'More Than I Can Say' the only unequivocal smashes as his 1983 chart swansong (with 'Till You Come Back To Me') loomed nearer. Nevertheless, even 1979's fallow period for singles was mitigated by huge returns for a compilation. By the late 80s Sayer was bereft of a recording contract, having severed his longstanding relationship with **Chrysalis Records** and was reduced to self-financing his UK tours. A legal wrangle with his former manager, Adam Faith, resulted in Sayer reportedly receiving £650,000 in lost royalties. Although a financial settlement was agreed, it was nowhere near the figure quoted, although Sayer did get back the ownership of his masters and song publishing. His recording career recommenced in 1990 after signing to **EMI** and was reunited with producer Alan Tarney. Indications of a revival in his chart fortunes remain to be seen; however, this artist has been written off twice before, in 1973 and 1979, and critics should not be so quick to do so again.

Albums: *Silver Bird* (1974), *Just A Boy* (1974), *Another Year* (1975), *Endless Flight* (1976), *Thunder In My Heart* (1977), *Leo Sayer* (1978), *Here* (1979), *Living In A Fantasy* (1980), *World Radio* (1982), *Have You Ever Been In Love* (1983), *Cool Touch* (1990). Compilations: *The Very Best Of Leo Sayer* (1979), *All The Best* (1993).

Sayles, Charlie

b. 4 January 1948, Woburn, Massachusetts, USA. Sayles only became acquainted with the blues when he heard a record by **B.B. King** during his US military service in Vietnam, and began to take a serious interest in playing harmonica in 1971. During the 70s he played frequently on the streets in cities across the country, and was put on the bill of several folk festivals. His original blues compositions, raw, amplified harmonica and direct singing were captured on vinyl in 1976, when he was playing in New York. Sayles began working with a small band around 1980, but he still remains largely an uncompromising street and solo performer. In 1990 he recorded for the JSP label, to coincide with a British tour.

Albums: *The Raw Harmonica Blues Of Charlie Sayles* (1976), *Night Ain't Right* (1990).

Sayles, Johnny

b. 9 February 1937, Winnsboro, Texas, USA, d. 17 August 1993, Chicago, Illinois, USA. Sayles was arguably one of the finest 'tough-soul' singers of the earliest (early 60s) soul era, and several of his recordings for George Leaner's Chicago-based Mar-V-Lus label are as potent and telling as anything cut by far better-known singers, such as **Wilson Pickett** and **Otis Clay**. Sayles only had four sides released at the time, but several others were reissued later on a superb Japanese album. At the age of 18, he moved to St. Louis and worked with Eugene Neal's Rocking Kings, **Ike Turner**'s local Kings Of Rhythm, and fronted his own band at **Chuck Berry**'s Paradise Club. After quitting music for a time to study in Houston, in 1963 he joined the **Five Dutones** Review tour, playing the role of **Little Johnny Taylor**, who had a current R&B number 1 hit with 'Part Time Love'. His first recording for Leaner, the fine uptempo 'Don't Turn Your Back On Me', featured Sayles' driving tough-soul vocal, and was coupled with 'You Told A Lie', a great **Bobby 'Blue' Bland**-style, 'bluesoul' track. His second release, 'You Did Me Wrong' (May 1964), with its metronomic slow, plodding beat, appeals equally to both blues and deep-soul lovers. It was backed by 'Got You On My Mind', an even slower and more bluesy number. Further Mar-V-Lus releases, included the mid-paced 'Tell Me Where I Stand' and 'The Girl That I Love', Subsequently, Sayles joined a **Lou Rawls** show in Alaska, and his later Leaner recordings were not available until the 80s Japanese P-Vine album. After leaving Rawls, Sayles joined ex-Leaner producer Monk Higgins, and recorded the outstanding 'Nothing But Hard Rocks', which was released on Chi-Town. He worked for several other labels, including St Lawrence, **Chess** and Minit, where his 'Anything For You' became a UK northern-soul favourite when it was issued on **Liberty**. For the Dakar label, Sayles cut 'Somebody's Changing My Sweet Baby's Mind', which had been intended as a follow-up to **Tyrone Davis**' first hit for the label 'Can I Change My Mind'; and *Man On The Inside*, but continued to eschew recording in favour of live performances. Reported to have always wanted to sing 'sweet' like **Roy Hamilton**, his vocal power was immense, and, at times, his stage presence is said to have rivalled even that of **James Brown**.

Album: *Man On The Inside* (c.80s). Compilation: *Soul On Fire* (1981, 9 tracks).

Sbarbaro, Tony

b. 27 June 1897, New Orleans, Louisiana, USA, d. 30 October 1969. After playing drums in several local bands in his home town, Sbarbaro moved to Chicago where, in 1916, he became a member of the **Original Dixieland Jazz Band**. In 1925 he took over leadership of the band and was involved in various

ODJB recreations and reformations for much of the next three decades, often playing kazoo as well as drums. Although he did not have the polished jazz technique of his black counterparts from New Orleans, or indeed of some of the better white dixieland drummers, Sbarbaro (who frequently used the name **Tony Spargo**) was a lively drummer who brought great enthusiasm to his performances.
Album: *The Original Dixieland Jazz Band (1918-36)* (1979).

SBK Records

Formed in the summer of 1989 as an outgrowth of a production company also called SBK (among whose clients was folk singer **Tracy Chapman**), this US record company had already become a major player in the music industry within its first year. The company was formed in 1986 by Stephen Swid (who left the firm before the record division was launched), former real estate lawyer Martin Bandier (b. 1941) and Charles Koppelman (b. 1940), the latter a 30-year music business veteran who had produced records for artists including **Dolly Parton**, **Neil Diamond** and **Barbra Streisand**. In 1986 the firm purchased the **CBS** music publishing division for $125 million, giving it ownership of some 200,000 songs. In 1989 they sold that catalogue to UK entertainment company Thorn-**EMI** for $295 million. Of that sum, $30 million went toward the establishment of the record company. SBK Records released less than 20 albums in its first year, but among those were **Wilson Phillips**, a US number 1 which became one of the largest selling debut album's of all time (8 million), the soundtrack of hit film *Teenage Mutant Ninja Turtles* and Technotronic's *Pump Up The Jam*. SBK had placed over 12 singles on the US pop charts by mid-1990 and had grossed over $50 million worldwide.

Scafell Pike

An electric folk band with English and Swedish members. They displayed dubious taste by covering essential folk classics such as 'The Roast Beef Of Old England'. Despite this, they earned a contract with both Epic and Phonogram.
Selected album: *Lord's Rake* (1974).

Scaffold

Formed in Liverpool, England in 1962, the Scaffold was the unlikely confluence of two concurrent 'booms' - satire and Merseybeat. Poet Roger McGough (b. 9 November 1937) and humorist John Gorman (b. 4 January 1937) joined **Mike McGear** (b. Michael McCartney, 7 January 1944), younger brother of **Paul McCartney**, to create an act not solely reliant on pop for success. They contributed material to *Gazteet*, a late-night programme on ABC-Television and following an acclaimed residency at London's Establishment club, took their 'Birds, Marriages and Deaths' revue to the 1964 Edinburgh Festival, where they would return on several occasions. Although the trio enjoyed major hits with 'Thank U Very Much' (1967) and 'Lily The Pink' (1968) - the latter of which was a massive Christmas UK number 1 - these tongue-in-cheek releases contrasted the group's in-concert revues and albums. Here McGough's poetry and Gorman's comedy routines were of equal importance and their versatility was confirmed on *The Scaffold* and *L The P*. The schoolboy-ish 'Gin Gan Goolie' gave the group a minor chart entry in 1969, before the unit was absorbed by **Grimms**, a larger, if similarly constituted, act which also featured members of the **Liverpool Scene**. On its demise McGear recorded *Woman*, before agreeing to resurrect Scaffold for *Fresh Liver* on which **Zoot Money** (keyboards) and Ollie Halsall (guitar) joined the **Average White Band** horn section to help bring a rock-based perspective to the trio's work. The haunting 'Liverpool Lou' provided another UK Top 10 hit in 1974, but the founder members embarked on separate paths following *Sold Out*. McGear resumed his solo career, and became a credible photographer, while McGough returned to writing poetry. Gorman pursued a career in television, principally on the cult UK television children's show *Tiswas* and was back in the UK charts alongside Sally James, Chris Tarrant and Lenny Henry as the **Four Bucketeers** with 'The Bucket Of Water Song' in 1980.
Albums: *The Scaffold* (1967), *L The P* (1968), *Lily The Pink* (1969), *Fresh Liver* (1973), *Sold Out* (1974). Compilation: *The Singles A's And B's* (1984).

Scaggs, Boz

b. William Royce Scaggs, 8 June 1944, Ohio, USA. Scaggs was raised in Dallas, Texas, where he joined fellow guitarist **Steve Miller** in a high-school group, the Marksmen. The musicians maintained this partnership in the Ardells, a group they formed at the University of Wisconsin, but this early association ended when Scaggs returned to Texas. Boz then formed an R&B unit, the Wigs, whom he took to London in anticipation of a more receptive audience. The group broke up when this failed to materialize and the guitarist headed for mainland Europe where he forged a career as an itinerant folk-singer. Scaggs was particularly successful in Sweden, where he recorded a rudimentary solo album, *Boz*. This interlude in exile ended in 1967 when he received an invitation from his erstwhile colleague to join the fledgling Steve Miller Band. Scaggs recorded two albums with this pioneering unit but left for a solo career in 1968. *Boz Scaggs*, recorded at the renowned Fame studios in **Muscle Shoals**, was a magnificent offering and featured sterling contributions from **Duane Allman**, particularly on the extended reading of Fenton Robinson's 'Loan Me A Dime'. Over the next five years, Boz forged an exemplary soul/rock direction with several excellent albums, including *My Time* and *Slow Dancer*. Skilled production work from **Glyn Johns** and **Johnny Bristol** reinforced a high quality, but it was not until 1976, and the smooth *Silk Degrees*, that this was translated into commercial success. A slick session band, which later became **Toto**, enhanced some of Scaggs' finest compositions, including 'Lowdown' (a US chart number 3 hit), 'What Can I Say?' and 'Lido Shuffle', each of which reached the UK Top 30. The album also featured 'We're All Alone', which has since become a standard. Paradoxically the singer's career faltered in the wake of this exceptional album and despite enjoying several hit singles during 1980, Scaggs maintained a low profile during the subsequent decade. It was eight years before a new selection, *Other Roads* appeared and a further six before *Some Change*. The latter was an uninspired collection.

Albums: *Boz* (1966), *Boz Scaggs* (1969), *Moments* (1971), *Boz Scaggs And Band* (1971), *My Time* (1972), *Slow Dancer* (1974), *Silk Degrees* (1976), *Two Down Then Left* (1977), *Middle Man* (1980), *Other Roads* (1988), *Some Change* (Virgin 1994). Compilation: *Hits!* (1980).

Scala, Primo

Primo Scala was a best-seller on Rex records with his Accordion Band but he did not really exist. The name was a pseudonym for musical director/producer Harry Bidgood (b. 1898, London, England, d. 1955), who recorded much anonymous dance music in the 20s and 30s. He was pianist with De Groot's salon orchestra at the Piccadilly Hotel, and recorded on **HMV** with its offshoot, the Piccadilly Dance Band. When De Groot left the hotel, his light music was replaced by an orthodox dance band with Bidgood as pianist. After visiting Berlin in 1924, where the band recorded for Vox, Bidgood resigned, going to Vocalion Records as recording manager and musical director. He made records with his house band, releasing them on the various Vocalion labels (Aco, Beltona, Guardsman, Broadcast, Coliseum, etc) under names such as the Midnight Merrymakers, Riverside Dance Band and Kentucky Revellers. In the late 20s his regular pool of musicians included **Ted Heath**, who played for him at the Ritz Hotel and Ciro's Club. Vocalion dropped all their other labels and concentrated on Broadcast, a more expensive product with a retail price of 2/- (10p). In 1932 the company was taken over by Crystalate, who inaugurated the Imperial, Rex and Eclipse labels, the latter sold by Woolworth's at 6d each (two-and-a-half pence). Bidgood built up an all-accordion band for Imperial as Roma's Accordion Band, whose records were also issued on Eclipse under the name of Don Porto. When he decided Rex too should have some of this music, it was released under the name of Primo Scala's Accordion Band; then Crystalate discontinued Eclipse Records and introduced Crown, another 6d

record label, on which Bidgood/Porto/Scala/Roma became Rossini's Accordion Band. Though they were all the same band it was Scala on whom Bidgood concentrated his efforts, taking the band on radio and music-hall tours. In a more musically ambitious and challenging vein he spent part of the World War II years conducting the London Symphony Orchestra in film music in his capacity as Musical director for British Columbia Pictures. He disappeared from the music scene soon afterwards.

Albums: *Primo Scala And His Accordion Band* (1981), *Strike Up The Band* (1983), *Shoe Shine Boy* (1988).

Scales, Harvey, And The Seven Sounds

An R&B band formed in Milwaukee, Wisconsin, USA, in 1961. Members were lead vocalist and guitarist Harvey Scales (b. 1941, Arkansas, USA), Monny Smith, Bill Purtie, Rudy Jacobs, Al Vance, Bill Stonewall, and Ray Armstead. Superstar **James Brown** was sweeping the charts in the late 60s with a new kind of harder soul called 'funk', and under his influence Harvey Scales And The Seven Sounds, like numerous other groups then, made their presence felt recording new funk sounds. The group's one hit, 'Get Down' (number 32 R&B, 1967), was recorded on Lenny LeCour's Magic Touch label. The b-side, 'Love-itis', was later recorded by the rock group **J. Geils Band**. After signing with **Chess Records**, Scales and his group had a regional hit with the LeCour-produced 'The Yolk' in 1969. Later under the aegis of Detroit producer Don Davis the group recorded for **Stax Records** with little success. In 1976, for southern soul hit-maker **Johnnie Taylor**, Scales co-wrote the massive hit, 'Disco Lady'. That success landed Scales a recording deal with Casablanca, in which the artist released two albums. Scales was still recording in the early 90s.

Albums: *Confidential Affair* (Casablanca 1978), *Hot Foot* (Casablanca 1979), *All In A Night's Work* (Earthtone 1991).

Scandal (featuring Patty Smyth)

The USA rock band Scandal were originally formed by guitarist Zack Smith (b. Westport, Connecticut, USA) who had previously played in outfits with Dee Murray and Davey Johnson of the **Elton John** band. By 1982, Scandal consisted of Ivan Elias (bass), Benji King (keyboards), and Frankie La Rocka (drums). They were auditioning for a singer when they came across Patty Smyth (b. 26 June 1957, New York City, USA), who was the daughter of a manager of a Greenwich Village Club. Once teamed up they undertook lucrative tours with **Hall And Oates** and the **Kinks**, releasing their debut single, 'Goodbye To You', in 1982. This was followed by a self-titled mini-album and *The Warrior*. The title track was a US Top 10 hit, written by former Sweeney Todd vocalist **Nick Gilder**, with **Spider**

(USA) keyboardist Holly Knight. It would be Scandal's only success and they subsequently split around 1985. Smyth has since married **Richard Hell** and released her own solo album in 1987.

Albums: *Scandal* (1982), *The Warrior* (1984). Solo album: Patty Smyth *Never Enough* (1987).

Scanner

This German rock quintet rose from the ashes of Lion's Breed in 1987. Comprising Tom S. Sopha (guitar), Michael Knoblich (vocals), Wolfgang Kolorz (drums), Axel A.J. Julius (guitar) and Martin Bork (bass), their brand of metal-thrash identified them with fellow countrymen, **Helloween**. Signing to Noise Records in 1988, Scanner released *Hypertrace*, a science-fiction concept album. The storyline revolved around extra-terrestrial robots preventing war between the superpowers and, although far from original, it found an appreciative and appreciable audience. Knoblich quit the group in 1989 and was replaced by ex-Angel Dust vocalist S.L. Coe. They recorded *Terminal Earth*, another concept album, centred this time on the aforementioned robots' concern for planet Earth, and the damage that the human race has inflicted upon it. Not suprisingly, it bore a strong musical resemblance to its predecessor.

Albums: *Hypertrace* (Noise 1988), *Terminal Earth* (Noise 1990).

Scanner (Dance)

Named after the hand-held device which can intercept telephone and radio calls, Scanner comprise the UK-based duo of Robin Rimbaud (b. c.1964) and Steve Williams - who are regularly on patrol to pick up conversations on mobile phones, replaying them alongside their own studio sounds. In turn their recordings were adorned with some of the more memorable/bizarre findings they had tuned in to with their own scanner, from aural pornography to static and more everyday conversation. These delights had graced two albums for Ash International by 1994. The equipment was originally purchased from a group of fellow hunt sabateurs who were using it to monitor police movements. Rimbaud also runs the Electronic Lounge, a monthly 'event' in the ICA bar, and lectured on the art of 'scanning' at London University. The duo have also remixed for **Autechre** and **Reload**.

Scarbury, Joey

b. 7 June 1955, Ontario, California, USA. Joey Scarbury made his mark on the US pop charts in 1981 with 'Theme From Greatest American Hero (Believe It Or Not)', from the American television series of the same name. Scarbury began singing as a child and was later discovered by the father of songwriter **Jimmy Webb**. Scarbury first recorded in 1968, cutting a Webb song', She Never Smiles Anymore'. He

continued to record for numerous record labels, including Dunhill, Bell, Big Tree and **Columbia Records** but managed only one minor chart single, 'Goodbye To You', in 1971 on Lionel Records. For the next nine years Scarbury sang backing vocals for **Loretta Lynn** and for sessions produced by **Mike Post**. His break came when he recorded the television theme, written by Post and Stephen Geyer, on **Elektra Records**. It reached number 2 in the US, but Scarbury returned to the singles charts just once more, with the minor hit 'When She Dances', later that year. His *America's Greatest Hero* just missed the Top 100 albums list in 1981. Scarbury recorded for **RCA Records** with no luck and later switched careers to become a baseball player.

Album: *America's Greatest Hero* (1981).

Scarface

b. Brad Jordan, USA. Formerly a member of Houston's nastiest, the **Geto Boys**, Scarface's 'official' solo debut (an album of sorts had prefigured *Mr Scarface Is Back*) was a familiar roll-call of sex and street violence, with the titles reading like a litany of horror movies ('Body Snatchers', 'Born Killer', Diary Of A Madman'). The follow-up repeated the formula to an ever greater degree of success, eventually going platinum. Though there was much skullduggery and blatant misogyny apparent again, there was at least light to lift the shade. The hardcore rapper was not too hardcore to include tracks like 'Now I Feel Ya', which spoke openly of his relationship with his son and parents. In real life he suffers from depression, which was also documented on bloodcurdling tracks like 'The Wall'. His suicide attempt, triggered by his girlfriend announcing she was leaving him, had been depicted on the sleeve of a previous Geto Boys album. The first single from a projected fourth album was 'Hand Of The Dead Body', a duet with **Ice Cube** which defended rap against various charges laid at its door in the 90s. The key to Scarface's craft can be located in the fact that he boasts of first seeing the film *The Warriors* at age eight. Sadly, he never quite grew out of it.

Album: *Mr. Scarface Is Back* (Rap-A-Lot 1991), *The World Is Yours* (Rap-A-Lot 1993), *The Diary* (Virgin 1995).

Scarlet

This acoustic band were formed in Hull, Humberside, and belong in the tradition of **Marine Girls** and **Everything But The Girl**, also from that city. They crashed into the charts in 1995 with the treacly 'Independent Love Song', although the suddenness of their arrival did not reflect the length of pianist Joe Youle and singer Cheryl Parker's (both b. c.1971) apprenticeship. Seven years previously they had consulted Paul Heaton (then leader of the **Housemartins** and later the **Beautiful South**) over

the quality of two songs they had composed. He apparently said: 'If only my first song had been as good as this, but one of you can sing and one of you can't.' However, he left the duo to make up their minds about to whom this comment was directed. Eventually, Youle concentrated solely on the keyboard, and at age 17, and the duo contacted Gary Crowley at **Island Records**. Six years later they approached him again, on his first day in a new A&R post at **Warner Brothers Records**, and he signed them. 'I don't think he even listened to our music, he just thought we had the balls to make it.' Songs on their debut album ran the gamut of relationship issues, with men in particular given short shrift for their insensitivities and improprieties, notably on the track about an MP's 'love child', 'Man In A Cage'.
Album: *Naked* (Warners 1995).

Scarlet Party

The short-lived **Beatles**que quartet were formed in 1981 by brothers Graham Dye (b. 2 August 1961, Barking, Essex, England; vocals/guitar), Steven Dye (b. 17 September 1963, Barking, Essex, England; bass/vocals/keyboards) and were joined by Sean Heaphy (drums) and Mark Gilmour (guitar), younger brother of **Pink Floyd**'s **David Gilmour**. Their strong composing ability led them to recording an album at the legendary Abbey Road studios, and performing live at the studio's 50th anniversary party. Much media attention was given to their debut '101 Damn-nations', which was released on the re-activated **Parlophone**, label 20 years after the **Beatles**' debut. Graham Dye's **John Lennon**-influenced vocals was another talking point and the band seemed set for stardom. This immaculate record surprisingly only reached the lower regions of the UK Top 50, and even more disappointing was that their strong follow-up 'Eyes Of Ice' failed to chart. Although they toured, supporting **Steve Hackett**, **Huey Lewis** and **Sad Cafe**, the band disintegrated through lack of commercial success. Graham returned in 1985 singing lead vocal on the **Alan Parsons Project** track 'Light Of The World', from *Stereotomy*, and again in 1990 with 'Little Hans' from Parsons' *Freudiana*. In 1995, the brothers were working on new material to submit to the record company that failed to capitalize on their remarkably fresh talent a decade earlier.

Scars

The Scars formed in Scotland - Bobby King (vocals), Paul Research (guitar), John Mackie (bass) and Calumn Mackay (drums) - evolved out of Edinburgh's late 70s punk milieu. Early live appearances were enthusiastic rather than accomplished, revealing the group's youthfulness, but they gradually asserted a competence and individuality. 'Adultery', released on the city's Fast Product label, showed an undoubted grasp of melody,

and in 1981 the Scars were signed to **Charisma Records**' short-lived Pre subsidiary. *Author! Author!* was an excellent art/punk selection, but this highly promising set was the group's final recording, and they split up soon after its release.
Album: *Author! Author!* (Pre 1981).

Scat Opera

Formed in the UK during the late 80s by Ernie Brennan (vocals), Steve Yates (guitar), John O'Reilly (bass) and Mark Diment (drums), Scat Opera recorded several well-received demos before picking up prestigious support slots with **Faith No More** in the autumn of 1989. Though comparisons to that band followed, in truth Scat Opera played at greater velocity and with more precise musical definition. The pieces, however, were not entirely in place until they signed a contract with **Music For Nations** in the spring of 1990. They made their debut a year later with *About Time*, recorded at Slaughterhouse Studios and produced by Colin Richardson. A UK tour as support to **Gaye Bykers On Acid** ensued, before returning to the studio (this time Windings Studio in Wales) with Richardson for a second set, *Four Gone Confusion*, to be released in October 1992. Again the music incorporated elements drawn from funk (particularly apparent in bass player O'Reilly's slapping technique), jazz and metal.
Albums: *About Time* (Music For Nations 1991), *Four Gone Confusion* (Music For Nations 1992).

Scatterbrain

A New York, USA band who have experienced at first hand the swings and roundabouts of the modern music industry, Scatterbrain drew original members Tommy Christ (vocals) and Paul Nieder (guitar) from hardcore outfit Ludichrist. This group, who released two albums for Relativity, *Immaculate Deception* in 1987 and *Powertrip* in 1989, were never accepted by the hardcore community, whose low tolerance threshold for humour militated against Ludichrist's flippancy. Scatterbrain was consequently invoked as the duo's new home, featuring additional members Guy Brogna (bass) and Mike Boyko (drums). However, early songs like 'Goodbye Freedom, Hello Mom' indicated that their sense of fun had not deserted them in the transition. Their debut, *Here Comes Trouble*, boasted two minor hits, 'Down With The Ship' and 'Don't Call Me Dude', both of which also had memorable videos. Touring the US and Europe, Scatterbrain discovered a rich vein of support for their efforts in Australia, where 'Don't Call Me Dude' would go Top 10. *Scumbuggery* followed in 1991, though this would be their last tenure with their label. For *Mundis Intellectuals* the group moved over to **Music For Nations**' subsidiary Bulletproof Records, with opening track 'Write That Hit' addressing the group's problems with industry executives (some of the lyrics, including 'How about hip hop?', were legendarily taken from real suggestions made to them by their former record company).

Albums: *Here Comes Trouble* (In-Effect 1990), *Scumbuggery* (In-Effect 1991), *Mundis Intellectuals* (Bulletproof 1994).

Schenker, Michael

b.10 January 1955, Savstedt, Germany. Schenker began his musical career in 1971 at the age of 16, when, along with brother Rudolf, he formed the **Scorpions**. After contributing impressive guitarwork on the band's *Lonesome Crow* debut, he was offered the chance to replace **Bernie Marsden** in **UFO**. Schenker joined the group in June 1973 and their resultant musical direction swung to hard rock. *Phenomenon*, released in 1974, featured the metal classics 'Doctor, Doctor' and 'Rock Bottom', with Schenker's performance on his Gibson 'Flying V' hammering home the band's new identity. A series of excellent albums followed before Schenker eventually quit in 1978 after the recording of *Obsession*. The split had been predicted for some time following personal conflicts between Schenker and vocalist Phil Mogg. The guitarist moved back to Germany and temporarily rejoined the Scorpions, contributing to *Lovedrive*, released in 1979. Soon afterwards he formed his own band, the Michael Schenker Group, which was later abbreviated to **MSG**. MSG's personnel has remained in a constant state of flux, with Schenker hiring and firing musicians seemingly at will. In 1991 Schenker also took time out between MSG albums to contribute to the Contraband project, a one-off collaboration between members of Shark Island, **Vixen**, **Ratt** and **L.A.Guns**.

Albums: With the Scorpions: *Action/Lonesome Crow* (Brain 1972), *Lovedrive* (EMI 1979). With UFO: *Phenomenon* (Chrysalis 1974), *Force It* (Chrysalis 1975), *No Heavy Pettin'* (Chrysalis 1976), *Lights Out* (Chrysalis 1977), *Obsession* (Chrysalis 1978), *Strangers In The Night* (Chrysalis 1979, double album). With MSG: *The Michael Schenker Group* (Chrysalis 1980), *MSG* (Chrysalis 1981), *One Night At Budokan* (Chrysalis 1982), *Assault Attack* (Chrysalis 1982), *Built To Destroy* (Chrysalis 1983), *Rock Will Never Die* (Chrysalis 1984), *Perfect Timing* (EMI 1987), *Save Yourself* (Capitol 1989), *MSG* (EMI 1992). With Contraband: *Contraband* (Impact/EMI 1991).

Schertzer, Hymie

b. 2 April 1909, New York City, New York, USA, d. 22 March 1977. After playing alto saxophone in a number of bands around the New York area, Schertzer became lead alto for **Benny Goodman**. In 1938 he joined **Tommy Dorsey**, switching a number of times back and forth between the two bands. In the 40s he played in the band led by **Bunny Berigan** and also appeared on a number of record dates with such luminaries as **Lionel Hampton** and **Billie Holiday**. In the mid-40s he went into studio work where he remained for the next 30 years, making numerous record dates with such artists as **Ella Fitzgerald** and **Louis Armstrong**. Schertzer (who sometimes spelled his name Shertzer) was one of the unsung heroes of the swing era, soloing only rarely, but his solid and skilful playing made him one of the most sought-after lead altos of his time.

Album: *Hymie Shertzer* (1957).

Schertzinger, Victor

b. 8 April 1880, Mahanoy City, Pennsylvania, USA, d. 26 October 1941, Hollywood, California, USA. A leading composer, conductor and director for movies, from the early days of silents, through the 30s and 40s. A gifted violinist as a child, Schertzinger toured as a concert soloist and studied music in Europe before returning and becoming a well-known conductor by the time he was 30. A few years later he began to compose the music for popular songs such as 'Marchetta' and 'My Wonderful Dream', and in 1916 moved to Hollywood to write scores for a series of silent movies, including Thomas Ince's revolutionary *Civilization*. Almost immediately he began to direct as well, and from then, throughout his career, he successfully combined the two occupations. With the advent of sound in the late 20s, Schertzinger contributed complete scores or individual songs to musicals such as **The Love Parade**, *Heads Up*, **One Night Of Love**, *Love Me Forever*, *Follow Your Heart*, *The Music Goes 'Round*, *Something To Sing About*, **Road To Singapore**, *Rhythm On The River*, **Kiss The Boys Goodbye**, and **The Fleet's In**. Several of his most appealing songs, with lyrics by **Johnny Mercer**, came from that last movie which was released in 1942, shortly after his death. These included 'I Remember You', 'Tangerine', 'If You Build A Better Mousetrap', 'Arthur Murray Taught Me Dancing In A Hurry', 'When You Hear The Time Signal', and 'The Fleet's In'. Among his other songs from that period were 'Magnolias In The Moonlight', 'Life Begins When You're In Love', 'Captain Custard', 'The Moon And The Willow Tree', 'I Don't Want To Cry Anymore', 'Kiss The Boys Goodbye', 'Sand In My Shoes', and 'I'll Never Let A Day Pass By'. Schertzinger also directed several of the above musicals, as well as numerous dramatic features. After directing **Bing Crosby**, **Bob Hope**, and **Dorothy Lamour** in *Road To Singapore*, the first of the popular 'Road' pictures, Schertzinger worked again with the 'Old Groaner' on *Road To Zanzibar* - arguably the best of the series - *Rhythm On The River*, and **Birth Of The Blues**. As well as Mercer, Schertzinger's songwriting collaborators included Clifford Grey, **Johnny Burke**, **Gus Kahn**, and **Frank Loesser**. They all shared his ability to write lively, optimistic and amusing numbers, with the occasional memorable ballad as well.

Schickele, Peter

b. 17 July 1935, Ames, Iowa, USA. Peter Schickele was a composer and humorist who, although he also wrote serious classical music, gained popularity through his satirical compositions recorded as the fictitious character P.D.Q. Bach. Schickele and his family moved to Washington, DC, when he was eight-years-old and there he became exposed to the satirical jazz of **Spike Jones**. At the age of 12, Schickele moved to North Dakota where he became involved in theatre, learnt to play the bassoon and studied classical music. He became a classical composer while attending college in New York, where he settled in his 20s. He also discovered jazz, folk and rock music while at school, all of which he would later draw on in his composing. Schickele developed the concept of P.D.Q. Bach in 1953. While experimenting with a primitive tape recorder, he taped the first movement of Bach's second *Brandenburg Concerto* performing all of the wind parts on bassoon. Inspired by one of Bach's few humorous pieces, *Coffee Cantata*, Schickele wrote his own *Sanka Cantata* and assigned the pseudonym P.D.Q. Bach to the piece as author. By 1959, Schickele (who became known as 'Professor' Peter Schickele) and some of his musical associates began performing humorous classical music in concert at New York's Juilliard music college and in Aspen, Colorado. The event became an annual affair, and in 1965 he performed his first non-university public concert at New York's Town Hall. It was recorded and released on **Vanguard Records** as *Music Of P.D.Q. Bach (1807-1742)*. Schickele concocted an entire 'biography' for the phony composer and published it in a book, *The Definitive Biography Of P.D.Q. Bach*. Although he continued to write and record serious music, which was performed by several respected orchestras, and worked as an arranger for such pop-folk artists as **Joan Baez** and **Buffy Sainte-Marie**, Schickele's P.D.Q. Bach albums for Vanguard, and, later Telarc Records, have remained his most recognized works. They have served to introduce many non-classical music fans to that style of music.

Albums: *Music of P.D.Q. Bach (1807-1742)* (1965), *P.D.Q. Bach At Carnegie Hall (An Hysteric Return)* (1966), *P.D.Q. Bach On The Air* (1967), *The Stoned Guest* (1970), *Intimate P.D.Q. Bach* (1973), *Portrait Of P.D.Q. Bach* (1977), *Black Forest Bluegrass* (1979), *Silent Running* (1979, film soundtrack), *Leibesleider Polkas* (1980), *Music You Can't Get Out Of Your Head* (1982), *A Little Nightmare Music (An Opera In One Irrevocable Act)* (1983), *1712 Overture And Other Musical Assaults* (1989), *Oedipus Tex And Other Choral Calamities* (1990).

Schifrin, Lalo

b. 21 June 1932, Buenos Aires, Argentina. Schifrin was taught classical piano from the age of six but later studied sociology and law at university. He won a scholarship to the Paris Conservatoire where he studied with Olivier Messiaen. In 1955 he represented Argentina in the Third International Jazz Festival in Paris. He met **Dizzy Gillespie** first in 1956 when the trumpeter was touring South America. Schifrin had founded the first Argentine big band in the **Count Basie** tradition and in 1957 wrote his first film music. He moved to New York in 1958 and toured Europe in 1960 with a **Jazz At The Philharmonic** ensemble which included Dizzy with whom he played between 1960 and 1962. He had become increasingly interested in large-scale compositions and wrote two suites for Gillespie - *Gillespiana* and *New Continent*. He worked with **Quincy Jones** when he left Gillespie, but became more and more involved in scoring for television and feature films including *The Cincinatti Kid* (1965), *Bullitt* (1968) and *Dirty Harry* (1971). His more than 150 scores over a period of nearly 30 years also have included *The Liquidator, Cool Hand Luke, The Fox, Coogan's Bluff, Kelly's Heros, Hit!, Magnum Force, Voyage Of The Damned, The Eagle Has Landed, Rollercoaster, The Amityville Horror, The Competition, The Sting II, Hollywood Wives* (television mini-series), *The Fourth Protocol, F/X2 - The Deadly Art Of Illusion, The Dead Pool, Return From The River Kwai, A Woman Called Jackie* (1992 television series), and *The Beverly Hillbillies* (1993). He lectured in composition at the University of California, Los Angeles (1968-71), and has spent a good deal of his career searching for common ground between jazz and classical music. In 1995, he conducted the London Philharmonic Orchestra at London's Festival Hall, in *Jazz Meets The Symphony*, 'an evening of jazz-symphonic fusion'.

Selected albums: *Bossa Nova - New Brazilian Jazz* (1962), *New Fantasy* (1966), *Music From 'Mission: Impossible'* (1967), *Towering Toccata* (1977), *Black Widow* (1976), *Free Ride* (1979), *Guitar Concerto* (1985), *Anno Domini* (1986), with Jimmy Smith *The Cat Strikes Again* (1986).

Schmidt, Harvey

b. 12 September 1929, Dallas, Texas, USA. An important composer for the musical theatre from the early 60s, Schmidt was majoring in art at the University of Texas when he met lyricist Tom Jones (b. 17 February 1928, Littlefield, Texas, USA). Jones was studying to be a stage director, and the two men collaborated on college shows before joining the US Army. They subsequently met up again in New York, where Schmidt was working as a commercial artist while Jones was directing a series of night club revues produced by Julius Monk. In 1959, Schmidt and Jones contributed several songs to one of these revues, *Demi-Dozen*, and in the following year, on 3 May 1960, the show for which they will always be remembered, ***The Fantasticks***, opened Off Broadway at the Sullivan Street Playhouse. With music and lyrics by Schmidt and Jones, and a book by Jones, this simple, romantic comedy, with two memorable songs, 'Try To

Remember' and 'Soon It's Gonna Rain', was still in residence 35 years later, making it the world's longest running musical, and New York's answer to London's *The Mousetrap*. After writing the scores for two successful mainline Broadway productions, *110 In The Shade* (1963) and *I Do! I Do!* (1966), Schmidt and Jones turned their attention to the allegorical *Celebration* (1960), which folded after some three months. Since then their innovative and often experimental work has been presented Off Broadway and in regional theatre. These productions have included *Philemon* (1975), *Grover's Corners* (1987), and several attempts to musicalise the stories of the French author Colette. A national tour of *Grover's Corners*, which was based on Thornton Wilder's play *Our Town*, was announced with a full page advertisment in *Variety* in 1989, but had to be called off because of the illness of its star, **Mary Martin**. In 1992, Schmidt and Jones led an English-speaking tour of *The Fantasticks* throughout the Japanese mainland, with Jones reprising the role he played in the 1960 production, and Schmidt playing the piano. In the same year, Schmidt's 'Monteargentario: Seven Dances For Solo Piano' was released on Bay Cities' *Classical Broadway*.

Further reading: *The Fantasticks: The 30th Anniversary Edition*, Tom Jones and Harvey Schmidt. *The Amazing Story Of The Fantasticks: America's Longest Running Play*, Robert Viagas and Donald C. Farber.

Schmidt, Irmin

b. 29 May 1937, Germany. Schmidt studied under modern classical composer Karlheinz Stockhausen before becoming a founder-member of **Can** in 1968. The band's organist and synthesizer player, Schmidt made a major contribution to Can's 12 albums recorded over eight years. In 1976 the band was dissolved and Schmidt, now based in France, turned to composing and recording film and television music. On many of these projects he was accompanied by fellow Can members Michael Karoli and Jaki Liebezeit (drums). Much of his work appeared on albums issued by Spoon, a label owned by the four members of Can. Schmidt rejoined his former colleagues for the Can reunion album, *Rite Time* in 1988.
Albums: *Film Musik 3/4* (1983), *Toy Planet* (1990).

Schneider, John

b. 8 April 1954, Mount Kisco, Westchester County, New York, USA. Schneider, a gifted musician and actor, has appeared in musicals from the age of 14. He played Bo Duke in the long-running US television series about a disaster-prone, hillbilly family, *The Dukes Of Hazzard* from 1979-85. He is featured on the 1982 cast album of the same name. In 1981 he had his first US hit (pop chart number 14, country number 4) with a revival of **Elvis Presley**'s 'It's Now Or Never', and proved himself to be one television star who could sing.

However, despite other successes on the US country chart, he was not accepted as a bona fide artist by country disc jockeys. In 1984, the disc jockeys were given unmarked copies of 'I've Been Around Enough To Know', and many of them played the record believing it to be by **George Strait**. Schneider's identity was revealed and the single topped the US country chart. He had further number 1's with 'Country Girls', 'What's A Memory Like You (Doing In A Love Like This)?' and 'You're The Last Thing I Needed Tonight'. Schneider though, unlike most country stars, did not care for touring and his final US Top 10 country hit was in 1987 with 'Love, You Ain't Seen The Last Of Me', at a time when he was planning to do just that. He returned to acting and was in a successful series, *Grand Slam*, in 1990.
Albums: *Now Or Never* (1981), *Dukes Of Hazzard* (1982, television cast), *White Christmas* (1981), *Quiet Man* (1982), with Jill Michaels *If You Believe* (1983), *Too Good To Stop Now* (1984), *Trying To Outrun The Wind* (1985), *A Memory Like You* (1986), *Take The Long Way Home* (1986), *You Ain't Seen The Last Of Me* (1987).

Schneider, Mary

b. c.1933, Rockampton, Queensland, Australia. From a German family, she grew up in Brisbane and began performing with elder sister Rita (b. c.1928) after being influenced by radio broadcasts of **Carson Jay Robison** And His Pioneers. They played local venues and entertained troops before finally establishing themselves by an appearance on *Australia's Amateur Hour* in 1945. Their act, which contained singing, yodelling and comedy, eventually included their 'schneiderphone' - a one-man band contraption that consisted of a washboard with horns, bells, cymbals and various other noise making gadgets attached. They recorded eight sides for Regal-Zonophone in 1950 and during the 50s and 60s, they toured extensively throughout Australia, New Zealand, Asia and the Far East. They appeared on countless television programmes and even recorded an EP of rock 'n' roll music called *Rockin' With The Schneider Sisters* for Magnasound. In 1970, they did a major tour of American bases in the Far East that, at one stage, saw them play no less than 170 shows (including 20 in 12 days), during a four and a half-month period that comprised only part of the tour. In 1972, after further tours, they decided amicably to stop performing as a duo. Rita (who later recorded an EP, *Country Fun*, for Hadley) had developed an interest in writing and began working within the television industry, whilst Mary went on to develop her solo act. She even experimented with jazz and blues but soon began to place more and more emphasis on her yodelling and quickly became very proficient in varying styles of the art. She had been initially attracted to yodelling after hearing recordings of Harry Torrani and the Austrian yodeller, Minna Reverelli, as well as her natural interest in such country yodellers as Elton Britt. Her busy schedules seemingly left little time for recording, in spite of many requests for her to do so from her fans. Surprisingly, with many rating her as one of the finest yodellers, she herself at one stage modestly doubted her own abilities and for a time, seemed reluctant to make recordings. Always in demand, she toured for almost 10 years before eventually she decided to record some yodel numbers. When record companies told her 'there is no demand for yodelling', she ignored them and financed her own, Magic Of Yodelling. Initially released on the Bluebell label, it received extensive airplay on 2KY Sydney and after being taken over by KTel, it soon went platinum. In 1984, she recorded a double album, *Can't Stop Yodelling*, which did well until the record company ran into difficulties. Two years later, it was reissued on Colstal and after television exposure, it also became a big seller. In 1994, after working with Rita to produce lyrics for popular classics such as 'The Skater's Waltz', 'In A Monastery Garden' and 'Tritsch Tratsch Polka', she demonstrated her amazing abilities by recording what knowledgeable experts of the art have described as 'a yodelling masterpiece'. She is constantly in demand for live appearances and tours extensively usually accompanied by her talented daughter, Melinda, a modern performer in her own right. Her much talked about version of Toranni's 'Mockingbird Yodel' was released in the UK on *Yodelling Crazy* by EMI in 1992. The early duet recordings and the Magnasound EP (for which it is reported they never received payment) are now collector's items.

Albums: *Magic Of Yodelling* (Bluebell/KTel 1981), *Can't Stop Yodelling* (KTel 1984, double album, reissued Colstal 1986), *Sound Of Yodelling* (Paganini 1991), *Yodelling The Classics* (Dino 1994).

Schoebel, Elmer

b. 8 September 1896, East St. Louis, Illinois, USA, d. 14 December 1970. His first professional work was as a pianist in silent-movie theatres. By the early 20s he was well known in Chicago where he worked with the **New Orleans Rhythm Kings** and also led his own band. In New York later in the 20s he played in the **Isham Jones** band but was also busy as an arranger and composer. He then settled into studio work until the mid-40s when he became active as a pianist in clubs and also continued to write. His compositions and co-compositions include 'Nobody's Sweetheart', 'Prince Of Wails' and two jazz standards, 'Farewell Blues' and 'Bugle Call Rag'.

Schofield, Phillip

b. 1962, Oldham, Lancashire, England. When Schofield took over the leading role of *Joseph And The Amazing Technicolor Dreamcoat* at the London Palladium while **Jason Donovan** went on holiday early in 1992, it proved to be one of **Andrew Lloyd Webber**'s most (commercially) inspired decisions. Having been obsessed with broadcasting from an early age, Schofield eventually got a job as a bookings clerk with the BBC in 1979. Later that year he emigrated to New Zealand with his family, and began his television career there on a pop show called *Shazam!*. He stayed in New Zealand for three and a half years, and, on his return, landed a late-night spot on Capital Radio in London. During the 80s he became one of the most popular presenters on children's television, especially on the Saturday morning programme *Going Live!*, and other shows such as the travelogue, *Schofield's Europe*, and *Television's Greatest Hits*. He also had his own record programmes on BBC Radio One. In October 1991, while hosting the *Smash Hits Pollwinners Party* on live television, he was 'assaulted' by the guitarist Fruitbat, a member of the eccentric pop group **Carter USM**. When he recovered, he revealed that **Jason Donovan** had been voted best male singer - and, just under three months later, took over from Donovan in *Joseph* at the Palladium on 13 January 1992. After receiving a five-minute standing ovation on the first night, he was offered the part full-time from May, when Donovan's contract ended. The theatre's box-office was besieged, and, from then on, until Donovan came back for the last few weeks before the show closed in January 1994, Scofield played the role for extended periods, and was widely acclaimed - particularly by the young girls who arrived by the coachload. Many of them must also have bought his record of 'Close Every Door', one of the songs from the show, enabling it reach the UK Top 30. Since then, Schofield has headed a UK regional tour of *Joseph*, as well as fronting a new television 'investigative series,' *Schofield's Quest*.

Schon And Hammer

This was a short-lived partnership between **Journey**'s Neal Schon (b. 27 February 1954, San Mateo, California, USA; guitar/vocals) and **Jan Hammer** (b. 17 April 1948, Prague, Czechoslovakia; keyboards/drums). The fusion of styles between Schon's AOR and Hammer's jazz-rock produced *Untold Passion*, a record which largely consisted of virtuoso performances from both musicians duelling against each other. The innovative British electric jazz bassist Colin Hodgkinson, previously with **Back Door**, accompanied the duo in the studio on the first album and Schon's vocal contributions proved to be particularly satisfying. By the time of the second release many of Schon's comrades from Journey had been enlisted, resulting in a lighter collection of songs and a departure from Schon And Hammer's *raison d'être*. The partnership was soon dissolved, with Schon returning full-time to Journey and Hammer moving to television work, enjoying particular success with the *Miami Vice* series.

Albums: *Untold Passion* (CBS 1981), *Here To Stay* (CBS 1982).

Schönberg, Claude-Michel

b. 1944, France. A composer, author, and record producer, Schönberg began his collaboration with **Alain Boublil** in 1973 with the first-ever staged French rock opera *La Revolution Francaise*, which played to capacity audiences and sold over 350,000 double-albums. A year later he sang his own music and lyrics on an album which spawned the hit single 'Le Premier Pas'. In 1978, he and Boublil started work on the musical *Les Misérables* which was presented at the Palais des Sports in Paris in September 1980. The concept album won two gold discs in 1981. *Les Misérables* (with English lyrics by **Herbert Kretzmer**) opened at the Barbican Theatre in London on 30 September 1985, and transferred to the Palace Theatre in December of that year before settling in for a long run. When the show was produced on Broadway in 1987, Schönberg won **Tony Awards** for best score and book, and a Grammy for Best Original Cast recording. In January 1994, *Les Misérables* became the third longest-running musical in London theatre history. Schonberg and Boublil's next project, *Miss Saigon*, was acclaimed both in London (1989) and New York (1991), and has been successfully presented in many countries throughout the world. In December 1994, it became the longest-running musical ever at the Theatre Royal, Drury Lane, eclipsing the 2,281-performance record set by *My Fair Lady*. Two more of the partners' compositions, 'Rhapsody For Piano And Orchestra' and 'Symphonic Suite', were premiered at London's Royal Albert Hall in 1992.

Schoof, Manfred

b. 6 April 1936, Madgeburg, Germany. This innovative jazz trumpet and flügelhorn player wrote his first arrangements for his school band. From 1955-58 he studied at the Musikakademie at Kassel and from 1958-63 at the Cologne Musikhochschule where he took a course in jazz run by the West German bandleader **Kurt Edelhagen**. After writing arrangements for Edelhagen's Radio Big Band and touring with **Gunter Hampel**, he led his own pioneering free jazz quintet in 1965, which included **Alex Von Schlippenbach** and **Gerd Dudek**. The quintet later formed the nucleus of the Manfred Schoof Orchestra in 1969, which brought together some of the leading exponents of European improvised music, such as **Evan Parker**, **Derek Bailey**, **Peter Brötzmann**, **Irène Schweizer** and **Han Bennink**. Schoof was also a member of **George Russell**'s orchestra from 1969-71. During the 70s and 80s he toured throughout Europe, recording with the New Jazz Trio, the **Globe Unity Orchestra**, **Jasper Van't Hof**, **Albert Mangelsdorff** and others. In 1987, he performed and recorded with the **George Gruntz** Concert Jazz band in Fort Worth, Texas. Schoof has also composed in a contemporary classical vein, most notably for the Berlin Philharmonic.

Albums: *The Early Quintet* (1966), *European Echoes* (1969), with New Jazz Trio *Alternate Takes* (1970), with the Globe Unity Orchestra *Pearls* (1975), *Scales* (1977), *Light Lines* (1977), with Peter Brötzmann a.o. *In A State Of Undress* (1989), *Shadows And Smiles* (Wergo 1989).

School Of Violence

This New York hardcore quartet was formed in 1985 by Stegmon Von Heintz (guitar), Karl Axell (vocals), Rick Stone (bass) and M.S. Evans (drums). Their recorded debut came on a compilation album, *The People Are Hungry*. This led to a contract with Metal Blade Records and the release of *We The People* in 1988. Assimilating influences drawn from punk and thrash bands like **Bad Brains**, **Anthrax** and **D.O.A.**, it featured vitriolic lyrics addressing social and political injustices. The production was very ragged however, and the messages were swamped beneath the drum and bass-laden tumult.

Album: *We The People* (Metal Blade 1988).

Schoolboys

An R&B vocal group from Harlem, New York City, New York, USA. With a series of remarkable series of pleading ballads in 1957, the Schoolboys typified the east coast pre-teen soprano sound, but like most such groups their career was short-lived. Members were Leslie Martin (lead), Roger Hayes (tenor), James McKay (baritone), and Renaldo Gamble (bass), and their entry into the recording business was facilitated by famed New York disc jockey Tommy 'Dr. Jive' Smalls, who was introduced to the group at the behest of their manager. Smalls then arranged for the group to be signed to **OKeh Records**. The Schoolboys' first success was a double-sided hit, 'Please Say You Want Me' (number 13 R&B)/'Shirley' (number 15 R&B), in early 1957. The group broke up soon after, but 'Carol' made a strong impression later in the year on the east coast, even though it failed to make the national charts. The Schoolboys' last record on OKeh, 'Pearl', featured Martin in the lead who was supported by some members of the **Cadillacs**. Gamble had gone to join the **Kodaks** (another pre-teen group) and Hayes joined the Collegians of 'Zoom Zoom Zoom' fame. The Schoolboys made one more record, for Jaunita, 'Angel Of Love', in 1958, before ending their career.

Compilation: *Little Joe And The Thrillers Meet The Schoolboys* (Collectables 1991, contains six tracks by the Schoolboys).

Schoolly D

b. Jesse B. Weaver Jnr., Baltimore, Philadelphia, USA. Posturing street rapper who, together with his DJ Code Money (b. Lance Allen, USA), was an early pioneer in 'gun rap', a format which featured an abundance of violence and vendettas, and the glorification of the MC's personal armoury. Allied to the usual sexual declamation, it was a limited worldview but a partially effective one. Following 1984 singles 'Maniac' and 'Gangster Boogie', Schoolly D released an independent, eponymous album that was notable for the track 'PSK - What Does It Mean'. PSK transpired to be an acronym for Park Side Killers, a gang of Schoolly's aquaintence in Philadelphia. Though this breakthrough album will ensure Schoolly D's name remains hallowed in the annals of gangsta rap, he has done little since that would otherwise justify his inclusion. Still rapping over the basic, unadventourous scratching of Money, Schoolly D has not been seen to move on; whereas greater intellects have explored gang violence as a means of illustrating the big picture, Schoolly D has proved happy merely to indulge in, admittedly horrific, reportage. Song titles like 'Mr Big Dick' and 'Where's My Bitches' speak volumes about the lyrical insight displayed on the vast majority of his output. The first light at the end of the tunnel came with *Am I Black Enough For You?*, which at least incorporated a few more socio-political concerns, with cuts like 'Black Jesus' opening up new, potentially much more interesting, avenues of provocation. The title-track, too, was more insightful than previous fare had led us to expect: 'All I need is my blackness, Some others seem to lack this.'. By the time of his 'comeback' album of 1994, Schoolly had progressed further still. Renouncing the basic samples that had underscored most of his career, he now employed a full live band, including Urge Overkill's Chuck Treece, Joe 'The Butcher' Nicolo and co-producer Mike Tyler.

Albums: *Schoolly D* (Schoolly-D 1986), *Saturday Night - The Album* (Schoolly-D 1987), *The Adventures Of Schoolly D* (combining both *Schoolly D* and *Saturday Night - The Album*) (Rykodisc 1987), *Smoke Some Kill* (Jive 1988), *Am I Black Enough For You?* (Jive 1989), *How A Black Man Feels* (Capitol 1991), *Welcome To America* (Ruffhouse/Columbia 1994).

Schroeder, Gene

b. 5 February 1915, Madison, Wisconsin, USA, d. 16 February 1975. Schroeder's parents were musicians and, growing up in a musical atmosphere, he learned to play piano at an early age. He continued his studies through high school and university before turning professional. In the late 30s he arrived in New York, where he led his own small bands and also worked with leading jazzmen such as Joe Marsala and Wild Bill Davison. By the early 40s he was a familiar figure at several clubs in Boston, Chicago and New York; this is how he met Eddie Condon, with whom he formed a long-lasting musical friendship. He played in the house band at Condon's club for 17 years, occasionally touring with them too. In the 50s he appeared on a number of essential recording dates with Condon and with Bobby Hackett and Jack Teagarden. Eventually, Schroeder left Condon to join the Dukes Of Dixieland. Late in the 60s he was briefly with Tony Parenti, but ill-health curtailed his career and he was musically inactive during the last years of his life. Schroeder was an unspectacular, rock-solid supportive player, ideally suited to the role in which he was cast by Condon.

Selected albums: with Eddie Condon *At The Jazz Band Ball* (1955), with Bobby Hackett and Jack Teagarden *Jazz Ultimate* (1957).

Schroeder, John

b. 1935, London, England. Schroeder became assistant to EMI's Columbia label chief Norrie Paramor in 1958. His first production was 'Sing Little Birdie' by Pearl Carr & Teddy Johnson, which finished second in the Eurovision Song Contest in the following year. Subsequently Schroeder supervised recording sessions by numerous Columbia artists including Cliff Richard and the Shadows. In 1961, he discovered the 14-year-old Helen Shapiro and when Paramor could find no suitable material for her, Schroeder wrote his first song and her first hit, 'Please Don't Treat Me Like A Child'. A subsequent Shapiro song, 'Walking Back To Happiness' won the Ivor Novello award for Schroeder and co-writer Mike Hawker. He next spent two years as label manager for Oriole, the UK's only significant independent record company. There he produced hits by Marion Evans, Clinton Ford and Swedish instrumental group the Spotniks. Oriole was also the first British label to issue material from Berry Gordy's Tamla Motown labels. Schroeder left Oriole shortly before it was purchased by CBS to become head of Pye Records' Piccadilly label. There, he had immediate success with the Rockin' Berries, the Ivy League and Sounds Orchestral, an instrumental studio group he formed with keyboards player Johnny Pearson who had a major success in 1965 with the lilting 'Cast Your Fate To The Wind'. Schroeder and Pearson went on to record 14 Sounds Orchestral albums and were planning to revive the group in the early 90s. During a seven year tenure with Pye, he wrote for and produced artists as diverse as Status Quo, Geno Washington and Shapiro. For a period during the 70s, Schroeder ran his own Alaska Records whose roster included Afro-rock band Cymande, rock 'n' roll revivalists Flying Saucers and Joy Sarney, whose 'Naughty Naughty Naughty' was a minor hit in 1977. Schroeder was also a pioneer in the video business before moving to Vancouver, Canada in 1978 where he was active throughout the 80s as an independent producer.

Schubert

Many European commentators maintain that Schubert represent Austria's pop-rock equivalent of **Bon Jovi**, not only in sound but popularity. The group were formed in 1987 by ex-No Bros members Klaus Schubert (guitar), Nikki P. Opperer (keyboards) and UB vocalist Lem Enzinger. Several albums and hard touring later, 1994 brought the world *Toilet Songs*, the title reflecting their view on the long-term future of the planet. As well as the group's more traditional AOR/mainstream approach, 'Reflections Of The Past', saw them encompass a vaguely industrial feel. Elsewhere, however, it was business as usual with largely disappointing renderings of **Deep Purple** and **Magnum**-inspired heavy rock.
Selected album: *Toilet Songs* (Mausoleum 1994).

Schuller, Gunther

b. 22 November 1925, New York City, New York, USA. After studying several instruments together with arranging and composition and music theory, Schuller played in several symphony orchestras before turning to jazz. He recorded with **Miles Davis** in the late 40s and early 50s and subsequently was a prime mover in what he termed 'third stream' music, a form which sought to blend jazz with appropriate aspects of western classical music. Schuller continued to combine his interests in classical music and jazz in his playing, composing and teaching career. Among the jazz musicians for whom he has written special pieces, and in some cases has recorded with, are **Ornette Coleman**, **Eric Dolphy**, **Bill Evans** and **John Lewis**. His teaching has included spells at the Lennox School of Jazz, of which he was a co-founder, and the New England Conservatory. He has also been active in music publishing and recording, forming his own companies in both fields. He has also written extensively on jazz and, apart from numerous magazine articles, he is the author of an important trilogy of which the first two volumes are *Early Jazz: Its Roots And Musical Development* (1968) and *The Swing Era: The Development Of Jazz, 1930-1945* (1989).
Selected albums: *Three Little Feelings* (1956), *The Gunther Schuller Orchestra* i (1957), with Miles Davis *Porgy And Bess* (1958), *Jazz Abstractions* (1960), *The Gunther Schuller Orchestra* ii (c.1966), *Ellington's Symphony In Black* (1980), *Vintage Dolphy* (1986).
Further reading: *Early Jazz: Its Roots And Musical Development*, Gunther Schuller. *The Swing Era: The Development Of Jazz 1930-1945*, Gunther Schuller.

Schulze, Klaus

Born in Germany, Schulze is one of the fathers of modern electronic music. Originally a drummer, he was a founder member of **Tangerine Dream** in 1967 and played on the group's debut. His debut solo album was on the Ohr subsidiary of Hansa Records but much of his later work appeared on his own Brain label. During the late 70s he recorded on synthesizer with **Stomu Yamash'ta** (*Go Two*) and was the first musician to perform live at the London Planetarium. He also toured with **Arthur Brown**, who sang on *Dune*, an album inspired by Frank Herbert's cult science fiction novel. In the 80s Schulze concentrated on recording albums whose titles and mesmeric synthesized compositions were the essence of 'new age' music. In 1987, he recorded the soundtrack for the film *Babel* with Andreas Grosser.
Albums: *Irrlicht* (1972), *Cyborg* (1973), *Blackdance* (1974), *Picture Music* (1974), *Timewind* (1975), *Moondawn* (1976), *Body Love* (1977), *Mirage* (1977), *Body Love II* (1977), *X* (1978), *Blanche* (1979), *Dune* (1979), *Live* (1980), *Dig It* (1980), *Trancefer* (1981), *Rock On* (1981), *Audentity* (1983), *Drive Inn* (1984), *Aphrica* (1984), *Angst* (1985), *Dreams* (1987), *Babel* (1987, film soundtrack), *En=Trance* (1988), *The Dresden Performance* (1991), *The Dome Event* (1993).

Schutt, Arthur

b. 21 November 1902, Reading, Pennsylvania, USA, d. 28 January 1965. After playing piano in silent-movie theatres, Schutt joined a band led by Paul Specht. During the 20s Schutt played piano in several of the more popular society bands, including those of Specht, **Roger Wolfe Kahn** and **Freddy Rich**. Towards the end of the decade he was involved in recording sessions with several of the leading white jazzmen of the day, notably **Bix Beiderbecke**, **Red Nichols**, **Frank Trumbauer** and **Benny Goodman**. Throughout the 30s and early 40s he was mostly active in the studios but found time for occasional club dates in New York. Later in the 40s and on through the 50s he continued with studio work but was now based in Hollywood, where he played clubs only rarely.

Schutze, Paul

b. Australia. With a background in industrial/*avant garde* music, notably the Melbourne jazz artists Laughing Hands and film scores, Schutze was quick to see the possibilities in the artistic marketplace opened up by techno. Although *More Beautiful Human Life* was his first recording for **R&S** subsidiary Apollo, it was in fact his sixth album in total. This was a collage of sounds and noises melded into a cinematic narrative, underpinned by his studies of Indian percussion and tabla music. Schutze has also undertaken remixing chores for guitar bands like **Main** and **Bark Psychosis**, in an attempt to broaden both his and their musical palates.
Selected albums: *New Maps Of Hell* (Extreme 1994). As Uzect Plaush: *More Beautiful Human Life* (Apollo 1994).

Schuur, Diane

b. Tacoma, Washington, USA. Schuur is a top-selling **GRP** artist of long standing, and one of jazz's most popular vocalists. Born in Tacuma, but growing up in Auburn, she took to jazz with prodigious enthusiasm, learning **Dina Washington**'s repertoire at the age of three and four, and listening to her mother's **Duke Ellington** records and her father at the piano. Astonishingly, she was singing professionally at the age of nine, and began performing her own tunes at 16. In 1975, she won a place in drummer Ed Shaughnessy's big band (of *Late Show* fame), and travelled with the group to the **Monterey Jazz Festival**, where she met and jammed with the great **Dizzy Gillespie**. Her biggest break, however, came at the same festival four years later, when she was discovered by an enthusiastic **Stan Getz**, who began to spread the word about Schuur's obvious talent, and even invited her to perform with him at the White House in 1982. Two years later, she was invited back by Nancy Reagan, and the broadcast recording of this concert won her a contract with the GRP label. She has been with GRP ever since, winning Grammys in 1986 and 1987, and releasing almost an album per year ever since, some of them featuring other top jazz and blues stars, including **B.B. King** and the **Count Basie** Orchestra. Schuur has a pleasant, musical voice, but tends toward the bland sound of jazz-pop.

Albums: *Deedles* (GRP 1984), *Schuur Thing* (GRP 1985), *Timeless* (GRP 1986), *Deedles And Basie: Diane Schuur & The Count Basie Orchestra* (GRP 1987), *Talkin' Bout You* (GRP 1988), *Pure Schuur* (GRP 1990), *In Tribute* (GRP 1992), *Love Songs* (GRP 1993), with B.B. King *Heart To Heart* (GRP 1994). Compilation: *Diane Schuur Collection* (GRP 1989).

Video: *Diane Schuur And The Count Basie Orchestra* (GRP 1992).

Schwartz, Arthur

b. 25 November 1900, New York City, New York, USA, d. 3 September 1984. A distinguished composer and film producer, Arthur Schwartz was prohibited by his family from learning music, so he began composing while still a teenager at high school. He studied law and continued to write as a hobby, but in 1924 he met **Lorenz Hart**, with whom he immediately began to collaborate on songs. They enjoyed some modest success but not enough to turn Schwartz from his path as a lawyer. In the late 20s he practised law in New York City, continuing to write songs in his spare time with a string of lyricists as collaborators, until Hart convinced him that he could make a career in music. He took time off from his practice and was advised to seek a permanent collaborator. He was introduced to **Howard Dietz**, with whom he established immediate rapport. Among their first joint efforts to the revue *The Little Show* (1929), was one of the songs that Schwartz had written with Hart, 'I Love To Lie Awake In Bed'. After being given a new lyric by Dietz, it became 'I Guess I'll Have To Change My Plan' - also known as 'The blue pajama song'. Later songs for revues included 'Something To Remember You By' and 'The Moment I Saw You'. In 1931, Schwartz and Dietz had a major success with *The Band Wagon*, which starred **Fred Astaire** and his sister Adele. The partners' score included their most important song success, 'Dancing In The Dark'. Other shows of the 30s were less successful but there were always excellent songs: 'Louisiana Hayride', 'Alone Together', 'A Shine On Your Shoes', 'What A Wonderful World', 'Love Is A Dancing Thing' and 'You And The Night And The Music'. The pair also wrote for radio and interspersed their collaborations with songs written with other partners. Schwartz wrote songs for shows such as *Virginia* (1937) and *Stars In Your Eyes* (1939). During the 40s and 50s he wrote songs with various collaborators for several film musicals, including *Navy Blues*, *Thank Your Lucky Stars* ('They're Either Too Young Or Too Old' with **Frank Loesser**), *The Time, The Place And The Girl* ('Gal In Calico', 'A Rainy Night In Rio' with **Leo Robin**), and *Excuse My Dust* (1951). He also served as producer on pictures such as *Cover Girl*, *Night And Day*, and *The Band Wagon*. Schwartz was reunited with Dietz in 1948 on a revue *Inside USA*, and in 1953 they wrote a new song, 'That's Entertainment', for the screen version of *The Band Wagon*. In 1951, Schwartz collaborated with **Dorothy Fields** on *A Tree Grows In Brooklyn*, from which came 'Love Is The Reason' and 'I'll Buy You A Star'. Schwartz and Fields also wrote *By The Beautiful Sea* (1954), which included 'Alone Too Long'. Later Broadway shows by Schwartz and Dietz proved unsuccessful and although their songs, such as 'Something You Never Had Before' and 'Before I Kiss The World Goodbye', were pleasant and lyrically deft, they were not of the high standard they had previously set themselves. In the late 60s Schwartz settled in London, England, for a while where he wrote *Nicholas Nickleby* and *Look Who's Dancing* (a revised version of *A Tree Grows In Brooklyn* with several new songs). He also recorded an album of his own songs, *From The Pen Of Arthur Schwartz*, before returning to live in the USA.

Album: *From The Pen Of Arthur Schwartz* (1976).

Schwartz, Stephen

b. 6 March 1948, New York, USA. One of the few new theatrical composers and lyricists to emerge in the 70s, Schwartz studied at the Carnegie-Mellon University before deciding to make a career as a songwriter. In 1969 he contributed the title song to Leonard Gershe's play *Butterflies Are Free*, which ran on Broadway for more than 1,000 performances, and was filmed in 1972. In 1976 Schwartz had a smash hit with his rock-pop score for the Off Broadway 'biblical' musical *Godspell*, which ran for over 2,500 performances in New York, and produced the hit song 'Day By Day'. Also in 1971, Schwartz collaborated with **Leonard Bernstein** on additional text for the composer's 'theatre piece', *Mass*, which was commissioned for the opening of the John F. Kennedy Center for the Performing Arts. During the early 70s, Schwartz enjoyed more success with *Pippin* (1972), which had another agreeable song, 'Magic Do', and *The Magic Show* (1974). Each show ran for nearly five years in New York. Since then he seems to have lost the magic formula. *The Baker's Wife* (1976) closed out of town although it has since become something of a cult item, and *Working* (1978), *Rags* (1986), and *Children Of Eden* (London 1991), could only manage 132 performances between them. However, most theatre observers feel that, like **Charles Strouse**, with whom he collaborated on *Rags*, Stephen Schwartz will almost certainly be back. In 1995, Schwartz turned his attention to the screen, and collaborated with **Alan Manken** on the score for the **Walt Disney** animated feature *Pocahontas*.

Schwarz, Brinsley

(see **Brinsley Schwarz**)

Schweizer, Irène

b. 2 June 1941, Schaffhausen, Switzerland. Her interest in music sparked by the dance bands who played in her parents' restaurant, Schweizer began to play folk songs on the accordion at the age of eight and took up the piano four years later. By her late teens she was playing hard bop in a student band, but a brief stay in England in the early 60s alerted her to the more modern approaches of **Joe Harriott** and **Tubby Hayes**. Settling in Zurich she formed a trio, whose recordings show her music was still relatively conservative - **Junior Mance** and **Bill Evans** were early heroes - but by the time she recorded with **Pierre Favre**'s groups in the late 60s (*Santana*, *This Is Free Jazz*) she was investigating the freer music that has since remained her chief focus of interest (and was partly inspired by hearing **Cecil Taylor** in the mid-60s). One of the first members of Berlin's FMP organization, Schweizer released most of her recordings on their label for the next 15 years, many featuring her in partnership with saxophonist Rüdiger Carl, though other associates included **Manfred Schoof, John Martin Tchicai** and **Louis Moholo**, plus a guest appearance with the group, **Henry Cow** (*Western Culture*). In 1978, **Lindsay Cooper** invited her to join the newly-formed Feminist Improvising Group (FIG) and in 1983 Schweizer set up the European Women's Improvising Group (EWIG); she has remained a committed advocate for women's music, helping to organize the Canaille Festival of Women's Improvised Music in Zurich in 1986. In the mid-80s, with FMP in financial crisis, she was instrumental in setting up Switzerland's annual, three-city Taktlos Festival of improvised music plus its associated label, Intakt, on which many of her own recent releases have appeared. Prominent among these have been two CD releases of solo music and a series of duets - with drummers Moholo, Günter Sommer and **Andrew Cyrille** (Schweizer herself is a capable drummer), plus bassist **Joëlle Léandre** (a frequent collaborator) and pianist **Marilyn Crispell**. One of Europe's premier improvisers, Schweizer can play the entire gamut of piano, from dynamic, percussive attack to delicate and humorous interplay. Her latest UK tour was in 1991 with the **London Jazz Composers' Orchestra**, whose leader **Barry Guy** wrote 'Theoria' for her, a 'kind of piano concerto' to celebrate her 50th birthday.

Selected albums: *Jubilation* (rec. 1962), *Brandy* (rec. 1964), *Willem's Fun Feast* (1973), *Ramifications* (1975, rec. 1973), with Rüdiger Carl *Goose Pannee* (1975), with Carl, Louis Moholo *Messer* (1976), with John Tchicai *Willi The Pig* (1976), *Wilde Señoritas* (1976), *Hohe Ufer Konzerte* (1977), *Early Tapes* (1978, rec. 1967), *Hexensabbat* (1978), with Carl, Moholo *Tuned Boots* (1978), with Carl *The Very Centre Of Middle Europe* (1979), with Carl *Die V-Mann Suite* (1981), *Live At Taktlos* (1986, rec. 1984), with Joëlle Léandre *Cordial Gratin* (1987), *Irène Schweizer - Louis Moholo* (1987), with others *Canaille* (1988, rec. 1986), *The Storming Of The Winter Palace* (1988), *Irène Schweizer - Günter Sommer* (1988), *Irène Schweizer - Andrew Cyrille* (1989), *Piano Solo Volume One* (Intakt 1991), *Irene Schweizer And Pierre Favre* (Intakt 1990), *Piano Solo Volume Two* (Intakt 1991), with Marilyn Crispell *Overlapping Hands: Eight Segments* (1991).

Scientist

b. Jamaica. Scientist (real name Overton Brown) burst onto the reggae scene in the early 80s with a reckless mixing style that seemed to outdo even **King Tubbys** wildest extravaganzas. He began his career as an engineer at **Studio One** in 1978, mixing the dub to **Sugar Minott**'s 'Oh Mr DC' among others. Shortly after this he became a protegé of King Tubby, and swiftly gained a reputation with his fresh mixing style. In 1980 the UK-based record company **Greensleeves** began to release the productions of then hot-shot Jamaican producer, **Henry 'Junjo' Lawes**. Lawes, hitting big with new singing sensation **Barrington Levy**, used Tubby's studio for his voicing and final mix-downs and offered Greensleeves a couple of dub albums mixed by Tubby's sensational young engineer. *Scientist v Prince Jammy* (1980), mostly consisting of dub mixes of Barrington Levy tracks, was presented as a 'Big Showdown' between the two dubmasters, the first track mixed by Scientist, the second by **Prince Jammy**, and so on. The combination of heavyweight **Roots Radics** rhythms pitted against one another - the cover upping the ante by depicting the two protagonists cartoon style, sitting at their mixing desks in a boxing ring surrounded by a crowd of dreads - made for exciting listening, and gave the dub idiom a much needed shot in the arm.

Greensleeves followed this with an album proclaiming Scientist to be the *Heavyweight Dub Champion*, a similar brew of Roots Radics/Barrington Levy rhythms. Soon, dub albums mixed by Scientist began to appear with bewildering regularity from various sources. Greensleeves in particular continued to issue album after album which, despite their increasingly unlikely sounding titles and garish covers, remain essential listening. Scientist moved from Tubby's four-track studio to **Joe Joe Hookim**'s sixteen-track **Channel One** studio in 1982, where he also learned to record live. His popularity resurrected dub's fading fortunes for a few years, but the form had lost ground in the Jamaican dancehalls to the new breed of **dancehall** DJs and vocalists, and by the mid-80s few Jamaican producers felt it prudent to spend money on producing dub albums. He continued as resident engineer at Channel One until the mid-80s when he moved to New York to continue his production career.

Albums: *Introducing* (JB Music/Greensleeves 1979), *Scientist v Prince Jammy* (Greensleeves 1980), *Heavyweight Dub Champion* (Greensleeves 1980), *Scientist Meets The Space Invaders* (Greensleeves 1981), *Dub Landing Vol 1 & 2* (Starlight 1981), *Scientist Rids The World Of The Evil Curse Of The Vampires* (Greensleeves 1981), *Scientist Encounters Pacman* (Greensleeves 1982), *Scientist Wins The World Cup* (Greensleeves 1983), *The People's Choice* (Kingdom 1983), *Dub Duel At King Tubbys* (Kingdom 1983), *High Priest Of Dub* (Kingdom 1983), *In The Kingdom Of Dub* (Kingdom 1983), *King Of Dub* (Kingdom 1987), *1999 Dub* (Heartbeat 1988). Compilation: *Crucial Cuts* (Kingdom 1984).

Scientists Of Sound

Boasting four different birth locations (Nigeria, Maruitius, St Lucia, Jamaica), the Scientists Of Sound are based in England, and comprise J-Blast 'The Weak Rhyme Wrecker' (ex-**J-Blast And The 100% Proof**), DJ Aybee 'The Underground Nigga', Kool Sett and Cherokee 'Mr Mibian'. A colourful press release claimed they were originally one person, travelling through the universe, when they were split into four component parts and spread around the globe. After adapting the personas of indigenous creatures, they reunited in England as a result of influencing their parents to travel to the UK. This unwieldy ethos was continued in their live shows (a choerographed approach often compared to **Leaders Of The New School**) and embraced in the way each member as regarded as a different anatomical appendage of the central being: J-Blast the mouthpiece, Kool Sett the heart, etc. Signed to the **Underdog**'s Bite It! label after

debuting with a 1992 EP, their first release for their new employer was 1994's 'Bad Boy Swing'.

Sclavis, Louis

b. 2 February 1953, Lyon, France. Louis Sclavis specializes in soprano saxophone, clarinet and bass clarinet; when he plays the clarinets, in particular, he does so with an authority very few modern jazz players can even approximate. Sclavis first came to attention with the group Workshop de Lyon, with whom he recorded five albums between 1975 and 1985. In 1976, he was a founder member of the Association à la Récherce d'un Folklore Imaginaire which proposed (amongst other things) that rather than be constrained by musical 'roots', a group of musicians should be free to dream up their own culture. Correspondingly, Sclavis's own recordings cover a wide and colourful terrain. Still much in demand as a sideman, Sclavis has played with **Anthony Braxton**, **Cecil Taylor**, **Chris McGregor**'s Brotherhood Of Breath and others. On *Alms/Tiergarten (Spree)* by the Cecil Taylor European Orchestra, Sclavis emerges as one of the most powerful voices in a power-packed band.

Albums: with Jean Bolcato *Champ De Frigg* (1975), *Ad Augusta Per Angustia* (Nato 1981), *Rencontres* (Nato 1985), *Clarinettes* (IDA 1985), *Chine* (IDA 1987), *Chamber Music* (IDA 1989), with André Ricros *Le Partage Des Eaux* (1989), with Evan Parker, Hans Koch, Wolfgang Fuchs *Duets (Dithyrambische)* (1990), *Rouge* (ECM 1992), *Ellington On The Air* (Ida 1993), *Acoustic Quartet* ECM 1993).

Scobey, Bob

b. 9 December 1916, Tucumcari, New Mexico, USA, d. 12 June 1963. In the 30s Scobey played trumpet in several dance bands, mostly in California where he grew up. In 1938, he began a long-lasting musical association with **Lu Watters**, which brought him to the forefront of the jazz revival movement. During the 50s, he led his own traditional band, which attained a level of popularity similar to those of Watters and **Turk Murphy**, another companion in the west coast dixieland revival. In the 60s Scobey ran his own club in Chicago and remained a popular figure at festivals of traditional jazz. A sound, if unspectacular, trumpet player, Scobey's great enthusiasm for his music rubbed off on the sideman in any band of which he was a member.

Selected albums: *Bob Scobey's Alexander's Jazz Band* (Dawn Club 1986, 1946-47 recordings), *Bob Scobey's Frisco Band Vol. 1* (1950-51), *Vol. 2* (1952-53), *Direct From San Francisco* (Good Time 1993).

Scofield, John

b. 26 December 1951, Ohio, USA. From an early background of playing with local R&B groups, guitarist Scofield attended the renowned **Berklee College Of Music** in Boston during the early 70s. He recorded

with **Gerry Mulligan** and **Chet Baker** and eventually received an invitation to join **Billy Cobham** as replacement for **John Abercrombie**. Following a two-year stint he played with **Charles Mingus**, **Gary Burton**, and **Dave Liebman**. His early solo work built slowly and steadily into a style that is uniquely his. *Shinola* was recorded live and is a mellow album, bordering on the lethargic, and features the bass playing of Scofield's acknowledged mentor **Steve Swallow**. Between 1983 and 1985 Scofield was an integral part of **Miles Davis**' band, playing on a number of recordings including *Decoy* and *You're Under Arrest*. Following this exposure, Scofield had accumulated a considerable following. During the mid-80s he played with **McCoy Tyner**, Marc Johnson and the French National Orchestra. *Electric Outlet* showed that Scofield had now created his own uniquely rich and creamy sound, and *Still Warm* capitalized on this burst of creativity and became the first of a series of outstanding albums on Gramavision. Great excitement preceded its release, following a giveaway record in *Guitar Player* magazine. The album became a big seller and was a flawless work. He continued in a similar funky, though less jazzier, vein for *Blue Matter* and *Loud Jazz*, the former featuring some impressive drum work from Dennis Chambers. *Flat Out* featured diverse and interesting arrangements of standards like **Sammy Fain/Paul Francis Webster**'s 'Secret Love' and **Jerome Kern/Oscar Hammerstein II**'s 'All The Things You Are'. A live offering, *Pick Hits*, brilliantly encapsulated the best of Scofield's recent work, and demonstrated his growing importance as a class player. *Time On My Hands* was a critics' favourite and another strong seller. For many, it was the jazz album of 1990. Scofield's playing had now reached a point where he was regarded as one of the world's top guitarists. His compositional skills continued to blossom; his interplay with **Charlie Haden** and **Jack DeJohnette** was imaginative and uplifting. Maintaining an extraordinarily prolific musical peak, he delivered another exciting record in the shape of *Meant To Be* and toured with the **Mike Gibbs** Orchestra during 1991, where his accessible and rich jazz guitar blended harmoniously with Gibbs' innovative compositions. *Grace Under Pressure* and *What We Do* continued his run of first-rate and highly popular albums, still showing Scofield full of fresh ideas. *Hand Jive* was his return to funk and soul/jazz with some excellent contributions from the saxophone of Eddie Harris. Jim Ferguson, writing in *Guitar Player*, perceptively stated that Scofield's solos are 'like the chase scene in *The French Connection* - incredibly exciting, intense and constantly flirting with disaster, but rarely out of control'. Scofield is one of the most original and talented guitarists currently playing.
Albums: *John Scofield Live* (Enja 1977), *Rough House* (Enja 1978), *Who's Who* (Novus 1979), *Bar Talk* (Enja 1980), *Shinola* (Enja 1981), *Out Like A Light* (Enja 1981), *John Scofield - John Abercrombie* (c.80s), *More Sightings* (c.80s), *Electric Outlet* (Gramavision 1984), *Still Warm* (Gramavision 1987), *Blue Matter* (Gramavision 1987), *Loud Jazz* (Gramavision 1987), *Flat Out* (Gramavision 1989), *Pick Hits Live* (Gramavision 1989), *Time On My Hands* (Blue Note 1990), *Slo Sco* (Gramavision 1990) *Meant To Be* (Blue Note 1991), *Grace Under Pressure* (Blue Note 1992), *What We Do* (Blue Note 1993), with Pat Metheny *I Can See Your House From Here* (Blue Note 1994), *Hand Jive* (Blue Note 1994).

Scorn

A synthesis of new technology and the traditional grindcore logarithms of pounding bottom end drums and bass, Scorn are a UK duo of ex-**Napalm Death** personnel Mick Harris (drums; also a member of Painkiller) and Nick Bullen (bass/vocals) - initially helped out by a further former member of that band, Justin Broadrick (guitar). A debut album and attendant single, *Vae Solis* and 'Lick Forever Dog', were produced by John Wakelin at Rhythm Studios in Birmingham. Setting out on the road with **Cancer** and **Pitch Shifter** to promote this primeval slab of white noise, the group were joined by Candiru guitarist Pat McCahan, who replaced Broadrick (now fully occupied with **Godflesh**). A five-track, 40-minute 12-inch single emerged in October 1992, 'Deliverance', followed by the *White Irises Blind* EP. *Colossus* was the group's second full length affair and once more saw them working with Wakelin. If anything, *Evanescence* surpassed previous exercises in extremity, with a bass sound so deep that the term dub was widely invoked. This sonic marginalism led them in to contact with musicians outside of their own tribe, and 1995 saw the release of a remix album, with contributors including **Coil**, **Scanner**, **Meat Beat Manifesto** and **Bill Laswell** among others.
Albums: *Vae Solis* (Earache 1992), *Colossus* (Earache 1993), *Evanescence* (Earache 1994).

Scorpions

This German hard rock group was formed by guitarists Rudolf and **Michael Schenker** (b.10 January 1955, Savstedt, Germany) in 1971. With Klaus Meine (b. 25 May 1948; vocals), Lothar Heinberg (bass) and Wolfgang Dziony (drums), they exploded onto the international heavy rock scene with *Lonesome Crow* in 1972. This tough and exciting record was characterized by Schenker's distinctive, fiery guitarwork on his **Gibson** 'Flying V' and Klaus Meine's dramatic vocals. Soon after the album was released Heinberg, Dziony and Schenker left, the latter joining **UFO**. Francis Buchholz and Jurgen Rosenthal stepped in on bass and drums respectively for the recording of *Fly To The Rainbow*. Ulrich Roth was recruited as Schenker's replacement in 1974 and Rudy Lenners took over the drum stool from Rosenthal the following year. The following releases, *Trance* and *Virgin Killer*, epitomized the Scorpions new-found confidence and unique style; a fusion of intimidating power-riffs, wailing guitar solos and melodic vocal lines. Produced by Dieter Dierks, the improvements musically were now matched technically. Their reputation began to grow throughout Europe and the Far East, backed up by exhaustive touring. *Taken By Force* saw Herman Rarebell replace Lenners, with the band branching out into anthemic power-ballads, bolstered by emotive production, for the first time. Although commercially successful, Roth was not happy with this move, and he quit to form **Electric Sun** following a major tour to support the album. *Tokyo Tapes* was recorded on this tour and marked the end of the first phase of the band's career. This was an electrifying live set populated by top form renditions of their strongest numbers. Mathias Jabs was recruited as Roth's replacement, but had to step down temporarily in favour of Michael Schenker, who had just left UFO under acrimonious circumstances. Schenker contributed guitar on three tracks of *Lovedrive* and toured with them afterwards. He was replaced by Jabs permanently after collapsing on stage during their European tour in 1979. The band had now achieved a stable line-up, and shared the mutual goal of breaking through in the USA. Relentless touring schedules ensued and their albums leaned more and more towards sophisticated hard-edged melodic rock. *Blackout* made the US **Billboard** Top 10, as did the following *Love At First Sting* which featured the magnificent 'Still Loving You', a fine and enduring hard rock ballad. *World Wide Live* was released in 1985, another double live set, but this time only featuring material from the second phase of the band's career. Superbly recorded and produced, it captured the band at their melodic best, peaking at number 14 in a four-month stay on the US chart. The band took a well-earned break before releasing *Savage Amusement* in 1988, their first studio album for almost four years. This marked a slight change in emphasis again, adopting a more restrained approach. Nevertheless it proved a huge success, reaching number 5 in the USA and number 1 throughout Europe. The band switched to **Phonogram Records** in 1989 and ended their 20-year association with producer Dieter Dierks. *Crazy World* followed and was to become their most successful album to date. The politically poignant 'Wind Of Change', lifted as a single, became their first million-seller as it reached the number 1 position in country after country around the world. Produced by **Keith Olsen**, *Crazy World* transformed the band's sound, ensuring enormous crossover potential without radically compromising their identity or alienating their original fanbase. Buchholz was sacked in 1992, at which time investigators began to look into the band's accounts for alleged tax evasion. His replacement

would be classically trained musician Ralph Heickermann, who had previously provided computer programming for **Kingdom Come**, as well as varied soundtrack work.

Albums: *Action/Lonesome Crow* (Brain 1972), *Fly To The Rainbow* (RCA 1974), *In Trance* (RCA 1975), *Virgin Killers* (RCA 1976), *Taken By Force* (RCA 1978), *Tokyo Tapes* (RCA 1978), *Lovedrive* (EMI 1979), *Animal Magnetism* (EMI 1980), *Blackout* (EMI 1982), *Love At First Sting* (EMI 1984), *World Wide Live* (EMI 1985), *Savage Amusement* (EMI 1988), (1990), *Crazy World* (Vertigo 1990), *Face The Heat* (Vertigo 1993), *Love Bites* (Mercury 1995). Compilations: *The Best Of The Scorpions* (RCA 1979), *The Best Of The Scorpions, Volume 2* (RCA 1984), *Gold Ballads* (Harvest 1987), *CD Box Set* (EMI 1991). Herman Rarebell solo: *Nip In The Bud* (Harvest 1981). Videos: *World Wide Live* (1985), *Crazy World Tour* (1991).

Scott, Bobby

b. 29 January 1937, New York City, USA, d. 5 November 1990, New York City, New York, USA. Scott was a pianist, singer, composer, arranger, teacher and record producer. He also played several other instruments such as cello, bass, vibes, accordion and clarinet, but was mainly known for his jazz piano work and vocals. He attended Dorothea Anderson Follette's School of Music, and then in 1949 studied composition with Edward Moritz, a former pupil of Claude Debussy. Despite his early classical training, Scott turned to jazz in his teens, and played with small bands led by such as **Louis Prima**, **Tony Scott** and **Gene Krupa**, with whom he cut some sides for **Verve Records**. From 1954, he recorded under his own name for labels such as Bethlehem, Savoy, **Atlantic** and **ABC**, and in 1956 had a US Top 20 hit with 'Chain Gang', written by Sol Quasha and Hank Yakus (not the **Sam Cooke** song). In 1960, Scott wrote the title theme for Shelagh Delaney's play *A Taste Of Honey*, which became popular for pianist Martin Denny and, when Ric Marlow added a lyric, for **Tony Bennett**. It was also included on the **Beatles**' first album (UK). The song won a Grammy in 1962, and three more when **Herb Alpert** took it into the US Top 10 in 1965. In the early 60s Scott was the musical director for **Dick Haymes** for a while, and, as a pianist, arranger and record producer for **Mercury Records**, also maintained a close working relationship with **Quincy Jones**. Scott played piano on most of Jones's Mercury albums, and accompanied Tania Vega and **John Lee Hooker** on Jones's soundtrack music for the film, *The Colour Purple* (1986). As a producer, Scott supervised sessions for important artists such as **Aretha Franklin**, **Marvin Gaye**, **Bobby Darin**, **Harry Belafonte** and **Sarah Vaughan**. He discovered and recorded guitarist/vocalist Perry Miller, who changed his name to **Jesse Colin Young**, and is also credited with taking singer **Bobby Hebb** back to Mercury, although Scott left the label before Hebb released his biggest hit, 'Sunny', in 1966. Scott's compositions included 'He Ain't Heavy, He's My Brother', (written with Bob Russell), a hit for **Neil Diamond** in 1970 and a UK number 1 for the **Hollies** that same year and later in 1988, when it featured impressively in a UK television commercial for Miller Lite Lager; 'Where Are You Going?' (with Danny Meehan), sung by Joe Butler in the film *Joe* (1970); and 'Slaves (Don't You Know My Name?)', performed by **Dionne Warwick** in the movie *Slaves* (1969). Scott also composed incidental music for the play *Dinny And The Witches*, and several pieces for harp and string trios, including 'The Giacometti Variations', so-called because it was part-used as a radio advertisement for the Giacometti Exhibition held at the New York Museum of Modern Art. His compositions for guitar included 'Solitude Book' and 'The Book Of Hours', the latter recorded with Brazilian guitarist Carlos Barbosa-Lima. *For Sentimental Reasons*, displays Scott simply as an accomplished pianist, who also sang. He died, of lung cancer, in the year of its release, in 1990.

Albums: *The Jazz Keyboard Of Bobby Scott* (1953), *Great Scott* (1954), *The Compositions, Volume 1* (1954)), *The Compositions, Volume 2* (1954), *The Compositions* (1955), *Scott Free* (1956), *Bobby Scott And Two Horns* (1957), *Bobby Scott And His Orchestra* (1959), *Bobby Scott With Friends* (1960), *The Complete Musician* (1960), *A Taste Of Honey* (1960), *Joyful Noises* (1962), *When The Feeling Hits You* (1963), *108 Pounds Of Heartache* (1963), *Bobby Scott With Michel Legrand* (1964), *For Sentimental Reasons* (1990). Compilation: *The Compositions Of Bobby Scott* (1988).

Scott, Buddy

b. Kenneth Scott, 9 January 1935, Jackson, Mississippi, USA, d. 5 February 1994, Chicago, Illinois, USA. Scott is typical of the lesser-known Chicago bluesmen who played a supporting role to more famous names in the music's post-war heyday. With the increasing number of deaths of these more famous names, some of the attention has been focused upon men such as Scott in the twilight of their years. He was born into a large musical family which moved north to Chicago in 1940. John Lee **'Sonny Boy' Williamson** was a frequent visitor and Scott's mother, Ida, played guitar behind him at the Piccadilly bar. He took up the guitar at 16 and joined his brother Howard's band, the Masqueraders. During the 50s and 60s, he worked in a succession of family bands and recorded with **Syl Johnson**, Little Mack and Lee 'Shot' Williams, and worked live with a number of blues and jazz bands. He also made a number of singles for the Biscayne, PM and Capri labels. In 1978, Alligator recorded his band, Scotty And The Rib Tips, for its Living Chicago Blues series, after **Queen Sylvia Embry** requested his presence on her own session. Scott remained a jobbing musician for the rest of his life, usually in bands that featured one or more of his children. His son, Kenneth Jnr., played rhythm guitar on *Bad Avenue*, a collection of blues standards and just two original songs, recorded in 1992 and released a year later. Entertaining although hardly innovative, it illustrated Scott's enduring appeal.

Albums: Scotty And The Rib Tips: *Living Chicago Blues Vol. 3* (Alligator 1978/1991). Buddy Scott: *Bad Avenue* (Verve/Gitanes 1993).

Scott, Casey

As a fourteen-year old in her home town of Portland, Oregon, USA, Scott was ejected from her first punk rock band which she formed two years previously, when she was told that they 'weren't going to play like the **Clash**'. She was also kicked out of her drama course at Boston University after protesting at the limitations of the female roles she was offered. Choosing instead to tour Europe as a singer/songwriter, she was immediately detained and imprisoned in London because she did not have a work permit. Her solo work, reminiscent of **Patti Smith** or **Elvis Costello**, soon convinced her she needed a proper band to get the message across. Hence the recruitment of Justin McCarthy (bass), Patrick Julius (drums), and Greg Cartwright (lead guitar). The band are entitled the Creeps, and their debut was recorded in three weeks under the production tutelage of Thom Panunzio (who had also worked with **U2**).

Album: *Creep City* (1993).

Scott, Cecil

b. 22 November 1905, Springfield, Ohio, USA, d. 5 January 1964. Scott began playing clarinet and saxophones as a child and had his own band while still a teenager. His bandleading career lasted throughout the 20s and by the end of that decade he was resident in New York, where he made a big impression on audiences and rival bands. His sidemen included his brother, drummer Lloyd Scott, plus **Dicky Wells**, **Johnny Hodges**, **Chu Berry** and a succession of distinguished trumpeters, such as **Bill Coleman**, **Joe Thomas**, **Frankie Newton** and **Roy Eldridge**. Scott continued to lead a band until the early 30s, when a bad leg injury interrupted his career. From the mid-30s into the early 40s he played with various small groups, mostly in the New York and Chicago areas. In 1942, he returned to leading a big band and subsequently a series of small groups, activities which continued throughout the 50s and into the early 60s. During this late period he worked with **Willie 'The Lion' Smith** and was recorded with the encouragement of **Chris Barber**. A driving, gutsy player on clarinet and tenor saxophone, Scott was a forceful leader who demanded and received enthusiastic support from his sidemen. At its peak his band was one of the best of the New York-based black bands and had it not been for his enforced layoff just as the swing era was getting under way he might well have achieved greater recognition.

Selected album: *Chris Barber Presents Harlem Washboard: Cecil Scott And His Washboard Band* (1959).

Scott, Freddie

b. 24 April 1933, Providence, Rhode Island, USA. Scott was a contract songwriter with Screen Gems/**Columbia**, and had also recorded for a score of minor New York labels. His 1963 hit, 'Hey Girl', was issued on Colpix, but after two lesser hits, Freddie signed to Shout Records. 'Are You Lonely For Me', later recorded by **Chuck Jackson**, was a US R&B number 7 in 1966. Scott subsequently issued emotional versions of **Solomon Burke**'s 'Cry To Me', **Van Morrison**'s 'He Ain't Give You None' and a powerful **Bert Berns/Jeff Barry** composition, 'Am I Grooving You'. Shout latterly folded and the singer moved between several companies. His last chart hit came on Probe in 1970 with 'I Shall Be Released'.

Albums: *Freddie Scott Sings* (Colpix 1964), *Everything I Have Is Yours* (Columbia 1964), *Lonely Man* (Columbia 1967), *Are You Lonely For Me?* (Shout 1967), *I Shall Be Released* (Probe 1970).

Scott, Isaac

b. 11 June 1945, Pine Bluff, Arkansas, USA. Scott's family moved to the west coast in the late 40s, settling in Portland, Oregon, and Isaac was exposed to both gospel music and blues as a youngster. Until the 70s he worked with gospel groups, but in 1974 he chose to concentrate on blues, while he was living in Seattle, Washington. His guitar playing reflects the influence of **Albert Collins**, and his singing and repertoire reveal strong elements of blues, soul, and gospel. Scott has had two albums released by Red Lightnin' and live material has been issued by Solid Smoke and Criminal.

Albums: *Isaac Scott Blues Band* (1978), *Big Time Blues Man* (1983).

Scott, Jack

b. Jack Scafone Jnr., 24 January 1936, Windsor, Ontario, Canada. This distinctive deep voiced rock 'n' roll and ballad singer/songwriter moved to Michigan at the age of 10 and fronted the Southern Drifters from 1954. He signed to **ABC** in 1957 and his first release was the rocker 'Baby She's Gone'. Scott joined Carlton in 1958 and had a transatlantic Top 10 hit with his double-sided debut for the label 'My True Love'/'Leroy'. Always backed on records by session vocal group, the Chantones, he had a further seven US Top 40 successes over the next two years, including the Top 10 hits 'Goodbye Baby' in 1958, 'What In The World's Come Over You' (a UK Top 20 hit) and 'Burning Bridges' both in 1960 (the latter two released on Top Rank). He achieved a couple of minor hits on **Capitol** in 1961 and later recorded on various labels

including Groove, Guaranteed, **RCA**, Jubilee, GRT, **Dot** (where he notched up a country hit in 1974) and Ponie. He remains a top drawing act on the rock 'n' roll club circuit around the world.

Albums: *Jack Scott* (1958), *What Am I Living For* (1958), *I Remember Hank Williams* (1960), *What In The World's Come Over You?* (1960), *The Spirit Moves Me* (1961), *Burning Bridges* (1964), *Scott On Groove* (1980), *Greaseball* (1985). Compilation: *Grizzly Bear* (1986).

Scott, John

b. Patrick John Michael O'Hara Scott, 1 November 1930, Bristol, England. After being very active in the 60s pop scene, Scott has developed into a respected film music composer, now living in London and Hollywood. During his early career he acted as staff arranger with the **Ted Heath** band, playing saxophone, clarinet, harp and flute; for many years he was regarded as one of England's foremost jazz flautists. 'Johnny' Scott (as he was then known) also played in the **Woody Herman** orchestra, and arranged for Bert **Ambrose**. He claimed to have learned a lot from **Henry Mancini**, when playing for him on flute and saxophone in London sessions for films including *Charade* and *Arabesque*. For a while he worked closely with **John Barry** in The John Barry Seven, and played on Barry's scores for *Beat Girl* (1959), and *The Whisperers* (1967), as well as on several early James Bond movies. In the record studios Scott accompanied **Cilla Black**, **Tom Jones**, **Matt Monro**, the **Hollies**, **Shirley Bassey**, **Elkie Brooks**, **Gerry And The Pacemakers**, **P.J. Proby**, **Edward Woodward**, the **Mike Sammes** Singers, **Freddie And The Dreamers**, Spike Milligan and Charlie Drake. In the mid-60s he formed his own jazz combo - the Johnny Scott Quintet - playing flute with Duncan Lamont on saxophone, Barry Morgan drums, David Snell harp and Arthur Watts on bass. His growing interest in composition led him to offer his work to mood music publishers for their recorded music libraries, for the use of radio, film and television companies. Scott's music was published by Keith Prowse, Peer International and Boosey & Hawkes. His score for a 1965 promotional film *Shellarama* brought offers for his first feature film *A Study In Terror* (1965) which he wrote as 'Patrick John Scott'. He was persuaded to change it to 'Johnny', but as his film work grew he decided that 'John' seemed more suitable. His next assignments included *Doctor In Clover* (1966), *Rocket To The Moon* (1966) and *The Long Duel* (1967). In 1971 an operation on his lower jaw forced him to give up playing, since when he has concentrated on composition. Major film scores followed: *Jerusalem File* (1971), *Antony And Cleopatra* (1972), *England Made Me* (1973), *Penny Gold* (1973), *The Final Countdown* (1980), *Greystoke* (1984), *The Shooting Party* (1984), *King Kong Lives* (1986), *Deadly Pursuit* (US title *Shoot To Kill*) (1987), *Man*

On Fire (1987), *The Deceivers* (1988), *Winter People* (1989), *Black Rainbow* (1990). His work on *Inseminoid* (1980) received the 1981 award for Best Musical Score at the International Festival of Horror and Science Fiction films in Madrid, Spain. Television credits include themes for *Thames Report* (ITV), *Tonight* (BBC), *Midweek* (BBC), *Nationwide* (BBC) and episodes for *The World About Us* (BBC), *The Queen's Garden* (1985) and *Survival* (Anglia Television). Recent work has included numerous Jacques Cousteau specials such as *Clipperton - The Island Time Forgot* (1981), *The Warm Blooded Sea* (1983), *The Amazon* (1983) and the Cousteau 75th Birthday tribute (1985). His television work has been rewarded with two Emmys - *Wild Dogs Of Africa* (a 1972 documentary) and *Little Vic* (a 1978 mini-series). After years of making recordings with many record companies, Scott has established his own label JOS Records to promote his own scores.

Selected albums: *A Study In Terror* (Polydor 1965, film soundtrack), *Rocket To The Moon* (Polydor 1966, film soundtrack), *Antony And Cleopatra* (Polydor 1972, film soundtrack), *England Made Me* (DJM 1973, film soundtrack), *Inseminoid* (Citadel 1980), *The Shooting Party* (Varese 1984, film soundtrack), *Greystoke* (Warners 1984, film soundtrack), *The Winter People/Prayer For The Dying* (JOS 1989), *Cousteau - Rediscovery Of The World* (JOS 1989), *Cousteau - Amazon Parts 1 & 2* (JOS 1989), *Parc Oceanique Cousteau* (JOS 1989), *Cousteau - Saint Lawrence, Stairway To The Sea/Australia - The Last Barrier* (JOS 1989), *Cousteau - The First 75 Years/The Warm Blooded Sea* (JOS 1989), *King Of The Wind* (JOS 1990), *William The Conqueror* (JOS 1990), *John Scott Conducts His Own Favourite Film Scores* (JOS 1991).

Scott, Linda

b. Linda Joy Sampson, 1 June 1945, Queens, New York, USA. Linda Scott recorded 11 US Top 100 singles in the early 60s, including two Top 10 hits. She began singing in 1959, releasing her first single for Epic Records and appearing on the Arthur Godfrey radio show. In 1961, she signed with Canadian-American Records and recorded a remake of a song from the 1932 musical *Music In The Air*, 'I've Told Every Little Star', which reached number 3. She continued recording older material and repeated her first success with the follow-up 'Don't Bet Money Honey' also in 1961. Later singles also drew from films and stage music. Scott released four albums for Canadian-America, Congress and Kapp Records, and toured as part of the **Dick Clark** 'Caravan of Stars' road show. Clark later hired her as co-host of the syndicated rock television show *Where The Action Is* in the mid-60s, by which time her chart success had ended. She left show business in 1973 to devote time to raising a family.

Albums: *Starlight, Starbright* (1961), *Linda* (1962), *Hey, Look At Me Now* (1965). Compilations: *Great Scott! (Her Greatest Hits)* (1962)Films: *Don't Knock The Twist* (1962).

Scott, Little Jimmy

b. James Victor Scott, 17 July 1925, Cleveland, Ohio, USA. An influential figure to popular singers as stylistically diverse as **Nancy Wilson**, **Ray Charles**, and **Frankie Valli**, the highly acclaimed balladeer 'Little' Jimmy Scott nevertheless found it extremely difficult to transcend his enduring cult status among only the most knowledgeable of jazz aficionados until quite recently when he mounted a successful comeback after suffering decades of undeserved obscurity. Scott's wavering, other-worldly contralto vocal range, much closer in pitch to that of a woman than a man, was a result of a rare hereditary condition called Kallmann's Syndrome which restricted Scott's height to 4'11" until he was in his mid-30s (when he suddenly grew to 5'7"), blocked his sexual development, and stopped his voice from lowering into a conventional masculine register - thereby creating one of the most unusual and stunning vocal deliveries in post-war music history. He was one of 10 children, all of whom sang along heartily to their mother Justine's spirited piano playing at Hagar's Universal Spiritual Church in Cleveland. After her death (she was struck down while pushing her daughter out of the way of a speeding car), Scott was raised in various foster homes from age 13. While in his teens, he ushered at Cleveland's Metropolitan Theater, where he heard the bands of **Buddy Johnson**, **Erskine Hawkins** and **Lucky Millinder**. He received his first chance to sing in front of an audience in Meadsville, Pennsylvania, in the mid-40s, backed by jazz saxophone legends **Ben Webster** and **Lester Young**. Scott toured from 1945 to 1949 with shake dancer Estelle 'Caledonia' Young. Comedian Redd Foxx, actor Ralph Cooper, and heavyweight boxing champion Joe Louis helped the promising young singer land a job in 1948 at the Baby Grand nightclub on 125th Street in New York City. Scott joined **Lionel Hampton**'s band the next year, with whom he made his debut recordings. In 1950, he sang the hit 'Everybody's Somebody's Fool' on **Decca** Records as Hampton's featured vocalist (the song reached number 6 on **Billboard**'s R&B charts). Scott was also spotlighted vocally on 'I Wish I Knew', a popular but non-charting 1950 Decca side credited to the Lionel Hampton Quintet that featured Doug Duke's organ accompaniment, and 'I've Been A Fool'. Scott soon left Hampton's band to join forces with New Orleans R&B mainstay **Paul Gayten**'s band (which also featured vocalist **Annie Laurie**) in 1951. Scott made some live recordings for Fred Mendelsohn's Regal label that year with Gayten's band (trumpeter John Hunt, tenor saxist Ray Abrams, baritone saxist Pee Wee Numa-Moore, pianist Teddy Brannon, bassist Thomas Legange, and drummer Wesley Landis) that were captured for posterity at Rip's Playhouse, a New Orleans nightspot. Those long-buried tapes belatedly saw the light of day in 1991 on a Specialty Records disc. Mendelsohn sold Scott's contract to Teddy Reig and Jack Hook's Roost Records, where he recorded 16 sides under his own name (including his first classic rendition of 'The Masquerade Is Over') before signing with Herman Lubinsky's larger Savoy label in 1955. Four ballad-heavy sessions were held that year for Savoy, surrounding Scott with top-notch bandsmen including pianist/arranger Howard Biggs, saxist Budd Johnson, guitarists Mundell Lowe, George Barnes, and Everett Barksdale, bassist **Charles Mingus**, and drummer **Kenny Clarke**. Scott was unhappy with the skimpy financial rewards he received while under contract to Newark, New Jersey-based Savoy (more dates ensued in 1956 and 1958). But under Mendelsohn's astute supervision, Scott did manage to create numerous classic ballads for the company despite the fiscal discord. 'When Did You Leave Heaven', 'Imagination', and the bluesy 'Don't Cry Baby' are among Scott's finest performances for Savoy. Although his early years were artistically enriching, Scott's offstage existence was apparently another matter. The singer endured multiple divorces and suffered from a reported drinking problem. Scott temporarily switched over to Syd Nathan's King Records in 1957 for a dozen sides supervised by Henry Glover before returning to Savoy in 1960 for one more session. Finally, in 1962, Scott received what appeared to be his big break: a contract with Ray Charles' fledgling Tangerine label. With Marty Paich and Gerald Wilson supplying lush arrangements and Charles himself deftly handling the keyboards, the resulting album, *Falling in Love is Wonderful*, would have most likely boosted Scott's national profile considerably. Unfortunately, Lubinsky quashed the set's distribution shortly after its release, claiming that Scott remained under contract to Savoy. In 1969, **Atlantic** Records producer Joel Dorn recorded an album with Scott, *The Source*, with arrangements by Arif Mardin and sporting a varied set that included 'Day By Day', 'This Love Of Mine', and 'Exodus', but it failed to further Scott's fortunes. He returned to Savoy one last time in 1975 for a Mendelsohn-produced album that made little impact. For a lengthy period prior to his triumphant return to live performance in 1985 (which was spurred by the urging of his fourth wife, Earlene), Scott toiled as a shipping clerk at Cleveland's Sheraton Hotel, forgotten by all but his most loyal fans. Scott has engineered quite an amazing comeback in the years since. In 1992, his **Blue Horizon** album *All The Way* (listed as by Jimmy Scott, with no mention of his height) found him backed by an all-star jazz aggregation that included saxophonist **David 'Fathead' Newman**, pianist **Kenny Barron**, bassist **Ron Carter**, and drummer **Grady Tate** and string arrangements by **Johnny Mandel**. Scott followed in 1994 with another set for Sire/Blue Horizon, *Dream*. Jimmy Scott's reputation as

a unique vocal master is assured, but his status definitely has not come easily.

Selected albums: *Fabulous Songs Of Little Jimmy Scott* (Savoy), *The Soul Of Little Jimmy Scott* (Savoy), *Falling In Love Is Wonderful* (Tangerine 1962), *The Source* (Atlantic 1969), *Can't We Begin Again* (Savoy 1975), *Little Jimmy Scott* (Savoy Jazz 1984), *All Over Again* (Savoy Jazz 1985), *Regal Records: Live In New Orleans!* (Specialty 1991), *All The Way* (Blue Horizon 1992), *Lost And Found* (Rhino/Atlantic 1993), *Dream* (Sire/Blue Horizon 1994), *All Over Again* (Denon/Savoy Jazz 1994).

Scott, Marylin

Other than her records, almost nothing is known about Marylin Scott. One of her record companies had an address for her in Norfolk, Virginia, USA, and her first recording session was held in Charlotte, North Carolina, so an origin in the South Eastern states of the USA seems probable. Between 1945 and 1951 she recorded blues and R&B as Scott, and gospel as Mary Deloach. There was also a further gospel record in the mid-60s. Some of her records feature acoustic instruments and a fairly traditional sound, while others are in a more contemporary vein, with a small band for the R&B numbers, and organ and backing vocals for the gospel. In whatever setting, she performed with skill and conviction, and seemed to have few problems reconciling the sacred and secular sides of her musical personality.

Albums: *The Uneasy Blues* (1988), *I Got What Daddy Like* (1988).

Scott, Peggy, And Jo Jo Benson

Peggy Scott (b. 1948, Pensacola, Florida, USA) and Jo Jo Benson (b. 1940, Columbia, Ohio, USA). Scott, a former gospel singer, toured with **Ben E. King**, until a car accident forced her to seek a residency in a local group, the Swinging Sextet. Here she met Benson, who had sung with the **Chuck Willis** show, the **Upsetters** and the Enchanters. Scott and Benson scored a major US hit in 1968 with the powerful 'Lover's Holiday', but despite other success with 'Pickin' Wild Mountain Strawberries' and 'Soul Shake', the partners were unable to sustain a career together. Both subsequently recorded as solo acts, with Scott in particular cutting some fine performances for Old Town, **Mercury**, Malaco, RCA and SSS-International, for whom her cover of **Brenda Holloway**'s 'Every Little Bit Hurts' was outstanding.

Albums: *Soul Shake* (1969), *Lover's Heaven* (1969), *Nothing Can Stand In Our Way* (early 80s). Compilation: *Soul Shake* (1986).

Scott, Raymond

b. Harry Warnow, 10 September 1909, Brooklyn, New York, USA, d. 8 February 1994. After extensive studies, Scott became popular on radio as pianist, composer and leader of a small band. Playing mostly dance music and popular songs of the day plus a smattering of novelty numbers, many of which were his own compositions, his radio exposure had made him one of the best known names in the USA by the end of the 30s. Although most of his radio work had been with a polished sextet, he decided to exploit his popularity by forming a big band. After some limited touring he was persuaded back into the studios, where he formed one of the first mixed-race bands to be heard regularly on American radio. From the mid-40s onwards he worked in many areas of music; arranging, composing and directing orchestras on radio and television, and running recording companies. For several years in the 50s, he led the orchestra on NBC's *Your Hit Parade*. However, by the early 70s he had become involved in the pioneering of electronic music, and was head of electronic research and development for **Motown Records** for a time. He later retired to California.

Albums: *Business Man's Bounce (1939-40)* (1982), *Popular Music* (1984), *Raymond Scott And His Orchestra (1944)* (1988), *Reckless Nights And Turkish Twilights (1937-39)* (1993).

Scott, Robin

(see **M**)

Scott, Roger

b. 23 October 1943, Barnet, England, d. 31 October 1989. In 1961 Scott joined the Merchant Navy, travelling frequently to the USA. The style of music broadcasting there was unlike anything available (legally) in the UK. He was employed first in New York and subsequently in Montreal as a 'Brit' disc jockey, before being lured back to the UK in the early 70s by the prospect of legal commercial radio. Initially he worked for the United Biscuits Network, a factory broadcasting system which spawned several successful disc jockeys. In 1972 he spent two months with Radio 1 under the pseudonym Bob Baker, before joining Capital Radio, London's first commercial music station, in 1973. He stayed with Capital for 15 years. He was approached to be London anchor for the American radio syndication of **Live Aid** and the Nelson Mandela concerts. He then moved to Radio 1 in 1988 and took over from Johnnie Walker on the *Saturday Sequence*, and also hosted a late-night Sunday show. However, Scott was diagnosed with stomach cancer in the summer of 1989, but worked on until two weeks before his death.

Scott, Ronnie

b. 28 January 1927, London, England. Scott began playing on the soprano saxophone but switched to tenor in his early teens. After playing informally in clubs he joined the Johnny Claes band in 1944, before spells with **Ted Heath**, Bert **Ambrose** and other popular British dance bands. Scott also played on transatlantic liners in order to visit the USA and hear bebop at first hand. By the late 40s he was a key figure in the London bop scene, playing at the Club Eleven, of which he was a co-founder. During the 50s he led his own band and was also co-leader with **Tubby Hayes** of the Jazz Couriers. In 1959, he opened his own club in Gerrard Street, London, later transferring to Frith Street. During the 60s he divided his time between leading his own small group and running the club, but also found time to play with the **Clarke-Boland Big Band**. In the 70s and 80s he continued to lead small bands, usually a quartet, occasionally touring but most often playing as the interval band between sessions by the modern American jazz musicians he brought to the club. As a player, Scott comfortably straddles the mainstream and modern aspects of jazz. His big tone lends itself to a slightly aggressive approach, although in his ballad playing he displays the warmth which characterized the work of **Zoot Sims** and late-period **Stan Getz**, musicians he admires, but does not imitate. Although a gifted player, Scott's greatest contribution to jazz lies in his tireless promotion of fine British musicians and in his establishment of his club, a venue which has become renowned throughout the world for the excellence of its setting and the artists on display. In 1981, Scott was awarded an OBE in recognition of his services to music.

Albums: *Battle Royal* (Esquire 1951), *The Ronnie Scott Jazz Group* i (1952), *Live At The Jazz Club* (1953), *The Ronnie Scott Jazz Group* ii (1954), *The Jazz Couriers In Concert* (1958), *The Last Word* (1959), *The Night Is Scott And You're So Swingable* (1965), *Live At Ronnie's* (1968), *Scott At Ronnie's* (1973), *Serious Gold* (1977), *Great Scott* (1979), with various artists *Ronnie Scott's 20th Anniversary Album* (1979), *Never Pat A Burning Dog* (Jazz House 1990).

Further reading: *Jazz At Ronnie Scott's*, Grime, Kitty (ed.) (1979), *Let's Join Hands And Contact The Living* , Fordham, John (1986), *Jazz Man: The Amazing Story Of Ronnie Scott And His Club*, Fordham, John (1994).

Scott, Shirley

b. 14 March 1934, Philadelphia, Pennsylvania, USA. Although she had studied both piano and trumpet as a child, Scott's breakthrough occurred when she switched to organ in the mid-50s. Mostly working in small groups with a saxophone leader and a drummer, she became very popular. Her musical associates have included such outstanding jazzmen as **Eddie 'Lockjaw' Davis**, **Stanley Turrentine** (to whom she was married for a while), **Jimmy Forrest** and **Dexter Gordon**. A gifted player with an eclectic style that encompasses the blues and bebop, Scott is one of only a handful of organists to satisfactorily fit a potentially unsuitable instrument into a jazz setting. Her career received a boost in the 90s when the Hammond organ became fashionable once more.

Albums: *Shirley's Sounds* (1958), *The Eddie Lockjaw Davis Cookbook* (1958), *Great Scott!* (1958), *Scottie* (1958), *Shirley Scott Plays Duke* (1959), *Soul Searching* (1959), *The Shirley Scott Trio* i (1960), *Soul Sisters* (1960), *Mucho Mucho* (1960), *Like Cozy* (1960), *Satin Doll* (1961), *Stompin'* (1961), *Hip Soul* (1961), *Blue Seven* (1961), *Shirley Scott Plays Horace Silver* (1961), *Hip Twist* (1961), with Stanley Turrentine *Dearly Beloved* (1961), *Happy Talk* (1962), *The Soul Is Willing* (1963), *Drag 'Em Out* (1963), *Soul Shoutin'* (1963), *Travellin' Light* (1964), *Blue Flames* (Original Jazz Classics 1964), *Shirley Scott And Her Orchestra* i (1964), *The Great Live Sessions* (1964), *The Shirley Scott Sextet* (1965), *Queen Of The Organ* (Impulse 1965), *The Shirley Scott Trio* ii (1966), *The Shirley Scott Trio* iii (1966), *Shirley Scott And Her Orchestra* ii (1966), *The Shirley Scott Quintet* (1972), *One For Me* (1974), *Oasis* (Muse 1990), *Blues Everywhere* (Candid 1993).

Scott, Tom

b. 19 May 1948, Los Angeles, California, USA. Scott's mother - Margery Wright - was a pianist, his father - Nathan Scott - a film and television composer. Scott played clarinet in high school and won a teenage competition with his Neoteric Trio at the Hollywood Bowl in 1965. He learned all the saxophones and played in the studios for TV shows such as *Ironside*. He performed on **Roger Kellaway**'s *Spirit Feel* in 1967, playing fluent alto and soprano over a proto-fusion encounter of hard bop and rock music. As a member of Spontaneous Combustion in 1969, he played on *Come And Stick Your Head In*, an experimental record in the jazz-rock idiom. His own records - *Honeysuckle Breeze* (1967) and *Rural Still Life* (1968) - presented a tight, forceful jazz funk. From his early 20s he wrote prolifically for television and films (including *Conquest Of The Planet Of The Apes*), his sound becoming the blueprint for LA copshow soundtracks: urgent, funky, streamlined. His band, the LA Express, became one of the most successful fusion bands of the 70s. **Joni Mitchell** used them as her backing band on *Miles Of Aisles* (and guested on 1975's *Tom Cat*) and **George Harrison** played slide guitar on *New York Connection*. 1987's *Streamlines* showed that Scott had not lost his sound, but an interest in samples of ethnic instruments had given his music a more world-music feel.

Albums: *Honeysucle Breeze* (1967), *Rural Still Life* (1968), with Spontaneous Combustion *Come And Stick Your Head In* (1969), *Tom Scott & the LA Express* (1974), *Tom Cat* (1975), *New York Connection* (1975), *Blow It Out* (1977), *Apple Juice* (1981), *Desire* (1982), *Streamlines* (1987), *Target* (1993)

Films: *Americation* (1979).

Scott, Tommy

An integral part of Glasgow's early beat scene, Scott later moved to London where he joined the staff of **Decca Records**. He not only produced much of

Them's output, but contributed three songs to the group's second album. One of these, 'I Can Only Give You Everything', written with **Phil Coulter** was later recorded by the **Troggs**. In 1967, Them's former manager, **Phil Solomon**, founded Major Minor Records for which Scott became producer and A&R manager. He thus supervised releases by such disparate acts as the **Dubliners** and **Taste**, while licensing material from the USA, including the rights to **Tommy James And The Shondells**. However, the label latterly folded; Scott has enjoyed a lucrative career recording Scottish country dance band music since.

Albums: *Pipes And Strings Of Scotland* (1983), *Pipes And Strings Of Scotland Volume 2* (1984), *Scotland: 14 All-Time Scottish Favourites* (1986), *Tommy Scott's Scotland* (1986), *The Tommy Scott Collection* (1987), *Tommy Scott's Royale Highland Showband* (1987).

Further reading: *Van Morrison: A Portrait Of The Artist*, Johnny Rogan.

Scott, Tony

b. Anthony Sciacca, 17 June 1921, Morristown, New Jersey, USA. Scott learned to play clarinet as a child, later studying formally at the Juilliard School in Manhattan. During the late 40s and beyond, he made his living playing in big bands and as a sideman in mainstream groups, sometimes playing tenor saxophone. Fascinated by the new jazz sounds emerging from Minton's Playhouse and other New York venues, he became a strongly committed bop musician. Unfortunately for the development of his career, bop and the clarinet were uneasy bedfellows, although Scott was one of the tiny number of clarinettists to achieve some recognition, building a reputation through the 50s as one of the best new players on his instrument. He was also active as an arranger and musical director for several singers, including **Harry Belafonte**, **Billie Holiday** and **Sarah Vaughan**. In 1959 he recorded the remarkably forward-looking *Sung Heroes*, with **Bill Evans**, **Scott La Faro** and **Paul Motian**, but the same year left America, tired of music business racism and despairing of the fact that so many of his close friends - **Oran 'Hot Lips' Page**, **Charlie Parker**, **Art Tatum**, **Sid Catlett**, **Lester Young**, Billie Holiday - had recently died. Scott spent six years travelling, both in Europe and (mostly) the Far East, and began to incorporate into his repertoire elements of ethnic music, especially from India and the Orient, creating a personal precedent for world music long before the genre was acknowledged. The records he made in the mid-60s as aids to meditation proved to be popular and consistent sellers - 'a godsend' he said of them in 1988, claiming that their royalties were still his main source of income. In the early 70s Scott settled in Italy, playing at festivals and touring, often to the far east, making occasional records and as often as not anticipating trends and fashions in music - even if, as so often happens with pioneers, his work has been overshadowed by that of other less-talented musicians. His latest project to date has been a double album consisting entirely of different versions of **Billy Strayhorn**'s standard, 'Lush Life'. 'No one has sung it right yet', Scott told *Wire* in 1988, 'including **Nat 'King' Cole**, Sarah Vaughan, everybody - they all goof it'.

Albums: *A Touch Of Tony Scott* (1956), *Scott's Fling* (1957), *The Modern Art Of Jazz* (1957), *A Day In New York* (Fresh Sound 1958), *South Pacific Jazz* (1958), *52nd Street Scene* (1958), *Golden Moments* (1959), *Sung Heroes* (1959), *Dedications* (Core 1957-59 recordings), *Music For Zen Meditation* (Verve 1964), *Music For Yoga Meditation And Other Joys* (c.1967), *Tony Scott* (c.1969), *Prism* (1977), *Boomerang* (1977), *African Bird: Come Back! Mother Africa* (Soul Note 1984), *Lush Life Vols 1 and 2* (Core 1989), *Astral Meditation: Voyage Into A Black Hole 1-3* (Core 1989), *The Clarinet Album* (Philology 1993).

Scott-Heron, Gil

b. 1 April 1949, Chicago, Illinois, USA. Raised in Jackson, Tennessee, by his grandmother, Scott-Heron moved to New York at the age of 13 and had published two novels (*The Vulture* and *The Nigger Factory*) plus a book of poems by the time he was 12. He met musician Brian Jackson when both were students at Lincoln University, Pennsylvania, and in 1972 they formed the Midnight Band to play their original blend of jazz, soul and prototype rap music. *Small Talk At 125th And Lenox* was mostly an album of poems (from his book of the same name), but later albums showed Scott-Heron developing into a skilled songwriter whose work was soon covered by other artists: for example, **Labelle** recorded his 'The Revolution Will Not Be Televised' and **Esther Phillips** made a gripping version of 'Home Is Where The Hatred Is'. In 1973 he had a minor hit with 'The Bottle'. *Winter In America* and *The First Minute Of A New Day*, for new label **Arista**, were both heavily jazz-influenced, but later sets saw Scott-Heron exploring more pop-oriented formats, and in 1976 he scored a hit with the disco-based protest single, 'Johannesburg'. One of his best records of the 80s, *Reflections*, featured a fine version of **Marvin Gaye**'s 'Inner City Blues'; but his strongest songs were generally his own barbed political diatribes, in which he confronted issues such as nuclear power, apartheid and poverty and made a series of scathing attacks on American politicians. Richard Nixon, Gerald Ford, Barry Goldwater and Jimmy Carter were all targets of his trenchant satire and his anti-Reagan rap, 'B-Movie', gave him another small hit in 1982. An important precursor of today's rap artists, Scott-Heron once described Jackson (who left the band in 1980) and himself as 'interpreters of the black experience'.

However, by the 90s his view of the development of rap had become more jaundiced: 'They need to study music. I played in several bands before I began my career as a poet. There's a big difference between putting words over some music, and blending those same words into the music. There's not a lot of humour. They use a lot of slang and colloquialisms, and you don't really see inside the person. Instead, you just get a lot of posturing'. In 1994 he released his first album for ten years, *Spirits*, which began with 'Message To The Messenger', an address to today's rap artists: '. . . Young rappers, one more suggestion before I get out of your way, But I appreciate the respect you give me and what you got to say, I'm sayin' protect your community and spread that respect around, Tell brothers and sisters they got to calm that bullshit down, 'Cause we're terrorizin' our old folks and we brought fear into our homes'.

Albums: *Small Talk At 125th And Lenox* (Flying Dutchman 1972), *Free Will* (Flying Dutchman 1972), *Pieces Of A Man* (Flying Dutchman 1973), *Winter In America* (Strata East 1974), *The First Minute Of A New Day* (Arista 1975), *From South Africa To South Carolina* (Arista 1975), *It's Your World* (Arista 1976), *Bridges* (Arista 1977), *Secrets* (Arista 1978), *1980* (Arista 1980), *Real Eyes* (Arista 1980), *Reflections* (Arista 1981), *Moving Target* (Arista 1982), *Spirits* (TVT Records 1994). Compilations: *The Revolution Will Not Be Televised* (Flying Dutchman 1974), *The Mind Of Gil Scott-Heron* (1979), *The Best Of Gil Scott-Heron* (Arista 1984). *Tales Of Gil* (Essential 1990; double album), *Glory: The Gil Scott-Heron Collection* (Arista 1990). Video: *Tales Of Gil* (1990).

Scotty

b. c.1950, Jamaica. A singer and DJ, David Scott aka Scotty started out in late 1967 as a member of the Federals vocal group, gaining a massive local hit with 'Penny For Your Song' for producer **Derrick Harriott** the same year. They also recorded 'By The River' and 'Shocking Love' for Harriott, the original group breaking up after the Jamaican Song Festival in 1969. Scotty then joined the original line-up of the Chosen Few with Noel Brown and Franklin Spence, again at the instigation of Harriott. In July 1970, Scotty recorded his first DJ title, 'Musical Chariot'; this was followed by 'Sesame Street' (1970, Jamaican chart number 3), 'Riddle I This'/'Musical Chariot' (1970, Jamaican chart number 1), 'Jam Rock Style' (1971), later featured in the film *The Harder They Come*, 'Draw Your Brakes'. Scotty and Harriott had followed the trend set by DJs like **U-Roy** and **Dennis Alcapone** for **Duke Reid**, combining witty lyrics with classic **rocksteady** rhythms. He continued recording with Harriott until 1972. He later worked under the supervision of **Harry 'J' Johnson**. (the original DJ version of 'Breakfast In Bed'), Lloyd Charmers and **Sonia Pottinger**. Scotty moved to the USA during the mid-70s. During the late 80s, having returned to live in Jamaica, he began recording in a **ragga** style, with considerable local success.

Albums: *Schooldays* (1972), *Unbelievable Sounds* (Trojan 1988).

Scratch Acid

Formed in Austin, Texas, USA in 1982, Scratch Acid originally comprised of Steve Anderson (vocals), David Wm. Sims (guitar), Brett Bradford (guitar), David Yow (bass) and Rey Washam (drums), although Anderson was quickly ousted. The reshaped quartet made their live debut as an instrumental act, supporting the **Butthole Surfers**, following which Yow switched to vocals with Sims taking up bass. Scratch Acid established a reputation as one of the state's leading post-hardcore noise exponents, creating a sound inspired by **Killdozer** and **Big Black**. They issued *Scratch Acid* in 1984, but it was two years before the group began recording a full-length album. Although *Just Keep Eating* lacked the arresting power of its predecessor, it confirmed the group's ambition and originality. *Berserker*, completed later the same year, reaffirmed their influential status and is chiefly recalled for its opening track, 'Mary Had A Little Drug Problem'. Scratch Acid then undertook extended tours of the Europe and the USA, but relations within the group had become strained and they split up in May 1987 following a live date at Austin's Cave Club. Sims and Washam then joined Steve Albini (ex-Big Black) in **Rapeman**, following which Sims was reunited with Yow in the **Jesus Lizard**.

Albums: *Scratch Acid* (1984), *Just Keep Eating* (1986), *Berserker* (1986). Compilation: *The Greatest Gift* (1991).

Scream

Not to be confused with the Washington, DC punk band of the same name, this group took shape from the ashes of LA favourites **Racer X** when in-demand Philadelphian vocalist/guitarist John Corabi joined Bruce Bouillet (lead guitar) and John Alderete (bass) in that band's final line-up. With the departure of Scott Travis to **Judas Priest**, the drumstool was filled by Walt Woodward III (ex-**Americade** and **Shark Island**), and the band became the Scream. In contrast to the complex guitar-orientated metal of the old act, the Scream played in a variety of styles, from the gentle ballad, 'Father, Mother, Son' and the witty acoustic blues of 'Never Loved Her Anyway' to the electric hard rock of 'Outlaw' and the atmospheric 'Man In The Moon'. They even tackled funk-rock with 'Tell Me Why', revealing influences as diverse as the **Rolling Stones**, **Van Halen**, **Led Zeppelin**, **Humble Pie** and **Aerosmith**. However, the resultant debut, *Let It Scream*, was a highly cohesive work with a powerful Eddie Kramer production and a charismatic performance from Corabi. The album and subsequent live work were well-received, and with priority backing from Hollywood Records, the Scream seemed set for stardom, until Corabi was tempted away to replace Vince Neil in **Mötley Crüe**. A lengthy search for a new singer ensued, with Billy Scott eventually being recruited, but the band subsequently changed their name to Stash, with a new direction reportedly in the vein of **Sly And The Family Stone**.

Album: *Let It Scream* (Hollywood 1991).

Screaming Blue Messiahs

Rising from the ashes of Motor Boys Motor, the Screaming Blue Messiahs were essentially a vehicle for shaven-headed American singer/songwriter and guitarist Bill Carter. Supported by Kenny Harris (drums) and Chris Thompson (bass), Carter churned out a tight, venomous rock formula drawn from R&B and new wave, first heard on the well-received mini-album, *Good And Gone*. Originally issued on Ace's Big Beat label in July 1984, it made sufficient noise to attract **WEA Records**, who duly re-promoted it a year later. 'Twin Cadillac Valentine' (1985), was a razor-sharp slab of dynamic guitar rock and paved the way for the Screaming Blue Messiahs' most impressive album, *Gun Shy*, the following year. A session previously recorded for BBC disc jockey **John Peel** in 1984 saw the light of day nearly three years later on the Strange Fruit 'Peel Sessions' series. This preceded the the Screaming Blue Messiahs' relatively low key *Bikini Red* in September 1986. This spawned the closest thing to a hit single the Messiahs ever achieved with the eccentric 'I Wanna Be A Flintstone', which broached the Top 30 in February 1988. It was two years before a new Screaming Blue Messiahs set and when *Totally Religious* (on **Atlantic Records**) was released in October 1989, it failed to ignite an apathetic public. Although Carter's bite was still evident, the album disappointed in relation to past achievements and they disbanded soon after release. Harris and Thomas would go on to form Lerue.

Albums: *Good And Gone* (Big Beat 1984, mini-album), *Gun Shy* (WEA 1986), *Bikini Red* (WEA 1987), *Totally Religious* (Atlantic 1989). Compilation: *BBC Radio 1 Live In Concert* (Windsong 1992, rec. 1988).

Screaming Trees

Hard-drinking rock band from the rural community of Ellensburg, near Seattle, USA. The Screaming Trees blend 60s music (the **Beach Boys** being an obvious reference point) with psychotic, pure punk rage. Not to be confused with the Sheffield, England, synthesizer group of the same name who were also operational in the mid-80s, the Connor brothers (Gary Lee; guitar and Van; bass) are among the largest men in rock, rvialled in their girth only by fellow Seattle heavyweights **Poison Idea**. The rest of the line-up comprises Mark Lanegan (vocals) and Barrett Martin (drums - replacing original encumbent Mark Pickerell in 1991). *Even If And Especially When*, the best of three strong albums for **SST Records**, included notable compositions like the live favourite, 'Transfiguration', which typified the group's blend of punk aggression and 60s mysticism. Major label debut *Uncle Anaesthesia* brought production from Terry Date and **Soundgarden**'s Chris Cornell. By the time Screaming Trees moved to **Epic Records** they had embraced what one *Melody Maker* journalist called 'unashamed 70s Yankee rock', straddled by bursts of punk spite. Lanegan had by now released a solo, largely acoustic album, *The Winding Sheet*, for **Sub Pop** in 1990. This affecting, intensely personal collection included a cover of **Leadbelly**'s 'Where Did You Sleep Last Night', which Kurt Cobain would later employ as the trump card in **Nirvana**'s *MTV Unplugged* session. Other extra-curricular activities included Gary Lee Conner's Purple Outside project, and his brother Van fronting Solomon Grundy (one album each in 1990).

Albums: *Clairvoyance* (Velvetone 1986), *Even If And Especially When* (SST 1987), *Invisible Lantern* (SST 1988), *Buzz Factory* (SST 1989), *Uncle Anaesthesia* (Epic 1991), *Sweet Oblivion* (Epic 1992), *Change Has Come* (Epic 1993). Compilation: *Anthology* (SST 1991).

Scritti Politti

Scritti Politti was founded by a group of Leeds art students in 1978. By the time of their first single, 'Skank Bloc Bologna', the nucleus of the band was Green Gartside (b. 'Green' Strohmeyer-Gartside, 22 June 1956, Cardiff, Wales; vocals - who prefers not to reveal his actual first name), Matthew Kay (keyboards/manager) and Tom Morley (drums/programming) and Nial Jinks (bass, departed 1980). At this stage, the group was explicitly political (Green had been a Young Communist), encouraging listeners to create their own music in the face of the corporate record industry. Gartside also gained a reputation for convoluted word-play within his lyrics. This early *avant garde* phase gave way to a smooth sound which brought together elements of pop, jazz, soul and reggae on songs like 'The Sweetest Girl' (with **Robert Wyatt** on piano) and 'Asylums In Jerusalem'/'Jacques Derrida', which appeared on their debut album for **Rough Trade Records**, produced by Adam Kidron. Morley quit the group in November 1982, by which time Gartside *was* Scritti Politti. *Songs To Remember* became Rough Trade's most successful chart album; number 1 in the UK independent and, in the national chart, peaking at number 12 (beating **Stiff Little Fingers**' previous effort at number 14). After moving on to **Virgin Records**, Green linked up with New York musicians David Gamson (guitar) and Fred Maher (drums), who formed the basis of the group that made a series of UK hits in the years 1984-88.

Produced by **Arif Mardin**, these included 'Wood Beez (Pray Like Aretha Franklin)' (number 10), 'Absolute' (number 17) and 'The Word Girl' (number 6). A three-year silence was broken by 'Oh Patti (Don't Feel Sorry For Loverboy)', lifted from *Provision*, and boasting a trumpet solo by **Miles Davis**. Gartside again maintained a low-profile for two years after 'First Boy In This Town (Love Sick)', failed to break into the UK Top 60 in late 1988. He returned in 1991 with a revival of the **Beatles**' 'She's A Woman', featuring leading reggae star **Shabba Ranks** while another Jamaican star, Sweetie Irie, guested on a version of **Gladys Knight And The Pips**' 1967 hit, 'Take Me In Your Arms And Love Me'.

Albums: *Songs To Remember* (Rough Trade 1981), *Cupid And Psyche* (Virgin 1985), *Provision* (Virgin 1988).

Scrooge

By all accounts, Albert Finney was by no means the first choice to play the lead in this musical version of Charles Dickens's celebrated novel *A Christmas Carol* which was released in 1970. As it turns out, he makes a wonderfully crotchety Ebenezer Scrooge, the miserable miser who becomes a totally reformed character following eerie visitations by his late partner, Jacob Marley (Alec Guinness), and the ghosts of Christmases Past, Present and Yet To Come (Edith Evans, Kenneth More and Paddy Stone). The main beneficiaries of this new-found munificence are Scrooge's clerk, Bob Cratchit (David Collings) and his son Tiny Tim (Richard Beaumont). Also taking part in this extremely good looking production which was designed by Terry Marsh and photographed in Technicolor and Panavision by Oswald Morris, were Michael Medwin, Laurence Naismith, Anton Rodgers, Suzanne Neve, Frances Cuka, Roy Kinnear and Gordon Jackson. **Leslie Bricusse**, who co-produced the film with Robert Solo in the UK for Cinema Center, also wrote the screenplay and the songs. His rather uninspired score included the lively 'Thank You Very Much', 'Father Christmas', 'I'll Begin Again', 'A Christmas Carol', 'December The 25th', 'Happiness', 'I Like Life', and 'The Beautiful Day'. Paddy Stone staged the dances and the director was Ronald Neame. British reference books record another seven screen versions of *Scrooge* from 1901 onwards, starring such distinguished actors as Seymour Hicks, Bransby Williams, and Alastair Sim. There was also a more contemporary interpretation of *A Christmas Carol* entitled *Scrooged*, which was made in the USA in 1988 and starred Bill Murray and Karen Allen. Four years after that, Bricusse adapted his screen musical for the stage. It had its world premiere in November 1992 in Birmingham, England, with Bricusse's old writing partner **Anthony Newley** in the leading role.

Scruggs, Earl

b. 6 January 1924, Cleveland County, North Carolina, USA. Scruggs was raised in the Appalachian Mountains, and learned to play banjo from the age of five. In 1944, he joined **Bill Monroe**'s Bluegrass Boys, where he perfected his three- finger banjo technique. He later left with fellow member **Lester Flatt**, to form the Foggy Mountain Boys in 1948. They enjoyed a long career spanning 20 years, and were reportedly only outsold during the 60s, on **CBS Records**, by **Johnny Cash**. The duo became synonymous with their recordings of 'Foggy Mountain Breakdown', which was used in the film *Bonnie And Clyde* and 'The Ballad Of Jed Clampett', which was the theme tune for the television series *The Beverly Hillbillies*. In 1969, after Flatt and Scruggs parted company, the Earl Scruggs Revue was formed featuring Earl (banjo/vocals), and his sons, Randy (lead guitar/slide guitar/bass/vocals), Gary (bass/harmonica/vocals), Steve (guitar), plus Josh Graves (dobro/guitar/vocals) and Jody Maphis (drums/vocals). The Earl Scruggs Revue performed to great acclaim at the Wembley International Festival of Country Music in 1972. *His Family And Friends*, which comes from a 1971 National Educational Television Soundtrack, included guest appearances by **Bob Dylan**, **Joan Baez** and the **Byrds**. *Anniversary Special, Volume 1*, included a veritable who's who of the music scene, including **Roger McGuinn** and **Dan Fogelberg**. Graves left the group during the mid-70s to pursue a solo career. Scruggs' innovation in taking traditional fiddle tunes and transposing them for playing on banjo helped push back the boundaries of bluegrass, and paved the way for the later 'Newgrass' revival.

Albums: *Nashville's Rock* (c.1970), *Earl Scruggs Performing With His Family And Friends* (1972), *I Saw The Light With Some Help From My Friends* (1972), *Live At Kansas State* (1972), *Duelling Banjos* (1973), *The Earl Scruggs Revue* (1973), *Where Lillies Bloom* (c1970), *Rocking Across The Country* (1973), *Anniversary Special, Volume 1* (1975), *The Earl Scruggs Revue, Volume 2* (1976), *Family Portrait* (1976), *Earl Scruggs, 5-String Instructional Album* (1976), *Live From Austin City Limits* (1977), *Strike Anywhere* (1977), *Bold And New* (1978), *Today And Forever* (1979), *Rockin' 'Cross The Country* (1974), *Top Of The World* (1983).

Further reading: *Earl Scruggs And The 5-String Banjo*, Earl Scruggs

Sea Hags

Purveyors of all things degenerate and of definite 'wrong side of the tracks' orientation, Sea Hags were formed in San Francisco, California, in 1985. With a line-up comprising ex-rock photographer Ron Yocom (guitar/vocals), Frankie Wilsey (guitar), Chris Schlosshardt (bass) and Adam Maples (drums), their own manager would famously describe their trajectory thus: 'there's only so far you can get with three junkies and one alcoholic'. Their first and only album was recorded for **Chrysalis** by **Guns N' Roses** producer, Mike Clink (after the **Cult**'s Ian Astbury had expressed an interest). This collection, which aped the group's obvious inspiration, **Aerosmith**, riff for riff, caught the attention of the press, a situation exacerbated by the media-friendly antics of the subjects. However, the sadly predictable death of Chris Schlosshardt from a suspected drug overdose killed the band's momentum. Maples was briefly rumoured to be replacement for Steven Adler in Guns N'Roses, while Wilsey joined **Arcade**.

Album: *Sea Hags* (Chrysalis 1989).

Sea Urchins

The Sea Urchins were formed in West Bromwich, England, during 1986 by James Roberts (b. 4 March 1970, West Bromwich, West Midlands, England; vocals), Simon Woodcock (b. 2 December 1969, West Bromwich, West Midlands, England; guitar), Mark Bevin (b. 21 January 1970; bass), Bridget Duffy (b. 28 June 1970, Birmingham, England; tambourine, ex-drummer for the Velvet Underwear), Patrick Roberts (drums) and Robert Cooksey (b. 14 November 1969, Solihull, West Midlands, England; guitar). Two flexi-discs in the summer of 1987, 'Clingfilm' and 'Summershine', were available with several fanzines, and revealed the band's love of **Byrds** harmonies and the more tranquil aspects of the 60s. After Mark was replaced by Darren Martin (b. 25 March 1967) and Bridget had moved onto Vox organ, the Sea Urchins unleashed their first single, and the first for Bristol's **Sarah Records** in November 1987. The EP, *Pristine Christine*, was a well-received slice of jangly-guitar pop, but the following year's 'Solace' was stronger, the start of their self-confessed mod-rock phase. Both singles had fared well, but Sarah were reluctant to issue a complete album, and Bridget and Darren soon left, Simon switching to bass and James moving to guitar. Eventually, 'A Morning Odyssey' surfaced in the summer of 1990, but when the label refused to issue the rockier 'Low Scene', the band left Sarah for good. In the meantime, Welsh label Fierce issued a Sea Urchins ballad from 1988. The band signed to the Cheree label early in 1991 for 'Please Don't Cry', and were joined on stage by Andy Ellison (ex-**John's Children** and **Radio Stars**). In fact, John's Children's John Hewlett was to produce their next single, until Woodcock quit and the Sea Urchins split up after a particularly dismal gig in the summer of 1991. James, Patrick and Robert Cooksey were provisionally working as the Low Scene by the end of the year.

Seal

b. Sealhenry Samuel, 19 February 1963, London, England. Seal has established himself at the forefront of a British soul revival which looks set firm for the 90s. The second eldest of six brothers, his ancestry mixed Nigerian, Brazilian and Afro-Caribbean blood. Seal's first performance was at school at the age of 11, but it would be much later before his tentative musical plans came to fruition. Despite making many demos, he found it difficult to break into the music industry. After six months in Asia, he returned to England to find it entrenched in the Summer Of Love House Explosion. As the result of a chance encounter with rap artist Chester he was introduced to techno wizard **Adamski**. Seal happily contributed lyrics to his embryonic dance track, 'Killer', which eventually took the UK's dance floors by storm. However, the partnership did not last and Seal released his debut solo single, 'Crazy'. The first thing he had ventured to write on the guitar, the lyrics were imbued with the sort of new age mysticism given vent by 90s dance culture: 'Science is coming to a standstill, there's a swing more to the spiritual that gives me hope'. With production handled by **Trevor Horn**, Seal went on to record a magnificent debut album in Los Angeles with **Wendy And Lisa** which proved a huge commercial success (3 million copies worldwide). This was compounded when 1992's BRIT Awards saw him walk away with nearly every conceivable category. The high-profile campaign launched by **WEA** for his second album, once again an eponymous affair, saw sales of 2 million, worldwide, in its first year of release. Album: *Seal* i (1991), *Seal* ii (WEA 1994).

Seals And Crofts

A duo consisting of Jim Seals (b. 17 October 1941, Sidney, Texas, USA) and Dash Crofts (b. 14 August 1940, Cisco, Texas, USA), Seals And Crofts were one of the most popular soft rock-pop acts of the 70s. The pair first worked together in 1958 as guitarist (Seals) and drummer (Crofts) for Texan singer Dean Beard, with whom they recorded a number of singles that did not chart. When Beard was asked to join the **Champs**, of 'Tequila' fame, Seals and Crofts came along, relocating to Los Angeles. They stayed with the Champs until 1965, when Crofts returned to Texas. The following year, Seals joined a group called the Dawnbreakers, and Crofts returned to Los Angeles to join as well. Both Seals and Crofts converted to the Baha'i religion in 1969 (10 years later they would leave the music business to devote themselves to it full-time). Following the split of the Dawnbreakers, Seals and Crofts continued as an acoustic music duo (Seals played guitar, saxophone and violin, Crofts guitar and mandolin), recording their first album, which did not chart, for the Talent Associates label. Meanwhile, the pair performed live and built a following. In 1970 *Down Home*, made the charts and led to a label change to **Warner Brothers Records**. Their second album for that company, 1972's *Summer Breeze*, made number 7 on the US charts and the title single reached number 6.

('Summer Breeze' also provided the **Isley Brothers** with a UK Top 20 hit in 1974.) It was followed in 1973 by their best-selling *Diamond Girl*, which also yielded a number 6 title single. They maintained their popularity throughout the mid-70s, coming up with yet another number 6 single, 'Get Closer', in 1976. Following the release of the 1978 album *Takin' It Easy* and the same-titled single, which became their final chart entries, Seals And Crofts became less involved in music and devoted themselves to their faith.

Albums: *Seals And Crofts* (TA 1970), *Down Home* (TA 1970), *Year Of Sunday* (Warner 1972), *Summer Breeze* (Warner 1972), *Diamond Girl* (Warner 1973), *Unborn Child* (Warner 1974), *I'll Play For You* (Warner 1975), *Get Closer* (Warner 1976), *Sudan Village* (Warner 1976), *One On One* (Warner 1977, film soundtrack), *Takin' It Easy* (Warner 1978), *The Longest Road* (1980). Compilations: *Greatest Hits* (Warner 1975).

Seals, Dan

b. 8 February 1950, McCamey, Texas, USA. Leaving successful pop duo **England Dan And John Ford Coley** was, at first, a disastrous career move for Dan Seals. His management left him with unpaid tax bills and mounting debts and he lost his house, his van and his money. He says, 'I was bankrupt, separated and living at friends' places. My kids were with friends. It was a real bad time'. Furthermore, the two albums that he made for **Atlantic Records** as a solo artist, *Stones* and *Harbinger*, meant little. However, Kyle Lehning, who produced his hits with England Dan And John Ford Coley, never lost faith and helped to establish him on the US country charts with 'Everybody's Dream Girl' in 1983. Further country hits followed and he had a US number 1 hit with 'Meet Me In Montana', a duet with **Marie Osmond**, in 1985. Seals then had an extraordinary run of eight consecutive US number 1 country singles: the dancing 'Bop', the rodeo story 'Everything That Glitters (Is Not Gold)', 'You Still Move Me', 'I Will Be There', 'Three Time Loser', the wedding song 'One Friend', 'Addicted' and 'Big Wheels In The Moonlight', many of which he wrote himself. *Won't Be Blue Anymore*, sold half a million copies in the USA, while another big-selling record, *On The Front Line*, included an exquisite duet with **Emmylou Harris**, 'Lullaby'.

Albums: *Stones* (1980), *Harbinger* (1982), *Rebel Heart* (1983), *San Antone* (1984), *Won't Be Blue Anymore* (1985), *On The Front Line* (1986), *Rage On* (1988), *On Arrival* (1990), *Walking The Wire* (1992). Compilation: *The Best Of Dan Seals* (1987).

Seals, Son

b. Frank Seals Jnr., 13 August 1942, Osceola, Arkansas, USA. Son Seals was one of 13 children of Jim Seals, an entertainer and club owner in rural Arkansas. Son began his musical education on the drums and worked with many of the later famous musicians who travelled through the area. Having taught himself to play the guitar, he formed his own band to work around the city of Little Rock. He moved to Chicago in 1971, initially to work outside music, although he soon began to appear at local clubs. In 1973, he signed to the Alligator label and recorded his first album. Since then, he has become well-known on the blues scene both in the USA and in Europe. Edging towards the 'soul blues' category his career has gained strength, particularly with the release of the well-received album *Bad Axe*, although he has not yet fully-achieved the attention he deserves.

Albums: *Son Seals* (1973), *Midnight Son* (1975), *Chicago Fire* (1980), *Bad Axe* (1984), *Live 'N' Burnin'* (1988), *Living In The Danger Zones* (1991).

Seals, Troy

b. 16 November 1938, Big Hill, Kentucky, USA. Seals, a cousin to **Dan Seals**, began playing guitar in his teens and formed his own rock 'n' roll band. In 1960, he was working in a club in Ohio with **Lonnie Mack** and Denny Rice, where he befriended a visiting performer, **Conway Twitty**. Twitty introduced him to Jo Ann Campbell, who had had a few successes on the US pop charts. Seals married Campbell and they worked as a duo, making the US R&B charts with 'I Found A Love, Oh What A Love' in 1964. After some time working as a construction worker, Seals moved to Nashville to sell his songs. 'There's A Honky Tonk Angel (Who'll Take Me Back In)', written by Seals and Rice, was a US country number 1 for Conway Twitty, while **Cliff Richard**'s version for the UK market was withdrawn when he discovered what honky tonk angels were (!). **Elvis Presley** also recorded the song, along with Seals' 'Pieces Of My Life'. Seals' most recorded song is 'We Had It All', written with Donnie Fritts, which has been recorded by **Rita Coolidge**, **Waylon Jennings**, **Brenda Lee**, **Stu Stevens** and **Scott Walker**. His songwriting partners include Don Goodman and Will Jennings, a university professor in English literature, and together they all wrote 'Feelins'', a US country number 1 for Conway Twitty and **Loretta Lynn**; with Mentor Williams 'When We Make Love', a US country number 1 for **Alabama**; with Max D. Barnes 'Don't Take It Away' (another US country number 1 for Conway Twitty) and 'Storms Of Life' (**Randy Travis**). One of his best songs is the mysterious 'Seven Spanish Angels', written with Eddie Setser, a US country number 1 for **Willie Nelson** and **Ray Charles**. Seals has done much session work as a guitarist and has had a few minor country hits himself.

Albums: *Now Presenting Troy Seals* (1973), *Troy Seals* (1976).

Seamen, Phil

b. 28 August 1928, Burton-on-Trent, Staffordshire, England, d. 13 October 1972. Seamen first attracted attention when he played drums with post-war British dance bands, including those led by **Nat Gonella** and **Joe Loss**. By the early 50s he was a key figure in the nascent London bop scene, working with **Ronnie Scott**, **Tubby Hayes**, **Joe Harriott** and other leading musicians. Later in the decade he recorded with **Stan Tracey**, on *Little Klunk* (1959) and the following year with Harriott, on the saxophonist's *Free Form*. In the early 60s Seamen tried his hand in blues bands, including those of **Georgie Fame** and **Alexis Korner**. In the late 60s he was back with Scott but also played in rock bands, including Air Force which was led by one of his students, **Ginger Baker**. The range of Seamen's musical interests is apparent from the company he kept, and he brought to everything he did enormous enthusiasm and vitality. His dynamic playing enhanced countless club and pub sessions in and around London, a handful being captured on record. Sadly, for all his skills, Seamen's career and ultimately his life were blighted by drug addiction. Seamen's virtuosity was remarkable: his work with Harriott was noteworthy for the manner in which he adapted to free jazz, and he coped admirably with the very different demands required by his performances in rock and blues bands. Despite such performances, however, it is a bop drummer that he made his most notable mark on the British jazz scene.

Albums: *Third Festival Of British Jazz* (1956), *Now!...Live!* (1968), *Phil On Drums! A Jam Session At The Hideaway* (1971), *Phil Talks And Plays/The Phil Seamen Story* (1972).

Searchers

One of the premier groups from the mid-60s Merseybeat explosion, the Searchers comprised: Chris Curtis (b. Christopher Crummey, 26 August 1941, Oldham, Lancashire, England; drums), Mike Pender (b. Michael John Prendergast, 3 March 1942, Liverpool, England; lead guitar), **Tony Jackson** (b. 16 July 1940, Liverpool, England; vocals/bass) and John McNally (b. 30 August 1941, Liverpool, England; rhythm guitar). Having previously backed Liverpool singer Johnny Sandon, they broke away and took their new name from the 1956 John Ford western, *The Searchers*. During 1962, they appeared in Hamburg and after sending a demo tape to A&R representative **Tony Hatch** were signed to Pye Records the following year. Their **Doc Pomus/Mort Shuman** debut 'Sweets For My Sweet' was a memorable tune with strong harmonies and a professional production. By the summer of 1963, it climbed to number 1 establishing the Searchers as rivals to **Brian Epstein**'s celebrated stable of Liverpool groups. *Meet The Searchers*, was swiftly issued and revealed the group's R&B pedigree on such standards as 'Farmer John' and 'Love Potion Number 9'. Meanwhile, Tony Hatch composed a catchy follow-up single, 'Sugar And Spice', which just failed to reach number 1. It was their third single, however, that won them international acclaim. The **Jack Nitzsche/Sonny Bono** composition 'Needles And Pins' was a superb melody, brilliantly arranged by the group and a striking chart-topper of its era. It also broke the group in the USA, reaching the Top 20 in March 1964. It was followed that same year with further US success; including 'Ain't That Just Like Me' (US number 61), 'Sugar And Spice' (US number 44), and 'Some Day We're Gonna Love Again' (US number 34).

Earlier that year the band released their superbly atmospheric cover of the **Orlons**' 'Don't Throw Your Love Away', which justifiably gave the group their third UK number 1 single. The pop world was shocked by the abrupt departure of bassist Tony Jackson whose falsetto vocals had contributed as much to the group's early sound and identity. He was replaced in the autumn by Frank Allen (b. Francis Renaud McNeice, 14 December 1943, Hayes, Middlesex, England), a former member of **Cliff Bennett And The Rebel Rousers** and close friend of Chris Curtis. A strident reading of **Jackie DeShannon**'s 'When You Walk In The Room' was another highlight of 1964 which showed their rich **Rickenbacker** guitar work to notable effect. The **Malvina Reynolds**' protest song, 'What Have They Done To The Rain?' indicated their folk-rock potential, but its melancholic tune and slower pace was reflected in a lower chart placing. A return to the 'old' Searchers sound with the plaintive 'Goodbye My Love', took them back into the UK Top 5 in early 1965, but the number 1 days were over. For a time, it seemed that the Searchers might not slide so inexorably as rivals **Billy J. Kramer And The Dakotas** and **Gerry And The Pacemakers**. They enjoyed further US success where their cover of the **Clovers**' 'Love Potion Number 9' was a Top 10 hit at the end of 1964 and on into 1965. This continued with 'Bumble Bee (US number 21), 'Goodbye My Lover Goodbye' (US number 52). The Curtis/Pender hit, 'He's Got No Love' (US number 79, UK number 12) showed that they could write their own hit material but this run could not be sustained. The release of **P.F. Sloan**'s 'Take Me For What I'm Worth' (US number 76, UK number 20) suggested that they might become linked with the **Bob Dylan**-inspired folk-rock boom. Instead, their commercial fortunes rapidly declined and after Curtis left in 1966, they were finally dropped by Pye. Their last UK hit was a version of **Paul And Barry Ryan**'s 'Have You Ever Loved Somebody', this proved to be their penultimate success in the USA which ended with 'Desdemona' (number 94) in 1971. Cabaret stints followed but the Searchers continued playing and in the circumstances underwent minimal line-up changes. They threatened a serious resurgence in 1979 when **Sire** issued a promising comeback album. The attempt to reach a new wave audience was ultimately

unsuccessful, however, and after the less well received *Play For Today* (titled *Love's Melodies* in the USA), the group stoically returned to the cabaret circuit. To their credit, their act does not only dwell on 60s hits and they remain one of the most musically competent and finest surviving performing bands from the 60s golden age. Albums: *Meet The Searchers* (1963), *Sugar And Spice* (1963), *Hear! Hear!* (1964, US release, live recording at the Star Club, Hamburg), *It's The Searchers* (1964), *This Is Us* (1964, US release), *The New Searchers LP* (1965, US release), *The Searchers No. 4* (1965, US release), *Sounds Like Searchers* (1965), *Take Me For What I'm Worth* (1965), *Second Take* (1972), *Needles And Pins* (1974), *The Searchers* (1979), *Play For Today* (1981). Compilations: *100 Minutes Of The Searchers* (1982), *The Searchers Hit Collection* (1987), *The EP Collection* (1989), *30th Anniversary Collection* (1992), *The EP Collection Vol. 2* (1992), *Rare Recordings* (1993).

Sears, Al

b. 21 February 1910, Macomb, Illinois, USA, d. 23 March 1990. After playing alto and baritone saxophones in various bands in the north-eastern states, Sears switched to tenor saxophone and moved to New York, where he was soon in demand. In the late 20s he was with **Chick Webb** and Zack Whyte, then briefly played with **Elmer Snowden** before forming his own band. In 1941 he folded his band and joined **Andy Kirk**, then **Lionel Hampton**, and, in 1944, succeeded **Ben Webster** in the **Duke Ellington** band. Sears remained with Ellington until 1949 and soon thereafter joined **Johnny Hodges**'s band, which had a successful record with Sears's composition 'Castle Rock'. Sears subsequently ran his own music publishing business in partnership with **Budd Johnson**, playing occasionally in R&B bands and using the name Big Al Sears. A forceful player with enormous drive and energy, Sears needed only a slight coarsening of his naturally rasping tone to adapt readily into the R&B fold. Despite such later manifestations, however, his recorded solos with Ellington indicate a musician of considerable sophistication, and his recordings, which include 'Hiawatha' from Ellington's 'The Beautiful Indians', frequently offer fine examples of his craft. Selected albums: *Duke Ellington At Carnegie Hall* (1946), *Duke Ellington And His Orchestra 1946* (1946), with Ellington *Liberian Suite* (1947), with Johnny Hodges *Rabbit On Verve Vol. 1* (1951), *Al Sears And His Orchestra* (1960), *Swing's The Thing* (1960), *Sear-iously* (Bear Family 1992).

Sears, Zenas 'Daddy'

b. c.1914, d. 4 October 1989, Atlanta, Georgia, USA. A respected white Atlanta, Georgia, jazz and pop disc jockey, Sears began programming jump blues and R&B records in January 1946. Two years later he took a job at the state-owned radio station WGST, on the condition that he would be allowed a nightly blues show, *The Blues Caravan*. Owing to his success with this format, he was able to expand the show to include talent shows which he broadcast live from Atlanta theatres such as Decatur Street's 81 Theatre. Here he discovered local singers such as **Tommy Brown**, Billy Wright, **Chuck Willis** (whom he managed in the early to mid-50s, and got him his first recording contract with **OKeh Records**) and **Little Richard**. These artists were invariably backed by the Blues Caravan All Stars, a group of local musicians which included John Peek and Roy Mays. In 1954, Georgia's new governor banned Sears' programme from the WGST, and Sears formed WAOK. He continued with his policy to play the best of black music - in 1959 he recorded **Ray Charles**' set at the WAOK 5th Anniversary Party which **Atlantic** issued as the best-selling *Ray Charles In Person*. In the late 50s and 60s, Sears became involved with Dr Martin Luther King and the SCLC, and his position with the radio station allowed him to spread his views on integration and equal rights.

Seatrain

The original Seatrain line-up - John Gregory (guitar/vocals), Richard Greene (violin), Donald Kretmar (saxophone/bass), Andy Kulberg (bass/flute) and Roy Blumenfeld (drums) - evolved from the New York-based **Blues Project** and this particular quintet completed the previous group's contractual obligations with the *Planned Obsolescence* album. The unit's first official self-titled album was released in 1969. By this point the group had been augmented by lyricist James T. Roberts and this imaginative collection fused such seemingly disparate elements as rock, bluegrass and Elizabethan-styled folksiness. Internal problems sadly doomed this quirky line-up, and after approximately 25 members had passed through the band, a stable Seatrain line-up emerged with only Kulberg and Greene remaining from the initial band. The three newcomers were Lloyd Baskin (keyboards/vocals), Larry Atamanuk (drums) and former **Earth Opera** member Peter Rowan (guitar/vocals). A second album, also entitled *Seatrain*, was recorded in London under the aegis of **George Martin**, as was their third collection, *The Marblehead Messenger*. Both albums displayed an engaging, eclectic style, but were doomed to commercial indifference. The departure of Rowan and Greene to the critically acclaimed **Muleskinner** was a severe blow and although Kulberg and Baskin persevered by bringing Peter Walsh (guitar), Bill Elliott (keyboards) and Julio Coronado (drums) into the group, a fourth release, *Watch*, was a major disappointment. When Seatrain latterly disbanded, Kulberg pursued a career composing for numerous television shows.
Albums: *Seatrain* (A&M 1969), *Seatrain* (Capitol 1970), *The Marblehead Messenger* (Capitol 1971), *Watch* (1973).

Sebastian, John

b. 17 March 1944, New York, USA. The son of the famous classical harmonica player John Sebastian. John Jnr. is best known for his seminal jug band/rock fusion with the much-loved **Lovin' Spoonful** in the 60s, which established him as one of the finest American songwriters of the era. When the Spoonful finally collapsed Sebastian started a solo career that was briefly threatened when he was asked to become the fourth member of **Crosby, Stills And Nash**, but he declined when it was found that **Stephen Stills** wanted him to play drums. In 1969 his performance was one of the highlights of the **Woodstock Festival**, singing his warm and friendly material to a deliriously happy audience. His tie-dye jacket and jeans appearance, warm rapport, and acoustic set (aided by copious amounts of LSD) elevated him to a star. Sebastian debuted in 1970 with an outstanding solo work *John B Sebastian*, containing much of the spirit of Woodstock. Notable tracks such as the autobiographical 'Red Eye Express' and the evocative 'How Have You Been', were bound together with one of his finest songs, the painfully short 'She's A Lady'. Less than two minutes long, this love song was perfect for the times, and was a lyrical triumph with lines like 'She's a lady, and I chance to see her in my shuffling daze, she's a lady, hypnotised me there that day, I came to play in my usual way, hey'. Simply accompanied by Stills' and Crosby's mellow guitar, it remains a modern classic. Sebastian faltered with the uneven *Four Of Us*, a travelogue of hippie ideology but followed a few months later with *Real Live*, an engaging record, recorded at four gigs in California. At that time Sebastian was performing at a punishing rate throughout Europe and America. *Tarzana Kid* in 1974 sold poorly, but has latterly grown in stature with critics. At this time Sebastian was working with the late **Lowell George**, and a strong **Little Feat** influence is shown. The album's high point is a Sebastian/George classic, the beautiful 'Face Of Appalachia'. Two years later Sebastian was asked to write the theme song for a US comedy television series, *Welcome Back Kotter*. The result was a number 1 hit, 'Welcome Back'. Astonishingly, since then, no new album had appeared until 1992, when a Japanese label released his most recent songs. Throughout that time, however, Sebastian never stopped working. He accompanied **Sha Na Na** and **NRBQ** on many lengthy tours, appeared as a television presenter, wrote a children's book and among other commissions he composed the music for the *Care Bears* television series. Severe problems with his throat threatened his singing career at one point. He declined to be part of the 1992 reformed Lovin' Spoonful. Sebastian was, is and always will be the heart and soul of that band. He returned with the delightful *Tar Beach* in 1993. Although long-term fans noted that his voice was slightly weaker, the album contained a varied mixture of rock, blues and country. Many songs he had written more than a decade earlier were included, the most notable being his uplifting tribute to **Smokey Robinson**; 'Smokey Don't Go. Hardly prolific, Sebastian remains one of the best American songwriters of the 60s. It is a great pity that he is not more active .

Albums: *John B. Sebastian* (1970), *The Four Of Us* (1971), *Real Live* (1971), *Tarzana Kid* (1974), *Welcome Back* (1976), *Tar Beach* (Shanachie 1993).

Secada, Jon

US disco balladeer of some merit whose rapid expansion in to the singles and albums charts owes a good deal to the production team Emilio Estefan Jnr., Clay Oswald and Jorge Casas. They had previously shaped the career of **Gloria Estafan And The Miami Sound Machine**. The similarities do not end there; as well as the distinctive Latin rhythm, Secada is likewise of Latin American descent. His hits, each formulaic but successful expositions of romantic dance, include 'Just Another Day', 'Do You Believe Us' and 'Angel'.

Albums: *Jon Secada* (1992), *Heart, Soul & A Voice* (SBK 1994).

Secombe, Harry

b. Harold Donald Secombe, 8 September 1921, Swansea, West Glamorgan, Wales. Harry Secombe's development as an all-round entertainer began as a product of the post-war 'fair play' policy of London's West End Windmill Theatre. This ensured that men recently, or soon-to-be demobbed from the armed forces, were given the chance to prove themselves to an audience and get noticed by agents. Secombe worked at the theatre before becoming a regular on the variety circuit in the late 40s. In 1949 he teamed up with Peter Sellers, Spike Milligan and Michael Bentine to form the highly-influential British radio comedy team, the **Goons**, taking on characters, created by Spike Milligan, such as the popular Neddy Seagoon. With his large build, gentle humour and resonant Welsh baritone, which he put to good effect on light operatic arias as well as popular tunes, Secombe became a regular fixture at the London Palladium, including Royal Command performances, from the 50s through to the 80s. His frequent screen appearances, in both comedy and 'straight' roles, came in films such as *Helter Skelter* (1949, his debut), *Fake's Progress* (1950), *Down Among The Z Men* (1952), *Davy* (1957), *Oliver!* (1968), *The Bedsitting Room* (1968), *Song Of Norway* (1969), *Rhubarb* (1969) and *The Magnificent Seven Deadly Sins* (1971). He appeared regularly on UK television screens, in variety shows and his own series in the 60s and 70s. In 1963, Secombe created the leading role in the musical *Pickwick*, which had a book by Wolf Mankowitz, and

music and lyrics by **Leslie Bricusse** and **Cyril Ornadel**. He took the show's big ballad, 'If I Ruled The World', into the UK Top 20, and it has since become indelibly associated with him. Four years later he played the role of D'Artagnan in *The Four Musketeers*, which had a score **by Laurie Johnson** and **Herbert Kretzmer**, and ran for over a year. He had scored his first solo UK chart hit with 'On With The Motley' in 1955, and achieved his biggest record success to date in 1967 with Charlie Chaplin's 'This Is My Song', which was prevented from reaching the number 1 slot by **Petula Clark**'s version of the very same song.

Following a massive reduction in his weight (for medical reasons) a trimmed-down Secombe has in recent years carved out a career since 1983 as the presenter of Independent Television's religious programme *Highway*, which required him to master another skill, that of the interview technique. He has over the years been actively involved in charity organizations and fund-raising and after being awarded the CBE in 1963, Harry Secombe was knighted in 1981. In 1993, 30 years after creating the leading role in *Pickwick*, he appeared in a UK revival of the show with his old friend Roy Castle.

Albums (excluding Goons and other comedy albums): *At Your Request* (late 50s), *Operatic Arias* (late 50s), *Richard Tauber Favourites* (late 50s), *Secombe Sings* (1959), *Harry Secombe Showcase* (1960), *Sacred Songs* (1961), *Vienna, City Of My Dreams* (early 60s), *Show Souvenirs* (early 60s), *Immortal Hymns* (early 60s), *Secombe's Personal Choice* (1967), *If I Ruled The World* (1971), *Songs For Sunday* (1972), *This Is Harry Secombe, Volume Four* (1974), *A Man And His Dreams* (1976), *Far Away Places* (1977), *Twenty Songs Of Joy* (1978), *Bless This House* (1979), *Songs Of My Homeland* (1979), *These Are My Songs* (1980), with Moira Anderson *Golden Memories* (1981, reissued as *This Is My Lovely Day* on CD), *A Song And A Prayer* aka *How Great Thou Art* (1981), *The Musical World Of Harry Secombe* (1983), *Highway Of Life* (1986), *The Highway Companion* (1987), *Onward Christian Soldiers* (1987), *Yours Sincerely* (1991), *Sir Harry* (1993). Compilations: *Spotlight On Harry Secombe* (1975), *The Harry Secombe Collection* (1976), *Portrait* (1978).

Further reading: *Arias And Raspberries*, Sir Harry Secombe.

Second Chorus

This 1940 film is an enjoyable piece of hokum about two swing band trumpeters, **Fred Astaire** and Burgess Meredith, vying for the affections of Paulette Goddard. The musicians play with **Artie Shaw**'s band and there are some excellent musical sequences featuring the leader's clarinet, backed in a performance of 'Concerto For Clarinet' by **Nick Fatool**'s drums, and the trumpets of **Bobby Hackett** and **Billy Butterfield** ghosting for Astaire and Meredith.

Second Vision

After he left the **Albion Band** in 1979, **Ric Sanders** joined ex-**Soft Machine** colleague **John Etheridge** in the jazz fusion, Second Vision. Although they improvised, they were equally liable to end up reeling. Their sole album showed much promise, which sadly remained untapped. The band also included ex-**Gryphon** and future **Home Service** bassist Jon Davie and keyboardist Dave Bristow.

Album: *First Steps* (1980).

Secret Affair

Led by Ian Page (b. Ian Paine, 1960, England; vocals/trumpet/piano/organ), and Dave Cairns (b. 1959, England; guitar/vocals), Secret Affair, one of the most creative neo-mod groups of the late 70s, emerged out of the lightweight UK new wave band New Hearts who folded in 1978. New Hearts released two lacklustre singles. The Secret Affair line-up was completed by Dennis Smith (bass/vocals, ex-Advertising), and Chris Bennett (drums, ex-**Alternative TV**). Bennett did not work out and was replaced by Seb Shelton (ex-Young Bucks). They debuted supporting the **Jam** (as the New Hearts had once done), but made their name at the Bridge House Tavern in Canning Town, London, centre of the mod revival. They appeared on the *Mods Mayday* live compilation but then set up their own I-Spy label through **Arista Records**. Subsequently they toured with **Purple Hearts** and Back To Zero under the banner 'March Of The Mods'. Their first single, 'Time For Action', was an immediate success for both band and label, featuring Chris Gent (of the Autographs) on saxophone. They also signed Squire to the I-Spy label. Further singles in differing styles charted and the debut album was well received, particularly the epic title track which referred to their fan following. However, Shelton left late in 1980 to join the Up-Set, then **Dexy's Midnight Runners** and was replaced by Paul Bultitude. After two singles from the final Secret Affair album failed commercially, they disbanded. Dave Cairns went on to form the duo Flag, with Archie Brown, his former colleague from the Young Bucks. He subsequently formed another band called Walk On Fire with Dennis Smith. Page, who now writes fantasy books, formed Ian Page and Bop whose single 'Unity Street' created some interest. Bultitude joined the **Mari Wilson**'s Wilsations and later founded the Dance Network label. Smith threw in his lot with **Nik Kershaw**'s Krew, and Seb Shelton went on to manage, amongst others, the **Woodentops**.

Albums: *Glory Boys* (1979), *Behind Closed Doors* (1980), *Business As Usual* (1982).

Secret Garden, The

This charming and stylish musical was welcomed by one critic as 'one of the most aggressively pretty shows ever to grace a Broadway stage' when it opened at the St. James Theatre in New York on 25 April 1991. Marsha Norman's book was based on the much-loved Edwardian children's novel by Frances Hodgson Burnett, and tells of Mary Lennox (Daisy Eagan), who returns to England and the custody of her hunchbacked uncle, Archibald Craven (**Mandy Patinkin**), after her family, who were in the Colonial Service in India, are wiped out by an outbreak of cholera. Mary discovers Craven's sickly young son Colin (John Babcock), who is being left to wither and die in a secluded room in the large, dreary mansion on the Yorkshire moors. She also finds the key to the secret walled garden which has been locked up since Craven's wife, Lily (Rebecca Luker), died in childbirth some 10 years earlier. Lily returns to the scene in saintly form, and has one of the show's most effective numbers, 'Come To My Garden'. Several other departed souls also materialise, including Mary's parents and several of the young victims of the cholera outbreak who form the chorus. The spirits lead Mary, Colin, and Craven 'towards vitality and joy' in such captivating numbers as 'I Hear Someone Crying' and 'Come Spirit, Come Charm'. The remainder of composer Lucy Simon and lyricist Marsha Norman's 'sentimental and old-fashioned' score included 'Opening Dream', 'There's A Girl', 'The House Upon A Hill', 'A Girl In the Valley', 'Lily's Eyes', 'The Girl I Mean To Be', 'A Bit Of Earth', 'Letter Song', 'Where In The World', and 'How Could I Ever Know?'. General opinion was that the whole show was 'warm and wonderful', especially the gorgeous costumes, and designer-producer Heidi Landesman's ingenious placing of the action inside a toy theatre complete with drops and wings. She won a **Tony Award** for her dazzling effects, as did 11-year old Daisy Eagan for her lovely open performance. For a children's story *The Secret Garden* did pretty well - even with a $60 top price - and ran until January 1993, a total of 706 performances. A touring company broke records in several US cities, and was also highly sucessful in other countries such as Japan. Another, much smaller adaptation of Frances Hodgson Burnett's story, with a book and lyrics by Diana Morgan and music by Steven Markwick, was presented more than once in the early 90s at the King's Head, Islington, on the London Fringe, and other, regional venues. The novel has been filmed at least three times: as a feature film with Margaret O'Brien in 1949, a television movie with Gennie James and Derek Jacobi in 1987, and another feature film in 1993 with Maggie Smith, Kate Maberly, John Lynch, and Haydon Prowse.

Secret Knowledge

Dance collective featuring the writing skills of singer Wonder (b. West Virginia, USA) and Kris Needs, a man with a long and shady history. His chequered past includes stints in treaseball pub rockers the **Vice Creems**, and a part-time position as **John Otway**'s bongo player. He began writing for *ZigZag* magazine in 1975 going on to take over the editorship in 1977. In the 80s and 90s he concentrated on writing dance reviews for *Echoes* and other magazines. Wonder meanwhile had formerly fronted a Munich, Germany-based jazz/blues band titled Strange Fruit. Unlike many of the predominantly soul-based female vocalists who regularly add their voices to house/trance cuts, Wonder is responsible for writing lyrics as well as the occasional melody (including 'Sugar Daddy'). The duo met together in the late 80s in New York, recording a one-off rap single together, 'Rap Too Tight'. Once they had returned to the UK, and Needs had discovered the burgeoning Acid House movement, they cut their first track under the Secret Knowledge flag: 'Your Worst Nightmare'. Influenced by the deep house of New York's **Strictly Rhythm** label, they followed their debut with 'Ooh Baby', one of the first releases on **Andy Weatherall**'s **Sabres Of Paradise** label. Next up came one of the biggest club hits of 1993, 'Sugar Daddy'. It has been reported that this 'orgasmic' track was used widely to help stimulate sexual relief in prisons and detention centres throughout Britain. In its wake Secret Knowledge were elevated to the status of hot producers/remixers. Among their other collaborative monikers are Delta Lady (Secret Knowledge under a different name reflecting a more urbane, funk-based side to their nature), Four Boy One Girl Action (whose 'Hawaiian Death Stomp' combined Needs with **David Holmes** and members of the Sabres enclave), the Rabettes (featuring Weatherall's girlfriend Nina's assorted rabbits and guinea pigs), Hutchbern, The Pecking Order (featuring various impersonations of chickens) and Codpeace (with Alex Paterson of the **Orb**). Needs has also stepped out as a remix artist, converting artists from many fields incuding the **Boo Radleys**. They clashed with the compilers of the excellent *Trance Europe Express 2* in mid-1994 over their contribution, 'Afterworld'. The lyrics addressed Wonder's cousin, an AIDS sufferer, but the track was deemed to be out of context on an otherwise instrumental set. While compromises were still being discussed a vocal-less version was 'inadvertently' included instead, as Needs discovered after returning from touring with **Primal Scream**. They issued the 'correct' version on Kris' Stolen Karots label instead.

Secret Life

Secret Life initially consisted of Charton Antenbring (disc jockey and reporter for UK magazine *The Big Issue*), Andy Throup (classically trained pianist and studio owner) and Paul Bryant (vocals). Secret Life was officially an umbrella organisation with a number of producers and musicians (notably Throup's studio co-owner, Jim Di Salvo) also contributing. They made headlines with 1992's 'As Always' cut for **Cowboy Records** (whose Charlie Chester manages the band), which was among that label's biggest successes. It was based on **Stevie Wonder**'s 'Songs In The Key Of Life' (which had previously been issued in a 'house' version by Chicago-based Ricky Dillard of Nightwriters' fame). However, after **Masters At Work** remixed 1994's 'Borrowed Time', which was on the first demo the band passed to Chester, their manager realised their potential might extend beyond the dance frontier and into the pop market. As a result Chester moved them over to **Pulse 8 Records** in an eight-album deal that year, with the group reduced to a core duo of Bryant and Throup. With a radio-friendly single, 'Love So Strong', and an album following in 1995, Secret Life looked well set to make the transition into the pop charts.
Album: *Sole Purpose* (Pulse 8 1995).

Secrets

This US vocal group was formed in the early 60s in Cleveland, Ohio, USA, and comprised of Pat Miller, Kragen Gray, Josie Allen and Carole Raymont. The quartet's closest brush with national fame was a number 18 hit single, 'The Boy Next Door', issued on the Philips label in 1963. The girl group was managed by Redda Robbins, who arranged a recording contract with Philips, a subsidiary of **Mercury Records**. The Secrets were given 'The Boy Next Door', written by Johnny Madara and David White, and it became their sole hit. The group continued to record on small labels for a while but never repeated their initial success.

Section 25

The nucleus of this Blackpool, Lancashire, England group started in November 1979 with brothers Vincent Cassidy (electronics/drum machine) and Larry Cassidy (guitar/vocals). In April 1978, a guitarist called Phil joined and Section 25 performed their first gig on 1 June. November of that year saw Phil replaced by Paul Wiggin. The group then introduced a second drummer, John and, since they were unable to find a suitable keyboard player, the appropriate passages were recorded on a tape machine, having first been constructed at SSRU, the group's rehearsal studio. The sound engineer, John Hurst, played a decisive role in the group's live sound. Their first single, 'Girls Don't Count', came out in early 1980. Over the next two years they toured Europe extensively and frequently supported **New Order**. After the release of their first album, Wiggin left after a gig in Helsinki. Lee Shallcross (drums) joined in February 1982 and toured with them in the USA. After their second album emerged on the **Factory** Benelux label, in February 1983, the Cassidys decided to cancel further live shows, drop all their old material and re-think their approach. By August 1983 they returned as a five piece with

Angela Flowers (vocals/keyboards) and Jenny Ross (vocals/keyboards), with a first gig in December 1983. Two further albums followed in the mid-80s, but by then Section 25 had become very much the forgotten band at Factory, alongside the similarly unheralded **Stockholm Monsters**.

Albums: *Always Now* (Factory 1981), *The Key Of Dreams* (Factory 1982), *From The Hip* (Factory 1984), *Love And Hate* (Factory 1986).

Secunda, Tony

b. 1940, London, England. d. 12 February 1995, San Anselmo, California, USA. The son of a Russian emigrant who had relocated from New York to London, Secunda was educated at public school, then dropped out to work for magazine publishers Fleetway Press. A regular visitor to the 2 I's coffee bar, he was intrigued by British rock 'n' roll but seemed too young to take an active part as an entrepreneur. After a period in the merchant navy, during which time he visited Hollywood, he returned to London and began booking gigs in youth clubs. His first management job was with **Johnny Kidd And The Pirates**, one of the most respected musical ensembles of their period. Unfortunately for Secunda, his partner Stanley Dale ousted him from the managerial throne. Recoiling from that setback Secunda then teamed up with songwriter **Chris Andrews** for a brief spell before becoming a wrestling promoter. Ever on the move, Secunda next moved to South Africa, returned to London again in 1964 and took over the management of **Lesley Duncan**. No successes were forthcoming but later that year Secunda's luck changed when he acquired the Birmingham-based **Moody Blues**. The group hit number 1 early the following year with the atmospheric 'Go Now'. Financial bickering soon ensued, however, and Secunda parted from the group amid considerable acrimony. He departed with singer **Denny Laine**, as his sole supporter. Secunda stayed with the Birmingham beat boom for his next find, the **Move**. An inveterate lover of media sensationalism, he used stock shock tactics to introduce his charges to the world. They were photographed in gangster suits, with a stripper and made no apologies for their self-professed violent stage act. Their sparkling run of hits testified both to their talent and Secunda's mastery of media manipulation. As with many Secunda stunts, however, the outrage went a little too far. In 1968, he concocted the idea of protesting against Britain's Prime Minister by creating a whimsical postcard of the leader naked in a bath tub. Harold Wilson duly sued for libel and the group lost a substantial amount of their royalties to charity. Secunda moved on, then managed the doomed Birmingham supergroup, **Balls**. For a brief period it was rumoured that he might manage **Paul McCartney**'s **Wings** (formed in 1971), which (like Balls) included his former protégé Denny Laine,

but nothing came of the proposed match. Instead, Secunda became more involved in the label Regal Zonophone, with partner **Denny Cordell**. He became a short-term manager for **T Rex** before **Marc Bolan** (who left Regal Zonophone in 1970) set off in search of other entrepreneurs. A 60s legend, Secunda effectively retired from management during the early/mid-70s. He settled in America, married an heiress, and his only notable excursion into pop during the period was some work with the **Dwight Twilley** Band. Returning to England, he worked with **Gary Shearston** and, more oddly, **Steeleye Span**. The folk group received a taste of Secunda's publicity-making when he arranged for one of their gigs to be littered with pound notes. Although Secunda seemed the perfect manager during the early days of punk, he instead took on the heavy metal group **Motorhead**, but that relationship soon ended. With **Malcolm McLaren** stealing the limelight for his group the **Sex Pistols**, Secunda was convinced that his own powers as a media sensationalist could be put to use with the right group. The comeback proved anti-climactic. Secunda found the right group in the **Pretenders**, but appeared to lose interest in backing them at a crucial time, just before they broke through. As a managerial buccaneer, Secunda was one of the most colourful figures in pop during the mid-late 60s but declined or neglected to traverse into top artist management in the harsher climate of the 80s.

Sedaka, Neil

b. 13 March 1939, Brooklyn, New York, USA. Pianist Sedaka began his songwriting career with lyricist Howard Greenfield in the early 50s. During this high school period, Sedaka dated Carol Klein (later known as **Carole King**). For a brief period, Sedaka joined the **Tokens**, then won a scholarship to New York's Juilliard School of Music. In 1958, the pianist joined **Don Kirshner**'s **Brill Building** school of instant songwriters. Sedaka's first major hit success came with 'Stupid Cupid', which was an international smash for **Connie Franci**s. The following year, Sedaka signed to **RCA** as a recording artist and enjoyed a minor US hit with 'The Diary'. The frantic follow-up 'I Go Ape' was a strong novelty record, which helped establish Sedaka. This was followed by one of his most famous songs, 'Oh Carol', a lament directed at his former girlfriend Carole King, who replied in kind with the less successful 'Oh Neil'. Sedaka's solid voice and memorable melodies resulted in a string of early 60s hits, including 'Stairway To Heaven', 'Calendar Girl', 'Little Devil', 'King Of Clowns', 'Happy Birthday Sweet Sixteen' and 'Breaking Up Is Hard To Do'. These songs summed up the nature of Sedaka's lyrical appeal. The material subtly dramatized the trials and rewards of teenage life and the emotional upheavals resulting from birthdays, break-ups and incessant speculation on the qualities of a loved one. Such songs of neurotic love had their distinct time in the early 60s, and with the decline of the clean-cut teen balladeer and the emergence of groups, there was an inevitable lull in Sedaka's fortunes. He abandoned the pop star role but continued writing a fair share of hits over the next 10 years, including 'Venus In Blue Jeans' (**Jimmy Clanton/Mark Wynter**), 'Working On A Groovy Thing' (**Fifth Dimension**), 'Puppet Man' (**Tom Jones**) and 'Is This The Way To Amarillo?' (**Tony Christie**). In 1972, Sedaka effectively relaunched his solo career with *Emergence* and relocated to the UK. By 1973, he was back in the British charts with 'That's When The Music Takes Me' from *Solitaire*. The third album of the comeback, *The Tra-La Days Are Over*, was highly regarded and included 'Our Last Song Together', dedicated to Howard Greenfield. With *Laughter In The Rain*, Sedaka extended his appeal to his homeland. The title track topped the US charts in 1975, completing a remarkable international comeback. That same year, the **Captain And Tennille** took Sedaka's 'Love Will Keep Us Together' to the US number 1 spot and the songwriter followed suit soon after with 'Bad Blood'. The year ended with an excellent reworking of 'Breaking Up Is Hard To Do' in a completely different arrangement which provided another worldwide smash. He enjoyed his last major hit during 1980 in the company of his daughter Dara on 'Should've Never Let You Go'. Sedaka continues to tour regularly, performing hits from two different decades.

Albums: *Rock With Sedaka* (1959), *Emergence* (1972), *Solitaire* (1972), *The Tra-La Days Are Over* (1973), *Laughter In The Rain* (1974), *Live At The Royal Festival Hall* (1974), *Overnight Success* (1975), *The Hungry Years* (1975), *Steppin' Out* (1976), *A Song* (1977), *In The Pocket* (1980), *Come See About Me* (1984), *Love Will keep Us Together: The Singer And His Songs* (1992). Compilations: *Neil Sedaka Sings His Greatest Hits* (1963), *Sedaka's Back* (1975), *Laughter And Tears: The Best Of Neil Sedaka Today* (1976), *Neil Sedaka's Greatest Hits* (1977), *Timeless* (1991), *Originals: The Greatest Hits* (1992).
Further reading: *Breaking Up Is Hard To Do*, Neil Sedaka.

Sedric, Gene

b. 17 June 1907, St. Louis, Missouri, USA, d. 3 April 1963. Sedric began playing clarinet in local bands, later taking up the tenor saxophone, as well. His first important jobs were with Charlie Creath, Fate Marable and other bandleaders playing in the region and on the riverboats. In the early 20s he arrived in New York with a touring band and there joined **Sam Wooding**, with whom he visited Europe. In 1934, he became a member of **Fats Waller**'s small group, remaining there until the leader's death in 1943. Subsequently he led his own small bands, also playing and recording with other leaders. In the early 50s he again visited Europe, playing with **Mezz Mezzrow**, **Buck Clayton** and others. In 1953 he joined a band led by Conrad Janis and at the end of the decade freelanced until ill-health forced him into retirement. Although he was not an exceptional performer on either instrument, Sedric fitted well into the cheerful music that Waller's accompanists offered. Thanks to this association he enjoyed a long and successful career.
Compilation: *Fats Waller And His Rhythm 1934-36 (Classic Years In Digital Stereo)* (1988).

Seducer

This hard rock group was formed in Amsterdam, Netherlands, in 1980 by vocalists/guitarists Frans Phillipus and Jerry Lopies. After a series of false starts, the line-up stabilized with the recruitment of bassist Eppie Munting and drummer Rene van Leersum. Specializing in blues-based hard rock and boogie, the band contributed their first tracks to a compilation, *Holland Heavy Metal Vol. 1*, in 1982. A deal with the independent Universe label followed and a self-titled debut appeared in 1983. This was poorly received, and a line-up re-shuffle ensued with Van Leersum and Lopies departing in favour of ex-**Hammerhead** guitarist Erik Karreman, drummer Jan Koster and vocalist Thijs Hamelaers. They contributed two further numbers to the *Dutch Steel* compilation in 1984, but the group disbanded shortly afterwards as Koster and Karreman formed Highway Chile, while Hamelaers went on to Germane and later the Sleez Beez.
Album: *Seducer* (Universe 1983).

See For Miles

See For Miles was founded in 1982 by Colin Miles, previously head of EMI's reissue division, where he masterminded the **Harvest** Heritage and 'NUT' series. He established his new venture with repackages drawn from EMI's archives, notably a string of compilations featuring British Beat acts. Mark Rye, former manager of ex-**Be Bop Deluxe** singer/guitarist **Bill Nelson**, subsequently became Miles' partner as the label expanded into one of the UK's most prolific reissue outlets. Its catalogue reflects its founder's eclectic taste in music, ranging from early rock 'n' roll (**Cliff Richard**), through acid rock (**Quicksilver Messenger Service**) to 70s pop. It also released 'various artists' sets, notably *The Sixties: Lost And Found* and *The Great British Psychedelic Trip*, and 'EP Collections', which compile the contents of these 50s/60s artefacts by a particular artist. The **Kinks**, **Donovan**, **Muddy Waters** and **Howlin' Wolf** are among the many acts issued in this series. Miles and Rye also inaugurated a budget-priced C5 subsidiary and during the 90s instigated a highly-successful mail-order outlet, Magpie. In doing so Miles confirmed the success of his highly-individual enterprise.

Seeds

Formed in 1965, the Seeds provided a pivotal link between garage/punk rock and the emergent underground styles. They were led by **Sky Saxon** (b. Richard Marsh), a charismatic figure already established on the fringes of a budding Los Angeles scene through a handful of low-key releases. Jan Savage (guitar), Darryl Hooper (keyboards) and Rick Andridge (drums) completed his newest venture which scored a US hit the following year with the compulsive 'Pushin' Too Hard'. Its raw, simple riff and Saxon's howling, half-spoken, intonation established a pattern which remained almost unchanged throughout the group's career. The Seeds enjoyed minor chart success with 'Mr. Farmer' and 'Can't Seem To Make You Mine', while their first two albums, *The Seeds* and *A Web Of Sound*, were also well-received. The latter featured the 14-minute 'Up In Her Room', in which Saxon's free-spirited improvisations were allowed to run riot. The quartet embraced 'flower-power' with *Future*. Flutes, tablas, cellos and tubas were added to the basic Seeds' riffs while such titles as 'March Of The Flower Children' and 'Flower Lady And Her Assistant' left little doubt as to where Saxon's sympathies lay. This release was followed by a curious interlude wherein the group, now dubbed the Sky Saxon Blues Band, recorded *A Full Spoon Of Seedy Blues*. This erratic and rather unsatisfactory departure came replete with a testimonial from **Muddy Waters**, but it later transpired that the project was a ploy, that failed, by the group to escape their recording contract. Their last official album, *Raw And Alive At Merlin's Music Box*, marked a return to form. Subsequent singles charted a collapsing unit and psyche, although Saxon later re-emerged as Sky Sunlight, fronting several aggregations known variously as Stars New Seeds or the Universal Stars Band. Jan Savage, meanwhile, joined the Los Angeles Police Department.

Albums: *The Seeds* (1966), *A Web Of Sound* (1966), *Future* (1967), *A Full Spoon Of Seedy Blues* (1967), *Raw And Alive At Merlin's Music Box* (1967). Compilations: *Fallin' Off The Edge* (1977), *Evil Hoodoo* (1988), *A Faded Picture* (1991).

Seefeel

An intriguing combination of introspective ambient textures (although they abhor the term) and propulsive guitars have distinguished Seefeel's nascent career. Guitarist and songwriter Mark Clifford answered an advert which Justin Fletcher (drums) had placed on a noticeboard at Goldsmith's College, London. They added Darren 'Delores Throb' Seymour (bass) and set about auditioning over 70 hopefuls for the singer's job. In the end Clifford responded to another ad, 'Wanting to join or form band into **My Bloody Vlanetine** and **Sonic Youth**', and called ex-animation student Sarah Peacock, who had placed it. As her tastes reflected Seefeel's personal creed, a distillation of MBV's guitar abuse with ambient's drone, she was immediately taken on board. The made their recording debut with the *More Like Space* EP - which confused BBC Radio 1 DJ John Peel as to whether to play it at 33rpm or 45rpm. Two EPs and an album for **Too Pure Records** quickly followed, 'Pure, Impure' featuring a spectral **Aphex Twin** remix. They also collaborated and toured with heroes the **Cocteau Twins** (the question Clifford asked Sarah when he rang her up was whether or not she liked them). Another EP in 1994, *Starethrough*, was their first for **Warp Records**, and again provoked interest, coinciding with and reflecting a move from indie to dance coverage in the UK music weeklies.

Album: *Quique* (Too Pure 1993), *Succour* (Warp 1995).

Seeger, Mike

b. 15 August 1933, New York City, New York, USA. Mike is the son of well-known musicologist Charles Seeger, and Ruth Crawford Seeger, composer and author. From his youngest days he was surrounded by traditional music, and learned to play the autoharp at the age of 12. A few years later, he started to play guitar, mandolin, fiddle, dulcimer, mouth harp, and dobro. Together with his sister **Peggy Seeger**, he played with local square dance bands in the Washington area. His first involvement with country music came about while serving 'time' for conscientious objection, working in a hospital, when he teamed up with Hazel Dickens and Bob Baker. Mike formed the **New Lost City Ramblers** in 1958, with John Cohen and Tom Paley. That year, Seeger won the Galax Old Time Fiddlers Convention in Virginia for banjo work. It was during the late 50s that Mike started the first of his many recordings of other singers, including **Elizabeth 'Libba' Cotten**, and **Dock Boggs**. With changes in the personnel of the New Lost City Ramblers, Mike worked a great deal more in a solo capacity, but still recorded with the New Lost City Ramblers for the **Folkways** label. Among other projects, Mike was involved with the Newport Folk Festival in Rhode Island, and was a director of the Smithsonian Folklife Company from 1970. By the late 60s, he had formed the Strange Creek Singers with Alice L. Gerrard, Lamar Grier and Hazel Dickens. On 16 August 1970 he married Gerrard, but they were later divorced. Mike has recorded numerous albums with the various line-ups, with sister Peggy, and solo, and has continued to perform at festivals in the same capacity at home and throughout the world. His earlier work as a collector has also helped to keep alive a great deal of Southern traditional music.

Albums: *Oldtime Country Music* (Folkways 1962), *Mike Seeger* (Vanguard 1964), *Tipple, Loom And Rail: Songs Of The Industrialization Of The South* (Folkways 1965), *Mike And Peggy Seeger* (Argo 1966), *Strange Creek Singers* (1968), with Peggy Seeger *American Folksongs For Children* (1970), *Mike And Alice Seeger In Concert* (1970), *Music From True Vine* (Mercury 1971), *Second Annual Farewell Reunion* (Mercury 1973), *Alice And Mike* (Greenhays 1980), as A. Roebic And The Exertions *Old Time Music Dance Party* (Flying Fish 1986), *Fresh Old Time-String Band Music* (Rounder 1988), with Peggy and Penny Seeger and members of their families *American Folksongs For Christmas* (Rounder 1989), *Solo-Oldtime Country Music* (Rounder 1990), *Third Annual Farewell Reunion* (Rounder 1995).

Seeger, Peggy

b. Margaret Seeger, 17 June 1935, New York City, New York, USA. Seeger was accomplished on guitar, banjo, Appalachian dulcimer, autoharp and concertina. Her parents, Ruth Crawford and Charles Seeger were both professional musicians and teachers. They insisted that their daughter receive a formal musical education from the age of seven years. At the same time they encouraged her interest in folk music and, at the age of 10 Peggy started to learn guitar. A few years later she began to play 5-string banjo. After majoring in music at college, she started singing folksongs professionally. In 1955, Seeger relocated to Holland and studied Russian at university. Peggy first came to the UK in 1956 as an actress, to take part in a television film, *Dark Side Of The Moon*, and also joined the Ramblers, a group which included **Ewan MacColl**, **Alan Lomax** and **Shirley Collins**. In 1957, together with MacColl and Charles Parker, she worked on a series of documentaries for the BBC which are now commonly known as *The Radio Ballads*. These programmes were highly innovative and, together with music, brought the thoughts and views of a whole range of workers to a large listening public. In 1959, Peggy became a British subject, since she has been in much demand at folk clubs and festivals. In addition, she holds workshops and seminars, both at home and abroad. Along with **Frankie Armstrong**, Seeger has long championed women's rights through many of her songs. One such song, 'Gonna Be An Engineer' is possibly her best-known on the subject of equal rights for women. Due to her knowledge of folk music, Peggy was a leading-light in the English folk song revival. After Ewan died in 1989, Peggy again launched a solo career, touring both the USA and Australia. Her collaboration with MacColl, produced hundreds of songs and she has recorded a substantial number of albums in her own right, as well as with Mike and Penny Seeger. *The New Briton Gazette No.3* and *Fields Of Vietnam*, both recorded on **Folkways** in the USA, with Ewan MacColl and the Critics Group, were never released.

Selected albums: with Ewan MacColl *Two Way Trip* (1961), with MacColl *The Amorous Muse* (1966), with MacColl *The Long Harvest, Vol. 1* (1966), with MacColl *The Long Harvest, Vol. 2* (1967), with MacColl *The Long Harvest, Vol. 3* (1968), with MacColl *The Angry Muse* (1968), with Sandra Kerr and Frankie Armstrong *The Female Frolic* (1968), with MacColl *The Long Harvest, Vol. 4* (1969), with MacColl *The Long Harvest, Vol. 5* (1970), with Mike Seeger *American Folksongs For Children* (1970), with MacColl *The Long Harvest, Vol. 6* (1971), with MacColl *The Long Harvest, Vol. 7* (1972), with MacColl *The Long Harvest, Vol. 8* (1973), with MacColl *The Long Harvest, Vol. 9* (1974), with MacColl *The Long Harvest, Vol. 10* (1975), with MacColl *Penelope Isn't Waiting Anymore* (1977), with MacColl *Saturday Night At The Bull And Mouth* (1977), *Cold Snap* (1977), *Hot Blast* (1978), *Different Therefore Equal* (1979), with Ewan MacColl *Kilroy Was Here* (1980), *From Where I Stand* (1982), *Familiar Faces* (1988, with Seeger & MacColl families *American Folksongs For Christmas* (Rounder 1989)), with Ewan MacColl *Naming Of Names* (1990), with Irene Scott *Almost Commercially Viable* (1993). Compilations: *The Best Of Peggy Seeger* (1962), *The World Of Ewan MacColl And Peggy Seeger* (1970), *The World Of Ewan MacColl And Peggy Seeger, Vol. 2* (1972), *The Folkways Years 1955-92 - Songs Of Love And Politics* (1992).

Further reading: *Who's Going To Shoe Your Pretty Little Foot, Who's Going To Glove Your Hand?*, Peggy Seeger with Tom Paley. *Folk Songs Of Peggy Seeger*, Peggy Seeger. *Travellers Songs Of England And Scotland*, Peggy Seeger and Ewan MacColl. *Doomsday In The Afternoon*, Peggy Seeger and Ewan MacColl.

Seeger, Pete

b. 3 May 1919, New York City, New York, USA. Educated at Harvard University, he is the brother of **Peggy Seeger** and half brother of **Mike Seeger**. Pete Seeger's mother was a violin teacher, and his father a renowned musicologist. While still young Pete Seeger learned to play banjo and ukulele, and shortly afterwards he developed his interest in American folk music. Seeger took his banjo round the country, playing and learning songs from the workers and farmers. He served in the US Army during World War II. In addition to being a member of the **Weavers** from 1949-58, he had earlier been in a group called the Almanac Singers. The group included **Woody Guthrie**, Lee Hays and Millard Lampell. The Almanac Singers had frequently given free performances to union meetings and strikers' demonstrations. Despite such apparent diversions, Seeger maintained a successfully high profile in his own solo career. The era of McCarthyism put a blight on many live performances, owing to the right-wing political paranoia that existed at the time. It was in 1948 that Seeger was blacklisted and had to appear before the House of Un-American Activities Committee for his alleged communist sympathies. This did not stop Seeger from performing sell-out concerts abroad and speaking out on a wide range of civil rights and environmental issues. He became known for popularizing songs such as 'Little Boxes', 'Where Have All The Flowers Gone' and, 'We Shall Overcome'. In more recent times Seeger also performed and recorded with **Arlo Guthrie**. Seeger was also involved with the Clearwater Sloop project on the Hudson River, attempting to publicize the threat of pollution. He has always worked and campaigned for civil rights, peace and equality, and has never compromised his ideals. By the mid-70s, Seeger had released in excess of 50 albums, several of which were instructional records for banjo playing. In addition to these albums Seeger has appeared on the work of many other artists providing either vocal or instrumental back-up. The 1993 release, *Live At Newport*, consisted of previously unreleased recordings made at the Newport Folk Festival between 1963 and 1965. Seeger is one of the most important figures ever in the development of free speech and humanitarian causes through folk music.

Albums: with the Almanac Singers *Songs For John Doe* (Keynote/Almanac 1941), with the Almanac Singers *Talking Union And Other Union Songs* (Keynote 1941), with the Almanac Singers *Sod Buster Ballads, Deep Sea Shanties* (General Records 1941), with the Almanac Singers *Dear Mr. President* (Keynote 1942), *Songs Of The Lincoln Bridge* (Asch 1943), *Songs For Political Action* (CIO-Political Action Commitee 1946), *Bawdy Ballads And Real Sad Songs* (Charter 1947), *We Sing Vol.1* (bootleg 1950, recorded live in concert), *Darling Corey* (1950), *Pete Seeger Concert* (1953), *Pete Seeger Sampler* (1954), *Goofing-Off Suite* (1954), *How To Play The Five String Banjo* (1954), *Frontier Ballads, Vol. 1* (1954), *Frontier Ballads, Vol. 2* (1954), *Birds, Beasts, Bugs And Little Fishes* (1954), *Birds, Beasts, Bugs And Bigger Fishes* (1955), *The Folksinger's Guitar Guide* (1955), *Bantu Choral Folk Songs* (1955), *Folksongs Of Our Continents* (1955), *With Voices Together We Sing* (1956), *American Industrial Ballads* (1956), *Love Songs For Friends And Foes* (1956), *American Ballads* (1957), *American Favorite Ballads* (1957), *Gazette With Pete Seeger, Vol. 1* (1958), *Sleep Time* (1958), *Pete Seeger And Sonny Terry* (1958), *We Shall Overcome* (1958), *Song And Play Time With Pete Seeger* (1958), *American Favorite Ballads, Vol. 2* (1959), *Sing Out! Hootenanny* (Folkways 1959), *Hootenanny Tonight* (1959), *Folk Songs For Young People* (1959), *Folk Festival At Newport, Vol. 1* (1959), *Pete Seeger In Concert Vols. 1 & 2* (Folklore 1959), with Mike Seeger, Rev. Larry Eisenberg *American Playparties* (1959), with Frank Hamilton *Nonesuch* (1959), *American Favorite Ballads, Vol. 3* (1960), *Songs Of The Civil War* (1960), *Champlain Valley Songs* (1960), *At Village Gate, Vol. 1* (1960), *The Rainbow Quest* (1960), *Highlights Of Pete Seeger At The Village Gate With Memphis Slim And Willie Dixon* (Folkways 1960), *Sing Out With Pete* (1961), *American Favorite Ballads, Vol. 4* (1961), *Gazette, Vol. 2* (1961), *Pete Seeger: Story Songs* (1961), *At Village Gate, Vol. 2* (1962), *American Favorite Ballads, Vol. 5* (1962), *In Person At The Bitter End* (1962), *American Game And Activity Songs For Children* (1962), *The Bitter And The Sweet* (1963), *Pete Seeger, Children's Concert At Town Hall* (1963), *We Shall Overcome*

(1963), *Little Boxes And Other Broadsides* (1963), *The Nativity* (1963), *In Concert, Vol. 2 (St. Pancras Town Hall)* (1964, rec. 1959), *Broadsides Songs And Ballads* (1964), *Broadsides 2* (1964), *Freight Train* (1964), *Little Boxes* (1964), *Pete Seeger And Big Bill Broonzy In Concert* (1964), *Strangers And Cousins* (1965), *The Pete Seeger Box* (1965), *Songs Of Struggle And Protest* (1965), *WNEW's Story Of The Sea* (Folkways 1965), *Pete Seeger On Campus* (Verve/Folkways 1965), *Broadside Ballads, Vol. 2* (1965), *I Can See A New Day* (1965), *God Bless The Grass* (1966), *Dangerous Songs!?* (1966), *Pete Seeger Sings Woody Guthrie* (1967), *Waist Deep In The Big Muddy* (1967), *Traditional Christmas Carols* (1967), *Pete Seeger Sings Leadbelly* (1968), *American Folksongs For Children* (1968), *Pete Seeger Sings And Answers Questions At The Ford Hall Forum In Boston* (1968), *Where Have All The Flowers Gone* (1969), *Leadbelly* (1969), *Pete Seeger Now* (1969), *Pete Seeger Young Vs. Old* (1971), *Rainbow Race* (1973), *America's Balladeer* (Everest/Olympic 1973), *Banks Of Marble* (1974), *Pete Seeger And Brother Kirk Visit Sesame Street* (1974), *Pete Seeger And Arlo Guthrie Together In Concert* (1975), with Ed Renehan *Fifty Sail On Newburgh Bay* (1976), *Tribute To Leadbelly* (1977), *Circles And Seasons* (1979), *American Industrial Ballads* (1979), *Singalong-Sanders Theater 1980* (1980), *Pete Seeger Live At Newport* (1993). Compilations: *The World Of Pete Seeger* (1974), *The Essential Pete Seeger* (1978), *Live At The Royal Festival Hall* (1986), *Can't You See This System's Rotten Through And Through* (1986).

Further reading: *How Can I Keep From Singing*, David King Dunaway, *The Foolish Frog*, Seeger, Pete (1973), *How Can I Keep From Singing?*, Dunaway, David King (1981), *Everbody Says Freedom*, Reiser, Bob (1989), *Carry It On!: History In Song And Pictures Of The Working Men & Women Of America*, Seeger, Pete & Reiser, Bob (1991), *Where Have All The Flowers Gone?*, Pete Seeger, *Incompleat Folksinger*, Schwartz, Jo Metcalf (1993).

Seekers

Founded in Australia in 1963, the original Seekers comprised Athol Guy (b. 5 January 1940, Victoria, Australia, vocals/double bass), Keith Potger (b. 2 March 1941, Columbo, Sri Lanka, vocals/guitar), Bruce Woodley (b. 25 July 1942, Melbourne, Australia, vocals/guitar) and Ken Ray (lead vocals/guitar). After a year with the above line-up, Athol Guy recruited Judith Durham (b. 3 July 1943, Melbourne, Australia) as the new lead singer and it was this formation which won international success. Following a visit to London in 1964, the group were signed to the Grade Agency and secured a prestigious guest spot on the televised *Sunday Night At The London Palladium*. Tom Springfield, of the recently-defunct **Springfields**, soon realized that the Seekers could fill the gap left by his former group and offered his services as songwriter/producer. Although 1965 was one of the most competitive years in pop, the Seekers strongly challenged the **Beatles** and the **Rolling Stones** as the top chart act of the year. A trilogy of folk/pop smashes: 'I'll Never Find Another You', 'A World Of Our Own' and 'The Carnival Is Over' widened their appeal, leading to lucrative supper club dates and frequent television appearances. Apart from Tom Springfield's compositions, such as 'Walk With Me', they also scored a massive chart hit with **Malvina Reynolds**' 'Morningtown Ride' and gave **Paul Simon** his first UK success with a bouncy adaptation of 'Someday One Day'. Meanwhile, Bruce Woodley teamed up with Simon to write some songs, including the **Cyrkle** hit 'Red Rubber Ball'. In early 1967, the breezy 'Georgy Girl' (written by Tom Springfield and **Jim Dale**) was a transatlantic Top 10 hit but thereafter, apart from 'When Will The Good Apples Fall' and 'Emerald City', the group were no longer chart regulars. Two years later they bowed out in a televised farewell performance, and went their separate ways. Keith Potger oversaw the formation of the **New Seekers** before moving into record production; Bruce Woodley became a highly successful writer of television jingles; Athol Guy spent several years as a Liberal representative in the Victoria parliament; and Judith Durham pursued a solo singing career. She had a minor UK hit in 1967 with 'Olive Tree', and her 1973 album *Here I Am* contained songs by **Rod McKuen**, **Nilsson** and **Elton John**, as well as some folksy and jazz material. In 1975, the Seekers briefly reformed with teenage Dutch singer Louisa Wisseling replacing Judith Durham. They enjoyed one moment of chart glory when 'The Sparrow Song' topped the Australian charts. In 1990 Judith Durham was involved in a serious car crash and spent six months recovering. The experience is said to have inspired her to reunite the original Seekers, and they played a series of 100 dates across Australia and New Zealand, before appearing in several 1994 Silver Jubilee Reunion Concerts in the UK at venues which included London's Royal Albert Hall and Wembley Arena.

Albums: *The Seekers* (1965), *A World Of Our Own* (1965), *The New Seekers* (1965, US release), *Come The Day* (1966), *Seen In Green* (1967), *Georgy Girl* (1967, US release), *Live At The Talk Of The Town* (1968), *Four And Only Seekers* (1969), *The Seekers* (1975). Compilations: *The Sound Of The Seekers* (1967), *Love Is Kind* (1967), *Seekers Golden Collection* (1969), *A World Of Their Own* (1969), *The Very Best Of The Seekers* (1974), *An Hour Of The Seekers* (1988), *The Seekers Greatest Hits* (1988), *A Carnival Of Hits* (1994). Further reading: *Colours Of My Life*, Judith Durham.

Seely, Jeannie

b. Marilyn Jeanne Seely, 6 July 1940, Titusville, Pennsylvania, USA. Seely had studied banking but she had been singing in public from 11 years old. She gained valuable experience by working as a secretary in Los Angeles for **Liberty Records**. In 1965 with encouragement from the man she later married, **Hank Cochran**, she came to Nashville. She worked for **Ernest Tubb** and then for **Porter Wagoner**. In 1966, she went to number 2 on the US country charts with Cochran's 'Don't Touch Me', and won a Grammy as the Best Country Female Vocalist. She had success with more of Cochran's songs, notably 'I'll Love You More', 'Welcome Home To Nothing' and 'Just Enough To Start Me Dreaming', and dedicated an album to him, *Thanks, Hank*. Being a small blonde in a miniskirt, she was a distinctive partner for the six-foot **Jack Greene** and they had a succession of US country hits, including a number 2, 'I Wish I Didn't Have To Miss You'. Seely wrote 'It Just Takes Practice' (**Dottie West**), 'Senses' (**Willie Nelson** and **Connie Smith**) and 'Leavin' And Sayin' Goodbye' (Jack Greene, **Faron Young** and **Norma Jean**). In 1973 she had success with 'Can I Sleep In Your Arms Tonight, Mister?', a parody by Hank Cochran of the old-time 'May I Sleep In Your Barn Tonight, Mister?'. She also made a bid for the outlaw country market with a song addressed to **Jessi Colter**, 'We're Still Hangin' In There, Ain't We, Jessi?'.

Selected albums: *Thanks, Hank* (1967), *I Love You More* (1968), *Little Things* (1968), *Jeannie Seely* (1969), *Please Be My New Love* (1970), *Make The World Go Away* (1972), *Can I Sleep In Your Arms?* (1973), *Seely Style* (1976), *Greatest Hits On Monument* (1993); with Jack Greene *I Wish I Didn't Have To Miss You* (1969), *Jack Greene And Jeannie Seely* (1970), *Two For The Show* (1971), *Live At The Grand Ole Opry* (1978).

Seger, Bob

b. 6 May 1945, Detroit, Michigan, USA. Seger began his long career in the early 60s as a member of the Decibels. He subsequently joined Doug Brown and the Omens as organist, but was installed as their vocalist and songwriter when such talents surfaced. The group made its recording debut as the Beach Bums, with 'The Ballad Of The Yellow Beret', but this pastiche of the contemporaneous **Barry Sadler** hit, 'The Ballad Of The Green Beret', was withdrawn in the face of a threatened lawsuit. The act then became known as Bob Seger and the Last Heard and as such completed several powerful singles, notably 'East Side Story' (1966) and 'Heavy Music' (1967). Seger was signed by **Capitol Records** in 1968 and the singer's new group, the Bob Seger System, enjoyed a US Top 20 hit that year with 'Ramblin' Gamblin' Man'. Numerous excellent hard-rock releases followed, including the impressive *Mongrel* album, but the artist was unable to repeat his early success and disbanded the group in 1971.

Having spent a period studying for a college degree, Seger returned to music with his own label, Palladium and three unspectacular albums ensued. He garnered considerable acclaim for his 1974 single, 'Get Out Of Denver', which has since become a much-covered classic. However, Seger only achieved deserved commercial success upon returning to Capitol when *Beautiful Loser* reached the lower reaches of the US album charts (number 131). Now fronting the Silver Bullet Band - Drew Abbott (guitar), Robyn Robbins (keyboards), Alto Reed (saxophone), Chris Campbell (bass) and Charlie Allen Martin (drums) - Seger reinforced his in-concert popularity with the exciting *Live Bullet*, which was in turn followed by *Night Moves*, his first platinum disc. The title track reached the US Top 5 in 1977, a feat 'Still The Same' repeated the following year. The latter hit was culled from the triple-platinum album, *Stranger In Town*, which also included 'Hollywood Nights', 'Old Time Rock 'N' Roll' and 'We've Got Tonight'. By couching simple sentiments in traditional, R&B-based rock, the set confirmed Seger's ability to articulate the aspirations of blue-collar America, a feature enhanced by his punishing tour schedule. *Against The Wind* also topped the US album charts, while another live set, *Nine Tonight*, allowed the artist time to recharge creative energies.

He recruited **Jimmy Iovine** for *The Distance* which stalled at number 5. While Seger is rightly seen as a major artist in the USA he has been unable to appeal to anything more than a cult audience in the UK. Among his later hit singles were the **Rodney Crowell** song 'Shame On The Moon' (1983), Old Time Rock 'n' Roll (from the film Risky Business), Understanding (from the film Teachers) and the number 1 hit 'Shakedown', taken from the soundtrack of *Beverly Hills Cop II*. Seger released his first studio album for five years in 1991. Co-produced by Don Was, it was a Top 10 hit in the USA clearly showing his massive following had remained. A highly successful greatest hits collection issued in 1994 (with copious sleeve notes from Seger) also demonstrated just what a huge following he still has.

Albums: *Ramblin' Gamblin' Man* (1968), *Noah* (1969), *Mongrel* (1970), *Brand New Morning* (1971), *Back In '72* (1973), *Smokin' O.P.'s* (1973), *Seven* (1974), *Beautiful Loser* (1975), *Live Bullet* (1976), *Night Moves* (1976), *Stranger In Town* (1978), *Against The Wind* (1980), *Nine Tonight* (1981), *The Distance* (1982), *Like A Rock* (1986), *The Fire Inside* (1991). Compilation: *Bob Seger And The Silver Bullet Band Greatest Hits* (Capitol 1994).
Films: *American Pop* (1981).

Segure, Roger

b. 22 May 1905, Brooklyn, New York, USA. Segure studied at university in Nevada and California. He worked as a pianist on boats to the East and played in both China and Japan in the 30s. He settled in New York in the late 30s doing arrangements for the bands of **Louis Armstrong**, **Andy Kirk**, **John Kirby** and **Jimmy Lunceford** whose full-time arranger he became between 1940-42. He wrote the score for the film *Blues In The Night* for Lunceford. Segure was an influential arranger who wrote several very forward looking pieces. In the late 40s he moved to Los Angeles and in time became the musical director for various television shows. He spent some time teaching before retiring.

Seifert, Zbigniew

b. 6 June 1946, Cracow, Poland, d. 15 February 1979, Munich, Germany. Seifert studied violin from the age of six and took up the alto saxophone in his teens. He studied music at the Chopin School of Music in Cracow and graduated from the Higher School of Music in 1970. In 1965 he had started his own quartet modelled on the style of **John Coltrane**'s classic quartet. By the time he played with **Tomasz Stanko**'s band (1969-73) he was playing a freer form of jazz, gradually incorporating more violin and dropping the alto altogether in 1971. The free style was well served by his passionate, tough and technically adept playing which measured up to his desire to 'play as Coltrane would if he played the violin'. He moved to Germany in 1973 and worked with **Hans Koller**'s Free Sound (1974-75) and appeared at the Montreux Jazz Festival with **John Lewis** in 1976. Hamburg Radio commissioned a large scale piece from him and he played and recorded with **Oregon**. He died from cancer at the age of 32.

Albums: with Tomasz Stanko *Purple Sun* (1973), *Man Of The Light* (1976), with Oregon *Violin* (1977), with Charlie Mariano *Helen 12 Trees* (1977), *Passion* (1978).

Seldom Scene

Formed in late 1971, as a Washington DC based semi-professional newgrass bluegrass band. A fellow musician, most probably Charlie Waller of the Country Gentlemen, was responsible for the name, when he suggested that since the members had to fit their musical appearances around their daily employment, they would be seldom seen playing in the area. The founder members were John Duffey (b. 4 March 1934, Washington DC, USA; mandolin/guitar/vocals) and Tom Gray (b. c.1946, Chicago, Illinois, USA; string bass/guitar/mandolin/vocals), who had both previously played with Waller in the Country Gentlemen, Mike Auldridge (b. 1938, Washington DC, USA; dobro/vocals), Ben Eldridge (banjo/guitar/vocals) and John Starling (guitar/lead vocals). All had daily work outside the music industry, although Duffey actually repaired musical instruments through an Arlington, Virginia music store. Gray worked for the National Geographical magazine as a cartographer, Eldridge was a mathematician, whilst Starling was a US Army surgeon, then working at a local hospital. Auldridge, now one of country music's finest dobro players, who has also played on countless recordings as a session musician, as well as recording solo albums, was working as a commercial artist. (Auldridge's uncle,

Ellsworth T. Cozens, a talented multi-instrumentalist, had played steel guitar, mandolin and banjo on **Jimmie Rodgers**' recordings in 1928.) Seldom Scene first played a residency at the Red Fox Inn, Bethesda, in January 1972. This soon led to festival and concert appearances and by 1974, their fine harmonies and musicianship had seen them achieve a popularity almost equal to that of the long established Country Gentlemen. They recorded a series of albums for Rebel in 1972, before moving to **Sugar Hill** in 1980. There were no personnel changes until 1977, when Phil Rosenthal, who had already written material for the band, including their popular 'Willie Boy' and 'Muddy Water', replaced Starling. (Starling, an exceptional bluegrass vocalist and songwriter, subsequently become a popular artist in his own right, recording several very successful albums for Sugar Hill.) In 1986, Rosenthal (who also recorded solo albums) left and was replaced by Lou Reid (fiddle, guitar, dobro, mandolin, lead vocals), who had previously worked with **Ricky Skaggs** and Doyle Lawson. Tom Gray finally left the group soon afterwards, his place being taken by T. Michael Coleman, who had played previously with **Doc Watson**. This change also saw an instrumental variation, since Coleman played an electric bass guitar instead of the acoustic stand up bass that Gray had always used. The band played a special concert, on 10 November 1986, at Washington's John F. Kennedy Center For The Performing Arts, to commemorate their 15 years in the music business, which was recorded as a double album and included several guest appearances by artists such as **Emmylou Harris**, **Linda Ronstadt,** John Starling, **Jonathan Edwards** and Charlie Waller. The album actually contained a liner note from President Ronald Reagan. Five years later, all the eight artists who had been members over the years played together to record another live album, this time at Birchmere, to commemorate the 20th anniversary of the Seldom Scene's formation.
Albums: *Seldom Scene-Act 1* (Rebel 1972), *Seldom Scene-Act 2* (Rebel 1973), S*eldom Scene-Act 3* (Rebel 1974), *Old Train* (Rebel 1974), *Live At The Cellar Door* (Rebel 1976, double album), *The New Seldom Scene Album* (Rebel 1977), *Baptizing* (Rebel 1978), *Seldom Scene-Act 4* (Sugar Hill 1980), *After Midnight* (Sugar Hill 1981), *At The Scene* (Sugar Hill 1984), *Jonathan Edwards & The Seldom Scene* (Sugar Hill 1985), *A Change Of Scenery* (Sugar Hill 1988), *15th Anniversary Celebration* (Sugar Hill 1988, double album), *Scenic Roots* (Sugar Hill 1991), *Scene 20* (Sugar Hill 1992, double album).

Selecter

When Coventry's **Specials** needed a b-side for their own debut, 'Gangsters', they approached fellow local musician Noel Davies. With the assistance of John Bradbury aka Prince Rimshot (drums), and Barry Jones

(trombone), Davies concocted the instrumental trac,k 'The Selecter'. Released on the Specials own 2-Tone label, the single took off with both sides receiving airplay. This meant that a band had to be formed to tour. Bradbury was busy drumming for the Specials and Jones had returned to his newsagent business so Davies assembled the Selecter Mk II. This consisted of Pauline Black (vocals), Noel Davis (guitar), Crompton Amanor (drums/vocals), Charles H. Bainbridge (drums), Gappa Hendricks, Desmond Brown (keyboards) and Charlie Anderson (bass). Anderson claims the original **ska** superstar, **Prince Buster**, amongst his ancestors. The Debut album featured the renowned ska trombonist **Rico Rodriquez**. Like many of the bands who first found fame on 2-Tone, the Selecter departed for pastures new - in this case 2-Tone's distributors, **Chrysalis**. They managed a string of successful singles such as 'On My Radio', 'Three Minute Hero', and 'Missing Words'. Black left in 1981 and recorded the single, 'Pirates Of The Airwaves', with Sunday Best before concentrating on acting. She would reappear to the general public as hostess of the children's pop/games show, *Hold Tight*. However, more impressive performances included a one-woman show, *Let Them Call It Jazz*, plus portrayals of Cleopatra and **Billie Holiday**, the latter bringing her the *Time Out* award for best actress in 1990. Black rejoined Selector on tour in 1991 as signs of a ska revival in London gained ground, though she also found time to host Radio 5's *Black To The Future* and complete her first novel, *The Goldfinches*. A phone call from Doug Trendle (aka Buster Blood Vessel from **Bad Manners**) had prompted the Selecter's reformation, which culminated in the release of their first new material for over a decade in 1994.
Albums: *Too Much Pressure* (1980), *Celebrate The Bullet* (1981), *Out On The Streets* (1992), *The Happy Album* (1994). Compilation: *The Selecter & The Specials: Live In Concert* (1993).

Sellers, Brother John

b. 27 May 1924, Clarksdale, Mississippi, USA. Raised by his godmother after his family broke up in the following a terrible flood, Sellers moved to Chicago in the 30s, and began his professional music career in gospel. He subsequently toured with **Mahalia Jackson** in the 40s. His religious convictions never excluded blues music from, and he recorded in both genres from 1945. He was quick to see the growing market among whites for black music, and was working festivals and white clubs by the early 50s. In 1957 he came to Europe with **Big Bill Broonzy**. After Broonzy's death his star began to wane as research uncovered more intuitive blues singers, whose approach was regarded as more 'authentic' than Sellers' stagey and rather inflexible singing. He has continued to make solo appearances, and has been with the Alvin Ailey Dance Company (as a musician) since the early 60s.

Albums: *Brother John Sellers Sings Blues And Folk Songs* (1954), *In London* (1957), *Big Boat Up The River* (1959), *Baptist Shouts And Gospel Songs* (1959).

Selvin, Ben

b. 1898, d. 15 July 1980, New York, USA. The Bar Harbor Society Orchestra, Southampton Serenaders, the Broadway Syncopators, Roy Carroll and Lloyd Keating - all were among the many pseudonyms which hid the identity of various Selvin dance bands. His first hit, 'I'm Forever Blowing Bubbles' (this later became the adopted anthem of the West Ham United Football Club), in 1919, was credited to Selvin's Novelty Orchestra, and his 1920 version of 'Dardanella', with its 'boogie woogie' bass pattern, is reportedly the first record to sell over five million copies. Although his were basically just recording bands, Selvin employed some top sidemen including **Jimmy** and **Tommy Dorsey**, **Benny Goodman**, **Red Nichols**, and **Bunny Berigan**. During the 20s and 30s his output was prodigious. Estimates vary wildly, but it would seem that he recorded several thousand tracks, including 'Happy Days Are Here Again', 'When It's Springtime In The Rockies', 'Oh How I Miss You Tonight', 'Manhattan', 'Blue Skies' and 'I Only Have Eyes For You'. He also provided accompaniment for other big stars of the day such as **Ethel Waters** ('Three Little Words'), **Ruth Etting** ('Dancing With Tears In My Eyes'), **Irving Kaufman** ('Yes, We Have No Bananas' and 'Dirty Hands, Dirty Face'), and **Kate Smith** ('When The Moon Comes Over The Mountain'). His own last hit was in 1938 with 'Born To Be Kissed'. Selvin was also a recording executive for **Columbia** into the 40s, and later worked for the Muzak Corporation and as an advisor to other recording companies.

Album: *Cheerful Little Earful 1929-32* (1984).

Semenya, Caiphus

b. 21 June 1941, Alexandra Township, Johannesburg, South Africa. An occasional recording artist under his own name, Semenya has played a major role in the development of South African popular music, mainly as a producer and composer. He has produced or co-produced albums for fellow South Africans **Letta Mbulu**, **Hugh Masekela** and **Myriam Makeba**, and has composed material recorded by a host of artists including Mbulu, Masekela, Makeba, **Cannonball Adderley**, **Lou Rawls**, **Stanley Turrentine**, **Herb Alpert**, **Nina Simone**, **Quincy Jones** and **Harry Belafonte**. With Quincy Jones he composed and arranged all the African music heard in the television series *Roots*. Semenya first became involved with the South African music scene at the age of 13 when he was hired as an assistant by the legendary itinerant township disc jockey Mabaso. A year later his family moved from Alexandra to Benoni Township in the East Rand, where in 1955 he joined a vocal quartet known as the Dining Brothers (later known as the Katsenjammer Kids). Within three years the group became one of black South Africa's leading line-ups, performing at township functions throughout the country. In 1959 Semenya left the group to pursue a solo career, and was hired as a singer/actor in the original production of the seminal township musical *King Kong*. In 1961 at the conclusion of *King Kong's* hugely successful tour of the UK, Semenya returned to South Africa and from 1962 to 1964 took part in many concerts, operas and plays sponsored by the black musicians' trade union/cultural pressure group the Union of South African Artists.

In 1964, he joined the cast of the musical *Sponono*, which followed its Johannesburg season with a short run on Broadway. When the company returned to South Africa, Semenya, who had by this time had as much as he could stomach of working conditions under apartheid, decided to stay behind in the USA. In 1970, with fellow South African expatriates Masekela and Jonas Gwanga, he co-founded the group **Union Of South Africa** (a memorable but short-lived band which folded following the lengthy hospitalization of Gwanga after he was injured in a hit-and-run car accident). In 1980, he formed his own production company, Munjale, whose first release was Mbulu's *Sound Of A Rainbow*. In 1983, he released his first own-name album, *Listen To The Wind*, a brilliant combination of a wide variety of musical styles, including black South African mbaqanga, American blues, traditional Zulu folk songs and reggae.

Albums: *Listen To The Wind* (1983), *Caiphus Semenya* (1988).

Semien, 'Ivory' Lee

b. 13 September 1931, Washington, Louisiana, USA. Having played music from his early years, Ivory Lee settled in Houston in his teens and began to play in the blues clubs in that city, making his first records as a vocalist in the early 50s. He took up as drummer with the great slide guitarist **Hop Wilson**, and they made a number of records together, some with Wilson as leader, others - including his best known song 'Rockin' In The Coconut Top' with Semien himself on vocals. In the early 60s, he started his own record label, Ivory Records, whose best known releases featured some magnificent blues by Wilson. He remained an active musician in Houston, at least on a semi-professional basis, although making little impact outside.

Albums: *Rockin' Blues Party* (1987), *Steel Guitar Flash* (1988).

Semple, Archie

b. 1 March 1928, Edinburgh, Scotland, d. 26 January

1974. After first playing clarinet in bands in his homeland, Semple moved to London in the early 50s. There he became an important voice in the burgeoning traditional jazz scene, playing with the bands of **Mick Mulligan**, **Freddy Randall** and **Alex Welsh**, with whom he remained until the early 60s. During that decade he played with various bands, led his own small groups and made many records, despite the fast-encroaching effects of a severe drinking problem. A very distinctive player with a rich and quirky musical imagination, Semple was one of the most strikingly individualistic musicians to emerge from the sometimes predictable British trad scene. His presence in the already formidable Welsh band helped create much memorable music. He died in 1974.

Albums: *The Clarinet Of Archie Semple* (1957-58), with Welsh *It's Right Here For You* (1960), *The Archie Semple Trio* (1960), *Archie Semple And His Orchestra* (1962), *The Archie Semple Quartet* (1963).

Senator Bobby

Senator Bobby was a studio concoction of writer/producer of **Chip Taylor** (b. James Wesley Voight, 1940, Yonkers, New York, USA). Using voice impersonator Bill Minkin and a demo of the **Troggs'** garage-band classic, 'Wild Thing', he created in 1967 a comedic take-off of Senator Robert Kennedy and his Massachusetts accent. With the single going to number 20 pop, a follow-up album was produced joining Minkin in a comedy troupe called the Hardly Worthit Players with Dennis Wholey, Steve Baron, and Carol Morley. Typical of most novelty acts, the group could not follow up, scraping the bottom of the chart at 99 with a take-off on **Donovan**'s 'Mellow Yellow' in 1967, which was a dual take-off of senators Kennedy and Everett McKinley Dirksen. Whorley went on to become a highly successful television talk-show host. Taylor, prior to his Senator Bobby project, was a one-hit-wonder in a duo called **Just Us**. He became a moderately successful country and western singer in the 70s.

Album: *The Hardly Worthit Report* (1967).

Sensational Alex Harvey Band

Formed in 1972 when veteran vocalist **Alex Harvey** (b. 5 February 1935, Glasgow, Scotland, d. 4 February 1981) teamed with struggling Glasgow group, **Tear Gas**. Zal Cleminson (b. 4 May 1949; guitar), Hugh McKenna (b. 28 November 1949; keyboards), Chris Glen (b. 6 November 1950, Paisley, Renfrewshire, Scotland; bass) and Ted McKenna (b. 10 March 1950; drums) gave the singer the uncultured power his uncompromising rasp required and were the perfect foil to the sense of drama he created. Armed with a musical and cultural heritage, Harvey embarked on a unique direction combining elements of rock, R&B and the British music hall. He created the slum-kid Vambo,

celebrated pulp fiction with 'Sergeant Fury' and extolled a passion for 'b-movie' lore in 'Don't Worry About The Lights Mother, They're Burning Big Louie Tonight'. *Framed*, SAHB's debut, was accompanied by a period of frenetic live activity. *Next*, reflected a consequent confidence which was especially apparent on the title track, a harrowing, atmospheric rendition of a **Jacques Brel** composition. The quintet continued their commercial ascendancy with *The Impossible Dream* and *Tomorrow Belongs To Me*, while enhancing their in-concert reputation with a series of excellent and increasingly ambitious stage shows. Harvey's presence was a determining factor in their visual appeal, but Cleminson's intelligent use of clown make-up and mime brought yet another factor to the unit's creative think-tank. *Live* encapsulated this era, while SAHB's irreverence was made clear in their exaggerated reading of **Tom Jones**' hit 'Delilah', which gave the group a UK Top 10 single. Its success inspired *The Penthouse Tapes*, which featured such disparate favourites as 'Crazy Horses' (the **Osmonds**) 'School's Out' (**Alice Cooper**) and 'Goodnight Irene' (**Leadbelly**). The group enjoyed another hit single with 'Boston Tea Party' (1976), but the rigorous schedule extracted a toll on their vocalist. He entered hospital to attend to a recurring liver problem, during which time the remaining members recorded *Fourplay* as SAHB (Without Alex). Hugh McKenna was then replaced by Tommy Eyre and in August 1977 Harvey rejoined the group to complete *Rock Drill*. However, three months later he walked out on his colleagues during a rehearsal for BBC's *Sight And Sound* programme and despite the ill-feeling this caused, it was later accepted that his return had been premature given the extent of his illness. Despite pursuing a solo career at a more measured pace, Harvey died as a result of a heart attack on 4 February 1981. Ted McKenna, Cleminson and Glen had meanwhile formed the short-lived Zal, with Billy Rankin (guitar) and Leroi Jones (vocals), but this ill-starred ensemble struggled in the face of punk and split up in April 1978. McKenna later joined **Rory Gallagher** and **MSG**, while Cleminson was briefly a member of **Nazareth**. In 1992 members of the original band were reunited as the Sensational Party Boys. The band became very popular once more, in their native Glasgow and surrounding areas. They officially changed their name in August 1993 back to the Sensational Alex Harvey Band with the original line-up (less Alex). Their credible front man is ex Zero Zero and Strangeways vocalist Stevie Doherty (b. 17 July 1959, Coatbridge, Scotland). He is able to perform the catalogue with great presence and power, without attempting to emulate Harvey.

Albums: *Framed* (1972), *Next* (1973), *The Impossible Dream* (1974), *Tomorrow Belongs To Me* (1975), *Live* (1975), *The Penthouse Tapes* (1976), *SAHB Stories* (1976), *Rock Drill* (1978). Compilations: *Big Hits And Close Shaves* (1977),

Collectors Items (1980), *The Best Of The Sensational Alex Harvey Band* (1984), *The Legend* (1985), *Anthology - Alex Harvey* (1986), *Collection - Alex Harvey* (1986). SAHB (Without Alex): *Fourplay* (1977).
Video: *Live On The Test (Windsong)* (1994).

Sensations

This Philadelphia R&B ensemble featured the warm chirpy lead of Yvonne Mills Baker (b. Philadelphia, Pennsylvania, USA). The group was formed in 1954, and in 1956 they scored with two minor ballad hits, a remake of the old standard, 'Yes Sir That's My Baby' (US R&B number 15) and 'Please Mr. Disc Jockey' (US R&B number 13) for the **Atlantic** subsidiary label **Atco**. The group included lead Yvonne Mills, alternate lead Tommy Wicks and bass Alphonso Howell. The Sensations failed to register further hits and disbanded. In 1961 Howell persuaded Baker to reform the group and they added Richard Curtain (tenor) and Sam Armstrong (baritone). Through their mentor and producer, Philadelphia disc jockey Kae Williams, the Sensations won a contract with the **Chess** subsidiary label, Argo. Singing with greater robustness and at a faster clip the group hit first with a remake of the **Teresa Brewer** oldie, 'Music Music Music' (US R&B number 12 in 1961). The following year they struck gold with 'Let Me In' (US R&B number 2 and pop number 4). The last chart record for the Sensations was a remake of the **Frankie Laine** hit, 'That's My Desire' (US pop Top 75 in 1962). The group disbanded around 1964 and Baker continued making records for a few more years in the soul idiom.
Album: *Let Me In* (1963).

Senseless Things

The Senseless Things formed around the enduring musical partnership of songwriter Mark Keds (vocals/guitar) and Morgan Nicholls (bass, originally guitar), who as 11 year old Twickenham, London, England schoolboys put together Wild Division in the early 80s. With the addition of drummer Cass 'Cade' Browne they became the Psychotics, playing various venues in their local area despite still being at school. Their first gig together as the Senseless Things followed at the subsequently demolished Clarendon in Hammersmith, London, in October 1986. Auxiliary members at this stage included a keyboard player Ben, then a guitarist, Gerry, who deputised for Nicholls while the latter was studying for his 'O' Levels. The definitive Senseless Things line-up finally evolved in summer 1987 when Nicholls returned to take over bass, with new recruit, former BBC clerk Ben Harding acquiring the vacant guitarist's role. Taking their musical cue from the **Ramones** and the **Dickies**, and their spiritual lead from fellow guitar outfit **Mega City Four**, the quartet embarked upon a hectic touring schedule which unveiled their roguish charm and

obvious potential. Their youthful zest initially outshone their musical achievements, which were first aired for public consideration on a 7-inch compilation single given away with issue 6 of London fanzine *Sniffin' Rock*. By March 1988 the band had attracted the attention of BBC disc jockey **John Peel**, who invited them to record the first of two sessions for his programme. Following another fanzine release, three tracks headed by 'I'm Moving', a friend offered to finance a 'proper' release. The impressive 'Up And Coming' 12-inch followed, then 'Girlfriend'/'Standing In The Rain', for Way Cool Records. The musical imbalance which had seen them sacrifice melody for speed had, by the time, been thoroughly redressed. The band's debut mini-album, entitled *Postcard C.V.*, arrived in November 1989. It comprised 22 minutes of scratchy, boisterous punk pop now imbued with more shading and subtlety. Continuing to trawl the independent wasteland, the band joined What Goes On Records just as it collapsed, but the situation was rescued by Vinyl Solution subsidiary Decoy Records, who released the four track EP, *Is It Too Late?*, in May 1990. The group stayed with Decoy for 'Can't Do Anything', which prefaced an appearance at the **Reading Festival**, but the ground swell of live support eventually saw them snapped up by **Epic Records** at the start of 1991. The subsequent *The First Of Too Many* introduced acoustic guitars and gentler moods to the punky blitzes of yore, and 'Got It At The Delmar' scuttled into the Top 60 of the UK singles chart. Two further Top 20 singles followed in 1992, 'Easy To Smile' and 'Hold It Down'. The first single from 1993's *Empire Of The Senseless*, 'Homophobic Asshole', was a brave statement but one which ultimately alienated radio programmers. Despite continuing to write quality songs (becoming more reminiscent of the **Replacements** as time passed by) the momentum had been irretrievably lost. Rumours circulated in March 1995 of the band's impending collapse, having been dropped by their record company. Of the band's new album, *Taking Care Of Business*, guitarist Mark Keds would remark: 'We've achieved a very rounded and accomplished rock record, which is what we always set out to do. We're not going to repeat it. Obviously, we'll be touring the album... after that, I think it's going to be all change. Whatever comes next is going to be completely different.' Keds was falsely rumoured to be joining the **Wildhearts**, with whom he had formerly appeared, while it was also suggested that drummer Cass might link with friends **Urge Overkill**.
Albums: *Postcard C.V.* (Way Cool 1989, mini-album), *The First Of Too Many* (Epic 1992), *Empire Of The Senseless* (Epic 1993), *Taking Care Of Business* (Epic 1995).

Senser

This multi-ethnic seven-piece south London band were conceived in 1987. Their *metier* is the synthesis of

numerous styles of music into a format which at once stimulates both the feet and grey matter. Fronted by Heitham Al-Sayed (raps/vocals/percussion), Senser proved the only band of their generation to see features in magazines dedicated to heavy metal, hip hop and indie music - and few were in any way grudging. The other members of the band are Nick Michaelson (guitar), Andy 'Awe' (a DJ who once held the national high score on the Asteroids video game), Haggis (engineer), James Barrett (bass), John Morgan (drums) and Kersten Haigh (vocals/flute). This line-up was cemented in 1992, as they began the first of two tours supporting **Ozric Tentacles**, plus low-key squat and benefit gigs. The first seeds of the band were sewn when Michaelson and Barrett met at a guitarist competition at the Forum, in London. Ex-school friend Haigh fronted the band from 1988 onwards, before the Senser name had been invoked, bringing vocals inspired from her journeys in India. Wimbledon resident Al-Sayed joined in 1991 as a drummer, but soon progressed to rapping duties as the band attempted to tackle their own version of **Public Enemy**'s 'She Watch Channel Zero'. Their 1993 singles, 'Eject' and 'The Key', brought rave reviews across dance and indie periodicals, with their ferocious musical clatter evading categorisation. 'Switch', entering the UK Top 40, in turn announced a Top 5 debut album, *Stacked Up*, and a widely applauded appearance on the 1994 Glastonbury Festival stage. Al-Sayed, meanwhile, was particularly vocal in espousing the cause of the travelling community, under threat in 1994 from a new Criminal Justice bill. Although his throat problems prevented the band from building on their impact for much of 1994, *Stacked Up* would go on to over 80,000 sales.
Album: *Stacked Up* (Ultimate 1994).
Video: *States Of Mind* (1995).

Sentinals

Formed in San Luis Obispo, California, USA, the Sentinals rose to become a popular surf group. They made their debut in 1962 with 'Latin'ia', and were later signed to leading surf outlet Del-Fi for which they completed *Big Surf* and *The Surfer Girl*. However, the sextet is better recalled for the future careers of its personnel. Guitarist/vocalist Mike Olsen later found fame as **Lee Michaels**, while guitarists **Merrell Fankhauser** and **Bill Dodd** subsequently formed HMS Bounty, an acclaimed pop/psychedelic act. Drummer Johnny Barbata resurfaced in the **Turtles**, **Crosby, Stills, Nash And Young** and **Jefferson Airplane/Starship**, while Tommy Nunes (guitar) and Kenny Hinkel (bass) joined **Johnny Rivers**.
Albums: *Big Surf* (1963), *The Surfer Girl* (1963), *Vegas A Go-Go* (1964).

Sentinel Beast

This thrash metal group was formed in Sacramento, California, USA, in 1984 by bassist Mike Spencer, vocalist Debbie Gunn and drummer Scott Awes. Adding guitarists Barry Fischel and Mark Koyasako, they debuted with their theme tune, 'Sentinel Beast', on the *Metal Massacre VII* compilation in 1986. This opened the door to a full contract with Metal Blade Records and the emergence of *Depths Of Death* the same year. This was standard **Anthrax**-style heavy metal, poorly produced and notable only for the high-speed cover of **Iron Maiden**'s 'Phantom Of The Opera'. The album was a commercial flop and founder member Spencer left to join **Flotsam And Jetsum** soon after its release. The band subsequently disintegrated, with Debbie Gunn re-appearing later in **Znowhite** and Ice Age.
Albums: *Depths Of Death* (Metal Blade 1986).

Sepultura

Formed in Belo Horizonte, Brazil, in 1984 by brothers Igor (b. 24 September 1970, Brazil; drums) and Max Cavalera (b. 4 August 1969, Brazil; vocals/guitar), with Paulo Jnr. (b. 30 April 1969, Brazil; bass) and guitarist Jairo T, who was replaced in April 1987 by Andreas Kisser (b. 24 August 1968) of fellow Brazilian metal act Pestilence. Sepultura is the Portuguese word for grave, and this is a strong clue as to the nature of a music which deals with themes of death and destruction, originally influenced by bands such as **Slayer** and **Venom**. In 1985 Sepultura recorded an album with Brazilian band **Overdose** (whom Sepultura had supported on their very first gig), but this debut, *Bestial Devastation*, was of poor quality and had limited circulation. Their first solo effort, *Morbid Visions*, was released in 1986, followed a year later by *Schizophrenia*. The music on both was typified by speed, aggression and anger, much of which stemmed from the band's preoccupations with the poor social conditions in their native land. It was Monte Conner of American record label Roadrunner who brought the band to international notice in 1989 when they released *Beneath The Remains*, which had been recorded in Rio with Scott Burns as producer. In 1990 Sepultura played at the Dynamo Festival in Holland where they met Gloria Bujnowski, manager of **Sacred Reich**; their relationship with her led to the re-release of *Schizophrenia*. Despite European and American success, Sepultura have not deserted Brazil, and they played at the Rock in Rio festival in 1990. *Arise*, released in 1991, proved the best selling album in the history of the Roadrunner label. The sessions for *Chaos A.D.* saw the group strip down their music in a more minimalist approach, which mirrored the punk ethos, especially evident on a cover of **New Model Army**'s 'The Hunt' (they had previously cut the **Dead Kennedys**' 'Drug

Me' for an **Altnerative Tentacles** compilation). 1994, meanwhile, would see Cavalera branch out to release the *Point Blank* CD, working alongside **Fudgetunnel**'s Alex Newport under the name **Nailbomb**.

Albums: *Bestial Devastation* (Cogumelo 1985, split LP with Overdose), *Morbid Visions* (Cogumelo 1986), *Schizophrenia* (Cogumelo 1987), *Beneath The Remains* (Roadracer 1989), *Arise* (Roadracer 1991), *Chaos A.D.* (Roadrunner 1993). Max Cavalera in Nailbomb: *Point Blank* (Roadrunner 1994).

Sequel Records

An 'out-of-house' subsidiary of the **Castle Communications** empire, the reissue label Sequel was founded in September 1987 and is headed by former music journalist and **Motown Records** press officer, Bob Fisher. His introduction to the reissue market came with the *History Of Rock* compilations. He went on to work with **Charly Records** before talking to Castle's Jon Beecher about the possibility of launching a collector's label dedicated to repackaging the more obscure items in their catalogue. By the mid-90s under Fisher's tasteful eye Sequel had successfully orchestrated over 200 reissues, including material culled from the **Pye, Bronze**, Buddah, All Platinum and Bearsville Records' catalogues. Most commercially successful have been the *Blues Guitar Box Sets*, the *Alternative Captain Beefheart Compilation, Under The Influence* - an album of songs covered by the **Beatles**, and two albums by jazz rockers **Colesseum**. Other notable issues have included the *Surf Box Set, The Pye International Story* and *The Piccadilly Story*. One of the best received anthologies was the collection documenting the rise of rap's founding fathers, **Sugarhill Records**. With lavish sleevenotes from **David Toop** (a luxury not afforded to most reissues on parent label, Castle), it typified the meticulous approach to Sequel's craft. In the 90s Fisher entered into the realms of new albums and released works by such varied artists as **Calvin Owens** and Chris Jagger. In the reissue department, 90s product includes the **Jazz Butcher** catalogue, the **Black Oak Arkansas** catalogue and an excellent series from the Josie and Jubilee labels. Like Ace Records it is apparent that the choice of material is based upon a genuine love and knowledge of the music.

Serendipity Singers

This nine piece group was formed at the University of Colorado, USA, in the wake of the success of the **New Christy Minstrels**. The line-up was based around Mike Brovsky (vocals), Brooks Hatch (vocals), and Bryan Sennett (vocals). To these were added Jon Arbenz (guitar), John Madden (guitar), Bob Young (bass), Diane Decker (vocals), Tommy Tieman (vocals) and Lynne Weintraub (vocals). Their material, though not strictly folk, encompassed a range of songs from traditional through to pop music. From performing on college campuses, they moved outside of the confines of university and sang at the Bitter End in New York. As a result, the group were offered a recording deal with Philips and a spot on the influential *Hottenanny* television show. *The Serendipity Singers* contained the group's one big hit, 'Don't Let The Rain Come Down (Crooked Little Man)', which reached the US Top 10 in 1964. The album scaled the US Top 20 the same year. A follow-up 'Beans In My Ears' made the US Top 30, but despite regularly touring at home, mainly on the college circuit, and touring abroad, the group never repeated their earlier success.

Albums: *The Serendipity Singers* (1964), *The Many Sides Of The Serendipity Singers* (1964), *Take Your Shoes Off With The Serendipity Singers* (1965), *We Belong Together* (1966).

Sergeant

This predominantly Swiss, six-piece group was formed from the ashes of the Steve Whitney Band. Comprising Pete Prescott (vocals), Rob Seales (guitar), Chrigi Wiedemeier (guitar), Urs Amacher (keyboards), Rolf Schlup (bass) and Geri Steimer (drums) they specialized in Americanized hard-rock with melodic undercurrents. Signing to Mausoleum Records, they debuted in 1985 with *Sergeant*, a workman-like rock record that paid respect to **Van Halen**, **Kiss** and **Foreigner**. *Streetwise*, released the following year, was a major disappointment, as it merely regurgitated and reprocessed the riffs of their debut. Disillusioned by the media and public response, the band went their separate ways shortly after the album was released. In 1988 Seales and Amacher re-formed the band with new members Romy Caviezel (vocals), Harry Borner (bass) and Urs Rothenbuhler (drums), but this collaboration has yet to release any new material.

Albums: *Sergeant* (Mausoleum 1985), *Streetwise* (Mausoleum 1986).

Serious Drinking

Formed after attendance at the University Of East Anglia, Norwich, England in February 1981, this motley assortment of ex-students carved a niche for themselves in the independent charts of the early 80s by injecting their songs with comedic candour. Jem (bass) was an outspoken member of the Socialist Workers Party, although Lance (the only one not to attend UEA, drums), Martin Simon (ex-**Higsons**) and Eugene (the two singers) and Andy (ex-**Farmers Boys**; guitar) were more concerned with football and alcoholic beverages. The explanation for the presence of two singers was typically straightforward: 'Eugene is in the band because Martin wanted a lift to a practice and Eugene had a car and he's just stayed ever since'. They took their name from a headline announcing an interview with the **Cockney Rejects** in *Sounds*. Pigeonholed as leaders of some mythical 'herbert' movement, they did nevertheless have a penchant for traditional British leisure pursuits. The singles 'Love On The Terraces' and 'Hangover' both fared well in the independent charts, the former produced by Mark Bedford of **Madness.** The latter included the impressive 'Baby I'm Dying A Death' as its b-side, culled from the band's popular **John Peel** radio session. 1983's *The Revolution Begins at Closing Time* and *They May Be Drinkers Robin, But They're Still Human Beings* fully displayed their eccentricity. The band's philosophy was still crystal clear, 'Basically what we're saying is go out, get drunk and enjoy yourself, and don't be nasty to other people.' Unfortunately, after 'Country Girl Became Drugs And Sex Punk' (another borrowed headline), both Gem and Lance departed. Karen Yarnell (ex-**Gymslips**) joined on drums and they released *Love On The Terraces*, a collection of favourite tracks and new recordings to coincide with the World Cup in 1990. *Stranger Than Tannadice* followed and was accompanied by sporadic live appearances.

Albums: *The Revolution Begins At Closing Time* (1983), *They May Be Drinkers Robin, But They're Still Human Beings* (1984), *Love On The Terraces* (1990), *Stranger Than Tannadice - The Hits, Misses and Own Goals Of Serious Drinking* (1991).

Serpent Power

Serpent Power was formed in November 1966. Their debut performance, at a benefit concert for the Telegraph Group Neighbourhood Centre, resulted in a recording deal with the prestigious **Vanguard** label. This experimental ensemble was a musical outlet for David Meltzer, one of several poets active in San Francisco's North Beach enclave. An accomplished guitarist, Meltzer led several bluegrass groups during the early 60s including the Snopes County Camp Followers, which featured his wife, Tina (vocals/autoharp) and J.P. Pickens (banjo). Two former members of the **Grass Roots**, Denny Ellis (rhythm guitar) and David Stenson (bass), joined David, Tina, John Payne (organ) and Clark Coolidge (drums) for the group's first album, which successfully amalgamated softer, almost good-time music with the free-association style exemplified on the lengthy 'Endless Tunnel'. A new line-up - David Meltzer, Bob Cuff, Jim Moscoso, David Moore plus Coolidge - forged an even more radical direction, but this departure was rejected by their record company. Instead David and Tina recorded *Poet Song*, a haunting collection of poems and songs augmented by a string quartet. However, when a third collection, *Green Morning*, was cancelled, David Meltzer resumed his literary career.

Albums: *Serpent Power* (1967), *Poet Song* (1969 - credited to David And Tina Meltzer).

Servants

David Westlake's carefully crafted guitar pop tunes were the central attraction of west London's Servants. Accompanied by John Mahon (guitar), Philip King (bass - later with **Felt**, **Biff Bang Pow!**, the Apple Boutique and See See Rider), and John Wills (drums), the band featured on the *New Musical Express C86* cassette ('Transparent'). Their first single, 'She's Always Hiding', surfaced around the same time on the Head label, followed by a four-track EP, *The Sun, A Small Star*. But Westlake left soon after, joining **Creation Records**, forming Westlake and releasing a self-titled mini-album in 1987. The Servants second line-up featured Luke Haines (b. 7 October 1967, Walton-On-Thames, Surrey, England; vocals/guitar) and Alice Readman (b. 1967, Harrow, Middlesex, England; bass), alongside former **Housemartins**' drummer Hugh Whitaker. The results were restricted to a one-off single, 'It's My Turn', and a lone album. Haines and Readman would go on to greater success in the **Auteurs**.

Album: *Disinterested* (Paperhouse 1990).

Sessions, Ronnie

b. 7 December 1948, Henrietta, Oklahoma, USA. Sessions grew up in Bakersfield, California. His first record, in 1957, was a novelty version of **Little Richard**'s 'Keep A-Knockin'' made with Richard's band. Through a schoolboy friend he knew the host, Herb Henson, of a television series, *Trading Post*, and he became a regular performer. He studied to be a vet but he also recorded for local labels and, joining **Gene Autry**'s Republic label in 1968, he had regional hits with 'The Life Of Riley' and 'More Than Satisfied'. He moved to Nashville and his songwriting talent was recognized by **Hank Cochran**. However, his first country hits were with revivals of pop songs, 'Never Been To Spain' and 'Tossin' And Turnin''. Over at MCA, he had major country hits in 1977 with 'Wiggle, Wiggle' and **Bobby Goldsboro**'s 'Me And Millie (Stompin' Grapes And Gettin' Silly). He failed to consolidate his success and, after being dropped by MCA in 1980, he has hardly recorded since. His last US country chart entry was in 1986 with 'I Bought The Shoes That Just Walked Out On Me'.

Album: *Ronnie Sessions* (1977).

Sevåg, Øystein

b. 1957, Norway. A composer and keyboard player whose forays into contemporary instrumental music have attracted a surfeit of critical acclaim, Sevåg produces these recordings from his 250-year old home in Sandefjord, 120 kilometres to the south west of Oslo. His first piano lessons came at the age of five, though he listened to everything from the **Beatles** to classical music as a child. By the age of 12 he was playing bass in a rock band, before going on to study classical piano, flute and composition at the Music Conservatory of Oslo. His first works were written here for string quartets and wind quintets, and he became a prominent member of the Norwegian Society For Contemporary Music during the 80s. By this time the arrival of synthesizers and electronic music had awakened his interests in the possibilities therein, and he embarked on the construction of his own studio (Bogen Lydstudio, in Stokke). He initially released his debut album, *Close Your Eyes And See*, on his own label in 1989. It immediately took up residence in **Billboard**'s New Age chart, remaining in the Top 25 for 17 weeks, earning the *Gavin Report*'s nomination for Top Adult Alternative album of 1991, two years after initial release. However, such endurance was symptomatic of the album's development - it had been no less than five years in creation. The follow-up was slightly more speedy, however. *LINK* was a collaborative effort with various associates, and drew critical comparisons to **Vangelis** and **Christopher Franke**. Five of its tracks were used in coverage of the 1994 Winter Olympics in Lillehammer by CBS television, ensuring a rising demand for soundtrack work for television and film. For *Global House*, Sevåg declined his now familiar electronic approach, favouring instead a reliance on ethnic musicianship. Prominent in this process were elements such as Afro-Cuban percussion, Australian didjeridoo and the Vestavo String Quartet. Several musicians present on earlier recordings also returned, including saxophonist Bendik Hofseth, guitarist Lakki Patey, trumpeter Nils Petter Molvaer and bass player Audun Erlien. It also saw him organise a full-scale touring band to export his music beyond Scandinavia, and build on his already considerable success in the US new age market.

Albums: *Close Your Eyes And See* (Own label 1989), *LINK* (Windham Hill 1994), *Global House* (Windham Hill 1995).

Seven Brides For Seven Brothers

Adapted from Stephen Vincent Benet's short story, *The Sobbin' Women*, which was 'inspired' by Plutach's *Rape Of The Sabine Women*, this film was released by MGM in 1954 and, somewhat surprisingly, turned out to be one of the hit screen musicals of the decade. Frances Goodrich, Albert Hackett, and Dorothy Kingsley wrote the screenplay which told of Adam Pontipee (**Howard Keel**), who leaves his six scruffy brothers to the squalor of their farmhouse in Oregon (c.1850s) to go into town in search of a hard-working wife. He finds her in the shape of Milly (**Jane Powell**), and their subsequent life together, during which Milly successfully advises the slovenly sextet on how to live and love, makes for an endearing and entertaining film. Her first 'lesson' is 'Goin' Co'tin', just one of the many musical highlights in **Gene De Paul** and **Johnny Mercer**'s spirited and exuberant score. Others included the optimistic 'Bless Your Beautiful Hide' (Keel), 'Wonderful, Wonderful Day' (Powell), 'When You're In Love' (Powell-Keel),

'Sobbin' Women' (Keel-brothers), 'June Bride' (Powell-brides), and 'Spring, Spring, Spring' (Powell-brothers-brides). The six virile brothers, named by their god-fearing mother as Benjamin, Caleb, Ephram, Daniel, Frankincense, and Gideon, were played by Russ Tamblyn, Tommy Rall, Jeff Richards, Marc Platt, Matt Mattox, and Jacques d'Amboise. In the end, they all got their brides (Virginia Gibson, Julie Newmeyer, Betty Carr, Nancy Kilgas, Norma Doggett, and Rita Kilmonis) by somewhat unconventional methods, after displaying exceptionally brilliant dancing skills in the contrasting languorous 'Lonesome Polecat' and spectacular 'barn-raising' scenes. The choreography for those, and rest of the innovative dance numbers was designed by **Michael Kidd**. **Saul Chaplin** and **Adolph Deutsch** won Academy Awards for 'scoring of a musical picture'. **Stanley Donen** directed with style and vigour. George Folsey was responsible for the breathtakingly beautiful photography in Amsco and CinemaScope. This film is considered by many to be among the all-time great musicals, but a 1982 stage version was not welcomed in New York and folded after five performances. Four years later a West End production fared a little better.

Severinson, Doc

b. Carl Hilding Severinson, 7 July 1927, Arlington, Oregon, USA. After playing trumpet in several name bands during the late years of the swing era, Severinson began a long career as a studio musician in New York in 1949. By 1967 he was leading the orchestra on the popular *Tonight* television show. In addition to leading the band and playing trumpet, he frequently wisecracked with host Merv Griffin, all of which helped to make him one of the best-known musicians in the USA. A sound if occasionally over-spectacular trumpeter, Severinson's later work on the west coast displayed an interest in jazz-rock.

Albums: *Tempestuous Trumpet* (1960), *Doc Severinson And His Orchestra* i (1965), *Doc Severinson And His Orchestra* ii (1965-66), *Doc Severinson And His Orchestra* iii (1966), *Doc Severinson And His Orchestra* iv (1967), *Doc Severinson And His Orchestra* v (1967), *Doc Severinson And His Orchestra* vi (c.1967), *Doc Severinson And His Orchestra* viii (c.1968), *Night Journey* (1975), *The Tonight Show Orchestra With Doc Severinson* (1986), *Good Medicine* (1992).

Seville, David

b. Ross Bagdasarian, 27 January 1919, Fresno, California, USA, d. 16 January 1972. This singer/songwriter/conductor and actor is best remembered as the creator of the **Chipmunks**. He first appeared on Broadway in the late 30s and was drafted to Britain during the war. His first musical success came in 1951 when a song he had co-written a decade earlier, 'Come On-A My House', topped the chart in a version by **Rosemary Clooney**. He

recorded on Coral in 1951 and joined **Mercury** two years later. Seville made the UK top 20 in 1956 under the name Alfi & Harry with 'The Trouble With Harry' (inspired by the film of the same name, in which he appeared), and he was successful again later that year with 'Armen's Theme' (inspired not by his Armenian descent but by his wife, singer Kay Armen). His biggest 'solo' hit came in 1958 with the transatlantic novelty smash 'Witch Doctor', which topped the US chart. He extended the idea of a speeded-up voice (as used on that hit) to produce a trio which he called the Chipmunks. They sold millions of records and had a top-rated cartoon television show before he retired them in 1967. After his death in 1972, his son Ross Jnr. brought the Chipmunks back and they have since enjoyed more success on both sides of the Atlantic.
Album: *The Music Of David Seville* (1958).

Seward, Alec

b. 16 March 1902, Charles City, Virginia, USA, d. 11 May 1972, New York City, New York, USA. Raised in Newport News, Virginia, Seward was a semi-professional blues singer and guitarist from the age of 18. In 1923, he moved to New York, where he became an associate of **Sonny Terry** and **Brownie McGhee**. He recorded with Louis Hayes under a variety of colourful pseudonyms, including Guitar Slim & Jelly Belly, the Blues King and the Back Porch Boys, and with Terry and **Woody Guthrie** for the nascent folk audience. His music was typical of the southeast, being gentle, relaxed, and ragtime influenced. By 1960, when mental illness ended Hayes' musical career, Seward was also largely retired. He recorded again in the mid-60s, but was little heard of thereafter.
Albums: *Creepin' Blues* (1965), *Carolina Blues* (c.1972), *Late One Saturday Evening* (1975).

Sex Gang Children

This London based post punk/gothic band were briefly in vogue in the early 80s. They were built around vocalist Andi Sex Gang, who talked himself into support slots for which he needed to quickly assemble a new band. He eventually settled on Dave Roberts (bass), Terry McLeay (guitar) and Rob Stroud (drums), who played their first gig under the name Panic Button. The name Sex Gang Children was lifted from a William Burroughs book and was actually on a list of names that fellow King's Road fashion victim **Boy George** was toying with. It later transpired that Boy George had in turn taken it from **Malcolm McLaren**'s original suggestion for a moniker for the band which would become **Bow Wow Wow**. By 1982 a number of bands in the same mould began breaking through in the capital. Sex Gang Children's first vinyl release was a 12-inch titled 'Beasts', produced by Nicky Garrett (ex-**UK Subs**), after which Tony James (**Generation X**, later **Sigue Sigue Sputnik**) began

to take an interest in the band. Their most fondly remembered release, 'Into The Abyss', closed 1982 with their debut long player arriving early the next year. The single lifted from it, 'Sebastiane', featured Jinni Hewes from **Marc And The Mambas** on violin. Andi then performed a debut with **Marc Almond** ('The Hungry Years') for the compilation *The Whip*, which also included a contribution from Roberts' other band, Car Crash International. Stroud left to join Pink And Black (featuring future **All About Eve** bass player Andy Cousins), and was replaced by Nigel Preston (ex-**Theatre Of Hate**). He stayed long enough to record the single 'Mauritia Mayer', before he took part in a bizarre 'drummers' swop with Ray Mondo of Death **Cult**. Events took a further strange turn when the latter was deported back to Sierra Leone for passport irregularities after a USA tour. Roberts also departed, leaving Andi and McLeay to recruit Cam Campbell (bass), and Kevin Matthews (drums). However, only one single, 'Deiche', was released before the band disintegrated and Andi set out on a solo career.
Albums: *Song And Legend* (Illuminated 1983), *Beasts* (Illuminated 1983), *Live* (Arkham 1984), *Re-enter The Abyss* (Dojo 1986), *Blind* (Jungle 1993).

Sex Pistols

This incandescent UK punk group came together under the aegis of entrepreneur **Malcolm McLaren** during the summer of 1975. Periodically known as the Swankers, with lead vocalist Wally Nightingale, they soon metamorphosed into the Sex Pistols with a line up comprising: Steve Jones (b. 3 May 1955, London, England; guitar), Paul Cook (b. 20 July 1956, London, England; drums), Glen Matlock (b. 27 August 1956, Paddington, London, England; bass) and Johnny Rotten (b. John Lydon, 31 January 1956, Finsbury Park, London, England; vocals). By 1976 the group was playing irregularly around London and boasted a small following of teenagers, whose spiked hair, torn clothes and safety pins echoed the new fashion that McLaren was transforming into commodity. The group's gigs became synonymous with violence, which reached a peak during the 100 Club's Punk Rock Festival when a girl was blinded in a glass-smashing incident involving the group's most fearful follower, **Sid Vicious**. The adverse publicity did not prevent the group from signing to **EMI Records** later that year when they also released their first single, 'Anarchy In The UK'. From Rotten's sneering laugh at the opening of the song to the final seconds of feedback, it was a riveting debut. The Pistols promoted the work on London Weekend Television's *Today* programme, which ended in a stream of four-letter abuse that brought the group banner headlines in the following morning's tabloid press. More controversy ensued when the group's 'Anarchy' tour was decimated and the single suffered distribution problems and bans from shops. Eventually, it peaked at number 38 in the UK charts. Soon after, the group was dropped from EMI in a blaze of publicity. By February 1977, Matlock was replaced by punk caricature Sid Vicious (b. John Simon Ritchie, 10 May 1957, London, England, d. 2 February 1979). The following month, the group was signed to **A&M Records** outside the gates of Buckingham Palace. One week later, A&M cancelled the contract, with McLaren picking up another parting cheque of £40,000. After reluctantly signing to the small label **Virgin Records**, the group issued 'God Save The Queen'. The single tore into the heart of British Nationalism at a time when the populace was celebrating the Queen's Jubilee. Despite a daytime radio ban the single rose to number 1 in the *New Musical Express* chart (number 2 in the 'official' charts, though some commentators detected skullduggery at play to prevent it from reaching the top spot). The Pistols suffered for their art as outraged royalists attacked them whenever they appeared on the streets. A third single, the melodic 'Pretty Vacant' (largely the work of the departed Matlock) proved their most accessible single to date and restored them to the Top 10. By the winter the group hit again with 'Holidays In The Sun' and issued their controversially-titled album, *Never Mind The Bollocks - Here's The Sex Pistols*. The work rocketed to number 1 in the UK album charts amid partisan claims that it was a milestone in rock. In truth, it was a more patchy affair, containing a preponderance of previously released material which merely underlined that the group was running short of ideas. An ill-fated attempt to capture the group's story on film wasted much time and revenue, while a poorly received tour of America fractured the Pistols' already strained relationship. In early 1978, Rotten announced that he was leaving the group after a gig in San Francisco. According to the manager Malcolm McLaren he was fired. McLaren, meanwhile, was intent on taking the group to Brazil in order that they could be filmed playing with the train robber, Ronnie Biggs. Vicious, incapacitated by heroin addiction, could not make the trip, but Jones and Cook were happy to indulge in the publicity stunt. McLaren mischievously promoted Biggs as the group's new lead singer and another controversial single emerged: 'Cosh The Driver'. It was later retitled 'No One Is Innocent (A Punk Prayer)' and issued as a double a-side with Vicious's somehow charming rendition of the **Frank Sinatra** standard, 'My Way'. McLaren's movie was finally completed by director Julien Temple under the title *The Great Rock 'n' Roll Swindle*. A self-conscious rewriting of history, it callously wrote Matlock out of the script and saw the unavailable Rotten relegated to old footage. While the film was being completed, the Pistols' disintegration was completed. Vicious, now the centre of the group, recorded a lame version of **Eddie Cochran**'s 'C'mon Everybody' before returning to

New York. On 12 October 1978, his girlfriend Nancy Spungen was found stabbed in his hotel room and Vicious was charged with murder. While released on bail, he suffered a fatal overdose of heroin and died peacefully in his sleep on the morning of 2 February 1979. Virgin Records continued to issue the desultory fragments of Pistols work that they had on catalogue, including the appropriately titled compilation, *Flogging A Dead Horse*. The group's impact as the grand symbol of UK punk rock has ensured their longevity. The unholy saga appropriately ended in the High Court a decade on in 1986 when Rotten and his fellow ex-Pistols won substantial damages against their former manager.

Albums: *Never Mind The Bollocks - Here's The Sex Pistols* (Virgin 1977). Compilations: *The Great Rock 'N' Roll Swindle* (Virgin 1979), *Some Product - Carri On Sex Pistols* (Virgin 1979), *Flogging A Dead Horse* (Virgin 1980), *Kiss This* (Virgin 1992).

Further reading: *Sex Pistols Scrap Book*, Ray Stevenson. *Sex Pistols: The Inside Story*, Fred & Judy Vermorel. *Sex Pistols File*, Ray Stevenson. *The Great Rock 'N' Roll Swindle: A Novel*, Michael Moorcock. *The Sid Vicious Family Album*, Anne Beverley. *The Sex Pistols Diary*, Lee Wood. *I Was A Teenage Sex Pistol*, Glen Matlock. *12 Days On The Road: The Sex Pistols And America*, Neil Monk & Jimmy Guterman. *Chaos: The Sex Pistols*, Bob Gruen. *England's Dreaming: Sex Pistols And Punk Rock*, Jon Savage. *Never Mind The B*ll*cks: A Photographed Record Of The Sex Pistols*, Dennis Morris. *Sex Pistols: Agents Of Anarchy*, Tony Scrivener. *Sid's Way: The Life And Death Of Sid Vicious*, Keith Bateson & Alan Parker. *Rotten: No Irish, No Blacks, No Dogs*, Johnny Rotten.

Sex, Love And Money

Formed in Greenville, North Carolina, USA, by Chuck Manning (vocals/guitar), John Bateman (guitar), Jim Bury (bass) and Jon Chambliss (drums), this metal outfit took its name from a local expression. 'It's a term that people call other people around here - SLAM babies - their primary concerns are Sex, Love and Money. To us it's a deeper, darker, and more realistic view of what we think everybody's invisible engine is'. Bateman graduated from Greenville's highly regarded Art School, after spending much of his life in Columbia, South America. This bred an early interest in both metal and flamenco. He hooked up with the remaining members who were participating in a **Ramones**-influenced punk band in April 1991. Songwriting within the band is arranged on a democratic principle with each member writing their own parts in isolation, Manning adding the lyrics. A creative process which first saw fruition in January 1995 with the release of a self-titled debut album for **Music For Nations**' subsidiary Bulletproof Records.

Album: *Sex, Love And Money* (Bulletproof 1995).

Sexton, Ann

b. 5 February 1950, Greenville, South Carolina, USA. One of several lesser-known southern-soul female artists, Sexton made a string of quality records for legendary Nashville soul DJ/label-owner, the late John Richbourg aka John R. Born into a South Carolina family steeped in gospel music, she married young, and, with her husband Melvin Burton (who later played saxophone in **Moses Dillard**'s band), soon progressed from gospel to secular club singing, where she was spotted in 1971 by songwriter David Lee. In a local studio, Sexton recorded Lee's impassioned 'You're Letting Me Down' coupled with the future UK northern-soul favourite 'You've Been Gone Too Long'. Released initially on Lee's tiny Impel label, it was later issued by John R on his Seventy-Seven outlet. After a couple of Nashville sessions, Sexton's records were then chiefly cut in Memphis, some produced by Lee and John R and others by Gene 'Bowlegs' Miller, who had earlier discovered **Ann Peebles**. By 1976, John R was recording Sexton's versions of songs by the fine southern-soul writer/singer Frank O (Johnson) at Clayton Ivey's Wishbone studio in Muscle Shoals. After John R's Seventy Seven label folded, Sexton recorded the highly regarded *The Beginning* in 1977 for the Monument subsidiary, Sound Stage 7, but to no commercial effect.
Album: *The Beginning* (1977). Compilations: *Love Trials* (1987), *You're Gonna Miss Me* (1993).

Sexton, Charlie

b. 1968, San Antonio, Texas, USA. This singing multi-instrumentalist became a professional musician in early adolescence, joining **Joe Ely**'s band as a guitarist in 1981. Both on stage and in the studio, he accompanied the **Bob Dylan** and **Don Henley** (notably on *Building The Perfect Beast*), and collaborated with **Keith Richards** and **Ron Wood** on the *Easy Street* film soundtrack. His debut on MCA Records (*Pictures For Pleasure*) and its 1986 single ('Beat's So Lonely') hovered between numbers 15 and 20 in their respective US charts. Entries as moderate have followed, and the precocious Sexton's success has yet to be sealed with a major hit.
Album: *Pictures For Pleasure* (1985).

Sgt. Pepper's Lonely Hearts Club Band

Arguably one of the greatest follies in cinematic pop history, this 1978 feature was a flawed attempt to take themes and lyrics from the **Beatles**' catalogue and transform them into a musical. Directed by Michael Schultz and produced by **Robert Stigwood** it was produced in the USA by Universal Films. The plot, which echoes that of *Yellow Submarine*, involved Sgt. Pepper's grandson, Billy Shears, who assists Heartland in its fight with the Future Villain Band,

played by **Aerosmith**. The **Bee Gees** and **Peter Frampton**, at that point among the most popular acts in the USA, headed a star-studded cast which included **Donovan**, **Robert Palmer**, **Curtis Mayfield**, **Al Stewart**, **Johnny Winter**, **George Benson** and **Jack Bruce**. Michael Schultz, who directed the much-superior *Car Wash*, seemed powerless to control a top-heavy project, flimsy on premise and overburdened by performers. Despite the presence of Beatles' producer **George Martin** as musical arranger, the soundtrack was equally flawed, with few interpretations showing either empathy or originality. Aerosmith did bring a swaggering panache to 'Come Together', **Billy Preston**, who played on the original version, provided a strong 'Get Back' while **Earth, Wind And Fire** bestowed 'Got To Get You Into My Life' with undeniable swing. However, the remaining selections were poor, leaving the viewer to wonder why the participants had bothered at all.

Sha Na Na

Spearheading the US rock 'n' roll revivalism that began in the late 60s, the group emerged from Columbia University in 1968 with a repertoire derived exclusively from the 50s, and a choreographed stage act that embraced a jiving contest for audience participants. Looking the anachronistic part - gold lame, brilliantine cockades, drainpiped hosiery *et al* - the initial line-up consisted of vocalists Scott Powell, Johnny Contardo, Frederick Greene, Don York and Richard Joffe; guitarists Chris Donald, Elliot Cahn and Henry Gross; pianists Scott Symon and John Bauman, plus Bruce Clarke (bass), Jocko Marcellino (drums) and - the only musician with a revered past - saxophonist Leonard Baker (ex-**Danny And The Juniors**). Surprisingly, there were few personnel changes until a streamlining to a less cumbersome 10-piece in 1973. The band were launched internationally by a show-stealing appearance at 1969's **Woodstock Festival** (that was included in the subsequent film and album spin-offs) but their onstage recreations of old sounds did not easily translate on disc - especially if the original versions had emotional significance for the listener. From 1972's *The Night Is Still Young*, 'Bounce In Your Buggy' - one of few self-composed numbers - was the closest the outfit ever came to a hit (though Gross would enjoy a solo US smash in 1976 with 'Shannon'). Nevertheless, the approbation of the famous was manifest in **Keith Moon**'s compering of a Sha Na Na bash in 1971 and **John Lennon**'s choice of the band to open his One-For-One charity concert in New York a year later. By 1974, however, their act had degenerated to a dreary repetition that took its toll in discord, nervous breakdowns and more unresolvable internal problems culminating in a fatal heroin overdose by Vincent Taylor, a latter-day member. Yet Sha Na Na's early example enabled archivist-performers such as **Darts**,

Shakin' Stevens and the **Stray Cats** to further the cause of a seemingly outmoded musical form.

Selected albums: *The Night Is Still Young* (1972), *Rock And Roll Revival* (1977), *Sha Na Na Is Here To Stay* (1985), *Rockin' And A Rollin'* (1987). Compilation: *20 Greatest Hits* (1989)

Films: *Grease* (1978).

Shabazz, Lakim

At the forefront of the Nation Of Islam movement, Shabazz entered the stage with *Pure Righteousness*, an early production by **DJ Mark the 45 King**, which submitted a powerful blow for the Afrocentricity movement. Shabazz began his rapping whilst still at school, his interest initially awakened through an appetite for poetry. He took part in a succession of low-key, competitive MC clashes, until meeting the 45 King, who had recently relocated from New Jersey to New York. After losing contact for a while, he heard Mark mentioned on the radio, and called him up. Together they put together a handful of tracks, and Shabazz was subsequently signed to Tuff City via label boss, Aaron Fuchs. The second of his albums for the latter featured a more oppressively pro-Muslim stance, especially the unequivocal 'When You See A Devil Smash Him'.

Albums: *Pure Righteousness* (Tuff City 1988), *The Lost Tribe Of Shabazz* (Tuff City 1990).

Shack

Formed in 1986 by brothers Mick (b. 28 November 1961, Liverpool, England) and John Head (b. 4 October 1965), Shack emerged from the ashes of the **Pale Fountains**. Having had their fingers burnt by the major records industry - the Pale Fountains reached number 46 in the UK charts with 'Thank You', but were generally misunderstood by their employers - Shack joined up with independent label the Ghetto Recording Company. Experts at the cleverly understated melodic guitar pop song, 1988 saw the release of their acclaimed debut album, *Zilch*. Yet instead of persevering with their commercial instincts, Shack laid low until reappearing with a single in 1991 and a planned second album for the year after, which never materialised.

Album: *Zilch* (Ghetto 1988).

Shad, Bob

b. 12 February 1920, New York City, New York, USA, d. 13 March 1985, Los Angeles, California, USA. Shad entered record production in the 40s, producing jazz (including **Charlie Parker**) and blues and R&B (including **Dusty Fletcher**) for Savoy, National and other companies. In 1948 he founded Sittin' In With, initially recording jazz, but concluded that there was a bigger market for blues, which the majors were neglecting; he cut material by **Lightnin' Hopkins**,

Sonny Terry and **Brownie McGhee**, and the last sides by **Curley Weaver**. On field trips to the South, Shad recorded **Smokey Hogg** and **Peppermint Harris** (including his hit 'Rainin' In My Heart') on portable equipment. In 1951, he joined Mercury as A&R director, producing **Patti Page**, **Vic Damone** and the **Platters** as well as blues sessions by Hopkins, **Big Bill Broonzy** and others, and launching the jazz marque Emarcy, for which he made important sessions with **Sarah Vaughan**, **Maynard Ferguson**, **Dinah Washington** (her first with strings) and many others. After leaving Mercury, Shad founded Mainstream, which issued, besides his Sittin' In With material, jazz by such as **Shelly Manne** and **Dizzy Gillespie**, and Sarah Vaughan's collaborations with **Michel Legrand**. Shad also produced rock artists, making the first recordings of **Janis Joplin** and **Ted Nugent**, and remained active with Mainstream through the 70s.

Shade, Will

b. 5 February 1898, Memphis, Tennessee, USA, d. 18 September 1966, Memphis, Tennessee, USA. Although named after his father, Will Shade was raised by his grandmother Annie Brimmer and was often known around Memphis as Son Brimmer. He took an early interest in music and played guitar and harmonica. He worked as a musician in and around Memphis, sometimes joining the medicine shows which visited the city. Sometime in the 20s he formed the Memphis Jug Band, a shifting conglomeration of local talent that included at different times **Charlie Burse**, **Will 'Casey Bill' Weldon**, **Furry Lewis**, **Jab Jones**, and **Ben Ramey**. The popularity of this group, whose work ranged from knock-about, good-time dance numbers to moving blues performances, was at its peak during the years 1927-34 after which they ceased to record but remained mainstays of the local scene. The group often supported singers such as **Jenny Mae Clayton**, Shade's wife, and **Memphis Minnie**, at one time married to Will Weldon. Shade enjoyed a brief second career when, in the company of Charlie Burse, he recorded for the Folkways and Rounder labels in the early 60s. He death was due to pneumonia.

Albums: *Memphis Jug Band 1927-1930 (3 volumes)* (1991), *Memphis Jug Band 1932-34* (1991).

Shades Of Blue

Vocal group from Detroit, Michigan, USA. Shades Of Blue are known for just one hit, 'Oh How Happy', which with its sing-a-long simplicity and good cheer raced up the chart in 1966 reaching number 12. Members of the group were Nick Marinelli, Linda Allan, Bob Kerr and Ernie Dernai. They were discovered and produced by soul singer **Edwin Starr**, who was looking for a white group to record 'Oh How Happy', a song he had written years earlier. After having the group turned down by another Detroit company, Starr took them to Harry Balk's small Impact operation, and with 'Oh How Happy' Impact got its only national hit. The group could not give Balk another big record, as their two subsequent records in 1966 - 'Lonely Summer' and 'Happiness' - stalled on the lower reaches of charts.

Album: *Happiness Is The Shades of Blue* (Impact 1966).

Shades Of Joy

Although based in San Francisco, California, the founders of this jazz-rock unit were Texan emigres. Leader Martin Fierro (horns/vocals) was a former member of the **Sir Douglas Quintet** and **Mother Earth**, while Millie Foster (vocals), Jackie King (guitar/sitar), Jym Young (keyboards), Edward Adams (bass) and Jose Rodrigues (drums) were veterans of various *avant garde* and blues bands. The group's albums were undeniably competent, but their dexterity was hampered by unexceptional material. Rodrigues was latterly replaced by George Rains who, with Jym Young, joined the **Boz Scaggs** Band when Shades Of Joy split up. Fierro meanwhile returned to the Sir Douglas fold.

Albums: *Shades Of Joy* (1969), *Music From El Topo* (1971).

Shadow King

Following Lou Gramm's departure from **Foreigner** in 1988 he pursued a relatively less successful solo career for three years. In 1991 his desire to be part of a band once more led to the formation of Shadow King. Named after one of the band's songs, and based on the description of a huge, decadent and apocalyptic city; the band is completed by Vivian Campbell (guitar; ex-**Dio** and **Whitesnake**), Bruce Turgon (bass) and Kevin Valentine (drums). Signing to **Atlantic Records**, they debuted with a self-titled album in 1991. This was a strong collection of hi-tech, hard-edged AOR characterized by Gramm's soulful vocal delivery. Campbell's guitar work was surprisingly economical and restrained, marking a distinct change from his previous flamboyant output. Superbly produced by Keith Olsen, it was one of the year's most accomplished and mature rock releases. Afterwards Campbell moved on to join **Def Leppard**.

Album: *Shadow King* (Atlantic 1991).

Shadowfax

Taking their name from Gandalf's horse in *The Lord Of The Rings*, this Windham Hill band pursued a path of new-age inspired folk, bringing in strong elements of jazz and medieval music. The unit was formed in near Chicago, Illinois, USA during the winter of 1972 by Chuck Greenberg (b. 1950, Chicago, Illinois, USA; saxophone/lyricon), Greg Stinson (b. August 1949, Oklahoma, USA; guitars) and Phil Maggini (b. March 1949, Chicago, Illinois, USA; bass), later adding Stuart Nevitt (b. March 1953, Elizabeth, New Jersey, USA; drums/percussion) in 1974. Their debut *Watercourse Way* made little impression upon release in 1976 and it was not until *Shadowfax* in 1982 that the group received both success and acclaim. This album reached a high placing on the Billboard jazz chart and won the top new jazz band award in *Cashbox*. The band added Jamii Szmadzinski (b. 1954, Michigan, USA; violin) and Jared Stewart (b. February 1956, Los Angeles, California, USA; piano/synthesizers) for *Shadowdance*. Additional personnel who have passed through this truly idealistic aggregation include Emil Richards, Michael Spiro, Mike Lehocky, Adam Rudolph, David Lewis and Charlie Bisharat.

Albums: *Watercourse Way* (1976), *Shadowfax* (1982), *Shadowdance* (1983), *Dreams Of the Children* (1985), *Too Far To Whisper* (1986), *Folksongs For A Nuclear Village* (1988).

Shadows

The UK's premier instrumental group, the Shadows evolved from the Five Chestnuts to become **Cliff Richard**'s backing group, the Drifters. By late 1958 the line-up had settled and under their new name the Shadows, the group comprised: **Hank B Marvin** (b. Brian Robson Rankin, 28 October 1941, Newcastle-upon-Tyne, England; lead guitar), Bruce Welch (b. 2 November 1941, Bognor Regis, Sussex, England; rhythm guitar), Jet Harris (b. Terence Hawkins, 6 July 1939, London, England; bass) and Tony Meehan (b. Daniel Meehan, 2 March 1943, London, England; drums). Soon after backing Cliff Richard on his first single, they were signed as a group by **EMI** Columbia's A&R manager **Norrie Paramor**. After two singles under their old name, the Drifters, they issued the vocal 'Saturday Dance', which failed to sell. An abrupt change of fortune came in 1960 when they met singer/songwriter **Jerry Lordan**, who presented them with 'Apache'. Their instrumental was one of the finest of its era and dominated the UK number 1 position for six weeks, as well as being voted single of the year in several music papers. It was duly noted that they had knocked their singer's 'Please Don't Tease' off the top of the charts and, in doing so, firmly established themselves as important artists in their own right. The Shadows' influence on the new generation of groups that followed was immense. Marvin was revered as a guitarist, and although the group were firmly part of the British show-business establishment, their musical credibility was beyond question. A wealth of evocative instrumentals followed, including 'FBI', 'The Frightened City', 'The Savage' and 'Guitar Tango'. These Top 10 singles were interspersed with four formidable UK number 1 hits: 'Kon Tiki', 'Wonderful Land', 'Dance On' and 'Foot Tapper'. Despite such successes, the group underwent personnel shifts. Both Tony Meehan and Jet Harris left the group to be replaced by drummer Brian Bennett (b. 9 February

1940, London, England) and bassist Brian Locking. Ironically, the Shadows soon found themselves competing against the combined forces of **Jet Harris And Tony Meehan**, who recorded some startling instrumentals in their own right, including the chart-topping 'Diamonds'.

The Shadows continued to chart consistently during 1963-64 with 'Atlantis', 'Shindig', 'Geronimo', 'Theme For Young Lovers' and 'The Rise And Fall Of Flingel Bunt', but it was clear that the Mersey beat boom had lessened their appeal. Throughout this period, they continued to appear in films with Cliff Richard and undertook acting and musical roles in *Aladdin And His Wonderful Lamp* at the London Palladium, which spawned the hit 'Genie With The Light Brown Lamp'. An attempted change of direction was notable in 1965 with the minor vocal hits, 'The Next Time I See Mary Ann' and 'Don't Make My Baby Blue'. Further movie and pantomime appearances followed, amid a decline in chart fortunes. At the end of 1968, the group announced that they intended to split up. In late 1969, a streamlined Shadows featuring Marvin, Rostill, Bennett and pianist Alan Hawkshaw toured Japan. Marvin then pursued some solo activities before reuniting with Welch for the **Crosby, Stills & Nash**-influenced **Marvin, Welch & Farrar**. The early 70s coincided with numerous personal dramas. Marvin became a Jehovah's Witness, Welch had a tempestuous relationship with singer **Olivia Newton-John** and Rostill was fatally electrocuted while playing his guitar. In 1974, the Shadows reconvened for *Rockin' With Curly Leads*, on which they were joined by bassist/producer Alan Tarney. Several live performances followed and the group were then offered the opportunity to represent the United Kingdom in the Eurovision Song Contest. They achieved second place with 'Let Me Be The One', which also provided them with their first UK Top 20 hit in 10 years. The stupendous success of an accompanying *20 Golden Greats* compilation effectively revitalized their career. By 1978, they were back in the UK Top 10 for the first time since 1965 with an instrumental reading of 'Don't Cry For Me Argentina'. That feat was repeated several months later with 'Theme From The Deer Hunter (Cavatina)'. Regular tours and compilations followed and in 1983, the group received an **Ivor Novello** Award from the British Academy of Songwriters, Composers and Authors to celebrate their 25th anniversary. Long regarded as one of the great institutions of British pop music, the Shadows have survived a generation of musical and cultural changes in fashion yet continue to please audiences with their instrumental abilities. It is however, for their massive influence over five decades of budding young guitarists, ready to afford a **Fender** Stratocaster, that they will be remembered. No UK 'beat combo' has ever been or is ever likely to be more popular.

Albums: *The Shadows* (1961), *Out Of The Shadows* (1962), *Dance With The Shadows* (1964), *The Sound Of The Shadows* (1965), *Shadow Music* (1966), *Jigsaw* (1967), *From Hank, Bruce, Brian And John* (1967), *Established 1958* (1968), *Shades Of Rock* (1970), *Rockin' With Curly Leads* (1974), *Specs Appeal* (1975), *Live At The Paris Olympia* (1975), *Tasty* (1977), *Thank You Very Much* (1978), *Change Of Address* (1980), *Hits Right Up Your Street* (1981), *Life In The Jungle/Live At Abbey Road* (1982), *XXV* (1983), *Guardian Angel* (1984), *Moonlight Shadows* (1986), *Simply Shadows* (1987), *Stepping To The Shadows* (1989), *Reflections* (1991). Compilations: *The Shadows Greatest Hits* (1963), *More Hits* (1965), *Somethin' Else* (1969), *20 Golden Greats* (1977), *String Of Hits* (1980), *Another String Of Hot Hits* (1980), *At Their Very Best* (1989), *Themes And Dreams* (1991). Films: *Carnival Rock* (1957), *Expresso Bongo* (1959), *Summer Holiday* (1963), *Finders Keepers* (1967).

Further reading: *The Shadows By Themselves*, Shadows (1961), *Foot Tapping: The Shadows 1958-1978*, Geddes, George Thomson (1978), *The Shadows: A History And Discography*, Geddes, George Thomson (1981), *The Story Of The Shadows: An Autobiography*, Shadows as told to Mike Reed (1983), *Rock 'N' Roll: I Gave You The Best Years Of My Life: A Life In The Shadows*, Welch, Bruce (1990), *Funny Old World: The Life And Times Of John Henry Rostill*, Bradford, Rob (1991).

Shadows Of Knight

Formed in Chicago in 1965, the original line-up comprised of Jim Sohns (vocals), Warren Rogers (lead guitar), Jerry McGeorge (rhythm guitar), Norm Gotsch (bass) and Tom Schiffour (drums). As the houseband at the city's Cellar club, the Shadows were already highly popular when they secured a recording contract. Their debut single, a cover version of the classic **Them** track, 'Gloria', was the climax to the quintet's stage act, but when the group toned down its mildly-risque lyric, they were rewarded with a US Top 10 hit. By this point Gotsch had been replaced, with Rogers switching to lead to accommodate new guitarist Joe Kelly. Their best-known line-up now established, the Shadows enjoyed another minor chart entry with 'Oh Yeah', before completing their debut album. *Gloria* comprised of several Chicago R&B standards which, paradoxically, were patterned on British interpretations of the same material. Two excellent group originals, 'Light Bulb Blues' and 'It Happens That Way', revealed an emergent, but sadly under-used, talent. *Back Door Men* offered a slightly wider perspective with versions of 'Hey Joe' and 'Tomorrow's Gonna Be Another Day' (also recorded by the **Monkees**), but the highlight was an inspired interpretation of 'Bad Little Woman', originally recorded by Irish group the Wheels. Dave 'The Hawk' Wolinski replaced Warren Rogers when the latter was drafted in late 1966. This was the prelude to wholesale changes when, on 4 July 1967, Sohns fired the entire group. The singer subsequently reappeared fronting a new line-up - John Fisher, Dan Baughman, Woody Woodfuff and Kenny Turkin - and a new recording deal with the bubblegum Super K label. 'Shake' gave the group a final US Top 50 entry, but its unashamed pop approach owed little to the heritage of the 'old'. Further releases for the same outlet proved equally disappointing, while an attempt at recreating the past with 'Gloria 69' was unsuccessful. Sohns has led several versions of his group over the ensuing years, McGeorge found fleeting notoriety as a member of **H.P. Lovecraft**, while Wolinski found fame as a member of **Rufus** and his work with **Michael Jackson**.

Albums: *Gloria* (1966), *Back Door Men* (1967), *The Shadows Of Knight* (1969). Compilations: *Gloria* (1979), *Gee-El-O-Are-I-Ay* (1985), *Raw And Alive At The Cellar: 1966* (1992).

Shadz Of Lingo

Hailing from Atlanta, Georgia, rappers Lingo and Kolorado alongside DJ Rocco have won plaudits for their furious mix of hip hop, dancehall reggae and jazz styles, only occasionally lapsing into the cool groove of geographical neighbours like **Arrested Development**. Their background as jingle writers partially explains this eclecticism. Having met at high school in Virginia, the trio decided to make a career in music, after several abortive attempts at rapping, by forming their own production company in 1988. When they launched Shadz Of Lingo they hit on an effective old school style, inviting producers of note such as Erick Sermon (**EPMD**), **Diamond D**. and Solid Productions in to help them. Live, the band are noted for their freestyle approach, with Kolorado claiming never to write lyrics down, tailoring them instead for each individual occason.

Album: *A View To A Kill* (ERG 1993).

Shaggs

Formed in Freemont, New Hampshire, USA, the Shaggs comprised of the Wiggin sisters, Helen (guitar), Dorothy (guitar) and Betty (drums). Their father, Austin, financed the recording, manufacture and distribution of the trio's 1972 set, *Philosophy Of The World*, which revealed a group of startling ineptitude. Out-of-tune guitars, off-key harmonies and naive lyrics marked an album which quickly attained cult status by lovers of the genre. The initial pressing of 2,000 copies quickly sold out and it remained a cherished collector's item for 10 years until re-released by the folk specialist label, Rounder. The Shaggs then undertook further recordings on which their grasp of music proved equally unsure.

Albums: *Philosophy Of The World* (1972), *Shaggs' Own Thing* (1982), *The Shaggs* (1988).

Shaggy

Shaggy (b. Orville Richard Burrell, 22 October 1968, Kingston, Jamaica, West Indies) is, effectively, the man who put New York reggae on the map, thanks to his world-wide hit, 'Oh Carolina'. The same record also helped start the **ragga** boom of 1993, an explosion that also carried the likes of **Shabba Ranks**, **Chaka Demus & Pliers** and **Snow** to the international pop charts. An amusing vocal stylist who can be as rude as the next man without ever descending into a leer, Shaggy cut his lyrical teeth on Brooklyn's Gibraltar Musik **sound system**. He'd moved there at 18 with his parents, and at 19 he'd joined the Marines, based at Lejeune, North Carolina. Following active service in the Gulf War, Shaggy began to cut singles for a variety of labels, among them 'Man A Me Yard'/'Bullet Proof Baddie' for Don One, and 'Big Hood'/'Duppy Or Uglyman' for Spiderman. A chance meeting with Sting, a radio DJ at KISS-FM/WNNK, led to Shaggy's first New York reggae chart number 1, 'Mampie', a version of the 'Drum Song' rhythm produced by Sting for New York reggae ruler Phillip Smart's Tan-Yah label.

His next 45, 'Big Up', released on Sting International and recorded in tandem with singer Rayvon, also hit number 1, as would 'Oh Carolina'. A mighty cover of the **Folks Brothers** classic, replete with samples of the original, the record became a huge hit on import charts wherever reggae was sold. At the time Shaggy was still in the Marines, meaning an 18-hour round trip to Brooklyn for dates and studio sessions. At the end of 1992, Greensleeves picked up 'Oh Carolina' for UK release, and by Spring 1993 Shaggy had scored a pop chart hit all over Europe with the song, reaching number 1 in the UK and several other countries. His next single, the slow, raucous 'Soon Be Done' failed, however, to capitalise on his success. Apparently unruffled by this, a liaison with **Maxi Priest** for 'One More Chance' led to a **Virgin** contract, and the *Pure Pleasure* album. A third single from the LP, 'Nice And Lovely', again failed to garner the necessary airplay to repeat the sales of 'Oh Carolina' (which by now had made it on to the soundtrack of Sharon Stone's film, *Sliver*), but it was a fine, light-hearted record in its own right. The album also contained a version of his earlier 'Duppy Or Uglyman' cut, re-styled as 'Fraid To Ask'. Where Shaggy goes from here is a hard call to make: his *Pure Pleasure* world tour, taking in dates as diverse as Russia and South Africa, was an unqualified success, but Shaggy needs more chart action to maintain his status and to rival his great idol, **Sammy Davis Jnr**.

Album: *Pure Pleasure* (Virgin 1993).

Shah

Formed in Moscow, Russia, in 1985, Shah comprise Antonio Garcia (vocals/guitar), Anatoly Krupnov (bass) and Andrei Sazanov (drums). The group were pioneers of thrash metal in the USSR and attracted the attention of Velerie Gaina, guitarist with fellow Soviet band, Kruiz. Gaina helped Shah record their first demo, which he then took to the West and German independent label Atom H Records. Suitably impressed, the label signed the band, resulting in a debut collection, *Beware*, which betrayed the obvious influence of **Anthrax**. Bearing in mind the cultural and political hurdles the band had to overcome, it was a considerable achievement. In 1990 Shah played at the Public Against Violence Festival in Ostava, Czechoslovakia, along with German melodic rockers **Bonfire** and UK thrash metal band **Talion** and was a huge success. They continue to perform regularly and extensively in their own country.

Album: *Beware* (Atom H 1989).

Shakatak

This UK group were one the original benefactors of the early 80s British jazz/funk boom (alongside contemporaries **Level 42**). The group comprised Bill Sharpe (keyboards), George Anderson (bass), Keith Winter (guitar), Roger Odell (drums), Nigel Wright (keyboards/synthesizers) and Gil Seward (vocals). Between 1980 and 1987, Shakatak had 14 UK chart singles. Since their chart debut with 'Feels Like The First Time' on the **Polydor** label (a long standing partnership), other notable hits have been 'Easier Said Than Done' (1981), 'Night Birds' (UK Top 10 - 1982), 'Dark Is The Night' (1983) and 'Down On The Street' (UK Top 10 - 1984). This understated group proved their reputation as one of the finest purveyors of classy jazz/funk with the successful **K-Tel** compilation, *The Coolest Cuts*. The later half of the 80s have shown Shakatak leaving behind the demands of instant pop chart hits and they allowed themselves to mature, honing their jazz influences. - most evident on the 1989 set, *Turn The Music Up*, their first studio effort in almost five years. In addition to releasing a solo album in 1988, Sharpe has also collaborated with **Gary Numan** on, what was a one-off single, 'Change Your Mind' in 1985. On reaching the UK Top 20, it was not until four years later the duo released a full album, *Automatic*.

Albums: *Drivin' Hard* (1981), *Nightbirds* (1982), *Invitations* (1982), *Out Of This World* (1983), *Down On The Street* (1984), *Live!* (1985), *Turn The Music Up* (1989), *Bitter Sweet* (1991), *Street Level* (1993). Compilations: *The Coolest Cuts* (1988), *The Remix Best Album* (1992). Solo albums: Bill Sharpe *Famous People* (1988), Sharpe with Gary Numan *Automatic* (1989).

Shake, Rattle And Roll

Taking its title from a best-selling single by **Bill Haley And The Comets**, this 1956 'B' film attempted to capitalise on rock 'n' roll. In a plot which would quickly

become world-weary, conservative adults attempt to ban the new music, but are challenged to a television trial by teenagers. R&B singer **Joe Turner** performs 'Lipstick, Powder And Paint' and 'Feelin' Happy', **Fats Domino** adds 'Ain't That A Shame', 'Honey Chile' and 'I'm In Love Again'; otherwise *Shake, Rattle And Roll* is largely forgettable. Clumsily scripted hip parlance - 'dig', 'dad', 'man' and 'the most' - renders the youth's arguments laughable while the use of subtitles as translation verges on spiteful. It is difficult to imagine the motives behind director Edward Cahn's ideas, but the final sensation is of a film desperate to exploit a genre while at the same time belittle it and its adherents.

Shakespear's Sister

Formed by Siobhan Marie Deidre Fahey-Stewart (b. 10 September 1958, Dublin, Eire) who was better known simply as Siobhan Fahey, and **Marcella Detroit** (b. Marcella Levy, 21 June 1959, Detroit, Michigan, USA) with producer and writer Richard Feldman keeping a low profile as third member. Siobhan, who had left Ireland for the UK to become a press officer at **Decca**, was a member of the top 80s girl group **Bananarama**. She left in early 1988, although Detroit, too, had previously released solo material and worked as songwriter to **Al Jarreau** and **Chaka Khan** (having co-penned 'Lay Down Sally' with **Eric Clapton** whilst touring as his backing singer). Taking their name from a **Smiths**' song and keeping the spelling mistake made by a designer, one of their first gigs took place in Leningrad, USSR, in January 1989. Their debut, 'Break My Heart (You Really)', was not a hit. However, 'You're History' reached the UK Top 10, while the debut album made number 9. 1991 finally saw the unveiling of a follow-up with *Hormonally Yours*, much of it recorded while both participants were pregnant: 'It's self-deprecating but yet its very female without being militant or apologetic. Its just...what we are.' The group recorded in Los Angeles where Siobhan lives with husband **Dave Stewart**. In February 1992 Shakespear's Sister achieved a spectacular UK number 1 coup with 'Stay' (remaining there for eight weeks, ostensibly through a powerful, melodrmatic hookline and video) and follwed it with 'I Don't Care' (UK number 7), 'Goodbye Cruel World' (number 32) and 'Hello, 'Turn Your Radio On' (number 14). Seemingly destined for great things, the group was nevertheless disbanded by Fahey, without warning to Detroit, live on stage at an awards ceremony in 1993. Detroit (reportedly 'not bitter') was the first to launch a solo career.

Albums: *Sacred Heart* (London 1989), *Hormonally Yours* (London 1991).

Shakey Jake

b. James D. Harris, 12 April 1921, Earle, Arkansas,

USA, d. 2 March 1990, Pine Bluff, Arkansas, USA. A professional gambler when not playing harmonica (his nickname was derived from the crapshooters' call 'Shake 'em, Jake'), Harris began playing in Chicago blues bands during the late 40s. He recorded a single in 1958, on which his contribution was overshadowed by that of his nephew **Magic Sam**. During the 60s he recorded two albums that did not do him justice, as club recordings with Sam make evident. His encouragement of younger musicians brought about the recording debut of, among others, **Luther Allison**, with whom Jake recorded his best album after moving to Los Angeles. In later years, occasional recordings appeared, including some on his own label, and Harris ran a blues club for a while, but was dogged by poor health, and isolated by neighbourhood gang violence.

Albums: *Good Times* (1960), *Mouth Harp Blues* (1961), *Further On Up The Road* (1969), *The Devil's Harmonica* (1972), *Magic Rocker* (1980), *Magic Touch* (1983), *The Key Won't Fit* (c.1985).

Shakin' Stevens

b. Michael Barrett, 4 March 1948, Ely, South Glamorgan, Wales. A rock 'n' roll singer in the style of the early **Elvis Presley**, Stevens brought this 50s spirit to a long series of pop hits during the 80s. In the late 60s he was lead singer with a Welsh rock revival group, the Backbeats which became Shakin' Stevens And The Sunsets. During 1970-73 the band recorded unsuccessful albums for **EMI**, **CBS** and Dureco in Holland, where the Sunsets had a large following. In 1976, they recorded a cover version of the **Hank Mizell** hit 'Jungle Rock' before disbanding. Shakin' Stevens now began a solo career appearing on stage in **Jack Good**'s West End musical *Elvis* and on UK television in a new series of *Oh Boy!*, Good's 50s live music show. His recording career still faltered, however, when a 1977 album for Track was followed by commercially unsuccessful revivals of such 50s hits as **Roy Head**'s 'Treat Her Right' and **Jody Reynolds**' death song 'Endless Sleep', produced by ex-**Springfields** member Mike Hurst at CBS. A change of producer to **Stuart Colman** in 1980 brought Stevens' first Top 20 hit, 'Marie Marie', first recorded by the Blasters and the following year Colman's infectious rockabilly arrangement of the 1954 **Rosemary Clooney** number 1 'This Ole House' topped the UK chart. The backing group was revival band **Matchbox**.

Over the next seven years, Stevens had over 20 Top 20 hits in the UK, although he made almost no impact in the USA. Among his hits were three number 1 - a revival, of Jim Lowe's 1956 song 'Green Door' (1981), Stevens' own 'Oh Julie' (1982) and 'Merry Christmas Everyone' (1985). With an audience equally divided between young children and the middle-aged, his other

recordings included brief excursions into soul (the **Supremes**' 'Come See About Me' in 1987) and ballads (the **Bing Crosby**/Grace Kelly film theme 'True Love', 1988), while he duetted with fellow Welsh artist **Bonnie Tyler** on 'A Rockin' Good Way (To Mess Around And Fall In Love)' (1984), which was first recorded in 1960 by **Dinah Washington** and **Brook Benton**.

At the dawn of the 90s, there were signs that Stevens' hold over his British audiences was faltering. For while the Pete Hammond-produced 'I Might' reached the Top 20, his subsequent records in 1990/1 made little impact. A major promotion for the compilation *The Epic Years* (billed as Shaky) failed to dent the UK top 50. 1993 started badly for Stevens as litigation with his former band the Sunsets was resolved, both **Dave Edmunds** and Shaky had to pay out £500,000 in back royalties.

Albums: *A Legend* (1970), *I'm No J.D.* (1971), *Shakin' Stevens* (1977), *Take One!* (1980), *This Ole House* (1981), *Shaky* (1981), *Give Me Your Heart Tonight* (1982), *The Bop Won't Stop* (1983), *Lipstick, Powder And Paint* (1985), *Let's Boogie* (1987), *A Whole Lotta Shaky* (1988), *Rock 'N' Roll* (1990), *Merry Christmas Everyone* (1991). Compilations: *Greatest Hits* (1984), *The Track Years* (1988), *The Epic Years* (1992), *This Ole House* (1993).

Shakin' Street

This rock 'n' roll quintet was influenced by the **Stooges**, **Rolling Stones** and **Blue Öyster Cult**, and took their name from a song by the **MC5**. Formed in Paris in 1975 by Fabienne Shine (b. Tunisia; vocals) and her songwriting partner, Eric Lewy (guitar/vocals), the group was completed by Mike Winter (bass), Armik Tigrane (guitar) and Jean Lou Kalinowski (drums). Signing to **CBS**, they debuted with the average *Vampire Rock*, a selection of predominantly uptempo rockers, notable only for Shine's unusual vocals. Ross The Boss (ex-**Dictators**) replaced Tigrane for the second album. This was a vast improvement, with a denser sound and more abrasive guitar work brought through in the final mix. Ross The Boss subsequently left to form **Manowar** with Joey De Maio in 1981, but Shakin' Street carried on for a short time with ex-**Thrasher** guitarist Duck McDonald, before finally disbanding. Their second album proved an undiscovered classic of the metal genre and is much sought after by collectors.

Albums: *Vampire Rock* (CBS 1978), *Shakin' Street* (CBS 1980), *Skin 'Em* (Virgin 1981).

Shalamar

This group was created by Dick Griffey, booking agent for US television's *Soul Train* show, and Simon Soussan, a veteran of Britain's 'northern soul' scene. The latter produced 'Uptown Festival', a medley of popular Tamla/**Motown** favourites, which was issued on Griffey's Solar label. Although credited to 'Shalamar', the track featured session musicians, but its success inspired Griffey to create a performing group. **Jody Watley** (b. 30 January 1959, Chicago, Illinois, USA), Jeffrey Daniels and Gerald Brown were recruited via *Soul Train* in 1977, although Brown was replaced the following year by Howard Hewitt (b. Akron, Ohio, USA). 'The Second Time Around' gave the trio an R&B chart topper in 1979, but subsequent releases were better received in the UK where lightweight soul/disco offerings, including 'I Can Make You Feel Good', 'A Night To Remember' and 'There It Is', provided three Top 10 entries in 1982. Daniels and Watley then left the group to pursue solo careers. Their replacements, Delisa Davis and Micki Free, joined in 1984. The group won a Grammy award for 'Don't Get Stopped In Beverly Hills', a track from *Heartbeat* used in the Eddie Murphy film *Beverly Hills Cop*, but Hewitts' departure in 1976 eroded any newfound confidence. Sidney Justin restored the group to a trio, continuing to score further, albeit minor hit singles. By now Shalamar's golden, if brief period had ended; nevertheless the Shalamar name had survived into the late 80s when Justin, along with newcomers Micki Free and Delisa Davis recorded *Circumstantial Evidence*.

Albums: *Uptown Festival* (1977), *Disco Gardens* (1978), *Big Fun* (1979), *Three For Love* (1981), *Go For It* (1981), *Friends* (1982), *The Look* (1982), *Heartbreak* (1984), *Circumstantial Evidence* (1987). Compilations: *Greatest Hits* (1982), *The Greatest Hits* (1986), *Here It Is - The Best Of* (1992), *Wake Up* (1993).
Film: *Footloose* (1984).

Shall We Dance

Screenwriter Allan Scott, whose name was a familiar feature on the credits of **Fred Astaire** and **Ginger Rogers** movies, excelled himself with the plot for this 1937 vehicle for the popular duo's delightful dance routines. Together with Ernest Pagano, Scott fashioned a story in which ballet dancer Pete Rogers (Astaire) falls for Broadway musical star Linda Keen (Rogers) in Paris. He serenades her on the liner back to New York, and later, with her help, fulfills his lifetime ambition by mixing his beloved ballet with modern tap-dancing. Before that happens - and this is where Scott and Pagano really score - the couple dispel constant rumours that they are married by *getting* married - so that that they can divorce! There was nothing as complicated as that about the sublime songs by **George** and **Ira Gershwin**. They were all simply terrific, and included three of the composers' all-time standards, 'They All Laughed', 'Let's Call The Whole Thing Off' (Fred and Ginger on roller-skates), and 'They Can't Take That Away From Me'. Also present were with the lively '(I've Got) Beginner's Luck', 'Slap That Bass', the rhythmic title song, and a catchy little instrumental piece, 'Walking The Dog', set on the deck of the liner. Directed by Mark Sandrich, with dance

sequences choreographed by **Hermes Pan** and Harry Losee, *Shall We Dance* was the seventh Fred Astaire-Ginger Rogers film, and, while they were as great as ever, and the supporting cast which included Edward Everett Horton and Eric Blore were always amusing, somehow things were beginning to pall a little. In fact, to some, this picture marked the beginning of their decline.

Sham 69

Originally formed in London, England, in 1976, this five-piece skinhead/punk-influenced group comprised Jimmy Pursey (vocals), Albie Slider (bass), Neil Harris (lead guitar), Johnny Goodfornothing (rhythm guitar) and Billy Bostik (drums). Pursey was a fierce, working-class idealist, an avenging angel of the unemployed, who ironically sacked most of the above line-up within a year due to their lack of commitment. A streamlined aggregation featuring Dave Parsons (guitar), Dave Treganna (bass) and Mark Cain (drums) helped Pursey reach the UK charts with a series of anthemic hits including 'Angels With Dirty Faces', 'If The Kids Are United', 'Hurry Up Harry' and 'Hersham Boys'. Although Pursey championed proletarian solidarity, his rabble-rousing all too often brought violence and disruption from a small right-wing faction causing wary promoters to shun the group. After a troubled couple of years attempting to reconcile his ideals and their results, Pursey elected to go solo, but his time had passed. The group reformed in the early 90s and performed at punk nostalgia/revival concerts.

Albums: *Tell Us The Truth* (Polydor 1978), *That's Life* (Polydor 1978), *Adventures Of The Hersham Boys* (Polydor 1979), *The Game* (Polydor 1980), *Volunteer* (Legacy 1988), *Kings & Queens* (CMP 1993). Compilations: *The First, The Best And The Last* (Polydor 1980), *Angels With Dirty Faces - The Best Of* (Receiver 1986), *Live And Loud* (Link 1987), *Live And Loud Vol. 2* (Link 1988), *The Best Of The Rest Of Sham 69* (Receiver 1989), *Complete Live* (Castle 1989), *Live At The Roxy* (Receiver 1990, rec. 1977), *BBC Radio 1 Live In Concert* (Windsong 1993).

Shamblin, Eldon

b. 24 April 1916, Weatherford, Oklahoma, USA. He learned to play guitar in his early teens and at 17, was playing in Oklahoma City honky tonks. In 1935, he moved to Tulsa with a western swing band, the Alabama Boys, but soon left them to become the staff guitarist playing swing music on KTUL. In November 1937, **Bob Wills** persuaded Shamblin to join his Texas Playboys. His rhythm guitar work and previous experience of swing groups quickly became a prime factor of Wills' music. Shamblin not only reorganised the rhythm section but also became the band's arranger and made his first recordings with Wills in 1938. Early in 1940, Shamblin took to playing electric lead guitar and his clever abilities to blend with steel guitarist,

Leon McAuliffe, set standards that future musicians have tried to emulate. They recorded their noted 'Twin Guitar Special' in February 1941. He stayed with Wills until called up for World War II Army service which saw him attain the rank of captain. In 1947, he rejoined a much changed Wills' band in Texas and acted as manager as well as playing rhythm and occasional lead guitar until 1954. In 1954, he left to join Hoyle Nix's western swing band but in 1956, Shamblin went back to Wills. In 1957, he returned to Tulsa and though playing locally, he worked as a piano tuner and electric organ repairer. In 1970, **Merle Haggard** persuaded him and former Texas Playboys to play on his tribute album to Wills, *A Tribute To The Best Damn Fiddle Player In The World*. Following this, he and nine other old Playboys made further recordings at Haggard's home. The experience rekindled his interest and between 1975 and 1981, he played as a member of Haggard's band, the Strangers, until he retired to Tulsa. Shamblin's earlier work may be heard on many Wills' recordings, particularly **Columbia**'s Special Products and Historical Series, while some post-war recordings are captured on the first three volumes of the Kaleidoscope labels *Tiffany Transcriptions*. In the late 70s, he also recorded on the *Reunion* album made by a western swing band led by **Johnnie Lee Wills**. Shamblin made few solo recordings but he did also record an highly acclaimed album of country jazz for Flying Fish with the legendary jazz violinist **Joe Venuti**, **Curly Chalker**, a leading country jazz and western swing steel guitarist and mandolin expert Jethro Burns who for years had been one half of the comedy duo **Homer And Jethro**. In 1993, Shambling played with **Asleep At The Wheel** on their Grammy winner 'Red Wing'. Shambling has been rated by many experts as the world's best and most influential rhythm guitarist.

Albums: with Joe Venuti, Curly Chalker, Jethro Burns *S'Wonderful (4 Giants Of Swing)* (Flying Fish 1977), *Guitar Genius* (Delta c.1980).

Shamen

From the ashes of the moderately successful Alone Again Or (named after the track from **Love**'s *Forever Changes*) in 1986, the Shamen had a profound effect upon contemporary pop music over the next half decade. Formed in Aberdeen by Colin Angus (b. 24 August 1961, Aberdeen, Scotland; bass), Peter Stephenson (b. 1 March 1962, Ayrshire, Scotland), Keith McKenzie (b. 30 August 1961, Aberdeen, Scotland) and Derek McKenzie (b. 27 February 1964, Aberdeen, Scotland; guitar), the Shamen's formative stage relied heavily on crushing, psychedelic rock played by a relatively orthodox line-up. Their debut album, *Drop*, captured a sense of their colourful live shows and sealed the first chapter of the band's career.

Soon after, Colin Angus became fascinated by the nascent underground hip hop movement. Derek McKenzie was rather less enamoured with the hardcore dance explosion and departed, allowing William Sinnott (b. 23 December 1960, Glasgow, Scotland, d. 23 May 1991; bass) to join the ranks and further encourage the Shamen's move towards the dancefloor. In 1988, their hard-edged blend of rhythms, guitars, samples, sexually explicit slideshows and furious rhetoric drew anger from feminists, politicians and - after the scathing 'Jesus Loves Amerika' single - religious groups. That same year the band relocated to London, slimmed down to the duo of Angus and Sinnott who concentrated on exploring the areas of altered states with mind-expanding psychedelics. By 1990 the Shamen's influence - albeit unwitting - was vividly realised as the much-touted indie-dance crossover saw bands fuse musical cultures with the likes of **Jesus Jones** openly confessing to the Shamen's groundbreaking lead. By this time the Shamen themselves had taken to touring with the 'Synergy' show, a unique four hour extravaganza featuring rappers and designed to take the band even further away from their rock roots. After four years of such imaginative adventures into sound, 1991 promised a huge breakthrough for the Shamen and their fluctuating creative entourage. Unfortunately, just as the group inexorably toppled towards commercial riches, Will Sinnott drowned off the coast of Gomera, one of the Canary Islands, on the 23rd of May. With the support of Sinnott's family, the Shamen persevered with a remix of 'Move Any Mountain (Pro Gen '91)' which climbed into the Top 10 of the UK chart, a fitting farewell to the loss of such a creative force. Mr C (b. Richard West), a cockney rapper, DJ and head of the Plink Plonk record label, had joined the band for a section of 'Move Any Mountain (Pro Gen '91)'. Although many found his patois ill-fitting, his rhymes founded the spring board for UK chart success 'LSI', followed by the number 1 'Ebeneezer Goode' - which was accused in many quarters for extolling the virtues of the Ecstasy drug ('E's Are Good, E's Are Good, E's Are Ebeneezer Goode'). The Shamen denied all, and moved on with the release of *Boss Drum*. Its title track provided a deeply affecting dance single, complete with lyrics returning the band to their original, shamanic ethos of universal rhythms. Placed next to the teen-pop of 'LSI' and 'Ebeneezer Goode', such innovative work reinforced the Shamen's position as the wild cards of the UK dance scene.

Albums: *Drop* (Moshka 1987), *In Gorbachev We Trust* (Demon 1989), *Phorward* (Moshka 1989), *En-Tact* (One Little Indian 1990), *En-Tek* (One Little Indian 1990), *Progeny* (One Little Indian 1991), *Boss Drum* (One Little Indian 1992), *Different Drum* (One Little Indian 1992), *The Shamen On Air* (Band Of Joy 1993).

Shampoo

Adorned in ra ra skirts, pigtails and dayglo t-shirts, Shampoo's arrival on the 1994 British pop scene brought kitsch back to centre stage with a bang. 'The Kylie and Dannii of Baby Tears Punk Rock Pop', as the *New Musical Express* decreed, Jacqui Blake (b. c.1977) and Carrie Askew (b. c.1975) arrived fresh from school in Plumstead, London. The duo's early endeavours included writing a fanzine, *Last Exit*, about the **Manic Street Preachers**, appearing in one of their videos and earning a reputation for being 'around town'. They then met **St. Etienne**'s Bob Stanley at a party and talked him into giving them a deal on his Icerink label. The resultant single, 'Blisters & Bruises', earned a *Melody Maker* Single Of The Week award for its naive, spunky charm. They wrote the lyrics, while Lawrence of **Felt/Denim** wrote the music and produced. Shampoo were fully launched with the release of the delinquent 'Trouble' and hopelessly amateur 'Viva La Megababes', the latter a cheap and unruly take on the **Voodoo Queens**' 'Supermodel': 'Riot girls, diet girls, who really gives a fuck'. 'Trouble', meanwhile, was bizzarely used by BBC television to publicise a Frank Bruno boxing fight, and sold over 150,000 copies. Fabulously popular in Japan, their lyrical concerns for their debut album had expanded to encompass video games, throwing up after dodgy kebabs and sentimental love songs.
Album: *We Are Shampoo* (Food 1994).

Shanghai

Formerly known as **Spider**, they changed their name to Shanghai in 1981 to avoid confusion with the other groups using the same name at the time. Signing to **Chrysalis**, the band comprised Amanda Blue (vocals), Keith Lentin (guitar), Beau Hill (keyboards), Jimmy Lowell (bass) and Anton Fig (drums). They debuted with a self-titled album in 1982, a keyboard dominated, melodic pop-rock opus that received favourable reviews at the time of release. The band soon splintered with Hill moving into the production side, Anton Fig worked with **Glen Burtnick** and Amanda Blue started a solo career under the guidance of **Gene Simmons**. Given time to develop, Shanghai could have been a major force on the American AOR scene.
Albums: *Shanghai* (1982).

Shangri-Las

Late entrants in the early 60's school of 'girl groups', the Shangri-Las comprised two pairs of sisters, Mary-Ann and Margie Ganser and Betty and Mary Weiss. During 1963 they were discovered by **George 'Shadow' Morton** and recorded two singles under the name Bon Bons before signing to the newly formed **Red Bird** label. Relaunched as the Shangri-Las, they secured a worldwide hit with 'Remember (Walkin' In The Sand)', a delightful arrangement complete with the sound of crashing waves and crying seagulls. It was the sound-effect of a reving motorbike engine which opened their distinctive follow-up, 'Leader Of The Pack', which was even more successful and a prime candidate for the 'death disc' genre with its narrative of teenage love cut short because of a motorcycle accident. By 1966, Margie Ganser had left the group, though this had little effect on their popularity or output. They had already found a perfect niche, specializing in the doomed romanticism of American teenage life and unfolding a landscape filled with misunderstood adolescents, rebel boyfriends, disapproving parents, the foreboding threat of pregnancy and, inevitably, tragic death. This hit formula occasionally wore thin but Shadow Morton could always be relied upon to engineer a gripping production. During their closing hit phase in 1966/67, the group recorded two songs, 'I Can Never Go Home Anymore' and 'Past Present And Future' which saw the old teenage angst transmogrified into an almost tragic, sexual neuroticism. The enduring commercial quality of their best work was underlined by consistent repackaging and the successive chart reappearances of the biker anthem, 'Leader Of The Pack'.
Albums: *Leader Of The Pack* (1965), *'65* (1965).
Compilation: *Golden Hits* (1984), *16 Greatest Hits* (1993).
Further reading: *Girl Groups: The Story Of A Sound*, Alan Betrock.

Shank, Bud

b. Clifford Everett Jnr., 27 May 1926, Dayton, Ohio, USA. After studying and gigging on most of the reed instruments, Shank concentrated on alto saxophone, later doubling on flute and baritone saxophone. From 1947 he was resident on the west coast, playing in the big bands of **Charlie Barnet**, **Alvino Rey**, **Art Mooney** and **Stan Kenton** but making his greatest impact in small groups. With **Shorty Rogers**, Milt Bernhardt, **Bob Cooper**, **Art Pepper** and **Shelly Manne**, he was one of the tightly-knit group of Los Angeles-based musicians who formed the nucleus of the white west coast jazz scene of the 50s. As a member of the Lighthouse All-Stars and groups recording under the names of one or another of the leaders of the movement, Shank built a substantial reputation. He also recorded with **Laurindo Almeida**, beginning an association which was renewed several years later with the formation of the LA Four. Although active in the film and television studios during the 50s and 60s, Shank continued to make jazz dates, and with increasing frequency. In 1974 he was a founder-member of the LA Four. In the early 80s, by then wholly engaged in jazz, he toured as a single and also with Rogers, appearing in the UK with the **Vic Lewis** big band and recording with the Royal Philharmonic Orchestra. Shank's extensive recorded output over four decades allows an interesting examination of his development as a musician. His early alto playing was derivative of **Charlie Parker** and **Art Pepper**, while his flute playing, taken up during his stint with Kenton, was highly original and greatly advanced the use of the instrument in bebop settings. In later years his alto style became highly personalized and no longer showed influences outside of his own creative impulse. Indeed, by the mid-80s he had reputedly abandoned his other instruments in order to concentrate fully on alto.

Selected albums: with Shorty Rogers *Cool And Crazy* (1953), with Shelly Manne *The West Coast Sound* (1953), *The Bud Shank Quintet* i (1953), *The Bud Shank-Laurindo Almeida Quartet: Brazilliance Vol. 1* (1953), *The Bud Shank-Shorty Rogers Quintet* (1954), *Bud Shank And Three Trombones* (1954), *Bud Shank And Strings* (1955), *The Bud Shank-Bill Perkins Quintet* (1955), *The Bud Shank-Bob Cooper Quartet* (1956), *Live At The Haig* (1956), *The Bud Shank Quartet* i (1956), *The Bud Shank-Russ Freeman Quartet* (1956), *The Bud Shank Quartet* ii (1956), *Sessions, Live* (1956), *The Bud Shank-Bob Cooper Quintet* (1956), *The Bud Shank Quartet* iii (1957), *The Bud Shank-Laurindo Almeida Quartet: Brazilliance Vol. 2* (1958), *I'll Take Romance* (1958), *Misty Eyes* (West Wind 1958), *The Bud Shank Quartet* iv (1958), *The Bud Shank Quartet* v (1959), *The Bud Shank Quintet* ii (1961), *The Bud Shank Sextet* ii (1961), *New Groove* (1961), *The Bud Shank Septet* i (1962), *The Bud Shank Septet* ii (1963), *The Bud Shank Quartet* vi (1963), *Bud Shank And His Brazilian Friends* (c.1965), *Brazil '65* (1965), *Bud Shank-Chet Baker* i (1966), *Bud Shank-Chet Baker* ii (1966), *Bud Shank And His Orchestra* i (1966), *Bud Shank And His Orchestra* ii (1966), *Bud Shank And His Orchestra* iii (1967), *Bud Shank And His Orchestra* iv (1967), *Bud Shank-Chet Baker* iii (1968), *The Windmills Of Your Mind* (1969), *Bud Shank And The Bob Alcivar Singers* (1969-70), *The LA Four Scores!* (1975), *Sunshine Express* (Concord 1976), *Heritage* (1977), with LA Four *Watch What Happens* (1978), *Crystal Moments* (1979), *Explorations 1980* (Concord 1979), *Shades Of Dring* (1981), with Rogers *Yesterday, Today, And Forever* (1983), with Rogers, Vic Lewis *Back Again* (1984), *This Bud's For You* (1984), *California Concert* (1985), *Concert For Alto Saxophone And Symphony Orchestra* (c.1987), *Serious Swingers* (Contemporary 1987), *Tomorrow's Rainbow* (Contemporary c.1987), *At Jazz Alley* (JVC 1987), *Tales Of The Pilot* (1989), *Lost In The Stars* (Fresh Sound 1991), *The Doctor Is In* (1992), with Laurindo Almeida *Baa-Too-Kee* (1993), *I Told You So* (Candid 1994).

Shankar, Lakshminarayana

b. 26 April 1950, Madras, India. The son of noted violinist, V. Lakshminarayana, Shankar was taught to sing ragas at the age of two and began studying violin with his father at five. At his father's insistence he also studied a South Indian drum, the mridangam. It was his father, too, who encouraged him to learn from the North Indian (Hindustani) as well as his native South Indian (Carnatic) tradition. In 1969 he moved to the

USA to take a Ph.D in ethnomusicology at the Wesleyan University. Subsequently, while working at the University, he began to meet jazz and rock musicians such as **Ornette Coleman**, Jimmy Garrison and **John McLaughlin**. From 1973 he and McLaughlin studied together and between 1975-78 they co-led Shakti, an acoustic fusion of free jazz and Indian music, which grew out of Turyanandha Sangeeth, a duo with McLaughlin. He has continued to lead bands which cross the boundaries of music, including Peshkar, Shankar and the less adventurous, rock-based Epidemics. In 1988 the Epidemics took part in a world tour for human rights along with **Sting**, **Tracy Chapman**, **Bruce Springsteen** and **Peter Gabriel**. A remarkable, compelling musician who can carry an audience with him through Hindustani, Carnatic and jazz-based music in a single concert, Shankar plays an impressive-looking and sounding 10-string double-necked violin which he designed himself. He is much in demand for rock sessions requiring his unique sound, and can be heard (sometimes very briefly) on albums by Gabriel, **Lou Reed**, **Talking Heads**, **Frank Zappa**, **Phil Collins**, **Echo And The Bunnymen** and the **Pretenders**. He also played on the soundtrack of Martin Scorcese's *The Last Temptation Of Christ* and joined **Bill Laswell**'s movable feast of a band, **Material**, for its 'come-back' *Seven Souls*.

Albums: *Shakti* (1975), *A Handful Of Beauty* (1976), *Natural Elements* (1977), *Touch Me There* (1979), *The Epidemics, Who's To Know* (1981), *Song For Everyone* (1984), as the Epidemics *Vision, Caroline* (1986), with Material *Seven Souls* (1989), *Nobody Told Me* (1990), *Pancha Nadai Pallavi* (1990), *M.R.C.S.* (1991).

Shankar, Ravi

b. 7 April 1920, Benares, India. The foremost exponent of Indian music, Shankar was largely responsible for introducing the sitar to western audiences. He began his career as a member of elder brother Uday's music company, but in 1938 gave up an interest in dance to study classical music under Guru Ustad Allauddin Khan of Mahair. An intensive eight-year period ensued, following which Shankar began performing in his own right. He contributed music to film-maker Satyajit Ray's trilogy: *Pather Panchali, Aparajito* and *The World Of Apu*. A US tour in 1957 ignited interest in both the artist and the syncopated raga. This position was enhanced by subsequent appearances under the sponsorship of the Asia Society Performing Arts Program. Shankar also enjoyed the approbation of fellow musicians, recording *West Meets East* with violinist Yehudi Menuhin and parts of *Portrait Of A Genius* with flautist **Paul Horn**, but drew greater recognition when **Beatles** guitarist **George Harrison** professed his admiration. The sitar thus appeared in pop, notably on the former group's

'Norwegian Wood', but while Harrison's interest was undoubtedly genuine - he studied under the maestro in Bombay - the short-lived 'raga-rock' genre was marked by expediency. Although initially sceptical, Shankar later enjoyed his newfound status although he was dismissive of rock's temporal trappings, in particular its drug culture, disowning his excellent soundtrack to *Chappaqua* upon discovering the film's hedonistic content. In May 1967, Shankar opened the Kinnara School Of Music in Los Angeles and within weeks was one of the star attractions at the **Monterey Pop Festival**. By this point the artist had been joined by longstanding tabla player Alla Rakha, a disciple of Lahore musician Ustad Quader Bax. His dexterous technique inspired Shankar to even greater artistic heights, as evinced on *Portrait Of A Genius* and *Ravi Shankar In New York*. In 1969, the sitarist appeared at the **Woodstock Festival**, and was one of the artists signed to the Beatles' Apple label. Galvanized by Shankar's concern over famine in Bangla Desh, George Harrison organized an all-star concert in New York's Madison Square Garden. The ensuing *Concert For Bangla Desh* (1971), featured the master musician's contribution to the performance. He subsequently recorded for the ex-Beatle's Dark Horse label and in 1974 toured the US with Harrison to promote *Ravi Shankar, Family And Friends*. Such appearances brought Shankar's spell within the 'rock' community to an end, but he remains a highly-respected and popular figure on the international concert circuit and has contributed greatly to the now-burgeoning 'world music' movement.

Selected albums: *Ravi Shankar In Concert* (1962), *Portrait Of A Genius* (1965), *Chappaqua* (1966, film soundtrack), *Ravi Shankar In New York* (1967), *Ravi Shankar At The Monterey International Pop Festival* (1968), *Ravi Shankar At Woodstock* (1970), *Raga* (1971), *In Concert 1972* (1973), *Transmigration Macbre* (1973, film soundtrack of *Viola*), *Ravi Shankar, Family And Friends* (1974), *Sounds Of India* (1974), *Ravi Shankar In San Francisco* (1974), *Sitar Recital* (1974), *The Genius Of Ravi Shankar* (1974), *Ahmedjaw Thirakhwa* (1976), *Music Festival From India* (1976), *Genesis* (1986, film soundtrack), *Pandit Ravi Shankar* (1988), *RGS. Kamshwari/Gangshwari* (1989, reissue), *RGS. S Kaylan/S Sarang* (1989, reissue), *Inside The Kremlin* (1989), with Yehudi Menuhin *West Meets East* (1989, reissue), *Farewell, My Friend* (1992), *Sound Of The Sitar* (1993).

Shannon

b. Shannon Greene, 1958, Washington, DC, USA. Shannon was best known for her 1984 US Top 10/UK Top 20 dance single 'Let The Music Play'. She grew up in Brooklyn, New York, and studied both singing and dance as a child. Shannon was attending York University when she recorded 'Let The Music Play', originally for Emergency Records, in 1983. Mirage Records, a division of the larger **Atlantic Records**,

picked up distribution of the single and it made its way to number 2 on the US R&B charts and number 8 pop. The follow-up, 'Give Me Tonight', also reached the R&B Top 10 but did not make the pop Top 40. In the UK, she gained two further chart hits with 'Give Me Tonight' and 'Sweet Somebody' both reaching the Top 30 in 1984. Shannon had one final pop chart single, 'Do You Wanna Get Away', in 1985, but continued to land on the R&B charts for another year, finally placing a total of seven singles on that chart. Her debut album, *Let The Music Play*, also charted but by the late 80s Shannon's name had disappeared from the US music scene.

Albums: *Let The Music Play* (1984), *Do You Wanna Get Away* (1985).

Shannon, Del

b. Charles Westover, 30 December 1934, Coopersville, Michigan, USA, d. 8 February 1990. From the plethora of clean, American, post doo-wop male vocalists to find enormous success in the early 60s, only a small handful retained musical credibility. Shannon was undoubtedly from this pedigree. More than 30 years after his chart debut, Shannon's work is still regularly played. His early musical interests took him under the country influence of the legendary **Hank Williams.** Shannon's first record release however was pure gutsy pop; the infectious melody was written by accident while rehearsing in the local Hi-Lo club with keyboard player Max Crook (Maximillian). The song was 'Runaway', a spectacular debut that reached the top of the charts in the USA and UK, and was subsequently recorded by dozens of admiring artists. The single, with its shrill sounding Musitron (an instrument created by Crook) together with Shannon's falsetto, was irresistible. **Johnny Bienstock**, who was running **Big Top Records** in New York, received a telephone order following a Miami radio station playing the track once. The order was for an unprecidented 39,000 copies. It was at that stage that Bienstock knew he had unleashed a major star. What is not known generally known is that Shannon sang flat on all the recordings of the song. Bienstock and a colleague went into the studio overnight sped up and redubbed the master tape so that Shannon's voice was correct. The record was released a full 10 seconds shorter, and nobody, including Shannon ever noticed. He succeeded however, where others failed, due to his talent as a composer and his apparent maturity, appealing to the public with a clear youthful strident voice. This paradox was cleared up many years later, when it was discovered that he was five years older than stated. Had this come out in 1961, it is debatable whether he would have competed successfully alongside his fresh-faced contemporaries. His teenage tales of loneliness, despair, broken hearts, failed relationships, infidelity and ultimate doom, found a receptive audience. Shannon would rarely use the word 'love' in his lyrics. Even the plaintive, almost happy, 1962 hit 'Swiss Maid' combined his trademark falsetto with yodelling, ending with the heroine dying, forlorn and unhappy. Over the next three years Shannon continued to produce and write his own material with great success, especially in Britain, where his run of 10 consecutive hits ended with 'Sue's Gotta Be Mine' in October 1963. In the interim, he had produced several memorable Top 10 successes, including the bitingly acerbic 'Hats Off To Larry' and 'Little Town Flirt', which betrayed an almost misogynistic contempt. The re-worked themes of his songs were now beginning to pale, and together with the growth of Merseybeat, Shannon's former regular appearances in the charts became sporadic, even though he was the first American artist to record a **Beatles**' song, 'From Me To You'.

Shannon worked steadily for the next 25 years, enjoying a few more hit singles including a cover version of **Bobby Freeman**'s 'Do You Wanna Dance', followed by 'Handy Man', formerly a hit for **Jimmy Jones**, from whom he 'borrowed' his famous falsetto. In 1965 'Keep Searchin'' was Shannon's last major success The song had an elegiac feel, recalling an era of innocence already passed. Throughout the 60s and 70s Shannon was a regular visitor to Britain where he found a smaller but more appreciative audience. He acquired many professional admirers over the years including **Jeff Lynne**, **Tom Petty** and **Dave Edmunds**, who variously helped him rise above his sad decline into a nether world of alcohol and pills. The 1981 Petty produced *Drop Down And Get Me* was critically well-received but sold poorly. Ironically, he received a belated hit in America with 'Sea Of Love', which found favour in 1982. This led to a brief renaissance for him in the USA. Although Shannon was financially secure through wise property investment, he still performed regularly. Ultimately however, he was branded to rock 'n' roll revival tours which finally took their toll on 8 February 1990, when a severely depressed Shannon pointed a .22 calibre rifle to his head and pulled the trigger, ending the misery echoed in his catalogue of hits.

Albums: *Runaway With Del Shannon* (1961), *Hats Off To Del Shannon* (1963), *Little Town Flirt* (1963), *Handy Man* (1964), *Del Shannon Sings Hank Williams* (1965), *1,661 Seconds With Del Shannon* (1965), *This Is My Bag* (1966), *Total Commitment* (1966), *The Further Adventures Of Charles Westover* (1968), *Live In England* (1972), *Drop Down And Get Me* (1981), *Rock On* (1991). Selected compilations: *The Best Of Del Shannon* (1967), *The Vintage Years* (1979), *Runaway Hits* (1990), *I Go To Pieces* (1990), *Looking Back, His Biggest Hits (*1991).
Films: *It's Trad, Dad a.k.a. Ring-A-Ding Rhythm* (1962).

Shannon, Sharon

b. 8 June 1968, Corrofin, County Clare, Eire. A solo performer on accordion and fiddle, both Shannon's parents were dancers, and her brothers and sisters all played musical instruments. Initially she too played locally with them. While still in her teens she joined Disirt Tola, with her sister Mary, the group then heading to the USA for live engagements. She was then asked to provide the music for Brendan Behan's play, *The Hostage*, at the Druid Theatre. She later joined Arcady, along with Frances Black, James Delaney, Patsy Broderick and Ringo McDonagh (formerly with **De Dannan**). Sharon remained with them for about a year, and in 1989 went to the Glastonbury Festival, as a guest of Mike Scott of the **Waterboys**, as their accordion player. She remained with the group for 18 months, recording and touring worldwide in the process. On leaving the Waterboys she commenced a solo tour with **Christy Moore**. Finally, she released her long awaited debut album, *Sharon Shannon*. The album was well-received, and featured a number of respected musicians, including Donal Lunny, Mike Scott and Adam Clayton (**U2**). Although largely a solo performer, her current band includes former Waterboys member Trevor Hutchinson (bass), Mary Custy (fiddle) and Gerry O'Beirne (guitar/ukelele). As a performer she has quickly captured the imagination of the folk scene.
Albums: *Sharon Shannon* (Solid 1991), *Out The Gap* (Solid 1994).

Shanty Crew

The Shanty Crew were formed in 1976 with the group specializing in both traditional and modern sea songs. They are the longest established group singing traditional sailor shanties, in Britain. Two of the founder members, Chris Roche and Gerry Milne, survived the changes to record *Let The Wind Blow Free*. The release included such standards as 'Rolling Down To Old Maui' and 'Haul Away For Rosie-O'. In 1986 the group appeared at the Liverpool and Douarnenez Sea Festivals. Inevitably, the line-up fluctuated again until Roche, teamed with Steve Belsey (the other founder member), Tony Goodenough, Phil Jarrett, Phil Money and Dominic Magog to record *Stand To Yer Ground*. With the addition of Goodenough, they have added French shanties to the group's repertoire, as Tony speaks fluent French. In addition to researching and performing, Roche is editor of the *Journal Of The Cape Horner Association*, and holds the largest private collection of books and records of shanties and sailors songs in the world.
Albums: *Let The Wind Blow Free* (1984), *Stand To Yer Ground* (1990).

Shapiro, Helen

b. 28 September 1946, Bethnal Green, London, England. Helen Shapiro drew considerable attention when, as a 14 year old schoolgirl, she scored a UK Top 3 hit with 'Don't Treat Me Like A Child'. A deep intonation belied her youth, and by the end of 1961 the singer had scored two chart-topping singles with 'You Don't Know' and 'Walkin' Back To Happiness'. This success was maintained the following year with 'Tell Me What He Said' (number 2) and 'Little Miss Lonely' (number 8), as Helen won concurrent polls as 'Best British Female Singer' and was voted 'Best Newcomer' by the Variety Club of Great Britain. However, having recorded the original version of 'It's My Party' during an artistically fruitful session in Nashville, Helen was disappointed when an acetate reached **Lesley Gore**, who enjoyed a massive international hit using a similar arrangement. Shapiro's producer, **Norrie Paramor**, also vetoed the opportunity to record 'Misery', composed with Helen in mind by **John Lennon** and **Paul McCartney**. Indeed the advent of the **Beatles** helped undermine the singer's career. Despite being younger than many beat group members, Shapiro was perceived as belonging to a now-outmoded era and despite a series of excellent singles, was eclipsed by 'newcomers' **Cilla Black** and **Dusty Springfield**. The late 60s proved fallower still and, barring one pseudonymous release, Helen did not record at all between 1970-75. A **Russ Ballard** song, 'Can't Break The Habit' became a minor hit in Europe during 1977 and in turn engendered *All For The Love Of The Music*, a set sadly denied a UK release. Six years later Shapiro resurfaced on writer **Charlie Gillett**'s Oval label. *Straighten Up And Fly Right* showed the singer had lost none of her early power and this excellent collection of standards was rightly acclaimed. An equally confident collaboration with jazz musician **Humphrey Lyttelton** ensued, since which Helen Shapiro has maintained a high profile through radio, television and live appearances, singing jazz-influenced big band material and gospel songs. She also made an impressive London cabaret debut at the Café Royal in 1995.

Albums: *Tops With Me* (1962), *Helen's Sixteen* (1963), *Helen In Nashville* (1963), *Helen Hits Out* (1964), *All For The Love Of The Music* (1977), *Straighten Up And Fly Right* (1983), *Echoes Of The Duke* (1985), *The Quality Of Mercer* (1987), *Nothing But The Best* (1995). Compilations: *Twelve Hits And A Miss Shapiro* (1967), *The Very Best Of Helen Shapiro* (1974), *The 25th Anniversary Album* (1986), *The EP Collection* (1989).

Further reading: *Walking Back To Happiness*, Helen Shapiro, *Helen Shapiro: Pop Princess*, John S. Janson.

Films: *It's Trad, Dad a.k.a. Ring-A-Ding Rhythm* (1962).

Shark Island

This five-piece, melodic hard rock group was formed in

1986 from the ashes of Los Angeles glam rockers, the Sharks. Comprising Richard Black (vocals), Spencer Sercombe (guitar), Tom Rucci (bass), Michael Guy (guitar) and Walt Woodward (drums; ex-**Americade**), they recorded an album of demos in 1987 which saw **A&M Records** step in with a development deal. As a result of which, two of the band's songs were aired on the soundtrack to *Bill And Ted's Excellent Adventure*. Losing second guitarist Guy and replacing their rhythm section with Chris Heilman (ex-**Bernie Tormé**; bass) and Gregg Ellis (drums), they then moved over to **Epic Records** for a second album and first release proper in 1988. This showed the band to have matured considerably, with the material displaying new-found confidence in better production surroundings. Black had developed into an accomplished vocalist and songwriter, with a style that married the best elements of **Jon Bon Jovi** and David Coverdale (**Whitesnake**). It is an oft-repeated rumour that Axl Rose of **Guns N'Roses** leaned heavily on his style in developing his own delivery. Black was also involved in the Contraband project of 1991, which featured **Michael Schenker** and members of **L.A. Guns**, **Ratt** and **Vixen**. This one-off collaboration recorded an album of cover versions, including Shark Island's 'Bad For Each Other'. Sercombe would also work on various **MSG** dates.

Albums: *S'Cool Bus* (Shark 1987), *Law Of The Order* (Epic 1989).

Sharkey, Feargal

b. 13 August 1958, Derry, Northern Ireland. Sharkey first found fame as the lead singer of the Irish pop-punk group, the **Undertones**, whose singles provided some of the best pop of the late 70s. The group's reign lasted from 1976-83 after which Sharkey teamed up with **Vince Clarke** in the short-lived **Assembly**. The plaintive 'Never Never' was a Top 10 hit for the group and highlighted the power of Sharkey's distinctive, quavering vocal style. In 1984, Sharkey recorded the underrated 'Listen To Your Heart' for **Madness**' label Zarjazz and this was followed by his biggest success, 'A Good Heart'. This insistent tune established him as a potential major act by reaching number 1 in the UK charts. The Top 10 follow-up 'You Little Thief' was almost equally distinctive and Sharkey's debut album, produced by the **Eurythmics**' **David A. Stewart** was very well received. Sharkey subsequently moved to America, where he recorded *Wish*. A long-delayed third album, *Songs From The Mardi Gras*, continued Sharkey's slow drift away from the mainstream, although it did spawn a surprise Top 20 hit, 'I've Got News For You'. In 1993 Sharkey was working as an A&R manager for **Polydor Records** and in 1995 it was announced that he was forming a new UK record label.

Albums: *Feargal Sharkey* (1985), *Wish* (1987), *Songs From The Mardi Gras* (1991).

Sharman, Dave

b. c.1970, England. Dave Sharman first rose to prominence in 1989 when he featured on a session for BBC Radio 1 DJ Tommy Vance's *Friday Rock Show*. Comprising four instrumental selections, this proved such a success that producer Tony Wilson was allegedly alerting labels during recording. His debut album, titled after its year of release, saw rave reviews from both the metal and musician fraternities, with US magazine *Guitar For The Practising Musician* declaring Sharman 'Guitar God In Waiting'. Later, he was invited on the 'Night Of The Guitars' tour, where he shared a stage with **Rick Derringer**, **Ronnie Montrose** and others. A second album, *Exit Within*, was conceived when the guitarist met ex-**Whitesnake** bass player Neil Murray at an **Ian Gillan** audition, the duo linking with German vocalist Thomas Brache. The resultant 'Trucker' and 'Frantic' tracks were utilized by Radio 1's *Rock Show* and used as theme music. A more solid band aggregation was sought for *Here 'N' Now*, with Sharman joined by Steve Wood (drums), Tom Jeffreys (bass) and a retained Brache on vocals. Titling the new band Graphic, they debuted with a set which comprised seven band compositions and three instrumentals.

Albums: *1990* (1990), *Exit Within* (1992). With Graphic: *Here 'N' Now* (Bleeding Hearts 1995).

Sharon, Ralph

b. 17 September 1923, London, England. Sharon came to prominence as pianist with the **Ted Heath** band in the years immediately after World War II. He also played, and sometimes recorded, with British bop musicians of the late 40s, including **Ronnie Scott** and **Victor Feldman**. In the early 50s he moved to the USA, became an American citizen, and continued to play piano in a variety of settings, frequently in distinguished company. He also established a reputation as a sympathetic accompanist to singers, notably **Tony Bennett** and **Chris Connor**. On one of his albums with Bennett, Sharon wrote arrangements for the **Count Basie** band, playing piano on most tracks, while on another album, three decades later, he arranged songs by **Irving Berlin** for his own small group, with added guests who included **George Benson**, **Dexter Gordon** and **Dizzy Gillespie**. Sharon's habitual diffidence has kept him hidden from the spotlight he clearly deserves. Among his early American recordings were some with his wife, the singer Sue Ryan.

Selected albums: *The Ralph Sharon Sextet i* (1955), *The Ralph Sharon Trio i* (1956), *Mr & Mrs Jazz* (Fresh Sounds 1956), *The Ralph Sharon Sextet ii* (1957), *The Ralph Sharon Quartet* (1958), with Tony Bennett *Bennett/Basie* (1959), *Ralph Sharon With The Rolena Carter Chorale* (c.1962), *The Ralph Sharon Trio ii* (c.1965), with Bennett *Bennett/Berlin*

(1987), *The Magic Of George Gershwin* (Horatio Nelson 1988), *The Magic Of Irving Berlin* (Horatio Nelson 1989), *The Magic Of Cole Porter* (Horatio Nelson 1989).

Sharp Nine

Formed in 1993, Sharp Nine relocated Seattle's grunge sound to their home base of Sweden on their dark and hypnotic debut album, *Untimed*. With Jesper Starander (vocals), Joacim Starander (guitar), Andreas Jonasson (guitar), Dan Hansson (bass) and Frederick Lindehall (drums), this recording following intensive gigging around Stockholm where they honed live favourites such as 'No Tiles Free' and 'Unload' into a distinctive, neo-industrial metal hybrid.

Album: *Untimed* (Mausoleum 1994).

Sharp, Cecil

b. Cecil James Sharp, 22 November 1859, Denmark Hill, London, England, d. 23 June 1924. Sharp is most commonly remembered for his collecting of folk songs and dance tunes in order to preserve the tradition of popular music. He collected a wealth of material, both in Britain and the USA, where he made regular trips to the Appalachian Mountains, often with his assistant Maud Karpeles (b. 12 November 1885, London, England). Sharp was the third child of nine, having four brothers and four sisters. Cecil, always a weak child, left school in 1874. His early hay-fever turned to asthma in later life. His interest in music was largely inherited from his mother, though both parents encouraged him. He entered Clare College, Cambridge, in October 1879, where he read Mathematics. Leaving in 1882, he went to Australia, where he took a job washing Hansom cabs in Adelaide. There followed various jobs as a bank clerk and violin teacher, and eventually he became assistant organist at St. Peter's Cathedral, Adelaide. During one trip to England, a bout of typhoid caused paralysis in Sharp's legs. In early 1891 he tried unsuccessfully to get his compositions published, and returned to England the following year. He taught in England until 1896, and was Principal of Hampstead Conservatory until 1905. In 1911 Sharp founded the English Folk Dance Society, which later became the English Folk Dance And Song Society (EFDSS), having amalgamated with the English Folk Song Society. The first song Sharp collected was 'The Seeds Of Love', which he heard his gardener, John England, singing. This song was the first to be included in his book *Folk Songs From Somerset*. Between 1916 and 1918, often accompanied by his long time assistant Karpeles, Sharp spent one year in the Southern Appalachian Mountains of America. He collected a wealth of material and produced numerous notes, books and articles on song and dance music. It is impossible to imagine what would have gone undiscovered, had it not been for his enthusiasm and knowledge of the subject. Sharp died on 23 June 1924, in Hampstead, London, and was cremated at Golders Green, London on 25 June. A memorial service was held at St. Martin-in-the-Fields, Trafalgar Square. A year earlier, his university had conferred on him the degree of Master of Music. Maud Karpeles died on 1 October 1976 at the age of 91. Sharp left his manuscript collection of songs, tunes and dance notes to Clare College, and his library to the English Folk Dance Society. The foundation stone for Cecil Sharp House, the London Headquarters of the English Folk Dance And Song Society, was laid on 24 June 1929.

Further reading: *Folk Songs From Somerset*, with C.L. Marson. *Songs Of The West*, with S. Baring Gould. *English Folk Songs For Schools*, with S. Baring Gould. *English Folk Carols*, Cecil Sharp. *English Folk Chanterys*, Cecil Sharp. *English Folksongs From The Southern Appalachian Mountains*, Cecil Sharp, edited by Maud Karpeles. *Cecil Sharp*, A.H.Fox Strangeways with Maud Karpeles. *Cecil Sharp-His Life And Work*, Maud Karpeles. *The Crystal Spring: English Folk Songs Collected By Cecil Sharp*, edited by Maud Karpeles.

Sharp, Dee Dee

b. Dione LaRue, 9 September 1945, Philadelphia, Pennsylvania, USA. A backing vocalist for the **Cameo-Parkway** labels, Dee Dee Sharp was the uncredited voice on **Chubby Checker**'s 'Slow Twistin'' single. Her own debut, 'Mashed Potato Time', was recorded at the same session and thanks to the power of **Dick Clark**'s *American Bandstand* television show this energetic, excited song became an immediate success. Cameo sadly chose to milk its dance-based appeal and releases such as 'Gravy (For My Mashed Potatoes)' and 'Do The Bird' packaged her as a temporary novelty act at the expense of an untapped potential. Dee Dee resurfaced in the 70s on the TSOP/**Philadelphia International** labels. Married to producer Kenny Gamble, she scored two minor soul hits with 'I'm Not In Love' (1976 - a cover of the **10cc** hit) and 'I Love You Anyway' (1981).

Albums: *It's Mashed Potato Time* (1962), *Down To Earth* (1962), *Do The Bird* (1963), *All The Hits* (1963), *Down Memory Lane* (1963), *What Color Is Love* (1978). Compilation: *18 Golden Hits* (mid-60s) Films: *Don't Knock The Twist* (1962).

Sharp, Jonah

Ambient artist lcoated in San Francisco who records as Space Time Continuum on his own Reflective Records. In 1993 he undertook an album with **Peter Namlock** for Fax, and a second collection with Californian hippy mystic Terrence McKenna for Caroline. Originally a jazz and session drummer in the UK, he played at several London parties as a DJ before relocating to the US. He has since set up a new studio in San Francisco. As well as his own *Flourescence* EP, other Reflective releases have included a Namlock

remix CD and a techno-flavoured 12-inch by emiT ecapS.

Sharpees

Vernon Guy (b. 21 March 1945), Stacy Johnson (b. 13 April 1945), Herbert Reeves (b. 1947, d. 1972), and early member Horise O'Toole (b. 1943); all from St. Louis, Missouri, USA. George Leaner's Chicago-based One-derful label recruited several acts from the St. Louis area via local representatives, A&R man Mack McKinney and house writer/arranger Eddie Silvers. One of them was the Sharpees, named after the St. Louis guitarist/bandleader/revue-director, Benny Sharp. Johnson was the first to be recruited by in 1961 after Sharp heard him perform solo with the Arabians. He was joined by Vernon Guy (ex-Seven Gospel Singers and Cool Sounds), and O'Toole, then with the Originals. They first worked as the New Breed, but had become the Sharpees by the time they backed (Little Miss) Jessie Smith in 1961 on 'My Baby's Gone' for the Mel-O label. Then, in late 1962, Guy and Johnson left Sharp to join the **Ike And Tina Turner** Review and to cut solo singles for Ike Turner's Teena, Sonja and Sony labels in 1963. They both also appeared on the 1964 Kent live album, *The Ike & Tina Turner Review*, before Johnson moved to LA. Later that year, while on the west coast, Johnson was back with Turner, who produced his 'Consider Yourself' for the Modern label. By the time the Sharpees arrived at Oliver Sain's St. Louis studio to record their first single, 'Do The 45', which was released on George Leaner's One-derful label, the line-up consisted of two of the original members, Guy and O'Toole, plus a new man, Herbert Reeves, ex-leader of the Arabians. The record was similar to Junior Walker's 'Shotgun', and was a strong 'dance' seller in northern US markets. While on tour, O'Toole contracted tuberculosis, and was replaced by the other founder member, Stacy Johnson. The Sharpees' 'Tired Of Being Lonely' (1965), recorded in Chicago with Reeves' strong but soulful lead, made the upper reaches of the Hot 100 early in 1966. After two flop singles, the Sharpees remained a very popular live act on the chitlin' circuit through to 1967, with Johnson cutting a solo single for another of Leaner's labels, M-Pac, in 1966 under the aegis of **Harold Burrage**. The group effectively split up in 1967, although a new pact with Sharp resulted in one more record a year later, on Midas, another Leaner label. They stayed together until 1972, when Herbert Reeves was tragically shot dead. In the early 80s, Guy and Johnson formed a new Sharpees group with Bobby Wilson and Guy's nephew, Paul Grady, and they continued to gig around the St. Louis area.

Sharrock, Sonny

b. Warren Hardin Sharrock, 27 August 1940, Ossining, New York, USA, d. 26 May 1994, Ossining, New

York, USA. Now regarded as one of the most remarkable guitarists in contemporary jazz, Sharrock was a late starter, teaching himself the instrument at the age of 20. Before that he sang in a doo-wop group, the Echoes. He recorded with them for **Alan Freed** but the tracks were never released. When he was 21 he spent a few months studying formally at **Berklee College Of Music**. Starting in 1965 he worked with a succession of major names in the *avant garde* (including **Pharoah Sanders**, **Don Cherry**, **Sunny Murray** and Olatunji, **John Gilmore** and **Byard Lancaster**) then from 1967-73 provided the 'outside' element in **Herbie Mann**'s band. In 1970 he contributed to 'Yesternow', the second part of **Miles Davis**'s *Jack Johnson*. In 1973 he formed a band with his then wife, Linda Sharrock (Chambers), and made his solo debut in 1986 with *Last Exit*. At the time of its release he was playing with **Peter Brötzmann**, **Bill Laswell**, and **Ronald Shannon Jackson**. After a fascinating and innovative solo album, *Guitar*, he established a more conventional band which toured successfully with packages organized by New York's Knitting Factory club. In 1991 he released *Ask The Ages*, with an all-star quartet containing Sanders, Charnett Moffett and **Elvin Jones**. Sharrock died of a heart attack in May 1994.

Selected albums: with Pharoah Sanders *Tauhid* (1967), with Herbie Mann *Memphis Underground* (1968), with Wayne Shorter *Super Nova* (1969), *Black Woman* (1970), with Miles Davis *Jack Johnson* (1970), *Monkie Pockie Boo* (Affinity 1974), *Paradise* (1974), with Material *Memory Serves* (1981), *Guitar* (Enemy 1986), with Last Exit *Last Exit* (1986), *The Noise Of Trouble, Cassette Tapes* (1987), *Seize The Rainbow* (Enemy 1987), *Live In New York* (Enemy 1990), *Iron Path, The Cologne Tapes* (1990), *Ask The Ages* (1991), *Highlife* (Highlife 1991), with Nicky Skopelitis *Faith Moves* (1991), *Ask The Ages* (Axiom 1991).

Shaver, Billy Joe

b. 15 September 1941, Corsicana, Texas, USA. Shaver was raised in Waco, Texas and lost two fingers in a saw-mill accident. In typically contradictory fashion, he took up bronc-busting as a safer job and started to learn guitar. An early song, 'Two Bits Worth Of Nothing', was written about his wife - a lady he has both married and divorced three times! Shaver spent some years in Nashville before **Bobby Bare** discovered him. He and Bare co-wrote his first single, 'Chicken On The Ground', for **Mercury Records** in 1970. Bare hit the US country charts with the simple, gutsy philosophy of 'Ride Me Down Easy' in 1973. **Johnny Rodriguez** did well with 'I Couldn't Be Me Without You', while **Tom T. Hall** favoured 'Old Five And Dimers' and a song about **Willie Nelson**, 'Willy The Wandering Gypsy And Me'. **Waylon Jennings**' important album *Honky Tonk Heroes* contained nine Shaver songs including their co-written 'You Ask Me To', which was

subsequently recorded by **Elvis Presley**. Shaver's first album, produced by **Kris Kristofferson**, contained his gruff-voiced versions of many excellent songs including his first country hit, 'I Been To Georgia On A Fast Train'. His Texan influences (blues, jazz, Mexican) and his themes (life on the road, brief encounters, how it used to be) fitted in with outlaw country music. His best song, 'Black Rose', tells of his love for a black girl and contains the dubious line, 'The Devil made me do it the first time, The second time I done it on my own.' Shaver hated live performances and he fell prey to ulcers, alcoholism and drug-addiction, so much so that an album for **MGM Records** was never made. Other songwriters wrote about him, including Kris Kristofferson's 'The Fighter' and Tom T. Hall's 'Joe, Don't Let The Music Kill You'. In 1976, Shaver released his second album and followed it with a glittering line-up (Willie Nelson, **Ricky Skaggs**, **Emmylou Harris**) for 'Gypsy Boy'. He turned to religion and 'I'm Just An Old Chunk Of Coal (But I'm Gonna Be A Diamond Someday)' was recorded by both **Johnny Cash** and **John Anderson**. Perhaps there were too many outlaw singers and Shaver, with his lack of product, was overlooked. His output of six studio albums in 17 years, with several songs repeated, is astonishingly low, particularly for a country singer.

Albums: *Old Five And Dimers Like Me* (1973), *When I Get My Wings* (1976), *Gypsy Boy* (1977), *I'm Just An Old Chunk Of Coal* (1981), *Billy Joe Shaver* (1982), *Salt Of The Earth* (1987), *Live In Australia* (1989), as Shaver *Tramp On Your Street* (Praxis/Zoo 1993), *Honky Tonk Heroes* (Bear Family 1994).

Shavers, Charlie

b. 3 August 1917, New York City, New York, USA, d. 8 July 1971. Shavers took up trumpet in his teens and played with various minor bands before joining **Tiny Bradshaw** in 1937. In the same year he played with **Lucky Millinder**, **Jimmie Noone** and **John Kirby**. The Kirby sextet proved an ideal setting for him, both as trumpeter and arranger, and he stayed for seven years. Among his compositions written while with Kirby are 'Pastel Blue', which with lyrics added became 'Why Begin Again', and 'Undecided', which became a jazz standard in its own right and with added lyrics a hit for **Ella Fitzgerald**. In 1944 he left Kirby for the **Tommy Dorsey** orchestra, where for a decade he was featured soloist. He made records throughout these years with various leaders, including a session under the nominal guidance of Herbie Haymer that featured **Nat 'King' Cole** and **Buddy Rich**. This set was issued, fluffs, retakes, off-microphone comments and all, under the title *Anatomy Of A Jam Session*. Another admirable date from this period was a Gene Norman concert at Pasadena, California, issued under **Lionel Hampton**'s name. In the 50s and 60s Shavers played mostly in small groups, often as leader, touring extensively as a single and with **Jazz At The Philharmonic**. A masterly musician, Shavers was capable of adapting to almost any mainstream setting. In the right company he would produce emotionally powerful playing; with Kirby he played with the elegance and finesse this group demanded, and in his later years with JATP he would deliver wildly exciting bravura solos, all with remarkable ease and overt good humour.

Selected albums: with Nat 'King' Cole and Buddy Rich *Anatomy Of A Jam Session* (1945), with Lionel Hampton *Stardust* (1945), *Jazz At The Philharmonic: Hartford 1953* (1953), *The Charlie Shavers Sextet* (1954), *The Most Intimate Charlie Shavers* (1955), *Gershwin, Shavers And Strings* (1955), *We Dig Cole!* (1958), *Art Ford's Jazz Party* (1958), *The Charlie Shavers Quartet* i (1958-59), *The Charlie Shavers Quartet* ii (1959), *Memorial* (1959), *The Charlie Shavers Quartet* iii (1960), *The Charlie Shavers Quartet* iv (1961), *Swing Along* (1961) *Swinging With Charlie* (1961), *The Charlie Shavers-Wild Bill Davis Combo* (1961), *A Man And His Music* (c.1962), *Live At The London House* (1962), *Live From Chicago* (1962), *Charlie Shavers And His Orchestra* (1963), *Charlie Shavers At Le Crazy Horse Saloon In Paris* (c.1964), *The Last Session* (1970), *Live!* (Black And Blue 1970). Compilations: *November 1961 & March 1962* (1980), *Trumpet Man (1944-58)* (1981).

Shaw, Allen

b. c.1890, Henning, Tennessee, USA, d. 1940, Tipton County, Tennessee, USA. A travelling man, remembered all through western Tennessee and in Memphis, Shaw played forceful steel guitar, and sang the blues in an exultant voice on his one issued record, cut in 1934 with **Willie Borum** on second guitar. On one title, Shaw played impeccably sensitive yet very powerful slide guitar. Shaw and Borum also backed **Hattie Hart** at this session. Shaw's son, Willie Tango, reckoned to be a better guitarist than his father, never recorded (though he was the subject of a song recorded by **Memphis Minnie**).

Compilation: *Memphis Blues* (1990).

Shaw, Artie

b. Arthur Jacob Arshawsky, 23 May 1910, New York City, New York, USA. Shaw took up the alto saxophone at the age of 12 and a few years later was playing in a Connecticut dance band. In 1926, he switched to clarinet and spent the next three years working in Cleveland, Ohio, as arranger and musical director for Austin Wylie. He also played in **Irving Aaronson**'s popular band, doubling on tenor saxophone. In New York from the end of 1929, Shaw became a regular at after-hours sessions, sitting in with leading jazzmen and establishing a reputation as a technically brilliant clarinettist. He made numerous record dates with dance bands and jazz musicians

including **Teddy Wilson**, with whom he appeared on some of **Billie Holiday**'s sessions. In 1936, Shaw formed a band which included strings for a concert and, with the addition of regular dance band instruments, secured a recording contract. The band did not last long and in April 1937 he formed a conventional big band that was an immediate success, thanks in part to melodic arrangements by **Jerry Gray**. The band made several records including 'Begin The Beguine', which was a huge popular success. Musically, Shaw's band was one of the best of the period and, during the first couple of years of its existence, included Johnny Best, **Cliff Leeman**, Les Robinson, **Georgie Auld**, **Tony Pastor** and **Buddy Rich**. During 1938 Shaw briefly had Holiday as the band's singer; but racial discrimination in New York hotels and on the band's radio shows led to a succession of disagreeable confrontations which eventually compelled the singer to quit. Other singers Shaw used were **Kitty Kallen** and **Helen Forrest**. Always uneasy with publicity and the demands of the public, Shaw abruptly folded the band late in 1939, but a featured role in the 1940 **Fred Astaire**-Paulette Goddard film, *Second Chorus*, brought another hit, 'Frenesi', and he quickly reformed a band. The new band included a string section and a band-within-a-band, the Gramercy Five. The big band included **Billy Butterfield**, **Jack Jenney**, **Nick Fatool** and **Johnny Guarnieri**. In the small group, Guarnieri switched from piano to harpsichord to create a highly distinctive sound. More successful records followed, including 'Concert For Clarinet', 'Summit Ridge Drive' and 'Special Delivery Stomp'. Shaw's dislike of celebrity caused him to disband once again, but he soon reformed only to be forced to fold when the USA entered the war. In 1942 he headed a band in the US Navy which included several leading jazzmen. After the war he formed a new band that featured **Roy Eldridge**, **Dodo Marmarosa**, **Barney Kessel**, **Chuck Gentry**, Stan Fishelson and other top musicians. This band, like all the others, was short-lived and during the rest of the 40s Shaw periodically formed bands only to break them up again within a few months. At the same time he also studied classical guitar and began to develop a secondary career as a writer. By the mid-50s he had retired from music and spent much of his time writing. He lived for a number of years in Spain but in the late 60s returned to the USA, where he continued to expand his writing career. In the 80s he reformed a band, under the direction of Dick Johnson, and performed at special concerts. In 1985 a film documentary, *Time Is All You've Got*, traced his career in detail. In June 1992 he appeared in London at a concert performance where **Bob Wilber** recreated some of his music.

During the late 30s and early 40s Shaw was set up as a rival to **Benny Goodman**, but the antagonism was a creation of publicists; in reality the two men were amicable towards one another. Nevertheless, fans of the pair were divided, heatedly arguing the respective merits of their idol. Stylistically, Shaw's playing was perhaps slightly cooler than Goodman's, although his jazz sense was no less refined. Like Goodman, Shaw was a technical marvel, playing with remarkable precision yet always swinging. His erratic bandleading career, allied as it was to a full private life - amongst his eight wives were some of Hollywood's most glamorous stars - militated against his ever achieving the same level of success as Goodman or many other bandleading contemporaries. Nevertheless, his bands were always musicianly and his frequent hiring of black musicians, including Holiday, Eldridge and **Oran 'Hot Lips' Page**, helped to break down racial barriers in music.

Selected compilations: *Artie Shaw Recreates His Great '38 Band* (1963), *The 1938 Band In Hi-Fi (1938)* (1979), *Swinging Big Bands, 1938-45, Volume 1* (1981), *Melody And Madness Vols. 1-5 (1938-39)* (1982), *This Is Artie Shaw* (1983), *Traffic Jam* (1985), *The Indispensable Artie Shaw Vols 1/2 (1938-39)* (1986), *The Indispensable Artie Shaw Vols 3/4 (1940-42)* (1986), *The Rhythmakers Vols 1-3 (1937-38)* (1987), *Thou Swell (1936-37)* (1988), *Gloomy Sunday* (Pickwick 1992), *Frenesi* (Bluebird 1992), *The Last Recordings, Rare And Unreleased* (S&R 1992), *Let's Go For Shaw* (1993), *Lets Go For Shaw* (Avid 1993).

Further reading: *The Trouble With Cinderella: An Outline Of Identity*, Artie Shaw.

Shaw, Arvell

b. 15 September 1923, St. Louis, Missouri, USA. Although he had previously studied other instruments, Shaw began playing bass while working with the Fate Marable band in the early 40s. Shortly after this, military service interrupted his career but soon after World War II ended he joined **Louis Armstrong**, a job which, on and off, lasted for a quarter of a century. First, he was with Armstrong's big band; he rejoined when the All Stars were formed in 1945, staying until 1953 (with a short break to study in Switzerland). In the mid-to-late 50s and in the 60s he made frequent return visits to Armstrong but found time for appearances with **Benny Goodman**, **Teddy Wilson** and others. After Armstrong's death in 1971, Shaw worked with a number of mainstream jazz artists, including **Buddy Tate**, **Dorothy Donegan** and **Earl Hines**, freelanced in the USA and Europe and then, in the 80s, re-entered the Armstrong fold by joining **Keith Smith**'s *Wonderful World Of Louis Armstrong* concert package. A solid and thoroughly dependable member of the rhythm section, Shaw is also an energetic and accomplished soloist whose playing always commands attention.

Albums: with Louis Armstrong *Satchmo At Symphony Hall* (1947), *Louis Armstrong Plays W. C. Handy* (1954), *Louis*

Armstrong At The Crescendo (1955), *The Many Faces Of Dorothy Donegan* (1975).

Shaw, Charles 'Bobo'

b. 15 September 1947, Pope, Mississippi, USA. Shaw studied with a string of drummers and also learned bass and trombone with Frank Mokuss. He played drums in R&B bands, backing soul saxophonist **Oliver Sain**, singers **Ike And Tina Turner** and bluesman **Albert King**. He moved to St. Louis, Missouri, and was a founder of BAG (**Black Artists Group**). There he met and played with altoist **Oliver Lake** as well as playing in the St. Louis Symphony Orchestra. In the early 70s he moved with other BAG members to Europe, where he played with **Anthony Braxton**, **Steve Lacy**, **Frank Wright** and **Alan Silva**. He calls his bands the Human Arts Ensemble or (more recently) the Red, Black & Green Solidarity Unit. In 1972 the Human Arts Ensemble made its debut recording with *Whisper Of Dharma*, followed a year later by *Under The Sun*, which featured Lake and **Lester Bowie** as guest artists. In 1974 Shaw moved to New York, and in the next few years recorded with **Frank Lowe** (*Fresh*, *The Flam*), Bowie (*Fast Last*, *Rope-A-Dope*) and Lake (*Heavy Spirits*). In 1977 he recorded a duo album with Bowie (*Bugle Boy Bop*), although this was not released until 1983. He also teamed up with Bowie's trombonist brother, **Joseph Bowie**, in a new line-up of the Human Arts Ensemble and in the next two years released *P'nk J'zz; Trio Performances Vol 1*, which featured guitarist James Emery (from **String Trio Of New York**); *Vol 2*, which featured Luther Thomas on alto and John Lindberg (also from STONY) on bass; and *Junk Trap*, which combined all five players. Shaw also played on two Human Arts Ensemble dates led by Thomas (*Funky Donkey Vol 1*, *Poem Of Gratitude*) and as a member of the St Louis Creative Ensemble, which played Europe in 1979 and recorded *I Can't Figure Out*. Since this burst of activity little has been heard from him, apart from appearances with **Marion Brown** and Bowie's punk-funk group **Defunkt**.

Albums: with the Human Arts Ensemble *Whisper Of Dharma* (1973), *Streets Of St Louis* (1974), with HAE *Under The Sun* (1975, rec. 1973), with Luther Thomas/HAE *Poem Of Gratitude* (70s), with Luther Thomas/HAE *Funky Donkey Vol 1* (1977), with HAE *P'nk J'zz* (1977), with HAE *Trio Performances Vols 1 and 2* (1978), with HAE *Junk Trap* (1978), with St Louis Creative Ensemble *I Can't Figure Out* (1979), with Lester Bowie *Bugle Boy Bop* (1983, rec. 1977).

Shaw, Eddie

b. 20 March 1937, Benoit, Mississippi, USA. Shaw grew up in neighbouring Greenville and learned to play clarinet and trombone before choosing the saxophone. He played with local jump-blues bands (including one led by **Ike Turner**) and sat in with **Muddy Waters** in 1957. Muddy hired him immediately and he moved to Chicago. Once there he associated with **Howlin' Wolf** and **Magic Sam**, and recorded with both. He also fronted his own band on vocals and saxophone. Eddie also ran the 1815 Club in Chicago, wrote and arranged songs for other artists, learned to play blues harmonica, and has recorded as bandleader for **Mac Simmons**' label, for Alligator's *Living Chicago Blues* project, and for the Isabel and Rooster companies.

Albums: *Have Blues - Will Travel* (1979), *Movin' And Groovin' Man* (1982), *Blues Is Good News* (1993).

Shaw, Eddie 'Vaan'

b. 8 November 1955, Greeville, Mississippi, USA. When **Howlin' Wolf**'s your babysitter and your father leads his band, it is hardly surprising if, like Vaan Shaw, you grow up to play the blues yourself. He spent his childhood in and around the band, learned the mechanics of guitar playing from **Magic Sam** and **Hubert Sumlin**, and actually backed Wolf at the tender age of 11, substituting for an absent Sumlin. The following year, he joined the houseband when his father bought the 1815 Club (renaming it Eddie's Place) and backed **Muddy Waters**, Wolf, **Freddie King** and **James Cotton**. After Wolf's death, Eddie Shaw formed the Wolf Gang with his former sidemen and Vaan as guitarist. His first album, *Morning Rain*, would have been more impressive if there had been less reliance upon standard Chicago fare. That was remedied by *The Trail Of Tears*, of which more than half consisted of songs written by Shaw *fils et père*.

Albums: *Morning Rain* (Wolf 1993), *The Trail Of Tears* (Wolf 1994).

Shaw, Ian

b. 2 June 1962, St. Asaph, North Wales. Shaw studied piano and music theory at Kings College, London, where he gained a Bachelor of Music in 1983. He later encountered **Mel Tormé** in Amsterdam, a stimulus which still informs his performances. In 1987 he returned to London, forming the soul/rock band Brave New World with keyboard player Adrian York. He appeared at **Ronnie Scott**'s, and toured Europe with virtuoso blues and jazz vocalist **Carol Grimes**. This association yielded 1990's *Lazy Blue Eyes*. He won a Perrier Award, was nominated Best British Jazz Singer by *The Guardian*, and guested on **Fairground Attraction**'s *First Of A Million Kisses*. In 1992 he released *Ghostsongs*, recorded at Ronnie Scott's. The set showcased Shaw's catholic taste from **Duke Ellington** to **Charles Mingus**, including a haunting interpretation of 'Danny Boy'. It captured his astounding vocal range, dipping into scat and occasionally applied as an additional instrument. Touring to promote the album, Shaw guested with **Kenny Wheeler** and **John Taylor,** and contributed to **Yello**'s *Zebra*. He became a staple of the London

jazz scene, sometimes playing alone at the piano, sometimes with full backing band, but always to packed houses. *Taking It To Hart*, a tribute to **Richard Rodgers** and **Lorenz Hart,** was released in 1995, featuring appearances by **Guy Barker**, **Mari Wilson**, **Iain Ballamy** and Carol Grimes. A 'big band' album *Setting Standards* and a first US tour are scheduled for 1995/6, with a **Joni Mitchell** tribute album also probable.

Albums: with Carol Grimes *Lazy Blue Eyes* (1990), *Ghostsongs* (1992), *Taking It To Hart* (1995).

Shaw, Marlina

b. Marlina Burgess, 1944, New Rochelle, New York, USA. Shaw was basically a cocktail lounge-type jazz singer who occasionally ventured onto the soul music charts. She began her career in 1963, and was discovered by **Chess Records** in 1966 while singing on the Playboy lounge circuit. On Chess's Cadet subsidiary, under the aegis of producer Richard Evans, she performed vocal counterparts of jazz hits such as 'Mercy Mercy Mercy' (number 33 R&B, number 58 pop) by **Cannonball Adderley** and 'Wade In The Water' by **Ramsey Lewis Trio**. Chess released two albums and a bunch of singles of Shaw before she left the company in 1968. For the next five years she performed periodically with **Count Basie**, and after signing with **Blue Note** in 1972 built a solidly-based jazz recording career. Her most popular album for the company was *Who Is This Bitch, Anyway?*, but her last Blue Note release in 1976, *Just A Matter Of Time*, saw a more disco-driven result that yielded a modest chart single, 'It's Better Than Walkin' Out' (number 74 R&B). A move to **Columbia** in 1977 got her biggest chart success with *Sweet Beginnings* and a hit single 'Go Away Little Boy' (number 21 R&B), a remake of **Steve Lawrence**'s 'Go Away Little Girl'. From an album for South Bay, *Let Me In Your Life*, she achieved her last chart single, 'Never Give Up On You' (number 91 R&B).

Selected albums: *Out Of Different Bags* (Cadet 1967), *Spice Of Life* (Cadet 1968), *From The Depths Of My Soul* (Blue Note 1973), *Who Is This Bitch Anyway?* (Blue Note 1975), *Just A Matter Of Time* (Blue Note 1976)**,** *Sweet Beginnings* (Columbia 1977), *Acting Up* (Columbia 1978), *Take A Bite* (Columbia 1979), *Let Me In Your Life* (South Bay 1983), *Love Is In Flight* (Polydor 1988).

Shaw, Pat, And Julie Matthews

Pat (b. 1 August 1958, South Yorkshire, England), and Julie (b. 2 April 1963, South Yorkshire, England) met while performing on the local folk circuit. After being brought together on a session by a local radio station, they continued to perform together occasionally. Matthews' background lay in her travels, writing songs and playing in bars in Europe. Shaw however had taken up teaching, but the two got back together on

Matthews' return home. In 1990 Matthews joined the **Albion Band**, as lead vocalist, with many of her compositions being used by the group. One such song, 'The Thorn Upon The Rose', was recorded in 1991 by **Mary Black** for her album, *Babes In The Wood*. Following the success of the song in Ireland and Japan, Matthews started to become recognised as a writer of note. In 1992 she left the Albion Band, and Shaw left her teaching job, the two now performing together full-time. By this time Shaw was already a sought after session singer. Shortly afterwards they released their first album, *As Long As I Am Able*. The following year saw the release of the highly acclaimed *Lies And Alibis*. All 12 songs featured were Matthews' originals, and the album was produced by **Clive Gregson**. The duo also featured on another 1993 release, *Intuition*. This album featured the talents of Shaw and Matthews, as well as four other women from South Yorkshire; Kate Rusby, Kathryn Roberts and Kathleen and Rosalie Deighton from the **Deighton Family**. The balance provided by the duo's voices, and Matthews' songs, suggests a bright future lays ahead.

Albums: *As Long As I Am Able* (1992), *Intuition* (1993), *Lies And Alibis* (Fat Cat 1993).

Shaw, Robert

b. 9 August 1908, Staffons, Texas, USA. One of the great Texas barrelhouse piano players, Shaw was raised on his father's cattle ranch. His mother played piano and guitar. From his mid-20s he started playing for local parties. Eventually he left home to work as an itinerant pianist in bordellos, juke-joints and barrelhouses throughout Texas and up as far as Kansas City, Missouri. In 1935 he settled in Austin, Texas working outside music running a food market, with occasional private party work, into the 70s. He played the Berlin Jazz Festival in 1974 and Montreux in 1975. Nat Hentoff referred to him as a 'gruff easeful blues singer telling stories that came out of his audience's lives.

Album: *Texas Barrelhouse Piano* (1980), *The Ma Grinder* (1993).

Shaw, Sandie

b. Sandra Goodrich, 26 February 1947, Dagenham, Essex, England. Discovered by singer **Adam Faith**, Shaw was taken under the imperious wing of his manager Eve Taylor and launched as a teenage pop star in 1964. Her first single, 'As Long As You're Happy', proved unsuccessful but the follow-up, an excellent reading of **Burt Bacharach** and **Hal David**'s '(There's) Always Something There To Remind Me' reached number 1 in the UK. A striking performer, known for her imposing height, model looks and bare feet, Shaw's star shone for the next three years with a series of hits, mainly composed by her songwriter/producer **Chris Andrews**. His style,

specializing in abrupt, jerky, oom-pah rhythms and plaintive ballads, served Sandie well, especially on the calypso-inspired 'Long Live Love', which provided her second UK number 1 in 1965. By the following year, Shaw's chart placings were slipping and Taylor was keen to influence her towards cabaret. Chosen to represent Britain in the 1967 Eurovision Song Contest, Shaw emerged triumphant with the Bill Martin/**Phil Coulter** composed 'Puppet On A String', which gave her a third UK number 1. After one further Martin/Coulter hit, 'Tonight In Tokyo', she returned to Andrews with only limited success. By 1969 she was back on the novelty trail with Peter Callender's translation of the French 'Monsieur Dupont'. Attempts to launch Shaw as a family entertainer were hampered by salacious newspaper reports and during the 70s, troubled by a failed marriage to fashion entrepreneur Jeff Banks, she effectively retired. In the early 80s she was rediscovered by **Heaven 17** offshoots **BEF**, and recorded a middling version of 'Anyone Who Had A Heart', previously a number 1 for her old rival **Cilla Black**. The Shaw resurgence was completed when she was heavily promoted by **Smiths**' vocalist **Morrissey**, one of whose compositions, 'Heaven Knows I'm Miserable Now' was clearly inspired by the title of Shaw's failed 60s single, 'Heaven Knows I'm Missing You Now'. With instrumental backing from the Smiths, Shaw enjoyed a brief chart comeback with 'Hand In Glove' in 1984. In 1986, she reached the lower regions of the UK chart with a cover of **Lloyd Cole**'s 'Are You Ready To Be Heartbroken?'. Her comeback album, on **Rough Trade**, featured songs by Morrissey, the Smiths and **Jesus And Mary Chain**.

Albums: *Sandie* (1965), *Me* (1965), *Puppet On A String* (1967), *Love Me, Please Love Me* (1967), *Reviewing The Situation* (1969), *Hello Angel* (1988). Compilations: *A Golden Hour Of Sandie Shaw - Greatest Hits* (1974), *20 Golden Pieces* (1986), *The Sandie Shaw Golden CD Collection* (1989), *The EP Collection* (1991), *The 64/67 Complete Sandie Shaw Set* (1993), *Nothing Less Than Brilliant: The Best Of Sandie Shaw* (Virgin 1994)

Further reading: *The World At My Feet*, Shaw, Sandie (1991).

Shaw, Thomas

b. 4 March 1908, Brenham, Texas, USA, d. 24 February 1977, San Diego, California, USA. Shaw was taught harmonica and guitar by relatives while still quite young, developing his blues style through his collaborations with more famous artists of the day, **Blind Lemon Jefferson** and **Ramblin' Thomas**. Having spent much of his youth travelling throughout Texas, he settled in California in 1934. There he continued his musical activities, appearing on radio and setting up his own club, which ran for many years. In the 60s, he became a minister at a San Diego church, but he was also taken up by the blues revival, and made his first recordings, in which the Jefferson influence was especially notable. He appeared at folk festivals and toured in Europe in 1972.

Album: *Born In Texas* (1974).

Shaw, Tommy

After **Styx** broke up in 1983 former vocalist Tommy Shaw embarked on a solo career. Signing to **A&M Records**, he released *Girls With Guns* the following year. This proved a big disappointment to Styx fans, who had high hopes for Shaw, and were not impressed with the strictly average melodic pop-rock on offer. The pomp and ceremony of old appeared to have vanished overnight. *What If* followed the same pattern and was another commercial disappointment. Moving to **Atlantic Records**, Shaw teamed up with ex-Charlie vocalist/guitarist Terry Thomas. This produced *Ambition* and marked a return to form, both in the standard of songwriting and the singer's delivery. Rather than build on this and develop a successful solo career, he declared his intention to become part of a band set-up once more. Teaming up with guitarist **Ted Nugent**, bassist Jack Blades (ex-**Night Ranger**) and drummer Michael Cartellone, he would go on to multi-platinum success as part of **Damn Yankees**.

Albums: *Girls With Guns* (A&M 1984), *What If* (A&M 1985), *Ambition* (A&M 1987).

Shaw, Woody

b. Herman Shaw II, 24 December 1944, Laurinburg, North Carolina, USA, d. 11 May 1989. Shaw was raised in Newark, New Jersey, where his father sang in a gospel group. Taking up the trumpet at the age of 11, he quickly attained a level of proficiency which allowed him to sit in with visiting jazzmen. He left school when he was 16 years old to work in New York with **Willie Bobo** in whose band he played alongside **Chick Corea** and **Joe Farrell**. He also met **Eric Dolphy**, recording with him on 1963's *Iron Man*. The following year Dolphy invited Shaw to join his European tour, but died before the trumpeter had arrived. Shaw decided to go to Europe anyway, and stayed for a while in France, playing with **Kenny Clarke**, **Bud Powell** and others. Back in the USA in the mid-60s he joined **Horace Silver**, recording *The Cape Verdean Blues* (1965) and *The Jody Grind* (1966) and also worked with **McCoy Tyner** and **Art Blakey**. In the late 60s and early 70s he was busy as a studio musician and to some extent his jazz reputation suffered through his absence from the scene. He began recording for the Muse label in 1974 and this heralded a revival of interest in his work. He again played with Corea and Blakey and his group backed **Dexter Gordon** on his return to the USA, recording *The Homecoming* (1976). In the early 80s Shaw's band was in constant flux and amongst the musicians he used were Teri Lyne Carrington and Larry Willis. In 1984 he was featured with the Paris

Reunion Band, appearing on two fine albums, *French Cooking* and *For Klook*. Shaw suffered periods of severe illness, mostly induced through problems of drug addiction. He was going blind when, early in 1989, he visited the Village Vanguard to hear **Max Roach**. On the way home, he appeared to stumble down the steps at a New York subway station and fell under an approaching train, which severed an arm. Though rushed to hospital, he remained in a coma and died three months later. Shaw's playing was filled with the crackling brilliance of a post-**Dizzy Gillespie** trumpeter and yet he had the warmth which characterized musicians such as **Clifford Brown** and **Freddie Hubbard**, in whose shadow he laboured. Given a slight shift in time, and a major change in his personal habits, Shaw could well have been one of the great names of contemporary jazz.

Selected albums: *Blackstone Legacy* (1971), *Cassandranite* (Muse 1972), *Song Of Songs* (1973), *The Moontrane* (1974), *Love Dance* (1976), *At The Berliner Jazztage* (1977), *Little Red's Fantasy* (1978), *Stepping Stones* (1978), *Rosewood* (1978), *Woody III* (1979), *The Iron Men* (1981, rec. 1977), *United* (1981), *Lotus Flower* (1982), *Master Of The Art* (1982), *Time Is Right* (Red 1983), *Setting Standards* (1985), *Woody Shaw With The Tone Jansa Quartet* (Timelss 1986), *Imagination* (Muse 1987), *Solid* (Muse 1987), *The Eternal Triangle* (1987), *In My Own Sweet Way* (In And Out 1989).

Shay, Dorothy

b. Dorothy Sims, 1923, Jacksonville, Florida, USA, d. 22 October 1978. A popular country style comedienne, she became known as the Park Avenue Hillbilly and regularly appeared on the **Spike Jones** radio series in 1947. She appeared in the 1951 film *Comin' 'Round The Mountain* and later made appearances on *The Waltons* television series. She recorded for **Columbia** and is perhaps best remembered for her 1947 recording of 'Feudin' And Fightin'' (from the Broadway musical *Laffing Room Only*), which became a number 4 hit in both the country and pop charts. She died in 1978 following a heart attack.

She

Female MC who debuted with 'Miss DJ (Rap It Up!)', on the Clappers Record label, produced by Dennis Weedon. However, she would go on to record under sundry other titles, including Ms DJ and her own name, Sheila Spencer. Before her break in the music world she had sung in Brooklyn choirs from the age of five, and trained as an actress. Her resumé is undoubtedly a varied one. She would later become a national figure via her role as Thomasina in NBC's soap, *Another World*. She also previously sung backing vocals for **Kurtis Blow**'s debut album, and was Muhammed Ali's cheerleader.

She Done Him Wrong

Mae West's second - and some say her best - film was adapted by screenwriters Harvey Thew, John White, and West herself from her own play, *Diamond Lil*, which was set in the late 19th century. The trio toned down the erotic element somewhat, but with West's laconic delivery and skin-tight gowns, wholesomeness was just not possible - and not even desirable. Ironically, as saloon hostess Lady Lou, she directed her first invitation to 'Come up and see me . . . ?' to Cary Grant ('Mr. Clean'), who played a federal agent masquerading as a church mission man intent on terminating her various nefarious activities. Among the accomplished cast were Noah Beery, Owen Moore, Gilbert Roland, Fuzzy Knight, Grace La Rue, and Rochelle Hudson. The songs came from various composers and included 'I Like A Guy What Takes His Time', 'Maisie', and 'Haven't Got No Peace Of Mind' (all with words and music by **Ralph Rainger**); 'Silver Threads Among The Gold' (Eben E. Rexford-Hart Pease Danks), 'I Wonder Where My Easy Rider's Gone' (**Shelton Brooks**), and 'Frankie And Johnny' (traditional). Directed by Lowell Sherman, *She Done Him Wrong* shocked and disgusted some sections of the public in 1933, but still took a remarkable $3 million at the box-office.

She Loves Me

This chamber musical set in Budapest in the mid-30s, was the first to be both produced and directed by **Harold Prince**. It was based on the play *Parfumerie*, by Miklos Laszlo, which had been filmed twice, as *The Shop Around The Corner* and *In The Good Old Summertime*. *She Loves Me* opened at the Eugene O'Neill Theatre in New York on 23 April 1963, with music and lyrics by **Jerry Bock** and **Sheldon Harnick**. Jose Masteroff's book concerns certain members of the sales staff at Maraczek's Parfumerie, particularly the shop's manager, Georg Nowack (Daniel Massey), and the new salesgirl, Amalia Balash (**Barbara Cook**). They bicker with each other all day long, little knowing that each is the other's penfriend. Georg is the first to realize that they have been pouring their hearts out to each other via the US Mail, but he keeps it to himself. He finally reveals the true situation - and his feelings for her - by presenting her with some 'Ice Cream' (vanilla), and then reading aloud one of the letters she has written to her 'correspondent', whom she always refers to as 'Dear Friend'. The charming and tender story was perfectly complemented by the score, which has become one of the most cherished of all Broadway musicals. The songs included 'Days Gone By', 'No More Candy', 'Tonight At Eight', 'I Don't Know His Name', 'Will He Like Me?', 'Dear Friend', 'Try Me', 'Ice Cream', 'She Loves Me', 'A Trip To The Library', 'Grand Knowing You', 'Twelve Days To Christmas'.

She Loves Me ran for 301 performances, and gained one **Tony Award** for featured actor (Jack Cassidy), but lost out in the remainder of the categories to the brash and brassy *Hello, Dolly!* The 1964 London production, with Anne Rogers, Gary Raymond, and the popular singer **Gary Miller**, lasted for nearly six months. In 1993, a 30th anniversary revival starring Judy Kuhn and Boyd Gaines, was welcomed with open arms by Broadway audiences starved of good, original American musicals. A 1994 West End production, starring Ruthie Henshall and John Gordon-Sinclair, also received a warm reception. It won a remarkable five **Laurence Olivier Awards**, and the London Critics Circle Award for best musical.

She Rockers

Comprising school mates Donna McConnell and Antonia Jolly, who formerly worked with Alison Clarkson (later **Betty Boo**) before that artist broke solo. Originally intending to become a news journalist and tennis pro respectively, their discovery of rap, particularly the work of **Run DMC**, **LL Cool J** and other B-boys, turned them onto the hip hop bug. They decided to form the band with Clarkson after seeing **Salt 'N' Pepa** play live at London's Astoria venue. They took their name from an extension of McConnell's stage name (She-Rock), and saw their debut recording, 'First Impressions', housed on the compilation *Known To Be Down*. Unlikely though they viewed it to be at the time, the track came to the attention of none other than Chuck D of **Public Enemy**. The result was a collaboration with **Professor Griff** called 'Give It A Rest', which also featured DJ Streets Ahead. However, on returning to England from the US, Clarkson chose the solo route leaving her former partners as a duo. Two singles, 'Jam It Jam' and 'Do Dat Dance', marked out their new territory - cultured hip-house. The latter was produced by no less than **Technotronic**. Their roots in pop, dance and rap were given equal billing on the attendant album, which brought a blend of mellow, often humourous raps, with an undertow of house music and the disco strains of **Chic**. There were conscious raps among allusions to their love life, 'How Sweet It Is' pointing out how violence at hip hop shows was overexposed compared to much greater outbreaks elsewhere. The set was neutered, they claimed, by pressure from their record company. They had wanted it to be a hardcore hip hip set. A public disclaimer about the album being only half good, and not having had any say on the track listing, did not help its sales profile.

Albums: *Rockers From London* (Jive 1990).

Shear, Jules

b. 7 March 1952, Pittsburgh, Pennsylvania, USA. Singer-songwriter Jules Shear recorded numerous

albums both solo and with groups beginning in the late 70s, and wrote for such artists as **Cyndi Lauper**, the **Bangles**, **Art Garfunkel** and **Olivia Newton-John**. Shear moved from Pittsburgh to Los Angeles in the 70s. His first recorded work was with the band Funky Kings in 1976, also featuring singer-songwriter Jack Tempchin, who had written previously with the **Eagles**. Two years later Shear fronted Jules And The Polar Bears, a pop group that critics lumped in with the emerging new wave movement. The group debuted with the excellent *Got No Breeding*, which featured some of Shear's finest work, most notably 'Lovers By Rote'. After one more album, however, they disbanded in 1980. Shear next surfaced with the solo *Watch Dog* in 1983 and released three further albums under his own name. He briefly fronted the band Reckless Sleepers in 1988, which released one album, but Shear has yet to make a major commercial impact. In 1988, **Iain Matthews** recorded an entire album of Shear compositions, *Walking A Changing Line*, for **Windham Hill Records**. It was alleged that many of the lyrics of Aimee Mann's *Whatever* in 1994 were directed to Shear, following the break-up of their relationship.
Albums: *Funky Kings* (1976), *Got No Breeding* (1978), *Fenetiks* (1979), *Watch Dog* (1983), *The Eternal Return* (1985), *Demo-itis* (1986), *Big Boss Sounds* (1988), *The Third Party* (1989).

Shearing, George

b. 13 August 1919, London, England. Shearing was born blind but started to learn piano at the age of three. After limited training and extensive listening to recorded jazz, he began playing at hotels, clubs and pubs in the London area, sometimes as a single, occasionally with dance bands. In 1940 he joined Harry Parry's popular band and also played with **Stéphane Grappelli**. Shortly after visiting the USA in 1946, Shearing decided to settle there. Although at this time in his career he was influenced by bop pianists, notably **Bud Powell**, it was a complete break with this style that launched his career as a major star. Developing the locked-hands technique of playing block-chords, and accompanied by a discreet rhythm section of guitar, bass, drums and vibraphone, he had a succession of hugely popular records including 'September In The Rain' and his own composition, 'Lullaby Of Birdland'. With shifting personnel, which over the years included **Cal Tjader**, **Margie Hyams**, **Denzil Best**, **Israel Crosby**, **Joe Pass** and **Gary Burton**, the Shearing quintet remained popular until 1967. Later, Shearing played with a trio, as a solo and increasingly in duo. Amongst his collaborations have been sets with the Montgomery Brothers, **Marian McPartland**, Brian Torff, **Jim Hall**, **Hank Jones** and **Kenny Davern** (on a rather polite dixieland selection). Over the years he has worked fruitfully with singers, including **Peggy Lee**,

Ernestine Anderson, **Carmen McRae**, and, especially, **Mel Tormé**, with whom he performed frequently in the late 80s and early 90s at festivals, on radio and record dates. Shearing's interest in classical music resulted in some performances with concert orchestras in the 50s and 60s, and his solos frequently touch upon the musical patterns of Claude Debussy and, particularly, Erik Satie. Indeed, Shearing's delicate touch and whimsical nature should make him an ideal interpreter of Satie's work. As a jazz player Shearing has sometimes been the victim of critical indifference and even hostility. Mostly, reactions such as these centre upon the long period when he led his quintet. It might well be that the quality of the music was often rather lightweight but a second factor was the inability of some commentators on the jazz scene to accept an artist who had achieved wide public acceptance and financial success. That critical disregard should follow Shearing into his post-quintet years is inexplicable and unforgivable. Many of his late performances, especially his solo albums and those with Torff, bassist Neil Swainson, and Tormé, are superb examples of a pianist at the height of his powers. Inventive and melodic, his improvisations are unblushingly romantic but there is usually a hint of whimsy which happily reflects the warmth and offbeat humour of the man himself.
Selected albums: *Great Britain's* (Savoy 1947 recordings), *Latin Escapade* (1956), *Velvet Carpet* (1956), *Black Satin* (1957), *Burnished Brass* (1958), with Peggy Lee *Americana Hotel* (1959), *Shearing On Stage* (1959-63), *White Satin* (1960), *San Francisco Scene* (1960), *The Shearing Touch* (1960), with the Montgomery Brothers *Love Walked In* (1961), *Satin Affair* (1961), *Nat 'King Cole' Sings/George Shearing Plays* (1962), *Jazz Concert* (1963), *My Ship* (1974), *Light, Airy And Swinging* (1974), *The Way We Are* (1974), *Continental Experience* (1975), with Stéphane Grappelli *The Reunion* (1976), *The Many Facets Of George Shearing* (1976), *500 Miles High* (MPS 1977), *Windows* (1977), *On Target* (1979), with Brian Torff *Blues Alley Jazz* (Concord 1979), *Getting In The Swing Of Things* (1979), *On A Clear Day* (1980), with Carmen McRae *Two For The Road* (Concord 1980), with Marian McPartland *Alone Together* (Concord 1981), with Jim Hall *First Edition* (Concord 1981), *An Evening With Mel Tormé And George Shearing* (1982), with Mel Tormé *Top Drawer* (1983), *Bright Dimensions* (1984), *Live At The Cafe Carlyle* (Concord 1984), *Grand Piano* (Concord 1985), with Tormé *An Elegant Evening* (1985), *George Shearing And Barry Treadwell Play The Music Of Cole Porter* (Concord 1986), *More Grand Piano* (Concord 1986), *Breakin' Out* (Concord 1987), *Dexterity* (Concord 1987), *A Vintage Year* (1987), with Ernestine Anderson *A Perfect Match* (Concord 1988), with Hank Jones *The Spirit Of '76* (Concord 1988), *Piano* (Concord 1989), *George Shearing In Dixieland* (Concord 1989), with Tormé *Mel And George 'Do' World War II* (1990), *I Hear A Rhapsody* (Telarc 1992). Compilations:

The Young George Shearing (1939-44) (1983), *The Best Of George Shearing* (MFP 1983), *White Satin - Black Satin* (Capitol 1991), *The Capitol Years* (Capitol 1991). Films: *The Big Beat* (1957).

Shearston, Gary

b. 9 January 1939, Inverell, New South Wales, Australia. This singer/songwriter was also proficient on guitar and harmonica. Shearston moved with his family to Sydney at the age of 12, after his father's farm was destroyed by drought. By the time Gary was 19 he was a professional singer performing traditional Australian music in pubs, clubs and on radio and television. In the late 50s Gary made his first recording, for the Festival label, and this was followed by a number of albums for **CBS** in the early to mid-60s. Two of these albums were described as 'among the best records of traditional music ever made in Australia'. In 1965, Shearston received an award for the best composition of the year when 'Sometime Lovin'' was covered by a number of artists including **Peter Paul And Mary**. In the mid-60s, together with **Martin Wyndham-Read**, he recorded a live album on the Australian Score record label, although CBS would not let Shearston appear on the album. In addition, Shearston had his own folk music television programme. He then travelled to the US in 1968 and lived there for the next four years. During the mid-70s Gary travelled to Britain, where he recorded two albums for **Charisma**. Shearston's one major hit in the UK came in 1974, when 'I Get A Kick Out Of You' made the Top 10. This single made Shearston the first Australian artist to have a simultaneous hit in Britain and Australia. Despite the long gap between albums he carried on and worked the folk clubs of Europe. Returning to Australia from England in 1988, Shearston was made a Deacon of the Anglican Church in December 1991.
Albums: *Folk Songs And Ballads Of Australia* (CBS 1964), *Songs Of Our Time* (CBS 1964), *Australian Broadside* (CBS 1965), *The Springtime It Brings On The The Shearing* (CBS 1965), *Bolters, Bushrangers And Duffers* (CBS 1966), *Gary Shearston Sings His Songs* (CBS 1966), *Abreaction* (Festival 1967), *Dingo* (Charisma 1974), *The Greatest Stone On Earth And Other Two Bob Wonders* (Charisma 1975), *Aussie Blue* (Larrikin 1989). Compilations: *Gary Shearston Revisited* (CBS 1975), *I Get A Kick Out Of You* (Pickwick 1976).

Shed Seven

York, England band Shed Seven comprise Rick Witter (b. c.1973; lead vocals), Tom Gladwin (b. c.1973; bass), Paul Banks (b. c.1973; guitar) and Alan Leach (b. c.1970; drums). Together they brought a flash of domesticity and anti-glamour to the independent scene of the mid-90s - their interests including slot machines, bad television (Banks allegedly writes songs while watching *Prisoner Cell Block H*) and cheap alcohol. There was a refreshingly parochial atmosphere to their profile

- best symbolised by the fact that Leach is the boyfriend of Witter's sister - despite the fact that their primary influences included **Happy Mondays** and **Stone Roses**. The only hint of celebrity, aside from Witter once coming second in a karaoke competition in Cyprus, involved their vocalist's dalliance with Donna Matthews from **Elastica**. However, as their recorded output demonstrated, and many critics suggested, it remained a thin line between level-headedness and mundanity. To their credit, Shed Seven were unconcerned with the trappings of cool, happily signing to a major, **Polydor Records**, and making their debut with 'Mark': 'We chose to put Polydor on the middle of our records - like the **Who** and the **Jam**, two of the best British bands ever. That's what we aspire to, not to some crap indie credibility'. After playing the *New Musical Express*' On Into 94 gig, they would make two appearances on *Top Of The Tops*, and score two Top 30 singles and a Top 20 album. The band was clearly at their best live, though, and their 1994 sell-out tours cemented a strong following.
Album: *Change Giver* (Polydor 1994).

Sheila

b. Anna Chancel, 16 August 1946, Paris, France. Some of her parents' humble earnings as confectioners in a city market were set aside for their daughter's ballet, piano and singing lessons which were not, perhaps, put to their intended use when she performed **Petula Clark** numbers with Les Guitars Brothers. During after-hours rehearsals in a local cinema, their repertoire broadened to embrace the **Elvis Presley**, **Johnny Hallyday** and **Brenda Lee** selections that dominated a 1962 appearance at a Gallic rock 'n' roll stronghold, Le Golf Druout where pop composer Claude Carrere asked Chancel to sing on his adaptation of **Tommy Roe**'s 'Sheila'. This debut also gave its vocalist a *nom de theatre*. Co-written by Carrere, her second independently-produced single, 'L'Ecole Est Fini', was a national hit, and numerous promotional slots on television established Sheila as an enduring star. Widespread copying of her hairstyle and wardrobe by schoolgirls encouraged the exploitation of associated 'Sheila merchandise' and the opening of a chain of Sheila boutiques. She was also the central character in the first of many movies with musical interludes that attended her astonishing string of French chart-toppers; among them 'Chaque Instant De Chaque Jour', 'C'est Toi Que J'aime' and translated covers of **Cher**'s 'Bang Bang' and **Wayne Fontana**'s 'Pamela Pamela'. In 1967, her rags-to-riches story was serialized in *France-Soir* and, by the 70s, tit-bits about her romantic entanglements were more intriguing to her ageing fans than her latest record.

Sheldon, Jack

b. 30 November 1931, Jacksonville, Florida, USA.

After studying trumpet as a child, Sheldon played professionally while still in his early teens. In the late 40s, now relocated in the Los Angeles area, he played with many leading west coast musicians, including **Art Pepper**, **Dexter Gordon** and **Wardell Gray**. He was also closely associated with comedian Lenny Bruce. In 1955 he was one of the first of the west coast school to record for the Pacific Jazz label. In the mid-50s he recorded with the **Curtis Counce** group, which included **Harold Land**, and later in the decade with Dave Pell and Pepper. He also toured with Gray, **Stan Kenton** and **Benny Goodman**. In the 60s Sheldon's natural wit brought him work as a stand-up comedian and he also took up acting, playing the lead in a US television series, *What Makes Sammy Run?* In the 70s he worked with various bands, big and small, including Goodman's, **Woody Herman**'s and **Bill Berry**'s and also led his own small bands for club and record dates. Sheldon's trumpet playing is deeply rooted in bebop but he ably adapts it to the mainstream settings in which he often works. His live appearances always include examples of his engaging singing style and his sparkling, frequently abrasive wit. Much less well-known internationally than his talent deserves, Sheldon has survived many problems, including drug addiction and alcoholism, which would have ended the careers of less durable men.

Albums: *The Jack Sheldon Quartet* (1954), *The Jack Sheldon Quintet* (1956), *The Curtis Counce Group* (1956), *You Get More Bounce With Curtis Counce* (1957), *Jack Sheldon And His Orchestra* i (1957), *Jack's Groove* (1957-59), *Art Pepper Plus Eleven* (1959), with Pepper *Smack Up* (1960), *Jack Sheldon And His Orchestra* ii (1962), *Jack Sheldon With Orchestra Conducted By Don Sebesky* (1968) with Bill Berry *Hello Rev* (1976), *Singular* (1980), *Angel Wings* (1980), *Playin' It Straight* (1980), *Stand By For The Jack Sheldon Quartet* (Concord 1983), *Blues In The Night* (Phontastic 1984), *Hollywood Heroes* (Concord 1988), with Ross Tomkins *On My Own* (Concord 1992).
Video: *In New Orleans* (Hendring 1990).

Shellac

Rock *enfant-terrible* Steve Albini (ex-**Big Black/Rapeman**) formed this USA trio on an informal basis in 1993. Bouyed by the attention garnered in the wake of his producing *In Utero* for **Nirvana**, Albini (velocity), Bob Weston (mass) and Todd Turner (time) issued 'The Rude Gesture A Pictorial History', the first of two limited-issue singles to appear on the trio's own label. It offered all the trademarks of Albini's previous groups - awkward time changes, thundering bass lines, screaming guitar and frantic vocals. Weston was ex-**Volcano Suns**, while Trainer had worked with **Rifle Sport** and **Breaking Circus**. 'Uranus' followed in similar, exciting fashion. A third single, 'The Admiral', came in a sleeve still showing Albini's caustic remarks referring to how it

should be designed. A different version of the 'A' side appeared on *At Action Park*, which developed Albini's distinctive style without subverting its power and direction. His work remains as challenging as ever.
Album: *At Action Park* (Touch And Go 1994).

Shelley, Pete

b. Peter McNeish, 17 April 1955, Leigh, Lancashire, England. When the **Buzzcocks** disbanded in 1981, Shelley soon embarked on a variety of solo projects. In fact, his solo history extended before, and during, the Buzzcocks career. As one of the Invisible Girls, he helped out on **John Cooper Clarke** albums while the Buzzcocks were still active. Around the same time he also launched his own independent label, Groovy. On this he released *Free Agents* (subtitled *Three Pounds And Three Pounds Thirty Three R.R.P.*, which was also its original price). This consisted primarily of tape loops and feedback, and general free-for-all improvisation. Meanwhile on New Hormones (the Buzzcocks original label) came *The Tiller Boys* EP, another of Shelley's pet projects. The second release on Groovy was *Sky Yen*, a solo album originally recorded by Shelley in 1974 using electronic instruments. Much akin to work by **Kraftwerk**, it prefaced the electro dance feel of his later solo work. However, it was 1982's *Homosapien*, a weighty slice of electro-pop concerning bisexuality, which marked the high point in Shelley's solo career. It was produced by Martin Rushent as a launch for his Generic label, and caused much discussion of Shelley's sexuality, and a re-examination of his Buzzcocks lyrics. *XL1* in 1983 was more tame, although it did boast the novelty of including a Sinclair computer programme that reproduced the lyrics. One review compounded matters by mentioning no less than five Buzzcocks titles in comparison, which was perhaps a trifle unfair. Again, it was produced by Rushent, this time with a predominantly disco feel. After 1986's *Heaven And The Sea* Shelley sought the comfort of a band again, and attempted to retain anonymity in Zip.
Albums: *Free Agents* (1980), *Sky Yen* (1980), *Homosapien* (1982), *XL1* (1983), *Heaven And The Sea* (1986).

Shelleyan Orphan

It was in 1980 that Caroline Crawley (vocals/clarinet) and Jemaur Tayle (acoustic guitar/vocals) first got together in their hometown of Bournemouth, England, and discovered they had a mutual appreciation of the poet Shelley. Consequently they took the name of their band from his poem, 'Spirit Of Solitude'. Neither of them could read or write music, or play any of their chosen instruments so, in 1982, Crawley quit her A-Level studies and they moved to London in search of a string section and oboist, with the intention of using these traditionally classical instruments along with the guitar and their two voices in a pop context. Inspired by **T-Rex**, **Nick Drake** and **Van Morrison**, the self-taught duo found their musicians and touted themselves around London, until in June 1984 they won a Kid Jensen BBC radio session. Following a baffling support to the **Jesus And Mary Chain** at the ICA, where their classical ensemble shocked the assembled crowd, they were swiftly signed up by **Rough Trade Records**. Two sweet and mellow singles followed, 'Cavalry Of Cloud' and 'Anatomy Of Love', both to ecstatic reviews, and after a memorable appearance on *The Tube* television programme, their controversial debut, *Helleborine*, was released in May 1987. Its swirling romanticism was promptly dubbed 'pretentious' by the music press, gaining Shelleyan Orphan the title of 'Pre-Raphaelite Fruitcakes'. The next two years were spent writing, recording and maturing their sound, and with the addition of more traditional rock instruments to their string orientated line-up, the band produced the more immediate and accessible *Century Flower*. The album was a significant step forward, using unusual time signatures and baroque instrumentation to spectacular effect. The richly harmonic 'Shatter' and superb 'Timeblind' were among the highlights. Supporting the **Cure** across Europe and America, they showed another side to their gentle image and betrayed a new found energy and exuberance.

Albums: *Helleborine* (Rough Trade 1987), *Century Flower* (Rough Trade 1989), *Humroot* (1993).

Shells

This US Brooklyn-based R&B vocal group was formed in 1957. The Shells were noted for their typical New York doo-wop stylings, in which the use of a prominent bass, piercing falsetto, and strong vocal riffing supported a romantic lead, made for one of the great folk acts of the 50s. The group cut their first record, 'Baby Oh Baby' in 1957, which did not do anything upon its release on the local Johnson label. The Shells broke up, but the following year lead Nathaniel 'Little Nate' Bouknight formed a new ensemble bringing in Bobby Nurse (first tenor), Shade Randy Alston (second tenor), Gus Geter (baritone), and Danny Small (bass). Subsequent records did nothing, but as a result of the resurgence of doo-wop on the charts in the early 60s from the promotion efforts of record collectors Wayne Stierle and Donn Fileti, the career of the Shells was far from dead. Stierle and Fileti began promoting 'Baby Oh Baby' in 1960 and was able to make it a Top 20 hit on the national pop charts (on *Cash Box*'s R&B chart it went to number 11). The group reformed and Stierle started acting as producer coming out with some great sides, notably two excellent ones with new lead Ray Jones, 'Happy Holiday' (1962) and 'Deep In My Heart' (1962). But the Shells could not hit the charts again and broke up. In 1966, Stierle got the group together for one last **a cappella** session using the four remaining members without a lead.

Compilations: *Acappela Session With The Shells* (1972), *The Greatest Hits Of The Shells* (1973), *Baby Oh Baby: Golden Classics* (1989).

Shelter Records

Founded in 1969 by record producer Denny Cordell-Laverack (b. 1 August 1943, Argentina, d. 18 February 1995, Dublin, Eire) and performer **Leon Russell**. Cordell had already achieved notable success with his work for **Procol Harum** and **Joe Cocker**, and it was through his relationship with Cocker that the idea for the label evolved. Russell had written 'Delta Lady', Cocker's major international hit, and interest in its composer resulted in his debut album, Shelter's first major release. The label, which was based in Leon's hometown, Tulsa, originally concentrated on artists within its immediate circle. The catalogue included **J.J. Cale** and **Don Nix**, two long-standing Russell associates, the former became one of the company's most successful acts. Blues artist **Freddie King** was another important signing, but Russell's subsequent departure robbed Shelter of a vital asset. They did acquire the **Dwight Twilley** Band and, more crucially, **Tom Petty And The Heartbreakers**, but although the latter group became immensely popular, their period with Shelter was marred by litigation. Despite a comparative lull during the 80s, the label is now actively re-promoting its considerable back catalogue by way of licensing deals.

Shelton, Anne

b. Patricia Sibley, 10 November 1923, Dulwich, London, England, d. 31 July 1994, East Sussex, England. One of the most important and popular of UK popular singers, Anne Shelton came to prominence as the 'Forces sweetheart' during World War II and remained a fondly-regarded figure thereafter. She made her first BBC radio broadcast on 30 May 1940 in *Monday Night At Eight*, in which she sang 'Let The Curtain Come Down'. Her performance was heard by top UK bandleader **Bert Ambrose**, who signed her to sing with his band, and with whom she appeared on radio in *School Uniform*. Her own radio show, *Introducing Anne*, aimed mainly at British troops in the North African Desert, ran for four years, and she co-hosted *Calling Malta* with comedy actor Ronald Shiner; the programme was the only link with British troops on the Island during the air bombardment and siege during the early months of 1942. In that same year, Shelton started her recording career, and in 1944 had an enormous hit with her signature tune, 'Lili Marlene', a German song which was equally popular with the armed forces of 'both sides', and to which UK songwriter **Tommie Connor** added an English lyric. Also in 1944, she was one of the UK 'guest' vocalists who sang in concerts and on broadcasts with the American Band of the Supreme Allied Command and the American Band of the Allied Expeditionary Force, directed by **Glenn Miller**. Shelton also worked on radio with **Bing Crosby**. She appeared in several films, a mixture of musicals and comedies, including **Miss London Ltd.**, *Bees In Paradise*, and *King Arthur Was A Gentleman* (each starring diminutive comedian Arthur Askey) and *Come Dance With Me* (with comedians Derek Roy and Max Wall). After the war, she toured the UK variety circuit, and in 1949 updated her wartime hit by recording 'The Wedding Of Lilli Marlene'. In the same year she had two US hits with 'Be Mine' and 'Galway Bay', and in 1951, became the first British artist to tour the USA coast to coast, staying there for almost a year. In the UK she appeared extensively on radio and television during the 50s, and had several successful records, including 'I Remember The Cornfields', 'My Yiddishe Momma', 'Once In A While', ' I'm Praying To St. Christopher', 'Arrivederci Darling', 'Seven Days', 'Lay Down Your Arms' (a Swedish song with an English lyric by **Paddy Roberts**, which spent several weeks at the top of the UK chart), and 'Village Of Bernadette'. Her last chart entry, in 1961, was 'Sailor', a song of Austrian origin, which was a UK number 1 for **Petula Clark**. Albums around this time included *The Shelton Sound*, which contained impressive readings of standards such as 'Happiness Is Just A Thing Called Joe', 'Tangerine' and 'I'll Never Smile Again'. Throughout her career she worked with the cream of musical directors, including **Percy Faith**, **Wally Stott**, **Stanley Black**, **George Melachrino**, Frank Cordell, **Ken Mackintosh**, **Robert Farnon**, **Reg Owen**, **David Rose**, **Jerry Gray** and many more. In later years Shelton continued to feature on television and tour various parts of the world, including the UK, Europe, USA and Hong Kong. In 1978 she appeared in cabaret when 1,200 US veterans revisited the the D-Day Normandy beaches, and in the following year, performed one of her most popular 40s songs, 'I'll Be Seeing You', in John Schlesinger's film *Yanks*, which starred Richard Gere. In 1980 she sang 'You'll Never Know' for the Queen Mother on the occasion of her 80th birthday, and during the rest of the decade took part in charity and reunion affairs in aid of the British Legion and British Services organizations. These included occasions such as the 40th anniversary of D-Day, when she sang on UK television with a contemporary 'Glenn Miller' Band, and the 50th anniversary of the start of World War II. Anne Shelton also held the important post of Entertainments Officer for the Not Forgotten Association, which looks after disabled ex-servicemen and women from as far back as World War I. In 1990 she was awarded the OBE for services to the Association, and in the same year, her husband, Lieutenant Commander David Reid, died. They had met when she was only 17 years of age.

Selected albums: *Favourites Volumes 1 and 2* (Decca 1955), *The Shelton Sound* (Philips 1958), *Songs From Her Heart* (Philips 1959), *Anne* (ACL early 60s), *Captivating Anne* (Encore early 60s), *Anne Shelton Showcase* (Philips 1961), *A Souvenir Of Ireland* (Philips 1962), *My Heart Sings* (Wing 1967), *Irish Singalong* (Fontana late 60s), *The World Of Anne Shelton* (1971), *I'll Be Seeing You* (Decca 1977), *I'll Be There* (Decca 1977), *The Anne Shelton Collection* (Encore 1979), *Anne Shelton's Sentimental Journey* (President 1982), *Sing It Again, Anne* (President 1983), *Anne Shelton Sings With Ambrose And His Orchestra* (Recollections 1984), *The Magic Of Anne Shelton* (MFP 1984), *EMI Years* (1990), *Wartime Memories* (EMI 1993), with Ambrose and his Orchestra *Let There Be Love* (1994), *Lili Marlene* (ASV Living Era 1995).

Shelton, Ricky Van

b. 1952, Grit, near Lynchburg, Virginia, USA. Shelton was raised in a church-going family and he learned to love gospel music. His brother worked as a musician and through travelling with him, he also acquired a taste for country music. He worked as a pipefitter but his soon-to-be wife, Bettye, realized his singing potential and, in 1984, suggested that they went to Nashville where she had secured a personnel job. In 1986 he impressed producer Steve Buckingham during a club performance, and his first recording session yielded a US Top 30 country hit in 'Wild-Eyed Dream'. He then made the country Top 10 with one of his best records, the dramatic story-song, 'Crimes Of Passion'. In 1987 he had a US country number 1 by reviving a song from a **Conway Twitty** album, 'Somebody Lied'. In 1988 he had another number 1 by reviving **Harlan Howard**'s song, 'Life Turned Her That Way', which, unlike **Merle Tillis**, he performed in its original 4/4 tempo. His revival of an obscure **Roger Miller** song, 'Don't We All Have The Right', also went to number 1, thus giving him five country hits from his first album. Since then, he has had US country number 1's with revivals of 'I'll Leave This World Loving You', 'From A Jack To A King' and a new song, 'Living Proof'. Although Shelton has much in common with his hard-nosed contemporaries, he succumbed to a middle-of-the-road album of familiar Christmas songs. He recorded a duet of 'Sweet Memories' with **Brenda Lee**, whilst 'Rockin' Years' with **Dolly Parton** was a number 1 country single in 1991. To help his career, Shelton's wife has been studying law, whilst he knows that he must conquer his fear of flying. In 1992, Shelton recorded an album of semi-spiritual material, *Don't Overlook Salvation*, as a gift to his parents, before scoring more hits with the new recordings included on *Greatest Hits Plus*.

Albums: *Wild-Eyed Dream* (1987), *Loving Proof* (1988), *Ricky Van Shelton Sings Christmas* (1989), *Ricky Van Shelton III* (1990), *Backroads* (1991), *Don't Overlook Salvation* (1992), *Greatest Hits Plus* (1992), *A Bridge I Didn't Burn* (1993), *Love And Honor* (Columbia 1994).

Videos: *Where Was I* , *Live* (1993), *To Be Continued...* (1993).

Shelton, Roscoe

b. 22 August 1931, Lynchburg, Tennessee, USA. Based in Nashville, Shelton with his high tenor voice made his mark in the mid-60s with a style that reflected both gospel and country music influences and modestly rode the popularly for southern-style deep soul. Shelton served a long apprenticeship singing for the Fireside Gospel Singers and more importantly for the famed Fairfield Four, before recording blues for Excello in the 50s. For John Richbourg's Sound Stage 7 operation, he released two deep-soul ballads, 'Strain On My Heart' (number 25 R&B, 1965) and 'Easy Going Fellow' (number 32 R&B, 1965), both written by New Orleans Allen Orange. An appealing album followed, *Soul In His Music, Music In His Soul*, which featured more fine compositions of Orange. Shelton, however, could not sustain his career despite later recording some outstanding songs, notably **Dan Penn**'s 'There's A Heartbreak Somewhere'.
Album: *Music In His Soul, Soul In His Music* (Sound Stage 7 1966). Compilation: *Strain On Your Heart* (Charly 1987).

Shenandoah (Stage Musical)

This musical was based on the critically acclaimed movie of the same name which starred James Stewart and was released in 1965. James Lee Barrett, the author of the screenplay, collaborated with Philip Rose and Peter Udell on the libretto for the stage adaptation which opened at the Alvin Theatre in New York on 7 January 1975. Set in the Shenandoah Valley at the time of the American Civil War, the strongly anti-war story concerns a widowed Virginian farmer, Charlie Anderson (John Cullum), who refuses to allow the North versus South conflict to intrude upon his life until some Yankee troops abduct his youngest son (Joseph Shapiro) because he is wearing a Rebel cap. Several members of Anderson's family are killed in tragic circumstances in the days that follow. The score, by Peter Udell (lyrics) and Gary Geld (music), had a rousing 'wide open spaces' feel about it, with numbers such as 'Raise The Flag Of Dixie', 'I've Heard It All Before', 'Why Am I Me', 'Over The Hill', 'The Pickers Are Comin'', 'Meditation', 'We Make A Beautiful Pair', 'Freedom', 'Violets And Silverbells', 'Papa's Gonna Make It Alright', and 'Meditation'. Two of the most appealing numbers were the exuberant 'Next To Lovin' (I Like Fightin')', and the tender ballad 'The Only Home I Know'. It is sometimes said that *Shenandoah*'s remarkably long run of 1,050 performances owed something to the feelings of revulsion towards war in general - and Vietnam in particular - that were prevalent in America around that time. At any rate, the show won **Tony Awards** for its book, and for John Cullum's fine, sensitive performance. He recreated his original role when *Shenandoah* was revived for a limited period on Broadway in 1989. In 1994, a 20th anniversary production was presented by the Goodspeed Opera House in Connecticut.

Shep And The Limelights

This R&B vocal group came from New York, New York, USA. James Sheppard (b. c.1936, Queens, New York, USA, d. 24 January 1970) was lead and songwriter successively for two R&B groups, the Heartbeats and Shep and the Limelights. He created the first 'song cycle' (i.e.; a string of songs constituting a musical and literary unit) in rock 'n' roll. With the Limelights he got his only Top 10 pop success with 'Daddy's Home' making him a one-hit-wonder. But that song was part of a long cycle of songs, among the most distinctive being 'A Thousand Miles Away' (US R&B number 5 and pop Top 60 in 1956) and '500 Miles To Go' (1957) recorded with the Heartbeats, and 'Daddy's Home' (US R&B number 4 and pop number 2 in 1961), 'Ready For Your Love' (US pop Top 50 in 1961), 'Three Steps From The Altar' (US pop Top 60 in 1961), 'Our Anniversary' (US R&B number 7 in 1962), and 'What Did Daddy Do' (1962). The song-cycle first emerged in the 19th century as part of the German *lied* tradition, and many critics have thought that the **Beatles** with their *Sgt. Pepper's Lonely Heart's Club Band* from 1967 had created the first rock 'n' roll song cycle. The Heartbeats were formed in New York City in 1953, and first recorded the following year. Members on the first record were James Sheppard (tenor/baritone lead), Albert Crump (first tenor), Vernon Seavers (baritone), Robby Tatum (baritone), and Wally Roker (bass). The group distinguished itself with smooth tight harmony and a knack for creating great nonsense vocal riffs. Their sound was the ultimate in romantic doo-wop balladry. In 1960 the group broke up, and the following year Sheppard formed a new group, Shep And The Limelights, with two veterans of the New York doowop scene, first tenor Clarence Bassett and second tenor Charles Baskerville. A rarity among doowop groups, using no bass and relying on two-part harmony, Shep and the Limelights magnificently continued the great smooth romantic sound of the Heartbeats, albeit with less flavourful harmonies. The group broke up in 1966. Sheppard was shot dead on 24 January 1970. Bassett continued singing, firstly in the **Flamingos**, and later in Creative Funk. Wally Roker became a successful executive in the music business.
Album: *Our Anniversary* (1962), Compilations: *Echoes Of The Rock Era* (1972), with the Heartbeats *The Best Of The Heartbeats Including Shep & The Limelights* (1990).

Shepard, Jean

b. Imogene Shepard, 21 November 1933, Pauls Valley, Oklahoma, USA. Shepard was one of 11 children in a family, which moved to Visalia, California in 1946. Shepard learned to sing by listening to **Jimmie Rodgers**' records on a wind-up Victrola. She joined the Melody Ranch Girls, in which she played string bass and sang, and recorded for **Capitol** while still at school. The record was not successful but she subsequently played on the same bill as **Hank Thompson**, who reminded Capitol of her talent. In 1953 a single for the Korean war, 'Dear John Letter', with a narration from **Ferlin Husky**, topped the US country charts for 23 weeks. Because she was under 21, she could not legally leave the State on her own and the problem was making Husky her guardian. Shepard followed 'Dear John' with 'Forgive Me, John' while the original was satirized by **Stan Freberg**. Shepard had further country hits with 'Satisfied Mind' and 'Beautiful Lies' and she has been a regular member of the *Grand Ole Opry* since 1955. She worked with **Red Foley** from 1955-57 on his television show, *Ozark Jubilee*. Her 1956 *Songs Of A Love Affair* was a concept album, one side from the single woman's view, the other from the wife's. She was married to **Hawkshaw Hawkins**, who was killed in 1963 in the plane crash which also took the lives of **Patsy Cline** and **Cowboy Copas**. At the time Shepard was eight months pregnant with their second child. She returned to country music in 1964 with 'Second Fiddle To An Old Guitar' and she named her road band, The Second Fiddles. She also had success with 'Happy Hangovers To You', 'If Teardrops Were Silver', and two duets with Ray Pillow, 'I'll Take The Dog' and 'Mr. Do-It-Yourself'. Shepard was one of the first artists to be produced by crossover producer Larry Butler. In the 70s, she did well on the US country charts with **Bill Anderson**'s songs, 'Slippin' Away', 'At The Time', 'The Tips Of My Fingers' and 'Mercy' and recorded an album of his songs, *Poor Sweet Baby*. In 1975 she recorded a tribute to Hawkshaw Hawkins, 'Two Little Boys', which was written by their sons. Shepard was opposed to **Olivia Newton-John**'s award from the Country Music Association and she helped to found the Association Of Country Music Entertainers to 'keep it country'. To the public, it looked like sour grapes, especially as she had recorded 'Let Me Be There' and several pop hits. In recent years Shepard has recorded duets with **Gerry Ford**, and often plays UK country clubs, accompanied by her guitarist/husband, Benny Birchfield.

Albums: *Songs Of A Love Affair* (1956), *Lonesome Love* (1959), *This Is Jean Shepard* (1959), *Got You On My Mind* (1961), *Heartaches And Tears* (1962), *Lighthearted And Blue* (1964), *It's A Man Everytime* (1965), with Ray Pillow *I'll Take The Dog* (1966), *Many Happy Hangovers* (1966), *Hello Old Broken Heart* (1967), *Heart, We Did All That We Could* (1967), *Your Forevers Don't Last Very Long* (1967), *A Real Good Woman* (1968), *Heart To Heart* (1968), *Seven Lonely Days* (1969), *I'll Fly Away* (1969), *A Woman's Hand* (1970), *Declassified Jean Shepard* (1971), *Just As Soon As I Get Over Loving You* (1972), *Just Like Walking In The Sunshine* (1972), *Here And Now* (1971), *Slippin' Away* (1973), *Poor Sweet Baby* (1975), *For The Good Times* (1975), *I'm A Believer* (1975), *The Best Of Jean Shepard* (1975), *Mercy, Ain't Love Good* (1976), *I'll Do Anything It Takes* (1978), *Slippin' Away* (1982).

Shepherd Sisters

A quartet consisting of sisters Martha, Mary Lou, Gayle and Judy Shepherd, this group is best-remembered for the 1957 Top 20 hit 'Alone (Why Must I Be Alone)'. Hailing from Middletown, Ohio, USA, the girls sang in four-part harmony and were originally called the La-La Quartet when a booking agent discovered them. They were signed to the small Melba Records with no success. The label's owner, Morty Craft, next gave the sisters a song he had written, 'Alone', which he placed on his Lance label. The single, an upbeat, if melancholy number, reached number 18 in the US chart and number 14 in the UK. The Shepherd Sisters recorded further singles for such labels as **MGM** and United Artists without any luck. 'Alone' was later covered by the **Four Seasons**, who had a moderate hit with it in the 60s.

Shepherd, Dave

b. 7 February 1929, London, England. In the years following World War II, Shepherd took up the clarinet and quickly developed into one of the UK's most respected and admired musicians. An eclectic performer, ranging from Dixieland through most aspects of the mainstream to the fringes of bop, he has played with many British and American musicians. These include artists as diverse as **Freddy Randall** and **Billie Holiday**. Despite a short spell in the USA in the mid-50s and appearances at international festivals, Shepherd's career has centred on the UK and he works regularly with the Pizza Express All Stars, with **Digby Fairweather**, **Roy Williams**, **Len Skeat** and others. A superbly professional musician, Shepherd's ability to recreate the immaculate styling of **Benny Goodman** has led to an unfair tendency to narrow the focus of critical attention. In fact, when allowed free rein to his talent, he consistently demonstrates unfailing swing and a quality of musical elegance conspicuously absent in many better-known players.

Albums: *Shepherd's Delight* (1969), *Freddy Randall/Dave Shepherd Live At Montreux* (1973), *Benny Goodman Classics* (1975), *Dixieland Classics* (1976), *Airmal Special* (Chevron 1984), *Tribute To Benny Goodman* (Music Masters 1992).

Shepp, Archie

b. 24 May 1937, Fort Lauderdale, Florida, USA. Shepp was raised in Philadelphia. While studying dramatic literature at college he began playing on various instruments including the alto saxophone. His first professional engagement was on clarinet and he later played tenor saxophone with R&B bands. Settling in New York he tried to find work as an actor but was obliged to make a living in music, playing in Latin bands. He also played jazz with **Cecil Taylor**, **Bill Dixon**, **Don Cherry**, **John Tchicai** and others during the early 60s. With Cherry and Tchicai he was co-leader of the New York Contemporary Five. Shepp's musically questing nature drew him into the orbit of **John Coltrane**, with whom he established a fruitful musical relationship. Through Coltrane, Shepp was introduced to **Bob Thiele** of **Impulse! Records** and began recording under his own name for the label. Shepp's collaborations with Coltrane included an appearance at the 1965 *Down Beat* Festival in Chicago. That same year he appeared at the Newport Festival and had a play staged in New York. Although closely associated with the free jazz movement of the 60s, Shepp's music always included elements that were identifiably rooted in earlier forms of jazz and blues and he was very conscious of the importance of the music's roots. In an article in *Down Beat*, he wrote of the *avant garde*, 'It is not a movement, but a state of mind. It is a thorough denial of technological precision and a reaffirmation of *das Volk.*' With his name and reputation established by 1965, Shepp embarked upon a period of successful tours and recordings. He was busily writing music and occasionally stage plays, many of which carried evidence of his political convictions and concern over civil rights issues. At the end of the 60s he played at the Pan African Festival in Algiers, recorded several albums during a brief stop-over in Paris, then returned to the USA, where he became deeply involved in education, teaching music and literature, and was eventually appointed an associate professor at the University of Massachusetts. Over the next decade Shepp expanded his repertoire, incorporating aspects of jazz far-removed from his earlier freeform preferences, amongst them R&B, rock, blues and bop. Some of his recordings from the late 70s and early 80s give an indication of his range: they include improvised duo albums with **Max Roach**, sets of spirituals and blues with **Horace Parlan** and tribute albums to **Charlie Parker** and **Sidney Bechet**. In the 80s Shepp had matured into an all-round jazz player, impossible to pigeon-hole but capable of appealing to a wide audience through the heart and the mind. Although he has added the soprano saxophone to his instrumental arsenal, Shepp still concentrates on tenor, playing with a richly passionate tone and developing commanding solos shot through with vigorous declamatory phrases that emphasize his dramatic approach.

Selected albums: *Archie Shepp-Bill Dixon Quartet* (1962), *Archie Shepp And The New York Contemporary Five* (1963), *Four For Trane* (1964), *Fire Music* (Impulse 1965), *On This Night* (1965), *New Thing At Newport* (Impulse 1965), *Archie Shepp Live In San Francisco* (1966), *Mama Too Tight* (1966), *Freedom* (JMY 1968), *The Way Ahead* (1968), *Yasmina & Poem For Malcolm* (Affinity 1969), *Blase* (Charly 1970), *Attica Blues* (1972), *Montreux One/Two* (1975), *There's A Trumpet In My Soul* (Freedom 1975), *A Sea Of Faces* (1975), *Steam* (Enja 1976), *Montreaux One* (Freedom 1976), *Hi Fly* (1976), *Ballads For Trane* (Denon 1977), *On Green Dolphin Street* (Denon 1977), *Goin' Home* (1977), *Day Dream* (Denon 1978), with Abdullah Ibrahim *Duet* (Denon 1978), *Perfect Passions* (West Wind 1978), with Max Roach *The Long March* (1979), with Roach *Sweet Mao* (c.1979), *Lady Bird* (Denon 1979), *Bird Fire* (West Wind 1979), *The Long March Part 1* (Hat Art 1980), *Trouble In Mind* (1980), *Tray Of Silver* (Denon 1980), *I Know About The Life* (1981), *My Man* (1981), *Looking At Bird* (Steeplechase 1981), *Soul Song* (Enja 1982), *Mama Rose* (Steeplechase 1982), *African Moods* (1984), *I Know About the Life* (Sackville 1984), *Down Home In New York* (Soul Note 1984), *Live On Broadway* (Soul Note 1985), *The Fifth Of May* (1987), *Reunion* (L&R 1988), with Chet Baker *In Memory Of* (1988), *First Set* (52 Rue Est 1988), *Second Set* (52 Rue Est 1988), *Splashes* (L&R 1988), *Lover Man* (Timeless 1988), *In Memory Of First And Last Meeting 1988* (L&R 1989), *Art Of The Duo* (Enja 1990), *I Didn't Know About You* (Timelss 1991), *Black Ballad* (Timelss 1993).

Sheppard, Andy

b. 20 January 1957, Bristol, Avon, England. Sheppard attempted to learn saxophone at school, but was told he would have to take up clarinet first. In disgust he bought a guitar instead, but began on tenor saxophone after hearing **John Coltrane**. He also played the flute and sang solo in the choir while at school. He later discovered that he had perfect pitch, and only learned to read music in his late 20s. He took up the soprano under the influences of **Steve Lacy** and alcohol, having sold his tenor to a friend when drunk. Before moving to London Sheppard played with Sphere (not to be confused with the US band of the same name). He also played in Klaunstance, then spent two years in Paris working with Laurent Cugny's big band, Lumiere, and Urban Sax. Returning to the UK he played with Paul Dunmall and **Keith Tippett**. In early 1987 Sheppard formed his own small band, recording two acclaimed albums and undertaking several successful tours. He also became a regular performer in bands led by **Carla Bley**, **Gil Evans** and **George Russell**. In 1990 he set up the Soft On The Inside big band, which produced an album and a video, and he also recorded an acclaimed set of duo improvisations with Tippett. Since early 1991 Sheppard has run an electric small group, In Co-Motion (featuring the fine trumpeter Claude Deppa), alongside the big band, and he recently composed a piece for ice-dancers Torville and Dean. He also played in an occasional trio with Bley and **Steve Swallow** (producer on most of his albums). Sheppard is one of the most assured and versatile (and least flashy) saxophonists on the scene today.

Albums: *Andy Sheppard* (Antilles 1987), with Sphere *Sphere* (1988), *Present Tense* (1988), *Introductions In The Dark* (Antilles 1989), *Soft On The Inside* (Antilles 1990), with Keith Tippett *66 Shades Of Lipstick* (1990), *In Co-Motion* (Antilles 1991), *Rhythm Method* (Blue Note 1993), *Delivery Suite* (Blue Note 1994).

Sheppard, T.G.

b. William Browder, 20 July 1944, Humboldt, Tennessee, USA. Sheppard is a nephew of old-time country performer, Rod Brasfield, and his mother was a piano teacher who gave him lessons. Sheppard began his professional musical career in Memphis in the early 60s working as a backup vocalist for **Travis Wammack** and then performing as Brian Stacey, having a regional hit with 'High School Days'. After his marriage in 1965, Sheppard became a record promoter for **Stax** and **RCA**. In 1974, he was signed by **Motown**'s country arm, Melodyland, and had two number 1 country records with 'The Devil In The Bottle' and 'Trying To Beat The Morning Home'. He took his name from The German Shepherd dogs but many have thought his name represents The Good Shepherd. Sheppard merged his Memphis soul background with country music, which included revivals of the **Four Tops**' 'I Can't Help Myself' and **Neil Diamond**'s 'Solitary Man'. Over at Warners, Sheppard had a US country number 1 with 'Last Cheater's Waltz' and followed it with another 10. In 1981 Sheppard made the US Top 40 with 'I Loved 'Em Every One'. His duets include 'Faking Love' with Karen Brooks, 'Home Again' with **Judy Collins** and 'Make My Day' with Clint Eastwood.

Albums: *T.G.Sheppard* (1975), *Motels And Memories* (1976), *Solitary Man* (1976), *T.G.* (1978), *Daylight* (1978), *Three-Quarters Lonely* (1979), *Smooth Sailin'* (1980), *I Love 'Em All* (1981), *Finally* (1982), *Perfect Stranger* (1982), *Slow Burn* (1983), *One Owner Heart* (1984), *Livin' On The Edge* (1985), *It Still Rains In Memphis* (1986), *One For The Money* (1987), *Crossroads* (1988).

Sheppards

This R&B vocal group was formed in 1959 in Chicago, Illinois, USA. The Sheppards created a marvellous transitional style of R&B during the early 60s, drawing much of its character from earlier doo-wop yet incorporating instrumentation and vocal stylings that in later years would inform soul music. They were named after their producer Bill 'Bunky' Sheppard. The members were lead and bass Millard Edwards, lead and top tenor Murrie Eskridge, baritone Jimmy Allen, bass and fifth tenor James Dennis Isaac bass, second tenor O.C. Perkins and guitarist Kermit Chandler. The group's most famous song was the doo-wop ballad 'Island Of Love' (1959), but later tracks included 'The Glitter In Your Eyes' (1961) and 'Tragic' (1962). All the members had been veterans of the R&B scene for several years before joining together as the Sheppards. Eskridge and Perkins were members of the Palms on United in 1957, and Edwards, Allen and Isaac were members of the Bel Aires on **Decca** in 1958. Edwards left the group in 1967 to join the **Esquires**, another Sheppard-produced group. The Sheppards broke up in 1969. Jimmy Allen died in 1980; Kermit Chandler in 1981.

Albums: *The Sheppards* (1964), *The Sheppards* (1980), *Golden Classics* (1989).

Sherbet

Formed in Sydney, Australia in 1969, Sherbet became an Antipodean pop phenomenon, Sherbet dominated the Australian charts throughout the 70s achieving massive success with the teenage and pre-teen audience. The band became so well known that it seemed they could not put a foot wrong. The group comprised of musicians with experience in various 'second division' Sydney bands and utilized the British influence of **Slade** and the **Sweet**. The band performed an impressive stage show, with a more than adequate vocalist in **Daryl Braithwaite** (b. 11 January 1949, Melbourne, Australia) and a strong writing team in Garth Porter (keyboards/vocals) and Clive Shakespeare (b. 3 June 1957, Australia; guitar/vocals). The initial line-up was completed with Alan Sandow (b. 28 February 1958, Australia; drums) and Bruce Worrall (bass). The band's management also worked overtime courting the media, arranging tours to every far-flung population centre in Australia, including many that had never had a pop or rock band visit before. The band achieved 10 Australian Top 10 hit singles with 10 making the Top 40 and enjoyed similar success with their albums. Tony Mitchell (b. 21 October 1951, Australia) replaced Worrall in 1972. An attempt at the UK market was successful with the 'Howzat' single reaching number 4 in 1976, but they were unable to capitalize further on this success. In 1976 Clive Shakespeare departed and was briefly replaced by ex-**Daddy Cool** member Gunther Gorman, who in turn was supplanted by Harvey James. A favourite amongst their fans was 'You've Got The Gun' (1976) which had been a minor hit before they made the big time, a song that displayed their English influences. They also attempted to crack at the US market with their 1979 album going under the name *Highway*. Making little progress they returned to

Australia, renamed themselves the Sherbs and changed direction to a more mature, heavier AOR sound. This alienated them from their teen following and also failed to attract the older audience which now regarded them with suspicion. In the period 1980-84 they released ten singles and three albums to good critical reviews but few sales, although *The Skill* did reach the US Top 100. Shakespeare and Porter are now involved in production work, while Braithwaite has had two very successful solo albums, demonstrating his expressive vocals and songwriting.

Albums: *Time Change Natural Progression* (1972), *On With The Show* (1973), *Slipstream* (1974), *In Concert* (1975), *Life* (1975), *Howzat!* (1976), *Caught In The Act* (1978), *Photoplay* (1977), *Sherbet/Highway* (1979). As the Sherbs: *The Skill* (1980), *Defying Gravity* (1981), *Shaping Up* (1982).

Sheridan, Tony

b. Anthony Sheridan McGinnity, 21 May 1940, Norwich, Norfolk, England. Sheridan formed his first band, the Saints, in 1955, before relocating to London. There he joined **Vince Taylor And The Playboys** in early 1959, going on to spearhead the English Invasion in Hamburg (Germany). A popular attraction at clubs such as the Kaiserkeller with the Jets, that group soon evolved into the Beat Brothers with a line-up of Sheridan (vocals/guitar), Ken Packwood (guitar), Rick Richards (guitar), Colin Melander (bass), Ian Hines (keyboards) and Jimmy Doyle (drums), though their various formations changed almost constantly. Some of the more interesting personnel to pass through the Beat Brothers in these nebulous days at the Kaiserkeller were **John Lennon**, **Paul McCartney**, **George Harrison**, **Stuart Sutcliffe** and **Pete Best**. This line-up recorded with producer Bert Kaempfert at the controls, though by later in 1962 the Beat Brothers had been joined by **Ringo Starr**, Roy Young (keyboards) and Rikky Barnes (saxophone). Sheridan's first appearance at the infamous Star Club arrived on 12 May 1962, fronting the Tony Sheridan Quartet, who were later retitled the Star Combo. By 1964 he had teamed up with Glaswegian expatriates Bobb Patrick Big Six. However, with the Hamburg beat boom all but over by 1964, Sheridan travelled to Vietnam to play US army bases, accompanied by Volker Tonndorf (bass), Jimmy Doyle (drums) and vocalist Barbara Evers. He eventually returned to Hamburg to turn solo in 1968, where his cult status had not diminished - a reputation that endures to this day. Sheridan then converted to the Sannyasin religion, re-titled himself Swami Probhu Sharan, living with his family in Wuppertal, Germany.

Albums: *My Bonnie* (1962), *The Beatle's First Featuring Tony Sheridan* (1964), *Just A Little Bit Of Tony Sheridan* (1964), *The Best Of Tony Sheridan* (1964), *Meet The Beat* (1965), *Rocks On* (1974), *On My Mind* (1976), *Worlds Apart* (1978).

Sherman, Al

b. 7 September 1897, Kiev, Russia, d. 15 September 1973, Los Angeles, California, USA. A popular songwriter who enjoyed success mainly in the 20s and 30s, Sherman's his first songs, 'Save Your Sorrow', in 1925, was successful for the Shannon Four, **Ray Miller** and **Gene Austin**. Al Sherman's other well-known numbers included 'I Must Be Dreaming', 'He's So Unusual', 'You Gotta Be A Football Hero', 'No, No, A Thousand Times No!,' 'Now's The Time To Fall In Love' and 'On The Beach At Bali Bali'. He wrote the occasional song during the 40s and 50s, such as 'Pretending'. 'The Pigskin Polka' and 'Comes A-Long-A-Love'. His chief collaborator was Al Lewis; he also wrote with Abner Silver, Buddy de Silva, Jack Meskill, Ed Heyman and Harry Tobias. Back in 1930 Sherman wrote 'Livin' In The Sunlight, Lovin' In The Moonlight' for **Maurice Chevalier** to sing in one of his first Hollywood films, *The Big Pond*, in which he co-starred with Claudette Colbert. Just over 30 years later his sons, **Richard M. And Robert B. Sherman** provided Chevalier with 'Merci Beaucoup', 'Enjoy It' and 'Grimpon'. These songs featured on the soundtrack of *In Search Of The Castaways*, one of the great French entertainer's last screen appearances.

Sherman, Allan

b. Allan Copelon, 30 November 1924, Chicago, Illinois, USA, d. 21 November 1973. Allan Sherman enjoyed a lucrative career during the 60s with his self-penned parodies of popular and folk songs. After his parents' 1930 divorce, Sherman lived with his mother and attended 21 different schools in Chicago, Los Angeles, New York and Miami. After attending college in the early 40s and serving in the army, he began writing. One of his first works was a musical parody in which the Jewish Sherman starred himself as Adolf Hitler. In 1947 he began working in the fledgling television medium, writing jokes for variety programmes. He joined the popular US *I've Got A Secret* show in 1951, with which he stayed for seven years. Sherman then wrote for the **Steve Allen** programme but in 1960 found himself unemployed. His career took an upswing when he entertained guests at neighbour Harpo Marx's party with witty send-ups of show tunes. Talent scout Bullets Durgom, who had nurtured the success of **Jackie Gleason**, took an interest and convinced **Warner Brothers Records** to sign Sherman. Originally the label wanted him to record his show tune parodies but decided on folk songs instead, as folk was the music of the moment. Sherman's *My Son, The Folk Singer*, was issued in October 1962 and became the fastest-selling album in Warners' history at that time. The rotund Sherman capitalized on Jewish suburban humour by turning folk songs such as **Harry Belafonte**'s 'Matilda' into 'My Zelda', and the folk

song 'The Streets Of Laredo' into 'The Streets Of Miami'. The French standard 'Frere Jacques' became 'Sarah Jackman' and the USA patriotic number 'The Battle Hymn Of The Republic' was turned into 'The Ballad Of Harry Lewis', the story of a garment salesman. The debut and the following two albums all reached number 1 in the US album charts, this record, for a comedian, is unlikely to be beaten. Sherman's success was immediate, with numerous appearances on major USA television programmes and a headlining concert at Carnegie Hall. The formula of the first album was repeated on the subsequent *My Son, The Celebrity* and *My Son, The Nut*. The third album also produced a number 2 single, 'Hello Muddah, Hello Fadduh! (A Letter From Camp)', based on Ponchielli's 'Dance Of The Hours'. By 1964 the phenomenal novelty had diminished although Sherman continued to record for Warner Brothers until 1967, hosted television specials, acted on the stage and even wrote humour books, but never regained that initial blast of fame. He died in Los Angeles, due to respiratory illness caused by his obesity.
Albums: *My Son, The Folk Singer* (1962), *My Son, The Celebrity* (1963), *My Son, The Nut* (1963), *Allan In Wonderland* (1964), with Arthur Fiedler And The Boston Pops *Peter And The Commissar* (1964), *For Swingin' Livers Only* (1964), *My Name Is Allan* (1965), *Live! (Hoping You Are The Same)* (1966), *Togetherness* (1967). Compilations: *Best Of Allan Sherman* (1979), *A Gift Of Laughter (Best Of Volume II)* (1986).

Sherman, Bim

b. Jarrett Tomlinson, 1952, Kingston, Jamaica, West Indies. His earliest recordings include 'Mighty Ruler' and 'Ever Firm', which appeared on the Love and Ja-Man labels in late 1976/early 1977. Around the same time, a series of singles began appearing on his own Scorpio label. Because of restricted finances, he would often use each rhythm track for two different songs, but his writing skills and plaintive vocals ensured that every record sounded fresh. Several Jah Stone DJ versions of his songs were also issued at this time. In 1978 eight of his Scorpio singles together with 'Mighty Ruler' and 'Ever Firm' were compiled for *Love Forever*, which was released in the UK on the Tribesman label. It is a classic set which he has never equalled. In 1979 he issued *Lovers Leap* which, while not hitting the heights of its predecessor, is a consistently strong collection. A year later he was featured on one side of *Bim Sherman Meets Horace Andy And U Black*, a minor but enjoyable set. Shortly after this he settled in the UK, where he met producer Adrian Sherwood. Sherwood subsequently produced *Across The Red Sea* (1982), but it was not the sensation for which followers of both had hoped. Despite having written some excellent songs, the record loses many of the nuances of the vocals by submerging them in the mix.

In 1984 *Love Forever* was re-released as *Danger*, and he issued his self-produced *Bim Sherman And The Voluntary*, a very disappointing work. This was followed by *Haunting Ground*, an uneven set that boasts an excellent Adrian Sherwood-produced title track. Even though his voice could be haunting, he was let down by slight songs and uninspired accompaniments, a trend that continued on *Exploitation* and *Too Hot*. All through the 80s and early 90s he was a featured vocalist on the highly-acclaimed Sherwood produced Singers And Players series of albums. Fragments of his vocals together with some complete songs also appear in works by Fats Comet, Keith LeBlanc and **Gary Clail**. He remains a very talented artist with enormous potential.
Selected albums: *Love Forever* (Tribesman 1978, reissued as *Danger* Century 1984), *Lovers Leap* (Scorpio 1979), *Across The Red Sea* (On-U-Sound 1982), *Bim Sherman And The Voluntary* (Century 1984), *Haunting Ground* (RDL/Revolver 1986), *Exploitation* (RDL/Revolver 1989), *Too Hot* (Century 1990), *Crazy World* (Century 1992). As The Discoverers: *The Justice League Of Zion* (1994). As Bim Sherman & The Allstars: *African Rubadub* (RDL 1987). With Horace Andy and U Black: *Bim Sherman Meets Horace Andy And U Black* (Yard International 1980). With Dub Syndicate: *Reality* (Century 1992), *Lion Heart Dub* (Century 1993).

Sherman, Richard M., And Robert B.

Richard M. Sherman (b. 12 June 1928, New York, USA) and Robert B. Sherman (b. 19 December 1925, New York, USA) followed in their father, **Al Sherman**'s footsteps as songwriters who collaborated on complete scores, mainly for **Walt Disney** movies of the 60s and 70s. After providing **Johnny Burnette** with the hit song 'You're Sixteen', they contributed to several films in the early 60s, including *The Parent Trap*, *In Search Of The Castaways*, *Summer Magic* and *The Sword In The Stone*. Massive success came in 1964 with the music and lyrics for **Mary Poppins**. The Oscar-winning score included 'A Spoonful Of Sugar', 'Feed The Birds', 'Jolly Holiday', 'Let's Go Fly A Kite' and 'Chim Chim Cher-ee' (which won the Academy Award for 'Best Song'). When the brothers accepted their award they commented: 'There are no words. All we can say is: "Supercalafragelisticexpialidocious"' - which was the title of another famous song from the film. *Mary Poppins* was dubbed the 'best and most original musical of the decade', and 'the best live-action film in Disney's history'. The soundtrack album went to number 1 in the US and remained in the charts for 18 months. **Julie Andrews**, appearing in her first feature film, was voted 'Best Actress' for her performance in the title role. Another British performer, **Tommy Steele**, was not so fortunate in *The Happiest Millionaire*. It was called 'miserable and depressing' despite a lively score by the Shermans, which included 'Fortuosity'. The film was the last to be personally supervised by Walt Disney before he died in 1966. Much more to the critics' liking was the delightful animated feature, *The Jungle Book*, which was inspired by the Rudyard Kipling *Mowgli* stories. The Shermans' songs, including 'I Wan'na Be Like You' and 'That's What Friends Are For', were amusingly delivered by the voices of **Phil Harris**, Sebastian Cabot, **Louis Prima**, George Sanders and Sterling Holloway. The songs and much of the dialogue were released on a lavishly illustrated album.

The late 60s were extremely fertile years for the Sherman brothers. Among the films to which they contributed music and lyrics were *The One And Only Genuine Original Family Band* (another highly acclaimed animal animation), *The Aristocats*, *Bedknobs And Broomsticks*, and **Chitty Chitty Bang Bang**. In 1974 the Sherman brothers' score for the Broadway musical *Over Here*, starred the two survivors from the **Andrews Sisters**, Maxene and Patti. The show, which echoed the styles and sounds of World War II and the swing era, ran for a year. Throughout the 70s, and beyond, the Shermans continued to write songs and scores for films, including *Charlotte's Web*, *Tom Sawyer*, *Huckleberry Finn*, **The Slipper And The Rose** and *The Magic Of Lassie*. Several songs from those films were nominated for Academy Awards, and the Sherman brothers were also involved in writing some of the screenplays. In 1995, a show for which they wrote the music and lyrics, *Stage Door Charley* (sometimes known as *Busker Alley*), a musical adaptation of the 1938 Vivien Leigh-Charles Laughton movie *St. Martin's Lane*, was out of town in the US en route to Broadway.

Sherock, Shorty

b. Clarence F. Cherock, 17 November 1915, Minneapolis, Minnesota, USA, d. 19 February 1980. As a child Sherock played cornet, switching later to trumpet when he worked in local bands. In 1936 he was hired by **Ben Pollack** and subsequently played in numerous bands, including those important units led by **Seger Ellis**, **Jimmy Dorsey**, **Bob Crosby**, **Gene Krupa**, **Tommy Dorsey** and **Alvino Rey**. Immediately following World War II he formed and led his own band and played with **Jazz At The Philharmonic**. He then worked in film studios for much of his remaining career, although he did play with **Georgie Auld** and **Matty Matlock** in the 50s and with **Benny Carter** during the 60s. A skilful, highly-respected musician, Sherock was able to communicate his enthusiasm to his fellows and in his earlier years frequently played exciting solos. He died in 1980.

Albums: with others *Session At Midnight* (1955), with Matty Matlock *And They Called It Dixieland* (1958), with Benny Carter *BBB & Co.* (1962).

Sherriff

This Canadian melodic rock quintet was formed in 1981 by Arnold Lanni (vocals/keyboards) and bassist Wolf Hassel (bass). With the addition of Freddy Curci (vocals), Steve De Marchi (guitar) and Rob Elliot (drums), they signed to **Capitol Records** and released a self-titled debut the following year. Their approach was characterized by grandiose sweeping melodies, which drew inspiration from **Kansas**, **Foreigner** and **Styx**, but with a smattering of their own ideas to authenticate the songs. The album failed to attract the media's attention and the band parted company. Lanni and Hassel later formed Frozen Ghost, while Curci and De Marchi teamed up in Alias. In 1988, quite unexpectedly, 'When I'm With You' from the debut Sherriff album became a number 1 US hit 5 years after it first charted (at number 61). The album was re-released and also did well; resulting in pressure to re-form Sherriff. Lanni and Hassel declined as they retained rights to the name and wanted to continue with Frozen Ghost.

Album: *Sherriff* (Capitol 1982).

Sherrill, Billy

b. Philip Campbell, 5 November 1936, Winston, Alabama, USA. Sherrill's father was a travelling evangelist - he is shown on horseback on the cover of **Charlie Rich**'s album *Silver Linings* - and Sherrill played piano at his meetings. He also played saxophone in a local rock 'n' roll band, Benny Cagle and the Rhythm Swingsters. In 1956 he left to work with Rick Hall in the R&B-styled Fairlanes. His 1958 Mercury single, 'Like Making Love', was covered for the UK market by **Marty Wilde**, and he had some success in Alabama with an instrumental, 'Tipsy', in 1960. He worked for Sun Records' new Nashville studios from 1961 to 1964; in particular, he brought out Charlie Rich's talent as a blues singer. He and Rick Hall then established the Fame studios in Nashville. In 1964 he started working for Columbia Records and he produced R&B records by **Ted Taylor** and the **Staple Singers** as well as an album by **Elvis Presley**'s guitarist, **Scotty Moore**, *The Guitar That Changed The World*. He co-wrote and produced **David Houston**'s US number 1 country hit, 'Almost Persuaded', and his subsequent hits with Houston include a duet with **Tammy Wynette**, 'My Elusive Dreams'. It was Sherrill who discovered Wynette and in 1968 they wrote 'Stand By Your Man' in half an hour and recorded it immediately. Although Sherrill's records crossed over to the pop market, he did not avoid country music instruments such as the steel guitar, although he did favour lavish orchestrations. He also discovered **Tanya Tucker**, **Janie Frickie** and **Lacy J. Dalton**, and has made successful records with Charlie Rich ('Behind Closed Doors', 'The Most

Beautiful Girl'), **George Jones**, **Marty Robbins** and **Barbara Mandrell**. He became a freelance producer in 1980 but he continued to work with many of the same artists. He has produced over 10 albums apiece for **David Allan Coe**, George Jones and Tammy Wynette; other credits include *The Baron* for **Johnny Cash** and the soundtrack for the film, *Take This Job And Shove It*. His best works include two all-star country albums, *My Very Special Guests* with George Jones, and *Friendship* with **Ray Charles**. The friction between him and **Elvis Costello** whilst making the album, *Almost Blue*, was shown on a UK television documentary, but the album did very well and yielded a Top 10 hit, 'A Good Year For The Roses'.
Album: *Classical Country* (1967).

Sherrys

This 'girl group' came from Philadelphia, Pennsylvania, USA. It was formed in the early 60s by Little Joe Cook, who had sung the hit single, 'Peanut', as lead in his group the Thrillers in 1957. The Sherrys consisted of his two daughters, lead Delthine Cook and Dinell, his niece Charlotte Butler, and a friend of the girls Delores 'Honey' Wylie. Their first record, 'Pop Pop Pop-Pie' (US R&B number 25 and pop number 36 in 1962), was a lightweight song, but because it came out in the midst of a Philadelphia-manufactured dance craze the record became a national hit. 'Slop Time' (1963) was the equally banal follow-up. The group broke up soon afterwards, but Charlotte Butler later married a Swedish rock 'n' roll star and appeared with her husband on their own television show.
Album: *At The Hop With The Sherrys* (1962).

Shertzer, Hymie

(see **Schertzer, Hymie**)

Shervington, Pluto

b. Leighton Shervington, August 1950, Kingston, Jamaica, West Indies. In his early twenties Shervington joined a show band called Tomorrows Children. Fellow performers Ernie Smith and Tinga Stewart had enjoyed commercial success with 'Duppy Or A Gunman' and 'Play De Music' respectively. Both songs were sung in a heavy patois and enjoyed chart status. Inspired by this, Shervington sang the hit 'Ram Goat Liver', and the follow-up 'Dat'. Two paradoxical stories of poverty disguised as comedy tunes, which went over the heads of many listeners. In 1976 when released in the UK the song was a Top 5 hit for the newly formed Opal label. **Trojan Records** realised that they had licensed his earlier hit 'Ram Goat Liver' and gave Shervington his second UK chart entry peaking at number 35 two months after the success of 'Dat'. He moved to Miami, Florida where he began recording and in 1982 returned to the international market for the release of 'Your Honour', which entered the UK

Top 20. His follow-up 'I Man Bitter' and an album were not commercial successes.
Album: *Pluto Again* (KR 1982).

Sherwood, Adrian

b. c.1958. A pioneering force in UK reggae, Sherwood's first attempts to set up labels in the late 70s were disastrous, and cost him a small fortune in the process. Despite such misadventures, he couldn't resist having a further try, and set up the On-U-Sound label to house ex-**Pop Group** singer **Mark Stewart**'s New Age Steppers project. Over a hundred albums and 45s have subsequently been released, including music by **Bim Sherman**, Dub Syndicate and Mothmen (an embryonic **Simply Red**). Sherwood styled On-U-Sound after the reggae model of 'house bands' (Revolutionaries, **Soul Syndicate** etc.). The label/organisation also played out as a **sound system**, in a similar fashion to its Jamaican counterparts. Among the notable long-term protagonists at On-U-Sound have been Bonjo (African Head Charge), Bim Sherman and Skip McDonald, Doug Wimbush and Keith LeBlanc (**Tackhead**). However, Sherwood is just as well known for his production skills, which he learned at first hand from **Prince Far-I** and Dr Pablo. The **Fall**, **Depeche Mode** and **Ministry** having been among his notable clients. On-U-Sound came to the attention of the public outside reggae circles when self-styled 'white toaster' **Gary Clail** entered the charts. However, neither this, nor any other individual release, can be described as representative of the rock-reggae-dance fusion which On-U-Sound have fostered. On-U-Sounds' eclecticism remains rampant, but as Sherwood himself concedes: 'I'm first and foremost a passionate fan of reggae music'.
Selected albums: New Age Steppers: *Vol. 1* (Statik 1979). Dub Syndicate: *Pounding System* (On-U-Sound 1988). Gary Clail & Tackhead: *Tackhead Sound System* (On-U-Sound 1988). African Head Charge: *Songs Of Praise* (On-U-Sound 1984). Various: *On-U-Sound Present Pay It All Back Vol. 4* (On-U-Sound 1993).

Sherwood, Bobby

b. 30 May 1914, Indianapolis, USA. Self-taught on several instruments, Sherwood first appeared on stage as a child when he became a member of a vaudeville troupe. In the mid-30s he was hired by **Bing Crosby** as accompanist following the death of guitarist **Eddie Lang**. Through his association with Crosby, Sherwood readily secured work in Hollywood, mostly with MGM. In 1941, by this time mostly playing trumpet, he formed his own big band. Although he was also an accomplished arranger, again self taught, Sherwood lacked the qualities needed for band leadership; despite hiring outstanding young musicians such as **Zoot Sims**, his band was often under-rehearsed and, according to critic George T. Simon, 'one of the most slovenly-looking crews' he ever saw on a bandstand. Thanks to the popularity of records such as 'Sherwood's Forest' and 'Elk's Parade', both of which he composed, he managed to keep the band afloat until the end of the 40s. Sherwood then became an actor, working in both the theatre and films. Towards the end of the 50s he again tried his hand at bandleading, forming a small group and later a big band to work in hotels and casinos in Las Vegas and other gambling resorts.

Albums: *Pal Joey* (c.1957). Compilations: *Out Of Sherwood's Forest* (1942-47), *Sherwood Swing* (1944), *Bobby Sherwood And His Orchestra 1944-1946* (1944-46), *One Night Stand With Bobby Sherwood* (1947).

Shew, Bobby

b. 4 March 1941, Albuquerque, New Mexico, USA. Shew taught himself to play trumpet and was playing semi-professionally as he entered his teens. During military service he decided to make music his career and soon in 1964, after his discharge became a member of the **Tommy Dorsey** Orchestra. The following year he moved on to **Woody Herman**, then **Buddy Rich**, and thereafter took a succession of jobs with bands in hotels and casinos in Las Vegas. In the early 70s he settled in Los Angeles, playing in the studios but also working jazz gigs, including a sustained period with the **Toshiko Akiyoshi-Lew Tabackin** big band. His spell with the band produced many fine albums, notably *Kogun* (1974), *Tales Of A Courtesan* (1975) and *Insights* (1976). Also during the 70s he played in many Los Angeles-based rehearsal bands, including **Don Menza**'s and **Juggernaut**. He played, too, in small groups, as well as teaching privately and directing clinics and workshops. In the late 70s he toured Europe and the UK with **Louie Bellson**'s big band, appearing on some of the live recordings: *Dynamite!* (1979) and *London Scene* (1980). During these tours he expanded his teaching activities wherever he went. In the 80s Shew's playing was mostly in small groups, as both sideman and leader, but he made occasional appearances with youth bands including the UK's Wigan Youth Jazz Orchestra, with whom he recorded *Aim For The Heart* in 1987. In the late 80s and early 90s Shew's teaching role developed still further and he remains in great demand around the world. In performance he rarely uses his spectacularly wide range simply for its own sake. The soft, warm sound he creates from his instrument is especially suitable for ballads and lends a distinctive quality to any trumpet section in which he appears. An important influence through his teaching activities, Shew is ensuring that in a period when dazzling technical proficiency is becoming almost commonplace the emotional qualities of jazz are not forgotten.

Albums: *Telepathy* (1978), *Outstanding In His Field* (1978-79), *Class Reunion* (1980), *Parallel 37* (1980), *Play Song* (1981), *Trumpets No End* (1983), *Breakfast Wine* (1984), with Wigan Youth Jazz Orchestra *Aim For The Heart* (1987).

Shields

This R&B vocal group came from Los Angeles, California, USA. The Shields were an *ad hoc* group formed in 1958 by producer George Motola to record a cover song of the Slades' 'You Cheated'. Membership of that particular group has always been conjectural, but it is generally accepted as comprising lead Frankie Ervin (b. 27 March 1926, Blythe, California, USA), falsetto **Jesse Belvin** (b. 15 December 1932, San Antonio, Texas, USA), **Johnny 'Guitar' Watson** (b. 3 February 1935, Houston, Texas, USA), Mel Williams, and Buster Williams. 'You Cheated', which went to number 11 R&B and number 12 pop in 1958, was the group's only hit, and the song remains one of the most enduring legacies of the age of doo-wop.

Shields, Lonnie

b. 17 April, 1956, West Helena, Arkansas, USA. From some of his statements, it would be easy to cast Shields as a reluctant bluesman. His early musical experience centred around the church, although he never joined his church's choir. He was 11 when he acquired his first guitar and took some instruction from Eddie Smith, a local multi-instrumentalist. Two years later, he bought his first amplified model and joined a band which changed its name from the Checkmates to the Shades Of Black, to reflect its repertoire drawn from the **Isley Brothers** and **Earth, Wind And Fire**. He became a multi-instrumentalist himself, playing saxophones in school, and guitar, bass and harmonica with the band. In his late teens, he spent some time with a gospel group, the Christian Stars. His first exposure to blues came through drummer Sam Carr, who worked with **Frank Frost** and **Big Jack Johnson** as the Jelly Roll Kings. His major debut as a blues player came at the inaugural 1986 King Biscuit Blues Festival, where he met Jim O'Neal of Rooster Blues. Shields recorded a single for O'Neal, 'Strong Woman', the following year, but kept his job as a shoe repairman which he had had from the age of 15. *Portrait* was recorded over a number of years and featured men like Johnson, **Lucky Peterson** and **Vaan Shaw**. It showed Shields to be a capable songwriter and guitarist with the promise of development in future projects.

Album: *Portrait* (Rooster Blues 1993).

Shihab, Sahib

b. Edmund Gregory, 23 June 1925, Savannah, Georgia, USA, d. 24 October 1989. After learning to play several reed instruments, Shihab concentrated on alto saxophone and played professionally while still in his early teens. At the age of 19 he was lead alto with

Fletcher Henderson and also played in **Roy Eldridge**'s big band. After 1947, the year in which he adopted the Muslim faith and changed his name, Shihab played with several of the leading bop musicians, including **Thelonious Monk**, with whom he made the first recording of "Round Midnight', **Tadd Dameron**, **Art Blakey** (playing in the first of the drummer's **Jazz Messengers** groups to record), **Dizzy Gillespie** and **John Coltrane**, the last performing on the tenorman's first recording date as leader. In the 50s Shihab began to play baritone saxophone and at the end of the decade travelled to Europe with **Quincy Jones**. He remained on the Continent for several years, playing with the **Clarke-Boland Big Band** for almost a decade. During this period he added soprano saxophone and flute to his instrumental armoury, and in 1965 he composed a jazz ballet based on Hans Christian Andersen's *The Red Shoes*. In the early 70s Shihab returned to the USA to work in film studios, but was frequently back in Europe during the remaining part of the decade and into the early 80s. He finally settled in the USA in 1986, which is where he died in 1989. Over the years, Shihab's inventiveness when playing flute and soprano surpassed his earlier work on alto. It was, however, on baritone that he made his most distinctive contribution, weaving thoughtfully agile solos with a remarkably light sound.
Selected albums: with Thelonious Monk *Genius Of Modern Music Vol. 1* (1947), *Jazz Sahib* (Savoy 1957 recordings), *The Jazz We Heard Last Summer* (1957), *Jazz-Sahib* (1957), *Companionship* (1964-65), *Sahib Shihab And The Danish Radio Jazz Group* (1965), *Seeds* (1968), *Sentiments* (1971), *Sahib Shihab And The Jef Gilson Unit* (1972), with others *Flute Summit* (1973), *Conversations* (1992).

Shilkret, Jack

b. 13 October 1896, New York, USA, d. 16 June 1964, New York, USA. The younger brother of **Nathaniel Shilkret**, Jack was a pianist and danceband leader in the 20s and 30s. He worked on the radio show *Bond Bread Tea Shop* with Julia Sanderson and **Frank Crumit**, wrote the music for some minor films, and composed several popular songs, including 'Make Believe', 'Lazy Summer Moon', 'April Showers Bring May Flowers', 'Just Another Kiss', 'Copenhagen Love Song', and 'She's The Daughter Of K-K-K-Katy'.
Selected album: *Strauss Waltzes For Dancing* (c.50s).

Shilkret, Nat

b. Nathaniel Schüldkraut, 25 December 1889, New York, USA, d. 18 February 1982, Long Island, New York, USA. A clarinettist, composer, arranger, conductor and an executive with Victor Records for many years. Shilkret was also an accomplished classical violinist. Early in his career he played with the New York Symphony, the New York Philharmonic, and the Metropolitan Opera House Orchestra. He also worked in the concert bands of **John Philip Sousa** and Arthur Pryor before joining Victor, eventually becoming their Director of Light Music. From 1924-32 he conducted his Victor Orchestra on over 50 US chart hits, including 'Tell Me You'll Forgive Me', 'June Brought The Roses', 'Rio Rita', 'On The Riviera', 'All Alone Monday', 'One Alone', 'The Riff Song', 'I Know That You Know', 'Flapperette', 'When Day Is Done', 'What Does It Matter Now?', 'The Doll Dance', 'Hallelujah!', 'Me And My Shadow', 'It's A Million To One You're In Love', 'Paree (Ca C'est Paris)', 'Diane', 'Thinking Of You', 'Did You Mean It?', 'Why Do I Love You?', 'The Sidewalks Of New York', 'Out Of The Dawn', 'One Kiss', 'Marie', 'You Were Meant For Me', 'Pagan Love Song', 'Love Me', 'Chant Of The Jungle', 'Get Happy' and 'Delishious'. 'Dancing With Tears In My Eyes' was his most successful record, reaching number 1 in the US chart. Vocalists on some of those tracks included Vernon Dalhart, Lewis James, Carl Mattieu, Johnny Marvin, the Revellers, Elliott Shaw, Franklyn Baur, and Paul Small. Shilkret also provided the orchestral accompaniment for many other Victor artists, such as **Allan Jones**, who had a big hit with 'The Donkey Serenade' from the film *The Firefly* (1937). He was the conductor on 'Indian Love Call', a hit for **Jeanette MacDonald** with **Nelson Eddy**, *Nelson Eddy Favorites* and **Jane Froman**'s *Gems From Gershwin*. Some of his own compositions, too, were recorded successfully, by **Bunny Berigan** and **Jimmie Lunceford** ('The First Time I Saw You'), the Hilo Hawaiian Orchestra ('Down The River Of Broken Dreams'), and **Ben Selvin** and **Gene Austin** ('Jeannie, I Dream Of Lilac Time'). With Austin, Shilkret wrote his best remembered song, 'The Lonesome Road', which was included in the **Jerome Kern/Oscar Hammerstein II** score for the part-talking movie version of *Show Boat* (1927). Thirty years later **Frank Sinatra** remembered it on his **Capitol** release, *A Swingin' Affair*. Shilkret also composed several classical pieces, such as 'New York Ballet' and 'Southern Humoresque'. Throughout the 30s he worked extensively on radio in such shows as *Hall Of Fame*, *Camel Caravan*, *Relaxation Time*, *Palmolive Beauty Box Theatre* and his own programmes. In 1935 he moved to Hollywood, and for the next 20 or so years, as an arranger, conductor and musical director, contributed to a great many movies, including *The Plough And The Stars* (starring Barbara Stanwyck), 'Mary Of Scotland' (an historical drama, with Katharine Hepburn, John Ford and Frederic March), *The Toast Of New York* (with Cary Grant), *She Went To The Races*, *The Hoodlum Saint*, *Kentucky Derby Story* and *Airline Glamour Girls*. One of the last films he worked on, in 1953, was a short about fishing entitled *Flying Tarpons*. He also contributed the occasional film song, such as 'Heart Of A Gypsy' (with Robert Shayon) for *The Bohemian Girl*, and 'King Of The Road' (with Eddie Cherkose) for *Music For Madame*.

Shillelagh Sisters

This UK north London all-woman rockabilly group was formed in 1983. The group found themselves mixed-up with the emerging 'country cow-punk' scene which included **Yip Yip Coyote** and the **Boothill Foot-Tappers**. The Sisters, who as legend has it, first decided to form while congregated in a gent's toilet-room at a party, comprised Trisha (b. Patricia O'Flynn; saxophone), Jacqui Sullivan (vocals), Mitzi (drums) and Lynder (double bass). Having completed one album for **CBS** in 1984, they disappeared from view soon afterwards, leaving some observers debating to the present day whether or not they ever managed to spell 'Shillelagh' correctly or not! Jacqui later joined **Bananarama** as the replacement for Siobhan Fahey, while O'Flynn played in the original line-up of **Coming Up Roses**.
Album: *The Shillelagh Sisters* (1984).

Shimmy-Disc

This idiosyncratic label was founded in New York in 1987 by Mark **Kramer**, formerly of **Shockabilly** and the **Butthole Surfers**. Having built his own studio, Noise New York, Kramer set about recording acts of a similar irascible nature. The label's first release, *20th Anniversary Of The Summer Of Love*, was a various artists' compendium which included contributions by Krackhouse, Men & Volts, Allen Ginsberg, **Half Japanese** and **Tuli Kupferberg**, many of whom would later record for Shimmy-Disc. The set also featured **Bongwater**, the group Kramer forged with performance artist Ann Magnuson, whose enthralling double set, *Breaking No New Ground*, was the label's second release. Shimmy-Disc allowed Kramer to indulge his musical fantasies; it provided the vehicle for another of his own bands, **B.A.L.L.** and several collaborative projects, notably with **Jad Fair** and John S. Hall. Shimmy Disc reissued albums by Shockabilly and allowed mavericks exposure which might otherwise have been denied them. Zany Brooklyn sextet, When People Were Shorter And Lived Near The Water, unleashed their 15-song 'tribute' to pop crooner **Bobby Goldsboro** (*Bobby*), before doing the same to *Porgy And Bess* with *Porgy*. Kramer also made international signings, releasing albums by British acts the **Walkingseeds** and Jellyfish Kiss and Japanese hardcore act, the Boredoms. A highlight of the label's catalogue was *Rutles Highway Revisited*, a various artists' tribute to **Beatles**' spoof, the **Rutles**. **Das Damen**, **Galaxie 500** and Peter Stampfel of the **Holy Modal Rounders** were among the assembled cast; the liner notes were written by Rutles' creator **Neil Innes** in his guise as 'Ron Nasty'. Late-period Shimmy-Disc signings include the sublime **Lydia Husik** but,

following the release of *The Guilt Trip*, Kramer's solo debut, the label's future was thrown into doubt when Ann Magnuson took out legal action on the acrimonious break-up of Bongwater. Kramer did begin two subsidiary company's, See Eye and Kokopop, in 1993, but at the time of writing all outlets are in limbo.

Shindig

A pivotal television programme which ran on the ABC network in the USA from 1964-66, *Shindig* was one of the first national prime time shows to feature live rock 'n' roll music as its main focus. Hosted by disc jockey Jimmy O'Neill, *Shindig* debuted on 16 September 1964, with a half-hour programme featuring performances by **Sam Cooke**, the **Everly Brothers**, the **Righteous Brothers** and **Bobby Sherman** (who reached massive fame as a 'teen idol' as the result of his *Shindig* appearances). Sherman was a 'regular' on the weekly show, as were **Donna Loren**, the Wellingtons, **Glen Campbell**, and **Sonny And Cher**. The show had its own 'house band', the Shindogs, among whose members were **Leon Russell**, **James Burton** and Campbell. Virtually every major rock music artist of the era appeared on at least one episode of *Shindig*, including the **Beatles**, the **Rolling Stones**, the **Beach Boys**, the **Supremes** and **James Brown**. In addition, it featured non-rock guest hosts in order to try to woo the adult viewers. Among these were Zsa Zsa Gabor, Mickey Rooney and Boris Karloff. The show became so popular that in its second season, beginning in September 1965, it was expanded to two nights a week. That proved to be its last season, however, and *Shindig* was cancelled. Its final programme was aired on 8 January 1966. In 1991, Rhino Home Video began releasing large series of compilation videotapes of *Shindig* appearances.

Shinehead

b. Edmund Carl Aitken, Kent, England. Although born in the UK, Aitken's family moved to Jamaica when he was two years old, then emigrated to New York in 1976 where he settled permanently. Counting among his influences a diverse array of artists including the **Jackson 5** and **Otis Redding**, together with numerous reggae performers, Shinehead began singing at the age of 19, mixing the Jamaican toasting style with the more urbanized hip-hop which was developing in New York. After studying electrical and computer engineering his first musical activity came with Downbeat International in 1981, with **Brigadier Jerry** becoming a formative influence. He quickly developed a reputation for an astonishing range of dancehall skills; mimicking, singing, DJing, selecting, rapping and even whistling to great effect over Downbeat's stock-in-trade **Studio One** dub plates. It was there he gained his name: by virtue of his distinctive, closely cropped hairstyle. In late 1983 he

joined forces with Claude Evans, who ran the African Love **sound system**-cum-label in Brooklyn. Evans managed to procure a rhythm track the **Wailers** had reputedly played for **Bob Marley**, who had died before using it. In 1984 Shinehead voiced 'Billie Jean'/'Mama Used To Say' over two sides of the rhythm and scored a massive hit for African Love. The debut album, *Rough And Rugged*, which followed in 1986 showcased his remarkably varied talents with a blend of dancehall, ballads, rap and reggae that yielded further hits in the shape of 'Know How Fi Chat', 'Hello Y'All' and 'Who The Cap Fits'. That same year he guested on **Sly And Robbie**'s popular 'Boops' and was signed to **Elektra** in 1987. Their alliance has proved to be a disappointing one. The second album, *Unity*, was merely the first set re-arranged (some by **Run DMC**'s Jam Master Jay), and contained many of the same tracks, some of which were by then four years old. Increasingly new material was aimed at the US crossover market, and despite the success of 'Strive' with his fading roots audience in 1990, his fortunes have taken a distinctly downward turn. *Sidewalk University* again assembled the services of assorted pop/rap/dance personnel in a bid for commercial reward, with the single 'Jamaican In New York' selling reasonably well. It is a long way removed from the dazzling attributes shown on his earlier work, although he continues to make combative appearances on sound systems both in the US and Jamaica.
Selected albums: *Rough And Rugged* (African Love Music 1986), *Unity* (African Love/Elektra 1988), *The Real Rock* (African Love/Elektra 1990), *Sidewalk University* (African Love/Elektra 1993), *Troddin'* (Elektra 1994).

Shines, Johnny

b. 26 April 1915, Frayser, Tennessee, USA, d. 20 April 1992. Johnny Shines was taught to play the guitar by his mother and sometimes worked the streets of Memphis for tips with a group of other youths. In 1932 he set up as a sharecropper in Hughes, Arkansas, but still worked part time as a musician. During the 30s he hoboed around the work camp and juke joint circuit in the company of such men as **Robert Johnson**, with whom he appeared on a radio show in 1937. His ramblings took him as far as Canada. In 1941 he took the trail north to Chicago where he sometimes performed in the famous Maxwell Street market before forming his own group to play the clubs; he sometimes doubled as house photographer. Despite being respected by his fellow musicians and occasionally recording under the name Shoe Shine Johnny, his career did not take off until the 60s when his slide guitar and strong, emotive vocals were seen as a direct link with Delta blues, then much in vogue. From then on Johnny Shines went from strength to strength, touring the USA, Europe and Japan, with great success often in the company of **Robert Lockwood**. Shines

was an intelligent and articulate man who was fully aware of his position in the blues world and made the most of his late opportunities. Concerned about the quality of life offered to his children in the northern cities, he moved back to the south where he suffered a heart attack that affected his playing. His recovery was slow and although still played guitar he was unable to return to the dazzling proficiency of his earlier days.
Selected albums: *Masters Of The Modern Blues* (1966), *Last Night Dream* (1968), *With Big Walter Horton* (1970), *Standing At The Crossroads* (1970), *Sitting On Top Of The World* (1972), *Nobody's Fault But Mine* (1973), *Hey Ba Ba Re Bop* (1978), *Johnny Shines Live 1974* (1989), with Snooky Pryor *Back To The Country* (1993).

Shirati Jazz

While the majority of African countries have developed a variety of styles clearly rooted in their own traditional folk musics, Kenya, home of Shirati Jazz, has been more outward-looking, drawing ideas from across the continent and calling the resultant mixture benga. An electric dance music that appeared in the early 60s, the benga rhythm could be heard in Sierra Leone, Ghana, Nigeria and Zimbabwe, and reached Kenya around the middle of the decade, where bands like Victoria Kings Jazz and Shirati Jazz grafted on elements of the folk music of their own Luo people and gave some national identity to the style. Shirati were formed in 1965 by guitarist Daniel Owino Misiani, also known as D.O. Misiani, and occasionally D07 after the number of letters in his surname. He went into music in 1961 as a maraccas player for two acoustic guitarists, Obonyo Waru and Odira Jombo Ngareya, before taking up the guitar himself. In Kenya, as elsewhere throughout Africa, musicians are traditionally looked upon as shiftless degenerates - a view that Misiani's father, a highly religious man, held with a vengeance. He broke Misiani's first guitar, confiscated the second and then lobbied the village authorities to arrest his rebellious son and give him a salutary spell in the local jail. For his part, Misiani did his best to live up to the stereotype, travelling with extremely young female singers and, on at least one occasion, being thrown into jail at the behest of outraged parents. It was only after he had become successful, and gave his father lavish presents, that family peace and some semblance of public propriety was established. By the start of the 70s, Shirati were the biggest stars on the Kenyan scene, a position they retained until well into the latter half of the 80s. In 1987 they undertook their first European tour, during the British leg of which they recorded the *Benga Beat* for local specialist label World Circuit.
Albums: *East African Hit Parade* (1975), *Shirati Jazz* (1981), *Benga Beat* (1987), *My Life And Loves* (1988).

Shire

This American hard rock quartet was formed in 1983

by David Anthony (vocals), Alan St. Lesa (guitar), Mick Adrian (bass) and Steve Ordyke (drums). They secured a record deal with Enigma the following year. Influenced by **Dokken**, **Kiss** and **Van Halen**, their debut was a somewhat formularized collection of mid-paced rockers that ultimately lacked distinction. Produced by Don Dokken and Michael Wagner, the album was eagerly anticipated, but proved a major disappointment when it arrived. Little more was heard of Shire in its wake.

Album: *Shire* (Enigma 1984).

Shire, David

b. 3 July 1937, Buffalo, New York, USA. A prolific composer for films, television and the stage, Shire studied piano as a youngster, and played in his father's dance band at local functions. While at Yale he majored in music, and wrote two musicals, one of which was entitled *Cyrano*. He subsequently studied briefly at Brandeis University where he was the first recipient of the **Eddie Fisher** Fellowship Award. In 1961, together with another former Yale student, Richard Maltby Jnr., Shire wrote some songs for the Off Broadway revue *Sap Of Life*, and the new team also had two of their numbers, 'Autumn' and 'No More Songs For Me', recorded by the up-and-coming **Barbra Streisand**. This led to Shire spending nearly two years playing piano in the orchestra pit for *Funny Girl*, and serving as assistant arranger on Streisand's early television specials. In the late 60s, after his stage musical *Love Match* failed to reach Broadway, Shire began to write the scores for popular television programmes such as *The Virginian*, and eventually moved out to Hollywood in 1969. The majority of his more than 40 feature film scores - for a wide variety of genre such as westerns, comedies, thrillers, melodramas and love stories - were written in the 70s, and included *One More Train To Rob* (1971), *Summertree, Skin Game, Drive, He Said, Two People, Showdown, Class Of '44, The Conversation, Farewell, My Lovely, The Hindenburg, All The President's Men, The Big Bus, **Saturday Night Fever**, Straight Time*, and *Norma Rae* (1979). Throughout the 80s and early 90s he continued to write the background music for movies such as *Only When I Laugh* (1981), *The Night The Lights Went Out In Georgia, Paternity, Max Dugan Returns, Oh, God! You Devil, 2010, Return To Oz, Short Circuit, 'Night Mother, Backfire, Vice Versa, Monkey Shines, Paris Trout*, and *Bed And Breakfast* (1992). Shire has also scored numerous television films, and miniseries such as *Echoes In The Darkness* (1987), *The Women Of Brewster Place* (1989), and *The Kennedys Of Massachusetts* (1990). In 1979 he won an Oscar for the song 'It Goes Like It Goes' (lyric by Norman Gimbel) which was sung on the soundtrack of the film *Norma Rae* by **Jennifer Warnes**. He was also awarded two Grammys for his contributions to the *Saturday Night Fever* soundtrack album. As well as Streisand, his songs have been

recorded by numerous other artists, including **Johnny Mathis**, **Melissa Manchester**, and **Judy Collins**, and he has had several US chart successes, including 'Washington Square' (written with Bob Goldstein, and a US number 2 in 1963 for the dixieland-styled band, the Village Stompers), and 'With You I'm Born Again' (lyric by Carol Connors), an international hit in 1980 for **Billy Preston** and **Syreeta**. Shire has also composed songs and incidental music for Joe Papp's New York Shakespeare Festival Theatre, and other acclaimed theatrical productions. He was married for a time to actress Talia Shire, the sister of director Francis Ford Coppola, and star of several *Rocky* movies.

Richard Maltby Jnr. (b. 6 October 1937, USA), Shire's main collaborator and the son of the celebrated composer and bandleader **Richard Maltby**, worked as a director in the legitimate theatre during the 70s before collaborating with Shire on two successful Off Broadway revues, *Starting Here, Starting Now...* (1977) and *Closer Than Ever* (1989), both of which became cult attractions and have been presented in several countries, including Britain; and the Broadway musical *Baby* (1983) which ran for 241 performances. Maltby directed all three projects. He also won a Tony Award in 1978 as 'Outstanding Director' for ***Ain't Misbehavin'***, a musical celebrating songs written and associated with **Fats Waller**, which he conceived with Murray Horwitz. His other Broadway credits include directing, adapting, and providing extra lyrics for ***Song And Dance*** (1985); and writing the lyrics (with **Alain Boublil**) for *Miss Saigon* (1989), and for the spectacular 1991 Broadway flop *Nick And Nora*. Maltby is also known for the 'fiendishly difficult' crosswords he contributes to *Harpers* magazine.

Selected album: with Maureen McGovern *David Shire At The Movies* (Bay Cities 1992), and soundtrack and Original Cast albums.

Shirelles

Formed in Passaic, New Jersey, USA, the Shirelles are arguably the archetypal 'girl-group'; Shirley Owens (b. 10 June 1941), Beverly Lee (b. 3 August 1941), Doris Kenner (b. 2 August 1941) and Addie 'Micki' Harris (b. 22 January 1940, d. 10 June 1982) were initially known as the uncomfortably named Poquellos. School-friends for whom singing was simply a pastime, the quartet embarked on professional career when a classmate, Mary Jane Greenberg, recommended them to her mother. Florence Greenberg, an aspiring entrepreneur, signed them to her Tiara label, on which the resultant single, 'I Met Him On A Sunday', was a minor hit. This inspired the inauguration of a second outlet, Scepter, where the Shirelles secured pop immortality with 'Will You Love Me Tomorrow'. Here Alston's tender, aching vocal not only posed the ultimate question, but implied she already had decided 'yes' to her personal dilemma. One of pop's most treasured recordings, it was followed by a series of exceptional singles, 'Mama Said' (1961), 'Baby It's You' (1962) and 'Foolish Little Girl' (1963), which confirmed their exemplary position. The Shirelles' effect on other groups, including those in Britain, is incalculable, and the **Beatles**, the **Merseybeats**, and **Manfred Mann** are among those who covered their work. The quartet's progress was dealt a crucial setback when producer and arranger Luther Dixon left to take up another post. Newer Scepter acts, including **Dionne Warwick**, assumed the quartet's one-time prime position while a punitive record contract kept the group tied to the label. By the time the Shirelles were free to move elsewhere, it was too late to enjoy a contemporary career and the group was confined to the 'oldies' circuit. Micki Harris died aged 42, on 10 June 1982. By combining sweetening strings with elements of church music, the group provided a pivotal influence on the direction of popular music.

Albums: *Baby It's You* (1962), *Twist Party* (1962), *Trumpets And Strings* (1963), *Foolish Little Girl* (1963). Solo albums: Shirley Alston (Owens) *With A Little Help From My Friends* (1975), *Lady Rose* (1977). Compilations: *Soulfully Yours* (1985), *Sha La La* (1985), *Lost And Found* (1987), *Greatest Hits* (1987), *The Collection* (1990), *The Best Of* (1992), *16 Greatest Hits* (1993), *Lost And Found: Rare And Unissued* (1994).

Further reading: *Girl Groups: The Story Of A Sound*, Alan Betrock.

Shirley And Lee

New Orleans-based duo Shirley Goodman (b. 19 June 1936, New Orleans, Louisiana, USA) and Leonard Lee (b. 29 June 1936, d. 23 October 1976) began recording together in 1952. Billed as 'The Sweethearts Of The Blues', they enjoyed a series of US R&B hits, including 'I'm Gone' (1952) and 'Feel So Good' (1955), marked by the juxtaposition of Shirley's shrill, child-like intonation and Lee's bluesy counterpoint. In 1956 they crossed over into the pop US Top 20 with 'Let The Good Times Roll', a charming, infectious performance, written and arranged by Lee. The song became the first million-seller for the Aladdin label and is now regarded as an R&B standard. Shirley And Lee enjoyed minor hits with 'I Feel Good' (1956) and 'When I Saw You' (1957), before parting company in 1963. Shirley moved to the west coast, where she appeared on sessions for producer **Harold Battiste** and **Dr. John**, while Lee pursued a low-key solo career. His death in 1976 paradoxically coincided with Goodman's newfound popularity as leader of **Shirley And Company**.

Albums: *Let The Good Times Roll* (1956, Aladdin label), *Let The Good Times Roll* (1962, Imperial label). Compilations: *Legendary Masters Shirley & Lee* (1974), *The Best Of Shirley & Lee* (1982), *Happy Days* (1985), *Respectfully Yours* (1985).

Shirley, Roy

b. c.1948, Kingston, Jamaica, West Indies. Perhaps one of the most eccentric performers (in a business peopled almost exclusively with eccentric performers), Roy Shirley is known to reggae fans world-wide on the strength of a handful of superb releases and some of the most electrifying stage shows ever. He first recorded for **Beverley's** in 1964, working in the same territory as luminaries of the **ska** scene such as **Ken Boothe** and Joe White. He was also a member of the original **Uniques** but his breakthrough came one night in 1966 after watching a Salvation Army band parade down Orange Street. Their beat, Roy claims, formed the basis of one of the best known records ever made in Jamaica, and one that many class as the first **rocksteady** outing - 'Hold Them', produced by **Joel 'Joe Gibbs' Gibson** - it was his first record too. The record was huge but Roy still feels bitter about the treatment he received from **Coxsone Dodd** who 'versioned' Roy's tune with Ken Boothe and renamed it 'Feel Good', the sales seriously damaging those of Roy's original.

Undeterred Roy continued his musical career recording in the rock steady and reggae style for Sir JJ, Caltone, Joe Gibbs and most notably **Bunny Lee**, whose first big hit was 'Music Field' with Roy Shirley. Another big hit followed in 1971 when Roy released 'A Sugar' through Randys. He first toured the UK in 1972 with **U-Roy** and many of the latter's fans were forced to admit that Roy Shirley was a nearly impossible act to follow. Roy has remained in the UK on and off ever since and he set up the All Stars Artistic Federated Union in London in 1976 in order to 'seek promotion and to gain satisfaction for all kinds of artists'. He wanted up-and-coming performers to avoid the pitfalls that had dogged his career, and to put something back into a business that he feels has never really paid him his due rewards. He still possesses the same incredibly intense delivery, and he took 1982's Reggae Sunsplash in Jamaica by storm with his outrageous stage act. His records still promote the virtue of music and living good and despite his setbacks Roy still remains optimistic that, one day, the tide will turn for him.

Shirts

This US pop-rock act were formed from the ashes of the Lackeys and Schemers, who played several low-key gigs in the early 70s. The line-up featured Annie Golden (b. c.1953; vocals), Ronnie Ardito (guitar), Artie La Monica (guitar), Robert Racioppo (bass), John Piccolo (keyboards) and John 'Zeeek' Criscioni (drums). All members provided songs either on their own or in partnership with other personnel. Golden also worked as an actor, having a leading role in the screen adaptation of *Hair* in 1979. Other names which were suggested for the assembly included the Pants and the

Sleeves. Shirts was the eventual choice, with the proviso that it should be pronounced Shoits in a thick New York accent. Unsurprisingly this tradition has lapsed with time. They initially earned a crust as a Top 40 covers band playing in bars, before graduating to clubs like **CBGB's** in 1975. Their first single, 'Tell Me Your Plans', was a surprise hit in Europe. Their big break came with a **Peter Gabriel** tour, before further singles and albums including the single 'Laugh And Walk Away'. Golden released a solo single in 1984, but the band disappeared from the annals of rock taking their pronunciation with them. They did reunite, however, for one night in 1993 to celebrate the 20th anniversary of their spiritual home, CBGB's.

Albums: *The Shirts* (Capitol 1978), *Street Light Shine* (Capitol 1979), *Inner Sleeve* (Capitol 1980).

Shiva

This UK rock trio, which combined both progressive rock and metal traditions, was formed in 1981 by multi-instrumentalist John Hall (vocals/guitar/keyboards). Adding Andy Skuse (bass/keyboards) and Chris Logan (drums) they signed to Heavy Metal Records in 1982. Together they debuted with *Fire Dance*, a complex and inventive album which brought to mind memories of **Rush**, **Deep Purple** and **Uriah Heep** to its generally sympathetic reviewers. Instrumentally, the album was faultless, but the vocals were less impressive. Phil Williams replaced Logan in 1984, but this new line-up failed to make any recordings.

Album: *Fire Dance* (Heavy Metal 1982).

Shiva's Headband

Founded in Austin, Texas in 1967 by violinist/vocalist Spencer Perskin. Susan Perskin (vocals/percussion), Bob Tonreid (guitar), Kenny Parker (bass) and Jerry Barnett (drums) completed the original line-up which was buoyed the following year with the addition of Shawn Siegal (keyboards). The sextet completed their debut single, 'Kaleidoscoptic', before moving to San Francisco to record *Take Me To The Mountains*. Robert Gladwin and Richard Finnel replaced Tonreid and Barnett prior to recording, but the group remained a vehicle for Perskin's violin dexterity and his frazzled vision of psychedelic country. Shiva's Headband then returned to Texas where a revitalized line-up completed *Comin' To A Head*, before becoming an integral part of the state's vibrant live circuit. Spencer Perskin continued to lead the group into the 80s, although his wife Susan and Shawn Siegal were the only members to remain from the 1968 line-up.

Albums: *Take Me To The Mountains* (1970), *Comin' To A Head* (1982), *Psychedelic Yesterday* (1977), *In The Primo Of Life* (1985).

Shockabilly

Formed in 1982 by guitarist **Eugene Chadbourne**, bassist Kramer and drummer Dave Licht, Shockabilly produced music that sounded like an unholy combination of the **Electric Prunes** and Karlheinz Stockhausen. They specialized in outrageous covers - 'Psychotic Reaction', '19th Nervous Breakdown', 'Day Tripper', 'Purple Haze' - and also more obscure items by **John Lee Hooker**, **John Fogerty** and **Syd Barrett**. When the song appears familiar it gives the listener a thread on which to hang the power trio-chaos they liked to indulge in. Chadbourne's background was in rock, blues, late 60s free jazz and free improvisation - he put it all into Shockabilly with an energy and spleen that gained a response from the more adventurous post-punk audiences. After they folded in 1985 Chadbourne, an inspired songwriter, pursued a solo career while Kramer set up Shimmy Disk, one of the great radical rock labels of the 80s and 90s.

Albums: *The Dawn Of Shockabilly* (1982), *Earth Versus Shockabilly* (1983), *Colosseum* (1984), *Vietnam* (1984), *Heaven* (1985). Compilation: *Greatest Hits* (1983).

Shocked, Michelle

b. 1962, Dallas, Texas, USA. This roots singer/songwriter's music draws on frequently tough experiences of a nomadic lifestyle. Her childhood had been divided between a religiously inclined mother (Catholic then Mormon), and her estranged father, a some-time mandolin player. She originally came to prominence via a Walkman recorded gig, taped around a campfire, complete with crickets on backing vocals. *Short Sharp Shocked* highlighted more varied and less self-conscious stylings than the more mainstream **Suzanne Vega**/**Tracy Chapman** school. *Captain Swing* was her 'big band' record, where she was joined once more by **Dwight Yoakam**'s producer/guitarist Pete Anderson, as well as a plethora of famous extras (**Fats Domino**, **Bobby 'Blue' Bland**, **Randy Newman**). Despite songs with titles like 'God Is A Real Estate Developer', its jazzy rhythms and swishing brass made it her most commercially accessible. The album's title was taken from the 19th Century leader of a farm labourer's revolt, the type of subject matter which put her in good company with touring companion **Billy Bragg**. The recording of *Arkansas Traveller* was completed by travelling across the US and further afield with a portable studio. Hence musicians like **Taj Mahal**, **Doc Watson**, Levon Helm (the **Band**), **Clarence 'Gatemouth' Brown** and **Hothouse Flowers** made their contributions in Ireland, Australia and elsewhere. Shocked had spent time researching the origins of American music and in particular the black-faced minstrel legacy, which she attacked with her own traditional songs. Shocked is one of the most interesting of the new generation of folk artists.

Albums: *The Texas Campfire Tapes* (1987), *Short Sharp Shocked* (1988), *Captain Swing* (1989), *Arkansas Traveller* (1992).

Shocking Blue

Formed in 1967 by ex-Motions guitarist Robbie van Leeuwen (b. 1944), this Dutch quartet originally featured lead vocalist Fred de Wilde, bassist Klassje van der Wal and drummer Cornelius van der Beek. After one minor hit in their homeland, 'Lucy Brown Is Back In Town', there was a major line-up change when the group's management replaced De Wilde with Mariska Veres (b. 1949). With her solid vocals, long dark hair, heavy make-up and low-cut garments Veres brought the group a sexy image and another Netherlands hit 'Send Me A Postcard Darling'. Next came 'Venus', a massive European hit, which went on to top the US charts in February 1970 after **Jerry Ross** had signed the group to his Colossus label. With the talented Van Leeuwen dominating the composing and production credits, Shocking Blue attempted to bridge the gap between the pop and progressive markets. Their *Shocking Blue At Home* contained such lengthy cuts as 'California Here I Come', 'The Butterfly And I' and featured a sitar on the innovative 'Acka Raga'. They remained largely a pop unit in the UK market however, where they enjoyed another minor hit with 'Mighty Joe', which had reached number 1 in Holland. Thereafter, the transatlantic hits evaporated although they managed another Dutch chart topper with 'Never Marry A Railroad Man'. Within four years of their international fame, they split in 1974, with Van Leeuwen later re-surfacing in the folk/jazz group, Galaxy Inc. His most famous song 'Venus' was frequently covered and was back at number 1 in the USA in 1981 and 1986 by **Stars On 45** and **Bananarama**, respectively.
Albums: *The Shocking Blue* (1970), *Shocking Blue At Home* (1970), *Scorpio's Dance* (early 70s), *Beat With Us* (early 70s).

Shocking Miss Pilgrim, The

Difficult to believe in these more enlightened times, that the lady was shocking because she had the temerity to work in an office. After Mr. Remington came up with his new-fangled invention in 1874, the thoroughly modern Miss Cynthia Pilgrim (**Betty Grable**) comes top of her class at a New York business school and takes a position as a 'typewriter' (typist) with the Pritchard Shipping Company in Boston. After overcoming initial opposition from her boss, John Pritchard (**Dick Haymes**), and the office manager (Gene Lockhart), Miss Pilgrim then compounds the felony by becoming leader of the local suffragette movement. However, this only postpones the inevitable romantic union between worker and management. Somewhat unusually, audiences were accorded only a very brief glimpse of the famous Grable legs - when she lifted her skirt to check a run in her stockings. The charming score had lyrics by **Ira Gershwin** to what he called 'posthumous' music. He and the composer-musician **Kay Swift** spent several weeks going through his late brother **George Gershwin**'s manuscripts, and the result was several delightful songs which included two outstanding duets for Grable and Haymes, 'For You, For Me, For Evermore' and 'Aren't You Kind Of Glad We Did?', along with several other appropriate items such as 'The Back Bay Polka', 'One Two Three', 'Waltz Me No Waltzes', Demon Rum', 'Changing My Tune', 'But Not In Boston', 'Waltzing Is Better Than Sitting Down', 'Sweet Packard', and 'Stand Up And Fight'. **Hermes Pan** staged the dances, and the screenplay, which was adapted from a story by Ernest and Frederica Maas, was written by George Seaton who also directed. The splendid supporting cast included Ann Revere, Allyn Joslyn, Elizabeth Patterson, Elizabeth Risdon, Arthur Shields, Charles Kemper, and Roy Roberts. *The Shocking Miss Pilgrim* was photographed in Technicolor by Leon Shamroy and produced for 20th Century-Fox by William Perlberg.

Shoes

Formed in Zion, Illinois, USA, this group comprised Jeff Murphy (vocal/guitar), brother John Murphy (bass/vocal), Gary Klebe (guitar/vocal) and Skip Meyer (drums). They preferred composing and recording on a TEAC four-track machine in the Murphy's living room to concert performances. When an architecture scholarship took Klebe to France in 1974, the others taped *One In Versailles* and pressed 300 copies to surprise him. On his return, this privatized policy continued with *Bazooka*, a tape circulated among immediate fans. Containing 15 original compositions, *Black Vinyl Shoes* reached a wider public that included Greg Shaw, who signed them to his Bomp label for a one-shot double a-side, 'Tomorrow Night'/'Okay'. The former was re-made in 1979 in England during sessions for *Present Tense*, the group's debut on **Elektra Records**. Subsequent product did not, however, include the hits needed to walk the Shoes into the pop mainstream.
Albums: *One In Versailles* (1974), *Black Vinyl Shoes* (1977), *Present Tense* (1979), *Tongue Twister* (1980), *Silhouettes* (1984).

Shok Paris

Hailing from Ohio State, USA, Shok Paris were formed in 1982 by the three-man nucleus of drummer Bill Sabo and guitarists Eric Manderwald and Ken Erb. With vocalist Vic Hix and bassist Kel Bershire completing the line-up, they debuted with 'Go Down Fighting' on the *Cleveland Metal* compilation. This opened the door to a deal with Auburn Records and they recorded *Go For The Throat* in less than two days.

Musically, with their high-energy, aggressive songs they were very much in the **Riot**, **Kiss** and **Accept** mould. Jan Roll took over the drumstool on *Steel And Starlight*, but this proved to be simply a repeat performance, played under different titles with less conviction than the debut.

Albums: *Go For The Throat* (Auburn 1984), *Steel And Starlight* (Auburn 1987).

Sholes, Steve

b. Stephen Henry Sholes, 12 February 1911, Washington DC, USA, d. 22 April 1968, Nashville, Tennessee, USA. Sholes' father worked in the music industry and in 1920, he moved the family to Merchantville, New Jersey, in order that he could work for **Victor** at their Camden recording studio. The boy inherited his father's love of music and learned to play clarinet and saxophone and after graduating, he worked for a time as a professional musician. In 1935, realising he would never reached the heights to which he aimed as a musician, he also gained employment with Victor. In 1939, he was appointed A&R man dealing with popular, jazz and big band music. He soon proved successful in this post and in the early 40s, he was allotted the task of overseeing all of **RCA**'s country and R&B recordings. This work led to him making regular visits to Nashville, where he quickly spotted the potential recording talents of **Eddy Arnold**. His career was interrupted for Army service in World War II but on his discharge in 1945, he concentrated more and more on recording artist in Nashville. It was through Sholes' careful guidance that RCA became the first major label to have permanent recording facilities in Music City. He was subsequently responsible for managing the recording careers of several major stars including **Hank Snow**, **Jim Reeves**, **Skeeter Davis** and **Chet Atkins**. In 1955, he signed **Elvis Presley** from **Sun Records.** He also groomed Atkins in the business side of the industry, appointing him as his assistant in 1952 and in 1957, he named Atkins the chief of RCA's country music operations in Nashville. In the early 60s, Sholes was one of the prominent members of the country music world who worked hard to see the foundation of Nashville's **Country Music Hall Of Fame**. In 1967, he was himself honoured with membership of that institution. The plaque erected on his induction stated 'Record Company executive and giant influence toward making country music an integral part of cultural America'. Sholes died following a heart attack in 1968.

Shondell, Troy

b. 14 May 1944, Fort Wayne, Indiana, USA. Shondell's 'This Time', a typical teen heartthrob song of the era, went to number 6 in the US charts, but he failed to build an enduring career in pop music when his follow-up, 'Tears From An Angel', got no higher than number 77. In the UK, 'This Time' went to number 22. Shondell was a music major at Valparaiso University when he recorded Chips Moman's 'This Time' in a Fort Wayne studio. After he released the record on his own Goldcrest label, the record started getting considerable airplay and he was signed to **Liberty Records**, which put the song on the national charts. When his pop career proved fleeting, Shondell moved to Nashville to pursue a career in country and western music. During the 80s he scored modestly with several songs on the country charts.

Album: *Many Sides Of Troy Shondell* (1963).

Shonen Knife

Japanese sisters Atsuko Yamano (b. 22 February c.1960, Osaka, Japan) and Naoko Yamano (b. 18 December c.1961, Osaka, Japan) with Michie Nakatani (b. 8 October c.1961, Osaka, Japan) play buzzsaw, distinctly **Ramones**-derived, pop. Shonen Knife means 'Boy Knife', the brand name of a small Japanese pocket knife. They formed in December 1981, their sporadic recording career starting in Osaka before relocating to the west coast of America. There they came to the attention of US punk pop fans in general, and **Nirvana** in particular. The latter took them under their wing with support slots, which brought them international recognition. However, they had long been a cult delicacy in American punk circles, made evident when 30 bands each contributed to an album's worth of covers of Shonen Knife songs (*Every Band Has A Shonen Knife Who Loves Them*). Although their charm may be limited in the long-term, a suitable epitaph for their appeal comes from Nirvana's Kurt Cobain: 'They play pop music, pop, pop, pop music'.

Albums: *Burning Farm* (Zero 1983, mini-album), *Yamano Atchan* (Zero 1984, mini-album), *Pretty Little Baka Guy* (Zero 1986, mini-album), *712* (Nippon Crown 1991), *Let's Knife* (MCA Victor 1992), *Rock Animals* (August Records 1993). Compilation: *Shonen Knife* (Giant 1990).

Shooters

The Shooters' leader is Walt Aldridge (guitar/vocals) and the other members are Gary Baker (bass), Barry Billings (guitar), Chalmers Davis (keyboards) and Michael Dillon (drums). They had US country hits with 'They Only Come Out At Night', 'Tell It To Your Teddy Bear', 'Borderline' amongst others in the late 80s. Their albums combine various forms of music with *Solid As A Rock* being recorded in Muscle Shoals.

Albums: *Shooters* (1987), *Solid As A Rock* (Epic 1989).

Shooting Star

One of the greatest exponents of pomp rock, Shooting Star exploded onto the scene during the 80's. An American outfit with a strong line-up of Van McLain (vocals/guitar), Gary West (guitar/vocals/keyboards),

Charles Waltz (vocals/violin), Ron Vernin (bass) and Steve Thomas (drums), they have consistently released solid albums, arguably reaching a peak with *Ill Wishes*. The music is full-blooded with magnificent harmonies and enormous choruses. Following their 1985 release the band seemed to go into hibernation, during which time Gary West and Charles Waltz left for pastures new. Their 1991 offering continues where they left off, with the title seeming to be particularly apt.

Albums: *Shooting Star* (1980), *Hang On For Your Life* (1981), *Ill Wishes* (1982), *Burning* (1983), *Silent Scream* (1985), *It's Not Over* (1991).

Shop Assistants

Formed in Edinburgh, Scotland, during 1984, this pop band used guitar inflections enthusiastically borrowed from the **Buzzcocks**. They were originally titled Buba And The Shop Assistants and released a solitary single, 'Something To Do', under that name. With only 500 pressings on the obscure Villa 21 independent, it has gained a reputation amongst record collectors for its monetary value as well as the spirited songwriting. Mainman David Keegan (guitar) was joined by Alex Taylor (vocals), Sarah Kneale (bass) and twin drummers Ann Donald (replaced in 1986 by Joan Bride) and Laura McPhail. 'All Day Long', on the Subway Organisation label, was allegedly **Morrissey**'s favourite single of 1985, but by this time they had garnered adequate plaudits from their exposure in fanzines and magazines. The following year's release on the 53rd & 3rd label (jointly set up by Keegan with Stephen of the **Pastels**), 'Safety Net', reached number 1 on the UK independent chart. Signing to the major **Chrysalis Records** label saw the release of their debut album, which made a brief appearance in the Top 100 and then disappeared - as did the band. When Taylor left in 1987 to form the **Motorcycle Boy** the critical acclaim dried up. Keegan also left, taking up a post as skiing instructor, while Kneale and McPhail went back to college. They reformed in 1990, with McPhail switching to bass and Margarita taking her place on drums. One of the singles produced, 'The Big E', was, typically, a tribute to the guitar chord rather than the fashionable drug of the period. By this time they had signed to Andrew Tulley's Avalanche label, although their status in the independent scene has been somewhat eroded by the passing years. Keegan would eventually make a permanent commitment to the Pastels.

Album: *Shop Assistants* (Chrysalis 1986).

Shore, Dinah

b. Frances Rose Shore, 1 March 1917, Winchester, Tennessee, USA, d. 24 February 1994, Los Angeles, California, USA. One of her country's most enduring all-round entertainers, Shore staked her first claim to fame, while still at school, on Nashville radio. Further broadcasting and theatre engagements in New York soon followed. She she recorded with **Xaviar Cugat** and **Ben Bernie**, and sang on some of Cugat's early 40s hits, such as 'The Breeze And I', 'Whatever Happened To You?', 'The Rhumba-Cardi', and 'Quierme Mucho (Yours)', initially under the name Dinah Shaw. Shore was one of the first vocalists to break free from the big bands (she had been rejected at auditions for **Benny Goodman** and **Tommy Dorsey**) and become a star in her own right. She became extremely popular on both radio, and made her solo recording debut in 1939. Her smoky, low-pitched voice was especially attractive on slow ballads, and from 1940-57 she had a string of some 80 US chart hits, including 'Yes, My Darling Daughter', 'Jim', 'Blues In The Night', 'Skylark', 'You'd Be So Nice To Come Home To', 'Murder, He Says', 'Candy', 'Laughing On The Outside (Crying On The Inside)', 'All That Glitters Is Not Gold', 'Doin' What Comes Natur'lly', 'You Keep Coming Back Like A Song', 'I Wish I Didn't Love You So', 'You Do', 'Baby, It's Cold Outside' (with Buddy Clark), 'Dear Hearts And Gentle People', 'My Heart Cries For You', 'A Penny A Kiss', 'Sweet Violets'; and number 1's, 'I'll Walk Alone', 'The Gypsy', 'Anniversary Song', and 'Buttons And Bows'. She made a number of film appearances, including *Thank Your Lucky Stars* (1943), **Up In Arms** (1944), *Follow The Boys* (1944), *Belle Of The Yukon* (1945), **Till The Clouds Roll By** (1946), and *Aaron Slick From Punkin Crick* (1952). She also lent her voice to two **Walt Disney** animated features, *Make Mine Music* (1946) and *Fun And Fancy Free* (1957), and was last seen on the big screen in the George Burns comedy *Oh God!* (1977), and Robert Altman's quirky political satire *H.E.A.L.T.H.* (1979). In 1951 Shore began appearing regularly on television, making several spectaculars. Later, it was her continuing success on the small screen that brought about a career change when she became host on a highly rated daytime talk show, a role she maintained into the 80s. Her popularity on television barely declined throughout this period, and she won no less than 10 Emmys in all. The late 80s saw her performing on stage once more, though she returned to the television format for *Conversation With Dinah*, which ran from 1989-91.

Selected albums: *Blues In The Night* (1952), with Buddy Clark 'S*Wonderful* (c.50s), *Holding Hands At Midnight* (1955), *Moments Like These* (c.50s), *Buttons And Bows* (1959), *Dinah, Yes Indeed!* (1959), with André Previn *Dinah Sings, Previn Plays* (1960), *Lavender Blue* (1960), with the Red Norvo Quintet *Some Blues With Red* (1962), *Dinah, Down Home!* (1962), *Lower Basin St. Revisted* (1965), *Make The World Go Away* (1987), *Oh Lonesome Me* (c.80s). Further reading: *Dinah!*, Cassidy, B. (1979).

Short, Bobby

b. Robert Waltrip, 15 September 1926, Danville, Illinois, USA. A self-taught pianist, Short worked in vaudeville as a child and sang in clubs and on radio in Chicago. In mid-1937 he went to New York where he played and sang for audiences unprepared for smart-suited sophistication from a pre-teenager. Short went back to school, but influenced by the stylish performances of such night-club artists as **Hildegarde**, continued to hone his act. When he returned to show business he toured extensively, eventually spending some time on the west coast. By the early 50s he had matured into a sophisticated singer-pianist. Whether in Los Angeles, New York or Paris, he played the best night-clubs, establishing a reputation as a witty purveyor of songs. His vocal range is limited, and accordingly he sings with engaging restraint. His club appearances over the years at such places as the Café Carlyle and 21, have earned him a following.

Further reading: *Black And White Baby*, Bobby Short.

Short, J.D.

b. 26 December 1902, Port Gibson, Mississippi, USA, d. November 1962. Short grew up in various parts of Mississippi where he learned guitar from Willie Johnson and piano from Son Harris. In 1923, Short moved to St Louis where he was discovered by **Jessie Stone**. He recorded country blues for Paramount (1930) and Vocalion (1932), but spent most of the 30s playing clarinet in a St Louis jazz group. Short was crippled by a wartime injury but continued performing after 1945, often as a guitar/harmonica/bass drum one-man-band and sometimes with his cousin **Big Joe Williams**. The duo worked together on Short's final recording for **Sonet**, recreating on tracks like 'Starry Crown Blues', the music of their early years in the South. Short died a few months later, in November 1962.

Albums: *The Legacy Of The Blues Vol 8* (1962).

Shorter, Wayne

b. 25 August 1933, Newark, New Jersey, USA. Shorter first played clarinet, taking up the tenor saxophone during his late teens. He studied music at New York University during the mid-50s before serving in the US army for two years. During his student days he had played with various bands, including that led by **Horace Silver**, and on his discharge encountered **John Coltrane**, with whom he developed many theoretical views on music. He was also briefly with **Maynard Ferguson**. In 1959 he became a member of **Art Blakey**'s **Jazz Messengers**, remaining with the band until 1963. The following year he joined **Miles Davis**, staying until 1970. Late that year he teamed up with **Joe Zawinul**, whom he had first met in the Ferguson band, to form **Weather Report**. During his stints with Blakey and Davis Shorter had written extensively and his compositions had also formed the basis of several increasingly experimental record sessions under his own name for the **Blue Note** label. He continued to write for the new band and also for further dates under his own name and with **V.S.O.P.**, with whom he worked in the mid- and late 70s. In the mid-80s he was leading his own band and also recording and touring with other musicians, thus reducing his activities with Weather Report.

As a player, Shorter developed through his period with Blakey into a leading proponent of hard bop. His fiery, tough-toned and dramatically angular playing was well-suited to the aggressive nature of the Blakey band. During his time with Davis another side to his musical personality emerged, in which a more tender approach greatly enhanced his playing. This side had made its appearance earlier, on *Wayning Moments*, but was given greater scope with Davis. On Davis's *Bitches Brew*, Shorter also played soprano saxophone: two weeks later he employed this instrument throughout on his own *Super Nova*, playing with exotic enthusiasm. The years with Zawinul broadened his range still further, highlighting his appreciation of freer forms and giving rein to his delight in musical exotica. Although laying ground rules for many later fusion bands, Weather Report's distinction lay in the way the group allowed the two principals to retain their powerful musical personalities. Later, as the band began to sound more like other fusion bands, Shorter's exploratory nature found greater scope in the bands he formed away from Weather Report. As a composer, Shorter was responsible for some of the best work of the Blakey band of his era and also for many of Davis's stronger pieces of the late 60s. A major innovator and influence on hard boppers and fusionists alike, Shorter remains one of the most imaginative musicians in jazz, constantly seeking new horizons but - thanks to his broad musical knowledge - retaining identifiable links with the past.

Selected albums: *The Vee Jay Years* (Affinity 1959), *Wayne Shorter* (1959-62), *Wayning Moments* (Affinity 1961-62), *Night Dreamer* (1964), *Juju* (1964), *Speak No Evil* (Blue Note 1964), *Night Dreamer* (Blue Note 1964), *The Best Of Wayne Shorter* (1964-67), with Miles Davis *Live At The Plugged Nickel* (1965), *The Soothsayer* (1965), *The All-Seeing Eye* (1965), *Etcetera* (1965), *Adam's Apple* (Blue Note 1966), *Schizophrenia* (1967), *Super Nova* (Blue Note 1969), *Odyssey Of Iska* (1970), *Moto Grosso Feio* (c.1971), *Native Dancer* (Columbia 1974), *Atlantis* (CBS 1985), *Endangered Species* (1985), *Phantom Navigator* (CBS 1986-87), *Joy Ryder* (CBS 1987), *Second Genesis* (Affinity 1993), with Herbie Hancock, Ron Carter, Wallace Roney, Tony Williams *A Tribute To Miles* (QWest/Reprise 1994), *All Seeing Eye* (Connoisseur 1994).

Shortino, Paul

Former **Quiet Riot** vocalist Shortino found musical ambition early in life, coming from a talented family and taking vocal lessons before his teens. Later came a series of bands on Hollywood's Sunset Strip playing club gigs. It was in this scene that he first encountered Wendy and Ronnie Dio (of **Dio**), through whose auspices Shortino was engaged as vocalist for **Rough Cutt**. After that band sundered he would join Quiet Riot in 1989, but not before he had written songs for the television series *Fame*, and played the part of Duke Fame in *Spinal Tap*. The 90s saw him elect to pursue a solo career, joining with guitarist Jeff Northrup. The first results of this collaboration would arrive with the release of the agenda-setting *Back On Track* in March 1994.

Album: *Back On Track* (Bulletproof 1994).

Shotgun Messiah

This Swedish act began life as **Kingpin**, with Harry K. Cody (guitar), Tim Skold (bass) and Stixx Galore (drums) joined by ex-**Easy Action** vocalist Zinny J. San, releasing *Welcome To Bop City* in 1988. A subsequent relocation to Los Angeles, USA, saw a name change for both band and (remixed) album. *Shotgun Messiah* was set apart from other glam albums by the quality of musicianship, Cody evoking **Steve Vai** and **Joe Satriani** with his fluid soloing. San departed after touring was complete, with Skold taking the vocalist slot while Bobby Lycon joined as bassist for *Second Coming*, which offered promising songwriting progression and gruff, powerful vocals from Skold. However, the band failed to expand beyond their cult status despite enthusiastic press support, and both Lycon and Stixx left after *I Want More*, an EP of covers (**Ramones**, **New York Dolls**, **Iggy Pop**) and acoustic reworkings of older material. Cody and Skold (now bassist/vocalist) took the bold step of industrializing Shotgun Messiah, using drum machines, synthesizers and samples on *Violent New Breed*, and creating a new sound by blending commercial songwriting with abrasive delivery for an excellent album, although the transformation was viewed with cynicism in some quarters. However, this effort still could not enhance Shotgun Messiah's fortunes, and Cody and Skold called it a day soon after.

Albums: *Shotgun Messiah* (Relativity 1989), *Second Coming* (Relativity 1991), *I Want More* (Relativity 1992, mini-album), *Violent New Breed* (Relativity 1993).

Shout

This US melodic rock group was put together by ex-**Joshua** guitarist/vocalist Ken Tamplin and ex-**Idle Cure** guitarist Chuck King in 1988. Recruiting bassist Loren Robinson, they entered the studio with session drummers Dennis Holt and Mark Hugenberger to record *It Won't Be Long*. This featured highly sophisticated arrangements and classy songs in the **Journey**, **Boston** and **Styx** mould. Joey Galletta was added as a permanent drummer for *In Your Face*, which leaned towards a significantly heavier direction. The album also featured guest appearances from guitarists Alex Masi, **Marty Friedman** and Lanny Cordola and was notable for some exciting six-string duels on many of the songs. The band became inactive in 1990, when Tamplin teamed up with Cordola (ex-**House Of Lords**) to form **Magdallan**.

Albums: *It Won't Be Long* (1988), *In Your Face* (1989).

Show Boat

A major theatrical triumph of the 20s which has never lost its original magic, *Show Boat* opened at the Ziegfeld Theatre in New York on 27 December 1927. **Oscar Hammerstein II** based his libretto on the Edna Ferber novel about the life and loves of the resident family and the travelling entertainers on a particular Mississippi riverboat in the late 19th century. With music by **Jerome Kern** and book and lyrics by **Oscar Hammerstein II**, the magnificent score included many songs which have become an integral part of American popular music. Perhaps the best known is 'Ol' Man River', sung in the original staging by Jules Bledsoe as Joe, but made internationally famous by **Paul Robeson** who played Joe in the 1932 Broadway production. This had basically the original cast, except for Robeson, and Dennis King, who replaced Howard Marsh. Other fine songs included 'Make Believe', 'You Are Love', 'Can't Help Lovin' Dat Man', 'Life Upon The Wicked Stage', 'Till Good Luck Comes My Way', 'I Might Fall Back On You', 'After The Ball', and 'Why Do I Love You?'. Another number, 'Bill' (lyric with **P.G. Wodehouse**) had been discarded from at least two of Kern's earlier shows, was revived for **Helen Morgan** in the role of Julie. It became one of the hits of the production and was ever afterwards associated with the singer. Also among the cast were Norma Terris, Charles Winninger, Edna May Oliver, Tess, Gardella, Eva Puck, Sammy White, and Charles Ellis. *Show Boat* ran on Broadway for 572 performances. When it was staged in London in 1928, the cast included Robeson, Edith Day, Howett Worster, Cedric Hardwicke, Marie Burke, Viola Compton, and **Alberta Hunter**. London audiences saw it again in 1943 and 1971. For the 1946 Broadway revival, which ran for 418 performances, Kern and Hammerstein added a new song, 'Nobody Else But Me', which is said to have been Kern's last composition. The show was produced in 1966 at the Lincoln Center with **Barbara Cook**, Stephen Douglass, David Wayne, Constance Towers, and William Warfield, and in 1983 by the Houston Grand Opera with a cast that included **Donald O'Connor**, Sheryl Woods, and Ron Raines. In 1990, a version by Opera North and the Royal

Shakespeare Company toured the UK and played a limited season at the London Palladium. Four years later, in October 1994, an 'enormously affecting production', directed by **Hal Prince**, which had previously been well received in Toronto, opened on Broadway to excellent reviews. It won **Tony Awards** for best musical revival, director, choreography (Susan Stroman), and featured actress (Gretha Boston). Several film versions have been made, the first in 1929 as a silent with sound added. The 1936 release starred Morgan, Robeson, **Allan Jones** and Hattie McDaniel, and in the 1951 remake the leads were sung by **Howard Keel** and **Kathryn Grayson**. In 1988, EMI Records in the UK released what they claimed was 'the first ever complete recording of Jerome Kern and Oscar Hammerstein II's great musical'. It featured Frederica von Stade, Jerry Hadley, Teresa Stratas, Bruce Hubbard, Karia Burns, Lillian Gish, and the London Sinfonietta conducted by John McGlinn. Further reading: *Show Boat: The Story Of A Classic American Musical*, M. Kreuger.

Show Boat (Film Musical)

The first screen adaptation of **Jerome Kern** and **Oscar Hammerstein II**'s Broadway show was a part-talkie released in 1929. Seven years later, Hammerstein himself wrote the screenplay which retold the familiar story of life on the Mississippi showboat operated by Captain Andy Hawks. This version starred several of the artists who had, at one time or another, appeared on stage in this beloved American classic. Irene Dunne and **Allan Jones** play the young ingenue Magnolia Hawks and Gaylord Ravenal, her no-good gambler of a husband; **Helen Morgan** is the mulatto Julie (she also took the role in the 1929 film), with Donald Cook as her husband Steve; Charles Winninger plays the jovial and understanding Captain Hawks, and **Paul Robeson**, as Joe, sings the immortal 'Ol' Man River'. Most of the songs from the original score were retained, including 'Make Believe' (Dunne and Jones), 'Can't Help Lovin' Dat Man' (Morgan), 'Bill' (lyric also with **P.G. Wodehouse**) (Morgan), and 'You Are Love' (Dunne and Jones). In addition, Kern and Hammerstein wrote three new ones, 'Ah Still Suits Me' (Robeson), 'Gallivantin' Around' (Dunne), and the lovely 'I Have The Room Above Her' (Dunne and Jones). LeRoy Prinz choreographed the spirited and imaginative dance sequences, and the film was produced for Universal by Carl Laemmle Jnr. and directed by James Whale. From the opening titles with their cardboard cut-out figures and models on a carousel, through to the film's final moments when Ravenal, reduced to working as theatre doorman, is reunited with Magnolia and their daughter Kim, this picture is a total delight.

Show Boat was remade in 1951 by the renowned **Arthur Freed** Unit at MGM. This extremely satisfying version starred **Kathryn Grayson** (Magnolia), **Howard Keel** (Ravenal), Ava Gardner (Julie, singing dubbed by Annette Warren), and Joe E. Brown (Captain Hawks). William Warfield sang 'Ol' Man Man River', and Marge and **Gower Champion**'s song-and-dance routines based around 'I Might Fall Back On You' and 'Life Upon The Wicked Stage' were utterly charming. Those two songs were from the 1927 stage show, and another of the original numbers, 'Why Do I Love You?', which not used in the 1936 film, was sung here by Grayson and Keel. John Lee Mahin's screenplay differed in some respects from Hammerstein's earlier effort, but remained generally faithful to the spirit of the piece. The choreography was the work of Robert Alton, the film was directed by George Sidney.

Show Is On, The

One of the last of the smart and sophisticated Broadway revues that were so popular in the late 20s and early 30s. This one, which was a vehicle for the extravagant comedic talents of Beatrice Lillie and Bert Lahr, opened at the Winter Garden in New York on 25 December 1936. David Freedman and **Moss Hart** wrote the sketches which emphasised the production's celebration of 'show business', and lampooned contemporary figures such as John Gielgud and Leslie Howard, who were both offering their 'Hamlets' in New York. The songs came from a variety of composers and lyricists, but 'Little Old Lady' (**Hoagy Carmichael** and Stanley Adams) and 'By Strauss' (**George Gershwin-Ira Gershwin**) are probably the best-remembered items from the score. There were several other appealing numbers, including 'Long As You've Got Your Health' (Will Irwin-**E.Y. 'Yip Harburg**-Norman Zeno), 'Song Of The Woodman' (**Harold Arlen**-Harburg), 'Now' (**Vernon Duke**-Ted Fetter), 'Rhythm' (**Richard Rodgers-Lorenz Hart**), and 'Buy Yourself A Balloon' (**Herman Hupfield**). During the latter, Beatrice Lillie distributed garters to gentlemen members of the audience while perched on a 'moon seat', which was swung out into the auditorium. The show was stylishly directed by Edward Clark Lilley and **Vincente Minnelli**, several years before the beginning of Minnelli's distinguished Hollywood career. It ran for 237 performances, and, in some ways, marked the end of an elegant and rather special era.

Showaddywaddy

When two promising Leicestershire groups fused their talents in 1973, the result was an octet comprising Dave Bartram (vocals), Billy Gask (vocals), Russ Fields (guitar), Trevor Oakes (guitar), Al James (bass), Rod Teas (bass), Malcolm Allured (drums) and Romeo Challenger (drums). Showaddywaddy personified the easy-listening dilution of rock 'n' roll and rockabilly and their visual appeal and showmanship won them talent contests and, more importantly, a contract with Bell Records. Initially penning their own hits, they charted steadily, but after reaching number 2 with **Eddie Cochran's** 'Three Steps To Heaven', the cover version game was begun in earnest. Fifteen of their singles reached the UK Top 20 during the late 70s but the seemingly foolproof hit formula ran dry in the following decade when the rock 'n' roll revival had passed.

Albums: *Showaddywaddy* (Bell 1974), *Step Two* (Bell 1975), *Trocadero* (Bell 1976), *Red Star* (Arista 1977), *Crepes And Drapes* (Arista 1979), *Bright Lights* (Arista 1980), *Good Times* (1981), *Jump Boogie And Jive* (President 1991), Compilations: *Greatest Hits* (Arista 1976), *The Very Best Of* (Arista 1981), *Living Legends* (1983), *The Best Steps To Heaven* (Tiger 1987), *20 Steps To The Top* (Repertoire 1991), *20 Greatest Hits* (IMD 1992).

Showbiz And AG

Bronx-based compatriots of **Diamond D**, **Showbiz And AG** were forced to make their mark in hip hop by establishing their own independent label, Showbiz Records, to house their debut EP, *Soul Clap*. This emerged in late 1991, and immediately created a buzz, leading them into a deal with **London** Records. AG had previously worked freestyle battles with **Lord Finesse** in high school, who introduced him to Showbiz. The partnership formed, they hustled through New York in a failed bid to get a contract. However, when their debut EP landed, particularly through the sucess of the 'Diggin' In The Crates' cut, they were hot news on the scene. Their profile was galvanised by Showbiz's highly successful remix of **Arrested Development**'s 'Tenessee'. He has gone on to foster the careers of Big L and Deshawn.

Album: *Represent* (London 1992).

Showers, 'Little' Hudson

b. 6 September 1919, Anguilla, Mississippi, USA. Little Hudson (as he was known on records) had been playing guitar for some years when he moved to Chicago at the age of 20. There he began to play on the flourishing blues scene, and eventually started his own group, the Red Devils Trio. He made some records in 1953, for the JOB label with his band including pianist Lazy Bill Lucas, but otherwise remained obscure. A very short recording, originally made as a radio advertisement, has been unearthed and issued in more recent years.

Albums: *John Brim And Little Hudson* (1981), *Southside Screamers* (1984).

Showmen

An R&B vocal group from Norfolk, Virginia, USA. The Showmen were a classic early 60s transitional group that represented some of the dying gasps of doo-wop and the first stirrings of the soul revolution.

Members were General Norman Johnson (b. 23 May 1943, Norfolk, USA), Milton Wells, Gene and Dorsey Wright, and Leslie Felton. The group signed with the New Orleans-based Minit label in 1961 and had a hit immediately with a perky anthem for rock 'n' roll and R&B called 'It Will Stand' (number 40 R&B, number 61 pop). The b-side, 'Country Fool', received solid airplay in many parts of the country. The staying power of 'It Will Stand' was most evident when it made a modest return to the charts in 1964 (number 80 pop). In 1963 the Showmen found success in many markets with the delightful '39-21-46', and this too proved to have staying power over the years. The Showmen moved to the Philadelphia-based Swan label in 1965, but the singles they released were uninspired. The group's last record was in 1967, recorded in the Carolinas for the tiny Jokers Three label. In 1968 Johnson moved to Detroit and formed the **Chairman Of The Board** to record on the Invictus label. The Showmen's legacy lived on in the Carolinas where their classic hits, 'It Will Stand' and '39-21-46' have become Beach standards. Johnson for decades pursued a lucrative career down there as a Beach artist long after his popularity in the black community had faded.

Compilation: *Some Folks Don't Understand It* (Charly 1991).

Showstoppers

This US group was formed in Philadelphia by the younger brothers of R&B singer **Solomon Burke**. The unit comprised, Laddie Burke (b. 1950, Philadelphia, Pennsylvania, USA) and Alex Burke (b. 1949, Philadelphia, Pennsylvania, USA). The group was completed by another set of brothers, Earl Smith (b. 1949, Massachusetts, USA) and Timmy Smith (b. 1950, Massachusetts, USA). Having met while studying at Germantown High School, this electrifying unit, initially influenced by the vocal group, the **Vibrations**, is best recalled for 'Ain't Nothing But A Houseparty' (1968), a vibrant, infectious song beloved in discotheques. A minor pop hit in the US, the single proved far more popular in Britain, reaching number 11 on its first release before re-entering the charts in 1971. The backing musicians on this song included Carl Chambers, who was later drummer to **Gladys Knight And The Pips**, and Joe Thomas, who went on to become the guitarist with the **Impressions**. Two equally exciting tracks, 'Eeny Meeny' a UK Top 40 entry in 1968, and 'Shake Your Mini', followed, but the Showstoppers were unable to repeat their early success.

Shriekback

Shriekback originally evolved around a three-man nucleus of ex-**Gang Of Four** member Dave Allen, Carl Marsh (fresh from his own band, Out On Blue Six), plus Barry Andrews, previously with **XTC**,

League Of Gentlemen and Restaurant For Dogs. The trio fused funk and rock with a unique and complex rhythmic approach, creating a distinctive and influential sound. The first fruits of this project came in 1982 with the EP *Tench* and then 'Sexthinkone' on the Y label, but it was the next two singles, 'My Spine Is the Bassline' (1982) and 'Lined Up' (1983) that established the band. Two further singles, 'Working On The Ground' and 'Accretions', were enough to secure a deal with **Arista Records**, releasing *Jam Science* in 1984. The album also spawned two excellent singles, 'Hand On My Heart' and 'Mercy Dash'. The following year saw the release of *Oil And Gold*, which included 'Nemesis' and 'Fish Below The Ice'. Although more commercially based, the band had lost that hard, infectious funk vein that was previously so predominant. A move to **Island** yielded *Big Night Music*, early in 1987, accompanied by 'Gunning For Buddha' a month earlier. 'Get Down Tonight' followed in 1988, but this presaged the last Shriekback album proper, *Go Bang*. Those looking for an introduction to Shriekback might opt for *The Infinite*, a collection of the Y singles released on the Kaz label. Since then, there have been two further collections, summarising the band's time with Arista and Island respectively.

Albums: *Care* (1983), *Jam Science* (1984), *Oil And Gold* (1985), *Big Night Music* (1987), *Go Bang* (1988), *Sacred City* (Shriek 1994). Compilations: *The Infinite - The Best Of Shriekback* (1985), *The Best Of Shriekback, Volume 2* (1988), *The Best Of Shriekback* (1990).

Shuffle Along

This show started its life in America as a vaudeville sketch, and was then adapted into the 'longest-running musical to be produced, directed, written, and acted by Negroes'. Naturally, given the era in which it was created and the kind of people who were concerned with it, *Shuffle Along* was not invited to occupy a prime site. Rather it was shuffled off to the 63rd St. Music Hall at the northern end of Broadway, where it opened on 23 May 1921. Much to everyone's surprise, the show was a big hit, and ran for 504 performances. This was not neccessarily due to the book, which was written by Flournoy Miller and Aubrey Lyles, and provided the authors with two of the leading roles. Their story of political corruption in Jimtown, Dixieland, tells of how the leading candidates for the office of mayor, Steve Jenkins (Miller) and Sam Peck (Lyles), fix it so that whichever one of them wins - the other cannot lose. Eventually they are both kicked out of office by a knight in shining armour, the high-principled Harry Walton (Roger Matthews). **Noble Sissle** and **Eubie Blake** also took part in the show, but their main role was to write the score which contained one enormous hit, 'I'm Just Wild About Harry', as well as a varied selection of songs including the charming 'Love Will Find A Way', 'Bandana Days', 'If You've Never Been Vamped By a Brownskin (You've Never Been Vamped At All)', 'Everything Reminds Me Of You', 'Low Down Blues', 'Shuffle Along', and several more. **Paul Robeson** joined the Broadway cast for a time in as member of a vocal group, and, when the show eventually went on the road, **Joséphine Baker** was a member of the chorus. This was a tremendous, fast moving production, with a lot of style, humour, and pulsating music. Subsequent attempts to recreate the formula in 1928, 1932, and 1952, were all unsuccessful. Eubie Blake lived to be over 100, and a musical anthology of some of his work, entitled *Eubie!*, played on Broadway in 1978.

Shuman, Mort

b. 12 November 1936, Brooklyn, New York, USA, d. 2 November 1991, London, England. After studying music, Shuman began writing songs with blues singer **Doc Pomus** in 1958. Early in 1959 two of their songs were Top 40 hits: 'Plain Jane' for **Bobby Darin**, and **Fabian**'s 'I'm A Man'. During the next six years, their catalogue was estimated at over 500 songs, in a mixture of styles for a variety of artists. They included 'Surrender', 'Viva Las Vegas', 'Little Sister' and 'Kiss Me Quick' (**Elvis Presley**), 'Save The Last Dance For Me', 'Sweets For My Sweet' and 'This Magic Moment' (the **Drifters**), 'Teenager In Love' (**Dion And The Belmonts**), 'Can't Get Used To Losing You' (**Andy Williams**), 'Suspicion' (**Terry Stafford**); 'Seven Day Weekend' (**Gary 'U.S.' Bonds**) and 'Spanish Lace' (**Gene McDaniels**). Around the time of the team's break-up in 1965, Shuman collaborated with several other writers. These included John McFarland for **Billy J. Kramer**'s UK number 1, 'Little Children', Clive Westlake for 'Here I Go Again' (the **Hollies**), ex-pop star, **Kenny Lynch**, for 'Sha-La-La-La-Lee' (**Small Faces**), 'Loves Just A Broken Heart' (**Cilla Black**), producer **Jerry Ragavoy** for 'Get It While You Can' and 'Look At Granny Run, Run' (**Howard Tate**). Subsequently, Shuman moved to Paris, where he occasionally performed his own one-man show, and issued solo albums such as *Amerika* and *Imagine...*, as well as writing several songs for **Johnny Hallyday**. In 1968 Shuman translated the lyrics of French composer **Jacques Brel**; these were recorded by many artists including **Dusty Springfield**, **Scott Walker** and **Rod McKuen**. Together with Eric Blau, he devised, adapted and wrote lyrics for the revue *Jacques Brel Is Alive And Well And Living In Paris*. Shuman also starred in the piece, which became a world-wide success. In October 1989, *Budgie*, a musical set in London's Soho district, with Schuman's music and **Don Black**'s lyrics, opened in the West End. It starred former pop star, turned actor and entrepreneur, **Adam Faith**, and UK soap opera actress, Anita Dobson. The show closed after only three months, losing more than £1,000,000. Shuman wrote several other shows, including *Amadeo, Or How To Get Rid Of It*, based on an Ionesco play, a Hong Kong portrayal of *Madame Butterfly* and a re-working of Bertolt Brecht and **Kurt Weill**'s opera *Aufstieg Und Fall Der Stadt Mahogonny*. None has yet reached the commercial theatre. After undergoing a liver operation in the spring of 1991, he died in London.

Shusha

b. Shusha Guppy, 7 January 1940, Teheran, Iran. This songwriter, singer and author emigrated to France at the age of 16, and was educated at the Sorbonne in Paris, studying Oriental Languages and Philosophy. Having married an English author during the 60s, she relocated to London. Although she had trained and studied as an opera singer, her interest lay in a range of musical styles from medieval folk through 16th century ballads, to the works of writers such as **Jacques Brel** and **Joan Baez**. Shusha garnered a good deal of critical praise for a number of her recordings during the 70s, and made a number of television and radio appearances. In 1973, she travelled with the nomadic Bakhtiari tribe in Iran, making two films. The first, *People Of The Wind*, a documentary about the migration of the tribe across the mountains, won an Oscar nomination for best documentary in 1977. A soundtrack album from the film was later released in the USA. The second film was a short of Shusha singing during the journey. Never predictable, her albums varied in content. *From East To West* saw a collaboration with arranger **Paul Buckmaster**, setting traditional Persian songs to a jazz/rock setting. *Here I Love You*, by comparison, was an album of her own songs, while. *Durable Fire* featured songs by English poets, including William Shakespeare and Ted Hughes. Albums: *Song Of Long-Time Lovers* (1972), *Persian Love Songs And Mystic Chants* (1973), *Shusha* (1974), *This Is The Day* (1974), *Before The Deluge* (1975), *From East To West* (1978), *Here I Love You* (1980), with various artists *Lovely In The Dances-Songs Of Sydney Carter* (1981), *Durable Fire* (1983), *Strange Affair* (1987).
Further reading: *The Blindfold Horse-Memories Of A Persian Childhood*, Shusha Guppy, *A Girl In Paris*, Shusha Guppy, *Looking Back*, Shusha Guppy.

Shut Up And Dance

Hip hop/house artists PJ and Smiley (both b. c.1969) comprise this duo, who are also producers and owners of the Shut Up And Dance Rerord label (run from a bedroom in Stoke Newington). The group formed in Spring 1988, the record label coming a year later. This has saw releases by the Ragga Twins ('Spliffhead'), **Nicolette** and Rum & Black. Shut Up And Dance all began with the intoxicating club cut '5678', which eventually moved over 14,000 copies. This helped fund Shut Up And Dance as a full-scale label enterprise, with a penchant for the absurd. Their own '£10 To

Get In' and 'Derek Went Mad' being good examples. One 12-inch, 'Lamborghini', stitched together **Prince** and Annie Lennox (**Eurythmics**), and though it made the UK Top 60 radio stations refused to play it fearing punitive writs. The duo had originally recorded a novelty single under the name Private Party which featured various characters from the *Thunderbirds* and *Muppets* television programmes. Their anonymity was enhanced by the lack of detail which usually accompanied their releases, helping them become leaders in the UK's underground dance scene. Musically they spliced their recordings with samples drawn from a myriad of sources; predictable dub reggae through to techno beats. However, it was the number 2 chart smash 'Ravin' I'm Ravin'' (sung by **Peter Bouncer**) which brought them real commercial attention, more than they either envisaged or welcomed. It also sent copyright lawyers into apopletic overdrive. They spent almost two years struggling in court following action taken by the MCPS on behalf of six major record companies for uncleared use of samples. Although they returned with an EP in 1994, the appropriately titled *Phuck The Biz*, their legal problems were far from over, their business having long since been declared bankrupt. It would be a shame if their brushes with the law overshadowed classic records like 1992's 'Autobiography Of A Crack Head'.
Albums: *Dance Before The Police Come* (Shut Up And Dance 1990), *Death Is Not The End* (Shut Up And Dance 1992).

Shy

This quintet were founded in Birmingham, England, and specialized in Americanized, melodic heavy rock. Formed in 1982, they released their debut album the following year on the independent Ebony label. The songs were excellent, characterized by the silver-throated purr of Tony Mills, but the album was let down by a slight production. New bassist Roy Stephen Davis joined in 1984, and along with vocalist Mills, guitarist Steve Harris, drummer Alan Kelly and keyboard player Pat McKenna, they secured a new deal with **RCA Records**. Two quality albums of sophisticated pomp-metal followed, with 1987's *Excess All Areas* being the band's finest work. This included a melodramatic version of **Cliff Richard**'s 'Devil Woman' given a true heavy metal revision. They gained the support slot on **Meat Loaf**'s 1987 UK tour, but the album still failed to sell in large quantities. RCA dropped the band, but they were rescued by **MCA Records**, which allocated a large budget to record *Misspent Youth*, with Roy Thomas Baker as producer. This album was a major disappointment as the band's naturally aggressive approach had been tempered. The songs were geared for Stateside FM-radio consumption and the group's identity was suffocated in the clinically sterile production. In 1993 new vocalist, Los Angeles-based, Birmingham-born John 'Wardi' Ward, replaced Tony Mills, who had departed in 1990. The new line-up played at the White Knights Festival in Russia in 1992, and signed to Parachute Records. They launched their comeback in 1994 with a cover of the **Rolling Stones**' 'It's Only Rock 'n' Roll'.

Albums: *Once Bitten, Twice...* (Ebony 1983), *Brave The Storm* (RCA 1985), *Excess All Areas* (RCA 1987), *Misspent Youth* (MCA 1989), *Welcome To The Madhouse* (1994).

Shyheim

b. Shyheim Franklin, c.1979, Statten Island, New York, USA. Child prodigy who does not take kindly to comparisons to **Kriss Kross** *et al*, whose debut album emerged when he was only 14. He had first come to hip hop via the sounds of **LL Cool J** and **Run DMC**, and as a child learnt to rap along with them before graduating to verses of his own. His break came when producer RNS heard him rapping on the street in front of his block in Stapleton Projects, a dwelling he also shared with the young Shyheim. Together they worked on demos in RNS' studio, before attracting the interest of **Virgin Records**. More talented than most, Shyheim's depiction of inner ghetto violence did strike a chord, and was not related in the tedious 'my gun's bigger than your gun' mantra of too many artists. His 'On And On' single, for example, contained the somehow touching line: 'Ain't never had a good Christmas, So who's Santa Claus?'. Compared by many to a young Rakim (**Eric B And Rakim**), Shyheim's posse of homeboys (Do Lil's, Rubberbandz, KD, the Down Low Wrecker) were all present on his debut album, as were his 'brother artists', the **Wu Tang Clan** (Prince Rakeem of that crew being his next-door neighbour).

Album: *Aka The Rugged Child* (Virgin 1994).

Siberry, Jane

b. 12 October 1955, Toronto, Canada. This singer/composer stands outside the traditional boundaries of folk music, being compared to such artists as **Laurie Anderson**, **Joni Mitchell** and **Suzanne Vega**. Having graduated from the University of Guelph with a degree in Microbiology, Siberry began by performing on the local coffee house circuit in Canada. Her first, independently produced album, in 1981, was followed by a Canadian tour. She financed the project by earning tips as a waitress. *No Borders Here* included 'Mimi On The Beach', an underground hit at home in Canada. *The Speckless Sky* went gold in Canada, and won two CASBYS, Canada's People Choice Award, for both album and producer of the year. Siberry made her first live appearance in Europe, following the release of *The Walking*, at the ICA in London. *The Walking* marked her recording debut for **Reprise**. Having recorded her earlier production demos in a 16-track studio located in

an apple orchard near Toronto, she decided to record the whole of *Bound By The Beauty* at Orchard Studio. For the task, a 24-track unit was parachuted into the studio. The whole album was recorded in a matter of weeks, and included Teddy Borowiecki, who had played with **k.d. lang** (piano/accordion), Stich Winston (drums), John Switzer (bass), and Ken Myhr (guitar). The album was mixed by Kevin Killen, known for work with both **Kate Bush** and **Peter Gabriel** and was greeted with considerable critical acclaim. The belated follow-up saw her work with **Brian Eno** on two tracks. Commenting on its distinctive title and character, she noted: 'I think this record is more whole in a funny way... It is also more masculine. Before, my work has always had a sense of graciousness and hospitality, like the good mother. I don't think I could be called a female singer/songwriter with this record'.

Albums: *Jane Siberry* (1981), *No Borders Here* (1984), *The Speckless Sky* (1985), *The Walking* (1988), *Bound By The Beauty* (1991), *When I Was A Boy* (1993). Compilation: *Summer In The Yukon* (1992).

Sidi Bou Said

Formed in 1990, Sidi Bou Said (pronounced Siddy Boo Sigh) consist of four women from Lewisham, London, England, who were keen to escape the then prevalent 'Riot Grrrl' movement. Indeed, they declined to appear in a documentary about women in rock music because of their fear of becoming categorised regardless of their music. The group's multi-layered sound was influenced by the folk rock of **Soft Machine** as well as the all-out guitar assault of the **Pixies** and was introduced on two fine EPs, *Twilight Eyes* and *Three Sides*, where Claire Lemmon (vocals/guitar) and Lou Howton (vocals/guitar), both classically trained guitarists, shared songwriting credits. After playing dates with **Belly** they returned to Lincolnshire with the producer Tim Friese-Green to produce *Brooch* which included re-workings of their earlier singles and strong tracks such as 'Big Yellow Taxidermist', which seemingly advocated disembowelling a loved one. However, the rest of their debut disappointed somewhat, and it was left to 1995's *Bodies*, produced by Tim Smith of the **Cardiacs**, to restore their reputation. This mixture of unusual song constructions, including string sections, harpsichord and flute, embellished highly original lyrics from the pen of Lemmon, backed once again by the rhythm section of Gayl Harrison (bass) and Melanie Woods (drums). Howton had departed in the summer of 1994.

Albums: *Brooch* (Ultimate 1993), *Bodies* (Ultimate 1995).

Sidran, Ben

b. 14 August 1943, Chicago, Illinois, U.S.A. A Ph.D. in musicology and philosophy, Sidran became embroiled in rock music upon joining the Ardells, a popular attraction at the University of Wisconsin which also featured **Steve Miller** and **Boz Scaggs**. Sidran later travelled to London to complete a doctoral thesis on the development of black music in America. This was published as *Black Talk* in 1971. Here he became reacquainted with Miller during the recording of the latter's *Brave New World*, an album marked by Sidran's memorable piano work and compositional skills. He remained an associate member of Miller's band, contributing to *Your Saving Grace* and *Number 5* before making numerous session appearances. The artist's solo career began in 1971 with the release of *Feel Your Groove*; he has since pursued an idiosyncratic, jazz-based path, eschewing commercially-minded motives in favour of a relaxed, almost casual, approach. His best work, captured on *Puttin' In Time On Planet Earth* (1973) and *The Doctor Is In* (1977), reveals a laconic wit redolent of **Mose Allison**, but elsewhere Sidran's under-achievements suggest lethargy rather than control. He nonetheless remains a highly-respected musician and is best-known in the UK as host to *On The Live Side*, a perennial favourite of late-night television. In 1991 he released *Cool Paradise* to favourable reviews and helped re-launch the career of **Georgie Fame**, now a stable-mate on the new jazz label Go Jazz.

Albums: *Feel Your Groove* (1971), *I Lead A Life* (1972), *Puttin' In Time On Planet Earth* (1973), *Don't Let Go* (1974), *Free In America* (1976), *The Doctor Is In* (1977), *A Little Kiss In The Night* (1978), *The Cat And The Hat* (1979), *Live At Montreaux* (1979), *Old Songs For The New Depression* (Antilles 1982), *Bop City* (1984), *On The Live Side* (Windham Hill 1987), *Too Hot To Touch* (Windham Hill 1988), *Cool Paradise* (Go Jazz 1991), *Enivre D'Amour* (Go Jazz 1992), *Heat Wave* (Go Jazz 1992), *A Good Travel Agent* (Go Jazz 1992), *Life's A Lesson* (Go Jazz 1993). Compilation: *That's Life I Guess* (1988).

Further reading: *Black Talk*, Sidran, Ben (1995).

Siebel, Paul

b. c. 1945, Buffalo, New York, USA. For many years Paul Siebel was a popular performer in Greenwich Village clubs. His blend of country and folk music pre-dated its more widespread appeal following the release of **Bob Dylan**'s *Nashville Skyline* album. Although actively pursuing a musical career thoughout most of the 60s, it was not until the following decade that the singer made his recording debut. *Woodsmoke And Oranges* was a critically acclaimed collection and featured 'Louise', Siebel's original composition which was later covered by several acts, including **Linda Ronstadt** and **Iain Matthews**. The artist's *Jack-Knife Gypsy* was equally meritorious and an excellent supporting group, including Richard Greene (fiddle) and David Grisman (mandolin), enhanced Siebel's evocative delivery. Public indifference sadly undermined his development although he has remained a popular live attraction.

Albums: *Woodsmoke And Oranges* (1970), *Jack-Knife Gypsy* (1971), *Paul Siebel Live* (1981).

Siegal-Schwall Blues Band

Corky Siegel (vocals/harmonica) and Jim Schwall (guitar/vocals) began working as a duo in April 1965. As such they made several appearances in Chicago's south-side clubs, prior to securing a date at the prestigious *Pepper's*. Here they used a temporary rhythm section - Bob Anderson (bass) and Billy Davenport (drums) before replacing them with Jos Davidson and Russ Chadwick. Although an electric ensemble, the group's early albums were less intense than those of contemporaries, the **Paul Butterfield** Blues Band and **Charlie Musselwhite**'s South Side Blues Band. Siegal-Schwall offered a lighter perspective, reliant on a collective effort rather than virtuoso soloing. Siegal was, nonetheless, an accomplished harmonica player and the group retained an in-concert popularity throughout the 60s. The two founder members remained at the helm through several line-up alterations, but the band split up in 1974 following the release of the highly unusual *Three Pieces For Blues Band And Orchestra* by William Russo. Siegal and Schwall were reunited 14 years later to celebrate the 15th anniversary of radio station WXRT-FM, on which the group had performed during its inauguration.

Albums: *The Siegal-Schwall Band* (1966), *Say Siegal-Schwall* (1967), *Shake!* (1968), *Siegal-Schwall 70* (1970), *Siegal-Schwall Band* (1971), *Sleepy Hollow* (1972), *953 West* (1973), *Three Pieces For Blues Band And Orchestra* (1973), *Live Last Summer* (1974), *RIP Siegal-Schwall* (1974), *Siegal-Schwall Reunion Concert* (1988). Compilation: *The Best Of The Siegal-Schwall Band* (1974).

Sieges Even

This German 'techno-thrash' quartet was put together by vocalist Franz Herde and guitarist Markus Steffen in 1986. After recording three demos they were picked up by the Steamhammer label in 1988. They debuted with *Life Cycle*, a complex and inventive speed-metal fusion of jazz, rock and classical styles. The material was characterized by a multitude of quick-fire time changes, that ultimately fragmented the songs and made them difficult to distinguish from one another. The album was generally well-received, but made little impact outside Germany.

Album: *Life Cycle* (Steamhammer 1988).

Siffre, Labi

Siffre was born and brought up in Bayswater, London, England to an English mother and Nigerian father. He first took employment as a mini-cab driver and delivery man but practised guitar whenever he could, going on to study music harmonics. He played his first gigs as one of a trio of like-minded youngsters, before taking up a nine-month residency at Annie's Rooms. His tenure completed, he travelled to Cannes, France, and played with a variety of soul musicians and bands. He

returned to the UK in the late 60s to score solo hits in 1971 with 'It Must Be Love' (later covered by **Madness**) and 'Crying Laughing, Loving, Lying'. Although 'Watch Me' in 1972 was his last hit of the 70s, he made a spectacular comeback in 1987 with the anthemic '(Something Inside) So Strong'.
Album: *Labi Siffre* (1970), *Singer And The Song* (1971), *Crying, Laughing, Loving, Lying* (1972), *So Strong* (1988), *Make My Day* (1989). Compilation: *The Labi Siffre Collection* (1986).

Sigler, Bunny

b. Walter Sigler, 27 March 1941, Philadelphia, Pennsylvania, USA. Sigler first made a name for himself singing a medley of old R&B hits, hitting in 1967 with 'Let The Good Times Roll & Feel So Good' (number 20 R&B and number 22 pop) and 'Lovey Dovey & You're So Fine'. Earlier in his career he had belonged to a doo-wop vocal group, the Opals, which recorded in 1959 for the Philadelphia V-Tone label, with little success. After his late 60s records, Sigler dropped out of recording for several years to concentrate on songwriting, and wrote songs for **Jackie Moore**, **Joe Simon**, the **Three Degrees**, **O'Jays**, **Intruders**, and **Billy Paul**, most of whom were Philadelphia International Records (PIR) artists. In 1973 Sigler returned to the charts on PIR with a remake of **Bobby Lewis**'s old hit 'Tossin' And Turnin'' (number 38 R&B). By the late 70s he had moved into disco on the Gold Mine label and in 1978 got his biggest hits with 'Let Me Party With You' (number 8 R&B and number 43 pop) and 'Only You' (number 11 R&B and number 87), the latter recorded with Loleatta Holloway.
Album: *Let The Good Times Roll* (1967), *That's How Long I'll Be Loving You* (1974), *Keep Smilin'* (1975), *My Music* (1976), (with Barbara Mason) *Locked In This Position* (1977), *Let Me Party With You* (1978), *I've Always Wanted To Sing...Not Just Write Songs* (1979), *Let It Snow* (1980).

Signal

This group was formed in 1988 by ex-**King Kobra** frontman Mark Free, together with one time **Alice Cooper** rhythm section, Eric Scott (bass/keyboards) and Jan Uvena (drums), with Danny Jacobs (guitar) completing the line-up. Their only album, the Kevin Elson-produced *Loud And Clear*, was released in the USA in 1989 on **EMI Records**. The commercial, melodic style of rock was aimed specifically at the American market, and highlighted the undoubted talents of Free to full effect, especially on tracks such as 'Liar' and 'My Mistake' which featured a duet with **Mr. Big**'s Eric Martin. The more sensitive side to Free is exhibited on 'This Love, This Time', a ballad in the mould of classic **Foreigner**. The album was critically well received, but despite impressive sales on import in the UK and modest sales in the USA, EMI dropped the band soon after its release. Mark Free has recently resurfaced working alongside former **Stone Fury** and World Trade guitarist Bruce Gowdy in Unruly Child.
Album: *Loud And Clear* (1989).

Signorelli, Frank

b. 24 May 1901, New York City, USA, d. 9 December 1975. Playing piano from childhood, Signorelli became a founder-member of the **Original Memphis Five** while still a teenager. He also played with the **Original Dixieland Jazz Band** and during the 20s was ceaselessly active. During this decade he worked with **Joe Venuti**, **Eddie Lang**, **Adrian Rollini**, **Bix Beiderbecke** and a host of leading white jazzmen of the day. He also played with **Paul Whiteman**, but he remained most closely associated with **Phil Napoleon**, a friend and musical companion from his youth. During the 30s he resumed his connection with the ODJB and in the 50s with the OMF, recording with them and with **Connee Boswell**. A sound if unexceptional pianist, Signorelli also composed a number of tunes that became standards, amongst which are 'I'll Never Be The Same' and 'Stairway To The Stars'.
Album: *Connee Boswell And The Original Memphis Five In Hi-Fi* (1956).

Sigue Sigue Sputnik

These UK punk/glam revivalists engineered themselves a briefly prosperous niche in the mid-80s. The creation of Tony James (ex-**Chelsea**, **Generation X**), Sigue Sigue Sputnik artlessly copied the shock tactics of **Sex Pistols** manager **Malcolm McLaren**. Instead of taking on board the Pistols' nihilism, James poached from cyberpunk novels and films (particularly *Blade Runner*) for their image. This consisted of dyed hair piled high, bright colours and an abundance of eye-liner. James had also recruited clothes designer Martin Degville (vocals), Neal X (b. Neil Whitmore; guitar), Ray Mayhew (drums) and Chris Cavanagh (drums), taking pride in their apparent lack of musical experience. Taking their name from a Moscow street gang, they set about a publicity campaign which resulted in **EMI Records**, understandably keen not to let the next Pistols slip through their hands again, signing them for a reported £4 million pounds. The figure was deliberately exaggerated in order to provoke publicity. Their first single was 'Love Missile F1-11', which soared to number 3 in the UK charts in February 1986. However, though 'Twenty-First Century Boy' also made the Top 20, and a debut album sold advertising space between tracks, James' money-making ruse soon ended. Despite an avalanche of intentionally lurid press, the band dissolved, and Tony James subsequently, albeit briefly, joined the **Sisters Of Mercy** in 1991. Kavanagh would go on to **Big Audio**

Dynamite, though James would make another attempt at ressurecting Sigue Sigue Sputnik later in the 90s. Degville recorded a dreadful solo album in the interim.

Albums: *Flaunt It* (Parlophone 1986), *Dress For Excess* (EMI 1988). Compilation: *First Generation* (Jungle 1990). Further reading: *Ultra*, No author listed (1986).

Silber, Irwin

b. 17 October 1925, New York City, New York, USA. Silber has been involved in the music business as an editor, publisher, author and producer. His involvement in folk music started with the formation of the Folksay Group at Brooklyn College, from where he graduated with a BA in 1945. Soon afterwards, he formed People's Songs Inc, in an attempt to use the music to promote causes both social and political. Just a few years later, People's Songs Inc was declared bankrupt. Not to be outdone, Silber, along with a group which included **Alan Lomax**, **Paul Robeson**, and **Pete Seeger**, founded People's Artists Inc. The organization, acting as an agency, secured bookings for folk artists and performers who were regarded as 'political'. The following year, 1950, the publication of *Sing Out!* magazine started, and Silber remained its editor until 1967. In 1964, Silber published an open letter to **Bob Dylan**, criticizing Dylan's musical change of direction, away from political comment. The letter, naturally, brought forth complaints galore. Silber later teamed-up with **Moses Asch**, who founded both Asch and **Folkways** Records. Together they formed Oak Publications, and published books about folk music, and folk music books. They produced books by such performers and writers as **Tom Paxton**, **Jean Ritchie** and many more. In 1967, Oak Publications was bought out by Music Sales Limited, London, at which point Silber resigned as editor, joining the *National Guardian* newspaper the following year. He continued to produce a number of albums, as well a numerous articles and books on the subject of folk music.

Further reading: *Lift Every Voice. Reprints From The People's Songs Bulletin. Songs Of The Civil War. Hootenanny Song Book. Songs Of The Great American West. Folksong Festival. Great Atlantic And Pacific Songbook. The Vietnam Songbook*, with Barbara Dane. *The Season Of The Year. Songs America Voted By. Songs Of Independence. The Folksinger's Wordbook*, with Fred Silber.

Sileás

This Celtic harp and vocal duo, pronounced Sheelis, comprises of Patsy Seddon (b. 12 January 1961, Edinburgh, Scotland) and Mary MacMaster (b. 22 November 1955, Glasgow, Scotland). The name Sileás is taken from a 17th century Gaelic poet, Sileás Na Ceapaich. Seddon learnt violin and Scottish harp as a child, studied music at school, and achieved an honours degree in Celtic Studies at university. MacMaster also learnt piano, recorder, cello, and guitar whilst young. Mary, however, spent time busking with the guitar and dulcimer, not taking up the harp until the age of 22. She studied Scottish History and Gaelic at Edinburgh University, receiving an honours MA in 1985. Both were members of the all woman group Sprangeen from 1982-86, but it was in 1985, that the duo started playing professionally together. Sprangeen recorded only one album for Springthyme records in 1984.

In 1986, after leaving the group, they released their debut album as a duo, *Delighted With Harps*. Together they have toured Germany, Switzerland, and the USA, and have also played festivals in the UK, Europe and Scandinavia, in addition to travelling to the Sudan for the British Council. In Scotland they have been selected twice in the Top 10 folk albums category. In 1991, they formed the Poozies with **Sally Barker** and Karen Tweed. The same year Patsy and Mary were also asked by **Dick Gaughan** to join Clan Alba. The other members include Brian MacNeill, Davy Steele, Gary West, Mike Travis, and Dave Tulloch. In this outfit the two are featured on electric harps.

With Sileás, as with the other line-ups, they have successfully managed to span both traditional and contemporary music forms. Their imaginative and innovative playing has made them in demand on other artists recordings, including those of **June Tabor** and **Maddy Prior** (the Silly Sisters), and Sally Barker.

Albums: *Sprangeen* (1984), *Delighted With Harps* (1986), *Beating Harps* (1988), *Harpbreakers* (1990).

Silent Rage

This Californian hard rock quartet was formed in 1986 by Mark Hawkins (vocals/guitar/synthesizer), Timmy James Reilly (vocals/guitar), E.L. Curcio (bass) and Jerry Grant (drums). They debuted with 'Make it Or Break It' on the *Pure Metal* compilation. This led to producer/guitarist **Paul Sabu** taking an interest in the band. He produced *Shattered Hearts* and co-wrote three numbers on the album. This collection followed a direction similar to **Y&T**, **Kiss** and **Van Halen** but featured extensive use of keyboards, which added a strong melodic undercurrent to the songs. Moving to **Kiss** bassist **Gene Simmons**' self-titled label, a subsidiary of **RCA Records**, *Don't Touch Me There* materialized in 1990. This built on the strong foundations of their debut and was immaculately produced, but blatantly geared for Stateside FM radio playlists.

Albums: *Shattered Hearts* (Chameleon 1987), *Don't Touch Me There* (Simmons/RCA 1990).

Silent Records

San Francisco label headed by managing director Kim Cascone, who had previously been in charge of sound on two David Lynch movies, *Twin Peaks* and *Wild At*

Heart. Formed in 1989 (the first release being PGR's 'Silent', which gave the label a name), the company is the ultimate ambient/subsconscious operation, based on a desire to experiment with the dynamics and properties of sound. Cascone's own Heavenly Music Corporation is but one of the names on the catalogue, whose discography included over 50 records by 1994. Others include Cosmic Trigger, **Michael Mantra**, Spice Barons and Thessolonians. The label is best sampled on the popular compilation series, *From Here To Eternity*. 'What we're about is open systems, an inclusive kind of nurturing of ideas, and of using people who have some kind of a different spin on the genre'.

Silhouettes

Formed in 1956 in Philadelphia, Pennsylvania, USA, the Silhouettes recorded one of the classics of the doo-wop era of rock 'n' roll, 'Get A Job'. The song was written by tenor Rick Lewis while he was in the USA Army, stationed in Germany. Upon returning home Lewis joined a singing group called the Parakeets. He left them to front a band called the Gospel Tornadoes, comprising lead singer Bill Horton, bass singer Raymond Edwards and baritone Earl Beal. When the gospel group changed to secular music it took on a new name, the Thunderbirds. A disc jockey, Kae Williams, signed the group to his own Junior Records in 1958 and 'Get A Job' was recorded, as the b-side to the ballad 'I'm Lonely'. The group's name was changed to the Silhouettes and the record was released on the larger Ember label. 'Get A Job' received more attention than the ballad side and ultimately found its way to number 1 in the USA, becoming in time one of the best known uptempo doo-wop records. The nonsense phrase 'sha-na-na-na', part of its lyric, was taken in the late 60s by the rock 'n' roll revival group **Sha Na Na**. The Silhouettes recorded a number of follow-ups but were never able to reach the charts again. With numerous personnel changes the group managed to stay afloat until 1968. Four original members reunited in 1980 and were still working the revival circuit in the early 90s.
Album: *The Original And New Silhouettes - '58-'68 Get A Job* (1968).

Silk Stockings

Cole Porter's final Broadway show was based on the 1939 film *Ninotchka*, which starred Greta Garbo. During the out-of-town try-outs, Abe Burrows' name was added to those of librettists **George S. Kaufman** and Leueen McGrath, and Kaufman was replaced as director by Cy Feur. *Silk Stockings* opened at the Imperial Theatre in New York on 24 February 1955. In this musical version of the by now familiar story, Ninotchka (Hildegarde Neff) is seduced by a glib Hollywood talent agent, Steve Canfield (**Don Ameche**), who is trying to persuade a famous Russian

composer, Peter Ilyich Boroff (Philip Sterling), to expand his 'Ode To A Tractor' into the score for a ritzy movie version of *War And Peace*. The score was not top-drawer Porter by any means, but there were some worthwhile numbers especially the gorgeous ballad, 'All Of You', the amusing and contemporary 'Stereophonic Sound', and several more varied and entertaining items including 'Paris Loves Lovers', 'Without Love', 'It's A Chemical Reaction, That's All', 'Too Bad', 'Silk Stockings', 'The Red Blues', 'As On The Seasons We Sail', 'Satin And Silk', 'Josephine', and 'Siberia'. The show enjoyed a run of 478 perormances and was filmed in 1957 with **Fred Astaire** and **Cyd Charisse**.

Silk Stockings (Film Musical)

Two years after *Silk Stockings* began its successful run on Broadway, MGM released this screen version which reunited **Fred Astaire** with one of his most thrilling dancing partners, **Cyd Charisse**. Leonard Gershe and Leonard Spigelgass's screenplay was adapted from the show's libretto, which itself was based on the 1939 Greta Garbo movie *Ninotchka* and a story by Melchior Lengyel. The plot concerns a beautiful Russian emissary, Nina (Ninotchka), played by Charisse, who eventually falls for an American businessman (Astaire) after being sent to the US in an effort to discover why three previous 'comrades' have failed to retrieve a Russian composer who is believed to be contemplating defection to the West. However, by then, the trio of messengers, Jules Munshin, Peter Lorre and Joseph Buloff, are themselves well on the way to capitulating to the capitalist way of life. Most of **Cole Porter**'s songs from the stage show were retained and two new ones, 'Fated To Be Mated' and 'The Ritz Roll And Rock', added. The dancing, predictably, was 'out of this world', and Astaire was his usual charming vocal self on numbers such as 'All Of You', 'Paris Loves Lovers' and 'It's A Chemical Reaction, That's All' (with Charisse, dubbed by Carol Richards), and 'Stereophonic Sound' (with Janis Paige). Other numbers included 'Too Bad', 'Silk Stockings', 'Satin And Silk', 'Without Love', 'Josephine', and 'The Red Blues'. After helping themselves to generous portions of Western liquid hospitality, the three reluctant Reds, Munshin, Lorre and Buloff, were hilarious as they muse - musically - on the subject of 'Siberia'. *Silk Stockings*, which turned out to be Fred Astaire's last musical film (apart from the generally unsatisfactory *Finian's Rainbow*, made when he was nearly 70), was a fine affair. The choreographers were **Hermes Pan** and Eugene Loring (with Fred Astaire, as usual, uncredited) and the director was Rouben Mamoulian. The musical director was **André Previn**, and the film was photographed in Metrocolor and Cinemascope.

Silk, Garnett

b. Garnett Smith, c.1967, Manchester, Jamaica, West

Indies, d. 9 December 1994, Mandeville, Jamaica. One of the most significant singer/songwriters to emerge from Jamaica in recent times, Silk began his involvement in music by DJing as Little Bimbo from the tender age of 12. Formative years spent on the Destiny Outernational, Pepper's Disco, Stereophonic and Soul Remembrance **sound systems** led to his first recording, 'Problem Everywhere', for Delroy 'Callo' Collins in 1987. The following year he moved to Kingston and voiced for **Sugar Minott**'s Youth Promotion label, recording one song, 'No Disrespect'. Next came sessions with the late **King Tubby**, as well as **King Jammy** and **Penthouse**, before he signed a two-year deal with **Steely And Clevie**. Despite recording an album with them only one track, a duet with Chevelle Franklin on 'We Could Be Together', was released during this period. Disillusioned, he returned to the country parish where he grew up, concentrating instead on writing songs, often in the company of his childhood friend, Anthony Rochester. **Tony Rebel** then introduced him to Courtney Cole, whose Roof International studio was based in Ocho Rios on Jamaica's north coast. From there the hits flowed, with 'I Can see Clearly Now' (a duet with dub poet Yasus Afari) and 'Seven Spanish Angels' proving especially popular. During 1992 he voiced the first of his output for **Bobby Digital**, who was to produce his debut album, *It's Growing,* by the end of the year. It was immediately hailed as a masterpiece of contemporary roots music and revealed a lyricist of rare depth and originality. Given his consistent emphasis on cultural themes - typified by 'I Am Vexed', 'The Rod' and the best-selling title song - and a fluid vocal style which imbues all his work with an almost religious intensity, comparisons were inevitably drawn with the late **Bob Marley**. By mid-1993 he had signed to **Atlantic** and seen many of his past recordings either reissued or released for the first time. These included further tracks for Roof, Steely And Clevie, Danny Browne, Black Scorpio, Phillip Smart, Top Rank, Jahmento, Star Trail - for whom 'Hello Africa' made number 1 on the UK reggae charts - and **Sly And Robbie**. Silk died with his mother when they were trapped in a fire that destroyed her home in Mandeville, Jamaica.
Selected albums: *It's Growing* (Blue Mountain/VP 1992), *Gold* (Charm 1993), *100% Silk* (VP 1993).

Silkie

Sylvia Tatler (vocals), Mike Ramsden (guitar/vocals), Ivor Aylesbury (guitar/vocals) and Kevin Cunningham (double bass) were students at Hull University, England, when they were 'discovered' by **Beatles**' manager **Brian Epstein**. The Silkie's folk credentials were established with their debut single, 'Blood Red River', but they achieved a commercial success with 'You've Got To Hide Your Love Away', which clipped the UK Top 30 in October 1965. This engaging release was produced by its composers - **John Lennon** and **Paul McCartney** - but the group was unable to repeat its charm and lost any prevailing pop/folk battle to the **Seekers**.
Albums: *The Silkie Sing The Songs Of Bob Dylan* (1965), *You've Got To Hide Your Love Away* (1965, US release).

Silkworm

Seattle trio whose literate rock dynamic was initially propelled by Tim Midgett (bass/vocals), Andrew Cohen (guitar/vocals) and Joel Phelps (guitar/vocals). The group were formed in their hometown of Missoula, Montana, in the mid-80s, evolving into Silkworm in 1987. It wasn't until 1990, however, that Silkworm crystallised as a unit, adding drummer Michael Dahlquist and relocating to Seattle. A series of singles followed on a variety of indie labels, before the release of *In The West* in 1993. Their second album, *Libertine*, was the first to grace Seattle indie El Recordo. Both sets were produced by maverick producer Steve Albini (**Big Black/Rapeman** etc.), while obvious musical reference points included the **Minutemen**, **Mission Of Burma** and **Gang Of Four**. However, Phelps would depart following the release of *Libertine*. Having previously been one of three central songwriters (alongside Cohen and Midgett) in the band, this inevitably shifted the group's creative axis.
Albums: *In The West* (C/Z 1993), *Libertine* (El Recordo 1994).

Sill, Judee

b. c.1949, Los Angeles, USA, d. 1974. This Los Angeles-based artist first attracted attention for her work with the city's folk-rock fraternity. An early composition, 'Dead Time Bummer Blues', was recorded by the **Leaves**, whose bassist, Jim Pons, later joined the **Turtles**. He introduced Sill to Blimp, the group's publishing company, the fruit of which was 'Lady O', their finest late-period performance. The song also appeared on *Judee Sill*, the artist's poignant debut, which was largely produced by Pons in partnership with another ex-Leave, John Beck. **Graham Nash** supervised the sole exception, 'Jesus Was A Crossmaker', which drew considerable comment over its lyrical content and was one of the songs Sill featured on a rare UK television appearance. *Heart Food* continued this uncompromising individual's quest for excellence and deftly balanced upbeat, country-tinged compositions with dramatic emotional ballads. A gift for melody suggested a long, successful career, but Judee Sill subsequently abandoned full-time music and died in mysterious circumstances in 1974.
Albums: *Judee Sill* (1971), *Heart Food* (1973).

Silly Sisters

During the lull which followed the commercial high point of **Steeleye Span**'s *All Around My Hat* album, vocalist **Maddy Prior** performed an abrupt volte face and plunged back into pure folk song recording with a traditional album recorded with **June Tabor,** a librarian in Swindon, England. Despite its 'awful' cover, *Silly Sisters* undoubtedly helped launch Tabor. It contained an all-star band of musicians, on the sometimes chaotic, though always jovial set. It has since become something of a legend, with Prior's high soaring voice, contrasted by Tabor's more earthy tones. The whole escapade attracted a great deal of media attention and quite naturally there was clamour for a follow up. In 1988 the Silly Sisters did reunite for *No More To The Dance* for the folkist Topic label. More touring followed, this time selective and considered, and whilst this set is still a fine record, backed by musicians of reputation and note, it hasn't the charm and innocence of the debut. However, neither singer has ruled out another collaboration.

Albums: *Silly Sisters* (1976), *No More To The Dance* (1988).

Silly Wizard

This Scottish band was formed in 1972 by Gordon Jones (b. 21 November 1947, Birkenhead, Liverpool, England; guitar/mandolin), Bob Thomas (b. 28 July 1950, Robroyston, Glasgow, Scotland; guitar), and Chris Pritchard (b. Edinburgh, Scotland; vocals). Pritchard left within a matter of months and was replaced by John Cunningham (b. 27 August 1957, Edinburgh, Scotland; fiddle/mandolin), and Madelaine Taylor (b. Perth, Scotland; vocals/guitar/bodhran/spoons). This line-up recorded for Transatlantic Records, but with Taylor's departure, to join Witches Promise, the recording was never issued. Silly Wizard continued with this line-up until late 1974, when Neil Adams (b. England; bass) joined the group. **Andy M. Stewart** (vocals/banjo), then joined, and shortly afterwards, Adams left. The four were then augmented by Freeland Barbour (accordion), and Alasdair Donaldson (bass). By the time of *Silly Wizard*, Donaldson had left to join the **Rezillos**, while Barbour had taken up with the Wallochmore Ceilidh Band. Phil Cunningham (b. 27 January 1960, Edinburgh, Scotland; keyboards), and Martin 'Mame' Hadden (b. 23 May 1957, Aberdeen, Scotland; bass/vocals) arrived in late 1976, recording *Caledonia's Hardy Sons*. Following the release of *So Many Partings*, John Cunningham joined the US-based group Raindogs, but performed occasionally solo, and with brother Phil. **Dougie MacLean** (b. 27 September 1954, Dunblane, Scotland; guitar/fiddle/vocals), then joined the line-up temporarily, in 1979. He, along with Stewart and Hadden, had previously been with the group Puddock's Well. Phil had earlier won several Scottish accordion championships and, in 1977, both he and John received the Heretic Award for services to Scottish Tradition. In 1980, the group recorded 'Take The High Road', the original theme from the Scottish

television series. During the early 80s, a bootleg recording, tentatively titled *Live In Edinburgh*, was intercepted before it could be released, and the ensuing court case, being the first bootleg recording case in Scottish history, saw the group win the right for it to remain unreleased. The group helped to popularize Scottish traditional music among a wider audience, particularly in the USA. The final line-up saw all the various members involved in projects outside of the group.

Gordon Jones and Bob Thomas formed Harbourtown Records, Hadden teamed up with Allan Carr and Jane Rothfield to form Hadden Rothfield and Carr, while Stewart started working with Manus Lunny. Meanwhile, Phil went on to work and record with Relativity. Silly Wizard played their last date in 1988, in New York State.

Albums: *Silly Wizard* (1976), *Caledonia's Hardy Sons* (1978), *So Many Partings* (1979), *Wild And Beautiful* (1981), *Kiss The Tears Away* (1983), *Fair Warning* (1983), *Live In America* (1985), *Golden Golden* (1985), *A Glint Of Silver* (1987), *Live Wizardry - The Best Of Silly Wizard In Concert* (1988). Compilations: *The Best Of Silly Wizard* (1985). Solo albums: Phil Cunningham *Airs And Graces* (1984), *Relativity* (1987), *Palomino Waltz* (1989); John Cunningham *Fair Warning* (1988); Phil and John Cunningham: *Against The Storm* (1980).

Silva, Alan

b. 22 January 1939, Bermuda. Silva grew up in New York, studying piano and violin from the age of 10. He also took trumpet lessons from **Donald Byrd** for three years. He only started playing double bass at the age of 23. His acute musical ear and interest in new sounds made him ideal for some of **Cecil Taylor**'s most demanding music: he played on the classic **Blue Note** releases of 1966, *Unit Structures* and *Conquistador!* Together with Burton Greene he formed the Free Form Improvisation Ensemble. He played with Taylor until 1969, and also worked for other key innovators: **Sun Ra** (1965-70), **Albert Ayler** (1966-70), **Sunny Murray** (1969) and **Archie Shepp** (1969). In 1970 he moved to France and formed the Celestial Communication Orchestra to play free jazz with various instrumentations. He also played in smaller groups with tenor saxophonist **Frank Wright**, pianist Bobby Few and drummer Muhammad Ali. From the mid-70s he lived and taught in both New York and Paris, recording with Taylor, trumpeter **Bill Dixon** and pianist **Andrew Hill**. In 1982 he recorded with the **Globe Unity Orchestra**. In the mid-80s he dropped out of performance, declaring that the scene had become sterile (though 1986's *Take Some Risks* makes one question that judgement). In 1990 he returned to performance with the pioneering British percussionist Roger Turner and tenor saxophonist Gary Todd, playing at the Crawley Outside In Festival in 1990 and touring in 1991. On this last tour he played only keyboards - a Roland U-20 - declaring that he found his bass playing no longer surprised him. An intensely involving and visual performer, Silva is a great educationalist and communicator. He needs to be witnessed live to appreciate the energy and passion of his playing.

Albums: *Lunar Surface* (1969), *Seasons* (1970), *Desert Mirage* (1973), with Bobby Few, Frank Wright *Solos, Duos* (1975), with Roger Turner *Take Some Risks* (1986), *My Country* (1989, rec. 1971).

Silver Convention

This studio group was created by Munich-based producers Silvester Levay and Michael Kunze. After scoring a UK hit in 1975 with 'Save Me', they went on to reach number 1 in the USA with 'Fly, Robin, Fly'. The international fame persuaded the duo to audition some female singers to adopt the Silver Convention name and the lucky trio were Linda Thompson (ex-Les Humphries Singers), Ramona Wulf (formerly a solo artist) and Penny McLean. This 'second generation' Silver Convention proved more than a match for their anonymous studio counterparts and achieved transatlantic Top 10 success with the infectious 'Get Up And Boogie (That's Right)', one of the most distinctive disco numbers of the period. A significant line-up change followed with the departure of Thompson, replaced by Rhonda Heath. Further minor hits followed until the group quietly disbanded in the late 70s.

Albums: *Save Me* (1975), *Silver Convention* (1976), *Madhouse* (1976), *Golden Girls* (1977). Compilation: *Silver Convention: Greatest Hits* (1977).

Silver Dream Racer

David Essex starred in this 1980 film in which he portrayed a garage storeman given a newly-designed motorcycle with which he attempts to win a championship race at the Silverstone circuit. Some excellent action sequences apart, *Silver Dream Racer* is as antiquated as its plot and it failed to recreate the success of earlier Essex ventures **That'll Be The Day** and **Stardust**. The singer wrote most of the soundtrack material with some help from John Cameron, formerly of the rock band **CCS**, and he was rewarded when the title song reached number 4 in the UK singles chart.

Silver Jews

Silver Jews is essentially a vehicle for David Berman (b. Virginia, USA) with the backing of friends drawn from **Pavement**, with whom he had previously co-written songs (he had done the same with **Royal Trux**). Silver Jew's 1994 set earned admiring glances throughout the underground community, earning comparisons to the **Palace Brothers** and **Violent Femmes** despite its

billing as a concept album. Fans of Pavement's askew narratives would certainly not be disappointed with the track selection - ranging from improvisational pieces like 'The Moon Is Number 18' to charming, anecdotal dioramas 'Advice To The Graduate' and 'Trains Across The Sea'. Arguably the best composition, 'Secret Knowledge Of Back Roads', would also be played by Pavement on a **John Peel** session for BBC Radio, ensuring the continued cult growth of Berman's concern.

Album: *Starlite Walker* (Domino 1994).

Silver Mountain

This melodic heavy metal group was formed in Malmo, Sweden, in 1978, taking their name from a song on **Rainbow**'s debut album, 'Man On The Silver Mountain'. Not surprisingly, the band's sound proved to be an amalgam of **Deep Purple**, **Rainbow** and **Judas Priest** influences. Silver Mountain have been through an endless series of line-up changes, with the only constant being founder member Jonas Hansson (guitar/vocals). It took almost five years before the band secured a record deal, with **Roadrunner Records**. They went on to release four quality, if slightly dated metal albums, and built up strong followings in Scandinavia, Greece and Japan. The most recent line-up comprised Johan Dahlstrom (vocals), Jonas Hansson (guitar/vocals), Erik Bjorn Nielsen (keyboards), Per Stadin (bass) and Kjell Gustavson (drums).

Albums: *Shakin' Brains* (Roadrunner 1983), *Universe* (Roadrunner 1985), *Live In Japan '85* (SMS 1986), *Roses And Champagne* (Hex 1988).

Silver, Horace

b. 2 September 1928, Norwalk, Connecticut, USA. Silver studied piano and tenor saxophone at school, settling on the former instrument for his professional career. Early influences included Portuguese folk music (from his father), blues and bop. He formed a trio for local gigs which included backing visiting musicians. One such visitor, **Stan Getz**, was sufficiently impressed to take the trio on the road with him in 1950. The following year Silver settled in New York, playing regularly at Birdland and other leading venues. In 1952 he began a long-lasting association with **Blue Note**, recording under his own name and with other leaders. In 1953 he formed a band named the **Jazz Messengers** with **Art Blakey**, who would later adopt the name for all his own groups. By 1956 Silver was leading his own quintet, exploring the reaches of bop and becoming a founding father of the hard bop movement. Silver's line-up - trumpet, tenor saxophone, piano, bass and drums - was subject to many changes over the years, but the calibre of musicians he hired was always very high. Amongst his sidemen were **Donald Byrd**, **Art Farmer**, **Michael** and **Randy**

Brecker, **Woody Shaw**, **Blue Mitchell**, **Hank Mobley** and **Joe Henderson**. He continued to lead fine bands, touring and recording extensively during the following decades, and in the late 80s and early 90s could still be heard at concerts around the world performing to an impressively high standard. As a pianist Silver is a powerful, thrusting player with an urgent rhythmic pulse. As a composer, his early musical interests have constantly reappeared in his work and his incorporation into hard bop of elements of gospel and R&B have ensured that for all the overall complexities of sound his music remains highly accessible. Several of his pieces have become modern standards, amongst them 'Opus de Funk', 'Doodlin'', 'Nica's Dream' and 'The Preacher'. The introduction on **Steely Dan**'s 'Ricki Don't Lose That Number' was strongly influenced by Silver's memorable 'Song For My Father'. During the 70s Silver experimented with compositions and recordings which set his piano playing and the standard quintet against larger orchestral backing, often achieving far more success than others who have written and performed in this way.

Selected albums: *Horace Silver Trio* (Blue Note 1954), *Horace Silver And The Jazz Messengers* i (Blue Note 1954), *Horace Silver Quintet Vols 1 & 2* (1955), *Horace Silver And The Jazz Messengers* ii (1955), *Six Pieces Of Silver* (1956), *Silver's Blue* (1956), *The Stylings Of Silver* (1957), *Finger Poppin'* (1959), *Blowin' The Blues Away* (Blue Note 1959), *Horace-Scope* (Blue Note 1960), *The Tokyo Blues* (1962), *Song For My Father* (Blue Note 1964), *Live 1964* (1964), *Cape Verdean Blues* (Blue Note 1965), *The Jody Grind* (Blue Note 1967), *Serenade To A Soul Sister* (1968), *You Gotta Take A Little Love* (1969), *That Healin' Feelin'* (*The United States Of Mind, Phase I*) (1970), *Total Response (Phase II)* (c.1971), *All (Phase III)* (c.1973), *Silver 'N' Brass* (1975), *Silver 'N' Wood* (1976), *Silver 'N' Voices* (1976), *Silver 'N' Percussion* (1977), *Silver 'N' Strings Play The Music Of The Spheres* (1978), *Guides To Growing Up* (1981), *Spiritualizing The Senses* (1983), *There's No Need To Struggle* (1983), *It's Got To Be Funky* (Columbia 1993), *Pencil Packin' Papa* (1994). Compilation: *The Best Of Horace Silver - The Blue Note Years* (Blue Note 1988).

Silver, Mike

b. 12 September 1945, Uffington, Berkshire, England. Silver began playing guitar at the age of 15. It was later during the 60s that he first wrote seriously and took an interest in acoustic music. He became a regular in the folk clubs of London and Cornwall during this period. In 1971, Silver formed Daylight, with Steve Hayton (guitar/mandolin/vocals) and Chrissie Quayle (guitar). They were signed to **RCA** the same year and produced one album. He then signed to **Elton John**'s Rocket Records, and toured the USA, in 1973. At this time, Silver was in demand as a session guitarist, and recorded with **Charles Aznavour**, and Ray Thomas

of the **Moody Blues**. In 1973, Silver recorded *Troubadour*, but this failed to bring him to a wider audience. However, that same year, he gained exposure when he supported **Dory Previn** and **Ashford And Simpson** at a number of concert appearances in the USA. Silver then appeared as guitarist for Brenda Wootton at the Norwich Folk Festival in 1976, in addition to playing a number of large festivals throughout the UK, Germany and Denmark. **Justin Hayward** recorded Mike's composition 'Maybe It's Just Love', on his solo *Night Flight*, in 1980. During the early part of the 80s, Mike appeared in concert on radio with **Randy Newman** and also worked on recordings with **Allan Taylor**, and Fiona Simpson. The number of other performers that he has worked with is considerable. In 1991, Silver formed Road Dog, which included Kit Morgan (guitar/guitar synthesizer), Paul Cleaver (drums/percussion) and Dave Goodier (bass guitar). Silver continues to play solo concerts in addition to working with the band.

Albums: *The Applicant* (1969), *Daylight* (1971), *Troubadour* (early 70s), *Come And Be My Lady* (1976), *Midnight Train* (1980), *Silver Songs* (1981), *Let's Talk About You* (1983), *Free* (1984), *No Machine* (1986), *Roadworks* (1990).

Silverfish

Silverfish were instigated in 1988 by budding guitarist and regular London gig-goer Andrew 'Fuzz' Duprey (b. 14 June 1963, Kent, England), who thought of the band name and had a desperate urge to play 'noise you could dance to'. Stuart Watson (b. 10 November 1962, Northamptonshire, England; drums) and Chris Mowforth (b. 30 May 1964, Middlesex, England; bass) joined up to start - literally - 'bashing around ideas', until Duprey realised he could not sing and play bass simultaneously. Thus Lesley Rankine (b. 11 April 1965, Edinburgh, Scotland) was discovered b(r)awling at a hardcore gig and subsequently became the vocalist. The title for their first album was derived from an early live review which compared her singing to that of a 'fat Axl Rose' (of **Guns N'Roses**). Silverfish were confrontational, to say the least: early EP titles included *Total Fucking Asshole* and *Fuckin' Drivin' Or What*, and the expletives were aligned with a suitably ferocious splatterpunk sound which gouged a uniquely noisy niche for itself in the British scheme of things, despite a brief spell spent under the unwanted umbrella of 'Camden Lurch' - a 'scene' half-invented by the ever-imaginative UK music press in an attempt to catagorize the burgeoning state of alternative music in north London. In 1991 Silverfish took a potentially major step up the ladder by switching labels, to **Creation Records**, prior to causing havoc on their first tour of America. However, the band would grind to a premature halt on their return, with Lesley Rankine stated to be working on a solo project in 1995.

Albums: *Fat Axl* (Wiiija 1990), *Organ Fan* (Creation 1992). Compilation: *Cockeye* (Wiiija 1990).

Silverhead

The first real band to be fronted by actor/singer **Michael Des Barres**, Silverhead formed in 1971 with Steve Forest (guitar), Rod Davies (guitar), Nigel Harrison (bass) and Pete Thompson (drums). They were signed to **Deep Purple**'s record label in 1982 by Tony Edwards and their debut album soon followed. Although quite mild on record their stage presence and raucous glam rock style won them a lewd reputation. This did little to help and Forest quit. Adopting a heavier approach they enlisted Robbie Blunt as Forest's replacement and recorded an album, *16 & Savaged*, and toured, mainly in America. By 1974 they had found an audience in Japan and in New York where glam had its home with the **New York Dolls**. It was during this time that Des Barres met up with 'super groupie' Pamela Miller. Not long after the band split. While Des Barres married Miller, Harrison joined Ray Manzarek form the **Doors** for his solo outings before they both formed Nite City (Harrison later found fame with **Blondie**), Blunt joined the reformed **Chicken Shack** but would later be remembered for playing guitar on **Robert Plant**'s hit single, 'Big Log'. Des Barres went on to **Detective** and a solo career. A little insight in to Silverhead circa 1974 can be discovered in Pamela Des Barres' book, *I'm With The Band*.
Albums: *Silverhead* (Purple 1972), *16 & Savaged* (Purple 1973).

Silverstein, Shel

b. Shelby Silverstein, 1932, Chicago, Illinois, USA. A former artist with *Stars And Stripes* magazine, Silverstein joined the staff of *Playboy* at its inception during the early 50s and for almost two decades his cartoons were a regular feature of the publication. He later became a successful illustrator and author of children's books, including *Uncle Shelby's ABZ Book*, *Uncle Shelby's Zoo* and *Giraffe And A Half*. Silverstein was also drawn to the folk scene emanating from Chicago's Gate Of Horn and New York's Bitter End, latterly becoming a respected composer and performer of the genre. Early 60s collaborations with **Bob Gibson** were particularly memorable and in 1961 Silverstein completed *Inside Folk Songs* which included the original versions of 'The Unicorn' and '25 Minutes To Go', later popularized, respectively, by the Irish Rovers and **Brothers Four**. Silverstein provided 'novelty' hits for **Johnny Cash** ('A Boy Named Sue') and **Loretta Lynn**, ('One's On The Way'), but an association with **Dr. Hook** proved to be the most fruitful. A series of successful singles ensued, notably 'Sylvia's Mother' and 'The Cover Of *Rolling Stone*', and a grateful group reciprocated by supplying the backing on *Freakin' At The Freaker's Ball*. This ribald set included many of Silverstein's best-known

compositions from this period, including 'Polly In A Porny', 'I Got Stoned And I Missed It' and 'Don't Give A Dose To The One You Love Most', the last-named of which was adopted in several anti-venereal disease campaigns. *The Great Conch Robbery*, released on the traditional music outlet Flying Fish, was less scatological in tone, since which Silverstein has adopted a less-public profile.
Albums: *Hairy Jazz* (1959), *Inside Folk Songs* (1961), *I'm So Good I Don't Have To Brag* (1965), *Drain My Brain* (1966), *A Boy Named Sue* (1968), *Freakin' At The Freaker's Ball* (1969), *Songs And Stories* (1972), *The Great Conch Train Robbery* (1979).

Silvertones

The Silvertones were a vocal trio consisting of Carl Grant, Delroy Denton and Keith Coley. The name was given to the trio to describe the tone of their combined voices. An unusual feature about the group is that they did not serve their apprenticeship at **Coxsone Dodd**'s Studio One, although they are remembered as Studio One legends. In 1975 they released *Silver Bullets* which won critical acclaim but failed to make any impression on the charts through inadequate marketing. Four years later they achieved an enormous hit with, 'I Want To Be There'. This was followed by the equally successful releases 'Smile', 'Stop Crying', 'Have A Little Faith' and 'Come Forward', the latter track being credited with the Brentford Rockers, recorded in 1979. The Brentford rockers featured an all star line-up including **Jackie Mittoo**, Pablove Black, Leroy Sibbles, Leroy 'Horsemouth' Wallace, Cleveland and Dalton Brownie, **Ernest Ranglin**, **Roland Alphonso** and Johnny Moore. Whilst at Downbeat's they also contributed to *Sir Coxsone's Family Christmas Album Stylee* performing, 'Merry Merry Christmas'.
Album: *Silver Bullets* (Trojan 1975).

Silvester, Victor

b. Victor Marlborough Silvester, 25 February 1900, Wembley, Middlesex, England, d. 14 August 1978, Le Lavandou, France. This important dance orchestra leader in the UK for over 30 years originated 'strict tempo' ballroom dancing. The second son of a vicar in Wembley, north London, Silvester learned to dance and play the piano as a child. He studied music at the Trinity College of music and the London College of Music, but ran away from school and joined the British Army just before he reached the age of 15. After some bitter experiences during World War I, including being a member of a firing squad which shot 12 deserters at Boulogne, he was sent home when his real age was discovered. He returned to the Front, and was awarded the Italian Bronze Medal for Valour. After the War, legend has it that he attended that very British institution, a 'tea dance' at Harrod's, the 'top people's store', which revived his interest in the terpsichorean side of life. After further involvement with the army, including a spell at Sandhurst, he decided to devote himself to a career in dancing. For over two years he partnered Phyllis Clarke, and they won the World's Dancing Championship in 1922. In the same year, he married beauty queen Dorothy Newton, and opened a dance school (the first of a chain) in London's Bond Street. Frustrated by the lack of suitable dance records, he formed his first orchestra in 1935, and persuaded **EMI** to allow him to record Al Bryan and **George M. Meyer**'s 'You're Dancing On My Heart', which sold 17,000 copies, and became his signature tune. Two years later he made the first of over 6,500 broadcasts, the most popular of which, the BBC *Dancing Club* series, started in 1941. From 1943-44, influenced by the influx of GI'S into the UK, he directed a series of recordings made especially for 'jive dancing'. The seven piece group included top musicians such as trombonist **George Chisholm**, trumpeter **Tommy McQuater**, pianist Billy Munn (who did most of the arrangements) and multi-instrumentalist E.O. 'Poggy' Pogson, who played lead saxophone doubling clarinet, and stayed with Silvester for 26 years. Twenty of those early tracks were released by EMI on *Victor Silvester's Jive Band*, in 1985. They were a long way from the general public's conception of the suave, distinctive Silvester sound, prefaced by his introduction: 'Slow, slow, quick, quick, slow', which accompanied the dancing in the nation's ballrooms and on television when the *Dancing Club* transferred to the small screen in the 50s, and ran for 17 years. By the end of the run Silvester's failing health meant that his son, Victor Jnr., was sometimes leading the Orchestra; in the 70s he took over full-time direction. A phenomenon in popular music, Silvester withstood the radical changes in dance music through the years, especially the rock 'n' roll 50s and the beat boom of the 60s, and survived with his high standards intact. For world-wide audiences his name was synonymous with the best in ballroom dancing, and his *Record Request* programme on the BBC World Service reflected this fact. He was awarded an OBE in 1961 for Services To Ballroom Dancing. One of his books, *Modern Ballroom Dancing*, sold over a million copies and went through 50 editions. He made so many albums that even he found it difficult to remember the precise number. His affection for 30s music was demonstrated on the 16 track *The Tuneful Thirties*, while, *Let's Dance To Some More Favourite Melodies* and *Up Up And Away* contained material from the 60s and 70s. In 1978 his total record sales were estimated at over 75 million. Early in that year he released a rarity: a collection of old favourites entitled *The Song And Dance Men*, on which his orchestra accompanied a singer, **Max Bygraves**. Later in 1978 Victor Silvester died while on holiday in the South of France. His son, Victor Jnr, continued to direct the Orchestra into the 90s.

Selected albums: *Spotlight On Victor Silvester* (1981), *Spotlight On Victor Silvester, Volume 2* (1984), *Get Rhythm In Your Feet* (1985), *Slow, Slow, Quick, Quick, Slow* (1988), *In Strict Tempo* (1988), *Victor Silvester And His Silver Strings* (1992).

Further reading: *Dancing Is My Life*, Silvester, Victor (1958).

Silvestri, Alan

b. New York, USA. A prolific composer of film music, from the 70s through to the 90s. Silvestri studied at the **Berklee College Of Music** in Boston, Massachusetts, before scoring some low-budget movies and working on the US television series *Chips* In the late 70s and early 80s he composed the music for *Las Vegas Lady*, *The Amazing Dobermans* (starring **Fred Astaire** in an off-beat role), and *Par Ou Tes Rentre?* (1984). Subsequently he scored blockbuster productions such as *Romancing The Stone*, *Back To The Future*, and the remarkable live-action *Who Framed Roger Rabbit* (1988). His other credits during the 80s included *Fandang*, *Summer Rental*, *Delta Force*, *Flight Of The Navigator*, *No Mercy*, *Outrageous Fortune*, *Predator*, *Overboard*, *My Stepmother Is An Alien*, *She's Out Of Control*, *The Abyss*, and *Back To The Future Part II* (1989). In the following year, Silvestri also scored the third and final episode of director Robert Zemeckis' time-travel series, *Back To The Future Part III*, starring Michael J. Fox. During the early 90s Silvestri continued to compose for highly commercial movies such as *Young Guns II*, *Predator 2*, *Dutch*, *Soapdish*, *Ricochet*, *Shattered*, *Driving Me Crazy*, *Father Of The Bride* (a re-make of the 1950 classic starring Steve Martin), *Stop! Or My Mom Will Shoot*, *Death Becomes Her*, *The Bodyguard*, *Cop And A Half*, *Super Mario Brothers*, *The Abyss: Special Edition*, *Grumpy Old Men*, *Blown Away*, *Forrest Gump*, and *Richie Rich* (1994). In 1992, following Ashman and Menken's recent success with *The Little Mermaid* and *Beauty And The Beast*, Silvestri composed the music for the animated feature, *Ferngully...The Last Rainforest*, based on Diana Young's stories, *Ferngully*. In 1995, he was honoured by BMI with its Richard Kirk Award for career achievement.

Simeon, Omer

b. 21 July 1902, New Orleans, Louisiana, USA, d. 17 September 1959. Although taught clarinet by fellow New Orleanian **Lorenzo Tio**, Simeon's musical education took place in Chicago where he lived from 1914. After playing in various bands he joined **Charlie Elgar**'s popular Chicago-based danceband, where he remained for several years. During his stint with Elgar he appeared on a number of record dates with **Jelly Roll Morton** and also left the band for a short engagement with **Joe 'King' Oliver**. In the late 20s he played with **Luis Russell** in New York and then resumed his association with Morton. Back in Chicago in 1928 he spent a couple of years with Erskine Tate and then joined **Earl 'Fatha' Hines** for a six-year spell at the Royal Gardens. In the 40s he played with various bands, including **Jimmie Lunceford**'s, and he spent most of the 50s with **Wilbur De Paris** in New York. A bold and imaginative clarinettist, Simeon's long periods in big bands afforded him only limited opportunities to solo, although his recordings with small groups give frequent if tantalizing hints of a gifted musician.

Album: with Wilbur De Paris *Rampart Street Ramblers* (1952). Compilations: *The Complete Jelly Roll Morton Vols 1/2 (1926-27)* (1983), *Omer Simeon 1926-29* (Hot n' Sweet 1993).

Simeone, Harry, Chorale

b. 9 May 1911, Newark, New Jersey, USA. An arranger, conductor and composer Simeone studied at the Juilliard School of Music, before working for **CBS**, where he was spotted by bandleader **Fred Waring**. He took him onto his staff as an arranger in 1939, and from there Simeone moved to Hollywood and worked for Paramount with the legendary composer-conductor **Victor Young** on several **Bing Crosby** movies, including *Here Come The Waves* and the 'Road' series with Hope and Lamour. In 1945 he re-joined Waring and became the editor of Waring's *Shawnee Press*. From 1952-59 he served as the conductor and chorale arranger for the popular weekly *Firestone Hour* on television. In 1958 Simeone released the chorale album *Sing We Now Of Christmas*, a collection of sacred songs and carols. It also contained 'The Little Drummer Boy', written by Simeone with Henry Onorati and Katherine Davis. The tune was taken from the Spanish song 'Tabolilleros'. Issued as a single, the Harry Simeone Chorale version entered the US charts each December for five consecutive years, from 1958-62. In the UK Top 20 there were additional versions by the **Beverley Sisters** and **Michael Flanders** in 1959, and in 1972 the songs was again successful in Britain in a version by the Pipes And Drums And Military Band Of The Royal Scots Guards. In 1970, estimated sales from some 150 versions were in the order of 25 million. The original *Sing We Now Of Christmas* was re-titled *The Little Drummer Boy* in 1963, and remained in catalogues throughout the 80s.

Selected album: *The Little Drummer Boy* (1984).

Simmons, 'Little' Mack

b. 25 January 1934, Twist, Arkansas, USA. Simmons is one of the stalwarts of the Chicago club scene; he taught himself harmonica as a youngster and in the early 50s sometimes worked with bluesman on the Saint Louis, Missouri, club circuit, before settling in Chicago in 1954. Since the late 60s he has recorded for many small local labels, and occasionally larger companies such as Checker. He has run his own label and club from time to time and has recorded blues, gospel (he was known for a time as Reverend Mac

Simmons) and soul. His version of 'Rainy Night In Georgia', performed as a harmonica instrumental, was a local hit in the early 70s. He toured Europe in 1975. Album: *Blue Lights* (1976).

Simmons, Gene

One of the most charismatic characters in the world of heavy rock, Simmons (b. Chaim Witz, 25 August 1949, Haifa, Israel) is bass player with **Kiss**. Indeed, he was a founder member of the band in 1971 along with Paul Stanley. Simmons's first involvement with the music industry was in producing radio jingles, but it was not long before Kiss became a worldwide phenomenon. Simmons, along with his band mates, donned complete make-up (in his case a blood dripping, fire eating demon) and it was not until 1983 when Kiss unmasked that the 'real' Gene Simmons was revealed. Simmons has recorded some 20 albums with Kiss and has penned a great deal of the material either solely or in partnership with Paul Stanley. In 1978, while still in full demonic make-up, he released a credible solo album as did all his then band mates. A star-studded number of guest stars featured, including **Bob Seger**, **Cher**, **Donna Summer**, **Helen Reddy** and **Cheap Trick** guitarist Rick Neilsen and it reached number 22 on the US chart. A single was released at the same time, 'Radioactive' which was marketed in red vinyl together with a free Gene Simmons Kiss mask. It reached number 41 in the UK charts. During the 80's Simmons expanded his talents into production, films and set up his own record label, Simmons Records. In 1989 he took rock vocalist King Diamond to court for using facial make-up similar to what he had worn in Kiss. Simmons won the case. The 90s sees Kiss still recording under the guidance of Simmons and Stanley while the former's other music business activities continue.

Album: *Gene Simmons* (1978).

Simmons, Jeff

Jeff Simmons's rock career is really only a footnote to the **Frank Zappa** story, but he did manage to release one highly-regarded album. In 1969, Zappa had set up the Straight label in order to 'present musical and sociological material which the important record companies would probably not allow you to hear'. In among **Captain Beefheart**, **Wild Man Fischer**, **Lord Buckley**, Lenny Bruce and the **GTO's**, Jeff Simmons looked like the straight guy: what was remarkable was how good the album was. *Lucille Has Messed My Mind Up* of 1970 was psychedelic R&B, a combination of tightly crafted **Cream**-like songs and Simmons's plaintive, jazzy vocals. Zappa wrote the title song, a kind of 50s doo-wop number (reprised by Zappa on *Joe's Garage* ten years later) and played guitar on two numbers. 'Wonderful Wino' also got an airing (later to reappear on *Zoot Allures* in 1976). Production was by Zappa under the name La Marr Bruister. Simmons played bass and sang backing on Zappa's *Chunga's Revenge* (1971), but left under a cloud. Though he is thanked on the cover of *200 Motels*, his pretensions to superstardom are guyed in the movie. He recorded the soundtrack to the film *Naked Angels* - fuzz guitar instrumentals - and then vanished from sight.

Albums: *Lucille Has Messed My Mind Up* (1970), *Naked Angels* (1971).

Simmons, John

b. 14 June 1918, Haskell, Oklahoma, USA, d. 19 September 1979. While living in California Simmons took up the bass when a sporting injury affected his trumpet playing. He advanced quickly on his new instrument and worked with **Nat 'King' Cole** and **Teddy Wilson** in the mid-to-late 30s. In the early 40s he moved to Chicago, playing with **Roy Eldridge**, **Benny Goodman**, **Louis Armstrong** and other leading jazzmen. In the remaining years of the decade he appeared on countless small group recording dates, backing distinguished artists such as **Hot Lips Page**, **Ben Webster**, **Billie Holiday**, **Erroll Garner**, **Coleman Hawkins**, **Benny Carter** and **Ella Fitzgerald**. Although essentially a mainstream musician with a robust sound and unflagging swing, Simmons also coped comfortably with the demands of playing with beboppers, who included **Thelonious Monk**. In the 50s he toured and recorded with **Harry Edison**, **Tadd Dameron**, **Phineas Newborn Jnr.** and others but these and his later years were dogged by poor health. He died in 1979.

Album: with Phineas Newborn *I Love A Piano* (1959).

Simmons, Norman

b. 6 October 1929, Chicago, USA. Simmons studied piano at the Chicago School of Music (1945-49) and then worked as house pianist in various Chicago clubs - the BeeHive (1953-56) and the C&C Lounge (1957-59). In the late 50s he became the accompanist to vocalists **Dakota Staton** and **Ernestine Anderson** and then settled in New York. He worked as an arranger for Riverside Records. He recorded with **Johnny Griffin** and worked with the **Eddie 'Lockjaw' Davis**/Johnny Griffin Quintet. He rarely solos but is an accomplished accompanist who worked with **Carmen McRae** throughout the 60s and with **Joe Williams** ever since. He has also played with vocalists **Anita O'Day**, **Helen Humes** and **Betty Carter** and with **Roy Eldridge** and **Scott Hamilton** and **Warren Vaché**. He taught for Jazzmobile (1974) and joined the faculty of Paterson State College in 1982.

Albums: with Griffin *Big Soul Band* (1960), with Davis *Battle Stations* (1960), *Ramira The Dancer* (1976), *Midnight Creeper* (1981), *13th Moon* (1986), *I Am The Blues* (1988).

Simmons, Patrick

b. 23 January 1950, Aberdeen, Washington, USA. A former student at San Jose State University, Simmons was playing guitar in Scratch, a country-folk trio, when he joined the embryonic **Doobie Brothers** in 1970. He remained with this highly successful act throughout the ensuing decade, penning during that time much of the repertoire, including the 1975 US number 1 hit single 'Black Water'. He secured a solo recording deal 1981 and began work on a debut album when the group was dissolved the following year. *Arcade* was a competent, if unexceptional collection, although one of the tracks, 'So Wrong', reached number 30 in the US when released as a single. The guitarist rejoined several former colleagues for a 1987 concert in aid of Vietnam Veterans, which in turn inspired a full-scale Doobie Brothers reunion.

Album: *Arcade* (1983).

Simmons, Russell

b. c.1958, Hollis, Queens, New York, USA. Simmons' artistic and business sense has seen him become the ultimate B-Boy millionaire, bullet-proof Rolls Royce notwithstanding. His entrepreneurial interests began by promoting disco parties while he was studying sociology at City College Of New York. Rush management was formed in 1979, and quickly escalated following the success of **Kurtis Blow** and **Fearless Four**. His first writing credit came with Blow's 'Christmas Rap'. However, no one can accuse Simmons of having fortune fall in his lap. He was part of the Rush team who picketed MTV in order to get them to play black videos (Run DMC's 'Rock Box', although **Michael Jackson** was the first to be played), and has maintained his commitment to black development. Throughout the 80s **Def Jam**, the label, would be the dominant force in the music, via the work of **Run DMC** and **Public Enemy**. Though he would eventually split from Rick Rubin, Simmons' stature in the eyes of the hip hop audience has hardly decreased. In 1993 Rush Management was valued at $34 million, with seven record labels, management, fashion (the Phat line) and broadcasting interests. The president of the company is Carmen Ashurst-Watson, but Simmons remains responsible for the company ethos: 'My only real purpose is managing and directing. I sacrifice all the time for my artists. It's my job to make sure they have rich black babies'.

Simmons, Sonny

b. Huey Simmons, 4 August 1933, Sicily Island, Louisiana, USA. Simmons's family moved to Oakland, California when he was eight years old. Though he was interested in music, his parents could not afford to pay for lessons for him, and it was not until 1950 that he was able to buy his own alto saxophone. A few years later he met Prince Lasha and worked with him for a decade. In 1960 they appeared on television together in Sacramento, and in 1962 Simmons made his recording debut as part of Lasha's quintet with *The Cry* for the west coast label Contemporary. Initially inspired by **Charlie Parker**, Simmons found that **Ornette Coleman**'s freedom from the chord changes 'worked out' for him. He married the trumpeter **Barbara Donald** in 1964 and they frequently appeared together. In 1964 he was playing with **Eric Dolphy**. In 1966 he cut *Staying On Watch* for ESP, a masterpiece of new jazz. In the late 60s Simmons and Donald moved to Woodstock, New York, where they started the Woodstock Music Festival and in 196, made a movie. In 1970 they returned to California. Despite formidable playing skill and a strong set of compositions - including 'City Of David', 'Interplanetary Travellers', 'Dolphy's Days' and 'Burning Spirits' - Simmons dropped out of sight in the 70s. He and Donald split up towards the end of that decade. Still based in San Francisco, Simmons continues to play: his latest recording is the track 'Ballad For My Friend', included on the 1990 compilation CD *Beets*.

Albums: with Prince Lasha *The Cry* (1962), with Elvin Jones *Illumination!* (1963), with Eric Dolphy *Conversations* (1964), with Dolphy *Iron Man* (1964), *Staying On The Watch* (1966), with Lasha *Firebirds* (1967), *Music Of The Spheres* (1967), *Manhattan Egos* (1969), *Ruma Suma* (1970), *Burning Spirits* (1971).

Simms, Ginny
(see **Kyser, Kay**)

Simon And Garfunkel
This highly successful vocal duo first played together during their early years in New York. **Paul Simon** (b. 13 October 1941, Newark, New Jersey, USA) and **Art Garfunkel** (b. Arthur Garfunkel, 5 November 1941, Forest Hills, New York, USA) were initially inspired by the **Everly Brothers** and under the name Tom And Jerry enjoyed a US hit with the rock 'n' roll styled 'Hey Schoolgirl'. They also completed an album which was later reissued after their rise to international prominence in the 60s. Garfunkel subsequently returned to college and Simon pursued a solo career before the duo reunited in 1964 for *Wednesday Morning 3AM*. A strong, harmonic work, which included an acoustic reading of 'The Sound Of Silence', the album did not sell well enough to encourage the group to stay together. While Simon was in England the folk rockboom was in the ascendant and producer Tom Wilson made the presumptuous but prescient decision to overdub 'Sound Of Silence' with electric instrumentation. Within weeks, the song was number 1 in the US charts, and Simon and Garfunkel were hastily reunited. An album titled after their million-selling single was rush-released early in 1966 and proved a commendable work. Among its major achievements was 'Homeward Bound', an evocative and moving portrayal of life on the road, which went on to become a transatlantic hit. The solipsistic 'I Am A Rock' was another international success with such angst-ridden lines as, 'I have no need of friendship, friendship causes pain'. In keeping with the social commentary that permeated their mid-60s' work, the group included two songs whose theme was suicide: 'A Most Peculiar Man' and 'Richard Cory'. Embraced by a vast following, especially among the student population, the duo certainly looked the part with their college scarves, duffle coats and cerebral demeanour. Their next single, 'The Dangling Conversation', was their most ambitious lyric to date and far too esoteric for the Top 20. Nevertheless, the work testified to their artistic courage and boded well for the release of a second album within a year: *Parsley, Sage, Rosemary And Thyme*. The album took its title from a repeated line in 'Scarborough Fair', which was their excellent harmonic weaving of that traditional song and another, 'Canticle'. An accomplished work, the album had a varied mood from the grandly serious 'For Emily, Whenever I May Find Her' to the bouncy '59th Street Bridge Song (Feelin' Groovy)' (subsequently a hit for **Harpers Bizarre**). After two strong but uncommercial singles, 'At The Zoo' and 'Fakin' It', the duo contributed to the soundtrack of the 1968 film, *The Graduate*. The key song in the film was 'Mrs Robinson' which provided the group with one of their biggest international sellers. That same year saw the release of *Bookends*, a superbly-crafted work, ranging from the serene 'Save The Life Of My Child' to the personal odyssey 'America' and the vivid imagery of 'Old Friends'. *Bookends* is still felt by many to be their finest work.

In 1969 the duo released 'The Boxer', a long single that nevertheless found commercial success on both sides of the Atlantic. This classic single reappeared on the group's next album, the celebrated *Bridge Over Troubled Water*. One of the best-selling albums of all time (303 weeks on the UK chart), the work's title track became a standard with its lush, orchestral arrangement and contrasting tempo. Heavily gospel-influenced, the album included several well-covered songs such as 'Keep The Customer Satisfied', 'Cecilia' and 'El Condor Pasa'. While at the peak of their commercial success, with an album that dominated the top of the chart listings for months, the duo became irascible and their partnership abruptly ceased. The release of a *Greatest Hits* package in 1972 included four previously unissued live tracks and during the same year the duo performed together at a benefit concert for Senator George McGovern. In 1981 they again reunited. The results were captured in 1981 on *The Concert In Central Park*. After a long break, a further duet occurred on the hit single 'My Little Town' in 1975. Although another studio album was undertaken, the sessions broke down and Simon transferred the planned material to his 1983 solo *Hearts And Bones*. In the autumn of 1993 Paul Simon and Art Garfunkel settled their differences long enough to complete 21 sell-out dates in New York.

Albums: *Wednesday Morning 3AM* (Columbia 1968), *The Sound Of Silence* (Columbia 1966), *Parsley, Sage, Rosemary And Thyme* (Columbia 1966), *The Graduate* (Columbia 1968, film soundtrack), *Bookends* (Columbia 1968), *Bridge Over Troubled Water* (Columbia 1970), *The Concert In Central Park* (Geffen 1981). Compilations: *Simon And Garfunkel's Greatest Hits* (Columbia 1972), *The Simon And Garfunkel Collection* (1981), *The Definitive Simon And Garfunkel* (1992).

Further reading: *Simon & Garfunkel: A Biography In Words & Pictures*, Michael S. Cohen. *Paul Simon: Now And Then*, Spencer Leigh. *Paul Simon*, Dave Marsh. *Simon And Garfunkel*, Robert Matthew-Walker. *Bookends: The Simon And Garfunkel Story*, Patrick Humphries. *The Boy In The Bubble: A Biography Of Paul Simon*, Patrick Humphries. *Simon And Garfunkel: Old Friends*, Joseph Morella and Patricia Barey.

Simon Chase

This Canadian melodic pop-rock partnership comprised vocalist Andy Michaels and guitarist Sil Simone. Formed in 1987, they made their debut with *Thrill Of The Chase*, which utilized session help from bassist Pete Cardinali and drummer Greg Loates. Produced by **Triumph**'s Rik Emmett it was an impressive debut of lightweight but infectious AOR, tailor-made for Stateside FM radio playlists. However, partly due to poor promotion, the album never took off and little has been heard from them since.

Album: *Thrill Of The Chase* (1988).

Simon, Carly

b. 25 June 1945, New York City, New York, USA. Simon became one of the most popular singer-songwriters of the 70s and achieved equal success with film music in the 80s. In the early 60s she played Greenwich Village clubs with her sister Lucy. As the Simon Sisters they had one minor hit with 'Winkin' Blinkin And Nod' (Kapp Records 1964) and recorded two albums of soft folk and children's' material. After the duo split up, Carly Simon made an unsuccessful attempt to launch a solo career through **Albert Grossman** (then **Bob Dylan**'s manager) before concentrating on songwriting with film critic Jacob Brackman. In 1971, two of their songs, the wistful 'That's The Way I've Always Heard It Should Be' and the **Paul Samwell-Smith** produced 'Anticipation' were US hits for Simon. Her voice was given a rock accompaniment by **Richard Perry** on her third album which included her most famous song, 'You're So Vain', whose target was variously supposed to be

Warren Beatty and/or **Mick Jagger**, who provided backing vocals. The song was a million-seller in 1972 and nearly two decades later was reissued in Britain after it had been used in a television commercial. *No Secrets* remains her most applauded work, and featured among numerous gems, 'The Right Thing To Do'.

Simon's next Top 10 hit was an insipid revival of the **Charlie And Inez Foxx** song 'Mockingbird' on which she duetted with **James Taylor** to whom she was married from 1972-83. Their marriage was given enormous coverage in the US media, rivalling that of Richard Burton and Elizabeth Taylor. Their divorce received similar treatment as Carly found solace with Taylor's drummer Russell Kunkel. *Hotcakes* became US Top 3 album in 1972. During the latter part of the 70s, Simon was less prolific as a writer and recording artist although she played benefit concerts for anti-nuclear causes. Her most successful records were the James Bond film theme. 'Nobody Does It Better', written by **Carole Bayer Sager** and **Marvin Hamlisch** and 'You Belong To Me', a collaboration with **Michael McDonald**, both in 1977. During the 80s, Simon's worked moved away from the singer-songwriter field and towards the pop mainstream. She released two albums of pre-war Broadway standards (*Torch* and *My Romance*) and increased her involvement with films. Her UK hit 'Why' (1982) was written by **Chic** and used in the movie *Soup For One* while she appeared in *Perfect* with **John Travolta**. But her biggest achievement of the decade was to compose and perform two of its memorable film themes. Both 'Coming Around Again' (from *Heartburn*, 1986) and the Oscar-winning 'Let The River Run' (from *Working Girl*, 1989) demonstrated the continuing depth of Simon's songwriting talent while the quality of her previous work was showcased on a 1988 live album and video recorded in the open air at Martha's Vineyard, Massachusetts. In 1990, her career came full circle when Lucy Simon was a guest artist on *Have You Seen Me Lately?* After a lengthy gap in recording *Letters Never Sent* was released in 1995. This was a perplexing album lyrically nostalgic and sad with lush arrangements which peaked outside the Top 100 in the USA.

Albums: as the Simon Sisters *The Simon Sisters* (1964), *Cuddlebug* (1965); solo *Carly Simon* (1971), *Anticipation* (1972), *No Secrets* (1972), *Hotcakes* (1974), *Playing Possum* (1975), *Another Passenger* (1976), *Boys In The Trees* (1978), *Spy* (1979), *Come Upstairs* (1980), *Torch* (1981), *Hello Big Man* (1983), *Spoiled Girl* (1985), *Coming Around Again* (1987), *Greatest Hits Live* (1988), *My Romance* (1990), *Have You Seen Me Lately?* (1990), *Letters Never Sent* (Arista 1994). Compilation: *The Best Of Carly Simon* (1975).

Further reading: *Carly Simon*, Morse, Charles (1975).

Simon, Joe

b. 2 September 1943, Simmesport, Louisiana, USA. Simon's professional career began following his move to Oakland, California, where a 1962 release, 'My Adorable One' was a minor hit. In 1964, Joe met John Richbourg, a Nashville-based disc jockey who began guiding the singer's musical path, initially on the Sound Stage 7 label. 'Let's Do It Over' (1965), Simon's first R&B hit, emphasized Richbourg's preference for a blend of gentle soul and country, and the singer's smooth delivery found its niche on such poignant songs as 'Teenager's Prayer', 'Nine Pound Steel' (both 1967) and 'The Chokin' Kind', a US R&B number 1 in 1969. The following year Simon moved to the **Polydor** subsidiary, Spring. He maintained his ties with Richbourg until 1971, when a **Gamble And Huff** production, 'Drowning In The Sea Of Love' was an R&B Number 3. Further success came with 'The Power Of Love' (1972), 'Step By Step' (1973 - his only UK hit), 'Theme From Cleopatra Jones' (1973) and 'Get Down Get Down (Get On The Floor)' (1975), but the artist increasingly sacrificed his craft in favour of the dancefloor. His late 70s releases were less well received and in 1980 he returned to Nashville. Since then Joe's work has been restricted to local labels.

Albums: *Simon Pure Soul* (1967), *No Sad Songs* (1968), *Simon Sings* (1969), *The Chokin' Kind* (1969), *Joe Simon - Better Than Ever* (1969), *Sounds Of Simon* (1971), *Drowning In The Sea Of Love* (1972), *Power Of Love* (1973), *Mood, Heart And Soul* (1974), *Simon Country* (1974), *Get Down* (1975), *Joe Simon Today* (1976), *Easy To Love* (1977), *Bad Case Of Love* (1978), *Love Vibration* (1979), *Happy Birthday Baby* (1979), *Soul Neighbors* (1984), *Mr. Right* (1985). Compilations: *Joe Simon* (c.1969, 1962/3 Hush/VeeJay recordings), *Joe Simon's Greatest Hits* (1972), *The Best Of Joe Simon* (1972), *The World Of ...* (1973, double album), *The Chokin' Kind/Better Than Ever* (1976, double album), *The Best Of ...* (1977), *Lookin' Back - The Best Of Joe Simon 1966-70* (1988).

Simon, John

b. 11 August 1941, Norwalk, Connecticut, USA. Having studied music at college, Simon joined **Columbia Records** where he initially worked on documentary material. He switched to pop in 1966 and produced 'Red Rubber Ball', a US Top 3 hit for the **Cyrkle**. This led to involvement with other acts, including **Simon And Garfunkel** and **Leonard Cohen**, and his score for the off-beat movie, *You Are What You Eat*. One of Simon's songs from the film, 'My Name Is Jack', became a major hit for **Manfred Mann**. The artist's relationship with the **Band** was especially fruitful. He not only produced the group's first two albums but also acted as an auxiliary member on piano, tuba and horns. Simon's first solo album featured reciprocal help from several Band members and included 'Davy's On The Road Again', a song he composed with **Robbie Robertson**. However, despite successful work with **Gordon Lightfoot**, **Bobby Charles** and **Seals And Crofts**, John Simon

later drifted out of favour as both producer and performer.

Albums: *You Are What You Eat* (1968, film soundtrack), *The John Simon Album* (1971), *The Journey* (1972).

Simon, Paul

b. Paul Frederic Simon, 13 October 1941, Newark, New Jersey, USA. Simon first entered the music business with partner **Art Garfunkel** in the duo Tom and Jerry. In 1957, they scored a US hit with the rock 'n' roll influenced 'Hey Schoolgirl'. After one album, they split up in order to return to college. Although Simon briefly worked with **Carole King** recording demonstration discs for minor acts, he did not record again until the early 60s. Employing various pseudonyms, Simon enjoyed a couple of minor US hits during 1962-63 as Tico And The Triumphs ('Motorcycle') and Jerry Landis ('The Lone Teen-Ranger'). After moving to Europe in 1964, Simon busked in Paris and appeared at various folk clubs in London. Upon returning to New York, he was signed to **CBS Records** by producer Tom Wilson and reunited with his erstwhile partner Garfunkel. Their 1964 recording *Wednesday Morning 3 AM*, which included 'The Sound Of Silence' initially failed to sell, prompting Simon to return to London. While there, he made *The Paul Simon Songbook*, a solo work, recorded on one microphone with the astonishingly low budget of £60. Among its contents were several of Simon's most well-known compositions, including 'I Am A Rock', 'A Most Peculiar Man' and 'Kathy's Song'. The album was virtually ignored until Tom Wilson altered Simon's artistic stature overnight. Back in the USA, the producer grafted electric instrumentation on to **Simon And Garfunkel**'s acoustic recording of 'Sound Of Silence' and created a folk-rock classic that soared to the top of the US charts. Between 1965 and 70, Simon And Garfunkel became one of the most successful recording duos in the history of popular music. The partnership ended amid musical disagreements and a realization that they had grown apart.

After the break-up, Simon took songwriting classes in New York and prepared a stylistically diverse solo album, *Paul Simon* (1972). The work incorporated elements of latin, reggae and jazz and spawned the hit singles 'Mother And Child Reunion' and 'Me And Julio Down By The Schoolyard'. One year later, Simon returned with the much more commercial *There Goes Rhymin' Simon* which enjoyed massive chart success and included two major hits, 'Kodachrome' and 'Take Me To The Mardi Gras'. A highly successful tour resulted in *Live Rhymin'*, which featured several Simon And Garfunkel standards. This flurry of creativity in 1975 culminated in the chart-topping *Still Crazy After All These Years* which won several Grammy awards. The wry '50 Ways To Leave Your Lover', taken from the album, provided Simon with his first number 1 single as a soloist, while the hit 'My Little Town' featured a tantalizing duet with Garfunkel. A five-year hiatus followed during which Simon took stock of his career. He appeared briefly in Woody Allen's movie *Annie Hall*, recorded a hit single with Garfunkel and **James Taylor** ('Wonderful World'), released a *Greatest Hits* package featuring the catchy 'Slip Slidin' Away' and switched labels from CBS to **Warner Brothers**. In 1980, he released the ambitious *One Trick Pony*, from his film of the same name. The movie included cameo appearances by the **Lovin' Spoonful** and **Tiny Tim** but was not particularly well-received even though it was far more literate than most 'rock-related' films. In the wake of that project, Simon suffered a long period of writer's block, which was to delay the recording of his next album.

Meanwhile, a double-album live reunion of Simon And Garfunkel recorded in Central Park was issued and sold extremely well. It was intended to preview a studio reunion, but the sessions were subsequently scrapped. Instead, Simon concentrated on his next album, which finally emerged in 1983 as *Hearts And Bones*. An intense and underrated effort, it sold poorly despite its evocative hit single 'The Late Great **Johnny Ace**' (dedicated to both the doomed 50s star and the assassinated **John Lennon**). Simon was dismayed by the album's lack of commercial success and critics felt that he was in a creative rut. That situation altered during 1984 when Simon was introduced to the enlivening music of the South African black townships. After an appearance at the celebrated USA For Africa recording of 'We Are The World', Simon immersed himself in the music of the Dark Continent. *Graceland* (1986) was one of the most intriguing and commercially successful albums of the decade with Simon utilizing musical contributions from **Ladysmith Black Mambazo**, **Los Lobos**, **Linda Ronstadt** and **Rockie Dopsie And The Twisters**. The project and subsequent tour was bathed in controversy due to accusations (misconceived according to the United Nations Anti-Apartheid Committee) that Simon had broken the cultural boycott against South Africa. The success of the album in combining contrasting cross-cultural musical heritages was typical of a performer who had already incorporated folk, R&B, calypso and blues into his earlier repertoire. The album spawned several notable hits, 'The Boy In The Bubble' (with its technological imagery), 'You Can Call Me Al' (inspired by an amusing case of mistaken identity) and 'Graceland' (an oblique homage to **Elvis Presley**'s Memphis home). Although *Graceland* seemed a near impossible work to follow up, Simon continued his pan-cultural investigations with *The Rhythm Of The Saints*, which incorporated African and Brazilian musical elements. He married **Edie Brickell** in 1994.

Albums: *The Paul Simon Songbook* (1965), *Paul Simon* (1972), *There Goes Rhymin' Simon* (1973), *Live Rhymin'*

(1974), *Still Crazy After All These Years* (1975), *One Trick Pony* (Warner 1980, film soundtrack), *Hearts And Bones* (Warner 1983), *Graceland* (Warner 1986), *The Rhythm Of The Saints* (Warner 1990), Paul Simon's Concert In The Park (Warner 1991). Compilations: *Greatest Hits, Etc.* (1977), *Paul Simon 1964/1993* (1993, 3 CD boxed-set). Video: *Paul Simon: Born At The Right Time* (1993). Further reading: *The Boy In The Bubble*, Patrick Humphries. Film: *One Trick Pony* (1980).

Simone, Nina

b. Eunice Waymon, 21 February 1933, Tyron, North Carolina, USA. An accomplished pianist as a child, Nina later studied at New York's Juilliard School Of Music. Her jazz credentials were established in 1959 where she secured a hit with an emotive interpretation of **George Gershwin**'s 'I Loves You Porgy'. Her influential 60s work included 'Gin House Blues', 'Forbidden Fruit' and 'I Put A Spell On You', while another of her singles, 'Don't Let Me Be Misunderstood', was later covered by the **Animals**. The singer's popular fortune flourished upon her signing with **RCA**. 'Ain't Got No - I Got Life', a song lifted from the mock-hippie musical, *Hair*, was a UK number 2, while her searing version of the **Bee Gees**' 'To Love Somebody' reached number 5. In America, her own composition, 'To Be Young, Gifted And Black', dedicated to her late friend and playwright, Lorraine Hansberry, reflected Nina's growing militancy. Releases then grew infrequent as her political activism increased. A commanding, if taciturn live performer, Simone's appearances were increasingly focused on benefits and rallies, although a fluke UK hit, 'My Baby Just Cares For Me', a resurrected 50s master, pushed the singer, momentarily, into the commercial spotlight when it reached number 5 in 1987. Tired of an America she perceived as uncaring, Simone has settled in France where her work continues to flourish. An uncompromising personality, Nina Simone's interpretations of soul, jazz, blues and standards are both compulsive and unique.

Albums: *Little Girl Blue* (1959 - later issued as *The Original Nina Simone*), *The Amazing Nina Simone* (1959), *Nina Simone At The Town Hall* (1959), *Nina Simone At Newport* (1960), *Forbidden Fruit* (1961), *Nina Simone At The Village Gate* (1961), *Nina Simone Sings Ellington* (1962), *Nina's Choice* (1963), *Nina Simone At Carnegie Hall* (1963), *Folksy Nina* (1964), *Nina Simone In Concert* (1964), *Broadway ... Blues ... Ballads* (1964), *I Put A Spell On You* (1965), *Tell Me More* (1965), *Pastel Blues* (1965), *Let It All Out* (1966), *Wild Is The Wind* (1966), *Nina With Strings* (1966), *This Is* (1966), *Nina Simone Sings The Blues* (1966), *High Priestess Of Soul* (1967), *Sweet 'N' Swinging* (1967), *Silk And Soul* (1967), *'Nuff Said* (1968), *And Piano!* (1969), *To Love Somebody* (1969), *Black Gold* (1970), *Here Comes The Sun* (1971), *Heart And Soul* (1971), *Emergency Ward* (1972),

It Is Finished (1972), *Gifted And Black* (1974), *I Loves You Porgy* (1977), *Baltimore* (1978), *Cry Before I Go* (1980), *Nina Simone* (1982), *Fodder On My Wings* (1982), *Live At Vine Street* (1987), *Live At Ronnie Scott's* (1988), *Nina's Back* (1989), *In Concert* (1992), *A Single Woman* (1993). Compilations *Fine And Mellow* (1975), *The Artistry Of Nina Simone* (1982), *Music For The Millions* (1983), *My Baby Just Cares For Me* (1984), *Lady Midnight* (1987), *The Nina Simone Collection* (1888), *The Nina Simone Story* (1989), *16 Greatest Hits* (1993)

Further reading: *I Put A Spell On You: The Autobiography Of Nina Simone*, Simone, Nina with Cleary, Stephen (1991).

Simonelli, Victor

b. c.1967, USA. Brooklyn-based producer of the early 90s who learnt his craft at the knee of **Arthur Baker**, working in his Shakedown Studio. After editing work on tracks by **Al Jarreau** and **David Bowie**, he joined Lenny Dee to establish Brooklyn Street Essentials, a remix team. He has worked widely in this territory ever since. His own nom de plumes included Groove Committee (cutting 'Dirty Games' for **Nu Groove**), Solution, Ebony Soul and the Street Players. Throughout he has maintained his belief in working with fully-fledged songs rather than simply strong rhythmic tracks. He has recently recorded with **Tommy Musto** as part of Colourblind.

Simper, Nick

b. 3 November 1946, Southall, Middlesex, England. Bassist Simper was initially a member of Buddy Britten And The Regents, a popular Middlesex beat group which completed two singles in 1965. He subsequently joined **Johnny Kidd And The Pirates**, a tenure which ended with the singer's tragic death, before touring in exploitative hit group the **Flowerpot Men**. A founder member of **Deep Purple**, Simper appeared on this successful unit's first three albums, before leaving in March 1968. Spells with **Marsha Hunt** and **Screaming Lord Sutch** then ensued, following which the bassist formed **Warhorse** whom he led for four years until 1974. A career as a session musician was interrupted in 1978 by Nick Simper's Fantango, with Jim Proops (vocals), Peter Parks (guitar/vocals) and Ron Penney (drums), which completed *Slipstreaming* in 1979. The bassist then reverted to studio work.

Simple Aggression

Formed on the first day of October 1989 in the hills of Independence, Kentucky, USA, Simple Aggression subsequently relocated to Cincinnati to establish their reputation. Comprising Doug Carter (vocals), James Carr (guitar), Darrin McKinney (guitar), Dave Swart (bass) and Kenny Soward (drums), the group took a name which prophesied a high velocity metal attack. However, the quintet were more than a simple 'thrash'

band, preferring instead to work a steady groove at the core of their sound (the influence of the **Red Hot Chili Peppers** was certainly at work). A latent commercial instinct was also unveiled on their long playing debut by the inclusion of a strong ballad, 'Of Winter'.

Album: *Formulations In Black* (Bulletproof 1994).

Simplé E

Talented female rapper who broke through in 1994 with her debut single 'Play My Funk', a Top 20 US R&B chart success. Taken from the *Sugar Hill* motion picture soundtrack, and produced by Dwayne Wiggins of **Tony Toni Tone!**, it revealed her to be able to switch from sung passages to gripping raps without missing a beat. Her debut album was aided by the production of Terry T and S.I.D. Reynolds.

Album: *The Colourz Of Sound* (Beacon 1994).

Simple Minds

This Scottish group was formed in 1978 by Jim Kerr (b. 9 July 1959, Glasgow, Scotland; vocals), Charlie Burchill (b. 27 November 1959, Glasgow, Scotland; guitar), Tony Donald (bass) and Brian McGee (drums), former members of Glasgow punk group Johnny And The Self-Abusers. A second guitarist, Duncan Barnwell, was recruited following a newspaper advertisement. The unit was augmented by keyboard player Mick McNeil (b. 20 July 1958) before Derek Forbes (b. 22 June 1956) replaced a disaffected Donald. The upheavals of this initial era were completed with Barnwell's departure. Having established themselves as one of Scotland's leading live attractions, Simple Minds were signed to Zoom, an Edinburgh-based independent label marketed by **Arista Records**. 'Life In A Day', the group's debut single, broached the UK Top 50 in March 1979 while the attendant album reached number 30. Critics were divided over its merits, although a consensus deemed the set derivative. Within weeks the quintet began decrying their creation and embarked on a more radical direction. *Real To Real Cacophony* unfolded within the recording studio in an attempt to regain an early spontaneity and while this largely experimental collection was a commercial flop, it reinstated the group's self-respect and won unanimous music press approbation.

Empires And Dance, was released in September 1980. The set fused the flair of its predecessor to a newly established love of dance music and reflected influences garnered during European tours. It included 'I Travel', a pulsating travelogue which became a firm favourite throughout the club circuit and helped engender a new sense of optimism in the group's career. Now free of Arista, Simple Minds were signed to **Virgin Records** in 1981, and paired with producer **Steve Hillage**. The resultant sessions spawned two albums, *Sons And Fascination* and *Sister Feelings Call*, which were initially released together. It became the group's first UK Top 20 entrant, spawning three minor hit singles with 'The American', 'Love Song' and 'Sweat In Bullet' and began Simple Minds' transformation from cult to popular favourites. This very success unnerved Brian McGee, who abhorred touring. In August 1981 he was replaced by former **Slik** and **Skids** drummer Kenny Hyslop (b. 14 February 1951, Helensburgh, Strathclyde, Scotland), although the newcomer's recorded contribution was confined to 'Promised You A Miracle'. This powerful song reached number 13 in Britain, and proved popular in Europe and Australia where the group enjoyed an almost fanatical following. Although Mike Ogletree joined on Hyslop's departure, a former musician, Mel Gaynor (b. 29 May 1959), eventually became the quintet's permanent drummer. Both musicians were featured on *New Gold Dream*, Simple Minds' most successful album to date which peaked at number 3. Here the group was harnessing a more commercial sound, and they achieved a series of hits with its attendant singles, 'Glittering Prize' and 'Someone, Somewhere In Summertime'. A sixth collection, *Sparkle In The Rain*, united the quintet with producer **Steve Lillywhite**, inspiring comparisons with his other proteges, **U2**. 'Waterfront', a brash, pulsating grandiose performance, and 'Speed Your Love To Me', prefaced its release, and the album entered the UK chart at number 1. The set also featured 'Up On The Catwalk', a further Top 30 entrant, and a version of **Lou Reed**'s 'Street Hassle', a long-established group favourite.

Jim Kerr married **Pretenders**' singer Chrissie Hynde in 1984, but their relationship did not survive the rigours of touring. The following year Simple Minds chose to record in America under the aegis of Jimmy Iovine and Bob Clearmountain. It was during this period that the group contributed 'Don't You (Forget About Me)' to the soundtrack of the film *The Breakfast Club*. The quintet remained ambivalent about the song, which was written by Keith Forsey and Steve Schiff, but it paradoxically became a US number 1 when issued as a single. Although the group initially vetoed a world-wide release, they reneged in the light of this achievement whereupon the record became a massive international hit and confirmed the group's world-beating status. However, the track did not appear on the ensuing *Once Upon A Time* which, despite international success, drew considerable criticism for its bombastic approach. Three tracks, 'Alive And Kicking', 'Sanctify Yourself' and 'All The Things She Said' nonetheless reached the UK Top 10 while a concurrent world tour, documented on *Live In The City Of Light*, was one of the year's major events. The proceeds of several dates were donated to Amnesty International, reflecting a growing politicization within the group. In 1988 they were a major inspiration behind the concert celebrating Nelson Mandela's 70th birthday, but although a new composition, 'Mandela Day', was recorded for the event, Simple Minds refused to release it as a single, fearful of seeming opportunistic. The song was later coupled to 'Belfast Child', a lengthy, haunting lament for Northern Ireland based on a traditional folk melody, 'She Moved Through The Fair'. This artistically ambitious work topped the UK chart in February 1989 and set the tone for the group's subsequent album, *Street Fighting Years*, their first studio set in four years. Although it achieved platinum status within five days, sales then dropped rather dramatically, reflecting the uncompromising nature of its content. Three further singles entered the UK Top 20, while *The Amsterdam EP*, which included a version of **Prince**'s 'Sign 'O' The Times', reached number 18 at the end of the year. This contradictory period closed with the rancorous departure of Mick McNeil, replaced by Peter Vitesse, and the ending of the group's ten-year association with Schoolhouse Management. Simple Minds entered the 90s with an official line-up of Jim Kerr and Charlie Burchill and a development almost impossible to predict. *Real Life* saw the band re-introducing more personal themes to their songwriting after the political concerns of previous albums. The new material recaptured the grand, epic sound that is Simple Minds' trademark. Kerr married **Patsy Kensit** in January 1992. The highly commercial 'Shes A River' came in advance of *Good News From The Next World* in 1995, just as the next world was beginning to think Simple Minds were from an age past, this timely album re-awoke memories of the early 80s.

Albums: *Life In A Day* (1979), *Real To Real Cacophony* (1979), *Empires And Dance* (1980), *Sons And Fascination/Sister Feelings Call* (1981), *New Gold Dream (81, 82, 83, 84)* (1982), *Sparkle In The Rain* (1984), *Once Upon A Time* (1985), *Live In The City Of Light* (1987), *Street Fighting Years* (1989), *Real Life* (1991), *Good News From The Next World* (Virgin 1995). Compilations: *Celebration* (1982), *Themes For Great Cities* (1982), *Glittering Prizes 81/92* (1992).

Further reading: *Simple Minds: Glittering Prize*, Thomas, Dave (1985), *Simple Minds*, Sweeting, Adam (1988), *Simple Minds: A Visual Documentary*, Wrenn, Mike (1990), *Simple Minds: Street Fighting Years*, Bos, Alfred (1990).

Simple Simon

One of America's most cherished clowns, Ed Wynn, brought his fumbling style, nervous laugh, and excruciating puns to this **Florenz Ziegfeld** production which opened at the impresario's own Broadway theatre on 18 February 1930. Wynn also collaborated with **Guy Bolton** on the book in which he was cast a a newspaper vendor who, rather than accept that bad news exists, spends his time in a kind of fairy-tale land. This gave Ziegfeld and his designer Joseph Urban the opportunity to display the lavish sets and costumes for which he was justifiably famous.

Richard Rodgers and **Lorenz Hart** wrote the score, and it contained one of their most enduring numbers, 'Ten Cents A Dance', which was emphatically introduced by **Ruth Etting**. She had a big record hit with the song, and it figured prominently in her film biography, *Love Me Or Leave Me*, in which she was played by **Doris Day**. Ironically, the song 'Love Me Or Leave Me' (**Gus Kahn-Walter Donaldson**) was added to the score of *Simple Simon* a couple of months after the show opened. One of the numbers that was cut during the Broadway try-out, 'Dancing On The Ceiling', was later sung by **Jessie Matthews** in the London production of ***Ever Green***, and became forever associated with her. The remainder of the score for *Simple Simon* included 'I Can Do Wonders With You', 'Don't Tell Your Folks', 'Send For Me', and 'I Still Believe In You'. The show ran for 135 performances, and returned early in 1931 for a further brief engagement.

Simplice, Sery

b. February 1949, Touba, Cote D'lvoire. One of Cote D'lvoire's most popular roots modernizers, vocalist and guitarist Simplice is the leading exponent of the country's gbegbe style, a traditional dance rhythm that has spread far beyond its village origins to the clubs and dancehalls of the capital, Abidjan. Simplice spent 1964 and 1965 moving from village to village, playing traditional songs on a guitar made from a petrol can. In 1966, he moved to Abidjan, where he joined the band led by one of the pioneers of modern Ivoirian music, Amedee Pierre, 'Le Dope National', who was singing traditional proverbs and stories over a mix of Ivoirian and Zairean rhythms. As his guitarist, Simplice decided to go further and transpose an entire traditional music into modern form. Leaving Amedee Pierre in 1978, he set up his own unit, Les Freres Djatys. The band's mixture of heavy rhythms and harsh vocals carried the full flavour of the old rural music ; although Abidjan audiences at first rejected the sound as 'backward' and 'reactionary', by 1983 the sheer vigour and power of the music had won Simplice a substantial following. That year he was crowned the King Of Gbegbe Music on national television. In 1985, he made his first European tour.

Albums: *Gbolou* (1981), *Gbolou Vol.2* (1983), *King Of Gbegbe* (1985), *Paris Concert* (1987), *Gbegbe Universal* (1989).

Simply Red

This 80s soul-influenced group was led by Manchester born vocalist Mick Hucknall (b. Michael James Hucknall, 8 June 1960, Denton, Gt. Manchester, England). Hucknall's first recording group was the punk-inspired Frantic Elevators, who recorded a handful of singles, including an impressive vocal ballad, 'Holding Back The Years'. When they split up in 1983,

the vocalist formed Simply Red with a fluid line-up that included Ojo, Mog, Dave Fryman and Eddie Sherwood. After signing to **Elektra** the group had a more settled line-up featuring Hucknall, Tony Bowers (bass), Fritz McIntyre (b. 2 September 1958; keyboards), Tim Kellett (brass), Sylvan Richardson (guitar) and Chris Joyce (drums). Their debut album *Picture Book* climbed to number 2 in the UK charts, while their enticing cover of the **Valentine Brothers**' 'Money's Too Tight To Mention' was a Top 20 hit. Although the group registered a lowly number 66 with the follow-up 'Come To My Aid', they rediscovered the hit formula with a sterling re-recording of the minor classic 'Holding Back The Years' which peaked at number 2. The song went on to top the US charts, which ushered in a period of international success. Their next album, *Men And Women*, included collaborations between Hucknall and former **Motown** composer Lamont Dozier (of **Holland/Dozier/Holland** fame). Further hits followed with 'The Right Thing', 'Infidelity' and a reworking of the **Cole Porter** standard, 'Ev'ry Time We Say Goodbye'. Having twice reached number 2 in the album charts, Simply Red finally scaled the summit in 1989 with the accomplished *A New Flame*. The album coincided with another hit, 'It's Only Love', which was followed by a splendid reworking of **Harold Melvin And The Bluenotes**' 'If You Don't Know Me By Now', which again climbed to number 2 in the UK. Since then, Simply Red have consolidated their position as the one of the most accomplished blue-eyed soul outfits to emerge from the UK in recent years. The 1991 album *Stars* showed them pursuing hip-hop inspired rhythms, alongside their usual soul-inspired style. It topped the British charts over a period of months, outselling much-hyped efforts by **Michael Jackson**, **U2**, **Dire Straits** and **Guns N' Roses**. Their momentum has seemingly collapsed, as over four years have elapsed since the multi-million selling *Stars*, maybe the fear of failure has gripped them, or the songs that flowed effortlessly have dried up.

Albums: *Picture Book* (1985), *Men And Women* (1987), *A New Flame* (1989), *Stars* (1991).

Further reading: *Simply Mick: Mick Hucknall Of Simply Red. The Inside Story*, Robin McGibbon and Rob McGibbon. *The First Fully Illustrated Biography*, Mark Hodkinson.

Simpson, Martin

b. 5 May 1953, Scunthorpe, South Humberside, England. Having started playing guitar at the age of 12, Simpson played the proverbial 'floor spots' at local folk clubs, and received his first paid booking at the age of 14. By the age of 18 Simpson had become a full-time professional on the folk club circuit. He came to the attention of a number of influential people, one of whom was Bill Leader who recorded Martin's debut

Golden Vanity for his own Trailer label. The album mixed such folk standards as 'Pretty Polly' and 'Soldiers Joy', with contemporary works such as **Bob Dylan**'s 'Love Minus Zero/No Limit'. That same year, Simpson opened for **Steeleye Span** on their UK tour, and, not long after became an accompanist for **June Tabor**. In 1979 he joined the **Albion Band** at the National Theatre and played with them on two subsequent tours. *A Cut Above*, recorded with Tabor on **Topic**, is still highly regarded. There followed a succession of fine albums, but without a great degree of commercial success. Since 1987, Simpson has lived in the USA with his American wife Jessica Radcliffe Simpson (b. 18 February 1952, Los Angeles, California, USA). The two also work as a duo, having released *True Dare Or Promise* in 1987. *The Pink Suede Bootleg* was released as a limited edition. Noted for his style of playing, Simpson is not as often in the limelight as he was in the 70s and 80s, but a tour of the UK in 1991 showed that he was still a talent of great merit. In addition to solo and duo work, Simpson played briefly with Metamora in the USA, and has also been working with Henry Gray, the Louisiana born blues pianist. Simpson also played on *Abbyssinians* and *Aqaba* by June Tabor, and *Earthed In Cloud Valley* and *'Til The Beasts Returning* by **Andrew Cronshaw**. In 1991, Martin was made honorary guitarist of the American Association of Stringed Instrument Artisans (A.S.I.A). A new album from Martin and Jessica was released, featuring their New York based band of Eric Aceto (violect), Hank Roberts (cello), Doug Robinson (bass), and Tom Beers (harmonica).
Albums: *Golden Vanity* (1976), with June Tabor *A Cut Above* (1981), *Special Agent* (1981), *Grinning In Your Face* (1983), *Sad Or High Kicking* (1985), *Nobody's Fault But Mine* (1986), with Jessica Radcliffe Simpson *True Dare Or Promise* (1987), *Leaves Of Life* (1989), *When I Was On Horseback* (1991), *A Closer Walk With Thee* (Gourd 1994), with Jessica Radcliffe Simpson *Red Roses* (Rhiannon 1994).

Simpson, Valerie
b. 26 August 1948, The Bronx, New York, USA. This career of this superior singer and songwriter is inexorably linked to that of her partner Nicholas Ashford. Billed as Valerie And Nick, the couple made their recording debut in 1964 with 'I'll Find You', but achieved greater distinction for a series of excellent compositions, often in partnership with **'Joshie' Jo Armstead**. Among the many artists to record the team's songs were **Ray Charles**, **Maxine Brown** and **Chuck Jackson**. In 1966 Ashford And Simpson were signed to the staff of Tamla/**Motown**. The latter supposedly deputized, uncredited, for singer **Tammi Terrell** while she was too ill to complete duets with **Marvin Gaye**. Valerie's voice, she controversially claims, was featured on 'The Onion Song', a UK Top

10 hit, which in part inspired the resumption of her recording career. 'Silly Wasn't I' reached the R&B Top 30 in 1972, but the following year she and Nicholas rekindled their performing partnership and, as **Ashford And Simpson**, enjoyed a prolonged spell of chart success.
Albums: *Valerie Simpson Exposed* (1971), *Valerie Simpson* (1972), *Keep It Comin'* (1977).

Sims, Clarence 'Guitar'
b. New Orleans, Louisiana, USA. Sims was initially inspired to sing the blues on hearing **Tommy McClennan**'s recording of 'Bottle Up And Go', and later vocal influences included **Nappy Brown**, **Fats Domino**, **Louis Jordan** and **Lloyd Price**. In 1955 Sims moved to Los Angeles, where he appeared on talent shows and in clubs. Two years later, he moved to San Francisco's Fillmore district and assumed the profession name 'Fillmore Slim' and recorded for the Dooto, Kent, and Dore labels. In the late 60s he also appeared on disc as 'Ron Silva'. However, Sims was incarcerated between 1980 and 1985; it was during this time that he began to play guitar seriously. Following his release, he recorded a promising album for **Troyce Keys**'s label in February 1987 and continues to play around the west coast. His age at the time of recording was given as 53 years old.
Album: *Born To Sing The Blues* (1987).

Sims, Frankie Lee
b. 30 April 1917, New Orleans, Louisiana, USA, d. 10 May 1970. Despite his birthplace, Sims' music is very much in the blues vein of Texas, where he moved in childhood. On his earliest records, for the Blue Bonnet label, in 1947-48, he played a traditional fingerstyle guitar, but later developed an electric style of his own, riffing behind the vocals, filling the breaks with exciting, often distorted flashes of lead. His best known song was 'Lucy Mae', which he recorded several times, most successfully with Specialty in 1953. Later recordings on Ace and Vin developed his rocking style still further with a small band, but they marked the end of his brief period of success. A New York session in 1960 remained unissued until well after his death.
Albums: *Lucy Mae Blues* (1970), *Walking With Frankie* (1985).

Sims, Zoot
b. John Haley Sims, 29 October 1925, Inglewood, California, USA, d. 23 March 1985. Sims played clarinet in grade school but took up the tenor saxophone to work with singer **Kenny Baker** in 1941. He played with Bobby Sherwood from 1942-43, Sonny Durham in 1943 and the **Benny Goodman** big band in 1944. His recording debut was with **Joe Bushkin**'s small group in 1944. The years 1944-46 were spent in the army. On discharge Sims rejoined Goodman,

playing alongside his brother Ray until 1947 when he joined **Woody Herman**, becoming famous as one of the 'Four Brothers' (the other saxophonists were **Stan Getz**, **Herbie Steward** and **Serge Chaloff**). He left to play with **Artie Shaw** from 1949-50, then toured Europe with Goodman at regular intervals (1950, 1958, 1972 and 1976) and also toured with **Stan Kenton** and **Gerry Mulligan**. In the early 70s Sims started playing soprano saxophone as well as tenor, and later in the decade embarked on a prolific period of recording for **Norman Granz**'s Pablo label, making approximately 15 albums between 1975-84. In 1972 and 1978 he took part in re-union concerts with Herman. He also liked to freelance, especially in company with tenor saxophonist **Al Cohn**, with whom he had first worked in the early 50s. Sims was the first American to play a residency at Ronnie Scott's following the lifting of the embargo on visiting musicians in 1961, and he returned there many times, his last visit being in 1982. He toured Scandinavia in 1984, but the doctors had diagnosed terminal cancer, of which he died in 1985. Zoot Sims was a redoubtable exponent of the tenor style developed by **Lester Young** and contributed swinging, lithe solos to countless big band arrangements.

Selected albums: *Zoot Swings The Blues* (1950), *Tenorly* (Vogue c.1954), with Gerry Mulligan *The Concert Jazz Band Live* (1955), *Zoot!* (Original Jazz Classics 1956), *Tonite's Music Today* (Black Lion 1956), *Morning Fun* (Black Lion 1957), *Zoot Sims In Paris* (EMI/Pathe 1957), *Al And Zoot* (1957), *Down Home* (1960), *Jive At Five* (1960), *Either Way* (Evidence 1962),*Suitably Zoot* (1965), with Joe Venuti *Joe & Zoot* (1968), with Count Basie *Basie And Zoot* (1975), *Hawthorne Nights* (1976), *Zoot Sims And The Gershwin Brothers* (Original Jazz Classics 1976), *Soprano Sax* (1976), *If I'm Lucky* (Original Jazz Classics 1978), *Warm Tenor* (Pablo 1979), *Just Friends* (Original Jazz Classics 1979), *Passion Flower* (1980), with Joe Pass *Blues For Two* (Original Jazz Classics 1982), *I Wish I Were Twins* (1983), *Suddenly Its Spring* (Original Jazz Classics 1984), *Quietly There* (Original Jazz Classics 1984), *In A Sentimental Mood* (1984), *I Hear A Rhapsody* (1992), *A Summer Thing* (1993). Compilation: *The Best Of Zoot Sims* (Pablo 1982).

Further reading: *The John Haley Sims (Zoot Sims) Discography*, Astrup, Arne, *The John Haley Sims (Zoot Sims) Discography Supplement*, Astrup, Arne.

Sinatra, Frank

b. Francis Albert Sinatra, 12 December 1915, Hoboken, New Jersey, USA. After working for a while in the office of a local newspaper, *The Jersey Observer*, Frank Sinatra decided to pursue a career as a singer. Already an admirer of **Bing Crosby**, he was impelled to pursue this course after attending a 1933 Crosby concert, and sang whenever and wherever he could, working locally in clubs and bars. Then, in 1935 he entered a popular US radio talent show, *Major Bowes Amateur Hour*. Also on the show was a singing trio, and the four young men found themselves teamed together by the no-nonsense promoter. The ad-hoc teaming worked, and the group, renamed 'The Hoboken Four', won first prize. Resulting from this came a succession of concert dates with the Major Bowes travelling show, along with club and occasional radio dates. By 1938 Sinatra was singing on several shows on each of a half-dozen radio stations, sometimes for expenses - often for nothing. The experience and especially the exposure were vital if he was to be recognised. Among the bands with which he performed was one led by songwriter **Harold Arlen** but in 1939, shortly after he married his childhood sweetheart, Nancy Barbato, he was heard and hired by **Harry James** who had only recently formed his own big band. James recognised Sinatra's talent from the start and also identified the source of his determination to succeed, his massive self-confidence and powerful ego. During their brief association, James remarked to an interviewer, 'His name is Sinatra, and he considers himself the greatest vocalist in the business. Get that! No one's even heard of him! He's never had a hit record, and he looks like a wet rag, but he says he's the greatest.' In 1939 and early 1940 Sinatra made a number of records with James and began to develop a small following. His records with James included 'My Buddy' and 'All Or Nothing At All'.

In 1940 Sinatra was approached with an offer by **Tommy Dorsey**, then leading one of the most popular swing era bands. Only some six months had expired on Sinatra's two-year contract with James, who must have realised he was parting with a potential goldmine but he was a generous-spirited man and let the singer go. Sinatra had many successful records with Dorsey including 'Polka Dots And Moonbeams', 'Imagination', 'Fools Rush In', 'I'll Never Smile Again', 'The One I Love', 'Violets For Your Furs', 'How About You?' and 'In The Blue Of Evening', some of which became fixtures in his repertoire. One record from this period became a major hit a few years later when the USA entered World War II. This song, recorded at Sinatra's second session with Dorsey in February 1940, was 'I'll Be Seeing You', and its lyric gained a special significance for servicemen, and the women they had left behind. Sinatra's popularity with the young female population, achieved despite or perhaps because of his gangling unheroic and rather vulnerable appearance, prompted him to leave Dorsey and begin a solo career. In spite of the tough line taken by Dorsey over the remaining half of his five-year contract (Dorsey allegedly settled for 43% of the singer's gross over the next 10 years), Sinatra quit.

Within months his decision proved to be right. He had become the idol of hordes of teenage girls, his public appearances were sell-outs and his records jostled with one another for hit status. In the early 40s he had appeared in a handful of films as Dorsey's vocalist, but by the middle of the decade he began appearing in feature films as an actor-singer. These included lightweight if enjoyable fare such as **Higher And Higher** (1944), **Anchors Aweigh** (1945), **It Happened In Brooklyn** (1947), **The Kissing Bandit** (1948) and *Double Dynamite* (1951). By the 50s, however, Sinatra's career was in trouble; both as singer and actor he appeared to have reached the end of the road. His acting had suffered in part from the quality of material he was offered, and accepted. Nevertheless, it was his film career that was the first to revive when he landed the role of Angelo Maggio in *From Here To Eternity* (1953) for which he won an Academy Award as Best Supporting Actor. Thereafter, he was taken seriously as an actor even if he rarely was given the same standard of role or achieved the same quality of performance.

He continued to make films, usually in straight acting roles, but occasionally in musicals. Among the former were *The Man With The Golden Arm* (1955), one of the roles which matched his breakthrough performance as Maggio, *Johnny Concho* (1956), *Kings Go Forth* (1958), *A Hole In The Head* (1959), *The Manchurian Candidate* (1962), *Von Ryan's Express* (1965), *Assault On A Queen* (1966), *Tony Rome* (1967) and *The Detective* (1968). His musicals included **Guys And Dolls** (1955), **High Society** (1956), **Pal Joey** (1957), **The Joker Is Wild** (1957), **Can-Can** (1960) and *Robin And The 7 Hoods* (1964). Later, he appeared in an above average television movie, *Contract On Cherry Street* (1977), and *The First Deadly Sin* (1980).

Soon after his Oscar-winning appearance in *From Here To Eternity*, Sinatra made a comeback as a recording artist. He had been recording for Columbia where he fell out of step when changes were made to the company's musical policy and in 1953 he was signed by **Capitol Records**. Sinatra's first session at Capitol was arranged and conducted by **Axel Stordahl** whom Sinatra had known in the Dorsey band. For the next session, however, he was teamed with **Nelson Riddle**. Sinatra had heard the results of earlier recording sessions made by **Nat 'King' Cole** at Capitol on which Riddle had collaborated. Sinatra was deeply impressed by the results and some sources suggest that on joining Capitol he had asked for Riddle. The results of this partnership set Sinatra's singing career firmly in the spotlight. Over the next few years classic albums such as *Songs For Young Lovers*, *This Is Sinatra*, *A Swingin' Affair*, *Come Fly With Me*, *Swing Easy*, *In The Wee Small Hours* and the exceptional *Songs For Swingin' Lovers* set standards for popular singers which have been rarely equalled and almost never surpassed. The two men were intensely aware of one another's talents and although critics were unanimous in their praise of Riddle, the arranger was unassumingly diffident,

declaring that it was the singer's 'great talent that put him back on top'. For all Riddle's modesty, there can be little doubt that the arranger encouraged Sinatra's latent feeling for jazz which helped create the relaxed yet superbly swinging atmosphere which epitomised their work together. On his albums for Capitol, his own label **Reprise**, and other labels, sometimes with Riddle, other times with **Robert Farnon**, **Neal Hefti**, **Gordon Jenkins**, **Quincy Jones**, **Billy May** or Stordahl, Sinatra built upon his penchant for the best in American popular song, displaying a deep understanding of the wishes of composer and lyricist.

Fans old and new bought his albums in their tens of thousands and several reached the top in the **Billboard** charts. The 1955 album, *In The Wee Small Hours*, was in for 29 weeks reaching number 2; the following year's *Songs For Swingin' Lovers* charted for 66 weeks, also reaching the second spot. *Come Fly With Me*, from 1958, spent 71 weeks in the charts reaching number 1 and other top positions were attained by 1958's *Only The Lonely*, 120 weeks, 1960's *Nice 'N' Easy*, 86 weeks, and in 1966, *Strangers In The Night*, 73 weeks. The title song from this last album also made number 1 in **Billboard**'s singles charts as did the following year's 'Something Stupid' on which he duetted with his daughter, **Nancy Sinatra**. At a time in popular music's history when ballads were not the most appealing form, and singers were usually in groups and getting younger by the minute, these were no mean achievements for a middle-aged solo singer making a comeback. The secret of this late success lay in Sinatra's superior technical ability, his wealth of experience, his abiding love for the material with which he worked and the invariably high standards of professionalism he brought to his recordings and public performances. During his stint with Dorsey, the singer had taken a marked professional interest in the band leader's trombone playing. He consciously learned breath control, in particular circular breathing, and the use of dynamics from Dorsey. Additionally, he employed Dorsey's legato style which aided the smooth phrasing of his best ballad work. Complementing this, Sinatra's enjoyment of jazz and the company of jazz musicians prompted him to adopt jazz phrasing which greatly enhanced his rhythmic style. More than any other popular singer of his or previous generations, Sinatra learned the value of delayed phrasing and singing behind the beat, and he and his arrangers invariably found exactly the right tempo. His relaxed rhythmic style contrasted strikingly with the stiffer-sounding singers who preceded him. Even Crosby, whose popularity Sinatra eventually surpassed, later accommodated some of Sinatra's stylistic devices. (Crosby's habitual lazy-sounding style was of a different order from Sinatra's and until late in his career he never fully shook off his 2/4 style while Sinatra, almost from the start, was completely at home with the 4/4 beat of swing.)

Sinatra's revived career brought him more attention even than in his heyday as the bobby-soxers' idol. Much of the interest was intrusive and led to frequently acrimonious and sometimes violent clashes with reporters. With much of what is written about him stemming from a decidedly ambivalent view, the picture of the man behind the voice is often confused. Undoubtedly, his private persona is multi-faceted. He has been described by acquaintances as quick-tempered, pugnacious, sometimes vicious and capable of extreme verbal cruelty and he has often displayed serious misjudgement in the company he keeps. In marked contrast, others have categorically declared him to be enormously generous to friends in need and to individuals and organizations he believes can benefit from his personal or financial support. His political stance has changed dramatically over the years and here again his judgement seems to be flawed. At first a Democrat, he supported Roosevelt and later Kennedy with enormous enthusiasm. His ties with the Kennedy clan were close, and not always for the best of reasons. Sinatra was unceremoniously dropped by the Kennedys following revelations that he had introduced to John Kennedy a woman who became simultaneously the mistress of the President of the United States and a leading figure in the Mafia. Sinatra then became a Republican and lent his support as fund-raiser and campaigner to Richard Nixon and Ronald Reagan, apparently oblivious to their serious flaws.

An immensely rich man, with interests in industry, real estate, recording companies, film and television production, Sinatra has chosen to continue working, making frequent comebacks and presenting a never-ending succession of 'farewell' concerts which, as time passed, became less like concerts and more like major events in contemporary popular culture. He continued to attract adoring audiences and in the late 80s and early 90s, despite being in his mid- to late seventies, could command staggering fees for personal appearances. Ultimately, however, when an assessment has to be made of his life, it is not the money or the worship of his fans that matters; neither is it the mixed quality of his film career and the uncertainties surrounding his personal characteristics and shortcomings. What really matters is that in his treatment of the classics from the Great American Songbook, Sinatra has made a unique contribution to 20th-century popular music. Despite an occasional lapse, when he replaces carefully-crafted lyrics with his own inimitable (yet all-too-often badly imitated) phrases, over several decades he fashioned countless timeless performances. There are some songs which, however many singers may have recorded them before or since Sinatra, or will record them in the future, have become inextricably linked with his name: 'I'll Walk Alone', 'It Could Happen To You', 'I'll Never Smile Again', 'Violets For Your Furs', 'How About You?',

'Jeepers Creepers', 'All Of Me', 'Taking A Chance On Love', 'Just One Of Those Things', 'My Funny Valentine', 'They Can't Take That Away From Me', 'I Get A Kick Out Of You', 'You Make Me Feel So Young', 'Old Devil Moon', 'The Girl Next Door', 'My One And Only Love', 'Three Coins In The Fountain', 'Love And Marriage', 'Swingin' Down The Lane', 'Come Fly With Me', 'Fly Me To The Moon', 'The Tender Trap', 'Chicago', 'New York, New York', 'Let Me Try Again', 'Night And Day', 'Here's That Rainy Day', 'You Make Me Feel So Young', 'Strangers In The Night', 'I Thought About You', 'Lady Is A Tramp', 'Anything Goes', 'Night And Day', 'All The Way', 'One For My Baby', 'I've Got You Under My Skin'.

Not all these songs are major examples of the songwriters' art yet even on lesser material, of which 'My Way' is a notable example, he provides a patina of quality the songs and their writers may not deserve and which no one else could have supplied. Since the 70s Sinatra's voice has shown serious signs of decay. The pleasing baritone had given way to a worn and slightly rusting replica of what it once had been. Nevertheless, he sang on, adjusting to the changes in his voice and as often as not still creating exemplary performances of many of his favourite songs. In these twilight years he was especially effective in the easy swinging mid-tempo he had always preferred and which concealed the inevitable vocal deterioration wrought by time. He made records into the 80s, *LA Is My Lady* being the last although with so many farewell concerts and television spectaculars who can say if the last record has yet been released. In assessing Sinatra's place in popular music it is very easy to slip into hyperbole. After all, through dedication to his craft and his indisputable love for the songs he sang, Sinatra became the greatest exponent of a form of music which he helped turn into an art form. In so doing he became an icon of popular culture which is no mean achievement for a skinny kid from Hoboken. Writing in the *Observer*, when Sinatra's retirement was thought, mistakenly, to be imminent, music critic Benny Green observed: 'What few people, apart from musicians, have never seemed to grasp is that he is not simply the best popular singer of his generation . . . but the culminating point in an evolutionary process which has refined the art of interpreting words set to music. Nor is there even the remotest possibility that he will have a successor. Sinatra was the result of a fusing of a set of historical circumstances which can never be repeated.' Sinatra himself has never publicly spoken of his work in such glowing terms, choosing instead to describe himself simply as a 'saloon singer'. Deep in his heart, however, Sinatra must know that Green's judgement is the more accurate and it is one which will long be echoed by countless millions of fans all around the world.

Musically at least, it is a world better for the care which Frank Sinatra has lavished upon its popular songs. In 1992, a two-part television biography, *Sinatra*, was transmitted in the US, produced by Tina Sinatra, and starring Philip Casnoff in the leading role. Almost inevitably, it topped the weekly ratings. In 1993 Capitol Records re-signed Sinatra after 30 years with Reprise Records and announced a new album as 'the recording event of the decade'. The title *Duets* was a brilliant piece of marketing; it had Sinatra teamed with a varied all-star cast including **Aretha Franklin**, **Carly Simon**, **Barbra Streisand**, **Tony Bennett**, **Natalie Cole**, **Kenny G** and **U2**'s Bono. A subsequent volume, *Duets II*, featuring artists such as **Stevie Wonder**, **Antonio Carlos Jobim**, Chrissie Hynde, **Willie Nelson**, **Lena Horne**, **Gladys Knight**, and **Patti LaBelle**, was released in 1994.

Selected albums: *Sing And Dance With Frank Sinatra* (1950), *Songs For Young Lovers* (1955), *Swing Easy* (1955), *In The Wee Small Hours* (1955), *Songs For Swingin' Lovers* (1956), *High Society* (1956, film soundtrack), *Close To You* (1957), *A Swingin' Affair!* (1957), *Where Are You?* (1957), *Pal Joey* (1957, film soundtrack), *A Jolly Christmas From Frank Sinatra* (1957), *Come Fly With Me* (1958), *Frank Sinatra Sings For Only The Lonely* (1958), *Come Dance With Me!* (1959), *No One Cares* (1959), *Can-Can* (1960, film soundtrack), *Nice 'N' Easy* (1960), *Sinatra's Swinging Session!!!* (1961), *Ring-A-Ding Ding!* (1961), *Sinatra Swings* (1961), *Come Swing With Me!* (1961), *I Remember Tommy...*(1961), *Sinatra And Strings* (1961), *Point Of No Return* (1961), *Sinatra And Swingin' Brass* (1962), *All Alone* (1962), with Count Basie *Sinatra-Basie* (1962), *The Concert Sinatra* (1963), *The Select Johnny Mercer* (1963), *Sinatra's Sinatra* (1963), *Come Blow Your Horn* (1963, film soundtrack), *Days Of Wine And Roses, Moon River, And Other Academy Award Winners* (1964), with Bing Crosby and Fred Waring *America I Hear You Singing* (1964), with Basie *It Might As Well Be Swing* (1964), *Softly As I Leave You* (1964), *Sinatra '65* (1965), *September Of My Years* (1965), *My Kind Of Broadway* (1965), *Moonlight Sinatra* (1965), *A Man And His Music* (1965), *Strangers In The Night* (1966), *Sinatra At The Sands* (1966), *That's Life* (1966), *Francis Albert Sinatra And Antonio Carlos Jobim* (1967), *Frank Sinatra (The World We Knew)* (1967), with Nancy Sinatra *Frank And Nancy* (1967), with Duke Ellington *Francis A. And Edward K.* (1968), *Cycles* (1968), *The Sinatra Family Wish You A Merry Christmas* (1968), *My Way* (1969), *A Man Alone And Other Songs By Rod McKuen* (1969), *Watertown* (1970), with Antonio Carlos Jobim *Sinatra And Company* (1971), *Ol' Blue Eyes Is Back* (1973), *Some Nice Things I've Missed* (1974), *Sinatra - The Main Event Live* (1974), *Trilogy: Past, Present, Future* (1980), *She Shot Me Down* (1981), *LA Is My Lady* (1984), *Duets* (1993), *Sinatra And Sextet: Live In Paris* (Reprise 1994), *From Hoboken NJ To The White House* (1994), with Dean Martin *A Swingin' Night At The Sabre Room* (1994), *Old Gold Shows* *1946* (1994), *Duets II* (1994). Compilations: *This Is Sinatra!* (1956), *That Old Feeling* (1956) *Frankie* (1957), *Adventures Of The Heart* (1957), *This Is Sinatra, Volume 2* (1958), *The Frank Sinatra Story* (1958), *Look To Your Heart* (1959), *All The Way* (1961), *Sinatra Sings...Of Love And Things* (1962), *Tell Her You Love Her* (1963), *Sinatra: A Man And His Music (1960-65)* (1965), *The Movie Songs (1954-60)* (1967), *Frank Sinatra's Greatest Hits!* (1968), *Frank Sinatra's Greatest Hits, Vol. 2* (1972), *Round # 1* (1974), *Portrait Of Sinatra* (1977), *Radio Years* (1987), *Rare Recordings 1935-70* (1989), *Gold Collection* (1993), *Sings The Songs Of Cahn And Styne* (1993), *This Is Frank Sinatra 1953-57* (1994), with Tommy Dorsey *The Song Is You* (1994, 5-CD set), *The Soundtrack Sessions* (Bravura 1994), *Two From Sinatra* (Capitol 1995).

Further reading: *The Voice: The Story Of An American Phenomen*, Kahn, E.J. (1946), *Sinatra And His Rat Pack: A Biography*, Gehman, Richard (1961), *Sinatra*, Douglas-Home, Robin (1962), *Sinatra: Retreat Of The Romantic*, Shaw, Arnold (1970), *The Films Of Frank Sinatra*, Ringold, Gene (1971), *Sinatra And The Great Song Stylists*, Barnes, Ken (1972), *Songs By Sinatra, 1939-1970*, Hainsworth, Brian (1973), *Frank Sinatra*, Taylor, Paula (1976), *On Stage: Frank Sinatra*, Lake, Harriet (1976), *Frank Sinatra*, Scaduto, Anthony (1977), *The Sinatra File: Part One*, Ridgway, John (1977), *Sinatra: An Unauthorized Biography*, Wilson, Earl (1978), *The Sinatra File: Part Two*, Ridgway, John (1978), *Sinatra*, Frank, Alan (1978), *The Revised Compleat Sinatra: Discography, Filmography And Television Appearenc*, Lonstein, Albert I. (1979), *Frank Sinatra*, Howlett, John (1980), *Sinatra In His Own Words*, Sinatra, Frank (1981), *The Frank Sinatra Scrapbook: His Life And Times In Words And Pictures*, Peters, Richard (1982), *Frank Sinatra: My Father*, Sinatra, Nancy (1990), *His Way: The Unauthorized Biography Of Frank Sinatra*, Kelly, Kitty (1990), *Frank Sinatra*, Hodge, Jessica (1992), *Frank Sinatra: A Complete Recording History*, Ackelson, Richard W. (1992).

Sinatra, Frank, Jnr.

b. 10 January 1944, New Jersey, USA. Frank Sinatra Jnr. was encouraged by his legendary father *not* to pursue a career in music. Despite this, he sang along to his father's records, and, by the early 60s had decided on a singing career of his own. In 1963, just like Frank Snr. he joined the **Tommy Dorsey** band (whose namesake was long dead), with an act similar to that of his father. However, the younger Sinatra's main claim to fame is not for his singing, but for being the victim of a kidnapping on 9 December 1963. Ransomed for nearly a quarter of a million dollars, paid by his father, Frank Jnr.'s reputation was hurt when the kidnappers claimed they had been hired by the younger Sinatra as a publicity stunt. They were convicted of the crime and the money returned. Sinatra Jnr. toured the following year and recorded his debut album, *Young Love For Sale*, for his father's **Reprise Records** label. He performed on many television programmes during the 70s and recorded for Daybreak Records. In the early 70s he was accompanied on *Spice* and *His Way*, by the **Nelson Riddle** Orchestra. Riddle had arranged and conducted several of his father's finest albums. Sinatra went on to record a country album, and a tribute to arranger **Billy May**. In the late 80s and early 90s Sinatra played nightlubs in Las Vegas, backed by the potent big band of Buddy Childers. He has also conducted the orchestra for his father's concerts and tours.

Albums: *Young Love For Sale* (1964), *Spice* (1971), *His Way* (1972), *It's Alright* (1978), *Billy May For President* (1983).

Sinatra, Nancy

b. 8 June 1940, Jersey City, New Jersey, USA. Determined not to rest on the laurels of famous father, **Frank Sinatra**, Nancy spent several years taking lessons in music, dance and drama. She made an impressive appearance on the Frank Sinatra/**Elvis Presley** television special (1959), and two years later made her recording debut with 'Cuff Links And A Tie Clip'. From 1960-65, she was married to pop singer **Tommy Sands**. Further releases were combined with a budding acting career until 1966 when, having teamed with producer/songwriter **Lee Hazelwood**, Nancy enjoyed an international smash with the sultry number 1 'These Boots Are Made For Walkin''. It's descending bass line on every verse made it one of the most recognisable hits of 1966. 'How Does That Grab You Darlin'', 'Friday's Child', and 'Sugar Town', all entered the US Top 40, before 'Somethin' Stupid', a duet with her father, gave the singer a second UK and US chart topper. Her other mostly country-styled record hits during the 60s included 'Love Eyes', 'Jackson' and 'Lightning's Girl' (both with Hazelwood), 'Lady Bird', 'Highway Song', and 'Some Velvet Morning'. In 1971, she joined Hazelwood again for the slightly risqué 'Did You Ever'. She also made nightclub appearances, and starred in television specials and feature films such as *Get Yourself A College Girl*, *The Wild Angels* and **Elvis Presley**'s *Speedway*, and sang the theme song to the *James Bond* film *You Only Live Twice*. After spending some years away from the limelight, in 1985 she published a biography entitled *Frank Sinatra: My Father*. A decade later she embarked on a major comeback, releasing her first solo album for more than 15 years, and posing *au naturel* for a six-page pictorial in *Playboy* magazine.

Albums: *Boots* (1966), *How Does That Grab You Darlin'* (1966), *Nancy In London* (1966), *Sugar* (1967), *Country My Way* (1967), *Movin' With Nancy* (1968), with Lee Hazelwood *Nancy And Lee* (1968), *Nancy* (1969), *Woman* (1970), *This Is Nancy Sinatra* (1971), with Hazelwood *Did You Ever* (1972). Compilations: *Nancy's Greatest Hits* (1970), *All-Time Hits* (1988), *Lightning's Girl* (c.80s), with Mel Tillis *Mel And Nancy* (Elektra c.80s), *The Very Best Of Nancy Sinatra* (1988), *One More Time* (Cougar 1995).

Films: *Get Yourself A College Girl* (1964), *The Ghost In The Invisible Bikini* (1966).

Sindecut

North London rap collective Sindecut spent their early days performing at the Swiss Cottage Community Centre, before releasing an eponymous debut single in 1986. Other members congregated around the nucleus of rapper Crazy Noddy and DJ Fingers, including Lyne Lyn (rapper), DJ Don't Ramp (producer), Mix Man G, Mad P and, later, Spike Tee and Louise Francis. Various members travelled to America in 1987/88 to get a deal with **B-Boy** Records, but lost out on the chance of a deal when label boss Bill Kamarra was sent to prison. They elected to set up their own label, Jgunglelist, instead (an interesting use of the term before it was hijacked by the 'jungle' club movement). The Sindecut made their name with the infectious rhythms of 'Posse'. It was an imposing stew of ragga vocals and hip hop breaks. Their first club hit, though, was 'Sindecut Kickin' Yeah', on another independent label, Baad. They grew up with the similarly formulated **Soul II Soul**, merging soul and reggae with rap: 'Its just our influences really. Americans have a lot of influences but they tend to make one type of music. We want to make music that we are influenced by and put it together into a new sound'. Their debut album showcased raps backed by orchestrated strings and frantic live drums - an almost 'new age' hip hop affair.

Album: *Changing The Scenery* (Virgin 1990).

Sing As We Go

Regarded by many as the best of the films that the popular Lancashire entertainer **Gracie Fields** appeared in, *Sing As We Go* was presented to highly appreciative audiences in 1934 courtesy of producer-director Basil Dean and Associated Talking Pictures. Not just an amusing and tuneful musical, this picture was also something of a social document as well, touching as it did on the difficulties of unemployment in the north of England. Grace Platt (Fields) leads her fellow workers out in style when the Greybeck Mill is forced to close. Not one to sit around and wait for something to happen, Grace 'gets on her bike' and cycles to Blackpool where she (briefly) works as a waitress in a boarding house, a palmist's assistant and 'The Human Spider' in a magician's show at the Pleasure Beach. She is delighted when her new-found friend, Phyllis (Dorothy Hyson), wins first prize in the Bathing Belles competition, but less than pleased when Phyllis becomes attracted to her friend from the mill, assistant manager Hugh Phillips (John Loder), who is also in Blackpool trying to drum up business. Not one to hold a grudge, Grace helps Hugh in his efforts to re-open the mill, and, as the new Welfare Officer, is at the head of the exultant march back to work, singing (not unexpectedly) 'Sing As We Go'. That song, and 'Just A Catchy Little Tune', were the work of the Welsh songwriter Harry Parr-Davies who wrote several other numbers for Gracie Fields, and was her accompanist for a time. The other songs in *Sing As We Go* were 'Thora' (Stephen Adams-Frederick E. Weatherly) and 'Little Bottom Drawer' (Will Haines-Jimmy Harper). As usual with these small but significant British films, the supporting parts were beautifully cast. In this instance the players included Frank Pettingell as Grace's fun-loving Uncle Murgatroyd, **Stanley Holloway** as a policeman, Lawrence Grossmith, Arthur Sinclair, Morris Harvey, Maire O'Neill, Ben Field, Norman Walker, Margaret Yarde, and Olive Sloane. Gordon Wellesley and the distinguished English author, J.B. Priestley, adapted the screenplay from an original story by Priestley.

Sing You Sinners

One of the screen's all-time favourite song-and-dance men, **Donald O'Connor**, made his debut - at the age of 13 - in this Paramount release of 1938. In Claude Binyon's heart-warming story, he plays the kid brother of **Bing Crosby** and Fred MacMurray, two guys who never see eye-to-eye - except for music. MacMurray is a thrifty 'small town Galahad, the breakfast-eating, four button type' (as Sky Masterson says in *Guys And Dolls*), while Crosby is a gambler who continually wastes the family's money until one day he manages to buy a horse, which, with O'Connor aboard, romps home first in the big race. Ellen Drew provided the love interest, and Elizabeth Patterson was amusing (and patient) as the trio's mother. Also in the cast were William Haade, Irving Bacon, and Harry Barris. **Johnny Burke** and **Jimmy Monaco** contributed several agreeable songs including 'Laugh And Call It Love', 'Where Is Central Park?', 'I've Got A Pocketful Of Dreams', and 'Don't Let That Moon Get Away', the last two of which became hits for Crosby, and endured. However, the film's musical highspot was probably **Hoagy Carmichael** and **Frank Loesser**'s 'Small Fry', which the three brothers (who gig together in the evenings) turned into an easy-going, charming routine. Bing Crosby and his friend, lyricist **Johnny Mercer**, also made a popular recording of the number. *Sing You Sinners*, which was directed by Wesley Ruggles, went on to make beautiful music at the box-office.

Singer, Harold 'Hal'

b. 8 October 1919, Tulsa, Oklahoma, USA. After beginning his musical tuition on the violin at the age of eight, Singer switched to clarinet and, finally, tenor saxophone which he played with various big bands in the 40s - notably **Ernie Fields** and **Tommy Douglas** (both 1941), Nat Towles (1942), **Jay McShann** (1942-43), Roy Eldridge (1944) and **Lucky**

Millinder and **Oran 'Hot Lips' Page** (both 1947). After appearing on various jazz and R&B records in the late 40s - he played tenor on **Wynonie Harris**' 'Good Rocking Tonight' - he was recommended to Savoy Records by his close friend, Don Byas, and began a run of instrumental hits in 1948 with a tune that would furnish him with a life-long nickname - 'Cornbread'. He later went to **Mercury** (1950), Coral (1951-52), returning to Savoy in 1952 to play as both session musician and to usher in the new musical era with his own 'Rock & Roll' and 'Hot Rod'. In the late 50s he recorded R&B for Time, DeLuxe and King and blues and jazz for Prestige and in the 60s recorded a jazz album for Strand before moving to France where he maintained a steady, if unexciting, living recording for French **Polydor**, Black & Blue and Futura. In the 80s, Hal made a comeback with guest spots on records by **Booker T. Laury**, **Jimmy Witherspoon**, and **Rocket 88**, as well his own excellent *Swing On It*, on England's JSP Records.

Selected albums: with Charlie Shavers *Blue Stompin'* (1959), *Shades Of Blue* (1963), with Milt Buckner *Milt And Hal* (1966), *Paris Soul Food* (1969), *Blues And News* (1971), with Paul Williams, Big Jay McNeely, Sam 'The Man' Taylor and Lee Allen *Honkers & Screamers - Roots Of Rock 'N' Roll Vol. 6* (1979), *Swing On It* (1981), *Rent Party* (1984), *No Rush* (1993).

Singin' In the Rain

Regarded by many as the most entertaining film musical of all time, this MGM classic was released in 1952. **Betty Comden** and **Adolph Green**'s witty screenplay parodies that momentous and painful period in Hollywood movie history when talkies took over from silent pictures. Don Lockwood (**Gene Kelly**) and Lina Lamont (Jean Hagen) are Monumental Studio's brightest silent stars. Lockwood, encouraged by his ex-dancing partner Cosmo Brown (**Donald O'Connor**), has no problem making the transition, while Lina's voice is so squeaky and sharp it could break glass. Luckily, aspiring actress Kathy Selden (**Debbie Reynolds**) pops out of a giant cake and provides a dubbing service - and Kelly's love interest. The team's first attempt at a sound film is a total disaster, but Kelly and O'Connor turn it into a musical, and, at the triumphant premiere, Reynolds is revealed as the hidden starlet, while Hagen is hilariously disgraced. *Singin' In The Rain* is indeed one of the greatest film musicals of all time, and its comedy exists apart from, and within the musical numbers. The scenes poking fun at the changeover to sound are very effective, particularly when irate director Roscoe Dexter (Douglas Fowley) is attempting to place Hagen's microphone in a strategic position - desperate to find a place on the set ('It's in the bush!') or on her person where a consistent level of sound can be obtained. Most of the score consisted of a collection of songs written by

Arthur Freed and **Nacio Herb Brown** for early MGM musicals, and every one of them is performed brilliantly. O'Connor is marvellously athletic and funny on 'Make 'Em Laugh' (most critics noted the similarities with **Cole Porter**'s 'Be A Clown'), and on two duets with Kelly, 'Fit As A Fiddle' (Al Goodhart-**Al Hoffman**) and 'Moses Supposes' (**Roger Edens**-Comden-Green). Reynolds joins both of them for the uplifting 'Good Morning', and then, just with Kelly, milks the lovely 'You Were Meant For Me' for all its worth. Other highlights include the spectacular 'Broadway Ballet' which is presented as part of the film within a film featuring **Cyd Charisse** and Kelly, and 'All I Do Is Dream Of You', 'Beautiful Girl', 'I've Got A Feelin' You're Foolin'', 'Should I', and 'Would You?'. Yet the moment from the film people always remember, and the clip that most frequently crops up in nostalgia programmes, is the one in which Kelly splashes around in the teeming rain, viewed by a rather bemused and soaking-wet policeman. Truly a memorable moment from a memorable film, which was photographed in Technicolor by Harold Rosson and produced by Arthur Freed's MGM unit. The director-choreographers were Gene Kelly and **Stanley Donen**.

In 1983 Comden and Green adapted the film into a stage musical which ran at the London Palladium for over three years, breaking all theatre records. It starred **Tommy Steele** (who also directed), Roy Castle, Sarah Payne and Danielle Carson, and featured several additional songs. A 1985 Broadway production failed to recover its costs. Ten years later, Steele directed a highly successful UK revival tour, with **Paul Nicholas** in the leading role.

Singing Fool, The

According to the American trade paper *Variety*, this part-talkie film - **Al Jolson** and Warner Brothers' follow-up to *The Jazz Singer* - grossed nearly $4 million in the US and Canada alone following its release in 1928. C. Graham Baker's screenplay was even more schmaltz-laden than Jolson's previous trail-blazing effort, with that film's tear-jerking 'My Mammy' being more than matched on the maudlin scale by 'Sonny Boy', which Jolson croons to his three-year-old screen son (Davey Lee) when he knows the boy is dying. Songwriters **De Sylva, Brown And Henderson** are said to have written the cliché-ridden number for a laugh, but there was nothing funny about the character who sang it. Even before his son's illness, the successful singer's wife (Josephine Dunn) had walked out on him, and he was going rapidly downhill before a nightclub cigarette girl (Betty Bronson) gave him some loving and self respect. Once again Jolson was tremendous, his magnetic personality overwhelming every other aspect of the production as he punched out song after song. These included 'It All

Depends On You' and 'I'm Sitting On Top Of The World' (De Sylva, Brown And Henderson), 'There's a Rainbow 'Round My Shoulder' (Dave Dreyer-**Billy Rose**-Al Jolson), 'Golden Gate' (Dreyer-**Joseph Meyer**-Rose-Jolson), 'Keep Smiling At Trouble' (Jolson-De Sylva-Lewis Gensler), and 'The Spaniard That Blighted My Life' (Billy Merson). The dance director for *The Singing Fool* was Larry Ceballos, and the film was directed by Lloyd Bacon and produced by Darryl F. Zanuck.

Singing Nun

b. Janine Deckers, 1928, d. 31 March 1985. Better known as Sister Luc-Gabrielle of the Fichermont convent in Brussels, this guitar-playing vocalist came to prominence after signing to Philips Records in 1961. Their Belgium branch issued her album *Soeur Sourire* (Sister Smile), which sold well on the Continent. One of the songs, the French sung 'Dominique', a breezy tribute to the founder of the Dominican order, captured the imagination of the international record-buying public and became a worldwide hit, reaching number 1 in the USA during the Christmas of 1963. Her album also reached the top of the US charts in the same month and she received the Grammy Award for 'Best Gospel or Religious Recording' of 1963. Revenue for the sales of her work was contributed to foreign missions. Although the Singing Nun appeared on the prestigious *Ed Sullivan* Show, she failed to secure a hit follow-up. However, Debbie Reynolds starred in a 1966 film of the nun's life and the movie was advertised with a shot of Sister Sourire riding a scooter and playing an acoustic guitar. Worldly trappings eventually enticed Deckers from the convent in October 1966 and she later recorded the controversial 'Glory Be To God For The Golden Pill'. In 1985 she committed suicide in a Belgium convent.

Albums: *Soeur Sourire* (1962), *The Singing Nun* (1963).

Singing Postman

One of the most implausible stars of the swinging 60s, the Singing Postman (aka Allan Smethurst, b. c.1925, Sheringham, Norfolk, England) nevertheless crafted one of the better examples of novelty pop in 'Hev Yew Gotta Loight, Boy?'. A legend on his own delivery route, Smethurst was an authentic Norfolk postie, who extolled life's simple pleasures and misfortunes with judicious stressing of the East country vernacular. Tracks on his recordings were all notated in the relevant 'patois', 'Oi Can't Git A Noice Loaf Of Bread', 'They're Orl Playing' Dommies In The Bar' and 'A Miss From Diss' offering huge insights into the life cycle of the Fenland citizen. Many were written from the point of view of a bygone, golden era, as Smethurst has moved to Grimsby during World War II. Such mildly comic, rural anecdotage may have forever remained a secret to Norfolk had it not been for

the merest brush with the pop charts. 'Hev Yew Gotta Light' picked up radio play in the mid-60s, and the Singing Postman was soon engaged in promotional duties on television shows *Nationwide* and the *Des O'Connor Show*. Sadly, what otherwise might have been a long, if somewhat secular career, was hampered by celebrity. He continued to release records until the end of the decade, but by the turn of the 70s he was penniless, his name dragged through the courts via an alleged assault. His fingers had become arthritic too, and he was forced to give up his career in 1970. That may very well have been that, until, in late 1993, a video advertisement for Ovaltine Light used 'Hev Yew Gotta Light' as its soundtrack, and reminded the world of the cheery grin and Woolworths guitar which used to accompany the original version. Sadly for Smethurst the attention arrived a little late in the day. His royalty cheque was eventually posted to a Salvation Army hostel in Grimsby, where reporters discovered him.
Albums: *The Singing Postman's Year* (late 60s).

Singing Stockmen

Norm Scott III (b. 1 January 1907, Sydney, New South Wales, Australia) and brother Arthur (b. 1903, Sydney, New South Wales, Australia, d. 1968), the eldest of nine Scott children. A pioneer duo of Australian country music, Norm played guitar and banjo-mandolin and was singing professionally in 1924. In the late 20s, after hearing recordings of **Jimmie Rodgers**, he was probably the first Australian singer to perform in the style of Rodgers. Around 1928, he opened his Hawaiian Club, where he built up a business that saw him teach five guitar classes, including hillbilly, to over 100 pupils each every week. (The business eventually extended to other cities and towns, later employing 32 teachers and at one time having over 4,000 students in Sydney alone). He also formed his Hawaiian Club Band, which commenced a series of broadcasts on 2GB, lasting until the mid-50s. During the early days several later famous artists, including **Buddy Williams** played at the club, whilst **Tim McNamara** and the **McKean Sisters** actually had guitar lessons there. After noting the success of **Tex Morton**'s early recordings, Norm and Arthur began performing as the Singing Stockmen and cut two sides, 'Night Time In Nevada' and 'Hillbilly Valley' for Regal-Zonophone in October 1938 that led to six further recordings on 12 May 1939. Realising that the Hawaiian Band, who were used on the recordings, was unsuited for country music work, Norm formed an hillbilly band. It comprised Dick Carr (b. 1911, Melbourne, Australia, a steel guitarist who later had solo success before becoming the leader of **EMI**'s noted studio band. It was Carr and his band the Bushlanders who provided the backing for **Slim Dusty**'s 1957 hit 'The Pub With No Beer), George Raymond (a fiddler who later forged a solo career as a novelty

instrumentalist) and Hal Carter (an accordionist and later the leader of a popular old time dance band). Scott's hopes for further recordings with his new band floundered, when Carr and Raymond left to join Tex Morton's Roughriders. The Singing Stockmen never recorded again and Arthur, who had first sung successfully as a boy soprano around 1913, retired from the music scene. Norm Scott continued in the business until he finally sold his interest in the Hawaiian Club in the 50s and nominally retired from music.

Singleton, Shelby

b. 16 December 1931, Waskom, Texas, USA. Based in Shreveport, Louisiana, Singleton, worked as a record plugger for the **Mercury** label before becoming sales manager. He began producing country acts in the late 50s, and was responsible for bringing the **Big Bopper** and **Johnny Preston** to the company. Singleton's later productions included **Brook Benton** and **Clyde McPhatter**, and in 1961 he assumed responsibility for Smash, Mercury's subsidiary pop outlet. **James Brown**, **Charlie Rich** and **Jerry Lee Lewis** were three of his most prestigious signings.
Shelby left the label in 1967, purchased the extensive **Sun** catalogue, and inaugurated a series of new companies, including Plantation (for country) and SSS International (for soul). 'Harper Valley PTA', a massive international hit for **Jeannie C. Riley**, established the former outlet, while the latter enjoyed success with **Peggy Scott And Jo Jo Benson** and **Johnny Adams**. Singleton remains active in the music industry, administering his wide and varied catalogue.

Singleton, Zutty

b. Arthur James Singleton, 14 May 1898, Bunkie, Louisiana, USA, d. 14 July 1975. Playing drums from his early childhood, Singleton first worked professionally in 1915. After military service in World War I he played in several leading New Orleans bands, including those of **Oscar 'Papa' Celestin** and **Louis Nelson**, then worked the riverboats with **Fate Marable** in the early 20s. After spending time in New Orleans and St Louis, where he played with Charlie Creath (whose sister he married), Singleton moved to Chicago where he played in bands led by **Dave Peyton** and **Jimmie Noone**, then teamed up with **Louis Armstrong** and **Earl 'Fatha' Hines** for record dates and a brief spell as co-owners of a club. As a member of the **Carroll Dickerson** band he went to New York, where he subsequently played with many leading jazzmen of the day. He also led his own band, securing residencies at several clubs and recording extensively throughout the 30s with musicians such as **Roy Eldridge**, **Mezz Mezzrow** and **Sidney Bechet.** In the 40s he worked in bands that played in a startlingly wide range of styles, accompanying musicians as diverse as **T-Bone Walker** and **Charlie**

Parker, **Wingy Manone** and **Dizzy Gillespie**. In the 50s he toured Europe, teaming up with **Bill Coleman**, **Oran 'Hot Lips' Page**, Mezzrow again and also leading his own bands. He recorded extensively in this period and throughout the 60s. A stroke in 1970 effectively ended his playing career, but he remained a father-figure in the jazz community, especially in New York where he and his wife made their home. Although Singleton had all the fundamental skills displayed by **Baby Dodds**, generally regarded as the master of New Orleans drummers, he was far more flexible, as the range of his musical companions demonstrates. His joyously springy playing style enhanced numerous recording sessions and his solo excursions managed the usually impossible task of being highly musical, even melodious, while being compellingly rhythmic. He appeared in several films, including *Stormy Weather* (1943) and *L'Aventure Du Jazz* (1969).

Albums: *Zutty And The Clarinet Kings* (1967), *L'Aventure Du Jazz* (1969, film soundtrack). Compilations: *Louis Armstrong Classics Vol. 3* (1928), with Mezz Mezzrow *Clarinet Marmalade* (1951), with Bill Coleman *Rarities* (1952).

Sinitta

b. Sinitta Renay Malone, 19 October 1966, Seattle, Washington, USA. The daughter of singer **Miquel Brown**, Sinitta's brand of manufactured disco-pop was aided by competent studio production and songwriting assistance by a variety of talent, namely the **Stock, Aitken And Waterman** team, plus, at various times, Ralf Rene Maue, **Paul Hardcastle** and James George Hargreaves. Sinitta's pleasant appearance went a long way in securing, for a while, constant coverage in the British teen pop magazines. This was reflected her run of UK hits on the Fanfare label in the latter half of the 90s which was launched by 'So Macho'/'Cruising (number 2, 1986) and was distinguished by three further Top 10 hits, 'Toy Boy' (1987), 'Cross My Broken Heart' (1988), 'Right Back Where We Started From' (1989). Later chart positions boasted a Top 20 hit with a cover version of the 1973 **Robert Knight** hit 'Love On A Mountain Top' (number 20, 1989). In early 1993 Sinitta released *The Supremes EP*, which as the name suggests is a collection of **Supremes** covers.

Albums: *Sinitta!* (1987), *Wicked!* (1989).

Sinner

This German hard rock/thrash metal group was formed by Matthias Lasch in 1980. Lasch later became known as Mat Sinner, adding guitarists Wolfgang Werner and Calo Rapallo, drummer Edgar Patrik (later of **Bonfire**) and keyboardist Franky Mittelbach to complete the band's initial line-up. Influenced by **Accept**, **Judas Priest**, **Iron Maiden** and later **Metallica**, they released six workman-like, but ultimately uninspiring albums between 1982 and 1987. The personnel was in a constant state of flux, with Sinner the only constant. Their early career was dominated by **New Wave Of British Heavy Metal** style material, reminiscent of **Angelwitch** and **Tygers Of Pan Tang**, then moved towards a thrashier direction as **Slayer** and **Anthrax** arrived on the scene. The band have never made any impression outside Germany and after *Dangerous Charm* in 1987 they were dropped by their record company.

Albums: *Wild 'n' Evil* (SL 1982), *Fast Decision* (Noise 1983), *Danger Zone* (Noise 1984), *Touch Of Sin* (Noise 1985), *Comin' Out Fighting* (Noise 1986), *Dangerous Charm* (Noise 1987).

Siouxsie And The Banshees

Siouxsie Sioux (b. Susan Dallion, 27 May 1957, London, England) was part of the notorious 'Bromley contingent', including Steve Severin (b. Steven Bailey, 25 September 1955), which followed the **Sex Pistols** in their early days. Siouxsie had also taken part in the 100 Club Punk Festival, singing an elongated version of 'The Lord's Prayer' with a group that included **Sid Vicious** on drums. The fledgling singer also achieved some minor fame after a verbal exchange with television presenter Bill Grundy which unwittingly prompted the Sex Pistols' infamous swearing match on the *Today* programme. Within months of that incident Siouxsie put together her backing group the Banshees, featuring Pete Fenton (guitar), Steve Severin (bass) and Kenny Morris (drums). Siouxsie flirted with Nazi imagery, highlighted by black make-up and frequently exposed breasts. By mid-1977 Fenton was replaced by John McGeogh, and the group supported **Johnny Thunders And The Heartbreakers** as well as recording a session for the BBC disc jockey, **John Peel**. By 1978, the group had signed to **Polydor Records** (the last of the important punk bands of the era to be rounded up by a major) and released their first single, the sublime 'Hong Kong Garden', which reached the UK Top 10. *The Scream* soon followed, produced by **Steve Lillywhite.** Less commercial offerings ensued with 'The Staircase (Mystery)' and 'Playground Twist', which were soon succeeded by *Join Hands*. During a promotional tour, Morris and McKay abruptly left, to be replaced by former **Slits** drummer Budgie (b. Peter Clark, 21 August 1957) and temporary Banshee Robert Smith, on leave from the **Cure**. Siouxsie's Germanic influences were emphasized on the stark 'Mittageisen (Metal Postcard)', which barely scraped into the Top 50. Both 'Happy House' and 'Christine' were more melodic offerings, deservedly bringing greater commercial success. After the success of *Kaleidoscope*, the group embarked on a world tour, including a concert behind the 'Iron Curtain'. Another Top 10 album, *Juju*, was followed by some extra-curricular activities. Siouxie and Budgie formed an occasional offshoot group, the **Creatures**, who enjoyed Top 10 success in their own right, as well as recording an album. Smith and Severin also recorded successfully together as the **Glove**. After the string-accompanied *A Kiss In The Dreamhouse*, the group reconvened in the autumn of 1983 to play a concert for Italy's Communist Party. A highly commercial version of the **Beatles**' 'Dear Prudence' provided the group with their biggest UK hit, peaking at number 3. Early in 1984 the evocative 'Swimming Horses' maintained their hit profile, while further personnel changes ensued with the enlistment of John Carruthers from **Clock DVA**. He, in turn, was replaced by Jon Klein. Regular albums during the mid-80s showed that the group had established a loyal cult following and could experiment freely in the studio without a significant loss of commercial appeal. Having already enjoyed success with a cover version, Siouxsie then tackled **Bob Dylan**'s 'This Wheel's On Fire', which reached the UK Top 20. An entire album of cover versions followed though *Through The Looking Glass* received the most awkward reviews of the band's career. A change of direction with *Peep Show* saw the band embrace a more sophisticated sound, maintaining the eastern nuances of yore but doing so within an elaborate musical scheme. 1991 returned them to the charts with the evocative 'Kiss Them For Me' and *Superstition*, an album of light touch but contrastingly dense production. Arugably their greatest achievement of the 90s, however, was the much-delayed *The Rapture*. Adding musical adventurism (notably the heavily orchestrated three movements of the title-track) to familiar but entertaining refractions from their earlier career ('Not Forgotten'), the approach of middle age had evidently not weakened their resolve.

Albums: *The Scream* (Polydor 1978), *Join Hands* (Polydor 1979), *Kaleidoscope* (Polydor 1980), *Juju* (Polydor 1981), *A Kiss In The Dreamhouse* (Polydor 1982), *Nocturne* (Polydor 1983), *Hyaena* (Polydor 1984), *Tinderbox* (Polydor 1986), *Through The Looking Glass* (Polydor 1987), *Peep Show* (Polydor 1988), *Superstition* (Polydor 1991), *The Rapture* (Polydor 1995). Compilations: *Once Upon A Time - The Singles* (Polydor 1981), *Twice Upon A Time* (Polydor 1992).
Video: *Greetings From Zurich* (1994)
Films: *Jubilee* (1978).
Further reading: *Siouxsie And The Banshees*, West, Mike (1982), *Entranced: The Siouxsie & The Banshees Story*, Johns, Brian (1989).

Sir Douglas Quintet

Formed in 1964, the quintet was fashioned by a Houston-based producer, **Huey P. Meaux** and former teenage prodigy, **Doug Sahm** (b. 6 November 1941, San Antonio, Texas, USA). The name, Sir Douglas Quintet, first used on 'Sugar Bee' (1964), was fashioned to suggest Anglo credentials in the midst of the British Invasion, but Sahm's southern accent soon put paid to such attempted deception. **Augie Meyers** (b. 31 May 1940; organ), Francisco (Frank) Morin (b. 13 August 1946; horns), Harvey Kagan (b. 18 April 1946; bass) and John Perez (b. 8 November 1942; drums) completed the line-up which scored an international hit with 'She's About A Mover', an infectious blend of Texas pop and the **Beatles**' 'She's A Woman', underscored by Meyers' simple, insistent keyboards. This charming style continued on several further singles and the band's debut album, prematurely entitled *The Best Of The Sir Douglas Quintet*. In keeping with several Texans, including **Janis Joplin** and the **Thirteenth Floor Elevators**, the Quintet sought the relaxed clime of San Francisco following an arrest on drugs charges in 1966. However, it was two years before the band resumed recording with *Honky Blues*, although only Sahm and Morin were retained from the earlier unit which was bolstered by other Lone Star state exiles Wayne Talbert (piano), Martin Fierro (horns) and George Rains (drums).

The original Quintet was reconstituted for *Mendocino*. This superb selection remains their finest offering and includes the atmospheric 'At The Crossroads', a fiery remake of 'She's About a Mover' and the compulsive title track, which became the group's sole million-seller when released as a single. This commercial peak was not sustained and despite delivering several other excellent albums, the unit broke up in 1972 when Sahm embarked on a solo career. It was, however, a temporary respite and since reforming in 1976 the group has been resurrected on several occasions, in part to tour and capitalise on a continued European popularity.

Albums: *The Best Of The Sir Douglas Quintet* (1965), *Sir Douglas Quintet + 2 - Honkey Blues* (1968), *Mendocino* (1969), *1+1+1 = 4* (1970), *The Return Of Doug Salanda* (1971), *Rough Edges* (1973), *Quintessence* (1982), *Border Wave* (1983), *Rio Medina* (1984), *Very Much Alive/Love Ya, Europe* (1988), *Midnight Sun* (1988), *Day Dreaming At Midnight* (Elektra 1994). Compilations: *The Sir Douglas Quintet Collection* (1986), *Sir Doug's Recording Trip* (1988).

Sir Mix-A-Lot

Seattle based DJ/MC and producer (b. Anthony Ray) who broke with 'Posse On Broadway', a statement of intent released on his own label in 1986, which would go on to sell over a million copies. Further crossover success arrived with rap's second great rock/rap coalition: a cover of **Black Sabbath**'s 'Iron Man', performed in conjunction with Seattle thrash outfit **Metal Church**. By the time of his second album Sir Mix-A-Lot was sampling **Prince**'s 'Batdance', and maintaining his sharp, political edge - though he is too light-hearted and deft of touch to be considered truly gangsta. His Rhyme Cartel is signed to Def American records, and he can boast a platinum and gold album for *Swass* and *Seminar*, respectively. Sir-Mix-A-Lot's use of unlikely sources, the synthesized pop of **Devo** and **Kraftwerk** measured against the conscious lyrics of rappers like **Public Enemy**, was a unique combination. However, there were some crude sexual japes on tracks like 'Mack Daddy', and he was hardly shown in the best light by the pro-gun swagger of 'No Rods Barred'. He did enjoy another huge hit in 'Baby Got Back', however.

Albums: *Swass* (Nastymix 1988), *Seminar* (Nastymix 1989), *Mack Daddy* (Def American 1992), *Chief Boot Knocka* (American Recordings 1994).

Sire Records

Through its involvement with artists from the **Climax Blues Band** to **Madonna**, Sire has been a force in the music business for over two decades. The company was formed in 1966 in New York by Seymour Stein and songwriter/producer **Richard Gottehrer**. Stein had been chart compiler for *Billboard* magazine, personal assistant to Sid Nathan of King Records and a plugger for the Red Bird label. To begin with, Sire concentrated on releasing such underground artists as the **Deviants** and the **Purple Gang** as well as the stable of blues artists signed to **Mike Vernon**'s **Blue Horizon** records. In the early 70s Sire licensed from Vernon records such artists as the **Climax Chicago Blues Band** and **Focus**. The first US signing had been Martha Velez but after Gottehrer left the company, Stein plunged into the New York new wave scene releasing the debut albums by the **Ramones**, **Talking Heads** and **Richard Hell** and the Voidoids. From the UK punk scene, the label had the **Rezillos** and later the **Pretenders**. In 1978 Sire signed a distribution agreement with **Warner Bros** and was eventually wholly-owned by the Warner Music Group. However, Stein retained creative control and while the most important Sire artist of the 80s was **Madonna**, he also signed rock band **Modern English** and rap artist **Ice-T**. He maintained the UK link by releasing material from the **Smiths**, **James**, the **Soup Dragons** and **Morrissey**.

Sirone

b. Norris Jones, 28 September 1940, Atlanta, Georgia, USA. Master bassist and occasional trombonist Sirone (it's 'Norris' backwards, almost) has one of the most exceptional resumés of any New Jazz musician, having played with **John Coltrane**, **Cecil Taylor**, **Ornette Coleman**, **Albert Ayler**, **Sun Ra**, and **Bill Dixon** - that's to say *all* of the most important innovators. In the 70s he commuted between the Cecil Taylor Unit and the **Revolutionary Ensemble** and was the pivot of innumerable New York 'loft scene' sessions but, by the mid-80s, work opportunities had shrunk greatly. (Even improvisation has its fashion cycles.) Since 1986,

Sirone's major gig has been with the group Phalanx, an all-star aggregate also featuring **James 'Blood' Ulmer**, **George Adams**, and **Rashied Ali**.

Albums: *Artistry* (1978), *Live* (1980), *Original Phalanx* (1987), with Phalanx *In Touch* (1988).

Sissle, Noble

b. 10 July 1889, Indianapolis, Indiana, USA, d. 17 December 1975. Sissle's early career was spent largely in vaudeville as a singer and he also sang with the orchestra of **James Reese Europe**. However, his talents as a songwriter gradually drew him to Broadway where, in collaboration with **Eubie Blake**, he achieved a major breakthrough. Before Sissle and Blake it was rare for a black entertainer to gain acceptance along the 'Great White Way', but the success of their 1921 show, *Shuffle Along*, changed all that. *Shuffle Along* starred Florence Mills and among its memorable tunes were 'In Honeysuckle Time', 'Love Will Find A Way' and the hit of the show, 'I'm Just Wild About Harry'. In this and succeeding shows, such as *Chocolate Dandies*, the collaborators presented a succession of songs, dances and sketches that were attuned to the new musical sounds of the day - unlike most other Broadway shows which also performed by all-black casts, had ignored ragtime and the emergence of jazz. In these and later years Sissle led a number of fine orchestras that featured some of the best musicians available, among them **Sidney Bechet**, **Otto 'Toby' Hardwicke**, **Tommy Ladnier** and **Buster Bailey**. In the late 20s Sissle led a band in Paris and London and during the 30s led successful bands in New York and elsewhere in the USA. He continued touring during the 40s and 50s but gradually directed his attention to music publishing.

Albums: *Sissle And Blake's 'Shuffle Along' (1921)* (80s), *Sissle And His Sizzling Syncopators (1930-31)* (80s).

Sister Carol

b. 1959, Kingston, Jamaica, West Indies. From her upbringing of outright poverty in Denham Town Ghetto, Sister Carol has emerged as a new star of US **dancehall**. She met her mentor, **Brigadier Jerry**, at the age of 20, and he inspired her to try the DJ style rather than straight singing. However, she emigrated to Brooklyn, New York, in the late 70s, feeling disaffected by the 'punany' or 'slackness' that had overtaken traditional roots reggae concerns. In America her musical pursuits would run in parallel to a film career, which was initiated when she was spotted duetting with **Judy Mowatt** on 'Screwface'. This won her a featured role in *Something Wild*, followed by *Married To The Mob*.

Selected albums: *Jah Disciples* (RAS 1991), *Call Mi* (Heartbeat 1995).

Sister Sledge

Debra (b. 1955), Joan (1957), Kim (1958) and Kathie

Sledge (1959) were all born and raised in Philadelphia, Pennsylvania, USA. They started their recording career in 1971 and spent a short time working as backing singers before enjoying a series of minor R&B hits between 1974 and 1977. Two years later they entered a fruitful relationship with **Chic** masterminds Nile Rodgers and Bernard Edwards which resulted in several sparkling singles including 'He's The Greatest Dancer', 'We Are Family' and 'Lost In Music', each of which reached the the the UK Top 20 in 1979. The Sisters then left the Chic organization and began to produce their own material in 1981. Although success in the USA waned, the quartet retained their UK popularity and two remixes of former hits served as a prelude to 'Frankie', a simple but irrepressible song which reached number 1 in 1985. Since then however, Sister Sledge have been unable to maintain this status.

Albums: *Circle Of Love* (1975), *Together* (1977), *We Are Family* (1979), *Love Somebody Today* (1980), *All American Girls* (1981), *The Sisters* (1982), *Bet Cha Say That To All The Girls* (1983), *When The Boys Meet The Girls* (1985). Compilations: *Greatest Hits* (1986), *The Best Of...* (1993).

Sister Souljah

b. Lisa Williamson, USA. Rapper who became something of a *cause celebre* when President-elect Bill Clinton verbally attacked her during his campaign. On June 13 1992 he declared that Souljah had made 'racist remarks' and 'advocated violence against whites' in an interview with *Rolling Stone* magazine. As if having such political heavyweights on her case were not enough, she also found herself being sued by former producer Michael Shinn, after she listed him as a 'two-faced backstabber' on the sleevenotes to her 1992 **Epic** album. The source of their inital disagreement was not disclosed, but she was dropped from the label after its release in any case. The album is still worth investigating however, notably on cuts like 'State Of Accomodation: Why Aren't You Angry?' and 'Killing Me Softly: Deadly Code Of Silence', which featured guest shots from Chuck D and **Ice Cube** respectively. She also worked with **Public Enemy**, joining the band in late 1990 after accompanying them on their US lecture tour. However, her contribution (rapping on 'By The Time I Get To Arizona' from *The Enemy Strikes Black*) was disappointing and her tenure with the band was a brief one. She had already appeared on **Terminator X**'s single, 'Wanna Be Dancin' (Buck Whylin')', and would also guest on his debut solo album.

Album: *360 Degrees Of Power* (Epic 1992).

Sisters Of Mercy

A post-punk rock outfit whose flirtations with gothic imagery would dog the public and media perception of them throughout an eclectic career. They formed in Leeds, Yorkshire, England in 1980, when Leeds and Oxford University drop-out Andrew Eldritch (b. Andrew Taylor, 15 May 1959, East Anglia, England; vocals) teamed up with Gary Marx (guitar) and a drum machine. After releasing 'The Damage Done' (on which Eldritch plays drums and guitar) on their own Merciful Release label, the band expanded to include Ben Gunn (guitar) and Craig Adams (bass) for supports with **Clash**, **Psychedelic Furs** and the **Birthday Party**. A cult reputation in the North of England was augmented by excellent press, and further enhanced by the release of 'Alice'. A magnificent gothic dance saga, together with the subsequent 'Temple Of Love', it hallmarked the band's early musical character. Inbetween these two landmark 45s Gunn left to be replaced by Wayne Hussey (ex-**Pauline Murray**, **Dead Or Alive**). **WEA** picked up the distribution for Merciful Release as the band's reputation continued to grow throughout 1983 and 1984. However, despite the release of their debut album, the following year brought a creative watershed. Continuing rivalries between Marx and Eldritch forced the former to depart. This was only a stop-gap treaty with the band announcing a final split in April 1985 after a concert at the Royal Albert Hall. The rest of the year witnessed extraordinary legal wrangles between Eldritch on one hand and Adams and Hussey on the other, each claiming use of the name Sisters Of Mercy. Eldritch went as far as releasing a record under the title Sisterhood simply to prevent Adams and Hussey from adopting this halfway-house title. The duo eventually settled on the **Mission** as their new home, while Eldritch moved to Berlin, West Germany. Still operating under the Sisters Of Mercy title, Eldritch recruited Patricia Morrison (b. 14 January 1962, ex-**Gun Club**) for hit singles 'This Corrosion' and 'Dominion', and the album *Floodland*. A two year spell of inactivity was broken in 1990 with 'More', showcasing another new line-up; Tony James (ex-**Generation X**, **Sigue Sigue Sputnik**; bass), Tim Bricheno (b. 6 July 1963, Huddersfield, Yorkshire, England; guitar - ex-All About Eve) and Andreas Bruhn (guitar). The *Vision Thing* indulged Eldritch's penchant for deep rooted, esoteric metaphor, which occasionally makes his lyrics futile and impenetrable. 1991 saw a loss-making, aborted tour with **Public Enemy**, though this has done little to erase the confidence of the self-confessed 'world's greatest lyricist'.

Albums: *First And Last And Always* (1985), *Floodland* (1988), *Vision Thing* (1990), *Some Girls Wander By Mistake* (1992).

Videos: *Wake, The* (1987), *Shot Rev 2.0* (1994).

Further reading: *Heartland: Anthology Of Issues 1, 11 And 111*, Pinell, Andrew (1991).

Sisters Unlimited

This group formed initially when the various members

all lived in London. The line-up comprised **Janet Kerr** (b. 11 January 1958, Buckhaven, Fife, Scotland), **Peta Webb**, (b. 23 August 1946, Woodford Green, Essex, England), Rosie Davis (b. 30 July 1948, Woolton, Liverpool, England) and Sandra Kerr (b. 14 February 1942, Romford, Essex, England). They got together when requested for special events, such as International Women's Day, and worked in various combinations of two and three at festivals running voice and harmony workshops for women. Much of the song content in their work is from a woman's perspective. In August 1989, they appeared in concert in the Purcell Room, on London's South Bank. Despite individual commitments limiting the time the four have to play together, they are working on a new album for 1992, and are arranging a short British tour with the French female **a cappella** group Roulez Fillettes.
Album: *No Limits* (Harbourtown 1991).

Six Feet Under

This Swedish power-metal quintet modelled themselves on **Deep Purple**, **Rainbow** and **Whitesnake**. The band were formed in 1982 by vocalist Bjorn Lodin and guitarist Thomas Larsson. Recruiting Peter Ostling (keyboards), Kent Jansson (bass) and Claus Annersjo (drums), they signed to the Europa Film label the following year. This contract resulted in two albums which featured few original ideas. Larsson's guitar style was based almost exclusively on **Ritchie Blackmore**'s, which imbued the songs with too strong a sense of *deja vu*. Marcus Kallstrum took over the drumstool on *Eruption*, which sold fewer copies than their debut. Disillusioned, the band went their separate ways in 1985.
Albums: *Six Feet Under* (Europa Film 1983), *Eruption* (Europa Film 1984).

Six Teens

An R&B vocal group from Los Angeles, California, USA. In the wake of the success of **Frankie Lymon And The Teenagers**, many east coast groups emerged with the pre-teen lead sound. The Six Teens diverged slightly from the pattern by the fact of their west coast origin and the use of a female to sing the 'adolescent teen boy' part. Members were Trudy Williams (lead), Ed Wells (lead), Richard Owens, Darryl Lewis, Beverly Pecot, and Louise Williams. Their one hit was the fetching 'A Casual Look' (number 7 R&B, number 25 pop), from 1956, on which Williams's youth was most telling and appealing. The group's follow-up, 'Send Me Flowers', was a regional hit in Hawaii, and 'Only Jim' and 'Arrow Of Love' likewise achieved regional sales. The group's last recordings were made in 1958, and Owens became a member of the **Vibrations**.
Compilation: *A Casual Look* (Official 1989).

Sizemore, Asher, And Little Jimmy

Asher Sizemore (b. 6 June 1906, Manchester, Kentucky, USA, d. c.1973) and his eldest son Jimmy (b. 29 January 1928, Paintsville, Kentucky, USA). Sizemore initially worked as a bookkeeper for a mining company in Pike County but longed to be a singer. In 1931, Singing old time and cowboy songs, he first appeared on radio in Huntington, West Virginia, before moving to WCKY Cincinnati and then WHAS Louisville, where he was first joined on air by his five-year-old son. In 1933, the duo were hired by the *Grand Ole Opry*, where they remained a popular act for about 10 years. Jimmy, at the age of five, allegedly had a repertoire of over 200 songs and understandably because of his extreme youth, his *Opry* and radio performances gained him a considerable following. He sang duets with his father but is remembered for his youthful renditions of such numbers as 'Chewing Gum' and 'The Booger Bear'. In 1934, he achieved recording success with a maudlin rendition of 'Little Jimmy's Goodbye To **Jimmie Rodgers**'. The Sizemores toured regularly but to augment their income, Asher established a very successful mail order service for their annual books of *Health & Home Songs* and they also made transcription disc recordings that Asher syndicated to stations throughout the south and midwest. By the late 30s, the act also included Jimmy's younger brother Buddy. Drawing mainly on sentimental numbers that contained regular references to mother, home, death, heaven and righteousness, with some interruption for part of World War II, they maintained a successful career throughout the 40s, mainly in the mid-west. In 1950, now joined by daughter Nancy Louise, Asher returned to WKLO Louisville. Jimmy and Buddy both served in the US Forces in Korea, Buddy being killed in action in November 1950. Asher and Jimmy later moved to Arkansas where they both worked on radio. Asher Sizemore died in the 70s but Jimmy was still working on radio in an executive capacity into the 80s.
Albums: *Mountain Ballads & Old Hymns* (1966), *Songs Of The Soil* (1984).

Ska

A generic title for Jamaican music recorded between 1961-67, ska emerged from Jamaican R&B, which itself was largely based on American R&B and doo-wop. The difference being that while the US style smoothed out and became soul, the Jamaican sound, if anything, became wilder and more jerky, in what is commonly assumed to be an exaggeration of the 'jump' beat played on the black radio stations of Miami and New Orleans in the late 50s, and readily heard in Jamaica. Ska was fuelled by the **sound systems**, the over-amplified mobile discos which were (and still are) Jamaica's preferred method of enjoying music. At first, from the start of the 50s onwards, sound systems used American records. By the mid-to-late 50s competition had become so fierce between rival systems that finding an exclusive record by an American act had become a preoccupation - if you had the right song, your rivals could do little to stop your pre-eminence. Eventually, as the wild beat of the likes of **Amos Milburn**, **Wynonie Harris** *et al* began to fade into the past, sound system owners formed an alliance with indigenous Jamaican singers and musicians, which resulted in a hybrid of doo-wop, R&B and jazz that eventually precipitated ska, the jump-up sound where the jump took precedence over everything else.

The sound system bosses became Jamaica's first record producers, and included Sir **Coxsone Dodd**, **Duke Reid** and King Edwards: their names reflecting the showmanship and drive for supremacy of the sound systems. The singers numbered **Delroy Wilson**, Jiving Juniors (see **Derrick Harriott**), **Alton** (**Ellis**) and Eddy, **Lord Creator** and many more. These artists quickly became Jamaica's first stars. The instrumental outings of the bands, under the leadership of talents such as trombonist **Don Drummond**, tenor saxman **Roland Alphonso**, and alto sax player **Tommy McCook**, if anything, outshone the vocal records, with a frequently freewheeling, heavy-jazz philosophy that many have since tried, but failed, to imitate. By 1964 ska had become popular amongst mods in England, where it was known as Blue Beat, the name of the foremost UK licensing label. British acts such as **Georgie Fame And The Blue Flames**, and The Migil 5 had hits in the ska style, while more authentically Jamaican acts such as **Millie**, **Prince Buster** and the **Skatalites** all scored chart entries. By 1966 ska was beginning to burn out in Jamaica, to be replaced by the more sedate and perhaps more exclusively indigenous sound of **rocksteady**. However, ska has remained intermittently popular, demonstrated by several 'ska revivals', the most successful of which was the UK **2 Tone** movement in the late-70s. It seems that the beat will never truly exhaust itself. At any given time, somewhere in the world from Japan to Germany, a would-be Skatalites can be unearthed, making a nightclub jump to the infectious rhythms of this most animated of musics.

Selected albums: Various: *Ska Authentic* (Studio One), *The History Of Ska* (Bamboo 1969), *Club Ska '67* (Mango/Island 1980), *Intensified Vols 1 & 2* (Mango/Island 1979).

Video: *Ska Explosion 2 (Visionary)* (1994).

Skagarack

This Danish melodic hard rock quintet were formed in 1985 by vocalist Torben Schmidt and guitarist Jan Petersen. With the addition of Tommy Rasmussen (keyboards), Morten Munch (bass) and Alvin Otto (drums), they incorporated elements of **Whitesnake**,

Night Ranger and **Boston** into their music. From AOR beginnings, they have gradually evolved into a heavier and more powerful group than their self-titled debut might have suggested. Schmidt's vocals are reminiscent of David Coverdale's: melodic, powerful and emotive, and Skagarak remain a fine band whose obvious potential has yet to cross the Scandinavian frontier.

Albums: *Skagarack* (Polydor 1986), *Hungry For A Game* (Polydor 1988), *A Slice Of Heaven* (Medley 1990).

Skaggs, Ricky

b. Ricky Lee Skaggs, 18 July 1954, Brushey Creek, near Cordell, Kentucky, USA. His father, Hobert, was a welder, who enjoyed playing the guitar and singing gospel songs with Skaggs' mother, Dorothy. Skaggs was to record one of her songs, 'All I Ever Loved Was You'. Hobert came back from a welding job in Ohio with a mandolin for the five-year-old Skaggs, but had to return before he could show him how to play it. Within two weeks, Skaggs had figured it out for himself. In 1959 he was taken on stage during one of **Bill Monroe**'s concerts and played 'Ruby' on Monroe's mandolin to rapturous applause. At the age of seven, he played mandolin on **Flatt And Scruggs**' television show, and then learnt guitar and fiddle. Whilst working at a square dance with his father, he met **Keith Whitley**; they were to form a trio with Whitley's banjo-playing brother, Dwight, recording bluegrass and gospel shows for local radio. In 1970 they opened for Ralph Stanley, formerly of the **Stanley Brothers**, who was so impressed that he invited them to join his band, the Clinch Mountain Boys. They both made their recording debuts on Stanley's *Cry From The Cross*. The youngsters made two albums together, but Skaggs soon left in 1972, discouraged by the long hours and low pay.

Skaggs married Stanley's cousin and worked in a boiler room in Washington DC. However, he returned to music by joining the Country Gentlemen, principally on fiddle. Then, from 1974 to 1975, he played in the modern bluegrass band, J.D. Crowe And The New South. He later recorded a duet album with another member of the band, Tony Rice. Skaggs' first solo, *That's It*, includes contributions from his own parents. He formed his own band, Boone Creek, and recorded bluegrass albums, although they also touched on western swing and honky tonk. He was then offered a job in **Emmylou Harris**' Hot Band. 'Emmy tried to get me to join three times before I went. I wanted to stay in bluegrass and learn as much about the music as I could, but when **Rodney Crowell** left, I had an incentive to join her because I knew I'd be able to sing a lot.' From 1977 to 1980, Skaggs was to encourage Harris' forays into traditional country music via her *Blue Kentucky Girl, Light Of The Stable* and, especially, *Roses In The Snow*. Although Skaggs had rarely been a lead vocalist, his clear, high tenor was featured on an acoustic-based solo album, *Sweet Temptation*, for the North Carolina label, Sugar Hill. Emmylou Harris and **Albert Lee** were amongst the guest musicians. While he was working on another Sugar Hill album, *Don't Cheat In Our Hometown*, Epic Records took an interest in him. He switched to Epic and made his debut on the US country charts with a revival of Flatt And Scruggs' 'Don't Get Above Your Raising', which he later re-recorded in concert with **Elvis Costello**. *Rolling Stone* likened Skaggs' first Epic release, *Waitin' For The Sun To Shine*, to **Gram Parsons**' *Grievous Angel* as they both represented turning-points in country music.

Skaggs was putting the country back into country music by making fresh-sounding records which related to the music's heritage. As if to prove the point, he had US number 1 country hits by reviving Flatt and Scrugg's 'Crying My Heart Out Over You' and **Webb Pierce**'s 'I Don't Care'. He was the Country Music Association Male Vocalist of the Year for 1982, and became the 61st - and youngest - member of the *Grand Old Opry*. Despite the old-time feeling, he appealed to rock fans in a sell-out concert at London's Dominion Theatre, which was released on a live album. Skaggs had played on **Guy Clark**'s original version of 'Heartbroken' and his own recording of the song gave him another country chart-topper. He also completed his *Don't Cheat In Our Hometown*, which was released, after much negotiation, by Epic. Skaggs is a principled performer who leaves drinking or cheating songs to others, but he justified the title track, originally recorded by The Stanley Brothers, by calling it a 'don't cheat' song. Skaggs played on Albert Lee's first-class solo *Hiding*, and he had another number 1 with his own version of Lee's 'Country Boy', although the whimsical lyric must have baffled American listeners. With a revival of Bill Monroe's 'Uncle Pen', Skaggs is credited as being the first performer to top the country charts with a bluegrass song since Flatt And Scruggs in 1963, although he says, "Uncle Pen' would not be a bluegrass single according to law of Monroe because there are drums and electric instruments on it.' Skaggs won a Grammy for the best country instrumental, 'Wheel Hoss', which was used as the theme music for his BBC Radio 2 series, *Hit It, Boys*. In 1981 Skaggs, now divorced, married Sharon White of the **Whites**. They won the Vocal Duo of the Year award for their 1987 duet, 'Love Can't Ever Get Better Than This'. He also recorded a playful duet of 'Friendship' with **Ray Charles**, and says, 'The people who call me Picky Ricky can't have met Ray Charles. He irons out every wrinkle. I would sing my lead part and he'd say, "Aw, honey, that's good but convince me now: sing to your ol' daddy." Skaggs has worked on albums by the **Bellamy Brothers**, **Rodney Crowell**, **Exile** and **Jesse Winchester**. **Johnny Cash** had never previously used a fiddle player until Skaggs worked on

Silver. Skaggs' busy career suffered a setback when his son Andrew was shot in the mouth by a drug-crazed truckdriver, but returned in 1989 with two fine albums in the traditional mould: *White Limozeen*, which he produced for **Dolly Parton**, and his own *Kentucky Thunder*. *My Father's Son* in 1991 was his most consistent album in years, but its poor sales led Columbia to drop him from their roster in 1992. Skaggs is modest about his achievements, feeling that he is simply God's instrument. He has rekindled an interest in country music's heritage, and many musicians have followed his lead. He remains one of the best performers in country music today.

Albums: with Keith Whitley *Tribute To The Stanley Brothers* (1971), with Keith Whitley *Second Generation Bluegrass* (1972), *That's It* (1975), as Boone Creek *Boone Creek* (1977), as Boone Creek *One Way Track* (1978), with Tony Rice *Take Me Home Tonight In A Song* (1978), *Sweet Temptation* (1979), with Tony Rice *Skaggs And Rice* (1980), *Waitin' For The Sun To Shine* (1981), *Family And Friends* (1982), *Highways And Heartaches* (1982), *Don't Cheat In Our Hometown* (1983), *Country Boy* (1984), *Live In London* (1985), *Love's Gonna Get Ya!* (1986), *Comin' Home To Stay* (1988), *Kentucky Thunder* (1989), *My Father's Son* (1991).

Skatalites

The Skatalites were formed in June 1964, drawing from the ranks of session musicians then recording in the studios of Kingston, Jamaica. The personnel included **Don Drummond** (trombone), **Roland Alphonso** (tenor sax), **Tommy McCook** (tenor sax), Johnny 'Dizzy' Moore (trumpet), Lester Sterling (alto Sax), Jerome 'Jah Jerry Hines (guitar), **Jackie Mittoo** (piano), Lloyd Brevett (bass), and Lloyd Knibbs (drums). The band name was a Tommy McCook pun on the Soviet space satellite of 1963. The Skatalites' music, reputedly named after the characteristic 'ska' sound made by the guitar when playing the 'after beat', was a powerful synthesis; combining elements of R&B and swing jazz in arrangements and solos, underpinned by the uniquely Jamaican-stressed 'after beat', as opposed to the 'down beat' of R&B. Many of the musicians had learnt music at Alpha Boys' School in Kingston, then honing their talent in the Jamaican swing bands of the 40s and early 50s, and in numerous 'hotel bands' playing for the tourist trade. Most of the musicians thereby developed recognisable individual styles. Repertoire was drawn from many sources, including adaptations of Latin tunes, movie themes and updated mento, a Jamaican folk song form. Perhaps their most famous and identifiable tune is 'Guns Of Navarone' recorded in 1965 and a big club hit in the UK in the mid-60s. They recorded hundreds of superb instrumentals for various producers, either under the group name or as bands led by the particular musician who had arranged the session. Under the Skatalite name they made important music for **Coxsone Dodd** and **Duke Reid**, as well as for Justin and Philip Yap's Top Deck record label. They stayed together for just over two years until August 1965, when a combination of financial, organisational and personal problems caused the break-up of the band after their last gig, a police dance at the Runaway Bay Hotel. Of the main protagonists, Jackie Mittoo and Roland Alphonso were persuaded by Coxsone Dodd to form the Soul Brothers band, who would make many instrumentals and supply backing tracks at **Studio One** until 1967. Tommy McCook worked principally for Duke Reid, where he formed the studio band known as the Supersonics, and was musical co-director for Reid's Treasure Isle label with alto saxophonist Herman Marques. The tragically wayward Don Drummond suffered from severe depression and died on 6 May 1969 in Bellevue Asylum, Kingston. The Skatalites had backed virtually every singer of note in the studios, at the same time laying the musical foundation for subsequent developments in Jamaican music. They released a reunion album in 1975; not ska, but high quality instrumental reggae. In 1984 the band played the Jamaican and London 'Sunsplash' concerts to rapturous acclaim. The reformed group also toured Japan with vocalists **Prince Buster** and Lord Tanamo in 1989, recording live and in the studio.

Albums: *Ska Authentic* (Studio One 1967), *Ska Boo Da Ba* (Top Deck/Doctor Bird 60s), *The Skatalites* (Treasure Isle 1975), *Return Of The Big Guns* (Island 1984), *Live At Reggae Sunsplash* (Synergy 1986), *Stretching Out* (ROIR 1987), *Celebration Time* (Studio One 1988). Compilations: *Best Of The Skatalites* (Studio One 1974), *Scattered Lights* (Top Deck 1984).

SKB

(see **SKO**)

Skeat, Len

b. 9 February 1937, London, England. After playing bass with the **Ted Heath** band, Skeat began widening his musical foundation by working in numerous contexts. Among the artists with whom he has worked are singers **Tom Jones** and **Peggy Lee**, tenor saxophonists **Al Cohn**, **Spike Robinson** and **Tommy Whittle**, the Pizza Express All Stars, trumpeters **Ruby Braff** and **Digby Fairweather** and violinist **Stéphane Grappelli**. A master technician, Skeat exemplifies the great tradition of mainstream bass-playing and the invariably high quality of his performances ranks with the best. His heavy workload throughout the 70s and 80s led to ill health but, after a major operation in 1990, he was back at work, effortlessly providing the immaculate timekeeping and rhythmic pulse for which he is known.

Albums: with Stéphane Grappelli *I Got Rhythm* (1973), *Spike Robinson At Chesters* (1984), with Spike Robinson

The Gershwin Collection (1987), *The Pizza Express All Star Jazz Band* (1988).

Skeletal Family

No doubt influenced by the emergence of gothic punk in the early 80s, the Skeletal Family emerged from Bingley in Yorkshire towards the end of 1982. Early demos recorded in September and December featured the input of Anne Marie Hurst (lead vocals), Trotwood (b. Roger Nowell; bass), Stan Greenwood (guitar), Steve Crane (drums) and Karl Heinz (synthesizer). After a debut single, 'Just A Friend', on the Luggage label in March 1983, the band signed to Yorkshire's established indie, **Red Rhino Records**. By this time Howard Daniels had taken over on drums. 'The Night' shared the same influences championed by the band's 'goth' counterparts - the **Cramps**, **Bauhaus** and the **Birthday Party**. 'Alone She Cries' in January 1984 featured new drummer Martin Henderson, and was followed by 'So Sure' in June, alongside *Recollect*, a 12-inch EP comprising early demos. By the advent of *Burning Oil* in August, Skeletal Family had attracted a sizeable following, principally through support slots to the **Sisters Of Mercy**. This ascent continued with 'Promised Land' in February 1985, where they were aided by Graham Pleeth on synthesizer, the a-side backed by a cover of **Ben E. King**'s 'Stand By Me'. *Futile Combat* fared well in the UK independent charts, securing a deal with **Chrysalis Records**, but singer Anne Marie had left to join **Ghost Dance**. Recruiting drummer Kevin Phillips and Katrina on vocals, it was a new, more commercial Skeletal Family that issued 'Restless' in March 1986 and 'Just A Minute' in August, but neither made significant headway and the band were soon dropped (a fate that Ghost Dance would soon come to share).

Albums: *Burning Oil* (Red Rhino 1984), *Futile Combat* (Red Rhino 1985), *Ghosts* (Chrysalis 1986).

Skellern, Peter

b. 14 March 1947, Bury, Lancashire, England. A composer, singer, and musician, Skellern played trombone in a school band and served as organist and choirmaster in a local church before attending the Guildhall School of Music, from which he graduated with honours in 1968. Because 'I didn't want to spend the next 50 years playing Chopin', he joined March Hare which, as Harlan County, recorded a country-pop album before disbanding in 1971. Married with two children, Skellern worked as a hotel porter in Shaftesbury, Dorset, before striking lucky with a self-composed UK number 3 hit, 'You're A Lady'. *Peter Skellern, Not Without A Friend* was all original, bar **Hoagy Carmichael**'s 'Rockin' Chair', and another hit single with the title track to 1975's *Hold On To Love* established Skellern as a purveyor of wittily-observed if homely love songs of similar stamp to **Gilbert O'Sullivan**.

He earned the approbation of the ex-**Beatle** coterie which, already manifested in **Derek Taylor**'s production of *Not Without A Friend*, was further demonstrated when **George Harrison** assisted on *Hard Times*; the title number was later recorded by Starr. A minor hit in 1978 with 'Love Is The Sweetest Thing' (featuring Grimethorpe Colliery Band) was part of a tribute to **Fred Astaire** that won a Music Trades Association award for Best MOR Album of 1979. Skellern subsequently wrote and performed six autobiographical programmes for BBC television, followed by a series of musical plays (*Happy Endings*) and also hosted the chat show *Private Lives* in 1983. A year later he formed Oasis with Julian Lloyd Webber, **Mary Hopkin** and guitarist Bill Lovelady in an attempt to fuse mutual classical and pop interests, but the group's recordings failed to make a major impact. In 1985 he joined **Richard Stilgoe** for *Stilgoe And Skellern Stompin' At The Savoy*, a show in aid of The Lords Taverners charity organization. This led to the two entertainers working together on several successful tours, and in their two-man revue, *Who Plays Wins*, which was presented in the West End and New York. After becoming disenchanted with the record business for a time, in 1995 Skellern issued his first album for nearly eight years. Originally conceived as a tribute to the **Ink Spots**, it eventually consisted of a number of songs associated with that legendary group, and a few Hoagy Carmichael compositions 'just to break it up'.

Selected albums: *Peter Skellern With Harlan County* (1971), *Peter Skellern* (1972), *Not Without A Friend* (1973), *Holding My Own* (1974), *Hold On To Love* (1975), *Hard Times* (1976), *Skellern* (1978), *Astaire* (1979), *Still Magic* (1980), *Happy Endings* (1981), *A String Of Pearls* (1982), *Lovelight* (1987), *Stardust Memories* (1995 Warner). Compilations: *Introducing...Right From The Start* (1981), *Best Of Peter Skellern* (1985), *The Singer And The Song* (1993).

Ski Party

Released in 1965, *Ski Party* was another in a succession of exploitation films made under the American International Pictures banner. Having begun the series with several 'beach' features, AIP tinkered with the formula by taking similar plots and stars into slightly different locations. Borrowing a leaf from Billy Wilder's *Some Like It Hot*, **Frankie Avalon** and Dwayne Hickman dress in drag in order to stay with their girlfriends when they go on a skiing holiday to Sun Valley. The results are as predictable as ever, although it is true to say that the initial appeal of the genre was waning given the innovative nature of many contemporary pop films, notably *A Hard Day's Night*. Yet AIP were astute enough to garnish the flimsy premise with popular acts. Singer **Lesley Gore** famed for her teen-trauma classic 'It's My Party', made an appearance in *Ski Party*, as did Californian surf combo, the **Hondells**. More improbably, the film also featured **James Brown**, at that point largely unknown outside R&B circles. His sensational performance on the *TAMI Show* the previous year had helped popularise his impassioned style, but this was essentially an in-concert revue. *Ski Party* pitched the singer into a white teenage vehicle and this is perhaps the film's lasting testament.

Skibberean

A Swiss folk/rock band, whose members sing British traditional material. Their accents lead to some confusing lyrical moments, especially when they tackle traditional Geordie songs such as 'Byker Hill'.

Album: *Get Up And Dance* (1980).

Skid Row (Eire)

This blues-based rock band was put together by **Gary Moore** in Dublin, Eirre, in 1968, when the guitarist was only 16 years old. Recruiting **Phil Lynott** (vocals/bass), Eric Bell (guitar) and Brian Downey (drums) the initial line-up only survived 12 months. Lynott, Bell and Downey left to form **Thin Lizzy**, with Brendan Shiels (bass/vocals) and Noel Bridgeman (drums) joining Moore as replacements in a new power-trio. The group completed two singles, 'New Places, Old Faces' and 'Saturday Morning Man' - only released in Ireland - before securing a UK deal via **CBS Records**. Skid Row was a popular live attraction and tours of the US and Europe, supporting **Canned Heat** and **Savoy Brown**, augered well for the future. Their albums were also well-received, but Moore's growing reputation as an inventive and versatile guitarist outstripped the group's musical confines. He left in 1971 to work with the folk-rock band **Dr. Strangely Strange** and later on to the Gary Moore Band. Although Paul Chapman proved an able replacement, Skid Row's momentum now faltered and the trio was disbanded the following year. Sheils has, on occasion, revived the name for various endeavours, while Chapman later found fame with **UFO**.

Albums: *Skid Row* (CBS 1970), *34 Hours* (CBS 1971), *Alive And Kicking* (CBS 1978). Compilation: *Skid Row* (CBS 1987).

Skid Row (USA)

Hailing from New Jersey, USA, Skid Row were formed in late 1986 by Dave 'The Snake' Sabo (guitar) and Rachel Bolan (bass). Sebastian Bach (b. 3 April 1968, Canada; vocals; ex-**Madam X**), Scotti Hill (b. 31 May 1964; guitar) and Rob Affuso (drums) were soon added and the line-up was complete. Influenced by **Kiss**, **Sex Pistols**, **Ratt** and **Mötley Crüe**, the band's rise to fame was remarkably rapid. The break came when they were picked up by **Bon Jovi**'s management (Sabo was an old friend of Jon Bon Jovi) and offered the support slot on their US stadium tour of 1989. Bach's wild and provocative stage antics established the band's live reputation. Signed to **Atlantic Records**, they released their self-titled debut album to widespread critical acclaim the same year. It peaked at number 6 on the *Billboard* album chart and spawned two US Top 10 singles with '18 And Life' and 'I Remember You'. *Slave To The Grind* surpassed all expectations, debuting at number 1 in the US charts. Their commercial approach had been transformed into an abrasive and uncompromising barrage of metallic rock 'n' roll, delivered with punk-like arrogance. Afterwards, however, progress was halted by a period of inter-band squabbling which threatened to break the group. As Bach admitted to the press: 'I know I can be overbearing. But that's all changed now. Now people are in my face, giving their two cents' worth, making sure that everybody's vision is realised'. 1994 found them working on a new album, *Subhuman Race*, with production by Bob Rock.

Albums: *Skid Row* (Atlantic 1989), *Slave To The Grind* (Atlantic 1991), *Subhuman Race* (Atlantic 1994). Videos: *Oh Say Can You Scream?* (1991), *No Frills Video* (1993), *Roadkill* (1993).

Skidmore, Alan

b. Alan Richard James Skidmore, 21 April 1942, Kingston-on-Thames, London, England. 'Skid' plays soprano and tenor saxophones, flutes and drums. He is the son of Jimmy Skidmore, who gave him a discarded tenor which Alan ignored until he was about 15. At that time he decided to teach himself to play. A muscular and versatile player himself, the musicians he particularly admires include **Sonny Rollins**, **Dexter Gordon**, **Michael Brecker**, **Ronnie Scott**, **Andy Sheppard** and, above all, **John Coltrane**. Skid began playing professionally in 1958, and did various commercial engagements, including tours with comedian Tony Hancock and singer **Matt Monro** and five years in the house band at London's Talk Of The Town night club. In 1961 he made the first of many appearances on BBC radio's *Jazz Club*, and also met his idol, Coltrane. In the following years Skidmore worked with numerous important and/or successful bands, including Eric Delaney where he replaced his father when Jimmy decided to leave (in 1963), **Alexis Korner** (1964), **John Mayall**'s Blues Breakers (1964), Ronnie Scott (1965), **Georgie Fame** And The Blue Flames (1970), **Mike Westbrook** (1970-71), **Michael Gibbs** (1970-71), and **Chris McGregor**'s Brotherhood Of Breath (1971). In 1969 he had formed his own quintet, with which he won the best soloist and best band awards at the **Montreux Jazz Festival** and gained a scholarship to Berklee, though he did not take this up. In 1973 he co-founded S.O.S., probably the first all-saxophone band, with **Mike Osborne** and **John Surman**. He has subsequently had various small groups of his own, including El Skid (co-led with **Elton Dean**), SOH, and Tenor Tonic, and has worked with

the **George Gruntz** Concert Band, the **Elvin Jones** Jazz Machine, the Charlie Watts Orchestra, **Stan Tracey**, **Van Morrison**, Georgie Fame again, and with the West German Radio Band as featured soloist from 1981-84. In April 1991 he was reunited with Surman when they played as a duo at a benefit for Osborne.

Selected albums: *Once Upon A Time* (1969), with Mike Westbrook *Marching Song* (1969), *TCB* (1970), with Michael Gibbs *Michael Gibbs* (1970), *Tanglewood 63* (1971), with Chris McGregor *Brotherhood Of Breath* (1971), *S.O.S.*(1975), *El Skid* (1977), *SOH* (Ego 1979), *SOH Live* (1981), with Charlie Watts *Live At Fulham Town Hall* (1986), *Tribute To Trane* (Miles Music 1988), with Peter King *Brother Bernard* (1988), *From East To West* (Miles Music 1993). Compilations: *Jazz In Britain 68-69* (1971), *Alexis Korner And... 1961-72* (1986).

Skidmore, Jimmy

b. 8 February 1916, London, England. After teaching himself to play tenor saxophone, Skidmore played with Harry Parry, **George Shearing** and others, becoming especially active in the years immediately following World War II. He attracted attention as a member of the **Vic Lewis** Jazzmen and in the 50s played with **Kenny Baker** and **Humphrey Lyttelton**. During the 60s and 70s he continued to appear in clubs but with diminishing frequency. A combination of changing musical times and his own casual approach to his music militated against the success his talent deserved. In the mid-80s he was still playing in the London area and apparently taking the jazz world a little more seriously than in the past. His son, **Alan Skidmore**, also plays tenor saxophone.

Albums: *Humphrey Lyttelton Plays Standards* (1960), *Skid Marks!* (mid-70s).

Skids

A Scottish new wave band founded in Dunfermline in 1977 by Stuart Adamson (guitar/vocals, b. 11 April 1958, Manchester, UK), **Richard Jobson** (vocals) Tom Kellichan (drums) and Willie Simpson (bass). After issuing 'Reasons' on their own No Bad label, the group were signed by **Virgin**. David Batchelor produced 'Sweet Suburbia' and 'The Saints Are Coming' before 'Into The Valley' reached the UK Top 10 in 1979. Despite criticism of Jobson's lyrics as pretentious, the Skids enjoyed a further year of chart success as 'Masquerade' and 'Working For The Yankee Dollar' reached the Top 20. Both came from the second album, which was produced by **Bill Nelson** of **Be-Bop Deluxe**. Soon afterwards the band was hit by personnel changes. Russell Webb and Mike Baillie replaced Simpson and Kellichan and more crucially, the Skids' songwriting team was split when Adamson left after the release of the third album, which proved to be the group's most commercial, reaching the Top

10 and containing the minor hit 'Circus Games'. Without Adamson, *Joy*, an exploration of Celtic culture, was more or less a Jobson solo effort. The Skids dissolved in 1982, with *Fanfare* issued by Virgin as a mixture of greatest hits and unreleased tracks. In 1983, Stuart Adamson launched the career of his new band, **Big Country**. Richard Jobson recorded one album with a new band, the Armoury Show before pursuing a solo career as poet, songwriter and broadcaster. He released albums on Belgian label Les Disques Crepuscules and **Parlophone**.

Albums: *Scared To Dance* (1979), *Days In Europa* (1979), *Absolute Game* (1980), *Joy* (1981), *Fanfare* (1982). Compilation: *Dumferline* (1993).

Skillet Lickers

One of the most popular of string bands of early country music. The original members were James Gideon Tanner (b. 6 June 1885, near Monroe, Georgia, USA, d. 1962, Winder, Georgia, USA; fiddle/vocals), Riley Puckett, Clayton McMichen (b. 26 January 1900, Allatoona, Georgia, USA, d. 3 January 1970, Battletown, Kentucky, USA; fiddle/vocals) and Fate Norris (banjo/harmonica/vocals). The members had been performing in various combinations around Atlanta before 1924 but it was in that year that Tanner (a fiddle playing chicken farmer) and the blind guitarist Puckett recorded to become **Columbia**'s first hillbilly talent. In 1926, with McMichen and Norris they recorded for the first time as Gid Tanner And The Skillet Lickers. Over the years there were line-up variations and other important members included Lowe Stokes, Bert Layne (both outstanding fiddlers), Hoke Rice (guitar), Gid's brother Arthur (banjo/guitar) and teenage son Gordon (fiddle). By 1931, in some combination or other, they had cut 88 sides for Columbia - all but six being released. Their material included fiddle tunes, traditional ballads and pop songs plus little comedy skits such as their noted 'A Corn Licker Still In Georgia'. In 1934, Gid Tanner And The Skillet Lickers were credited with a million-selling record for their recording of 'Down Yonder' (Gordon Tanner was the featured fiddler on the recording). (In 1959 pianist **Del Wood** also sold a million with her version of this tune.) After the Skillet Lickers disbanded in the 30s, Tanner returned to chicken farming until his death in 1962. McMichen went on to a successful career with his own band the Georgia Wildcats (which at one time included Puckett) and held the title of National Fiddling Champion from 1934-49. Gordon Tanner who later led the Junior Skillet-Lickers, died following a heart attack on 26 July 1982. Bill C. Malone suggests that 'much of the band's popularity can be attributed to the energetic personality and showmanship of Tanner who whooped, sang in falsetto and in general played the part of the rustic fool'. McMichen is reputed to have suggested that 'Tanner's

fiddle playing was just as unrestricted and tended to detract from the overall quality of the band'. In the 80s, Tanner's grandson, Phil, led a band known as the Skillet Lickers II.

Albums: *Gid Tanner* (70s), *Gid Tanner & His Skillet Lickers* (1973), *Gid Tanner & His Skillet Lickers, Volume 2* (1975), *Kickapoo Medicine Show* (1977), *A Day At The County Fair* (1981), *A Corn Licker Still In Georgia* (80s).

Skin

The collapse of **Jagged Edge** led Myke Gray (b. 12 May 1968, Fulham, London, England) to form Taste with Jagged Edge bassist Andy Robbins, ex-**Kooga** vocalist/guitarist Neville MacDonald and drummer Dickie Fliszar, previously with **Bruce Dickinson**'s live band, in 1991. **Rory Gallagher**'s previous use of the Taste name soon led to a name-change to Skin. The band were content to ignore grunge trends and instead developed a more traditional melodic hard rock style, at times reminiscent of mid-80s **Whitesnake**, but with a fresh contemporary edge both musically and lyrically. Near-constant touring, including support stints with **Thunder** and **Little Angels**, helped the band develop a strong UK fan base, and Skin built on this, with the *Skin Up* EP and 'House Of Love' both doing well before 'Money' pushed them into the UK Top 20. Their self-titled debut album displayed the band's songwriting and musicianship to the full, with strong, bluesy vocals from MacDonald, and it deservedly hit the UK Top 10. The band successfully transferred their electric live show to the second stage at Donington in 1994, and scored another Top 20 single with 'Tower Of Strength', confirming their status as one of Britain's most popular rising rock bands.

Album: *Skin* (Parlophone 1994).

Skin Alley

This UK rock quartet - Bob James (guitar/saxophone), Krzysztof Henryk Juskiewicz (keyboards), Thomas Crimble (bass/vocals) and Alvin Pope (drums) - released their debut album in 1969. The set was produced by Dick Taylor, formerly of the **Pretty Things**, however, the group's workmanlike approach undermined any potential this pairing offered. Nick Graham (vocals/keyboards/bass/flute) joined the line-up for their second album, *To Pagham And Beyond*. Crimble subsequently left the group, as did Pope, who was replaced by Tony Knight. However, despite securing a lucrative deal with the American label, **Stax**, Skin Alley broke up following the release of a fourth collection, *Skintight*.

Albums: *Skin Alley* (1969), *To Pagham And Beyond* (1970), *Two Quid Deal* (1972), *Skintight* (1973).

Skin The Peeler

Based in Bristol, England, Skin the Peeler Bristol operated during 1984 as an excellent jazz/rock, Celtic slanted unit. Long time members, Terry Barter (mandolin) and Rod Salter (saxophone), revived the unit in 1989, and joined with Rose Hull (cello) to become an acoustic world beat band. The recent esoteric *World Dance* album contains influences from Eire, Africa, and Java, amongst others.

Albums. *Skin The Peeler* (1984), *Facing The Sun* (1989), *World Dance* (1991).

Skinner, Jimmie

b. 29 April 1909, Blue Lick, near Berea, Kentucky, USA, d. 27 October 1979. He relocated with the family to Hamilton, near Cincinnati, Ohio in 1926, where he found work in a factory. In 1928, he heard recordings by **Jimmie Rodgers** that so impressed him that he bought a guitar and set out to be a singer. He first broadcast on WCKY Covington and in the early 30s with his brother Esmer, he recorded two instrumentals for Gennett, though neither was released. Skinner began to write songs and continued to perform in his local area. In 1941, he was signed by **RCA** but again due to war-time material shortages he had no releases. During the next few years, he played regularly on several stations including WHPD Mt.Orab, Ohio and WHTN Huntingdon, West Virginia. He finally had record releases after recording for Red Barn Records although he had to handle distribution himself. His recording of 'Will You Be Satisfied That Way' was popular enough in Knoxville to get him a regular spot on WROL. In the late 40s, he and a partner took over the Cincinnati Radio Artist label and he issued several of his recordings including 'Don't Give Your Heart To A Rambler' (revived by Travis Tritt in 1991) and 'Doin' My Time'. The same year **Ernest Tubb** had major US country chart success with his song 'Let's Say Goodbye Like We Said Hello'.

In 1949, Skinner achieved his first chart hit with 'Tennessee Border'. In 1951, he was working both as a disc jockey on WNOP Covington and as an entertainer. He decided that there should be a special shop for the wants of country music followers and accordingly, with Lou Epstein, he opened *The Jimmie Skinner Music Center* in Cincinnati. The shop, which sold records, instruction manuals, song books and magazines by mail order, proved a tremendous success. He publicized the shop in trade publications and even presented live radio programmes from it. Other artists quickly realised the value and contributed adverts for their own records. He also later formed his own Vetco record label. The resultant publicity saw Skinner become a nationally known artist, although he had no major chart success during several years with **Capitol** and **Decca**. He joined **Mercury** in 1956 and the following year had a Top 10 country hit with 'I Found My Girl In The U.S.A.'. He had written the song as his answer to the **Bobby Helms** hit 'Fraulein'. Skinner then wrote an answer called 'I'm The Girl In The

U.S.A', which was recorded by fellow Mercury artist, **Connie Hill**. Between 1958 and 1960, he had 8 further country hits including 'What Makes A Man Wander', 'Dark Hollow' and 'Reasons To Live'. Skinner never became a major star but he was always busily connected with the industry through his music store and his radio and touring work. In 1974, he decided to move to Nashville; he thought it more suited to his songwriting ideas but he still continued to tour his beloved Kentucky and Ohio. It was on such an occasion that, following a show near Louisville, he complained of pains in his arm and immediately headed for his Henderson, Nashville home, where he died on 27 October 1979, presumably as the result of an heart attack. Noted writer John Morthland described his style as 'Unusually eloquent. He was probably the most underrated of those who sought to follow in the footsteps of Jimmie Rodgers and always less maudlin than most white country blues singers'.

Albums: *Songs That Make The Jukebox Play* (1957), *Country Singer* (1961), *Sings Jimmie Rodgers* (1962), *Jimmy Skinner (The Kentucky Colonel)* (1963), *Country Blues* (1964), *Jimmie Skinner's Number One Bluegrass* (1966), *Sings Bluegrass* (1968), *Have You Said Hello To Jesus Today* (c.1969), *Sings The Blues* (1975), *Bluegrass Volume 2* (1976), with Joe Clark *Old Joe Clark* (1976), *Jimmie Skinner And His Country Music Friends* (1976), *Number 1 Bluegrass* (1977), *Requestfully Yours* (c.1977), *Another Saturday Night* (1988).

Skinny Boys

Comprising brothers MC Shockin' Shaun (b. Shaun Harrison, Bridgeport, Connecticut, USA) and DJ Super Jay (b. James Harrison, Bridgeport, Connecticut, USA), plus their cousin Jock Box (b. Jacque Harrison, Bridgeport, Connecticut, USA). After first being drawn to the funk of **James Brown** and **George Clinton**, these young men were invigorated by the East Coast rap phenomenon. Super Jay grew particularly enamoured of **Grandmaster Flash**, and ditched his previous instruments (accordion and organ) to concentrate on DJing with a local partner. He was subsequently joined first by his brother, then cousin Jock Box, whose 'human beatbox' style resembled that of the **Fat Boys**' Darren Robinson. Indeed, the Skinny Boys moniker was a tongue-in-cheek reference to the latter band. Playing local skating rinks, they eventually came to the attention of Mark and Rhonda Bush. The former would offer the trio production, while the latter managed them and wrote their raps ('based on our ideas', the Skinny Boys claimed). In 1985, their first 12-inch single emerged, 'We're Skinny Boys'/'Awesome', on their manager's Bush label. A second single, 'Feed Us The Beat'/'Jock Box' saw them switch to Warlock, which also released their debut album. On the back of this exposure the trio were eventually signed to the Jive imprint. They would tour with the likes of **Jazzy Jeff And The Fresh Prince**, **Kool Moe Dee**, **Salt 'N'**

Pepa and, suitably, the Fat Boys, building a strong local following. Their second album, once again helmed by the Bushes, included 'I Wanna Be Like', which namechecked Prince, **Michael Jackson** and Bill Cosby as suitable role models. Despite the good intentions and strong start, the title of their final album for Jive in 1988 proved sadly ironic.

Albums: *Weightless* (Warlock 1986), *Skinny & Proud* (Jive 1987), *Skinny, They Can't Get Enough* (Jive 1988).

Skip And Flip

This US pop duo **Skip Battin** (b. Clyde Battin, 2 February 1934, Galipolis, Ohio, USA) and Flip (b. Gary Paxton, b. Mesa, Arizona, USA) met whilst attending the University of Arizona in the late 50s. Once known as the Rockabillies, they recorded on Rev as the Pledges and then as Gary & Clyde. Time Records picked up their Rev master 'Why Not Confess'/'Johnny Risk' and then moved them to its Brent label, with the more distinctive name Skip & Flip. Their recording of Paxton's song 'It Was I' went into the US Top 20 in 1959 and the follow-up 'Fancy Nancy' also charted. Their next release, a revival of Marvin & Johnny's R&B hit 'Cherry Pie' made the Top 20 but proved to be their last chart entry together. Paxton has since recorded under several names (including the chart topping **Hollywood Argyles**) for many labels. He has also had hits as a producer and label owner, including the two time charter 'Monster Mash' by **Bobby 'Boris' Pickett**. Paxton went into country music in the 70s and is now a noted personality in the gospel music world. Battin recorded on Indigo, May, Groove, Audicon and Signpost and played in the **Byrds**, **New Riders Of The Purple Sage** and the **Flying Burrito Brothers**.

Skip Bifferty

John Turnbull (guitar/vocals), Mickey Gallagher (keyboards), Colin Gibson (bass) and Tommy Jackman (drums) were all members of the Chosen Few, a popular beat group initially based in Newcastle-upon-Tyne, England. Vocalist Graham Bell was added to the line-up which assumed the name Skip Bifferty in the spring of 1966. The quintet made their energetic debut in August the following year with the excellent 'On Love', a song from their previous incarnation's repertoire. It was followed by two memorable examples of pop psychedelia, the last of which, 'Man In Black' was produced by the **Small Faces**' team of **Steve Marriott** and **Ronnie Lane**. Skip Bifferty's first album continued the melodic craftsmanship of those singles. Bell's assured voice soared over a rich tapestry of sound, resulting in one of the late 60s' most rewarding collections. The group's potential withered under business entanglements and an astonishing conflict with their proprietorial manager **Don Arden**. Although they tried to forge an alternative career as

Heavy Jelly, litigation over the rights to the name brought about their demise. Bell, Turnbull and Gallagher were later reunited in **Bell And Arc**, but while the singer then embarked on an ill-fated solo career, his former colleagues found success in **Ian Dury's Blockheads**. The band have subsequently become a cult item for UK record collectors.

Album: *Skip Bifferty* (1968).

SKO

In 1986 three top Nashville songwriters, Thom Schuyler, **Fred Knobloch** and **Paul Overstreet** formed the group, SKO. They were signed to Mary Tyler Moore's MTM label and had US country hits with 'You Can't Stop Love' and 'Baby's Got A New Baby', which was a number 1. Overstreet went solo the following year and Schuyler and Knobloch recruited Craig Bickhardt, but SKB only released one album in 1987, *No Easy Horses*, before they disbanded, their most successful singles being 'No Easy Horses' and 'Givers And Takers'.

Album: *SKO* (1986).

Skrew

Once described by *Alternative Press* magazine as 'the soundtrack to the Apocalypse', Texan industrial metal crew Skrew's unsettling take on atavism is concocted by Adam Grossman (vocals/guitar), Opossum (guitar), Brandon Workman (bass), Mark Dufour (drums), Jim Vollentine (keyboards) and Doug Shappuis (guitar). The band's origins can be traced back to the city of Austin in 1991 where they originally emerged as a duo, before expanding the group after the first album for live commitments. Singer, guitarist and lyricist Grossman remained the core of both incarnations. Tours with **Corrosion Of Conformity** and **Prong** in Europe followed, before a domestic jaunt prefaced studio work on a second album, this time as the full sextet. *Dusted* thus arrived with a three-guitar frontal assault, with outstanding tracks including the sharpened hardcore stance of 'Jesus Skrew Superstar', while the equally disturbing 'Godsdog' took a more experimental route.

Albums: *Burning In Water, Drowning In Flame* (Devotion 1992), *Dusted* (Devotion 1994).

Skull

This USA hard rock quartet was put together by ex-**Meat Loaf** guitarist Bob Kulick in 1991. Recruiting vocalist Dennis St. James, bassist Kjell Benner and drummer Bobby Rock, they adopted an approach that bridged the musical styles of **Kiss** and **Styx**. Signing to the independent **Music For Nations** label, they released *No Bones About It* to a mixed reception. The songs were strong and adequately performed, but were ultimately too derivative in their musical approach.

Album: *No Bones About It* (Music For Nations 1991).

Sky

A UK instrumental group founded in 1979 and devoted to fusing classical, jazz and rock music, Sky was led by virtuoso classical guitarist **John Williams** (b 24 April 1941, Melbourne, Victoria, Australia). Having already played concerts at **Ronnie Scott**'s jazz club, Williams formed the group with rock guitarist Kevin Peek, classical percussionist **Tristram Fry**, ex-**Curved Air** keyboards player Francis Monkman and **Herbie Flowers**, a versatile session bass player and composer of the novelty UK number 1 'Grandad'. In 1981, Monkman was replaced by Steve Gray. The group made an instant impact in Britain. Mixing original compositions with inventive adaptations of classical pieces, each of the first four albums reached the UK Top 10. *Sky 2* even headed the UK chart in 1980, aided by 'Toccata' a hit single taken from a Bach theme. European and Japanese concert tours were equally successful. *Cadmium* was more pop-orientated, containing the Alan Tarney compositions 'The Girl In Winter' and 'Return to Me'. After its release, Williams left the group which continued to record sporadically until 1987 when the group folded.
Albums: *Sky* (1979), *Sky 2* (1980), *Sky 3* (1981), *Forthcoming* (1982), *Sky 5 Live* (1983), *Cadmium* (1983), *The Great Balloon Race* (1985), *Mozart* (1987). Compilation: *Masterpieces - The Very Best Of Sky* (1984).

Sky Cries Mary

Formed in Seattle, their sound has often been descibed as sponge, as opposed to grunge. The 1995 line-up consists of Anisa Romero, vocals; DJ Fallout, ambient mix and turntables; Bennett James, drums; Gordon Raphael, keyboards; Marc Olsen, guitar and vocals; Joseph E. Howard, bass, sitar and mellotron; Roderick, vocals and lyrics. Two early members now perform with the **Posies** but this unit prefer a softer mantric approach quite unlike their obvious Hendrixisms. Their creative and original debut *A Return To The Inner Experience* contained mystic lyrics and tribal rhythms together with interestingly different versions of Iggy Pop's 'We Will Fall' and the Rolling Stones' '2000 Light Years'.
Album: *A Return To The Inner Experience* (World Domination, 1994).

Sky, Patrick

b. 2 October 1940, Live Oak Gardens, nr. Atlanta, Georgia. Sky's folksinging career flourished upon meeting fellow Native American **Buffy Sainte-Marie**. They toured together for three years, eventually arriving in New York's Greenwich Village during the early 60s. Sky's own recordings followed his appearance on Buffy's early work and one of his songs, 'Many A Mile', became the title track to her second album. Sky's debut featured both original songs and traditional material, a feature continued on his second collection. Pat was also actively involved in assisting the recently 'rediscovered' **Mississippi John Hurt** and his guitar work can be heard on several of the veteran bluesman's 60s sessions. It was not until 1968 that Sky released a third album, since when his recordings have been sporadic, partly through choice and partly because of the uncompromising nature of his later compositions. Unhappy with modern music, Sky has since restricted his performances to traditional and small-scale venues.
Albums: *Patrick Sky* (1965), *A Harvest Of Gentle Clang* (1966), *Reality Is Bad Enough* (1968), *Photographs* (1969), *Songs That Made America Famous* (1973), *Two Steps Forward One Step Back* (1976).

Skyclad

This innovative UK thrash-folk-rock crossover group were put together in 1991 by former **Sabbat** vocalist Martin Walkyier. Enlisting the services of Steve Ramsey (guitar), Graeme English (bass) and Keith Baxter (drums), they were signed by European label Noise. The debut, *Wayward Sons Of Mother Earth*, combined pagan lyrics, crashing powerchords and electric violin (curtesy of Fritha Jenkins) to startling effect. Press descriptions included citing them as the 'heavy metal equivalent of **Fairport Convention**', but they certainly offered a welcome alternative to run of the mill trad-rock.
Albums: *The Wayward Sons Of Mother Earth* (Noise 1991), *A Burnt Offering For The Bone Idol* (Noise 1992), *Jonah's Ark* (Noise 1993), *The Silent Whales Of Lunar Sea* (Noise International 1995).

Skyhooks

The amazing local success of Skyhooks can be attributed mainly to their sense of fun, strong local lyrics, excellent stage presence and well recorded albums produced by Ross Wilson. The band was formed in Melbourne, Australia in 1973 and immediately gathered attention with their stage act and songs. Fronted by a natural showman, Graham 'Shirley' Strachan (b 2 January 1952, Malvern, Australia; lead vocals), the band showcased the songwriting of Greg Macainish (b. 30 December 1951, Australia; bass) who used typically Australian anecdotes (not often seen in Australian work before) as well as the lead guitar work of Red Symons (b. 13 June 1949, Brighton, Australia). Symons had also perfected the comic use of his tongue in his stage act long before the arrival of Gene Simmons of **Kiss**. The line-up also included Bob Starkie (b. 26 July 1956, Australia) and Freddie Strauks (b. 21 October 1950, Melbourne, Victoria, Australia). The banning of six out of the ten tracks on the debut album from radio airplay, due to their sexual content and drug references, helped the band gain considerable free publicity. The second album saw them perform stronger instrumentally, with 'Love's Not Good Enough', but the highest charting single was the country-influenced 'All My Friends Are Getting Married', a theme with which many young adults could associate. Interestingly, the band now appealed to a wider cross-section of listeners rather than just the teenagers who idolized Strachan. The band's use of make-up and costumes made for good television and they were often featured on the national network. Although the band toured the USA with some success, they eventually lost their audience through apathy and the departure of a couple of original members. The loss of vocalist Strachan and replaced by Tony Williams at the beginning of 1979 was a setback the band never managed to overcome. Following their break-up, Strauks was the only member to keep playing regularly (with Jo Jo Zep And The Falcons, **Sports** and the **Bushwackers**), although Strachan had some solo success. Macainish went into production work while Symons has kept a high profile as the resident cynic and intellectual thug on various television shows. The band was reformed several times, each time resulting in a positive response and renewed record sales.

Albums: *Living In The Seventies* (1974), *Ego Is Not A Dirty Word* (1975), *Straight In A Gay World* (1976), *Tapes* (1977), *Guilty Until Proven Insane* (1978), *Live! Be In It* (1978), *Hot For The Orient* (1980), *Live In The 80s* (1983), *Latest And Greatest* (1990). Compilation: *Best Of Skyhooks* (1979).

Skyliners

This white vocal quintet comprised of members drawn from two Pittsburgh, USA groups. Jimmy Beaumont (lead vocals), Wally Lester (tenor) and Jackie Taylor (bass) had sung with the Crescents, while Janet Vogel and Joe VerScharen (baritone) were formerly of the El Rios. The new act reached number 12 in the US charts in 1959 with the poignant 'Since I Don't Have You', a much-covered classic marked by Beaumont's superb, sweeping delivery. The Skyliners later enjoyed two Top 30 entries with 'This I Swear' (1959) and 'Pennies From Heaven' (1960), but were quickly overtaken by newer, more contemporary acts. They did enjoy minor success in 1965 with 'The Loser', but the Skyliners became increasingly confined to the nostalgia circuit. Although Vogel retained a professional self-confidence, she was latterly beset by personal problems and committed suicide on 21 February 1980.

Albums: *The Skyliners* (1959), *Since I Don't Have You* (1963), *Once Upon A Time* (1971). Compilation: *Since I Don't Have You* (1991).

SL2

SL2 consist of two Essex-based DJs, Slipmatt (b. Matthew Nelson, c.1967) and Lime (b. John Fernandez, c.1968), joined by video 'stars' Jo and Kelly for live appearances. Already well established as DJs on the rave circuit, they introduced themselves to a wider audience with debut single 'Do That Dance', a more acid-influenced cut, and 'The Noise'. The impact proved to be small beer against that of the subsequent 'DJ's Take Control', which disappeared from its original 1,000 pressing on Awesome within two hours, before being picked up by **XL**. The song was built around a keyboard line from the Nightwriter's 1987 underground house cut, 'Let The Music Use You'. The b-side, 'Way In My Brain', hoisted one of reggae's most profligate bass lines, 'Under Me Sleng Ten'. It predicted the chart breakthrough of their next single, 'On A Ragga Tip', which brought the jungle style into the charts for the first time, and gave SL2 a Top 10 placing in their own right. This time it was built over a rhythm based on Jah Screechie's 'Walk And Skank'.

Slack, Freddie

b. Frederic Charles Slack, 7 August 1910, La Crosse, Wisconsin, USA, d. 10 August 1965, Hollywood, California, USA. A composer, pianist and bandleader, prominent from the late 30s until the mid-40s, who specialized in the jazz rhythm style, boogie-woogie. After attending the American Conservatory of Music in Chicago, Slack worked as a pianist and arranger with **Ben Pollack** and **Jimmy Dorsey** during the late 30s, before joining trombonist **Will Bradley**'s band in 1939. Together with drummer **Ray McKinley** (he was the band's co-leader) and arranger Leonard Whitney, Slack was instrumental in changing the band's style from ballads to boogie-woogie, and a year later they had their biggest hit with 'Beat Me, Daddy, Eight To The Bar'. Other successful recordings included 'Scrub Me, Mama, With A Boogie Beat', 'Down the Road A Piece', 'Rock-Bye-Boogie', 'Bounce Me, Brother, With A Solid Four', 'Fry Me, Cookie, With A Can Of Lard'. Slack left Bradley early in 1941 and started his own outfit on the west coast. In 1942 he had a big hit with 'Cow Cow Boogie', which had a vocal by the orchestra's regular singer, **Ella Mae Morse**. The record was the first of two initial releases on the brand new **Capitol** label; the other was 'Strip Polka' sung by one of the label's co-owners, **Johnny Mercer**. In the following year, Slack provided the backing for another Mercer hit, 'I Lost My Sugar In Salt Lake City', while his own successful records, through until 1946, included 'Hit The Road To Dreamland', 'That Old Black Magic' and 'Silver Wings In The Moonlight', the latter two with vocals by Slack's protégé, **Margaret Whiting**. 'Mr. Five By Five', 'Get On Board, Little Chillun'' and 'The House Of The Blue Lights', all featured vocals by Ella Mae Morse. The latter song was written by Slack; his other compositions included 'Cuban Sugar Mill', 'Riffette', 'A Cat's Ninth Life', 'Mr. Freddie's Boogie', 'Rib Joint', 'Rock-A-Bye The Boogie', 'A Kiss Goodnight' (a hit for Slack, and **Woody Herman**); and Slack's theme,

'Strange Cargo'. During the early 40s the orchestra featured in several musical movies, including *Reveille With Beverly* (in which **Frank Sinatra** had his first starring role); *Hat Check Girl, The Sky's The Limit, Seven Days Ashore, Follow The Boys, Babes On Swing Street* and *High School Hero*. In the early 50s Slack gave up the orchestra, and for the next decade played in a piano-duo team and with his own trio, in clubs and lounges, mostly around Nevada and the San Fernando Valley. In 1965 he died, of 'inconclusive causes', in his Hollywood apartment.

Albums: *Boogie-Woogie On The Eighty-Eight* (EmArcy), *The Hits Of Ella Mae Morse And Freddie Slack* (Capitol), with Will Bradley *Boogie Woogie* (Epic) (all c.50s).

Slade

Originally recording as the 'N Betweens, this UK quartet comprised Noddy Holder (b. Neville Holder, 15 June 1950, Walsall, West Midlands, England; vocals/guitar), Dave Hill (b. 4 April 1952, Fleet Castle, Devon, England; guitar), Jimmy Lea (b. 14 June 1952, Wolverhampton, West Midlands, England; bass) and Don Powell (b. 10 September 1950, Bilston, West Midlands, England; drums). During the spring of 1966 they performed regularly in the Midlands, playing an unusual mixture of soul standards, juxtaposed with a sprinkling of hard rock items. A chance meeting with producer **Kim Fowley** led to a one-off single, 'You Better Run', released in August 1966. Two further years of obscurity followed until their agent secured them an audition with **Fontana Records**' A&R head Jack Baverstock. He insisted that they change their name to Ambrose Slade and it was under that moniker that they recorded *Beginnings*. Chaff on the winds of opportunity, they next fell into the hands of former **Animals**' bassist turned manager, **Chas Chandler**. He abbreviated their name to Slade and oversaw their new incarnation as a skinhead group for the stomping 'Wild Winds Are Blowing'. Their image as 'bovver boys', complete with cropped hair and Dr Marten boots, provoked some scathing press from a media sensitive to youth culture violence. Slade persevered with their skinhead phase until 1970 when it was clear that their notoriety was passé. While growing their hair and cultivating a more colourful image, they retained their aggressive musicianship and screaming vocals for the bluesy 'Get Down Get With It', which reached number 20 in the UK. Under Chandler's guidance, Holder and Lea commenced composing their own material, relying on distinctive riffs, a boot-stomping beat and sloganeering lyrics, usually topped off by a deliberately misspelt title. 'Coz I Luv You' took them to number 1 in the UK in late 1971, precipitating an incredible run of chart success which was to continue uninterrupted for the next three years. After the average 'Look Wot You Dun' (which still hit number 4) they served up a veritable beer barrel of frothy chart-toppers including 'Take Me Bak 'Ome', 'Mama Weer Al Crazee Now', 'Cum On Feel The Noize' and 'Skweeze Me Pleeze Me'. Their finest moment was 1977's 'Merry Xmas Everybody', one of the great festive rock songs. Unpretentious and proudly working class, the group appealed to teenage audiences who cheered their larynx-wrenching singles and gloried in their garish yet peculiarly masculine forays into glam rock. Holder, clearly no sex symbol, offered a solid, cheery image, with Dickensian side whiskers and a hat covered in mirrors, while Hill took tasteless dressing to marvellous new extremes. Largely dependent upon a young, fickle audience, and seemingly incapable of spreading their parochial charm to the USA, Slade's supremacy was to prove ephemeral. They participated in a movie, *Slade In Flame*, which was surprisingly impressive, and undertook extensive tours, yet by the mid-70s they were yesterday's teen heroes. The ensuing punk explosion made them virtually redundant and prompted in 1977 the appropriately titled, *Whatever Happened To Slade*. Undeterred they carried on just as they had done in the late 60s, awaiting a new break. An appearance at the 1980 Reading Festival brought them credibility anew. This performance was captured on the *Slade Alive At Reading '80* EP which pushed the group into the UK singles chart for the first time in three years. The festive 'Merry Xmas Everybody' was re-recorded and charted that same year (the first in a run of seven consecutive years, subsequently in it's original form). Slade returned to the Top 10 in January 1981 with 'We'll Bring The House Down' and they have continued to gig extensively, being rewarded in 1983 with the number 2 hit, 'My Oh My', followed the next year with 'Run Run Away', a UK number 7 and their first US Top 20 hit, and the anthemic 'All Join Hands' (number 15). Slade are one of the few groups to have survived the heady days of glitter and glam with their reputation intact and are regarded with endearing affection by a wide spectrum of age groups. Which makes it seem churlish to point out that their creative peak is behind them.

Albums: As Ambrose Slade: *Ambrose Slade - Beginnings* (Fontana 1969). As Slade: *Play It Loud* (Polydor 1970), *Slade Alive* (Polydor 1972), *Slayed* (Polydor 1972), *Old, New, Borrowed And Blue* (Polydor 1974), *Stomp Your Hands, Clap Your Feet* (Warners 1974, US title), *Slade In Flame* (Polydor 1974, film soundtrack), *Nobody's Fools* (Polydor 1976), *Whatever Happened To Slade?* (Barn 1977), *Slade Alive Vol. 2* (Barn 1978), *Return To Base* (Barn 1979), *We'll Bring The House Down* (Cheapskate 1981), *Till Deaf Us Do Part* RCA (1981), *Slade On Stage* (RCA 1982), *Slade Alive* (Polydor 1983, double album), *The Amazing Kamikaze Syndrome* (RCA 1983), *On Stage* (RCA 1984), *Rogues Gallery* (RCA 1985), *Crackers - The Slade Christmas Party Album* (Telstar 1985), *You Boyz Make Big Noize* (RCA 1987). Compilations: *Sladest* (Polydor 1973), *Slade Smashes* (Barn 1980), *Story Of* (Polydor 1981, double

album), *Slade's Greats* (Polydor 1984), *Keep Your Hands Off My Power Supply* (CBS 1984, US title), *Wall Of Hits* (Polydor 1991), *Slade Collection 81-87* (RCA 1991).
Videos: *Slade In Flame* (1990), *Wall Of Hits* (1991).
Films: *Flame* (1974).
Further reading: *The Slade Story*, Tremlett, George (1975), *Slade In Flame*, Pidgeon, John (1975), *Slade: Feel The Noize*, Charlesworth, Chris (1984).

Slade, Julian

b. 28 May 1930, London, England. A composer, lyricist, librettist and pianist, Slade began to write when he was at Cambridge University, and his first two musicals, The *Meringue* and *Lady May* were presented by the Cambridge Amateur Dramatic Club. He then went to the Bristol Old Vic Theatre School, and in 1952 was invited by Denis Carey to join the company as a small part actor and musical director. In the same year he composed the music for a highly successful version of Sheridan's *The Duenna*, and it was at Bristol that he met Dorothy Reynolds, a leading actress, who collaborated with him on libretto and lyrics. Their long association began with *Christmas In King Street* and *The Merry Gentlemen*, written for the Theatre Royal, Bristol, and then, in 1954, *Salad Days*, which transferred to the Vaudeville Theatre in London. It continued to delight audiences until 1960, becoming the longest running British musical of its era. Slade played the piano in the pit for the first 18 months, while onstage, a magic piano in a London park caused passers-by to dance uncontrollably. The piece was typical Slade - a simple plot and inconsequential humour, accompanied by charming, hummable songs, such as 'We Said We Wouldn't Look Back', 'I Sit In The Sun', 'It's Easy To Sing', 'The Time Of My Life' and 'Cleopatra'. In 1956, *The Comedy Of Errors*, a comic operetta adapted from Shakespeare's play, for which Slade wrote the music, played a season at the Arts Theatre. It had originally been performed on BBC Television two years earlier. In 1957, Slade and Reynolds wrote *Free As Air*, which lasted for a over a year. This was succeeded by *Follow That Girl*, *Hooray For Daisy* and *Wildest Dreams*, which even contained a 'rock' number. However, these shows seemed out of place in the theatre of the 'angry young men'. 'Our shows went well out of town, but London didn't seem to want them,' Slade recalled. *Vanity Fair*, with lyrics by Roger Miller, faded after 70 performances at the Queen's Theatre, and Slade's first solo effort, *Nutmeg And Ginger* (1963), based on Francis Beaumont's 1609 comedy, *The Knight Of The Burning Pestle*, did not play the West End. Neither did some of the others, such as *The Pursuit Of Love* and *Out Of Bounds* (1973), although *Trelawney* (1972) stayed at the Prince of Wales Theatre for over six months. Slade received his warmest reviews for that show, the last time London saw his work until 1991, when a revival of his *Nutmeg And Ginger* opened to enthusiastic reviews on the Fringe,
at the Orange Tree Theatre in Richmond, Surrey, England.

Slam

Like so many techno operations, Glasgow-based Slam are a duo, comprising Orde Meikle and Stuart McMillan. And, again like others in the field, they do not limit themselves to one activity. They DJ regularly at the Arches and Sub Sub clubs in Glasgow, and are also responsible for running the pre-eminent **Soma** label, as well as remixing for **A Man Called Adam**, **Sunscreem** ('Love You More'), Perception, Mark Bell, **Botany 5**, **DSK** ('What Could We Do'), **Joey Negro** and **Kym Sims** ('Too Blind To See'). Slam took clubland by storm in 1992 with 'Eterna', repeating the feat in 1994 via their no-holds-barred revision of **Jean Michel Jarre**'s 'Chronologie 6'. After attending outdoor raves in Berlin, Holland, and Belgium, Jarre confessed he rather liked what they had done to his opus. Slam were less charitable: 'I read an interview with Jarre which gave me the impression that he's very excited about the European dance scene, but doesn't quite understand it and doesn't have the right contacts. So we had no qualms about ripping his track to pieces'.

Slapp Happy

Formed in Wumme, Germany in 1971, Slapp Happy was the confluence of three *avant garde* musicians; British-born **Anthony Moore** (piano/vocals), New Yorker **Peter Blegvad** (guitar/clarinet/vocals) and German vocalist/pianist **Dagmar Krause**. The trio enjoyed the patronage of art-rock outfit **Faust**, and recorded *Sort Of* at the latter group's studio, a converted schoolhouse. *Slapp Happy*, released on **Virgin Records**, offered an enthralling range of musical styles as the three individuals drew on their respective, contrasting heritages. Brecht, melodic pop and European literature abounded in a set which nonetheless remained highly accessible. The ebullient 'Casablanca Moon' proved highly enduring, while 80s' mavericks **Bongwater** revived 'The Drum' on *Too Much Sleep*. Slapp Happy became closely allied with the adventurous **Henry Cow** and the two units collaborated on *Desperate Straights* and *In Praise Of Learning*. However, both Moore and Blegvad became disenchanted with this arrangement and split from the collective in 1975, taking the Slapp Happy appellation with them. They then severed their partnership and embarked on equally fascinating solo careers. Krause meanwhile remained with Henry Cow until their disintegration later in the decade. She recorded *Babble* with **Kevin Coyne**, before recording several albums in her own right.
Albums: *Sort Of* (1972), *Slapp Happy* (1974), with Henry Cow *Desperate Straight* (1974), with Henry Cow *In Praise Of Learning* (1975).

Slater, Luke

b. c.1968, St Albans, Hertfordshire, England. Techno guru Slater mixes hair-raising darkside nuances with somnambulist ambient doodlings, occasionally revisiting the 303 sound with releases like 'Sea Serpent'. Of half-American, half-Korean descent, he is now based in Crawley, Sussex. Slater has recorded under a multitude of pseudonyms (Marganistic, Clementine, Planetary Assault System, Offset) for a variety of labels (**D-Jax Up Beats**, Spacehopper, **Loaded**, his own Jelly Jam). He has been heralded in some quarters as the UK torch bearer for the Detroit sound, particularly through his work with Planetary Sound Assault. However, as 7th Plain his music has mined a deeper shaft, and is in many ways divorced from dance music in any previous convention, alluding instead to classical textures. The presence of a strong strings quotient on the *Four Cornered Room* set prefigured the rise of the classical ambient movement that was beginning to take hold in the mid-90s.

Album: *X-Tront - Volume 2* (1993). As 7th Plain: *Four Cornered Room* (General Productions 1994).

Slaughter

When Vinnie Vincent's Invasion disintegrated in 1988, vocalist Mark Slaughter and bassist Dana Strum decided to start a new group under the name Slaughter. Recruiting guitarist Tim Kelly and drummer Blas Elias, they soon secured a deal with **Chrysalis Records** and recorded *Stick It To Ya*. With an approach that fused elements of **Kiss**, **Mötley Crüe** and **Bon Jovi**, their style was ultimately derivative, yet distinctive due to the stratospheric-like vocals of Mark Slaughter. Three minute blasts of memorable metallic pop, complete with rousing anthemic choruses was the usual recipe. Following support slots to Kiss on their American tour, the album took off and peaked at number 18, during its six-month residency on the *Billboard* album chart. A live mini-album followed, which featured live versions of songs from their debut release.

Albums: *Stick It To Ya* (Chrysalis 1990), *Stick It To Ya Live* (Chrysalis 1990), *The Wild Life* (Chrysalis 1992). Video: *From The Beginning* (1991).

Slaughter And The Dogs

Formed in Manchester, England, in 1976, this punk quartet comprised Wayne Barrett (vocals); Howard Bates (bass), Mike Rossi (guitar) and Mad Muffet (drums). One of the first groups to sign to Manchester's independent Rabid Records, the group subsequently won a contract with **Decca Records** for whom they released the glam/punk influenced debut album, *Do It Dog Style*. A dispute with their record company, combined with the departure of Barrett, saw them marooned back in Manchester. Adding Billy Duffy on guitar, they auditioned **Morrissey** as their new vocalist, before deciding to stay as a four-piece with Rossi singing. An unsuccessful relaunch as Slaughter convinced them to change their name to the Studio Sweethearts, but they fell apart in the summer of 1979. For a time they soldiered on with Barrett briefly returning as vocalist. He was later replaced by Ed Banger (Eddie Garrity) but soon after the unit folded. Duffy went on to form **Theatre Of Hate** and later joined the **Cult**. Slaughter And The Dogs did at least leave behind three enduring punk classics; their Rabid debut, 'Cranked Up Really High', and the terrace anthems, 'Where Have All The Bootboys Gone' and 'You're Ready Now'.

Albums: *Do It Dog Style* (Decca 1978), *Live At The Belle Vue* (Rabid 1979). As Slaughter: *Bite Back* (DJM 1980). Compilations: *The Way We Were* (Thrush 1983), *The Slaughterhouse Tapes* (Link 1989), *Rabid Dogs* (Receiver 1989).

Slave Raider

Formed in America in 1987 around the antics of vocalist Chainsaw Caine and his cohorts Nicci Wikkid (guitar), Letitia Rae (bass), Lance Sabin (guitar) and a drummer who called himself The Rock. At best they could be described as a poor man's **Twisted Sister** but lacked the talent to move off the bottom rung. Having recorded their debut album to be used as a demo **Jive Records** picked them up and Caine set his sights on taking the UK by storm. This included live performances where he would 'chainsaw' a large cardboard cut-out of **Rick Astley** in half. As a stage *coup de grace* it was neither particularly funny nor particularly original. Jive however pushed them hard with promotional videos and press coverage to little avail. They then put them in a London recording studio with Chris Tsangarides, but even the legendary producer could do little to help them and soon after the release of their second album Jive dropped them and they broke up.

Albums: *Take The World By Storm* (Jive 1988), *What Do You Know About Rock 'N' Roll* (Jive 1989).

Slayer

This intense death/thrash metal quartet was formed in Huntington Beach, Los Angeles, USA, during 1982. Comprising Tom Araya (bass/vocals), Kerry King (guitar), Jeff Hanneman (guitar) and Dave Lombardo (drums) they made their debut in 1983, with a track on the compilation *Metal Massacre III*. This led to Metal Blade signing the band and releasing their first two albums. *Show No Mercy* and *Hell Awaits* were undiluted blasts of pure white metallic noise. The band played at breakneck speed with amazing technical precision, but the intricacies of detail were lost in a muddy production. Araya's lyrics dealt with death, carnage, satanism and torture, but were reduced to an

indecipherable guttural howl. **Rick Rubin**, producer and owner of the **Def Jam** label teamed up with the band in 1986 for the recording of *Reign In Blood*. Featuring 10 tracks in just 28 minutes, it took the concept of thrash to its ultimate conclusion. The song 'Angel Of Death' became notorious for its references to Joseph Mengele, the Nazi doctor who committed atrocities against humanity (ironic, given that Araya has obvious non-Aryan origins). They themselves admitted to a right wing stance on matters of society and justice, despite being the subject of virulent attacks from that quarter over the years. *Hell Awaits* saw Rubin achieve a breakthrough in production with a clear and inherently powerful sound, and opened the band up to a wider audience. *South Of Heaven* was Slayer applying the brakes and introducing brain-numbing bass riffs similar to **Black Sabbath**, but was delivered with the same manic aggression as before. The guitars of Hanneman and King screamed violently and Araya's vocals were clearly heard for the first time. *Seasons In The Abyss* pushed the band to the forefront of the thrash metal genre, alongside **Metallica**. A state-of-the-art album in every respect, although deliberately commercial it is the band's most profound and convincing statement. A double live album followed, recorded in London, Lakeland and San Bernadino between October 1990 and August 1991. It captured the band at their brutal and uncompromising best and featured definitive versions of many of their most infamous numbers. However, it saw the permanent departure of Lombardo after many hints of a separation, with ex-**Forbidden** drummer Paul Bostaph stepping in. Lombardo would on to form Grip, working with **Death** mainman Chuck Shuldiner. 1994 saw the group work alongside **Ice-T** on a cover of the **Exploited**'s 'Disorder' for the *Judgement Night* soundtrack, before the unveiling of their long-anticipated sixth studio album, *Divine Intervention*.
Albums: *Show No Mercy* (Metal Blade 1984), *Hell Awaits* (Metal Blade 1985), *Reign In Blood* (Def Jam 1986), *Live Undead* (Enigma 1987), *South Of Heaven* (Def American 1988), *Seasons In The Abyss* (Def American 1990), *Decade Of Aggression-Live* (Def American 1991), *Divine Intervention* (American 1994).

Sledd, Patsy

b. Patsy Randolph, 29 January 1944, Falcon, Missouri, USA. One of ten children, she began to play the guitar and sing at the age of 10. She entertained locally when 15, performing as the Randolph Sisters with one of her sisters but soon followed a solo career. She was featured on the *Ozark Opry* and worked with a band on Austin's *Nashville Opry* before moving to Nashville in 1965. She joined **Roy Acuff** and toured with him all over the States, to the Caribbean and to Vietnam. Her performances led to solo spots on *Hee-Haw* and the *Mid-Western Hayride*. In 1961, she recorded for United Artists and in 1971 for Epic but failed to chart on either

label. She moved to Mega in 1972 and gained her first US country chart hit with 'Nothing Can Stop My Loving You'. Her biggest chart hit 'Chip Chip' came in 1974, the year she made her British debut at London's Wembley Festival as a support member of the **George Jones-Tammy Wynette** Show. When Jones' mother died suddenly and the two stars returned to the States without appearing at the Festival, she found herself more the star than the support and gained respect from the crowd for her fine performance with the Jones Boys. Surprisingly very little seems to have been heard from her since that time. After a minor hit with 'The Cowboy And The Lady' in 1976, her name was missing from the charts until 1987 when, recording on Showtime Records, she briefly charted with 'Don't Stay If You Don't Love Me'. It rather seems to have been she that didn't stay.
Albums: *Yours Sincerely* (1973), *Chip Chip* (1974).

Sledge, Percy

b. 25 November 1941, Leighton, Alabama, USA. An informal, intimate singer, Sledge led a popular campus attraction, the Esquires Combo, prior to his recording debut. Recommended to Quin Ivy, owner of the Norala Sound studio, Percy arrived with a rudimentary draft of 'When A Man Loves A Woman'. A timeless single, its simple arrangement hinged on **Spooner Oldham**'s organ sound and the singer's homely, nasal intonation. Released in 1966, it was a huge international hit, setting the tone for Percy's subsequent path. A series of emotional, poignant ballads followed, poised between country and soul, but none would achieve the same commercial profile. 'It Tears Me Up', 'Out Of Left Field' (both 1967) and 'Take Time To Know Her' (1968) nonetheless stand amongst southern soul's finest achievements. Having left **Atlantic Records**, Sledge re-emerged on Capricorn in 1974 with *I'll Be Your Everything*. Two 80s collections, *Percy* and *Wanted Again*, confirm the singer's intimate yet unassuming delivery. Released in Britain following the runaway success of a resurrected 'When A Man Loves A Woman', they are not diminished by comparison. In 1994 Sledge recorded his first all-new set for some time, the excellent *Blue Night* on Sky Ranch/**Virgin**, which majored on the Sledge 'strong suit', the slow-burning countrified soul-ballad, even though the sessions were cut in Los Angeles. The appearance of musicians such as **Steve Cropper** and **Bobby Womack** helped ensure the success of the album.
Albums: *When A Man Loves A Woman* (1966), *Warm And Tender Soul* (1966), *The Percy Sledge Way* (1967), *Take Time To Know Her* (1968), *I'll Be Your Everything* (1974), *If Loving You Is Wrong* (1986), *Percy* (1987), *Wanted Again* (1989), *Blue Night* (1994). Compilations *The Best Of Percy Sledge* (1969), *Any Day Now* (1984), *When A Man Loves A Woman (The Ultimate Collection)* (1987), *It Tears Me Up: The Best Of ...* (1992), *Greatest Hits* (1993).

Sledgehammer

Formed in Slough, Middlesex, England, by former school teacher Mike Cooke (guitar/vocals) in 1978, with Terry Pearce (bass) and Ken Revell (drums), the trio's first live appearance came as support to **Motörhead**. In 1979 they recorded the single, 'Sledgehammer', which proved to be their only hit and was reissued at least three times on different labels. To promote the single they toured with **April Wine** and **Budgie** and played the Reading Festival. They re-recorded the track for the *Metal For Muthas* compilation album and then spent much of the year on the road with **Def Leppard** and various **New Wave Of British Heavy Metal** packages. Their debut album, released in 1984, had been recorded during 1981 with help from John McCoy (**Gillan**). This failed to sell, as did the single, 'In The Queue'. Again, both suffered from comparisons to 'Sledgehammer', with the band unable to shake off the 'one hit wonder' syndrome. They soon faded away from the landscape, though they turned to matters more serious a couple of years later with 'Porno Peat' (an anti-pornography single) and concentrated on raising both money and awareness for women's rape centres and child abuse groups.
Album: *Blood On Their Hands* (Illuminated 1984).

Sleep

This San Jose, California doom metal trio draw from 60s and 70s influences including **Black Sabbath, Jimi Hendrix** and **Pink Floyd** to produce their own retro-styled brand of 'stoner' metal, a term derived from the band's smoking habits, even using suitably ancient amplifiers for an authentic early Sabbath sound. Al Cisneros (bass/vocals), Mat Pike (guitar) and Chris Hakius (drums) made their recorded debut with a cover of 'Snowblind' on the *Masters Of Misery* Sabbath tribute. After which they produced an awesomely heavy debut in *Sleep's Holy Mountain*, built on intense, weighty riffs and slow, lengthy song structures similar to early Sabbath, although, like contemporaries such as **Monster Magnet** and **Cathedral**, the delivery had a distinctly modern edge. Sleep's live performances continued the tradition of fearsomely heavy guitars as they toured the UK and Europe with Cathedral, **Cannibal Corpse** and **Fear Factory**, and played US dates with **Nik Turner**'s **Hawkind Experience**. A second album, *Dope Smoker*, was slated for release in Spring 1995, and remarkably comprises a single 37 minute long track.
Albums: *Sleep's Holy Mountain* (Earache 1993), *Dope Smoker* (Earache 1995).

Sleeper

Launched on the UK media primarily by dint of the provocative sexual statements of lead vocalist/guitarist Louise Wener (b. Enfield, Middlesex, England), these have somewhat eclipsed the contribution of fellow members Jon Stewart (b. c.1967; guitar), Andy McClure (b. c.1970, Liverpool, Merseyside, England; drums) and Diid (pronounced Deed) Osman (b. c.1969, Somalia, Africa; bass). The latter pair were recruited by creative axis, Wener and Stewart, after arriving in London from Manchester, where both had studied degrees in politics (and also become romantically linked). Their first gigs were played in October 1992, eventually signing to the newly invoked indie label Indolent the following year. Their debut EP, *Alice In Vain*, was recorded with **Boo Radleys/My Bloody Valentine** producer Anjeli Dutt at the helm. This set the group's agenda, Wener expressing her disenchantment with the austerity of feminism: 'Really women are as shitty and horrible and vindictive as men are'. Sleeper's musical perspective revealed urgent, stop-go punk pop close in construction to **Elastica**. February 1994 saw the release of *Swallow*, with a third EP, *Delicious*, following in May. However, it was 'Inbetweener' which brought them to the UK Top 20 the following year. The group's excellent debut album continued the fascination with matters anatomical, 'Swallow' and 'Delicious', which both reappeared, hardly requiring further exposition.
Album: *Smart* (Indolent 1995).

Sleeping Bag Records

New York City based rap label who first brought the world **Mantronix** and **Todd Terry**. The label was inaugurated by Willie Socolov and Arthur Russell when they released the latter's 'Go Bang' as Dinosaur L. The second single was 'Weekend' by Class Action. While that 45 was being plugged by Juggy Gayles, Socolov met with Gayles' son, Ron Resnick. Resnick would become vice-president of the company, as they went on to establish a rap platform which boasted **EPMD** before they defected to Def American. Other acts included **Joyce Sims** and **Cash Money And Marvellous**. Socolov and Russell were no musical purists, and were happy to describe themselves as: 'Two white, middle-class, Jewish hucksters'. Incidentally, Sleeping Bag was named after Socolov's ultimate bachelor behaviour - having a sleeping bag over his mattress to save making the bed. They opened a UK office through **Rough Trade** in 1990, but afterwards their influence waned.
Selected albums: Mantronix: *Mantronix* (Sleeping Bag 1985). Cash Money And Marvellous: *Where's The Party At* (Sleeping Bag 1988). T La Rock: *On A Warpath* (Sleeping Bag 1990).

Sleeping Beauty
(see **Disney, Walt**)

Slick

(see **Fat Larry's Band**)

Slick Rick

b. Richard Walters, South Wimbledon, London, England. Of Jamaican parentage, Walters moved to the USA at the age of 14, going on to attend New York's High School of Music & Art. By the time his solo career started, Slick had already enjoyed his five minutes of rap fame (as MC Ricky D) by backing **Doug E. Fresh** on his masterpiece, 'The Show'. Not the most enlightened of hip hop's rappers, as 'Treat Her Like A Prostitute' on his debut album confirmed, Slick Rick does, however, live up to his name on his more impressive numbers. These included his standard, 'The Ruler'. It was also impossible to argue with the superb production by Rich himself alongside Jam Master Jay (**Run DMC**) and Hank Shocklee and Eric Sadler (the **Bomb Squad**). His second album was recorded in just three weeks while he was out of jail on bail, and facing up to ten years for attempted murder (shooting his cousin and his friend, then undergoing a high speed car chase which ended in both him and his girlfriend breaking legs). It continued the jazzy rhythms of his debut, which would attain platinum status in his adopted US homeland. Rick's confident, efficient half-sung delivery also proved a powerful influence on subsequent rappers, including **Snoop Doggy Dogg**.

Albums: *The Great Adventures Of Slick Rick* (Def Jam 1988), *The Ruler's Back* (Def Jam 1991), *Behind Bars* (Island 1995).

Slick, Grace

b. Grace Wing, 30 October 1939, Evanston, Illinois, USA. A former fashion model, Grace Slick began a career in music by contributing recorder and piano soundtracks to husband Jerry's films. This experience was later enhanced by an interest in the nascent San Francisco rock scene and in August 1965 the couple formed the **Great Society**. This short-lived group combined melodic and experimental styles, but Grace quickly tired of their endearing amateurism, and joined **Jefferson Airplane** the following year, taking two renowned songs, 'Somebody To Love' and 'White Rabbit' with her. Slick's powerful, distinctive voice established her as the unit's focal point, as well as one of the era's best-known figures. Now separated from her husband, Slick began a personal and professional relationship with band guitarist **Paul Kantner**. Together they recorded *Blows Against The Empire* (1970 - credited to Kantner), *Sunfighter* (1971) and *Baron Von Tollbooth And The Chrome Nun* (1973) which many commentators feel superior to concurrent Airplane releases. Indeed commitment to such projects may have undermined the parent group, although *Manhole*, Slick's experimental solo debut, boasted a largely idiosyncratic

content. Dour and self-indulgent, the set's disappointments were deflected by the formation of **Jefferson Starship** whom Slick fronted until 1978 when alcohol-related problems resulted in her departure. *Dreams* nonetheless displayed a rekindled creativity and its success resulted in the singer rejoining her former colleagues in 1981. Grace maintained her own career with *Welcome To The Wrecking Ball*, but this heavy-handed collection merely reflected Jefferson Starship's slide towards AOR rock, rather than assert an independence. Despite the release of *Software*, Slick became increasingly committed to the parent group, now known simply as Starship. They enjoyed a series of highly-successful releases, including three US chart toppers, 'We Built This City (On Rock 'N' Roll)', 'Sara' and 'Nothing's Gonna Stop Us Now', the latter of which also reached number 1 in Britain. However, internal dissent culminated in 1989 with Grace leaving the line-up for a second time; she has since maintained a relatively low profile. Slick nonetheless remains one of the most charismatic artists to emerge from San Francisco's 'golden era'.

Albums: with Paul Kantner *Sunfighter* (1971), with Paul Kantner and David Freiberg *Baron Von Tollbooth And The Chrome Nun* (1973), *Manhole* (1974), *Dreams* (1980), *Welcome To The Wrecking Ball* (1981), *Software* (1984).

Further reading: *Grace Slick - The Biography*, Barbara Rowe.

Slik

A teenybop quartet who burnt brightly, and briefly, immediately before punk swept the slates clean. Slik may well have been long forgotten but for the fact that two of it's key members: **Midge Ure** (b. James Ure, 10 October 1953, Cambuslang, Lanarkshire, Scotland) and Kenny Hyslop (b. Kenneth John Hyslop, 14 February 1951, Braeholm, Helensburgh, Scotland) went on to take important roles in the new wave movement. Slik's origins were in the group Salvation, formed in Glasgow in 1970 by brothers Kevin and Jim McGinlay (b. James Anthony McGinlay, 9 March 1949, Lennoxtown, Scotland). Salvation started out as a blues rock band in the vein of **Ten Years After** but, in 1972, the brothers dropped all the other members and formed a new band using Ure, Hyslop, and Billy McIsaac (b. William McIsaac, 12 July 1949, Rothesay, Scotland; keyboards). Only drummer Hyslop had any real experience prior to Salvation having recorded an album with the group, Northwind, while working in Germany. McIsaac had been employed as a telephone engineer while Ure was an engineering apprentice by day and guitarist in several semi-pro bands by night, most notably Stumble. In April 1974, Kevin McGinlay left Salvation and later in the year they changed their name to Slik. Through their management company they became involved with songwriters Bill Martin and **Phil Coulter** and signed a contract with **Polydor**

Records. In January 1975, their debut single, 'The Boogiest Band In Town' was released and though it missed the charts, it also turned up on the soundtrack to 'teensploitation' film *Too Young To Rock* in July on which Slik appeared. By the end of the year the band were signed to Bell Records. The second single, an almost Gregorian chant-like song 'Forever And Ever' hit the top of the charts in February 1976. Dressed in their distinctive baseball shirts and with boyish good looks, Slik were plastered over the covers of teenage girls magazines and widely heralded as the Next Big Thing. However, their third single, 'Requiem', limped to number 24 to become Slik's final hit. A further single on Bell, 'The Kids A Punk', disappeared without trace as did one for **Arista** at the end of 1976. In March 1977, the remaining McGinlay brother departed for a career in cabaret and was replaced on bass by Russell Webb though he had only been in the band for a few months when they split. Ure and Hyslop put out a single, 'Put You In The Picture', under the pseudonym PVC2. The song later turned up on the only album by punk supergroup the **Rich Kids** - who featured Midge Ure as a guitarist. Meanwhile, Hyslop and Webb formed the Zones with Willi Gardner. They then formed the **Skids** with Hyslop eventually moving into the **Simple Minds** drum seat. Ure made a habit of appearing in various line-ups before making a notable impression upon **Visage** then, more successfully, **Ultravox** before stepping out on a solo career.
Album: *Slik* (1986).
Further reading: *Slik*, Tremlett, George (1976).

Slim Chance
(see **Lane, Ronnie**)

Slim Harpo
b. James Moore, 11 January 1924, Lobdel, Louisiana, USA, d. 31 January 1970. The eldest of an orphaned family, Moore worked as a longshoreman and building worker during the late 30s and early 40s. One of the foremost proponents of post-war rural blues, he began performing in Baton Rouge bars under the name Harmonica Slim. He later accompanied **Lightnin' Slim,** his brother-in-law, both live and in the studio, before commencing his own recording career in 1957. Christened 'Slim Harpo' by producer Jay Miller, the artist's solo debut coupled 'I'm A King Bee' with 'I Got Love If You Want It'. Influenced by **Jimmy Reed**, he began recording for Excello and enjoyed a string of popular R&B singles which combined a drawling vocal with incisive hamonica passages. Among them were 'Raining In My Heart' (1961), 'I Love The Life I Live', 'Buzzin'' (instrumental) and 'Little Queen Bee' (1964). These relaxed, almost lazy, performances, which featured an understated electric backing, set the tone for Moore's subsequent work. His warm, languid voice enhanced the sexual metaphor of 'I'm A King Bee',

which was later recorded by the **Rolling Stones**. The same group also covered the pulsating 'Shake Your Hips', which Harpo first issued in 1966, while the **Pretty Things**, the **Yardbirds** and **Them** featured versions of his songs in their early repertoires.
Harpo scored a notable US Top 20 pop hit in 1966 with 'Baby Scratch My Back' (also a number 1 R&B hit), which revitalized his career. Never a full-time musician, Harpo had his own trucking business during the 60s although he was a popular figure during the late 60s blues revival, with appearances at several renowned venues including the Electric Circus and the Fillmore East, but suffered a fatal heart attack on 31 January 1970.
Albums: *Rainin' In My Heart* (1961), *Baby Scratch My Back* (1966), *Tip On In* (1968). Compilations: *The Best Of Slim Harpo* (1969), *He Knew The Blues* (1970), *Blues Hangover* (1976), *Got Love If You Want It* (1980), *Shake Your Hips* (1986), *I'm A King Bee* (1989).

Slingsby, Xero
b. Matthew Coe, 23 November 1957, Skipton, Yorkshire, England, d. 16 August 1988. Coe's name change came in the mid-70s when punk rock made colourful stage-names *de rigueur*. He grew up in Bradford, where an accident at the age of 10 damaged his left hand: he took up the bass guitar as an alternative to therapeutic rubber-ball squeezing. He fell in with a motorbike crowd and played electric bass in numerous heavy rock bands. Sick of endless guitar indulgence, **Ornette Coleman**'s *New York Is Now!* was a revelation to him. He sold his **Fender** and **Marshall** amps and bought a double bass. He also acquired an alto saxophone. After spells as a grave-digger and a tractor-driver for Bradford Council, he attended a two-year course at Harrogate Music School, supplemented by gigs with tenor player Richard Ward. In 1979 Xero played in Ghent, the first of many visits to the more receptive European audiences. After a long apprenticeship playing Monk standards and free jazz, he formed a band called Xero Slingsby And The Works with bassist Louis Colan and drummer Gene Velocette. The idea was to present free jazz with punk-type brevity and was remarkably successful: the Works became part of the 'punkjazz' flowering in England that included **Blurt**, **Rip, Rig And Panic** and **Pigbag**. Baritone saxophonist **Alan Wilkinson** and drummer **Paul Hession** readily acknowledge their debt to Xero's inspirational belief in musical communication. After fighting brain cancer for three years - probably caused by his childhood accident - he died in 1988. The obituary in *The Wire* concluded: 'As jazz at the end of the 80s faces the twin temptations of purist pessimism or commercial betrayal, Xero's scorched alto sound, his booting lines and clamorous compositions, as well as his understanding of music as

event and spectacle, could well become the crucial lessons.'

Albums: *Shove It* (1985), *Up Down* (1986).

Slip 'N' Slide Records

Slip 'N' Slide was launched in the UK as a subsidiary of **Kickin' Records** for less hardcore tastes in 1993. The first record to cause a major ripple was Adonte's house track 'Dreams', mixed by Pete Lorimer. In the year of their inception they continued to plough a bold furrow with hits by Diggers ('Soweto', produced by Lyndsay Edwards of **Disco Evangelists** fame), the trance house of H.A.L.F. ('I Don't Need You Any More') and Soundscape ('Amoxa'), while club hits were provided by Boomshanka ('Gonna Make You Move', though the duo also record for their own Can Can imprint as Avarice) and Rock & Kato ('Jungle Kisses'). The label also licensed a compilation from German imprint Suck Me Plasma! (**Dance 2 Trance**, Norman etc.), and scored with Vivian Lee's 'Music Is So Wonderful' (remixed by **Fire Island**). Other artists include 3 Man Jury ('Digital Autopsy'), Decoy ('Open Your Mind'), John Bullock (whose 'Hendrix' sampled one of the great man's riffs), Men Of Faith ('Dance') and more.

Selected album: *Dance & Trance* (Slip 'N' Slide 1993).

Slipper And The Rose, The

Generally regarded as a disappointing attempt to musicalize the traditional *Cinderella* fairy tale, this film was made in the UK by Paradine Co-Productions (Executive producer David Frost; producer Stuart Lyons). Director Bryan Forbes's screenplay (written with **Richard M. and Robert B. Sherman**) had some delightful and endearing moments, but there were more than a few dull periods too in the running time of nearly two and a half hours. **Richard Chamberlain** was a suitably regal Prince Edward, and Gemma Craven gave a charming performance as the young girl who did - eventually - go to the ball. The list of supporting players contained some of the best and most distinguished actors in British films, theatre and television, including Annette Crosbie (Fairy Godmother), Edith Evans (Dowager Queen), Michael Hordern (King of Euphrania), Margaret Lockwood (Stepmother), Kenneth More (Chamberlain), and Christopher Gable, Julian Orchard, John Turner, Roy Barraclough, Valentine Dyall, and André Morell. The talented and prolific Sherman Brothers provided the score, which consisted of 'Why Can't I Be Two People?', 'What Has Love Got To Do With Getting Married?', 'Once I Was Loved', 'What A Comforting Thing To Know', 'Protocoligorically Correct', 'A Bride-Finding Ball', 'Suddenly It Happens', 'Secret Kingdom', 'He/She Danced With Me', 'Position And Positioning', 'Tell Me Anything (But Not That I Love Him)', and 'I Can't Forget The Melody'. It all looked beautiful, due in no small part to production designer

Ray Simm and the Technicolor and Panavision photography by Toni Imi. It was reissued in 1980 with 20 minutes cut.

Slits

This UK feminist punk group formed in 1976 with a line-up featuring Ari-Up (b. Arianna Foster; vocals), Kate Korus (guitar), Palmolive (drums; ex-**Raincoats**) and Suzi Gutsy (bass). Korus soon left to form the **Modettes** and Gutsy quit to team up with the Flicks. They were replaced by guitarist Viv Albertine and bass player Tessa Pollitt and it was this line-up that supported the **Clash** during the spring of 1977. The group were known for their uncompromising attitude and professed lack of technique, but their music was as aggressive and confrontational as the best of the punk fraternity. Their failure to secure a record contract during the first wave of the punk explosion was surprising. By the time they made their recording debut, Palmolive had been ousted and replaced by **Big In Japan** percussionist, Budgie (b. Peter Clark, 21 August 1957). Signed to **Island Records**, they worked with reggae producer **Dennis Bovell** on the dub-influenced *Cut*. The album attracted considerable press interest for its sleeve, which featured the group naked, after rolling in the mud. The departure of Budgie to **Siouxsie And The Banshees** (replaced by the **Pop Group**'s Bruce Smith) coincided with the arrival of reggae musician Prince Hammer and trumpeter **Don Cherry** (father of **Neneh Cherry**). A series of singles followed, including a memorable version of **John Holt**'s 'Man Next Door'. By 1981, the Slits had lost much of their original cutting edge and it came as little surprise when they disbanded at the end of the year.

Albums: *Cut* (Island 1979), *Bootleg Retrospective* (Rough Trade 1980), *Return Of The Giant Slits* (CBS 1981). Compilation: *The Peel Sessions* (Strange Fruit 1988).

Sloan

This Canadian grunge band originated at the Nova Scotia College Of Art in Halifax, where drummer Andrew Scott and bassist Chris Murphy linked with Northern Ireland-born guitarist Patrick Pentland and guitarist/vocalist Jay Ferguson. Sloan developed their own sound from a mixture of hardcore and grunge influences, producing a guitar-fuelled battery of short, sharp songs, releasing the *Peppermint* EP, recorded at a friend's house in Halifax, through their own Murderecords label. A lively performance at Canada's East Coast Music Conference brought the band to the attention of **Geffen Records**, who liked the EP and promptly signed Sloan. *Smeared* impressed reviewers and public alike, with the pop songwriting and vocal melodies counterpointed by Pentland's raw, aggressive guitar work. In spite of a low-key promotional approach, the record performed well as North American college radio picked up on 'Underwhelmed'.

Album: *Smeared* (Geffen 1992).

Sloan, P.F.

b. Phillip Gary Schlein, 1944, New York City, New York, USA. Sloan moved to Los Angeles as a teenager and in 1959 recorded his first single, 'All I Want Is Loving', for the ailing **Aladdin** label. When a second release, 'If You Believe In Me' failed to sell, Sloan began a career as a contract songwriter. In 1964 he joined **Lou Adler**'s Trousdale Music where he was teamed with fellow aspirant **Steve Barri**. Together they wrote singles for **Shelly Fabares**, **Bruce And Terry** and Terry Black, as well as Adler-protégés, **Jan And Dean**. Sloan and Barri composed several of the duo's hits and contributed backing harmonies under a pseudonym, the Fantastic Baggys. The pair recorded a much-prized surf album under this sobriquet.

The emergence of folk-rock had a profound influence on Sloan. By 1965 he was writing increasingly introspective material. The **Turtles** recorded three of his songs, 'You Baby', 'Let Me Be' and 'Can I Get To Know You Better', but passed on 'Eve Of Destruction', which became a US number 1 for the gruff-voiced **Barry McGuire**, despite an extensive radio ban. Folk purists balked at Sloan's perceived opportunism, but he was embraced by many as the voice of youth and a spokesman for a generation. The singer rekindled his own recording career with 'The Sins Of A Family' and the brilliant *Songs Of Our Times*. His poetic lyrics and love of simile provoked comparisons with **Bob Dylan**, but Sloan's gift for pop melody was equally apparent. The set included 'Take Me For What I Am Worth', later a hit for the **Searchers**. *Twelve More Times* featured a much fuller sound and featured two of Sloan's most poignant compositions, 'This Precious Time' and 'I Found a Girl'. He also enjoyed success, with Barri, as part of another 'backroom' group, the **Grass Roots**. When 'Where Were You When I Needed You' reached the US Top 30 in 1966, the pair put an official band together to carry on the name. By this point the more altruistic Sloan was growing estranged from his commercially minded partner and they drifted apart the following year. 'Karma (A Study Of Divination's)', credited to Philip Sloan, showed an artist embracing the trinkets of 1967, although the subsequent *Measure Of Pleasure* was rather bland. A lengthy break ensued, broken only by the singer/songwriter-styled *Raised On Records*, Sloan's last recording to date. Without a contract, he wound down music business commitments, prompting no less a personage than **Jim Webb** to mourn his absence with the moving tribute 'P.F. Sloan' from the 1977 album, *El Mirage*.

Sloan re-emerged from seclusion in 1985 with an appearance at New York's Bottom Line club. Here he was supported by Don Ciccone (ex-**Critters**; **Four Seasons**) and future **Smithereens**' member Dennis Dikem. In 1990 the singer re-wrote 'Eve Of Destruction' as 'Eve Of Destruction, 1990 (The Environment)', which was recorded by the equally-reclusive Barry McGuire. In November that year Sloan played at the annual National Academy Of Songwriters' convention. He received a standing ovation from an audience comprised of the best-known songwriters of a generation.

Albums: *Songs Of Our Times* (1965), *Twelve More Times* (1966), *Measure Of Pleasure* (1968), *Raised On Records* (1972). Compilation: with the Grass Roots *Songs Of Other Times* (1988).

Slowdive

Thames Valley indie band formed in 1989 by Rachel Goswell (b. 16 May 1971, Hampshire, England; vocals/guitar), Neil Halstead (b. 7 October 1970, Luton, Bedfordshire, England; vocals/guitar), Brook Christian Savill (b. 6 December 1977, Bury, Lancashire, England; guitar), Nicholas Chaplin (b. 23 December 1970, Slough, Berkshire, England; bass) and Adrian Sell (drums), who departed after six months to go to University. His replacement was Neil Carter, who also played with local Reading band the Colour Mary, until Simon Scott (b. 3 March 1971, Cambridge, England) joined permanently, having drummed for the Charlottes. While this was happening, Slowdive were creating a dreamy sound which frequently escaped analysis, but the main ingredients were floating harmonies and ripples of guitar effects within a traditional three-minute pop framework. Signed by a revitalized **Creation Records** on the basis of one demo tape, Slowdive made a surprising number of friends with what seemed to be a blatantly esoteric sound; indeed, by the summer of 1991 they had reached number 52 in the UK charts with the *Holding Our Breath* EP. However, something of a press backlash ensued over the following two years, as the 'Thames Valley' scene and 'shoe gazing', a name invoked to describe the motionless, effects-pedal driven dreamy pop of a welter of bands, fell from fashion. Contrary to expectations Slowdive's second album, *Souvlaki*, was named after a Jerky Boys' sketch in which a hotel receptionist is enrolled in an imaginary *ménage-à-trois*. Despite this, and **Brian Eno**'s production of three tracks, Slowdive remained widely perceived to be perennial **Cocteau Twins**' apprentices. Scott was lost at the end of 1993 because 'he got into acid jazz'. *Pygmalion*, created at Halstead's home studio, saw the group move into ambient soundscapes, including two tracks ('I Believe' and 'Like Up') for an American art house film.

Albums: *Just For A Day* (Creation 1991), *Souvlaki* (Creation 1993), *Pygmalion* (Creation 1995).

Sly And Robbie

Sly Dunbar (b. Lowell Charles Dunbar, 10 May 1952, Kingston, Jamaica; drums) and Robbie Shakespeare (b. 27 September 1953, Kingston, Jamaica; bass). Dunbar, nicknamed 'Sly' in honour of his fondness for **Sly And The Family Stone**, was an established figure in Skin Flesh & Bones when he met Shakespeare. They have probably played on more reggae records than the rest of Jamaica's many session musicians put together. The pair began working together as a team in 1975 and they quickly became Jamaica's leading, and most distinctive, rhythm section. They have played on numerous releases, including those by **U-Roy**, **Peter Tosh**, **Bunny Wailer**, **Culture** and **Black Uhuru**, while Dunbar also made several solo albums, all of which featured Shakespeare. They have constantly sought to push back the boundaries surrounding the music with their consistently inventive work. Sly drummed his first session for Upsetter **Lee Perry** as one of the **Upsetters**; the resulting 'Night Doctor' was a big hit both in Jamaica and the UK. He next moved to Skin, Flesh & Bones, whose variations on the reggae-meets-disco/soul sound gave them lots of session work and a residency at Kingston's Tit for Tat club. Sly was still searching for more however, and he moved onto another session group in the mid-70s, the Revolutionaries. This move changed the course of reggae music through their work at **Joseph 'Joe Joe' Hookim**'s Channel One Studio and their pioneering **rockers** sound. It was with the Revolutionaries that he teamed up with bass player Robbie Shakespeare who had gone through a similar apprenticeship with session bands, notably **Bunny Lee**'s **Aggrovators**. The two formed a friendship that turned into a musical partnership that was to dominate reggae music throughout the remainder of the 70s, 80s and on into the 90s.

Known now simply as Sly And Robbie (and occasionally Drumbar & Basspeare), they not only formed their own label Taxi, which produced many hit records for scores of well known artists but also found time to do session work for just about every important name in reggae. They toured extensively as the powerhouse rhythm section for **Black Uhuru** and, as their fame spread outside of reggae circles, they worked with **Grace Jones**, **Bob Dylan**, **Ian Dury** and **Joan Armatrading** among a host of other rock stars. In the early 80s they were among the first to use the burgeoning 'new technology' to musical effect; they demonstrated that it could be used to its full advantage without compromising their musicianship in any way. In a genre controlled by producers and 'this week's star', reggae musicians have never really been given their proper respect, but the accolades heaped on Sly And Robbie have helped to redress the balance. The fact that both have their feet planted firmly on the ground has ensured that they have never left the grass roots of the music behind, either. At the time of writing Taxi's latest beat/sound is tearing up the reggae world again. Sly And Robbie's mastery of the digital genre coupled with their abiding love and respect for the music's history has placed them at the forefront of Kingston's producers of the early 90s, and their 'Murder She Wrote' cut for **Chaka Demus & Pliers** set the tone for 1992, while 'Tease Mi' for the same duo, built around a sample from the **Skatalites** 60s hit, 'Ball Of Fire', was another significant UK chart success in 1993. Quite remarkable for a team whose successful career has already spanned three decades, with the promise of yet more to come.

Albums: *Disco Dub* (Gorgon 1978), *Gamblers Choice* (Taxi 1980), *Raiders Of The Lost Dub* (Mango/Island 1981), *60s, 70s Into The 80s* (Mango/Island 1981), *Dub Extravaganza* (CSA 1984), *A Dub Experience* (Island 1985), *Language Barrier* (Island 1985), *Electro Reggae* (Island 1986), *The Sting* (Taxi 1986), *Rhythm Killers* (4th & Broadway 1987), *Dub Rockers Delight* (Blue Moon 1987), *The Summit* (RAS 1988), *Silent Assassin* (4th & Broadway 1990). Compilations: *Reggae Greats* (Island 1985), *Hits 1987-90* (Sonic Sounds 1991). Productions: Various: *Present Taxi* (Taxi 1981), *Crucial Reggae* (Taxi 1984), *Taxi Wax* (Taxi 1984), *Taxi Gang* (Taxi 1984), *Taxi Connection Live In London* (Taxi 1986), *Taxi Fare* (Taxi 1987), *Two Rhythms Clash* (RAS 1990), *DJ Riot* (Mango/Island 1990), *Sound Of The 90s* (1990), *Carib Soul* (1990), *Present Sound Of Sound* (Musidisc 1994), *Present Ragga Pon Top* (Musidisc 1994). Black Uhuru: *Showcase* (Taxi 1979), *Sinsemilla* (Mango/Island 1980), *Red* (Mango/Island 1981), *Chill Out* (Mango/Island 1982), *Anthem* (Mango/Island 1983). Dennis Brown: *Brown Sugar* (Taxi 1986). Gregory Isaacs *Showcase* (Taxi 1980). Grace Jones: *Warm Leatherette* (Island 1980), *Nightclubbing* (Island 1981), *Livin' My Life* (Island 1982). Ini Kamoze: *Ini Kamoze* (Island 1984), *Statement* (Island 1984), *Pirate* (Island 1986). Sugar Minott: *Sugar And Spice* (Taxi 1986).

Sly And The Family Stone

This US group was formed in San Francisco, California in 1967. Sly Stone (b. Sylvester Stewart, 15 March 1944, Dallas, Texas, USA), Freddie Stone (b. 5 June 1946, Dallas, Texas, USA; guitar), Rosie Stone (b. 21 March 1945, Vallejo, California, USA; piano), Cynthia Robinson (b. 12 January 1946, Sacramento, California, USA; trumpet), Jerry Martini (b. 1 October 1943, Colorado, USA; saxophone), **Larry Graham** (b. 14 August 1946, Beaumont, Texas, USA; bass), Greg Errico (b. 1 September 1946, San Francisco, California, USA; drums). Sly Stone's recording career began in 1948. A child prodigy, he drummed and added guitar to 'On The Battlefield For My Lord', a single released by his family's group, the Stewart Four. At high school he sang harmony with the Vicanes, but by the early 60s he was working the bars and clubs on San Francisco's North Beach enclave. Sly learned his trade with several bands, including Joe Piazza And The Continentals, but he occasionally fronted his own. 'Long Time Away', a single credited to Sylvester Stewart, dates from this period. He also worked as a disc jockey at stations KSOL and KDIA. Sly joined Autumn Records as a songwriter/house-producer, and secured a 1964 success with **Bobby Freeman**'s 'C'mon And Swim'. His own opportunistic single, 'I Just Learned How To Swim', was less fortunate, a fate which also befell 'Buttermilk Pts 1 & 2'. Stone's production work, however, was exemplary; the **Beau Brummels**, the Tikis and the **Mojo Men** enjoyed a polished, individual sound. In 1966 Sly formed the Stoners, a short-lived group which included Cynthia Robinson. The following year Sly And The Family Stone made its debut on the local Loadstone label with 'I Ain't Got Nobody'. The group was then signed to Epic, where their first album proclaimed itself *A Whole New Thing*. However, it was 1968 before 'Dance To The Music' became a Top 10 single in the US and UK. 'Everyday People' topped the US chart early the following year, but Sly's talent was not fully established until a fourth album, *Stand!*, was released. Two million copies were sold, while tracks including the title song, 'I Want To Take You Higher' and 'Sex Machine', transformed black music forever. Rhythmically inventive, the whole band pulsated with a crazed enthusiasm which pitted doo-wop, soul, the San Francisco sound, and more, one upon the other. Contemporaries, from **Miles Davis** to **George Clinton** and the **Temptations**, showed traces of Sly's remarkable vision.

A sensational appearance at the **Woodstock Festival** reinforced his popularity. The new decade began with a double-sided hit, 'Thank You (Falettinme Be Mice Elf Agin)'/'Everybody Is A Star', an R&B and pop number 1, but the optimism suddenly clouded. Sly began missing concerts, those he did perform were often disappointing and when *There's A Riot Goin' On* did appear in 1971, it was dark, mysterious and brooding. This introverted set nonetheless reached number 1 in the US chart, and provided three successful singles, 'Family Affair' (another US R&B and pop number 1), 'Running Away' and 'Smilin'', but the joyful noise of the 60s was now over. *Fresh* (1973) lacked Sly's erstwhile focus while successive releases, *Small Talk* and *High On You*, reflected a waning power. The Family Stone was also crumbling, Larry Graham left to form **Graham Central Station**, while Andy Newmark replaced Greg Errico. Yet the real undermining factor was the leader's drug dependency, a constant stumbling block to Sly's recurrent 'comebacks'. A 1979 release, *Back On The Right Track*, featured several original members, but later tours were dogged by Stone's addiction problem. Jailed for possession of cocaine in 1987, this innovative artist closed the decade fighting further extradition charges.

Albums: *A Whole New Thing* (1967), *Dance To The Music* (1968), *Life* (1968), *M'Lady* (1968), *Stand!* (1969), *There's A Riot Going On* (1971), *Fresh* (1973), *Dance To The Music* (1973), *Small Talk* (1974), *High Energy* (1975), *High On You* (1975), *Heard You Missed Me, Well I'm Back* (1976), *Back On The Right Track* (1979), *Ain't But The One Way* (1983). Compilations: *Greatest Hits* (1970), *Ten Years Too Soon* (1979, a collection of re-mixes), *Anthology* (1981, compiles the group's Epic singles up to 1973), *The Best Of* (1992).

Small Faces

Formed in London during 1965, this mod-influenced group initially comprised: Steve Marriott b. 30 January 1947, Bow, London, England, d. 20 April 1991; vocals/guitar), **Ronnie** 'Plonk' **Lane** (b. 1 April 1946, Plaistow, London, England; bass), Jimmy Winston (b. James Langwith, 20 April 1945, Stratford, London, England; organ) and Kenny Jones (b. 16 September 1948, Stepney, London, England; drums). Fronted by former child actor Marriott, the group were signed to **Don Arden**'s Contemporary Records management and production and their product was licensed to **Decca**. Their debut, 'Whatcha Gonna Do About It', an in-house composition/production by Ian Samwell (formerly of Cliff Richard's Drifters) was a vibrant piece of **Solomon Burke**-influenced R&B that brought them into the UK Top 20. Within weeks of their chart entry, organist Smith was replaced by **Ian McLagan** (b. 12 May 1945, London, England), a former member of Boz And The Boz People. While their first release had been heavily hyped, the second, 'I Got Mine', failed to chart. Arden responded to this setback by recruiting hit songwriters **Kenny Lynch** and **Mort Shuman**, whose catchy 'Sha-La-La-La-Lee' gave the group a UK Top 3 hit. The Marriott/Lane composed 'Hey Girl' reinforced their chart credibility, which reached its apogee with the striking, Arden produced 'All Or Nothing'. The latter was their most raucous single to date; its strident chords and impassioned vocal ensuring the disc classic status in the annals of mid-60s UK white soul. The festive 'My Mind's Eye' brought a change of style, which coincided with disagreements with their record company.

By early 1967, the group were in litigation with their manager and found themselves banned from the prestigious television programme *Top Of The Pops* after Marriott insulted its producer. A final two singles for Decca, 'I Can't Make It' and 'Patterns' proved unsuccessful. Meanwhile, the group underwent a series of short term management agreements with Harold Davison, Robert Wace and **Andrew Oldham**. The **Rolling Stones**' manager signed them to his label Immediate and this coincided with their metamorphosis into a quasi-psychedelic ensemble. The drug influenced 'Here Comes The Nice' was followed by the experimental and slightly parodic 'Itchycoo Park' With their Top 10 status reaffirmed, the group returned to their blues style with the powerful 'Tin Soldier', which featured **P.P. Arnold** on backing vocals. For 'Lazy Sunday' the group combined their cockney charm with an alluring paean to hippie indolence; it was a strange combination of magnificent music hall wit and drug influenced mind expansion. Those same uneasy elements were at work on their chart-topping *Ogden's Nut Gone Flake*, which won several design awards for its innovative round cover in the shape of a tobacco tin. For their final single, the group bowed out with the chaotic 'The Universal' and the posthumous hit 'Afterglow Of Your Love'. By February 1969, Marriott decided to join **Peter Frampton** of the **Herd** in a new group, which emerged as **Humble Pie**. The Small Faces then disbanded only to re-emerge as the **Faces**. Successful reissues of 'Itchycoo Park' and 'Lazy Sunday' in the mid-70s persuaded Marriott, Jones, McLagan and new boy Rick Wills to revive the Small Faces name for a series of albums, none of which were well received. Subsequently, Jones joined the **Who**, Wills teamed up with **Foreigner**, McLagan played live with the Rolling Stones and Marriott reverted to playing small pubs in London. In 1989, Marriott recorded *30 Seconds To Midnight*, but was unable to forge a fully successful solo career. He perished in a fire in his Essex home in 1991.

Albums: *The Small Faces* (1966), *Small Faces* (1967), *There Are But Four Faces* (1968), *Ogden's Nut Gone Flake* (1968). Compilations: *From The Beginning* (1967), *The Autumn Stone* (1969), *Early Faces* (1972), *Playmates* (1977), *78 In The Shade* (1978), *For Your Delight* (1980). Films: *Dateline Diamonds* (1965). Further reading: *The Young Mods' Forgotten Story*, Paolo Hewitt.

Small, Drink

b. c.1934, Bishopville, South Carolina, USA. Small began playing guitar at the age of four and began his musical career while in high school, playing in secular groups and singing bass in a church choir. In the 50s he worked and recorded with the Spiritualaires of Columbia, South Columbia and *Metronome* magazine voted him Top Gospel Guitarist during his time with the group. In 1959 he returned to South Carolina and began working as a blues musician, recording the same year for the Sharp label. He has since recorded for his own Bishopville label, and for the Southland company, and he enjoyed a lot of attention following the release of a cassette album (from folk-blues to disco-blues), and followed it up with another well-received set a year later.

Albums: *The Blues Doctor* (1990), *Round Two* (1991).

Smalls, Cliff

b. 3. March 1918, Charleston, South Carolina, USA. Smalls graduated from Kansas Conservatory and worked for seven years with the Carolina Cotton Pickers before joining **Earl Hines**'s band (1942-46). In 1948 he worked as accompanist/musical director for **Billy Eckstine** and has over the years worked with many vocalists often on the R&B circuit he knew from his time with **Earl Bostic** in the early 50s. These vocalists have included **Clyde McPhatter**, **Brook Benton** and **Smokey Robinson** and the **Miracles** in the 60s. Since the 70s he has done more work in jazz with musicians like **Sy Oliver** and the New York Jazz Repertory Company, **Paul Gonsalves** and **Roy Eldridge**, **Buddy Tate** and the **Oliver Jackson** Trio.

Albums: with Sy Oliver *Yes Indeed* (1973), with Buddy Tate *The Texas Twister* (1975), with Oliver Jackson *Le Quartet* (1982), *Swing And Things* (1976), *Cliff Smalls* (1978).

Smalltown Parade

London, England indie quartet comprising Robert Moore (b. 1 November 1963, Haverhill, Suffolk, England; bass), Paul Bevoir (b. 29 May 1960, Islington, London, England; vocals/guitar), Simon Smith (b. 3 December 1958, Merton Park, London, England; drums) and Simon Taylor (b. 28 December 1960, Redhill, Surrey, England; keyboards). The band convened first in April 1980 when sleeve designer Bevoir invited Smith (ex-**Mood Six**) to see his collection of Corgi toy cars. Smalltown Parade were formed thereafter, though the original bass and guitar incumbents, drawn from San Francisco and Berlin, proved temporary. Just two months later the band's 'The Sunday Way Of Life' won Gary Crowley's BBC GLR Demo Clash for five consecutive weeks. In July this was released as a limited edition single on **Captain Sensible**'s Deltic Records, by which time the band had been augmented by the addition of Moore. Following a publishing deal signed in February 1991 with Japanese organization NTVM, 'And We Dance On' was released to strong critical acclaim. By May Taylor (also ex-Mood Six) had introduced himself to the band, and also befriended **Rolf Harris** at a party. The Australian master of the bilabong duly agreed to appear on the video to third single 'Watching Mary Go Round', painting a 20ft canvas of the group as they performed. A series of gigs ensued as 'token indie pop band' on *Number One* magazine road shows, Moore at one point being mistaken for a member of **Take That**, before a charity appearance alongside **Dannii Minogue** at London's Empire Ballroom. However, some of the band's impetus dissipated until in 1993 'Watching Mary Go Round' became a rejuvenated club hit in Japan, prompting Polystar Records to sign

the band for a debut album, *Get Beautiful*. Rave reviews in the Orient were commonplace but the band were unable to capitalise due to Bevoir's fear of flying. A second album followed a year later, again to an encouraging response, though by this time the sound was much leaner and more direct. It was followed by a Bevoir solo album, while 1995 saw work begin on a third Smalltown Parade set. Odds and ends were collected on a compilation by Tangerine Records.
Albums: *Get Beautiful* (Polystar 1993), *Faces* (Polystar 1994). Compilation: *Best Of* (Tangerine 1995). Paul Bevoir solo: *Paul Bevoir* (Polystar 1994).

Smart, Leroy

b. Jamaica. A distinguished vocalist of the hard-working, soulful school, Leroy Smart - the self-styled 'Don' - was orphaned at the age of two and brought up in Kingston's Alpha Catholic Boys School & Home - the first home for many of Jamaica's musical talents. His reputation precedes him as one of Jamaica's most outrageous and colourful characters and he is held in high esteem by the reggae fraternity, to the point where his name is often discussed not only in reverence but in awe. Consquently the stories of his struggles in life have assumed far greater importance over the years than his manifest vocal talents. He began recording in the early 70s and made the usual rounds of Kingston producers achieving success first with Jimmy Radway/Rodway and then with **Bunny Lee**, **Gussie Clarke** and **Joseph 'Joe Joe' Hookim** and many others. His stage shows were truly outrageous and were as famed as much for their acrobatic displays as his vocal pyrotechnics, while his agonised, mannered singing defied categorisation. He achieved classic status on a number of records throughout the 70s, including 'Pride And Ambition', 'Ballistic Affair', 'God Helps The Man' and 'Mr Smart'/'Happiness Is My Desire'. He continued to record in the 80s and on into the 90s too, hitting again with 'She Just A Draw Card' and 'I Am The Don'. His vocal power and forceful personality have always ensured that he is never far from the forefront of reggae music.
Selected albums: *Jah Loves Everyone* (Burning Sounds 1978), *Dread Hot In Africa* (Burning Sounds 1978), *Impressions Of* (Burning Sounds 1978), *She Love It In The Morning* (GG's 1984), *She Just A Draw Card* (Worldwide Success 1985), *Showcase* (Fatman 1985), *Live Up Roots Children* (Striker Lee 1985), *Bank Account* (Powerhouse 1985), *Musical Don* (Skengdon 1988), Propaganda (Burning Sounds 1988), *Talk About Friends* (1993).

S*M*A*S*H

Formed in Welwyn Garden City, Hertfordshire, England, this trio comprising Ed Borrie (vocals/guitar), Rob (drums) and Salvador (bass), actually date back to 1984, when the UK Miners strike was on and irrevocably altered Ed and Sal's political ideals

(although both were still schoolboys). Taking on Rob from a nearby squat, Sal moved over from singing to playing bass when the original bass player failed to turn up for rehearsals. To this day Sal still plays the instrument 'wrong side up'. Their first gig did not take place until early 1992, and by the following year the **New Musical Express** had decided they sounded like 'the **Stone Roses** on PCP', while two singles, 'Real Surreal'/'Drugs Again' and 'Shame'/'Lady Love Your Cunt' were released on their own Le Disques De Popcor Records. The second single was Single Of The Week in both the *New Musical Express* and **Melody Maker**. Its b-side was a repetition of Germaine Greer's celebrated feminist remark. Showcases like the 100 Club's New Art Riot gig in December 1993 and the NME's On Into 94 event placed them within the New Wave Of The New Wave movement, a description which the band thought of as 'bollocks'. In truth their reputation was built on tireless touring, and their popularity was enhanced by a cheap entry price policy. The 'buzz' was such that admirers included Billy Corgan (**Smashing Pumpkins**) and **Joe Strummer**, while the American label, **Sub Pop Records**, responsible for much of the grunge movement that S*M*A*S*H detested, tried to sign them. Instead they moved to Hi-Rise Records, releasing a mini-album six weeks later (compiling the first two 7-inch singles). A Top 30 hit, it saw them appear on *Top Of The Pops*, and the band later played the London Anti-Nazi Carnival on the back of a float with **Billy Bragg**. Censorship proved a problem over July's '(I Want To) Kill Somebody', which reached the Top 30 despite being on sale for only one day. Its impact was scuppered by BBC Radio 1 (the song included a hit list of Tory MP's, and was independently edited by the corporation to avoid offence). Their debut album was produced by Chris Allison (**Wedding Present**) in September 1994.
Albums: *S*M*A*S*H* (Hi-Rise 1994, mini-album), *Self Abused* (Hi-Rise 1994).

Smash Records

Founded in 1961 as a subsidiary of the Chicago-based **Mercury Records**, Smash enjoyed early success with **Joe Dowell**'s rendition of 'Wooden Heart', a US chart topper that year. **Bruce Channel**'s 'Hey! Baby' equalled that feat in 1962 while reaching number 2 in the UK. This engaging single featured a memorable harmonica sound later adopted by the **Beatles** on 'Love Me Do'. Smash enjoyed further chart entries in 1963 with the **Angels** ('My Boyfriend's Back') and British signing the **Caravelles** ('You Don't Have To Be A Baby To Cry'), before finding a consistent success with **Roger Miller** the following year. His homespun, laconic C&W was heard in a string of best-selling singles, including 'Dang Me', 'King Of The Road' (a UK number 1), 'England Swings' and 'Little Green

Apples'. Smash also enjoyed pop success with the **Left Banke**, whose original, baroque-styled, version of 'Walk Away Renee' reached the US Top 5 in 1966. However, the label was, by then, used increasingly as an outlet for 'southern' recordings, principally those by Houston-based producer **Huey P. Meaux**. Former rockabilly star **Charlie Rich** enjoyed fleeting chart success with 'Mohair Sam', but his spell at Smash is better recalled for the two exceptional albums he recorded while there; *Charlie Rich* and *The Many New Sides Of Charlie Rich*. **Jerry Lee Lewis** rekindled his failing career with several country-styled recordings including 'High-Heeled Sneakers' (1964), 'Detroit City' (1967) and 'What Made Milwaukee Famous' (1968), while Meaux subsequently brought protégés the **Sir Douglas Quintet** to Smash. They enjoyed a minor hit with 'Mendocino' (1969) as well as releasing several excellent 'Tex-mex'/blues albums. However, by 1970 Mercury had decided to discontinue Smash, assimilating options on those acts it wished to retain and dropping the remainder.

Smashing Orange

This initially promising band from Wilmington, Delaware, USA, specialized in loud garage group material flavoured with hardcore. Vocalists Rob Montejo and Sara Montejo were sibling college dropouts, though guitarist Rick Hodgson actually graduated in marketing. They all worked at a record store in Delaware, and established their permanent line-up only five days before their live debut. The other members were Tim Supplee (drums) and Steve Wagner (bass). Their first single was the critically lauded 'My Deranged Heart' on Native Records, while they made a deep impression on domestic audiences supporting **Lush** at the Marquee Club in New York. Their debut album arrived in the summer of 1991, confirming the band's potential, but when Native Records collapsed in the early 90s it left Smashing Orange in something of a quandry from which they have yet to emerge.
Album: *Smashing Orange* (Native 1991).

Smashing Pumpkins

Once widely viewed as poor relations to **Nirvana**'s major label alternative rock, Chicago, USA's Smashing Pumpkins, led by vocalist/guitarist Billy Corgan (b. 17 March 1967, Chicago, Illinois, USA) have persevered to gradually increasing acceptance and press veneration. Corgan's inspirations, the **Beatles**, **Led Zeppelin**, **Doors** and **Black Sabbath**, as well as a professional jazz musician father, add up to a powerful musical cocktail over which his lyrics, which frequently cross the threshold of normality and even sanity, float unsettlingly. The rest of the band comprises D'Arcy Wretzky (bass), James Iha (guitar) and Jimmy Chamberlain (drums). Smashing Pumpkins made their official debut with a drum machine at the Avalon club

in Chicago. Chamberlain was then drafted in from a ten-piece showband (JP And The Cats) to fill the percussion vacancy (Corgan had previously played in another local band, the Marked). The group made its debut in early 1990 with the release of 'I Am The One' on local label Limited Potential Records. Previously they had included two tracks on a Chicago compilation, *Light Into Dark*. This led the band to the attention of influential Seattle label **Sub Pop**, with whom they released 'Tristess'/'La Dolly Vita' in September 1990, before moving to Caroline Records. *Gish*, produced by **Butch Vig**, announced the group to both indie and metal audiences, and went to number 1 on the influential Rockpool College Radio Chart. Ironically, given the Nirvana comparisons, this came before Vig had produced *Nevermind*. However, it was *Siamese Dream* which launched the band to centre stage with its twisted metaphors and skewed rhythms. A Top 10 success in the US *Billboard* charts, it saw them joined by mellotron, cello and violin accompaniment to give the sound extra depth. However, these remained secondary to the pop hooks and rock atmospherics which have defined the band's sound.
Albums: *Gish* (Caroline 1991), *Siamese Dream* (Virgin 1993).
Video: *Vieuphoria* (1994).
Further reading: *Smashing Pumpkins*, Nick Wise.

Smif N Wessun

Brooklyn, New York, USA-based outfit, named after the famous gun-making duo, Smif N Wessun arrived as the second act on **Nervous** Records' subsidiary, Wreck, in 1993. Rappers Tek and Steele first broke vinyl cover with two tracks, 'Black Smif n Wessun' and 'U da Man', housed on **Black Moon**'s *Enta Da Stage* album. The association with the latter began when they used dancer Tracy Allan, who turned out to be Buckshot's sister, on stage in their early days. They would go on to support their mentors on their national tour with **Das EFX**. The production team responsible for *Enta Da Stage*, DJ Evid Dee and his brother Mr. Walt (aka Da Beatminerz), were also present for Smif N Wessun's debut single, 'Bucktown'. It would move over 75,000 units in its first three weeks of release.
Album: *The Shining* (Wreck 1994).

Smiley Culture

b. David Emmanuel, c.1960, London, England, of a Jamaican father and South American mother. Smiley gained his nickname at school where his method of chatting up girls was simply to ask for a smile. He served his apprenticeship with a number of local sounds before hitting the big time with south London's Saxon **sound system**, the home of a formidable amount of British reggae talent including **Maxi Priest**, **Tippa Irie** and **Phillip 'Papa' Levi**. His live reputation attracted the attention of record producers and his first recording for **Fashion** Records, 'Cockney Translation', featuring Smiley slipping effortlessly from Jamaican patois to a south London accent, touched a nerve and sold an unprecedented 40,000 copies. His follow-up 'Police Officer', again featuring the cockney and 'yardy' voices, did even better and reached the national Top 20 in early 1985. Appearances on BBC television's *Top Of The Pops* followed - a first for a reggae DJ - and Smiley was a 'star'. A major recording deal with **Polydor Records** followed. As well as hosting his own television show *Club Mix*, Smiley also found the time for a cameo appearance in the film *Absolute Beginners* singing **Miles Davis**' 'So What'. He continued to record, including some interesting collaborations with American hip hop artists. Smiley's importance is that he was among the first English based reggae artists to challenge the Jamaicans and succeed. The British public also took him to their hearts while the lyrics of 'Cockney Translation' are now used by teachers and lecturers to illustrate the effects and influence of immigration on the 'mother tongue'.

Albums: *The Original* (Top Notch 1986), *Tongue In Cheek* (Polydor 1986).

Smiley, Red

(see **Reno, Don**)

Smith

This Los Angeles-based group, initially called the Smiths, comprised of Gayle McCormick (b. 1949; vocals), Rick Cliburn (guitar), Alan Parker (guitar), Larry Moss (keyboards), Jerry Carter (bass) and Robert Evans (drums). Their brand of folksy pop is best heard on *A Group Called Smith*, which included their 1969 US Top 5 hit, a cover of the **Shirelles** hit, 'Baby It's You', produced pseudonymously by **Del Shannon**. The sextet also contributed their version of 'The Weight' to the million-selling soundtrack of *Easy Rider* when rights to the **Band**'s original version, as featured in the film, were withheld from the attendant album. By 1970 McCormick, Moss and Carter had been joined by Jade Hass (bass) and Ed Beyer (keyboards), but the group's short-lived fame was fading and they broke up soon afterwards, leaving McCormick to pursue a solo career.

Albums: *A Group Called Smith* (1969), *Minus Plus* (1970).

Smith And Mighty

Duo from Bristol, Avon, England, comprising Rob Smith and Ray Mighty who broke through in 1988 with two memorable cover versions of **Burt Bacharach/Hal David** songs, 'Anyone' and 'Walk On By'. Both were effortless, breezy interpretations of the originals, tuned up via dub house and hip hopt sylings, garnished with the sensitive addition of female vocals. **London Records** were first off the mark in signing them up, having previously worked on their own Three Stripe imprint (which also issued records

like Tru Funk's '4AM (The Lucid Phase)'. However, the momentum was lost when the debut LP for Bristolian artist Carlton bombed. Smith and Mighty's reputation for the Midas touch went down with that album, and in the fast-changing world of dance music they became yesterday's men. However, they persevered in relative silence (as well as fathering six children between them), re-emerging in 1994 with a new album and single, a cover of **Diana Ross**'s 'Remember Me', featuring their new vocal discovery, Marilyn. Their highly individual breakbeat style, which remained with them over the years, was to be sampled on the **U2** cover, 'Drowning Man', while elsewhere the album contained denser material akin to the 'jungle' movement. Underpinning it all, however, was the seismic bass which had characterised their early recordings, their philosophy on low frequency incorporated into the album' title.

Album: *Bass Is Maternal - When It's Loud, I Feel Safer* (London 1994).

Smith, Arthur 'Fiddlin"

b. 1898, Bold Springs, Humphreys County, Tennessee, USA, d. 1973. One of the 14 children of an old-time fiddle player, he started to play the fiddle at the age of four, and later the banjo, began playing locally in his teens. He seriously thought of a musical career around 1925, when he worked as a lineman for the railroad. Several of his siblings also played instruments and around 1929, he first played on the *Grand Ole Opry* with his guitar playing brother, Homer. In 1930, he teamed with brothers **Sam** and **Kirk McGee** and played the *Opry* as the Dixieliners, soon after giving up his railroad work and becoming a full-time professional musician. His excellent playing, coupled with the McGees' guitar and banjo, soon made the Dixieliners one of the most influential of the *Opry* bands, who even through the Depression were in great demand. Surprisingly they did not record together until reunited in the 60s. Smith recorded under his own name and was accompanied by the **Delmores**, probably because the record company initially thought that their name would attract even more attention.

He first recorded fiddle tunes for Bluebird Records in 1935, including his now famous 'Mocking Bird'. At the time they were not successful and to keep his contract, his next recordings featured vocals, with 'More Pretty Girls Than One' being very successful. He left both the *Opry* and the McGees in 1938 and relocated to Hollywood, where he appeared in b-westerns and toured with **Jimmy Wakely** and the **Sons Of The Pioneers**, played all over the States and wrote songs. In the early 50s 'Beautiful Brown Eyes', co-written by Smith and Alton Delmore, was a US country and pop hit for Jimmy Wakely and also for pop singer **Rosemary Clooney**. He eventually returned to Nashville in the late 50s, where he rejoined his old friends the McGees. This time they did record together and played numerous folk festivals and other concert appearances. Noted authority Charles K. Wolfe in *The Grand Ole Opry, The Early Years 1925-35* comments that 'Arthur Smith's fiddling style was more influential in the South than that of any other fiddler except possibly, Clayton McMichen'. This artist should not be confused with **Arthur** 'Guitar Boogie' **Smith** or Arthur Q. Smith (real name James A. Pritchett), a Knoxville songwriter, who sometimes co-wrote songs with **Jim Eanes**.

Albums: with Sam & Kirk McGee *Fiddlin'* (early 60s) *Arthur Smith & His Dixieliners* (1962), *Rare Old Fiddle Tunes (Fiddlin' Arthur Smith & His Dixieliners)* (1962), with Sam & Kirk McGee *Old Timers Of The Grand Ole Opry* (1964), McGee Brothers and Arthur Smith *Milk 'Em In The Evening Blues* (1965), *Fiddlin' Arthur Smith, Volume 1 & 2* (1978).

Smith, Arthur

b. 1 April 1921, Clinton, South Carolina, USA. After the family moved to Kershaw when he was four years old, his father ran the town band and his son played trumpet with it. A few years later, by now playing guitar, mandolin and banjo, he formed a country band with two of his brothers. He graduated with honours in the late 30s but turned down lucrative employment, deciding instead to form a Dixieland Jazz Band, the Crackerjacks, which played on WSPA Spartanburg. After his brothers were drafted, he worked on WBT Charlotte, until joining the Navy in 1944. He played in the Navy band, wrote songs and on his return to civilian life organised variety shows featuring country and gospel music on WBT and WBT-TV and in 1947, also gave bible classes. In 1948, he achieved Top 10 US country chart success with his **MGM** recordings of 'Guitar Boogie' and 'Banjo Boogie', with the former crossing over to the US pop chart, introducing many people to the potential of the electric guitar. (***Billboard*** initially seemed unsure in which chart to place the recording.) **Fender** began to produce his 'Broadcaster' model, soon changing the name to 'Telecaster', the start of that instrument's popularity. The following year 'Boomerang', another guitar instrumental, became a country hit. (In 1959, 'Guitar Boogie' was a US and UK pop hit for the **Virtues** and the same year became British guitarist **Bert Weedon**'s first UK pop hit, although both recorded it as 'Guitar Boogie Shuffle'.) *The Arthur Smith Show* on television started in the 50s and became so popular that by the mid-70s, it was still networked to most of the States; artists from all fields were eager guests. Smith and the Crackerjacks (no longer a jazz band) recorded regularly over the years for various labels with gospel music always prominent. Smith later became a deacon in a Baptist church.

By the 70s, he had also extended his business interests to include record, show and commercial productions and was also a director of a large insurance company. For a time in the mid-70s, he even ran a chain of supermarkets and formed the Arthur Smith Inns Corporation. In 1973, he and banjoist Don Reno instigated legal action against **Warner Brothers** over the use of 'Duellin' Banjos' as the theme music for the film *Deliverance*. They claimed that the music was based on a tune called 'Feudin' Banjos', written by Smith and recorded by them in 1955. After approximately two years of legal wrangling they won the case, received damages and legal rulings about future royalties. 'Duellin' Banjos' was named 'Best Country Music Song Of The Year' in 1973. The following year **George Hamilton IV** recorded his Bluegrass Gospel album at Smith's recording studio in Charlotte, North Carolina. Smith has copyrighted more than 500 songs, only one of which, 'Our Pilot Knows The Sea', is co-authored. In 1991, he published his first book, *Apply It To Life*. It includes the words and music to 10 of his best-known hymns, which have also been released as an album with vocals by **Johnny Cash**, George Beverly Shea, George Hamilton IV and Smith himself with the Crossroads Quartet. This artist should not be confused with **Fiddlin' Arthur Smith** or with Arthur Q. Smith (real name James A. Pritchett), a Knoxville songwriter, who sometimes co-wrote songs with **Jim Eanes**.

Albums: *Foolish Questions* (1955), *Specials* (1955), *Fingers On Fire* (1958), *Mr Guitar* (1962), *Arthur Smith And The Crossroads Quartet* (1962), *Arthur 'Guitar Boogie' Smith Goes To Town* (1963), *In Person* (1963), *Arthur 'Guitar' Smith And Voices* (1963), *The Arthur Smith Show* (1964), *Original Guitar Boogie* (1964), *Down Home With Arthur 'Guitar Boogie' Smith* (1964), *Great Country & Western Hits* (1965), *Arthur Smith & Son* (1966), *Presents A Tribute To Jim Reeves* (1966), *Guitar Boogie* (1968), *The Guitars Of Arthur 'Guitar Boogie' Smith* (1968), *Arthur Smith* (1970), *Battling Banjos* (1973), with George Hamilton IV *Singing On The Mountain* (1973), *Guitars Galore* (1975), *Feudin' Again* with Don Reno (1979), *Jumpin' Guitar* (1987), with Johnny Cash, George Beverly Shea and George Hamilton IV *Apply It To Life* (1991).

Further reading: *Apply It To Life*, Arthur Smith.

Smith, Bessie

b. 15 April 1894, Chattanooga, Tennessee, USA, d. 26 September 1937. In her childhood, Smith sang on street corners before joining a touring black minstrel show as a dancer. Also in the show was **Ma Rainey** and before long the young newcomer was also singing the blues. The older woman encouraged Smith, despite the fact that even at this early stage in her career her powerful voice was clearly heralding a major talent who would one day surpass Rainey. By 1920 Smith was headlining a touring show and was well on the way to becoming the finest singer of the blues the USA would ever hear. Despite changing fashions in music in the northern cities of New York and Chicago, Smith was a success wherever she performed and earning her billing as the Empress of the Blues. For all her successes elsewhere, however, her real empire was in the South, where she played theatres on the Theatre Owners' Booking Association circuit, packing in the crowds for every show. Although she was not among the first blues singers to make records, when she did they sold in huge numbers, rescuing more than one recording company from the brink of bankruptcy. The records, on which her accompanists included **Louis Armstrong** and **Joe Smith**, consolidated her position as the leading blues singer of her generation, but here too fashion dictated a shift in attitude. By 1928 her recording career was effectively over and personal problems, which stemmed from drink and poor judgement over her male companions, helped begin a drift from centre-stage. It was during this fallow period that she made her only film appearance, in *St Louis Blues* (1929), with **James P. Johnson** and members of the recently disbanded **Fletcher Henderson** Orchestra. She continued to perform, however, still attracting a faithful if diminished following. In 1933 **John Hammond** organized a record date, on which she was accompanied by, amongst others, **Jack Teagarden** and **Coleman Hawkins**, which proved to be her last. The following year she was in a highly successful touring show and in 1935 appeared at the **Apollo** Theatre in New York to great acclaim. In her private life she had a new companion, a showbiz-loving bootlegger named Richard Morgan, an uncle of **Lionel Hampton**, who brought her new stability. With the growing reawakening of interest in the earlier traditions of American music and another film planned, this should have been the moment for Smith's career to revive, but on 26 September 1937 she was fatally injured while being driven by Morgan to an engagement in Mississippi.

Smith's recordings range from uproarious vaudeville songs to slow blues; to the former she brought a reflection of her own frequently bawdy lifestyle, while the latter are invariably imbued with deeply felt emotions. All are delivered in a rich contralto matched by a majestic delivery. Every one of her recordings is worthy of attention, but especially important to an understanding of the blues and Smith's paramount position in its history are those made with Armstrong and Smith. Even in such stellar company, however, it is the singer who holds the attention. She was always in complete control, customarily refusing to work with a drummer and determinedly setting her own, usually slow, tempos. Indeed, on some recordings her entrance, after an opening chorus by her accompanists, noticeably slows the tempo. On her final record date she makes a gesture towards compromise by recording with musicians attuned to the imminent swing era, but she is still in charge. Her influence is impossible to

measure, so many of her contemporaries drew from her that almost all subsequent singers in the blues field and in some areas of jazz have stylistic links with the 'Empress of the Blues'. Many years after her death she was still the subject of plays and books, several of which perpetuated the myth that her death was a result of racial prejudice or used her to promulgate views not necessarily relevant to the singer's life. Fortunately, one of the books, Chris Albertson's *Bessie*, is an immaculately researched and well-written account of the life, times and music of one of the greatest figures in the history of American music.

Selected albums: *Any Woman's Blues (1923-30)* (1974), *Nobody's Blues But Mine (1925-27)* (1979), *St Louis Blues (1929)* (1981, film soundtrack), *The Bessie Smith Collection - 20 Golden Greats* (1985), *The Empresss (1924-28)* (1986), *Jazz Classics In Digital Stereo* (1986), *The World's Greatest Blues Singer* (1987), *The Bessie Smith Story (1924-33)* (1989).

Further reading: *Bessie Smith*, Oliver, Paul (1961), *Somebody's Angel Child: The Story Of Bessie Smith*, Moore, Carman (1969), *Bessie*, Albertson, Chris (1972), *Bessie Smith: Empress Of The Blues*, Feinstein, Elaine (1990).

Smith, Betty

b. 6 July 1929, Sileby, Lincolnshire, England. After studying piano and tenor saxophone as a child, Smith concentrated on the latter instrument at the start of her professional career. In the early 50s she played in **Freddy Randall**'s popular traditional band, but her real forte was in the mainstream. From the late 50s she regularly led her own small group and also played and sang with the **Ted Heath** band. Her solo career continued through the next two decades and in the 70s she was one of the highlights of the touring package, 'The Best Of British Jazz'. In the 80s she was still active and playing as well as ever. An outstanding performer, Smith is one of only a few women of her generation to successfully overcome the offensive yet seemingly immovable prejudice against women instrumentalists in jazz. The quality of her playing and the high standards she has set herself reveal the absurdity of such prejudices.

Albums: with others *The Best Of British Jazz* (1981), with others *The Very Best Of British Jazz* (1984).

Smith, Bill

b. 12 May 1938, Bristol, England. A jazz fan from childhood, Smith began to learn trumpet and drums, turning to soprano saxophone only in 1966, three years after he had moved to Toronto. Influenced by 60s free jazz and by the new music from Chicago's **AACM**, Smith played a prominent role in Canada's contemporary jazz scene of the 70s, working with various ensembles such as the All Time Sound Effects Orchestra, the *avant garde* Jazz Revival Band, the CCMC and Air Raid. In 1976 he recorded a set of duos with pianist Stuart Broomer, then in the late 70s formed a trio with David Lee (bass, cello) and David Prentice (violin). Originally called the New Art Music Ensemble (N.A.M.E.), they later became the Bill Smith Ensemble, recording two albums themselves and one each with guests **Leo Smith** and **Joe McPhee**. Also a well-known photographer and writer, Smith has long been co-publisher and editor of *Coda*, since the 60s one of the world's leading jazz magazines; is co-owner of Sackville Recordings; and was a founder of the Onari label (named after his wife, who co-runs it with him). He is also the originator of *Imagine The Sound* - a series of five (to date) projects that have included two photographic exhibitions, a set of jazz postcards, a film (featuring **Paul Bley**, **Bill Dixon**, **Archie Shepp** and **Cecil Taylor**) and a book of his photographs and writings. In 1988, he toured and recorded with the international saxophone sextet, Six Winds, but was not with them on their second album. (This artist should not be confused with the USA saxophonist/clarinettist Bill Smith, best known for his work with **Dave Brubeck**.)

Albums: with Stuart Broomer *Conversation Pieces* (1976), *Pick A Number* (1980), *The Subtle Deceit Of The Quick Gloved Hand* (1981), with Leo Smith *Rastafari* (1984), with Joe McPhee *Visitation* (1985, rec 1983), with Six Winds *Elephants Can Dance* (1988).

Further reading: *Imagine The Sound*, Bill Smith.

Smith, Bill 'Major'

b. Checotah, Oklahoma, USA. 'Major' Bill Smith (the nickname was due to a stint in the US Army) was a top record producer in Texas during the early 60s. His career started as a songwriter ('Twenty Feet Of Muddy Water', a country hit for **Sonny James**). In 1957 Smith went to work for Don Robey, owner of the Duke Records group of labels, producing rockabilly and R&B records, most notably the hit 'So Tough' by the Casuals. He formed his own LeCam label in 1959 and produced his first major hit in 1962 with **Bruce Channel**'s 'Hey Baby' (featuring a young **Delbert McClinton** on harmonica). Other popular Smith productions included **Paul And Paula**'s 'Hey Paula' in 1962 and 'Last Kiss' by **J. Frank Wilson And The Cavaliers** in 1964. Smith continued producing into the early 80s but registered no further hits.

Albums: Both collections involving various artists recorded by Smith - *Major Bill's Texas Rock 'N' Roll* (1979), *Major Bill's Texas Soul* (1988).

Smith, Brian

b. 3 January 1939, Wellington, New Zealand. Smith is a self-taught saxophonist. He played in rock, dance and jazz bands at home and in Australia before coming to England in 1964, when he first played with **Alexis Korner**'s Blues Incorporated (1964-65). In the late 60s he worked with the big bands of **Tubby Hayes** and **Maynard Ferguson**, with whom he worked until 1974. He also worked with the bands of **Graham Collier**, **Gordon Beck**, **Mike Westbrook**, **Mike Gibbs**, **Keith Tippett** and **John Stevens**. In 1969 he was a founder member of the successful band **Nucleus** with whom he stayed until he returned home to New Zealand in 1982. Since then he has played with his own quartet and won the Australian Jazz Record of the Year Award with *Southern Excursions* in 1984. He is a player with a formidable technique and the ability to fit into any music from rock and blues right through to free improvisation.

Albums: with Nucleus *Elastic Rock* (1970), *Belladonna* (1972), *Roots* (1973), *Awakening* (1980), with Neil Ardley *Kaleidoscope Of Colours* (1976), *Southern Excursions* (1984).

Smith, Broderick

b. 17 February 1948, England. With his no-nonsense approach and solid, distinctive voice, Smith remains one of the most unpretentious lead singers in Australia. Honing his skills via the blues and R&B bands early in his career (Adderley Smith Blues Band, Sundown and Carson), it was with the **Dingoes** (1973-79) that provided Smith with the vehicle to national acclaim. His two solo albums have since given some insight into his talent but he has not acquired the fame he deserves. Following on from the demise of the Dingoes he has led a series of different bands, the Hired Hand, the Big Combo, Doors Of Perception and the Noveltones. All featured excellent musicians, and his own harmonica playing ensured that his name has remained in the gig guides for the Melbourne pub-rock scene. Unfortunately his excellent blues/soul voice has remained unrecognized in the mass market.

Albums: *Smith's Big Combo* (1981), *Broderick Smith* (1984).

Smith, Buster

b. Henry Smith, 24 August 1904, Aldorf, Texas, USA, d. 10 August 1991. Smith first taught himself to play clarinet, working professionally in Texas in the early 20s. He then added alto saxophone and in 1925 joined **Walter Page**'s Blue Devils in Oklahoma City. Smith was one of several Blue Devils who left *en masse* to join **Bennie Moten** in Kansas City and briefly led this band after Moten's sudden death. He then co-led a band with **Count Basie**, but bowed out when the band left the familiar surroundings of Kansas City. Whatever the motive behind his decision to stay in Kansas City, when the band he had helped form went on to greatness, his career thereafter achieved less than earlier potential had promised. Forming a new band in 1937, Smith employed **Jay McShann**, the excellent if almost forgotten trombonist Fred Beckett, and a teenage saxophonist named **Charlie Parker**. During his career Smith had also written many arrangements for the bands in which he worked and also for other leaders. In the late 30s and early 40s his bandleading activities suffered when his attempts to break into the New York scene failed, a circumstance which diverted him more and more to arranging. In the early 40s he returned to his home state, settling in Dallas and leading small bands there for the greater part of the next four decades. Generally credited as being a major influence on Parker, Smith's own playing career has thus been overshadowed and his few recordings do little to confirm his legendary status.

Album: *The Legendary Buster Smith* (1959). Compilations: with others *Kansas City 1926 To 1930* (1926-30), with others *Original Boogie Woogie Piano Giants* (1938-41), with others *Kansas City Jazz* (1940-41).

Smith, Byther

b. 17 April 1933, Monticello, Mississippi, USA. Smith began playing guitar in church, but after settling in Chicago in 1958 he started singing blues and was tutored on guitar by **Herbert Sumlin** and **Freddie Robinson**. He recorded for several local labels (including, reputedly, Cobra and **VeeJay**), and worked with numerous gospel and blues groups, occasionally sitting in with his cousin **J.B. Lenoir**. In the late 60s he left music, returning in the early 70s as house guitarist at the famed Theresa's Lounge in Chicago, and enjoying a minor hit for CJ Records with 'Give Me My White Robe'. In 1983, Smith recorded an acclaimed album for Grits, with the follow-up two years later being reissued in 1991; Byther has also recorded for JSP. Smith is a modern, though traditionally-rooted Chicago bluesman with a very large repertoire.

Selected albums: *Tell Me How You Like It* (1985), *Addressing The Nation With The Blues* (1989), *Housefire* (1991, reissue).

Smith, Cal

b. Calvin Grant Shofner, 7 April 1932, Gans, Oklahoma, USA. The family moved to California, where he met the rodeo-rider Todd Mason, becoming his stooge for knife and bullwhip tricks. Mason taught him how to play the guitar and at the age of 15 he was a vocalist with the San Francisco country band, Kitty Dibble And Her Dude Ranch Wranglers. After military service, he played bass for Bill Drake, whose brother Jack was a prominent member of **Ernest Tubb**'s Texas Troubadours. This led to him becoming master of ceremonies under the name of Grant Shofner, for Ernest Tubb and the Texas Troubadours from 1962-68. His first appearance on one of Tubb's recordings was 'The Great Speckled Bird' in 1963. Tubb arranged a record contract with Kapp and Smith's first record on the US country charts was 'The Only Thing I Want' in 1967. Two years with **Decca** followed and he finally broke through with 'I've Found Someone Of My Own' and a chart-topping **Bill Anderson** song, 'The Lord Knows I'm Drinking'. He joined MCA in 1973 and had further chart-toppers with the Don Wayne

songs, 'Country Bumpkin' and 'It's Time To Pay The Fiddler'. A 1974 hit, also written by Bill Anderson, was called 'Between Lust And Watching TV' and he recorded a popular 'mother' song, 'Mama's Face'. His last Top 20 hit on the US country charts was 'I Just Came Home To Count The Memories' in 1977. Although Smith has a good voice, he was often landed with mediocre material he subsequently left the business for several years. He joined Ernest Tubb on his double-album *The Legend And The Legacy* although it's bizarre to hear two men singing 'Our Baby's Book'.

Albums: *All The World Is Lonely Now* (1966), *Goin' To Cal's Place* (1967), *Travellin' Man* (1968), *At Home With Cal* (1968), *It Takes Me All Night Long* (1969), *Drinking Champagne* (1969), *Country Hit Parade* (1970), *I've Found Someone Of My Own* (1972), *Swinging Doors* (1973), *Country Bumpkin* (1974), *It's Time To Pay The Fiddler* (1975), *My Kind Of Country* (1975), *Jason's Farm* (1976), *I Just Came Home To Count The Memories* (1977), *Stories Of Life* (1986).

Smith, Carl

b. 15 March 1927, Maynardsville, Tennessee, USA. The legendary **Roy Acuff** also came from Maynardsville and was Smith's hero. Smith sold seeds to pay for his first guitar and then cut grass to pay for lessons. He became a regular on a Knoxville country radio station, served in the navy in World War II, and was discovered by the 40s country singer, Molly O'Day, which led to a recording contract with **Columbia Records**. In 1951 he made his US country chart debut with 'Let's Live A Little', had a double-sided success with 'If Teardrops Were Pennies'/'Mr. Moon' and followed it with a number 1, 'Let Old Mother Nature Have Her Way'. His impressive tally of 41 chart records during the 50s included four more chart-toppers, 'Don't Just Stand There', 'Are You Teasing Me?' (both 1952), 'Hey, Joe' (1953) and 'Loose Talk' (1955) as well as having success with 'This Orchid Means Goodbye', 'Cut Across Shorty' and 'Ten Thousand Drums'. Smith was a ballad singer with a rich, mature voice and, as he preferred steel guitars and fiddles to modern instrumentation, he did not cross over to the pop market. Known as the Tall Gentleman, he was a natural for television and for several years he hosted a very successful country series in Canada, *Carl Smith's Country Music Hall*. He also appeared in the westerns, *The Badge Of Marshal Brennan* (1957) and *Buffalo Gun* (1961), the latter with **Webb Pierce** and **Marty Robbins**. Smith had a tempestuous marriage to **June Carter** from the **Carter Family**; their daughter, **Carlene Carter**, is also a recording artist. After their divorce and in 1957, Smith married Goldie Hill, who had had her own number 1 country single with 'I Let The Stars Get In My Eyes' (1953). Although Smith rarely made the US country Top 10 after the 50s, he had hits until well into the 70s and his total of 93 has rarely been passed. In the 80s, Carl re-recorded his hits for new albums, but it was only a half-hearted comeback. His main interest is in his prize-winning quarter-horses, which he raises on a 500-acre ranch outside Nashville.

Albums: *Carl Smith* (1956), *Softly And Tenderly* (with the Carter Sisters) (1956), *Sentimental Songs* (1957), *Smith's The Name* (1957), *Sunday Down South* (1957), *Let's Live A Little* (1958), *The Carl Smith Touch* (1960), *Easy To Please* (1962), *Tall, Tall Gentleman* (1963), *There Stands The Glass* (1964), *I Want To Live And Love* (1965), *Kisses Don't Lie* (1965), *Man With A Plan* (1966), *Satisfaction Guaranteed* (1967), *Country Gentleman* (1967), *The Country Gentleman Sings His Favourites* (1967), *Country On My Mind* (1968), *Deep Water* (1968), *Gentleman In Love* (1968), *Take It Like A Man* (1969), *A Tribute To Roy Acuff* (1969), *Faded Love And Winter Roses* (1969), *Carl Smith And The Tunesmiths* (1970), *Anniversary Album* (1970), *I Love You Because* (1970), *Knee Deep In The Blues* (1971), *Carl Smith Sings Bluegrass* (1971), *Don't Say You're Mine* (1972), *The Great Speckled Bird* (1972), *If This Is Goodbye* (1972), *The Girl I Love* (1975), *The Way I Lose My Mind* (1975), *This Lady Loving Me* (1977), *Silver Tongued Cowboy* (1978), *Greatest Hits, Volume 1* (1980), *Legendary* (1981), *Old Lonesome Times* (1988).

Smith, Carrie

b. 25 August 1941, Fort Gaines, Georgia, USA. Smith appeared at the 1957 **Newport Jazz Festival** as a member of a New Jersey church choir, but her solo professional career did not take off until the early 70s. An appearance with **Dick Hyman** and the **New York Jazz Repertory Orchestra** at Carnegie Hall in 1974 should have alerted audiences to her exceptional qualities, but for the rest of the decade she was much better received in Europe than in the USA. Her tours of festivals and concert halls were sometimes as a single, but also in company with NYJRO, **Tyree Glenn**, the **World's Greatest Jazz Band** and others. Smith's style is rooted in the blues and gospel but her repertoire is wide, encompassing many areas of 20th-century popular music. Her voice is deep and powerful and she is especially effective in live performances. Although her reputation has grown throughout the 80s, she still remains far less well-known than her considerable talent warrants.

Albums: with Dick Hyman *Satchmo Remembered* (1974), *Do Your Duty* (1976), *When You're Down And Out* (1977), *Carrie Smith* (1978), with others *Highlights In Jazz Anniversary Concert* (1985).

Smith, Clara

b. c.1894, Spartanburg, South Carolina, USA, d. 2 February, 1935. Singing professionally from her mid-teens in theatres and tent shows throughout the Deep South, by 1923 Smith was a big name in New York. She sang in Harlem clubs, opening her own very popular and successful Clara Smith Theatrical Club.

She was signed by **Columbia** to make records, on some of which she duetted with **Bessie Smith**. Her instrumental accompanists on record included **Louis Armstrong**, **Lonnie Johnson** and **James P. Johnson**. She worked constantly throughout the late 20s and into the early 30s, mostly in New York but with occasional short tours and residencies at clubs in other cities. She died suddenly from a heart attack on 2 February 1935. Smith sang the blues in a lowdown, dragging manner, creating dirge-like yet often deeply sensual interpretations.

Album: *Clara Smith, Vols. 1-7 (1923-32)* (1974).

Smith, Clarence 'Pine Top'

b. 11 January 1904, Troy, Alabama, USA, d. 15 March 1929, Chicago, Illinois, USA. Often considered to be the founder of the boogie woogie style of piano playing, 'Pine Top' Smith was actually a vaudeville performer. From his mid-teens, Smith toured tent shows and theatres as a pianist and dancer. He gradually concentrated on piano and, encouraged by **Charles 'Cow Cow' Davenport**, made a handful of records. Smith's style was largely in the mould of humorous songs backed up by vigorous two-handed playing. His small list of recordings also included blues but his fame rests, more than anything, on his recording of 'Pine Top's Boogie Woogie' (1928). This song represents, possibly, the first documented use of the term. His work on the circuits took him all over the south in the company of such artists as **Butterbeans And Susie**, and **Ma Rainey** but it was in Chicago that his promising career was cut short when he was accidentally shot by a man named David Bell during a skirmish in a dance hall. He was 25 and left a wife and two children. He has been recorded by many artists over the years, 'Pine Top's boogie woogie' remains as satisfying today as it was when it made its initial impact in 1928.

Selected albums: *Compilation 1928-29-30* (Oldie Blues 1986), *Pine Top Smith And Romeo Nelson* (1987), *Compilation 1929-30* (Oldie Blues 1988).

Smith, Connie

b. Constance June Meadows, 14 August 1941, Elkhart, Indiana, USA but was raised in West Virginia and Ohio. One of 14 children, she longed to be a country singer and taught herself to play the guitar whilst in hospital recovering from a leg injury, caused by an accident with a lawn mower. She sang at local events as a teenager and appeared on several radio and television shows. She married and for a time settled to the life of a housewife but after the birth of her first child, again, took to singing. Her break came in 1963, when she was booked to sing at the Frontier Ranch, a park near Columbus. Headlining the show was **Bill Anderson**, who was so impressed with her performance that he invited her to Nashville to appear on the *Ernest Tubb*

Record Shop live show. Two months later, she returned to make demo recordings, which won her an **RCA** contract. In 1964, her recording of Anderson's song 'Once A Day' became her first hit, spending 8 weeks at number 1 and 28 weeks in the US country charts. She became an overnight success and in the next five years added more Top 10 hits including 'If I Talk To Him', 'The Hurtin's All Over', 'Cincinnati, Ohio' and 'Baby's Back Again'. She later recorded an album of Anderson's songs, although she did not work with him. She became a member of the *Grand Ole Opry* in 1965, was much in demand for tours and concert appearances and appeared in such films as *Road To Nashville*, *Las Vegas Hillbillies* and *Second Fiddle To An Old Guitar*. In the early 70s, further Top 10 hits included 'I Never Once Stopped Loving You', 'Just One Time' and 'Just For What I Am' and tours included Europe, Australia and the Far East. She moved to **Columbia** in 1973, where her first hit came with a recording of her own song 'You've Got Me Right Where You Want Me' and in 1977 to Monument, where her biggest hit was a country version of 'I Just Want To Be Your Everything' (a pop number 1 for **Andy Gibb**). From 1979-85, she was absent from the charts as she retired from active participation in music, apart from some *Opry* appearances, as she devoted her time to raising her family. A born-again Christian (her eldest son Darren is a missionary), she has performed gospel music on the *Opry* and recorded an album of **Hank Williams**' gospel songs. She regularly plays the *Opry*, network radio and television shows and delighted her British fans by her appearance in Britain in 1990.

Albums: *Cute 'N' Country* (1965), *The Other Side Of Connie Smith* (1965), *Born To Sing* (1966), *Miss Smith Goes To Nashville* (1966), *Sings Great Sacred Songs* (1966), *Connie In The Country* (1967), *Downtown Country* (1967), *Sings Bill Anderson* (1967), *I Love Charley Brown* (1968), *Sunshine And Rain* (1968), *Soul Of Country Music* (1968), *Back In Baby's Arms* (1969), *Connie's Country* (1969), with Nat Stuckey *Young Love* (1969), *I Never Once Stopped Loving You* (1970), *Sunday Morning* (1970), *Come Along And Walk With Me* (1971), *My Heart Has A Mind Of Its Own* (1971), *Just One Time* (1971), *Where Is My Castle* (1971), *If It Ain't Love (And Other Great Dallas Frazier Songs)* (1972), *Ain't We Havin' Us A Good Time* (1972), *City Lights-Country Favorites* (1972), *A Lady Named Smith* (1973), *Love Is The Look You're Looking For* (1973), *Dream Painter* (1973), *God Is Abundant* (1973), with Nat Stuckey *Even The Bad Times Are Good* (1973), *Collections* (1974), *Connie Smith Now* (1974), *That's The Way Love Goes* (1974), *I Never Knew (What That Song Meant Before)* (1974), *Joy To The World* (1975), *Sings Hank Williams Gospel* (1975), *I Got A Lot Of Hurtin' Done Today* (1975), *I Don't Want To Talk It Over Anymore* (1976), *The Song We Fell In Love To* (1976), *Pure Connie Smith* (1977), *New Horizons* (1978), *Live In Branson, MO, USA* (1993).

Smith, Derek

b. 17 August 1931, London, England, England. After starting to play piano as a tiny child, Smith quickly developed until he was playing professionally at the age of 14. He began playing jazz and in the early 50s, working with **Kenny Graham**, **John Dankworth**, **Kenny Baker** and other leading British bands. In the mid-50s he moved to New York where he was soon in demand as a session musician, playing in studio orchestras and on record dates. However, he also played jazz with **Benny Goodman**, **Connie Kay** and others. During the 60s, Smith's career followed similar lines, mixing studio work with jazz, and towards the end of the decade he became a long-serving member of the *Tonight* show orchestra. In the 70s he again played with Goodman, touring overseas, and also worked with **Scott Hamilton** and in bands led by **Nick Brignola**, **Arnett Cobb** and others. As the 80s progressed Smith became steadily more active on the international jazz festival circuit, sometimes as soloist, other times in a trio with **Milt Hinton** and **Bobby Rosengarden**. A stylish player with a wide-ranging repertoire and a gift for elegantly presenting a constant fund of ideas, Smith is very much a musician's musician but by the early 90s was deservedly becoming better known to audiences.

Albums: *Love For Sale* (Progressive 1978), *The Man I Love* (Progressive 1978), *Plays The Music Of Jerome Kern* (Progressive 1981), *Dark Eyes* (East Wind 1985), *Plays Passionate Piano* (Hindsight 1992).

Smith, George

b. 22 April 1924, Helena, Arkansas, USA, d. 2 October 1983, Los Angeles, USA. A master of amplified and chromatic blues harmonica, Smith made a stunning debut in 1954 with 'Telephone Blues'/'Blues In The Dark', but failed to capture the audience which elevated **Little Walter** to stardom. This may have been because his west coast record label tended to back him with saxophones rather than the guitar-based sound of Chicago. Smith had worked in Chicago and Kansas City, but resided in Los Angeles from 1955, where he worked as a name act and accompanied Big Mama Thornton for many years. He continued to make recordings of variable quality, and was briefly a member of the **Muddy Waters** band. He toured Europe, during the 70s and was a member with **J.D. Nicholson** of the mainly white blues band **Bacon Fat**.

Albums: *Blues With A Feeling* (1969), *Arkansas Trap* (1970), *No Time For Jive* (1970), *Blowin' The Blues* (c. 1979), *Boogiein' With George* (c. 1983), *Harmonica Ace* (1991).

Smith, Gulliver

b. Kevin Smith, Australia. Smith appeared as a child

performer in Melbourne in the early 60s, covering golden oldies from the 50s. Eventually he left this scene to concentrate on his growing love of R&B and soul, with his band the Children in 1966. Dr Kandy's Third Eye followed in 1967-68; in the vanguard of Sydney's 'flower-power' psychedelic music period, their strange performances attracted Australian press attention. A series of short-lived, but interesting bands followed, but it was with **Company Caine** that his lyric writing became noticed and the band, despite poor media attention and no radio airplay, remains one of the great Australian cult bands of the 70s. Both their albums are now regarded as collector's items. Smith's solo album was well received, but it did not bring him a new audience. He moved back to Melbourne and led several more bands of variable quality which did not gather a following outside their small bohemian scene. Later Smith lived in the UK and New Zealand for many years, before returning to Australia in 1989. His song writing was noticed by **John Farnham** who included one of his co-written songs on a recent album. Album: *The Band's Alright But The Singer Is....*(1973).

Smith, Huey 'Piano'

b. 26 January 1934, New Orleans, Louisiana, USA. Pianist Smith drew his pulsating style from a variety of musical sources, including the boogie-woogie of **Albert Ammons** and jazz of **Jelly Roll Morton**. Having served in bands led by **Earl King** and Eddie '**Guitar Slim**' Jones, Huey became a respected session musician before embarking on an independent recording career. Leading his own group, the Clowns, which at its peak included Gerry Hall, Eugene Francis, Billy Roosevelt and vocalist **Bobby Marchan**, he scored two million-selling singles in 1957 with 'Rockin' Pneumonia And The Boogie Woogie Flu' and 'Don't You Just Know It'. Both releases showcased classic New Orleans rhythms as well as the leader's vibrant, percussive technique. The pianist was also featured on 'Sea Cruise', a 1959 smash for **Frankie Ford**, whose speeded-up vocal was overdubbed on an existing Clowns' tape. However, despite other excellent releases, Huey Smith did not enjoy another substantial hit and, having become a Jehovah's Witness, forsook music in favour of preaching.
Albums: *Having A Good Time* (1959), *For Dancing* (1961), *T'was The Night Before Christmas* (1962), *Rock 'N' Roll Revival* (1963). Compilations: *Rockin' Pneumonia And The Boogie Woogie Flu* (1965), *Huey 'Piano' Smith's Rock And Roll Revival* (1974), *Rockin' Pneumonia And The Boogie Woogie Flu* (1978, different from previous entry), *Rockin' And Jivin'* (1981), *The Imperial Sides 1960/1961* (1984), *Somewhere There's Honey For The Grizzly* (1984), *Pitta Pattin'* (1987).

Smith, J.B.

Johnnie B. Smith was recorded in the Texas State Penitentiary in the 60s while serving his fourth prison term, one of 45 years for murder. He was a powerful worksong leader, but his most important recordings were nine long unaccompanied solos, which he thought of as parts of a single song. Their 132 stanzas use essentially the same melody, at varying tempos, and with varying amounts of decoration. This melody, which appears to be unique to Smith, carries a four-line stanza, usually ABB'A' with B'A' a reversal of AB, leading to some striking poetic effects. Indeed, Smith was a remarkable poet of the prison experience, using some traditional lines and verses, but working them into songs that are largely original compositions, thematically coherent, and full of poignant images of confinement, loneliness and the slow passage of time. Smith was paroled in 1967, and did some preaching in Amarillo, but returned to prison for a parole violation.
Albums: *Ever Since I Have Been A Man Full Grown* (c.1970), *I'm Troubled With A Diamond* (1990), *Old Rattler Can't Hold Me* (1990).

Smith, J.T. 'Funny Papa'

b. c.1890, Texas, USA. Very little is known about the life of this blues guitarist and singer, although he reportedly played in New York in 1917, and worked in Texas and Oklahoma in the 20s and 30s. In 1930, he recorded. One of his albums provided him with a nickname (or possibly reflected an existing one), 'The Howling Wolf', pre-dating the more famous blues artist of that name by about 20 years, on record. His steady, rhythmic picking and warm baritone helped sell sufficient albums for him to record again the following year, including another 'Howling Wolf' track, and a dozen more. Following this, he served a prison sentence for murder. In 1935, he recorded at four long sessions in Fort Worth, Texas, along with **Black Boy Shine** and **Bernice Edwards**, although almost nothing from these was released. Smith's date of death is unrecorded.
Selected album: *The Original Howling Wolf* (1971).

Smith, Jabbo

b. Cladys Smith, 24 December 1908, Pembroke, Georgia, USA, d. 16 January 1991. Smith was taught trumpet and trombone while still a small child and later toured with a youth band. At the age of 16 he was working professionally as a trumpeter (although he would periodically play trombone in later years). In New York from about 1925 he played with **Charlie 'Fess' Johnson**, **Duke Ellington**, **James P. Johnson** and others. Stranded in Chicago when a show in which he was playing folded, he worked in bands led by **Carroll Dickerson**, **Earl 'Fatha' Hines**, **Erskine Tate** and Charlie Elgar. During the 30s he played with **Fess Williams**, Dickerson, led his own band, then returned to New York with **Claude Hopkins** and also played with **Sidney Bechet**. By the mid-40s, reputedly exhausted through high-living, he was leading his own band in the comparative musical backwater of Milwaukee and for the next dozen years mostly played in that city. He also worked outside music, for a car rental company, into the late 50s. Thereafter, he played less and less until he was brought to New York in 1975 to receive an award at Carnegie Hall. This event prompted him to begin practising again and he was soon touring internationally, playing and singing with **Sammy Rimington**, Orange Kellin and others. In the early 80s he suffered a series of heart attacks but kept on playing, often working in harness with seemingly unlikely musical companions such as **Don Cherry**. In these later years he increasingly turned to composing, writing music for the **Mel Lewis** orchestra, often in collaboration with **Keith Ingham**. Despite his remarkable durability and longevity, Smith remains a little-known figure in jazz and, given the extremely high regard in which he is held by fellow musicians, he is also very much under-recorded. In his youth he was often considered to be a potential rival to **Louis Armstrong** and although he has none of Armstrong's creative genius, his recordings display many flashes of spectacular brilliance.

Selected albums: *Jabbo Smith Vols 1 & 2* (1927-29), *Jabbo Smith Vols 1 & 2* (1928-38), *The Ace Of Rhythm* (1929), *Jabbo Smith And The Hot Antic Band* (1982), *Sweet 'N' Lowdown* (Affinity 1986, 1927-29 recordings), *Jabbo Smith Vol 1 1928-29* (Retrieval 1990), *Complete 1928-38 Sessions* (Jazz Archives 1993).

Smith, Jack

b. c.1918, USA. An actor and singer with a smooth tenor voice, Smith got a big break in 1933 when he joined the **Three Ambassadors** vocal group with **Gus Arnheim**'s Band, which was resident at the Coconut Grove, in the Ambassador Hotel, Los Angeles. Earlier, the Rhythm Boys, featuring **Bing Crosby**, had sung with the band there. When **Phil Harris** replaced Arnheim with his own extremely entertaining band, the Ambassadors stayed on, and later toured with him. During the late 30s the trio appeared regularly on **Kate Smith**'s radio programme in New York, until they disbanded in 1939. Jack Smith stayed in New York and sang in vocal groups on radio, including *Your Hit Parade*. In the early 40s he was a soloist on several radio shows, with bandleader **Raymond Scott** and the *Prudential Show*. He then had his own radio programme until the early 50s. From 1947-49 he had several record hits for **Capitol**, including 'Jack! Jack! Jack!', 'Civilization (Bongo, Bongo, Bongo)', 'Big Brass Band From Brazil', 'Shaunty O'Shea', 'Baby Face', 'Takin' Miss Mary To The Ball', 'Tea Leaves', 'You Call Everybody Darling', 'Cuanto Le Gusta (La Parranda)', 'Lavender Blue (Dilly Dilly)', 'Cruising Down The River' and 'Sunflower'.

On most of these he was accompanied by the **Clark Sisters**, a classy vocal quartet, who formerly sang under the name of the Sentimentalists with the **Tommy Dorsey** Orchestra. Smith also appeared in two movie musicals, *Make Believe Ballroom* (1949); and *On Moonlight Bay* (1951), in which he dueted 'Love Ya', with **Doris Day**. In the 50s, he sang on US television, but eventually concentrated more and more on acting.

Smith, Jimmy

b. James Oscar Smith, 8 December 1925, Norristown, Pennsylvania, USA. The sound of the Hammond Organ in jazz was popularized by Smith, often using the prefix monicker 'the incredible' or 'the amazing'. Smith has become the most famous jazz organist ever and arguably the most influential. Brought up by musical parents he was formally trained on piano and bass and combined the two skills with the Hammond while leading his own trio. He was heavily influenced by **Wild Bill Davis**. By the mid-50s Smith had refined his own brand of smoky soul jazz which epitomized laid-back 'late night' blues-based music. His vast output for the 'soul jazz' era of **Blue Note Records** led the genre and resulted in a number of other Hammond B3 maestro's appearing, notably, **Jimmy McGriff**, **'Brother' Jack McDuff**, **'Big' John Patten**, **Richard 'Groove' Holmes** and 'Baby Face' Willette. Smith was superbly complemented by outstanding musicians. Although **Art Blakey** played with Smith, Donald Bailey remains the definitive Smith drummer, while Smith tackled the bass notes on the Hammond. The guitar was featured prominently throughout the Blue Note years and Smith used the talents of Eddie McFadden, Quentin Warren and **Kenny Burrell**. Further immaculate playing came from **Stanley Turrentine** (tenor saxophone), **Lee Morgan** (trumpet) and **Lou Donaldson** (alto saxophone). Two classic albums from the late 50s were *The Sermon* and *Houseparty*. On the title track of the former, Smith and his musicians stretch out with majestic 'cool' over 20 minutes, allowing each soloist ample time. In 1962 Jimmy moved to **Verve Records** where he became the undisputed king, regularly crossing over into the pop best-sellers and the singles charts with memorable titles such as 'Walk On The Wild Side', 'Hobo Flats' and 'Who's Afraid Of Virginia Woolf'. These hits were notable for their superb orchestral arrangements by **Oliver Nelson**, although they tended to bury Smith's sound. However, the public continued putting him in the charts with 'The Cat', 'The Organ Grinder's Swing' and, with Smith on growling vocals 'Got My Mojo Working'.

His albums at this time also made the best-sellers and between 1963 and 1966 Smith was virtually ever present in the album charts with a total of 12 albums, many making the US Top 20. Smith's popularity had much to do with the R&B boom in Britain during the early 60s. His strong influence was found in the early work of **Steve Winwood**, **Georgie Fame**, **Zoot Money**, **Graham Bond** and **John Mayall**. Smith's two albums with **Wes Montgomery** were also well received; both allowed each other creative space with no ego involved. As the 60s ended Smith's music became more MOR and he pursued a soul/funk path during the 70s, using a synthesizer on occasion. Organ jazz was in the doldrums for many years and although Smith remained its leading exponent, he was leader of an unfashionable style. During the 80s after a series of low-key and largely unremarkable recordings Smith delivered the underrated *Off The Top* in 1982. Later in the decade the Hammond organ began to come back in favour in the UK with the **James Taylor Quartet** and the **Tommy Chase** Band and in Germany with **Barbara Dennerlein**. Much of Smith's seminal work has been re-mastered and reissued on compact disc since the end of the 80s almost as vindication for a genre which went so far out of fashion, it disappeared. A reunion with Kenny Burrell produced a fine live album *The Master* featuring re-workings of classic trio tracks.

Selected albums: *Jimmy Smith At The Organ Vol 1* (Blue Note 1956), *Jimmy Smith At The Organ Vol 2* (Blue Note 1956), *The Incredible Jimmy Smith At The Organ Vol 3* (Blue Note 1956), *The Incredible Jimmy Smith At Club Baby Grand Vol 1* (Blue Note 1956), *The Incredible Jimmy Smith At Club Baby Grand Vol 2* (Blue Note 1956), *The Champ* (Blue Note 1956), *A Date With Jimmy Smith Vol 1* (Blue Note 1957), *A Date With Jimmy Smith Vol 2* (Blue Note 1957), *The Sounds Of Jimmy Smith* (Blue Note 1957), *Plays Pretty Just For You* (Blue Note 1957), *Groovin' At Small's Paradise Vol 1* (Blue Note 1958), *Groovin' At Small's Paradise Vol 2* (Blue Note 1958), *The Sermon* (Blue Note 1958), *House Party* (Blue Note 1958), *Cool Blues* (Blue Note 1958), *Home Cookin'* (1958), *Crazy Baby* (Blue Note 1960), *Midnight Special* (Blue Note 1960), *Open House* (Blue Note 1960), *Back At The Chicken Shack* (Blue Note 1960), *Peter And The Wolf* (1960), *Plays Fats Waller* (Blue Note 1962), *Bashin'* (Verve 1962), *Hobo Flats* (Verve 1963), *I'm Movin' On* (Blue Note 1963), *Any Number Can Win* (Verve 1963), *Rockin' The Boat* (Blue Note 1963), with Kenny Burrell *Blue Bash!* (1963), *Prayer Meetin'* (Blue Note 1964), *Christmas '64* (Blue Note 1964), *Who's Afraid Of Virginia Woolf* (Verve 1964), *The Cat* (Verve 1964), *Organ Grinder's Swing* (Verve 1965), *Softly As A Summer Breeze* (Blue Note 1965), *Monster* (Verve 1965), *'Bucket'!* (Blue Note 1966), *Peter And The Wolf* (Verve 1966), *Get My Mojo Workin'* (Verve 1966), *Christmas Cookin'* (Verve 1966), *Hoochie Coochie Man* (Verve 1966), with Wes Montgomery, *Jimmy & Wes The Dynamic Duo* (Verve 1966), with Montgomery *Further Adventures Of Jimmy And Wes* (Verve 1966), *Respect* (Verve 1967), *Stay Loose* (Verve 1968), *Livin' It Up* (Verve 1968), featuring George Benson *The Boss* (Verve 1969), *Groove Drops* (Verve 1969), *Mr Jim* (Manhattan 1981), *Off The Top*

(Elektra 1982), *Keep On Comin'* (1983), *Go For Whatcha Know* (Blue Note 1986), *Jimmy Smith At The Organ* (1988), *The Cat Strikes Again* (Laserlight 1989), *Prime Time* (Milestone 1991), *Fourmost* (Milestone 1991), *Sum Serious Blues* (Milestone 1993), *The Master* (Blue Note 1994). Selected compilations: *Compact Jazz: The Best Of Jimmy Smith* (Verve 1968), *Jimmy Smith's Greatest Hits* (1968), *Compact Jazz: Jimmy Smith Plays the Blues* (Verve 1988).

Smith, Joe

b. 28 June 1902, Ripley, Ohio, USA, d. 2 December 1937. With his father, six brothers and a cousin all playing trumpet, it is hardly surprising that Smith too played this instrument. By his late teens, Smith was playing in New York, where he became a big attraction as musical director and featured soloist with a **Noble Sissle** and **Eubie Blake** show. He also established a reputation as a sensitive accompanist to singers, playing and recording with **Bessie Smith**, **Mamie Smith**, **Ma Rainey** and **Ethel Waters**. He was hired by **Fletcher Henderson** in 1925, staying three years, later rejoining the band for occasional club and recording dates. (During this period his brother, Russell Smith, was Henderson's lead trumpeter). In the late 20s and early 30s, he was also frequently in and out of **McKinney's Cotton Pickers**. He was one of the first trumpeters to intelligently explore the possibilities of mutes other than to create barnyard effects. Despite a reputation for leading a wild lifestyle, Smith's playing was always tasteful and often deeply moving. Preferring to remain in the middle register, he rarely used the spectacular high notes with which his contemporaries pleased their audiences. In his introspective approach to his solos, and his habitually relaxed and unhurried accompaniments to singers, he prefigured the manner in which trumpet players of a later generation would conceive of the instrument. In 1930, while touring with the Cotton Pickers, he was driving a car which was involved in an accident. A passenger in the car, his only close friend, George 'Fathead' Thomas, was killed. Subsequently, Smith's mental state deteriorated and in 1933 he was confined to an institution, where he died in December 1937.

Selected albums: with Ethel Waters *Oh Daddy!* (1921-24), with Waters *Jazzin' Baby Blues* (1921-27), with Fletcher Henderson *A Study In Frustration* (1923-38), with Ma Rainey *Blame It On The Blues* (1920s), *The Bessie Smith Story* (1925-27).

Smith, Johnny

b. John Henry Smith Jnr., 25 June 1922, Birmingham, Alabama, USA. After first playing trumpet and violin, Smith took up the guitar on which he became best known, although he continued to play trumpet in later years. In New York in the 40s Smith maintained steady employment as a studio musician, but also took part in after-hours bop sessions. In the early 50s a recording under his own name of 'Moonlight In Vermont', with **Stan Getz**, was greeted with great popular and critical acclaim. He also recorded with **Bennie Green**, **Kenny Clarke** and others on *Jazz Studio*, using the pseudonym Sir Jonathan Gasser, and made albums under his own name. In the 60s Smith moved west, remaining active in music as a teacher and occasional performer.

Albums: *Moonlight In Vermont* (c.50s), *The New Quartet* (unk.).

Smith, Johnny 'Hammond'

b. John Robert Smith, 16 December 1933, Louisville, Kentucky USA. Not be confused with the legendary swing promoter and talent spotter **John Hammond Jnr.**, Johnny 'Hammond' Smith (sometimes known simply as Johnny Hammond) is one of the giants of the soul jazz Hammond organ. Born the year the instrument was invented, he studied piano, trying to emulate the intricate jazz styles of **Art Tatum** and **Bud Powell**, before devoting himself to the Hammond during the 50s. His naturally funky approach and feel for the instrument established him as one of the leaders in a movement of bluesy, soul jazz organists who were mixing the sound of church gospel and hard-bop; and he began recording sessions under his own name for the Prestige (throughout the 60s) and, later, Kudu labels. Later in his career he added a range of synthesised and electronic sounds to his palette, but he remains most associated with the original Hammond. Recent years have witnessed a resurgence in popularity for the Hammond in jazz, and the soul jazz genre in general, and Johnny 'Hammond' Smith has once again been in demand in the studio and on the international jazz circuit.

Albums: with Oliver Nelson *Taking Care Of Business* (Original Jazz Classics 1960), with Gene Ammons *Greatest Hits, Vol. 1: The Sixties* (Original Jazz Classics 1961-69), *Wild Horses Rock Steady* (Kudu 1971), with Hank Crawford *Portrait* (Milestone 1990).

Albums: *That Good Feelin'* (New Jazz 1959), *All Soul* (New Jazz 1959), *Talk That Talk* (New Jazz 1960), *Gettin' The Message* (Prestige 1961), *Stimulation* (Prestige 1961), *Look Out!* (New Jazz 1962), *Mr Wonderful* (Riverside 1963), *Black Coffee* (Riverside 1963), *The Stinger* (Prestige 1965), *A Little Taste* (Riverside 1965), *Open House!* (Riverside 1965), *Opus De Funk* (Prestige 1966), *Ebb Tide* (Prestige 1967), *Love Potion No. 9* (Prestige 1967), *The Stinger Meets The Golden Thrush* (Prestige 1967), *Nasty* (Prestige 1968), *Dirty Grape* (Prestige 1968), *Soul Flowers* (Prestige 1968), *Soul Talk* (Prestige 1969). Compilations: *The Best Of Johnny 'Hammond' Smith* (Prestige 1969).

Smith, Kate

b. Kathryn Elizabeth Smith, 1 May 1907, Greenville, Alabama, USA, d. 17 June 1986. Smith is best remembered for her dynamic, belted rendition of **Irving Berlin**'s American patriotic anthem 'God Bless America', recorded in 1938 for Victor Records and a hit on three separate occasions. Her career spanned 50 years. She began singing professionally in the early 20s and moved to New York during that decade to appear in vaudeville presentations and on the Broadway stage. Large-framed and possessing a booming soprano voice, she quickly gained attention and was recording hit records for **Columbia Records** by 1927, the first being 'One Sweet Letter From You' with **Red Nichols**' Charleston Chasers. Her first major hit came in 1931 with 'When The Moon Comes Over The Mountain', her own radio theme song. In the following year she recorded the immensely successful 'River, Stay 'Way From My Door' (later a hit for **Frank Sinatra**), with **Guy Lombardo** And His Royal Canadians. Smith's association with patriotic causes began during World War II, when she helped to raise money for the US war effort. 'God Bless America' (written in 1918 and discarded by Berlin until he deemed it appropriate for Smith to record) first charted in 1939, before USA involvement in the war began, but returned to the best-seller lists twice more during the war. Smith also acted in several films during the 30s and 40s, including ***The Big Broadcast*** *Of 1932* and *This Is The Army*, along with budding actor Ronald Reagan. Kate Smith continued to record successfully for Columbia until 1946 and then switched to **MGM Records** two years later. She starred in her own television programme in the early 50s but retired from show business, save for sporadic appearances, in 1954. She died as a result of diabetes in 1986.

Albums: *Kate Smith At Carnegie Hall* (1963), *The Sweetest Sounds* (1964), *How Great Thou Art* (1966), *The Kate Smith Anniversary Album* (1966), *Kate Smith Today* (1966) *Songs Of The Now Generation* (1969). Compilations: *The Best Of Kate Smith* (1968), *The Best Of Kate Smith (Sacred)* (1970), *A Legendary Performer* (1978).

Smith, Keely

b. 9 March 1932, Norfolk, Virginia USA, Smith was a jazzy singer who worked with her husband, bandleader **Louis Prima**. She made her professional debut in 1950, joining Prima three years later. As well as her solo spots with the big band, she frequently dueted with Prima on stylized versions of well-known songs. In 1958 one of these, **Johnny Mercer** and **Harold Arlen**'s 'That Old Black Magic' became a surprise US Top 20 hit. The duo followed up with the minor successes 'I've Got You Under My Skin' and 'Bei Mir Bist Du Schoen', a revival of the 1937 **Andrews Sisters** hit. Smith appeared with Prima in the movie *Hey Boy, Hey Girl* (1959), singing 'Fever' and she also sang on the soundtrack of *Thunder Road* (1958). In the early 60s, Smith separated from Prima and signed to **Reprise**, where her musical director was **Nelson Riddle**. In

1965, she had Top 20 hits in the UK with an album of **Beatles**' compositions and a version of 'You're Breaking My Heart'.

Selected albums: *I Wish You Love* (1957), *Politely* (1958), *Swinging Pretty* (1959), *Because You're Mine* (1959), *Be My Love* (1959), *Twist With Keely Smith* (1962), *Little Girl Blue, Little Girl New* (1963), *Lennon-McCartney Songbook* (1964).

Smith, Keith

b. 19 March 1940, London, England. Taking up the trumpet in his youth, Smith originally favoured New Orleans style and established a considerable reputation in this field. In the late 50s and through to the mid-60s he played with several bands, leading his own in Europe and the USA, where he performed and recorded with **George Lewis** and **'Captain' John Handy**. Smith was also a member of the New Orleans All Stars, a package of mostly American musicians who toured Europe in the 60s. After a spell in Denmark with **Papa Bue Jensen**'s band in the early 70s, he again formed his own band in the UK. He named the band Hefty Jazz, a name he also gave to his own record company and booking agency, and established a practice of touring with well-conceived thematic package shows. Among these were 'The Wonderful World Of **Louis Armstrong**', for which he hired such ex-Louis Armstrong sidemen as **Arvell Shaw** and **Barrett Deems**, '100 Years Of Dixieland Jazz' and 'The Stardust Road', a tribute to the music of **Hoagy Carmichael**, which was headlined by **Georgie Fame**. A dedicated musician who also combines effective business and entrepreneurial skills, Smith remains at the forefront of the UK's traditional jazz scene in the 90s.

Albums: *Keith Smith's American All Stars In Europe* (1966), *Way Down Yonder In New Orleans, Then And Now* (1977), *Ball Of Fire* (Hefty Jazz 1978), *Up Jumped The Blues* (Hefty Jazz 1978), *Keith Smith's Hefty Jazz* (Jazzology 1988).

Smith, Larry

b. Hollis, Queens, New York, USA. Smith formed Orange Crush (which also featured Davey DMX - or **Davey D** - and Trevor Gale), in his first foray into hip hop. After which he would go on to become one of rap music's most important producers. His credits included work with **Jimmy Spicer** and early **Kurtis Blow**, before he oversaw the first two **Run DMC** albums. In the process he helped to create the spare, minimalist rhythm tracks and sound which would define the 'new school'. His influence waned as the 80s progressed, though he did helm three albums by **Whodini**.

Smith, Leo

b. 18 December 1941, Leland, Mississippi, USA. Smith's stepfather was blues guitarist Alex 'Little Bill' Wallace and in his early teens Smith led his own blues band. He was already proficient on trumpet, which he later studied in college and continued to play in various army bands. In 1967 he moved to Chicago, where he joined the **AACM**, recording with **Muhal Richard Abrams** and **'Kalaparusha' Maurice McIntyre** and becoming a member of **Anthony Braxton**'s trio. In 1969, the group moved to Paris, but broke up a year later. Smith returned to the USA and settled in Connecticut. He recorded again with Abrams and Braxton in the Creative Construction Company and also worked with **Marion Brown** in the Creative Improvisation Ensemble and in a duo format. Smith continued to play occasionally with AACM colleagues such as Braxton and **Roscoe Mitchell** ('L-R-G') during the 70s, but his chief focus of interest now was his own music. He set up a label, Kabell, formed a group, New Dalta Ahkri, and also began to develop his solo music in a series of concerts and records (*Creative Music-1, Solo Music/Ahkreanvention*). New Dalta Ahkri, whose members included **Anthony Davis**, **Oliver Lake** and Wes Brown, made a handful of albums renowned for their spacious, abstract beauty, as did Smith's trio (with Bobby Naughton and Dwight Andrews). *Divine Love* also featured guest artists **Lester Bowie**, **Charlie Haden** and **Kenny Wheeler**, while *Spirit Catcher* had one track ('The Burning Of Stones') on which Smith played with a trio of harpists. Smith's trumpet style blended the terseness of **Miles Davis** with the lyricism of **Booker Little** (his two chief influences), while his music was based on the innovatory concepts of 'ahkreanvention' and 'rhythm units', alternative methods of structuring improvisation which he had been refining since the late 60s. A writer too, his *Notes (8 Pieces)* set out his views on African-American music history and included scathing attacks on jazz journalism and the mainstream music business. The late 70s found him making several trips to Europe, playing at **Derek Bailey**'s **Company** Week (*Company 5, 6, 7*) and in 1979 recording both the big band *Budding Of A Rose* and the first of two trio discs with **Peter Kowald** and drummer Gunter Sommer.

In 1983 he recorded *Procession Of The Great Ancestry*, with Naughton and Kahil El'Zabar among the players ('a music of ritual and blues, of space and light,' enthused *Wire*). The same year he visited Canada to record *Rastafari* with the **Bill Smith** trio, the title signalling a conversion to Rastafarianism that led him, on later albums, to explore more popular forms, including reggae (*Jah Music, Human Rights* - though the latter also has one side of free improvisation with Kowald and Sommer from 1982). At the end of the 80s Smith was still playing in the New York area, but was also working as a teacher and had released no new recordings for several years. Hailed by Braxton as 'a genius' and by Anthony Davis as 'one of the unsung heroes of American music', the belated appearance of his *Procession Of The Great Ancestry* in 1990 prompted many to lament his long absence from the recording studio: as writer Graham Lock put it, 'such a silence hurts us all'.

Albums: *Creative Music-1* (1972), *Reflectativity* (1975), with Marion Brown *Duets* (1975, rec. 1970), with Anthony Braxton *Trio And Duet* (1975), with Creative Construction Company *CCC* (1975, rec 1970), with CCC *CCC-2* (1976, rec 1970), *Song Of Humanity* (1977), *The Mass On The World* (1978), *Divine Love* (ECM 1979), *Solo Music/Ahkreanvention* (1979), *Spirit Catcher* (Nessa 1979), *Budding Of A Rose* (1980), with Peter Kowald, Gunter Sommer *Touch The Earth* (1980), *Go In Numbers* (Black Saint 1982, rec 1980), with Kowald, Sommer *Break The Shells* (1982), with Bill Smith Trio *Rastafari* (1983), *Jah Music* (1986, rec. 1984), *Human Rights* (Gramm 1986, rec 1982-85), *Procession Of The Great Ancestry* (Chief 1990, rec. 1983), *Kulture Jazz* (ECM 1993).

Further reading: *Notes (8 Pieces)*, Leo Smith.

Smith, Lonnie Liston

b. 28 December 1940, Richmond, Virginia, USA. Born into a very musical family, Smith seemed destined from a very early age to make music his career. His father and two brothers were all vocalists, but it was the keyboard that attracted Lonnie. After studying at Morgan State University, he moved to New York and immersed himself in the city's thriving jazz scene. Accompanying **Betty Carter** for a year in 1963, Smith soon became a highly sought-after pianist, working with successive jazz stars, from **Roland Kirk** (1964-65), **Art Blakey** (1966-67), and **Joe Williams** (1967-68), through to **Pharoah Sanders** (1969-71), **Gato Barbieri** (1971-73), and finally **Miles Davis** (1972-73). In 1974, Smith formed the Cosmic Echoes with his brother Donald as vocalist. Playing a very popular soft fusion, they recorded a highly successful album in 1975, and remained popular throughout the decade. In 1991, after some time out of the spotlight, Smith recorded a high quality album *Magic Lady* and embarked on a European tour (including the UK).

Albums: with Pharoah Sanders *Karma* (1969), with Miles Davis *Big Fun* (1972); solo (with the Cosmic Echoes) *Expansions* (1975), *Visions Of A New World* (1975), *Reflections Of A Golden Dream* (1976), *Renaissance* (1977); solo *Live!* (1977), *Loveland* (1978), *Exoctic Myteries* (1979), *Dreams Of Tomorrow* (1983), *Silhouettes* (1984), *Rejuvenation* (1988), *Magic Lady* (1991). Compilation: *The Best Of Lonnie Liston Smith* (1981).

Smith, Mamie

b. 26 May 1883, Cincinnati, Ohio, USA, d. 30 October 1940. Despite beginning her show business career as a dancer, before the outbreak of World War I Smith was established as a singer. Although she was, essentially, a vaudeville singer, in 1920 she recorded 'Crazy Blues', thus becoming the first black singer to record the blues as a soloist. The enormous success of this and her subsequent recordings established her reputation and thereafter she was always in great demand. Her accompanying musicians, on record and on tour, included **Willie 'The Lion' Smith**, **Joe Smith**, Johnny Dunn, **Bubber Miley** and **Coleman Hawkins**. She lived extravagantly, squandering the enormous amount of money she earned, and when she died on 30 October 1940 after a long illness, she was bankrupt.

Compilations: with others *Jazz Sounds Of The Twenties Vol. 4: The Blues Singers* (1923-31).

Smith, Margo

b. Betty Lou Miller, 9 April 1942, Dayton, Ohio, USA. Smith began her singing career while still at school as a member of the Apple Sisters vocal group. She trained as a teacher but also had hopes of a singing career. She wrote songs in her spare time and eventually made some unsuccessful recordings for Chart Records. In 1975, after changing labels to 20th Century, she made her US country chart debut with her own song, 'There I've Said It' and quit her job as a teacher. She moved to **Warner** the following year and immediately had two Top 10 country hits with 'Save Your Kisses For Me' and 'Take My Breath Away'. By 1981, she had 20 chart entries including two number 1s, 'Don't Break The Heart That Loves You' and 'It Only Hurts For A Little While'. Several others such as 'If I Give My Heart To You' and 'My Guy' were versions of songs that had already had pop chart success for other singers. She duetted with Norro Wilson ('So Close Again') and **Rex Allen Jnr.** ('Cup Of Tea'). She was dropped by Warner in 1981 but managed a few minor hits on indie labels (the last being 'Echo Me' on Playback in 1988), but recorded an album for **Dot**/MCA in 1986. Traditionalists would rate much of her work as country-pop but she is a brilliant yodeler and usually features this now unusual talent for lady vocalists in her stage show.

Albums: *Margo Smith* (1975), *Song Bird* (1976), *Happiness* (1977), *Don't Break The Heart That Loves You* (1978), *Just Margo* (1979), *A Woman* (1979), *Diamonds And Chills* (1980), *Margo Smith* (1986), *The Best Yet* (1988).

Smith, Moses 'Whispering'

b. 25 January 1932, Union Church, Mississippi, USA, d. 19 April 1984, Baton Rouge, Louisiana, USA. Smith is more associated with the blues of Louisiana, where he moved in his 20s, than that of his birth state. He learned harmonica in his teens and was playing regularly while still in Mississippi, but it was following his relocation in Baton Rouge, and taking up with **Lightnin' Slim**, that he made his first records. His harmonica work was uncomplicated but effective, and his voice had a distinctive, almost hoarse quality, with an extraordinary power that gave him his sardonic nickname. The handful of singles recorded in 1963 and 1964, earned him a reputation that he was able to capitalize on during the blues revival some years later. There were a few more recordings on albums in the 70s, and a single in the early 80s showed he was still a convincing blues performer.

Album: *Louisiana Blues* (1984).

Smith, O.C.

b. Ocie Lee Smith, 21 June 1932, Mansfield, Los Angeles, USA. O.C. Smith was raised in Los Angeles, where he began singing jazz and standards in clubs at the end of the 40s. After serving five years in the US Air Force, he signed with Cadence Records in 1956, enjoying some success the following year with the sophisticated 'Lighthouse'. He remained predominantly a club performer until 1961, when he replaced **Joe Williams** in the **Count Basie** Band. He resumed his solo career in 1963, finally attaining a commercial breakthrough in 1968 with **Dallas Frazier**'s unusual story-song, 'The Son Of Hickory Holler's Tramp', recorded at Fame Studios in Muscle Shoals and a major hit in Britain. In the USA, this record was overshadowed by his rendition of Bobby Russell's 'Little Green Apples', which outsold a rival hit version by **Roger Miller**, though it lost out to a home-grown release by **Leapy Lee** in Britain. 'Daddy's Little Man' in 1969 provided O.C. Smith's final taste of US Top 40 success, though the soul-flavoured 'La La Peace Song' proved popular in 1974, and 'Together' was an unexpected chart entry in 1977. During the decade in which he was most successful, Smith issued a series of impressive albums, which showcased his fluent, soulful vocal style.

Albums: *The Dynamic O.C. Smith* (1966), *Hickory Holler Revisited* (1968), *For Once In My Life* (1969), *At Home* (1969), *Help Me Make It Through The Night* (1971), *La La Peace Song* (1974), *Together* (1977). Compilation: *The O.C. Smith Collection* (1980, double album).

Smith, Patti

b. 31 December 1946, Chicago, Illinois, USA. Smith was raised in New Jersey and became infatuated by music, principally the **Rolling Stones**, the **Velvet Underground**, **Jimi Hendrix** and **James Brown**. Her initial talent focused on poetry and art, while her first major label recording was a version of a Jim Morrison poem on Ray Manzarek's (both **Doors**) solo album. Her early writing, captured on three anthologies, *Seventh Heaven* (1971), *Kodak* (1972) and *Witt* (1973), was inspired by Arthur Rimbaud and William Burroughs, but as the 70s progressed she was increasingly drawn towards fusing such work with rock. In 1971, Smith was accompanied by guitarist Lenny Kaye for a reading in St Mark's Church, and this informal liaison continued for three years until the duo was joined by Richard Sohl (piano) in the first Patti

Smith Group. Their debut recording, 'Hey Joe'/'Piss Factory', was in part financed by photographer Robert Mapplethorpe, later responsible for many of the artist's striking album portraits. By 1974 the unit had become one of the most popular acts at New York's pivotal **CBGB's** club. Ivan Kral (bass) and J.D. Daugherty (drums) were then added to the line-up featured on *Horses*. This highly-lauded set, produced by **John Cale**, skilfully invoked Patti's 60s' mentors but in a celebratory manner. By simultaneously capturing the fire of punk, Smith completed a collection welcomed by both old and new audiences. However, *Radio Ethiopia* was perceived as self-indulgent and the artist's career was further undermined when she incurred a broken neck upon falling offstage early in 1977. A lengthy recuperation ensued but Smith re-emerged in July with a series of excellent concerts and the following year scored considerable commercial success with *Easter*. This powerful set included 'Because The Night', co-written with **Bruce Springsteen**, which deservedly reached the UK Top 5, but *Wave* failed to sustain such acclaim. She had previously collaborated on three **Blue Öyster Cult** albums, with then partner Allen Lanier. Patti then married former **MC5** guitarist Fred 'Sonic' Smith, and retired from active performing for much of the 80s to raise a family. She resumed recording in 1988 with *Dream Of Life*, which contained the artist's customary call-to-arms idealism ('People Have The Power') and respect for rock and poetic tradition.

Albums: *Horses* (Arista 1975), *Radio Ethiopia* (Arista 1976), *Easter* (Arista 1978), *Wave* (Arista 1979), *Dream Of Life* (Arista 1988).

Further reading: *A Useless Death*, Smith, Patti, *The Tongue Of Love*, Smith, Patti, *Seventh Heaven*, Smith, Patti (1972), *Witt*, Smith, Patti (1973), *Babel*, Smith, Patti (1974), *The Night*, Smith, Patti & Verlaine, Tom (1976), *Ha! Ha! Houdini!*, Smith, Patti (1977), *Patti Smith: Rock & Roll Madonna*, Roach, Dusty (1979), *Patti Smith: High On Rebellion*, Muir (1980), *Early Work: 1970-1979*, Smith, Patti (1994).

Smith, Rex

b. 19 September 1956, Jacksonville, Florida, USA. Smith scored one Top 10 single under his own name, and also achieved recognition as co-host of the US music television programme *Solid Gold* and as a performer, along with **Linda Ronstadt**, in the stage and film productions of *The Pirates Of Penzance*. Smith was raised in Atlanta, Georgia, where he performed in rock bands as a teenager and in various stage productions. Moving to New York in the 70s, he became leader of a band called Rex, which recorded two albums for **Columbia Records** that were unsuccessful. His break came in 1979 when he recorded 'You Take My Breath Away', from the soundtrack of the television movie *Sooner Or Later*, in

which he also starred. The single reached number 10 on Columbia and the *Sooner Or Later* album made the Top 20. Smith only returned to the singles chart one more time, in 1981, with 'Everlasting Love', a duet with **Stiff Records** artist **Rachel Sweet**, which reached number 32. Two other albums made the bottom of the charts in the early 80s, but Smith by then had found work hosting *Solid Gold*, the television dance show, with **Marilyn McCoo**, formerly of the **Fifth Dimension**. Smith also appeared in the television series *Street Hawk* and in Broadway productions of *Headin' For Broadway* and *Grease*. His last major notices came in 1983 when he, along with Ronstadt and actor Kevin Kline, appeared in *The Pirates Of Penzance*, first on Broadway and then on film.
Albums: *Rex* (1976), *Where Do We Go From Here?* (1977), *Sooner Of Later* (1979), *Forever, Rex Smith* (1980), *Everlasting Love* (1981).

Smith, Robert Curtis
b. c.1930, Mississippi, USA. This accomplished guitarist, was influenced by **Big Bill Broonzy**. A wistful but committed blues singer, Smith was encountered by chance in **Wade Walton**'s barber shop. Smith worked as a farm labourer, and raised a large family in considerable poverty. He was recorded again in 1962, but failed to achieve success with the new white audience. In 1969 he was reported to have joined the church and abandoned the blues.
Albums: *The Blues Of Robert Curtis Smith* (1963), *I Have To Paint My Face* (1969).

Smith, Russell
b. 1890, Ripley, Ohio, USA, d. 27 March 1966, Los Angeles, California, USA. The Smiths were a musical family though the two trumpeters Joe and Russell could scarcely have been less similar. Russell was a sober, ordered man who long outlived his more volatile brother. Russell became a professional musician in 1906 and moved to New York in 1910. He first played in Army Bands and then in reviews. He joined **Fletcher Henderson**'s band in 1925 and stayed for 15 years. He was very much the straight musician willing to leave the jazz to others and perfectly suited to playing lead in a big band. After Henderson he played with **Cab Calloway** (1941-46) and then with **Noble Sissle** (1946-50) before retiring to California in the 50s.
Albums: with Fletcher Henderson *A Study In Frustration* (1923-38).

Smith, Sammi
b. 5 August 1943, Orange, California, USA. As her father was a serviceman, the family moved around, and when aged only ll, she was singing pop standards in night clubs. She was discovered in 1967 by **Johnny Cash**'s bass player, Marshall Grant. Minor US country hits followed with 'So Long, Charlie Brown' and 'Brownsville Lumberyard'. She toured with **Waylon Jennings** and befriended a janitor at **Columbia Records**, **Kris Kristofferson**. Her warm, husky version of his song, 'Help Me Make It Through The Night', sold two million copies and was voted the Country Music Association's Single of the Year for 1971. Ironically, her record label, Mega, had been formed as a tax write-off and the last thing the owner wanted was a hit record. Smith had further country hits with 'Then You Walk In', 'For The Kids', 'I've Got To Have You', 'The Rainbow In Daddy's Eyes' and 'Today I Started Loving You Again', but she never topped 'Help Me Make It Through The Night' because, as she says, 'It was like following a Rembrandt with a kindergarten sketch'. Smith wrote 'Sand-Covered Angels', recorded by **Conway Twitty**, and 'Cedartown, Georgia' by Waylon Jennings. At Elektra, she recorded 'As Long As There's A Sunday' and 'Loving Arms' but in the 80s she only had limited US country chart success. Smith's former husband is **Willie Nelson**'s guitarist Jody Payne and, being part Apache herself, she has adopted two Apache children and has an all American Indian band, Apache Spirit. In 1978 she set up the Sammi Smith Scholarship for Apache Advance Education, the aim being to increase the number of Apache lawyers and doctors.
Albums: *He's Everywhere* (1970), *The World Of Sammi Smith* (1971), *Lonesome* (1971), *Something Old, Something New, Something Blue* (1972), *The Toast Of '45* (1973), *The Best Of Sammi Smith* (1974), *Rainbow In Daddy's Eyes* (1974), *Sunshine* (1975), *Today I Started Loving You Again* (1975), *The Very Best Of Sammi Smith* (1975), *As Long As There's A Sunday* (1976), *Help Me Make It Through The Night* (1976), *Her Way* (1976), *New Winds, All Quadrants* (1978), *Mixed Emotions* (1979), *Girl Hero* (1979), *Better Than Ever* (1986), *Here Comes That Rainbow Again* (1990).

Smith, Slim
b. Keith Smith, c.1948, Jamaica, West Indies, d. 1973. Smith first came to prominence as a member of the Victors Youth Band who were highly praised at the 1964 Jamaican Festival. He subsequently became a founding member and lead vocalist of the **Techniques** who secured a recording contract with **Duke Reid**'s Treasure Isle label. From 1964-65 they recorded several hits, two of which, 'I Am In Love' and 'Little Did You Know', are included on the Techniques' *Classics* compilation. After leaving the group in 1965, he visited Canada where he recorded his first solo album, *Toronto '66*, which almost instantly sunk into obscurity. On his return to Jamaica, he commenced recording for **Prince Buster** and **Coxsone Dodd**'s **Studio One** label, the main rival to Duke Reid. His Studio One recordings brilliantly highlight his passionate, soulful voice, shot through with an almost manic edge, and confirm him to be one

of Jamaica's greatest singers. His hits from this period include 'I've Got Your Number', 'Hip Hug' and 'Rougher Yet', many of which were later compiled for *Born To Love*.

In 1967 he formed a new group, the **Uniques**, and commenced his association with producer **Bunny Lee**. They topped the Jamaican hit parade with 'Let Me Go Girl', but after recording one album, *Absolutely The Uniques*, Slim left the group, but stayed with Lee to concentrate on a solo career. He had a hit almost immediately with 'Everybody Needs Love'. An album of the same name quickly followed, as did many further hits. By 1972 personal problems led him to be detained at Bellevue sanatorium, and the following year he committed suicide. His death stunned Jamaica. Still widely regarded as one of Jamaica's great vocalists, his lasting popularity has thankfuly resulted in the reissue of the bulk of his work.

Albums: *Toronto '66* (1966), *Everybody Needs Love* (1969, reissued Pama 1989), *Just A Dream* (c.1971, reissued Pama 1989). Compilations: *The Time Has Come* (Pama 1984), *Memorial* (Trojan 1985), *Dance Hall Connection* (Third World 1986), *Born To Love (1966-68)* (Studio One 1979), *20 Super Hits* (Sonic Sounds 1991), *Rain From The Skies* (Trojan 1992), *20 Rare Grooves* (Rhino 1994).

Smith, Stuff

b. Hezekiah Leroy Gordon Smith, 14 August 1909, Portsmouth, Ohio, USA, d. 25 September 1967. Smith began playing violin as a child; he had some formal tuition but left home at the age of 15 to make his way as a professional musician. In 1926 he became a member of the popular **Alphonso Trent** band, where he remained, with side trips to other bands, for four years. In 1930 he settled in Buffalo, where he formed his own group, and in 1936 he took to New York for a long and highly successful residency at the Onyx Club. This band, which included **Jonah Jones** and **Cozy Cole**, established Smith's reputation as forceful, hard-swinging jazzman with an anarchic sense of humour (he performed wearing a battered top hat and with a stuffed parrot on his shoulder). Off-stage he was an aggressive and disorganized individual, and in the late 30s he was forced to disband because of trouble with his sidemen, bookers, club owners and the union. Following **Fats Waller**'s death in 1943, Smith took over the band but this too was a short-lived affair. By the late 40s his career was in decline, but a series of recordings for **Norman Granz** in the late 50s, in which he was teamed, improbably but successfully, with **Dizzy Gillespie**, brought him back in to the spotlight. He began to tour, especially in Europe where he was extremely popular, settled in Denmark and continued to record. Perhaps the most exciting and dynamic of all the jazz fiddlers, Smith concentrated on swinging, attacking his instrument with wild fervour and

producing a rough-edged, almost violent sound. His performance of 'Bugle Call Rag' at a New York Town Hall concert in 1945 vividly demonstrates his all-stops-out approach to jazz and is a remarkable bravura display. Despite his swing era roots, Smith's recordings with Gillespie are filled with interesting explorations and he never seems ill-at-ease. A hard-drinker, Smith's later years were beset by hospitalizations, during which parts of his stomach and liver were removed. A visit to a Paris hospital resulted in his being declared a 'medical museum' and he was placed on the critical list, but within a few days he was back on the concert platform. He died in September 1967.

Albums: *Swingin' Stuff* (1956), *Have Violin, Will Swing* (1957), *Soft Winds* (1957), *Dizzy Gillespie With Stuff Smith* (1957), *Violins No End* (1957), *Sessions, Live* (1958), *Stuff Smith* (1959), *Cat On A Hot Fiddle* (1959), *Blues In G* (1965), with Stéphane Grappelli *Stuff And Steff* (1965), with Grappelli and Jean-Luc Ponty *Violin Summit* (1966), *Black Violin* (1967). Compilations: *Stuff Smith And His Onyx Club Orchestra* (1936), *The Varsity Sessions* (1938-40), with others Town Hall Concert Vol. 2 (1945).

Further reading: *Stuff Smith: Pure At Heart*, Anthony Barnett and Evan Logager, *Desert Sands: The Recordings And Performances Of Stuff Smith*, Anthony Barnett.

Smith, Tab

b. Talmadge Smith, 11 January 1909, Kinston, North Carolina, USA, d. 17 August 1971. After learning to play piano and C melody saxophone, Smith settled on alto and soprano saxophones. It was on alto that he made his name, working in bands led by **Fate Marable**, **Lucky Millinder** and **Frankie Newton** during the 30s. He also played in **Teddy Wilson**'s ill-fated big band, at this time often playing tenor. In 1939 and into the early 40s he was in great demand, recording with **Billie Holiday**, **Earl Hines**, **Charlie Shavers**, **Coleman Hawkins**, playing with **Count Basie** and Millinder again, and also leading his own band. In the late 40s and early 50s he played only part time but, after making some popular R&B recordings, he was soon back leading a band, which he continued to do throughout most of the 50s. Late in the decade he again dropped out of full-time music, ending his career playing organ in a St. Louis restaurant. Smith was a forceful player on both alto and soprano, his solos having an attractively restless urgency. His sound was burred and possessed a surging intensity that helped him make the transition into R&B. Under-recorded in his lifetime and largely overlooked since his death, Smith's contribution to jazz was inevitably if unjustly overshadowed by better-known contemporaries such as **Benny Carter**, **Willie Smith** and, perhaps, his closest musical counterpart, **Pete Brown**.

Selected albums: *Tab Smith i* (1959), *Tab Smith ii* (1960). Selected compilations: *Lucky Millinder And His Orchestra 1941-1943* (1941-43), with Coleman Hawkins *Swing*

(1944), with Charlie Shavers incl. on *Hawkins And Hines* (1944), *Because Of You* (1951-55), *I Don't Want To Play In Your Kitchen* (Saxophonograph 1987), *Jump Time 1951-52* (Delmark 1987), *Joy At The Savoy* (Saxophonograph 1987), *Because Of You* (Delmark 1989), *Worlds Greatest Altoist - These Foolish Things* (Saxophonograph 1989), *Aces High* (Delmark 1992).

Smith, Tommy

b. 27 April 1967, Luton, England. Smith grew up in Edinburgh and started playing saxophone at the age of 12. He wowed the jazz clubs with his precocious brilliance and appeared on television in 1982, backed by pianist **Gordon Beck** and bassist **Niels-Henning Ørsted Pedersen**. The next year, aged only 16, he recorded *Giant Strides* for Glasgow's GFM Records. It was an astonishing debut. The young tenor made mistakes, but the stark recording honed in on his major assets: a full, burnished tone and a firm idea of the overall shape of his solos. It shone out of the British jazz of the time like a beacon, a herald of the 'jazz revival' among younger players. In 1983 he played the Leverkusen Jazz Festival in Germany. The Scottish jazz scene helped to raise the money to send him to **Berklee College Of Music**, where he enrolled in January 1984. **Jaco Pastorius** invited him to join his group for club dates, as did vibist **Gary Burton**. In 1985 Smith formed Forward Motion, with Laszlo Gardonyi (piano), Terje Gewelt (bass) and Ian Froman (drums), and began international tours, playing a spacious, reflective jazz. It was no surprise when **ECM** producer Manfred Eicher asked him to play on Burton's *Whiz Kids* in 1986, as Smith was sounding more and more like the label's established saxophone maestro, **Jan Garbarek**. In 1988 he toured under his own name with Froman from Forward Motion, pianist **John Taylor** and bassist **Chris Laurence**. In 1989 he introduced a series of 10 jazz television broadcasts and in 1990 worked with pop band **Hue And Cry**. In May 1990 he premiered a concerto for saxophone and string ensemble commissioned by the Scottish Ensemble. Signed to **Blue Note** in the late 80s, he has so far released three albums on the label.
Albums: *Giant Strides* (GFM 1983), with Forward Motion *Progressions* (1985), with Forward Motion *The Berklee Tapes* (1985), *Step By Step* (Step By Step 1989), *Peeping Tom* (Blue Note 1990), *Standards* (Blue Note 1991), *Paris* (Blue Note 1992), *Reminiscence* (Linn 1994), *Misty Morning & No Time* (Linn 1995).

Smith, Trixie

b. 1895, Atlanta, Georgia, USA, d. 21 September 1943. Unlike many of her contemporaries, Smith attended university before going on the road as a singer. She worked the vaudeville circuit, singing popular songs of the day interspersed with blues songs. By the early 20s she was making records and had

embarked upon a parallel career as an actress. A highly polished performer, her records include several outstanding examples of the blues on which she is accompanied by artists such as **James P. Johnson**, **Fletcher Henderson** and **Freddie Keppard**.
Selected album: *Trixie Smith And Her Down Home Syncopators* (1925).

Smith, Willie

b. 25 November 1910, Charleston, South Carolina, USA, d. 7 March 1967. Smith began playing clarinet while still at school, performing professionally in his mid-teens. While at Fisk University he met **Jimmie Lunceford**, joining him in an orchestra there which eventually became a full-time professional organization. By now playing alto saxophone, Smith became a key member of the Lunceford band, meticulously drilling the saxophone section into perfection. He was with Lunceford until 1942, shortly before entering the US Navy where he directed a band. After the war he joined **Harry James**, bringing with him a level of commitment and dedication similar to that he had brought to Lunceford's band. He was with James until 1951, then played briefly with **Duke Ellington** and **Billy May**, then joined **Jazz At The Philharmonic**, touring internationally. During the remainder of the 50s he was with the ill-fated **Benny Goodman/Louis Armstrong** all-star package, followed by James and May again, then he did film studio work while combating a drink problem. In the early 60s Smith worked in various minor show bands in Los Angeles, Las Vegas and, briefly, led his own band in New York. Before the arrival of **Charlie Parker**, Smith, along with **Benny Carter** and **Johnny Hodges**, was one of the three major alto saxophonists in jazz. As a section leader he was outstanding, as almost any record by the Lunceford band will testify. As a soloist he had a sinuously beautiful tone, marked by a definitive hard edge that prevented him from ever slipping into sentimentality.
Albums: *Jazz At The Philharmonic* (1944-46), *Jazz At The Philharmonic 1946 Vol. 2* (1946), *Jazz History Vol. 12: Harry James* (1959-62), *Alto Saxophonist Supreme* (1965). Compilation: *The Complete Jimmie Lunceford* (1939-40).

Smith, Willie 'The Lion'

b. 25 November 1897, Goshen, New York, USA, d. 18 April 1973. Smith began playing piano at the age of six, encouraged by his mother. He continued with his informal musical education and by his mid-teenage years, he had established a formidable reputation in New York as a ragtime pianist. During World War I Smith acquired his nickname, apparently through acts of great heroism. In the post-war years he quickly developed into one of Harlem's best-known and feared stride pianists. Despite his popularity in Harlem and the respect of his fellows, including **Fats Waller**,

James P. Johnson and **Duke Ellington**, he made few records and remained virtually unknown outside the New York area. In the 40s he travelled a little further afield, and during the 50s and 60s gradually extended his audience, playing and reminiscing at the keyboard, and recording numerous albums which demonstrated his commanding style.

Selected albums: *The Lion Roars* (1957), *Music On My Mind* (1966), *Pork And Beans* (Black Lion 1966), *The Memoirs* (1967), *Live At Blues Alley* (1970), *The Lion's In Town* (Vogue 1993, 1959 recording). Selected compilations: *The Original 14 Plus Two* (1938-39), *Tea For Two* (Jazz Live 1981), *Memoirs Of Willie The Lion* (RCA 1983), *Memorial* (Vogue 1988, 1949-50 recordings) *Reminiscing The Piano Greats* (1950).

Further reading: *Music On My Mind*, Willie 'The Lion' Smith and George Hoefer (ed.)

Smith, Willie Mae Ford

b. c.1904, d. 2 February 1994. Gospel music stalwart, widely known in the music's parlance as 'Mother Smith'. Smith was also widely remembered for her role in the 1982 gospel music documentary, *Say Amen, Somebody*.

Smither, Chris

b. 11 November 1944, Miami, Florida, USA. Smither began his music career, during the 60s, by performing in the coffee houses and clubs in New Orleans where he had relocated from the age of 2. His first real blues influence came after listening to a **Lightnin' Hopkins**' recording, *Blues In My Bottle*, at the age of 17. He moved to Boston, Massachusetts in 1966, where he continued playing the lucrative coffee house/folk circuit. He also started associating with artists such as **Bonnie Raitt**, **John Hammond**, and **Mississippi Fred MacDowell**. After a promising start, with two albums on the Poppy label, the label folded. He recorded *Honeysuckle Dog*, for United Artists, which featured Raitt, but this was never released. Smither has had his songs covered by numerous performers, including Bonnie Raitt, who included his 'Love Me Like A Man', and 'I Feel The Same' on two of her albums and **John Mayall** who used 'Mail Order Mystics' as the title track on his recent album. He has performed at various times with many musicians including **Nanci Griffith**, **Jackson Browne**, **Van Morrison**, and also at numerous major festivals throughout the US.

Smithers' smooth, lyrical guitar style encompasses elements of folk, blues, country and rock and his voice is capable of sounding soft one minute and gruff the next. Having fought off the demon alcohol Smither faces the 90s as a survivor fresh and enthusiastic for his work. The live *Another Way To Find You*, on Flying Fish records was recorded over two nights in a studio with an invited audience. *Happier Blue* shows the artist really coming into his own. This excellent set includes **Lowell George**'s 'Rock And Roll Doctor' and **J.J. Cale**'s 'Magnolia' in addition to the original title track 'Happier Blue'. The powerful lyric of this song is but one example of his emotional talent; 'I was sad and then I loved you, it took my breath, now I think you love me and it scares me to death, cause now I lie awake and wonder, I worry I think about losing you, I don't care what you say, maybe I was happier blue'. Smither's guitar playing is worthy of noting (Bonnie Raitt calls him her Eric Clapton) as he is able to be percussive and rhythmic, together with a fluid busy style that is as breathtaking as it is effortless.

Albums: *I'm A Stranger Too* (1970), *Don't it Drag On* (1972), *It Ain't Easy* (1984, reissued 1990), *Another Way To Find You* (Flying Fish 1991), *Happier Blue* (1993), *Up On The Lowdown* (Hightone 1995).

Smithereens

Influenced by the 60s pop of the **Beatles**, **Beach Boys** and the **Byrds**, the Smithereens formed in New Jersey in 1980. Members Jim Babjak (guitar) and Dennis Diken (drums) had played together since 1971; Mike Mesaros (bass) was recruited in 1976 and finally Pat DiNizio (vocals). After recording two EPs, they backed songwriter **Otis Blackwell** ('Great Balls Of Fire') on two obscure albums. In 1986 the group signed to Enigma Records and released their first full album, *Especially For You*, which fared well among both college radio and mainstream rock listeners, as did the single 'Blood And Roses'. After a lengthy tour, the Smithereens recorded their second album, *Green Thoughts*, in 1988, this time distributed by **Capitol Records**. *Smithereens 11*, was their biggest selling album to date reaching number 41 in the US chart. The group's music has also been featured in several movie soundtracks including the teen-horror film, '*Class Of Nuke 'Em High*'. Their career faltered in 1991 with the poorly received *Blow Up* (US number 120) leaving critics to ponder if the band have run out of ideas.

Albums: *Especially For You* (1986), *Green Thoughts* (1988), *Smithereens 11* (1990), *Blow Up* (1991), *A Date With The Smithereens* (RCA 1994).

Smiths

Acclaimed by many as the most important UK group of the 80s, the Smiths were formed in Manchester during the spring of 1982. **Morrissey** (b. Steven Patrick Morrissey, 22 May 1959, Davyhulme, Manchester, England) and Johnny Marr (b. John Maher, 31 October 1963, Ardwick, Manchester, England) originally combined as a songwriting partnership, and only their names appeared on any contract bearing the title 'Smiths'. Morrissey had previously played for a couple of months in the Nosebleeds and also rehearsed and auditioned with a late version of **Slaughter And The Dogs**. After that he wrote reviews for *Record Mirror* and penned a couple of booklets on the **New York Dolls** and James Dean. Marr, meanwhile, had played in several Wythenshawe groups including the Paris Valentinos, White Dice, Sister Ray and Freaky Party. By the summer of 1982, the duo decided to form a group and recorded demos with drummer Simon Wolstencroft and a recording engineer named Dale. Wolstencroft subsequently declined an offer to join the Smiths and in later years became a member of the **Fall**. Eventually, Mike Joyce (b. 1 June 1963, Fallowfield, Manchester, England) was recruited as drummer, having previously played with the punk-inspired Hoax and Victim. During their debut gig at the Ritz in Manchester, the group was augmented by go-go dancer James Maker, who went on to join **Raymonde** and later RPLA. By the end of 1982, the group appointed a permanent bassist. Andy Rourke (b. 1963, Manchester, England), was an alumnus of various past groups with Marr. After being taken under the wing of local entrepreneur Joe Moss, the group strenuously rehearsed and after a series of gigs, signed to **Rough Trade Records** in the spring of 1983. By that time, they had issued their first single on the label, 'Hand In Glove', which failed to reach the Top 50. During the summer of 1983, they became entwined in the first of several tabloid press controversies when it was alleged that their lyrics contained references to child molesting. The eloquent Morrissey, who was already emerging as a media spokesperson of considerable power, sternly refuted the rumours. During the same period the group commenced work on their debut album with producer Troy Tate, but the sessions were curtailed, and a new set of recordings undertaken with John Porter. In November 1983 the group issued their second single, 'This Charming Man', a striking pop record that infiltrated the UK Top 30. Following an ill-fated trip to the USA at the end of the year, the quartet began 1984 with a new single, the notably rockier 'What Difference Does It Make?', which took them to number 12. *The Smiths* ably displayed the potential of the group, with Morrissey's oblique genderless lyrics coalesing with Marr's spirited guitar work. The closing track of the album was the haunting 'Suffer Little Children', a requiem to the child victims of the 60s Moors Murderers. The song later provoked a short-lived controversy in the tabloid press, which was resolved when the mother of one of the victims came out on Morrissey's side. A series of college gigs throughout Britain established the group as a cult favourite, with Morrissey displaying a distinctive image, complete with National Health spectacles, a hearing aid and bunches of gladioli. A collaboration with **Sandie Shaw** saw 'Hand In Glove' transformed into a belated hit, while Morrissey dominated music press interviews. His celibate stance provoked reams of speculation about his sexuality and his ability to provide good copy on subjects as various as animal rights, royalty, Oscar Wilde and 60s films, made him a journalist's dream interviewee. The singer's celebrated miserabilism was reinforced by the release of the autobiographical 'Heaven Knows I'm Miserable Now', which reached number 19 in the UK. Another Top 20 hit followed with 'William, It Was Really Nothing'. While the Smiths commenced work on their next album, Rough Trade issued the interim *Hatful Of Hollow*, a bargain-priced set that included various flip sides and radio sessions. It was a surprisingly effective work, that captured the inchoate charm of the group. By 1984 the Smiths found themselves feted as Britain's best group by various factions in the music press. The release of the sublime 'How Soon Is Now?' justified much of the hyperbole and this was reinforced by the power of their next album, *Meat Is Murder*. This displayed Morrissey's increasingly tendency towards social commentary, which had been indicated in his controversial comments on **Band Aid** and the IRA bombings. The album chronicled violence at schools ('The Headmaster Ritual'), adolescent thuggery ('Rusholme Ruffians'), child abuse ('Barbarism Begins At Home') and animal slaughter ('Meat Is Murder'). The proseletyzing tone was brilliantly complemented by the musicianship of Marr, Rourke and Joyce. Marr's work on such songs as 'The Headmaster Ritual' and 'That Joke Isn't Funny Anymore' effectively propelled him to the position of one of Britain's most respected rock guitarists. Despite releasing a milestone album, the group's fortunes in the singles charts were relatively disappointing. 'Shakespeare's Sister' received a lukewarm response and stalled at number 26, amid ever growing rumours that the group were dissatisfied with their record label. Another major UK tour in 1985 coincided with various management upheavals, which dissipated the group's energies. A successful trek across the USA was followed by the release of the plaintive summer single, 'The Boy With The Thorn In His Side' which, despite its commerciality, only reached number 23. A dispute with Rough Trade delayed the release of the next Smiths album, which was preceded by the superb 'Big Mouth Strikes Again', another example of Marr at his best. During the same period, Rourke was briefly ousted from the group due to his flirtation with heroin. He was soon reinstated, however, along with a second guitarist Craig Gannon, who had previously played with **Aztec Camera**, the **Bluebells** and **Colourfield**. In June 1986 *The Queen Is Dead* was issued and won immediate critical acclaim for its diversity and unadulterated power. The range of mood and emotion offered on the album was startling to behold, ranging from the epic grandeur of the title track to the overt romanticism of 'There Is A Light That Never Goes Out' and the irreverent comedy of 'Frankly Mr Shankly' and 'Some Girls Are Bigger Than Others'. A superb display of Morrissey/Marr at their apotheosis, the album was rightly placed alongside *Meat Is Murder* as one of the finest achievements of the decade. A debilitating stadium tour of the USA followed and during the group's absence they enjoyed a formidable Top 20 hit with the disco-denouncing 'Panic'. The sentiments of the song, coupled with Morrissey's negative comments on certain aspects of black music, provoked further adverse comments in the press. That controversy was soon replaced by the news that the Smiths were to record only one more album for Rough Trade and intended to transfer their operation to the major label, **EMI Records**. Meanwhile, the light pop of 'Ask' contrasted with riotous scenes during the group's 1986 UK tour. At the height of the drama, the group almost suffered a fatality when Johnny Marr was involved in a car crash. While he recuperated, guitarist Craig Gannon was fired, a decision that prompted legal action. The group ended the year with a concert at the Brixton Academy supported by fellow Mancunians, the Fall. It was to prove their final UK appearance. After another hit with 'Shoplifters Of The World Unite' the group completed what would prove their final album. The glam rock inspired 'Sheila Take A Bow' returned them to the Top 10 and their profile was maintained with the release of another sampler album, *The World Won't Listen*. Marr was growing increasingly disenchanted with the group's musical direction, however, and privately announced that he required a break. With the group's future still in doubt, press speculation proved so intense that an official announcement of a split occurred in August 1987. *Strangeways, Here We Come*, an intriguing transitional album, was issued posthumously. The work indicated the different directions that the major protagonists were progressing towards during their final phase. A prestigious television documentary of the group's career followed on *The South Bank Show* and a belated live album, *"Rank"*, was issued the following year. The junior members Rourke and Joyce initially appeared with Brix Smith's **Adult Net**, then backed **Sinead O'Connor**, before Joyce joined the **Buzzcocks**. Morrissey pursued a solo career, while Marr moved from the **Pretenders** to **The The** and **Electronic**, as well as appearing on a variety of sessions for artists as diverse as **Bryan Ferry**, **Talking Heads**, **Billy Bragg**, **Kirsty MacColl**, the **Pet Shop Boys**, Stex and Banderas. In 1992 there was renewed interest in the Smiths following the furore surrounding Johnny Rogan's controversial biography of the group, and Warner Brothers acquisition of the group's back-catalogue from Rough Trade.

Albums: *The Smiths* (Rough Trade 1984), *Meat Is Murder* (Rough Trade 1985), *The Queen Is Dead* (Rough Trade 1986), *Strangeways, Here We Come* (Rough Trade 1987), *"Rank"* (Rough Trade 1988). Compilations: *Hatful Of Hollow* (Rough Trade 1984), *The World Won't Listen* (Rough Trade 1987), *Louder Than Bombs* (Rough Trade 1987), *The Peel Sessions* (Strange Fruit 1988), *Best...2* (WEA 1992), *Singles* (WEA 1995).

Video: *The Complete Picture*.

Further reading: *The Smiths*, Mick Middles. *Morrissey & Marr: The Severed Alliance*, Johnny Rogan. *The Smiths: The Visual Documentary*, Johnny Rogan.

Smoke

Mick Rowley (vocals), Mal Luker (lead guitar), Phil Peacock (rhythm guitar), John 'Zeke' Lund (bass) and Geoff Gill (drums) were initially known as the Shots. This Yorkshire, England, group was groomed for success by Alan Brush, a gravel pit owner and self-made millionaire who harboured dreams of pop management. His ambitions faltered when the Shots' lone single, 'Keep A Hold Of What You Got', failed to sell. Phil Peacock then dropped out of the line-up, but within months the remaining quartet approached producer Monty Babson with several new demos. The most promising song, 'My Friend Jack', was released in February 1967 under the group's new name, the Smoke. Although irresistibly commercial, problems arose when the line 'my friend Jack eats sugar lumps' was construed as celebrating drug abuse. The record was banned in Britain, but became a massive hit on the continent and on the **pirate radio** ships, inspiring a release for the group's only album, *It's Smoke Time*. Later singles continued their quirky-styled pop, but they failed to garner a significant breakthrough. Having toyed with yet another appellation, Chords Five, Lund, Luker and Gill began work as resident musicians at Babson's Morgan Sound studios. Several more singles, credited to the Smoke, appeared on various labels during the late 60s/early 70s. These often throwaway efforts featured sundry variations on the above triumvirate, accompanied by any other backroom staff present.

Album: *It's Smoke Time* (1967). Compilation: *My Friend Jack* (1988).

Smokey Babe

b. Robert Brown, 1927, Itta Bena, Mississippi, USA, d. 1975, Louisiana, USA. Smokey Babe led a hard life of farmwork and migrant labour before and after settling in Baton Rouge, Louisiana. Here he entertained, and jammed with, his neighbours and friends, and was recorded in the early 60s. He was one of the most talented acoustic blues guitarists located by folkloric research, singing and playing both swinging, energetic dance music and moving personal blues. However, he never achieved the acclamation and wider exposure his talent merited.

Selected Albums: *Country Negro Jam Session* (1960), *Hot Blues* (1961), *Hottest Brand Goin'* (1963).

Smokey Joe's Cafe: The Songs Of Leiber And Stoller

This celebratory musical revue devoted to the works of the immensely influential songwriting team of the 50s and early 60s, was originally conceived by Stephen Helper and Jack Viertel, with assistance from Otis Sallid. It opened at the Virginia Theatre in New York on 2 March 1995. Nine singers - five men and four women - perform nearly 40 songs on Heidi Landesman's glitzy set, reminding those who needed reminding, that two white men, Jerry Leiber and Mike Stoller, who were seeped in black music, wrote and produced some of the greatest blues-influenced records of their time. One of them, 'Hound Dog', which was written for **Willie Mae 'Big Mama' Thornton**, and later popularized by **Elvis Presley**, was given the full treatment by the marvellous B.J. Thornton, who also had a ball with 'Fools Fall In Love'. Other outstanding performances came from DeLee Lively ('Teach Me How To Shimmy'), Victor Trent Cook ('I Who Have Nothing' and 'Searchin''), Pattie Darcy Jones ('Pearl's A Singer'), and Adrian Bailey ('Love Me'). Together with the rest of the splendid cast, which included Ken Ard, Brenda Baxton, Frederick B. Owens, and Michael Park, they evoked memories of legendary groups such as the **Coasters** and the **Drifters**, together with so many other artists who had hits with Leiber and Stoller's terrific songs. Among the rest of the nearly 40 songs on display were 'Love Potion Number Nine', 'Jailhouse Rock', 'Spanish Harlem', 'On Broadway', 'Yakety Yak', 'Charley Brown', 'Poison Ivy', 'Keep On Rollin'', 'There Goes My Baby', and, of course, 'Smokey Joe's Cafe'. Jerry Zaks was the director, and the show received seven **Tony** nominations, but failed to win one award: it was the year of *Sunset Boulevard* and *Show Boat*. An earlier tribute to Leiber and Stoller was devised by the British producer and author Ned Sherrin, and presented at the Roundhouse Theatre in London in 1980. Among the cast was Clarke Peters, who later conceived the long running **Louis Jordan** musical anthology, *Five Guys Named Moe* in 1990.

Smokie

This UK pop band from Bradford, Yorkshire, featured Chris Norman (vocals), Terry Utley (guitar), and Alan Silson (bass). The three were previously together in 1966 with a band titled the Elizabethans. Pete Spencer replaced their original drummer shortly afterwards. Turning professional in 1968, they changed their name to Kindness, performing at holiday camps and ballrooms. A variety of record company contracts failed to ignite any hit singles, however. Along the way they changed their name to Smokey, but it was not until they joined **Rak Records**, where **Mickie Most** introduced them to songwriters **Chinn And Chapman**, that they saw any success. They then scored frequently with 'If You Think You Know How To Love Me' and 'Don't Play Your Rock 'n' Roll To Me' in 1975, after which they changed the spelling of their name to Smokie. Their 1976 version of the Chinn/Chapman composition 'Living Next Door To Alice', originally recorded by New World, became a hit in the face of opposition from the burgeoning punk scene. Norman, meanwhile, joined fellow Rak artist **Suzi Quatro** on the 1978 hit duet 'Stumblin' In'. By 1978 and *The Montreux Album*, the band, through Norman and Spencer, were taking a greater share of writing credits, but this coincided with a drop in their fortunes. They bounced back briefly in 1980 with a cover of **Bobby Vee**'s 'Take Good Care Of My Baby', but this proved to be their last hit. Norman and Spencer moved on to writing for other artists including fellow Rak teenybop groups, and both Kevin Keegan's 'Head Over Heels' and the England World Cup Squad's 'This Time We'll Get It Right'.

Albums: *Smokie/Changing All The Time* (1975), *Bright Lights And Back Alleys* (1977), *The Montreux Album* (1978). Compilations: *Greatest Hits* (1977), *Smokie's Hits* (1980), *Greatest Hits Live* (1993).

Smooth, Joe

b. Joseph Welbon, USA. One of early house music's most distinctive vocalists, recording material like 'Time To Jack' and working with **Fingers Inc**. He actually started out as a DJ in 1983 at the Smart Bar in Chicago. There the staff were so impressed by his mixing that they dubbed him Joe Smooth for the first time. A genuine musician, he insisted on bringing his keyboards and drum machine on stage with him for his live shows. He went on to produce two house classics in 'You Can't Hide' (with **Frankie Knuckles**) and 'Promised Land' (later covered by the **Style Council**). His debut album featured guest vocals rather than his own as he concentrated on his musicianship. The singers included Anthony Thomas, former backing vocalist to the **Ohio Players**. The set included both 'Promised Land' and an unlikely **Jimi Hendrix** cover in 'Purple Haze'.

Smothers, Little Smokey

b. Abraham Smothers, 2 January 1939, Tchula, Mississippi, USA. Ten years younger than his brother, **Otis 'Big Smokey' Smothers**, the teenaged Abe arrived in Chicago in the mid-50s and because of his 'younger brother' status, received help from many established bluesmen. His first gig was with **Big Boy Spires**, who had already helped his brother and cousin, **Lester Davenport**. **Magic Sam** was also a major influence in the development of his guitar playing. He spent two years in **Howlin' Wolf**'s band and played on the July 1959 session which produced 'Mr Airplane Man' and 'Howlin' For My Darling'.

Smothers then formed his own band, the Wrench Crew, with another cousin, Lee 'Shot' Williams as vocalist. Beginning in 1962, he also nurtured the respective talents of **Paul Butterfield** and **Elvin Bishop**, giving tuition and allowing them to sit in at his gigs. When they were offered a record deal, Smothers took to the road with **Earl Hooker** and then spent the 70s working with **Jimmy Rogers**. Although he appeared on the *American Blues Legends '79* album, his job as a construction worker prevented him from joining the ensuing tour. During the 80s, he worked with the **Legendary Blues Band** and guitarist Billy Flynn from the band was involved in the making of *Bossman*, along with Elvin Bishop, Lee 'Shot' Williams and Tony Zamagni. Typically, Smothers surrendered his spotlight to others on a record that displayed a worthy but minor talent.
Albums: (Big Bear 1979), *Bossman* (Black Magic 1993).

Smothers, Otis 'Big Smokey'

b. 21 March 1929, Lexington, Mississippi, USA, d. 23 July 1993. Raised in the Tchula area, Smothers learned harmonica and guitar from an aunt before moving north to Chicago in 1946. His first stage appearance came five years later, with **Johnny Williams** and **Johnny Young** at the Square Deal Club. Other musicians with whom he played, on and off the street, included **Big Boy Spires**, **Earl Hooker**, Henry Strong and cousin, Lester Davenport. He also played with **Bo Diddley,** and claimed to be on 'Bring It To Jerome'. In 1956 he joined **Howlin' Wolf**'s band, playing second guitar on 'The Natchez Burning' and 'I Asked For Water'. Later, he was in a **Muddy Waters'** junior band, along with **Freddie King**, Mojo Elem and drummer T.J. McNulty. Having been refused by **Chess,** he recorded for Federal in August 1960. Encouraged by producer **Sonny Thompson** to emulate **Jimmy Reed**, he recorded 'Honey, I Ain't Teasin'' as part of a marathon 12-title session whose second half was immeasurably improved by the addition of Freddie King, the day before his own Federal debut. Another 1962 Federal session, with harmonica player Little Boyd, produced 'Twist With Me Annie', a bizarre updating of **Hank Ballard's** original. Sometime later, while a member of Muddy Waters' band, he recorded 'I Got My Eyes On You' for the obscure Gamma label. By the 70s, he had almost forsaken music, saying with more equanimity than some in his position, 'Everybody can't be president'.
Album: *The Complete Sessions* (1982).

Smurfs (Father Abraham And The)

If ever popular music veers too close to being a serious topic of academic cultural discussion, one only has to remember episodes like those of the Smurfs in the late 70s. While the punk wars raged around them, Father Abraham And The Smurfs mounted their chart bid with 'The Smurf Song', released on **Decca Records** in May 1978. Conducted in a semi-duet fashion, with Father Abraham leading the assembled midget characters in call-response chants, delivered in their eminently silly, high-pitched voices, it served to introduce the concept of Smurf culture to the nation. The Smurfs, also depicted in a cartoon series, lived in forests and promoted pre-environmental awareness good while hiding from human beings. Similar to the **Wombles** concept of a few years earlier, Father Abraham And The Smurfs enjoyed two further UK charts hits, 'Dippety Day' (number 13) and 'Christmas In Smurfland' (number 19). This prompted music business maverick **Jonathon King** to release his own cash-in novelty record, 'Lick A Smurp For Christmas (All Fall Down)', credited to Father Abraphart And The Smurfs. There were also a total of three albums for the more masochistic fans.
Albums: *Smurfing Sing Song* (Decca 1979), *Merry Christmas With The Smurfs* (Dureco 1983), *Smurf's Party Time* (Dureco 1983).

Smythe, Pat

b. 2. May 1923, Edinburgh, Scotland, d. 6. May 1983, London, England. Smythe practised as a lawyer in Edinburgh before moving to London in the late 50s. He played with trumpeter **Dizzy Reece** before joining **Joe Harriott**'s Quintet (1960-64). Harriott was developing the beginnings of a European free jazz quite unlike **Ornette Coleman**'s American form. Smythe was able to help both as pianist in the band and with suggestions to organize the new ideas. He stayed on with Harriott in the Indo Jazz Fusions which again organized improvization along new lines. Throughout the 70s he worked in a variety of contexts with **Kenny Wheeler**. He was a skilled accompanist especially of singers like **Anita O'Day**, **Blossom Dearie**, **Tony Bennett**, **Annie Ross**, **Elaine Delmar** and **Mark Murphy**. So respected a musician was he that after his death the Pat Smythe Memorial Trust and Award was established in his memory.
Albums: with Joe Harriott *Free Form* (1960), *Abstract* (1961-62), *Movement* (1963), *High Spirits* (1964), *Indo Jazz Suite* (1966), *Indo Jazz Fusions* (1966), *Personal Portrait* (1967), *Sandra King In A Concert Of Vernon Duke* (1982).

Snafu

Formed in 1973 by former **Freedom** vocalist and percussionist **Bobby Harrison** (b. 28 June 1943, East Ham, London, England) using the nucleus of the musicians who appeared on his solo album *Funkest* (1970). The name of the band came from an old Royal Air Force expression; Situation Normal - All Fucked Up. The original members were Colin Gibson (b. 21 September 1949, Newcastle-Upon-Tyne, Tyne & Wear, England; bass), Peter Solly (b. 19 October 1948, Hampstead, London, England; keyboards/

synthesizers), Terry Popple (b. 21 July 1946, Stockton On Tees, Co Durham, England; drums) and Mick Moody (b. 30 August 1950, Middlesbrough, Cleveland, England; guitar). Snafu played solidly constructed heavy rock, and fitted well into the receptive music scene of the early 70s. All the members had previously made names as reputable session musicians, particularly the north-east trio of Gibson, Popple and Moody who would later show up on albums by such artists as **Alan Hull** and **Graham Bonnet**.

Albums: *Snafu* (1974), *Situation Normal* (1974), *All Funked Up* (1975).

Snakefinger

Snakefinger was an appellation adopted by British guitarist Phil Lithman. A member of mid-60s' act Junior's Blues Band, Lithman subsequently moved to San Francisco for a career as a folk and blues singer, before returning to the UK in the early 70s to join former colleague Martin Stone (guitar) in Chilli Willi. The duo subsequently expanded this acoustic-based act and, as **Chilli Willi And The Red Hot Peppers**, became one of the finest acts of the UK 'pub rock' genre. The group split up in 1975, following which Lithman returned to California where he re-established links with the arcane **Residents**. Although Lithman became known as Snakefinger while with Chilli Willi, his exceptional dexterity and skills were apparent on several Residents' recordings, including their reconstructed rendition of 'Satisfaction' (1976) and the ambitious *Eskimo* (1979). The quartet backed Snakefinger on his debut single, 'The Spot' (1978) and over the ensuing three years co-wrote and produced his enthralling solo albums. Each release offered the same surreal qualities of the parent act, combining dismembered melody lines with quite startling guitar work. Later Snakefinger releases appeared outside the Residents' sphere although the artist still retained links with the group, contributing to *Stars And Hank Forever* (1986). His solo recordings continued to be both imaginative and compelling, but this talented musician succumbed to a fatal heart attack in 1988.

Albums: *Chewing The Hides Of Sound* (1979), *Greener Postures* (1981), *Manuel Of Errors* (1982), *Against The Grain* (1984), *History Of The Blues* (1984), *Night Of Desirable Objects* (1987).

Snakes Of Shake

This 80s Scottish group comprised Seori Burnette (guitar/lead vocals/harmonica), Tzen Vermillion (guitar), Sandy Brown (piano/accordion/vocals), Robert Renfrew (bass/slide guitar/vocals) and Rhod 'Lefty' Burnett (drums). Their debut album's highlight was the title-track, 'Southern Cross', a slice of cajun-influenced folk pop which was persistently promoted to break the band, without success. Seori Burnette's songwriting talent was often over-shadowed by his excessively dramatic singing style. By the time a second album was released, the line-up comprised Burnette, Brown, Renfrew, Neil Scott (guitar) and Iain Shedden (drums), the last-named previously of pop/punk act, the Jolt. *Gracelands And The Natural Wood* highlighted prefectly the group's blend of folk and rock styles. However, any progress was irretrievably undermined when the group's outlet, Making Waves, went into receivership, and they subsequently split up. Burnett and Shedden quickly resurfaced in a new act, Summerhill.

Albums: *Southern Cross* (Tense But Confident 1985), *Gracelands And The Natural Wood* (Making Waves 1986).

Snap!

Durron Butler (b. Maurice Durron Butler, 30 April 1967, Pittsburgh, Pennsylvania, USA) was initally a drummer with a heavy metal band in his hometown. Later he joined the army and was posted to Germany where he became a bomb disposal expert. Whilst there he teamed up with Rico Sparx and Moses P. for several musical projects. After his discharge he returned to the States but went back to Germany to tour with the **Fat Boys**. German based producers Benito Benites (b. Michael Munzing) and John Garrett Virgo III (b. Luca Anzilotti), operating under pseudonyms, had put together a project they would call Snap!, after a function on a sequencing programme. Previously the producers had recorded widely in their Frankfurt studio, for their own label, **Logic Records** (whose former A&R man, Mark Spoon, is now part of **Jam And Spoon**). They also ran their own club, Omen. Notable successes prior to Snap included the 16-Bit Project ('Where Are You' and 'High Score') and Off's 'Electric Salsa', which featured **Sven Vath** as frontman and singer. They then recorded a song called 'The Power' which was built from samples of New York rapper **Chill Rob G**'s 'Let The Rhythm Flow'. They added the powerful female backing vocals of Penny Ford, who had previously worked with **George Clinton**, **Chaka Khan** and **Mica Paris**, amongst others. Jackie Harris (b. Jaqueline Arlissa Harris, Pittsburgh, USA) was also credited for providing 'guide' vocals, and appeared in press interviews. The record was first released on the **Wild Pitch** label in America with the credit 'Snap featuring **Chill Rob G**'. However, after the first 30,000 sales problems with Chill Rob G (b. Robert Frazier) began to manifest themselves and they sought a replacement. They chose Butler, who was now rechristened Turbo G. He had already recorded for Logic as back-up rapper for Moses P. Chill Rob G was allowed to release his own version of 'The Power' in America. Around the rest of the world a new cut, featuring Turbo G, topped the charts. To promote the record Ford and Turbo G. toured widely, before the former embarked on a solo career.

She was replaced by Thea Austin. Throughout Benites and Garrett utilised Turbo G as the public face of Snap!, remaining shadowy figures back in their Frankfurt studio, which was now a hugely impressive complex. Though they continued to score collossal hits with 'Oops Upside Your Head' and 'Mary Had A Little Boy', dissent had set in within their ranks. Turbo wanted more artistic imput, and hated 'Rhythm Is A Dancer' the projected lead-off single for the band's second album. When a substitute, 'The Colour Of Love', crashed, the duo went ahead without his agreement. Their judgement was proved correct when 'Rhythm Is A Dancer' became another international smash (the biggest selling UK single of the year). But by now the rift between the parties was irreconcilable. Turbo G had signed up for a solo career (debuting with 'I'm Not Dead' on **Polydor**) while the Snap! single was still climbing in several territories. Austin too found herself a solo contract. The producers proved that they could survive without a front man when 'Exterminate', the first record not to feature Turbo G, became another million-seller.

Albums: *World Power* (Arista 1990), *The Madman's Return* (Arista 1992).

Video: *World Power* (1990).

Snapper

This New Zealand band specialising in 60s garage punk rock were formed in Dunedin, a college town at the bottom of South Island, in 1988. Veteran singer/guitarist Peter Gutteridge was a founder member of both the **Chills** and the Clean, the island's two most inspired outfits of the late 70s and early 80s. Their debut album emerged on the tiny Avalanche label, based in Edinburgh, Scotland, a country which has long harboured a predilection for Antipodean pop. Songs like 'Death And Weirdness In The Surfing Zone' were typical fuzz guitar workouts with Christine Voice's organ augmenting. Gutteridge's love of the **Velvet Underground** and **Stooges** shone through much of this work.

Album: *Shotgun Blossom* (Avalanche 1991).

Sneetches

This US group comprised Mike Levy (vocals/guitar), Matt Carges (guitar/vocals), Alec Palao (bass) and Daniel Swan (drums/vocals). Fanatical admirers of all that is best in classic pop music, the San Francisco-based Sneetches produced three highly-rated albums of guitar-based music in the late 80s and early 90s. *Sometimes That's All We Have* was noticeable for their rare ability to juxtapose joyous melodies with introspective, often depressive, lyrics. *Slow* gave further evidence of their capabilities. Both on record and on stage (the latter often with **Cyril Jordan** of the **Flamin' Groovies**) they displayed a fondness for exuberant cover versions; the fact that Palao and Swan

both came from England gave them the ability to celebrate the riches of two cultures.

Albums: *Lights Out* (1988), *Sometimes That's All We Have* (1989), *Slow* (1990), *Think Again* (1993).

SNFU

From Edmonton, Alberta, Canada, SNFU are a hardcore punk band who took obvious influence from both the **Subhumans** and **D.O.A.** Their line-ups have always centred around Mr Chi Pig (vocals), and Brent (guitar), with the rhythm section changing with almost every successive album. One of their early drummers, John Card, would later join D.O.A. SNFU have persevered over the years with a formula encompassing largely headlong addrenalin rushes. The most significant interlude was *If You Swear You'll Catch No Fish*, slick titles such as 'Better Homes And Gardens' indicating a growing maturity in the way they conveyed their lyrical gaze. Previously, overtly obvious joke anthems like 'Cannibal Cafe' had been their let-down. By the next album, they were speeding along at a furious rate once more, though some of the early angst had disappeared; 'It's hard to be angry when you live in an environment like this; the physical aspect of Edmonton is so comfortable'. They had definitely not grown in self-importance however; 'We're still the same awful band we were in '81'. Still active, SNFU encapsulate the best traditions of Canadian hardcore; energy, verve and humour. They moved over to Epitaph Records in 1995 for another splintering punk rock album.

Albums: *And No One Else Wanted To Play* (BYO 1984), *If You Swear You'll Catch No Fish* (BYO 1986), *Better Than A Stick In The Eye* (BYO 1988), *Last Of The Big Time Suspenders* (Skullduggery 1992), *The Ones Most Likely To Succeed* (Epitaph 1995).

Sniff 'N' The Tears

This London group was formed from the Ashes of Moon in 1974 only to disband within months after thwarted attempts to gain a recording contract. Its principal composer, Paul Roberts (vocals), returned to the world of art where his paintings had been exhibited in many European capitals. However, with the advent of the late 70s new wave, drummer Luigi Salvoni listened again to the 1974 demos and persuaded Roberts (then resident in France) to try again with Mick Dyche (guitar), Laurence Netto (guitar), Keith Miller (keyboards) and Nick South (bass). After another self-financed studio session, they were signed to Chiswick Records in the summer of 1978. One of Roberts' magnificent paintings graced the sleeve of *Fickle Heart* (produced by Salvoni) from which the catchy 'Driver's Seat' was a hit in the USA and Australasia while faltering just outside the UK Top 40. 1980's *The Game's Up* compounded *Billboard*'s comparison of them to **Dire Straits**. They began a downward spiral with

Ride Blue Divide (with **Lew Lewis** on harmonica) the last album to make a moderate commercial impact.

Albums: *Fickle Heart* (Chiswick 1978), *The Game's Up* (Chiswick 1980), *Love Action* (Chiswick 1981), *Ride Blue Divide* (Chiswick 1982). Compilations: *Retrospective* (Chiswick 1988), *A Best Of Sniff 'N' The Tears* (Chiswick 1991).

Sniper

This Japanese heavy metal group was formed in 1981 by guitarist Mansanori Kusakabe. Enlisting the services of Shigehisa Kitao (vocals), Romy Murase (bass) and Shunji Itoh (drums), their brand of heavy metal drew strongly on the styles of **UFO** and **Deep Purple**. Debuting with the single 'Fire' in 1983, they contributed 'Crazy Drug' to the *Heavy Metal Forces* compilation album the following year. Their first album was recorded live at the Electric Ladyland Club in Nagoya in 1984 and featured new recruit Ravhun Othani (ex-**Frank Marino** Band) as a second guitarist. The album was a limited edition of 1,000, which sold out, only to be re-pressed twice, with similar success. The band disintegrated shortly after its release, but was resurrected in 1985 by Kusakabe. The new line-up included Noburu Kaneko (vocals), Takeshi Kato (keyboards), Tsukasa Shinohara (bass) and Toshiyuki Miyata (drums). They produced *Quick And Dead*, but it made little impact outside Japan. A proposed tour of Holland to support it was cancelled and the band have been inactive since.

Albums: *Open The Attack* (Electric Ladyland 1984), *Quick And Dead* (Megaton 1985).

Snoman

b. LeBaron Frost, Alexandria, Virginia. An alternative to the rural langour of fellow Atlanta, Georgia-based rappers **Arrested Development** or **Gumbo**, Snoman's ruse is to retreat to the East Side old school artistry of the pioneering hip hop artists and B-Boys. He began writing his first poetry at the age of nine, and was subsequently inspired by the imported sounds of **Run DMC**. Following an appearance on the *Conquest Of A Nation* compilation he made his personal bow with the single, 'Money'. Backed by DJ Nabs, Snoman created a smooth, flowing blend of hip hop with intelligent, often introspective rhymes: 'It's very important to me that I write good, strong lyrics especially since I found it hard to express myself when I was growing up'.

Album: *The Exceptional One* (Conquest/Ichiban 1993).

Snoop Doggy Dogg

b. Calvin Broadus, 1971, Long Beach, California, USA. Snoop Doggy Dogg's commercial rise in 1993 was acutely timed, riding a surge in hardcore rap's popularity, and smashing previous records in any genre. *Doggy Style* was the most eagerly anticipated album in rap history, and the first debut album to enter the ***Billboard*** chart at number 1. With advance orders of over one and a half million, media speculators were predicting its importance long before a release date. As is *de rigeur* for gangsta rappers such as Snoop, his criminal past casts a long, somewhat romanticised shadow over his current achievements. He was busted for drugs after leaving high school in Long Beach, and spent three years in and out of jail. He first appeared in 1990 when helping out **Dr Dre** on a track called 'Deep Cover', from the film of the same title. Dogg was also ubiquitous on Dr Dre's breakthrough album, *The Chronic*, particularly on the hit single 'Nuthin' But A 'G' Thang', which he wrote and co-rapped on. After presenting a gong to **En Vogue** in September 1993 at the MTV video awards, Dogg surrendered himself to police custody after the show, on murder charges. This was over his alleged involvement in a driveby shooting. Inevitably, as news spread of Dogg's involvement interest in his vinyl product accelerated, and this played no small part in the eventual sales of his debut album. Critics noted how closely this was styled on **George Clinton**'s *Atomic Dog* project. Many also attacked the abusive imagery of women Dogg employed, particularly lurid on 'Ain't No Fun'. His justification: 'I'm not prejudiced in my rap, I just kick the rhymes'. If the US press were hostile to him they were no match for the sensationalism of the English tabloids. During touring commitments to support the album and single, 'Gin And Juice', he made the front page of the *Daily Star* with the headline: 'Kick This Evil Bastard Out!'. It was vaguely reminiscent of the spleen vented at the **Sex Pistols** in their heyday, and doubtless a good sign. He was asked to leave his hotel in Milestone, Kensington on arrival, and Terry Dicks, a bastion of Tory good taste, also objected to his presence in the country. A more serious impediment to Snoop's career is his imminent trial on charges of accessory to the murder of Phillip Woldermarian, shot by his bodyguard McKinley Lee.

Album: *Doggy Style* (Death Row 1993).

Videos: *Murder Was The Case (Warner)* (1994).

Snow

b. Darrin O'Brien, 1971, Toronto, Canada. Snow is the most commercially successful white DJ ever, whose debut UK single, 'Informer', reached the UK Top 3 in March 1993. Snow was raised in the Allenbury projects of Toronto and became a frequent visitor to reggae blues parties, where he assimilated the styles of **Junior Reid**, **Eek A Mouse**, **Tenor Saw** and **Nitty Gritty**. Considered a 'problem child', he spent 18 months in prison on a murder charge at the age of 19, before finally being acquitted; an experience which inspired the lyrics of 'Informer'. Rap mixer DJ Prince introduced him to MC Shan in New York who in turn recommended the East West label. They signed him in late 1992; his debut studio sessions resulting in *12 Inches Of Snow*, released in spring 1993. 'Lonely Monday Morning' subsequently became his first US single. Despite adverse criticism his gift for mimicry is a keen one, and by virtue of 'Informer' he has already entered reggae's record books.

Selected album: *12 Inches Of Snow* (East West 1993).

Snow White And The Seven Dwarfs
(see **Disney, Walt**)

Snow, Hank
b. Clarence Eugene Snow, 9 May 1914, Brooklyn, near Liverpool, Nova Scotia, Canada. After his parents divorced when he was eight years old, Snow spent four unhappy years with his grandmother, finally running away to re-join his mother when she re-married. His already miserable childhood worsened when he was cruelly ill-treated by his stepfather, which led him to abscond again. This time, though only 12 years old, it was to sea and he spent the next four years working on fishing boats in the Atlantic where, on several occasions, he almost lost his life. An early interest in music, gained from his mother who had been a pianist for silent films before he was born, led him to sing for fellow crew members. He left the sea and returned home, working wherever he could but seeking a singing career. He gained great inspiration listening to his mother's recordings of **Jimmie Rodgers**, and, acquiring a cheap guitar, practiced the Rodgers' blue yodel, guitar playing and delivery and set out to emulate his idol. He began to sing locally and eventually, through the help of Cecil Landry the station announcer and chief engineer, obtained a weekly unpaid spot on CHNS Halifax on a programme called *Down On The Farm*, where he became known as 'Clarence Snow and his Guitar' and 'The Cowboy Blue Yodeller'. It was Landry who, in 1934, first suggested the name of Hank, since he reckoned the boy needed a good western name. Snow became a talented guitarist and in the following years always played lead guitar for his own recordings. He met and married his wife Minnie in 1936 and for a long time the couple struggled to earn enough money to live on. Eventually through sponsorship, he was given a programme on the network *Canadian Farm Hour*.

In October 1936, by now known as 'Hank the Yodelling Ranger', he persuaded Hugh Joseph of **RCA**-Victor, Montreal, to allow him to record two of his own songs, 'Lonesome Blue Yodel' and 'The Prisoned Cowboy'. This marked the start of a recording career destined to set the record of being the longest one that any country artist ever spent with the same record company. Jimmie Rodgers' influence remained with him and when their only son was born in 1937, he was named Jimmie Rodgers Snow. In 1944, after further recordings and regular work in Canada, and having become 'Hank The Singing Ranger', due to the fact that as his voice deepened he found he could no longer yodel, he extended his career to the USA. He played various venues, including the *Wheeling Jamboree* and in Hollywood, usually appearing with his performing horse, Shawnee. The anticipated breakthrough did not materialize and during the late 40s, he struggled to achieve success. RCA, New York, guardedly informed him that they could not record him until he was known in America but eventually they relented and in 1949 his recording of 'Brand On My Heart' gained him success in Texas. In December 1949, he achieved his first minor country chart hit with 'Marriage Vow'. At the recommendation of fellow Jimmie Rodgers' devotee, **Ernest Tubb**, he made his debut on the *Grand Ole Opry* in January 1950, without making a great impression and seriously considered abandoning thoughts of a career in the USA. This idea was forgotten when his self-penned million-seller, 'I'm Moving On', established him for all-time. It spent 44 weeks in the US country charts, 21 at number 1 and even reached number 27 on the US pop charts. In the late 40s, Snow worked on tours with **Hank Williams** later stating 'I found Hank to be a fine person but the stories about him have been blown completely out of proportion. Take it from me, Hank Williams was okay'. Williams can actually be heard introducing Snow on the 1977 *A Tribute To Hank Williams*.

Snow formed a booking agency with **Colonel Tom Parker** and in 1954, they were responsible for **Elvis Presley's** only *Opry* performance. Presley sang 'Blue Moon Of Kentucky' but failed to make any impression with the audience that night. Parker, to Snow's chagrin, took over Presley's management, but Presley recorded material associated with Snow including 'A Fool Such As I', 'Old Shep' and later 'I'm Movin' On'. 'I don't mean to brag but Elvis was a big fan of mine and he was always sitting around singing my songs', says Snow. After his initial breakthrough, Snow became an internationally famous star whose records sold in their millions and between 1950 and 1980, he amassed 85 country chart hits. Further number 1 records were 'The Golden Rocket', 'I Don't Hurt Anymore', 'Let Me Go, Lover', 'Hello Love' and the tongue-twisting 'I've Been Everywhere'. The last, which gave him his second million-seller, was an Australian song originally naming Australian towns but Snow reckoned it would not mean much to Americans and requested the writer to change it to suit. He was later proud to state he recorded it on the sixth take, in spite of the fact that there were 93 place names to memorize. Hank Snow's penchant for wearing a toupee that does not always appear to fit correctly, has at times caused mirth and many people believe he deliberately emphasizes it. Legend has it that, humorously for the audience, one night his fiddler player removed it with his bow on stage and understandably received instant dismissal from his boss. Some album sleeves clearly indicate the toupee, others such as *My Nova Scotia Home* are most beautiful designs, while the noose on *Songs Of Tragedy* easily makes it one of the most remembered.

It is generally assumed that the character played by Henry Gibson in Robert Altman's controversial 1975 film *Nashville* was modelled on Snow. Over the years his melodic voice, perfect diction and distinctive guitar playing make his recordings immediately identifiable and his band, the Rainbow Ranch Boys, has always contained some of country music's finest musicians. His songwriting gained him election to the *Nashville Songwriters International Hall Of Fame* in 1978 and the following year he was inducted to the *Country Music Hall Of Fame*, the plaque rightly proclaiming him as one of country music's most influential entertainers. In 1981, after a 45-year association, he parted company from RCA stating it was 'because I would not record the type of things that are going today'. Snow has not recorded since, feeling that 'I have done everything in the recording line that was possible'. He resisted over-commercializing country music during his long career and says of the modern scene that '80% of today's would be country music is a joke and not fit to listen to - suggestive material and a lot of it you can't even understand the words, just a lot of loud music'. Snow has played in many countries all over the world, being a particular favourite in the UK. An ability to handle all types of material has led to him being classed among the most versatile country artists of all time. Remembering his own unhappy childhood he set up a foundation in Nashville to help abused children. He rarely tours now but maintains his regular *Opry* appearances and still is readily recognized by his flamboyant stage costumes, which have been his hallmark over the years.

Albums: *Hank Snow Sings* (1952), *Country Classics* (1952), *Salutes Jimmie Rodgers* (1953), *Country Guitar* (1954), *Just Keep A-Moving* (1955), *Old Doc Brown & Other Narrations* (1955), *Country & Western Jamboree* (1957), *Sacred Songs* (1958), *The Hank Snow E-Z Method of Spanish Guitar* (c.1958), *When Tragedy Struck* (1959), *Sings Jimmie Rodgers Songs* (1959), *The Singing Ranger* (1959), *Souvenirs* (1961), *Big Country Hits (Songs I Hadn't Recorded Till Now)* (1961), *Southern Cannonball* (1962), *One & Only Hank Snow* (1962), with Anita Carter *Together Again* (1962), *Railroad Man* (1963), *I've Been Everywhere* (1963), *The Last Ride* (1963), *More Hank Snow Souvenirs* (1964), *Old & Great Songs by Hank Snow* (1964), *Songs Of Tragedy* (1964), with Chet Atkins *Reminiscing* (1964), *Gloryland March* (1965), *Heartbreak Trail* (1965), *Highest Bidder And Other Favorites* (1965), *Your Favorite Country Hits* (1965), *Gospel Train* (1966), *This Is My Story* (1966), *The Guitar Stylings Of Hank Snow* (1966), *Gospel Stylings* (1966), *Travelin' Blues* (1966), *Spanish Fireball* (1967), *My Early Country Favorites* (1967), *Snow In Hawaii* (1967), *Christmas With Hank Snow* (1967), *My Nova Scotia Home* i (1967), *My Nova Scotia Home* ii (1968), *Lonely And Heartsick* (1968), *Somewhere Along Life's Highway* (1968), *Tales of The Yukon* (1968), *I Went To Your Wedding* (1969), *Snow In All Seasons* (1969), *Hits Covered By Snow* (1969), *Cure For The Blues* (1970), *In Memory Of Jimmie Rodgers* (1970), *Memories Are Made Of This* (1970), with Chet Atkins *C.B. Atkins & C.E. Snow By Special Request* (1970), *Wreck Of The Old 97* (1971), *Award Winners* (1971), *Tracks & Trains* (1971), *Lonesome Whistle* (1972), *The Jimmie Rodgers Story* (1972), *Legend Of Old Doc Brown* (1972), *Snowbird* (1973), *When My Blue Moon Turns To Gold Again* (1973), *Grand Ole Opry Favorites* (1973), *Hello Love* (1974), *I'm Moving On* (1974), *Now Is The Hour - For Me To Sing To My Friends In New Zealand* (1974), *That's You And Me* (1974), *You're Easy To Love* (1975), *All About Trains* (1975, one side Jimmie Rodgers), with Rodgers *Live From Evangel Temple* (1976), *#104 - Still Movin' On* (1977), *Living Legend* (1978), *Mysterious Lady* (1979), *Instrumentally Yours* (1979), with Kelly Foxton *Lovingly Yours* (1980), *By Request* (1981), with Foxton *Win Some, Lose Some, Lonesome* (1981), with Willie Nelson *Brand On My Heart* (1985). Compilations: *Hits, Hits & More Hits* (1968), *Hank Snow, The Singing Ranger Volume 1 (1949-1953)* (1989), *Hank Snow, The Singing Ranger Volume 2 (1953-1958)* (1990), *Hank Snow, The Thesaurus Transcriptions (1950-1956)* (1991), *Hank Snow, The Singing Ranger Volume 3 (1958-1969)* (1992, 12-CD set), *The Yodelling Ranger 1936-47* (1993, 6-CD box set), *The Singing Ranger Volume 4* (Bear Family 1994, 9 CD set).

Further reading: *The Hank Snow Story*, Snow, Hank with Jack Ownby & Bob Burris (1994).

Snow, Phoebe

b. Phoebe Laub, 17 July 1952, New York City, USA, Phoebe Snow was a singer with jazz and folk influences who released a string of popular albums in the 70s that showcased her versatile, elastic contralto vocals. Snow and her family moved to Teaneck, New Jersey where she studied piano during her childhood. She switched to guitar while in her teens. She wrote poetry and fashioned songs around them, which led her into performing at New York clubs in the early 70s. She was signed to **Leon Russell**'s Shelter Records label in 1974 and released her self-titled debut album, which reached the US Top 5, as did the single 'Poetry Man'. The album included jazz greats **Stan Getz** and **Teddy Wilson** guesting. Snow duetted with **Paul Simon** on his song 'Gone At Last' in 1975 and toured with him as well. She switched to **Columbia Records** for *Second Childhood*, in 1976, and stayed with that company throughout the decade, although her album sales lessened with each new release. In 1981 she switched to Mirage Records, distributed by **Atlantic Records**, and rebounded with *Rock Away*, which reached number 51 in the USA. In 1989 she reappeared on **Elektra Records** and in 1990-91 made numerous club appearances in the New York area, performing with a makeshift band that also included ex-**Steely Dan** member **Donald Fagen** and former **Doobie Brothers** singer **Michael McDonald**.

Albums: *Phoebe Snow* (1974), *Second Childhood* (1976), *It Looks Like Snow* (1976), *Never Letting Go* (1977), *Against The Grain* (1978), *Best Of* (1981), *Rock Away* (1981), *Something Real* (1989).

Snow, Valaida

b. 2 June 1905, Chattanooga, Tennessee, USA, d. 30 May 1956. Born into an intensely musical family, Snow was taught by her mother to play cello, bass, violin, banjo, mandolin, harp, accordion, clarinet, saxophone and trumpet. She also sang and danced. By the time she was 15 years old she was entertaining professionally and had decided to concentrate on trumpet and vocals. Her sisters Lavaida, Alvaida and Hattie were also professional singers, as was a brother, Arthur Bush. In 1924 Snow was attracting favourable attention in New York in the **Noble Sissle** and **Eubie Blake** show, *In Bamville (The Chocolate Dandies)*. Soon thereafter she was in London with *Blackbirds*, recording with Johnny Claes, Derek Neville, Freddy Gardner and others. She then worked in China for a time; on her return to the USA she headlined in Chicago and Los Angeles, then rejoined the cast of *Blackbirds*, this time in Paris. Tireless, she played in *Liza* across Europe and in Russia. In the early 30s she was performing in, and involved with the production of, the **Ethel Waters** show, *Rhapsody In Black*, in New York. In the mid-30s she returned to London and then to Hollywood, where she made films with her husband Ananais Berry, one of the famed Berry Brothers dancing troupe. After playing New York's **Apollo** Theatre she revisited Europe for more shows and films, then toured the Far East. In 1939 she was in Scandinavia, where she was arrested by the invading Germans and interned in a concentration camp at Wester-Faengle. After 18 months she was released as an exchange prisoner and returned to New York. Her experiences had severely damaged her both physically and psychologically, but she began performing again, remarried, and played several prestigious engagements. Sadly, the spark and vitality that had made her one of the outstanding American entertainers of the 30s had begun to dim. Snow played and sang the blues with deep feeling and could more than hold her own on up-tempo swingers. She had perfect pitch and was also a skilled transcriber and arranger. In short, she was a phenomenal musician yet, because she was a woman, in the jazz world of the 30s and 40s she was regarded as something of a curiosity. Fortunately, Rosetta Records' owner Rosetta Reitz has recently instigated a comprehensive reissue programme of Snow's excellent recorded legacy, and this clearly shows that as a trumpet player she was at least the equal of many of her more famous male contemporaries.

Albums: with others *Harlem Comes To London* (1929-38), *Valaida: Swing Is The Thing* (1936-37), *Hot Snow: Valaida Snow* (1937-50).

Snowblind

This UK melodic hard rock quintet was formed in 1982 by guitarist Andy Simmons. With Tony Mason (vocals), Ross Bingham (guitar/keyboards), Geoff Gilesoie (bass) and Kevin Baker (drums) completing the line-up, they were one of the few non-speed metal/thrash bands signed to the Belgian Mausoleum label. Using **Magnum**, **Rush** and **Grand Prix** as their musical blueprint, they debuted with a self-titled album in 1985. This comprised grandiose epics, punctuated by explosive guitar runs in places. The only drawback was Mason's vocals, which lacked the necessary warmth and range to give the songs real distinction. The album fared badly and little has been heard from them since.

Album: *Snowblind* (Mausoleum 1985).

Snowden, Elmer

b. 9 October 1900, Baltimore, Maryland, USA, d. 14 May 1973. Snowden was playing banjo professionally in the Washington DC area while still in his teens and in 1919 teamed up with **Duke Ellington** in a trio. A little while later, in New York, Snowden needed a piano player and sent for Ellington. Soon thereafter the rest of the band, the Washingtonians, parted company with Snowden, forming the nucleus of the orchestra Ellington was to lead with such success. Snowden formed a new band, and also began acting as a band contractor and musicians' agent. Through the late 20s and early 30s he was a popular bandleader in the New York area, employing many fine jazzmen. After a brief hiatus due to union problems he resumed bandleading, continuing to do so into the early 60s when he also taught and briefly enjoyed some success on the jazz festival circuit. During this period he played and sometimes recorded with **Turk Murphy**, **Lonnie Johnson** and **Darnell Howard**. Snowden died in May 1973.

Albums: *Harlem Banjo* (1960), with Lonnie Johnson *Blues And Ballads* (1960).

Snuff

Formed in London in 1988 by Andy (b. 4 July 1963, London England), Duncan (b. 22 August 1964, Louth, England) and Simon (b. 11 December 1966, London, England), Snuff started off as 'a joke' with a hectic mixture of implausibly fast guitars and exquisite melodies. The threesome soon created their own niche in a British music scene sorely lacking the hardcore hardware to rival the host of angry American bands. Next to their own creations such as 'Not Listening' Snuff added a litany of thrashed-up cover versions, ranging from **Tiffany** to **Simon And Garfunkel** and numerous British television commercial jingles in between. Such was the band's sense of economy, they once managed to squeeze over 30 tracks onto one 12-inch single! Had the band's ambition matched their liberal taste for cover versions, Snuff's potential would have been huge. However, by conscientiously adhering to a post-punk manifesto Snuff managed to stay resolutely independent in the face of large financial offers from the corporates. Somewhat fittingly given their stance, when Snuff tired of the demands of the band and the threat of a 'cabaret punk' tag, they immediately called it a day. Their farewell gig was at London's Kilburn National Ballroom in 1991, a great highpoint for any band to depart on. Simon and Duncan started working together on a new project, while bassist Andy joined fellow hardcore band Leatherface.

Album: *SnuffSaidButGorBlimeyGuvIfHeDidn'tThrowA-WobblerChaChaChaChaChaChaChaChaChaChaChaYou'reGoingHomeInACosmicAmbience* (1989).

Social Distortion

Formed in Fullerton, Orange County, California, USA, in the summer of 1978, Social Distortion initially featured Mike Ness (guitar), Casey Royer (drums), and the Agnew brothers, Rikk (vocals/guitar) and Frank (bass). That line-up only lasted until the following year, at which point the Agnews departed for fellow Fullerton band, the **Adolescents**. Dennis Danell then joined on bass, and Ness took over vocals (following experiments with a singer titled Dee Dee), and 'Carrott' replaced Royer. However, this remains a simplification of the band's early line-up shuffles, with other members including Tim Mag (later **DI**) and Danny Furious (ex-**Avengers**). After impressing Robbie Fields of Posh Boy Records at a party in Fullerton in 1981, the band booked studio time through him to record their 'Mainliner' 7-inch. This was a one-off affair, however, and afterwards the group moved on to their own 13th Floor Records imprint, also picking up a new and more permanent drummer and backing vocalist, Derek O'Brien (also DI). By this time Danell had switched to rhythm guitar, with Brent Liles becoming the new bass player (making the band a quartet once more). This line-up would last until 1984, spanning the recording of *Mommy's Little Monster*. A superb punk rock debut, this collection revealed more cohesion and tradition than the band's immediate peers, with a sound tracing its heritage back to the **Rolling Stones** as much as the **Sex Pistols**. It seemed that Social Distortion had all the ingredients to popularise hardcore ('Another State Of Mind' was achieving plays on **MTV** long before punk bands were fashionable in that medium), but their breakthrough was delayed by Ness's increasing use of hard drugs. The band practically disintegrated as a result. O'Brien joined DI permanently, while Liles fled

for Agent Orange in 1985. Their replacements were John Maurer (bass) and Chris Reece (drums; ex-**Lewd**). After attending detox clinics Ness finally made a comeback with 1988's *Prison Bound*. A mature, less strident effort, it saw the band flirt with country on tracks such as 'Like An Outlaw', returning to a revved-up Rolling Stones' blueprint for a cover of 'Backstreet Girl' as well as sharp original songs. It also signalled a move towards conventional blues rock which would come to fruition with successive albums for **Epic** and **Sony Records**. The best of these was 1992's *Between Heaven And Hell*, by which time the multi-tattooed Ness had moved into prime rockabilly mode, with lyrical inspiration taken from his battles with drink and drugs, ' I live my life for six months as well as I know how, then I sit down with my guitar and it kind of comes out.' In the light of this, songs such as 'Born To Lose' undercut their potential for cliché with the kind of hard-hitting authenticity which had always surrounded the band.

Albums: *Mommy's Little Monster* (13th Floor 1983), *Prison Bound* (Restless 1988), *Social Distortion* (Epic 1990), *Between Heaven And Hell* (Sony 1992).

Soda, Frank

This eccentric Canadian vocalist/guitarist is widely known for his warped sense of humour. He appeared on stage kitted out in strange outfits and the climax of the show usually involved making a television set explode on his head, Backed by the Imps, a two-piece rhythm section comprising Charles Towers (bass) and John Lechausser (drums), they recorded two hard rock albums characterized by frenzied, **Frank Zappa**-like guitar and Soda's shallow vocals. *Saturday Night Getaway* used session musicians instead of the Imps and featured four cuts from *In The Tube*, with the remaining new songs sounding second-rate in comparison. He built up a small but loyal cult following in Canada, but failed to make an impression elsewhere. He did, however, help singer **Lee Aaron** launch her career in 1982.

Albums: *In The Tube* (Quality 1979), *Frank Soda And The Imps* (Quality 1980), *Saturday Night Getaway* (Quality 1981), *Adventures Of Sodaman* (Visual 1983).

Sodom

This black metal/thrash trio was formed in 1983 by Angel Ripper (bass/vocals), Aggressor (vocals/guitar) and Witchhunter (drums). They drew inspiration from bands such as **Motörhead**, **Anvil** and **Venom**, making their debut with an agenda-setting EP, *Sign Of Evil*. By the time *Obsessed By Cruelty* emerged in 1986, Aggressor had quit to be replaced firstly by the similarly-pseudonymous Grave Violator, then Destructor and finally Blackfire. *Persecution Mania* followed in 1987 and marked a vast improvement over their debut, though lyrics had not moved on from obsessions with war, bloodlust and the black arts.

Produced by Harris Johns, it had a crisp and powerful sound and was to become their best-selling release. They toured Europe in 1988 with Whiplash and recorded *Mortal Way Of Life*, the first ever double live thrash album. *Agent Orange* followed in 1989 and they were supported by **Sepultura** on a European tour to help promote it. Michael Hoffman was recruited as the new guitarist when Blackfire left for **Kreator** in 1990.

Albums: *Obsessed By Cruelty* (Steamhammer 1986), *Persecution Mania* (Steamhammer 1987), *Mortal Way Of Life* (Steamhammer 1988, double album), *Agent Orange* (Steamhammer 1989), *Ausgebombt* (Steamhammer 1990), *Better Off Dead* (Steamhammer 1991), *Tapping The Vein* (Steamhammer 1993).

Soft Boys

When **Syd Barrett** gave up music for art, another Cambridge musician emerged to take on his mantle. **Robyn Hitchcock** started out as a solo performer and busker before becoming a member of B.B. Blackberry And The Swelterettes, then the Chosen Few, the Worst Fears, and Maureen And The Meatpackers. It was with the last named that Hitchcock first recorded (in 1976), although the results were not released until much later. His next group, Dennis And The Experts became the Soft Boys in 1976. The Soft Boys first recording session was in March 1977 by which point the line-up was Hitchcock (vocals/guitar/bass), Alan Davies (guitar), Andy Metcalfe (bass), and Morris Windsor aka Otis Fagg (drums). The original sessions remain unreleased but the same line-up also recorded a three track single - known as the *Give It To The Soft Boys* EP - for the notorious local Cambridge label, Raw Records (or rip-off records, to those who knew its owner well). This was released in the autumn of 1977 after which Davies left and Kimberley Rew was installed on guitar, harmonica, and vocals. The Soft Boys, now signed to Radar Records, released the single '(I Wanna Be An) Anglepoise Lamp', but it was not considered representative of their innovative live work. Forming their own Two Crabs label they released *Can Of Bees* in 1979 after which they replaced Metcalfe with Matthew Seligman. Jim Melton, who had been playing harmonica for a while, also left. Their remaining releases came on the Armageddon label and included *Underwater Moonlight*, which is considered amongst Hitchcock's finest moments. They broke up early in 1981 and Hitchcock went on to enjoy an erratic solo career, recruiting along the way Metcalfe and Windsor to form the Egyptians. Rew joined **Katrina And The Waves** and wrote the classic 'Going Down To Liverpool', while Seligman joined Local Heroes SW9 and continued to contribute to Hitchcock's solo efforts.

Albums: *A Can Of Bees* (Two Crabs 1979), *Underwater Moonlight* (Armageddon 1980), *Two Halves For The Price Of One* (Armageddon 1981), *Invisible Hits* (Midnight 1983), *Live At The Portland Arms* (Midnight 1987, cassette only). Compilations: *Raw Cuts* (Overground 1989, mini-album), *The Soft Boys 1976-81* (Rykodisc 1994).

Soft Cell

Formed in Leeds, England, in 1980 this duo featured vocalist **Marc Almond** (b. Peter Marc Almond, 9 July 1956, Southport, Lancashire, England) and synthesizer player David Ball (b. 3 May 1959, Blackpool, Lancashire, England). The art school twosome came to the attention of the **Some Bizzare** label entrepreneur **Stevo** following the release of their self-financed EP *Mutant Moments*. He duly included their 'Girl With The Patent Leather Face' on the compilation *Some Bizzare Album* and negotiated a licensing deal with Phonogram Records in Europe and **Sire** in the USA. Their debut single, 'Memorabilia', produced by **Mute Records** boss Daniel Miller, was an underground hit paving the way for the celebrated 'Tainted Love'. Composed by the **Four Preps**' Ed Cobb and already well known as a northern soul club favourite by **Gloria Jones**, 'Tainted Love' topped the UK charts, became the best selling British single of the year and remained in the US charts for an astonishing 43 weeks. Produced by the former producer of **Wire**, Mike Thorne, the single highlighted Almond's strong potential as a torch singer, a role which was developed on subsequent hit singles including 'Bedsitter', 'Say Hello Wave Goodbye', 'Torch' and 'What'. Almond's brand of erotic electronic sleaze could only partially be realized in the Soft Cell format and was more fully developed in the offshoot **Marc And The Mambas**. Implicit in Soft Cell's rise was a determined self-destructive streak, which meant that the group was never happy with the pop machinery of which it had inevitably became a part. The title of *The Art Of Falling Apart*, indicated how close they were to ending their hit collaboration. At the end of 1983 the duo announced their proposed dissolution and undertook a final tour early the following year, followed by a farewell album, *This Last Night In Sodom*. Almond embarked on a solo career, while Ball would eventually become one half of the **Grid**.

Albums: *Non-Stop Erotic Cabaret* (1981), *Non-Stop Ecstatic Dancing* (1982), *The Art Of Falling Apart* (1983), *This Last Night In Sodom* (1984). Compilations: *The Singles 1981-85* (1986), *Their Greatest Hits* (1988), *Memorabilia* (1991, also contains Marc Almond solo material).

Further reading: *Soft Cell*, Tebbutt, Simon (1984).

Soft Machine

Founded in 1966, the original line-up was **Robert Wyatt**, **Kevin Ayers**, Daevid Allen, Mike Ratledge and, very briefly, guitarist Larry Nolan. By autumn 1967 the classic line-up of the Softs' art-rock period (Ayers, Wyatt and Ratledge) had settled in. They toured with **Jimi Hendrix**, who, along with his producer, ex-**Animals** member **Chas Chandler**, encouraged them and facilitated the recording of their first album. (There had been earlier demos for **Giorgio Gomelsky**'s Marmalade label, but these were not issued until later, and then kept re-appearing in different configurations under various titles.) From the end of 1968, when Ayers left, until February 1970, the personnel was in a state of flux (Lyn Dobson, Marc Charig and Nick Evans were members for a while), and the music was evolving into a distinctive brand jazz-rock. Arguably, *Volume Two* and *Third* contain their most intriguing and exciting performances. Highlighted by Wyatt's very English spoken/sung vocals, the group had still managed to inject some humour into their work. The finest example is Wyatt's mercurial 'Moon In June'. By mid-1970 the second definitive line-up (Ratledge, Wyatt, Hugh Hopper and **Elton Dean**) was finally in place. It was this band that Tim Souster showcased when he was allowed a free hand to organise a late-night Promenade Concert in August 1970. In autumn 1971, Wyatt left to form Matching Mole (a clever pun on the French translation of Soft Machine; Machine Molle), and Phil Howard came in on drums until John Marshall became the permanent drummer. For the next few years, through a number of personnel changes (farewell Dean and Hopper, welcome **Roy Babbington**, Karl Jenkins) the Soft Machine were, for many listeners, the standard against which all jazz-rock fusions, including most of the big American names, had to be measured. However, with Ratledge's departure in January 1976 the group began to sound like a legion of other guitar-led fusion bands, competent and craftsmanlike, but, despite the virtuosity of **Allan Holdsworth** and **John Etheridge**, without the edge of earlier incarnations, and certainly without the dadaist elements of Wyatt's time. In 1984, Jenkins and Marshall brought together a new edition of the band (featuring Dave Macrae, Ray Warleigh and a number of new Jenkins compositions) for a season at **Ronnie Scott**'s club. It is their first three albums which contain the best of their work which clearly shows they were one of the most adventurous and important progressive bands of the late 60s and one that gently led their followers to understand and appreciate jazz.

Albums: *Soft Machine* (1968), *Soft Machine Volume Two* (1969), *Third* (1970), *Fourth* (1971), *Fifth* (1972), *Six* (1973), *Seven* (1973), *Bundles* (1975), *Softs* (1976), *Triple Echo* (1977, a 3-album set, mainly a compilation but including some previously unissued material), *Live At The Proms 1970* (1988), *The Peel Sessions* (1990), *The Untouchable* (1990), *As If . . .*(1991).

Further reading: *Gong Dreaming*, Allen, Daevid (1995).

Soho

Identical twin sisters Jackie (Jacquie Juanita Cuff) and Pauline (Pauline Osberga Cuff) were both born on 25 November 1962 in Wolverhampton, England.

Together with guitarist Tim London (b. Timothy Brinkhurst, 20 November 1960) they comprised the briefly successful dance band Soho. They started singing in the early 80s as student nurses in St Albans. After meeting London they became Tim London's Orgasm, and Tim London and the Soho sisters before settling on Soho. London had left school in 1977 and played in several small punk bands. Another early member was Nigel Dukey 'D' who left in 1989. They signed to **Virgin** for early singles 'You Won't Hold Me Down' (1988), and 'Message From My Baby' (1989). However, these and their first LP proved flops. Despite garnering lots of press, their brand of dance was a little less frenetic than the burgeoning Acid House scene and they were dropped from the label in 1989. They spent the next year singing covers in an Italian disco, before signing a new deal with Savage Tam Records. Their breakthrough came with their second single for the label, 'Hippychick', which sampled Johnny Marr's guitar effervescence from the **Smiths** 'How Soon Is Now'. Lyrically, it challenged the prevailing new age ethos of blissful hegemony ('Got no flowers for your gun'). However, Soho proved unable to capitalise on the Transatlantic success of the single. Tim and Jacqueline had a daughter in 1993, Charlie, and they were finally encouraged back into the studio for a new album to celebrate his arrival. The band re-emerged, as Oosh, in 1994, with a single and album entitled 'The View'.

Albums: *Noise* (Virgin 1989), *Goddess* (Savage 1991), *The View* (Magnet 1994).

Sojourn

This USA melodic rock quintet was formed in 1983 by Kevin Bullock (vocals/guitar/keyboards) and Doug Robinson (guitar/vocals). Enlisting the services of Kevin Stoker (keyboards), Doug Pectol (bass) and Dane Spencer (drums), they secured a deal with the Mad Cat label in 1985. They debuted with *Lookin' For More*, a melodic rock album with rough edges. It incorporated abrasive guitar work within a pomp-rock framework, and drew comparisons with **Triumph**, **Journey** and **UFO**. *Different Points Of View* consolidated their style before they went out on tour with **Mr. Mister** to promote the work, but nothing was heard from them afterwards.

Albums: *Lookin' For More* (Mad Cat 1985), *Different Points Of View* (Mad Cat 1988).

Solal, Martial

b. 23 August 1927, Algiers, Algeria. Solal was taught to play the piano from the age of seven by his opera singing mother. He worked with local bands in Algiers before moving to Paris in 1950. There he played with all the prominent French musicians as well as the visiting Americans - **Don Byas**, **Lucky Thompson**, **Sidney Bechet**. In 1968, he began a long association with alto saxophonist **Lee Konitz**. He occasionally leads a big band. Solal has a prodigious technique at the piano and an extensive harmonic knowledge. He has often worked as a solo performer when he rarely plays in a constant tempo and his melodic improvisation can be at its most remote. He wrote the score for Jean-Luc Godard's film *Breathless* (1959) and has since produced more than 20 film scores.

Albums: *Jazz A Gareau* (1970), *Martial Solal At Newport* (1963), *Impressive Rome* (1968), *Suite For Trio* (1970), *Nothing But Piano* (1975), *Big Band* (1981), *Bluesine* (1983); with Lee Konitz *Duplicity* (1977); with Stéphane Grappelli *Happy Reunion* (1980), *Martial Solal Plays Andre Hoideir* (1984).

Soldiers Of The King

Although the popular British actress, singer and comedienne **Cicely Courtneidge** was not accompanied on the screen in this 1933 Gainsborough release by her husband, **Jack Hulbert**, he did co-write the screenplay with W. P. Lipscomb and John Horton, and is said to have assisted Maurice Elvey with the direction. In this adaptation of an original story by Douglas Furber, Courtneidge plays the dual roles of retired music hall artist Jenny Marvello and her daughter Maisie, the reigning queen of a variety troupe. In the latter part she runs through her impressive range of male impersonations and comic business, while as the older woman she demonstrates an hitherto unseen dramatic acting ability. There were several well-known names such as Edward Everett Horton, Anthony Bushell, Bransby Williams, Dorothy Hyson, Frank Cellier, and **Leslie Sarony** in a the supporting cast which also included Rebla, Herschel Henlere, Arty Ash, Ivor McLaren, David Deveen, and Olive Sloan. The two most memorable songs were 'The Moment I Saw You' (**Noel Gay**-Clifford Grey) and the rousing 'There's Something About A Soldier' (Gay). This solo outing for Courtneidge enjoyed considerable success, but, even so, the old team were back together again later in the same year with *Falling For You*.

Solitaires

An R&B vocal group from Harlem, New York City, New York, USA. The Solitaires like no other vocal group of the 50s sang lushly harmonized doo-wop with a dreamy romantic feeling, and rank as one of the great groups of the 50s. The original members, formed in 1953, were veterans of the doo-wop scene and consisted of lead Herman Curtis (ex-**Vocaleers**), tenor Buzzy Willis and bass Pat Gaston (both ex-**Crows**), tenor/guitarist Monte Owens and baritone Bobby Baylor (both who had recorded with the **Mellomoods**), and pianist Bobby Williams. They signed with Hy Weiss's Old Town label in 1954, and with Curtis's haunting falsetto on 'Wonder Why', 'Blue

Valentine', 'Please Remember My Heart', and 'I Don't Stand A Ghost Of A Chance' the group quickly established themselves locally if not nationally. Their deep R&B sound, yet crisp and clean, set a standard for other groups. Curtis left in 1955 and, with the wonderfully flavourful tenor of new recruit Milton Love, the group entered their most commercially successful period. With such great records as 'The Wedding' (1955), 'The Angels Sang'(1956), 'You've Sin' (1956), and 'Walking Along' (1957), the latter covered by the **Diamonds**, they became a rock 'n' roll phenomenon. By the time the Solitaires left Old Town in 1960, however, they had metamorphosed into a **Coasters**-sounding group, and by the time of their last recording in 1964 personnel changes had left little that was recognizable with the classic group. The following the decades various ensembles of the Solitaires would appear on revival shows.

Compilation: *Walking Along With* (Ace 1992).

Solitude

Solitude were formed by Mike Hostler (drums) and Dan Martinez (guitar) in Delaware, USA, in 1985. With the addition of Keith Saulsbury (vocals/guitar) and Rodney Cope (bass) they released their first demo, *Focus Of Terror*, in 1987, their second, *Sickness*, following a year later. Increasingly strong reviews were maintained by their third and final demo, *Fall Of Creation*. Red Light then stepped in and signed the band in 1993 (**Music For Nations** offering a UKcontract). *From This Life*, their debut album, saw them combine diverse influences, taking **Black Sabbath**, **Slayer** and **Pantera** as a traditional metal foundation, but adding also elements of blues and progressive rock. Lyrically, targets included the death of communism ('After The Red'), betrayal ('In This Life') and growing old ('The Empty'), all dealt with in bold, primary colours and language. Touring with **Death Angel**, **Sacred Reich**, **Forbidden**, **Celtic Frost** and other death metal/thrash bands has not helped them escape the death metal category which somewhat inadequately describes their sound.

Album: *From Within* (Red Light 1994).

Solitude Aeturnus

Formed in 1988 by Texan guitarist John Perez, Solitude Aeturnus set out to revive the 'heavy groove orientated' style of **Black Sabbath**. The results were slow, epic, guitar-based heavy metal with a definite ethereal edge. Solitude Aeturnus secured a deal in 1991 and released *Into the Depths of Sorrow*. This established them as a part of the doom metal movement, which was a more atmospheric, grinding counterpart to the frantic aggression of death metal. While many of the bands in the doom genre were interested in creating sweeping vistas of tragic horror, Solitude Aeturnus have a more grandiose, dreamlike quality. Much of this is due to the semi-operatic vocals of Robert Lowe which contrast effectively with the maudlin power of the lumbering guitar riffs of John Perez and Edgar Rivera (the rhythm section comprises Lyle - bass, and Wolf - drums). Unfortunately, while they are good at what they do, Solitude Aeturnus have a tendency to be somewhat one-dimensional. Their third album, *Through the Darkest Hour*, followed a label change and has seen the band's material develop a little more punch.

Albums: *Into the Depths of Sorrow* (Roadracer 1991), *Beyond The Crimson Horizon* (Roadracer 1992), *Through The Darkest Hour* (Bullet Proof 1994).

Soloff, Lew

b. Lewis Michael Soloff, 20 January 1944, New York City, New York, USA. After studying piano, trumpet and music theory at several colleges of music, Soloff played jazz trumpet with several leaders, notably **Maynard Ferguson** and **Gil Evans** and the Latin groups of **Machito**, **Tito Puente**, and **Chuck Mangione**. In the late 60s he moved into jazz/rock, joining **Blood, Sweat and Tears** with whom he remained for five years. During this same period he also played jazz, recording with the **Thad Jones-Mel Lewis** band and **Clark Terry**'s big band. Throughout the 70s and early 80s, Soloff continued to mix pop and jazz work, playing and recording with musicians as diverse as Evans, **Sonny Stitt**, **George Russell**, **Jon Faddis** and with **Spyro Gyra**. He also demonstrated his versatility by playing classical music. A fiery, gutsy player, Soloff's broad repertoire has caused some jazz fans to overlook his work. He is, nevertheless, a musician of considerable depth, integrity and flair.

Albums: with Clark Terry *Live On 57th Street* (1970), with Sonny Stitt *Stomp Off, Let's Go* (1976), with Gil Evans *Parabola* (1978), *Yesterdays* (Paddle Wheel 1986), *Gil Evans And The Monday Night Orchestra Live At The Sweet Basil vols 1+2* (1988), *But Beautiful* (Paddle Wheel 1988), *My Romance* (Paddle Wheel 1989), *Little Wing* (Sweet Basil 1992).

Solomon, King

b. 12 October 1940, Tallulah, Louisiana, USA. Solomon enjoyed singing in the local church choir and for 10 years he was a member of the popular Friendly Brothers Spiritual Quartet. It was while touring with them that he made the switch to blues singing, subsequently appearing on the same bills as artists such as **B.B. King** and **Etta James**. He made his first record in 1959 and he has appeared on numerous small labels since then, with records occasionally being leased to larger companies such as Checker and Kent. He has been based in California for most of his recording career and has made one album, although the Dutch label Diving Duck did release a well-received compilation of his older material. Solomon continues to sing occasionally in the small clubs in Los Angeles.

Album: *Energy Crisis* (1978). Compilation: *Non Support Blues* (1988).

Solomon, Phil

b. 1924, Northern Ireland. One of the most controversial and well-known managers of mid-60s British pop, Solomon's speciality was overseeing the careers of aspiring Irish artists. The son of Morris Solomon, who owned the record distributors Solomon/Peres and was an important shareholder at **Decca**, Philip initially seemed an unlikely candidate for the family business. After a very inauspicious period in Australia he returned to Northern Ireland, traversed to England, and became a promoter during the 50s. Among the acts associated with him were **Nina And Frederick** and **Ruby Murray**, but it was the **Bachelors** who proved to be his first important discovery. Solomon introduced the group to Decca's A&R head **Dick Rowe** and watched as they became celebrated hitmakers and cabaret stars during the 60s. Their career development was a testament to the industry of Solomon's wife Dorothy, who emerged as one of the most respected agents in the music business. By contrast, Philip was the big time entrepreneur, always in the news with his latest scheme - whether it be a new record label, the latest Irish sensation, a new comedy star, a pirate radio station or a publicized feud with a managerial rival. In terms of rock history, Solomon may be best remembered for nurturing the early career of **Van Morrison**. After visiting the group **Them** at Belfast's Maritime Hotel, he duly signed the troublesome ensemble and even secured the services of **Bert Berns** as their producer. After a disastrous USA tour, Them disbanded and Morrison fell out with Solomon, a dispute that prompted legal redress. Of all Morrison's managers, however, Solomon was the most influential and the only true match for the temperamental singer/songwriter. One of Solomon's strengths was his ability to find important backroom talent to bolster his organization. **Tommy Scott** was employed as producer for many of Solomon's acts, while arranger **Phil Coulter** gained his first experiences in the music industry as part of the Solomon stable. The abilities of both these men can be discovered on the recordings of several Solomon acts, not least **Twinkle**, who enjoyed a couple of UK hits for Decca in 1965.

In 1966 Solomon became a director at Radio Caroline, a base that enabled him to publicize his artists with fresh aplomb. The following year he launched the independent label Major Minor which enjoyed a number of hits, mainly with Irish artists like **Frankie McBride**, but also with some imported hits including **Crazy Elephant**'s 'Gimme Gimme Good Lovin'' and **Jane Birkin** And **Serge Gainsbourg**'s 'Je T'Aime Moi Non Plus'. A known gambler, Solomon found himself in the bankruptcy court when he overreached himself in business. Yet, he returned as strong as ever. During the Major Minor period, he signed the **Dubliners** who recorded a number of albums for his label as well as enjoying unexpected chart success with such songs as 'Seven Drunken Nights' and 'Black Velvet Band'.

The singer that Solomon had greatest faith in, however, was to prove a disappointment. **David McWilliams** was regarded by his mentor as superior to Van Morrison and Solomon duly launched the biggest publicity campaign in the history of British pop music to launch the Northern Ireland singer's career. For all the hype, which included pages of advertisements in the music press and ceaseless plugging on Radio Caroline, McWilliams' 'The Days Of Pearly Spencer' failed to dent the charts, although Solomon recouped much of his investment on the Continent.

By the end of the 60s, Solomon's once great power in the British music business declined and he moved into other entrepreneurial areas. At his peak, however, he was the match of any manager of his era and remains the most historically neglected of the 60s pop power brokers.

Further reading: *Van Morrison: A Portrait Of The Artist*, Johnny Rogan.

Soma Records

Scottish record label based in Otago Street, Glasgow, opened in July 1991 and championed by Orde Meikle and Stuart McMillan, better known as the duo behind **Slam**. Other members of the team are Dave Clark, Nigel Hurst, Jim Muotone and Glen Gibbons. The latter two are Slam's studio engineers, played the major role in starting the Soma imprint, and also record for the label as Rejuvenation (*Work In Progress* 1992, 'Requiem' 1993, 'Sychophantasy' 1994). Slam had originally been an all-night party convention which evolved into an umbrella remix-production team. A record label was the obvious next step: 'Soma was set up to fill a void in Scottish music', noted Meikle. 'No one was paying attention to dance music here, so the label is a medium or catalyst for some of these people who are very talented, but don't have the confidence to approach a major record company down south'. Early signings included Rejuvenation, Dove and G7. Dove released 'Fallen' for them, before becoming **One Dove** and moving to **Boys Own**. Amongst other triumphs, the label housed Otaku's 'Percussion Obsession', the first vinyl outing for Back To Basic's Ralph Lawson, Sharkimaxx's 'Clashback' (aka **Felix Da Housecat**) and Piece & Jammin's *One For The Road* EP.

Some Bizzare Records

Founded by the eccentric teenage entrepreneur, **Stevo**, the UK-based **Some Bizzare Records** was one of the most challenging and enterprising labels of the 80s. The pioneering *Some Bizzare Album* brought together an array of fringe groups including **Throbbing Gristle**, **Classix Noveaux**, **Clock DVA**, **Cabaret Voltaire**, **Blancmange**, **Depeche Mode**, **Soft Cell** and **The The**. It was the last two acts that were to continue with the label and enable Stevo to continue mining for arcane talent. Cabaret Voltaire also returned for a spell, as did Genesis P. Orridge's **Throbbing Gristle** offshoot, **Psychic TV**. Stevo's interest in industrial music saw the signing of the first foreign group to the label, **Einsturzende Neubaten**. They were soon followed by London's **Test Department**. Mischievously subversive, sleazy and often controversial, Some Bizzare was a welcome haven for Jim Thirlwell and his various releases under the banner **Foetus**. By the end of the 80s Stevo had lost a major signing, The The, and, not for the first time, the label's financial future was a matter of conjecture. The power of Some Bizzare lay in its wilful obscurity aligned with Stevo's remarkable capacity to bring unlikely acts to critical and occasionally acclaim. Whether new signings such as Stex, Tim Hutton and Kandis King will re-invigorate the label's catalogue is part of the test for the 90s.

Some Like It Hot
(see *Sugar*)

Some People

Clive Donner directed this 1962 feature, the profits from which were donated to the Duke Of Edinburgh's Award Scheme. This is hardly the stuff of rebellious cinema. The plot of *Some People* did offer hint of excitement; three bikers who have lost their respective licences form a rock 'n' roll group to play at a youth club only to have one of their number leave to lead a gang which attacks them. However, any potential drama is wasted during what evolves into an antiseptic view of teenage life. Kenneth More stars as the patrician figure watching over rising stars Ray Brooks and David Hemmings, while musical interludes are provided by British instrumental unit the **Eagles**. Singer **Carol Deene**, famed for the hits 'Short Movies' and 'Norman', performed the title song to *Some People* and in so doing garnered her final UK chart entry.

Somerville, Jimmy
(see **Bronski Beat**; **Communards**)

Sommers, Joanie

b. 24 February 1941, Buffalo, New York, USA. Joanie Sommers is best remembered for her 1962 US Top 10 single 'Johnny Get Angry', although millions more would probably better recall her uncredited singing on several commercials for Pepsi Cola in the 60s.

Sommers and her family moved to Santa Monica, California when she was 13 years old and she sang in her high school band. In 1959 she was discovered by an executive from **Warner Brothers Records** and made an inauspicious debut as the duet partner of **Edd** 'Kookie' **Byrnes** on the latter's *Kookie*. Sommers finally charted in 1960 with 'One Boy' but her biggest hit was the **Hal David**-Sherman Edwards-penned 'Johnny Get Angry', which reached number 7 in the USA in 1962. Although Sommers continued to cut singles and albums for Warners during the 60s, and was still making records in the mid-70s, she never again came close to the success of that one hit single. Sommers did some acting in the late 60s, then semi-retired from performing in the 70s. She returned to entertaining in the 80s.

Albums: *Positively The Most* (1960), *Voice Of The Sixties!* (1961), *For Those Who Think Young* (1962), *Johnny Get Angry* (1962), *Let's Talk ABout Love* (1962), *Sommers' Seasons* (1963), *Softly, The Brazilian Sound* (1964), *Come Alive!* (1966).

Son House

b. Eddie James House Jnr., 21 March 1902, Riverton, Mississippi, USA, d. 19 October 1988, Detroit, Michigan, USA. Brought up in a religious home, Son House was drawn to the ministry in his youth, and only took up the guitar, and the blues, as late as 1927. Throughout his life there was to be a tension between his religious feelings and his secular way of life (including the playing of blues). In 1928 he served a year in jail for manslaughter (in self-defence). In 1930, he met **Charley Patton** at Lula, where he was spotted by a Paramount talent scout. House, Patton, **Willie Brown** and **Louise Johnson** travelled north to a memorable recording session, at which House recorded three two-part blues (together with one untraced record, and a test located in 1985). All were the work of an extraordinary musician. House was no virtuoso, but he brought total conviction to his performances: his ferocious, barking voice, driving bass ostinato, and stabbing bottleneck phrases blended into an overwhelming totality that, for all its impact on the listener, was fundamentally introspective. In the 30s, House and Brown played widely through Mississippi, Arkansas and Tennessee, and House taught both **Muddy Waters** and **Robert Johnson** some guitar technique and the 'Walking Blues' theme.

In 1941, following a tip from Waters, **Alan Lomax** of the Library of Congress located House at Lake Cormorant and made a number of recordings, including some hollers and three pieces which invaluably preserve House and Brown playing in a band with **Fiddlin' Joe Martin** (mandolin) and Leroy Williams (harmonica). Lomax returned the following year to supplement the single House solo recorded in 1941; the results document the breadth of House's repertoire, and catch him at the peak of his powers. In 1943, he moved to Rochester, New York, and had retired from music by 1948. When re-discovered in 1964, House was infirm, alcoholic, and barely able to play, but was fired by the admiration of his young white fans, and regained most of his abilities, recording a splendid album for **Columbia**, and providing an unforgettable experience for all who saw him in concert. All the intensity of his early recordings remained, and even when he was clearly in renewed physical and mental decline, it was a privilege to witness his music. He retired from performing in 1974, and lived in Detroit until his death.

Selected albums: *The Real Delta Blues* (1974), *Son House & The Great Delta Blues Singers* (1990), *The Complete Library Of Congress Sessions* (1990), *Death Letter Blues* (1991).

Son Of Bazerk

Flavor Flav protégé rapper backed by a six-piece No Self Control troupe whose employment of the **Bomb Squad** on their long playing debut drew favourable comparisons to the masters, **Public Enemy**, themselves. Likewise hailing from Long Island, New York, he is best known for the single, 'Change The Style'. Chuck D went so far as to describe him as the 'hardest rapper' he had ever heard. The band's second single was 'Bang (Get Down, Get Down)', housed on Bill Stephney and Hank Shocklee's SOUL label.

Album: *Bazerk Bazerk Bazerk* (MCA 1991).

Sondheim, Stephen

b. Stephen Joshua Sondheim, 22 March 1930, New York, USA. Sondheim is generally regarded as the most important theatrical composer of the 70s and 80s - his introduction of the concept musical (some say, anti-musical) or 'unified show', has made him a cult figure. Born into an affluent family, his father was a prominent New York dress manufacturer, Sondheim studied piano and organ sporadically from the age of seven. When he was 10 his parents divorced, and he spent some time at military school. His mother's friendship with the **Oscar Hammerstein II** family in Philadelphia enabled Sondheim to meet the lyricist, who took him under his wing and educated him in the art of writing for the musical theatre. After majoring in music at Williams College, Sondheim graduated in 1950 with the Hutchinson Prize For Musical Composition, a two-year fellowship, which enabled him to study with the innovative composer Milton Babbitt. During the early 50s, he contributed material to television shows such as *Topper*, and wrote the songs for a proposed Broadway musical, *Saturday Night* (1955), which was never staged due to the death of producer Lemuel Ayres. Sondheim also wrote the incidental music for the play *Girls Of Summer* (1956). His first major success was as a lyric writer, with **Leonard Bernstein**'s music, for the 1957 Broadway hit musical

West Side Story. Initially, Bernstein was billed as co-lyricist, but had his name removed before the New York opening, giving Sondheim full credit. The show ran for 734 performances on Broadway, and 1,039 in London. The songs included 'Jet Song', 'Maria', 'Something's Coming', 'Tonight', 'America', 'One Hand, One Heart', 'I Feel Pretty', 'Somewhere' and 'A Boy Like That'. A film version was released in 1961 and there were New York revivals in 1968 and 1980. Productions in London during in 1974 and 1984 were also significant in that they marked the first of many collaborations between Sondheim and producer **Harold Prince**.

It was another powerful theatrical personality, David Merrick, who mounted *Gypsy* (1959), based on stripper Gypsy Rose Lee's book, *Gypsy: A Memoir*, and considered by some to be the pinnacle achievement of the Broadway musical stage. Sondheim was set to write both music and lyrics before the show's star **Ethel Merman** demanded a more experienced composer. **Jule Styne** proved to be acceptable, and Sondheim concentrated on the lyrics, which have been called his best work in the musical theatre, despite the critical acclaim accorded his later shows. *Gypsy's* memorable score included 'Let Me Entertain You', 'Some People', 'Small World', 'You'll Never Get Away From Me', 'If Momma Was Married', 'All I Need Is The Girl', 'Everything's Coming Up Roses', 'Together, Wherever We Go', 'You Gotta Have A Gimmick' and 'Rose's Turn'. Merman apparently refused to embark on a long London run, so the show was not mounted there until 1973. **Angela Lansbury** scored a personal triumph then as the domineering mother, Rose, and repeated her success in the Broadway revival in 1974. In 1989, both the show and its star, Tyne Daly (well known for television's *Cagney and Lacey*), won **Tony Awards** in the 30th anniversary revival, which ran through until 1991. Rosalind Russell played Rose in the 1962 movie version, which received lukewarm reviews. For *Gypsy*, Sondheim had interrupted work on *A Funny Thing Happened On The Way To The Forum* (1962), to which he contributed both music and lyrics. Based on the plays of Plautus, it has been variously called 'a fast moving farce', 'a vaudeville-based Roman spoof' and 'a musical madhouse'. Sondheim's songs, which included the prologue, 'Comedy Tonight' ('Something appealing, something appalling/Something for everyone, a comedy tonight!') and 'Everybody Ought To Have A Maid', celebrated moments of joy or desire and punctuated the thematic action. The show won several Tony Awards, including 'Best Musical' and 'Best Producer' but nothing for Sondheim's score. The show was revived on Broadway in 1972 with Phil Silvers in the leading role, and had two London productions (1963 and 1986), both starring British comedian Frankie Howerd. A film version, starring Zero Mostel and Silvers, dropped several of the original songs. *Anyone Can Whistle* (1964), 'a daft moral fable about corrupt city officials', with an original book by Laurents, and songs by Sondheim, lasted just a week. The critics were unanimous in their condemnation of the musical with a theme that 'madness is the only hope for world sanity'. The original cast recording, which included 'Simple', 'I've Got You To Lean On', 'A Parade In Town', 'Me And My Town' and the appealing title song, was recorded after the show closed, and became a cult item.

Sondheim was back to 'lyrics only' for *Do I Hear A Waltz?* (1965). The durable Broadway composer **Richard Rodgers**, supplied the music for the show that he described as 'not a satisfying experience'. In retrospect, it was perhaps underrated. Adapted by Arthur Laurents from his play, *The Time Of The Cuckoo*, the show revolved around an American tourist in Venice, and included 'Moon In My Window', 'This Week's Americans', 'Perfectly Lovely Couple', 'We're Gonna Be All Right', and 'Here We Are Again'. Broadway had to wait until 1970 for the next Sondheim musical, the first to be directed by Harold Prince. *Company* had no plot, but concerned 'the lives of five Manhattan couples held together by their rather excessively protective feelings about a 'bachelor friend'. Its ironic, acerbic score included 'The Little Things You Do Together' ('The concerts you enjoy together/Neighbours you annoy together/Children you destroy together...'), 'Sorry-Grateful', 'You Could Drive A Person Crazy', 'Have I Got A Girl For You?', 'Someone Is Waiting', 'Another Hundred People', 'Getting Married Today', 'Side By Side By Side', 'What Would We Do Without You?', 'Poor Baby', 'Tick Tock', 'Barcelona', 'The Ladies Who Lunch' ('Another chance to disapprove, another brilliant zinger/Another reason not to move, another vodka stinger/I'll drink to that!') and 'Being Alive'. With a book by George Furth, produced and directed by Prince, the musical numbers staged by **Michael Bennett**, and starring Elaine Stritch and Larry Kert (for most of the run), *Company* ran for 690 performances. It gained the New York Drama Critics' Circle Award for Best Musical, and six Tony Awards, including Best Musical, and Best Music and Lyrics for Sondheim, the first awards of his Broadway career. The marathon recording session for the original cast album, produced by Thomas Z. Shepard, was the subject of a highly-acclaimed television documentary.

The next Prince-Bennett-Sondheim project, with a book by James Goldman, was the mammoth *Follies* (1971), 'the story of four people in their early 50s: two ex-show girls from the *Weismann Follies*, and two stage-door-Johnnies whom they married 30 years ago, who attend a reunion, and start looking backwards...'. It was a lavish, spectacular production, with a cast of 50, and a Sondheim score which contained 22 'book' songs, including 'Who's That Woman?' (sometimes referred to as the ('the mirror number'), 'Ah Paris!', 'Could I Leave You?', 'I'm Still Here' ('Then you career from career, to career/I'm almost through my memoirs/And I'm here!'); and several 'pastiche' numbers in the style of the 'great' songwriters such as **George Gershwin** and **Dorothy Fields** ('Losing My Mind'); **Cole Porter** ('The Story Of Lucy and Jessie'); **Sigmund Romberg** and **Rudolph Friml** ('One More Kiss'); **Jerome Kern** ('Loveland'); **Irving Berlin** (the prologue, 'Beautiful Girls') and **De Sylva, Brown, And Henderson** ('Broadway Baby'). Although the show received a great deal of publicity and gained the Drama Critics Circle Award for Best Musical, plus seven Tony awards, it closed after 522 performances with the loss of its entire $800,000 investment. A spokesperson commented: 'We sold more posters than tickets'. *Follies In Concert*, with the New York Philharmonic, played two performances in September 1985 at the Lincoln Center, and featured several legendary Broadway names such as **Carol Burnett**, **Betty Comden**, **Adolph Green**, Lee Remick, and **Barbara Cook**. The show was taped for television, and generated a much-acclaimed **RCA** album, which compensated for the disappointingly truncated recording of the original show. The show did not reach London until 1987, when the young **Cameron Mackintosh** produced a 'new conception' with Goldman's revised book, and several new songs replacing some of the originals. It closed after 600 performances, because of high running costs. *A Little Night Music* (1973), was the first Sondheim-Prince project to be based on an earlier source; in this instance, Ingmar Bergman's film *Smiles Of A Summer Night*. Set at the turn of the century, in Sweden it was an operetta, with all the music in three quarter time, or multiples thereof. The critics saw in it echoes of Mahler, Ravel, Rachmaninoff, Brahms, and even Johann Strauss. The score contained Sondheims's first song hit for which he wrote both words and music, 'Send In The Clowns'. Other songs included 'Liaisons', 'A Weekend In The Country', 'The Glamorous Life', 'In Praise Of Women', 'Remember' and 'Night Waltz'. The show ran for 601 performances, and was a healthy financial success. It gained the New York Drama Critics Award for Best Musical, and five Tony awards, including Sondheim's music and lyrics for a record third time in a row. The London run starred Jean Simmons, while Elizabeth Taylor played Desiree in the 1978 movie version.

On the back of the show's 1973 Broadway success, and the composer's increasing popularity, a benefit concert, *Sondheim: A Musical Tribute*, was mounted at the Shubert Theatre, featuring every available performer who had been associated with his shows, singing familiar, and not so familiar, material. *Pacific Overtures* (1976), was, perhaps, Sondheim's most daring and ambitious musical to date. John Weidman's book purported to

relate the entire 120 years history of Japan, from Commodore Perry's arrival in 1856, to its emergence as the powerful industrial force of the 20th century. The production was heavily influenced by the Japanese Kabuki Theatre. The entire cast were Asian, and Sondheim used many Oriental instruments to obtain his effects. Musical numbers included 'Chrysanthemum Tea', 'Please Hello', 'Welcome To Kanagawa', 'Next', 'Someone In A Tree' and 'The Advantages Of Floating In The Middle Of The Sea'. The show closed after 193 performances, losing its entire budget of over half-a-million dollars, but it still won the Drama Critics Circle Award for Best Musical. It was revived Off-Broadway in 1984.

The next Broadway project bearing Sondheim's name was much more successful, and far more conventional. *Side By Side By Sondheim* (1977), an anthology of some of his songs, started out at London's Mermaid Theatre the year before. Starring the original London cast of Millicent Martin, **Julia McKenzie**, David Kernan and Ned Sherrin, the New York production received almost unanimously favourable notices, and proved that many of Sondheim's songs, when presented in this revue form and removed from the sometimes bewildering librettos, could be popular items in their own right. In complete contrast, was *Sweeney Todd, The Demon Barber Of Fleet Street* (1979), Hugh Wheeler's version of the grisly tale of a 19th century barber who slits the throats of his clients, and turns the bodies over to Mrs Lovett (**Angela Lansbury**), who bakes them into pies. Sondheim's 'endlessly inventive, highly expressive score', considered to be near-opera, included the gruesome, 'Not While I'm Around', 'Epiphany', 'A Little Priest', the more gentle 'Pretty Women' and 'My Friends'. Generally accepted as one of the most ambitious Broadway musicals ever staged ('a staggering theatrical spectacle'; 'one giant step forward for vegetarianism'), *Sweeney Todd* ran for over 500 performances, and gained eight Tony Awards, including Best Musical, Score and Book. In 1980, it played in London for four months, and starred Denis Quilley and Sheila Hancock, and was successfully revived by the Royal National Theatre in 1993.

According to Sondheim himself, *Merrily We Roll Along* (1981), with a book by George Furth, was deliberately written in 'a consistent musical comedy style'. It was based on the 1934 play by **George S. Kaufman** and **Moss Hart**, and despite a run of only 16 performances, the pastiche score contained some 'insinuatingly catchy numbers'. It also marked the end, for the time being, of Sondheim's association with Harold Prince, who had produced and directed nearly all of his shows. Depressed and dejected, Sondheim threatened to give up writing for the theatre. However, in 1982, he began working with James Lapine, who had attracted some attention for his direction of the off-Broadway musical, *March Of The Falsettos* (1981).

The first fruits of the Sondheim-Lapine association, **Sunday In The Park With George** also started off-Broadway, as a Playwrights Horizon workshop production, before opening on Broadway in 1984. Inspired by George Seurat's 19th century painting, *Sunday Afternoon On The Island Of La Grande Jatte*, with book and direction by Lapine, the two-act show starred **Mandy Patinkin** and **Bernadette Peters**, and an 'intriguingly intricate' Sondheim score that included 'Finishing The Hat', 'Lesson No.8', and 'Move On'. The run of a year-and-a-half was due in no small part to energetic promotion by the *New York Times*, which caused the theatrical competition to dub the show, *Sunday In The Times With George*. In 1985, it was awarded the coveted Pulitzer Prize for Drama, and in 1990 became one of the rare musicals to be staged at London's Royal National Theatre. In 1987, Sondheim again received a Tony award for **Into the Woods,** a musical fairy tale of a baker and his wife, who live under the curse of a wicked witch, played by Bernadette Peters. The critics called it Sondheim's most accessible show for many years, with a score that included 'Cinderella At The Grave', 'Hello, Little Girl' and 'Children Will Listen'. It won the New York Drama Critics Circle, and Drama Desk Awards, for Best Musical, and a Grammy for Best Original Cast album. 'Angry', rather than accessible, was the critics' verdict of **Assassins**, with a book by John Weidman, which opened for a limited run Off Broadway early in 1991, and played the Donmar Warehouse in London a year later. Dubbed by *Newsweek*: 'Sondheim's most audacious, far out and grotesque work of his career', it 'attempted to examine the common thread of killers and would-be killers from John Wilkes Booth, the murderer of Lincoln, through Lee Harvey Oswald to John Hinckley Jnr, who shot Ronald Reagan'. The pastiche score included 'Everybody's Got The Right', 'The Ballad Of Booth' and 'The Ballad Of Czolgosz'. In 1993, a one-night tribute *Sondheim: A Celebration At Carnegie Hall*, was transmitted on US network television in the 'Great Performers' series, and, on a rather smaller scale, the Off Broadway revue *Putting It Together*, which was packed with Sondheim songs, brought **Julie Andrews** back to the New York musical stage for the first time since **Camelot**. In May 1994, **Passion**, the result of Sondheim's third collaboration with James Lapine, opened on Broadway and ran for 280 performances.

Besides his main Broadway works over the years, Sondheim provided material for many other stage projects, such as the music and lyrics for *The Frogs* (1974), songs for the revue *Marry Me A Little* and a song for the play *A Mighty Man Is He*. He also contributed the incidental music to *The Girls Of Summer*, 'Come Over Here' and 'Home Is the Place' for **Tony Bennett**. In addition, Sondheim wrote the incidental music for the play *Invitation To A March*, the score for the mini-musical

Passionella, the lyrics (with Mary Rodgers' music) for *The Mad Show* and new lyrics for composer Leonard Bernstein's 1974 revival of **Candide**. Sondheim's film work has included the music for *Stravinsky*, *Reds*, and *Dick Tracy*. He received an Oscar for his 'Sooner Or Later (I Always Get My Man)', from the latter film. Sondheim also wrote the screenplay, with Anthony Perkins, for *The Last Of Sheila*, a film 'full of impossible situations, demented logic and indecipherable clues', inspired by his penchant for board games and puzzles of every description. For television, Sondheim wrote the music and lyrics for *Evening Primrose*, which starred Perkins, and made his own acting debut in 1974, with Jack Cassidy, in a revival of the **George S. Kaufman**-Ring Lardner play *June Moon*. While never pretending to write 'hit songs' (apparently the term 'hummable' makes him bristle), Sondheim has nevertheless had his moments in the charts with songs such as 'Small World' (**Johnny Mathis**); 'Tonight' (**Ferrante And Teicher**); 'Maria' and 'Somewhere' (**P.J. Proby**); 'Send In The Clowns' (**Judy Collins**), and 'Losing My Mind' (**Liza Minnelli**). Probably Sondheim's greatest impact on records, apart from the Original Cast albums which to date have won seven Grammys, was **Barbra Streisand**'s *The Broadway Album* in 1985. Seven tracks, involving eight songs, were Sondheim's (two in collaboration with Bernstein), and he re-wrote three of them for Streisand, including 'Send In The Clowns'. *The Broadway Album* stayed at number 1 in the US charts for three weeks, and sold over three million copies. Other gratifying moments for Sondheim occurred in 1983 when he was voted a member of the American Academy and the Institute of Arts and Letters, and again in 1990, when he became Oxford University's first Professor of Drama. As for his contribution to the musical theatre, opinions are sharply divided. John Podhoretz in the *Washington Times* said that 'with *West Side Story*, the musical took a crucial, and in retrospect, suicidal step into the realm of social commentary, and created a self-destructive form in which characters were taken to task and made fun of, for doing things like bursting into song'. Others, like Harold Prince, have said that Stephen Sondheim is simply the best in the world.

Albums: various artists *Sondheim: A Celebration At Carnegie Hall* (RCA Victor 1994), various artists *Putting It Together* (RCA Victor 1994, original cast recording).

Further reading: *Sondheim & Co.*, Craig Zadan. *Sondheim And The American Musical*, Paul Sheran and Tom Sutcliffe. *Song By Song By Sondheim (The Stephen Sondheim Songbook)*, edited by Sheridan Morley. *Sunday In the Park With George*, Stephen Sondheim and James Lapine. *Sondheim*, Martin Gottfried, *Art Isn't Easy: Theatre Of Stephen Sondheim*, Joanne Gordon, *Sondheim's Broadway Musicals*, Stephen.

Sonet Records

One of the more enterprising of the UK independent labels of the 70s and 80s, Sonet's roots lay in the Storyville label, founded in 1951 by Danish jazz enthusiasts. Renamed Sonet in 1955, the company imported US jazz albums from Savoy and Roulette and in the 60s became the Scandinavian distributor for such notable UK labels as **Island**, **Chrysalis** and **Virgin**. Now based in Stockholm, under the direction of Dag Haeggqvist, Sonet began to record local artists, the most successful of whom included Jerry Williams and Ola And The Janglers. In the 90s, Sonet signed Swedish group Army Of Lovers and Finnish rock band 22-Pistepirkko. Among its few US recordings were albums with **Bill Haley And His Comets** in 1968-69. The company also had a strong jazz and blues catalogue, recording visiting US artists as well as licensing material from such companies as Alligator, Flying Fish, Cypress and the impressive folk-blues catalogue of Kicking Mule. With companies in all four Scandinavian countries, Sonet set up a UK branch in 1968. It had numerous hits from artists as diverse as **Terry Dactyl And The Dinosaurs**, **Sylvia**, **Pussycat** and **Hank C. Burnette**. The UK company also had a thriving publishing division and during the 80s acted as licensee for the **Mute** label. In 1991, the Scandinavian holdings of Sonet were purchased by PolyGram. The UK company maintained its independence under the name of Habana Music.

Song And Dance

A 'concert for the theatre', consisting of the 'song cycle' *Tell Me On Sunday*, with music by **Andrew Lloyd Webber** and lyrics by **Don Black**, and *Variations*, composed by Lloyd Webber on a theme of Paganini for his 'cellist brother Julian. *Tell Me On Sunday* was first performed at Lloyd Webber's Sydmonton Festival in 1979. When it subsequently played to an invited audience at London's Royalty Theatre in January 1980, and was broadcast by BBC television during the following month, the piece was sung by **Marti Webb**. In the same year, she had UK chart hits with two of the songs, 'Tell Me On Sunday' and 'Take That Look Off Your Face'. The latter number also won an **Ivor Novello** Award. She was cast again when *Tell Me On Sunday* was expanded to 50 minutes and became the first part of *Song And Dance*, while Wayne Sleep, with his team of eight dancers, performed *Variations* in the second half. The complete work opened at the Palace Theatre in London on 7 April 1982. *Tell Me On Sunday* is a simple tale of a young English woman in New York, and the trials and tribulations she experiences during a series of unhappy love affairs. The songs are considered to be among the composer's - and Don Black's - very best work, and included 'You Made Me Think You Were In Love', 'I Love New York', 'Come Back With The Same Look In Your Eyes', 'I'm Very You, You're Very Me', 'Let's Talk About Me', and 'When You Want To Fall In Love'. Black, who had spent some time in America, came up with what he thought was an apposite song title that apparently pleased him considerably - 'Capped Teeth And Caesar Salad'. *Song And Dance* enjoyed a run of 781 performances, closing in March 1984. During the run, Marti Webb was replaced by several actresses including Gemma Craven, **Lulu**, and Liz Robertson. **Sarah Brightman** played the lead when the show was transmitted on UK television in August 1984. In 1985, much to the reported chagrin of Don Black, *Song And Dance* was expanded even further (adaptation and new lyrics by **Richard Maltby Jnr.**) and presented at the Royale Theatre in New York, where it stayed for over a year. **Bernadette Peters** won a **Tony Award** for her performance in the leading role. Singer/songwriter **Melissa Manchester** was an interesting choice to play the lead in a 1987 Dallas production of the show, but the two original stars, Marti Webb and Wayne Sleep, recreated their roles in a new production which toured the UK and played a six-week season at London's Shaftesbury Theatre in 1990.

Song Is Born, A

A lame remake, seven years later, by director Howard Hawks of his own 1941 film, *Ball Of Fire*. A group of professors, locked away for years writing an encyclopedia, discover that the world of music has moved on and send one of their number out to discover what has been going on. Unfortunately for the dramatics, **Danny Kaye** and Virginia Mayo are no match for the original's Gary Cooper and Barbara Stanwyck. Fortunately for jazz lovers, there is rather a lot of talent on display. As might be expected, who you see on the screen is not always who you hear on the soundtrack but, amongst others, there are the considerable presences of **Louis Armstrong**, **Lionel Hampton**, **Tommy Dorsey**, **Charlie Barnet**, **Mel Powell** and **Louie Bellson**. **Benny Goodman** has an acting role as one of the professors who is also a dab hand on the clarinet.

Song Of Norway

The first of several shows in which **Robert Wright** and **George Forrest** adapted works by classical composers for Broadway. In this case they turned to the life and music of Edvard Grieg. *Song Of Norway* played in the San Francisco and the Los Angeles Opera companies, before opening at the Imperial Theatre in New York on 21 August 1944. The book by Milton Lazarus, based on a play by Homer Curran, tells a fanciful story in which Grieg (Lawrence Brooks) and his poet friend, Rikard Nordraak (Robert Shafer), are diverted from their work by the tempestuous Italian prima donna Louisa Giovanni (Irra Petina). After the poet's death, Grieg is supposedly inspired to write the A-Minor Piano Concerto. Wright and Forrest's music and lyrics combined with Grieg's music in a score which included 'Freddy And His Fiddle', 'Midsummer's Eve', 'Three Loves', 'Hill Of Dreams', 'The Legend', 'Strange Music', 'Now!', 'Hymn Of Betrothal', and 'I Love Thee'. *Song Of Norway* was one of Broadway's biggest wartime hits, running for 860 performances. The 1946 London production, with John Hargreaves, ran for over a year. A film version, starring Florence Henderson and Toralv Maurstad was released in 1970. In 1981, the show was revived on Broadway by the New York City Opera. Many recordings have been issued over the years, but the complete score was not available until 1992, when a version with Valerie Masterson, Diana Montague, David Rendall, and Donald Maxwell, was released on two CDs.

Song Remains The Same, The

By 1976 **Led Zeppelin** were unquestionably one of the most popular acts in rock history. Mindful of heritage, the group was inspired to make a feature film having watched the seminal rock 'n' roll vehicle, *The Girl Can't Help It*. *The Song Remains The Same* centres on a live concert at New York's Madison Square Gardens, while providing glimpses of the attendant hoopla. The opening sequences document preparations as the quartet assemble in the UK and travel to the venue. Bouyed by sterling camera work and sound by Peter Clifton and Joe Massot, the film captures the power and dynamics of a Led Zeppelin concert, showcasing some of their best-known material including 'Rock'n'Roll', 'Whole Lotta Love' and 'Stairway To Heaven'. However periods of 70s-styled excess undermine the proceedings and the live sections blend fantasy sequences reflecting each individual member and manager **Peter Grant**. Sword and sorcery and Celtic images are unquestionably part of the group's lore, but the self-indulgent 'dreams' detract, rather than enhance, the music. Yet if guitarist **Jimmy Page** finds his pyrotechnic skills undermined on 'Dazed And Confused', little could be done to salvage John Bonham's 'Moby Dick'. There is small doubt he is one of rock's finest-ever drummers, but his marathon solo taxes the most fervent admirer. Indeed the self-satisfied aura generated by the proceedings became a brickbat used against the group during the reactionary punk era. A soundtrack double album nonetheless topped the UK chart for one week in November 1976. Yet given the genuinely adventurous inroads exposed on predecessors *Physical Graffiti* and *Presence*, *The Song Remains The Same* reinforces stereotypical images of the group, rather than challenging them.

Songhai

One of the most rewarding, and musically polyglot, groups to emerge during the world music boom of the late 80s, Songhai brought together the *nuevo flamenco* of Spanish band **Ketama** (through guitarists/vocalists Juan Carmona, Jose Soto, Antonio Carmona and Jose Miguel Carmona), Malian kora player Toumani Diabate and British-born jazz/folk acoustic bass maestro, **Danny Thompson**. In late 1987, Ketama were in London for a series of club dates, and through a mutual friend were introduced to Diabate. A jam session followed in a London West End club patronized by Spanish expatriates, and the participants were so excited by the results that Ketama's producer **Joe Boyd** arranged a recording session in Madrid in spring 1988, augmenting the line-up with Thompson, with whom he had worked regularly since the late 60s. The name Songhai refers to the ancient Malian empire of the same name, while the band's music achieved an exquisite balance of African, Spanish and Anglo-American ingredients.
Album: *Songhai* (1988).

Sonia

b. 13 February 1971, Liverpool, Merseyside, England. Another **Stock, Aitken And Waterman** (SAW) pop protegee, Sonia had been singing around Liverpool clubs since leaving school and was a well known starlet in Merseyside having appeared as Adrian Boswell's girlfriend in the hit UK television situation comedy *Bread*. She also regularly hosted the *Stars Of The Future Show* at the Liverpool Empire in aid of underprivileged children. In her bid to make it as a singer she cajoled Waterman in to allowing her to sing live on his regular *Radio City* programme. He was impressed enough to get her on his televison show *The Hitman And Her* and shortly afterwards she recorded her debut single, 'You'll Never Stop Me Loving You'. Written and produced by the entire SAW team it was a UK number 1. Follow-up singles included 'Can't Forget You', 'Listen To Your Heart', and a cover of the **Skeeter Davis** hit 'End Of The World'. In 1990 she recorded a version of **James Taylor**'s 'You've Got A Friend' with new SAW heroes **Big Fun**. In 1993 Sonia represented Britain in the Eurovision Song Contest, with 'Better The Devil You Know', but was beaten to the number one position by the Irish entry.
Albums: *Everybody Knows* (1990), *Sonia* (1991), *Better The Devil You Know* (1993).

Sonic Boom

b. Peter Kember, 19 November 1965. UK-based Sonic Boom's solo project was originally planned as an aside for his main love, the **Spacemen 3**. Signing to the Silvertone label, Sonic issued 'Angel' (a drug-related tale not dissimilar both lyrically and musically to the

Velvet Underground's 'Heroin') in 1989. This was followed by *Spectrum* for which Sonic was helped by fellow Spacemen Jason and Will Carruthers, plus the **Jazz Butcher** and the **Perfect Disaster**'s Phil Parfitt. Spectrum's hypnotic blend of repetitive guitar riffs and keyboard runs betrayed his love of New York duo **Suicide**, but nevertheless possessed a definite if quiet charm. It even sported a psychedelic, gatefold revolving sleeve. Early buyers could send away for an orange vinyl 10-inch, 'Octaves'/'Tremeloes', which featured two elongated, synthesized notes! Unfortunately, the Spacemen 3 split in his wake to form **Spiritualized**, although their swan-song appeared later, ironically charting. Sonic re-emerged in the summer of 1991 with a low-key instrumental demo single, '(I Love You) To The Moon And Back', distributed free at gigs.
Album: *Spectrum* (1990).

Sonic Youth

A product of New York's experimental 'No-Wave' scene, Sonic Youth first recorded under the auspices of *avant garde* guitarist **Glenn Branca**. Thurston Moore (guitar), Lee Ranaldo (guitar) and Kim Gordon (bass) performed together on Branca's *Symphony No. 3*, while the group debuted in its own right on his Neutral label. *Sonic Youth* was recorded live at New York's Radio City Music Hall in December 1981 and featured original drummer Richard Edson. Three further collections, *Confusion Is Sex*, *Sonic Death* and a mini-album, *Kill Yr Idols*, completed the quartet's formative period which was marked by their pulsating blend of discordant guitars, impassioned vocals and ferocious, compulsive drum patterns, courtesy of newcomer Jim Sclavunos, or his replacement, Bob Bert. *Bad Moon Rising* was the first Sonic Youth album to secure a widespread release in both the USA and Britain. This acclaimed set included the compulsive 'I'm Insane' and the eerie 'Death Valley '69', a collaboration with **Lydia Lunch**, which invoked the horror of the infamous Charles Manson murders. Bob Bert was then replaced by Steve Shelley, who has remained with the line-up ever since. In 1986 the group unleashed *Evol*, which refined their ability to mix melody with menace, particularly on the outstanding 'Shadow Of A Doubt'. The album also introduced the Youth's tongue-in-cheek fascination with **Madonna**. 'Expressway To Yr Skull' was given two alternative titles, 'Madonna, Sean And Me' and 'The Cruxifiction Of Sean Penn', while later in the year the band were joined by Mike Watt from **Firehose** in a spin-off project, **Ciccone Youth**, which resulted in a mutated version of 'Into The Groove(y)'. (In 1989 this *alter ego* culminated in *Ciccone Youth*, which combined dance tracks with experimental sounds redolent of German groups **Faust** and **Neu**.) Sonic Youth's career continued with the highly-impressive *Sister*, followed in 1988 by *Daydream Nation*, a double set which allowed the group to expand themes when required. Once again the result was momentous. The instrumentation was powerful, recalling the intensity of the **Velvet Underground** or **Can** while the songs themselves were highly memorable. In 1990 Sonic Youth left the independent circuit by signing with the **Geffen Records** stable, going on to establish a reputation as godfathers to the alternative US rock scene. Thurston Moore was instrumental in the signing of **Nirvana** to Geffen Records, while Kim Gordon was similarly pivotal in the formation of **Hole**. Steve Shelley would also work closely with Geffen on a number of acts. Successive stints on **Lollapalooza** tours helped to make Sonic Youth the nation's best known underground band, while the group's members continued to collaborate on music and soundtrack projects to a degree which ensured the continuance of an already vast discography.
Albums: *Confusion Is Sex* (Neutral 1983), *Kill Yr Idols* (Zensor 1983), *Sonic Death* (Ecstatic Peace 1984), *Bad Moon Rising* (Homestead 1985), *Evol* (SST 1986), *Sister* (SST 1987), *Daydream Nation* (Blast First 1988), *Goo* (Geffen 1990), *Dirty Boots* (Geffen 1991, mini-album), *Dirty* (Geffen 1992), *Experimental Jet Set, Trash And No Star* (Geffen 1994), *Washing Machine* (Geffen 1995), *Made In USA* (Rhino/WEA 1995; film soundtrack, rec. 1986). Compilation: *Screaming Fields Of Sonic Love* (Blast First 1995). Lee Renaldo solo: *From Here To Infinity* (SST 1987). Thurston Moore solo: *Psychic Hearts* (Geffen 1995).
Further reading: *Confusion Is Next*, Alec Foego (1995).

Sonics

Formed in Tacoma, Washington, USA. The Sonics were one of several exemplary groups, including the Wailers (not the Jamaican group), **Kingsmen** and **Paul Revere And The Raiders**, to emerge from the Pacific north-west circuit. Gerry Roslie (vocals/keyboards), Larry Parypa (lead guitar), Rob Lind (saxophone), Andy Parypa (bass) and Bob Bennett (drums) continued the region's music traditions, blending 50s rock and blues with British-influenced beat. *Here Are The Sonics* included the regional hits, 'The Witch' and 'Psycho', but their frantic, driving sound was equally suited to the album's exciting cover versions, 'Good Golly Miss Molly', 'Do You Love Me' and 'Roll Over Beethoven'. A Rosalie original, 'Strychnine', was later recorded by the **Cramps**. *The Sonics Boom* offered a similar mixture, but was notable for the quintet's reading of 'Louie Louie', where they inverted the song's classic C-F-G chord progression to E-G-A. The group was signed to the nationally-distributed Jerden label for *Introducing The Sonics*, but the power of their early work was noticeably muted on this somewhat disappointing set. Their momentum was now waning, and despite completing a creditable version of **Frank Zappa**'s 'Any Way The Winds

Blows', the Sonics began to disintegrate. A group entitled Brady Hyatt and the Sonics was active in 1973, but it took the late 70s punk explosion to prompt a concerted revival. However, the new Roslie-led line-up, as featured on *Sinderella*, failed to match the excitement of the original and the group was latterly disbanded.

Albums: *Here Are The Sonics!!!* (1965), with the Wailers *Merry Christmas* (1965), *The Sonics Boom* (1966), *Introducing The Sonics* (1966), *Sinderella* (1974), *Original Northwest Punk* (1977), *Live Fanz Only* (1987), *Psycho-Sonic* (1993). Compilations: *Explosives* (1974), *Unreleased* (1981), *Fire And Ice* (1983), *Full Force* (1988), *The Ultimate Sonics* (Etiquette 1994).

Sonnier, Jo-el

b. 2 October 1946, Rayne, Louisiana, USA. The son of sharecroppers, Sonnier (pronounced Sawn-ya) was working in cottonfields from the age of five. He began singing and playing accordion, worked on local radio and recorded his first single, 'Tes Yeaux Bleus' (Your Blue Eyes) when aged 13. He recorded his 'white roots cajun music' for the Swallow and Goldband labels, and when 26 years old, moved to California and then to Nashville in search of national success. In 1976 he recorded **Lefty Frizzell**'s 'Always Late (With Your Kisses)' for Mercury and then formed a band called Friends, which included **Albert Lee**, David Lindley and Garth Hudson. His session work has included 'Cajun Born' for **Johnny Cash** and 'America Without Tears' for **Elvis Costello**. In 1987 Sonnier was signed to **RCA** and **Steve Winwood** guested on 'Rainin' In My Heart', a track on *Come On Joe*. He had a country hit with a frenzied version of **Richard Thompson**'s 'Tear-Stained Letter'. He has toured the USA with **Alabama** and the **Charlie Daniel**'s Band and, by all accounts, his UK debut at the Mean Fiddler in 1989 was electrifying. He was once known as the 'Cajun Valentino'.

Selected albums: *Cajun Life* (1980), *Come On Joe* (1988), *Have A Little Faith* (1989), *Tears Of Joy* (1991), *Hello Happiness Again* (1992), *The Complete Mercury Sessions* (1992), *Cajun Roots* (Rounder 1994).

Sonny And Cher

Although touted as the misunderstood young lovers of 1965 folk rock **Sonny Bono** and **Cher** were not as fresh and naive as their image suggested. Salvatore Bono (b. 16 February 1935, Detroit, Michigan) already had a chequered history in the music business stretching back to the late 50s when he wrote and produced records by such artists as **Larry Williams**, **Wynona Carr** and **Don And Dewey**. Bono also recorded for several small labels under an array of aliases such as Don Christy, Sonny Christy and Ronny Sommers. With arranger **Jack Nitzsche**, he co-wrote 'Needles And Pins', a UK number 1 for the **Searchers** in 1964. That same year, Sonny married

Cherilyn Sarkasian La Pier (b. 20 May 1946, El Centro, California) whom he had met while recording with the renowned producer **Phil Spector**. Although the duo recorded a couple of singles under the exotic name Caeser And Cleo, it was as Sonny and Cher that they found fame with the transatlantic number 1 'I Got You Babe'. Arranged by the underrated **Harold Battiste**, the single was a majestic example of romanticized folk rock and one of the best produced discs of its time. Bono's carefree, bohemian image obscured the workings of a music business veteran and it was no coincidence that he took full advantage of the pair's high profile. During late 1965, they dominated the charts as both a duo and soloists with such hits was 'Baby Don't Go', 'All I Really Want To Do', 'Laugh At Me', 'Just You' and 'But You're Mine'. Although their excessive output resulted in diminishing returns, their lean periods were still punctuated by further hits, most notably 'Little Man' and 'The Beat Goes On'. By the late 60s, they had fallen from critical grace, but starred in a couple of low budget movies, *Good Times* and *Chastity*. A brief resurgence as MOR entertainers in the 70s brought them their own television series, although by that time they had divorced. Eventually, extra-curricular acting activities ended their long-standing musical partnership.

While Cher went on to achieve a phenomenally successful acting and singing career, Bono also continued to work as an actor, but adopted a completely different role in 1988 when he was voted mayor of Palm Springs.

Albums: *Look At Us* (1965), *The Wondrous World Of Sonny And Cher* (1966), *In Case You're In Love* (1967), *Good Times* (1967), *Sonny And Cher Live* (1971), *All Ever Need Is You* (1972), *Mama Was A Rock And Roll Singer - Papa Used To Write All Her Songs* (1974), *Live In Las Vegas, Vol. 2* (1974). Compilations: *Baby Don't Go* (1965, early recordings), *The Best Of Sonny And Cher* (1967), *Greatest Hits* (1974), *The Sonny And Cher Collection: An Anthology Of Their Hits Alone And Together* (1991). Film: *Good Times* (1967).

Further reading: *Sonny And Cher*, Braun, Thomas (1978).

Sonora Matancera, La

This remarkable musical institution was founded on 12 January 1924 in the Cuban province of Matanzas by tres guitarist Valentín Cané. A horn-led string and percussion group, they were initially called Tuna Liberal and included guitarist/singer Rogelio Martínez (b. 1898, Matanzas, Cuba), who became the band's director, bassist Pablo Vázquez 'Babú' (d. 1969) and timbales player Jimagua. Following two name changes (Septeto Soprano and Estudiantina Matancera) and numerous personnel changes, they renamed themselves Septeto Sonora Matancera in late 1926 and relocated to Havana on 12 January 1927, where Caíto (b. Carlos Manuel Díaz Alonso, 8 November 1905, Matanzas,

Cuba, d. 27 September 1990, New York, USA; maracas player/third vocalist) joined shortly after the group's arrival in the capital. (Caíto's falsetto *voz de vieja* 'old woman's voice' in the chorus became one of the group's unique ingredients.) They soon established themselves and performed at many of Havana's prestigious venues, including the Alhambra Theatre, Galician Centre, Havana Sports Club and the fabled night meccas La Tropical and Marte y Belona, as well as on several radio stations. Their pioneering use of uniforms was at first ridiculed, but soon became the trend. They were one of Cuba's first co-operative bands, which helped underpin their internal cohesion and longevity, and have never felt the need for written contracts within their organization.

The group made their recording debut in mid-1928 on **RCA**-Victor. In 1932 they finally settled for the name La Sonora Matancera (The Matanzas Group). In 1929 timbalero José Rosario Chávez 'Manteca' replaced Jimagua. Between 1929 and 1932 they were frequently hired to perform by the Cuban ruler General Gerardo Machado Morales. In 1935, ex-Septeto Nacional member Calixto Leicea (b. 1910, Matanzas, Cuba; trumpeter/composer) replaced the deceased cornet player Ismael Goberna (an early member of the group) as the Sonora's first trumpeter. Popular singer Bienvenido Granda (b. 30 August 1915, Cuba, d. 9 July 1983, Mexico) joined in the early 40s and remained until disagreements with Martínez obliged him to leave in 1951. Between 1937 and 1939 future mambo popularizer Pérez Prado played piano with the group. In 1942 the Sonora was joined by distinctive piano stylist, composer and arranger Lino Frías (d. April 1983, New York, USA), who retired from the band in July 1977 due to arthritis; he was followed by the established New York salsa pianist, bandleader, arranger, composer and producer Javier Vázquez (b. 8 April 1936, Matanzas, Cuba), a son of early group member Pablo Vázquez 'Babú'.

To compete with other groups (using three trumpets), the Sonora added second trumpeter Pedro Knight on 6 January 1944. Knight later married **Celia Cruz**, singer with the group between 1950 and 1965, on 14 July 1962 in Mexico City and retired from the Sonora on 30 April 1967. In 1952 Raimundo Elpidio Vázquez replaced his father Babú on bass. In 1960, **Papaíto** took over as the Sonora's timbalero after the death of Manteca. Between 1976 and 1980 **Alfredo 'Chocolate' Armenteros** played trumpet alongside Leicea.

Their repertoire comprises various Cuban and other Latin rhythms; and over the decades they have possibly recorded about 4000 songs for a number of labels, including RCA-Victor, Panart, Seeco/Tropical, Ansonia, Orfeón, Barbaro (part of the Fania family) and Fania. During the 50s the Sonora enjoyed considerable pan-Caribbean and pan-Latin American

prominence. In 1957 they went on a major tour of South America. On 15 June 1960 the band left Cuba to fulfil a four week contract in Mexico, but remained nearly two years and never returned to Cuba. In 1962 they took up permanent residence in New York.

In addition to Granda and Cruz, an illustrious cavalcade of over 60 singers (both Cuban and non-Cuban) have worked with them, including:- Daniel Santos (b. 16 June 1916, Tras Talleres, San Juan, Puerto Rico, d. 27 November 1992, Ocala, Florida, USA), Myrta Silva (b. 11 September 1923, Arecibo, Puerto Rico, d. 2 December 1987, San Juan, Puerto Rico), Miguelito Valdés (b. 6 September 1910, Belén district, Havana, Cuba, d. 8 November 1978, Bogotá, Colombia), Bobby Capó (b. 1 January 1921, Coamo, Puerto Rico, d. 18 December 1989), Vicentico Valdés (b. 10 January 1921, Cayo Hueso district, Havana, Cuba), Nelson Pinedo (b. 10 February 1928, Barranquilla, Colombia), Alberto Beltrán (b. 5 May 1923, La Romana, Dominican Republic), Carlos Argentino (b. 23 June 1929, Buenos Aires, Argentina), Leo Marini (b. 23 August 1920, Mendoza, Argentina), Celio González (b. 29 January 1924, Camajuanillas, Las Villas, Cuba), Elliot Romero (b. San Juan, Puerto Rico, d. 1990), **Justo Betancourt**, Wuelfo Gutiérrez (b. Santiago de Las Vegas, Cuba), Yayo el Indio (b. Puerto Rico), **Roberto Torres**, Jorge Maldonado (b. 24 September 1950, Río Piedras, Puerto Rico), Cali Aleman (b. Nicaragua) and **Ismael Miranda**.

The band made an appearance accompanying Celia Cruz in the BBC2 *Arena* film profile *My Name Is Celia Cruz* broadcast on 12 February 1988. In June 1989, 13 former lead singers reunited with the Sonora for a series of three concerts to celebrate their 65th anniversary; a recording of their 1 June 1989 concert was issued on the double album *Live! From Carnegie Hall: 65th Anniversary Celebration*. They made their extremely belated UK debut in November 1993.

Selected albums: *Se Formó La Rumbantela* (rec. 1948-50; reissued 1994), *Algo Especial* (50s), *Grandes Exitos* (50s), *50 Años* (1975, 24 tracks from 1949-59), with Justo Betancourt *Sonora Matancera con Justo Betancourt* (1981), with Celia Cruz *Feliz Encuentro* (1982), *65 Aniversario* (1989, hits from 1951-58), *Live! From Carnegie Hall: 65th Anniversary Celebration* (1989).

Sons Of Adam

The Sons Of Adam were a superior Los Angeles garage band, active in both their home city and San Francisco during 1966. The quartet - which included Randy Holden (guitar), Mike Port (bass) and Michael Stuart (drums) - made their recording debut with 'Feathered Fish', a song written by **Arthur Lee** but never recorded by his own group, **Love**. The Sons Of Adam then completed two more singles, which included their versions of 'Tomorrow's Gonna Be Another Day', later popularized by the **Monkees**, and a gripping reading of the **Yardbirds**' 'You're A Better Man Than I'. Frustrated with the group's commercial impasse, Stuart subsequently joined the aforementioned Love, while Holden and Port resurfaced in the **Other Half**. The guitarist later found fame in **Blue Cheer**.

Sons Of Blues

This young, Chicago-based band (aka S.O.B. Band) originally comprised **Lurrie Bell**, **Billy Branch**, bassist Freddie Dixon (son of **Willie Dixon**), and drummer Jeff Ruffin. They garnered international acclaim for their recordings on Volume Three of the Alligator label's ground-breaking *Living Chicago Blues* series. Bell left in the early 80s and so Branch assumed leadership. The band's 1983 album for the Red Beans label included solid Chicago blues and some contemporary R&B. The line-up of Branch, guitarist Carlos Johnson, bassist J.W. Williams and drummer Moses Rutues was augmented by several guests, including **Jimmy Walker**. In recognition of William's own former band, the group is now known as the Sons Of Blues/Chi-Town Hustlers, under which name they recorded in 1987.

Album: *Where's My Money* (1983).

Sons Of Champlin

Bill Champlin (vocals/trumpet) and Tim Caine (saxophone) formed this enigmatic white-soul aggregation in 1965. They were initially joined by Terry Haggerty (lead guitar), Al Strong (bass) and Jim Myers (drums), but when a horn player, Geoff Palmer, was added, Champlin switched to guitar. Draft victim Myers was then replaced by Bill Bowen. Originally dubbed the Masterbeats, then, the Sons Of Father Champlin, the group adopted their more familiar name in 1966. A confident debut single, 'Sing Me A Rainbow', preceded their transformation from besuited aspirants to chemical proselytizers. Now established on the San Francisco scene, a sprawling double-album, *Loosen Up Naturally*, encapsulated their unique blend of love, peace, happiness and funk.

A second album, named after the group's now truncated title, the Sons, refined a similar mixture before they embarked on one of their periodic implosions, during which time various members joined, and left such ensembles as the Rhythm Dukes and the Nu-Boogaloo Express. A reconstituted line-up, shorn of its horn-section, reappeared on *Follow Your Heart*. Champlin, Haggerty and Palmer were joined by David Shallock (guitar) and Bill Vitt (drums) in a new venture, Yogi Phlegm, but this unfortunate/wonderful appellation was then abandoned. The quintet later reclaimed the Sons Of Champlin name, but although they secured some commercial success, it was tempered by mis-management and misfortune. Bill Champlin embarked on a solo career during the late 70s. He appeared as a backing singer on a score of releases and

co-wrote 'After The Love Is Gone' for **Earth, Wind And Fire**. Having completed two solo albums, *Single* and *Runaway*, this expressive vocalist joined **Chicago** in 1982.

Albums: *Loosen Up Naturally* (1969), *The Sons* (1969), *The Sons Minus Seeds And Stems* (1970), *Follow Your Heart* (1971), *Welcome To The Dance* (1973), *The Sons Of Champlin* (1975), *A Circle Filled With Love* (1976), *Loving Is Why* (1977). Compilation: *Marin County Sunshine* (1988).

Sons Of The Pioneers

The Sons Of The Pioneers was founded in 1933 by Leonard Slye (aka **Roy Rogers**), when he recruited two friends - Bob Nolan (b. Robert Clarence Nobles, 1 April 1908, New Brunswick, Canada) and Tim Spencer (b. Vernon Spencer, 13 July 1908, Webb City, Missouri, USA) - to reform a singing trio, known originally as the O-Bar-O Cowboys, and to undergo a name change to the Pioneer Trio. When they found regular radio work in Los Angeles, they added fiddle player Hugh Farr (b. 6 December 1903, Llano, Texas, USA). Someone suggested that they looked too young to be pioneers so they became the Sons Of The Pioneers. They were signed to US **Decca** Records in 1935, and Hugh's brother, Karl (b. Karl Marx Farr, 25 April 1909, Rochelle, Texas, USA) joined as a guitarist. The Sons Of The Pioneers sang in numerous western films and when Rogers was groomed as a singing cowboy in 1937, he was replaced as lead singer by Lloyd Perryman (b. Lloyd Wilson Perryman, 29 January 1917, Ruth, Arkansas, USA). Their best-selling records include 'Cool Water' and 'Tumbling Tumbleweeds', both written by Nolan. Spencer wrote the country standards, 'Cigarettes, Whisky And Wild, Wild Woman' and 'Room Full Of Roses'. Owing to throat problems, Tim Spencer retired from performing in 1949 but managed the group for some years. He died on 26 April 1974. Lloyd Perryman, who became the leader of the group when Spencer and Nolan left in 1949, died on 31 May 1977. On 20 September 1961, Karl Farr collapsed and died on stage after being agitated when a guitar-string broke, while his brother survived until 17 April 1980. Nolan died on 16 June 1980, requesting that his ashes be scattered across the Nevada desert. Other members of The Sons Of The Pioneers include Pat Brady, Ken Carson, Ken Curtis, Tommy Doss and Shug Fisher. Many critics rate the Perryman, Curtis and Doss recordings, which include the 1949 versions of 'Riders In The Sky' and 'Room Full Of Roses', as the best. Despite personnel changes, The Sons Of The Pioneers' recordings reflect a love of God, the hard-working life of a cowboy, and an admiration for 'home on the range'. The legacy of the Hollywood cowboys is still with us in the work of Ian Tyson but his songs paint a less romantic picture.

Albums: *Cowboy Hymns And Spirituals* (1952), *Western Classics* (1953), *25 Favourite Cowboy Songs* (1955), *How*

Great Thou Art (1957), *One Man's Songs* (1957), *Wagons West* (1958), *Cool Water (And 17 Timeless Favourites)* (1959), *Room Full Of Roses* (1960), *Lure Of The West* (1961), *Westward Ho!* (1961), *Tumbleweed Trail* (1962), *Good Old Country Music* (1963), *Trail Dust* (1963), *Country Fare* (1964), *Down Memory Lane* (1964), *Legends Of The West* (1965), *The Sons Of The Pioneers Sing The Songs Of Bob Nolan* (1966), *The Sons Of The Pioneers Sing Campfire Favorites* (1967), *San Antonio Rose And Other Country Favorites* (1968), *South Of The Border* (1968), *The Sons Of The Pioneers Visit The South Seas* (1969), *Riders In The Sky* (1973), *A Country And Western Songbook* (1977), *Sons Of The Pioneers - Volumes 1 & 2* (previously unissued radio transcriptions) (1980), *Let's Go West Again* (1981). Compilations: *The Sons Of The Pioneers - Columbia Historic Edition* (1982), *20 Of The Best* (1985), *Radio Transcriptions, Volumes 1-4* (1987), *Cool Water, Vol. 1 (1945-46)* (1987), *Teardrops In My Heart, Vol. 2 (1946-47)* (1987), *A Hundred And Sixty Acres, Vol. 3 (1946-47)* (1987), *Riders In The Sky, Vol. 4 (1947-49)* (1987), *Land Beyond The Sun, Vol. 5 (1949-50)* (1987), *Wagons West* (1993, 4 CD boxed set). Further reading: *Hear My Song: The Story Of The Celebrated Sons Of The Pioneers*.

Sons Of The San Joaquin

A western vocal trio formed in the San Joaquin Valley of California, comprising brothers Joe Hannah (b. 1 February 1931; bass/vocals) and Jack Hannah (b. 25 October 1933; guitar/vocals) both at Marshfield, Missouri, USA and Joe's son, Lon Hannah (b. 10 April 1956, Pasadena, California, USA; lead guitar/vocals). The brothers had always been attracted by the singing of the **Sons Of The Pioneers**, but it was Lon, at the time singing as a solo artist, who convinced them in 1987, that they should form a trio. At the time, the brothers worked as teachers and on occasions even worked cattle on local ranches. They made their performing debut at the major Clovis Rodeo and in 1989 appeared at the *Cowboy Poetry Gathering* in Elko, Nevada, where they proved an immediate hit and have become an expected regular act ever since. **Michael Martin Murphey**, present at the event, took them to Nashville to provide harmony vocals for *Cowboy Songs*, his noted western revival album. The Sons Of The San Joaquin went on to tour in their own right, soon building up a reputation for their close harmonies and authentic western sounds. Along with Texas singer **Don Edwards** and cowboy poet Waddie Mitchell, they were the first artists signed by the new Warner Western label. They began to write much of their own material, which portrayed the western life style and with **Riders In The Sky**, they do much to continue to popularise the sounds started many years ago by the Sons Of The Pioneers. They toured to Saudi Arabia and Pakistan in 1993 as goodwill ambassadors for the United States Information Service. The following year, they proved very successful when they performed with the Fresno Philharmonic Symphony Orchestra. The show consisted of selections from their recordings arranged in symphony setting and was accompanied by a video screen, which showed scenes from some classic westerns whilst they performed. They became associated with Edwards and Mitchell, to form *The Cowboy Jubilee*, a travelling show of western music and verse.

Albums: *Bound For The Rio Grande* (1989), *Great American Cowboy* (1991), *A Cowboy Has To Sing* (Warner Western 1992), *Songs Of The Silver Screen* (Warner Western 1993).

Sony Broadway

The Masterworks division of **Columbia Records** under the leadership of **Goddard Lieberson**, dominated the recording of Original Broadway Cast albums from the early 50s onwards. By that time, Columbia Records had become part of the Columbia Broadcasting System (**CBS**), having been bought out in 1938 for the sum of $700,000. Exactly 50 years later, the Japanese conglomerate, Sony Music, reportedly paid $2 billion for CBS. That is how, in the early 90s, the Sony Broadway label was in a position to begin to re-release all those (mostly) marvellous musicals from the genre's vintage years on mid-price CDs. By 1994 the list was substantial, and included *Goldilocks*, *Miss Liberty*, *Mr. President*, *Candide*, *West Side Story*, *Wonderful Town*, *The Apple Tree*, *The Rothschilds*, *On The Twentieth Century*, *The Girl Who Came To Supper*, *1776*, *Ballroom*, *Dear World*, *70, Girls, 70*, *The Most Happy Fella*, *Bajour*, *Irma La Douce*, *Out Of This World*, *Do I Hear A Waltz?*, *Flower Drum Song*, *The Sound Of Music*, *South Pacific*, *Two By Two*, *A Tree Grows In Brooklyn*, *Over Here*, *All American*, *It's a Bird, It's a Plane, It's Superman*, *Gentlemen Prefer Blondes*, *Hallelujah, Baby!*, *Irene*, *Here's Love*, *Dames At Sea*, and *Raisin*. The CD booklet covers are reconstructions of the original album sleeve graphics, but the liner notes are all newly written by contemporary experts such as Ken Mandelbaum. As well as those recording of the originals casts, the label has also released several studio recordings of Broadway shows, and various compilations such as *There's No Business Like Show Business - Broadway Showstoppers*, *There's Nothing Like A Dame - Broadway's Broads*, *Embraceable You - Broadway In Love*, *The Party's Over - Broadway Sings The Blues*, and tributes to leading songwriters, including **Stephen Sondheim**, **Richard Rodgers** and **Oscar Hammerstein II**, and **Betty Comden** and **Adolph Green**. Another label devoted to re-issuing Broadway musicals, most of which have only been available for many years, second-hand and at inflated collectors' prices, is **Broadway Angel**.

Sophisticated Ladies

This revue which celebrated the music of the great

American composer **Duke Ellington**, was conceived by Donald McKayle and opened at the Lunt-Fontanne Theatre in New York on 1 March 1981. McKayle was also one of the choreographers, along with director Michael Smuin and Henry LeTang, for what was essentially a dynamic song and dance show with an awful lot of class. From a large on-stage orchestra led by **Mercer Ellington**, Duke's son, there flowed a constant stream of classics from the world of popular music and jazz, such as 'I'm Beginning To See The Light', 'Satin Doll', 'Mood Indigo', 'Take the 'A' Train', 'I Got It Bad (And That Ain't Good)', 'It Don't Mean A Thing (If It Ain't Got That Swing)', and some 30 more. Tap dancer extraordinaire, Gregory Hines, headed a cast of dedicated singers and dancers including Gregg Burge, Judith Jamison, Hinton Battle, P.J. Benjamin, **Phyllis Hyman**, and Terri Klausner. The original book was dispensed with, and it was left to the superb music to carry the evening. This it did - and for a remarkable 767 performances. For some reason, it was 1992 before the show reached London, and by that time the West End was full of tributes to icons such as **Buddy Holly**, **Louis Jordan**, and **Cole Porter**. *Sophisticated Ladies* joined them for just three months.

Soprano Summit
(see **Davern, Kenny**; **Wilber, Bob**)

Sopwith Camel

Formed in San Francisco, California in 1965, Sopwith Camel originally consisted of Peter Kraemer (guitar/vocals), Terry McNeil (guitar/keyboards), Rod Albin (bass) and Fritz Kasten (drums). This embryonic line-up faltered with the loss of its rhythm section, but the arrival of William Sievers (guitar), Martin Beard (bass) and former **Mike Bloomfield** drummer Norman Mayell heralded the beginning of the group's most successful era. Their debut single, 'Hello Hello', reached the US Top 30 in January 1967, and its charming simplicity recalled the good-time music of the **Lovin' Spoonful**. The two groups shared the same label and Sopwith Camel were promoted as a surrogate, denying them the guitar-based direction their live show offered. *Sopwith Camel* was, nonetheless, a fine collection, highlighted by the enthralling 'Frantic Desolation'. The group split, though, when the record was not as successful as they had hoped. However, in 1972 the 'hit' line-up, bar Sievers, was reunited for *The Miraculous Hump Returns From The Moon*. This showcased a jazz-based emphasis, but failed to rekindle past glories and in 1974 the band split again. Kraemer did attempt to resurrect the name three years later, but when a van containing all of their equipment was destroyed by fire, Sopwith Camel was officially grounded.

Albums: *Sopwith Camel* (1967 - reissued in 1986 with one extra track as *Frantic Desolation*), *The Miraculous Hump Returns From The Moon* (1972).

Sorrels, Rosalie

b. Rosalie Ann Stringfellow, 24 June 1933, Boise, Idaho, USA. Absorbing many of her influences at an early age via her parents, Nancy Kelly and Walter Pendleton Stringfellow, and her grandparents, Rosalie developed a taste for Anglo-American music. During the 50s, and by then living in Salt Lake City and raising a family of five children alone, she took a course in American folk music which eventually led to her becoming involved in collecting traditional songs. Later, she took up the guitar, and this, coupled with the invaluable background she had been given, as well as the break-up of her marriage, encouraged her to take up singing professionally. Rosalie was taken on by Lena Spencer, to sing at the famous Caffe Lena, in 1966, and for a time Sorrels and her family lived with Spencer. Sorrels had never had an easy life, with an abortion at the age of 16, a baby given up for adoption at 17, and then, in 1976, Sorrel's eldest son, David, took his own life.

Lonesome Roving Wolves, on Green Linnet, was produced by **Patrick Sky** who recorded for the Philo and **Folkways** labels. 'The Baby Tree', recorded by Sorrels on *Rosalie's Songbag*, was covered by **Paul Kantner** on *Blows Against The Empire* by **Jefferson Starship**. Known for her storytelling, as well as her songs, Sorrels has played virtually every major festival in the USA during her career, in addition to the many colleges and coffee houses on the circuit. *Then Came The Children* was recorded live, in 1984, at the East Cultural Center in Vancouver, Canada. In 1988, Sorrels was afflicted by a cerebral aneurysm which, fortunately, she recovered from. Thanks to **Bruce 'Utah' Phillips**, she was soon working again. *Be Careful, There's A Baby In The House* includes the **Billie Holiday** classic 'God Bless The Child, a song that Rosalie is well qualified to sing. She now lives on Grimes Creek, in the family cabin, near Boise, and continues to tour and record.

Albums: *Folksongs Of Utah And Idaho* (1959), *The Unfortunate Rake* (1960), *Rosalie's Songbag* (1963), *Songs Of The Mormon Pioneers* (1964), *Somewhere Between* (1964), *If I Could Be The Rain* (1967), *Travelling Lady* (1972), *Whatever Happened To The Girl That Was* (1973), *Always A Lady* (1976), *Moments Of Happiness* (1977), *Travelling Lady Rides Again* (1978), *The Lonesome Roving Wolves-Songs And Ballads Of The West* (1980), with Terry Garthwaite, Bobby Hawkins *Live At The Great American Music Hall* (1981), *Miscellaneous Abstract Record #1* (1982), live with Bruce Carver *Then Came The Children* (1984), *Be Careful, There's A Baby In The House* (1990), *Report From Grimes Creek* (Green Linnet 1991), *What Does It Mean To Love?* (Green Linnet 1994).

Further reading: *Way Out In Idaho*, Rosalie Sorrels.

Sorrows

Formed in Coventry, England in 1963, the Sorrows

consisted of Don Maughn (vocals), Pip Whitcher (lead guitar), Wez Price (rhythm guitar), Philip Packham (bass) and Bruce Finley (drums). They achieved minor fame with 'Take A Heart', a pulsating, brooding performance wherein a rolling drum pattern and throbbing bass create a truly atmospheric single. Their fusion of R&B and mod-pop continued on several ensuing releases, but the quintet was unable to secure a consistent success. Maughn, who was later known as **Don Fardon**, left the group for a solo career in 1967. A restructured Sorrows, Price, Packham, Finley and Chris Fryers (vocals/organ/guitar), then moved to Italy, where 'Take A Heart' had become a substantial hit. The group completed several further recordings exclusive to that country, before breaking up at the end of the decade.

Albums: *Take A Heart* (1965), *Old Songs New Songs* (1968). Compilation: *Pink Purple Yellow And Red* (1987 - compiles all of the original group's singles).

Sortilege

This French heavy metal band was formerly known as Blood Wave. Sortilege were formed in 1981 by vocalist Christian Augustin and guitarist Stephanne L'Anguille Dumont. Adding Didier Dem (guitar), Daniel Lapp (bass) and Bob Snake (drums) they secured a contract with the Dutch Rave On label in 1983. They specialized in a persistent metallic boogie which recalled other French acts such as **Trust** and **Telephone**. *Metamorphose* was also released as *Metamorphosis*, complete with English lyrics, but it still failed to make any impact outside France. *Hero Tears* saw the band running short of ideas. They broke up shortly after it's release.

Albums: *Sortilege* (Rave On 1983), *Metamorphose* (Steamhammer 1984), *Hero Tears* (Steamhammer 1985).

Soul Asylum

Originally a Minneapolis, Minnesota, USA, garage hardcore band, Soul Asylum spent their early years under the yoke of comparisons to the more feted **Replacements** and **Husker Du**. Indeed, **Bob Mould** has been known to fondly describe Soul Asylum as 'our little brothers', and was on hand as producer for their first two long playing sets. Their roots in hardcore are betrayed by the choice of their original name, Loud Fast Rules. Their first formation in 1981 centred around the abiding creative nucleus of Dave Pirner (b. c.1965; vocals/guitar) and Dan Murphy (b. c.1963; guitar), alongside Karl Mueller (b. c.1965; bass) and Pat Morley (drums). Together they specialised in sharp lyrical observations and poppy punk. Morley left in December 1984 to be replaced, eventually, by Grant Young (b. c.1965), who arrived in time for *Made To Be Broken*. As their music progressed it became easier to trace back their heritage to the 60s rather than 70s. *Hang Time*, their third album proper, was their first for a major. It saw them move into the hands of a new production team (Ed Stasium and Lenny Kaye), with a very apparent display of studio polish. The mini-album which was meant to have preceded it (but didn't), *Clam Dip And Other Delights*, included their dismantling of a **Foreigner** song, 'Jukebox Hero', and a riotous reading of **Janis Joplin**'s 'Move Over'. When playing live they have been known to inflict their renditions of **Barry Manilow**'s 'Mandy' and **Glen Campbell**'s 'Rhinestone Cowboy' on an audience. Though *The Horse They Rode In On* was another splendid album, the idea of Soul Asylum breaking into the big league was becoming a progressively fantastic one (indeed band members had to pursue alternative employment in 1990, during which time Pirner suffered a nervous breakdown). However, largely thanks to the MTV rotation of 'Somebody To Shove', that was about to change. In its aftermath they gained a prestigious slot on the *David Letterman Show* before support billing to **Bob Dylan** and **Guns N'Roses**, plus a joint headlining package with **Screaming Trees** and the **Spin Doctors** on a three-month Alternative Nation Tour. Soon they were appearing in front of a worldwide audience of 400 million at the 1993 MTV Awards ceremony, where they were joined by **R.E.M.**'s Peter Buck and **Victoria Williams** for a jam of their follow-up hit, 'Runaway Train'. With Pirner dating film starlet Winona Ryder, the profile of a band who seemed destined for critical reverence and public indifference could not have been more unexpectedly high. However, in 1995 the band announced that their next studio sessions would avoid the overt commercial textures of their previous album. They also recruited their fourth drummer, Stirling Campbell, to replace Grant Young. The album was their most commercial offering to date.

Albums: *Say What You Will* (Twin Tone 1984), *Made To Be Broken* (Twin Tone 1986), *While You Were Out* (Twin Tone 1986), *Hang Time* (Twin Tone/A&M 1988), *Clam Dip And Other Delights* (What Goes On 1989, mini-album), *Soul Asylum And The Horse They Rode In On* (Twin Tone/A&M 1990), *Grave Dancers Union* (A&M 1993), *Let Your Dim Light Shine* (A&M 1995). Compilations: *Time's Incinerator* (Twin Tone 1984, cassette only), *Say What You Will Clarence, Karl Sold The Truck* (Twin Tone 1989).

Soul Children

This group was formed as a vehicle for the song writing talents of **Isaac Hayes** and **David Porter** in Memphis, Tennessee, USA. Comprising of Anita Louis (b. 24 November 1949, Memphis, Tennessee, USA), Shelbra Bennett (b. Memphis, Tennessee, USA), John 'Blackfoot' Colbert (b. 20 November 1946, Greenville, Mississippi, USA) and Norman West (b. 30 October 1939, Monroe, Louisiana, USA), they first surfaced in 1968 with 'Give 'Em Love'. This excellent

Hayes/Porter composition established their startling vocal interplay which, at times, suggested a male/female **Sam And Dave**. Although artistically consistent, only three of the group's singles, 'The Sweeter He Is' (1969), 'Hearsay' (1970) and 'I'll Be The Other Woman' (1973), reached the US R&B Top 10. The Soul Children were later reduced to a trio and moved to Epic when their former outlet, **Stax**, went into liquidation. Colbert later found fame under the name J. Blackfoot when one of his releases, 'Taxi', was a 1983 hit in both the US and UK.

Albums: *Soul Children* (1969), *Best Of Two Worlds* (1971), *Genesis* (1972), *Friction* (1974), *The Soul Years* (1974), *Finders Keepers* (1976), *Where Is Your Woman Tonight* (1977), *Open Door Policy* (1978). Compilations: *Soul Children/Genesis* (1990), *Friction/Best Of Two Worlds* (1992), *The Singles Plus Open Door Policy* (1993).

Soul II Soul

Highly succesful rap, soul and R&B group primarily consisting of Jazzie B (b. Beresford Romeo, 26 January 1963, London, England; rapper), Nellee Hooper (musical arrangement) and Philip 'Daddae' Harvey (multi instrumentalist). The name Soul II Soul originally described Jazzie B and Harvey's company supplying DJs and PA systems to dance acts. They also held a number of warehouse raves, particularly at Paddington Dome, near Kings Cross, before setting up their own venue. There they met Hooper, formerly of the **Wild Bunch** and currently a member of **Massive Attack**. Joining forces, they took up a residency at Covent Garden's African Centre before signing to **Virgin** subsidiary Ten. Following the release of two singles, 'Fairplay' and 'Feel Free', the band's profile grew with the aid of fashion T-shirts, two shops and Jazzie B's slot on the then pirate Kiss-FM radio station. However, their next release would break not only them but vocalist **Caron Wheeler** (b. 19 January 1963) as 'Keep On Movin' reached number 5 in the UK charts. The follow-up, 'Back To Life (However Do You Want Me)' once more featured Wheeler, and was taken from their debut *Club Classics Volume One*. The ranks of the Soul II Soul collective had swelled to incorporate a myriad of musicians, whose input was evident in the variety of styles employed. Wheeler soon left to take up a solo career, but the band's momentum was kept intact by 'Keep On Movin' penetrating the US clubs and the album scaling the top of the UK charts. 'Get A Life' was a further expansion on the influential stuttering rhythms which the band had previously employed on singles, but Jazzie B and Hooper's arrangement of **Sinead O'Conners** UK number 1 'Nothing Compares To You' was a poignant contrast. Other artists who sought their services included **Fine Young Cannibals** and **Neneh Cherry**. The early part of 1990 was spent in what amounted to business expansion, with a film company, a talent agency and an embryonic record label all branching out from the Soul II Soul organisation. The band's second album duly arrived half way through the year, incorporating **Courtney Pine** and **Kym Mazelle** amongst a star studded cast. However, despite entering the charts at number 1 it was given a frosty reception by some critics who saw it as comparitively conservative. Mazelle would also feature on the single 'Missing You', as Jazzie B unveiled the (ill-fated) new label 'Funki Dred', backed by **Motown**. As for a definition of what Soul II Soul are, Jazzie B is uncomplicated: 'Its a sound system . . . an organisation (which) came together to build upon making careers for people who had been less fortunate within the musical and artistic realms'.

Albums: *Club Classics Volume I* (Ten 1989), *Volume II: 1990 A New Decade* (Ten 1990), *Just Right Volume III* (Ten 1992), *Volume V Believe* (Virgin 1995). Compilation: *Volume IV - The Classic Singles* 88-93 (Virgin 1993).

Soul Sonic Force

With **Cosmic Force**, the Soul Sonics were part of **Afrika Bambaataa**'s ever-expanding Zulu Nation enclave. Alongside scratch DJ **Jazzy Jay**, Pow Wow and G.L.O.B.E., they featured rapper Mr Biggs, who had been working with Bambaataa as far back as 1974. Pow Wow, in turn, had a hand in producing 'Planet Rock', while G.L.O.B.E. was responsible for patenting the 'MC popping' technique, a desription he preferred to rapping, which saw him dropping in and out of rhymes at short notice, producing an effect not unlike a faulty microphone. He was also responsible for may of the group's lyrics. He had met Bambaataa while he was attending Bronx River High School, and was already friends with Pow Wow, who had perfected his rapping skills in nearby parks. Soul Sonic Force began as a nine-piece affair, which MC's gradually dropping out, including Lisa Lee who would remain with Bambaataa as part of Cosmic Force. In tandem with their mentor they would appear on four hugely influential singles, 'Zulu Nation Throwdown Part 2', 'Planet Rock', 'Looking For The Perfect Beat' and 'Renegades Of Funk'. Their impetus was interrupted in 1983 when both Mr Biggs and Pow Wow were convicted for armed robbery. When Bambaataa resurrected the name again in 1991 for *Return To Planet Rock*, it was merely a disguise for the Jungle Brothers.

Album: With Afrika Bambaataa: *Planet Rock: The Album* (Tommy Boy 1986).

Soul Stirrers

One of gospel's renowned vocal groups, the Soul Stirrers first performed in the early 30s, but their ascendancy began the following decade under the leadership of Rebert H. Harris. Eschewing the accustomed quartet format, Harris introduced the notion of a fifth member, a featured vocalist, thus infusing a greater flexibility without undermining traditional four-part harmonies. Harris left the group in 1950, tiring of what he perceived as non-spiritual influences. His replacement was **Sam Cooke**, late of the Highway QCs, a singer already groomed as a likely successor by Soul Stirrer baritone R.B. Robinson. This particular line-up was completed by Silas Roy Crain, Jesse J. Farley, T.L. Bruster and Paul Foster, although Bob King replaced Bruster in 1953. Cooke's silky delivery brought the group an even wider appeal while his compositions, including 'Nearer To Thee' and 'Touch The Hem Of His Garment', anticipated the styles he would follow on embracing secular music in 1956. Sam's replacement, **Johnnie Taylor**, was also drawn from the ranks of the Highway QCs. The newcomer bore an obvious debt to the former singer as the group's work on Cooke's Sar label attested. Taylor also embarked on a solo career, but the Stirrers continued to record throughout the 60s with Willie Rogers, Martin Jacox and Richard Miles assuming the lead role in turn. Like the **Staple Singers** before them, the veteran group latterly began to include material regarded as inspirational (for example 'Let It Be'), as opposed to strictly religious. In the late 80s and early 90s UK Ace issued a series of fine CD reissues of Specialty material, chiefly featuring Sam Cooke as lead singer.

Selected albums: *The Soul Stirrers Featuring Sam Cooke* (1964), *The Wonderful World Of Sam Cooke* (1965, featuring the Soul Stirrers), *Strength, Power And Love* (1974), *In the Beginning* (1989), *Sam Cooke With The Soul Stirrers* (1991), *The Soul Stirrers Featuring R.H. Harris* (1992), *Jesus Gave Me Water* (1993), *Heaven Is My Home* (1993), *The Last Mile Of The Way* (1994).

Soul Survivors

Vocalists Kenneth Jeremiah, Richard Ingui and Charles Ingui were a New York-based singing group, the Dedications, prior to adding backing musicians Paul Venturini (organ), Edward Leonetti (guitar) and Joey Forgione (drums). The sextet took the name the Soul Survivors in 1966 and secured an US Top 5 hit the following year with 'Expressway To Your Heart'. This all-white group was produced by the emergent **Gamble And Huff** team, but subsequent releases, including the like-sounding 'Explosion In Your Soul', were less successful and they split up. The Ingui brothers resurrected the name during the 70s, but despite signing to their former mentor's TSOP label, were unable to rekindle their former profile. Jeremiah later joined Shirley Goodman in Shirley & Company.

Albums: *When The Whistle Blows Anything Goes* (1967), *Take Another Look* (1968), *Soul Survivors* (1975).

Soul Syndicate

Yet another of the crack session teams that determined the sound and feel of reggae music at any given time in its evolution, the Soul Syndicate were hugely influential in the early to mid-70s. Their work with **Winston 'Niney' Holness**, **Duke Reid**, **Keith Hudson** and many others was brash and exciting and added a different dimension to the roots sound of the period. The hardcore members were the supremely talented Earl 'Chinna' Smith on guitar, Carlton 'Santa' Davis on drums, George 'Fully' Fullwood on bass, Tony Chin on rhythm guitar and Bernard 'Touter' Harvey, who later joined the **Wailers**, on keyboards. At one stage their featured vocalist was **Freddie McGregor**. This nucleus of talent, give or take a few members, also recorded for **Bunny Lee** as the **Aggrovators** as the decade wore on. Like so many of the musicians that have actually made reggae music over the years their names and work remain relatively unknown outside of the genre's cogniscenti, but perhaps, one day, their work (and that of so many others) will be given its proper recognition.

Selected album: *Harvest Uptown* (Soul Syndicate 1978).

Soul, David

b. David Solberg, 28 August 1943, Chicago, Illinois, USA. Under his *nom de theatre*, this handsome blond was a folk singer before trying his hand at acting. In 1966, he combined both talents with 30 appearances on US television's Merv Griffin Show as a masked vocalist ('The Covered Man') before less anonymous roles in *Here Comes The Bride*, *Streets Of San Francisco* and *Encyclopaedia Britannica Presents*. He is, however, best remembered as 'Ken Hutchinson' in *Starsky And Hutch*. A spin-off from this 70s television detective series was the projection of Soul as a pop star via a recording career which began with 1976's 'Don't Give Up On Us' - composed and produced by **Tony Macauley** - at number 1 both at home and in the UK. Though a one-hit-wonder in the USA, Britain was good for another year or so of smashes which included another chart-topper in 'Silver Lady' (co-written by Geoff Stephens). Most of Soul's offerings were in a feathery, moderato style with limpid orchestral sweetening and sentimental lyrics. His name remains synonymous with the mid-late 70s.

Albums: *David Soul* (1976), *Playing To An Audience Of One* (1977).

Soul, Jimmy

b. James McCleese, 24 August 1942, Weldon, North Carolina, USA, d. 25 June 1988. A former boy preacher, McCleese acquired his 'Soul' epithet from his congregations. He subsequently toured southern US states as a member of several gospel groups, including the famed Nightingales, wherein Jimmy was billed as 'The Wonder Boy', before discovering a forte for pop and R&B. He became a popular attraction around the Norfolk area of Virginia where he was introduced to songwriter/producer Frank Guida, who guided the career of **Gary 'U.S.' Bonds**. Soul joined Guida's

S.P.Q.R label and scored a Top 20 US R&B hit with his debut single, 'Twistin' Matilda', before striking gold with his second release, 'If You Wanna Be Happy', which topped the US pop chart in 1963. Both songs were remakes of popular calypso tunes, reflecting Guida's passion for West Indian music. The song also became a minor hit in Britain, and was latterly covered by the Peter B's, a group which included **Peter Bardens**, **Peter Green** and **Mick Fleetwood**. It sadly proved Soul's final chart entry although he nonetheless remained a popular entertainer. Jimmy Soul died in June 1988.

Albums: *If You Wanna Be Happy* (1963), *Jimmy Soul And The Belmonts* (1963).

Souled American

Formed in Chicago, Illinois in 1987, this idiosyncratic quartet featured Chris Crigoroff (guitars/vocals), Scott Tuma (guitars/vocals), Joe Edduci (bass/vocals) and Jamey Barnard (drums). Their unusual mixture of folk, blues and country has drawn many comparisons, including the **Band**, **Mike Hurley** and the **Cowboy Junkies**, but Souled American's lazed tempos, erratic voices and somnambulist playing remains unique. *Fe* inspired several positive reviews while *Flubber*, with its lurching interpretation of **John Fahey**'s 'Cupa Cowfee', saw the group fully establish its oeuvre. *Around The Horn* continued their campfire excursions into American roots music, but in offering slight variations on their basic approach, Souled American have shown a willingness to progress.

Albums: *Fe* (1989), *Flubber* (1989), *Around The Horn* (1990).

Souls Of Mischief

Part of **Del Tha Funkee Homosapien**'s Oakland-based Heiroglyphics enclave, Souls Of Mischief debuted with some panache on their 1993 album. With samples drawn from a selction of artists as diverse as **Grover Washington**, **Curtis Mayfield** and **Main Source**, it demonstrated their ability to blend mellow beats without the jive pimp talk so readily available in their neck of the woods from **Too Short**. The group comprises Tajal (b. c.1977), A-Plus (b. c.1976), Opio (b. c.1976) and Phesto (b. c.1977). Their recording career began when Del's cousin, **Ice Cube**, sorted him out with a recording contract, he in turn suggesting the Souls Of Mischief should be next up. They recorded a song with Del entitled 'Burnt' (featured on the b-side to 'Mistadobalina'), from whence they were spotted. Tajal and A-Plus were kickin' lyrics alongside label-mate **Spice-I** while still in eighth grade, and their vocal dexterity was a standout feature on their debut album, with combatitive rhymes overlaying the production work of A-Plus, Del, and Heiroglyphics production guru, Domino. This group certainly operate well together, hardly suprising since: 'We all went to the same elementary school, junior high, and most of us went into the same high school'.

Album: *'93 Till Infinity* (Jive 1993).

Soulsonics

Seen as a west coast answer to the **Brand New Heavies**, Soulsonics are one of the first native American flowerings of what that continent terms 'urban alternative' (more specifically **Acid Jazz** in UK parlance). The group were formed by Willie McNeil (b. Kansas, Misouri, USA; drums, ex-**Animal Dance**, formerly a cohort of **Joe Strummer**) and Jez Colin (b. England; bass). Primarily a live attraction, the band were inaugurated after Colin had returned home to London and caught the energy of the **Talkin' Loud** movement at Dingwalls nightclub. Determined to export that culture to Los Angeles, he formed the King King club with McNeil. The Soulsonics grew out of the club, initially as a quartet, with regular jamming sessions slowly extending the band's roster. Rather than a direct copy of UK groups like **Galliano**, Soulsonics tempered their fusion with a more specifically Latin flavour of Jazz, a style that has always been popular within California.

Album: *Jazz In The Present Tense* (Chrysalis 1993).

Sound

Prior to the Sound's formation Adrian Borland (vocals/guitar) had already released *Calling On Youth* and *Close Up*, and the *One To Infinity* EP as leader of UK's Outsiders from 1977-78. Towards the end of 1978 Graham Green joined the band, replacing the original bass player, Bob Lawrence, and Michael Dudley (drums) was recruited to play alongside Jan (percussion). The new line-up recorded three tracks, which emerged on the Torch label as the *Physical World* EP in December 1979, credited not as the Outsiders but as the Sound. They had progressed musically from their punk roots and were anxious to leave behind a name that still conjured up the atmosphere of 1977. After the critical acclaim of the debut EP, they signed to Korova Records, releasing a string of singles, 'Heyday', 'Sense Of Purpose', 'Hothouse' and two albums, *Jeopardy* and *From The Lions Mouth*. These stirred a great deal of interest from both critics and public alike, establishing Borland as one of the most creative and mature writers of the post-punk scene. During 1979, Borland and Green created Second Layer, a harder, more experimental project that ran parallel with the Sound, releasing two EPs and an album. Sporadic releases continued throughout the 80s for several different labels with varying degrees of quality and success, but never managing to equal the halcyon days of 1980-81. In addition to the singles 'Counting The Days', 'One Thousand Reasons', 'Temperature Drop', 'Hand Of Love' and 'Iron Years', they also collaborated with singer **Kevin Hewick** on

the *This Cover Keeps* EP in 1984. The band was to finally fragment in late 1987. Borland, however, continued to record for Play It Again Sam as Adrian Borland And The Citizens, as well as resurrecting Second Layer.
Albums: *Jeopardy* (Korova 1980), *From The Lions Mouth* (Korova 1981), *All Fall Down* (Korova 1982), *Heads And Hearts* (Statik 1985), *In The Hothouse* (Statik 1985), *Thunder* (Statik 1987).

Sound Barrier

Formerly known as Colour, Sound Barrier were a black heavy metal band from the United States formed in 1980 by Spacey T. (guitar), Bernie K (vocals), Stanley E. (bass) and Dave Brown (drums), who signed to **MCA Records** in 1982. They made their debut with *Total Control*; a highly complex fusion of metal, soul, funk and blues influences that defied simple pigeon-holing. Despite or because of this it sold poorly and they were subsequently unceremoniously dropped by their label. They bounced back energetically with a mini-album on the independent Pitbull label, which consolidated the style laid down on their debut release. This led to a contract with Metal Blade, but the resulting *Speed Of Light* proved to be very disappointing. It adopted a rather simpler, more mainstream approach and proved a rather unsuccessful attempt to widen their appeal. Emil Lech had taken over on bass by this stage, but the band was to splinter shortly after the album's release. Bernie K. went on to Masi, Spacey T. and Stanley E. joined Liberty, while bass-player Emil Lech teamed up with **Joshua**.
Albums: *Total Control* (MCA 1983), *Born To Rock* (Pit Bull 1984), *Speed Of Light* (Metal Blade 1986).

Sound Factory

Sound Factory boasts in its line-up writer/producer Emil Hellman, long renowned as one of Sweden's best and most influential dance remixers, and the vocals of St James. Sound Factory have proved to be one of the very few club acts to break out of their native territory, establishing themselves particularly in the United States, where 'Understand This Groove' sold over 140,000 copies. The duo was put together in 1992 and is signed to Cheiron (formerly **Swemix**). Sound Factory followed the success of their debut single with further house cuts 'To The Rhythm' and 'Bad Times'.

Sound Of Jazz, The

An outstanding achievement in the presentation of jazz on US television, this 1957 film was conceived and produced by Robert Herridge with the advice of the jazz writers Nat Hentoff and Whitney Balliett. Directed by Jack Smight, the film shows the musicians playing in an atmosphere of complete relaxation and thereby achieving an exceptionally high standard of performance. Regardless of who the musicians might have been, the concept and format would have been commendable. The fact that the musicians on display are indisputably some of the greatest figures in the history of jazz make this film an hour of continuous joy. The all-star bands led by **Count Basie** and **Red Allen** feature **Doc Cheatham**, **Freddie Green**, **Coleman Hawkins**, **Jo Jones**, **Roy Eldridge**, **Joe Newman**, **Gerry Mulligan**, **Rex Stewart**, **Earle Warren**, **Dicky Wells**, **Ben Webster**, **Lester Young**, singer **Jimmy Rushing**, **Vic Dickenson**, **Danny Barker**, **Milt Hinton**, **Nat Pierce** (who also contributed the arrangements played by the Basie-led band) and **Pee Wee Russell**. Also on hand is the **Jimmy Giuffre** trio with **Jim Hall** and Jim Atlas playing 'The Train And The River', and **Thelonious Monk** plays 'Blue Monk' accompanied by **Ahmed Abdul-Malik** and Osie Johnson. If all these riches were not enough there is **Billie Holiday** accompanied by **Mal Waldron**. Holiday sings her own composition, 'Fine And Mellow', in what must be this song's definitive performance, backed by many of the listed musicians with Lester Young contributing a poignant solo. Four decades after its making, this film remains a highwater mark in jazz and its standards remain those to which all other film-makers must aspire.

Sound Of Miles Davis, The

Produced and directed by the same team responsible for *The Sound Of Jazz* (Robert Herridge and Jack Smight), this 1959 film was originally entitled *Theater For A Song*. Miles Davis is presented with his quintet (**John Coltrane**, **Wynton Kelly**, **Paul Chambers** and **Jimmy Cobb**) and also with **Gil Evans** And His Orchestra. The performance captures Davis in outstanding and eloquent form and the contribution from the other musicians on hand helps make this an important filmed record of one of jazz music's most important and influential figures.

Sound Of Music, The

Even before its Broadway opening at the Lunt-Fontanne Theatre on 16 November 1959, *The Sound Of Music* was set to become a financial success. Advance sales exceeded three million dollars and with numerous touring versions, best-selling albums and a blockbuster film, it made a fortune for its composers, **Richard Rodgers** and **Oscar Hammerstein II**. The show had a strong narrative book, by Howard Lindsey and Russel Crouse, which was based upon the real-life story of Maria Rainer, her marriage to George von Trapp and her relationship with his family of singing youngsters. The family's evasion of capture by the Nazis during World War II gave the story a tense dramatic core and the fact that the family became professional singers meant that music and song blended well into the narrative, even if, at times, there seemed to be rather more sentiment than reality would have allowed. Starring **Mary Martin** as Maria, **Theodore Bikel** and Patricia Neway, the show was filled with songs which became very popular, including the title song, 'Do-Re-Mi', 'My Favorite Things', 'Edelweiss', 'So Long, Farewell', 'Sixteen Going On Seventeen', 'How Can Love Survive?', 'Maria', 'The Lonely Goatherd', and 'Climb Ev'ry Mountain'. Sentimental or not, it is hard to imagine that at the time he was working on this show, Hammerstein was a sick man; less than a year after the Broadway opening he was dead. *The Sound Of Music* played for 1,443 performances, and won **Tony Awards** for best musical (tied with *Fiorello!*), actress (Martin), featured actress (Neway), musical director (Frederick Dvonch), and scenic design (Oliver Smith). Jean Bayliss and Roger Dann headed the cast of the 1961 London production which surpassed the original and ran for 2,385 performances. New York revivals included one in 1967 at the City Centre, and another in 1990, presented by the New York City Opera, in which the ex-chart-topper **Debby Boone** played Maria. London audiences saw the show again in 1992 when it was presented at Sadlers Wells, with Liz Robertson and Christopher Cazenove. The 1965 film version, which starred **Julie Andrews**, won three Oscars and spawned one of the best-selling soundtrack albums of all-time.

Sound Of Music, The (Film Musical)

Dubbed 'The Sound Of Mucus' by some for its almost overwhelming sentimentality and sweetness, in the early 90s this film was still hovering around the Top 40 highest-earning movies of all-time in the USA, and that level of success has been reiterated around the world. Ernest Lehman's screenplay, which was based on the 1959 Broadway musical and the real-life story of the Austrian Von Trapp family of folk singers. Maria (**Julie Andrews**), a postulant nun in a Saltzburg convent, whose unconventional ways drive her fellow nuns to despair, is engaged by widower Captain Von Trapp (Christopher Plummer) as governess to his seven children. After one or two domestic disagreements (such as when she cuts up the curtains to make clothes for the children), they eventually fall in love and marry. Their happiness is disturbed by the imminence of World War II and the presence of the Nazi army in Austria. When Von Trapp is required to report for military service, the whole family escape from the soldiers' clutches at the end of a concert performance,

just as the real Von Trapp family did. Some of the film's most charming moments came when Maria is teaching the children music, and also when they are operating a marionette theatre together. Julie Andrews gave a tender, most appealing performance as the young girl maturing into a woman, and Plummer was bombastic and tender in turns. Eleanor Parker (as the Captain-hungry Baroness) and Richard Haydn (in the role of Max Detweiler, a man who would go anywhere in the world for a free bed and breakfast), led a supporting cast which included Peggy Wood, Charmian Carr, Anna Lee, Portia Nelson, and Marni Nixon. Most of **Richard Rodgers** and **Oscar Hammerstein II**'s songs from the stage show were retained, along with two new ones, 'Something Good' and 'I Have Confidence In Me', in a score that consisted of 'The Sound Of Music', 'Maria', 'Sixteen Going On Seventeen', 'My Favourite Things', 'Climb Ev'ry Mountain', 'The Lonely Goatherd', 'Do-Re-Mi', 'Edelweiss', and 'So Long, Farewell'. Bill Lee dubbed Plummer's vocals. Marc Breaux and Dee Dee Wood choreographed the delightful dance sequences, and the producer-director for 20th Century-Fox was Robert Wise. The memorable opening alpine aerial shot was credited to Ted McCord, who photographed the film superbly in DeLuxe Color and Todd-AO. *The Sound Of Music* won Academy Awards for best film, director, and music scoring (Irwin Kostal), and became the highest-grossing film in the USA during the 60s. Its soundtrack album spent a total of 70 weeks at number 1 in the UK, and was over a year in the US chart.

Sound System

It is impossible to overstate the importance of sound systems to the development of reggae music as just about every record producer, singer and DJ from the 50s onwards has been closely involved with them in one way or another. They were the forerunners of today's mobile disco but the amount and weight of their amplification equipment has always ensured that you felt the sound of the music as much as hearing it. In the 50s, R&B radio stations from southern American cities beamed their music to a responsive Jamaican audience and the popularity of R&B prompted enterprising locals to start their own sound systems. Operators such as **Coxsone Dodd** 'Sir Coxsone The Down Beat' and **Duke Reid** 'The Trojan', became stars in Jamaica on the strength of their sounds - both for the records that they played and for the way they presented them. The top outfits would play out in competition against each other and the rivalry was frequently violent and bloody. Records were hunted out in the USA where small fortunes were spent on the right tunes - the label details would be then scratched out to stop their rivals finding out what these top tunes actually were.

The sound system operators started to make their own R&B based recordings as the supply of hard R&B

records began to dry up in the late 50s, and the black American audiences moved towards a smoother style of music which the Jamaicans were not interested in. At first these recordings were intended solely for exclusive use (on acetate disc or **dub plate**) of the sound that made them but they proved so popular that the top 'sounds' began to release these records and **ska** and the Jamaican recording industry were born. From here on the development of Jamaican music through ska, **rocksteady**, reggae, **rockers**, **dub**, **dance hall** and **ragga** has always been inextricably linked with sound systems both as the testing ground for new records but, more importantly, for singers and DJs to test out the crowd's response as they took their turn at the microphone. Their popularity meant the proliferation of sound systems in New York, London and Toronto - at first anywhere with an expatriate Jamaican community - but later their influence was to spread outside and away and the importance of Jamaican Sounds to the development of hip hop and rap in America, for instance, has yet to be fully credited. The Sounds have gone through as many changes in styles and fashion as reggae music and have become a cultural rallying point across the globe. The current fashion is for playing 'specials' - one-off acetate discs recorded exclusively by current big names extolling the virtues of whatever particular sound the 'special' has been voiced for, usually to the tune and rhythm of a popular 'commercial' hit record. DJs' live contributions are kept to a minimum where once they dominated the sound. In many ways the wheel has turned full circle but to hear a top sound system playing out either in the warmth of a Kingston open air dance under the stars or crowded together in a small club in London or New York is to understand fully the strength and power of Jamaican music and to experience its direct and very real influence on its own committed following.

Soundgarden

This Seattle-based US quartet fused influences as diverse as **Led Zeppelin**, the **Stooges**, **Velvet Underground** and most particularly early UK and US punk bands into a dirty, sweaty, sexually explicit and decidedly fresh take on rock 'n' roll. The group; Chris Cornell (b. Seattle, Washington, USA; vocals/guitar), Kim Thayil (guitar), Hiro Yamamoto (bass) and Matt Cameron (drums), proffer a sound characterized by heavy-duty, bass-laden metallic riffs that swings between dark melancholia and *avant garde* minimalism. Cornell's ranting vocal style and articulate lyrics complete the effect. The group's first recording, the *Screaming Life* EP, was the second release on the hugely influential **Sub Pop** label, and marked out their territory. Indeed, Thayil had brought together the label's owners Bruce Pavitt and Jonathan Poneman in the first place. After signing to **SST** Records and releasing *Ultramega OK*, they attracted the attention of

A&M Records and eventually released *Louder Than Love*, one of the most underrated and offbeat rock albums of 1989. This also meant that they were the first of the Sub Pop generation to sign to a major. After its release Cameron and Cornell would also participate in the two million selling **Temple Of The Dog** album, which co-featured **Pearl Jam** members Eddie Vedder, Stone Gossard and Jeff Ament laying tribute at the door of deceased **Mother Love Bone** singer Andrew Wood. However, following the recording sessions for *Louder Than Love* Yamamoto would be replaced by Jason Everman (ex-**Nirvana**), though he would record on only one track, a cover of the **Beatles**' 'Come Together', before departing for **Mindfunk** via **Skunk**. His eventual replacement would be band friend Ben 'Hunter' Shepherd. *Badmotorfinger* built on the group's succesful formula but added insistent riffs, the grinding but melodious guitar sound which would come to define 'grunge', and their own perspectives on politics, religion and society. Among its many absorbing moments was the MTV-friendly single, 'Jesus Christ Pose'. Landing the support slot to **Guns N'Roses**' US *Illusions* tour deservedly opened Soundgarden up to a much wider audience. This was capitalized on by their fourth long player, which debuted at number 1 on the ***Billboard*** chart on 19 March 1994. Produced by Michael Beinhorn (**Soul Asylum**, **Red Hot Chili Peppers** etc.) and the band themselves, it was a magnum opus clocking in at more than 70 minutes and featuring 15 songs. Eventually selling over three million copies, it was promoted by an Australasian tour in January 1994, headlining the 'Big Day Out' festival package above the **Ramones**, **Smashing Pumpkins** and **Teenage Fanclub**, before moving on to Japan.

Albums: *Ultramega O.K.* (SST 1989), *Louder Than Love* (A&M 1990), *Badmotorfinger* (A&M 1991), *Superunknown* (A&M 1994). Compilation: *Screaming Life/FOPP* (Sub Pop 1990).
Video: *Motorvision* (1993).

Sounds Nice

When **Decca Records**' A&R representative Tony Hall heard Jane Birkin and **Serge Gainsbourg**'s 'Je T'Aime ... Moi Non Plus' at the Antibes festival in the South of France, he immediately recognized the potential of an instrumental version. When the song was duly banned in Britain in 1969 this newly formed and as yet unnamed group recorded a non-sexy version retitled 'Love At First Sight' which later became a Top 20 hit. After the recording session, Hall played a finished tape to **Paul McCartney** who casually remarked, 'sounds nice', thereby giving the group a name. Although the hit duo never charted again, their line-up was particularly interesting. Tim Mycroft, after stints with the Freewheelers, the **Third Ear Band** and **Gun** had decided to concentrate on writing and teamed up with arranger Paul Buckmaster. The third man behind the hit was producer **Gus Dudgeon**, who had recently enjoyed hits with **David Bowie**, **Locomotive** and the **Bonzo Dog Doo-Dah Band**. Following their pledge to create 'instrumentals with a difference' Buckmaster and Dudgeon went on to work successfully with **Elton John**.

Sounds Of Blackness

Led by bodybuilder Gary Hines, a former Mr Minnesota, Sounds Of Blackness are a gospel/soul 40-piece choir whose work has also torn up the dance charts. Stranger still, perhaps, was the fact that they broke though so late in their career. They were 20 years old as an outfit when they came to prominence in 1991. Hines took them over from their original incarnation as the Malcalaster College Black Choir in January 1971, running the group on a strict code of ethics and professional practices. The rulebook is sustained by the long waiting list of aspiring members, and Hines' self-appointed role as 'benevolent dictator'. They first made the charts under the aegis of **Jimmy Jam** and **Terry Lewis**, who had spotted the band and used them for backing vocals on their productions for **Alexander O'Neal**. In turn they used the choir to launch their new record label, Perspective, scoring almost immediately with 'Optimistic'. Released in 1991, it single-handedly sparked off a revival in the fortunes of gospel music. The album which housed it went on to win a Grammy award, as 'The Pressure' and 'Testify' also charted. Recent singles have again, via remixes from the likes of **Sasha**, and hugely emotive vocals from Ann Bennett-Nesby, proved extremely popular in the thoroughly secular arena of the club scene. Hines is ecstatic rather than hesitant about this, insisting that their message can seep through despite the environment. Sounds Of Blackness also sang 'Gloryland', alongside **Daryl Hall**, as the official theme to the 1994 World Cup.

Albums: *The Evolution Of Gospel* (Perspective/A&M 1991), *The Night Before Christmas - A Musical Fantasy* (Perspective/A&M 1992), *Africa To America* (Perspective/A&M 1994).

Sounds Orchestral

Led by pianist **John Pearson** (b. 18 June 1925, London, England), Sounds Orchestral was a conglomeration of session musicians who included in their ranks **Kenny Clare** (ex-drummer with **Johnny Dankworth**) and bass player/producer Tony Reeves (ex-**Colosseum**). The orchestral concept was conceived by renowned producer **John Schroeder**. 'People are looking for a change from the incessant beat and I intend Sounds to fulfil that demand', he told the pop press in early 1965. The group went someway towards fulfilling that ambition with their cover of the Vince Guaraldi Trio's 1960 recording 'Cast Your Fate

To The Wind'. With its melodic arrangement and subtle jazz rhythm, the song took the UK charts by storm in January 1965, climbing into the Top 3. Surprisingly, this unlikely pop hit also reached the US Top 10, paving the way for a number of instrumental hits during 1965, courtesy of artists ranging from **Horst Jankowski** to **Marcello Minerebi** and **Nini Rosso**.

Selected albums: *Cast Your Fate To The Wind* (1970), *Dreams* (1983), *Sleepy Shores* (1985). Compilation: *Golden Hour Of Sounds Orchestral* (1973).

Soup Dragons

The Soup Dragons emerged from Glasgow, Scotland, as one of a clutch of bands championed by the *New Musical Express* via their *C86* project. The group evolved around Sean Dickson (lead vocals/guitar/songwriter). In early 1985, he met up with Jim McCulloch (guitar), Ross A. Sinclair (drums) and Sushil K. Dade (bass), the collective taking their name from characters in the cult children's television programme, *The Clangers*. A flexi-disc, 'If You Were The Only Girl In The World', emerged at the end of the year, by which time the band were circulating a demonstration tape, *You Have Some Too*. The Subway Organisation label issued the Soup Dragons' first single, 'Whole Wide World' (1986), a tight, exciting slab of **Buzzcocks**-styled pop, performed at breakneck pace. This attracted ex-**Wham!** manager Jazz Summers, who set up a new label for them, Raw TV Products, in time for 'Hang-Ten!' (1986). In the meantime, Sean and later Jim had left another group they were serving time with, the **BMX Bandits**. 'Head Gone Astray' (1987), revealed a marked change away from new wave, towards 60s rock. 'Can't Take No More' and 'Soft As Your Face' fared well commercially but the latter's serene sound was at odds with the band's direction. 'The Majestic Head' (1988) lured **Sire Records** into a deal, but the next single, 'Kingdom Chairs' flopped. A subsequent debut album, *This Is Our Art*, emerged without fanfare. The **Stooges**'-influenced 'Backwards Dog' and 'Crotch Deep Trash', introduced a rockier feel and this was followed by the dance-orientated 'Mother Universe' (1990). Hinging around a **Marc Bolan** riff, the single was typical of the tracks on *Lovegod*, the band's second album. By this time, Sinclair had been replaced by new drummer Paul Quinn. After discovering an obscure **Rolling Stones** track from their 1965 *Out Of Our Heads* collection, the Soup Dragons teamed up with reggae singer **Junior Reid** and DJ/remixer **Terry Farley** to create a formidable crossover between white 'indie' rock and dance music. The single was a massive hit, something that had previously eluded the band. *Lovegod* was re-promoted and a remixed 'Mother Universe' was reissued, giving them further chart success. However, accusations of bandwagon-jumping continued to haunt the band (the press uniting on the fact that **Primal Scream** had got there first in whichever direction the group pursued). As the 90s progressed diminishing returns became the order of the day, and eventual dissolution with it. Quinn would go on to replace Brendan O'Hare in **Teenage Fanclub** in 1994, while Sushil joined BMX Bandits and Jim McCulloch moved to **Superstar**.

Albums: *This Is Our Art* (Sire 1988), *Lovegod* (Raw TV 1990), *Hotwired* (Big Life 1992), *Hydrophonic* (Phonogram 1995).

Source

Essentially UK born John Truelove, whose 'You Got The Love' (React), featuring Candi Station, was a classic summer of love piece, though it originally came out in 1991 on his own label. It was built on **Frankie Knuckles**' house classic, 'Your Love', and did more than any other record to catapult the coda 'Throw your hands in the air' into the nation's lexicon, hitting number 4 in the UK charts. The Source label was relaunched in 1993 as well as a new techno offshoot, Truelove Electronic Coalition. Source's other big number was 'Sanctuary Of Love', which led to him breaking from his original agreement with **Food Records** after its success.

Sousa, John Philip

b. 6 November 1854, Washington, DC, USA, d. 6 March 1932, Reading, Pennsylvania, USA. At the age of 13 Sousa joined the US Marine band of which his father (born in Spain of Portuguese parents) was a member. Here he mostly played the violin but in 1873 he left the band and resumed his studies, particularly of harmony and composition. In 1876 he joined a symphony orchestra in Philadelphia and also began to direct musical productions. In 1880 he returned to the US Marine band, this time as its director. After 12 years he formed his own band and embarked on a hugely successful career. Sousa employed first class musicians, among them the outstandingly gifted trombonist Arthur Pryor. In the late 19th century, touring bands, usually bright and brassy, played a mixture of European light classical music, newly-popular rags and other popular pieces. Sousa included all such items in his repertoire alongside cakewalks and music which bore the hallmarks of early jazz, but he arranged everything in a highly personal style. He also featured his own compositions, many of which were marches and which earned him the soubriquet, 'The March King'. Before World War I Sousa and his band had made several tours to Europe and one around the world. The band remained in existence for almost four decades, building a reputation for Sousa as a musical director and composer. In both capacities he had an enormous influence upon popular musical taste in the USA. His first major work was an operetta, *El Capitan*

(1895), and he also wrote several vocal pieces, ranging from minstrelsy to grandiose national pageants. It was, however, his marches which made his name. Among the best known are 'The Washington Post', 'Hands Across The Sea', 'Semper Fidelis', 'El Capitan', 'The Thunderer' and 'The Stars And Stripes Forever'.

Compilation: *The Sousa And Pryor Bands (1901-26)* (1987).

South Central Cartel

Fronted by MC Havoc Da Mouthpiece, whose father was a member of the **Chi-Lites**, the ranks of South Central Cartel are also inhabited by rappers Prodeje, Havikk Da Rymesman, LV Da Voice (the group's 'singer') and DJ's Kaos #1 and Gripp. Formed in 1986, the group which evolved into SCC had originally titled themselves Mafia Style and New Authority. The group hail from Los Angeles, as made explicit in the choice of their title, and released material on their own GWK (Gangstas With Knowledge) label. Like **Compton's Most Wanted** before them, they peddled hard street narratives, best displayed on singles like the self-explanatory 'Gang Stories'. They managed to sell over 200,000 copies of their debut album on GWK, before flirting with a contract to the Quality emporium. Eventually Havoc contacted **Russel Simmons**, whom he had met while at a Black Music convention, which led to the band joining Sony's RAL/**Def Jam** stable for *'N' Gatz We Trust*. As with previous work this boasted live musician backing, the advantages of which were tempered by the fact that they largely stuck to recreations of generic **George Clinton** riffs. However, in the wake of South Central Cartel's success Prodoje, who helmed the production, has gone on become a successful mixer and producer, working with **Public Enemy**, **LL Cool J** and **Spice I**. SCC themselves also scripted and starred in a public service film encouraging young people to use their vote.

Albums: *South Central Messages* (GWK 1992), *'N Gatz We Trust* (RAL/Def Jam 1994).

South Pacific (Stage Musical)

Opening on Broadway at the Majestic Theatre on 7 April 1949, *South Pacific* became one of the best-loved and most successful of the fruitful collaborations between **Richard Rodgers** and **Oscar Hammerstein II**. The libretto, by Hammerstein and Joshua Logan, was based on stories in James Michener's book *Tales Of The South Pacific*. Its story was set during World War II and dealt in part with racism, a subject not exactly commonplace in American musical comedies. **Mary Martin** starred as Nellie Forbush, an American nurse who falls in love with a middle-aged French planter, Emil de Becque (Ezio Pinza), but is disturbed by the fact that he has two children by a Polynesian woman who is now dead. Meanwhile, a US Navy lieutenant, Joe Cable (William

Tabbert), is attracted to an island girl, Liat (Betta St. John), but, like Nellie, his underlying racial fears cause him to reject her (or it could just be that is is scared stiff of her mother, Bloody Mary [Juanita Hall]). In any event, Joe dies in action and Nellie comes to terms with the colour issue and is reunited with Emile. The marvellous score, which contained several big hits, included 'Some Enchanted Evening', 'Younger Than Springtime', 'Wonderful Guy', 'I'm Gonna Wash That Man Right Outa My Hair', 'Honey Bun', 'There Is Nothin' Like A Dame', 'A Cockeyed Optimist', 'You've Got To Be Carefully Taught', 'This Nearly Was Mine', and two songs which were sung by Juanita Hall, 'Bali Ha'i' 'Dites-moi', and 'Happy Talk'. Myron McCormick played the endearing character of US marine Luther Billis, and he was the only member of the cast to appear in every one of *South Pacific*'s 1,925 performances. The show scooped the Tony Awards, winning for best musical, score, libretto, actress (Martin), actor (Pinza), supporting actress (Hall), supporting actor (McCormick), and director (Joshua Logan). It also became only the second musical (not counting **Oklahoma!**'s special award) to win the prestigious Pulitzer Prize for Drama. Mary Martin reprised her role in 1951 at the Drury Lane Theatre, with Wilbur Evans as de Becque. London audiences were delighted with her performance, and were particularly intrigued by her nightly ritual of washing her hair on-stage. Over the years American revivals have proliferated, but the 1988 London production, with a cast headed by Gemma Craven, which ran for over 400 performances, was said to be the first since 1951. The enormously popular 1958 screen version starred Mitzi Gaynor and Rossano Brazzi, and its soundtrack album spent over five years in the UK chart.

South Pacific (Film Musical)

This immensely successful screen version of the **Richard Rodgers** and **Oscar Hammerstein**'s 1949 Broadway hit musical was released by 20th Century-Fox in 1958. Paul Osborn's screenplay, which was adapted from the stage production and James A. Michener's *Tales Of The South Pacific*, told the by now familiar story of life on a South Sea island which is temporarily occupied by American troops during World War II. Two love stories run in parallel: that between the mature, sophisticated French planter, Emile de Becque (Rossano Brazzi), and a young nurse, Nellie Forbush (**Mitzi Gaynor**); and the other, which involves Lt. Joe Cable (John Kerr) and Liat (France Nuyen), the Polynesian daughter of Bloody Mary (Juanita Hall). Some felt that Oscar Hammerstein and Joshua Logan, who wrote the original libretto, fudged the 'racial issue' by allowing Cable to be killed in action so that he could not marry Liat. On the other hand, Nellie, after much personal torment and heart-

searching, found herself able to accept de Becque's ethnic children from a previous marriage. The supporting cast was excellent, with Ray Walston outstanding as Luther Billis. Early on in the film he led a group of fellow marines in the rousing, but poignant 'There Is Nothing Like A Dame', one of the songs in Rogers and Hammerstein's marvellous score that came from Broadway intact - with the addition of one other number, 'My Girl Back Home', which had been written, but not used, for the 1949 show. The remainder of the film's much-loved songs were 'Dites-moi', 'A Cockeyed Optimist', 'Twin Soliloquies', 'Some Echanted Evening', 'Bloody Mary', 'Bali Ha'i', 'I'm Gonna Wash That Man Right Outa My Hair', 'A Wonderful Guy', 'Younger Than Springtime', 'Happy Talk', 'Honey Bun', 'Carefully Taught', and 'This Nearly Was Mine'. The singing voices of Rossano Brazzi, John Kerr, and Juanita Hall were dubbed by Giorgio Tozzi, Bill Lee, and Muriel Smith respectively. The choreographer was LeRoy Prinz, and Joshua Logan directed, as he had done on Broadway. *South Pacific* was photographed by Leon Shamroy in Technicolor and the Todd-AO wide-screen process. There was a good deal of adverse criticism regarding the use of colour filters in the various musical sequences. The sountrack album proved to be one of the best-sellers of all time, spending an unprecedented (to date) total of 115 weeks at the top of the UK chart, and 31 weeks at number 1 in the USA.

South Shore Commission

A R&B funk band from Chicago, Illinois, USA. Members were Frank McCurry (vocals), Sheryl Henry (vocals), Sidney 'Pinchback' Lennear (guitar), Eugene Rogers (rhythm guitar), David Henderson (bass), and Warren Haygood (drums). The South Shore Commission played a modest role in the rising funk revolution in the 70s when many such outfits which started out as backing groups for vocalists emerged as recording groups in their own right. The unit was formed in 1960 in Washington, D.C. as the Exciters. In 1965 they became the back-up band for the **Five Dutones** and were signed to the One-derful label in Chicago. Members of the Exciters moved to Chicago and to nearby Gary, Indiana. When the Five Dutones broke up in 1967, the Exciters became the South Shore Commission with McCurry from the Five Dutones becoming one of the band's vocalists. The group charted locally in 1970 with 'Right On Brother' on **Atlantic Records** and in 1971 with 'Shadows' on Nickel. National success came when the South Shore Commission signed with New York-based **Scepter Records**, recording for their **Wand** subsidiary. Their biggest hit was 'Free Man' (number 9 R&B, number 61 pop), from 1975, and they charted twice more in the next year with 'We're On The Right Track' (number 30 R&B, number 94 pop) and 'Train Called Freedom' (number 35 R&B, number 86 pop). The latter two singles came from their only album, *South Shore Commission*, recorded in Philadelphia under producer **Bunny Sigler** and in Hollywood under producer Dick Griffey.

Album: *South Shore Commission* (Wand 1975).

South Side Movement

A funk band from Chicago, Illinois, USA. Original members were vocalist Melvin Moore, guitarist Bobby Pointer, bassist Ronald Simmons, keyboardist Morris Beeks, drummer Willie Hayes, trumpeter Steve Hawkins, trombonist Bill McFarland, and alto saxophonist Milton Johnson. The group began as the back-up band for the Chicago duo, Simtec And Wylie, and when that act fell into disarray in 1972 the band took the name South Side Movement. In 1973 they were signed to New York-based **Wand** label and achieved two chart singles with 'I've Been Watching You' (number 14 R&B, number 61 pop) and 'Can You Get To That' (number 56 R&B). They also recorded an album for the label, *I've Been Watching You*. The group moved to 20th Century Records in 1974 and recorded two more albums and a spate of singles, none of which charted. In 1975 the South Side Movement disbanded.

Albums: *I've Been Watching You* (Wand 1973), *Movin'* (20th Century 1974), *Moving South* (20th Century 1975).

South, Eddie

b. 27 November 1904, Louisiana, Missouri, USA, d. 25 April 1962, Chicago, Illinois, USA. Taught violin as a child, South was educated for a career as a classical musician. Sadly, this goal proved overly optimistic; in the USA in the 20s there was no place on concert stages for black performers. Inevitably, therefore, he became a danceband musician, mainly in Chicago, at first working with artists such as **Jimmy Wade**, Charlie Elgar and **Erskine Tate**. In the late 20s he teamed up with **Mike McKendrick** and then led his own band, the Alabamanians, recording with both. In 1928 he visited Europe, proving extremely popular, and during a visit to Budapest he resumed his studies and also established an interest in eastern-European gypsy music which remained with him for the rest of his life. In the early 30s he was again leading a band in Chicago, but did not enjoy the popular success of many of his contemporaries. In 1937 he returned to Europe to play at the International Exhibition in Paris. During this visit he recorded some outstanding sides with **Django Reinhardt**. From 1938 onwards he worked in the USA, mostly in a small group context but briefly led a big band. He played clubs and radio dates throughout the 40s and 50s, usually as leader but also with artists such as **Earl Hines**. He had his own radio show for a while and also appeared on television. The most stylish and melodic of all the jazz violinists,

South's classical training is evident on all his recorded work. Nevertheless, he played with a powerful swing and the neglect shown by record companies in the years since his death in April 1962 is regrettable.

Albums: *The Dark Angel Of The Fiddle* (1958). Compilations: *No More Blues* (1927-33), *Django Reinhardt And His American Friends* (1937-38), *Earl 'Fatha' Hines* (1947).

South, Joe

b. Joe Souter, 28 February 1940, Atlanta, Georgia, USA. South was obsessed with technology and, as a child, he developed his own radio station with a transmission area of a mile. A novelty song, 'The Purple People Eater Meets The Witch Doctor', sold well in 1958, and he became a session guitarist in both Nashville and Muscle Shoals. South backed **Eddy Arnold**, **Aretha Franklin**, **Wilson Pickett**, **Marty Robbins** and, in particular, **Bob Dylan** (*Blonde On Blonde*) and **Simon And Garfunkel** (most of *The Sounds Of Silence* LP). His 1962 single, 'Masquerade', was released in the UK, but his first writing/producing successes came with the **Tams**' 'Untie Me' and various **Billy Joe Royal** singles including 'Down In The Boondocks' and 'I Knew You When'. In 1968, he sang and played several instruments on Royal's *Introspect*. One track, 'Games People Play', made number 12 in the US charts and number 6 in the UK, and he also played guitar and sang harmony on **Boots Randolph**'s cover version. The song's title was taken from Eric Berne's best selling book about the psychology of human relationships. Another song title, '(I Never Promised You A) Rose Garden' came from a novel by Hannah Green, and was a transatlantic hit for country singer, **Lynn Anderson**. 'These Are Not My People' was a US country hit for Freddie Weller, 'Birds Of A Feather' was made popular by **Paul Revere And The Raiders**, but, more significantly, 'Hush' became **Deep Purple**'s first US Top 10 hit in 1968. South himself made number 12 in the US with 'Walk A Mile In My Shoes', which was also featured by **Elvis Presley** in concert, but his own career was not helped by a drugs bust, a pretentious single 'I'm A Star', and a poor stage presence. He told one audience to 'start dancing around the hall, then when you come in front of the stage, each one of you can kiss my ass.' South's songs reflect southern life but they also reflect his own insecurities and it is not surprising that he stopped performing. He had heeded his own words, 'Don't It Make You Want To Go Home'.

Albums: *Introspect* (1968 - released in the UK as *Games People Play*), *Don't It Make You Want To Go Home* (1969), *Walkin' Shoes* (1970), *So The Seeds Are Growing* (1971), *Midnight Rainbows* (1975), *Joe South, You're The Reason, To Have, To Hold And To Let Go* (1976), *Look Inside* (1976). Compilations: *Joe South's Greatest Hits* (1970), *The Joe South Story* (1971).

Souther, J.D.

b. John David Souther, 2 November 1945, Detroit, Michigan, USA. Souther's family migrated to Amarillo, Texas, where he was courted by local bands for his precocious talent as a singing guitarist. However, he committed himself to **Longbranch Pennywhistle**, a duo with future **Eagles**' guitarist, **Glenn Frey** who shared his admiration for **Hank Williams**, **Ray Charles** and **Buddy Holly**. While sharing a Los Angeles apartment with **Jackson Browne**, the pair recorded an album before going their separate ways in 1970 - though Souther would later collaborate on songs for the Eagles. His compositions were also recorded by **Bonnie Raitt** and **Linda Ronstadt**. After *John David Souther* for **Asylum Records**, he became a linchpin of the Souther-Hillman-Furay Band with ex-members of the **Byrds**, **Buffalo Springfield**, the **Flying Burrito Brothers** and **Manassas** for two albums prior to his discontent over the group's musical direction. A subsequent excellent second solo offering, *Black Rose*, was produced by **Peter Asher** and included performances by **Joe Walsh**, **Lowell George** and other country-rock luminaries. Souther's promotional tour drew encouraging responses, but it failed to live-up to market expectations. Disappointed, Souther withdrew into session work for artists including **Outlaws**, **Warren Zevon** and **Christopher Cross**. In 1979, Souther tried again with *You're Only Lonely* which contained the expected quota of guest stars; among them Jackson Browne, **John Sebastian** and Phil Everly. Following critically-acclaimed concerts in New York and California, his tenacity was rewarded when the tie-in single of the albums title track climbed into the US pop Top 10, selling even better in the country chart. Two years later a Souther/James Taylor composition 'Her Town Too' almost reached the US Top 10. Since then, Souther's output as a songwriter has been considerable.

Albums: *John David Souther* (1971), *Black Rose* (1976), *You're Only Lonely* (1979), *Home By Dawn* (1984).

Southern Pacific

When the **Doobie Brothers** broke up in 1982, guitarist/fiddler John McFee and drummer Keith Knudsen went into session work. Both of them are featured on **Emmylou Harris**' *White Shoes*, and McFee is particularly known for his contribution, playing both lead and steel guitar, on **Elvis Costello**'s *Almost Blue*. With vocalist Tim Goodman from **New Grass Revival** and two of **Elvis Presley**'s musicians, Jerry Scheff and Glen D. Hardin, they made some demos and were signed to **Warner Brothers Records** by Jim Ed Norman. They originally thought of calling themselves the Tex Pistols but decided on Southern Pacific. Their first album was a continuation of the soft rock and country that was pioneered by the **Eagles**. For touring purposes, Scheff and Hardin were replaced by Stu Cook from **Creedence Clearwater Revival** and session musician Kurt Howell. Emmylou Harris sang on an early hit, 'Thing About You', in 1985 and, by way of thanks, they recorded 'A Girl Like Emmylou'. In 1988, Tim Goodman was replaced by David Jenkins, the former lead singer from **Pablo Cruise**, and they sang 'Any Ole Wind That Blows' on the soundtrack of the Clint Eastwood film, *Pink Cadillac*. The permanence of the group was put into question when the Doobie Brothers decided to reform, but a final album was made in 1990. It included a revival of 'GTO' with the **Beach Boys**.

Albums: *Southern Pacific* (Warners 1985), *Killbilly Hill* (Warners 1986), *Zuma* (Warners 1988), *Country Line* (Warner 1990).

Southern, Jeri

b. Genevieve Hering, 5 August 1926, Royal, Nebraska, USA, d. 4 August 1991, Los Angeles, California, USA. A warm, 'smokey' voiced, jazz-influenced singer/pianist, Southern studied at the Notre Dame Academy, Omaha, and later played piano at the local Blackstone Hotel. After touring with a US Navy recruiting show, where she began singing, she worked at several venues in Chicago in the late 40s. These included the Hi Note Club, where she supported stars such as **Anita O'Day**. After obtaining a nightly spot on television, Southern was signed to **Decca Records** and had US Top 30 hits with 'You Better Go Now' (1951) and 'Joey' (1954). Her wistful version of 'When I Fall In Love' established her as a favourite in the UK, where she also had a Top 30 hit with 'Fire Down Below' (1957). She then switched to the **Capitol** label and made the highly-acclaimed *Jeri Southern Sings Cole Porter*, which featured a set of humourous arrangements by **Billy May**, including a 20s setting of 'Don't Look At Me That Way'. One of her many album releases, *When I Fall In Love*, which was released by MCA Records in 1984, contained several numbers closely identified with Southern including 'An Occasional Man'. She retired from performing in the mid-60s to become a vocal and piano coach for professional artists. She subsequently moved to Hollywood, and worked on arrangements with the film music composer **Hugo Friedhofer**, and later, cared for him. She also published a book, *Interpreting Popular Music At The Keyboard*. Her last public performance was at the Vine Street Bar And Grill in Los Angeles, where she was persuaded by Anita O'Day to emerge from the audience and play a medley of **Jerome Kern** songs. She died of pneumonia six months later.

Albums: *You Better Go Now* (50s), *When Your Heart's On Fire* (50s), *Warm* (1955) *Jeri Gently Jumps* (1958), *Prelude To A Kiss* (1958), *Southern Hospitality* (1959), *Jeri Southern Meets Cole Porter* (1959), *At The Crescendo* (1960), *Southern Breeze* (1959), *Coffee, Cigarettes And Memories* (1959), *Jeri*

Southern Meets Johnny Smith (1959), *Coffee, Cigarettes And Memories* (60s), *You Better Go Now* (1989). Compilation: *When I Fall In Love* (1984).

Southernaires

Formed in 1929, the Southernaires were a black gospel vocal quartet which found success via the radio, without making much of an impact in the area of phonograph record sales. The group consisted of tenor singer Homer Smith (b. 1902, Florence, Alabama, USA), second tenor Lowell Peters (b. 3 March 1903, Cleveland, Tennessee, USA), baritone Jay Stone Toney (b. September 1896, Columbia, Tennessee, USA) and bass singer/narrator William W. Edmunson (b. 15 October 1902, Spokane, Washington, USA). They made their first radio appearance in October 1930 in New York City and gradually built a large following for their regular programmes. In 1933 they added pianist Clarence Jones (b. c.1880s, Wilmingon, Ohio, USA) to the group. That year they started to perform in a dramatic radio series called *The Little Weatherbeaten, Whitewashed Church*, which lasted over 10 years and was syndicated nationwide. Although they recorded for **Decca Records** beginning in 1939 the recordings did not sell very well. Following World War II, the group shifted its emphasis from radio to concert appearances, with Ray Yeates replacing Smith. They briefly had their own television programme in 1948 and by 1951 were down to one original member, Edmunson.

Southlanders

This male vocal quartet, which claims to be the longest lasting vocal group in British pop music history, was formed by Vernon Nesbeth (b. c.1933, Jamaica, West Indies) in 1954. Nesbeth had won an *Opportunity Knocks* contest in his native country, and travelled to England in 1950 intent on making a career as a singer. He studied at the Royal College of Music, and took lessons from the renowned black actor, singer and teacher, Edric Connor. When Connor needed some backing singers for two Caribbean albums, Nesmith recruited Frank Mannah, and brothers Alan and Harry Wilmot. Harry was the father of the popular contemporary UK entertainer Gary Wilmot. After changing their name from the Caribbeans to the Southlanders, the group was signed by the Grade Organization, and toured the UK variety circuit. On a broadcast with **Geraldo**, they sang 'Earth Angel', and this song became their first record release in 1956. It was produced by **George Martin**, several years before he came to prominence with Peter Sellers' comedy albums and the **Beatles'** recordings. The Southlanders' other sides, through to 1961, included 'The Crazy Otto Rag', 'Ain't That A Shame', 'Have You Ever Been Lonely', 'Hush-A-By-Rock', 'The Wedding Of The Lucky Black Cat', 'Swedish Polka', 'I Never Dreamed', 'Peanuts', 'Penny Loafers And Bobby Socks', 'Put A Light In The

Window', 'Down Deep', 'Wishing For Your Love', 'I Wanna Jive Tonight', 'Torero', 'Coo-Choo-Choo Cha-Cha-Cha', 'Roma Rockarolla', 'Down Deep', 'Charlie', and 'Imitation Of Love'. They had their biggest hit in 1957 with the beautiful 'Alone', which is said to have sold 750,000 copies in the first few weeks of release, but the group is most identified with the novelty, 'Mole In A Hole' ('I am a mole and I live in a hole'), which they are required to include in every performance (they can even sing a version in Japanese). In the late 50s and early 60s the Southlanders were regulars on top-rated television programmes such as *6.5 Special* and *Crackerjack*, and had their own show with **Emile Ford And The Checkmates**. They were among the first entertainers to join Jimmy Saville's Mecca dance hall shows, which were the cradle of what became the disco boom. Since then, they have appeared in concerts and cabaret throughout the world, with a classy, highly entertaining act which combines their record hits with a weave of traditional calypso, spiritual rhythms and soul classics. Harry Wilmot died in 1961, and Alan retired in 1974; Frank Mannah died three years later. Nesbeth is still the lead singer and focal point in the 1995 line-up of baritone Randolph Patterson, bass Julian John Lewis, and tenor Joseph Servie. Over more than 40 years of the group's existence, he has also done some solo work. In 1975, he appeared with Michael Denison in *The Black Mikado* at London's Cambridge Theatre, and in 1982 he sang in the opera, *A Great Day In The Morning*, with Jesse Norman and Robert Wilson in Paris.

Southside Johnny And The Asbury Jukes

R&B fanatic Southside Johnny (b. John Lyons, 4 December 1948, New Jersey, USA) sang with the Blackberry Booze Band in the late 60s before teaming up with the Asbury Jukes with school friends Billy Rush (guitar), Kevin Kavanaugh (keyboards), Kenneth Pentifallo (bass) and Alan 'Doc' Berger (drums), plus transient members of a horn section. Popular in Upstage, Stone Poney and other parochial clubs, they sought a wider audience via a 1976 promotional album, *Live At The Bottom Line*, which helped facilitate a contract with Epic. Like another local lad, **Bruce Springsteen**, the outfit bolstered their reputation with practical demonstrations of credible influences by enlisting **Ronnie Spector**, **Lee Dorsey**, and black vocal groups of the 50s on *I Wanna Go Home* and its follow-up, *This Time It's For Real*. Both were weighted further with Springsteen sleeve notes and songs as well as production supervision by his guitarist (and ex-Juke) **Steven Van Zandt**. After *Hearts Of Stone* failed to reach a mass public, Epic let the band go with the valedictory *Having A Party* - essentially a 'best of' compilation.

Mitigating this setback were increasing touring fees that permitted sensational augmentation with saxophonists

Carlo Novi and Stan Harrison, trumpeters Ricki Gazda and Tony Palligrosi, and ex-**Diana Ross** trombonist Richard Rosenberg, as well as an additional guitarist in Joel Gramolini and replacement drummer Steve Becker. A debut on **Mercury**, 1979's *The Jukes* sold well as did *Love Is A Sacrifice* in 1980 but, for all the polished production by Barry Beckett many felt that much nascent passion had been dissipated. Possibly, this was traceable to the borrowing of the horns by Van Zandt for his Disciples Of Soul, and the exits of Pentifallo - and Berger, writer (with Lyons and Rush) of the band's original material. The in-concert *Reach Out And Touch The Sky* (with its fiery **Sam Cooke** medley) halted a commercial decline that resumed with later studio efforts - though radio interest in a revival of **Left Banke**'s 'Walk Away Renee' (from *At Least We Got Shoes*) and a Jersey Artists For Mankind charity single (organized by Lyons) suggests that all might not yet be lost. They halted the decline in 1991 with *Better Days*. This lyrically nostalgic album contained a Springsteen song 'Walk You All The Way Home' in addition to Van Zandt's numerous contributions.

Albums: *I Don't Wanna Go Home* (1976), *This Time It's For Real* (1977), *Hearts Of Stone* (1978), *The Jukes* (1979), *Love Is A Sacrifice* (1980), *Reach Out And Touch The Sky* (1981), *Trash It Up! Live* (1983), *In The Heat* (1984), *At Least We Got Shoes* (1986), *Better Days* (1991). Compilations: *Having A Party* (1979), *The Best Of* (1993).

Sovine, Red

b. Woodrow Wilson Sovine, 17 July 1918, Charleston, West Virginia, USA, d. 4 April 1980. Sovine was taught the guitar by his mother and was working professionally by the time he was 17 on WCHS Charleston with Johnny Bailes and then as part of Jim Pike And His Carolina Tarheels. In 1948 Sovine formed his own band, The Echo Valley Boys, and became a regular on *Louisiana Hayride*. Sovine acquired the nickname of 'The Old Syrup Sopper' following the sponsorship by Johnny Fair Syrup of some radio shows, and the title is apt for such narrations as 'Daddy's Girl'. Sovine recorded for US **Decca** Records and first made the country charts with 'Are You Mine?', a duet with Goldie Hill. Later that year, a further duet, this time with **Webb Pierce**, 'Why Baby Why', made number 1 on the US country charts. They followed this with the tear-jerking narration, 'Little Rosa', which became a mainstay of Sovine's act. From 1954 Sovine was a regular at *Grand Ole Opry* and, in all, he had 31 US country chart entries. He particularly scored with maudlin narrations about truckdrivers and his successes include 'Giddyup Go' (a US country number 1 about a truckdriver being reunited with his son), 'Phantom 309' (a truck-driving ghost story!) and his million-selling saga of a crippled boy and his CB radio, 'Teddy Bear' (1976). Sequels and parodies of 'Teddy Bear' abound, Sovine refused to record 'Teddy Bear's Last Ride',

which became a US country hit for Diana Williams. He retaliated with 'Little Joe' to indicate that Teddy Bear was not dead after all. Among his own compositions are 'I Didn't Jump The Fence' and 'Missing You', which was a UK hit for **Jim Reeves**. Sovine recorded 'The Hero' as a tribute to John Wayne and his son, Roger Wayne Sovine, was named in his honour. The young Sovine was briefly a country singer, making the lower end of the US country charts with 'Culman, Alabam' and 'Little Bitty Nitty Gritty Dirt Town'. Sovine's country music owed nothing to contemporary trends but his sentimentality was popular in UK clubs. He had no big-time image and, whilst touring the UK, he made a point of visiting specialist country music shops. In 1980 Sovine died of a heart attack at the wheel of his car in Nashville. The following year, as CB radio hit the UK, a reissue of 'Teddy Bear' reached number 5, his first UK chart entry.

Albums: *Red Sovine* (1957), *Country Music Time* (1957), *The One And Only Red Sovine* (1961), *Golden Country Ballads Of The 60's* (1962), *Red Sovine* (1964), *Red Sovine - Fine* (1964), *Little Rosa* (1965), *Town And Country Action* (1965), *Country Music Time* (1966), *Giddyup Go* (1966), *I Didn't Jump The Fence* (1967), *Farewell So Long Goodbye* (1967), *Phantom 309* (1967), *The Nashville Sound Of Red Sovine* (1967), *Sunday With Sovine* (1968), *Tell Maude I Slipped* (1968), *The Country Way* (1968), *Classic Narrations* (1969), *Closing Time 'Til Dawn* (1969), *Who Am I?* (1969), *I Know You're Married* (1970), *Ruby, Don't Take Your Love To Town* (1970), *The Greatest Grand Ole Opry* (1972), *It'll Come Back* (1974), *Teddy Bear* (1976), *Woodrow Wilson Sovine* (1977), *16 New Gospel Songs* (1980).

Spacemen 3

Spacemen 3 were instigated in Rugby, Warwickshire, England, in 1982 by **Sonic Boom** (b. Pete Kember, 19 November 1965) and regional soulmate Jason Pierce (also, strangely enough, b. 19 November 1965). Augmented by the rhythm section of Rosco and Pete Baines, it took Spacemen 3 fully four years to blossom onto record. Initially crying shy of sounding too much like the **Cramps**, the band carefully evolved into one-chord wonders; masters of the hypnotic, blissed-out groove. Such was their languid approach to working, and so dream-inspiring was their music, Spacemen 3 made a habit of sitting down for the entirety of their gigs. 1989's *Playing With Fire* included the intensely repetitive blast of 'Revolutions'. By this time Baines and Rosco had formed what was tantamount to a Spacemen 3 spin-off in the Darkside, allowing Will Carruthers and John Mattock to step into their places, and although this was the peak of the band's career, fundamental problems were still inherent: Sonic Boom made no secret of his drug dependency, having replaced heroin with methadone, and he and Jason Pierce were gradually growing apart to the point where they were chasing different goals. The relationship became so strained that *Recurring*, although still a Spaceman 3 effort, saw the two forces working separately, Boom being attributed with side one and Pierce with side two. By this stage Boom had embarked upon a solo career and Pierce was working with Mattock and Carruthers in another band, **Spiritualized**, a situation which further fanned the flames. When *Recurring* finally saw the light of day Spaceman 3's creative forces refused to even be interviewed together. A petty demise to what was, for some time, a creatively intense band.

Albums: *Sound Of Confusion* (Glass 1986), *The Perfect Prescription* (Glass 1987), *Performance* (Glass 1988), *Playing With Fire* (Fire 1989), *Recurring* (Fire 1991).

Spand, Charlie

Details on Spand's early history and later life is scant. What is known is that he recorded in excess of 20 tracks for the Paramount label between 1929 and 1931 and a further eight for **OKeh Records** in 1940. He was a friend and working partner of **Blind Blake**, with whom he recorded the classic 'Hastings Street' and appeared on the Paramount sampler disc 'Home Town Skiffle'. Spand's piano work was in the powerful Detroit style and his writing skills were considerable. His first recording 'Soon This Morning' became something of a staple for blues pianists. Working mainly in Chicago he was known to artists such as **Little Brother Montgomery** and **Jimmy Yancey** but after the war he disappeared. It is speculated, by Francis Wilford Smith, that Spand was born around the turn of the century in Ellijay, Georgia and retired to Los Angeles.

Compilations: *Piano Blues, Vol. 1* (1977), *Piano Blues, Vol. 5* (1978), *Piano Blues, Vol. 16* (1981).

Spandau Ballet

Evolving from a school group, the Makers, this UK New Romantic group was founded in 1979 with a line-up comprising Gary Kemp (b. 16 October 1960, London, England; guitar), his brother Martin Kemp (b. 10 October 1961, London, England; bass), Tony Hadley (b. 2 June 1960, London, England), John Keeble (b. 6 July 1959, London, England; drums) and Steve Norman (b. 25 March 1960, London, England; rhythm guitar/saxophone/percussion). Another school colleague, Steve Dagger, became the group's long-standing manager. The group originally came to prominence as part of the new romantic scene revolving around a handful of fashionable London clubs, at which the habitues would dress in outlandish clothes and make-up. Such was the interest in this unknown group that Spandau Ballet were offered a contract by **Island Records**' proprietor **Chris Blackwell**. This was rejected and, instead, the group set up their own label, Reformation. During early 1980, they were filmed for a television documentary

and soon after licensed their label through **Chrysalis Records**. Their powerful debut, the harrowing 'To Cut A Long Story Short' reached the UK Top 5. With their kilts and synthesizers, it was easy to assume that the group were just part of a passing fashion and over the next year their singles 'The Freeze' and 'Musclebound' were average rather than exceptional. The insistent 'Chant Number 1 (I Don't Need This Pressure On)' revealed a more interesting soul/funk direction, complete with added brass and a new image. The single reached the UK Top 3, but again was followed by a relatively fallow period with 'Paint Me Down' and 'She Loved Like Diamond' barely scraping into the charts. The group completed a couple of albums and employed various producers, including **Trevor Horn** for 'Instinction' and **Tony Swain** and **Steve Jolley** for 'Communication'. By 1983 the group pursued a more straightforward pop direction and pushed their lead singer as a junior **Frank Sinatra**. The new approach was demonstrated most forcibly on the irresistibly melodic 'True', which topped the UK charts. The album of the same name repeated the feat, while the follow-up 'Gold' reached number 2. The obvious international appeal of a potential standard like 'True' was underlined when the song belatedly climbed into the US Top 10. During the mid-80s, the group continued to chart regularly with such hits as 'Only When You Leave', 'I'll Fly For You', 'Highly Strung' and 'Round And Round'. A long-running legal dispute with Chrysalis forestalled the group's progress until they signed to **CBS/Columbia** in 1986. The politically-conscious *Through The Barricades* and its attendant hit single 'Fight For Yourselves' partly re-established their standing. Their later work, however, was overshadowed by the acting ambitions of the Kemp brothers, who appeared to considerable acclaim in the London gangster movie, *The Krays*.

Albums: *Journey To Glory* (1981), *Diamond* (1982), *True* (1983), *Parade* (1984), *Through The Barricades* (1986), *Heart Like A Sky* (1989). Compilation: *The Singles Collection* (1985). Solo: Tony Hadley *State Of Play* (1993).

Spaniels

This vocal ensemble was formed in 1952 in Gary, Indiana, USA. The Spaniels were universally recognized as one of the great R&B vocal harmony groups of the 50s, whose magnificent body of work was not truly reflected in their moderate chart success. The group originally consisted of Roosevelt High students James 'Pookie' Hudson (lead), Ernest Warren (first tenor), Opal Courtney (baritone), Willis C. Jackson (baritone), and Gerald Gregory (bass). In 1953 the quintet enjoyed an R&B Top 10 hit with 'Baby, It's You', but the following year achieved their biggest success when 'Goodnite Sweetheart, Goodnite' reached the US pop Top 30 despite competition from an opportunistic pop-style version by the **McGuire**

Sisters. The Spaniels' delicate doo-wop harmonies turned this ballad into one of the era's best-loved performances with an emotional pull outweighing its intrinsic simplicity. The Spaniels in 1955 followed with two fine regional hits, 'Let's Make Up' and 'You Painted Pictures'. The Spaniels reorganized in 1956, and Hudson and Gregory were now augmented by James Cochran (baritone), Carl Rainge (tenor), and Don Porter (second tenor). Top recordings of this group included the 'You Gave Me Peace Of Mind' (1956) and 'Everyone's Laughing' (number 13 R&B 1957), and 'I Lost You' (1958). Another reorganization in 1960 in which Hudson and Gregory brought in Andy McGruder, Billy Cary, and Ernest Warren, yielded the group's last hit featuring the classic Spaniels sound, 'I Know' (US R&B number 23 in 1960). Hudson went solo in 1961, but formed a soul-styled Spaniels group in 1969 that brought 'Fairy Tales' to the charts in 1970.

Albums: *Goodnite, It's Time To Go* (1958), *The Spaniels* (1960), *Spaniels* (1968). Compilations: *Hits Of The Spaniels* (1971), *Great Googley Moo!* (1981), *16 Soulful Serenades* (1984), *Stormy Weather* (1986), *Play It Cool* (1990), *40th Anniversary 1953-1993* (1993).

Spanier, Muggsy

b. Francis Joseph Spanier, 9 November 1906, Chicago, Illinois, USA, d. 12 February 1967, Sausalito, California, USA. Spanier began playing cornet while barely in his teens and within a couple of years was a professional musician. His first job was with **Elmer Schoebel**. By the end of the 20s he had established a reputation mostly in and around Chicago and had been hired by **Ted Lewis** for his popular band. He remained with Lewis until the mid-30s, then joined **Ben Pollack**. After a short period of serious illness he formed his own band, the Ragtimers, for a hotel residency in 1938 and also recorded with the band the following year. Although short-lived, the Ragtimers made an enormous impact on the public. During the 40s Spanier mingled leading his own bands with working for other artists such as **Bob Crosby**, **Pee Wee Russell**, **Art Hodes** and **Miff Mole**. In the 50s he worked frequently with **Earl Hines**, playing at numerous hotels, clubs and festivals all across the USA. Highly regarded by his fellow musicians, as much for his personal qualities as for his playing, Spanier's style was simple and direct, akin in these respects to that of earlier jazzmen. In spirit, however, he was very much a product of his home town. The 16 tracks recorded by Spanier's Ragtimers in 1939 are classics of a kind of jazz which retains its popularity, even if his successors rarely achieve their quality. Spanier's last years were dogged by poor health; he was forced to retire in 1964, and died three years later.

Albums: *Hot Horn* (1957), *Spanier In Chicago* (1958). Compilations: *Francis Joseph Muggsy Spanier* (1926-29), *The Great Sixteen* (1939), with Pee Wee Russell *Muggsy And Pee Wee* (1941-57), *Muggsy Spanier And His V-Disc All Stars* (1944).

Spanky And Our Gang

The original line-up of this engaging US harmony group - Elaine 'Spanky' McFarlane (tambourine/washboard), Nigel Pickering (12-string guitar) and Oz Bach (stand-up bass/kazoo) - began performing together in Chicago's folk clubs. Within months they were joined by Malcolm Hale (guitar/vocals) and John George Seiter (drums) and this restructured line-up scored a US Top 10 hit with its debut release, 'Sunday Will Never Be The Same'. This evocative song bore traces of the **Mamas And The Papas** and the more conservative **Seekers**, a style maintained on its follow-up, 'Lazy Day'. Bach was then replaced by Geoffrey Myers, who in turn made way for Kenny Hodges. Sixth member Lefty Baker (vocals/guitar) expanded the group's harmonic range, but while the haunting 'Like To Get To Know You' suggested a more mature direction, Spanky And Our Gang seemed more content with a bubbly, good-time, but rather lightweight approach. The premature death of Malcolm Hale in 1968 undermined the group's inner confidence, and any lingering momentum faltered when 'Give A Damn', a campaign song for the Urban Coalition League, incurred an airplay ban in several states. The remaining quintet broke up in 1969 although McFarlane and Pickering retained the name for the country-influenced *Change*. In 1981 the former joined a rejuvenated Mamas And The Papas, before touring with an all-new Spanky And Our Gang.

Albums: *Spanky And Our Gang* (1967), *Like To Get To Know You* (1968), *Anything You Choose/Without Rhyme Or Reason* (1969), *Spanky And Our Gang Live* (1970), *Change* (1975). Compilations: *Spanky's Greatest Hits* (1969), *The Best Of Spanky And Our Gang* (1986).

Spann, Lucille

b. Mahalia Lucille Jenkins, 23 June 1938, Bolton, Mississippi, USA. Lucille sang gospel to start with, both in Mississippi and later in Chicago, where she moved in her early teens. In the 60s, she met the great blues pianist **Otis Spann**, and they began a musical partnership and later married. They recorded together, but tragically their collaboration came to an end with Otis's early death in 1970. Lucille continued to work in music and made a number of further recordings.

Album: *Cry Before I Go* (1974).

Spann, Otis

b. 21 March 1930, Jackson, Mississippi, USA, d. 24 April 1970, Chicago, Illinois, USA. One of the finest pianists of post-war blues, Spann learned the instrument as a child. He initially played in his step-father's church, but by the age of 14 was a member of a small, local combo. Having pursued careers in football and boxing, Otis moved to Chicago where he returned to music through work with several established attractions, including **Memphis Slim** and **Roosevelt Sykes**, before fronting the houseband at the city's Tick Tock club. In 1952 the pianist made his first recordings with **Muddy Waters** and the following year he became a permanent member of this seminal artist's group, where he remained for most of his professional life. Spann did complete a solo session in 1955 with the assistance of **Willie Dixon** and **Robert Lockwood**, but session appearances for **Bo Diddley** and **Howlin' Wolf** apart, is recalled for the subtle yet complimentary support he imparted on Waters' music. Otis supported the singer on his ground-breaking UK tour of 1958 and was an integral part of the group which appeared at the 1960 Newport Jazz Festival. He subsequently completed an album for the Candid label, before resuming his association with Waters with a series of successful tours. British concerts during 1963 and 1964 proved highly influential on the emergent R&B scene and on the second visit Spann recorded two tracks, 'Pretty Girls Everywhere' and 'Stirs Me Up', with **Yardbirds**' guitarist **Eric Clapton**. Otis began a thriving solo career on returning to the US, completing a series of albums for several different labels, including Prestige and Bluesway. These releases not only showcased his remarkable talent on piano, they also offered a skilled composer and vocalist and featured sterling support from such contemporaries as Waters, **James Cotton** (harmonica) and S.P. Leary (drums). The latter also appeared on *The Biggest Thing Since Colossus*, Spann's collaboration with **Fleetwood Mac** stalwarts **Peter Green**, **Danny Kirwan** and **John McVie**. Barring contributions to a session by **Junior Wells** and the film *Blues Like Showers Of Rain*, this excellent set was the artist's last significant work. Increasingly debilitated by illness, Otis Spann entered Chicago's Cook County Hospital, where he died of cancer in 1970.

Selected albums: *Otis Spann Is The Blues* (1960), *Blues Is Where It's At* (1963), *Portrait In Blues* (1963), *Piano Blues* (1963), *The Blues Of Otis Spann* (1964), *Chicago Blues* (1964), *Nobody Knows My Troubles* (1967), *Bottom Of The Blues* (1968), *Raw Blues* (1968), *Cracked Spanner Head* (1969), *Blues Never Die* (1969), *Cryin' Time* (1970), *The Everlasting Blues* (1970), *Walking Blues* (1972), *Candid Spann, Volume 1* (1983), *Candid Spann, Volume 2* (1983), *Nobody Knows Chicago Like I Do* (1983), *Rarest* (1984), *Take Me Back Home* (1984), *Walking The Blues* (1987), *The Biggest Thing Since Colossus* (1993), *The Blues Of Otis Spann...Plus* (See For Miles 1994).

Spanos, Danny

This American vocalist/composer performed and recorded under his own name, always preferring the services of hired hands to a conventional band set-up. He recorded three albums during the early 80s, using a variety of session musicians, including **Earl Slick**, **Rick Derringer**, **Carmine Appice**, Dana Strum and Frankie Banali. His style fell somewhere between **Jimmy Barnes** and **Bryan Adams**; easily accessible hard rock with gritty vocals and infectious hooklines. Ultimately, the songs lacked real character and he failed to break into the big time.

Albums: *Danny Spanos* (Windsong 1980), *Passion In The Dark* (Epic 1983), *Looks Like Trouble* (Epic 1984).

Spargo, Tony

(see **Sbarbaro, Tony**)

Sparks

Ex-child actors and veterans of Los Angeles' Urban Renewal Project, vocalist Russell Mael and his elder brother Ron (keyboards) led Halfnelson in 1968 (with renowned rock critic John Mendelssohn on drums). By 1971, this had evolved into Sparks in which the Maels were joined by Earle Mankay (guitar), Jim Mankay (bass) and Harley Fernstein (drums). At the urging of **Todd Rundgren** - their eventual producer - **Albert Grossman** signed them to Bearsville. While it emitted a regional US hit in 'Wonder Girl,' Sparks' debut album sold poorly - as did the subsequent *A Woofer In Tweeter's Clothing*. A stressful club tour of Europe - during which they were often heckled - amassed, nonetheless, a cult following in glam-rock England where the Maels emigrated in 1973 to gain an **Island** recording contract and enlist a new Sparks from native players. Drummer 'Dinky' Diamond from Aldershot's Sound Of Time was a mainstay during this period but among many others passing through the ranks were guitarist Adrian Fisher from Toby and Jook's bass player Ian Hampton. Overseen by **Muff Winwood**, this Anglo-American edition of Sparks notched up eight UK chart entries, starting with 1974's unprecedented and startling 'This Town Ain't Big Enough For Both Of Us' from *Kimono My House*. With eccentric arrangements in the **Roxy Music** vein, 'Amateur Hour' and later singles were also notable for Ron's lyrical idiosyncracies as well as wide stereo separation between the bass guitar section and Russell's twittering falsetto. Their appeal hinged visually on the disparity between creepy Ron's conservative garb and 'Hitler' moustache, and Russell's bubbly androgyny. *Propaganda* was a stylistic departure but the basic formula was unaltered. Sparks' over-dependence on this combined with an unsteady stage act to provoke fading interest in further merchandise - despite strategies like hiring **Tony Visconti** to supervise 1975's *Indiscreet*, and the Maels' return to California to make *Big Beat* with expensive LA session musicians.

Sparks engineered a transient comeback to the British Top 20 in 1977 with two singles from *Number One In Heaven*, produced by **Giorgio Moroder** - and 1981's

'When I'm With You' (from *Terminal Jive*) sold well in France. Later, the brothers succeeded in the US Hot 100 - particularly with 1983's 'Cool Places,' a tie-up with the **Go-Go's**' guitarist **Jane Wiedlin** - which intimates that their future may hold more surprises. They were still active and receiving plenty of media attention in the 90s and their recent work has been well received, especially *Gratuitous Sax And Senseless Violins*.

Albums: *Sparks* (1971), *A Woofer In Tweeter's Clothing* (1972), *Kimono My House* (1974), *Propaganda* (1974), *Indiscreet* (1975), *Big Beat* (1978), *Number One In Heaven* (1979), *Terminal Jive* (1980), *Whoop That Sucker* (1981), *Angst In My Pants* (1982), *Sparks In Outer Space* (1983), *Half Nelson* (1993), *Gratuitous Sax And Senseless Violins* (Arista 1994). Compilation: *Best Of Sparks* (1979).

Sparks Brothers

Twin brothers, Aaron 'Pinetop' Sparks and Marion (aka Milton) 'Lindberg' Sparks (b. 22 May 1910, Tupelo, Mississippi, USA) were constantly in trouble with the law for fighting, gambling and theft, although Milton gradually reformed after a jail sentence for manslaughter in 1937. Pinetop was an accomplished pianist, equally adept at slow numbers and mid-tempo boogies, in which his style recalls **Big Maceo**. Lindberg's singing was more nasal, but equally attractive. Maceo and Lindberg played the rowdy houseparties of St. Louis, and recorded, separately and together, from 1932-35, leaving an impressive body of work, including what appear to be the original versions of '61 Highway' and 'Every Day I Have The Blues'. Their lyrics make poetry from the realities of their lives: travel, lowlife, prison and sex. Aaron died in c.1938, while Milton passed away on 25 May 1963, St. Louis, Missouri, USA.

Album: *Sparks Brothers* (1989).

Sparrow

Formed in Toronto, Canada, in 1965, Sparrow evolved from an earlier incarnation, Jack London and the Sparrows. The original line-up - Jack London (vocals), Dennis Edmonton (nee McCrochan, guitar), Jerry Edmonton (nee McCrochan, drums), Nick St. Nicholas (bass) and Art Ayre (organ) - enjoyed a No.1 hit in Canada with 'If You Don't Want My Love', before London left to pursue a poppier direction. Former folksinger John Kay (nee Joachim Krauledat) took his place and with the arrival of Goldy McJohn in favour of Ayre, the definitive Sparrow was established. The quintet quickly became a leading attraction in Toronto's Yorkville district, playing a gruff-styled R&B, perfect for Kay's growled vocals. By contrast, the Sparrow's singles, 'Tomorrow's Ship' and 'Green Bottle Lover', were, respectively, folk/rock and garage/punk. The group moved to Los Angeles in 1967, but split up when neither band nor producer (David Rubinson) were happy with their final series of

recordings. Kay, McJohn and Jerry Edmonton then formed **Steppenwolf**, whose best-known song, 'Born To Be Wild', was composed by Dennis Edmonton, under his newly-assumed name, Mars Bonfire. Nick St. Nicholas was a member of Steppenwolf between 1969 and 1970 and the success of this group inspired the release of *John Kay And The Sparrow*, which comprised of demo recordings made to secure their recording deal with **CBS**.

Albums: *John London And The Sparrows* (1964), *John Kay And The Sparrow* (1968). Compilation: *Tighten Up Your Wig: The Best Of John Kay And The Sparrow* (1993).

Spartan Warrior

This UK heavy metal group was formed in 1983 by Dave Wilkinson (vocals) Neil Wilkinson (guitar), Paul Swaddle (guitar), Tom Spencer (bass) and Gordon Webster (drums), making their debut with two cuts on the *Guardian* compilation in 1984. This opened the door to a contract with **Roadrunner Records**, which resulted in two non-descript, poorly produced metal albums. These incorporated elements of **Rush**, **Deep Purple** and **Led Zeppelin**, but few original ideas of their own. Failing to make any impact, the band returned to their day jobs in 1986.

Albums: *Spartan Warrior* (Roadrunner 1984), *Steel 'N' Chains* (Roadrunner 1985).

Spaulding, James

b. 30 July 1937, Indianapolis, Indiana, USA. In the mid-50s Spaulding studied at Chicago's Cosmopolitan School of Music, specializing in alto saxophone and flute, and also played in **Sun Ra**'s Arkestra and in **Sonny Thompson**'s R&B group. In 1962, Spaulding moved to New York and came to prominence playing as a sideman on numerous **Blue Note** releases, particularly on dates led by **Freddie Hubbard** (*Hubtones* and *Breaking Point*) but also on albums by **Stanley Turrentine**, **Horace Silver** and **Wayne Shorter**. Later work saw him playing with many leading post-bop artists, among them **Max Roach**, **Woody Shaw** and **Randy Weston**. In the 70s he played in the **Duke Ellington** Orchestra under **Mercer Ellington** and his debut as a leader was a tribute to Duke. Astonishingly, Spaulding has only made three albums in his own name in over 30 years as a player: the second, *Brilliant Corners*, was also a tribute - this time to **Thelonious Monk**. In the 80s he worked with **Ricky Ford** and later joined the **David Murray** Octet, touring and recording *Hopescope* with them. His latest, *Gotstabe A Better Way*, comprises tunes from a longer, ongoing project called 'The Courage Suite'.

Selected albums: *Plays The Legacy Of Duke Ellington* (1977), *Brilliant Corners* (1989), *Gostabe A Better Way* (1990), *Songs Of Courage* (1993 re. 1991).

Spear

(see **Pukwana, Dudu**)

Spear Of Destiny

Formed from the ashes of **Theatre Of Hate** in early 1983, Spear Of Destiny took their name from the mythological weapon which pierced the body of Christ, and was supposedly acquired over the years by Attila The Hun, Napoleon and Hitler. This helped the band to attract quite a volume of destructive commentary in the press. The original line-up featured mainstay Kirk Brandon (b. 3 August 1956, Westminster, London, England; vocals/guitar), Chris Bell (drums), Lasettes Ames (saxophone) and Stan Stammers (ex-Theatre Of Hate; bass). They signed to **CBS**, but maintained their own label design, 'Burning Rome', which had appeared on previous Theatre Of Hate releases. The first single 'Flying Scotsman' arrived in 1983, and was featured on *The Grapes Of Wrath* alongside the relentless single 'The Wheel'. Critical response to the group was divided. By July, Bell and Ames had left, for reasons described by Bell as personal and religious. Brandon and Stammers brought in former Theatre Of Hate saxophonist John Lennard (b. Canada, ex-Diodes) and Nigel Preston (ex Theatre Of Hate, **Sex Gang Children**). A third line-up added Alan St Clair (guitar) and Neil Pyzor (ex-Case; keyboards, saxophone), Dolphin Taylor (ex-**Tom Robinson Band** and **Stiff Little Fingers**; drums) and Nicky Donnelly (ex-Case; saxophone). It was this formation which recorded *One Eyed Jacks*, arguably the band's best album, and the singles 'Rainmaker', 'Liberator' and 'Prisoner Of Love', the latter signalling a change in direction which would be more fully realized on the follow-up album. When *World Service* arrived, there was considerable disappointment from fans and critics alike. Having built an enviable reputation as a lyricist of considerable vigour, tracks like 'Mickey' seemed grotesque and clumsy. Further personnel changes became commonplace, and by 1987 and *Outlands* the line-up comprised Pete Barnacle (drums), Volker Janssen (keyboards) and Chris Bostock (bass) alongside Brandon. The summer of that year saw Brandon incapacitated for six months with an ankle injury that left him unable to walk, an affliction from which he still carries a limp. However, the band were soon back in the charts with 'Never Take Me Alive', and a support tour with **U2**. Their 1988 singles 'So In Love With You' and 'Radio Radio' saw them switch from Epic to **Virgin**. By December 1990, old colleague Stan Stammers returned on bass, alongside new drummer and guitarist Bobby Rae Mayhem and Mark Thwaite. 1991 opened with Brandon touring once more under the joint Theatre Of Hate/Spear Of Destiny banner.

Albums: *The Grapes Of Wrath* (1983), *One Eyed Jacks* (1984), *World Service* (1985) *Outlands* (1987), *The Price You Pay* (1988), *S.O.D.'s Law* (1992), *Live At The Lyceum* (1993).

Spear, Roger Ruskin

b. England. A founder member of the **Bonzo Dog Doo-Dah Band**, Spear's use of robots and electric props provided enduring visual images to accompany the musical, lyrical and humorous antics of his colleagues. His creations were similar to another great eccentric, Professor Bruce Lacey, a former member of the Alberts, a group whose approach anticipated that of the Bonzos. In 1970, Spear briefly joined **Viv Stanshall**'s new unit, biG GRunt, before embarking on a solo career. He toured as a one man show with his *Giant Kinetic Wardrobe* and recorded two solo albums which were as entertaining as they were bizarre. *Electric Shocks* contained a cast which included *Melody Maker* journalists Chris Welch and Roy Hollingsworth, rock group the **Flamin' Groovies** and former Bonzos, Sam Spoons and Dave Clague, while *Unusual* featured assistance from **Help Yourself**, a quartet signed to the same label as Spear. However, although this extraordinary artist continued to make sporadic appearances, his profile diminished as the 70s progressed.

Albums: *Electric Shocks* (1972), *Unusual* (1973).

Spears, Billie Jo

b. 14 January 1937, Beaumont, Texas, USA. Discovered by songwriter **Jack Rhodes**, Billie Jo's first record, as Billie Jo Moore, 'Too Old For Toys, Too Young For Boys', earned her $4,200 at the age of 15. Despite appearances on *Louisiana Hayride*, she did not record regularly until she signed with United Artists in 1964. Following her producer, Kelso Herston, to **Capitol Records**, she had country hits with 'He's Got More Love In His Little Finger' and 'Mr. Walker, It's All Over'. After time off, following the removal of a nodule on her vocal cords, she recorded briefly for Brite Star and Cutlass. In 1974, Spears returned to United Artists where producer **Larry Butler** was developing a successful country roster. Her trans-Atlantic smash, 'Blanket on the Ground', was controversial in America. 'It sounded like a cheating song,' says Spears 'and the public don't think girls should sing cheating songs!' In actuality, it was about adding romance to a marriage and its success prompted other records with a similar theme and tempo - 'What I've Got In Mind' (which had originally been a rhumba) and "57 Chevrolet'. The traditional 'Sing Me An Old-Fashioned Song' sold well in the UK, whilst her cover of **Dorothy Moore**'s ballad 'Misty Blue' was successful in the USA. She is also known for her cover of **Gloria Gaynor**'s 'I Will Survive'. She maintains, 'It is still a country record. I am country. I could never go pop with my mouthful of firecrackers.' A duet album with **Del Reeves** *By Request* and a tribute to her producer *Larry Butler And Friends* with **Crystal Gayle** and **Dottie West** were not released in the UK. A single of her blues-soaked cover of 'Heartbreak Hotel' was cancelled in 1977 because she did not want to exploit **Elvis Presley**'s death. Billie Jo Spears has performed prolifically including over 300 concerts in the UK and her ambition is to make a live album at the Pavillion, Glasgow. Among her UK recordings are a duet with **Carey Duncan** of 'I Can Hear Kentucky Calling Me' and an album *B.J. - Billie Jo Spears Today* with her stage band, Owlkatraz. Of late, she has recorded husky-voiced versions of familiar songs for mass-marketed albums. A true ambassador of country music, she signs autographs and talks to fans after every appearance. She buys all her stage clothes in the UK and refuses to wear anything casual. 'If I didn't wear gowns,' she says, 'they'd throw rotten tomatoes.'

Albums: *The Voice Of Billie Jo Spears* (1968), *Mr.Walker, It's All Over* (1969), *Miss Sincerity* (1969), *With Love* (1970), *Country Girl* (1970), *Just Singin'* (1972), *Blanket On The Ground* (1974), *Billie Jo* (1975), *What I've Got In Mind* (1976), with Del Reeves *By Request* (1976), *If You Want Me* (1977), *Everytime I Sing A Love Song* (1977), *Lonely Hearts Club* (1978), *Love Ain't Gonna Wait For Us* (1978), *I Will Survive* (1979), *Standing Tall* (1980), *Special Songs* (1981), with Reeves *Del And Billie Jo* (1982), *B.J. - Billie Jo Spears Today* (1983), *We Just Came Apart At The Dreams* (1984), *Misty Blue* (1992), *Unmistakably* (1992). Compilations: *Singles - Billie Jo Spears* (1979), *17 Golden Pieces Of Billie Jo Spears* (1983), *20 Country Greats* (1988), *50 Original Tracks* (1993), *Stand By Your Man* (1993), *The Queen Of Country Music* (MFP 1994).

Special Ed

b. Edward Archer, c.1973, Brooklyn, New York, USA. Special Ed debuted with a superb, precise album, produced with numbing ferocity by Hitman Howie Tee. Archer had previously practised his lyrics in junior high school, perfecting his rhymes until he hooked up with Tee who agreed to produce some tracks for him. These were promptly delivered to **Profile Records** who immediately expressed an interest and sanctioned Special Ed's debut album. Though he was only 16 when this was released, the rhymes were mature and supremely confident. Over half a million sales confirmed his arrival. There was a more romantic discourse evident on the follow-up, which while less abrasive, was still an examplory introduction. Still largely with Tee, he produced four of the tracks himself. He also introduced a number of his friends, including his brother Drew Archer and homeboys 40-Love, Little Shawn and DJ Akshan. There was, however, a three year hiatus between *Legal* and his third album, proposed for 1993 release. The time was spent: 'Working with groups and putting together a studio and office in Brooklyn'. He also produced a track for **Tupac Shakur**'s *Strictly For My Niggaz*. He was

reported to be working with **Gang Starr**'s **DJ Premier**, Large Professor and **A Tribe Called Quest**'s Q-Tip on sessions for the new album, while further collaborations placed him alongside **Master Ace** and Buckshot (**Black Moon**) in the highly successful Crooklyn Dodgers project ('Crooklyn'). Albums: *Youngest In Charge* (Profile 1989), *Legal* (Profile 1990).

Special EFX

Formed in New York in 1982 by George Jinda (b. 4 June, Hungary; drums/percussion) and Chieli Minucci (b. 17 April; guitar), Special EFX blend African and Latin rhythms and produce a mixture of light rock and MOR jazz. Their music is perfect for the GRP label and consequently their output is prolific. They employ additional musicians to give them a rich and, in keeping with GRP's policy, state-of-the-art recording sound. Session players include **Mark Egan**, **McCoy Tyner**, **Dave Grusin** and **Omar Hakim**. All the albums up until *Just Like Magic* were basically the same sensitive mixture of accessible jazz/pop. That album is more acoustic and Jinda's electronic percussion was replaced by 'wooden world music'.

Albums: *Modern Manners* (1985), *Slice Of Life* (1986), *Mystique* (1987), *Double Feature* (1988), *Confidential* (1989), *Just Like Magic* (1990), *Peace Of The World* (1991), *Play* (1993).

Specials

This Coventry, England, ska-influenced group was formed in the summer of 1977 as the Special AKA, with a line-up comprising Jerry Dammers (b. Gerald Dankin, 22 May 1954, India; keyboards), Terry Hall (b. 19 March 1959, Coventry, England; vocals), Neville Staples (vocals/percussion), Lynval Golding (b. 24 July 1951, Coventy, England; guitar), Roddy Radiation (b. Rodney Byers; guitar), Sir Horace Gentleman (b. Horace Panter; bass) and John Bradbury (drums). Following touring with the **Clash**, they set up their own multi-racial 2-Tone label and issued the **Prince Buster**-inspired 'Gangsters', which reached the UK Top 10. After signing their label to **Chrysalis Records**, the group abbreviated their name to the Specials. Their **Elvis Costello** produced debut album was a refreshing, exuberant effort which included the Top 10 single 'A Message To You, Rudi'. The group spearheaded what became the 2-Tone movement and their label enjoyed an array of sparkling hits from **Madness**, the **Beat** and the **Selecter**. In January 1980 the Specials were at their peak following the release of their live EP, *The Special AKA Live*. The pro-contraceptive title track, 'Too Much Too Young', propelled them to number 1 in the UK charts. Further Top 10 hits with 'Rat Race', 'Stereotype' and 'Do Nothing' followed. The Specials ability to 'capture the moment' in pop was most persuasively felt with 'Ghost

Town', which topped the charts during the summer of 1981 while Britain was suffering inner-city riots. At this new peak of success, the group fragmented. Staples, Hall and Golding went on to form the intriguing **Fun Boy Three**, leaving Dammers to continue with a new line-up, which reverted to the old name, the Special AKA. After the minor success of 'Racist Friend' and the anthemic Top 10 hit, 'Nelson Mandela', Dammers became more politically active with Artists Against Apartheid. He was also a major force behind the Nelson Mandela 70th Birthday Party concert at London's Wembley Stadium on 11 June 1988. The retitled 'Free Nelson Mandela (70th Birthday Remake)' was issued to coincide with the show. However, Dammers was reluctant to record again due to outstanding debts over the *In The Studio* album, which would have to be cleared before he was free of contract. In 1993, with the 2-Tone revival in evidence, **Desmond Dekker** joined Staples, Golding, Radiation and Gentleman on *King Of Kings*, released on the **Trojan Records** label. Dammers, meanwhile, had a new band, Jazz Odyssey, but he would soon retire to DJing and studio projects after he developed tinnitus.

Albums: as the Specials *The Specials* (2-Tone/Chrysalis 1979), *More Specials* (2-Tone/Chrysalis 1980), as the Special AKA *In The Studio* (2-Tone/Chrysalis 1984), with Desmond Dekker *King Of Kings* (Trojan 1993). Compilations: *Singles* (Chrysalis 1991), *The Selecter & The Specials: Live In Concert* (Windsong 1993).

Specialty Records

Formed in 1946 in Los Angeles, California, USA by **Art Rupe**, originally from Pittsburgh, Pennsylvania. Specialty Records gave rise to some of the most powerful early R&B and rock 'n' roll performers, particularly **Little Richard**. Rupe had briefly run the small-time label Juke Box Records and with money earned there launched Specialty. Among the label's first signing were blues singers **Percy Mayfield** and **Joe Liggins**. He also signed gospel artists including the **Soul Stirrers**. In 1952 Rupe expanded his artist roster beyond the west coast and signed New Orleans R&B singer **Lloyd Price**, who was the label's greatest success to that time with his number 1 R&B hit 'Lawdy Miss Clawdy'. Other New Orleans acts on Specialty included **Art Neville** and **Ernie K-Doe**. In 1955, Rupe signed **Little Richard** (Penniman), who became the label's greatest success and one of the pioneers of early rock 'n' roll. All of Little Richard's hits, including 'Tutti Frutti', 'Good Golly Miss Molly' and 'Lucille', were on the Specialty label. Other Specialty rock 'n' roll/R&B artists included **Larry Williams** and **Don And Dewey**. The label was wound down during the 60s, but later revived in the 80s by Beverly Rupe, daughter of Art, who launched a reissue campaign making much of the classic Specialty material available

again.
Album: *The Specialty Story Volume One* (1985).

Spector, Phil

b. Harvey Phillip Spector, 26 December 1940, Bronx, New York, USA. Arguably pop's most distinctive record producer. Spector became involved in music upon moving to Fairfax, California in 1953. While there, he joined a loosely-knit community of young aspirants, including **Lou Adler**, Bruce Johnson and **Sandy Nelson**, the last of whom played drums on Spector's debut recording, 'To Know Him Is To Love Him'. This million-selling single for the **Teddy Bears** - Spector, Annette Kleibard and Marshall Leib - topped the US chart in 1958, but further releases by the group proved less successful. The artist's next project, the Spectors Three, was undertaken under the aegis of local entrepreneurs **Lee Hazelwood** and Lester Sill, but when it too reaped little commercial rewards, the latter recommended Phil's talents to New York production team **Leiber And Stoller**. In later years Spector made extravagant claims about his work from this period which have been rebuffed equally forcibly by his one-time mentors. He did contribute greatly as a composer, co-writing 'Spanish Harlem' and 'Young Boy Blues' for **Ben E. King**, while adding a notable guitar obligato to the **Drifters**' 'On Broadway'. His productions, although less conspicuous, included releases by **LaVern Baker**, **Ruth Brown** and Billy Storm, as well as the Top Notes' original version of the seminal 'Twist And Shout'. Spector's first major success as a producer came with Ray Petersen's version of 'Corrina Corrina', a US Top 10 in 1960, and **Curtis Lee**'s 'Pretty Little Angel Eyes', which reached number 7 the following year. Work for the **Paris Sisters** not only engendered a Top 5 hit, ('I Love How You Love Me') but rekindled an association with Lester Sill, with whom Spector formed Philles Records in 1961.

Within months he bought his partner out to become sole owner; this autocratic behaviour would mark all subsequent endeavours. It nonetheless resulted in a string of classic recordings for the **Crystals** and **Ronettes** including 'He's A Rebel' (1962), 'Then He Kissed Me', 'Be My Baby' and 'Baby I Love You' (all 1963) which were not only substantial international hits, but defined the entire 'girl-group' genre. Imitative releases supervised by **David Gates**, **Bob Crewe** and **Sonny Bono**, although excellent in their own right, failed to recapture Spector's dense production technique, later dubbed the 'wall of sound', which relied on lavish orchestration, layers of percussion and swathes of echo. Recordings were undertaken at the Gold Star studio in Los Angeles where arranger **Jack Nitzsche** and engineer Larry Levine worked with a team of exemplary session musicians, including Tommy Tedeso (guitar), Larry Knechtal (piano, bass),

Harold Battiste, **Leon Russell** (keyboards) and **Hal Blaine** (drums). Although ostensibly geared to producing singles, Phil did undertake the ambitious *A Christmas Gift To You*, on which his label's premier acts performed old and new seasonal favourites. Although not a contemporary success - its bonhomie was made redundant following the assassination of President Kennedy - the set is now rightly regarded as a classic. Spector's releases also featured some of the era's finest songwriting teams - **Goffin And King**, **Barry And Greenwich** and **Barry Mann** and Cynthia Weil - the last of which composed 'You've Lost That Lovin' Feelin'' for the **Righteous Brothers**, the producer's stylistic apogee. Several critics also cite 'River Deep Mountain High', a 1966 single by **Ike And Tina Turner** as Spector's greatest moment. It represented Spector's most ambitious production, but although his efforts were rewarded with a UK Top 3 hit, this impressive release barely scraped the US Hot 100 and a dispirited Spector folded his label and retired from music for several years.

He re-emerged in 1969 with a series of releases for **A&M** which included 'Black Pearl' a US Top 20 hit entry for **Sonny Charles And The Checkmates**. Controversy then dogged his contribution to the **Beatles**' *Let It Be* album. Spector assembled the set from incomplete tapes, but his use of melancholic orchestration on 'The Long And Winding Road' infuriated the song's composer, **Paul McCartney**, who cited this intrusion during the group's rancorous break-up. Spector nonetheless became installed at their Apple label, where he produced albums by **John Lennon** (*The Plastic Ono Band*, *Imagine*, *Sometime In New York City*), **George Harrison** (*All Things Must Pass* and the commemorative *Concert For Bangla Desh*). However, his behaviour grew increasingly erratic following the break-up of his marriage to former Ronette **Ronnie Spector** and his relationship with Lennon was severed during sessions for the nostalgic *Rock 'N' Roll* album (1974). In the meantime Phil had established the Warner-Spector outlet which undertook new recordings with, among others, **Cher** and **Nilsson**, as well as several judicious re-releases. A similar relationship with UK **Polydor** led to the formation of Phil Spector International, on which contemporary singles by **Dion**, **Darlene Love** and Jerri Bo Keno vied with 60s' recordings and archive material. As the 70s progressed so Spector became a recluse, although he emerged to produce albums by **Leonard Cohen** (*Death Of Ladies Man* - 1977) and the **Ramones** (*End Of The Century* - 1980), the latter of which included a revival of 'Baby I Love You', the group's sole UK Top 10 hit. Despite undertaking abortive sessions with the **Flamin' Groovies**, Phil remained largely detached from music throughout the 80s, although litigation against Leiber and Stoller and biographer Mark Ribowsky kept his name in the news. Spector was inducted into the Rock 'n' Roll Hall Of Fame in 1989, and having adopted **Allen Klein** as representative, completed negotiations with **EMI** for the rights to his extensive catalogue. The interest generated by this acquisition is a tribute to the respect afforded this producer whose major achievements were contained within a brief, three-year, period.

Compilations: *A Christmas Gift To You* (1963), *Phil Spector Wall Of Sound, Volume 1: The Ronettes* (1975), *Phil Spector Wall Of Sound, Volume 2: Bob B. Soxx And The Blue Jeans* (1975), *Phil Spector Wall Of Sound, Volume 3: The Crystals* (1975), *Phil Spector Wall Of Sound, Volume 4: Yesterday's Hits Today* (1976), *Phil Spector Wall Of Sound, Volume 5: Rare Masters* (1976), *Phil Spector Wall Of Sound, Volume 6: Rare Masters Volume 2* (1976), *The Phil Spector Story* (1976), *Echoes Of The Sixties* (1977), *Phil Spector 1974-1979* (1979), *Wall Of Sound* (1981), *Phil Spector: The Early Productions 1958-1961* (1984), *Twist And Shout: Twelve Atlantic Tracks Produced By Phil Spector* (1989), *Back To Mono* (CD box set, 1991).

Further reading: *The Phil Spector Story: Out Of His Head*, Williams, Richard (1972), *The Phil Spector Story*, Finnis, Rob (1974), *He's A Rebel*, Ribowskys, Mark (1989), *Collecting Phil Spector: The Man, The Legend, The Music*, Fitzpatrick, Jack & Fogerty, James E. (1991).

Spector, Ronnie

b. Veronica Bennett, 10 August 1943, New York, USA. The distinctive lead singer in the **Ronettes** first embarked on a solo career in 1964 with two low-key singles credited to 'Veronica'. Her marriage to her producer, **Phil Spector**, effectively forestalled Ronnie's career and a three-year hiatus followed her group's 1966 offering, 'I Can Hear Music'. 'Try Some Buy Some', a then-unreleased **George Harrison** song, marked the recording debut of 'Ronnie Spector' in 1971. By this point her marriage was crumbling and the ensuing divorce allowed Ronnie to pursue the career her erstwhile husband struggled to deny her. She put together a new Ronettes with Denise Edwards and Chip Fields and began recording for the **Buddah** label in 1973. Ronnie subsequently spent much of the 70s working in New York's clubs. During the latter part of the decade she made several appearances backed by **Southside Johnny And The Asbury Dukes**, while a 'comeback' single, 'Say Goodbye To Hollywood' was written by **Billy Joel** and produced by **Bruce Springsteen** and **'Miami' Steven Van Zandt**. Despite such pedigree, the record failed to ignite Ronnie's career and her later work has been marred by inconsistency.

Albums: *Siren* (1980), *Unfinished Business* (1987).

Further reading: *Be My Baby*, Ronnie Spector with Vince Waldron.

Spectrum

Formed in Melbourne, Australia in 1969, Spectrum

have often been compared in style to England's early 70s 'Canterbury' scene groups such as the **Soft Machine** and **Egg**, and later traces of an influence by **Traffic** could be detected. Performing in concert rather that at the traditional dances and clubs, Spectrum catered to the indigenous 'stoned' audience. The band was formed in Melbourne in 1969 and was based around the nucleus of writer **Mike Rudd** (guitar/vocals) and Bill Putt (bass), alongside Lee Neale (keyboards) and Mark Kennedy (drums, later replaced by Ray Arnott in 1970). Its music consisted of long instrumentals and jams with obtuse lyrics. Rudd's anthem 'I'll Be Gone', the band's only charting single, was lifted from its second album which contained the band's most important work. The band was one of the mainstays of the annual outdoor rock festival at Sunbury, near Melbourne. Its latter recordings were live renditions of previous material. The band had an alter-ego, **Murtceps**, which catered for the dance market and provided the money for Spectrum's more esoteric musings. After breaking-up in 1973, the band reform occasionally for live gigs despite the archaic material. Rudd and Putt have continued to perform and occasionally record with various other groups since the demise of Spectrum in 1973.
Albums: *Spectrum Part 1* (1971), *Miles Ago* (1972), *Terminal Buzz* (1973). Compilation: with the Murtceps *Testimonial* (1973).

Spedding, Chris

b. 17 June 1944, Sheffield, Yorkshire, England. An underestimated talent, this inventive guitarist began his career in a beat group, the Vulcans, prior to following a haphazard path touring in country bands and supporting cabaret attractions on the cruise ship Himalaya. Spells backing **Alan Price** and **Paul Jones** preceded Spedding's involvement in the **Battered Ornaments** where he established a reputation for technique and imagination. The guitarist was subsequently heard on **Jack Bruce**'s *Songs For A Tailor*, and on early releases by **Nucleus**, a leading jazz-rock ensemble. Session work for **Lulu**, **John Cale**, **Dusty Springfield** and others was interspersed by two low-key solo albums, *Backward Progression* and *The Only Lick I Know*. Spedding also formed the much-touted Sharks with former **Free** bassist **Andy Fraser**, but internal ructions undermined the group's potential. The guitarist resumed studio work in 1975, but also joined **Roy Harper** in Trigger, the singer's short-lived backing band. Spedding's clinical approach resulted in several career-based anomalies. He donned the requisite costume to perform with the **Wombles** and contrived an ill-fitting leather-boy image for a series of pop punk singles under the guidance of producer **Mickie Most**. 'Motor-Biking', in 1975, provided the UK Top 20 single the guitarist doubtlessly deserved, but these unusual interludes have discoloured perception of his other work.
Albums: *Backward Progression* (1971), *The Only Lick I Know* (1972), *Chris Spedding* (1976), *Hurt* (1977), *Guitar Graffiti* (1978), *I'm Not Like Everybody Else* (1980), *Friday The 13th* (1981), *Enemy Within* (1986), *Mean And Moody* (1993). Compilations: *Motorbikin': The Best Of Chris Spedding* (1991), *Just Plug Him In!* (1991)
Films: *Give My Regards To Broad Street* (1985).

Speedway Boulevard

This short-lived US group featured a *pot-pourri* of musical styles. Formed in 1979, the band comprised Ray Herring (vocals/piano), Gregg Hoffman (guitar/vocals), Jordan Rudes (keyboards), Dennis Feldman (bass/vocals) and Glenn Dove (drums). They signed to **Epic Records** and debuted in 1980 with a self-titled album that defied simple categorization. It featured a solid foundation of heavy-duty symphonic rock, modified by blues, funk, soul and Carribbean influences. In places, it courted comparisons with **Led Zeppelin**'s more experimental phases. Sadly, the band broke up before their true potential could be realized. Feldman went on to play with **Balance** and later **Michael Bolton**. Rudes guested on **Vinnie Moore**'s *Time Odyssey*.
Album: *Speedway Boulevard* (Epic 1980).

Speedy J

b. Jochem Paap, c.1969, Rotterdam, The Netherlands. Speedy J is a successful solo artist who started DJing in the early 80s and earned his nickname through his fast mixing and scratching technique. After picking up the house bug from America, he began to extend his musical set-up with drum machines and synthesizers and made the evolutionary leap to recording artist. His first efforts, 'Lift Off' and 'Take Me There', were released on a 12-inch compilation on **Hithouse** Records. Afterwards he hooked up with Detroit label **Plus 8** for the *Intercontinental* EP. Between this and a second EP for the label, *Evolution*, he also recorded a 12-inch for **R&S** (as Tune), and worked with Holland label Stealth. A track on the Plus 8 compilation *From Our Minds To Yours Volume 1*, 'Pullover', might have proved just another footnote had it not been picked up in the clubs and given subsequent release by Music Man. It eventually went Top 40 in several territories. A third Plus 8 EP, *Rise*, featured another big club hit in the live track, 'Something For Your Mind'. However, he was beginning to become stereotyped as a conventional, basic house operator, where his vision was originally broader. Consequently he developed the Public Energy pseudonym for such hard house material, from thence forward recording more divergent, experimental work as Speedy J. He was largely quiet during recording sessions for his debut album, aside from remixes for the **Shamen** and **Björk**. When 'Pepper', the album's promotional single

emerged it was housed on **Warp**, except for Benelux territories where Paap invoked his own Beam Me Up! label in association with Gijs Vroom (Vroom and Beyond) and Rene Van Der Weyde (TFX, Atlantic Ocean's 'Waterfall', etc.), and on Plus 8 in the US and Canada. Other releases on Beam Me Up! include Resonant Interval's 'Memory'. Paap also records as Country And Western. This moniker was utilised to house the first 'Positive Energy' release, which was originally a dancefloor hit for Speedy J on the Canadian techno label, **Plus 8**. It was remixed under this title with the aid of Effective's Simon Hannon and Lawrence Nelson. Paap went on to remix for **Killing Joke** in continuance of his hectic career.
Album: *Intrusion* (Warp 1993).

Spellbinders

An R&B vocal group from Jersey City, New Jersey, USA. Members were Bob Shivers, Jimmy Wright, Ben Grant, McArthur Munford, and Elouise Pennington. The Spellbinders delighted audiences in the mid-60s with a series of hits that epitomized the soft-soul vocal group sound of the era. Their first and biggest national hit, 'For You' (number 23 R&B) is a sublime piece of work written, arranged, and produced by **Van McCoy**, as was their only album, *The Magic Of The Spellbinders*. Two other chart hits followed in 1966, namely 'Chain Reaction' (number 36 R&B), which was a mediocre **Temptations** sound, and 'We're Acting Like Lovers' (number 27 R&B), a delightful mid-tempo number and the group's second most impressive achievement. The Spellbinders' last single before breaking up was a 1967 remake of the **Skyliners**' hit, 'Since I Don't Have You'.
Album: *The Magic Of The Spellbinders* (Columbia 1966).

Spellbound

This Swedish metal quintet was assembled in 1984 by Hans Froberg (vocals), J.J.Marsh (guitar), Al Strandberg (guitar/keyboards), Thompson (bass) and Ola Strandberg (drums), marking their debut with a track on Sonet's *Swedish Metal* compilation. This led to a full contract with Sonet, with the band delivering *Breaking The Spell* in 1984. Their style, based on an amalgam of **Van Halen**, **Led Zeppelin** and **Europe**, was given some degree of distinction by Froberg's powerful vocals. *Rockin' Reckless* followed, a virtual carbon copy of their debut, and suggested that the band were running out of ideas after just one album. Their association with Sonet ended in 1987, and nothing has been heard from them since.
Albums: *Breaking The Spell* (Sonet 1984), *Rockin' Reckless* (Sonet 1986).

Spellman, Benny

b. 11 December 1931, Pensacola, Florida, USA. Although a minor hit by chart standards, Benny Spellman's 'Lipstick Traces (On A Cigarette)' is one of the most fondly recalled New Orleans R&B hits of the early 60s and was subsequently revived by the **O'Jays**. It's b-side, 'Fortune Teller', impressed the young **Rolling Stones** enough for them to cover it. Spellman won a talent contest at college and, after a stint in the army, went professional, joining **Huey Smith And The Clowns** in New Orleans. In 1959, Spellman was signed to Minit Records but had little luck with his first few releases. To make ends meet he took jobs as a background studio vocalist, appearing on **Ernie K-Doe**'s 'Mother-In-Law', among others. Spellman's two-sided hit came in 1962, both songs having been penned by famed producer/writer **Allen Toussaint**. Benny was unable to follow with further hits and left music in 1968. He returned to the profession in the late 80s, appearing locally in New Orleans, but prior to that made his living in the 70s as a public relations executive for Miller Beer. He never recorded an album, although the singles sessions have been compiled.
Album: *Calling All Cars* (1984), *Fortune Teller* (1988).

Spencer, John B.

b. 1942, London, England. A highly praised songwriter in the rock tradition, Spencer has yet to achieve commercial success. He worked in book publishing before playing solo gigs at colleges and folk clubs during the early 70s. In 1974 he formed John Spencer's Louts with multi-instrumentalist Johnny G (John Gotting) and keyboards player Chas Ambler. Spencer himself played lead guitar. Performing his wry, literate and passionate compositions such as 'Mary Lou And The Sunshine Boy' and 'Bye Bye 69', the Louts built up a following on the London pub and club circuit. Recording contracts were signed and broken by three labels before **Beggar's Banquet** issued the group's only album. Spencer's evocative, gravelly voice and the quality of his lyrics brought favourable reviews but poor sales. Soon afterwards the Louts disbanded with Gotting and Ambler pursuing other projects. Spencer formed Spencer's Alternative with ex-**Gryphon** members Graeme Taylor (guitar) and Malcolm Bennett (bass). This group released 'Mumbo Jumbo' (1980) but was not heard to full effect on record until Dutch label Any Time issued *Out With A Bang*. In the meantime, Spencer's 'Cruisin'' had been a Swedish hit for Jerry Williams and had been covered by Texan artist **Augie Meyers**.
With Taylor the only survivor from the original line-up of his group, Spencer recorded the tougher-sounding *Break And Entry* which was issued by Irish-based Round Tower Records. The same label reissued all Spencer's earlier recordings in 1991 when John Spencer himself produced an album of cover versions of his own songs featuring **Martin Simpson** and **Danny Thompson**. Spencer is also a fiction writer, having published *The Electric Lullabye Meat Market* (1974), *A Case For Charlie*

(1978) and *Charlie Gets The Picture* (1979).
Albums: *The Last LP* (1978), *Out With A Bang* (1985), *Break And Entry* (1990), *Parlour Games* (1991), *Blue Smarties* (1991), *Judas And The Obscure* (1991), *Sunday Best* (1991).

Spencer's, John, Blues Explosion

Guitarist/vocalist Jon Spencer was the founding member and guiding force behind **Pussy Galore**, one of the most controversial acts to emerge from the US hardcore scene of the 1980s. Tiring of this stance - "If the whole thing is about 'Fuck you', there is just no hope" - Spencer formed temporary attachments with a variety of groups, including Boss Hogg, which featured ex-Pussy Galore foil Cristina Martinez, the Gibson Brothers and the Honeymoon Killers. The last-named band enjoyed a similar, if more restrained, trash culture fixation as Spencer's former vehicle, and their drummer, Russell Simmins was the first recruit for Blues Explosion. Eschewing a bassist, Spencer opted for a second guitarist, Judah Bauer, making verbal reference to the style of **Hound Dog Taylor**'s band. The trio's debut single, 'Son Of Sam', issued in 1992, was followed by a 'bootleg' album, *A Reverse Willie Horton*. Their self-titled official first LP appeared soon afterwards, but both it and *Extra Width* showed intriguing promise rather than realisation. *Orange*, however, is a fully-defined masterpiece, blending blues and soul, theremin and late 60s rock riffs. It confirms the group's position as one of the leading acts to emerge from the US independent scene of the 90s.
Albums: *A Reverse Willie Horton* (1992), *Jon Spencer's Blues Explosion* (1992), *Extra Width* (1993), *Orange* (1994).

Spencer, Tim

b. Vernon Spencer, 13 July 1908, Webb City, Missouri, USA, d. 26 April 1974, Apple Valley, California, USA. An important member of the **Sons Of The Pioneers**. The large Spencer family relocated as homesteaders to New Mexico in 1913, which initiated his love for the West. In 1921, a difference of opinion with his father about the purchase of a banjo ukulele on credit without permission, saw the 13-year-old leave home and find work in Texas until his father fetched him home to finish his education. After leaving school, he worked in the mines until an accident left him hospitalized with a cracked vertebra. Unable to return to the mines, he began singing in local venues. A yearning to be in western films saw him relocate to his brother Glenn's home in Los Angeles, where he took a daytime job in Safeway's warehouse and sought musical work in the evenings. He sang and yodelled with Leonard Slye (**Roy Rogers**) and Bob Nicholls as a replacement for **Bob Nolan** in the Rocky Mountaineers and later in the International Cowboys. In 1934, he and Slye were rejoined by Nolan to become the Pioneer Trio which eventually became the Sons Of The Pioneers. Spencer, who had not written songs previously, like Nolan, soon

began to contribute many of the group's most successful numbers. His own songs include 'The Everlasting Hills Of Oklahoma', 'Gold Star Mother With Silvery Hair', 'Room Full Of Roses' and the comedy standard 'Cigareetes, Whuskey And Wild Women'. He also co-wrote with brother Glenn and with Nolan. In late 1936, he left after a difference of opinion but returned in 1938, by which time Rogers had been replaced by **Lloyd Perryman**. Owing to voice problems, he retired from performing in 1949 (finding his own replacement, **Ken Curtis**) but acted as the group's manager for several years. After finally leaving the Pioneers, he ran his own gospel publishing company, Manna Music, until illness forced him to hand over to his son, Hal.

Spice I

b. Byron, Texas, USA. Part of the new wave of Oakland rappers., Spice I was discovered by his neighbourhood's most imposing figure, **Too Short**. Though he was born in Texas, he was raised in Hayward, before spending the final years of his adolesence in Oakland. A second album, *187 He Wrote*, contained plenty of the funky beats for which that area is renowned. This was gangsta rap in its most primal form, including cuts like 'I'm The Fuckin' Murderer', and the single, 'Dumpin' 'Em In Ditches'. Despite its simplistic formula, the album proved a runaway success. going from number 97 to number 1 in *Billboard*'s R&B chart in one week.
Album: *Spice I* (Jive 1992), *187 He Wrote* (Jive 1993).

Spice Trade

Taking their musical starting point as 'Newgrass', an American term for the cross-fertilisation of folk and bluegrass styles in an improvisational, free-flowing hybrid, UK's Spice Trade are built around former cajun swinger Chris Haigh (ex-**Zumzeaux**; fiddle). He has been joined in this new venture by several staples of the folk and jazz scene; Frank Kilkelly (also Companions Of The Rosy House; rhythm guitar), Rick Bolton (ex-Mike Westbrook and The Happy End; lead guitar), and Dudley Phillips (ex-**June Tabor**, **Mary Coughlan**, **Womaks**, **John Etheridge**; double bass). The band's first appearance outside of London came with the 1992 Shetland Folk Festival, and the heated critical reception afforded them there looks set to continue as they tour the mainland prior to their debut LP release.

Spider (UK)

This British boogie group was formed on Merseyside in 1976 by the Burrows brothers. The band comprised bassist/vocalist Brian Burrows, drummer Rob E. Burrows and guitarists Sniffa and Col Harkness. After incessant gigging around the north west, they relocated to London and were eventually signed by **RCA**

Records in 1983. They debuted with *Rock 'N' Roll Gypsies*, a fuel-injected collection of boogie-based rockers, identical in almost every respect to the style of **Status Quo**. From then on, they were regarded as a poor-man's 'Quo. The album sold miserably and RCA dropped them. Picked up by **A&M Records**, they released *Rough Justice*, a semi-concept affair concerning a courtroom trial. Spider were the defendants, being accused of playing heavy metal rock 'n' roll. Another flop, it left the band without a label once more. Undaunted they plodded on, with Stu Harwood replacing Sniffa on guitar in 1986. Moving to the Mausoleum label, they produced *Raise The Banner* the same year. Musically they had not progressed, and the market for low-tech, three-chord boogie proved an ever contracting one. Out-dated, and out of luck, they broke up shortly after the album was released. Brian Burrows is now a cartoonist and record sleeve designer.
Albums: *Rock 'N' Roll Gypsies* (RCA 1983), *Rough Justice* (A&M 1984), *Raise The Banner* (Mausoleum 1986).

Spider (USA)

Prior to the formation of Spider in New York during 1978, Amanda Blue (vocals), Keith Lentin (guitar) and Anton Fig (drums) had worked together six years previously in the South African based Hammak. Adding keyboardist Holly Knight and ex-**Riff Raff** bassist Jimmy Lowell, they soon negotiated a contract with the Dreamland label. This was made possible by **Ace Frehley**'s (**Kiss** guitarist) recommendation, following Anton Fig's appearance on the guitarist's solo album. Specializing in commercial American rock, with pop-rock overtones, they released two classy albums and scored minor US single successes with 'New Romance' and 'Better Be Good To Me'. They changed name to **Shanghai** in 1982 to avoid confusion with the British group of the same name.
Albums: *Spider* (Dreamland 1980), *Between The Lines* (Dreamland 1981).

Spiders

An R&B vocal group from New Orleans, Louisiana, USA. Members were lead Hayward 'Chuck' Carbo, first tenor Joe Maxon, baritone Matthew 'Mac' West, bass Oliver Howard, and bass/alternate lead Leonard 'Chick' Carbo. The Spiders brought a unique bluesy sound and added the lilting swing of their New Orleans heritage to create a one-of-a-kind style of 50s vocal harmony. The group began in the mid-40s singing gospel as the Zion Harmonizers. In 1953 they were still singing gospel when they were discovered by recording studio owner **Cosimo Matassa**. Under his encouragement they revamped themselves as a R&B group under the name Spiders. The group had three sizable R&B hits on the charts during their first year, 1954, namely the syncopated 'I Didn't Want To Do It' (number 3 R&B), the bluesy 'You're The One' (number

8 R&B), and the swinging 'I'm Slippin' In' (number 6 R&B). Maxon and West had both left by 1955, and were replaced with new members tenor Bill Moore and baritone Issacher Gordon. The new line-up hit the charts with 'Twenty One' (number 9 R&B) and one of their most superb records, the bouncy 'Witchcraft' (number 5 R&B). The group split in 1956, and the Carbo brothers worked to establish solo careers. Chuck Carbo was the more successful brother, recording many singles and albums *Life's Ups And Downs* (504 1989) and *Drawers Trouble* (Rounder 1993).
Compilations: *I Didn't Want To Do It* (Imperial 1961), *The Imperial Sessions* (Bear Family 1992).

Spikes Brothers

Benjamin J. 'Reb' and John Spikes were musical entrepreneurs who combined a fine sense of musical fashion with a sharp nose for business. They had their own musical touring shows in the early years of the century, working mostly in the American west. Amongst the performers who worked for them were blues singer Hattie McDaniel, later to become the first black artist to win an Oscar for her performance in *Gone With The Wind* (1939), and **Jelly Roll Morton**. The brothers settled in California before the 20s, establishing a flourishing band-contracting business and also operating a a band agency, a music store and a recording company. Amongst the musicians who played in their Los Angeles-based bands were **Les Hite**, **Lionel Hampton**, William Woodman Snr. and George Orendorff. In 1922 the brothers recorded **Edward 'Kid' Ory**'s band, using the name Spike's Seven Pods Of Pepper, which thus became the first black jazz group to record. The brothers' own band made a handful of records, some in 1924 and others three years later. The brothers expanded into music publishing, and were themselves responsible for writing lyrics to some early jazz standards, including 'Froggie Moore' and 'Wolverine Blues'. They also wrote words and music for 'Someday Sweetheart', a song which enjoyed long and lucrative popularity. By the end of the 20s the Spikes brothers were wealthy men with their interests now extending into restaurant ownership, while John was also busy as an arranger and music teacher. By the mid-30s John Spikes was forced into premature retirement through failing sight, although he continued to write music. Reb stayed in the business for many more years, working as a promoter and talent scout.

Spillane, Davy

A founding member of **Moving Hearts**, Spillane has stamped his own identity onto the music he plays. *Atlantic Bridge* was an album of crossover material, in parts fusing folk and country themes. The musicians on the recording included **Bela Fleck**, **Albert Lee**, **Jerry Douglas**, and **Christy Moore** among others.

For *Out Of The Air*, he had formed the Davy Spillane Band comprising Anthony Drennan (guitar), James Delaney (keyboards), Paul Moran (drums/percussion), and Tony Molloy (bass), as well as himself on Uilleann pipes and whistle. **Rory Gallagher** guested on a number of tracks on the album, including 'One For Phil', a tribute to **Phil Lynott**, written by Spillane and Gallagher. Currently, Spillane and the band are touring and the line-up now includes Greg Boland (guitar), Eoghan O'Neill (bass), as well as Delaney, Moran and Spillane, the others having left.

Albums: *Atlantic Bridge* (1987), *Out Of The Air* (1988), *Shadow Hunter* (1990), *Pipedreams* (1991), with Andy Irvine *East Wind* (1992), *A Place Among The Stones* (Columbia 1994).

Spin

Formed in the UK during the summer of 1989 by Lee Clark (b. 20 January 1963, Cleethorpes, England; vocals), Steve Mason (b. 17 April 1971, Pontypridd, Wales; bass), John Mason (b. 8 August 1967, Bristol, England) and Matt James (b. 20 September 1967, Deptford, London, England). Spin emerged from the ashes of the Go-Hole to claim a place in the legendary Camberwell squat scene in south London. Their first EP, released in the autumn of 1990, was a comfortably contemporary blend of guitars and danceable beats which put Spin in vogue alongside the successes of the Manchester 'Baggy' movement (a phrase culled from the bands' predilection for flared trousers). The quartet's career continued smoothly into 1991 until their first British tour at the end of March, when the tour van - broken down on the hard shoulder of the motorway - was hit by an articulated lorry. Three members of the Spin entourage were hospitalized in intensive care, with bassist John Mason still insufficiently recovered six months later and thus temporarily replaced by Kev Miles. Vocalist Lee Clark meanwhile, ironically the only person not injured in the accident, moved to Paris to become a poet and vowed to never travel by transit again. His post was filled by Martin T. Falls (b. 15 May 1970, Cardiff, Wales) whereupon Spin proved their resoluteness by completing and subsequently releasing their debut album to sympathetic acclaim.

Album: *In Motion* (Foundation 1991).

Spin Doctors

This four-piece group came together in 1989 when vocalist Christopher Barron and guitarist Eric Schenkman met drummer Aaron Comess at the New School of Jazz in New York. With the line-up completed by bassist Mark White, the band signed a record deal the following year. *Pocket Full Of Kryptonite* was a varied collection of well-crafted, tuneful rock songs flavoured with funk rhythms and witty, intelligent lyrics, and displayed the band's considerable musical ability, playing in a wide range of styles from the light, jazzy feel of the more balladic numbers to hard funk reminiscent of the **Red Hot Chili Peppers**, with almost nonchalant ease, while retaining a recognisable sound of their own. Undeterred by the album's lack of initial success, the Spin Doctors took to the road in the US, touring to the point of physical and financial exhaustion. When a Vermont radio station began to plug the album heavily, others soon followed, and the band's popularity spiralled upwards. *Pocket Full Of Kryptonite* became a major hit, producing a US Top 10 single in 'Little Miss Can't Be Wrong', despite the small storm caused by the track's opening line, 'Been a whole lot easier since the bitch left town' (the lyric was in fact aimed satirically at Barron's former step-mother rather than an exercise in rock misogyny). A live set, *Homebelly Groove*, was released to satisfy the new demand. By this time, comparisons were being drawn between the rise of the Spin Doctors and that of **Nirvana**, both being the people's choice, but the band simply stayed on the road, maintaining their impressive live reputation, while another single, 'Two Princes', led to worldwide success. However, late 1994 saw their first major setback, when news filtered through that guitarist Eric Shenkman had been ousted in favour of Anthony Krizan (b. New Jersey, USA). *Turn It Upside Down* was but a pale shadow of the multi-million selling *Pocket Full Of Kryptonite*. There were a few highlights ('Cleopatra's Cat, 'Mary Jane' and 'You Let Your Heart Go Too Fast') and maybe the band were pressured to follow-up quickly. After such a superb debut it was a bitter disappointment and would-be purchasers stayed away in their millions.

Albums: *Pocket Full Of Kryptonite* (Epic 1991), *Homebelly Groove* (Epic 1992), *Turn It Upside Down* (Epic 1994).

Spinal Tap

The concept for Spinal Tap - a satire of a fading British heavy metal band - was first aired in a late 70s' television sketch. Christopher Guest, formerly of parody troupe *National Lampoon*, played the part of lead guitarist Nigel Tufnell, while Harry Shearer (bassist Derek Smalls) and actor Michael McKean (vocalist David St. Hubbins) had performed with the Credibility Gap. Their initial sketch also featured **Loudon Wainwright** and drummer Russ Kunkel, but these true-life musicians dropped out of the project on its transformation to full-length film. *This Is Spinal Tap*, released in 1984, was not a cinematic success, but it has since become highly popular through the medium of video. Its portrayal of a doomed US tour is ruthless, exposing incompetence, megalomania and sheer madness, but in a manner combining humour with affection. However, rather than incurring the wrath of the rock fraternity, the film has been lauded by musicians, many of whom, unfathomably, claim inspiration for individual scenes. The contemporary

UK comedy team, the Comic Strip, used elements of Spinal Tap's theme in their second film, *More Bad News*. Spinal Tap reunited as a 'real' group and undertook an extensive tour in 1992 to promote *Break Like The Wind*, which featured guest appearances by **Jeff Beck**, **Nicky Hopkins** and Slash (**Guns N'Roses**). At this stage it seems Spinal Tap's jokes at metal's expense are too deep rooted in truth to ever wear thin.

Albums: *This Is Spinal Tap* (Polydor 1984), *Break Like The Wind* (MCA 1992).

Video: *This Is Spinal Tap* (1989).

Further reading: *Inside Spinal Tap*, Peter Occhiogrosso.

Spinners (UK)

This popular folk group was formed in 1958 with the following line-up: Tony Davis (b. 24 August 1930, Blackburn Lancashire, England; banjo/tin whistle/guitar/kazoo), Mick Groves (b. 29 September 1936, Salford. Lancashire, England; guitar), Hughie Jones (b. Hugh E. Jones 21 July 1936, Liverpool, England, guitar/harmonica/banjo) and Cliff Hall (b. 11 September 1925, Oriente Pourice, Cuba, guitar/harmonica). Hall was born to Jamaican parents who returned to Jamaica in 1939. He came to England after joining the Royal Air Force in 1942. The group was often augmented in concert by 'Count' John McCormick (double bass), who is generally regarded as the fifth 'Spinner'. Occasionally rebuked by folk 'purists' as bland and middle-of-the-road, the Spinners nevertheless brought many people into folk music. The regular sell-out attendances at their concerts are a testimony to this. Songs that are now covered by other performers and often mistakenly referred to as 'traditional' are in fact Hughie Jones originals: 'The Ellan Vannin Tragedy', 'The Marco Polo' and 'The Fairlie Duplex Engine'. In 1990, Hughie Jones produced *Hughie's Ditty-Bag*, a book of songs and stories. He is still performing occasionally as a soloist. After a 30 year career, the Spinners decided to call it a day, and released the double album *Final Fling*. Since retiring, the group have made a number of re-union tours, proving that both their interest, and the public's enthusiasm, have not waned.

Albums: *Quayside Songs Old And New* (1962), *The Spinners* (1963), *Folk At The Phil* (1964), *More Folk At The Phil* (1965), *The Family Of Man* (1966), *Another LP By The Spinners* (1967), *The Spinners Clockwork Storybook* (1969), *Not Quite Folk* (1969), *The Spinners Are In Town* (1970), *Love Is Teasing* (1972), *Sing Out, Shout With Joy* (1972), *By Arrangement* (1973), *The Spinners At The London Palladium* (1974), *The Spinners English Collection* (1976), *All Day Singing* (1977), *Songs Of The Tall Ships* (1978), *Your 20 Favourite Christmas Carols* (1978), *Around The World And Back Again* (1981), *Here's To You...From The Spinners* (1982), *Final Fling* (1988), *Hughie's Ditty Bag* (1991). Compilations: *Meet The Spinners* (1981), *18 Golden Favourites* (1982), *This Is The Spinners* (1982), *20 Golden*

Folk Songs (1984), *The Singing City* (1984).

Further reading: *The Spinners*, David Stuckey.

Spinners (USA)
(see **(Detroit) Spinners**)

Spinout

'Singing-swinging-racing-romancing-hitting the curves with no brakes on the excitement,' proclaimed the publicity machine about this 1966 **Elvis Presley** film. If only. In truth *Spinout* (UK title *California Holiday*) was another sub-standard, routine feature in which the singer played a bandleader and sports-car driver trying to avoid the attentions of four star-struck admirers. As if to confirm the unadventurous nature plaguing Presley's films, singer **Shelley Fabares** made yet another appearance as his co-star. Nine largely unremarkable tracks were recorded for the soundtrack, but the resultant album was bolstered by three numbers not featured in the film. The best of these was a haunting version of **Bob Dylan**'s 'Tomorrow Is A Long Time', the inclusion of which suggested that Presley was not immune from the changes occurring in contemporary pop. It is an awareness that could not be gleaned from the meagre fare offered in this feature.

Spiral Starecase

Formed c.1963 in Sacramento, California, USA, Spiral Starecase consisted of Pat Upton (lead singer/guitarist), Harvey Kaye (keyboardist), Dick Lopez (saxophonist), Bobby Raymond (bassist) and Vinny Parello (drums). The band was discovered in 1969 by **Sonny Knight** ('Confidential') while working in Las Vegas, and introduced by him to **Columbia Records**. After one flop single, they recorded Upton's 'More Today Than Yesterday', an upbeat soul tune with prominent horn backing in the **Chicago** style. It made number 12 in the US charts and the group released an album which also charted. Follow-up singles did not fare as well, however, and the group disappeared from the national scene by the dawn of the 70s.

Album: *More Today Than Yesterday* (1969).

Spiral Tribe

At the forefront of alternative culture and its attempts to embrace the new sounds of the 90s, Spiral Tribe will probably never leave their crusty-techno reputation far behind. Not that it would seem to unduly worry them. As part of the free festival movement, members have personal injunctions against them in most parts of England. Indeed, they headed to Europe in mid-1993 where legislation against travelling musicians is much more relaxed. They see music as a fluid, evolving medium, going to the extent of sampling the sound of their parties and feeding it back into the mix - thereby giving the audience an active role in proceedings. They came to the attention of the populace at large, *Sun*

readers notwithstanding, by staging two huge outdoor raves: the first at Castlemorton, the second at Canary Wharf. Their first single, 'Breach Of The Peace', arrived in August 1992, followed by 'Forward The Revolution' in November. They were helped in no small part by the financial assistance of Jazz Summers, former manager of **Wham!** and **Yazz**. A debut album, *Tecno Terra*, was recorded during commital proceedings at Malvern Magistrates Court concerning the Castlemorton affair - one of the most notorious live music events of recent years, and one which saw any number of media reports bearing false witness to what really happened. Via draconian legal rulings Spiral Tribe were forced to stay within 10 miles of the court, and managed to squat a deserted farmhouse where they could record. The resulting album was perhaps a less worthy cause than the plight of travelling sound systems themselves, especially where it embodied the cod-mysticism of 'chaos theory' (ie references to the number 23). Elsewhere Spiral Tribe's philosophy is well worth investigating: 'If industrialisation had to happen in order for us to get Technics desks and Akai samplers, so be it - in the same way that the blues grew out of the pain and suffering of the slaves that built the American railways'. Their membership is fluid, numbering about fifteen DJ's and musicians at any given time.
Album: *Tecno-Terra* (1993).

Spirea X

In 1988, tired of touring incessantly, Jim Beattie (vocals/guitar) left **Primal Scream** and moved back to Glasgow. Recharged, he formed Spirea X in the summer of 1990, their name taken from a Primal Scream b-side. He had been instrumental in Primal Scream's 'jangly' period, writing the classic 'Velocity Crescent', and he would continue to share Gillespie's nonchalant arrogance: 'We're going to do it. . . by having better songs, better melodies, better arrangements, better everything. By sheer force of ideas'. After a demo in July 1990, which attracted interest almost across the board, they played their first live gig in September at Queen Margaret Student Union. Despite heated competition to get Beattie's signature he eventually settled for the independent label **4AD Records**. The band quickly lost their original bass player and guitarist, and by May 1991 featured Andy Kerr (drums), Judith Boyle (Beattie's girlfriend, vocals/guitar), Jamie O'Donnell (bass) and Thomas McGurk (rhythm guitar). Two well received EPs followed, *Chlorine Dream* and *Speed Reaction*, before a debut album titled after a collection of Rimbaud's poetry. Here Beattie's grasp of melody and a fixation with **Byrds**-styled harmonies was allowed full rein, resulting in a mesmerising selection. The set also included an enthralling rendition of **Love**'s 'Signed D.C.'. Alas *Fireblade Skies* was not a commercial success and the group - now reduced to a duo of Beattie and

Boyle was dropped by their label in 1993.
Album: *Fireblade Skies* (4AD 1991).

Spires, Arthur 'Big Boy'

b. 6 November 1912, Yazoo City, Mississippi, USA. One of eight children in a family that, save for his uncle Robert, was unmusical, Spires remembers watching **Henry Stuckey** perform around his hometown. Teaching himself guitar in his late teens, he accompanied **Lightnin' Hopkins** when the latter made forays into Mississippi in the early 40s, playing in Yazoo City's Beer Garden. Spires moved to Chicago in 1943, studied guitar with Eddie El, and played in a group with El and fellow guitarist Earl Dranes. In 1952 the group submitted demos to Leonard Chess, who made one single (Checker 752) with Spires' vocals; 'Murmur Low' is a faithful reworking of **Tommy Johnson's** 1928 recording of 'Big Fat Mama', the vibrato in Spires' voice akin to that of **Arthur 'Big Boy' Crudup,** indicating the provenance of his nickname. The following year, he recorded 'About To Lose My Mind' (Chance 1137) which featured **John Lee Henley** on harmonica. A further session for United (referred to below) was split between Spires and Willie 'Long Time' Smith. Putting aside music at the end of the 50s, Spires didn't record again until 1965, taping a session for Pete Welding's Testament label with **Johnny Young,** which remains largely unissued.
Album: *Wrapped In My Baby* (1989).

Spirit

'Out of Topanga Canyon, from the Time Coast' stated the **CBS** publicity blurb for one of their finest acts of the late 60s. The rock band with a hint of jazz arrived with their self-titled debut album. Formerly Spirits Rebellious, the new band comprised: **Randy California** (b. Randolph Wolfe, 20 February 1951, Los Angeles, California, USA; guitar), Ed 'Mr Skin' Cassidy (b. 4 May 1931, Chicago, Illinois, USA; drums), John Locke (b. 25 September 1943, Los Angeles, California, USA; keyboards), **Jay Ferguson** (b. 10 May 1947, Burbank, California, USA; vocals) and Mark Andes (b. 19 February 1948, Philadelphia, Pennsylvania, USA; bass). Media interest was assured when it was found out that not only had the band a shaven-headed drummer who had played with many jazz giants including, **Gerry Mulligan**, **Cannonball Adderley** and **Thelonious Monk**, but that he was also the guitarist's father (later amended to step-father). The quality of the music however needed no hype. The album's tasteful use of strings mixed with Locke's stunning electric piano blended well with California's mature hard-edged guitar. Ferguson's lyrics were quirky and brilliant. 'Fresh Garbage', for example, contained the lines; 'Well look beneath your lid some morning, see the things you didn't quite consume, the world's a can for your fresh garbage.' The album reached number 31 in the US chart and stayed for over seven months. The following year's *The Family That Plays Together* in 1969, was a greater success and spawned a US Top 30 hit single 'I Got A Line On You'. Ferguson had to share the songwriting credits with the fast-developing California. The **Lou Adler**-produced set flowed with perfect continuity and almost 25 years later, the album sounds fresh. *Clear Spirit* contained Locke's instrumental music for the film *The Model Shop*, including the beautifully atmospheric 'Ice'. As a touring band they were most impressive, with Cassidy's massive drum kit sometimes dwarfing the stage. California would often use a clear perspex Stratocaster, while tinkering with his echoplex device which emitted the most colourful sound. The band's fourth collection, *The Twelve Dreams Of Dr Sardonicus* was arguably their finest work with Ferguson and California's songwriting reaching a peak. Although it was their lowest charting album to date (failing to make the Top 50 in the USA), it has subsequently and deservedly become their best- selling record. Randy's awareness for environmental and ecological issues was cleverly linked into his song 'Nature's Way', while Ferguson put in strong contributions including 'Animal Zoo'. At this time Spirit had their legendary album *Potatoland* rejected (it was eventually released after active petitioning from the UK rock magazine, *Dark Star*). The tensions within the band were mounting and Ferguson and Andes left to form **Jo Jo Gunne**. Surprisingly, California also departed to be replaced by Al and Christian Staehely. The John Locke dominated *Feedback* was not a commercial or critical success. The remains of Spirit disintegrated, while Jo Jo Gunne prospered and Randy attempted a solo career.

In 1976 Spirit returned with a new recording contract and a rejuvenated California. During the recent past it was found that Randy had jumped off London's Waterloo Bridge into the polluted River Thames and was miraculously rescued. The new nucleus of California, Cassidy and bassist Larry Knight toured regularly and built up a loyal following in Britain and Germany. The albums, whilst delighting the fans, sold poorly and the band became despondent. Nevertheless, there were some spectacular highlights, most notably the stunning yet perplexing double album *Spirit Of '76*. While Ferguson was enjoying great success as a solo artist, Mark Andes was with **Firefall**. A depressed California interviewed in London in 1978-79 stated that Spirit would not rise and that he would *never* play with Ed Cassidy again. Fortunately California was wrong as the original five were back together in 1984 for *The Thirteenth Dream*. They attempted re-workings of vintage Spirit numbers and sadly the album failed. California still attempts to keep the Spirit name alive with various assorted line-ups, usually together with the fatherly hand of Ed Cassidy. Both *Rapture In the Chambers* and *Tent Of Miracles* were disappointing works.

The Staehely brothers continue to work in the business, Christian as a session musician and Al has become one of the leading music business lawyers in the USA. Cassidy and California have since continued into the 90s using the Spirit moniker. Ultimately though it is only California who can continue as the moral owner of the name, as he is and has always been the true spirit of the band.

Albums: *Spirit* (1968), *The Family That Plays Together* (1969), *Clear Spirit* (1969), *The Twelve Dreams Of Dr. Sardonicus* (1970), *Feedback* (1972), *Spirit Of '76* (1975), *Son Of Spirit* (1976), *Farther Along* (1976), *Future Games (A Magical Kahuana Dream)* (1977), *Live* (1978), *Journey To Potatoland* (1981), (1984), *The Thirteenth Dream (Spirit Of '84)* (1984), *Rapture In The Chamber* (1989), *Tent Of Miracles* (1990), *Live At La Paloma 1993* (1995). Compilations: *The Best Of Spirit* (1973). *Chronicles* (1991), *Time Circle* (1991), *Spirit - The Collection* (1991).

Spirit Level

Spirit Level was a British jazz quartet formed in the early 80s. Playing excellent, fiery, free-ranging music, they were unfortunately not young enough - and lacked the requisite designer appearance - to benefit from the 80s jazz revival. Members were: Paul Dunmall (tenor saxophone), a powerful player often cited as one of the cream of British saxophonists and whose experience includes spells with **Alice Coltrane** and **Johnny 'Guitar' Watson**; Tim Richards (piano); Paul Anstey (bass); Tony Orrell (drums). For albums, they would often invite along a guest trumpeter: *Proud Owners* had Dave Holdsworth, *Killer Bunnies* featured Jack Walrath. In 1989, Paul Dunmall left to form Mujician with pianist **Keith Tippett** and Tony Orrell dropped out to form the delightful improvising trio MOR, with altoist Pete McPhail and bassist **Paul Rogers**. Reconstituted as Tim Richards' Spirit Level, the group now comprised a quartet of pianist Richards, Jerry Underwood (tenor saxophone), Ernest Mothle (bass) and **Mark Sanders** (drums), and released *New Year* in 1991.

Albums: *Mice In The Wallet* (1983), *Proud Owners* (1984), *Killer Bunnies* (1986), *The Swiss Radio Tapes* (1989), as Tim Richards's Spirit Level *New Year* (1991).

Spirit Of The West

Formed in 1983, this acoustic, but rock-minded trio, consisting of long-time Canadian friends, John Mann (vocals, guitar), Geoffrey Kelly (flute), J. Knutson (vocals, guitar), completely revived the Vancouver folk scene. In 1986, their *Tripping Upstairs* brilliantly demonstrated a use of airs and jigs to spice up their own protest compositions. Knutson left shortly afterwards, and the band recruited Hugh McMillan (bass) and Linda McRae (accordion). They toured Britain frequently during 1989-1990, and their association with the pop group, **The Wonder Stuff,**

noticeably influenced *Go Figure*, which was more or less an indie rock album, featuring ethnic instruments.
Selected albums: *Tripping Upstairs* (1986), *Go Figure* (1991).

Spirits

Seemingly a UK duo comprising Beverley Thomas and Osmond Wright, the real power behind the Spirits are in fact the production powerhouse of Damon Rochefort (b. c.1965, Cardiff, Wales; ex-**Nomads**, etc.) and Aaron Friedman. The group's debut single, 'Don't Bring Me Down', featured soaring gospel vocals with bright piano interludes and instantly became a favourite on the UK dancefloors. It also became that rarity in UK dance terms: it successfully crossed over to the US charts where it climbed to number 1. This came as a pleasant surprise to Thomas and Wright, the latter having been plucked from semi-obscurity in a gospel group where he had been writing his own material. The follow-up single, 'Spirit Inside', saw them repeat their success in the early 90s.

Spirits Of Rhythm

First formed in the late 20s by the brothers Wilbur and Douglas Daniels, the group performed under various names. By 1930 the band was making its way in New York City, having added **Leo Watson** to its ranks. In 1932, with **Teddy Bunn** on hand, the name was changed from the Five Cousins to the Spirits Of Rhythm and the group quickly established a reputation for highly entertaining performances. The instrumentation of the group was unusual. The Daniels brothers and Watson all sang and played the tiple - a stringed instrument, rather like a small guitar, of South American origin which has ten strings with pairs and triples tuned in octaves. The instrument has an interesting and melodious sound not unlike a rather classy mandolin. Bunn played guitar and drummer Virgil Scroggins used whisk brooms on a paper-wrapped suitcase. Despite the apparent eccentricity such a line-up implies, the band was a fine rhythmic band, with Bunn and Watson its outstanding members. In addition to a residency at the Onyx Club, the band also enjoyed success in Los Angeles and its records were immensely popular. With occasional changes in personnel the Spirits Of Rhythm remained together until 1946. Latterday reissues of their records underline the fact that they were far more than an easily-forgotten novelty band.
Album: *Rhythm Personified - 1933-34* (1985).

Spiritualized (Electric Mainline)

Dark, neo-psychedelic band formed by Jason Pierce (b. 19 November 1965; vocals/guitar) after his messy break up from former writing partner and **Spacemen 3** cohort Pete 'Sonic Boom' Kember. Based in Rugby, Midlands, they were actually inaugurated while

Spacemen 3 were still officially active. Pierce took the remnants of that band with him (Will Carruthers; bass and Jon Mattock; drums) and added his girlfriend Kate Radley (organ) and Mark Retoy (guitar). Their first release was a cover of the **Troggs**' 'Anyway That You Want Me', then 'Feel So Sad', a sonic opera lasting 13 minutes and 20 seconds. Headliners at ICA's 'Irn Bru' Rock week, their familiar **Velvet Underground** guitar noise/dream pop found favour with old Spacemen 3 fans as well as new converts. Singles such as 'Why Don't You Smile', however, were something of a departure from Pierce's morbid and moribund legacy. Notoriously shy and reticent in interviews, he had a preference for sitting down while playing gigs, which an impressionable audience eagerly imitated. A mail order live album arrived in 1993, after which sessions began on a second album proper. In the meantime Pierce discovered an affinity with some of the 90s ambient house artists, working on remixes for **LFO**, **Global Communications** and others. *Pure Phase* finally arrived in 1995 to the usual critical fanfare, going some way to accommodating its protagonist's assertion that he wanted to 'make a record so beautiful it brings a tear to your eye'. The best example of this approach to creating elegiac pop was 'All Of My Tears', with strings provided by the **Balanescu Quartet**. By this time Pierce had renamed the band Spiritualized Electric Mainline.
Albums: *Lazer Guided Melodies* (Dedicated 1992), *Fucked Up Inside* (Dedicated 1993), *Pure Phase* (Dedicated 1995).

Spirogyra (Folk)

Formed in Canterbury, England, Spirogya was one of a group of young bands signed to B&C Records at the same time as **Steeleye Span**. Writer Martin Cockerham and vocalist **Barbara Gaskin** - later to enjoy a hit with **Dave Stewart** - are the best known members. Their sound was similar to early **Strawbs**, and their records sounded whimsically English. Gaskin's voice gave them a pure, unsullied air.
Selected album: *Old Boot Wine* (1972).

Spitfire

Formed in 1990, this post-**My Bloody Valentine** UK guitar pop group made rapid progress. The band consisted of Jeff Pitcher (vocals), younger brother Nick (bass), Simon Walker (guitar), Matt Wise (guitar) and Justin Welch (drums). Original drummer Scott Kenny decided to join his other group Ever, while guitarist Steve White also left because he did not want to tour. They leapt into the fray with two EPs, *Translucent* and *Superbaby*. Their debut included a daring cover of the *Six Million Dollar Man* theme, and 'Superbaby' was produced by **That Petrol Emotion**'s Steve Mack. A tour with **Blur** helped bring them to national prominence, but more newsworthy were their infamous 'Back Stage' passes. Designed specifically to cater for

groupies, their tongues were firmly in cheek, but the press latched on to them as misogynists. It was 1993 before their first full length album emerged, though this still featured all the familiar swagger on the title-cut and 'Firebird', which included the intrusion of a flute.
Album: *Sex Bomb* (Fire 1993).

Spivak, Charlie

b. 17 February 1907, Kiev, Ukraine, d. 1 March 1982, Greenville, North Carolina, USA. Spivak learned to play trumpet as a small child growing up in the USA. In his mid-teens he joined Paul Specht's orchestra where he remained until 1930, moving on to the **Ben Pollack** band. Later, he was with the **Dorsey Brothers** orchestra, artists such as **Ray Noble**, **Raymond Scott**, **Bob Crosby** and **Jack Teagarden**, and also played in the New York studios. In 1939 he formed his own big band which, after a shaky start, became very successful. Thereafter, with only a short break through illness, he led the band for much of the next four decades. A skilled trumpeter, on the sweeter side of the swing era, Spivak's musical longevity owes much to his ability to see what the public wanted and then make sure that he delivered. His last residency, in Greenville, South Carolina, began in 1967 and continued until shortly before his death in 1982.
Albums: *Charlie Spivak And His Orchestra* i (1958), *Charlie Spivak And His Orchestra* ii (1962), *Charlie Spivak And His Orchestra* iii (1967), *Charlie Spivak And His Orchestra* iv (1968), *Charlie Spivak And His Orchestra* v (1972), *Charlie Spivak And His Orchestra* vi (1973), *1n9o8w1! (Now!)* (1981). Compilations: *Charlie Spivak And Jimmy Joy (1945)* (1979), *One Way Passage* (1979), *Charlie Spivak 1942* (1988), *Charlie Spivak And His Orchestra (1943-46)* (1988).

Spivey, Addie 'Sweet Peas'

b. 22 August 1910, Houston, Texas, USA, d. 1943, Detroit, Michigan, USA. Like her sister Elton ('The Za Zu Girl'), Addie probably owed her recording career to the success of the third sister, **Victoria Spivey**. A less-mannered singer than Victoria, Sweet Peas possessed a big, rich voice that was deployed to good effect, accompanied by a quartet led by **Henry 'Red' Allen**. Later recordings were less successful, and in the late 30s Addie Spivey retired from showbusiness.
Albums: Henry *'Red Allen Volume 2* (1975), *Blues Box 2* (1976), *Super Sisters* (1982).

Spivey, Victoria

b. 15 October 1906, Houston, Texas, USA, d. 3 October 1976, New York City, New York, USA. Spivey was recording at the age of 19, and had early hits 'Black Snake Blues' and 'T.B. Blues', sung in her unmistakable nasal, acidic tones. She recorded until 1937, appeared in the early black film musical

Hallelujah, and worked in vaudeville until her retirement in the early 50s. In 1960, she made a comeback, still writing remarkable songs, which she usually accompanied on piano or - less happily - ukulele. She founded the Spivey label in 1962, issuing some valuable recordings, and the first featured **Bob Dylan** as an accompanist Others were by inferior artists and/or poorly recorded. She was invaluable in coaxing her contemporaries like **Lucille Hegamin** and **Alberta Hunter** back to recording. Self-styled 'The Queen', Spivey was the **Madonna** of the blues, hyper-energetic, propelled by total self-belief, always performing, and drawn to themes of drugs, violence and sexual deviance.
Albums: *Idle Hours* (1961), *Songs We Taught Your Mother* (1962), *Basket Of Blues* (1962), *Victoria And Her Blues* (1963) *The Queen And Her Knights* (1965), *The Victoria Spivey Recorded Legacy Of The Blues* (c.1970), *Victoria Spivey* (1990).

SPK

This industrial noise band from Germany has advocated that their name stands for Surgical Penis Klinik, Systems Planning Korporation and other connotations at various points in their career. They began in 1978 when percussionist Derek Thompson was working in a mental hospital looking after brief SPK member Neil, a patient. Together they joined female banshee Sinan, the original conception of SPK being an alias for Sozialistiche Patienten Kollective. This evolved out of homage to the German movement of the same name trying to force improved rights for mental patients. They gained notoriety at early gigs by parading slides and films of medical operations, though later they would embrace flame throwers, oil drums etc. as part of their stage act. In so doing they shared links with the 'metal dance' outfits whose dealings were mainly in metallic percussion; **Test Department** and **Einsturzende Neubaten**. However, at a London Venue gig in December 1983, one of their members almost hit members of the audience (including one particularly unimpressed journalist) by swinging a metal chain out in to the auditorium. Such activities would do little to endear them to a largely cynical press, who had already collared them as being too eager to draw any sort of reaction. The situation was exaserbated by the dire mutant industrial creation, 'Metal Dance'. Earlier recordings, notably the inhospitable climate of searing noise and pain which was 1982's *Lichenschrei*, snapped at the heels of what **Throbbing Gristle** were doing without ever capturing the essence. However, things improved with the arrival of Graham Revell, who brought them to a recorded peak with *Zamia Lehmanni*, which deliberately evoked the sounds of fifth century Byzantium. By the 90s Revell had turned to soundtrack composition and using 'insect' sounds.

Albums: *Leichenschrei* (1982), *From Science To Ritual* (Plasma 1984), *Information Overload* (Normal 1985), *Zamia Lehmanni* (Side Effects 1986), *Auto-Da-Fe* (Walter Ulbright 1984), *Digitalis, Ambigua, Gold & Poison* (Nettwerk 1988), *Oceania* (Side Effects 1988).

Splinter

Splinter were a duo of **Beatles** fanatics from north-east England, comprising Bob Purvis (b. c.1950, Newcastle-upon-Tyne, Tyne & Wear, England), Bill Elliot (b. c.1950, Newcastle-upon-Tyne, Tyne & Wear, England), who played in a variety of Tyneside groups. Purvis had also worked with producer **Tony Visconti**, and Elliot sang on the **John Lennon** produced 'God Save Oz' record, in defence of *Oz* magazine when it was faced with obscenity charges in the early 70s. Fellow Beatle **George Harrison** became the duo's mentor and signed them to his Dark Horse label, where they had their sole hit, 'Costafine Town', in 1974. In 1979 they released a single, 'Danger Zone', on **Chas Chandler**'s Barn label, but otherwise have remained silent.
Album: *Splinter* (1974).

Split Beaver

This somewhat offensively titled heavy metal quartet was formed in Wolverhampton, England, during 1982 by Darrel Whitehouse (vocals), Mike Hoppet (guitar), Alan Rees (bass) and Mick Dunn (drums). They signed to the local Heavy Metal Records label the same year. The band specialized in plodding and clichéd British rock, influenced by **Deep Purple** and **Thin Lizzy** but without either the wit nor technique. They debuted with *When Hell Won't Have You*, a pedestrian and disappointing collection of uptempo rockers, after which they split up. It seems Hades was not the only place unwilling to entertain Split Beaver.
Album: *When Hell Won't Have You* (Heavy Metal 1982).

Split Enz

Originally formed in Auckland, New Zealand in 1972 as Split Ends, this expansive group evolved around the duo of **Tim Finn** (b. 25 June 1952, Te Awamuta, New Zealand; vocals/piano) and Jonathan 'Mike' Chunn (b. New Zealand; bass/keyboards) with Geoff Chunn (b. New Zealand; drums - later replaced by Paul Emlyn Crowther), Paul 'Wally' Wilkinson (b. New Zealand; guitar), Miles Golding (b. New Zealand; violin), Rob Gillies (b. New Zealand; saxophone), Michael Howard (b. New Zealand; flute) and Phil Judd (b. New Zealand; vocals/guitar/mandolin). Their reluctance to perform on the traditional bar circuit, left only the college and university venues, as well as the occasional open-air park concert, to enact their brand of theatrical-pop. They featured an eclectic set, wore unusual costumes, facial make-up (which drew comparisons in their homeland to **Skyhooks**), and even featured a spoons player (percussionist/costume designer Noel Crombie). After three singles released in New Zealand, the band were well established in their homeland, particularly after reaching the final of a national television talent show. After moving to Australia in early 1975, and altering their name, the group recorded their first album for the Mushroom label. At the invitation of **Phil Manzanera** who had seen the band when they supported **Roxy Music** on tour in Australia, the band flew to the UK. Signed to the **Chrysalis** label in Europe, Manzanera recorded the band's second album which included some re-working of their earlier material. Unfortunately, the band's arrival in England coincided with the punk movement and they found acceptance difficult. Returning to Australia in 1977, Split Enz recruited Tim Finn's brother Neil (b. 27 May 1958, Te Awamutu, New Zealand) to replace Judd. The departure of Wilkinson, Crowther and Chunn also made way for Nigel Griggs (b. 18 August 1949, New Zealand; bass) and Malcolm Green (b. 25 January 1953, England; drums). The 1979 album *True Colours*, on **A&M Records** contained their most successful single, Neil Finn's glorious 'I Got You' with reached number 12 in the UK. Follow-up releases saw the band reach modest positions in the US album charts, but they ran into trouble in the UK when their 'Six Months In A Leaky Boat' was banned by the BBC as its title was considered too provocative at a time when the British were fighting the Falklands war. While Tim Finn recorded a solo album, the group lost their momentum, eventually dissolving in 1985 after the release of *Conflicting Emotions* Tim Finn continued his solo career, while Neil went on to form **Crowded House** (also with Tim until 1992), with latter years group member Paul Hester (drums). Griggs, Judd and Crombie formed Schnell Fenster. Phil Judd released a solo album in 1983, *Private Lives*, on the Mushroom label.
Albums: *Mental Notes* (1975), *Second Thoughts* (1976), *Dizrhythmia* (1977), *Frenzy* (1979), *True Colours* (1980), *Waiata* (1981), *Time And Tide* (1982), *Conflicting Emotions* (1982), *See Ya Round* (1984), *Livin' Enz* (1985). Compilation: *The Beginning Of The Enz* (1980).

Splodgenessabounds

The origins of this UK group are heavily tinged with apochrypha. Max (then a drummer) replaced Gerry Healy in **Alien Sex Fiend** in 1978 and stayed for a few months before forming a duo called the Faber Brothers with guitarist Pat Thetic. They performed at Butlins Holiday Camp in Bognor, Sussex, but were sacked and returned to London to start a band. As Splodgenessabounds, the group started gigging in March 1979 and though various members came and went the line-up briefly comprised Max Splodge (vocals), his girlfriend Baby Greensleeves (vocals), Miles Flat (guitar), Donkey Gut (b. Winston Forbe;

keyboards), Whiffy Archer (paper and comb), Desert Island Joe Lurch Slythe and a dog. Robert Rodent joined on bass in early 1980 and Miles Flat left. They came to the public's attention when, to the eternal annoyance of publicans everywhere, they had a freak hit with 'Two Pints Of Lager And A Packet Of Crisps Please' in 1980. Other memorable songs in their repertoire included 'I've Got Lots Of Famous People Living Under The Floorboards Of My Humble Abode', 'Simon Templar', and a savage re-working of **Rolf Harris**' 'Two Little Boys'. Max was also reputed to be working on a rock opera called *Malcolm*, and appeared in the play *Camberwell Beauty*. His stage performances were somewhat spoiled due to wolf-whistles from his girly fan club (numbering three) throughout the evening. After falling out with Deram in 1982, the band signed to Razor under the shortened title Splodge, where they released *In Search Of The Seven Golden Gussets*, a tribute to mythical items of ladies' underwear. By this time the line-up included the following miscreants; Ronnie Plonker (guitar), Smacked Arse O'Reardon (bass), Poodle (drums) and Tone Tone The Garden Gnome (guitar). Max later recorded solo on Neat releasing the Tony James (**Sigue Sigue Sputnik**) single 'Phut Phut Splodgenik'.
Albums: *Splodgenessabounds* (1981), *In Search Of The Seven Golden Gussets* (1982).

Spoelstra, Mark

b. 30 June 1940, Kansas City, Missouri, USA. Originally based in California, 12-string folk/blues guitarist Spoelstra's songwriting career burgeoned following a move to New York where he realized the potential of original material. A confirmed pacifist and a conscientious objector to military service, his songs often reflected such themes and he was a regular contributor to *Broadside*, a magazine founded as an outlet for topical and protest material. Having completed two albums for the **Folkways** label, Spoelstra joined **Elektra Records**. His debut *Five And Twenty Questions*, featured 12 original songs and introduced his quiet, unassuming style. Mark later returned to California where he has continued to perform, but this committed individual has preferred to concentrate on social and community projects.
Albums: *The Songs Of Mark Spoelstra* (early-60s), *Mark Spoelstra At The Club 47, Inc.* (early 60s), *Five And Twenty Questions* (1964), *State Of Mind* (1965), *The Times I've Had* (mid-60s), *Mark Spoelstra At Club 47* (mid-60s), *The Songs Of Mark Spoelstra* (late 60s), *Mark Spoelstra* (1969), *Mark Spoelstra* (1972), *This House* (1972), *Mark Spoelstra* (1974).

Spontaneous Music Ensemble

Formed in 1965 by drummer **John Stevens**, SME was a group dedicated to free interplay between musicians. Early members included **Trevor Watts**, **Kenny Wheeler**, **Dave Holland**, and **Derek Bailey**, with guest appearances from artists such as **Paul Rutherford** (*Challenge*), **Evan Parker** (*Karyobin*), **Johnny Dyani** (*Oliv*) and **Bobby Bradford**. Rather like **Company** with Bailey, SME became a name for any improvised music project that John Stevens became involved in (though, unlike Bailey, Stevens also had other group names for 'less spontaneous' music: the Septet, Splinters, Away, Freebop etc). In 1970 Stevens formed the Spontaneous Music Orchestra to explore improvisation in larger groups, and SME became a core quartet of Stevens, Watts, singer **Julie Tippetts** and bassist Ron Herman (*Birds Of A Feather, 1, 2, Albert Ayler*). The *SME For CND* album featured Stevens and Watts with a workshop group, while *Bobby Bradford Plus SME* initiated a long association between Stevens and the west coast trumpeter. *Face To Face* was a particularly successful duo encounter between Stevens's drums and the soprano saxophone of Watts. As his interest turned to more structured musics, Stevens's SME projects became less frequent but the group was still playing on an occasional basis into the early 90s. Stevens seems to have little time for the 'no leader' aspect of many freely improvised encounters: unlike Company, whatever the line-up of SME, the instigator is well in charge.
Albums: *Challenge* (1966), *Karyobin* (Chronoscope 1968), *Oliv* (1969), *The Source* (Tangent 1971), *SME For CND For Peace And You To Share* (1971), *Birds Of A Feather* (1971), *So What Do You Think?* (Tangent 1971), *Bobby Bradford Plus SME* (1971), *Face To Face* (1975), with SMO "+=" (1975), *Biosystem* (Incus 1977), *Live - Big Band And Quartet* (1979, rec. 1977), *1,2, Albert Ayler* (1982, rec. 1971), *85 Minutes, Parts 1 & 2* (Emanem 1986, rec. 1974), *Live At Notre Dame Hall* (Sweet Folk All 1987).

Spooky

London-based progressive/ambient dance duo comprising Charlie May (b. 7 March 1969, Gillingham, Kent, England) and Duncan Forbes (b. 29 January 1969, Yeovil, Somserset, England). They signed to **Guerilla** for their first release, 'Don't Panic', in May 1992. The name came about as a 'last minute decision, which just seemed to fit in with the sound of our music'. May had previously worked as a sound engineer and caffeine research analyst, seeing service in Psi'Jamma and as keyboardist for **Ultramarine**. His partner Forbes had played in a variety of indie bands, including Red Ten, and enjoyed temporary positions as a school chef, van driver and bar tender. Influenced by a variety of musical media (**Cocteau Twins**, Detroit techno, **Underworld** etc), Spooky have won their spurs as much for their remixing talents as their own product (which includes the well received singles 'Land Of Oz', 'Schmoo' and 'Little Bullet'). Recent clients include Ultramarine, **William Orbit**, **Sven Vath** and Billie Ray Martin (ex-**Electribe 101**). As with work

recorded under their own name, these remixes offer a textured, tranquil shimmer to proceedings.
Album: *Gargantuan* (Guerilla 1993).

Spooky Tooth

Formed in 1967 as a blues group, they quickly moved into progressive rock during the heady days of the late 60s. Formerly named Art, they released a ponderous version of **Buffalo Springfield**'s 'For What It's Worth', as 'What's That Sound'. The original band comprised **Gary Wright** (b. 26 April 1945, Englewood, New Jersey, USA; keyboards/vocals), Mike Kellie (b. 24 March 1947, Birmingham, England; drums), Luther Grosvenor (b. 23 December 1949, Worcester, England; guitar), Mike Harrison (b. 3 September 1945, Carlisle, Cumberland, England; vocals) and Greg Ridley (b. 23 October 1947, Cumberland, England; bass). Their hard work on the English club scene won through, although their only commercial success was in the USA. They combined hard-edged imaginative versions of non-originals with their own considerable writing abilities. *Its All About* was a fine debut; although not a strong seller it contained their reading of 'Tobacco Road', always a club favourite and their debut single 'Sunshine Help Me', which sounded uncannily similar to early **Traffic**. It was *Spooky Two* however that put them on the map; eight powerful songs with a considerable degree of melody, this album remains as one of the era's finest. Their self-indulgent excursion with Pierre Henry on *Ceremony* was a change of direction that found few takers, save for the superb cover painting by British artist John Holmes. *The Last Puff* saw a number of personnel changes; Ridley had departed for **Humble Pie**, Gary Wright left to form Wonderwheel and Grosvenor later emerged as 'Ariel Bender' in **Stealers Wheel** and **Mott The Hoople**. Three members of the **Grease Band** joined; **Henry McCullough**, Chris Stainton and Alan Spenner. The album contained a number of non-originals, notably **David Ackles**' 'Down River' and a superb version of **Elton John**'s 'Son Of Your Father'. The band broke up shortly after its release, although various members eventually re-grouped for three further albums which, while competent, showed no progression and were all written to a dated formula. **Judas Priest** recorded 'Better By You, Better Than Me', which resulted in a court case following the death of two fans. The band were accused of inciting violence, causing the two fans to shoot themselves.
Albums: *It's All About* (Island 1968), *Spooky Two* (Island 1969), *Ceremony* (Island 1970), *The Last Puff* (Island 1970), *You Broke My Heart So I Busted Your Jaw* (Island 1973), *Witness* (Island 1973), *The Mirror* (Island 1974). Compilation: *That Was Only Yesterday* (1976 - features Gary Wright with Spooky Tooth, plus solo recordings), *The Best Of Spooky Tooth* (Island 1976).

Spoonie Gee

b. Gabe Jackson, Harlem, New York, USA. Spoonie-Gee was so-called because he only ever ate with that utensil when he was a child. As a youngster he proved adept at poetry, and was often to be found hanging out at the Rooftop Club, where early DJs like **DJ Hollywood** and Brucie B held sway. His recording career began at **Enjoy** Records, whose owner, Bobby Robinson, was his uncle. His most notable records included 'New Rap Language' with the **Treacherous 3**, backed by his own standard, 'Love Rap', on the flip. It featured his brother, Pooche Costello, on congos. They had grown up together in the same house as Bobby Robinson, his wife acting as surrogate mother when her sister died when Spoonie was just 12. Later he cut the family ties to join the growing band of deserters housed on the competing **Sugarhill** imprint. His hits for the label included 'Spoonie's Back' and 'Monster Jam', plus a reissue of his debut for Peter Brown's Sound Of New York USA label, 'Spoonin' Rap'. His career slowed in the mid-80s, and in 1984 he was to be found working in a rehabilitation centre for the mentally disabled. Three years later he once again found success, this time on Aaron Fuchs' Tuff City label, with the **Marley Marl/Teddy Riley**-produced *The Godfather*.
Album: *The Godfather* (Tuff City 1987).

Sports

Formed in Melbourne, Australia in 1976, the Sports featured Steve Cummings (lead vocals) Martin Armiger (guitar), Andrew Pendlebury (guitar), Jim Niven (keyboards/vocals), Robert Glover (bass) and Paul Hutchins (drums). Influenced by rock, rockabilly, country and new wave, the band recorded several exquisite pop songs in the new wave style which charted well, particularly in Melbourne. National success followed but as the original members left the band had less impact. After supporting **Graham Parker** on his tour of Australia during 1978, the Sports were invited to tour with him in Europe and England. Records were released but did not make a big impact in either Europe or the States. They undertook several large tours around Australia, released several more singles and the fourth album, but were no longer progressing. Personnel upheavals during the early 80s, saw Hutchins replaced in turn by Ian McLennan then Freddie Strauks (ex-**Skyhooks**). The Sports eventually broke-up at the end of 1981. After they disbanded Cummings ventured into a solo career, occasionally collaborating with Pendlebury who has also recorded three instrumental guitar albums. Armiger moved into production in television and stage as well as rock music.
Albums: *Reckless* (1978), *Don't Throw Stones* (1979), *Suddenly* (1980), *Sondra* (1981). Compilation: *All Sports* (1982).

Spotnicks

A Swedish instrumental group of the late 50s and early 60s, their career actually continued well into the 80s. Originally they consisted of Bo Winberg (b. 27 March 1939, Gothenburg, Sweden), Bob Lander (b. Bo Starander, 11 March 1942, Sweden), Bjorn Thelin (b. 11 June 1942, Sweden) and Ole Johannsson (b. Sweden). They were assembled by Winberg in 1957 as the Frazers, with Lander on guitar and vocals, Thelin on bass, Johannsson on drums, with Winberg himself playing lead guitar and building most of the bands equipment; including a guitar transmitter that allowed primitive flex-free playing. Spotted by Roland F. Fernedorg in 1960 they became the Spotnicks in 1961 and had several hit singles in their homeland. They were signed to **Oriole** in the UK in 1962 and toured the country, gaining instant notoriety for their gimmick of wearing spacesuits on stage. They played a mixture of instrumentals and Lander vocals, and first hit with 'Orange Blossom Special' in 1962. That same year they toured Russia and were introduced to Cosmonaut Yuri Gagarin.

They had further UK hits with 'Rocket Man', 'Hava Nagila' and 'Just Listen To My Heart' during 1962-63. In 1963 they made their cinematic debut in the pop film *Just For Fun*. A cover of the **Tornados**' 'Telstar' was released in Sweden under the pseudonym the Shy Ones. Johannsson left in 1963 to become a priest and was replaced by Derek Skinner (b. 5 March 1944, London, England). In 1965 they added organist Peter Winsens to the line-up and in September Skinner left to be replaced by Jimmy Nicol. Nicol was the drummer famed for having deputized for **Ringo Starr** on a 1964 World Tour when he was hospitalized after having collapsed with tonsillitis. Nicol had also played with the **Blue Flames** and his own band the Shubdubs. After much touring Nicol left in early 1967 and was replaced by Tommy Tausis (b. 22 March 1946). In October Thelin was called up for National Service and replaced by Magnus Hellsberg. Several further line-up changes occurred over the following years as the band continued to tour and record prolifically in Europe. Winberg was the only constant member although Lander was normally in the band until he left to form the Viking Truckers. The band were still active as of the mid-80s.

Selected albums: *Out-A-Space* (1963), *The Spotnicks In Paris* (1964), *The Very Best Of The Spotnicks* (1982), *In The Middle Of The Universe* (1984), *Music For The Millions* (1985), *Highway Boogie* (1986), *Love Is Blue* (1988).

Sprague, Carl T.

b. 1895, near Houston, Texas, USA, d. 1978. Sprague, possibly the first of the singing cowboys, was born on a ranch where he learned western songs around the camp fire. Although he attended college to study ranching, he accepted a coaching post in the college's athletic department. In 1925, impressed by **Vernon Dalhart**'s success, he wrote to Victor Records and suggested that they record his cowboy songs. 'When The Work's All Done This Fall', a story of a cowboy killed in a night stampede, sold nearly a million copies. Despite its success, he was unwilling to give up his college post but he continued to make records, sometimes accompanied by two fiddle players from the college band. Amongst his records are 'Following The Cow Trail', 'The Girl I Loved In Sunny Tennessee', 'Rounded Up In Glory' and 'Roll On Little Dogies' as well as such familiar cowboy songs as 'Home On The Range' and 'Red River Valley'. In 1937 he left his coaching post and ran a general store before being recalled to the army. During World War II, he was involved with recruitment in the Houston and Dallas areas and became a Major. After selling insurance and various other jobs, he retired to Bryan, Texas but during the 60s he donned a working cowboy's clothes for television appearances and university lectures. Between 1972 and 1974, he recorded 29 tracks, which have been released by Bear Family. Sprague died in Bryan in 1978 - his singing was a hobby but his knowledge has been a guideline for students of western music.

Albums: *The First Popular Singing Cowboy* (1975), *Cowboy Songs From Texas* (1978).

Spread Eagle

This New York metal band came together when vocalist Ray West joined Paul DiBartolo (guitar), Rob DeLuca (bass) and Tommi Gallo (drums), who had previously been together in a Boston band. The band were signed at a very early stage, and were forced to complete their songwriting in the studio while recording their debut. *Spread Eagle* comprised wonderfully raucous and raw metal built on vicious chainsaw guitar, although some typically sex-orientated lyrics provoked criticism, despite their tongue-in-cheek nature. The band tended to be slow starters live, taking time to build up a real head of steam, but otherwise their raw power and aggression transferred well to the stage. *Open To The Public* was more refined, as the band had matured and were able to spend more time on songwriting and recording, although much of the drumming was provided by session players as Gallo flitted in and out of the band. However, Spread Eagle have yet to improve upon their minor league status.

Albums: *Spread Eagle* (MCA 1990), *Open To The Public* (MCA 1993).

Spriguns

Mike and Mandy Morton formed Spriguns Of Tolgus at their own folk club in Cambridge, England. On their first two, self-financed albums, the Mortons were joined by Rick Thomas (fiddle) and Chris Russon (electric guitar). Playing soft focus electric folk, the band signed with **Decca**, and were encouraged by **Steeleye Span**'s Tim Hart, who produced *Revel, Weird & Wild* in 1976. By then known as the Spriguns, the group enlisted Dick Powell (keyboards), Tom Ling (fiddle), and Chris Woodcock (drums). Mandy Morton's songs reworked traditional ballads, making them difficult to distinguish from the original folk material. Powell was retained for *Time Will Pass*, and Australians Wayne Morrison (guitar) and Dennis Dunstan (drums) were recruited. Mandy Morton became the group's focus, and later releases were credited to her. *Magic Lady* involved several important folk guest artists, and when Morton signed for **Polydor** Scandinavia in 1979, she released her best work for some time. 'Scandinavia is great,' she said in 1980, 'they just turn up and listen to the music and don't think about categories or pigeon holes.' During the early 80s she toured with a straight rock band, and included a tribute on one of her albums to her all-time heroine Grace Slick (**Jefferson Airplane** etc.) - a paisley version of 'Somebody To Love'. The warm feyness of Morton's vocals fired the Spriguns, although they failed to break through despite a major recording deal. Mandy Morton was subsequently a presenter at BBC Radio Cambridge. The Spriguns releases later became the target of serious record collectors.

Albums: *Rowdy, Dowdy Day* (1974), *Jack With A Feather* (1975), *Revel, Weird & Wild* (1976), *Time Will Pass* (1977). as Mandy Morton *Magic Lady* (1978), *Sea Of Storms* (1979), *Valley Of Light* (1983).

Spring Parade

Remembered particularly for the joyous 'Waltzing In The Clouds' (Robert Stolz and **Gus Kahn**), this **Deanna Durbin** vehicle was released by Universal in 1940. A 'veteran' of eight films in the space of four years - and still only 19 years old - Durbin was cast as a baker's assistant in old Vienna. She falls for a handsome would-be composer (Robert Cummings), who plays the drums in the army while waiting for his music to be appreciated. S. K. Sakall, as the baker, and Henry Stephenson, in the role of Emperor Franz Joseph, turned Bruce Manning and Felix Jackson's light-hearted (and lightweight) screenplay into an amusing and entertaining movie. Also contributing to the pleasure were Mischa Auer, Henry Stephenson, Anne Gwynne, and the lively duo, Butch And Buddy. The music helped a lot, too. As well as 'Waltzing In the Clouds', which was nominated, but beaten for the Oscar that year by 'When You Wish Upon A Star' (from *Pinocchio*), Stolz and Kahn wrote 'When April Sings' and another catchy bit of nonsense, 'It's Foolish But It's Fun'. The other numbers were 'In A Spring Parade' (Charles Previn-Kahn), 'The Dawn Of Love' (Previn-Ralph Freed), and 'Blue Danube Dream' (Johann Strauss II-Kahn). Henry Koster directed yet another in the long line of Durbin hits which would continue for a few years to come.

Spring, Bryan

b. 24 August 1945, London, England. Spring was one of a handful of young drummers, others included Bobby Orr and **Phil Seamen**, who emerged in the 50s to give the lie to the cliche 'English rhythm sections don't swing'. Initially self-taught since the age of six, Spring also studied with **Philly Joe Jones**. After freelancing through the early 60s, he began a fruitful collaboration with **Stan Tracey**, playing and recording with the pianist's bands for eight years. In the late 60s and early 70s Spring played with **Frank Ricotti** and Klaus Doldinger's band, Passport, as well as spending several months with the group **Nucleus**. In 1975 the drummer formed his own band, co-led by saxophonist, **Don Weller**, an association that lasted into the 80s. Great energy and drive linked to a fine technique have made Spring the perfect drummer in many different settings, from big band to duet, and often the drummer of choice for visiting Americans of the stature of **George Coleman** and **Charlie Rouse**.

Albums: with Tracey *The Bracknell Connection* (1976), with Don Weller *Commit No Nuisance* (1979).

Springfield, Dusty

b. Mary Isabel Catherine Bernadette O'Brien, 16 April 1939, London, England. A long-standing critical favourite but sadly neglected by the public from the early 70s until the end of the 80s, the career of Britain's greatest ever white soul singer has been a turbulent one. Formerly referred to as 'the White Negress', Dusty began as a member of the cloying pop trio the Lana Sisters in the 50s, and moved (with her brother Tom) into the **Springfields**, one of Britain's top pop/folk acts of the early 60s. During the Merseybeat boom she made a bold move and went solo. Her 1963 debut with 'I Only Want To Be With You' removed any doubts the previously shy convent girl may have had; this jaunty, endearing song is now a classic of 60s' pop. She joined the swinging London club scene and became a familiar icon for teenage girls with her famous beehive blonde hairstyle and her dark 'panda' eye make-up. Over the next three years Springfield was constantly in the best-selling singles chart and consistently won the top female singer award, beating off stiff opposition from **Lulu**, **Cilla Black** and **Sandie Shaw**. During this time she campaigned unselfishly on behalf of the then little known black American soul and **Motown** artists; her mature taste in music made her different from many of her contemporaries.

Springfield's early albums were strong sellers, although they now appear to have been rushed works. Her pioneering choice of material by great songwriters such as **Burt Bacharach**, **Hal David**, **Randy Newman** and **Carole King** was exemplary. The orchestral arrangements of Ivor Raymonde and Johnny Franz drowned Dusty's voice at times, and her vocals appeared thin and strained due to poor production. She made superb cover versions of classics such as 'Mockingbird', 'Anyone Who Had A Heart', 'Wishin' And Hopin'', 'La Bamba', 'Who Can I Turn To' and 'Sunny'. Her worldwide success came, when her friend Vicki Wickham, and **Simon Napier-Bell** added English words to the Italian hit 'Io Che Non Vivo (Senzate)' and created 'You Don't Have To Say You Love Me'; this million selling opus proved her sole UK chart topper in 1966. By the end of the following year she was becoming disillusioned with the show business carousel on which she found herself trapped. The comparatively progressive *Where Am I Going* was an artistic success but it flopped, and the following year a similar fate awaited the excellent *Dusty...Definitely*. Her continuing exquisite choice of songs was no longer getting through to the fans. On the last mentioned album album she executed a fine version of **Herb Alpert**'s 'This Girl's In Love', and the definitive interpretation of **Randy Newman**'s 'I Think It's Going To Rain Today'.

In 1968, as Britain was swamped by the progressive music revolution, the uncomfortable split between what was underground and hip, and what was pop and unhip, got under way. Dusty, well aware that she could be doomed to the variety club circuit in Britain, moved to Memphis, one of the music capitals of the world, and immediately succeeded in recording her finest work, *Dusty In Memphis*. The production team of **Tom Dowd**, **Jerry Wexler** and **Arif Mardin** were the first people to recognize and allow her natural soul voice to be placed up-front, rather than competing with full and overpowering string arrangements. The album remains a classic and one of the finest records of the 60s. The single 'Son Of A Preacher Man' became a major hit, but the album failed in Britain and reached a derisory number 99 in the US chart. Following this bitter blow Dusty retreated and kept a lower profile, although her second album for **Atlantic**, *A Brand New Me*, was a moderate success. Released in the UK as *From Dusty With Love*, the **Thom Bell/Kenny Gamble** credited production boosted her failing popularity in Britain, where she still resided. *Cameo*, from 1973, exuded class and a superlative cover of **Van Morrison**'s 'Tupelo Honey', but produced no hit singles.

Dusty had now disappeared from the charts, and following a veiled admission in an interview in the London *Evening Standard* in 1975 that she was bisexual, she moved to Los Angeles. For the next few years she recorded sporadically, preferring to spend her time with tennis players like Billie Jean King and to campaign for animal rights (she is an obsessive cat lover). Following the release of the inappropriately titled *It Begins Again*, she was propelled towards a comeback, which failed. The strong disco-influenced *White Heat* in 1982 was her best album during these musically barren times yet it failed to gain a release outside the USA. A further attempt to put her in the public eye was orchestrated by club owner Peter Stringfellow, but after one single 'Just Like Butterflies' she fluttered out of sight again.

Her phoenix-like return at the end of the 80s was due entirely to Neil Tennant and Chris Lowe of the **Pet Shop Boys** who persuaded her to duet with them on their hit single 'What Have I Done To Deserve This?'. They then wrote the theme for the film *Scandal*, which Dusty took into the best-sellers. That song 'Nothing Has Been Proved' was ideal for her as the lyrics cleverly documented an era that she knew only too well. In the early 90s she moved back from America and for a time resided in Holland, surrounded by her beloved cats. At present she is recording and living back in Britain, and is less insecure, older and wiser but still plagued by ill-luck. In 1994 she underwent chemotherapy for breast cancer. This held up the release and promotion of her long-awaited new album with Columbia. In the spring of 1995 it was announced that the treatment had been carried out successfully and the album *A Very Fine Love* arrived in the wake of the single 'Wherever Would I Be'. This **Diane Warren** big production ballad featured a duet with **Daryl Hall**. The rest of the album showed that Springfield still retained a singing voice that could chill the spine and warm the heart, and with modern recording techniques she can, and hopefully health permitting, will now be heard to greater effect.

Albums: *A Girl Called Dusty* (Philips 1964), *Ev'rything's Coming Up Dusty* (Philips 1965), *Where Am I Going* (Philips 1967), *Dusty...Definitely* (Philips 1968), *Dusty In Memphis* (Philips 1969), *A Brand New Me (From Dusty With Love)* (Philips 1970), *See All Her Faces* (Philips 1972), *Cameo* (1973), *Dusty Sings Burt Bacharach And Carole King* (Philips 1975), *It Begins Again* (Mercury 1978), *Living Without Your Love* (Mercury 1979), *White Heat* (Casablanca 1982), *Reputation* (Parlophone 1990), *A Very Fine Love* (Columbia 1995).

Selected compilations: *Golden Hits* (Philips 1966), *Stay Awhile* (Wing 1968), *This Is Dusty Springfield Vol 2: The Magic Garden* (Philips 1973), *Greatest Hits* (1981), *Dusty: Love Songs* (Philips 1983), *The Silver Collection* (Philips 1988), *Dusty's Sounds Of The 60's* (Pickwick 1989), Love Songs (Pickwick 1989), *Dusty Springfield Songbook* (Pickwick 1990), *Blue For You* (1993), *Goin' Back: The Very Best Of Dusty Springfield* (Philips 1994), *The Legend Of Dusty Springfield* (Philips 1994; 4 CD box set).

Further reading: *Dusty*, Lucy O'Brien.

Springfield, Rick

b. Richard Springthorpe, 23 August 1949, Sydney, Australia. The son of an army officer, Springfield's

musical interests developed while living in England in the early 60s; on his return to Australia he played guitar and piano in the house band of a Melbourne club. At the end of the 60s, Springfield played with the Jordy Boys, Rock House and the MPD Band before joining Zoot. The group had several hits with Springfield compositions before he turned solo with the number 1 single 'Speak To The Sky'. He moved to the USA in 1972 where he was groomed to become a new teenybop idol and a new version of 'Speak To The Sky' was a Top 20 US hit. After contractual dispute kept him inactive for two years, he joined **Wes Farrell's** Chelsea label where **Elton John's** rhythm section Dee Murray (bass) and Nigel Olsson (drums) backed him on *Wait For The Night*. Soon afterwards the label collapsed and Springfield began a new career as a television actor. After guest appearances in *The Rockford Files*, *Wonder Woman* and *The Six Million Dollar Man*, he landed a leading role in the soap opera *General Hospital*. This exposure helped to give him a series of big hits on **RCA Records** in 1981-82 including 'Jessie's Girl' which reached number 1 and the Top 10 records 'I've Done Everything For You', and 'Don't Talk To Strangers'. The later hit 'Love Somebody' came from the 1984 film *Hard To Hold* in which Springfield played a rock singer. The next year a reissue of one 1978 track, ('Bruce'; a tale about being mistaken for **Bruce Springsteen**) was a Top 30 hit and later Springfield albums were equally popular in America.
Albums: *Beginnings* (1972), *Comic Book* (1974), *Heroes* (1974), *Wait For The Night* (1976), *Working Class Dog* (1981), *Success Hasn't Spoiled Me Yet* (1982), *Living In Oz* (1983), *Tao* (1985), *Rock Of Life* (1988).

Springfields

Formed in 1960, this popular UK folk-based attraction was based around singer/songwriter Tom O'Brien (b. 2 July 1934, Hampstead, London, England) and his sister Mary (b. 16 April 1939, Hampstead, London, England), who accompanied him on guitar. Better known as Tom and **Dusty Springfield**, the duo was later joined by the former's partner, Tim Field, and the following year the revitalized unit became one of Britain's top vocal groups. The trio enjoyed UK Top 5 singles with 'Island Of Dreams' (1962) and 'Say I Won't Be There' (1963), by which time Field had been replaced by Mike Longhurst-Pickworth, who took the less-cumbersome professional name Mike Hurst. The Springfields enjoyed success in America with 'Silver Threads And Golden Needles', a country standard which paradoxically failed to chart in Britain. However, although the single went on to sell in excess of one million copies, it was the group's only substantial US hit. The group split up in 1963 with each member then pursuing solo ventures. Dusty Springfield became one of the Britain's leading female singers, brother Tom continued his songwriting career while Hurst

established himself as a leading pop producer through work with **Cat Stevens**.
Albums: *Silver Threads And Golden Needles* (1962), *Folk Songs From The Hills* (1963), *Kinda Folksy* (1963). Compilation: *The Springfields Story* (mid-60s). Film: *It's All Over Town* (1964).

Springsteen, Bruce

b. 23 September 1949, Freehold, New Jersey, USA. As the world's greatest living rock 'n' roll star, Springsteen has unconsciously proved former ***Rolling Stone*** critic Jon Landau totally correct. Landau appeared smug and brave when he made the arrogant statement in 1974, 'I saw rock 'n' roll future, and its name is Bruce Springsteen'. Prior to that, Bruce had paid his dues, playing in local bands around New Jersey, notably with the Castiles, Earth, Steel Mill and Dr Zoom & The Sonic Boom, before he settled as the Bruce Springsteen Band with David Sancious (keyboards), Gary Tallent (bass,) Clarence Clemmons (saxophone,) **Steven Van Zandt** (guitar), Danny Federici (keyboards) and Vini Lopez (drums). Following an introduction to **CBS** A&R legend **John Hammond**, Springsteen was signed as a solo artist; the company sensed a future **Bob Dylan**. Springsteen ignored their plans and set about recording his debut with the band *Greetings From Asbury Park*. The album sold poorly, although critics in the USA and UK saw its potential. The follow-up only 10 months later was a much stronger collection, *The Wild, The Innocent And The E. Street Shuffle*. Future classics were on this similarly low-selling album, including 'Rosalita' and 'Incident On 57th Street'. It also contains the beautiful 'Asbury Park Fourth Of July (Sandy)', later recorded by the **Hollies**. His musicians were re-named the E. Street Band after its release and during the following May, Landau saw the band and made his now famous statement. He eventually became Springsteen's record producer and manager.
During this time, the first two albums began to sell steadily, following a heavy schedule of concerts, as word got out to the public that here was something special. Springsteen wrote directly to his fans in a language which they understood. Here was a working-class American, writing about his job, his car/bike, his girlfriend and his hometown. *Born To Run* came in 1975 and immediately put him into rock's first division. This superb album contained a wealth of lyrical frustration, anger and hope. The playing was faultless and the quality of the songs are among his best. Critics and fans loved it, and the album was a significant hit on both sides of the Atlantic. During the accompanying tour Bruce collected rave reviews and appeared as cover feature in both *Newsweek* and *Time*. Throughout his European tour the UK press were similar in their praise and exhaustive coverage, which led to a backlash of Bruce Springsteen jokes. Springsteen's recording career was then held up for three years as he and

Landau entered into litigation with Mike Appel, with whom Springsteen had struck a management deal in 1972. Other artists kept the torch burning brightly, with **Manfred Mann's Earth Band** releasing a sparkling version of his song 'Blinded By The Light' and **Patti Smith** recording a definitive cover of his 'Because The Night'. Other artists like ex-Hollie Allan Clarke, Robert Gordon, and the **Pointers Sisters** recorded his material. With the lawsuits successfully completed the anti-climactic *Darkness On The Edge Of Town* arrived in 1978. The album reflected the problems of the past years and is a moody album, yet 15 years later it still stands as a great work. The show-stopping 'Badlands' and 'The Promised Land' were two of the album's masterpieces. From the moment the record was released in June, Bruce and the band embarked on a gruelling tour which took them into 1979.

On his 30th birthday he played at the historic MUSE concert; the subsequent *No Nukes* album and video captured a vintage Springsteen performance of high-energy and humour. After feigning collapse onstage, he cheekily got the audience to beg for an encore having previously pointed out to them that he could not carry on like this as he is 30 years old! The audience loved the banter and together with the great Clarence Clemmons, he roared into an encore of 'Rosalita'. The next months were spent recording the double-set *The River*, which received almost as much praise as *Born To Run*. All shades of Springsteen are shown; it is brooding, depressing, pensive, uplifting, exciting and celebratory. In 20 songs, he covers every aspect of his life, and more importantly he covers aspects of the listener's life. It is hard to pick out any single tracks, but 'Hungry Heart', 'The River' and 'Fade Away' were all released and became hit singles. The following year he toured Europe again, and helped to resurrect **Gary 'U.S.' Bonds'** career by producing and writing some of his comeback *Dedication*. 'This Little Girl' is one of Springsteen's finest songs and US Bonds found himself back in the charts after almost 20 years' absence.

In September 1992 *Nebraska* arrived. This stark acoustic set was recorded solo, directly onto a cassette recorder. It is raw Springsteen, uncompromising and sometimes painful; Bruce without his clothes on. At one point on the album he imitates a wolf cry, but to many it was a genuine howl, that struck terror when turned up loudly. *Nebraska* was yet another major achievement. After a further lengthy wait for a new album, *Born In The USA* arrived in 1984. As is often the case, the album that is the most commercially accessible, best selling and longest resident in the charts, is not always the artist's best work. *Born In The USA* was a prime example. Selling over 12 million copies, it stayed in the UK charts for two-and-a-half years, in the country of origin it stayed even longer. Numerous hit singles were released including the title anthem, 'Cover Me' and

'I'm On Fire'. During one bout of Springsteen-mania on his 1985 European tour, all seven albums to date were in the UK charts. That year also saw him marry Julianne Phillips, and support political and social issues. He participated in the **USA For Africa**'s 'We Are The World' and joined former E. Street Band member Steven Van Zandt on the Artists United Against Apartheid song 'Sun City'. In festive style his perennial 'Santa Claus Is Coming To Town' made the UK Top 10 in December. Along with Bob Dylan, Springsteen is the most bootlegged artist in history. In order to stem the flow he released a five-album boxed set at the end of 1986. The superbly recorded *Live 1975-1985* entered the US charts at number 1.

The following year *Tunnel Of Love* was released; the advance orders took it to number 1 on the day of release in the UK and USA. It was another exceptionally strong work. Springsteen followed it with another major tour and visited the UK that summer. After months of speculation and paparazzi lens' intrusions, Springsteen's affair with his back-up singer Patti Scialfa was confirmed, with his wife filing for divorce. Bruce continued to be political by supporting the Human Rights Now tour for Amnesty International in 1988, although from that time on he has maintained a lower profile. During the late 80s he performed numerous low-key gigs in bars and clubs and occasional worthy causes as well as his own *Tunnel Of Love* tour. Springsteen's successful European tour was clouded by the press's continuing obsession with his divorce. In 1989 he recorded 'Viva Las Vegas' as part of a benefit album, and reached the age of 40. During the inactivity of that year the E. Street Band disintegrated upon Bruce's suggestion. During the early 90s the press followed his every move, anxiously awaiting signs of action as Springsteen continued to enjoy life, occasionally appearing with other famous musicians. It is a testament to Springsteen's standing that he can maintain his position, having released only eight albums of new material in almost 20 years. In 1992, he issued two albums simultaneously: *Human Touch* and *Lucky Town*, both scaled the charts in predictable fashion and both fans and critics welcomed him back, although not with quite the fervour of the past. He composed 'Streets Of Philadelphia' the title track for the film *Philadelphia* in 1994. In 1995 it was reported that he was working with the E. Street Band (including Clemmons) again. His *Greatest Hits* collection also included two new tracks and two previously unreleased oldies.

Albums: *Greetings From Asbury Park* (1973), *The Wild, The Innocent And The E. Street Shuffle* (1973), *Born To Run* (1975), *Darkness On The Edge Of Town* (1978), *The River* (1980), *Nebraska* (1982), *Born In The USA* (1984), *Live 1975-85* (1986), *Tunnel Of Love* (1987), *Human Touch* (1992), *Lucky Town* (1992), *In Concert - MTV Plugged* (1993), *Prodigal Son* (Dare International 1994).

Compilations: *Greatest Hits* (Columbia 1995).
Further reading: *Springsteen: Born To Run*, March, Dave (1979), *Bruce Springsteen*, Gambaccini, Peter (1979), *Springsteen: Blinded By The Light*, Humphries, Patrick & Hunt, Chris (1985), *Springsteen: No Surrender*, Lynch, Kate (1987), *Bruce Springsteen Here & Now*, MacInnis, Craig (1988), *The E. Street Shuffle*, Heylin, Clinton & Gee, Simon (1989), *Glory Days*, Marsh, Dave (1990), *Backstreets: Springsteen - The Man And His Music*, Cross, Ed. Charles R. (1990), *Down Thunder Road*, Eliot, Mark (1992), *Bruce Springsteen In His Own Words*, Duffy, John (1993).

Spud

A largely under-rated Irish electric folk group, who were active through the mid to late 70s. Their debut album was produced by the noted Irish fiddler, Donal Lunny, and the line-up consisted of Don Knox (fiddle), Michael Smith (bass), Austin Kenny (guitar) and Dermot O'Connor (guitar, vocals). By the time they recorded their most significant work, *Smoking On The Bog*, O'Connor had departed, to be replaced by multi-instrumentalist Ken Wilson and Dave Gaynor (drums). The album, recorded at Sawmills Studio in Cornwall, had a good time, boozy 'feel', and included an excellent cover of **Richard Thompson**'s 'Shame Of Doing Wrong'. A further Irish-only single release signified the end of Spud, and its ex-members have been absent from the music scene for some time.
Albums: *A Silk Purse* (1975), *The Happy Handful* (1975), *Smoking On The Bog* (1977).

Spy

This six-piece symphonic US rock group was formed in 1979 by David Nelson (guitar), John Vislocky (vocals), Danny Seidenberg (violin), Michael Visceglia (bass), Dave Le Bolt (keyboards) and Rob Goldman (drums). Spy were a highly versatile and talented band in the **Boston**, **Styx** and **Kansas** vein. Their self-titled debut, released in 1980, was an undiscovered classic of the pomp-rock genre. Saturated with keyboards, stunning vocal harmonies and fluid guitar work it is still difficult to explain why the album sold so poorly. They had more songs in preparation, but **CBS** dropped them before they could be fully completed. Spy disintegrated as most of the band members returned to session work.
Album: *Spy* (Kirshner 1980).

Spyro Gyra

Formed in 1975 by saxophonist Jay Beckenstein and pianist Jeremy Wall, the original Spyro Gyra comprised Chet Catallo (electric guitar), David Wolford (electric bass), Eli Konikoff (drums), and Gerardo Velez (percussion). After a modest start in Buffalo, New York, and an album on a small independent label, Beckenstein's hard work and commitment through countless changes of personnel resulted in appearances at major international jazz festivals in the 80s, and several gold albums. In addition to having four hits in the USA the band found considerable success in the UK with the infectious 'Morning Dance'. The band's mainstream treatment of a mixture of funk, Latin, and jazz remains popular today.
Albums: *Spyro Gyra* (Infinity 1978), *Morning Dance* (Infinity 1979), *Catching The Sun* (MCA 1980), *Carnival* (MCA 1980), *Freetime* (MCA 1981), *Incognito* (MCA 1982), *City Kids* (MCA 1983), *Access All Areas* (MCA 1984), *Breakout* (MCA 1986), *Stories Without Words* (MCA 1987), *Point Of View* (MCA 1989), *Fast Forward* (GRP 1990), *Alternating Currents* (GRP 1992), *Three Wishes* (GRP 1992), *Rites Of Summer* (GRP 1992), *Dreams Beyond Control* (GRP 1993). Compilation: *The Collection* (GRP 1991).
Video: *Graffiti* (GRP 1992).

Spys

This US pomp-rock quintet was formed in 1981 by ex-**Foreigner** duo Al Greenwood (keyboards) and Ed Gagliardi (bass). Enlisting the services of John Blanco (vocals), John Digaudio (guitar) and Billy Milne (drums), they signed to **EMI** the following year. They debuted with a self-titled album, produced by Neil Kernon (of **Dokken** and **Michael Bolton** fame). This featured some upfront, punchy guitar work amid the sophisticated, keyboard dominated arrangements. On *Behind Enemy Lines*, they became a little self-indulgent, utilizing a Russian male voice choir on several tracks. The album flopped and with growing legal and contractual problems, SPys disintegrated in 1983. Greenwood went on to work with **Joe Lynn Turner** and later N.Y.C.
Albums: *Spys* (EMI 1982), *Behind Enemy Lines* (EMI 1983).

Squadronaires

During World War II the British military forces created dance and show bands. As their name implies, The Squadronaires were members of the Royal Air Force. Originally, several members of the band were ex-sidemen of Bert **Ambrose**. Among the founder-players were leading British danceband musicians such as **Tommy McQuater**, **George Chisholm**, Sid Colin, Jock Cummings, and Jimmy Miller who was the leader for much of the band's life. The Squadronaires played a mixture of contemporary dance music and jazz numbers familiar through American records. In the post-war years the band maintained its popularity, touring extensively in the UK and broadcasting frequently. For many years the band's leader was **Ronnie Aldrich**, a fine pianist and arranger. By the early 60s, as musical tastes changed, the band's days were numbered and the Squadronaires were soon merely a fond memory. However, in 1987, a group of musicians, led by Harry Bence, decided to revive the band, and soon the New Squadronaires were attracting audiences with their mix of nostalgic oldies and contemporary pop music.

Compilations: *Flying Home* (Decca 1982), *Big Band Spectacular* (1987), *There's Something In The Air* (Decca 1994).

Squeeze

Formed in the south east London area of Deptford in 1974, Squeeze came to prominence in the late 70s riding on the new wave created by the punk movement. Original members Chris Difford (b. 4 November 1954, London, England; guitar/lead vocals), Glenn Tilbrook (b. 31 August 1957, London, England; guitar/vocals) and Julian **'Jools' Holland** (b. 24 January 1958; keyboards) named the group after a disreputable **Velvet Underground** album. With the addition of Harry Kakoulli (bass), and original drummer Paul Gunn replaced by sessions drummer Gilson Lavis (b. 27 June 1951, Bedford, England), Squeeze released an EP, *Packet Of Three*, in 1977. on the Deptford Fun City label. It was produced by former Velvets member **John Cale**. The EP's title in itself reflected the preoccupation of the group's main songwriters, Chris Difford and Glenn Tilbrook, with England's social underclass. It led to a major contract with **A&M Records** and a UK Top 20 hit in 1978 with 'Take Me I'm Yours'. Minor success with 'Bang Bang' and 'Goodbye Girl' that same year was followed in 1979 by two number 2 hits with 'Cool For Cats' and 'Up The Junction'. Difford's lyrics were by now beginning to show an acute talent in capturing the flavour of contemporary south London life with a sense of the tragi-comic. This began to fully flower with the release of 1980's *Argy Bargy* which spawned the singles 'Another Nail In My Heart' (UK Top 20) and the sublime 'Pulling Mussels (From A Shell)'. The set was Squeeze's most cohesive album to date; having finally thrown off any remaining traces of a punk influence they now displayed some of the finest 'kitchen sink' lyrics since **Ray Davies**' peak. The album also featured the group's new bass player, John Bentley (b. 16 April 1951). In 1980 Holland left for a solo career that included performing and recording with his own band, Jools Holland And The Millionaires (which displayed his talent for the 'boogie-woogie' piano style) and, to a larger extent, hosting the UK television show *The Tube*. His replacement was singer/pianist **Paul Carrack**, formerly with pub-rock band **Ace**. He appeared on *East Side Story* which was co-produced by **Elvis Costello**. Carrack stamped his mark on the album with his performance on 'Tempted' and with the success of 'Labelled With Love' a UK Top 5 hit, the album became the band's most successful to date. Carrack departed soon after to join **Carlene Carter**'s group and was replaced by Don Snow (b. 13 January 1957, Kenya; ex-**Sinceros**). The follow-up, *Sweets From A*

Stranger, was an uneven affair, although it did spawn the superb 'Black Coffee In Bed'. At the height of the group's success, amid intense world tours, including selling out New York's Madison Square Garden, Difford And Tilbrook dissolved the group. However, the duo continued to compose together releasing an album in 1984. The following year they re-formed the band with Lavis, the returning Holland and a new bass player, Keith Wilkinson. *Cosi Fan Tutti Frutti* was hailed as a return to form, and although not supplying any hit singles, the tracks 'King George Street', 'I Learnt How To Pray' and Difford/Holland's 'Heartbreaking World' stood out. In 1987 Squeeze achieved their highest position in the UK singles chart for almost six years when 'Hourglass' reached number 16 and subsequently gave the group their first US Top 40 hit, reaching number 15. '853-5937' repeated the transatlantic success. The accompanying album, *Babylon And On*, featured contributions from former **Soft Boy** Andy Metcalfe (horns/keyboards/moog). After the release of 1989's *Frank*, which contained one of the most sensitive lyrics ever written by a man about menstruation ('She Doesn't Have To Shave'), Holland departed once again to concentrate on television work. With Matt Irving joining as a second keyboard player, Squeeze released a live album, *A Round And A Bout*, on their old Deptford Fun City label in 1990, before signing a new record deal with **Warner Brothers**. The release of *Play* confirmed and continued Chris Difford and Glenn Tilbrook's reputation as one of the UK's finest songwriting teams, with 'Gone To The Dogs' and 'Wicked And Cruel' particularly resonant of earlier charms. *Some Fantastic Place* saw them reunited with A&M Records, although there was some critical carping about their insistence on a group format which did not always augur well for their more adroit and sober compositions.

Albums: *Squeeze* (A&M 1978), *Cool For Cats* (A&M 1979), *Argy Bargy* (A&M 1980), *East Side Story* (A&M 1981), *Sweets From A Stranger* (A&M 1982), *Cosi Fan Tutti Frutti* (A&M 1985), *Babylon And On* (A&M 1987), *Frank* (A&M 1989), *A Round And About* (Deptford Fun City 1990), *Play* (Reprise 1991), *Some Fantastic Place* (A&M 1993). Compilation: *Singles 45 And Under* (A&M 1982).

Squier, Billy

Having gained valuable experience as guitarist in the power-pop group **Sidewinders**, Billy Squier (b. Boston, USA), who had also appeared in the less-celebrated Magic Terry and the Universe, formed his own band under the name of Piper and recorded two albums for **A&M** during the late 70s. He dissolved Piper in 1979 and signed a solo deal with **Capitol Records** thereafter. *Tale Of The Tape* was released the following year and helped establish Squier's reputation as a sophisticated and talented songwriter/guitarist. Drawing inspiration from **Led Zeppelin**, **Queen**,

Fleetwood Mac and **Genesis** amongst others, he has continued to release quality albums of hard rock/pop crossover material. In the UK Squier has largely been ignored, even though he toured with **Whitesnake** in 1981 and played the Reading Festival. The story in the US is entirely different. There he has scored major successes with *Don't Say No* and *Emotions In Motion*, both of which made number 5 in the *Billboard* album chart. The former also produced hit singles in 'The Stroke' and 'My Kinda Lover'. By the time he released his eighth studio album, *Tell The Truth*, in 1993, Squier could reflect on worldwide sales of over 11 million records.

Albums: *Tale Of The Tape* (Capitol 1980), *Don't Say No* (Capitol 1981), *Emotions In Motion* (Capitol 1982), *Signs Of Life* (Capitol 1984), *Enough Is Enough* (Capitol 1986), *Hear And Now* (Capitol 1989), *Creatures Of Habit* (Capitol 1991), *Tell The Truth* (Capitol 1993).
Video: *Live In The Dark* (1986).

Squire, Chris

b. 4 March 1948, Wembley, London, England. An accomplished bass player who has made his name with supergroup **Yes**, having played with them for over 20 years. Yes was formed after Squire, then a member of the Syn, met **Jon Anderson** in a London music club. The original line-up consisted of Anderson (b. 25 October 1944, Accrington, Lancashire, England; vocals), an extremely gifted vocalist and composer; Peter Banks (b. England; guitar), also a former member of the Syn; **Bill Bruford** (b. 17 May 1948, London, England; drums); Tony Kaye (b. England; organ), and Squire. Anderson, Banks and Squire had been in a band called Mabel Greer's Toyshop in the last years of the 60s. Yes endured various personnel changes throughout the 70s, with Squire acting as a solid foundation for the band. By the mid-80s the line-up had been completely revamped by Squire with Anderson's help. In 1977, Squire and another band member, Alan White (b. 14 June 1949, Pelton, Co. Durham, England; drums), appeared on **Rick Wakeman**'s solo, *Criminal Record*. Their music matured as the decade progressed, Squire quickly becoming one of the best bassists to emerge from England. Some of the material the band put out could be described as pretentious, such as the highly esoteric *Tales From Topographic Oceans* which was based on Shastric Scriptures. In the mid-70s, each member of Yes undertook a solo project, Squire releasing the successful *Fish Out Of Water*. In 1981 the break-up of the band was confirmed. Although Squire and White rehearsed with **Robert Plant** and **Jimmy Page**, formerly of **Led Zeppelin**, nothing came of this project apart from Squire and White releasing 'Run With The Fox' which failed to chart. The following year Squire and White formed Cinema with South-African guitarist **Trevor Rabin** and Tony Kaye. Rabin was an unsatisfactory

vocalist, being replaced by Jon Anderson. Since the band was virtually identical to one of the early Yes line-ups, it was decided that they should call themselves by that name once more. However, by 1988 Yes had split into two warring factions with Squire owning the name, thereby forcing the other members to tour under the rather longer-winded title of **Anderson, Bruford, Wakeman And Howe**. It was Squire's version of Yes which released *Big Generator* in 1988 and he was very much part of the 90s Yes with the underrated *Talk*.
Album: *Fish Out Of Water* (1975).

Squires, Dorothy

b. Edna May Squires, 25 March 1918, Llanelli, Dyfed, Wales. A dynamic, dramatic and highly emotional singer, who has retained an army of fans throughout a career spanning over 50 years. At her 'live' performances, especially during the 70s, the audience came, not just to be entertained, but to pay homage. At the age of 18 she moved to London to become a singer, and worked at the Burlington Club, where she was discovered by American pianist and bandleader **Charlie Kunz**. She sang with his band at the Casani Club, and made her first radio broadcast from there. In 1938 she joined songwriter **Billy Reid** and his Orchestra, beginning a partnership which lasted until 1951, when she left to concentrate on a solo career. In between, she recorded many of Reid's songs, such as 'The Gypsy', 'It's A Pity To Say Goodnight', 'A Tree In A Meadow', and 'When China Boy Meets China Girl'. During the 40s Reid and Squires teamed up to become one of the most successful double acts on the UK variety circuit, and she made frequent appearances on BBC Radio's *Melody Lane, Band Parade, Variety Fanfare* and *Henry Hall*'s *Guest Night*. In 1953 Squires had a UK chart hit with one of Reid's biggest hit songs, 'I'm Walking Behind You' and, in the same year, married the young actor Roger Moore. They settled in California for most of the 50s, sometimes playing cabaret engagements. After the couple's acrimonious split in 1961, Squires made the UK Top 30 in collaboration with personality pianist **Russ Conway**, with her own composition 'Say It With Flowers'. She also became the first British artist to play London's Talk Of The Town. In 1968, after several unfruitful years, she financed her own album, *Say It With Flowers*, for President Records. This was followed by a version of the **Stevie Wonder** hit 'For Once In My Life', along with 'Till' and 'My Way' (an anthem which fitted her as perfectly as it did **Frank Sinatra**). During 1970, her version spent nearly six months in the UK chart, and inspired her to hire the London Palladium for a sell-out comeback concert, which she played to an ecstatic reception; a double album was released on **Decca**.

In the 70s Squires was headlining again throughout the UK, in concerts and cabaret, and also returned to the

USA to play New York's Carnegie Hall. She hired the Palladium again in 1974 for a concert in memory of Billy Reid, and in 1979 released another double album, *With All My Heart*. During the 80s she became semi-retired, giving a few concerts, one of which became *We Clowns - Live At The Dominion* (1984), on her own Esban label; she also released *Three Beautiful Words Of Love* on Conifer. Squire's career was bathed in controversy and she became one of the most notoriously prolific libel litigants in show-business history. In 1989 she was evicted from her 17-bedroom Thames-side mansion that once belonged to the celebrated actress Lily Langtry, and in 1995 her habitat was reportedly under threat once again. During the early 90s, Squires was still performing occasionally and in 1991 she released *The Best Of The* **EMI** *Years*, a 20-track compilation of her work with Billy Reid, some of her own compositions, and several of the other recordings she made for Columbia during the early 60s.

Album: *Dorothy Squires Sings Billy Reid* (Nixa 1958), *Say It With Flowers* (President 1968), *This Is My Life* (Ace Of Clubs late 60s), *Reflections* (Marble Arch late 60s), *Rain, Rain Go Away* (Decca 1977), *Golden Hour Presents Dorothy Squires* (1977), *With All My Heart* (2-LP set Decca 1979), *We Clowns - Live At The Dominion* (Esban 1984), *Three Beautiful Words Of Love* (Conifer 1988). Compilation: *The Best Of The EMI Years* (1991), *Best Of* (1994).

Squires, Rosemary

b. Joan Rosemary Yarrow, 7 December 1928, Bristol, Avon, England. This civil servant's daughter underwent vocal, piano and guitar lessons before and during study at Salisbury's St Edmund's Girls School. In 1940, a broadcast on the BBC Home Service's *Children's Hour* created demand for her in local venues that embraced US army bases. With an endearing west country burr, she sang in various combos formed within these camps, as well as in the Polish Military Band while employed in an antique bookshop and then an office. After becoming a professional performer, she was employed by **Ted Heath**, **Geraldo**, **Cyril Stapleton** and other big band conductors as well as smaller jazz bands led by **Max Harris**, **Kenny Baker** and **Alan Clare** - with whose trio she appeared at a BBC Festival of Jazz at the Royal Albert Hall. She has long been known to Britain at large, having been omnipresent since the late 40s on BBC radio light entertainment programmes - including *Melody Time*, *Workers' Playtime* and many of her own series. In 1962, she hovered just outside the UK chart with a version of 'The Gypsy Rover'. Currently reported to be living again in Salisbury, she remains an active musician, with Tibetan culture among her extra-mural interests. She was secretary of Britain's Tibet Society from 1972-75.

In 1991, she surprised her friends (and herself) by marrying for the first time, although it was far from being the first occasion on which she has changed her name. She recorded one of her most successful titles, 'Frankfurter Sandwiches', under the *nom de plume* of Joanne And The Streamliners, and in the 90s she still continues with her 'second career' - singing for television jingles. She also plays the role of DJ on her own Sunday afternoon programme on Radio Wiltshire. Selected albums: *My One And Only* (C5 1989), *A Time For Rosemary* (c.90s).

SRC

Based in Michigan, USA. SRC evolved out of the area's turbulent garage-band scene and local groups the Tremelos, the Chosen Few and the Fugitives. Initially known as the Scott Richard Case, the group - Scott Richardson (vocals), Gary Quackenbush (lead guitar), Steve Lyman (second lead guitar), Glenn Quackenbush (organ), Robin Dale (bass) and E.G. Clawson (drums) - recorded a handful of local releases before truncating their name to SRC and signing with **Capitol Records**. The six members, at first, all lived together and the group's self-titled debut album reflected their collective spiritual aims. The best-known track, 'Black Sheep', became an underground hit when released as a single, while a love of British rock, in particular **Procol Harum** and the **Pretty Things**, was apparent on some of the other performances. This unusual blend was undermined on subsequent albums as SRC attempted a more basic rock style. Personnel upheavals hampered their progress. Robin Dale replaced Al Wilmot in 1969, but a fundamental change occurred prior to a third album. Both Lyman and Gary Quackenbush were forced to leave, the latter taking with him the simple, yet distinctive fills, which provided the group's musical trademark. Newcomer Ray Goodman was a less satisfying substitute and although SRC continued into the 70s, briefly flirting with a new name, Blue Sceptre, on the way, they broke up without matching the strength of that first collection.

Albums: *SRC* (1968), *Milestones* (1969), *Traveller's Tale* (1970).

St Louis Blues

One of the first talkies, and one of few early films to feature jazz or blues artists, this offers the only screen appearance of **Bessie Smith**, the Empress of the Blues. Directed by Dudley Murphy (who in the same year made *Black And Tan*), this 1929 film features an extended performance of the title song built around a thin story which fully exploits elements of pathos in the lyrics. There is an excellent accompanying band, including **Joe Smith** and Kaiser Marshall, mostly drawn from the ranks of **Fletcher Henderson**'s band but led on this occasion by **James P. Johnson**. For all such attractions, however, this film's value lies in this solitary opportunity to see Smith, one of the greatest figures in the history of American popular music and through it to glean some fleeting but coherent understanding of the outstanding and memorable manner in which she commanded attention and dignified the whole genre of blues in the 20s and 30s. NB: the same title was used for a 1939 feature film, which includes, amongst others, performances by **Maxine Sullivan**. It was also used for the 1958 biopic based upon the life of **W.C. Handy** and starring **Nat 'King' Cole**.

St. Clair, Isla

Isla St. Clair was born Isabella Margaret Dice, 2 May 1952, Grangemouth, Stirling, Scotland. While still only 10 years old, St. Clair was already a highly popular singer at the Aberdeen Folk Club. She had her radio and television debut at the young age of 12, soon becoming popular through her appearances on programmes such as *Stories Are For Singing*, and *My Kind Of Folk*. She had always been called Isla, but adopted the original version of her mother's maiden name Sinclair, when her mother re-married. St. Clair's mother, Zetta, already a well respected singer and writer in the folk fraternity, was a big influence on her. Meeting such established traditional singers as **Jeannie Robertson**, helped further still to fuel the fire of enthusiasm in Isla. After leaving high school aged 17, St. Clair became a professional folk singer. She then went on to present the series *The Song And The Story* for BBC television, singing songs to highlight aspects of traditional ways of life that were gradually disappearing. On 18 August 1971, at the Sir Walter Scott Bicentenary Ceilidh, St. Clair sang her own version of the song 'Annie Of Lochroyan'. For the album *Isla St.Clair Sings Traditional Scottish Songs*, she was backed by Tom Ward (English concertina). For the recording, she received a paltry £50.00 advance, and since that time has never received any money, despite the album's sales at the time. In later years Isla St. Clair was to become well known to a far wider audience as the assistant to Larry Grayson on the highly popular and long-running BBC television game show *The Generation Game*. The album *Inheritance* saw her return to singing again.
Albums: *Isla St.Clair Sings Scottish Traditional Songs* (Tangent Records 1972), *Inheritance* (Moidart Music 1993).

St. John, Barry

In the wake of **Barry McGuire**'s 'Eve Of Destruction', this vocalist reached the UK Top 50 in 1965 with a less bombastic 'protest' song in 'Come Away Melinda', issued on **Columbia**. Barry St. John could not, however, capitalize on this modest triumph with further successful chart entries. Nevertheless, he was to find gainful employment as a session singer for significant artists such as **Alexis Korner**, **Long John Baldry**, **Duster Bennett** and other titans of the late 60s 'blues boom'. The next decade brought a wider spectrum of work in both mainstream pop (with **Bryan Ferry**, **Cockney Rebel**, **Andy Fairweather-Low**, and **Elton John**) and off-beat projects involving **Viv Stanshall**, **Kevin Coyne**, **John Cale** and Daevid Allen. By the 80s, he was standing in the shadows with **Pink Floyd**, **Tom Robinson** and **Whitesnake** among his illustrious clients.

St. John, Bridget

b. c.1950, England. Bridget St. John was one of the first acts to be signed to Dandelion, the independent label inaugurated by the BBC disc jockey **John Peel** in 1969. Her debut album *Ask Me No Questions*, was a folksy selection, but the artist's deep, assured voice compensated for the occasional immaturity of the lyrics. **John Martyn**, who contributed guitar on two of the tracks, donated an original composition, 'Back To Stay', to Bridget's second album, *Song For The Gentle Man*. This excellent collection confirmed the promise of her debut; string and woodwind sections added an engagingly pastoral effect and enhanced the cultivated, yet gentle, atmosphere. Her third album release, *Thank You For*, featured several folk-rock musicians, as well as Tim Renwick, Willie Wilson and Bruce Thomas from the group **Quiver**. Bridget then moved outlets to **Chrysalis Records** for her next album *Jumblequeen*. This, easily her most commercial offering, was produced by **Ten Years After** bassist Leo Lyons, but unfortunately sales were again deeply discouraging. The singer then dropped out of music for a period, before re-emerging in New York where she performed on a semi-professional basis.
Albums: *Ask Me No Questions* (1969), *Song For The Gentle Man* (1971), *Thank You For* (1972), *Jumblequeen* (1974).

St. John, Jeff

b. Jeff Newton, 22 April 1946, Australia. Jeff St. John was responsible for forming various bands in the Sydney area of Australia. From 1965, St. John covered soul hits from America which were at the time relatively unknown in Australia. The best-known bands he formed were Jeff St. John And The Id, Copperwine and Yama, (every one of which had good live followings, but whose records were not big hits); his charting songs were 'Big Time Operator' (1967) and 'Teach Me How to Fly' (1971). His voice was powerful and strong, providing an obvious focus for his bands but disputes about direction lead to St. John following a solo career in 1972. After visiting the UK and the USA he was finally offered a recording contract with **Asylum Records**, and became the first Australian to record with that label. The single 'A Fool In Love' reached the Top 10 in 1977 in Australia. Despite releasing a number of singles since and performing in front of several excellent bands, his career, hindered since he became wheelchair-bound in the late 60s, has maintained a low profile.

Albums: with Wendy Saddington (Copperwine) *Joint Effort* (1970), with Copperwine *Live* (1971), *Live* (1972), *So Far So Good* (1978). Compilations: *The Best Of* (1972), *Survivor 1965-75* (1977).

St. Louis Union

Initially based in Manchester, England, the St. Louis Union - Tony Cassiday (vocals), Keith Miller (guitar), Alex Kirby (tenor saxophone), David Tomlinson (organ), John Nichols (bass) and Dave Webb (drums) - attracted attention as winners of the 1965 *Melody Maker* beat group contest. Their prize was a recording contract with **Decca Records**, the first fruits of which was a version of 'Girl', plucked from the **Beatles**' album *Rubber Soul*. The sextet took the song into the UK Top 30, despite competition from the **Truth**. They later enjoyed a role in *The Ghost Goes Gear*, a film which also featured the **Spencer Davis Group**. However, the chart failure of subsequent singles, 'Behind The Door' and 'East Side Story', brought their brief career to an end.

St. Louis Woman

After collaborating with **Hoagy Carmichael** on the flop *Walk With Music* (1940), lyricist **Johnny Mercer** teamed with **Harold Arlen** on this musical which opened at the Martin Beck Theatre in New York on 30 March 1946. Although it ran only a little longer than his previous effort, it did contain at least one song that is still remembered nearly 50 years later. Arna Bontemps and Countee Cullen wrote the book which was based on Bontemps novel *God Sends Sunday*. The setting is St. Louis in 1898, where Della Green (Ruby Hill), is happily in harness with saloon owner Biglow Brown (Rex Ingram) before jockey Little Augie (Harold Nicholas) experiences a phenomenal winning streak. Della is impressed, and switches her affections to the jockey. However, Biglow puts a curse on them both just before he dies, which ruins both the racing and their relationship for a time. 'Come Rain Or Come Shine' is the song from the show that has endured more than any other, but **Pearl Bailey**, who played the comical character, Butterfly, also delighted audiences with the witty 'Legalize My Name' and 'A Woman's Prerogative'. The remainder of a fine score included 'Any Place I Hang My Hat Is Home', 'I Had Myself A True Love', 'Ridin' On the Moon', 'Sleep Peaceful, Mr. Used-To-Be', 'Lullabye', 'Leavin' Time', and 'Cakewalk My Lady'. The **Nicholas Brothers**, Harold and Fayard, the acrobatic dancers who featured in several Hollywood musicals during the 40s, performed some extraordinary feats, but, for some reason - certainly not because of the score - the public just would not turn up, and *St. Louis Woman* closed after only 113 peformances. Arlen and Mercer persevered, and adapted some of the material into a 'blues opera', *Free And Easy*, which spent a brief time in Europe in 1959. The original score - totalling only 29 minutes - was released on CD in 1993.

St. Paradise

This short-lived US hard rock group was formed in 1978 by ex-**Ted Nugent** band duo Derek St. Holmes (vocals/guitar) and Rob Grange (bass/vocals). Recruiting ex-**Montrose** drummer Denny Carmassi, the line-up looked very promising. Signed by **Warner Brothers**, they released a self-titled debut in 1979. Comprising of power-metal, the album lacked both drive and individuality and compared unfavourably with everything that the band's members had been associated with before. Following a European tour supporting **Van Halen**, which failed to win new fans for St. Paradise, the band disintegrated. Carmassi joined **Gamma** and St. Holmes worked with **Aerosmith**'s Brad Whitford for a short time, before rejoining Nugent once more.

Album: *St. Paradise* (Warners 1979).

St. Peters, Crispian

b. Robin Peter Smith, 5 April 1943, Swanley, Kent, England. Originally a member of UK pop group the Beat Formula Three, Smith was plucked from obscurity by manager Dave Nicolson, rechristened Crispian St. Peters and signed to a 10 year management and production contract. After two unsuccessful singles for **Decca** ('At This Moment' and 'No No No') Nicolson persuaded him to cover **We Five**'s US hit 'You Were On My Mind'. Although the single was almost buried in the pre-Christmas sales rush of 1965, it continued to sell into the New Year and took Crispian into the UK Top 10. Under Nicolson's tutelage, the shy star was momentarily transformed into arrogance incarnate and astonished the conservative music press of the period by his suggestion that he had written 80 songs of better quality than those of the **Beatles**. Other stars were also waved aside as Crispian announced that he was better than **Elvis Presley**: 'I'm going to make Presley look like the Statue of Liberty . . . I am sexier than **Dave Berry** and more exciting than **Tom Jones** . . . and the Beatles are past

it'. Outraged readers denounced him in letters columns, but St. Peters returned stronger than ever with the sprightly 'Pied Piper', a Top 10 hit on both sides of the Atlantic. Thereafter he was remembered more for his idle boasts than his music. After successive chart failures, he switched to country, a form that better suited his singing style. Serious psychological problems hampered his remote chances of a comeback and he fell into obscurity, reappearing irregularly on the flickering revivalist circuit.
Album: *Simply...Crispian St Peters* (1970).

Stabile, Dick

b. 1909, Newark, New Jersey, USA. Stabile studied saxophone while still at school and was a professional musician in his early teens. In 1926 he moved to New York to join the orchestra of George Olsen, moving then into **Ben Bernie**'s popular band where he remained until 1936. That year he formed his own outfit which became popular at New York hotels and ballrooms. His band remained in business while he served in the armed forces during World War II, his wife, singer **Gracie Barrie**, leading it in his absence. After the war Stabile continued to appeal to dancers and adjusted his repertoire to accommodate the growing number of radio listeners as the dance halls declined. After moving to the west coast he became musical director for **Dean Martin** and Jerry Lewis, appearing regularly with them on television and in some of their films. Stabile subsequently led bands in west coast and Las Vegas clubs and hotels before resettling in New Orleans where he fronted the house band at the Roosevelt Hotel.
Selected albums: *At The Statler* (Tops c.50s), *On Sunset Strip* (King 1959), *This Cat Really Blows* (Dot 1960).

Stackhouse, Houston

b. 28 September 1910, Wesson, Mississippi, USA, d. 1981. Despite his colourful name and his reputation among his peers, Stackhouse only received interest and acclaim towards the end of his life, although he played a contributory role in the development of delta blues. He became an active musician in his teens, learning first harmonica, violin, then mandolin and guitar. Moving to Crystal Springs, Mississippi, he came under the influence of **Tommy Johnson** and his brothers, Clarence and Mager. He in turn taught his first cousin, **Robert Nighthawk,** and on one occasion the pair worked with **Jimmy Rodgers** in Jackson, Mississippi. During the 30s, with Carey 'Ditty' Mason and Cootsie Thomas, he worked in a band modelled on the **Mississippi Sheiks**, with whom he occasionally played. In April 1946, Nighthawk summoned him to Helena, Arkansas, where he was advertising Mother's Best flour on station KFFA, with a band that included **Pinetop Perkins** and **Kansas City Red**. Stackhouse then became a member of the King Biscuit Boys, led by **Peck Curtis** when **Sonny Boy Williamson (Rice Miller)** was out of town. A day job with Chrysler and gigs with the Biscuit Boys continued through the 50s. He was not recorded until August 1967, in a session that also included Nighthawk and Curtis. A week later, he recorded with 'Ditty' Mason. Tracks from these sessions appeared on anthologies released by Testament, Arhoolie, Matchbox and Flyright. During the 70s, Stackhouse became a regular participant in blues festivals throughout the USA. As befitted the station he'd taken for himself, his death in 1981 went unrecorded.
Album: *Mississippi Delta Blues Vol. 1* (1968).

Stackridge

Using a bizarre mixture of dustbin lids and rhubarb stalks as stage props, Stackridge were once acclaimed as the 'West Country **Beatles**' and enjoyed a brief vogue in the early 70s. The group was formed in Bristol in 1969 as Stackridge Lemon by Jim 'Crun' Walter (bass) and Andy Davis (b. Andrew Cresswell-Davis; keyboards) who recruited James Warren (guitar) and Billy Sparkle (drums) through a newspaper advertisement. Lead singer and flautist Mike 'Mutter' Slater had been in a local folk duo. Adding violinist Mike Evans, they developed an idiosyncratic folk-rock style with whimsical lyrics on songs like 'Dora The Female Explorer', their debut single for MCA Records in 1971. Over the next three years, Stackridge toured throughout Europe and appeared at the 1972 Reading Festival with a troupe of St. Trinians-style dancers. Slater invented a dance craze, 'Do The Stanley' but left the group shortly before the release of the **George Martin**-produced *The Man In The Bowler Hat*. Stackridge now added session player Keith Bowkett (keyboards) and former **Audience** and Sammy member Keith Gemmell on saxophone and flute. They changed labels to **Elton John**'s Rocket in 1974 but despite Slater's return for *Mr Mick*, lack of commercial success caused the band to split in 1976. While Slater left the music business, Evans toured with visiting country stars and later played in the trio at Bath Pump Room. Davis played guitar on two albums by ex-**String Driven Thing** vocalist Kimberley Beacon and in 1979 formed the **Korgis** with Warren. The group made three albums for Rialto and had UK hits with 'If I Had You' (1979) and 'Everybody's Got To Learn Sometime' (1980). Warren later made *Burning Questions* (Sonet 1987) while Davis toured with **Tears For Fears** before recording the 'new age'-style *Clevedon Pier* for MMC, the label owned by Peter Van Hooke, who had played drums with Stackridge in the mid-70s.
Albums: *Stackridge* (1971), *Friendliness* (1972), *The Man In The Bowler Hat* (1974), *Extravaganza* (1974), *Mr Mick* (1976).

Stackwaddy

This group was formed in Manchester, England in 1969 by Mick Stott (lead guitar) and Stuart Banham (bass), previously of the New Religion. John Knail (vocals/harmonica) and Steve Revell (drums) completed the new act's line-up which first drew attention to an impressive appearance at Buxton's 1969 Progressive Blues Festival. Stackwaddy were later signed to UK disc jockey **John Peel**'s Dandelion label. Both *Stackwaddy* and *Bugger Off* revealed aspirations similar to British 60s' R&B groups, played in an uncluttered, irreverent, but exciting style. Included were versions of the **Pretty Things**' 'Rosalyn', **Frank Zappa**'s 'Willie The Pimp' and the wryly-titled 'Meat Pies Have Come But The Band's Not Here Yet', but Stackwaddy's guttural music proved unfashionable and the original group split up. However, between 1973 and 1976 Barnham led a revamped line-up comprising of Mike Sweeny (vocals), Wayne Jackson (bass) and Kevin Wilkinson (drums).
Albums: *Stackwaddy* (1971), *Bugger Off* (1972).

Stacy, Jess

b. 11 August 1904, Bird's Point, Missouri, USA, d. 1 January 1995, Los Angeles, California, USA. After teaching himself to play piano, Stacy worked the riverboats for a number of years, arriving in Chicago in the mid-20s. There, he played with numerous bands, including that of Paul Mares, on through into the early 30s. In 1935, **John Hammond** brought him to the attention of **Benny Goodman** and for the next four years Stacy was a member of the latter's band, playing at the 1938 Carnegie Hall concert during which he contributed a remarkable if out-of-context solo in the middle of the gallery-pleasing excesses of 'Sing Sing Sing'. He was with **Bob Crosby** from 1939-42, then returned to Goodman for a couple of years. He recorded with **Lee Wiley**, to whom he was married for a while, and directed her accompanying orchestra for a number of years. By the late 40s he was playing in west coast bars. Although he made a few return appearances with Goodman, he drifted towards the edges of the music business and by 1963 had abandoned playing altogether. In 1974, he performed again, this time at the **Newport Jazz Festival**, where he was rapturously received by audiences and critics. Thereafter, he resumed his playing career and continued to delight audiences. A distinctive and accomplished pianist, Stacy was capable of playing fearsome, two-fisted stride piano and contrastingly delicate solos, all marked by striking inventiveness.
Albums: with Benny Goodman *Carnegie Hall Concert* (1938), one side only *Stacy 'N' Sutton* (1953), *Tribute To Benny Goodman* (1955), *The Return Of Jess Stacy* (c.1962), *Stacy Still Swings* (1974). Compilations: *Jess Stacy And Friends* (1944).

Stafford, Jim

b. 16 January c.1946, Florida, USA. Stafford had a series of novelty hits in the mid-70s, but his career began as a member of the Legends which also included **Gram Parsons** and **Lobo** (Kent Lavoie). Working with Miami producer Phil Gernhard, Stafford signed to **MGM** as a solo singer, releasing 'Swamp Witch' in 1973. A minor hit, it was followed by the million-selling 'Spiders And Snakes', which used a swamp-rock sound reminiscent of **Tony Joe White** to tell a humorous tale. The song was composed by David Bellamy of the **Bellamy Brothers**. In 1974, Stafford tried a soft ballad with a twist, 'My Girl Bill' (his biggest UK hit) and another zany number, 'Wildwood Weed' which reached the US Top 10. Both were co-produced by Lobo. The same strand of humour ran through Stafford's 1975 singles 'Your Bulldog Drinks Champagne' and 'I Got Drunk And Missed It'. By now a minor celebrity, Stafford hosted a networked summer variety show from Los Angeles, where he met and married **Bobbie Gentry**. Such later records as 'Jasper' (**Polydor** 1976), co-written with Dave Loggins, and 'Turns Loose Of My Leg' (**Warner Brothers**/Curb 1977) were only minor hits but Stafford continued to record into the 80s for labels such as **Elektra**, Town House and **CBS**.
Albums: *Jim Stafford* (1974), *Spiders And Snakes* (1974), *Not Just Another Pretty Fool* (1975).

Stafford, Jo

b. 12 November 1920, Coalinga, near Fresno, California, USA. Although the birth date above is the one that has been accepted for some time, the alternative year of 1917 is given in the booklet accompanying the 1991 CD in the **Capitol** *Collectors Series*. One of the most popular female singers of the 40s, while still at high school Stafford studied serious music with the intention of making a career as a classical soprano. After five years of intensive work, she abandoned the idea and joined her two older sisters in their country music act, but later left to freelance on radio with the seven-man vocal group, the **Pied Pipers**. In 1939, after appearing on radio with **Tommy Dorsey**, they reduced the group to a quartet and joined Dorsey permanently. A large part of their appeal was Stafford's pure, almost academic tone, her distinctive vocal timbre and the complete lack of vibrato which provided a rock-steady lead. While with Dorsey she had solo success with 'Little Man With A Candy Cigar', 'Manhattan Serenade' and a 12-inch disc of 'For You'. She also duetted with Dorsey arranger **Sy Oliver** on his own composition, 'Yes Indeed'. When the Pipers left Dorsey in 1942 and started recording for **Capitol Records**, Stafford was soon out on her own as one of the top stars of the 40s. She stayed with the label until 1950, having hits such as

'Candy' (with **Johnny Mercer**), 'That's For Me', 'Serenade Of The Bells', 'Some Enchanted Evening' and 'Tennessee Waltz'. There were also several duets with **Gordon MacRae**, including 'My Darling, My Darling' from the Broadway musical *Where's Charley*, and 'Whispering Hope' an old religious song also recorded by **Pat Boone**. In 1950 she switched to **Columbia**, immediately having further success with 'Make Love To Me', 'Shrimp Boats', 'Keep It A Secret', 'Jambalaya' and her biggest seller 'You Belong To Me'. Just as important as the singles were a series of high-class albums of standards scored by her husband, ex-Dorsey arranger **Paul Weston**, who had become her musical alter-ego. Her reputation in some quarters as being a purely academic singer was given the lie on two notable occasions. The first was when she recorded pseudonymously as the lunatic Cinderella G. Stump on **Red Ingle** and the Natural Seven's 1947 comedy hit 'Temptation'; and the second a decade later when, with her husband, she made a series of albums as 'Jonathan And Darlene Edwards', in which they wickedly sent up amateur pianists and singers. In 1959 Stafford retired from public performing, but recorded until the mid-60s, sometimes for **Frank Sinatra**'s **Reprise** label. Dissatisfied with their former recording companies' neglect of their output, Stafford and Weston acquired the rights themselves and released them on their own Corinthian label.

Albums: with Gordon MacRae *Sunday Evening Songs* (1953), with Gordon MacRae *Memory Songs* (mid-50s), with Frankie Laine *Musical Portrait Of New Orleans* (mid-50s), *Happy Holiday* (mid-50s), *Ski Trails* (1956), *Once Over Lightly* (mid-50s), *Swingin' Down Broadway* (1958), *I'll Be Seeing You* (1959), *Ballad Of The Blues* (1959), *Jo + Jazz* (1960), *Jo + Blues* (early 60s, reissued 1980), *Jo + Broadway* (early 60s, reissued 1979), with Gordon MacRae *Old Rugged Cross* (early 60s), *Songs Of Faith Hope And Love* (early 60s, reissued 1978), *American Folk Songs* (1962, reissued 1978), with Gordon MacRae *Whispering Hope* (1962), with Gordon MacRae *Peace In The Valley* (1963), *Sweet Hour Of Prayer* (1964), *Joyful Season* (1964), *Getting Sentimental Over Tommy Dorsey* (mid-60s), *Do I Hear A Waltz?* (1966), *This Is Jo Stafford* (1966), *G.I. Joe - Songs Of World War II* (1979), *Broadway Revisited - Romantic Ballads From The Theater* (1983), *Fan Favorites Through The Years* (1984), *International Hits* (1988). Compilations: *Jo Stafford's Greatest Hits* (1959), *Jo Stafford Showcase* (1960), *The Hits Of Jo Stafford* (1963), *Jo Stafford's Greatest Hits - Best On Columbia* (1977), *Hits Of Jo Stafford* (1984), *Stars Of The 50s* (1984), *Introducing Jo Stafford* (1987), *Broadway Revisited* (1988), *Capitol Collectors Series* (1991). As Jonathan And Darlene Edwards *Sing Along With Jonathan And Darlene Edwards - Only The Chorus Is For Real* (50s/60s), *Jonathan And Darlene's Original Masterpiece* (50s/60s), *In Paris - Grammy Award Winning Album* (1960). Compilation: *Jonathan And Darlene's Greatest Hits* (80s).

Stafford, Terry

b. Amarillo, Texas, USA. This tall, local sports champion was also a fan of **Elvis Presley** and **Buddy Holly**, artists whose repertoires he would dip into when singing with his school group. With his parents' blessing, he began a showbusiness career in Hollywood where, after two years as a night-club entertainer, he was spotted by John Fisher and Les Worden who had just founded Crusader Records. His first record, 'Suspicion' - later a hit for Presley - was issued in February 1964 and, despite the onset of Beatlemania, scrambled to number 3 in the US chart, and beat a cover by Millicent Martin to Britain's Top 40. Further hits proved harder to come by, and a transfer to **MGM** in 1971 did not improve his fortunes.

Albums: *Suspicion!* (1964), *Dr. Goldfoot And The Girl Bombs* (1966, film soundtrack), *Born Losers* (1966, film soundtrack).

Films: *Dr Goldfoot And The Girl Bombs* (1966).

Stage Dolls

This melodic power-trio emerged from Trondheim, Norway. Formed in 1983, the original line-up comprised Torstein Flakne (vocals/guitar; ex-Kids), Terje Storli (bass) and Erlend Antonson (drums; ex-**Subway Sect**), the latter eventually replaced by Steinar Krokstad. Their three albums combine high-tech production with superbly crafted AOR, the songs heavily infused with melody and a keen sense of dynamics. 'Love Cries', lifted as a single from their self-titled 1988 album, became a minor Stateside hit in 1989. On the strength of this, they secured the support slots on the **Blue Murder** and **Warrant USA** tours the same year, but failed to build on the initial momentum.

Albums: *Soldier's Gun* (Polygram 1985), *Commandoes* (Polygram 1986), *Stage Dolls* (Polydor 1988).

Stage Door Canteen

Released in 1943, this film was a paper-thin excuse for Hollywood to bring onto the screen a stream of mostly front-rank entertainers to brighten war-time gloom. Alongside screen stars are leading figures from Broadway, vaudeville, popular music and jazz. **Benny Goodman** And His Orchestra, including **Jack Jenney**, **Conrad Gozzo**, **Jess Stacy**, **Louie Bellson** and **Peggy Lee**, perform two numbers. **Count Basie** And His Orchestra, including **Buck Clayton**, **Freddie Green**, **Walter Page**, **Harry Edison**, **Dicky Wells**, **Buddy Tate**, **Don Byas**, **Earle Warren** and **Jo Jones**, perform one number backing **Ethel Waters**.

Staines, Bill

b. 6 February 1947, Medford, Massachusetts, USA. This singer/songwriter's early influences were **Gordon**

Lightfoot, the **Weavers**, **Woody Guthrie**, **Ian And Sylvia Tyson**, and Peter La Farge. Bill grew up in the Boston area absorbing and listening to the music of the early 60s, and started playing professionally in 1965. Although largely playing guitar in concert, Staines also uses autoharp and banjo for recording work. In 1975, Bill won a National Yodelling contest at the Kerrville Folk Festival, Texas. The contest was built around the fact that **Jimmie Rodgers**, the singing and yodelling brakeman, was from Kerrville. Staines has successfully blended traditional and contemporary themes into a style that is highly original. His songs have been recorded by other artists, including **Nanci Griffith**, who included 'Roseville Fair' on her *The Last Of The True Believers*. In addition to touring regularly, Staines is currently working on a project to produce a complete book of all of his songs.

Albums: *Miles* (1976), *Old Wood And Winter Wine* (1977), *Just Play One More Tune* (1977), *Whistle Of The Jay* (1978), *Rodeo Rose* (1981), *Sandstone Cathedrals* (1983), *Bridges* (1984), *Wild, Wild Heart* (1985), *Redbird's Wing* (1988), *Tracks And Trails* (1991), *Going To The West* (1993). Compilations: *The First Million Miles* (1989).

Further reading: *If I Were A Word, Then I'd Be A Song*, Bill Staines, 1980. *Moving It Down The Line*, Bill Staines, 1987. *All God's Critters Got A Place In The Choir*, Bill Staines & Margot Zemach.

Stallone, Frank

b. Philadelphia, Pennsylvania, USA. The younger brother of actor Sylvester Stallone, Frank Stallone placed three singles in the US charts during the early 80s, including one Top 10 single. Stallone began singing and writing songs while in high school, and, living in New York City after graduating, worked with a band called Valentine, which recorded one poor-selling album. Frank appeared in his brother's first *Rocky* film in 1976, but did not receive a recording contract until 1980, when he signed with the Scotti Brothers label. One minor chart single, 'Case Of You', resulted. Stallone next surfaced in 1983 on RSO Records, for which he recorded the US Top 10 'Far From Over', which was heard in his brother's *Staying Alive* film. A third single, 'Darlin'', appeared in the charts in 1984.

Album: *Frank Stallone* (1988), *Close Your Eyes* (1993).

Stamey, Chris

b. Chapel Hill, North Carolina, USA. Singer/guitarist Stamey first rose to prominence as a member of the **Sneakers**, a short-lived pop/rock act which split up in 1976. Having become domiciled in New York, he was briefly associated with a group fronted by erstwhile **Box Tops** member, **Alex Chilton**, who in turn produced Stamey's solo debut single, 'The Summer Sun'. The artist subsequently formed the **dBs**, who completed a series of excellent, melodic albums.

However, despite critical approbation, the group was not a commercial success and Stamey left to resume his solo career during the 80s. A period involved with the **Golden Palominos**, an informal attraction loosely-based on available, like-minded musicians, punctuated his albums, but although unprolific, Stamey has continued to enjoy cult popularity. In 1991 he undertook live appearances in London, accompanied by former dBs partner Peter Holsapple.

Albums: *In The Winter Of Love* (1984), *It's Alright* (1987), with Peter Holsapple *Mavericks* (1991).

Stamm, Marvin

b. 23 May 1939, Memphis, Tennessee, USA. After studying trumpet at school and later at North Texas State University, Stamm joined the **Stan Kenton** Mellophonium Orchestra. In the mid-60s he was with **Woody Herman**, then became a studio player based in New York. During the next few years he also played many jazz dates, including work with the **Thad Jones-Mel Lewis** Jazz Orchestra, **Frank Foster**, **Chick Corea** and with **Duke Pearson**'s rehearsal band. In the 70s and on into the 80s he continued mixing studio work with jazz, playing with **Benny Goodman**, leading his own small groups and working with the American Jazz Orchestra and with **George Gruntz**. Stamm's decision to spend a substantial part of his career to date working in the studios has limited the number of opportunities for the jazz audience to hear him. When those occasions have arisen he has proved to be an interesting and enthusiastic player whose best work is always precise and controlled.

Albums: with Stan Kenton *Adventures In Time* (1962), with Woody Herman *Jazz Hoot* (1966), *Machinations* (1968), *Stammpede* (1982), with Benny Carter *Central City Sketches* (1987).

Stampede

This melodic UK hard rock band was formed in 1981 by ex-**Wild Horses** trio Reuben Archer (vocals), Laurence Archer (guitar) and Frank Noon (drums). Recruiting bassist Colin Bond, they signed to **Polydor Records** the following year. Noon left for Tormé and was replaced by Eddie Parsons before they debuted with *The Official Bootleg*, recorded live at the Reading Festival. Their music at this point incorporated elements of **Deep Purple** and **UFO**, particularly the guitar style of Laurence Archer which appeared to be a composite of the techniques of **Michael Schenker** and **Ritchie Blackmore**. *Hurricane Town* followed, but was a disappointment. It featured disposable, mid-paced rockers reminiscent of **Thin Lizzy**. Unable to attract media attention, Stampede split up in 1983. Laurence Archer joined **Grand Slam** and later recorded a solo album, *L.A.*

Albums: *The Official Bootleg* (Polydor 1982), *Hurricane Town* (Polydor 1983).

Stampley, Joe

b. 6 June 1943, Springhill, Louisiana, USA. Stampley met **Hank Williams** when he was 7 years old, who gave him the advice to 'just be yourself and act like yourself and maybe later on it will pay off for you'. He became friends with local disc jockey **Merle Kilgore**, when he was 15 and they began to write songs together. In 1958, Kilgore obtained for him the chance to record for Imperial. This led to the release of a single, 'Glenda', which sold well in his own locale but failed elsewhere. In 1961 a further recording on **Chess Records**, 'Teenage Picnic', also failed. He later recorded a tribute to his labelmate **Chuck Berry**, 'The Sheik Of Chicago'. Stampley, influenced in his early days by artists such as **Jerry Lee Lewis**, chose the piano as his instrument and in his high school years turned his interests to rock music. In the mid-60s, he was the lead singer of a rock group, the Cut-Ups, who soon became the Uniques. In 1966, they had minor local successes with 'Not Too Long Ago' (a Kilgore/Stampley song), 'Will You Love Me Tomorrow' and 'All These Things', but in 1969 the Uniques disbanded. In the early 70s, he decided to return to country music and moved to Nashville, where initially he worked as a staff writer for Gallico Music. He signed with **Dot Records** and achieved minor chart success in 1971 with 'Take Time To Know Her'. The following year he gained his first US country number 1 with his own 'Soul Song'. (It also became his only US pop chart success peaking at number 37). This proved the start of a very successful period for him as a recording artist. By 1979, he had taken his total of country chart entries to 32 including two more number 1 hits with 'Roll On Big Mama' (1975) and a solo version of the song that he had recorded ten years previously in the rock band, 'All These Things' (1976). Other Top 5 hits included 'I'm Still Loving You', 'Take Me Home To Somewhere' and 'Do You Ever Fool Around'.

He moved to Epic in 1975, working with Norro Wilson as his producer until 1978, when **Billy Sherrill** took over. It was during 1979, as a result of touring together in Europe, that Stampley joined forces with **Moe Bandy** and a single release of 'Just Good Ole Boys' became a number 1 country hit and led to a continuation of the partnership over the following years. The idea of Moe and Joe came to them in the Hard Rock Cafe, London during their appearance at the Wembley Festival. It was perhaps not too surprising that they proved a successful double act; they sounded a little alike when they sang and on stage they looked alike. Between 1979 and 1985 their further hits were to include 'Holding The Bag', 'Tell Ole I Ain't Here', 'Hey Joe (Hey Moe)'. In 1984, they ran into copyright problems with their parody about pop singer **Boy George** called 'Where's The Dress', when they used

the intro of **Culture Club**'s hit 'Karma Chameleon'. Quite apart from their single successes they recorded several albums together. During the 80s, Stampley continued to make solo **Billboard** chart entries but many critics, perhaps unfairly, suggested they came because of the publicity achieved by his association with Bandy. Recordings with Bandy apart, his only Top 10 hits in the 80s were 'I'm Gonna Love You Back To Loving Me Again' and 'Double Shot Of My Baby's Love'. He also had a minor hit with a duet recording with Jessica Boucher of 'Memory Lane'. His overall total of 57 US **Billboard** country chart entries is impressive but few traditional country fans would be too enthusiastic with some of his recordings. Perhaps his contributions were accurately summed up by the critic who wrote 'Joe Stampley and **Billy 'Crash' Craddock** led a field of country rockers, who in the 70s, injected a 50s flavour into their songs'. During his career Stampley claims to have played every state in the union and a lot of other countries as well. He played the *Grand Ole Opry* in the 70s, in the days when it was centred at the Ryman Auditorium but has never been a regular member. He once stated his regret was that he had never had a million-selling record.

Albums: *If You Touch Me* (1972), *Soul Song* (1973), *Take Me Home To Somewhere* (1974), *I'm Still Loving You* (1974), *Joe Stampley* (1975), *Billy, Get Me A Woman* (1975), *All These Things* (1976), *Ten Songs About Her* (1976), *The Sheik Of Chicago (Chuck Berry)* (1976), *Saturday Nite Dance* (1977), *Red Wine And Blue Memories* (1978), *I Don't Lie* (1979), with Moe Bandy *Just Good Ole Boys* (1979), *After Hours* (1980), *I'm Gonna Love You Back To Loving Me Again* (1981), with Moe Bandy *Hey Joe, Hey Moe* (1981), *Encores* (1981), *Backslidin'* (1982), *I'm Goin' Hurtin'* (1982), *Memory Lane* (1983), with Bandy *The Good Ole Boys Alive And Well* (1984), with Bandy *Live From Bad Bob's In Memphis* (1985), *I'll Still Be Loving You* (1985).

Stand Up And Sing

After their tremendous successs together in *That's A Good Girl* (1928), **Jack Buchanan** and Elsie Randolph teamed up again for this delightful musical comedy which was presented at the London Hippodrome on 5 March 1931. The score was by Phil Charig and **Vivian Ellis** (music) and Douglas Furber (lyrics). Furber also collaborated with Buchanan on a book which turned out to be the story of a mini-world tour. Much of the action takes place on the cruise ship S.S. Ambrosia and in Egypt where Buchanan, who is pretending to be a valet but is really a toff, goes to retrieve some important papers for his girl's father. The ingénue was played by **Anna Neagle** in her first important stage role before launching into a long and distinguished stage and film career. She duetted with Buchanan on 'There's Always Tomorrow', the show's big ballad, but he and Elsie Randolph (who rather conveniently was a maid to his valet) handled most of the other songs, which included 'Take It Or Leave It', 'Mercantile Marine', 'I Would If I Could', 'It's Not You', 'Nobody To Take Care Of Me', 'Keep Smiling', 'Night Time', and Buchanan's speciality 'inebriated dance' routine, 'Hiccup Time In Burgundy'. Also in the cast were familar names such as Sylvia Leslie, Richard Dolman, Richard Murdoch, Vera Pearce, Morris Harvey, and Anton Dolin who occasionally brought his brilliant brand of dancing from the ballet theatre to revue and musical comedy. *Stand Up And Sing* was an instant hit - West End audiences rejoiced in having Buchanan back on stage after a break of three years. The show ran for 325 performances at the Hippodrome and then toured successfully. During the run the entire second act was broadcast by the BBC, and several years later, in 1945, the complete show, still with Jack Buchanan and Elsie Randolph, was adapted for radio.

Standells

Tony Valentino (guitar/vocals) and Larry Tamblyn (organ) formed the Standells in 1962. The early line-up included drummer Gary Leeds, who later found fame in the **Walker Brothers**, Gary Lane (bass) and former Mousketeer Dick Dodd (drums). The quartet became a leading teen-based attraction in plush Los Angeles night-spots. This conformist image was shattered on their association with producer Ed Cobb who fashioned a series of angst-cum-protest punk anthems in 'Sometimes Good Guys Don't Wear White', 'Why Pick On Me' and the exceptional 'Dirty Water', a US number 11 hit in 1966. In 1966 Gary Lane left the group during a tour of Florida. He was initially succeeded by Dave Burke who in turn was replaced the following year by John Fleck (nee Fleckenstein). The latter, who co-wrote 'Can't Explain' on **Love**'s debut album, has since become a leading cinematographer. The Standells also appeared in the exploitation film, *Riot On Sunset Strip* (1967), but by this time their career was waning. Unfashionable in the face of San Francisco's acid-rock, the group's career was confined to the cabaret circuit as original members drifted away. **Lowell George**, later of **Frank Zappa**'s **Mothers Of Invention** and **Little Feat**, briefly joined their ranks, but by 1970 the Standells had become an oldies attraction.
Albums: *The Standells Live At PJs* (1964), *Live And Out Of Sight* (1964), *Dirty Water* (1966), *Why Pick On Me* (1966), *The Hot Ones* (1966), *Try It* (1967). Compilation: *The Best Of The Standells* (1984)
Films: *Get Yourself A College Girl* (1964).

Stanko, Tomasz

b. 11 July 1942, Rzeszow, Poland. Stanko learnt the violin and piano at school and studied trumpet at the music high school in Cracow (1969). He has a wide range and formidable technique. He formed the group Jazz Darings (1962) with **Adam Makowicz** and played with various other local musicians. In the early 70s he played with the **Globe Unity Orchestra** and the European Free Jazz Orchestra at Donaueschingen. He then formed a quintet which included **Zbigniew Seifert** who switched from alto saxophone to violin while he was with the band. Later on he formed the Unit again with Makowicz and this band earned widespread praise being described as a 'white **Ornette Coleman**'. In fact the band was more traditionally based, though there was an element of free playing in the music. He has since also played as an unaccompanied soloist at the **Taj Mahal** and Karla Caves Temple as well as performing with **Chico Freeman**, **James Spaulding**, **Jack DeJohnette**, **Gary Peacock** and the **Cecil Taylor** Big Band.
Albums: *Music For K* (1970), *We'll Remember Komeda* (1973), *Balladyna* (ECM 1975), *Music From The Taj Mahal And Karla Caves* (1980), with Gary Peacock *A Voice From The Past* (1981), with Cecil Taylor *Winged Serpent* (1985), *The Montreaux Performance* (ITM 1988), *Tales For A Girl 12/A Shakey Chica* (Jam 1992), *Bluish* (Power Bros 1992), *Bosanossa And Other Ballads* (GOWI 1994).

Stanley Brothers

Carter Glen Stanley (b. 27 August 1925, McClure, Dickenson County, Virginia, USA) and his brother Ralph Edmond Stanley (b. 25 February 1927, Big Spraddle Creek, near Stratton, Dickenson County, Virginia, USA). Their father Lee Stanley was a noted singer and their mother played banjo. They learned many old-time songs as children and soon began to sing at church and family functions. In 1941, with two school friends, they formed the Lazy Ramblers and played some local venues. In 1942, with Carter playing guitar and Ralph the banjo, they appeared as a duo on WJHL Johnson City, Tennessee. After graduation, Ralph spent eighteen months in the Army, mainly serving in Germany. In 1946, after a brief spell with Roy Sykes' Blue Ridge Mountain Boys, they formed their own Clinch Mountain Boys and began playing on WNVA Norton. Soon after they moved to WCYB Bristol, Tennessee, to appear regularly on *Farm And Fun Time*. Their intricate harmony vocal work (Carter sang lead to Ralph's tenor harmony) and their variety of music, with styles varying from the old-time to bluegrass, then being popularized by **Bill Monroe**, proved a great success. In 1947, they made their first recordings for the Rich-R-Tone label and later moved to WPTF Raleigh, North Carolina. With their standard five instrument line-up, they became one of the most renowned bluegrass bands and were much in demand for concert appearances.
Between 1949 and 1952 they made some recordings for **Columbia** which are now rated as classic bluegrass. These included many of Carter's own compositions, such as 'The White Dove', 'Too Late To Cry', 'We'll

Be Sweethearts In Heaven' and 'The Fields Have Turned Brown'. They disbanded for a short time in 1951. Ralph briefly played banjo with Bill Monroe before being injured in a car crash. During this time, Carter played guitar and recorded with Bill Monroe. However, they soon reformed their band and returned to *Farm And Fun Time* on WCYB. After leaving Columbia, they first recorded a great many sides for **Mercury**. The material included more self-penned numbers, honky-tonk songs, instrumentals and quite a lot of of gospel songs recorded with quartet vocal harmonies. Ralph Stanley has always maintained that this period produced their best recordings and experts have rated the mid-50s as the Stanley Brothers' 'Golden Era'. Later recordings were issued on Starday, King, Wango, Rimrock and Cabin Creek. (Over the years Copper Creek records have released a series taken from radio shows, which at the time of writing already totals 10 albums.) Their only US country chart success came in 1960; a Top 20 hit for the novelty number 'How Far To Little Rock'.

Through the 50s and up to the mid-60s, they played at venues and festivals all over the States and made overseas tours. It was during a European tour in March 1966 that they appeared in concert in London. The hectic schedules caused Carter to develop a drink problem; his health was badly affected and he died in hospital in Bristol, Virginia, on 1 December 1966. After his brother's death, Ralph Stanley reformed the Clinch Mountain Boys and continued to play and recorded bluegrass music. In 1970, he started the annual Bluegrass Festival (named after his brother), an event which attracted large numbers of musicians and bluegrass fans. Over the years, his style of banjo playing has been copied by many young musicians and he has become respected (like Monroe) as one of the most important artists for popularizing bluegrass music. During the 70s and 80s, the Clinch Mountain Boys have included within their ranks such country artists as **Ricky Skaggs**, **Keith Whitley** and Larry Sparks and others including **John Conlee** and **Emmylou Harris** have recorded Stanley Brothers songs. British bluegrass followers were delighted to see Ralph Stanley live at the 1991 Edale Festival.

Albums: by the Stanley Brothers *Country Pickin' & Singin'* (1958), *The Stanley Brothers* (1959), *Everybody's Country Favorites* (1959), *Mountain Song Favorites* (1959), *Hymns & Sacred Songs* (1959), *Sacred Songs From The Hills* (1960), *For The Good People* (1960), *Old Time Camp Meeting* (1961), *Sing Everybody's Country Favorites* (1961), *The Stanley Brothers* (1961), *In Person* (1961), *Sing The Songs They Like The Best* (1961), *Live At Antioch College-1960* (1961), *Award Winners At The Folk Song Festival* (1962), *The Mountain Music Sound* (1962), *Good Old Camp Meeting Songs* (1962), *Five String Banjo Hootenanny* (1963), *The World's Finest Five String Banjo* (1963), *Just Because (Folk Concert)* (1963), *Hard Times* (1963), *Country-Folk Music Spotlight*

(1963), *Old Country Church* (1963), *Bluegrass Songs For You* (1964), *Hymns Of The Cross* (1964), *The Stanley Brothers - Their Original Recordings* (1965), *The Angels Are Singing* (1966), *Jacob's Vision* (1966), *Bluegrass Gospel Favorites* (1966), *The Greatest Country & Western Show On Earth* (1966), *A Collection Of Original Gospel & Sacred Songs* (1966), *The Stanley Brothers Go To Europe* (1966), *An Empty Mansion* (1967), *Memorial Album* (1967), *The Best Loved Songs Of Carter Stanley* (1967), *The Legendary Stanley Brothers Recorded Live, Volume 1* (1968), *The Legendary Stanley Brothers Recorded Live, Volume 2* (1969), *On Stage* (1969), *How Far To Little Rock* (1969), *Deluxe Album* (1970), *Together For The Last Time* (1971), *Rank Strangers* (1973), *The Stanley Brothers* (1974), *The Stanley Brothers On The Air* (1976), *A Beautiful Life* (1978), *I Saw The Light* (1980), *The Columbia Sessions, Volume 1* (1981), *Shadows Of The Past* (1981), *The Columbia Sessions, Volume 2* (1982), *The Stanley Brothers* (1983, 6-album set), *Stanley Brothers On Radio, Volume 1* (1984), *Stanley Brothers On Radio, Volume 2* (1984), *The Starday Sessions* (1984), *The Stanley Series* (80s, 10-album set), *On WCYB Bristol Farm & Fun Time* (1988), *Gospel Songs From Cabin Creek* (1990), *The Stanley Brothers And The Clinch Mountain Boys* (Bear Family 1994).

Albums By Ralph Stanley: *The Bluegrass Sound* (1968), *Brand New Country Songs By* (1968), *Over The Sunset Hill* (1968), *Old Time Music* (c.1969), *Hills Of Home* (1970), *Cry From The Cross* (1971), *Ralph Stanley Live In Japan* (1971), *Sings Michegan Bluegrass* (1971), *Something Old Something New* (1972), *Plays Requests* (1973), *Old Country Church* (1973), *I Want To Preach The Gospel* (1973), *The Stanley Sound Around The World* (1973), *Gospel Echoes Of The Stanley Brothers* (1973), *A Man And His Music* (1975), *Let Me Rest On A Peaceful Mountain* (1975), *Live at McClure* (1976), *Old Home Place* (1977), *Clinch Mountain Gospel* (1978), *Down Where The River Bends* (1979), *I'll Wear A White Robe* (1980), *Hymn Time* (1980), with Jimmy Martin *First Time Together* (1980), *The Stanley Sound Today* (1981), *The Memory Of Your Smile* (1982), *Child Of The King* (1983), *Bluegrass* (1983), *Sings Traditional Bluegrass And Gospel* (1983), *Live At The Old Home Place* (1983), *Snow Covered Mound* (1984), *Singing Sixteen Years* (c.1984), *Shadows Of The Past* (c.1984), *I Can Tell You The Time* (1985), *Live In Japan* (1986), *Lonesome & Blue* (1986), *I'll Answer The Call* (1988), *Ralph Stanley & Raymond Fairchild* (1989), *(Clawhammer) The Way My Mama Taught Me* (1990), *Like Father Like Son* (1990), *Pray For The Boys* (1991), *Saturday Night And Sunday Morning* (Freeland 1993), *The Stanley Brothers And The Clinch Mountain Boys 1953-59* (Bear Family 1994, double CD set).

Albums issued on Wango in early 60s as John's Gospel Quartet: *John's Gospel Quartet* (reissued 1973 as *The Stanley Brothers of Virginia Volume.1*), *John's Country Quartet* (reissued 1973 as *The Long Journey Home*), *John's Gospel Quartet Volume 2* (reissued 1973 as *The Stanley Brothers Volume 4*), *John's Gospel Quartet Songs Of Mother & Home* (reissued 1973 as *The Little Old Country Church House*).

Stansfield, Lisa

b. 11 April 1966, Rochdale, Greater Manchester, England. Stansfield started her musical career singing in her early teens, entering and winning several talent contests. She gained valuable experience presenting the Granada television children's programme, *Razzamatazz* in the early 80s. After quitting the programme Stansfield teamed up with former school friends and budding songwriters Andy Morris and (Lisa's boyfriend) Ian Devaney to form the white-soul group, Blue Zone in 1983. With backing from **Arista Records**, the group released *Big Thing* (1986), and several singles on the Rockin' Horse label but achieved little success outside the club circuit. In 1989, the trio were invited by the dance-music production team, **Coldcut** (Matt Black and Jonathan Moore) to record the single 'People Hold On'. The single reached the UK Top 20 and prompted former Blue Zone/**Wham!** manager Jazz Summers to sign Stansfield as a solo act while retaining Morris and Devaney in the capacity as composers, with Stansfield, musicians and producers. The first single, on Arista, 'This Is The Right Time' reached number 13 in the UK chart while the follow-up, 'All Around This World' emerged as one of best singles of 1989, hitting the UK number 1 spot and becoming an international hit. Her debut *Affection*, reached number 2, eventually selling five million copies worldwide. Stansfield, with her infectious smile, a disarming broad Lancastrian/Rochdale accent, down-to-earth nature and kiss-curled hair emerging from an collection of hats, became one of the top pop personalities of the year and collected a variety of awards including the Best British Newcomer at the 1990 BRIT awards. That same year, the Blue Zone songwriting team of Stansfield, Morris and Devaney were also acknowledged by being presented the prestigious **Ivor Novello** award for their number 1 hit as Best Contemporary Song. While 'Live Together' was peaking at number 10 in the UK singles chart, plans were afoot to break into the US chart. *All Around This World* then reached number 3 topped the ***Billboard*** R&B listing while *Affection* reached the US Top 10. Her success in the US was followed by 'You Can't Deny It' (number 14) and 'This Is The Right Time' (number 21). The following years' BRIT awards were notable for Stansfield winning the Best British Female Artist award. She also succeeded in offending organizer **Jonathan King**, by speaking out against the Gulf War. *Real Love*, which allowed Stansfield free range to express herself, won over previously reticent admirers and promoted a more mature image.

Albums: *Affection* (1989), *Real Love* (1991), *Lisa Stansfield In Session* (1992), *So Natural* (1993).

Stanshall, Vivian

b. 21 March 1943, Shillingford, Oxfordshire, England, d. 5 March 1995. Stanshall's love of pre-war ephemera, trad jazz and an art school prankishness was instrumental in shaping the original tenor of the **Bonzo Dog Doo-Dah Band**. This satirical unit was one of the most humourous and inventive groups to emerge from the 60s, but fell foul of the eclectic pursuits of its divergent members. Stanshall's first offering following the Bonzo's collapse was 'Labio Dental Fricative', a single credited to the Sean Head Showband, an impromptu unit which included guitarist **Eric Clapton**. A second release, a brazenly tongue-in-cheek rendition of **Terry Stafford**'s 'Suspicion', featured Vivian Stanshall And His Gargantuan Chums, and was coupled to 'Blind Date', the singer's only recording with biG GRunt, the group he had formed with **Roger Ruskin Spear**, Dennis Cowan and 'Borneo' Fred Munt, three refugees from the immediate Bonzo Dog circle. Each band member, bar Munt, appeared on *Let's Make Up And Be Friendly*, the album the Bonzos belatedly completed to fulfil contractual obligations. Despite a handful of excellent live appearances, biG GRunt's undoubted potential withered to a premature end when Stanshall entered hospital following a nervous breakdown.

Men Opening Umbrellas, Stanshall's debut album, was released in 1974. **Steve Winwood** was one of the many musicians featured on the record, inaugurating a working relationship which continued with the excellent 'Vacant Chair' on Winwood's solo debut *Steve Winwood* and major lyrical contributions to *Arc Of A Diver*, his 1980 release. Indeed, despite recording a punk-inspired version of **Cliff Richard**'s 'The Young Ones', Stanshall achieved notoriety for his contributions to other outside projects, narrating **Mike Oldfield**'s *Tubular Bells* and as a contributor to the BBC Radio 4 programme, *Start The Week*. It was while deputizing for the Radio 1 disc jockey **John Peel** that Stanshall developed his infamous monologue, *Rawlinson End*. This later formed the basis for the artist's 1978 release, *Sir Henry At Rawlinson End*, which later inspired a film of the same title and starred Trevor Howard. Stanshall continued to tread his idiosyncratic path throughout the 80s. An album of songs, *Teddy Bears Don't Knit* was followed by another spoken-word release, *Henry At Ndidis Kraal*. In 1991, he continued the Rawlinson saga by staging at London's Bloomsbury Theatre, *Rawlinson Dogends*, which included in the show's backing band former Bonzo colleagues, Roger Ruskin-Spear and Rodney Slater. In the 90s Stanshall carved out a separate career using his voice in advertising, making full use of his luxurious, stately tones. Until his tragic death, caused by a fire at his home, Stanshall was one of England's most cherished eccentrics. At his memorial service which was attended by a host of professional admirers, Steve Winwood sang an impassioned 'Arc Of A Diver' accompanied by his acoustic guitar. Neil Innes made a moving speech which contained the poignant line 'did he (Stanshall) fear that nobody would love him if he allowed himself to be ordinary?'

Albums: *Men Opening Umbrellas* (1974), *Sir Henry At Rawlinson End* (1978), *Teddy Bears Don't Knit* (1981), *Henry At Ndidis Kraal* (1984).

Further reading: *Mojo* magazine, May 1995.

Staple Singers

This well-known US family gospel group consisted of Roebuck 'Pops' Staples (b. 28 December 1915, Winona, Mississippi, USA) and four of his children, **Mavis Staples** (b. 1940, Chicago, Illinois, USA), Pervis Staples (b. 1935), Cleotha Staples (b. 1934) and Yvonne Staples (b. 1939). The quintet fused an original presentation of sacred music, offsetting Mavis Staples' striking voice against her father's lighter tenor, rather than follow the accustomed 'jubilee' or 'quartet' formations, prevalent in the genre. Pops' striking guitar work, reminiscent of delta-blues, added to their inherent individuality. Singles such as 'Uncloudy Day', 'Will The Circle Be Unbroken' and 'I'm Coming Home', proved especially popular, while an original song, 'This May Be The Last time' provided the inspiration for the **Rolling Stones**' hit 'The Last Time'.

During the early half of the 60s, the group tried to broaden its scope. Two singles produced by **Larry Williams**, 'Why (Am I Treated So Bad)' and 'For What It's Worth', a **Stephen Stills**' composition, anticipated the direction the Staples would take on signing with **Stax** in 1967. Here they began recording material contributed by the label's established songwriters, including **Homer Banks** and Bettye Crutcher, which embraced a moral focus, rather than a specifically religious one. Reduced to a quartet following the departure of Pervis, a bubbling version of **Bobby Bloom**'s 'Heavy Makes You Happy' (1970) gave the group their first R&B hit. This newfound appeal flourished with 'Respect Yourself' (1971) and 'I'll Take You There' (1972 - a US pop number 1), both of which expressed the group's growing confidence. Their popularity was confirmed with 'If You're Ready (Come Go With Me)' (1973), 'City In The Sky' (1974), and by appearances in two films, *Wattstax* and *Soul To Soul*. The Staple Singers later moved to the Curtom label where they had an immediate success with two songs from a **Curtis Mayfield**-penned film soundtrack, 'Let's Do It Again' (another US pop number 1) and 'New Orleans'. These recordings were the group's last major hits although a series of minor R&B chart places between 1984 and 1985 continued the Staples' long-established ability to be both populist and inspirational.

Albums: *Gospel Program* (1961), *Hammers And Nails* (1962), *Great Day* (1963), *25th Day Of December* (1962), *Spirituals* (1965), *Amen* (1965), *Freedom Highway* (1965), *Why* (1966),

This Little Light (1966), *For What It's Worth* (1967), *Staple Singers* (1968), *Pray On* (1968), *Soul Folk In Action* (1968), *We'll Get Over* (1970), *I Had A Dream* (1970), *Heavy Makes You Happy* (1971), *The Staple Swingers* (1971), *Beatitude: Respect Yourself* (1972), *Be What You Are* (1973), *Use What You Got* (1973), *City In The Sky* (1974), *Let's Do It Again* (1975), *Pass It On* (1976), *Family Tree* (1977), *Unlock Your Mind* (1978), *Hold On To Your Dream* (1981), *Turning Point* (1984). *The Staple Singers* (1985). Compilations: *Swing Low* (1961, early recordings), *Uncloudy Day* (1961, early recordings), *Tell It Like It Is* (1972, early recordings), *Great Day* (1975, early recordings), *Stand By Me* (1977, early recordings), *Respect Yourself: The Best Of The Staple Singers* (1988), *Freedom Highway* (1991), *Staple Swingers* (1991), *Soul Folk In Action/We'll Get Over* (1994). Pop Staples solo: with Steve Cropper, Albert King *Jammed Together* (1970), *Peace To The Neighborhood* (1992).

Staples, Mavis

b. 1940, Chicago, Illinois, USA. The exceptional lead voice of the **Staple Singers** began a simultaneous solo career when the group was signed to the **Stax** label in 1968. Here she began recording distinctly secular material including songs by **Otis Redding** ('Good To Me', 'Security'), **Sam Cooke** ('You Send Me') and **Joe Simon** ('The Chokin' Kind'). The singer's gospel fervour enhanced such compositions although her first R&B hit came with an original song, 'I Have Learned To Do Without You'. This progress was waylaid in the wake of the Staples' own success with 'Heavy Makes You Happy' and her career was only resumed in 1977. 'A Piece Of The Action' was a fine collaboration with **Curtis Mayfield**, but later releases swamped her magnificent voice in disco and electro-pop beat. In 1987 the singer was signed to **Prince**'s Paisley Park organization, the fruits of which appeared on *Time Waits For No-One*, released two years later. Mavis also made a guest appearance on **Aretha Franklin**'s gospel set, *One Lord, One Faith, One Baptism*.

Albums: *Mavis Staples* (1969), *Only For The Lonely* (1970), *A Piece Of The Action* (1977), *Time Waits For No One* (1989), *The Voice* NPG 1995). Compilation: *Don't Change Me Now* (1990).

Staples, Pops

b. Roebuck Staples, 2 December 1914, Winona, Mississippi, USA. Despite spending most of his life (very successfully) performing gospel music, Pops Staples had a solid grounding in blues in his teenage years. Brought up on Will Dockery's Plantation outside Drew, he watched **Charley Patton** playing guitar on the boss's porch. He took up the guitar at 16, learning by ear and playing church songs for his father. But at weekends, he sneaked off to chittlin' feasts to earn some change playing the blues. Married at 18, he moved his growing family to Chicago in 1935, taking menial jobs and at weekends singing with the Silver Trumpets. In

1952, he bought a cheap guitar and taught his children to sing gospel songs. Five years later, the **Staples Singers** went professional. Staples was 77 when he recorded his first solo album, which brought together **Ry Cooder**, **Bonnie Raitt**, **Jackson Browne** and **Willie Mitchell**. The songs ranged from Browne's title track to Cooder-produced versions of 'Down In Mississippi' and 'I Shall Not Be Moved'. *father father* continued in the same vein, combining 'Jesus Is Going To Make Up (My Dying Bed)' with **Bob Dylan**'s 'You Got To Serve Somebody' and **Curtis Mayfield**'s 'People Get Ready'. Though hardly blues, Pops Staples' music represents a gentle voice of reason in a strident world.

Albums: *Peace To The Nieghborhood* (PointBlank 1992), *father father* (PointBlank 1994).

Stapleton, Cyril

b. 31 December 1914, Nottingham, England, d. 25 February, 1974. Stapleton played the violin at the age of 11, and served in pit orchestras for silent movies before joining **Henry Hall** as a violinist in the early 30s. By 1939, and the outbreak of World War II, he had moved on to working under Billy Ternent, via **Jack Payne**, and married impressionist Beryl Orde. He joined the Royal Air Force, initially as an air-gunner, later conducting the RAF Symphony Orchestra at the Potsdam Summit Conference. At the end of the war he formed a band to play at Fisher's Restaurant in London's New Bond Street. In the late 40s, the band, plus strings, was featured on BBC radio programmes such as *Hit Parade* and *Golden Slipper*. In the 50s he became known as the UK's 'Mr. Music' when he became the leader of the all-star BBC Show Band which made its first broadcast on the Light Programme on 2 October 1952, and was featured three nights a week thereafter. He led the band for five years, playing host to star US artists such as **Frank Sinatra**, and **Nat 'King' Cole**, along with residents Janie Marlow and the **Stargazers** vocal group. With his own band he had a string of UK chart hits for **Decca**, from 1955-57 including 'Elephant Tango', 'Blue Star' (theme from the US television series, *The Medics*), 'The Italian Theme', 'The Happy Whistler' and 'Forgotten Dreams'. In the USA Stapleton made the Top 30 with 'The Children's Marching Song' (from the movie, *The Inn Of The Sixth Happiness*) which, along with 'Blue Star', sold a million copies. In 1966 the Stapleton band moved to Pye Records, and later, he became A&R controller and an independent producer, master-minding the multi-million-selling *Singalong* series of albums by **Max Bygraves**. In the last few years of his life Stapleton began to tour with a big band, attempting to recreate the sounds of his heyday.

Albums: *Songs Of The Golden West* (1958), *Music For Dancing In The Dark* (1958), *Just For You* (1959), *Italy After Dark* (1959), *New York After Dark* (1959), *Come 'N' Get It* (1959), *Big Hits From Broadway* (1960), with Don Rendell *All-Time Big Band Hits* (1960), with his Concert Orchestra *'Congress Dances'* (1960), with Brian Johnson, Ray Merrell, Joy Worth *'Gigi' And 'South Pacific'* (1960), *Great Movie Hits* (1960), *Great Movie Hits Volume 2* (1961), *Top Pop Instrumentals* (1961), *Songs You Won't Forget* (1962), *My Fair Lady/King And I* (1969). Compilations: *The Big Band's Back* (1974), *Golden Hour Of Strict Tempo* (1974).

Star Is Born, A

Over the years, several films have attempted to strip the veneer of glamour from Hollywood, the film capital of the world, and expose the sadness and bitterness that sometimes lies beneath. *Sunset Boulevard* (1950) is, perhaps, the prime example of the genre, and, more recently, *The Player* (1992) dwelt on the greed and double-dealing inherent in the movie business. Adela Rogers St. John's original story, which eventually evolved into the 1954 Warner Brothers musical picture, *A Star Is Born*, first came to the screen in 1932 under the title of *What Price Hollywood?* Then, five years later, it was adapted for an Academy Award winning dramatic film entitled *A Star Is Born*, which had a story by William A. Wellman, a screenplay by Dorothy Parker, Alan Campbell and Robert Carson, and starred Janet Gaynor and Fredric March. **Moss Hart**'s superbly crafted screenplay for the 1954 musical version, which stayed fairly closely to the plot of the previous film, tells of Norman Maine (James Mason), a has-been movie actor, whose temperamental and brutish behaviour result in him being ostracised from Hollywood studios and society. While taking solace in the bottle, he is forced to become dependent on his wife, Esther Blodgett (professional name Vicki Lester), played by **Judy Garland**. Mainly through his influence (and her talent), she has become a big star herself. Eventually, unable to cope with life at the bottom of the barrel, he drowns himself. Garland was outstanding throughout - this was probably her greatest film role - and Mason, who is said to have been about fifth choice for the part, was wonderful, too. Charles Bickford as the studio head who is reluctant to let Maine go, and Jack Carson in the role of the studio's publicity chief who is only too glad to get rid of him, were in a fine supporting cast along with Lucy Marlow, Grady Sutton, Tommy Noonan, Amanda Blake, Irving Bacon, and James Brown. **Harold Arlen** and **Ira Gershwin** wrote most of the songs, including the compelling 'The Man That Got Away', 'Gotta Have Me Go With You', 'Someone At Last', 'It's A New World' and two that were cut because of the film's excessive length, 'Lose That Long Face' and 'Here's What I'm Here For'. The remainder were 'Swanee' (**George Gershwin-Irving Caesar**), and 'Born In A Trunk' (Leonard Gershe-**Roger Edens**) which effectively topped and tailed a medley of old songs. The choreographer was Richard

Barstow, and the film was produced by Sidney Luft (Garland's then husband), directed by George Cukor, and photographed in Technicolor and CinemaScope. One of the all-time great film musicals, *A Star Is Born* was re-released in the 80s complete with the two songs that were cut from the original print, and some other scenes restored.

In the 1976 remake of *A Star Is Born*, starring **Barbra Streisand** and **Kris Kristofferson**, screenwriters John Gregory Dunne, Frank Pierson and Joan Didion set their new plot in the world of rock music, with an appropriate score which included such numbers as 'Lost Inside Of You' (Streisand-**Leon Russell**), 'I Believe In Love' (**Kenny Loggins-Alan And Marilyn Bergman**), 'Queen Bee' (**Rupert Holmes**), and 'The Woman In The Moon' (**Paul Williams**-Kenny Ascher). Barbra Streisand and Paul Williams also collaborated on 'Love Theme (Evergreen)', which won an Academy Award and topped the US chart. The film was released by Warner Brothers and photographed in Metrocolor and Panavision. The director was Frank Pierson, and *A Star Is Born* (Mark III) was a smash hit, grossing nearly $40 million in the USA and Canada alone.

Star Spangled Rhythm

Just the thing for the troops - a rousing, star-studded spectacle that must have raised the spirits of war-weary forces and civilians alike when it was released by Paramount in December 1942. For what it was worth, Harry Tugend's screenplay had the Paramount gatekeeper (Victor Moore) pretending to be an important studio executive in order to impress the buddies of his sailor son (Eddie Bracken). The latter's efforts to organize a massive show is the perfect hook on which to hang a bundle of songs and sketches performed by many of Paramount's principal players. Joining in the fun and games were **Betty Hutton**, **Bing Crosby**, **Bob Hope**, **Dorothy Lamour**, Franchot Tone, Vera Zorina, Fred MacMurray, Jerry Colonna, Veronica Lake, Alan Ladd, Marjorie Reynolds, Eddie 'Rochester' Anderson, Paulette Goddard, Arthur Treacher, Cass Daley, Susan Hayward, Macdonald Carey, William Bendix, Sterling Holloway, Marjorie Reynolds, Gil Lamb, Edward Fielding, Walter Abel, and many more. **Harold Arlen** and **Johnny Mercer**'s appealing score contained two of their all time standards, 'That Old Black Magic', introduced by Johnny Johnston, and 'Hit The Road To Dreamland' which was given a fine treatment by **Mary Martin**, **Dick Powell** and the Golden Gate Quartet. The rest of the songs were 'I'm Doing It For Defence', 'On The Swing Shift', 'A Sweater, A Sarong And A Peek-A-Boo Bang', 'He Loved Me Till The All-Clear Came', 'Sharp As A Tack', and 'Old Glory'. Danny Dare and George Ballanchine staged the dances, and the director of this lively and entertaining affair was George Marshall. Joesph Sistrom produced, and it was photographed in black and white by Leo Tover.

Star!

While this 1968 movie biography of London-born actress **Gertrude Lawrence** failed to even nearly recoup its massive $12 million investment, and was generally considered to be far too long, it is by no means a poor picture mainly because the central role is played by **Julie Andrews**. Wisely, she does not attempt an impersonation, but rather gives an impression of what this darling of London and Broadway musical shows and revues, from the 20s through to the 50s, must have been like. William Fairchild's screenplay begins with Lawrence's childhood days in Clapham when she was part of the family music hall act along with her father (Bruce Forsyth) and his 'lady friend' (Beryl Reid). Director Robert Wise places the adult Lawrence in a projection room watching (and commenting on) the rushes of a biography being compiled about her career and the men in her life, including Richard Crenna as her second husband Richard Aldrich. **Noël Coward** was probably her greatest influence, and Daniel Massey's portrayal of 'The Master' as an amiable and sophisticated character is one of the movie's most appealing features. His elegant version of 'Forbidden Fruit' which Coward often used as his 'audition song', is a delight. The two stars combine for the 'Red Peppers' sequence from Coward's play *Tonight At 8.30*, and Andrews handles most of the remaining songs with great flair and panache. They included 'Someone to Watch Over Me', 'Do Do Do', and 'Dear Little Boy' (all **George Gershwin-Ira Gershwin**), ''N' Everything' (**Buddy De Sylva-Gus Kahn-Al Jolson**), 'Limehouse Blues' (Douglas Furber-Philip Braham), 'Burlington Bertie From Bow' (William Hargreaves), 'Jenny' and 'My Ship' (both **Kurt Weill**-Ira Gershwin), 'The Physician' (**Cole Porter**), and 'Parisian Pierrot', 'Someday I'll Find You' and 'Has Anybody Seen Our Ship?' (all Coward). The brand new title number was by **James Van Heusen** and **Sammy Cahn**. Also among the cast were Michael Craig, Robert Reed, Garrett Lewis, Don Knoll, John Collin, and Alan Oppenheimer, Richard Anthony, and J. Pat O'Malley. **Michael Kidd** was the choreographer and the film was superbly photographed by Ernest Laszlo in Deluxe Color and Todd-AO. It was directed by Robert Wise and produced for 20th Century-Fox by **Saul Chaplin**. *Star!* was eventually cut from nearly three hours to just over two, and re-released under the title of *Those Were The Happy Times*. That version lost money too.

Starcastle

This AOR rock group was formed in Illinois, USA, in 1972 by Stephen Hagler (guitar/vocals), Herb Schildt (keyboards) and Gary Strater (bass). The six-piece line-up was completed by ex-**REO Speedwagon** vocalist Terry Luttrell, guitarist Matt Stuart and drummer Steve Tassoer. After being championed by the local WGPU Radio Station in Champaign, Illinois, they were signed by **Epic Records** in 1974. Their music, which incorporated elements of **Yes**, **Emerson, Lake And Palmer** and **Rush**, was characterized by multi-vocal harmonies and complex, but carefully executed time-changes. They released four albums before splitting up, but never achieved the recognition their talents deserved.

Albums: *Starcastle* (Epic 1975), *Fountains Of Light* (Epic 1977), *Citadel* (Epic 1978), *Reel To Reel* (Epic 1979).

Starcher, Buddy

b. Oby Edgar Starcher, 16 March 1906, Kentuck, Jackson County, West Virginia, USA. He first learned to play banjo but later became an outstanding guitarist. In 1928, he was probably the first hillbilly artist to appear on radio in the Baltimore area. Between 1930 and 1960, he continually moved around, not only playing venues in his home State, Virginia and Kentucky (especially Charleston and Fairmont), but further afield to Miami, Iowa and Philadelphia. In 1946, he recorded in Chicago for Four Star, including his best-known song 'I'll Still Write Your Name In The Sand'. Now a much recorded bluegrass standard, it reached number 8 in the country charts. Later he recorded for other labels including **Columbia**, Starday, **Decca**, Bluebonnet and Bear Family. In 1960, his television show in Charleston had higher local ratings than NBC's *Today*. In 1966, he had a number 2 country and number 39 pop hit with 'History Repeats Itself' - his cleverly written narration detailing the many similarities between the assassinations of Presidents Lincoln and Kennedy. In the late 60s, he returned to radio and for some years managed radio stations, being usually brought in as a troubleshooter to pick up ailing stations - once they were running successfully, he moved on to the next challenge. He has written many fine songs including 'Song Of The Water Wheel' (a hit for **Slim Whitman**) and also some prose. In the late 30s, he married fellow artist, Mary Ann (Vasas) who in 1941, took over from **Patsy Montana** on WLS Chicago.

Albums: *Buddy Starcher & His Mountain Guitar* (1962), *History Repeats Itself* i (1966), *History Repeats Itself* ii (1966), *Buddy Starcher Volume 1* (1967), *Country Soul & Inspiration* (c.60s), *Country Love Songs* (1978), *The Boy From Down Home* (1984), *Pride Of The West Virginia Hills* (1984), *Me And My Guitar* (1986).

Further reading: *Buddy Starcher - Biography*, Robert H. Cagle.

Starchild

This Canadian hard rock quartet, formed in 1977 by Richard Whittie (vocals), Robert Sprenger (guitar), Neil Light (bass) and Gregg Hinz (drums), debuted with *Children Of The Stars* the following year. Influenced by **Triumph**, **Rush** and **Styx**, the album was characterized by Sprenger's inventive guitar work and Whittie's distinctive vocals. Hinz quit to join **Helix** shortly after the album's release, with ex-**Lone Star** drummer Dixie Lee stepping in as replacement. The band continued for a short time, but split up before any further recordings were made.

Album: *Children Of The Stars* (Axe 1978).

Stardust

Directed by Michael Apted in 1974 and starring **David Essex**, *Stardust* continued the exploits of popsinger Jim Maclaine, first unveiled on the superior *That'll Be The Day*. This follow-up charted Maclaine's inexorable rise from member of 60s' beat group the Stray Cats to solo star in the early part of the subsequent decade. A life of selfish hedonism - sex, drugs and calculated misanthropy - leaves the star in lonely isolation at the film's close, but the predictable outcome undermines any implied moral statement. **Adam Faith** co-stars memorably as Maclaine's long-suffering associate, providing much-needed warmth in several scenes. **Dave Edmunds**, who appears as a member of the Stray Cats, provided a portion of the soundtrack music, creating empathetic renditions of several pop staples, including 'Some Other Guy' and 'A Shot Of Rhythm 'n' Blues' while the remainder is culled from original material by a variety of 60s acts.

Stardust, Alvin

b. Bernard William Jewry, 27 September 1942, London, England. Jewry first enjoyed pop fame during the early 60s under the name **Shane Fenton**. When the arrival of the **Beatles** and the subsequent Mersey beat explosion occurred, Fenton effectively retired from singing. In one of the more unlikely comebacks in British pop history, he re-emerged in 1973 as hit singer Alvin Stardust. Bedecked in menacingly black leather, with an image that fused **Gene Vincent** with **Dave Berry**, Stardust returned to the charts with the UK number 2 hit 'My Coo-Ca-Choo'. It was followed by the chart-topping 'Jealous Mind' which, like its predecessor, was composed by songwriter Peter Shelley. Two further UK Top 10 hits followed, with 'Red Dress' and 'You You You' before his chart career petered out with 'Tell Me Why' and 'Good Love Can Never Die'. The indomitable Stardust revitalized his career once more during the early 80s with the Top 10 successes 'Pretend' and the commemorative ballad 'I Feel Like **Buddy Holly**', which also mentioned **Paul McCartney**. Stardust ended 1984 with two further hits 'I Won't Run Away' and 'So Near Christmas' before once again falling from chart favour. He remains a popular star on the British showbusiness scene and in recent years, as a born-again Christian, presented and performed on BBC television with Christian pop and rock acts.

Albums: *It's All Happening* (1963), *Good Rockin' Tonight* (1974), *I'm A Moody Guy* (1982), *I Feel Like... Alvin Stardust* (1984). Compilation: *Greatest Hits: Alvin Stardust* (1977), *20 Of The Best* (1987).

Further reading: *The Alvin Stardust Story*, Tremlett, George (1976).

Starfighters

This UK hard rock/boogie quintet was formed in 1980 by ex-**Suburban Studs**' vocalist Steve Burton and guitarist Stevie Young (cousin of **AC/DC**'s Angus Young). With Pat Hambly (guitar), Doug Dennis (bass) and Steve Bailey (drums; ex-**Holly And The Italians**) completing the line-up, they were picked up by **Jive Records** in 1981, after having toured with AC/DC. Produced by Tony Platt, their debut album was characterized by raunchy rock 'n' roll, with abrasive, up-front guitar work from Young. However, at best they were a poor man's AC/DC, specializing in second-hand riffs, hackneyed vocals and a predictable backbeat. On *In Flight Movie*, they tried desperately to move away from this approach, concentrating instead on more traditional blues-based hard rock. Unfortunately this new style had even less to commend it, and they broke up soon after its release.

Albums: *Starfighters* (Jive 1981) *In Flight Movie* (Jive 1983).

Stargard

This inter-racial female soul/disco trio consisted of Rochelle Runnells, Debra Anderson and Janice Williams from Los Angeles, California, USA. Runnells and Anderson had been in various groups together, including Virgin Spring, before Anderson joined Masters Children, and Runnells founded Nature's Gift. They worked together again as backing singers for **Anthony Newley** and when Anderson left she was replaced by Williams. Runnells was asked by top producer **Norman Whitfield**'s right hand man Mark Davis to form a trio and she and Williams brought back Anderson (who had recorded some unsuccessful solo records on TK and **Columbia**). The trio, who had an intergalactic image, made the title song from Richard Pryor's film *Which Way Is Up* an R&B number 1 and a transatlantic Top 20 hit in 1978. They returned to the R&B Top 10 later that year with the title track from *What You Waitin' For* but that was their last real taste of success. They appeared in the ill-fated *Sgt. Pepper* film as the Diamonds and joined **Warner Brothers** in 1980. Anderson left shortly after and the act continued for a while as a duo.

Albums: *Stargard* (1978), *What You Waitin' For* (1978).

Stargazers

Formed in 1949, they developed into Britain's most popular vocal group in the early 50s. The original line-up consisted of **Dick James**, **Cliff Adams**, Marie Benson, Fred Datcheler, and Ronnie Milne. They first attracted attention on radio programmes such as *The Derek Roy Show* and *The Family Hour*, later moving to *Top Score*, the *Goon Show* and *Take It From Here*. The Stargazers began recording towards the end of 1949, working for a variety of labels, including **Decca**, **HMV**, **Columbia** and Polygon, backing artists such as **Steve Conway** and Benny Lee, and later, **Dennis Lotis** and **Jimmy Young**. Their own releases included 'Me And My Imagination', 'Red Silken Stockings', 'A-Round The Corner' and 'Sugarbush'. In April 1953, they became the first British act to reach number 1 in the infant *New Musical Express* chart, with 'Broken Wings'. Amost a year later, they hit the top spot again, with **Meredith Willson**'s 'I See The Moon'. They continued to record into the late 50s, and made the UK chart with 'Happy Wanderer', 'Somebody', 'Crazy Otto Rag', 'Close The Door', 'Twenty Tiny Fingers' and 'Hot Diggity' (1956). They worked constantly in radio, and their own series, *The Stagazers' Music Shop*, opened for business on **Radio Luxembourg** in 1952, crossing to the BBC nearly five years later. The group also had a regular slot on the BBC's *Show Band Show* with **Cyril Stapleton**, and toured the UK variety circuit. Their first permanent personnel change came in 1953, when David Carey replaced Ronnie Milne. Milne emigrated to Canada and took up a post in the Canadian Army, training young musicians. Two years later, the group appeared in the Royal Variety Performance, and, in the same year, Eula Parker took over from her fellow Australian, Marie Benson, who embarked on a solo career, armed with a two year contract with Philips Records. Parker herself was later succeeded by June Marlow. After being replaced by Bob Brown, Dick James, the Stargazers' original leader, had solo hits with 'Robin Hood' and 'Garden Of Eden' before becoming a successful music publisher and the proprietor of **DJM Records**. Cliff Adams went on to devise the radio programme, *Sing Something Simple* in 1959, and he and his Singers have remained with the show ever since. Fred Datcheler became a member of the Polka Dots, a vocal group bearing some resemblance to the **Hi-Lo's**. Datcheler's son, Clark, was a founder member of the 80s vocal/instrumental band **Johnny Hates Jazz**.

Selected albums: *Make It Soon* (1955), *South Of The Border* (1960).

Starjets

This band was formed in Belfast, Northern Ireland, in June 1976 with a line-up composed of Paul Bowen (guitar/vocals), Terry Sharpe (guitar/vocals), John Martin (bass/vocals) and Liam L'Estrange (drums/vocals). Since their school days each member had been involved with various bands of different

musical tastes. Their paths often overlapped with Spike, a small rock band that included John, Paul and Liam. However, the limitations of the Irish rock circuit ultimately resulted in the Starjets leaving their native shores and heading across the water to England. In the first months of 1978 they were put into the 'power-pop' category which was influenced musically by the 60s, with a leaning towards punk. Their live set included cover versions such as the **Beatles**' 'Please Please Me' and the **Archies**' 'Sugar Sugar', as well as a series of self-penned songs: 'No Politics', 'Smart Boys', 'Top Of The World', 'Run With The Pack' and 'War Stories'. Their 1978 debut 'It Really Doesn't Matter' was closely followed by 'Run With The Pack'. Both received excellent reviews and had all the ingredients of a power-pop hit but due to lack of promotion, neither had any commercial success. *God Bless The Starjets* spawned three singles: 'Ten Years', 'War Stories' and 'School Days'. Critics and the public showed only a lukewarm response, 'War Stories' being the only one to achieve any success, reaching number 51 in the UK charts. 'Shireleo', suffered the same fate as previous offerings. Soon after the band broke up, but not before the release of a single under the pseudonym Tango Brigade called 'Donegal'. Some of the members went on to find success with the **Adventures**.
Album: *God Bless The Starjets* (1979).

Stark, Bobby

b. 6 January 1906, New York City, New York, USA, d. 29 December 1945, New York, USA. After learning to play several instruments Stark settled on trumpet, and by the mid-20s he was well-known on the New York club scene. He played briefly with **McKinney's Cotton Pickers** and **Chick Webb**, then joined **Fletcher Henderson** for five years. He followed this with another five-year job, this time with Webb. After Webb's death he continued for a while under **Ella Fitzgerald**'s leadership, then entered the US Army during the early part of World War II. In 1943 he was with **Garvin Bushell**, then played in various bands, including **Benny Morton**'s, until his early death in December 1945. A strikingly individualistic soloist, Stark's playing changed over the years from a forceful extrovert style, to one that was thoughtfully melodic.

Starland Vocal Band

A quartet based in the Washington, DC, USA. Starland Vocal Band took one single, the novelty disco hit 'Afternoon Delight', to the top of the US charts in 1976. The band comprised of the husband-wife team Bill Danoff (b. 7 May 1946, Springfield, Massachusetts; USA) and Taffy Danoff (b. Kathleen Nivert, 24 October 1944, Washington, DC, USA), Jon Carroll (b. 1 March 1957, Washington, DC, USA) and Margot Chapman (b. 7 September 1957, Honolulu, Hawaii, USA). The group had its roots in a band called **Fat City** which included the Danoffs. The Starland Vocal Band were formed in late 1974 and opened for **John Denver** on his 1975 tour (Bill had earlier co-written the John Denver hit 'Take Me Home, Country Roads'); Denver subsequently signed them to his Windsong Records label. The dance song 'Afternoon Delight', about the pleasures of mid-day sex ('Sky rocket's in flight - afternoon delight'), was the band's breakthrough in May 1976 and spent 14 weeks in the US charts, peaking at number 1. They placed a self-titled album at number 20 and three other singles charted but nothing came close to repeating the debut's success. Despite winning the Best New Artist and Best Vocal Arrangement Grammy awards, and being given a six-week television show of their own, the band's popularity declined and they broke up in 1980. Carroll later wrote the **Linda Ronstadt** hit, 'Get Closer', and eventually married Chapman; while the Danoffs divorced, but still worked together under the Fat City banner.
Albums: *Starland Vocal Band* (1976), *Rear View Mirror* (1977), *Late Nite Radio* (1978).

Starlets

An R&B female group from Chicago, Illinois, USA. Members were Liz 'Dynetta Boone' Walker, Jane Hall, Mickey McKinney, and Maxine Edwards. The Starlets with their strident rock 'n' roll sound reflected the early 60s era when African-American girl groups seemed to dominate the pop and R&B charts. Their one hit was 'Better Tell Him No' (number 24 R&B, number 38 pop, 1961), in which their mentor/composer Bernice Williams shared the lead with Edwards. The record in retrospect sounds harsh and unappealing, and most later listeners would favour the soul-style ballad b-side led by Walker, 'You Are The One'. Another 1961 release produced the excellent Walker-led 'My Last Cry', which received only local play in Chicago. In 1962 the Starlets on a tour of east coast cities violated their contract by recording 'I Sold My Heart To The Junkman' for Newtown Records in Philadelphia. Label owner Harold Robinson saw in Maxine Edwards' strident lead a voice that could give tremendous drive to a song. The record was released under the name Bluebelles, and it became **Patti Labelle And The Bluebelles** first hit in 1962, launching their career, even though ironically they did not sing on it. The Starlets in 1962 were dropped by their company, and shortly thereafter disbanded.

Starlight Express

Andrew Lloyd Webber is quoted as saying that this show, which was nick-named 'Squeals On Wheels' by one unkind critic, started out in 1975 as an entertainment intended for children. In 1983 he rewrote it for the benefit of his own children, Imogen and Nicholas, and then, with the help of lyricist

Richard Stilgoe, it became the full-blown musical which opened at the Apollo Victoria in London on 27 March 1984. The theatre's interior had to be completely re-designed to accommodate a series of racetracks, gantries, ramps, and bridges which encircled and dominated the auditorium. More than 20 rollerskaters, pretending to be trains, zoom along the tracks enacting a story in which, after a number of races, Rusty (Ray Shell), a shy little steam engine, triumphs over Greaseball (Jeff Shankley) the flashy diesel locomotive, and gets hitched up to his favourite carriage, Pearl (Stephanie Lawrence). The high-tech effects, plus Arlene Phillips' imaginative choreography and **Trevor Nunn**'s direction, created what seemed almost like a giant computer game. The loudly amplified score contained elements of rock, blues, country, and many other influences, in songs such as 'Call Me Rusty', 'Only He (Has The Power To Move Me)', 'Pumping Iron', 'U.N.C.O.U.P.L.E.D', 'AC-DC', 'Right Place, Right Time', 'One Rock 'N' Roll Too Many', and 'Light At The End Of The Tunnel'. The show proved to be a consistently popular attraction, and, in April 1992, became the second longest-running British musical after *Cats*. Later in the year the production was revised and re-choreographed, and five new songs added, before it resumed its record-breaking journey. One member of the new cast, Lon Satton, had played Poppa the old steam locomotive since the first night in 1984. *Starlight Express* was also reworked for its Broadway run which began in March 1987 and lasted for 761 performances. In September 1993, a 90 minute edition of the show opened at the Las Vegas Hilton, the first major legitimate production ever to play the US gambling capital.

Starr, Edwin

b. Charles Hatcher, 21 January 1942, Nashville, Tennessee, USA. The brother of soul singers Roger and Willie Hatcher, Edwin Starr was raised in Cleveland, where he formed the Future Tones vocal group in 1957. They recorded one single for Tress, before Starr was drafted into the US Army for three years. After completing his service, he toured for two years with the **Bill Doggett** Combo, and was then offered a solo contract with the Ric Tic label in 1965. His first single, 'Agent Double-O-Soul', was a US Top 30 hit and Starr exploited its popularity by appearing in a short promotional film with actor Sean Connery, best-known for his role as James Bond. 'Stop Her On Sight (SOS)' repeated this success, and brought Starr a cult following in Britain, where his strident, gutsy style proved popular in specialist soul clubs. When **Motown Records** took over the Ric Tic catalogue in 1967, Starr was initially overlooked by the label's hierarchy. He re-emerged in 1969 with '25 Miles', a Top 10 hit which owed much to the dominant soul style of the **Stax** label. An album of duets with **Blinky** brought

some critical acclaim, before Starr resumed his solo career with the strident, politically-outspoken, 'War', a US number 1 in 1970. Teamed with writer/producer **Norman Whitfield**, Starr was allowed to record material which had been earmarked for the **Temptations**, who covered both of his subsequent Motown hits, 'Stop The War Now' and 'Funky Music Sho Nuff Turns Me On'.

Starr's own credentials as a writer had been demonstrated on 'Oh How Happy', which had become a soul standard since he first recorded it in the late 60s. He was given room to blossom on the 1974 soundtrack *Hell Up In Harlem*, which fitted into the 'blaxploitation' mould established by **Curtis Mayfield** and **Isaac Hayes**. Tantalized by this breath of artistic freedom, Starr left the confines of Motown in 1975, recording for small labels in Britain and America before striking a new commercial seam in 1979 with two major disco hits, 'Contact' and 'HAPPY Radio'. In the 80s, Starr was based in the UK, where he collaborated with the **Style Council** on a record in support of striking coalminers, and enjoyed a run of club hits on the Hippodrome label, most notably 'It Ain't Fair' in 1985. Between 1989 and 1991 Starr worked with Ian Levine's Motor City Records, recording a re-make of '25 Miles' in a modern style and releasing *Where Is The Sound*.

Albums: *Soul Master* (1968), *25 Miles* (1969), with Blinky *Just We Two* (1969), *War And Peace* (1970), *Involved* (1971), *Hell Up In Harlem* (1974), *Free To Be Myself* (1975), *Edwin Starr* (1977), *Afternoon Sunshine* (1977), *Clean* (1978), *HAPPY Radio* (1979), *Stronger Than You Think I Am* (1980), *Where Is The Sound* (1991). Compilation: *20 Greatest Motown Hits* (1986).

Starr, Jack

After quitting the heavy metal band **Virgin Steele** in 1984, guitarist Jack Starr teamed up with ex-**Riot** vocalist Rhett Forrester and former **Rods**' rhythm section Gary Bordonaro and Carl Canedy. They delivered *Out Of The Darkness* in 1984, a subtle combination of aggression, melody and dynamics. Starr dissolved the band soon after the album came out, preferring instead to use a new set of backing musicians on each subsequent release. Over the next four albums he moved away from his metallic roots, towards more commercial, arena-style rock typified by **Bon Jovi** and **Dokken**. Starr is one of the more original new-style, techno-wizard guitarists, but has yet to receive the recognition his talents undoubtedly deserve. He has recently opted to record under the band name of Burning Starr.

Albums: *Out Of The Darkness* (Music For Nations 1984), *Rock The American Way* (Passport 1985), *No Turning Back* (US Metal 1986), *Blaze Of Glory* (US Metal 1987), *Burning Starr* (US Metal 1989).

Starr, Kay

b. Katherine LaVerne Starks, 21 July 1922, Dougherty, Oklahoma, USA. While she was still a child Starr's family moved to Dallas, Texas, where she made her professional debut on local radio before she had left school. In 1939 she was hired briefly by **Glenn Miller** when his regular singer, **Marion Hutton**, was sick. Starr made records with Miller, but was soon on the move. She spent brief spells with the bands of **Bob Crosby** and **Joe Venuti**, and attracted most attention during her mid-40s stint with **Charlie Barnet**. Among the records she made with Barnet was 'Share Croppin' Blues', which was modestly successful. However, the record sold well enough to interest **Capitol Records**, and, from 1948-54, she had a string of hits with the label, including 'So Tired', 'Hoop-Dee-Doo', 'Bonaparte's Retreat', 'I'll Never Be Free', 'Oh, Babe!', 'Come On-AaMy House', 'Wheel Of Fortune' (US number 1 1952), Comes A-Long A-Love' (UK number 1 1952), 'Side By Side', 'Half a Photograph', 'Allez-Vous-En', 'Changing Partners', 'The Man Upstairs', 'If You Love Me (Really Love Me)' and 'Am I A Toy Or A Treasure?'. In 1955 she switched to **RCA**, and went straight to the top of the charts in the US and UK with 'Rock And Roll Waltz'. Her last singles hit to date was 'My Heart Reminds Me' (1957). Starr sang with controlled power and a strong emotional undertow, which made her an appealing in-person performer. In the 60s she became a regular attraction at venues such as Harrah's, Reno, and, as recently as the late 80s, she returned there, and also played New York clubs as a solo attraction and as part of nostalgia packages such as *3 Girls 3* (with **Helen O'Connell** and **Margaret Whiting**), and *4 Girls 4* (add Kaye Ballard). In the spring of 1993, she joined **Pat Boone**, another popular 50s survivor, on *The April Love Tour* of the UK.

Selcted albums: *In A Blue Mood* (1955), *Blue Starr* (1955), *Movin'* (1959), *Rockin' With Kay* (c.1959), *I Hear The Word* (1959), *Just Plain Country* (1959 reissued 1987), *Movin' On Broadway* (1960), *Kay Starr* (1960), *Losers Weepers* (1960), *One More Time* (1960), *Jazz Singer* (1961), *Cry By Night* (1962), *Tears And Heartaches* (1966), *Kay Starr And Count Basie* (1968). Compilations: *Pure Gold* (1981), with Bob Crosby *Suddenly It's 1939* (1985), *1947; Kay Starr* (1986), *Wheel Of Fortune* (1989), *Capitol Collectors Series* (1991).

Starr, Kenny

b. Kenneth Trebbe, 21 September 1953, Topeka, Kansas, USA. Starr grew up in Burlingame, Kansas and, according to publicity, was fronting his own band, the Rockin' Rebels, from the age of nine. As a teenager, he played clubs as part of a pop act, Kenny and the Imperials. Starr switched to country music in 1969 and won a talent contest in Wichita. A promoter invited him to appear on a forthcoming show with **Loretta Lynn** and **Conway Twitty**, where he won a standing ovation. Lynn suggested he moved to Nashville and gave him a job with her roadshow. With her support, he recorded for MCA from 1973-78 and had a US country Top 10 hit with 'The Blind Man In The Bleachers'. He had further success with 'Tonight I Face The Man Who Made It Happen', 'Hold Tight', 'Slow Drivin'' and 'Me And The Elephant', but he was soon forgotten.

Album: *The Blind Man In The Bleachers* (1975).

Starr, Maurice

b. 1954. Starr is a Boston-based entrepreneur who was the svengali behind **New Kids On The Block** and **New Edition**. Described in one newspaper article as 'a cross between **Berry Gordy** and P.T. Barnum', Starr was a failed R&B singer when he decided instead to create, manage and produce an act which would perform his songs. He assembled New Edition in 1982, hand picking the five black teenagers that comprised the group. They went on to have 11 US Top 10 R&B hits (one of which also made the pop Top 10) before its key members split, most notably **Bobby Brown**, who has had a successful solo career. In 1984 Starr applied the same formula to a quintet of white teenagers and by 1989, New Kids On The Block were the fastest-rising group in the USA. Starr also handled the group's lucrative marketing of posters, T-shirts, and other spin-offs. In 1990 he was hoping to repeat the success of his first two creations with artists such as Rick Wes, Perfect Gentlemen, Homework, the Superiors, Tommy Page and Ana.

Starr, Ringo

b. Richard Starkey, 7 July 1940, Dingle, Liverpool, England. Starkey established his reputation on the nascent Merseybeat circuit as drummer with **Rory Storm** And The Hurricanes. He later became acquainted with the **Beatles**, and having established a lively rapport with three of the group, became the natural successor to the taciturn **Pete Best** upon his firing in 1962. Ringo - a name derived from his many finger adornments - offered a simple, uncluttered playing style which formed the ideal bedrock for his partners' sense of melody. Although overshadowed musically, a deadpan sense of humour helped establish his individuality and each album also contained an obligatory Starr vocal. The most notable of these was 'Yellow Submarine', a million-selling single in 1966. Ringo's success in the group's attendant films, *A Hard Day's Night* and *Help!*, inspired an acting career and comedy roles in *Candy* and *The Magic Christian* ensued. His solo recording career started with *Sentimental Journey*, a collection of standards, and *Beaucoups Of Blues*, a country selection recorded in Nashville, both predated the Beatles' demise. Fears that his career would then falter proved unfounded. Starr's debut single, 'It Don't Come Easy', co-written with **George Harrison**, topped the US charts and sold in excess of 1 million copies while the same pair also created 'Back Off Boogaloo' (UK number 2) and 'Photograph'. *Ringo* featured songs and contributions from each of his former colleagues, although none were recorded together. Buoyed by strong original material and judicious rock 'n' roll favourites, the album later achieved platinum status and was rightly lauded as one of the strongest ex-Beatles' collections. 'You're Sixteen' topped the US chart in 1974, but despite further success with 'Oh My My', 'Snookeroo' (penned by **Elton John** and **Bernie Taupin**) and 'Only You', Ringo's momentum then waned. A highly-praised role in the film *That'll Be The Day* (1973) was followed by the poorly-received movie *Caveman*, while the albums *Ringo The 4th* and *Bad Boy* showed an artist bereft of direction. A 1983 album, *Old Wave*, was denied a release in both the US and UK, while the period was also marred by alcoholism and chronic ill-health. During this nadir, Ringo reached a completely new audience as narrator of the award winning children's television series, *Thomas The Tank Engine*, but signalled his return to active performing with a guest appearance on **Carl Perkins**' tribute show. However, an album recorded with US producer Chips Moman in 1987 was abandoned when sessions were blighted by excessive imbibing. Ringo then underwent highly-publicized treatment at an alcohol rehabilitation clinic with his wife, actress Barbara Bach, before reasserting his musical career with the All-Starr Band. **Levon Helm**, **Billy Preston**, **Joe Walsh** and **Dr. John** were among those joining the drummer for a successful 1989 US tour, later the subject of an album and video. The stellar cast Ringo was able to assemble confirmed the respect he is still afforded. Ringo received a high-profile in 1992 with a new album and tour. The record coincided with the 25th anniversary of *Sgt Pepper's* which was a timely reminder that Ringo's playing on that album was quite superb, and, in addition to his equally fine performance on *Abbey Road* begs for a re-appraisal of his standing as a drummer which appears grossly underrated.

Albums: *Sentimental Journey* (1969), *Beaucoups Of Blues* (1970), *Ringo* (1973), *Goodnight Vienna* (1974), *Ringo's Rotogravure* (1976), *Ringo The 4th* (1977), *Bad Boy* (1977), *Stop And Smell The Roses* (1981), *Old Wave* (1985), *Ringo Starr And His All-Starr Band* (1990), *Time Takes Time* (1992), *Live From Montreux* (1993). Compilations: *Blasts From Your Past* (1975), *StarrStruck: Ringo's Best (1976-1983)* (1989).

Further reading: *Ringo Starr Straightman Or Joker*, Alan Clayson.

Films: *A Hard Day's Night* (1964), *Help* (1965), *Give My Regards To Broad Street* (1985).

Starry Eyed And Laughing

This promising UK group formed in May 1973 as a duo: Tony Poole (b. 28 July 1952, Northampton, England; vocals/12 string guitar) and Ross McGeeney (b. 22 December 1950, Northamptonshire, England; vocals/lead guitar). Taking their name from a line in **Bob Dylan**'s song 'Chimes Of Freedom', the group were initially hugely influenced by the **Byrds**, with **Roger McGuinn**-style jingle-jangle **Rickenbacker** guitar-work and vocals. After briefly performing with bassist Steve Hall and drummer Nick Brown, the group found more suitable replacements in the form of Iain Whitmore (b. 5 October 1953, Shoreham, Sussex, England) and Mike Wackford (b. 6 February 1953, Worthing, Sussex, England). After securing a contract with **CBS Records** in April 1974, the quartet issued a self-titled debut album the following September. The work was dominated by Poole/McGeeney compositions and critics duly noted the striking Byrds' flavouring. After a year on the road, the group completed *Thought Talk*, which was issued in October 1975. Although the title was taken from the Byrds' song 'I See You', the album was a less derivative, more mature work, with Poole showing his melodic excellence on 'One Foot In The Boat' and Whitmore emerging as a highly-talented writer on the orchestrated 'Fools Gold'. Following a promotional tour of the USA that autumn, the group suddenly fragmented. McGeeney was replaced by Roger Kelly, and Whitmore quit in the spring of 1976. A valedictory gig for the German television show *Rockpalast* saw McGeeney return, playing alongside Kelly. Later that year, Poole briefly shortened the group title to Starry Eyed and recorded a couple of commercial singles produced by **Flo And Eddie**, but the anticipated radio hits were not forthcoming and so the story ended.

Albums: *Starry Eyed And Laughing* (1974), *Thought Talk* (1975).

Stars On 45

(see **Starsound**)

Starship

(see **Jefferson Starship**, **Jefferson Airplane** and **Hot Tuna**)

Starsound

The credit for the Starsound phenomenon arguably belongs to an unknown European bootlegger who created a medley of songs by original artists for use in discotheques during 1980. One of the tunes in the sequence was **Shocking Blue**'s 'Venus' and its appearance so outraged publisher William van Kooten that he was determined to record a rival legal version. Producer Jaap Eggermont, fo'merly a drummer in **Golden Earring**, elected to retain 'Venus' followed

by the **Archies**' 'Sugar Sugar' and a wealth of **Beatles** oldies. Three Fab Four soundalikes, Bas Muys, Okkie Huysdens and Hans Vermoulen took on the roles of **John Lennon**, **Paul McCartney** and **George Harrison**, respectively. In the UK, the track was titled 'Stars On 45' and credited to **Starsound**, but in the USA, Stars On 45 were the registered artists and the song sub-title was the longest in chart-topping history: 'Medley: Intro/Venus/Sugar Sugar/No Reply/I'll Be Back/Drive My Car/Do You Want To Know A Secret/We Can Work It Out/I Should Have Known Better/Nowhere Man/You're Going To Lose That Girl/Stars On 45'. In the UK, 'Stars On 45, Volume 2' featured a medley of **Abba** songs and, like its predecessor, reached number 2. Before long, the idea was ruthlessly milked and other record companies took note by releasing medley tributes by such artists as the **Beach Boys** and **Hollies**. A decade later, the medley art was resurrected and perfected by the multi-chart topping **Jive Bunny** And The Mastermixers.
Albums: *Stars On 45* (1981), *Stars On 45 - Volume 2* (1981), *Stars Medley* (1982).

Start

This Icelandic pop-rock group was formed in 1980 by vocalist Petur Kristjansson and guitarist Kristjan Edelstein. Enlisting the services of Eirikur Haukson (guitar/vocals), Nikulas Robertson (keyboards), Jon Olafsson (bass/vocals) and David Karlsson (drums), they signed to the Steinar label the following year. They debuted with *En Hun Snyst Nu Samt*; a predictable collection of soft-rock anthems with Icelandic vocals. They disappeared into oblivion, after representing Iceland in the Eurovision Song Contest.
Album: *En Hun Snyst Nu Samt* (Steinar 1981).

Starz

New York band formed in 1975 by guitarist Brendan Harkin, drummer Joey X Dube and bassist Peter Sweval. Whilst looking for musicians to complete their line-up they worked as session men and also recorded a soundtrack to the porn film, *Divine Obsession*. The following year they recruited guitarist Richie Ranno and vocalist Michael Lee Smith and signed to **Capitol Records**, who released the hit single, 'She's Just A Fallen Angel', and the album, *Starz*. Two more albums followed in 1977 before Harkin and Sweval left to be replaced by Bobby Messano and Orville Davies respectively. This line-up recorded the monumental *Coliseum Rock* set which took them to a worldwide audience. What followed was two years of touring but no new recordings. After a farewell tour they split in 1980. Ranno and Dube formed a new band with bassist Oeter Scance. A year later Ranno and Scance reunited with Smith and together with ex-**Prism** drummer Doug Madick, formed Hellcats. This band continued in the Starz vein of anthemic rock with

melody. Indeed, they even included much Starz material in their live set, their success leading to a series of Starz live albums and compilations being released. Messano had spent his time working with various bands associated with **Atlantic Records** including **Fiona**, and in 1989 formed his own band.
Albums: *Starz* (Capitol 1976), *Violation* (Capitol 1977), *Attention Shoppers* (Capitol 1977), *Colisseum Rock* (Capitol 1978). Compilations: *Live In America* (Violation 1983), *Live In Canada* (Heavy Metal 1985), *Piss Party* (Heavy Metal 1985), *Brightest Starz* (Heavy Metal 1985), *Starz To Colisseum Rock* (Heavy Metal 1985), *Do It With The Lights On* (Performance 1987), *Live In Action* (Roadrunner 1989). Hellcats: *Hellcats* (King Klassic 1982), *Hellcats Kids* (King Klassic 1987). Bobby Messano: *Messano* (Strategic 1989).

State Fair

This warm-hearted, idealistic slice of Americana came to the screen in 1945 courtesy of producer William Perlberg and 20th Century-Fox. It contained the only score that **Richard Rodgers** and **Oscar Hammerstein II** wrote especially for a film, and Hammerstein also contributed the screenplay (based on the novel by Phil Stong) which was short on narrative and seemed to consist simply of a series of relationships. Abel Frake (Charles Winninger) and his wife Melissa (Fay Bainter) of Brunswick, Iowa, spend a few days at the state fair with their children, Margie (Jeanne Crain), Wayne (**Dick Haymes**), and Abel's temperamental boar, Blue Boy. By the time they return to their farm, Blue Boy has won the prestigious blue ribbon, Melissa's sour pickle and mincemeat have both gained first prize, Margie has fallen for a small-time (soon to be a Chicago columnist) newspaper reporter Pat Gilbert (Dana Andrews), and Wayne is serenading band singer Emily Edwards (**Vivian Blaine**) with 'It's A Grand Night For Singing' in the middle of the day. Blaine had two nice songs, 'That's For Me' and 'Isn't It Kinda Fun?', (with Haymes), but the best number in the score was the lovely 'It Might As Well Be Spring', which was introduced by Jeanne Crain (dubbed by Louanne Hogan) and went on to win the Oscar for best song. Other numbers were the celebratory 'Our State Fair' and 'All I Owe Ioway'. The film's charming and affectionate style extended to the supporting cast which contained many familiar faces including Donald Meek, Frank McHugh, Percy Kilbride, William Marshall, and Harry Morgan. Leon Shamroy photographed it beautifully in Technicolor, and the director, Walter Lang, captured the mood of the times perfectly. There had been a previous (non-musical) film of *State Fair* in 1933 starring **Will Rogers** and Janet Gaynor, and there was a further musical version in 1962. This featured Tom Ewell, **Alice Faye**, Pamela Tiffin, **Bobby Darin**, **Pat Boone**, Ann-Margret, and some additional songs with both music and lyrics by Richard

Rodgers. The premiere of a new stage version of *State Fair* took place at the Stevens Centre in Winston-Salem, North Carolina, in July 1992, and was later presented at the Long Beach Civic Light Opera. A Broadway production was expected early in 1996.

Statetrooper

After leaving UK band **MSG** vocalist Gary Barden formed Statetrooper in 1986 with Martin Bushell (guitar), Jeff Summers (guitar; ex-**Weapon**), Steve Glover (keyboards), Jeff Brown (bass; ex-**Wildfire**) and Bruce Bisland (drums; ex-Wildfire/Weapon). They debuted the following year with a self-titled album of melodic AOR, which featured extensive keyboards with a production from Phil Chilton. It courted comparisons with **Foreigner**, **Styx** and **Thin Lizzy**, but lacked consistency in terms of songwriting. The album sold poorly and following a short period with Brian Robertson (ex-**Motörhead** and Thin Lizzy) on guitar, the band broke up.
Album: *Statetrooper* (FM Revolver 1987).

Statler Brothers

The Statler Brothers hail from Staunton, a town on the edge of Shenandoah Valley, Virginia, USA. In 1955 Harold W. Reid (bass, b. 21 August 1939, Augusta County, Virginia, USA), Philip E. Balsley (baritone, b. 8 August 1939, Augusta County, Virginia, USA), Lew C. DeWitt (tenor, b. 8 March 1939, Roanoke County, Virginia, USA) and Joe McDorman formed a gospel quartet. Although McDorman never became a Statler, he has worked with them occasionally. In 1960 he was replaced by Harold's brother, Donald S. Reid (b. 5 June 1945, Staunton, Virginia, USA), who is now the group's lead singer. Originally the quartet was called The Kingsmen, but they changed it to avoid confusion with a US pop group. The Statler Brothers was chosen from the manufacturer's name on a box of tissues, and the group point out that they might have been the Kleenex Brothers. In 1963, they auditioned for **Johnny Cash**, who invited them to be part of his road show. He also secured a record contract with Columbia, but the label was disappointed with the poor sales of their first records. Having been refused further studio time, they recorded Lew DeWitt's song, 'Flowers On The Wall', during a break in one of Johnny Cash's sessions. The infectious novelty made number 4 on the US pop charts (number 2, country) and, despite the American references, also entered the UK Top 40. The Statler Brothers continued with Cash's roadshow and recorded both with him ('Daddy Sang Bass') and on their own ('Ruthless', 'You Can't Have Your Kate And Edith Too'). Dissatisfied by the promotion of their records and by the lukewarm material they were given, they switched to Mercury Records in 1970 and their records have been produced by Jerry Kennedy since then.

With such US country hits as 'Bed Of Roses', 'Do You Remember These?', 'I'll Go To My Grave Loving You' and the number 1 'Do You Know You Are My Sunshine?', they established themselves as the number 1 country vocal group. They left Cash's roadshow in 1972, but they recorded a tribute to him, 'We Got Paid By Cash', as well as tributes to their favourite gospel group ('The Blackwood Brothers By The Statler Brothers') and their favourite guitarist ('**Chet Atkins**' Hand'). DeWitt was incapacitated through Crohn's disease and left in 1982. He released the solo *On My Own*, in 1985, but he died in Waynesboro, Virginia, on 15 August 1990. Many of their songs relate to their love of the cinema - 'The Movies', 'Whatever Happened To Randolph Scott?' and 'Elizabeth', a country number 1 written, inspired by watching the film *Giant*, by Jimmy Fortune, who replaced DeWitt. Fortune also wrote two other number 1 US country records for them, 'My Only Love' and 'Too Much On My Heart'. They also had considerable success with a spirited revival of 'Hello Mary Lou', which was praised by its composer, **Gene Pitney**. Their stage act includes the homespun humour of their alter egos, Lester 'Roadhog' Moran And The Cadillac Cowboys, and they gave themselves a plywood disc when the first 1,250 of the resulting album were sold. On the other hand, The Statler Brothers' Old-Fashioned Fourth Of July Celebration in Staunton attracts 70,000 a year. The Statler Brothers are managed from office buildings, which used to be a school which Dewitt and The Reids attended.
Albums: *Flowers On The Wall* (1966), *Big Hits* (1967), *Oh Happy Day* (1969), *Bed Of Roses* (1971), *Pictures Of Moments To Remember* (1971), *Interview* (1972), *Country Music Then And Now* (1972), *Symphonies In E Major* (1973), *Thank You World* (1974), *Alive At Johnny Mack Brown High School* (as by Lester 'Roadhog' Moran And His Cadillac Cowboys) (1973), *Carry Me Back* (1973), *Sons Of The Motherland* (1975), *The Holy Bible - Old Testament* (1975), *The Holy Bible - New Testament* (1975), *Harold, Lew, Phil And Don* (1976), *The Country America Loves* (1977), *Short Stories* (1977), *Entertainers, On And Off The Record* (1978), *The Originals* (1979), *Christmas Card* (1979), *Tenth Anniversary* (1980), *Years Ago* (1981), *The Legend Goes On* (1982), *Country Gospel* (1982), *Today* (1983), *Atlanta Blue* (1984), *Partners In Rhyme* (1985), *Christmas Present* (1985), *Four For The Show* (1986), *Radio Gospel Favourites* (1986), *Maple Street Memories* (1987), *Live* (1990), *Music, Memories And You* (1990), *All American Cowboy* (1991), *Words And Music* (1992), *Home* (1993).

Staton, Candi

b. Hanceville, Alabama, USA. A former member of the Jewel Gospel Trio, Staton left the group, and her first husband, for a secular career. She was then discovered performing at a club by **Clarence Carter**, who took the singer to the Fame label. Carter wrote her debut hit, the uncompromising 'I'd Rather Be An Old Man's

Sweetheart (Than A Young Man's Fool)', and helped guide the singer's early releases. She later began pursuing a country-influenced path, especially in the wake of her successful version of **Tammy Wynette**'s 'Stand By Your Man'. Staton and Carter were, by now, married, although this relationship subsequently ended in divorce. Candi left Fame for **Warner Brothers** in 1974 but it was two years before 'Young Hearts Run Free', an excellent pop-styled hit, consolidated this new phase. 'Nights On Broadway', written by the **Bee Gees**, then became a UK Top 10 single, although it unaccountably flopped in America. The singer has continued to enjoy intermittent UK success but US hits have been restricted to the R&B chart. 'You Lost The Love' a collaboration with the Force was a popular dancefloor track and a UK Top 40 hit in 1991. In the 90s Staton has been recording in the gospel field.

Albums: *I'm Just A Prisoner* (1969), *Stand By Your Man* (1971), *Candi Staton* (1972), *Candi* (1974), *Young Hearts Run Free* (1976), *Music Speaks Louder Than Words* (1977), *House Of Love* (1978), *Chance* (1979), *Candi Staton* (1980), *Nightlites* (1982), *Make Me An Instrument* (1985), *Sing A Song* (1986), *Love Lifted Me* (1988), *Stand Up And Be A Witness* (1990). Compilations: *Tell It Like It Is* (1986, shared with Bettye Swann), *Nightlites* (1992), *Candy* (1992, Japan), *Young Hearts Run Free* (1992, Japan).

Staton, Dakota

b. 3 June 1932, Pittsburgh, Pennsylvania, USA. After singing in clubs in a style modelled on that of such diverse artists as **Dinah Washington** and **Sarah Vaughan**, Staton began to attract wider attention in the mid-50s. She extended her repertoire to include popular songs, R&B, soul and gospel and made a number of successful record albums. In the mid-60s she took up residence in the UK and Europe, but was back in the USA early in the following decade. She is at her best with mainstream jazz accompaniment, whether a big band, such as **Manny Albam**'s or **Kurt Edelhagen**'s, or a small group, such as those led by **George Shearing** and **Jonah Jones**. Staton's R&B material is less attractive, often performed at feverish tempos and with a deliberate coarsening of her powerful voice.

Albums: *The Late, Late Show* (1957), *Dakota Staton* i (1958), *Dakota Staton* ii (1959), *Dakota Staton* iii (1960), *Dakota Staton* iv (1960), *Dakota Staton* v (1960), *Dakota Staton At Storyville* (1961), *Dakota Staton* vi (1963), *Dakota Staton At Newport* (1963), *Dakota Staton* vii (c.1964), *Dakota Staton* viii (1967), with Richard 'Groove' Holmes *Let Me Off Uptown* (c.1972), *Dakota Staton With The Manny Albam Big Band* (1973), *Darling, Please Save Your Love* (1992).

Status Quo

The origins of this durable and now-legendary attraction lie in the Spectres, a London-based beat group. Founder members Mike (later Francis) Rossi (b.

29 May 1949, Peckham, London, England; guitar/vocals) and Alan Lancaster (b. 7 February 1949, Peckham, London, England; bass) led the act from its inception in 1962 until 1967, by which time Roy Lynes (organ) and John Coughlan (b. 19 September 1946, Dulwich, London, England; drums) completed its line-up. The Spectres' three singles encompassed several styles of music, ranging from pop to brash R&B, but the quartet took a new name, Traffic Jam, when such releases proved commercially unsuccessful. A similar failure beset 'Almost But Not Quite There', but the group was nonetheless buoyed by the arrival of Rick Parfitt aka Rick Harrison (b. 12 October 1948, Woking, Surrey, England; guitar/vocals), lately of cabaret attraction, the Highlights. The revamped unit assumed their 'Status Quo' appellation in August 1967 and initially sought work backing various solo artists, including **Madeline Bell** and **Tommy Quickly**. Such employment came to an abrupt end the following year when the quintet's debut single, 'Pictures Of Matchstick Men', soared to number 7. One of the era's most distinctive performances, the song's ringing guitar pattern and *de rigueur* phasing courted pop and psychedelic affectations. A follow-up release, 'Black Veils Of Melancholy', exaggerated latter trappings at the expense of melody, but the group enjoyed another UK Top 10 hit with the jaunty 'Ice In The Sun', co-written by former 50s singer, **Marty Wilde**. Subsequent recordings in a similar vein struggled to emulate such success, and despite reaching number 12 with 'Down The Dustpipe', Status Quo was increasingly viewed as a *passé* novelty. However, the song itself, which featured a simple riff and wailing harmonica, indicated the musical direction unveiled more fully on *Ma Kelly's Greasy Spoon*. The album included Quo's version of **Steamhammer**'s 'Junior's Wailing', which had inspired this conversion to a simpler, 'boogie' style. Gone too were the satin shirts, frock coats and kipper ties, replaced by long hair, denim jeans and plimsolls. The departure of Lynes *en route* to Scotland - 'He just got off the train and that was the last we ever saw of him' (Rossi) - brought the unit's guitar work to the fore, although indifference from their record company blighted progress. Assiduous live appearances built up a grass roots following and impressive slots at the Reading and Great Western Festivals (both 1972) signalled a commercial turning point. Now signed to the renowned **Vertigo** label, Status Quo scored a UK Top 10 hit that year with 'Paper Plane' but more importantly, reached number 5 in the album charts with *Piledriver*. A subsequent release, *Hello*, entered at number 1, confirming the group's emergence as a major attraction. Since that point their style has basically remained unchanged, fusing simple, 12-bar riffs to catchy melodies, while an unpretentious 'lads' image has proved equally enduring. Each of their 70s albums reached the Top 5, while a consistent

presence in the singles' chart included such notable entries as 'Caroline' (1973), 'Down Down' (a chart topper in 1974), 'Whatever You Want' (1979) and 'Lies'/'Don't Drive My Car' (1980). An uncharacteristic ballad, 'Living On An Island' (1979), showed a softer perspective while Quo also proved adept at adapting outside material, as evinced by their version of **John Fogerty**'s 'Rockin' All Over The World' (1977). That song was later re-recorded as 'Running All Over The World' to promote the charitable *Race Against Time* in 1988. The quartet undertook a lengthy break during 1980, but answered rumours of a permanent split with *Just Supposin'*. However, a dissatisfied Coughlan left the group in 1981 in order to form his own act, Diesel. Pete Kircher, (ex-**Original Mirrors**), took his place, but Quo was then undermined by the growing estrangement between Lancaster and Rossi and Parfitt. The bassist moved to Australia in 1983 - a cardboard cut-out substituted on several television slots - but he remained a member for the next two years. Lancaster's final appearance with the group was at *Live Aid*, following which he unsuccessfully took out a High Court injunction to prevent the group performing without him. Rossi and Parfitt secured the rights to the name 'Status Quo' and reformed the act around John Edwards (bass), Jeff Rich (drums) and keyboard player **Andy Bown**. The last-named musician, formerly of the **Herd** and **Judas Jump**, had begun his association with the group in 1973, but only now became an official member. Despite such traumas Quo continued to enjoy commercial approbation with Top 10 entries 'Dear John' (1982), 'Marguerita Time' (1983), 'In The Army Now' (1986) and 'Burning Bridges (On And Off And On Again)' (1988), while *1+9+8+2* was their fourth chart-topping album. Status Quo celebrated its silver anniversary in October 1991 by entering *The Guinness Book Of Records* having completed four charity concerts in four UK cities in the space of 12 hours. This ambitious undertaking, the subject of a television documentary, was succeeded by a national tour which confirmed the group's continued mass-market popularity. 1994 brought another number 1 single with 'Come On You Reds', a musically dubious project recorded with the league football champions, Manchester United. The much-loved Status Quo have carved a large niche in music history by producing uncomplicated, unpretentious and infectious rock music. Their track-record is incredible - just two statistics worthy of consideration are: worldwide sales of over 100 million, and just one short of 50 British hit singles (more than any other band).

Albums: *Picturesque Matchstickable Messages* (Pye 1968), *Spare Parts* (Pye 1969), *Ma Kelly's Greasy Spoon* (Pye 1970), *Dog Of Two Head* (Pye 1971), *Piledriver* (Vertigo 1972), *Hello* (Vertigo 1973), *Quo* (Vertigo 1974), *On The Level* (Vertigo 1975), *Blue For You* (Vertigo 1976), *Status Quo Live!* (Vertigo 1977, double album), *Rockin' All Over The World* (Vertigo 1977), *If You Can't Stand The Heat* (Vertigo 1978), *Whatever You Want* (Vertigo 1979), *Just Supposin'* (Vertigo 1980), *Never Too Late* (Vertigo 1982), *1+9+8+2* (Vertigo 1982), *Back To Back* (Vertigo 1983), *In The Army Now* (Vertigo 1986), *Ain't Complaining* (Vertigo 1988), *Perfect Remedy* (Vertigo 1989), *Rock 'Til You Drop* (Vertigo 1991), *Live Alive Quo* (Vertigo 1992), *Thirsty Work* (Polydor 1994).

Compilations: *Status Quo-tations* (Marble Arch 1969), *The Best Of Status Quo* (Pye 1973), *The Golden Hour Of Status Quo* (Golden Hour 1973), *Down The Dustpipe* (Golden Hour 1975), *The Rest Of Status Quo* (Pye 1976), *The Status Quo File* (Pye 1977, double album), *The Status Quo Collection* (Pickwick 1978, double album), *Twelve Gold Bars* (Vertigo 1980), *Spotlight On Status Quo Volume 1* (PRT 1980, double album), *Fresh Quota* (PRT 1981), *100 Minutes Of Status Quo* (PRT 1982), *Spotlight On Status Quo Volume 2* (PRT 1982), *From The Makers Of...* (Phonogram 1983, triple album), *Works* (PRT 1983), *To Be Or Not To Be* (Contour 1983), *Twelve Gold Bars Volume 1 & 2* (Vertigo 1984, double album), *Na Na Na* (Flashback 1985), *Collection: Status Quo* (Castle 1985), *Quotations, Volume 1* (PRT 1987), *Quotations, Volume 2* (PRT 1987), *From The Beginning* (PRT 1988), *C.90 Collector* (Legacy 1989), *B-Sides And Rarities* (Castle 1990), *The Early Works 1968 - '73* (Essential 1990, CD box set).

Videos: *Live At The NEC* (1984), *Best Of Status Quo*, *Preserved* (1986), *End Of The Road* (1986), *Rocking All Over The Years* (1987), *The Anniversary Waltz* (1991), *Rock Til You Drop* (1991)

Further reading: *Status Quo: The Authorized Biography*, Shearlaw, John (1979), *Status Quo*, Hibbert, Tom (1981), *Status Quo: Rockin' All Over The World*, Jeffries, Neil (1985), *25th Anniversary Edition*, Shearlaw, John (1987), *Just For The Record: The Autobioography Of Status Quo*, Rossi, Francis, And Rick Parfitt (1993).

Stax Records

Stax Records was founded in Memphis, Tennessee, USA, by brother and sister Jim (St) Stewart (b. 1930) and Estelle (ax) Axton (1918). Stewart, an aspiring fiddler, began recording local C&W artists in 1957, using a relative's garage as an improvised studio. The following year Estelle funded the purchase of an Ampex recorder and the siblings newly-named company, Satellite, was relocated in the nearby town of Brunswick. By 1960, however, they had returned to Memphis and established themselves in a disused theatre on McLemore Avenue. Local talent was attracted to the fledgling label and national hits for **Carla Thomas** and the **Mar-Keys** followed before the Satellite name was dropped in favour of Stax to avoid confusion with another company. These early successes were distributed by **Atlantic Records**, a relationship which soon proved mutually beneficial. 'Green Onions', the hypnotic instrumental by **Booker**

T. And The MGs, was another best-seller and defined the sound which established the studio's reputation. A subsidiary outlet, Volt, secured success with **Otis Redding** and the Stax empire flourished with releases by **Eddie Floyd**, **Johnnie Taylor** and **Rufus Thomas**. However, relations between the company and Atlantic became strained and the sessions which produced **Wilson Pickett**'s 'In The Midnight Hour' were the last recorded at Stax to bear Atlantic's imprint. Future releases bore the studio's distinctive logo (the Clicking Fingers), the most notable songs of which were those by **Sam And Dave**.

The two sides began renegotiations in 1967. The sale of Atlantic to **Warner Brothers** and the premature death of Otis Redding undermined Stewart's confidence, but a final twist proved irrevocable. Under the terms of the parties' original agreement, Atlantic owned every Stax master, released or unreleased, leaving the latter with a name and roster, but no back catalogue. In 1968 Stax signed a distribution deal with the Gulf/Western corporation, although it resulted in Estelle Axton's departure and the promotion of former disc jockey Al Bell to company vice-president. Although the immediate period was fruitful; releases by Johnnie Taylor, Booker T. Jones. and **Judy Clay** and **William Bell** were major hits, an ill-advised move into the album market proved over-ambitious. Nonetheless, Stax enjoyed considerable success with **Isaac Hayes** and in 1970 Stewart and Al Bell brought it back into private ownership through the financial assistance of the European classical label, Deutsche Grammophon. Within a year Stewart relinquished control to Bell, who then secured a lucrative distribution deal with **Columbia**. Despite a series of successful releases during the early 70s, including 'If Loving You Is Wrong (I Don't Want To Be Right)' (**Luther Ingram**) and 'Woman To Woman' (**Shirley Brown**), Stax grew increasingly troubled. Audits from the Internal Revenue Service and the Union Planters band revealed serious discrepancies and resulted in the indictment of several employees. In 1973, Columbia was granted an injunction preventing Stax from breaking its distribution arrangement; two years later the company was unable to meet its January payroll. Artists began seeking other outlets, Isaac Hayes sued for non-payment of royalties and despite Stewart's best efforts, Stax was closed down on 12 January 1976 on the order of the bankruptcy court judge. The feelings of the musicians at the label was summed up later when Donald 'Duck' Dunn, the label's longstanding session bassist commented, 'I knew it was over when they signed **Lena Zavaroni**.'

Although the bank attempted to salvage the situation, the label was sold to **Fantasy Records** in June the following year. Since then the new owners have judiciously repackaged the company's heritage and during the late 80s, secured the rights to all unreleased material from the Atlantic era.

Compilations: *The Stax Story Volume 1* (1975), *The Stax Story Volume 2* (1975), *Stax Blues Masters* (1978), *Stax Gold* (1979), *Stax Greatest Hits* (1987), *Stax Sirens And Volt Vamps* (1988), *The Complete Stax-Volt Singles, 1959-1968* (1991), *The Complete Stax-Volt Singles 1968-1971* (1993).

Stay Away Joe

By the time this **Elvis Presley** vehicle appeared in 1968, it was abundantly clear his Hollywood treadmill had undermined his entire career. Only die-hard aficionados welcomed a plot wherein the singer portrayed a Native American rodeo rider who returns to his reservation to help fight unwanted federal interference. Only five songs were featured on the soundtrack. That two of them are entitled 'Stay Away' and 'Stay Away Joe' indicates the ambivalent attitude present in Presley's 60s' Hollywood work. Fortunately, *Stay Away Joe* was quickly eclipsed later in the year by the *Elvis* television special, which completely revived a too-long moribund artist.

Steady B

b. Warren McGlone, c.1970, Philadelphia, USA. Steady B boasts distinguished lineage, he is the cousin of Lawrence Goodman, owner of the **Pop Art** label. Perhaps Steady B's lack of headline reviews has more to do with his decision to stay in his native Philadelphia rather than any lack of talent or forbearance. Originally inspired by old school rappers **Run DMC** and **Whodini**, his debut release was infact a direct answer record to another big influence, **LL Cool J**. 'I'll Take Your Radio' being a challenge to the originator of 'I Can't Live Without My Radio'. He was just 15 years old, and a steady stream of hits would follow: 'Fly Shante', 'Just Call Us Def' and 'Do Tha Filla'. On the back of these cult items he won himself a contract with **Jive**, which has seen the release of five albums in as many years. Although none have brought great commercial reward, each has seen workmanlike performances straddling both the pop-rap and hardcore markets. He has now launched a new group, C.B.E.

Albums: *Bring The Beat Back* (Jive 1987), *What's My Name?* (Jive 1987), *Let The Hustlers Play* (Jive 1988), *Going Steady* (Jive 1990), *Steady B V* (Jive 1991).

Steagall, Red

b. Russell Steagall, 22 December 1937, Gainesville, Texas, USA. In 1954, he contacted polio, which badly affected the use of his left hand and arm. Realising his hoped for football career was no longer a possibility, he turned his attention to music. During his convalescence, as part of the therapeutic treatment, he first began to play the mandolin and then, as his fingers strengthened, the guitar. By playing local dances and clubs, he financed his course at West Texas State

University, where he got a degree in Agriculture and Animal Science and then for five years worked for Sand Mark Oil as a soil analyst. He moved to California in 1965, sang locally and for a year worked as a salesman of industrial chemicals. Working first with his friend, Don Lanier, he began to develop his songwriting and in 1966, **Ray Charles** recorded their song 'Here We Go Again'. He concentrated on his writing, later claiming that by 1969 sixty of his songs had been recorded by other artists. In 1969, Ray Sanders had a hit with his song 'Beer Drinkin' Music' and Steagall himself made his first recordings on Dot. In 1971, **Del Reeves** had a hit with 'A Dozen Pairs Of Boots' and the following year, having moved to Nashville and joined Capitol, Steagall gained his own first country chart hit with 'Party Dolls And Wine'. During the 70s, later recording for **ABC**/Dot and **Elektra** and with his continued strong leaning towards Western-Swing and honky tonk songs, Steagall charted a steady succession of country chart entries, though none made the Top 10. His biggest came with 'Lone Star Beer And Bob Wills Music' - a number 11 in 1976. His love for **Bob Wills'** music saw him also chart a tribute song 'Bob's Got A Swing Band In Heaven'. For years, with his band the Coleman County Cowboys, he played dance halls and rodeos all over the West. Steagall became a genuine singing cowboy with his own Texas ranch and his keen interest in things Western saw him become one of the top entertainers on the US rodeo circuit, playing some 250 dates a year for many years. In 1974, he was instrumental in **Reba McEntire** becoming a star, after hearing her sing the national anthem at the National Rodeo Finals. In the 80s, he cut down touring drastically but remained active in various ventures, including his publishing house. He also cut out most of his songwriting to concentrate on writing poetry about the West and breeding quarter horses on his ranch. In 1987, he made his debut as an actor in a children's film called *Benji, The Hunted* - a dog story with the animal perhaps getting the best lines. Somewhat surprisingly, his last chart entry was 'Hard Hat Days And Honky Tonk Nights' back in 1980.
Albums: *Party Dolls And Wine* (1972), *Somewhere My Love* (1972), *If You've Got The Time I've Got The Song* (1973), *Finer Things In Life* (1975), *Lonestar Beer And Bob Wills Music* (1976), *Texas Red* (1976), *For All Our Cowboy Friends* (1977), *Hang On Feelin'* (1978), *It's Our Life* (c.1980), *Cowboy Favorites* (1985), *Red Steagall* (1986), *Born To This Land* (1993).

Stealers Wheel

The turbulent, acrimonious and comparatively brief career of Stealers Wheel enabled the two main members **Gerry Rafferty** and **Joe Egan** to produce some memorable and inventive, relaxed pop music. During the early 70s. Rafferty (b. 16 April 1946, Paisley, Scotland) and long-time friend Joe Egan (b. c.1946 Scotland) assembled in London to form a British **Crosby, Stills And Nash**, together with **Rab Noakes**, Ian Campbell and Roger Brown. After rehearsing and negotiating a record contract with **A&M Records**. The band had already fragmented, before they entered the studio to meet with legendary producers **Leiber And Stoller**. Paul Pilnick (guitar), Tony Williams (bass) and ex-**Juicy Lucy** member Rod Coombes (drums) bailed out Rafferty and Egan; the result was a surprising success, achieved by the sheer quality of their songs and the blend of the two leaders' voices. 'Stuck In The Middle With You' is an enduring song reminiscent of mid-period **Beatles**, and it found favour by reaching the Top 10 on both sides of the Atlantic. While the song was high on the charts Rafferty departed and was replaced by former **Spooky Tooth** lead guitarist Luther Grosvenor (aka Ariel Bender). Rafferty had returned by the time the second album was due to be recorded, but the musical chairs continued as all the remaining members left the band, leaving Rafferty and Egan holding the baby. Various session players completed *Ferguslie Park*, astonishingly another superb, melodic and cohesive album. The album was a failure commercially and the two leaders set about completing their contractual obligations and recording their final work *Right Or Wrong*. Even with similarly strong material, notably the evocative 'Benidictus' and the arresting 'Found My Way To You', the album failed. Rafferty and Egan, disillusioned, buried the name forever. Management problems plagued their career and lyrics of these troubled times continued to appear on both Egan and Rafferty's subsequent solo work. 'Stuck In The Middle' was used prominently in the film *Reservoir Dogs* in 1993.
Albums: *Stealers Wheel* (1973), *Ferguslie Park* (1974), *Right Or Wrong* (1975). Compilation: *The Best Of Stealers Wheel* (1978).

Stealin' Horses

Formerly known as Radio City, Stealin' Horses were a melodic USA pop-rock group established in 1985 around the nucleus of Kiya Heartwood (vocals/guitar) and Kopana Terry (drums). Utilizing an impressive array of guest musicians who included **Toto**'s Steve Lukather and Mike Porcano, they released their self-titled debut in 1985. It comprised a commercial *pot-pourri* of styles and featured blues, rock, funk, soul, R&B and even country numbers. Unfortunately, they were unable to find an audience for such diverse material and split up shortly after the album was released.
Album: *Stealin' Horses* (1985).

Steam

Formed in 1969 in Bridgeport, Connecticut, USA, Steam recorded a single, 'Na Na Hey Hey Kiss Him Goodbye', that went to number 1 in the US during

1969. The group had roots in an early 60s band called the Chateaus, which recorded a number of singles for **Coral Records** and **Warner Brothers Records** which were unsuccessful. Two of the members of that band, pianist Paul Leka and drummer Gary DeCarlo, met up again in 1969, the year after Leka had co-written the hit 'Green Tambourine' for the **Lemon Pipers**. Leka then went to work for **Mercury Records**; he and DeCarlo teamed up with another ex-Chateau, Dale Frashuer, to update the song that became 'Na Na Hey Hey Kiss Him Goodbye', which they had written in 1961. They had not intended to let the finished version with the 'na na hey hey' chorus go out as a finished product, but Mercury released it on its Fontana subsidiary. The group quickly adapted the name Steam and watched as the single went to the top. Leka assembled a touring version of Steam which did not include the other two originators of their hit. A second single, 'I've Gotta Make You Love Me', was issued but missed the Top 40, while the sole Steam album fizzled at number 84, causing a quick end to this one-hit group. The popularity of their sole transatlantic hit was emphasized when **Bananarama** took 'Na Na Hey Hey Kiss Him Goodbye' back into the UK Top 10 in 1983.
Album: *Steam* (1970).

Steam Packet

The idea for this 60s revue-styled package, encompassing R&B, soul, jazz and instrumentals, came from **Giorgio Gomelsky**, impresario and manager to several of Britain's leading beat groups. Determined to find a strong vocalist for one of his acts, **Brian Auger And The Trinity**, Gomelsky adopted three: **Long John Baldry**, **Rod Stewart** and **Julie Driscoll**. Auger (organ), Vic Briggs (guitar), Rick Brown (bass) and Mickey Waller (drums) provided the instrumental muscle, while each singer was apportioned a slot in a show which culminated in a rousing, gospel-like fervour. Indeed, Steam Packet's live appearances were received with great enthusiasm, but their progress was hampered by inter-management bickering. Stewart was fired in March 1966, and Baldry walked out some months later, leaving Auger and Driscoll to pursue a career which reaped due commercial rewards later in the decade. The Steam Packet's sole recorded legacy was recorded one morning in December 1965. It was intended solely as a demonstration tape, but the results were released in the wake of the participants' subsequent success.
Album: *First Of The Supergroups* (1977).

Steamhammer

Kieran White (vocals/harmonica), Martin Pugh (lead guitar), Martin Quittenton (rhythm guitar), Steve Davy (bass) and Michael Rushton (drums) made their recording debut in 1969 with the excellent *Steamhammer*.

The set featured an impressive group original, 'Junior's Wailing', which was later adopted by **Status Quo** during their transformation from pop group to boogie band. Pugh and Quittenton also contributed to **Rod Stewart**'s first debut, *An Old Raincoat Won't Let You Down*, and the latter guitarist subsequently remained with the singer, co-writing the million-selling 'Maggie May', and adding the song's distinctive mandolin sound. Pugh, White and Davy were then joined by Steve Jollife (saxophones/flute) and Mick Bradley (drums) for *Steamhammer Mk. II* which, although offering the blues-base of its predecessor, showed an increased interest in improvisation, as evidenced in the extended 'Another Travelling Tune'. This propensity for a more progressive direction was maintained on ensuing releases, the last of which was only issued in Europe, where the group had amassed a considerable following. Defections, sadly, undermined their potential and Steamhammer broke up during the mid-70s.
Albums: *Steamhammer* (1969), *Steamhammer Mk. II* (1970), *Mountains* (1970), *Speech* (1972). Compilation: *This Is Steamhammer* (1972).

Steel Forest

This Dutch quintet was formed in Amsterdam during 1981 by Sunny Hays (vocals), Fred Heikens (guitar), Appie van Vliet (keyboards), Ron Heikens (bass) and Joop Oliver (drums). They negotiated a deal with the Dureco label the following year. They made their debut with *First Confession*, a clichéd and formularized Euro-rock opus, which failed to find an audience. Hays was replaced by Thijs Hamelaers (later of Sleez Beez) and William Lawson (ex-Angus) took over the drumstool after the album was released, but this line-up disintegrated before entering the studio.
Album: *First Confession* (Dureco 1982).

Steel Pulse

Probably the UK's most highly-regarded roots reggae outfit, Steel Pulse originally formed at Handsworth School, Birmingham, and comprised David Hinds (lead vocals, guitar), Basil Gabbidon (lead guitar, vocals) and Ronnie McQueen (bass). However, it is Hinds who, as songwriter, has always been the engine behind Steel Pulse, from their early days establishing themselves in the Birmingham club scene onwards. Formed in 1975, their debut release, 'Kibudu, Mansetta And Abuku', arrived on the small independent label Dip, and linked the plight of urban black youth with the image of a greater African homeland. They followed it with 'Nyah Love' for Anchor. Surprisingly, they were initially refused live dates in Caribbean venues in the Midlands because of their Rastafarian beliefs. Aligning themselves closely with the Rock Against Racism organisation, they chose to tour instead with sympathetic elements of the punk movement, including the **Stranglers**, **XTC** etc.: 'Punks had a way of enjoying themselves - throw bottles at you, beer, spit at you, that kind of thing'. Eventually they found a more natural home in support slots for **Burning Spear**, which brought them to the attention of **Island** Records.

Their first release for Island was the 'Ku Klux Klan' 45, a considered tilt at the evils of racism, and one often accompanied by a visual parody of the sect on stage. By this time their ranks had swelled to include Selwyn 'Bumbo' Brown (keyboards), Steve 'Grizzly' Nesbitt (drums), Fonso Martin (vocals, percussion) and Michael Riley (vocals). *Handsworth Revolution* was an accomplished long playing debut and one of the major landmarks in the evolution of British reggae. However, despite critical and moderate commercial success over three albums, the relationship with Island had soured by the advent of *Caught You* (released in the US as *Reggae Fever*). They switched to **Elektra**, and unveiled their most consistent collection of songs since their debut with *True Democracy*, distinguished by the Garvey-eulogising 'Rally Around' cut. A further definitive set arrived in *Earth Crisis*. Unfortunately, Elektra chose to take a leaf out of Island's book in trying to coerce Steel Pulse into a more mainstream vein, asking them to emulate the pop-reggae stance of **Eddy Grant**. *Babylon Bandit* was consequently weakened, but did contain the anthemic 'Not King James Version', which was a powerful indictment on the omission of black people and history from certain versions of the Bible. Their next move was to MCA for *State Of Emergency*, which retained some of the synthesized dance elements of its predecessor. Though it was a significantly happier compromise, it still paled before any of their earlier albums. *Centennial* was recorded live at the Elysee Montmarte in Paris, and dedicated to the hundred year anniversary of the birth of Haile Selassie. It was the first recording since the defection of Fonso Martin, leaving the trio of Hinds, Nesbitt and Selwyn. While they still faced inverted snobbery at the hands of British reggae fans, in America their reputation was growing, becoming the first ever reggae band to appear on the *Tonight* television show. Their profile was raised further when, in 1992, Hinds challenged the New York Taxi and Limousine Commission in the Supreme High Court, asserting that their cab drivers discriminated against black people in general and Rastas in particular.

Albums: *Handsworth Revolution* (Island 1978), *Tribute To The Martyrs* (Island 1979), *Caught You/Reggae Fever* (Mango/Island 1980), *True Democracy* (Elektra 1982), *Earth Crisis* (Elektra 1984), *Babylon Bandit* (Elektra 1985), *State Of Emergency* (MCA 1988), *Victims* (MCA 1992), *Rastafari Centennial* (MCA 1992). Compilation: *Reggae Greats* (Mango/Island 1985).

Steele, Chrissy

This Canadian 'heavy metal goddess' linked up with former **Headpins** guitarist, songwriter and producer Brian MacLeod to concoct *Magnet To Steele* in 1991. The album was recorded on Macleod's power yacht whilst cruising along the coast of British Columbia. Steele has a powerful and characteristic style, but the derivative and commercial structure to the material did her no favours. The bravado and sexual imagery of the press releases appeared more interesting than the actual music.

Album: *Magnet To Steele* (Chrysalis 1991).

Steele, Tommy

b. Thomas Hicks, 17 December 1936, Bermondsey, London, England. After serving as a merchant seaman, Hicks formed a skiffle trio called the Cavemen, with **Lionel Bart** and Mike Pratt, before being discovered by entrepreneur John Kennedy in the 2I's coffee bar in Soho, London. A name change to Tommy Steele followed, and after an appearance at London's Condor Club, the boy was introduced to manager **Larry Parnes**. From thereon, his rise to stardom was meteoric. Using the old 'working-class boy makes good' angle, Kennedy launched the chirpy cockney in the unlikely setting of a debutante's ball. Class conscious Fleet Street lapped up the idea of Tommy as the 'Deb's delight' and took him to their hearts. His debut single, 'Rock With The Caveman' was an immediate Top 20 hit and although the follow-up 'Doomsday Rock'/'Elevator Rock' failed to chart, the management was unfazed. Their confidence was rewarded when Steele hit number 1 in the UK charts with a cover of **Guy Mitchell**'s 'Singing The Blues' in January 1957. By this point, he was Britain's first and premier rock 'n' roll singer and, without resorting to sexual suggestiveness, provoked mass teenage hysteria unseen since the days of **Johnnie Ray**. At one stage, he had four songs in the Top 30, although he never restricted himself to pure rock 'n' roll. A bit part in the film *Kill Me Tomorrow*, led to an autobiographical musical *The Tommy Steele Story*, which also spawned a book of the same title. For a time, Steele combined the twin roles of rock 'n' roller and family entertainer, but his original persona faded towards the end of the 50s. Further movie success in *The Duke Wore Jeans* (1958) and *Tommy The Toreador* (1959) effectively redefined his image. His rocking days closed with covers of **Ritchie Valens**' 'Come On Let's Go' and **Freddy Cannon**'s 'Tallahassee Lassie'. The decade ended with the novelty 'Little White Bull', after which it was goodbye to rock 'n' roll.

After appearing on several variety bills during the late 50s, Steele sampled the 'legit' side of show business in 1960 when he played Tony Lumpkin in *She Stoops To Conquer* at the Old Vic, and he was back in the straight theatre again in 1969, in the role of Truffaldino in *The Servant Of Two Masters* at the Queen's Theatre. In the years between those two plays, he experienced some of the highlights of his career. In 1963, he starred as Arthur Kipps in the stage musical *Half A Sixpence*, which ran for 18 months in the West End before transferring to Broadway in 1965. Steele re-created the role in the 1967 film version. A year later, he appeared in another major musical movie, *Finan's Rainbow*, with **Fred Astaire** and **Petula Clark**. His other films included *Touch It Light*, *It's All Happening*, *The Happiest Millionaire* and *Where's Jack?* In 1974, Steele made one of his rare television appearances in the autobiographical *My Life, My Song*, and appeared at the London Palladium in the musical *Hans Andersen*. He also starred in the revival three years later. In 1979/80 his one-man show was resident at London's Prince of Wales Theatre for a record 60 weeks - the Variety Club Of Great Britain made him their Entertainer Of The Year. He was also awarded the OBE. Steele was back at the Palladium again in 1983 and 1989, heading the cast of the highly popular *Singin' In The Rain*, which he also directed. In the latter capacity he tried - too late as it transpired - to save impresario Harold Fielding's *Ziegfeld* (1988) from becoming a spectacular flop. Fielding had originally cast Steele in *Half A Sixpence* some 25 years earlier. Off-stage in the 80s, Steele published a thriller called *The Final Run*, had one of his paintings exhibited at the Royal Academy, was commissioned by Liverpool City Council to fashion a bronze statue of 'Eleanor Rigby' as a tribute to the **Beatles**, and composed two musical pieces, 'A Portrait Of Pablo' and 'Rock Suite - An Elderly Person's Guide To Rock'. After *Hans Andersen* and *Singin' In The Rain*, the third, and least successful of Steele's stage adaptations of memorable musical movies, was *Some Like It Hot* (1992). A hybrid of Billy Wilder's classic film, and the Broadway stage musical *Sugar* (1972), it received derisory reviews ('The show's hero is Mr Steele's dentist'), and staggered along for three months in the West End on the strength of its star's undoubted box-office appeal. In 1993, Steele was presented with the Hans Andersen Award at the Danish Embassy in London, and two years later he he received the Bernard Delfont Award from the Variety Club of Great Britain for his 'outstanding contribution to show business'. By that time, Tommy Steele was back on the road again with 'A Dazzling New Song & Dance Spectacular' entitled *What A Show!* Albums: *The Tommy Steele Stage Show* (1957), *The Tommy Steele Story* (1957), *Stars Of 6.05* (late 50s), *The Duke Wore Jeans* (1958, film soundtrack), *Tommy The Toreador* (1959, film soundtrack), *So This Is Broadway* (1964), *Light Up The Sky* (1959), *Cinderella* (1959, stage cast), *Get Happy With Tommy* (1960), *It's All Happening* (1962), *Half A Sixpence* (1963, London stage cast), *Everything's Coming Up Broadway* (1967), *The Happiest Millionire* (1967), *My Life My Song* (1974), *Hans Andersen* (1978, London stage cast), with Sally Ann Howes *Henry Fielding's Hans Andersen* (1985). Compilations: *The Happy World Of Tommy Steele*

(1969), *The World Of Tommy Steele, Volume 2* (1971), *Focus On Tommy Steele* (1977), *The Family Album* (1979), *20 Greatest Hits* (1983), *Tommy Steele And The Steelmen - The Rock 'N' Roll Years* (1988), *Handful Of Songs* (1993).
Films: *Kill Me Tomorrow* (1955), *The Tommy Steele Story* (1957), *The Duke Wore Jeans* (1959), *Light Up The Sky* (1959), *Tommy The Toreador* (1960), *It's All Happening* (1962), *The Happiest Millionaire* (1967), *Half A Sixpence* (1967), *Finian's Rainbow* (1968), *Where's Jack* (1969).
Further reading: *Tommy Steele: The Facts About A Teenage Idol And An Inside:Picture Of Show Busin*, Kennedy, John (1958), *Quincy's Quest*, Tommy Steele, based on the children's television programme he scripted.

Steeler (Germany)

This German heavy metal quintet, formerly known as **Sinner**, emerged as Steeler in 1981. The band were formed in Bochum, Westphalia, by Peter Burtz (vocals) and virtuoso guitarist **Axel Rudi Pell**. With the addition of Volher Krawczak (bass), Bertram Frewer (backing vocals) and Volker Jakel (drums), they signed to the independent Earthshaker label in 1984. They debuted the same year with a self-titled album of uptempo hard-rockers which recalled the **Scorpions**. However, the strong material was discredited somewhat by the budget production. After *Rulin' The Earth*, the band moved to Steamhammer Records and replaced Krawczak with new bass player Herve Rossi. *Strike Back* saw the band move towards an Americanized arena-rock approach, typical of **Ratt**, **Dokken** and **Kiss**. After *Undercover Animal* a series of line-up changes ensued, with Pell leaving to build a solo career. In consequence the future of the band was sealed, and no further releases accrued.
Albums: *Steeler* (Earthshaker 1984), *Rulin' The Earth* (Earthshaker1985), *Strike Back* (Steamhammer 1986), *Undercover Animal* (Steamhammer 1988).

Steeler (USA)

This US hard rock quartet was formed in Nashville, Tennessee, in 1982 by vocalist Ron **Keel**. Recruiting Rik Fox (bass) and Mark Edwards (drums), the line-up was completed when Shrapnel label boss, Mike Varney, introduced Swedish guitarist **Yngwie Malmsteen** to the band. They relocated to Los Angeles and gigged incessantly on the bar and club circuit. Varney offered them a deal and they delivered a self-titled debut the following year. It was pure Americana bar-rock; chest-beating anthems, punctuated by shrill guitar work. Malmsteen quit just as the album was released, joining **Alcatrazz** and later forming his own outfit, Rising Force. Keel formed a new outfit under his own name, while Fox formed Sin.
Album: *Steeler* (Shrapnel 1983).

Steeleyard Blues

Although made several years after such classic 'outlaw'

statements as *Easy Rider* or *Two Lane Blacktop*, this 1972 Warner Brothers feature contained elements of anti-establishment rhetoric. Donald Sutherland starred as a mischievous ex-criminal and demolition derby driver while Jane Fonda, at that point viewed as the scourge of US society, played a genial call-girl. Their exploits to bring an ageing Catolina flying boat out of disrepair and into working order forms the core of the film's plot, while Sutherland's continued harassment of his brother, a district attorney, provides the mild protest theme. Peter Boyle is memorable as their deranged accomplist, while the presence of Howard Hessmen provides a link between the feature's visual and aural dimensions. The latter was formerly associated with two radical troupes, the San Francisco Mime Company and the Committee, both of which occasionally shared bills with Bay Area rock acts. One such group, the **Electric Flag**, had already scored Peter Fonda's drug-orientated vehicle, *The Trip*, and their vocalist/composer **Nick Gravenites**, was commissioned to provide a soundtrack for *Steelyard Blues*. He in turn introduced former Flag guitarist **Michael Bloomfield** to the project. An inventive musician, Bloomfield's blues-based technique added colour and atmosphere to the film and the attendant album proved popular in its own right. Yet neither musician was able to capitalise on *Steelyard Blues'* success. Gravenites returned to his first love; performing, while Bloomfield, plagued by personal problems, undertook an erratic career path. He did continue to write music for films, although his services were confined to pornographic features.

Steeleye Span

The roots of this pivotal English folk-rock group lay in several ill-fated rehearsals between Ashley 'Tyger' Hutchings (b. January 1945, London, England; bass, ex-**Fairport Convention**), Irish trio **Sweeny's Men** - Terry Woods (vocals, guitar, mandolin), Johnny Moynihan (vocals, fiddle) and Andy Irvine (vocals, mandolin) - and Woods' wife Gay (vocals, concertina, autoharp). When Moynihan and Irvine subsequently retracted, the remaining musicians were joined by **Tim Hart** (vocals, guitar, dulcimer, harmonium) and **Maddy Prior** (vocals), two well-known figures in folk circles. Taking their name from a Lincolnshire waggoner celebrated in song, Steeleye Span began extensive rehearsals before recording the excellent *Hark, The Village Wait*. The set comprised of traditional material, expertly arranged and performed to encompass the rock-based perspective Hutchings helped create on the Fairport's *Liege And Lief*, while retaining the purity of the songs. The Woods then left to pursue their own career and were replaced by **Martin Carthy** (vocals, guitar) and Peter Knight (vocals, fiddle) for *Please To See The King* and *Ten Man Mop*. This particular line-up toured extensively, but the departure of Hutchings for the purist **Albion Country Band** signalled a dramatic realignment in the Steeleye camp. Carthy resumed his solo career when conflict arose over the extent of change and two musicians of a rock-based persuasion - Bob Johnson (guitar) and Rick Kemp (bass) - were brought in. The quintet also left manager/producer Sandy Robertson for the higher-profile of Jo Lustig, who secured the group's new recording deal with **Chrysalis Records**. Both *Below The Salt* and *Parcel Of Rogues*, displayed an electric content and tight dynamics, while the punningly-entitled *Now We Are Six*, which was produced by **Jethro Tull**'s Ian Anderson and had **David Bowie** playing saxophone on 'Thomas The Rhymer', emphasized the terse drumming of newcomer Nigel Pegrum. The group enjoyed two hit singles with 'Gaudete' (1973) and 'All Around My Hat' (1975), the latter of which reached the UK Top and was produced by **Mike Batt**. On *Commoners Crown* the group recruited actor/comedian Peter Sellers to play ukelele on 'New York Girls'. However, the charm of Steeleye's early work was gradually eroding and although their soaring harmonies remained as strong as ever, experiments with reggae and heavier rock rhythms alienated rather than attracted prospective audiences. The group was 'rested' following the disappointing *Rocket Cottage* (1976), but reconvened the following year for *Storm Force Ten*. However, Knight and Johnson were otherwise employed and this line-up was completed by John Kirkpatrick (accordion) and the prodigal Martin Carthy. Although their formal disbanding was announced in March 1978, Steeleye Span has been resurrected on subsequent occasions. Hart, Prior and Carthy have also pursued successful solo careers.

Albums: *Hark, The Village Wait* (1970), *Please To See The King* (1971), *Ten Man Mop (Or Mr. Reservoir Strikes Again)* (1971), *Below The Salt* (1972), *Parcel Of Rogues* (1973), *Now We Are Six* (1974), *Commoners Crown* (1975), *All Around My Hat* (1975), *Rocket Cottage* (1976), *Storm Force Ten* (1977), *Live At Last* (1978), *Sails Of Silver* (1980), *Back In Line* (1986), *Tempted And Tried* (1989), *In Concert* (Park 1995). Compilations: *Individually And Collectively* (1972), *Steeleye Span Almanac* (1973), *Original Masters* (1977). *Time Span* (1978), *Best Of Steeleye Span* (1984), *Steeleye Span* (1985), *Portfolio* (1988), *The Early Years* (1989).

Steely And Clevie

This Jamaican studio 'band' comprises Wycliffe 'Steely' Johnson and Cleveland 'Clevie' Browne. Every five years or so Jamaica produces a rhythm section that dominates reggae. In the 70s it was the Barrett Brothers, who drove the **Upsetters** and **Bob Marley**'s Wailers. The late 70s/early 80s belonged to **Sly And Robbie**, but by 1986 reggae required a team fully conversant with computerized music: Steely & Clevie. Wycliffe 'Steely' Johnson first surfaced with **Sugar Minott**'s Youth Promotion organisation, playing keyboards on Sugar's classic *Ghetto-ology* (1978). After a period with the Generation Gap, he joined the **Roots Radics**, earning a reputation for hard work and innovation. When the Radics became *the* band for the new dancehall music of the early 80s, it gave Steely a perfect understanding of a minimal, raw-basics kind of reggae. Drummer Cleveland 'Clevie' Browne (pronounced *Brown-ie*) began playing as part of the Browne Bunch in the 70s with brothers Dalton and Danny. During the late 70s he played sessions at **Studio One**, backing **Freddie McGregor** amongst others. In the early 80s McGregor hired Clevie for his road group, known as the Studio One Band, and on tour Clevie would come into contact with equipment that was not yet *de rigeur* in Jamaican studios and became interested in drum machines, while his fellow-drummers declared them an abomination. Prior to that, Clevie had cut tracks with Bob Marley in 1979 where the singer was using a primitive drum machine in the studio, and Clevie had always kept one ear open for them ever since. In the mid-80s Clevie's brothers Danny & Dalton were the musical pulse of the Bloodfire Posse, the first all-electronic reggae group. By the time 'digital' music arrived, Clevie was ready for it. At some point in the late 70s Steely & Clevie met during sessions for **Augustus Pablo** at **Lee Perry**'s Black Ark studio, working on **Hugh Mundell**'s *Africa Must Be Free By 1983*. The pair clicked with a kind of yin and yang relationship: Clevie the studious, mild musician, Steely the louder, ragga character. When they took up residence as house 'band' at **King Jammy**'s Studio in 1986, they were clearly on the verge of something big.

Jammy's was the engine of mid-80s reggae; from there Steely & Clevie worked with everyone, cutting 10 singles a week at its peak in 1987 and a stream of albums from various artists such as **Cocoa Tea**, **Dennis Brown**, **Admiral Bailey** and **Lieutenant Stitchie**. Jammy's had the best **ragga** sound going and although producer King Jammy got the glory, much of the work was done by Steely & Clevie, engineers **Bobby Digital** and Squingie Francis, and the arranger, Mikey Bennett. They also gigged for most of the other producers in Jamaica; hence they knew virtually everyone when they began their own label - Steely & Clevie - in 1988. They immediately hit with a debut release from Johnny P., making the DJ a star. The formula of brash, unusual beats and strong melodies also worked for Foxy Brown, relaunched **Tiger**'s career, scored with Anthony Red Rose, Anthony Malvo and Little Twitch and revived older acts **Dillinger** and **Johnny Osbourne**. Sessions for **Gussie Clarke** helped establish his studio as the major technological force in late-80s' reggae, and Steely & Clevie cut a series of inimitable 'one rhythm' albums on their own label: *Limousine, Bursting Out, Real Rock Style, Can't Do The Work*. Broader attention

followed with work for former **Soul II Soul** singer Caron Wheeler, **Maxi Priest**, **Aswad** and **J.C. Lodge**. While they have not yet been inclined to sign to a major label, it seems that, despite competition from the Firehouse Crew and **Mafia & Fluxy**, Steely & Clevie will continue their dominance of the reggae studio for the foreseeable future.

Selected albums: Various: *Bursting Out* (S&C 1988), *At The Top* (Black Solidarity 1988), *Can't Do The Work* (S&C 1989), *Limousine* (S&C 989), *Real Rock Style* (S&C/Jet Star 1989), *Godfather* (VP 1990), *Lion Attack* (VP 1990), *More Poco* (VP 1990), *Girl Talk* (VP 1991), *Present Soundboy Clash* (Profile 1991), *Play Studio One Vintage* (Heartbeat 1992).

Steely Dan

The seeds of this much-respected rock group were sewn at New York's Bard College where founder members **Donald Fagen** b. 10 January 1948, Passaic, New Jersey, New York, USA (keyboards/vocals) and Walter Becker b. 20 February 1950, Queens, New York, USA (bass/vocals) were students. They subsequently forged a songwriting team and their many demos were later collected on several exploitative compilations. Formative versions of 'Brooklyn', 'Berry Town' and 'Parker's Band' - each of which were re-recorded on official Steely Dan releases - were recorded during this period. The duo also enjoyed a contemporaneous association with pop/harmony act **Jay And The Americans**, for which they adopted the pseudonyms Gus Marker and Tristan Fabriani. Becker and Fagen appeared on the group's last US Top 20 hit, 'Walkin' In The Rain' (1969), the albums *Wax Museum* and *Capture The Moment*, and accompanied the unit on tour. Group vocalist Jerry Vance and drummer John Discepolo joined the pair for *You Gotta Walk It Like You Talk It (Or You'll Lose That Beat)*, the soundtrack to a low-key movie. Denny Dias (guitar) also contributed to these sessions and he joined Fagen and Becker on their next project which evolved following an alliance with producer Gary Katz. Taking the name 'Steely Dan' from the steam-powered dildo in William Burroughs' novel *The Naked Lunch*, the trio was quickly expanded by the arrival of David Palmer b. Plainfield, New Jersey, New York (vocals ex-Myddle Class), Jeff 'Skunk' Baxter b. 13 December 1948, Washington DC, USA (guitar ex-**Ultimate Spinach**) and Jim Hodder b. Boston, Massachusetts (drums). The accomplished *Can't Buy A Thrill* was completed within weeks, but drew considerable critical praise for its deft melodies and immaculate musicianship. The title track and 'Do It Again' reached the US Top 20 when issued as singles and this newfound fame inspired the sarcasm of 'Show Biz Kids' on *Countdown To Ecstacy*.

Their second album was another undoubted classic of the 70s, and featured such bittersweet celebrations as 'The Boston Rag' and 'My Old School'. By this point

Palmer had left the line-up following an uncomfortable US tour, but although Baxter declared the set superior to its predecessor, the same commercial approbation did not follow. This was reversed with the release of *Pretzel Logic*, Steely Dan's first US Top 10 album. Here Fagen and Becker drew more fully on their love of jazz, acquiring the riff of 'Rikki Don't Lose That Number' from **Horace Silver**'s 'Song Of My Father' and recreating **Duke Ellington**'s 'East St. Louis Toodle-O'. The former reached number 4 in the US charts. The group's clarity of purpose and enthralling dexterity was never so apparent, but internal conflicts simmered over a reluctance to tour, shown by Becker and, especially, Fagen who was unhappy with the in-concert role of front-man. Steely Dan's final live appearance was on 4 July 1974 and ensuing strife resulted in the departures of both Baxter and Hodder. The guitarist resurfaced in the **Doobie Brothers**, with whom he was already guesting, while the drummer reverted to session work. The faithful Dias joined newcomers **Michael McDonald** (keyboards/vocals) and Jeff Porcaro (drums) for *Katy Lied* which also featured cameos by guitarist **Rick Derringer** and saxophonist Phil Woods. At the time of issue the set was, however, greeted with disquiet as the transformation from active unit to purely studio creation resulted in crafted anonymity. In recent years the album has shown its strengths and is now highly rated.

The Royal Scam redressed the commercial balance and in its title track offered one of the group's most impressive tracks to date. Becker and Fagen were, by now, the sole arbiters of Steely Dan, McDonald having followed Baxter into the Doobie Brothers and Dias and Porcaro opting for studio employment. The new collection boasted another series of sumptuous tunes and included 'Haitian Divorce', the group's lone Top 20 hit in Britain. *Aja* continued in a similar vein where an array of quality musicians - including **Wayne Shorter**, Jim Horn and **Tom Scott** - brought meticulousness to a set notable for the seemingly effortless, jazz/disco sweep evinced on 'Peg'. A similar pattern was unveiled on the immaculately recorded *Gaucho*, the release of which was marred by conflict between the group and record label over escalating recording costs. The latter's nervousness was assuaged when the album achieved platinum sales and an attendant single, 'Hey Nineteen', reached the US Top 10. However, Becker and Fagen had now tired of their creation and in June 1981 they announced the break-up of their partnership. The following year Fagen released *The Nightfly*, a superb collection which continued where his erstwhile group had ended. Producer Katz supervised the accustomed cabal of Los Angeles session musicians to create a sound and texture emphasizing the latter's dominant role in later Steely Dan releases. Becker meanwhile produced albums for **China Crisis** and **Rickie Lee Jones**, but in May

1990 the pair were reunited in New York's Hit Factory studio to collaborate on material for a forthcoming Fagen project. 'We're not working as Steely Dan,' stated Becker, but aficionados were undoubtedly heartened by news of their rekindled partnership. Although it took a further three years, the partnership worked together on Donald Fagen's impressive *Kamakiriad* and played together as Steely Dan to delighted fans in their homeland.

Albums: *Can't Buy A Thrill* (1972), *Countdown To Ecstasy* (1973), *Pretzel Logic* (1974), *Katy Lied* (1975), *The Royal Scam* (1976), *Aja* (1977), *Gaucho* (1980). Compilations: *You Gotta Walk It Like You Talk It (Or You'll Lose That Beat)* (1974, early recordings), *Greatest Hits* (1979), *Gold* (1982), *A Decade Of Steely Dan* (1985), *Reelin' In The Years* (1985), *Berry Town* (1986), *Sun Mountain* (1986, early Becker/Fagen material), *Old Regime* (1987, early Becker/Fagen material), *Stone Piano* (1988, early Becker/Fagen material), *Gold (Expanded Edition)* (1991), *Citizen Steely Dan, 1972-80* (1993, 4-CD box set). Donald Fagen: *The Nightfly* (1982), *Kamakiriad* (1993).

Further reading: *Steely Dan: Reelin' In The Years*, Sweet, Brian (1994).

Steeplechase

This nondescript melodic US rock quartet was formed in 1980 by Joe Lamente (vocals), Tony Sumo (guitar), Bob Held (bass) and Vinny Conigliaro (drums). They were signed to the local BCR label the following year. Drawing inspiration from the mid-west rock scene, their music incorporated elements of **Petra**, **Starz** and **Spy**. Their debut and sole album failed to take off and the band disintegrated soon after its release. Lamente joined **Shelter** and later recorded the solo set, *Secrets That You Keep*, in 1986.

Album: *Steeplechase* (BCR 1981).

Stegall, Keith

b. 1 November 1954, Wichita Falls, Texas, USA. Keith is the son of Bob Stegall, who played steel guitar for **Johnny Horton.** He made his stage debut when only eight years old and performed in a variety of folk and country groups during his adolescence. He formed his own band, the Pacesetters, when only 12 and toured overseas with the folk group, the Cheerful Givers. He moved to Nashville and became a staff writer for CBASS. He wrote 'Sexy Eyes' (**Dr Hook**), 'We're In This Love Together' (**Al Jarreau**) and 'Hurricane' (**Leon Everette**). He had a few minor US country hits with **Capitol Records** but had more success with Epic, making the Top 10 with 'Pretty Lady'. Stegall co-produced **Alan Jackson**'s landmark album, *Here In The Real World*, and also sang harmony vocals on it. He writes with Alan and Roger Murrah and their songs have included 'Blue Blooded Woman' (Alan Jackson) and 'If I Could Make A Living' (Clay Walker).

Album: *Keith Stegall* (Epic 1985).

Stegmeyer, Bill

b. 8 October 1916, Detroit, Michigan, USA, d. 19 August 1968, Long Island, New York, USA. Stegmeyer began playing clarinet and saxophones while still at school, then joined the Austin Wylie band. A colleague there was **Billy Butterfield**, a friend from his university days. While with the Wylie band Stegmeyer also arranged and worked on local radio. In 1938 he joined **Glenn Miller** and the following year played in **Bob Crosby**'s band. His interest in arranging gradually superseded his playing and in later decades he worked extensively in radio in Detroit and New York. From time to time he made appearances with jazz groups, among them the band co-led by **Yank Lawson** and **Bob Haggart**. Very highly regarded by fellow musicians, the direction taken by Stegmeyer in his career resulted in his being little known by fans.
Album: *The Best Of Dixieland: The Legendary Lawson-Haggart Jazz Band 1952-3* (1975).

Steig, Jeremy

b. 23 September 1942, New York, USA. Steig began on the recorder when he was six, took up the flute aged 11 and first played professionally when he was 15 while he was still at the High School of Music and Art. Early in his career he played in a band including **Paul Bley** and **Gary Peacock**. In the late 60s he played with **Richie Havens** before joining **Tim Hardin**'s backing band and then forming his own rock-influenced band - Jeremy And The Satyrs. Steig has great technical ability on the whole range of flutes on which he employs a wide performance technique. He has been especially adept at incorporating the use of all sorts of electronics into his music making employing devices such as the wah wah peddle and ring modulator. He has continued to work as a soloist and with his own groups, although he has also performed with **Eddie Gomez**, **Art Blakey** and Pierre Courbois' Association PC in 1974.
Albums: *Flute Fever* (1963), *Jeremy And The Satyrs* (1967), *Temple Of Birth* (1974), *Firefly* (1977), with Eddie Gomez *Outlaws* (1976), *Lend Me Your Ears* (1978), *Rain Forest* (1980).

Steiner, Max

b. Maximilian Raoul Steiner, 10 May 1888, Vienna, Austria, d. 28 December 1971, Hollywood, California, USA. A composer and conductor for some 300 films, from the late 20s through to the 60s, Steiner was often called the leader in his field. He studied at the Imperial Academy Of Music in Vienna, and was awarded the Gold Medal. In his teens he wrote and conducted his own operetta before travelling to London in 1904, and conducting in music halls in England and on the Continent. He moved to the USA in 1914 and conducted on Broadway, for concert tours, and spent some time as chief orchestrator for the Harms music publishing house. Steiner joined RKO in Hollywood in 1929, a couple of years after the movies began to talk, and worked, uncredited on *Rio Rita*, a 'lavish musical Western', starring Bebe Daniels and John Boles. From then, until 1934, his name appears on the titles of over 80 productions, mostly as the composer of the background music. They included *Check And Double Check* (film debut of Amos 'n' Andy), *Cimarron*, *Beau Ideal*, *A Bill Of Divorcement*, *The Half Naked Truth*, *The Lost Squadron*, *Little Women* and *Morning Glory*, both starring the young Katharine Hepburn, and *King Kong* 'the greatest monster movie of all'. In 1934, Steiner was nominated for an Academy Award for his score to *The Lost Patrol*, and, in the following year, won the Oscar for his work on John Ford's *The Informer*. His other scores in 30s included *Of Human Bondage*, *Alice Adams* (Hepburn again), *The Charge Of The Light Brigade*, (1936, Steiner's first, in a long series of films for **Warner Brothers**), *A Star Is Born* (1937), *The Garden Of Allah*, *The Life Of Emile Zola*, *Tovarich*, *Jezebel*, *The Adventures Of Tom Sawyer*, *Crime School*, *The Amazing Dr Clitterhouse*, *Four Daughters*, *The Sisters*, *Angels With Dirty Faces*, *The Dawn Patrol*, *The Oklahoma Kid*, *Dark Victory*, *We Are Not Alone*, and *Gone With The Wind*. Steiner's memorable score for the latter film included the haunting 'Tara's Theme', which became a hit for Leroy Holmes and his Orchestra, and as 'My Own True Love' with a lyric by **Mack David**, for **Johnny Desmond** as well.
During the 30s, Steiner also served as musical director on several classic RKO **Fred Astaire-Ginger Rogers** musicals, such as *The Gay Divorcee*, *Follow The Fleet*, *Roberta*, and *Top Hat*. In the 40s, especially during the years of World War II, Steiner scored some of the most fondly remembered films in the history of the cinema, such as *Now Voyager* (1942, Steiner's second Academy Award), which included the persuasive theme, 'It Can't Be Wrong' (lyric Kim Gannon, a smash hit for **Dick Haymes**), *Casablanca*, *The Corn Is Green*, *Johnny Belinda*, and *The Letter*. Other significant 40s films for which Steiner provided the music were *All This And Heaven Too*, *Sergeant York*, *They Died With Their Boots On*, *In This Our Life*, *Desperate Journey*, *Mission To Moscow*, *Watch On The Rhine*, *Passage To Marseilles* (including 'Someday I'll Meet You Again'), *The Adventures Of Mark Twain*, *Since You Went Away* (1944, starring Claudette Colbert and Joseph Cotton - Steiner's third Academy Award), *Arsenic And Old Lace*, *The Conspirators*, *Mildred Pearce*, *Saratoga Trunk* (including 'As Long As I Live'), *The Big Sleep*, *My Wild Irish Rose*, *Life With Father*, *The Treasure Of The Sierra Madre*, *Key Largo*, *The Adventures Of Don Juan*, and *White Heat* (1949). In 1950, Steiner received another of his 22 Academy Award nominations for his work on *The Flame And The Arrow*, starring Burt Lancaster, and, in the same year, he scored Tennessee Williams' *The Glass Menagerie*, with the vivacious UK

musical comedy star **Gertrude Lawrence**. His other 50s film music included *Operation Pacific*, *On Moonlight Bay*, *The Miracle Of Our Lady Fatima*, *The Jazz Singer*, *By The Light Of The Silvery Moon*, *The Caine Mutiny*, *Battle Cry* (including 'Honey-Babe'), *Marjorie Morningstar*, *The F.B.I. Story*, and *A Summer Place* (1959, the theme was a US hit for **Percy Faith** and his Orchestra, and, with a lyric by Mack Discant, for the **Lettermen** in 1965). Even though he was over 70, Steiner continued to work into the 60s on such movies as *The Dark At The Top Of The Stairs*, *Spencer's Mountain*, *Youngblood Hawk*, and *Two On A Guillotine*, although demand for his kind of romantic, powerful, yet tender, background music had declined. His contributions to television included the theme music for the popular *Perry Mason* series which starred Raymond Burr.
Selected albums: *Now Voyager-The Classic Film Scores Of Max Steiner* (RCA 1973) *King Kong* (1980), *Revisited* (1988).

Steinman, Jim

American songwriter/producer/musician Steinman first came to the public's attention in 1975 as musical arranger for the comedy company National Lampoon. He was also a playwright and it was at an audition that he first met Dallas singer/actor **Meat Loaf**. Together they conceived one of the biggest rock albums of all time, *Bat Out Of Hell*. Steinman's unique Wagnerian production technique was later to grace countless other artists from **Bonnie Tyler** to **Barry Manilow**. With Meat Loaf unable to record a follow-up Steinman grew impatient and decided to record the album himself. Released in 1981, *Bad For Good* lacked the vocal impact of Meat Loaf and was not a best-seller - it was, however, still a superb album featuring **Todd Rundgren** as guitarist and co-producer. Many of the songs would later appear on the *Bat Out Of Hell 2* album which heralded a reunion with Meat Loaf, having parted company after the latter's *Deadringer* set, also from 1981. Perhaps the most stunning track from *Bad For Good* was a spoken-word piece titled 'Love And Death And An American Guitar', where Steinman proclaims in a style reminiscent of Jim Morrison's 'Horse Latitudes', that 'I once killed a Fender guitar'. He was also the mastermind for the 1990 double album project, *Original Sin*, a concept piece based on sexuality - at times almost operatic in construction it would not be taken seriously and so he returned to production work where he remains most in demand.
Albums: *Bad For Good* (Epic 1981), *Original Sin* (Virgin 1990, double album).

Stephenson, Martin

b. c.1965, Durham, England. This singer/songwriter's reputation has been bolstered by virtue of searing live performances throughout the UK. His early love of literature and music led to the formation of the first Daintees line-up in his early teens. With a regular turnover of staff and lack of proper gigs the band nevertheless became something of a busking sensation, on the evidence of which Newcastle record label Kitchenware sent them into the studio. After two singles, notable amongst which was the intoxicating 'Roll On Summertime', a debut album was embarked upon. The Daintees line-up at this time comprised Stephenson (guitar/vocals), Anthony Dunn (bass/acoustic guitar/vocals), John Steel (keyboards/harmonica/bass/vocals) and Paul Smith (drums/percussion). *Boat To Bolivia* was praised by the *New Musical Express* because it 'builds bridges between love and hate, between cradle and grave, between folk and pop, between the past and present'. An example of the candidness and honesty of Stephenson's lyrics is best portrayed on 'Caroline' and 'Crocodile Cryer'. He also revealed his appreciation of the folk/blues rag guitar style with 'Tribute To The Late Rev. Gary Davis' as well as regular live performances of **Van Dyke Parks**' 'High Coin'. However, a lengthy hiatus delayed the arrival of the follow-up until 1988. *Gladsome, Humour & Blue* contained the superb 'Wholly Humble Heart'. Once again reviews were excellent, and Stephenson already held an impressive reputation for hearty live shows. *Salutation Road* became the songwriter's most politicized work in 1990, prefaced by the single 'Left Us To Burn' which directly attacked Margaret Thatcher. He continues to be a consistent live draw, often appearing solo, or with the Daintees, who comprise any musician who fits the bill. Not yet considered a major songwriter, his elevation to that status may only be a matter of time and *Yogi In My House* is an excellent starting point for an introduction to this highly talented writer.
Albums: *Boat To Bolivia* (1985), *Gladsome, Humour & Blue* (1988), *Salutation Road* (1990), *The Boys Heart* (1992), *High Bells Ring Thin* (1993), *Yogi In My House* (Demon 1995) Compilation: *There Comes A Time: The Very Best Of Martin Stephenson & The Daintees* (1993).

Steppenwolf

Although based in southern California, Steppenwolf evolved out of a Toronto act, the Sparrow(s). John Kay (b. Joachim F. Krauledat, 12 April 1944, Tilsit, Germany; vocals), Michael Monarch (b. 5 July 1950, Los Angeles, California, USA; lead guitar), Goldy McJohn (b. 2 May 1945; keyboards), Rushton Moreve (bass) and Jerry Edmonton (b. 24 October 1946, Canada; drums) assumed their new name in 1967, inspired by the novel of cult author Herman Hesse. John Morgan replaced Moreve prior to recording. The group's exemplary debut album included 'Born To Be Wild' which reached number 2 in the US charts. This rebellious anthem was written by Dennis Edmonton (Mars Bonfire), guitarist in Sparrow and brother of drummer Jerry. It was featured in the famous opening sequence of the film, *Easy Rider*, and has since acquired classic status. Steppenwolf actively cultivated a menacing, hard rock image, and successive collections mixed this heavy style with blues. 'Magic Carpet Ride' and 'Rock Me' were also US Top 10 singles yet the group deflected any criticism such temporal success attracted by addressing such contemporary issues as politics, drugs and racial prejudice. Newcomers Larry Byrom (guitar) and Nick St. Nicholas (b. 28 September 1943, Hamburg, Germany; bass), former members of Time, were featured on *Monster*, Steppenwolf's most cohesive set. A concept album based on Kay's jaundiced view of contemporary (1970) America, it was a benchmark in the fortunes of the group. Continued personnel changes undermined their stability, and later versions of the band seemed content to further a spurious biker image, rather than enlarge on earlier achievements. John Kay dissolved the band in 1972, but his solo career proved inconclusive and within two years he was leading a reconstituted Steppenwolf. The singer has left and reformed his creation several times over the ensuing years, but has been unable to repeat former glories.

Albums: *Steppenwolf* (Dunhill 1968), *The Second* (Dunhill 1968), *Steppenwolf At Your Birthday Party* (Dunhill 1969), *Early Steppenwolf* (Dunhill 1969 - Sparrow recordings from 1967), *Monster* (Dunhill 1969), *Steppenwolf 'Live'* (Dunhill 1970), *Steppenwolf 7* (Dunhill 1970), *For Ladies Only* (Dunhill 1971), *Slow Flux* (Mums 1974), *Hour Of The Wolf* (Epic 1975), *Skullduggery* (Epic 1976), *Live In London* (Attic 1982), *Wolf Tracks* (Attic 1982), *Rock & Roll Rebels* (Qwil 1987), *Rise And Shine* (IRS 1990). Compilations: *Steppenwolf Gold* (Dunhill 1971), *Rest In Peace* (Dunhill 1972), *16 Greatest Hits* (Dunhill 1973), *Masters Of Rock* (Dunhill 1975), *Golden Greats: Steppenwolf* (MCA 1985).

Stepper, Reggie

DJ considered to be among the better examples of the new Jamaican 'chatters'. His album for Tommy 'Pipper' Mason was cut with the help of rhythms donated by Mixing Lab, Music Works and **Penthouse**. Reggie had arrived at Mason's studio a relative unknown, but emerged as a new **dancehall** star, going on to work with production team **Steely & Clevie**.
Selected album: *Kim Bo King* (King Dragon 1990).

Steppin' Out

Lyndall Hobbs directed, and appeared in, this 1979 short which was based around concurrent London teen sub-cultures. Roller disco enthusiasts, punks and mods are presented in favoured haunts with music provided by a variety of acts including **Ian Dury** And The Blockheads, **Bryan Ferry**, **Sylvester** and the **Who**. Two Mod revival groups are featured live in-concert. The **Merton Parkas** offer their insouciant paean to

scooters, 'You Need Wheels', while **Secret Affair** perform their debut hit, 'Time For Action'. However, as both punk and disco were better-served elsewhere, any laurels *Steppin' Out* possesses rests on the questionable contributions of these short-lived bands.

Steps Ahead

Formed in 1979 under the name Steps, this group was seen by founder and vibes player **Mike Mainieri** as a way of bringing together some of the virtuoso musicians working in the New York studio scene. Originally comprising of **Michael Brecker** (tenor saxophone), Don Grolnick (keyboards), **Eddie Gomez** (bass), and **Peter Erskine** (drums), Steps toured Japan and recorded three albums there. With the departure of Grolnick in 1983, Steps became Steps Ahead, and a series of changes of personnel ensued including the passing through of David Sancious. By 1987, the group, now led by Brecker, had stabilized, and included **Mike Stern** (electric guitar), **Darryl Jones** (bass), and **Steve Smith** (drums). Steps Ahead has defined the New York fusion sound for some time, and has been an important vehicle for the hugely influential Michael Brecker.
Albums: *Step By Step* (1980), *Steps Ahead* (1983), *Magnetic* (1986), *Yin-Yang* (1992), *Vibe* (NYC 1995).

Stept, Sam

b. Samuel H. Stept, 18 September 1897, Odessa, Russia, d. 1 December 1964, Los Angeles, California, USA. A popular composer during the 30s and 40s, Stept was taken to the USA in 1900 and grew up in Pittsburgh, Pennsylvania. After playing the piano for a local music publishing house, he served as an accompanist in vaudeville for artists such as **Mae West**, Ann Chandler and Jack Norworth, and then led a dance band in Cleveland, Ohio, in the early 20s. A few years later he started composing, and in 1928, in collaboration with Bud Green, had a big hit with 'That's My Weakness Now', which **Helen Kane** made into one of her special numbers. It was featured in **Rouben Mamoulian**'s critically acclaimed movie *Applause* (1929), and has since become a standard. During the late 20s and early 30s, Stept and Green combined on several songs for films, including 'Love Is A Dreamer', 'For The Likes O' You And Me', 'When They Sing "The Wearing Of The Green" In Syncopated Blues' (all from *Lucky In Love*), 'The World Is Yours and Mine' (*Mother's Boy*), 'There's A Tear For Every Smile In Hollywood' (*Showgirl*), and 'Tomorrow Is Another Day' and 'Liza Lee' (*Big Boy*). With Green and Herman Ruby, Stept contributed 'Do Something' and 'I'll Always Be In Love With You' to the RKO backstage movie *Syncopation* (1929).

During the 30s his other compositions included 'Congratulations', 'Please Don't Talk About Me When I'm Gone' (popular for **Gene Austin** and later,

Johnnie Ray), 'I Beg Your Pardon', 'Mademoiselle', 'London On A Rainy Night', 'I'm Painting The Town Red', 'Tiny Little Fingerprints' and 'My First Impression Of You'. He also wrote songs for films with Sidney Mitchell, such as 'All My Life', 'Laughing Irish Eyes' (title track); 'Recollections Of Love' (*Dancing Feet*), and 'How Am I Doin' With You?' (*Sitting On The Moon*). Stept's other collaborators around this time included Ted Koehler, with whom he wrote 'We've Come A Long Way Together' (*Hullabaloo*), and 'Goodnight My Lucky Day', 'We Happen To Be In The Army', 'Now You're Talking My Language', and 'It Must Be Love' (all from *23 And 1/2 Hours To Leave*). Stept also worked with Sidney Mitchell on 'All My Life' (*Johnny Doughboy*) and 'And Then' (*Twilight On The Prairie*); **Ned Washington** for 'Sweet Heartache' (*Hit Parade*); and Charles Newman on 'The Answer Is Love' (*That's Right - You're Wrong*). For 30s stage shows Stept wrote 'Swing Little Thingy' (with Bud Green) for *Shady Lady*, 'So I Married The Girl' (with **Herb Magidson**) for *George White*'s *Music Hall Varieties*, and most of the songs, with **Lew Brown** and **Charles Tobias**, for the 1939 hit, *Yokel Boy*. The score included 'I Can't Afford To Dream', 'Let's Make Memories Tonight', and 'Comes Love'. *Yokel Boy* was filmed in 1942, with Eddie Foy Jnr in the title role. In the same year Stept, again with Brown and Tobias, wrote 'Don't Sit Under The Apple Tree' for the **Andrews Sisters** to sing in *Private Buckaroo*. The song became a big record hit for the Sisters, as well as **Glenn Miller**. Stept also contributed numbers to other early 40s movies such as *When Johnny Comes Marching Home* ('This Is Worth Fighting For', lyric by **Eddie De Lange**) and *Stars On Parade* ('When They Ask About You'). In the late 40s he was less active, but was still composing ballads such as 'I Was Here When You Left Me', and 'Next Time I Fall In Love'. He also contributed 'Yo Te Amo Mucho' to the movie *Holiday In Mexico* in 1946. In 1950, with Dan Shapiro, he wrote several numbers for the Broadway revue, *Michael Todd's Peep Show*, including 'We've Got What It Takes', and 'A Brand New Rainbow In The Sky'. After composing songs such as 'If You Should Leave Me', 'Star-Gazing' and 'Don't You Care A Little Bit About Me?' in the early 50s, Stept concentrated on his music publishing interests. In 1961 his 'Please Don't Talk About Me When I'm Gone' received a carefree rendering from **Frank Sinatra** on *Swing Along With Me*, the singer's second album for his own **Reprise** label.

Stereo MC's

This UK rap/dance outfit's commercial breakthrough has been the result of both sustained hard work and an original talent. The band comprise three women and three men; Rob Birch (b. Robert Charles Birch, 11 June 1961, Ruddington, Nottinghamshire, England; vocals), Nick 'The Head' Hallam (b. 11 June 1962, Nottingham, England; synthesizers, computers, scratching), and Owen If (b. Ian Frederick Rossiter, 20 March 1959, Newport, Wales; percussion; ex-**Bourbonese Qualk**), plus Cath Coffey (b. Catherine Muthomi Coffey, c.1965, Kenya - 'I can't tell you my real age because I act and tell different casting directions various different ages), Andrea Bedassie (b. 7 November 1957, London, England), and Verona Davis (b. 18 February 1952, London, England) on backing vocals. Hallam and Birch had been friends in Nottingham since the age of six. There they formed a rock duo titled Dogman And Head, before moving to London in 1985 when they were 17 years old. Together they started recording rap music, though keeping intact their original love of soul, and set up their own label **Gee Street** with John Baker and DJ Richie Rich, from their base in Clapham. They were given a cash windfall when they were each handed £7,000 by a property developer to move out of their adjacent flats. This allowed them to establish the Gee St studio in a basement on the London street of the same name. The Stereo MC's first recording was 'Move It', released before the duo recruited Italian-British DJ Cesare, and formed their alter-ego remix team, Ultimatum. In the meantime, **Island Records** signed up Gee St for distribution, re-releasing 'Move It' in March 1988. Their first remix as Ultimatum arrived shortly afterwards (**Jungle Brothers**' 'Black Is Black'). Cesare left after a tour supporting **Jesus Jones**, stating that he was unhappy with the band's direction and financial arrangements. He would go on to produce in his own right. Hallam and Birch pressed on, recording a debut album, *Supernatural*, with Baby Bam of the Jungle Brothers. They also recruited Owen If, originally for live percussion, who had previously been employed at Pinewood Studios as a special effects trainee, working on films like *Batman* and *Full Metal Jacket*. A support tour with **Living Colour** turned out to be a disaster, however. 1991 brought their first crossover hit with 'Lost In Music', based on the Ultimatum remix of the Jungle Brothers' 'Doin' Your Own Dang'. Their remixes have since encompassed artists like **Aswad** ('Warrior Re-Charge'), **Definition Of Sound** ('Wear Your Love Like Heaven'), **Disposable Heroes Of Hiphoprisy** ('Television - The Drug Of The Nation', 'Language Of Violence'), **Dreams Warriors** ('Follow Me Not'), **Electronic** ('Idiot Country Two'), **Mica Paris** ('Stand Up', 'Contribution'), **Monie Love** ('It's A Shame', 'Monie In The Middle'), **PM Dawn** ('Reality Used To Be A Friend Of Mine'), **Queen Latifah** ('Dance 4 Me') and **U2** ('Mysterious Ways'). Coffey was added to the line-up for 'Elevate My Mind', her two female compatriots joining shortly after. She enjoys a concurrent career as an actor and dancer, mainly in black theatre productions. She was even in the famed Broadway flop version of *Carrie*. 'Elevate Your Mind' actually gave the group a Top 40 hit in the

US - a first for UK hip hop. Bedassie arrived as a qualified fashion designer, while Davis had formerly worked in a hip hop act with Owen If, titled Giant. The powerful *Connected* was released in September 1992 to mounting acclaim; previous albums had all been well received, but this was comfortably their most rounded and spirited effort. However, it was not until the title track and the exquisite rhythms of 'Step It Up' hit the UK charts that it was brought to the wider audience it richly deserved. In its wake the Stereo MC's collared the Best Group category at the 1994 BRIT Awards ceremony, part of a growing volume of evidence that locates the band within the commercial dance field rather than their roots in hip hop.

Albums: *33, 45,78* (4th & Broadway 1989), *Supernatural* (4th & Broadway 1990), *Connected* (4th & Broadway 1992).

Video: *Connected* (1993).

Stereolab

From south London, Stereolab wear their **John Cage** and **John Cale** influences on their sleeves, but within a short time span have amassed an impressive body of work. The principal mover is Tim Gane (ex-**McCarthy**), who was at first joined by his girlfriend Laetitia Sadier (b. 1968, Paris, France), Martin Kean (ex-New Zealand band the **Chills**), and **Th' Faith Healers**' drummer Joe Dilworth, also a *Melody Maker* photographer. Tim gave the band their name; after an obscure offshoot of 60s folk label, Vanguard (it has also been stated that the title was taken from a hi-fi testing label). At their early gigs they were joined by Russell Yates (**Moose**) on guitar and Gina Morris (*New Musical Express* journalist) on vocals. Too Pure signed them, allowing them to keep the Duophonic imprint. By the time of the release of the 'Low-Fi' 10-inch in September 1992, Mary Hansen had arrived to lend keyboard and vocal support, and Andy Ramsay replaced Dilworth on drums. 'John Cage Bubblegum', which some critics have noted as an adequate description of their sound, was released in the US only, on Slumberland, via a limited edition version containing a stick of gum. By the time *The Groop Played Space Age Bachelor Pad Music* was released in March 1993, further line-up changes had occurred, with Duncan Brown joining on bass and ex-**Microdisney** guitarist Sean O'Hagan also joining. This set was the closest to ambient soundscapes, similar to **Martin Denny** or **Arthur Lyman**, that they had yet come. The group left Too Pure for **Elektra Records** at the end of 1993, once again retaining the Duophonic Ultra High Frequency Disks imprint for their domestic releases. Duophonic would also issue material by Arcwelder and Herzfeld, the latter featuring another former McCarthy member, Malcolm Eden. The double LP, *Transient Random Noise-Bursts With Announcements*, straddled both indie and dance markets.

This was more minimalist than ambient, and maintained their reputation not only as a competent rock outfit, but also a fixture of the experimental dance music axis. 1995's addictive *Music For The Amorphous Body Study Centre* continued to embrace subjects outside of pop music convention, on this occasion acting as a soundtrack to the work of artist Charles Long for an exhibition at New York's Tanya Bonakdar Gallery.

Albums: *Peng!* (Too Pure 1992), *The Groop Played Space Age Bachelor Pad Music* (Too Pure 1993), *Transient Random Noise-Bursts With Announcements* (Duophonic 1993, double album), *Mars Audio Quintet* (Duophonic 1994), *Music For The Amorphous Body Study Centre* (Duophonic 1995, mini-album).

Stereos

An R&B vocal group from Steubenville, Ohio, USA. Members were lead Bruce Robinson, first tenor Nathaniel Hicks, second tenor Sam Profit, baritone George Otis, and bass Ronnie Collins. The Stereos were typical of the early 60s transition from doo-wop to soul singing in a style that utilized doo-wop harmonies but propelled by a gospelized lead vocals. The genesis of the group were the Buckeyes, who recorded several tracks for Deluxe Records in 1956. Three members of the group - Robinson, Collins, and first tenor Leroy Swearingen - joined with Profit and Otis to form the Stereos in 1959. After they made an unsuccessful record for **Otis Blackwell**'s Gibralter label, Swearingen left and was replaced with Hicks. The group was signed to **MGM**'s Cub subsidiary in 1961, and immediately found success with the Swearingen-penned 'I Really Love You' (number 15 R&B, number 29 pop). The Stereos were not able to successfully follow-up with their two further singles on Cub, or later singles on **Columbia**, World Artists, and Val. The group broke up in 1965, but came together again as a self-contained band in 1967. After two singles on **Chess Records**' Cadet subsidiary during 1967-68, the Stereos disbanded for good.

Sterling Cooke Force

This **Jimi Hendrix**-inspired US group was put together by guitarist/vocalist Sterling Cooke in 1983. Recruiting Gino Cannon (vocals), Harry Shuman (bass) and Albie Coccia (drums), they recorded two unspectacular albums during the mid-80s. *Force This* saw Cooke rescind the vocals to Cannon and the music adopted a more melodic and restrained style. Second-hand riffs, bridges and solos were the order of the day, which left the band with a serious identity crisis. After losing their recording contract they were consigned to the status of minor club circuit band from then on.

Albums: *Full Force* (Ebony 1984), *Force This* (Ebony 1986).

Stern, Joseph W.

b. 11 January 1870, New York City, New York, USA, d. 31 March 1934. A self-taught but somewhat amateurish pianist, Stern was a travelling salesman when he met another salesman, Edward B. Marks (1865-1944). Marks had already dabbled with song lyrics. One evening, when the two men were stormbound in a small hotel they whiled away the time making up a song about an item in the local newspaper. With foresight, Stern and Marks set up their own publishing company for their 'The Little Lost Child' and soon found themselves rich. The song's popularity with vaudeville audiences led to the two men deciding to make songwriting and publishing their full time work. The next few years saw them write songs such as 'No One Ever Loved More Than I', 'My Mother Was A Lady', 'Games We Used To Play' and 'Don't Wear Your Heart On Your Sleeve'. Their style of song became a little dated after the turn of the century and soon Stern decided to retire. Marks continued publishing songs and worked briefly in national government.

Stern, Mike

b. 1954, Boston, Massachusetts, USA. Whilst always a rock-orientated electric guitarist, Stern's forays into contemporary jazz have never lacked edge or excitement. A student of **Pat Metheny** whilst at **Berklee College Of Music**, his first break came in 1976, when he joined **Blood, Sweat And Tears**. He worked with seminal fusion drummer **Billy Cobham** towards the end of the 70s, before being hired by legendary trumpeter **Miles Davis**. Following Davis' band, Stern worked with bass virtuoso **Jaco Pastorius**' Word Of Mouth, and began touring and recording as a leader in the early 80s. Some of his most exciting recent work has been with extraordinary tenor saxophonist **Michael Brecker**, in Brecker's own band or with the fast-fingered fusion group **Steps Ahead**. Recommended recordings include *Time In Place*, which features some of the New York fusion/studio virtuosi with whom Stern has become associated, including Michael Brecker and **Bob Berg** on tenor saxophones, keyboardist **Don Grolnick**, fusion drummer **Peter Erskine** and sought after percussionist Don Alias. He plays some subtle guitar on Michael Brecker's *Don't Try This At Home*, amongst a line-up that includes pianist **Herbie Hancock**, drummer **Jack DeJohnette** and bassist **Charlie Haden**.

Albums: with Miles Davis *The Man With The Horn* (1981), with Davis *We Want Miles* (1981), with Billy Cobham *Stratus* (1981), with Davis *Star People* (1983), *Upside Downside* (1985), with Harvie Swartz *Urban Earth* (1985), with Swartz *Smart Moves* (1986), with Lew Soloff *Yesterdays* (1986), *Time In Place* (1987), with Michael Brecker *Don't Try This At Home* (1988), *Jigsaw* (1989),

with Bob Berg *Cycles* (1989), with Berg *In The Shadows* (1990), with Berg *Back Roads* (1991), with Berg *Short Stories* (1992).

Stetsasonic

Among rap's elder statesmen with origins in 1981, Brooklyn's Stetsasonic were hugely influential on a number of fronts. They were one of the few bands of their generation to promote the use of live instruments, and there was simply no hip hop comparison to their onstage power. Via their 'A.F.R.I.C.A.' 45 (1985) they helped usher in a new wave of black consciousness and ethnocentricity/positivity, which both **De La Soul** and the **Jungle Brothers** would further streamline. Proceeds from the song were handed over to the Africa Fund for humanitarian relief projects. Alongside **Run DMC**, Stetsasonic were instrumental in promoting the rock/rap crossover, yet maintained an articulate rap narrative, best sampled on their classic second album, *In Full Gear*. 'This Is A Hip Hop Band' they announced on its cover - it was, but not like any hip hop band had sounded before. They were joined by the **Force MD's** on an exemplory version of the **Floaters**' 'Float On', and also tackled the contextual rap history lesson of 'Talkin' All That Jazz', which would pre-date the jazz/rap phenomenon by at least three years. Their third album included direct political point-making exercises like 'Free South Africa'. Fittingly, it was Stetsasonic who were chosen to represent rap at the Nelson Mandela concert in London. DJ **Prince Paul** (b. Paul Huston) and lead rapper **Daddy-O** (b. c.1961, Brooklyn, New York, USA) were the lynchpins behind the group, who also included Delite, Fruitkwan (aka Fuquan) and DBC. The split came in 1990 when Daddy-O decided, not entirely unilaterally, that Statsasonic were beginning to exhaust their possibilities. Both Prince Paul and Daddy-O subsequently become in-demand producers and remixers. The former has produced **Fine Young Cannibals**, in addition to underscoring **De La Soul**'s *3 Feet High And Rising*, while **Boo-Yaa Tribe** adopted his hard funk drum effect. Daddy-O, meanwhile, remixed for **Mary J. Blige**, also working with artists as diverse as **Queen Latifah**, **Big Daddy Kane** (notably *It's A Big Daddy Thing*) and the **Red Hot Chilli Peppers**. DBC recorded a handful of tracks for independent labels. Any bad blood which may have existed at the time of their dissolvement would appear to have been forgotten when the news broke that the original line up recorded together again in 1993, with a view to a release the following year. 1994 also saw Prince Paul collaborating with Fruitkwan as part of the **Gravediggaz**.

Albums: *On Fire* (Tommy Boy 1986), *In Full Gear* (Tommy Boy 1988), *Blood Sweat And No Tears* (Tommy Boy 1991).

Stevens', Steve, Atomic Playboys

Steve Stevens first attracted attention as lead guitarist in **Billy Idol**'s band, where his flash and fiery style brought Idol's hard rock to life. Stevens also accompanied **Michael Jackson** on 'Dirty Diana' and has worked with Ric Ocasek of the **Cars**, Steve Lukather of **Toto** and the **Thompson Twins**. He broke ranks from Idol's band in 1988 to form Steve Steven's Atomic Playboys with vocalist Perry McCarty, drummer Thommy Price and keyboard player Phil Ashley. Released in 1989, their self-titled debut was a major disappointment. With the exception of the title-cut, the songs were derivative and overtly commercial. Following an unsuccessful US club tour in 1990, the band broke up.
Album: *Steve Steven's Atomic Playboys* (Warners 1989).

Stevens, Cat

b. Steven Georgiou, 21 July 1947, London, England. For Yusuf Islam, the constant search for the meaning of life that littered his lyrics and arose in interviews, seems to have arrived. Those who criticized his sometimes trite espousing of various causes now accept that his conversion to the Islamic faith and his retirement from a music world of 'sin and greed' was a committed move that will not be reversed. His legacy as Cat Stevens is a considerable catalogue of timeless songs, many destined to become classics. In 1966, producer Mike Hurst spotted Cat performing at the Hammersmith College, London; he was so impressed that he arranged to record him and his song, 'I Love My Dog'. Tony Hall at **Decca Records** was similarly impressed and Stevens became the first artist on the new **Deram** label. The record and its b-side 'Portobello Road' showed great promise and over the next two years Stevens delivered many perfect pop songs. Some were recorded by himself but many other artists queued up for material from this precociously-talented teenager. His own hits; 'Matthew And Son', 'I'm Gonna Get Me A Gun' and 'Bad Night' were equalled by the quality of his songs for others; the soulful 'First Cut Is The Deepest' by **P.P. Arnold** and the addictive 'Here Comes My Baby' by the **Tremeloes**. His two Decca albums were packed full of short, infectious songs, although they suffered from dated accompaniments. Stevens contracted tuberculosis and was absent for some time. During his convalescence he took stock of his life. Over the next eight years and 11 albums, the astute listener can detect a troubled soul.
Mona Bone Jakon was the first in the series of albums known as bedsitter music. It was followed by two hugely successful works: *Tea For The Tillerman* and *Teaser And The Firecat*. These revealed the solitary songwriter, letting the listener into his private thoughts, aspirations and desires. Stevens was the master of this genre and produced a wealth of simplistic, yet beautiful songs.

Anthems like 'Wild World', 'Peace Train' and 'Moon Shadow', love songs including 'Lady D'Arbanville', 'Hard Headed Woman' and 'Can't Keep It In', are all faultless and memorable compositions. Stevens was at his sharpest with his posing numbers that hinted of dubiety, religion and scepticism. Two of his finest songs are 'Father And Son' and 'Sitting'. The first is a dialogue between father and son, and gives the listener an insight into his lonely childhood in Soho. The line 'How can I try to explain, when I do he turns away again, its always been the same, same old story' the child continues with 'from the moment I could talk, I was ordered to listen, now there's a way that I know, that I have to go, away, I know I have to go'. The song is astonishingly powerful in relating Stevens' own turmoil to virtually every person that has ever heard the song. 'Sitting' is similarly powerful, although it is a song of great hope. It opens confidently, 'Ooh I'm on my way I know I am, somewhere not so far from here, all I know is all I feel right now, I feel the power growing in my hair'. Few were unmoved by these two songs. In his time Stevens had eight consecutive gold albums and 10 hit singles in the UK and 14 in the USA. In recent years he has been very active teaching and spreading the word of Islam; in 1991 prior to the Gulf War he travelled to Baghdad to seek the freedom of hostages. Reports in 1994 suggested that he was ready to return to the world of the recording studio, albeit only to offer a spoken word narrative on *Mohammed - The Life Of The Prophet*.
Albums: *Matthew & Son* (1967), *New Masters* (1968), *Mona Bone Jakon* (1970), *Tea For The Tillerman* (1970), *Teaser & The Firecat* (1971), *Very Young And Early Songs* (1972), *Catch Bull At Four* (1972), *Foreigner* (1973), *Buddha And The Chocolate Box* (1974), *View From The Top* (1974), *Numbers* (1975), *Izitso* (1977), *Back To Earth* (1978). Compilations: *Greatest Hits* (1975), *Footsteps In The Dark* (1984), *The Very Best Of Cat Stevens* (1990) Video: *Tea For The Tillerman Live - The Best Of* (1993). Further reading: *Cat Stevens*, Charlesworth, Chris (1985).

Stevens, Connie

b. Concetta Ann Ingolia, 8 August 1938, Brooklyn, New York, USA. Stevens was an actress and singer, whose antecedents are said to have been Italian, Irish, English and Mohican. Stevens entered show-business at the age of 16 and in 1959, after making several appearances on the Warner Brothers' hit television series *77 Sunset Strip*, had a chart hit with the novelty, 'Kookie, Kookie, (Lend Me Your Comb)', in collaboration with one of the show's stars, **Edd Byrnes**. The record sold over a million copies, as did Stevens' first and only solo hit, 'Sixteen Reasons' (1960). Her other 60s releases included 'Why'd You Wanna Make Me Cry?', 'Mr. Songwriter' and 'Now That You've Gone', *Connie Stevens* and *Sings The **Hank***

Williams Songbook. Stevens' other television work included the drama, *The Littlest Angel*, with Fred Gwynne, E.G. Marshall and **Cab Calloway**; and *Wendy And Me*, a series in which she co-starred with comedian George Burns, shortly after his wife Gracie, retired. From 1959-62, Stevens starred with Robert Conrad, Anthony Eisley and Grant Williams in another Warner 'episodic/action' series, *Hawaiian Eye*. She also appeared in the theatre, and shortly after starring on Broadway with Tony Perkins in Neil Simon's play, *Star Spangled Girl*, she followed Debbie Reynolds and Elizabeth Taylor, and became singer **Eddie Fisher**'s third wife - they later divorced. After making her big screen debut in 1959 with *Eighteen And Anxious*, she appeared with Jerry Lewis and Marilyn Maxwell in *Rock-A-Bye-Baby*, with songs by the unusual combination of **Harry Warren** and **Sammy Cahn**. Her other movies included a couple of 1961 soap operas, *Parrish* and *Susan Slade*, the ghostly *Two On A Guillotine* (1965), a film version of the hit Broadway play *Never Too Late* (1965), a re-make of the 1948 UK film *No Orchids For Miss Blandish* and television movies, such as *Mr. Jericho*, and *The Sex Symbol*. The latter project was plagued by legal action because of its similarity to **Marilyn Monroe**'s life story. Stevens' other television projects, in the 80s and early 90s, included an appearance on *Bob Hope's Christmas Show* from the Persian Gulf (1988), *Bring Me The Head Of Dobie Gillis*, *Tape Heads* and *Murder She Wrote*. In 1987 she was reunited with Edd Byrnes, this time on the big screen, in *Back To The Beach*, a nostalgic look back at the surf/beach-type movies of the 60s, with several of the original stars, such as **Frankie Avalon** and **Annette** Funicello.

Albums: *Conchetta* (1958), *Hawaiian Eye* (1959, television soundtrack), *Connie Stevens From 'Hawaiian Eye'* (1960), *Connie* (1961), *The Hank Williams Songbook* (1962), *Palm Springs Weekend* (1963, film soundtrack), *The Littlest Angel* (1969, television soundtrack).

Stevens, Dodie

b. Geraldine Ann Pasquale, 17 February 1947, Chicago, Illinois, USA. Stevens moved with her family to Temple City in California when she was three years old. As a child, in the 50s, she performed at USO shows and Army and Navy hospitals and, at the age of 10, was 'discovered', while singing on a local television show. Signed to Crystallette Records, it was 18 months before the company recorded her. Her first release, Mickie Grant's 'Pink Shoelaces', went to number 3 in the US charts in 1959. It was one of the first records to be produced by the prolific H.B. Barnum. Subsequent singles such as 'Yes-sir-ee' and 'No' failed to repeat that initial success, as did the three albums, released on the **Dot** label. She appeared in several movies, including *Hound Dog* (with **Fabian**), *Convicts Four* and *Alakazam The Great* (an animated feature in which Stevens

provided the voice of a monkey). She retired at 16 to get married, and had a child at 19, but was divorced in 1968. She returned to singing, and joined **Sergio Mendes** for a while, toured with rock 'n' roll revival shows, and became an in-demand session singer, working with **Mac Davis** and others.

Albums: *Dodie Stevens* (1960), *Over The Rainbow* (1960), *Pink Shoelaces* (1961).

Stevens, Garry

b. 21 October 1916, Los Angeles, California, USA. An excellent band singer during the 40s, early in his career Stevens worked as a trumpeter-vocalist with various bands on the US east coast, and spent some time with combos led by Paul Kain and Don Bestor. In the late 30s he became a staff musician-singer on radio in Washington, DC before joining **Charlie Spivak**'s outfit as vocalist in late 1941. He stayed with Spivak until 1943, and sang on several of his hit records including 'This Is No Laughing Matter', 'My Devotion', 'I Left My Heart At The Stage Door Canteen' and 'White Christmas'. The Stardusters vocal group, featuring one of the best girl band singers, **June Hutton**, was with the band at the same time. After military service in World War II, Stevens joined **Tex Beneke**'s **Glenn Miller** Orchestra in the late 40s, and sang on two of the band's successful sides, 'Anniversary Song' and 'As Long As I'm Dreaming' in 1947. His other records included 'But Beautiful', 'Beyond The Sea' and 'Poinciana' (with Beneke), 'At Last', and 'It's So Peaceful In The Country' (with Spivak).

Stevens, Guy

b. c.1940, d. 29 August 1981. This enigmatic figure first came to prominence during the early 60s as a disc jockey at London's influential Scene club. His collection of soul and R&B releases was one of the finest in Britain and compilation tapes culled from this remarkable archive supplied several groups, including the **Who** and the **Small Faces**, with their early live repertoires. Having helped assemble several anthologies culled from the **Chess** label, Stevens joined **Island Records** in order to mastermind their Sue subsidiary. He also began work as a producer and following a successful debut with *Larry Williams On Stage*, took control of the **VIPs**, a new signing to the parent company. This Carlisle-based group accompanied Guy on a 1967 album, *Hapshash And The Coloured Coat*, which also featured designers Michael English and Nigel Weymouth. The VIPs later evolved into **Spooky Tooth**. Stevens' best-known collaboration came with **Mott The Hoople**. He produced their first four albums but, more crucially, shaped the sound and attitude of this early work. **Free**, **Traffic** and **Mighty Baby** also benefited from Guy's involvement, but by the early 70s, his persona had become too erratic.

Chronic alcoholism debilitated his abilities and few now considered using his talents. Stevens did produce some early demos for the **Clash** and in 1979 they invited him to work on what became *London Calling*. Arguably the group's definitive release, its success should have engendered a renewed career for its producer, but considerable resistance still remained. On 29 August, 1981, Guy Stevens was found dead in his south London home, the victim of a heart attack. His influence on music, although not of the highest profile, remains incalculable.

Stevens, John

b. 10 June 1940, Brentford, Middlesex, England, d. 13 September 1994, London, England. Stevens, whose father was a tap dancer, studied at Ealing Junior Art School and Ealing College of Higher Education. In 1958 he joined the Air Force, where he played drums in various bands after studying at the RAF's Music School. He spent three and a half years in Cologne, where he was able to see concerts by modern players such as **John Coltrane** and **Eric Dolphy**; there he also played with future German *avant gardists*, **Manfred Schoof** and **Alex Von Schlippenbach**. The late 50s skiffle boom had awakened his interest in blues and jazz - both New Orleans and modern - and back in England he played with **Joe Harriott**, **Ellsworth 'Shake' Keane** and **Tubby Hayes**. By 1964 he was centrally involved with modern jazz in London, playing with **Ronnie Scott** and **Stan Tracey**, then joining a quartet that comprised **Jeff Clyne**, **Ian Carr** and **Trevor Watts**, whom he had met in the RAF in 1958 and who would become one of his most frequent collaborators over the next 10 years. In 1965 he formed a septet that included **Kenny Wheeler**, **Alan Skidmore** and **Ron Mathewson** and, together with Watts and **Paul Rutherford** (another ex-RAF colleague), he also initiated the **Spontaneous Music Ensemble**, a launchpad for many free improvising musicians. In 1966, Stevens began organizing concerts at the Little Theatre Club, which rapidly became the epicentre of the new British jazz. Stevens moved back into more mainstream areas with the group Splinters in 1971, which he co-led with fellow-drummer **Phil Seamen**. In 1971, he formed the John Stevens Dance Orchestra and, in 1974, Away, his jazz-rock group. During this time he recorded and toured with **John Martyn**. In 1982, he formed Freebop and Folkus (their musical inclinations can be read from their names). In 1985, he published a book of workshop techniques, something he had been involved with since the mid-60s, winning the 1972 Thames Television award for community work. From 1983 he directed the UK Jazz Centre Society's Outreach Community Project, nurturing the talents of prominent figures in the mid-80s jazz revival, including **Courtney Pine**. In 1988, *Live Tracks* brought together many of his

collaborators, including Pine, USA trumpeter **Bobby Bradford**, UK saxophonists **Pete King** and **Evan Parker** and trombonist **Annie Whitehead**, in a celebration of the joys of untrammelled bop-based improvisation.

Albums: *Springboard* (1967), with Evan Parker *The Longest Night Vols 1 & 2* (1976), *Somewhere In Between* (1976), *Application, Interaction And ...* (Spotlite 1979), with Folkus *The Life Of Riley* (Affinity 1983), *Freebop* (Affinity 1983), with Dudu Pukwana *Radebe - They Shoot To Kill* (1987), with Free Bop *Live Tracks* (1988).

Stevens, Jon

b. New Zealand. Stevens became the number one teen idol of the 70s in New Zealand and recorded two successful albums of covers and standards there. He was enticed to Australia to broaden his horizons and to prove his talent to a wider audience. There he joined the Fraser brothers from the Change, a young hard-rock band. As **Noiseworks** they recorded two well received albums. His clean strong voice is a good vehicle for the stadium rock music played by the band. Albums: *Jezebel* (1980), *Jon Stevens* (1982).

Stevens, Ray

b. Ray Ragsdale, 24 January 1941, Clarksdale, Georgia USA. A prolific country-pop writer and performer, Stevens' novelty hits of the 70s and 80s form a history of the fads and crazes of the era. He became a disc jockey on a local station at 15 and the following year recorded 'Five More Steps' on the Prep label. Stevens' first nonsense song, 'Chickie Chickie Wah Wah' was written in 1958 but it was not until 1961, with **Mercury Records** that he had a Top 40 hit with the tongue-twisting 'Jeremiah Peabody's Poly Unsaturated Quick Dissolving Fast Acting Pleasant Tasting Green And Purple Pills'. This was followed by 'Ahab The Arab' (1962) and 'Harry The Hairy Ape' (1963). Stevens also had a penchant for social comment which came through in songs like 'Mr Businessman' (1968), 'America Communicate With Me' and the first recording of **Kris Kristofferson**'s 'Sunday Morning Coming Down'. However, the zany songs were the most successful and in 1969 he sold a million copies of 'Gitarzan' and followed with a version of **Leiber And Stoller**'s **Coasters**' hit 'Along Came Jones' and 'Bridget The Midget (The Queen Of The Blues). His first number 1 was the simple melodic ballad 'Everything Is Beautiful' in 1970. All of these however, were outsold by 'The Streak' which topped the charts on both sides of the Atlantic in 1974. Stevens' softer side was evident in his version of Erroll Garner's 'Misty' which won a Grammy in 1976 for its bluegrass-styled arrangement. Later novelty efforts, aimed principally at country audiences included 'Shriner's Convention' (1980), 'It's Me Again Margaret' (1985), 'I Saw Elvis In A UFO' (1989) and 'Power Tools'.

Albums: *1,837 Seconds Of Humor* (1962), *Ahab The Arab* (1962), *This Is Ray Stevens* (1963), *Gitarzan* (1969), *Unreal!!!* (1970), *Everything Is Beautiful* (1970), *Turn Your Radio On* (1972), *Boogity Boogity* (1974), *Misty* (1975), *Just For The Record* (1975), *Feel The Music* (1976), *Shriner's Convention* (1980), *Don't Laugh Now* (1982), *Me* (1983), *He Thinks He's Ray Stevens* (1985), *Surely You Joust* (1988), *I Have Returned* (1988), *Beside Myself* (1989). Compilations: *Ray Stevens' Greatest Hits* (1971), *The Very Best Of Ray Stevens* (1975), *Both Sides Of Ray Stevens* (1986), *Greatest Hits* (1987).

Videos: *Comedy Video Classics* (1993), *Live* (Club Video 1994).

Stevens, Shakin'
(see **Shakin' Stevens**

Stevens, Stu
b. Wilfrid Pierce, 25 September c.1937, Annesley Woodhouse, Kirkby-In-Ashfield, Nottinghamshire, England. He drove tractors on the farm at the age of eight, but his ambition to be a farmer was never fully realised. When he was about 13 years old, his father, a miner, died so Wilfrid left school to work down the mines to keep the family. His first singing experience came after his brother entered him in a local talent show around 1965. He won and his powerful deep voice found him a regular paid singing spot at the club. It seemed to him much easier than farming so he bought himself a guitar (later learned piano) and began to put together a repertoire of songs. In the late 60s, as Stuart Stevens, he made his first recordings for **EMI**, including the release of a single ('Soft Is The Night'/'Tender Hearted'). He also appeared on the **Lonnie Donegan** television show. In March 1970, he was booked to entertain at a reception for the American country stars of the Wembley Festival. Performing as Willard Pierce, he created such an impression that it led to him appearing on the Festival itself the following day - seemingly the first British artist to do so. He made a noteworthy appearance on *Opportunity Knocks* in 1972 (unfortunately falling foul of the 'never work with children or animals' adage and lost by three votes to a child drummer). He recorded for the Youngblood label in 1972, with the subsequent album, *Stories In Song*, selling some 12,000 copies. In 1973, he performed at a disc jockey Convention in Nashville, subsequently appearing at many major venues, including the *Grand Ole Opry* and on network television. He was signed by **Cliffie Stone** to the US Granite label in 1974, who released his Youngblood album in the USA and in Europe. His recording of 'My Woman My Woman My Wife' became popular on both sides of the Atlantic, even drawing praise from the song's writer **Marty Robbins**.

Further trips to the States followed until, sadly for him, both Granite and Youngblood ceased record production, leaving him without a label in either country. He had continued to play the British clubs, first with his band Silver Mist, then with Pat and Roger Johns, before eventually appearing with his two sons Stuart (bass guitar) and Steven (keyboards). He also opened his own recording studios and worked on production with other artists. He formed his own Major Oak, Eagle and Ash labels and released albums, which proved popular with his British fans. Twelve out of 28 unissued Youngblood tracks later appeared on his album *The Loner*. In 1979, he almost made the British Top 40 with 'The Man From Outer Space' which, after initially being released on his own Eagle label, was picked up by MCA Records and received air-play and jocularity from Terry Wogan on BBC radio. Further singles followed, including 'If I Heard You Call My Name', 'One Red Rose' and 'Hello Pretty Lady', which sold well for country records, but not well enough for a major label seeking pop record sales. This resulted in him parting company with MCA.

Stu's national popularity increased and he regularly played the theatre and concert hall circuit, always doing it his way and always refusing to perform anything he did not wish to sing. Many think, no doubt correctly, that had he become a 'yes' man and allowed himself to be type-cast, he would undoubtedly have become a major star. In 1984, Stu and his wife were devastated by the death, from a rare heart disease, of their youngest son. Steven (19), a keyboard player of very outstanding abilities, had appeared on stage from the age of seven. Although Stu played out his immediate special bookings, he soon tended to withdraw from active participation in the music scene. In recent years, he has made infrequent appearances but in the main 'The Voice', as he was affectionately known to his fans, has been silent - a great, if understandable, loss to British country music.

Albums: *Stories In Song* (1973), *Command Performance* (1976), *Together Again* (1977), *Stu Stevens - Country Music Volume 7* (1977, cassette only), *Stories In Song Volume 2 - The Loner* (1978), *The Man From Outer Space* (1979), *Stu* (1979), *Emma And I* (1980), *Old Rugged Cross* (1981, cassette only), *Songs That Made Stu Stevens* (1981), *The Voice - Live* (1982, cassette only), *In Memory Of Steven (Live)* (1986, cassette only), *The Man And His Music* (1986, cassette only).

Stevenson, B.W.
b. Louis C. Stevenson, 5 October 1949, Dallas, Texas, USA, d. 28 April 1988, USA. B.W. Stevenson (the initials stood for Buckwheat) is now best remembered for his 1973 *Billboard* Top 10 single 'My Maria'. Stevenson performed with many local Texas rock bands as a teenager, before attending college and then joining the US Air Force. Upon being discharged from the Air Force, Stevenson returned to the thriving club scene, particularly in the burgeoning Austin, Texas

area. Although he considered himself a blues and rock singer, he was signed to **RCA Records** as a country artist and released 'Shambala', a song which charted but did not fare as well as the version by rockers **Three Dog Night**. Stevenson and Daniel Moore's 'My Maria' became a number 9 pop hit (oddly missing the country charts), and the album of the same title reached number 45, also in 1973. Stevenson continued to record, placing two further singles on the charts in the 70s (the latter, 'Down To The Station', for **Warner Brothers Records**). He also recorded for MCA Records. Stevenson died following heart surgery in April 1988.

Albums: *B.W. Stevenson* (1972), *Lead Free* (1972), *My Maria* (1973), *Calabasas* (1974), *Lost Feeling* (1977), *Lifeline* (1980).

Stevenson, Mickey

b. William Stevenson. Having spent his formative years recording R&B and gospel music, Stevenson joined the nascent Tamla/**Motown** organization in 1959, later co-producing and arranging singles by **Marv Johnson**. As the company's first A&R director, he was responsible for supervising all facets of recording, assigning acts to producers and songwriters, and enlisting notable musicians like **Choker Campbell**, Benny Benjamin and James Jamerson. He brought **Martha Reeves** to the label, where she was also employed as his secretary, and later co-wrote 'Wild One' and 'Dancing In The Streets' for her group, **Martha And The Vandellas**. Stevenson's compositional and/or production credits included 'Beechwood 4-5789' and 'Playboy' for the **Marvelettes**, 'Needle In A Haystack' for the **Velvelettes** and 'Stubborn Kind Of Fellow' and 'Pride And Joy' for **Marvin Gaye**, who also recorded with Stevenson's wife, **Kim Weston**. Their singing partnership was sundered prematurely when she and her husband left Motown in January 1967 to join **MGM Records**. Although Mickey later founded his own label, People, he was unable to recapture the considerable success he enjoyed earlier in the decade.

Stevo

b. Steven Pearse, 26 December 1962, Dagenham, Essex, England. One of the most outspoken, adventurous and original discoverers of arcane talent, Stevo came to the fore of the British music scene during the early 80s. A misfit and underachiever at school, he was virtually illiterate and underwent a self-improving course which coincided with his rise to prominence in the music industry. Originally a disc jockey, he compiled an 'electronic music' and 'futurist' chart for the music press which led to him being bombarded with roughly-hewn demos from unknown artists. During 1980, Stevo packaged the best of this material as the *Some Bizzare Album* (its misspelling was

unintentional but apposite). Among the artists included were **Throbbing Gristle**, **Classix Noveaux**, **Clock DVA**, **Cabaret Voltaire**, **Blancmange**, **Depeche Mode**, **Soft Cell** and **The The**. The latter two artists came under Stevo's management and joined his innovative **Some Bizzare** record label. Stevo received instant recognition for his brusque behaviour and eccentric business dealings. After the chart-topping success of Soft Cell, major record companies anxious to license his acts were forced to endure the teenage entrepreneur's strange whims, which included signing a contract in the pouring rain while sitting on one of the lions in Trafalgar Square. With similar eccentricity, the contract for the hand of **Psychic TV** included a clause demanding a year's supply of baby food. It said much for Stevo's power and persuasion that he managed to license so many wilfully uncommercial acts to the major labels. His strength lay in an ability to capture innovative acts at an early stage when they were merely regarded as weird. In the case of Soft Cell and later The The, Stevo showed that he had the ear to nurture potentially major artists. Many other acts were a testament to his love of the unusual. Berlin's **Einsturzende Neubaten** decried conventional rock instruments in favour of industrial sounds, and the scream of clanging metal as percussion could also be heard via **Test Department**. The unremitting aural depravity of **Foetus** threatened to complete Stevo's journey into the darker areas of the soul, and with commercial acts on the wane the future of his label was perpetually in doubt. In the early 90s, however, Stevo is still stalking the musical boundaries with a stream of new signings including Stex, Tim Hutton, Kandis King and Vicious Circle.

Further reading: *Starmakers And Svengalis: The History Of British Pop Management*, Johnny Rogan.

Steward, Herbie

b. 7 May 1926, Los Angeles, California, USA. Steward took up clarinet and alto and tenor saxophones while still a youth, but later concentrated on tenor. In the early and mid-40s he gigged in the Los Angeles area, playing with **Barney Kessel** and then signing on with a succession of big bands, including those of **Artie Shaw**, **Alvino Rey** and Butch Stone. In the latter band he played alongside **Stan Getz**, **Shorty Rogers** and **Don Lamond**. In 1947 he played in the **Gene Rowland** rehearsal band, in which the leader experimented with unusual saxophone voicings using the talents of Steward, Getz, **Zoot Sims** and **Jimmy Giuffre**. When the entire section was hired by **Woody Herman**, Steward became one of the original 'Four Brothers' saxophone team but stayed only three months before moving on. Later in the 40s and in the early 50s he played with more big bands. including those led by **Tommy Dorsey**, **Harry James** and **Claude Thornhill**. During the remainder of the 50s and on through the 60s he worked in show and studio bands, by now usually preferring the alto to the tenor. In these decades and in the 70s he made occasional returns to the jazz scene for record dates. From the early 70s he was resident in San Francisco and could still be heard playing with rehearsal bands. In 1987, he returned to centre stage with appearances on the international festival circuit, playing alto, tenor and soprano saxophones. A highly-regarded player, Steward's coolly elegant tone fitted well into the Four Brothers concept and the more introspective small groups. His early work showed few signs of major influences and although his later work displays his awareness of musical developments in jazz, everything is filtered through his highly personal and eminently tasteful style.

Albums: *Passport To Pimlico* (1950), with Zoot Sims, Serge Chaloff, Al Cohn *Four Brothers Together Again* (1957), *So Pretty* (1962), *Herbie Steward With Orchestra Directed By Dick Hazard* (1962), *Barney Plays Kessel* (1975), *The Three Horns Of Herbie Steward* (1981). Compilation: *The Best Of Woody Herman* (1945-47).

Stewart, Al

b. 5 September 1945, Glasgow, Scotland. Stewart first came to prominence during the folk boom of the mid-60s. His musical career began in Bournemouth, where he played guitar, backing **Tony Blackburn** in the Sabres. In 1965, he moved to London, played at various folk clubs and shared lodgings with **Jackson C. Frank**, **Sandy Denny** and **Paul Simon**. Stewart was signed to **Decca** in 1966 and released one unsuccessful single, 'The Elf', featuring **Jimmy Page** on lead guitar. The following year, he joined **CBS** and released the acoustic, string-accompanied, introspective *Bedsitter Images*. The succeeding *Love Chronicles*, a diary of Stewart's romantic life, was most notable for the lengthy title track and the fact that it used a contentious word ('fucking') in an allegedly artistic context. The singer's interest in acoustic folk continued on *Zero She Flies*, which featured the historical narrative 'Manuscript'. Stewart's interest in the confessional love song reached its conclusion on *Orange*, with the impressive 'Night Of The 4th Of May'. This was followed by his most ambitious work to date, *Past, Present And Future*. Pursuing his interest in historical themes, Stewart presented some of his best acoustic workouts in the impressive 'Roads To Moscow' and epic 'Nostradamus'. A considerable gap ensued before the release of *Modern Times*, which saw Stewart making inroads into the American market for the first time. After leaving CBS and signing to **RCA**, he relocated to California and surprised many by the commercial power of his celebrated *Year Of The Cat*, which reached the US Top 10. The title track also gave Stewart his first US hit. Another switch of label to **Arista** preceded *Time Passages*, which suffered by comparison with its

predecessor. The underrated *24 P Carrots* was succeeded by a part studio/part live album, which merely consolidated his position. With *Russians And Americans*, Stewart embraced a more noticeable political stance, but the sales were disappointing. Legal and contractual problems effectively deterred him from recording for four years until the welcome, if portentous, *The Last Days Of The Century*. During that time he had re-located to France and set about expanding his impressive cellar of vintage wines. Stewart remains one of the more underrated performers, despite his commercial breakthrough in the 70s.

Albums: *Bedsitter Images* (1967), *Love Chronicles* (1969), *Zero She Flies* (1970), *The First Album (Bedsitter Images)* (1970), *Orange* (1972), *Past, Present And Future* (1973), *Modern Times* (1975), *Year Of The Cat* (1976), *Time Passages* (1978), *24 P/Carrots* (1980), *Indian Summer/Live* (1981), *Russians And Americans* (EMI 1984), *Last Days Of The Century* (1988), *Rhymes In Rooms - Al Stewart Live Featuring Peter White* (1992), *Famous Last Words* (Permanent 1993), with Laurence Juber *Between The Wars* (EMI 1995). Compilations: *The Early Years* (1978), *Best Of Al Stewart* (1985), *Chronicles ... The Best Of Al Stewart* (1991), *To Whom It May Concern 1966-70* (EMI 1994).

Stewart, Andy

b. 20 December 1933, Scotland, d. 11 October 1993, Arbroath, Angus, Scotland. This singer/comedian rose to fame initially as the presenter of *Dance Party Roof*, which was shown on Scottish television. He subsequently became a national figure as a member of the resident cast of *The White Heather Club*, a long-running BBC television show. Stewart eventually the programme's compere, a role he combined with a recording career which bore fruit in 1960 when the blithe 'Donald Where's Your Trousers' reached the UK Top 20. Other whimsical singles, including 'Campbeltown Loch' and 'Dr. Findlay', contrasted with releases of a more romantic nature, the best-known of which was 'A Scottish Soldier' (1961). An ever-present kilt and homely fare ensured the artist's popularity among home-based Scots and expatriots and his career flourished in Australia, New Zealand and Canada. In 1976 he was awarded the MBE. Recurrent ill-health gave Stewart a lower profile and he underwent triple by pass surgery. He enjoyed a surprise return to the UK chart when 'Donald Where's Your Troosers' was re-released in 1989. Stewart received a series of glowing obituaries following his death in 1993, having been forgiven by all, outside his homeland, for spoiling Sassenachs' New Year's Eve television entertainment. In Scotland his music touched many as his pride and sheer joy at being born a Scot shone through.

Albums: *Andy Stewart* (1962), *Songs Of Scotland* (c.60s),

Andy The Rhymer (c.60s), *Scotch Corner* (1973), with Jimmy Blue And His Band *Brand New With Andy* (1975), with Ann Williamson *Country Boy* (1975), *I Love To Wear The Kilt* (1977), with Jimmy Blue And His Band *Andy's Hogmanay Party* (1978), *Scotland Is Andy Stewart* (1978), *Sing A Song Of Scotland* (1979), *20 Golden Scottish Greats* (1979), *100 Best Scottish Songs* (1979), *Come In Come In* (1983), *Legends Of Scotland* (1986), *Fire In The Glen* (1986), *For Auld Land Syne* (1987), *My Scotland* (1988), *Dublin Lady* (1988), *Back From The Bothy* (1988). Compilations: *The Very Best Of Andy Stewart* (1973), *Andy Stewart's Greatest Hits* (1977), *The Best Of Andy Stewart* (1987), *Forever In Song, 80 All-Time Scottish Favourites* (1993).

Stewart, Andy M.

b. Andrew McGregor Stewart, 8 September 1952, Alyth, Perthshire, Scotland to a father who had a large collection of traditional songs, and a mother who wrote poetry and songs and music. He started playing in the early 70s, having previously sung at sessions and get-togethers. In 1973, Stewart joined the already established duo of **Dougie MacLean** (b. 27 September 1954, Dunblane, Scotland; guitar/fiddle/vocals), and Ewan Sutherland (guitar/vocals). These three, together with Martin Hadden (b. 23 May 1957, Aberdeen, Scotland; bass/vocals), formed Puddock's Well. In 1974 Andy joined **Silly Wizard** on tenor banjo and vocals, with whom he toured and recorded. It was with Silly Wizard in 1980 that he recorded a single, 'Take The High Road', the original theme for the television series of the same name. *Take The High By The Hush* featured half traditional ballads and half original Stewart compositions. The album was well received, being voted **Melody Maker**'s Folk Album Of The Year. In 1984 Stewart teamed up with Manus Lunny (b. 8 February 1962, Dublin, Eire; bouzouki/guitar/vocals), regularly working as a duo, but adding Phil Cunningham (b. 27 January 1960, Edinburgh, Scotland; piano/accordion/whistles/vocals), to record *Fire In The Glen*. This album for **Topic Records** featured virtually all original material. As well as being featured on a number of compilation albums which include other artists, and having recorded with others, Andy still works with Lunny, and Gerry O'Byrne (guitar/vocals) from the group Patrick Street.
Albums: *By The Hush* (1982), with Manus Lunny, Phil Cunningham *Fire In The Glen* (1986), with Lunny *Dublin Lady* (1987), with Lunny *At It Again* (1990), *Andy M. Stewart Sings The Songs Of Robert Burns* (1990). Compilations: various artists *Flight Of The Green Linnet* (1988), with Lunny and various artists *The Celts Rise Again* (1990), various artists *The Irish Folk Festival-Back To The Future* (1990), various artists *The Irish Folk Festival Jubilee* (1991).

Stewart, Billy

b. 24 March 1937, Washington, DC, USA, d. 17 January 1970. Introduced to music by his family's Stewart Gospel Singers, Billy embraced a more secular direction with the Rainbows, a group which also included **Don Covay** and **Marvin Gaye**. From there Stewart joined **Bo Diddley**'s band on piano. His solo debut, 'Billy's Blues', was released on **Chess** in 1956, after which he worked with the Marquees. A second single, 'Billy's Heartaches' (1957), appeared on the **OKeh** label, but a return to Chess in the early 60's proved decisive. A succession of melodic songs, including 'I Do Love You' and 'Sitting In The Park' (both 1965), established a crafted style which blended R&B jazz and the singer's distinctive vocal delivery. These elements were prevalent in his radical interpretation of **George Gershwin** and DuBose Heyward's 'Summertime', a Top 10 US hit in 1966. Stewart's subsequent releases were less successful although he remained a popular live attraction. In January 1970, while touring in North Carolina, Billy's car plunged into the River Neuse, killing him and three of his musicians.
Albums: *I Do Love You* (Chess 1965), *Unbelievable* (Chess 1966). Compilation: *One More Time* (Chess/MCA 1990).

Stewart, Bob

b. 3 February 1945, Sioux Falls, Dakota, USA. Stewart played trumpet for eight years, then switched to tuba in his second year at the Philadelphia College of Performing Arts. He learned to play in dixieland bands (where the tuba occupies the role taken in later jazz by the string bass), including a residency at Your Father's Moustache. After graduating with a teaching degree in 1968 he relocated to New York, where he taught and led a junior high school band. He had been jamming with tuba-player **Howard Johnson** for years, now he joined his tuba ensemble Substructure and was also a founder member of Gravity. In 1971 he worked with the Collective Black Artists Ensemble and in the early 70s with a variety of artists, including **Freddie Hubbard** and **Taj Mahal**. He formed a trio with **Arthur Blythe** and cellist Abdul Wadud, showing that the tuba could operate at the forefront of post-free explorations of tradition, particularly gripping as he interpreted Monk's left-hand bass lines on the tribute record *Light Blue*. He worked with **Gil Evans** (recording the tuba solo on **Hendrix**'s `Voodoo Chile' on *Live At Royal Festival Hall*) and with **Carla Bley**. He became a founder member of **Lester Bowie**'s Brass Fantasy. Indeed, Stewart was there whenever a tuba was needed - as it increasingly was during the 80s period of consolidation, when arrangers looked to jazz history for inspiration. He has also played with the **Globe Unity Orchestra** and co-leads (with French-horn player John Clark) the Clark-Stewart Quartet. In

1987 he formed his own band, First Line, with guitarist Kelvyn Bell from **Defunkt**, touring in 1988 and 1991. The band play an amalgam of New Orleans, free jazz and fusion that Stewart calls 'dixie funk'.

Albums: *First Line* (1988), with First Line *Going Home* (1990).

Stewart, Dave, And Barbara Gaskin

One of the surprise hits of the early 80s was a UK number 1 cover of **Leslie Gore**'s 'Its My Party' by two former members of several UK progressive bands. Dave Stewart was originally organist in Uriel in late 1967 (with **Steve Hillage**). When Hillage left, Stewart and Uriel's other members Clive Brooks and Mont Campbell formed **Egg** who released a couple of albums in the late 60s and early 70s. At the same time Stewart often guested on keyboards with Steve Hillage's new band Khane. In 1973 he replaced David Sinclair in **Hatfield And The North** who included a female backing group, the Northettes, consisting of Barbara Gaskin (ex-Spyrogyra; not the chart act of the late 70s but a Canterbury folk-rock assembly), Amanda Parsons, and Ann Rosenthal. Hatfield And The North metamorphosed into National Health in 1975 but eventually folded later in the decade. Stewart formed his own record label Broken Records and recorded a version of the **Jimmy Ruffin** hit, 'What Becomes Of The Broken Hearted', featuring **Colin Blunstone** on vocals. The record (and label) were picked up by **Stiff Records** and became a Top 20 UK hit. For the follow-up Stewart chose his former Hatfield And The North colleague (and by now, lover) Barbara Gaskin to sing lead with Northette Amanda Parsons on backing vocals. The record - 'It's My Party' - reached number 1. Subsequent singles 'Johnny Rocco', and 'The Siamese Cat Song' (from *Lady And The Tramp*) flopped, though 'Busy Doin' Nothin' (from *A Connecticut Yankee In The Court Of King Arthur*) made the Top 50. 'Leipzig' and 'I'm In A Different World' were further failures but in 1986 they returned with another oldie - **Little Eva**'s 'The Locomotion', which reached the bottom end of the charts.

Album: *The Big Idea* (1991).

Stewart, David A.

b. 9 September 1952, Sunderland, Tyne & Wear, England. At the age of 15, the fledgling guitarist Stewart introduced himself to the world of rock music by stowing away in the back of **Amazing Blondel**'s tour van, after the group had given a performance in Stewart's home town of Newcastle. He later teamed up with guitarist Brian Harrison to form a duo, which after releasing *Deep December* went on to form **Longdancer** on **Elton John**'s Rocket label in 1973. During this time, Stewart had met ex-Royal Academy of Music student **Annie Lennox** in London, where the couple

co-habited. In 1977, together with friend Peter Coombes, they first recorded as a trio, the Catch, which developed into the **Tourists**. After establishing a following on the European continent, the Tourists achieved fame in the UK with minor hit singles, culminating in the number 4 hit cover version of **Dusty Springfield**'s 1979 'I Only Want To Be With You' and 'So Good To Be Back Home Again'. This popularity with the public, however, was at odds with the particularly virulent and antagonistic attitude of the popular music press who viewed the band as 'old wave' cashing in on the 'new wave'. When the band split in late 1980, Stewart and Lennox, who had now ended their romantic relationship, continued working together and formed the **Eurythmics**. After a spell spent shaking off their reputation left over from the Tourists, the duo gradually won favourable reviews to eventually emerge as one of the world's major pop acts of the 80s. They were awarded the **Ivor Norvello** award for Songwriter Of The Year in 1984 and Stewart received the Best British Producer award at the BRIT ceremony in 1986. He increased his role and reputation as a producer by working with, amongst others, **Bob Dylan**, **Feargal Sharkey** and **Mick Jagger**. A flurry of awards followed the next year for songwriting and production and in August, Stewart married Siobhan Fahey of **Bananarama**. In 1989 **Boris Grebenshikov**, the first Russian rock artist to record and perform in the west, travelled to the US and UK to record *Radio Silence* with Stewart. After the recording of the Eurythmics' *We To Are One*, the group's activities were put on hold while the duo allowed themselves time to rest and indulge in other projects. For Stewart, this included forming his own record label, Anxious, working with saxophonist **Candy Dulfer** on the UK Top 10 hit 'Lily Was Here' (1990), and the formation of his new group, the Spiritual Cowboys who achieved a minor UK chart placing for 'Jack Talking' (1990). Comprising Martin Chambers (drums, ex-**Pretenders**), John Turbull (guitar) and Chris James (bass), the group tour and record as a full time project, and their debut album reached the UK Top 40. Stewart is now regarded as one of the major figures of the pop establishment, and despite the attacks of a personal and artistic nature from the more radical quarters of the British press, it can be said that he has been responsible for some of the finest pop music produced throughout the 80s and early 90s. On his solo album in 1994 he enlisted the services of a wide-ranging group of artists including, **Carly Simon**, **Lou Reed**, **Bootsy Collins**, **David Sanborn**, **Laurie Anderson**, Mick Jagger and his wife Siobhan Fahey.

Albums: *Lily Was Here* (1990, film soundtrack), with the Spiritual Cowboys *Dave Stewart And The Spiritual Cowboys* (1990), with the Spiritual Cowboys *Honest* (1991), *Greetings From The Gutter* (East West 1994).

Stewart, Gary

b. 28 May 1945, Jenkins, Kentucky, USA. Stewart's family moved to Florida when he was 12, where he made his first record for the local Cory label and played in a beat group called the Amps. Teaming up with a policeman, Bill Eldridge, he wrote **Stonewall Jackson**'s 1965 US country hit, 'Poor Red Georgia Dirt'. Several songwriting successes followed including chart entries for **Billy Walker** ('She Goes Walking Through My Mind', 'When A Man Loves A Woman (The Way I Love You)', 'Traces Of A Woman', 'It's Time To Love Her'), **Cal Smith** ('You Can't Housebreak A Tomcat', 'It Takes Me All Night Long') and **Nat Stuckey** ('Sweet Thang And Cisco'). Gary recorded an album for Kapp, *You're Not The Woman You Used To Be*, and then moved to **RCA**. He had his first US country hit with a country version of the **Allman Brothers**' 'Ramblin' Man' and then made the Top 10 with 'Drinkin' Thing'. For some years Stewart worked as the pianist in **Charley Pride**'s roadband and he can be heard on Pride's *In Concert* double-album. He established himself as a hard driving, honky-tonk performer with *Out Of Hand* and a US country number 1, 'She's Actin' Single (I'm Drinkin' Doubles)', although his vibrato annoyed some. His 1977 *Your Place Or Mine* included guest appearances from **Nicolette Larson**, **Emmylou Harris** and **Rodney Crowell**. His two albums with songwriter Dean Dillon were not commercial successes, and Stewart returned to working in honky-tonk clubs. However, drug addiction got the better of him and his life collapsed when his wife left him and his son committed suicide. In the late 80s, he returned to performing, carrying on in the same musical style as before.

Albums: *You're Not The Woman You Used To Be* (1973), *Out Of Hand* (1975), *Steppin' Out* (1976), *Your Place Or Mine* (1977), *Little Junior* (1978), *Gary* (1979), *Cactus And Rose* (1980), with Dean Dillon *Brotherly Love* (1982), with Dean Dillon *Those Were The Days* (1983), *Brand New* (1988), *Battleground* (1990), *I'm A Texan* (1993).

Stewart, John

b. 5 September 1939, San Diego, California, USA. Stewart's musical career began in the 50s when, as frontman of the Furies, he recorded 'Rocking Anna' for a tiny independent label. Having discovered folk music, Stewart began performing with college friend John Montgomery, but achieved wider success as a songwriter when several of his compositions, including 'Molly Dee' and 'Green Grasses', were recorded by the **Kingston Trio**. Indeed, the artist joined this prestigious group in 1961, following his spell in the like-sounding **Cumberland Three**. Stewart left the Kingston trio in 1967. His reputation was enhanced when a new composition, 'Daydream Believer', became a number 1 hit for the **Monkees** and this dalliance

with pop continued when the artist contributed 'Never Goin' Back' to a disintegrating **Lovin' Spoonful** on their final album.

In 1968 Stewart was joined by singer Buffy Ford, whom he would marry in 1975. Together they completed *Signals Through The Glass*, before the former resumed his solo path with the excellent *California Bloodlines*. This country-inspired collection established Stewart's sonorous delivery and displayed a view of America which, if sometimes sentimental, was both optimistic and refreshing. It was a style the performer would continue over a series of albums which, despite critical approval, achieved only moderate success. Stewart's fortunes were upturned in 1979 when a duet with **Stevie Nicks**, 'Gold', became a US hit. The attendant *Bombs Away Dream Babies*, featured assistance from **Fleetwood Mac** guitarist, **Lindsay Buckingham** and although markedly different in tone to its predecessors, the set augured well for the future. However, despite contributions from **Linda Ronstadt** and **Phil Everly**, the follow-up, *Dream Babies Go To Hollywood*, proved an anti-climax. Stewart subsequently turned from commercial pursuits and resumed a more specialist direction with a series of low-key recordings for independent companies.

Albums: *Signals Through The Glass* (1968), *California Bloodlines* (1969), *Willard* (1970), *The Lonesome Picker Rides Again* (1971), *Sunstorm* (1972), *Cannons In The Rain* (1973), *The Phoenix Concerts - Live* (1974), *Wingless Angels* (1975), *Fire In The Wind* (1977), *Bombs Away Dream Babies* (1979), *Dream Babies Go Hollywood* (1980), *Blondes* (1982), *Trancas* (1984), *Centennial* (1984), *The Last Campaign* (1985), *Neon Beach* (1991), *Bullets In The Hour Glass* (1993), *Greetings From John Stewart* (1993). Compilation: *Forgotten Songs Of Some Old Yesterday* (1980), *California Bloodlines Plus...* (1987).

Stewart, Louis

b. 5 January 1944, Waterford, Eire. After playing guitar in a succession of show bands, Stewart began playing jazz in the early 60s. By the end of the decade he had achieved a substantial reputation and had worked with such leading jazzmen as **Tubby Hayes** and **Benny Goodman**. Throughout the 70s he continued to enhance his standing in both the UK and the USA, recording with **Peter Ind** and others. He also toured Europe, attracting considerable attention everywhere he played. In the 80s his reputation grew apace, despite his preference for spending a substantial part of his time in his homeland, and he made well-received albums with **Martin Taylor**, Brian Dunning, **Spike Robinson** and others. A brilliant sound allied to a crystal-clear tone has helped make Stewart one of the outstanding guitarists in jazz. A virtuoso technique allows him to realize fully his endless inventiveness.

Albums: *Louis Stewart In Dublin* (1975), with Peter Ind *Baubles, Bangles And Beads* (1975), *Out On His Own* (Livia

1976-77), *Milesian Source* (1977), with Brian Dunning *Alone Together* (Livia 1979), *I Thought About You* (Lee Lambert 1979), with Martin Taylor *Acoustic Guitar Duets* (1985), *Good News* (Villa 1986), with Spike Robinson *Three For The Road* (1989).

Stewart, Mark, And The Maffia

When the **Pop Group** split up in the early 80s, vocalist Mark Stewart joined forces with master mixer, Adrian Sherwood. The rhythm team of the Sugarhill label, the pioneers of rap, were making records for Sherwood under the name of Fats Comet. Skip McDonald (guitar), Doug Wimbush (bass) and Keith LeBlanc (drums) unleashed a creative madness that had not been required for their ubiquitous session work for artists such as **Bill Laswell**, **Mick Jagger** and **Will Downing**. On paper, it should not have worked: the anguished voice of English post-punk radicalism howling over black pop's finest musicians, but a tour in 1986 proved that it did: a harbinger of the black rock movement led by **Living Colour**. Their debut of 1985, *As The Veneer Of Democracy Starts To Fade*, powerfully fused Stewart's paranoic, apocalyptic vision with state-of-the-art, heavy techno-funk. 1987's *Survival* sounded even more like a Pop Group record, but it packed a punch that group had never achieved.
Albums: *As The Veneer Of Democracy Starts To Fade* (1985), *Survival* (1987).

Stewart, Redd

b. Henry Redd Stewart, 21 May 1921, Ashland City, Tennessee, USA. After the family relocated to Kentucky, Stewart while still at school learned piano, fiddle and guitar and by the mid-30s, was performing in the Louisville area. He joined **Pee Wee King**'s Golden West Cowboys on WHAS in 1937, first as a musician but also became featured vocalist when **Eddy Arnold** left to pursue his solo career. Stewart moved with King to the *Grand Ole Opry* until he was called up for military service during which he wrote 'A Soldier's Last Letter', which became a hit for **Ernest Tubb**. He rejoined King after the war and from 1947-57, they appeared on a popular weekly radio and television show on WAUE Louisville and toured extensively. The two were to enjoy some 30 years of successful songwriting collaboration. Their successes included 'Tennessee Waltz' (Stewart added lyrics to King's signature tune the 'No Name Waltz'), the song becoming a hit for both King and **Cowboy Copas** in 1948, a million-seller for Patti Page in 1950 and charted again by **Lacy J. Dalton** in 1980. Other million-sellers were 'Slowpoke', a 1951 hit for King, and 'You Belong To Me' for **Jo Stafford** in 1952. Stewart also wrote the **Jim Reeves** winner 'That's A Sad Affair'. He sang on all of King's hits but never charted with his solo recordings, although he recorded for several labels. After King retired in 1969, Stewart

continued to be active in the music world.
Solo albums: *Sings Favorite Old Time Songs* (1959), *I Remember* (1974). (See also album listing for Pee Wee King).

Stewart, Rex

b. 22 February 1907, Philadelphia, Pennsylvania, USA, d. 7 September 1967, Los Angeles, California, USA. Stewart began playing cornet in his early teens, having previously tried several other instruments. By 1921 he was in New York where he played in a succession of bands over the next three or four years. A spell with **Elmer Snowden** in the mid-20s was followed by a job with **Fletcher Henderson**. Over the next few years he worked in a number of bands, frequently returning to Henderson, and then, in 1934, joined **Duke Ellington**. He remained with Ellington until 1945, with spells out of the band for engagements with **Benny Carter** and others. In the late 40s and 50s he led his own bands in the USA and Europe, and was the driving force behind the reformed Henderson All Stars band at the South Bay Jazz Festival in 1957. In the 60s Stewart developed a parallel career as broadcaster and writer. One of the most distinctive cornetists in jazz, Stewart developed the half-valve style of playing into an art form. His featured numbers with Ellington, especially 'Boy Meets Horn', have been frequently imitated but never surpassed. The biting, electrifying solos he played on numerous record dates, notably with the Henderson All Stars reunion band, have enormous energy and constantly display a strikingly original mind.
Albums: *Boston 1953* (1953), *The Irrepressible Rex Stewart* (c.1954), *The Big Challenge* (1957), with Henderson All Stars *The Big Reunion* (1957), *Rendezvous With Rex* (1958), *Porgy And Bess Revisited* (1958), *Rex Stewart-Dickie Wells* (1959), *The Rex Stewart Quintet* (1959), *The Rex Stewart Sextet* i (1960), *The Happy Jazz Of Rex Stewart* (1960), *The Rex Stewart Sextet* ii (1960), *Rex Stewart Meets Henri Chaix* (1966), *Rex Stewart Memorial* (1966). Compilations: with Fletcher Henderson *Swing's The Thing Vol. 2* (1931-34), *The Indispensable Duke Ellington Vols 5/6* (1940), with Ellington *The Blanton-Webster Band* (1940-42), *Rex Stewart's Big Eight* (1940), *Hollywood Jam* (1945).
Further reading: *Jazz Masters of the Thirties*, Rex Stewart with Stanley Dance.

Stewart, Rod

b. Roderick David Stewart, 10 January 1945, Highgate, London, England. The leading British rock star of the 70s started his career as an apprentice professional with Brentford Football Club (over the years Stewart has made it known that football is his second love). Following a spell roaming Europe with folk artist **Wizz Jones** in the early 60s he returned to join Jimmy Powell And The Five Dimensions in 1963. This frantic R&B band featured Rod playing furious harmonica, reminiscent of **James Cotton** and **Little Walter**. As word got out, he was attracted to London and was hired by **Long John Baldry** in his band the Hoochie Coochie Men (formerly **Cyril Davies**' All Stars). Without significant success outside the club scene, the band disintegrated and evolved into the **Steampacket**, with Baldry, Stewart, **Brian Auger**, **Julie Driscoll**, Mickey Waller and Rick Brown. Following a television documentary on the swinging mod scene, featuring Stewart, he collected his monicker 'Rod the Mod'. In 1965, he joined the blues-based Shotgun Express as joint lead vocalist with **Beryl Marsden**. The impressive line-up included **Peter Green**, **Mick Fleetwood** and **Peter Bardens**. By the following year, Stewart was well-known in R&B and blues circles, but it was joining the **Jeff Beck** Group that gave him national exposure. During his tenure with Beck he recorded two important albums, *Truth* and *Cosa Nostra-Beck Ola* and made a number of gruelling tours of America.

When the group broke up (partly through exhaustion) Stewart and **Ron Wood** joined the **Faces**, now having lost their smallest face, **Steve Marriot**. Simultaneously, Rod had been signed as a solo artist to **Phonogram**, and he managed to juggle both careers expertly over the next six years. Though critically well-received, his first album sold only moderately; it was *Gasoline Alley* that made the breakthrough. In addition to the superb title track it contained the glorious 'Lady Day'. This album marked the beginning of the 'mandolin' sound supplied by the talented guitarist Martin Quittenton. Stewart became a superstar on the strength of his next two albums, *Every Picture Tells A Story* and *Never A Dull Moment*. Taken as one body of work, they represent Stewart at his best. His choice and exemplary execution of non-originals gave him numerous hits from these albums including; 'Reason To Believe' (**Tim Hardin**), 'I'm Losing You' (**Temptations**), 'Angel' (**Jimi Hendrix**). His own classics were the irresistible chart-topping magnum opus 'Maggie May' and the wonderful 'You Wear It Well', all sung in his now familiar frail, hoarse voice. In the mid-70s, following the release of the below average *Smiler*, Rod embarked on a relationship with the actress, Britt Ekland. Besotted with her, he allowed her to dictate his sense of dress, and for a while appeared in faintly ludicrous dungarees made out of silk and ridiculous jump suits. At the same time he became the darling of the magazine and gutter press, a reputation he has unwillingly maintained through his succession of affairs with women. *Atlantic Crossing* was his last critical success for many years; it included the future football crowd anthem and number 1 hit, 'Sailing' (written by Gavin Sutherland), and a fine reading of **Dobie Gray**'s 'Drift Away'. His albums throughout the second half of the 70s were patchy affairs although they became phenomenally successful, selling millions, in

many cases topping the charts world-wide. The high-spots during this glitzy phase, which saw him readily embrace the prevalent disco era, were 'The Killing Of Georgie', **Cat Stevens**' 'First Cut Is The Deepest', 'Tonight's The Night' and 'You're In My Heart'. Other hits included 'Hot Legs' and the superbly immodest but irresistible number 1, 'D'Ya Think I'm Sexy'. His 'Ole Ola', meanwhile, was adopted by the Scottish World Cup football team, an area in which his popularity has always endured.

He entered the 80s newly married, to **George Hamilton IV**'s ex-wife, Alana, and maintained his momentum of regular hits and successful albums; his large body of fans ensured a chart placing irrespective of the quality. The 80s saw Stewart spending his time jet-setting all over the world, with the press rarely far from his heels (covering his marriage break-up, his long relationship with Kelly Emberg, and the unceasing round of parties). Behind the jack-the-lad persona was an artist who still had a good ear for a quality song, a talent which surfaced throughout the decade with numbers like 'How Long' (**Paul Carrick**), 'Some Guys Have All The Luck' (**Robert Palmer**) and, reunited with Jeff Beck, a superb performance of **Curtis Mayfield**'s 'People Get Ready'. His biggest hits of the 80s were 'What Am I Gonna Do', 'Every Beat Of My Heart' and his best of the decade, 'Baby Jane'. As the 90s got under way Stewart, now re-married, indicated that he had settled down, and found an enduring love at last. His new guise has not affected his record sales; in April 1991 he was high on the UK chart with 'Rhythm Of My Heart' and had the best selling *Vagabond Heart*. *Unplugged And Seated* in 1993 boosted his credibility with an exciting performance of familiar songs. A new album in 1995 was his best for some years and during the launch Stewart undertook some interviews which were both revealing and hilarious. The once seemingly pompous rock star, dressed to the nines in baggy silks is really 'Rod the Mod' after all. Rod Stewart, one of the biggest 'superstars' of the century, has now turned 50 without his audience diminishing in any way. Rarely has his credibility been higher than now.

Albums: *An Old Raincoat Won't Ever Let You Down* (Vertigo 1970), *Gasoline Alley* (Vertigo 1970), *Every Picture Tells A Story* (Mercury 1971), *Never A Dull Moment* (Mercury 1972), *Smiler* (Mercury 1974), *Atlantic Crossing* (Warners 1975), *A Night On The Town* (Riva 1976), *Foot Loose And Fancy Free* (Riva 1977), *Blondes Have More Fun* (Riva 1978), *Foolish Behaviour* (Riva 1980), *Tonight I'm Yours* (Riva 1981), *Absolutely Live* (Riva 1982, double album), *Body Wishes* (Warners 1983), *Camouflage* (Warners 1984), *Out Of Order* (Warners 1988), *Vagabond* (1991), *Unplugged And Seated* (1993). Compilations: *Sing It Again Rod* (Mercury 1973), *The Vintage Years* (Mercury 1976, double album), *Recorded Highlights And Action Replays* (Phillips 1976), *The Best Of Rod Stewart* (Mercury

1977, double album), *The Best Of Rod Stewart Volume 2* (Mercury 1977, double album), *Rod Stewart's Greatest Hits Volume 1* (Riva 1979), *Hot Rods* (Mercury 1980), *Maggie May* (Pickwick 1981), *Rod Stewart* (Pickwick 1982), *Jukebox Heaven* (Pickwick 1987), *The Best Of Rod Stewart* (Warners 1989), *Storyteller* (Warners 1989), *The Early Years* (1992), *Lead Vocalist* (1993).

Videos: *Live At The Los Angeles Forum* (1984), *Tonight He's Yours* (1984), *Video Biography* (1988)

Further reading: *The Rod Stewart Story*, Tremlett, George (1976), *Rod Stewart And The Faces*, Pidgeon, John (1976), *Rod Stewart: A Biography In Words & Pictures*, Cromelin, Richard (1976), *Rod Stewart*, Jasper, Tony (1977), *Rod Stewart: A Life On The Town*, Burton, Peter (1977), *Rod Stewart*, Rockl, Gerd and Sahner, Paul (1979), *Rod Stewart*, Nelson, Paul & Bangs, Lester (1981), *Rod Stewart: A Biography*, Ewbank, Tim & Hildred, Stafford (1991), *Rod Stewart: Vagabond Heart*, Guiliano, Geoffrey (1993).

Stewart, Slam

b. Leroy Stewart, 21 September 1914, Englewood, New Jersey, USA, d. 10 December 1987. He studied bass at Boston Conservatory, having earlier played violin. Almost from the start of his career Stewart was experimenting with his distinctive style in which he bowed the bass while humming in unison, an octave higher. **John Chilton** suggests that the concept was originally violinist Ray Perry's but certainly Stewart developed this technique into a fine art. In New York in 1937, Stewart met **Slim Gaillard** and together they became hugely popular on radio and records, their 'Flat Foot Floogie' being an enormous hit. During the late 30s and through the 40s he worked mostly in small groups, accompanying Gaillard, **Art Tatum**, **Lester Young**, **Benny Goodman** and others. In the 50s he played with Tatum, **Roy Eldridge** and also became a regular accompanist to singer **Rose Murphy**. In the 60s he added classical music to his repertoire. He continued to tour extensively in the 70s and 80s, playing with a wide range of artists, mostly in the mainstream of jazz. Stewart consistently displayed a comprehensive technique yet always played in an intensely rhythmic manner which he was never afraid to temper with wit.

Albums: *Slam Stewart* (Black And Blue 1971), *Slamboree* (1975), *Slam Stewart/Georges Delerue* (1975), *Fish Scales* (Black And Blue 1975), *Two Big Mice* (Black And Blue 1977), with Bucky Pizzarelli *Dialogue* (1978), with Major Holley *Shut Yo' Mouth* (1981). *New York New York* (Stash 1981). Compilation: with Slim Gaillard *Original 1938 Recordings, Volume 1* (1989).

Stewart, Tinga

b. *c.* 1959, Kingston, Jamaica, West Indies. Stewart came to prominence when he won the 1974 Jamaican Song Festival singing 'Play De Music' which became a reggae hit in both Jamaica and the UK. In 1975 Stewart composed 'Hooray Festival' the winning entry for his brother Roman Stewart and inspired by these consecutive conquests the Opal label in the UK released Roman's track 'Oh But If I Could Do My Life Again'. Stewart became involved with **Lloyd Charmers** and Ernie Smith on their Wildflower project, a commitment to producing quality sounds much of which later surfaced through Opal. The brothers success at the Festival resulted in them being branded with the image of 'festival singers', which had an unhelpful effect on their early careers. Stewart continued to release singles through the 80s including 'Gypsy Rasta', 'Key To Your Heart' and his version of 'Red Red Wine'. He eventually revived his roots credibility when he recorded 'Take Time To Know' with **Ninjaman**. Their recording is widely acknowledged as being the first combination tune which led to a plethora of singer and DJ hits. Previously the DJs voiced over an old master tape whereas in combination style the artists recorded together. He continued recording in combination: 'Knock Out Batty' with Tinga Love and 'I Wanna Take You Home' with Little Twitch. His revival resulted in a tour of Japan in 1989 as part of the Reggae Sunsplash world tour. On his return he became involved in production work, licensing his output to the RAS label in the US. He also continued to record his own tracks, including 'Gonna Fall In Love', 'In The Mood', 'Street Dancing' and the rootsy 'Son Of A Slave'.

Albums: *With The Dancehall DJs* (RAS 1993), *Aware Of Love* (VP 1994).

Stewart, Wynn

b. Wynnford Lindsey Stewart, 7 June 1934, on a farm near Morrisville, Missouri, USA, d. 17 July 1985, Hendersonville, Tennessee, USA. Stewart's uncle was a major league pitcher, which gave him thoughts of a baseball career, until told that he would never be big enough. He became interested in songwriting, learned to play the guitar and, at the age of 13, appeared regularly on KWTO Springfield. A year later the family moved to California, where Stewart became friendly and for a time ran a band, with Ralph Mooney, the now legendary steel guitarist. Stewart first recorded for Intro in 1954 and local success with his own song 'Strolling' led to him signing for **Capitol**. In 1956, his recording of 'Waltz Of The Angels' became his first hit, further minor ones followed but it was not until 1959, after he moved to the Challenge label, that he achieved major success with 'Wishful Thinking' and also recorded with **Jan Howard**. In the late 50s, he moved to Las Vegas, where he opened the Nashville Nevada Club and hosted his own television series on KTOO. In 1959, **Miki And Griff** had a UK pop chart hit with Stewart's song 'Hold Back Tomorrow'. Competition for places in his band was fierce and in

1962, Stewart gave **Merle Haggard** the job of playing bass and singing the odd song during his own breaks. A year later he provided Haggard with 'Sing A Sad Song', which became his first chart hit. He returned to California in the mid-60s, toured with his band the Tourists and also rejoined Capitol, where between 1965 and 1971 he had 17 country chart hits including 'It's Such A Pretty World Today', his only number 1. He moved to **RCA** in 1972, but achieved his next Top 20 hits in 1976 with 'After The Storm' and his own version of 'Sing A Sad Song', after moving to Playboy Records. Stewart's reputation became somewhat marred by problems, his private life suffered (he was married three times) and at times drinking caused him to miss bookings. He eventually moved to Nashville, where he believed he could achieve another breakthrough with a special come-back tour. At 6 pm on 17 July 1985, the evening the tour was due to start, he suffered a heart attack and died. Stewart was a fine singer, who should have been a bigger star, for, as John Morthland later wrote, 'He may not have been as consistent as Haggard or **Buck Owens** but at his best, he was their equal as a writer'.

Albums: with Jan Howard *Sweethearts Of Country Music* (1961), *Wynn Stewart* (1962), *Songs Of Wynn Stewart* (1965), *Above And Beyond* (1967), *It's Such A Pretty World Today* (1967), *Wynn Stewart And Jan Howard Sing Their Hits* (1968), *In Love* (1968), *Love's Gonna Happen To Me* (1968), *Something Pretty* (1968), *Let The Whole World Sing With Me* (1969), *Yours Forever* (1969), *You Don't Care What Happens To Me* (1970), *It's A Beautiful Day* (1970), *Baby It's Yours* (1971), *After The Storm* (1976), *Wishful Thinking (The Challenge Years 1958-1963)* (1988).

Stidham, Arbee

b. 9 February 1917, Devalls Bluff, Arkansas, USA. In his childhood he learnt to play harmonica, clarinet and alto saxophone and formed his own band. When Stidham moved to Chicago he met Lester Melrose who signed the young blues singer to **RCA**-Victor in 1947. His biggest hit, `My Heart Belongs to You', was recorded at the first session in September of that year, and Stidham spent the rest of his career trying to emulate its success. After Victor (1947-50), he recorded for Sittin' In With (1951), Checker (1953), Abco (1956) and States (1957) as a vocalist, but took up the guitar in the 50s under the tutelage of **Big Bill Broonzy**. In 1960-61, Stidham recorded one album for Bluesville (which included a remake of his big hit) and two for Folkways, in which his singing was accompanied by his guitar. He also accompanied **Memphis Slim** on one of the pianist's Folkways sessions. In 1965 Stidham again recut `My Heart Belongs To You' for Sam Phillips. In the 70s a single was released on Blues City and a brace of albums on Mainstream and Folkways.

Selected albums: *There's Always Tomorrow* (70s), *My Heart Belongs To You* (1982).

Stiff Little Fingers

This Irish punk band were formed from the ashes of cover group Highway Star. Taking their new name from a track on the **Vibrators'** *Pure Mania* debut, Stiff Little Fingers soon attracted one of the most fervent fan bases of the era. Present at the **Clash**'s Belfast gig in 1977, Jake Burns (vocals/lead guitar) led Henry Cluney (rhythm guitar), Ali McMordie (bass) and Brian Falloon (drums) as Ireland's first new wave cover band. The original drummer, Gordon Blair, had gone on to play with **Rudi**. When journalist Gordon Ogilvie saw the band live he urged them to concentrate on their own material, quickly becoming their manager and co-lyricist. They recorded their first two original songs, 'Suspect Device'/'Wasted Life' soon after, on their own Rigid Digits label. The first pressing of 350 copies sold out almost as soon as BBC disc jockey **John Peel** span it. **Rough Trade** quickly picked up the distribution, and released the band's second single, 'Alternative Ulster', in conjunction with Rigid Digits. After a major tour supporting the **Tom Robinson Band**, the group were almost signed to **Island**, but remained on Rough Trade for their long playing debut, *Inflammable Material*. With songs concentrating on personal experiences in the politically charged climate of Northern Ireland, the album still managed to surprise many with its inclusion of diverse rock patterns and a flawed love song. The release marked the departure of Falloon who was replaced by Jim Reilly. The follow-up, *Nobodys Heroes*, revealed great strides in technique and sophistication with the band branching out into dub, reggae and pop. The dialogue with the audience was still direct, however, urging tolerance, self-respect and unity, and rejecting the trappings of rock stardom. They would still come in for criticism, however, for Ogilvie's patronage. After a disappointing live album, the impressive *Go For It!* saw the band at the peak of their abilities and popularity. Reilly left for the USA, joining Red Rockers shortly afterwards, with Brian 'Dolphin' Taylor (ex-Tom Robinson Band) drafted in as his replacement. 1982's *Now Then* embraced songs of a more pop-rock nature, though in many ways the compromise was an unhappy one. Burns left at the beginning of the following year, forming The Big Wheel. However, live and on record he was unable to shake off comparisons to Stiff Little Fingers, and he soon opted instead for a career as trainee producer at BBC Radio 1. McMordie formed Fiction Groove and contributed to **Sinead O'Conner**'s *The Lion And The Cobra*, while Cluney taught guitar back in Ireland. Taylor returned for a brief stint of drumming with TRB, but the spectre of Stiff Little Fingers remained. One reunion gig gave birth to further events, until 1990 when they re-formed on a permanent basis. McMordie had grown tired of the rock circuit, however, and his replacement was the group's old friend **Bruce Foxton** (ex-**Jam**). In the early 90s they embarked on further major tours and recorded two respectable albums, *Flags And Emblems* and *Fly The Flag*, but lost the long-serving Henry Cluney amid much acrimony.

Albums: *Inflammable Material* (Rough Trade 1979), *Nobody's Heroes* (Chrysalis 1980), *Hanx!* (Chrysalis 1980), *Go For It!* (Chrysalis 1981), *Now Then* (Chrysalis 1982), *Flags And Emblems* (Essential! 1991), *Fly The Flag* (Essential! 1993), *Get A Life* (Castle Communications 1994). Compilations: *All The Best* (Chrysalis 1983, double album), *Live And Loud* (Link 1988, double album, reissued as *No Sleep Till Belfast*, Kaz, 1988), *See You Up There* (Virgin 1989, double album), *Live In Sweden* (Limited Edition 1989), *The Peel Sessions* (Strange Fruit 1989), *Greatest Hits Live* (Link 1991), *Alternative Chartbusters* (Link 1991).

Stiff Records

Britain's premier 'new wave' label of the 70s was founded in 1976 by pub-rock producer and promoter, Dave Robinson, and Andrew Jakeman, tour manager of **Dr Feelgood**. The first release, 'Heart Of The City' by **Nick Lowe**, was financed by a £400 loan from Dr Feelgood's singer, Lee Brilleaux. From 1976-77, the label released material by a range of London-based pub and punk rock bands such as **Roogalator**, **Lew Lewis**, the **Adverts** and the **Damned**. Stiff also signed **Elvis Costello** whose fourth single, 'Watching The Detectives', was the label's first hit. Costello had achieved prominence as a member of Stiff's first package tour of numerous British cities. Like its 1978 successor, the tour served to publicise and popularise the label and its artists. During the early days it was extremely hip to be seen wearing a Stiff T-shirt bearing its uncompromising slogan, 'If it ain't Stiff it ain't worth a fuck'. Towards the end of 1977, Stiff suffered a setback when Jakeman, Costello and Nick Lowe left to join the Radar label. However, Stiff's fortunes were transformed by the success of **Ian Dury** whose anthem, 'Sex And Drugs And Rock 'n' Roll', had made little impact when first issued in 1977. A year later, however, 'What A Waste' inaugurated a run of four hit singles. **Lene Lovich**, **Jona Lewie** and **Madness** also provided Top 20 records for the label in 1978-80, when Robinson switched distribution from **EMI** to **CBS Records**. In the early 80s Stiff flirted with reggae (**Desmond Dekker**) and soul (various productions by **Eddy Grant**), but the bulk of its releases still came from artists on the eccentric fringe of the new wave such as **Tenpole Tudor** and **Wreckless Eric**. The company also issued one album from **Graham Parker** before he moved to the larger **RCA Records** label. There were also hits from the **Belle Stars** and Dave Stewart with Barbara Gaskin. From the outset, Robinson had been interested in new wave developments in America and over the years Stiff licensed material by such artists as **Rachel Sweet**,

Devo, the **Plasmatics** and **Jane Aire**. In 1984 Stiff was merged with **Island Records** and Robinson became managing director of both companies. This coincided with the departure of Madness to start their own label (Zarjazz), although Stiff's new signing, the **Pogues**, provided hits throughout the mid-80s. The merger was not a success, however, and in 1986 Robinson resumed control of an independent Stiff, only to see it suffer an immediate cash-crisis. The assets of the company, which had a turnover of £4m at its peak, were sold to **ZTT Records** for a reputed £300,000. Under the new ownership there were initial releases from the Pogues, hard bop drummer **Tommy Chase** and female vocal group the **Mint Juleps**. But by the 90s the pioneering Stiff had become simply a reissue label.

Further reading: *Stiff, The Story Of a Record Label, 1976-1982*, Muirhead, Bert (1983).

Stigers, Curtis

b. c.1968, Boise, Idaho, USA. Stigers originally started out playing in punk and blues bands in his local music community. However, his classical training was in clarinet, before he decided to switch to saxophone in high school. It was then he took the decision to move to New York in search of rock 'n' roll. There, he moved back to familiar waters: 'When I got there I started out in the Blues scene. I wanted to play with other people and they had the best jams!' Despite having worked hard to attract record company interest on the club circuit, it was in the unfamiliar world of jazz he would be discovered. He was playing saxophone and singing in a jazz-influenced trio with piano and bass, when spotted by the son of record company mogul Clive Davies (**Arista** head). 'I could have gone to other companies and had unfettered freedom. But I wanted the guidance. I had to learn to collaborate'. Since then Stigers has become an MOR airwaves favourite, likened disparagingly to **Michael Bolton**, but with his true influences **Ray Charles** and **Otis Redding**. Hits such as 'Never Saw A Miracle', if not delineating a bold new talent, have at least marked him as an adequate commercial balladeer.

Albums: *Curtis Stigers* (1992), *Time Was* (Arista 1995).
Video: *Live In Concert* (1993).

Stigwood, Robert

After relocating from Australia at the end of the 50s, this famous entrepreneur set up a theatrical agency. When one of his clients, **John Leyton**, traversed into the pop field with the chart-topping 'Johnny Remember Me', Stigwood branched out into pop management. His expansionism thereafter was extreme and embraced music publishing, promotion and even record production. For a time he worked for the **Tremeloes**' manager **Peter Walsh** at Starlite Artists, and as a rock manager/agent boasted **Cream** and

Graham Bond among his clientele. An overreacher by nature, Stigwood suffered the indignity of a much-publicized bankruptcy, which left many questioning his standing in the mid-60s pop world. With the **Bee Gees** among his roster, Stigwood established a new company, the Robert Stigwood Organization. Ever the controversialist, he became involved in a contretemps with **Don Arden**, who suspected that he was intent on poaching the **Small Faces** and frightened him off. Stigwood was luckier in his involvements with **Brian Epstein**, who recognized his business acumen and imagination and offered him a controlling interest in his company NEMS for the ludicrously low figure of £500,000. Epstein died before Stigwood could exercise that option and he met strong resistance from the **Beatles** and others. Eventually, he left NEMS accompanied by the Bee Gees, Cream and the **Foundations**. Stigwood next moved his operation to America and astonished the world in the late 70s by transforming the unfashionable Bee Gees into one of pop's biggest selling acts. His involvement in the film and theatrical world also brought lucrative success, courtesy of *Grease* and *Saturday Night Fever*. The chart-topping feats of **John Travolta/Olivia Newton-John**, ensured that RSO retained a high profile as one of the most successful record labels of the late 70s. Although Stigwood's Midas touch deserted him with the ill-fated film of *Sgt Pepper's Lonely Hearts Club Band* and *Times Square*, his capacity for entrepreneurial reinvention cannot be underestimated. His involvements in TV-AM broadcasting added another outlet to an evolving business empire.

Stiles, Danny

b. USA. Stiles played trumpet and flügelhorn in New York in the late 60s and early 70s, in a studio band for the Merv Griffin and Dick Cavett shows. On the former, he met **Bill Watrous**, with whom he began an important musical relationship. He also played lead trumpet in Watrous's Manhattan Wildlife Refuge big band.
Album: with Watrous *Manhattan Wildlife Refuge* (1974).

Stilgoe, Richard

b. 28 March 1943, Camberley, Surrey, England. Now known as a television presenter and entertainer, Richard Stilgoe came into showbusiness via the Cambridge Footlights. He also played piano in a 60s beat group called Tony Snow And The Blizzards. Arriving at the BBC in the 70s, he appeared regularly on shows such as *A Class By Himself*, *Nationwide*, *That's Life*, and *Stilgoe's Around*, often performing a self-written, highly topical little ditty. Extremely talented - he plays 14 instruments and sings in opera - Stilgoe broke new ground in the 80s when he teamed up with composer **Andrew Lloyd Webber**, and wrote the lyrics for the hit musical *Starlight Express*, and contributed additional lyrics to *Cats* and *The Phantom Of The Opera*. In 1985, he joined **Peter Skellern** for *Stilgoe And Skellern Stompin' At The Savoy*, a show in aid of The Lords Taverners charity organization. This led to the two entertainers working together on several successful tours, and in their two-man revue, *Who Plays Wins*, which was presented in the West End and New York. Stilgoe has also had his own BBC 1 children's series, and is a patron of the National Youth Music Theatre, for whom has written the words and music for *Bodywork*, a musical that takes place inside the human body. It had its premiere at the Brighton Festival in 1987. In 1991, Stilgoe was also devoting much of his time to a small forest which he is growing for the sole purpose of making musical instruments.
Albums: *Live Performance* (1977), *Bodywork* (1988).

Stills, Stephen

b. 3 January 1945, Dallas, Texas, USA. The often dubbed 'musical genius' is better known for his work with the pivotal **Buffalo Springfield**, and for many years his association with **David Crosby**, **Graham Nash** and **Neil Young**. After the Springfield's break-up, Stills, at a loose end, joined with **Al Kooper** and **Mike Bloomfield** for the million-selling *Super Session*. His contributions included **Donovan**'s 'Season Of The Witch', on which he played one of the decade's most famous wah-wah guitar solos. His solo career began during one of **Crosby, Stills And Nash**'s many hiatuses. Then living in England at **Ringo Starr**'s former home, Stills enlisted a team of musical heavyweights to play on his self-titled debut which reached the US Top 3 in 1970. This outstanding album remains his best work, and is justifiably still available. In addition to the irresistible hit single 'Love The One You're With' the album contains a healthy mixture of styles, all demonstrating his considerable dexterity as a songwriter, guitarist and singer. The solo acoustic 'Black Queen' for example, was reputedly recorded while Stills was completely drunk, and yet his mastery of the (**C.F.**) **Martin** acoustic guitar still prevails. All tracks reach the listener, from the infectious 'Old Times Good Times', featuring **Jimi Hendrix** to 'Go Back Home', featuring **Eric Clapton**; it is unfair to single out any track for they are all exemplary. On this one album, Stills demonstrated the extent of his powers. *Stephen Stills 2* was a similar success containing the innocently profound 'Change Partners', a brass re-working of the Springfield's 'Bluebird' and the brilliant yet oddly-timed blues number 'Nothing To Do But Today'. For a while it appeared that Stills' solo career would eclipse that of his CSNY involvement. His superbly eclectic double album with **Manassas** and its consolidating follow-up made Stills an immensely important figure during these years. Ultimately Stephen was unable to match his opening pair of albums. While *Stills* was an admirable effort, the subsequent live album and *Illegal Stills* were patchy. His nadir came in 1978 when, following the break up of his marriage to French chanteuse **Veronique Sanson** he produced *Thoroughfare Gap*, a collection riddled with uninspired songs of self-pity. Only the title track was worthy of his name. No official solo release came until 1984, when **Ahmet Ertegun** reluctantly allowed Stills to put out *Right By You*. While the slick production did not appeal to all Stills aficionados, it proved to be his most cohesive work since *Stephen Stills 2*, although appealing more to the AOR market. The moderate hit 'Can't Let Go' featured both Stills and Michael Finnigan, exercising their fine voices to great effect. Since then the brilliant but erratic Stills has continued his stop-go career with Crosby, Nash, and occasionally Young. Stills released a solo acoustic self-financed work in 1991. *Stills Alone* was an excellent return to his folk and blues roots and featured hoarse-voiced versions of the **Beatles** 'In My Life' and **Bob Dylan**'s 'Ballad Of Hollis Brown'. As a guitarist, his work in 1992 with a rejuvenated Crosby, Stills And Nash was quite breathtaking, demonstrating that those early accolades were not mis-judged. It is a great pity that his songwriting which was so prolific in the early 70s has seemingly deserted him.

Albums: with Al Kooper, Mike Bloomfield *Super Session* (1969), *Stephen Stills* (1970), *Stephen Stills 2* (1971), *Stills* (1975), *Illegal Stills* (1976), *Stephen Stills Live* (1975), *Thoroughfare Gap* (1978), *Right By You* (1984), *Stills Alone.* (1991).

Stills-Young Band

Former cohorts in both **Buffalo Springfield** and **Crosby, Stills, Nash And Young**, **Stephen Stills** (guitar/vocals) and **Neil Young** (guitar/vocals) began this brief association in 1975 when the latter made several impromptu appearances during one of the former's promotional tours. An album followed on which the duo was joined by Stills' regular band - Jerry Aeillo (keyboards), George Perry (bass), Joe Vitale (drums/flute) and Joe Lala (percussion) - and although initial sessions also featured **David Crosby** and **Graham Nash**, their contributions were latterly wiped, causing friction between the four former colleagues. A proposed reunion was scuppered and **Crosby And Nash** returned to their duet recordings. *Long May You Run* did contain several worthwhile songs, including the title track and 'Black Coral', but it lacked a sense of cohesion and was generally viewed as a disappointment. A promotional tour ended in disarray when Young abandoned the group after a handful of dates, leading the enigmatic note: 'Dear Stephen, funny how some things that start spontaneously end that way. Eat a peach, Neil'.

Album: *Long May You Run* (1976).

Stiltskin

Authors of the most distinctive riff of 1994, few knew who Stiltskin were at the time, yet millions recognised the instrumental section of 'Inside' which accompanied a lavish Levi's television advertisement. Picked up by the jeans manufacturer when it was overheard playing at the group's publishers, 'Inside' shot to number 1 in the UK charts when finally released as a single in the summer of 1994. The band had actually formed in 1989 when Peter Lawlor (guitar) and James Finnigan (bass) met for the first time in London. Finnigan had previously spent two years working alongside the Kane brothers in **Hue And Cry**, before electing to pursue a rockier direction. His new partner, meanwhile, had just returned from New York, dismayed with the dominance of dance and rap music. The duo began working on songs together in Lawlor's demo studio, recruiting an old friend of Finnigan's, Ross McFarlane, as drummer. However, unable to find a suitable singer or arouse record company interest, McFarlane relocated to Glasgow to drum with several bands, including Slide and Fireball. There were few further developments until the summer of 1993, when Lawlor and Finnigan were driving along the M8 between Edinburgh and Glasgow and passed a figure 'frantically retrieving objects which resembled guitars from a van engulfed in flames on the motorway's hard shoulder'. That distressed figure would turn out to be Ray Wilson, who accepted an offer of a lift from the pair in order to make the gig he was playing that night. When he walked off stage, Lawlor and Finnigan offered him the job as Stiltskin vocalist. The new formation persuaded McFarlane to return to the fold, shortly after which they were approached to use 'Inside'. Their management team set up White Water records to house their releases, with a second single, 'Footsteps', also charting, before a debut album in late 1994.

Album: *The Mind's Eye* (White Water 1994).

Sting

b. Gordon Sumner, 2 October 1951, Wallsend, Tyne & Wear, England. Sting's solo career began in 1982, two years before the break-up of the **Police**, for whom he was lead singer and bassist. In that year he starred in the film *Brimstone And Treacle* and from it released a version of the 30s ballad, 'Spread A Little Happiness', composed by Vivian Ellis. Its novel character and Sting's own popularity ensured Top 20 status in Britain. While continuing to tour and record with the Police, he also co-wrote the **Dire Straits** hit 'Money For Nothing' and sang harmonies on **Phil Collins'** *No Jacket Required*. By 1985, however, the other members of the Police were pursuing solo interests and Sting formed a touring band, the Blue Turtles. It included leading New York jazz figures such as **Branford Marsalis** (alto saxophone), **Kenny Kirkland** (keyboards) and **Omar Hakim** (drums). The group recorded his first solo album at **Eddy Grant**'s studio in Jamaica before Marsalis and Sting performed at the **Live Aid** concert with Phil Collins. *Dream Of The Blue Turtles* found Sting developing the more cerebral lyrics to be found on the final Police album, *Synchronicity*. It also brought him three big international hits with 'If You Love Somebody Set Them Free', 'Fortress Around Your Heart' and 'Russians'. 'An Englishman In New York' (inspired by English eccentric Quentin Crisp) became a UK hit in 1990 after being remixed by Ben Liebrand. In 1985, Michael Apted directed *Bring On The Night*, a film about Sting and his group.

After touring with the Blue Turtles, Sting recorded *Nothing Like The Sun* (a title taken from a Shakespeare sonnet) with Marsalis and Police guitarist **Andy Summers** plus guests **Ruben Blades**, **Eric Clapton** and **Mark Knopfler**. The album was an instant success internationally and contained 'They Dance Alone', Sting's tribute to the victims of repression in Argentina, in addition to a notable recording of **Jimi Hendrix**'s 'Little Wing'. This track featured one of the last orchestral arrangements by the late **Gil Evans**. In 1988, Sting took part in Amnesty International's *Human Rights Now!* international tour and he devoted much of the following two years to campaigning and fundraising activity on behalf of environmental causes, notably highlighting the plight of the Indians of the Brazilian rainforest. In 1991, Sting released his third studio album, from which 'All This Time' was a US Top 10 hit, and featured strong tracks including the beautifully evocative 'They Dance Alone (Gueca Solo)' and Hendrix's 'Little Wing', one of Gil Evans' last arrangements. He set up his own label, Pangaea, in the late 80s to release material by jazz and *avant garde* artists and returned in 1991 with the autobiographical *The Soul Cages*. He continued in a similar vein with *Ten Summoner's Tales*, which contained further high quality hit singles including 'If I Ever Lose My Faith In You' and 'Fields Of Gold'. Gordon 'Mr Sheer Profundity' Sumner has become one of the finest quality songwriters to appear out of the second UK 'new wave' boom (post 1977). The collection *Fields Of Gold* highlights his considerable accomplishment.

Albums: *Dream Of The Blue Turtles* (A&M 1985), *Bring On The Night* (A&M 1986), *Nothing Like the Sun* (A&M 1987), *The Soul Cages* (A&M 1991), *Acoustic - Live In Newcastle* (A&M 1991), *Ten Summoner's Tales* (A&M 1993). Compilation: *Fields Of Gold 1984-1994* (A&M 1994). Videos: *Bring On The Night* (1987), *The Videos* (1988), *The Soul Cages* (1991), *Live At The Hague* (1991), *Fields Of Gold: The Best Of Sting 1984-94* (1994). Further reading: *Sting: A Biography*, Sellers, Robert (1989).

Stingray

This South African melodic heavy rock group was formed in 1978 by Dennis East (vocals), Mike Pilot (guitar), Danny Anthill (keyboards), Allan Goldswain (keyboards), Eddie Boyle (bass) and Shaun Wright (drums). Together they based their style firmly on American rock giants such as **Styx**, **Boston**, **Kansas** and **Journey**. They released two technically excellent albums, characterized by the heavy use of keyboards and multi-part vocal harmonies, but failing to attract attention outside their native South Africa, the band broke up in 1981.

Albums: *Stingray* (Carrere 1979), *Operation Stingray* (Nitty Gritty 1980).

Stitt, Sonny

b. Edward Stitt, 2 February 1924, Boston, Massachusetts, USA, d. 22 July 1982. Starting out on alto saxophone, Stitt gained his early experience playing in the big bands led by **Tiny Bradshaw** and **Billy Eckstine**. Influenced by **Charlie Parker** and by the many fine young beboppers he encountered on the Eckstine band, Stitt quickly developed into a formidable player. He played with **Dizzy Gillespie**, **Kenny Clarke** and others but by the late 40s was concerned that he should develop a more personal style. In pursuit of this he switched to tenor saxophone and formed the first of many bands he was to lead and co-lead over the years. Amongst his early collaborators was **Gene Ammons**, whom he had met during the Eckstine stint. In the late 50s he was with **Jazz At The Philharmonic** and in 1960 was briefly with **Miles Davis**. Throughout the 60s and 70s Stitt maintained a high level of performances at home and abroad, despite periodic bouts of ill-health generated by his drug addictions. In the early 60s he recorded with **Paul Gonsalves**, *Salt And Pepper*, and in the early 70s toured with Gillespie as a member of the Giants Of Jazz, continuing to make many fine record albums. His early 80s albums included *Sonny, Sweets And Jaws*, with **Harry Edison** and **Eddie 'Lockjaw' Davis**, and a fine set made just weeks before his death. Although his early career was overshadowed by Parker, Stitt was never a copyist. Indeed, his was a highly original musical mind, as became apparent after he switched to tenor and forged a new and appreciative audience for his work. In later years he played alto saxophone as often as he played tenor, by which time it was plain to see that the likening to Parker was largely a result of critical pigeon-holing.

Selected albums: *Sonny Stitt/Bud Powell/J. J. Johnson* (1949), *A Very Special Concert* (1950), *Symphony Hall Swing* (1952-56), *Super Stitt! Vols 1 & 2* (1954), *Tenor Battles* (1954), *Sonny Stitt With The New Yorkers* (1957), *Only The Blues* (1957), *Sonny Stitt* (c.1957-58), *Newport* (1958), *Burnin'* (1958), *The Hard Swing* (1959), *Sonny Stitt Sits In With The Oscar Peterson Trio* (1959), *Sonny Stitt At The D.J. Lounge* (1961), *Low Flame* (1962), *Autumn In New York* (1962-67), with Jack McDuff *Sonny Stitt Meets Brother Jack*

(Original Jazz Classics 1962), *Sonny Stitt Plays Bird* (1963), *Salt And Pepper* (1963), *My Main Man* (1964), *Interaction* (1965), *Sonny* (1966), *Stardust* (1966), *What's New!!! Sonny Stitt Plays The Varitone* (1966), *Night Work* (1967), *Autumn In New York* (Black Lion 1968), *Night Letter* (1969), *Black Vibrations* (c.1971), *So Doggone Good* (1972), *Constellation* (Muse 1972), *Tune Up!* (Muse 1972), *The Champ* (Muse 1973), *Satan* (1974), *In Walked Sonny* (1975), *I Remember Bird* (1976), *Moonlight In Vermont* (1977), *Back To My Old Home Town* (Black And Blue 1979), *Groovin' High* (1980), *Sonny, Sweets And Jaws* (1981), *At Last* (1982), *The Last Stitt Sessions* (Muse 1982).

Stiv Bators

b. Stivin Bator, 22 October 1949, Cleveland, Ohio, USA, d. June 1990. Bators formed his first bands Mother Goose and Frankenstein, who were transmuted into a seminal US 'no wave' band the **Dead Boys**. They moved to New York in 1976. Although they officially split in 1978 there would be frequent reunions, as Bators moved to Los Angeles where he recorded demos with friend Jeff Jones (ex-Blue Ash). He also gigged with Akron band Rubber City Rebels. The first release from the demos was a version of the **Choir**'s (later the **Raspberries**) 60s single 'It's Cold Outside', which was released on Greg Shaw's Bomp label. A second guitarist and debut album (USA only) followed in 1980 on which the duo was augmented by guitarist Eddy Best and drummer David Quinton (formerly in Toronto's the Mods). After appearing in John Walter's cult movie *Polyester*, Bators formed a touring band with Rick Bremner replacing Quinton. By 1981, Bators had become a permanent member of the Wanderers. The Stiv Bators Band played a final American tour in February 1981 with Brian James of the **Damned** guesting on guitar, after which Bators would concentrate on the Wanderers until September 1981. After the impressive *Only Lovers Left Alive* (1981), Bators took Dave Treganna (ex-**Sham 69**) with him to join James and Nicky Turner (ex-**Barracudas**) in **Lords Of The New Church**. Following the Lords' demise, Bators resurfaced in London in 1989 for a 'Return Of The Living Boys' gig. This time his cohorts were drawn from a variety of local personnel, and it was not until he returned to Paris that he entered a recording studio once more. A new line-up included Dee Dee Ramone (**Ramones**), who had to be replaced by Neil X (**Sigue Sigue Sputnik**) before the sessions began, Kris Dollimore (ex-**Godfathers**) and guest appearances from **Johnny Thunders**. With six songs completed, Bators was hit by car in June 1990, and died the day after. There are hopes that his sessions will receive a posthumous release.
Album: *Where The Action Is* (1980).

Stivell, Alan

b. Alan Cochevelou, 1943, Brittany, France. The son of a harp maker, Cochevelou was given his first harp at the age of nine. He later chose the professional name of Stivell, the Breton translation meaning fountain, spring or source. Having started out as a solo performer playing traditional Breton music on the wire-strung Celtic harp, Stivell explored the music of Ireland, Scotland, Wales and the west country of England. In 1967, he formed a group comprising of himself on harp, bagpipes, Irish flute and Dan Ar Bras on electric guitar, as well as adding percussion and bass. In 1976, Stivell left the group, and soon after released the solo *E. Langonned*. By integrating rock elements in traditional numbers such as 'She Moved Thro' The Fair', Stivell began to influence the growing folk rock movement. He put folk music in the UK charts for a while with a successful run of hits in the 70s. Stivell makes occasional appearances at festivals and continues to tour. **Kate Bush** and Shane MacGowan guested on his 1994 album.
Albums: *Reflections* (1971), *A L'Olympia* (1972), *Renaissance Of The Celtic Harp* (1972), *Chemins De Terre* (1972), *Celtic Rock* (1972), *Alan Stivell Reflections* (1973), *From Celtic Roots* (1974), *A Longonnet* (1975), *In Dublin* (1975), *E. Langonned* (1976), *Trema'n Inis/Vers I'lle* (1976), *Before Landing* (1977), *Suzi MacGuire* (1978), *Journée A La Maison* (1978), *Tro Ar Bed* (1979), *Celtic Symphony/Symphonie Celtique* (1980), *Legend* (1984), *Harpes Du Nouvel Age* (1986), *Again* (Disques Dreyfus 1993), *Brian Boru* (Dreyfus 1995).

Stobart, Kathy

b. 1 April 1925, South Shields, Co. Durham, England. Stobart in her long career as a leading jazz saxophonist has recorded and played with countless top musicians, yet her own recorded output is comparatively sparse. From her professional debut at the age of 14 she eventually moved to London where work was more plentiful, playing with **Art Pepper** (then a serviceman) while posted in the UK during the war. Following a spell with the **Vic Lewis** Big Band during the late 40s Stobart married trumpeter Bert Courtley and formed her own band in the early 50s. Her work over many years with **Humphrey Lyttelton** has produced some of her finest playing and Lyttelton rightly regards her as a world-class musician. Her other credits include work with **Johnnie Griffin, Al Haig, Earl 'Fatha' Hines, Buddy Tate, Zoot Sims, Harry Beckett** and **Dick Hyman**. Stobart topped the bill at the first British women's jazz festival in 1982 and was a member of Gail Force 17 (the women's big band) during the mid-80s. Additionally she has made a reputation as a music teacher. Still refusing to retire from the road, she was on tour with Lyttelton again throughout the 90s.
Albums: *Arderia* (1983), *Saxploitation* (1983).

Stock, Aitken And Waterman

Modelling themselves on the **Motown** hit factory of the 60s, Mike Stock (b. 3 December 1951), Matt Aitken (b. 25 August 1956), and Pete Waterman (b. 15 January 1947) were the most successful team of UK writer/producers during the 80s. Waterman had been a soul disc jockey, promoter man producer and remixer (**Adrian Baker**'s 'Sherry', Susan Cadogan's 'Hurts So Good'). In 1984, he joined forces with Stock and Aitken, members of pop band Agents Aren't Aeroplanes. The trio first designed records for the thriving British disco scene, having their first hits with singles by *Dead Or Alive* ('You Spin Me Round', UK number 1, 1984) **Divine**, **Hazell Dean** and **Sinitta** ('So Macho', 1986). The team specialized in designing songs for specific artists and they gained further UK number 1s in 1987 with 'Respectable' by **Mel And Kim** and **Rick Astley**'s 'Never Gonna Give You Up'. In that year, too, they released a dance single under their own names. 'Roadblock' reached the UK Top 20. In 1988, SAW, as they were now referred to, launched their own PWL label and shifted their attention to the teenage audience. Their main vehicles were Australian soap opera stars **Kylie Minogue** and **Jason Donovan**. Minogue's 'I Should Be So Lucky' was the first of over a dozen Top 10 hits in four years and the epitome of the SAW approach, a brightly produced, tuneful and highly memorable song. Donovan had similar success both with SAW compositions like 'Too Many Broken Hearts' and revivals (**Brian Hyland**'s 'Sealed With A Kiss'). The Stock, Aitken Waterman formula was applied to other artists such as **Sonia**, Brother Beyond, **Big Fun** and **Donna Summer**, but by 1991, a change of direction was apparent. Following Astley's example, Jason Donovan had left the fold in search of artistic freedom. Equally significantly, the SAW team was hit by the departure of its main songwriter Matt Aitken. Meanwhile, Waterman was busy with three new labels, PWL America, PWL Continental and PWL Black. The list of further hits goes on and on, clearly they now command enourmous respect.

Albums: *Hit Factory* (1987), *Hit Factory, Volume 2* (1988), *Hit Factory, Volume 3* (1989), *The Best Of Stock, Aitken And Waterman* (1990).

Stockard, Ocie

b. Ocie Blanton Stockard, 11 May 1909, Crafton, Texas, USA, d. 23 April 1988, Fort Worth, Texas, USA. A talented musician and stalwart of western swing music. He learned guitar from his sister's boyfriend, fiddle breakdowns from his father and played at dances at the age of 10. He later learned to read music, improved his fiddle playing as well as becoming an accomplished banjo and tenor guitar player. Whilst working as a barber in Fort Worth, he began to play on KTAT. In 1930, often alternating instruments, he played in a band known as the High Fliers and also at dances with **Milton** and **Derwood Brown**, **Bob Wills** and Herman Arnspiger. When Milton Brown formed his Musical Brownies, Stockard became a regular band member playing banjo on their first recordings in April 1934. Throughout his time with Brown, he played different instruments as the occasion demanded and also added harmony vocals. After Milton Brown's death, he continued with the band under Derwood Brown's leadership making **Decca** recordings (including vocals) in February 1937. Soon afterwards, Stockard formed his own band, the Wanderers and made recordings for Bluebird. It proved a popular Texas band until it folded in the late 40s, when Stockard relocated to California and for some years played with Bob Wills' Texas Playboys. He also played with **Tommy Duncan**'s Western All Stars in Los Angeles, until he finally tired of the business and returned to Fort Worth. He ran a bar until his retirement and subsequently died in a nursing home there in April 1988.

Stockhausen, Markus

b. 1957, Cologne, Germany. Son of the composer Karlheinz Stockhausen, Markus studied piano and trumpet at the Cologne Musikhochschule. He also plays flügelhorn and synthesizer. In 1981 he won the German Music Competition. Since 1974 he has worked regularly with his father, who has written a number of works for him, including 'Sirius'. In particular, the solo trumpet parts in Stockhausen perés massive opera cycle, Licht, were created for Markus. Outside of the contemporary 'classical' field he has played free improvised music with various groups, and currently has a band, Aparis, with his brother Simon on saxophones and keyboards.

Albums: with Gary Peacock: *Cosi Lotano...Quasi Dentro* (ECM 1989), *Aparis* (ECM 1990), *Tagtraum* (New Note 1992), *Despite The Fire Fighters' Efforts* (ECM 1993).

Stockton's Wing

Formed in 1978, this rigid, traditionalist Irish band featured banjo, fiddles, whistles and mandolins, before they enlisted the didgeridoo player/bassist Steve Coone. Subsequently, whilst still jigging and reeling, they recruited a rhythm section and aimed for commercial acceptance. They even gained British radio play with the nagging 'Beautiful Affair'. *Light In The Western Sky* was a best seller, although their next album, *Take One, Live* is a more balanced and representative set. When it was recorded group's line-up was Paul Roche (whistle), Tony Molloy (bass), Mike Hanrahan (guitar), Keran Hanrahan (mandolin), Maurice Lennon (fiddle) and Fran Breen (drums). Breen later went on to play with **Nanci Griffith**. Through the 80s the band's membership fluctuated, but they still released some pleasant albums. In 1992 they adopted a 'back to basics' acoustic line-up of Peter Keenan (keyboards) and Dave McNevin (banjo, mandolin) joining Roche, Mike Hanrahan and Lennon in a reduced five-piece unit.

Selected albums: *Light In The Western Sky* (1982), *Take One, Live* (1984), *Full Flight* (1986), *The Crooked Rose* (Tara 1992). Compilation: *The Stockton's Wing Collection* (Tara 1991).

Stokes, Frank

b. 1 January 1888, Whitehaven, Tennessee, USA, d. 12 September 1955, Memphis, Tennessee, USA. Stokes was raised in Mississippi, taking up the guitar early. He worked on medicine shows, and in the streets of Memphis in the bands of **Will Batts** and **Jack Kelly**. By 1927, when Stokes and his fellow guitarist **Dan Sane** made their first records as the Beale Street Sheiks, they were one of the tightest guitar duos in blues, much influenced by ragtime, and also performing medicine show and minstrel songs. Stokes was the vocalist, and played second guitar. They recorded together until 1929. However, Stokes also recorded solo, and with Will Batts on fiddle. Stokes' recorded personality is that of the promiscuous rounder, by turns macho and pleading for another chance. His singing is forthright, with impressive breath control. Stokes and Sane worked together until illness forced Stokes to retire from music in 1952.

Albums: *The Beale Street Sheiks* (1990), *Frank Stokes* (1990).

Stoller, Alvin

b. 7 October 1925, New York City, USA, d. 19 October 1992. Taking up the drums as a child, Stoller's dues were paid while he was still a teenager with stints in bands led by **Raymond Scott**, **Teddy Powell**, **Benny Goodman** and **Charlie Spivak**. In 1945 he followed **Buddy Rich** into the vacated drum stool with the **Tommy Dorsey** band, bringing with him much of his predecessor's enthusiasm - and not a little of his fiery temperament. Through the late 40s and 50s, Stoller's career found him playing in name bands such as those led by **Georgie Auld**, **Harry James**, **Billy May**, **Charlie Barnet**, **Claude Thornhill** and **Bob Crosby**. This same period saw him in constant demand as a studio musician, especially for **Norman Granz**, backing artists such as **Erroll Garner**, **Billie Holiday**, **Ben Webster**, **Ella Fitzgerald** and **Benny Carter**, with whom he appeared on *Additions To Further Definitions*. Tastefully discreet when backing singers or in a small group setting and powerfully propulsive when driving a big band, Stoller was one of the best late swing era drummers even if he was sometimes overlooked thanks to his long service in film and television studios in late years.

Albums: with Harry Edison *Sweets At The Haig* (1953), *The Art Tatum-Roy Eldridge-Alvin Stoller-John Simmons*

Quartet (1955), *Around The Horn With Maynard Ferguson* (1955-56), *The Genius Of Coleman Hawkins* (1957), with Benny Carter *Additions To Further Definitions* (1966).

Stoller, Mike

(see **Leiber And Stoller**)

Stone City Band

Kenny Hawkins, Tom McDermott, Levi Ruffin Jnr, Daniel Le Melle, Jerry Livingston, Jerry Rainer and Nat Hughes formed the Stone City Band in the USA during 1978. The following year, they were co-opted by rising funk star **Rick James** as his backing band. They worked with James for four years, supporting him on albums such as *Garden Of Love* and *Street Songs*. In return, James helped them record three albums in their own right, though there was little conceptual or musical difference between their work and his own. Songs like 'Strut Your Stuff', 'Little Runaway' and 'Bad Lady' demonstrated that they had adopted James' one-dimensional view of human relations, and their hard, funk-based style was also heavily-derivative of their mentor's style.

Albums: *In 'N' Out* (1980), *The Boys Are Back* (1981), *Out From The Shadow* (1983).

Stone Fury

Moving from Hamburg, Germany, to Los Angeles, USA, in 1983, vocalist Lenny Wolf teamed up with Bruce Gowdy (guitar) to form Stone Fury. Adding Rick Wilson (bass) and Jody Cortez (drums), they signed to **MCA Records** and debuted the following year with *Burns Like A Star*. The album offered traditional blues-based hard rock, similar in construction to **Led Zeppelin**. Wolf's vocals were modelled very closely on **Robert Plant**'s, both in pitch and phrasing, which provoked accusations of imitation. *Let Them Talk* was more restrained and employed a greater use of melody and atmospherics. Unable to make a breakthrough in the USA, Wolf went back to Germany and later formed **Kingdom Come** on his return to the States in 1987. Gowdy, in the meantime, formed World Trade.

Albums: *Burns Like A Star* (MCA 1984), *Let Them Talk* (MCA 1986).

Stone Poneys

Formed in 1964, the Stone Poneys are remembered today almost exclusively for the fact that their lead singer was **Linda Ronstadt**. The group came together in Tucson, Arizona, USA, and originally consisted of Ronstadt (b. 15 July 1946, Tucson, Arizona, USA), who had performed with a sister and brother as the Three Ronstadts, Bob Kimmel (guitar) and Kenny Edwards (keyboards/guitar). Moving to Los Angeles in 1965, the group was booked into folk clubs such as the Troubadour. A record offer by **Mercury Records** was declined (the label had demanded the group perform surf music!), and they signed instead with Sidewalk Records, releasing the rare single 'So Fine'/'Everybody Has Their Own Ideas'. They were next signed to **Capitol Records**. The group's debut album, a self-titled effort, was unsuccessful in 1966, but a single, 'Different Drum', written by future **Monkees** member **Michael Nesmith** and taken from the Stone Poneys' *Evergreen* album, broke the group in late 1967. The single reached number 13 in the USA and the album climbed to number 100. One further single, 'Up To My Neck In High Muddy Water', barely made the charts in 1968 and after another Nesmith composition, 'Some Of Shelley's Blues', failed to chart, Edwards left the group and Ronstadt began her highly successful solo career.

Albums: *Stone Poneys* (1967), *Evergreen* (1967), *Different Drum* (1974).

Stone Roses

A classic case of an overnight success stretched over half a decade, the UK band Stone Roses evolved through a motley collection of Manchester-based non-starters such as the Mill, the Patrol and English Rose before settling down as Stone Roses in 1985. Acclaimed for their early warehouse gigs, at this time the line-up consisted of Ian Brown (b. Ian George Brown, 20 February 1963, Ancoats, Gt. Manchester, England; vocals), John Squire (b. 24 November 1962, Broadheath, Gt. Manchester, England; guitar), Reni (b. Alan John Wren, 10 April 1964, Manchester, England; drums), Andy Couzens (guitar) and Pete Garner (bass). In their hometown, at least, the band had little trouble in working up a following, in spite of their predilection for juxtaposing leather trousers with elegant melodies. In 1987 guitarist Andy Couzens left, later to form the **High**, and Pete Garner followed soon after, allowing Gary 'Mani' Mounfield (b. 16 November 1962, Crumpsall, Gt. Manchester, England) to take over bass guitar. By this time the band had already made a low-key recording debut, with the ephemeral 45, 'So Young'. By the end of the year the reconstituted foursome were packing out venues in Manchester, but finding it difficult to get noticed in the rest of the country. A contract with Silvertone Recordsl in 1988 produced 'Elephant Stone', and showed its makers to be grasping the essence of classic 60s pop. A year later they had carried it over the threshold of the independent scene and into the nation's front rooms. When the follow-up, 'Made Of Stone', attracted media attention, the Stone Roses' ball started rolling at a phenomenal pace. Their debut album was hailed in all quarters as a guitar/pop classic, and as the Manchester 'baggy' scene infiltrated Britain's consciousness, Stone Roses - alongside the funkier, grubbier **Happy Mondays** - were perceived to be leaders of the flare-wearing pack. By the close of 1989, the Roses had moved from half-filling London's dingiest clubs to playing to 7,500 people at Alexandra Palace. Having achieved such incredible success so quickly, when the band vanished to work on new material, the rumour mongers inevitably came out in force. In 1990 'One Love' reached the UK Top 10, but aside from this singular vinyl artefact, the media was mainly concerned with the Roses' rows with a previous record company, who had reissued old material accompanied by a video made without the band's permission. This resulted in the group vandalising the company's property, which in turn led to a much-publicized court case. As if this was not enough, Stone Roses were back in court when they tried to leave Silvertone, who took an injunction out against their valuable proteges. This prevented any further Stone Roses material from being released, even though the band eventually won their case and signed to **Geffen Records** for a reported $4 million.

By the end of 1991, their eagerly awaited new product was still stuck somewhere in the pipeline while, in true Stone Roses fashion, after their live extravaganzas at Spike Island, Glasgow, London and Blackpool, plans were afoot for a massive open air comeback gig for the following spring. It never happened that year, nor the next. In fact the Stone Roses absence from the limelight - initially through contractual problems with Silvertone and management squabbles - then seemingly through pure apathy, became something of an industry standing joke. Had their debut album not had such a huge impact on the public consciousness they would surely have been forgotten. Painstaking sessions with a series of producers finally saw the immodestly titled *Second Coming* released in 1995. It was announced in an exclusive interview given to the UK magazine dedicated to helping the homeless, *The Big Issue*, much to the chagrin of a slavering British music press. Almost inevitably, it failed to meet expectations, despite the fact that the US market was now opening up for the band. They also lost drummer Reni, who was replaced within weeks of its release by Robbie Maddix, who had previously played with Manchester rapper **Rebel MC**. Promotional gigs seemed less natural and relaxed than had previously been the case, while Silvertone milked the last gasp out of the band's legacy with them to compile a second compilation album (from only one original studio set). Their loyal fans' patience was pushed to the limit when after much excitement caused by the announcement that 'Yes they will be playing the 25th Glastonbury Festival' a few days before they pulled out. The Stone Roses could well go into the record books for having cancelled more gigs than they have actually played. And so the legend grows.

Album: *The Stone Roses* (Silvertone 1989), *Second Coming* (Geffen 1995). Compilations: *Turns Into Stone* (Silvertone 1992), *The Complete Stone Roses* (Silvertone 1995).

Stone Temple Pilots

The Stone Temple Pilots are the result of a chance

meeting between vocalist Scott Weiland (who prefers to be known by his surname only) and bassist Robert DeLeo at one of **Black Flag**'s final shows in Los Angeles. After discovering that they both went out with the same girl, a songwriting partnership led to the formation of a full band, originally known as Mighty Joe Young, and later renamed Stone Temple Pilots, with drummer Eric Kretz and DeLeo's guitarist brother Dean joining the duo. Moving away from the **Guns N'Roses**-crazed Los Angeles scene of the time to San Diego, the band were able to play club shows and develop hard rock material given an alternative edge by their varied influences. Although the sound of the band brought many others to mind, from **Led Zeppelin** to Seattle bands such as **Pearl Jam** and **Alice In Chains**, and Weiland's deep voice bore a passing resemblance to that of Eddie Vedder, it was very much Stone Temple Pilots' own sound, and there was no denying the quality of *Core*. The dense wall of muscular guitar over a tight, precise rhythm section provides a powerful setting for Weiland's emotive vocals and challenging lyrics. 'Sex Type Thing', perhaps the band's best-known song, deals with sexual harassment from the viewpoint of a particularly brutish male, and the singer was initially concerned that the message would be misinterpreted. His fears proved unfounded and, helped by heavy touring, *Core* would reach the US Top 20 by the summer of 1993, eventually selling over four million copies in the US. The follow-up, *Purple*, would debut at number 1 in the US album charts, staying there for three weeks. This time the band purposely avoided any material which could be construed as derivative of Pearl Jam, having tired of the unfair criticism, and their second effort proved to be an atmospheric and rewarding experience as STP produced a quasi-psychedelic sound which confirmed their own identity and considerable talents.
Albums: *Core* (Atlantic 1992), *Purple* (Atlantic 1994).

Stone The Crows

Singer **Maggie Bell** and guitarist Leslie Harvey (younger brother of **Alex Harvey**), served their musical apprenticeships in Glasgow's Palais dancebands. In 1967 they toured American bases in Germany with a group which also included Bill and Bobby Patrick. The following year Bell and Harvey formed Power, houseband at the Burns Howff bar, which included Jimmy Dewar (bass) and John McGuinness (organ). Leslie subsequently toured America, augmenting another Glasgow-based group, Cartoone. This newly-formed quartet was managed by **Peter Grant**, whom the guitarist then brought to Scotland to view Power. Grant duly signed the group, who were renamed Stone The Crows on the addition of former **John Mayall** drummer, Colin Allen. The quintet's early blues-based albums were notable for both Bell and Dewar's expressive vocals and Harvey's textured, economic guitar work. However, an inability to match their live popularity with record sales led to disaffection and both McGuinness and Dewar left on completing *Ode To John Law*. Steve Thompson (bass) and Ronnie Leahy (keyboards) joined Stone The Crows for *Teenage Licks*, their most successful album to date. Bell was awarded the first of several top vocalist awards but this new-found momentum ended in tragedy. On 3 May 1972, Leslie Harvey died after being electrocuted onstage at Swansea's Top Rank Ballroom. Although the group completed a fourth album with Jimmy McCulloch from **Thunderclap Newman**, they lacked the heart to continue and broke up the following year.
Albums: *Stone The Crows* (1970), *Ode To John Law* (1970), *Teenage Licks* (1971), *'Ontinuous Performance* (1972). Compilation: *Flashback - Stone The Crows* (1976).

Stone, Cliffie

b. Clifford Gilpin Snyder, 1 March 1917, Burbank, California, USA. In the early 30s Stone played bass and trombone in dance bands before becoming a country music compere and disc jockey in 1935. During the 40s he was bandleader and host of the CBS network *Hollywood Barn Dance* and from 1943-47 he compered almost thirty other country radio shows weekly. He joined **Capitol Records** in 1946, working on production as well as recording and had chart hits in 1947-48, including 'Peepin' Through The Keyhole' and 'When My Blue Moon Turns To Gold Again'. In 1949, he hosted the famed *Hometown Jamboree* and, from 1953 to its closure in 1960, the radio and television show *Town Hall Party*. These shows did much to popularize country music over a wide area and many artists benefited from their appearances on them. One prominent regular on *Hometown Jamboree* was Stone's father, a banjo playing comedian who performed as Herman The Hermit. Stone discovered **Tennessee Ernie Ford** in 1949 and was his manager for many years; he also worked with many other artists including Spade Cooley, **Lefty Frizzell**, **Hank Thompson** and Molly Bee. During the 60s he cut back on his own performing, concentrating on management, a booking agency and several music publishing firms including Central Songs, which he sold to Capitol in 1969. Throughout the 60s-70s he was involved in production, formed Granite records, did committee work for the Country Music Association and ATV Music before retiring in the late 70s. Over the years he wrote many songs and worked with **Merle Travis** on such classics as 'Divorce Me C.O.D', 'So Round So Firm So Fully Packed' and 'No Vacancy'. Stone, who rarely left his native California during his illustrious career, was elected to Nashville's Country Music Hall Of Fame in 1989 for his services to the music in the non-performer category.
Albums: *Blue Moon Of Kentucky* (Capitol 1954), *The*

Party's On Me (Capitol 1958), *Cool Cowboy* (Capitol 1959), *Square Dance Promenade* (Capitol 1960), *Original Cowboy Sing-a-long* (Capitol 1961), *Together Again* (Tower 1967).

Stone, Doug

b. 1956, Newnan, Georgia, USA. Stone, the product of a broken home, was encouraged to become a musician by his mother. Stone, who can sing and play guitar, keyboards, fiddle and drums, worked as part of a trio around Georgia for several years without finding commercial success. He then auditioned for the producer Bob Montgomery who immediately signed him to Epic Records. In 1990, Stone had his first US country hit with 'I'd Be Better Off In A Pine Box'. Like many other 'new country' singers, he was a throwback to the honky tonk tradition of **George Jones** and **Merle Haggard**. His other successes have included 'I Thought It Was You', 'A Jukebox With A Country Song' and one of the slickest country songs of recent years, 'Warning Labels'.
Albums: *Doug Stone* (1990), *I Thought It Was You* (1991), *From The Heart* (1992), *More Love* (1993), *Faith In Me, Faith In You* (Columbia 1995).
Video: *I Never Knew Love* (1993).

Stone, Jesse

b. 1901, Atchison, Kansas, USA. As a young man, pianist Stone worked extensively in the southwest playing in numerous bands. During the greater part of the 20s he led his own **territory band** but at the end of the decade became arranger and musical director for other leading territory bands including those of **Terrence Holder**, **George E. Lee** and Thamon Hayes. He returned to bandleading in the mid-30s, continuing in this capacity throughout the next decade before becoming an A&R man. Stone, who made very few recordings, was one of the lesser, but still important, figures in the development of **Kansas City Jazz**. His arrangements and expertise as leader and director helped fashion the propulsive swing which marked the style.

Stone, Kirby, Four

This vocal quartet comprised Kirby Stone (b. 27 April 1918, New York, USA), Eddie Hall, Larry Foster and Mike Gardner. They had a hip brand of humour and a distinctive, upbeat, swinging style. Originally an instrumental quintet, the group became a vocal foursome before making a name for themselves in nightclubs and local television shows. They came to prominence in 1958 with an appearance on the *Ed Sullivan* Show, which led to a contract with **Columbia Records**, and the release of *Man, I Flipped...When I Heard The Kirby Stone Four*. It was a mixture of standards, such as 'S'Wonderful' and 'It Could Happen To You', and special material written by Stone and Gardner. Their programme included 'Juke Box Dream', a vehicle for Foster's uncanny vocal impressions. In the same year they also had a Top 30 single with their extremely original conception of 'Baubles, Bangles And Beads', from the 1953 Broadway musical *Kismet*. The accompanying album reached the US Top 20. Amongst their other album releases, *Guys And Dolls (Like Today)* (1962) included a 'liberetto-ture' (a combination of libretto and overture) by Kirby Stone and the group's frequent arranger and conductor, **Dick Hyman**, as an attempt to present the Abe Burrows/Jo Swerling/**Frank Loesser** masterpiece as a 'show for the ear alone'. Stone added some extra lyrics for his 'guys', who were augmented by the 'dolls' - a female vocal chorus - plus a 25 piece orchestra which included such luminaries as **Alvino Rey**, **Shelly Manne** and **Al Klink**. Subsequently, the Kirby Stone Four continued to flourish, and went forward, armed with this common credo: 'A pox on all harmonica players, nightclub owners named Rocky, and juveniles who win contests by playing 'Lady Of Spain' on white accordions.'
Albums: *Man, I Flipped...When I Heard The Kirby Stone Four* (1958), *Baubles, Bangles And Beads* (1958), *The Kirby Stone Touch* (1960), *Guys And Dolls (Like Today)* (1962).

Stone, Lew

b. Louis Stone, 28 June 1898, London, England, d. 13 February 1969, London, England. A self-taught musician, Stone developed into a first-class pianist and arranger, and led one of the leading dance bands of the 30s. His book, *Harmony And Orchestration For The Modern Dance Band*, became the standard work for 20 years. In 1925, Stone played piano for the London Aeolian Band, and worked for **Bert Ralton** shortly before Ralton's death on an African safari. From 1927-31 he was a freelance arranger for many name bands including **Ambrose** and **Jack Payne**, before joining **Roy Fox** at the Monseigneur Restaurant in London's Piccadilly. When Fox left in 1932, Stone took over and formed his own band from a nucleus of Fox personnel, including Joe Ferrie and Lew Davis (trombones), Joe Crossman and Ernest Ritte (saxophones), **Nat Gonella** and Alfie Noakes (trumpets), Bill Harty (drums), Tiny Winters (bass), and vocalist **Al Bowlly**. Ferrie, Gonella and Winters also sang regularly with the band. They broadcast regularly on Tuesday nights, introduced by the band's theme, 'Oh Susannah', and throughout the 30s recorded a selection of 'hot' titles including 'White Jazz/Blue Jazz', 'Tiger Rag', 'Milenbourg Joys', 'Call Of The Freaks', comedy numbers such as 'Annie Doesn't Live Here Any More', and, most significantly, sentimental ballads of the day sung by Al Bowlly. Bowlly stayed with Stone until 1934, and contributed some of what is regarded as his best work on songs such as 'I'll Never Be The Same', 'Just Let Me Look At You', 'What A Little Moonlight

Can Do', 'Easy Come, Easy Go', 'How Could We Be Wrong?' and 'With My Eyes Wide Open I'm Dreaming'. He also sang on Stone's only US hit, 'Isle Of Capri', and returned to the band for a spell in the late 30s. Besides playing clubs such as the Hollywood Restaurant and the Café De Paris in between provincial theatre tours, Stone was the musical director for British and Dominion Films, and worked on over 40 movies including **Goodnight Vienna** with **Jack Buchanan**, *Bitter Sweet* and *The Little Damozel* both starring **Anna Neagle** and featuring the Stone Band. He also served as musical director for several West End shows such as **Richard Rodgers And Lorenz Hart**'s **On Your Toes**, as well as *Hide And Seek* and **Under Your Hat**, both starring **Cicely Courtneidge**. During World War II, Stone led several small groups including the Novatones and the Stonecrackers as well as his big band which he used for touring dancehalls, military camps and variety theatres. From 1947-49, he led the theatre orchestra for **Irving Berlin**'s big hit, **Annie Get Your Gun**, at the London Coliseum. During the 50s he continued to play top clubs such as the Pigalle and Oddenino's besides appearing at big Mecca ballrooms in Scotland and the north of England. In 1959 he disbanded the orchestra and assembled a sextet for broadcasting, which he led until 1967, although he devoted most of his time in the 60s to the Lew Stone Entertainment Service agency. Unlike many of the successful bandleaders who came to prominence in the 30s Stone was not a showman and never sought the limelight. Today he is remembered as one of the most skilful, innovative and imaginative arrangers of his era.

Albums: *10.30 Tuesday Night* (1963), *Al Bowlly And Lew Stone And His Band* (1964), *My Kind Of Music* (1967), *The Golden Age Of British Dance Bands* (1969), *The Bands That Matter* (1970), *Presenting Lew Stone 1934-35* (1973), *The Echo Of A Song (1932)* (1977), *Get Happy* (1981), *The Echo Of A Song* (1983), *Coffee In The Morning* (1983), *Right From The Heart* (1985), *The Golden Age Of Lew Stone* (1985), *Sing Me A Swing Song* (1988), *Pop Goes Your Heart* (1988), *Dinner And Dance* (1990)

Further reading: *Lew Stone: A Career In Music.*, Trodd, K..

Stone, Sly
(see **Sly And The Family Stone**)

Stoneground

This large-scale communal group was originally formed in Walnut Creek, California, USA. Initially a trio, by 1970 the line-up had been expanded to include Tim Barnes (guitar), John Blakely (guitar), Luthor Bildt (guitar), Alan Fitzgerald (bass) and Mike Mau (drums). This quintet was invited to back **Sal Valentino**, formerly of the **Beau Brummels**, in a touring revue, the Medicine Ball Caravan. Sal was also accompanied

by four women vocalists, Annie Sampson, Deidre La Porte, Lynn Hughes and Lydia Moreno. The newly constituted 10-piece crossed America and Europe between 1970 and 1971. Stoneground's debut album consolidated the material performed on tour, but its successor, *Family Album*, is the group's definitive collection. This appealing double-set showcased the contrasting vocal styles and informal playing which made their music so appealing, but internal friction doomed the group's potential and by 1973 only Barnes and Sampson remained from the trailblazing, large-scale unit. Subsequent versions were less cumbersome, but equally unstable, and three later members, Cory Lerios, Steve Price and David Jenkins left to form **Pablo Cruise** who ironically found the commercial success the parent group was denied. Sampson, however, remains a popular attraction on the Bay Area circuit while Valentino maintains his individualistic path.

Albums: *Stoneground* (1971), *Family Album* (1972), *Stoneground III* (1973), *Flat Out* (1976), *Hearts Of Stone* (1978), *Play It Loud* (1980), *Bad Machines And Limousines* (1982), *I'm Nervous* (1982).

Stoneman Family

The Stoneman Family originated with Ernest V. 'Pop' Stoneman (b. 25 May 1893, in a log cabin near Monarat, Carroll County, Virginia, USA, d. 14 June 1968, Nashville, Tennessee, USA), who learned to play guitar, autoharp, banjo and harmonica and showed a talent to quickly learn songs that he either heard or read in early song books. He worked in cotton mills, coal mines and as a carpenter in various parts of the area. It was while working as the last at Bluefield, West Virginia that he heard the first recordings of fellow Virginian, **Henry Whitter**. Ernest was unimpressed by Whitter's singing and like others, believed that he could do better. He travelled to New York where, providing his own autoharp and harmonica backings, he auditioned for **Columbia** and **OKeh**. The former showed no interest, but he made his first recordings for OKeh in September 1924, including his million seller, 'The Sinking Of The Titanic'. It proved to be one of the biggest hits of the 20s and has since been recorded by many artists, including **Roy Acuff**. The records sold well enough and further sessions soon followed; on one he was accompanied by Emmett Lundy, a noted Virginian fiddler and on occasions, he recorded with his fiddle-playing wife, Hattie Stoneman (b.1900, d. 22 July 1976, Murfreesboro, Tennessee, USA).

In 1926, he recorded for **RCA**-Victor with his first band the Dixie Mountaineers and later with the Blue Ridge Cornshuckers. In the following years many recordings were made, which saw release on various labels, some under pseudonyms such as Slim Harris, Ernest Johnson, Uncle Ben Hawkins and Jim Seaney. In July 1927, he recorded at the noted sessions at

Bristol, Tennessee, where **Ralph Peer** also recorded the **Carter Family** and **Jimmie Rodgers**. Due to the Depression, he did not record between 1929 and 1933, but even so he had proved so popular that between 1925 and 1934, he had still recorded over two hundred songs. Some recordings were with other musicians, including his banjoist cousin George Stoneman (1883-1966), fiddlers Alex 'Uncle Eck' Dunford (c.1978-1953) and Kahle Brewer (b.1904) and on his last pre-World War II session in 1934, he was accompanied by his eldest son Eddie (b.1920), who played banjo and took some vocals. In 1931, financially insecure in spite of the earnings from record sales, he moved to Washington, DC where, to support his family (he and his wife had 23 children in all), he worked as a carpenter in a naval gun factory. Some of the children learned to play some instrument during childhood and when after the War he gradually began to return to entertaining, his band was made up of his wife and their own children.

A winning appearance on a television quiz show in 1956 led to him to reactivate his career. With his wife and five of his children, he recorded again (on **Folkways**) in 1957. After adding some contemporary country and bluegrass music to the old time and folk songs that he had always performed, the Stoneman Family became a popular touring act. They played on the *Grand Ole Opry* in 1962 and even appeared at *Fillmore West* in San Francisco, America's first psychedelic ballroom. In 1964, they moved their home to California, where they became active on the west coast folk scene and appeared at the prestigious Monterey Folk Festival. They also played on various network television shows in the 60s, including that of Jimmy Dean and between 1966 and 1968, they hosted their own series. At this time, the group consisted of Pop (autoharp/guitar), Calvin 'Scotty' Scott (fiddle), Van Haden (b. 1941, d. June 3 1995; guitar), Donna (mandolin), Roni (Veronica) (banjo) and Jim (bass). They had five minor hits with recordings on **MGM** in the late 60s but later recorded for other labels including Starday and **RCA**. In 1967, the CMA voted the Stoneman Family the Vocal Group Of The Year. Ernest Stoneman made his last recordings on 11 April 1968, and continued to perform with the group almost up to his death.

He was in all probability the first person ever to record using an autoharp and he is well remembered by exponents for his ability to play the melody line, instead of merely playing chords, the standard method of playing the instrument, even by its inventor. (This ability is demonstrated on some of his recordings, including 'Stoney's Waltz'.) He is also accepted as being the only country musician to record on both Edison cylinders and modern stereo albums and he was also the leading performer of string-band music in the Galax area of Virginia. After 'Pop' Stoneman's death,

Patti (autoharp) gave up her solo career to join with Donna, Roni, Van and Jim and as the Stoneman Family, they continued to play his music and toured all over the USA and Europe. In 1972, they recorded a live album, *Meet The Stonemans,* at London's Wembley Festival. Scotty Stoneman who also worked with the Blue Grass Champs and the **Kentucky Colonels**, won many fiddle competitions, including the National on several occasions and at the time of his death, in 1973, he was rated one of the world's finest bluegrass fiddle players. Hattie Stoneman, who first recorded in 1925, died in hospital aged 75. In later years, Donna left to concentrate on gospel music, Roni became a featured star of the television show *Hee-Haw.* Patti, Jim and Van continued to play as the Stoneman Family. Twin brothers Gene and Dean (b.1931) performed for a time in the Maryland area as the Stoneman Brothers, until Dean formed his Vintage Bluegrass band. In 1981, several members of the family reunited to record a special album. Dean Stoneman died of a lung complaint in Lanham, Maryland on 28 February 1989.

Albums by Ernest V. Stoneman: *Cool Cowboy* (Capitol 1958), *Ernest V.Stoneman & His Dixie Mountaineers (1927-1928)* (Historical 1968), *Pop Stoneman Memorial Album* (MGM 1969), *Ernest V.Stoneman & the Blue Ridge Corn Shuckers* (Rounder c.1975), *Round The Heart Of Old Galax* (County c.1976), *Ernest V.Stoneman Volume 1* (Old Homestead 1986), *Ernest V.Stoneman Volume 2* (Old Homestead 1986), *Ernest V.Stoneman Volume 3* (Old Homestead c.1988), *A Rare Find* (Stonehouse c.80s, covers early 60s).

Albums by the Stoneman Family: *American Banjo Tunes & Songs* (Folkways 1957), *Old Time Tunes Of The South* (Folkways 1957), *Bluegrass Champs* (Starday 1963), *Big Ball In Monterey* (World Pacific 1964), *White Lightning* (Starday 1965), *Those Singin', Swingin', Stompin', Sensational Stonemans* (MGM 1966), with the Tracy Schwarz Band *Down Home* (Folkways c.1966), with the Tracy Schwarz Band *The Stoneman Family* (Folkways c.1966), *All In The Family* (MGM 1967), *Stoneman's Country* (MGM 1967), *The Great Stonemans* (MGM 1968), *A Stoneman Christmas* (MGM 1968), *The Stoneman Family Live* (Sunset 1968), *Tribute To Pop Stoneman* (MGM 1969), *In All Honesty* (RCS-Victor 1970), *Dawn Of The Stoneman's Age* (RCA-Victor 1970), *The Stonemans* (MGM 1970), *California Blues* (RCA-Victor 1971), *Live At Wembley* (NAL 1972, UK only), *Meet The Stonemans* (1972), *Cuttin' The Grass* (CMH 1976), *On The Road* (CMH 1977), *Country Hospitality* (Meteor 1977), *Hot And Gettin' Hotter* (Stonehouse c.80s, cassette only), *Live At The Roy Acuff Theater* (Stonehouse c.80s, cassette only), *The Stoneman Family Volume 1; Live From Their T.V. Shows* (Stonehouse c.80s, cassette only), *First Family Of Country Music* (CMH 1981, double album), *Family Bible* (Rutabaga 1988), *For God And Country* (Old Homestead c.1990).

Solo albums by Scotty Stoneman: *Mr Country Fiddler*

(Design 1967), with the Kentucky Colonels *1965 Live In L.A.* (Sierra-Briar 1978), with Bill Emerson *20 Fiddlin' Banjo Hits* (Country Music Legends 1980). By Donna Stoneman: *I'll Fly Away* (Temple c.70s), *Donna Stoneman And Family - Gospel* (No Label c.80s, cassette only), *Donna Stoneman And Family - Old Rugged Cross* (No Label c.80s, cassette only). By Roni Stoneman: *First Lady Of Banjo* (Stone Ray c.1989, cassette only), *Pure And Country* (Stone Ray c.1989, cassette only).

Further reading: *The Stonemans*, Tribe, Ivan M. (1993).

Stooges

Purveyors, with the **MC5**, of classic, high-energy American rock, the Stooges' influence on successive generations is considerable. They were led by the enigmatic James Jewel Osterberg (aka Iggy Stooge and **Iggy Pop**, b. 21 April 1947, Ann Arbor, Michigan, USA) who assumed his unusual sobriquet in deference to the Iguanas, a high-school band in which he drummed. Iggy formed the Psychedelic Stooges with guitarist Ron Asheton. Scott Asheton (drums) and Dave Alexander (bass) completed the line-up which quickly became a fixture of Detroit's thriving underground circuit. By September 1967, the group had dropped its adjectival prefix and had achieved a notoriety through the onstage behaviour of its uninhibited frontman. The Stooges' first album was produced by **John Cale** although the group's initial choice was veteran soul svengali, **Jerry Ragovoy**. This exciting debut matched its malevolent, garage-band sneer with the air of nihilism prevalent in the immediate post-summer of love era. Iggy's exaggerated, **Mick Jagger**-influenced swagger swept over the group's three-chord maelstrom to create an enthralling and compulsive sound. The band were augmented by saxophonist Steven Mackay for *Funhouse*. This exceptional release documented a contemporary live set, opening with the forthright 'Down On The Street' and closing with the anarchic, almost free-form 'LA Blues'. This uncompromising collection proved uncommercial and the Stooges were then dropped by their record label. A second guitarist, Bill Cheatham joined in August 1970, while over the next few months two bassists, Zeke Zettner and Jimmy Recca, passed through the ranks as replacements for Dave Alexander. Cheatham was then ousted in favour of James Williamson, who made a significant contribution to the ensuing Stooges' period. Long-time Iggy fan, **David Bowie**, brought the group to the Mainman management stable and the singer was also responsible for mixing *Raw Power*. Although it lacked the purpose of its predecessors, the set became the Stooges' most successful release and contained two of their best-known performances, 'Gimme Danger' and 'Search And Destroy'. However, the quartet - Iggy, Williamson and the Asheton brothers - were dropped from Mainman for alleged drug dependence. In 1973, Scott Thurston (keyboards) was added to the line-up,

but their impetus was waning. The Stooges made their final live appearance on 9 February, 1974 at Detroit's Michigan Palace. This tawdry performance ended with a battle between the group and a local biker gang, the results of which were captured on *Metallic KO*. Within days a drained Iggy Pop announced the formal end of the Stooges.

Albums: *The Stooges* (1969), *Funhouse* (1970), as Iggy And The Stooges *Raw Power* (1973), *Metallic KO* (1976), *Rubber Legs* (1988, rare recordings from 1973/4). Compilations: as Iggy Pop and James Williamson *Kill City* (1977), *No Fun* (1980), as Iggy And The Stooges *I'm Sick Of You* (1981), *I Gotta Right* (1983).

Stop The Violence Movement

Set up by prominent members of the New York hip hop community in 1989, the Stop The Violence Movement was just that - a lobby to bring about a ceasefire in the endless gang warfare in the black ghettos. Numbering amongst its contributors **Kool Moe Dee**, **Public Enemy**, **Stetsasonic**, **Boogie Down Productions** and many others, a single was released on the **Jive** imprint, 'Self Destruction', in 1989. It would become the movement's anthem.

Stop The World - I Want To Get Off

This fresh, novel - some say unique - entertainment, with book music and lyrics by the new team of **Anthony Newley** and **Leslie Bricusse**, opened at the Queen's Theatre in London on 20 July 1961. Newley also directed, and played the leading role of Littlechap whose travels through the Seven Ages of Man - from factory teaboy to an Earldom - inevitably end in disillusionment. After taking the first step by marrying his boss's daughter, Evie (Anna Quayle), Littlechap's rise to fame and power is swift. His new life-style brings him into contact with other women (all played by Quayle), including an athletic Russian, Anya ('I will come to your room at two o'clock. Please be ready - I'm playing football at half past'), the American nightclub singer Ginnie, and Ilse, an au pair from Germany. Throughout it all, he is unable to find true happiness for himself and his family, or father the son he constantly yearns for. All the action took place on a set designed by Sean Kenny, which resembled a section of a circus tent with bare planks representing the seating. Newley, dressed like a clown with white face, and wearing baggy pants held up by big braces, sang the show's three big numbers, 'Gonna Build A Mountain', 'Once In A Lifetime', and 'What Kind Of Fool Am I?', and he also had the amusing 'Lumbered', and a lovely ballad, 'Someone Nice Like You'. The score also included 'I Wanna Be Rich', 'Glorious Russia', 'Meilinki Meilchick', 'Typische Deutsche', 'Nag Nag Nag', 'All-American', and 'Mumbo Jumbo'. The London run of 556 performances was followed by an almost identical stay in New York, where Anna

Quayle won a **Tony Award**, but Newley was beaten by Zero Mostel's bravura performance in *A Funny Thing Happened On The Way To The Forum*. **Sammy Davis Jnr**., who had a hit with 'What Kind Of Fool Am I?' in the US and UK, starred in a revised revival of the show on Broadway in 1978, and Newley recreated his original role in a 1989 West End production which lasted for five weeks and reportedly lost £600,000. There have been two unsuccessful film versions: in 1966 with Tony Tanner and Millicent Martin; and a 1979 'disaster' entitled *Sammy Stops The World*, with Sammy Davis Jnr. and Marian Mercer.

Stordahl, Axel

b. 8 August 1913, New York City, New York, USA, d. 30 August 1963, Encino, California, USA. Early in his career Stordahl played trumpet with the Bert Block band, but joined **Tommy Dorsey** in 1936, and was allowed to develop his arranging talents. Although he could write effective big band swingers, Stordahl was most effective with sensitive interpretations of ballad, which suited the singing style of another Dorsey employee, **Frank Sinatra**. After his stint with Dorsey, Stordahl arranged for and led studio bands on radio and television. He was also in demand by record companies, where he again encountered Sinatra. In collaboration with **Paul Weston**, Stordahl wrote the music for 'Day By Day' (lyrics by **Sammy Cahn**).

Stories

This US pop group came together in the wake of the disbandment of the **Left Banke**. Multi-instrumentalist Michael Brown was searching for a strong, harmonic unit and brought together Ian Lloyd (b. Ian Buoncocglio, Seattle, USA; vocals), Steve Love (guitar) and Bryan Medley (drums). However, after completing their self-titled debut album in 1972, founding member Michael Brown dramatically quit. Determined to soldier on, the group recruited two new members, Kenny Aaronson (bass) and Ken Bichel (piano) and in 1973 recorded *About Us*. An opportune cover of **Hot Chocolate**'s UK hit 'Brother Louie' (itself inspired from the **Richard Berry/Kingsmen** classic 'Louie Louie') brought the Stories a surprise US number 1 hit. Two further US hits followed, 'Mammy Blue' and 'If It Feels Good, Do It', before the group abruptly split up. Lloyd alone registered some further success with the minor hit 'Slip Away' in 1979.
Albums: *Stories* (1972), *About Us* (1973).

Storm

This Los Angeles-based quartet, formed in 1978 by Jeanette Chase (vocals), Lear Stevens (guitar), Ronni Hansen (bass) and David Devon (drums), played hi-tech hard-rock, characterized by Lear's **Brian May**-like guitar sound and the powerful vocals of Chase. They incorporated elements of **Queen**, **Van Halen** and **Styx** within complex, and at times classically styled arrangements. Their second album moved more towards AOR, with the inclusion of more lightweight material and even folk influences.
Albums: *Storm* (MCA 1979), *Storm* (Capitol 1983).

Storm, Gale

b. Josephine Cottle, 5 April 1922, Bloomington, Texas, USA. A dynamic singer who came to fame mainly through covering the hits of others, Storm arrived in Hollywood in 1939 after winning a 'Gateway To Hollywood' contest in her home state. She was soon working for the Universal and RKO studios, though she ultimately achieved popularity playing Margie Albright in *My Little Margie* (1952-54), a television series, credited as being the first of its kind to be screened five days a week. By 1955, she was recording for Randy Wood's **Dot** label, getting into the US Top 5 with her cover of **Smiley Lewis**'s 'I Hear You Knocking', followed by 'Teen Age Prayer', Memories Are Made Of This' (both 1955), 'Why Do Fools Fall In Love?', 'Ivory Tower' (both 1956) and 'Dark Moon' (1957). During 1956-59, she had her own 125-segment television series which is considered a precursor for *Love Boat*. By the late 70s, Storm was living in the San Fernando Valley, but still working with local theatre companies. In 1987 Storm was appearing on the west coast with two other veterans, **Betty Garrett** and Sheree North, in Terry Kingsley-Smith's comedy *Breaking Up The Act*.
Albums: *Gale Storm* (1956), *Sentimental Me* (1956), *Soft And Tenderly* (1959), *Gale Storm Sings* (1959). Compilation: *Gale Storm Hits* (1958).

Storm, Rory

b. Alan Caldwell, 1940, Liverpool, England, d. 28 September 1972. Vocalist Caldwell began performing as a member of the Texan Skiffle Group, before forming one of the city's first beat groups with Johnny Byrne (alias Johnny Guitar), Lou Walters, Ty Brian and Ritchie Starkey, later known as **Ringo Starr**. The quintet employed several names - the Raving Texans, Al Caldwell And His Jazzmen - before becoming Rory Storm And The Hurricanes in 1960, with Caldwell assuming the lead persona. They enjoyed a fervent local popularity, in part because of the singer's showmanship, and were placed third behind **Beatles** and **Gerry And The Pacemakers** in a poll undertaken by the *Mersey Beat* newspaper in 1962. Ringo's switch to the Beatles in August that year precipitated a recurrent drumming problem, and a stand-in was required on the Hurricanes' contributions to *This Is Merseybeat*. Spirited but unoriginal, the three tracks they completed revealed a barely adequate vocalist, while a later version of 'America', produced by **Brian Epstein**, failed to capture an in-concert fire. The premature death of Ty Brian and the departure of

Lou Walters ended any lingering potential, and the Hurricanes were disbanded in 1966 following their appearance at the last night of the famed Cavern club. Rory then pursued a career as a disc jockey but, increasingly prone to ill-heath, he died following an accidental overdose of alcohol and medication. His grief-stricken mother committed suicide on discovering his body.

Stormbringer

This Swiss quintet was formed in 1984 by Dave Barreto (vocals), Angi Schilero (guitar), Fabian Emmenger (keyboards), Urs Hufschmid (bass) and Laurie Chiundinelli (drums). Taking their name from **Deep Purple**'s 1974 album, they specialized in melodic power-metal, evidently based on the works of the latter group. However, it proved to be a rather non-descript tribute, and attracted few supporters. Disillusioned by the lack of media and public response, they split up soon after the album was released. Schilero went on to play with **China** for a short time, before starting his own band.
Album: *Stormbringer* (Musk 1985).

Stormtroopers Of Death

More commonly known as S.O.D., this band initially came into existence as a one-off side project for **Anthrax** musicians Scott Ian (guitar) and Charlie Benante (drums). Taking time out during the recording of Anthrax's *Spreading The Disease* in 1985, they asked **Nuclear Assault** bassist Dan Lilker and roadie Billy Milano (vocals; ex-Psychos) to join them, to make use of three day's free studio time. The result was *Speak English Or Die*, a manic fusion of thrash and hardcore styles, that had both humour and considerable crossover appeal. Milano went on to form **Method Of Destruction**, using exactly the same musical blueprint (indeed, some of Scott Ian's S.O.D. lyrics would be re-used in this project). A posthumous release, *Live From Budokan*, emerged in 1992, while sporadic reunions have also occurred over recent years.
Albums: *Speak English Or Die* (Megaforce 1985), *Live From Budokan* (Megaforce 1992).

Stormwitch

This German heavy metal quintet, who employed a strong satanic/gothic horror image, were formed by guitarist Lee Tarot (b. Harold Spengler) in 1981, together with Andy Aldrian (vocals), Steve Merchant (guitar), Ronny Pearson (bass) and Pete Lancer (drums). These were all fellow Germans, who nevertheless altered their names in order to sound American. Their first three albums offered undistinguished Euro-metal, reminiscent of **Running Wild**, and made little impact outside Germany. A lack of success saw them change direction on 1987's *The Beauty And The Beast*, adopting a more straightforward hard rock approach. All to little avail, however, with the band disintegrating shortly afterwards.
Albums: *Walpurgis Night* (Powerstation 1984), *Tales Of Terror* (Powerstation 1985), *Stronger Than Heaven* (Powerstation 1986), *The Beauty And The Beast* (Gama 1987).

Stormy Weather

Hollywood being what it was then, director Andrew Stone led an almost 'all-white' team behind the cameras for this otherwise 'all-black' musical. Never mind the routine and rather trite backstage storyline, the cast is superb. Led by **Bill 'Bojangles' Robinson** and **Lena Horne**, they romp through some magnificent musical numbers including spots by **Cab Calloway** and his Orchestra, including **Shad Collins**, **Illinois Jacquet** and **J.C. Heard**, Katharine Dunham and her dancers, and the fabulous **Nicholas Brothers**. For all this remarkable talent, however, the show is stolen by **Fats Waller**. In addition to acting in a couple of scenes he and an all-star band, including **Slam Stewart**, **Benny Carter**, the film's musical director (and the only black person in an off-camera role), and **Zutty Singleton**, the band's nominal leader, back Ada Brown for one number and are featured in two: 'Ain't Misbehavin'' and 'Moppin' And Boppin''. It was while returning east from Hollywood after appearing in this film that Waller died. Adding to this 1943 film's many marvels is the fact that at the time of its making Robinson, who was born around 1873, was long past his youthful prime.

Story Of Vernon And Irene Castle, The

All good things must come to an end, and this picture, which was released in 1939, was **Fred Astaire** and **Ginger Rogers**' last for RKO, although they reunited for MGM's *The Barkleys Of Broadway* some 10 years later. The 'Barkleys' were a product of writers **Betty Comden** and **Adolph Green**'s fertile imagination, but **Vernon** and **Irene Castle** were the famous real-life dance team who became all the rage in America during World War I. The screenplay, by Richard Sherman, **Oscar Hammerstein II**, and Dorothy Yost, traced the couple's tremendously successful career from their first meeting until Vernon's tragic death in an aircraft training accident in 1918. There was only one new song in the film's score, the charming 'Only When You're In My Arms', by **Harry Ruby**, Con Conrad and **Bert Kalmar**. The remainder consisted of carefully selected numbers from the dancing duo's heyday, and included several of their specialities such as 'Too Much Mustard (Castle Walk)', 'Rose Room (Castle Tango)', 'Little Brown Jug (Castle Polka)', 'Dengoza (Maxixe)', 'When They Were Dancing Around', 'Pretty Baby (Trés Jolie)', 'Millicent Waltz', 'Night Of Gladness', 'Missouri Waltz', and numerous other memories of bygone days. Astaire and

Rogers excelled, especially in the ballroom dancing sequences, and Edna May Oliver as the couple's agent, was also outstanding. However, the sight of Fred Astaire dying in a film was not most people's idea of fun, and the film reportedly lost some $50,000 dollars. Ever-present dance director **Hermes Pan** was still there at the end, but producer Pandro S. Berman and director Mark Sandrich, who had contributed so much to the historic series, were replaced this time by George Haight and H.C. Potter. As one legendary dance team (Fred Astaire and Ginger Rogers) portrayed another (Vernon and Irene Castle), one half of a future highly talented duo was waiting to pick up the torch. Marge Belcher (later Marge Champion), who danced so delightfully with her husband **Gower Champion** in films such as *Show Boat* (1951), had a small part in *The Story Of Vernon And Irene Castle*.

Story, Carl

b. 29 May 1916, Lenoir, Caldwell County, North Carolina, USA, d. 30 March 1995. Story followed his musical father by playing the fiddle and he was fronting his own band when only 19 years old. He played fiddle with **Bill Monroe** in 1942-43, but was then enlisted for the War. After demobilisation, he turned to guitar and reformed his own band, the Rambling Mountaineers, becoming popular on several radio stations. His records for **Mercury** were a mixture of mainstream country and bluegrass, and his many excellent musicians include Clarence 'Tater' Tate (fiddle), Bobby Thompson (banjo) and the brothers Bud and Willie Brewster (mandolin and banjo, respectively). Story's own bass-baritone was not the most natural voice for bluegrass music but he developed a countertenor which was ideally suited to the music. He co-wrote 'I Overlooked An Orchid', later a country hit for Mickey Gilley, as well as many gospel songs - 'Lights At The River', 'My Lord Keeps A Record' and 'Are You Afraid To Die?'. Many of Story's early recordings have been reissued by the German Cattle label.
Albums: *Gospel Quartet Favorites* (1958), *America's Favorite Country Gospel Artist* (1959), *Preachin', Prayin', Shoutin' and Singin'* (1959), *Everybody Will Be Happy* (1961), *Get Religion* (1961), *Gospel Revival* (1961), *Mighty Close To Heaven* (1963), *All Day Singing With Dinner On The Ground* (1964), *Good Ole Mountain Gospel Music* (1964), *There's Nothing On Earth That Heaven Can't Cure* (1965), *Sacred Songs Of Life* (1965), *Glory Hallelujah* (1966), *Songs Of Our Saviour* (1966), *From The Altar To Vietnam* (1966), *Carl Story Sings The Gospel Songs You Asked For* (1966), *The Best Of Country Music* (1967), *My Lord Keeps A Record* (1968), *Daddy Sang Bass* (1969), *Precious Memories* (1969), *'Neath The Tree Of Life* (1971), *Precious Memories* (1971), *Light At The River* (1974), *Mother's Last Word* (1975), *Mountain Music* (1976), *The Bluegrass Gospel Collection* (1976), *Live At Bill Grant's Bluegrass Festival* (1977), with the Brewster Brothers *Just*

A Rose Will Do (1977), *Lonesome Wail From The Hills* (1977), *Songs From The Blue Ridge Mountains* (1979), *Bluegrass Sound In Stereo* (1980), *The Early Days* (1980), *It's A Mighty Hard Road To Travel* (1980), *Bluegrass Time* (1980), *A Beautiful City* (1982), *Country And Bluegrass Classics* (1983).

Story, Liz

b. 1957, Southern California, USA. Fascinated and attracted to pianos from an early age Story has produced a series of excellent solo piano albums over the past decade. Her debut in 1983 with *Solid Colours* showed considerable promise, having been influenced by both Mozart and **Bill Evans**. her music became identified with the new-age music that her record company Windham Hill were pioneering at that time. She recorded two albums with Novus in the late 80s but returned to Windham Hill in 1990 having developed a fuller, chordal sound which was showcased on *Escape Of The Circus Ponies*. Her unashamedly romantic My Foolish Heart was a collection of standards and showcased excellent versions of Rogers and Hart's 'My Romance' and Ellington/Webster's 'I Got It Bad (And That Aint Good)'. The Gift was an atmospheric album of Christmas music and following the project Story re-examined her Spanish Catholic childhood and her own religious beliefs.
Albums: *Solid Colours* (1983), *Unaccountable Effect* (1985), *Part Of Fortune* (1988), *Speechless* (1989), *Escape Of The Circus Ponies* (1991), *My Foolish Heart* (1993), *The Gift* (Windham Hill 1994).

Storyteller

This UK folk-based quintet - Caroline Attard, Terry Durham, Mike Rogers (all vocals), Rodney Clark (bass/vocals) and Roger Moon (guitar/vocals) - released their debut album in 1970. The album was produced by two former members of the **Herd**, **Peter Frampton** and **Andy Bown**, the latter of whom maintained his association with the group as a songwriter and auxiliary member. Rogers was replaced by Chris Belshaw prior to the release of *Empty Pages*. A further acolyte from the Herd, drummer Henry Spinetti, contributed to this promising album, but Storyteller broke up soon after its completion. Attard, a former singer with pop duo the Other Two, later appeared, alongside Belshaw, on Bown's *Sweet William* collection.
Albums: *Storyteller* (1970), *Empty Pages* (1971).

Stott, Wally
(see **Morley, Angela**)

Stovall, Jewell 'Babe'
b. 4 October 1907, Tylertown, Mississippi, USA, d. 21 September 1974, New Orleans, Louisiana, USA. More properly regarded as a songster in the tradition of

Mance Lipscomb, Stovall emerged in the blues revival of the mid-60s. The last of 12 children in a sharecropping family, he taught himself to play the guitar, encouraged by his schoolteacher. He learned his first tune, later twice recorded as 'Maypole March', from oldest brother Myrt Holmes. During the 20s, Stovall became part of a group of musicians, congregated around an older man, Herb Quinn, that played for both black and white audiences. In the mid-30s, **Tommy Johnson** married a local girl, Rosa Youngblood, and stayed in the area for some years. Stovall, along with Arzo Youngblood, O.D. Jones and **Roosevelt Holts,** learned Johnson's 'Big Road Blues' and copied his style. Around this time, he married, and moved to Franklinton, Louisiana. In 1957, he began to play on the streets of New Orleans' French Quarter. He was recorded, twice in 1958, and once with brother Tom on mandolin in 1961, by Larry Borenstein. The tapes remaining unissued until 1988. A full session, with accompaniment from banjo and string bass, was recorded in 1964, and issued but poorly distributed by Verve. Stovall joined the folk circuit thereafter, appearing at the first five New Orleans Jazz & Heritage Festivals from 1970 to 1974.
Album: *Babe Stovall 1958 - 1964* (1990).

Stovepipe No.1
b. Sam Jones. Stovepipe was a Cincinnati-based, one-man band, playing guitar, rack harmonica, and the length of chimney that gave him his nickname, which produced booming, fruity bass lines. He recorded as early as 1924, with a repertoire of gospel, blues, ballads and white dance tunes. Jones was associated with the guitarist and harmonica player David Crockett, who accompanied Jones on recordings in 1927, and led King David's Jug Band; Jones was the band's lead singer on its 1930 recordings, and his stovepipe provided the 'jug' sound.
Album: *Stovepipe No. 1 & David Crockett* (1988).

Stowaway
Alice Faye had the two best songs, **Mack Gordon** and **Harry Revel**'s 'Goodnight My Love' and 'One Never Knows, Does One?', but it was **Shirley Temple**'s picture - clutching a pooch- that appeared on the sheet music for both numbers. Actually, she does flirt with 'Goodnight My Love' in the film - but not to any great effect. As usual, she plays her 'orphan of the storm' character, this time accidentally stowing away on a luxury yacht out of Shanghai. During the voyage, millionaire playboy Robert Young takes such a shine to her that he actually marries fellow passenger Alice Faye so that he can adopt the little darling - although the impression is given that the nuptials would probably have taken place anyway, even if the curly-headed one had not been around. Naturally, she speaks Chinese fluently, although best wishes such as 'May the bird of prosperity continue to nest in your rooftop' are purveyed in English. When the ship reaches Hong Kong she becomes involved in a kind of Oriental talent contest, taking off **Al Jolson** and **Ginger Rogers** (complete with **Fred Astaire** dummy) while singing 'You've Gotta S-M-I-L-E If You Want To Be H-A-Double P-Y'. It all ends in suitably sentimental style around the festive tree as Shirley gives forth with 'That's What I Want For Christmas' (**Irving Caesar**-Gerald Marks). Also involved in the shenanigans are Eugene Pallette, Helen Westley, Arthur Treacher, J. Edward Bromberg, Allan Lane, Astrid Allwyn, and Jayne Regan. William Conselman, Arthur Sheekam, and Nat Perrin wrote the screenplay from a story by Samuel G. Engel, and director William A Seiter kept it all moving along at good pace. Darryl F. Zanuck was in charge of production (executive producers **Earl Carroll** and Harold Wilson) and Arthur Miller photographed the film splendidly in black and white. It was released by 20th Century-Fox in 1936, and went on to become one of the year's biggest money-spinners.

Strachey, Jack
b. 25 September 1894, London, England, d. 27 May 1972, London, England. Achieved great success with the international hit 'These Foolish Things', which was composed for the London show *Spread It Abroad*. Strachey's other claim to fame is 'In Party Mood', used for many years by the BBC as the *Housewives' Choice* signature tune. Strachey liked to work in the theatre, and was also a talented writer of mood music - 'In Party Mood' was originally written for London publishers Bosworths, and was recorded by them for the sole use of radio, television and film companies. His other main works include 'Ascot Parade', 'Eros In Piccadilly', 'Knights Of Malta', 'Mayfair Parade', the revue 'New Faces', 'Overture And Beginners March', 'Pink Champagne', 'Shaftesbury Avenue', 'Song Of The May Tree', 'Starlight Cruise', 'Theatreland' and 'Up With The Curtain'. Strachey collaborated with H.D. Hedley on the musical plays *Dear Little Billy* and *Lady Luck*. His other songs never recaptured the success of 'These Foolish Things', but 'A Boy A Girl And The Moon' and 'Give Them A Waltz Tune' were modest hits.

Stradlin, Izzy, And The Ju Ju Hounds
Tired of the pressures of working with one of the world's high-profile acts, Stradlin left **Guns N'Roses** in the autumn of 1991 to work on a solo project. With himself on guitar and lead vocals, and the former **Burning Tree** rhythm section of Mark Dutton and Doni Grey, Stradlin added a Ju Ju Hounds line-up of former **Georgia Satellites** guitarist Rick Richards, ex-**Broken Homes** bassist Jimmy Ashhurst, and drummer Charlie Quintana, for the band's 1992 recording debut. Axl Rose's description of the band as

'Izzy's **Keith Richards** thing' was apt, as the influence of the **Rolling Stones** guitarist on Stradlin's songwriting and vocal style was obvious, even incorporating their shared taste for reggae with a furious cover of **Toots And the Maytals'** 'Pressure Drop'. However, far from being a mere homage, the album was excellent, and generally well-received. Subsequent live shows were electric affairs, with Stradlin appearing more relaxed, and Richards, in particular, contributing some stunning slide/lead guitar work, and vocals. Somewhat surprisingly, Stradlin made a brief return to the Guns N'Roses camp for some open-air European shows in the summer of 1993, ironically standing in for his replacement, Gilby Clarke, after the latter broke his wrist.
Album: *Izzy Stradlin And The Ju Ju Hounds* (Geffen 1992).

Straight, Charley

b. 16 January 1891, Chicago, USA, d. 21 September 1940. On leaving Wendell Phillips High School, Straight was a pianist in vaudeville before entering the band business. Together with Roy Bargy (on second piano) and a saxophonist he formed Straight's Trio aka the Imperial Three, doing unsuccessful recording tests for Victor and **Columbia** on consecutive days in November 1919. However, a month later the Emerson label released the trio's first records. In 1923, Straight and his new nine-piece band were recording for Paramount, the tracks being simultaneously issued on subsidiary labels as the Frisco Syncopators, Harmograph Dance Orchestra, Manhattan Imperial Orchestra, Broadway Melody Makers and Rendezvous Dance Orchestra. Long resident at the Rainbow Gardens in Chicago, the band was joined by **Bix Beiderbecke** in 1924. **Joseph 'Wingy' Manone** also played with Straight, and in 1926, **Miff Mole** and **Wild Bill Davison** were on a **Brunswick** session which produced 'Hobo's Prayer'/'Minor Gaff', also issued on Vocalion as by the Tennessee Tooters. Most of Straight's 1926-27 sides went out on Brunswick under his own name but some were also issued on Vocalion as the Tuxedo Orchestra. He never worked as a leader after his last Brunswick sessions of August 1928, though he is known to have recorded with the **Benson Orchestra** of Chicago, run by the agency which handled his own band. Straight was a prolific songwriter, though none of his work seems to have endured; he was also musical director of a company making piano rolls, to which he undoubtedly contributed himself. He was born, lived, worked, seldom left, and finally died, in Chicago, in September 1940.

Strait, George

b. 18 May 1952, Poteet, Texas, USA. Strait, the second son of a school teacher, was raised in Pearsall, Texas. When his father took over the family ranch, he

developed an interest in farming. Strait heard country music throughout his youth but the record which cemented his love was **Merle Haggard**'s *A Tribute To The Best Damn Fiddle Player In The World (Or, My Salute To Bob Wills)*. Strait dropped out of college to elope with his girlfriend, Norma, and then enlisted in the US Army. Whilst there, he began playing country music. Then, at university studying agriculture, he founded the Ace In The Hole band. (His 1989 US country number l, 'Ace In The Hole', was not about his band, nor did it feature them.) In 1976, he briefly recorded for Pappy Daily's D Records in Houston, one title being 'That Don't Change The Way I Feel About You'. Starting in 1977, Strait made trips to Nashville, but he was too shy to do himself justice. Disillusioned, he was considering a return to Texas but his wife urged him to keep trying. A club owner he had worked for, Erv Woolsey, was working for MCA Records: he signed him to the label and then became his manager. In 1981, Strait's first single, 'Unwound', made number 6 in the US country charts. After two further hits, 'Fool Hearted Memory', from the film in which he had a cameo role, *The Soldier*, went to number l. Strait was unsure about the recitation on 'You Look So Good In Love', but it was another chart-topper and led to him calling a racehorse, Looks Good In Love. Strait's run of 18 US country number 1 hits also included 'Does Fort Worth Ever Cross Your Mind?' (1985), 'Nobody In His Right Mind Would've Left Her' (1986), 'Am I Blue' (1987), 'Famous Last Words Of A Fool' (1988) and 'Baby's Gotten Good At Goodbye' (1989). Strait was a throwback to the 50s honkytonk sound of country music. He used twin fiddles and steel guitar and his strong, warm delivery was similar to Haggard and **Lefty Frizzell**. He made no secret of it as he recorded a fine tribute to Frizzell, 'Lefty's Gone'. Strait suffered a personal tragedy when his daughter, Jennifer, died in a car accident in 1986. Managing to compose himself, *Ocean Front Property*, became the first album to enter **Billboard**'s country music chart at number l, and it included another classic single, 'All My Ex's Live In Texas', which also demonstrated his love of western swing. The white-stetsoned Strait, who also manages to run   large farm, became one of the USA's top concert attractions, winning many awards from the Country Music Association, but it was only in 1989 that he became their Entertainer of the Year. After the impressive *Chill Of An Early Fall*, Strait scored a major commercial success with a starring role in the film *Pure Country*.
Albums: *Strait Country* (1981), *Strait From Your Heart* (1982), *Right Or Wrong* (1983), *Does Fort Worth Ever Cross Your Mind?* (1984), *Something Special* (1985), *Merry Christmas Strait To You* (1986), *No. 7* (1987), *Ocean Front Property* (1987), *If You Ain't Lovin' (You Ain't Livin')* (1988), *Beyond The Blue Neon* (1989), *Livin' It Up* (1990), *Chill Of An Early Fall* (1991), *Holding My Own* (1992), *Pure Country*

(1992, soundtrack), *Easy Come, Easy Go* (1993), *Lead On* (MCA 1994). Compilations: *Greatest Hits* (1986), *Greatest Hits, Volume 2* (1987).

Strange Creek Singers

This group was formed during the late 60s by **Mike Seeger** (b. 15 August 1933, New York City, New York, USA). The rest of the group were Lamar Grier (banjo), Tracy Schwartz, who had formerly been with Seeger's **New Lost City Ramblers**, (fiddle/guitar/banjo), Hazel Dickens (guitar), and Alice Gerrard (guitar). The name of the group is taken from Strange Creek, West Virginia, and the group played a mixture of bluegrass and old-time musical styles, both traditional and contemporary. It was very much a hobbyist's affair, given the commitments outside of the group of all concerned. Nevertheless, they toured both Europe and the USA, playing a number of major festivals in the process. Seeger is still recording, while Schwartz performs and tours with the Tracy Schwartz Cajun Trio. Dickens, in the meantime, has recorded a number of albums in her own right.
Album: *Strange Creek Singers* (Arhoolie 1968).

Strange Folk

An eccentric, knockabout UK group, which included Mike Willoughby and Mike Gavin playing a mixture of skiffle environmental protest material. They discovered the folk scene for two summers, played the festivals, drove about in an old van, made music on anything available, recorded an album, and then split up.
Album: *Unhand Me You Bearded Loon* (1988).

Strange, Pete

b. 19 December 1938, London, England. Strange is a self-taught trombonist who started his career with Eric Silk's Southern Jazz Band. He played with a variety of bands before joining Bruce Turner's Jump Band. When that folded he played semi-professionally for a number of years before joining **Keith Nichols'** **Midnite Follies Orchestra** in the late 70s. He wrote arrangements for, and played with the band of trumpeter **Digby Fairweather**. Strange also organized his own unusual five trombone band Five-A-Slide and played with **Alan Elsdon**'s band. In 1983 he moved on to **Humphrey Lyttelton**'s band for which he has written many fine arrangements as well as providing stylish trombone playing derived principally from **Lawrence Brown** and **Dicky Wells**.
Albums: with Bruce Turner *Going Places* (1963), with Humphrey Lyttelton *It Seems Like Yesterday* (1983), *Echoes Of The Duke* (1984), *Humph At The Bull's Head* (1985).

Strangeloves

Formed in 1964 in New York City, the Strangeloves consisted of songwriters and record producers Bob Feldman, Jerry Goldstein and **Richard Gottehrer**.

Although they left their mark under the name Strangeloves with only four singles and one album, their fascinating story extends both before and beyond the group's brief tenure. Feldman and Goldstein had been childhood friends in Brooklyn, New York and sang in street corner doo-wop groups. They began writing songs together and had their first success with 'Big Beat', which disc jockey **Alan Freed** used as the theme song of his television show. By 1960 they had recorded some unsuccessful singles as Bob and Jerry when they met Bronx native Gottehrer, who was also writing songs. Before long the trio's compositions were being recorded by such major artists as **Dion**, **Pat Boone**, **Freddy Cannon**, **Bobby Vee** and the Jive Five. Their greatest success came in 1963 when Feldman, Goldstein and Gottehrer wrote and produced 'My Boyfriend's Back', which became a number 1 hit for the **Angels**. By the following year, however, the landscape of pop music had changed with the arrival of the **Beatles**, and the trio had to rethink its approach. They created the Strangeloves (taking their name from the Stanley Kubrick/Peter Sellers film, *Dr. Strangelove*) and a mythical story to go with them. Wearing bizarre costumes, they said they were from the Australian outback and put on phony accents. Their names became Niles, Miles and Giles Strange.
In 1965, they released their first single, 'Love Love Love', on Swan Records, which failed to chart. They then signed to Bang Records and released 'I Want Candy', a **Bo Diddley**-like rocker that reached number 11. Three further singles charted: 'Cara-Lin' (number 39 in 1965), 'Night Time' (number 30 in 1966) and 'Hand Jive' (number 100 in 1966). Their only album also made the charts.
In addition to their recordings as the Strangeloves, Goldstein and Feldman recorded as the Kittens, as Rome and Paris, as Bobby and the Beaus and as Ezra and the Iveys. The trio produced the **McCoys**' hit 'Hang On Sloopy' and recorded as the Sheep.
Following the break-up of the Strangeloves, Goldstein worked for Uni Records, and later produced the group **War**. Feldman continued to write music and produce, working with artists such as **Jay and the Americans**, **Johnny Mathis**, Freddy Cannon and **Link Wray**. Gottehrer became a partner in **Sire Records** and a successful record producer during the punk era, producing the first two albums by the **Go-Go's**, the debut album by **Blondie** and many others. Feldman recently formed a new Strangeloves group.
Album: *I Want Candy* (1965).

Stranger

This melodic pop-rock quartet was formed in Florida, USA, during 1981 by Greg Billings (vocals), Ronnie Garvin (guitar), Tom Cardenas (bass) and John Price (drums). With the line-up stabilized, they signed to **CBS Records** the following year. Produced by Tom

Werman (of **Ted Nugent** and **Mötley Crüe** fame), their debut album was a highly impressive collection of anthemic rockers, punctuated by some fiery guitar work from Garvin. Despite its seemingly obvious commercial potential the album failed to make an impact, and little was heard of the band until a second album, a full nine years later.

Albums: *Stranger* (Epic 1982), *No Rules* (Thunderbay 1991).

Strangeways

This Scottish quartet was put together in 1985 by brothers Ian (guitar) and David Stewart (bass). With Jim Drummond (drums) and Tony Liddell (vocals), they debuted with a self-titled album in 1985. This offered a blend of Americanized, melodic AOR comparable with the work of **Boston**, **Journey** or **Kansas**. Produced by Kevin Elson (of Journey fame), it surpassed many expectations, but was ignored by the British public. Terry Brock (from Atlanta, USA) replaced Liddell on *Native Sons*, which saw the band consolidate their style and progress significantly as songwriters. It remains one of the sadly neglected albums of the pomp-rock/AOR genre. *Walk In The Fire* was not as immediate, with Brock's vocals sounding hoarse and less sophisticated. He left to audition for **Deep Purple** in 1989, but was unsuccessful. Strangeways have been inactive since.

Albums: *Strangeways* (Bonaire 1986), *Native Sons* (RCA 1987), *Walk In The Fire* (RCA 1989).

Stranglers

One of the longest-surviving groups from the British new wave explosion of the late 70s, the Stranglers first rehearsed in Guildford as early as 1974. Two years later, the full line-up emerged comprising: **Hugh Cornwell** (b. 28 August 1949, London, England; vocals/guitar), **Jean Jacques Burnel** (b. 21 February 1952, London, England; vocals/bass), Jet Black (b. Brian Duffy, 26 August 1943; drums) and Dave Greenfield (keyboards). Following a tour supporting **Patti Smith** during 1976 and some favourable press reports (the first to bring comparisons to the **Doors**), the group were signed by United Artists Records. Courting controversy from the outset, they caused a sensation and saw their date at London's Roundhouse cut short when Cornwell wore an allegedly obscene T-shirt. In February 1977 the Stranglers' debut single, '(Get A) Grip (On Yourself)' reached number 44 in the UK charts and inexplicably dropped out after only one week. According to the chart compilers, the sales were inadvertently assigned to another record, but it was too late to rectify the damage. 'Grip' saw the group at their early best. Bathed in swirling organ and backed by a throbbing beat, the single displayed Cornwell's gruff vocal to strong effect. The b-side, 'London Lady', was taken at a faster pace and revealed the first signs of an

overbearing misogynism that would later see them fall foul of critics. Initially bracketed with punk, the Stranglers owed as much to their pub-rock background and it soon emerged that they were older and more knowing than their teenage contemporaries. Nevertheless their first album, *Rattus Norvegicus*, was greeted with enthusiasm by the rock press and sold extremely well. The blasphemous lyrics of 'Hanging Around' and the gruesome imagery of 'Down In The Sewer' seemingly proved less acceptable than the women-baiting subject matter of their next single, 'Peaches'. Banned by BBC radio, the song still charted thanks to airplay offering up the b-side, 'Go Buddy Go'. Rather than bowing to the feminist criticisms levelled against them, the group subsequently compounded the felony by introducing strippers at a Battersea Park, London concert (though male strippers were also present). Journalists were treated even more cavalierly and the group were renowned for their violent antics against those who opposed them (karate black belt Burnel would attack writer John Savage after one unhelpful review). Having initially alienated the press, their work was almost universally derided thereafter. The public kept faith, however, and ensured that the Stranglers enjoyed a formidable run of hits over the next few years. The lugubrious protest, 'Something Better Change', and faster paced 'No More Heroes' both reached the UK Top 10, while 'Five Minutes' and 'Nice 'N Sleazy' each entered the Top 20. In the background there were the usual slices of bad publicity. Burnel and Black were arrested for being drunk and disorderly before charges were dropped. Cornwell was not so fortunate and found himself sentenced to three months' imprisonment on drugs charges in January 1980. Within two months of his release, the group found themselves under arrest in Nice, France, after allegedly inciting a riot. Later that year they received a heavy fine in a French court. The group's uncompromising outlaw image tended to distract from subtle changes that had been occurring in their musical repertoire. Their brave cover of the **Burt Bacharach/Hal David** standard, 'Walk On By', reached number 21 in spite of the fact that 100,000 copies of the record had already been issued *gratis* with *Black And White*. Equally effective and contrasting was the melodic 'Duchess', which displayed the Stranglers' plaintive edge to surprising effect. Their albums also revealed a new diversity from *The Raven* (with its elaborate 3-D cover) to the genuinely strange *Themeninblack*. The latter was primarily Cornwell's concept, and introduced the idea of extra-terrestrial hit-men who silence individuals that have witnessed UFO landings - an ever vengeful music press delighted in pulling it to pieces. For their next album, *La Folie*, the group were accompanied on tour by a ballet company. The album spawned the group's biggest hit, the evocative 'Golden Brown', with its startling, classical-influenced harpsichord arrangement. It reached the UK number 2 spot, resting just behind **Buck Fizz**'s 'Land Of Make Believe'. Even at their most melodic the Stranglers ran into a minor furore when it was alleged that the song was concerned with heroin consumption. Fortunately, the theme was so lyrically obscure that the accusations failed to prove convincing enough to provoke a ban. Another single from *La Folie* was the sentimental 'Strange Little Girl', which also climbed into the UK Top 10. The melodic influence continued on 'European Female', but in spite of the hits, the group's subsequent albums failed to attract serious critical attention. As unremittingly ambitious as ever, the Stranglers' 1986 album, *Dreamtime*, was inspired by Aboriginal culture and complemented their outsider image. Just as it seemed that their appeal was becoming merely cultish, they returned to their old style with a cover of the **Kinks**' 'All Day And All Of The Night'. It was enough to provide them with their first Top 10 hit for five years. Increasingly unpredictable, the group re-recorded their first single, 'Grip', which ironically fared better than the original, reaching the Top 40 in January 1989. Despite their small handful of collaborative ventures, it seemed unlikely that either Cornwell or Burnel would ever consider abandoning the group for solo careers. Perpetual derision by the press finally took its cumulative toll on the lead singer, however, and in the summer of 1990 Cornwell announced that he was quitting the group. The lacklustre *10* was written specifically for the American market, but failed to sell, in light of which Cornwell called time on his involvement. Burnel, Black and Greenfield were left with the unenviable problem of finding an experienced replacement and deciding whether to retain the name Stranglers. The band recruited vocalist Paul Roberts and guitarist John Ellis (formerly of the **Vibrators** and a veteran of Burnel's Purple Helmets side project). *Stranglers In The Night* was arguably a return to form, but still failed to recapture old glories. A second set *About Time* with the band's new line-up emerged in 1995. Although there were strong instrumental performances on tracks such as 'Golden Boy', Cornwell's absence was sorely missed as ultimately the songwriting was unadventurous.

Albums: *Rattus Norvegicus* (United Artists 1977), *No More Heroes* (United Artists 1977), *Black And White* (United Artists 1978), *Live (X Cert)* (United Artists 1979), *The Raven* (United Artists 1979), *The Meninblack* (Liberty 1981), *La Folie* (Liberty 1981), *Feline* (Epic 1983), *Aural Sculpture* (Epic 1984), *Dreamtime* (Epic 1986), *All Live And All Of The Night* (Epic 1988), *10* (Epic 1990), *Stranglers In The Night* (China 1992), *About Time* (When 1995).
Compilations: *The Collection* (Liberty 1982), *Off The Beaten Track* (Liberty 1986), *The Singles* (EMI 1989), *Greatest Hits: 1977-1990* (Epic 1990), *The Old Testament (The UA Recordings 1977- 1982)* (EMI 1992), *The Early Years 74/75/76 Rare, Live And Unreleased* (Newspeak 1992), *Saturday Night Sunday Morning* (Castle 1993), *The Stranglers And Friends: Live In Concert* (Receiver 1995, rec. 1980).
Further reading: *Inside Information*, Cornwell, Hugh (1980), *Much Ado About Nothing*, Black, Jet (1981).

Strapps

This UK hard rock quartet was formed in 1975 by Ross Stagg (vocals/guitar), Noel Scott (keyboards), Joe Read (bass) and Mick Underwood (drums), and were picked up by **EMI Records** the following year. Drawing their inspiration from **Deep Purple**, **Thin Lizzy** and **Uriah Heep**, they released four albums over a five-year period. These met with very limited success, except in Japan, where they maintained a cult following. Strapps never graduated from support act status in Europe, which was a fair summation of their true potential. The band finally disintegrated in 1979, when Underwood joined **Gillan**.
Albums: *Strapps* (EMI 1976), *Secret Damage* (EMI 1977), *Sharp Conversation* (EMI 1978), *Ball Of Fire* (EMI 1979).

Stratton-Smith, Tony

b. 1935, d. March 1987. A sports journalist on several local and national newspapers, Stratton-Smith first came to prominence writing football annuals in the 50s. A chance meeting with **Antonio Carlos Jobin** convinced him to switch careers and he emerged as a music publisher and later pop manager. A good friend of **Brian Epstein**, he was originally asked to ghost-write the **Beatles** manager's autobiography but turned down the project to complete a work on the martyr Mother Maria Skobtzova. By 1965, Stratton-Smith was back in the pop business managing **Paddy, Klaus And Gibson**, who were soon followed by **Beryl Marsden**, the **Koobas** and **Creation**. All of them under achieved, in spite of some crafty chart hyping from their desperate manager. It was not until the end of the decade that Tony found his true niche managing such 'progressive' artists as the **Nice**, **Rare Bird** and **Van Der Graaf Generator.** The new phase coincided with the launching of **Charisma Records** whose roster included **Genesis**, **Lindisfarne**, **Audience** and **Bell And Arc**, all of whom were managed by Stratton-Smith at one time. By the mid-80s, Tony wound down his interests and Charisma was sold to **Virgin Records** in 1986. The following year, this most-liked of British music business entrepreneurs died of stomach cancer. A service in his memory attracted a 'telephone directory' of musicians and music business friends.
Further reading: *Starmakers & Svengalis: The History Of British Pop Management*, Johnny Rogan.

Stratus

When former **Iron Maiden** drummer Clive Burr

joined **Praying Mantis** in 1985 the new band became known as Stratus - the remaining personnel comprising Bernie Shaw (vocals), Tino Troy (guitar), Alan Nelson (keyboards), and Chris Troy (bass). Moving away from the formularized **New Wave Of British Heavy Metal** approach, Stratus employed the extensive use of keyboards and multi-part vocal harmonies. They debuted with *Throwing Shapes*, a lacklustre pomp-rock album lacking in both in energy and quality songs. The album fared badly and the band split up soon after it was released. Bernie Shaw went on to join **Uriah Heep**.
Album: *Throwing Shapes* (Steeltrax 1985).

Strawberry Alarm Clock

Based in California and originally known as the Sixpence, the Strawberry Alarm Clock enjoyed a US number 1 in 1967 with the memorable 'Incense And Peppermints'. This euphoric slice of 'flower-power' bubblegum was initially intended as a b-side and the featured voice was that of a friend on hand during the session, rather than an official member. The group - Mark Weitz (organ), Ed King (lead guitar), Lee Freeman (rhythm guitar), Gary Lovetro (bass) and Randy Seol (drums) - added a second bassist, George Bunnell, prior to recording a debut album. The new arrival was also an accomplished songwriter, and his contributions enhanced a set which coupled hippie trappings with enchanting melodies and some imaginative instrumentation. Such features were maintained on successive Strawberry Alarm Clock albums, while 'Tomorrow' and 'Sit With The Guru' continued their reign as chart contenders. The group supplied much of the music for the film *Psyche-Out*, in which they also appeared. Gary Lovetro left the line-up prior to *Wake Up It's Tomorrow*, and several subsequent changes undermined the band's direction. *Good Morning Starshine*, released in 1969, introduced a reshaped unit where Jimmy Pitman (guitar) and Gene Gunnels (drums) joined Weitz and King, the latter of whom was relegated to bass. Although undoubtedly professional, this particular quartet lacked the innovation of its predecessor and although they remained together until 1971, the Strawberry Alarm Clock was unable to regain its early profile. Ed King later joined **Lynyrd Skynyrd**, while several of his erstwhile colleagues were reunited during the 80s for a succession of 'summer of love revisited' tours.
Albums: *Incense And Peppermints* (1967), *Wake Up It's Tomorrow* (1967), *The World In A Seashell* (1968), *Good Morning Starshine* (1969). Compilations: *The Best Of The Strawberry Alarm Clock* (1970), *Changes* (1971), *Strawberries Mean Love* (1987).

Strawberry Statement, The

A real life sit-in and subsequent riot by students at Columbia University inspired this 1970 film. The one-dimensional plot and pacing leaves no doubt as to where director Stuart Hagmann expects sympathies to fall, resulting in a feature which, while worthy, remains dull. Its graphic ending, wherein the forces of authority exact vengeance with billy-club and boot, while powerful, is cliched. The soundtrack includes contributions from **Buffy Sainte-Marie** ('The Circle Game'), **Thunderclap Newman** ('Something In The Air') and **Crosby, Stills Nash And Young** ('Our House' and 'Helpless'). The same group, without Young, supply 'Long Time Gone' while two solo **Neil Young** songs, 'The Loner' and 'Down By The River', are also featured. Such quality music ensured that the soundtrack album, released by **Reprise Records** in the UK and US, enjoyed a popularity greater than the film itself.

Strawberry Switchblade

This colourful UK duo, comprising Jill Bryson (vocals/guitar) and Rose McDowell (vocals/guitar), emerged as a product of the late 70s Glasgow, Scotland punk scene. Their appearance in polka-dotted frocks with frills, ribbons, flowers and cheap jewellery unfortunately distracted attention from their songwriting. Despite sounding like a happy pop band, their lyrics expressed sadness. The debut single in 1983, 'Trees And Flowers', was written as a result of Jill's agoraphobia. Signed to the independent Ninety-Two Happy Customers label (under the aegis of producers **David Balfe** and **Bill Drummond**), this melancholy song was given a pastoral feel by the oboe playing of former Ravishing Beauties member Kate St. John. With added studio assistance from Roddy Frame (guitar) of **Aztec Camera** and **Madness**'s Mark Bedford (bass), the single reached number 4 in the UK Independent chart. The duo found national success in late 1984 with the chirpy 'Since Yesterday' and were feted by the music media. An over-produced debut album, far removed from the simplicity of 'Trees And Flowers', entered the UK Top 25 but failed to supply the duo with the expected run of hit singles. Their last hit came in 1985 with a cover of **Dolly Parton**'s classic, 'Jolene'. Following the break-up of the group, Rose attempted to revive her career without Jill in the late 80s for a time working under the name Candy Cane, but met with little success.
Album: *Strawberry Switchblade* (Korova 1985).

Strawbs

This versatile unit was formed in 1967 by guitarists Dave Cousins (b. 7 January 1945; guitar/banjo/piano/recorder) and Tony Hooper. They initially worked as a bluegrass group, the Strawberry Hill Boys, with mandolinist Arthur Phillips, but later pursued a folk-based direction. Truncating their name to the Strawbs, the founding duo added Ron Chesterman on bass prior to the arrival of singer

Sandy Denny whose short spell in the line-up is documented in *All Our Own Work*. This endearing collection, released in the wake of Denny's success with **Fairport Convention**, features an early version of her exemplary composition, 'Who Knows Where The Time Goes'. Cousins, Hooper and Chesterman released their official debut, *Strawbs*, in 1968. This excellent selection featured several of the group's finest compositions, including 'Oh How She Changed' and 'The Battle', and was acclaimed by both folk and rock audiences. *Dragonfly*, was less well-received, prompting a realignment in the band. The original duo was joined by former **Velvet Opera** members John Ford (b. 1 July 1948, Fulham, London, England; bass/acoustic guitar) and Richard Hudson (b. Richard William Stafford Hudson, 9 May 1948, London, England; drums/guitar/sitar), plus **Rick Wakeman** (keyboards), a graduate of the Royal Academy of Music. The Strawbs embraced electric rock with *Just A Collection Of Antiques And Curios*, although critical analysis concentrated on Wakeman's contribution.

Such plaudits continued on *From The Witchwood* but the pianist grew frustrated within the group's framework and left to join **Yes**. He was replaced by Blue Weaver (b. 11 March 1947, Cardiff, South Glamorgan, Wales; guitar/autoharp/piano) from **Amen Corner**. Despite the commercial success generated by the outstanding *Grave New World*, tension within the Strawbs mounted, and in 1972, Hooper was replaced by Dave Lambert (b. 8 March 1949, Hounslow, Middlesex, England). Relations between Cousins and Hudson and Ford were also deteriorating and although 'Lay Down' gave the band its first UK Top 20 single, the jocular 'Part Of The Union', written by the bassist and drummer, became the Strawbs' most successful release. The group split following an acrimonious US tour. The departing rhythm section formed their own unit, **Hudson-Ford** while Cousins and Lambert brought in pianist John Hawken (ex-**Nashville Teens** and **Renaissance**), Chas Cronk (bass) and former **Stealers Wheel** drummer Rod Coombes. However, a series of poorly-received albums suggested the Strawbs had lost both direction and inspiration. Cousins nonetheless presided over several fluctuating line-ups and continued to record into the 80s despite a shrinking popularity. In 1989, the group reunited, including the trio of Cousins, Hooper And Hudson, for the *Don't Say Goodbye*.

Albums: *Strawbs* (1969), *Dragonfly* (1970), *Just A Collection Of Antiques And Curios* (1970), *From The Witchwood* (1971), *Grave New World* (1972), as Sandy Denny And The Strawbs *All Our Own Work* (1973), *Bursting At The Seams* (1973), *Hero And Heroine* (1974), *Ghosts* (1975), *Nomadness* (1976), *Deep Cuts* (1976), *Burning For You* (1977), *Dead Lines* (1978), *Don't Say Goodbye* (1988). Compilations: *Strawbs By Choice* (1974), *Best Of The Strawbs* (1978), *A Choice Collection* (1992), *Preserves Uncanned* (1993), *Greatest Hits Live* (Goes On Forever 1994).

Strawhead

This UK folk group comprised Chris Pollington (b. Christopher Harvey Pollington, 1948, Manchester, England; organ/vocals/recorder/guitar), Malcolm Gibbons (b. 1949, Chorley, Lancashire, England; bass drum/vocals/guitar), and Gregg G. Butler (b. 1946, Brixton, London, England; cornett, vocals, recorder, snare drum), evolving from a four piece, in 1974, who were all members of the Garstang Morris Men. They became a trio in 1976, the same year they played the Fylde Folk Festival. Strawhead represented Britain for the BBC in an international folk festival in Belgium. They were involved in a project commemorating Preston Guild in 1992. It featured the history of Preston, Lancashire in song up to 1900. The project also included a show, 'The Old Lamb And Flag', for which a book and album are planned. The group's sense of history is evident in most of their work, accentuated by their effective use of instrumentation. This was demonstrated on *Sedgemoor*, the story of Monmouth's rebellion in 1685.

Albums: *Farewell Musket, Pike And Drum* (1977), *Fortunes Of War* (1979), *Songs From The Book Of England* (1980), *Through Smoke And Fire* (1982), *Gentlemen Of Fortune* (1984), *Sedgemoor* (Dragon 1985), *Law Lies Bleeding* (Dragon 1988), *Tiffin* (Dragon 1990), *Victorian Ballads* (Dragon 1993). Compilation: *A New Vintage* (1987).

Stray Cats

With high-blown quiffs and 50s 'cat' clothes, Brian Setzer (b. 10 April 1959, New York; guitar/vocals), Lee Rocker (b. Leon Drucher, 1961; double bass) and Slim Jim Phantom (b. Jim McDonnell, 20 March 1961; drums) emerged from New York's Long Island as the most commercially viable strand of the rockabilly resurgence in the early 80s - though they had to migrate to England to find a short but intense period of chart success. Their exhilarating repertoire was dominated by the works of artists such as **Carl Perkins** and **Eddie Cochran** in addition to some stylized group originals, but their taste was sufficiently catholic to also acknowledge the influence of later rock 'n' roll practitioners such as **Creedence Clearwater Revival** and **Joe Ely**. Probably their most iconoclastic re-working, however, was their arrangement of the **Supremes**' 'You Can't Hurry Love' that appeared on the b-side of their second single, 1981's 'Rock This Town'. This shared the same UK chart position as their earlier, debut hit, 'Runaway Boys', reaching number 9. 'Stray Cat Strut', produced by **Dave Edmunds**, was a similar success - as was the trio's debut album, but 1981 closed with the comparative failure of both *Gonna Ball* and 'You Don't Believe Me' - as well as 'The Race Is On', a joint effort with Edmunds. When the group split shortly after '(She's) Sexy And 17' reached only number 29 in 1983, Rocker and Phantom amalgamated - as 'Phantom, Rocker And Slick' - with guitarist Earl Slick with whom they appeared on a star-studded televised tribute to Carl Perkins, organized by Edmunds in 1985. The band returned to the lower reaches of the charts in 1989 with 'Bring It Back Again'.

Albums: *Stray Cats* (1981), *Gonna Ball* (1981), *Built For Speed* (1982, US release - mixture of tracks from first two albums), *Rant 'N' Rave With The Stray Cats* (1983), *Blast Off* (1989), *Choo Choo Hot Fish* (1993), *Original Cool* (Essential 1994). Solo album: Brian Setzer *The Knife Feels Like Justice* (1984), *Live Nude Guitars* (1988); Phantom, Rocker And Slick *Phantom, Rocker And Slick* (1985).

Stray Dog

This blues-based US heavy metal group started life as a power-trio in 1973. Formed by the nucleus of Snuffy Walden (vocals/guitar), Alan Roberts (bass/vocals) and Leslie Sampson (b. 1950; drums), their style incorporated elements of **Grand Funk**, **Jimi Hendrix** and **Led Zeppelin**. Timmy Dulaine (guitar/vocals) and Luis Cabaza (keyboards) were added in 1974, with rather negative results. The aggression and power of the three-piece had been dissipated amongst needlessly intricate arrangements. *While You're Down There* was a major disappointment and following management and contractual problems, the band went their separate ways in 1975. Walden later reappeared as theme composer to popular US television soap opera *30 Something*.

Albums: *Stray Dog* (Manticore 1973), *While You're Down There* (Manticore 1974).

Strayhorn, Billy

b. 29 November 1915, Dayton, Ohio, USA, d. 31 May 1967. After studying music at school and privately, Strayhorn began writing music and late in 1938 submitted material to **Duke Ellington**. Early the following year Ellington recorded the first of these works, and Strayhorn was soon involved in writing original material and arrangements for the Ellington band. The association with Ellington largely excluded all other musical activity during the rest of Strayhorn's life. When he did write arrangements for and play piano with other artists, they were usually present or former Ellingtonians. Although he played piano on record dates with various Ellingtonians and on piano duets with Ellington himself, Strayhorn's greatest contribution to jazz must be the many superb compositions immortalized by the Ellington orchestra. The best known of these might well be the Ellington theme, 'Take The "A" Train', but his other masterpieces are almost all sumptuous ballads and include 'Day Dream', 'Passion Flower', 'Lotus Blossom', 'Raincheck', 'Chelsea Bridge' and 'Lush Life'. This last piece was written in 1938 but Strayhorn

withheld publication for many years, preferring to wait until a singer emerged capable of interpreting the song as he imagined it. The first recording was by **Nat 'King' Cole** in 1949 but, good as this was, Strayhorn later remarked that he had still to hear the song sung right. The intertwining of Strayhorn's writing with that of Ellington complicates a thorough understanding of his importance, and **Brian Priestley** is one of several musicians/writers who have indicated the value of intensive research in this area. When Strayhorn was hospitalized in 1967, he continued working almost to the end on his final composition, 'Blood Count'. A few months after his death in May 1967, Ellington recorded a tribute album of Strayhorn compositions, *And His Mother Called Him Bill*.

Selected albums: *Ellington-Strayhorn Duets* (1950), by Duke Ellington *Historically Speaking, The Duke* (1956), by Ellington *Such Sweet Thunder* (1956-57), *Cue For Saxophones* (Affinity 1958), *Billy Strayhorn And The Paris String Quartet* (1961), by Ellington *Far East Suite* (1966), *The Billy Strayhorn Project* (Stash 1991), *Lush Life* (Red Baron 1992). Compilation: by Ellington *The Blanton-Webster Band* (1940-42).

Street, Mel

b. King Malachi Street, 21 October 1933, near Grundy, West Virginia, USA, d. 12 October 1978. Street began performing on local radio in the 50s and then he moved to Niagara Falls and New York, making his living on building sites. He later wrote and recorded the song, 'The High Line Man', about working on radio station masts. He returned to West Virginia and worked in car repairs. He also played clubs and honky tonks, and he recorded his song, 'Borrowed Angel', for a small label in 1970. Two years later it was reissued and became a US country hit. He had further hits with 'Lovin' On Back Streets' and 'I Met A Friend Of Yours Today'. Street became an alcoholic and, beset by personal problems, he shot himself on his 45th birthday in Hendersonville, Tennessee. His US single at the time was 'Just Hangin' On'. **George Jones** sang 'Amazing Grace' at his funeral. Since his death, he has had country hits with 'The One Thing My Lady Never Puts In Words' and, a duet with Sandy Powell, 'Slip Away'. In 1981, his television-advertised, *Mel Street's Greatest Hits*, sold 400,000 copies.

Albums: *Borrowed Time* (1972), *Mel Street* (1973), *Two Way Street* (1974), *Smokey Mountain Memories* (1975), *Country Colours* (1976), *Mel Street* (1977, Polydor release), *Mel Street* (1978, Mercury release), *Country Soul* (1978). Compilations: *Greatest Hits* (1976), *The Very Best Of Mel Street* (1980), *The Many Moods Of Mel Street* (1980).

Streetband

This UK rock band of the late 70s were notable mainly for the membership of **Paul Young** (b. 17 January 1956, Luton, Bedfordshire, England). Having played in

local group, Kat Kool And The Kool Kats, Young formed Streetband in 1977 with John Gifford (guitar/vocals), Mick Pearl (bass/vocals), Roger Kelly (guitar) and Vince Chaulk (drums, ex-Mr Big, whose biggest hit was 'Romeo' in 1977). The group's R&B-tinged music brought a recording deal with Logo Records. The debut album was produced by Chas Jankel, **Ian Dury**'s songwriting partner. The first single, 'Hold On' had a novelty b-side, 'Toast' which gained airplay and became a Top 20 hit in 1978. Streetband returned to their hard-rocking approach for later singles and a second album which included **Jools Holland** playing keyboards. Lack of further commercial success precipitated the break-up of the group in 1979 when Young, Gifford and Pearl formed the soul group **Q-Tips**.
Albums: *London* (1979), *Dilemma* (1979).

Streets

This melodic USA heavy rock quartet was formed in 1982 by ex-**Kansas** vocalist Steve Walsh and Mike Slamer (guitar; ex-**City Boy**). Drafting in Billy Greer (bass) and Tim Gehrt (drums), they adopted a much more straightforward AOR approach than their former employers, concentrating on infectious hooklines and memorable choruses, rather than intricate keyboard fills and complex arrangements. Their self-titled debut was received very favourably by the music media, but failed to win over a large audience, partly due to poor promotion. *Crimes In Mind* saw the band maturing as songwriters, but **Atlantic Records** were guilty of indifference once more, and the album failed to take off. Disillusioned, Streets broke up in 1986, with Walsh and Greer joining the re-vamped Kansas.
Albums: *Streets* (Atlantic 1983), *Crimes In Mind* (Atlantic 1985).

Streetwalkers

After **Family**'s farewell tour in autumn 1973, vocalist Roger Chapman and guitarist Charles Whitney, collaborated on *Streetwalkers* with help from guitarist Bob Tench (from the **Jeff Beck** Group) and members of **King Crimson**. These were among the *ad hoc* UK aggregation that backed Chapman and Whitney for a brief promotional tour - and Tench became the nucleus of a more fixed set-up when the pair recommenced operations as 'Streetwalkers'. With Jon Plotel (bass, ex-Casablanca) and Nicko McBain (drums), the group recorded *Downtown Flyers* which, like its predecessor, was far less self-consciously 'weird' than Family's output had been and, with Chapman's vibrato moderated, drew much inspiration from R&B and soul stylings. A popular attraction on the college circuit - especially in Germany - the quartet's *Red Card* reached the UK Top 20 but this triumph was dampened by internal difficulties. In July 1976, Plotel and Nicko were replaced by Michael Feat and David Dowie.

Augmented by Brian Johnson on keyboards, Streetwalkers released the undistinguished *Vicious But Fair* before bowing out with a concert album in late 1977. However, the group survived in spirit via Chapman's subsequent stage performances with a new band, his three solo albums and his characteristically agonized singing in a television commercial for Brutus jeans.
Albums: *Streetwalkers* (1974), *Downtown Flyers* (1975), *Red Card* (1976), *Vicious But Fair* (1977), *Live* (1977).

Strehli, Angela

b. 22 November 1945, Lubbock, Texas, USA. A lynch-pin in the Austin blues scene from its inception in the 70s, Strehli had hung out with Lubbockites **Joe Ely** and **Jimmie Dale Gilmore** and learned harmonica and bass before becoming a singer. As the Texas representative of the YWCA, she visited Chicago in 1966 and spent her free time visiting blues clubs to see **Muddy Waters**, **Howlin' Wolf** and **Buddy Guy**. In her final years at university, she formed the Fabulous Rockets with Lewis Cowdrey; an attempt to establish the band in California failed after a few months. Returning to Austin, she sang backup for James Polk And The Brothers and sat in with Storm, formed by Cowdrey and **Jimmie Vaughan**. In 1972 she formed Southern Feeling with W.C. Clark and Denny Freeman. Three years later she took a job as stage manager and sound technician for the Antone's club. Strehli went back to full-time singing in 1982 and in 1986 recorded *Stranger Blues*, an EP that inaugurated the Antones label. *Soul Shake* followed a year later. In 1992, along with **Marcia Ball** and **Lou Ann Barton**, she recorded *Dreams Come True*, an album of original songs along with **Ike Turner**'s 'A Fool In Love' and 'I Idolize You' and **Etta James**' 'Something's Got A Hold On Me'. In 1990, Strehli dissolved her band and moved to San Francisco. *Blonde And Blue* combined **Little Walter** and **Elmore James** songs with her own material and a duet with **Don Covay** on 'Um, Um, Um, Um, Um, Um'.
Albums: *Soul Shake* (Antone's 1987), with Marcia Ball, Lou Ann Barton *Dreams Come True* (Antone's 1990), *Blonde And Blue* (Rounder 1994). Compilation: *Antone's Women* (Antone's 1992).

Streisand, Barbra

b. 24 April 1942, New York City, New York, USA. A celebrated actress, singer, and film producer, from childhood Streisand was eager to make a career in show business, happily singing and 'playacting' for neighbours in Brooklyn, where she was born and raised. At the age of 15, she had a trial run with a theatrical company in upstate New York and by 1959, the year she graduated, was convinced that she could make a success of her chosen career. She still sang for fun, but was set on being a stage actress. The lack of opportunities in straight plays drove her to try singing instead and she entered and won a talent contest at The Lion, a gay bar in Greenwich Village. The prize was a booking at the club and this was followed by more club work, including an engagement at the Bon Soir which was later extended and established her as a fast-rising new singer. Appearances in Off-Broadway revues followed, in which she acted and sang. Towards the end of 1961 she was cast in *I Can Get It For You Wholesale*, a musical play with songs by **Harold Rome**. The show was only moderately successful but Streisand's notices were excellent (as were those of another newcomer, Elliott Gould), and she regularly stopped the show with 'Miss Marmelstein'. She was invited to appear on an 'original cast' recording of the show, which was followed by another record session, to make an album of Rome's *Pins And Needles*, a show he had written 25 years earlier. The records and her Bon Soir appearances brought a television date, and in 1962, on the strength of these, she made her first album for **Columbia Records**. With arrangements by Peter Matz, who was also responsible for the charts used by **Noël Coward** at his 1955 Las Vegas appearance, the songs included 'Cry Me A River', 'Happy Days Are Here Again' and 'Who's Afraid Of The Big, Bad Wolf?'. Within two weeks of its release in February 1963, Streisand was the top-selling female vocalist in the USA. Two Grammy Awards followed, for Best Album and Best Female Vocalist (for 'Happy Days Are Here Again'). Streisand's career was now unstoppable.

She had more successful club appearances in 1963 and released another strong album, and then opened for **Liberace** at Las Vegas, and appeared at Los Angeles's Coconut Grove and the Hollywood Bowl. That same remarkable year she married Elliott Gould, and she was engaged to appear in the Broadway show *Funny Girl*. Based upon the life of **Fanny Brice**, *Funny Girl* had a troubled pre-production history, but once it opened it proved to have all the qualities its principal producer, Ray Stark, (who had nurtured the show for 10 years), believed it to have. **Jule Styne** and **Bob Merrill** wrote the score, which included amongst which were 'People' and 'Don't Rain On My Parade', the show was a massive success, running for 1,348 performances and giving Streisand cover stories in *Time* and *Life* magazines. Early in 1966 Streisand opened *Funny Girl* in London but the show's run was curtailed when she became pregnant. During the mid-60s she starred in a succession of popular and award-winning television spectaculars. Albums of the music from these shows were big-sellers and one included her first composition, 'Ma Premiere Chanson'. In 1967, she went to Hollywood to make the film version of *Funny Girl*, the original Styne-Merrill score being extended by the addition of some of the songs Fanny Brice had performed during her own Broadway career. These included 'Second-Hand Rose' and 'My Man'. In addition to *Funny Girl*, Streisand's film career included roles in **Hello, Dolly!** and **On A Clear Day You Can See Forever**. The film of *Funny Girl* (1968) was a hit, with Streisand winning one of two Oscars awarded that year for Best Actress (the other winner was Katharine Hepburn).

By the time she came to the set to make her second Hollywood film, *Hello, Dolly!* (1969), Streisand had developed an unenviable reputation as a meddlesome perfectionist who wanted, and usually succeeded in obtaining, control over every aspect of the films in which she appeared. Although in her later films, especially those which she produced, her demands seemed increasingly like self-indulgence, her perfectionism worked for her on the many albums and stage appearances which followed throughout the 70s. This next decade saw changes in Streisand's public persona and also in the films she worked on. Developing her childhood ambitions to act, she turned more and more to straight acting roles, leaving the songs for her record albums and television shows. Among her films of the 70s were *The Owl And The Pussycat* (1970), *What's Up, Doc?* (1972), *The Way We Were* (1973), **Funny Lady** (1975), a sequel to *Funny Girl*, and *A Star Is Born* (1976). For the latter she co-wrote (with **Paul Williams**) a song, 'Evergreen', which won an Oscar as Best Song. Streisand continued to make well-conceived and perfectly executed albums, most of which sold in large numbers. She even recorded a set of the more popular songs written by classical composers such as Debussy and Schumann.

Although her albums continued to attract favourable reviews and sell well, her films became open season for critics and were markedly less popular with fans. The shift became most noticeable after *A Star Is Born* was released and its damaging self-indulgence was apparent to all. Nevertheless, the film won admirers and several Golden Globe Awards. She had an unexpected number 1 hit in 1978 with 'You Don't Bring Me Flowers', a duet with **Neil Diamond**, and she also shared the microphone with **Donna Summer** on 'Enough Is Enough', a disco number which reached Platinum, and with **Barry Gibb** on the album, *Guilty*. Her film career continued into the early 80s with *All Night Long* (1981) and *Yentl*, (1983) which she co-produced and directed. By the mid-80s Streisand's career appeared to be on cruise. However, she starred in and wrote the music for *Nuts* (1987), a film which received mixed reviews. Growing concern for ecological matters revealed themselves in public statements and on such occasions as the recording of her 1986 video/album, *One Voice*. In 1991 she was criticized for another directorial assignment on *Prince Of Tides*. As a performer, Streisand was one of the greatest showbiz phenomenons of the 60s. Her wide vocal range and a voice which unusually blends sweetness with strength, helps make Streisand one of the outstanding dramatic singers in popular music. Her insistence upon perfection has meant that her many records are exemplars for other singers. Her 1991 movie, *Prince Of Tides*, which she also directed, was nominated for seven Oscars. Two years later, she was being talked of as a close confidante and advisor to the newly elected US President Clinton, although she still found the time to return - on record at least - to where it all started, when she released *Back To Broadway*. In November 1993 it was reported that the singer had given away her £10 million Californian estate 'in an attempt to save the earth'. The 26 acres of landscaped gardens with six houses and three swimming pools would become the Barbra Streisand Centre For Conservancy Studies. She recouped the money early in January 1994, by giving two 90-minute concerts at MGM's new Grand Hotel and theme park in Las Vegas for a reported fee of £13 million. Later in the year she received mixed critical reviews for the four British concerts she gave at Wembley Arena in the course of a world tour. Her share of the box-office receipts - with tickets at an all-time high of £260 - and expensive merchandise is reported to have been in the region of £5 million.

Selected albums: *The Barbra Streisand Album* (1962), *The Second Barbra Streisand Album* (1963), *Barbra Streisand: The Third Album* (1964), *Funny Girl* (1964), *People* (1964), *My Name Is Barbra* (1965), *Color Me Barbra* (1966), *Je M'Appelle Barbra* (1967), *What About Today?* (1969), *Stoney End* (1970), *Greatest Hits* (1970), *Barbra Joan Streisand* (1971), *Classical Barbra* (1974), *Butterfly* (1975), *Lazy Afternoon* (1975), *Streisand Superman* (1977), *Songbird* (1978), *Wet* (1979), *Guilty* (1980), *Memories* (1981), *Yentl* (1983, soundtrack), *Emotion* (1984), *The Broadway Album* (1985), *One Voice* (1986), *Nuts: Original Motion Picture Soundtrack* (1987), *Til I Loved You* (1988), *A Collection: Greatest Hits...And More* (1989), *Just For The Record...* (1991), *The Prince Of Tides* (1991, film soundtrack), *Butterfly* (1992), *Back To Broadway* (1993), *The Concert* (1994).

Further reading: *Streisand: The Woman and the Legend*, James Spada. *Barbra Streisand, The Woman, The Myth, The Music*, Shawn Considine. *Barbra: An Actress Who Sings Volume 1*, James Kimbrell

Videos: *Barbra - The Concert* (1994), *One Voice* (1994).

Further reading: *Barbra Streisand*, Eldred, Patricia Mulrooney (1975), *On Stage Barbra Streisand*, Keenan, Debra (1976), *Streisand: Unauthorized Biography*, Jordan, Rene (1976), *The Films Of Barbra Streisand*, Castell, David (1977), *Barbra Streisand: An Illustrated Biography*, Brady, Frank (1979), *Barbra: A Biography Of Barbra Streisand*, Zec, Donald (1982), *Streisand Through The Lens*, Teti, Frank (1982), *Streisand: The Woman And The Legend*, Spada, James (1983), *Barbra Streisand, The Woman, The Myth, The Music*, Considine, Shawn (1986).

Stress Records

A UK-based division of DMC Ltd, who are also responsible for the early 90s magazines *Mixmag* and *Mixmag Update*, and artist management. DMC was originally set up as a DJ club, providing exclusive megamix albums in the 80s for DJs. It was an operation that evolved into releasing remix albums every month. In the process DMC gave a lot of young producers a break as these reached the ears of A&R staff. They thus discovered the likes of **Sasha**, who like many artists made his first recordings on DMC. Stress grew out of a younger element, like Dave Seaman (half of **Brothers In Rhythm**), getting involved in DMC. After entering the DMC chamionships he was invited over to New York to play at the New Music Seminar and was offerred a job in the late 80s. Rather than merely 'passing on' their trained-up production discoveries to the major labels and talent scouts, Stress was inaugurated to provide them with an in-house outlet, should they prefer it. Nick Gordon Brown and Seaman remain the prime movers behind Stress, which exists as a separate, independent entity within the DMC umbrella, having the final say on A&R decisions. Records like Rusty (David Syon and Andrea Gemelotto)'s 'Everything's Gonna Change', **Hustlers Convention**'s *Groovers Delight* EP and Last Rhythm's 'Last Rhythm (Sure Is Pure '92 remix) established the label. Some of their bigger hits over the 1993/1994 period included Chris & James' 'Club For Life', Reefa's 'Inner Fantasy', Bubbleman's 'Theme' and Brothers In Rhythm's 'Forever And A Day'. The same duo also remixed Voices Of 6th Avenue's 'Call Him Up' for the label. In 1994 Reefa! contributed 'Inner Fantasy'/'Get Up Stand Up', while other releases included Masi's 'Apache', Mindwarp's 'Too' (the Boston, USA-based crew's follow-up to 'One') and Coyote's 'Jekyll & Hyde'.

Selected album: Various: *DJ Culture* (Stress 1993), *Club Culture* (Stress 1994).

Stressball

New Orleans sludge metal specialists, formed in 1989, whose name is derived from drummer and part-time chef Joe Fazzio's own 'stressball' - 'it takes batteries and it's supposed to be like a paper-weight or something, and when you get pissed off, you throw it at the wall and it sounds like glass breaking'. The rest of the group comprises Lennon Laviolette (guitar), Steven Gaille (vocals) and Eddy Dupuy (bass). Fazzio is also a good friend of **Pantera**'s Phil Anselmo, and the two play together in the side-band, Both Legs Broken (along with Kirk Windstein from **Crowbar** and Mark Schultz from **Eyehategod**). Stressball was inaugurated while Fazzio and friends practised at a 100 year old warehouse in the centre of New Orleans, where bands such as Graveyard Rodeo (who practically invented the slow, torturous sound associated with the scene), Eyehategod and stablemates Crowbar also emerged. Fazzio himself had previously played in a band called

Crawlspace with Mike Williams from Eyehategod, with whom they have toured widely.
Album: *Stressball* (Pavement 1993).

Stretch

This UK rock band first took shape in 1974, when singer Dave Perry (who more frequently used the alias Elmer Gantry, drawn from Sinclair Lewis' novel of the same title), former **Curved Air** members Kirby Gregory (guitar) and Jim Russell (drums), and session player Steve Emery (bass) put the act together. Perry had previously fronted Elmer Gantry's Velvet Opera between 1967 and 1968 and, in 1973, the band had played as 'bogus' **Fleetwood Mac** impersonators (they were sent to the USA in this capacity by Fleetwood Mac manager Clifford Davis). Stretch recorded three albums between 1975 and 1977 (with Jeff Rich replacing Russell in 1976), all of these recalling a classic, hard-edged British blues-rock style, dominated by Gantry's excellent vocal contributions. The first of these albums included the UK chart hit, 'Why Did You Do It?'. However, the birth of punk deprived Stretch of their initial momentum and they never reaped any sustained commercial harvest for their efforts. With three albums behind them Gantry dissolved the band in 1977. Without him there was little abiding interest and a follow-up album was ignored. Gantry shortly reappeared on **Cozy Powell**'s 1981 album, *Tilt*.
Albums: *Elmer Gantry's Velvet Opera* (Anchor 1968), *Elastique* (Anchor 1975), *You Can't Beat Your Brain For Entertainment* (Anchor 1976), *Life Blood* (Anchor 1977), *Forget The Past* (Anchor 1978).

Strickland, Napoleon

b. c.1920, probably Como, Mississippi, USA. Self-described as 'the fife-blowingest man in the state of Mississippi', Strickland also played harmonica, guitar and the one-stringed 'diddley-bow'. Not regarded as a good singer, he was nevertheless highly esteemed by the community around Como for the intensity of his commitment and the force of his playing. His piercing fife, accompanied by the thundering syncopation of the bass and snare drums, was central to the success of the picnics that were the chief community entertainment in the summer months.
Albums: *Traveling Through The Jungle* (1974), *Afro-American Music From Tate And Panola Counties, Mississippi* (1978).

Stricklin, Al

b. Alton Meeks Stricklin, 29 January 1908, Antioch, Johnson County, Texas, USA, d. 15 October 1986, Cleburne, Texas, USA. He started to play piano at the age of five so that he could accompany his fiddle playing father. By the age of 12, he was a competent pianist. He worked his way through college by playing for functions and by giving piano lessons. He left college because of the Depression, in order to help with the family finances. He found employment as staff pianist with KFJZ Fort Worth, and met **Bob Wills** for the first time when he auditioned Wills and **Milton Brown** for the station. In 1933, he lost his job at KFJZ and for a time worked as a teacher but, in 1935, he returned to the station playing on a daily programme with the High Flyers. Soon after, when Bob Wills formed his Texas Playboys, he asked Stricklin to play piano for him. He stayed with Wills for seven years, during which time he played on some of Wills' most respected recordings. In the late 40s, he worked with several bands even, on occasions, rejoining Wills. He played on the session made at **Merle Haggard**'s home in 1971 and on the famous last recordings made by Wills in December 1973. In the late 70s, when **Leon McAuliffe** fronted a line-up of ex-Texas Playboys, Stricklin played and recorded with them. He recorded a solo album and also left a graphic account of his years with Wills in a book. Stricklin was undoubtedly a founder of western swing piano playing and highly respected by experts on the genre.
Further reading: *My Years With Bob Wills*, Al Stricklin.

Strictly Ballroom

Made in Australia, this film was the hit of the 1992 Cannes Festival, and is probably the most enjoyable dance film to emerge since **John Travolta** strutted his extravagant stuff in *Saturday Night Fever* (1977). It was the brainchild of Baz Luhrmann who is better known 'down under' as the wunderkind of the Sydney Opera House. As director and screenwriter (with Craig Pearce), he presented the original 30 minute, and then 50 minute versions on stage before reshaping the concept for the screen. In this form it tells the story of Scott Hastings (Paul Mercurio) who has been preparing for the Australian Ballroom Dance Federation Championships since he was a young child. Having reached the semi-finals, he blows his chances by breaking the rules and improvising his own steps on the dance floor. This infuriates Scott's partner, Liz Holt (Gia Carides), and she walks away. Also fuming are his domineering mother, Shirley, and coach, Les Kendall (Pat Thompson and Peter Whitford), who together run the local dance school, and the powerful Federation President, Barry Fife (Bill Hunter). Out in the cold, Scott finds a new partner in Fran (Tara Morice), an unattractive beginner, and together, with the help of Fran's Spanish father and grandmother, they perfect a flamenco routine for the Pan-Pacific Grand Prix. As expected, it proves anathema to the judges, but the audience love the sequence and go wild, joining the couple - who by now are preparing to dance off into the sunset together - on the floor for a spectacular celebration. It is not quite as simple as that - there are darker aspects involving Scott's father, Doug (Barry Otto), who, it turns out, was quite an innovative dancer himself in the old days, a fact which led to his wife Shirley turning to the cosy safety of Les Kendall. Also among the cast were John Hannan, Sonia Kruger, Kris McQuade, Pip Munshin, Leonie Page, Antonio Vargas (as Fran's father, Rico), Armonia Benedito, Jack Webster, and Lauren Hewett. John 'Cha Cha' O'Connell was the choreographer and the music score was composed by musical director David Hirschfelder. The songs used ranged from 'Perhaps, Perhaps, Perhaps (Quizas, Quizas, Quizas)' (Osvaldo Farres), 'La Cumparsita' (Rodriguez Ravern), 'Espana Carne' (Pascual Narro-Marquina), and 'Rhumba De Burros' (Baz Luhrmann), to 'Time After Time' (**Cyndi Lauper**), 'Happy Feet' (**Jack Yellen-Milton Ager**), and 'Love Is In The Air' (Harry Vanda-George Young). It was beautifully photographed in Eastman Color by Steve Mason, and produced by Tristram Maill. This immensely likeable, charming and amusing film, with fine performances, especially from Scott Hastings, principal dancer and choreographer with the Sydney Dance Company, proved to be a box-office winner, not only in Australia, but worldwide.

Strictly Rhythm
Manhattan, New York, house stable which, whilst still remaining a cult taste in their native country, has become the most popular of all foreign labels in the UK. The Strictly Rhythm boss is one Mark Finkelstein, who established the company in 1989. An unlikely source of cult idolatory, the be-suited Finkelstein has an MSC in Aeronautics and an MBA from Harvard in finance. 'Everybody's heard of the label but few can name three acts on it. If you ask me if I'm happy with that then I'd have to say yes, because at the end of it the philosophy and vision are mine. But I'd be equally happy if one act came along and blew that away'. He also insists on a blanket ban on sampling, pointing out that 'it's just theft of somebody else's idea, when we should be creating our own'. Finkelstein originally entered the music business by taking over Spring Records for three years (home to various earlier dance artists like Isis - or **Todd Terry** in disguise. He recruited Gladys Pizarro from the latter as his A&R right hand. The label went on to score enormous cult success with their weekly releases (accelerating to two a week in 1993), with each pressed on superior quality Europadisc vinyl. Records like Logic's 'The Warning', Underground Solution's 'Luv Dancing', Slam Jam's 'Tech Nine' (Todd Terry), the Untouchables' debut EP (**Kenny 'Dope' Gonzalez**) and others set the tone. Pizarro left in 1991, joining **Nervous**, her role taken by **DJ Pierre** and George Morel (ex-2 In A Room). However, when Pierre elected to return to his own recording projects, Pizarro swtiched back. The change did little to interrupt the flow of hits, with Photon Inc's 'Generate Power', Simone's 'My Family Depends On Me' and New Jersey duo William Jennings and Eddie

Lee Lewis' Aly-Us project (whose 'Follow Me' became a massive club staple). It is important not to underestimate the role DJ Pierre played in Strictly Rhythm's development. As an artist and musician Pierre offerred 'Annihilating Rhythm' by Darkman, the aforementioned 'Generate Power' by Photon Inc. (with **Roy Davis Jnr**), 'Love And Happiness' by Joint Venture alongside Morel, and dozens more. Gonzalez continued his ascendency by providing material like Total Ka-Os' 'My Love'. **Erick 'More' Morillo**, too, was just as prolific - claiming to have released over 25 records on Strictly Rhythm during 1993 alone (the best of which included the Smooth Touch sequence). Morillo was also behind 'I Like To Move It' (Reel 2 Real), which, like **Barbara Tucker**'s 'Beautiful People', was licensed to **Positiva** in the UK. 1993 saw the label set up a rap/hip hop subsidiary, Phat Wax. Widely revered, and often imitated, Strictly Rhythm has enjoyed a longevity in musical fashion which defies the short shelf-life usually afforded house styles. One of the few UK based acts on the stable was Caucasian Boy ('Northern Lights'), but generally it was a one-way import deal for British dance fans. In 1994 Hardheads' 'New York Express' broke big for the label, with its escalating BPM count once again sucking the dance fraternity in. Others from more recent times include 2 Direct (Anthony Acid and 'Brutal' Bill Marquez)'s 'Get Down'/'Free' and Morel's Grooves Part 5, with 'I Feel It' (Morel with vocalist Zhana Saunders). But this is merely the tip of the iceberg. It would be possible to spend an entire encyclopedia merely documenting the Stictly Rhythm discography. They remain the connoiseur's house label, with its name as close to a guarantee of quality as the music comes.

Strictly Underground
Record label based in Romford, Essex, England, and run by Mark Ryder, who records on the imprint as Fantasy UFO. Under the latter title his first single was 'Fantasy' for **XL**, which just missed the Top 40. The second, 'Mind Body And Soul', with a hip house rap from Jay Groove (b. London), and vocals from Stella Mac, was lincensed to East West via Strictly Underground. Ryder liased with DJ Hype for 1991's Sound Clash record, 'The Burial'. Their other major artists include/included M-D-Emm, Warrior, Tigers In Space and Sonic Experience.

Strife
Blues-based British hard rock trio who formed in 1972. The band - John Reid (vocals/guitar), Gordon Rowley (bass/vocals) and David Williams (drums/vocals) - gigged incessantly and earned a reputation as a perennial support act, but lacked the individuality to reach headline status. Strife built up a small but loyal cult following during the mid-70s, with their honest, no-frills, good-time rock 'n' roll. They released two

average rock albums, with *Back To Thunder* featuring **Don Airey** on keyboards and Paul Ellison in place of Williams on drums. After one last stab at success with the EP, *School*, the band gave up in 1979. Rowley went on to form **Nightwing**.

Albums: *Rush* (Chrysalis 1975), *Back To Thunder* (Gull 1978).

Strike Up The Band

Regarded by some as having been ahead of its time, this somewhat bitter satirical spoof on war, big business, and politics in America at the time of the Depression, proved too much for the public to take first time round. In 1927, it closed during out-of-town tryouts, and only made Broadway in a revised and toned-down version some three years later. By the time the show opened at the Times Square Theatre on 14 January 1930, **George S. Kaufman** and his acerbic book about a 'cheese tariff' war between the US and the Swiss, had been replaced by Morrie Ryskind and a sweeter plot about chocolate. Nevertheless, it was still a radical departure from the usual 'moon and June' style of musical comedy, and paved the way for other more socially relevant shows such as *Of Thee I Sing*, *I'd Rather Be Right*, and *Let 'Em Eat Cake*. The comedy team of Bobby Clark and Paul McCullough led the cast, along with Blanche Ring, Jerry Goff, Dudley Clements, and Doris Carson. **George** and **Ira Gershwin** wrote the score which contained at least three enduring items: the rousing title song; 'Soon', which has received many memorable readings over the years, including one by **Ella Fitzgerald** on her tribute album to the composers; and 'I've Got A Crush On You', affectionately remembered in 1993 by **Frank Sinatra** and **Barbra Streisand** on the album *Duets*. The rest of the numbers, which included 'Madamoiselle In New Rochelle', 'Hanging Around With You', 'If I Became President', 'I Mean To Say', and the highly amusing 'A Typical Self-Made American', were played in fine style by **Red Nichols** Orchestra, whose personnel included **Glenn Miller**, **Gene Krupa**, **Jimmy Dorsey**, **Jack Teagarden** and **Benny Goodman**. Given the show's innovative and original approach, a run of 191 performances was probably as much as the producers could have expected.

Strike Up The Band (Film Musical)

(see **Babes In Arms** Film Musical)

Striker

This versatile hard rock quartet was formed in 1977 by the multi-talented Rick Randle (vocals, keyboards, guitar). Enlisting the services of Scott Roseburg (vocals/bass/guitar), Rick Ramirez (guitar) and Rick Taylor (drums/vocals), Striker signed with **Arista Records** the following year. Their music incorporated

rock, funk, boogie, blues and soul influences, and although this eclecticism avoided press pigeon-holing, it also served to severely limit their potential audience. A debut album featured impressive guitar and vocal harmonies, but ultimately lacked identity because of the varied styles employed. Failing to win an appreciative audience, Randle dissolved the band in 1979. Rick Ramirez went on to join Bruzer.

Album: *Striker* (Arista 1978).

String Trio Of New York

Formed in October 1977 by violinist **Billy Bang**, James Emery (guitar) and John Lindberg (bass), this was an unlikely proposition: three members of the New York *avant garde*, associates of **Anthony Braxton**, **Frank Lowe** and **Leroy Jenkins**, playing cafe music that ransacked gypsy music, blues, jazz and ragtime for inspiration. During the solos the players would get as 'out' as anything to be heard in New York, but their tunes provided entry points for the listener. They proved to be very popular and recorded prolifically. In May 1986 Bang was replaced by violinist Charles Burnham, a former accomplice of **James Blood Ulmer**. They had not lost their invention or swing, as was proved by 1990's *Ascendant*.

Albums: *String Trio Of New York* (1978), *Area Code 212* (1980), *Common Goal* (1982), *Rebirth Of A Feeling* (1984), *Natural Balance* (1987), *Ascendant* (1990).

String-a-Longs

Keith McCormack (vocals/guitar), Richard Stevens (guitar), James Torres (guitar), Aubrey Lee de Cordova (bass) and Don Allen (drums) were a Texan high school group with a bias towards instrumentals. Encouraged by audience reaction to their act at local dances and parties, they auditioned for **Norman Petty** in his studio in Clovis, New Mexico. Impressed, Petty collaborated with Stephens and Torres on the writing of 1961's 'Wheels', the String-a-Longs first single and only hit. Inconsequential but maddeningly catchy, it entered international Top 10s, but lack of further similar success brought the group back to parochial engagements and impending disbandment within two years.

Album: *Pick-A-Hit Featuring 'Wheels'* (Warwick 1961).

String-Driven Thing

With animated, shock-headed violinist Graham Smith their visual selling-point, Pauline Adams (vocals), her husband Chris (guitar/vocals) and Colin Wilson (guitar/bass) trod an idiosyncratically British rock path in the early 70s. Like acts of similar stamp, they were later augmented by a drummer, when Billy Fairley toughened up the sound on their second album featuring new recruits Clare Sealey (cello) and Bill Hatje (who took over Wilson's bass duties). The band's performances on children's television proved surprisingly popular, and a wider fame was predicted. The departure of the Adamses and Hatje in 1974 was seen as unfortunate but by no means disastrous as the group were able to continue in recognizable form with, respectively, Kimberley Beacon, Graham White and James Exell for *Please Mind Your Head*, on which Henry McDonald (keyboards) and jazz saxophonist **Alan Skidmore** (then one of **Georgie Fame**'s Blue Flames) were heard too. Even more iconoclastic was the appearance of *Oh Boy* regular Cuddley Dudley on mouth organ for their final album before Smith's defection to **Van Der Graaf Generator** in 1976 and String-Driven Thing's correlated break-up.

Albums: *String-Driven Thing* (1972), *Machine That Cried* (1973), *Please Mind Your Head* (1974), *Keep Yer 'And On It* (1975).

Stringbean

b. David Akeman, 17 June 1914, Annville, Jackson County, Kentucky, USA, d. 10 November 1973. Akeman was raised on a farm and received his first banjo by trading a pair of his prized bantams. Between 1935-39 he worked with several bands including that of local celebrity Asa Martin, who, because of his gangling appearance, first gave him the nickname of String Beans. Akeman's baseball pitching attracted the attention of **Bill Monroe**, who signed him for his private team, not knowing that he was also a banjo player. During his time with Monroe, Akeman also worked with Willie Egbert Westbrooks as String Beans and Cousin Wilbur. In 1945 he left Monroe, being replaced by **Earl Scruggs** and for three years worked with **Lew Childre**, the two becoming a popular *Grand Ole Opry* act. Akemen, now known as Stringbean, also adopted the strange stage attire, probably based on one worn by old time comedian Slim Miller, which gave the effect of a tall man with very short legs. He married Estelle Stanfill in 1945, who shared his love of the outdoor life and acted as his chauffeur since Akemen had two cars but never learned to drive. In 1946, he formed a lasting friendship with **Grandpa Jones** and by 1950 was an established solo star of the *Opry*, which he remained to his death. Akeman recorded for Starday in the 60s, achieving success with songs such as 'Chewing Gum', 'I Wonder Where Wanda Went' and 'I'm Going To The Grand Ole Opry And Make Myself A Name'. In 1969, along with Jones, he also became a regular on the network television show *Hee-Haw*. His love of the quiet country life and his distrust of banks had fatal consequences when, on returning to their farm at Goodlettsville after his *Opry* performance on 10 November 1973, the Akemans surprised two intruders. Stringbean was shot on entering the house and his wife, then parking the car, was pursued and shot down on the lawn. The killers fled with $250 leaving the bodies to be discovered early next morning by Grandpa Jones. John and Douglas Brown were arrested, charged with murder and in spite of the public outcry for the death penalty, were sentenced to life imprisonment.

Albums: *Old Time Pickin' & Singin' With Stringbean* (1961), *Stringbean* (1962), *Kentucky Wonder* (1962), *A Salute To Uncle Dave Macon* (1963), *Old Time Banjo Picking And Singing* (1964), *Way Back In The Hills Of Old Kentucky* (1964), *Hee-Haw Cornshucker* (1971), *Me & Old Crow (Got A Good Thing Goin')* (1972), *Stringbean Goin' To The Grand Ole Opry* (1977).

Strip, The

A would-be jazz drummer, **Mickey Rooney**, fresh out of the army, tangles with criminals. As directed by Leslie Kardos in this 1951 movie, all is very predictable but the pleasures in this film centre upon the band he joins, no less than **Louis Armstrong** And His All Stars. To meet some Hollywood executive's misconceived ideas on racial integration, apart from Rooney another white face appears on-screen in the band, behind the string bass. However, part of what you see and all of what you hear is the real All Stars back in the days when Armstrong's group truly merited the term: **Jack Teagarden**, **Barney Bigard**, **Earl Hines**, **Arvell Shaw** and **William 'Cozy' Cole** (the last two dubbing for their on-screen counterparts).

Armstrong recorded one of the film's songs, 'A Kiss To Build A Dream On', which became a minor hit for him. He also sings 'Shadrack' and the band plays a handful of other 'good old good ones' including 'Ole Miss'/'Bugle Call Rag' which is a feature for Rooney/Cole. In some scenes without the band Rooney may have played drums himself, something at which he was rather good although he was no Cozy Cole.

Stritch, Elaine

b. 2 February 1925, Detroit, Michigan, USA. A highly individual actress and singer, with a magnetic appeal, Elaine Stritch has been called caustic, sardonic, witty, tough, and much else besides. She is said to have sung for the first time on stage in the Long Island revue *The Shape Of Things!*, in June 1947, and a few months later she introduced 'Civilization (Bongo, Bongo, Bongo)' on Broadway, in another revue, *Angels In The Wings*. Stritch subsequently understudied **Ethel Merman** in **Irving Berlin**'s hit musical *Call Me Madam*, and played Merman's role of ambassador Sally Adams in the 1952/3 US tour. Also in 1952, she was Melba Snyder in a revival of ***Pal Joey*** at the Broadhurst Theatre, and gave a memorable reading of the amusing 'Zip'. During the remainder of the 50s, Stritch appeared on Broadway in short-lived versions of ***On Your Toes*** and ***Goldilocks***, and in 1961, sang 'Why Do The Wrong People Travel?', amongst other songs, in **Noël Coward**'s *Sail Away*. In the following year she went with the latter show to London. Although she starred as Vera Charles in the US tour of ***Mame***, and appeared in a US television version of the legendary revue *Pins And Needles*, Stritch did not appear on Broadway again until *Company* (1970), the show which gave her cult status. The television programme documenting the agonies involved in recording its Original Cast album, particularly the sequence in which a weary Stritch struggles to lay down a **Stephen Sondheim**-pleasing version of 'The Ladies Who Lunch', proved to be riveting viewing, and was eventually released on videotape and laserdisc. After starring in the 1972 London production of *Company*, Stritch lived in England for about 10 years, appearing in various plays, and co-starring with Donald Sinden in the top-rated television series *Two's Company*. In 1985, she returned in triumph to New York for the two-performance *Follies In Concert* at the Lincoln Centre. She played Hattie, and very nearly stopped the show with her sensational rendering of 'Broadway Baby'. In the early 90s, she was back at the Lincoln Center with the original cast of *Company* for benefit concerts, made her cabaret debut at New York's Rainbow and Stars, and played the role of Parthy in the 1994 **Tony Award**-winning revival of *Show Boat* on Broadway. All the foregoing has been achieved in parallel with a distinguished career in the straight theatre.

Selected album: *Stritch* (Dolphin 1955), Original and Studio Cast recordings, and Painted Smiles *Revisited* albums.

Strong, Barrett

b. 5 February 1941, Westpoint, Mississippi, USA. The cousin of two members of the R&B vocal group the Diablos, Barrett Strong launched his own singing career with **Berry Gordy**'s fledgling Tamla label in 1959. At the end of that year, he recorded the original version of Gordy's song 'Money', a major US hit which became a rock standard after it was covered by the **Beatles** and the **Rolling Stones**. Strong also wrote **Eddie Holland**'s US hit 'Jamie' in 1961. Later that year, he briefly joined **VeeJay Records**, but he returned to the **Motown** stable in the early 60s to work as a writer and producer. He established a partnership with **Norman Whitfield** from 1966-73; together, the pair masterminded a series of hits by the **Temptations**, with Strong contributing the powerful lyrics to classics like 'Cloud Nine', 'Just My Imagination' and 'Papa Was A Rolling Stone'. Strong left Motown in 1973 to resume his recording career, scoring some success with 'Stand Up And Cheer For The Preacher' on Epic, and 'Is It True' on **Capitol** in 1975. He lacked the distinctive talent of the great soul vocalists, however, and seems destined to be remembered for his behind-the-scenes work at Motown rather than his own sporadic releases.

Albums: *Stronghold* (1975), *Live And Love* (1976), *Love Is You* (1988).

Strouse, Charles

b. 7 June 1928, New York City, New York, USA. A composer who has experienced the sweet taste of Broadway success - but not for some considerable time. When Strouse graduated from the Eastman School of Music he intended to make a career in the classical field, and studied for a time with Aaron Copland. After meeting lyricist **Lee Adams** in 1949 he changed course, and during the early 50s they contributed songs to revues at the popular Green Mansions summer resort, and in 1956 they had some numbers interpolated into the Off Broadway shows *The Littlest Revue* and *Shoestring '57*. Their big break came in 1960 with *Bye Bye Birdie*, which is often cited as the first musical to acknowledge the existence of rock 'n' roll. It starred Dick Van Dyke and **Chita Rivera** and ran for 607 performances. The witty and tuneful score included 'Kids!', 'A Lot Of Livin' To Do', and 'Put On A Happy Face'. Ironically, two years earlier, Strouse, with Fred Tobias, had written a bona fide rock 'n' roll hit, 'Born Too Late', which the Poni-Tails took to number 7 in the US chart. As for Strouse and Adams' shows, *All American* (1962), a musical about college football, failed to score heavily, but *Golden Boy* (1964) lasted for 569 performances on the sheer strength of **Sammy Davis Jnr.**'s appeal. *It's A Bird, It's A Plane, It's Superman* (1966), which was based on the syndicated comic-strip, came down to earth with a bump after only 129 performances. It was four years before Strouse and Adams took off again with *Applause*, their second big hit which ran for over two years, and, like *Golden Boy*, had a gilt-edged box office star in Lauren Bacall. In 1971 Strouse wrote his own lyrics for *Six* - which ran for eight - performances, that is, Off Broadway. The composer collaborated once again with Adams for *I And Albert* in 1972 - presented in London only - but audiences there were definitely not amused. Strouse's hit-of-a-lifetime came five years later - but not in collaboration with Lee Adams. **Martin Charnin** provided the lyrics for another Strouse show that was based, like *It's A Bird, It's A Plane*, on a comic-strip - in this case Little Orphan Annie. Together with librettist Thomas Meehan they turned it into *Annie* (1977), the hottest Broadway ticket of the 70s which ran for 2,377 performances. Since then, over a period of some 15 years, Strouse has had a string of flops - and some real beauties at that: *A Broadway Musical* (one performance), *Flowers For Algernon* (London 28 performances) - adapted for New York as *Charley And Algernon* (17), *Bring Back Birdie* (four), *Dance A Little Closer* (one), *Mayor* (268, but still a failure), *Rags* (four), *Lyle* (didn't reach Broadway), *Annie 2*, the follow-up to his mega-hit (closed in Washington), and *Nick And Nora* (nine). In 1991, the 1986 disaster, *Rags* - which has a truly delectable score - was revived Off Broadway, and two years later a scaled-down version of

Annie 2, retitled *Annie Warbucks*, was also presented there. Experienced Broadway watchers say that in spite of all the setbacks, the musical theatre has not seen the last of Charles Strouse.

Structure

Structure is an umbrella organisation based in Germany for a series of labels which includes Monotone, Trance Atlantic and Digitrax Int. After an initial flurry of acid tracks in 1988, Trance Atlantic was the first of these associated labels to make a name for itself in 1991, by reinstating the 303 sound. In the process mainman J. Burger became one of the first to predict the re-emergence of that musical format. The most notable examples were to be found in Bionaut's 'Science Wonder' and Mike Inc's 'Trance Atlantic Express', an 11-minute epic. Structure was formed in early 1992, releasing just over a dozen releases in its first two years with pressings limited to 2,500 copies. Artists included the aforementioned Bionaut and Mike Inc, alongside Air Liquide (Ingmar Koch and Jammin' Unit) and Walker. The labels in the group are organised to represent differing musical approaches: Structure (acid), Blue (ambient), Digitrax (ambient/techno) and Monotone (hardcore).

Strunk, Jud

b. Justin Strunk, Jnr., 11 June 1936, Jamestown, New York, USA. Strunk was a story-telling banjo player who was popular in both the country and pop markets at the time he died in a plane crash on 15 October 1981. He was raised in Farmington, Maine and was entertaining locals even as a child. He performed as a one-man show for the US Armed Forces and appeared in an off-Broadway musical production titled *Beautiful Dreamer*. He relocated to California in the early 70s and appeared on television with his story-songs. In 1973 he signed to **MGM Records** and released 'Daisy A Day', a song that appeared on both the pop and country charts. He returned to the country charts three more times, with other humorous tales such as 'Next Door Neighbor's Kid' and 'The Biggest Parakeets In Town'.
Albums: *Jud Strunk's Downeast Viewpoint* (1970), *Daisy A Day* (1973).

Stryper

Christian heavy metal quartet from Los Angeles, California, formed by the Sweet brothers in 1981. Originally known as Roxx Regime, this group featured Michael Sweet (vocals), Robert Sweet (drums), Timothy Gaines (bass) and Oz Fox (guitar), playing standard, Americanized hard rock. Devising a carefully constructed image and marketing strategy, they subsequently changed their name to Stryper and dressed in matching yellow and black outfits. They were now a band with a mission - to spread the word of God through rock music, and become the total antithesis of the satanic metal movement. Signing to Enigma Records, they attracted widespread media attention which generally focused on the 'novelty' factor of their spiritual inclinations. A debut mini-album, *Yellow And Black Attack*, featured standard hard rock, with simple lyrics and high-pitched harmonies, while live shows climaxed with the band throwing bibles into the audience. By their third album they had built up a loyal army of fans and the excellently-produced melodic rock contained within widened their appeal. *To Hell With The Devil* peaked at number 32 on its three month stay on the **Billboard** album charts. *In God We Trust* saw the band mellow with more emphasis on pop-rock singalong numbers and the resultant exclusion of driving rock. The album was a commercial disappointment, failing to build on the success of the previous release. It did reach number 32, but only stayed on the *Billboard* chart for five weeks. The band took time off for a radical re-think, before entering the studio again. Oz Fox ventured into production during this time and oversaw the recording of the debut album by fellow Christian-rockers **Guardian**. *Against The Law* emerged in 1990, marking a return to a more aggressive style. The yellow and black stage costumes had been jettisoned and the lyrics were considerably less twee. However, by this time, most of their original fans had moved on and the album sold poorly. When Michael Sweet quit in 1992 it seeemed only divine intervention could rescue Stryper's career.
Albums: *The Yellow And Black Attack* (Enigma 1984), *Soldiers Under Command* (Enigma 1985), *To Hell With The Devil* (Enigma 1986), *In God We Trust* (Enigma 1988), *Against The Law* (Enigma 1990).
Video: *Live In Japan* (1988).

Stuart, Alice

b. 15 June 1942, Seattle, Washington, USA. Stuart began performing at the Pamir House, or P-House, a folk club based in her home city. She befriended several local performers, notably Don McAllister and Steve Lolar (both later of the **Daily Flash**), before securing a residency on the weekly KING-TV *Hootenanny*. She moved to Los Angeles in 1963, and the following year was featured at the famed Berkeley Folk Festival, an appearance which inspired her solo debut. *All The Good Times*, issued on the specialist **Arhoolie** label, drew material from Charlie Poole, **Mississippi John Hurt** and **Tom Paxton**, and remained on catalogue for many years. Alice joined the **Mothers Of Invention** at the end of 1965, but finding their music too eclectic, quickly resumed her solo career. This blossomed with the accomplished *Full Time Woman*, the title track of which became a local 'standard' and was recorded by contemporaries **Grootna**. Stuart then formed Snake with Karl Sevareid (bass) and Bob Jones (drums), but *Believing* sadly failed to match the regional success of its predecessor. The singer later expanded her repertoire to include material from **Boz Scaggs** and **Jimmy Cliff**, but her popularity was confined to the Bay Area club circuit.

Albums: *All The Good Times* (1964), *Full Time Woman* (1970), *Believing* (1971).

Stuart, Marty

b. 1958, Philadelphia, Mississippi, USA. Stuart learned the mandolin and played with the Sullivan Family Gospel Singers, and went on the road with **Lester Flatt** when only 13 years old. After Flatt's death in 1979, Stuart became part of **Johnny Cash**'s band. He married Cash's daughter, Cindy, although they were soon divorced. Cash was among the guests on his *Busy Bee Cafe*. Stuart had a US country hit with 'Arlene' in l985. When his first album for US **Columbia**, *Marty Stuart*, did not sell they shelved plans to release a second, *Let There Be Country*, which featured **Emmylou Harris** and **Mark O'Connor**. He has appeared on many albums, including all-star gatherings such as *Will The Circle Be Unbroken, Vol.2*, *Class Of '55* and *Highwaymen*. In 1988 he returned to playing mandolin for Jerry Sullivan's gospel group and he subsequently produced their highly acclaimed album, *A Joyful Noise*. He revitalized his own career with a powerful mixture of country and rockabilly called *Hillbilly Rock* for MCA. His duet with **Travis Tritt**, 'The Whiskey Ain't Workin'', was a US country hit and they worked together on the 'No Hats' tour. He was part of Mark O'Connor's influential 1991 album, *The Nashville Cats*. Stuart collects rhinestone suits, owns one of **Hank Williams**' guitars, tours in **Ernest Tubb**'s bus and follows his dictum of 'Hillbilly rules, OK?'

Albums: *Marty* (1979), *Busy Bee Cafe* (Rounder 1982), *Marty Stuart* (Columbia 1985), *Hillbilly Rock* (MCA 1989), *Tempted* (MCA 1991). Compilation: *Marty Stuart* (MCA 1995).

Videos: *Hillbilly Rock* (1994), *Kiss Me, I'm Gone (Scene Three)* (1994).

Stuckey, Henry

b. 11 April 1897, Bentonia, Mississippi, USA, d. 9 March 1966, Jackson, Mississippi, USA. Stuckey is best known as the apparent originator of a local style of blues guitar playing and singing, mostly associated with **Skip James**, also from Bentonia. He had taught himself guitar in childhood, which may account partly for the rather odd uses of open tunings that James was to exploit so effectively on his records. The two men played together frequently in the 20s, but Stuckey did not make any records when James did in 1931. He claimed later to have recorded in 1935, but no trace of these has been found. He remained sporadically active in music, mainly on a local basis, although he also worked for a while in Omaha, Nebraska.

Stuckey, Nat

b. Nathan Wright Stuckey II, 17 December c.mid-30s, Cass County, Texas, USA (his actual date of birth has been variously given as 1933, 1934, 1937 or 1938), d. 24 August 1988. After studying for and obtaining a degree in radio and television, he worked as a disc jockey, first on KALT Atlanta, Texas and then moving to KWKH Shreveport, Louisiana. He began to entertain and between 1958 and 1959; fronting his own band the Cornhuskers, he played the local clubs until his performances won him a spot on KWKH's *Louisiana Hayride*, which he played from 1962-66. After first recording for Sim, he joined the Paula label and in 1966, 'Sweet Thang', which reached number 4, gave him his first US country chart entry. He named his band after the song and during the late 60s, he registered further hits on Paula, before moving in 1968 to **RCA**, when he also relocated to Nashville. His Top 20s included 'Oh Woman', 'My Can Do Can't Keep Up With My Want To', 'Plastic Saddle', 'Joe And Mabel's 12th Street Bar And Grill', 'Cut Across Shorty', 'Sweet Thang And Cisco' and a duet with **Connie Smith** of the **Sonny James**' 1957 country and the pop number 1 'Young Love'. (**Gary Stewart** played piano in Stuckey's band for some time). He recorded three albums with Connie Smith, including in 1970, an all gospel album with one track, 'If God Is Dead (Who's That Living In My Soul)', making the *Billboard* charts. During the 60s, he also had success as a songwriter with his songs becoming hits for other artists such as 'Waitin' In Your Welfare Line' (a country number 1 for **Buck Owens**) and 'Pop A Top' (a country number 3 for Jim Ed Brown). His name continued to appear in the charts in the 70s and he had major success with 'She Wakes Me With A Kiss Every Morning' and 'I Used It All On You'. In 1976, he moved to MCA but by the end of the decade his career had begun to fade and his name had disappeared from the charts, the last entry being 'The Days Of Sand And Shovels' in 1978. He continued to tour but could not maintain his earlier successes and was reduced to mainly playing minor venues. In his later years, he was even working as a jingle singer and doing commercials. In 1985, he made a final trip to Europe (he had toured several times previously), when he appeared in London at the Wembley Festival. He formed his own publishing company in Nashville but died of lung cancer in August 1988.

Albums: *Nat Stuckey Really Sings* (1966), *All My Tomorrows* (1967), *Country Favorites* (1967), *Nat Stuckey Sings* (1968), *Keep 'Em Country* (1969), *New Country Roads* (1969), with Connie Smith *Young Love* (1969), *Old Man Willis* (1970), *Sunday Morning With Nat Stuckey And Connie Smith* (1970), *Country Fever* (1970), *Only A Woman Like You* (1971), *She Wakes Me With A Kiss Every Morning* (1971), *Forgive Me For Calling You Darling* (1972), *Is It Any Wonder That I Love You*

(1972), *Take Time To Love Her* (1973), *Nat Stuckey* (1973), with Connie Smith *Even The Bad Times Are Good* (1973), *In The Ghetto* (1974), *Independence* (1976).

Student Prince In Heidelberg, The

The geographical qualification 'In Heidelberg' was dropped from the title after the original production which opened at the Al Jolson Theatre in New York on 2 December 1924, and went on to become the longest-running Broadway musical of the 20s. With music by **Sigmund Romberg** and book and lyrics by Dorothy Donnelly, this operetta was based on the play *Old Heidelberg*, by Rudolf Bleichman, which was adapted from Wilhelm Meyer-Forster's *Alt Heidelberg*. Set in 1860, the story concerns Prince Karl-Franz of Karlsberg (Howard Marsh), who takes lodgings at the Inn of the Three Golden Apples while he is studying at Heidelberg University. He falls in love with a waitress there, Kathie (Ilse Marvenga), and is about to elope with her when he hears that his father, the king, is dying. Karl-Franz must leave to assume his regal responsibilites. Re-united two years later, they realise that, although they still love each other, their lives will be better spent apart. Romberg and Donnelly's score was in the grand operetta style, and contained several memorable numbers, including 'The Drinking Song', 'Serenade', 'Deep In My Heart, Dear', 'Just We Two', and 'Golden Days'. After an impressive run of 608 performances, Ilse Marvenga recreated her role in the 1926 London production which folded after less than three months. Rather more successful revivals were presented in 1929, 1944, and particularly in 1968 when a revised version, with extra songs, and starring the highly popular actor-manager **John Hanson**, played at the Cambridge Theatre. Broadway audiences saw the show again in 1931 and 1943, and there was a production by the New York City Opera in 1980. Film versions were released in 1927, with Ramon Navarro and Norma Shearer, and in 1954, with Edmund Purdom (sung by **Mario Lanza**) and Ann Blyth.

Student Prince, The

Mario Lanza walked out on MGM producer Joe Pasternak before filming had even started on **Sigmund Romberg** and Dorothy Donnelly's epic operetta which eventually reached the screen in 1954. Fortunately for all concerned, Lanza had recorded all the songs before he left, so it was simply a matter of matching his voice to the performing style of Edmund Purdom, the British actor chosen to co-star with Ann Blyth in this tale located in Old Heidelberg. Set in the late 1800s, Sonia Levien and William Ludwig's screenplay, which was based on Donnelly's Broadway libretto and Wilhelm Meyer-Forster's play, told the familiar story of the brief romance between the Student Prince Karl Franz (Purdom) and the waitress Kathy (Blyth) to the accompaniment of immortal songs from the 1924 hit stage production such as 'Serenade', 'Deep In My Heart, Dear', 'Drinking Song', 'Come Boys, Let's All Be Gay Boys', and 'Golden Days'. To these were added three new ones by **Nicholas Brodszky** and **Paul Francis Webster**, 'I Walk With God', Summertime In Heidelberg', and 'Beloved'. Louis Calhern, S.Z. Sakall, Edmund Gwenn, John Williams, Evelyn Vardon, Richard Anderson, and John Hoyt were among those taking part in this lavish production which was expertly photographed in Ansco Color and CinemaScope by Paul Vogel and directed by Richard Thorpe. An earlier, silent film of *The Student Prince*, directed by **Ernst Lubitsch** and starring Ramon Navarro and Norma Shearer, was released in 1927.

Studer, Fredy

b. 16 June 1948, Lucerne, Switzerland. Studer is a self-taught musician who started playing drums when he was 16 years old and appeared in a wide range of bands from rock through jazz to experimental. In 1970, he moved to Rome with a rock trio. He became a consultant for the development of Paiste cymbals. Throughout the 70s he was with the jazz/rock band Om and then played in the rock band Hand In Hand. Studer formed a trio with **Rainer Bruninghaus** and **Markus Stockhausen** between 1981 and 1984 and then played in the **Charlie Mariano/Jasper Van't Hof** band. He also performed in the percussion group Singing Drums with **Pierre Favre**, **Paul Motian** and **Nana Vanconcelos**. Studer has toured extensively including trips to the USA, Central and South America, the Carribbean, North Africa and Japan.
Albums: with George Gruntz *Percussion Profiles* (1977), *Om With Dom Um Romao* (1977), *Continuum* (1983), with Singing Drums *Singing Drums* (1985), as Doran, Studer, Minton, Bates, Ali *Play The Music Of Jimi Hendrix* (Call It Anything 1994).

Studio One

(see **Dodd, Coxsone**)

Stump

Of all the quirky, **Captain Beefheart**-indebted groups to reside at Manchester's Ron Johnson label, Stump were not only the most distinctive, but also the most endearing. Unlike their manic stablemates, mad-eyed Mick Lynch (vocals), Chris Salmon (guitar), Kev Hopper (bass) and Rob McKahey (drums) avoided an aggressive, staccato-guitar onslaught, opting instead for awkward chord and rhythm changes and a wacky, humorous lyrical content, first heard on the charming EP *Mud On A Colon* in March 1986. BBC disc jockey **John Peel** was an early admirer and while Stump's Peel session of that year would eventually surface on vinyl the following January, the band were caught up in the *C86* programme organized by the ***New Musical Express*** and turned up on *The Tube* television show with the offbeat video for their contribution, 'Buffalo'. A debut album, *Quirk Out*, was issued on the Stuff label as Ron Johnson ran into financial problems, and it was not long before Ensign Records lured the band into major territory. 'Chaos' preceded a second album, *A Fierce Pancake*, revealing a Stump that had lost none of their individuality, but it was 'Charlton Heston' (1988), with its 'lights camel action' line and frog-dominated video, that attracted most attention. A full-scale single release for the excellent 'Buffalo' looked set to chart in November, but after it failed, the band all but disappeared.

Albums: *Quirk Out* (Stuff 1987), *A Fierce Pancake* (Ensign 1988).

Style Council

Founded in 1983 by Paul Weller (b. 25 May 1958, England) and Mick Talbot (b. 11 September 1958). Weller had been lead singer of the **Jam** while Talbot was the former keyboards player with the Merton Parkas and the Bureau. Another constant collaborator was singer D.C. Lee, whom Weller married. Weller's avowed aim with the group was to merge his twin interests of soul music and social comment. In this his most important model was **Curtis Mayfield**, who appeared on Style Council's 1987 album. The continuing popularity of the Jam ensured that Style Council's first four releases, in 1983, were UK hits. They included the EP, *Paris*. 'Speak Like A Child' and 'Long Hot Summer'. Tracey Thorn from **Everything But The Girl** was a guest vocalist on the band's first album. Perhaps the most effective Style Council song was the evocative 'My Ever Changing Moods', the first of three Top 10 hits in 1984 and the band's only US hit. During the mid-80s, Weller's political activism was at its height as he recorded 'Soul Deep' as the Council Collective with **Jimmy Ruffin** and **Junior** (Giscombe) to raise funds for the families of striking coal miners and became a founder member of Red Wedge, an artists' support group for the Labour Party. Style Council appeared at **Live Aid** in 1985 and in 1986 made a short film, *JerUSAlem*, a satirical attack on the pop music industry. There were continuing British hits, notably 'The Walls Come Tumbling Down' (1985), 'Have You Ever Had It Blue' (featured in the 1986 film *Absolute Beginners*) and 'Wanted' (1987). With its eclectic mix of soul, classical and pop influences, the 1988 album was less of a commercial success and by 1990, Style Council was defunct. Weller re-emerged the next year with a new band, the Paul Weller Movement, recording for his own Freedom High label.

Albums: *Café Bleu* (1984), *Our Favourite Shop* (1985), *Home And Abroad* (1986), *The Cost Of Loving* (1987), *Confessions Of A Pop Group* (1988), *Here's Some That Got Away* (1993).

Stylistics

The Stylistics were formed in 1968 from the fragments of two Philadelphia groups, the Monarchs and the Percussions, by Russell Thompkins Jnr (b. 21 March 1951, Philadelphia, Pennsylvania, USA), Airrion Love (b. 8 August 1949, Philadelphia, Pennsylvania, USA), James Smith (b. 16 June 1950, New York City, USA), Herbie Murrell (b. 27 April 1949, Lane, South Carolina, USA) and James Dunn (b. 4 February 1950, Philadelphia, Pennsylvania, USA). The quintet's debut single, 'You're A Big Girl Now' was initially issued on a local independent, but became a national hit following its acquisition by the Avco label. The Stylistics were then signed to this outlet directly and teamed with producer/composer **Thom Bell**. This skillful musician had already worked successfully with the **Delfonics** and his sculpted, sweet soul arrangements proved ideal for his new charges. In partnership with lyricist Linda Creed, Bell fashioned a series of immaculate singles, including 'You Are Everything' (1971), 'Betcha By Golly Wow' and 'I'm Stone In Love With You' (both 1972), where Simpkins' aching voice soared against the group's sumptuous harmonies and a cool, yet inventive accompaniment. The style reached its apogee in 1974 with 'You Make Me Feel Brand New', a number 2 single in both the US and UK. This release marked the end of Bell's collaboration with the group who were now pushed towards the easy listening market. With arranger **Van McCoy** turning sweet into saccharine, the material grew increasingly bland, while Thompkins' falsetto, once heartfelt, now seemed contrived. Although their American fortune waned, the Stylistics continued to enjoy success in Britain with 'Sing Baby Sing', 'Can't Give You Anything (But My Love)' (both 1975) and '16 Bars' (1976), while a compilation album that same year, *The Best Of The Stylistics*, became one of the UK's best-selling albums. Despite this remarkable popularity, purists labelled the group a parody of its former self. Ill-health forced Dunn to retire in 1978, whereupon the remaining quartet left Avco for a brief spell with **Mercury**. Two years later they were signed to the TSOP/**Philadelphia International** stable, which resulted in some crafted recordings reminiscent of their heyday, but problems within the company undermined the group's progress. Subsequent singles for Streetwise took the Stylistics into the lower reaches of the R&B chart, but their halcyon days now seem to be over.

Albums: *The Stylistics* (1971), *Round 2: The Stylistics* (1972), *Rockin' Roll Baby* (1973), *Let's Put It All Together* (1974), *Heavy* (UK title: *From The Mountain*) (1974), *Thank You Baby* (1975), *You Are Beautiful* (1975), *Fabulous* (1976), *Once Upon A Juke Box* (1976), *Sun And Soul* (1977), *Wonder Woman* (1978), *In Fashion* (1978), *Black Satin* (1979), *Love Spell* (1979), *Live In Japan* (1979), *The Lion Sleeps Tonight* (1979), *Hurry Up This Way Again* (1980), *Closer Than Close* (1981), *1982* (1982), *Some Things Never Change* (1985), *Love Talks* (1993). Compilations: *The Best Of The Stylistics* (1975), *Spotlight On The Stylistics* (1977).

Styne, Jule

b. Julius Kerwin Stein, 31 December 1905, London, England, d. 20 September 1994, New York, USA. A highly distinguished composer for the musical theatre, films, and Tin Pan Alley, Styne spent his early life in the east London district of Bethnal Green, where his father ran a butter and egg store. He used to do **Harry Lauder** impressions, and when he was five, he was taken by his parents to see the great entertainer at the London Hippodrome. He climbed up on stage, and Lauder lent him his crook and encouraged him to sing 'She's My Daisy'. Something of a child prodigy, he was a competent pianist even before he emigrated with his family to the USA at the age of eight. They settled in Chicago, and Styne studied harmony and composition, and played with the Chicago Symphony Orchestra, but had to abandon a classical career because 'my hands were too small - my span was inadequate'. While he was still at high school, Styne played the piano at burlesque houses, and composed his first two songs, 'The Guy In the Polka-Dot Tie' and 'The Moth And The Flame'. After graduating, he worked in nightclubs and for various pickup groups, and in 1927, had a hit with the catchy 'Sunday' (written with Ned Miller, Chester Conn and Bennie Kreuger). In the late 20s, Styne was a member of **Ben Pollack**'s big-time Chicago Band, which at various times included legendary names such as **Benny Goodman**, **Glenn Miller**, and **Charlie Spivak**. By 1932, he had formed his own band, which played at the night clubs and speakeasies in Chicago. During the 30s he moved to Hollywood, via New York, and worked as vocal coach at 20th Century Fox ('I taught **Shirley Temple** and **Alice Faye** how to sing!', and wrote some songs for low budget movies such as *Hold That Co-Ed* (1938, 'Limpy Dimp' with Sidney Clare and Nick Castle). He transferred to Republic Studios, the home of **Gene Autry** and **Roy Rogers**, and continued to contribute to shoestring productions such as *Hit Parade Of 1941* ('Who Am I?', with Walter Bullock), *Melody Ranch*, *Rookies On Parade*, and *Angels With Broken Wings*. On loan to Paramount, Styne teamed with **Frank Loesser** for 'I Don't Want To Walk Without You' and 'I Said No', which were featured in the Eddie Bracken movie *Sweater Girl* (1942). The former number was an enormous wartime hit, particularly for **Harry James** and his Orchestra, with a vocal by **Helen Forrest**. While at Republic, Styne met lyricist **Sammy Cahn**, and during the 40s they collaborated on numerous appealing songs, mostly for films, including 'I've Heard That Song Before', 'Five Minutes More', 'Victory Polka', 'Poor Little Rhode Island', 'Saturday Night (Is The Loneliest Night Of The Week)', 'Zuyder Zee', 'Guess I'll Hang My Tears Out To Dry' (from the 1944 flop musical *Glad To See You*), 'Anywhere', 'Can't You Read Between The Lines?', 'When The One You Love

(Simply Won't Come Back)', 'I've Never Forgotten', 'The Things We Did Last Summer', 'Let It Snow! Let It Snow! Let It Snow!', 'I Gotta Gal I Love In North And South Dakota', 'It's Been A Long, Long Time', 'Ev'ry Day I Love You (Just A Little Bit More)', 'I'm In Love', 'It's Magic', 'It's You Or No One', 'Put 'Em In A Box (Tie It With A Ribbon And Throw 'Em In the Deep Blue Sea' (last three from **Doris Day**'s first movie, *Romance On The High Seas*), 'Give Me A Song With A Beautiful Melody', and 'It's A Great Feeling' (1949). During that period, Styne also collaborated with others, including **Herb Magidson** ('Barrelhouse Bessie From Basin Street' and 'Conchita, Marquita, Lolita, Pepita, Rosita, Juanita Lopez') and Walter Bishop ('Bop! Goes My Heart'). Many of those songs were immensely successful for **Frank Sinatra**, and Styne and Cahn wrote the scores for three of the singer's most successful films of the 40s, *Step Lively* ('As Long As There's Music', 'Come Out, Wherever You Are', 'Some Other Time'), *Anchors Aweigh* ('The Charm Of You', 'I Fall In Love Too Easily', 'I Begged Her'), and *It Happened In Brooklyn* ('It's The Same Old Dream', 'Time After Time', 'I Believe', 'The Brooklyn Bridge'). Sinatra also introduced Styne and Cahn's Oscar-winning 'Three Coins In The Fountain' in 1954. Some years before that, Styne and Cahn had moved to New York to work on the score for the stage musical *High Button Shoes* ('Papa, Won't You Dance With Me', 'I Still Get Jealous', 'Can't You Just See Yourself?'). It starred Phil Silvers and Nanette Fabray, and ran for 727 performances. After returning briefly to Hollywood, at the age of 44, Styne embarked on an illustrious Broadway career, composing the music for a string of mostly highly successful shows, including *Gentlemen Prefer Blondes* (1949, 'Diamonds Are A Girl's Best Friend', 'Bye, Bye, Baby'), *Two On The Aisle* (1951, 'Hold Me-Hold Me-Hold Me', 'If You Hadn't But You Did'), *Hazel Flagg* (1953, 'Ev'ry Street's A Boulevard', 'How do You Speak To An Angel?'), *Peter Pan* (1954, 'Never Never Land', 'Distant Melody'), *Wake Up Darling* (1956, a five performance flop, 'L'il Ol' You And L'il Ol' Me'), *Bells Are Ringing* (1956, 'Just In Time', 'The Party's Over', 'Long Before I Knew You'), *Say, Darling* (1958, 'Dance Only With Me'), *Gypsy* (1959, 'Small World', 'Everything's Coming Up Roses', 'Rose's Turn', 'All I Need Is The Girl'), *Do Re Mi* (1960, 'Make Someone Happy', 'Fireworks'), *Subways Are For Sleeping* (1961, 'I Just Can't Wait', 'Comes Once In A Lifetime', 'Be A Santa'), *Funny Girl* (1964, 'The Music That Makes Me Dance', 'Sadie, Sadie', 'People', 'Don't Rain On My Parade'), *Fade Out-Fade In* (1964, 'You Mustn't Feel Discouraged'), *Hallelujah, Baby!* (1967, 'My Own Morning', 'Now's The Time'), *Darling Of The Day* (1968, 'Let's See What Happens', 'That Something Extra Special'), *Look To The Lilies* (1970, 'I! Yes, Me! That's Who!'), *Prettybelle* (1971, closed out of town), *Sugar*

(1972, 'It's Always Love', 'We Could Be Close' [revised for London as *Some Like It Hot* in 1992]), *Lorelei* (1974, a revised version of *Gentlemen Prefer Blondes*), *Hellzapoppin'!* (1976, closed out of town, 'Only One To A Customer'), **Bar Mitzvah Boy** (London 1978, 'You Wouldn't Be You', 'The Sun Shines Out Of Your Eyes', 'Where The Music Is Coming From'), *One Night Stand* (1980, closed during previews, 'Too Old To Be So Young', 'Long Way From Home'), *Pieces Of Eight* (1985, closed during regional tryout in Canada), and **The Red Shoes** (1993, closed after three days). Styne's chief collaborators for Broadway were **Betty Comden** and **Adolph Green**, and he also worked with **Leo Robin**, **E.Y 'Yip' Harburg**, Sammy Cahn, **Bob Hilliard**, amongst others. His two longest-running (and legendary) shows were written with **Bob Merrill** (*Funny Girl*) and **Stephen Sondheim** (*Gypsy*). Styne also co-produced several musicals, and composed the scores for television specials, and films such as *West Point Story*, *Two Tickets To Broadway*, and *My Sister Eileen*.

One of the most talented, and prolific ('I believe in perspiration - not inspiration') all-round songwriters in the history of American popular music, Styne won many awards and honours, and was inducted into the Songwriters Hall of Fame and the Theatre Hall of Fame. Several artists have devoted complete albums to his songs, and in 1995, *Everything's Coming Up Roses-The Overtures Of Jule Styne*, played by the National Symphony Orchestra conducted by Jack Everly, was released. **ASCAP**'s memorial tribute to Styne in February of that year included a Stephen Sondheim lyric which ran: 'Jule/You never took things cooly/Your syntax was unduly/Unruly/But Jule/I love you truly.'

Selected albums: *My Name Is Jule* (United Artists 50s), with Michael Feinstein *Michael Feinstein Sings The Jule Styne Songbook* (Elektra Nonesuch 1991).

Further reading: *Jule*, Theodore Taylor.

Styx

This Chicago-based quintet are widely believed to be responsible for the development of the term pomp-rock (pompous, overblown arrangements, with perfect-pitch harmonies and a very full production). Styx evolved from the bands Tradewinds and T.W.4, but re-named themselves after the fabled river from Greek mythology, when they signed to Wooden Nickel, a subsidiary of **RCA Records**, in 1972. The line-up comprised Dennis De Young (vocals/keyboards), James Young (guitar/vocals), Chuck Panozzo (bass), John Panozzo (drums) and John Curulewski (guitar). Combining symphonic and progressive influences they released a series of varied and highly melodic albums during the early 70s. Success was slow to catch up with them; *Styx II*, originally released in 1973, spawned the Top Ten **Billboard** hit 'Lady' in 1975. The album then made similar progress, eventually peaking at number 20. After signing to **A&M Records** in 1975,

John Curulewski departed with the release of *Equinox*, to be replaced by Tommy Shaw. This was a real turning point in the band's career as Shaw took over lead vocals and contributed significantly on the writing side. From here on Styx albums had an added degree of accessibility and moved towards a more commercial approach. *The Grand Illusion*, released in 1977, was Shaw's first major success, peaking at number 6 during its nine-month stay on the *Billboard* album chart. It also featured the number 8-peaking single, 'Sail Away'. *Pieces Of Eight* and *Cornerstone* consolidated their success, with the latter containing 'Babe', the band's first number 1 single in the USA. *Paradise Theater* was the Styx's *tour de force*, a complex, laser-etched concept album, complete with elaborate and expensive packaging. It generated two further US Top 10 hits in 'The Best Of Times' and 'Too Much Time On My Hands'. The album became their most successful ever, and also stayed at number 1 for three weeks on the album chart. *Kilroy Was Here* followed, yet another concept album, which brought them close to repetition. A watered down pop-rock album with a big-budget production, its success came on the back of their previous album rather than on its own merits. *Caught In The Act* was an uninspired live offering. They disbanded shortly after its release. Styx re-formed in 1990 with the original line-up, except for pop-rock funkster Glenn Burtnick, who replaced Tommy Shaw (who had joined **Damn Yankees**). *Edge Of The Century* indicated that the band still had something to offer, with a diverse and classy selection of contemporary AOR. As one of the tracks on the album stated, the group were self-evidently 'Not Dead Yet'.

Albums: *Styx* (Wooden Nickel 1972), *Styx II* (Wooden Nickel 1973), *The Serpent Is Rising* (Wooden Nickel 1973), *Man Of Miracles* (Wooden Nickel 1974), *Equinox* (A&M 1975), *Crystal Ball* (A&M 1976), *The Grand Illusion* (A&M 1977), *Pieces Of Eight* (A&M 1978), *Cornerstone* (A&M 1979), *Paradise Theater* (A&M 1980), *Kilroy Was Here* (A&M 1983), *Caught In The Act* (A&M 1984), *Edge Of The Century* (A&M 1990). Compilation: *The Best Of Styx* (A&M 1979).

Video: *Caught In The Act* (1984).

Sub Pop Records

Based in Seattle, Washington, USA, the Sub Pop label has served as the natural focus for local acts since the late 80s. It has become closely associated with several noise/guitar bands fusing heavy riffs to a sound influenced by the **Stooges**. Releases by **Mudhoney** and **Tad** helped establish a cult following, while the subsequent success of **Nirvana** focused attention on the group's tenure with the company. Sub Pop was also noted for 'one-off' recordings and **Dinosaur Jr**, **Rapeman** and **Thin White Rope** were among those taking advantage of this practice. The label also established the Sub Pop Singles Club, whereby an

annual subscriber would receive an exclusive, limited edition release each month. The idea was later adopted by **Rough Trade Records** in 1991 as well as several other labels.
Album: *Sub Pop Grunge Years* (Sup Pop 1990).

Sub Sub

Pop dance crew from Manchester, England who have been together since 1989, originally comprising Melanie Williams (vocals), Jimi Goodwin, Jezz Williams and Andy Williams. Their earliest releases were based more in the DIY-bedroom techno mode than that which would bring them to *Top Of The Pops* and the Top 10. 'Space Face' was a white-label release hawked via the boot of their cars, followed by the instrumental *Coast* EP. This was the only result of a deal they inked with **Virgin Records**, before transferring to **New Order** manager Rob Gretton's **Robsrecords**, who reissued it in August 1992. Their breakthrough hit arrived with the stirring 'Ain't No Love (Ain't No Use)', with a particularly virulent mix from DJ **Graeme Park**. In its wake they were invited to produce remixes for a range of artists (including **Take That** and, insult of insults, **Sinitta**). They have thus far kept their credits to more credible productions. Their 1994 album was preceded by a single, 'Respect', which introduced their new vocalist, Nina Henchion.
Album: *Full Fathom Five* (Robsrecords 1994).

Subdudes

This four-piece R&B band are from New Orleans, Louisiana, USA, although they have since relocated to Denver, Colorado. They are fronted by singer/guitarist Tommy Malone with notable stylistic help from John Magnie's accordion. The Subdudes' eclectic songs fuse the best traditions of their hometown's black music influences - be they blues, funk, Mardi Gras or gospel, with an earthy, punchy delivery. Otherwise the most distinctive attributes to their sound are the rich harmonies and lack of a conventional 'drummer'. Drawing heavily on the New Orleans/Memphis soul spirit, the group is made up of accomplished musicians who have previously backed **Roseanne Cash** and **Joni Mitchell**. Their debut was completed with the aid of Don Gehman, and introduced strong songs such as 'Need Somebody', 'Any Cure' and 'Got You On His Mind' (as well as traditional covers such as 'Big Chief'). A version of **Al Green**'s 'Tired Of Being Alone' graced a second set in 1991, while **Glyn Johns** (**Beatles** and **Rolling Stones** producer) was drafted in for the group's third album, which some critics described as an amalgam of the **Neville Brothers** and **Eagles**.
Albums: *The Subdudes* (Atlantic 1990), *Lucky* (Atlantic 1991), *Annunciation* (High Street 1994).

Subhumans (Canada)

Influential Vancouver punk band who did much of the groundwork for later Canadian left field outfits. However, the Subhumans are possibly more famous for their contribution and inclusion in 'ecological terrorism' activities. Charges included bombing a plant making guidance systems for nuclear missiles, dynamiting a hydro-power station and fire-bombing pornography shops. Gerry 'Useless' Hannah (bass) was the band member implicated and tried, along with four others. He would receive a 10 year custodial sentence. The Subhumans had already marked out their ability to challenge the conventions of the punk movement with *Incorrect Thoughts*' 'Slave To My Dick', an indictment of male stupidity which went against the grain of the macho ethos of 'hardcore' music. The rest of the original band featured; Brian 'Wimpy Boy' Goble (vocals; ex-Skulls), Mike Graham (guitar) and Greg 'Dimwit' James (drums). James was replaced by Jim Iwagama on drums when he joined Pointed Sticks, until he returned on that band's split. Gerry Useless would quit the band after his sentence as he became more interested in environmental issues (he wanted to become a forest warden). Iwagama chose this moment to depart also, for reasons of pure lethargy. The returning James was joined by a new bass player, Ron, again from Vancouver. Goble and James would go on to pursue a lengthy career in **D.O.A.**. James is the elder brother of original D.O.A. drummer Chuck Biscuits (later **Circle Jerks**, **Black Flag**, **Danzig** etc). Historically, the 'guerilla' activities overshadowed the career of one of the few hardcore bands capable of writing bracing, fully realised songs with a rare lyrical poignancy.
Albums: *Incorrect Thoughts* (Friends 1980), *No Wishes, No Prayers* (SST 1983).

Subhumans (UK)

One of the most popular and entertaining of the 80s anarcho punk bands influenced by the cottage industry approach of **Crass**. The most significant departure from their bretheren would be in the use of music which traced its heritage more to **Led Zeppelin** than the **Damned**. Lyrically, the Subhumans trod familiar territory (vegetarianism, human rights, anti-government sloganeering) though they did so with more humour than many. For instance, 'Are you prepared to die for you beliefs, or just to dye your hair' from 'Work Rest Play Die' questioned the authenticity of the movement they were a part of. The band comprised Dick (b. Richard Lucas; vocals), Bruce (guitar), Grant (bass) and Trotsky (drums), though for *29:29 Split Vision* Phil would replace Grant. On later recordings the Subhumans continued to expand in to other musical areas, largely leaving behind their original thrash based formula (although their debut EP had anticipated such ecelcticism with a reggae number). Members of the band would go on to form Citizen Fish, whose blend of punk and ska would be popularised throughout the UK on the free festival circuit. **Dick Lucas** stayed true to the band's anarcho roots by continuing to operate his own Bluurg label for releases by both his own bands plus many others.

Albums: *The Day The Country Died* (Spiderleg 1981), *Time Flies But Aeroplanes Crash* (Bluurg 1983), *From The Cradle To The Grave* (Bluurg 1984), *Worlds Apart* (Bluurg 1985), *EP-LP* (Bluurg 1986), *29:29 Split Vision* (Bluurg 1987).

Subramaniam, Dr. L.

b. 23 July 1947, Madras, India. A child prodigy, Subramaniam was taught by his father, a renowned Indian violinist, and his mother, an Indian classical singer. He gave his first violin concert performance at the age of eight, and by 15 was being hailed as 'violin Chakravati' ('world emperor' of violinists). A year later he received the prestigious President's Award in India. His *Violin Trio*, which included his brother, **Lakshminarayana Shankar**, became a principal attraction at the Madras Festival during the 60s. In 1973 he toured Europe and the USA with **George Harrison** and sitarist **Ravi Shankar**. While teaching at California Arts University in the USA, he developed a lasting interest in jazz-ethnic fusions which led to performances with **Herbie Hancock**, **Stéphane Grappelli**, **Larry Coryell**, **Stanley Clarke** and **Stu Goldberg**. In 1980, he formed Rainbow with saxophonist **John Handy** and sarod master Ali Akbar Khan. Since 1983 his compositions have been influenced by the western classical tradition; 'Spring Rhapsody' has been described as a polyrhythmic homage to Bach and baroque music. Subramaniam is also a graduate in medicine from the Madras Medical College.

Albums: *The Virtuoso Violin Of South India* (70s), *L'Archet Magnétique de L. Subramaniam* (1980), *Blossom* (1982), *Fantasy Without Limit* (1982), *Indian Classical Music* (1986), *Garland* (1986), with Stu Goldberg *Solos-Duos-Trios* (nda), *In Praise Of Ganesh* (1993).

Subsonic 2

Include Me Out was widely praised as one of the most impressive debuts of 1991, a legitimate compliment to one of UK rap's most inriguing new formations. DJ Docta D and MC Steel provide the hands on the steering wheel, which veers wildly from R&B to funk and Motown, taking in breakbeats and some of the smarter rhymes heard in the parish. The pair met after Steel addressed a demo, recorded on his own portable studio, to Heatwave Radio. This pirate station, helmed by Docta D, took to the tape in a big way, with continued requests urging him to seek out the cassette's creator. Afterwards they spent three years working together on new material, with cuts like 'Dedicated To The City', with its captivating jazz saxophone, boosted by the literacy of English and Russian graduate Steel. While the title recalled many hardcore rappers

concerns about authenticating themselves with tales of urban mayhem, 'Dedicated' is merely a delightful nod to the lyricist's direct environment, a celebration of its vibrancy and variety. Or 'Unsung Heroes Of Hip-Hop', which cleverly mocks the sheepish competition between hardcore crews which too often merely produces imitation: 'Well, do you really wanna base a career, On an '84 **Run DMC** idea?'.

Album: *Include Me Out* (Columbia 1991).

Subterfuge

An alias for Thomas Barnett (b. c.1967), who once held down a day job alongside Chez Damier, a friend of **Juan Atkins** and **Derrick May**, who had recorded for the former's **KMS** label. Through these connections Barnett met May and recorded 'Nude Photo' with him for **Transmat** (as Rhythim Is Rhythim). The duo fell out when Barnett received no monies for the track and his name disappeared from the credits. After dropping out and working in his own home-studio he re-emerged on **Infonet** with the *Liquid Poetry* EP. He also worked for the Dutch label Prime, putting out a set of 'Nude Photo' remixes. A series of EPs then the *Synthetic Dream* album followed, a set overshadowed by the poverty he was experiencing while recording it, which is evident throughout its tough, remorseless grooves.

Album: *Synthetic Dream* (Prime 1993).

Subterraneans, The

This adaptation of a Jack Kerouac novel came too early for it to be successful. When this film was released in 1960, Hollywood was then still hidebound by its own peculiar code of sexual ethics. What could and could not be shown on the screen was a tangle which this film, directed by Ranald MacDougall, fails to unravel. Jazz fans have an excuse for watching it, however, as there are good moments from musicians such as **André Previn**, the film's musical director, Dave Bailey, **Chico Hamilton**, **Art Farmer**, **Art Pepper**, Bob Enevoldson, Russ Freeman, **Red Mitchell**, **Shelly Manne**, **Bill Perkins** and **Gerry Mulligan**, who also has an acting role.

Suburban Base

This label is the home of hardcore techno and breakbeats, and was established by Dan Donnelly in Romford, Essex, England, in 1990 as an offshoot of his record shop, Boogie Times (which is also called Suburban Base). Good examples of the Suburban Base sound are Sonz Of A Loop Da Loop Era's 'Far Out', which transferred from the Boogie Times label, or Aston And DJ Rap, who also worked on a production basis under the alias Rhythm for **Perfecto** records. They released the 'Vertigo' single in May 1993. Earlier worthy samples of the label's product came with Q Bass's 'Hardcore Will Never Die'. Danny Breaks (with

the rave anthem 'Far Out'), Timebase (aka DJ Krome and Mr Time), M&M, Austin Reynolds (an in-house studio operative who recorded 'I Got High' under his own name and as the Phuture Assasins with the *Future Sound* EP) filled out the artist roster. The homegrown talent also included E Type (studio engineer Mike James) and Run Tings (shop worker Winston Meikle). Rachel Wallace (once a star of a *South Bank Show* talent contest), who featured on the remix of M&M's 'I Feel This Way', was given full billing on her own single, 'Tell Me Why'. However, their biggest hit came with the 'kiddie techno' novelty, 'Sesame's Treet', by the Smarte's (Chris Powell, Tom Orton and Nick Arnold). Suburban Base set up an offshoot, **Fruit Tree**, for house productions, hiring Luke Coke as its A&R man. This was because they were so pleased with his work on their material through his job at Phuture Trax Promotions. That imprint's life began with Vibe Tribe's 'Rock It', which again was Austin Reynolds, who also remixed for **Andronicus** and **East 17**. A further subsidiary was launched as an outlet for compilations, Breakdown Records. This does not involve exclusively Suburban Base tracks, but also scans the shelves for important hardcore tunes which may have escaped the net. In 1992 the label had signed a US deal with **Atlantic** worth a reported $500,000.
Selected albums: Various: *Base For Your Face* (Suburban Base 1992), *Drum & Bass* (Breakdown 1994).

Sudden, Nikki

Following the dissolution of premier UK art punk band **Swell Maps**, former lead singer and driving force Sudden joined the Abstract label to release *Waiting On Egypt*. He had continued to make music erratically before this. Among these recordings were sessions with Another Pretty Face (later Mike Scott's **Waterboys**) in Christmas 1980. His first solo single was 'Back To The Start' on Rather Records, before the release of 'Channel Steamer', which would form part of the debut album. He was pleased with the results: 'Nearly everyone I know thinks it's the best thing I've ever done and I must admit when I listen to it I get a pleasant surprise'. Also included were 'Forest Fire' and 'New York', both unreleased Swell Maps songs. The nucleus of musicians that he employed included Scott (guitar), Steve Burgess (bass), Anthony Thistlethwaite (saxophone) and Empire (ex-**TV Personalities**) on drums. Following *The Bible Belt* in 1983 Sudden would work extensively with Dave Kusworth as the **Jacobites**, releasing over half a dozen albums for Glass and **Creation Records**. He also wrote for several music magazines including the later issues of *Zig Zag* during this period, later collaborating on projects with **Roland S. Howard**. His most recent album, *The Jewel Thief*, saw him work with his long-time fans, **R.E.M.**
Albums: *Waiting On Egypt* (Abstract 1982), *The Bible Belt* (Flicknife 1983), with Rowland S. Howard *Kiss You Kidnapped Charabanc* (Creation 1987), with the French Revolution *Groove* (Creation 1989), *The Jewel Thief* (Creation 1991).

Suddenly, Tammy!

Based in Pennsylvania, USA, this pop rock group comprise Beth Sorrentino (vocals/piano), brother Jay Sorrentino (drums) and Ken Heitmueller (bass/vocals). Formed in 1990, the group spent several years developing their uncluttered brand of melodic pop, with clever songwriting from the Sorrentino siblings giving them much of their impetus. Such originality brought the group several admirers, including UK press darlings **Suede** who invited them to support as opening act on their US tour in the summer of 1994. The group went on to perform with artists as diverse as **Jackson Browne**, **David Byrne** and the **Cranberries**. Their debut album was released by US indie label Spin Art in the spring of 1994, before **WEA Record**s picked it up for wider distribution. It was produced and engineered by the group in their own studio - the 'Cat Box' - in Lancaster County, Pennsylvania, and comprised 13 songs drawing from pop, rock and jazz traditions, with strong tunes such as 'Disease' and 'Lamp' distinguished by Beth Sorrentino's expressive vocals.
Album: *Suddenly, Tammy!* (Spin Art 1994).

Sudhalter, Dick

b. 28 December 1928, Boston, Massachusetts, USA. Sudhalter played as an amateur while engaged in a career in journalism. Playing cornet in various parts of the USA and UK, he established a quiet reputation mostly amongst musicians. As he expanded his career in music, Sudhalter's virtues as a player and a tireless organizer became more widely apparent. He was involved in the creation of the New **Paul Whiteman** Orchestra and also worked with **Bobby Hackett**, **Keith Nichols**, the **New York Jazz Repertory Orchestra** and others in faithful but undogmatic re-creations of early jazz, in particular the music of **Bix Beiderbecke**. His interest in the life and career of Beiderbecke led him to write the biography, *Bix: Man And Legend* and his other writings have extended into the *New York Post*. His late 80s and early 90s playing ventures include performances with **Dick Wellstood** and **Marty Grosz** in the band known as the Classic Jazz Quartet, and with Loren Schoenberg and singers Barbara Lea and Daryl Sherman in the group named Mr Tram Associates.
Albums: *Friends With Pleasure* (Audiophile 1981), with Mr Tram Associates *Getting Some Fun Out Of Life* (1988), *Get Out And Get Under The Moon* (1989), *Dick Sudhalter And Connie Jones* (Stomp Off 1992).

Sue And Sunny

b. Madras, India. Sisters Yvonne and Heather Wheatman made their recording debut in 1963 under the name the Myrtelles. Their unsuccessful reading of **Leslie Gore**'s 'Just Let Me Cry' was followed by two singles as Sue And Sunshine, before the duo settled on the above appellation in 1966. When several soul-styled releases failed to chart, Sue And Sunny embarked on a more remunerative career as session backing singers. Their most notable appearance was on **Joe Cocker**'s international hit, 'With A Little Help From My Friends', but they also contributed to **Love Affair**'s 'Rainbow Valley'. Sue And Sunny later formed part of the original **Brotherhood Of Man**, but their involvement ended prior to this act's ascendancy. Sunny (Heather) enjoyed a UK Top 10 hit in her own right with 'Doctor's Orders' (1974) while Sue (Glover) completed an album, enterprisingly entitled *Solo*. Together the duo have remained in demand as backing singers, particularly as part of the **James Last** entourage.

Sue Records

Former real estate entrepreneur Henry 'Juggy Murray' Jones incorporated the Sue label in New York City on 2 January 1957. Initially sited on West 125th Street, close to the fabled **Apollo** Theatre, the company was well-placed to sign aspiring R&B talent. Sue scored its first hit single the following year with its seventh release, Bobby Hendricks' 'Itchy Twitchy Feeling', which reached the US Top 30. This exciting performance featured the **Coasters** on backing vocals and helped establish the label as one of the earliest successful, black-owned companies, pre-empting **Tamla/Motown**'s first hit by some six months. By 1960 Murray had relocated to West 54th Street, near to Bell Sound Studios where many of the label's recording sessions were undertaken. His early signings included **Don Covay**, but it was with **Ike and Tina Turner** that Juggy found consistent success. Two of the duo's finest singles, 'A Fool In Love' and 'It's Gonna Work Out Fine', were released on Sue and their success allowed Murray to expand his company. Soul and R&B remained at its core, but the label also featured several jazz-based acts, including **Jimmy McGriff**, **Bill Doggett** and Hank Jacobs. Subsidiary companies were also established, including Symbol, the roster of which included **Inez and Charlie Foxx**, who enjoyed considerable success with 'Mockingbird' (number 2 R&B) and 'Hurt By Love'. Famed R&B songwriter **Bert Berns** also recorded for this outlet under the pseudonym 'Russell Byrd'. A.F.O. provided a short-lived association with a New Orleans-based collective headed by producer **Harold Battiste**. 'I Know' (**Barbara George**) and 'She Put The Hurt On Me' (**Prince La La**) were issued on this outlet, while

the Crackerjack imprint included **Derek Martin**'s 'Daddy Rollin' Stone', cited by **George Harrison** as one of his favourites of the era and later covered by the **Who**.

A handful of Sue recordings were initially issued in Britain on **Decca**'s **London/American** outlet, but in 1964 Murray struck a licensing deal with **Island**'s Chris Blackwell. Responsibility for British Sue was passed to disc-jockey/producer **Guy Stevens** who, after seventeen singles, decided to use it for product leased from other sources. Murray felt this diminished Sue's individual identity, withdrew from the arrangement and reverted to London/American for future releases. Stevens retained the Sue name, and thereafter the path of both companies was entirely different. In Britain, the label issued material by, among others, **James Brown**, **Freddy King**, **B.B. King** and **Elmore James**. It proved instrumental in introducing acts to a UK audience and many musicians, including **Stevie Winwood**, **Steve Marriott** and **Eric Clapton**, expressed a debt to Stevens' interest. British Sue folded in February 1967 as the Island label switched priorities from black music to white rock. The entire catalogue was deleted in 1969, but was briefly revived in the 1983 with a series of commemorative EPs.

Juggy Murray continued to administer Sue but failed to meet the changes evolving during the mid-60s. He claims to have signed **Jimi Hendrix** prior to the guitarist's departure for England, although no tracks were recorded. A proposed distribution deal with **Stax** fell through, the latter company eventually opting for **Atlantic**. In 1968 Murray sold his remaining masters and publishing to United Artists. He produced several former Sue acts for their Veep and Minit subsidiaries including the **Soul Sisters**, **Baby Washington** and Tina Britt. Murray retained the rights to the Sue name, reactivating it on occasions over the ensuing years. He enjoyed a 'comeback' hit in 1969 when one-man band **Wilbert Harrison** re-recorded his own 'Let's Stick Together' as 'Let's Work Together'. The latter was then popularised by **Canned Heat**. Murray then founded another short-lived outlet, Juggernaught, before moving to Los Angeles to launch Jupiter Records. It was here he found belated success as an artist. 'Inside America', credited to Juggy Murray Jones, issued in Britain via the Contempo label, climbed to 39 in 1976. It is, however, for his pioneering Sue label that he will be best remembered. An indispensible box set was compiled by Alan Warner in 1994.

Compilations: *The Sue Story: Volumes One to Three* (UK-only) (1966), *The Sue Records Story: The Sound Of Soul* (4CD box set) (EMI 1994).

Suede

This hugely promoted UK band broke through in 1993

by merging the lyrical perspective of **Morrissey** with the posturings of **David Bowie** and the glam set. Though Brett Anderson (vocals) does have a rare gift for brilliantly evocative mood swings and monochrome diaramas, there is so far little to suggest that the sum of their talents add up to anything approaching those of these celebrated forefathers. Just as much was made of guitarist Bernard Butler's similarities to Johnny Marr (**Smiths**, **Electronic**). The rest of the band comprised Matt Osman (bass) and Simon Gilbert (drums), a position which Mike Joyce (ex-Smiths) would try out for. However, it was Anderson's arrogant wit and seedy, sexually ambivalent narratives that fascinated the music press. Their first release, 'The Drowners', arrived in March 1992, and 'My Insatiable One', on the b-side, was a brooding low-life London tale of 'shitting paracetamol on the escalator', which so impressed Morrissey he would later cover it live. Anderson would also get to meet his other spiritual forefather in a two-part joint interview with David Bowie in the *New Musical Express*. By this time, the mainstream music media, starved of an adequate figurehead for the 90s, had latched on to the band in a quite disconcerting manner. *Q* magazine put them on their front cover before the release of their debut album, a previously unthinkable concession. Their appearance at the 1993 televised *Brits* awards gave them massive exposure. On the back of this high profile their debut album went straight to number 1 in the UK charts, going gold on the second day of release. Again, much of the lyrical imagery was deliberately homo-erotic, reflected in the sleeve art work. The picture of two naked women kissing, taken by Tee Corrine, was cut to head and shoulders to hide the identity of those involved. All seemed rosy in the graden until the eve of the group's second album in 1994, when it was announced that Butler had left the band (recent interviews had hinted at rancour between Anderson and the guitarist). He would be replaced by 17-year old 'unknown' Richard Oakes. However, as the writing for *Dog Man Star* (which emerged to mixed reviews) had already been completed, there was little immediate evidence to guage the reshuffled Suede on until 1995. Chart returns, on the other hand, suggested the band's chart thunder may have been stolen by **Blur** and **Oasis**. Butler, meanwhile, would go on to write well-regarded new material with **McAlmont**.

Albums: *Suede* (Nude 1993), *Dog Man Star* (Nude 1994).
Videos: *Love & Poison* (1993), *Bootleg 1* (1993).
Further reading: *Suede: The Illustrated Biography*, Membrey, York (1993).

Suesse, Dana

b. 3 December 1910, Kansas City, Missouri, USA, d. 16 October 1987, New York, USA. Not many female composers of popular music were around in the 30s, but Suesse was one of that select band, and a few of her songs have endured over the years. A classically trained pianist, she moved to New York with her mother, an opera singer, and was commissioned by **Paul Whiteman** to compose two jazz concertos for piano and orchestra. Turning from serious to popular music, a modest hit in 1932 with 'Have You Forgotten?' (written with **Leo Robin**), was followed by a collaboration with lyricist **Edward Heyman** which produced a few popular items such as 'Ho Hum', 'My Silent Love', and 'You Oughta Be In Pictures'. The duo also contributed 'Love Makes The World Go Round', 'Take This Ring', 'I'm So Happy I Could Cry', 'The Day You Were Born', and 'Twenty-Four Hours A Day' to the 1935 film musical *Sweet Surrender*. Also among Suesse's relatively small catalogue were 'Whistling In The Dark' (with Allan Boretz), the delightful 'The Night Is Young And You're So Beautiful' (with **Billy Rose** and **Irving Kahal**), 'Moon About Town', 'It Happened In Chicago', 'Blue Moonlight', 'You Have To Live A Little', 'He's A Man I Adore', 'Yours For A Song' (with Rose and Ted Fetter, introduced at New York's World Fair in 1939 in *Billy Rose's Aquacade*), and several classical pieces. In later years she performed frequently as a piano soloist.

Sugar

In the aftermath of **Nirvana**'s commercial breakthrough unhinging a flood of loud, powerful and uncompromising USA-based music, **Bob Mould** (guitar/vocals) found himself subject to the somewhat unflattering representation 'Godfather of Grunge'. The ex-**Hüsker Dü** songwriter has earned this accolade on the back of his former group's considerable influence, but with Sugar he seemed set to continue to justify the critical plaudits which have followed his every move. Joined by David Barbe (ex-Mercyland; bass/vocals), and Malcolm Travis (ex-Zulus; drums), he found another powerful triumvirate to augment his own muse. Barbe proved particularly complementary, a talented songwriter in his own right, his presence as a forthright and intelligent counterpoint mirrored the contribution **Grant Hart** made to Hüsker Dü. Sugar's breakthrough, most visibly in the UK, came with the arrival of *Copper Blue* in 1992. Populated by energetic, evocative, and determinedly melodic pop noise, the album found critics grasping for superlatives. The Hüsker Dü comparisons were inevitable, but Mould was now viewed as an all-conquering prodigal son. Singles like 'Changes' tied the band's musical muscle to a straightforward commercial skeleton, and daytime radio play became an unlikely but welcome recipient of Sugar's crossover appeal. The historically contrary Mould responded a few months later with *Beaster*, in which the melodies and hooks, though still present, were buried under layers of harsh feedback and noise. Ultimately as rewarding as previous work, its appearance nevertheless reminded long-term Mould watchers of his brilliant but pedantic nature. *F.U.E.L.* offered a hybrid of the approaches on the two previous albums, and again saw Mould venerated in the press, if not with the same fawning abandon that *Copper Blue* had produced. Afterwards, however, Mould ruminated widely about his doubts over the long-term future of Sugar, suggesting inner-band tensions between the trio. Albums: *Copper Blue* (Creation 1992), *Beaster* (Creation 1993), *F.U.E.L. (File Under Easy Listening)* (Creation 1994).

Sugar (Stage Musical)

Based on the enormously popular 1959 film, *Some Like It Hot*, this musical, which had a score by the *Funny Girl* team of **Jule Styne** and **Bob Merrill**, opened at the Majestic Theatre in New York on 9 April 1972. Peter Stone's book stayed closely to the original story of two musicians who, having accidentally witnessed the notorious St. Valentine's Day Massacre in Chicago, flee to Miami disguised as members of an all-female orchestra. Robert Morse and Tony Roberts played the roles that were taken in the film by Jack Lemmon and Tony Curtis, Cyril Ritchard was the eccentric millionaire who found himself completely beguiled by Morse in drag, and Elaine Joyce did her best to make people forget the unforgettable **Marilyn Monroe**. The score was suitably 20s in style, and included numbers such as 'When You Meet A Man In Chicago', '(Doing It For) Sugar', 'Sun On My Face', 'What Do You Give To A Man Who's Had Everything?', 'Beautiful Through And Through', 'We Could Be Close', 'It's Always Love', 'Hey, Why Not!', and 'Penniless Bums'. **Gower Champion** contributed some slick choreography, and *Sugar* stayed around for 505 performances. Twenty years later a revised edition with the orginal film title, *Some Like It Hot*, reached London's West End. The emphasis was switched from the character of Sugar to the show's star, **Tommy Steele**, and when he had to leave the cast for a time following an on-stage accident, the production went rapidly downhill and closed after a run of three months with losses estimated at around £2 million.

Sugar Babies

This celebration of the golden age of American burlesque entertainment between 1905 and 1930, opened at the Mark Hellinger Theatre in New York on 8 October 1979. It was conceived by Ralph G. Allen and Harry Rigby, two students of the burlesque form, who based several of the numbers directly on famous historic routines. Most of the music came from the catalogue of the distinguished American composer **Jimmy McHugh**, with lyrics by **Dorothy Fields**, **Harold Adamson**, and **Al Dubin**. Additional music and lyrics were by Arthur Malvin. The obvious choice for the role of comedian and song-and-dance man, to follow in the oversized footsteps of legendary burlesque

comics such as Bert Lahr, Bobby Clark, and W.C. Fields, was one of America's most cherished clowns, **Mickey Rooney**. His co-star was **Ann Miller**, whose long legs and precision dancing style showed no noticeable signs of deterioration since she appeared in movies such as *Kiss Me, Kate* and *On The Town* more than 25 years previously. The sketch material was strictly 'adults only', but the songs, which included classics such as 'Exactly Like You', 'I Feel A Song Comin' On', 'I'm In The Mood For Love', and 'On The Sunny Side Of The Street', appealed to young and old alike. The show ran for a remarkable 1,208 performances and then undertook succcessful US road tours. The 1988 London production, with Rooney and Miller, appealed at first, but then went under after a run of just over three months.

Sugar Hill Records (country)

An independent label founded in 1978 by Barry Poss, who had previously worked with County Records. Sugar Hill particularly specialises in bluegrass music but has also done much to popularise recordings of acoustic music. In the 60s, some independent labels including King and Starday released bluegrass material by such as the **Stanley Brothers** but when these labels folded, bluegrass music tended to become a neglected genre. The major labels rarely covered the music (**Bill Monroe**'s work on **Decca**, later MCA, excepted) and it was left to labels like County to provide the recordings of acoustic music. In the 70s, **Rounder Records** appeared and later Rebel became a noted bluegrass label. When Sugar Hill was launched, they neatly bridged a gap between such labels as Rounder and the major labels.

Their first release was *One Way Track* by Boone Creek, a short lived five-piece bluegrass band, whose members included **Ricky Skaggs** and Jerry Douglas. It was also Skaggs who gave the label its first real boost with *Sweet Temptation* (SH3706). It was an album that drew glowing praise from the critics, both for the artist and the label, for the clever way it combined bluegrass and country. It also sent Skaggs on the way to major stardom albeit not with Sugar Hill, although he did make further recordings for the label. From that point Sugar Hill moved on and using their 3000 series, they have built an enviable reputation with recordings by such as **Seldom Scene**, **Country Gentlemen**, Doyle Lawson, John Starling, **Doc Watson**, **Peter Rowan** and the excellent Nashville Bluegrass Band, to name but few of the artists whose careers have been founded around their recordings for Sugar Hill. Later the label launched other series such as the 1000, which issued recordings by artists ranging from Texas singer/songwriters **Townes Van Zandt** and **Guy Clark** to the more folk country songs of Robin And Linda Williams. Gospel music fans may find some excellent examples on the 9100 series. Over the years, the label's production staff have built a reputation for their excellent sound reproduction. Their catalogue is perhaps smaller than some indie labels but they have never allowed attempts at quick sales to deter them from producing the highest possible standard of recordings as witness the Grammy awards their recordings have won.

Sugarcreek

This top class pomp-rock group emerged from North Carolina, USA. The band were formed in 1981 by vocalist Tim Clark and guitarist Jerry West. Recruiting Rick Lee (keyboards), Robbie Hegler (bass) and Lynn Samples (drums), they drew inspiration from the popular AOR rock artists of the day (**Journey**, **Styx** and **Kansas**). They made a significant breakthrough with *Fortune*, a highly melodic album swathed in keyboards and silky-smooth vocal harmonies. Michael Hough was added as a second guitarist for *Rock The Night Away*, which marked a more commercial slant to the band's songwriting. He quit shortly after the album was released and the band subsequently shortened their name to **Creek** in 1986.
Albums: *Live At The Roxy* (Beaver 1981), *Fortune* (Beaver 1982), *Rock The Night Away* (Ripete 1984), *Sugarcreek* (Music For Nations 1985).

Sugarcubes

This offbeat pop band was formed in Reykjavik, Iceland on 8 June 1986, the date taken from the birth of **Björk**'s son, Sindri. The settled line-up featured Björk Gundmundsdottir (b. 1966, Reykjavik, Iceland; vocals/keyboards), Bragi Olaffson (bass), Einar Orn Benediktsson (vocals/trumpet), Margret 'Magga' Ornolfsdottir (keyboards, replacing original keyboard player Einar Mellax) Sigtryggur 'Siggi' Balduresson (drums) and Thor Eldon (guitar). Björk's step-father was in a rock showband, and after early stage appearances she completed her first album at the age of 11. She was also the singer for prototype groups Toppie Tikarras then Theyr, alongside Siggi Balduresson. The latter band shot to prominence when Jaz Coleman and Youth (**Killing Joke**) mysteriously appeared in Iceland in March 1982, paranoid about an impending apocalypse, and collaborated on several projects with Theyr. Björk, Einar and Siggi then went on to form Kukl, who toured Europe and released two records on the **Crass** label, establishing a link with the UK anarcho-punk scene which would be cemented when the band joined UK independent label **One Little Indian Records**. Their debut single, 'Birthday', and album, *Life's Too Good*, saw the band championed in the UK press almost immediately. In particular, praise was heaped on Björk's distinctive and emotive vocals. The Sugarcubes ran their own company in Iceland called Bad Taste, an organization which encompassed an art gallery, poetry bookshop, record label, radio station

and publishing house. Björk's ex-husband, Thor, a graduate in Media Studies from London Polytechnic and the band's guitarist, sired their son Sindri under a government incentive scheme to boost the island's population, the financial rewards for this action allowing him to buy a pair of contact lenses. He then married Magga Ornolfsdottir (ex-the Giant Lizard), who joined the band in time for their second album. In addition, Siggi Balduresson and Bragi Olaffson, the band's rhythm section, were brother-in-laws, having married twin sisters. Most bizarre of all, however, was the subsequent marriage of Einar and Bragi in Denmark in 1989, the first openly gay marriage in pop history. *Here Today, Tomorrow, Next Week*, its title taken from a line in Kenneth Graeme's book *Wind In The Willows*, was a much more elaborate album, with a full brass section on 'Tidal Wave' and strings on the single, 'Planet'. However, compared with the rapturous reception granted their first album, *Here Today* took a critical pasting. Even label boss Derek Birkett conceded that it was far too deliberate. The press was also quick to seize on the fact that Einar's vocal interjections detracted from the band's performance. After much touring the group returned to Reykjavik, where they followed their own interests for a time. Björk collaborated on the Bad Taste album *Glimg Glo*; 'Just Icelandic pop songs from the 50s with jazz influences'. Balduresson also contributed drums. Members of the band spent time as an alternative jazz orchestra. The band then played a concert for President Mitterand of France, in Reykjavik, and Björk joined **808 State** on their *Ex:El* album and single, 'Oops'. The group's third album found them back in favour with the music press and back in the charts with 'Hit', but the inevitable happened shortly afterwards, with Björk heading for a critically and commercially rewarding solo career.
Albums: *Life's Too Good* (One Little Indian 1988), *Here Today, Tomorrow, Next Week* (One Little Indian 1989), *It's It* (One Little Indian 1992, remixes), *Stick Around For Joy* (One Little Indian 1992).

Sugarhill Gang

Englewood, New Jersey troupe, whose 'Rapper's Delight' was hip hop's breakthrough single. They gave the music an identity and a calling card in the first line of the song: 'A hip-hop, The hi-be, To the hi-be, The hip-hip-hop, You don't stop rockin'. Master Gee (b. Guy O'Brien, 1963), Wonder Mike (b. Michael Wright, 1958) and Big Bank Hank (b. Henry Jackson, 1958) saw massive international success in 1979 with 'Rappers Delight', based on the subsequently widely borrowed rhythm track from **Chic**'s 'Good Times', over which the trio offered a series of sly boasts which were chatted rather than sung. Joe Robinson remembers the song's elevation to commercial status: 'Sylvia brought this to me, a 15 minute record on a 12-inch disc. No 15 minute record has ever got played on the radio, so I said, what am I gonna do with this? But all I had to do with it was get one play anywhere and it broke'. Considered at the time to be something of a novelty item, 'Rapper's Delight' was significantly more than that. Sylvia and Joe Robinson had recruited the three rappers on an *ad hoc* basis. Hank was a former bouncer and pizza waiter, and brought fresh rhymes from his friend Granmaster Caz (see **Cold Crush Brothers**). The backing was offered by Positive Force, a group from Pennsylvania who enjoyed their own hit with 'We Got The Funk', but became part of the Sugarhill phenomenon when 'Rapper's Delight' struck. They would go on to tour on the Gang's early live shows, before the Sugarhill house band took over. Smaller hits followed with 'The Love In You' (1979) and 'Kick It Live From 9 To 5' (1982), before the group faded and fell apart in the early 80s. The Sugarhill Gang were already assured of their place in hip hop's history, even if reports that Big Bank Hank was working as a Englewood garbage man in the 90s are correct.

Albums: *Rappers Delight* (Sugarhill 1980), *8th Wonder* (Sugarhill 1982).

Sugarhill Records

Joe Robinson Jnr. and Sylvia Robinson were behind this label, named after the comparatively affluent locale in Harlem, though they themselves had moved to Englewood in New Jersey. It was not necessarily the first rap label, but by far the biggest and most important. The inspiration came from their teenage children's enthusiasm for the hip hop movement and its celebrity MCs, particularly the 'live jam' tapes. Sylvia already had a music legacy. It is widely recalled that she had scored a Top 20 hit in 1973 with 'Pillow Talk'. However, she had also scored as Little Sylvia for Savoy, and duetted with her guitar tutor Houston 'Mickey' Baker', at which time she also met Joe, on the duet 'Love Is Strange'. Joe's background, conversely, was in real estate, but he gained an introduction to music via his wife. Together they opened a club entitled the Blue Morocco in the Bronx, and by the end of the 60s had started the All Platinum label. This housed soul and funk records by **George Kerr**, **Linda Jones**, the Universal Messengers and others. Joe also owned the rights to the **Chess** back-catalogue. They convinced Morris Levy to assist them in a new venture and, in 1979, Sugarhill's rap agenda was launched with 'Rapper's Delight'. By sampling the huge **Chic** hit 'Good Times', it effectively gave birth to the debate over artistic authorship which has dominated rap since. It did, however, have precedents, one of which Sylvia Robinson was only too aware of: 'Strange Love' had also been subject to disputes over plagiarism. Their reputation as financially irascible operators is enshrined in rap legend, though so is their contribution to the development of the music. Employing the Sugarhill house band (**Keith LeBlanc**, Skip

McDonald, Doug Wimbush - who had met as part of Wood Brass & Steel, a funk outfit who had also performed regular duties for the Robinsons' former label All Platinum - later to move to the UK and become **Tackhead**), a steady stream of rap classics followed. These included **Four Plus One**'s 'That's The Joint', and 'The Message' and 'White Lines' by **Grandmaster Flash** and **Grandmaster Melle Mel** respectively. The success was rapid, but led to complications over finance. Specifically, they were accused of not paying their artists' royalties, a charge they defend vehemently. Despite the acrimony over the Grandmaster Flash And The Furious Five in-fighting debacle, Joe Robinson Jnr., for one, does not countenance their widely read press statements: 'Who gives a fuck what those fuckin' bums think? Them guys was drug addicts using crack when it first came out. Flash never wrote a song, never did a rap - son of a bitch was never in the studio when a record was made out of here. It's all in the court records'. He was referring to the 1983 case, which, although they won, forced Sugarhill into financial difficulties. They linked up with **MCA** but to no avail. Sugarhill would eventually go under in the mid-80s following problems with distributors. They had been left behind by new technology - their policy of never hiring outside producers severely damaging them when sequencers and samplers were introduced, as no-one in the company knew how to use them. They eventually sold their ownership of Chess, but the Robinsons remain in the music business, and currently run publishing and licensing companies in New York (Sylvia had made a brief return to recording with 'Good To Be The Queen', an answer record to Mel Brooks' 'Good To Be The King' rap). As for the late lamented Sugarhill, it is nice to see at least one label with as colourful a history as the music it played such a major role in advancing.

Selected compilations: *Rapped Uptight Vol. 1* (Sugarhill 1981), *Rapped Uptight Vol. 2* (Sugarhill 1982), *Old School Rap: The Sugarhill Story* (Sequel 1992), *The Sugarhill 12-inch Mixes* (Castle 1994).

Suicidal Tendencies

Vocalist Mike Muir formed Suicidal Tendencies in the early 80s in the Venice Beach area of Los Angeles, California, USA, enlisting Grant Estes (guitar), Louiche Mayorga (bass) and Amery Smith (drums). Despite an inauspicious start, being voted 'worst band and biggest assholes' in *Flipside* magazine's 1982 polls, the band produced a hardcore classic in *Suicidal Tendencies*, and although they initially fell between hardcore punk and thrash stools, MTV's support of 'Institutionalized' helped the group take off. *Join The Army* was recorded with respected guitarist Rocky George and drummer R.J. Herrera replacing Estes and Smith, and the skateboarding anthem, 'Possessed To Skate', kept the group in the ascendancy. *How Will I Laugh*

Tomorrow...When I Can't Even Smile Today? marked the debut of Mike Clark (rhythm guitar) as the group's sound exploded, extending from a balladic title-track to the furious 'Trip At The Brain'. This progression continued on *Controlled By Hatred/Feel Like Shit...Deja Vu*, but as the band's stature increased, so did their problems. Their name and image were easy targets for both the PMRC and the California police, with the former blaming teenage suicides on a band who were unable to play near their home town due to performance permit refusals from the latter, who feared Suicidal Tendencies were an LA gang. Naturally, the outspoken Muir fought vehemently against these bizarre accusations and treatment. Talented bassist Robert Rujillo, with whom Muir formed **Infectious Grooves** in tandem with Suicidal, made his debut on the excellent *Lights...Cameras...Revolution*, which produced hits in the defiant 'You Can't Bring Me Down' and 'Send Me Your Money', a vitriolic attack on televangelist preachers. The band also re-recorded their debut during these sessions for release as *Still Cyco After All These Years*. The Peter Collins-produced *The Art Of Rebellion*, with new drummer Josh Freece, was a more ambitious, diverse work, and rather more lightweight than previous albums. Any fears that the band were mellowing were dispelled by furious live shows. *Suicidal For Life*, with Jimmy DeGrasso (ex-**White Lion/Y&T**) replacing Freece, emphasized the point as the band returned in fast-paced and profanity-peppered style, while continuing to extend individual talents to the full. Shortly after its release news filtered through that the band were no more, and a chapter in hardcore history slammed shut behind them.

Albums: *Suicidal Tendencies* (Frontier 1983), *Join The Army* (Caroline/Virgin 1987), *How Will I Laugh Tomorrow...When I Can't Even Smile Today* (Epic 1988), *Controlled By Hatred/Feel Like Shit...Deja Vu* (Epic 1989), *Lights...Camera...Revolution* (Epic 1990), *The Art Of Rebellion* (Epic 1992), *Still Cyco After All These Years* (Epic 1993), *Suicidal For Life* (Epic 1994). Compilation: *FNG* (Virgin 1992).

Suicide

This US band were an influence on **Birthday Party**, **Soft Cell**, **Sigue Sigue Sputnik** and the **Sisters Of Mercy** with a potent fusion of rockabilly and electronic music on cheap equipment. Singer Alan Vega (b. 1948) and multi-instrumentalist Martin Rev polarized audiences in Max's Kansas City and other New York clubs in the early 70s, remaining unheard on vinyl until the advent of the new wave when their arrangement of 'Rocket 88' was included on *Max's Kansas City* (1976) compilation. **Ramones** associates Craig Leon and Martin Thau oversaw the duo's early recording career (on Thau's Red Star label) until a support spot on a **Cars** tour brought them to the notice of vocalist Ric Ocasek who produced *Alan Vega And Martin Rev* for Ze

Records, as well as 'Hey Lord', Suicide's contribution to a 1981 Ze sampler. Ocasek was also involved in the pair's respective solo albums. Of these, Vega's vocal-dominated efforts elicited most public interest - particularly with 1981's *Vega* (containing the European hit 'Juke Box Baby') and *Sunset Strip* with its revival of **Hot Chocolate**'s 'Everyone's A Winner'. Vega also mounted a one-man sculpture exhibition in New York and, with **David Bowie** and **Philip Glass**, had a hand in David Van Teighem's collage for the ballet *Fair Accompli* before Suicide resumed corporate activities in 1986.

Albums: *Suicide* (1977), *24 Minutes Over Brussels* (1978), *Live* (1979), *Half Alive* (1981), *Alan Vega And Martin Rev* (1981), *A Way Of Life* (1989). Solo albums: Martin Rev *Martin Rev* (1979), *Clouds Of Glory* (1985), *Cheyanne* (1992); Alan Vega *Vega* (1981), *Sunset Strip* (1983), *Just A Million Dreams* (1985), *Deuce Avenue* (1990), *New Race Is On* (1993).

Sulieman, Idrees

b. Leonard Graham, 7 August 1923, St. Petersburg, Florida, USA. After playing trumpet for a number of years with **territory bands**, in 1943 Sulieman joined **Earl 'Fatha' Hines**. After some more dues-paying in minor bands, he came to New York where he played with **Thelonious Monk** and then began a tour through an impressive succession of big bands, including those led by **Cab Calloway**, **Count Basie** and **Lionel Hampton**. He also played in small groups led by **Mal Waldron**, **Randy Weston** and others. In the 60s he moved to Sweden, then settled in Denmark where he has remained. From the mid-60s he played with the **Clarke-Boland Big Band** and also took up alto saxophone. In the 70s he continued to work in Denmark, mostly with radio big bands, but made occasional record dates as leader and with musicians such as **Horace Parlan**. Despite being one of the first jazz musicians to play bop, Sulieman's long residency away from the international spotlight has meant that he has had little influence upon others.

Albums: with Mal Waldron *Mal 1* (1956), with Horace Parlan *Arrival* (1973), *Now Is The Time* (1976).

Sullivan, Big Jim

b. c.1940, London, England, he worked in a sheet-metal factory before joining a skiffle group as a guitarist. Sullivan was soon hired by **Marty Wilde** as a member of his backing group, the Wildcats. In 1959, the group backed **Eddie Cochran** on his final UK tour, and later recorded the instrumentals 'Trambone' and 'Samovar' as the Krew Kats. After that group split up, Sullivan became a session musician and teacher, giving lessons to young hopefuls like **Ritchie Blackmore** and **Jimmy Page**. During the 60s he played on thousands of recordings, backing such artists as **Michael Cox**, the **Kinks**, **Small Faces**,

Jonathan King, Donovan, the Rolling Stones, Nancy Wilson and Sarah Vaughan. In 1969 he accompanied Tom Jones on a world tour. Sullivan made occasional records under his own name at this time. 'You Don't Know What You've Got' (1961) was a cover version of Ral Donner's hit while 'She Walks Through The Fair' was a traditional Irish tune. Sullivan also studied Indian music with Ustad Vilayat Khan and in 1968 made a sitar album for Mercury. Two years later, he played with Blackmore and Albert Lee as Green Bullfrog, a studio group reproduced by Derek Lawrence. In 1974 he made a rare vocal album for Lawrence's Retreat label, following this by forming Tiger with Dave Macrae (keyboards), Phil Curtis (bass) and Billy Rankin (drums). The band made albums for Retreat and EMI (*Going Down Laughing*, 1976). During the 80s, Sullivan remained in demand for session work and made more solo recordings, among which was *Test Of Time* produced by Mike Vernon.

Albums: *Sitar Beat* (1968), *Jim Sullivan* (1972), *Big Jim's Back* (1974), *Sullivan Plays O'Sullivan* (1977), *Rock 'n' Roll Wrecks* (1983), *Test Of Time* (1983).

Sullivan, Ed

b. 28 September 1902, New York City, New York, USA, d. 13 October 1974. Sullivan hosted the most popular variety programme on US television during the 50s and 60s. He presented hundreds of the most important musical acts of the era to a wide audience; it was on *The Ed Sullivan Show* that most of America first saw Elvis Presley and the Beatles. Guest musical acts nearly always performed live, some backed by Sullivan's orchestra, led by Ray Bloch. Sullivan was one of seven children, and grew up in New York's Harlem section until the age of five, when his family moved to the suburb of Port Chester, New York, north of the city. He had no particular desire to be an entertainer and took a job as a sportswriter with a Port Chester newspaper as a teenager. In the early 20s he was hired by the *New York Evening Graphic* newspaper in the city, and then by the larger *New York Daily News* in 1932.

While at that paper he began hosting vaudeville shows, which led, in 1947, to an offer by CBS Television to host a new programme (at that time *all* television programmes were new, the medium having opened up at the close of World War II) called *Toast of The Town*. It debuted on 20 June 1948; he held on to his newspaper column as well. On 25 September 1955 the programme's name was changed to *The Ed Sullivan Show*. On his show, Sullivan featured any kind of entertainment he thought would grab a portion of the viewing audience, from opera singers to jugglers, dancing chimps to pop groups. The programme became one of the highest-rated on American television, and was a Sunday night ritual for millions of

Americans. Sullivan became a celebrity himself while his mannerisms and way of speaking became fodder for many comedians and impressionists. Among the hundreds of musical artists to have appeared on the show, in addition to Presley and the Beatles, were Louis Armstrong, Judy Garland, Liberace, the Rolling Stones, the Doors and Ella Fitzgerald. (In 1990, the audio and video rights to some of those performances were leased, and compilation albums featuring music from *The Ed Sullivan Show* began to appear in the USA.) The programme was broadcast for the last time on 6 June 1971.

Sullivan, Ira

b. 1 May 1931, Washington, USA. Sullivan is that rare thing, a true multi-instrumentalist, capable of improvising statements of worth on all his instruments. He was taught trumpet by his father, saxophone by his mother and played both in 50s' Chicago with such seminal figures as Charlie Parker, Lester Young, Wardell Gray and Roy Eldridge, garnering a reputation as a fearsome bebop soloist. After playing briefly with Art Blakey (1956), and mastering alto and baritone saxophone, Sullivan moved south to Florida and out of the spotlight in the early 60s. His reluctance to travel limited his opportunities to play with musicians of the first rank, but Sullivan continued to play in the Miami area, often in schools and churches. Contact with local younger players, notably Jaco Pastorius and Pat Metheny lead to teaching and to a broadening of his own musical roots to include the lessons of John Coltrane's music and elements of jazz rock. With the addition of flute and soprano saxophone to his armoury, Sullivan moved to New York and in 1980 formed a quintet with legendary bop trumpeter Red Rodney. Resisting the temptation to follow current trends and play the music of their youth, Sullivan and Rodney worked on new material and fostered young talent to produce some of the freshest and most stimulating music of the decade.

Albums: *Nicky's Tune* (Delmark 1958), *Ira Sullivan Quartet* (Delmark 1974), *Ira Sullivan* (Flying Fish 1976), *Peace* (1978), with Red Rodney *Live At The Village Vanguard* (1980), *Bird Lives* (Affinity 1981), *Horizons* (Discovery 1983), *Does It All* (Muse 1988), *Tough Town* (Delmark 1992).

Sullivan, Joe

b. 4 November 1906, Chicago, Illinois, USA, d. 13 October 1971. After studying piano formally, Sullivan began working in theatres and clubs in and around Chicago while still a teenager. Throughout the 20s he was one of the busiest musicians in Chicago, playing at clubs and on numerous record dates with leading jazzmen, mostly in small groups. He also worked as accompanist to Bing Crosby during the early 30s. At various times in that decade he played in several larger ensembles, among them bands led by **Roger Wolfe Kahn** and **Bob Crosby**. Ill health drove him from the Crosby band just as it hit the bigtime. In the 40s he played with **Bobby Hackett** and **Eddie Condon** and also frequently worked as a single. He continued playing alone, not from choice, and in small jazz groups through the 50s. From the early 60s onwards his career was dogged by both poor health and critical disregard. An eclectic pianist, Sullivan's robust style displayed elements of stride but he was at his propulsive best playing in a lively Chicago-style band. Among his compositions are 'Gin Mill Blues' and 'Little Rock Getaway'.

Albums: *Fats Waller First Editions* (1952), *New Solos By An Old Master* (1953), *Mr Piano Man* (1955), *Gin Mill* (Pumpkin 1963). Selected compilations: *Joe Sullivan And The All Stars (1950)* (Shoestring 1981), *At The Piano* (Shoestring 1981), *Piano Man (1935-40)* (1988).

Sullivan, Maxine

b. Marietta Williams, 13 May 1911, Homestead, Pennsylvania, USA, d. 7 April 1987. Sullivan began singing in and around Pittsburgh, Pennsylvania, before travelling to New York in 1937. She joined the **Claude Thornhill** band and made a hugely successful record of 'Loch Lomond'. The popularity of this recording led to her making several more jazzed-up folk songs, including 'Annie Laurie', which, for all their frequent banality, she sang with effortless charm. In the late 30s and early 40s she made several feature films and also worked and recorded with her husband **John Kirby**. After a brief retirement she began appearing again in New York and also travelled to Europe. In the mid-50s she quit singing to take up nursing but returned in 1958. In addition to singing she also played flügelhorn, valve-trombone and pocket trumpet. She continued to work through the 60s, often with **Cliff Jackson**, who had become her second husband, and with **Bob Wilber**. Her career blossomed in the late 70s and throughout most of the 80s, thanks to performances with the **World's Greatest Jazz Band** and **Scott Hamilton**. In her later years she devoted some of her considerable energy to running the 'House that Jazz Built', a museum she created at her home and dedicated to Jackson's memory. The hallmarks of her singing were charm and delicacy, qualities which were often out of favour and probably accounted for the ups and downs of her career. Her later work, especially the recordings with Wilber, proved that her talent was far greater than public taste had allowed.

Albums: with others *Seven Ages Of Jazz* (1958), *Maxine Sullivan i* (1969), *Close As Pages In A Book* (1969), *Queen Of Song* (1970), *Maxine Sullivan ii* (1971), *Maxine* (1975), *Harlem Butterfly* (1975-77), *We Just Couldn't Say Goodbye* (1978), *Maxine Sullivan And Ike Isaacs* (1978), *Sullivan, Shakespeare, Hyman* (Audiophile 1979), *Maxine Sullivan And Her Swedish Jazz All Stars* (1981), *It Was Great Fun!*

(1983), *Good Morning, Life* (1983), *The Queen; Something To Remember Her By* (Kenneth 1985), *The Great Songs From The Cotton Club By Harold Arlen And Ted Koehler* (Mobile Fidelity 1985), *Uptown* (Concord 1985), *The Lady's In Love With You* (1985), *I Love To Be In Love* (c.1986), *Maxine Sullivan And Scott Hamilton* (1986), *Songs Of Burton Lane* (1986), *Together: Maxine Sullivan Sings Julie Styne* (c.1986), *Swingin' Street* (Concord 1987), *Spring Isn't Everything* (Audiophile 1987). Compilations: *It's Wonderful* (1992), *1944 To 1948* (1993).

Sultans Of Ping FC

Formed in 1989 in Cork, Eire, and titled after the **Dire Straits'** song of similar title, the Sultans Of Ping FC have built up a rabid live following for their cross-dressing antics and tales of the totally unexpected. They chose their name in mock admiration of **Mark Knopfler**'s outfit, being virulently anti-stadium rock 'n' roll 'baloney'. The band comprise Niall O'Flaherty (vocals), Paddy O'Connell (guitar), Morty McCarthy (drums) and Dat (b. Alan McFeely; bass). Their gigs quickly became legend after a local affair in which the promoter asked the crowd to sit down. The band joined them in solidarity, leading to audience participation of a bizarre nature: a series of floor gymnastics, with kicks to the air from a prone position. The gig that launched them nationally came when taking part in an Irish rock open, where they were the token local Cork entrants. Home support pushed them in to the winner's enclosure. The first single endorsed this lunacy: 'Where's Me Jumper' on **Rhythm King Records**, revolved around the tale of Niall having his jumper pinched at a dance. In the best traditions of **Serious Drinking** and **Half Man Half Biscuit,** the Sultans are a band sharing the esoteric conviction of fellow Cork residents the **Frank And Walters**. However, their debut album was more than a barrage of jokes; with string and harmonica arrangements backing the strange lyrical observations. These included songs about Jesus' second coming (in a tracksuit), and a pole vaulter unhindered by arms, legs or head. Titles like 'Give Him A Ball And A Yard Of Grass' and 'Riot At The Sheepdog Trials' still gave a fairly strong indication of which planet in the pop universe the Sultans pinged from. *Teenage Drug* emerged to less flattering reviews, but was ultimately no less endearing in its humour, a strain which is often more complex than has been portrayed in some sections of the media. Album: *Casual Sex In The Cineplex* (Rhythm King 1992), *Teenage Drug* (Rhythm King 1993).

Sulzmann, Stan

b. 30 November 1948, London, England. From his mid-teens Sulzmann was playing saxophones on the blues circuit, but in 1964 he joined the first edition of **Bill Ashton**'s **National Youth Jazz Orchestra**. Following this he worked on the Queen Mary crossing to New York and then returned to London to study at the Royal Academy of Music. Subsequently, as well as winning the **Melody Maker** New Star award, he played with **Mike Gibbs**, **Graham Collier**, **John Dankworth**, **John Taylor** (with whom he also established a quartet in 1970), John Warren, **Clark Terry**, Brian Cooper, **Alan Cohen**, the **Clarke-Boland Big Band**, **Kenny Wheeler**, **Gordon Beck**'s Gyroscope and **Gil Evans**' early 80s London band. Equally adept on soprano, alto and tenor saxophones and flutes and clarinet, Sulzmann was one of the earliest of several distinguished graduates from the NYJO, and his influences range from **Frank Zappa**, through to Kenny Wheeler (whose compositions he showcased on *Everybody's Song But My Own*) and **Miles Davis** to Debussy and Delius.

Selected albums: with Michael Gibbs *Tanglewood '63* (1971), *On Loan With Gratitude* (1977), *Krark* (1979), with John Taylor *Everybody's Song But My Own* (1987), with Tony Hymas *Flying Fortress* (1991), *Feudal Rabbits* (Ah-Um 1991), with Marc Copland *Never At All* (Future 1993).

Sumac, Yma

b. Emperatriz Chavarri, 10 September 1927, Ichocan, Peru. A flamboyant singer, of striking appearance, who was the subject of a series of publicity campaigns designed to shroud her origins in mystery: was she an Inca princess, one of the chosen 'Golden Virgins'? Or a Brooklyn housewife named Amy Camus (Yma Sumac spelt backwards)? Whatever the doubts as to her heritage, what is abundantly clear is her four octave range, ascending from 'female baritone, through lyric soprano, to high coloratura'. The rest of the story goes like this: she was the sixth child of a full-blooded Indian mother and a mixed Indian and Spanish father, and was raised a Quechuan. After performing in local Indian festivals, she moved with her family to Lima, and joined the Compania Peruana de Arte, a group of 46 Indian dancers, singers and musicians. In 1942, Sumac married the Compania's leader, musician and composer, Moises Vivanco, and, four years later, travelled to New York with him, and her cousin, Cholita Rivero, as the Inca Taqui Trio. In the late 40s the Trio played nightclubs such as New York's Blue Angel, and appeared on radio programmes and Arthur Godfrey's television show. Other work included an eight week tour of the Borscht Circuit in the Catskill mountains. Signed for **Capitol Records**, her first album, *Voice Of Xtabay*, was released in 1950. It featured Sumac 'imitating birds and kettledrums, and singing a selection of strangely compelling songs, such as 'Chant Of The Chosen Maidens' and 'Virgin Of The Sun God', which were written for her by Moises Vivanco, and based on ancient Peruvian folk music'. With only the advantage of minimum publicity (at first), and the notorious 'phony biography', the 10-inch album sold

half a million copies 'overnight'. It was followed by several more in the same vein, and led to an enormously successful concert appearance at the Hollywood Bowl. In 1951, Sumac made her Broadway debut in the short-lived musical, *Flahooley*, singing three songs written for her by Vivanco 'with no lyrics and no real relevance to the story'. During the 50s she continued to be 'hot', playing Carnegie Hall, the Roxy Theatre with **Danny Kaye**, Las Vegas nightclubs and concert tours of South America and Europe. She also appeared in the movie, *Secret Of The Incas* (1954), with Charlton Heston and Robert Young. By the end of the decade she was beginning to be regarded by some as 'passe', and, eventually, as a 'nostalgic camp icon'. She retired in the early 60s, but is reported to have performed in 1975 at the Chateau Madrid club in Manhattan. In 1987 she hit the comeback trail with a three week engagement at New York's Ballroom, and, a year later, gained favourable reviews in Los Angeles for 'charming and frequently breathtaking performance'. In her set she featured well-know Latin songs such as 'La Molina' as well as the ethereal material 'that I recorded for Capitol 2,000 years ago!'. In 1992, a German documentary film, *Yma Sumac: Hollywood's Inca Princess*, mapped out her exotic career, and attempted to examine her remarkable range with the aid of computer technology. The lady herself declined to co-operate with the venture, thereby leaving the mystery, and the legend, intact.

Selected albums: *Voice Of The Xtabay* (1950), *Legend Of The Sun Virgin* (1951), *Mambo* (1953), *Inca Taqui* (1955), *Legend Of The Jivaro* (1957), *Feugo Del Ande* (1959), *Live In Concert* (1961).

Sumlin, Hubert

b. 16 November 1931, Greenwood, Mississippi, USA. Renowned for his guitar work, particularly in support of his mentor **Howlin' Wolf**, Hubert Sumlin began his career in the Mississippi juke joints. He joined **Jimmy Cotton** and met Wolf in Memphis where he worked with him briefly before following him to Chicago in 1954. His occasional stormy relationship with Wolf lasted until the latter's death although on Wolf's obsequies he is listed as a son. He was in Europe with Wolf on the AFBF of 1964 and later worked with other bluesmen including **Eddie Taylor** and **Muddy Waters**. Since Wolf's death Hubert has pursued his career under his own name, often working with alumni of Wolf's band. Never a strong singer, he has relied on his guitar playing prowess to see him through, but his work has been patchy and some feel that he has yet to regain his original stature.

Albums: *The Rocking Chair Album (Howlin Wolf)* (1962), *Blues Party* (1987), *Healing Feeling* (Black Top 1990), *Blues Guitar Boss* (1991), *My Guitar And Me* (Evidence 1994).

Summer Holiday (1948)

Another wallow in turn-of-the-century small-town Americana of the kind that hardly ever failed at the US box-office. This one was based on Eugene O'Neill's comedy *Ah, Wilderness!*, and was released by MGM in 1948. Frances Goodrich and Albert Hackett's screenplay retained much of the warmth and gentleness which had made the original so appealing, and **Mickey Rooney**, as a youngster making the often bewildering transition into manhood, was superb. **Gloria De Haven** was fine as his girlfriend, and so were parents Walter Huston and Selena Royle. The remainder of a strong cast included Frank Morgan, Agnes Moorehead, Jackie 'Butch' Jenkins, Marilyn Maxwell, and Anne Francis. **Harry Warren** and **Ralph Blane**'s score was skilfully integrated into the story, and included 'Our Home Town', 'Independence Day', 'Afraid To Fall In Love', 'Weary Blues', 'I Think You're The Sweetest Kid I've Ever Known', 'All Hail Danville High', and the lively 'Stanley Steamer'. **Charles Walters**, who was renowned for his exuberant choreography, staged the dances, and **Rouben Mamoulian**, who set the standard for movie musicals with his *Love Me Tonight* (1933), directed with his usual flair and attention for detail and character. It was photographed brilliantly in Technicolor by Charles Schoenbaum, and produced by the famous Arthur Freed Unit. The modestly successful 1959 Broadway musical, *Take Me Along*, which had a score by **Bob Merrill**, was also based on O'Neill's *Ah, Wilderness!*

Summer Holiday (1962)

Cliff Richard's second 'teenage' feature, released in 1962, maintained the light-hearted nature of its successful predecessor, *The Young Ones*. *Summer Holiday* revolves around four London Transport mechanics who borrow a double-decker bus and embark for the Continent. Pursuit, love, capture and an inevitable happy ending ensue, but Peter Yates' snappy direction and location shots result in a film no less slight than much British light comedy of its time. Indeed, the appearance of the singer's backing group, the **Shadows**, in various different guises, was one of the films endearing features. However, the presence of established stalwarts Ron Moody and David Kossoff alongside Richard, Una Stubbs and Mervyn Hayes help place the musical within the framework of all-round entertainment. Winter season pantomime was the next logical step. *Summer Holiday* contained some of the singer's most enduring hit singles, including the double-sided chart topper, 'Bachelor Boy'/'The Next Time' and the title track itself, which also reached number one in the UK. Cliff Richard (and the Shadows), were arguably at the peak of their collective popularity at this point. In February 1963 the *Summer Holiday* album took over the number 1 spot on the album list from *Out Of The Shadows*. It reigned there for 14 unbroken weeks, until being replaced, prophetically, by the **Beatles**' *Please Please Me*.

Summer Stock

Of the three films in which **Judy Garland** and **Gene Kelly** starred together, their final project, *Summer Stock*, is the least impressive. Yet this 1950 MGM release still remains a favourite for many, and has some genuinely charming moments. It tells the tale of the two Falbury sisters - Jane (Garland) has remained at home in New England to run the farm, while Abigail (**Gloria DeHaven**), has left the roost to pursue a showbiz career. To her sister's horror, Abigail brings the people, props and paraphernalia of a whole new show, written and organised by Joe D. Ross (Kelly), to rehearse on the farm. Jane insists that if the whole gang is going to live there and use the barn for rehearsals, they had better earn their keep. This results in some amusing shenanigans, with cows, chickens and an accident with a brand new tractor - disasters which Phil Silvers normally has something to do with. When Abigail suddenly leaves the production, Jane steps into her place, and does so with a hard working attitude and passion that her sister never displayed. When Abigail returns to apologise half way through the opening night of the show, she not only finds that Jane's performance has been a triumph, but that Jane and Joe have fallen in love. Jane's fiancé, Orville (Eddie Bracken), is left out in the cold, but it looks like Abigail is going to help him recover from the blow. George Wells and Sy Gomberg's screenplay is a happy bundle of clichés - let's put a show on in a barn . . . you've only got a few days to learn the part etc. Not that anyone cared much, because *Summer Stock*, directed by **Charles Walters** and produced by Joe Pasternak, was good fun, and indeed, several of the sequences are still quite memorable. Garland's singing and dancing in 'Get Happy' (**Harold Arlen**/Ted Koehler) combine to create one of her all-time best and sophisticated performances. During the rest of the film she was obviously overweight, but 'Get Happy' was shot two months after filming had officially ended, and by then she was back in fine condition. Whatever her physical problems, Garland's voice did not seem to be affected on the uplifting 'If You Feel Like Singing, Sing' and the poignant 'Friendly Star'. They were both written by **Harry Warren** and **Mack Gordon**, who also contributed 'Happy Harvest', 'Blue Jean Polka', 'Dig-Dig-Dig For Your Dinner' and 'Mem'ry Island'. Garland and Kelly were perfect together, and Kelly and Silvers also had a great time with the more comical material, as they did in *Cover Girl* some six years earlier. Kelly's own personal mark of genius showed itself in the sequence when, while walking on the stage, he stepped on a squeaky floorboard. Simply by using this, a sheet of newspaper and the accompaniment of 'You Wonderful You' (Warren-Jack Brooks-**Saul Chaplin**), he devised one of the film's most enchanting dances. Nick Castle handled the rest of the choreography, and the film was shot in Technicolor by Robert Planck. For UK audiences the title was changed to *If You Feel Like Singing*.

Summer, Donna

b. Ladonna Gaines, 31 December 1948, Boston, Massachusetts, USA, Summer's 'Love To Love You Baby' made her the best-known of all 70s disco divas. Having sung with rock bands in Boston, Summer moved to Europe in 1968 and appeared in German versions of *Hair* and *Porgy And Bess* and married Austrian actor Helmut Sommer, from whom she took her stage name. Summer's first records were 'Hostage' and 'Lady Of The Night' for Giorgio Moroder's Oasis label in Munich. They were local hits but it was 'Love To Love You Baby' (1975) which made her an international star. The track featured Summer's erotic sighs and moans above Moroder's hypnotic disco beats and it sold a million copies in the US on Neil Bogart's Casablanca label. In 1977, a similar formula took 'I Feel Love' to the top of the UK chart and 'Down Deep Inside', Summer's theme song for the film *The Deep* was a big international success. Her own film debut came the next year in *Thank God It's Friday* in which she sang another million-seller 'Last Dance'. This was the peak period of Summer's career as she scored three more US number 1s in 1978-79 with a revival of **Jim Webb**'s 'MacArthur Park', 'Hot Stuff', 'Bad Girls' and 'No More tears (Enough Is Enough)' a duet with **Barbra Streisand**. The demise of disco coincided with a legal dispute between Summer and Bogart and in 1980 she signed to **David Geffen**'s new company.

Her work now took on a more pronounced soul and gospel flavour - she had become a born-again Christian. Her only big hit during the early 80s was 'Love Is In Control (Finger On The Trigger)' in 1982, produced by **Quincy Jones**. After a three year absence from music, Summer returned in 1987 with a US and European tour. Her best-selling 1989 album for **Warner Brothers** was written and produced by **Stock Aitken And Waterman** while Clivilles & Cole worked on *Love Is Gonna Change*.

Albums: *Love To Love You Baby* (1975), *A Love Trilogy* (1976), *Four Seasons Of Love* (1976), *I Remember Yesterday* (1977), *Once Upon A Time* (1977), *Live And More* (1978), *Bad Girls* (1979), *The Wanderer* (1980), *Donna Summer* (1982), *She Works Hard For The Money* (1983), *Cats Without Claws* (1984), *All Systems Go* (1987), *Another Place And Time* (1989), *Love Is Gonna Change* (1990), *Mistaken Identity* (1991), *This Time I Know It's For Real* (1993). Compilations: *On The Radio - Greatest Hits, Volumes 1 And 2* (1979), *Walk Away - Collector's Edition (The Best Of 1977-1980)* (1980), *The Best Of Donna Summer* (1990)

Further reading: *Donna Summer: An Unauthorized Biography*, Haskins, James (1983).

Summerfield, Saffron

Singer/songwriter b. 29 August 1949, Weston Favel, Northamptonshire, England. Playing guitar and piano, Saffron enjoyed a good deal of popularity during the mid to late 70s. Having studied classical and modern guitar with Vic Jacques, in the early 70s, she went on to play support to **Fairport Convention** in Holland, **Long John Baldry** in the UK, **Joan Armatrading** in Holland, and Alquin in Holland and Germany, during the period 1976 to 1979. Despite working a great deal, and her style of combining blues/jazz influences, her career never took off, in England, as well as it should have done. However, she regularly toured in Holland and Belgium, where she was extrememly popular, and played Ireland and Scotland a great deal. Both her albums were released on her own Mother Earth label in the UK, but in Holland were released on **Polydor**. From 1984/85, she was the "musician in residence" at Battersea Arts Centre, in London, and in 1986/87, she was musical director for two documentaries, under the series title "Six Of Hearts", on Channel 4 television. From 1987, Saffron took a temporary lay-off from performing, but has now returned to live appearances, with a new album, for Brewhouse Records, being recorded for release in 1994.

Albums: *Salisbury Plain* (1975), *Fancy Meeting You Here* (1976).

Summerhill

Arising from the ashes of the **Snakes Of Shake**, the UK band Summerhill looked to the early **Byrds**' sound for inspiration, their brand of folk-rock first heard on *I Want You* on the Rocket label in 1988. Their prolific live schedule, often as support act, made the team of Seori Burnette (vocals/guitar), Neil Scott (guitar/vocals), Keith Gilles (bass/vocals) and Ian Shedden (drums) a popular live act and a move to Demon's Diablo label came in time for a mini-album, *Lowdown*, later that year. Signed to **Polydor Records**, it was a year before the partnership was fruitful, during which time Michael Sturgis had replaced Shedden. 'Here I Am' was an obvious stab at the mainstream and it was March 1990 before *West Of Here*, was released. From it came 'Don't Let It Die' that same month and then a one-off single cover of the **Rolling Stones**' 'Wild Horses'. Despite some encouraging reviews Summerhill failed to make a sufficient impact on the charts and disbanded later that year. Keith Gilles later joined Sumishta Brahm's group, 13 Frightened Girls, appearing on the **Jazz Butcher** produced 'Lost At Sea' (1991).

Albums: *I Want You* (1988), *Lowdown* (1988), *West Of Here* (1990).

Summers, Andy

b. Andrew Somers, 31 December 1942, Poulton-le-Fylde, Lancashire, England. Raised in Bournemouth, Dorset, Summers was performing in the city's clubs and coffee-bars while still a teenager. He first encountered **Zoot Money** in the Don Robb Band, a local cabaret attraction, and later joined the ebullient singer in his Big Roll Band. This excellent soul/R&B group became one of the leading acts of the London club circuit during the mid-60s. Summers retained his association with Money in **Dantallion's Chariot** and the US-based New **Animals**. When the latter broke up in 1968, the guitarist remained in California where he studied classical styles, joined a latino-rock band and acted with various Hollywood theatre groups. He returned to England in 1973 and over the next four years Summers toured with several contrasting artists, including **Neil Sedaka**, **David Essex**, **Kevin Coyne** and **Kevin Ayers**. In May 1977, he played guitar in a temporary unit, Strontium 90, which also included **Sting** (bass) and Stewart Copeland (drums). Summers so impressed the duo they asked him to join their full-time group, the **Police**, with whom the guitarist remained until they disbanded. A superbly inventive musician, he did much to popularize the use of the 'flanging' effect, Summers' embarked on several projects; his finely-honed skills were more fully developed on *I Advance Unmasked*, a collaboration with **King Crimson**'s **Robert Fripp**. Ensuing solo albums have enhanced the guitarist's reputation for both excellence and imagination.

Albums: with Robert Fripp *I Advance Unmasked* (1982), *Bewitched* (1984), *XYZ* (1987), *The Golden Wire* (1989), *Charming Snakes* (1990), with John Etheridge *Invisible Threads* (Mesa 1994).

Sun Dial

The Sun Dial's well-received debut album from 1990, *Other Way Out*, re-created the psychedelic sound of the late 60s with an unnerving accuracy. A myriad of soaring vocals (and trippy lyrics to match), progressive chord changes and some delightful acid rock guitar (plus other strange instruments), the album's limited run on the Tangerine label soon expired and the trio signed with the UFO label early the following year. Hailing from south London, Sun Dial's roots lay with frontman Gary Ramon (guitar/vocals), previously with Modern Art. He joined up with Anthony Clough (bass/bamboo flutes/organ) and Dave Morgan (drums/percussion). Alongside a reissue/repackage of *Other Way Out*, UFO released its most upfront moment, 'Exploding In My Mind'. By the summer, the band had recruited a second guitarist for live work, while Clough took a smaller role; this was felt on a new single, 'Fireball', treading a mellower, more traditional rock sound. *Acid Yantra* saw better distribution through the

auspices of **Beggars Banquet Records**, and also broadened the band's sound with the addition of a mellotron.

Albums: *Other Way Out* (Tangerine 1990), *Libertine* (UFO 1993), *Acid Yantra* (Beggars Banquet 1995).

Sun Ra

b. Herman P. Blount, 22 May 1914, Birmingham, Alabama, USA, d. 30 May 1993, Birmingham, Alabama, USA. One of the most extraordinary figures in 20th century music, Sun Ra claims to have arrived here from the planet Saturn on a date that can't be revealed because of its astrological significance! More down-to-earth researchers have suggested the birthdate above, although this remains unconfirmed. There is a similar uncertainty about his original name: while he sometimes went under the name of Herman 'Sonny' Blount in the 30s and 40s, he also used the name Sonny Lee and has claimed that his parents' name was Arman. However, for approximately 40 years he was known as Sun Ra - or, as he's announced to countless concert audiences, 'Some call me Mr Ra, some call me Mr Re. You can call me Mr Mystery.' His first musical memories are of hearing classic blues singers such as **Bessie Smith** and **Ethel Waters** and he grew up a fan of the swing bands, especially those led by **Fletcher Henderson**. His early work experience as pianist, arranger and composer included stints with Fess Wheatley and Oliver Bibb in the Chicago area in the mid-30s, but this period of his life remains largely undocumented. In 1946 he was at Chicago's Club DeLisa, playing behind visiting jazz and blues artists such as **Joe Williams** and **LaVern Baker** and writing arrangements for his idol, Henderson, who had a 15-month residency at the club. Ra then worked with bassist Eugene Wright's Dukes Of Swing in 1948 and also played with **Coleman Hawkins** and **Stuff Smith**. In the early 50s he began to lead his own small groups, which soon featured **Pat Patrick** and **John Gilmore**, and by the middle of the decade he had assembled a 10-piece big band, the Arkestra, who recorded their debut, *Sun Song*, in 1956. Originally playing an idiosyncratic bebop, with arrangements that also showed the influence of **Duke Ellington** and **Tadd Dameron**, the Arkestra had developed by the early 60s into possibly the era's most advanced and experimental group. Ra was one of the first jazz leaders to use two basses, to employ the electric bass, to play electronic keyboards, to use extensive percussion and polyrhythms, to explore modal music and to pioneer solo and group freeform improvisations.

In addition, he made his mark in the wider cultural context: he proclaimed the African origins of jazz, reaffirmed pride in black history and reasserted the spiritual and mystical dimensions of music (all important factors in the black cultural/political renaissance of the 60s). In the late 50s Ra set up his own label, Saturn Records (aka Thoth), one of the first musician-owned labels, and most of his 100-plus recordings have been released on Saturn, although many have been issued or reissued on other labels (notably Impulse! in the 60s and 70s). Nearly all Saturn albums have been limited-edition pressings that appear in plain white or hand-drawn sleeves and are now valued collector's items. (The facts that they are extremely rare, that they often contain no recording details, that they are sometimes reissued under different titles and that some 'new' releases actually comprise a side each from two older albums, all mean that a complete and accurate Sun Ra discography is almost impossible to compile.)

Despite years of severe poverty and relocations from Chicago to New York (1961) and then to Philadelphia (1968), Sun Ra kept the Arkestra in existence for over three decades, though they played under a different name almost every year: examples include the Astro-Infinity Arkestra, the Blue Universe Arkestra, the Cosmo Jet Set Arkestra and the Year 2000 Myth Science Arkestra. The list of illustrious band members over the years takes in **Ahmed Abdullah**, **Marion Brown**, **Richard Davis**, Robin Eubanks, **Craig Harris**, **Billy Higgins**, **Frank Lowe**, **Julian Priester**, **Pharoah Sanders** and **James Spaulding**, (there are dozens more), while occasional guest performers have included **Lester Bowie**, **Don Cherry** and **Archie Shepp**. Many players returned for further stints, though the financial rewards were never great, and a handful remained virtually without a break since the very beginning - notably Gilmore and **Marshall Allen**. Several core band members lived together in a communal house where Ra reportedly imposed strict discipline: he allowed no drugs, no alcohol and was fond of waking everyone up in the middle of the night for extra rehearsals: music was everything. (He was also credited as the person who persuaded **John Coltrane** to give up drugs: and Coltrane took saxophone lessons from Gilmore.) Almost from the outset the band wore exotic costumes, usually with Ancient Egyptian or outer space motifs, and used elements of spectacle in their stage act: light shows, dance, mime and an endearing habit of winding through the audience chanting about their exploits on other planets ('we travel the spaceways, from planet to planet'). In the 70s Ra began to expand their repertoire to include more traditional material, especially big band numbers by the likes of Ellington, Henderson, **Jimmie Lunceford** and **Jelly Roll Morton**. At the same time he kept abreast of jazz-funk and also continued to perform his ear-splitting, freeform synthesizer solos; so any live concert by the Arkestra was likely to span the entire gamut of black creative music. Their recordings proved more erratic (and often very low-fi) but over the years they had accumulated a set of indisputable masterpieces, with apparent creative peaks coming in the early/mid-60s (*Jazz In Silhouette*, *Rocket Number Nine Take Off For The Planet Venus*, *The Heliocentric Worlds Of Sun Ra, Volumes 1 & 2*, *Nothing Is*, *The Magic City*) and the late 70s (*Media Dreams*, *Disco 3000*, *Omniverse*, *Sleeping Beauty*, *Strange Celestial Road*, *Sunrise In Different Dimensions*). The Arkestra made occasional guest appearances (for example, they played on three tracks of Phil Alvin's *Unsung Stories* and contributed 'Pink Elephants' to Hal Willner's Disney tribute, *Stay Awake* - an episode that led to them playing entire sets of Disney tunes in the late 80s) and selected members have occasionally made small-group recordings with Ra: for instance, both *New Steps* and *Other Voices, Other Blues* feature Ra, Gilmore, Michael Ray (trumpet) and Luqman Ali (percussion). Sun Ra himself released a handful of solo piano albums - *Monorails & Satellites, Vols 1 & 2*, *Aurora Borealis*, *St Louis Blues Solo Piano* - and the duo *Visions* with **Walt Dickerson**: his piano style ranged across a variety of influences, including blues, **Count Basie**'s bounce, **Thelonious Monk**'s dissonance and a degree of European impressionism.

A stroke in 1990 left Ra with impaired movement, but the Arkestra's 1991 London concerts proved there had been no diminution of musical quality. His influence has been enormous and has seeped through into every nook and cranny of modern music, from **Funkadelic** to Karlheinz Stockhausen to the **Art Ensemble Of Chicago**. 'Musically,' said drummer Roger Blank, 'Sun Ra is one of the unacknowledged legislators of the world.' A poet and philosopher too, Ra published several volumes of writings. In fact, while a few critics have seized on items such as the Arkestra's glitzy costumes and space chants to dismiss them as a circus and Ra himself as a freak or charlatan, most of his ideas and proclamations made perfect sense when viewed in the context of African-American culture. Taking a new name, for instance, is a venerable blues tradition (think of **Muddy Waters**, **Howlin' Wolf**, **Leadbelly**) and Ra's emphasis on Ancient Egypt was just one of the means he used to focus attention on black history and black achievement. More detailed expositions can be found in the chapters on his music and thought in Chris Cutler's *File Under Popular*, John Litweiler's *The Freedom Principle*, Graham Lock's *Forces In Motion* and Valerie Wilmer's *As Serious As Your Life*. A documentary film, *Sun Ra: A Joyful Noise* directed by Robert Muge, was released in 1980. Sun Ra was one of the great modern visionaries: he not only had a dream, but lived it to the full for the last 40 years. He showed that, with imagination, commitment and a love of beauty, you can create your own future and make the impossible real. Sun Ra left planet Earth in May 1993.

Albums: *Sun Song* (1957), *Super-Sonic Jazz* (Evidence 1957), *Angels And Demons At Play* (Evidence 1958), *Sun Ra & His Solar Arkestra Visit Planet Earth* (1958), *We Travel The Space Ways* (1960), *Jazz In Silhouette* (1960), *Fate In A*

Pleasant Mood (1961), *The Nubians Of Plutonia* aka *The Lady With The Golden Stockings* (1962), *Rocket Number Nine Take Off For The Planet Venus* aka *Interstellar Low Ways* (1962), *Bad & Beautiful* (1963), *The Futuristic Sounds Of Sun Ra* aka *We Are In The Future* (1963), *Art Forms Of Dimensions Tomorrow* (Evidence 1964), *Secrets Of The Sun* (1965), *When Angels Speak Of Love* (1965), *The Heliocentric Worlds Of Sun Ra, Vol 1* (ESP 1965), *Cosmic Tones For Mental Therapy* (Evidence 1966), *The Heliocentric Worlds Of Sun Ra, Vol 2* (ESP 1966), *The Magic City* (Evidence 1966), *Nothing Is* (ESP 1967), *Other Planes Of There* (1967), *Sound Of Joy* (1968, rec. 1957), *Holiday For Soul Dance* (Evidence 1968), *Atlantis* (Evidence 1968), *When Sun Comes Out* (1969), *Sound Sun Pleasure* (1969), *My Brother The Wind* (1970), *The Night Of The Purple Moon* (1970), *Continuation* (1970), *Pictures Of Infinity* (1971, rec. 1967), *Nuits De La Fondation Maeght, Vols 1 & 2* (1971), *The Solar Myth Approach, Vols 1 & 2* (Affinity 1971), *It's After The End Of The World* (1971), *Song Of The Stargazers* (1971), *Strange Strings* (1972, rec. 1968), *To Nature's God* aka *Sun Ra In Egypt* (1972), *Horizon* (1972), *Nidhamu* (1972), *Monorails & Satellites, Vol. 1* (1973, rec. 1967), *Astro Black* (1973), *Space Is The Place* (Evidence 1973), *Monorails & Satellites, Vol. 2* (1974, rec. 1967), *Discipline 27 - 11* (1974), *Pathways To Unknown Worlds* (1974), *Dreams Come True* (1975, rec. 50s-60s), *My Brother The Wind, Vol. 2* (1975), *The Antique Blacks* (1975), *Cosmo Earth Fantasy* aka *Temple U* aka *Sub-Underground* (1975), *Taking A Chance On Chances* (1975), *The Invisible Shield* (1976, rec. 50s-70s), *Featuring Pharoah Sanders And Black Harold* (1976, rec. 1964), *Live In Paris* aka *Live At The Gibus* (1976), *Outer Spaceways Incorporated* (Black Lion 1977), *Primitone* (1977), *Universe In Blue* (1977), *Discipline 99* aka *Out Beyond The Kingdom Of* (1977), *What's New* (1977), *Over The Rainbow* (1977), *Celebrations For Dial Tunes* (1978), *Cosmos* (1978), *Live At Montreux* (1978), *Solo Piano* (1978), *Unity* (1978), *New Steps* (1978), *Other Voices, Other Blues* (1978), *Media Dreams* (1978), *Sound Mirror* (1978), *Disco 3000* (1978), *Lanquidity* (1978), *St Louis Blues* (1979), *The Soul Vibrations Of Man* aka *Soul Vibrations* (1979), *The Other Side Of The Sun* (1980), *Blithe Spirit Dance* (1980), *Omniverse* (1980), *Seductive Fantasy* (1980), *Of Mythic Worlds* (1980), *Strange Celestial Road* (1980), *Sleeping Beauty* (1980), *Dance Of Innocent Passion* (1980), *Rose Hued Mansions Of The Sun* aka *Voice Of The Eternal Tomorrow* (1981), *Sunrise In Different Dimensions* (1981), *Aurora Borealis* (1981), *I Pharoah* (1981), *Some Blues But Not The Kind That's Blue* aka *My Favourite Things* (1981), *Beyond The Purple Star Zone* (1981), *Journey Stars Beyond* (1981), *Otherness Blue* aka *Just Friends* (1983, rec. 50s-80s), *Hiroshima* (1984), *Sun Ra Meets Salah Ragab In Egypt* (1984), *Ra To The Rescue* (1984), *Live At Praxis '84, Vols 1 - 3* (1984), *A Fireside Chat With Lucifer* (1985), *Cosmo Sun Connection* (1985), *Celestial Love* (1985), *Children Of The Sun* (1986), *Stars That Shine Darkly* (1986), *A Night In East Berlin* (1987), *Reflections In Blue* (1987), *Love In Outer Space* (1988, rec. 1983), *Live At Pit-Inn, Tokyo* (1988), *Blue Delight* (A&M 1989), *Hours After* (1989), *Cosmo Omnibus Imaginable Illusion* (DIW 1989), *Out There A Minute* (1989, rec. 60s), *John Cage Meets Sun Ra* (1989), *Purple Night* (A&M 1990), *Sun Ra & His Year 2000 Myth Science Arkestra - Live In London 1990* (1990), *Mayan Temples* (Black Saint 1992), *Destination Unknown* (Leo 1992), *Friendly Galaxy* (Leo 1993), *Pleiades* (Leo 1993).

Further reading: *The Immeasurable Equation*, Sun Ra.

Sun Records

The Sun Record Company was founded in Memphis, Tennessee in February 1952. It evolved out of the Memphis Recording Service, a small studio installed two years earlier by **Sam Phillips**, a former disc jockey on stations WMSL and WREC. Although early work often comprised of social occasions, Phillips' ambitions focused on an untapped local blues market. Completed masters were leased to a variety of independent outlets, including **Chess**, Duke and RPM, in the process launching the careers of **B.B. King**, **Howlin' Wolf** and **Bobby 'Blue' Bland**. The Sun label was the natural extension of this success and its early reputation for superior R&B was established with hits by **Rufus Thomas** ('Bear Cat') and **'Little' Junior Parker** ('Feelin' Good'). In 1954 Phillips began recording country music, and the confluence of these two styles resulted in rockabilly. Its most vocal proponent was **Elvis Presley**, signed by Phillips that year, who completed five exceptional singles for the label before joining **RCA** Victor. Presley's recordings, which included 'That's Alright Mama', 'Good Rockin' Tonight' and 'Mystery Train', featured **Scotty Moore** on guitar and Bill Black on bass, whose sparse, economical support enhanced the singer's unfettered delivery. The crisp production defined Sun rockabilly, a sound the singer was unable to recapture following his move to a major label. Although many commentators questioned Phillips' decision, he retorted that he could now develop the careers of **Carl Perkins** and **Johnny Cash**. The former's exemplary releases included 'Blue Suede Shoes', (Sun's first national pop hit), 'Matchbox' and 'Boppin' The Blues', but a near-fatal car crash undermined his progress. His mantle was taken up by other rockabilly singers - **Warren Smith**, **Sonny Burgess** and **Billy Lee Riley** - but these lesser acts failed to establish a consistent career. **Roy Orbison** and **Charlie Rich** enjoyed limited success on Sun, but found greater acclaim elsewhere. The aforementioned Cash then became Sun's most commercial property and he enjoyed several hits, including 'I Walk The Line' (1957), 'Ballad Of A Teenage Queen' and 'Guess Things Happen That Way' (both 1958), thus emphasizing the label's country heritage. Four million-sellers - 'Whole Lotta Shakin' Goin' On', 'Great Balls Of Fire', 'Breathless' and 'High School Confidential' - by the exuberant **Jerry Lee Lewis**, closed a highly-productive decade, but the same singer's rapid fall from grace, coupled with the loss of Cash and Perkins, proved hard to surmount.

Sun's simple, rhythmic sound - the only device used to enhance a performance was echo - now proved anachronistic, yet a move to new, larger premises in 1960 paradoxically meant it was lost forever. The label was never Phillips' sole business investment; radio stations, mining and the Holiday Inn Hotel chain vied for his attention, while new record companies, **Hi** and **Stax**, seemed better able to capture the now-changing Memphis music scene. Paradoxically, this allowed Sun's achievements to remain untarnished and thus its legend is still undiminished. On July 1 1969, Sam Phillips sold the entire company to country music entrepreneur **Shelby Singleton** who, with the able assistance of British licensees **Charly Records**, have completed a series of judicious repackages.

Compilations: *The Roots Of Rock Volumes 1-13* (1977), *Sun Golden Hits* (1981), *The Sun Box* (1982), *Sun: The Blues* (1985), *Sun Country Box* (1986), *Sun Records - The Rocking Years* (1987), *The Sound Of Sun* (1988), *The Sun Story Vols 1 & 2* (1991), *The Very Best Of Sun Rock 'N' Roll* (1991).

Further reading: *Sun Records*, Colin Escott and Martin Hawkins.

Sun Valley Serenade

Such was the popularity of the **Glenn Miller** Band by 1941 that it just had to appear in a film, even if the story was as light as a feather and Miller himself was definitely no actor. Robert Ellis and Helen Logan's screenplay (from a story by Art Arthur and Robert Harari) was about a cute Norwegian refugee (Sonja Henie) whose arrival in America startles the band's pianist (John Payne) simply because he had agreed to sponsor a child. Inevitably, surprise turns to love on the snowy slopes of Sun Valley, Idaho. The musical sequences were tremendous, especially choreographer **Hermes Pan**'s staging of 'Chattanooga Choo-Choo' (**Harry Warren-Mack Gordon**) which begins conventionally enough with **Tex Beneke**, **Paula Kelly** and the Modernaires singing with the band, and then segues into a spectacular song-and-dance routine featuring the amazing **Nicholas Brothers** and Dorothy Dandridge. Warren and Gordon contributed three other popular numbers, 'The Kiss Polka', 'I Know Why (And So Do You)', and 'It Happened In Sun Valley', while Joe Garland's 'In The Mood' also got an airing. Milton Berle supplied the wisecracks, and Lynn Bari and Joan Davis were in it too. Henie's big moment came in the impressive 'black ice' finale when, accompanied by numerous white-clad couples, she gave a stunning display of ballet-style ice dancing. H. Bruce Humberstone directed, and *Sun Valley Serenade* was produced by Milton Sperling for 20th Century-Fox. Not much footage of the Miller Band exists, so this film and *Orchestra Wives* are continually re-viewed by lovers of the Swing Era.

Sun, Joe

b. James J. Paulson, 25 September 1943, Rochester, Minnesota, USA. Sun says, 'I grew up on a farm and, like almost everyone else in the middle of nowhere, listened to the radio.' Sun listened to country and blues stations, hence the strong blues edge to his country music. In the early 70s, he moved to Chicago for a job in computers but he attended folk clubs along Wells Street and was further influenced by John Prine and Steve Goodman. He built up the confidence to become a performer himself, first working as Jack Daniels and then with a group, the Branded Men. During a stint as a disc jockey in Minneapolis, he was mesmerised by **Mickey Newbury**'s 'Are My Thoughts With You?' and decided to move to Nashville. He arrived in 1972 and formed his own graphics company, The Sun Shop, and then used his disc jockey experience to become a record-plugger. He helped to re-establish **Bill Black**'s Combo. In 1977 he worked for the newly-formed country division of Ovation Records, defiantly promoting a b-side the **Kendalls**' 'Heaven's Just A Sin Away', which went to number 1 in the US country chart. Ovation invited him to record some records and he quickly went to number 14 in the US country charts with **Hugh Moffatt**'s song, 'Old Flames (Can't Hold A Candle To You)'. He had further hits with 'High And Dry', 'I Came On Business For The King' and, with Sheila Andrews, 'What I Had With You'. 'Shotgun Rider' also made the US pop charts, while his cover of 'The Long Black Veil' includes an introduction from its writer, Danny Dill and Marijohn Wilkin. After Ovation went bankrupt, he moved to **Elektra** but his hard-rocking country style was poorly promoted. With his group, the Solar System, he took to touring Europe two or three times a year. His album, *Hank Bogart Still Lives*, is a tribute to his heroes. His favourite of his own compositions is 'The Sun Never Sets': 'I don't think I'll do much better than that.'

Albums: *Old Flames (Can't Hold A Candle To You)* (1978), *Out Of Your Mind* (1979), *Livin' On Honky Tonk Time* (1980), *Storms Of Life* (1981), *I Ain't Honky Tonkin' No More* (1982), *The Sun Never Sets* (1984), *Twilight Zone* (1987), *Hank Bogart Still Lives* (1989), *Dixie And Me* (1992), *Some Old Memories 1988-1993* (Crazy Music 1994).

Sunday In The Park With George

Stephen Sondheim and his librettist and director James Lapine, used a painting by the 19th century impressionist painter, Georges Seurat, as the basis for this innovative musical which opened at the Booth Theatre in New York on 2 May 1984. 'A Sunday Afternoon On The Island Of La Grande Jatte' has been described as 'a multi-layered panorama of Parisian life and a masterpiece of pointillism - the method of building a painting from minute dots of blending colours'. In the show's first act the painting gradually comes to life as George (**Mandy Patinkin**) obsessively creates the characters and places them on the canvas, eventually progressing to the complete tableau. Meanwhile, the relationship with Dot (**Bernadette Peters**), his mistress-model, falls apart, and although they are expecting a child, she leaves him to marry someone else. The second act advances the plot by 100 years. The setting is now present-day New York, and Seurat and Dot's great-grandson, also named George, is 'an American mulitmedia sculptor likewise bedevilled by a philistine society'. Sondheim and Lapine's point of view about 'the angst of artistic creation' comes over loud and clear throughout. Sondheim's score was complex and intricate, and included 'Sunday In The Park With George', 'No Life', 'Colour And Light', 'Gossip', 'The Day Off', 'Everybody Loves Louis', 'Finishing The Hat', 'We Do Not Belong Together', 'Beautiful', 'Sunday', 'It's Hot Up Here', 'Chromolume No. 7', 'Putting It Together', 'Children And Art', 'Lesson No. 8', and 'Move On'. Considering the quality of the piece, a run of 604 performances was somewhat disappointing. There were **Tony Awards** for the brilliant scenic design (Tony Straiges) and lighting (Richard Nelson), and the show was voted best musical by the New York Drama Critics Circle. It also won the 1985 Pulitzer Prize for Drama. Five years later, *Sunday In The Park With George* was presented in London by the Royal National Theatre. That production gained **Laurence Olivier** Awards for best musical and actor (Philip Quast).

Sundays

Fragrant indie band formed in London, England, in the summer of 1987, by songwriters David Gavurin (b. 4 April 1963, England; guitar) and Harriet Wheeler (b. June 26 1963, England; vocals), who had already gained prior singing experience in a band called Jim Jiminee. Later joined by the rhythm section of Paul Brindley (b. 6 November 1963, England; bass) and Patrick Hannan (b. 4 March 1966, England; drums), the Sundays' first ever live performance at the seminal Falcon 'Vertigo Club' in Camden Town, London, in August 1988, sparked off abnormally excessive interest from both media and record business circles. Playing what many perceived to be a delicate, flawless mix of the **Smiths**' guitars and the **Cocteau Twins**' vocal acrobatics, the band's high profile ensured a Top 50 place in the UK charts for their debut single, 'Can't Be Sure', in January 1989. Despite this dramatic arrival, the Sundays did not capitalize on their success until exactly a year later, when *Reading, Writing, Arithmetic* took everyone by surprise by entering the UK charts at number 4. Despite these rapid advances, the Sundays are notorious for being slow songwriters - legend has it that their label, **Rough Trade Records**, wanted to release a single from the album but the band did not have any other material for a b-side. This was to be

their last release for two years, as touring commitments took the quartet to Europe, Japan and the equally reverential America, where **Rolling Stone** magazine had voted the Sundays' Best Foreign Newcomer. Financial difficulties at their label also held up proceedings while they sought a new record deal during 1991, eventually signing to **Parlophone Records** in January 1992. A second album was not completed before October of that year, and reactions, though not unkind, lacked the fervour that had greeted their debut. Albums: *Reading, Writing, Arithmetic* (Rough Trade 1990), *Blind* (Parlophone 1992).

Sundowners

Eric Tutin (b. c.1914, near Childers, Queensland, Australia; piano/accordion/vocals), Joan Martin (b. 1924, Queensland, Australia; guitar/vocals). An early Australian country music duo, formed in Toowoomba in 1939, they worked locally before moving first to 4BK Brisbane and then to Sydney. They made their only recordings for Regal-Zonophone on 30 June 1942, being joined by fiddler Ted McMinn as they recorded six original songs, which proved very popular. In 1944, Martin decided without warning to quit the business to marry. She reputedly moved to America but in the 60s, she was rumoured to be living in Victoria. Tutin first played piano with a dance band, before forming a country quartet, which included Aphra Lorraine, whom he married. Between 1946 and 1950, they toured extensively with Lester's Follies, before forming their own touring show, the Vanities. In 1952, they gave up the touring to run a music shop in Gympie, Queensland, from where they established a popular radio country show on 4GY called *Tutin's Tune Time*, which proved so popular it ran for many years. They eventually retired to Toowoomba.

Sunny

After Marilyn Miller's great success in **Florenz Ziegfeld**'s *Sally* (1920), another distinguished American producer, Charles Dillingham, arranged for her to board this vehicle for her singing and dancing talents which arrived at the New Amsterdam Theatre in New York on 22 September 1925, and stayed for 517 performances. **Otto Harbach** and **Oscar Hammerstein II** wrote the more than fanciful book in which Sunny Peters (Miller), a star equestrian performer in an English circus, stows away on an ocean liner to be near her beloved, Tom Warren (Paul Frawley). Almost 70 years later, it is difficult to understand why Sunny has to marry - not Tom - but his best friend, Jim Deming (Jack Donahue), in order to disembark in the USA. Also in the cast were Clifton Webb, Mary Hay, Joseph Cawthorn, **Cliff Edwards**, and George Olsen And His Orchestra. The score, with music by **Jerome Kern** and lyrics by Harbach and Hammerstein, included 'Let's Not Say Goodnight Till

It's Morning', 'Sunny', 'D'Ye Love Me?', 'Two Little Bluebirds', 'I Might Grow Fond Of You', and 'Who'. **Jack Buchanan** made the latter number his own when *Sunny* opened in London at the Hippodrome in 1926. Joining him in the West End production which ran for 363 performances, were Elsie Randolph, **Binnie Hale**, Maidie Hope, and Claude Hulbert. An early 'talkie' version of *Sunny* released in 1930 starred Marilyn Miller, Lawrence Grey, and Jack Donahue, and there was a remake in 1941 with **Anna Neagle** and **Ray Bolger**.

Sunny And The Sunglows

This Mexican-American group came from San Antonio, Texas, USA. The group was formed in 1959 and originally consisted of Sunny Ozuna, Jess, Oscar, and Ray Villanueva, Tony Tostado, Gilbert Fernandez, and Alfred Luna. Sunny and the Sunglows (who also recorded as Sunny And The Sunliners) were one of the few Hispanic acts to succeed in the pop and soul markets, in which they sang old R&B hits with a typical Hispanic approach, laid-back and soulful. Their hits were a remake of **Little Willie John**'s classic 'Talk To Me' (US R&B number 12 and pop number 11, 1963), a remake of **Tony Bennett**'s 'Rags To Riches' (1963), and a remake of the **Five Keys**' 'Out Of Sight Out Of Mind' (1964). In 1965, the group scored a minor pop hit with a saxophone-dominated polka instrumental, 'Peanuts (La Cacahuata)' and much of the group's subsequent recordings were brassy polka instrumentals for the Mexican-American community.
Albums: *Talk To Me/Rags To Riches* (1963), *All Night Worker* (1964), *The Original Peanuts* (1965), *Smile Now Cry Later* (1966), *Live In Hollywood* (1966), *This Is My Band* (1977), *Sky High* (1966).

Sunnyboys

This Australian band successfully combined the new wave energy of the early 80s with the guitar sounds of the 60s. They came on to the Sydney scene in 1980, with a softer sound, a refreshing change from the heavy rock sound that dominated Sydney at the time. They were popular in New South Wales, but were unable to match this elsewhere with only three singles making the lower reaches of the Australian charts, perhaps due to their inconsistent live performances. By their third album the band had lost its way, and went to the UK to re-assess their career. There they produced a strong album which did not do well, and so they disbanded in 1984. Jeremy Oxley reformed the group in 1987, with Peter Hiencenberg (drums), Nick Freedman (guitar) and Phil Smith (bass), and completed one album for **RCA**.
Albums: *The Sunnyboys* (1981), *Individuals* (1982), *Get Some Fun* (1983), *Days Gone By* (1985), *Real Live* (1985), *Too Young To Despair* (1989).

Sunnyland Slim

b. Albert Luandrew, 5 September 1907, Vance, Mississippi, USA, d. 17 March 1995. A seminal figure in the development of the post-war Chicago blues, Sunnyland Slim taught himself piano and organ as a child in Mississippi and spent many years playing around the south, before settling in Chicago in 1942. There he established his reputation with older musicians such as **Lonnie Johnson**, **Tampa Red** and **Peter J. 'Doctor' Clayton** (some of his earliest records were issued under the pseudonym Doctor Clayton's Buddy), but more importantly with the new breed of blues singers and musicians that included figures such as **Muddy Waters** and **Little Walter**. In the company of artists such as these, his powerful piano work was to set the standard for underpinning the hard, electric sound associated with Chicago blues in the 50s. He recorded extensively under his own name for many important labels of the period, like **Chess**, J.O.B., **VeeJay** and Cobra, as well as smaller labels, producing such classic Chicago blues sides as 'Johnson Machine Gun', 'Going Back To Memphis' and 'Highway 51'. He was also to be heard accompanying many other important artists of the time, including **Robert Lockwood**, **Floyd Jones** and **J.B. Lenoir**, as well as those already mentioned. He is often credited as having helped younger musicians to get their careers started. Throughout the 60s and 70s, he recorded prolifically and toured widely both in the US and overseas. In the 80s he produced albums on his own Airway label, and lent assistance to young players such as Eddie Lusk and **Lurrie Bell**.
Albums: *Devil Is A Busy Man* (1989), *Be Careful How You Vote* (1989), *House Rent Party* (1992).

Sunnysiders

Freddy Morgan (b. 7 November 1910, New York City, New York, USA, d. 1970), formed the Sunnysiders in the mid-50s with **Margie Rayburn**, Norman Milkin and Jad Paul. Morgan was a banjoist and songwriter and a member of **Spike Jones**'s City Slickers between 1947-58. The group signed with Kapp Records and their first single, 'Hey, Mr. Banjo', penned by Morgan and Milkin, reached number 12 in the USA. They followed it up with other banjo-related songs, including 'The Lonesome Banjo' and 'Banjo Picker's Ball', but were unable to return to the charts. Rayburn (who married Milkin) did have her own US Top 10 single in 1957 with 'I'm Available'.
Album: *Motor City Bluegrass* (1970).

Suns Of Arqa

Exceedingly pleasant, sitar-soaked, cross-cultural house music, often to be caught live at **Planet Dog** events. The main man behind Suns Of Arqa is Lancashire-based Mick Ward, whose fusion of flute, violin, keyboards and sitar in highly original in the dance music sphere. Previous to their celebrity in the dance scene, Suns Of Arqa had already recorded a set for ROIR in association with **Prince Far I**. In 1994 they had 'Govinda's Dream' remixed by **A Guy Called Gerald**.

Albums: *Cradle* (Earthsounds 1992), *Kokoromochi* (Arqa 1993).

Sunscreem

Lucia Holmes, from Maidstone, Kent, England, but of half-Swedish parentage, is the vocalist and programmer with this band, who developed an affinity for the nether regions of the UK pop charts in the 90s. They have their own Essex based studio, and were touted as the first live band playing rave music, scoring with singles like 'Luv U More' and 'Perfect Motion' (which went Top 20). Their version of **Marianne Faithfull**'s 'Broken English', performed live on television show *The Word*, also won them admirers. The other main mover behind the band is technical guru Paul Carnell, along with Darren Woodford, Rob Fricker and Sean Wright. However, that self-same studio he had played a major role in building brought them grief in 1993 when they left some of their friends in charge while they went on holiday, returning to discover that they had made use of their time by recording an album, *Panarama*, for the Big Fish label.

Album: *03* (Sony 1993).

Sunset Boulevard

Composer **Andrew Lloyd Webber**'s long awaited musical adaptation of Billy Wilder's classic black and white movie which starred Gloria Swanson and William Holden, finally surmounted a host of technical problems and opened at the refurbished Adelphi Theatre in London on 12 July 1993. The book and lyrics were by **Don Black**, who had previously collaborated with Lloyd Webber, and the author Christopher Hampton who was making his debut in the musical theatre. Their libretto, which stayed closely to the original screenplay, told the familiar story of Norma Desmond (**Patti LuPone**), the ageing silent movie queen, who enlists the help of the failed and penniless scriptwriter Joe Gillis (Kevin Anderson) in her efforts to make a comeback. Too late he finds that he is hopelessly trapped. The score contained several powerful ballads, particularly 'With One Look' and 'As If We Never Said Goodbye', and there were others which could prove just as durable such as 'Surrender', 'New Ways To Dream', 'The Perfect Year', and 'Too Much In Love To Care'. There were also a couple of amusing comedy numbers, 'The Lady's Paying' and 'Let's Have Lunch'. The £3 million production received generally good, if not enthusiastic reviews. Most critics thought that Patti LuPone looked too young for the role, but there were no reservations about

her voice. There was also praise for John Napier's 'wonderfully elaborate rococo set'. Going against convention, *Sunset Boulevard* had its US premiere, not on Broadway, but in Los Angeles. By the time the show opened there in December 1993, it had been drastically reworked, and a new song, 'Every Movie's A Circus', added. There was a first night standing ovation for film actress Glenn Close who played Norma, and the lavish post-premiere party was held at Paramount Studios where the original 1950 film was made. Lloyd Webber subsequently closed the London production down for a '$1.5 million revamp'. When it reopened, **Betty Buckley** and John Barrowman had taken over the leading roles. Buckley was replaced by **Elaine Paige** in May 1995. Glenn Close reaffirmed her position as the 'definitive' Norma (to date) when the show opened on Broadway in November 1994. She took the 'best actress in a musical' **Tony Award**, and the show also won for best musical, book and score (both unopposed), featured actor (George Hearn), scenic design (Napier), and lighting design (Andrew Bridge).

Further reading: *Sunset Boulevard - From Movie To Musical*, George Perry.

Sunshine Company

Formed in Los Angeles, California, USA in February 1967, the Sunshine Company was a pop-psychedelic group that made a minor impact during its two-year existence. The quintet consisted of Mary Nance (vocals), Douglas 'Red' Mark (guitar/vocals), Maury Mansea (guitarist/pianist/vocalist), Larry Sims (bass) and Merel Bregante (drums). As their name would suggest, the group specialized in lightweight 'flower-power' music and dressed the hippie role to the hilt. Shortly after forming the group was signed to **Imperial Records**. Similar in style to the **Mamas And The Papas** and **Spanky And Our Gang**, the Sunshine Company did not share their commercial success. Their first single, 'Happy', made it to number 50 in the USA, while the follow-up, 'Back On The Street Again', reached number 36. One more single, 'Look, Here Comes The Sun', ended their run in that chart during 1968. It was that year that they became a sextet with the inclusion of Dave Hodgkins (acoustic guitar). The Sunshine Company recorded three albums during 1967-68, only the first of which, *Happiness Is The Sunshine Company*, reached the charts. By 1969, the group had dissolved, with Mark going on to form **Redeye** and Merel Bregante joining **Loggins And Messina**.

Albums: *Happiness Is The Sunshine Company* (1967), *The Sunshine Company* (1968), *Sunshine & Shadows* (1968).

Sunshine, Monty

b. 8 April 1928, London, England. After teaching himself to play clarinet, Sunshine became involved in the UK trad jazz scene of the late 40s. He was a founder member of the Crane River Jazz Band and later teamed up with **Chris Barber** to form a co-operative group. For a while this band was under the nominal leadership of **Ken Colyer**, but later reverted to its original democratic status. Sunshine was featured on several records, notably 'Petite Fleur', and helped the band to establish a reputation as one of the best of the UK trad outfits. In 1960 he left Barber to form his own band which, while retaining a high level of popularity for a number of years, never achieved the success of the Barber/Sunshine band. However, Sunshine established a name in Europe, especially in Germany. In the 70s he had occasional reunions with the reformed Crane River Jazz Band and with Barber. Although a proponent of New Orleans jazz, Sunshine's playing style has always favoured the full, romantic sound of musicians such as **Sidney Bechet** and **Barney Bigard**. In the 80s he was often on tour as a single, still popular with the audience he had known from his earliest days in the business.

Selected albums: *A Taste Of Sunshine* (1976), *Magic Is The Moonlight* (1978), *Sunshine In London* (Black Lion 1979), *On Sunday* (1987). Compilations: *Monty Sunshine And The Crane River Jazz Band, 1950-53* (1988), *Gotta Travel On* (Timeless 1992).

Super Diamono De Dakar

Almost immediately after 'mbalax' star **Youssou N'Dour** burst onto the international scene in the mid-80s with his inspired electric updating of traditional Senegalese music, his hottest domestic competition - Super Diamono - joined the global running with their 1987 album *People*. Although both sets of performers had their foundation in mbalax, their approaches could hardly have been more different. Where N'Dour featured frenetic rhythms, loud bursts of talking drum and time signatures of mind-boggling complexity, Super Diamono adopted a leaner, more powerful approach, keyed around heavy bass guitar and murderous kit drums. The group was founded in the Senegalese capital Dakar in 1975. Like other bands of the time, they played in Afro-Cuban style, before forging their own brand of modernized Senegalese roots music towards the end of the decade. The stimulus came from a two-year expedition through rural Senegal, listening to and recording local musicians while supporting themselves by performing in village squares and market town dancehalls. In 1977, the band returned to Dakar with the fruits of their work. Among the early albums, *Ndaxona* is remarkable for its wailing vocals from lead singer Omar Pene, rasping guitars and roots-flavoured horn charts. Diamono then introduced traditional percussion instruments into the line-up. A string of cassette-only album releases followed, before the release of the live album *Mam* in 1984 and the studio productions *Geddy Bayam* and *Ndakami* in 1985. While *People* remains the

band's chef d'oeuvre, the more recent *Sabar* runs it a close second.

Albums: *Ndaxona* (1979), *Mam* (1984), *Geddy Bayam* (1985), *Ndakami* (1985), *People* (1987), *Sabar* (1990).

Super Etoile De Dakar
(see **N'Dour, Youssou**)

Superbs

An R&B vocal group from California, USA. The Superbs were one of the best mid-60s sweet soul groups that melded doo-wop harmonies into the sound of soul. Members were Eleanor 'Punkin' Green' (lead), Walter White, Bobby Swain, Gordy Harmon, and Ronny Cook. Green possessed a soprano lead that sounded much like a male falsetto and it was an era when falsetto-led groups were regularly on the charts. After their first record in 1964 on Lew Bedell's Dore label, 'Storybook Of Love', flopped, Harmon left to form the **Whispers**. (The Whispers were the Superbs labelmates and were likewise outstanding in merging doo-wop with soul). The next record, 'Baby Baby All The Time', with its relaxed lope, proved a success in 1964. Similar sounding and equally appealing follow-ups were 'Sad Sad Day' (1964) and 'Baby's Gone Away' (1965). Around this time Swain left the group to form the Entertainers Four, who also recorded for Dore. He was replaced by Lawrence Randall. Green left in 1966 to get married and the group regrouped, but the magic was gone and by the 70s the group had broken up. Lawrence Randall formed a new Superbs group in the mid-80s to play the southern California revival circuit.

Supercat

b. William Maragh, Kingston, Jamaica, West Indies. Of East Indian extract and the son of a construction worker, Supercat grew up in Sievright Gardens joining Soul Imperial Hi-Fi as a teenage DJ apprentice to Early B. From there he went on to Crystal Blue Flames, Supreme Love, Studio Mix, King Majesty and finally Kilimanjaro. Known as Catarack, he replaced the late Jim Brown as principal DJ in 1980. Two years later he voiced his debut tune, 'Mr Walker', in combination with Bruck Back for **Winston Riley**. After a break from recording he returned in 1985 with a vengeance, having now been dubbed Supercat. 'Boops' was a massive seller, spawning countless other versions whilst 'Cry Fe De Youth' revealed a more serious side to his nature. Work began on his debut album which was released in 1986. **King Jammys**, George Phang, Tuff Gong and Ranking Joe had all recorded him by then. That year he left for Miami with the Stur-Mars **sound system**, being the first artist to voice for their affiliated Skengdon label. They released his second album and the singles 'Vineyard Party', 'Mind Up', 'Sweets For My Sweets' and 'Wild Apache', the latter featuring a prototype **ragga**/hip hop beat and inspiring the title of his own label.

Resident in Brooklyn from 1988, 'Cabin Stabbin' (with Nicodemus and Junior Demus), 'Nuff Man A Dead', 'Ghetto Red Hot' and his trademark 'Don Dada' all demonstrated his often fiercely militant stance to be undiminished. Further hits with Trevor Sparks ('Dolly My Baby') and **Frankie Paul** and **Heavy D** ('Big And Ready') in 1990 eventually led to a deal with **Columbia**, who released the *Don Dada* album in 1992. That year he produced artists like Private P, Sugar D, **Tiger**, **Papa San**, **Cutty Ranks** and the late Alton Black on his own Wild Apache imprint, as well as guesting on rap duo **Kriss Kross**' hit, 'Jump Up'. In 1993 'Dolly My Baby' was chosen for the soundtrack of the *Cool Runnings* movie.

Selected albums: *Si Boops Deh* (Techniques 1986), *Sweets For My Sweets* (Skengdon 1986), *Don Dada* (Columbia 1992).

Supereal

A London-based duo of Peter Morris and Paul Freegard who branched out to cult dancefloor status following their origins in **Meat Beat Manifesto**. Their music incorporated the more forboding elements which were always associated with their former employers, as well as rich breakbeats and informed treatments of house styles. Tracks such as 'Terminal High RIP' seem to have been provoked by a restless, playful spirit, which was somewhat lacking in MBM. Their career had begun in 1990 with 'Body Medusa', before 'United State Of Love' for **Guerilla** in 1992. The first of these was remixed by **Leftfield**, the second by **Slam**.

Album: *Elixir* (Guerilla 1992).

Superfly

This 1972 release was one of several films starring African-American actors in a genre dubbed 'blaxpolitation'. The first, and best, of these was *Shaft*, which featured a taught score by **Isaac Hayes**. *Superfly* featured the less-feted Jeff Alexander as its musical director, but he proved astute in signing former **Impressions**' leader **Curtis Mayfield** to contribute several excellent compositions. Two powerful songs, 'Freddy's Dead' and the title track itself, reached the US Top 10, providing a boost to their creator's solo career. Their success helped promote *Superfly* and gave it a prominence the one-dimensional plot did not deserve. Ron O'Neal starred as a drugs' pusher looking for the one big deal which would enable him to retire, but the ambivalent script suggested that violent New York cocaine dealers possess the air of noble outlaws. Indeed several black self-help groups picketed several cinemas showing the film. Mayfield himself later expressed disquiet about the theme, preferring the cautionary 'Freddy's Dead' than other, more celebratory, inclusions. The singer later scored *Claudine* and *Short Eyes*, neither of which enjoyed the commercial approbation of *Superfly*. The film itself inspired an even more lacklustre follow-up, *Superfly TNT*.

Supergrass

Highly regarded new entrants in the UK's indie guitar band movement of the mid-90s, Oxford's Supergrass comprise Danny Goffey (b. c.1975; drums), Gary Coombes (b. c.1976; vocals/guitar) and Mickey Quinn (b. c.1970; bass). Previously Goffey and Coombes had been part of the Jennifers, who recorded one single for **Suede**'s label, Nude Records. With the addition of Quinn rehearsals took place in various bedrooms in early 1994, with inspiration garnered from the **Pixies**, **Sonic Youth** and **Buzzcocks**. They eventually worked their way up to a ramshackle half hour live set which made up in rakish enthusiasm what it lacked in musical accomplishment. Their debut single, 'Caught By The Fuzz', about being lifted by the constabulary for cannabis possession, brought them to much wider attention, though not before it had been released on three separate occasions. Bedroom label Backbeat first supplied 250 copies in the summer of 1994. Fierce Panda then included it as part of a six-track EP of various teenage bands on the advent of the group signing to **Parlophone Records**. Re-released by the major in October, it climbed to number 42 in the UK charts, and by the close of the year it was voted number 5 in DJ **John Peel**'s Festive 50 selection. They also toured with **Shed Seven** and supported **Blur** at their Alexandra Palace gig, before the release of a second single, 'Man Size Rooster', in early 1995. Their debut album was produced at Sawmills Studios, Golant, with Mystics' singer Sam Williams, while the band also contributed to the **Sub Pop Records** Singles Club with 'Lose It'. 'Alright', another instantly likeable single taken from the album, entered the UK charts at number 2 in July 1995 following the band's enthusiastically-received appearance at the Glastonbury festival.

Album: *I Should Coco* (Parlophone 1995).

Supersax

Formed in Los Angeles in 1972 by **Buddy Clark** and **Med Flory**, the band's original purpose was to recreate the music of **Charlie Parker** through sparkling orchestrations of Parker's solos scored for a five-piece saxophone section. The original saxophone line-up comprised Flory, **Bill Perkins**, **Warne Marsh** and Jay Migliori with trumpeter **Conte Candoli** and a rhythm section of Ronnell Bright (piano), Clark, and **Jake Hanna**. Clark left the band in the mid-70s and other changes took place but under Flory's direction they continued to make club appearances in Los Angeles and to record into the late 80s.

Albums: *Supersax Plays Bird* (1972), *Supersax Plays Bird, Volume 2* (1973), *Salt Peanuts* (1974), *Supersax Plays Bird With Strings* (1974), *Chasin' The Bird* (1977), *Dynamite!* (1978), *Supersax & LA Voices Vols 1-3* (1982-86), *Straighten Up & Fly Right* (1986).

Supersuckers

Originally from Austin, Texas, but now relocated to Seattle via Tucson, the Supersuckers are Dan Seigal (drums), Ron Heathman (guitar), Eddie Spaghetti (bass/vocals) and Dan Bolton (guitar). They have recorded for a variety of other outlets since their formation in the late 80s, using eMpTy for their 1991 debut long player, *The Songs All Sound The Same*. This reprised some of their earlier, hard to source 7-inch records for Sympathy For The Record Industry, Lucky and eMpTy themselves. Their debut for new Seattle home **Sub Pop Records** came with 'Like A Big Fuckin' Train', then 'Hell City Hell'/'Dead Homiez' (the latter a bizarre **Ice Cube** cover). *The Smoke Of Hell* became their first long player proper in 1992, with a glorious and somewhat attention-grabbing jacket drawn by comic artist Daniel Clowes. It was produced by 'grunge supremo' **Jack Endino**. Following a first visit to Britain with **Reverend Horton Heat** in 1993, the Supersuckers entered the studio to work on a follow-up set. *La Mano Cornuda* duly arrived the following year and expanded on previous lyrical and musical themes - hard rocking songs about hard drinking hard men being the overwhelming impression. Albums: *The Smoke Of Hell* (Sub Pop 1992), *La Mano Cornuda* (Sup Pop 1994). Compilation: *The Songs All Sound The Same* (eMpTy 1991).

Supertramp

Many aspiring musicians would have envied the opportunity which was given to Supertramp in 1969. They were financed by the Dutch millionaire Stanley August Miesegaes, which enabled Richard Davies (b. 22 July 1944, Swindon, Wiltshire, England; vocals/keyboards) to recruit, through the *Melody Maker*, the band of his choice. He enlisted Roger Hodgson (b. 21 March 1950, Portsmouth, Hampshire, England; guitar), Dave Winthrop (b. 27 November 1948, New Jersey, USA; saxophone), Richard Palmer (guitar) and Bob Miller (drums). The debut *Supertramp* was an unspectacular affair of lengthy self-indulgent solos. The follow-up, *Indelibly Stamped* was similarly unsuccessful and meandering; the controversial cover created most interest, depicting a busty, naked tattooed female. The band were in dire straits when their fairy godfather departed, along with Winthrop and Palmer. They recruited ex-**Alan Bown** band members, John Helliwell (b. 15 February 1945, Todmorden, Yorkshire, England) and Dougie Thompson (b. 24 March 1951, Glasgow, Scotland) and from **Bees Make Honey**, Bob Benberg. They had a remarkable change in fortune as *Crime Of The Century* became one of the top-selling albums of 1974. The band had refined their keyboard-dominated sound and produced an album that was well-reviewed. Their debut hit 'Dreamer' was taken from the album, while 'Bloody Well Right' was a Top 40 hit in the USA, going on to become one of their classic live numbers. The subsequent *Crisis? What Crisis?* and *Even In The Quietest Moments* were lesser works, being erratic in content. The choral 'Give A Little Bit', with its infectious acoustic guitar introduction was a minor transatlantic hit in 1977. Supertramp were elevated to rock's first division with the faultless *Breakfast In America*. Four of the tracks became hits, 'The Logical Song', 'Take The Long Way Home', 'Goodbye Stranger' and the title track. The album stayed on top of the US charts for six weeks and became their biggest seller, with over 18 million copies to date. The obligatory live album came in 1980 and was followed by the R&B influenced *Famous Last Words*. Hodgson left shortly afterwards, unhappy with the bluesier direction the band were taking and made two respectable solo albums, *In The Eye Of A Storm* and *Hai Hai*. Supertramp continued with occasional tours and infrequent albums. Their recent releases, however, have only found minor success.

Albums: *Supertramp* (1970), *Indelibly Stamped* (1971), *Crime Of The Century* (1974), *Crisis? What Crisis?* (1975), *Even In The Quietest Moments* (1977), *Breakfast In America* (1979), *Paris* (1980), *Famous Last Words* (1982), *Brother Where You Bound* (1985), *Free As A Bird* (1987), *Supertramp Live 88* (1988). Compilations: *The Autobiography Of Supertramp* (1986), *The Very Best Of* (1992).

Further reading: *The Supertramp Book*, Melhuish, Martin (1986).

Supremes

America's most successful female vocal group of all time was formed by four Detroit schoolgirls in the late 50s. **Diana Ross** (b. 26 March 1944, Detroit, USA), Betty Hutton, **Florence Ballard** (b. 30 June 1943, Detroit, USA) and **Mary Wilson** (b. 4 March 1944, Greenville, Mississippi, USA) named themselves the **Primettes** in tribute to the local male group, the Primes - who themselves found fame in the 60s as the **Temptations**. Having issued a solitary single on a small local label, the Primettes were signed to **Berry Gordy**'s **Motown** stable, where they initially found public acceptance hard to find. For more than two years, they issued a succession of flop singles, despite the best efforts of top Motown writer/producer **Smokey Robinson** to find them a suitable vehicle for their unsophisticated talents. Only when Diana Ross supplanted Florence Ballard as the group's regular lead vocalist, at Gordy's suggestion, did the Supremes break into the US charts. The dynamic 'When The Lovelight Starts Shining In His Eyes', modelled on the production style of **Phil Spector**, was the group's first hit in 1963. The follow-up single flopped, so Gordy handed the group over to the newly-formed **Holland/Dozier/Holland** writing and production team. They concocted the slight, but effervescent, 'Where Did Our Love Go' for the Supremes, which topped the US charts and was also a major hit in Britain.

This achievement inaugurated a remarkable run of success for the group and their producers, as their next four releases - 'Baby Love', 'Come See About Me', 'Stop! In The Name Of Love' and 'Back In My Arms Again' - all topped the US singles charts, while 'Baby Love' became the only record by an American group to reach number 1 in Britain during the beat-dominated year of 1964. All these singles were hinged around insistent, very danceable rhythms with repetitive lyrics and melodies, which placed no great strain on Ross's fragile voice. With their girl-next-door looks and endearingly unsophisticated demeanour, the Supremes became role models for young black Americans and their name was used to promote a range of merchandising, even (ironically) a brand of white bread.

The rather perfunctory 'Nothing But Heartaches' broke the chart-topping sequence, which was immediately restored by the more ambitious 'I Hear A Symphony'. As Holland/Dozier/Holland moved into their prime, and Ross increased in confidence, the group's repertoire grew more mature. They recorded albums of Broadway standards, played residencies at expensive night-clubs, and were expertly groomed by Motown staff as all-round entertainers. Meanwhile, the hits kept coming, with four more US number 1 hits in the shape of 'You Can't Hurry Love', 'You Keep Me Hanging On', 'Love Is Here And Now You're Gone' and 'The Happening' - the last of which was a blatant attempt to cash in on the psychedelic movement. Behind the scenes, the group's future was in some jeopardy: Florence Ballard had grown increasingly unhappy in the supporting role into which Berry Gordy had forced her, and her occasionally erratic and troublesome behaviour was ultimately used as an excuse to force her out of the group. Without fanfare, Ballard was ousted in mid-1967, and replaced by Cindy Birdsong; most fans simply did not notice. At the same time, Diana Ross's prime position in the group's hierarchy was confirmed in public, when she was given individual credit on the group's records, a move which prompted a flurry of similar demands from the lead singers of other Motown groups.

'Reflections', an eerie, gripping song that was one of Motown's most adventurous productions to date, introduced the new era. Motown's loss of Holland/Dozier/Holland slowed the group's progress in 1968, before they bounced back with two controversial slices of overt social commentary, 'Love Child' and 'I'm Livin' In Shame', the first of which was yet another US number 1. The Supremes also formed a successful recording partnership with the Temptations, exemplified by the hit single 'I'm Gonna Make You Love Me'.

During 1969, there were persistent rumours that Berry Gordy was about to launch Diana Ross on a solo career. These were confirmed at the end of the year, when the Supremes staged a farewell performance, and Ross bade goodbye to the group with the elegiac 'Someday We'll Be Together' - a US chart-topper on which, ironically, she was the only member of the Supremes to appear. Ross was replaced by Jean Terrell, sister of heavyweight boxer Ernie Terrell. The new line-up, with Terrell and Mary Wilson alternating lead vocal duties, found immediate success with 'Up The Ladder To The Roof' in early 1970, while 'Stoned Love', the group's biggest UK hit for four years, revived memories of their early successes with its rhythmic base and repetitive hook. The Supremes also tried to revive the atmosphere of their earlier recordings with the Temptations on a series of albums with the **Four Tops**. Gradually, their momentum was lost, and as Motown shifted its centre of activity from Detroit to California, the Supremes were left behind. Lynda Laurence replaced Cindy Birdsong in the line-up in 1972; Birdsong returned in 1974 when Laurence became pregnant. The latter move coincided with the departure of Jean Terrell, whose place was taken by **Scherrie Payne**. With the group recording only rarely, Birdsong quit again, leaving Mary Wilson - at last established as the unchallenged leader - to recruit Susaye Greene in her place. This trio recorded the self-explanatory *Mary, Scherrie And Susaye* in 1976, before disbanding the following year. Mary Wilson attempted to assemble a new set of Supremes for recording purposes, and actually toured Britain in 1978 with Karen Rowland and Karen Jackson in the line-up. The termination of her Motown contract stymied this move, however, and since then the use of the Supremes' name has legally resided with Motown. They have chosen not to sully the memory of their most famous group by concocting an ersatz Supremes to cash in on their heritage. Jean Terrell, Scherrie Payne and Lynda Laurence won the rights to use the Supremes' name in the UK. Payne began recording disco material with producer Ian Levine in 1989, for the Nightmare and Motor City labels. Levine also signed Laurence, Wilson and ex-Supreme Susaye Greene to solo deals and recorded Terrell, Lawrence and Greene for a remake of 'Stoned Love'. The career of Mary Wilson has also continued with a starring role in the Toronto, Canada production of the stage musical *The Beehive* in 1989 and the publication of the second volume of her autobiography in 1990.

Albums: as the Supremes *Meet The Supremes* (1963), *Where Did Our Love Go?* (1964), *A Bit Of Liverpool* (1964), *The Supremes Sing Country, Western And Pop* (1964), *We*

Remember Sam Cooke (1965), *More Hits By The Supremes* (1965), *Merry Christmas* (1965), *The Supremes At The Copa* (1965), *I Hear A Symphony* (1966), *Supremes A-Go-Go* (1966), *The Supremes Sing Holland, Dozier, Holland* (1967), *Right On* (1970), with the Four Tops *The Magnificent Seven* (1970), *New Ways But Love Stays* (1970), with the Four Tops *The Return Of The Magnificent Seven* (1971), *Touch* (1971), with the Four Tops *Dynamite* (1971), *Floy Joy* (1972), *The Supremes* (1975), *High Energy* (1976), *Mary, Scherrie And Susaye* (1976).

Albums: as Diana Ross & the Supremes *Diana Ross And The Supremes Sing Rodgers And Hart* (1967), *Reflections* (1968), *Diana Ross And The Supremes Sing And Perform 'Funny Girl'* (1968), *Diana Ross And The Supremes Live At London's Talk Of The Town* (1968), with the Temptations *Diana Ross And The Supremes Join The Temptations* (1968), *Love Child* (1968), with the Temptations *TCB* (1968), *Let The Sunshine In* (1969), with the Temptations *Together* (1969), *Cream Of The Crop* (1969), *Diana Ross And The Supremes On Broadway* (1969), *Farewell* (1970).

Further reading: *Reflections*, Johnny Bond, *Dreamgirl: My Life As A Supreme*, Mary Wilson. *Girl Groups: The Story Of A Sound*, Alan Betrock. *Supreme Faith: Someday We'll Be Together*, Mary Wilson and Patricia Romanowski.

Sure Is Pure

Remix team probably best known for their work with the **Doobie Brothers**, an unlikely teaming which saw the soft rockers back in the charts after several years absence. Based in Stoke On Trent, Staffordshire, England, Sure Is Pure are built around lynchpin DJ Kelvin Andrews, and they have also undertaken remixing chores for **INXS**, **Yothu Yindi** ('Treaty') and other major league outfits. They have recorded in their own right, including the 1991 EP *Proper Tunes* for their own imprint Gem. The same label would also be the first home to their 'Is This Love Really Real?' single, featuring vocalist Aphrique, before it transferred to **Union City** in 1992. Again for Gem they picked up and remixed Unique featuring Kim Cooper's 'Danube Dance'. In 1994 Andrews formed an indie rock band called Camp Carnival, who recorded a version of Sure Is Pure's 'Grind Zone Blues' (from the *Out To Lunch* EP), and signed to **Vinyl Solution**.

Surf Party

Released in 1963, *Surf Party* was an early entrant into the 'beach' genre largely propagated by American International Pictures. This was not one of their vehicles, but it featured a similarly asinine plot. Three girls arrive in California from Arizona, hoping to find one of their number's drop-out brother. Pop singer **Bobby Vinton** ('Blue Velvet') stars as a surfer aiding their quest, but in now-accustomed fashion, interest lies in the film's musical content. Prolific composer/performer **Jackie DeShannon** contributed the *de rigeur* 'Glory Wave', one-hit wonders the

Routers (Let's Go') offered 'Crack Up', while surf act the Astronauts added 'Fire Water' as well as the title track.

Surface

This Birmingham, England-based hard rock group was formed in 1986 by Gez Finnegan (vocals), Mark Davies (guitar), Loz Rabone (guitar), Dean Field (keyboards), Ian Hawkins (bass) and Jamie Hawkins (drums). They styled themselves on the successful US AOR formula of groups such as **Journey**, and signed to the independent Killerwatt label, where they debuted with *Race The Night*, which was recorded live. The album failed and the band returned to their former part-time status.
Album: *Race The Night* (Killerwatt 1986).

Surfaris

Formed in Glendale, California in 1962, the Surfaris - Jim Fuller (b. 1947; lead guitar), Jim Pash (b. 1949; guitar), Bob Berryhill (b. 1947; guitar), Pat Connolly (b. 1947; bass) and Ron Wilson (b. 1945; drums) - achieved international success the following year with 'Wipe Out'. This frantic yet simplistic instrumental, originally envisaged as a throwaway b-side, is recognized as one of the definitive surfing anthems, although some of its lustre has been removed in the wake of a protracted allegation of plagiarism. **Merrell Fankhauser**, former guitarist with the Impacts, successfully claimed the piece infringed his composition of the same title. Further controversy arose when the Surfaris discovered that the music gracing their debut album was, in fact, played by a rival group, the Challengers. However, despite their understandable anger, such backroom machinations remained rife throughout the quintet's career. Their third album, *Hit City '64*, introduced a partnership with producer **Gary Usher**, who employed a team of experienced session musicians on ensuing Surfaris' releases.

In 1965 the group abandoned beach and hot-rod themes for folk rock. Wilson had developed into an accomplished lead singer and with Ken Forssi replacing Connolly on bass, the Surfaris completed the promising *It Ain't Me Babe*. However, Usher then severed his relationship with the band and they broke up when the last remaining original member, Jim Pash, left the line-up. Wilson died in 1989 from a brain haemorrhage. Newcomer Forssi then joined **Love**, and although no other member achieved similar success, Berryhill resurrected the Surfaris' name in 1981.

Albums: *Wipe Out* (1963), *The Surfaris Play Wipe Out And Others* (1963), *Hit City '64* (1964), *Fun City, USA* (1964), *Hit City '65* (1965), *It Ain't Me Babe* (1965), *Surfaris Live* (1983). Compilations: *Yesterday's Pop Scene* (1973), *Surfers Rule* (1976), *Gone With The Wave* (1977).

Surgin

This US melodic hard rock group was founded in 1984 by former Rest members Tommy Swift (drums) and Jack Ponti (guitar/vocals). Enlisting the services of Russel Arcara (vocals), John Capra (keyboards), Gay Shapiro (keyboards) and Michael King (bass/vocals), they debuted in 1985 with *When Midnight Comes*. This featured the **Bon Jovi** track, 'Shot Through The Heart', which was written by Ponti and Jon Bon Jovi, while they were both part of Rest. Elsewhere the album comprised infectious hard rock anthems, underscored by strong melody lines, and was critically acclaimed at the time of release. In spite of tours supporting **Aerosmith** and **Ratt**, Surgin failed to achieve commercial success. As Ponti concentrated on session work and composing for other artists, Surgin became redundant.
Album: *When Midnight Comes* (Music For Nations 1985).

Surman, John

b. John Douglas Surman, 30 August 1944, Tavistock, Devon, England. Surman, a remarkable player on soprano and baritone saxophones, bass clarinet, bamboo flutes and sometimes tenor saxophone and synthesizers. He was a member of the Jazz Workshop at Plymouth Arts Centre with **Mike Westbrook** whilst still at school, and came to London with Westbrook's band in 1962. He studied at London College of Music (1962-65) and London University Institute of Education (1966). By the time he ceased to be a regular member of Westbrook's band in 1968 he was also working in **Ronnie Scott**'s nine-piece outfit (the Band) with **Humphrey Lyttelton** and had twice been voted the world's best baritone saxophone player by *Melody Maker* readers as well as top instrumentalist at the 1968 **Montreux International Jazz Festival**. Since then various of his albums have collected awards from all over the world. From 1968-69 he led a group, varying from a quartet to an octet, centring round **Mike Osborne**, Harry Miller and Alan Jackson. During the 60s and 70s he also played with **Alexis Korner**'s New Church, **Mike Gibbs**, **Graham Collier**, **Chris McGregor**, **Dave Holland**, **John McLaughlin** (on the guitarist's acclaimed *Extrapolation*), John Warren and **Harry Beckett**. Owing to lack of work in the UK, he emigrated to Europe where he formed the Trio with **Barre Phillips** and Stu Martin. Surman next worked with **Terje Rypdal** (*Morning Glory*), before the Trio briefly reformed, augmented by **Albert Mangelsdorff** to become MUMPS. At this time he first met **Jack DeJohnette** with whom he was to work regularly in the 80s and 90s. In 1973 he formed another highly impressive and influential trio, S.O.S., with Osborne and **Alan Skidmore**. He began experimenting with electronics during this period, a facet of his work explored in depth on his albums of the late 70s and 80s. He formed duos with **Stan Tracey** and **Karin Krog**, in 1978 (the latter becoming a regular musical associate), and from 1979-82 worked with **Miroslav Vitous**. In 1981, Surman formed the Brass Project, and during the 80s he was a member of **Gil Evans**' British band and later of his New York band. He also worked with **Paul Bley** and **Bill Frisell** and, in 1986, toured with **Elvin Jones**, Holland and Mangelsdorff. A powerful and resourceful improviser, Surman also composes for all sizes of jazz groups, as well as writing pieces for choirs and for dance companies, notably the Carolyn Carlson Dance Theatre at the Paris Opera, with whom he worked from 1974-79.

Albums: with Mike Westbrook *Celebration* (1967), *Release* (1968), *John Surman* (1968), *How Many Clouds Can You See* (1969), with John McLaughlin *Extrapolation* (1969), *Marching Song* (1969), *Where Fortune Smiles* (1970), *The Trio* (1970), with Mike Gibbs *Michael Gibbs* (1970), with Gibbs *Tanglewood '63* (1971), with Chris McGregor *Brotherhood Of Breath* (1971), *Conflagration* (1971), with John Warren *Tales Of The Algonquin* (1971), *Westering Home* (1972), *Morning Glory* (1973), *S.O.S.* (1975), *Live At Woodstock Town Hall* (1975), *Live At Moers Festival* (1975), *Citadel/Room 315* (1975), with Stan Tracey *Sonatinas* (1978), *Surman For All Saints* (1979), *Upon Reflection* (ECM 1979), *The Amazing Adventures Of Simon Simon* (ECM 1981), with Karin Krog *Such Winters Of Memory* (ECM 1983), with Barry Altschul *Irina* (1983), *Withholding Pattern* (ECM 1985), with Paul Bley *Fragments* (1986), with Alexis Korner *Alexis Korner And... 1961-72* (1986), with the Trio *By Contact* (1987, rec. 1971), *Private City* (ECM 1988), *The Paul Bley Quartet* (1988), *The Road To St. Ives* (ECM 1990), with John Taylor *Ambleside Days* (1992), *Adventure Playground* (ECM 1992), with Albert Mangelsdorff *Room 1220* (1993), with Warren *The Brass Project* (ECM 1993), with John Abercrombie, Marc Johnson, Peter Erskine *November* (1994), *Stranger Than Fiction* (ECM 1994), *Nordic Quartet* (ECM 1995).

Surrender

This Canadian hard rock quintet was formed in 1978 by Alfie Zappacosta (vocals/guitar), Steve Jenson (guitar), Peter Curry (keyboards), Geoff Waddington (bass) and Paul Delaney (drums). Incorporating elements of **Rush**, **Triumph** and **Yes** in their music over the course of two excellent albums characterized by extended guitar-keyboard interplay, they nevertheless failed to find an appreciative audience. Curry and Waddington quit in 1983 and the remaining trio continued as Zappacosta.
Albums: *Surrender* (Capitol 1979), *No Surrender* (Capitol 1982). As Zappacosta: *Zappacosta* (Capitol 1984), *A To Z* (Capitol 1987).

Survivor

This sophisticated melodic US rock group was put together by guitarists Jim Peterik (formerly of **Ides Of March**) and Frankie Sullivan in 1978. Recruiting vocalist Dave Bickler, they recorded their self-titled debut as a three-piece. This featured a *pot-pourri* of ideas that had no definite direction or style. They expanded the band to a quintet in 1981, with the addition of Marc Doubray (drums) and Stephen Ellis (bass). From this point on, the band were comparable in approach to the AOR rock styles of **Styx**, **Foreigner** and **Journey**, but never achieved the same degree of recognition or success. Their first short-lived affair with glory came with the song 'Eye Of The Tiger', used as the theme to the *Rocky III* film. The single, with its heavy drum beat and rousing chorus, became a worldwide number 1 hit, and is still a staple of FM radio and various advertising campaigns. Unfortunately, the rest of the songs on the album of the same name were patchy in comparison. Nevertheless, the work succeeded on the strength of the title cut, peaking at number 2 and 12 on the US and UK album charts, respectively. *Caught In The Game*, released the following year, was a more satisfying album. It adopted a heavier approach and featured a more up-front guitar sound from Sullivan, but did not find favour with the record-buying public. Bickler was fired at this stage and replaced by ex-**Cobra** vocalist Jimi Jamison, whose vocals added an extra, almost soulful dimension to the band. The resulting *Vital Signs* gave the band their second breakthrough. It enjoyed a six-month residency on the ***Billboard*** album chart, attaining number 16 as its highest position, and also spawned two Top 10 hits with 'High On You' and 'The Search Is Over'. They recorded 'Burning Heart' (essentially a re-tread of 'Eye Of The Tiger') as the theme song to *Rocky IV* in 1986 and achieved another international hit, reaching number 5 on the UK singles chart. Surprisingly, the song was not included on *When Seconds Count*, which pursued a heavier direction once more. The band had contracted to a three-piece nucleus of Jamison, Sullivan and Peterik at this juncture and had used session musicians to finish the album. *Too Hot To Sleep* was probably the most consistent and strongest album of the band's career, featuring a magnificent collection of commercially-minded, hard rock anthems. The album made little commercial impact and the band finally disbanded in 1989.

Albums: *Survivor* (Scotti Bros 1979), *Premonition* (Scotti Bros 1981), *Eye Of The Tiger* (Scotti Bros 1982), *Caught In The Game* (Scotti Bros 1983), *Vital Signs* (Scotti Bros 1984), *When Seconds Count* (Scotti Bros 1986), *Too Hot To Sleep* (Scotti Bros 1988). Compilation: *Best Of* (Scotti Bros 1989).

Suso, Foday Musa

b. 9 December 1953, Banjul, The Gambia. Bandleader, vocalist, kora player. Born into a long-established and distinguished line of Gambian jalis or griots - traditional musicians who combine the functions of entertainer and tribal historian (in a society where history is passed down by word of mouth rather than the printed page) - Suso is a master of authentic-roots kora (a West African version of the harp) and a pioneer of its Western-informed fusion possibilities. In 1975, keen to explore rock and jazz music while also introducing the kora to non-African audiences, Suso settled in Germany, where he gigged with local musicians in Berlin, Hamburg and Munich. The experience was stimulating, but in the mid-70s the German music scene lacked the vitality of those in the UK or USA, and in 1977 he moved again, this time to Chicago. Once settled in the city, Suso formed the **Mandingo Griot Society**, a loose aggregation of like-minded African, Caribbean and American musicians playing a dance-based fusion of rock, funk, reggae and traditional Gambian styles. Two albums followed: *Mandingo Griot Society* and *Mighty Rhythm*.

During the early 80s, Suso began to be noticed by some of the more adventurous producers and musicians in the New York funk and jazz fields, who had heard the Mandingo Griot Society albums and were aware of the solo work he had contributed to the soundtrack of Alex Haley's television series *Roots* (which traced a modern day American black man's family tree back to its origins in The Gambia). Notable among these figures were the producer **Bill Laswell** and the keyboard player **Herbie Hancock**. With Laswell and Hancock, he worked on the official theme tune for the American team at the 1984 Los Angeles Olympics. The collaboration continued with Suso guesting on one track, 'Junku', on Hancock's Laswell-produced 1984 album *Sound System*. Later that year, Hancock returned the compliment, guesting on Suso's *Watto Sitta*, produced by Laswell and presenting a blistering fusion of hot electro-funk and traditional Gambian songs and instrumentation. Also in 1984, Suso played a major role in the Laswell-produced collaborative album *Deadline*, which also featured P-funk keyboard star **Bernie Worrell** and saxophonist **Manu Dibango**. Two years later, Suso collaborated with Hancock on an acoustic duo album, *Herbie Hancock And Foday Musa Suso*: an exquisite blend of jazz piano and kora which, sadly, was only released (on **CBS**) in Japan. Suso now divides his time between Chicago, New York and The Gambia, combining the roles of traditional griot and hi-tech Western fusionist.

Albums: *Mandingo Griot Society* (1978), *Mighty Rhythm* (1981), *Watto Sitta* (1984), *Herbie Hancock And Foday Musa Suso* (1986).

Sutch, Screaming Lord

b. 10 November 1940, Middlesex, England. David Sutch rose to prominence in 1960 as the first long-haired pop star, with tresses in excess of 18 inches. His recording career peaked with such early releases as 'Til The Following Night', 'Jack The Ripper' and 'I'm A Hog For You Baby', all produced by the late **Joe Meek**. Although never registering a chart entry, Sutch boasted one of the most accomplished live acts of the era in the Savages, whose ranks included such luminaries as **Ritchie Blackmore**, **Nicky Hopkins** and **Paul Nicholas**. For 30 years, Sutch has sustained his flagging recording career with a plethora of publicity stunts ranging from dramatic marriage proposals to standing for Parliament and founding his own radio station. In 1970, he enjoyed some minor success in the US album charts with *Lord Sutch And Heavy Friends*, which featured Blackmore, **Jimmy Page**, **Jeff Beck**, **Keith Moon**, Nicky Hopkins, Noel Redding and John Bonham. He now combines regular club work with the presidency of the Monster Raving Loony Party.

Albums: *Lord Sutch And Heavy Friends* (1970), *Hands Of Jack The Ripper* (1972), *Rock And Horror* (1982), *Alive And Well* (1982).

Further reading: *Life As Sutch: The Official Autobiography Of Monster Raving Looney*, Lord David Sutch with Peter Chippindale (1991).

Sutcliffe, Stuart

b. 1940, Edinburgh, Scotland, d. 10 April 1962. Though born in Scotland, Sutcliffe's family moved to Liverpool during his infancy. At the city's art college, Sutcliffe's yardstick of 'cool' was Modigliani rather than **Elvis Presley**, and he became an idol of **John Lennon**, a friend in the same year. With a cash prize for a painting in the 1959 John Moores Exhibition, Sutcliffe purchased a bass guitar to join Lennon's Johnny And The Moondogs - who would evolve by 1960 into the **Beatles**, a choice of name attributed to Sutcliffe. His decision to leave his studies to join the group in their earliest expeditions was not greeted with enthusiasm by his tutors, lecturer Arthur Ballard recalling that he was 'a brilliant potential artist lured away from what he was most serious about and really wanted to do - for £20 a week'. During the group's first season in Hamburg, he became engaged to photographer Astrid Kirchherr, one of a local bohemian faction, whose sartorial style and *pilzenkopf* haircuts he and most of the group would emulate. In late 1961, he left the Beatles to recommence his studies at Hamburg's State School of Art under Edouardo Paolozzi - but not for long. In April 1962, Sutcliffe died of a cerebral haemorrhage. None of the Beatles attended his funeral. His association with the group, however, led to many posthumous exhibitions of his

work and a 1990 documentary about him on British television. Yet, beyond morbid mystique, visual evidence suggests that, had he lived, Stuart Sutcliffe would have been recognised as an outstanding artist even without his former Beatlehood opening doors. In April 1994 a film entitled *Backbeat* opened, which depicted Sutcliffe's life, the central role taken by Stephen Dorff. A biography of the same title, co-authored by Sutcliffe's sister, was published at the same time.

Further reading: *Backbeat*, Alan Clayson and Pauline Sutcliffe (1994).

Sutherland Brothers (And Quiver)

Basically a duo from the outset, comprising brothers Iain Sutherland (b. 17 November 1948, Ellon, Aberdeenshire, Scotland; vocals/guitar/keyboards), and Gavin Sutherland (b. 6 October 1951, Peterhead, Aberdeenshire, Scotland; bass/guitar/vocals). The two had been signed to **Island Records**, releasing *The Sutherland Brothers Band*. It was during this period that they wrote and recorded the song 'Sailing', later a UK number 1 for **Rod Stewart**. Having completed their second album with the use of session musicians, they began seeking a permanent backing group. A meeting between their manager Wayne Bordell, and **Quiver** showed a mutual need for each others talents. The Sutherland Brothers needed a band, and Quiver needed new songs, so the Sutherland Brothers And Quiver were born, comprising Iain and Gavin, Tim Renwick (b. 7 August 1949, Cambridge, England; guitar/vocals/flute), Willie Wilson (b. John Wilson, 8 July 1947, Cambridge, England; drums, vocals, percussion), Bruce Thomas (b. 14 August 1948, Middlesbrough, Cleveland, England; bass), Cal Batchelor (vocals/guitar/keyboards), and Pete Wood (b. Middlesex, England, d. 1994, New York, USA; keyboards). Within a few months they released *Lifeboat*. In the USA, the release was credited as the Sutherland Brothers And Quiver, but in the UK as the Sutherland Brothers. There were also variations in the track listing between the UK and American releases. The band recorded three tracks, 'I Don't Want To Love You But You Got Me Anyway', 'Have You Had A Vision', and 'Not Fade Away', prior to playing a support tour, of the USA, to **Elton John**, in 1973. After recording, Cal Batchelor announced that he was going to leave the band as he could no longer see a future for him in it. So the subsequent of the USA went ahead without him. *Dream Kid*, produced by **Muff Winwood**, saw bassist Bruce Thomas leave shortly afterwards. (He later joined **Elvis Costello** And **The Attractions.**) Terry 'Tex' Comer from **Ace**, took over the role of bass player to play on half the recordings for *Beat Of The Street*. In fact, the song 'How Long', often thought to be a love song, was actually written about how the group had been trying to persuade Comer to join them for some time. Taking on Mick Blackburn as manager, they got a deal with **CBS**, and *Reach For The Sky* was released on 7 November 1975. Produced by Ron and Howie Albert, it featured Dave Gilmour on pedal steel guitar on one track. Gilmour had produced 'We Get Along', the b-side of 'Arms Of Mary'. Wood left to become **Al Stewart**'s keyboard player. By the time *Slipstream* was released, the line-up was Wilson, Renwick, Gavin, and Iain., although shortly afterwards Renwick left. Produced by **Bruce Welch**, the recording of *Down To Earth* was augmented by a number of respected session musicians, including Ray Flacke (guitar), and Brian Bennett (percussion). By the time of *When The Night Comes Down*, Wilson had left. More recently Gavin has spent time writing and editing books, as well as continuing to write songs, and playing with local musicians in Scotland. Iain has also been composing, but with only occasional performances.

Albums: *The Sutherland Brothers Band* (Island 1972). With Quiver *Lifeboat* (Island 1972), *Dream Kid* (Island 1974), *Beat Of The Street* (Island 1974), *Reach For The Sky* (CBS 1975), *Slipstream* (CBS 1976), *Down To Earth* (CBS 1977), *When The Night Comes Down* (CBS 1978). Compilation: *Sailing* (Island 1976).
Further reading: *The Whaling Years, Peterhead 1788-1893*, Gavin Sutherland.

Sutherland, Nadine

b. 1968, Kingston, Jamaica, West Indies. She began performing in 1980 and balanced her recording career alongside her education commitments. Supported by the family, her parents managed her career and being a naive performer in a perilous occupation, acted as her guardians. She studied business administration at college and when **Bob Marley** heard her work she was recruited to Tuff Gong. Following on from his unsuccessful Wail 'N' Soul venture, a determined Marley put all his energies into the 'Gong' and signed newcomers Sutherland and Dallol along with **Rita Marley**, **Tyrone Taylor** and the Melody Makers. Sutherland's live appearances helped to groom her for stardom and she performed outside of Jamaica in 1982 at a memorial concert for Bob Marley alongside, **Ziggy Marley And The Melody Makers**, the I Threes and the **Wailers**. Viewed by many as a soft alternative to the ghetto sounds Sutherland was not to make an impression in the reggae charts. In 1986 she toured supporting **Bunny Wailer** in the USA along with Leroy Sibbles of the **Heptones**. Aware of her *carte blanche* reputation she found work as a backing vocalist at **Gussie Clarke**'s Music Works studio thereby earning respect. By the late 80s she recorded over **Gregory Isaacs** 'Mind You Dis' rhythm on the song, 'Mr Hard To Please', featured on the one rhythm, *Music Works Showcase '89*. By the early 90s she worked with the current top producer in Jamaica, **Donovan Germain** whose Penthouse studios carried the swing.

Her 1993 hit with Terror Fabulous, 'Action', was used by the Jamaican Labour Party as their campaign theme (without her consent). The same year she enjoyed number 1 on the reggae chart when DJ legend **Buju Banton**'s 1992 hit 'Dickie' was re-released featuring Sutherland's vocals as 'Wicked Dickie'.
Album: *Until* (1994).

Sutton, Ralph

b. 4 November 1922, Hamburg, Missouri, USA. After playing piano locally for several years, Sutton joined **Jack Teagarden** in 1941. During the 40s he attracted widespread attention, thanks to his participation in a series of radio shows hosted by jazz writer Rudi Blesh. From the late 40s through to the mid-50s he played regularly at **Eddie Condon**'s club in New York. In the 60s he worked mostly as a single, but also played in a number of traditional bands and towards the end of the decade was a founder-member of the **World's Greatest Jazz Band**. Thereafter, Sutton's star rose and remained in the ascendancy with a series of record albums and world tours, solo and in a variety of settings. His musical partners in these ventures included **Ruby Braff**, **Jay McShann**, **Kenny Davern** and **Peanuts Hucko**.

He continues to perform with great panache and a seemingly undiminished level of invention into the early 90s. An outstanding pianist in the great tradition of stride giants such as **James P. Johnson** and **Fats Waller**, Sutton's style is both forceful and lightly dancing, as the needs of his repertoire demand. Although drawing from the century-old tradition of jazz piano, from ragtime through the blues to Harlem stride, Sutton brings to his playing such inventive enthusiasm that everything he does seems freshly-minted.

Selected albums: *Ralph Sutton Plays The Music Of Fats Waller* (1951), *Ralph Sutton At The Piano* (1952), one side only *Stacy 'N' Sutton* (1953), with Lee Collins *The Hangover All Stars Live 1953* (1953), *Ralph Sutton's Jazzola Six* (1953), *Ralph Sutton And The All Stars* (1954), *The Ralph Sutton Quartet* i (1959), *Ragtime USA* (1962-63), *The Ralph Sutton Trio* (1966), with Ruby Braff *On Sunnie's Side Of The Street* (1968), *The Night They Raided Sunnie's* (1969), with Yank Lawson and Bob Wilber *The Ralph Sutton Trio And Guests* (1969), *Piano Moods* (1975), *Off The Cuff* (1975), *Suttonly It Jumped* (1975), *Live!* (1975), *Changes* (1976), *Jazz At The Forum* (1976), *Live At Haywards Heath* (Flyright 1976), *The Ralph Sutton Quartet* ii (1977) with Wild Bill Davison *Together Again* (1977), *Stomp Off, Let's Go* (1977), *The Other Side Of Ralph Sutton* (1980), with Braff *Quartet* (1980), *Ralph Sutton & Ruby Braff: Duets* (1980), with Jay McShann *The Last Of The Whorehouse Piano Players Vols 1 & 2* (Chiaroscuro 1980), *Ralph Sutton & Kenny Davern Trio Vols 1 & 2* (1980), *Ralph Sutton And The Jazz Band* (1981), with Eddie Miller *We've Got Rhythm* (1981), *Ralph Sutton & Jack Lesberg* (1981), *The Big*

Noise From Wayzata (1981), *Great Piano Solos And Duets* (1982), *Live At Hanratty's* (1982), *Blowin' Bubbles* (1982), *Partners In Crime* (Sackville 1983), *At Cafe Des Copains* (Sackville 1987), Bix Beiderbecke Suite (Commodore Class 1987), with the Sackville All Stars *A Tribute To Louis Armstrong* (1988), *Alligator Crawl* (Jazzology 1989), *Eye Opener* (J&M 1990), *Maybeck Recital Hall Series Vol 30* (Concord 1993). Selected compilations: *Piano Solos In The Classic Jazz Tradition* (1949-52), *Piano Solos/Beiderbecke Suite* (1950), *The Ralph Sutton Trio* (1950).

Suzuki, Kenji

This Japanese child prodigy and virtuoso guitarist first came to prominence after winning a national competition for guitarists at the age of 14. Resembling a Japanese version of **Elvis Costello**, his mastery of the fretboard was quite astonishing. After a low-key mini-album of mainly Japanese-style instrumentals, he teamed up with ex-**Cream** bassist **Jack Bruce** and **Frehley's Comet**'s drummer Anton Fig. This association recorded as a power-trio, playing Cream classics and *avant garde*, blues-based rock, fused with Japanese classical pieces.
Album: *Jack Bruce, Anton Fig & Kenji Suzuki - Inazuma Supersession* (1988).

Sven Gali

This Toronto, Canada-based group was formed in 1988 by guitarists Dee Cernile and Andy Frank, vocalist Dave Wanless (b. London, England), and bassist Shawn Maher after the members had accumulated professional experience as backing musicians for a number of Canadian acts, but had tired of their anonymous status. Enlisting New York session drummer Gregg Gerson, the band spent their formative years on the domestic club circuit, honing an accessible, yet raw metal sound which would serve them well. Their self-titled debut and ensuing live shows, including a UK tour with **Wolfsbane**, drew comparisons to **Skid Row** (USA) in terms of style, delivery and stage performance, and the band's ability and genuine enthusiasm suggests that they may be able to overcome the difficulties facing traditional metal in post-grunge times.
Album: *Sven Gali* (Ariola/BMG 1993).

Sven Klang's Kvintett

Based upon a stage play by Henric Holmberg and Ninne Olsson, this film made in 1976, directed by Stellan Olsson, tells the story of an amateur, and not-very-good, traditional jazz band in Sweden in the late 50s. The band is joined by an alto saxophonist who is not only a vastly superior musician but is also eagerly experimenting with bop. This character, portrayed by Christer Boustedt (who really does play alto), is loosely based upon alto and baritone saxophonist **Lars Gullin** who died in the year of the film's release. The

film offers one of the best accounts of life on the road for jazz musicians, whatever their nationality.

SVT

This US band was fronted by bassist Jack Casady, formerly of **Jefferson Airplane** and **Hot Tuna**, who dubbed his venture from a medical term - supra ventricular techycardia - for excessive heart-beat and pulse-rate. Brian Marnell (guitar), Nick Buck (keyboards) and Bill Gibson (drums) completed a line-up inspired by the punk/new wave movement, although Paul Zahl subsequently replaced Gibson when the latter joined **Huey Lewis And The News**. Two locally-issued singles enhanced the group's standing on San Francisco's thriving concert circuit before the re-shaped unit completed *Extended Play*. Casady and Zahl formed a new act, Yanks, following the release of *No Regrets*, but the bassist abandoned this project on rejoining former Airplane colleagues **Paul Kantner** and **Marty Balin** in the KBC Band. Zahl later surfaced in the **Flamin' Groovies**.
Albums: *Extended Play* (1980), *No Regrets* (1981).

SWA

Formed in Los Angeles, California, USA in 1985, SWA featured Merrill Ward (vocals), Richard Ford (guitar), Chuck Dukowski (ex-**Black Flag**; bass) and Greg Cameron (drums). Musically the quartet continued the hardcore thrash of Dudowski's previous group, but an unsettled lead guitar slot hampered progress. Sylvia Juncosa replaced Ford for *XCIII*, while *Winter* marked the arrival of Phil Van Duyane. A two-year hiatus ensued before the release of *Volume*, but the set showed no real development from its predecessors, a fact which confirmed SWA's limited appeal.
Albums: *Your Future If You Have One* (1985), *Sex Doctor* (1986), *XCIII* (1987), *Winter* (1989), *Volume* (1991). Compilation: *Evolution* (1987).

Swain, Tony

b. 20 January 1952, London, England. Record producer, musician and songwriter Swain started his career as a television cameraman, where he met Steve Jolley in 1975. They worked together on the *Muppet Show* until Tony left to work in a recording studio as a writer/producer. In 1981 reunited with Jolley they built a reputation when their song 'Body Talk' became a major hit for **Imagination**. The formula continued through a run of eight further hit singles, including 'Just An Illusion' which narrowly missed the UK number 1 spot. In addition to four albums with Imagination, their high standing in the music business gave them an impressive list of productions with major success with **Bananarama**, **Spandau Ballet** and **Alison Moyet**, including the multi-million selling number 1 albums *True*, *Parade* (Spandau Ballet) and *Alf* (Moyet). Swain co-wrote all the tracks bar one on the last, and played keyboards on this classic pop album including the major hit 'Love Resurrection'. Swain with Jolley were nominated for a BPI award following its success. Since then they have worked with the Truth, **Diana Ross**, **Tom Robinson**, **Errol Brown**, **Wang Chung** and Louise Goffin, and following their mutual break Tony went on to produce **Kim Wilde**'s *Close* which became another million-seller. Towards the end of a highly lucrative decade, Swain saw the completion of his own 'state of the art' recording studio at his home in Hertfordshire. He was a major contributor to quality British pop music throughout the 80s.

Swallow, Steve

b. 4 October 1940, New York City, New York, USA. Swallow started out on trumpet, then took up the double bass at the age of 18. At college he played bebop with Ian Underwood (later saxophonist with **Frank Zappa**). In 1960, he joined the **Paul Bley** Trio, later working with **Jimmy Giuffre**, **Art Farmer** and **George Russell** and winning the *Downbeat* critics' poll as new star in 1964. In June 1965 he joined the **Stan Getz** Quartet, with which he played until 1967. Between 1967 and 1970, he was in **Gary Burton**'s quartet and between 1970 and 1973 he played in San Francisco with pianists Art Lande and **Mike Nock** before returning to work with Burton. Since the early 70s he has played intermittently with **Mike Gibbs**, but has worked most regularly with **Carla Bley** (his current partner), playing in her various groups of the late 70s and 80s. In 1980 he set music to poems by Robert Creeley for the album *Home*. By the mid-70s he was playing nothing but electric bass, using a pick, and producing a sound that was popular with the current arrangers. He is also a prolific composer, with credits on Gibbs, Burton and **Chick Corea** albums for titles such as 'Arise Her Eyes', 'Chelsea Bells', 'Como En Vietnam' and 'Hotel Hello'. **John Scofield**, who has recorded and played with Swallow over many years, regards him as his mentor. In the late 80s Swallow recorded a set of duos with Bley and also began to work with UK saxophonist **Andy Sheppard**, producing his first three albums as a leader and playing with him in 1991 in a trio that also featured Bley. Swallow remains a hugely underrated and highly talented figure in recent jazz.
Selected albums: with Gary Burton *Hotel Hello* (1973), *Home* (ECM 1980), with Carla Bley *Carla* (Xtrawatt 1988), with Carla Bley *Duets* (1989), *Swallow* (Xtrawatt 1991), with Bley *Go Together* (1993), *Real Book* (Xtrawatt 1994).

Swallows

An R&B vocal group from Baltimore, Maryland, USA, which line-up comprised Eddie Rich (lead), Irving Turner (tenor/baritone), Earl Hurley (tenor), Herman 'Junior' Denby (second tenor/baritone), Frederick 'Money' Johnson (baritone), and Norris 'Bunky' Mack (bass). The Swallows were one of the classiest of the early 50s vocal harmony groups, recording sleepy ballads much in the style of their Baltimore counterparts, the **Orioles**, but also recording outstanding jump and bluesy tunes in the style of **Charles Brown**. The group was formed in 1946 and signed with **King Records** in 1951. Their first recordings were largely Rich-led sweet ballads, best exemplified by their first hit 'Will You Be Mine' (number 9 R&B) from 1951. The Swallows developed some notoriety for a 1952 song, the risque 'It Ain't The Meat (It's The Motion)', an uptempo number led by their bass Mack in the same style of the **Dominoes**' 'Sixty Minute Man'. Another 1952 song set a new style for the group, 'Beside You' (number 8 R&B), in which lead Denby captured perfectly the sound of the urbane blues singer Charles Brown. Much of the Swallows subsequent material was in this style, but by 1953 that sound had come to sound dated next to up-and-coming groups such as the **Drifters** and **Clovers**. The Swallows left King and made one more recording, for the After Hours label in 1954, and then began to fall apart. Rich kept a group together with new members until he disbanded the Swallows in 1956. In 1958 a new Swallows group consisting of three original members - Rich, Hurley, and Johnson - plus new recruits Buddy Bailey and Calvin Kollette got together. They signed with King Record's Federal subsidiary and recorded mostly uptempo songs. When their excellent recording of 'Itchy Twitchy Feeling' failed to compete with Bobby Hendrick's hit version the new group disbanded.
Compilation: *Dearest* (Charly 1991).

Swamp Dogg

b. Jerry Williams Jnr., 12 July 1942, Portsmouth, Virginia, USA. This eccentric performer first recorded, as Little Jerry, during the 50s. His subsequent releases were as varied as the outlets they appeared on, although Williams did achieve a minor hit in 1966 with 'Baby You're My Everything'. He later forsook a conventional direction by assuming his 'Swamp Dogg' *alter ego*. Although the artist is well-known for his production and/or songwriting work for **Irma Thomas**, **Patti LaBelle**, **Doris Duke**, **Z.Z. Hill** and **Solomon Burke**, his solo work is equally of value. His first album, *Total Destruction Of Your Mind*, has become a soul classic, incorporating the sound of early **Stax** recordings with the rock style of the late 60s and early 70s. The artist embraced the bayou inflections of **Tony Joe White** and **John Fogerty**, while his songs betrayed a lyrical wit and oblique perception rendering them unique. Such titles as 'Mama's Baby - Daddy's Maybe', 'Eat The Goose (Before The Goose Eats You)' and 'The Love We Got Ain't Worth Two Dead Flies' (a duet with **Esther Phillips**) provide a taste of this performer's vision.

Albums: *Total Destruction Of Your Mind* (1970), *Rat On* (1971), *Cuffed, Collared And Tagged* (1972), *Gag A Maggot* (1973), *Have You Heard This Story* (1974), *Never Too Old To Boogie* (1976), *Finally Caught Up With Myself* (1977), *An Opportunity ... Not A Bargain* (1977), *Doing A Party Tonight* (1980), *I'm Not Selling Out, I'm Buying In* (1981). Compilations: *Swamp Dogg's Greatest Hits* (1976), *The Best Of* (1982). In addition there have been numerous collections compiled from Williams' extensive tape archive, including: *Uncut And Classified 1A* (1981), *Unmuzzled* (1983), *I Called For A Rope And They Threw Me A Rock* (1989).

Swan Arcade

Formed in Bradford, Yorkshire, England, in 1970, this group comprised Dave Brady (vocals), Heather Brady (vocals) and Jim Boyes (b. 14 November 1945, Bridlington, Yorkshire, England; vocals/guitar). The group take their name from a local landmark that was demolished during re-planning of the city. Renowned for their powerful unaccompanied vocals and strong harmonies, and their arrangements of both traditional and contemporary material, *Together Forever*, included songs such as the **Beatle**'s 'Paperback Writer', and the **Kink**s' 'Lola'. In 1972, Boyes left the group, having moved to Sheffield, and his place was taken by Royston Wood from the **Young Tradition**, and later Brian Miller, who provided bass harmonies. They appeared at most of the major British festivals and on BBC disc jockey **John Peel**'s radio show. By 1974, Boyes had returned and there followed tours of Europe and Britain, with a concert performance for Dutch television with **Kate and Anna McGarrigle**. *Matchless* stayed in the Belgian folk charts for three years, while later, in 1977, the group provided backing vocals on *We Are Like The Ocean* for **Barry Melton** of **Country Joe And The Fish**. Swan Arcade have also provided backing vocals for **Richard And Linda Thompson**, **Ashley Hutchings** and the **Albion Band**. Swan Arcade broke up in 1978, Jim joining Jiggery Polkary, and Dave and Heather running a hotel in the Lake District. Eventually, they were persuaded to get back together, and in 1985, the appropriately entitled *Together Forever* received good reviews from the folk music press, and radio and festival appearances followed. 1987 saw the formation of Blue Murder, comprising Swan Arcade with the **Watersons** (not to be confused with the heavy rock group of the same name). This line-up has proven successful at a number of festivals, but commitments for both groups prevent them from working together more often. 1988 saw further tours of Europe and Britain by Swan Arcade.

Albums: *Swan Arcade* (Trailer 1973), *Matchless* (Shanachie 1977), *Together Forever* (1985), *Diving For Pearls* (1986), *Nothing Blue* (1988), *Full Circle* (1990). Compilations: (all with various artists) *Flash Company* (1987), *Square Roots* (1987), *Fellside Song Sample* (1987), *Circle Dance* (1990). Solo album: Jim Boyes *Out Of The Blue* (1991).

Swan, Billy

b. Billy Lance Swan, 12 May 1942, in Cape Giradeau, Missouri, USA. Swan grew up listening to country stars like **Hank Williams** and **Lefty Frizzell** and then fell under the spell of 50s rock 'n' rollers. At the age of 16, he wrote 'Lover Please', which was recorded by a local plumber who also had an early morning television show (!), *Mirt Mirley And The Rhythm Steppers*. **Elvis Presley**'s bass player, **Bill Black**, approved and recorded it with his Combo in 1960 before passing it to **Clyde McPhatter**. McPhatter's version went to number 7 on the US charts, but was overshadowed in the UK by the **Vernons Girls**, whose version made number 16. Swan, who had insurance money as a result of losing an eye in an accident, moved to Memphis, primarily to write for Bill Black's Combo. He befriended Elvis Presley's uncle, Travis Smith, who was a gate guard at Graceland. Soon, Swan was also minding the gate and attending Elvis' late night visits to cinemas and funfairs. Swan decided that he would be more likely to find work as a musician in Nashville, but the only employment he found was as a janitor at **Columbia**'s studios. He quit while **Bob Dylan** was recording *Blonde On Blonde*, offering his job to **Kris Kristofferson** who had entered the building looking for work. Billy swanned around for some time, mainly working as a roadie for **Mel Tillis**, before meeting **Tony Joe White** and producing demos of his 'swamp rock'. Swan was invited to produce White officially and their work included *Black And White* with its million-selling single, 'Polk Salad Annie'.

By now Kristofferson had his own record contract and he invited Swan to play bass with his band. They appeared at the Isle of Wight Festival in 1970 where Kristofferson's song 'Blame It On The Stones' was taken at face value. While Kristofferson was being jeered, Swan leaned over and said, 'They love you, Kris.' Billy then joined **Kinky Friedman** in his band, the Texas Jewboys: he appears on his albums and Friedman recorded 'Lover Please'. Kristofferson invited him to join his band again and producer Chip Young, noticing that Swan's voice was similar to **Ringo Starr**'s, invited him to record for Monument. The first single was a revival of **Hank Williams**' 'Wedding Bells'. Swan was given an electric organ as a wedding present by Kristofferson and **Rita Coolidge**. He was fooling around and the chords to 'I Can Help' appeared. Within a few minutes, he also had the lyrics. On the record, Chip Young's guitar effectively balances Billy's swirling organ and, with its heavy echo, the production was very 50s. The tune was so infectious that it topped the US charts for two weeks and made number 6 in the UK.

The subsequent album was a cheerful, good-time affair, almost as though **Sun Records** had decided to modernize their sound. Billy had a similar song prepared for the follow-up single, 'Everything's The Same (Ain't Nothin' Changed)' but Monument preferred to take something from the album to promote its sales. 'I'm Her Fool', with its humorous barking ending was released but it was banned by several radio stations because of the line, 'She pets me when I bury my bone'. A slow version of 'Don't Be Cruel' made number 42 in the UK. Elvis Presley recorded a full-blooded version of 'I Can Help' in 1975, which became a UK Top 30 hit in 1983. Apparently, Presley was amused by the line, 'If your child needs a daddy, I can help', and he sent Swan the socks he wore on the session as a souvenir. Elvis died before he could record Swan's 'No Way Around It (It's Love)'. One of the many asides on **Jerry Lee Lewis**' version of 'I Can Help' is 'Think about it, Elvis'. Billy Swan released three more albums for Monument and then one each for **A&M** and Epic, but he failed to recapture the overall quality of his first. Amongst his guest musicians were **Carl Perkins**, who joined him on remakes of 'Blue Suede Shoes' and 'Your True Love' and an unreleased 'Matchbox', and **Scotty Moore** and **Otis Blackwell**. The Kristoffersons recorded 'Lover Please', also a song by Billy and his wife, Marlu, 'Number One'. Swan and Kristofferson co-wrote 'Nobody Loves Anybody Anymore' on Kristofferson's *To The Bone*. Swan has also played on albums by **Barefoot Jerry**, **Harry Chapin**, **Fred Frith** and **Dennis Linde**. He has worked with **T-Bone Burnett** on several of his albums and they co-wrote 'Drivin' Wheel' (later recorded by **Emmylou Harris**), 'The Bird That I Held In My Hand'. Swan briefly worked with **Randy Meisner** of the **Eagles** in a country-rock band, Black Tie, who released *When The Night Falls* in 1986. The album includes a tribute to rock 'n' roll's wildman, 'Jerry Lee', as well as familiar songs like 'If You Gotta Make a Fool of Somebody' and 'Chain Gang'. Since then, Swan has preferred the security of touring with Kris Kristofferson.

Albums: *I Can Help* (1975), *Billy Swan* (1975), *Rock 'N' Roll Moon* (1976), *Billy Swan - Four* (1977), *You're OK, I'm OK* (1978), *I'm Into Lovin' You* (1981), *When The Night Falls* (as part of Black Tie) (1986).

Albums: with Martin Carthy and Diz Disley *Rags, Reels And Airs* (1967), with Carthy *But Two Came By* (1968), with Carthy *Prince Heathen* (1969), *Selections* (1971), *Swarbrick* (1976), *Swarbrick 2* (1977), *Dave Swarbrick And Friends* (1978), *Lift The Lid And Listen* (1978), *The Ceilidh Album* (1978), *Smiddyburn* (1981), with Simon Nicol *Live At The White Bear* (1982), *Flittin'* (1983), with Nicol *In The Club* (1983), with Nicol *Close To The Wind* (1984), with Carthy *Life And Limb* (1990), with Carthy *Skin & Bone* (1992).

Swann, Bettye

b. Betty Jean Champion 24 October 1944, Shreveport, Louisiana, USA. This superior singer first recorded during the early 60s as a member of the Fawns. A **Carolyn Franklin** song, 'Don't Wait Too Long', provided Bettye with a solo hit in 1965, but her career was more fully launched two years later with an US R&B chart-topper, the beautiful 'Make Me Yours'. Subsequent recordings established the singer's reputation as an imaginative interpreter of country/soul. Her versions of **Merle Haggard**'s 'Today I Started Loving You Again' (1972) and **Tammy Wynette**'s "Til I Get It Right" (1973) are superb. Swann continued this direction under the aegis of **Millie Jackson** producer Brad Shapiro, but her last hit to date was in 1975 with 'All The Way In Or All The Way Out', which reached the lower regions of the *Billboard* R&B chart.

Albums: *Make Me Yours* (1967), *The Soul View Now!* (1968), *Don't You Ever Get Tired (Of Hurting Me)?* (1969), with Candi Staton *Tell It Like It Is* (1986).

Swann, Donald

b. Donald Ibrahim Swann, 30 September 1923, Llanelli, Wales, d. 23 March 1994, London, England. Swann was the progeny of a union between a Russian doctor and Turkoman nurse who fled St. Petersburg, Russia, during the Revolution. He attended school at Westminster where he proved a popular member of the revue team alongside Michael Flanders (see **Flanders And Swann**) and stage manager and future UK MP Tony Benn, before beginning studies at Oxford University. While working with the Friends' Ambulance Unit he visited Greece, whose serenity and sense of community, alongside his Russian heritage, greatly influenced his music. However, he soon returned to London to contribute material to West End revues, linking again with Michael Flanders. Both were soon buoyed by the success of ventures like *Penny Plain* (1951), *Airs On A Shoestring* (1953) and *Fresh Airs* (1956). However, it was their own two-man show, *At The Drop Of A Hat*, which propelled them to nationwide fame after it opened on New Year's Eve in 1956. A massive hit, the show ran for over two years in London, before playing on Broadway and touring the USA and Canada. It was followed in 1963 by *At The Drop Of Another Hat*. However, Swann grew discontented with the endless cycle of engagements and touring which followed, destroying his first marriage. He remained in his house in Battersea, collaborating with Flanders on an album of animal songs for children, and scoring adaptations of the works of his friends C.S. Lewis and J.R.R. Tolkien. He also composed music as a backdrop to his favourite poet, Emily Dickinson, and formed less successful partnerships with John Amis, Frank Topping, Ian Wallace and Lili Malandraki, following the death of Flanders in 1975. Thankfully he was able to complete his autobiography with the help of second wife Alison Smith before he succumbed to cancer at the age of 70. At that time he was also working on material for a new revue, *Swann Amongst The Sirens*, based on his wartime experiences in Greece (to have been staged by the Cherub Theatre Company).

Further reading: *Swann's Way: A Life In Song* (1994).

Swans

Like many early 80s American bands determined to stretch the boundaries of musical cacophony, the Swans were drawn to the thriving New York underground that has also produced **Jim Thirlwell**, **Lydia Lunch** and **Sonic Youth** over the years. Although the band have endured numerous line-up changes, the Swans always centred on singer Michael Gira and, later, Jarboe. After a raucous debut EP in 1982, *Speak*, the band released the influential *Filth* on the German Zensor label, which attracted a strong European audience. In 1984 they announced *Cop* on their own Kelvin 422 label, their first record to appear in the UK. Although *Cop* was awash with harsh guitars and awkward, dirge-like sounds, it was easily more accessible than *Filth*, as was the subsequent EP, *Raping A Slave*, in March 1985 (despite the title). 'Time Is Money (Bastard)' kicked off 1986 with a typically uncompromising title, preceding *Greed* in February. Themes of depravity, sex, death and the more sinister aspects of human nature prevailed, also to be heard on *Holy Money* and 'A Screw' later that year. 1987 saw the band move to Product Inc. for a double album, *Children Of The God*, although another less official effort, *Public Castration Is A Good Idea*, also surfaced that year. Most of 1987 was taken up with Jarboe's new project, Skin, although there was a limited German-only Swans release, *Real Love*. Another double album, 1988's *Feel Good Now*, emerged on the **Rough Trade Records**-distributed Love label. Meanwhile, a sinister cover of **Joy Division**'s 'Love Will Tear Us Apart' climbed the indie charts in June, resulting in a deal with **MCA Records**. 'Saved', the Swans' first single for the major label in April 1989, revealed a definite shift towards mainstream rock, further evident on *The Burning World*: the sombre, Wagnerian approach was still there, but the ingredients were certainly more palatable. The band also seemed to have worked out of their collective system their monstrous live assaults on an audience, which were generally too painful and horribly loud to be anything other than an exercise in art-house shock tactic indulgence. August's 'Can't Find My Way Home' was far more melodic than earlier singles and it seemed that Swans were on the brink of crossing to a much wider audience. But for the next two years they concentrated on reissues of early material on Gira's own Young God label. In May 1991 the band issued *White Light From The Mouth Of Infinity*, which was both commercial and innovative, illustrating the way in which Gira and companions could always command the attention of those willing to experiment a little in their listening tastes. In 1995 Gira released his first book, *The Consumer And Other Stories*, through **Henry Rollins**' 21/3/61 publishing house, in tandem with the Swans' latest recording venture; a relatively restrained and accessible collection dubbed *The Great Annihilator*.

Albums: *Filth* (Zensor/Neutral 1983), *Cop* (K.422 1984), *Greed* (PVC 1986), *Holy Money* (PVC 1986), *Children Of The God* (Product Inc/Caroline 1987, double album), *Feel Good Now* (Love 1988, double album), *The Burning World* (Uni-MCA 1989), *White Light From The Mouth Of Infinity* (Young God 1991), *The Great Annihilator* (Young God 1995).

Further reading: *The Consumer And Other Stories*, Michael Gira, 1995.

SWAPO Singers

Like South Africa's ANC, Namibia's liberation organisation SWAPO has from time to time put together agit-prop bands or choirs, to bolster the morale of the troops or attract overseas media attention. One generation of the SWAPO Singers came to Western attention in the mid-80s, when **Jerry Dammers** and **Robert Wyatt** respectively produced and collaborated on *Wind Of Change*.

Album: *Wind Of Change* (1986).

Swarbrick, Dave

b. 5 April 1941, New Malden, Surrey, England. Violinist and vocalist Swarbrick has played with many well-known groups and performers both in the folk and other areas of music. He is usually best remembered for his time with **Fairport Convention**, whom he first joined in 1969. In his earlier days he played fiddle and mandola for the **Ian Campbell Folk Group**. Additionally, Swarbrick has recorded and toured with **Simon Nicol** and **Martin Carthy**. Swarbrick first teamed up with Carthy in 1966 and when he played on Carthy's debut album for **Fontana** in 1968, was fined by his own record company Transatlantic for performing without their permission. Continual playing of the electric violin had a detrimental effect on Swarbrick's hearing; he is virtually deaf in one ear. This, however, has not stopped him working. Swarbrick left Fairport Convention in 1984, and shortly after formed **Whippersnapper** with Martin Jenkins, Chris Leslie and Kevin Dempsey. After two accomplished albums, Swarbrick left the band in the middle of a tour. In 1990, he once more teamed up with Martin Carthy to record the excellent *Life And Limb*. Swarbrick is now a member of the **Keith Hancock** Band, which includes long-time associate Martin Carthy and Rauri McFarlane.

Albums: with Martin Carthy, Diz Disley *Rags, Reels And*

Airs (1967), with Carthy *But Two Came By* (1968), with Carthy *Prince Heathen* (1969), *Selections* (1971), *Swarbrick* (1976), *Swarbrick 2* (1977), *Dave Swarbrick And Friends* (1978), *Lift The Lid And Listen* (1978), *The Ceilidh Album* (1978), *Smiddyburn* (1981), with Simon Nicol *Live At The White Bear* (1982), *Flittin'* (1983), with Nicol *In The Club* (1983), with Nicol *Close To The Wind* (1984), with Carthy *Life And Limb* (1990), *Live At Jackson's Lane* (1991), with Carthy *Skin & Bone* (1992).

Sweaty Nipples

Unattractively-titled heavy metal band, whose name legendarily arrived from the following scenario: 'The temperature was 198 degrees in a bakery. Olga, a 240lb dominating boss, had just finished chastising Davey, Brian and Dave for make bread loaves in a phallic form when her shirt sleeve got caught in a mixer'. This hapless misogynist tale continues until it results in Dave (rechristened Davey Nipples; bass) burrowing his head into the lady's mammaries to disengage her from the machine. An inauspicious start for the band, which also featured the aforementioned Brian Lehfeldt (vocals/percussion) and Dave Merrick (vocals/samples), as well as Ryan Moore (guitar). The group have built a healthy following in their native North West America on the back of compulsive live performances not seen in that region since the heyday of **Poison Idea**. In the process they have picked up awards at the 1991 Portland Music Association ceremony (best alternative/metal act) and the 1992 PMA equivalent for best live show. With this behind them they joined the North West leg of the 1992 **Lollapalooza** tour, sharing a stage with **Faith No More**, **Bad Brains** and others. Their debut album was recorded for Nastymix (predominantly a rap outlet) with Rick Parashar (**Alice In Chains**, **Pearl Jam**) and Kelly Gray (**Candlebox**) at the controls. Scheduled for release in October 1991, Nastymix subsequently entered receivership and the resulting mire of lawyers and officialdom placed Sweaty Nipples in stasis. They persevered by playing live and adding two new members, Scott Heard (vocals/guitar) and Hans Wagner (drums), eventually gaining a new deal with Megaforce (**Music For Nations** in the UK). After an eponymous single, the group made their long-playing debut with *Bug Harvest*. This, despite the group's grisly moniker, weighed in with a highly effective, and somewhat fearsome three guitar/two drummers attack. Album: *Bug Harvest* (Megaforce 1994).

Sweeney Todd

A 'Musical Thriller' which is often regarded as **Stephen Sondheim**'s most satisfying work to date - certainly his most grisly - *Sweeney Todd* opened at the Uris Theatre in New York on 1 March 1979. Sondheim and librettist Hugh Wheeler based their musical adaptation of the legendary 'demon barber of

Fleet Street' on Christopher Bond's play, *Sweeney Todd*, which played at the Theatre Royal, Stratford East in 1973. As Wheeler's story begins, the barber Sweeney Todd (Len Cariou) is just returning to London after 15 years in enforced exile. He discovers that his wife has been driven to her death (or so he thinks) and his daughter made a ward of court by the man who sentenced him - the evil Judge Turpin (Edmund Lyndeck). Intent on revenge, he rents a room above a shop run by Mrs. Lovett (**Angela Lansbury**), who sells 'The Worst Pies In London'. While waiting for his chance to dispose of Judge Turpin, Todd lures other unsuspecting victims to his barbers' chair. He slits their throats, before passing them over to Mrs. Lovett, who uses her meat grinder and oven to turn them into pies. Although he gets the Judge in the end, justice is seen to be done when Sweeney Todd is slain with one of his own razors, and lies beside the body of his wife whom he has inadvertently murdered. Sondheim's superb 'near-operatic' score, which has been called 'Grand Guignol' and 'quasi-Brechtian' in style, ranged from the witty list song 'A Little Priest', to tender ballads such as 'Not While I'm Around' and 'Johanna', along with other numbers such as 'Pretty Women', 'By The Sea', 'Epiphany', 'Poor Thing', 'God, That's Good', and 'The Ballad Of Sweeney Todd'. The show ran for 558 performances and won eight **Tony Awards**, including best musical, book, score, actor (Cariou), actress (Lansbury) and director (**Harold Prince**). A New York revival was presented at the Circle In the Square in 1989, with Bob Gunton and Beth Fowler, and the Paper Mill Playhouse, New Jersey, offered a version with George Hearn and Judy Kaye in 1992. The 1980 London production at Drury Lane, with Denis Quilley and Sheila Hancock, was generally held to be unsatisfactory. However, the 1993 'chamber version', presented by the Royal National Theatre and starring **Julia McKenzie** and Alun Armstrong, was widely acclaimed, and won **Laurence Olivier** Awards for best musical revival, actress (McKenzie). actor (Armstrong), and director (Declan Donnellan).

Sweeney's Men

This band were the forerunner of many bands to come out of Ireland, such as **Planxty** and **Moving Hearts**, and highly-influential in the field of electric folk, although they only lasted from 1966 to 1969. The group, formed by Terry Woods(guitar/mandolin/vocals/five-string banjo/concertina), included **Andy Irvine** (b. Eire;vocals/mandolin/guitar/bouzouki/harmonica), and Johnny Moynihan (vocals/bouzouki/tin whistle). Traditional Irish material, jigs, shantys and American ballads were bound together in an innovatory manner, and the band soon became an influence on other folk acts. Irvine left after *Sweeney's Men 1968*. His replacement, the guitarist Henry McCulloch, was with the band only a few months, but his influence can be heard on *Tracks of Sweeney*. It included his composition 'A Mistake No Doubt' which he also introduced to his next group, the **Grease Band**. By 1969 plans were afoot to expand the line-up. Former **Fairport Convention** bassist **Ashley Hutchings** wished to join, as did Woods' wife, Gay. Instead the trio formed **Steeleye Span**. Terry Woods formed a duo with his wife Gay, as Gay and Terry Woods, and supported **Ralph McTell** in 1975. Irvine and Moynihan formed Planxty, and Irvine also later ventured into solo work, occasionally with **Paul Brady**.

Albums: *Sweeney's Men 1968* (Transatlantic 1968), *Rattlin' And Roarin' Willy* (1968), *Tracks Of Sweeney's Men* (Transatlantic 1969). Compilations: *The Legend Of Sweeney's Men* (Demon/Transatlantic 1988), *Time Was Never Here 1968-9* (1993).

Sweet

The nucleus of the Sweet came together in 1966, when drummer Mick Tucker (b. 17 July 1949, Harlesden, London, England) and vocalist Brian Connolly (b. 5 October 1949, Hamilton, Scotland) played together in Wainwright's Gentlemen, a small-time club circuit band whose repertoire comprised a mixture of **Motown**, R&B and psychedelia. The pair broke away to form Sweetshop, later shortened to just Sweet, with Steve Priest (b. 23 February 1950, Hayes, Middlesex) on bass and Frank Torpey on guitar. After releasing four unsuccessful singles on Fontana and **EMI**, Torpey was replaced by Andy Scott (b. 30 June 1951, Wrexham, Wales) and the new line-up signed to **RCA**. The band were introduced to the writing partnership of **Chinn And Chapman**, who were to provide the band with a string of hit singles. Their initial success was down to bubblegum pop anthems such as 'Funny, Funny', 'Co-Co', 'Poppa Joe' and 'Little Willy'. However, the band were writing their own hard-rock numbers on the b-sides of these hits. This resulted in Chinn/Chapman coming up with heavier pop-rock numbers, most notably the powerful 'Blockbuster', which reached number 1 in the UK at the beginning of 1973. The group's determinedly effete, glam-rock image was reinforced by a succession of Top 10 hits, including 'Hell Raiser', 'Ballroom Blitz', 'Teenage Rampage' and 'The Six Teens'.

Sweet decided to take greater control of their own destiny in 1974 and recorded the album *Sweet Fanny Adams* without the assistance of Chinn and Chapman. The album charted at number 27, but disappeared again after just two weeks. The work marked a significant departure from their commercially-minded singles on which they had built their reputation. 'Set Me Free', 'Restless' and 'Sweet F.A.' epitomized their no-frills hard-rock style. *Desolation Boulevard* included the self-penned 'Fox On The Run' which was to hit number 2 in the UK singles chart. This gave the band

confidence and renewed RCA's faith in the band as a commercial proposition. However, as Sweet became more of an albums band, the hit singles began to dry up, with 1978's 'Love Is Like Oxygen' being their last Top 10 hit. Following a move to **Polydor**, they cut four albums with each release making less impact than its predecessor. Their brand of melodic rock, infused with infectious hooks and brutal riffs, now failed to satisfy both the teenybopper and the more mature rock fan. Since 1982, various incarnations of the band have appeared from time to time, with any number from one to three of the original members in the line-up. The most recent of these was in 1989, when they recorded a live album at London's Marquee Club, with Paul Mario Day (ex-More) handling the vocals. Brian Connolly now suffers from a muscular disorder. However, his grim situation was warmed in 1992 with the incredible success of the film *Ballroom Blitz* and the subsequent renewed interest in the Sweet.

Albums: *Funny How Sweet Co Co Can Be* (1971), *Sweet* (1973), *Sweet Fanny Adams* (1974), *Desolation Boulevard* (1974), *Strung Up* (1975), *Give Us A Wink* (1976), *Off The Record* (1977), *Level Headed* (1978), *Cut Above The Rest* (1979), *Water's Edge* (1980), *Identity Crisis* (1982), *Live At The Marquee* (1989), *Blockbusters* (1989). Compilations: *Biggest Hits* (1972), *Sweet's Golden Greats* (1983), *Sweet 16 - It's, It's The Sweet's Hits* (1984), *Hard Centres - The Rock Years* (1987), *The Collection* (1989), *Ballroom Blitz - Live 1973* (Dojo 1993).

Sweet Adeline

Following her tremendous success in **Show Boat** (1927), **Jerome Kern** and **Oscar Hammerstein II** wrote the score for this 'Musical Romance Of the Gay Nineties' for **Helen Morgan**, the torch singer who could wring a tear from even the most innocuous ballad. Not that there were any of those in this show. 'Why Was I Born?', one of the composers' most heartfelt and enduring numbers, was introduced by Morgan, along with 'Here Am I', 'Don't Ever Leave Me', and ''Twas Not So Long Ago'. *Sweet Adeline* opened at the Hammerstein Theatre in New York on 3 September 1929, with a book by Hammerstein set in 1898, and concerns Addie Schmidt who leaves her father's beer garden in Hoboken, New Jersey, for singing stardom on Broadway. There were several more appealing numbers in what is accepted as one of the loveliest of Kern's early scores, including a bluesy piece, 'Some Girl Is On Your Mind' which was sung by a group of Addie's boyfriends, the waltz ballad 'The Sun Is About To Rise', 'Spring Is Here', 'Out Of The Blue', and the lively 'Play Us A Polka Dot'. *Sweet Adeline* was an immediate success and looked set for a long run. Then came the Wall Street Crash, and although the show rode out the storm for a while, it was forced to close in April 1930 after a total of 234 performances. The 1935 film version had a revised book, and Irene Dunne.

Sweet And Low-Down

Only one good reason for staying up late to watch this 1944 film (if it is ever shown on television) and that is **Benny Goodman**. Fortunately, he and his orchestra and quartet are on-screen rather a lot in this tale of a swing band on tour. Although this was not Goodman's best band, there are still several good musicians on hand. Some are seen, others only heard while actors mime their instruments. Amongst the musicians are **Bill Harris**, **Zoot Sims**, Morey Feld, **Jess Stacy**, **Sid Weiss**, Allan Reuss, **Heinie Beau** and **Al Klink**. (Alternative title: *Moment For Music*).

Sweet Beat

This low-budget 1959 British film was produced by Jeff Kruger who co-owned London's fabled Flamingo nightclub and subsequently operated the Ember label. It starred Julie Amber as a beauty queen turned singer who is offered a lucrative spot in a New York venue by a promoter seeking sexual favours in return. The title song was performed by **Tony Crombie** who, as leader of Tony Crombie And His Rockets, was one of the first UK musicians to embrace nascent rock 'n' roll earlier in the decade. Fred Parris And His Satins, Cindy Mann, Jeri Lee and Lee Allen And His Band were among the other acts featured in a film which promptly sank with little trace.

Sweet Charity

Veteran lyricist **Dorothy Fields** teamed with the much younger composer **Cy Coleman** on the score for this warm-hearted musical which opened at the Palace Theatre in New York on 29 January 1966. Neil Simon's book, which was based on the Federico Fellini film *Nights Of Cabiria*, changed the movie's main character from a prostitute to a dance hall hostess, named Charity (**Gwen Verdon**). In her desperate quest for love, marriage, and respectability, she becomes romantically involved with an Italian film star, Vittorio Vidal (James Luisi), and a neurotic accountant, Oscar Lindquist (John McMartin) whom she is set to marry until her job comes between them. **Bob Fosse** won a **Tony Award** for his innovative and exciting choreography, and there was not a dull moment in a score that contained a whole range of marvellous songs, including 'Big Spender', 'Rich Man's Frug', 'If My Friends Could See Me Now', 'Too Many Tomorrows', 'There's Gotta Be Something Better Than This', 'Rhythm Of Life', 'Baby, Dream Your Dream', 'Where Am I Going?', 'I'm A Brass Band', and 'I Love to Cry At Weddings'. Gwen Verdon's portrayal of the loveable Charity was funny and tender, but she was edged out of the Tonys by **Angela Lansbury** who triumphed for her performance in *Mame*. *Sweet Charity* ran for 608 performances and was revived on Broadway in 1986 with Debbie Allen in the lead. The 1967 London production starred the South African actress Juliet Prowse, and two years later a film version was released with Shirley MacLaine, John McMartin, **Chita Rivera**, and **Sammy Davis Jnr**.

Sweet Charity (Film Musical)

Director-choreographer **Bob Fosse**'s 1969 screen adaptation of the hit Broadway musical was heavily criticized at the time of release in 1969, for its over-use of gimmicky cinematic trickery and the over-the-top central performance of Shirley MacLaine. However, in retrospect many observers feel that it wasn't so bad after all. Peter Stone's screenplay stayed closely to Neil Simon's stage libretto which told of dance hall hostess Charity Hope Valentine (MacLaine) who is all set achieve her ambition and marry strait-laced Oscar Lindquist (John McMartin) until he finds out where she works. At first he appears to be coming to terms with Charity's somewhat unconventional lifestyle, but after attending her rowdy farewell party at the Fan-Dango ballroom, he finds that he can't go through with the ceremony and jilts her at the very last minute. There were strong supporting performances from Ricardo Montalban as film star Vittorio Vidal, **Sammy Davis Jnr.** in the role of Big Daddy, an hilarious hippy evangelist, **Stubby Kaye** as the owner of the Fan-Dango, and Paula Kelly, **Rita Moreno** and the rest of the girls at the club who all want to get out themselves, but still hate to see Charity go. Also among the cast were Barbara Bouchet, Suzanne Charney, Alan Hewitt, Dante D'Paulo, Bud Vest, Ben Vereen, Lee Roy Reams, Al Lanti, John Wheeler, and Leon Bing. Most of **Cy Coleman** and **Dorothy Fields**'s outstanding songs survived the journey from Broadway to Hollywood, and the team added some new ones to form a score which consisted of 'Big Spender', 'If My Friends Could See Me Now', 'My Personal Property', 'Rhythm Of Life', 'There's Gotta Be Something Better Than This', 'I'm a Brass Band', 'Rich Man's Frug', 'The Hustle', 'Where Am I Going?', 'I Love To Cry At Weddings', 'It's a Nice Face', and the title number. In spite of the carping of the critics, much of Bob Fosse's choreography and direction was superb and stands repeated viewing. Robert Arthur was the producer for Universal, and the picture was photographed in Technicolor and Panavision by Robert Surtees.

Sweet Exorcist
(see **Cabaret Voltaire**)

Sweet Inspirations

The Sweet Inspirations' career reached back into the Drinkards, a formative gospel group whose fluid line-up included **Dionne Warwick** and **Cissy Houston**. The unit dropped this name on pursuing a secular path as session singers. Houston remained at the helm during several subsequent changes, (**Doris Troy** and

Judy Clay were among the former members), and the group emerged from its backroom role with a recording deal of its own. Now dubbed the Sweet Inspirations by **Atlantic Records** producer **Jerry Wexler**, the line-up of Cissy Houston, Sylvia Shemwell, Myrna Smith and Estelle Brown secured a minor hit with 'Why (Am I Treated So Bad)' (1967), but it was a self-titled composition, 'Sweet Inspiration' which gave the group its best-remembered single, reaching the US Top 20 in 1968. When Cissy Houston left for a belated solo career in 1970, the remaining trio, Myrna Smith, Estelle Brown and Sylvia Shemwell, joined **Elvis Presley**'s concert retinue, and cut a further album on their own, a good 1973 outing for **Stax**. After a hiatus from the recording scene, Smith and Shemwell were joined by Gloria Brown in place of Estelle Brown who had quit earlier, and a final album appeared on RSO in 1979, though Brown herself was replaced on the actual recording by Pat Terry. In 1994 Estelle, Sylvia and Myrna reunited for a special series of shows, including a tribute to Presley.

Albums: *The Sweet Inspirations* (1967), *Songs Of Faith And Inspiration* (1968), *What The World Needs Now Is Love* (1968), *Sweets For My Sweet* (1969), *Sweet, Sweet Soul* (1970), *Estelle, Myrna And Sylvia* (1973), *Hot Butterfly* (1979). Compilations: *Estelle, Myrna And Sylvia* (1991), *The Best Of ...* (1994).

Sweet Love, Bitter

Directed by Herbert Daniels in 1966, this is an uneven and slightly self-conscious attempt to examine racial problems in the USA through the life of a jazz musician. Based upon the novel, *Night Song*, by John Alfred Williams, the story is very loosely based upon **Charlie Parker**'s final years Dick Gregory stars as the saxophone player, dubbed by Charles McPherson, and also heard are **Chick Corea** and **Steve Swallow**. The film's musical director is **Mal Waldron**. (Alternative title: *It Won't Rub Off, Baby*).

Sweet Pain

This UK studio group comprised of several of the country's leading blues musicians. Saxophonist **Dick Heckstall-Smith** was a veteran of Blues Incorporated, the **Graham Bond Organisation** and **John Mayall**'s Bluesbreakers before becoming a founder-member of **Colosseum**, while John O'Leary (harmonica) and Keith Tillman (bass) were concurrently members of the **John Dummer Blues Band**. Stuart Cowell (guitar), Sam Crozier (piano), Junior Dunn (drums) and vocalists Annette Brox and Alan Greed completed the Sweet Pain line-up featured on the unit's lone album. Its tough blend of jazz-based R&B was marked by the free-playing associated with informal 'jam' sessions, and on its completion the individual members resumed their respective careers. This release, dubbed *England's Heavy Blues Super Session*

for America, is a testimony to their short-lived collective ambition.

Album: *Sweet Pain* aka *England's Heavy Blues Super Session* (1969).

Sweet Savage

This melodic hard rock quartet was formed in Belfast, Northern Ireland, in 1979 by guitarists Vivian Campbell and Trevor Fleming. Recruiting bassist David Haller and drummer David Bates, they achieved their first break by landing the support slots on 1981 tours by **Motörhead** and **Wishbone Ash**. Debuting the same year with 'Take No Prisoners'/'Killing Time', the future looked very bright for the band. A UK tour supporting **Thin Lizzy** was followed by an impressive session on UK DJ **Tommy Vance**'s *Friday Rock Show* ('Eye of The Storm' appeared on the compilation, *Friday Rock Show II*). Two further singles, 'Straight Through The Heart' (1981) and 'The Raid' (1981), were released, before Campbell accepted the offer to join Ronnie James **Dio**. Four re-written Sweet Savage tracks appeared on Dio's *Holy Diver*. The band continued for a short time with Ian Wilson as Campbell's replacement. However, he proved an inadequate substitute and the band folded in 1984, after the re-release of 'Straight Through The Heart'.

Sweet Sister

Spanish heavy metal band formed in 1990 with a line-up of Tete (vocals/guitar), Pedro (guitar/keyboards), Toni (bass) and Jordi (drums). They recorded their first demo in 1992. Two others followed before they entered the studio in 1994 to record 22 tracks of which 12 were selected for their debut album with **Music For Nations**' subsidiary Under One Flag. Reflecting varied musical tastes running from the **Cure** to **Guns N'Roses** via **U2**, the album attracted a degree of press support but sales were limited outside their native territory.

Album: *Flora And Fauna* (Under One Flag 1994).

Sweet Talks

The Sweet Talks were more than just a band, they were an institution, a training-ground for Ghanaian highlifers. The name has been imitated, taken in vain, stolen; there have been Sweet Beans and Talkative Sweets, but there was only one - or at the most, two - Sweet Talks. The band was formed in late 1973, and shortly afterwards took up an extended residency at the Talk Of The Town Hotel in Tema. The key founder members were Pope Flynn and A.B.Crentsil (vocals) and Smart Nkansah (guitar). In the next few years, other major talents would join, including vocalist **Jewel Ackah** and guitarist Eric Agyeman.

The band's early music had two distinct styles. One was a throwback to colonial days, with the band playing cover versions of European and North American chart hits, sung by Flynn. The other was Ghanaian cultural music, sung by Crentsil in a uniquely husky, red-blooded voice. Born in the Western region, Crentsil had spent his early years listening to such roots styles as osode and palm wine. He worked as a railwayman, singing part-time with local bands such as the Eldoradoes and the Medican Lantics. He first met Nkansah when the latter was touring with Yamoah's Guitar Band in 1972; the two became friends and, recruiting Flynn, decided to form the Sweet Talks. The group's first hit was the single 'Adam And Eve' in 1975, which was followed by the successful album *The Kusum Beat* in 1976, an update of northern Ghanaian traditional music based around percussion and xylophones. In 1977, the band repeated this success with *Spritual Ghana*, this time based on osode highlife rhythms.

In 1979, when the band were about to set off on a tour of the USA, Nkansah left, to be replaced by another of Ghana's leading roots guitarists, Eric Agyeman, previously a member of Dr. K. Gyasi's Noble Kings. He had started his career in 1963, playing **Beatles** and **Rolling Stones** covers in Afro Boateng's Midnight Movers, and had joined Gyasi in 1972, combining the roles of lead guitarist and arranger. The new Sweet Talks line-up spent autumn 1979 in the USA, recording *Party Time In Hollywood* with Wayne Henderson of the **Crusaders** (for whom they also recorded some album backing tracks) and *Sweet Talks*. Deeply unhappy with the Californian winter, they then returned to Ghana, where they had a dispute with their manager and disbanded. Agyeman and Crentsil formed Super Brain, which lasted only a short time. Agyeman then returned to Gyasi and later went solo; Crentsil picked up the pieces with a new line-up, Super Sweet Talks International, and released *The Lord's Prayer*, which included 'Area Special', a hymn of praise to palm wine drinking. He then took the band to Ivory Coast, where they recorded *Tantie Alaba*, which included another drinking classic in 'Akpetchi Seller' (akpetchi being a form of Ghanaian gin).

In 1984, Crentsil moved temporarily to the UK, where - together with Agyeman, also visiting - he fronted a band put together by Mac Tontoh of **Osibisa**, which recorded *Highlife Stars*, released on Osibisa's own Flying Elephant label.

Tontoh, Crentsil and Agyeman had hoped that *Highlife Stars* - also the name of the band which recorded it and gigged behind it - would make a major impact in the UK, then in the throes of a substantial explosion of interest in African music, but while the album made a huge impact on specialist audiences it failed to make any mainstream impression. Crentsil and Agyeman accordingly returned to Ghana towards the end of 1984, Crentsil to form Ahenfo and Agyeman to form Kokroko. By this time, Ackah had formed a second, short-lived incarnation of the Sweet Talks, based in the

Ivory Coast. The most successful ex-original Sweet Talks was Nkansah who, following his departure from the band in 1979, formed the popular, highlife-based Sunsum Band, and enjoyed two top-selling albums with *Disco Spiritual* (1981) and the rootsier *Odo* (1985).

Selected albums: *Adam And Eve* (1975), *The Kusum Beat* (1976), *Spiritual Ghana* (1977), *Party Time In Hollywood* (1979), *Sweet Talks* (1979).

Sweet Tee

b. Toi Jackson, Queens, New York, USA. Female MC, re-discovered by **Salt 'N' Pepa**'s producer **Hurby Lovebug**, whose breakthrough single was 'I Got Da Feelin''. She had originally recorded for her father, **Paul Winley**, ('Vicious Rap', 'It's Like That Y'All') and Champion Records ('Its My Beat' with Jazzy Joyce). 'Vicious Rap', produced by her mother, carried a false arrest narrative, and was one of the prototype conscious rap singles. Her father remembers because 'Everytime I look at her she had her head in her notebook'. Rather than concentrating on her homework, however, she was instead busy manufacturing her rhymes. However, there was little to be heard from her following a singular album for **Profile** in 1989, and two singles, 'On The Smooth Tip' and 'Let's Dance'.

Album: *It's Tee Time* (Profile 1989).

Sweet, Matthew

b. c.1964, Nebraska, USA. After working with the **Golden Palominos** in the late 80s, Sweet rapidly found himself thrust into the spotlight with his third album, 1991's *Girlfriend*, a *tour de force* of power pop flavoured with a captivating lyrical slant manifested by the singer/guitarist's highly personal narratives. The collection saw him accompanied by New York luminaries including **Material** drummer Fred Maher, Robert Quine (ex-**Lou Reed** and **Richard Hell And The Voidoids**) and Richard Lloyd (ex-**Television**), plus the UK's **Lloyd Cole**. The mature rock sound visited therein quickly saw rave critical comparisons to **Neil Young** and **Big Star**, despite the shoestring recording budget. It evolved at a troubled time for Sweet, coinciding with his divorce and the loss of most of his musical equipment and records through a boiler flood. Also dropped by his record company (his two previous albums had been released on **Columbia** and **A&M Records** respectively), Sweet was about to take employment at a 'Toys R Us' children's store before he found a new label who accepted his unreleased third album. *Girlfriend* quickly went on to sell over half a million copies in the US. One of the most notable tracks, 'Does She Talk?', was a tribute to porn Channel 23, but this was only one strand of a powerful armoury of moods and highly affecting, plangent guitar work. *Son Of* remixed arguably the best track from the lauded follow-up album, *Altered Beast*, 'Devil With The Green

Eyes', and added five unavailable live tracks recorded in October 1993 and January 1994, with Lloyd and Quine guesting. For *100% Fun* Sweet was joined once more by Quine and Lloyd, with **Velvet Crush** drummer Rick Menck and **kd Lang** associate Greg Leisz on pedal steel and mandolin, with Brendan O'Brien (**Pearl Jam**, **Bob Dylan**, **Soundgarden**) producing. Bearing in mind his popularity in the Far East, it was accompanied by a 20 page 'manga' comic (the most popular cultural phenomenon of Japan in the 90s), starring Sweet. The touring band for 1995 added Tony Marsico (bass) and Stuart Johnson (drums).
Albums: *Inside* (Columbia 1986), *Earth* (A&M 1989), *Girlfriend* (Zoo 1991), *Altered Beast* (Zoo 1993), *Son Of Altered Beast* (Zoo 1994, mini-album), *100% Fun* (Zoo 1995).

Sweet, Rachel

b. 1963, Akron, Ohio, USA. Rachel Sweet sang professionally at the age of five, working as a child model for television commercials in New York and as a support act to Mickey Rooney. At the age of 12 she recorded her first single, the country song 'Faded Rose', on the Derrick label which, along with her follow-up, 'We Live In Two Different Worlds' reached the lower regions of the *Billboard* Country charts. Under the tutelage of manager and songwriter Liam Sternberg, Rachel landed a contract with the pioneering independent UK label **Stiff Records**. The company had previously distributed a compilation album of Akron acts which included two tracks by the singer. For the Stiff 78 Tour with fellow labelmates **Lene Lovich**, **Wreckless Eric**, **Jona Lewie** and **Mickey Jupp**, Rachel's backing band were the **Records**. The single, a version of the **Isaac Hayes/David Porter** song 'B-A-B-Y', reached the UK Top 40. Sweet possessed a mature voice for someone still in her mid-teens. *Fool Around* saw her tackling **Del Shannon**'s 'I Go To Pieces' and **Elvis Costello**'s 'Stranger In The House' as well as several Sternberg originals. Rachel's obvious talents were dogged by persistent, but tenuous, accusations of her being marketed as 'jail-bait'. After parting with Sternberg in 1979, her second album presented Rachel with a harder image, complete with an advertising campaign bizarrely depicting her as a leather-jacketed, sullen child abductor. Backed by **Fingerprintz**, the songs on the album contained cover versions of **Lou Reed**'s 'New Age', **Graham Parker**'s 'Fool's Gold' and the **Damned**'s 'New Rose' as well as the usual quota of country rock. As with the first album, *Protect The Innocent* was a commercial failure, although this time it did not enjoy critical approbation. Her departure from Stiff to **CBS** saw the release of *...And Then He Kissed Me* which included the UK and US Top 40 hit duet with **Rex Smith**, 'Everlasting Love' in 1981. Despite this encouraging start, the mismanaged talents of Rachel Sweet saw her fade from the scene.
Albums: *Fool Around* (1978), *Protect The Innocent* (1980), *...And Then He Kissed Me* (1981).

Sweethearts (Film Musical)

Jeanette MacDonald and **Nelson Eddy**'s fifth film together, which was released by MGM in 1938, eschewed the familiar costumes and wigs for a far more contemporary setting. Dorothy Parker and Alan Campbell's screenplay cast them as a successful musical comedy team in the long-running Broadway hit show, *Sweethearts*. Like so many stars in those days, the duo are attracted by the big money that Hollywood has to offer, but, in their case, it all goes sour, and they soon return to the theatre. Also among the strong cast were **Ray Bolger**, Frank Morgan, Herman Bing, Reginald Gardiner, Mischa Auer, and Florence Rice. The plot bore no relationship to the book of the real Broadway show called *Sweethearts*, which opened in 1913, although four of **Victor Herbert**'s lovely songs were retained for the film version, albeit with new lyrics by **Robert Wright** and **George Forrest**. These were 'Pretty As A Picture', 'Wooden Shoes', 'Every Lover Must Meet His Fate', and the title number. The same team also contributed 'Summer Serenade', 'On Parade', and 'Game Of Love', and there were several other songs by various composers such as 'Little Grey Home In The West' (Herman Loehr-D. Eardly Wilmott) and 'Happy Day' (Herbert Stothart-Wright-Forrest). Albertina Rasch was the choreographer, and W.S. Van Dyke directed what was an effervescent and good natured affair in which MacDonald and Eddy were at their peak. It was the first MGM picture to be photographed in three-colour Technicolor, and Oliver T. Marsh and Allen Davey were awarded a special Oscar for their cinematography.

Sweethearts (Stage Musical)

Most operettas are cherished for their sometimes glorious music, and gently mocked for their 'you cannot be serious' librettos. *Sweethearts*, which opened at the New Amsterdam Theatre in New York on 8 September 1913, was typical of the genré. Even so, Harry B. Smith and Fred De Gresac's book for this show stretched credibilty to breaking point and beyond. The romantic story begins when the infant Sylvia (Christie MacDonald) is found in a tulip garden by Dame Paula (also known as Mother Goose) who is in charge of the Laundry of the White Geese. Sylvia is raised as her daughter until one day, purely by chance, she meets Prince Franz (Thomas Conkey) and they fall in love. Everything works out well because Sylvia is really the Crown Princess of the Kingdom of Zilania, so there is a big royal wedding and the couple ascend the vacant throne together. In contrast to that somewhat bizarre tale, the score, by **Victor Herbert** (music) and Robert B. Smith (lyrics), was rich and grand. Christie

Macdonald introduced the gorgeous waltz, 'Sweethearts', and there were other numbers almost as fine, including 'The Angelus', 'Every Lover Must Meet His Fate', 'Pretty As A Picture', 'The Cricket On the Hearth', and 'Jeannette And Her Little Wooden Shoes'. The show ran for 136 performances and returned to New York briefly in 1929. A far more successful Broadway revival was mounted in 1947, when, following the successful resuscitation of Herbert's **The Red Mill** two years before, *Sweethearts* enjoyed a run of 288 performances at the Shubert Theatre. With a revised book by John Cecil Holm, the show was now a vehicle for comedian Bobby Clark, whose own particular brand of mayhem gave the piece a lighter and funnier touch. The 1938 film version starred **Jeanette MacDonald** and **Nelson Eddy**.

Sweethearts Of The Rodeo

Sisters Janis and Kristine Oliver grew up in California and spent much time harmonising. In 1973 they started working as an acoustic duo, taking their name from a **Byrds** album. Although they mostly performed contemporary country-rock songs, they also had some traditional country leanings. They both were married, becoming Janis Gill and Kristine Arnold. Janis went to Nashville with her husband, **Vince Gill**, who became one of the first of the 'new country' singers. Janis invited her sister to Nashville, where they won a major talent contest. In 1986, they recorded their first album, *Sweethearts Of The Rodeo*, which yielded five US country singles including 'Hey Doll Baby'. By and large, Kristine is the lead singer and Janis the songwriter, although their wide repertoire includes 'I Feel Fine' and 'So Sad (To Watch Good Love Go Bad)'. The long delay before Columbia released *Sisters* led to rumours that the duo's time at the label was drawing to a close. The 1993 album was released on the Sugar Hill label.
Albums: *Sweethearts Of The Rodeo* (1986), *One Time One Night* (1988), *Buffalo Zone* (1990), *Sisters* (1992), *Rodeo Waltz* (Sugar Hill 1993).

Sweetie Irie

West London DJ who kickstarted his career impressively with the tough-talking 45s 'Meggaman' and 'New Talk', the latter duetted with Spar Joe 90. He followed these up with a debut album featuring covers of **Sugar Minott** and **Aswad** standards, plus a strong selection of originals.
Selected album: *DJ For The Future* (Mango/Island 1991).

Swell Maps

Although associated with the immediate post-punk aftermath, UK group Swell Maps was formed in 1972. Five years later **Nikki Sudden** (guitar/vocals), **Epic Soundtracks** (drums/vocals), Jowe Head (bass), Richard Earl (vocals) and David Barrington (vocals)

founded their own Rather label, which issued material in conjunction with **Rough Trade Records**. Although their debut single, 'Read About Seymour', became a cult favourite, the group steadfastly refused to become categorized. Despite the pop element of successive singles - 'Dresden Style', 'Real Shocks' and 'Let's Build A Car' - their albums offered a bewildering array of sounds ranging from garage-band simplicity to new-age styled piano instrumentals. Although Swell Maps broke up in 1980, a series of reissues, some of which include archive material, has kept their reputation alive. So too have the fortunes of ex-members Sudden and Epic, who have both begun fruitful solo careers.
Albums: *A Trip To Marineville* (Rather/Rough Trade 1979), *Jane From Occupied Europe* (Rather/Rough Trade 1980). Compilations: *Whatever Happens Next* (Rather/Rough Trade 1981), *Collision Time* (Rather/Rough Trade 1984), *Train Out Of It* (Antar 1987).

Swemix Records

Swedish dance label which was inaugurated in 1989 by a group of local DJ's headed by Jackmaster Fax (Rene Hedemyr) and JJ (Johan Jarpsten). The latter pairing also recorded for the label as Dynamic Duo. Once described as the Nordic equivalent to the UK's DMC enclave, each month Swemix released a Remixed Records double album package of the hottest club hits. Other staples of the Swemix catalogue included the Stonebridge remix team (who recorded as Mr Magic) and artists like Frankie LaMotte and Terry Leigh, on the Basement Division subsidiary. The idea for the label was first mooted because the collective thought they could remix better and more suitable cuts than they were being handed by the major record companies. Thus their roster grew to accomodate major clients like **Milli Vanilli**, **Neneh Cherry**, **Pasadenas** and **Gloria Estefan**. In so doing they revolutionised the Swedish, and to some extent, mainland Europe, dance music scene. Among their higher profile signings were **Da Yeene** (who hit in the 90s with cuts like 'Alright' and 'Good Thing') and **Dr Alban**, whom they had watched setting up the Alphabet Street club in Gothenburg, a frequent haunt of many of the Swemix principals. It was this artist more than any other which established both the label and a new style of euro-dance in the 90s, signing to **Arista** via Germany's **Logic**. There were also two further subsidiary operations, B-Tech and Energy (who released Clubland's 'Hold On' and Paradise Orchestra's 'Colour Me', later licensed to **Pulse 8**). Swemix has subsequently metamorphosised into Cheiron, and no longer deals exclusively in dance.

Swervedriver

Previously known as Shake Appeal, Swervedriver came

into being at the end of 1989 when Adam Franklin (b. 7 October 1966, Billericay, Essex, England; vocals, formerly of Oxford hopefuls Satan Knew My Father), Jimmy Hartridge (b. 27 November 1965, Oxfordshire, England; guitar) and Adrian Vines (b. 25 January 1968, Yorkshire, England; bass) moved from the Home Counties to London and linked up with Graham Bonnar (b. 28 April 1967, Scotland) who had previously drummed for British hardcore group, Ut. The collective's sound changed accordingly from **Stooges**-style grunge-rock to a more contemporary American stylisation - a definition which was hardly weakened by the band's apparent lyrical obsession with highways, pick-up trucks and several other things mid-Western. In spite of the unfavourable comparisons, Swervedriver and their effects-driven guitars battled their way from beneath the shadow of their supposedly more credible transatlantic counterparts, reaching number 63 in the UK charts with their third EP, *Sandblasted*. However, Bonnar left in early 1992. By March 1993 his replacement, Jez (b. 17 February 1966, Gateshead, England), had arrived. Vines had also left, in September 1992, but the bass position was still free a year later. A second album, produced by Alan Moulder, who had worked on the band's 'Never Lose That Feeling' single, emerged to little fanfare, with the bass parts shared between Franklin and Hartridge. Vines would go on to work with **Skyscraper**. The quartet was completed with Steve George, b. 23 September 1966 in time for their excellent 1995 album.

Album: *Raise* (Creation 1991), *Mezcal Head* (Creation 1993), *Ejector Seat Reservation* (Creation 1995).

Swift, Kay

b. Kay Faulkner Swift, 19 April 1897, New York City, New York, USA, d. 28 January 1993, Southington, Connecticut, USA. A composer, lyricist and writer for Broadway, whose small but impressive catalogue of work is often overshadowed by her close association with the composer **George Gershwin**. After studying at Juilliard, Swift became an accomplished pianist and often performed on the concert platform, before making her breakthrough on Broadway in 1929 with the song 'Can't We Be Friends?', which was introduced by **Libby Holman** in the hit revue *The Little Show*. The sophisticated sombre lyric to what is essentially a spirited, jaunty tune, was written by Paul James, a *nom de plume* for Swift's first husband, banker James P. Warburg. The duo repeated their success in the following year with the score for the musical *Fine And Dandy*, which included 'Let's Go Eat Worms In The Garden', 'Jog Hop', the appealing title number, and Swift's best-remembered song, 'Can This Be Love'. Her relationship with George Gershwin, which eventually led to the breakup of her marriage, was intense and fruitful. As a rich socialite, she made his

transition from Tin Pan Alley to concert hall all the smoother, and they spent many hours working together at the piano. In June 1937, after spending nine months in Hollywood with his brother Ira, George told Swift he was returning so that they could be together, but shortly afterwards he died before he could make the trip. Swift subsequently collaborated with **Ira Gershwin** in turning the best of George's unpublished - and often only partly finished - manuscripts into complete songs. Several of these comprised the score for the 1947 film musical *The Shocking Miss Pilgrim*, starring **Betty Grable** and **Dick Haymes**, the best known of which are 'For You, For Me, For Evermore' and 'Aren't You Kind Of Glad We Did?'. Swift's own credits included 'Up Among The Chimney Pots' for the *9:15 Revue* (1930), 'I'm All Washed Up With Love' (with Albert Silverman) for the left-wing musical *Parade* (1935), music and lyrics for Cornelia Otis Skinner's one-woman revue *Paris 90*, the score for celebrated choreographer George Balanchine's ballet *Alma Mater* - a spoof on the Harvard-Yale football game (1935), and the song cycle *Reaching For The Brass Ring*. Among her other songs for revues and shows were 'A Moonlight Memory', 'One Little Girl' ('Campfire Girls' 50th Anniversary Song'), the 1962 Seattle World's Fair song 'Century 21', 'Calliope', 'Sagebrush Lullaby' and 'Forever And A Day'. Swift's second husband was rodeo cowboy Faye Hubbard, and details of their life together were revealed in her memoir *Who Could Ask For Anything More?*, published in 1943. It was filmed in 1950 with Irene Dunne and Fred MacMurray. Swift's third marriage, which also ended in divorce, was to radio announcer Hunter Galloway.

Further reading: *Who Could Ask For Anything More?*, Kay Swift.

Swing Out Sister

A string of sparkling pop hits beginning with 'Breakout' marked a fine opening for Swing Out Sister in 1987 and *It's Better To Travel* became a UK number 1 on the strength of the singles. Originally a trio, the band comprised Corinne Drewery (vocals), Andrew Connell (keyboards) and Martin Jackson (drums). Connell had played for many years in the respected Manchester jazz/new-wave group **A Certain Ratio** while Jackson had drummed with various Manchester bands including **Magazine** and the **Chameleons**. A management link-up saw the pair join forces with Drewery whose father had been a member of a Nottingham group the Junco Partners. Jackson left the group soon after *It's Better To Travel* and did not play on the follow-up, *Kaleidoscope World*, although he helped programme drum machines on several tracks. Connell, a grade eight pianist and fan of **Burt Bacharach** and **Herb Alpert**, injected an orchestrated, spacious element into songs like 'Forever Blue' and 'Masquerade', assisted by producer Paul O'Duffy. It did not contain as much commercial punch as *It's Better To Travel* but was warmly received by critics. The duo rarely take on a heavy workload and seem happy releasing records intermittently on their own idiosyncratic terms. 1994 saw them put together a full band, featuring Derick Johnson (bass), Myke Wilson (drums), Tim Cansfield (guitar), John Thrikell (trumpet) and Gary Plumey (saxophone) for the release of *The Living Return*.

Albums: *It's Better To Travel* (1987), *Kaleidoscope World* (1989), *Swing Out Sister* (1992), *The Living Return* (Mercury 1994).

Swing Time

Released in August 1936, just a few months after **Follow the Fleet**, *Swing Time* gave **Fred Astaire** and **Ginger Rogers** fans another feast of sensational dance routines and marvellous songs. Screenwriters Howard Lindsay and Allan Scott's vivid imagination resulted in a story in which dancer and gambler John 'Lucky' Garnett (Astaire) goes to New York to make his fortune after his future in-laws have rejected him as financially unsuitable for their daughter Margaret (Betty Furness). After meeting dance instructress Penny Carrol (Ginger Rogers), Margaret and money are forgotten, and the new team sing and dance their way to stardom. **Jerome Kern** and **Dorothy Fields**'s score was full of outstanding numbers such as 'Pick Yourself Up', 'A Fine Romance', 'Never Gonna Dance', 'Waltz In Swing Time', and 'Bojangles Of Harlem' for which Astaire donned blackface for the only time in his long career. The lovely, tender ballad 'The Way You Look Tonight', which Fred sang to Ginger while she was shampooing her hair, won the Academy Award for best song. Most of the laughs were provided by the bumbling ex-vaudevillian Victor Moore and two of the comical characters from previous Astaire-Rogers extravaganzas, Helen Broderick and Eric Blore. *Swing Time*, which was another big box-office hit for RKO, was directed by George Stevens. The dance director - almost inevitably - was **Hermes Pan**.

Swingbeat

A musical format often titled New Jack Swing (or indeed New Jill Swing when it concerns female performers). Swingbeat's origins lay in the 80s and **Teddy Riley**, who remains the music's most important figurehead to this day. As a Harlem based hip hop DJ, Riley began to experiment with rap's beats, adding soul vocals to produce a more upfront, demanding blend of R&B. The hybrid quickly picked up the title swingbeat, the derivation of which is obviously onomatopaeic. Although it was initially accepted by neither hip hop nor soul purists, the music found a keen, and predominantly young audience, with early supergroups including **Today** and **Guy**. In the 90s, by now rechristened New Jack Swing by the American media, the format continued its commercial ascendency. The first of the 'New Jill Swing' groups were **Gyrlz**, another of Teddy Riley's protégés. After which would come the highly succesful **TLC**, **Jade** and **SWV**. Prime swingbeat movers now include **Jodeci**, **Wreckx-N-Effect**, **Mary J. Blige** and **Bobby Brown** (plus other former members of **New Edition**). English outfits like **Rhythm Within**, and, on the female front, **TCW** (Twentieth Century Women), have also picked up the trail.

Swingin' Medallions

Formed in 1962 as the Medallions in South Carolina, USA, the group consisted of John McElrath (keyboards), Carroll Bledsoe (trumpet), Joe Morris (drums), Jimbo Doares (guitar), Charles Webber (trumpet), Brent Forston (keyboard/saxophone/flute), Steven Caldwell (saxophone) and James Perkins (bass), half of whom played rhythm instruments and the other half horns. By 1966, calling themselves the Swingin' Medallions, they had achieved some success in their live act performing a 1958 local recording by Dick Holler and the Holidays, 'Double Shot (Of My Baby's Love)'. After several abortive attempts at recording the song, the group invited its friends into the studio to make background noises, thus creating one of the all-time great 'party' songs. Issued on Smash Records 'Double Shot' reached number 17 in the US chart, but the group were never able to follow it successfully, and they disbanded in 1970. Before that time, Forston and Caldwell had split from the group in 1967 to record on **A&M** under the name of the Pieces Of Eight. McElrath has since been working with a new group of Swingin' Medallions into the late 80s. Once every year, since 1983, all the original members meet up for a reunion concert.

Album: *Double Shot (Of My Baby's Love)* (1966).

Swinging Blue Jeans

Determined to concentrate on rock 'n roll, several leading figures in Liverpool's skiffle scene founded the Bluegenes in 1958. They were singer and lead guitarist Ray Ennis (b. 26 May 1942), rhythm guitarist Ray Ellis (b 8 March 1942), bass-player Les Braid (b 15 September 1941), drummer Norman Kuhlke (b 17 June 1942) and Paul Moss (banjo). All were born in Liverpool. Minus Moss, the group became one of the leading attractions in the Merseyside beat group scene and also played in Hamburg. Following the **Beatles**' first successes, the Swinging Blues Jeans (as they had been renamed) signed a recording deal with EMI's HMV label. The **Beatles**'-sounding 'It's Too Late Now', was a minor hit the following year, but it was the group's third single, 'Hippy Hippy Shake', which provided their biggest success when it reached number 2. This rasping rendition of a Chan Romero song remains one of the era's finest performances, invoking a power the Blue Jeans never quite recaptured. Their version of 'Good Golly Miss Molly' nonetheless peaked at number 11, while the reflective rendition of **Betty Everett**'s soul ballad 'You're No Good' reached number 3. An excellent reading of **Dionne Warwick**'s hit 'Don't Make Me Over' stalled outside the Top 30. It was, however, the quartet's last substantial hit despite a series of highly-polished other singles, including 'Promise You'll Tell Her' (1964), 'Crazy 'Bout My Baby' (1965). The Blue Jeans were unfairly dubbed anachronistic. Several personnel changes also ensued, including the induction of two former **Escorts**, Terry Sylvester and Mike Gregory, but neither this, nor a brief change of name to Music Motor, made any difference to their fortunes. In 1968, the band was briefly renamed Ray Ennis and the Blue Jeans but when Sylvester was chosen to replace **Graham Nash** in the **Hollies,** the remaining members decided to split up. However, the revival of interest in 60s music persuaded Ennis to re-form the Swinging Blue Jeans in 1973. He re-recorded 'Hippy Hippy Shake' for an album on Dart Records and continued leading the band on the UK scampi-and-chips revival circuit for the next two decades. A 1992 reissue album included nine previous unreleased tracks among them were versions of **Little Richard**'s 'Ready Teddy' and & 'Three Little Fishes', the novelty song first recorded in 1939 by US bandleader Kay Kyser.

Albums: *Blue Jeans A' Swinging* aka *Swinging Blue Jeans* aka *Tutti Frutti* (1964), *The Swinging Blue Jeans: La Voce Del Padrone* (1966), *Hippy Hippy Shake* (1973), *Brand New And Faded* (1974), *Dancin'* (1985). Compilations: *Hippy Hippy Shake* (1964), *Shake: The Best Of The Swinging Blue Jeans* (1986).

Swinging UK

Swinging UK was the first of two shorts directed by Frank Gilpin in 1964; the second was *UK Swings Again*. The premise of both features was identical; disc jockeys Kent Walton, Alan Freeman and Brian Matthews introduced several popular acts, all bar one of whom mimes to a current hit and a less-feted selection. Thus the **Four Pennies** offer the chart-topping 'Juliet', **Millie** sings the perennial 'My Boy Lollipop' and the **Merseybeats** play 'Don't Turn Around'. The Wackers are the sole exception, their version of 'Love Or Money' failed to chart and on this evidence, it is not hard to fathom why. Both of Gilpin's features were amalgamated with a third film, *Mods And Rockers* for US release. The composite was entitled *Go, Go Big Beat*, with actors Marlon Brando and Rod Steger improbably standing in for the British disc jockeys.

Swingle Singers

The commercial success of this French choir undermined many ingrained prejudices by pop consumers against serious music, preparing them for **Walter Carlos**' *Switched-On Bach*, **Deep Purple**'s *Concerto For Group And Orchestra* and the promotion of the Portsmouth Sinfonia as a pop act. In 1963, the Singers were assembled by Ward Lamar Swingle (b. 21 September 1927, Mobile, Alabama, USA), a former conductor of Les Ballets De Paris. Addressing themselves to jazzy arrangements of the classics - particularly Bach - their wordless style had the novel effect of predetermined mass scat-singing. After *Jazz Sebastian Bach* and *Bach's Greatest Hits* made respective inroads into the UK and US Top 20, the outfit was catapulted into an arduous schedule of television and radio appearances during back-to-back world tours that embraced over 2,000 concerts by 1991. While the main choir continued to earn Grammy awards for 1965's *Going Baroque* and similar variations on his original concept, Swingle formed a smaller unit (Swingles II) for more contemporary challenges such as Luciano Berio's *Sinfonia* which was premiered in New York in 1973 - and for *Cries*, *A-Ronne* and other increasingly more complex works by the same composer.

Selected albums: *Bach's Greatest Hits* (1963), *Jazz Sebastian Bach* (1963), *Going Baroque* (1964), *Anyone For Mozart?* (1965), *Folio* (1980), *Swingle Singers Christmas Album* (1980), *Place Vendome* (1985), *Anyone For Mozart, Bach, Handel, Vivaldi?* (1986). Compilation: *Best Of The Swingle Singers* (1987).

Swingmen In Europe

A film with a succession of bandstand performances by visiting American jazzmen. Directed by Jean Mazeas, this 1977 film features **Milt Buckner**, **Teddy Buckner**, Gene **'Mighty Flea'** Conner, **Illinois Jacquet**, **Jo Jones**, **Sammy Price**, **J.C. Heard** and **Doc Cheatham**.

Switch

Bobby DeBarge (keyboards), Greg Williams (keyboards) and Jody Sims (drums) first collaborated in the Ohio-based funk band White Heat in the early 70s. After recording a self-titled album in 1975 produced by **Barry White**, the trio left the band, enlisting Philip Ingram (vocals), Tommy DeBarge (bass) and Eddie Fluellen (guitar) to form First Class. **Jermaine Jackson** helped them secure a deal with **Motown Records**, and produced their first album on the label, for which they were renamed Switch. The band's dance-oriented brand of soul proved popular in clubs and discos, and they enjoyed three major hits in the late 70s, 'There'll Never Be', 'I Call Your Name' and 'Love Over And Over Again'. They were unable to break into the mainstream pop market however, and decreasing returns for their efforts led them to quit Motown in 1982. Bobby DeBarge left the group to join other members of his family in *DeBarge*, before his career was cut short in the late 80s when he was convicted of cocaine trafficking. Meanwhile, Switch moved to the Total Experience label, where they scored a belated UK hit with 'Keeping Secrets' in 1984.

Albums: *Switch* (1978), Switch II (1979), *Reaching For Tomorrow* (1980), *This Is My Dream* (1980), *Switch V, Am I Still Your Boyfriend?* (1985).

Sword

This Canadian heavy metal quartet was formed in Montreal in 1981 by vocalist Rick Hughes and drummer Dan Hughes. Augmented by Mike Plant (guitar) and Mike Larock (bass), it took the band five years to secure a record deal. Finally signing to Aquarius in 1986, in the same year they released *Metalized*, which paid respect to both the early 80s British scene and older groups such as **Black Sabbath** and **Rainbow**. Sword then secured support slots on the **Alice Cooper** and **Metallica** tours of 1987, regaling audiences with a primal example of early power metal. *Sweet Dreams*, released in 1988, consolidated this approach: monstrously aching riffs and gut-wrenching guitar breaks, encased within dynamic and melodic arrangements. Sword were an excellent unit, but through a lack of image and record company backing, their commercial prospects were ultimately compromised, and they broke up in 1991.

Albums: *Metalized* (Aquarius 1986), *Sweet Dreams* (Aquarius 1988).

SWV

Standing for Sisters With Voices, these 'ghetto sisters' from Brooklyn and the Bronx comprise the talents of Coko (b. Cheryl Gamble, c.1974) Taj (b. Tamara Johnson, c.1974) and Lelee (b. Leanne Lyons, c. 1976). Shaped by producer **Teddy Riley** to reflect streetwise dress and attitude, the band's sound is somewhat harder than that which might be expected of 'New Jill Swingers'. On tracks like 'Downtown' they revealed themselves as happy to engage in intimate details of the sex wars. Their debut album also encompassed both rap and a capella, and included the hit single 'I'm So Into You', which crossed over into the Billboard Top 20.

Album: *It's About Time* (RCA 1993).

Sye

This Canadian hard rock group was formed in 1981 by Phillipino-born vocalist/guitarist Bernie Carlos. Based in Toronto, Carlos joined forces with bassist and fellow countryman Phillipino Gunner San Augustin. The duo joined the Metal Blade label and debuted with *Turn On The Night* in 1985. Session musician Ray Cincinnato played drums on the album, but Steve Ferguson was recruited as a permanent addition after the work was released. Sye's music featured some impressive guitar parts, but was ultimately hampered by the weak and indistinct vocals. It would be four years before a follow-up appeared, by which time their name had largely been forgotten.

Albums: *Turn On The Fire* (Metal Blade 1985), *Winds Of Change* (Loudspell 1989).

Sykes, Roosevelt

b. 31 January 1906, Elmar, Arkansas, USA. Sykes learned piano at 12 and by the early 20s was playing in local barrelhouses. Sykes moved to St. Louis in 1928 and his first records for **Okeh** and Victor were in 1929-31. During the 30s, Sykes recorded for **Decca** and acted as a talent scout for the label. Among his most popular compositions were 'Night Time Is The Right Time' and 'The Honeydripper', which was Sykes' nickname. He settled in Chicago in the early 40s, becoming the piano accompanist on numerous city blues records by artists such as St Louis Jimmy and **Lonnie Johnson**. In 1954, he moved to New Orleans continued to record prolifically for Decca, Prestige, Spivey, **Folkways**, **Delmark** and other labels. The Prestige album, *Honeydripper*, included **King Curtis** on saxophone. His versatility in different piano styles made Sykes well placed to take advantage of the increased European interest in blues and he made his first visit to the UK in 1961, performing with **Chris Barber**'s jazz band. He returned in 1965 and 1966 with the Folk Blues Festival package and he played many US blues and jazz festivals in the 70s. As a result of his popularity with these new audiences, much of his pre-1945 work was reissued in the 70s and 80s.

Albums: *Big Man Of The Blues* (1959), *Return Of Roosevelt Sykes* (1960), *Honeydripper* (1961), *Blues* (1963), *Blues From Bar Rooms* (1967) *Feel Like Blowing My Horn* (1973), *Dirty Double Mother* (1973).

Sylvain Sylvain

Although a founder member of the rock band Actress with **Johnny Thunders** and Billy Murcia, Sylvain only joined his colleagues in their next venture, the pivotal, glam-rock group, the **New York Dolls**, as a replacement for original guitarist Rick Rivets. He remained with the group until their break-up in 1977, following which the artist formed the Criminals with Bobby Blain (keyboards), Michael Page (bass) and Tony Machine (drums). This highly-respected quartet completed one single, 'The Kids Are Back', for their own Sing Sing label, but progress was hampered by Sylvain's concurrent commitment to former Dolls' vocalist **David Johansen**. Ties as a composer and backing musician were severed in 1979 when Syl established a new act, Sylvain Sylvain And The Teenage News, with two further refugees from the Johansen band, Johnny Rao (guitar) and Buz Verno (bass). Both *Sylvain Sylvain* and it's follow-up, *And The Teardrops* confirmed the artist's gift for classic pop melody, but were not a commercial success and the artist was subsequently dropped by his label, **RCA**. He resurrected his independent Sing Sing label for 'Out With The Wrong Woman' (1983), but its creator has since failed to sustain the profile he enjoyed throughout the 70s.

Albums: *Sylvain Sylvain* (1979), *And The Teardrops* (1980). Compilation: *'78 Criminals* (1985).

Sylvester

b. Sylvester James, 1946, Los Angeles, California, USA, d. 1988. Having moved to San Francisco in 1967, James joined the Cockettes, an androgynous theatrical group with whom he made his debut on New Year's Eve 1970. He subsequently pursed a career as 'Ruby Blue' before putting together the Hot Band with James Q. Smith (guitar), Bobby Blood (trumpet), Chris Mostert (saxophone), Kerry Hatch (bass) and Travis Fullerton (drums). The line-up later included vocalists Izora Rhodes and Martha Wash, now better known as the **Weather Girls**. Early recordings for the Blue Thumb label, coupled with an outrageous live show, secured James' local reputation, but his 'discovery' by former **Motown** producer **Harvey Fuqua** led to a much wider audience. In 1978 Sylvester scored two massive disco hits with 'You Make Me Feel (Mighty Real)' and 'Dance (Disco Heat)', performances marked by an unswerving urgency and the singer's soaring falsetto. The artist was adopted by the city's gay community, where later releases proved especially popular. Sylvester's excellent voice and skilled arrangements bestowed a lasting quality on his work, but he died of an AIDS-related illness in 1988. **Jimmy Somerville** subsequently recorded a version of *Mighty Real* as a tribute to this imaginative performer's talent.

Albums: With the Hot Band; *Sylvester And The Hot Band - Scratch My Flower* (1973), *Bazaar* (1973). Solo; *Sylvester* (1977), *Step II* (1978), *Stars* (1979), *Living Proof* (1979), *Sell My Soul* (1980), *Mighty Real* (1980), *Too Hot To Sleep* (1981), *Sylvester And Griffin* (1982), *All I Need* (1983), *Call Me* (1984), *M1015* (1984), *Mutual Attraction* (1987). Compilations: *Star - The Best Of Sylvester* (1989), *The Original Hits* (1989), *Greatest Hits* (1993).

Sylvia

b. Sylvia Kirby Allen, 9 December 1956, Kokomo, Indiana, USA. Sylvia was singing in a church choir from a young age and always wanted to be a professional singer. She took a secretarial job for producer Tom Collins in Nashville in 1976 and he was soon using her on songwriting demos. She worked as a backing vocalist on sessions for **Ronnie Milsap** and **Barbara Mandrell** and went on the road with **Janie Frickie**. She was signed to **RCA** and worked as an opening act for **Charley Pride**. She had US country hits with 'Tumbleweed', 'Drifter' (a number l), 'The Matador' and 'Heart On The Mend', which all came from her first album. In 1982 she had her second US country number l and a Top 20 pop hit with 'Nobody', which had only been completed hours before the session. She did not develop her style of merging country music with a disco beat as, in 1985, she took time out to write more personal material. Her duet with Michael Johnson, 'I Love You By Heart', was on the US country chart for 25 weeks, but her most unusual success was with **James Galway** on a revival of 'The Wayward Wind'.

Albums: *Drifter* (1981), *Just Sylvia* (1982), *Snapshot* (1983), *Surprise* (1984), *One Step Closer* (1985).

Sylvian, David

b. David Batt, 23 February 1958, Beckenham, Kent, England. Sylvian first established himself as a singer with **Japan**. His androgynous image and ethereal vocals made him a prominent figure in that group. Just before their break-up in late 1982, he branched out into a new venture recording with **Ryûichi Sakamoto** of the Yellow Magic Orchestra. The duo's 'Bamboo House' reached the UK Top 30 and the collaboration continued the following year with 'Forbidden Colours', the haunting theme to the **David Bowie** film *Merry Christmas Mr Lawrence*. Sylvian's own 'Red Guitar' also reached the Top 20 and he soon gained a reputation as an uncompromising artist, intent on working at his own pace, and to his own agenda. The atmospheric *Brilliant Trees*, reached the UK Top 5 and was widely acclaimed. Over two years elapsed before the double album follow-up *Gone To Earth*, which fared less well. By the time of *Let The Happiness In*, Sylvian had virtually returned to the pop fringe but his love of experimentation was still present. A collaboration with former **Can** member **Holgar Czukay** on the atmospherically ambient *Plight And Premonition* and *Flux And Mutability* emphasized this point. Sylvian subsequently joined his former Japan colleagues for their 1991 reunion project under the guise of Rain Tree Crow. Following his collaboration with Ryûichi Sakamoto in 1992, Sylvian was back in the charts with 'Heartbeat (Tainai Kaiki II)', after which he worked on an album with Robert Fripp (**King Crimson**).

Albums: *Brilliant Trees* (1984), *Words With The Shamen* (1985), *Alchemy (An Index Of Possibilities)* (1985, cassette release), *Gone To Earth* (1986, double album), *Secrets Of The Beehive* (1987), with Holgar Czukay *Plight And Premonition* (1988), *Flux And Mutability* (1989), *The Weather Box* (1990), *Ember Glance* (1991), with Robert Fripp *The First Day* (Virgin 1993), with Robert Fripp *Damage* (Damage 1994).

Further reading: *David Sylvian: 80 Days*, Zornes, D, Sawyer, H. & Powell H. (1990).

Symarip

(see **Pyramids**)

Symphony In Black

A very short but musically fascinating film made in 1934 which offers an opportunity to see and hear **Duke Ellington** And His Orchestra and **Billie Holiday**. Ellington's musicians include **Artie Whetsol**, **Cootie Williams**, **Joe Nanton**, **Lawrence Brown**, **Johnny Hodges**, **Harry Carney** and **Sonny Greer**. Holiday, in the first of her few film appearances, sings 'Saddest Tale'.

Syms, Sylvia

b. Sylvia Blagman, 2 December 1917, Brooklyn, USA, d. 10 May 1992, New York, USA. One of America's most distinguished cabaret and jazz singers with a profound appreciation of lyrics, Sylvia Syms overcame polio as a child, and in her teens discovered the delights of jazz in the clubs of New York's 52nd Street. Inspired and trained by **Billie Holiday**, she made her singing debut in 1941 at Kelly's Stable, and in 1948 was spotted while performing at the Cinderella Club in Greenwich Village by Mae West, who gave her the part of Flo the Shoplifter in a revival of *Diamond Lil*. She subsequently appeared in the regional theatre on many occasions as Bloody Mary in *South Pacific* and as Dolly Levi in *Hello, Dolly!*, and also acted in straight roles. Signed to **Decca**, she had a million-selling record in 1956 with an up-tempo version of 'I Could Have Danced All Night' from *My Fair Lady*, and enjoyed further success with 'English Muffins And Irish Stew' and 'It's Good To Be Alive'. **Frank Sinatra** called her the 'Buddha' on account of her short 'beer barrel' stature, but he was one of her greatest admirers, hailing her as 'the best saloon singer in the world'. He also produced her 1982 album *Syms By Sinatra*. In the late 80s and early 90s, Syms still performed occasionally at intimate venues such Eighty Eight's, Michael's Pub, and Freddy's in New York, where sensitive audiences thrilled to her tasteful selections, which included such delights as 'Skylark', 'You Are Not My First Love', 'I Want To Be Yours', 'Fun To Be Fooled', 'I Guess I'll Hang My Tears Out To Dry', 'It Amazes Me', and 'Pink Taffeta'. She died of a heart attack while performing a tribute programme to Frank Sinatra in the Oak Room of the Algonquin Hotel in Manhattan.
Selected albums: *Sings* (Atlantic 50s), *That Man* (Kapp 1961), *Sylvia Syms Is* (Prestige 60s), *In A Sentimental Mood* (Movietone (1967), *For Once In My Life* (Prestige 1967), *Syms By Sinatra* (Reprise 1982), *Along Came Bill* (80s), *You Must Believe In Spring* (Cabaret 1992), *A Jazz Portrait Of Johnny Mercer* (Koch 1995, rec. 1984).

Syncopation

Directed by William Dieterle, this 1942 film offers a Hollywood-eye view of the story of jazz. Predictably, accuracy goes out the window but there are some nice musical moments from a band of winners of a poll held by the *Saturday Evening Post*, whose readers seem to have heard of **Benny Goodman** and a few other swing era musicians but very little else. Apart from Goodman there are **Harry James**, **Jack Jenney**, **Charlie Barnet**, **Joe Venuti**, **Bob Haggart** and **Gene Krupa**. Stan Wrightsman dubbed the soundtrack for Bonia Granville, **Bunny Berigan** for Jackie Cooper, **Rex Stewart** for Todd Duncan.

Syndicate Of Sound

Formed in San Jose, California, USA in 1964, the Syndicate Of Sound were known for one classic garage-band/punk single, 'Little Girl', a US Top 10 hit on Bell Records in 1966. The group consisted of Don Baskin (b. 9 October 1946, Honolulu, Hawaii, USA; vocals/saxophone), John Sharkey (b. 8 June 1946, Los Angeles, California, USA; guitar/keyboards), Jim Sawyers (lead guitar), Bob Gonzales (bass) and John Duckworth (b. 18 November 1946, Springfield, Missouri, USA; drums). After an unsuccessful single for the Scarlet label, they recorded 'Little Girl' for the local Hush Records. It was a regional hit and picked up for national distribution by Bell, for which the group also recorded an album. The group placed two other minor singles on the charts, one later that year for Bell and another in 1970 on **Buddah**. They also recorded unsuccessfully for **Capitol** and disbanded in 1970.
Album: *Little Girl* (1966).

Syreeta

b. Rita Wright, Pittsburgh, Philadelphia, USA. Like **Martha Reeves**, Syreeta joined the staff of **Motown Records** as a secretary rather than a recording artist. In the mid-60s she sang occasional backing vocals on Motown sessions, and in 1967 **Ashford** and **Simpson** produced her debut single, 'I Can't Give Back The Love I Feel For You', which became a cult record among British soul fans. In 1968 she met **Stevie Wonder**, who encouraged her to begin songwriting. She co-wrote his 1970 hit 'Signed, Sealed, Delivered (I'm Yours)', and also commenced work on the song-cycle which became *Where I'm Coming From*. The couple were married on 14 September 1970, and although they were divorced just 18 months later, they continued to work together for several years. In 1972, Wonder produced *Syreeta*, a stunning collection of soft-soul and light-funk which showcased her fluent, joyous vocals. The collaboration allowed Stevie to experiment with studio techniques that he perfected on his own later projects, and also inspired one of his earliest pronouncements of black pride on the affecting ballad 'Black Maybe'. *Stevie Wonder Presents Syreeta* in 1974 continued the pair's close musical partnership, and produced a British hit in the reggae-flavoured 'Your Kiss Is Sweet'. The couple's last joint recording, 'Harm Our Love' in 1975, was also their most commercial, and its success in the UK and USA gave Syreeta a

platform from which to build. She teamed up with **G.C. Cameron** for a disappointing album of duets before completing a more fulfilling partnership with **Billy Preston**, which produced the soundtrack for the film *Fast Break*, and a US and UK Top 10 hit, the sentimental love song, 'With You I'm Born Again'. Syreeta and Preston completed a further album project in 1981. Her solo recordings were less successful, and after the **Jermaine Jackson**-produced *The Spell* in 1983, she abandoned her career to concentrate on raising a family. In the late 80s, Syreeta recorded several tracks for Ian Levine's Motor City label, including a solo rendition of 'With You I'm Born Again' and new duets with Billy Preston.
Albums: *Syreeta* (1972), *Stevie Wonder Presents Syreeta* (1974), *One To One* (1977), with G.C. Cameron *Rich Love, Poor Love* (1977), with Billy Preston *Fast Break* (1979), *Syreeta* (1980), *Billy Preston And Syreeta* (1981), *Set My Love In Motion* (1981), *The Spell* (1983).

System 7

Ambient dance duo featuring Miquette Giraudy (b. 9 February 1953, Nice, France; synthesizers, samples) and the more celebrated **Steve Hillage** (b. Stephen Simpson Hillage, 2 August 1951, Walthamstow, London, England; guitars, samplers, synthesizers). Giraudy is a former film-maker from the south of France, where she met up with Hillage's band, the cult synth prog rockers **Gong**. Her films had included *More* and *La Vallee*, both of which featured **Pink Floyd** on their soundtracks. Fascinated by synthesisers, she became a self-taught musician and in the current format writes most of the material before Hillage adds a layer of guitar work. Hillage enjoys his own cult following through his work with **Kevin Ayers**, Gong and the Steve Hillage Group, and had become enveloped in the ambient house explosion via the work of **Spooky**, the **Drum Club**, **Orbital**, **Black Dog** and **Fluke**, before collaborating with another listening favourite, the **Orb**. In turn System 7 have been joined on vinyl by a host of rock, pop and dance stars; Alex Paterson (Orb), Youth (**Killing Joke/Brilliant**), Mick McNeil (**Simple Minds**) **Paul Oakenfold** and **Derrick May**. Their recording career started in August 1991 with 'Miracle' on Ten Records, after which they moved to **Big Life** but sought their own Weird & Unconventional imprint. Singles of the quality of 'Freedom Fighters' and 'Sinbad' have helped them garner a considerable reputation among both their peers and late-night ravers searching for the perfect chill-out tune.
Albums: *System 7* (Ten 1991), *777* (Weird And Unconventional/Big Life 1993).

Syzygy

Syzygy are London, England-based duo Dominic Glynn and Justin McKay, who first met at the end of the 80s, when Glynn was working part-time providing BBC Television's *Doctor Who* series with incidental music. Mutually inspired by Detroit techno (**Derrick May**, **Juan Atkins**, etc.), their first recordings emerged on the Infonet record label, before they adopted the names Mind Control and Zendik for two further 12-inch releases. They subsequently signed more permanently to **Rising High Records** as Syzygy. Two EPs, *Discovery* and *Can I Dream*, began to push their profile in the 'intelligent techno' club scene. A debut double album, meanwhile, drew its title from 'the collective consciousness of the planet, a phenomenon for which there is no easy explanation'. An extended concept ambient album, it took as its theme a musical fable of the earth's development.
Album: *The Morphic Resonance* (Rising High 1994, double album).

Szabo, Gabor

b. 1936, Budapest, Hungary, d. 26 February 1982. Guitarist Azabo emigrated to the USA in 1956 to study at the **Berklee College Of Music**. He came to notice playing with **Chico Hamilton** and **Charles Lloyd**. In the late 60s he began to explore a fusion of jazz with the kind of rock which was superficially influenced by Indian music. He introduced a number of Eastern styles into his playing. Although his Hungarian roots probably pre-disposed him to an empathy with these elements they were often seen as mere gimmicks, and he was generally dismissed by the critics. The eclectic albums made under his own name were very much of their time, and he was not an important figure, but in his work with Lloyd and Hamilton, he showed himself capable of being a warm-toned and subtle player.
Albums: with Charles Lloyd *Of Course Of Course* (1965), *Spellbinder* (1967), *The Sorcerer* (1967), *Bacchanal* (1968), *Gabor Szabo 1969* (1969), with Lena Horne *Lena & Gabor* (1970), *Nightflight* (1976), *Rambler, Wind, Sky And Diamonds* (1977), *Macho* (1978), *Mizra* (1978), *Belsta River*, (Four Leaf Clover 1988), with Bobby Womack *High Contrast* (Affinity 1988), *Small World* (Four Leaf Clover 1988). Compilation: *His Greatest Hits* (1977).

Szymczyk, Bill

b. 13 February 1943, Muskegon, Michigan, USA. After studying electronics in the US Armed Forces, Szymczyk journeyed to New York in 1964 and worked as a junior recording engineer on some tracks by folk singers **Phil Ochs**, **Eric Andersen** and **Tom Rush**. By 1967, he had produced his first album, Harry Brooks' *How To Play Electronic Bass* and from there he signed with ABC Records. As a house producer he worked with Boston band, Ford Theatre, before collaborating on **B.B. King**'s *Love And Well*. By the end of the 60s, he had produced several King albums plus his biggest US hit single 'The Thrill Is Gone', on which

Szymczyk had employed tasteful orchestration. The first successful rock act to be discovered and produced by Szymczyk were the **James Gang**, featuring guitarist **Joe Walsh**. Szymczyk's early work is arguably best captured on their album, *Thirds*, where Walsh's phased guitar echoes menacingly on the excellent 'Walk Away'. Szymczyk stuck with Walsh for his solo *Barnstorm*, and also spent five years working with the **J. Geils Band** until they finally elected to produce themselves. Although Walsh was intent on doing the same, he decided to use Szymczyk's talents as co-producer on his more successful albums *The Smoker You Drink, The Player You Get* and *So What*, before again allowing him full control on the excellent *...But Seriously Folks*. Throughout this period, Szymczyk had found a more lucrative post after being called upon to complete the **Eagles**' *On The Border*. Initially, Bill was reluctant to take the offer for fear of offending their producer **Glyn Johns**, but finally he received his rival's blessing and the sessions produced a hit album. From there, the Eagles went on to become one of the most commercially successful acts in the world and gradually moved away from their country roots to a rockier sound. The arrival of Joe Walsh in the Eagles camp had working advantages for Szymczyk, although he was strangely against the move. The combination worked to spectacular effect on *Hotel California*, however, in which Walsh's hard edge merged brilliantly with the group's sweeter melodies and harmonic blend. By this point Szymczyk was an in-demand producer, having worked on albums by **Jo Jo Gunne**, **Rick Derringer**, **Wishbone Ash**, **Elvin Bishop**, **Jay Ferguson** and **REO Speedwagon**. After completing the Eagles' final album, *The Long Run*, Szymczyk was at last offered the opportunity to work with an already established major group, the **Who**. The work in question was *Face Dances*, their first since the death of **Keith Moon**. It says much for Szymczyk's reputation at the time that he was called to England to work in an alien environment with such an established act. Like many producers, Szymczyk was largely associated with a particular sound at a key time. In his case, the sound was FM-orientated American, late 70s, AOR rock.

Further reading: *The Rock Producers*, John Tobler.

T

10,000 Maniacs

This American group emerged on the wave of popularity caused by the interest in world music. Lead vocalist Natalie Merchant is backed by Jerome Augustyniak (drums), Robert Buck (guitar), Dennis Drew (keyboards), Steven Gustafson (bass). The group started playing together in Jamestown, New York, in 1981. They initially specialized in cover versions of songs by such bands as **Joy Division**, and **Gang Of Four**. rock music. BBC disc jockey **John Peel** endorsed the group's 'My Mother The War', and it appeared in his Top 50 for 1983. Shortly afterwards, in 1984, the Maniacs toured the UK. The group were signed to **Elektra Records** in 1985, and after a UK tour, recorded *The Wishing Chair* with **Joe Boyd** as producer. Original member John Lombardo (guitar) left the group in 1986 following a great deal of touring. 1987 saw a change of producer for *In My Tribe*, with **Peter Asher** stepping in, as he did with the subsequent release *Blind Man's Zoo*. The production change obviously worked as the album went into the US Top 40 in 1987, going gold in 1988, and platinum the following year. 'Peace Train', taken from the former album, received a great deal of airplay, but following the alleged death threat declarations to American servicemen by Yusuf Islam, formerly **Cat Stevens**, the writer of the song. The group insisted that any re-pressing of the album should exclude the aforementioned track. *Blind Man's Zoo* went into the US Top 20 in 1989, achieving gold status the same year. Following the release of *Blind Man's Zoo*, the group were on the road from June to December of 1989. The band consolidated their standing, now as a highly original group, albeit using other musical influences. This was superbly demonstrated with *Our Time In Eden* including the lilting 'Noah's Dove and the punchy brass of 'Few And Far Between'. Merchant's 'Jezabel' had the strings arranged by Paul Buckmaster. *Hope Chest* is a compilation, re-mixed, of the group's first two independently released albums. In September 1993 Merchant departed to develop her solo career, commenting 'There is no ill will between the members of the group, this is a natural passage'.

Albums: *Human Conflict Number 5* (Christian Burial 1982), *Secrets Of The I Ching* (Christian Burial 1983), *The Wishing Chair* (Elektra 1985), *In My Tribe* (Elektra 1987), *Blind Man's Zoo* (Elektra 1989), *Our Time In Eden* (1992), *10,000 Maniacs MTV Unplugged* (1993). Compilation: *Hope Chest* (Elektra 1990).

Video: *MTV Unplugged* (Elektra 1994).

10cc

The formation of 10cc in 1970 represented the birth of a Manchester supergroup. The line-up - Eric Stewart (b. 20 January 1945, Manchester, England; vocals/guitar), Lol Creme (b. Lawrence Creme, 9 September 1947, Manchester, England; vocals/guitar), Kevin Godley (b. 7 October 1945, Manchester, England; vocals/drums) and **Graham Gouldman** (b. 10 May 1945, Manchester, England; vocals/guitar) - boasted years of musical experience stretching back to the mid-60s. Stewart was a former member of both **Wayne Fontana And The Mindbenders** and the **Mindbenders**; Gouldman had played in the **Mockingbirds** and written many hits for such artists as **Herman's Hermits**, the **Yardbirds**, the **Hollies** and **Jeff Beck**; **Godley And Creme** had worked in various session groups, including **Hotlegs**, which had spawned 10cc. After working with **Neil Sedaka**, the 10cc ensemble launched their own recording career on **Jonathan King**'s UK label with the 50s doo-wop pastiche 'Donna'. The song reached number 2 in the UK chart, spearheading a run which continued almost uninterrupted until the end of the decade. 10cc specialized in reinterpreting pop's great tradition by affectionately adopting old styles and introducing them to new teenage audiences. At the same time, their wit, word play and subtle satire appealed to an older audience, who appreciated mild irony, strong musicianship and first rate production. The chart-topping 'Rubber Bullets', the high school romp 'The Dean And I', the sardonic 'Wall Street Shuffle', zestful 'Silly Love' and mock-philosophical 'Life Is A Minestrone' were all delightful slices of 70s pop and among the best singles of their time. In 1975, the group achieved their most memorable hit with the tragi-comic UK chart-topper 'I'm Not In Love', a song that also brought them success in the USA. The group continued its peak period with the mischievous 'Art For Art Sake' and bizarre travelogue 'I'm Mandy Fly Me' before internal strife undermined their progress. In 1976, the group split in half as Godley And Creme pursued work in video production and as a recording duo. Stewart and Gouldman retained the 10cc tag and toured with a line-up comprising Tony O'Malley (keyboards), Rick Fenn (guitar) and Stuart Tosh (drums). The streamlined 10cc continued to chart with the over-sweetened 'The Things We Do For Love' and the mock-reggae chart topper 'Dreadlock Holiday'. Nevertheless, it was generally agreed that their recordings lacked the depth, invention, humour and charm of the original line-up. The hits ceased after 1982 and Stewart and Gouldman went on to pursue other ventures. The former produced **Sad Cafe** and collaborated with **Paul McCartney**, while the more industrious Gouldman produced **Gilbert O'Sullivan** and the **Ramones** before forming the duo **Wax**, with **Andrew Gold**. 10cc issued a new album in 1992 after Gouldman and Stewart began writing songs with each other after a long break. Godley and Creme joined in during the recording, although they did not participate in any writing. The moderate reception the album received seemed to indicate that a full-scale renunion would not take place. Their back catalogue of quality pop songs will continue to be highly respected, although the 1994 live album was a reunion that sounded as though they were doing it as penance.

Albums: *10cc* (1973), *Sheet Music* (1974), *The Original Soundtrack* (1975), *How Dare You* (1976), *Deceptive Bends* (1977), *Live And Let Live* (1977), *Bloody Tourists* (1978), *Look Hear!* (1980), *Ten Out Of 10* (1981), *10cc In Concert* (1982), *Window In The Jungle* (1983), *Meanwhile* (1992), *10CC Live* (Creative Man 1994). Compilations: *10cc - The Greatest Hits* (1975), *Greatest Hits 1972-1978* (1979), *The Early Years* (1993), *Food For Thought* (1993). Videos: *Live In Concert* (1986), *Live At The International Music Show* (1987), *Changing Faces, The Very Best Of* (1988).

Further reading: *The 10cc Story*, Tremlett, George (1976).

2 Live Crew

Rap headline-makers from Miami, Florida (via California), who formed in 1985 around central figure **Luther Campbell**. 2 Live Crew became unlikely figures in a media censorship debate when, in June 1990, *As Nasty As They Wanna Be* was passed sentence on by a judge in Broward County, Florida. In the process it became the first record in America to be deemed legally obscene (a federal appeal court overturned the decision in 1993). Their right to free speech saw them defended by sources as diverse as **Sinead O'Connor**, **Bruce Springsteen** and **Motley Crue**, but the overbearing impression remained that 2 Live Crew were a third-rate rap outfit earning first division kudos by little more than circumstance. Their debut set, recorded before Campbell became an actual member, marked out the band's territory. To this end, 2 Live Crew have several times expressed themselves to be an adult comedy troupe, 'The Eddie Murphys of Rap', in the best traditions of crude party records by **Blowfly** and others. Hence 'We Want Some Pussy' and other, inconsequential, mildly offensive tracks. Campbell was

the founder of the band's record label, Luke Skywalker Records (shortened to Luke Records when film-maker George Lucas, who created the Luke Skywalker character in the film *Star Wars*, filed suit), while Campbell's compatriots in 2 Live Crew numbered rappers Trinidad-born Chris Wong Won, New Yorker Mark Ross and California DJ David Hobbs (under the psuedonyms Brother Marquis and Fresh Kid Ice on the 'clean' version of *Move Somethin'*). Their music was underpinned by the familiar 'Miami Bass' sound, of synthesised, deep backbeats. *As Nasty As We Wanna Be*, replete with 87 references to oral sex *alone*, included the notorious 'Me So Horny', built around a sample from *Full Metal Jacket*. It is an unquestionably offensive lyric, but not any more so than that by the **Geto Boys** or others. There are probably worse examples within the 2 Live Crew's own songbook - 'The Fuck Shop', which samples **Guns N'Roses** guitar lines, or 'Head Booty And Cock' which became almost a battle-cry, notably when repeated, Nuremburg-like, by chanting fans on the Phoenix, Arizona-recorded live album. Advocates of record stickering such as the Parents Music Resource Center (PMRC) and Forida attorney/evangelist Jack Thompson, argued strongly that the group's records should not be available for sale to minors. A retail record store owner arrested for selling a copy of their *Move Somethin'* - albeit to an adult - was later acquitted. The group itself was then arrested for performing music from the *Nasty* album in an adults-only club, sparking charges by anti-censorship groups that the law enforcement officials were becoming over-zealous. There is not much doubt that this was true - Miami has one of the biggest pornography industries in the country, and it was obvious the moguls behind it were not being pursued with equal vigour, if they were being pursued at all. Not that the band were going out of their way to help improve their public image (whilst doubtless realising the commercial advantages of such notoriety). Luther Campbell claimed on CBS network TV show *A Current Affair* during 1992 that he had had oral sex on stage with female fans in Japan. Campbell had been aquitted a year previously for giving an obscene performance in his home state, Florida. In 1993 they became legal ground-breakers again, this time over their 1989 parody of **Roy Orbison**'s 'Pretty Woman'. For the first time, Acuff Rose Music Inc were suing an artist on the grounds that their version tarnishes the image of the original. On top of all the heat Campbell released a solo album, *Banned In The USA*. The scandal abated somewhat, and as 2 Live Crew's otherwise unremarkable career progressed, there was even an AIDS awareness ditty on *Nasty Weekend* - 'Who's Fuckin' Who'. They also promoted safe sex with their own brand of Homeboy Condoms, one of their more acceptable acts of mysoginist titilation.

Albums: *The 2 Live Crew Is What We Are* (Luke

Skyywalker 1986), *Move Somethin'* (Luke Skyywalker 1988), *As Nasty As They Wanna Be* (Luke Skyywalker 1989), *As Clean As They Wanna Be* (Luke Skyywalker 1989), *Live In Concert* (Effect 1990), *Sports Weekend (As Nasty As They Wanna Be Part II)* (Luke 1991), *Sports Weekend (As Clean As They Wanna Be Part II)* (Luke 1991). Compilation: *Best Of* (Luke 1992). As Luther Campbell Featuring The 2 Live Crew: *Banned In The USA* (Luke 1990). As The New 2 Live Crew: *Back At Your Ass For The Nine-4* (Luke 1994). Luther Campbell solo: *Luke In The Nude* (Luke 1993).
Video: *Banned In The USA* (1990).

2 Live Jews

A crude spin-off from the ranks of **2 Live Crew**, this was Miami-based MCs 'Moisha' Lambert and Joe 'Easy Irving' Stone's idea of a good joke. The song titles gave the game away very quickly: 'Oui! It's So Humid', 'Accountant Suckers' and 'Beggin' For A Bargain'.
Album: *As Kosher As They Wanna Be* (Kosher 1990).

2 Too Many

West Philadelphia act sponsored by local boys made good **DJ Jazzy Jeff And The Fresh Prince**. 2 Too Many's debut single, 'Where's The Party', was hugely reminiscent of their better-known colleagues' style, with a penchant for fun over gangsta or soicio-political concerns. The duo comprise Jazz (b. Armique Shartez Wyche, c.1972), L'il Troy (b. Troy Carter, c.1973) and Ant Live (b. Anthony Fontenot, c.1974). They had been rapping together since the late 80s, before Jazz and Troy linked up in the 9th Grade, bringing aboard cousin Ant to finalise the band's line-up. They took their name from their high-school poverty; whenever they would attempt to embark on an evening's entertainment or activity, they always found enough to pay for one, and thus became: 2 Too Many. However, fortunes changed when they met Will Smith (aka the Fresh Prince) when he was recording next door to their rehearsal room. They introduced themselves and invited him to see them play. The result was a contract with his own Willjam Productions through **Jive** Records. He teamed them up with Hula and Fingers, the producton duo behind his huge 1991 success, 'Summertime'. They envisaged long careers on the strength of this, spending many hours researching the music business in libraries to make sure they would not be taken advantage of, and acquainting themselves with management and production disciplines.
Album: *Chillin' Like A Smut Villain* (Jive 1992).

2 Tribes

Funk metal crossover aggregation formed in London during 1990, the mixed-race line-up giving them their name. The band, who, predictably, were often said to represent the UK's answer to **Living Colour**, comprised Ashton Liburd (vocals), Paul Gold (bass),

Rod Quinn (b. Dublin, Eire; drums) and John McLoughlin (guitar). The group's efforts were spearheaded by a single, 'The Music Biz', which had that same legend scrawled over a pig on its jacket. Their uncompromising live sets, meanwhile, included a cover of **Public Enemy**'s '911 Is A Joke', the American rap stars' vicious attack on emergency response times in black communities, borrowed after a relative of the band died waiting three hours for an ambulance. Signed to **Chrysalis** subsidiary Compulsion, they made their long playing debut with a self-titled album in early 1992 which met with a degree of enthusiasm from the rock press. Especially notable was the agenda-setting 'File Under Rock (Bite The Hand That Bleeds Us)' single, which bemoaned the fact that their records were always housed under the 'black' sections in stores, despite 2 Tribes being an authentic rock act. It included the lines: 'This ain't **Soul II Soul**, It's rock 'n' roll'. However, despite earning a Single Of The Week plaudit in the *New Musical Express*, it was not enough to avert their descent into obscurity, with the band splitting soon after its release.
Album: *2 Tribes* (Compulsion 1992).

2 Unlimited

Cod-house act from Holland who enjoyed two weeks at the top of the UK charts with 'No Limits', featuring Anita Dels' diva vocals and Ray Slijngaard's hilarity-inducing chorus of 'Techno! Techno! Techno! Techno!'. It was mangificently parodied in an episode of television series *Spitting Image*, where the puppet Anita recited 'No lyrics, no no no no, no no there's no lyrics'. An album of the same name contained further variations on the formula, though arguably of an even lower quality threshold. Slijngaard rejoices in the distinction of having previously been a chef at Amsterdam airport - affording snide journalists the opportunity of comparing 2 Unlimited's brand of Euro-pop with greasy fast-food. Dels previously worked as a secretary, singing part-time with the Trouble Girls. The men behind the group are Jean-Paul De Coster and Phil Wilde, of Byte Records (who previously tasted success with Bizz Nizz's 'Don't Miss The Party Line'). Their philosophy is redolent of the Euro-techno axis, but anathema to traditional British views of artistic imput: '2 Unlimited is trendy music that appeals to the youths, it's not aggressive so the kids kids can enjoy it. There's also a strong melody that stays in the head, and the visuals are good too'. They readily admit to creating music to satiate a market rather than attempting to build a fan base around any creative vision. The statistics, whilst not exonerating them, did prove them to be entirely correct in their suppostion - in 1993 2 Unlimited sold over a million singles in Britain alone. 'No Limits' was also the biggest selling European record of the year, while their second album sold nearly three million copies. Earlier success had included the arguably more interesting 'Workaholic'.

Album: *Get Ready* (PWL 1992), *No Limits* (PWL 1992), *Real Things* (PWL 1994).

Video: *No Limits* (1993).

20/20

This US group was formed in Los Angeles, California, in 1978 by Steve Allen (guitar/vocals) and Ron Flynt (bass/vocals), two ex-patriot musicians from Tulsa, Oklahoma. Drummer Mike Gallo completed the line-up featured on the group's early work for Bomp!, a leading independent label, which in turn inspired a major deal with **Columbia Records**' subsidiary Portrait. *20/20* was produced by former **Sparks**' vocalist Earl Mankey and featured newcomer Chris Silagyi (keyboards). Despite commercial indifference, its superior brand of power-pop was a critical success, and drew favourable comparisons with the **Dwight Twilley** Band. Gallo was later replaced by Joel Turrisi (ex-Gary Valentine And The Know), but when successive, meritorious albums failed to further the group's career, 20/20 was disbanded.

Albums: *20/20* (1979), *Look Out* (1981), *Sex Trap* (1983).

200 Motels

Rock iconoclast **Frank Zappa** wrote the story, screenplay and music for this 1971 film. Tony Palmer, famed for his documentaries *All My Loving* and *Cream's Last Concert*, directed the project with considerable aplomb, shooting the scenes on video before transferring the results onto film using newly-discovered optical effects. The result was a surreal pantomime based around the on-the-road experiences of a touring band staying at a motel in Centreville, USA. The freewheeling imagery centred on Zappa's group, the **Mother Of Invention**, which he reinaugurated for this project with several new members, including **Aynsley Dunbar** and two former **Turtles**, Mark Volman and Howard Kaylan. The latter pair, known as the Phlorescent Leech And Eddie (or **Flo And Eddie**) to escape contractual wrangles brought a new visual/verbal aspect to the band, one this madcap film exploits to great effect. Former Mother Jimmy Carl Black stars as the Lonesome Cowboy, folksinger **Theodore Bikel** drifts in and out of the proceedings, **Keith Moon** of the **Who** features dressed as a nun and **Ringo Starr** appears memorably as Frank Zappa. In-concert footage, including the Mothers' collaboration with the Royal Philharmonic Orchestra, crosscuts satirical scenes of sexual conquest and hedonism and in the manner of many of Zappa's 'documentary' projects, the attendant soundtrack album, which includes material not in the film and omits some that is, mixes dialogue with music. Disjoined and self-indulgent, *200 Motels* articulates the madness surrounding rock' first generation.

21 Guns

This melodic hard rock quartet were assembled in 1991 by ex-**Thin Lizzy** guitarist Scott Gorham. Recruiting fellow Americans Leif Johansen (bass), Michael Sturgis (drums) and Tommy La Verdi (vocals) to complete the line-up, they were soon offered a contract by **RCA** Records. They debuted in the summer of 1992 with *Salute*, a highly polished album which met with positive reviews in the press. Influences such as **Foreigner**, **White Lion** and **Journey** were prevalent throughout the album, though Gorham's distinctive style held any accusations of plagiarism in check.

Album: *Salute* (RCA 1992).

24-7 Spyz

This multi-faceted South Bronx, New York, hardcore quartet formed in 1986, playing a mixture of ska, punk and funk until they began to incorporate hardcore aggression in the manner of **Fishbone** and **Bad Brains,** progressing like the former in particular towards an eclectic but accessible sound. Founder Jimi Hazel (guitar), Peter Fluid (vocals), Rick Skatore (bass) and Anthony Johnson (drums) made their debut with *Harder Than You*, mixing rap and reggae into their funk and thrash melting pot, with stunning performances from the **Jimi Hendrix**-worshipping Hazel and the energetic Fluid. *Gumbo Millenium* continued in similar genre-blending fashion as the band began to attract press attention for their wild live act, but musical differences saw both Fluid and Johnson depart as touring ended. Jeff Brodnax (vocals) and Joel Maitoza (drums) made their debut on *This Is...24-7 Spyz*, with the band surprisingly maintaining a continuity of style both live and in the studio, despite the drastic line-up change. *Strength In Numbers* contained 24-7 Spyz's most consistent material, but like Fishbone, the band's diversity seemed to hold them back, and commercial success remained distant. A reunion of the original line-up seemed to be on the cards in mid-1994, but came to nothing after Temporarily Disconnected.

Albums: *Harder Than You* (In-Effect 1989), *Gumbo Millenium* (In-Effect 1990), *This Is...24-7 Spyz* (East West 1991, mini-album), *Strength In Numbers* (East West 1992), *Temporalily Disconnected* (Enemy 1994).

25th Of May

This controversial and short-lived rap act from Liverpool, England, courted trouble with singles like 'Fuck The Right To Vote' and 'It's Alright', which extolled the virtues of shoplifting. Inaugurated at the Sefton Park Trade Union Centre, the band comprised Steve Swindells (vocals), Jimmy Mathias (DJ) and Nigel Cope (bass). They came to prominence at the same time as Merseyside was swaying to the sounds of 60s retro pop acts like **Rain** and the **Real People**. This was anathema to Swindells in a period when he judged black hip hop to be 'eclipsing all other forms of music'. They signed to **Arista** Records just as Mathias and Cope were busted for drug possession in May 1991. Overcoming the contradictions of being a 'white' **Public Enemy** proved a big stumbling block, however, and their media blitz had cooled by the following year.

Album: *Lenin And McCarthy* (Arista 1992).

29th Street Saxophone Quartet

Jim Hartog (baritone saxophone), Ed Jackson (alto saxophone), Rich Rothenburg (tenor saxophone), **Bobby Watson** (alto saxophone). The 29th Street Saxophone Quartet first came together for a European tour in 1983, though the idea for the group had been mooted by Hartog and Jackson in the late 70s, and partly put into practice in the early 80s, when the pair had jammed with other New York-based saxophonists both in and outside Hartog's 29th Street loft apartment. In 1983 the arrival of Watson, already a player with a growing international reputation and several years' experience of working with **Art Blakey**, really launched the group on the road to worldwide success. A popular live act, the quartet's core allegiance to hard bop secured them their particular niche among comparable ensembles (such as the World and **ROVA Saxophone Quartet**'s) and also helped to fuel their direct emotional power and danceability. All four are outstanding soloists, but their records are also characterized by what one writer has called 'a state of integrated motion', the horns threading together in quickfire counterpoint or complex rhythmic interweavings. As early as *Watch Your Step*, the group had introduced rap onto one track and their recent *Underground* leavens or dilutes (according to one's point of view) the original saxophone quartet concept with guest appearances by vocalist Pamela Watson, pianist **Benny Green** and trumpeter **Hugh Masekela** among others.

Albums: *Pointillistic Groove* (1984), *Watch Your Step* (1985), *Live* (1987), *The Real Deal* (1989), *Underground* (1991), *Your Move* (1992).

2Pac

b. Tupac Amaru Shakur, 16 June 1971. A controversy-laced former **Digital Underground** hip hop star, Tupac has enjoyed a degree of crossover success with 'I Get Around'. The album which housed it, *Strictly 4 My N.I.G.G.A.Z.* offered a rare degree of insight, with glints of wisdom like 'Last Wordz' - 'United we stand, divided we fall, they can shoot one nigga, but they can't shoot us all'. To further his views he ran the Undreground Railroad network for troubled teenagers in his native Oakland, California. However, such a statement did not mention any of the less strenuous lengths the law might go to in silencing him. He was accused in 1993 of involvement in the shooting of two plain clothes policemen and one count of forceful sodomy. He was already on bail for an outstanding battery charge for allegedly striking a woman who asked for his autograph. He had also been arrested in Los Angeles for carrying a concealed weapon and assaulting a driver. After appearing in director John Singleton's film *Poetic Justice*, alongside **Janet Jackson**, he was dropped from the same director's *Higher Learning*. Shakur took things into his own hands when he was also removed from the set of Allen Hughes *Menace II Society*, attacking the director, for which charges were also laid. He did however, make it on to the final cut of *Above The Rim*, and had already turned in a memorable performance in *Juice*. Further controversy followed when a tape of *2Pacalypse Now* was found in the possession of a man arrested for murder. All of which added to the resonance of the title of his third album.

Album: *2Pacalypse Now* (Interscope 1992), *Strictly 4 My N.I.G.G.A.Z.* (Interscope 1993), *Me Against The World* (Interscope 1994).

3 Mustaphas 3

This pseudo-Balkan group have often been included under the 'World Music' banner. Each group member has adopted 6 August as an official birthday in order to avoid confusion. Niaveti Mustapha III (flutes/German bagpipes), Hijaz Mustapha (violin/bouzouki), Houzam Mustapha (drums), Sabah Habas Mustapha (bass/percussion), Kemo "Kem Kem" Mustapha (accordion/piano), and Daoudi Mustapha (clarinet) made their UK debut in August 1982. They hail from Szegerley, and their major breakthrough was going from Balkan Beat Bastard Bad Boys to Godfathers Of World Music, without changing their direction. The Mustaphas are occasionally joined by Expensive Mustapha (trumpet). The humorous ensemble was first brought to public attention by **John Peel**. The group have attracted a degree of criticism for not taking their music seriously, but the end product is still extremely popular with audiences both in Europe and the USA. As an indication of this, *Soup Of The Century* was number 1 in the **Billboard** World Music charts, and was voted the 'Best World Music/International' album for 1990 by NAIRD (National Association of Independent Record Distributors), in the USA. For *Heart Of Uncle*, on Globestyle Records, the group were joined by their sister Laura Tima Daviz Mustapha (vocals). They have backed a number of other artists, such as **Ofra Haza** where they sang 'Linda Linda' and managed to offend some people by singing half the lyrics in Hebrew and half in Arabic.

Albums: *Bam! Mustaphas Play Stereo* (1985), *From The Balkans To Your Heart-The Radio Years* (1985), *L'Orchestre Bam de Grand Mustapha International & Party Play "Local Music"* (1986), *Shopping* (1987), *Heart Of Uncle* (1989), *Soup Of The Century* (1990). Compilation: *Friends, Fiends & Fronds* (1991).

38 Special

38 Special were formed in 1977 by guitarist and vocalist Donnie Van Zant (brother to Johnny of the Van Zant Band and **Lynyrd Skynyrd**'s Ronnie), with Jeff Carlisi (guitar), Don Barnes (guitar), Larry Junstrom (bass) and drummers Steve Brookins and Jack Grodin. In keeping with fraternal tradition the band proffered Southern boogie/rock, though their sound later slipped in to AOR. Signed to **A&M Records** they had little impact outside of the southern states but in 1979 scored a minor hit with 'Rocking Into The Night', which was followed by an album and major tour. With fame eluding them (despite a further single success in 1980 with 'Hang On Loosely') they dropped out of the scene in 1984 but made a comeback in 1986 and recorded the film theme, *Revenge Of The Nerds 2*. Barnes left soon after as did Brookins, both in an attempt to launch their own bands. Danny Clancy joined on guitar while Brookins was replaced by keyboard player Max Carol. 1988's *Rock N Roll Strategy* earned strong reviews, but after release the group lost their contract with A&M. *Bone Against Steel*, meanwhile, saw them return to a southern boogie framework without the AOR trappings and won many new supporters.
Albums: *38 Special* (A&M 1977), *Special Delivery* (A&M 1978), *Rockin' Into The Night* (A&M 1979), *Wild-Eyed Southern Boys* (A&M 1980), *Special Forces* (A&M 1982), *Tour De Force* (A&M 1983), *Strength In Numbers* (A&M 1987), *Rock N Roll Strategy* (A&M 1988), *Bone Against Steel* (Charisma 1991).

3Phase

Signed to **Novamute**, 3Phase is essentially Sven Roehrig (b. Berlin, Germany) plus his various associates and technological aides. He in turn is part of the Berlin-based Tresor club and label, which has achieved lots of good press (not least via the patronage of the **Orb**'s Alex Paterson). His debut album (*Schlangenfarm* translates as 'Snake Farm') revealed Roehrig's debt to his industrial music past - he had formerly been a member of Justice League, Tox Movement and Boom Factory, and his earliest major influence was **Throbbing Gristle**. The 3Phase banner had first been invoked as his interests in techno grew, and also reflected the post-Wall Berlin spirit which gave birth to a regenerated club scene. In 1992 he collaborated with DJ Dr. Mottke for 'Der Klang Der Familie', which became the theme song to Berlin's third annual Techno festival - the Love Parade. It also provided the title of Tresor's first compilation album, and became a massive European-wide hit in its own right.
Albums: *Schlangenfarm* (Novamute 1993), *Rota* (Novamute 1993).

3rd Bass

Comprising **MC Serch** (b. Michael Berrin, 6 May 1967, Queens, New York, USA), **Prime Minister Pete Nice** (b. Peter Nash, 5 February 1967, Brooklyn, New York, USA) and DJ Richie Rich, 3rd Bass were one of the few white US rap teams to maintain any degree of credibility. **Def Jam**'s second white Jewish act (after the Beastie Boys), they were a million miles apart from their better known precursors. At their best they combined raw intelligence with strong humour and a powerful musical delivery. Their debut album, produced with the help of **Prince Paul** (**Stetsasonic**) and Sam Sever (who originally encouraged the then solo Nice and Serch to team up), was bolstered by mighty cuts like 'Steppin' To The AM', with its melange of TV samples and urban paranoia. Nice was a particularly effective mic. man, whose classes in modern poetry at Columbia University clearly shone through. However, the extent to which 3rd Bass seemed to be anxious about their skin colour was reflected by two tracks on *Derelicts Of Dialect* which both pilloried **Vanilla Ice** (notably 'Pop Goes The Weasel'). Elsewhere they could be assured and effective, 'Product Of The Environment' on their debut being a case in point. Nice would go on to a successful new career alongside Rich, while Serch would become A&R Vice-President of **Wild Pitch** Records.
Albums: *The Cactus Album* (Def Jam 1989), *The Cactus Revisited: 3rd Bass Remixes* (Def Jam 1990), *Derelicts Of Dialect* (Def Jam 1991).

T La Rock

b. c.1961, Bronx, New York, USA. Although he did not gain prominence until the 90s, old school rapper T La Rock can boast quite a heritage. His brother, **Special K**, was signed to the original **Sugarhill** label. He had also met Rick Rubin of **Def Jam**, before the latter had got his label underway. Together the duo recorded 'It's Yours' on Party Time records. La Rock fell out with Rubin when he discovered that he was also fostering the career of **LL Cool J**, who would inherit his king of the B-boys title. He cut one album, produced by himself, DJ Doc and **DJ Mark The 45 King** in 1987 for **Virgin** subsidary Ten. When he resurfaced in the 90s with *On The Warpath* **Todd Terry** was in the producer's chair. The original version of the record, which had taken four months to record, was scrapped in favour of a new Terry production. He had initially come to the **Sleeping Bag** offices to offer La Rock the chance to rap over one of his productions. The resulting album, which was originally to have included on stage banter and was vaunted to the press as *On Tour*, contained a much less hardcore, more commerical slant than expected. As a concession to his long-term supporters it also included 'Its Yours', which had previously been a much sought after and unobtainable old school classic. Alongside this were excursions into swingbeat, and a return to old B-boy stylings in 'Warpath'.

Albums: *Lyrical King* (Ten 1987), *On A Warpath* (Sleeping Bag 1990).

T'Pau

Formed in 1986, this UK group began as a songwriting partnership between vocalist Carol Decker (b. 10 September 1957, London, England) and guitarist Ronnie Rogers (b. 13 March 1959, Shrewsbury, England). While recording a demonstration disc, they were joined by session musicians Michael Chetwood (b. 26 August 1954, Shrewsbury, England; keyboards), Paul Jackons (b. 8 August 1961; bass) and Tim Burgess (b. 6 October 1961, Shrewsbury, England; drums). The group then signed to Siren Records as T'Pau, the name being taken from a character in the science fiction television series *Star Trek*. Having acquired the services of producer Roy Thomas Baker, T'Pau recorded their first sessions in Los Angeles. The group's first two singles failed to make any impact in the UK market, until 'Heart And Soul' abruptly established them in the US charts, where it climbed to number 4 in 1987. The song was re-promoted in Britain and repeated that chart placing. In order to bolster the line-up, lead guitarist Dean Howard was recruited and a major UK tour followed. Decker's strong, expressive vocals were highlighted on 'China In Your Hand', which topped the UK charts, a feat repeated by *Bridge Of Spies*. Further Top 20 hits with 'Valentine', 'I Will Be With You' and 'Secret Garden' and two more albums consolidated their standing, without threatening a return to peak form. Following their break up Decker embarked on a solo career in 1994.

Albums: *Bridge Of Spies* (1987), *Rage* (1988), *Promise* (1991). Compilation: *Heart And Soul - The Very Best Of* (1992).

T-Bones (UK)

Formed in 1964, the T-Bones - **Gary Farr** (vocals/harmonica), Winston Whetherall (lead guitar), Andy McKechnie (rhythm guitar), Stuart Parks (bass) and Andy Steele (drums) - were one of several groups active on London's R&B circuit. They made their recording debut in November that year with an uncompromising reading of 'How Many More Years', a powerful **Howlin' Wolf** song later popularized by **Led Zeppelin**. Two further singles and an excellent EP completed the T-Bones' catalogue, but the group was unable to make a significant commercial breakthrough. Steele, who later joined the **Herd**, was subsequently replaced by Brian Walkeley, and by 1966 only Farr remained from the unit's original line-up. The singer continued to front the T-Bones until early 1967. This late-period version included **Keith Emerson** (keyboards) and Lee Jackson (bass), but their sole recorded legacy rests with 'It I Had A Ticket', on which they backed jazz trombonist **Chris Barber**. Emerson and Jackson were later reunited in the **Nice**, while Farr embarked on a solo career.

Compilations: *London 1964-1965* (1980), *One More Chance* (1987).

T-Bones (USA)

This studio instrumental group came from Los Angeles, California. The group was conceived in 1964 by **Liberty Records** to record albums of surf instrumentals, and the company hired Joe Saraceno (b. 16 May 1937, Utica, New York, USA) to produce the group because of his previous experience with another studio instrumental hitmaker, the **Routers** (of 'Let's Go' fame). By its very nature the T-Bones's personnel changed from session to session. Their only Top 10 hit, 'No Matter What Shape (Your Stomach's In)' (US number 3), in 1965 was based on a jingle of an Alka Seltzer commercial. It yielded the group's fourth album, *No Matter What Shape* (1966), and its personnel included guitarist Danny Robert Hamilton (b. Spokane, Washington, USA), bassist Frank Carollo (b. Leland, Mississippi, USA), and drummer Tommy Clark Reynolds (b. New York, New York, USA). The group's follow-up, 'Slippin' 'N' Chippin' (number 62) in 1966, was based on a jingle from a Nabisco Sip 'N' Chip commercial, and produced an album of the same name. After one more album the T-Bones emerged as a vocal/instrumental group Hamilton, Joe Frank & Reynolds, hitting most notably with 'Fallin' In Love' in 1975.

Albums: *Boss Drag* (1964), *Boss Drag At The Beach* (1964), *Doin' The Jerk* (1965), *No Matter What Shape* (1966), *Slippin' And Chippin'* (1966), *Everyone's Gone To The Moon* (1966).

T-Empo

One of the major proponents of what has been fetchingly described as 'handbag house' is Tim Lennox (b. c.1966, Birmingham, Midlands, England). Lennox, like many before him, has stepped out from behind the decks to switch from being DJ to producer. He had been DJing for ten years, starting at a gay club called Heroes, in Manchester, before helping set up the notorious Flesh events at the Hacienda in 1991, settling on current home Paradise Factory shortly afterwards. His first recorded effort, featuring a typically striking vocal from Sharon D. Clark and help from producer Aron Friedman and Damon Rochefort (of **Nomad** fame), was a cover of Cuba Gooding's 'Happiness', released under the title Serious Rope. A second cover, this time of Barbara Mason's 'Another Man', also sustained critical approval. This diarama of a Brooklyn housewife dumped by her man for another lover, also male, had the camp, heightened sense of drama intrinsic to the 'handbag house' style. This was released as Shy One, after which he switched to the T-Empo name in order to engender a more structured approach to making music. Hence his band evolved, featuring Adam Clough, session singer Loretta and engineer Simon Bradshaw. After the huge success of 'Another Man' several record companies were fighting to sign Lennox, and he eventually opted for **ffrr**, based on their good record with gay/hi-NRG/house acts. However, a third release, 'Saturday Night Sunday Morning', the first to use the pseudonym T-Empo, arrived jointly with the exclusive gay record label Out On Vinyl, on which Lennox holds a director's chair. His remixing skills also rose in popularity, and, again under the name T-Empo, included the **Brand New Heavies** ('Dream On Dreamer'), **RuPaul** ('House Of Love'), **Grace Jones** ('Slave To The Rhythm'), **Joe Roberts** ('Lover') and **K Klass** ('Rhythm Is A Mystery'). The Joe Roberts mix was a particular triumph, when ffrr promoted it to a-side status over a version from Lennox's long-time hero, **David Morales**.

T-Ride

This innovative trio originated in Santa Clara, California, where childhood friends Eric Valentine (drums) and Dan Arlie (bass/vocals) linked up with guitarist Jeff Tyson to produce an effective blend of musical influences and styles. Signed to Hollywood Records, the band rejected the label's offers of major production names like Eddie Kramer in favour of their drummer, who had already amassed considerable production experience with a variety of acts, in addition to producing the excellent demo which clinched their deal. Valentine duly made a sterling job of *T-Ride*. The band were compared most obviously to **Queen** and **Van Halen** due to the sheer variety of the material, quality musicianship and songwriting, and stunning vocal harmonies, but the delivery also had sufficient humour and individuality to give the band their own identity. The debut attracted a succession of positive reviews, moving **Joe Satriani** to describe the band as the future of metal, and T-Ride were equal to the task of transferring their songs to the live arena, but the album simply disappeared, and the band have been quiet since.
Album: *T-Ride* (Hollywood 1992).

T. Rex

Although initially a six-piece group, formed by **Marc Bolan** (b. Mark Feld, 30 July 1947, Hackney, London, England; vocals/guitar) in 1967 on leaving **John's Children**, the new venture was reduced to an acoustic duo when a finance company repossessed their instruments and amplifiers. Steve 'Peregrine' Took (b. 28 July, 1949, London, England; percussion) completed the original line-up which was originally known as **Tyrannosaurus Rex**. Nurtured by disc jockey **John Peel**, the group quickly became an established act on the UK 'underground' circuit through numerous live appearances. Bolan's quivering voice and rhythmic guitar-playing were ably supported by Took's frenetic bongos and the sound created was one of the most distinctive of the era. 'Debora', their debut single, broached the UK Top 40, while a follow-up, 'One Inch Rock', reached number 28, but Tyrannosaurus Rex found a wider audience with their albums. *My People Were Fair...* and *Prophets, Seers & Sages* encapsulated Bolan's quirky talent and while his lyrics, made obtuse by a sometimes impenetrable delivery, invoked pixies, fawns, the work of J.R.R. Tolkien and the trappings of 'flower-power', his affection for pop's tradition resulted in many memorable melodies. Bolan also published *The Warlock Of Love*, a collection of poems which entered the best-selling book lists.

Unicorn (1969) introduced a much fuller sound as Tyrannosaurus Rex began to court a wider popularity. Long-time producer **Tony Visconti** emphasized the supporting instruments - organ, harmonium, bass guitar and drumkit - while adding piano on 'Catblack', one of the more popular selections. However, tension between Bolan and Took led to the latter's departure and Mickey Finn (b. 3 June 1947), formerly with **Hapshash And The Coloured Coat**, took his place in 1970. The ensuing *A Beard Of Stars* completed the transformation into a fully-fledged electric group and while the lyrical content and shape of the songs remained the same, the overall sound was noticeably punchier and more direct. The most obvious example, 'Elemental Child', featured Bolan's long, almost frantic, guitar solo. The duo's name was truncated to T. Rex in October 1970. The attendant single, 'Ride A White Swan', rose to number 2, a success which confirmed an irrevocable change in Bolan's music. Steve Currie (bass) and Bill (Fifield) Legend (drums) formerly of **Legend**, the Epics and Bateson And Stott, were added to the line-up for 'Hot Love' and 'Get It On', both of which topped the UK charts, and *Electric Warrior*, a number 1 album. *T. Rextacy* became the watchword for pop's new phenomenon which continued unabated when 'Jeepster' reached number 2. However, the track was issued without Bolan's permission and in retort the singer left the Fly label to found his own T. Rex outlet. The pattern of hits continued throughout 1972 with two polished chart-toppers, 'Telegram Sam' and 'Metal Guru', and two number 2 hits, 'Children Of The Revolution' and 'Solid Gold Easy Action', while the now-anachronistic 'Debora' reached the Top 10 upon re-release. A documentary, *Born To Boogie*, filmed by **Ringo Starr**, captured this frenetic period, but although '20th Century Boy' and 'The Groover' (both 1973) were also substantial hits, they were the group's last UK Top 10 entries. Bolan's relationship with Visconti was severed following 'Truck On (Tyke)' and a tired predictability crept into the singer's work.

Astringent touring of Britain, America, Japan and Australia undermined his creativity, reflected in the disappointing *Zinc Alloy...* and *Bolan's Zip Gun* albums. American soul singer **Gloria Jones**, now Bolan's girlfriend, was added to the group, but a series of departures, including those of Currie, Legend and Finn, emphasized an internal dissent. Although 'New York City' bore a 'T. Rex' credit, the group had been officially declared defunct with session musicians completing future recordings. A series of minor hits - 'Dream Lady', 'London Boys' and 'Laser Love' - was punctuated by 'I Love To Boogie', which reached the UK Top 20, but its lustre was removed by charges of plagiarism. However unlike many contemporaries, Bolan welcomed the punk explosion, championing the **Damned** and booking **Generation X** on his short-lived television show, *Marc*. The series featured poignant reunions with **David Bowie** and John's Children singer Andy Ellison and helped halt Bolan's sliding fortunes. A working unit of **Herbie Flowers** (bass) and Tony Newman (drums) was formed in the wake of a new recording deal with **RCA**, but on 16 September 1977, Marc Bolan was killed when the car in which he was a passenger struck a tree. The first of several T. Rex related deaths, it was followed by those of Took (1980) and Currie (1981). A vociferous fan-club has kept Bolan's name alive through multiple reissues and repackages and the singer has retained a cult popularity. Although his spell as a top-selling act was brief, he was instrumental in restating pop values in the face of prevailing progressive trends.

Albums: as Tyrannosaurus Rex *My People Were Fair And Had Sky In Their Hair But Now They're Content To Wear Stars On Their Brows* (1968), *Prophets Seers & Sages, The Angels Of The Ages* (1968), *Unicorn* (1969), *A Beard Of Stars* (1970); as T. Rex *T. Rex* (1970), *Electric Warrior* (1971), *The Slider* (1972), *Tanx* (1973), *Zinc Alloy And The Hidden Riders Of Tomorrow Or A Creamed Cage In August* (1974), *Bolan's Zip Gun* (1975), *Futuristic Dragon* (1976), *Dandy In The Underworld* (1977), *T. Rex In Concert - The Electric Warrior Tour 1971* (1981). Compilations: *The Best Of T. Rex* (1971, contains Tyrannosaurus Rex material), *Bolan Boogie* (1972), *Great Hits* (1973), *Light Of Love* (1974), *Marc - The Words And Music 1947-1977* (1978), *Solid Gold T. Rex* (1979), *The Unobtainable T. Rex* (1980), *Children Of Ranr Suite* (1982), *Across The Airwaves* (1982), *Beyond The Rising Sun* (1984), *The Best Of The 20th Century Boy* (1985), *Dance In The Moonlight* (1985), *Billy Super Duper* (1985), *Till Dawn* (1985), *The T. Rex Collection* (1986), *Get It On* (1986), *A Crown Of Jewels* (1986), *The Singles Collection* (1987), *The Marc Shows* (1989).

Further reading: *Tyrannosaurus Rex*, Stevenson, Ray (1991).

T.A.S.S.

German heavy metal trio who combine the industrial approach of **Front 242** with more conventional metal riffing for a result not unlike that produced in recent years by **Machine Head**. Formed in Berlin by ex-Voodoo Club members 'The Voodoo' and 'Dr. Rabe', they expanded to a trio in the summer of 1992 with the addition of American singer and lyricist Collier. Their combination of monolithic guitars, pounding dance rhythms and intelligent sampling recalled **Nine Inch Nails** at their most pummelling.

Album: *Maniafesto* (Gun 1994).

T.O.B.A.

The Theatre Owners Booking Association was an organization which booked black acts into US black theatres for black audiences between 1911 and 1930. Thus, TOBA was formed for reasons rooted in prejudice and racism and the majority of the people behind the organization were white. At the height of the era the organization had a circuit of some 80 theatres strung between Philadelphia and Dallas. The association was known among entertainers as 'Tobytime' although some thought that 'Tough On Black Acts' might be a more appropriate explanation of the acronym. An unfortunately large number who felt they had been badly treated considered 'Tough On Black Asses' to be even more apt. Among the entertainers who worked on the Tobytime circuit were, the brilliant dance teams the Nicholas Brothers and the Berry Brothers, and **Bessie Smith**, **Bill 'Bojangles' Robinson**, **Ida Cox**, **Bert Williams**, dancer Rubberlegs Williams, comedian Moms Mabley, **Ethel Waters**, **Beulah 'Sippie' Wallace**, **Fletcher Henderson**, **Joe 'King' Oliver**, **Alphonso Trent**, **Bennie Moten**, **Luis Russell**, **Count Basie**, dancers Buck and Bubbles, comedians and singers Butterbeans And Susie, **Ma Rainey**, **Victoria Spivey**, **Sammy Price**, **Duke Ellington** and **Louis Armstrong**. For all the deficiencies in management which prompted criticism from performers, TOBA was extremely important in providing a focus for the emerging sense of identity of Afro-American culture in the 20s. There is little doubt that it was also an invaluable organization in advancing, admittedly for its own profit, the development of performers of the highest quality. Those who saw the leading acts during their Tobytime days, also the time when many were at their peak, were convinced that those whose names are now forgotten were at least the equal of the tiny handful of black acts which broke through the barrier and entertained on white stages in the 20s.

T.S. Monk

This funk group was formed by New Yorker Thelonious Sphere Monk Jnr., the son of the legendary and revolutionary jazz pianist. Jazz greats **Max Roach** and **Art Blakey** started him on the road to being a drummer by giving him his first drum kit. He played in his father's group for a couple of years in the early 70s and can be heard on two of tenor man **Paul Jeffrey**'s albums. In 1974 he recorded on **Atlantic** with Natural Essence, which is where he met singer Yvonne Fletcher. Together with Yvonne and his sister Boo Boo he formed the group Cycles in 1976 and did backing sessions for hit producer Sandy Linzer. Linzer, known for his work with **Odyssey**, then worked with the trio and placed them (with the new name T.S. Monk) on Mirage Records. Their first single 'Bon Bon Vie' made the R&B Top 20 and hit the UK charts as did the follow-up 'Candidate For Love', both being taken from their US Top 100 album *House Of Music*. Despite the encouraging start their sophomore album *More Of The Good Life* made a lesser impact and the act, which also included an eight-piece band, soon vanished from sight. Albums: *House Of Music* (1981), *More Of The Good Life* (1982), *Take One* (1992).

T.V. Slim

b. Oscar Wills, 10 February 1916, Houston, Texas, USA. d. 21 October 1969, Kingman, Arizona, USA. A musician from the late 30s, Wills was resident and recording in Louisiana during the 50s, playing guitar (and harmonica, though not on record), and singing blues in a voice that was rich and laidback on slow songs, hoarse and exciting on uptempo ones. He operated his own Speed label, but recorded the humorous tale of 'Flat Foot Sam' ('always in a jam') for Cliff; when Cliff went out of business, Slim acquired the tape and leased it to Checker, for whom it was a novelty hit. Wills moved to California in 1959, and did some touring and recording, but was chiefly occupied running the television repair shop that gave him his nickname. He died in a car crash while returning from a gig in Chicago.
Albums: *Goin' To California* (1979), *Flat Foot Sam* (c.1984).

T99

This group, whose roots were in Belgian new beat, produced one of 1991's biggest rave tunes with 'Anasthasia', after which they moved from **XL** to **Columbia**. The followed it up with 'Nocturne', sung by Perla Den Boer with a rap from Zenon Zevenbergen. Their debut album saw them add a further, more speedy rapper for several of the cuts, but they were still some way short of the artistic mark set by the Detroit stalwarts, which they were desperately trying to emulate. However, the resonant 'Anasthasia' was later sampled by both **2 Unlimited** and even **Kylie Minogue**. T99 is a duo of Patrick De Meyer and Oliver Abeloos.
Album: *Children Of Chaos* (Columbia 1992).

Tabackin, Lew

b. 26 March 1940, Philadelphia, Pennsylvania, USA. Tabackin studied music extensively - at high school, the Philadelphia Conservatory and privately - before beginning his playing career in 1965. He played tenor saxophone and flute with various bands in and around New York, including those led by **Tal Farlow**, **Maynard Ferguson**, **Clark Terry**, **Cab Calloway**, the band led by **Larry** and **Les Elgart**, the **Thad Jones-Mel Lewis** Jazz Orchestra and the rehearsal bands of **Duke Pearson** and **Chuck Israels**. He also led his own small group and was also active in the east coast television studios. In the late 60s he was briefly in Europe, playing and teaching in Germany and Denmark. In 1970 he began a musical, and eventually personal relationship with **Toshiko Akiyoshi**. After their marriage he was principal soloist with their orchestra, which was based in Los Angeles during the 70s and in New York from the early 80s. In the late 80s and early 90s he was frequently on tour around the world, usually as a single. A superb technician on tenor saxophone, Tabackin's powerful playing style contains echoes of several of his influences, most strikingly **Sonny Rollins**. He is, however, a distinctive and accomplished performer in his own right. His solos, often dazzling and lengthy unaccompanied cadenzas interpolated into Akiyoshi's frequently complex charts, are filled with extraordinarily fluent and brilliantly executed ideas. In contrast Tabackin's flute playing gleams with softly executed yet vivid concepts. In addition to his albums with the Akiyoshi-Tabackin band, he has also recorded with **Bill Berry** (who was instrumental in introducing Tabackin and Akiyoshi to one another), with **Louie Bellson**, fellow tenorist **Warne Marsh**, Toshiyuki Miyama and his New Herd on *Vintage Tenor*, and with his own small groups.
Albums: *Tabackin* (1974), *Dual Nature* (1976), *Trackin'* (1976), *Tenor Gladness* (1976), *Rites Of Pan* (1977), *Vintage Tenor* (1978), *Black And Tan Fantasy* (1979), *Lew Tabackin Quartet* (1983), *Angelica* (1984), *Desert Lady* (Concord 1989), *I'll Be Seeing You* (Concord 1992).

Tabor, June

b. 31 December 1947, Warwick, England. Tabor is a fine interpreter of both contemporary and traditional songs. Her acclaimed debut, *Airs And Graces*, immediately made her a favourite singer for numerous session appearances. She has collaborated with **Martin Simpson** on several occasions, resulting in *A Cut Above*, as well as with **Maddy Prior** from **Steeleye Span** with whom she has recorded as the Silly Sisters. *Freedom And Rain* was recorded with the **Oyster Band**, which saw Tabor departing into more of a rock format which many felt was long overdue. In addition, following a period of working with Huw Warren (piano), Tabor recorded *Some Other Time*, which included jazz standards such as 'Round Midnight'. Other collaborations utilizing her exceptional voice have been with **Nic Jones**, **Martin Carthy**, **Peter**

Bellamy, the **Albion Band** and **Fairport Convention**. A number of her earlier albums have recently been re-released, and the excellent Conifer compilation *Aspects* was well-received.

Albums: *Airs And Graces* (Topic 1976), *Ashes And Diamonds* (1977), *Bees On Horseback* (1977), with Martin Simpson *A Cut Above* (1980, *Abyssinians* (Topic 1983), *Theme From 'Spy Ship'* (1983), *The Peel Sessions* (1986), with Maddy Prior *Silly Sisters* (1986), *Aqaba* (Topic 1988), *Some Other Time* (1989), with Maddy Prior *No More To The Dance* (1990), *Angel Tiger* (Cooking Vinyl 1992), *Against The Streams* (Cooking Vinyl 1994). Compilation: *Aspects* (Conifer 1990), *Anthology* (1993).

Tackhead

A UK dub/hip hop/dance outfit who formed in 1987 and released a remarkable first single, 'The Game', with a Brian Moore (football commentator) sample and backbeat which comprised metal guitar and electro 'Hi-NRG' attack, together with football chants. The band comprised **Keith LeBlanc** (previously behind the groundbreaking 'Malcolm X' single; percussion, keyboards), plus Doug Wimbush (bass) and Skip McDonald (guitar). Together they had previously operated as the **Sugarhill Gang** house band, in their home town of Bristol, Connecticut, USA, performing on the likes of 'Rapper's Delight', 'The Message' and 'White Lines'. Before which they had also been major contributors, as Wood Brass & Steel, to many of the recordings which emerged from another Sylvia Robinson label, All Platinum. Migrating to London in 1984, they became a central component in **Adrian Sherwood**'s **On U Sound** label. Sherwood became the mixmaster who would take the trio's basic tracks and add a little club magic. Although they all appeared on LeBlanc's solo work, their first recording as Tackhead came with **Gary Clail** as vocalist in 1987 - *Tackhead Tape Time* - which was jointly credited. They subsequently recruited Bernard Fowler, who appeared on their best album, *Friendly As A Hand Grenade*. Its follow-up set, *Strange Things*, was an unfortunate shot at crossover success, following the band's relocation to the US. Guest contributions from **Melle Mel**, **Lisa Fancher** and even **Mick Jagger** on harmonica did little to elevate a dour reading of dance-rock. In 1991 Leblanc joined with Tim Simenon (**Bomb The Bass**) in a new project titled Interference.

Albums: As Gary Clail's Tackhead Sound System: *Tackhead Tape Time* (Nettwerk/Capitol 1987). As Tackhead: *Friendly As A Hand Grenade* (TVT 1989), *Strange Things* (SBK 1990).

Tacuma, Jamaaladeen

b. Rudy MacDaniel, 11 June 1956, Hempstead, New York, USA. Tacuma grew up in Philadelphia and sang doo-wop as a teenager. He has named his youthful inspirations as **James Brown**, the **Temptations** and **Stevie Wonder**. He started playing double bass at the age of 13 and his first professional gig was with organist **Charles Earland**. He was brought to the world's attention by his participation in **Ornette Coleman**'s seminal *Dancing In Your Head* in 1977 (his name was still listed as Rudy MacDaniel since this was before his conversion to Islam). He had the ability to combine slick, dance-oriented riffs with an ear open to Ornette's harmolodic weaving of contrasting keys and tempi. He also appeared on *Body Meta* (1978, rec. 1975) and *Of Human Feelings* (1979) as part of Prime Time, Ornette's electric band. In 1978 he played on **James Blood Ulmer**'s thunderous masterpiece *Tales Of Captain Black*. In 1981 he received the highest number of votes ever received for an electric bassist in the 'Talent Deserving Wider Recognition' category of the *downbeat* critics' poll. His debut for Gramavision in 1983, *Showstopper*, presented his own sleek, airbrushed version of harmolodics. The follow-up, *Renaissance Man* (1984), had a disco version of the 'Dancing In Your Head' theme (on which Ornette guested), a poem for **Paul Robeson** and an extended suite for string quartet and fretless bass; the album lived up to its name. Having produced the excellent '(I Want To) Squeeze You Hold You' for Willy (**Mink**) **DeVille** in 1983, he went on to form a pop/dance band, Cosmetic, that released a cover of **Smokey Robinson**'s 'Get Ready' for **Rough Trade Records** and a (stunning) album of out-and-out commercial music, *So Tranquilizin'*. Such attention to the commercial jugular caused **Bill Laswell** to call him the 'pimp' of harmolodics; Tacuma preferred to call it a 'Trojan horse' operation. In April 1985 he presented his music at Carnegie Recital Hall with the Ebony String Quartet, drummer Anton Fier and an orchestra led by **Anthony Davis**. The same year he was back with Prime Time for *Opening At The Caravan Of Dreams* and he also played on the harmolodic half of Coleman's 1987 *In All Languages* double set. *Music World* (1987) and *Juke Box* (1989) confirmed his ability to flit between genres while maintaining his own special flavour. Other involvements have been as a founder member of **Golden Palominos**, and backing both guitarist **Jeff Beck** and poet Jayne Cortez.

Albums: *Showstopper* (1983), with Cosmetic *So Tranquilizin'* (1984), *Renaissance Man* (1984), *Music World* (1987), *Juke Box* (1989), *Boss Of The Bass* (1993).

Tad

The monolithic noise engine which is Tad was formed in Seattle, USA, in 1988, by Tad Doyle (b. Idaho; vocals/guitar) and Kurt Danielson (bass), who had previously been working together with the delightfully titled Bundles Of Piss. Fellow miscreants Gary Thorstensen (guitar) and Josh Sinder (drums) joined later. With the rise of the American north west and the **Sub Pop** imprint in particular, Tad became pre-

eminent among that label's bands - though in truth there was always a strong metallic undercurrent which set them aside from the traditional hardcore-rooted sound of grunge. Lyrically too, as *God's Ball* all too clearly demonstrates, they were closer in style to **Black Sabbath** than **Black Flag** (song titles included 'Nipple Belt' and 'Satan's Chainsaw'). Whatever, the career of Tad has always proved entertaining. Sharing a touring van with **Nirvana** in 1989 on their first European jaunt they were ideally placed to see the destruction of the Berlin wall, though on a later European excursion they were offered the perfect contrast when the Belfast hotel in which they were staying was bombed by the IRA (the explosive device malfunctioned). *Salt Lick* saw production from Steve Albini (**Big Black**, **Rapeman**, **Shellac**) and, understandably, was even noisier as a result. *8-Way Santa* earned much of its notoriety from a sleeve which featured a man fondling a woman's breast - an endearing picture found in a garage-sale photo album. However, this prompted a legal suit in 1991 by the woman concerned (and her second husband) which forced its removal. That was hardly the end of the group's travails, however. On their US tour with **Primus** in the summer of the same year they narrowly missed being struck by lightning. The following year in Canada further calamity was averted when a mountain boulder descended and crashed through their van, just behind the driver's seat. *Inhaler* would be the group's first album for a major, though bad-tempered songs like 'Grease Box' and 'Lycanthrope' hardly suggested a relaxing of attitudes. Tad Doyle, meanwhile, enjoyed a little celebrity with a small part in Cameron Crowe's *Singles* film, before his band made their debut for a major label with 1995's *Infrared Riding Hood*.
Albums: *God's Balls* (Sub Pop 1989), *Salt Lick* (Sub Pop 1990), *8-Way Santa* (Sub Pop 1991), *Inhaler* (Music For Nations 1993), *Live Alien Broadcast* (Music For Nations 1994), *Infrared Riding Hood* (East West 1995).

Taffola, Joey

b. c.1965, USA. Beginning his career on the guitar at the age of 14, Joey Taffola served his apprenticeship with the unremarkable speed-metal outfit **Jag Panzer**. In 1987 he left the band and returned to California to take instruction from guitar guru **Tony Macalpine**. Moving to the Guitar Institute Of Technology, Taffola studied jazz, rock and classical styles alongside Paul Gilbert (later of **Racer X**). After recording a series of demos, Shrapnel boss Mike Varney signed Taffola to produce a guitar instrumental album. With the help of former Jag Panzer drummer Reynold Carlson and ex-**Rising Force** bassist Wally Voss, *Out Of The Sun* appeared in 1987. Although the album featured guest appearances by Paul Gilbert (guitar) and Tony Macalpine (keyboards), it lacked both direction and individuality. Taffola's style proved a characterless

hybrid of **Yngwie Malmsteen**'s, Macalpine's and **Vinnie Moore**'s styles. After an aborted band project featuring ex-Rising Force vocalist Mark Boals, Taffola started work on his second album, *Infa Red*.
Album: *Out Of The Sun* (Roadrunner 1987), *Infa Red* (Roadrunner 1991).

Taggart, Blind Joe

Joel 'Blind Joe' Taggart was second in popularity to only **Blind Willie Johnson** as a 'guitar evangelist'. Like Johnson he often employed a female voice on his sessions and although he did not have Johnson's vocal range or his guitar skills, he did produce many recordings that are as effective today as when they were recorded. These range from his earlier, often unaccompanied duets with his wife Emma (some made before Johnson got to record) to his later days when his own guitar work had much improved and he was often aided by a very young **Josh White**. He also used the voices of his son James and daughter Bertha and had his work issued under the pseudonyms Blind Jeremiah Taylor, Blind Tim Russell and Blind Joe Donnell. It is generally accepted that the singer who recorded 'C and O Blues' at one of his sessions in 1927 under the name of Blind Joe Amos was also Taggart disguising his involvement with the 'devil's music'.
Selected albums: *Blind Joe Taggart: A Guitar Evangelist* (1972), *Blind Joe Taggart 1926 - 1934* (1984).

Tairrie B

Tairrie (pronounced Terry) was one of executive producer **Eazy-E**'s less successful protégés. Heralded as the rap **Madonna**, she failed to achieve sales with her debut album. This despite having two tracks produced by **Schoolly D** and the eloquence of cuts like 'Ruthless Bitch'. Some critics suggested that the delivery, though tidy and competent, lacked power.
Album: *The Power Of A Woman* (Comptown 1990).

Tait, Lynn

b. c.1946, Jamaica. Lynn didn't take up the guitar until his fourteenth year - until then he'd been seriously involved in steel pan music. However, he was soon fronting his own band in Trinidad who were booked to play the Independence celebrations in 1962 in Jamaica by **Byron Lee**. Lynn liked Jamaica so much that he decided to stay there, working his way through the Sheiks, the Cavaliers and the Comets - all 'live' bands that didn't actually make any recordings - although he had recorded with the **Skatalites**. His next group, Lynn Tait & The Jets, which included Hux Brown, Headley Bennett, Hopeton Lewis, Gladstone Anderson and **Winston Wright**, were contracted to Federal Records in 1967. Their recording of 'Take It Easy' with Hopeton Lewis as featured vocalist was one of the first **rocksteady** records - (although many others lay claim to that honour) - and it went straight to number

1. Many see the rocksteady period in Jamaican music as one of the most creative and musically adventurous, and Lynn Tait & The Jets were the rocksteady session band at the eye of the storm. They recorded hit after hit for Federal, Wirl, **Derrick Harriott**, **Bunny Lee & Beverley's**, **Sonia Pottinger** and **Duke Reid**, sometimes doing up to five sessions a day for different producers. Lynn's modesty about his part in this musical evolution is as gentle as his guitar playing, and he felt that to have the public liking what he did was more than enough, indeed a 'great gift'. All he was interested in was 'creating beautiful music'. Some of his recordings with **Johnny Nash**, such as 'Cupid' and 'Hold Me Tight', even stole into the UK national charts, and he will always be fondly remembered as a musical giant of the rocksteady era.
Selected album: *Rock Steady Greatest Hits* (Merritone).

Taj Mahal

b. Henry Saint Clair Fredericks, 17 May 1940, New York City, New York, USA. The son of a jazz arranger, Mahal developed his early interest in black music by studying its origins at university. After graduating, he began performing in Boston clubs, before moving to the west coast in 1965. The artist was a founder member of the legendary **Rising Sons**, a respected folk-rock group which also included **Ry Cooder** and **Spirit** drummer Ed Cassidy. Mahal resumed his solo career when the group's projected debut album was shelved. His first solo album, *Taj Mahal*, released in 1968, was a powerful, yet intimate compendium of electrified country blues which introduced an early backing band of **Jesse Davis** (guitar), Gary Gilmore (bass) and Chuck Blakwell (drums). A second album, *The Natch'l Blues*, offered similarly excellent fare while extending his palette to include interpretations of two soul songs. This early period reached its apogee with *Giant Steps/The Ole Folks At Home*, a double-album comprising a traditional-styled acoustic album and a vibrant rock selection. Mahal continued to broaden his remarkable canvas. *The Real Thing*, recorded in-concert, featured support from a tuba section, while the singer's pursuit of ethnic styles resulted in the African-American persuasion of *Happy Just To Be Like I Am* and the West Indian influence of *Mo Roots*. He has maintained his chameleon-like quality over a succession of cultured releases, during which the singer has remained a popular live attraction at the head of a fluctuating backing group, known initially as the Intergalactic Soul Messengers, then as the International Rhythm Band.
Albums: *Taj Mahal* (1968), *The Natch'l Blues* (1968), *Giant Steps/The Ole Folks At Home* (1969), *The Real Thing* (1971), *Happy Just To Be Like I Am* (1971), *Recycling The Blues And Other Related Stuff* (1972), *The Sounder* (1973), *Oooh So Good 'N' Blues* (1973), *Mo' Roots* (1974), *Music Keeps Me Together* (1975), *Satisfied 'N Tickled Too* (1976), *Music Fuh Ya'*

(1977), *Brothers* (1977), *Evolution* (1977), *Taj Mahal And The International Rhythm Band Live* (1979), *Going Home* (1980), *Live* (1981), *Take A Giant Step* (1983), *Taj* (1987), *Live And Direct* (1987), *Mule Bone* (1991), *Like Never Before* (Private Music 1991), *Dancing The Blues* (Private Music/BMG 1994, *An Evening Of Acoustic Music* (Tradition and Moderne 1995). Compilation: *Going Home* (1980), *The Taj Mahal Collection* (1987).

Take 6

Initially a quartet known as the Sounds Of Distinction then the Alliance, this highly-rated ensemble first formed in northern Alabama, USA in 1980. The group evolved into a six-piece **a cappella** gospel group of breathtaking ability. The members are Alvin Chea, Cedric Dent, David Thomas, Mervyn Warren, Mark Kibble and Claude V. McKnight. The combination of their Seventh-day Adventist beliefs and their appreciation of jazz and R&B has enabled them to make inroads into both record buying markets, winning Grammies for best Soul Gospel and best Jazz Vocal categories. Their 1990 appearance with **k.d. lang** in the movie *Dick Tracy* singing 'Ridin' The Rails' has given them further valuable exposure. Additionally they have recorded with **Dianne Reeves**, **Quincy Jones** and **Joe Sample**. *Join The Band* marked a new direction for the group as it incoporated live musicians including **Greg Phillinganes**, Gerald Albright and **Herbie Hancock**. It also featured lead vocals from **Ray Charles**, **Stevie Wonder** and a rap from **Queen Latifah**. Music writer David Okamota aptly described Take 6 as 'winning over a loyal congregation of secular fans with a soothing, uplifting sound that stirs the soul without twisting the arm'.
Albums: *Take 6* (Reprise 1988), *So Much 2 Say* (Reprise 1990), *He Is Christmas* (Reprise 1992), *Join The Band* (Reprise 1994).

Take A Chance

The stories of the changes that are made to shows on the road during their pre-Broadway or West End try-outs are legendary, but not many can have undergone such radical reforms as this one. In September 1932 it was a revue entitled *Humpty Dumpty* with sketches and songs that dealt in an amusing way with certain aspects of American history. The material was linked by two members of the company seated in one of the theatre boxes, but the remainder of the audience in Pittsburg, Pennsylvania did not see the joke, and *Humpty Dumpty* had a great fall after just five days up there on the wall. However, when the show - re-titled *Take A Chance* - opened at the Apollo Theatre on Broadway on 26 November, it had been turned into a conventional book musical, in which the stars, Jack Whiting and June Knight, are appearing together in a revue called *Humpty Dumpty* with songs and sketches - that naturally enough - deal in an amusing way with certain aspects of

American history. The original score by **Richard Whiting** and **Nacio Herb Brown** (music) and **Buddy De Sylva** (lyrics) had been supplemented by several numbers by the composer **Vincent Youmans**. There were also some important changes in the cast, but fortunately **Ethel Merman** survived to sing (clearly and fairly loudly) the pick of the output from this impressive array of songwriters. She introduced the show's three big hits, 'Eadie Was A Lady' (De Sylva-Whiting-**Roger Edens**), 'Rise 'n' Shine' (De Sylva-Youmans), and 'You're An Old Smoothie' (De Sylva-Whiting-Brown) on which she duetted with 'innocent-abroad' comedian Jack Haley. The love-interest, Jack Whiting and June Knight, shared most of the other numbers which included 'Should I Be Sweet?', 'Oh, How I Long to Belong To You' and 'So Do I' (all three by De Sylva and Youmans), along with 'Turn Out The Lights' (De Sylva-Whiting-Brown), for which Whiting and Knight were joined by Haley and the show's other funny man, Sid Silvers. He also collaborated on the book with De Sylva and Laurence Schwab. With America emerging slowly from the Depression, *Take A Chance* was just the tonic that Broadway audiences needed, and they kept on coming for 243 performances. Towards the end of the run, Haley and Silvers were replaced by Olsen and Johnson, the vaudeville comedy team, who were making their debut in a legitimate Broadway musical. June Knight appeared in the 1933 film version, which came up with yet another variation on the original theme, along with Lillian Roth, James Dunn, and **Cliff Edwards** ('Ukelele Ike').

Take Me Along

Bob Merrill, the composer and lyricist for a host of pop hits during the 50s, wrote his first Broadway score in 1957 for *New Girl In Town*, a musical adaptation of Eugene O'Neill's classic drama *Anna Christie*. Two years later, for *Take Me Along*, he tackled another of the playwright's works, but one with a much lighter theme - *Ah, Wilderness!* It opened at the Shubert Theatre in New York on 22 October 1959 with a strong cast which was headed by a legendary Hollywood leading man of the 30s and 40s, Walter Pidgeon, and **Jackie Gleason**, whose main claim to fame at that time was as a comedian on US television. Joseph Stein and Robert Russell wrote the book which was set in the homely town of Centerville, Connecticut in 1910. Pidgeon plays Ned Miller, the publisher of the local newspaper, and the father of Richard, whose adolescent problems with his girlfriend, Muriel Macomber (Susan Luckey), and the devil drink, are resolved when he enters the hallowed halls of Yale University. The sub-plot concerns Sid Davis (Jackie Gleason), a far more serious drinker, who would like to settle down with Ned's sister, Lily (Eileen Herlie), but he will have to sober up before she will have him.

Pidgeon and Gleason duetted on the the lively 'Take Me Along', and the rest of Merrill's score, which has been called 'wistful and enchanting', included 'I Would Die', 'Staying Young', 'I Get Embarrassed', 'Sid Ol' Kid', 'We're Home', 'Promise Me A Rose', 'Nine O'Clock', and 'But Yours'. Walter Pidgeon and Jackie Gleason were both nominated for the **Tony Award** for best actor, and Gleason won for the most satisfying stage role of his career. He was succeeded during the show's run of 448 performances by William Bendix, the movie tough-guy with a heart of gold; it sounds like perfect casting. *Take Me Along* returned to Broadway during the 1984/5 season, which, according to experienced Broadway watchers, was one of the worst in living memory. The climate was not right for the show's warm and charming approach, and it closed after only one performance.

Take Me High

Following a period of reticence, **Cliff Richard** re-entered the world of celluloid with this 1973 exercise. However, the plot of *Take Me High* suggested the singer had learned nothing from the years since *The Young Ones* and *Summer Holiday*. The story revolves around the exploits of a merchant banker as he attempts to defeat a rival for a prized account but in the meantime opens a hamburger restaurant in Birmingham. Respite cannot be salvaged from Richard's musical contributions which reach a nadir with 'The Brumburger Duet'. *Take Me High* has barely nothing to commend it, few artists of Cliff's standing and experience have made such a professional blunder and yet survived with career intact.

Take Me Out To The Ball Game

A kind of a rehearsal for the historic *On The Town*, which was also released in 1949, except that **Frank Sinatra**, **Gene Kelly** and Jules Munshin are dressed mostly in baseball gear in this one, instead of their more familiar sailor suits. Actually, at the beginning of the film, Dennis Ryan (Sinatra) and Eddie O'Brien (Kelly), are clad in natty striped suits and straw boaters while engaging in their off-season occupation as a song-and-dance team in vaudeville. When they re-join Nat Goldberg (Munshin) and the rest of their Wolves team-mates at the Florida training camp, it is to find that the team has a new boss - Miss K.C. (Katharine) Higgins (**Esther Williams**). She takes the job so seriously that she is only spotted in the hotel swimming pool once. Under her strict supervision, the team is well on the way to winning the pennant when a bunch of racketeers try to knobble O'Brien, and his performance suffers. However, a little love and affection from Katharine soon raises his batting average again, and the Wolves go on to glory. **Betty Garrett** chases (and catches) Sinatra - as she does in *On The Town* - and their duet, 'It's Fate Baby, It's Fate' (**Roger Edens**), is one of the film's highspots. Sinatra is suitably romantic with 'The Right Girl for Me' (**Betty Comden-Adolph Green**-Edens), and Kelly has his moments - along with other members of the cast - in 'Yes Indeedy', 'O'Brien To Ryan To Goldberg', 'Strictly USA', (all Comden-Green-Edens), 'The Hat My Father Wore Upon St. Patrick's Day' (Jean Schwartz-William Jerome), and 'Take Me Out To The Ball Game' (**Albert Von Tilze**r-Jack Norworth). Also involved in Harry Tugend and George Wells's turn-of-the-century screenplay (adapted from a story by Kelly and **Stanley Donen**) were Edward Arnold, Richard Lane, Sally Forrest, Murray Alper, William Graff, and the Blackburn Twins. Kelly and Donen also staged some nifty dance routines, and the whole affair was presided over by another ace choreographer, director **Busby Berkeley**. George Folsey photographed the picture splendidly in Technicolor, and it was produced by **Arthur Freed**'s MGM unit. It was re-titled *Everybody's Cheering* in the UK.

Take My Tip

Billed as a musical, but more of a farce, this immensely entertaining vehicle for the husband-and-wife team of **Cicely Courtneidge** and **Jack Hulbert** was produced by Gaumont-British Pictures in 1937. Lord and Lady Pilkington, otherwise known as George and Hattie (Hulbert and Courtneidge), have fallen on hard times due to George's extravagance and naiveté. The crunch finally comes when he purchases a non-existent oil well for £15,000 from a cove called Buchan (Harold Huth), after meeting him in a Turkish Bath. Happily, help is at hand in the person of George and Hattie's trusted servant, Paradine (Frank Cellier), who has recently bought an hotel in Dalmatia with the money he has made backing horses that his boss (George) *didn't* fancy. He offers his former employers jobs in the hotel as head waiter (George) and hostess (Hattie). While there they adopt various disguises (and somewhat devious means) to retrieve their money from Buchan - complete with a handsome £5,000 profit. All ends satisfactorily (and democratically) with Paradine, George and Hattie going into partnership together. Incidentally, Hattie is an ex-musical comedy actress and George is a nifty hoofer, so there is plenty of excuse for the inclusion of songs such as, 'Birdie Out Of A Cage', 'Colonel Bogey' (Kenneth J. Alford), 'The Sleepwalker', 'Sentimental Agitation', 'I'm Turning The Town Upside Down', 'Everybody Dance', and the delightful duet, 'I Was Anything But Sentimental' (Sammy Lerner-**Al Hoffman**-Al Goodhart). Also taking part in the fun and games were Frank Pettingell, comedian Robb Wilton, Philip Buchel, H.F. Maltby, Elliot Makeham, and Paul Sheridan. In charge of the mayhem was director Herbert Mason.

Take That

Formed in Manchester, England, Take That have, in commercial terms at least, come closest to emulating the **Beatles**' legacy of phenomenal mass popularity in the 90s. Teen pop can be a fickle career, but their rise has thus far shown no signs of abating, and one similarity they display in common with their Liverpool cousins is the rare ability to unite both young and middle-aged music fans. The group is led by lead vocalist Gary Barlow (b. 20 January 1971, Frodsham, Cheshire, England), with Mark Anthony Owen (b. 27 January 1974), Howard Paul Donald (b. 28 April 1968, Droylsden, Manchester, England), Jason Thomas Orange (b. 10 July 1970, Manchester, England) and Robbie Williams (b. 13 February 1974, Port Vale, England). As a child Barlow was a talented musician, and backed **Ken Dodd** shows on the organ by the time he was 14. His first break came when he submitted a song, 'Let's Pray For Christmas', which was short-listed and played on the 'A Song For Christmas' competition on BBC television's *Pebble Mill*. Owen had failed soccer trials for Manchester United before taking work at an Oldham bank, while Orange was a former breakdancer brought up as a Mormon. Williams' mother was singer and his father a comedian and prior to the commencement of Take That he had a small role in Channel 4's *Brookside* soap opera. Donald's parents, too, had a musical background, before he took up work in a garage and joined Orange in a breakdancing unit, Street Beat. Barlow, Owen and Williams were formerly part of The Cutest Rush. Take That released their debut single, 'Do What U Like', on their own Dance U.K. label in July 1991. Much of the publicity they initially attracted surrounded the risqué video which accompanied it, featuring the band revealing their buttocks. The furore helped to make up the minds of **RCA Records**, who signed the band in September, and 'Promises' subsequently reached number 38 in the UK charts two months later. In February 1992 'Once You've Tasted Love' reached number 47, coinciding with a 'Safe Sex' club tour undertaken with the support of the Family Planning Association, before June brought their UK chart breakthrough with a cover of the **Tavarés**' 'It Only Takes A Minute'. By the time it reached number 7 in the UK charts the country's pop press swooped on them for their clean-cut (with the exception of the bearded Orange) good looks, dance routines and simple, catchy songs. Barlow also stepped up his reputation as a songwriter for the ensuing *Take That And Party*, which debuted at number 5 in the UK album charts. October's *A Million Love Songs* EP, led off by its powerful ballad title-track originally written by Barlow aged 16, also reached number 7. Their popularity was confirmed by the receipt of seven trophies at the *Smash Hits* Readers Poll Party Awards in December, as effective a barometer as any of the prevailing tastes of the UK's youth. By the following year the fortunes of the group's debut album were resuscitated as it climbed to number 2 in the UK charts, following the number 3 success of their cover of **Barry Manilow**'s 'Could It Be Magic'. This also won them a BRIT Award for Best British Single in February, before 'Why Can't I Wake Up With You' rose to number 2 at the end of the same month. By April the group's debut album and 'It Only Takes A Minute' had been launched in the US, with the help of a Take That cereal box, but initial forays into the American market proved unsuccessful. 'Pray' became their first UK number 1 in July 1993, a feat repeated with 'Relight My Fire', featuring a guest appearance from **Lulu**, in October. In the meantime the band were concentrating on recording their second album, and when *Everything Changes* duly emerged on 23 October 1993 it debuted at number 1 in the UK charts. Proving that their popularity was not impinging on their prolific release schedule, 'Babe' became a third successive UK number 1 in December, though it eventually lost the coveted Christmas number 1 spot to **Mr Blobby**. The group's success continued throughout 1994, and into 1995, when 'Sure' and 'Back For Good' earned them two more UK number 1 placings. The latter song demonstrated much more substance than their usual lightweight pop. There were strong signs that Take That were finally being accepted by the music critics. Younger fans were shocked when Williams announced his departure for a solo career in mid-1995, although the writing had been on the wall for some time as his participation in *Nobody Else* had been minimal.

Albums: *Take That And Party* (RCA 1992), *Everything Changes* (RCA 1993), *Nobody Else* (RCA 1995).
Videos: *Take That And Party* (1992), *Take That: The Party-Live At Wembley* (1993).
Further reading: *Take That: Our Story*, Morgan, Piers (1993), *Everything Changes*, Take That (1994).

Talas

This US hard rock outfit was masterminded by bass virtuoso Billy Sheehan. Enlisting the services of former **Chain Reaction** vocalist Phil Naro, guitarist Mitch Perry and drummer Mark Miller, they specialized in melodic, guitar-orientated rock with a strong commercial edge. After the release of a self-financed debut album in 1980 the band began to build up a small, but loyal fanbase. This attracted the attention of Food For Thought Records. Enjoying a larger budget, Talas delivered *Sink Your Teeth Into That* in 1982. This was a showcase for Sheehan's amazing bass work and featured 'Shyboy', which he later re-recorded with **Dave Lee Roth**. At this point the band were put on hold, as Sheehan helped out **UFO** on their European tour. After an unfruitful association with **Steve Stevens**, Sheehan put Talas back on the road and

recorded *Live Speed On Ice* in 1983. The album did not sell and the band became redundant as Sheehan then left to join Dave Lee Roth's band and later formed **Mr. Big**.

Albums: *Talas* (Relativity 1980), *Sink Your Teeth Into That* (Food For Thought 1982), *Live Speed On Ice* (Important 1983). Compilation: *The Talas Years* (Combat 1990).

Talion

This UK speed-metal quartet, formerly known as Trojan, formed in 1988, the line-up comprising Graeme Wyatt (vocals), Pete Wadeson (guitar), Phil Gavin (bass) and Johnny Lee Jackson (drums). Influenced by **Metallica**, **Megadeth** and **Judas Priest**, their niche was uninspired and at times amateurish speed metal. Signed to the independent Major Records, they debuted with *Killing The World* in 1989. This was a fairly lacklustre recording which ensured that the band did not progress beyond pub-rock status.

Album: *Killing The World* (Major 1989).

Talisman

This Swedish melodic heavy metal band was founded in 1989 by ex-**Rising Force** bassist Marcel Jacob. Recruiting vocalist Jeff Scott Soto and guitarist Christopher Stahl, they joined Airplay Records and made their debut the following year with a self-titled album, incorporating elements of **Europe**, **Yngwie Malmsteen** and **TNT**. High-pitched vocal harmonies and bursts of fiery guitar were the band's trademarks, but they failed to make an impression outside Sweden.

Album: *Talisman* (Airplay 1990).

Talk Talk

Formed in 1981, this UK pop group comprised Mark Hollis (b. 1955, Tottenham, London, England; vocals), Lee Harris (drums), Paul Webb (bass), Simon Brenner (keyboards). They were soon signed to **EMI** who were intent on moulding them into the same league as stablemates **Duran Duran**. In fact they could not have been more different. They went along with their company's ideas for the first album which produced a number of hit singles including, 'Talk Talk' and 'Today'. Labelled as a 'New Romantic' band, they were very keen to shake off the tag and dismissed their keyboard player to make them a looser, more flexible creative unit. For the next couple of years Hollis spent the time writing new material and assembling a pool of musicians to record a second album. The format was repeated with the highly accessible *The Colour Of Spring*, both records were critically acclaimed and showed the band as a more creative and imaginative act than their debut had suggested. It was their fourth album *Spirit Of Eden* that showed their true musical preferences. A solemn six-track record, it had no commercial appeal, and no obvious single. Its poor showing led to EMI dropping the band who signed with Polydor. It was three years before a new studio album appeared, and to fill in the gap a greatest hits compilation was issued without the band's permission. It nevertheless managed to sell over a million copies and give them three more hit singles. Ironically, their biggest success so far was an EMI reissue of their previous hit 'Its My Life'. *Laughing Stock* picked up where they had left off although to date they have failed to match the catchy commercial appeal of *The Colour Of Spring*.

Albums; *The Party's Over* (1982), *Its My Life* (1984), *Its My Mix* (1984), *The Colour Of Spring* (1986), *Spirit Of Eden* (1988), *Laughing Stock* (1991). Compilations: *Natural History: The Very Best Of Talk Talk* (1990), *History Revisited* (1991, remixes of greatest hits).

Talkin' Loud

Gilles Peterson's extension of the original **Acid Jazz** empire, which has, if anything, gone on to outshine that UK imprint. Peterson originally ran a jazz funk pirate station from his own garden shed. He subsequently gained his own show on the leading Invicta pirate in exchange for lending them his transmitter. Taking a residency as the jazz room of the Electric Ballroom in Camden, North London, he was invigorated by the legendary atmosphere and freeform dancing that occurred there. The formula was relocated to Soho's Wag Club, then Camden's legendary Dingwalls Club . The first Talkin' Loud nights began at the Fridge. He had returned to piracy after his Mad On Jazz show had been axed after encouraging people to join the anti-Gulf War marches, and he eventually settled at Kiss-FM. In the meantime he was also working alongside Eddie Piller at Acid Jazz, before splitting to form his own label, named after his Talkin' Loud nights, when the finance was put forward by Phonogram. Signings include **Galliano**, **Young Disciples**, **Omar** (before he departed for **RCA**), **Urban Species** (probably the label's biggest hopes for the future) and others. Talkin' Loud's greatest moments so far have included the triology of Galliano releases which culminated in 1994's *The Plot Thickens*, which at last saw the band doing the business for the label, the Young Disciples' 'Apparently Nothin'' 45 with **Carleen Anderson**'s unmistakable vocal, and Omar's 'There's Nothing Like This' cut. The Urban Species debut album was also widely applauded. New signings include hip hop/jazz fusioners the Roots, from Philadelphia, as Talkin' Loud continues to explore a number of new musical horizons. Peterson has also started a new club, The Way It Is, with James Lavelle of **Mo Wax**.

Selected albums: Young Disciples: *Road To Freedom* (Talkin' Loud 1991). Urban Species: *Listen* (Talkin' Loud 1994). Galliano: *The Plot Thickens* (Talkin' Loud 1994).

Talking Heads

One of the most critically acclaimed groups of the past two decades, Talking Heads pursued an idiosyncratic path of (often) uncompromising brilliance. After graduating from the Rhode Island School of Design, students **David Byrne** (b. 14 May 1952, Dumbarton, Scotland; vocals/guitar), Chris Frantz (b. Charlton Christopher Frantz, 8 May 1951, Fort Campbell, Kentucky, USA; drums) and Tina Weymouth (b. Martina Weymouth, 22 November 1950, Coronado, California, USA; bass) relocated to New York. In 1975, they lived and rehearsed in Manhattan and named themselves Talking Heads. After appearing at the club CBGBs, they were approached by Seymour Stein of **Sire Records**, who would eventually sign the group. Early in 1976, the line-up was expanded to include pianist Jerry Harrison (b. Jeremiah Harrison, 21 February 1949, Milwaukee, Wisconsin, USA), a former member of **Jonathan Richman**'s **Modern Lovers**. The group's art school background, witty invention and musical unorthodoxy was evident on their intriguingly titled debut, 'Love Goes To Building On Fire'. After touring extensively, they issued *Talking Heads '77*, an exhilarating first album, which was widely praised for its verve and intelligence. The highlight of the set was the insistent 'Psycho Killer', a *tour de force*, in which singer Byrne displayed his deranged vocal dramatics to the full. His wide-eyed stare, jerky movements and onstage cool reminded many commentators of Anthony Perkins, star of Hitchcock's movie *Psycho*.

For their second album, the group turned to **Brian Eno** as producer. *More Songs About Buildings And Food* was a remarkable work, its title echoing Talking Heads' anti-romantic subject matter. Byrne's eccentric vocal phrasing was brilliantly complemented by some startling rhythm work and the songs were uniformly excellent. The climactic 'The Big Country' a satiric commentary on consumerist America, featured the scathing aside: 'I wouldn't live there if you paid me'. The album also featured one cover version, an interesting reading of **Al Green**'s 'Take Me To The River', which was a minor hit. Eno's services were retained for the more opaque *Fear Of Music*, which included the popular 'Life During Wartime'. Byrne next collaborated with Eno on *My Life In The Bush Of Ghosts*, before the group reunited for *Remain In Light*. The latter boasted the superb 'Once In A Lifetime', complete with 'found voices' and African polyrhythms. An edited version of the song provided one of the best hit singles of 1981. During the early 80s, the group's extra-curricular activites increased and while Byrne explored ballet on *The Catherine Wheel*, Franz and Weymouth found success with their spin-off project, **Tom Tom Club**. The live double *The Name Of This Band Is Talking Heads* served as a stop-gap until *Speaking In Tongues* appeared in the summer of 1983. As ambitious as ever, the album spawned the group's UK Top 10 single, 'Burning Down The House'. While touring with additional guitarist Alex Weir (formerly of the **Brothers Four**), the group were captured on film in *Stop Making Sense*, the soundtrack of which sold well. The excellent *Little Creatures*, a more accessible offering than their more experimental work, featured three strong singles in the title track, 'And She Was' and 'Road To Nowhere'. The latter brought the group their biggest chart hit and was accompanied by an imaginative and highly entertaining video. In 1986, Byrne moved more forcibly into movies with *True Stories*, for which Talking Heads provided the soundtrack; it was two more years before the group reconvened for *Naked*. Produced by Steve Lillywhite, the work included musical contributions from **Level 42** producer Wally Badarou and guitarists Yves N'Djock and Johnny Marr (from the **Smiths**). Since then Talking Heads have branched out into various offshoot ventures; there was an official announcement of their break-up at the end of 1991. The single- and double-album retrospectives released in October 1992 provided a fairly definitive assessment of their career, including some interesting rarities, but without doing justice to a band rightly regarded as one of the best and most influential of their time.

Albums: *Talking Heads '77* (1977), *More Songs About Buildings And Food* (1978), *Fear Of Music* (1979), *Remain In Light* (1980), *The Name Of This Band Is Talking Heads* (1982), *Speaking In Tongues* (1983), *Stop Making Sense* (1984), *Little Creatures* (1985), *True Stories* (1986, film soundtrack), *Naked* (1988). Compilations: *Once In A Lifetime: The Best Of* (1992), *Popular Favorites 1976 - 1992 (Sand In The Vaseline)* (1992)

Videos: *Stop Making Sense* (1986), *Storytelling Giant* (1988).

Further reading: *Talking Heads*, Miles (1981), *The Name Of This Book Is Talking Heads*, Reese, Krista (1983), *Talking Heads: The Band And Their Music*, Gans, David (1986), *Talking Heads: A Biography*, Davis, Jerome (1987).

Tall Stories

This cult AOR band was formed in New York in 1988 by vocalist/guitarist Steve Augeri. The Tall Stories line-up settled with the addition of lead guitarist Jack Morer and the experienced rhythm section of Tom DeFaria (drums) and Kevin Totoian (bass). The latter had replaced Anthony Esposito (bass), who would join **Lynch Mob**, while numerous early drummers included the **Damn Yankees**' Michael Cartellone. The band's abilities developed as they played the clubs around the tri-state area of New York, New Jersey and Connecticut, and they were signed by **Epic**. The Frank Fillipetti-produced *Tall Stories* was universally hailed as an AOR classic, with an artful guitar-based delivery reminiscent of **Tyketto**. Augeri's vocals evoked **Journey**'s **Steve Perry** and **Strangeways**' Terry Brock in addition to Tyketto's Danny Vaughn.

However, like many good 90s AOR albums, *Tall Stories* remains an undiscovered gem, and the band have been quiet since.

Album: *Tall Stories* (Epic 1991).

Talmy, Shel

b. c.1940, Chicago, Illinois, USA. Having spent his early career in television, Talmy took up a post as engineer at Conway Recorders, an independent studio in Los Angeles. Here he made uncredited contributions to several 'surfing' hits, notably by the Castells and Marketts. In 1963 Talmy arrived in the UK where he successfully persuaded **Decca** to provide work on a freelance basis, making him the country's first independent producer. His early work was strictly MOR, but early hits with the homely **Bachelors** allowed a freedom to place groups with different labels and explore new styles of music. In 1963 he began a fruitful partnership with the **Kinks** which, over the next four years, resulted in a series of seminal 60s singles, including 'You Really Got Me' (1964), 'Sunny Afternoon' (1966) and 'Waterloo Sunset' (1967). Such success inspired his relationship with the **Who**, which included two highlights of the exciting group's early work, 'I Can't Explain' and 'My Generation'. However, relations between the two parties were severed, rancorously, in 1966, when Talmy refused to renegotiate the group's percentage royalty. An out-of-court settlement ended their agreement, but the producer continued to earn a royalty from the band's records until 1970. Talmy also produced material for the **Easybeats**, notably the startling 'Friday On My Mind', as well as releases by Davy Jones (later **David Bowie**), the **Zephyrs** and Rockin' Vickers.

His skills lay in an ability to bring out a special performance and equip it with a requisite punch, rather than create a homogeneous sound which was moulded irrespective of the act's ability. In 1965 he founded the Planet label, but although its catalogue boasted the excellent **Creation**, arguably his exemplary act, the company's other work was largely undistinguished. Talmy continued his commercial success with **Manfred Mann** and **Amen Corner**, but by the late 60s switched to the album market with **Roy Harper** and the **Pentangle**. During the early 70s Talmy produced work for **String Driven Thing** and Fumble, but found little artistic satisfaction in the era's prevalent progressive rock style. Punk offered a return to quicker, simpler recording, as evidenced in a brief collaboration with the **Damned**, but Talmy had now become restricted by gradual blindness. He subsequently returned to California and although undertaking several production projects, including work for surf-revivalists **Jon And The Nightriders** (1983) and the **Fuzztones** (1989), has pursued concurrent interests in publishing. Talmy also retains the rights to many of his 60s masters, which have

become the subject of judicious re-releases.
Recommended listening - the Who *My Generation* (1966), the Kinks *The Hit Singles Collection* (1987), the Creation *How Does It Feel To Feel* (1982).

Talulah Gosh

Formed in Oxford, England, in February 1986, the much-maligned Talulah Gosh emerged in the aftermath of the *New Musical Express*'s influential *C86* promotion. Taking their name from an *NME* **Clare Grogan** interview headline, the group came to symbolize a movement that would come to be tagged 'shambling'. Its hard-core followers indulged themselves by wearing asexual basin hair-cuts (boys) or straight short fringes (girls), plain anoraks, plus the affectation of a child-like innocence. The music borrowed a great deal from the **Ramones**, **Velvet Underground** and US 60s girl-groups while the lyrics dealt with boy/girl relationships but barely mentioned sex in obvious 'rock 'n' roll' terms, and their un-elitist sense of fun endeared them to many. These particular exponenents consisted of Peter Momtchiloff (b. 10 March 1962, Weybridge, Surrey, England; guitar), Pebbles (b. Elizabeth Price, 6 November 1966, Bradford, Yorkshire, England; vocals/tambourine), Robert Pursey, replaced early on by Chris Scott (b. 31 October 1961, Hemel Hempstead, Hertfordshire, England; bass), Marigold (b. Amelia Fletcher, 1 January 1966, London, England; vocals/guitar) and her brother Mathew Fletcher (b. 5 November 1970, London, England; drums). One of the group's most popular early songs was 'The Day She Lost Her Pastels Badge', which combined the movement's tweeness with a nod to the band many identified as its figureheads. They scored two UK Independent Top 5 singles with 'Steaming Train'/'Just A Dream' and 'Beatnik Boy'/'My Best Friend', both on the Edinburgh-based 53rd & 3rd label, which were later compiled on the best-selling *Steaming Train* EP in 1987. Elizabeth Price, who left in December 1986, was replaced by Eithne Farry (b. 21 May 1965, Chelsea, London, England) as second vocalist. Price later created the Cosmic English Music label with Gregory Webster (formerly of the **Razorcuts**) and as a duo also formed the Carousel. One final UK Independent chart hit ensued for Talulah Gosh with 'Bringing Up Baby' the following year and a later album, *They've Scoffed The Lot*, released on **Sarah Records**, contained tracks from various BBC Radio 1 sessions from both line-ups. The group split in early 1988, due to university commitments and a consensus that the group had run its course. Farry and Scott later appeared in Saturn 5, while Momtchilof, who had briefly played in the final line-up of the Razorcuts, joined the Fletcher siblings in a successful revival of the 'Gosh formula as **Heavenly** in 1990.
Albums: *They've Scoffed The Lot* (Sarah 1991).

Compilation: *Rock Legends Volume 69* (Sarah 1987, collects single releases).

Tamam Shud

Evolving in 1967 out of a series of bands which had developed a cult following along the New South Wales coastline in Australia, Tamam Shud were led by Lindsay Bjerre (lead vocals/guitar) and comprised Peter Baron (bass), Daniie Davidson (drums), Larry Duryrea (congas), Alex 'Zac' Zytnik (guitar). The band took up the mantle of a progressive blues-based concert band, renowned for performing long instrumentals. Initially adopted by the burgeoning psychedelic and drug scene, their popularity rapidly took in the surfing fraternity and the college circuit. Their two albums are considered progressive and adventurous, featuring the guitar work of Tim Gaze, who joined in 1970. After the band petered out in 1972, Bjerre continued an undistinguished solo career with two lightweight albums. Gaze ventured to the UK with his new band Khavas Jute before re-uniting with Shud drummer Nigel Maccara in **Ariel**.
Albums: *Evolution* (1969), *Gooluntionites And The Real People* (1970).

Tamla-Motown Records

(see **Motown Records**)

Tamlins

Among reggae music's most accomplished but least widely-acknowledged backing-singers, the Tamlins comprise Carlton Smith, Junior Moore and Derrick Lara. Together they spent several years touring in support of **Peter Tosh**, and also backed **John Holt**, **Delroy Wilson**, **Pat Kelly** and **Marcia Griffiths** in the studio. They branched out on their own in the 80s, with Lara's high-pitched vocals gaining deserved recognition for its Philly-soul stylings.
Selected album: *Love Devine* (Heartbeat).

Tampa Red

b. Hudson Woodbridge aka Whittaker, c.8 January 1904, Smithville, Georgia, USA; d. 19 March 1981, Chicago, Illinois, USA. Tampa Red was raised in Tampa, Florida by his grandmother Whittaker's family, hence his nickname. By the time of his 1928 recording debut for Vocalion, he had developed the clear, precise bottleneck blues guitar style that earned him his billing, 'The Guitar Wizard'. He teamed with **Thomas A. Dorsey** in Chicago in 1925, and they were soon popular, touring the black theatre circuit. 'It's Tight Like That', recorded in late 1928, was a huge hit, fuelling the hokum craze. They recorded extensively, often in *double entendre* vein, until 1932, when Dorsey finally moved over to gospel. Tampa also recorded with his Hokum Jug Band, featuring **Frankie Jaxon**, and alone, in which capacity he cut a number of exquisite guitar solos. By 1934, when Tampa signed with Victor, he had ceased live work outside Chicago. He was with Victor for nearly 20 years, recording a great many titles. During the 30s, many of them were pop songs with his Chicago Five, often featuring his kazoo. Usually a live solo act, he worked on record with various piano players. He was also an accomplished pianist, in a style anticipating that of **Big Maceo**, who became his regular recording partner in 1941. In the late 40s, Tampa was still keeping up with trends, leading a recording band whose rhythmic force foreshadows the post-war Chicago sound.

Tampa Red's wife Frances was his business manager, and ran their home as a lodging house and rehearsal centre for blues singers. Her death in the mid-50s had a devastating effect on Tampa, leading to excessive drinking and a mental collapse. In 1960, he recorded two under-produced solo albums for Bluesville, also making a few appearances. However, he had no real wish to make a comeback, and lived quietly with a woman friend, and from 1974 in a nursing home. In a career that ranged from accompanying **Ma Rainey** to being backed by **Walter Horton**, he was widely admired and imitated, most notably by **Robert Nighthawk**, and wrote many blues standards, including 'Sweet Black Angel', 'Love Her With A Feeling', 'Don't You Lie To Me' and 'It Hurts Me Too' (covered respectively by **B.B. King**, **Freddy King**, **Fats Domino** and **Elmore James** among others).

Selected albums: *Don't Tampa With The Blues* (1960), *Don't Jive Me* (1961), *Bottleneck Guitar* (1974), *Guitar Wizard* (1975), *The Guitar Wizard* (c.1976), *Crazy With The Blues* (1981), *Tampa Red i* (1982), *Tampa Red ii* (1983), *Midnight Blues* (1988), *Get It Cats'* (1989), *Volume 2* (1990), *Bottleneck Guitar 1928 - 1937* (1993), *Complete Recorded Works 1934-53 Vol. 6* (Document 1994).

Tams

This US group was formed in 1952 as the Four Dots in Atlanta, Georgia, USA. Their line-up featured Joseph Pope (b. 6 November 1933), Charles Pope (b. 7 August 1936), Robert Lee Smith (b. 18 March 1936), and Horace Kay (b. 13 April 1934). Although such an early origin suggests longevity, it was not until 1960 that the group emerged with a single on Swan. Now dubbed the Tams (derived by their wearing of Tam O'Shanter hats on stage), they added a further member, Floyd Ashton, (b. 15 August 1933), prior to signing with Bill Lowery, an Atlanta song publisher and entrepreneur. Among those already on his books were **Joe South** and Ray Whitley, two musicians who would work closely with the group. 'Untie Me', a South composition, was recorded at Fame and leased to Philadelphia's Arlen Records. The song became a Top 20 US R&B hit, but follow-up releases failed until 1963 when Lowery secured a new deal with **ABC** Paramount. The Tams' first single there, 'What Kind Of Fool (Do You Think I

Am)', reached the US Top 10 and established a series of Whitley-penned successes. His compositions included 'You Lied To Your Daddy' and 'Hey Girl Don't Bother Me', ideal material for Joe Pope's ragged lead and the group's unpolished harmonies. After 1964, the group preferred Atlanta's Master Sound studio, by which time Albert Cottle (b. 1941, Washington, DC, USA) had replaced Ashton. South and Whitley continued their involvement, writing, playing on and producing various sessions, but the Tams only further US hit in 1968 with the bubbling 'Be Young, Be Foolish, Be Happy', which peaked on the ***Billboard*** R&B chart at 26 and reached the UK Top 40 in 1970. By the end of the 60s their mentors had moved elsewhere while the Master Sound houseband was breaking up. Dropped by ABC, the Tams unsuccessfully moved to 1-2-3 and **Capitol** until a chance reissue of 'Hey Girl Don't Bother Me' became a surprise UK number 1 in 1971. They were not to chart again until 16 years later when their association with the Shag, a dance craze and subsequent 80s film, secured a further lifeline to this remarkable group, giving the group a UK Top 30 with 'There Ain't Nothing Like Shaggin''.

Albums: *Presenting The Tams* (ABC 1964), *Hey Girl Don't Bother Me* (ABC 1964), *Time For The Tams* (ABC 1967), *A Portrait Of The Tams* (ABC 1969), *Be Young, Be Foolish, Be Happy* (Stateside 1970). Compilations: *A Little More Soul* (ABC 1968), *The Best Of The Tams* (1-2-3 Capitol 1971), *The Mighty Mighty Tams* (Sounds South 1978), *Greatest Hits - Beach Party Vol. 1* (Carousel South 1981), *Atlanta Soul Connection* (Charly 1983), *Beach Music From The Tams* (Compleat 1983), *Reminiscing* (Wonder 1982), *There Ain't Nothing Like...The Tams* (Virgin 1987).

Tana, Akira

b. 14 March 1952, San Jose, California, USA. A self-taught drummer, Tana played semi-professionally while still at college. He attended Harvard University where he gained a degree in East Asian Studies/Sociology. He then studied at the New England Conservatory of Music, also taking private tuition from percussionists with the Boston Symphony and Boston Pops Orchestras and from jazz drummer **Alan Dawson**. During his studies he had the opportunity of working with **Helen Humes**, **Milt Jackson**, **Sonny Rollins**, **George Russell**, **Sonny Stitt** and other leading jazz musicians. He also played with the Boston Symphony Orchestra and several of the classical music ensembles at the New England Conservatory. In the early 80s he continued to accompany major artists such as **Al Cohn**, **Art Farmer**, **Benny Golson**, **Jim Hall**, **Jimmy Rowles**, **Zoot Sims** and **Cedar Walton**. He also performed with artists outside the jazz world, including **Charles Aznavour** and **Lena Horne**. Tana recorded extensively during these years and in addition to albums with some of the foregoing also appeared with **Ran Blake**, **Chris Connor**, **Carl Fontana**, **Jimmy Heath**, **Tete Montoliu**, **Spike Robinson**, **Warne Marsh** and many others. In the early 90s Tana worked with **James Moody**, **Dizzy Gillespie**, **Frank Wess**, **Ray Bryant** and **J.J. Johnson**. With **Rufus Reid** he formed the band TanaReid and, with Reid and Kei Akagi, the Asian American Jazz Trio. A technically accomplished drummer, Tana's wide range is hinted at by the musicians with whom he has worked. Comfortably at home accompanying singers and instrumental ballads, Tana is equally in his element playing hard bop. In the bands he co-leads with Reid he generates an excitingly propulsive rhythmic drive. In addition to playing, Tana has also produced and co-produced several albums including those by TanaReid, the Asian American Jazz trio and Project G-7. He regularly conducts workshops and clinics at colleges and universities, including **Berklee College Of Music**, and is an adjunct professor at two colleges.

Albums: with Zoot Sims *I Wish I Were Twins* (1983), with TanaReid *Yours And Mine* (1990), with Sumi Tonooka *Taking Time* (1990), with Asian American Jazz Trio *Sound Circle* (1991), with Project G-7 *A Tribute To Wes Montgomery Vol. 1* (1991), with TanaReid *Passing Thoughts* (1992).

Tanega, Norma

b. 30 January 1939, Vallejo, California, USA. Her Filipino parents actively encouraged their daughter's interest in music and art, both of which she studied. Although classically-trained, Tanega quickly showed a preference for guitar. She moved to New York to work as a graphic artist, but quickly became immersed in the city's folk enclave. She drew encouragement from **Bob Dylan** and **Tom Paxton** and her prolific songwriting resulted in a recording deal. Tanega's debut single, 'Walkin' My Cat Named Dog' (1966), reached number 22 both in the US and UK charts, and she was optimistically categorized alongside other lyrical artists, including **Janis Ian** and **Bob Lind**. Sadly, Tanega's hit proved to be her strongest composition; further releases were unsuccessful and the first phase of the singer's career ended almost as quickly as it had begun. She briefly re-emerged in 1977 with an album recorded for **RCA Records**.

Albums: *Walkin' My Cat Named Dog* (1966), *I Don't Think It Will Hurt* (1977).

Tangerine Dream

Like **Amon Duul** and **Can**, Tangerine Dream were German-based purveyors of imaginative electronic music. There have been numerous line-ups since the band's formation in 1968, although Edgar Froese (b. 6 June 1944, Tilsit, East Prussia) has remained at the head of affairs throughout. After playing with college band the Ones, who released a single and performed for Salvador Dali at his villa, Froese put together Tangerine Dream with himself on guitar, Voker Hombach (flute/violin), Kirt Herkenber (bass) and Lanse Hapshash (drums). Heavily influenced by US bands like the **Doors**, **Jefferson Airplane** and the **Grateful Dead**, they performed live at various student counter culture events. By 1969 they had split and remained inactive until Froese recruited Steve Jollife (electric flute). He departed soon after, although he would return to the fold later. A debut album was recorded, for which Froese brought in Konrad Schnitzler and **Klaus Schulze**, who would later embark on a solo career for **Virgin Records**. Jazz drummer Christoph Franke (ex-Agitation Free) joined in 1971, as did organist Steve Schroyder. This line-up recorded *Alpha Centauri*, which combined space age rock in the style of **Pink Floyd** with classical structures. Peter Baumann (ex-Ants) replaced Schroyder, and this became the band's first stable line-up, staying together until 1977.

Zeit saw the band's instrumentation incorporate new synthesizer technology, while *Atem* focused on atmospheric, restrained passages. Influential BBC disc jockey **John Peel** elected it the best album of 1983. *Phaedra* established their biggest foothold in the UK market when it reached number 15 in the album charts in 1974. Their attentions turned, however, to a series of film soundtracks, while Froese released his first solo, *Aqua*. At the height of punk, and as one of the named targets of the insurrection, *Stratosfear* emerged. It was their most commercial album so far. Guitar, piano and harpsichord were all incorporated, taking the edge off the harsh electronics. After the hectic touring schedule of the following year, Baumann left to pursue his solo career. He would go on to form his own Private Music label, and, ironically, sign Tangerine Dream for releases in the USA. He was replaced by former member and multi-instrumentalist Jollife, as well as drummer Klaus Kreiger. The ensuing *Cyclone* featured vocals and lyrics for the first time, although they returned to instrumental work with *Force Majeure*. As the new decade dawned, the band became the first western combo to play in East Berlin. *Tangram* and *Exit* relied on melody more than their precursors, the latter featuring the emotive 'Kiev Mission', which included a message from the Russian Peace Movement. *Le Parc* used advanced sampling technology, which seemed to be a little at odds with the band's natural abilities. Schmoelling became the next to depart for a solo career in 1985, replaced by classically trained Paul Haslinger. Three years later Chris Franke, after 17 years service, followed Schmoelling's example. Computer programmer Ralf Wadephal took his place but when he left the band elected to continue as a duo. Although often criticized, the band was pivotal in refining a sound which effectively pioneered new-age ambient electronic music more than a decade later.

Their importance in this field should not be underestimated.

Albums: *Electronic Meditation* (1970), *Alpha Centauri* (1971), *Zeit* (1972), *Atem* (1973), *Phaedra* (1974), *Rubycon* (1975), *Ricochet* (1975), *Stratosfear* (1976), *Encore* (1977), *Sorcerer* (1977, soundtrack), *Cyclone* (1978), *Force Majeure* (1979), *Thief* (1980, soundtrack), *Tangram* (1980), *Quichotte* (1980), *Exit* (1981), *White Eagle* (1982), *Wavelength* (1983, soundtrack), *Risky Business* (1983, soundtrack), *Hyperborea* (1983), *Firestarter* (1984, soundtrack), *Flashpoint* (1984, soundtrack), *Le Parc* (1985), *Legend* (1986, soundtrack), *Underwater Sunlight* (1986), *Near Dark* (1987, soundtrack), *Tyger* (1987), *Three O'Clock High* (1987, soundtrack), *Shy People* (1987, soundtrack), *Optical Race* (1988), *Lily On The Beach* (1989), *Melrose* (1990), *Rockoon* (1992), *Canyon Dreams* (1993), *Turn Of The Tides* (Miramar 1994). Compilation: *The Collection* (1987)

Videos: *Three Phase* (1993).

Tangier

This US hard rock outfit have adopted a different style on each of their albums to date. Formed in 1984 by vocalist Bill Matson and guitarist/songwriter Doug Gordon, they initially played blues-based hard rock, which paid respect to **Free**, **Molly Hatchet** and **Bad Company**. With Rocco Mazella (guitar), Mike Kost (bass) and Mark Hopkins (drums) completing the line-up, they toured frequently but failed to make a breakthrough. Five years after formation, Matson and Gordon returned with Gari Saint (guitar), Garry Nutt (bass) and Bobby Bender (drums) to record *Four Winds*. The first act to be signed to Atco, the band offered a sophisticated sound which leaned towards mainstream AOR with blues undercurrents. Matson and Saint quit in 1990, with Mike Le Compte taking over vocal duties and the band contracting to a four-piece in the process. *Stranded* emerged the following year and saw the band diversifying their approach and toughening their act. The hybrid was a little awkward at times, but more often achieved the desired end result of producing radio-friendly material with memorable choruses.

Albums: *Four Winds* (Atco 1989), *Stranded* (Atco 1991).

Tangled Feet

UK act Tangled Feet are the brainchild of Jason Relf, who is responsible for guitars, keyboards, bass, programming as well as vocals. Relf began his career at the age of 16, writing, arranging and playing bass in a 12-piece funk band, Zoock, which kindled his interest in production after he oversaw their three studio sessions. Beginning to use sequencers for the first time in mid-1989, he released his first single under the name of Solar Plexus which had some strong reviews from the dance music press and which received support from top DJ's such as **Sasha**. He then moved on to **Astralasia**, and played keyboards on their first single,

'Celestial Ocean', and co-wrote and performed on their second single and album, 'Politics Of Ecstasy'. While still a member of the band he began to collaborate with Scott James, DJ at the well-known 'Shave Yer Tongue' club. Together they released two singles under the name S.Y.T., 'Cairo Eclipse', on the **Sabres Of Paradise** label, and 'Blooma', on **Leftfield**'s Hard Hands imprint. Relf was joined in Tangled Feet by his friend and associate Paul Douglas (vocals/guitar/programming) in late 1993. Their first release together was 'Messiah', which also featured the Rays, a band Relf was producing at the same time. It was remixed by the Pylon King (who gained excellent reviews for releases such as 'The Voices Of Khwan' and 'Zexos Empire'). Strangely, Tangled Feet found themselves signed to heavy metal label **Music For Nations**' subsidiary, Devotion.

Tania Maria

b. 9 May 1948, São Luis, Maranhao, Brazil. An excellent pianist, powerful singer and enchanting live performer, Tania Maria combines in her staccato vocal style the rhythmic virtues of bebop and Latin dance, with a strong commitment to spontaneity. She learned classical piano at first, discovered the work of **Nat 'King' Cole** and **Oscar Peterson**, and moved to Paris in 1974. Maria's vitality won her a contract at a Paris nightclub for a three-month residency, and she stayed in the city for the next seven years, recording several albums that emphasized her Brazilian roots. She played the 1975 **Newport Jazz Festival** opposite **Sarah Vaughan**, was encouraged by the guitarist **Charlie Byrd**, and in 1981 she recorded *Piquant* for the USA label Concord, moved to the USA and began to develop a successful recording career there. Live recordings have captured her essence best (1984's *Wild!* is one of her most impressive), and recent commercial funk outings have obscured her originality and vividness, but her concert performances still reveal an artist of energy, musicality and originality. *No Comment* is relaxing and smooth whilst exploring the outer fringes of dance and funk. A lyric sheet is not required to appreciate her work, merely an open mind and open ears.

Albums: *Brazil With My Soul* (1978), *Live* (1978), *Tania Maria Et Niels-Henning Ørsted Pedersen* (1979), *Piquant* (1981), *Taurus* (1982), *Come With Me* (1983), *Love Explosion* (1984), *Wild!* (1985), *Made In New York* (1985), *The Lady From Brazil* (1987), *Outrageous* (1993), *No Comment* (TKM 1995).

Tank

This UK band, led by Algy Ward (bass/vocals, ex-**Damned**) with brothers Peter (guitar) and Mark Brabbs (drums), were dogged throughout their career by a reputation as **Motörhead** copyists stemming from their *Filth Hounds Of Hades* debut. The band's early power trio stance obviously owed much to Motörhead, although their songwriting style and sense of humour set them apart, and they were given a very hot reception by the notoriously intolerant Motörhead crowd on the *Iron Fist* tour. *Power Of The Hunter* showed distinct progression and included a fun cover of the **Osmonds'** 'Crazy Horses', but the collapse of Kamaflage Records shortly after the release was a setback. Undaunted, Tank emerged as a quartet with ex-**White Spirit** guitarist Mick Tucker on *This Means War*, an impressive concept album inspired by the Falklands conflict, but this too was unsuccessful, and the Brabbs brothers departed. Tank recorded two further albums, adding Cliff Evans (guitar) and drummers Graeme Crallan (on *Honour And Blood*) and Gary Taylor (on *Tank*) without any upturn in their fortunes. Tucker departed prior to the release of the latter, and the band split in 1989 after an ill-fated US club tour.

Albums: *Filth Hounds Of Hades* (Kamaflage 1982), *Power Of The Hunter* (Kamaflage 1982), *This Means War* (Music For Nations 1983), *Honour And Blood* (Music For Nations 1985), *Tank* (GWR 1988).

Tankard

Formed in 1982, prolific German thrash metal band Tankard are determined to live up to their country's reputation as a nation of beer drinkers. To drink heavily while on tour, relaxing, or in the studio is hardly uncommon in the rock world, but Tankard's interest in alcohol borders on the obsessive. Always light-hearted and loud, typical Tankard song titles include 'The Morning After' and 'Beermuda', which are delivered in a drunken assault of punk-influenced thrash guitars. While they are something of a beery institution on the European mainland, this has never translated into acceptance in the UK or US markets. *Tankwart* is an oddity, released only in their domestic market, consisting of covers of traditional German drinking songs. The previous year's *Two Faced* had seen the band take a more conventional approach to their craft with the intention of producing 'serious' music. It was not a happy compromise.

Albums: *Zombie Attack* (Noise 1985), *Chemical Invasion* (Noise 1987), *The Morning After* (Noise 1988), *Hair Of The Dog* (Noise 1990), *The Meaning Of Life* (Noise 1990), *Fat, Ugly, Live* (Noise 1991), *Stone Cold Sober* (Noise 1992), *Alien* (Noise 1993), *Two Faced* (Noise 1993), *Tankwart* (Noise 1994).

Tanksley, Francesca

b. 21 November 1957, Vincenza, Italy. Although born in Italy she grew up in Munich, where she studied music from the age of seven. She went to Boston when she was 16 to study piano and composition at **Berklee College Of Music**; then two years later she returned to Munich. In 1980 she moved to New York, working

with Melba Liston until 1983, when she joined Billy Harper's quintet with whom she toured extensively. She has also worked with Clifford Jordan, Cecil Payne, Bill Hardman and Erica Lindsay, and has led her own quintet and co-leads the Erica Lindsay/Howard Johnson Quintet. She is a fine composer too.

Albums: with Billy Harper *Destiny Is Yours* (1990), with Erica Lindsay *Dreamer* (1990).

Tannahill Weavers

This group formed in Paisley, Scotland in 1968, and took their name from the town's weaving community. Over the years, the group have undergone numerous personnel changes, with John Cassidy (flute/guitar/whistles/vocals), Davie Shaw (bass/guitar), Stuart McKay (guitar/vocals) and Gordon Duncan (bagpipes), from the early line-ups, leaving before the group recorded. Initially the group played mainly in Scotland, but in 1974 they set out on a short tour of Germany, followed by their first major tour of England. *Are Ye Sleeping Maggie*, their debut, was the first to be released on the Plant Life label. The line-up on this recording was Roy Gullane (b. Maryhill, Glasgow, Scotland; guitar/tenor banjo/vocals), who joined in 1969, Phil Smillie (b. 22 December 1955, Kelvin Hall, Glasgow, Scotland; flute/bodhran/vocals), who joined in 1975, Hudson Swan (b. 31 August 1954, Paisley, Renfrewshire, Scotland; fiddle/guitar/bouzouki), who joined in 1972, and **Dougie MacLean** (b. 27 September 1954, Dunblane, Scotland; fiddle/guitar/vocals). Tours of Europe followed, and in 1978 the group played support to **Steeleye Span** on the latter's British tour. In complete contrast, later that same year the Tannahill Weavers played support to **Dire Straits** in Holland. The numerous personnel changes that have occurred over the years have included Willie Beaton (fiddle), Mike Ward (fiddle/mandolin), Alan McLeod (bagpipes/whistles), Bill Bourne (b. Red Deer, Alberta, Canada; bouzouki/vocals), Ross Kennedy (bouzouki/vocals), Iain MacInnes (bagpipes) and Stuart Morrison (fiddle). The current line-up includes Gullane and Smillie, plus John Martin (fiddle/cello/vocals), who joined in 1989 and was formerly with **Ossian**, **Contraband**, and the Easy Club and Kenny Forsythe (bagpipes), who joined in 1991. Les Wilson (bouzouki/keyboards), who originally joined in 1982, left within the year and returned in 1989. At one time the group changed their name, albeit briefly, to Faithless Nellie Grey. Most of the group's touring is done in the USA and Europe. 1991 saw the Tannahill Weavers' 10th annual tour of the USA, with further tours and recordings planned. Despite the various changes in the line-up, the strong Celtic flavour in the music, which combines bagpipes and electric instrumentation, remains consistent.

Albums: *Are Ye Sleeping Maggie* (1976), *The Old Woman's*

Dance (1978), *The Tannahill Weavers* (1979), *Tannahill Weavers 4* (1982), *Passage* (1984), *Land Of Light* (1986), *Dancing Feet* (1987), *Cullen Bay* (Green Linnet 1990), *The Mermaid's Song* (1992). Compilation: *The Best Of The Tannahill Weavers 1979-1989* (1989).

Tannen, Holly

b. New York City, New York, USA. Described as a singer, dulcimer and piano player, and writer, Tannen has become one of the better regarded exponents of the hammer, or hammered, dulcimer. From a well-educated background, having studied anthropology, zoology and psychology, Tannen learned to play the piano. After being given an Appalachian, or mountain, dulcimer, she fell in love with the instrument and set about teaching herself to play. Moving to Berkeley, California, she met up with singer Rita Weill and guitarist Janet Smith, and performed with them often. Later the idea of combining other instruments with the dulcimer took hold, and she set about putting this into practice. She had earlier worked with **Pete Cooper** in 1979, when they recorded *Frosty Morning*, and toured Britain, Europe and the USA. She returned to California from England, in 1981, releasing *Invocation* on Kicking Mule in 1983. She also appeared on two tracks on *All Around The World*, an album by Cooper in 1990. As well as performing, and recording the instrument, Holly has regularly written a column in the west coast magazine *Folkscene*, appropriately called 'Dulcimer Corner'. After moving to England she provided another column called 'Notes From England'. Albums: with Pete Cooper *Frosty Morning* (Plant Life 1979), *Invocation* (Kicking Mule 1983), *Between The Worlds* (Gold Leaf 1985), with others *Berkeley Farms* (c.80s).

Tanner, Gid

(see **Skillet Lickers**)

Tansads

Formed around the songwriting of guitarist John Kettle and members of his family, the Tansads dispense a mixture of English folk and pop influences, with a dash of funk. Coming together in the late 80s, Kettle, his long-term partner Janet Anderton (vocals), and his brothers Robert, and Ed (bass) formed the nucleus of the band. When his youngest brother, Andrew, was recruited, the twin lead vocal sound reminded some of the 70s folk/rock giants. With Dominic Lowe on accordion and brass, 'Bug' (drums) and 'Cudo' (percussion), the band recorded *Shandyland* in 1991. Lyrically homespun, and tongue-in-cheek, *Folk North West* wrote: 'They are our future . . . and they are absolutely brilliant.' The album attracted the attention of producer Phil Tennant, and the group was signed to Musidisc (which had released the **Levellers**). Subsequent sessions resulted in 'Brian Kant' and *Up*

The Shirkers, both of which gained national airplay, and featured in *Folk Roots* and the UK independent charts. By then the sound was harder, and the lyrics contemporary, but still humorous. Extensive touring followed, along with BBC Radio 1 sessions, and the release of *Up The Shirkers* in Europe and the USA.
Albums: *Shandyland* (1991), *Up The Shirkers* (1993), *Flock* (Transatlantic 1994).

Tapscott, Horace

b. 6 April 1934, Houston, Texas, USA. Tapscott moved to Los Angeles at the age of nine and, although taught piano by his mother (an accomplished stride player), he decided to concentrate on trombone. Helped by bandleader **Gerald Wilson**, Tapscott began to play professionally, but after army service in Korea, switched back to piano, jamming on LA's Central Avenue scene with musicians such as **Sonny Criss**, **Eric Dolphy**, **Red Callender**, **Charles Lloyd** and **Buddy Collette**. For 18 months he was accompanist to singer **Lorez Alexandria**, then toured briefly with **Lionel Hampton** before deciding to remain in Los Angeles where, in 1961, he co-founded the UGMA (the Underground Musicians Association) as a community self-help organization based in the Watts area. The UGMA later became the UGMAA (the Union of God's Musicians and Artists Ascension) but has otherwise survived intact for 30 years, providing a testing ground for generations of upcoming west coast musicians (alumni include **Arthur Blythe**, **David Murray**, Roberto Miranda) as has its offshoot big band, the Pan-Afrikan Peoples Arkestra (motto: 'Our music is contributive rather than competitive'). Although (or perhaps because) Tapscott and the UGMAA served the black community and celebrated the black cultural heritage in much the same way as **Muhal Richard Abrams** and the **AACM** would do in Chicago, they found themselves neglected by the media and the mainstream record industry. Until a cluster of albums suddenly appeared in the late 70s, Tapscott had only two appearances on record to show for nearly 20 years of making music. The first, in 1968, was on alto saxophonist Criss's *Sonny's Dream: The Birth Of The New Cool*, for which Tapscott wrote and arranged all the tunes and conducted the 10-piece ensemble; the second was his own *The Giant Is Awakened*, a fiercely exciting quintet session that also marked Arthur Blythe's recording debut. (Long a collector's item, it was reissued in 1991 as part of the Novus Series '70 CD, *West Coast Hot*.) The record's evident Black Power sympathies - the 'Giant' of the title was, said Tapscott, 'the New Black Nation' - perhaps helps to explain why it was almost a decade before Tapscott was able to record again; a sudden flurry of activity producing some small-group albums and, notably, a trio of releases with the Pan-Afrikan Peoples Arkestra (*Flight 17*, *The Call*, *Live At The IUCC*) on the small, independent Nimbus label, which also initiated a series of solo piano records (*The Tapscott Sessions*) in the 80s. A dramatic, lyrical pianist - he cites **Art Tatum**, **Thelonious Monk**, **Andrew Hill**, his mother and Vladimir Horowitz as major influences - Tapscott's compositions are, he says, inspired by 'the experience of black people in America'. His tunes celebrate their history, their community, their culture; filled with blues, dance, struggle, dream, they are - as the title of his first solo album declares - the songs of the unsung. By devoting himself to their cause, Tapscott has remained largely unsung himself.

Albums: *The Giant Is Awakened* (1969), *West Coast Hot* (Novus 1970), *Songs Of The Unsung* (1978), *Flight 17* (1978), *The Call* (1978), *In New York* (1979), *Live At The IUCC* (1979), with Everett Brown Jnr. *At The Crossroads* (1980), *Dial 'B' For Barbra* (1981), *Live At Lobero* (1982), *Live At Lobero Vol II* (1982), *The Tapscott Sessions Vols 1-8* (1985-91, rec. 1982-84), *The Dark Tree Vol 1* (Hat Art 1991, rec. 1989), *The Dark Tree Vol 2* (Hat Art 1991, rec. 1989).

Tarheel Slim

b. Alden Bunn, 24 September 1924, Bailey, North Carolina, USA, d. 21 August 1977. Tarheel Slim was a blues, gospel and doo-wop singer and guitarist who took his sobriquet from the popular nickname of North Carolina - Tarheel State. Bunn learned guitar at the age of 12 and sang in church by the age of 20. He began working with the Gospel Four following World War II and then joined the Selah Jubilee Singers, with whom he first recorded, in the late 40s. As the gospel group could not record secular music, they also worked under the names the Four Barons and the Larks, recording the R&B hits 'Eyesight To The Blind' and 'Little Side Car' for Apollo Records in 1951. Bunn recorded under his real name for Apollo and also with the group the Wheels in 1956 on Premium Records. That was followed by a partnership with his wife as the Lovers for Lamp Records in 1958. They then recorded for the Fire label as Tarheel Slim And Little Ann, a name they kept until 1962. After a spell outside the music business, Slim returned in 1970, when he recorded for Trix Records, an association which lasted until his death.

Album: *Lock Me In Your Heart* (1989).

Tarika Sammy

A roots music group from Madagascar, purveying a traditional blend that evolved from Indonesian, African and Arabic influences on the Indian Ocean island's culture. The band's founder is Sammy (b. Samoela Adriamalalaharijaona), who had run a loose musical collective since the early 80s, and also built many traditional instruments. When Madagascar was opened up to the West, the influence of musical imports like rock meant a lessening of interest in native forms.

However, the hidden benefit was that if local Madagascans weren't interested in traditional fare, then the outside world was. Ian Anderson of Rogue Records in Britain was impressed by what he had previously heard of the island's indigenous sound, and laid plans to produce an album with harmonising sisters Hantira (b. Hantrarivo Rasoanaivo) and Noro (b. Tina Norosoa Raharimalala). Having previously recorded Sammy on a trip in 1990, he suggested that he and his cousin Tiana (Solomon Ratianarinaivo) join with the aforementioned pair as a four-piece. Thus Tarika Sammy was put together, and by 1992 they were touring the UK to an ecstatic reaction (including an appearance on television show *Blue Peter*). Their debut album was recorded during their stay, featuring the **3 Mustaphas 3** rhythm section. For their follow-up, however, the group flew in bass and drums from Madagascar to produce an even more authentic roots feel.

Albums: *Fanafody* (Rogue/Green Linnet 1992), *Balance* (Rogue 1994), *Bibiango* (Xenophile 1995).

Tarleton's Jig

Formed in 1979, Tarleton's Jig were an offshoot from two other groups, the City Waites and Common Ground. With a membership rich in classical training, this talented group utilized a vast array of exotic instruments, such as recorders, shawms, flutes, curtals, Danish, Flemish and English bagpipes, the Rauchespfeife, cornet, baroque violin, recorders, crumhorns, rebecs, lutes, uilleann pipes, theorbo and guitars. Tarleton's Jig comprises James Bisgood (b. 3 March 1959, Isleworth, Middlesex, England; also vocals), Jeremy West (b. 29 November 1953, Sussex, England), David Miller (b. 13 April 1953, Glamorgan, Wales) and Keith Thompson (b. 7 August 1951, Whitstable, Kent, England). The group has performed a wide spectrum of popular English music from the Middle Ages to the mid-18th Century, with particular emphasis on 16th and 17th centuries. They regularly perform at stately homes and castles, and often in the presence of Royalty. *For King And Parliament* contained music from soldier's camps, taverns and street corners, as well as the battlefield. *A Fit Of Mirth For A Groat* was equally well-received. It was performed much as it would have been during the English Civil Wars. One of the musicians featured on this album, Sharon Lindo (b. 11 December 1959, Romford, Essex, England), left in 1989.

In 1990, Martin Pope (b. 22 June 1955, Kuala Lumpur, Malaysia) left the line-up, having joined in 1982. *Roaring Boys* was originally scheduled for release in 1990. With the departure of Lindo who had played on a substantial amount of the recordings, the release was shelved, but the tapes still exist, and subsequent release is not considered out of the question. Due to a large 'pool' of highly talented musicians, the group has managed to maintain its standards and continues to work, using authentic instruments of the period, and full costumes of the time. They have also provided soundtrack themes for a number of documentary television programmes, such as *The History Man*.

Other regular players in the now fluid line-up include, Nick Hayley (b. 5 April 1954, London, England), William Lyons (b. 13 May 1964, England), Jonathan Morgan (b. 21 April 1953, Birmingham, England), and Robert White (b. 10 March 1955, Lambeth, London, England).

Albums: *For King And Parliament* (1987), *A Fit Of Mirth For A Groat* (1989).

Tarleton, Jimmie

(see **Darby And Tarleton**)

Tarriers

Formed c.1954, the Tarriers are remembered for two primary reasons: their 1957 US Top 5 recording of 'The Banana Boat Song' and the fact that one of its members was Alan Arkin, who went on to become a highly successful actor. The folk group was put together by **Erik Darling** (b. 25 September 1933, Baltimore, Maryland, USA), who was influenced by the folk revivalists of the day. After performing briefly with a large troupe of vocalists, Darling hooked up with Arkin (b. 26 March 1934, Brooklyn, New York) and Bob Carey as the Tunetellers. The group changed its name to the Tarriers and wrote and recorded 'The Banana Boat Song' to capitalize on the calypso music craze then sweeping the USA. Simultaneously they recorded a similar song called 'Cindy, Oh Cindy' with singer **Vince Martin**. Both singles were released on Glory Records, 'Cindy' reaching number 9 and 'The Banana Boat Song' number 4. The Tarriers never again made the charts, however, and the original trio dissolved two years later. Darling joined the **Weavers** and later went on to form the **Rooftop Singers**, Arkin began his acting career and Carey kept a Tarriers group alive until 1964.

Albums: *The Tarriers* (1957), *Hard Travelin'* (1959), *Tell The World About This* (1960), *The Tarriers* (1962), *Gather 'Round* (1963), *The Original Tarriers* (1963).

Taste

A popular blues-rock attraction, Taste was formed in Cork, Eire in 1966 when Eric Kittringham (bass) and Norman Damery (drums) joined **Rory Gallagher** (b. 2 March 1949, Ballyshannon, Co. Donegal, Eire), erstwhile guitarist with the Impact Showband. The new group became a leading attraction in Ireland and in Germany, but in 1968 Gallagher replaced the original rhythm section with Charlie McCracken (bass) and John Wilson (ex-**Them**) on drums. The new line-up then became a part of London's burgeoning blues and progressive circuit. Their debut, *Taste*, was one of the

era's most popular releases, and featured several in-concert favourites, including 'Same Old Story' and 'Sugar Mama'. *On The Boards* was another commercial success, and the group seemed poised to inherit the power-trio mantle vacated by **Cream**. However, the unit broke up in October 1970 following a rancorous split between Gallagher and his colleagues. The guitarist then began a fruitful solo career until his untimely death in 1995.

Albums: *Taste* (1969), *On The Boards* (1970), *Live Taste* (1971), *Live At The Isle Of Wight* (1972). Compilation: *The Greatest Rock Sensation* (1978).

Tate, Baby

b. 28 January 1916, Elberton, Georgia, USA, d. 17 August 1972, Columbia, South Carolina, USA. Tate moved to Greenville, South Carolina at the age of 10, and there took up with **Blind Boy Fuller**. He learned guitar, and his music developed along similar lines to Fuller's, in the distinctively southeastern style. He continued to play, at least on a part-time basis, in the local area, broken only by military service in World War II. He partnered **Pink Anderson** for several years, and this connection led to his making an album in 1962, in which he demonstrated a wide traditional repertoire, although the Fuller sound also came across strongly. He recorded again 10 years later, with harmonica player Peg Leg Sam.

Album: *See What You Done* (1962).

Tate, Buddy

b. George Holmes Tate, 22 February 1915, Sherman, Texas, USA. One of the outstanding tenor saxophonists of his generation, Tate paid his dues in a succession of **territory bands** between 1927 and 1939. Having started out on alto, he quickly developed into a formidable tenor player, lending presence and distinction to the bands of Troy Floyd, **Terrence Holder**, **Andy Kirk** and Nat Towles, the latter always regarded by Tate as one of the best in which he ever worked. In 1939 he joined the **Count Basie** band, having briefly worked with Basie five years earlier. He stayed until the end of the 40s, then played with **Lucky Millinder**, **Oran 'Hot Lips' Page** and others, before taking his own band into a residency at the Celebrity Club in Harlem in 1953. He remained there until the mid-70s, taking time out to tour and record extensively with such artists such as **Jimmy Rushing** and **Buck Clayton**. In 1975 he briefly co-led a band with **Paul Quinichette**, but from then onwards worked mostly as a solo, occasionally teaming up with mainstream comrades such as **Illinois Jacquet**, **Al Grey**, **Scott Hamilton** and **Bobby Rosengarden**. Tate was seriously injured in 1981, scalded in a hotel shower, but returned to the fray only to be stricken with serious illness in the late 80s. The early 90s saw him return tentatively to playing again. His full-toned sound, robust 'Texas Tenor' styling and unflagging swing have earned him a significant place in the history of mainstream jazz. A thoroughly delightful individual, charming, sophisticated and thoughtful, he is a true gentleman of jazz and one of the music's most distinguished ambassadors.

Albums: *Buddy Tate's Celebrity Club Orchestra Vol. 1* (1954), *Swinging Like Tate* (1958), *Tate's Date* (1959), *Tate A Tate* (1960), *Groovin' With Tate* (1961), *The Buddy Tate-Milt Buckner Trio* (1967), *Buddy Tate's Celebrity Club Orchestra Vol. 2* (1968), *Unbroken* (1970), *Buddy Tate And Wild Bill Davis: Midnight Slows Vol. 2* (1972), *The Count's Men* (1973), *Buddy Tate And His Buddies* (1973), *Midnight Slows Vols 4 & 5* (1974), *Kansas City Woman* (1974), *The Texas Twister* (1975), *A Jazz Meeting* (1975), *After Midnight* (1975-76), *A Soft Summer Night* (1976), *Buddy Tate Meets Dollar Brand* (1977), *Sherman Shuffle* (1978), *The Buddy Tate Quartet* (1978), *Buddy Tate And The Muse All Stars Live At Sandy's* (1978), *Hard Blowin': Live At Sandy's* (1978), *The Ballad Artistry Of Buddy Tate* (1981), *The Great Buddy Tate* (1981), *Swingin' The Forties With The Great Eight* (1983), *Buddy Tate Meets Torsten Zwingenberger* (1983), *Just Jazz* (1984), *Long Tall Tenor* (1986). Compilations: with Count Basie *The Jubilee Alternatives* (1943-44), *Jumpin' On The West Coast* (1947).

Tate, Grady

b. 14 January 1932, Durham, North Carolina, USA. A self-taught drummer, Tate began playing while still a small child. During his military service he turned to jazz and subsequently worked with **Wild Bill Davis**. In the early 60s he played in the **Quincy Jones** big band and then spent time with **Count Basie**, **Duke Ellington** and a string of small groups, including those led by **Rahsaan Roland Kirk**, **Oscar Peterson**, **Zoot Sims**, **Red Rodney** and **Ray Brown**. He also made some albums as a singer. Tate's interest in singing made him especially sympathetic to vocalists' needs and he has recorded with **Ella Fitzgerald**, **Sarah Vaughan**, **Lena Horne**, as well as **Ray Charles** among many. Tate's drumming is suited to many areas of jazz and he invariably brings a lithe swing to any band of which he is a member. In recent years he appears to show a preference for singing, not in the jazz idiom but angled towards the popular field.

Albums: as singer *Feeling Life* (1969), as singer *Master Grady Tate* (1977), with Roland Kirk *Now Please Don't You Cry Beautiful Edith* (1967), with Pee Wee Russell, Oliver Nelson *The Spirit Of '67* (1967), with Quincy Jones *Walking In Space* (1969) with Oscar Peterson *Silent Partner* (1979), with Red Rodney *The 3 Rs* (1979), with Ray Brown *Don't Forget The Blues* (1985), *TNT: Grady Tate Sings* (1993).

Tate, Howard

b. 1943, Macon, Georgia, USA. A former member of the Gainors with **Garnet Mimms**, Tate also sang with **Bill Doggett**'s band. A solo act by 1962, he (like Mimms) was guided by producer/songwriter **Jerry Ragovoy**. Between 1966 and 1968, Howard secured four US R&B hits including 'Ain't Nobody Home', 'Look At Granny Run, Run' (later covered by **Ry Cooder**) and 'Stop' (later covered by **Mike Bloomfield** and **Al Kooper**). Tate's work provided material for several acts, most notably **Janis Joplin**, who recorded 'Get It While You Can'. After releasing two singles on the Turntable label, 'There Are The Things That Make Me Know You're Gone' (1969) and 'My Soul's Got A Hole In It' (1970), Tate moved to **Atlantic Records** where he enjoyed the production assistance of former mentor Ragavoy. From there he moved on to various other labels, but sadly, with little success.

Albums: *Get It While You Can* (1966), *Howard Tate's Reaction* (1970).

Tattoo Rodeo

Previously known as White Sister, an ultra-sophisticated funk-tinged hard-rock outfit. The band switched name and changed image somewhat during 1991, in order to land a major recording contract. With acoustic and blues influences replacing the soul/funk elements, the band aimed at the same market as **Tesla**, **Bon Jovi** and **Def Leppard**. Comprising Dennis Churchill-Dries (vocals/bass), Rick Chadock (guitar), Michael Lord (keyboards) and Rich Wright (drums), the band specialize in highly infectious and melodic song structures, characterized by an impassioned vocal delivery. Picked up by **Atlantic**, they debuted with *Rode Hard, Put Away Wet* and received a positive, if slightly guarded media response. This comprised thirteen, blues-based rock anthems that had both guts and style. Their image was rather understated and as a result, they failed to attract the degree of attention that their talents deserved.

Album: *Rode Hard, Put Away Wet* (1991).

Tattooed Love Boys

This streetwise UK rock quartet were formed in 1987 by vocalist Gary Mielle and drummer Mick Ransome (ex-**Praying Mantis**). With Cris C.J. Jagdhar (guitar) and Darayus Z. Kaye (bass) completing the line-up, they drew inspiration from the **New York Dolls**, **Ramones** and **Hanoi Rocks**. Debuting with *Bleeding Hearts And Needle Marks* in 1988, they proved they could write instant if ultimately disposable sleazy rock anthems, which possessed a degree of naive charm. The album sold poorly and the band disintegrated in 1989. They were resurrected in 1991 with the nucleus of Ransome and Mielle plus new recruits Dean Marshall (bass), Nick Singleton (guitar) and Chris Danby (rhythm guitar). *No Time For Nursery Rhymes'* attempt at a more sophisticated approach backfired somewhat. The result was an amateurish affair, which

hinted at plagiarism of **Guns N' Roses**.
Albums: *Bleeding Hearts And Needle Marks* (Razor 1988), *No Time For Nursery Rhymes* (Music For Nations 1990).

Tatum, Art

b. 13 October 1909, Toledo, Ohio, USA, d. 5 November 1956. Born into a musical family, Tatum was handicapped from birth by impaired sight. Blind in one eye and only partially sighted in the other, he nevertheless studied piano formally and learned to read music. By his mid-teens he was playing professionally in Toledo. He played briefly in the Speed Webb band, but was mostly active as a soloist or in small groups working in clubs and playing on radio. He was heard by singer Adelaide Hall, who took him on the road as her accompanist. With Hall he travelled to New York in 1932 and the following year made his first recordings. He spent the next few years playing clubs in Cleveland and Chicago but in 1937 was back in New York, where his playing in clubs, on radio and on record established his reputation as a major figure in jazz circles. He toured the USA and also played in the UK. In the early 40s he formed a trio with bassist **Slam Stewart** and guitarist **Tiny Grimes** which became extremely popular. For the next decade Tatum toured extensively, performing throughout North America. In the early 50s he was signed by **Norman Granz** who recorded him in a series of remarkable performances, both as soloist (*The Solo Masterpieces*) and in a small group context with **Benny Carter**, **Buddy De Franco**, **Roy Eldridge**, **Lionel Hampton**, **Ben Webster** and others (*The Group Masterpieces*). A matchless virtuoso performer, Tatum's impact on the New York jazz scene in the early 30s had extensive repercussions. Even **Fats Waller**, an acknowledged master and someone Tatum had listened to on record in his own formative years, was aware of the phenomenal talent of the newcomer, reputedly declaring onstage - when he spotted Tatum in the audience - 'God is in the house tonight'.

Tatum's dazzling extemporizations on themes from jazz and the classics but mostly from the popular song book, became bywords and set standards few of his successors matched and none surpassed. Capable of breathtaking runs, interspersed with striking single notes and sometimes unexpected chords, he developed a unique solo style. His powerful left-hand figures tipped a hat in the direction of stride whilst he simultaneously explored the limits of an orthodox keyboard like no other pianist in jazz (and few elsewhere). A playful habit of quoting from other melodies, a technique which in unskilled hands can be merely irritating, was developed into a singular stylistic device. Unlike some virtuoso performers, Tatum never sacrificed feeling and swing for effect. Although he continued to develop throughout his career, it is hard to discover any recorded evidence that he was never

poised and polished. His prodigious talent allowed him to achieve extraordinary recording successes: his solo sessions for Granz were mostly completed in two days - 69 tracks, all but three needing only one take. Ray Spencer, whose studies of the artist are extensive, has commented that Tatum achieved such a remarkable work rate through constant 'refining and honing down after each performance until an ideal version remained needing no further adjustments'. While this is clearly so, Tatum's performances never suggest a man merely going through the motions. Everything he did was fresh and vital, as if minted especially for the occasion in hand. Although he remains a major figure in jazz piano, Tatum is often overlooked in the cataloguing of those who affected the course of the music. He appears to stand to one side of the developing thrust of jazz, yet his creativity and the manner in which he explored harmonic complexities and unusual chord sequences influenced many musicians, including **Bud Powell** and **Herbie Hancock**, and especially non-pianists, amongst whom can be listed **Charlie Parker** and **John Coltrane**. The word genius is often used carelessly but, in assessing Tatum and the manner in which he transformed ideas and the imagined limitations of the piano in jazz, it is hard to think of a word that is more appropriate.

Selected compilations: *The Chronological Art Tatum* (1932-34), *The Chronological Art Tatum* (1934-40), *Pure Genius* (1934-45), *The Standard Sessions* (1935-43), *Get Happy!* (1938-39), *Pieces Of Eight* (1939-55), with Les Paul *Together* (early 40s), *The Complete Trio Sessions With Tiny Grimes And Slam Stewart Vols 1 & 2* (1944), *Moods* (1944-55), *Pieces Of Eight* (1945-55), *Art Tatum* (1949), *The Complete Capitol Recordings* (1949-52), *Art Tatum At The Piano Vols 1 & 2* (50s), *Art Tatum Piano Discoveries* (1950-55), *Piano Solo* (1952), *Piano Solo Private Sessions* (1952), *The Complete Pablo Solo Masterpieces* (Pablo 1953-56), with Roy Eldridge, Ben Webster and others *The Tatum Group Masterpieces* (1954-56), *Lasting Impressions* (1955-56), *Presenting The Art Tatum Trio* (1956), *Art Tatum On The Air* (Aircheck 1978), *Tatum Group Masterpices Vols 1-9* (Pablo 1978), *Tatum Solo Masterpieces Vols 1-12* (Pablo 1978), *The V Discs* (Black Lion 1979, 1944-46 recordings), *20th Century Piano Genius* (Emarcy 1987), *Complete Art Tatum Vols 1 and 2* (Capitol 1990), *Complete Brunswick And Decca Sessions 1932-41* (Affinity 1993).

Further reading: *Art Tatum, A Guide To His Recorded Music*, Laubich, Arnold (1982), *Too Marvellous For Words: The Life And Genius Of*, Lester, James (1994).

Taupin, Bernie

b. 22 May 1950, Sleaford, Lincolnshire, England. Taupin is recalled principally, as the title of his own memoirs affirms, as 'The One Who Writes The Words For **Elton John**', even though this lucrative partnership terminated in 1976, nearly a decade after the two independently answered a **Liberty Records** music press advertisement for new talent. Put together by A&R representative Ray Williams, John and Taupin (then fresh from school as a Lincolnshire farm labourer) were engaged as songwriters by **Dick James** Music. Initially, they collaborated by post; John putting melodies to Taupin's lines in which the sound of the words rather than their sense permeated early efforts such as 'When The First Tear Shows', an a-side by Brian Keith (ex-**Plastic Penny**).

As John's career as a singing pianist took off, Taupin's output exuded a strong romanticism, most notably on the reflective 'Your Song,' John's chart debut. Taupin went on to produce **David Ackles**' *American Gothic*, which was a minor US chart entry in 1972. A couple of prosaically-named Taupin solo albums were thought expedient, but despite tuneful vocals and sterling accompaniment from guitarists **Shawn Phillips** and Caleb Quaye, his prominence as a performer was infinitely less than that of flamboyant Elton, the 'Captain Fantastic' of the autobiographical 1975 album - with Taupin as the 'Brown Dirt Cowboy'.

By then, Taupin was exploring the stance of 'the-outsider-versus-society', epitomized by North American outlaw themes reminiscent of the **Band**, and prevalent on 1970's *Tumbleweed Connection*. An advantage of his comparative facelessness was freedom to roam abroad. Taupin's perceptive observations and self-projections often converted into skilful librettos, as in 'Snookeroo,' an overview of a squandered youth in Liverpool, made-to-measure for **Ringo Starr**'s *Goodnight Vienna*. Nevertheless, John's melodies saved the throwaway 'Your Sister Can't Twist,' and rendered unto trite couplets like 'Hollywood created a superstar/And pain was the price you paid' (from 'Candle In The Wind') an undeserved 'beautiful sadness'.

Free of John, Taupin's career became caught in the wealthy lethargy of Los Angeles. His own infrequent albums were overshadowed by additional collaborations with **Alice Cooper** (*From The Inside*) which featured 'How You Gonna See Me Now', an exorcism of the horrors of alcoholism. During this time he jointly composed the US number 1 'We Built This City' for **Starship**. During the 80s Taupin was reunited as Elton's principal lyricist and both the film *Two Rooms* and the accompanying album confirmed the John/Taupin musical partnership as one of the greatest of all time.

Albums: *Bernie Taupin* (1970), *Taupin* (1971), *He Who Rides The Tiger* (1980).

Further reading: *The One Who Writes The Words For Elton John*, Bernie Taupin. *Elton*, Philip Norman. *Elton John Bernie Taupin, The Complete Lyrics*.

Tavares

This US group was formed in 1964 in New Bedford, Massachusetts, USA. The line-up consisted of five brothers, Ralph, Antone 'Chubby', Feliciano 'Butch', Arthur 'Pooch' and Perry Lee 'Tiny' Tavares. Originally known as Chubby And The Turnpikes, the group assumed its family's surname in 1969. Although they lacked a distinctive lead voice or a characteristic sound, Tavares' undemanding blend of light soul and pop resulted in several commercial successes. The brothers' early run of R&B hits culminated in 1975 with 'It Only Takes A Minute', a soul chart-topper and a US pop Top 10 entry. The following year the group scored their sole million-seller in 'Heaven Must Be Missing An Angel' before enjoying further success with one of their strongest songs, 'Don't Take Away The Music'. Both of these singles reached number 4 in the UK where Tavares enjoyed an enduring popularity. 'Whodunit' (1977) was another major release, while 'More Than A Woman' (1978), a song from that year's box-office smash, *Saturday Night Fever*, gave the group their last significant hit. Tavares continued to reach the R&B lists until 1984, but their safe, almost old-fashioned style gradually fell from favour.

Albums: *Check It Out* (1974), *Hard Core Poetry* (1974), *In The City* (1975), *Sky High!* (1976), *Love Storm* (1977), *Future Bound* (1978), *Madam Butterfly* (1979), *Supercharged* (1980), *New Directions* (1982). Compilation: *The Best Of The Tavares* (1977).

Tawney, Cyril

b. 12 October 1930, Gosport, Hampshire, England. Most of this guitar-playing songwriter's work reflects his 12 years in the Royal Navy, during which time he started writing songs and singing. He took part in the English Folk Dance and Song Society's first National Folk Festival, in London, in October 1957. A fellow entrant was BBC producer Charles Parker, who booked Tawney for his Christmas broadcast *Sing Christmas*. Thus, with the attention of BBC West Region, Cyril started his radio and television career. Tawney is the only British career serviceman to have his own fully networked television programme, *Watch Aboard*, first broadcast in 1959. He made his recording debut in 1960, on *Rocket Along*, an anthology with other artists, on **HMV Records**. Turning to full-time singing in May 1959, he was initially employed solely by the BBC. He helped to pioneer the British folk revival in the 60s via the newly emerging folk clubs. His interest in west country and nautical songs, led him to found the Plymouth Folk Song Club in January 1962, and the West of England Folk Centre, in 1965. During the late 60s, Tawney presented *Folkspin*, a radio programme devoted solely to record requests for British traditional music. As time passed, his songwriting reflected more non-naval themes, and he maintained his singing career while gaining BA and MA degrees during the 70s.

A number of his earlier works, notably 'Sally Free And Easy', 'The Grey Funnel Line', 'The Oggie Man', and 'Sammy's Bar', have been recorded by numerous artists, and are performed regularly in folk clubs. It is a testament to their authenticity that they are often erroneously considered traditional, rather than self-penned. Tawney also appeared on a number of albums with other artists such as the *World Of Folk* series on **Decca**'s Argo label. Tawney stopped touring British folk clubs in 1985, and now concentrates on concerts, festivals and special appearances. His book, *Grey Funnel Lines*, featuring traditional songs of the 20th Century Royal Navy, was the result of over 30 years research. Together with his wife, Rosemary, he founded Neptune Tapes, a label dealing with all aspects of maritime song. Tawney is now engaged in writing a series of tales with a Royal Navy background.

Albums: with others *Rocket Along* (HMV 1960), with others *A Pinch Of Salt* (HMV 1960), *Between Decks* (DTS 1963), with others *Farewell Nancy* (1964), with others *Folksound Of Britain* (HMV 1965), *The Outlandish Knight* (Polydor 1969), *Children's Songs From Devon And Cornwall* (Argo 1970), *A Mayflower Garland* (Argo 1970), *This Is A Man's World* (1970), with others *World Of Folk* (1971), *In Port* (Argo 1972), *I Will Give My Love* (Argo 1973), with others *World Of The Countryside* (1974), *Down Among The Barley Straw* (Leader 1976), with others *The Transports* (1977), with others *Reunion* (1984), *In The Naval Spirit* (Neptune 1988), *Round The Buoy* (1989), *Sally Free And Easy* (1990), *Sailor's Delight* (Neptune 1991), *In Every Port* (Neptune 1991), *Down The Hatch* (Neptune 1994).

Further reading: *Grey Funnel Lines - Traditional Song And Verse Of The Royal Navy 1900-1970*, Cyril Tawney.

Taxi Records
(see **Sly And Robbie**)

Taylor, 'Little' Johnny

b. Johnny Young, 11 February 1943, Memphis, Tennessee, USA. After relocating to Los Angeles, Little Johnny Taylor (not to be confused with the excellent R & B singer, **Johnnie Taylor**, who followed **Sam Cooke** as lead singer with the **Soul Stirrers**) joined the gospel group the **Stars Of Bethel**, and later joined the **Mighty Clouds of Joy**, whereupon he struck up friendships with **Ted Taylor** and **Clay Hammond**. Taylor soon decided, however, to turn solo, and he struck gold with his second solo record, released by Galaxy Records. (His first single for Galaxy, 'You'll Need Another Favor' reached a respectable number 27 in the *Billboard* R & B chart in May 1963.) Taylor's friend Clay Hammond composed the hit single, 'Part Time Love', an emotional blues-ballad, which gave Young, now called 'Little' Johnny Taylor, a number 1 hit in the *Billboard* R&B chart in 1963. The song has since become a soul standard. Despite further accomplished releases, including 'Since I Found A New Love' (number 78 in the *Billboard* R&B chart in January 1964) and 'Zig Zag Lightning' (number 43 in the *Billboard* R&B chart in October 1966), each of which

were strikingly similar (perhaps too similar) to 'Part Time Love', it was not until November 1971 that 'Little' Johnny Taylor recaptured something of his erstwhile standing. Having recently moved from Galaxy Records to Ronn Records, he enjoyed a number 9 *Billboard* R&B hit with the suggestive 'Everybody Knows About My Good Thing'. Ronn continued to release his singles throughout the early 70s. Although 'Its My Fault Darling' reached number 41 (R&B) in March 1972, 'Open House At My House' reached number 16 (R&B) in August 1972 and 'I'll Make It Worth Your While' reached number 37 (R&B) in April 1973, his final single for Ronn, 'You're Savin' Your Best Loving For Me', released in July 1974, flopped badly and reached only number 83 (R&B). In the 70s he also sang a number of equally commercially unsuccessful duets with the soul singer **Ted Taylor** (no relation). 'Little' Johnny Taylor, although greatly talented, has never found it easy to live up to his tremendous early success as a solo artist. He does, however, continue to perform occasionally.

Album: *Part Time Love* (Galaxy 1962), *Little Johnny Taylor* (Galaxy 1963), *Everybody Knows About My Good Thing* (Ronn 1970), *Open House At My House* (Ronn 1973), with Ted Taylor *The Super Taylors* (1974), *L.J.T.* (1974), *Stuck In The Mud* (1988), *Ugly Man* (1989). Compilations: *I Should'a Been A Preacher* (1981), *Part-Time Love* (1981), *The Galaxy Years* (1991).

Taylor, 'Sam The Man'

b. Leroy Samuel Taylor, 12 July 1916, Lexington, Tennessee, USA. Taylor started on clarinet and played with Paul Taylor in Gary, Indiana, going on to play his tenor saxophone in the bands of Scat Man Crothers (1937-38), Sunset Royals/Doc Wheeler's Sunset Orchestra (1939-42; recording for **RCA**'s Bluebird subsidiary), **Cootie Williams** (1942-45; recording for Hit/Majestic and **Capitol**), **Lucky Millinder** (1945-46; recording for **Decca** and King/Queen) and **Cab Calloway** (1946-52; recording for **Columbia**, Bluebird, Hi-Tone, **London** and Regal). Leaving the Calloway band upon its demise in 1952, several of the band members, notably Taylor, **David 'Panama' Francis** and **Milt Hinton**, went on to carve out a lucrative career with their own units separately, and as ubiquitous session musicians together for the rest of the 50s and early 60s on the majority of New York R&B sessions. Taylor played with **Alan Freed**'s Rock 'n' Roll Orchestra, often battling on saxophone with his friend Big Al Sears, and settled into the 60s album market with his own albums on Metrojazz and **MGM**. In the 70s he took part in several festival tours of Europe and Japan, but little has been heard from him in recent years.

Album: with Hal Singer, Paul Williams, Lee Allen and

Big Jay McNeely *Honkers & Screamers - The Roots Of Rock N' Roll Vol. 6* (1989).

Taylor, Allan

b. 30 September 1945, Brighton, Sussex, England. This singer/songwriter/instrumentalist has achieved considerable acclaim on the UK folk circuit. After leaving school at the age of 16, he helped to organize local folk clubs, until turning professional five years later. Taylor attracted the interest of United Artists after supporting **Fairport Convention** on a national tour. *Sometimes* was released on the **Liberty** label, and aroused a degree of interest from the folk media. Backing musicians on the album were Fairport Convention members Dave Mattacks, Dave Pegg, and **Dave Swarbrick**. Following Taylor's move to New York from 1972-74, *The American Album* followed a different course, and included a wealth of respected Nashville and Los Angeles session musicians. In July 1975, Allan formed the group Cajun Moon in order to encompass traditional, Appalachian and cajun musical styles. The trio, which included Brian Golbey (fiddle), and Jon Gillaspie (keyboards), toured with **Steeleye Span** and Taylor signed a deal with **Chrysalis** resulting in *Cajun Moon* in May 1976. Due to overwork, Taylor damaged his vocal chords, and was forced to rest for three months. This more or less spelt the end of the group and, following an operation, Taylor recommenced solo work, signing a publishing deal with Chrysalis and a recording deal with Rubber Records. His first release, *The Traveller*, appeared in April 1978, and featured **John Kirkpatrick** on melodeon and accordion. Following an appearance at the Nylon Folk Festival in Switzerland, in July 1980, Allan was presented with the Grand Prix Du Disque De Montreux for the best European folk album of that year. Due to a greater influence of working on the continent, *Roll On The Day* presented a slightly different style of writing. *Circle Round Again* consisted of re-recordings of popular songs from previously deleted Taylor albums. Around the time of *Win Or Lose*, Allan received a BA from Leeds University, and was working on his MA at Lancaster University, when he completed his first novel. Taylor then spent two years touring and working on material for *Lines*, which was released in March 1988. 'It's Good To See You', written by Taylor, was recorded by **Don Williams**, and other artists such as **Frankie Miller**, **Françoise Hardy** and Fairport Convention have recorded Allan Taylor songs.

He has now been included in the *Oxford Book Of Traditional Verse* as one of the writers who has best furthered the folk tradition. Taylor, more recently, gained a PhD in Ethnomusicology in addition to continuing to tour as well as writing music for television.

Albums: *Sometimes* (Liberty 1971), *The Lady* (United Artists 1972), *The American Album* (United Artists 1973), *Cajun Moon* (1976), *The Traveller* (Rubber 1978), *Roll On The Day* (Rubber 1980), *Circle Round Again* (1983), *Win Or Lose* (1983), *Lines* (1988), *Out Of Time* (1990), *So Long* (1993).

Taylor, Art

b. 6 April 1929, New York City, New York, USA, d. 6 February 1995. As a teenager Taylor played drums with **Sonny Rollins**, **Howard McGhee** and other young bop musicians in New York. In the early 50s he was also to be heard in mainstream groups, playing with **Coleman Hawkins** and **Buddy De Franco**. He continued to play with leading beboppers, including **Bud Powell**, and later in the decade was with **Miles Davis** and **John Coltrane**. From time to time he led his own bands, and toured the USA and Europe with several groups. He became resident in Europe in the early 60s, playing with visiting fellow Americans including **Dexter Gordon** and **Johnny Griffin**. During this period, Taylor began recording interviews with musicians, the results of which, often acutely angled towards the racial and political circumstances surrounding jazz, were first published in 1977 under the title *Notes And Tones*. In the mid-80s Taylor returned to the USA and hosted a radio show.

Albums: *Taylor's Wailers* (Original Jazz Classics 1957), with Gene Ammons *Groove Blues* (1958), with John Coltrane *Soultrane* (1958), *Taylor's Tenors* (1959), with Coltrane *Giant Steps* (1959), *A.T.'s Delight* (Blue Note 1960), with Dexter Gordon *A Day In Copenhagen* (1969), *Mr A. T.* (Enja 1992), *Wailin' At The Vanguard* (Verve 1993).

Further reading: *Notes And Tones*, Arthur Taylor.

Taylor, Billy

b. 21 July 1921, Greenville, North Carolina, USA. After extensive formal studies, Taylor began playing piano with numerous leading jazzmen of the late swing era/early bebop period. These included **Ben Webster**, **Dizzy Gillespie**, **Stuff Smith** and **Charlie Parker**. By the early 50s Taylor's high reputation led to his being hired as house pianist at Birdland. His main contribution to jazz in the 50s was as leader of a trio, usually in New York, which continued more or less non-stop for the next three decades. He also appeared regularly on radio and television both as a performer and a presenter of programmes. During recent years he has developed an abiding interest in jazz education, writing piano tutors and forming Jazzmobile, the Harlem-based concert group. Taylor has frequently played and composed music which fuses jazz with the classical form. Among these works are his 'Suite For Jazz Piano And Orchestra', composed in 1973, and 'Homage', a chamber music piece first performed by the Billy Taylor Trio and the Juilliard String Quartet in 1990.

An inventive and technically facile player, Taylor's dedication to the development of interest in jazz in the community has sometimes led the wider audience to overlook his undoubted skills. (This artist should not be confused with either Billy Taylor Snr. or Billy Taylor Jnr., father and son bass players.)

Selected albums: *Piano Panorama* (1951), *The Billy Taylor Sextet* (1952), *Jazz At Storyville* (1952), *The Billy Taylor Trio* i (1952), *The Billy Taylor Trio* ii (1953), *The Billy Taylor Trio* iii (1954), *The Billy Taylor Trio With Candido* (Original Jazz Classics 1954), *Cross-Section* (Original Jazz Classics 1954), *Billy Taylor At Town Hall* (1954), *A Touch Of Taylor* (1955), *Billy Taylor* i (1956), *Billy Taylor* ii (1956), *The Billy Taylor Quartet* i (1956), *Billy Taylor At The London House* (1956), *My Fair Lady Loves Jazz* (1957), *Taylor Made Jazz* (1957), *The Billy Taylor Trio* iv (1957), *One For Fun* (1959), *Billy Taylor And Four Flutes* (Original Jazz Classics 1959), *Billy Uptown* (1960), *Warming Up* (1960), *Interlude* (1961), *Billy Taylor With Jimmy Jones And His Orchestra* (1961), *The Billy Taylor Quartet* ii (1962), *The Billy Taylor Septet* (1963), *Billy Taylor With Oliver Nelson's Orchestra* i (1963), *Billy Taylor With Oliver Nelson's Orchestra* ii (1963), *Billy Taylor And His Orchestra* i (1964), *Billy Taylor Today/A Sleeping Bee* (1969), *Billy Taylor And His Orchestra* ii (c.1970), *Live At Storyville* (1977), *Where've You Been?* (1980), *You Tempt Me* (Taylor Made 1985), *White Night And Jazz In Leningrad* (Taylor Made 1988), *Solo* (Taylor Made 1989), *Billy Taylor And The Jazzmobile All Stars* (Taylor Made 1989), *Dr T* (GRP 1993).

Further reading: *The History And Development Of Jazz Piano*, Taylor, Billy (1975).

Taylor, Bobby, And The Vancouvers

Bobby Taylor (lead vocals), Tommy Chong (guitar), Wes Henderson (guitar), Robbie King (keyboards), Ted Lewis (drums) and Eddie Patterson (bass) joined forces in Vancouver, Canada in the mid-60s. They were signed to **Motown Records** in 1967, supporting **Gladys Knight And The Pips** on a US tour. The following year, they issued their debut single, 'Does Your Mama Know About Me', an emotive ballad with a lyric that capitalized on the band's inter-racial make-up. The single reached the US Top 30, and was succeeded by two smaller hits, 'I Am Your Man' and 'Melinda'. After issuing an eponymous debut album, the Vancouvers split, and Tommy Chong formed the comedy double-act **Cheech And Chong**, who achieved great popularity in the early 70s with their drug-related humour. Taylor remained with Motown as a soloist, and was responsible for alerting the company to the talents of the Jackson Five, although **Diana Ross** was publicly credited with the signing. He left Motown in the early 70s and recorded spasmodically for several more years, registering one minor hit in 1975 with 'Why Play Games'. In 1988 Taylor signed to Ian Levine's Motor City label and was instrumental in renewing contact with dozens of ex-

Motown acts, many of which are now recording again.

Albums: *Bobby Taylor And The Vancouvers* (1968), Bobby Taylor solo *Taylor Made Soul* (1969), *Find My Way Back* (1990).

Taylor, Bram

b. Bramwell Taylor, 6 August 1951, Leigh, Lancashire, England. Both of Taylor's parents were musically-minded members of the Salvation Army. After initially learning to play cornet and tenor horn, he moved on to the guitar. Inspired by such artists as **Harvey Andrews** and Marie Little, he began playing at folk clubs. By 1975, in addition to playing to a wider audience, he was co-presenter/performer for BBC Manchester on the children's programme *Chatterbox*. In 1979, together with Dave Dutton (b. 19 August 1947, Atherton, Lancashire, England; vocals/ukulele/banjo), and Eric White (b. 2 October 1946, Leigh, Lancashire, England; ukelele/banjo/lap organ/melodeon/penny whistle/accordion/concertina), he formed the comedy group, Inclognito. Taylor released *The Haymakers*, in 1982, more to sound out interest than anything else. Generally traditional in feel, it suffered in terms of production, but provided a good platform for Taylor and his clear vocal style. In 1985, White was replaced by Jackie Finney (b. 26 October 1960, Salford, Lancashire, England; penny whistle/accordion/keyboards/guitar/vocals). In 1989 the group split, owing to Taylors solo commitments, and Dutton's acting involvement in the BBC situation comedy *Watching*. He signed to **Fellside Records**, an independent label run by Paul and Linda Adams on 1 August 1984. His first release, *Bide A While*, was well received by the folk music press. *Dreams And Songs To Sing* reflected a slight departure in style by the use of more contemporary material, but kept the same formula and the same musicians, including the strong vocal harmonies of Fiona Simpson. The album received the 1987 British Music Retailers award for excellence in the Folk and Country category. *Taylor Made* was evidence of his ability to take contemporary songs and record them with an underlying traditional feel, thus pleasing both sides of the folk music 'divide'.

Albums: *The Haymakers* (Freestyle Enterprises 1982), *Bide A While* (Fellside 1984), *Dreams And Songs To Sing* (Fellside 1986), *Taylor Made* (Fellside 1990), *Further Horizons* (Fellside 1993). Compilations: with various artists *Flash Company* (Fellside 1986), with various artists *Beyond The Seas* (Fellside 1988).

Taylor, Cecil

b. 15 March 1929, New York City, New York, USA. A towering figure in post-war *avant garde* jazz, Taylor has been hailed as the greatest piano virtuoso of the 20th century because of the phenomenal power, speed and intensity of his playing. 'We in black music think of the piano as a percussive instrument,' he told writer John

Litweiler: 'we beat the keyboard, we get inside the instrument. . . the physical force going into the making of black music - if that is misunderstood, it leads to screaming. . .' Taylor grew up in Long Island, studying piano from the age of five and percussion (with a classical tutor) soon afterwards. He attended the New York College of Music and the New England Conservatory in Boston, though he later claimed he had learned more by listening to **Duke Ellington** records. Despite an early interest in European classical composers, especially Stravinsky, Taylor's major influences come from the jazz tradition, notably big band leaders such as Ellington, drummers **Sonny Greer** and **Chick Webb** and a lineage of pianists that runs through **Fats Waller**, **Erroll Garner**, **Thelonious Monk** and **Horace Silver**. Although his first gigs were with swing era veterans **Hot Lips Page**, **Johnny Hodges** and **Lawrence Brown**, by the mid-50s Taylor was leading his own small groups and laying the basis for a musical revolution that is still in progress. His early associates included **Buell Neidlinger**, **Dennis Charles**, **Steve Lacy** and **Archie Shepp** (plus a fairly disastrous one-off encounter with **John Coltrane**) and his first recordings still bore a discernible, if carefully distanced, relationship to the jazz mainstream. By the early 60s, working with **Sunny Murray**, **Alan Silva** and his longest-serving colleague, **Jimmy Lyons**, Taylor's music had shed all direct reference to tonality and regular time-keeping and sounded almost purely abstract. However, the arrival of **Ornette Coleman** in New York in 1959, playing his own version of 'free jazz', rather overshadowed all other innovators and Taylor's more radical and complex music was largely ignored by the press and public, although a handful of fellow pioneers - the best-known of whom was **Albert Ayler** - embraced it enthusiastically. (Another admirer was **Gil Evans**, whose *Into The Hot* actually comprised one side of music by Taylor and one side by **Johnny Carisi**: Evans himself is not on the album!) Taylor lived in poverty for much of the 60s, even working as a dishwasher on occasion; but gradually his influence began to permeate the scene, particularly after **Blue Note Records** released two outstanding 1966 sessions. Both featured his regular partners Lyons, Silva, **Andrew Cyrille** and **Henry Grimes**: in addition, *Unit Structures* had **Ken McIntyre** and trumpeter Eddie Gale Stevens and *Conquistador!* had **Bill Dixon** (with whom Taylor had worked in the Jazz Composers' Guild). In 1968 Taylor made an album with the Jazz Composers' Orchestra and a 1969 concert with a new group of Lyons, Cyrille and **Sam Rivers** was released on the French label Shandar; but recording opportunities remained scarce. In the early 70s he became involved in education, teaching at Wisconsin University and colleges in Ohio and New Jersey; in 1973 he briefly ran his own label, Unit Core,

releasing *Indents (Mysteries)* and *Spring Of Two Blue-Js*. Finally, the trickle of other releases - on Trio in Japan, on Arista's Freedom label in the USA, on Enja in Europe - began to gather momentum and by the early 80s Taylor was recording regularly for the European **Soul Note** and Hat Hut labels, while later in the decade **Leo Records** and **FMP** also championed his work. During this period his ensembles included Lyons (always), Cyrille (often), Silva (occasionally) plus players such as **Sirone**, **Ronald Shannon Jackson**, violinist Ramsey Ameer, trumpeter Raphé Malik, **Jerome Cooper**, **William Parker** and percussionist Rashid Bakr: their characteristic sound was a torrential flood of full-tilt, densely-textured, swirling, churning, flying improvisation that could and usually did last for two to three hours without pause.

Taylor also recorded a series of stunning solo albums, notably *Fly! Fly! Fly! Fly! Fly!* and the live double-set *Garden*, which showed he was one of the most dazzling, dynamic pianists in jazz history, and released two memorable duo albums - *Embraced*, with **Mary Lou Williams**; *Historic Concerts*, with **Max Roach** - that further enhanced his reputation. In 1985 the first recording of Taylor's big band music, *Winged Serpent (Sliding Quadrants)*, was released by Soul Note. In 1986 Jimmy Lyons died of lung cancer; Taylor lost both a close friend and his most dedicated musical collaborator. In 1987 he toured with a new Unit (Parker, **Carlos Ward**, **Leroy Jenkins**, **Thurman Barker**: three of their concerts were released by Leo the following year) but since then has worked mostly in a trio format, usually with Parker and **Tony Oxley** (sometimes calling themselves the Feel Trio). In 1988, FMP brought 20 European improvisers to Berlin for a month-long festival of concerts and workshops that featured Taylor. Several of these were later released in the lavishly-packaged, 11-CD box-set *Cecil Taylor In Berlin '88*, which comprised two discs of Taylor's big band music, one of a big band workshop, one solo concert, one trio set with Tristan Honsinger and **Evan Parker**, a duo with **Derek Bailey** and five discs of duos with drummers - Oxley, Günter Sommer, **Paul Lovens**, **Han Bennink** and **Louis Moholo**. The set was released to worldwide acclaim in the music press and sealed Taylor's standing as one of the four or five leading innovators in post-bebop jazz. Although he has few direct imitators, he has proved an inspiration to free players everywhere and in particular to many jazz pianists, from **Alex Von Schlippenbach** to **Marilyn Crispell**.

The tremendous energy and sweep of his music has fooled many listeners into believing it has no structural underpinning, but Ekkehard Jost, both in his book *Free Jazz* and in one of the several essays in the booklet that accompanies the FMP box-set, has identified certain formal elements that recur in Taylor's work. (There are also useful chapters on his music in John Litweiler's *The*

Freedom Principle and Valerie Wilmer's *As Serious As Your Life*, plus a detailed account of his early career in A.B. Spellman's *Four Lives In The Bebop Business*. Taylor himself has always stressed the spiritual and mystical nature of African American music: 'It's about magic and capturing spirits.') A devotee of dance from Baby Lawrence to contemporary ballet (he once remarked 'I try to imitate on the piano the leaps in space a dancer makes'), Taylor has worked extensively in this field, for example on projects with choreographers/dancers Dianne McIntyre and Mikhail Baryshnikov. A poet too, whose writings often adorn his album sleeves, Taylor's *Chinampus* had him half-reciting, half-chanting a selection of sound-poetry and accompanying himself on various percussion instruments. For many years he has been working on a book about 'methodological concepts of black music', to be entitled *Mysteries*.

Albums: *Jazz Advance* (Blue Note 1956), with others *At Newport* (1957), *Hard Driving Jazz* (1958, reissued as John Coltrane *Coltrane Time*), *Looking Ahead!* (Original Jazz Classics 1959), *Love For Sale* (1959), *The World Of Cecil Taylor* (1960, reissued as *Air*), with Buell Neidlinger *New York City R&B* (1961, reissued as *Cell Walk For Celeste*), *Cecil Taylor All Stars Featuring Buell Neidlinger* (1961, reissued as *Jumpin' Punkins*), by Gil Evans *Into The Hot* (1961), *The Early Unit 1962* (1962), *Live At The Cafe Montmartre* (1963, reissued as *Innovations*), *Nefertiti The Beautiful One Has Come* (1963, reissued as *What's New*), *Charles Mingus/Cecil Taylor* (1965), *Unit Structures* (1966) *Conquistador!* (1967), *Cecil Taylor* (1967, reissued as *Student Studies*), *Soundtrack Ferrari* (1967), *The Jazz Composers' Orchestra* (1968), *Nuits De La Foundation Maeght, Vols 1-3* (1969, reissued as *The Great Concert Of Cecil Taylor*), *Cecil Taylor Quartet In Europe* (1970), *J For Jazz Broadcasts Present Cecil Taylor* (1971), *Indent (Mysteries)* (Arista 1973, reissued as *Indent*), *Akisakila* (Konnex 1973), *Cecil Taylor Solo* (1973), *Spring Of Two Blue-Js* (1974), *Silent Tongues* (Arista 1975), *Dark To Themselves* (1976), *Air Above Mountains (Buildings Within)* (1977), with Mary Lou Williams *Embraced* (1978), *Cecil Taylor Unit* (New World 1978), *3 Phasis* (New World 1979), *Live In The Black Forest* (1979), *One Too Many Salty Swift And Not Goodbye* (Hat Art 1980, rec. 1978), *Spots Circles And Fantasy* (FMP 1979), *It Is In The Brewing Luminous* (Hat Art 1981), *Fly! Fly! Fly! Fly! Fly!* (1981), *Garden Part One* (Hat Art 1982), *Garden Part Two* (Hat Art 1982), *Praxis* (1982, rec. 1968), *Live In Willisau '83* (1983), *Calling It The 8th* (1983, rec. 1981), with Max Roach *Historic Concerts* (1984, rec. 1979), *Winged Serpent (Sliding Quadrants)* (Soul Note 1985), *The Eighth* (1986, rec. 1981), *For Olim* (Soul Note 1987), *Live In Bologna* (Leo 1988), *Live In Vienna* (Leo 1988), *Chinampus* (Leo 1988), *Tzotzil Mummers Tzotzil* (1989), *Cecil Taylor In Berlin '88* (1989, 11-CD box-set, most discs also available singly), *Erzulie Maketh Scent* (FMP 1989), *Pleistozaen Mit Wasser* (FMP 1989), *Leaf Palm Hand* (FMP 1989), *Regalia* (FMP 1989), *Remembrance* (FMP 1989), *Riobec* (FMP 1989), *The Hearth*

(FMP 1989), *Legba Crossing* (FMP 1989), *Alms/Tiergarten* (FMP 1989), with Günter Sommer *In East Berlin* (1989), *Looking (The Feel Trio),* (FMP 1990), *In Florescence* (1990), with William Parker, Tony Oxley *Looking (Berlin Version) The Feel Trio* (1990), *Looking (Berlin Version) Corona* (1991), *Looking (Berlin Version) Solo* (1991), *Celebrated Blazons* (FMP 1991), *Double Holy House* (FMP 1991), with Art Ensemble Of Chicago *Thelonious Sphere Monk* (1991), *Olu Iwa* (Soul Note 1994, 1986 recording). Selected compilations: *In Transition* (1975, rec. 1955, 1959), with others *Masters Of The Modern Piano* (1976, rec. 1957), *The Complete Candid Recordings Of Cecil Taylor And Buell Neidlinger* (1989, rec. 1960-61, six-album box-set). Further reading: *Black Music: Four Lives*, A.B. Spellman. *The Freedom Principle: Jazz After 1958*, John Litweiler.

Taylor, Chip

b. James Wesley Voight, 1940, Yonkers, New York, USA. The younger brother of actor Jon Voight, Taylor began his recording career during the late 50s with several rockabilly-styled recordings. He subsequently formed **Just Us** with songwriting partner Al Gorgoni and produced material for local act the Flying Machine, which featured **James Taylor** and guitarist **Danny Kortchmar**. However Taylor became better-known as the composer of 'Wild Thing', a risque pop song popularized by the **Troggs** and, later, **Jimi Hendrix**. Other credits included 'Anyway That You Want Me', a follow-up hit for the former group, 'I Can't Let Go' (the **Hollies**), 'Angel Of The Morning' (**Merilee Rush/Juice Newton**) and 'Storybook Children' (**Billy Vera/Judy Clay**), many of which he shared with either Gorgoni, Trade Martin, or both. During the late 60s the trio began recording as Gorgoni, Martin And Taylor, but in 1971 the last named embarked on a solo career with *Gasoline*. *Chip Taylor's Last Chance* was the subject of effusive critical acclaim, but poor sales, although the artist's unerring grasp of country styles was maintained on *Some Of Us*. **Waylon Jennings**, **Bobby Bare** and **Tammy Wynette** were among those recording his songs, although a fourth collection, *This Side Of The Big River*, was less strong. Taylor's last solo release *Saint Sebastian* maintained the high quality of his recorded output. The continued popularity of his best-known work is a testament to his importance as a singer/songwriter.

Albums: *Gasoline* (1971), *Chip Taylor's Last Chance* (1973), *Some Of Us* (1974), *This Side Of The Big River* (1975), *Somebody Shot Out Of The Jukebox* (1976), *Saint Sebastian* (1979).

Taylor, Derek

b. Liverpool, England. As a London *Daily Express* showbusiness correspondent, he was briefed to do a 'hatchet job' on the **Beatles**' agreement to appear on 1963's Royal Variety Show but he could only praise them. Another *Express* commission to collate **George**

Harrison's weekly ruminations for 12 Fridays (Harrison was paid £150 for each one) was the foundation of a lasting friendship with the guitarist, strengthened when Taylor was put on the group's payroll as **Brian Epstein**'s personal assistant and ghost writer of his *Cellarful Of Noise* autobiography. In October 1964, he became the Beatles' press officer after his predecessor's outraged resignation. Conflicts with Epstein hastened Taylor's own exit in 1965. Emigrating to California, he gained employment as publicist for the **Byrds**, the **Beach Boys**, the **Mamas And The Papas**, **Buffalo Springfield** and other acts, and was on the steering committee of the celebrated **Monterey Pop Festival** in 1967. The following year found him back in London as the obvious choice to organize the Beatles' Apple Corps publicity department; his urbane, sympathetic manner winning many important contacts. While at Apple, he attempted to compose a stage musical with Harrison, but a more tangible legacy was his *As Time Goes By* memoir of two years 'in a bizarre royal court in a strange fairy tale'. Following Apple's collapse Derek moved to Los Angeles as Head of Special Projects for **Warner-Reprise** Records (later **WEA**) before transfer to Europe as the label's general manager. Further musical chairs ensued and then promotion to Vice-President of Creative Services back in Hollywood where he was honoured with a *This Is Your Life*-type citation with Harrison and **Ringo Starr** among leading entertainers walking on to tell some funny story from the past. By autumn 1979, the mercurial Taylor had gravitated back to England after Harrison's HandMade film company cried out for his unique skills. Extra-mural duties included penning scene-setting commentaries to the ex-Beatle's taped reminiscences for publication as *I Me Mine*. Happy with the result, George interceded on his hireling's behalf to convince Genesis Publications that Taylor's idiosyncratic account of his own life would be viable. In 1985, therefore, 2,000 hand-tooled copies of Taylor's witty yarn, *Fifty Years Adrift*, went on sale at £148 each. His sparkling book, *It Was Twenty Years Ago Today* was accompanied by a television film. They brilliantly encapsulated the essence of the 'summer of love'. Among Taylor's recent projects is the narrative to a collection of the late Michael Cooper's photographs. He also works occasionally for British regional television - and on Apple Records' 1991 reissue programme. Taylor is a gentle soul who is crucial to any student of the Beatles and the 60s.
Further reading; *As Time Goes By*, Derek Taylor. *Fifty Years Adrift*, Derek Taylor. *It Was Twenty Years Ago Today*, Derek Taylor.

Taylor, Eddie

b. 29 January 1923, Benoit, Mississippi, USA. A self-taught musician, Eddie 'Playboy' Taylor found early inspiration in the work of **Charley Patton**, **Son House** and **Robert Johnson**. His formative years were spent playing guitar at local social gatherings and clubs but in 1948 he travelled to Chicago to pursue a full-time career. Taylor's combo became a popular attraction and in 1953 he auditioned for the city's **VeeJay** label. Paradoxically, the company preferred the style of back-up guitarist **Jimmy Reed** and their roles were consequently reversed. Eddie appeared on the majority of masters Reed recorded between 1953 and 1964, including 'You Don't Have To Go' (1955), 'Ain't That Lovin' You Baby' (1956) and 'Honest I Do' (1957), each of which reached the R&B Top 10. Taylor's sessions as a leader commenced in 1955 and he later achieved a local hit with 'Big Town Playboy'. Despite such success, further recordings were sporadic, and only six more titles were issued, the last of those in 1964. Taylor meanwhile sought employment as an accompanist with other VeeJay acts, including **John Lee Hooker** and **Sunnyland Slim**. In 1968 he joined Hooker and Reed on a successful European tour, but positive reviews did not engender a new recording deal. The guitarist continued sporadic studio work until 1972 when he completed *I Feel So Bad* for a west coast independent label. This in turn inspired a second transatlantic tour, during which Taylor recorded *Ready For Eddie* for the Birmingham-based Big Bear company. He then endured a further low-key period, but a collection of masters from the VeeJay era, released in 1981, rekindled interest in this accomplished, yet underrated, bluesman's career. Eddie Taylor was never a self-promoter and he has probably sold more records since his death than while he was alive.
Albums: *I Feel So Bad* (1972), *Ready For Eddie* (1972), *My Heart Is Bleeding* (1988), *Still Not Ready For Eddie* (1988). Compilations: *Big Town Playboy* (1981), *Bad Boy* (1993).

Taylor, Eric

b. c.1947, USA. Taylor wrote stories as a child and later put his talent into narrative songs. He served in Vietnam, experiencing drug and alcohol problems, and then he befriended singer-songwriters, **Guy Clark** and **Townes Van Zandt**, in Houston, Texas in 1969. He and his ex-wife **Nanci Griffith** recorded albums for the small Featherbed label, *Shameless Love* and *Poet In My Window*, respectively. Each was featured on the other's album and Taylor's 'Only Lovers' is about their relationship. Despite his talents as a performer, Taylor decided to qualify as a psychologist and devote his time to helping addicts in Houston. He sang background vocals on Griffith's 1988 live album, *One Fair Summer Evening*, which included his song about the death of Crazy Horse, 'Deadwood, South Dakota', described by Griffith as 'one of the best pieces of writing I've ever heard'.
Album: *Shameless Love* (1981).

Taylor, Eva

b. Irene Gibbons, 22 January 1895, St. Louis, Missouri, USA, d. 31 October 1977, Mineola, New York, USA. On stage from the age of three, Taylor had toured the Antipodes and Europe before her teens. In 1921 she settled in New York and married the bandleader, pianist and composer **Clarence Williams**. She pursued a prolific career in musical theatre, recording and especially radio until 1942, when she virtually retired, although she made a few European appearances in the late 60s and 70s. Taylor's singing lacked much jazz or blues feeling; it seems likely that her husband's position as 'race' records manager for **OKeh Records** accounts for the frequency with which Taylor recorded. Not surprisingly, it was often a Clarence Williams composition that was selected.
Compilations: *Sidney Bechet Memorial Album* (c.1960), *Jazz Sounds Of The Twenties, Volume 4* (c.1962), *Clarence Williams* (c.1962), *Eva Taylor & Clarence Williams* (c.1985), *1925-26* (1988).

Taylor, Felice

b. 29 January 1948, Richmond, California, USA. Felice emerged from the burgeoning Los Angeles girl-group scene where she recorded with the Sweets, a trio which also featured her sisters Darlene and Norma. Signed as a solo act to the Mustang label, Taylor's three 1967 singles there were each produced and co-written by **Barry White**. 'It May Be Winter Outside (But In My Heart It's Spring)' was an R&B hit although the beatier 'I'm Under The Influence Of Love' unaccountably failed to chart. White later re-recorded both songs with **Love Unlimited**. Taylor meanwhile scored a substantial UK hit with her third release, 'I Feel Love Comin' On'. She then moved labels to Kent, but stripped of White's imaginative arrangements, her adenoidal delivery tended to grate. Her best latter-day offering was 'All I Want To Do Is Love You'. Recorded in Britain, it was written by Derv Gordon and arranged by **Eddy Grant**, two former members of the **Equals**.

Taylor, James

b. 12 March 1948, Boston, Massachusetts, USA. The embodiment of the American singer-songwriter from the late 60s and early 70s was the frail and troubled James Taylor. He was born into a wealthy family. His mother was a classically trained soprano and encouraged James and his siblings to become musical. As a child he wanted for nothing and divided his time between two substantial homes. He befriended **Danny 'Kootch' Kortchmar** at the age of 15 and won a local talent contest. As is often the case, boarding school education often suits the parents more than the child, and James rebelled from Milton Academy at the age of 16 to join his brother Alex in a rock band, the

Fabulous Corsairs. At only 17 he committed himself to the McLean Mental Institution in Massachusetts. Following his nine-month stay he re-united with 'Kootch' and together they formed the commercially disastrous Flying Machine. At 18, now being supported by his parents in his own apartment, the seemingly affluent James drew the predictable crowd of hangers-on and emotional parasites. He experimented and soon was addicted to heroin. He had the drive to move out, and after several months of travelling he arrived in London and found a flat in Notting Hill (which in 1968 was hardly the place for someone trying to kick a drug habit!). Once again 'Kootch' came to the rescue, and suggested Taylor take a demo tape to **Peter Asher**. 'Kootch' had supported **Peter And Gordon** on an American tour, and Asher was now looking for talent as head of the new Apple Records. Both Asher and **Paul McCartney** liked the work and the thin, weak and by now world-weary teenager was given the opportunity to record. *James Taylor* was not a success when released, even though classic songs like 'Carolina On My Mind' and 'Something In The Way She Moves' appeared on it.
Depressed and still hooked on heroin, Taylor returned to America, this time to the Austin Riggs Mental Institution. Meanwhile Asher, frustrated at the disorganized Apple, moved to America, and persevering with Taylor, he secured a deal with **Warner Brothers** and rounded up a team of supportive musician friends; 'Kootch', Leland Sklar, Russ Kunkel and **Carole King**. Many of the songs written in the institution appeared on the superlative *Sweet Baby James*. The album eventually spent two years in the US charts and contained a jewel of a song: 'Fire And Rain'. In this, he encapsulated his entire life, problems and fears; it stands as one of the finest songs of the era. Taylor received rave notices from critics and he was quickly elevated to superstardom. The follow-up *Mud Slide Slim And The Blue Horizon* consolidated the previous success and contained the definitive reading of Carole King's 'You've Got A Friend'. In 1972, now free of drugs, Taylor worked with the **Beach Boys'** **Dennis Wilson** on the cult drag-race film *Two Lane Blacktop* and released *One Man Dog* which contained another hit 'Don't Let Me Be Lonely Tonight'. Fortunately Taylor was not lonely for long; he married **Carly Simon** in the biggest show business wedding since Burton and Taylor. They duetted on a version of the **Charlie And Inez Foxx** hit, 'Mockingbird' which made the US Top 5 in 1974.
Taylor's albums began to form a pattern of mostly original compositions, mixed with an immaculately chosen blend of R&B, soul and rock 'n' roll classics. Ironically most of his subsequent hits were non-originals. **Holland Dozier And Holland**'s 'How Sweet It Is', **Otis Blackwell's** 'Handy Man', **Goffin And King**'s 'Up On The Roof'. Taylor was also

displaying confidence and sparkling onstage wit, having a superb rapport with his audiences, where once his shyness was excruciating. Simon filed for divorce a decade after their marriage, but Taylor accepted the breakdown and carried on with his profession. The assured Taylor is instrumentally captured by **Pat Metheny**'s joyous composition 'James' recorded on Metheny's *Offramp* album in 1982. In 1985 Taylor released the immaculate *That's Why I'm Here*. The reason he is here, as the lyric explains is; 'fortune and fame is such a curious game, perfect strangers can call you by name, pay good money to hear "Fire And Rain", again and again and again'. This one song says as much about James Taylor today as 'Fire And Rain' did many years ago. He has survived, he is happy, he is still creative and above all his concerts show that he is genuinely grateful to be able to perform. In recent years Taylor continues to add guest harmony vocals to all and sundry in addition to regularly touring. A double live album was issued in 1993 and is a necessary purchase for those who stopped buying his records when they moved out of their bedsitter in 1971. One autobiography crying to be written is this man's.

Albums: *James Taylor* (1968), *Sweet Baby James* (1970), *James Taylor And The Original Flying Machine - 1967* (1970), *Mud Slide Slim And The Blue Horizon* (1971), *One Man Dog* (1972), *Walking Man* (1974), *Gorilla* (1975), *In The Pocket* (1976), *JT* (1977), *Flag* (1979), *Dad Loves His Work* (1981), *That's Why I'm Here* (1985), *Never Die Young* (1988), *New Moon Shine* (1991), *Live In Rio* (CBS 1992, 1985 recordings), *Live* (1993). Compilations: *Greatest Hits* (1976), *Classic Songs* (1987), *The Best Of James Taylor - The Classic Years* (1990).

Videos: *James Taylor In Concert* (1991), *Squibnocket* (1993).

Taylor, James, Quartet

When the Medway Valley's psychedelic-mod hopefuls the **Prisoners** disbanded in 1986, organist James Taylor vowed to move into the realms of jazz, and away from rock. Assembling a quartet from Kent, England, comprising fellow Prisoner bassist Allan Crockford and ex-Daggermen personnel Simon Howard (drums) and Taylor's brother David (guitar), the band recorded a BBC session for disc jockey **John Peel**, before Taylor retired to Sweden for a break. But the broadcast made such an impression that the group were signed to new 'mod' label Re-Elect The President. A mini-album of cover versions, *Mission Impossible*, featured 'organ groovy' 60s soundtrack instrumentals like the single 'Blow Up', with **Jimmy Smith** and **Booker T. And The MGs** providing the strongest influences. *The Money Spyder* took the theme a stage further; while the **Damned** had mocked the psychedelic soundtrack as Naz Nomad And The Nightmares, the JTQ reminisced on the beat and jazz age. But Taylor become frustrated with the band's limitations and by the time *Wait A Minute* appeared on

Polydor's dance off-shoot, Urban, in September 1988, only his brother remained with him in the group. For a powerful remake of the 'Starsky And Hutch Theme', new jazz musicians and ex-**James Brown** horn-players were recruited, as the JTQ found themselves central to a new, London-based 'acid jazz' movement. Howard and Crockford, meanwhile, provided the rhythm section for ex-Prisoner Graham Day's new project, the Prime Movers. 1989 saw a further development for the JTQ with the recruitment of two rappers for May's 'Breakout'. The single hinted at a move away from jazz towards the dance charts, but *Do The Right Thing* combined both elements, alongside a continuing debt to the original fusion of jazz/dance and rare groove, not least on their rousing rendition of the 70s club favourite, 'Got To Get Your Own'. While ex-**Style Council** and **Jazz Renegades** drummer Steve White served in the JTQ for a time, Taylor himself has also made several guest performances, including appearances for the **Wonder Stuff**. 'See A Brighter Day' featuring Noel McKoy saw them bid for chart success in July 1993.

Albums: *Mission Impossible* (1987), *The Money Spyder* (1987), *Wait A Minute* (1988), *Get Organised* (1989), *Do The Right Thing* (1990), *Absolute* (1991), *Supernatural Feeling* (1993), *In The Hands Of The Inevitable* (Acid Jazz 1995).

Taylor, Jeremy

b. 24 November 1937, Newbury, Berkshire, England. Singer-songwriter Taylor went to Trinity College, Oxford, where he read French and Italian. He left England to take up a teaching post in Johannesburg, South Africa, where he spent his spare time singing in coffee bars, as well as writing short stories and plays. Painter Harold Rubin suggested that Taylor try his hand at songwriting, which he did, later composing original songs for the show *Wait A Minim!* The show became even more successful following Taylor's success with his single 'Ag Pleez Deddy' which reached number 1 in the South African charts. The show went on tour, so Taylor left his job, and toured South Africa and Rhodesia for two years. He then released a solo album, simply called *Jeremy Taylor*, which proved equally successful, despite being banned by the South African Broadcasting Corporation. Taylor then appeared in *Minim 'Bili* (Zulu for Minim The Second). The show came to London as *Wait A Minim!*, and the cast recording was released by **Decca**. Around the same time, Taylor released *Always Something New Out Of Africa*. This encompassed a range of musical styles and a variety of unusual African instruments. He left *Wait A Minim!* before it departed for the USA and with **Sydney Carter** he recorded *Live At Eton*, before leaving the college, where he was teaching at the time. Taking to the folk circuit full time, Taylor released *Jeremy Taylor His Songs*, and made regular appearances on *BBC 2's Late Night Line Up* and on BBC Television.

Granada television presented him in *At Last It's Friday*, a show featuring topical news items. His songs were used by Anglia television for the *Survival* series, while the BBC used his material for *Bird's Eye View* among other programmes. He was given his own television series, *Songs From The Two Brewers*, and together with John Wells, he wrote the music for Joan Littlewood's production of *Mrs. Wilson's Diary*. From 1974, after the double album release with Spike Milligan, the two toured for two years presenting their own show. After this period, Taylor recorded two albums, *Jobsworth*, and *Come To Blackpool*, the former containing the now classic title track. In 1980, Taylor was allowed back into South Africa, where he lived on his farm in Broederstroom, and during his time there wrote and presented a series of one-man shows. He moved back to Britain in June 1994 and is performing occasionally again.

Albums: *Wait A Minim* (Gallotone 1961), *Jeremy Taylor* (Gallotone 1962), *Minim 'Bili* (Gallotone 1962), *Wait A Minim!* (Decca 1963), *Always Something New Out Of Africa* (Decca 1964), *Jeremy Taylor And Sydney Carter Live At Eton* (Phillips Fontana 1966), *Jeremy Taylor And His Songs* (Phillips Fontana 1968), *Jeremy Taylor More Of His Songs* (Phillips Fontana 1969), *Jobsworth* (Jeremy Taylor Records 1971), *Piece Of Ground* (Jeremy Taylor Records 1972), *An Adult Entertainment-Spike Milligan And Jeremy Taylor Live At Cambridge University* (Spark Records 1974), *Come To Blackpool* (Spark Records 1975), *Jeremy Taylor Live At The New Vic* (Jeremy Taylor Records 1976), *Done At A Flash* (Jeremy Taylor Records 1977), *Back In Town* (Gallotone 1979), *Ag Pleez Deddy And Other Hits* (Plum Records 1980), *Safe My Mate !* (Teal Records 1981), *Jeremy Taylor Stuff-The L.P.* (Teal Records 1983), *Jeremy Taylor Live At The Cherrytrees* (Jeremy Taylor Records 1984).

Taylor, John

b. 25 September 1942, Manchester, England. A self-taught pianist, Taylor had established himself as one of the most respected British jazz pianists by the end of the 60s and has continued to consolidate his reputation ever since. He began his musical career with a dance band until 1964, when he moved to London, and began playing with other young lions of the time, such as **John Surman**, **Alan Skidmore** and Norma Winstone, whom he would later marry. He also worked with established stars like **Marian Montgomery**, **Cleo Laine** and **John Dankworth**. In the late 60s he began to lead his own trio and sextet with **Kenny Wheeler**, **Chris Pyne**, Stan Sulzmann, **Chris Laurence** and Tony Levin. He also played in Sulzmann's quartet, with Winstone in Edge Of Time and with **Mike Gibbs**. He was a member of Surman's outstanding but short-lived Morning Glory with **Terje Rypdal**. His collaboration with Surman, which produced some of the most inventive and original jazz-based music of the 70s and 80s, has continued to the present. In the mid-70s he spent some time with the **Ronnie Scott** quintet. In 1977, with Wheeler and Winstone, he formed Azimuth (not to be confused with Azymuth), for which he writes most of the music. At the end of the decade he played with **Jan Garbarek**, **Arild Andersen** and **Miroslav Vitous**. He has also worked with **Lee Konitz**, John Warren, **Graham Collier**, and **Harry Beckett**. His rich, fluid playing, inspired in part by **Bill Evans**, is especially distinctive on ballads. He is also an accomplished composer, and credits Gibbs with being a fundamental influence on his writing. In the 90s Taylor continues to work with Azimuth, to play in a regular duo with Winstone and to lead his own trio, with Mick Hutton and Steve Argüelles.

Albums: *Pause And Think Again* (1971), with Michael Gibbs *Michael Gibbs* (1971), with John Surman *Morning Glory* (1973), *Fragment* (1974), with Azimuth *Azimuth* (ECM 1977), with Azimuth *Touchstone* (1979), with Azimuth *Depart* (1980), with Miroslav Vitous *Journey's End* (1982), with Kenny Wheeler *Double Double You* (1983), *Azimuth '85* (1985), with Stan Sulzmann *Everybody's Song But My Own* (1987), with Lee Konitz *Songs Of The Stars* (1988), *Blue Glass* (Jazz House 1992), with Surman *Ambleside Days* (Ah Um 1992).

Taylor, Johnnie

b. 5 May 1938, Crawfordsville, Arkansas, USA. Having left home at the age of 15, Taylor surfaced as part of several gospel groups, including the Five Echoes and the Highway QCs. From there he joined the **Soul Stirrers**, replacing **Sam Cooke** on the latter's recommendation. Taylor switched to secular music in 1961; releases on Cooke's Sar and Derby labels betrayed his mentor's obvious influence. In 1965 he signed with **Stax** and scored several R&B hits before 'Who's Making Love' (1968) crossed over into *Billboard*'s pop Top 5. Further releases, including, 'Take Care Of Your Homework' (1969), 'I Believe In You (You Believe In Me)' and 'Cheaper To Keep Her' (both 1973), continued this success. Taylor maintained his momentum on a move to **Columbia**. The felicitous 'Disco Lady' (1976) was the first single to be certified platinum by the RIAA, but although subsequent releases reached the R&B chart they fared less well with the wider audience. Following a short spell with Beverley Glenn, the singer found an ideal niche on **Malaco**, a bastion for traditional southern soul. Taylor's first album there, *This Is The Night* (1984), reaffirmed his gritty, blues-edged approach, a feature consolidated on *Wall To Wall*, *Lover Boy* and *Crazy 'Bout You*. *Wanted: One Soul Singer*, *Who's Making Love* and *Taylored In Silk* encapsulate his lengthy period at Stax. *Somebody's Gettin' It* compiles several Columbia recordings while Taylor's early work on Sar is found on *The Roots Of Johnnie Taylor*.

Albums: *Wanted One Soul Singer* (1967), *Who's Making*

Love? (1968), *The Johnnie Taylor Philosophy Continues* (1969), *Rare Stamps* (1970), *One Step Beyond* (1971), *Taylored In Silk* (1973), *Super Taylor* (1974), *Eargasm* (1976), *Rated Extraordinaire* (1977), *Disco 9000* (1977), *Ever Ready* (1978), *Reflections* (197), *She's Killing Me* (1979), *A New Day* (1980), *Just Ain't Good Enough* (1982), *This Is Your Night* (1984), *Best Of The Old And The New* (1984), *Wall To Wall* (1985), *Lover Boy* (1987), *In Control* (1988), *Crazy 'Bout You* (1989), *Just Can't Do Right* (c.90s), *Real Love* (c.90s). Compilations: *The Roots Of Johnnie Taylor* (1969), *Rare Stamps* (1970), *The Johnnie Taylor Chronicle (1968-1972)* (1978), *The Johnnie Taylor Chronicle (1972-1974)* (1978), *Somebody's Getting It* (1989), *Chronicle: The 20 Greatest Hits* (c.1989), *Raw Blues/Little Bluebird* (1992), *The Johnnie Taylor Philosophy Continues/One Step Beyond* (1994), *The Best Of... On Malaco Vol. 1* (1994).

Taylor, Kingsize, And The Dominoes

Vocalist Taylor led one of the most exciting Liverpool beat groups during the early 60s, but approbation in their homeland was undermined by an almost perpetual residency in German clubs. Originally signed to Philips, they completed several singles not issued in the UK before compounding this anonymity by agreeing to record for **Polydor** as the Shakers. *Let's Do The Slop, Twist, Madison, Hully Gully With The Shakers* was a worthwhile resume of R&B/soul staples, but the unit's complex series of recordings is best exemplified in their rendition of **Solomon Burke**'s 'Stupidity'. This compulsive release, credited to Taylor and the Dominoes, was one of the finest of the genre, but the band ceased recording later that year following a live EP culled from a set at Hamburg's Star Club. Taylor achieved notoriety during the 70s when his reel-to-reel tape of a **Beatles**' performance at the same venue formed the basis for several archive packages. A Dominoes' set on the same spool - the prime reason for its initial recording - did not generate the same interest although their version of 'Hully Gully' has erroneously crept into several aforementioned Beatles' releases.

Album: *Let's Do The Slop, Twist, Madison, Hully Gully With The Shakers* (1963).

Taylor, Koko

b. Cora Walton, 28 September 1935, Memphis, Tennessee, USA. Taylor is one of the few major figures whom post-war Chicago blues has produced. Her soulfully rasping voice has ensured her popularity in the Windy City, and latterly further afield, for 30 years, since she recorded her first single for the local USA label. Pacted by the leading black music independent label **Chess**, she scored their last blues hit in 1966 with the **Willie Dixon** song 'Wang Dang Doodle', whose cast of low-life characters suited her raucous delivery (guitar work supplied by **Buddy Guy**). In the 70s and 80s a series of well-produced and sometimes exciting albums with her band the Blues Machine, as well as

such prestigious gigs as Carnegie Hall and the **Montreux International Jazz Festival**, have confirmed her position as the world's top-selling female blues artist. Though she admits that 'It's not easy to be a woman out there', she has succeeded on her own terms and without compromising the raunchy, barroom quality of her music.

Albums: *Koko Taylor* (1968), *Basic Soul* (c.1970), *Chicago Baby* (1974), *I Got What It Takes* (1975), *Earthshaker* (1978), *From The Heart Of A Woman* (1981), *Queen Of The Blues* (1985), *An Audience With The Queen - Live From Chicago* (1987), *Blues In Heaven* (1988), *Jump For Joy* (1990), *Force Of Nature* (Alligator 1993). Compilation: *Koko Taylor* (1990, rec. 1965-69).

Taylor, Livingston

b. 1951, Chapel Hill, North Carolina, USA. Taylor was the youngest of four singing and guitar-playing brother and sisters. With a home background of folk music, he played coffee houses in Boston and attracted the interest of rock critic Jon Landau. His first two albums for Phil Walden's Capricorn label were produced by Landau and contained the minor hits 'Carolina Day', and 'Get Out Of Bed', both written by Taylor. His acoustic style was reminiscent of the work of his brother, **James Taylor**, but retained a bluesier edge. James Taylor and **Carly Simon** sang on *Over The Rainbow*, but after its release Livingston was dropped by Capricorn. He continued to tour regularly throughout the 70s and after signing to Epic, he had Top 40 hits with the Nick de Caro-produced 'I Will Be In Love With You' (1979) and 'First Time Love' (1980), produced by John Boylan and Jeff 'Skunk' Baxter, formerly of the **Doobie Brothers**. He continued to record sporadically during the 80s, scoring a minor hit with 'Loving Arms', a duet with **Leah Kunkel** and also performed at US colleges and folk clubs.

Albums: *Livingston Taylor* (1970), *Liv* (1971), *Over The Rainbow* (1973), *Three Way Mirror* (1978), *Man's Best Friend* (1980), *Life Is Good* (1988), *Good Friends* (1993).

Taylor, Martin

b. 1956, England. Repeatedly referred to as 'the guitarists' guitarist', Taylor shows an extraordinary flair and natural feel for his instrument, that has enabled him to make subtle and profound contributions in a number of different musical styles, and has resulted in a keen and loyal international audience that makes its presence felt on each Taylor tour. An early starter at the age of four, he was playing his first professional performance (in a Harlow, Hertfordshire, music shop) at eight, and displaying his genuinely prodigious talent in trad and mainstream bands led by Sonny Dee and **Lennie Hastings** by 1968. Turning professional at the first opportunity three years later, Taylor spent much of the 70s honing his talents in swing bands and cafe residencies, and enjoying the occasional opportunity to sit in with and impress visiting Americans, including **Count Basie** (whom he met on a cruise ship) and **Barney Kessel**. His first album, a duo with bassist **Peter Ind**, was released on Ind's Wave label in 1978, and a year later he established his celebrated and continuing relationship with the legendary swing violinist **Stéphane Grappelli**, touring internationally, recording with Grappelli and classical violin virtuoso Yehudi Menuhin and broadcasting live on the BBC with Grappelli and popular composer Julian Lloyd Webber. Touring with Grappelli, whose previous guitar partners had included the brilliant **Django Reinhardt** and **Joe Pass**, helped introduce Taylor's talents to a wider audience, and appearances during 1981 at Carnegie Hall, the Hollywood Bowl, the Royal Opera House and on Johnny Carson's *Tonight Show* marked the beginning of a busy decade – as Taylor concurrently worked at perfecting his solo style while in the UK, and continued to steadily build a solid reputation amongst America's jazz musicians, touring with guitarist **Emily Remler**, and recording with **Toots Thielemans**, **Buddy De Franco** (their album *Groovin'* was voted Jazz Album of the Year by the British Music Retailers Association), Paulinho De Costa and **John Patitucci**, **Chet Atkins**, and finally replacing **Herb Ellis** in the Great Guitars trio with **Charlie Byrd** and Barney Kessel. Since 1990, Taylor has been touring increasingly under his own name, playing sell-out dates and televised concerts in Australia, Hong Kong and Israel, and enjoying greater recognition in the UK, partly as a result of a fruitful relationship with Linn Records. His 1993 *Artistry* was the culmination of years spent developing a 'complete' solo style. Performing on a custom-made 'stereo guitar' that separates the bass and treble strings into different channels, Taylor accompanies his own swinging improvisations with chords and walking bass lines, providing a record of the kind of performance that has left so many guitarists stunned in recent years.

Selected albums: *Taylor Made* (Wave 1978), with Stéphane Grappelli *At The Winery* (1980), with Grappelli, Yehudi Menuhin *Strictly For The Birds* (1980), with Grappelli, Menuhin *Top Hat* (1981), *Skye Boat* (Concord 1981), with Grappelli *Vintage '81* (1981), with Grappelli *Live In San Francisco* (1982), *A Tribute To Art Tatum* (1984), with Buddy De Franco *Groovin'* (1985), *Innovations* (1985), *Sarabanda* (Gala 1986), with Vassar Clements *Together At Last* (1987), *Don't Fret* (Linn 1990), *Matter Of Time* (1991), *Change Of Heart* (Linn 1991), *Artistry* (Linn 1993), with Grappelli *Reunion* (1993), *Spirit Of Django* (Linn 1994).

Taylor, Melvin

b. 13 March 1959, Jackson, Mississippi, USA. At three years old Taylor moved with his family to Chicago, and began playing guitar around the age of six, inspired by

an uncle who played blues. He was influenced by a variety of guitarists, including **B.B. King**, **Albert King**, **Jimi Hendrix**, and particularly **Wes Montgomery**. In the early 70s Taylor played on Maxwell Street, Chicago's open air street market, and in his mid-teens was with a group call the Transistors. He has also worked with **Carey Bell**, (and son **Lurrie Bell**), and was a member of **Eddie Shaw**'s group (he also recorded with Shaw) and the **Legendary Blues Band.** He made his debut recording for the French label in 1982, and a follow-up appeared in 1984. He also recorded on Alligator's 'New Bluebloods' anthology. Taylor is a fleet-fingered player who now plays with feel and technique.

Album: *Melvin Taylor Plays The Blues For You* (1984).

Taylor, Mick

b. Michael Taylor, 17 January 1948, Welwyn Garden City, Hertfordshire, England. A rock and blues guitarist, much influenced by **B.B. King, Muddy Waters** and jazz saxophone giant **John Coltrane**, Taylor taught himself to play after leaving school at 15. His first band, the Welwyn-based Gods, also featured Ken Hensley (later of **Uriah Heep**) and John Glascock (**Jethro Tull**). In August 1965, Taylor deputized for absentee **Eric Clapton** in **John Mayall**'s Bluesbreakers, and joined the band on a permanent basis from June 1967. He was the longest-serving of Mayall's guitarists by the time he left to join the **Rolling Stones** in 1969, as a replacement for Brian Jones. Taylor had minimal involvement with their *Let It Bleed*, but his controlled and tasteful blues playing brought a rare lyricism to the band's early 70s' releases. He left the Stones in December 1975, working initially with **Jack Bruce** and **Carla Bley,** and appearing on two albums by jazz-rockers **Gong**. The well-received *Mick Taylor* put him back in the limelight temporarily; he spent much of the early 80s as part of **Bob Dylan**'s band, appearing on three albums and touring with him in 1984. *Stranger In This Town* met with little success, and Taylor subsequently joined informal band the Bluesmasters (with **Junior Wells** and **Steve Jordan**) on *Win Or Lose* (1991), the debut release by American Brian Kramer. Taylor was reunited with John Mayall, guesting on his excellent *Wake Up Call* in 1993.

Albums: with John Mayall And The Bluesbreakers *Crusade* (1967), *Diary Of A Band Vol. 1* (1968), *Diary Of A Band Vol 2* (1968), *Bare Wires* (1968), *Blues From Laurel Canyon* (1969), *Back To The Roots* (1971); with the Rolling Stones *Let It Bleed* (1969), *Get Yer Ya-Ya's Out* (1970), *Sticky Fingers* (1971), *Exile On Main Street* (1972), *Goat's Head Soup* (1973), *It's Only Rock 'N' Roll* (1974); with Bob Dylan *Infidels* (1983), *Real Live* (1984); solo *Mick Taylor* (1979), *Stranger In This Town* (1990).

Taylor, Montana

b. Arthur Taylor, 1903, Butte, Montana, USA. Nicknamed after his birthplace, Taylor was raised in Indianapolis, where he learned piano in 1919. He played cafes and rent parties there and in Chicago, before recording two 78s for Vocalion in 1929. Although one record was partially spoiled by the vocal antics of the Jazoo Boys, Taylor's percussive, inventive piano playing was of the highest order. Shortly afterwards he stopped playing, discouraged by the absence of royalties. Located by jazz fans in 1946, Taylor made a series of recordings that not only showed he retained all his instrumental abilities, both solo and as accompanist to **Bertha 'Chippie' Hill,** but revealed him to be a moving singer as well, particularly on slow, introspective pieces like 'I Can't Sleep'. Discouraged anew, however, Taylor dropped out of sight again, and his subsequent whereabouts are unknown.
Album: *Montana's Blues* (1977).

Taylor, R. Dean

Toronto-born R. Dean Taylor remains the most successful white artist to emerge from the **Motown Records** stable. The protege of writer/producer **Brian Holland**, he worked on many of the mid-60s hits produced by the **Holland/Dozier/Holland** partnership, and later claimed to have helped compose several songs credited to them. He began his recording career in 1965, with 'Let's Go Somewhere', but found more success with two of his compositions for the **Supremes**, 'Love Child' and 'I'm Living In Shame', both of which brought a new realism into the group's work. In 1967, he recorded the classic soul number 'There's A Ghost In My House', which enjoyed cult status in Britain. A year later he released the evocative 'Gotta See Jane', which also charted in the UK that summer. His most memorable single was 'Indiana Wants Me', an effect-laden melodrama which climbed high in both the UK and US charts in 1970. Despite his popularity in Britain, where a revival of 'There's A Ghost In My House' reached the Top 3 in 1974, Taylor was unable to repeat this success with his subsequent recordings, either on his own Jane label in 1973, or with **Polydor** from 1974.
Albums: *I Think Therefore I Am* (1970), *Indiana Wants Me* (1971), *LA Sunset* (1975).

Taylor, Roger

b. Roger Meddows-Taylor, 26 July 1949, King's Lynn, Norfolk, England. Best known as the drummer in million-selling UK rock group **Queen**, Taylor has also recorded as a soloist. During 1977 he made his debut by releasing 'I Wanna Testify', which failed to chart but remains of cult interest to Queen fans. Four years later came 'Future Management' and *Fun In Space*, which received a scathing reception in the music press. The underrated 'Man On Fire' stalled at number 66 and was overshadowed by Queen product. Taylor's second solo album, *Strange Frontier*, featured songs by **Bob Dylan**, **Bruce Springsteen** and the **Spencer Davis Group**, and clipped the UK Top 30. With the demise of Queen in 1991 following the death of **Freddie Mercury**, Taylor's solo activities took on greater substance. He has in fact been the leader of his own band, the **Cross**, since 1987.
Albums: *Fun In Space* (1981), *Strange Frontier* (1984). With the Cros:s *Shove It* (1988), *Mad, Bad And Dangerous To Know* (1990), *Happiness?* (Parlophone 1994).

Taylor, Ted

b. Austin Taylor, 16 February 1934, Okmulgee, Oklahoma, USA, d. October 1987. Taylor was a veteran of several spiritual groups including the Mighty Clouds Of Joy and the Santa Monica Soul Seekers. This latter group then crossed over to R&B, where they worked a dual career both as the **Cadets** and the Jacks. Taylor embarked on his solo path in 1957 and scored with many regional hits. His most notable early singles were 'Be Ever Wonderful', for the Duke label in 1960 and 'Stay Away From My Baby', his first R&B chart hit for **OKeh** from 1965. Following a short spell with **Atco**, the singer joined Jewel/Ronn Records. He remained there until the mid-70s although his output never achieved the recognition it deserved. After that Taylor cut albums for Alarm, MCA and his own Solpugdits/SPG label. Tragically, Taylor was killed in a road accident in October 1987.
Albums: *Be Ever Wonderful* (1963), *Blues And Soul* (1965), *Shades Of Blue* (1970), *You Can Dig It* (1970), *Taylor Made* (1971), with Little Johnny Taylor *The Super Taylors* (1974), *Ted Taylor 1976* (1976), *Keepin' My Head Above Water* (1978), *Be Ever Wonderful* (1986), *Taylor Made For You* (1987). Compilations: *Greatest Hits* (1966), *Keep On Walking* (1980), *Somebody's Always Trying 1958-1966* (1988), *Taylor Made* (1991), *Be Ever Wonderful* (1991), *Steal Away* (1991).

Taylor, Theodore 'Hound Dog'

b. 12 April 1917, Natchez, Mississippi, USA, d. 17 December 1975, Chicago, Illinois, USA. Taylor had an apprenticeship playing guitar in Mississippi with musicians such as **Elmore James** and **John Lee 'Sonny Boy' Williamson**. In 1942 he moved to Chicago where he worked the clubs as well as the market on Maxwell Street. Two singles from the early 60s underlined the vitality of his music, especially the high-energy 'Five Take Five'. He won a following among young blues fans and toured Europe as well as north America. In 1971 he made an album for Alligator Records and this helped established a reputation for intense bottleneck guitar blues and R&B. He did not live long enough to exploit his reputation.

Album: *And His Houserockers* (1971), *Beware Of The Dog* (1975).

Taylor, Tyrone

b. 1957, Negril, Jamaica, West Indies. He recorded his first outing with producer, **Joe Gibbs** when he was only 12 years old. The result, 'Delilah' surfaced in the UK as the b-side to **Dennis Walks** hit, 'Having A Party'. As the song did not fulfil Taylor's musical ambition he drifted among some of Jamaica's top session men learning to play a number of instruments. One of his most influential benefactors was Willie Lindo who encouraged him to persevere with a career in the music business. Taylor was to record with a number of producers notably with Jack Ruby and **Winston 'Niney' Holness** and was signed to **Bob Marley**'s Tuff Gong enterprise. Taylor's sessions with Holness resulted in two Jamaican hits, 'Just A Feeling' and 'Sufferation', the latter featured a special **King Tubby** mix. By 1983 Taylor enjoyed international notoriety when he released the semi-autobiographical, 'Cottage In Negril' a self-production through his own, Love Time production company. The single surfaced at a time when dancehall ruled and despite his gentler approach he was able to earn the title of Best Selling Singer Of 1983. At the the following year's Sunsplash festival he appeared alongside **Bob Andy**, with whom his songwriting skills are often compared, **Edi Fitzroy** and **Dennis Brown**. His following release 'Come To Me' was not as successful, but the song was a hard act to follow. Undeterred by the minor hit, MCA, who had enjoyed a UK number one hit with **Musical Youth**, signed Taylor on the strength of 'Cottage In Negril'. The deal led to the release of 'Pledge To The Sun' which failed to generate sufficient enthusiasm for further output. He had recorded an album's worth of material which was not released. A tour of Europe was arranged without any support from the label and disillusionment from lack of promotion led to his premature departure from the contract. Following this setback little was heard from Taylor but he bounced back with the roots market releasing sporadic hits most notably in 1987 when he released 'Members Only' and 'Be For Real'. By 1993 he had returned to working with his original guiding mentor Willie Lindo, who produced *The Way To Paradise*, which featured mainly cover versions in Taylor's inimitable style. The following year he teamed up with producer Clive Hunt, returned to Bob Marley's Tuff Gong studio, and released the hit 'Rainy Sunset'.
Albums: *Sings For Members Only* (Techniques 1989), *Jamming In The Hills* (1990), *The Way To Paradise* (1994). Compilation: *Cottage In Negril* (1989).

Taylor, Vince

One of the first, and most authentic British rock 'n' rollers, Taylor was virtually ignored by his native Britons but managed to make a decent living in France where he spent most of his life. He started out in 1958 backed by his Playboys, who comprised Tony Harvey (guitar), Tony Sheridan (guitar/vocals), Brian 'Licorice' Locking (bass) and **Brian Bennett** (drums). They appeared regularly on the pioneering UK television rock show *Oh Boy!* and released a cover of a **Charlie Rich** song, 'Right Behind You Baby', on **Parlophone**. A second single in 1959, 'Brand New Cadillac', penned by Taylor, ranks alongside Ian Samwell's 'Move It' as one of *the* authentic British rock records. The **Clash** would later contribute a version which restored it to the British rock tradition. The band split in early 1959 (Locking and Bennett moved to various bands including the **Shadows**, Sheridan to Hamburg where he worked with the fledgling **Beatles**) and Taylor assembled a new backing band with Harvey plus Alan LeClaire on piano, Johnny Vance on bass, and Bobby Woodman on drums. This line-up of the Playboys also backed **Screaming Lord Sutch** in 1960. Taylor toured with Sutch, **Keith Kelly** and **Lance Fortune** on a '2 I's (coffee bar)' package tour. Around the Summer of 1961 Harvey joined Nero And The Gladiators, the rest of the Playboys went to France to back **Johnny Hallyday**, and Taylor followed their trail, becoming a minor celebrity in the process. He continued to record throughout the 60s, 70s and 80s, mostly doing covers of rock 'n' roll classics. He died in 1991.
Albums: *Le Rock C'est Ça!* (1961), *Vince* (1965), *Alive, Well & Rocking In Paris* (1972), *Cadillac* (1975), *Live 1977* (1979), *Luv* (1980), *Bien Compris* (1987), *Black Leather Rebel* (1993).

Tchaikovsky, Bram

Bram Tchaikovsky (b. Peter Bramall, 10 November 1950, Lincolnshire, England) started playing guitar in his teens and was already in a group by the mid-60s. In the 70s he formed the All-Time Heroes with James Roper (bass), Majo (keyboards) and Keith Line (drums). They recorded some demos and also landed themselves a spot supporting **Man** on tour, but by this time they had become Roper. They changed their name again, reverting to a shorter version of their first name - Heroes - and put out a cover version of **Bruce Springsteen**'s 'Growing Up'. Bram originally auditioned for the **Motors** in February 1977 and although he failed the first audition he was soon taken on, thus ending the career of Heroes. In 1978, whilst Andy McMaster and Nick Garvey had the Motors idling whilst they wrote songs, Tchaikovsky formed Battleaxe with Micky Broadbent (bass/guitar/keyboards) and Keith Boyce (drums, ex-**Heavy Metal Kids**). They put out a Garvey produced single 'Sarah Smiles', on the Criminal label before signing to Radar. Now known simply by the name of their leader (whose split from the Motors was permanent but highly amicable) Bram Tchaikovsky set about recording *Strange Man Changed Man* in November 1978. As well as Broadbent and Boyce, **Mike Oldfield** played tubular bells on the track 'Girl Of My Dreams', which breached the US Top 40. Co-producer Garvey provided backing vocals and former Heroes sideman Roper took some of the photography. By the time of the second album, Boyce had left and Heroes drummer Line had taken over. Denis Forbes had also been brought in to help Tchaikovsky and Broadbent with guitar, bass and vocals. Bob Andrews (of the **Rumour**) helped out with keyboards on the track 'Pressure', which was the title of the album in the USA. Broadbent had left by 1981 and the band themselves left the rapidly disintegrating Radar label and signed to **Arista**. Funland was recorded at Rockfield studios in January and February 1981 with a brand new line-up of Tchaikovsky, Forbes, Lord Richard Itchingham (bass), and Derek Ballard (drums). It would be the last album by the band and despite persistent rumours of a Motors reunion Bram remains out of the limelight.

Albums: *Strange Man, Changed Man* (1979), *The Russians Are Coming* (1980), *Funland* (1981).

Tchicai, John Martin

b. 28 April 1936, Copenhagen, Denmark. Tchicai, the son of a Danish mother and Congolese father, was the only major non-American figure in the free jazz movement of the early 60s. He had studied violin at first, but then took up alto saxophone and clarinet. Since 1983 he has switched primarily to tenor saxophone. He spent three years at the Aarhus Academy of Music and then moved to the Copenhagen Academy. In 1962 he met **Albert Ayler** during Ayler's stay in Copenhagen, led his band at the World Youth Jazz Festival in Helsinki, and worked with Jorgen Leth's quintet at the Warsaw Jazz Festival. As a result of his meeting in Helsinki with **Archie Shepp** and **Bill Dixon** he moved to New York in 1963 and joined the New York Contemporary Five, which included Shepp, Dixon (later replaced by **Don Cherry** for a tour of Europe), Don Moore and J.C. Moses. On his return to New York he founded the New York Art Quartet with **Roswell Rudd**, **Milford Graves** and Lewis Worrell (or sometimes **Steve Swallow** or **Eddie Gomez**) on bass. He also joined the Jazz Composers' Guild and worked with the **Jazz Composers' Orchestra** and **Carla Bley**. In 1965 he took part in **John Coltrane**'s controversial and epoch-making *Ascension*. On returning to Europe in 1966 he played with **Gunter Hampel** and Cherry as well as leading groups of his own, including Cadentia Nova Danica. CND was an extremely impressive nine-piece band which grew, reaching 26 pieces for its second recording, and finally split, some of its members forming the rock band Burning Red Ivanhoe. In the 70s he worked often with **Johnny Dyani**, who had

emigrated to Denmark, and with the Strange Brothers (1976- 81), the Instant Composers Pool, **George Gruntz** and **Irène Schweizer**. In the early 80s he played with Pierre Dørge, the New Jungle Orchestra, **Chris McGregor**'s Brotherhood Of Breath (*Yes, Please*), De Zes Winden (an all-saxophone group) and, again, Dyani, with whom he was touring at the time of the bassist's death. An impressive and personal improviser, he was a lyrical altoist with a rich tone, and his sound is equally distinctive since moving over to tenor. He also plays soprano sax and bass clarinet and has essayed occasional vocals and synthesizer programming on some recent sessions.

Selected albums: with Archie Shepp *Rufus* (1964), with the New York Contemporary Five *Consequences* (1964), *New York Eye And Ear Control* (1964), *New York Contemporary Five Vols. 1 & 2* (1964), with Shepp *Four For Trane* (1964), *New York Art Quartet* (1965), with the New York Art Quartet *Mohawk* (1965), with John Coltrane *Ascension* (1965), *John Tchicai And Cadentia Nova Danica* (Freedom 1969), with CND *Afrodisiaca* (1970), with Irène Schweizer *Willi The Pig* (1976), *Real Tchicai* (1977), with Strange Brothers *Darktown Highlights* (Storyville 1977), *Solo* (1977), *John Tchicai And Strange Brothers* (1978), with Andre Goudbeck *Duets* (1978), with Goudbeck *Barefoot Dance* (1979), with Hartmut Geerken *Continent* (Praxis 1981), *Live In Athens* (Praxis 1981), with Strange Brothers *Merlin Vibrations* (1983), *Put Up The Fight* (Storyville 1987), *Timo's Message* (Black Saint 1987, rec. 1984), *Clinch* (1991), with Vitold Rek *Satisfaction* (Enja 1992).

Tea And Symphony

Formed in Birmingham, England, this adventurous ensemble was part of the city's Big Bear management stable. Although Tea And Symphony originally consisted of James Langston (vocals/guitar), Jeff Daw (guitar) and Nigel Phillips (drums/'exotic' instruments), they were often augmented by musicians from the agency including Bob Lamb and Mick Hincks from the group **Locomotive**. Tea And Symphony's debut *An Asylum For The Musically Insane*, was an enchanting, if self-indulgent collection, but its period-piece madness was sadly jettisoned for the more formal follow-up, *Jo Sago*. Guitarists Bob Wilson and Dave Carroll were now part of the group's fluid line-up, but the ensemble broke up in 1971 when both of these artists, and drummer Bob Lamb, joined the **Idle Race**. The three individuals remained with their newfound outlet when it became known as the **Steve Gibbons** Band.

Albums: *An Asylum For The Musically Insane* (1969), *Jo Sago* (1970).

Teagarden, Charlie

b. 19 July 1913, Vernon, Texas, USA, d. 10 December 1984. A trumpet-playing member of the prodigious Teagarden family, Charlie played in several **territory**

bands during the 20s. At the end of the decade he was in **Ben Pollack**'s band and during the 30s played in bands led by **Red Nichols**, **Paul Whiteman** and others. In the 40s he was with **Harry James** and, most fruitfully, **Jimmy Dorsey**. Throughout these years he regularly played and recorded with his brother **Jack Teagarden**. In the 50s he mingled studio work in Hollywood with appearances in the **Bob Crosby** band and eventually settled in Las Vegas, playing in casino and hotel bands. A rich-toned trumpeter, with a joyous ring to everything he played, Little T's career was inevitably, if rather unfairly, overshadowed by that of his famous brother.

Albums: with Jimmy Dorsey *Dorseyland Band* (1950), *Big Horn* (1962).

Teagarden, Cub

b. Clois Lee Teagarden, 16 December 1915, Vernon, Texas, USA, d. 1969. Youngest of the noted Teagarden family of jazz musicians, Cub played drums in various **territory bands** in the 30s. He touched the edge of the big time with the big band led by his brother, **Jack Teagarden**, at the end of the 30s but this was a short-lived experience. Thereafter he gigged on the west coast until his retirement from full-time music at the end of the 40s.

Teagarden, Jack

b. Weldon L. Teagarden, 29 August 1905, Vernon, Texas, USA, d. 15 January 1964. One of the giants of jazz, Teagarden began playing trombone and singing in and around his home town, encouraged by his mother, Helen Teagarden, a pianist. From his early teens he was playing professionally, touring with various bands, notably that led by **Peck Kelley**. He continued to gain experience with a number of bands, his reputation spreading ahead of him until, by the time he reached New York City in the late 20s, he was ready for the big time. He joined **Ben Pollack** in 1928 and through his work with this band, and numerous record dates, he frightened just about every other trombone player in the country into either changing their approach or contemplating premature retirement. He recorded extensively with small bands and with **Paul Whiteman**, and appeared frequently on radio, sometimes forming his own small groups. An attempt at leading a big band was doomed to failure, due in part to Teagarden's casual and unbusinesslike manner and also to his fondness for drink. In 1946 he became a member of **Louis Armstrong**'s All Stars, touring extensively and reaching audiences who had long idolized him through his recordings. In 1951 he left Armstrong to form his own band. During the remainder of his life he led small groups, some of which included his brother and sister, **Charlie** and **Norma Teagarden**. He was also co-leader with **Earl Hines** of an all-star band, which included **Peanuts Hucko**,

Cozy Cole and **Max Kaminsky**. The ceaseless touring and drinking weakened him and he died suddenly in 1964.

Teagarden's trombone playing was smooth and stylish and quite unlike any player before him. Although his consummate skill affected the playing of numerous other trombone players, Teagarden's style was not really developed by his successors. When he played the blues he was much closer to the work of black musicians than any other white musician of his generation. His relaxed sound concealed a thorough command of his instrument and in retrospect it is easy to understand the fear he inspired in musicians like **Glenn Miller** and **Bill Rank**. A pointer to the awe with which he was regarded in the profession is the fact that even **Tommy Dorsey**, himself one of the most technically distinguished trombonists in jazz, refused to play a solo when he found himself on a record date with Teagarden. Heavily influenced by the black blues singers he heard as a child in Texas, Teagarden was also a remarkable singer. He sang in a sleepy drawl and formed a significant bridge in popular music, linking the blues to the white crooning style of **Bing Crosby**. Despite the success of his blues singing, his later performances with Armstrong inclined more towards the humour and easy-going charm which reflected his personality. Thanks to a succession of definitive recordings, on which he ably demonstrated his superlative trombone technique and lazy vocal charm, Teagarden made many songs his own. These include 'I'm Coming Virginia', 'If I Could Be With You One Hour Tonight', 'Aunt Hagar's Blues', 'The Sheik Of Araby' and, especially, 'Stars Fell On Alabama' and 'Basin Street Blues'.

Albums: with Louis Armstrong *Town Hall Concert Plus* (1947), with Armstrong *Satchmo At Symphony Hall* (1949), *Jack Teagarden In San Francisco* (1953), *Meet Me Where They Play The Blues* (1954), *Hangover Club, San Francisco, 1954* (1954), *Jack Teagarden And His Sextet* i (1954), *Jack Teagarden With Herb Geller's Orchestra* (1956), *Jack Teagarden With Van Alexander's Orchestra* (1956), *Jack Teagarden And His Sextet* ii (1957), *The Jack Teagarden-Earl Hines All Stars In England* (1957), *The Jack Teagarden-Earl Hines All Stars At The Olympia Theatre, Paris* (1957), *Jack Teagarden* i (1958), *Jack Teagarden* ii (1958), *Jack Teagarden And His Dixieland Band* (1958), *Jack Teagarden And His Sextet* iii (1959), *Jack Teagarden And His Orchestra* i (1961), *Jack Teagarden And His Orchestra* ii (1961), *Jack Teagarden With Russ Case And Bob Brookmeyer's Orchestra* (1962), *Jack Teagarden On Okinawa* (1959), *Jack Teagarden!!!* (1962), *The Jack Teagarden Sextet In Person* (1963), *Hollywood Bowl Concert* (1963). Compilations: *King Of The Blues Trombone* (1928-40), *I Gotta Right To Sing The Blues* (1929-34), *A Hundred Year From Today* (1931-34), *T 'N' T* (1933-34), *Jack Teagarden On The Air* (1936-38), *Jack Teagarden And His Orchestra* iii (1939), *Jack Teagarden's Big Eight* (1940), *Big Band Gems* (1940-41), *Big T And The Condon Gang*

(1944), with Armstrong *Satchmo Meets Big Tea* (1944-58), *Jack Teagarden And His Sextet* iv (1947), *Big T's Jazz* (1947-55), *The Swingin' Gate* (1960-63), *A Hundred Years From Today* (1931-34).

Further reading: *Jack Teagarden's Music*, Walters, H. Jnr. (1960), *Jack Teagarden: The Story Of A Jazz Maverick*, Smith, Jay D., & Guttridge, Len (1960).

Teagarden, Norma

b. 29 April 1911, Vernon, Texas, USA. Like her mother, Helen Teagarden, Norma took up piano, playing in local bands and later in south-west **territory bands**. She played briefly with her brother, **Jack Teagarden**, and also worked in bands led by **Ben Pollack,** Matty Matlock and others during the 40s and 50s. She continued playing, often as a single, during the following decades and in the mid-80s toured the UK. A highly-gifted musician, she only began to attract the attention and honours her talent deserved after Jack's death.

Albums: all with Jack Teagarden *Big T's Jazz* (1947-55 recordings), *The Swingin' Gate* (1960-63 recordings).

Teardrop Explodes

This Liverpool group was assembled by vocalist **Julian Cope** (b. 21 October 1957, Bargoed, Wales), a former member of the Crucial Three, which had featured **Ian McCulloch** (later of **Echo And The Bunnymen**) and Pete Wylie (later of **Wah!**). The Teardrop Explodes took their name from a page in a Marvel comic and the original group came together in late 1978 with a line-up featuring Cope, Michael Finkler (guitar), Paul Simpson (keyboards) and Gary Dwyer (drums). After signing to **Bill Drummond** and Dave Balfe's Liverpool record label Zoo, they issued 'Sleeping Gas' in early 1979. It was soon followed by the eccentric but appealing 'Bouncing Babies'. By then, Simpson had left to be replaced by Balfe, who had previously appeared in the short-lived **Lori And The Chameleons**. The exuberant 'Treason (It's Just A Story)' was the Teardrop Explodes' most commercial and exciting offering to date, and was unlucky not to chart. The shaky line-up next lost Finkler, who was replaced by Alan Gill, formerly of **Dalek I Love You**. A distribution deal with **Phonogram Records** coincided with a higher press profile for Cope, which was rewarded with the minor hit, 'When I Dream'. *Kilimanjaro* followed and displayed the group as one of the most inventive and intriguing of their era. A repromoted/remixed version of 'Treason' belatedly charted, as did the stirring 'Passionate Friend'. By late 1981, Cope was intent on restructuring the group; new members included Alfie Agius and Troy Tate. *Wilder* further displayed the wayward talents of Cope and revealed a group bristling with ideas, unusual melodies and strong arrangements influenced by late 60s psychedelia. When the sessions for a third album broke

down, Cope curtailed the group's activities and in 1984 embarked on an erratic yet often inspired solo career. The irreverently-titled *Everybody Wants To Shag The Teardrop Explodes* was posthumously exhumed for release in 1990, using the sessions for that projected third collection.

Albums: *Kilimanjaro* (Mercury 1980), *Wilder* (Mercury 1981), *Everybody Wants To Shag The Teardrop Explodes* (Fontana 1990). Compilations: *Piano* (Document 1990).

Teardrops

The Teardrops were an amalgamation of various stalwarts of the Manchester new wave scene. **Buzzcocks** bassist Steve Garvey was joined by original **Fall** bassist Tony Friel, who had played with Contact and the **Passage**, and drummer Karl Burns, also previously with the Fall and the Passage, plus **Public Image Limited**. The band's first outing, 'Seeing Double', on local label TJM, was what might have been expected from the members involved: a fairly robust but murky brand of post-punk. After featuring on TJM's *Identity Parade* sampler ('Colours'), the Teardrops released a 12-inch EP, *Leave Me No Choice*, before calling it a day with the appropriately-titled *Final Vinyl* in 1981. Burns rejoined the Fall in time for 'Lie, Dream Of Casino Soul'.

Album: *Final Vinyl* (TJM 1981).

Tears For Fears

Schoolfriends Roland Orzabal (b. 22 August 1961, Bath, England) and Curt Smith (b. 24 June 1961, Bath, England) formed Tears For Fears after they had spent their teenage years in groups together, including a ska revivalist combo called Graduate. The name Tears For Fears was drawn from a book written by Arthur Janov. They signed to Phonogram in 1981 while other synthesizer groups like the **Human League** and **Depeche Mode** were breaking through into the pop field. Their first two singles were unsuccessful but 'Mad World' made number 3 in the UK charts in 1982. Curt Smith, dressed in long overcoats and sporting a pig-tail, was touted in the UK as a vaguely alternative teen idol. *The Hurting* showcased a thoughtful, tuneful band and it topped the UK charts, supplying further Top 10 singles with 'Change' and 'Pale Shelter'. During this time the duo was augmented by Ian Stanley on keyboards and Manny Ellis on drums. By *Songs From The Big Chair* Orzabal was handling most of the vocal duties and had taken on the role of chief songwriter. 'Shout' and 'Everybody Wants To Rule The World' were number 1 hits in the US and the album also reached number 1. The song, 'Everybody Wants To Rule The World' was adopted as the theme tune for the Sport Aid famine relief event in 1986 (with a slight change in the title to 'Everybody Wants To Run The World') and it gave the group massive exposure. They took a lengthy break after 1985 and reappeared four years later with a highly-changed sound on *The Seeds Of Love*. They shunned their earlier electronic approach and attempted to weave together huge piano and vocal chords in a style reminiscent of the **Beatles**. Its release was delayed many times as the pair constantly re-mixed the material. Many top names played on the album including **Phil Collins** and **Oleta Adams**, whom Orzabal later produced. Both the album and single, 'Sowing The Seeds Of Love' were Top 10 hits in the US but in the UK the lavish arrangements did not receive the same critical and commercial approval. Smith left the band in the early 90s to begin a solo career. Retaining the name of the band Orzabal released *Elemental*, the first album after Smith's departure.

Albums: *The Hurting* (1983), *Songs From The Big Chair* (1985), *The Seeds Of Love* (1989), *Elemental* (1993). Compilation: *Tears Roll Down (Greatest Hits 82-92)* (1992). Curt Smith solo: *Soul On Board* (1993)

Further reading: *Tears For Fears*, Greene, Ann (1986).

Techniques

Formed by **Winston Riley** in 1962 while still at school, the Techniques original line-up additionally featured fellow vocalists **Slim Smith**, Franklyn White and Frederick Waite. Together they performed at future Jamaican prime minister Edward Seaga's club Chocomo Lawn, an important showcase for local talent at the time, appearing alongside **Byron Lee**, **Tommy McCook**, **Alton Ellis**, **Marcia Griffiths**, the Sensations, who included Riley's brother Buster. The group were spotted by talent scouts from British based **Columbia Records**, upon which their first single, 'No One', appeared. This was not released in Jamaica however, and it was not until 1965 when singer **Stranger Cole** introduced them to producer **Duke Reid** that they recorded their earliest Jamaican releases, 'Don't Leave Me', 'When You Are Wrong', and the popular 'Little Did You Know', featuring the peerless falsetto melisma of Slim Smith. With the advent of **rocksteady** in 1967 vocal harmony groups specialising in Chicago soul-style love songs really came into their own, and the Techniques, under the Duke's aegis, were perfectly placed to capitalise on the trend. Throughout 1967 the hits poured out of Reid's Treasure Isle studio, situated above his Orange Street liquor store. His classic productions on artists such as **Alton Ellis**, the **Paragons**, Phyllis Dillon, the **Melodians**, **Dobby Dobson**, and many others, all backed by **Tommy McCook** And the Supersonics, briefly toppled **Coxsone Dodd**'s dominance as Jamaica's leading hit maker.

In 1966 the group broke up, Smith leaving to pursue a solo career at **Studio One**, then later with producer **Bunny Lee** as part of the **Uniques** vocal trio, and ultimately on to a tragic end. Franklyn White's whereabouts remain obscure, but Frederick Waite migrated to the UK where he managed **Musical Youth**, whose number included several of his offspring, achieving a UK number 1 with 'Pass The Dutchie' in 1982. Slim's place was filled by **Pat Kelly**, who sang lead on some of their most popular records including their big hits 'You Don't Care', versions of **Curtis Mayfield**'s 'You'll Want Me Back' and 'Queen Majesty, the **Temptations**' 'I Wish It Would Rain' and 'Run Come Celebrate', 'I'm In The Mood', 'There Comes A Time' and the sublime 'It's You I Love'. Other hits from this period featuring different lead singers include 'My Girl', 'Drink Wine', 'Love Is Not A Gamble' and 'Travelling Man'. The Techniques left Treasure Isle in 1968 with Riley going on to set up his own Techniques label, producing other artists and further sides by the group, whose personnel during this period included Jackie Parris, ex-Termite **Lloyd Parks**, Morvin Brooks and Bruce Ruffin. These included another version of 'Travelling Man', 'Your Love's A Game' and 'Lonely Man' all featuring Dave Barker (**Dave And Ansell Collins**) on lead vocals, 'What Am I To Do', with Pat Kelly again as lead vocalist, 'What's It All About', and 'Go Find Yourself A Fool'. Riley went on to become one of the most successful producers of the 80s achieving massive hits with **General Echo**, **Tenor Saw**, **Supercat** and others. As a group, the Techniques recorded sporadically in the following years. A re-recording of 'Love Is Not A Gamble', with ex-**Paragon** Tyrone Evans on lead vocals appeared as a 12-inch in 1982, followed by an album of the same title, since which they have been silent.

Compilations: *Unforgettable Days* (Techniques 1981, covers 1965-72), *I'll Never Fall In Love* (Techniques 1982), *Classics* (Techniques 1991), *Run Come Celebrate - Their Greatest Reggae Hits* (Heartbeat 1993).

Techno

An easy definition of techno would be percussion based electronic dance music, characterised by stripped down drum beats and basslines. However, the real roots of techno can be traced back to the experimental musicologists like **Karl Heinz Stockhausen**. In terms of equipment there was no greater precedent than that set by Dr Robert Moog, who invented the synthesizer in California, and provoked the first fears of the 'death of real music' which have shadowed electronic recordings ever since. If **Chicory Tip**'s 'Son Of My Father' was the first to employ the Moog in 1972, then **Kraftwerk** were certainly the first to harness and harvest the possibilities of the synthesizer and other electronic instruments. Kraftwerk served as godfathers to UK electro pop outfits like the **Human League** (in their early experimental phase) and **Depeche Mode**. It is hard to imagine now but groups like these and even **Gary Numan** proved a huge influence on the US hip hop scene and the development of New York 'electro' in the early 80s (particularly **Afrika Bambaataa**'s 'Planet Rock'). But techno as we now know it descended from the Detroit region, which specialised in a stripped down, abrasive sound, maintaining some of the soulful elements of the **Motown** palate, over the innovations that hip hop's electro period had engendered. Techno also reflected the city's decline, as well as the advent of technology, and this tension was crucial to the dynamics of the sound. As **Kevin Saunderson** recounts: 'When we first started doing this music we were ahead. But Detroit is still a very behind city when it comes to anything cultural'. Techno as an umbrella term for this sound was first invoked by an article in *The Face* in May 1988, when it was used to describe the work of Saunderson (particularly 'Big Fun'), **Derrick May** (who recorded techno's greatest anthem, 'Strings Of Life') and **Juan Atkins** ('No UFO's'). The Detroit labels of note included May's **Transmat**, Juan Atkins' Metroplex, Saunderson's **KMS**, **Underground Resistance**, Planet E, Red Planet, Submerge and Accelerate. Much like house, the audience for techno proved to be a predominantly British/European one. Labels like **Rising High** and **Warp** in the UK, and **R&S** in Belgium helped build on the innovations of May, Atkins and **Carl Craig**. UK artists like the **Prodigy** and **LFO** took the sound to a new, less artful but more direct level. According to Saunderson, the difference between most Detroit techno and its English re-interpreters was that it lacked the 'spirituality' of the original. Had he wished to produce more controversy, he might have substituted 'blackness' - nearly all of the main Detroit pioneers were black. Most UK techno, conversely, at least until the advent of jungle, were white. Most techno utilises the establishment of a groove or movement by repetition, building a framework which does not translate easily into more conventional musical terms. Some obviously find this adjustment difficult, but the variations in texture and tempo are at least as subtle as those in rock music - often more so, due to the absence of a lyrical focus.

Technotronic

Belgian techno/house outfit created by producer Jo 'Thomas DeQuincey' Bogaert. He was looking for a female rapper to sing over a backing track he had produced, before stumbling upon **Ya Kid K** in the Antwerp rap group, Fresh Beat. Born Manuela Kamosi in Zaire, she moved to Belgium when she was 11. At 15 she spent some time in Chicago and was introduced to rap and Deep House, then currently in vogue. She returned to Belgium where she hooked up with Bogaert. Together they created 'Pump Up The Jam', though the cover shot actually featured a model named Felly and the record was credited to Technotronic featuring Felly. Ya Kid K was righteously indignant and by the time the first album was recorded care was

taken that the act was rebilled Technotronic featuring Ya Kid K. Her rapping partner was **MC Eric**, whose most notable contribution would be the chant sequence from 'This Beat Is Technotronik'. 'Pump Up The Jam' eventually reached the UK's number 2 spot in 1989. Follow-ups would include 'Get Up (Before The Night Is Over)' with Ya Kid K, 'This Beat Is Technotronik', 'Rockin' Over The Beat', 'Megamix' (Bogaert on his own) and 'Turn It Up' (Technotronic featuring Melissa and Einstein). Ya Kid K would go on to perform on Hi Tek's 'Spin That Wheel' in 1990 (a version of which is also included on Technotronic's *Trip On This* remix album), and enjoy her own solo career, as would her partner MC Eric. By the time of *Body To Body* Technotronic had recruited Reggie/Rejana Magloire (of Indeep fame, but not the singer on 'Last Night A DJ Saved My Life', who was Rose Marie Ramsey) as their female frontperson. Jo Bogaert would go on to record a solo album, *Different Voices*, for **Guerilla**.
Albums: *Pump Up The Jam* (Epic 1990), *Trip On This - The Remixes* (Epic 1990), *Body To Body* (Epic 1991). Jo Bogaert solo: *Different Voices* (Guerilla 1994).
Video: *Pump Up The Hits* (1990).

Technova

David Harrow was previously a London musician best known for his work with the **On-U-Sound** team on material by **Gary Clail**, **Lee Perry**, **Bim Sherman** and, under his own auspices, for **Jah Wobble**'s *Without Judgement* album. As Pulse 8 (not the record label) he also issued 'Radio Morocco', the first ever single on **Nation Records** in October 1989. His first UK release as Technova was 'Tantra', a 25-minute trance/ambient affair with a strong reggae undertow, released on the **Sabres Of Paradise** imprint. He had impressed the latter's **Andy Weatherall** with an appearance at the Sabres Christmas party, accompanied by naked (except for luminous paint) tattooed and pierced dancers. The single was actually taken from an album released in Australia on the Shock label in 1993, though Weatherfield quickly announced plans to re-release it on the Sabres imprint. 'The basic idea of the album is to simulate a long journey. It's totally seamless and it took a lot of prepartion to get it to flow the way that I wanted'. The project made plentiful use of DAT-recorded environmental sounds picked up on Harrow's own journey through Australasia.
Album: *Trantic Shadows* (Shock 1993).

Teddy Bears

Were it not for the fact that **Phil Spector** began as a member of the Teddy Bears, this one-hit-wonder trio would likely be a minor footnote in the history of rock. Spector moved to the USA with his family at the age of nine following the suicide of his father, whose tombstone bore the legend 'To know him is to love

him'. While in high school in Los Angeles, Spector sang at talent shows and assembled a group called the Sleepwalkers. He formed the Teddy Bears with singers Marshall Leib, Annette Kleinbard and Harvey Goldstein (who left the group shortly after its formation), after graduating from high school in June 1958. The group recorded a demo of Spector's composition, 'Don't You Worry, My Little Pet', which Dore Records released. For the b-side, Spector's 'To Know Him Is To Love Him' was recorded and it was that side which caught the ear of the public, rising to number 1 in the US charts in late 1958. Following that success, the group signed with the larger **Imperial Records** and recorded an album (which is very rare and valuable today) as well as further singles. No more were hits and the group disbanded after Kleinbard was seriously injured in a 1960 car accident. The striking 'To Know Him Is To Love Him' became a standard, and was later successfully revived by **Peter And Gordon** in 1965. The later career of Spector has been well-documented. Kleinbard, after her recovery, changed her name to Carol Connors and became a successful songwriter ('Hey Little Cobra' for the **Rip Chords**, **Vicki Lawrence**'s 'The Night The Lights Went Out In Georgia', and music for numerous films including two of the *Rocky* series). Marshall Leib joined the group the **Hollywood Argyles**, played guitar on some **Duane Eddy** records and produced records by the **Everly Brothers** and others.
Album: *The Teddy Bears Sing!* (1959).

Tee Set

With lead singer Peter Tetteroo its mainstay, this Dutch quintet's recording career began in 1966 with proficient covers of British hits. Growing their hair and catching up with the latest mod gear from London, they looked the part too - and a bona fide English guitarist Ray Fenwick (later of the **Spencer Davis Group**) passed through their fluctuating ranks. Work permit irregularities ended his stint with Tee Set just before Tetteroo and Hans Van Eyk composed 'Ma Belle Amie' which was released in 1969 on a European label before being taken up by North America's Colossus Records. The rise of this self-produced single in the Netherlands charts was a dry run for a climb to number 4 in the USA, and global sales of over a million. Although there was no follow-up of similar impact, the outfit remained a popular concert draw throughout Europe until a calculated disbandment in the late 70s.

Tee, Richard

b. 24 November 1943, New York, USA, d. 21 July 1993. Tee had 12 years of classical training on the piano and went to the High School of Music and Art. When he graduated a contact obtained him work as house pianist at **Motown Records**, which was then

turning out a string of hits. His first recording was with **Marvin Gaye**. In time Tee became a staff arranger and as well as playing the piano discovered the orchestral capabilities of the Hammond organ. When he returned to New York he continued to work in the studio. He described his playing thus: 'Chords and rhythm are my meat; even my solos are mostly chords. I try to be an orchestra and I feel most comfortable playing everything I can with 10 fingers.' He played on numerous records with musicians as diverse as **Roland Kirk**, **Carly Simon**, **Joe Cocker** and **Herbie Mann**. In 1976 he played in the influential funk band Stuff along with other session musicians including **Eric Gale** and **Steve Gadd**. The band recorded several well-received albums and Tee's solo career with **CBS** saw him marketed alongside contemporary 'smooth' jazz artists such as **Bob James** and **Lonnie Liston Smith**. Tee was one of the small core of musicians **Paul Simon** regularly used to record and perform with over the years. In 1991 Tee also played live with Paul Simon on the Rhythm Of The Saints tour. He ascribed his popularity on sessions to a willingness to keep things simple and not to restrict the leader's efforts: 'I play a constant rhythm that doesn't really change, and I try to keep it simple so that it gives others a chance to put their two cents in.'
Albums: with Stuff *Stuff* (1977), *Live In Japan* (1979); solo *Strokin'* (1979), *Natural Ingredients* (1980), *The Bottom Line* (1985).

Tee, Willie

b. Wilson Turbinton, 6 February 1944, New Orleans, Louisiana, USA. Willie Tee, although typical of the New Orleans soul sound, is best noted as a cult figure among Beach Music aficionados in the Carolinas. Tee came from a musical family and was taught piano at an early age. His father was a jazz trombonist and his brother is the famed jazz and R&B saxophonist Earl Turbinton. Tee first recorded in 1962 with a local record 'Always Accused' on AFO. His break came when he recorded a double-sided masterpiece, 'Teasin' You'/'Walking Up A One Way Street' for the Nola label. **Atlantic Records** picked up the record and made 'Teasin' You' (number 12 R&B) a national hit in 1965. Later in the year Atlantic picked up 'Thank You John'/'Dedicated To You', which although was equally outstanding never charted. In any case, Beach Music dancers in the Carolinas heard these Tee songs and made them favourites for their jukeboxes. In 1969 he joined **Capitol Records** but his three-year stay yielded a couple of unmemorable singles and a jazz album of instrumentals. He joined United Artists in 1976, but 'Liberty Bell', and *Anticipation*, were disappointments. A series of singles on his Gatur label (co-owned with Julius Gaines) produced some New Orleans play during the 70s. Increasingly, Tee became more involved in the production side, and produced

well-received albums by the **Wild Magnolias** and Carl Anderson. By 1988 Tee's own projects were more in a jazz vein and he recorded an album with his brother called *Turbinton Brothers* for Rounder.
Albums: *I'm Only A Man* (Capitol early 70s), *Anticipation* (United Artists 1976), *Turbinton Brothers* (Rounder 1988).

Teen Queens

This R&B duo of Betty and Rosie Collins came from Los Angeles, California, USA. Their entry into the recording business and signing to RPM Records in 1955 was facilitated by their older brother Aaron Collins of the Jacks/**Cadets**, who recorded for the same company. The youthful amateurishness of the singing of their one hit, 'Eddie My Love' (number 2 R&B and number 14 pop), probably helped make the record a hit in 1956. It was one of the first records to specifically direct its appeal to teenagers. It was an era of the cover record, and both the **Fontane Sisters** and the **Chordettes** also took the song high on the pop charts, but it is the Teen Queens' version that endures. The duo could not follow up with a hit, despite recording some excellent material over the years. Moves to **RCA** in 1958 and Antler in 1960 did not help and the duo broke up in 1961.
Albums: *Eddie My Love* (1956), *The Teen Queens* (1963), *Rock Everybody* (1986).

Teenage Fanclub

Formerly the bulk of infamous Glaswegian band the Boy Hairdressers, Teenage Fanclub, a more sober sobriquet than the original suggestion of 'Teenage Fanny', came into being after Norman Blake (b. 20 October 1965, Bellshill, Scotland; guitar/vocals), Raymond McGinley (b. 3 January 1964, Glasgow, Scotland; guitar/vocals) and Francis MacDonald (b. 21 November 1970, Bellshill, Scotland; drums) moved on from that pseudo-punk combo and linked up with Gerard Love (b. 31 August 1967, Motherwell, Scotland; bass/vocals). During 1989 the quartet recorded an entire album - completed three months before the band had even played live - until MacDonald (later to join the **Pastels**) made way for Brendan O'Hare (b. 16 January 1970, Bellshill, Scotland). As well as the historical connection with the Boy Hairdressers, members of Teenage Fanclub also had dealings with fellow Scots outfit, **BMX Bandits**. Thus brought up on a diet of fun, loud guitars and irreverence, Teenage Fanclub stamped their mark on 1990 with a series of drunken live shows and the erratic but highly promising Americanized rock debut, *A Catholic Education*. In October the band paid tribute to **John Lennon** by covering his 'Ballad Of John & Yoko', releasing and deleting the record on the same day. A year on and supplemented by the support of a vociferous music press, Teenage Fanclub toned down their sound, allowing the melodies to come through

more forcefully in a manner which self-consciously recalled the 70s guitar sound of **Big Star** and **Neil Young** (they became fundamental in instigating the former band's revival in the early 90s). Inevitably 'Starsign' - with a cover of **Madonna**'s 'Like A Virgin' on the b-side - threatened the UK charts on the back of the band's new impetus. *Bandwagonesque* arrived at the end of 1991 and became one of the year's most memorable albums. Laced with chiming guitar and irresistible melody, it suggested a band ready to outgrow their humble independent origins. A sense of disappointment accompanied the release of *Thirteen*, completed in eight months after touring the better-received *Bandwagonesque* (which sold 70,000 copies in the UK and 150,000 in the US, where the band are signed to **Geffen Records**). This resulted in a concerted effort to make the band's fifth studio album, *Grand Prix*, an exceptional album. The songs were rehearsed for three months before entering the studio, where everything was fine-tuned over a five week period at the Manor in Oxford with producer Dave Bianco (formerly **Black Crowes**' producer George Dracoulias' engineer). It also saw the introduction of new drummer Paul Quinn, formerly of the **Soup Dragons**. Reassuringly, the opening singles from these sessions, 'Mellow Doubt', and 'Sparkey's Dream' showed them still to be writing basic, heroically romantic and happy guitar pop songs. When it finally arrived *Grand Prix* did not disappoint, it was a stunning return to form
Albums: *A Catholic Education* (Paperhouse 1990), *The King* (Creation 1991), *Bandwagonesque* (Creation 1991), *Thirteen* (Creation 1993), *Grand Prix* (Creation 1995). Compilation: *Deep Fried Fanclub* (Paperhouse/Fire 1995).

Teenage Jesus And The Jerks

The 17-year-old **Lydia Lunch** formed Teenage Jesus And The Jerks in the UK during 1976 to channel her feelings of contempt towards a complacent music industry, but almost immediately clashed with founder members **James Chance** (b. James Siegfried) and Reck, both of whom left before any recordings were completed. Chance later formed the Contortions, Reck going on to front one of Japan's most successful punk acts, Friction. Lunch's distraught singing and atonal guitar cut against drummer Bradley Field and bassist Jim Sclavunos (later replaced by filmmaker Gordon Stevenson) to create an uncompromising, unholy noise labelled 'no wave', which was first heard on their single, 'Orphans', in 1978. 'Baby Doll' reared its ugly head nearly a year later, followed by a mini-album and 12-inch EP. *Pink* boasted seven excellent tracks, while *Pre*, on the Ze label, collected several early recordings. They disbanded in 1980 when Lydia Lunch progressed to the less violent, murkier sound of Beirut Slump. Field moved on to rejoin Chance as one of his Contortions.

However, the discordant, tortuous racket they exuded from Teenage Jesus And The Jerks has influenced a variety of distinguished names since then, from the **Birthday Party** to **Sonic Youth**. It is no coincidence that Lunch has worked with them both.

Album: *Pink* (Lust Unlust 1979, mini-album).

Telescopes

Quintessential English indie band formed in 1988 by Stephen Lawrie (b. 28 March 1969, East Hartford, Northumberland, England; vocals), Joanna Doran (b. Wednesbury, West Midlands, England; guitar/vocals), David Fitzgerald (b. 30 August 1966, Wellingborough, Northamptonshire, England; bass), Robert Brooks (b. 11 April 1969, Burton-upon-Trent, Staffordshire, England) and Dominic Dillon (b. 26 September 1964, Bolton, Lancashire, England). The Telescopes started out peddling a fearsome noise which owed much to the path laid earlier in the decade by the **Jesus And Mary Chain**. Their first release was on a flexidisc shared with **Loop** and sold with the *Sowing Seeds* fanzine, after which came two temperamental singles on Cheree records followed by a deal with the American What Goes On label. Unfortunately, after a further brace of singles and one album in 1989, What Goes On succumbed to bankruptcy, leaving the Telescopes to battle for the rights to their own songs and sign to **Creation Records**. The change of label coincided with a change in musical style as the group added lighter shades and harmonies to their intense guitar-based sound, a development which paid dividends when their eighth single, 'Flying', reached number 79 in the UK charts in 1991.

Albums: *Taste* (What Goes On 1989), *Untitled* (Creation 1992).

Television

Lead guitarist/vocalist **Tom Verlaine** (b. Thomas Miller, 13 December 1949, Mount Morris, New Jersey, USA) first worked with bassist **Richard Hell** (b. Richard Myers, 2 October 1949, Lexington, Kentucky, USA) and drummer Billy Ficca in the early 70s as the Neon Boys. By the end of 1973, with the addition of rhythm guitarist **Richard Lloyd,** they reunited as Television. Early the following year they secured a residency at the Bowery club, **CBGB's**, and found themselves at the forefront of the New York new wave explosion. Conflicts between Verlaine and Hell led to the departure of the latter who would soon re-emerge with the **Heartbreakers**. Meanwhile, Television found a replacement bassist in Fred Smith from **Blondie**. The new line-up recorded the raw but arresting 'Little Johnny Jewel', a tribute to **Iggy Pop**, for their own label, Ork Records. This led to their signing with **Elektra Records** for whom they recorded their debut album in 1977. *Marquee Moon* was largely ignored in their homeland, but elicited astonished, ecstatic reviews in the UK. where it was applauded as one of rock's most accomplished debut albums. Verlaine's sneering, nasal vocal and searing, jagged twin guitar interplay with Lloyd were the hallmarks of Television's work, particularly on such stand-out tracks as 'Torn Curtain', 'Venus' and 'Prove It'. Although the group looked set for a long and distinguished career, the follow-up, *Adventure*, was a lesser work and the group broke up in 1978. Since then both Verlaine and Lloyd pursued solo careers with mixed results. In November 1991, Verlaine, Lloyd, Smith and Ficca revived Television and spent the ensuing time rehearsing for a come back album for **Capitol Records**. They returned to Britain and made an appearance at the 1992 Glastonbury Festival.

Albums: *Marquee Moon* (Elektra 1978), *Adventure* (Elektra 1979), *The Blow Up* (ROIR 1983, rec. live 1978, cassette only), *Television* (Capitol 1993).

Television Personalities

A crass meeting of 60s pastiche and a tongue-in-cheek nod towards punk have characterised Dan Treacy's Television Personalities over their long, erratic career. Treacy teamed up with Edward Ball back in 1977, releasing the privately pressed '14th Floor' the following year. After Ball's solo single as O Level, the pair issued what was to be seen as a pivotal artefact of the time, the EP *Where's Bill Grundy Now?* (1978). BBC disc jockey **John Peel** latched onto one of the tracks, 'Part Time Punks' (a cruel send-up of a rapidly decaying London scene) and this exposure attracted the interest of **Rough Trade Records**. Ball spent some time working on his solo projects in the early 80s, the Teenage Filmstars and the **Times**. The TV Star's debut album, *And Don't The Kids Just Love It*, extended Treacy's exploration of 60s influences. From it came the whimsical 'I Know Where Syd Barrett Lives' as a single, their last for Rough Trade. Treacy then teamed up with Ed Ball to form the Whaam! label, for TVPs and Times products plus other signings, including the **Marine Girls**. 1982, the group's busiest recording year, saw *Mummy You're Not Watching Me* share the instant appeal of the group's debut. 'Three Wishes' followed, and coincided with a minor psychedelic revival in London. *They Could Have Been Bigger Than The Beatles* was a surprisingly strong collection of demos and out-takes. The band were soon expanded by Mark Flunder (bass), Dave Musker (organ) and Joe Foster (12-string guitar) for a tour of Italy, with Flunder replaced by ex-**Swell Maps** bass player Jowe Head for a similar tour of Germany. 1983's 'A Sense Of Belonging' saw a one-off return to Rough Trade and caused a minor scandal over its sleeve. But delays meant that *The Painted Word* was not issued until January 1985. Foster and Musker soon left to work at **Creation Records**. With a new drummer, Jeff Bloom, Treacy set up a new label, after Whaam! was folded due to pressure from pop duo **Wham!**. In the meantime, the German album, *Chocolat-Art (A Tribute To James Last)*, captured one of their European live gigs. It was not until early 1990 that the next album emerged. *Privilege* included the catchy 'Salvador Dali's Garden Party'. Then the band laid low for a further two years (punctuated by a live album for Overground Records) until the release of *Closer To God*.

Albums: *And Don't The Kids Just Love It* (Rough Trade 1980), *Mummy You're Not Watching Me* (Whaam! 1982), *They Could Have Been Bigger Than The Beatles* (Whaam! 1982), *The Painted Word* (Illuminated 1985), *Chocolat-Art (A Tribute To James Last)* (Pastell 1985), *Privilege* (Fire 1990), *Camping In France* (Overground 1991), *Closer To God* (1992), *I Was A Mod Before You Were A Mod* (Overground 1995).

Telex

This electro-pop outfit from Brussels, Belgium, was formed in 1978 by Marc Moulin (keyboards), a former member of Cos, and head of the Kamikazee label whose jazz/*avant garde* output could be aired on his weekend presentation on local Radio Cité. Telex's personnel was completed by Michael Moers (vocals), and the multi-talented Dan Lacksman, composer, architect, photographer and the country's first professional synthesizer player. Tearing a leaf from **Roxy Music**'s book, the group's records blended state-of-the-art technology and wilfully outmoded pop convention. Following a signing to **Sire Records**, a 1979 single, 'Twist A San Tropez', was taken from *Looking For San Tropez* which also included the 'Moskow Diskow' follow-up as well as diverting versions of **Plastic Bertrand**'s 'Ça Plane Pour Moi' and **Bill Haley**'s 'Rock Around The Clock' (issued as a single in Australasia). Another album was released the following year but little more from this promising trio has been heard since.

Albums: *Looking For San Tropez* (1979), *Neurovision* (1980).

Temiz, Okay

b. 11 February 1939, Istanbul, Turkey. Temiz first learned Turkish music from his mother and later studied classical percussion and tympani. He started to play drums professionally in 1955 and toured with Turkish show groups in Turkey and North Africa. During 1969-70 he played with the **Don Cherry** Trio and in 1970 he toured with the famous Turkish musician Binali Selman. He became a founder-member of the Swedish-Turkish group Sevda in 1971 and played with them until 1972. He then participated in the trio Music For Xaba together with **Johnny Mbizo Dyani** and **Mongezi Feza**. He rejoined Sevda in 1973 and started his own trio in 1974 with which he recorded Turkish Folk Jaz. In the mid-70s he formed the group Oriental Wind that has since been the main outlet for his activities. This group mixes modal jazz improvisation with Turkish and Oriental music forms in uneven time signatures. Temiz' drums are of his own design and are made of hand-beaten copper after the ideal of the Turkish drums Dumbuka's and Darbuka's.

Albums: *Turkish Folk Jazz* (1975), with Salih Baysal *The Myth* (1978), with Don Cherry *Live In Ankara* (1978), with Johnny Dyani and Mongezi Feza *Music For Xaba* (1972), *Music For Xaba Vol. II* (1979), with Oriental Wind *Oriental Wind* (1977), *Zikir* (1979), *Chila-Chila* (1979), *Sankirna* (1945), *Misket* (1991), with Percussion Summit *Percussion Summit* (19484), with Berndt Rosengren *Notes From Underground* (1974), with Sevda *Jazz I Sverige '72* (1972), *Live At Jazzhus Montmartre* (1972), *Live At Fregatten* (1973).

Temperance 7

Formed in 1955 to play 20s style jazz, the Temperance 7 consisted at various times of Whispering Paul McDowell (vocals), Captain Cephas Howard (trumpet/euphonium and various instruments), Joe Clark (clarinet), Alan Swainston-Cooper (pedal clarinet/swanee whistle), Philip 'Finger' Harrison (banjo/alto and baritone sax), Canon Colin Bowles (piano/harmonica), Clifford Beban (tuba), Brian Innes (drums), Dr. John Grieves-Watson (banjo), Sheik Haroun el John R.T. Davies (trombone/alto sax) and Frank Paverty (sousaphone). Their debut single, 'You're Driving Me Crazy' (producer **George Martin**'s first number 1), was followed by three more hits in 1961, 'Pasadena', 'Hard Hearted Hannah'/'Chili Bom Bom', and 'Charleston'. In 1963 they appeared in the play *The Bed Sitting Room* written by John Antrobus and Spike Milligan. They split in the mid 60s, but their spirit resurfaced in groups like the **Bonzo Dog Doo-Dah Band** and the **New Vaudeville Band**. The Temperance 7 were reformed in the 70s by Ted Wood, brother of the **Rolling Stones**' **Ronnie Wood**. At the time of writing in 1995, Colin Bowles is reported to have died several years ago, but the other members are said to be pursuing a variety of interests, including publishing, sound retreval, film set and graphic designing, acting, and antiques.

Albums: *Temperance 7* (1961), *Temperance 7 Plus One* (1961), *Hot Temperance 7* (1987), *Tea For Eight* (1990), *33 Not Out* (1990).

Temperley, Joe

b. 20 September 1929, Cowdenbeath, Scotland. After taking a few lessons on alto saxophone, Temperley began gigging at clubs in Glasgow. When he was 20 he joined the Tommy Sampson band, returning with them to London. He then worked with Harry Parry, **Joe Loss**, **Jack Parnell**, **Tony Crombie** and others, and during this period began playing tenor saxophone. A mid-50s stint with **Tommy Whittle** brought a further change of instrument, this time onto baritone saxophone. He then joined **Humphrey Lyttelton**, in whose band he remained for seven years. It was while he was with Lyttelton that he made his first big impression on the international jazz scene and in 1965 he settled in the USA, playing in the bands of **Woody Herman**, **Buddy Rich**, **Buck Clayton**, **Duke Pearson** and the **Thad Jones**-**Mel Lewis** Jazz Orchestra. During the 70s he played in **Clark Terry**'s band and in the **Duke Ellington** orchestra, which was continuing under the direction of **Mercer Ellington**. From the late-70s onwards he freelanced, mainly in New York City, but also finding time for touring and recording with several musicians, including **Jimmy Knepper**, **Kathy Stobart** and **Scott Hamilton**. A major saxophonist and one of the outstanding baritone players in jazz, Temperley plays with an enviable sonority, bringing wit and imagination to his solos. The fluidity of his playing shows that in skilled hands this most demanding of instruments is capable not only of power and drive but also of warmth and moving tenderness.

Albums: with Humphrey Lyttelton *Humph Plays Standards* (1960), *Le Vrai Buck Clayton* (1964), with Clark Terry *Live On 57th Street* (1970), with Mercer Ellington *Continuum* (1974-5), with Jimmy Knepper *Just Friends* (Hep 1978), *Nightingale* (Hep 1993).

Temple Of The Dog

This one-off project involved members of Seattle, USA-based bands **Mother Love Bone** and **Soundgarden**, and was recorded as a tribute to the late Andrew Wood, former Mother Love Bone vocalist. The 'band' comprised Chris Cornell (vocals), Matt Cameron (drums), Mike McCready (guitar), Stone Gossard (rhythm guitar) and Jeff Ament (bass). Signed to **A&M Records**, the album received widespread critical acclaim immediately following its release. The music fused elements of the **Doors/Joy Division/Stooges** with the harder, dirtier and at times funkier rhythms of Soundgarden. It was a moving, powerful and genuine tribute to the first casualty of the 90s Seattle scene. Gossard and Ament later formed **Pearl Jam**.

Album: *Temple Of The Dog* (A&M 1991).

Temple, Johnny

b. 18 October 1906, Canton, Mississippi, USA, d. 22 November 1968, Jackson, Mississippi, USA. Johnny Temple learned guitar from his stepfather Slim Duckett, a well known performer from the Jackson area who later recorded for **OKeh Records** in 1930. Temple could also play the mandolin and often worked at house parties and juke joints. In 1932 he moved to Chicago where he worked as a general all-round-musician and recorded blues for both **Decca** and Vocalion. He worked with the famous **McCoy** brothers and recorded as part of the knockabout jazz

group the **Harlem Hamfats.** He continued to work in Chicago until well into the post-war period, appearing with artists such as Billy Boy Arnold and **Walter Horton**, as well as forming his own group, the Rolling Four. In the mid-60s he returned to Jackson where, after a period of ill health, he died from cancer at the age of 62.

Compilations: *Chicago Blues* (1985), *Johnny Temple* (1986).

Temple, Shirley

b. 23 April 1928, Santa Monica, California, USA. By the time this actress, singer, and dancer was six years old, she was a movie star of the first magnitude. Four years later, she became 20th Century-Fox's - and Hollywood's - top box-office attraction, with reported annual earnings of $300,000. Her poise, acting and dancing, plus her incredible screen presence, even gave rise to scurrilous rumours to the effect that she was a dwarf. After taking dancing lessons from the age of three, she appeared in short films and played bit parts in several minor features before coming to prominence singing 'Baby Take A Bow' in the 1934 musical *Stand Up And Cheer*. Her nine pictures in 1934, including ***Little Miss Marker***, which made her a major film attraction, earned her a special (miniature) Academy Award 'in grateful recognition of her outstanding contribution to screen entertainment during the year'. Throughout the rest of the 30s she sparkled in musicals such as *Bright Eyes*, *Curly Top*, *The Littlest Rebel*, *Captain January*, ***Poor Little Rich Girl***, *Dimples*, ***Stowaway***, *Rebecca Of Sunnybrook Farm*, *Little Miss Broadway*, *Just Around The Corner*, *The Blue Bird*, and *Young People* (1940). From out of these simple, yet mostly enormously popular films, came songs such as 'On The Good Ship Lollipop', 'Animal Crackers In My Soup', 'When I Grow Up', 'Curly Top', 'At The Codfish Ball', 'Picture Me Without You', 'Oh, My Goodness', 'But Definitely', 'That's What I Want For Christmas', 'When I'm With You', 'We Should Be Together', 'Swing Me An Old-Fashioned Love Song' 'This Is a Happy Little Ditty', and 'I Want To Walk In The Rain'. By the end of the 30s Shirley Temple's career was in decline; the most successful child star of all-time could not sustain her appeal as a teenager. She left Fox and appeared throughout the 40s in a number of films for other studios - but only in straight roles. There were to be no more musicals. After marrying businessman Charles Black in 1950, she became known as Shirley Temple Black and retired from show business for a time, concentrating on her family and working extensively for charity. In the late 50s and into the early 60s, she appeared on US television in *The Shirley Temple Storybook* and *The Shirley Temple Show*. Later in the 60s she was prominent in politics and ran unsuccessfully for Congress as a Republican candidate. She subsequently served as US Ambassador to the United Nations and Ghana, and US Chief of Protocol. In 1990 she was appointed US Ambassador to Czechoslovakia, and, two years later, received a career achievement award at the annual D.W. Griffith Awards in Manhattan. In 1982, she attended a lavish retrospective tribute to her films organized by the Academy of Motion Picture Arts and Sciences, and was presented with a new, full-size Oscar to replace the miniature she received in 1934. In 1994 it was announced that some of her most popular films were being computer-coloured and released on video. Further reading: *Shirley Temple*, L.C. Eby. *Temple*, J. Basinger. *Films Of Shirley Temple*, R. Windeler. *Shirley Temple: American Princess*, Anne Edwards. *Child Star* (her autobiography).

Templeman, Ted

b. 24 October 1944. Templeman grew up in northern California, USA, where he drummed with various local groups. He subsequently joined the San Francisco-based Tikis, who evolved into **Harpers Bizarre** in 1966. Having switched to guitar and vocals, Templeman assumed an increased responsibility for arranging the group's close harmonies and ultimately assisted Lenny Waronker in his production capacity. When Harpers Bizarre broke up in 1970, Waronker invited the aspirant to join **Warner Brothers** as a staff producer. Templeman's first commission was the **Doobie Brothers**, with whom he built up a longstanding relationship. Others benefiting from his skills included **Van Morrison**, **Captain Beefheart**, **Little Feat** and **Montrose**, as Templeman forged a style which gave his charges a clarity and purpose without being over-fussy, allowing them to retain their individuality.

Tempo, Nino, and April Stevens

Nino Tempo, (b. 6 January 1935, Niagara Falls, New York, USA) forged a career as session musician and arranger/composer for **Rosemary Clooney** and **Steve Lawrence**, before forming a duo with sister April Stevens (b. 29 April, Niagara Falls, New York, USA). The latter had already enjoyed minor success as a solo act with 'Teach Me Tiger', but the siblings scored a major hit in 1963 when their revival of 'Deep Purple' which topped the US charts and secured a Grammy award as that year's 'Best Rock 'N' Roll Recording'. They also held the record for many years with the longest title, the b-side of 'Deep Purple' was 'I've Been Carrying A Torch For You For So Long That It's Burned A Great Big Hole In My Heart'. Reworkings of 'Whispering' and 'Stardust' also reached the best-sellers but Tempo achieved a more contemporary outlook following backroom and compositional work with **Phil Spector**. He and April embraced a folk-rock/girl group direction with 'All Strung Out' and 'I Can't Go On Living (Without You Baby)' which the former co-wrote with Jerry Riopelle. An excellent attendant album contained compositions

by **David Gates** and **Warren Zevon**, but the couple's *passe* image hindered potential interest. They later embarked on separate paths with Tempo resuming his association with Spector during the 70s, particularly with new protege Jerri Bo Keno.
Albums: *Deep Purple* (1963), *Nino & April Sing The Great Songs* (1964), *Hey Baby* (1966), *Nino Tempo, April Stevens Programme* (60s), *All Strung Out* (1967).

Temptations

The most successful group in black music history was formed in 1961 in Detroit, Michigan, USA, by former members of two local R&B outfits. **Eddie Kendricks** (b. 17 December 1939, Union Springs, Alabama, USA) and Paul Williams (b. 2 July 1939, Birmingham, Alabama, USA, d. 17 August 1973) both sang with the **Primes**; Melvin Franklin (b. David English, 12 October 1942, Montgomery, Alabama, USA, d. 23 February 1995, Los Angeles, California, USA), Eldridge Bryant and Otis Williams (b. Otis Miles 30 October 1941, Texarkana, Texas, USA) came from the Distants. Initially known as the Elgins, the quintet were renamed the Temptations by **Berry Gordy** when he signed them to **Motown** in 1961. After issuing three singles on the Motown subsidiary Miracle Records, one of them under the pseudonym of the Pirates, the group moved to the Gordy label. 'Dream Come Home' provided their first brief taste of chart status in 1962, though it was only when they were teamed with writer/producer/performer **Smokey Robinson** that the Temptations achieved consistent success. The group's classic line-up was established in 1963, when Eldridge Bryant was replaced by **David Ruffin** (b. 18 January 1941, Meridian, Mississippi, USA). His gruff baritone provided the perfect counterpoint to Kendricks' wispy tenor and falsetto, a contrast which Smokey Robinson exploited to the full. Over the next two years, he fashioned a series of hits in both ballad and dance styles, carefully arranging complex vocal harmonies which hinted at the group's doo-wop heritage. 'The Way You Do The Things You Do' was the Temptations' first major hit, a stunningly simple rhythm number featuring a typically cunning series of lyrical images. 'My Girl' in 1965, the group's first US number 1, demonstrated Robinson's graceful command of the ballad idiom, and brought Ruffin's vocals to the fore for the first time. This track, featured in the movie 'My Girl', was reissued in 1992 and was once again a hit.
'It's Growing', 'Since I Lost My Baby', 'My Baby' and 'Get Ready' continued the run of success into 1966, establishing the Temptations as the leaders of the Motown sound. 'It's Growing' brought a fresh layer of subtlety into Robinson's lyric writing, while 'Get Ready' embodied all the excitement of the Motown rhythm factory, blending an irresistible melody with a stunning vocal arrangement. **Norman Whitfield**

succeeded Robinson as the Temptations' producer in 1966 - a role he continued to occupy for almost a decade. He introduced a new rawness into their sound, spotlighting David Ruffin as an impassioned lead vocalist, and creating a series of R&B records that rivalled the output of **Stax** and **Atlantic** for toughness and power. 'Ain't Too Proud To Beg' introduced the Whitfield approach, and while the Top 3 hit 'Beauty Is Only Skin Deep' represented a throwback to the Robinson era, 'I'm Losing You' and 'You're My Everything' confirmed the new direction.

The peak of Whitfield's initial phase with the group was 'I Wish It Would Rain', a dramatic ballad which the producer heightened with delicate use of sound effects. The record was another major hit, and gave the Temptations their sixth R&B number 1 in three years. It also marked the end of an era, as David Ruffin first requested individual credit before the group's name, and when this was refused, elected to leave for a solo career. He was replaced by ex-**Contour** Dennis Edwards, whose strident vocals fitted perfectly into the Temptations' harmonic blend. Whitfield chose this moment to inaugurate a new production style. Conscious of the psychedelic shift in the rock mainstream, and the inventive soul music being created by **Sly And The Family Stone**, he joined forces with lyricist **Barrett Strong** to pull Motown brutally into the modern world. The result was 'Cloud Nine', a record which reflected the increasing use of illegal drugs among young people, and shocked some listeners with its lyrical ambiguity. Whitfield created the music to match, breaking down the traditional barriers between lead and backing singers and giving each of the Temptations a recognizable role in the group. Over the next four years, Whitfield and the Temptations pioneered the concept of psychedelic soul, stretching the Motown formula to the limit, introducing a new vein of social and political comment, and utilizing many of rock's experimental production techniques to hammer home the message. 'Runaway Child, Running Wild' examined the problems of teenage rebellion; 'I Can't Get Next To You' reflected the fragmentation of personal relationships (and topped the US charts with the group's second number 1 hit); and 'Ball Of Confusion' bemoaned the disintegrating fabric of American society. These lyrical tracts were set to harsh, uncompromising rhythm tracks, seeped in wah-wah guitar and soaked in layers of harmony and counterpoint. The Temptations were greeted as representatives of the counter-culture, a trend which climaxed when they recorded Whitfield's outspoken protest against the Vietnam War, 'Stop The War Now'. The new direction alarmed Eddie Kendricks, who felt more at home on the series of collaborations with the **Supremes** which the group also taped in the late 60s. He left for a solo career in 1971, after recording another US number 1, the evocative ballad 'Just My

Imagination'. He was replaced first by Richard Owens, then later in 1971 by Damon Harris. This line-up recorded the 1972 number 1, 'Papa Was A Rolling Stone', a production *tour de force* which remains one of Motown's finest achievements, belatedly winning the label its first Grammy award. After that, everything was an anti-climax. Paul Williams left the group in 1971, to be replaced by another former Distant member, Richard Street; Williams shot himself in 1973, after years of depression and drug abuse. Whitfield's partnership with Strong was broken the same year, and although he continued to rework the 'Papa Was A Rolling Stone' formula, the commercial and artistic returns were smaller. The Temptations still scored hits, and 'Masterpiece', 'Let Your Hair Down' (both 1973) and 'Happy People' (1975) all topped the soul charts, but they were no longer a leading force in black music.

Whitfield left Motown in 1975; at the same time, Glenn Leonard replaced Damon Harris in the group. After struggling on for another year, the Temptations moved to Atlantic for two albums, which saw Louis Price taking the place of Dennis Edwards. When the Atlantic deal brought no change of fortunes, the group returned to Motown, and to Dennis Edwards. 'Power' in 1980 restored them to the charts, before **Rick James** engineered a brief reunion with David Ruffin and Eddie Kendricks for a tour, an album, and a hit single, 'Standing On The Top'. Ruffin and Kendricks then left to form a duo, Ron Tyson replaced Glenn Leonard, and Ali-Ollie Woodson took over the role of lead vocalist from Edwards. Woodson brought with him a song called 'Treat Her Like A Lady', which became their biggest UK hit in a decade. Subsequent releases confirmed the quality of the current line-up, though without a strong guiding hand they are unlikely to rival the achievements of the late 60s and early 70's line-ups, the culmination of Motown's classic era.

Albums: *Meet The Temptations* (1964), *The Temptations Sing Smokey* (1965), *The Temptin' Temptations* (1965), *Gettin' Ready* (1966), *Live!* (1967), *With A Lot O' Soul* (1967), *In A Mellow Mood* (1967), *Wish It Would Rain* (1968), *Diana Ross And The Supremes Join The Temptations* (1968), with Diana Ross And The Supremes *TCB* (1968), *Live At The Copa* (1968), *Cloud Nine* (1969), *The Temptations' Show* (1969), *Puzzle People* (1969), with Diana Ross And The Supremes *Together* (1969), with Diana Ross And The Supremes *On Broadway* (1969), *Psychedelic Shack* (1970), *Live At London's Talk Of The Town* (1970), *Christmas Card* (1970), *Sky's The Limit* (1971), *Solid Rock* (1972), *All Directions* (1972), *Masterpiece* (1973), *1990* (1973), *A Song For You* (1975), *House Party* (1975), *Wings Of Love* (1976), *The Temptations Do The Temptations* (1976), *Hear To Tempt You* (1977), *Bare Back* (1978), *Power* (1980), *The Temptations* (1981), with Jimmy Ruffin and Eddie Kendricks *Reunion* (1982), *Surface Thrills* (1983), *Back To Basics* (1984), *Truly For You* (1984), *Touch Me* (1985), *To Be Continued . . .* (1986), *Together Again* (1987), *Special*

(1989), *Milestone* (1991). Compilations: *Greatest Hits* (1966), *Greatest Hits, Volume 2* (1970), *Anthology* (1973), *25 Anniversary* (1986), *Compact Command Performances* (1989), *The Original Lead Singers Of The Temptations* (1993), *Emperors Of Soul* 5CD set (1994).

Ten City

Consistent, sometimes spectacular Chicago house group, with Byron Stingily's falsetto always the focus. The other members were Byron Burke and Herb Lawson. They met in a rehearsal studio in Chicago in 1985, Herb being drawn from R&B band Rise, while Stingily was then fronting B Rude Inc. The trio recorded two singles as Ragtyme, 'I Can't Stay Away' and 'Fix It Man'. In 1986 they signed to **Atlantic** and made the name change. The debut single, 'Devotion', was an instant hit (it would later be revamped by **Nomad** for their '(I Wanna Give You) Devotion' hit). Their production was helmed by **Marshall Jefferson**, who was responsible for shaping much of their early character and sound. The band began making steady progress in the late 80s, going chartbound in the UK the following year with 'That's The Way Love Is'. Ten City, aside from the Jefferson connections (their union ended by the advent of Ten City's third album), are good writers in their own right, having provided for **Adeva** and **Ultra Nate** among others. Their sound is also distinguished by the live musicianship, and they claim to the 'the first true musicians to play house'. If plagiarism amounts to tribute, then their basslines, rhythms and melodies have re-appeared on enough occasions to suggest a lasting influence on dance music.
Albums: *Foundation* (East West 1988), *State Of Mind* (East West 1990), *No House Big Enough* (East West 1992), *Love In A Day* (Columbia 1994), *That Was Then, This Is Now* (Columbia 1994).

Ten Years After

Formed in Nottingham, England as the Jaybirds in 1965 they abandoned their pedestrian title for a name which slotted in with the booming underground progressive music scene. The quartet of **Alvin Lee** (b. 19 December 1944, Nottingham, England; guitar/vocals), Chick Churchill (b. 2 January 1949, Mold, Flint/Clwyd, Wales; keyboards), Ric Lee (b. 20 October 1945, Cannock, Staffordshire, England; drums) and Leo Lyons (b. 30 November 1943, Bedford, England; bass) played a mixture of rock 'n' roll and blues which kept them apart from the mainstream blues *cognoscenti* of **Fleetwood Mac**, **Chicken Shack** and **Savoy Brown**. Their debut album was largely ignored and it took months of gruelling club work to establish their claim. The superb live *Undead*, recorded at Klooks Kleek club, spread the word that Alvin Lee was not only an outstanding guitarist, but he was the fastest by a mile. Unfortunately for the other three

members, Alvin overshadowed them to the extent that they became merely backing musicians in what was described as the Alvin Lee show. The band began a series of US tours which gave them the record of more US tours than any other UK band. Lee's furious performance of 'Goin' Home' at the **Woodstock Festival** was one of the highlights, although that song became a millstone for them. Over the next two years they delivered four solid albums, which all charted in the UK and the USA. *Ssssh*, with its **Graham Nash** cover photography, was the strongest. 'Stoned Woman' epitomized their sound and style although it was 'Love Like A Man' from *Cricklewood Green* that gave them their only UK hit. *A Space In Time* saw them briefly relinquish guitar-based pieces in favour of electronics. By the time of *Rock 'N' Roll To The World* the band were jaded and they rested from touring to work on solo projects. This resulted in Alvin's *On The Road To Freedom* with gospel singer Mylon Le Fevre and a dull album from Chick Churchill, *You And Me*. When they reconvened, their spark and will had all but gone and remaining albums were poor. After months of rumour, Lee admitted that the band had broken up. In 1978 Lee formed the trio Ten Years Later, with little reaction, and in 1989 the original band reformed and released *About Time,* but only their most loyal fans were interested. The band was still active in the early 90s.
Albums: *Ten Years After* (1967), *Undead* (1968), *Stonedhenge* (1969), *Sssssh* (1969), *Cricklewood Green* (1970), *Watt* (1970), *A Space In Time* (1971), *Rock 'N' Roll Music To The World* (1972), *Recorded Live* (1973), *Positive Vibrations* (1974), *About Time* (1989). Compilations: *Alvin Lee & Company* (1972), *Goin' Home! - Their Greatest Hits* (1975), *Original Recordings Vol. 1* (1987), *The Essential* (1992).

Tenaglia, Danny

Italian-American Tenaglia has, together with keyboard player Peter Dauo, played host to an impressive slew of garage/house cuts emanating from New York in the 90s. He first turned to dance music when hearing a mix tape for the first time, subsequently selling them for the artist concerned. He was a keen enthusiast in the early disco boom, and played his first gig at a local club in Bayside, Queens, New York, when he was still 14. From there he picked up on musical trends as they occurred, being particularly influenced by the early innovations of **David Morales** and **Kevin Saunderson**. His productions of cuts like 'Glammer Girl' by the Look (a Jon Waters tribute), and the tehcno-jazz innovations of his partner Dauo, built an enviable reputation, as his profile grew alongside that of fellow New Yorkers **DJ Duke** and **Junior Vasquez**. Naturally this helped bring in the remix projects, including **Right Said Fred** and **Yothu Yindi**. Despite his obvious musical merits Tenaglia has yet to crack the US scene, which contrasts alarmingly with his popularity in Euorpe and even the Orient. In the UK his reputation has been franked by performances at the musically-sympathetic **Ministry Of Sound** club nights.

Tenneva Ramblers

Formed in 1924, they comprised Claude Grant (b. 1906, d. 1976; guitar/vocals), his brother Jack (b. 1903, d. 1968, mandolin), both from Bristol, Tennessee, USA and Jack Pierce (b. 1908; fiddle) of Smyth County, Virginia, USA, but were sometimes joined by Smokey Davis (a blackface comedian) and on recordings by Claude Slagle (banjo). In 1927, **Jimmie Rodgers** offered them work as his backing group. After initially refusing, they changed their name to the Jimmie Rodgers Entertainers and made some appearances with him. They were scheduled to back Rodgers on his first recordings but just prior to the session, they left him and reverted to their old name to pursue a recording career of their own. They remained active on various radio stations until 1954, sometimes being known as the Grant Brothers. They are remembered for their recording of 'The Longest Train'.
Album: *The Tenneva Ramblers* (c.70s).

Tennors, Clive

Clive was an original member of 70s reggae hit-makers the Tennors, who worked for the **Studio One** and **Treasure Isle** empires, scoring with tracks such as 'Cleopatra', 'Ride Yu Donkey' and 'Another Scorcher'. Though a solo career was widely mooted, it wasn't until the late 80s that any evidence of Clive Tennors' work came to light. In 1986 he appeared at a series of club dates in Miami. Following a brace of singles he released his debut long player, titled after one of the Tennors' most popular tunes, Ride Yu Donkey'.
Selected album: *Ride Yu Donkey* (Unicorn 1991).

Tenor Saw

b. Clive Bright, 1966, Kingston, Jamaica, West Indies, d. 1988, Houston, Texas, USA. One of the most influential singers of the early **digital** era, Tenor Saw's eerie, hypnotic wail was stamped with an almost religious fervour. He was raised in the Payne Avenue district of west Kingston; recording his debut 'Roll Call' in 1984 for George Phang's Powerhouse label after an introduction by **Nitty Gritty**. During 1985 he sang with **Sugar Minott**'s Youth Promotion **sound system** and label, recording 'Lots Of Sign' and 'Pumpkin Belly' (also versioned for **King Jammys**). 'Run Come Call Me' and 'Fever' too were sizeable hits. None, however, could compare to 'Ring The Alarm', which Tenor Saw voiced magnificently over **Winston Riley**'s 'Stalag' rhythm for the Techniques label. There was no bigger record that year and it continues to be regarded as an anthem in today's dancehalls. 'Golden Hen' for Uptempo continued the sequence of straight hits into 1986 when Minott released his debut

album, *Fever*. Tenor had already left for Miami and the Skengdon crew where 'Dancehall Feeling' and the posthumously released 'Bad Boys' was recorded. After a trip to England and the successful 'Never Work On A Sunday' for **Donovan Germain**, Tenor journeyed to New York in 1987. There he recorded the epic 'Victory Train' with **Freddie McGregor**'s **Studio One** Band, and further singles for Witty, Robert Livingston ('Come Me Just A Come'), and Jah Life. His duet with General Doggie on 'Chill Out Chill Out' for Digital English was this most enigmatic of singers' swan song. In August 1988 he was killed by a speeding car in Houston, Texas.
Selected albums: *Fever* (Blue Mountain 1986), *Lives On* (1992). With Cocoa Tea: *Meets Cocoa Tea* (Witty 1987). With Don Angelo: *Clash* (Witty 1985). Various: *Strictly Livestock* (Greensleeves 1986).

Tenpole Tudor

This theatrical UK punk-pop group was led by the inimitable Edward Tudor-Pole (b. 6 December 1955, London, England) who first took to the stage at the age of nine when he appeared in *A Christmas Carol*. After a course at Chiswick Polytechnic he went to train at the Royal Academy of Dramatic Arts. In 1977 he joined a band called the Visitors which also included future *Riverside* BBC televsion host Mike Andrews. Edward formed the band Tenpole Tudor with Visitors Gary Long (drums), Dick Crippen (bass) and Bob Kingston (guitar). Kingston came from a musical family and had previously been a member of Sta-Prest with his brother Ray, himself later in the Temper. His sister June would soon become a member of the **Mo-Dettes**. Tudor appeared in the film *The Great Rock 'N' Roll Swindle* (**Malcolm McLaren** had been an early mentor) and performed 'Who Killed Bambi', which appeared on the b-side of the **Sex Pistols**' 'Silly Thing'. Eddie also helped Paul Cook and Steve Jones write the title song to the film. His first single under their own name was 'Real Fun', which came out on Korova Records. After signing to **Stiff Records** the group released 'Three Bells In A Row'. Over the next few months they took part on the *Sons Of Stiff* tour, hit the charts three times starting with the raucous 'Swords Of A Thousand Men', recruited a second guitarist in the form of Munch Universe, and released two albums, before they suddenly went out of fashion again. In 1982 Eddie decided to split the band up. Crippen, Long, and Kingston became the Tudors and released 'Tied Up With Lou Cool' whilst Eddie formed a new cajun-style Tenpole Tudor and put out the 'Hayrick Song'. He then left Stiff and moved in to jazz and swing style bands whilst also reviving his acting career. In 1985 he formed an old style Tenpole Tudor and toured the country dressed in armour but left the following year to concentrate on acting. He subsequently appeared on stage (*The Sinking Of The Belgrano*), film (*Straight To Hell,*

Absolute Beginners and *Walker*) and television (in the comedy *Roy's Raiders*). He also reformed Tenpole Tudor again in 1989 and it seemed likely that he would continue to do so at regular intervals until his acting career took off. Memorably playing the narrator in stage play *The Road*, Tudor then took over the host's role in UK Channel 4 television's *The Crystal Maze*.

Albums: *Eddie, Old Bob, Dick And Gary* (Stiff 1981), *Let The Four Winds Blow* (Stiff 1981). Compilation: *Wunderbar* (Dojo 1992).

Terminator X

b. Norman Rodgers. One of the last of the **Public Enemy** fold to release a solo record, Terminator X's efforts reflect his work with his principal employers, minus the intrusion of Chuck D or **Flavor Flav**. Aimed squarely at the dance end of the hip hop market, *Valley Of The Jeep Beets* was primarily a collection of deep, bass-driven hip hop chops, and confirmed him as one of the finest DJs. It saw vocal contributions from Andrew 13 and **Sister Souljah**, on a combination of hard funk and scratchy raps. As Public Enemy prepared to tour in support of their 1994 album he was involved in a serious motorbike accident, breaking both his legs. However, that did not deter the release of his second solo outing. The highlight of this set was 'G'Damn Datt DJ Made My Day', on which he duelled on the turntable alongside **Grandmaster Flash**. Other old school legends like the **Cold Crush Brothers** and **Kool Herc** popped up elsewhere.

Album: *Terminator X And The Valley Of The Jeep Beets* (CBS/Columbia 1991). With The Godfathers Of Threatt: *Super Bad* (RAL 1994).

Ternent, Billy

b. 10 October 1899, Newcastle, England, d. 23 March 1977, London, England. A bandleader, arranger, multi-instrumentalist, and composer, Ternent was discovered by **Jack Hylton** while playing with the Selma Four in a Newcastle restaurant. Hylton took him to London where Ternent played in Al Starita's dance band at the Kit Kat Restaurant before joining Hylton's show band. From 1927 until the outbreak of World War II, Ternent wrote most of the Hylton band's familiar top-class arrangements, played several instruments, and served as the deputy leader on broadcasts, recordings and several extensive foreign tours. On leaving Hylton, he led various BBC orchestras for four years before forming his own band in 1944 and touring throughout the UK to enthusiastic audiences. His life-long signature tune was **Vivian Ellis'** 'She's My Lovely'. From the late 40s he conducted for numerous West End shows and visiting American artists (**Frank Sinatra** called him 'the little giant'), and spent five years, from 1962-67, as musical director at the London Palladium, participating in several Royal Command Performances. He was especially popular on radio, in programmes such as *Variety Bandbox*, where his versatility and superb musicianship were always in evidence. He made his first recordings with his Sweet Rhythm Orchestra in 1938, and among the top musicians and singers who were associated with his stylish and tasteful dance band were Harry Roche, **Don Lusher**, **Tommy Whittle**, Duncan Campbell, Stan Roderick, Duncan Lamont, Rick Kennedy, Tony Mercer, Shirley Norman, Margaret Rose, and Eva Beynon.

Selected albums: *She's My Lovely* (President 1960), *That Unmistakable Sound* (1969), *The Ternent Sound* (President 1986).

Terraplane

Terraplane evolved in the early 80s in south London as Nuthin' Fancy, the post-school band of Danny Bowes (vocals) and Luke Morley (guitar). By 1983 they had evolved into Terraplane with the addition of Nick Linden (bass) and Gary James (drums). The band soon became fixtures on the London circuit, playing at the Reading Festival before releasing an independent single, 'I Survive'. Suitably impressed, **Epic Records** signed Terraplane, but the young band perhaps took too much notice of advice about image and style from their label and management, who chose to emphasize a poppier direction, away from the band's melodic hard rock roots. When the debut finally emerged, the humorous original title of *Talking To God* (later You) *On The Great White Telephone* had been replaced by the bland *Black & White*. While the quality of Morley's songwriting was obvious, the production resulted in a slick pop sound in contrast to the band's rockier live approach, given a heavier edge with the addition of rhythm guitarist Rudi Riviere (ex-Sapphire). *Black & White* was only a moderate success but failed to break the lucrative pop market, and *Moving Target*, recorded without the departed Riviere (to America and session work), was rather directionless, with the band folding a year later. Morley, Bowes and James regrouped with much greater success in **Thunder**, perhaps demonstrating what might have been for Terraplane had the band been left to develop in their own right.

Albums: *Black & White* (Epic 1986), *Moving Target* (Epic 1987).

Terrell, Tammi

b. Thomasina Montgomery, 29 April 1945, Philadelphia, Pennsylvania, USA, d. 16 March 1970. Tammi Terrell began recording for Scepter/**Wand Records** at the age of 15, before touring with the **James Brown** Revue for a year. In 1965, she married heavyweight boxer Ernie Terrell, the brother of future Supreme Jean Terrell. Tammi's warm, sensuous vocals won her a contract with **Motown** later that year, and in 1966 she enjoyed a series of R&B hits, among them a soulful rendition of 'This Old Heart Of Mine'. In

1967, she was selected to replace **Kim Weston** as **Marvin Gaye**'s recording partner. This inspired teaming produced Gaye's most successful duets, and the pair issued a stream of hit singles between 1967 and 1969. 'Ain't No Mountain High Enough' and 'You're All I Need To Get By' epitomized their style, as Marvin and Tammi weaved around each other's voices, creating an aura of romance and eroticism which led to persistent rumours that they were lovers.

From the beginning, their partnership was tinged with unhappiness, Terrell collapsing in Gaye's arms during a performance in 1967. She was diagnosed as suffering from a brain tumour, and despite a series of major operations over the next three years, her health steadily weakened. By 1969, she was unable to perform in public, and on several of the duo's final recordings, their producer, **Valerie Simpson**, controversially claims to have taken her place. Ironically, one of these tracks, 'The Onion Song', proved to be the most successful of the Gaye/Terrell singles in the UK. Tammi Terrell died on 16 March 1970, her burial service attracting thousands of mourners, including many of her Motown colleagues. Her death has been the subject of much speculation, centred on rumours that her brain disorders were triggered by alleged beatings administered by a member of the Motown hierarchy. These accusations were given voice in *Number One With A Bullet*, a novel by former Gaye aide Elaine Jesmer, which included a character clearly based on Terrell.

Albums: *Early Show* (1969), *Irresistible* (1969). With Marvin Gaye: *United* (1968), *You're All I Need* (1968), *Easy* (1969).

Territory Bands

Many of the popular dance and jazz orchestras of the late 20s and 30s were based in New York. Even those bands that toured extensively started and ended their trips on the east coast found the accumulation of musicians in New York particularly helpful when hiring new men. Additionally, most of the leading recording and broadcasting companies had their headquarters in the city. However, New York was far from the whole story. Many fine bands rarely came there, some never at all. Many of the bands which worked extensively, sometimes exclusively in the mid-west, south and southwestern states, based themselves in other centres. These bands were referred to by people in the music business as territory bands, a term which should not regarded as having dismissive connotations. Perhaps the region with the most notable tradition in high quality dance and jazz orchestras was Texas. Based in Dallas were the fine **Alphonso Trent** band, generally regarded as the best of the territory bands, plus outfits led by Don Albert, **Terrence Holder** and Doc Ross, in whose band **Jack Teagarden** played. The Milt Larkins and Nat Towles units, both bands highly

regarded amongst musicians, were based in Houston; and San Antonio had Boots And His Buddies, led by drummer Clifford 'Boots' Douglas, and Troy Floyd. Even smaller towns, such as Amarillo, had exceptional bands, in this case Gene Coy's Happy Black Aces. Texas was not the only state with a musical tradition. In Denver, Colorado, George Morrison led an exceptional band which at times included musicians such as **Andy Kirk** and **Jimmie Lunceford**. St Louis, Missouri, was home-base for Charlie Creath, Dewey Jackson, **Frank Trumbauer**, the **Jeter-Pillars Orchestra**, and the **Missourians**, a band with which Blanche and **Cab Calloway** were associated. Oklahoma City boasted Eugene Crookes and the Blue Devils, a band led by **Walter Page** and whose sidemen, and leader, eventually became important in the development of the bands of **Bennie Moten** and **Count Basie**. Milwaukee, Wisconsin, had Grant Moore; Omaha, Nebraska, had Clarence Love, Lloyd Hunter and Red Perkins; and Cincinnati, Ohio, was home to Zack Whyte's Chocolate Beau Brummels. Salina, Kansas, was the base for Art Bronson's Bostonians. Although the southwest and mid-west is usually thought of as home for the territory bands, those from California and Massachusetts should not be overlooked. These included the Los Angeles-based bands of the **Spikes Brothers**, Charlie Echols and **Les Hite**, while outstanding on the northeast coast was Boston-based Sabby Lewis. For all the status and quality of bands such as these, however, Kansas City, Missouri was the single most important centre outside of New York. The city boasted an enviable roster of superb bands, many of which went on to national and international fame, while individual sidemen became important, and in some cases legendary, figures of jazz. Most of the bands already referred to passed through Kansas City (see **Kansas City Jazz**). A list of sidemen who played in territory bands during their formative years would be almost endless, but amongst those who have to be mentioned are **Lester Young**, **Ben Webster**, **Herschel Evans**, **Buddy Tate**, **Oran 'Hot Lips' Page**, **Jimmy Rushing**, **Harry Edison**, **Charlie Christian**, **Snub Mosley**, **Peanuts Holland**, **Gene Ramey**, **Budd Johnson**, **Arnett Cobb**, **Illinois Jacquet** and **Earl Bostic**. Numerous compilation albums have been released, most of which bear confusingly similar titles, such as *The Territory Bands*.

Further reading: *Jazz Style In Kansas City And The Southwest*, Ross Russell.

Terror Fabulous

b. c.1974. Jamaican DJ who became one of the fastest rising stars of the **dancehall** scene in the 90s. His skills were learned on local streets in his early teens, before he completed a course in electrical engineering and was

introduced to producer Dave Kelly. In tandem they produced a single, 'Dorothy', which brought both to wider fame and recognition. His growing profile saw him signed to **East West** in the UK, for whom his debut album included hit singles 'Action' (with **Nadine Sutherland**), 'Miss Goody Goody' (with **Maxi Priest**) and the title-track (with Gary Minott).
Selected albums: *Yaga Yaga* (East West 1994), *Glamorous* (New Sound 1994).

Terrorizer

This American quartet were more of a project than a real band, featuring the **Morbid Angel** rhythm section of Pete Sandoval (drums) and David Vincent (bass, vocals), in collaboration with the Californian-based duo of Oscar Garcia (vocals) and Jesse Pintado (guitar). Terrorizer broke up when Morbid Angel's emergence from the underground death metal scene meant that Sandoval and Vincent no longer had time to spare. *World Downfall*, however, was a definitive grindcore album, given a fierce sound by producer Vincent and engineer Scott Burns. Sandoval and Vincent produced their customary tight performance to ensure effective delivery of often highly paced material, while Pintado showed the ability and aggression which was to lead to his subsequent recruitment to the **Napalm Death** ranks. Which just left Garcia to growl and spit outrage through largely politicised, hardcore-influenced lyrics. A second album remains unreleased.
Album: *World Downfall* (Earache 1989).

Terrorvision

This Bradford, England, quartet formed in 1986 as Spoilt Brats, and quickly fused rock, funk and thrash influences into an infectiously upbeat pop-metal style. Singer Tony Wright, guitarist Mark Yates, bassist Leigh Marklew and drummer Shutty were signed by **EMI** on the strength of their 'Pump Action Sunshine' demo, and negotiated their own label name, Total Vegas. Two remixed demo tracks, 'Urban Space Crime' and 'Jason', appeared on the *Thrive* EP as Terrorvision followed a hectic touring schedule prior to the release of *Formaldehyde*. The debut produced minor hits in 'American TV' and 'New Policy One', and was backed by UK and European tours with the **Ramones** and **Motörhead** respectively, while **Def Leppard** frontman Joe Elliott was sufficiently impressed to invite Terrorvision to open Leppard's 1993 show at Sheffield's Don Valley Stadium. 1994 proved to be quite a year for Terrorvision, beginning with their UK Top 30 breakthrough with 'My House'. *How To Make Friends And Influence People* emerged to rave reviews and entered the UK Top 20, bringing the band their first silver disc, and produced four more Top 30 singles in 'Oblivion', 'Middleman', 'Pretend Best Friend' and 'Alice, What's The Matter?', the greatest number by any single band in 1994. They also played both the Reading and Donington Festivals, in addition to two sold-out UK tours and a series of European dates, before moving on to work on a new album in 1995.
Albums: *Formaldehyde* (Total Vegas 1992), *How To Make Friends And Influence People* (Total Vegas 1994).

Terry And The Pirates

This US rock band's complex history began in 1970 when the group's driving force, Terry Dolan, a former veteran of San Francisco's folk circuit, embarked on a recording career. Several local musicians, including **John Cipollina** and **Nicky Hopkins** from **Quicksilver Messenger Service**, and future **Steve Miller** Band guitarist Greg Douglas assisted a project which, although never released, established the idea of a part-time group. Terry And The Pirates would never boast a settled line-up, but its fluid concept, free from commercial restraints, evoked the spirit of the 'classic' San Franciscan era, particularly with respect to Cipollina's inventive, improvisational guitar work. During their constantly changing line-up they included: Lonnie Turner (Steve Miller Band), David Weber, Jim McPherson and Hutch Hutchinson (**Copperhead** and **Raven**) and Jeff Myer (**Savage Resurrection** and **Jesse Colin Young**'s band). Their albums feature material compiled from various sources, but it is for an in-concert prowess that the Pirates will be remembered. Cipollina's death in 1989 has robbed Dolan of his surest lieutenant; *Silverado Trail* was a fitting tribute to this excellent musician's talent.
Albums: *Too Close For Comfort* (1979), *The Doubtful Handshake* (1980), *Wind Dancer* (1981), *Rising Of The Moon* (1982), *Acoustic Rangers* (1988), *Silverado Trail* (1990).

Terry Dactyl And The Dinosaurs

This UK jugband-cum-skiffle group enjoyed a concurrent career as **Brett Marvin And The Thunderbolts**. Little effort was spared to hide this fact, even though each 'act' was signed to different recording companies. The Dinosaurs enjoyed the patronage of producer/entrepreneur **Jonathan King**, who signed them to his UK label. Their debut single, 'Seaside Shuffle', reached number 2 in 1972, while the following year the group scored a minor chart entry with 'On A Saturday Night'. The 'Brett Marvin' appellation was fully resurrected when further releases proved unsuccessful, while vocalist/keyboard player **Jona Lewie** later embarked on a solo career.

Terry, Clark

b. 14 December 1920, St. Louis, Missouri, USA. Terry gained invaluable experience playing trumpet in local bands, but developed his remarkable technique while in the US Navy. As he recalled for jazz writer Steve Voce, he practised using a clarinet book, preferring the more fluid sound this generated in his playing. After his military service he joined **Charlie Barnet**, then became a mainstay of the **Count Basie** band for three years until 1951, when he joined **Duke Ellington** for an eight-year stint. At the end of the 50s he went into studio work in New York City, becoming one of the first black musicians to be regularly employed in this way. For a dozen years he was featured in the **Doc Severinson** band, which played on the Johnny Carson television show. During this time he continued to play in jazz groups for club and record dates, working with **Bob Brookmeyer**, **J.J. Johnson** and others, and also leading his own 'Big B-A-D Band', which featured many leading New York session men. During the 70s Terry began playing flügelhorn, eventually making this his principal instrument. The 70s and 80s found him touring extensively, playing concerts, clubs and festivals around the world, usually as leader but ably blending in with almost any background from late swing style to post-bop. Terry's remarkable technical accomplishment has never overwhelmed the depth of emotion which imbues his playing, and neither of these characteristics has ever dampened his infectious humour. This quality is most readily apparent on his singing of 'Mumbles', for which he created a unique variation on scat. His duets with himself, during which he plays flügelhorn and trumpet, are remarkable displays of his astonishing skills yet never degenerate into mere bravura exercises. Terry remains a major figure in the history of jazz trumpet and is one of the music's most respected and widely-admired ambassadors.

Selected albums: *Introducing Clark Terry* (1955), *Swahili* (1955), with Duke Ellington *A Drum Is A Woman* (1956), *Serenade To A Bus Seat* (Original Jazz Classics 1957), *Duke With A Difference* (Original Jazz Classics 1957), *Out On A Limb* (1957), *In Orbit* (Original Jazz Classics 1958), *Top And Bottom Brass* (1959), *Clark Terry* (1960), *Color Changes* (Candid 1960), *Everything's Mellow* (1961), *The Night Life* (1962), *Three In Jazz* (1963), *Tread Ye Lightly* (1963), *What Makes Sammy Swing* (1963), *More* (1963), with Bob Brookmeyer *Tonight* (1964), *The Happy Horns Of Clark Terry* (1964), *Mumbles* (1965), *The Power Of Positive Swinging* (1965), *Gingerbread Men* (1966), *Spanish Rice* (1966), *It's What's Happenin'* (1967), *Clark Terry At The Montreux Jazz Festival* (1969), *Big B.A.D. Band Live On 57th Street* (1970), *Big B.A.D. Band Live at The Wichita Jazz Festival* (Vanguard 1974), *Clark Terry And His Jolly Giants* (1975), *Professor Jive* (1976), *Wham! Live At The Lighthouse* (1976), *Big B. A. D. Band Live At Buddy's Place* (Vanguard 1976), *Clark After Dark* (1977), *The Globetrotter* (1977), *Funk Dumplin's* (1978), *Clark Terry's Big Band In Warsaw* (1978), *Out Of Nowhere* (1978), *Brahms Lullaby* (1978), *Mother...! Mother...!* (1979), *Ain't Misbehavin'* (Pablo 1979), *Clark Terry At Buffalo State* (1979), *Memories Of Duke* (Original Jazz Classics 1980), *'Yes, The Blues'* (1981), with Red Mitchell *To Duke And Basie* (1986), *Take Double* (1986), with Mitchell *Jive At Five* (Enja 1988), *Portraits* (Chesky 1988), *The Clark Terry Spacemen* (1989),

with Oliver Jones *Just Friends* (1989), *Live At The Village Gate* (Chesky 1990), *Having Fun* (Delos 1991).

Terry, Sonny

b. Saunders Terrell, 24 October 1911, Greensboro, North Carolina, USA, d. 12 March 1986, New York City, New York, USA. By the age of 16, Sonny Terry was virtually blind following two accidents, which encouraged his concentration on music. After his father's death, Terry worked on medicine shows, and around 1937 teamed up with **Blind Boy Fuller,** moving to Durham, North Carolina, to play the streets with Fuller, Gary Davis and washboard player George Washington (Bull City Red). Terry made his recording debut in December 1937 as Fuller's harmonica player. His vocalized tones were interspersed with a distinctive falsetto whoop, and he continued in this fashion until Fuller's death in 1941. By Terry's good luck, Fuller was in jail when **John Hammond** came to recruit him for the 1938 *Spirituals To Swing* concert, and Terry took his place. His inextricably interwoven harmonica playing and singing were a sensation, but had little immediate effect on his career, although **OKeh Records** did record him as a name artist. In 1942, Terry was to appear at a concert in Washington, DC, and J.B. Long, who managed them both, suggested that **Brownie McGhee** should lead Terry. This led to a booking in New York, where both men relocated, and to the formation of their long-term musical partnership. In New York Terry recorded, as leader and sideman, for many black-orientated labels; but his first New York sides were made for Moses Asch of Folkways with accompaniment by **Woody Guthrie**, and this was a pointer to the future. By the late 50s, Terry and McGhee had effectively ceased to perform for black audiences, and presented their music as 'folk-blues'. This was seen as a sell-out by those who demanded uncompromisingly 'black' music from blues singers. However an objective examination of their repertoire shows a large number of songs that had been recorded for black audiences in an R&B setting, while the children's songs and country dance music Terry recorded for Asch remain a valuable documentation. Even so Terry's singing voice, (now no longer falsetto), was rather coarse, and sometimes badly pitched. McGhee and Terry were not close friends, and in the latter days actively disliked one another even to the point of bickering on stage; nevertheless, their partnership brought the blues to a vast audience worldwide.

Albums: *Harmonica And Vocal Solos* (c.1958), *Sonny Terry's New Sound* (1958), *On The Road* (c.1959), *Washboard Band Country Dance Music* (1963), *Sonny's Story* (1960), *Hometown Blues* (1969), *Wizard Of The Harmonica* (1972), *Whoopin'* (c.1985), *Whoopin' The Blues* (1986), *Old Town Blues Vol. 1* (1986), *Sonny Terry* (1987), *Toughest Terry And Baddest Brown* (1987), *Sonny Terry* (1988), *Brownie McGhee & Sonny*

Terry Sing (1990), *The Folkways Years* (1991).

Terry, Todd

Todd is a USA house production innovator and expert with a reputation second to none (in fact, some UK journalists from specialist magazines have taken to nicknaming him 'God' for easy reference). An established producer and DJ, he learned his trade playing early house and hip hop at parties in New York. 'Bongo (To The Batmobile)', a major signpost in the development of acid house, and further singles like 'Can You Party?' and 'A Day In The Life Of A Black Riot' were credited to the Todd Terry Project alias In addition to an album and singles on **Champion** (including the mighty 'Put Your Hands Together'), he has also cut records for **Strictly Rhythm, Nervous** and Freeze (SAX's 'This Will Be Mine'). His distinctive use of samples underpins all his production and remix work: "What I try to do is to make an art out of the samples'. This often involves multi-layers of creative theft without allowing a given example to offer its 'signature' to the listener. His remix clients have included **Bizarre Inc** ('I'm Gonna Get You') and **Snap!**, and he also collaborated with old friend **Tony Humphries** to remix **Alison Limerick**'s 'Make It On My Own'. 'Whenever I do a remix I strip the vocal right down and use just a little bit. That's why I don't do many remixes, they are a long way from the original'. A good example was the magic he worked on **PM Dawn**'s 'From A Watcher's Point Of View'. He partially became involved because members of that band had previously worked for him at Warlock Records. He owns his own home-studio, the Loudhouse, in his native Brooklyn.
Selected album: *This Is The New Todd Terry Project Album* (Champion 1992).

Teschemacher, Frank

b. 13 March 1906, Kansas City, Missouri, USA, d. 1 March 1932. Raised in Chicago, Teschemacher first took up violin then played various other instruments before settling on alto saxophone. He played with many of the young emergent Chicagoans, including **Jimmy McPartland**, making many jazz records while playing in dance bands for a living. In 1925 he began playing clarinet, the instrument on which he made his greatest mark. In the late 20s he played in the bands of **Ben Pollack**, **Ted Lewis** and **Red Nichols**, but continued to work in numerous minor groups. At the end of the 20s he resumed playing alto and violin and also occasionally played cornet. Although he appeared on many fine jazz recordings with **Red McKenzie**, **Eddie Condon** and others, usually on clarinet, his contributions here rarely support the enormously high regard in which he was held by his fellow musicians. Shortly after he joined a new band formed by **Wild Bill Davison** he was killed in a road accident in March 1932, just a few days short of his 26th birthday.
Compilation: with various leaders *Chicago Jazz Vol. 1* (1928-30).

Tesla

Originally known as City Kid, Tesla are a five-piece, blues-based, hard rock quintet from Sacramento, California, USA. Named after the scientist Nikola Tesla, the current line-up came together in 1985. The band comprises Jeff Keith (vocals), Tommy Skeoch (guitar/vocals), Frank Hannon (guitar/keyboards/vocals), Brian Wheat (bass/vocals) and Troy Lucketta (drums; ex-Eric Martin Band, Breathless). They signed to **Geffen Records** in 1986 and recorded *Mechanical Resonance*, a universally acclaimed debut that ranks alongside that of **Montrose**'s first album in terms of setting new standards. The title was taken from one of Tesla's theories and combined raunchy metallic rock with blues and rock 'n' roll influences. Jeff Keith's impassioned vocals gave the material an added dimension, as the songs alternated between passionate, gut-wrenching ballads and crazy, fuel-injected rockers. The album eventually took off in the US, reaching number 32 on the ***Billboard*** chart. *The Great Radio Controversy* saw the band rapidly maturing, with a highly polished, but no-less energetic collection of songs that were saturated with infectious riffs and subtle hook-lines. The ballad, 'Love Song', became a Top 10 hit, while the album climbed to number 18 on the US charts. Tesla's third collection created something of a precedent, a live album that was totally acoustic and included a number of inspired cover versions. It highlighted the band's humour, technical excellence and ability to entertain. *Psychotic Supper* showed they could easily switch back to power-mode, with a near 70-minute onslaught of high-energy hard rock numbers. Tesla defy convention and have no gimmicks, nor do they conform to any particular image, choosing instead to tour relentlessly (for over a year to support *Psychotic Supper*, playing over 138 shows in the process). *Bust A Nut*, meanwhile, included a cover of **Joe South**'s 'Games People Play', and offered a further blast of superbly declaimed traditional, neo-purist, heavy metal.
Albums: *Mechanical Resonance* (Geffen 1986), *The Great Radio Controversy* (Geffen 1989), *Five Man Acoustical Jam* (Geffen 1990), *Psychotic Supper* (Geffen 1991), *Bust A Nut* (Geffen 1994).
Video: *Five Man Video Band* (1991).

Test Department

This UK experimental/industrial band comprised Paul Jamrozy (b. 3 March 1959), Graham Cunnington (b. 23 August 1960), Alistair Adams (b. 5 October 1959), Tony Cudlip (b. 9 September 1959) and Gus Ferguson. Originally forming in 1982 as a loose collective in New

Cross, London, England, they were all co-directors of Test Department's stable, Ministry of Power Records. However, they liaised with a variety of other artists and musicians in order to empower their large-scale projects. The most recent and impressive of these was the huge *The Second Coming* show for Glasgow's 1990 Year Of Culture, set in the abandoned St. Rollox Railway Works. This served as the culmination of several years inaugurating spectacular musical events in unlikely settings. Others have included Cannon Street Station, Bishopsbridge Maintenance Depot, a sand quarry, a car factory in Wales and an ice rink in Friesland. 'From the beginning there was a realization that we wanted to make things pretty monumental', they concede. Allied to their innovative use of spectacle was the employment of instruments from the natural and unnatural environment; scrap metal and industrial cast-offs beating a rhythm to film and slide shows. Powered by a four-piece anvil chorus, the music splendidly complemented visuals drawn from 20s and 30s industrial monochromes. Originally signed up to **Stevo**'s **Some Bizzare** label, they came in the same wave as fellow travellers **SPK** and **Einsturzende Neubaten**. In early 1984 they published an open manifesto in a letter to the ***New Musical Express***: '...we will continue a disciplined attack on the official wall of ignorance both in music and in politics'. This remains a constant objective, as witnessed by their *Pax Britannica* album, recorded with the help of the Scottish Chamber Orchestra and Choir as a critique of Thatcherism.

Albums: *Beating The Retreat* (Some Bizzare 1984), *Shoulder To Shoulder With South Wales Striking Miners* (Some Bizzare 1985), *The Unacceptable Face Of Freedom* (Ministry Of Power/Some Bizzare 1986), *A Good Night Out* (Ministry Of Power/Some Bizzare 1988), *Terra Firma* (Sub Rosa/Ministry Of Power 1988), with Brith Gof *The Gododdin* (Ministry Of Power 1989), *Pax Britannica* (Ministry Of Power 1991), *Proven In Action* (Ministry Of Power 1991, live album). Compilation: *Legacy (1990-1993)* (Ministry Of Power 1994).

Testament

This thrash act was one of the first to emerge from San Francisco's Bay Area in **Metallica**'s wake in the 80s. Originally formed as Legacy in 1983, becoming Testament two years later, the line-up included vocalist Steve Souza alongside Alex Skolnick (lead guitar, replacing original guitarist Derek Ramirez), Eric Peterson (rhythm guitar), Greg Christian (bass), and Louie Clemente (drums). However, Souza soon departed for **Exodus** and was replaced by giant frontman Chuck Billy. *The Legacy* was a ferocious introduction, quickly establishing Testament at the forefront of the burgeoning thrash scene. Following a live mini-album recorded at Holland's Dynamo Festival, *The New Order* consolidated their popularity

with improved songwriting, producing one certifiable classic in 'Disciples Of The Watch'. Skolnick, however, was losing interest in pure thrash, extending his undoubted talents by moonlighting in Stuart Hamm's touring band at one point, and his influence brought a more considered melodic power metal approach to *Practice What You Preach*, which worked superbly. However, *Souls Of Black* was rushed to coincide with the European Clash Of The Titans tour with **Slayer**, **Megadeth** and **Suicidal Tendencies**, and was consequently disappointing. After *The Ritual*, Skolnick joined **Savatage** and Clemente also departed. *Return To Apocalyptic City* introduced Glen Alvelais (guitar, ex-**Forbidden**) and John Tempesta (drums, ex-**Exodus**), but Alvelais' tenure was short-lived, with journeyman guitarist James Murphy (ex-**Death/Obituary/Disincarnate/Cancer**) stepping in for *Low*, which saw a return to the glorious thrashing style of yore. Tempesta subsequently joined **White Zombie**, and was replaced by John Dutte (ex-**Evil Dead**).

Albums: *The Legacy* (Megaforce 1987), *Live At Eindhoven* (Megaforce 1987, mini-album), *The New Order* (Megaforce 1988), *Practice What You Preach* (Megaforce 1989), *Souls Of Black* (Megaforce 1990), *The Ritual* (Atlantic 1992), *Return To Apocalyptic City* (Atlantic 1993, mini-album), *Low* (East West 1994).

Tester, Scan

b. Lewis Tester, 1887, Chelwood Common, Sussex, England, d. 1972. Tester showed a penchant for music from a very young age, progressing quickly from tambourine to melodeon, concertina and fiddle. In addition to his early days busking in Brighton, Sussex, Scan played for dances in a number of local inns. After World War I, he continued playing for dances and formed Tester's Imperial Band which featured, in addition to Tester, his second wife Sarah on drums, and daughter Daisy on piano. Occasionally, Tester's brother Will would play on bandoneon. The band survived until 1931, after which Scan played at a pub called the Stone Quarry, until he died in 1972. In his lifetime, he had built an extensive repertoire of dance material. It was thanks to a collector, Mervyn Plunkett, that Tester's music, and the music of Sussex, came to the attention of a much wider audience in 1957. Plunkett recorded Tester and his music; *I Never Played Too Many Posh Dances*, is a double album featuring recordings from 1957-68.

Albums: *The Man In The Moon* (1975), *I Never Played Too Many Posh Dances* (1990); with other artists *Music Of The Sussex Weald* (1966), *Boscastle Breakdown* (1974), *Sussex Harvest* (1975).

Further reading: *I Never Played Too Many Posh Dances*, Reg Hall.

Tex, Joe

b. Joseph Arrington Jnr., 8 August 1933, Rogers, Texas, USA, d. 13 August 1982. The professional career of this popular singer began onstage at the **Apollo**. He won first place in a 1954 talent contest and duly secured a record deal. Releases on King, Ace and the Anna labels were derivative and disappointing, but Tex meanwhile honed his songwriting talent. **James Brown**'s version of 'Baby You're Right' (1962) became a US R&B number 2, after which Tex was signed by Buddy Killen, a Nashville song publisher, who in turn established Dial as a recording outlet. Although early releases showed promise, it was not until 1965 that Tex prospered. Recorded at Fame and distributed by **Atlantic**, 'Hold On To What You've Got' was a US Top 5 hit. The first of several preaching singles, its homely values were maintained on 'A Woman Can Change A Man' and 'The Love You Save (May Be Your Own)'. However, Joe was equally comfortable on uptempo songs, as 'S.Y.S.L.J.F.M. (The Letter Song)' (1966) and 'Show Me' (1967) proved. Later releases were less successful and although 'Skinny Legs And All' and 'Men Are Gettin' Scarce' showed him still capable of major hits, the singer seemed unsure of his direction. A fallow period ended with 'I Gotcha' (1972), an irresistibly cheeky song, but Tex chose this moment to retire. A convert to the Muslim faith since 1966, he changed his name to Yusuf Hazziez, and toured as a spiritual lecturer. He returned to music in 1975. Two years later he enjoyed a 'comeback' hit with the irrepressible 'Ain't Gonna Bump No More (With No Big Fat Woman)'. By the 80s, however, Joe had withdrawn again from full-time performing. He devoted himself to Islam, his Texas ranch and the Houston Oilers football team. He was tempted into a Soul Clan reunion in 1981, but in August 1982 he died following a heart attack.

Albums: *Hold What You've Got* (1965), *The New Boss* (1965), *The Love You Save* (1966), *I've Got To Do A Little Better* (1966), *Live And Lively* (1968), *Soul Country* (1968), *Happy Soul* (1969), *You Better Get It* (1969), *Buying A Book* (1969), *With Strings And Things* (1970), *From The Roots Came The Rapper* (1972), *I Gotcha* (1972), *Joe Tex Spills The Beans* (early 70s), *Another Man's Woman* (early 70s), *Bumps And Bruises* (1977), *Rub Down* (1978), *He Who Is Without Funk Cast The First Stone* (1979). Compilations: *The Very Best Of Joe Tex* (1988), *The Very Best Of Joe Tex - Real Country Soul . . . Scarce As Hen's Teeth* (1988), *Different Strokes* (1989), *Stone Soul Country* (1989), *Greatest Hits* (1992), *Ain't Gonna Bump No More* (1993), *I Gotcha (His Greatest Hits)* (1993), *Skinny Legs And All* (1994), *You're Right Joe Tex!* (1995).

Texas

This Glasgow-based group was established in 1988 by ex-**Altered Images**' bassist Johnny McElhone. Stuart Kerr (drums), formerly of **Love And Money**, completed its rhythm section, although the quartet's sound was shaped by two novices; Sharleen Spiteri and Ally McErlaine. Where the former offered a distinctive, expressive voice, the latter's plangent guitarwork provided Texas with a defintive sound, inspired by the 'slide' style of **Ry Cooder**. The group's debut, *Southside*, sold in excess of two million copies, while an attendant single, 'I Don't Want A Lover', reached the UK Top 10. Kerr was replaced by Richard Hynd for their second album, *Mother's Finest*, which also introduced keyboard player Eddie Campbell. Here Texas widened their musical palate to include drum samples and if a debt to 60s' icons the **Doors** and **Rolling Stones** is apparent, the group equally exhibits an undoubted self-confidence.

Albums: *Southside* (1989), *Mother's Finest* (1991), *Rick's Road* (1993).

Texas Tornados

Following the success of the Highwaymen (**Johnny Cash**, **Waylon Jennings**, **Kris Kristofferson**, **Willie Nelson**), four lesser-known Tex-Mex musicians formed the Texas Tornados and secured a contract with a major label, **Reprise/WEA**. Doug Sahm and organist **Augie Meyers**, who had been part of the **Sir Douglas Quintet** and had frequently worked together were joined by accordionist **Flaco Jiminez** and one-time country star, **Freddy Fender**. Their enthusiastic debut, *Texas Tornados*, was both a commercial success and a Grammy winner. In actuality, Fender and Jiminez were missing from several tracks and the album, with its mixture of country, blues and Mexican music, was similar to what Sahm and Meyers had been playing for years. Subsequent albums also sound like the Sir Douglas Quintet with friends: their excellent music has included an English/Spanish version of **Bob Dylan**'s 'To Ramona', **Butch Hancock**'s 'She Never Spoke Spanish To Me' and Sahm's standards, 'Who Were You Thinkin' Of' and 'Is Anybody Goin' To San Antone?'.

Albums: *Texas Tornados* (1990), *Zone Of Our Own* (1991), *Hangin' On By A Thread* (1992).

Thackray, Jake

b. 1938, Yorkshire, England. Thackray enjoyed a residency on a UK television series, *Jake Thackray And Songs*. His distinctive clipped intonation enhanced his repertoire of comic, romantic, traditional and serious songs. He became a regular guest on other television programmes, such as *The David Frost Show* and *On The Braden Beat*. Since his first job at the City Palace Of Varieties, in Leeds, Jake has toured the USA, Europe, Canada, Africa and other parts of the world. Unlike other folk performers who, having achieved a degree of commercial status, left the folk scene Thackray could still be seen playing small clubs, while filling engagements at the London Palladium, the Royal Albert Hall, and other large venues fulfiling the demand for old favourites such as 'Bantam Cock' and 'Sister Josephine'.

Albums: *The Last Will And Testament Of Jake Thackray* (1967), *Jake's Progress* (EMI 1969), *Live Performance - Jake Thackray* (EMI 1971), *Bantam Cock* (EMI 1972), *On Again, On Again* (EMI 1977), *Jake Thackray And His Songs* (1980), *Tramshed Forever* (1981). Compilations: *The Very Best Of Jake Thackray* (EMI 1975), *Lah-Di-Dah* (EMI 1991).

Thanks A Million

Taking a break from Warner Brothers, **Ruby Keeler** and the *Gold Diggers*, **Dick Powell** co-starred with the delightful Ann Dvorak in this bright and entertaining musical which was released by 20th Century-Fox in 1935. The distinguished writer, producer, and director Nunnally Johnson, came up with a pip of a satirical script in which Powell plays Eric Land, a crooner with a small troupe of travelling entertainers. They get stranded in a small town, and - just to pass the time - Powell reads the speech for the Commonwealth Party candidate for State Governor, A. Darius Culliman (Raymond Walburn), after the old boy is taken ill with indigestion (drunk). Powell is so impressive that leading members of the Party persuade him to run for the office himself. Naturally, they will expect cushy jobs for themselves after he wins. However, he will have no part in their corruption, and, after exposing them, is triumphantly elected on a four-point ticket - one of which is that none of his political addresses will last for more than 30 seconds. Ann Dvorak played Powell's adoring girlfriend of course, and radio star Fred Allen was fine as his manager - a bit of a hustler who is intent on bringing some pizzazz into politics. Also among the cast were Paula Kelly, Benny Baker, Alan Dinehart, Paul Harvey, Edwin Maxwell, and Margaret Irving. **Paul Whitman** and his Band with Zorina, and Rubinoff and the Yacht Club Boys made guest appearances. **Gus Kahn** and Arthur Johnston wrote the tuneful score which included 'Thanks A Million', 'Sittin' On A Hilltop', 'Pocketful Of Sunshine', 'New O'leans', 'Sugar Plum', 'Sing Brother', and 'The Square Deal Party'. Roy Del Ruth directed with verve and style, and it was nicely photographed in black and white by Peverell Marley. The producer was Darryl F. Zanuck. It was remade in 1946 as *If I'm Lucky*.

Tharpe, Sister Rosetta

b. 20 March 1915, Cotton Plant, Arkansas, USA, d. 9 October 1973. After first singing in a church choir, Tharpe quickly became a solo singer. In addition to her deeply-held religious views, she was influenced by blues singers and musicians and took up the guitar to help broaden her repertoire. By the late 30s she was a popular performer at sacred and secular functions, happily switching from gospel to jazz. She was featured at **John Hammond**'s 'Spirituals To Swing' concerts at Carnegie Hall and also worked at the Cotton Club with **Cab Calloway**. In the early 40s she spent a year with the **Lucky Millinder** band, recording several best-selling numbers which included 'I Want A Tall Skinny Papa' and a marvellous rendition of 'Trouble In Mind'. Apparently conscience-stricken at this venture into the seamier side of life, she returned to the safety of the church, rocking congregations to the roots of their souls with her ecstatic and sometimes frenzied singing. She continued to record and her duets with fellow gospel singer Marie Knight are classics of the form. Later in her career, she continued to sing in churches but returned regularly to the jazz scene, making enormously successful tours of Europe and the UK with **Chris Barber** and others in the 50s and 60s. One of the few gospel singers to become an effective jazz performer, her vitality and zeal won her a substantial following in both fields. She died in October 1973.

Albums: *Live In Paris* (1964). Compilations: with Lucky Millinder *Apollo Jump* (1941-42 recordings), *The Best Of Sister Rosetta Tharpe, Vols 1 & 2* (1940s-50s recordings).

That Night In Rio

One of the most familiar (and entertaining) plots in movie musicals - it was also the basis of *Folies Bergère De Paris* (1935) and *On The Riviera* (1951) - was utilised in this lively Technicolor 20th Century-Fox musical which burst on to the screen in 1941. Perhaps the reason why screenwriters George Seaton, Bess Meredyth, and Hal Long (and others before them) used Rudolph Lothar and Hans Adler's original play for their inspiration, is because it entails the (inevitably) good-looking leading man playing two roles. The story goes something like this: a nightclub entertainer (**Don Ameche**) resembles a philandering businessman (Don Ameche) so closely that he is hired to take the tycoon's place when he is out of town 'on business' with a 'client' (**Carmen Miranda**). The deception is so convincing that even the neglected wife (**Alice Faye**) does not know the difference. In only her second American film, Miranda had already got into the habit of stealing the honours from under the noses of the more established stars. In this particular case she was aided and abetted by songwriters **Harry Warren** and **Mack Gordon**, who presented her with two stunning numbers, 'I, Yi, Yi, Yi, Yi (I Like You Very Much)' and 'Chica Chica Boom Chic'; and director Irving Cummings who (as he had done in *Down Argentine Way*) gave her the opening number. Choreographer **Hermes Pan** helped her too, by designing some splendid settings in which to showcase her very individual talents. The rest of the score included 'They Met In Rio', 'Boa Noite', and 'The

Baron Is In Conference' (Warren-Gordon), along with 'Cae Cae' (Roberto Martins-Pedro Berrios). The admirable supporting cast contained some very familiar names, including S.Z. Sakall, J. Carrol Naish, Curt Bois, Leonid Kinskey, along with the Banda Da Lua (Carmen Miranda's orchestra), and guest artists the Flores Brothers.

That Petrol Emotion

This critically lauded and highly skilled pop group's efforts to break in to the mainstream were been consistently thwarted despite a splendid arsenal of songs. The band was originally formed when the O'Neill brothers (Sean; guitar, Damian; bass) parted from the fragmenting **Undertones**. A new approach was immediate with Sean reverting to his Irish name (having always appeared as John in his former band), and Damian switching to bass instead of guitar. They added Ciaran McLaughlin (drums), Reamann O'Gormain (guitar; ex-**Bam Bam And The Calling**), and, most importantly, dynamic Seattle-born front man Steve Mack (vocals). They debuted with a single, 'Keen', on the small independent label, Pink. Both that and the subsequent 'V2' proved radical departures for those clamouring for a re-run of the Undertones, with frothing guitar and a fuller sound. There was now a political agenda too, ironic in view of the press bombardment of the Undertones as to why they did not write songs about the troubles in Northern Ireland. The questioning of British imperialism, explored through factors like 'racist' jokes and the fate of political prisoners, would became a tenet of their music (and more particularly record sleeves). Both their pop-based debut and *Babble* were dominated by frantic guitar and Mack's wholehearted delivery. However, their one album deal with **Polydor Records** finished with *Babble* and they moved on to **Virgin Records** for the more diverse *End Of The Millenium Psychosis Blues*. This included the controversial but poignant ballad 'Cellophane', bone-shattering disco of 'Groove Check', and **Sonic Youth**-tainted 'Under The Sky'. Big Jimmy (trombone) and Geoff Barrett (saxophone), ex-**Dexy's Midnight Runners**, had been added to bolster the sound but finances could not stretch to take them on tour. McLaughlin was beginning to step out as a major songwriting force, as Sean O'Neill elected to give family matters more prominence and returned to Derry. His brother switched to guitar with John Marchini taking over on bass. *Chemicrazy* which followed was exceptionally strong, especially on singles 'Hey Venus' and 'Sensitize'. In the light of its commercial failure the group were dropped by Virgin, going on to release a final album on their own label, Koogat. However, its lack of sales again contrasted with its critical reception, and in March 1994 press announcements of the band's split reached the music press (though the group had already been inactive for

some time). Despite constant campaigning on their behalf by the press, 'Big Decision', a direct call to political activism which reached a paltry UK number 42, remained their biggest chart success.
Albums: *Manic Pop Thrill* (1986), *Babble* (1987), *End Of The Millenium Psychosis Blues* (1988), *Chemicrazy* (Virgin 1990), *Fireproof* (Koogat 1993).

That Summer

Genre movies hitched to passing fads are the stuff of pop's cinematic history. Rock 'n' roll, surfing and psychedelia all spawned corresponding, often quickie, films, and 70s punk was no different. Two hitherto unknown actors, Emily Moore and Julie Shipley, play factory hands escaping drudgery in Leeds for a summer of seasonal work in Torquay. Here they meet two Londoners, portrayed by Tony Winstone and Ray London, and encounter the usual travails associated with teenage life. Engaging performances coupled with sympathetically-paced direction from Harley Cokliss ensures *That Summer*, although hardly innovatory, rises above mere formula. The soundtrack, culled from music heard on jukeboxes, radios and in clubs, emphasises the 'new-wave' aspect of punk with songs by the **Boomtown Rats**, **Elvis Costello**, **Ian Dury** and **Nick Lowe**. US acts **Patti Smith**, **Richard Hell** and the **Ramones** are among the others featured in a low-key, but meritorious, film.

That'll Be The Day

One of the best British films of the early 70s, *That'll Be The Day* was a sometimes bitter look at teenage life in the pre-**Beatles** era. **David Essex** starred as the disaffected Jamie MacLean, an aspiring rock 'n' roll singer, who rejects the values of his parents in favour of fairgrounds and holiday camps. He meets and befriends Mike, memorably portrayed by **Ringo Starr**, who in real life spent a season at Butlins' with his early group, Rory Storme And The Hurricanes. **Billy Fury** plays vocalist Stormy Tempest, leading a group which included **Graham Bond** and **Who** drummer **Keith Moon**, who also collaborated on the soundtrack music with former Beatles road manager, Neil Aspinall, and Wil Malone, latterly of pop groups **Orange Bicycle** and the **Smoke**. The Essex character is inspired by Tempest's performance and shows little regard for others in his quest for fame. His affairs are causal and he shows little regard for Mike when the latter is severely beaten. A shallow individual, MacLean steps on the first rung of success as the film closes; his subsequent career is chronicled on a follow-up film, *Stardust*. *That'll Be The Day* blends strong characterisation with the drabness of British late 50s culture. This unflinchingly unsentimental feature contextualises the importance of concurrent pop as a release for pent-up frustration.

That's A Good Girl

The first of several highly popular and successful musical comedies in which **Jack Buchanan** and Elsie Randolph starred together, and delighted London theatre audiences with their elegant and graceful blend of song and dance - and the usual frothy plot. *That's A Good Girl* opened at the London Hippodrome on 5 June 1928 with a book by Douglas Furber in which Buchanan was pursued throughout England and the South of France by Randolph in the role of a detective who adopted so many disguises that she probably did not know who she was herself. There were plenty of smart and witty lines, but the audiences really came to see the 'dynamic duo' - Britain's answer to **Fred Astaire** and his sister Adele. The music for *That's A Good Girl* was composed by the Americans Phil Charig and **Joseph Meyer**, and another distinguished American, **Ira Gershwin**, provided some of the lyrics, along with Douglas Furber and Desmond Carter. The big hit song, introduced by the two stars, was 'Fancy Our Meeting', and this remained forever associated with Jack Buchanan. The rest of the numbers included another duet, 'The One I'm Looking For', along with 'Sweet So-And-So', 'Tell Me Why', 'Chirp, Chirp', 'Marching Song', 'Let Yourself Go', and 'Parting Time'. This show found Buchanan at the peak of his powers. It's sometimes difficult to realise how enormously popular and versatile he was. As well as performing in *That's A Good Girl*, he also presented the show, and choreographed and directed it as well. It ran for nearly a year, a total of 363 performances, and Jack Buchanan and Elsie Randolph recreated their roles for the film version which was released in 1933.

The Girl Can't Help It

Perhaps the finest film of the rock 'n' roll era, this 1956 outing has much to commend it. In a plot illiberally borrowed from Judy Holiday's *Born Yesterday*, struggling agent Tom Ewell is charged by mobster Edmund O'Brien to further the career of his girlfriend (Jayne Mansfield). Then-risqué references to the last-named's physical shape aside - a running gag throughout - the film is fired by comedy veteran Frank Tashlin's script and direction which, for once, matches the pace and rhythm of its musical interludes. **Gene Vincent** provides a memorable 'The Girl Can't Help It', the fledgling talent of **Eddie Cochran** is heard on 'Twenty Flight Rock' and **Fats Domino** adds a superb 'Blue Monday'. However, the star is undoubtedly **Little Richard**, who tears through the title song, 'She's Got It' and 'Ready Teddy'. *The Girl Can't Help It* not only showcased such acts without condescension, it was the first rock 'n' roll film shot in colour. However, the film's strength does not solely rest on these pivotal figures. Tom Ewell is superb as the long-suffering agent and his hallucination about a former client immortalised forever **Julie London**'s 'Cry Me A River'. Edmund O'Brien relished his rare excursion into comedy and the gangster-inspired composition he sang, 'Rock Around The Rock Pile', acted as a thinly-veiled sideswipe at exploitative releases made to cash-in on fads. Few films embraced rock'n'roll with understanding and respect.

The The

Formed in 1979, this UK group was centred on the activities of singer/songwriter **Matt Johnson**. Initially, the unit included Keith Laws and cartoonist Tom Johnston, but the line-up was continually changing and often featured Johnson alone. Following their debut at London's Africa Centre on 11 May 1979, The The's first single, 'Controversial Subject', was issued by **4AD Records**. Two years later, they signed with Stevo's **Some Bizzare Records** and released the excellent 'Cold Spell Ahead'. Since 4AD still had a one-record option, Johnson issued *Burning Blue Soul* for them under his own name. Manager Stevo found it difficult to license The The's material to a major label but eventually **Phonogram Records** invested £8,000 in 'Uncertain Smile' (a retitled version of 'Cold Spell Ahead'), produced in New York by Mike Thorne. It was an exceptionally impressive recording, but its impact was overshadowed by contractual machinations which saw Johnson move to another label, **CBS Records**. A projected album, *The Pornography Of Despair*, took longer to complete than expected and was vetoed by Johnson. It was eventually replaced by the superb *Soul Mining*, one of the most critically acclaimed albums of 1983. By now, Johnson was already known for his uncompromising attitude and lust for perfection. Three years passed before the release of *Infected*, but it was well worth the wait. The album served as a harrowing commentary on the sexual, spiritual, political and economic malaise of 80s Britain. The production was exemplary and emphasized Johnson's standing as one of the most important cult artists to emerge during the decade. In 1988, Johnson established a new version of The The featuring former **Smiths** guitarist Johnny Marr, bassist James Eller and drummer Dave Palmer. A worldwide tour coincided with the release of *Mind Bomb*, which garnered the least promising reviews of Johnson's career. The work was bombastic in tone and filled with lyrical diatribes and anti-religious rants allied to distinctly unmelodic songs. Johnson retained the new group for another album released in 1993, which recovered some of the lost ground. 1995's *Hanky Panky* saw Johnson deliver 11 cover versions of **Hank Williams**' songs to coincide with the publication of a new biography on the subject.
Albums: *Soul Mining* (Some Bizzare 1983), *Infected* (Epic 1986), *Mind Bomb* (Epic 1989), *Dusk* (Epic 1993), *Hanky Panky* (Epic 1995).
Videos: *Infected* (1989), *From Dawn 'Til Dusk* (1993).

Theatre Of Hate

Formed in September 1981, this UK post-punk group comprised Kirk Brandon (vocals; ex-Pack), John Lennard (saxophone), Stan Stammers (bass), Billy Duffy (guitar) and Nigel Preston (drums). This was in fact the band's second line-up, Brandon having ditched all his former Pack; Jonathan Werner (bass), Jim Walker (drums) and Simon Werner (guitar), following the release of the first of a series of live albums and three singles. After establishing a strong live reputation for their hard, uncompromising lyrics, and harrowing, martial rhythms, the group recorded their 1982 debut album, *Westworld*. Produced by Mick Jones of the **Clash**, the work proved commercial enough to infiltrate the UK Top 20. The attendant single, 'Do You Believe In The Westworld?' also gave the group their only Top 40 singles entry. Drummer Preston was replaced by Luke Rendle, while Duffy went on to form the **Cult**. Despite their promise and strong following, the group fell apart a year after their inception with Stammers and Brandon going on to form **Spear Of Destiny**.

Albums: *He Who Dares Wins Live At The Warehouse Leeds* (SS 1981), *Live At The Lyceum* (Straight 1982), *Westworld* (Burning Rome 1982), *He Who Dares Wins Live in Berlin* (SS 1982). Compilations: *Revolution* (Burning Rome 1993), *Ten Years After* (Burning Rome 1993).

Theatre Owners Booking Association

(see **T.O.B.A.**)

Thelin, Eje

b. Eilert Ove Thelin, 9 September 1938, Jonkoping, Sweden, d. 18 May 1990. Thelin was one of the strongest voices on the trombone to emerge from Europe in the 60s. His knowledge of every style of jazz helped him develop an identity for his own groups and gave him the opportunity of playing with illustrious visitors such as **George Russel**l. Thelin moved to Austria where he taught for five years, while still jointly leading a group with **Joachim Kuhn**; they both appeared on *Eternal Rhythm* by **Don Cherry**. On his return to Sweden Thelin continued to lead his own groups and obtained a government stipend for life as a leading artist. Sadly he died in his early 50s in 1990. He will be remembered as one of the most powerful trombonists in modal and free music to come from Europe.

Albums: with Don Cherry *Eternal Rhythm* (1969), with Jouck Minor and Pierre Favre *Candles of Vision* (1973), as leader *Live* (1976).

Them

Formed in Belfast, Northern Ireland in 1963, Them's tempestuous career spawned some of the finest records of their era. The original line-up - **Van Morrison** (b.

31 August 1945, Belfast, Northern Ireland; vocals/harmonica), Billy Harrison (guitar), Eric Wrixen (keyboards), Alan Henderson (bass) and Ronnie Millings (drums) - were stalwarts of the city's Maritime Hotel, where they forged a fiery, uncompromising brand of R&B. A demo tape featuring a lengthy version of 'Lovelight' engendered a management deal with the imposing **Phil Solomon**, who persuaded Dick Rowe to sign the group to **Decca Records**. The group then moved to London and issued their debut single, 'Don't Start Crying Now' which flopped. Brothers Patrick and Jackie McAuley had replaced Wrixen and Millings by the time Them's second single, 'Baby Please Don't Go', was released. Although aided by session musicians, the quintet's performance was remarkable, and this urgent, exciting single - which briefly served as the theme song to the influential UK television pop programme *Ready Steady Go* - deservedly reached the UK Top 10. It was backed by the Morrison-penned 'Gloria', a paean to teenage lust hinged to a hypnotic riff, later adopted by aspiring bar bands. The follow-up 'Here Comes The Night', was written and produced by R&B veteran **Bert Berns**. It peaked at number 2, and although it inferred a long career, Them's internal disharmony undermined progress. **Peter Bardens** replaced Jackie McAuley for the group's debut album which matched brooding original songs, notably the frantic 'Mystic Eyes' and 'You Just Can't Win', with sympathetic covers. Further defections ensued when subsequent singles failed to emulate early success and by the release of *Them Again*, the unit had been recast around Morrison, Henderson, Jim Armstrong (guitar), Ray Elliott (saxophone/keyboards) and John Wilson (drums). This piecemeal set nonetheless boasted several highlights, including the vocalist's impassioned reading of the **Bob Dylan** composition, 'It's All Over Now, Baby Blue'. Dave Harvey then replaced Wilson, but this version of Them disintegrated in 1966 following a gruelling US tour and dispute with Solomon. Posthumous releases included the extraordinary 'The Story Of Them' documenting the group's early days at the Maritime in Belfast. Morrison then began a highly prolific solo career, leaving behind a period of confusion which saw the McAuley brothers re-emerge with a rival unit known variously as 'Them', 'Them Belfast Gypsies', the 'Freaks Of Nature', or simply the 'Belfast Gypsies'. Meanwhile ex-**Mad Lads** singer Kenny McDowell joined Henderson, Armstrong, Elliott and Harvey in a reconstituted Them who moved to Los Angeles following the intervention of producer Ray Ruff. *Now And Them* combined garage R&B with the *de rigueur* west coast sound exemplified by the lengthy 'Square Room', but the new line-up found it hard to escape the legacy of its predecessors. Elliott left the group in 1967, but the remaining quartet completed the psychedelic *Time Out, Time In For Them* as a quartet before McDowell and Armstrong returned to

Belfast to form Sk'Boo. Henderson then maintained the Them name for two disappointing albums, on which he was supported by anonymous session musicians, before joining Ruff for a religious rock-opera, *Truth Of Truths*. He subsequently retired from music altogether, but renewed interest in his old group's heritage prompted a reunion of sorts in 1979 when the bassist recruited Billy Harrison, Eric Wrixen, Mel Austin (vocals) and Billy Bell (drums) for *Shut Your Mouth*. True to form both Harrison and Wrixen were fired prior to a tour of Germany; after which the Them appellation was again laid to rest.

Albums: *Them* aka *The Angry Young Them* (1965), *Them Again* (1966), *Now And Them* (1967), *Time Out, Time In For Them* (1968), *Them* (1970), *In Reality* (1971), *Shut Your Mouth* (1979). Compilations: *Here Comes The Night* (1965), *The World Of Them* (1969), *Them Featuring Van Morrison* (1973), *Backtrackin' With Them* (70s), *Rock Roots: Them* (1976), *Collection: Them* (1986), *The Singles* (1987).

Further reading: *Van Morrison: A Portrait Of The Artist*, Johnny Rogan.

Themen, Art

b. 26 November 1939, Manchester, England. A self-taught musician, Themen played tenor saxophone with a university jazz band while studying medicine at Cambridge. After qualifying as a doctor, he moved to London and in the early 60s played in several blues and R&B bands and also worked in the backing groups for numerous pop sessions. During this period he worked with **Alexis Korner**, **Phil Seamen**, **Dick Heckstall-Smith**, **Rod Stewart**, **Joe Cocker** and **Long John Baldry**. In the late 60s and early 70s his musical direction shifted towards jazz and he played with **Barbara Thompson**, **Michael Garrick**, **Henry Lowther** and **Graham Collier**. In 1974 he began a long and particularly fruitful association with **Stan Tracey**, which has continued into the 90s. He has also accompanied numerous visiting US jazzmen, including **Al Haig**, **Red Rodney**, **George Coleman** and **Nat Adderley**. A highly individual playing style marks Themen's performances and had he chosen to adopt music as a full-time career he would have doubtless been an international artist of considerable stature. That he has achieved his present high standing in the jazz world while at the same time pursuing his medical career as a consultant surgeon, is testimony to his remarkable gifts.

Albums: with Stan Tracey *Under Milk Wood* (1976), with Al Haig *Expressly Ellington* (1978), with Tracey *Spectrum* (1982), *Stan Tracey's Hexad Live At Ronnie Scott's* (1985).

Then Jerico

Titled, incorrectly, after the city whose walls fell to the trumpets of the Israelites in the Bible, UK group Then Jerico managed three Top 40 hits in 1989 before breaking up. Comprising Mark Shaw (b. 10 June 1961,

Chesterfield, Derbyshire, England; vocals), Jasper Stainthorpe (b. 18 February 1958, Tonbridge, Kent, England), Robert Downes (b. 7 December 1961, Cheadle Hulme, Cheshire, England; guitar), Scott Taylor (b. 31 December 1961, Redhill, Surrey, England; guitar) and Steve Wren (b. 26 October 1962, Lambeth, London, England), the band formed when Shaw and Stainthorpe met in a north London studio, where the latter was working as an engineer. Stainthorpe recommended Wren though it transpired that he had already turned down an offer from Shaw two years earlier. Scott Taylor, former guitarist in Belouis Some's backing band, completed the line-up. The band always received more press for Shaw's good looks than their inoffensive pop music, Their biggest hit was 'Big Area' which reached number 13. Shaw turned solo following the band's split, and released a poorly received solo album in 1991 on **EMI**.

Albums: *First (The Sound Of Music)* (1987), *The Big Area* (1989).

Theodorakis, Mikis

b. 29 July 1925, Khios, Greece. A poet, patriot, politician and composer of numerous film scores, Theodorakis was seven years old when he learned to sing Byzantine hymns and Greek folk songs. His first film music of note was for *Barefoot Battalion* (1954), the true story of Greek orphans' struggle against the Germans during World War II; an apt theme in view of his own subsequent strife. His other movie scores, during the 50s and early 60s, included *Night Ambush*, *The Shadow Of The Cat*, *The Lovers Of Tereul*, *Phaedra*, *Electra* and *Five Miles To Midnight*. In 1964, the composer's memorable score for *Zorba The Greek* contributed to the film's enormous success. It was to be one of his last projects before his life changed dramatically in April 1967. Following the fascist colonels' military *coup d'etat* in Greece, Theodorakis, as a Communist, was forced underground, and eventually imprisoned and tortured. By Army Order, the people were banned from listening to and performing his works, although his music became a symbol of resistance for the his fellow islanders. In 1969, **John Barry**, a fellow composer for films, smuggled out tapes of Theodorakis singing new songs, reciting his own poems and describing prison conditions, and sent them to U Thant, the then Secretary General of the United Nations. Theodorakis's own version of his appalling experiences were detailed in his book, *Journals Of Resistance*, in 1973. After his escape from Greece, the composer was exiled for several years in Paris, and started writing for films again in the early 70s. These included *Biribi*, *Serpico*, *State Of Seige*, *Sutjeska*, *Partisans*, *Letters From Marusia*, *Iphighenia* and *Easy Road*. For a number years Theodorakis was a Member of Parliament in Greece, but in the late 80s he began to give concerts in Europe and elsewhere, and resumed composing for projects such as the Turkish film *Sis* (1989). In 1992 it was reported that he had resigned his post as a minister without portfolio in the Greek government.

Selected albums: *Zorba The Greek* (1983), *The Bouzoukis Of Mikis Theodorakis* (1984), *Ballad Of Mauthausen* (1986), *Canto General* (1986), *All Time Greatest Hits* (1993).

Therapy

This UK group formed in 1970, when Fiona Simpson (b. 8 May 1952, Farnborough, Hampshire, England; guitar/vocals), joined the existing duo of Dave Shannon (b. 7 February 1947, Belfast, Northern Ireland; keyboards/guitar/vocals), and Sam Bracken (guitar/vocals). While the former duo had specialized in blues and ragtime, the addition of Fiona changed their repertoire to include songs by such writers as **James Taylor**, and **Joni Mitchell**. When Bracken left in 1971, Simpson and Shannon continued as a duo until 1983, touring Europe, playing venues as disparate as a folk club one night, and the Royal Albert Hall the next. One of the most requested songs at bookings was Joni Mitchell's 'Carey', which displayed Simpson's voice to startling effect. *Almanac*, released on **CBS**, featured all Dave Shannon originals. The album based a song around each sign of the Zodiac. The group undertook much television work during this period, and incorporated comedy into their act, opening shows for such acts as **Max Boyce**, **Jasper Carrott**, and the **Barron Knights**. *Bringing The House Down* included such diverse songs as 'Killing Me Softly With His Song', and the traditional 'Lord Franklyn'. Indeed, many of the songs featured in Therapy's live set came from outside the folk spectrum, much to the displeasure of some folk purists. 1977 saw the release of a single on **DJM Records**, 'The Most Important Part Of Me Is You', produced by Brian Bennett of the **Shadows**, followed by a remake of *Almanac*. Subsequent albums were released on their own label, Therapy Records. By financing and producing their own albums, largely for selling at gigs, they have encouraged other acts to pursue the same line in bypassing record companies, a practice that has now become commonplace on the folk scene. Shannon left to become a music producer for the BBC, while Fiona has continued to perform in a solo capacity, essentially in folk clubs and at festivals, both at home and abroad. She has also recorded in her own right and is a sought-after session singer on records and for BBC Radio.

Albums: *Almanac* (1971), *One Night Stand* (1973), *Bringing The House Down* (1975), *Supertrouper* (1980), *Schizophrenia* (1981). Fiona Simpson solo: *Then There Was One* (1984), *Cold Hands* (1987), *Beneath The Rose* (1989).

Therapy?

Northern Irish hard rock/indie metal trio comprising Andy Cairns (guitar/vocals), Michael McKeegan (bass) and Fyfe Ewing (drums). Cairns and Ewing first met by chance at a charity concert in the late 80s. At that time both were playing in covers bands, but decided to begin writing together. McKeegan was drafted in for live support (having originally lent his bass to the duo's bedroom sessions) and the enduring Therapy? line-up was in place. They played their first gig supporting **Decadence Within** at Connor Art College in the summer of 1989, by which time they had already composed some 30 songs. After two demos failed to ignite attention from suitable labels, the band released their debut single, 'Meat Abstract'/'Punishment Kiss', on their own Multifuckingnational imprint. Following approving plays from **John Peel** the group found their way on to **Wiiija Records**, via the intervention of **Silverfish**'s Leslie. Their debut single was then added to new material for a mini-album, *Baby Teeth*. This was followed in short order by a second abbreviated set, *Pleasure Death*. Both these collections went to number 1 in the UK indie charts, but the band remained hamstrung by lack of finance from their record company. Therapy? signed to **A&M** in 1992, and collected a much bigger budget for a new album, *Nurse*, and touring. However, at best the press were neutral about the record, which featured more complex arrangements and themes than the punk-descended speed burnouts of earlier releases. The band's career was revitalized in March 1993 when 'Screamager' made the UK Top 10. Almost a year later *Troublegum* was unveiled, which returned to more familiar Therapy? elements - buzzsaw guitar, harsh but persistent melodies and musical adrenalin - aided by a cleaner, leaner production than had previously been the case. Nominated for the **Mercury Prize** - alongside the **Prodigy** easily the most extreme record to be offered as a candidate - it enshrined Therapy?'s progress as the most commercially successful British band working in their territory. 1995's *Infernal Love* offered a significant departure. Alongside the trademark grinding hardcore sound came ballads, string quartets and upbeat lyrics, indicating a band able to shed their old skins musically and lyrically, where it might have been easier to retread former glories. How this transformation will sit with their existing audience, however, is another matter.

Albums: *Baby Teeth* (Wiiija 1991, mini-album), *Pleasure Death* (Wiiija 1992, mini-album), *Nurse* (A&M 1992), *Troublegum* (A&M 1994), *Infernal Love* (A&M 1995).

There's No Business Like Show Business

Incongruous is perhaps an appropriate word to describe the casting of the 'Nabob of Sob', pop singer **Johnnie Ray**, in this film, which was one of the last of the truly lavish screen musicals which was released by 20th Century-Fox in 1955. He plays one of the Donahues, a vaudeville act consisting of his brother and sister (**Mitzi Gaynor** and **Donald O'Connor**) and their parents (**Dan Dailey** and **Ethel Merman**).

Ray even manages to induce a few of his trademark tears, although in this instance they swell up in the eyes of his proud old Mom and Dad after he has announced his decision to become a priest. That scene, and his strangulated version of 'If You Believe', one of the two new songs in **Irving Berlin**'s otherwise entertaining score, should surely have won someone a bad-taste Oscar. Instead, the only whiff of an Academy Award was the nomination for Lamar Trotti's story (adapted for the screen by Henry and Phoebe Ephron). It deals with the triumphs and crises experienced by the family group, and O'Connor's initially ill-fated love affair with a cabaret singer played by **Marilyn Monroe**. After spending some time in the US Navy 'growing up', O'Connor joins the rest of the clan for the finalé and a rousing version of the title song. Before he went off to sea he had some of the best numbers, singing and dancing delightfully in 'A Man Chases A Girl (Until She Catches Him)' and (with Gaynor and Monroe) 'Lazy'. He also adopted a Scottish accent for his part in a spectacular setting of 'Alexander's Ragtime Band'. Gaynor gave the number a touch of the Parisian, Merman was gamely Germanic, and Johnnie Ray . . . well, his intended articulation was unclear. Other highlights of the film were Monroe's sizzling versions of 'Heat Wave' and 'After You Get What You Want You Don't Want It', and Merman and Dailey's 'Play A Simple Melody', 'A Pretty Girl Is Like A Melody', 'Let's Have Another Cup Of Coffee', and 'You'd Be Surprised'. Jack Cole, who had worked with Monroe on **Gentlemen Prefer Blondes** two years earlier, staged her dances, and the remainder of the film's spirited routines were choreographed by Robert Alton. Sol C. Siegel was the producer, and it was directed by Walter Lang. The impressive DeLuxe Color and CinemaScope photography was by Leon Shamroy.

These Animal Men

Essential but nevertheless relatively aged participants in the media-led New Wave Of The New Wave movement, These Animal Men's debut single was 'Speeed King', a tribute to the power of amphetamines. It arrived in a cover with a bowl of white powder and four straws, prompting Brighton MP Andrew Bowden to criticise their attitude to drugs as 'appalling'. The local council of Plymouth banned them full stop. Like an even more ill-mannered **Manic Street Preachers**, elsewhere their ten commandments included such errant nonsense as 'Get A Catholic Education' and 'Love's Good, But Not As Good As Wanking'. The latter statement got them into trouble when they offered to demonstrate its advantages live on a youth television show. The band was formed in Brighton by Hooligan (b. Julian; guitar) and bass player Patrick (b. Liverpool, Merseyside, England), who knew each other from nursery school. They added additional members Boag (vocals) and Stevie (drums), following

'Speeed King' with 'You're Not My Babylon'. A stop-gap release compiled both with a live version of the title-track, 'Too Sussed', recorded live for the last ever edition of BBC Radio 5's *Vibe* programme. Breaking the UK Top 40, it also brought the band to the ***Top Of The Pops*** stage. A full album, produced by Dave Eringa, was available before the end of the year, and replicated the punk-pop approach of the debut with some particularly virulent lyrics ('Flawed Is Beautiful' and 'Sitting Tenant' in particular).
Albums: *Too Sussed* (Hi-Rise 1994, mini-album), *(Come On, Join) The High Society* (Hi-Rise 1994), *Taxi For These Animal Men* (Hi-Rise 1995, mini-album).

They Might Be Giants

John Flansburgh and John Linnell formed this New York based duo in 1984 after an initial meeting in Massachusetts, USA. The group took their name from a 1972 George C. Scott movie. Their original intention to recruit a full band was abandoned, but Linnell learned the accordion and Flansburgh mastered the guitar. Following Linnell's broken wrist which decimated their early tour dates, they devised the 'Dial-A-Song Service', which still operates today, premiering their intelligent pop skills. A self-titled debut album collated many of these early songwriting ventures, gaining the band a considerable cult reputation. **MTV** picked up on their quirky visual appeal, and *Lincoln* became the biggest selling independent album of 1989 in the USA. With wry and perverse lyrics like 'I can't help but feel jealous each time she climbs on his knee' ('Santa's Beard') they struck an immediate chord with college radio. The UK independent label **One Little Indian Records** released the album before the group tied up a major deal with **Elektra Records**. *Flood* showcased their obtuse lyrical approach, contrasting influences as diverse as the **Ramones** and **Love**. The UK hit single, 'Birdhouse In Your Soul', was a beautifully crafted pop song highlighting the band's affection for the naive charm of the 60s ballad. While *Apollo 18* brought minor hits in 'The Statue Got Me High' and 'The Guitar (The Lion Sleeps Tonight)', *John Henry* saw them introduce a full band for the first time, including Brian Doherty (ex-Silos; drums), Tony Maimone (ex-**Pere Ubu**, **Bob Mould**; bass), Kurt Hoffman (ex-**Ordinaires**, Band Of Weeds; saxophone/keyboards) and Steven Bernstein (ex-Spanish Fly; trumpet). 1995 brought the band an unlikely appearance, with 'Sensurround', on the soundtrack to global kids film smash, *Mighty Morphin Power Rangers*.
Albums: *They Might Be Giants* (Elektra 1987), *Lincoln* (Elektra 1989), *Don't Let's Start* (Elektra 1989), *Flood* (Elektra 1990), *Apollo 18* (Elektra 1992), *John Henry* (Warners 1994).

They're Playing Our Song

After composer **Marvin Hamlisch**'s tremendous success with the long-running *A Chorus Line* (1975), he turned to his real-life partner, **Carole Bayer Sager**, for the lyrics to this miniscule musical which opened at the Imperial Theatre in New York on 11 February 1979. Miniscule that is, as regards the cast, for there were only two principal players, Lucie Arnaz and Robert Klein, although they each had three singing alter egos. Neil Simon's book, which is said to have been based on Hamlisch and Sager's own stormy relationship, concerns Vernon Gersch (Klein) and Sonia Walsk (Arnaz), two hip young songwriters whose developing romantic entanglement is hampered by Sonia's ex-boyfriend's telephone calls at any time of the day or night, and the feeling that they should keep things on a professional level anyway. The pleasing, melodic score included 'Fallin'', 'Workin' It Out', 'If He Really Knew Me', 'They're Playing My Song', 'Just For Tonight', 'When You're In My Arms', 'Right', and 'I Still Believe In Love'. No doubt the absence of a large chorus and similar overheads contributed to the show's abililty to last out for 1,082 performances. Subsequent road shows were equally successful, and the West End production with Tom Conti and Gemma Craven was the highlight of the 1980 London theatre season.

Thiele, Bob

b. 1923. Thiele has been one of the most important and prolific jazz and pop producers in US popular music. A teenage jazz fan, Thiele joined the US **Decca** company after World War II, and became head of A&R for the Coral label. There he supervised hundreds of records including hits by by the **McGuire Sisters** and **Jackie Wilson** as well as licensing **Buddy Holly** material from **Norman Petty**. In 1961, Thiele set up the **Impulse!** jazz label with Creed Taylor. Over the rest of the decade he signed and recorded many of the greatest names in the 'new wave' jazz scene including **John Coltrane**, **Archie Shepp** and **Albert Ayler**. His biggest hit, however, was with **Louis Armstrong**'s 'What A Wonderful World', which he co-wrote. Thiele's first independent label had been Signature, during whose brief career he had released jazz-and-poetry records by beat-poet Jack Kerouac. In the early 70s he set up Flying Dutchman with Bernard Purdie as musical director. Among its signings were **Gil Scott-Heron** and **Lonnie Liston Smith**, whose records Thiele continued to produce until the late 80s. After Flying Dutchman was closed down, Bob returned to freelance production but in 1983 he founded Dr. Jazz, a company devoted to mainstream jazz from the orchestras of **Duke Ellington** and **Count Basie** as well as singer **Teresa Brewer**, whom Thiele had married in 1972. In 1988, Dr. Jazz was sold to **CBS**

but Thiele returned three years later, launching Red Baron Records with albums from Brewer and **McCoy Tyner**.

Thielemans, Toots

b. Jean Baptiste Thielemans, 29 April 1922, Brussels, Belgium. A child prodigy, Thielemans played the accordion at the age of three (a home-made version; a real one would have considerably outweighed him), switching to harmonica in his mid-teens. A few years later he added the guitar to his instrumental roll-call and also became an accomplished whistler. The guitar apart, Thielemans's chosen instruments were not especially suited to jazz, but he displayed enough invention and assurance to be hired by **Benny Goodman** for a European tour in 1950 and by **George Shearing** in 1953 for a spell which lasted over five years. In the 60s his popularity increased with a successful recording of his own composition 'Bluesette', and he worked frequently in clubs in Europe and the USA and at international festivals. His activity continued throughout the following two decades and he played with leading artists such as **Oscar Peterson** and **Dizzy Gillespie**. He has also played on the soundtracks of many films. Most distinctive on harmonica, Thielemans has gone far to correcting the prejudice felt by many jazz fans towards this instrument. A momentary shift in the late 80s into jazz-rock fusion was less than wholly successful; he remains happiest in a bop setting, while displaying a fine command of ballads on his many recordings. Whilst the harmonica has only limited appeal in a jazz setting, Thielemans has made the genre his own.

Selected albums: *Man Bites Harmonica* (Original Jazz Classics 1957), with George Shearing *On Stage!* (1958), *Toots Thielemans And His Orchestra* (1958), *The Toots Thielemans Quartet* i (1959), *Toots Thielemans With Kurt Edelhagen And His Orchestra* (1960), *The Toots Thielemans Quartet* ii (1960), *The Toots Thielemans Quartet* iii (1961), *The Toots Thielemans Trio* (1961), *Toots Thielemans And Arne Domnerus* (1961), *Toots Thielemans And Dick Hyman* (1962), *Toots Thielemans* i (1965), *Contrasts* (c.1967), *Toots Thielemans With Herbie Hancock* (1968), *Toots Thielemans With Orchestra* (1969, overdubbed), *A Taste Of Toots* (1970), *Toots Thielemans* ii (1972), *Live* (1974), *Toots Thielemans And Friends* (1974), *Toots Thielemans Captured Alive* (Polydor 1974), *The Oscar Peterson Big Six At Montreux* (1975), *Live Two* (1975), *Old Friends* (1976), *Live Three* (1976), *Toots Thielemans* iii (1978), *Slow Motion* (c.1979), *Apple Dimple* (Denon 1979), *Live In The Netherlands* (1980), *Dizzy Gillespie At Montreux* (1980), *Jean 'Toots' Thielemans Live!* (1981), *Nice To Meet You* (c.1981), *Chiko's Bar* (1985), *Your Precious Love* (1985), *Just Friends* (Jazzline 1986), *Do Not Leave Me* (Stash 1986), *Only Trust Your Heart* (Concord 1988), *Footprints* (Emarcy 1989), *For My Lady* (Emarcy 1992), *The Brasil Project* (1992). Compilation: *The Silver Collection* (Polydor 1985).

Thigpen, Ed

b. 28 December 1930, Chicago, Illinois, USA. Following in the footsteps of his father Ben (who played drums with **Andy Kirk** for almost two decades), Thigpen began playing drums as a child. His first big-name engagement came in 1951 when he joined the **Cootie Williams** band. Later in the 50s he played with **Johnny Hodges**, **Lennie Tristano**, **John Coltrane**, **Bud Powell** and most often with **Billy Taylor**. In the 60s he followed his Taylor stint with another long spell accompanying a noted pianist, this time **Oscar Peterson**. His sensitive playing style endeared him to singers and he accompanied **Dinah Washington** in the early 50s and **Ella Fitzgerald** in the late 60s and early 70s. In 1972 he settled in Scandinavia, playing with visitors such as **Johnny Griffin** and **Art Farmer**, and teaching in Copenhagen and Malmo. Thigpen's neat and contained style is ideally suited to a small group setting while his inquiring mind has caused him to introduce many unusual effects into his performances, drawing on Eastern musical traditions. He has written several manuals on drumming techniques and is a tireless educator.

Albums: with John Coltrane *Cattin'* (1957), *The Oscar Peterson Trio: Live From Chicago* (1961), *Out Of The Storm* (1966), with Johnny Griffin *Blues For Harvey* (1973), *Ed Thigpen's Action-Re-Action* (Sonet 1974), with Art Farmer *Manhattan* (1980), *Young Men And Olds* (Timeless 1989), *Easy Flight* (Reckless 1990), *Mr. Taste* (Justin Time 1992).

Thin Lizzy

Formed in Dublin, Eire, in 1969, this fondly remembered hard-rocking group comprised **Phil Lynott** (b. 20 August 1951, Dublin, Eire, d. 4 January 1986; vocals/bass), Eric Bell (b. 3 September 1947, Belfast, Northern Ireland; guitar) and Brian Downey (b. 27 January 1951, Dublin, Eire; drums). After signing to **Decca Records**, they issued two albums, neither of which charted. A change of fortune occurred after they recorded a novelty rock version of the traditional 'Whiskey In The Jar'. The single reached the UK Top 10 and popularized the group's blend of Irish folk and strident guitar work. The group then underwent a series of line-up changes during early 1974. Bell was replaced by **Gary Moore** and two more temporary guitarists were recruited, Andy Gee and John Cann. The arrival of guitarists Brian Robertson (b. 12 September 1956, Glasgow, Scotland) and Scott Gorham (b. 17 March 1951, Santa Monica, California, USA) stabilized the group as they entered their most productive phase. A series of UK concerts throughout 1975 saw the group make considerable headway. 1976 was the breakthrough year with the acclaimed *Jailbreak* hitting the charts. The driving macho celebration of

'The Boys Are Back In Town' reached the UK Top 10 and US Top 20 and was voted single of the year by the influential **New Musical Express**. In early 1977 Robertson was forced to leave the group due to a hand injury following a fight and was replaced by the returning Moore. Another UK Top 20 hit followed with the scathing 'Don't Believe A Word', drawn from *Johnny The Fox*. Moore then returned to **Colosseum** and the recovered Robertson took his place. Both 'Dancin' In The Moonlight' and *Bad Reputation* were UK Top 10 hits and were soon followed by the excellent double album, *Live And Dangerous*. 1979 saw the group scaling new commercial heights with such Top 20 singles as 'Waiting For An Alibi' and 'Do Anything You Want To', plus the best-selling *Black Rose*. The torturous line-up changes continued apace. Robertson again left and joined **Wild Horses**. Moore returned, but within a year was replaced by **Midge Ure** (formerly of **Slik** and the **Rich Kids**). By late 1979, the peripatetic Ure had moved on to **Ultravox** and was replaced by Snowy White. In early 1980, Lynott married Caroline Crowther, daughter of the television personality Leslie Crowther. After recording some solo work, Lynott reunited with Thin Lizzy for *Chinatown*, which included the controversial Top 10 single, 'Killer On The Loose'. The heavily-promoted *Adventures Of Thin Lizzy* maintained their standing, before White bowed out on *Renegade*. He was replaced by John Sykes, formerly of the **Tygers Of Pan Tang**. One more album, *Thunder And Lightning*, followed before Lynott split up the group in the summer of 1984. A posthumous live album, *Life-Live*, was issued at the end of that year. Its title took on an ironically macabre significance two years later when Lynott died of heart failure and pneumonia after a drugs overdose. Four months later, in May 1986, Thin Lizzy reformed for the Self Aid concert organized in Eire by **Bob Geldof**, who replaced Lynott on vocals for the day. The 90s found Brian Robertson touring with tribute band, Ain't Lizzy, while the original group's name remained on the lips of many young groups as a primary influence.

Albums: *Thin Lizzy* (Decca 1971), *Shades Of Blue Orphanage* (Decca 1972), *Vagabonds Of The Western World* (Decca 1973), *Night Life* (Vertigo 1974), *Fighting* (Vertigo 1975), *Jailbreak* (Vertigo 1976), *Johnny The Fox* (Vertigo 1976), *Bad Reputation* (Vertigo 1977), *Live And Dangerous* (Vertigo 1978, double album), *Black Rose* (Vertigo 1979), *Renegade* (Vertigo 1981), *Thunder And Lightning* (Vertigo 1983), *Life-Live* (Vertigo 1983, double album), *BBC Radio 1 Live In Concert* (Windsong 1992, rec 1983).

Compilations: *Remembering - Part One* (Decca 1976), *The Continuing Saga Of The Ageing Orphans* (Decca 1979), *Rockers* (Decca 1981), *Adventures Of Thin Lizzy* (Vertigo 1981), *Lizzy Killers* (Vertigo 1983), *The Collection* (Castle 1985, double album), *The Best Of Phil Lynott And Thin Lizzy* (Telstar 1987), *Dedication - The Best Of Thin Lizzy* (Vertigo 1991).

Videos: *Live And Dangerous* (1986), *Dedication* (1991).
Further reading: *Songs For While I'm Away*, Lynott, Philip (1974), *Thin Lizzy*, Pryce, Larry (1977), *Philip*, Lynott, Philip (1977), *Thin Lizzy: The Approved Biography*, Salewicz, Chris (1979).

Thin White Rope

Formed in Sacramento, California, USA, in 1984, Thin White Rope initially comprised; Guy Kyser (vocals/guitar), Roger Kunkel (guitar), Kevin Stayhodor (bass/vocals) and Frank French (drums, ex-True West). However, by 1985 Stayhodor had been replaced by Steve Tesluk while the group's notoriously unsettled drumming position had been filled by Joe Becker. Taking their name from William Burroughs' slang description of male ejaculation, *Exploring The Axis* was an exceptionally powerful debut, marked by Kyser's distinctive voice and ragged guitar style. The balance between power and heavy-handedness was perfectly struck although subsequent releases, in particular *Moonhead* and *In The Spanish Cave*, have veered towards the latter. Two mini-albums, *Bottom Feeders* and *Red Sun*, show the group's quirkiness in a better light. The former was marked by a suitably idiosyncratic reading of blues singer **Jimmy Reed**'s 'Ain't That Lovin' You Baby', while the latter offers other cover versions, including 'Town Without Pity' (**Gene Pitney**) and 'Some Velvet Morning' (**Nancy Sinatra** and **Lee Hazelwood**). Despite limited commercial acceptance, Thin White Rope continued to record interesting, if erratic, music, which in 1991 included 'Ants Are Cavemen' on the **Sub Pop Records** label. However, the split came in the summer of the following year, ostensibly because they felt it was time to try their hands at something different. Kyser would go on to study for a degree, though he continued to write songs with his girlfriend.
Albums: *Exploring The Axis* (Frontier 1985), *Moonhead* (Frontier 1987), *In The Spanish Cave* (Frontier 1988), *Sack Full Of Silver* (Frontier 1990), *Squatter's Rights* (Frontier 1991, mini-album), *The Ruby Sea* (Frontier 1991), *The One That Got Away (live)* (Frontier 1992). Compilation: *Spoor* (Frontier 1995).

Think

New York songwriter Lou Stallman was the man behind many novelty hits including the unusual one by Think. Stallman, who had recorded on Rainbow in 1956, wrote 50s hits like **Clyde McPhatter**'s 'Treasure Of Love', **Perry Como**'s US number 1 'Round And Round' and Linda Laurie's novelty 'Ambrose'. In the 60s his novelty song 'Yogi' hit the Top 10 by the Ivy Three (who included Charles Koppelman - the 'K' of **SBK Records**) and the Royalettes scored with his 'It's Gonna Take a Miracle' (a Top 10 hit for **Deniece Williams** in 1982). In 1971, together with Bobby Susser, he recorded 'Once

You Understand', which was a dialogue between children and parents, highlighting the problems caused by the generation gap. It ended with a father being told his son had died of an overdose and dad (played by Stallman) sobbing his heart out! Despite being banned in half the country, the record hit the US Top 40 and three years later returned to the chart when the ban was dropped. Think (as the act was called) released a follow-up 'It's Not The World - It's The People' but it did nothing. Their hit resurfaced in 1990 when sampled on the dance record 'Mr. Kirk's Nightmare' by 4 Hero.

Third Ear Band

Described by founder Glenn Sweeny as 'electric-acid-raga', the music of the UK Third Ear Band employed the drone-like figures and improvisatory techniques beloved by fellow pioneers the **Soft Machine** and **Terry Riley**. However, the esoteric, almost preternatural sweep of their work gave the group its originality as they studiously invoked an aura of ley-lines, druids and cosmology. Sweeny (drums/percussion) had been part of London's free-jazz circle prior to forming two *avant garde* ensembles, the Sun Trolly and the Hydrogen Jukebox. Paul Minns (oboe) and Richard Koss (violin) completed the early Third Ear Band line-up, although cellist Mel Davis augmented the group on their debut *Alchemy*. The unit was later commissioned to compose a soundtrack to Roman Polanski's film, *Macbeth*. However, although their ethereal music provided the ideal accompaniment to this remarkable project, the group's highly stylized approach proved too specialized for mainstream acceptance. Despite record company indifference, Sweeny has pursued his vision into the 90s, while a late period member, Paul Buckmaster, has become a successful arranger.
Albums: *Alchemy* (1969), *Third Ear Band* (1970), *Music From Macbeth* (1972), *Magic Music* (1990). Compilation: *Experiences* (1976).

Third Rail

A studio group comprised of Artie Resnick (writer of the **Young Rascals**' 'Good Lovin'), his wife Kris and Joey Levine, the Third Rail recorded their first single, 'R Subway Train That Came To Life', in 1966 for **Cameo Records**. Switching to Epic Records the following year, they recorded an album, *Id Music*, which included a song called 'Run Run Run' which commented on the futility of the urban rat race to a punky psychedelic sound. That single became a minor chart hit and was later rediscovered via the compilation *Nuggets*, which collected mid-60s punk. The Third Rail released four more singles but failed to realize any further hits. Levine joined the **Ohio Express** in 1968.
Album: *Id Music* (1967).

Third World

Reggae band blending roots and soul, comprising Michael 'Ibo' Cooper (keyboards), Stephen 'Cat' Coore (guitar/cello), Richard Daley (bass), Willie 'Root' Stewart (drums), Irvin 'Carrot' Jarrett (percussion), William 'Bunny Rugs' Clarke (lead vocal/guitar) and Prilly Hamilton. Coore and Cooper first played together at the end of the 60s, and the early years of the band saw the line-up in a state of flux: Coore, Cooper and Daley, plus drummer Carl Barovier (later replaced by Cornell Marshall and Willie Stewart) had all played with **Inner Circle**, a band that pursued a similar 'uptown reggae' course. By 1975 the line-up had settled to the above, minus Bunny Rugs, who had been pursuing a soul-reggae direction in a series of solo projects, aided by a uniquely spirited voice. Their first album, *Third World*, found them signed to **Island** and supporting **Bob Marley** at his breakthrough concerts at London's Lyceum in the summer of 1975. It was a mellow, carefully-crafted debut. *96 Degrees In the Shade* found the band and new singer Clarke in fine form, and delivered a huge international hit in the shape of a cover of the **O'Jays**/Gamble-Huff song, 'Now That We've Found Love'. The *Journey To Addis* album offered more of the same: a mix of roots and sweet soul. Further hits, 'Cool Meditation' (1979), 'Dancing On The Floor' (1981) and 'Try Jah Love' (1982), the latter two for a new label, **CBS**, kept their name in the public eye. A lone record for **Winston 'Niney' Holness** in Jamaica, pretty much summed up their attitude: 'Roots With Quality'. The late-80s saw the band increasingly lauded in America, drawing album contributions from **Stevie Wonder**, **Stetsasonic**'s **Daddy O**, the **Brecker Brothers** and **Jamal-ski**. Third World still gig regularly, have the wisdom to continue working with their original producer, Geoffrey Chung, from time to time, and remain a name always worth watching out for, even if they haven't yet set the world alight on record.

Selected albums: *Third World* (Island 1976), *96 Degrees In the Shade* (Island 1977), *Journey To Addis* (Island 1978), *Prisoner In The Street* (Island 1980), *Rock The World* (CBS 1985), *Sense Of Purpose* (CBS 1985), *You've Got The Power* (CBS 1987), *Hold On To Love* (CBS 1987). Compilations: *Reggae Ambassadors* (Island 1985).

Thirlwell, Jim

(see **Foetus**)

Thirteenth Floor Elevators

Formed in Austin, Texas, USA in 1965, this influential group evolved from the nucleus of the Lingsmen, a popular local attraction. The original line-up included Stacy Sutherland (guitar), Bennie Thurman (bass), John Ike Walton (drums) and Max Rainey (vocals), but the latter was replaced by **Roky Erickson** (vocals/guitar).

The quartet retained their anachronistic name until adding lyricist and jug player Tommy Hall, whose wife Clementine, suggested their more intriguing appellation. The Elevators made their recording debut with 'You're Gonna Miss Me'. Erickson had recorded this acerbic composition with an earlier group, the Spades, but his new colleagues added an emphatic enthusiasm missing from the original version. Hall's quivering jug interjections, unlikely in a rock setting, suggested a taste for the unusual enhanced by the group's mystical air.

Their debut *The Psychedelic Sounds Of...*, combined this off-beat spiritualism with R&B to create some of the era's most compulsive music. However the group's overt drug culture proselytisation led to inevitable confrontations with the conservative Texan authorities. Several arrests ensued, the group's live appearances were monitored by the state police, while a management dispute led to the departure of Walton and new bassist Ronnie Leatherman. The Elevators briefly broke up during the summer of 1967, but Hall, Erickson and Sutherland regrouped around a new rhythm section of Danny Galindo and Danny Thomas. A second album, *Easter Everywhere*, maintained the high quality of its predecessor, but external pressures proved too strong to repel. Studio out-takes were overdubbed with fake applause to create the implausible *Live*, while a final collection, *Bull Of The Woods*, coupled partially-completed performances with older, unissued masters. Despite an occasional reunion, the Elevators disintegrated when Erickson was committed to a mental institution and Sutherland was imprisoned. Reissues and archive compilations have furthered their reputation, but the group's personal tragedies culminated in 1978 when Sutherland was shot dead by his wife.

Albums: *The Psychedelic Sounds Of The Thirteenth Floor Elevators* (1966), *Easter Everywhere* (1967), *Live* (1968), *Bull Of The Woods* (1968). Compilations: *Fire In My Bones* (1985), *Elevator Tracks* (1987), *I've Seen Your Face Before* (1988), *The Collection* (1991, contains the first four albums), *Out Of Order* (1993).

This Heat

This English group comprised Charles Bullen (guitar/clarinet/viola/vocals) Charles Heyward (drums/vocals/keyboards) and Gareth Williams (guitar/bass/vocals/keyboards). Bullen and Heyward had first met in 1972 when Heyward answered a *Melody Maker* ad from Liverpudlian guitarist Bullen and travelled down to London, where the duo briefly formed Radar Favourites. Heyward had previously been in Quiet Sun with **Phil Manzanera** (1968-70), the Amazing Band (1970-72) and **Gong** (1972). In February 1974 they formed the short-lived Dolphic Logic. Phil Manzanera's reformed Quiet Sun led to Heyward appearing on both Manzanera's solo stab,

Diamond Heat, and Quiet Sun's *Mainstream* in 1975. In January 1976 Gareth Williams joined the duo and they became This Heat. Williams had never played keyboards, which altered both the musical attitude and instrumental approach, allowing the unit space to improvise and compose more freely. Three weeks later, they played their first London gig. Between 1976 and 1977 they continued to rehearse, made home recordings and performed live, building up a solid reputation for their uncompromising sound. At times schizophrenic, it swung from moments of quiet beauty to an all-out wall-of-noise assault. This was no better exemplified than in two sessions they did for **John Peel's** BBC Radio 1 show which still defy description. Towards the end of 1977 they met and performed with Ghanaian percussionist Mario Boyar Diekvuroh, who in turn had an immense influence on them. Private recordings made at the time were eventually released on a limited edition cassette, through the y French Tago Mago label in 1981. At the same time, the group moved into rehearsal rooms and were able to record at their own convenience. Throughout 1977 and 1978 the pressure to release a record came from various labels but the group maintained an independent stance. *This Heat* was finally released in 1979, produced by David Cunninhams and **Slapp Happy** guitarist Antony More. It received unanimous acclaim, despite criticism being levelled at Heyward's **Robert Wyatt**-esque vocals. In July 1981 Williams played his last concert as a member of the group before travelling to India, but not before the excellent 12-inch EP, *Health & Efficiency*, was released. Later the same year *Deceit* was unveiled on **Rough Trade Records**. During 1981 Heyward also found time to play drums on both **Laura Logic**'s *Pedigree Charm* and the **Raincoats'** *Odyshape*, touring the UK with the latter as their drummer. In April 1982 Heyward and Bullen were joined by Trefor Goronwy (bass/vocals) and Ian Hill (keyboards/vocals). This formation was short-lived and played only a handful of European dates before returning to the UK to play their final gig on May 18 to enthusiastic reviews. Despite only two studio albums, a 12-inch single and two cassette-only releases, This Heat's influence remains, and the fact that their work still sounds as adventurous and daring today as it did when released is a testament to their originality. Following their demise, Bullen concentrated on working as a recording engineer, Heyward and Goronwy were joined by Stephen Rickard (tapes/autoharp) to form the sadly-ignored Camberwell Now, who utilized an early version of sampling called the tape switchboard, devised by Rickard. While the group never quite captured the intensity of their predecessors, they did stretch the melodic elements further. Their limited discography amounts to *The Ghost Trade*, and a 12-inch single, 'Green Fingers' (an old This Heat song). During a hiatus in Camberwell Now activity Heyward aligned

himself with two other drummers, Rick Brown and Guigou Chenebier to record *Noisy Champs* under the cheeky moniker, Les Batteries. After Camberwell Now's demise in 1986 Heyward went on to record a simple melodic album, *Survive The Gesture*. Two further collections followed, both equally diverse in their sound and subject matter: *Skew Whiff*, a tribute to American Abstract Expressionist painter Mark Rothko, and *Switch On War*, prompted by the 1991 Gulf War. Heyward has also been active playing live with ex-**Henry Cow** and **Art Bears** guitarist Fred Frith in group titled Keep The Dog, and also worked with Nick Doyne-Ditmus (ex-Pinski Zoo) on a project entitled Carol, Singing. Albums: *This Heat, This Heat* (Piano 1979), *Deceit* (Rough Trade 1981).

This Is The Army (Stage Musical)
Apart from **George M. Cohan**, no personality in American show business could wave the stars and stripes quite like **Irving Berlin**. He did it to great effect during World War I with the stage show *Yip Yip Yaphank*, and he rekindled the patriotic flames again in 1942 with *This Is The Army*. This all-soldier revue, which opened at the Broadway Theatre in New York on July 4 (naturally), was a mixture of songs and sketches designed to spread the belief that it was just a matter of time before the boys would all be home - and for good. Most of the songs were new, but Berlin himself sang one of fondly rememberd oldies, 'Oh, How I Hate To Get Up In the Morning', surrounded by his buddies dressed in 1917 soldiers' uniforms, just as he had in *Yip Yip Yaphank* all those years ago. The rest of the fine score included 'This Is The Army, Mr. Jones' ('You've had your breakfast in bed before/But you won't get it there anymore'), 'The Army's Made A Man Of Me', 'I'm Getting Tired So I Can Sleep', 'This Time', and 'American Eagles'. For the 'I Left My Heart At The Stage Door Canteen' number, male cast members impersonated female celebrities such as Gypsy Rose Lee and Lynn Fontanne, representing the stars who really did wait on members of the US Armed Services at the real-life Stage Door Canteen in New York. Among those taking part in the show at various times, were Ezra Stone, **Burl Ives**, Robert Sidney, Earl Oxford, Gary Merrill, and Alan Manson. The rousing finale, with everyone dressed in full uniform, was guaranteed to bring a tear to the eye every night. *This Is the Army* ran for 113 performances in New York, and then toured in the US and overseas until the end of the war. The 1943 film version starred George Murphy and Joan Leslie (and Irving Berlin).

This Is The Army (Film Musical)
Many of the same personnel, and most of **Irving Berlin**'s original songs, made the journey from Broadway to Hollywood when this screen version of the 1942 all-soldier stage revue was released in the

following year. Warner Brothers also linked the individual items with a story by Casey Robinson and Claude Binyon, which - guess what - was all about putting on a show that contained some of Berlin's most popular war-tinged and flag-waving numbers. The composer himself, dressed in his World War I uniform, sings 'Oh, How I Hate To Get Up In The Morning', and **Kate Smith** provides another of the highlights with her inspiring version of 'God Bless America'. The remaining songs are performed by the soldiers and a group of principals consisting of George Murphy, Joan Leslie, George Tobias, Charles Butterworth, Alan Hale, **Frances Langford**, Dolores Costello, and Gertude Nieson. These included 'I Left My Heart At The Stage Door Canteen', 'The Army's Made A Man Out Of Me', 'This Is The Army, Mr. Jones', 'We're On Our Way To France', 'I'm Getting Tired So I Can Sleep', 'How About A Cheer For The Navy?', 'American Eagles', 'With My Head In The Clouds', 'This Time', 'Poor Little Me, I'm On K.P.', 'Your Country And My Country', 'What The Well-Dressed Man In Harlem Will Wear', 'My Sweetie', and 'This Time Is The Last Time'. Future US President Ronald Reagan was in the cast, too. He plays Murphy's son who picks up the baton from his ageing producer father and puts on a US Forces revue in World War II - entitled *This Is The Army*. The show was an unqualified success, as was this picture, which thrilled everyone who saw it. Much of the credit for that must go to director Michael Curtiz, choreographers LeRoy Prinz and Robert Sidney, musical director Ray Heindorf who won an Oscar for 'scoring of a musical picture', and producers Jack L. Warner and Hal B. Wallis. According to *Variety*, the five most commercially successful film musicals of the 40s were all **Walt Disney** features. *This Is The Army* was in sixth place, but as a morale booster, the picture was in a league of its own. All the profits from a US box-office gross of $8.5 million went to the Army Relief Fund.

This Mortal Coil

This group was essentially the creation of Ivo Watts-Russell (b. c.1955, England), the co-owner of **4AD Records**, a highly successful Wandsworth, London-based independent label. This Mortal Coil was actually a collaboration of musicians recording in various permutations, overseen and directed by Ivo. The first single, an epic cover of **Tim Buckley**'s 'Song To The Siren', was originally intended as a b-side. However, bolstered by the considerable talents of Robin Guthrie and Elizabeth Fraser (**Cocteau Twins**), it saw its own release and became a near permanent fixture in the independent charts as a result. The album which followed set the pattern for the occasional outings to come. Featuring a selection of artists from the 4AD roster plus various outsiders, the albums included several covers of Ivo's favourite songwriters (Buckley,

Alex Chilton, **Roy Harper**, **Gene Clark** and **Syd Barrett**). At times shamefully indulgent, the series has nevertheless highlighted the occasional stunning performance and breathtaking arrangement. The most recent outing, which Ivo promises to be final, continues this tradition. In addition to label favourites Kim Deal (**Pixies**), Tanya Donelly (**Throwing Muses/ Breeders/Belly**) and **Heidi Berry**, also recruited was Caroline Crawley (**Shelleyan Orphan**). Previous encumbents have included **Howard Devoto** and Gordon Sharp (Cindytalk).

Albums: *It'll End In Tears* (4AD 1984), *Filigree And Shadow* (4AD 1986), *Blood* (4AD 1991).

This Year Of Grace!

One of the most popular of the **Noël Coward - Charles B. Cochran** revues, *This Year Of Grace!* opened at the London Pavilion on 22 March 1928. The book, music and lyrics were by Coward, and the all-star cast included **Sonnie Hale**, Douglas Byng, Maisie Gay, Tilly Losch, **Jessie Matthews**, Lance Lister, and Moya Nugent. The score contained several memorable numbers, such as 'Dance, Little Lady', 'A Room With A View', 'Teach Me To Dance Like Grandma', 'Lorelei', 'Mary Make-Believe', 'I'm Mad About You', and 'Try To Learn To Love'. It ran for 316 performances in London, and Coward himself starred in the Broadway edition which began its run of 158 performances in November 1928. With him in the New York cast were Florence Desmond, and Beatrice Lillie who introduced an extra Coward composition, 'World Weary'.

This'll Make You Whistle

After appearing in various films such as *Brewster's Millions*, *Come Out Of The Pantry*, and *When Knights Were Bold*, with the glamorous Hollywood actresses Fay Wray and Lili Damita, **Jack Buchanan** was reunited with his best-known partner, the very English Elsie Randolph, for this 1937 General Film Distributors' screen adaptation of the hit West End musical. In **Guy Bolton** and Paul Thompson's screenplay, which was based on their original book, Bill Hopping (Buchanan) splits from his fiancé, Laura (Marjorie Brooks), because she is more passionate about horses than she is about him. Laura wants him back, and despatches her guardian uncle (Antony Holles) to look him over and give his approval. Having made alternative romantic arrangements with Joan (Jean Gillie), Bill and his pals Reggie and Archie (William Kendall and David Hutcheson), throw a 'Bohemian' party in order to put the uncle off. Unfortunately, this particular uncle entirely approves of this kind of behaviour; even the presence of Bobbie Rivers (Elsie Randolph), an artist's model who is in the habit of removing her clothes even when she isn't working, fails to put him off. However, after the action moves to Le Touquet, Reggie is the one who ends up with Laura. Maurice Sigler, Al Goodhart, and **Al Hoffman** were responsible for the lively and tuneful score which included 'I'm In Dancing Mood', 'There Isn't Any Limit To My Love', 'Without Rhythm', and 'This'll Make You Whistle'. The producer-director was **Herbert Wilcox**.

Thistlethwaite, Anthony

Part of the **Waterboys**' line-up when they recorded their two greatest albums, *Pagan Place* and *This Is The Sea*, Thistlethwaite enjoyed two career highs with his contributions to the band - the saxophone climax on 'The Whole Of The Moon', and the mandolin playing which underpinned 'Fisherman's Blues' both bore his signature. The Waterboys, however, are just one strand of a prolific recording and performance career. Among his other employers have been **Bob Dylan**, the **Mission**, **Donovan**, **Fairground Attraction** and the **Psychedelic Furs**. His first solo album arrived in 1992. Given a generally warm reception by critics, it saw him touring widely in the UK with the support of backing band the Blue Stars. At the same time he became a semi-permanent fixture in the **Saw Doctors**, which led to extensive British, US and Australian tours. It wasn't until late in 1994 that Thistlewaite found the time to return to the studio to record *Cartwheels*. This featured 11 new compositions written by the artist, with musical guests including **Kirsty MacColl**, **Sharon Shannon**, former **Rolling Stones** member Mick Taylor, **Youth**, **Donal Lunny**, Dave Mattocks of **Fairport Convention** and **Ralph McTell**. It successfully invoked electric, acoustic and horn elements to accomplish its propulsive fusion of folk and rock.
Albums: *Aesop Wrote A Fable* (Rolling Acres 1992), *Cartwheels* (Rolling Acres 1995).

Thomas, B.J.

b. Billy Joe Thomas, 7 August 1942, Hugo, Oklahoma, USA. B.J. Thomas maintained a sturdy career in the USA in both the pop and country fields from the mid-60s into the late 80s. After getting experience by singing in church during his youth, Thomas joined the Triumphs in Houston, Texas, who released a number of unsuccessful singles on small labels. Collaborating with songwriter Mark Charron, a member of the Triumphs, the group recorded an original song, 'Billy And Sue', and released it on the Bragg label without national success. (It was re-released on **Warner Brothers Records** in 1964 but again failed to take off.) Thomas then recorded a cover of **Hank Williams**' 'I'm So Lonesome I Could Cry' for Texas producer **Huey P. Meaux**. It was released on Scepter Records, a New York company and vaulted to number 8 on the national singles chart in the USA. Thomas enjoyed further Top 40 hits with 'Mama' (also recorded successfully by **Dave Berry**), 'Billy And Sue' and 'The

Eyes Of A Woman'. In 1968, Thomas returned to the US Top 10 with the soft-rock 'Hooked On A Feeling', written by Mark James, who also penned 'Suspicious Minds' and 'Always On My Mind' for **Elvis Presley**. In late 1969, Thomas reached number 1 in the US with 'Raindrops Keep Falling On My Head', a song by **Burt Bacharach** and **Hal David** which was featured in the hit film *Butch Cassidy And The Sundance Kid*. 1970 ended with another Top 10 success, 'I Just Can't Help Believing', written by **Barry Mann** and **Cynthia Weil**. Thomas's last significant single for Scepter was 1972's 'Rock And Roll Lullaby', another Mann and Weil composition, which reached number 15 and featured **Duane Eddy** on guitar and the **Blossoms** on backing vocals. After that, the company folded, and it was not until 1975, now signed to **ABC Records** (after a brief, unproductive stint at Paramount), that Thomas enjoyed another hit. '(Hey Won't You Play) Another Somebody Done Somebody Wrong Song' provided his second number 1 and also topped the country charts. That record provided a second career for Thomas as a country star. Although he switched record company affiliations often, moving from ABC to MCA in 1978, to Cleveland International in 1983, and to **Columbia Records** in 1985, Thomas maintained his status in that field until the late 80s. Featuring gospel material in his act as well as straight country, he drew a new audience and continued to sell records. Thomas enjoyed a particularly strong string of country singles in 1983-84, beginning with two number 1 records, 'Whatever Happened To Old Fashioned Love' and 'New Looks From An Old Lover'. 'Two Car Garage' and 'The Whole World's In Love When You're Lonely' also made the Top 10, while a duet with **Ray Charles**, 'Rock And Roll Shoes', reached number 15. Simultaneous with his country career, Thomas recorded a number of gospel-inspired albums for the Myrrh label.
Selected albums: *I'm So Lonesome I Could Cry* (1966), *Tomorrow Never Comes* (1966), *Songs For Lovers And Losers* (1967), *On My Way* (1968), *Young And In Love* (1969), *Raindrops Keep Fallin' On My Head* (1969), *Everybody's Out Of Town* (1970), *Most Of All* (1970), *Billy Joe Thomas* (1972), *B.J. Thomas Country* (1972), *Songs* (1973), *Longhorn And London Bridges* (1974), *Reunion* (1975), *Help Me Make It To My Rockin' Chair* (1975), *B.J. Thomas* (1977), *Home Where I Belong* (1977), *B.J. Thomas* (1977), *Everybody Loves* (1978), *Happy Man* (1979), *New Looks* (1983), *Throwin' Rocks At The Moon* (1985). Compilations: *Greatest Hits, Vol. 1* (1969), *Greatest Hits, Vol. 2* (1971), *ABC Collection* (1976).

Thomas, Carla

b. 21 December 1942, Memphis, Tennessee, USA. The daughter of **Rufus Thomas**, Carla first performed with the Teen Town Singers. "Cause I Love You', a duet with her father, was released on Satellite (later

Stax) in 1960, but the following year she established herself as a solo act with 'Gee Whiz (Look At His Eyes)'. Leased to **Atlantic**, the song became a US Top 10 hit. 'I'll Bring It Home To You' (1962), (an answer to **Sam Cooke**), 'What A Fool I've Been' (1963) and 'Let Me Good To You' (1965) then followed. 'B-A-B-Y', written by **Isaac Hayes** and **David Porter**, reached the US R&B Top 3, before a series of duets with **Otis Redding** proclaimed her 'Queen of Soul'. An excellent version of **Lowell Fulson**'s 'Tramp' introduced the partnership. 'Knock On Wood' and 'Lovey Dovey' followed before Redding's premature death. Carla's own career was eclipsed as **Aretha Franklin** assumed her regal mantle. Singles with **William Bell** and **Johnnie Taylor** failed to recapture past glories, although the singer stayed with Stax until its bankruptcy in 1975. Since then Thomas has not recorded, although she does tour occasionally with the Stax revival shows, and she appeared, along with her father, at the Porretta Terme Soul Festival in 1991.
Albums: *Gee Whiz* (1961), *Comfort Me* (1966), *Carla* (1966), with Otis Redding *King And Queen* (1967), *The Queen Alone* (1967), *Memphis Queen* (1969), *Love Means Carla Thomas* (1971). Compilations: *The Best Of Carla Thomas* (1969), *Hidden Gems* (1992), *The Best Of - The Singles Plus 1968-73* (1993), *Sugar* (1994).

Thomas, Charles
(see **Davis, 'Maxwell Street' Jimmy**)

Thomas, Chris (UK)
b. 13 January 1947, Perivale, Middlesex, UK. This highly-regarded producer was originally a member of obscure UK 60s group Second Chance, which included in its ranks Patrick Campbell-Lyons, later of **Nirvana** and **Speedy Keen**, subsequently of **Thunderclap Newman**. After joining **George Martin**'s AIR production company, he contributed to the **Beatles**' self-titled double album, playing keyboards on several tracks. Four albums with the **Climax** Chicago **Blues Band** followed before Thomas moved on to **Procol Harum**. He worked on all their albums from *Home* to *Exotic Birds And Fruit* and won a reputation as a firm and punctilious producer. A particularly intense working period in the early 70s saw him produce two albums by the **Mick Abrahams** Band, **John Cale**'s *1919*, three albums by **Badfinger**, plus mixing duties on **Eno**'s *Here Come The Warm Jets* and **Pink Floyd**'s *Dark Side Of The Moon*. A long stint at the controls for **Roxy Music** resulted in *For Your Pleasure, Stranded, Siren* and *Viva Roxy Music* and for a time, there were even rumours that Thomas would collaborate with **Bryan Ferry** as a writing partner. It came to nothing.
1976 was a year of change in the music business and Thomas was caught in the maelstrom after being selected to produce the **Sex Pistols**. He recalls one

particular afternoon when they cut 'EMI', 'Pretty Vacant' and 'God Save The Queen' in a single session. Amid the punk explosion, Thomas still returned to the old guard, producing **Paul McCartney** on **Wings**' *Back To The Egg*. As well as brief tie-ups with **Frankie Miller** and **Tom Robinson**, Thomas oversaw the beginning of a very promising career when he produced the first two albums by the **Pretenders**. Equally at home with new wave acts and established artists, Thomas later worked with **Pete Townshend**, **Elton John** and the **Human League**. Thomas has often managed to stay in the vanguard of quality rock and pop, his productions associated with only the highest quality of acts.

Thomas, Chris (USA)
b. 14 October 1962, Baton Rouge, Louisiana, USA. The son of bluesman **Tabby Thomas,** Chris grew up with the music of his father and other local artists including **Slim Harpo**, **Silas Hogan**, and **Henry Gray**, Although he includes **Prince, Jimi Hendrix**, and **Bob Marley** among his major influences. He has toured and recorded with his father, and material under his own name has appeared on Bluebeat (his father's label), **Arhoolie,** and Wolf. He is now under contract to Hightone/**Warner Brothers Records.** *Living Blues* described Thomas as 'One of the most versatile young artists around, grounded in the blues...'.
Album: *The Beginning* (1986), with various artists *Louisiana Blues Live At Tabby's Blues Box* (1989, one track only).

Thomas, David
After the original **Pere Ubu** broke up, the group's central figure, David Thomas, embarked on a fascinating body of work with the Pedestrians that was both highly musical and experimental. Alongside veteran female jazz pianist **Lindsay Cooper**, Thomas stayed at **Rough Trade Records** for a 45rpm album, *The Sound Of The Sand And Other Songs Of The Pedestrians*. It continued Thomas' preferred furrow of *avant garde* rock, mingled with some of the strangest and most endearing vocal performances known to the rock/pop sphere (everything from animal impersonations to a full blown operatic tilt). A subsequent lull was broken by *Variations On A Theme* in 1984. The release of *More Places Forever* and *The Monster Walks On Winter Lake* (with the Wooden Buds) allowed Thomas to interact with a plethora of diverse talent; he has collaborated with Chris Cutler, Mayo Thompson, Ralph Harney, Scott Kraus, Ian Green, **Richard Thompson**, Anton Fier (**Golden Palominos**), Philip Moxham (**Young Marble Giants**), Eddie Thornton and Allen Ravinstein, among many others. After the issue of *Winter Comes Home* on the experimental label Recommended, followed by *Blame The Messenger* on Rough Trade (Twin/Tone in the USA), the

idiosyncratic Thomas later reformed Pere Ubu.

Albums: *The Sound Of Sand And Other Songs Of The Pedestrians* (Rough Trade 1981). With David Thomas & His Legs: *Winter Comes Home* (Re 1982). With the Pedestrians: *Variations On A Theme* (Sixth International 1984), *More Places Forever* (Twin/Tone 1985). With The Wooden Birds: *The Monster Walks On Winter Lake* (Twin/Tone 1985), *Blame The Messenger* (Twin/Tone 1987).

Thomas, David, And The Pedestrians

After the original **Pere Ubu** broke up, the group's central figure, David Thomas, embarked on a fascinating body of work with the Pedestrians that was both musical and experimental. Alongside veteran female jazz pianist **Lindsay Cooper**, Thomas stayed at **Rough Trade** for a 45rpm album, *The Sound Of The Sand And Other Songs Of The Pedestrians*. A subsequent lull was broken by *Variations On A Theme* in 1984, continuing Thomas's avenue of *avant garde* rock. The release of *More Places Forever* and *The Monster Walks On Winter Lake* (with the Wooden Buds) allowed Thomas to interact with a plethora of diverse talent; he has worked with Chris Cutler, Mayo Thompson, Ralph Harney, Scott Kraus, Ian Green, **Richard Thompson**, Anton Fier, Philip Moxham (**Young Marble Giants**), Eddie Thornton and Allen Ravinstein. After the issuing *Winter Comes Home* on the experimental label Recommended, followed by *Blame The Messenger* on **Rough Trade**, the idiosyncratic Thomas later reformed Pere Ubu.

Albums: *The Sound Of Sand And Other Songs Of The Pedestrians* (1981), *Variations On A Theme* (1984), *More Places Forever* (1985), *The Monster Walks On Winter Lake* (1986), *Winter Comes Home* (1986), *Blame The Messenger* (1987).

Thomas, Earl

b. Earl Thomas Bridgeman, 1950, Pikeville, Tennessee, USA. With a Navy officer for a father, Thomas grew up in Seattle, Guam and San Diego, before returning to Pikeville in 1965. He grew up listening to his father play blues guitar and harmonica. In 1983, he moved to Arcata, California, where he studied dentistry at Humboldt State University but before he had completed his studies, he had begun to sing at open-mike nights in local clubs. In 1987, he and co-writer Phillip Wooten moved to San Diego, where Thomas joined the Rhumboogies, performing 40s jump band music. In 1989, he recorded an album, *I Sing The Blues*, which he released on his own Conton label. He also formed a band, the Blues Ambassadors, which has featured musicians such as Zach Zunis, Joel Foy, Christopher Crepps and Michael Cherry. A copy of his album reached Herb Cohen, who signed him to Bizarre Records. *Blue ... Not Blues* consisted of remixed versions of the original album plus three new songs. Thomas has toured Europe with **Buddy Guy** and

appeared at the **Montreux Jazz Festival**. A lifelong fan of **Ike Turner**, his second album reflected his growing interested in both rhythm and the blues.

Albums: *I Sing The Blues* (Conton 1990), *Blue ... Not Blues* (Bizarre/Demon 1992), *Extra Soul* (Bizarre/Demon 1994).

Thomas, George

b. c.1885, Houston, Texas, USA, d. March 1930, Chicago, Illinois, USA (1936, Washington, DC, USA also cited). Thomas was the pianist head of an important Texas blues clan which included his daughter **Hociel Thomas**, his siblings **Beuluh 'Sippie' Wallace** and **Hersal Thomas**, plus Bernice Edwards, not a blood relative, but raised with the family. Thomas was an important composer (of 'New Orleans Hop Scop Blues' and 'Muscle Shoals Blues' among other tunes), and a publisher, for a time in partnership with **Clarence Williams**. On disc, he made 'The Rocks' in 1923 (as Clay Custer), a solo which contains the earliest recording of a walking bass, accompanied Sippie's friend Tiny Franklin, and made one record under his own name, and a few with his jazz group, the Muscle Shoals Devils.

Album: *The Thomas Family* (1977).

Thomas, Hersal

b. 1910, Houston, Texas, USA, d. 3 July 1926, Detroit, Michigan, USA. A child prodigy on piano, Thomas was tutored by his brother **George**, but soon exceeded him for invention. In mid-20s Chicago, his reputation, alike for technique and feeling, made other pianists wary of playing at parties where he was present. He cut 'Hersal Blues' and his celebrated 'Suitcase Blues', an enduring standard of blues piano, in 1925, and was accompanying his sister **Beuluh 'Sippie' Wallace** (with **Joe 'King' Oliver** and **Louis Armstrong**!) before he was 15. In 1925/6 he was heavily in demand for recording, backing his niece **Hociel Thomas** among others. He was working at Penny's Pleasure Inn in Detroit, an engagement arranged by Sippie, when he died of food poisoning, aged only 16.

Album: *The Thomas Family* (1977).

Thomas, Hociel

b. 10 July 1904, Houston, Texas, USA, d. 22 August 1952, Oakland, California, USA. Sister of **George Thomas**, and niece of **Beuluh 'Sippie' Wallace** and **Hersal Thomas**, Hociel Thomas was a direct and effective blues singer, as she showed when she recorded during 1925-26; her records always featured Hersal on piano, and his sudden death in 1926 devastated Hociel, who abandoned her musical career. Discovered in California by jazz fans, she recorded some fine sides in 1946 with her own capable Texas piano, and **Mutt Carey** on trumpet, and appeared with **Kid Ory** in 1948, but soon retired again. In about

1950, she was acquitted of manslaughter after a fight with a sister, in which the sister died and Hociel was blinded.

Albums: *Hot Society LP 1001* (untitled) (c.1970), *Louis And The Blues Singers* (1972), *The Piano Blues, Vol. 4* (1977), *The Thomas Family* (1977).

Thomas, Irma

b. Irma Lee, 18 February 1941, Ponchatoula, Louisiana, USA. The 'Soul Queen Of New Orleans' was discovered in 1958 by bandleader Tommy Ridgley. Her early records were popular locally, but an R&B hit came in 1960 with '(You Can Have My Husband But Please) Don't Mess With My Man'. The following year Thomas rejoined producer/writer **Allen Toussaint**, with whom she had worked on her first recordings. This reunion resulted in two of Irma's finest singles, 'It's Raining' and 'Ruler Of My Heart' (1962), the latter a prototype for **Otis Redding**'s 'Pain In My Heart'. After signing with the **Imperial** label in 1963 she recorded 'Wish Someone Would Care' (1964), which reached the US Top 20, while the follow-up, 'Anyone Who Knows What Love Is (Will Understand)', also entered the national chart. This single is better recalled for its b-side, 'Time Is On My Side', which was successfully covered by the **Rolling Stones**. Thomas continued to record excellent singles without achieving due commercial success. Her final hit was a magnificent interpretation of 'Good To Me' (1968), recorded at **Muscle Shoals** and issued on **Chess**. She then moved to Canyon, Roker and Cotillion, before appearing on **Swamp Dogg**'s short-lived Fungus label with *In Between Tears* (1973). Irma has continued to record fine albums and remains a highly popular live attraction. Her career continues into the 90s with new albums and a planned biography.

Albums: *Wish Someone Would Care* (1964), *Take A Look* (1968), *In Between Tears* (1973), *Irma Thomas Live* (1977), *Soul Queen Of New Orleans* (1978), *Safe With Me* (1979), *Hip Shakin' Mama* (1981), *The New Rules* (1986), *The Way I Feel* (1988), *Simply The Best* (1991), *True Believer* (1992), *Walk Around Heaven: New Orleans Gospel Soul* (Rounder 1994). Compilations: Irma Thomas Sings (c.70s), *Time Is On My Side* (1983), *Down At Muscle Shoals* i (1984), *Best Of: Breakaway* (1986), *Something Good: The Muscle Shoals Sessions* (1989), *Down At Muscle Shoals* ii (1989), *Ruler Of Hearts* (1989), *Down At Muscle Shoals* iii (1991), *Wish Someone Would Care* (1991), *Safe With Me/Irma Thomas Live* (1991), *Time Is On My Side: The Best Of Vol. 1* (1992), *The Soul Queen Of New Orleans* (1993).

Thomas, Jah

b. Nkrumah Thomas (named after nationalist leader Kwame Nkrumah), c.1958, Kingston Jamaica, West Indies. He began recording in the mid-70s supported by **Alvin Ranglin** and commencing with 'Midnight Rock'. Thomas' international success came when the newly formed Greensleeves label, set up by the owners of a record shop in Ealing, released his debut album in 1978. *Stop You Loafin'* was a popular release and introduced reggae fans to the artwork of Tony McDermott who has designed many covers for the label. The set was produced at Channel One by **Joseph 'Joe Joe' Hookim** and a host of top musicians provided the backing including **Sly Dunbar**, **Robbie Shakespeare** and **Ansell Collins**. Thomas' success led to a further outing *Dance Hall Style* from another specialist record shop which was unable to emulate Greensleeves success. Two albums with similar titles surfaced. The first a self-production on his own label, Midnight Rock, and the other produced by Jah Life which resulted in confusion and dwindling record sales for Thomas. His DJ career took a back seat when he decided to concentrate on producing other artists including Robin Hood, Robert French and the two Palmers. Triston Palmer enjoyed a massive hit with 'Joker Smoker' and **Michael Palmer** hit with, 'Ghetto Dance'. In the Christmas of 1985 his production of Michael Palmer's 'Happy Merry Christmas' was released on the b-side to 'Where Is Santa Claus' by Mr And Mrs Yellowman and proved to be the more favoured chant. Thomas continued enjoying hits as a DJ with 'Shoulder Move', 'Clean Your Teeth', 'Polka Dot' and 'Posse', the latter recorded in combination with Jim Brown.

Albums: *Stop You Loafin'* (Greensleeves 1978), *Dance Hall Style* (Silver Camel 1979), *Dance On The Corner* (Midnight Rock 1979), *Dance Pon De Corner* (Jah Life 1979), *Black Ash Dub* (Trojan 1980), *Tribute To The Reggae King* (Midnight Rock 1981/Vista 1983), *Shoulder Move* (Midnight Rock 1983), *Nah Fight Over Woman* (Vista 1983).

Thomas, James 'Son'

b. 14 October 1926, Eden, Mississippi, USA, d. 26 June 1993. Until his discovery by a blues music researcher in 1967, Thomas had never travelled more than 100 miles from Leland, Mississippi. As such, he was a valuable source of lore on the creative processes of Delta blues, and made a number of satisfying recordings, accompanying his dark singing with the typically hypnotic guitar of the region. In subsequent years, he travelled more widely, including Europe, and recorded again. This recognition enabled him to afford to give up his various jobs including those of gravedigger and removal man. Greater exposure revealed him to be a likeable performer, but one with few original themes, as is often typical of blues singers of his generation. Thomas was also a story teller and folk sculptor working in clay he dug from his local river. In 1991 he had an operation to remove a brain tumour. Two years later, while recovering from a stroke, he suffered a fatal cardiac arrest.

Albums: *The Blues Are Alive And Well* (1970), *Down On*

The Delta (1981), *Delta Blues Classics* (1981), *Highway 61 Blues* (1983), *Good Morning School Girl* (1986), *Bottomlands* (1990).

Thomas, Jesse 'Babyface'

b. 3 February 1911, Logansport, Louisiana, USA. Although he was the younger brother of blues guitarist Willard **Ramblin' Thomas**, Jesse was not influenced by his style. On his 1929 debut records, he imitated **Lonnie Johnson** and **Blind Blake** but by the time of his next recordings in 1948, he had developed an individual electric guitar style of great fluency. This stemmed from formal training, an acquaintance with jazz, and his serious attempts to transfer his piano playing to the guitar. His singing and playing were still firmly within Texan blues traditions. Thomas recorded intermittently on the west coast until 1957, when he returned to Louisiana. while there, he occasionally released records on his self-operated Red River label, a successor to Club, which had briefly traded in the early 50s. A mid-60s soul recording was less successful than a blues single released on Red River in 1989. This showed that Thomas remained a capable and sophisticated musician.

Selected albums: *Down Behind The Rise* (1979), *1948-53* (1993).

Thomas, Joe (saxophone)

b. Joseph Vankert Thomas, 19 June 1909, Uniontown, Pennsylvania, USA, d. 3 August 1986. After starting out on alto saxophone, on which instrument he played with **Horace Henderson** and others, Thomas switched to tenor saxophone. On this instrument he played with **Stuff Smith** in 1932 and then joined **Jimmie Lunceford** for a 14-year-long stay. Heavily featured as an instrumentalist and also as an occasional singer, he was one of several key figures in the band. On Lunceford's death Thomas co-led the band for a while but then formed his own small group. In the early 50s he dropped out of full-time music, but made sporadic appearances at festivals and on recording sessions into the late 70s. A forceful soloist, Thomas's playing steadily improved during his spell with Lunceford where the stern discipline exerted by section leader **Willie Smith** dramatically affected his work. NB. This musician should not be confused with several others of the same name in jazz, at least two of whom also play tenor saxophone: Joe Thomas (b. 23 December 1908), the brother of **Walter 'Foots' Thomas**, and Joe Thomas (b. 16 June 1933).

Album: *Raw Meat* (1979). Compilation: *The Complete Jimmie Lunceford* (1939-40).

Thomas, Joe (trumpet)

b. Joseph Lewis Thomas, 24 July 1909, Webster Groves, Missouri, USA, d. 6 August 1984. After playing trumpet in several obscure **territory bands** during the late 20s and early 30s, Thomas settled in New York City in 1933. There he played with the bands of **Fletcher Henderson**, **Fats Waller**, **Willie Bryant** and **Benny Carter**. At the start of the 40s he briefly led his own band, then worked with numerous other leaders, including **James P. Johnson**, **Teddy Wilson**, **Barney Bigard**, **Roy Eldridge**, **Don Byas**, **Cozy Cole** and **Bud Freeman**. He continued to play through succeeding decades, his appearances including a stint in the Fletcher Henderson Reunion band and engagements at **Eddie Condon**'s club and with **Claude Hopkins** and **J.C. Higginbotham**. He played into the 70s before ill-health prompted his retirement. A warm, full tone characterized Thomas's playing and the many small group recordings made during his career show a gifted instrumentalist with an inventive solo capacity.

Albums: with Henderson All Stars *Big Reunion* (1957), one side only *Mainstream* (1958). Selected compilations: *The Indispensable Fletcher Henderson* (1927-36 recordings), with Roy Eldridge *The Jazz Greats - Brass* (1944 recordings), *Don Byas - 1945* (1945 recordings), *Blowin' In From KC* (Uptown 1983), *Raw Meat* (Uptown 1983), *Jumping With Joe* (Swingtime 1987).

Thomas, Kenny

b. c.1969, London, England. Thomas is among the most popular of the UK's current soul dance vocalists. His biggest UK hit came in 1991 with 'Thinking About Your Love' (number 4), while his debut album sold more than 600,000 copies in the UK alone. Other hit singles spawned by that debut included 'Outstanding', 'The Best Of You' and 'Tender Love', and also resulted in a Brit Award nomination for Best British Male Vocalist and Best British Newcomer. The warm, relaxed dance grooves of that debut were replicated on a second album which continued Thomas' massive commercial success. Guest musicians this time round included the **Young Disciples**, **Nu Colours** and the **Reggae Philharmonic Orchestra**. This time some of the bonhomie of the original set was more restrained, with a slightly more mature lyrical vision reflecting more real-life experiences.

Albums: *Voices* (1991), *Wait For Me* (1993).

Thomas, Kid

b. Louis Thomas Watts, 20 June 1934, Sturgis, Mississippi, USA, d. 13 April 1970, Beverly Hills, California, USA. Watts was also known as Tommy Lewis/Louis. Chicago based from 1941, he played harmonica and sang blues from the end of the 40s, recording for Federal in 1955, and seeing occasional releases on small labels until the end of his life. This came shortly after his location by a music researcher in California, where Thomas had settled in 1960. He had killed a child in a road accident and was shot by the boy's father after manslaughter charges were dismissed.

The strong feelings this aroused among blues enthusiasts should not be allowed to mask the fact that Thomas was a minor and derivative performer, albeit an impressively energetic one, especially when imitating **Little Richard**.

Albums: *Rockin' This Joint Tonite* (1979), *Here's My Story* (1991).

Thomas, Lafayette Jerl

b. 13 June 1928, Shreveport, Louisiana, USA, d. 20 May 1977, Brisbane, California, USA. One of the few postwar guitarists to develop a personal style from an early admiration of **'T-Bone' Walker,** Thomas was encouraged by uncle, **Jesse 'Babyface' Thomas**. The family moved to San Francisco soon after his birth and there he learned to play both piano and guitar. His first gig in 1947 was with Al Simmons' Rhythm Rockers. In 1948 he replaced guitarist Robert Kelton in **Jimmy McCracklin**'s band, with whom he remained intermittently for the rest of his career. He made his first record while on tour with McCracklin. 'Baby Take A Chance With Me', recorded in Memphis in 1951 for **Sam Phillips,** was issued on **Chess** as by L.J. Thomas And His Louisiana Playboys. He also worked with **Bob Geddins,** playing on many **Jimmy Wilson** sessions leased to Aladdin, 7-11, Big Town and Irma. His own records were made for small labels such as Jumping, Hollywood (unissued) and Trilyte but more often he cut odd titles at McCracklin's 50s sessions for Modern, Peacock and Chess, to be discovered and issued on album three decades later. Moving briefly to New York in 1959, he made 'Lafayette's A-Comin'' for Savoy with pianist **Sammy Price,** before returning to the west coast. He worked outside music for most of the 60s, sharing one album session with pianist **Dave Alexander** and **L.C. 'Good Rocking' Robinson** in September 1968. The comeback was brief and he spent his last years working as a hose assembler. His best work is to be found on the records of McCracklin and Wilson, providing the biting solos for which he will be remembered.

Album: *Everybody Rock! The Best Of Jimmy McCracklin* (1989).

Thomas, Leone

b. 4. October 1937, East St. Louis, Illinois, USA. Thomas studied music at Tennessee State University but he had already started singing, sitting in with the band of Armando Peraza (congas) and bands including **Jimmy Forest** and **Grant Green**. During these early years he had been particularly inspired by seeing **John Coltrane** playing with **Miles Davis**. In 1959 Thomas moved to New York and sang in **Apollo** shows with **Dakota Staton** and **Art Blakey**'s **Jazz Messengers** among others. In 1961 he joined **Count Basie**'s Orchestra and only left when he was inducted into the army. When he was discharged he worked with

Pharoah Sanders with whom he was free to develop the more unusual elements of his style; in particular, the 'yodelling' he says is derived from the singing of Congo pygmies. It was most apparent at this stage that he sees music as social commentary: 'You just have to be more than an entertainer. How the blazes can you ignore what is happening?'. Since then he has worked solo and appeared with the bands of guitarist **Carlos Santana** and trumpeter **Freddy Hubbard**.

Albums: with Pharoah Sanders *Karma* (1969); with Santana *Spirits Known And Unknown* (1969), *Leon Thomas Album* (1970), *Three Shades Of Blue* (1971), *Blues And The Soulful Truth* (1972), *Full Circle* (1973).

Thomas, Nicky

b. 1949, Portland, Jamaica, West Indies, d. 1990. Working as a labourer on the same building site as Albert Griffiths, Clinton Fearon and David Webber, later to become the **Gladiators**, Nicky Thomas dreamed of success in the music business. He got his break with the **Derrick Harriot**-produced 'Run Mr Nigel Run'. He found greater success working with Joel Gibson (later to be known as **Joe Gibbs**) in 1969. The collaboration saw a number of hits including 'God Bless The Children' and 'Mama's Song', along with covers of 'Rainy Night In Georgia' and 'If I Had A Hammer'. In the summer of 1970 the release of 'Love Of The Common People' took Nicky into the UK Top 10 and a tour followed. Nicky decided to stay in the UK to promote a compilation, *Love Of The Common People*, which featured tracks recorded with Joe Gibbs in 1969. The release of 'Yesterday Man' almost took Nicky back into the UK chart, after being lifted from his self-produced set, *Tell It Like It Is*. One of the most significant tracks demonstrated his frustration with the derision reggae suffered at the hands of most Radio 1 presenters - 'BBC'. The song opens with his supporters chanting 'Nicky - Nicky - Nicky', before he states: 'Hold It - hold it - it's a long walk to the BBC but I'm gonna get there just the same'. Undeterred by such indifference he continued to record in a commercial vein, earning a minor hit with 'Images Of You'. He also released 'Suzanne Beware Of The Devil', produced by **Dandy Livingstone**. Unfortunately for Thomas it was the producer's own vocal version that secured a UK Top 20 hit when it was released in 1972 as the b-side to 'What Do You Wanna Make Those Eyes At Me For'. In 1974 he released a cover version of the **Kinks**' hit, 'Lola', and toured the UK, with backing supplied by a group who were to later find fame as **Misty In Roots**. The tour went well, playing to ecstatic audiences and Nicky proved to be especially popular with the girls. He was also featured in the television programme, *Aquarius*, recording at Chalk Farm studio, London, and the accompanying interview gave him the chance to express his opinions regarding reggae and the media. In 1983 **Paul Young**, inspired by Thomas' rendition of 'Love Of The Common People', enjoyed his third Top 10 hit with the song. **Trojan Records**, obliged public demand for the original version with its release on a 'maxi single', along with 'Yesterday Man' and the most requested tune at his live shows, 'Have A Little Faith'.

Albums: *Love Of The Common People* (Trojan 1970), *Tell It Like It Is* (Trojan 1971), *Images Of You* (Trojan 1973), *Doing The Moon Walk* (Trojan 1991, covers 1970-73).

Thomas, Pat

b. 1951, Kumasi, Ghana. The wave of disco and reggae that swept Africa in the mid-70s created differing responses: some musicians pulled away from playing imported music entirely, others adopted it and adapted it to their own purposes. One of the latter is highlife vocalist Thomas, who made his name with his band the Sweet Beans. He was brought up by his uncle, Onyina, a celebrated local bandleader and the owner of a record store in Kumasi. In 1969 he joined the Broadway Dance Band, leaving a year later to join the Uhuru Dance Band for a tour of the UK. Returning to Ghana, he played with Ebo Taylor's Blue Monks, spent a year in the Cote D'lvoire and then formed the Sweet Beans in 1973. Like many Ghanaian bands, the Sweet Beans received sponsorship from a government body, in this case the Cocoa Marketing Board. They released *False Lover* in 1974, then split and re-formed as Marijata, releasing *Marijata* and *Pat Thomas Introduces Marijata*, after which Thomas released two reggae-influenced solo albums, *Let's Think It Over* and *Asawado*. He then left for Berlin, where he recorded the classic *1980*, a hi-tech mix of reggae and disco-highlife that featured **George Darko** on lead guitar.

The albums that followed his return to Ghana abandoned electronic slickness in favour of a return to roots: *Sweeter Than Honey* dug into traditional dagomba rhythms. When Thomas does hit form he is hard to beat; his 1985 output included three hastily recorded albums, including the disastrously under-mixed *Pat Thomas And Ebo Taylor* and one blustering triumph, *Asanteman*, which combined a history of the Ashante kingdom, kicked off by a blast of traditional horn playing with solid production. By this time, Thomas had discovered football, which would provide lyrics and conceptual themes for his songwriting throughout the rest of the decade. In 1984, he had recorded the mini-album *Asante Kotoko*, dedicated to the Ghanaian club which had won the Africa Cup in 1983. The title track was played over the speakers at the club's home pitch and occasionally played live at half-time by a local highlife band. In 1985, Thomas went to work on a further Asante album, to commemorate the club's 50th anniversary.

Albums: with the Sweet Beans *False Lover* (1974), with Marijata *Marijata* (1975), *Pat Thomas Introduces Marijata* (1976), *Let's Think It Over* (1978), *Asawado* (1979), with George Darko *1980* (1980), with Ebo Taylor *Sweeter Than Honey* (1981), *Asante Kotoko* (1984), *Asanteman* (1985), *Pat Thomas And Ebo Taylor* (1985), *Highlife Greats* (1987), *Sike Ya Mogye* (1992).

Thomas, Ramblin'

b. Willard Thomas, 1902, Logansport, Louisiana, USA, d. c.1945, Memphis, Tennessee, USA. According to his younger brother **Jesse 'Babyface' Thomas**, Willard Thomas was nicknamed by Paramount when he recorded in 1928. He was peripatetic and spent much of his time between Dallas (where he played with **Blind Lemon Jefferson**) and Shreveport, where he probably acquired the slide guitar technique heard on many of his records. Thomas also travelled east of Shreveport into Louisiana, where he associated with **King Solomon Hill.** Although echoes of Jefferson, **Blind Blake** and **Lonnie Johnson** are audible, both Thomas's sour-edged playing and his cynical, hard-bitten singing are instantly recognizable. Thomas was an inventive lyricist who drew on his life for his songs, singing of being locked up for 'vag', of 'Hard Dallas', and of the alcoholism which may have hastened his death from tuberculosis.

Album: *Ramblin' Thomas* (1983).

Thomas, Rene

b. 25 February 1927, Liege, Belgium, d. 3 January 1975, Santander, Spain. Thomas was a self-taught guitarist at first much influenced by **Django Rheinhardt**. By the time he moved to Paris in the early 50s, he had adapted to the style of **Jimmy Raney**. In Paris he played with many visiting Americans including trumpeter **Chet Baker** in 1955. In 1958 he moved to New York where he worked with the groups of pianist **Toshiko Akiyoshi** and tenor saxophonist **Sonny Rollins**, who thought him 'better than any of the American guitarists of the day'. He was an excellent accompanist who soloed with long, flowing lines and a sharp attack. By 1963 he had returned to Paris and was working with **Kenny Clarke** and others. He played with tenor saxophonist **Stan Getz** from 1969-72. Thomas died of a heart attack in 1975.

Selected albums: with Sonny Rollins *Brass/Trio* (1958), *Guitar Groove* (1960), *Meeting Mr. T* (1963), with Stan Getz *Dynasty* (1971).

Thomas, Rufus

b. 26 March 1917, Cayce, Mississippi, USA. A singer, dancer and entertainer, Thomas learned his trade as a member of the Rabbit's Foot Minstrels, a vaudeville-inspired touring group. By the late 40s he was performing in several Memphis nightclubs and organizing local talent shows. **B.B. King, Bobby 'Blue' Bland** and **Little Junior Parker** were discovered in this way. When King's career subsequently blossomed, Thomas replaced him as a disc jockey at WDIA and remained there until 1974. He also began recording and several releases appeared on Star Talent, **Chess** and Meteor before 'Bear Cat' became a Top 3 US R&B hit. An answer to **Willie Mae Thornton**'s 'Hound Dog', it was released on **Sun** in 1953. Rufus remained a local celebrity until 1960 when he recorded with his daughter, **Carla Thomas**. Their duet, "Cause I Love You' was issued on the fledgling Satellite (later **Stax**) label where it became a regional hit. Thomas secured his reputation with a series of infectious singles. 'Walking The Dog' (1963) was a US Top 10 entry while several of his other recordings, notably 'Jump Back' and 'All Night Worker' (both in 1964) were beloved by aspiring British groups. His later success with novelty numbers – 'Do The Funky Chicken' (1970), '(Do The) Push And Pull, Part 1' (1970) and 'Do The Funky Penguin' (1971) – has obscured the merits of less brazen recordings. 'Sophisticated Sissy' (1967) and 'Memphis Train' (1968) are prime 60s' R&B. Rufus stayed with Stax until its 1975 collapse, from where he moved to AVI. His releases there included *If There Were No Music* and *I Ain't Getting Older, I'm Gettin' Better*. In 1980 Thomas re-recorded several of his older songs for a self-named collection on Gusto. The 80s saw him putting aside R&B and recording rap with *Rappin' Rufus*, on the Inchiban label and tackling blues with *That Woman Is Poison* on the Alligator label. He continues to perform regularly and appeared at several European soul festivals in the 90s.

Albums: *Walking The Dog* (1964), *Do The Funky Chicken* (1970), *Doing The Push And Pull Live At PJs* (1971), *Did You Hear Me* (1973), *Crown Prince Of Dance* (1973), *Blues In The Basement* (1975), *If There Were No Music* (1977), *I Ain't Gettin' Older, I'm Gettin' Better* (1977), *Rufus Thomas* (1980), *Rappin' Rufus* (1986), *That Woman Is Poison* (1988), *Timeless Funk* (1992). Compilation: *Jump Back - A 1963-67 Retrospective* (1984), *Can't Get Away From This Dog* (1991), *The Best Of - The Singles* (1993).

Thomas, Sam Fan

b. Samuel Thomas Ndonfeng, April 1952, Bafoussam, Cameroon. With the track 'African Typic Collection', vocalist and composer Thomas burst onto the international scene as one of the most promising performers to emerge in the mid-80s, further developing the hard-driving, electric makossa style first given an international profile by **Manu Dibango**. At the age of 13, he took up guitar, and five years later joined local group Les Tigres Noires, led by blind tchmassi star Andre Marie Tala. He stayed with the band until 1976, playing on both their singles, then left for Cotonou, where he recorded his debut, *Funky New Bell* with the Black Santiagos. In 1977, he recorded *Special Kwongne*, before working as a studio technician on the local Temba label. His third album, *Rikiaton* appeared in 1982, followed by *Makassi,* whose

outstanding 'African Typic Collection' confirmed his reputation as one of makossa's brightest new stars. With its acoustic guitar framework and medley of African dances, from the tchmassi to kavacha and the makossa, the track remains a remarkable and enduring piece of work, its crisp central melodies leading into a beautiful chanted extract of an old **OK Jazz** song, 'Boma L'Heure'. It is, however, not typical Sam Fan Thomas. Away from the polished acoustic swing of 'Typic' his more normal approach is to fill all available spaces with layers of tight guitar patterns and relentless percussion, reminiscent of the zouk musicians with whom he has worked sporadically since the early 80s. Thomas maintained his commercial momentum with *Neng Makassi* in 1985 and *Makassi Plus* in 1986, before being eclipsed by younger makossa musicians and falling out of the limelight in the latter half of the 80s.

Albums: with the Black Santiagos *Funky New Bell* (1976); solo *Special Kwongne* (1977), *Rikiaton* (1982), *Makassi* (1984), *Neng Makassi* (1985), *Makassi Plus* (1986).

Thomas, Tabby

b. 5 January 1929, Baton Rouge, Louisiana, USA. Thomas's first musical influences came from radio and records, and he started to play music himself while in the airforce. He sang with an R&B band during the early 50s and his first records were in that style, with strong touches of **Roy Brown**'s sound. A release on the Feature label in 1954 marked the beginning of a long, if intermittent association with producer **Jay Miller**, during which they tried a wide range of styles, including blues and soul. Their most successful collaboration was 'Hoodoo Party', on Excello in 1962. In 1981, Thomas opened the Blues Box in Baton Rouge to present local artists; this has achieved an international reputation for regular appearances by **Silas Hogan**, **Henry Gray** and others, including Thomas's own son Chris.

Album: *25 Years With The Blues* (1979), *Hoodoo Party* (1990).

Thomas, Timmy

b. 13 November 1944, Evansville, Indiana, USA. An accomplished singer, songwriter and keyboard player, Thomas first attracted attention for his work as an accompanist with jazz musicians **Donald Byrd** and **Cannonball Adderley**. He then embarked on a spell as a session musician, most notably with the Memhis-based Goldwax label, before his solo career blossomed in 1972 with 'Why Can't We Live Together?' (US number 3/UK Top 20). His simple, **Booker T. Jones**-like organ style came to the fore as a hypnotic pulse punctuates an understated, but heartfelt plea. This rhythmic song was later tastefully covered by the sophisticated British vocalist, **Sade** in 1984. Timmy's immediate releases continued in this vein, but he was unable to repeat that initial success. He nonetheless enjoyed a run of minor R&B hits culminating in 'Gotta Give A Little Love' (Ten Years After)', a US Top 30 soul entry in 1984.

Albums: *Why Can't We Live Together* (1972), *You're The Song I Always Wanted To Sing* (1975), *The Magician* (1977), *Touch To Touch* (1978), *Live* (1980).

Thomas, Walter 'Foots'

b. 10 February 1907, Muskogee, Oklahoma, USA, d. 26 August 1981. Accomplished on most of the saxophone family, as well as clarinet and flute, Thomas played professionally while still at high school. In the late 20s he played with several important New York-based musicians, including **Jelly Roll Morton** and **Luis Russell**. At the end of the 20s he joined the **Missourians**, the band later fronted by **Cab Calloway**. During several years with Calloway he also wrote many of the band's most popular arrangements. In the early 40s he played with **Don Redman** and led his own bands, but by the end of the decade had stopped playing to concentrate on other aspects of the music business. He died in August 1981. His brother, Joe Thomas (b. 23 December 1908), was also a saxophonist.

Compilations: *The Most Important Recordings Of Cab Calloway* (1930-49 recordings), one side only *The Walter 'Foots' Thomas All Stars* (1944-45 recordings).

Thomas, Willie B.

b. 25 May 1912, Lobdell, Mississippi, USA. Thomas was permanently disabled by a back injury he received in his early teens during his family's migration to Louisiana. He partnered the fiddler **James 'Butch' Cage** on kazoo for 10 years before taking up the guitar, on which he recorded with Thomas after their discovery in 1959. Thomas was unusual in seeing no conflict between his secular music and his activities as a street preacher. His guitar playing, though limited, was an ideal complement to Cage's fiddle, and they formed an unmistakable, raucous vocal duo.

Albums: *Country Negro Jam Session* (1960), *I Have To Paint My Face* (1969), *Raise A Rukus Tonight* (1979).

Thompson Twins

The origins of this UK synthesizer pop act were much less conventional than their chart material might suggest. Their name derived from the *Tin Tin* cartoon books of Herge. Formed in 1977, the line-up featured Tom Bailey (b. 18 June 1957, Halifax, Yorkshire, England; vocals/keyboards/percussion), Peter Dodd (b. 27 October 1953; guitar) and John Roog (guitar/vocals/percussion), who were friends living in Chesterfield when they decided to experiment with music. Several gigs later they relocated to London where they picked up drummer Chris Bell (later **Spear Of Destiny** and **Gene Loves Jezebel**). After sporadic gigs 1981 saw their line-up extended to include Joe Leeway (b. 15 November 1957, Islington, London, England; percussion/vocals), Alannah Currie (b. 20 September, 1959, Auckland, New Zealand; percussion/saxophone), and Matthew Seligman (ex-**Soft Boys**; bass). This seven-piece became a cult attraction in the capital, where their favourite gimmick involved inviting their audience on stage to beat out a rhythmic backdrop to the songs. Their motivation was similar to that of the punk ethos: 'We were angry with the world in general - the deceit and the lies'. However, when *A Product Of...* was released it showed a band struggling to make the transition from stage to studio. Producer Steve Lillywhite took them in hand for *Set*, and the Bailey-penned 'In The Name Of Love' saw them gain their first minor hit in the UK. It did much better in the US, staying at the top of the *Billboard* Disco charts for five weeks. Before this news filtered back, four of the band had been jettisoned, leaving just Bailey, Currie and Leeway. The cumbersome bohemian enterprise had evolved into a slick business machine, each member taking responsibility for either the music, visuals or production, in a manner not dissimilar to the original **Public Image Limited** concept. Reinventing their image as those of the Snap, Crackle and Pop characters of the Kelloggs' breakfast cereal, they set about a sustained assault on the upper regions of the UK charts. 1983's 'Love On Your Side' was their first major domestic hit, preceding *Quick Step And Side Kick*, their first album as a trio which rose to number 2 in 1983. Highly commercial singles 'Hold Me Now', 'Doctor Doctor' and 'You Take Me Up' put them firmly in the first division of UK pop acts. Further minor hits followed, most notably the anti-heroin 'Don't Mess With Doctor Dream'. However, when Leeway left at the end of 1986 the Thompson Twins became the duo their name had always implied. Bailey and Currie had been romantically involved since 1980, and had their first child eight years later. Unfortunately, success on the scale of their previous incarnation deserted them for the rest of the 80s although their songwriting talents earned **Deborah Harry** a UK Top 20 hit in 1989 with 'I Want That Man'.

Albums: *A Product Of...* (1981), *Set* (1982), *Quick Step And Side Kick* (1983), *Into The Gap* (1984), *Here's To The Future* (1986), *Close To The Bone* (1987), *Big Trash* (1989), *Queer* (1991). Compilations: *Greatest Mixes* (1988), *The Greatest Hits* (1990).

Further reading: *The Thompson Twins: An Odd Couple*, Rouce, Rose (1985).

Thompson, 'Lucky'

b. Eli Thompson, 16 June 1924, Columbia, South Carolina, USA. Thompson's professional career began in the early 40s as a sideman in **territory bands**. After moving to New York in 1943 he played in the bands of **Lionel Hampton**, **Don Redman**, **Billy**

Eckstine, **Lucky Millinder** and in 1944 joined **Count Basie**. On the west coast he recorded with **Dizzy Gillespie** and **Charlie Parker**, being hired by Gillespie for the famous engagement at Billy Berg's to help make up the numbers when Parker failed to turn up or was late. Indeed, Parker failed to show up for a record date with Ross Russell's Dial label and Thompson sat in. When Parker eventually made a date for Russell, this time with **Miles Davis**, Thompson was again present. Thompson played briefly with **Boyd Raeburn** and was also active in the studios. In 1946 he was a member of the Stars Of Swing, a co-operative band masterminded by **Charles Mingus** and **Buddy Collette** and which also featured **Britt Woodman** and John Anderson. This band lasted less than two months and unfortunately was never recorded. Back in New York at the end of the 40s, Thompson formed his own band and in the early 50s headlined at the Savoy Ballroom. After dabbling briefly in R&B he made several jazz albums with **Oscar Pettiford**, **Milt Jackson** and, notably, with Miles Davis on the famous Prestige session for which Davis hired Thompson, **J.J. Johnson**, **Horace Silver**, **Percy Heath** and **Art Blakey** and which resulted in superb performances of 'Walkin'' and 'Blue 'N' Boogie'. In 1956 he visited Europe, recording prodigiously in France under his own name and also touring with **Stan Kenton**. Thompson took a liking to Europe and resided there for several years in the late 50s/early 60s and again at the end of the 60s.

Between these two sojourns he played little, preferring life on a small farm in Michigan, and after his latest return from Europe in 1973 he taught for a while before retiring from music. Thompson's playing on tenor and soprano saxophone ably straddles the main strands favoured by musicians of his generation. Although identifiably influenced by **Coleman Hawkins** and **Don Byas** he had absorbed the stylistic departures of **Lester Young** and **Charlie Parker**. However, he possessed a fertile imagination and the characteristics of his playing were very much his own; indeed Thompson proved to be one of the most original and inventive saxophonists working in the post-bebop mainstream and his early retirement was a grievous loss to jazz. His departure from music was prompted by his growing dissatisfaction with the way in which musicians were treated by record companies, club owners, promoters and others in the business. He was especially dismayed by discriminatory practices he encountered from bigoted whites who were in positions of power and could control the careers of black musicians and his own relatively small legacy of recordings is probably not unconnected with the fact that he was never afraid to speak out when he felt injustice was being done.

Selected albums: *Lucky Thompson Featuring Oscar Pettiford* (1956), *Lucky Thompson & Gerard Pochonet Et Son Quartette* (1956), *Lucky Standards* (1956), *Lucky Thompson* (1963), *Lucky Thompson Plays Jerome Kern And No More* (1963), *Lucky Strikes* (Original Jazz Classics 1965), *Happy Days Are Here Again* (1965), *Lucky Thompson In Switzerland* (1969) *A Lucky Songbook In Europe* (1969), *I Offer You* (1973), *Brown Rose* (1985, rec. 1956). Compilations: *Dancing Sunbeam* (1975, rec. 1956), *Body And Soul* (1978, rec. 1970), *Paris 1956 Volume One* (1985, rec. 1956), *Illuminations* (1974), *Lucky Sessions* (Vogue 1993).

Thompson, Barbara

b. 27 July 1944, Oxford, England. Classically trained at the Royal College of Music in London, where she studied flute, clarinet, piano and composition between 1965 and 1968, Thompson had private tuition on the saxophone before joining **Neil Ardley**'s New Jazz Orchestra in 1965, her first professional jazz gig. She performed and recorded intermittently with the National Jazz Orchestra until 1978, and met her future husband, drummer **Jon Hiseman**, while both were members of the band. From 1969, Thompson lead various groups of her own, working with musicians including **John Dankworth**, **Don Rendell** and **Manfred Mann**. In 1975 she formed the jazz-rock group Paraphernalia, which has been the main outlet for her compositional and performing skills. Mixing a range of musics as diverse as Sri Lankan folk tunes, English country music and modern jazz, Paraphernalia has toured extensively throughout Europe and performed at many of the continent's major jazz festivals. Away from Paraphernalia, Thompson has been a member of the United Rock And Jazz Ensemble since 1975, and an active session musician - performing on the albums of **Andrew Lloyd Webber**'s *Variations*, *Cats* and *Requiem* - and from 1973-80 led a Latin-jazz outfit called Jubiaba. In 1988, her *Concert For Saxophone And Orchestra* was premiered in Germany; she has also written three long works for a 20-piece jazz orchestra. With Hiseman, she tours, she runs Temple Music, a music publishing company, and maintains a 24-track studio at their house in Surrey. Paraphernalia re-groups and tours occasionally, always to find a receptive following, especially in Germany where she is rightly appreciated.

Albums: *Barbara Thompson's Paraphernalia* (1978), *Jubiaba* (MCA 1978), *Wilde Tales* (MCA 1979), *Live In Concert* (1980), *Mother Earth* (Verabra 1983), *Ghosts* (1983), *Pure Fantasy* (TM 1984), *Shadowshow* (1984), *Heavenly Bodies* (Verabra 1986), *Lady Saxophone* (1986), *Special Edition* (Verabra 1987), *A Cry From The Heart* (Verabra 1987), *Breathless* (Verabra 1991), *Songs From The Center Of The Earth* (Black Sun 1991), *Everlasing Flame* (Verabra 1993).

Thompson, Butch

b. 28 November 1943, Marine, Minnesota, USA. Thompson began playing piano as a child and in his late teens became a member of a popular New

Orleans-style band in Minneapolis. The band regularly accompanied such leading New Orleans jazzmen as **George Lewis**, **Kid Thomas** and **Pops Foster**. Thompson also formed his own small group which worked extensively on radio, achieving considerable popularity. During the 70s Thompson began to tour internationally. He also worked with the New Orleans Ragtime Orchestra and his own band dedicated to the music of **King Oliver**. Thompson's dedication to a tradition that was vintage long before he was born, has ensured that an important strand of jazz piano history remains extant. A sparkling player in the idiom of New Orleans, Thompson regularly revives the music of **Jelly Roll Morton**, Oliver and other past masters. In recent years he has often worked with several unsung musicians with similarly dedicated concepts, including cornetist Charles DeVore and drummer Hal Smith.

Selected albums: *Kid Thomas At San Jacinto Hall* (1965), *A'Solas* (1981), *Echoes from Storyville* (1984), *Live From The Shattuck Hotel* (1985), *King Oliver's Centennial Band* (1988), *New Orleans Joys* (1989), *Chicago Breakdown* (1989), *Good Old New York* (1989), *Plays Favorites* (Solo Art 1993), *Minnesota Wonder* (Daring 1993).

Thompson, Charles, Sir

b. 12 March 1918, Springfield, Ohio, USA. After starting out on violin Thompson switched to piano and was playing professionally by his mid-teenage years. During the mid- to late 30s he played with several notable **territory bands** in the southwest, including that led by Nat Towles. In 1940 he was briefly with **Lionel Hampton**'s big band but preferred small group work, although he regularly wrote arrangements for musicians including **Count Basie** and **Jimmy Dorsey**. During the 40s and 50s he worked with leading jazzmen such as **Lester Young** (who bestowed upon him the title by which he was subsequently known), **Coleman Hawkins**, **Illinois Jacquet**, **Jimmy Rushing** and **Buck Clayton**, the last an especially important musical associate. Through the 60s he continued playing with **Roy Eldridge**, Clayton and other major artists, and also led his own groups, often switching to organ. Poor health slowed his career in the 70s but by the 80s he was back on the scene again, playing at numerous venues around the world. A particularly effective ensemble player, Thompson's work in the Clayton bands of the mid-50s ably demonstrated his understated skills. His solos display a calm assurance, a largely unused affinity for the blues and a delicate touch on ballads. 'Robbins' Nest', a jazz standard, is his composition.

Albums: *Bop This* (1953), *Buck Clayton Jam Sessions* (1953-54), *The Sir Charles Thompson Quartet/For The Ears* (1954-55), *Sir Charles Thompson With Coleman Hawkins* (1954), *The Sir Charles Thompson Trio* (1955), *The Sir Charles Thompson Quintet* (1960), with Buck Clayton *Kansas City Nights* (1960-61), *Rockin' Rhythm* (1961), with Roy Eldridge *Trumpet Summit* (1967), *Hey, There!* (1974), *Sweet And Lovely* (1977), *Portrait Of A Piano* (1984), *Robbins' Nest* (1993).

Thompson, Danny

b. April 1939, London, England. An expressive, inventive double bass player, Thompson became established in British jazz circles through his work with **Tubby Hayes**. In 1964 he joined **Alexis Korner**'s Blues Incorporated where he would forge an intuitive partnership with drummer Terry Cox. Three years later the duo formed the rhythm section in **Pentangle**, a folk 'supergroup' which featured singer Jacquie McShee and guitarists **John Renbourn** and **Bert Jansch**. Thompson remained with this seminal quintet until their demise in 1972 but had forged a concurrent career as a leading session musician. He appeared on releases by **Donovan**, **Cliff Richard** ('Congratulations') and **Rod Stewart** ('Maggie May'), but was acclaimed for peerless contributions to albums by folksingers **Nick Drake** and **John Martyn**. The bassist's collaborations with the latter were particularly of note (and their legendary drinking sessions) and their working relationship spanned several excellent albums, including *Solid Air*, *Inside Out* and *Live At Leeds*. A notorious imbiber, Thompson then found his workload and confidence diminishing. He successfully conquered his alcohol problem and resumed session work with typically excellent contributions to releases by **Kate Bush**, **David Sylvian** and **Talk Talk**. In 1987 the bassist formed his own group, Whatever, and recorded new age and world music collections. In the 90s his remarkable dexterity was heard on regular tours with **Richard Thompson**, the only criticism received was that Thompson (Danny) should have been given a microphone in addition to Thonmpson (Richard) as the inter-song banter was hilarious. He remains a leading instrumentalist, respected for his sympathetic and emotional style on the stand up bass. Thompson is a giant, both in stature and in his contribution to jazz and rock or whatever. Should the music ever desert him, Thompson could carve a career as a stand-up comic.

Albums: *Whatever* (1987), *Whatever Next* (1989), with Toumani Diabate and Ketama *Songhai* (1989).

Thompson, Eddie

b. 31 May 1925, London, England, d. 6 November 1986. Born blind, Thompson learned to play piano as a child. In the late 40s he was active in London clubs, playing with Carlo Krahmer, **Vic Feldman** and others. In the 50s he played on radio, in studio bands, made records under his own name and with **Tony Crombie**, **Tommy Whittle**, **Freddy Randall** and others and by the end of the decade was house pianist at **Ronnie Scott**'s club. In the early 60s he went to the USA to live, playing regularly at the Hickory House in

New York. Back in the UK in the early 70s, he led a trio which toured extensively and frequently backed visiting American jazzmen, including **Buddy Tate**, **Ruby Braff** and **Spike Robinson**. A dazzlingly inventive player in his early days, Thompson sometimes delivered bravura performances at the expense of feeling but in his maturity he made many memorable appearances at concerts around the UK. He had an enormous repertoire and when in musical sympathy with a guest he could be the best of accompanists. His solo playing was long overlooked by record companies but Alastair Robertson of Hep Records compensated for this with some excellent sessions in the early 80s. Thompson's death at the age of 61 came when he was at the height of his powers.

Selected albums: *I Hear Music* (Dormouse 1956), *By Myself* (77 1970), *Some Strings, Some Skins And A Bunch Of Keys* (c.1975), *Dutch Treat* (1976), *Ain't She Sweet* (1978), *When Lights Are Low* (1980), *Memories Of You* (1983), with Roy Williams *When The Lights Are Low* (Hep Jazz 1988).

Thompson, Errol

b. c.1952, Kingston, Jamaica, West Indies. Thompson began working for **Joel Gibson** following in the footsteps of **Lee Perry** who had ventured into his own Black Ark Recording Studio. Thompson was working alongside **Winston 'Niney' Holness** at Randy's Studio in North Parade as a recording engineer. With **Joe Gibbs** as the producer and Thompson as the engineer they had a run of hits for most of the 70s. Early in the 70s they had hits with, **Peter Tosh** ('Maga Dog'), **Dennis Brown** ('Money In My Pocket'), **Big Youth** ('Foreman Vs Frazier') and **Delroy Wilson** ('Pretty Girl'). The early hits were recorded in a two track studio at the back of Gibbs' record shop but the duo's success led to a relocation to North Parade, known as Joe Gibbs Record Globe. The site was used in the film *Rockers* when Leroy 'Horsemouth' Wallace tries to negotiate a deal with Gibbs at the studio to set up his own distribution network. At the new studio the duo became known as the Mighty Two and Thompson's more prominent role as the producer for Joe Gibbs productions was acknowledged by the formation of the Errol T and Belmont labels. By the mid-70s many artists had had hits produced by the Mighty Two, including **Culture** ('Two Sevens Clash'), Bobby Melody ('Jah Bring I Joy'), **Trinity** ('Three Piece Suit'), Ruddy Thomas ('Loving Pauper'), **Prince Far I** ('Heavy Manners'), Big Youth ('Equal Rights Style') and Dennis Brown ('Money In My Pocket'). Brown's remake entered the UK Top 20 in 1979, but was preceded in 1977 by the number 1 hit 'Up Town Top Ranking' by **Althea And Donna** which had 'Calico Suit' credited to the Mighty Two on the b-side. The duo continued to dominate the reggae charts with a number of Dennis Brown albums and a series of dub albums notably the *African Dub* series. By the late 70s/early 80s the duo worked with **Eek A Mouse** 'Virgin Girl' and **Yellowman** 'Which One A Dem A Wear De Ring'. Joe Gibbs left for Miami in the early 80s and by 1983 Thompson was found beaten to death in a Kingston alley. He had fathered three children with **Marcia Griffiths**.

Album: *The Mighty Two* (Heartbeat 1990).

Thompson, Hank

b. Henry William Thompson, 3 September 1925, Waco, Texas, USA. Thompson, as a young boy, was fond of records by **Jimmie Rodgers** and the **Carter Family**. He first learned the harmonica and then his parents gave him a guitar for his tenth birthday. He also played Hawaiian guitar, learned conjuring tricks and had a ventriloquist's doll. With his range of talents, he was a popular performer at Saturday morning stage shows in Waco. In 1942, he began his own local radio series, *Hank - The Hired Hand*. From 1943 Thompson served three years in the US navy. He worked as an electrical engineer and, in his spare time, he entertained his shipmates. He says, 'The navy enhanced my career as it gave the opportunity to perform all the time. When I was overseas, I knew the guys were getting tired of hearing the same songs and so I started writing.' In 1946, he returned to Waco, formed the Brazos Valley Boys (named after the river running through Waco), and began performing at dances throughout Texas. His own song, 'Whoa Sailor', was a regional hit on Globe Records. It was followed by 'A Lonely Heart Knows' on Bluebonnet. Country star **Tex Ritter** heard Thompson and recommended him to his label, **Capitol**. Almost immediately, Thompson had a number 2 country hit with '(I've Got A) Humpty Dumpty Heart'. In 1949 he had another country hit with a re-recorded 'Whoa Sailor'. Thompson was a tall, upright performer with a resonant voice not unlike Ritter's, who dressed himself and his band in expensive Nudie suits. Applying his engineering knowledge, he gave the band a powerful live sound and lighting, and soon he had the most successful western swing band in the USA.

In 1951 Thompson began a 13-year partnership with the Hollywood record producer Ken Nelson and recorded his most successful single, 'The Wild Side Of Life', in one take. (Ironically 'Crying In The Deep Blue Sea' was the original a-side). 'The Wild Side Of Life' stayed at the top of the US country charts for 15 weeks and won Thompson a gold record. **Kitty Wells** recorded an answer version, 'It Wasn't God Who Made Honky Tonk Angels', while Thompson himself answered 'Goodnight, Irene' with 'Wake Up, Irene'. Defying conventions, Thompson was permitted to repeat its snare drum sound on the *Grand Ole Opry*. Thompson had further country hits with 'Waiting In The Lobby Of Your Heart', 'Rub-A-Dub-Dub', 'Breakin' The Rules', 'Honky Tonk Girl', 'The

Blackboard Of My Heart', and 'Breakin' In Another Heart', which was co-written with his wife Dorothy. In 1957 Thompson parodied rock 'n' roll in 'Rockin' In The Congo' and became a successful performer in Las Vegas. He heard 'Squaws Along The Yukon' on a hunting trip in Alaska with **Merle Travis** and together they arranged and updated the song. In 1959 became the first country artist to record in stereo via the best-selling *Songs For Rounders*, and the first to record an 'in concert' album, *Live At The Golden Nugget*. He heard a band in a club in Holbrook, Arizona and was most impressed with their original song, 'A Six Pack To Go'. He turned the song into a country standard, later reviving it in duet with **George Strait**, and had further country hits with 'She's Just A Whole Lot Like You' and 'Oklahoma Hills'. Since Thompson left Capitol in 1964, he has recorded for several labels and his country hits have included 'Smokey The Bar', 'Where Is The Circus?', 'The Older The Violin, The Sweeter The Music' and, appropriately, 'Mr. Honky Tonk, The King Of Western Swing'. He has recorded tribute albums to the **Mills Brothers** (*Cab Driver*) and **Nat 'King' Cole**. In 1973 Thompson opened a school of country music in Claremore, Oklahoma, where he taught. He was elected to the *Country Music Hall Of Fame* in 1989, and still tours throughout the world, wearing his sequinned jackets: 'The public is entitled to something that is colourful and flashy. We're in show business and there's nothing colourful about a T-shirt and ragged jeans.'
Albums: *Songs Of The Brazos Valley* (1953), *North Of The Rio Grande* (1955), *New Recordings Of All Time Hits* (1956), *Favourite Waltzes* (1956), *Hank Thompson Favourites* (1957), *Hank!* (1957), *Dance Ranch* (1958), *Songs For Rounders* (1959), *Most Of All* (1960), *This Broken Heart Of Mine* (1960), *An Old Love Affair* (1961), *At The Golden Nugget* (1961), *A Six Pack To Go* (1961), *No. 1 Country And Western Band* (1962), *Live At The Cherokee Frontier Days Rodeo In Wyoming* (1962), *Live At The State Fair Of Texas* (1963), *It's Christmas Time With Hank* (1964), *Breakin' In Another Heart* (1965), *Breakin' The Rules* (1966), *The Countrypolitan Sound Of Hank Thompson's Brazos Valley Boys* (1967), *Just An Old Flame* (1967), *Country Blues* (1968), *Hank Thompson Sings The Gold Standards* (1968), *On Tap, In The Can Or In The Bottle* (1968), *Smokey The Bar* (1969), *Salutes Oklahoma* (1969), *The Instrumental Sound Of Hank Thompson's Brazos Valley Boys* (1970), *Next Time I Fall In Love (I Won't)* (1971), *Cab Driver - A Salute To The Mills Brothers* (1972), *1000 And One Nighters* (1973), *Kindly Keep It Country* (1973), *Movin' On* (1974), *Hank Thompson Sings The Hits Of Nat 'King' Cole* (1975), *Back In The Swing Of Things* (1976), *The Thompson Touch* (1977), with Roy Clark, Freddy Fender and Don Williams *Country Comes To Carnegie Hall* (1977), *Doin' My Thing* (1977), *Brand New Hank* (1978), *Take Me Back To Texas* (1980), *Hank Thompson* (1986), *Here's To Country Music* (1988). Compilations: *Where Is The Circus (And Other Heart Breakin' Hits)* (1966), *A Gold Standard Collection* (1967), *25th Anniversary Album* (1972), *Best Of The Best Of Hank Thompson* (1980), *Greatest Hits, Volumes 1 & 2* (1987).

Thompson, Joe And Odell

b. 9 December 1918 and 9 August 1911 respectively, Mebane, North Carolina, USA. Joe (fiddler) and Odell Thompson (banjoist) are first cousins whose fathers were musicians on the same instruments. Odell took up blues and the guitar in the 20s, but continued to play the older repertoire with his cousin in local stringbands until the 40s. As this style lost popularity, they retired until the early 70s, when a folklore researcher persuaded them to perform in public once more. Much of their repertoire was derived from their fathers, so that they preserved the music of the pre-World War I black string band; as possibly the last black fiddle-banjo duo performing, it was an unexpected bonus that they were still vigorous and skilful musicians.
Album: *Old Time Music From The North Carolina Piedmont* (1989).

Thompson, Linval

b. c.1959, Kingston, Jamaica. Thompson was raised in Queens, New York, and at the age of sixteen recorded 'No Other Woman'. On returning to Jamaica he began recording with Phil Pratt, although little surfaced on vinyl from these sessions. Having declined the opportunity to record with **Bunny Lee** following an introduction by his long time friend **Johnny Clarke**, he recorded a **dub plate** with Tippertone. Back in New York he resumed his studies in engineering but was soon drawn back towards the music business. Due to the increasing demand for reggae in the US Linval had a fruitful business in supplying fresh rhythms to record buyers, and his success led him back to Jamaica. On his return he recorded 'Kung Fu Fighting' with manic producer **Lee Perry**, which announced the onset of a prolific career. Encouraged by the sales of 'Don't Cut Off Your Dreadlocks', produced by **Bunny Lee**, the album, including the title-track, also appeared in the UK. Linval began to produce his own material and a contract with **Trojan Records** led to the release of *I Love Marijuana* and its dub version, *Negrea Love Dub*, both of which enjoyed healthy sales. Establishing his notoriety as a producer his services were enrolled by Cornell Campbell, the **Wailing Souls**, the **Viceroys, Tapper Zukie, Barrington Levy, Trinity, Ranking Dread** and Roman Stewart. Ranking Dread's set included DJ versions of Linval's own 'I Love Marijuana' as 'Marijuana In My Soul', and 'Africa Is For Blackman' as 'Africa'. The DJ was to hit the UK headlines following suggestions that he was a member of the 'Yardies', supposedly a criminal West Indian organisation, although Yardie simply refers to someone from Jamaica, i.e. 'Back A Yard'. Thompson was carving out quite a niche, with his productions appearing on a plethora of labels in the UK. His sessions with **Trinity** led to the release of *Rock In The Ghetto* through Trojan, whilst lifted from the same set **Greensleeves Records** released 'Don't Try To Use Me'. In 1983 the release of *Baby Father* included the classic 'Shouldn't Lift Your Hand', a track which condemned violence against women with lyrics stating: 'You shouldn't lift your feet to kick the young lady, You shouldn't lift your hand to lick the young girlie'. Further illustrating his entrepreneurial skills a partnership in the UK was formed with Mikey Scott for the Strong Like Sampson and Thompson Koos record labels to distribute his output.

Albums: *Don't Cut Off Your Dreadlocks* (Third World 1976), *I Love Marijuana* (Trojan 1978), *I Love Jah* (Burning Sounds 1979), *If I Follow My Heart* (Burning Sounds 1980), *Look How Me Sexy* (Greensleeves 1982), *Baby Father* (Greensleeves 1983) *Starlight* (Mango 1989).

Thompson, Richard

b. 3 April 1949, Totteridge & Whetsone, London, England. The incredibly talented Thompson forged his reputation as guitarist, vocalist and composer with **Fairport Convention** which, although initially dubbed 'England's **Jefferson Airplane**', later evolved into the seminal folk-rock act through such acclaimed releases as *What We Did On Our Holidays* (1968), *Unhalfbricking* (1968), *Liege And Leif* (1969) and *Full House* (1970). Thompson's sensitive compositions graced all of the above but none have been applauded more than 'Meet On the Ledge'. This simple lilting song oozes with restraint, class and emotion and is one of the most evocative songs to come out of the late 60's 'underground' music scene. Thompson's innovative guitar style brought a distinctive edge to their work as he harnessed such diverse influences as **Django Reinhart**, **Charlie Christian**, **Otis Rush**, **James Burton** and **Mike Bloomfield**. The guitarist left the group in 1971 and having contributed to two related projects, *The Bunch* and *Morris On*, completed an impressive solo debut, *Henry The Human Fly*. He then forged a professional partnership with his wife, Linda Peters and, as **Richard And Linda Thompson**, recorded a series of excellent albums, notably *I Want To See The Bright Lights Tonight* (1974), and *Hokey Pokey* which established the artist's reputation for incisive, descriptive compositions. Richard also collaborated with such disparate vocalists as **Sandy Denny**, **John Martyn**, **Iain Matthews**, **Elvis Costello** and **Pere Ubu**'s **David Thomas**, which in turn enhanced his already considerable reputation.

The Thompsons separated in 1982, although the guitarist had completed his second solo album, *Strict Tempo*, a compendium of styles based on hornpipes, jigs and reels, the previous year. An in-concert set, *Small Town Romance* followed, before the artist recorded the acclaimed *Hand Of Kindness* and *Across The Crowded Room*,

the latter of which featured the embittered 'She Twists The Knife Again'. In 1986 Thompson undertook extensive US and UK tours to promote *Daring Adventures*, leading a group which included (Clive) **Gregson And** (Christine) **Collister**. He then completed the soundtrack to *The Marksman*, a BBC television series, before joining John French, Fred Frith and **Henry Kaiser** for the experimental *Live, Love, Larf And Loaf*. In 1988 Thompson switched outlets to **Capitol Records**. Thompson recorded with the **Golden Palominos** in 1991 and the same year performed with **David Byrne**. *Watching The Dark* is a three CD set covering Thompson's career, it puts into perspective what an important figure was, is and will continue to be. His own painful modesty underlies a masterful lyricist an outstanding guitarist and a major songwriter. Quite what this man has to do to receive commercial success will forever remain a mystery.

Albums: *Henry The Human Fly* (1972), *Strict Tempo* (1981), *Small Town Romance* (1982), *Hand Of Kindness* (1984), *Across A Crowded Room* (1985), *Daring Adventures* (1986), *The Marksman* (1987), *Amnesia* (1988), *Rumour And Sigh* (1990), *Sweet Talker* (1992), *Mirror Blue* (Capitol 1994). Compilation: *Watching The Dark* 3CD box set (Hannibal 1993).

Further reading: *Meet On the Ledge*, Humphries, Patrick, *Richard Thompson: 21 Years Of Doom & Gloom*, Heylin, Clinton (1988), *Gypsy Love Songs & Sad Refrains: The Recordings Of Richard Thompson & Sandy Denn*, Heylin, Clinton (1989).

Thompson, Richard And Linda

This husband-and-wife folk/rock duo began performing together officially in 1972 although their association dated from the previous year. When **Richard Thompson** (b. 3 April 1949, Totteridge & Whetsone, London, England; guitar/vocals) left **Fairport Convention**, he pursued a generally low-key path, performing in folk clubs and on various sessions, including *Rock On*, a collection of rock 'n' roll favourites which featured several Fairport acolytes. 'When Will I Be Loved?' was marked by a duet between **Sandy Denny** and Linda Peters, the latter of whom then provided vocals on Thompson's *Henry The Human Fly*. Richard and Linda then began a professional, and personal, relationship, introduced on *I Want To See The Bright Lights Tonight*. This excellent album contained several of Richard's best-known compositions, including the title track, 'Cavalry Cross' and the despondent 'End Of The Rainbow': 'Life seems so rosy in the cradle, but I'll be a friend, I'll tell you what's in store/There's nothing at the end of the rainbow/There's nothing to grow up for anymore'. The Thompsons toured with former-Fairport guitarist **Simon Nicol** as Hokey Pokey, which in turn evolved into a larger, more emphatic unit, Sour Grapes. The former group inspired the title of a second enthralling album which blended humour with social comment. Its release was the prelude to a frenetic period which culminated in *Pour Down Like Silver*, the Thompson's second album within 12 months. It reflected the couple's growing interest in the Sufi faith, but despite a sombre reputation, the set included several excellent compositions.

A three year hiatus in the Thompson's career ensued, broken only in 1977 by a series of live performances accompanied by fellow converts Ian Whiteman, Roger Powell and Mick Evans, all previously with **Mighty Baby**. Now signed to the **Chrysalis** label, *First Light* provided a welcome return and many commentators rate this album as the duo's finest. The follow-up release, *Sunnyvista*, was in comparison, a disappointment, despite the inclusion of the satiric title track and the angry and passionate 'You're Going To Need Somebody'. However, it led to the duo's departure from their record label. This second, if enforced, break ended with the superb *Shoot Out The Lights*, nominated by **Rolling Stone** as the best album of 1982. Indeed such a response suggested the Thompsons would now secure widespread success and they embarked on a US tour to consolidate this newly-won recognition. Despite this, the couple's marriage was breaking up and in June 1982 the duo made their final appearance together at Sheffield's South Yorkshire Folk Festival. Richard Thompson then resumed his critically-acclaimed solo career, while Linda went on to record *One Clear Moment* (1985).

Albums: *I Want To See The Bright Lights Tonight* (1974), *Hokey Pokey* (1975), *Pour Down Like Silver* (1975), *First Light* (1978), *Sunnyvista* (1979), *Shoot Out The Lights* (1982).

Thompson, Sonny

b. Alphonso Thompson, 22 August 1916, Centreville, Mississippi, USA, d. 11 August 1989. This long-time Chicago-based R&B bandleader and pianist first recorded boogie woogies in 1946 for the Detroit-based Sultan label. After signing for the Miracle label in Chicago, he scored with 'Long Gone', which went to number 1 on the R&B chart in 1948. The gently rolling instrumental set the tone for his later hits, 'Late Freight' (R&B number 1, 1948), 'Blue Dreams' (R&B number 10, 1949) and 'Mellow Blues' (R&B number 8, 1952). His later chart records featured the vocals of his wife, Lulu Reed, notably 'I'll Drown In My Tears' and 'Let's Call It A Day', both from 1952. Thompson worked largely as a session musician during the 50s, and in 1959 succeeded Ralph Bass as an A&R director for King Records' Chicago office. After the closure of the King office in 1964, Thompson continued session work and made occasional tours of Europe.

Albums: *Moody Blues* (1956), *Mellow Blues For The Late Hours* (1959), with Freddy King and Lulu Reed *Boy, Girl, Boy* (1962), *Swings In Paris* (1974). Compilation: *Cat On The Keys* (1988).

Thompson, Sue

b. Eva Sue McKee, 19 July 1926, Nevada, Missouri, USA. Sue's earliest ambition was to be a singing cowgirl, and she sang at many local functions. She continued performing when the family moved to California and she appeared regularly on a Dude Martin's country television show in San Francisco. A single with Martin, 'If You Want Some Lovin'', led to a solo contract with **Mercury Records**. In 1960, she sang on **Red Foley**'s portion of the *Grand Ole Opry* and she signed with the country label, Hickory. **John D. Loudermilk** wrote 'Sad Movies (Make Me Cry)' and 'Norman', which went to numbers 5 and 3 respectively on the US pop charts and both became million-sellers. **Boudleaux** and **Felice Bryant** wrote another US hit, 'Have A Good Time', and Loudermilk returned with the novelties, 'James (Hold The Ladder Steady)' and 'Paper Tiger'. Despite her American success, Thompson only had two minor Top 50 entries in the UK, but she was unlucky as **Carol Deene** covered all three Loudermilk songs. Through her novelty songs she became known as 'the girl with the itty bitty voice', so she turned to more mature material. In the 70s she was teamed with **Don Gibson**, the two registering nine US country successes including 'The Two Of Us Together' and 'Oh How Love Changes'. Her last significant country success was with 'Big Mabel Murphy' in 1975. She married singer Hank Penny.

Albums: *Meet Sue Thompson* (1962), *Two Of A Kind* (1962), *Paper Tiger* (1962), *With Strings Attached* (1966), *Country Side Of Sue Thompson* (1966), *This Is Sue Thompson* (1969), *And Love Me* (1974), *Sweet Memories* (1974), *Big Mabel Murphy* (1975). With Don Gibson: *The 2 Of Us Together* (1973), *Warm Love* (1974), *Oh How Love Changes* (1975).

Thompson, Uncle Jimmie

b. James Donald Thompson, 1848, near Baxter, Smith County, Tennessee, USA. Little is known of his early life except that the family moved to Texas just before the Civil War, and by 1860 Thompson was already a capable fiddle player using a style described as the long bow technique, common to the state. He learned tunes from Civil War veterans and other sources and though generally described as a farmer, he travelled extensively. He returned to Smith County, Tennessee probably in the early 1880s, where he married a local girl. Around 1902 Thompson and his family returned to Texas. By this time he was playing more public performances and in 1907 he won an eight-day fiddling contest in Dallas. It was probably 1912, when he once more returned to Tennessee and bought a farm near Henderson. His wife died soon afterwards but in 1916 he remarried and moved to Laguardo, Wilson County. He acquired an old truck, which he adapted as a mobile caravan and began to tour the state playing his fiddle at fairs or wherever he could make a dollar. He was always a hard drinking man and stubborn in his ways. About 1923 he drove all the way back to Texas just to take part in a fiddling contest. At the age of 77 his wish to broadcast came true when **George D. Hay** made him the first artist on his new *WSM Barn Dance* programme that was to become the *Grand Ole Opry*. He boasted that he could play a thousand tunes and was deeply upset when he found that his niece Eva made him have his trousers pressed for the occasion. His comment was 'Hey, thar, who ironed them damn wrinkles im my britches? I like my britches smooth and round to fit my kneecaps.' Following his broadcast, Uncle Jimmie became somewhat of a celebrity, with his eccentricity endearing him to many people. Some of his habits did not endear him to George D. Hay, particularly his likeness for a jug of local moonshine 'just to lubricate his arm' nor his seeming inability to play to his allotted time without considerably over-running.

By 1927, with the emergence of many new artists, his *Opry* appearances were very limited. He first recorded in Atlanta for **Columbia** in 1926 and later in 1930 recorded in Knoxville for **Brunswick**/Vocalion. Experts comment that he was still a player of great ability when he made his last recordings. He died from pneumonia at his home in Laguardo, Tennessee on 17 February 1931. Eva Thompson Jones was the only member of the *Opry* cast to attend his funeral. He once stayed at Eva's house in Nashville and when later asked how he liked it he replied, 'I wouldn't have it, there ain't nowhere for to spit when I chew my tobacco'. Examples of his recorded work may be found on various compilation albums of early string band and country music.

Further reading: *The Grand Ole Opry (The Early Years 1925-35)*, Charles K. Wolfe.

Thoms, Shirley

b. 12 January 1925, Toowoomba, Queensland, Australia. She grew up on a farm and was singing and yodelling the songs of **Buddy Williams** and **Tex Morton**, that she heard on the radio, by her early teens. In 1940, she won a radio talent competition with her version of Harry Torrani's 'Mocking Bird Yodel'. This success led to her first six recordings for Regal-Zonophone, made in Sydney, on 27 May 1941. She wrote her own material and they included 'Where The Golden Wattle Blooms'. They soon proved popular and six more recordings quickly followed, including her version of 'Mother's Old Red Shawl'. She toured with various shows, including Sole Bros Circus and during World War II, she was also very popular as a member of an army entertainment unit. Between 1942 and 1946, she recorded 20 more sides, including her weepy 'The Faithful Old Dog' for the same label. She married John Sole in 1950 and nominally retired, although she recorded six sides for the Rodeo label in 1952. Her son Peter was born in 1956 but in 1958 her husband died. She later married a veterinary surgeon and although the marriage failed, she acquired an interest in veterinary science. She has also written on philosophy and designed and built herself a palatial home in Sydney. In 1970, she was persuaded to appear at the Tamworth Festival. She also returned to the recording studios, this time for Hadley, where she soon proved that her voice had lost none of its appeal, nor had she lost her ability to yodel with the best. (Her Austrian born grandfather had always stoutly maintained her ability to yodel was hereditary). Although her recorded output was not large, she has the unique distinction of being the first female Australian country singer to make solo recordings, as well as being the first Queenslander to make a record. She sang with a plaintiveness similar to **Kitty Wells** and her original 78 recordings are still highly sought after by collectors. However, during the 70s, all her original Regal-Zonophone recordings were re-issued (in recording order) on three albums. In 1980, she became the fifth artist but the first female performer to be elected to the Country Music Roll Of Renown (Australia's equivalent to Nashville's Country Music Hall Of Fame).

Albums: *Australia's Yodelling Sweetheart* (Hadley 1970), *Shirley Thoms* (Hadley 1972), *The Complete Shirley Thoms Collection Volumes 1, 2* and *3* (Hadley 70s, covers 1941-46).

Thor

b. Jon-Mikl Thor. This body builder turned singer who took his name from a Marvel comic character, was a former Mr. Teenage USA, Mr. Canada and Mr. North America. His band consisted of vocalist Pantera (b. Rusty Hamilton, a former model), Steve Price (guitar), Keith Zazzi (bass) and Mike Favata (drums). Their debut release, *Keep The Dogs Away*, appeared on the Three Hats Record label in 1978. This album was an uneventful affair of basic hard rock/heavy metal which, even at the time of its release, sounded dated. Thor then took quite a long break until returning with the release of a mini-album, *Unchained*, in 1984. Then came Thor's most successful album, *Only The Strong*, released on Roadrunner in 1985. Much attention was paid to Thor's live party-piece - where, by blowing into it, he expanded and burst a rubber hot-water bottle (often with the claim 'let's see **Michael Jackson** do this'). Other 'theatricals' included staged clashes between Norse gods, with Thor replendent in spiked body armour, wielding a mighty (plastic) sword or bearded axe. All conducted without the tiniest trace of irony, and an almost camp machismo from the group's frontman. 1985 proved an eventful year for Thor as not only did he have two singles, 'Let The Blood Run Red' and 'Thunder On The Tundra' (both from *Only The Strong*), released, but also a live album, *Live In Detroit*.

That year also saw him enter the film world appearing in and writing the soundtrack for *Recruits*. Part of the soundtrack formed the basis for Thor's next release, *Recruits: Wild In The Streets*. That marked the end of Thor's musical aspirations as he once again turned his attention to the movie business by appearing in *Zombie Nightmare* alongside original *Batman* star, Adam West.
Albums: *Keep The Dogs Away* (Three Hats 1978), *Unchained* (Ultra Noise 1984, mini-album), *Only The Strong* (Roadrunner 1985), *Live In Detroit* (Raw Power 1985), *Recruits: Wild In The Streets* (Roadrunner 1986). Video: *Live In London* (1985).

Thorn, Tracey

(see **Marine Girls** and **Everything But The Girl**)

Thornhill, Claude

b. 10 August 1909, Terra Haute, Indiana, USA, d. 1 July 1965. Thornhill studied piano formally, playing jazz with a friend, **Danny Polo**. In the early 30s he was resident in New York City, playing with **Hal Kemp**, Don Voorhees, **Paul Whiteman**, **Benny Goodman** and many other leaders. In the mid-30s he worked with **Ray Noble** and **Andre Kostelanetz**. Later in the decade he was busily writing arrangements for several bands and singers, and one song recorded by **Maxine Sullivan** ('Loch Lomond') was a huge hit. His successes for others led him to form his own band, hiring emerging talents such as **Lee Konitz**, **Red Rodney** and **Gerry Mulligan**, while his arranging staff included **Gil Evans**, who would later frequently assert how much his time with Thornhill had influenced his writing. In his 1940 band Thornhill sought perfect intonation from his musicians and balance between the sections. He urged his sidemen to eliminate vibrato, aiding this effect by adding French horns, themselves essentially vibratoless instruments. The resulting pastel-shaded musical patterns and sustained chords, against which Thornhill made delicate solo statements on piano, was in striking contrast to the sound of other big bands of the period. Ill health forced him to disband in 1948, but he returned to playing in the 50s and continued on an occasional basis until his sudden death in July 1965. Lasting testimony to Thornhill lies in the arranging styles of both Evans and Mulligan, both of whom long afterwards pursued concepts and sounds rooted in Thornhill's band of the early 40s.
Selected albums: *One Night Stand With Claude Thornhill* (1950), *Claude Thornhill And His Orchestra* i (1953), *Claude Thornhill And His Orchestra* ii (1956), *Claude On A Cloud* (1958), *Claude Thornhill And His Orchestra* iii (1959), *Claude Thornhill And His Orchestra* iv (1963). Compilations: *The Real Birth Of The Cool* (1942-47), *Claude Thornhill* (1947), *The Uncollected Claude Thornhill* (1947), *The Song Is You* (Hep Jazz 1981, 1948-49 recordings), *Tapestries* (Charly

1987, 1937-47 recordings), *Snowfall* (Fresh Sounds 1988).

Thornton, James

b. 5 December 1861, Liverpool, England, d. 27 July 1938. Growing up in the USA, where his family emigrated when he was eight-years-old, Thornton was raised in Boston. He worked there as a singing waiter before moving to New York to do much the same kind of thing. He married the singer Lizzie Cox, who inspired him to write many of his best songs. Unfortunately, Thornton's songwriting was interrupted by bouts of serious drinking which were themselves interspersed with periods drying out in New York's Bellevue Hospital. For a while Thornton worked in vaudeville in a double act with Charles Lawlor. Thornton's wife popularized some of his songs in her vaudeville act, among them 'My Sweetheart's The Man In The Moon' and 'When You Were Sweet Sixteen'. This last song was a huge popular success, sheet music sales running into a fortune. Sadly, Thornton's drinking habits frequently led him to sell his work outright for ready cash. This was the case with 'Sweet Sixteen' which, in fact, he sold to two different publishers at the same time, netting a grand total of $40 and a law suit. Thornton's sentimental ballads fell out of favour and although he had minor successes with 'The Bridge Of Sighs', 'On The Benches In The Park' and 'There's A Mother Waiting For You At Home, Sweet Home' his days as a songwriter waned after the turn of the century.

Thornton, Willie Mae 'Big Mama'

b. 11 December 1926, Montgomery, Alabama, USA, d. 25 July 1984. Thornton was the daughter of a minister and learned drums and harmonica as a child. By the early 40s she was singing and dancing in Sammy Green's Hot Harlem Revue throughout the southern states. Basing herself in Texas, she made her first records as Big Mama Thornton for Peacock in 1951. Two years later she topped the R&B charts with the original version of 'Hound Dog', the **Leiber** and **Stoller** song which **Elvis Presley** would later make world famous. The backing was by **Johnny Otis**' band with Pete Lewis contributing a memorable guitar solo. Thornton toured with Otis and recorded less successfully for Peacock until 1957 when she moved to California. There she made records for Bay-Tone (1961) Sotoplay (1963) and Kent (1964). Her career took a new turn when she joined the 1965 Folk Blues Festival troupe and entranced audiences in Europe. The next year, **Arhoolie** recorded her in Chicago with **Muddy Waters**, **James Cotton** and **Otis Spann**. A 1968 live album for the same label included 'Ball And Chain' which inspired **Janis Joplin**'s notable version of the song. She sang some pop standards on the 1969 **Mercury** album and in the 70s she recorded for Backbeat, **Vanguard** and Crazy Cajun. *On Jail*, recorded before prison audiences, she performed new versions of 'Hound Dog' and 'Ball And Chain'. Thornton died in Los Angeles in July 1984.

Selected albums: *In Europe* (1965), *Big Mama Thornton, Vol. 2* (1966), *With Chicago Blues* (1967), *She's Back* (1968), *Ball & Chain* (1968), *Stronger Than Dirt* (1969), *The Way It Is* (1970), *Maybe* (1970), *She's Back* (1970), *Saved* (1973), *Jail* (1975), *Sassy Mama* (1975), *Mama's Pride* (1978), *Live Together* (1979), *Hound Dog: The Peacock Recordings* (1993), *The Rising Sun Collection* (Just A Memory).

Thorogood, George

b. 31 December 1952, Wilmington, Delaware, USA. White blues guitarist George Thorogood first became interested in music, notably Chicago blues, when he saw John Paul Hammond performing in 1970. Three years later he formed the Destroyers in Delaware before moving them to Boston where they backed visiting blues stars. The Destroyers comprised Thorogood (guitar), Michael Lenn (bass), and Jeff Simon (drums). School friend Ron Smith played guitar on and off to make up the quartet. In 1974 they recorded some demos which were released later. They made their first album in 1975 after blues fanatic John Forward spotted them playing at Joe's Place in Cambridge, Massachusetts and put them in touch with the folk label Rounder. The album was not released immediately as Blough replaced Lenn and his bass parts had to be added. It was eventually released in 1978 (on **Sonet** in the UK) and the single 'Move It On Over' was Rounder's first release. Smith left in 1980 and was replaced by saxophonist Hank Carter. Thorogood, a former semi-professional baseball player, took time away from music that season to play ball but by 1981 was back in the fold as the band opened for the **Rolling Stones** at several of their American gigs. The venues were unfamiliar to Thorogood as normally he shunned large arenas for smaller clubs, even going to the extent of playing under false names to prevent the smaller venues being overcrowded. After three albums with Rounder they signed to **Capitol** and continued to record throughout the 80s. In 1985 they appeared at **Live Aid** playing with blues legend **Albert Collins**.

Albums: *George Thorogood And The Destroyers* (1978), *Move It On Over* (1978), *Better Than The Rest* (1979), *More George Thorogood And The Destroyers* (1980), *Bad To The Bone* (1982), *Maverick* (1985), *Live* (1986), *Born To Be Bad* (1988), *Killer's Bluze* (1993), *Haircut* (1993).

Thoroughly Modern Millie

This thoroughly entertaining pastiche of the 20s and the world of silent movies was released by Universal in 1967. **Julie Andrews** is Millie, the 'modern' of the title, and eager to marry one of New York's rich and eligible bachelors. She has a room at a boarding house which is reserved for single young women. Here she

meets, and takes under her wing, a new resident, Miss Dorothy Brown (Mary Tyler Moore), who immediately attracts the attention of the landlady Mrs. Meers (Beatrice Lillie), a sinister (but hilarious) character with a serious interest in white slave trading. Millie sets out to capture her granite-jawed boss, Trevor Graydon (John Gavin), but he falls for Miss Dorothy and Millie is happy to end up with Jimmy Smith (James Fox), who (by heck) makes up dance-steps like 'The Tapioca' (**Jimmy Van Heusen-Sammy Cahn**) right there on the spot. **Carol Channing** as the wealthy Muzzy (step-mother of Miss Dorothy and Jimmy, as it turns out), makes one of her rare screen appearances, and renders delightful versions of 'Jazz Baby' (M.K. Jerome-Blanche Merrill) and 'Do It Again' (**George Gershwin-Buddy De Sylva**). Julie Andrews was splendid as Millie, especially when handling 'period' numbers such as 'Jimmy' (**Kay Thompson**), 'Baby Face' (Harry Askst-Benny Davis), 'Poor Butterfly' (Raymond Hubbell-John Golden), and the scene-setting title song by Cahn and Van Heusen. Her delicious all-round performance is some indication of how impressive she must have been on Broadway in 1954 when she starred in **The Boyfriend** - a pastiche in a similar vein. This upbeat, jolly movie had a screenplay by Richard Morris and was directed by George Roy Hill. The choreographer was Joe Layton, and it was photographed in Technicolor and Panavision by Russell Metty. **Elmer Bernstein** won an Oscar for his background music score.

Thorpe, Billy

b. 29 March 1946, Manchester, England. Arriving in Sydney, via Brisbane, in 1964, Thorpe soon joined a band, the Vibratones and re-christened the Aztecs, with whom he could perform at dances in Sydney, playing the new beat music coming from England. Following the success of their first single in Sydney, they recorded 'Poison Ivy', after hearing the **Rolling Stones'** version, and the song became an Australian number 1 hit. Inexplicably, Thorpe broke up this band and started recording with a 'new' Aztecs, MOR ballads such as 'Somewhere Over The Rainbow', 'I Told The Brook', 'Twilight Time' and 'Love Letters', all cover versions which were Australian Top 10 hit singles. By 1966 he was fronting his own television show, but the hits dried up and the second Aztecs disbanded. Undeterred, Thorpe took up the guitar and grew his hair. He formed yet another new band, still called the Aztecs, which emerged as a heavy blues rock band claiming to be the loudest band in the land throughout the 70s. This music appealed to the beer-drinking dominions of pubs and outdoor festivals where Thorpe was undisputed king. The first half of the 70s saw line-up changes in the Aztecs, but nonetheless four albums and one single reached the Top 10. By late 1976 he had moved to the USA, where he concentrated on writing and producing a sci-fi/hi-tech album *Children Of The Sun* which had success in the USA, reaching the Top 40. His follow-up album, *21st Century Man*, released on **Elektra** also charted, albeit with a minor position. Unrecorded since 1982, Thorpe ran a business importing toys, although in 1991 he was again touring Australia with Mick Fleetwood and Zoo as his backing band.

Albums: *Billy Thorpe & The Aztecs* (1965), *I Got A Woman* (1968), *It's All Happening*, (1974), *Million Dollar Bill* (1974), *Pick Me Up And Play Me Loud* (1975), *Children Of The Sun* (1979), *Time Traveller* (1980), *21st Century Man* (1981), *Stimulation* (1981), *East Of Eden Gate* (1982).

Those Were The Happy Times
(see *Star!*)

Thought Industry
From Michigan, USA, Thought Industry comprise Brent Oberlin (vocals/bass), Dustin Donaldson (drums), Paul Enzio (guitar) and Chris Lee (guitar). Though often wrongly classified within the 'industrial' metal fraternity (the result not just of their name but also tours with **Godflesh** and **Skinny Puppy**), Thought Industry's sound is too relentlessly individual for either that or another pigeonhole, metal: 'To me most 'metal' bands rehash clichéd musical/lyrical ideas and are very conservative in their output and viewpoints. We use the power of metal or punk without it's parody or redundancy'. Any satisfactory description of the band's music would be hard pressed to deny the strong metallic undercurrent, however, which their dual guitar approach epitomises. Critical guesses over *Songs For Insects* spanned the **Jesus Lizard**, **Voivod** and **Primus**, with lyrics which dealt with hallucinogenic drugs, violence and social alienation. For the lugubriously titled follow-up subjects would be dealt with inside a more personal framework, but the musical onslaught continued unabated.

Albums: *Songs For Insects* (Music For Nations 1993), *Mods Carve The Pig: Assassins, Toads And God's Flesh* (Music For Nations 1994).

Thoumire, Simon
b. 11 July 1970, Edinburgh, Scotland. Concertina player Thoumire made his first big impact on the folk scene when winning the BBC Radio 2 Young Tradition Award in 1989. Thoumire, pronounced Toomere, is French in origin. His style fuses traditional folk and jazz music, creating a highly original sound. *Hootz* was extremely well received, as was the follow-up release, in tandem with Seannachie, *Devil's Delight*. In addition to teaching English concertina, both in the UK and America, Thoumire has toured the US and Canada, as well as making live appearances in Europe and on television and radio. For *Waltzes For Playboys*, the Simon Thoumire Three included Kevin MacKenzie (guitar) and Brian Sheils (bass).

Albums: with Seannachie *Take Note* (Raven 1988), *Devil's Delight* (Raven 1992), with Ian Carr: *Hootz* (Black Crow 1990), as the Simon Thoumire Three: *Waltzes For Playboys* (Celtic Music 1993), with Fergus MacKenzie *Exhibit A* (Iona 1995).

Thousand Yard Stare
Named, somewhat perplexingly, after the vacant look often associated with Vietnam veterans, Thousand Yard Stare are a qunitessentially English five-piece band from Slough, Berkshire. The band was formed in November 1988 by friends who knew each other from regular evenings at their local venue, Windsor's Psykik Dance Hall. The band comprise Stephen Barnes (vocals), Dominic Bostock (drums), Sean McDonough (bass), Giles Duffy (guitar) and Kevin Moxon (rhythm guitar). They released a 4 track EP on their own Stifled Aardvark label, 'Weatherwatching', and sold it at gigs from November 1990 onwards. The next year saw mounting music press interest and support slots with bands such as **Carter the Unstoppable Sex Machine**, **Ned's Atomic Dustbin**, **Milltown Brothers**, and **James**. In opposition to the dominant 'shoegazing' ethos, the band always proved themselves highly vivid live exponents, if not as inspired as some of those headlining acts. Signing to **Polydor** for their debut album, Barnes' lyrics proved the band's greatest asset; a little short of the stature of **XTC** whilst dealing in a similar, neo-Romantic English vein.

Albums: *Hands On* (1992), *Fair To Middling* (1993), *Mappamundi* (1993).

Thousands Cheer
Another lavish effort by Hollywood in 1943 to lighten the war years by parading many of the most popular entertainers across the screen with only the most tenuous storyline to hold things together. Paul Jarrico and Richard Collins's script concerns the love affair between a former circus aerialist (**Gene Kelly**), who becomes a US army private and falls for the colonel's daughter (**Kathryn Grayson**). John Boles and Mary Astor play her father and mother, and most of MGM's galaxy of stars perform a dazzling array of musical party pieces, including **Lena Horne** ('Honeysuckle Rose'), **Judy Garland**, with Jose Iturbi, ('The Joint Is Really Jumpin' In Carnegie Hall'), and Virginia O'Brien ('In A Little Spanish Town'). Gene Kelly danced 'The Mop Dance' delightfully, and Kathryn Grayson sang several numbers, notably 'Three Letters In A Mailbox', 'Daybreak', and 'Let There Be Music'. Also cast were **Mickey Rooney**, Red Skelton, **Eleanor Powell**, Margaret O'Brien, **June Allyson**, **Gloria De Haven**, Lucille Ball, and Frank Morgan. Guest stars included Marilyn Maxwell, Ann Sothern, and Marsha Hunt. Some of the best musical moments were provided by the bands of **Bob Crosby**, **Kay**

Kyser, and **Benny Carter**. There were Oscar nominations for George Folsey's colour cinematography, Herbert Stothart's 'scoring of a musical picture', and Cedric Gibbons and Daniel Cathcart's interior direction. George Sidney directed *Thousands Cheer*, which grossed $3.5 million at the box office in the US and Canada alone, making it one of the most successful musicals of the decade.

Thrasher

In June and July 1984 the US heavy metal label Combat funded a super session and enlisted Carl Canedy (drums) to write and produce an album's worth of material. Canedy formed a writing partnership with guitarist Andy MacDonald and they put the 'Thrasher' band together at the Music America Studios in New York. An impressive line-up was amassed: Kenny Aaronson (Derringer/**HSAS**; bass), Dickie Peterson (**Blue Cheer**; vocals), Billy Sheehan (**Talas**; bass), Mars Cowling (**Pat Travers Band**; bass), Maryann Scandiffio (**Black Lace**; vocals), Dan Spitz (**Anthrax**; guitar), Jack Starr (**Virgin Steel**; guitar), Rhett Forrester (**Riot**; vocals), Kim Simmonds (**Savoy Brown**; guitar), Gary Bordonaro (**Rods**; bass) and additional vocalists James Rivera, Leslie Dunn and Jackie Kenyon.
Album: *Thrasher* (Music For Nations 1985).

Threadgill, Henry

b. 15 February 1944, Chicago, Illinois, USA. At college Threadgill shared a saxophone teacher with **Anthony Braxton**. In the early 60s he played with **Roscoe Mitchell** and **Muhal Richard Abrams** in the Experimental Band, the precursor of the **AACM**. He missed the AACM's beginnings as he spent several years touring America with an Evangelist Camp, contributing saxophone to the gospel services. Two years in the army had him playing everything from marches to classical music to jazz. In the late 60s he returned to Chicago and his AACM colleagues, playing with **Amina Claudine Myers** and Abrams and also in the house band of a Chicago blues club. In 1971 he formed **Air**, a trio with **Fred Hopkins** (bass) and **Steve McCall** (percussion) though it was only after 1975 that the group became widely active. Adept on alto, tenor and baritone saxophones as well as clarinet, flute and bass flute, Threadgill's playing was characterized by a pliancy and exceptional freshness. In the late 70s he formed X-75, a nonet of strings and winds, which recorded *Volume One* for Arista/Novus. The unusual line-up bewildered promoters and there was no volume two. In 1977 he recorded on Braxton's *For Trio* and later played in **David Murray**'s Octet (1980-2). His X-75 ensemble evolved into his longstanding 'Sextet' (although it has seven members there are only *six parts*), with a fascinating deployment of Hopkins on bass, Deidre Murray on cello and two percussionists.

This group became the vehicle for some of the great jazz records of the 80s: *Just The Facts And Pass The Bucket* (1983), *You Know The Number* (1986) and *Rag, Bush And All* (1988). In December 1987 his composition for strings, percussion and voices, *Run Silent, Run Deep, Run Loud, Run High* (based on the laws of particle physics) was premiered at the Brooklyn Academy of Music. By the end of the 80s he had formed a 19-piece band that played dance tunes, a marching band and a septet, Very Very Circus, with an unusual line-up of two tubas, two electric guitars, trombone, drums plus the leader's alto saxophone and flute. In 1991, Very Very Circus released their debut recording, *Spirit Of Nuff...Nuff*, and in 1992 they toured the UK. Together with his AACM colleagues Abrams, Braxton and Mitchell, Threadgill remains on the cutting edge of musical exploration: he is a thrilling improviser and a boldly original composer.
Albums: with X-75 *Volume One* (1979), *When Was That* (1982), *Just The Facts And Pass The Bucket* (1983), *Subject To Change* (1985), *You Know The Number* (RCA 1986), *Easily Slip Into Another World* (RCA 1987), *Rag, Bush And All* (RCA 1988), with Very Very Circus *Spirit Of Nuff...Nuff* (Black Saint 1991), *Live At Koncepts* (Taylor Made 1992), *Too Much Sugar For A Dime* (1993), *Song Out Of My Trees* (Black Saint 1994).

Three Beat Records

Liverpool, England, dance label, headed by joint partner Hywel Williams, a local rave organiser, alongside Dave Nicoll, Jonathan Barlow and Phillip Southall. Three Beat is also responsible for running a series of club nights in and around Merseyside. They signed a licensing deal with **London/ffrr** in 1994, having built their reputation with records like New Atlantic's 'Take Off Some Time'. Although Three Beat reamined indepedent ffrr were to be given first choice over licensing any of their product. The first release under the new arrangement was 2 Cowboy's 'Everybody's Gonfi-Gon', a huge hit. Their mid-90s roster included Cordial, Neuro Project, Jeaney Tracey, Bong Devils, Supernatura, Bandito and Vicki Shepherd, in addition to the aforementioned New Atlantic.

Three Degrees

Protegees of producer/songwriter Richard Barrett; Fayette Pickney, Linda Turner and Shirley Porter scored a US hit with their first single, 'Gee Baby (I'm Sorry)', in 1965. This Philadelphia-based trio, sponsored by Kenny Gamble and Leon Huff, secured further pop success the next year with 'Look In My Eyes', but struggled to sustain this momentum until 1970, when their emphatic reworking of the **Chantels'** standard, 'Maybe', returned them to the chart. By this point Sheila Ferguson and Valerie Holiday had joined the line-up in place of Turner and Porter. The Three Degrees' golden period came on signing with **Philadelphia International**. They shared vocals with **MFSB** on 'TSOP', the theme song to television's successful *Soul Train* show. This US pop and R&B number 1 preceded the trio's international hits, 'Year Of Decision' and 'When Will I See You Again?' (both 1974). These glossy performances were particularly popular in the UK, where the group continued to chart, notably with the Top 10 hits, 'Take Good Care Of Yourself' (1975), 'Woman In Love' and 'My Simple Heart' (both 1979). Helen Scott appeared on the 1976 album *Standing Up For Love*. Now signed to Ariola Records, the Three Degrees' releases grew increasingly bland as they emphasized the cabaret element suppressed in their early work. Fêted by royalty - Prince Charles stated they were his favourite group after booking them for his 30th birthday party - the 80s saw the group resident in the UK where they were a fixture on the variety and supper-club circuit. Ferguson entered the 90s as a solo artist, heralded by the release of a remix of 'When Will I See You Again?'. As to their proud heritage as 70s hit-makers of stunning visual appearance, Valerie Holiday has this to add: 'They were wigs. You think anyone would really do that to their hair?'

Albums: *Maybe* (1970), *Three Degrees* (1974), *International* (1975), *So Much In Love* (1975), *Take Good Care Of Yourself* (1975), *Three Degrees Live* (1975), *Three Degrees Live In Japan* (1975), *Standing Up For Love* (1977), *The Three Degrees* (1978), *New Dimensions* (1978), *3D* (1979), *Three Degrees And Holding* (1989), *Woman In Love* (1993). Compilations: *Gold* (1980), *Hits Hits Hits* (1981), *20 Golden Greats* (1984), *The Complete Swan Recordings* (1992). Solo album: Fayette Pickney: *One Degree* (1979).

Three Dog Night

This highly successful US harmony rock trio formed in 1968 with a line-up comprising Danny Hutton (b. Daniel Anthony Hutton 10 September 1942, Buncrana, Eire), Cory Wells (b. 5 February 1942, Buffalo, New York, USA) and Chuck Negron (b. Charles Negron, 8 June 1942, New York, USA). The three lead singers were backed by Jim Greenspoon (b. 7 February 1948, Los Angeles, California, USA; organ), Joe Schermie (b. 12 February 1948, Madison, Wisconsin, USA; bass), Mike Allsup (b. 8 March 1947, Modesto, California, USA; guitar) and Floyd Sneed (b. 22 November 1943, Calgary, Alberta, USA; drums). With their distinctive and sometimes extraordinary harmonic blend, the group registered an impressive 21 **Billboard** Top 40 hits between 1969-75. Their startling version of **Lennon/McCartney**'s 'It's For You' typified the group at their best, but it was their original arrangements of the work of less well-known writers that brought welcome exposure and considerable royalties to fresh talent. Both **Nilsson**

and **Laura Nyro** first glimpsed the Top 10 courtesy of Three Dog Night's covers of 'One' and 'Eli's Coming', respectively. The risqué 'Mama Told Me Not To Come' provided the same service for **Randy Newman** while also giving the group their first number 1 in 1970. During the next two years they registered two further US chart toppers, 'Joy To The World' (composed by **Hoyt Axton**) and 'Black And White' (a UK hit for reggae group Greyhound). Always ready to record promising material and adapt it to their distinctive harmonic blend, they brought vicarious US chart success to **Russ Ballard**'s 'Liar' and **Leo Sayer**'s UK number 1 'The Show Must Go On'. By the early 70s, there were gradual changes in the trio's back-up musicians, with several members of **Rufus** joining during 1976. The departure of Danny Hutton (replaced by Jay Gruska) proved a body blow, however, and precipitated the group's decline and disbandment. During 1981, they reunited briefly with Hutton but failed to retrieve past chart glories. The strength of Three Dog Night lay in the power of their harmonies and the strength of the material they adapted. In the age of the singer/songwriter, they were seldom applauded by critics but their inventive arrangements struck a chord with the public to the tune of 10 million selling records. Three Dog Night brought a fresh approach to the art of covering seemingly uncommercial material and demonstrated how a strong song can be translated into something approaching a standard.

Albums: *Three Dog Night* (1969), *Suitable For Framing* (1969), *Captured Live At The Forum* (1969), *It Ain't Easy* (1970), *Naturally* (1970), *Golden Bisquits* (1971), *Harmony* (1971), *Seven Separate Fools* (1972), *Around The World With Three Dog Night* (1973), *Cyan* (1973), *Hard Labor* (1974), *Coming Down Your Way* (1975), *American Pastime* (1976), *It's A Jungle* (1983). Compilations: *Joy To The World - Their Greatest Hits* (1975), *The Best Of* (1983), *Celebrate: The Three Dog Night Story* (1993).

Three Johns

This UK pop punk band from Leeds, Yorkshire, formed on Royal Wedding Day in 1981, set themselves a characteristic precedent by being refused permission to play a 'Funk The Wedding' gig because they were drunk. The line-up featured John Brennan (ex-25 Rifles; bass), John Langford (ex-**Mekons**; guitar) and John Hyatt (ex-Sheeny And The Goys, Another Colour; vocals). They met in Leeds while they were at college, although individually they are from Wales, Belfast and Wolverhampton. A drum machine was used in preference to an extra member, although, ironically, all three musicians were competent percussionists. They signed to CNT Records in 1982 and released two singles, one of which, 'English White Boy Engineer', was a re-working of an old Mekons number. The lyrical focus of the song attacked

hypocritical attitudes towards South Africa and apartheid, and the group were quickly designated as left wing rockers, albeit heavy drinking ones: 'We all have socialist convictions and obviously that comes through ... but we're not a socialist band. We're a group of socialists who are in a band. It's a fine distinction but an important one'. They quickly made their reputation via frenetic and comic live shows, even performing a version of **Madonna**'s 'Like A Virgin'. A legacy of fine singles populated the independents charts, including 'Pink Headed Bug', 'Men Like Monkeys' and 'Do The Square Thing'. 1985's 'Death Of A European' was a *New Musical Express* Single Of The Week, although by misfortune it emerged in the aftermath of the Heysel football tragedy and hence achieved no airplay. Unfortunately, there was insufficient success to allow the band to give up their day jobs. Langford earned his living as a part-time graphic designer for the Health Education Service, and Hyatt (who designed the band's covers) was a teacher of Fine Art at Leeds Polytechnic. Their debut album, *Atom Drum Bop*, bore the legend 'Rock 'n' Roll versus Thaatchiism', and included contributions from schoolgirl Kate Morath on oboe. They worked with **Adrian Sherwood** on 1987's *Never And Always*, while 1988's *The Death Of Everything And More* was summed up by one critic as 'messy, snappy, guttural'. After that came a long break in their musical endeavours: 'We basically stopped working after our last gig in December 1988. We'd done a US tour which was a total disaster and we didn't speak to each other after that, we were all too busy having babies and things'. Hyatt produced an art exhibition at Liverpool's Tate Gallery, and Langford continued to work with the Mekons. They returned with *Eat Your Sons* in 1990, a concept album dealing with, of all things, cannibalism.
Albums: *Atom Drum Bop* (Abstract 1984), *The World By Storm* (Abstract 1986), *Live In Chicago* (Last Time Round 1986), *Deathrocker Scrapbook* (ROIR 1988, cassette only), *Death Of Everything* (Caroline 1988), *Eat Your Sons* (Tupelo 1990). Compilation: *Crime Pays...Rock 'n' Roll In The Democracy* (Abstract 1986).

Three O'Clock

Of all the early 80s west coast groups to profess a liking for psychedelia, the Three O'Clock were the most overtly pop-influenced. From Sun Valley, California, USA, Michael Quercio (lead vocals/bass), Louis Guttierez (guitar), Mike Mariano (keyboards) and Danny Benair (drums) had their debut, *Sixteen Tambourines*, released in Europe in 1984 by the French label Lolita. Riding on the crest of the so-called 'paisley underground' wave of publicity, the album created enough of a stir to clinch a deal with IRS, releasing *Arriving Without Travelling* (from which was drawn 'Hand

In Hand'). But like their debut, this only hinted at psychedelia and owed more if anything to that other late 60s musical form, bubblegum. The release of *Ever After* in 1987 saw Guttierez replaced Steven Altenberg, and though melodically strong, suffered from its stylized production. There was even a hint of **Prince** in there somewhere, not least on the single 'Warm Aspirations', so it was no surprise when the band teamed up with his Paisley Park operation in 1988. But since *Vermillion*, issued soon after, the Three O'Clock have kept a low profile.
Albums: *Sixteen Tambourines* (1984), *Arriving Without Travelling* (1985), *Ever After* (1987), *Vermillion* (1988).

Three's A Crowd

Just one year after they had appeared together in the legendary revue *The Little Show*, the main participants in that show were reunited for this similar kind of song and sketch entertainment which opened at the Selwyn Theatre in New York on 15 October 1930. Most of the numbers were written by **Arthur Schwartz** and **Howard Dietz**, who combined with the suave and sophisticated song-and-dance man Clifton Webb, deadpan comedian Fred Allen, and torch singer *extraordinaire* **Libby Holman**, to make this an amusing and innovative show. The sketches came from a variety of writers such as Dietz himself, Laurence Schwab, William Miles, Donald Blackman, Groucho Marx, and Arthur Sheekman. Schwartz and Dietz's musical numbers included 'The Moment I Saw You', 'Right At The Start Of It', and the gentle and wistful 'Something To Remember You By', which was introduced by Holman and which became popular through her own recording, and another, several years later, by **Dinah Shore**. Libby Holman also sang probably the most enduring song in the piece, the lovely ballad 'Body And Soul', which was the work of **Johnny Green**, Edward Heyman, Frank Eyton and Robert Sour. After early recordings by **Paul Whiteman**, **Leo Reisman** with **Eddy Duchin** at the piano, and **Ruth Etting**, it went on to become an all-time standard in the popular field, and has proved to be a particular favourite of jazz artists such as the pioneering tenor saxophonist **Coleman Hawkins**. The rest of the score for *Three's A Crowd* included 'Talkative Toes' (Dietz-**Vernon Duke**), 'Out In The Open Air' (Dietz-**Burton Lane**), 'All The King's Horses' (Dietz-Edward Brandt-**Alec Wilder**), and 'Yaller' (Richard Myers-Charles Schwab). The show ran for a total of 272 performances, and set the mood and style for many other musical productions of the 30s.